International Directory of
COMPANY
HISTORIES

International Directory of

COMPANY HISTORIES

VOLUME 15

Editor
Tina Grant

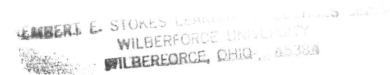
ST. JAMES PRESS

AN IMPRINT OF GALE

Detroit • New York • Toronto • London

STAFF

Tina Grant, *Editor*

Miranda H. Ferrara, *Project Manager*
Paula Kepos, Margaret Mazurkiewicz, Michael J. Tyrkus, *Contributing Editors*
Peter M. Gareffa, *Managing Editor, St. James Press*

The paper used in this publication meets the minimum
requirements of American National Standard for Information Sciences—
Permanence Paper for Printed Library Materials, ANSI Z39.48-1984.

This book is printed on recycled paper that meets Environmental Protection Agency Standards.

Library of Congress Catalog Number: 89-190943

British Library Cataloguing in Publication Data

International directory of company histories. Vol. 15
I. Tina Grant
338.7409

ISBN 1-55862-218-7

Printed in the United States of America
Published simultaneously in the United Kingdom

St. James Press is an imprint of Gale

Cover photograph of the Federal Trade Commission, Washington, D.C.

10 9 8 7 6 5 4 3 2 1

CONTENTS

Preface . . . . page ix

List of Abbreviations xi

Company Histories

A.S. Yakovlev Design Bureau 3
Abercrombie & Fitch Co. 7
Allianz Aktiengesellschaft Holding 10
American International Group, Inc. 15
Angelica Corporation 20
Aspen Skiing Company 23
Assicurazioni Generali SpA 27
Baby Superstore, Inc. 32
Badger Paper Mills, Inc. 35
Banco Espírito Santo e Comercial de
    Lisboa S.A. 38
Bank of Tokyo-Mitsubishi Ltd. 41
Bass PLC 44
Bekins Company 48
Bertelsmann AG 51
Blimpie International, Inc. 55
Boatmen's Bancshares Inc. 58
Borders Group, Inc. 61
Brach and Brock Confections, Inc. 63
British Telecommunications plc 66
Brooke Group Ltd. 71
California Pizza Kitchen Inc. 74
Callaway Golf Company 77
Carborundum Company 80
Carlton Communications plc 83
Carson Pirie Scott & Company 86
Caterpillar Inc. 89
Catherines Stores Corporation 94
Christie's International plc 98
Chromcraft Revington, Inc. 102
Cincom Systems Inc. 106
Coles Express Inc. 109
Columbia/HCA Healthcare Corporation 112
Commercial Metals Company 115

Community Psychiatric Centers 118
Comprehensive Care Corporation 121
Comverse Technology, Inc. 124
Continental Can Co., Inc. 127
Corel Corporation 131
Crown Equipment Corporation 134
Culbro Corporation 137
Daimler-Benz AG 140
Donna Karan Company 145
Electronics for Imaging, Inc. 148
English China Clays plc 151
Esterline Technologies Corp. 155
Farrar, Straus and Giroux Inc. 158
First Commerce Bancshares, Inc. 161
Fisher Companies, Inc. 164
Fleer Corporation 167
Flexsteel Industries Inc. 170
Fluke Corporation 173
Food Lion, Inc. 176
Fortis, Inc. 179
G.S. Blodgett Corporation 183
Greif Bros. Corporation 186
Grist Mill Company 189
GTE Corporation 192
Guccio Gucci, S.p.A. 198
Guess, Inc. 201
Gymboree Corporation 204
Hancock Holding Company 207
Handleman Company 210
Harman International Industries Inc. 213
HarperCollins Publishers 216
Hershey Foods Corporation 219
Ingersoll-Rand Company 223
Inter-Regional Financial Group, Inc. 231

International Paper Company 227
The Intrawest Corporation 234
Irvin Feld & Kenneth Feld
      Productions, Inc. 237
Jay Jacobs, Inc. 243
JG Industries, Inc. 240
Johnston Industries, Inc. 246
Joseph T. Ryerson & Son, Inc. 249
Kay-Bee Toy Stores 252
Kemper Corporation 254
King Kullen Grocery Co., Inc. 259
Knight-Ridder, Inc. 262
The Kroger Company 267
Laclede Steel Company 271
Lamonts Apparel, Inc. 274
Landry's Seafood Restaurants, Inc. 277
Levitz Furniture Inc. 280
Lockheed Martin Corporation 283
MagneTek, Inc. 287
Marisa Christina, Inc. 290
Matra-Hachette S.A. 293
Mike-Sell's Inc. 298
Moran Towing Corporation, Inc. 301
Mosinee Paper Corporation 304
Mr. Coffee, Inc. 307
Mr. Gasket Inc. 310
National City Corp. 313
Nature's Sunshine Products, Inc. 317
Netscape Communications Corporation 320
New England Confectionery Co. 323
Oakwood Homes Corporation 326
OfficeMax Inc. 329
Old National Bancorp 332
Ottaway Newspapers, Inc. 335
Otto-Versand (GmbH & Co.) 338
Pamida Holdings Corporation 341
Papa John's International, Inc. 344
Paychex, Inc. 347
Petrolite Corporation 350
Pirelli S.p.A. 353
Playtex Products, Inc. 357
Ponderosa Steakhouse 361
Precision Castparts Corp. 365
Prince Sports Group, Inc. 368
Progress Software Corporation 371
Pulitzer Publishing Company 375

Quixote Corporation 378
Recoton Corp. 381
Rexel, Inc. 384
Robbins & Myers Inc. 388
Robert Mondavi Corporation 391
Rollerblade, Inc. 395
Ronco, Inc. 399
Roper Industries Inc. 402
Rosemount Inc. 405
Roto-Rooter Corp. 409
The Rouse Company 412
Royal Appliance Manufacturing
      Company 416
Ryan's Family Steak Houses, Inc. 419
S&C Electric Company 422
S-K-I Limited 457
San Miguel Corporation 428
Sanderson Farms, Inc. 425
The Sanwa Bank, Ltd. 431
Sara Lee Corporation 434
Science Applications International
      Corporation 438
Scottish & Newcastle plc 441
Seattle Times Company 445
Seaway Food Town, Inc. 448
Sierra Health Services, Inc. 451
Sierra On-Line Inc. 454
Skis Rossignol S.A. 460
Smith Barney Inc. 463
Smith International, Inc. 466
Sportmart, Inc. 469
Standard Register Co. 472
Stanhome Inc. 475
Super Food Services, Inc. 479
Symbol Technologies, Inc. 482
Taco John's International Inc. 485
Tillotson Corp. 488
Timberline Software Corporation 491
The Tokai Bank, Limited 494
Toll Brothers Inc. 497
The Tranzonic Cos. 500
Trico Products Corporation 503
Turtle Wax, Inc. 506
TVI, Inc. 510
United Technologies Automotive Inc. 513
Varsity Spirit Corp. 516

Veba A.G. 519
Vitalink Pharmacy Services, Inc. 522
W.R. Berkley Corp. 525
Watkins-Johnson Company 528
Weis Markets, Inc. 531

Western Company of North America 534
WMS Industries, Inc. 537
Wyse Technology, Inc. 540
Zilog, Inc. 543

Index to Companies 549
Index to Industries 665
Notes on Contributors 681

PREFACE

The St. James Press series *The International Directory of Company Histories (IDCH)* is intended for reference use by students, business people, librarians, historians, economists, investors, job candidates, and others who seek to learn more about the historical development of the world's most important companies. To date, *IDCH* has covered over 2,500 companies in fifteen volumes.

Inclusion Criteria

Most companies chosen for inclusion in *IDCH* have achieved a minimum of US$100 million in annual sales and are leading influences in their industries or geographical locations. Companies may be publicly held, private, or non-profit. State-owned companies that are important in their industries and that may operate much like public or private companies also are included. Wholly owned subsidiaries and divisions are presented if they meet the requirements for inclusion.

Entries on companies that have had major changes since they were last profiled may be selected for updating.

The *IDCH* series highlights 10% private and non-profit companies, and features updated entries on approximately 25 companies per volume.

Entry Format

Each entry begins with the company's legal name, the address of its headquarters, its telephone number and fax number and a statement of public, private, state, or parent ownership. A company with a legal name in both English and the language of its headquarters country is listed by the English name, with the native-language name in parentheses.

Also provided are the company's founding or earliest incorporation date, the number of employees, and the most recent sales figures available. Sales figures are given in local currencies with equivalents in U.S. dollars. For some private companies, sales figures are estimates. The entry lists the exchanges on which a company's stock is traded, as well as the company's principal Standard Industrial Classification codes. American spelling is used throughout, and the word "billion" is used in its U.S. sense of one thousand million.

Sources

The histories were compiled from publicly accessible sources such as general and academic periodicals, books, annual reports, and material supplied by the companies themselves.

Cumulative Indexes

Following the entries are two indexes: the **Index to Companies**, which provides an alphabetical index to companies discussed in the text as well as companies profiled, and the **Index to Industries**, which allows researchers to locate companies by their principal industry. Both indexes are cumulative and specific instructions for using the indexes are found immediately preceding each index.

Special to This Volume

Volume 15 includes an entry for the A. S. Yakovlev Design Bureau, the first company profiled from the former U.S.S.R.

New Series Features

Beginning with Volume 15 *IDCH* features include:

- Expanded inclusion criteria. The inclusion criteria have been broadened to include a larger number of smaller, private, and emerging companies.

- Thoroughly revised **Index to Companies**. In response to comments by users of *IDCH*, the index has been reviewed and edited for consistency, ease of use, and better presentation.

Suggestions Welcome

Comments and suggestions from users of *IDCH* on any aspect of the product as well as suggestions for companies to be included or updated are cordially invited. Please write:

The Editor
International Directory of Company History
St. James Press
835 Penobscot Building
Detroit, Michigan 48226-4094

ABBREVIATIONS FOR FORMS OF COMPANY INCORPORATION

A.B.	Aktiebolaget (Sweden)
A.G.	Aktiengesellschaft (Germany, Switzerland)
A.S.	Atieselskab (Denmark)
A.S.	Aksjeselskap (Denmark, Norway)
A.Ş.	Anomin Şirket (Turkey)
B.V.	Besloten Vennootschap met beperkte, Aansprakelijkheid (The Netherlands)
Co.	Company (United Kingdom, United States)
Corp.	Corporation (United States)
G.I.E.	Groupement d'Intérêt Economique (France)
GmbH	Gesellschaft mit beschränkter Haftung (Germany)
H.B.	Handelsbolaget (Sweden)
Inc.	Incorporated (United States)
KGaA	Kommanditgesellschaft auf Aktien (Germany)
K.K.	Kabushiki Kaisha (Japan)
LLC	Limited Liability Company (Middle East)
Ltd.	Limited (Canada, Japan, United Kingdom, United States)
N.V.	Naamloze Vennootschap (The Netherlands)
OY	Osakeyhtiöt (Finland)
PLC	Public Limited Company (United Kingdom)
PTY.	Proprietary (Australia, Hong Kong, South Africa)
S.A.	Société Anonyme (Belgium, France, Switzerland)
SpA	Società per Azioni (Italy)

ABBREVIATIONS FOR CURRENCY

DA	Algerian dinar	Dfl	Netherlands florin
A$	Australian dollar	NZ$	New Zealand dollar
Sch	Austrian schilling	N	Nigerian naira
BFr	Belgian franc	NKr	Norwegian krone
Cr	Brazilian cruzado	RO	Omani rial
C$	Canadian dollar	P	Philippine peso
DKr	Danish krone	Esc	Portuguese escudo
E£	Egyptian pound	SRls	Saudi Arabian riyal
Fmk	Finnish markka	S$	Singapore dollar
FFr	French franc	R	South African rand
DM	German mark	W	South Korean won
HK$	Hong Kong dollar	Pta	Spanish peseta
Rs	Indian rupee	SKr	Swedish krona
Rp	Indonesian rupiah	SFr	Swiss franc
IR£	Irish pound	NT$	Taiwanese dollar
L	Italian lira	B	Thai baht
¥	Japanese yen	£	United Kingdom pound
W	Korean won	$	United States dollar
KD	Kuwaiti dinar	B	Venezuelan bolivar
LuxFr	Luxembourgian franc	K	Zambian kwacha
M$	Malaysian ringgit		

International Directory of
COMPANY
HISTORIES

A. S. Yakovlev Design Bureau

68 Leningradsky Prospekt
Moscow, 125315
Russia
7 (095) 157 17 34
Fax: 7 (095) 157 47 26

Joint Stock Company
Founded: 1935
Employees: 4,000
SICs: 3721 Aircraft

The A. S. Yakovlev Design Bureau, named for Aleksandr Sergeyevich Yakovlev, has gained a reputation as probably the most prolific and most versatile in the Soviet Union, producing virtually every type of aircraft from small gliders to massive helicopters. Since the first "Yak" flew in the 1920s the company has produced more than 70,000, more than any other Russian company. Yak gained particular distinction with its Yak-38, the second operational jet (after the Hawker Harrier) capable of taking off and landing vertically, and its Yak-141, the world's only supersonic V/STOL aircraft. The firm's designs are produced by Moskovskii Mashinostroitelnyy Zavod "Skorost" Imieni A. S. Yakovleva (Moscow Machine-Building Factory "Speed" Named after A.S. Yakovlev), an alliance of engine and aircraft manufacturers in the Commonwealth of Independent States. As the CIS aircraft industry struggles in a challenging environment, Yakovlev has earned a reputation as one of the most progressive design bureaus, entering into numerous cooperative agreements with CIS and Western aerospace firms.

Aleksandr Sergeyevich Yakovlev's first experience with an aircraft was at age six, when his grandmother took him to Khodynka Field to see an observation balloon. He recounted the disappointing experience in *Notes of an Aircraft Designer:* there were no balloons, and the French airplane that was there failed to get off the ground. Unimpressed, Yakovlev dreamt instead of following in the footsteps of his uncle, a railway designer.

At this time, Russian aviation itself was barely getting off the ground, although Igor Sikorsky's engineers had built the largest airplane in the world at the time, the four-engined *Ilya Muromets*. This set the precedent for a long line of Soviet behemoths. According to Yakovlev, the Tsarist government and investors preferred to assemble planes in Russia using foreign parts and foreign designs, another strategy that would see much use.

Before graduating from gymnasium in 1923, Yakovlev built his first glider out of pine, paper, nails, and glue. It flew 50 feet on its first flight. After diligently serving as fund raisers for the Society of Friends of the Air Fleet, he and some friends obtained a scrapped airplane (a captured Nieuport) for the purposes of reversing engineering—another common theme in Soviet aircraft design.

After persistent searching, Yakovlev secured a position assisting Nikolai Dmitriyevich Anoshchenko in building a glider for the country's first glider competitions. As a reward for his diligent work, he was allowed to accompany the pilot to the site of the competition, the Crimea. The glider proved tail-heavy and crashed. Another future prominent designer, Sergei Ilyushin, who had also traveled to the competition, helped Yakovlev engineer his own glider. The next year Yakovlev's glider, built by a team of schoolmates, won a 200-ruble prize in Crimea.

Unable to enter the Zhukovsky Air Force Academy, Yakovlev worked as an unskilled laborer, first unloading potatoes and then, in 1924, with help from Ilyushin, in an Air Force Academy training workshop. After two years he began working on the airfield crew and soon afterward was promoted to junior mechanic. While he had reached his goal, his job was strenuous. Towing, fueling, starting, and de-icing the planes all had to be done by hand; sometimes several mechanics had to run alongside the plane to hold its tail aloft on take-off.

In his spare time, Yakovlev worked to build his first powered aircraft with funds from the All-Union Voluntary Society for Support of the Air Force (Osoaviakhim). He was also assisted by his fellow enthusiasts and mechanics from the Moscow Central Airfield where he worked. The biplane's first flight was on May 12, 1927, the happiest day of Yakovlev's life. Not only was the design successful, it later set two world records for sports airplanes: non-stop flight distance (1420 km) and longest time aloft (15.5 hours). On the success of this design, Yakovlev was finally accepted into the Air Force Academy, where he continued designing and building.

After graduating in 1931, Yakovlev was assigned to work on the I-5 fighter, to be the fastest airplane of its day. Yakovlev persuaded the technical commission that the design would be faster as a monoplane. The completed plane flew ten kph faster than its goal speed of 320 kph, but a design error forced the plane to make a precarious crash landing during official testing. Yakovlev was forbidden to design any more aircraft.

In pleading his case, Yakovlev so impressed a bureaucrat with his four-place monoplane, capable of landing in a small field next to a *dacha,* that he was not only allowed to continue his work, he was given his own plant: a bed factory on the Leningradsky Prospekt in Moscow. The unfortunate incident, however, was mirrored in 1935, when another important Soviet designer, Ilyushin, had to make a forced landing in a swift three-seat liaison plane designed by Yakovlev. Yakovlev's reputation survived: the fault was with the mechanic, who had not filled the engine with oil.

The first product at the Yakovlev plant was the UT-2, a fast, two-seat monoplane trainer which won first place in a 5000-km tour of the Soviet Union in 1935. Another trainer, the UT-1, was designed later that year; the two models were built by the thousands.

Yakovlev recalled being visited by the already legendary designer Andrei Tupolev, who watched the test flights of Yakovlev's sports planes such as the UT-1 and UT-2. The UT-2 was later developed into the Yak-18, modified for improved spin characteristics, which was popular throughout the 1970s and 1980s and resumed production in 1993.

The success of these designs enhanced the reputation of Yakovlev and his crew, and a large, well-furnished factory was built on the site of their former workshops. Ahead of its day, the plant was spacious and well-lighted, featured a non-smoking atmosphere, and banned separate offices for supervisors. Designers also supervised the production of the parts they were responsible for. Yakovlev's first fighter, the Yak-1, began production in 1939 and earned the designer an incredible reward from Stalin: the Order of Lenin, an automobile, and 100,000 rubles.

During this period, Yakovlev built and tested the work of other Soviet design bureaus (known as OKBs, for opytno-konstruktorskoye byuro) including the MiG-3 fighter (Mikoyan and Gurevich), the Il-2 and Il-4 attack aircraft (Ilyushin), and the Pe-2 and Pe-8 bombers (Petlyakov). During a prewar tour of Europe, Yakovlev visited several European manufacturers, including Bleriot, Renault-Cauldron, de Havilland, Fiat, Messerschmitt, Heinkel, and Focke-Wulf.

The German invasion in 1941 necessitated increased production, which was hindered by the gargantuan task of evacuating the entire Yak design bureau and plant to Kamensk-Uralska, a thousand miles away. However, the thousands of employees were again working within a week of arrival.

Several new fighter designs were introduced during the war, meeting needs for a faster trainer (Yak-7) and for increased range (Yak-9), armament (Yak-9T), and speed (Yak-3). Approximately 30,000 of these types (two-thirds of Soviet fighter production) were manufactured during the war; 4,848 of these were Yak-3s.

The design bureau's first jet was the single-engine Yak-15, which was essentially a Yak-3 with a liquid jet engine installed. In 1947 this became the first Soviet jet plane to enter operational service in the Red Air Force. Another postwar product was the Yak-16, a ten-seat passenger plane closely resembling the Douglas DC-3/C-47.

In 1952 Yak was assigned the daunting test of designing, building, and testing a twin-engine 24-passenger aircraft in one year. This was multiplied by the fact that the aircraft in question was a helicopter, almost totally out of the group's expertise. Technical problems, such as cooling the engines of a stationary aircraft and minimizing vibration, took months of experience gained from sometimes heartbreaking testing to overcome.

The company produced other diverse products after the war, from ground attack aircraft to airliners. The Yak-40, a short-range, 32 passenger trijet, entered service in 1968 and was the first Soviet aircraft certified by American airworthiness standards. It remained popular; in 1992, 600 out of 1000 produced were still being operated, 450 of those in the CIS. In the 1990s an upgrade program was planned to convert the existing Yak-40s to a twin-engine business jet configuration. The Yak-42, a medium-range, 120-passenger trijet, was introduced in 1980, when production of the Yak-40 ceased. By 1992, 140 had been produced; 120 remained in service in the CIS. It gained a reputation as the quietest, most efficient, and most dependable Soviet jetliner. Yakovlev continued to produce approximately twenty per year in the early 1990s, and planned a freighter version, the Yak-42T. Cuba bought four Yak-42s in 1990 and China bought eight in 1991. India, Italy, Iran, Peru, and some Balkan states also expressed interest.

Aleksandr Yakovlev died at the age of 83 on August 22, 1989, a time of upheaval in the Soviet aircraft industry. Even before the bloodless revolution of 1992, many Soviet companies were developing joint ventures with Western firms. After the coup attempt in August 1991, the Soviet Ministry of Aviation Industry was disbanded, leaving the companies with much greater autonomy. At the same time, the loss of government price controls, subsidies, and orders left many companies scrambling for survival. Many factories were converted to produce civilian rather than military planes, and many others were forced to produce consumer goods (even pots and pans), which at this time represented approximately 40 percent of the output of Soviet aircraft plants. Although Yakovlev continued working on numerous aviation projects, it also found itself designing railway cars.

The design bureaus themselves tended to reject the idea of consolidation or joint ventures. Yakovlev was more open to cooperation among the other OKBs and with foreign companies, as its general designer, Aleksandr N. Dondukov, told *Aviation Week & Space Technology*. The company was already working on joint proposals with Antonov, Mikoyan, Sukhoi, and Ilyushin before the Soviet empire dissolved. It had also formed the alliance known as ''Skorost'' (Russian for ''speed'') with airframe manufacturing plants in Saratov, Smolensk, and Irkutsk and the ZMKB Progress engine design and Zaporozhye engine manufacturing plants, among others. Although the design bureau employed about 4,000, another five times as many workers constructed the planes.

This association reversed the Soviet tendency to maintain separate manufacturing facilities, which may have produced the designs of several different OKBs. The goal was a Western-style organization capable of performing all the steps of production, from research and development through after-sales support. The factories themselves were also obligated to provide the OKBs with a critical source of income (about five percent of the sale price of each order) to replace dwindling government subsidies, in order that they in turn might continue to produce new models.

Aleksandr Dondukov, who assumed leadership of the OKB in January, 1991, implemented its reorganization. According to *Aviation Week & Space Technology,* his goal was a single, privatized company capable of designing, manufacturing, marketing, and servicing its aircraft. The company would be known as the ''Yakovlev Air Corporation.'' To this end, several former Aeroflot maintenance factories were approached for inclusion in a joint stock company that would number 60,000 employees, 4,000 comprising the Yakovlev OKB itself. Dondukov assumed the role of Chairman of Yak Corporation.

While the volatility of Russian politics frightened many Western investors and regional conflicts hindered privatization, several factors weighed in Yakovlev's favor. The company had earned a reputation for versatility, and its expertise in short take-off/vertical landing technology left it with a marketable commodity. In fact, the only other company with extensive experience in this area was British Aerospace, which had acquired Hawker Aviation and its Harrier ''jump jet'' program. Although the Russian government Yakovlev's Yak-141 V/STOL aircraft had been designed for Navy use, in 1995 the American manufacturer Lockheed Martin, unable to use British Aerospace due to its long-term alliance with McDonnell Douglas, approached Yakovlev to help it field a bid for the U.S. Joint Advanced Strike Technology contract. Lockheed Martin particularly valued the company's computer modeling software. India and China also expressed interest in a joint V/STOL venture.

The fact that by 1991, 50 percent of the company's work already involved civil aviation helped as well. For a long time, the company had strived to reached Western standards: the Yak-40 gained U.S. and European certification in the early 1970s, making it the first Soviet airliner to do so (and the only one to do so for at least twenty years).

The Skorost group was negotiating with Hyundai in 1992. Israeli Aircraft Industries (IAI) was also negotiating with Yakovlev for possible cooperation on Yakovlev's new Yak-42M transport and its unmanned aircraft. Yakovlev offered a skilled workforce at a fraction the rate of Israel's: $30 to $40 per month in 1993. Another project under development in the mid-1990s was the Yak-48, a four to 19-seat jet also known as the IAI Galaxy.

The company was working on several other diverse products in the 1990s. Its largest civil project was the Yak-42M, a fly-by-wire three-engined transport with a maximum range of approximately 4,000 km (2500 miles) and a capacity of over 150 passengers. The company pinned much of its hopes on the Yak-46, based on the Yak-42M transport. It studied two- and three-engined versions.

Dondukov sought to form a unique association of approximately ten operators to finance the development of the Yak-46. In another innovative development, the company created the Yakovlev Air Service, comprised of a model fleet of four airplanes, in order to help the company better understand the needs of its air carrier customers.

Smaller projects included two general aviation aircraft, the Yak-112 four-seater and the Yak-58 multipurpose six-seater; the Yak-56 trainer to replace the Yak-52; the Yak-55M, an improvement of its aerobatic plane and the Yak-54, a trainer version; and the Shmel (''bumblebee''), a remote-controlled surveillance aircraft. The Yak-112, a high-wing, single-engine plane, incorporated American (Allied Signal) avionics and American (Teledyne) engines. Plans to fit domestic versions of the plane with Russian avionics and engines were canceled due to a lack of supplies. The company reported initial sales to CIS governments and private customers.

In 1993 Yakovlev OKB announced plans for a twin-engine business jet, the Yak-77, to be equipped with Western (Collins) avionics. The Yak-77 would boast a long range (10,000 km or 6,200 miles) and would undercut its primary competitor, the (French) Dassault Falcon 9000. The same year, Aermacchi of Italy announced its involvement in Yakovlev's bid (the Yak-130) to produce an advanced twinjet military trainer for the Russian government. Aermacchi, also experienced in building military trainers, would market the Yak-130 in the West. A version powered by a Western engine was being planned, as well as an armed attack version.

The company known for its innovation in design, marketing, and finance made one of its most unique offerings by revisiting its history. After the only surviving Yak-3 was shown at an airshow in Santa Monica, California, the Gunnell Company (USA) placed an order for new Yak-3s to sell to aviation enthusiasts and museums. Aircraft of this era had soared in price: an original British Spitfire could sell for more than $1 million. Twenty Yak-3s, equipped with American engines and propellers, were made in 1993; the first two sold at auction for $450,000 each.

Further Reading

Covault, Craig, ''Russia Debates Doctrine, Bomber, Fighter Decisions,'' *Aviation Week & Space Technology,* May 31, 1993, p. 23.
Dawson, Dorothy, ''There's Life Yet in the Round Engine,'' *Professional Engineering,* April 20, 1994, p. 16.
Dodds, Henry, ''Soviet Aviation: States of Chaos,'' *Interavia Aerospace Review,* November, 1991, pp. 14–15.

Duffy, Paul, "Design and Production: Finding Common Ground," *Air Transport World*, August, 1993, pp. 81–83.

"Italy Joins Yak-130," *Aviation Week & Space Technology*, June 28, 1993, p. 60.

Lambert, Mark, ed., *Jane's All the World's Aircraft, 1994–95*, New York: Jane's Publishing Co., 1994.

Morrocco, John D., "Lockheed Martin Taps Yakovlev for STOVL Skill," *Aviation Week & Space Technology*, June 19, 1995, pp. 74–77.

——, "Soviets Grope for Order with New Industry Alliances," *Aviation Week & Space Technology*, November 18, 1991, 42–44.

——, "Yakovlev Banks on New Transports to Ensure Design Bureau's Survival," *Aviation Week & Space Technology*, November 18, 1991, pp. 50–51.

"New From Old," *Air Transport World*, August 1993, p. 104.

O'Leary, Michael, "Gee, I Could've Had a Yak!" *Air Progress*, December, 1994, pp. 31–38.

"Russia to Test New Trainers," *Aviation Week & Space Technology*, June 26, 1995, p. 26.

Rybak, Boris, "Russia in Final Phase of Trainer Competition," *Aviation Week & Space Technology*, September 5, 1994, pp. 142–47.

——, and Jeffrey M. Lenorovitz, "Confusion Reigns in Trainer Contests," *Aviation Week & Space Technology*, September 12, 1994, p. 43.

"Two Russian Plants to Build Yak-112," *Aviation Week & Space Technology*, February 8, 1993, p. 52.

Yakovlev Aircraft, Moscow: A. S. Yakovlev Design Bureau, n.d.

Yakovlev, Aleksandr Sergeyevich, *Sovyetski samolety: Kratkii ocherk* (Soviet Aircraft: A Brief Outline). Moscow: Nauka, 1979.

——, *Rasskazy aviakonstruktora*, translated by Albert Zdornykh as *Notes of an Aircraft Designer*, Moscow: Foreign Languages Publishing House, 1960; reprint, New York: Arno Press, 1972.

—Frederick C. Ingram

Abercrombie & Fitch Co.

Four Limited Parkway East
P.O. Box 182168
Columbus, Ohio 43218-2168
U.S.A.
(614) 577-6500
Fax: (614) 577-6565

Wholly Owned Subsidiary of The Limited, Inc.
Incorporated: 1904
Sales: $165 million (1994)
Employees: 1,000
SICs: 5611 Men and Boys Clothing & Accessory Stores;
    5621 Women's Clothing Stores; 5632 Women's
    Accessory & Specialty Stores; 5947 Gift, Novelty &
    Souvenir Shops

During the first half of the 20th century Abercrombie & Fitch Co. was the definitive store for America's sporting elite, outfitting big-game hunters, fishermen, and other adventurers. After the chain went bankrupt in 1977, Oshman's Sporting Goods revived the Abercrombie & Fitch name but shifted its focus to more contemporary sporting goods and a wider array of apparel for men and women. The Limited, Inc., after acquiring the company in 1988, eliminated sporting goods entirely.

The Early Years

Abercrombie & Fitch Co. was founded in 1892 in New York City by David T. Abercrombie and Ezra H. Fitch. Abercrombie, a former prospector, miner, trapper, and railroad surveyor or engineer, owned a small shop and factory producing camping equipment in lower Manhattan. Fitch, one of his customers, was a successful lawyer in Kingston, New York, but the outdoors was his chief interest.

The partners were ill matched. Fitch was the visionary of the two, anticipating a clientele far broader than merely those who camped out in the course of earning a living. Furthermore, both men were hot-tempered. Following the latest of many long and violent arguments, Abercrombie resigned in 1907 to return to manufacturing camping equipment. Fitch continued with other partners. In 1909 he mailed out 50,000 copies of a 456-page catalogue. Since they cost a dollar each to produce, they almost bankrupted the company, but the subsequent flood of orders justified the expense. In 1917 Abercrombie & Fitch moved into a 12-story building on Madison Avenue at East 45th Street, a location the advertising department described as "Where the Blazed Trail Crosses the Boulevard." It included a luxuriously furnished log cabin that Fitch made his town house, with an adjoining casting pool.

By this time Abercrombie & Fitch's reputation as purveyor to the sporting elite already was well established. It had equipped Theodore Roosevelt for an African safari and also outfitted, or was soon going to outfit, polar expeditions led by Roald Amundsen and Admiral Richard Byrd and flights made by Charles Lindbergh and Amelia Earhart. Every president from Roosevelt to Gerald Ford eventually would buy something from the store.

Roaring Twenties and Depression Thirties

Fitch retired in 1928, selling his interest in the company to his brother-in-law, James S. Cobb, who became president, and an employee, Otis L. Guernsey, who became vice-president. In his first year at the helm, Cobb acquired a similar New York business, Von Lengerke & Detmold, respected for its European-made sporting guns and fishing tackle, and Von Lengerke & Antoine, the Chicago branch, which became a subsidiary of Abercrombie & Fitch but continued until 1959 under its own name. In 1930 Cobb bought Griffin & Howe, a gunsmith shop. The merchandise that Von Lengerke & Detmold and Griffin & Howe had in stock was added to the Madison Avenue store.

By this time Abercrombie & Fitch was selling outdoor and sporting equipment not only for hunting, fishing, camping, and exploration, but also for skating, polo, golf, and tennis. It also carried a variety of outdoor clothing, boots, and shoes for both men and women and cameras, pocket cutlery, and indoor games. In the 1920s Abercrombie & Fitch became the epicenter of the burgeoning mah-jongg craze and *the* place in New York to thumb one's nose at Prohibition by purchasing a hip flask. Also during the 1920s, Abercrombie & Fitch opened a summer-only store in Hyannis, Massachusetts, for the yachting set. Net sales and income, rising steadily in this decade, reached a record $6.3 million and $548,000, respectively, in 1929.

These figures would not be topped in the next decade. Sales, in the grip of the Great Depression, fell to $2,598,925 in fiscal year 1933 (ending January 31, 1933), when a loss of $521,118 was recorded, on top of a loss of $241,211 the previous year. During this period, Guernsey's negotiations with the firm's creditors probably saved it from collapse. Subsequent years were profitable, and in 1938 Abercrombie & Fitch resumed paying dividends. It also established golf and shooting schools in the store.

By 1939 Abercrombie & Fitch was calling itself "The Greatest Sporting Goods Store in the World." It boasted the world's largest and most valuable collection of firearms and the widest assortment of fishing flies obtainable anywhere (15,000 in all) to accompany its array of rods, reels, and other fishing tackle. Riders, dog fanciers, skiers, and archers all found every conceivable type of gear. Guns and camping and fishing equipment accounted for 30 percent of the New York store's sales volume in 1938. Sales of clothing, shoes, and furnishings accounted for 45 percent. Inventory on hand was valued at about 40 percent of annual sales, an extremely high ratio that reflected Abercrombie & Fitch's readiness to meet its customers' demands. Catalogue mail orders accounted for about ten percent of business.

Abercrombie & Fitch in Midcentury

Net profit during the 1940s was highest in fiscal year 1947, when it reached $682,894, which turned out to be an all-time record. In 1958 Abercrombie & Fitch opened a store in San Francisco. Soon after, it added small winter-only stores in Palm Beach and Sarasota, Florida, and summer stores in Bayhead, New Jersey, and Southampton, New York. Guernsey, who had succeeded Cobb as president, explained his firm's mission at this time in frankly elitist terms: "The Abercrombie & Fitch type does not care about the cost; he wants the finest quality."

The New York store remained, of course, the company's flagship. At the close of the 1950s the main floor sported heads of buffalo, caribou, moose, elk, and other big game, stuffed fish of spectacular size, and elephant's-foot wastebaskets. Here were sold a variety of contraptions for indoor and outdoor pursuits. One corner held dog and cat items. The basement was given over to the shooting range, while the mezzanine contained paraphernalia for skindiving, archery, skiing, and lawn games. Floors two through five were reserved for clothing suitable for any terrain or climate. On floor six was a picture gallery and bookstore concentrating on sporting themes, a watch repair facility, and the golf school, complete with a resident pro. On the seventh floor, the gun room, besides more stuffed game heads, held about 700 shotguns and rifles, constituting the most lavish assemblage of sporting firearms on earth. The eighth floor was devoted to fishing, camping, and boating, and reserved a desk for the company's fly- and bait-casting instructor, who gave lessons at the pool on the roof. He also handled mail and telephone inquiries on fishing, hunting, and skiing. The

fishing section alone stocked about 48,000 flies and 18,000 lures.

In fiscal 1960, net sales rose to a record $16.5 million, but net profit fell for the fourth straight year, to $185,649. The next year net sales fell below $15.5 million, and net profit dropped again, to $124,097. Nevertheless, Guernsey's successor as president, John H. Ewing, saw no cause for alarm, rejecting the idea of a budget shop or "splash ads for storewide sales." He told a *Business Week* interviewer in 1961 that Abercrombie & Fitch enjoyed a special niche "by sticking to our knitting; by not trying to be all things to all people."

A Disastrous Decade: 1968–1977

During the 1960s Abercrombie & Fitch opened new stores in Colorado Springs; Short Hills, New Jersey; Bal Harbour, Florida; and Troy, Michigan, a suburb of Detroit. It also opened small shops in other stores. And in 1968, a year in which riots in the ghettos, protests against the war in Vietnam, and the assassinations of Martin Luther King and Robert Kennedy seemed to be tearing the country apart, Abercrombie & Fitch was finally ready to shake up its way of doing business by holding a warehouse sale. More than 90,000 bemused customers sifted through the Manhattan store one summer day for bargains that included pop-up tents bought so far in the past that no one remembered how to pop them up, boots made of long-haired goatskin hide, miniature antique cannons, leather baby elephants, and Yukon dog sleds.

In early 1970 the store held another sale. A horde of hopefuls turned up to seize such bargains as a 15-foot inoperative hovercraft for $3 and eight $100 surfboards for $17 each. An offbeat newspaper advertising campaign followed that featured a single item, such as hunting shoes, accompanied by diagrams and copy that overwhelmed the reader with product information. If these antics indicated a measure of desperation, it was because Abercrombie & Fitch had recorded a loss of more than $500,000 in the latest fiscal year. In October 1970 William Humphreys, the new company president, said the ads would be changed and sales would cease because the people who showed up were not Abercrombie & Fitch's kind of customer.

In the ensuing years, Humphreys, a former Lord & Taylor executive, concentrated on cutting the company budget, improving inventory control and credit practices, and expanding into the suburbs. A new Abercrombie & Fitch store opened in Oak Brook, Illinois, north of Chicago. To win a broader range of clientele, the New York store moved its expensive sailboats upstairs from the main floor, expanded its gift and sportswear lines, added a discount clothing shop on the tenth floor, and hired new buyers for women's wear. Nevertheless, the company continued to lose money under Humphreys and his successor, Hal Haskell, its chief stockholder.

In August 1976, after a year in which the company had lost $1 million, Abercrombie & Fitch filed for Chapter 11 bankruptcy. When it closed its doors for good in November 1977, post-mortems pointed out the obvious: the company had failed to make the transition from supplying fat-cat sportsmen of the old school to the skiers, bikers, and backpackers of the 1970s. One advertising man described management as "ossified," and another said company officers had no faith in television's ability to draw in customers even after its first TV commercials, in 1969, filled the store.

The Oshman Decade: 1978–1987

Oshman's Sporting Goods, a Houston-based chain, bought the Abercrombie & Fitch name, trademark, and mailing list in 1978 and opened a store in 1979 under the A&F name in Beverly Hills, California. Featuring a 52-page catalogue and eclectic merchandise, including exercise machines, Harris-tweed jackets, and $70 pith helmets, it also outfitted actor Jack Lemmon for an Alaskan fishing trip and Dodger baseball star Steve Garvey for grouse hunting in Minnesota. A bigger Dallas store opened in 1980, complete with $40,000 elephant guns and an Abercrombie Runabout sports convertible for $20,775.

Abercrombie & Fitch returned to New York City in 1984, opening in the renovated South Street Seaport area of lower Manhattan. By the end of 1986 the chain had grown to 26 stores, including a second Manhattan outlet in midtown's glitzy Trump Tower. Net sales reached an estimated $40 million to $45 million in 1985. The Oshman-owned Abercrombie & Fitch chain stocked relatively few hunting and fishing supplies or exotic items, concentrating on exercise machines, tennis rackets, golf clubs, and other paraphernalia of more contemporary interest, much of it designed exclusively for the chain. Men's and women's clothing departments featured business and casual dress as well as sportswear, and the gift departments offered an array of goods, including gourmet edibles.

An upbeat assessment of the new Abercrombie & Fitch by *Chain Store Age Executive* in September 1986 was followed by a more skeptical appraisal by *Forbes* six months later, which described the chain's merchandise as a hodgepodge of unrelated items and concluded, "Sometimes it is better to bury the dead than to try reviving them." *Forbes* estimated sales for fiscal 1986 at $48 million and profits at "a so-so $1.5 million."

Expansion in the 1990s

In January 1988 The Limited, Inc. acquired 25 of the existing 27 Abercrombie & Fitch stores from Oshman's for about $45 million in cash. The organization was moved to corporate headquarters in Columbus, Ohio, and the inventory was cleared out. A stronger emphasis was placed on apparel, with 60 to 65 percent of the merchandise men's sportswear and furnishings, 20 to 25 percent women's wear, and the remaining 15 to 20 percent gifts, including grooming products and nature books. "We can't get caught up in guns and fishing rods," the chain's president, Sally Frame-Kasaks, a former women's-wear executive, told a *Daily News Record* reporter. Nearly all the goods were midpriced and bore an A&F label.

When Frame-Kasaks became chairman and chief executive officer of Ann Taylor in February 1992, she was succeeded as president of Abercrombie & Fitch by Michael Jeffries, a clothing merchandising executive. At this time the chain had 36 stores credited with annual sales of about $50 million. Sales grew to $85 million in 1992, $111 million in 1993, and $165 million in 1994. There were 67 Abercrombie & Fitch stores at the end of January 1995, compared to 49 a year earlier. A target of 102 stores, mostly in malls, was set for the end of 1995. The Abercrombie & Fitch division established new records for merchandise margin rate and profitability during 1994.

Further Reading

"Abercrombie & Fitch," *Fortune*, July 1939, pp. 124, 230, 232, 234.
"Abercrombie's Misfire," *Time*, August 23, 1976, p. 55.
"Caterer to the Outdoor Man," *Business Week*, December 16, 1961, pp. 84–86, 89.
"New Life for Troubled Chains," *Chain Store Age Executive*, September 1986, pp. 21, 24.
Palmieri, Jean E., "Abercrombie & Fitch Aim: 100 Units; $300M Sales," *Daily News Record*, June 14, 1991, p. 7.
Paris, Ellen, "Endangered Species?" *Forbes*, March 9, 1987, pp. 136–137.
Sayre, Joel, "The Twelve-Story Game Room," *Holiday*, December 1959.

—Robert Halasz

Allianz ⊕

Allianz Aktiengesellschaft Holding

Königinstrasse 28
D-80802 Munich 44
Germany
(89) 3 80 00
Fax: (89) 34 99 41

Public Company
Incorporated: 1890 as Allianz Versicherungs-Aktien-
    Gesellschaft
Employees: 68,000
Total Assets: DM 255.13 billion (1994)
Stock Exchanges: Berlin Bremen Düsseldorf Frankfurt
    Hamburg Hanover Munich Stuttgart London Zürich
    Geneva Basel
SICs: 6311 Life Insurance; 6321 Accident & Health
    Insurance; 6324 Hospital & Medical Service Plans;
    6331 Fire, Marine & Casualty Insurance; 6351 Surety
    Insurance; 6411 Insurance Agents, Brokers &
    Services; 6531 Real Estate Agents & Managers; 6719
    Offices of Holding Companies, Not Elsewhere
    Classified

In terms of gross premium income, Allianz Aktiengesellschaft Holding is the largest insurer in Europe and the second-largest insurer worldwide, behind only Japan's Nippon Life. In addition to its number one position in Germany, Allianz is the largest insurer in Hungary, the second-largest in Italy, the fourth-largest in Austria, and the fifth-largest in Switzerland. It is also a leading insurer in the United States through such subsidiaries as Allianz Life of North America and Fireman's Fund Insurance Company. Through a network of subsidiaries in 53 countries, more than 43 percent of Allianz's premium income comes from outside Germany.

The company was founded as Allianz Versicherungs-Aktien-Gesellschaft in 1890 by Carl Thieme, director of the Munich Reinsurance Company, and the private banker Wilhelm Finck, at the time when the German economy had gotten back into its stride after a long depression and was entering the

second phase of its industrial revolution. Taking advantage of the rapid spread of mechanization in the workplace and the steeply rising number of industrial and traffic accidents, Thieme and Finck began by concentrating on accident and liability insurance. From the 1890s until World War I, however, Allianz grew and prospered mainly through freight insurance, which with reinsurance has been fundamental to the Allianz story from its beginning. In the view of leading experts of the time, the freight insurance market was very overcrowded, but Paul von der Nahmer, Allianz's second company chairman who led the firm from 1894 with Carl Thieme and from 1904 alone, spotted the great possibilities offered by the rapid expansion in the volume of German trade. In 1913, when Allianz had already become by far the largest German freight insurer, this division produced almost 45 percent of the firm's premium income.

Before World War I, Allianz had already begun to extend its scope, although it was still far from offering a full composite range. In 1900 it received the first German license to sell plant insurance, and in 1911 it was also licensed to insure against mechanical breakdowns, a service available exclusively from Allianz until 1924. For three decades the role played in the firm's business by these two classes of insurance did not increase, but Allianz's expertise in this area due to its early involvement is one reason for the firm's present undisputed position as market leader in the field of engineering—that is, mechanical, plant, and equipment—insurance. In 1905 Allianz included direct fire insurance in its list of benefits.

Allianz's advance from medium size to the rank of largest insurance group in Germany took place within a few years, between the end of World War I and the mid-1920s. Before the war the Berlin-based firm had drawn only about 20 percent of its premium income from abroad. Afterward, like all German insurers, it was cut off from international markets almost completely but later, in a rise unparalleled in the history of German insurance, it came to dominate the whole industry. The foundation for this achievement had been laid by Paul von der Nahmer with his sound and farsighted financial strategy. As one of the few people to assess accurately the effects that war would have on the future of Germany's currency and its insurance industry, he had taken early steps to provide Allianz with substantial foreign currency reserves that helped it to achieve an almost proverbial stability amidst the chaos of inflation. After his death in 1921 his successor, Dr. Kurt Schmitt, used these financial reserves to enable Allianz to achieve the highest turnover of all German insurers.

In 1917, at the age of 31, Schmitt was made executive managing director. His innovations were to lead the company to the top of the German insurance industry and to a major global presence. He attempted to establish a foothold in all markets, to expand into all classes of insurance, and to extend the company's international activities. The conditions of the Treaty of Versailles had stood in the way of the latter aim, but his efforts to make the firm active in all classes of insurance were therefore all the more successful. In 1918 he established the motor insurance company Kraft-Versicherungs-AG (Motor Insurance AG), the first large company in Germany to specialize in motor vehicle risks. Immediately after the war ended he also sought collaboration with large life insurance companies. When these negotiations unexpectedly broke down early in 1922, Schmitt, by then chairman of the board of Allianz, founded within the space of ten days the Allianz Lebensversicherungsbank-AG (Allianz Life-Assurance Bank AG), which by 1927 had grown into the largest life insurance company in Europe.

During the hyperinflation of 1922–23, numerous mergers speeded the firm on its way to the top. Specialist insurance companies were finding it particularly hard to survive, and the German insurance market was hit by a wave of mergers. Allianz concentrated on absorbing only those companies that would fill existing gaps in its own range, both of services and of regions served.

In the years of rapid currency depreciation, Allianz's merger policy differed markedly from that of other companies. It succeeded because it was directed towards maximum rationalization. Whereas in other groups mergers tended to result in little more than a hodgepodge of individual companies, the Berlin group immediately welded all its member companies into an organic whole, created a new overall structure, and finally undertook radical rationalization at home and abroad. The latter task was achieved principally by Hans Hess, who had joined Allianz in 1918.

Until the early 1920s Allianz, in common with all other German insurance companies, employed outdated administration and organization techniques. The Allianz board was the first to realize that combating the effects of inflation and employee rationalization would have to be top priorities. Hess succeeded in introducing the basic principles of scientific management into the insurance business. By means of an assortment of technical and, even more importantly, organizational improvements, he managed a significant increase in productivity and a reduction in costs. He spread a network of branch offices across Germany and ensured that the latest equipment was installed. He replaced the old, strongly independent insurance agents, each working for several companies covering the most varied types of insurance, with agents trained in composite insurance and working solely for Allianz. He also set up a system of incentive schemes for employees, run with an element of sporting competition. Alongside this initiative came the extension of the social installations and services provided for staff. These measures gave the firm great stability in periods of crisis. Even during the world depression Allianz was able to maintain its volume of premiums and considerably increase the number of personnel.

Whereas during the inflation period the firm had concentrated on broadening its scope, after the stabilization of the currency in 1923–24 it set its sights on growth in volume. It was engaged in a major expansion of its capacities when in the mid-1920s a new wave of amalgamation policies hit German industry, and large groups formed for chemicals manufacture, electrical engineering, and heavy industry gave rise to a significant increase in risk potential.

In 1927 the group surprised the public by announcing a merger with the famous Stuttgarter Verein Versicherungs-AG, the market leader in accident and liability insurance. It was the largest merger to date in the history of German insurance. When in the summer of 1929 the Frankfurter Allgemeine Versicherungs-AG, the second-largest insurance group in Germany, collapsed as the result of illegal, loss-making noninsurance deals, Allianz decided within 24 hours to meet all of the Frankfurter's obligations to its clients. With Münchener Rückversicherungs-AG, Allianz immediately founded the Neue Frankfurter Allgemeine Versicherungs-AG to assume the Frankfurter's liabilities. This dramatic rescue operation saved the whole insurance industry from a serious loss of public confidence and from state intervention in its affairs.

The industry could not, however, escape government interference after Adolf Hitler came to power in 1933 and enlisted savers and insurance policy holders in his secret financial preparations for war. From 1935 onwards the regime obliged insurance companies to increase their subscriptions to government loans; from the summer of 1942 three-quarters of their investment capital was affected in this way.

It was in an attempt to protect the industry from this sort of encroachment that in 1933, after much hesitation, Kurt Schmitt agreed to become trade minister in Hitler's second cabinet. He was convinced he would be able to restrain National Socialism and lead it in the direction he wished to go. A few weeks were enough to make him regret his action; he gave up the attempt, and after a year took the first opportunity to withdraw from politics. In 1935 he became chairman of the supervisory board of Allianz Lebensversicherungs-AG and in 1938 he was made chairman of the board of directors of Münchener Rück. In 1933 he had been succeeded as chairman of Allianz Versicherungs-AG by his former deputy, Hans Hess, who during the whole of the Third Reich made no secret—even in public—of his profound dislike of Nazism and took part in the resistance movement against Hitler.

During the 1920s and 1930s Allianz expanded its range, venturing into completely new areas of insurance. Its innovations in the field of engineering insurance were particularly forward-looking. It was the first in Germany to offer installation and guarantee insurance, in 1923, and construction and civil engineering insurance, in 1934. While other insurers still saw their role purely and simply in terms of providing financial compensation for loss, Allianz built up an independent technical-advice and loss-prevention service. In 1920, using special engineers, it carried out the first regular inspection of power plants. From 1924 it also published *Der Maschinen-Schaden* (Mechanical Breakdown), a periodical that today continues to combine the utmost practicality with high scientific standards. In 1932 Allianz set up its first materials- and equipment-testing installation, which swiftly became a highly reputed center for loss research. The firm completed its activities in this area in 1938 with the introduction of a fire damage prevention service. Political conditions in the interwar years, however, meant that it could only scratch the surface of its international aspirations.

World War II hit Allianz hard. The head office in Berlin was completely demolished, and since it was situated in the eastern part of the city there could be no question of rebuilding it. The partition of Germany also meant the loss of a large part of its marketing area, together with several of its most successful branch offices. At the end of the war the various specialized sections of the company were scattered all over Germany in various locations. There were no longer any headquarters. With the difficulty of communications between the western zone of Germany and West Berlin, particularly after the Berlin blockade of 1948, it became clear that in the interest of the company as a whole, Berlin must now be ruled out as a future base. The seat of the central management was therefore moved to Munich, and that of Allianz Lebensversicherungs-AG to Stuttgart.

In October 1948 Hess relinquished the chairmanship of the board of management. He was succeeded by Hans Goudefroy, who made it his business to preserve the assets of the Allianz group and its internal stability even after the currency reform of 1948. In the mid-1950s, under his leadership, Allianz completed its second phase of rationalization. The adoption of electronic data processing—in 1956 the board of directors started using one of Europe's earliest computers—is a striking example of the many innovations embraced since then by Allianz. At the same time, by a rapid expansion of its foreign business network, the group regained its leading position in the German insurance market. Such dramatic growth was without precedent in Europe. Outstripping all other insurers, Allianz acquired a presence in every part of the Federal Republic of Germany, and owing to its new slogan, ". . . höffentlich Allianz versichert!" (I hope you're insured with Allianz!); created in the mid-1950s, it became known to virtually everybody.

During the 1950s and 1960s Allianz concentrated almost exclusively on the home market, with the emphasis on private insurance, though it did make some advances in the large-risk industrial sector, particularly in the area of engineering insurance. In February 1962, following the premature death of Goudefroy at the end of the preceding year, the chairmanship of the board of management was taken over by Alfred Haase, previously organization manager of the Allianz group. In a smooth transition, Haase carried on the work of his predecessor, further expanding the network of agents, developing the domestic private insurance business, and continuing internal rationalization. During his term of office the Allianz Allgemeine Rechtsschutzversicherungs-AG (Allianz General Patent Insurance A.G.) was founded; it commenced trading in 1970. Haase also presided over further developments in loss prevention. In 1969 the old testing installation was renamed the Allianz Center for Technology and in 1971 it was enlarged by the creation of the Institute of Motor Vehicle Technology.

At the turn of the 1970s the German insurance industry was faced with new problems, most notably a cost explosion due to steep wage rises throughout the whole economy. In addition a sharp increase in the accident rate had taken the motor insurance sector into the red. Competition throughout the industry was becoming much fiercer too. Although Allianz's turnover continued to climb, net yield began to fall. Into this very difficult situation stepped Wolfgang Schieren, who in 1971 came to the group as managing director. As had happened half a century before under Kurt Schmitt, there began a new phase in the firm's history. Schieren began by ordering a halt to staff recruitment and instigating a radical cost reduction program. While competitors' staff numbers continued to rise, the Munich group was already economizing in order to invest for the future.

A second consequence of Schieren's appointment was that Allianz ceased concentrating its acquisition activities primarily on private insurance and gave equal consideration to large-risk industrial and commercial business. Within a few years the firm became the foremost German concern in this increasingly important sector, in certain areas of which, such as engineering insurance, it became a world leader. Restructuring of the organization of industrial insurance formed part of this new orientation. In 1987 an operation began that was to extend over several years, aimed at simplifying the hitherto complicated classifications of large-risk industrial insurance.

Finally, under Wolfgang Schieren, Allianz evolved from a domestically focused business to an internationally oriented insurer. In 1970 the group's premium income was DM4 billion, only 3.2 percent derived from abroad; by 1989, out of a total income of DM31.8 billion, 40 percent came from foreign premiums. Allianz reacted promptly to the increasing internationalism of German industry as West Germany developed, from the beginning of the 1970s, from being a mere exporter to being a foreign investor. As Allianz expanded its services to industry, it wanted to offer its clients insurance coverage for their foreign investments too. It was realized early on at Allianz's Munich headquarters that dramatic changes were taking place in industry and that an insurer who was active only at a national level could no longer meet the needs of increasingly multinational enterprises.

During the first phase of these foreign activities Allianz tried to gain a foothold in foreign markets mainly by setting up new companies. The Allianz International Insurance Company Ltd. began trading in London in 1975, and similar companies were established in Spain and the Netherlands. In France the Paris board of directors was enlarged. In 1977 the firm ventured into the U.S. market for the first time, setting up the Allianz Insurance Company to deal in property insurance in Los Angeles. This development ended the first phase of Allianz's foreign expansion.

In 1974, constrained by the legal upper limit set for foreign investors, Allianz had bought a 30 percent share in a Brazilian insurance company which from then on traded under the name of Allianz Ultramar. In 1977 the group acquired from Commercial Union of London the Anglo-Elementar-Versicherungs-AG with headquarters in Vienna, and two years later, in the United States, the North American Life and Casualty Company, based in Minneapolis, Minnesota, as well as the Fidelity Union Life Insurance Company of Dallas. In the same period Allianz established a foothold in Australia, and in 1981 it moved into Chile.

The creation of this world network went almost unnoticed by the public until the beginning of the 1980s when Allianz, in a dramatic takeover attempt, tried to obtain a majority holding in the British Eagle Star Insurance Company. By June 1981 the German group had acquired almost 30 percent of Eagle Star's shares. At the end of 1983 there was a battle between Allianz and the conglomerate BAT Industries for the remaining shares. BAT emerged the victor, though Allianz made a profit of £156.5 million by selling off the Eagle Star shares bought in 1981.

In 1986 Allianz did succeed in establishing itself in the United Kingdom, however, when it acquired from BTR plc the Cornhill Insurance Company, founded in 1905. Cornhill's foreign interests afforded, among other advantages, an entry into the developing east Asian market. In 1984 Allianz had already taken a further step towards internationalism with the acquisition of a majority holding in the Riunione Adriatica di Sicurtá (RAS), the second-largest insurance company in Italy. Through RAS's wide foreign network Allianz gained entry into several countries in which it previously had had little or no representation.

Interests were acquired in Argentina, Spain, and Greece, and a new company was formed in Indonesia. In collaboration with local banks, life insurance companies were set up in Spain and Greece. In 1985 Allianz reorganized as Allianz Aktiengesellschaft Holding, to reflect its size and diversity. In September 1989, in the fight for control of the French insurance group VIA/ Rhin et Moselle, Allianz acquired—within the space of a few days—first 50 percent, then 65 percent of the shares as the previous owner, the conglomerate Compagnie de Navigation Mixte, with the help of Allianz managed to fend off a takeover attempt by the state insurance company AGF and the bank Paribas. Another sensational acquisition, this time in Budapest at the end of 1989, was that of a 49 percent interest in Hungary's former state insurance company Hungária Biztositó, which had come into being three years earlier when the state monopoly company was split into two parts. Allianz thus demonstrated its interest in any east European market willing to adapt to the free market economy. Finally, Allianz made a considerable stir at home by buying a 51 percent interest in Deutsche Versicherungs-AG, which was founded on July 1, 1990, to take over the business of the former East German state insurance service. Other German insurers raised objections, to no avail, about the monopolistic nature of the takeover, and about the fire sale price paid—DM270 million (US$162 million). As part of the takeover, Allianz also obtained the right to purchase the other 49 percent of the firm, which Allianz later proceeded to do.

The crowning achievement among all these foreign activities was undoubtedly the US$1.1 billion acquisition of the Firemen's Fund Insurance Company of Novato, California, a U.S. property and casualty insurance group whose 1989 premiums of US$3.4 billion made it the 14th largest insurer in the country. By this one move—which took place in Allianz's centennial year, 1990—the Allianz group almost quadrupled its premium income in the United States. Another significant move came in 1991 when Allianz received a license to sell insurance in Japan, the first German insurer to do so. With this spate of activity, Allianz became the most internationally active insurer in the world.

This unprecedented expansion would not have been possible without group restructuring. The dual functioning of Allianz Versicherungs-AG as a primary insurance company operating in the home market as well as a holding company, proved a hindrance to the expansion of international activities and increased industrial involvement as well as to the marked growth of its intergroup reinsurance company. In June 1985 the direct German property insurance business was transferred to a fully owned subsidiary under the name Allianz Versicherungs-AG (Allianz Insurance AG). The interest in Allianz Lebensversicherungs-AG (Allianz Life Assurance AG) and the foreign subsidiaries remained under the holding company now trading as Allianz AG, which has also taken over the reinsurance business passed on by the Allianz companies. In spite of all the group's business successes and new acquisitions, this reorganization must be seen as the most significant event in Allianz's history since World War II.

Just prior to his retirement, Schieren engineered an alliance with Dresdner Bank, the second-largest bank in Germany, through the purchase of a 23 percent stake in mid-1991. Anticipating the coming elimination of barriers in the banking and insurance markets in Europe, Schieren wished to build a Europe-wide network of banks and insurance offices that would send clients to each other. The move was also seen as a challenge to German financial giant Deutsche Bank, Germany's largest bank and a competitor to Allianz in the insurance industry.

Links between German companies, such as the ones between Allianz and Dresdner, became better known in the early 1990s. For example, both Dresdner Bank and Deutsche Bank each owned ten percent of Allianz. The power of Allianz, however, was shown by its US$230 billion in investments, including an average ten percent stake in every public company in Germany. Most of these investments were credited to Schieren, who upon his retirement in October 1991 was succeeded by Dr. Henning Schulter-Noelle, former chairman of Allianz Lebensversicherungs.

Schulter-Noelle's first challenge was to stem the hemorrhaging of Allianz's newly acquired East German subsidiary, Deutsche Versicherungs. Thanks in large part to the difficulty of integrating the East German offices into the Allianz network, Allianz suffered its first underwriting loss in two decades, posting a DM1.78 billion (US$1.17 billion) loss in 1992. In response, Allianz reorganized its German operations and cut its East German workforce in half. In 1993 the company took further action by forcing its industrial policyholders to either pay higher premiums, improve risk management, or retain more risk. Through such moves the underwriting losses were reduced to DM1.19 billion in 1993 and to DM348 million in 1994. At the same time, operating results at Deutsche Versicherungs were steadily improving, from a loss of more than DM550 million in 1991 to a loss of just DM38 million in 1994.

In 1994 Allianz increased its capital base more than 6 percent through a share offering. The cash was to be used for further expansion, this time focusing on small and medium-sized insurance firms in Europe that did not feel they would be able to deal with the coming deregulation of the European market. The first such acquisition occurred later that year when Allianz purchased the direct insurance units of Swiss Reinsurance Company. In the purchase, Allianz gained the Swiss-based Elvia group, which propelled Allianz to the number five position in Swiss insurance; Lloyd Adriatico, an Italian insurer particular strong in automobile insurance, which solidified Allianz's number two position in insurance in Italy; and Vereinte, a German insurance company which Allianz had to divest because of antitrust regulations.

In the United States, Allianz's Fireman's Fund acquisition was suffering from a property and casualty market that continued to be depressed. Although premium volume increased a modest 6.6 percent in 1994, earnings were greatly affected by catastrophic losses totaling US$116 million, more than US$57 million of which resulted from the January earthquake in Northridge, California, alone. In 1995 Fireman's Fund increased its reserve for environmental claims by US$800 million as a provision against liability damages it might incur as a result of Superfund lawsuits.

Since the company continuing to be nettled by underwriting losses, Allianz Versicherungs announced in mid-1995 that for large risks it would no longer abide by the quasi cartel rating system that held sway in Germany. Allianz's new system would be based on the individual risk of the policyholder, thus leading to reduced premiums for good risks, increased premiums for poor risks, and eliminated policies for the poorest risks. Allianz hoped to realize an underwriting profit within three years of the system's implementation.

With its dominance of the European insurance market and its position as the largest non-Japanese international insurer, Allianz was a powerful company as the 21st century approached. It had achieved steady growth through acquisitions and seemed well-positioned to take advantage of the deregulation of the European financial industries. Some observers had criticized Allianz for favoring growth over profitability, and net income in the early 1990s did in fact fluctuate. Nevertheless, Schulte-Noelle said in 1995 that profits were Allianz's top priority and he would work to make improvements in that area.

Principal Subsidiaries

Allianz Allgemeine Rechtsschutzversicherungs-AG (50%); Allianz Lebensversicherungs-AG (46.5%); Allianz Versicherungs-AG; Bayerische Versicherungsbank AG (45%); Deutsche Krankenversicherung AG; Deutsche Lebensversicherungs-AG; Deutsche Versicherungs-AG; Frankfurter Versicherungs-AG (49.9%); Anglo-Elementar Versicherungs-AG (Austria; 97.2%); Wiener Allianz Lebensversicherungs-AG (Austria; 36%); Wiener Allianz Versicherungs-AG (Austria); DKV International S.A. (Belgium); Allianz pojišt'ovna, a.s. (Czech Republic); Allianz Nordeuropa Forsikringsaktieselskabet (Denmark); Domus Forsikringsaktieselskabet A/S (Denmark); Allianz Via Assurances I.A.R.D.T. (France); Allianz Via Vie Compagnie d'Assurances sur la Vie (France); Compagnie Générale de Prévoyance Société Anonyme de Prévoyance et de Capitalisation (France); Rhin et Moselle Assurances Compagnie d'Assurances sur le Vie Société Anonyme (France); Rhin et Moselle Assurances Compagnie Générale d'Assurances et de Réassurances Société Anonyme (France); Allianz General Insurance Company S.A. (Greece); Allianz Life Insurance Company S.A. (Greece); Hungária Biztosító Rt (Hungary; 55.8%); Cornhill Insurance PLC (Ire-

land); Allianz Pace Assicurazioni e Riassicurazioni S.p.A (Italy; 56.1%); Lloyd Adriatico S.p.A. (Italy); Riunione Adriatica di Sicurtà S.p.A. (Italy); DKV-Luxembourg S.A.; International Reinsurance Company S.A. (Luxembourg); Allianz Nederland N.V. (Netherlands); N.V. Verzekeringsmaatschappij Rijnmond (Netherlands); Portugal Previdente Companhia de Seguros; Ost-West Allianz (Russia); Allianz poist'ov a.s. (Slovakia); Allianz RAS Seguros y Reaseguros S.A. (Spain); Eurovida, S.A. Compañia de Seguros y Reaseguros (Spain); Allianz Continentale Allgemeine Versicherung AG (Switzerland); Allianz Continentale Lebensversicherung AG (Switzerland); Elvia Reiseversicherungs-Gesellschaft (Switzerland); Elvia Schweizerische Lebensversicherungs-Gesellschaft (Switzerland); Elvia Schweizerische Versicherungs-Gesellschaft (Switzerland); Şark Hayat Sigorta A.Ş. (Turkey); Şark Sigorta T.A.Ş. (Turkery); Cornhill Insurance PLC (U.K.); Allianz RAS Argentina S.A. de Seguros Generales; Colón Compañia de Seguros Generales S.A. (Argentina); Allianz-Ultramar Companhia Brasileira de Seguros (Brazil); Allianz Insurance Company of Canada; Trafalgar Insurace Company of Canada; Allianz Bice Compañía de Seguros de Vida S.A. (Chile); Allianz Compañía de Seguros S.A. (Chile); Allianz México S.A. Compañía de Seguros; Allianz Insurance Company (U.S.A.); Allianz Life Insurance Company of North America (U.S.A.); Firemen's Fund Insurance Company (U.S.A.); Jefferson Insurance Company of N.Y. (U.S.A.); Adriatica de Seguros C.A. (Venezuela); Arab International Insurance Company (Egypt); Allianz Cornhill Insurance (Far East) Ltd. (Hong Kong); P.T. Asuransi Allianz Utama Indonesia; Allianz Fire and Marine Insurance Japan, Ltd.; Allianz Insurance of Namibia Ltd.; Allianz Insurance (Singapore) Pte. Ltd.; Allianz Insurance Ltd. (South Africa); The Navakij Insurance Public Company Ltd. (Thailand); Allianz Versicherungs-AG Dubai Branch (United Arab Emirites).

Further Reading

"Allianz, the First of the Few," *Economist*, August 11, 1990, pp. 79–80.

Arps, Ludwig, *Wechselvolle Zeiten: 75 Jahre Allianz Versicherung 1890–1965*, Munich: Allianz-Versicherungs-AG, 1975.

Borscheid, Peter, *100 Jahre Allianz 1890–1990*, Munich: Allianz Aktiengesellschaft Holding, 1990.

Fisher, Andrew, and Ralph Atkins, "Deceptive Image of Anonymity," *Financial Times*, December 15, 1994, p. 25.

Kirk, Don Lewis, "Allianz Goes Own Way in Setting Rates," *Business Insurance*, June 5, 1995, pp. 39–40.

Kirk, Don Lewis, "Allianz to Hike Rates: Policyholders Drafted into War on Underwriting Losses," *Business Insurance*, November 8, 1993, pp. 25, 27.

Kirk, Don Lewis, "Underwriting Loss Triggers Fall in Allianz Stock," *Business Insurance*, August 24, 1992, pp. 23, 25.

Steinmetz, Greg, "Bigger or Better? Allianz Wants Both," *Wall Street Journal*, May 30, 1995, p. A11.

Templeman, John, et. al., "A Challenger for Germany's Heavyweight Banking Title," *Business Week*, August 12, 1991, pp. 36–37.

"A Wholly German Empire," *Economist*, November 2, 1991, pp. 77–78.

—Peter Borscheid
Translated from the German by Olive Classe
—updated by David E. Salamie

American International Group, Inc.

70 Pine Street
New York, New York 10270
U.S.A.
(212) 770-7000
Fax: (212) 425-3499

Public Company
Incorporated: 1967
Employees: 32,000
Total Assets: $114.35 billion (1994)
Stock Exchanges: New York London Tokyo Paris Zürich
    Basel Geneva Lausanne
SICs: 6331 Fire, Marine & Casualty Insurance; 6311 Life
    Insurance; 6411 Insurance Agents, Brokers &
    Services; 6159 Miscellaneous Business Credit
    Institutions; 6719 Offices of Holding Companies, Not
    Elsewhere Classified

American International Group, Inc. (AIG) is a holding company for a network of subsidiaries primarily engaged in insurance and insurance-related activities, including property, casualty, marine, life, and financial services. AIG operates in more than 130 countries and jurisdictions, and its combined revenues make it the largest U.S.-based international insurance organization. The corporation, whose earliest roots were in Asia, has had an active history of mergers, acquisitions, and consolidations, which ultimately resulted in the formation of American International Group.

In 1919 a 27-year-old U.S. businessman, Cornelius Vander Starr, opened a two-room, two-clerk insurance agency in Shanghai and named it American Asiatic Underwriters (AAU). AAU, which later became part of American International Underwriters (AIU), initially served as an underwriter for insurance companies that had established branches in Shanghai. During a trip to New York in 1921 Starr added representation of other U.S. companies to his operations, including the Globe & Rutgers Company. Later that decade Starr brought representa-

tion of the Pittsburgh, Pennsylvania, company, National Union Fire Insurance, into his fold.

Starr's next quest was to gain general life insurance agency powers, but he found no U.S. companies willing to assume the risk because there were no life-expectancy statistics available for the Chinese population. In 1921 Starr overcame this obstacle by forming his own company, Asia Life Insurance Company (ALICO). ALICO's most popular product was a 20-year endowment policy, with rates established on the basis of Starr's personal observation that in general Chinese enjoyed longer life expectancies than their Western counterparts.

In 1926 Starr opened a New York office under the name American International Underwriters to serve as an insurance writer on U.S.-owned risks outside of North America. Like its Chinese counterpart, AIU also served as a general agent for U.S. insurers. By the end of the decade Starr's Chinese operations were seeing modest profits, and branch offices for both general and life insurance had been established throughout the Shanghai region. In 1931 Starr joined British and Chinese businessmen in a partnership and established the International Assurance Company (INTASCO).

AIU established a foundation for Latin American business in 1932 when George Moszkowski, who ran the company's New York office, negotiated the purchase of the Central American and Caribbean portfolios of an American insurer withdrawing from foreign operations. AIU's operations in Central America remained modest throughout the decade.

Before, during, and after World War II, AIU was able to capitalize on world economic and political situations. With much of the world on the brink of war, in 1939 Starr moved his headquarters to New York, temporarily closing the Shanghai office. After hostilities broke out, operations of dominant Italian, German, and British agencies were reduced, and AIU expanded in Central America. In 1940 AIU established a regional headquarters in Cuba, and a half dozen offices in South America soon followed. AIU's Central American business grew with the local economies of these neutral countries during the war years.

At the end of World War II, the Shanghai office was re-opened under the guidance of K. K. Tse. Several profitable years followed until the late 1940s, when the future of foreign activities in Shanghai grew dim. In 1949 key employees and documents were airlifted out of Shanghai and the regional headquarters moved to Hong Kong. In late 1950 operations in China were closed.

Meanwhile, many surrounding countries were recovering from war. With economic improvement underway, AIU entered Japan and West Germany by selling insurance to occupying U.S. troops. AIU's prewar operations in Europe had been limited to small agencies in France, Belgium, and the Netherlands, but postwar conditions, resulting in tight financing for local insurers, placed AIU in a position to expand its European business. At the same time, expansion of American business abroad created opportunities for AIU's "home-foreign" business.

In 1947 Starr began a reorganization designed to revive war-torn operations and lay the groundwork for future growth. Starr's first move was to announce the incorporation of a Philippine arm of the American Life Insurance Company, the Philippine American Life Insurance Company (Philam Life), in 1947. U.S. businessman Earl Carroll was named to head up the new company, which grew quickly, largely through the sale of endowment policies. These policies provided farmers and small merchants with the means to build their savings in a country with few banks. Sales revenue was frequently reinvested in the local economy.

Started as a partnership, INTASCO, which until this time had maintained a relatively small life insurance business, was reorganized in 1948 when Starr took control of the business. He added "American" to the company's name, changed the company's abbreviated name to AIA, and assigned it the Southeast Asian territories of Malaysia, Singapore, and Thailand and the home-base front of Hong Kong.

That same year Starr began uniting his somewhat fragmented network of insurance companies, beginning with the creation of two Bermuda-based entities. The first, American International Underwriters Overseas, Ltd. (AIUO), became the parent of all established AIU agency companies overseas. The second, American International Reinsurance Company, Inc. (AIRCO), was designed to hold companies dealing primarily in life insurance. AIRCO also took control of company investment programs and served as a reinsurer for these subsidiaries. The last of Starr's trio of new organizations was American International Underwriters Association (AIUA), established in 1949 to serve as a partnership of American insurance companies that were represented by AIU. AIUA provided for pooled business in stipulated percentages and shared assets that were kept overseas to meet local regulations.

Perhaps the most dramatic reorganization occurred within Starr's oldest life insurance company, ALICO. After lying dormant for a decade, the company was renamed American Life Insurance Company and assigned the Caribbean, Middle East, and some growing African nations. ALICO marketed life insurance to populations previously not attractive to insurers.

The 1950s were a period of rapid expansion for AIU. Branches were established in Western Europe, the Middle East, north Africa, and Australia. By the end of the decade AIU was operating in 75 countries. The 1950s also marked the emergence of Starr's companies in domestic markets.

In 1952 AIRCO acquired a majority interest in the Globe & Rutgers Insurance Company, a medium-sized American fire insurance company once represented by AIU. A Globe & Rutgers subsidiary, the Insurance Company of the State of Pennsylvania, came with the purchase. Founded in 1794, the Pennsylvania subsidiary was the second-oldest stock insurance company in the United States. American Home Assurance Company, which was founded in 1853, was also included in the package. Globe & Rutgers was later merged with American Home and took its name.

Starr and his colleagues joined the American Home board but left the company largely under old management. Earnings at the new subsidiary fluctuated greatly for several years. A net loss of $1.4 million was reported in 1957, followed by a net profit of better than $950,000 the following year. In an effort to stabilize earnings, AIRCO sold American Home's agency business to another insurer in 1962. That same year Starr named Maurice R. Greenberg as American Home president, and the company formed the American International Life Assurance Company of New York to specialize in term and group insurance. Greenberg had begun his insurance career ten years earlier with Continental Casualty Company. In 1960 he joined American International and was assigned the task of developing an overseas accident and health business.

In leading American Home, Greenberg focused on broker sales, allowing the company to issue its own policies and maintain underwriting control. The company concentrated on commercial and industrial risks, which involved negotiated rather than state-controlled rates. American Home also developed substantial reinsurance facilities in order to cover large shares of major risks and control insurance ratings. Greenberg initiated new products and services such as personal accident insurance, which emphasized deductibles. Meanwhile, American Home avoided medical insurance. The new sales system caught on, offering brokers the high deductibles that traditional insurers avoided but that some large corporations sought in order to cut costs.

During the late 1960s American International's corporate structure began to resemble its present form as it became an important commercial and industrial property and casualty insurer. While a new company organization was being forged through further acquisitions and reorganization, the insurance group began capitalizing on its innovative products and entrance into new markets.

Acquisitions during this period included controlling interests in the National Union Fire Insurance Company of Pittsburgh, Pennsylvania, which had been represented by AIU since 1927, and the New Hampshire Insurance Company. The former, which was threatened by high underwriting losses, was transformed much like American Home, and then linked with it in a pooling agreement. Commerce and Industry Insurance Company, a small property insurer specializing in highly protected risks, and Trans-atlantic Reinsurance Company were also acquired during this period.

The wholly owned American International Group was formed by AIRCO in 1967. AIG represented the beginning of a major corporate reorganization, with the company formed to hold shares of other domestic companies, including American Home and New Hampshire. ALICO was soon added to AIG's holdings. Greenberg was elected president and CEO of AIG in 1967. The following year Starr died, having seen only the beginning of a new era for the insurance empire he had created.

In 1969, after going public, AIG acquired majority interests in National Union, New Hampshire, and American Home, paying for its increased stake in the three companies with AIG stock. In 1970 AIU and its agencies and subsidiaries became wholly owned subsidiaries of AIG.

Throughout the 1960s AIU's overseas business grew, despite the loss of its large Cuban business following Fidel Castro's takeover of that country. Since it had entered most major markets a decade earlier, expansion during this time was limited to growth within areas with established territories. In an effort to strengthen AIG's overseas position, an 18-month program was initiated in 1972 creating a regional system of benefits managers for Europe, Africa, Central America, South America, the Middle East, the Far East, and United States. That same year the AIG subsidiary ALICO became the first foreign-owned company granted a license to sell insurance to Japanese nationals in Japan.

During the early 1970s AIG increased its specialization by forming a number of new groups. Subsidiaries created by AIG during this time included A.I. Credit Corporation to finance general insurance premiums written through both affiliate and nonaffiliate insurers; North American Managers, Inc., to sell insurance in the United States for foreign companies; AIG Oil Rig, Inc., to initiate and manage insurance for offshore oil- and gas-drilling rigs; AIG Risk Management, Inc., to provide worldwide risk management services; AIG Data Center, Inc.; and American International Insurance Company of Ireland, Ltd. During this period AIG also acquired all remaining shares of the New Hampshire and National Union companies.

AIG's profits took off in the 1970s, at a compounded growth rate of roughly 20 percent, with AIG's net income surpassing $50 million by 1975. High premiums in the new market areas of oil rigs and pension-fund management as well as the use of limited-partnership insurance for high risks contributed to the growth.

Consolidation and reorganization continued in 1976, when AIU stopped writing policies for insurance companies it did not own. That same year the company was organized into four broad categories: the foreign general insurance division, the brokerage division of domestic general insurance, the agency division of domestic general insurance, and a life insurance division. The following year the subsidiary Trans-atlantic Reinsurance was reorganized as a major reinsurer, with shares sold to seven other companies. AIG absorbed its parent company, AIRCO, in 1978, completing a nine-year consolidation plan to simplify corporate structure.

In 1979 AIG entered Eastern Europe and initiated joint ventures with state-owned insurers in Hungary, Poland, and Romania. In succeeding years similar operations were started in China and Yugoslavia. At the end of the 1970s AIG had 20 percent annual growth in revenues and had increased its size nearly tenfold. In 1979 AIG reported over $250 million in net income.

During the 1980s AIG ventured into health-care services, and acquired a variety of financial and investment sources as well as real estate holdings. Acquisitions included United Guaranty Corporation, a residential-mortgage insurance company; the Swiss bank Uberseebank A.G.; Ticino Societa d'Assicurazioni Sulla Vita, a Swiss-based life insurer; Southeastern Aviation Underwriters—later renamed AIG Aviation, Inc.—an airlines, aviation, and space-program insurer; and Jurgovan & Blair, a health maintenance organization consulting business. In 1981 AIG, in combination with Presidio Oil Company, purchased a majority interest in 109 natural gas wells.

In 1984 the company reported its first decline in profits, largely due to underwriting losses including those resulting from a major hurricane. Some of AIG's specialty companies, such as AIG Oil Rig, AIG Energy, AIG Entertainment, and AIG Political Risk, which were created during the preceding 15 years, were consolidated in 1984 under the name AIG Specialty Agencies, Inc. That same year AIG special services division was introduced to underwrite risks such as extortion, kidnapping, and ransom demand.

In 1985 AIG's profit margin rebounded, with the company exceeding 1983 earnings and posting a net income of $420 million. In 1987 AIG surpassed $1 billion in net income. That same year AIG was authorized by the South Korean government to begin life insurance operations, ending a 15-year struggle to break into the Korean market. AIG became the second foreign insurance company in South Korea, with its largest international competitor, CIGNA Corporation, given approval earlier in the year.

Two important AIG executives, National Union President Joseph P. DeAlessandro and American Home President Dennis Busti, left AIG in 1987 for other companies. Maurice Greenberg's son, Jeffrey W. Greenberg, was moved over from the presidency of AIU's North American division and named new president of National Union, while Joseph R. Wiedemann was named American Home president. Wiedemann had been president of AIG's Boston-based subsidiary Lexington Insurance Company.

AIG broadened its trading markets in 1987 when it became the first foreign insurance organization on the Tokyo Stock Exchange. The following year AIG was listed on the London International Stock Exchange. Additional listings include Paris and Switzerland, added in 1990.

AIG continued diversification moves in 1988, forming a Hong Kong-based venture to introduce American fast food franchises into the Asian market. The venture marked the first time an American institutional investor—AIG's Financial Investment Corporation of Asia—moved into an overseas franchise market.

That same year AIG also experienced some difficulty. It was involved in what is believed to be one of the largest insurance-related arbitration awards in history. Enron Corporation was awarded a $162 million claim from insurers for Peruvian properties that had been expropriated, and AIG was forced to pay nearly two-thirds of the judgment.

Throughout the 1980s AIG operated as one of two major sources of environmental-impairment-liability (EIL) insurance. Early in 1989 Maurice Greenberg proposed the creation of a hazardous-waste-cleanup tax funded through a 2 percent premium fee assessed on all commercial and casualty and property policies, with insurers matching that amount. Greenberg suggested the tax could help fund cleanup of Environmental Protection Agency Superfund sites and ultimately bring more insurers into EIL writing, but critics charged the plan was self-serving.

The late 1980s saw continued consolidation for AIG. The financial service group was formed in 1987 to consolidate specialized financial operations. UNAT, AIG's general insurance company on the European continent, was formed later that year to consolidate operations in Europe and prepare for the elimination of trade barriers among European nations in 1992. Headquartered in Paris, UNAT's expanding territory includes France, Belgium, the Netherlands, Sweden, Norway, and Denmark.

In 1989 AIGlobal was formed to provide a single source of comprehensive property and casualty, life, and group insurance, and facilitate corporate financial services for multinational companies. That same year International Healthcare and Jurgovan & Blair were merged to form American International Healthcare, Inc., an international consulting and management company for health-care services.

From 1987 into the mid-1990s AIG continued its diversification into financial services. In 1987 a joint venture, AIG Financial Products Corp., was established to structure complex financial transactions, including interest rate and currency swaps. In 1988 AIG acquired ownership of 30 percent of A.B. Asesores Bursatiles, a Spanish brokerage, and invested in certain investment management and venture capital operations in the United Kingdom and Hong Kong. AIG Trading Corporation, a joint venture engaging in commodity transactions, was established in early 1990, and later that year AIG acquired International Lease Finance Corporation, which was engaged primarily in the acquisition of new and used commercial jet aircraft and the leasing of such aircraft to domestic and foreign airlines. In 1994 AIG Combined Risks Ltd. was formed as a London-based investment bank providing risk management solutions involving corporate finance, reinsurance, and derivative instruments. All of these companies were placed under the umbrella of AIG's Financial Services Group. By 1994 operating income for the group had climbed to $404.9 million.

During 1990 Transatlantic Holdings, Inc., a holding company formed to hold Trans-atlantic Reinsurance Company and another reinsurer, Putnam Reinsurance Company, went public in a secondary offering. AIG continued to hold approximately 41 percent of Transatlantic Holdings after the public offering.

In June 1990 AIG agreed to buy Fischbach Corporation for $43 million. Fischbach, a Florida-based contractor, was an AIG performance-bond customer that had begun to experience financial difficulties. If Fischbach had failed, AIG could have been forced to pay hundreds of millions of dollars to companies with which Fischbach had contracted. After the purchase, AIG sold 51 percent of Fischbach to contractor Peter Kiewit Sons'.

In 1992 AIG garnered much bad publicity over a memo written by Jeffrey Greenberg, who by then had become an executive vice-president of AIG. Issued on the day that Hurricane Andrew reached the coast of Florida, the memo, sent to presidents of AIG subsidiary companies, seemed to suggest that AIG underwriters should be encouraged to push for premium increases in the wake of the hurricane: ''Begin by calling your underwriters together and explaining the significance of the hurricane. This is an opportunity to get price increases now. We must be the first and it begins by establishing the psychology with our own people. Please get it moving today.'' When the memo was made public it prompted investigations in both Florida and Louisiana, and denunciations from insurance watchdog groups, as well as consumer activist Ralph Nader who accused AIG of trying to start a cycle of ''price gouging.'' Maurice Greenberg maintained, however, that the contents of the memo were taken out of context and were part of a larger AIG discussion of long-needed rate increases for commercial insurance.

During the early 1990s AIG continued to expand outside the United States, thereby increasing its non-U.S. revenue to 52 percent of the total by 1994. Asia and the states of the former Soviet Union were particular targets during this period. Led by Maurice Greenberg's son Evan, AIG's Asia-Pacific Division reentered the Chinese market in 1992 when it became the first insurer to receive a license there since the Communist revolution in 1949. Two years later AIG also became the first insurer to return to Pakistan when it formed a subsidiary of ALICO to sell life and related types of insurance (the Pakistani government had nationalized all insurance companies in 1972). In early 1995, AIG reached an agreement with the Tata Group of India to jointly operate a life and nonlife insurance business in India once these insurance markets are opened to private and foreign investment. Meanwhile, AIG continued to be the largest foreign insurer in Japan.

To the west, Russia and Uzbekistan were added to AIG empire in 1994. Through joint ventures with local firms, AIG established commercial insurance and political risk insurance operations in Uzbekistan. Later in 1994 AIG received a license for its joint venture in Russia, the Russian American Insurance Company, which would offer commercial insurance to Russian companies and foreign firms operating in Russia.

1994 also saw AIG branch out into additional insurance lines within the U.S. market. AIG made an initial $216 million investment in 20th Century Industries, a private auto insurer in California which had incurred heavy losses as a result of the Northridge earthquake and was on the brink of insolvency. AIG pledged to invest additional capital if certain conditions were met. AIG also stepped in to rescue Alexander & Alexander Services, Inc. (A&A), a New York-based independent insurance broker. AIG's $200 million investment was intended to allow A&A to reorganize itself and improve profitability.

In the 27 years since Maurice Greenberg had taken over as CEO from the company founder, Greenberg had guided AIG into position as a leader in its industry with total assets reaching $114.35 billion in 1994. In an industry that had been rocked by several huge natural disasters in the late 1980s and early 1990s, AIG's return on equity remained remarkably stable throughout the period, ranging from 11.75 percent to 18.83 percent, thanks largely to the geographic and operational diversity engineered by Greenberg. During his reign at AIG, Greenberg became a legend in the insurance industry. Just about the only question that analysts had in regard to AIG's future as it neared the end of the century was who would succeed Greenberg (he turned 70 in 1995) and become only the third leader in AIG history. In fact, over the years several potential successors had left AIG to head up other firms, not willing to wait for Greenberg to retire. A new and louder round of speculation arose in mid-1995 when Jeffrey Greenberg, who had been widely rumored to be the latest heir apparent, abruptly resigned from the firm. Some observers then raised the possibility that Jeffrey's brother Evan was the new heir apparent, using his recent promotion to executive vice-president to support their theory. In any event, it was a tribute to AIG's strength and future prospects that most observers were unconcerned that Greenberg would not reveal the succession plan that he said was locked in an AIG safe.

Principal Subsidiaries

A.I. Credit Corp.; AIG Aviation, Inc.; AIG Claim Services, Inc.; AIG Consultants, Inc.; AIG Financial Products Corp.; AIG Global Investors, Inc.; AIG Investment Corporation; AIG Managed Care, Inc.; AIG Risk Management, Inc.; AIG Technical Services, Inc.; AIG Trading Group Inc.; American Home Assurance Company; American International Life Assurance Company of New York; American International Recovery, Inc.; AIG Life Insurance Company; Audubon Insurance Company; Commerce and Industry Insurance Company; International Lease Finance Corporation; Lexington Insurance Company; National Union Fire Insurance Company of Pittsburgh, Pa.;

New Hampshire Insurance Company; Transatlantic Holdings, Inc. (46%); United Guaranty Corporation; American International Reinsurance Company Limited (Bermuda); American International Underwriters Overseas, Limited (Bermuda); IPC Holdings, Ltd. (Bermuda; 24%); SELIC Holdings, Ltd. (Bermuda; 24%); AIU Canada Ltd.; Commerce and Industry Insurance Co. of Canada; AIG Europe, S.A. (France); American International Assurance Company, Ltd. (Hong Kong); Philippine American Life Insurance Company (Philippines); AIG Romania Insurance Company S.A.; Russian American Insurance Company (Russia); UeberseeBank AG (Switzerland); Nan Shan Life Insurance Company Ltd. (Taiwan); AIG Combined Risks Ltd. (U.K.); AIG Europe (UK) Limited; American International Underwriters (UK) Ltd.; American Life Insurance Company, UK; Landmark Insurance Company (U.K.).

Principal Divisions

Africa-Middle East Division; Asia-Pacific Division; Central Europe and Commonwealth of Independent States Division; Crisis Management Division; Energy Division; Group Management Division; Latin American Division; Mass Marketing Division; North American Division; Political Risk Division; Risk Management Division; Specialty Auto Division; Trade Credit Division; U.K./Ireland Division; Worldwide Accident and Health Division.

Further Reading

History of AIG, New York: American International Group, Inc., 1985.
''Local Hero: AIG,'' *Economist,* July 4, 1992, pp. 71–72.
McLeod, Douglas, ''Heir Apparent Leaves AIG,'' *Business Insurance,* June 12, 1995, p. 1.
Meakin, Thomas K., ''AIG Hits Home Run with 20th Century, Analysts Says,'' *National Underwriter Property & Casualty-Risk & Benefits,* October 17, 1994, pp. 29–30.
''Risky Business,'' *Chief Executive,* June 1993, pp. 34–37.
Wells, Chris, ''Insurers under Seige,'' *Business Week,* August 21, 1989, pp. 72–79.

—updated by David E. Salamie

Angelica Corporation

424 South Woods Mill Road
Chesterfield, Missouri 63017
U.S.A.
(314) 854-3800
Fax: (314) 386-5578

Public Company
Incorporated: 1904 as Angelica Jacket Company
Employees: 9,800
Sales: $472.8 million (1995)
Stock Exchanges: New York
SICs: 2329 Men's & Boys' Clothing, Not Elsewhere
Classified; 2339 Women's & Misses' Outerwear, Not
Elsewhere Classified; 7219 Laundry & Garment
Services, Not Elsewhere Classified; 7299
Miscellaneous Personal Services, Not Elsewhere
Classified

Angelica Corporation is the leading supplier of textile rental and laundry services in the United States and holds distinction in two other markets, ranking as the leading manufacturer and marketer of uniform apparel and the leading U.S. operator of specialty retail stores. During the mid-1990s these areas—Rental Services, Manufacturing and Marketing, and Retail Sales—constituted Angelica's key business segments. Originating as a manufacturer of uniforms in the late 19th century, the company broadened its roster of clientele over the years before diversifying into retail sales with the opening of its first Life Retail Store in 1965 and its move into textile rental services in 1968.

From its entrepreneurial beginnings in the late 19th century, Angelica established itself as a trendsetter, a characteristic that would describe the company more than a century later when it ranked as a dominant uniform apparel manufacturer and marketer. The company evolved from a fledgling upstart into a diversified, multinational concern by developing styles that became standard attire for service industry employees. Success

in one market spawned entry into another, eventually creating a multifaceted company with a chain of retail stores, a textile rental and laundry service business, and uniform apparel lines in a host of markets. However, it all began with one garment—the company's first original creation—a cook's uniform sewn by the wife of railroad chef Cherubino Angelica in St. Louis, Missouri, in 1878. From this first uniform, scores of original, trendsetting designs followed, making the Angelica label a pervasive fixture in the American workplace.

The cook's uniform created by Angelica's wife was distinctly different from his usual chef's attire and unlike the garments worn by other cooks in St. Louis and, presumably, anywhere else. The white hat was tall, resembling a crown with a pillow seated on top. The white coat was double-breasted, cloth buttons sewn to the sides, with two reversible layers of cloth in front to protect the wearer from direct heat and spattering grease. The cuffs, split on the sides, functioned as potholders when turned down. Although the white chef's uniform tailored by Cherubino Angelica's wife would become a ubiquitous, traditional garment worn by chefs a century later, in 1878 it was distinctly new and quickly drew comments from other railroad chefs, who were intrigued by its design and functionality. Cherubino Angelica attracted enough attention with his novel uniform to leave his job with the railroad and start his own company, an entrepreneurial venture that marked the beginning of Angelica Corporation's existence.

With his wife supplying the uniforms, Cherubino Angelica began soliciting orders from cooks for outfits identical to the one he had modeled while working as a cook himself, recording sufficient success to keep his small business afloat. By the 1890s, the Angelica family business had reached a respectable level of prominence, having created the uniforms worn by the glamorous Harvey Girls, the waitresses who worked at the Fred Harvey Restaurants located in train stations across the nation. In 1897 while en route to his native Italy, Cherubino Angelica was killed in the shipwreck of the *S.S. Burgoyne* off the coast of Newfoundland, leaving a firmly established business that was nearing its 20th year of operation.

Following Angelica's death, the company continued under the control of the Angelica family. In the early years of the new century, the Angelica family business diversified for the first time when it began competing in the nascent linen supply industry; then, in 1903, after 25 years of stewarding the company, the Angelicas sold their small enterprise to Alfred J. Levy. Levy paid $2,500 for the company and its six sewing machines; he then recruited his brother Mont, a recent graduate of the University of Michigan, to join him in managing the business.

Together, the Levy brothers endeavored to transform the image of uniforms from a "Badge of Servility" to a "Mark of Service," as their early advertising proclaimed, and toward this objective the pair were successful, at least in promoting greater attention to the garments worn by workers in the service industry. After incorporating their company as Angelica Jacket Company in 1904, the brothers expanded their production capabilities, amassing 32 sewing machines by 1910, when Angelica Jacket's roster of customers included employers in the hotel industry, the restaurant industry, the food processing industry, and the railroad industry. By this point, the innovative tradition first established by Cherubino Angelica's wife had remained alive within the company under the tutelage of the Levy brothers. Angelica Jacket had pioneered bandettes, tea aprons, and large wrap-around aprons worn by waitresses, and had promoted the adoption of white jackets instead of black coats for waiters.

A decade later, still pressing for the elimination of black mohair coats for waiters, which the company rightly charged were unsanitary because they were not washable, Angelica Jacket launched a campaign to promote its washable white uniforms with the slogan, "Sliding to Success on a Cake of White Soap." Two years later, in 1922, the company embraced a full spectrum of colors, offering for the first time a line of garments in fast-dyed colors and made from synthetic fibers. Concurrent with the introduction of this lively panoply of uniforms, the company opened an office and warehouse in New York City, as the breadth of its operations expanded.

As business grew and the demand for uniforms intensified, Angelica Jacket's marketing and distribution reach extended with the establishment of warehouses in Chicago in 1928 and in Los Angeles in 1932. With operations spread across country, Angelica Jacket moved forward through the 1930s, its progress fueled by the momentum generated by more than a half century of business. However, by the beginning of the 1940s, events outside of the company's control precipitated sweeping changes throughout its operations, bringing its traditional business shuddering to a temporary halt. By 1941, the United States was at war, bringing to a formal end the decade-long Depression and ushering in a period of sacrifice and concerted action by the American people and by American businesses. At Angelica Jacket, the manufacturing and marketing of uniforms gave way to a different product line, as the company did what it could to contribute to the war effort. During the war years, Angelica Jacket ranked as one of the largest manufacturers of combat jackets for the armed forces and served as a supplier for the Red Cross. On the domestic front, the company designed a line of uniforms called "Plantswear" for women thrust into manufacturing jobs previously held nearly exclusively by men.

After the conclusion of the Second World War, when annual sales for the company reached $3.5 million, Angelica Jacket faced the postwar years with renewed vigor, its sights set on fulfilling ambitious plans. Embodying this irrepressible optimism was the company's new objective: "to have our label on the back of every uniform used in the country." Though an unrealistic goal, the proclamation motivated employees and management to pursue the unattainable, giving the company the driving spirit to capitalize on the unprecedented prosperity to come in the decades ahead. In the late 1940s, the company strengthened its position in one of the markets that would enable it to take advantage of the lucrative economic times ahead when it bolstered its involvement in the health care industry. For years, Angelica Jacket had manufactured and marketed a line of hospital staff uniforms, but beginning in 1949 its participation in the growing health care market was entrenched with the introduction of a line of patient and operating apparel, foreshadowing its foray into the production of specialized protective apparel for contaminant-free environments 15 years later.

The 1950s, 1960s, and 1970s witnessed the explosive growth of service industries in the United States, a phenomenon that had a definitive affect on the magnitude of Angelica Jacket. More service personnel meant a greater need for uniforms and, not surprisingly, a greater demand for Angelica Jacket's line of men's and women's washable service apparel. The company broadened its marketing scope during the maturation of the service industries to include a variety of occupations, but it did so with a different corporate title. In 1950, as it prepared to meet the mounting apparel needs of service industry employers across the country, the company changed its name from Angelica Jacket Company to Angelica Uniform Company, then moved forward, expanding its manufacturing capabilities and increasing the ranks of its production personnel for the bright future ahead.

By the end of the 1950s, Angelica Uniform was a publicly-traded company, having made its initial public offering in 1958, when seven factories, eight warehouses, and 1,000 company employees comprised the growing Angelica empire. As the company entered the 1960s, with annual sales exceeding $10 million, it was regarded as the largest manufacturer of men's and women's washable service apparel for hospitals, restaurants and hotels. Angelica Uniform's enviable industry ranking became more domineering during the decade as it diversified its business, evolving into a well-rounded concern supported by burgeoning markets. The company entered the textile rental field in 1961, began production of protective apparel for "clean room" environments in 1964, then made several pivotal moves in 1965 to respond to the changing nature of its industry.

By the mid-1960s, workers in the service industries were required with increasing frequency to furnish their own uniforms, a shift in the composition of the company's customer base that Angelica Uniform's management sought to mirror by acquiring James G. Fast Company, a Chicago mail order firm, and by entering the retail uniform business with the opening of the company's first Life Uniform Shop. Concurrent with these two signal moves, both of which were made in 1965, Angelica Uniform acquired Kansas City White Goods Company, strengthening its textile product line for health care institutions, and crossed U.S. borders for the first time with the acquisition of a uniform company in Canada. On the heels of these important additions to the company's range of operations, Angelica Uniform Company changed its name in 1967 to Angelica Corporation.

In 1968 Angelica returned to diversifying its interests, acquiring the California-based Environmentals Incorporated, a provider of laundry and linen services to hospitals and other health care institutions. Angelica's involvement in the medical market, which dated back more than 20 years by this point, was fast becoming the primary engine driving the company's growth, as hospitals and other health care institutions increasingly sought outside laundry and linen service assistance. Newly constructed hospitals were no longer outfitted with laundry facilities, while older hospitals turned to companies like Angelica to realize significant cost savings, providing a substantial boost to Angelica's business.

Although Angelica's strong position in the medical market represented its most promising avenue of growth as the 1970s neared, the company's other businesses by no means remained idle. Angelica's international involvement in uniform production was deepened in 1970 with the acquisition of Whitewear Manufacturing Company, a Canadian manufacturer of uniforms. Its retail business—the operation of a chain of retail stores stocking uniforms and shoes—had recorded explosive growth, giving the company 100 Life Uniform Shops by 1973. Annual sales by this point had more than doubled since the name change in 1967, eclipsing $80 million during the early years of the 1970s. By the mid-1970s, Angelica's involvement in the medical market was propelling the company, accounting for more than half of the company's total sales for the first time in its history. As annual sales reached and then surpassed the $100 million mark during the latter half of the 1970s, the company's three primary business segments were each recording resolute growth. The company's Life Uniform Shops, with more than 150 units located in nearly every major U.S. city, had quickly become the largest specialty uniform chain in the nation. Its uniform business, after a century of development, was widely regarded as a venerable giant by industry observers, and its growing presence in the health care market buoyed prospects for the future, fueling optimism as Angelica entered the 1980s.

During the early 1980s, Angelica was the market leader in each of its three business segments: the rental of textile and garment services, the manufacture and marketing of uniforms, and the operation of a national chain of specialty apparel retail stores. Its linen rental business for the health care industry continued to be regarded as the company's major growth vehicle, helping Angelica generate more than $200 million a year in total sales by 1982. In the decade ahead, the company relied heavily on strengthening its resources through acquisitions, absorbing, in seven separate transactions between 1982 and the end of the decade, rental service facilities in Texas, Arizona,

California, Connecticut, Pennsylvania, New Jersey, and Rhode Island. Annual sales swelled as a result, increasing from roughly $200 million at the beginning of the decade to nearly $330 million by the decade's conclusion.

During the early 1990s, Angelica acquired a substantial number of laundry facilities in Florida through its purchase of Service Control Corp., and established a presence overseas for the first time with its 1991 acquisition of a uniform company based in England. In 1994, another English company was acquired, strengthening Angelica's ability to enter the European market on a direct basis. By the mid-1990s Angelica was considered an industry stalwart, its decades of growth having created a company of considerable magnitude. With more than 260 units composing Angelica's Life Uniform Shops retail chain and 36 manufacturing locations scattered across the country, Angelica comprised the market leader in its original line of business and ranked as the largest uniform seller in Canada. The company's nationwide network of linen processing plants and rental services facilities, however, represented the backbone supporting Angelica during the mid-1990s, accounting for $244.5 million of the $472 million it collected in sales in 1995 and generating the bulk of its earnings. As the company moved toward the 21st century, its three business segments were firmly rooted in stable, established markets, sparking hope that the future would afford as much success as the past.

Principal Subsidiaries

Angelica Healthcare Services Group Inc.; Angelica Realty Co.; Angelica International Ltd.; Southern Service Company; Angelica Uniform Company of Nevada; Industrias Textiles El Curu (Costa Rica); Angelica Holdings Limited (United Kingdom).

Principal Divisions

Rental Services; Manufacturing and Marketing; Life Retail Stores.

Further Reading

"Angelica Corp.," *Wall Street Journal*, November 2, 1990, p. B3.

"Angelica Corporation," *The Wall Street Transcript*, June 17, 1985, p. 78, 273.

"Angelica Corp.'s Young Is Named Chief Executive," *Wall Street Journal*, May 24, 1989, p. B13.

"Profitable Fields," *Financial World*, December 22, 1965, p. 14.

Roney, William C., "Angelica Corporation," *The Wall Street Transcript*, November 29, 1982, p. 67,873.

Willatt, Norris, "No Washday Blues," *Barron's*, September 27, 1963, p. 5.

"Women's Apparel a Growth Field," *Financial World*, March 1, 1961, p. 7.

—Jeffrey L. Covell

ASPEN
SKIING
COMPANY

Aspen Skiing Company

P.O. Box 1248
Aspen, Colorado 81612
U.S.A.
(970) 925-1220
Fax: (970) 920-0771

Private Company
Incorporated: 1946 as Aspen Skiing Corporation
Employees: 2,000
Sales: $78 million
SIC: 7011 Hotels & Motels; 7999 Amusement &
   Recreation, Not Elsewhere Classified

Founded in 1946, Aspen Skiing Company is headquartered in Aspen, Colorado, a small town in the Roaring Fork Valley of the Rocky Mountains. The company owns four ski resorts; Aspen Mountain, Aspen Highlands, Buttermilk Mountain, and Snowmass, all of which are located within a short distance of its headquarters. These four resorts, together referred to as "Aspen," form one of the world's most famous and popular ski areas. In 1978 the company was purchased by Twentieth Century Fox and subsequently underwent several changes in ownership, eventually coming under the control of the Crown family of Chicago.

Skiing became common in and around Aspen long before the mountains were developed as ski resorts. As early as 1879, when mining prospectors founded the town of Aspen, people were using skis for both transportation and recreation. Two of the original settlers were Swedish, and it was they who introduced "snowshoes," or skis, which were essential during that first winter, when 52 feet of snow fell in the valley of the Roaring Fork River. Bolstered by silver mining in the surrounding mountains, the town's population grew rapidly, from 300 in 1880 to 8,808 in 1890. This would be a golden era for Aspen.

Then, in 1893, when the population hit 12,000, came the great silver panic, which forced Congress to drop silver as a monetary standard. Silver's value plummeted. Aspen, once pre-

dicted to reach a population of 100,000, instead suffered an exodus of miners. By 1917 the town had only 700 people; some were still mining for silver, lead, and zinc, while others were ranchers and potato farmers. During these "quiet years," as they came to be known, people still skied, but more often for recreation, as other means of transportation were taking over. Skiing was most popular among kids, some of whom made their own skis from wood stolen out of old, abandoned houses.

The foundations for the Aspen Skiing Company were laid in the 1930s, when interest in the sport was growing in the United States, despite the Great Depression. The Winter Olympics were held in Lake Placid, New York, in 1932, and in 1936 a group of investors opened Sun Valley, a ski resort in Idaho, with surprising success. Also important were the increasing availability of manufactured skis, the development of safer bindings, and the immigration of noted European skiers, some of whom were escaping Hitler's new Germany.

The first attempt at developing a resort at Aspen came in 1936, when three men (T.J. Flynn, Ted Ryan, and Billy Fiske) formed the Highland Bavarian Corporation. Flynn, the only local of the three businessmen, remembered Scandinavian miners racing down the mountains for recreation. After announcing their resort plans to the Aspen Lions Club, the town enthusiastically backed the project. Although only a lodge had been constructed, the resort opened in December 1936. The lift, not built until the next year, would be called the "boat tow." It was made of an old car motor, two mine hoists, and two ten-person sleds. The resort's first slope, called Roch Run (after the Swiss mountaineer Andre Roch, who carried out many of the corporation's early goals, including surveying the mountain), was cut for free by the Aspen Ski Club, which Roch helped found. Aggressive advertising through brochures, films, and ski races brought attention to Aspen, and the Federal Government, through the Works Project Administration, helped construct a new warming hut, jumping hill, and clubhouse.

World War II interrupted the resort's development (Fiske himself died in the war), though the boat tow continued to be run, servicing local skiers as well as members of the famous Tenth Mountain Division (the U.S. military's ski soldiers, who were being trained at nearby Camp Hale, later called Ski

Cooper). The Tenth Mountain Division would eventually fight in Italy. Among the Tenth Mountain soldiers who skied at Aspen were Friedl Pfeifer, Johnny Litchfield, and Percy Rideout. After the war, many Tenth Mountain veterans returned to Colorado with the hope of opening their own resorts. Pfeifer, originally from Austria, moved to Aspen, and he was struck by its potential: "The sight was a match for anything in the Alps. I envisioned the runs cut naturally with the contours of the mountain, blending with the meadows, gorges, and glades. There would be terrain for any level skier."

Meanwhile, Walter Paepcke, a wealthy Chicago businessman, and his wife, Elizabeth, also had plans for Aspen, though for them the town had the potential to become a new cultural center. The Paepckes owned a home in Colorado, and in 1938 Elizabeth visited Aspen, where she skied and was awestruck by the scenery. Walter, who was not a skier, would later write: "Aspen had everything . . . it had fishing, climbing, skiing. Aspen had so much to add to leisure, to the renewal of the inner spirit. It was the perfect setting for music, art, education . . . all the things that make life worth living."

In 1945, Paepcke began acquiring property in Aspen, much of which could be bought simply by paying past taxes. Though not particularly interested in mixing his cultural plans with skiing, he was aware that Tenth Mountain veterans, including Pfeifer, had moved to Aspen to develop a resort. Thus he decided to meet with Pfeifer in September 1945, but no agreements were made. Meanwhile, Pfeifer was making substantial plans. After talking with the Aspen Ski Club, he made arrangements to take over the mountain's boat tow, establish a downhill ski event (the Roch Cup), and start a ski school. The school, which he codirected with Litchfield and Rideout, opened on December 18, 1945.

Pfeifer had hoped to develop the resort with Harold Klock, a mining engineer. But they were unable to raise the funds, so in late 1945 Pfeifer and Walter Paepcke again met, this time to make a deal. In exchange for Paepcke's help in raising money ($300,000 was necessary to capitalize the new corporation and build a chair lift), Pfeifer agreed to let Paepcke run the new ski resort. On January 21, 1946, with a board of Paepcke, Pfeifer, Paul Nitze, George Berger, and Robert Collins, Aspen Skiing Corporation was incorporated. A separate Aspen Company was established by Paepcke to manage his real estate holdings.

Many barriers still had to be hurdled. Aspen Mountain, with Roch Run and the boat tow, was chosen for the site of the new resort, but there were hundreds of mining claims on the mountain that needed to be located and purchased. Because the land was part of the White River National Forest, new lifts and trails also had to be approved by the U.S. Forest Service, though in those days the service was interested in promoting ski resorts (later it would be concerned with the environmental impact of resorts). Aspen's fame would be helped greatly by the Paepckes, who were able to attract to the resort influential people (including Illinois governor Adlai Stevenson, who had the misfortune of being tipped off the boat tow into a gully).

Lift 1 and the Sundeck (a lodge on the mountain) were completed by the end of 1946, and the company held an official opening of the chair lift on January 11, 1947. Colorado Gover-

nor F. Lee Knaus attended the event, as did U.S. Senator Ed Johnson. The mayor's daughter started the lift, and 2,000 spectators watched a slalom and jumping demonstration by some of the country's best skiers. The lift ticket that season was $3.75 a day. The company, in its first year, also established a ski patrol, placed safety telephones and toboggans on the mountain, and held three races. The resort thus began with much fanfare and quickly gained notoriety, in part for the difficulty of the mountain's terrain. It was this difficulty, however, that would slow the resort's early growth, as families tended to be attracted to more gentle slopes.

Dick Durrance, a former ski racer who became general manager in 1947, soon oversaw an expansion of the resort's terrain. He organized the cutting of Ruthie's Run, a wider and easier slope than Roch Run; again this was done by volunteers. His biggest coup, however, was convincing European organizers to bring to Aspen the 1950 FIS Championships. This, the first world skiing championship held in the United States, required new trails, telephone lines, and timing equipment. The company would spend $72,000 to complete the preparations and provide accommodations for skiers. Held in February 1950, some 1,500 racers, spectators, coaches, and officials came to Aspen. Many stayed with local residents.

Meanwhile, Paepcke was beginning, as one local Aspenite wrote, "the process of grafting culture onto an old mining town." In 1947 he founded the Goethe Bicentennial Foundation to plan a celebration in Aspen of the writer's 200th birthday. Held in June and July 1949, it attracted such noted intellectuals and artists as Albert Schweitzer and Arthur Rubinstein. The success of the event would spawn other cultural organizations in Aspen, including the Aspen Institute for Humanistic Studies, the Aspen Music Festival and Music School, and the International Design Conference of Aspen. The mix of culture and skiing, for which Aspen would become famous, would later be attempted by numerous competing ski resorts.

Despite the difficult terrain of Aspen Mountain, the resort's popularity grew over the 1950s, bringing with it a new problem of overcrowding. Even the company admitted there had been years when the "waiting lines sometimes exceeded 60 minutes." Other sources reported lines lasting as much as two hours. In response, the company built Lift 3 in 1954 and Lift 4 in 1956, and it also began to improve its trails with basic snow grooming.

From the 1960s forward, Aspen Skiing Corporation continued to increase the number of trails and lifts and to construct new facilities. The company would also expand through the development of three new, adjacent resorts: Buttermilk, Aspen Highlands, and Snowmass. None of those resorts were initiated by the company, though it was at least peripherally involved in all three.

Buttermilk was founded by Pfeifer, who during the 1950s ran the ski school at not only Aspen Mountain but also Sun Valley. The terrain at Aspen Mountain was particularly difficult for Pfeifer's students. In 1953, therefore, Pfeifer purchased about 300 acres at the bottom of a nearby mountain that was better suited for beginning and intermediate trails. He had hoped that Aspen Skiing Corporation would lease his land and help develop the resort, but it refused, claiming its hands were full running its own resort. Pfeifer then turned to Art Pfister, who owned land adjacent to Pfeifer's, and the two men began a new corporation to develop what became known as Buttermilk Mountain.

Pfeifer and Pfister agreed to share expenses for a restaurant at the base and a T-bar lift. Pfeifer sold his shares in Aspen Skiing Corporation to raise money. Opened for the 1958–59 ski season, Buttermilk began slowly, though by 1962 it had installed two chair lifts and a top-of-the-mountain restaurant, funded by Robert O. Anderson, president of Atlantic Richfield Oil Company, who had become a partner in Buttermilk with Pfeifer and Pfister. Although Buttermilk and Aspen Mountain were located close to each other, there was little competition between the two resorts, in part because Anderson and Pfister were also on the board of Aspen Skiing Corporation. In fact, Aspen Skiing Corporation handled Buttermilk's marketing and ticket sales, and in 1963 it purchased Buttermilk Mountain.

Aspen Highlands opened the same season as Buttermilk. It was the project of Whipple ("Whip") Van Ness Jones, a graduate of Harvard Business School. He attended the Goethe Foundation's celebration in Aspen in 1949 and in 1950 purchased a house from Paepcke's son-in-law. Several years later he bought land at the base of what became Aspen Highlands (close to both Aspen Mountain and Buttermilk), where he planned to live and raise horses. In 1957, though, three neighbors (Had Deane, Dick Wright, and Pat Henry) approached Jones and asked if he would invest in a new ski resort at nearby Sievers Mountain.

The project ultimately failed to materialize when the local forest ranger, Paul Hauk, determined that the site was unsuitable for skiing. So the partners looked to the mountain just behind Jones's property. Jones, Hauk, Durrance, Pfeifer, and Fred Iselin explored this new site. On April 16, 1958, Jones took a 30-year lease on 4,200 acres of National Forest land, which would be the terrain of the resort. Once again Aspen Skiing Company refused to get involved, but Jones had the resources to develop it himself. He hired Pete Seibert, a Tenth Mountain veteran and the future founder of Vail Mountain, as the mountain manager; Earl Eaton, the former head of Aspen Mountain's ski patrol, to organize the new resort's ski patrol; and Stein Erikson, a famous Norwegian ski racer, to help lay out trails and head the ski school. Erikson's fame would prove to be a draw for skiers. In 1958, its first season, Aspen Highlands registered some 30,000 "skier visits," compared with Aspen Mountain's 93,000 and Buttermilk's 16,400. It offered a lower-priced lift ticket than Aspen Mountain, and it had more snowfall and a better view. Aspen Highlands would not be purchased by Aspen Skiing Corporation until December 1993.

The popularity of all three resorts continued to grow in the 1960s, in part because of broader developments in the ski industry. The 1960 Winter Olympics in Squaw Valley, California, brought greater visibility to skiing in the United States. Furthermore, improved equipment, such as Head metal skis, was making the sport easier and safer. Airlines, seeing skiing as a source for greater travel, began promoting the sport. Legal changes made ownership of ski condominiums more practical. Even stretch pants contributed, as they made skiing appear more

fashionable. By 1965–66 ski visits had jumped to 174,000 at Aspen Mountain, 87,500 at Buttermilk, and 68,000 at Aspen Highlands. Three years later, in 1968–69, skier visits at Aspen Highlands more than doubled to 145,000.

Aspen's fourth mountain, Snowmass, opened in December 1967, though under much different circumstances. The resort was the idea of William Janss, a former Olympic skier whose family owned a business in California specializing in real estate, construction, and cattle. By 1961 Janss had purchased seven ranches in the Bush Creek Valley, below Baldy and Burnt mountains, totaling some 3,400 acres, and that year he announced his intention of developing a new resort. Unlike the previous three resorts, Snowmass would be planned and developed with "heavyweight corporate proficiency," as *Skiing* magazine observed. Experimental trails were cut as early as 1961, and the following year the trails were skied by people carried up the mountain on "snowcats"; these skiers provided feedback that was used in cutting other trails.

Aspen Skiing Corporation, through its Snowmass Skiing Corporation subsidiary, was contracted to build ski lifts and operate the ski area, while Janss Colorado Corporation was in charge of real estate (along with American Cement Corporation). Unlike Aspen Mountain, which began with an existing town at its base, Snowmass, which was about 13 miles from Aspen, had to create its own base village. In 1967 a Denver magazine reported that the resort had already constructed "five lodges, 120 condominium apartments, a dozen private residences; a conference center with a movie theater, outdoor ice rink and paddle tennis courts; four heated outdoor swimming pools, including one of Olympic size; 21 shops and boutiques; and six restaurants." The mountain itself had a restaurant, as well as five chair lifts. When it opened in December 1967, Snowmass had a village entirely focused on tourism.

In the 1970s and 1980s there were further changes in the ski industry. Most significant, skiers were beginning to shun small, basic ski areas for those that provided the largest number of trails, the most and fastest lifts, and the best facilities. Aspen Skiing Corporation, like other ski resort companies, would respond by providing additional services and constructing more luxurious accommodations. More trails were cut, slopes were groomed frequently for ease of skiing, and more lifts were built to reduce lift lines. The introduction of expensive high-speed quads (chair lifts carrying four people at speeds much faster than ordinary lifts) were increasingly installed at Aspen resorts and elsewhere. As Americans became more and more litigious, insurance costs for Aspen Skiing Corporation also rose. The ballooning cost of running a ski resort was reflected in the price of a lift ticket, which at Aspen Mountain jumped from $13.00 in the mid-1970s to $52.00 in 1995.

During this same period the company itself became a pawn in corporate deal making. In 1978 Twentieth Century Fox purchased Aspen Skiing Corporation, which became a subsidiary. Two years later, in June 1981, businessman Marvin Davis bought Twentieth Century Fox, and in the process he changed the status of Aspen Skiing Corporation from a public to a private company. He also changed its name to Aspen Skiing Company. This arrangement did not last long, as in September 1981 Aspen Skiing Company and other Twentieth Century Fox subsidiaries, including Pebble Beach, were transfered to a separate venture, 50 percent of which was acquired by Urban Investment and Development (a subsidiary itself of Aetna Life Insurance). The corporate shuffling continued in December 1983, when Urban Investment sold its 50 percent share to a management company headed by Davis, and then in July 1985, when Twentieth Century Fox sold its share to Bell Mountain Partnership, Ltd., owned by the Crown family of Chicago. Eight years later, in April 1993, Davis's management company sold its interest to the Crown family, which finally became the sole owner of Aspen Skiing Company.

In the 1990s Aspen Skiing Company's four resorts undoubtedly formed one of North America's premier ski areas, along with such "magaresorts" as Vail Mountain in Colorado and Whistler/Blackcomb in British Columbia. Aspen Mountain, Aspen Highlands, Buttermilk, and Snowmass together had 4,225 acres of skiable terrain, 41 lifts, and 15 on-mountain restaurants. The town of Aspen, which served all four, had long become a culturally sophisticated center known for its numerous visiting celebrities. At the Sundeck on Aspen Mountain skiers were even provided with fax machines and access to electronic databases that reported stock prices and other information.

Going into the mid-1990s, Aspen Skiing Company was in a strong position to compete in the changing world of ski resorts, which were increasingly being purchased by large corporations. Its ownership of four resorts allowed it to consolidate functions, such as purchasing, public relations, and marketing, to save money. A single lift ticket gave access to all four resorts, which were advertised together as one ski area. Equally important, it had the advantage of owning a ski area, "Aspen," with universal name recognition among skiers. In the history of skiing, Aspen had become a legend. With its investments in new lifts and facilities and other improvements, Aspen Skiing Company was doing all it could to maintain the resort's envious blend of great skiing and cultural sophistication.

Further Reading

Allen, James Sloan, *The Romance of Commerce and Culture: Capitalism, Modernism, and the Chicago-Aspen Crusade for Cultural Reform,* Chicago: The University of Chicago Press, 1983.

Barlow-Perez, Sally, *A History of Aspen,* Aspen, Colo.: Who Press, 1991.

Carlson, Lee, "Resorts Enter New, Corporate Age," *Skiing Trade News,* November 1994, pp. 22–23.

Dusenbery, Harris, *Ski the High Trail: World War II Ski Troopers in the High Colorado Rockies,* Portland, Ore.: Binford and Mort Publishing, 1991.

Gilbert, Anne, *Re-creation through Recreation: Aspen Skiing from 1870 to 1970,* Aspen, Colo.: Aspen Historical Society, 1995.

Gutner, Toddi, "Musical Chairlifts," *Forbes,* September 27, 1993, p. 20.

Markels, Alex, "As Business Stagnates at Chic Ski Areas, the Gloves Come Off," *Wall Street Journal,* December 8, 1995, p. A1.

Taylor, John N., "Aspen Adieu?," *Forbes,* February 15, 1993, p. 20.

—Thomas Riggs

Assicurazioni Generali SpA

Piazza Duca degli Abruzzi, 2
34132 Trieste
Italy
(040) 6711
Fax: (040) 671600

Public Company
Incorporated: 1831 as Assicurazioni Generali Austro-
   Italiche
Employees: 6,563
Total Assets: US$20.91 billion (1993)
Stock Exchanges: Milan Rome Turin Trieste Florence
   Genoa Bologna Tokyo New York Frankfurt Paris
   London
SICs: 6311 Life Insurance; 6321 Accident & Health
   Insurance; 6331 Fire, Marine & Casualty Insurance;
   6719 Holding Companies, Not Elsewhere Classified

Founded in Trieste in 1831, Assicurazioni Generali SpA is the largest insurance company in Italy and the fifth-largest in Europe. Very active outside its home market from the very beginning, Generali derives more than two-thirds of its premium income from outside Italy. Generali subsidiaries and agencies are located in more than 40 countries worldwide, with widespread coverage of Western Europe and North and South America and additional operations in Eastern Europe, Africa, the Middle East, and the Asia-Pacific region.

Trieste's position on the Adriatic and its role as chief port of the Austro-Hungarian Empire made it a center of shipping and commerce, when the first ventures in maritime insurance were established in the mid-1700s after the Hapsburg King Charles VI had declared it a free port. Following the upheavals of revolution and the Napoleonic Wars, Trieste experienced an economic boom. In 1825, some 20 insurance companies were active, chiefly in maritime insurance.

Generali was founded by Giuseppe Lazzano Morpurgo, a businessman from a leading family in Gorizia, who brought together a group of Trieste financiers and merchants in November 1831 to found the Ausilio Generale di Sicurezza. Their intention was to establish a company with sufficient capitalization to expand beyond the geographical territory reached by other Trieste houses. Like its chief competitor at the time, the Adriatico Banco d'Assicurazione—today known as Riunione Adriatica di Sicurtà or RAS—the Ausilio Generale founding members were drawn from Trieste's multiethnic business community, which included Austrians, Slavs, Italians, Germans, and Greeks.

At the first shareholders' assembly, conflicts among the partners over statutes led to the dissolution of Ausilio Generale. A month later the remaining partners formed the Assicurazioni Generali Austro-Italiche, with an initial capitalization of 2 million florins, divided into 2,000 shares of 1,000 florins each. Statutes were approved on December 26, 1831. Almost immediately, founding member Giuseppe Morpurgo left Trieste to establish the company's Venice headquarters, which was placed under the direction of Samuel della Vida from Ferrara.

Other Generali founders included Marco Parente, a businessman with ties to the Vienna Rothschild family, and Vidal Benjamin Cusin, grandfather of two future secretary-generals of Generali, Marco Besso and Giuseppe Besso. The company's other members included Giovanni Cristoforo Ritter de Zahony, a Frankfurt native with a Hungarian title; the shipbuilder Michele Vucetich; Alessio Paris, who in 1826 had been a founder of the competitor Adriatico Banco; and Giambattista Rosmini, an Italian lawyer who managed the new company in his role as legal adviser.

The adjective "Generali" was intended to convey the fact that the company's activities were not limited to maritime and flood insurance but, as Article 2 of the first charter indicated, "insurance of land [i.e., fire and shipping insurance] . . . security of the life of man in all its ramifications, pensions and whatever other area of insurance permitted by law." The first agencies were opened rapidly, amounting to some 25 in the principal cities of the Hapsburg Empire in the first two years. Branches, agencies, and affiliates were established in France in 1832, and in 1835 to the east in Switzerland and Germany, in Transylvania, and Galizia. Administration of the company was divided between the Trieste and Venice headquarters, with Venice in charge of operations in Italy and west Europe while the central management in Trieste handled operations elsewhere in Austria-Hungary and east Europe. In 1837, the Venice office began to operate in the field of credit insurance, while limiting its transport insurance solely to goods being shipped from Venice.

In 1835, a struggle for power developed between the president, Zahony, and legal administrator Giambattista Rosmini, with Morpurgo supporting the president. The board of directors sided with Rosmini, who succeeded in forcing Zahony and Morpurgo out of the company. At this time, the charter was rewritten and the position of president was abolished, to be reinstated in 1909. The dispute had a deleterious effect on business; four other board members left with Zahony and Morpurgo, and the directors compelled Rosmini to share power with Masino Levi, former agent in the Padua office, who was named general secretary.

The following 40 years under Levi's direction saw unprecedented growth for Generali. Expansion was effected according to the company's geographical division, with activity on the Italian peninsula overseen by the Venice office, while Trieste was responsible for other European operations. Generali was especially active in east and central Europe, where offices opened in Saxony, Prussia, and Silesia in 1837, expanding further in 1838 to Corfu, Bavaria, Russian Poland, Serbia, and Valacchia. The company's Hamburg operations center was run for many years by the mathematical prodigy Wilhelm Lazarus, who compiled the first mortality tables for Germany.

While growth was surging on the continent, expansion on the Italian peninsula was slower. Prior to the unification of Italy, protectionist laws in effect in the separate Italian states greatly restricted activity by foreign insurance companies. For example, until 1850 Generali representatives in the Bourbon kingdom of Naples frequently had to appeal to the throne to avoid suspension of their activity. In the Papal States, business was possible only in the Romagna region. In the kingdom of Piedmont, the Società Reale Mutua held a legal monopoly in fire insurance, and heavy legal hindrances existed in other fields until 1853. At Parma and Piacenza, Generali was only able to begin activity in 1837, when the Milan agency succeeded in winning monopoly rights in the region from the Bourbon duchess Maria-Luigia.

Expansion throughout Europe was carried out by means of a tiered system. Territories were grouped around a central general agency responsible for gradually increasing growth in new expansion zones. Where Generali was unable to establish an autonomous agency, an affiliate was authorized. From its lucrative Pest agency in Hungary, Generali extended operations to Bucharest in 1847 and to Belgrade in 1856. In the following decade, operations started in Bosnia and the remaining area of Turkish domination, enlarging Generali's territory to include the whole of the Middle East, especially in the branch of fire insurance. The first fire insurance policies in Alexandria were issued by Generali in 1851, limited to the city's European quarter.

Later in the 19th century, Generali's attention turned to eastern and other non-European countries. Between 1879 and 1882 Generali opened agencies or representative offices in the main ports of the Near East and the Far East, along the sea routes of the Lloyd Austriaco line which had its terminal in Trieste: Generali's territory was thus extended throughout Greece, to Beirut, Tunis, Bombay, Colombo, Shanghai, and Hong Kong. Across the Pacific Ocean, agencies were opened in San Francisco, California, and in Valparaiso, Chile. New kinds of insurance were initiated; in 1877, Generali began extending coverage to plate glass, in 1881 to injury, and by the end of the century to theft.

In 1878, Marco Besso replaced Masino Levi as secretary general, inaugurating a period of modernization and diversification. Besso had come to Generali in 1863 as the company's representative to Rome, where he successfully negotiated the acquisition of the Vatican's failing Pontificia insurance house. Taking over the company at the age of 35, Besso established Generali's life insurance activities and initiated a policy of real estate investment. During his period of tenure the company acquired the Procuratie Vecchie, one of the Renaissance palaces on Venice's Piazza San Marco, and built its imposing Rome headquarters in Piazza Venezia.

Also during this period Generali laid the groundwork for its future as a major European group with the constitution of its first wholly owned subsidiaries. It established Cassa Generale Ungherese di Risparmio (General Savings Bank of Hungary) in 1881, followed by Unfall (Austrian General Accident Insurance) in 1882, which today operates under the name Erste Allgemeine.

Marco Besso was replaced by his brother Giuseppe Besso in 1885, who served as secretary general until 1894. Marco Besso continued to guide Generali, however, acting as president from 1909, when the position was reinstated, until his death in 1920. During the years 1894 to 1909, he acted as consulting director while the post of secretary general was filled by Edmondo Richetti, who had joined the company ten years earlier as director of the Austrian Unfall branch.

During these years Besso formed what was to prove a fruitful long-term relationship with Italy's principal merchant bank, the Banca Commerciale Italiana (COMIT), which still exists today. Less than two years after COMIT was founded in 1894, Besso was installed on the board of directors where he remained for life. Except for a ten-year period coinciding with World War II, Generali and COMIT traditionally have held reciprocal seats on each other's boards. Also during this period, Franz Kafka was hired by the company's general agency in Prague as an office worker. However, the aspiring novelist left after nine months, suffering from nervous ailments.

In 1914, on the eve of World War I, Generali was enjoying a position of tremendous strength. Its assets totaled 12,600,000 crowns (L13,323,000). While the war brought unprecedented destruction to the very areas of Europe in which Generali was most active, the company suffered more from political pressures than from financial loss. At the outbreak of hostilities, Generali's two most important offices found themselves in opposing camps of warring nations. The Venice headquarters made every effort to be regarded as Italian, whereas Generali's Trieste office reaffirmed its loyalty to the Hapsburgs. The governments of France and England regarded Generali as a part of the Austro-Hungarian empire, and the company's activities were curtailed in both countries until 1916.

Generali, however, was viewed with equal suspicion in Vienna. The Trieste headquarters was relocated to the Austro-Hungarian capital, where activities were supervised by a substitute managing director, Emanuel Ehrentheil. Generali, like much of Trieste, had always divided its loyalties between Italy and the Hapsburgs. Since much of Generali's personnel transferred to Italy at the outbreak of fighting, the authorities placed most of Generali's officers on a list of suspected Italian nationalists. Claiming suspicion of foreign espionage, the Military Command investigated the directors and searched their homes. In 1916 the company's assets temporarily were sequestered under a decree to prevent the flight of foreign capital. Despite this, on May 31, 1918, a Generali life policy was written for the last Hapsburg emperor, Charles I.

In 1918, with the armistice, Trieste was united with the Italian republic and Generali assumed as its insignia the Lion of St. Mark, symbol of Venetian power and justice. After the collapse of the Hapsburg monarchy in central Europe, new nationalist states replaced the politically united territories that Generali had cultivated for nearly a century. In addition to the damage inflicted by the fighting, the new order resulted in complex monetary, legal, and economic problems in the insurance industry. Authorized to continue its activity in all the former Austro-Hungarian territories, Generali initially restricted itself to handling life insurance in Czechoslovakia and Yugoslavia.

Adjusting for the devaluation of the lire from its 1913 rates, the company estimated that its assets had fallen by 17 percent since the outbreak of war, but two years later Generali was on the road to an impressive recovery, and under the direction of Edgardo Morpurgo, from 1920, the company marked its 100th anniversary in extraordinarily good health.

Despite the economic crisis of 1929, Generali's capital rose from L13 million to L60 million in ten years, and gross premiums in life insurance rose from L1 billion to L6 billion. The company boasted 3,150 representatives in Italy and 5,765 in foreign countries. It had 30 subsidiaries and associated companies—6 in Italy and 24 abroad. Real estate holdings were valued at L292 million, which then included urban and agricultural property in 17 different countries. Faced with the effects of the Great Depression in the United States and the need to have strong liquid assets readily available, the company established a new department at its central headquarters, solely in charge of financing.

Notable events in the 1930s included the acquisition of Aleanza & Unione Mediterranea in 1933, which was merged with Securitas Esperia, already controlled by Generali, to form Alleanza-Securitas-Esperia (Allsecures), no longer a part of the Generali group. Life insurance activities absorbed from this group formed the basis for the Alleanza Assicurazioni company, which became the largest private life insurance company in Italy, second only to the state-run giant, INA. Significant

growth occurred, meanwhile, in Generali's French holding La Concorde, and the Austrian Erste Allgemeine. Benito Mussolini's alliance with Nazi Germany ensured that Italian interests in Austria were not lost after Adolf Hitler's *anschluss* in 1934.

The extension of Germany's anti-Semitic laws to Italy, however, had a devastating effect on the Generali group. With the rise of fascism in Italy, Morpurgo, who was Jewish, had struggled to maintain control, enrolling in the Fascist Party and appointing a staunch supporter of Mussolini as managing director. Gino Baroncini—who came to Generali from the Milan-based subsidiary Anonima Grandine, an insurer formed by Generali in 1890 to cover crop damage by hailstorms—was to determine the company's structure and course for much of the next 30 years. In 1938, however, Morpurgo was forced to leave the company, eventually fleeing to Argentina. He was replaced by Count Giuseppe Volpi di Misurata, who served until the fall of the Fascist government in 1943.

The company also lost 66 Jewish employees, including 20 directors. With Trieste under a German high command, Generali's central headquarters were moved to Rome, and its status as an Italian company was formalized by an official decree. Antonio Cosulich, a Trieste shipbuilder and member of the board, was named chairman and served until 1948, with Baroncini continuing as managing director.

The end of the war renewed prospects for a return to normal operating conditions in Western Europe, but in Eastern Europe all rights, property, and interests pertaining to Italy or Italian citizens were seized. Generali's agencies and affiliates in Hungary, Czechoslovakia, Poland, and Romania suffered the worst losses while those in Yugoslavia, Bulgaria, Albania, and east Germany fared slightly better. In all, the Generali group lost 14 subsidiaries as well as substantial real estate holdings in Eastern Europe. Efforts by Baroncini to recover some of the losses in Eastern Europe were only partly successful: L13 billion were eventually restored to the company in payments from various countries, about one-tenth of what was lost. There were further losses in the former Italian colonies, such as Libya and Ethiopia.

But in 1945 tensions did not immediately ease in Trieste, where a bloody campaign of terror was waged by Yugoslavia at the end of the war, when Yugoslavian nationalists tried to win control of the city. After the declaration of the Free Territory of Trieste, the city led a tense existence from 1947 to 1954, until a hard-won international compromise resulted in the city's being awarded to Italy.

Generali's solid asset base made the work of reconstruction possible, and already by 1948 the company's Western European operations were on the way to recovery. Spurred by the loss of Eastern and Central European markets, attention turned to Latin America, where a majority ownership was acquired in the Argentinian company Providencia. At the beginning of the 1950s, operations resumed in Greece and the Middle East and in Brazil, Guatemala, Venezuela, Ecuador, and Colombia. In South Africa, Generali acquired a controlling interest in the new Standard General Insurance, then in a phase of considerable expansion.

From 1948 to 1953, Senator Mario Abbate succeeded Cosulich as president of the company. Formerly Abbate had been chairman of the Milan subsidiary Anonima Grandine. Already elderly and in ill health, Abbate's was largely a titular presidency. Chief executive responsibility was shared by Baroncini and Michele Sulfina, a Generali manager who had served with Edgardo Morpurgo in the 1920s and 1930s. In 1950, during Abbate's tenure, direct operations resumed in the United States after Generali had obtained the necessary authorization to offer shipping and fire insurance as well as reinsurance. At this time, and as Italy entered its postwar economic boom, the company dedicated itself to reorganizing and restructuring its Italian assets. Thus in 1955 the two old Milan firms constituted to handle injury and hailstorm insurance in the 19th century, Anonima Infortuni and Anonima Grandine, were merged to form the Milan head office.

Mario Tripcovich, who succeeded the aging Senator Abbate as president in 1953, came from the Trieste shipbuilding concern founded in 1895 by his father, Diodato Tripcovich, himself a member of Generali's executive council for 20 years. The younger Tripcovich had spearheaded efforts to improve Generali's position in the United States, insisting on buying the Buffalo Insurance Company in 1950.

Tripcovich was succeeded in 1956 by Camillo Giussani, who acted for a period as simultaneous chairman of Generali and the Banca Commerciale Italiana. The strengthening of bonds between the two companies was to continue in the decades that followed. As the Italian economy surged ahead, so did Generali, achieving first place among foreign insurers operating in Austria and France, thanks to its considerable presence in both countries, through La Concorde in France and Erste Allgemeine in Austria. The company was active in 60 different countries, and was diversifying into previously unheard-of areas. When television came to Italy, Generali initiated policies covering equipment and antennae, fire, theft, and destruction of cathode tubes.

The decade was also characterized by the entrance of powerful shareholders into the elite group of Trieste financiers and industrialists who had traditionally occupied seats on Generali's executive council. In 1956 Mediobanca, Italy's largest semiprivate bank, acquired a 3.5 percent share. Guiding this move was Enrico Cuccia, president of the bank since 1949, who was to have a hand in Generali's course in decades to come.

Baroncini, the engineer of Generali's postwar recovery, was named chairman in 1960 and served until 1968 when he was succeeded by another former official of the COMIT bank, Cesare Merzagore. In 1966 an international cooperation agreement was reached with a leading U.S. insurer, Aetna Life and Casualty, under which each company provided reciprocal services to the other's clients while abroad.

In the 1970s Generali rationalized its foreign activities, aiming at greater local integration. Companies such as Generali France, Generali Belgium and, in West Germany, Generali Lebensversicherung were created as domestic companies governed by local laws, and often were strengthened by mergers with local companies. Reinsurance activity was increased. The Europ Assistance Service companies were also established, providing tourist assistance in the European market.

Enrico Randone became Generali's chairman in 1979, taking over from Merzagore, who remained as honorary chairman. By this time the company had assumed its present name. Two years later a robust Generali celebrated its 150th anniversary. Total premiums amounted to L1.395 trillion, real property was valued at L581 billion, and equity investments at L1.09 trillion. This marked the beginning of a significant decade for the company. The prospect of a unified European market in 1992 prompted an increase in mergers and acquisitions in the major European markets, as Europe's large insurers prepared for tough competition.

Generali had distinguished itself in the postwar decades as a slow-moving giant, too dignified for U.S.-style hostile takeover bids. In 1988, however, the Italian company tried to acquire Compagnie du Midi, one of the larger French insurance groups. This bid was ultimately unsuccessful, as the threat of takeover drove Midi to seek protection in a merger with its largest competitor in France, the Axa Group. The widely publicized adventure ended in a boardroom battle between the two French managers. Midi's president Bernard Pagezy was driven out by his younger partner Claude Bébéar, while Generali won no more than a joint partnership with Axa-Midi, in accordance with French regulations on foreign investment.

During this period, the large shareholders controlling nearly 23 percent of Generali stock proved to be influential in determining company strategy. Mediobanca headed this list, controlling 5.6 percent. Another 4.8 percent was held by the Euralux investment group whose members include Italy's powerful Agnelli family. The Banca d'Italia owned a similar portion of shares.

Generali closed the decade with the formation of AB Generali Budapest, the first mixed-ownership insurance company in Eastern Europe, 40 percent of the joint venture being owned by Generali and 60 percent by Allami Biztosito, a Hungarian state-owned insurer. In 1990, Generali made its first real entrance into the U.S. business world, buying the Kansas City, Missouri-based Business Men's Assurance Company of America from its parent BMA Corporation for about US$285 million, or less than L360 billion. Another significant achievement was Generali's link-up with Taisho Marine and Fire Insurance Company (now Mitsui Marine and Fire Insurance Company), the third-largest insurer in Japan, whereby Generali was able to open a liaison office and general agency through Taisho Marine and Fire in Tokyo, and Taisho was able to operate in Italy through the offices of Generali subsidiary la Navale.

In 1991, the 80-year-old chairman Enrico Randone retired, along with several other senior officers who had guided Generali's policy for the past few decades. Taking over the chairmanship was Eugenio Coppola di Canzano. Coppola continued to seek opportunities for Generali outside Italy. Asia was one area targeted for growth as Generali expanded its presence there by opening agencies in Hong Kong and Singapore. Another was North America where Generali and New York-based Continental Corp. signed an agreement in 1991, whereby Continental would service and underwrite the North American portion of multinational policies covering commercial and personal property and casualty risks.

Back in Europe, Generali was experiencing a difficult period in the early 1990s. Its operations in England were consistently unprofitable because of huge underwriting losses. The already poor ratio of underwriting losses to premium income of 113 percent in 1991 increased to 117 percent in 1992. Generali officials blamed the U.K. losses on several natural disasters, including Hurricane Andrew. Generali's French operations posted an overall loss in 1992 primarily due to large losses for the non-life insurance companies there. The problems were partially cyclical ones since the non-life underwriting markets in both countries were suffering a general downturn. Some analysts, however, pinned at least part of the blame on mismanagement. Overall, Generali was able to maintain a steady level of profits during this period because its home operations had benefited from a government crackdown on crime and from improved risk management by the company's underwriters.

Elsewhere in Europe, Generali's fairly small operation in Switzerland was significantly enhanced by the 1994 acquisition of 56 percent of the voting rights of Swiss insurer Fortuna Holding from TA Media AG. As a result, Generali's premium income in Switzerland increased 379.1 percent in 1994 over 1993 results and nearly six percent of Generali's total premium income in 1994 came from the Swiss market.

The chairmanship of the company once again changed hands in 1995 after Coppola resigned and Antoine Bernheim took over. By early 1996, Bernheim appeared to have resolved Generali's vexing relationship with the French insurer Axa, which stemmed from Generali's unsuccessful attempt to take over Midi in 1988. Since the attempted takeover, Generali had held an indirect 16.9 percent stake in Axa but was unable to exercise any influence in the company's decision-making process. Generali wanted to work together with Axa in foreign markets, particularly in Asia, but had consistently been ignored. After Generali threatened to sell its stake unless Axa cooperated with it, in early 1996 Axa finally gave Generali the greater voice it wanted by realigning the links between the two firms. Consequently, Generali gained a direct 11 percent stake in Axa, with voting rights equivalent to 15.6 percent.

Despite its difficulties in Europe, Generali enjoyed steady growth in the early 1990s. Gross premiums written increased 15.5 percent in 1994 to US$17.63 billion and profits increased from $374.4 million in 1993 to $393.2 million in 1994. Through these uncertain years the company had maintained its number five position in the European insurance market. As competition began to increase in anticipation of the deregulation of the European financial markets, Generali's long tradition of success outside its home market boded well for its future.

Principal Subsidiaries

Agricola San Giorgio S.p.A.; Agricoltura Assicurazioni; Alleanza Assicurazioni S.p.A. (57.86%); Aurora Assicurazioni

S.p.A. (99.78%); Friuli-Venezia Giulia Assicurazioni (61.1%); Gefina; Genagricola S.p.A.; La Venezia Assicurizioni S.p.A.; Navale Assicurazioni S.p.A. (98.17%); Società Italiana Assicurazioni Danni S.p.A.; Unione Mediterranea di Sicurtà S.p.A. (98.01%); Europ Assistance S.A. (France; 53.52%); Generali France S.A. (99.92%); La Concorde S.A. (France; 81.95%); La Fédération Continentale (France; 99.73%); La Lutèce S.A. (France; 99.26%); Deutscher Lloyd Lebensversicherung AG (Germany); Generali Versicherung (Germany); Deutscher Lloyd Versicherung (Germany; 70.18%); Northern Star Insurance Co. Ltd. (U.K.); Participatie Maatschappij Graafschap Holland (Netherlands); Banco Vitalicio de España Compañía Anonima de Seguros (Spain); Caja de Previsión y Socorro S.A. (Spain); Central Hispano Generali, Holding de Entidades de Seguros, S.A. (Spain); Generali Belgium Holding S.A.; Generali Hellas A.E. (Greece; 99%); Generali Life A.E. (Greece; 60%); Generali Luxembourg; Generali Vida Companhia de Seguros S.A. (Portugal; 99.99%); Generali Worldwide Insurance Co. (Guernsey); EA-Generali AG (Austria); Erste Allgemeine Versicherung AG (Austria); Generali Allgemeine Lebensversichering AG (Austria); Interunfall Versichering AG (Austria; 77.66%); Fortuna Holding (Switzerland; 36.07%); Holdux Beteilgungsgesellschaft (Switzerland); Union Suisse Compagnie Generale d'Assurances (Switzerland; 95.78%); Generali Sigorta A.S. (Turkey; 88.97%); Generali Budapest Biztosító Rt. (Hungary); Providencia Osztrák-Magyar Biztosító Rt. (Hungary; 78%); Anglická Business Center spol. (Czech Republic); Generali Asigurari S.A. (Romania); Business Men's Assurance Company of America (U.S.A.); Europ Assistance U.S. Holdings, Inc. (U.S.A.); Transocean Holding Corp. (U.S.A.); Worldwide Assistance Services Inc. (U.S.A.); Federation Insurance Company of Canada; Generali Argentina Vida Compañía de Seguros Patrimoniales (95.14%); Transocean do Brasil Partipacoes S.A. (Brazil); Seguros La Andina (Colombia; 72.71%); The Standard General Insurance Company Ltd. (South Africa; 95.32%).

Further Reading

Le Assicurazioni Generali: Cenni Storici, Trieste: Assicurazioni Generali, 1966.

An Introduction to Generali, Trieste: Generali Group, 1988.

Generali Group: The Insurer without Frontiers, Trieste: Generali Group, 1995.

Lindner, Claudio, and Giancarlo Mazzuca, Il leone di Trieste: il romanzo delle Assicurazioni Generali dalle origini austroungariche all'era Cuccia, Milan: Sperling & Kupfer, 1990.

Palladini, Giovanni, "Le Compagnie di assicurazioni di Trieste," Trieste Economica, December 1966.

Pitt, William, "Generali, Continental Venture Targets French Multinationals," Business Insurance, June 29, 1992, p. 95.

Schondelmeyer, Brent, "Generali Goliath Embraces BMA," Kansas City Business Journal, November 15, 1991, p. 19.

"Stumbling Abroad," Economist, July 17, 1993, pp. 71–72.

Sullivan, Ruth, "Gallic Blood Injects New Life into Generali," European, November 2, 1995, p. 28.

—Paul Conrad
—updated by David E. Salamie

Baby Superstore, Inc.

605 Haywood Rd.
Greenville, South Carolina 29607
U.S.A.
(803) 675-0299
Fax: (803) 675-0299

Public Company
Incorporated: 1970 as Carolina Baby Inc.
Employees: 1,662
Stock Exchanges: NASDAQ
Sales: $309 million (1995)
SICs: 5641 Children's & Infants' Wear Stores; 5712
    Furniture Stores; 5999 Miscellaneous Retail Stores,
    Not Elsewhere Classified

Baby Superstore, Inc., operates a chain of 60 stores in 16 southeastern and midwestern states. The stores sell clothing, supplies, toys, furniture, and other accessories for babies, and are distinguished by diverse inventory and low prices. The company plans to more than double in size during the mid-1990s.

Baby Superstore was founded by American entrepreneur and billionaire Jack Tate. In 1995 *Forbes* listed 51-year-old Tate as one of the 400 wealthiest people in the United States. Most of that wealth was generated through Tate's Baby Superstore venture, which he launched in the early 1970s and groomed into the most successful baby supplies business in history. Baby Superstore capitalized on the trend toward giant discount specialty outlets in the 1980s, expanded rapidly, and began growing at an even faster pace in the 1990s.

Tate was first exposed to the retail industry as a boy growing up in Greenville, South Carolina. His father, Jack Sr., operated a furniture store with his Uncle George. The business was moderately successful, but Tate's father didn't believe that it, or retail in general, promised a very bright future for his son. Instead, Jack Tate, Sr., wanted his son to become an attorney. Tate graduated from the University of North Carolina in 1966 and entered Harvard Law School. The intense desire to start his own business was ignited one day in March 1969 when he went shopping for baby supplies and furniture for his nine-month-old daughter and was struck with an inspiration: Why not put everything that you needed to buy for your baby under one roof and create a sort of one-stop-shop for parents? "It hit me with a force that I still don't understand," Tate recalled in the October 23, 1995, *Forbes*.

After his shopping trip, Tate wrote the name "Carolina Baby" on a legal pad and filed it away. Although he hesitantly started his own law practice after graduation from Harvard, he couldn't get his mind off of the idea. His attention quickly strayed from his law firm, and Tate began looking for capital to start a Carolina Baby shop. He approached some local bankers and was able to convince them to front about $200,000. Tate had hired a 20-year-old legal secretary named Lisa Robertson to help with his law practice part-time. Together, they opened the first Carolina Baby store in Greenville in March 1971, and Robertson remained president of the company, under Chief Executive Tate, into the mid-1990s. The shop, which provided furniture, clothing, and toys for babies and children through age 12, was a hit. Tate shuttered his law firm in April and never looked back.

Tate's ability to round up $200,000 in cash while still in his early 20s reflected his entrepreneurial traits, which included infectious enthusiasm and hard-driving ambition. Augmenting those personal qualities was a feeling that Tate had experienced since early childhood that he was destined to accomplish something significant with his life. "I remember feeling driven when I was six years old," Tate said in the *Forbes* article. "I can't describe it. It was just a feeling that I was supposed to do something." That "something" for the next few decades would be his baby supplies enterprise.

Tate opened his second Baby Superstore two years later in nearby Easly, South Carolina. That store spawned a gradual expansion of Carolina Baby shops throughout the Carolinas during the 1970s and early 1980s. Besides building more stores, Tate began experimenting with different concepts and formats to find the perfect recipe for his shops. He tried opening some stores in malls, for example, but discovered that the real estate was too expensive for him to fully stock a store and still generate sufficient profits. He eventually found that bigger, less expensive locations in strip shopping centers worked well. He also gradually narrowed his target market to younger and younger kids, finally focusing on babies and toddlers.

Hard work and persistence paid off for Tate and Robertson, who watched their venture slowly take off during the 1970s and early 1980s and build steam during the mid-1980s. The company began expanding outside of the Carolinas into neighboring southeastern states, where the concept was well received. By the mid-1980s Carolina Baby, Inc. was operating about 25 stores that averaged 6,000 square feet in size. The company was generating nearly $15 million in annual sales and realizing steady profits, and Tate was generally satisfied with the store format that had evolved—until 1987. In that year, Tate hit on a new concept that was destined to transform his company when he opened an experimental 20,000-square-foot superstore in Marietta, Georgia.

The giant store offered a wide range of goods and was an immediate hit. Sales-per-square-foot shot up an amazing 50 percent over the company's smaller stores. Tate suddenly realized that, after building his business for more than 15 years, he would have to effectively shut down his other stores and convert them into superstores. In 1987 Tate changed the name of the company to Baby Superstore, Inc., and began looking for cash to build Baby Superstore outlets. During the next five years he and fellow executives scrambled to open a total of 26 shops under the Baby Superstore banner. From $14.5 million in 1987, sales exploded to $26 million in 1989, $38 million in 1990, and then to a whopping $47 million in 1991.

Tate's gains at Carolina Baby and Baby Superstore during the 1970s, 1980s, and early 1990s were made even more impressive by the fact that he achieved them by utilizing a fiscally conservative growth strategy. Expansion was funded largely by internal cash flow, and Tate invested much of the company's profits back into the business. Tate himself was something of a maverick among successful entrepreneurs. For example, despite his multi-millionaire status, he lived simply in a two-bedroom A-frame house located in a remote mountain town near Greenville. He kept two pet goats and a pet sheep. The most conspicuous evidence of his success were a helicopter and a Lear jet, which he purchased and maintained with cash from his own pocket.

As the company opened new stores, it continued to tweak its format to maximize sales and profits. In one important innovation in 1992, Baby Superstore borrowed an idea from hardware superstore retailer Home Depot. Management began tearing out interior walls and ceilings and reducing backroom stock space. Long, wide aisles were created that were walled in by inventory piled high toward the ceiling. Stores were stocked with a wide range of furniture and supplies for babies, toddlers, and juveniles. The goal was to create an impressive store where shoppers knew that they could go to find nearly any item that they needed, wanted, or didn't even know existed for their children or grandchildren. The effort was hugely successful, as evidenced by a steady increase in per-store sales and profits.

The success of Baby Superstore didn't go unnoticed. Other retailers followed the company into the baby market. Among

the most notable new competitors in the early 1990s were KidSource and Lil' Things. Tate met the startups head on by opening Baby Superstore outlets across the street from some of the competitors' new stores. A more weighty contender was the massive Toys "R" Us chain, which announced in 1994 that it was going to open five Babies "R" Us stores in 1995. To contend with such threats to his market share, Tate opened new stores at a steady, rapid clip. By 1994 the company was operating a chain of about 40 stores, with plans to have roughly 50 shops in 13 states open by the end of 1995.

Even with the new competition, Baby Superstore executives were confident of their future. Demographic projections favored Baby Superstore's concept and suggested continued market growth, and Tate worked to boost the company's exposure through new marketing efforts. Baby Superstore began offering its own brand of clothing, for example, which was manufactured by some of the same Asian producers that supplied Baby Gap. At the same time, the company was expanding floor space and inventory to top its competitors. In 1994 it began opening 40,000-square-foot stores that stocked about 25,000 items from 500 suppliers—compared to about 15,000 items stocked by Toys "R" Us.

Indeed, over several years the company had developed a shrewd mix of products, prices, and service that generated its reputation as a savvy merchandiser. "Baby Superstore has struck a chord with consumers with its combination of great brand names and dominant assortments," surmised Doug Hyde, chief executive of OshKosh B'Gosh, in the June 19, 1995, *Discount Store News.* "They've been around for a long time, and they're very sophisticated merchants. . . . Baby Superstore is a long-term, significant player." Baby Superstore sold goods categorized into six major segments focused on babies through three-year-olds: furniture, which comprised its largest profit center; clothing; baby needs; toys; commodities; and shoes. The product mix within each segment was chosen to appeal to both broad markets and niches, such as premature babies or baby Christening accouterments. And, while prices were kept low through volume purchases, the company prided itself on a high level of customer service.

After more than two decades of funding growth largely from earnings, Tate finally decided to take Baby Superstore public. The decision was partly the result of a meeting between Tate and Kenneth Langone, a well-known New York investment banker. Langone was known for, among other deals, taking Ross Perot's Electronic Data Systems public in 1968 and engineering a successful initial public offering for Home Depot in 1978. In September 1994 Langone helped to take Baby Superstore public with a stock sale that raised $33 million. The company's stock price more than doubled to $25 on its first day of trading, reflecting investor enthusiasm over the company. A few months later, by which time the stock had vaulted to $38 per share, Baby Superstore raised another $29 million through a second offering.

Tate planned to use the cash to intensify expansion efforts. The company had already managed to boost sales to $63 million in 1992, $104 million in 1993, and then to a whopping $175 million in 1994. At the same time, profits swelled from about $500,000 annually during the early 1990s to a fat $2.32 million in 1994. By the end of 1994 the company was operating a chain of nearly 40 Superstores. Management planned to boost that number by about 40 during the next two years, moving into new markets including Chicago and New York. As a result of new stores, as well as increased revenues at existing units, the organization's sales surged to more than $300 million in 1995. "This is a company with tremendous growth prospects," said retail analyst Marcia Aaron. "Based on our estimates, we believe that Baby Superstore is capable of 50 percent compound annual growth over the next three years."

Further Reading

Alpert, Bill, "Growing Pains: Baby Superstore," *Barron's*, October 23, 1995, p. 20.

"Baby Superstore Founder Jack Tate to Speak in Charleston," *PR Newswire*, November 2, 1995.

Meeks, Fleming, "Catering to Indulgent Parents," *Forbes*, October 23, 1995, p. 148.

Reda, Susan, "Baby Superstore: Building Sturdy Stock," *Discount Store News*, June 19, 1995, p. A8.

—Dave Mote

Badger Paper Mills, Inc.

200 West Front Street
P.O. Box 149
Peshtigo, Wisconsin 54157
U.S.A.
(715) 582-4551
Fax: (715) 582-4853

Public Company
Incorporated: 1929
Employees: 435
Sales: $73.6 million (1994)
Stock Exchanges: NASDAQ
SICs: 2621 Paper Mills

Badger Paper Mills, Inc. is a leading producer of plain, printed, and waxed papers for the flexible packaging industry. Badger makes about two-thirds of the government butter wrap used in the United States and makes the specialty wrapping paper for many well-known products, including Tootsie Rolls, Dentyne gum, Nestle's candies, and Bit-O-Honey candy bars. Badger also produces soap wrappers, other candy wrappers, gum wrap, meat packaging, and fast food sandwich packaging. The company has been manufacturing bread wrapping since the 1930s. Badger also produces computer paper, copier paper and other writing and printing papers, marketed under the brand names Ta-Non-Ka, Copyrite, BPM, Envirographic, and Northern Brights. Badger Paper Mills additionally specializes in custom papers developed to suit such unique customer needs as odd sizes and colors, specially perforated or punched paper, or other custom designs. The company sells its writing papers through wholesale paper merchants and operates a direct sales force to market its packaging and specialty papers. The company manages about 17,000 acres of forest land and produces about 60 percent of its own pulp. Badger also operates a subsidiary, Plas-Techs, Inc. in Oconto Falls, Wisconsin, to print and process plastic and paper substrates.

Badger Paper Mills, Inc. was founded in 1929 by a group of investors who had taken over a failing mill called the Peshtigo Paper Company. The town of Peshtigo, Wisconsin, was the site of one of the nation's most horrific forest fires in 1871. Gale-force winds whipped flames through woods covering six counties of northeastern Wisconsin, and more than 800 people were killed in the fire. Overshadowed by the Great Chicago Fire, which occurred at the same time, the considerably more lethal Peshtigo fire left the town completely ruined. It was subsequently rebuilt, and because of its proximity to timberland and its ample waterway, the Peshtigo river, the area served as home to several paper mills. The Peshtigo Fibre Company was built in 1917, and the Peshtigo Pulp and Paper Company was built in 1918. These two were combined into the Peshtigo Paper Company in 1922, but Peshtigo Paper never did well. It was operating at only half capacity most of the time, and in November 1928, the company went bankrupt and shut down. The town of Peshtigo too was languishing. Unemployment was high, and homes were being sold for only a fraction of their value.

The failing mill was taken over in January 1929, by a group of seven entrepreneurs from Menasha, Wisconsin, led by Edwin A. Meyer. They purchased Peshtigo Paper for $250,000 and renamed the company Badger Paper Mills. Meyer and his group had expertise in the paper industry, and they believed they could revive the old plant. Meyer himself had been in the paper business for twenty years when he bought Peshtigo, and he brought with him investors experienced in every aspect of running a paper mill. When they arrived in Peshtigo, they found their newly acquired property in less than prime condition. Several carloads of obsolete equipment had to be thrown out. The tunnel crossing the river between the sulphite mill on the east side of the river and the paper mill on the west side needed to be reinforced, and up-to-date equipment had to be installed. However, the group from Menasha pooled their skills and came up with a viable plan to return the company to profitability.

Several members of the group had backgrounds in paper manufacturing equipment, and they oversaw the installation of new machinery. Badger decided to make waxed paper, and a wax machine and rewinder were installed immediately. In 1930, what had been the old boiler house was remade into the wax department, and the first wax paper printing press was installed.

The company's Fourdrinier paper machine was redesigned and rebuilt in 1931, and a second printing press was purchased in 1935. Badger improved its facilities year by year throughout the 1930s. Despite the nationwide depression that had begun in the year Badger was founded, the company prospered. Badger was able to turn a profit in its very first year.

Badger's success was due in part to the quality products its new equipment put out, but the company was able to find buyers for its products largely because its new owners had considerable marketing skill. From the beginning, the company set up a Sales and Advertising department, which was headed by Clarence Hoeper. In addition, company president Edwin Meyer had a wide acquaintance with the heads of paper distributing companies in Wisconsin and across the country. Meyer, Hoeper, and their associates traveled tirelessly to attract buyers for Badger paper products. Commercial bread baking had become big business beginning in the 1920s, when the development of bread wrapping and slicing machines made large-scale distribution possible. Badger Paper Mills marketed its waxed paper bread wrapper to this growing industry. Because Badger's work force was unionized, the company was allowed to print the ''union label'' on its wrapping. This apparently gave Badger's product a marketing edge. Bread wrap remained one of the company's leading products for over fifty years.

Badger's new owners also installed a cost accounting control system for the new corporation. Sales grew as new orders came in. The company was able to continue to make improvements to its facilities, constructing a new warehouse in 1938 and digging new wells in 1941 and 1948. Badger introduced a waxed paper called FRESHrap and installed special automatic equipment for this product in 1949 and 1950.

Over the ensuing years, Badger packaging papers were used for such nationally distributed brand foods as Red Star yeast, Pepperidge Farm bread, Pillsbury Space Food Sticks, Dream Whip, Pop Tarts, Hamburger Helper, Hall's cough drops, Sugar Daddy candy, Tootsie Pops, and myriad others. Fast food restaurants also used Badger papers to wrap and package their foods. Burger King used Badger paper to wrap its burgers, and Arby's purchased Badger pouch containers for its french fries. The company also sold many brands of imprinted butter wrap. In its fine paper division, Badger made several grades of copier paper, printing and writing paper, and mimeo paper.

Badger's customers were unusually loyal, and the company made a profit every year for its first fifty years. Labor relations were stable, and the company also had a good relationship with the town of Peshtigo, supplying the town's water until the 1960s. Badger completely rebuilt its Fourdrinier machine, which produced its fine grade papers, in 1964, then again in 1985. Major equipment improvements kept Badger's products competitive, and efficient marketing too paid off. Badger cultivated niche markets, offering special size and color paper, for example. Because Badger procured most of its pulp from its own trees, the company exercised a high degree of control over its product through each step of the manufacturing process. Badger was able to adapt quickly to customer needs, and could add or drop products with more flexibility than some of its larger competitors.

Badger decided to enter the fanfold computer paper market in 1983. Within a few years, its SHARPrint brand computer paper comprised 20 percent of its production. Badger's sales rose sharply in the 1980s, from $48 million in 1984 to over $72 million in 1988. The company also made a significant overhaul of its plant in the 1980s, prompted in part by air pollution problems identified by the Wisconsin Department of Natural Resources (DNR). Inspectors from the DNR discovered emergency levels of sulphur dioxide downwind from Badger's wood pulp digesters in August 1983. The emissions were the highest ever recorded in Wisconsin at the time, and eventually the DNR filed suit against the company. Through a loan from the city of Peshtigo and an industrial development bond issue, Badger raised $14.5 million for new construction. Twelve million dollars went to rebuild its Fourdrinier machine. The company also installed a new wet scrubber system and a continuous computer monitor to take care of the sulphur dioxide emission problem, at a cost of close to $1 million.

Sales in 1990 hit a record high of over $76 million. Badger expanded by acquiring a subsidiary, Plas-Techs, Inc., in 1991. Plas-Techs, located in Oconto Falls, Wisconsin, provided additional printing capabilities for Badger's flexible packaging papers. This market continued to improve for Badger. Badger had long made specialty papers for the fast food industry. Environmental concerns turned more and more of these companies away from polystyrene containers, to paper or paper laminate packaging, and Badger benefitted from this trend. Environmental concerns also made recycled papers increasingly popular, and Badger introduced a new line of recycled printing and writing papers under the Envirographic brand label.

The company made another acquisition in 1992, buying the Howard Paper Mill in Dayton, Ohio. The Howard Mill was able to produce higher grade printing and writing papers than Badger's Peshtigo plant. Badger intended to develop niche markets for high-grade papers, and the company designed more than 70 new products at the Dayton plant in the year following the acquisition. None of this paid off, however. Poor market conditions and high costs kept the Howard Mill from profitability, and Badger sold it off again in 1993. Badger continued to look for niche markets. It began operating a computerized color control system that allowed Badger to produce as many as 90 different colors, according to customer specifications. With this new technology in place, Badger was able to attract new customers and increase its share of the custom color paper market. Nevertheless, a depressed market in 1993 held down the company's profits and led to a loss at year-end of over $4 million.

The paper industry experienced erratic changes in 1994. The cost of paper fiber increased 90 percent over the year, though the price of standard uncoated free-sheet paper remained extremely depressed. Badger's packaging paper division had strong sales, but the company ended 1994 with another loss of net earnings, this time of just over $2.5 million. In August 1994, Badger sold its SHARPrint computer papers product line to an Illinois company, CST Office Products. Though computer papers had made up a large proportion of the company's sales in the 1980s, by 1994 Badger was refocused on its principal products, packaging and printing grade papers. By the end of 1994, the industry depression seemed to be ending, and demand for paper was on the rise again. Badger expected improved business conditions to help return the company to profitability. The company instituted an early retirement program to try to curb overstaffing and made improvements to various manufacturing processes to increase efficiency and reduce costs. Badger also made changes and improvements to some of its waste processing facilities. It redirected the waste water effluents from its mills from a settling lagoon into the city of Peshtigo waste water treatment facility. The company jointly operated this treatment facility with the city. The redirection actually resulted in less release of waste water, and Badger made plans to close its lagoon, as well as a landfill, in compliance with Department of Natural Resources regulations.

Principal Subsidiaries

Plas-Techs, Inc.

Principal Divisions

Fine Paper Division; MG Flexible Packaging Division.

Further Reading

"DNR Says Paper Mill Violated Pollution Laws." *Capital Times,* April 9, 1984.

Fifty Years of Progress, 1929–1979, Peshtigo, Wisc.: Badger Paper Mills, Inc., 1979.

"Management Shuffled by Paper Firm." *Milwaukee Journal,* April 22, 1976.

"Net Down, Sales Up at Paper Firm." *Milwaukee Journal,* February 16, 1976.

"Paper Mill Faces Pollution Suit." *Wall Street Journal,* June 30, 1984.

"Peshtigo Firm Starts Expansion Project." *Capital Times,* April 17, 1985.

Rooks, Alan. "Badger Paper: Small Town Story with a Happy Ending." *PIMA Magazine,* August 1989.

—A. Woodward

**BANCO
ESPIRITO SANTO**

Banco Espírito Santo e Comercial de Lisboa S.A.

Av. da Liberdade, 195
1250 Lisboa
Portugal
(351) 1 315 8331
Fax: (351) 1 355 5248

Public Company
Incorporated: 1920 as Banco Espírito Santo
Employees: 5,714
Revenues: Esc17.3 billion (US$23 million) (1994)
Stock Exchanges: New York Oporto Monaco
    Luxembourg London
SICs: 6021 National Commercial Banks

With total assets of US$15.6 billion, Banco Espírito Santo e Comercial de Lisboa S.A. is one of Portugal's largest, most profitable commercial banks. The history of this venerable financial institution—whose name means "Holy Spirit"—is closely linked to Portugal's volatile political and economic past. In 1992, after 16 years under government ownership, the bank was reprivatized by a group of institutional investors led by descendants of the founding Espírito Santo family. By the mid-1990s, the family-held Espírito Santo Financial Holding S.A. owned a controlling interest in Banco Espírito Santo (BESCL). While Luxembourg-based Espírito Santo Financial Holding is technically the parent company, the two entities are often referred to interchangeably. Other significant institutional investors included France's Caisse Nationale de Crédit Agricole and The Chase Manhattan Bank Clients AC. The Portuguese government retained a stake in Espírito Santo through the early 1990s as well.

While BESCL's activities are concentrated in its home country, it also has offices in twelve other countries around the world. The company's roster of services includes credit cards, stock brokerage, asset management, and leasing. In addition to its commercial banking operations, BESCL also controls Portugal's third-largest insurance company, Companhia de Seguros Tranquilidade Vida, S.A., and manages six Portuguese mutual funds.

The Espírito Santo family's banking odyssey began during the late 19th century, when patriarch José Maria de Espírito Santo Silva established Beirao, Pinto, Silva and Co., a bank in the national capital of Lisbon. The family changed the institution's name to Espírito Santo Silva and Banco Co. in 1918. Although the first two decades of the 20th century were a period of great political upheaval, during which time Portugal haltingly shifted via revolution from a monarchical form of government to a republican regime, the period between the two World Wars was one of dramatic growth in Portugal's banking industry. José Maria's eldest son, also named José, led Espírito Santo until 1931, when he was expelled from the Catholic country for getting a divorce.

José's younger brother Ricardo defied the global depression of the 1930s to build a European banking empire. He found a willing supporter in António de Oliveira Salazar, the prime minister who founded the "Estado Novo" (New State) in 1933. His virtual dictatorship endured over four decades, becoming Europe's most prolific authoritarian government. Salazar had acted as Portugal's finance minister in the late 1920s and had played an important role in the stabilization of the country's finances. The Espírito Santos expanded into insurance with the purchase of Tranquilidade during the early 1930s. In 1937, Banco Espírito Santo merged with the 62-year-old Banco Comercial de Lisboa, renaming the new entity Banco Espírito Santo e Comercial de Lisboa.

Salazar's strategies fostered Espírito Santo's growth during and after the Second World War. Portugal's neutrality during the war made it a haven for the wealthy of Europe, and postwar protectionism precluded foreign competition. Salazar's tenuous hold on Portugal's African colonies facilitated the Espírito Santo family's acquisition of major sugar, coffee, and palm oil plantations in Mozambique and Angola. The 1960s brought a veritable "boom" to what had historically been western Europe's poorest nation, as economic growth surged at an annual rate between 5 percent and 7 percent. By the early 1970s, the privately held, $2 billion-asset Banco Espírito Santo had become Portugal's largest bank, and its Tranquilidade subsidiary was the country's top insurance company. The family fortune was estimated to total $4 billion at its summit.

However, when Salazar suffered a debilitating heart attack in 1968, his successor, Marcelo Caetano, was unable to hold the Estado Novo together. By 1974, the pressure of colonial wars and deep economic recession precipitated a bloodless military coup. Although the new regime, the Movimento das Forças Armadas (Armed Forces Movement, or MFA), instituted what has been characterized as ``a moderate form of democracy,'' its communist leanings led to the nationalization of Portugal's biggest companies. Early that year, Chief Executive Officer Manuel Ricardo Espírito Santo was arrested at a meeting of the bank's board of directors and condemned to a 14-month prison sentence.

Battered but unbowed, the Espírito Santo family fled to Spain, then settled in London. The family took its meager settlement from the government and founded E.S. International Holding S.A. in Luxembourg with $20,000. They purchased a major stake in Florida's Biscayne Bank (later renamed Espírito Santo Bank of Florida) in 1978 and won a Brazilian banking license late in the decade. They began to reassert the well-recognized family name in 1983 with the creation of Bank Espírito Santo International Ltd. in the Cayman Islands. They also purchased equity in banks in London and Paris, and established a fund management company in Lausanne, Switzerland. By 1990, they had accumulated a $246 million enterprise.

In the meantime, the 1985 election of free-market Social Democrat Anibal Cavaco Silva heralded an era of reprivatization. When the new regime began to reprivatize financial institutions and insurance companies in 1986, Espírito Santo wasted no time in reentering its home country. That same year, Espírito Santo Financial Holding formed a commercial bank, Banco Internacional de Credito, as a joint venture with France's Credit Agricole. Espírito Santo used the proceeds of a Eurobond floatation to repurchase Tranquilidade in 1990. The family reacquired Banco Espírito Santo with the help of France's Caisse Nationale de Crédit Agricole and The Chase Manhattan Bank Clients AC.

While nationalization had weakened some of BESCL's competitors, Espírito Santo was fairly well managed throughout the period of state ownership. In 1993, Espírito Santo official Manuel Villas-Boas told *Euromoney* that ``To a large degree the bank kept to the philosophies of credit and the systems implemented before the period of nationalization. The bank was fortunate in the choice of management it had under nationalization, and the bank had a strong and well provided balance sheet when we took it back.''

That didn't mean that there was no room for improvement, however. For example, BESCL's employee roster had grown by 70 percent during the period of nationalization. Led by Chairman Ricardo Espírito Santo Silva Salgado, the family focused on restructuring the group and increasing efficiency. They called upon well-known management consultants McKinsey and Company to assist with the reorganization. The new management team increased productivity dramatically by reducing staffing levels from 6,800 in 1990 to 5,700 by 1994, while simultaneously increasing the number of branches from 177 to 332. The ratio of administrative costs to financial assets decreased by almost 18 percent and the number of employees per branch declined from 27 to 17 in the process. Assets per

employee doubled from 1991 to Esc 400 million in 1994. In 1993, BESCL boosted its technological efficiency with a US$12.8 million computer network upgrade from Unisys Corp.

The bank also shifted its strategic focus from corporate clients to the private customers, who had proven loyal patrons during the exile. Espírito Santo's commercial bank, Banco Internacional de Credito, sought to increase its share of Portugal's mortgage business to ten percent by the mid-1980s. In 1992, the financial group added a Spanish institution, Banco Industrial del Mediterraneo, to its growing roster of businesses, at an estimated price tag of 5.5 billion pesetas (US$55 million). The company's increasingly diverse interests—which included leasing, investment banking, and credit cards by the mid-1990s—allowed for cross-selling of products and services.

An unidentified Lisbon banker told *Euromoney* that ``Espírito Santo represents old money in Portugal. Their bank is the last of the old commercial banks that has retained its power.'' That name recognition factor helped impart ``an image of solidity and conservatism.'' BESCL continued to nurture that reputation in the early 1990s, employing a conservative lending policy and maintaining a highly diversified loan portfolio. That caution earned Espírito Santo the highest international credit rating given to a Portuguese bank. These strong appraisals, in turn, enabled BESCL to successfully float $76.9 million of its shares as American Depositary Receipts (ADRs) on the New York Stock Exchange in 1993. James R. Kraus of *American Banker* defined ADRs as ``negotiable receipts that are held in custody overseas and are traded in dollars.''

In 1993, *Euromoney* noted that ``Espírito Santo's biggest challenge is to adapt the style and organization of a bank which existed when Portugal was a small rural economy into one fit for a growing industrial and international environment.'' Merrill Lynch market analyst Sasha Serafimovski agreed, telling *Money* magazine in 1995 that ``Portugal is one of the fastest-growing and most profitable banking markets in Europe.'' After BESCL saw a five-year average annual earnings growth of 21.6 percent from 1989 to 1994, Serafimovski predicted that Espírito's annual earnings growth would slow somewhat, to 15 percent, in the years leading up to the turn of the 21st century, but forecast a 60 percent increase in the financial group's share price by the end of 1995. Indeed, the challenges facing Banco Espírito Santo e Comercial de Lisboa in the mid-1990s seemed meager at worst, in comparison with the hurdles it had already met and surmounted.

Late in 1995, Kraus reported in *American Banker* that Espírito Santo had entered negotiations with Chemical Banking Corp. to purchase Banco Chemical (Portugal) S.A. If completed, the transaction would dramatically expand Espírito Santo into a $300 billion (asset), 75,000-employee bank.

Principal Subsidiaries

MULTIGER—Sociedade de Compra, Venda e Administraç a. de Propriedades, S.A. (89.55%); BESSA—Banco Espírito Santo S.A. (Spain); Bescleasing—Sociedade de Locaç ao Financeira Mobiliária S.A. (72.02%); ESAF—Espírito Santo Activos Financeiros SGPS, S.A. (65%); Euroges Factoring S.A.

(98.5%); ESER—Sociedade Financeira de Corretagem, S.A. (57%); Crediflash—Sociedade Financeira para Aquisições a Crédito, S.A. (75%); Esger—Empresas de Servicos e Consultoria S.A. (81.8%); ESGP—Espírito Santo Gest ao de Patrimónios S.A. (64%); Esegur; BESNAC—Banco Espírito Santo North American Capital Corp.; ESOL—Espírito Santo Overseas Ltd. (Cayman Islands); Krediges—Sociedade de Servicos S.A. (50%); Banco Essi S.A. (34.42%); Europ Assistance—Companhia Portuguesa de Seguros de Assistencia S.A. (23%); Vendal (28.81%); Pextrafil (21.77%); SPGM—Sociedade de Investimentos S.A. (21.77%); Centralcontrol SGPS (25%); Banco Inter-Unido (49.85%); ESAF Espírito Santo Fundo de Pensoes (45.01%).

Further Reading

Gilbert, Nick, "Espírito Santo: Kindred Spirits," *Financial World*, March 1, 1994, p. 18.
"Home Free and Looking to the Future," *Euromoney*, June 1993, p. 149.
Kraus, James R., "More Banks Hopping on ADR Bandwagon," *American Banker*, September 7, 1993, p. 9.
——. "Big Foreign Banks Come Ashore to Raise Equity in U.S. Markets," *American Banker*, November 19, 1993, p. 24.
"Portugal: Espírito Santo's 16-Year Odyssey," *International Management*, August 1990, p. 19.
Satterfield, David, "Miami Bank Ruffles Legal Feathers over Use of Family Name," *American Banker*, March 10, 1987, p. 16.
Scherreik, Susan, "Looking Abroad for Stock Gains of 28 Percent or More," *Money*, January 1995, p. 68.

—April Dougal Gasbarre

Bank of Tokyo-Mitsubishi Ltd.

7-1, Marunouchi, 2-chome
Chiyoda-ku
Tokyo 100
Japan
(03) 240-1111
Fax: (03) 240-4197

Public Company
Incorporated: 1996
Employees: 24,000
Total Assets: ¥72 trillion (US$701.4 billion) (1995)
Stock Exchanges: Tokyo Osaka New York Basel Geneva
    London Paris Zurich
SICs: 6029 Commercial Banks, Not Elsewhere
    Classified; 6081 Branches & Agencies of Foreign
    Banks; 6082 Foreign Trade & International Banking
    Institutions; 6159 Miscellaneous Business Credit
    Institutions; 6211 Security Brokers, Dealers &
    Flotation Companies; 6282 Investment Advice; 6712
    Offices of Bank Holding Companies; 6799 Investors,
    Not Elsewhere Classified

Bank of Tokyo-Mitsubishi Ltd., the world's largest bank, was formed in April 1996 from the merger of The Mitsubishi Bank, Ltd. and Bank of Tokyo, Ltd. The new superbank combined Mitsubishi's extensive network of domestic branches with Bank of Tokyo's overseas strength, and includes operations in a wide range of banking and financial services. Prior to the merger, Mitsubishi Bank and Bank of Tokyo were two of the healthiest banks in Japan and had survived, relatively unscathed, the Japanese lending crisis of the early 1990s.

Mitsubishi Bank was only one of many companies that originated as a division of the giant Mitsubishi trading conglomerate and were later incorporated as independent companies. Before World War II, the various Mitsubishi companies were allowed to operate in concert as a large vertical monopoly called a *zaibatsu*. Postwar industrial legislation, however,

brought about the disintegration of the conglomerate and forced each Mitsubishi company, including Mitsubishi Bank, to endure success or failure without support from its sister companies. Industrial deregulation eventually allowed the group to re-form.

Mitsubishi Bank had its origin in the exchange office of the Mitsubishi Shoji, which was the original Mitsubishi company and one of the largest maritime shipping and warehousing enterprises in Japan. The exchange office added foreign-currency transactions to its business in 1890, and five years later was reorganized into a full-service banking department. By 1917, as the Mitsubishi group continued to grow, it became necessary that it reorganize. Several divisions were spun off into independent companies, including the bank, which became independent in 1919. The following year, Mitsubishi Bank opened offices in New York and London.

Business for the Mitsubishi group as a whole remained quite strong through the 1920s, largely because of a rapidly expanding economy. As the primary instrument for the group's financial needs, the bank grew accordingly, and from 1919 to 1929 doubled its capitalization, to ¥100 million.

Japan's tumultuous industrialization brought down many banks, even those connected with trading conglomerates. The Mitsubishi group, however, was the strongest group in Japan, and survived calamities such as the Kanto Earthquake in 1923 and several serious recessions.

Mitsubishi was one of the most active Japanese interests on the Asian mainland, particularly in Manchuria. The bank opened an office at Dairen, Manchuria's main port, in 1933. At this time, a group within the military was rising to power that advocated a neomercantilist Japanese domination of Asia. This led to war with China in 1937, and political isolation some years later. On the eve of World War II, Mitsubishi was forced to close its offices in both London and New York.

The war was at first a profitable venture for the Mitsubishi group, Japan's largest arms manufacturer. But after the United States joined the war against Japan, the entire nation's industrial organization had to be changed. In order to increase efficiency, the government ordered a massive centralization, which in 1943 resulted in the merger of Mitsubishi Bank and One Hundredth Bank. The following year, the bank opened another office in occupied Shanghai under a directive to assist Japanese commercial and military interests.

When the war ended in 1945, the Mitsubishi group had suffered devastating losses in virtually every area of its operation. This, coupled with the collapse of commerce and the currency, left the bank with little but its human capital. What remained of the organization was split into hundreds of smaller companies by the occupation authority. Mitsubishi Bank, renamed Chiyoda Bank in 1948, was reorganized and its ranks were purged of war criminals.

Chiyoda Bank, named for the Tokyo financial district in which it was headquartered, started over as a common city bank and was strictly forbidden to reestablish ties with the other former Mitsubishi companies. These regulations, however, were gradually relaxed over time until, in 1953, after reopening its offices in London and New York, the bank readopted the name Mitsubishi.

With the expertise of its remaining staff, Mitsubishi Bank quickly reestablished itself as a powerful trade coordinating entity and rebuilt its ties with the other Mitsubishi companies, particularly the four trading companies that had reemerged in 1954. The bank doubled its capitalization to ¥5.5 trillion between 1953 and 1956, and again to ¥11 trillion in 1960. Indeed, the bank had grown so spectacularly that its managerial ranks soon failed to keep pace. In an effort to place more experienced workers in the field, in 1957 the bank established a training center.

During the 1960s, Mitsubishi Bank opened offices in Los Angeles, Paris, and Seoul. As an institution increasingly involved in corporate finance, the bank followed its clients to both export and resource markets. It financed raw-material purchases, helped to build factories that turned out finished products, and participated in the distribution of those products worldwide. As such, Mitsubishi Bank became an integral contributor to Japan's export-led growth.

Still chartered as a city bank, Mitsubishi was prevented from engaging in certain foreign-exchange and long-term-financing activities. Individual banking, perhaps Japan's most stable business, was a low priority for Mitsubishi; the bank simply found greater opportunities in corporate business. Much of that opportunity grew from the influence the bank wielded inside the boardrooms of its clients.

During the 1970s, the bank established several more offices in Europe, the United States, and Asia. A subsidiary, Mitsubishi Bank of California, was opened in 1972. Later in the decade, however, as Japan became a capital-surplus nation, the lending market began to dry up as more and more companies elected to conduct their own financing. By the late 1970s, deregulation had narrowed profits on lending even further.

Recognizing the importance of information management, the bank established an information office in 1972, long before such intelligence units were popular. Such an office provided it the expertise with which to establish an investment-banking

operation. Also, Mitsubishi experimented in new areas of business, including leasing, asset management, and a number of other quasi-financial ventures.

Kazuo Ibuki initiated a broad corporate reorganization shortly after he was named president of Mitsubishi Bank in June 1986. In an effort to make Mitsubishi a universal, or full-service, international bank, Ibuki divided the company into five groups: international, merchant, corporate, national banking, and capital markets. A number of young, somewhat less stodgy employees were promoted to management positions, injecting new imagination and enthusiasm into the organization.

The bank also reorganized its New York-based trust and banking subsidiary, formerly affiliated with the Bank of California, which Mitsubishi purchased in 1984 because it held great promise for Mitsubishi's entry into trust banking and securities.

In the late 1980s, Japan's economy went through a period of extreme speculation as land prices and share prices soared beyond reason. When the "bubble" burst early in the 1990s, the banking industry in Japan was hit hard. Many banks had to take huge write-offs on unrecoverable loans. A very conservative operation, Mitsubishi was a known risk avoider, and, as a result, did not suffer much from the crisis. In fact, into the mid-1990s, Mitsubishi could boast of a lower than average ratio of nonperforming loans to total assets. The bank had wisely stayed away from speculative property loans and subsequently earned its rewards for its prudence.

One such reward came in 1994 and involved Mitsubishi's takeover of Nippon Trust Bank Ltd. One of the many victims of the burst bubble, and also one of the largest, Nippon Trust's loan portfolio included as much as ¥500 billion in unrecoverable loans. Because Mitsubishi owned a five percent stake in Nippon, Japan's finance ministry pressured Mitsubishi to bail the company out. So Mitsubishi paid ¥200 billion (US$2 billion) for 64 percent more of Nippon, bringing Mitsubishi's stake to 69 percent. Observers noted that Nippon Trust's bad loans exceeded its net asset value and therefore the acquisition could hardly be called a gain. However, the finance ministry rewarded Mitsubishi for taking on the Nippon burden by allowing the bank to begin managing pension funds ahead of the other city banks. Since all the city banks were anxious to move into various financial services and were frustrated at the slow pace of deregulation, this was a significant coup for Mitsubishi.

In March 1995, Mitsubishi Bank and Bank of Tokyo, Ltd. announced that they intended to merge. Compared with Mitsubishi's strength in retail and corporate banking in the domestic market, Bank of Tokyo (BOT) had a long history of involvement in overseas banking and finance since its founding in 1880 as Yokohama Specie Bank. The only bank in the country to employ more foreigners than Japanese, BOT developed into Japan's leading foreign exchange bank. This position led the bank to gain many foreign clients, as well as to successful operations in derivatives trading and overseas banking, notably its Union Bank based in California. In fact, in terms of branches, BOT's success as an international operator was clear—it had just 37 domestic branches at the time of the merger, compared to 363 overseas.

The merger was consummated in April 1996, resulting in the world's largest bank, Bank of Tokyo-Mitsubishi Ltd., with total assets of ¥72 trillion (US$701.4 billion), 40 percent more than its nearest rival. Because of the complementary nature of the merged banks holdings, there was remarkably little overlap in the new banking behemoth. Further, unlike in typical mergers in the United States, huge numbers of employee layoffs were not announced at the same time as the merger. Even one observer's estimate of the number of jobs to be shed (most likely through attrition and early retirements) was relatively small—2,000. This was due both to how well the two operations meshed and to the more paternalistic nature of Japanese business. Ironically, the one area in which significant overlap did exist was in California, where Mitsubishi's Bank of California and BOT's Union Bank were to be merged, with perhaps more typically American layoffs.

Before the creation of the Bank of Tokyo-Mitsubishi, Sanwa Bank was regarded as the top world bank and had set a goal in the late 1980s of becoming the world's leading universal bank. Given the various strengths of Mitsubishi and BOT, it now appeared quite possible that Bank of Tokyo-Mitsubishi would be the first to reach that lofty objective. In any case, its sheer size would certainly make it a force to be reckoned with.

Principal Subsidiaries

Bank of Australia Ltd.; MBA Securities Limited (Australia); Mitsubishi Bank of Australia Limited; Mitsubishi Bank (Europe) S.A. (Belgium); Banco de Tokyo S/A (Brazil); Banco Mitsubishi Brasileiro S.A. (Brazil); Tozan Leasing S/A Arrendamente Mercantil (Brazil); The Bank of Tokyo Canada; Mitsubishi Bank of Canada; Mitsubishi Finance (Cayman) Limited (Cayman Islands); Banque Europeenne de Tokyo S.A. (France); Bank of Tokyo (Deutschland) AG (Germany); Mitsubishi Bank (Deutschland) GmbH (Germany); BOT Finance (H.K.) Ltd. (Hong Kong); BOT International H.K. Limited (Hong Kong); Kincheng-Tokyo Finance Co., Ltd. (Hong Kong; 50%); Liu Chong Hing Bank Limited (Hong Kong); Mitsubishi Finance (Hong Kong) Limited; Worldsec Asset Management Limited (Hong Kong); Worldsec Corporate Finance Limited (Hong Kong); Worldsec International Limited (Hong Kong); P.T. Mitsubishi Buana Bank (Indonesia); BOT Finanziaria Italiana S.p.A. (Italy); The Bank of Tokyo (Luxembourg) S.A.; Amanah Merchant Bank Berhad (Malaysia); Sime Diamond Leasing (Malaysia) Sdn. Bhd.; The Bank of Tokyo (Holland) N.V. (Netherlands); MBE Finance N.V. (Netherlands); Bank of Tokyo (Curacao) Holding N.V. (Netherlands Antilles); MBL Finance (Curacao) N.V. (Netherlands Antilles); The Bank of Tokyo (Panama) S.A.; Mitsubishi Bank (Panama) S.A.; BOT International (Singapore) Ltd.; Diamond Futures (Singapore) Pte. Ltd.; MBL Merchant Bank (Singapore) Limited; Bank of Tokyo (Switzerland) Ltd.; Mitsubishi Bank (Switzerland) Ltd.; The Bangkok Tokyo Finance & Securities Co., Ltd. (Thailand); Thai-Mitsubishi Investment Corporation Limited (Thailand); Bank of Tokyo International Ltd. (U.K.; 95%); Mitsubishi Finance International Ltd. (U.K.); Saudi International Bank (U.K.; 5%); BanCal Tri-State Corporation (U.S.A.); Bank of California International Corporation (U.S.A.); The Bank of California, N.A. (U.S.A.); Bank of Tokyo Intl., U.S.A.; The Bank of Tokyo Trust Co. (U.S.A.); BOT Securities Inc. (U.S.A.); The Chicago Tokyo Bank (U.S.A.; 4.93%); Mitsubishi Bank Trust Company of New York (U.S.A); Mitsubishi Capital Inc. (U.S.A.); Mitsubishi Capital Market Services, Inc. (U.S.A.); Mitsubishi Financial Futures Inc. (U.S.A.); Mitsubishi Securities (USA), Inc.; Peter Piper, Inc. (U.S.A.); Tokyo Bancorp Intl. (Houston) Inc. (U.S.A.); Union Bank (San Francisco) (U.S.A.; 76%).

Further Reading

"The Big One," *Economist*, April 1, 1995, pp. 60–61.
Bremner, Brian, William Glasgall, and Kelley Holland, "Tokyo Mitsubishi Bank: Big, Yes. Bad, No," *Business Week*, April 10, 1995.
"Mitsubeautiful," *Economist*, February 9, 1991, p. 86.
"Nippon Entrusted," *Economist*, October 15, 1994, p. 104.
Sapsford, Jathon, and Robert Steiner. "Huge Japanese Merger Could Help Revitalize the Financial Sector," *Wall Street Journal*, March 29, 1995, pp. A1, A8.

—updated by David E. Salamie

Bass PLC

20 North Audley Street
London W1Y 1WEF
England
0171-409-1919
Fax: 0171-409-8502

Public Company
Incorporated: 1967 as Bass Charrington Ltd.
Employees: 90,000
Sales: £4.54 billion (US$7.22 billion) (1995)
Stock Exchanges: London Brussels Amsterdam
SICs: 2082 Malt Beverages; 2086 Bottled & Canned Soft
   Drinks & Carbonated Waters; 5812 Eating Places;
   7011 Hotels & Motels; 7999 Amusement &
   Recreation Services, Not Elsewhere Classified

Born in a brewery, Bass PLC has grown into a diversified leisure-oriented group of companies operating in five main areas: brewing, restaurants and pubs, entertainment and gambling, hotels, and soft drinks. Bass is the largest brewer in England with the top two beer brands: Carling Black Label and Tennent's Lager; operates more than 2,400 pubs and such restaurants as Toby and Harvester; runs 800 retail betting shops in the United Kingdom, Ireland, and Jersey; owns or franchises more than 2,000 hotels in more than 60 countries under the Holiday Inn, Crown Plaza, and Holiday Inn Express brands; and runs the second leading soft drink maker in England, Britvic Soft Drinks. This diversity—largely engineered during the latter decades of the 20th century—is a new development for Bass, which for most of its history focused on breweries and pubs.

The founding of Bass & Company dates back to 1777 in the ancient town of Burton-on-Trent in Staffordshire. Although monks had been brewing beer in this town since the twelfth century, it was William Bass who laid the foundation for securing Burton's status as the focal point of Britain's brewing activities. William Bass inhabited the house next to the gateway of his brewery; it was here that his son and grandson, both future company leaders, were born. By 1791 Michael Bass, William's son, was actively engaged in his father's business.

By the turn of the century the increased volume of brewing, now 2,000 barrels per year, compelled the family to expand the High Street brewery to twice its original size. In 1821 the company became one of the first brewers to export ale to India after discovering that it was a suitable product for warm climates. Thus was born the "East India Pale Ale" which many other brewers soon imitated.

Michael Thomas Bass, William's grandson, assumed control of the brewery in 1827 when brewing capacity had reached nearly 10,000 barrels per year. By 1837 the company was known by the name of Bass, Ratcliffe & Gretton, after two fellow businessmen—John Gretton and Richard Ratcliffe—who had formed a partnership with Bass. The expansion of the railways greatly benefited the growing business; Burton ales, transported across the nation, became widely recognized as premier brands. With Bass's output surpassing 140,000 barrels a year by 1853, a second brewery was needed. By 1860 volume had increased threefold; a third brewery was constructed.

Michael Thomas Bass became not only an important figure in the industry but also a widely recognized civic leader. He financed the construction of several churches, recreation facilities, and a public library. Moreover, he served in Parliament for 33 years as a member for Derby.

By 1876 Bass was recognized; it was now Britain's largest brewing company. Its bottled ale was so popular that the company was forced to become the first firm in England to make use of the Trade Marks Registration Act of 1875 to protect its red pyramid trademark. A few years prior to Michael Bass's death in 1884, the business was organized as a private limited company. The old brewery on the High Street was renovated, but now the Bass empire covered 145 acres of land, the largest ale and bitter beer brewery in the world.

In 1888, under the leadership of Michael Bass's eldest son, Michael A. Bass, later Lord Burton, the company was incorporated as Bass, Ratcliffe & Gretton Ltd. with a share capital of

£2.7 million. Output neared one million barrels a year; more than 2,500 men and boys were employed at the breweries.

In the same year that Lord Burton incorporated the company, Gretton's son, John Gretton, Jr., joined the firm. After assuming control of the malting department in 1893, Gretton went on to join the board of directors. Gretton also served as a Conservative MP between 1895 and 1943. Among his many political causes, Gretton opposed the Licensing Bill of 1908 and trade restrictions on the brewing industry during World War I. Upon Lord Burton's death in 1908, Gretton assumed the title of Bass's chairman.

During the next decades Bass's management, unlike that of many competitors, adhered to the free trade system whereby the company relied on small traders to bottle and stock its products. Increasingly, the more common practice for British brewers was to run their own "public houses" as outlets to retail their beer. Bass did own a few public houses, but preferred to depend on the continuing national popularity of its brands to achieve expansion. As long as Bass remained in such high demand, the retailing could be left to the free trade customers. While competitors chose to invest money in the improvement of their public houses, Gretton ignored the trend and neglected his properties.

During World War I overall consumption of beer decreased. The brewing industry (through taxation) was used by the government as a source of income. This led to an increase in the price of beer. The advent of radio, cinema, and other modern leisure activities drew patrons away from the public houses. These changes in social attitudes gave further impetus to the brewers to improve their properties. Public houses were increasingly converted to comfortable places where customers could enjoy an evening of food, drink, and conversation.

Yet Gretton chose to continue rejecting the general trend toward improved public houses. Instead, his company spent the decade of the 1920s acquiring several other breweries. In 1926 Bass purchased control of Worthington & Company Ltd., a long-established competitor also located in Burton-on-Trent. The Worthington label, like that of Bass, enjoyed a national reputation. This acquisition, however, did not lead to the kind of merger common in today's market; Worthington remained virtually an autonomous operation.

While Bass continued making acquisitions, including the purchase of a wine and spirit operation, further changes in the industry occurred that were at odds with Bass's traditional approach. The small but growing firm of Mitchells & Butler not only set an industry example by improving its public house properties, but also led a trend in initiating a policy of direct brewery management. Formerly most brewery-owned houses were run by tenants who were given a free hand to operate the business. Mitchells & Butler imposed new regulations on the tenant managers; it compelled them to sell more of the firm's own beer rather than national brands such as Bass and Worthington. This policy ensured higher earnings and therefore a greater return on their investment. Such actions undercut Bass's market position.

Bass's continuing reliance on the free trade system became increasingly anachronistic. But it was not only changing social attitudes and industry trends that contributed to Bass's declining sales in the postwar years; the economic conditions of the early 1930s created further obstacles. As a result of worldwide depression, factories shut down and unemployment increased, and Bass was forced to cut back production.

Gretton had become preoccupied with his nonbusiness activities. He was deeply involved in political life, a vocal advocate of conservative causes. Bass management was not entirely asleep, however. When awareness of hygiene and quality drew consumers to pasteurized and bottled products, Bass capitalized on the trend: it introduced its "Blue Triangle" brand in 1934. Sales of this bottled version of the older "Red Triangle" grew steadily.

After Gretton died in 1947, Arthur Manners, a long-time Bass executive, assumed the title of chairman. Like Gretton's, his management style was conservative. Yet between the late 1940s and the late 1950s Bass's net profits increased by 123 percent. Expansion took the form of share acquisitions in the equity of fellow brewers. Bass acquired holdings in William Hancock & Company and Wenlock Brewery Company.

Over the next few years, however, Bass's failure to adopt a more modern business approach helped to create competition that previously did not exist. Because of the "tied house" system, Bass beer lost popularity to more aggressively marketed national brands and regionally brewed pale ales. The company refused to update its pricing system or adjust to changing public tastes toward milder beers. Even Bass's holdings in other companies were mismanaged; integration was nonexistent and redundant operations put a strain on profits. Although Bass operated an extensive trading network, controlled 17 subsidiaries across the United Kingdom, and still manufactured a venerated beer, a major change was in order.

When Arthur Manners retired as chairman in 1952, his position was filled by C. A. Ball, a 65-year-old executive who had started his career as Manners's typist. While Ball recognized the need to modernize by hiring professional managers, Bass's decline had progressed too far. Ball died in 1959 and was succeeded by the nearly 70-year-old Sir James Grigg, a former cabinet minister under Churchill. Grigg's first action as chairman was to find a suitable merger to help the company solve growing financial difficulties.

H. Alan Walker, the dynamic chief executive director of Mitchells & Butler, approached Grigg, and an agreement was soon completed. Walker had built Mitchells & Butler into one of the most efficient and financially successful breweries in the industry. By closing down unprofitable operations, by modernizing marketing and production, and by acquiring other breweries, he had significantly improved the company's performance. Yet Walker's company was not large enough to protect itself against any potential takeover bid; he was looking for a merger of his own choosing. Bass, Ratcliffe & Gretton merged with Mitchells & Butler in 1961.

At virtually the same time, another industry merger occurred that would play an important role in Bass's future. In 1962 Charrington & Company Ltd., a London brewery whose history dates back to 1766, merged with United Breweries, the brewers of the national brands of Carling Lager and Jubilee Stout. While Charrington functioned in many ways as a family concern,

United was a new consortium of medium-sized brewers from various parts of the United Kingdom.

The formation of Charrington United Breweries created a well-balanced national company with strong ties to London and an established distribution network across the United Kingdom. Almost the exact same thing could be said of the Bass, Mitchells & Butler merger. With Walker assuming the title of chief executive and Grigg maintaining his position as chairman, the management began a program of rationalization to integrate and modernize the companies' operations.

By the late 1960s, however, the management of both newly formed companies recognized the unfulfilled potential in their firms' performance. While Charrington United Breweries controlled a variety of regional brands, the company lacked a premium draught beer such as Bass or Worthington. Bass, Mitchells & Butler lacked a spirit and soft drinks business as successful as that of Charrington United Breweries's Canada Dry subsidiary. Although the mergers improved the two companies' national distribution networks, areas of weakness existed for both firms. In 1967 a new merger was arranged between Charrington United Breweries and Bass, Mitchells & Butler.

Bass Charrington Ltd. was an immediate success. The easy integration process was followed by years of effort to improve market position. This improvement slowed for a short time between 1973 and 1974 as a result of rising inflation and economic recession. By 1975, however, company performance once again improved, and Bass Charrington began to garner the benefits from its investments and expansion.

By the early 1980s the newly renamed Bass PLC had registered an 18 percent increase in its earnings. Under the leadership of chairman Derek Palmar, Bass now managed more pubs in the United Kingdom than any other industry competitor. Furthermore, the company successfully capitalized on the growing market for lager. Yet in many ways Bass maintained its conservative management policies. A ''Bass package'' of regional ales continued to be distributed by the free trade system. Similarly, Bass's property improvements, while generous, were more concerned with promoting family establishments than catering to younger clients. A program of diversification led Bass to create a leisure division. While mostly profitable, their subsidiaries, which included a hotel business and betting shops, contributed less than 20 percent to profits. Bass remained one of the least diversified of the major brewers.

In the late 1980s, however, Bass's leisure activities assumed a greater role in the company. The hotel division, through its Coral and Crest subsidiaries, enjoyed healthy financial gains. Indeed, Crest became one of the fastest-growing British companies in Europe. In May 1987 Bass announced an agreement with the U.S.-based Holiday Corporation to purchase eight European Holiday Inn hotels for £152 million. Two years later, Bass dramatically increased its hotel holdings when it acquired the full Holiday Inn chain from Holiday Corporation in 1989 for $2.23 billion. Bass gained 55 company-owned Holiday Inn hotels, the Holiday Inn brand name, and franchise rights to the more than 1,400 Holiday Inn hotels that were franchised or based on joint ventures. The remainder of Holiday Corporation—which included Embassy Suites, Hampton Inns, and Homewood Suites properties and Harrah's casinos—was spun off to shareholders as Promus Companies Inc.

The initial years under Bass were difficult ones for Holiday Inn. Founded in Memphis in 1952 and named after the film *Holiday Inn,* the chain grew rapidly in the United States, mainly along the burgeoning highways of the 1950s and 1960s. By the time of its acquisition by Bass, Holiday Inns could be found in nearly 50 countries, but were beginning to show their age back home in America. Holiday Inn had built its empire in the middle of the lodging market, attracting both business customers and vacationers. As its properties aged and its service declined, the chain was being squeezed by a drop-off in business customers dissatisfied with the service and travelers not willing to pay rates that had crept higher and were ever more uncompetitive given the rise of newer, cut-rate chains such as Hampton Inn. To counter these trends, Bass in 1990 initiated a $1 billion renovation of the Holiday Inn chain to be completed over the course of several years. Bass also began to expand its top-of-the-line Crowne Plaza hotels to gain market share on the high end, while it simultaneously launched its own cut-rate chain called Holiday Inn Express in 1991 to win back budget-conscious customers. By 1995 Bass had more than doubled the number of Crowne Plaza properties to more than 100, while Holiday Inn Express reached the 350 mark. Another part of Bass's strategy was to aggressively expand all three of the chains outside North America, concentrating primarily on Europe and the Asia/Pacific region. During 1995, the number of countries with Holiday Inn properties exceeded 60 and the total number of Bass lodging properties passed 2,000. Finally, Bass in 1992 invested $60 million in technology upgrades, including a new Holiday Inn Reservation Optimization system to improve its reservations capability.

None of these moves paid off immediately, however, and the Holiday Inn division dragged down Bass's overall operating results with decreases in profits for the hotel operations in 1991 and 1992. Meanwhile, evidence of Bass's displeasure with its acquisition became evident from a 1992 lawsuit it filed against Promus. The suit alleged that Promus had intentionally withheld important information from Bass during the acquisitions negotiations, thus inflating the price Bass paid. Wishing to free itself from the suit in order to move forward with a split of the company, Promus settled with Bass in 1995 without admitting guilt and agreed to pay $49 million. While the suit was being contested, Holiday Inn seemed to turn the corner with an 18 percent increase in profits in 1993, followed by more modest four and 2.4 percent profit increases in 1994 and 1995.

The turnaround in lodging came just in time as Bass experienced difficulties in its brewery unit in the 1990s stemming from a decline in beer drinking in England. Beer sales for Bass declined 0.8 percent in 1994, then fell 5.1 percent in 1995. With the English beer market soft, Bass continued to expand its soft drinks holdings with the 1995 acquisition of Robinsons Soft Drinks from Reckitt & Colman plc for £103 million. The leisure retailing sector was bolstered through the purchase in 1995 of 78 Harvester pub restaurants and the Harvester brand from Forte Plc for £165 million. The brewery sector was not left out of the 1995 spending spree, however, as Bass increased its holdings in the Czech Republic with the purchase of majority stakes in the Czech brewing companies Vratislavice A.S. and

Ostravar A.S., and established a joint venture in China—the world's second-largest beer market—with the Ginsber Beer Group.

The mid-1980s to the mid-1990s was a period of enormous change for Bass with its systematic program of diversification into related and complementary areas of the leisure industry. By 1995, brewing accounted for only 32 percent of total profits, with taverns at 23 percent, entertainment/gambling at 21 percent, hotels at 13 percent, and soft drinks at 11 percent. Bass hoped that the diversity of these holdings would protect it from downturns in any one sector, such as it was experiencing in brewing. Bass's increasing geographic diversity also boded well for the firm's future.

Principal Subsidiaries

Barcrest Limited; Bass Beers Worldwide Limited; Bass Brewers Limited; Bass Developments Limited; Bass Holdings Limited; Bass Investments PLC; Bass Leisure Activities Limited; Bass Leisure Entertainments Limited; Bass Leisure Group Limited; Bass Leisure Limited; Bass Overseas Holdings Limited; Bass Taverns Limited; BLMS Limited; Britannia Soft Drinks Limited (50%); Britvic Soft Drinks Limited (90%); Coral Racing Limited; Gala Leisure Limited; Robinsons Soft Drinks Limited; Toby Restaurants Limited; Société Viticole de Château Lascombes SA (France; 97.5%); White Shield Insurance Company Limited (Gibraltar); Bass International Holdings NV (Netherlands); Bass America Inc. (U.S.); Holiday Corporation (U.S.); Holiday Inns Franchising Inc. (U.S.); Holiday Inns, Inc. (U.S.).

Principal Divisions

Bass Brewers; Bass Leisure; Bass Taverns; Britvic Soft Drinks; Holiday Inn Worldwide.

Further Reading

Bass: The Story of the World's Most Famous Ale, Burton-on-Trent: Bass, 1927.
Clark, Jack J., ''Holiday Inn: New Rooms in the Inn,'' *Cornell Hotel & Restaurant Administration Quarterly,* October 1993, p. 59.
DeMarco, Edward, ''Holiday Inn's Profits Surged in '94, Helping Bass,'' *Atlanta Business Chronicle,* February 24, 1995, p. 18B.
Hawkins, Chuck, Mark Maremont, and Alice Cuneo, ''Bass Can't Get Comfortable at Holiday Inns,'' *Business Week,* March 2, 1992, p. 42.
Rowe, Megan, ''Holiday Inn: From Fat and Sassy to Lean and Mean,'' *Lodging Hospitality,* July 1992, pp. 24–26.

—updated by David E. Salamie

Bekins Company

300 S. Mannheim Road
Hillside, Illinois 60162
U.S.A.
(708) 547-2000

Private Company
Incorporated: 1940 as Bekins Van Lines Company
Employees: 2,000
Sales: $200 million (1994)
SICs: 4214 Local Trucking with Storage; 4213 Trucking
   Except Local

The Bekins Company is a leader in the moving and storage industry. Originally specializing in transporting household goods, the company now also moves office furnishings, trade show exhibits, and company inventories, as well as providing storage facilities for a myriad of items.

The Company is Started

The company's founder, Martin Bekins, was the son of a Dutch immigrant, Sjoerd Bekius, who arrived in New Orleans and then made his way across land to eventually settle in a Michigan farming community in the mid-1800s. Sjoerd's migration probably entailed loading his belongings onto a horse or into a horse-drawn wagon and slowly making the trek to his destination; until the turn of the century, the moving and storage industry did not exist.

After leaving his father's farm and settling in Grand Rapids, Michigan, in 1880, Martin changed his last name to Bekins. His brother John soon followed and the two young men found jobs driving freight wagons during the day. In the evenings they completed their education. After graduation, the Bekins brothers decided to apply their job experiences in a practical manner, and in 1891 the Bekins Company opened for business in Sioux City, Iowa, offering moving services by horse and wagon. Their first financial statement listed assets and liabilities of $2,246.67.

Western Expansion Offers New Business Opportunities

As early as 1830, tales were circulating that fabulous riches in gold were free for the taking on the western frontier. Pioneers by the thousands began to make the treacherous trip across plains, deserts, and mountains in lumbering Conestoga wagons or "prairie schooners." Two main routes developed: the Oregon Trail along the Platte River, and the Santa Fe Trail from St. Louis to Sante Fe, New Mexico. Moving household possessions was a challenging venture as furniture and sentimental keepsakes were bounced over the rugged terrain.

Astutely noting the nation's migration to the west, the Bekins brothers quickly opened another office in Omaha, Nebraska. Two other brothers, Dan and Taeke, took over the management of the Sioux City location. In 1895, Martin decided to expand the business to Los Angeles. Bekins was the first company to use covered moving vans on the West Coast and to specialize in moving household goods.

The Locomotive and Automobile Bring New Changes

Although steam power had been harnessed for numerous purposes through the centuries, perhaps none was as significant as its use in the development of the locomotive in the late 19th century. The continental railroad system would greatly enhance opportunities for expansion and mobility. In anticipation of these changes, the Bekins brothers established the Bekins Household Shipping Company in Chicago in 1898 to serve as a link between the two coasts. Shipments were pooled from locations up and down the eastern seaboard for rail transport to California.

In the years following the turn of the century, particularly during Theodore Roosevelt's administration, the United States enjoyed an economic boom. A significant portion of the population was prosperous enough to own second homes or excess furniture that required storing. As a result, public warehousing emerged as an industry. Bekins' first warehouses featured a ramp that allowed the horse-drawn vans to be driven directly into the building for unloading.

However, like the Conestoga wagon, the horse-drawn van was destined for oblivion. By 1903 Bekins was replacing the old moving method, driving the first motor trucks on the West Coast. The initial Bekins trucks, powered by two-cylindered, air-cooled engines, were two of only 700 such trucks in the nation. By the end of World War I, Bekins had ceased to use horse-drawn vans altogether. There were now four additional Bekins organizations in the Northwest, Colorado, Iowa, and Nebraska, owned and operated by the children and grandchildren of John Bekins and Dan Bekins.

Bekins built the industry's first reinforced steel and concrete warehouse in Los Angeles in 1906. Later that same year, another Bekins warehouse was under construction on Mission Street in San Francisco, when the infamous and devastating earthquake and fire hit that city. The superior construction of the warehouse's foundation and walls allowed it to remain intact, and Bekins deployed its motor van to bring the newly homeless to the warehouse for temporary shelter.

Martin's children—Milo Sr., Reed, Floyd, and Ruth— purchased the company and installed Milo as president in 1918. The decade that followed saw Bekins introduce specially constructed shipping boxes called ''porto-vans'' for transporting household items by boat and rail. Warehouse companies created a national network to coordinate transportation. The network was aided by the National Moving and Storage Association, which Milo Bekins helped to found.

The network operated in this manner: a person who needed to move household belongings would contact a local warehouse company, which would in turn contact another warehouse company in the destination city. The local company would transport the crated possessions, either by electric or horse-drawn trucks, to its warehouse. Routing personnel would consult railroad schedules and arrange for hook-up on a particular train. The destination company would be advised of the expected arrival time by wire. When the train reached its destination, the destination warehouse company would pick up and store the contents until the owners arrived and arranged for its delivery to their new home. By the end of the 1920s, Bekins had nearly one thousand porto-vans crisscrossing the United States, until the construction of transcontinental highways changed the character of transportation once again.

Bekins adjusted its operations accordingly and the industry's first move by transcontinental motor van was accomplished in 1928. The padded moving van left Sioux City on June 23, driven by Bekins employee Gordon Mead and his son Wayne. Eschewing the newer U.S. routes 40 and 50, the Meads traveled the Santa Fe Trail and arrived in Los Angeles on July 8th of that year.

During the 1920s Bekins locations were opened in Berkeley, Sacramento, Fresno, Pasadena, and West Hollywood. Bekins extended its motor van operations into the northwestern and eastern regions of the United States in the 1930s. Moving and storage companies became federally regulated along with the trucking industry under the Interstate Commerce Act of 1935.

The Postwar Years Bring Further Growth

In 1940 the regional offices were combined to form Bekins Van Lines Company. At first the warehouses were concentrated in the center of major cities. With the end of World War II and the proliferation of suburban communities made possible by the automobile, however, Bekins moved its warehouses to the outlying areas as well. Two of Bekins' most noteworthy moving jobs during this time were the relocations of the Brooklyn Dodgers to Los Angeles and the New York Giants to San Francisco in 1958.

Bekins' growth accelerated in the 1960s. By 1963, the company was posting gross yearly revenues of $40 million with an after-tax net of $1.8 million. Four major areas of service developed: local moving and storage within communities; long distance moving of household and other valuable goods; international moving and storage for military personnel and civilians; and other related services, such as the storage of business records, records management, film storage, and office and industrial moving.

It was perhaps not surprising, with its geographic focus in California, that Bekins was able to cultivate business amid the Hollywood movie industry. From facilities in Hollywood and Los Angeles, Bekins' film centers were created to store, clean, repair, and distribute millions of dollars worth of film. Moreover, the company created a catalog system to allow for easy retrieval of the films. Bekins' electronic products division had its start during the 1960s as well and became one of the company's most profitable services, until computer mainframes and other electronic items became more manageable in size, and the retailers and consumers were able to handle the equipment themselves.

The Era of Deregulation Increases Competition

In the 1970s, federal deregulation of the moving and trucking industry generated an environment of intense competition. The Motor Carrier's Act of 1980 was designed to allow more opportunities for new businesses and to allow existing ones to expand their services. The act also provide for increased price flexibility. To survive, Bekins employed creative marketing techniques to retain and attract customers. With its ''No Excuse Move'' promotional campaign, Bekins became the first moving and storage company to offer guaranteed pricing, guaranteed pick-up and delivery dates, and full replacement protection coverage. As the world entered the computer age, the pressure to use state-of-the art information processing was also increasing. By 1987, Bekins was tracking 95 percent of its shipments in an integrated set of online computer systems.

Bekins was purchased by Minstar, Inc., in 1983, in that company's explosive rise to prominence under the leadership of corporate raider Irwin L. Jacobs. However, by 1987, the Bekins family was able to repurchase their company from Minstar and return it to its privately owned status. In the meantime, however, under Minstar's parentage Bekins had been transformed from a family-run business to one with over 2,000 employees, 470 independent agents, and more than 50 wholly owned moving and storage companies.

By the 1990s, the nature of the van line industry had changed dramatically. The moving of household goods settled into a cyclical pattern, with one-third of all household moves scheduled during the three summer months. Demographers also projected that the aging Baby Boomer population would create a decrease in U.S. mobility rates. Companies were forced to further diversify, and Bekins was characteristically in the vanguard. Although 60 percent of its business was still generated by moving household goods, a growing 40 percent was in specialty distributions, particularly equipment for the trade show industry. Another growing area was in catalog delivery and the delivery of large catalog orders for such retailers as Williams Sonoma, Neiman Marcus, and American Express. True to its strong customer service emphasis, Bekins not only delivered the furniture or appliances, but it uncrated them, set them up in the consumer's home, and promised to handle the return if any items were defective. Company executives predicted that 80 percent of Bekins's future growth will come from specialty distributions in the late 1990s.

The Close of the Twentieth Century Brings New Challenges

Perhaps Bekins' most innovative venture of the 1990s was its contract logistics operations, whereby it took over a retailer's entire transportation, delivery, warehousing, inventory control, installation, and billing operations. In the early 1990s, Bekins contracted with Eastman Kodak to provide this service for Kodak's high-end copiers and printers. To make this project possible, Bekins developed a national inventory management system called Distribution and Logistics System, or DLS, that employed discrete item tracking via bar coding.

Bekins also faced some challenges in the mid-1990s. During this time it became involved in a lawsuit brought by the U.S. Justice Department. Specifically, the 1995 suit charged that a Philadelphia affiliate of subsidiary Bekins Van Lines Co. had violated the Americans with Disabilities Act, when some movers allegedly refused to move the belongings of a customer whose friend was stricken with AIDs. The suit remained unsettled in early 1996.

During this time, the company also made an unsuccessful bid to acquire the moving division of Mayflower Group, Inc. Instead, Unigroup, the parent of Bekins's rival United Van Lines, took over Mayflower in 1995. This merger left six major carriers in the United States with more consolidations expected. A change in regulatory agencies due to the disbanding of the Interstate Commerce Commission was also expected to affect the industry. Nevertheless, its revered history of moving household goods and its willingness to keep pace with a changing industry by exploring and implementing new lines of business boded well for Bekins.

Principal Subsidiaries

Bekins Moving and Storage Company; Bekins Van Lines Company.

Further Reading

"Bekins History," company document, Hillside, Ill.: Bekins Company, 1978.

Bryant, Daniel P., *Journey to the Promised Land*, Los Angeles: Newcomen Society, 1964.

Harrington, Lisa, "Van Lines Change Their Stripes," *Transportation and Distribution*, December 1994, pp. 28–32.

Jackson, Gianna, "Moving? Prices Are Rising, So Get a Move On," *The New York Times*, April 22, 1995, p. 39.

Slobodzian, Joseph A., "Justice Department Sues Moving Company for Discrimination," *The Philadelphia Inquirer*, October 25, 1995.

Svaldi, Aldo, "Movers Stuck in Gridlock, Lack Drivers, Vans, Space," *The Denver Business Journal*, August 5–11, 1994, pp. 7–8.

—Mary McNulty

Bertelsmann AG

Carl-Bertelsmann-Strasse 270
Postfach 111
D-33311 Gütersloh
Germany
(5241) 800
Fax: (5241) 75166

Public Company
Incorporated: 1835 as Bertelsmann Verlag
Employees: 51,767
Sales: DM20.60 billion (US$13.90 billion) (1995)
Stock Exchanges: Hamburg Munich Düsseldorf Frankfurt
SICs: 2721 Periodicals: Publishing, or Publishing &
 Printing; 2731 Books: Publishing, or Publishing &
 Printing; 2741 Miscellaneous Publishing; 3652
 Phonograph Records & Pre-Recorded Audio Tapes &
 Discs; 4833 Television Broadcasting Stations; 5735
 Record & Prerecorded Tape Stores; 5961 Catalog &
 Mail Order Houses; 7812 Motion Picture & Video
 Tape Production

Bertelsmann AG is the largest media group in Germany and Europe, and the second-largest in the world to the U.S.-based Time Warner Inc. With operations in 40 countries, primarily in Europe and North America, Bertelsmann is active in four main areas: magazine and newspaper publishing; book publishing and book clubs; entertainment businesses in music, television, and multimedia; and industrial businesses in printing, paper production, and other media-related fields. Among its nearly 500 worldwide subsidiaries, the best known operations include Gruner + Jahr, publisher of magazines in Europe and the United States; Bantam Doubleday Dell, a major U.S. book publisher; and such record labels as RCA, Arista, BMG Ariola, and BMG Victor, which jointly make up BMG/Music, ranked number six worldwide among music companies.

The company was founded as a family business in the middle of the 19th century and had already grown to a consider-

able size before World War II. The significant expansion phase of the company, however, only began after the German currency reform of 1948, when Reinhard Mohn succeeded with the Bertelsmann book club (the Lesering) in introducing a revolutionary form of direct sales to the traditional German publishing market. Bertelsmann grew into an international force on the back of this great success. In 1995 17.9 percent of Bertelsmann's share capital was in the hands of the Mohn family and 10.7 percent belonged to the Hamburg publisher Dr. Gerd Bucerius, of *Die Zeit* fame; 71.4 percent of the capital stock was held by the Bertelsmann Foundation, established in 1977 by Reinhard Mohn and intended to take over the Mohn family's share in Bertelsmann and appoint the company's management.

Although a multiple media giant in the mid-1990s, the company began in 1835 as a small publisher of evangelical hymn books and devotional pamphlets in Pietist eastern Westphalia, where its headquarters have remained, resisting any suggestions of transferring to Hamburg or Munich. The founder of the company was Carl Bertelsmann, who was born in Gütersloh in 1791, two years after the French Revolution. His father died before he was two years old. His mother was to find him an apprenticeship in a bookbinder's business as she had done for his elder brother. To avoid conscription into Napoleon's Russian army, Carl Bertelsmann went traveling, going via Berlin to Upper Silesia.

When Carl Bertelsmann returned to Gütersloh in 1815, after Napoleon's defeat and exile, he found that his brother had taken on the position for which he had been trained. It was only after his brother's death in 1819 that Carl Bertelsmann was able to set up as a bookbinder in his home town. "The little Bertelsmann from Gütersloh," as he was known in the area, soon found a place in the Pietist movement that shaped the eastern Westphalian community, and discovered that it particularly needed hymn books for its services. Gradually Bertelsmann's bookbinding business became a book-printing business as well, and then developed into a full publishing house.

This development occurred during the mid-19th century Biedermeier period, a time in which German middle-class culture flourished and which was marked in Westphalia by Prussian government. Carl Bertelsmann was a conservative and a royalist faithful to the Prussian king. He supported the latter's cause during the revolution of 1848–49 in which he became politically involved. Generally, though, he dedicated himself to working industriously for his company which, while small, was expanding rapidly. By the time of his death, it employed 14 people.

When Carl Bertelsmann died in 1850, he left behind a wife and son and a considerable fortune. He had laid the foundations for the company's subsequent development, but he was not there to witness the success of the firm's bestseller, the *Missionsharfe* (Missionary Harp), a hymn book of which two million copies were printed. The first edition appeared in 1853. By this time Bertelsmann was publishing not only Christian literature, but also historical and philological books, as well as novels. It ran its own printing press as before. Heinrich Bertelsmann, who inherited the business from his father, was able, as a result, to build on a very wide foundation that prevented his company from remaining a small publisher of denominational literature.

The printing and publishing house grew considerably in the second generation, thanks in part to the acquisition of other publishing houses that could not hold their own against competition in the market. This tradition of buying up weaker competitors to modernize them and thus make them competitive once more is a policy that Bertelsmann still pursues. By the time Heinrich Bertelsmann died in 1887, his 60 employees had moved into a brand-new building.

The company consequently came under the ownership of the Mohn family in its third generation, after Heinrich Bertelsmann's only child, Friederike Bertelsmann, married Johannes Mohn in 1881. Johannes Mohn was a minister's son from the Westerwald who had learned about the book trade under Heinrich Bertelsmann. Although without personal means and an outsider in Gütersloh, Mohn immediately took on the responsibilities of the business after his father-in-law's death, showing considerable talent in its management. In particular, he expanded the printing side so that the book production could be increased steadily without incurring outside costs.

For this conservative company, with its strong allegiance to throne and church, the German defeat in World War I and the consequent revolution, bringing about the kaiser's abdication, was a painful break with the past. Disheartened by events, the 65-year-old Johannes Mohn passed on the responsibility for the business to his son Heinrich, only 26 years old at the time. Like his great-grandfather, grandfather, and father before him, Heinrich Mohn had had the best possible theoretical and practical training for his career as a publisher. Bad health and hard times would, however, prevent him from enjoying his position to the full.

Before the war, Johannes Mohn had already had a taxable income of 100,000 marks a year. He was a millionaire. Despite the family wealth, the Gütersloh printing and publishing house was almost forced to close, not long after Heinrich Mohn had taken it over, because of the effects of galloping inflation in Germany in 1923. For the first time in the company's history, no new employees were taken on, while valued staff had to be laid off. Scarcely had this crisis been overcome than an even greater world economic crisis broke out in 1930.

Heinrich Mohn countered these difficulties and the Third Reich with the help of his Christian convictions. Like his predecessors he was extremely close to the Evangelical Church and in particular to the part of that church, the Bekennende Kirche, or German Confessional Church, which stood by its faith in God in opposition to Hitler. This was the church to which Martin Niemöller and Dietrich Bonhoeffer, spiritual leaders of the German *Widerstand*, or anti-Hitler opposition, belonged. At the same time Mohn was successfully trading with the German air force, which he supplied with millions of cheap books and pamphlets. When World War II began in 1939, roughly 400 printers, typesetters, and publishers worked for Bertelsmann in Gütersloh. The company had a turnover of 8.1 million reichsmarks in 1941 and by this time had far outstripped its German competitors.

The Nazi authorities, however, disapproved of the company's publication of religious texts and after the war began, Mohn's right to print these works was removed. His printing works were provided with less and less paper by the authorities, making it increasingly difficult to operate. When the British forces bombed Gütersloh in March 1945, most of the company's buildings were destroyed. Although a few of the expensive printing machines remained intact so that the business was able to continue, the company's future looked uncertain because Heinrich Mohn's health was failing.

Good fortune came to Bertelsmann's aid, when Reinhard Mohn returned home from prisoner-of-war camp earlier than his elder but less-gifted brother, Sigbert Mohn. Neither was to have inherited the company originally, but when the eldest of the four brothers was killed on the sixth day of the war, the position fell to Sigbert. Since he was only to return from Russian prisoner-of-war camp in 1949, his younger brother Reinhard took charge of affairs in Gütersloh in 1947.

After his school-leaving exams at the Evangelical Foundation Grammar School in Gütersloh, Reinhard Mohn had wanted to become an aeronautical engineer, but when the war broke out, he was called up to join the German Africa Corps under General Erwin Rommel. After Reinhard was injured, he was taken prisoner by the American troops.

After his return to Gütersloh, Reinhard Mohn took the company helm with determination. When the West Germans suddenly stopped buying books after Germany's adoption of the deutsche mark in 1948, the young publisher made a daring decision. Instead of hoping for better times like the other publishers of the day, in 1950 he invited the West German retail booksellers to form the Lesering together with Bertelsmann. For a small sum, any reader could become a member of this book club. In return, the reader would receive a certain number of books from C. Bertelsmann Verlag every year.

There had already been book clubs in Germany. What was new about the Bertelsmann Lesering, however, was that the "corner bookshops" were made partners by the publishing house. With this type of direct sales the bookshops also profited, whereas previous book clubs had only created undesirable competition. Nevertheless there were still those who were critical. Many bookshop owners who did not acquire any Lesering members and consequently did not benefit from the club felt threatened. They were afraid that the Bertelsmann Lesering would take away their customers, but these fears proved to be exaggerated. In fact, the Bertelsmann Lesering won many people over to buying books who previously had not dared to go into bookshops for fear of being shown up for their lack of education.

The Bertelsmann Lesering proved highly successful. It gave the Gütersloh printing and publishing house two decisive advantages over its competitors—a certain guarantee of purchases of its own books and the high capacity use of its printing presses. These two factors combined to make Bertelsmann's turnover soar in the 1950s. Company turnover doubled each year between 1951 and 1953, going from DM7 million to DM30 million. This was a far greater turnover than that of any other book publisher in West Germany. In 1956–57, Bertelsmann was to break the DM100 million barrier. By 1973, Reinhard Mohn saw the figure reach DM1 billion. At the end of this 22-year period, the company employed a workforce of 11,000 at Gütersloh and elsewhere as opposed to an original 500 in 1951.

The success of the company could not be explained by the Bertelsmann Lesering alone. Two additional decisions taken by Reinhard Mohn were to be of great significance. The first, born from necessity, was to cover the company's enormous need for capital; Mohn made his employees shareholders, but without voting rights. This and other socially minded actions made the Gütersloh office, far from West Germany's glittering metropolis, a greatly envied workplace. Mohn's second decision was to branch out from books and invest in modern media such as records, magazines, and television to keep pace with changing consumer demands.

These changes all took place with breathtaking speed in the 1950s, 1960s, and 1970s. Most successful was the acquisition of a stake in the Hamburg publishing company Gruner + Jahr, which was gradually built up to a 74.9 percent shareholding in 1976. Not only did the Hamburg sister company bring in excellent results, owing to good management, but it also helped Bertelsmann achieve wider acceptance in the media world following a long period during which the Westphalian family business had been regarded as rather provincial.

The principle behind Bertelsmann's acquisitions was always the same. Reinhard Mohn bought firms that were active in related fields of business and which could be purchased relatively cheaply because of problems they could not solve themselves. He would place a couple of trusted colleagues in leading posts and leave them to work hard on their own. Delegation of responsibility and decentralization of business were his beliefs. For ambitious managers who valued a certain degree of independence, it was and remained a challenge. By 1994 Bertelsmann consisted of around 300 profit centers which operated virtually independently from one another and were coordinated from the group's headquarters in Gütersloh.

During the end of the 1960s, Bertelsmann reached the limits of its growth within the German-speaking world. Mohn decided to expand the business abroad. The first step was to introduce Bertelsmann's Lesering to Spain, with all the other sectors of operation—from the printing works to the book and magazine publishing companies—following at short intervals. As a result, turnover rose to DM5.5 billion by 1980 and the number of employees rose to 30,000 worldwide. Bertelsmann, transformed into a public limited company because of the colossal growth in its capital requirements, prepared to leap to the top of the media world league.

In 1981, after more than 30 years at the head of the company, Mohn moved from being chairman of the company to being chairman of the supervisory board. For the first time in Bertelsmann's history, Mohn left the operational running of the company to a manager who was not a member of the family. In taking this step he instituted a ruling which he applied to all members of the board and to himself and which would become company policy at Bertelsmann: employees may not remain in their jobs past 60 years of age.

Under its new boss Dr. Mark Wössner (a former assistant to Mohn, who had made his way to the top beginning in the late 1960s in the printing and industrial plant sectors), Bertelsmann AG held the position of the leading media group in the world for a time in the mid-1980s (until Time and Warner merged in 1989). This leadership role was made possible by several acquisitions in the United States, which stretched the Westphalian company to the limits of its capacity. Between 1985 and 1986 Bertelsmann acquired the publishing group Doubleday-Dell and turned the music section of RCA into the BMG (Bertelsmann Music Group). It was a massive package, for which Wössner paid more than US$800 million. This show of strength catapulted Bertelsmann AG's world turnover above DM9 billion, with the group employing more than 40,000 people worldwide.

Bertelsmann also looked to Eastern Europe, where possibilities had been revealed by the fall of the Berlin Wall and the Eastern Bloc. With world turnover of DM13.3 billion in 1989–90, Bertelsmann AG was well equipped to make the most of these developments. In 1990 alone, Bertelsmann spent DM1 billion in the newly opened eastern Germany, by starting a book club, buying the largest regional newspaper there, and acquiring in a joint deal with Maxwell, the publisher of Berlin's leading daily newspaper.

The company's major moves into the U.S. market did not immediately pay off. By 1992, 21 percent of Bertelsmann's sales originated in the United States, but only about ten percent of its profits. BMG's flagship RCA label was just breaking even, having gone through three presidents since the takeover and not having had a hit album since 1987's *Dirty Dancing* soundtrack. Although strong in the country and jazz niche markets, the label lacked a major performer in the contemporary music category, the most popular style of the time. Market share for RCA remained stagnant at about ten percent. BMG was helped by its Arista label, which was performing better than RCA and had a solid 1992 led by Whitney Houston's megahit soundtrack from *The Bodyguard*, which sold more than 20 million copies. Nevertheless, Bertelsmann was criticized for being too cautious when in early 1992 it was outbid by Britain's Thorn EMI in a battle for Virgin Records, which within two years could boast of signing such hit performers as Janet Jackson and Smashing Pumpkins. Other opportunities to bolster the BMG holdings were also missed, such as the bidding for A&M, Island Records, and Chrysalis Records.

In what became Bantam Doubleday Dell following the take-over, Bertelsmann had successfully turned around the Doubleday book club operations. Yet, overall, Doubleday had failed to turn a profit for Bertelsmann. Contributing to the book publishing operations difficulties, according to analysts, was Bertelsmann's haste in instituting changes at Doubleday, which alienated the industry establishment in the publishing capital of New York. Nevertheless, Doubleday author John Grisham had a string of best-selling suspense novels, one of which, *The Client*, became one of the fastest-selling books in publishing history.

In 1993 Bertelsmann restructured itself along product lines, reducing the number of divisions from seven to four: Books, which consisted of Doubleday and book and record clubs; Gruner + Jahr, which included all the magazine and newspaper publishing operations; BMG Entertainment, including music, television, and multimedia; and Bertelsmann Industry, which included printing, paper production, and other businesses. The goal of the restructuring was to instill more cooperation between different operations within the organization and to give the divisions more freedom to make decisions and increased investment authority. Each division was given its own board of directors, and with the exception of Gruner + Jahr the boards were of the British-American model—single boards comprised of insiders and outsiders—rather than the typical two-tier German model. This novel approach was intended as an attempt to combine the conservatism Bertelsmann had employed to cautiously build itself into a giant and the entrepreneurial freedom that its increasingly American competitors were so well known for.

Bertelsmann's debt remained very low into the mid-1990s, with a debt ratio of 16.3 percent for fiscal 1993–94. Cash would not be a problem for the divisions as they sought out growth opportunities. Overall, Bertelsmann spent DM1 billion (US$674 million) in acquisitions in 1995, most prominent of which were the purchases of a group of magazines from the New York Times Co. and the Italian music publisher Ricordi.

At the same time, in the area of multimedia, BMG Entertainment decided that rather than making acquisitions or developing products and services on its own, it would follow a strategy of partnering with the world's most innovative software developers. The earliest significant such venture was BMG's partnership with the leading American online service provider, America Online, to set up online services in Germany, France, and England. Bertelsmann financed the 50–50 venture with US$100 million and also gained a five percent stake in America Online with an additional US$50 million investment, while America Online agreed to contribute its knowledge gained through more than ten years in the business.

Overall, Bertelsmann was enjoying steady growth in sales and income and improving results in its U.S. operations in the mid-1990s. Moreover, on April 2, 1996, the company announced plans to merge its television and radio operations with those of Compagnie Luxembourgeoise de Télédiffusion (CLT), a Luxembourg-based broadcaster, prompting speculation that the resulting company would become Europe's largest television company and one capable of competing with Time Warner Inc. in Europe. With such merger plans in the making, Bertels-mann seemed poised to better its already enviable position in the media industry.

Principal Subsidiaries

Bertelsmann Club GmbH; Bertelsmann Lexikothek Verlag GmbH; Bertelsmann Online GmbH & Co. KG (50%); Blanvalet Verlag GmbH; EBG Verlags GmbH; Dr. Th. Gabler GmbH; GeoCenter Verlagsvertreib GmbH; Wilhelm Goldmann Verlag GmbH; Gruner + Jahr AG & Co.; Albrecht Knaus Verlag; Mosaik Verlag; Prisma Verlag GmbH; Prisma-Verlag GmbH & Co. KG; Reise-und Verkehrs Verlag GmbH; Schulverlag Vieweg GmbH; Ufa Film und Fernseh GmbH; Friedrich Vieweg & Sohn; Westdeutscher Verlag GmbH; Doubleday Australia Pty. Ltd.; Verlag Kremayr und Scheriau (Austria); BMG Ariola Belgium SA; BMG Ariola Music Ltda. (Brazil); BMG Music Canada; Doubleday Canada Ltd. (49%); BMG Ariola S.A. (France); BMG Ariola Musica S.p.A. (Italy); BMG Ariola S.A. de C.V. (Mexico; 75%); Doubleday New Zealand Ltd.; Circulo de Leitores (Portugal); Circulo de Lectores S.A. (Spain); Plaza y Janes S.A. (Spain); Bertelsmann Inc. (U.S.A.); BMG/Music (U.S.A.); Bantam Doubleday Dell Publishing Group, Inc. (U.S.A.); Bertelsmann Printing & Manufacturing Corp. (U.S.A.); Doubleday Book & Music Club (U.S.A.); Bertelsmann Music Group (U.S.A.).

Principal Divisions

Bertelsmann Industry Division; BMG Entertainment Divison; Books Divison; Gruner + Jahr Division.

Further Reading

Barnet, Richard J., and John Cavanagh, *Global Dreams: Imperial Corporations and the New World Order*, New York: Simon & Schuster, 1994, 480 p.
''Bertelsmann Gets Bigger,'' *Business Week*, April 15, 1996, p. 65.
''Bertelsmann: The Media Company that Makes Murdoch's Empire Look Small,'' *Economist*, April 9, 1988.
''Coming to America: The Sequel: Bertelsmann,'' *Economist*, November 16, 1991, p. 90.
Edmondson, Gail, and Patrick Oster, ''Waltz of the Media Giants,'' *Business Week*, September 12, 1994.
''Ich Bin ein Amerikaner,'' *Economist*, June 18, 1994, pp. 69–71.
Landler, Mark, ''An Overnight Success—After Six Years,'' *Business Week*, April 19, 1993, pp. 52, 54.
Lottman, Herbert R., ''Beyond Books at Bertelsmann: The World's Biggest Book Publisher Has Many Other Irons in the Fire, at Home and Abroad,'' *Publishers Weekly*, January 23, 1995, p. 17.
Morais, Richard C., ''The Latest U.S. Media Giant Isn't Even American,'' *Forbes*, April 25, 1988, p. 70.
Picaper, Jean-Paul, ''Bertelsmann: le géant allemand de l'edition,'' *Le Figaro*, February 20, 1989.
Schifrin, Matthew, ''The Betriebsergebnis Factor,'' *Forbes*, May 23, 1994, pp. 118–124.
Studemann, Frederick, ''Europe's Great Communicator,'' *International Management*, September 1992, pp. 34–37.

—Dirk Bavendamm
Translated from the German by Philippe A. Barbour
—updated by David E. Salamie

Blimpie International, Inc.

740 Broadway
New York, New York 10003
U.S.A.
(212) 673-5900
Fax: (212) 995-2560

Public Company
Incorporated: 1977 as International Blimpie Corporation
Employees: 67
Sales: $27 million (1995)
Stock Exchange: NASDAQ
SICs: 6794 Patent Owners & Lessors; 5812 Eating
  Places; 6719 Offices of Holding Companies, Not
  Elsewhere Classified

Blimpie International, Inc. is the franchisor for Blimpie restaurants, the second-largest submarine sandwich chain in the world. By autumn of 1995, there were about 1,100 Blimpie outlets in operation—one in Stockholm, Sweden, the rest in the United States—and the chain was growing at a rate of about 45 units per month. Of the 44 states in which Blimpie franchises are located, Georgia and Texas lead the way, with more than 100 outlets each. Unlike many restaurant chains, Blimpie does not generally operate "company stores." Virtually all of its income is derived from the various fees associated with franchise arrangements. In addition to free-standing outlets and locations in malls and store clusters, Blimpies can be found in a variety of nontraditional sites, such as inside convenience stores, schools, and hospitals. These nontraditional outlets represent one of the company's fastest growing segments.

The first Blimpie sub shop was opened in Hoboken, New Jersey, in 1964 by Tony Conza, Peter DeCarlo, and Angelo Bandassare, a trio of former high school buddies. Inspired by a successful Point Pleasant, New Jersey, operation called Mike's Submarines, Conza, DeCarlo, and Bandassare speculated that a similar restaurant would do well in Hoboken. They raised $2,500 in seed capital by borrowing from friends and began serving essentially the same sandwich for which people were lining up at Mike's. The original Blimpie was an instant hit, and, before long, customers began asking about starting up franchises. The first franchise was sold to a friend in western New York for $600 during the company's first year of operation.

In 1965 Bandassare left the company to start his own food service supply firm. Conza and DeCarlo decided to expand into New York City, beginning with a store on 55th Street in Manhattan, near Carnegie Hall. By 1967 there were ten Blimpies in the chain, four of which were owned by the company's two remaining founders. Unfortunately, Conza and DeCarlo were not experienced businessmen, and, in spite of the chain's rapid growth and good sales volume, profits were difficult to make. To keep the company afloat, the partners sold the four stores they owned and began to concentrate primarily on franchising.

By the mid-1970s, Conza felt the time was ripe to introduce Blimpie subs to the South. Partner DeCarlo, however, was against the move. This disagreement eventually led to a split between the two men. In 1976 Blimpie was divided into two separate entities, with both retaining rights to the Blimpie trademark. DeCarlo became head of a new, completely independent company, Metropolitan Blimpie (later renamed Blimpie's of New York, Inc.), which controlled franchising rights in New York, New Jersey, and other parts of the East Coast. Conza retained control of the original company, which was incorporated in 1977 as International Blimpie Corporation. Conza, a college dropout with no business credentials other than his experience with Blimpie, remained chairman and CEO of Blimpie into the 1990s.

During the late 1970s, Conza was willing to sell franchises anywhere there was an interested franchisee. Blimpie began selling franchises both for individual stores and for whole territories. Unfortunately, many of these new franchises were rather isolated from the rest of the chain, and some of the benefits of franchise arrangements—chainwide advertising, for example—had little effect in those locations. Although the chain was growing rapidly, several of the newer stores failed. By 1983, International Blimpie's annual revenues were approaching $1 million, and Blimpie's franchises totaled 150.

Conza took the company public that year, with a modest initial over-the-counter offering of 90 cents per share.

Over the next few years, Blimpie embarked on a diversification program that failed miserably. Conza began to feel that there was no future in submarine sandwiches. At the same time, he longed for the kind of respect that only comes to real restaurateurs, not fast food moguls. In 1984, Conza opened the Border Cafe, a tablecloth restaurant serving southwestern cuisine on Manhattan's swanky Upper East Side. Although the Border Cafe did reasonably well at first, this shift in focus proved to be a major blunder. While Conza was turning his attention away from the subs that had gotten him where he was, competitor Subway—which was founded in 1965, just a year after the first Blimpie's was opened—was beginning an expansion drive that would push it far ahead of Blimpie as the world's foremost submarine sandwich chain.

To reflect his increasing concentration on non-Blimpie activities, Conza changed the name of the company to Astor Restaurant Group, Inc. in 1985. Meanwhile, the Blimpie's chain was stagnating. The number of outlets was stalled at about 200. In Manhattan, the company's birthplace, the Blimpie name suffered severe image problems. In the early days, the company had not been particularly selective as to who could get a franchise. In addition, its early franchise contracts allowed operators quite a bit of latitude in how the restaurants were to be run. This led to a degree of uniformity among stores far below that of other national fast food chains, not to mention a reputation for questionable sanitation standards.

After the Border Cafe's initial success, Conza opened two more of them in 1986, one in Woodstock, New York, and the other—with New York Yankee Dave Winfield as a partner—on the Upper West Side of Manhattan. Unfortunately, the Border Cafe idea turned out to be a big money loser. Although Astor brought in $4.5 million in revenues for 1987 (its largest total yet), the company showed a net loss of $347,800 for the year. That year, only 30 new Blimpie restaurants were opened, and company stock was in free fall, bottoming out as low as 15 cents per share. Gradually, Conza's interest in his core business began to return. Over the next couple of years, Atlanta became the company's biggest target for new Blimpie's franchises. In 1987, the company celebrated the opening of the 50th Blimpie's store in the Atlanta area by giving away 25,000 free sandwiches to customers there.

By 1988 Conza had realized the error of his ways, and he quickly got out of the Tex-Mex business. Seeing the tremendous success of Subway, Conza decided to redouble his efforts in the hoagie arena. He began to address the Blimpie problem with renewed vigor and a more systematic approach than he had used before. The first step in Conza's revitalization program was to identify four fundamental problems plaguing the business: a lack of goals, poor use of financial resources, low employee morale, and procrastination. He then got together with a group of managers and drew up a list of "101 Small Improvements." Delegating to his senior staff much of the day-to-day managing he had always done himself, Conza went on the road in an attempt to open up the long-closed channels of communication between Blimpie and its franchisees.

Next, Blimpie launched a quality control program aimed at cleaning up its 140 New York restaurants, which had long been sources of embarrassment to the chain. At the same time, Conza continued in his efforts to improve relations with franchisees, many of whom had become disgruntled over the last decade. In addition to flying to dozens of cities to meet restaurant owners, Conza formed a franchisee advisory council to keep him apprised of important issues; he launched a newsletter called *No Baloney News* and a toll-free hotline to get important information out to franchisees; and he gave franchisees more control over advertising through the formation of regional advertising co-ops.

In 1989 Blimpie began testing a new low-calorie menu in the hope of attracting a bigger share of the increasingly fat-conscious American public. The new menu, called Blimpie Lite, included a variety of tuna-, crab-, chicken-, and turkey-based items, in both salad and pita-bread sandwich form. The following year, the company launched another test: gourmet salads sold under the name Blimpie Fresherie. Blimpie also began tinkering with its prototype restaurant design around this time, incorporating the company's signature lime-green and yellow colors into a sleeker look for new outlets. By 1990 the Blimpie turnaround was well underway, with systemwide sales reaching $120 million per year.

The Blimpie chain continued to grow steadily through the early 1990s. Much of this growth was fueled by the company's area developer program, in which franchise rights were sold for an entire area to a developer, who then subfranchised those rights to individual operators. The company continued testing new products throughout this period. In 1991 Blimpie unveiled its Quick Bite menu in response to the appearance of value menus in many fast food establishments, including arch-rival Subway. Items on the Quick Bite menu included 3-inch hero sandwiches for 99 cents, a 6-inch bacon, lettuce, and tomato sandwich for $1.59, and a veggie pocket pita sandwich, also priced at $1.59. The company also began testing pizza at a handful of locations in an effort to breathe some life into its dinner business. Conza's attempts to improve franchisee relations continued as well. The company's first annual franchisee convention was held in 1991.

By the beginning of 1992, there were Blimpie restaurants in 27 states. That year, the chain passed the 500-unit mark. In the spring of 1993, Blimpie began trading its stock on the up-and-coming NASDAQ exchange. Around this time, the company began to sink more resources into advertising than it had in the past, doubling its marketing budget to about $2 million per year. A new advertising campaign was launched, encompassing just about every medium available, including television, radio, print, and point-of-purchase. This campaign marked the introduction of the chain's new tag line: "Simply Blimpie for fresh-sliced subs." Some of the television spots featured people on the street struggling to repeat the tongue-twisting phrase, "Simply Blimpie."

Sales throughout the Blimpie system reached $132 million by 1993, and Blimpie International earned $1 million on $12 million in revenue. By autumn of that year, the chain had grown to 670 outlets. Improved marketing support from the parent company helped reduce the rate of franchise failures from ten percent to three percent. In some cases, such as in the brutally competitive Chicago market, Conza allowed franchisees to divert their six percent annual franchise fee to advertising.

As the 1990s continued, Blimpie came up with a new concept that accelerated the chain's growth even further. Blimpie's franchises began appearing in a variety of nontraditional locations. First it was convenience stores. As convenience store proprietors began to seek out new ways to compensate for declining cigarette sales, they started turning to fast food. Blimpie's was the natural choice for many, for two main reasons: a real kitchen was not required, and start-up costs were relatively low (as little as $35,000) compared with other fast food operations. Among the early nontraditional sites for Blimpie's outlets were the Des Moines, Iowa-based Kum & Go convenience store chain; Texaco Food Marts in Mississippi; and the food court at the University of Texas. Blimpie's also became part of the first Home Depot superstore restaurant section, located in Atlanta.

In 1994, the 800th Blimpie, in Iron City, Michigan, was opened. That year, the company launched several new concepts to further its drive for nontraditional venues. The Blimpie kiosk is a movable, condensed restaurant that can be fit into a 100-square-foot area. The kiosk, which can serve four types of sandwiches, drinks, and side orders, is designed for use at stadiums, fairs, and other special events. Another new idea was the movable display cart, suitable for high-traffic areas such as airports, college campuses, and concerts. Other new wrinkles included a special refrigerated case for convenience stores (Blimpie's fastest-growing market), and the Blimpie Bakery, offering a variety of baked goods aimed at boosting early morning business.

Blimpie reached two major milestones in 1995. Largely on the strength of its nontraditional location push, the chain passed the 1,000-outlet mark that year. Blimpie International also lived up to the second word in its name for the first time in company history, with the opening of a location in Stockholm, Sweden. As the 1990s continued, the company continued to look for more new ways to sell Blimpie sandwiches, including vending machines, outlets in supermarkets, and new types of carts and other mobile product delivery systems. Although Blimpie remained far behind Subway in the battle for hoagie supremacy, the renewed faith of founder and chairman Conza in the future of the submarine sandwich was helping the company realize gains in popularity and sales.

Further Reading

Bird, Laura, "Building a Lighter, Fresher Blimpie," *Adweek's Marketing Week,* August 6, 1990, p. 23.

"Blimpie's Starts Quality Drive in Manhattan," *Nation's Restaurant News,* April 4, 1988, p. 63.

Cohen, Andrew, " 'Blimpie' and 'Lite' May No Longer Be Contradictory Terms," *Wall Street Journal,* April 27, 1989, p. B5.

Edwards, Joe, "Astor Puts Blimpie in a Growth Mode," *Nation's Restaurant News,* November 9, 1987, p. F25.

Grimm, Matthew, "Blimpie Plans Winter Image Push," *Adweek's Marketing Week,* September 2, 1991, p. 7.

Howard, Theresa, "Now on Deck for Blimpie: NASDAQ, New Ad Campaign," *Nation's Restaurant News,* February 22, 1993, p. 16.

Keegan, Peter O., "Under New VP, Blimpie Int'l. Eyes Nontraditional Growth," *Nation's Restaurant News,* September 5, 1994, p. 7.

Kleinfield, N.R., "Trying To Build a Bigger Blimpie," *New York Times,* December 13, 1987, p. F4.

Richman, Louis S., "Rekindling the Entrepreneurial Fire," *Fortune,* February 21, 1994, p. 112.

Rigg, Cynthia, "Blimpie's Cuts Mustard With Convenience Stores," *Crain's New York Business,* October 11, 1993, p. 3.

Touby, Laurel, "Blimpie Is Trying To Be a Hero to Franchisees Again," *Business Week,* March 22, 1993, p. 70.

—Robert R. Jacobson

Boatmen's Bancshares Inc.

800 Market Street
St. Louis, Missouri 63101
U.S.A.
(314) 466-6100
Fax: (314) 456-7333

Public Company
Incorporated: 1847 as Boatmen's Savings Institution
Employees: 17,863
Assets: $33.4 billion (1995)
Stock Exchanges: NASDAQ
SICs: 6712 Bank Holding Companies; 6021 National
   Commercial Banks; 6022 State Commercial Banks;
   6091 Nondeposit Trust Facilities; Functions Related to
   Depository Banking, Not Elsewhere Classified; 6162
   Mortgage Bankers & Loan Correspondents; 6211
   Security Brokers, Dealers, & Flotation Companies;
   6351 Surety Insurance; 6411 Insurance Agents,
   Brokers, & Service

Boatmen's Bancshares Inc. is the oldest bank west of the Mississippi River, the largest commercial bank in Missouri, and one of the 30 largest bank holding companies in North America. In 1995 Boatmen's was operating 50 banks in more than 500 locations throughout the midwest and southwest United States. Its operations also included one of the largest trust companies in the nation, as well as a mortgage banking concern and various credit and insurance businesses. Boatmen's began expanding aggressively in the late 1980s.

Boatmen's began as the vision of banker, entrepreneur, and civic leader George Knight Budd. Budd was born in 1802 to George and Susanah Britton Budd, both of whom claimed prominent East Coast lineage. Before he arrived in St. Louis on a steamer in 1835, he had already traveled extensively in the United States, as well as in the Mediterranean and in South America. Budd brought with him a substantial fortune and cosmopolitan vision. Viewing the thriving commerce on St. Louis' Mississippi shore, Budd determined that the "Gateway" city was the place where he would settle.

Budd spent his first few years in St. Louis as a merchant before joining with a partner, Andrew Park, to form the private banking firm of Budd, Park & Co. Besides his business interests, Budd was a leader in his community. He sold U.S. bonds during the Civil War, for example, and served as financial editor of the *Missouri Democrat.* He was also a leader in the First Presbyterian Church and served as a city councilman and as city comptroller in the early 1850s. Budd's service as comptroller demonstrated how his far-reaching vision surpassed that of his peers. As comptroller, Budd arranged for the city to purchase a tract of land downtown for use as a park. Many citizens viewed the purchase as wildly extravagant, and Budd was even forced to resign because of opposition to his decision. But the purchase eventually proved to be one of the greatest bargains the city ever made; the site became the location of the City Hall and other municipal buildings.

By the time Budd was forced to resign from the comptroller position, he had already started the organization (Boatmen's Savings Institution) that would become Boatmen's Bancshares. Budd had faced a formidable wall of opposition to that venture, as well, because it was the first nonstate bank of its kind in Missouri. Budd was motivated to start Boatmen's Savings largely by his desire to help the industrial and working classes in St. Louis, many of whom were boatmen. Indeed, he saw that many of the rivermen were drinking and gambling their money away, rather than saving and investing it for their families and their future.

Budd wanted to start a bank that would cater to the needs of the working class rather than commercial enterprise. The entire city would benefit, he reasoned, because welfare and charitable needs would be reduced, a financial instrument would be put in place that would direct working people's money into more productive assets like homes and durable goods, and investment capital would be generated for St. Louis. Opposition to his proposal came from bureaucrats, many of whom wanted to protect the state's control of the commercial banking business. Those critics argued that a private bank would compete with Missouri's commercial bank. In fact, the Missouri legislature had shot down dozens of petitions from other people who wanted to start private, noncommercial banks.

Budd was able to overcome resistance to his plan. On February 16, 1847, the legislature passed an act granting a charter for Boatmen's Saving Institution; ''Whereas the boatmen and other industrious classes . . . need an institution in which they can safely deposit at interest, their earnings, and experience has proved that savings institutions have been productive and of great benefit to the laboring classes, inducing habits of economy and industry. . . .'' Shortly thereafter, Budd and fellow founders of the bank set up shop in an old jewelry store. Adam L. Mills was appointed president of the bank and served in that position until 1854.

Boatmen's started out offering an interest rate of three percent for cash deposits. The bank's trustees invested the cash in relatively conservative instruments. The first $1,000 of deposits, for example, was invested in a city bond that paid six percent interest. Thus, as Budd had predicted, the bank was supplying investment capital for the community. Within a year of opening its doors Boatmen's had accrued $26,000 in deposits and was struggling toward profitability. Encouraged by the success of the venture, the legislature gradually eased restrictions on the bank. In 1851, for instance, the state allowed Boatmen's to begin making real estate loans to individuals. By the early 1850s the bank was showing profits.

Boatmen's survival and growth toward profitability during the mid-1850s was nothing short of miraculous given the string of catastrophes that nearly quashed the fledgling financial institution. A cholera epidemic that raged through the city in 1849 took its toll on the working class, for example, killing more than 600 people in July alone. Even worse, a steamer caught fire in 1850 and ignited a blaze that devastated much of the city. 23 steamers and 430 buildings were destroyed. Fate spared the building that housed Boatmen's, which was damaged but still standing amidst the ashes of the structures immediately adjacent to it.

Despite the seriousness of the fire and the plague, by far the worst setback Boatmen's experienced during its first decade was a nearly ruinous event that transpired the night of April 5th, 1854. On April 6th, the bank's trustees were summoned to a meeting and told that the bank's safe had been robbed. Missing was $19,000 in gold and bank notes. The bank's safe had simply been opened with a key and emptied. It had taken the bank seven years to accrue a total surplus of $11,000. Now, that amount and $8,000 more was suddenly ripped from the company's balance sheet.

Suspicion for the theft quickly fell on Joseph Thornton, the bank's secretary. Thornton was one of the few people that knew that the key to the bank's small safe, which held the key to the larger safe, was hidden in the bank's chandelier the night of the theft. Furthermore, it was learned that shortly after the theft Thornton had deposited in the Bank of the State of Missouri a large package of bank notes that were water soaked and covered with mud, as though they had been buried. When questioned about the incident, Thornton withdrew the notes from the bank and was caught depositing similar water-soaked notes in smaller amounts at Boatmen's.

Despite damning circumstantial evidence, Thornton was eventually acquitted. He argued that the notes had been found under a stump by a steamboat deckhand, who thought the notes were worthless and sold them to Thornton. Justice prevailed a few years later after Thornton met Joseph Charless on the street in St. Louis. Charless, the president of the State Bank of Missouri, had testified against Thornton. Upon seeing his nemesis, Thornton drew a pistol and shot Charless. Thornton was found guilty of murder during a speedy trial and, to the delight of his detractors, promptly lynched.

Adding to Boatmen's woes was a run on its assets on January 13, 1855. Panicked depositors rushed to withdraw their money from the institution. Disaster loomed until the proprietress of one of the city's most expensive bordellos arrived in a carriage. She elbowed her way through the crowd standing outside the bank and conspicuously deposited $4,500 in gold. As the story goes, that giant deposit was enough to quell depositors' fears that Boatmen's would run out of money. The gold remained on deposit for one year, and is credited with having helped save the institution. Interestingly, another one of Boatmen's new depositors in that year was a young farmer and woodchopper named Ulysses S. Grant, the future president of the United States.

Having survived a rough start-up period, Boatmen's enjoyed healthy growth during much of the late 1800s. In the late 1850s, the state allowed the bank to begin issuing stock, lend money at higher rates of interest, execute trusts, and issue notes. Despite its humble beginnings, by the 1870s Boatmen's had emerged as a force in St. Louis banking. By the 1880s, moreover, Boatmen's had become known nationally as a strong financial institution. And by the early 1890s the bank was boasting nearly $7 million in deposits (That amount was temporarily reduced to about $5.4 million during the panic of 1893, however).

Under the presidency of Edwards Whitaker, Boatmen's remained a fiercely independent financial institution during the early 1900s. The Federal Reserve System had been organized in 1914 to, among other benefits, help protect banks from economic turbulence. But Whitaker was wary of federal intrusion and control and refused to allow Boatmen's to become a member. Boatmen's did finally join the Federal Reserve in 1926, following Whitaker's resignation. Other changes at the bank included the use of women tellers and the sale of investment securities, both of which were prompted by the demands of World War I.

Boatmen's experienced several name changes; it became Boatmen's Saving Bank in 1873, Boatmen's Bank in 1890, and Boatmen's National Bank of St. Louis in 1926. The name change in 1926 coincided with the initiation of a separate Trust Division, and reflected the organization's conversion to a national bank. By 1929 Boatmen's National Bank had about $28 million in assets, roughly $20.5 million of which were deposits. Unfortunately, Black Friday reduced that asset value to about $8.5 million and put Boatmen's, like many other banks of the era, on the brink of bankruptcy.

Boatmen's had merged with the investment firm of Kauffman, Smith & Co. shortly before the market collapse. Tom K. Smith, vice-president of the latter company, became president of Boatmen's. He helped steer the organization through the Great Depression and was even instrumental in helping the Federal Government establish the Federal Deposit Insurance Corporation (FDIC), which became an integral part of the American banking system following the Depression. Boatmen's was among the 25 St. Louis banks, of a total of 60, that survived the Depression.

Conservative financial practices and tight management allowed Boatmen's to emerge from the crises during the 1930s relatively unscathed. In fact, by 1942 Boatmen's was sporting more than $100 million in deposits and was established as a leading St. Louis bank. Five year later, in the midst of World War II, Boatmen's celebrated its 100th anniversary with deposits of more than $120 million. It was the fourth largest bank in St. Louis at the time. Boatmen's pulled its weight during the war by selling war bonds and opening special banking facilities for military personnel.

Boatmen's sustained moderate gains during the 1950s and 1960s, growing along with the city of St. Louis. It wasn't until the late 1960s, though, that Boatmen's began its drive to become a leading regional banking institution. Importantly, Boatmen's became a multi-bank holding company in 1969 through the formation of Boatmen's Bancshares. Boatmen's Bancshares was created as the parent company for Boatmen's National Bank to act as the instrument through which the bank would expand into new regions and markets.

Boatmen's Bancshares first expanded locally, purchasing four small suburban banks and a Springfield, Missouri mortgage banking company during the early 1970s. During the next five years Boatmen's aggressively chased regional opportunities to boost its exposure statewide. By 1978 the holding company had purchased eight Missouri banks as well as a mortgage banking operation in Illinois. By 1980, moreover, Boatmen's was boasting a portfolio of assets worth $2 billion and an organization comprised of 17 banks, a mortgage company, an insurance business, and 38 banking branches statewide.

Boatmen's continued to grow throughout the 1980s. A series of mergers and acquisitions included the 1983 purchase of Metro Bancholding Corporation, a prominent St. Louis bank. In 1984 Boatmen's added CharterCorp, a Kansas City-based holding company that had more than 45 banks with 100 branch locations and assets of more than $6 billion. Suddenly, Boatmen's was one of the largest commercial banking organizations in the Midwest. Adding to its muscle was the 1986 takeover of General Bancshares. That important buy gave Boatmen's access to markets in Illinois and Tennessee.

Boatmen's biggest expansion initiative was launched in 1988, when the holding company acquired Centerre Bancorporation. The giant merger nearly doubled the size of Boatmen's and made it the biggest bank in Missouri. Other acquisitions followed during the ongoing bank industry consolidation that permeated the 1980s and early 1990s. Boatmen's bought Community Federal Savings and Loan in 1990, giving it several hundred thousand new Missouri customers. In 1991 it moved westward with the purchase of First Interstate Bank of Oklahoma. Founders Bancorporation, also in Oklahoma, joined the Boatmen's portfolio in 1992. That buyout launched a flurry of acquisition during the year that gave Boatmen's an entry into Arkansas, Iowa, New Mexico, and Texas.

Among the most notable 1992 acquisitions was Sunwest Financial Services, which brought assets worth $3.8 billion to Boatmen's balance sheet. Combined, Boatmen's made acquisitions totaling $6.8 billion in 1991 and 1992, giving it a total asset base of more than $23 billion going into 1993. By early 1993, Boatmen's was operating in seven states with approximately 400 branch locations and about 175 automated teller machines. Later that year the bank initiated operations in Kansas with the purchase of First Continental Bank and Trust Company. By year's end Boatmen's had nearly $25 billion in assets and more than 425 locations in eight states.

Aggressive growth became Boatmen's hallmark for the early and mid-1990s. In 1994 the holding company made a big move in Arkansas with the acquisition of Worthen Banking Corporation, which encompassed approximately $3.5 billion in assets and 112 retail locations in Arkansas and Texas. Subsequent acquisitions were eclipsed by the announcement late in 1994 that Boatmen's had agreed to buy Fourth Financial Corporation of Wichita, Kansas. When that merger was completed in 1996, Boatmen's was expected to have a whopping $41 billion in assets.

By late 1995 Boatmen's was holding $33.4 billion in assets and operating more than 500 bank branches in nine states. It was among the 30 largest holding companies in the nation and one of the leading U.S. providers of trust services with more than $40 billion of assets under management. Importantly, Boatmen's posted net income for 1994 of $355 million, which was the culmination of an increase in earnings almost every year since the mid-1980s. For the remainder of the century, Boatmen's planned to sustain its growth and enhance its stature as a leading U.S. financial institution.

Principal Subsidiaries

Boatmen's Trust Company; Fourth Financial Corporation; Sunwest Bank; Superior Federal Bank, F.S.B.; FKF, Inc.; Security Bancshares, Inc.; Catoosa Bancshares, Inc.; Founders Bancorporation, Inc.; Eighth and Taylor Corp.

Further Reading

Boatmen's History of Growth and Expansion, St. Louis: Boatmen's Bancshares, September 1995.

Elbert, David, "Boatmen's Puts New Man in Charge," *Des Moines Register,* April 6, 1993, Bus. Sec.

Eubanks, Ben, and Dan Margolies, "Boatmen's Predicts Earning $137 million After Merger," *Kansas City Business Journal,* August 22, 1988, p. 12.

Eubanks, Ben, "At Boatmen's, the Craig Era Begins," *St. Louis Business Journal,* March 6, 1989, p. 1A.

——, "Boatmen's Climbs from Sixth to Become Largest Bank Firm," *St. Louis Business Journal,* December 25, 1989, p. 6A.

Gilmore, Casey, "What Will Merger Mean? Boatmen's, Bank IV Working on Details of Combined Forces," *The Kansas City Business Journal,* September 1, 1995, p. 1.

Palmeri, Christopher, "Softly to the Big Time," *Forbes,* May 10, 1993.

Ringer, Richard, "Can Boatmen's Steer to Bigger Profits," *United States Banker,* August 1991, p. 20.

Rule, W.G., *The Means of Wealth, Peace and Happiness: The Story of the Oldest Bank West of the Mississippi,* St. Louis: Boatmen's National Bank, 1947.

Schroeder, Amy and Gianna Jacobson, "Mercantile, Centerre Have Long Missouri History," *St. Louis Business Journal,* April 25, 1988, p. 18A.

—Dave Mote

BORDERS
GROUP, INC.

Borders Group, Inc.

500 E. Washington Street
Ann Arbor, Michigan 48104
U.S.A.
(313) 995-7262
Fax: (313) 995-9405

Public Company
Incorporated: 1971 as Borders Books
Employees: 10,000
Sales: $1.74 billion (1995)
Stock Exchanges: New York
SICs: 5735 Recorded & Prerecorded Tape Stores; 5942
    Book Stores

Borders Group, Inc. is the nation's second largest retailer of books, music, and other educational, informational, and entertainment products. Its Waldenbooks bookstores were in over 1,000 mall stores by 1995. Furthermore, it owned the rapidly expanding Borders Books & Music superstores and Planet Music stores. Throughout the country, the Borders name is associated with superstores catering to book and music lovers, with a wide selection of hard-to-find titles and tapes as well as a growing number of varied forms of electronic media. These superstores, which numbered 116 in early 1996, provided customers with plentiful sitting and browsing areas, a well-versed customer service team, and even espresso bars featuring live entertainment.

Borders Group, Inc. came into existence following the spin off from its parent Kmart Corporation in May 1995. But the Borders name dates back over two decades. Borders began as a single used bookstore in Ann Arbor, Michigan. The shop was founded by Louis and Tom Borders in 1971. Serving the bustling academic community of the University of Michigan and Ann Arbor's smaller colleges, the store held its own and became a popular neighborhood hangout. Within the next several years, the Borders brothers opened two more bookstores in Michigan, one in Atlanta, and another in Indianapolis. In addition, Louis and Tom started a wholesaling business they called

BIS (Book Inventory Systems), which experienced healthy growth.

Toying with the idea of a "superstore," the brothers opened their first prototype in 1985. Its success and the rise of similar competing stores set the retail book industry on its ear, shifting sales away from mall-based stores and into busy suburban areas (the areas that the Borders' bookstores had always targeted). By 1988, with their five Midwest bookstores and BIS's bustling service numbering 14 bookstore clients, the brothers' enterprise was bringing in a net income of $1.9 million from sales of $32.3 million. But the brothers wanted to expand in a big way.

To achieve their dream of taking the Borders name national, Louis and Tom put their faith in a young man named Robert DiRomualdo, a graduate of the Drexel Institute of Technology with a Harvard MBA. DiRomualdo had worked his way through several merchandising and marketing positions at Acme Markets and Little General Stores before becoming president and chief executive of Hickory Farms, the prominent food shop chain.

When DiRomualdo joined the Borders brothers' enterprise in 1988, the industry was ripe for the kind of expansion Louis and Tom had hoped for. The late 1980s and early 1990s were a time of unprecedented growth for book retailers, as industry sales mushroomed from $59 million in sales for the top two superstore chains with only 31 units in 1989, to nearly $1.4 billion by 1994 from 350 units; an astounding 87 percent compound annual rate. Taking advantage of these circumstances, DiRomualdo, who was named president and chief executive in 1989, opened 14 new stores in the next three years. Within a few short years DiRomualdo had turned Borders into a household name in the Midwest, and analysts considered Borders the premier book superstore chain of the 1990s.

By 1992, Borders had quadrupled its size and was beginning the complicated process of going public. Around the same time, the retailer attracted the attention of the huge Kmart Corporation, which had bought Waldenbooks in 1984 and was looking to expand its book retailing segment even further. In October of 1992, Louis and Tom Borders sold their business (though they remained investors), and Borders became a wholly owned subsidiary of Kmart. Sales from Borders' operations for 1993 reached $224.8 million, a 15.8 percent increase in net sales over the previous year. Several changes were implemented in 1993, including modernized cash registers, a human resources department, formal training programs for employees, and the introduction of music to the stores' stock.

In August 1994, Borders and sibling Waldenbooks formed a new company called Borders Group, Inc., with plans to eventually break free from Kmart. DiRomualdo joined with George Mrkonic, who ran Kmart's specialty stores division for four years (which included Builders Square, The Sports Authority, Pay Less Drug Stores, Waldenbooks, Borders, Kmart's in-store Reader's Market shops and others) and had jumped over to the Group in November. He had helped shape the company into a mechanized book and music mecca. By the end of the year Borders had acquired five CD Superstores and one Planet Music outlet. The company went on to add four Planet stores and 32 new Borders superstores.

The Group's overall sales for the year reached $1.5 billion. With what some analysts have called the industry's most sophisticated computer inventory management and sales system, Borders not only possessed the highest sales-per-foot ratio in the industry, but was able to track popular titles by selling season. Borders had identified as many as 55 separately defined seasonal patterns and programmed these into the computer system to keep better track of seasonal and regular bestselling titles, and to help maintain a supply of such titles with little or no interruption in prospective sales.

Though Kmart's ownership of Borders (and Waldenbooks) was to end with the formation of the Borders Group, Inc., finances were settled with the proceeds of a public offering of the new company's stock in May 1995. Two months later, Borders announced it would purchase Kmart's 13 percent stock share. DiRomualdo was installed as chairman and chief executive, while Mrkonic became vice-chairman and president. After a one-time write-off of $182 million, the Borders Group announced second quarter (1994) sales of nearly $364 million, representing an 11.7 percent gain over the previous year's posted sales of $327 million.

Though Borders' transition from small retailer to national chain wasn't completely smooth, many long-time employees remained with the company and were rewarded for their loyalty by generous benefits worked out during the Kmart acquisition. One sore point arose in 1994 with the proposed closure of Louis and Tom's original Borders store in Ann Arbor, set for relocation into an old department store building. Not only was the new store slated to be a Borders Books & Music (the previous was books-only), but its spacious 45,000-square foot interior (four times the size of the original) could in no way maintain the homey atmosphere of the first Borders book shop, despite the added benefits of much more space and extras like the popular new espresso bars.

Nevertheless, Borders new format was obviously giving customers what they wanted and needed. In addition to its unique, state-of-the-art inventory and ordering system, Borders' employee base was another of its major boons; most employees were full-time and college-educated, and all were tested for their knowledge of literature and music prior to hiring. Additionally, the bookstore chain prided itself on first-rate customer service, offering patrons a wide range of services from locating out-of-print titles to community activities like children's storytelling hours and poetry readings.

Rounding out Borders' offerings were growing varieties of alternative educational and informational media, from videos to CD-ROMs, a relaxing and comfortable environment which encouraged customers to linger, and the ubiquitous espresso bars. An industry-first that was quickly copied by competitors, Borders' espresso bars grew from a store add-on and overhead cost to a $20 million per year venture. 82 of the company's 88 superstores had espresso bars in 1995, and all new stores were scheduled to have them.

The Borders superstore prototype in 1996 was 30,000 square feet of space, substantially larger than major competitor Barnes & Noble's megastore. Averaging 128,000 book titles and about 57,000 prerecorded music titles at an initial cost of $2.6 million, most Borders superstores became profitable within 12 months of business. Since the majority of Borders' superstores were built following the early 1990s, the company's success by 1996 had been swift and immediate.

Revenue figures for year-end 1995 were just shy of $1.6 billion for the Borders Group as a whole, with Borders Books & Music stores contributing over $622.6 million (a 63.4 percent increase over 1994's sales). The superstores contributed a healthy 39.6 percent slice of the Group's overall sales, a welcome and expected 12.2 percent increase from their share in 1994. Analysts predicted 1996 sales to reach more than $2 billion, with Borders' superstores division hitting $950 million.

Second only to Barnes & Noble in sales, Borders' superstores were chosen over Barnes' by analysts as having a better variety of products, and most expected the bookseller to overtake its rival in the near future. Additionally, Borders planned to take advantage of Waldenbooks' status as a cash cow to finance expansion across the nation. Scheduled to open between 30 and 35 new Borders superstores in 1996 and to continue the trend (from 35 to 40 new superstores per year) until the end of the 1990s, Borders hoped to not only prove its mettle but to become the country's top book-retailing chain.

Principal Subsidiaries

Borders Inc.; Waldenbooks; Planet Music, Inc.

Further Reading

"Borders Group, Inc. Announces Year-End Results," *PR Newswire,* March 11, 1996, p. 311.
"Borders Group, Inc.—Booking Profits," *United States Equity Research—Retailing,* June 22, 1995.
"Kmart Sells Remaining 13% Stake in Borders Group," *New York Times,* August 17, 1995, p. C3.
McKenna, John F. and Buchanan, Robert F., "Strategic Assessment—Borders Group, Inc.," *NatWest Securities,* October 9, 1995.
Mutter, John, "Beyond Borders: Trimming Walden," *Publishers Weekly,* February 7, 1994, pp. 28–32.

—Taryn Benbow Pfalzgraf

Brach and Brock Confections, Inc.

P.O. Box 22427
Chattanooga, Tennessee 37422-2427
U.S.A.
(423) 899-1100
Fax: (423) 855-5505

Private Company
Incorporated: 1904 as E. J. Brach & Sons; 1906 as
  Brock Candy Company
Employees: 2,500
Sales: $600 million (1995 est.)
SICs: 2064 Candy & Other Confectionery Products

The 1994 merger of E. J. Brach & Sons and Brock Candy Company combined two venerable American candy makers into an industry powerhouse. With 1995 sales estimated to reach $600 million, Brach and Brock Confections, Inc. ranks with M&M/Mars, Hershey, and Nestlé at the top of the U.S. candy industry, while leading the industry in general line candy sales. Approximately 35 percent of the combined companies' sales come from Brach's "Pick-a-Mix" line of individually wrapped bulk candies; the company also continues to make Brock's chocolate-covered cherries and Starlite Mints, both perennial best-sellers, as well as a limited range of branded items. Corporate, sales, and marketing headquarters for the combined companies have been relocated to Brock's Tennessee headquarters. The company continues to operate the largest single-manufacturing candy plant in the country, Brach's 2.3 million square-foot facility in Chicago, which also houses Brach and Brock's research and development and purchasing operations.

Both Brach and Brock grew from small, turn-of-the-century storefronts. In 1904, German immigrant Emil J. Brach pulled together $1,000 to open the "Palace of Sweets," an 18 × 65-foot candy shop located on the corner of Chicago's North Avenue and Towne Street. Joined by sons Edwin, and later, Frank, Brach's store featured its own one-kettle candy kitchen. From the start, Brach sought methods for boosting production while reducing labor costs, and early on introduced not only a mechanized kettle-heating element, but also a device for dipping taffy, Brach's initial product. With these devices, Brach could sell his candy for 20 cents per pound, far lower than the typical retailer's price of 50 to 60 cents per pound. Brach soon began to sell his candy to retailers throughout Chicago, adding four new kettles and producing 3,000 pounds of candy per week.

By 1906, Brach's customers quickly included almost all of the city's large department stores. He was forced to expand production again, now moving to a larger facility. At the same time, Brach introduced peanut and hard candies to his product line. In the new plant, Brach's production soon passed 12,000 pounds per week, and three years later he was forced to move again to a still larger facility. With this move, Brach added coconut candies and expanded his line of hard candies. Within a year, however, the company had already outgrown the new plant. Additional space, doubling the size of the company's production area, was leased in a building next door, and Brach's product line grew to include cream, gum, fudge, and crystallized candies.

One year later, in 1911, with production topping 50,000 pounds per week, Brach expanded yet again, moving his offices to a building down the street and converting the old offices into additional floor space. Brach's candies were reaching farther and farther outside of the city, and, because the railroads were still the principal means of distribution, Brach faced new difficulties in transporting growing shipments of his candies. In 1913, Brach moved again, to a larger plant located on the railroad. The addition of chocolate and cream dipping and icing, as well as marshmallow confections, increased production to 250,000 pounds per week. At this point, Brach instituted product testing and quality control measures, creating a Laboratory of Control in the Brach plant.

Brach next moved into chocolate manufacturing, installing machinery to make chocolate from the bean in a second, 60,000-square-foot space. From 1915 to 1918, Brach's capacity grew to 1.1 million pounds per week. Incorporated in 1916, Brach added a third site in 1918, increasing production of his candy line to more than 2 million pounds per week. Four years later, Brach consolidated operations, building a $5 million facility on Chicago's West Side. Brach's sales grew to $7.9 million in 1925, with a net income of more than $1 million.

The onset of the Depression era hit the candy industry hard. Candy sales, which had reached nearly $448 million in 1914, fell to $211 million in 1933. Brach's sales dropped as well, to a low of $1.27 million in 1934. Nonetheless, the company remained profitable, posting a net income of $175,000 for that year. By then, Brach employed more than 1,000 people, making the company one of Chicago's largest employers. Sales climbed slowly through the 1930s, returning to $7.9 million in 1938. The candy industry was tested again by the outbreak of the Second World War and the resulting shortages of sugar and other raw products. Yet, emerging from the war, Brach's sales had tripled, to $21.5 million in 1945.

By the end of the next decade, Brach's sales more than doubled, reaching over $58 million in 1960. Its 23-acre Chicago plant was the largest candy factory in the country. A second, 30-acre site was purchased in New Brunswick, New Jersey in 1959. Brach's line had grown to 250 types of candy, including hard candies, chocolates, fudge, peanut, caramels, cremes, jellies, lozenges, and panned candies, with specialty items for Halloween, Christmas, Easter, and Valentine's Day. Production in the Chicago facility alone topped 4 million pounds per week, making Brach the country's largest candy producer.

Brach began to attract the interest of larger companies. In 1966, after rejecting a $19 million offer that would have given Consolidated Foods a 17 percent stake in the company, Frank Brach, by then company president and chairman, accepted American Home Products' $136 million offer to acquire the company. In 1977, Frank Brach turned over the presidency to Ned Mitchell, who would lead the company into the 1980s. At the time of American Home's acquisition, Brach's $83 million in sales held about 7 percent of the total candy market. Over the next 20 years, Brach's sales would grow to more than $700 million per year, and Brach would capture as much as two-thirds of the general line and bulk candy market.

A new trend in the candy industry, however, which began to develop especially in the postwar years, would erode Brach's long-time position as the nation's largest candymaker. Prior to the second world war, consumer candy purchases went largely to the penny candy and individual item variety; after the war, consumers turned more and more to a new type of candy, the candy bar, many of which would become household brand names. Candy bars held an advantage over general line candies such as Brach's, in that sales of candy bars could be made from a far wider variety of selling points, from vending machines to drug stores to convenience stores, and so on. Brach, especially with its Pick-a-Mix bin candies, was largely limited to grocery stores. The candy bar supported more successfully the impulse purchases important to the candy industry, and by the early 1980s Brach's share of the overall candy market shriveled, while other giants, particularly Hershey and M&M/Mars, emerged. Meanwhile, Brach's pegboard displays had changed little in the past decades, presenting an outdated look against the more modern packaging and advertising of its competitors. The candy industry was also growing; during the 1980s alone it would nearly double in size, from about $5 billion to nearly $10

billion in 1991. But the 1980s would see Brach's fortunes decline drastically.

In 1987, American Home sold Brach to Jacobs Suchard A.G., a Swiss coffee and candymaker with about $3.3 billion in sales in 1987. Run by Klaus Jacobs, Suchard hoped to use Brach to expand its European empire, and especially its Toblerone and Milka brands, into the United States.

Suchard and Brach ran into problems almost immediately. Management styles and goals clashed, and Jacobs quickly fired Brach's top officers and gutted the leadership of its sales, marketing, production, and finance departments as well. Some of these positions were filled with executives from Suchard's European operations; other positions, including a large percentage of Brach's sales and marketing department, were staffed by people with little experience in the candy industry. Under the European management, which failed to recognize many key differences between the U.S. and European candy markets, Brach faltered through a series of poor decisions. One of these involved the scaling back of Brach's line, which had reached 1,700 different candies and packaging types and sizes, to only 300 SKUs. This proved disastrous for Brach, because the bulk of its sales continued to be made at the grocery stores and through other vendors that required the flexibility of Brach's former range to realize the highest profit margins. To make matters worse, the Suchard-led company did not recognize the U.S. candy market's purchase pattern—in that the bulk of sales are made surrounding Valentine's Day, Easter, Halloween, and Christmas—and failed to promote and, at times, even produce the specialized holiday candies. Corporate headquarters were relocated to a Chicago suburb. Finally, Suchard changed Brach's name, which enjoyed recognition by as much as 77 percent of the U.S. candy-buying public, to Jacobs Suchard Inc.

Brach's customers, including major chains such as Walgreens, deserted the company for its competitors. Sales dropped, and the company began posting losses, reaching $50 million in operating losses in 1988, and more than $200 million over the next several years. By 1990, the company had gone through two CEOs in three years. Its new CEO and president, Peter Rogers, formerly with RJR Nabisco, attempted to turn the company around, restoring the Brach name and rebuilding its product line. When Philip Morris paid $3.8 million to acquire a majority stake in Jacobs Suchard A.G., however, it refused to take Brach as part of the package. Brach's losses mounted, and the company began a series of massive layoffs that would trim its employee rolls from nearly 3,000 workers to about 1,700. Production dropped to 50 percent capacity. Sales picked up slightly during the early 1990s, to about $430 million in 1993, but Brach continued to lose money.

Rogers was replaced by Kevin Martin, formerly of M&M/Mars and Pillsbury Co. Under Martin, Brach stepped up its new product development and worked to refine its packaging and point-of-sale design. Martin also brought the company's corporate headquarters back into its Chicago plant. By 1994, Brach posted its first operating profit—of about $1 million—since 1987, on sales of an estimated $475 million. In September of that year, Brach announced the acquisition of the Brock Candy Company for $140 million.

Unlike Brach, the Brock Candy Company had remained a privately held, family-run company through most of its history, only going public in 1993. Founded in 1906 by William E. Brock, Brock Candy would not reach the size of Brach, but achieved a strong reputation for the quality of its products.

William E. Brock, born in North Carolina, had been a traveling salesman for R. J. Reynolds Tobacco Co. when, in 1906, he decided to settle down in Chattanooga, Tennessee. Brock bought a small wholesale grocery shop, which also held a candy shop, the Trigg Candy Company. Brock continued the candy-making operation, which consisted of handmade penny and bulk candies, peanut brittle, peppermints, and fudge, changing the company's name to the Brock Candy Company in 1909. Brock's first major expansion came in the early 1920s, when it modernized its factory, installing automatic moguls. Next, Brock eliminated all slab confectionery items, such as peanut brittle and fudge, which were products already produced by many manufacturers, making that area extremely competitive. Instead, Brock concentrated on launching new lines of jelly and marshmallow candies, using its automated moguls equipment. During the 1920s, Brock also began packaging its candies in cellophane bags, making it one of the first to do so. During the 1930s, Brock introduced its Chocolate Covered Cherries, which not only helped the company survive the lean Depression era but would remain one of its biggest sellers for the next 60 years. During the Second World War, when rationing forced the company to cut back on much of its production, it introduced the Brock Bar, a coated nut roll using the still plentiful ingredients corn syrup and peanuts. William E. Brock went on to a career in the U.S. Senate, and his son, William, Jr., succeeded him to head the company.

Brock's next great expansion came in 1950, when it added 60,000 square feet to its plant, bringing its downtown Chattanooga plant to 180,000 square feet. By the end of that decade, however, Brock was again ready for further expansion, and it purchased a 30-acre site on the Jersey Pike outside of Chattanooga. In 1964, Brock constructed a 64,000-square-foot distribution warehouse on the new site. By the end of the 1960s, the warehouse was expanded by another 25,000 square feet. The company also made its first acquisition, of Schuler Chocolates in Winona, Minnesota, adding to its seasonal confection capacity.

By the mid-1970s the company was producing more than 30 million pounds of candies per year. It moved to a newly constructed production and office facility on its Jersey Pike site in 1976. By the early 1980s, and led by Pat Brock, William Brock, Jr.'s son, Brock's sales reached $34 million, and its product line included chocolates, jelly sweets, and hard candies. In 1981, Brock also became the first American producer of European-style gummi candies. Later in the decade, Brock introduced a line of fruit snacks, and then moved into contract and industrial production of its fruit-based products. In 1990, sales passed $72 million, bringing a net income of nearly $2.5 million. Production had grown to 70 million tons per year.

Brock made a second acquisition, of Shelly Brothers, Inc. of Souderton, Pennsylvania, for $600,000, in 1990. That purchase was followed by Brock's first international partnership, when the company bought a 30 percent share in Clara Candy, of Dublin, Ireland in 1993. By then, Brock had gone public, with an initial public offering of 2.3 million shares, for nearly 63 percent of the company's stock. Brock's sales continued to rise, to $102 million in 1993 and $112 million in 1994, for net incomes of $5.3 million and $6.5 million, respectively. In 1994, Brock accepted Brach's $140 million merger offer.

The combined company, renamed Brach and Brock Confections, marked the second attempt for the two companies to join forces. A first deal had been struck in the early 1980s, but American Home, fearing an antitrust suit, forced Brach to back out. The merger of the companies was seen as beneficial to both, offering Brach's strong production facilities, and Brock's strong distribution lines, which included its largest customer, Wal-Mart, accounting for nearly 40 percent of Brock's sales. By 1995, the merger allowed Brach to post its first profit in nearly a decade, with net income estimated to reach $20 million. Brach's troubled past seemed behind it, and for the combined candy companies, the future looked sweet.

Principal Subsidiaries

Schuler Chocolate, Incorporated; Shelly Bros., Inc.; Clara Candy (Ireland; 30%).

Further Reading

Klokis, Holly, ''The Palace of Sweets: Brach's Then and Now,'' *Candy Industry*, December 1983, p. 82.
Lazarus, George, ''A Sweet Development at Brach Duo,'' *Chicago Tribune*, August 31, 1995, p. B3.
——, ''Brach Acquiring Competitor To Sweeten Income,'' *Chicago Tribune*, September 2, 1994, p. B2.
Raffles, Richard, ''Brock Candy Move Marks the Dawn of a New Era,'' *Candy & Snack Industry*, June 1977, p. 79.
Shackleford, Chris, ''The Sweet Smell of Success,'' *Chattanooga Free Press*, September 4, 1994.
Stalter, Nedra, ''Believing in a Dream Brought Brock Success,'' *Candy Industry*, December 1983, p. 152.
Tiffany, Susan, ''Brock: Dedicated to 'Sweet Things in Life,' '' *Candy Industry*, May 1994, p. 20.

—M. L. Cohen

British Telecommunications plc

BT Centre
81 Newgate Street
London EC1A 7AJ
England
(0171) 356 5000
Fax: (0171) 356 5520

Public Company
Incorporated: 1984
Employees: 137,500
Sales:£13.89 billion (US$22.64 billion) (1995)
Stock Exchanges: London New York Toronto Tokyo
SICs: 4813 Telephone Communications, Except Radio
  Telephone; 4812 Radio Telephone Communications;
  6719 Holding Companies, Not Elsewhere Classified;
  4822 Telegraph & Other Message Communications;
  4899 Communication Services, Not Elsewhere
  Classified; 8711 Engineering Services; 8731
  Commercial, Physical & Biological Research

British Telecommunications plc, commonly known as BT, is the largest company in the United Kingdom. It came into being in early 1984 through the transformation of a former state utility, at a turning point in the development of U.K. and European telecommunications. Since being privatized, BT has maintained its position as the dominant provider of local and long-distance telephone service in the United Kingdom, but has faced increasing competition and seen its market share fall as the English government continues to deregulate the market. BT has subsequently looked abroad for its future growth and is in the process of developing a global telecommunications network for multinational companies.

British Telecommunications's administrative and technological roots are mingled with those of the U.K. Post Office and reach back into the second half of the 19th century, when inventors at home and abroad, such as Alexander Graham Bell, Thomas Edison, and Guglielmo Marconi, were applying elec-

tromagnetic principles to the development of practicable forms of telecommunications. Out of this the modern telegraph, followed by the telephone, was born. In 1850 the first submarine telegraph cable was laid across the English Channel. In 1878 Bell demonstrated his newly patented telephone to Queen Victoria, and in 1879 England's first telephone exchange opened in London. It was in the United Kingdom, too, that the first international telephone call was made, in 1891, between England and France. The telegraph and telephone were at first exploited by private enterprises, but they were gradually taken over by a U.K. government department, the General Post Office. The reversal of that nationalization process was completed in the early 1990s.

In 1869 the Postmaster General was granted the exclusive right to transmit telegrams within the United Kingdom. At first the telephone was slow to catch on and was not regarded by the Post Office as a serious threat to its telegraphic network. The first independent U.K. telephone service provider, Telephone Company Ltd., was set up in 1879 and in 1880 merged with its competitor, Edison Telephone Company, to form United Telephone Company. Seeing that the telephone was beginning to take customers away from its telegraph service, the Post Office embarked on a series of protective measures, and in 1880 the government brought an action against the recently formed United Telephone Company, claiming that it was operating in contravention of the Telegraph Act of 1869. The High Court subsequently decided that the telephone was a form of telegraph. The merger was revoked, and telephone companies were required to be licensed by the telegraph monopoly holder, the Post Office.

The next stage in the process of squeezing out competition and establishing a state telephone monopoly was the building up of the Post Office's own system. In 1896 the Post Office completed its improved telephone network by taking over the trunk lines of National Telephone Company, the largest of its licensees, and started to set up its own local telephone exchanges. It was then decided that more national licenses would be granted. National Telephone Company continued to operate a local service until its license expired in 1911, but in 1912 the Post Office was granted a monopoly on the supply of telephone services throughout the United Kingdom. It took over all of National Telephone Company's exchanges and opened an automatic exchange in Epsom, south of London.

Since 1899 several of the larger towns and cities, including Glasgow, Brighton, Swansea, Portsmouth, and Kingston upon Hull (Hull), had each been operating an independent local telephone service, but their number gradually dwindled as they were bought out by National Telephone Company or the Post Office. In 1913 only Hull was left. By cooperating with successive competitors—National Telephone Company and the Post Office—it survived, first as the Hull Corporation Telephone Department, a municipal enterprise run by the Hull City Council, and since 1987, as a limited company, Kingston Communications (Hull) PLC, wholly owned by Hull City Council and a licensed public telecommunications operator (PTO), with interconnection agreements with BT and BT's competitor, Mercury Telecommunications Limited.

A landmark in the prehistory of BT was the Post Office Act of 1969, which changed the status of the Post Office. This former government department became a state public corporation under the Secretary of State for Industry. The telecommunications services remained in the Post Office but were divided from the postal services into Post Office Telecommunications.

Three further events marked the telephone industry's move toward an environment of free competition. First came the passage of the 1981 British Telecommunications Act, which took Post Office Telecommunications out of the Post Office, turning it into an autonomous, though still state-owned, body known as British Telecommunications Corporation or, more familiarly, British Telecom. Second was the 1984 Telecommunications Act, by which BT was privatized, the telecommunications market was further liberalized, and a regulatory body was set up. Third, the Duopoly Review in 1990 resulted in the government's 1991 decision to further increase telecommunications competition. The government also decided to sell off its remaining shares in BT, although this decision was not influenced by the Duopoly Review.

In July 1981 the British Telecommunications Act which separated telecommunications from the Post Office and set up a new state public corporation to supply them also gave the government powers to license competitors in the operation of the domestic telephone network. As well as modifying the state company's statutory monopoly of the telephone network, this act took away its monopoly in the provision of telecommunication equipment, leaving it only with the right to supply and install a subscriber's first telephone. The act not only opened the market to competition in value-added services, such as data processing and storage, but also allowed other providers to use BT's lines.

In October 1981 Mercury Communications Limited was chosen to receive a 25-year renewable license to operate a national and international digital network—a system that encodes information as a series of on-off signals—to compete with BT's trunk traffic. Mercury had been set up early in 1981 by British Petroleum, Barclay's Merchant Bank, and Cable and Wireless plc to enter the business of long-distance communications, offering a customized service to companies. The license

allowed it to interconnect with the BT network and to enter the European and U.S. sectors. In 1983 the government undertook for seven years not to license any company but BT and Mercury to carry telecommunication services over fixed links. Under this duopoly policy, Mercury, which began operating in 1986, was to be BT's single serious network competitor until the early 1990s. Less than a year after the 1981 act, the government announced its intention to privatize the British Telecommunications Corporation.

At the end of 1982 the first telecommunications bill had reached the committee stage, when the general election of May 1983 was called. The bill immediately died, but was presented again in the new Parliament and finally became law in its second form, the Telecommunications Act of April 12, 1984. It had undergone 320 hours of debate and discussion, during which BT itself had briefed members of Parliament on its views and interests. By the act, BT lost its exclusive right to run telecommunications systems, and all PTOs had to be licensed. The new company was to be sold as an integrated organization. Fragmentation, similar to the breakup of American Telephone and Telegraph Company (AT&T) in the United States, would have left the resultant entities too small to defend the home market from foreign competition, to stand up to multinationals in the world markets, and to command the technology and the financial strength for adequate research and development. In November 1984, 3.01 billion ordinary shares of 25 pence were offered for sale at 130 pence per share, the first figure being the nominal or face value of the share, and the second its sale price, or market value, at the time of sale. The government retained a 48.6 percent stake in the new company, valued at the time of sale at £7.8 billion. All the offered shares were bought.

Under the terms of the 1984 act, BT's main activity was to supply telecommunication services in the U.K. market of 55 million people in accordance with a 25-year operating license from the Department of Trade and Industry. Starting in 1984, BT's performance and development were conditioned by an official regulatory body, the semi-independent Office of Telecommunications (Oftel), set up in August 1984 under the Secretary of State for Trade and Industry and headed by the Director General of Telecommunications (Bryan Carsberg being the first to hold the post). A major role of this body was, by simulating the effects of real competition, to prevent BT from abusing its inherited dominance of the U.K. telecommunications market during the process of deregulation. Nevertheless, the fairness of the competition was often disputed by interested parties. In its severely regulated environment, BT had lost the security of being a state monopoly, without gaining the freedom of action of a wholly autonomous business. Oftel monitored BT's pricing, accounting, investment policies, and quality of services; issued licenses to additional competitors; and continued to facilitate the interconnection of rival services to the BT network. Competitors, for their part, tended to feel that BT was favored by the regulator. The new British Telecommunications plc created by the 1984 act then shared its monopoly in telecommunication systems with Mercury as well as Kingston Communications (Hull) PLC, plus some general licensees.

When BT became a separate state corporation in 1981, before its rebirth in 1984 as a privatized company, it inherited from its Post Office days an evolved network. This network had to be brought up to date at the same time BT was taking on competition from operators starting from scratch. These competitors were using the latest technology, without public service obligations and were able, for example, to go straight to digital systems and cheaper and more efficient fiber-optic cable, while BT still had copper wire circuits to be amortized. BT kept technology in the forefront, however, and spent 2 percent of its turnover on research and development to keep it there. The domestic telephone services sector was by far BT's largest operating division in terms of assets, revenue, and number of employees. In 1990 it accounted for nearly 75 percent of turnover. Its core business was the public switched telephone network (PSTN). The 20 millionth U.K. telephone was installed in 1975, the system became fully automatic in 1976, and in the early 1990s BT, with more than 25 million lines, operated the world's sixth-largest telephone network, with nearly 100,000 public pay phones. In 1990 BTUK—the product of the 1987 merger of BT's local communications services and national networks divisions—was operating more than 7,000 local exchange units, of which nearly half were already digital.

Meanwhile, Mercury's market share in the early 1990s was variously estimated between 3.7 and 5 percent, but was increasing markedly. An efficiency and investment effort was BT management's response to this new competition and to growing demands and service expectations from its customers. Waiting times for connections and repairs were reduced, and new digital equipment was introduced into the network, including exchanges that use microchip technology to integrate the switching and transmission elements of the network, resulting in a higher quality of service and improved voice transmission. All trunk exchange units have been digital since June 1990. BT aimed to have a fully digital network by the year 2000. In addition, new products, such as microwave radio transmission in the city of London, were offered.

Another area within which BT faced stiff competition was the capricious mobile communications market. BT's Mobile Telephone System 4, a noncellular service introduced in 1981, with 7,000 subscribers at the beginning of 1990, had capacity problems at peak periods and was being replaced by a cellular network, Cellnet, shared by BT's 60 percent and Securicor Communications. Its rival, using another network, was Racal-Vodafone. In February 1989 BT bought, for £907 million, a 20 percent interest in McCaw Cellular Communications, Inc., a U.S. mobile cellular telephone and broadcasting systems provider and operator.

In the late 1980s, BT offered a wide range of VANS—value-added network services, including such electronic mailbox services as Telecom Gold and Message Handling Service—in the United Kingdom. In November 1989, in order to further its strategies in the home and international VANS market, BT bought, for £231 million, the U.S. company Tymnet, one of the largest VANS companies in the world, and consolidated some of its own international services under a new company, BT Tymnet Inc. BT started setting up an ISDN—integrated services digital network—that could eventually replace the other networks by offering all data, voice, text, and image network services at high speed, with circuit-switched digital connections from a single access point. Although ISDN was of primary importance in BT's plans for the future, like

other telecommunication firms, BT had to move slowly in this area, needing to await definition of international standards and to raise the consciousness of potential customers. A pilot service was launched by BT in June 1985 that by the end of 1989 was available to 75 percent of business users.

In the early 1990s BT faced major changes. The duopoly policy was reviewed in 1990, and a report issued in January 1991 was followed two months later by a government recommendation that both BT and Mercury should face greater competition in local, trunk, and international services. BT was still barred from offering entertainment services on cable television, but after some hard bargaining, Bryan Carsberg, director of telecommunications; Peter Lilley, secretary of state for trade and industry; and Iain Vallance, BT's chairman, agreed on amendments to BT's 25-year license. BT was then allowed to proceed with further rebalancing between telephone rentals and call charges and with customized tariffs. It was announced that the sale of a slice of the government's residual share in BT would take place in November 1991.

In the face of increasing competition, BT engaged in a rationalizing and restructuring operation. In the year ending March 31, 1990, a slimming-down and cost-control operation began, covered by an exceptional charge of £390 million. In the following year, 18,800 jobs were shed and overtime work was cut, while another 10,000 terminations were planned for the year 1991 to 1992. In April 1991 the reshaped company announced that the three former operating divisions, BTUK, comprising Local Communications Services and National Networks; BTI, British Telecom International; and CSD, Communication Services Division, would be replaced. In their stead were placed two major divisions that deal directly with customers: Personal Communications and Business Communications, both supported by a Products and Services Division. BT's international and U.K. networks were brought together into a new Worldwide Networks Division, and some business activities best managed separately, such as mobile communications and operator services, comprised a new Special Business Division.

Early in 1991 BT's intensified drive to consolidate its image as a smart, market-oriented world organization with a human face was signaled by its integration of the current BT acronym into a new blue and red logo, representing a dancing piper apparently delivering a sound message. A new designer image was commissioned for the group and was widely publicized; public telephones were replaced by newly designed models; and the bright yellow of BT vehicles began to be replaced, in a notoriously expensive replace-or-respray operation, by a stylish gray.

As the 1990s continued, BT's challenges became more intense. While at least 98 percent of its revenues and profits continued to come from its home market, the additional competition allowed under the 1991 review of the duopoly policy combined with continued moves by Oftel to reduce BT's monopoly began to seriously erode BT's position in the U.K. market. From 1991 to early 1996, some 150 firms started operations in the United Kingdom that were competitive with BT, several of the most important of which were cable firms owned by U.S. Baby Bell companies. As a result, BT's share of the U.K. telephone market tumbled, with its residential-customers market share falling from 99 percent in 1991 to 93 percent in

1995 and its business-customers market share falling from 94 percent in 1991 to 83 percent in 1995. Some analysts were predicting that by 2000 BT's share of the U.K. residential market would fall to as low as 65 percent.

In response, BT continued the cost-cutting program it began in 1990. More than 100,000 jobs had been eliminated by 1995, reducing the BT workforce from 239,000 in 1990 to 137,500 in 1995. The program was to be continued into the late 1990s, moving toward a goal of a 100,000-employee workforce with productivity levels in line with the Baby Bells. BT's upstart competitors also forced the company to upgrade its service and lower its prices since they were luring away BT customers by offering low prices and better service. In fiscal year 1995 BT reduced prices on both domestic and international long-distances calls, adding up to more than £800 million in savings for its customers for the year. That same year, BT increased capital expenditures 23 percent in order to improve customer service and upgrade its network.

Meanwhile, the often cantankerous relationship between BT and Oftel grew more confrontational in the mid-1990s. Perhaps not coincidentally, these BT-Oftel battles took place after 1993, the year in which the British government sold nearly all of its remaining stake in BT for US$7.43 billion. In 1995, BT expressed support for the development of number portability—the ability of customers to keep the same phone number even if they change telephone suppliers—but objected to a plan which the company felt would place a disproportionate share of the costs on BT. In response to BT's rejection of the plan, Oftel referred the matter to the Monopolies and Mergers Commission, the first time BT had been subjected to such a referral. Later in 1995, the regulator announced that it wanted to reduce BT's return on capital from the 15.6 percent of 1995 to as low as 8 percent. If forced to accept this, the company's ability to invest for future growth might be seriously damaged. Such a possibility sent BT stock plunging throughout 1995.

The overall impact of the competition and regulation showed clearly in BT's revenues and profits. The company revenue growth had stagnated with the £13.15 billion figure of 1991 only increasing to £13.89 billion in 1995. Profits fell in three of the four years from 1992 to 1995, and fell overall from £2.04 billion to £1.74 billion.

Embattled at home and certainly facing more and more pressure there for the foreseeable future, BT almost had no choice but to look overseas for its long-term survival. Early attempts at international expansion had failed, including the 1986 purchase of Mitel Corp., a Canadian phone equipment manufacturer which BT sold in 1992 at a loss of £120 million (US$200 million); and the company's stake in McCaw Cellular, which it sold in 1992 to AT&T (which had just purchased a larger stake in McCaw) at a profit exceeding £200 million (US$333 million). According to Vallance, these investments no longer fit into the company's international plans, which now centered around building a global telecommunications network offering comprehensive services to multinational corporations. Vallance's first attempt at this failed, however. In 1991 the company set up a subsidiary, Syncordia Corp., in Atlanta, Georgia, to start such a network on its own, but had little success attracting either customers or the telecommunications

partners it needed around the world to make the venture succeed.

Syncordia was shut down three years later, after BT realized it had erred attempting to go it alone. In mid-1993, BT's second attempt to go global began with the announcement of an alliance with the major U.S. telecommunications firm MCI Communications Corp. The alliance, which received final approval in mid-1994, involved BT purchasing a 20 percent stake in MCI for £2.86 billion (US$4.2 billion). The two firms set up a joint venture called Concert Communications Company, based in England, which was 75 percent owned by BT and 25 percent by MCI. Syncordia was folded into the new venture, which would inherit Syncordia's charge of providing telecommunications services for multinational corporations.

To make Concert work, however, BT needed additional partners in other areas of the world. Over the next few years, BT set up alliances with several European companies including Norwegian Telecom, Tele Danmark, Telecom Finland, and Banco Santander of Spain. A foothold in the important German market was also secured in a 1995 alliance with the German conglomerate Viag AG, in which the partners planned to start a joint venture that would offer Concert services. BT now had a solid network of partners in Europe and North America, but remained weak in the critical Asian market having allied only with International Telecom Japan Inc., a small international carrier. Meanwhile, AT&T was working furiously to set up its own system of global alliances through its WorldPartners program. By 1995, while AT&T had had more success than BT in Asia, having established partnerships with KDD of Japan and with Singapore Telecom, the American giant was having difficulties making inroads in Europe.

In the midst of the difficult 1995 BT endured, two top executives left the company, one retiring and one resigning. Vallance decided to step aside as CEO, while remaining chairman, and turned to an outsider, Peter L. Bonfield. Taking over as CEO in early 1996, Bonfield had been the chief executive of ICL PLC, a British computer company owned by Fujitsu Ltd. Observers noted that Bonfield's experience with Japanese business practices might help BT in its effort to enhance its alliances in Asia.

Heading into the turn of the century, British Telecommunications was certainly being squeezed in its still all-important home market. Its international activities were still very much in a start-up phase and needed time to turn the company's huge investments in them into profits. The question was whether its cash would be drained faster at home than its payoff abroad. Perhaps, therefore, needing to move faster than AT&T to secure a global network, it appeared in early 1996 that BT might try effecting a major merger to gain its missing Asian link. The most significant possibility was that BT would merge with Cable and Wireless plc (C&W), which owned 80 percent of the main home market competitor of BT, Mercury. Merger talks between C&W and BT began in late 1995. If it happened, the merged firm would have to sell off Mercury, but more importantly BT would have gained C&W's 57.5 percent stake in Hong Kong Telecommunications Ltd. and its telecommunication businesses in Japan and Australia. And BT might finally break free of its dependence on the U.K. market.

Principal Subsidiaries

BT (CBP) Limited; BT Cableships Limited; BT Property Limited; BT (Worldwide) Limited; Call Connections Limited (60%); Cellnet Solutions Limited (60%); Concert Communications Company (75%); International Maritime Satellite Organisation (9%); Manx Telecom Limited; Marshalls Finance Limited (31%); Telecom Securicor Cellular Radio Limited (60%); Westminster Cable Company Limited; Yellow Page Sales Limited; BT Australasia Pty Limited (Australia); BT France; European Telecommunications Satellite Organisation (France; 18%); BT Telecom (Deutschland) GmbH (Germany); Gibraltar Telecommunications International Limited (50%); BT (Hong Kong) Limited; BT Telecommunicaciones SA (Spain; 50%); BT North America Inc. (U.S.); International Telecommunications Satellite Organization (U.S.; 7%); MCI Communications Corporation (U.S.; 20%).

Further Reading

Competition and Choice: Telecommunications Policy for the 1990s, London: HMSO, March 1991.

Dwyer, Paula, ''The Sun Never Sets on British Telecom,'' *Business Week,* December 7, 1992, pp. 54–55.

Eglin, Roger, ''BT Prepares to Beat the World,'' *Management Today,* July 1993, pp. 9–10.

''Europe'' and ''The United Kingdom,'' *DATAPRO Reports on International Telecommunications 1990–91,* Delran, N.J.: McGraw-Hill, 1990–1991.

Flynn, Julia, Catherine Arnst, and Gail Edmondson, ''Who'll Be the First Global Phone Company?,'' *Business Week,* March 27, 1995, pp. 176–80.

Flynn, Julia, and Mark Lewyn, ''Why Telecom's Odd Couple Is Trying So Hard,'' *Business Week,* September 20, 1993, pp. 96, 98.

Flynn, Julia, Mark Lewyn, and Gail Edmondson, ''What a Time to Take Over at British Telecom,'' *Business Week,* January 29, 1996.

Hass, Nancy, ''The Whipping Boy: Meet British Telecom's Iain Vallance, the Rodney Dangerfield of Telecommunications,'' *Financial World,* September 15, 1992, pp. 48–49.

Hudson, Richard L., ''BT Faces a Line of Potential International Competitors,'' *Wall Street Journal,* April 29, 1993, p. B4.

''Major Telecommunications Companies in Europe,'' *Profile of the Worldwide Telecommunications Industry,* Oxford: Elsevier Advanced Technology, 1990.

Newman, Karin, *The Selling of British Telecom,* London: Holt, Rinehart and Winston, 1986.

Purton, Peter, ''Is BT Lost in the Fog of World Events?,'' *Telephony,* December 7, 1992, pp. 7–8.

''Shooting a Line,'' *Economist,* July 10, 1993, pp. 62–63.

—Olive Classe
—updated by David E. Salamie

Brooke Group Ltd.

100 S.E. Second Street
Miami, Florida 33131
U.S.A.
(305) 579-8000

Public Company
Incorporated: 1980 as Brooke Partners L.P.
Employees: 1,850
Sales: $479.3 million
Stock Exchanges: New York
SICs: 2111 Cigarettes

Brooke Group Ltd. is a holding company for a variety of companies, the most important being the Liggett Group Inc., the successor of the Liggett & Myers Tobacco Company. Liggett produces such branded cigarettes as L&M, Chesterfield, Lark, and Eve, as well as the value-price brand Pyramid.

Brooke Partners L. P. was founded in 1980 by financier Bennett S. LeBow as an investment vehicle. Bennett bought troubled companies that he considered undervalued and attempted to turn them around. LeBow had studied engineering, worked as a computer analyst for the U.S. military, and formed his own computer company in 1967. He took that company, DSI Systems Inc., public in 1969, but then pushed too hard to expand and nearly bankrupted the company. After selling DSI in 1971 he became an advisor to high-tech companies, frequently investing in them as well.

LeBow formed Brooke Partners with the assistance of investment firm Drexel Burnham Lambert Inc., which owned 15 percent. Brooke sold one of its early investments, computer display maker Information Displays Inc., in 1984. In 1985 Brooke bought 54 percent of computer maker MAI Basic Four, which sold software and hardware to small companies in highly specific markets like the hotel business. MAI had been losing money. As it usually did, Brooke quickly sent in its own managers and advisors to cut expenses, pare down the firm's

staff, and put a new business strategy in place. MAI was soon making money again.

Brooke also bought the microfilm division of Bell & Howell Co. and Brigham's Inc., an ice cream business. With its MAI success under its belt and a growing portfolio of companies, Brooke turned to a much bigger target; the Liggett Group, once one of the largest U.S. tobacco companies. At the time it was owned by British firm Metropolitan PLC. Liggett began as a manufacturer of snuff in Belleville, Illinois in 1822. In 1873 John Edmund Liggett, grandson of the firm's founder, joined with George S. Myers to form Liggett & Myers, which began producing cigarettes. Ligget eventually produced L&M, Chesterfield, and Lark cigarettes, which were some of the best-known brands in the industry for several decades.

While the firm remained profitable, it made many mistakes over the years. In the 1950s, with the use of filters becoming widespread on cigarettes, Liggett put its money into Chesterfields, which were not filtered. The decision cost Liggett market share in ensuing years. The company also missed opportunities related to the marketing potential of packaging changes. When crush-proof, flip-top boxes were introduced, for example, Liggett ignored the innovation. Likewise, with the health risks of cigarettes increasingly on the public's mind, competitors introduced low-tar cigarettes in 1967. Liggett did nothing as low-tar cigarettes became increasingly prevalent. Finally, in 1976, Liggett introduced Decade, its first low-tar cigarette, nearly 10 years after the competition.

Meanwhile, Liggett was diversifying. It bought or created brands in the liquor market including Wild Turkey, a prestigious bourbon put out through its Austin, Nichols & Co. subsidiary. The firm also imported table wines and liqueurs like Campari aperitif from Italy. Its Paddington Corp. subsidiary imported J&B Scotch. Liggett also put out Alpo, the best-selling canned dog food in the United States. Due to the decline of Liggett's tobacco profits, Alpo was one of the firm's biggest profit makers. By the early 1970s the company's president, Raymond J. Mulligan, had come from the Alpo division and had no background in the cigarette business. Liggett had profits of $80.4 million in 1973 on sales of $586 million.

Sales of Liggett's premium brands of alcohol grew at an annual rate of 20 percent over the next five years. In 1978 the company gave up on international cigarette sales, spinning off its foreign cigarette business to Philip Morris for $108 million. Liggett nearly sold its domestic cigarette business too, but could not quite work out a deal. By 1979 cigarettes had shrunk to 20 percent of Liggett's business, while wine and spirits accounted for 30 percent. The firm held only three percent of the cigarette market. Meanwhile, Alpo continued to grow and the company moved into the growing market for dry dog food. Liggett's Diversified Products Corp. was pumping up sales as well, becoming the largest maker of barbells and other physical fitness equipment.

Liggett also bought two leading Pepsi Cola bottling companies; one in Fresno, California, and the other in Columbia, South Carolina. Meanwhile, it cut its advertising for cigarettes by 45 percent, causing many industry observers to believe that the company was preparing for the eventual demise of its cigarette business. The following year, however, Liggett introduced generic cigarettes. Considered a risky move because cigarette marketing was so dependant on brand names, it nevertheless proved a successful one. None of its larger rivals produced generic cigarettes, so Liggett captured the market for them.

Also in 1980, Liggett Group was bought by Grand Metropolitan Ltd., the London-based liquor and entertainment company, for $575 million after a long takeover battle. Grand Metropolitan had already owned 9.5 percent of Liggett, and Liggett had imported Grand Met's J&B Scotch. Liggett initially opposed the purchase, and to dissuade Grand Met sold its Austin, Nichols subsidiary, which made the Wild Turkey bourbon Grand Met wanted to own, for $97.5 million.

With Grand Met, Liggett experienced some success with generic cigarettes over the next several years, but by 1984 larger rivals were challenging it. R.J. Reynolds began selling its Doral brand cigarettes at generic prices, for instance, while Brown & Williamson Tobacco Co. brought out a line of generic and private-label cigarettes. Liggett's management had been considering buying the firm from Grand Met for $325 million, but when Liggett's rivals brought out competing generic products, the group's financing fell through.

Liggett's sales and profits plummeted until it was bought by Brooke Partners in 1986 for $137 million. Brooke installed LeBow's partner William Weksel as chairman. Not content with its move into tobacco, Brooke bought 53 percent of telecommunications firm Western Union Corp. in 1987. Founded in 1851, Western Union had once been a communications giant. But the advent of the telephone slowly strangled the firm. By the time Brooke assumed control, the telegraph accounted for less than ten percent of Western Union's revenue. It made more money from its teletypewriter services, mailgrams, and money order service.

When the British shipbuilding concern that was building LeBow's private yacht went bankrupt, Brooke bought it for less than $5 million. In 1988, moreover, Brooke proposed a buyout of American Brands. When that didn't work, LeBow tried to persuade American Brands to buy the Liggett Group. That

effort failed as well. In the meantime, Liggett introduced the Pyramid brand of low-cost cigarettes, which proved to be one of the most successful cigarette introductions of the 1980s. Then, in 1989, Brooke Partners started SkyBox International Inc., a sports trading card company.

In 1990 the Liggett Group changed its name to Brooke Group Ltd. and announced it would emphasize its push to diversify into sports and entertainment products. Liggett already had a small football and basketball card business, and distributed chocolate mints made in Finland. The cards and candy used the same distribution channels used by the cigarette business. At about the same time, William Weksel resigned and LeBow was elected chair. Liggett's 1989 sales of $572.9 million accounted for the lion's share of Brooke Partners' total sales, but smoking was under increasing legal pressure. So, Liggett changed its name to Brooke Group and split into two subsidiaries; Liggett Group Inc. managed the firm's tobacco business, while Impel Marketing Inc. managed the group's other activities. Impel specialized in the sales and marketing needed to broaden sales of sports and entertainment products.

Later in 1990, LeBow restructured his companies. Brooke Group became the parent of Brooke Partners, which was suffering from the heavy debt it acquired as the result of its many leveraged buyouts. As a result, Brooke Group (formerly Liggett Group) became responsible for Brooke Partners' $300 million debt. The interest on the bonds paying for Brooke Partners' acquisition of MAI and Western Union came to $45 million a year, severely limiting Brooke Group's cash flow. Some investors were outraged. One portfolio manager told the *Wall Street Journal* that LeBow ''took an equity investment and turned it into a junk bond.'' The price of Brooke Group's shares plummeted.

Brooke Group had been managed by a nominally independent company called Brooke Management Inc., which was owned by LeBow and whose sole client was Brooke Group. In 1991 Brooke Group paid Brooke Management $10.2 million for services and expenses. LeBow decided to fold Brooke Management into Brooke Group, and in 1992 Brooke Group paid LeBow $12 million for Brooke Management, a firm whose assets comprised the managerial expertise of LeBow and his associates. LeBow had not drawn a salary as president of Brooke Group, but he did after the buyout.

In 1992 Brooke Group took a charge to restructure MAI and SkyBox International, its sports and trading-card subsidiary. SkyBox lost $80 million in 1991. Brooke Group lost $149.6 million in 1991 and $75.8 million in 1992. Furthermore, its English boat yard, renamed Brooke Yachts International Ltd., went under in 1992, leaving Brooke with a $4.8 million writeoff. Liggett's sales were declining, meanwhile, partly because of a decision to place more emphasis on its full-price brands of cigarettes like Chesterfield, Eve, and L&M. Liggett's cigarette market share had sunk to three percent from six percent since its 1986 takeover by Brooke.

Liggett named Edward Horrigan chairman and CEO in 1993. Horrigan, the former chairman of R.J. Reynolds Tobacco, said that Liggett would look again to the overseas market, try to hold market share of its branded cigarettes, and try to expand the market share of its discount cigarettes. At the same time, Philip Morris and RJR were announcing discounts on their leading brands, thus putting pressure on the discount cigarette market. Liggett restructured its headquarters and manufacturing operations in 1993. In 1994 it reduced its sales force by 150, using 300 part time sales people instead. It also cut employee benefits.

In 1993 Western Union (renamed New Valley) entered Chapter 11 bankruptcy. One of its last remaining profit makers, its telex business, had gone sour as fax technology made it obsolete. Brooke fought with New Valley's debt holders to keep control of New Valley's one remaining profitable business; money transfer. With its U.S. operations in turmoil, Brooke sought to invest in the former Soviet Union. One venture, a joint-venture with the Ducat tobacco company in Moscow, took years to produce a cigarette because of disagreements with the Russian government and other problems.

Fed up with the company's problems, a group of shareholders filed suit against LeBow and four other Brooke officers alleging that they had enriched themselves at the expense of the company, which had been stripped of assets. Soon after, the *Wall Street Journal* published an intensely critical article about Brooke Group in which it claimed that LeBow "has increasingly used the company as a kind of personal bank." The shareholder suit was settled in 1994 after LeBow repaid much of the $20 million that the lawsuit alleged he owed the company. The settlement linked LeBow's future salary to company performance, and required approval by outside directors of any transaction of more than $100,000 between Brooke Group and LeBow.

Despite Horrigan's efforts, the cigarette market share of Liggett continued to decline, falling to 2.3 percent of the U.S. market in 1994; Liggett held .9 percent of the branded market and 5.4 percent of the discount market. Liggett also sold 750 million cigarettes in the Middle East and Eastern Europe, and produced over 300 combinations of brands, lengths, styles and packages. Overall, Brooke had profits of $110.1 million in 1994 on sales of $479.3 million.

In November 1994, New Valley was forced to sell its money transfer services as part of its Chapter 11 bankruptcy reorganiza-tion. After it emerged from bankruptcy in 1995, it bought a 28.2 percent interest in Brazilian airplane manufacturer Empresa Brasileira de Aeronautica, S.A., for $12.8 million. In March 1995, Brooke sold its remaining 15 percent stake in SkyBox International. The firm also purchased 6.4 percent of the ShowBiz Pizza Time chain, and Ladenburg Thalmann, a 119-year-old New York securities firm that cost it $26.8 million.

By mid-1995 Brooke had improved enough for *Business Week* to conclude that LeBow was "finally paying attention to beefing up Brooke's quarterly performance and bottom-line results."

Principal Subsidiaries

New Valley Corp.; BGLS Inc.; Liggett Group Inc.; Impel Marketing Inc.

Further Reading

Atlas, Riva, "Blowing Smoke," *Forbes*, March 29, 1993, p. 60.

Cohen, Laurie P., "Ready Credit: Head of Brooke Group Draws on Its Coffers to Tune of Millions," *Wall Street Journal*, July 30, 1993, pp. A1, A4.

"Liggett's New Recipe," *Financial World*, February 1, 1980, pp. 48–49.

Cole, Robert J., "Grand Met Raises Bid for Liggett," *New York Times*, May 15, 1980, p. D1.

Finch, Peter, "Bennett LeBow: Up from Bottom-Fishing," *Business Week*, December 12, 1988, pp. 108, 110.

Gloede, William, "L&M Smokes Out Generic Competition," *Advertising Age*, August 13, 1984, pp. 4, 58.

Kansas, Dave, "Brooke Group to Settle Shareholder Suit Over Dealings with Chairman LeBow," *Wall Street Journal*, March 18, 1994.

"L&M Smokes Out Generic Competition," *Advertising Age*, August 13, 1984.

Lowenstein, Roger, "Why Some Holders of Tobacco Firm May Feel Burned," *Wall Street Journal*, November 30, 1990.

Ramirez, Anthony, "Liggett to Change Its Focus with Shift from Cigarettes," *New York Times*, June 22, 1990, pp. D1–D2.

Stevenson, Richard W., "Grand Metropolitan Sells Liggett to an Investor," *New York Times*, October 29, 1986.

—Scott M. Lewis

California Pizza Kitchen Inc.

1640 South Sepulveda Boulevard
Suite 200
Los Angeles, California 90025
U.S.A.
(310) 575-3000
Fax: (310) 575-5757

Private Company
Incorporated: 1985
Employees: 3,000
Sales: $120 million
SICs: 5812 Eating Places

California Pizza Kitchen Inc. is one of the most successful and fastest-growing chain restaurants that began operations in the United States within the last ten years. The company boasts one of the most innovative and distinctive menus of any eating establishment in America, including such items as Barbecue Chicken Pizza, Bacon-Lettuce-Tomato Pizza, and Moo Shu Chicken Calzone Pizza. Although California Pizza Kitchen offers more than just pizza, including pasta, salads, desserts, beer, wine, and soft drinks, it is the pizza that it is famous for. With sales in 1995 rapidly increasing over the 1994 figures, and with 78 restaurants operating in 18 states, the company intends to continue its aggressive expansion policy.

The founders of California Pizza Kitchen are Larry Flax and Rick Rosenfield. Flax, a native of Los Angeles, California, was educated at the University of Southern California Law School and served as an Assistant United States Attorney during the early 1970s. In that capacity, Flax worked as Chief of Civil Rights and as Assistant Chief of the Criminal Division for the United States Department of Justice. Rosenfield, a native of Chicago, worked as an attorney for the U.S. Department of Justice in Washington, D.C., and as Assistant U.S. Attorney for the Central District of California. Having met while pursuing their respective careers as assistant federal prosecutors, the two men struck up a friendship during the early 1970s and decided to form their own law firm. Concentrating on criminal defense

cases, in 1984 the two partners found themselves arguing a case before a Superior Court Judge in San Francisco. Flax and Rosenfield strongly believed that the facts of the case were in their favor, but the jury was unable to reach a verdict. Disillusioned by the hung jury, the two young men decided to leave the legal profession to seek a more rewarding career.

During their partnership, Flax and Rosenfield had offered legal services on a national basis, and in the course of their business travels they had sampled restaurants across the country and developed an enthusiasm for good food. Resolving to turn their enthusiasm into a business opportunity, they decided to open a restaurant. The two entrepreneurs took their lead from Wolfgang Puck, the master chef and owner of Spago restaurant in West Hollywood, who was known for creating pizzas with unusual toppings; the pair saw an opportunity to bring innovative pizza like Puck's to the mass market. The first California Pizza Kitchen was opened in Beverly Hills in 1985 and was an immediate success.

The strategy behind California Pizza Kitchen was simple. The owners wanted to provide a casual, upscale, family restaurant, with good food as the cornerstone of the enterprise. Most of the chain's kitchens are out in the open, so customers can watch the cooks preparing their pizzas. The restaurants are decorated with white tile to provide a clean, crisp atmosphere. The pizzas are baked in wood-burning ovens imported from Italy, whose designs had been perfected over a period of a few hundred years. The oven is fired to approximately 800 degrees Fahrenheit, and the pizza is cooked in three minutes in order to sear the ingredients. This results in a tastier—and, according to some cooks, a healthier—pizza. The partners were committed to creating designer pizzas with unusual toppings, such as duck sausage, Tandoori chicken, and goat cheese, an approach that not only attracted customers not normally inclined to eat pizza, but also enabled the company to take advantage of food trends within the industry. When the owners added pasta, salads, soft drinks, liquor, and desserts to the menu, California Pizza Kitchen was on the road to success.

Although the company struggled during its first few years of operation and incurred some debt, sales of its pizza were always increasing. The company's big break came in 1989 when the flamboyant chairman of Golden Nugget casinos, Steve Wynn, struck a deal with Flax and Rosenfield to put a California Pizza Kitchen in the Mirage Hotel and Casino. Located in Las Vegas, the heart of the U.S. gambling industry, the new restaurant garnered $5.5 million in sales during its first year of operation. On weekends, according to the restaurant's manager, tables were turning over between 16 to 25 times within a 13-hour period. Unfortunately for Flax and Rosenfield, they didn't own the restaurant in the Mirage Hotel and Casino. Wynn had arranged an unusual California Pizza Kitchen franchise. Yet the publicity that came from the success of the restaurant in Las Vegas opened doors to new opportunities in other parts of the country. Real estate developers were soon lobbying to place a California Pizza Kitchen in strategic locations for new malls and commercial developments.

In 1992 PepsiCo Inc., located in Purchase, New York, bought a 50 percent interest in California Pizza Kitchen, which it later increased to 67 percent. In addition to its line of soft drink products, PepsiCo owned Pizza Hut, KFC (formerly known as Kentucky Fried Chicken), and Taco Bell. Management at PepsiCo wanted to gain more experience in operating full-service, moderately priced, casual-dining restaurants. The deal was finalized for $97 million, with Flax and Rosenfield receiving $20 million apiece, and PepsiCo assumed two seats out of the four on California Pizza Kitchen's board of directors. Not surprisingly, two of Taco Bell's officers were chosen for the two seats on the board. Flax and Rosenfield remained as co-chairs of the board of directors with 50 percent voting control, and continued to direct the day-to-day operations of the company. The only change PepsiCo required in the agreement was for California Pizza to replace the sale of Coca-Cola products with PepsiCo's line of soft drinks.

The arrangement between PepsiCo and California Pizza Kitchen seemed to be a gift to Flax and Rosenfield. At the time of the deal, California Pizza Kitchen was generating approximately $60 million in annual sales from all its restaurants, with each one averaging a little over $3 million. The number of employees had reached 1,700, the number of operating restaurants had risen to 25, and the ambitious entrepreneurs were pursuing a strategy to open a new unit each month. Although the owners were contemplating a public stock offering in order to continue their expansion program, they decided to accept PepsiCo's offer due to the generous terms of the agreement. Flax and Rosenfield realized that PepsiCo management wanted to learn how to run an operation like theirs, and they were more than willing to teach people at PepsiCo what they knew in exchange for limitless expansion capital. Each new restaurant was costing nearly $1 million to open over an eight-month period, and Flax and Rosenfield did not want to interrupt their aggressive expansion plans.

California Pizza Kitchen was opening restaurants in upscale office buildings and pricey malls and as free-standing units in affluent areas. The company's restaurants were primarily located throughout the greater Los Angeles metropolitan area, but new units were opened on a monthly basis in major cities across the country, including Chicago and Atlanta. Except for two franchises in Las Vegas, and a limited partnership in Chicago, all of the restaurant units were owned by Flax and Rosenfield.

Delighted by the chain's success, PepsiCo management was especially intrigued by the part played by the waitstaff in California Pizza Kitchen's achievement. When PepsiCo officials visited a number of California Pizza Kitchen units located in various areas of the country, they discovered an inordinately friendly and helpful staff of waiters and waitresses at each restaurant. Impressed by the process of selection, training, and retainment of employees, PepsiCo was determined to learn how to apply these techniques to its own restaurant operations.

The partnership between PepsiCo and California Pizza Kitchen flourished from the very beginning. By the end of 1993, Flax and Rosenfield were operating 35 restaurants across the country, and were planning an ambitious expansion drive of 50 new units per year in both 1994 and 1995. In 1993 the restaurant industry honored Flax and Rosenfield with the Golden Chain award, one of the plaudits that the partners found most satisfying out of all the accolades they received.

As their successes multiplied, Flax and Rosenfield began to devote even more attention than before to the development of personnel, which included over 3,000 workers, 160 of whom were kitchen managers and general managers. Not only were the two men driving forces behind better service, but through their constant concern with internal coaching and promotion, they enhanced their employees' career opportunities. A former waiter and cook who had joined the company when it was only one month old was promoted to vice-president of back-of-the-house operations; a unit-level assistant manager became front-of-the-house operations vice-president; and the company's first waitress in the Beverly Hills restaurant became vice-president of training. The former lawyers also worked to improve the pay scale and benefits of their workers, securing, for example, a $2.3 million deal in special compensation and bonuses for company executives through negotiations with parent PepsiCo.

Throughout all of these developments, the focus of California Pizza Kitchen remained the food. The company offered 29 different pizza flavors, including duck sausage pizza, Thai chicken pizza, two-sausage pizza, tuna-melt pizza, mixed grill vegetarian pizza, goat cheese pizza, and eggplant Parmesan pizza, with prices ranging from $6.95 to $11.95.

The year 1994 was one of the best to date for the company. California Pizza Kitchen added 28 restaurants to reach a total of 70 units operating in 15 states and the District of Columbia. Sales also shot up to the $120 million milepost, a dramatic increase of 60 percent over the previous year. Surprisingly, only 40 percent of revenues were coming from the company's pizza menu: other items such as corn soup and barbecue chopped chicken salad were selling just as well. Per unit annual sales were still hovering around the $3 million mark.

By the beginning of 1995, California Pizza Kitchen was operating 78 restaurants in 18 states and in the District of Columbia. New food toppings and combinations were continually being added to the pizza menu, as were as a host of new items such as Chicken Tequila Fettucine and Tuscan Bean Soup. Although Larry Flax and Richard Rosenfield remained firmly in control of the day-to-day operations of the restaurant chain, new management personnel from PepsiCo were becoming more and more an integral part of the company's decision-making process.

Further Reading

Albright, William, "Everybody's Hot to Get in This Kitchen," *Houston Post,* December 9, 1994, p. 17.

Barret, Amy, "Detergents, Aisle 2, Pizza Hut, Aisle 5," *Business Week,* June 7, 1993, pp. 88–89.

——, "Pepsi Is Going after the Upper Crust," *Business Week,* June 7, 1993, p. 90.

"The Best of 1991," *Business Week,* January 13, 1992, p. 123.

Britt, Russ, "California Pizza Kitchen Sell Slice," *Daily News,* May 21, 1992, p. 12.

"California Dreamin'," *Restaurants & Institutions,* April 1985, p. 27.

Faust, Fred, "Chain's Winning Strategy: Top Pizza with Americans' Favorites," *St. Louis Dispatch,* August 26, 1991, pp. 1–4.

Howard, Theresa, "PepsiCo Acquires 50% of California Pizza Kitchen," *Nation's Restaurant News,* June 1, 1992, pp. 1–2.

Littlefield, Kinney, "Pretty Is Part of Pizza Picture at New Takeout Eatery in Irvine," *Orange County Register,* May 28, 1993, p. 6.

Martin, Richard, "Larry Flax and Rick Rosenfield: Courting a New Success," *Nation's Restaurant News,* September 20, 1993, p. 118.

McCarthy, Michael J., "PepsiCo Buys Its First Slice of Fancy Pizza," *Wall Street Journal,* May 21, 1992, p. B1(E).

—Thomas Derdak

Callaway Golf Company

2285 Rutherford Road
Carlsbad, California 92008
U.S.A.
(619) 931-1771
Fax: (619) 929-8120

Public Company
Incorporated: 1982
Sales: $448.7 million
Employees: 1,071
Stock Exchanges: New York
SICs: Sporting & Athletic Goods, Not Elsewhere
    Classified

Callaway Golf Company is the premier manufacturer of golf clubs in the United States. The company sells more golf clubs than any other firm, and has the lion's share of the $3 billion golf equipment industry, eclipsing the higher-profile brand names such as Wilson, Spalding, and MacGregor. Callaway's most famous club, the ''Big Bertha'' Driver, is the most popular piece of equipment sold to golfers, and more professionals use Callaway Drivers than any other competing brand. In 1995 Callaway Drivers were the number one brand used on the PGA, Senior PGA, LPGA, NIKE, and European PGA golf tours. With the company's products in such popular demand, it is not surprising that sales for 1995 rose a whopping 77 percent over the previous year, while profits increased 89 percent over the 1994 figures. The success of Callaway Golf Company can be solely attributed to one man: Ely Callaway.

Ely Reeves Callaway, Jr., was born in La Grange, Georgia, a small town about 60 miles southwest of Atlanta. Ely's grandfather, a Baptist preacher, owned and operated a plantation with approximately 20 slaves. When the Union forces defeated the Confederacy in the American Civil War during the 1860s, the Callaways lost their entire fortune. Ely's uncle, Fuller Callaway, was the primary force behind the family's resurgence. He first went into farming, then into dry goods, later into banking, and finally into the cotton mill trade. Ely's father worked for his uncle, but when the young Ely Reeves Jr. graduated from Emory University, his father advised him not to work for the family.

In June 1940 Ely was working as a runner in the factoring department of the Trust Company of Georgia, and decided to take an army reserve correspondence course. Commissioned six weeks later, Ely went to Philadelphia and began working in the apparel-procurement division of the quartermaster's depot. Callaway was soon promoted to major, a significant achievement for a young man of 24, and was in charge of 70 civilians and two lawyers. During this time, he was buying approximately 70 percent of the total wartime production of the U.S. cotton apparel industry, and was dealing with companies like Levi Strauss, Hart, Schaffner & Marx, and the Arrow Shirt Company on a daily basis. When the war ended, Callaway decided to go to work for Deering, Milliken & Company in order to continue a career in the textile and apparel industry.

Callaway rose quickly in his chosen profession. In 1954, after he became involved in a disagreement with Roger Milliken's brother-in-law, however, Milliken fired him unceremoniously. Undismayed, Callaway found a job at Textron Industries and, under the supervision of Royal Little, oversaw the merger of Robbins Mills and American Woolen, two large textile mills. When Textron sold Callaway's division to Burlington Industries, Callaway was part of the package deal. By 1968, Callaway was appointed president of Burlington Industries.

Callaway's appointment as president of the largest and most influential textile company in the world merely fueled his ambition. When he was passed over for the position of chairman in 1973, Callaway quit abruptly. Picking up his family, he moved from the East Coast to California in order to start a wine making company in the tiny town of Temecula. Although the land that Callaway had purchased was not prime grape growing country, nonetheless he persevered until his venture began to pay off. Callaway Vineyard & Winery was soon supplying its products to well-known restaurants such as the Four Seasons in New York City. He sold the operation to Hiram Walker in 1981 at a price of $14 million. In just a few short years, Callaway had posted a profit of over $9 million.

At the age of 60, Callaway thought it was time to relax, and, hearkening back to his youth and the years when he was a tournament champion, he began in earnest to resume his game of golf. One day on the golf course, he became acquainted with a hickory-shaft club that had a steel core. Callaway liked the golf club so much that he called up its manufacturers to tell them so. The golf club manufacturers, short of money and looking for someone to invest in their company, asked Callaway for help. Callaway immediately purchased the four-month-old enterprise at the bargain basement price of $2.5 million, and pinned his own name to the company.

Callaway Golf Company, under the direction of Callaway himself, immediately began to conceive of strategies to increase both its profile and its revenues in the highly competitive sports equipment market. Callaway decided the best way to achieve the above goals was to introduce new products, and within four years of acquiring the company he had his design staff come up with a new premium-priced item that did away with a large amount of the neck of the club, while extending the shaft through the clubhead. The response to Callaway's new design was nothing less than phenomenal. Golfers responded to the heavier-weighted clubheads that included a lower center of gravity, and sales shot up dramatically, as did the profile and reputation of Callaway's company. In 1988 company sales amounted to approximately $5 million. One year later, sales had doubled to $10.5 million. In 1990 sales doubled again, and by 1991, revenues skyrocketed to $54.7 million, an increase of nearly 150 percent.

In 1991 Callaway created the "Big Bertha" Driver, an oversized driver named for the huge gun used by the Germans during World War I to drop shells on Paris from six miles away. The principle behind Callaway's creation of the metal wood driver was that it put more weight around the perimeter of the head of the club, resulting in a thinner face. According to Callaway, this gave the golfer a greater "feel" at the time of impact with the ball. Moreover, the golfer didn't have to hit the ball precisely on the button to obtain directional control and good distance. Soon golfers were swearing by them, and sales surpassed all the other brands of golf clubs made in America.

With the company growing rapidly, Callaway decided to take it public in February 1992. With 2.6 million shares of stock offered on the New York Exchange at $20 per share, the stock had jumped to $36 per share by the end of the day. The capital provided by the stock offering enabled Callaway to expand his manufacturing capacity. The demand for the company's golf club was rising at unexpected rates, and management at the firm needed more cash to take advantage of what has always been regarded as a notoriously faddish market in the golf equipment industry. By the end of 1992, sales had reached $132 million. At the end of April 1993, the price per share of Callaway Golf Company stock had increased to an impressive $54. In 1993, when sales were reported at $255 million, the company had surpassed the better-known names in the sporting goods industry such as Wilson, Spalding, and MacGregor to become the revenue leader in the field. As sales and stock price continued to climb, Callaway's personal share rose to a hefty $86 million.

In 1994 Callaway Golf Company introduced a innovative design for irons that would accompany the highly successful "Big Bertha" Metal Wood Drivers. The new irons, created with the same principles in mind as Callaway's "Big Berthas," were an immediate hit on the golf course. Priced at $125, the steel-shafted irons were approximately 20 percent more costly than conventional premium clubs. For $175, a golfer could purchase the new design with a graphite shaft. Since nearly all the company's clubs relied on a new development in casting technology, supplies of the new clubs were limited and helped keep the price per iron high. A total set of nine irons and three woods purchased from Callaway Golf Company at the suggested retail price amounted to the small fortune of $2,325. Yet golfing enthusiasts, both amateur and professional, happily bought the company's wares. By the end of fiscal 1994, sales had risen to $449 million.

At the beginning of 1995, there were only three major companies in the golf equipment industry, including Callaway Golf, Cobra Golf, and Taylor Made, a division of Salomon, which was a prominent manufacturer of skis in France. These three firms were clobbering the remaining competition. Revenues at Callaway Golf in 1994 had increased substantially over the previous year, while revenues at Cobra Gold shot up an astounding 121 percent during the same period. There seemed to be no end to the prospects for these three companies. Nearly 400 golf courses were opened in the United States in 1994, with approximately 800 more under construction. The baby-boomer generation was approaching its golfing years, and the sport was gaining in popularity all over the world, especially in the countries of the Pacific Rim.

Yet trouble loomed on the horizon as increased competition among the three major companies and a gathering group of both new and old golf equipment firms threatened to cut into profit margins. Companies like Wilson and Spalding saw an opportunity to secure a share of the market with new products made from aerospace grade materials and composites. When a golfer swings a club, the wrists rotate, and the head and shaft of the club twist, creating a centrifugal force that tends to pull the club from the golfer's hands. When the golfer then hits the ball, for every millimeter the ball is hit off the center of the club's head, there is a corresponding penalty in distance. When Callaway's designers created "Big Bertha," they revolutionized the industry by taking advantage of a major technological innovation, namely, investment casting. This process is an improved technique for making metal club heads and enabled designers to shift the weight of the club around with greater precision than ever before. With other innovations, Callaway's people designed a club that allowed a golfer to actually control more of the centrifugal force of a swing directly onto the ball.

One company, Goldwin Golf, began to use 7075-T6 aluminum, an aerospace grade material, in its manufacture of golf clubs. Management at Goldwin guarded their production process as carefully as a national secret. Another development by the same company resulted in the design of a club head that used a mere 140 grams, approximately 30 percent less than the average weight. GolfGear, yet another firm on the cutting edge of golfing technology, began using an aluminum-vanadium alloy. Only three firms in the industry could forge the new metal. Some companies also began using titanium, which is lighter and denser than steel, resulting in a longer driving range. In Japan, over 60 percent of all drivers used are made of titanium, and the seemingly prohibitive cost of $700 for a club is not an insurmountable deterrent.

In spite of the competition, however, Callaway Golf Company continues as the leader in the golf equipment industry. The company has recently built a $9 million research, development, and test facility for the purpose of staying ahead of the game. The facility is a state-of-the-art complex, including a 260-yard driving range, which is peppered with hundreds of testing sensors, four kinds of bunkers, and three types of grass in order to simulate the golfing conditions at any course around the world. Ely Callaway expects the highly sophisticated setup to yield innovative golf club designs. Since the development of new technologies for designing and new material for manufacturing golf clubs has become so essential to keeping abreast of the industry, the inability to introduce a new product for even two or three years could spell disaster for any golf equipment company.

Callaway Golf Company is in an enviable position within the golf equipment industry. The company not only employs some of the brightest and most committed design engineers in the sport of golf, but has one of the world's most talented entrepreneurs, Ely Callaway. As long as Callaway continues to combine the results of new golfing technology with an uncanny ability to market products, his company will be assured of a bright and promising future.

Further Reading

"Callaway on Callaway," *Daily News Record*, June 22, 1995, p. 8.

"Heavy Artillery," *Fortune*, May 30, 1994, p. 167.

Impoco, Jim, "Ely Callaway Hits the Green," *U.S. News & World Report*, April 11, 1994, p. 47.

Jaffe, Thomas, "Big Bertha's Big Bucks," *Forbes*, December 21, 1992, p. 344.

Marcial, Gene G., "Jazzy Picks from the Common Fund's Motley Crew," *Business Week*, April 5, 1993, p. 78.

Perry, Nancy J., "How Golf's Big Bertha Grew," *Fortune*, May 18, 1992, p. 113.

Phalon, Richard, "Big Bertha's Sweet Spot," *Forbes*, May 11, 1992, p. 130.

Saporito, Bill, "Can Big Bertha Stay in the Driver's Seat?," *Fortune*, June 12, 1995, pp. 110–16.

Witford, David, "Opposite Attractions," *Inc.*, December 1994, pp. 60–68.

—Thomas Derdak

Carborundum Company

P.O. Box 156
Niagara Falls, New York 14302-0156
U.S.A.
(716) 278-2000
Fax: (716) 278-2900

Wholly Owned Subsidiary of Compagnie de Saint-Gobain
  S.A.
Incorporated: 1891
Employees: 3,200
Sales: $340.0 million (1994)
SICs: 3299 Nonmetallic Mineral Products, Not Elsewhere
  Classified

The Carborundum Company manufactures a diverse line of products focused on ceramic and composite technology. Throughout its history, Carborundum has been a worldwide leader in the development and application of materials such as silicon carbide, boron nitride, aluminum nitride, and other ceramics, with a special emphasis on abrasives and refractory and insulation compounds. Carborundum products have been put to use in virtually every industry, from steel to automotive to space exploration, and, beginning in the late 1980s, the semiconductor industry as well. Long based in Niagara Falls, New York, Carborundum operates divisions in more than 30 countries and employs over 3,000 people. In 1995 Carborundum was bought by Compagnie de Saint-Gobain S.A. of France.

Early in 1891, Edward Goodrich Acheson, a young scientist and inventor in Monongahela City, Pennsylvania, was attempting to create artificial diamonds using electricity. As a byproduct, his experiments produced small crystals that could cut glass, and even diamonds. On the assumption that the new crystals were formed from a combination of carbon and corundum (that is, natural aluminum oxide), Acheson called his product Carborundum; it was not until a year later that chemical analysis of the crystals showed them to be in fact silicon carbide—the world's first artificially produced mineral. Acheson's first sale of his new product, to a New York diamond cutter, brought him $60, at about 40 cents per carat, or $880 per pound.

The Carborundum Company—Acheson kept the name because he liked the sound of it—was formed in September 1891 with $150,000 raised by Acheson and a group of Monongahela investors, who paid $100 for each of 1,500 shares. Two years later Carborundum secured a $7,000 contract with George Westinghouse, who had been hired to light the Columbian Exposition Building in Chicago, for 60,000 of Carborundum's new grinding wheels. Acheson used this money to buy the company's first dynamo; however, he soon sought a cheaper and more plentiful source of electric power, and when a hydroelectric dam was constructed at Niagara Falls, Acheson proposed to move the company closer to this power source. When his board of directors objected, Acheson formed a new board and contracted with the Niagara Power Company for 1,000 horsepower. Acheson turned to Andrew Mellon for backing to finance the move, and the Mellon family retained 20 percent ownership in the company throughout the next century.

The new Carborundum plant opened in Niagara Falls in October 1895. With an abundant source of electrical power, Carborundum's next task was to develop a way to produce large quantities of the silicon carbide product. To this end the company built its first 1,000-horsepower furnaces. Using intense heat over a 24-hour cycle, chunks of silicon carbide could be formed from a mixture of sand, salt, sawdust, and coke. The resulting crystal chunks were crushed and applied to grinding wheels and other abrasive tools. The bricks used to build the furnaces, however, could not stand the intense heat. Recognizing the heat-resistant qualities of silicon carbide, Carborundum patented the mineral for use as a refractory material in 1898. The following year, the company's first international subsidiary opened, across Niagara Falls in Canada.

With the advent of industrialization, new manufacturing techniques created a demand for the new abrasives produced by Carborundum. Indeed, silicon carbide's abrasive and refractory qualities played a vital role in the growth of modern industry. Carborundum expanded rapidly. In 1905 it introduced a new abrasive, fused aluminum oxide, under the name Aloxite. At the same time, the company developed a process for producing fused silicon metal. In 1906 it opened the Deutsche Carborundum Werke near Düsseldorf, Germany, followed in 1910 by the opening of the Compagnie Française Aloxite in France. Sales in that year topped $2 million. By 1913, Carborundum was producing 15 million pounds of silicon carbide each year, and its Niagara Falls plant had grown to 13 acres using 13,000 horsepower. Its products were important to the development of many industries, including bicycle makers, the railroads, and the growing automobile and aviation industries. In 1913 a new subsidiary, The Carborundum Company Ltd., was formed in Manchester, England.

The outbreak of World War I provided a major boost to the company's growth, with Carborundum's silicon carbide output fueling the war effort. With the war's end, Carborundum formed a Refractories Division to develop this part of its business. A facility for the division was purchased in Perth Amboy, New Jersey; its products were given trademarks using the suffix ''frax.'' The first refractories—Carbofrax and Refrax—were soon joined by such trademarks as Silfrax, Mullfrax, Firefrax, and others. By the end of the war, Carborundum had quadrupled its staff, to 2,000, and its annual sales had reached $11 million.

Sales dropped somewhat immediately following World War I, but the postwar industrial boom soon renewed the demand for Carborundum products. Silicon carbide not only possessed heat resistance capabilities, but also could be used to conduct electricity at high and low temperatures. During the 1920s, the Wireless Resistor Company of America, based in Milwaukee, pioneered this use of silicon carbide in an electric heating element called ''Globar.'' In 1927 Carborundum purchased that company, by then called the Globar Corporation, and moved its production to Niagara Falls. The new Globar division soon branched out from producing heating elements for the metal, chemical, and ceramic industries to manufacturing resistors for the burgeoning electronics market. By the end of the decade, Carborundum had also acquired A/S Smetleverk of Norway and the Hutto Engineering Company of Detroit, and the company's annual sales had risen to $17.5 million.

Although growth slowed again during the Depression, Carborundum continued to expand its product line. Among its new products were the first grinding wheels to use crushed diamonds as an abrasive. Carborundum's foreign expansion continued with the acquisition in 1938 of the Australian Abrasive Pty., Ltd., in New South Wales. By 1940, annual sales topped $20 million, and the company employed more than 4,000 people.

Business boomed during the Second World War as Carborundum's production grew to support the war effort. By 1943, Carborundum's 6,000 employees produced $52 million in annual revenue. The slogan ''Illegitimi Non Carborundum''— often translated as ''Don't Let the Bastards Grind You Down''—helped make the Carborundum Company a household name during this time. By the end of the war, Carborundum employed roughly 20 percent of the Niagara Falls-area workforce.

After the war, Carborundum once again embarked on an ambitious expansion plan. The company announced a $20 million program to upgrade and expand facilities in order to make the company more competitive in the postwar era. The Niagara Falls facilities were modernized, and new facilities were built or purchased in Wheatfield, New York; Vancouver, Washington; and Falconer, New York. At this time, the company was decentralized into four primary operating divisions: Bonded Abrasives and Grains; Refractories; Coated Abrasives; and Globar.

Carborundum continued to develop new materials and products. During the war years, Carborundum had begun development of its Fiberfrax ceramic fiber, and in 1952 the company began to market the first commercial applications of the new material. Composed of aluminum oxide and silica, the cotton-like fiber's properties of high heat resistance, light weight, and low heat transmission made it extremely versatile. Fiberfrax was soon used not only as refractory insulation, but also in the aviation, chemical, papermaking, and electrical industries, and would one day be found in such products as papers, felts, ropes, and woven textiles, including blankets. To further its research capacity, in 1953 Carborundum built a 60,000-square-foot facility for its Research and Development Division, which by then had a budget of more than $1 million per year. Also in 1953, in response to a five-year contract with the Atomic Energy Commission, Carborundum began production of zirconium sponge metal. Within a year, its new Carborundum Metals Company plant in Akron, New York, produced 150,000 tons of the zirconium and hafnium sponge metals vital to the construction of nuclear power facilities. This marked Carborundum's first diversification beyond its traditional abrasives and refractories markets.

Diversification became essential for the company's further growth. Because Carborundum had long depended directly on the capital goods market for its revenues, when that market cycled through a decline, Carborundum's fortunes went with them. During the 1950s the company stepped up the pace of its acquisitions, while moving to diversify internally. The company spent some $15 million developing its zirconium and hafnium capacity. In 1954 it acquired Stupakoff Ceramic and Manufacturing Company of Latrobe, Pennsylvania, and the American Tripoli Corporation of Seneca, Missouri, followed in the next year by the acquisition of the Curtis Machine Corporation of Jamestown, New York. Between 1953 and 1959, new Carborundum plants opened in Brazil, Puerto Rico, Switzerland, New Zealand, India, and Belgium, bringing the company to a total of 30 plants in 10 countries. New materials developed during this time included boron nitride, KT silicon carbide, and synthetic diamonds. By 1956, annual sales reached $104 million.

Not all of the company's diversification efforts were successful, however. The zirconium and hafnium markets quickly became glutted, resulting in significant losses for the company. The newly acquired Stupakoff Ceramics, which manufactured ceramic seals for electrical components, had been riding high at the time of Carborundum's purchase due to business generated by the Korean War. When that war ended, so too did Stupakoff's growth. In 1957 the Stupakoff division was combined with the Refractories and Globar divisions into a single Refractories division. Over the next decade, despite the growth of revenues to $150 million per year, Carborundum's per-share earnings stagnated. By 1965, Carborundum had lost its leadership in the domestic abrasives market—which still accounted for some two-thirds of its sales—to the Norton Company of Massachusetts.

More acquisitions followed in the early 1960s, including the Tysaman Machine Company in Tennessee, Carborundum-Nederland N.V. in the Netherlands, Falls Industries in Ohio, Basic Carbon Corp. in New York, Lockport Felt Company in New York, W. T. Copeland & Sons in England, and Industrias Abrasives S.A. in Spain. By the mid-1960s Carborundum was under the direction of William Wendel, who remained company president until 1978. Under Wendel's leadership Carborundum acquisition policy followed a stricter adherence to the company's core ceramics technology while nonetheless moving beyond the capital goods market into the steel, paper, plastics, pollution control, and china industries. New plants, Toshiba Monofrax in Tokyo and a graphite electrode manufacturing plant in Kentucky, both built in 1966, exemplify Carborundum's new efforts to manufacture not only abrasives but also the machines and systems that use them. From 1963 to 1974, Carborundum's sales rose from $162 million to $557 million, while its earnings per share more than doubled. In 1974 there were nearly 18,000 Carborundum employees. Through the 1970s sales grew an average of 16 percent and net earnings at an average of 17 percent, reaching $32.8 million in 1976.

By the mid-1970s, Carborundum's success began to attract attention: after fighting off a hostile takeover attempt by Eaton Corp., Carborundum was purchased by Kennecott Copper Corporation for $571 million, which was the second-largest cash tender offer in U.S. history. Carborundum, with $713 million in sales and 19,000 employees, became a wholly owned subsidiary. William Wendel became president of Kennecott, which dropped the Copper from its name in 1980. Between 1978 and 1981 Carborundum went through three presidents.

Then, in 1981, Standard Oil of Ohio, popularly known as Sohio, purchased Kennecott and its Carborundum subsidiary for $1.77 billion. Through the 1980s, Carborundum's name was changed twice to Sohio Engineered Materials Company and Standard Oil Engineered Materials Company before returning the Carborundum name in 1988. Deeper changes were also made during this time. The company was once again reorganized, this time into three operating companies: Abrasives; Electro Minerals; and Resistant Materials. Silicon carbide continued to be one of the company's core minerals, now with the development of Hexoloy alpha silicon carbide products. The company also moved into development of materials for the growing semiconductor industry. An even more significant change occurred in 1983, when Carborundum's Niagara Falls bonded abrasives plant was closed and its coated abrasives plant sold to an independent investor, which later sold the plant to the Norton Company, although parts of Carborundum's abrasives business continued to operate under its own name. The following year, the Electro Minerals division was sold to Washington Mills Abrasive company, and all but Carborundum's Brazilian abrasives activities were sold off to Carborundum management

and other partners. Carborundum had all but left its original market.

In 1987 British Petroleum acquired Standard Oil and its Carborundum subsidiary. Carborundum was organized under British Petroleum's BP Chemicals division. That year also marked the first large-volume use of Carborundum's Hexoloy material, with a shipment of automotive water pump seals to Germany. In 1989 a new structural ceramics manufacturing facility was opened in Möchengladbach, Germany, to supply the European automotive market. The company's development of aluminum nitride substrates and ceramic packages for the semiconductor industry led to the organization of a Substrates Division in 1989. The company also opened a microelectronics development center in Phoenix, Arizona, and acquired Ceradyne Specialty Products; meanwhile, it continued developing new uses for its Fiberfrax technology, while maintaining global leadership in sales of its Globar heating elements. 1990 sales of $350 million and a payroll of 4,500 employees reflected the changes the past decade had brought to Carborundum.

The recession of the early 1990s cut into Carborundum's sales. By 1993 BP Chemicals reported an operating loss of over $100 million. British Petroleum then announced plans to divest its non-hydrocarbon-related businesses. Plans to sell off Carborundum were formulated by 1994 and early in 1995 BP announced its intention to sell most of Carborundum—with the exception of its ceramic fibers unit—to St. Gobain S.A., the huge French glass and ceramics manufacturer. In 1990 St. Gobain had already purchased the Norton Company and its Carborundum abrasives unit; after nearly fifty years of intense competition between the Norton and Carborundum, they were to be joined into the same company. Despite a last-minute attempt by Carborundum's management to purchase the company, the sale to St. Gobain went through late in 1995. At that time, BP was also preparing to sell Carborundum's ceramics fibers unit, possibly to Carborundum management.

The acquisition of Carborundum by St. Gobain, subject to approval by the Federal Trade Commission and the governments of Great Britain, France, and Germany, was expected to be completed in 1996. Because the overlap of the two companies was minimal, St. Gobain expected to keep most of Carborundum's manufacturing facilities open, while pursuing the expansion of Carborundum's Asian and Pacific presence. Nevertheless, the future of Carborundum's management, and its Niagara Falls headquarters, was uncertain.

Further Reading

Layman, Patricia, ''BP's Carborundum Sold to Saint-Gobain,'' *Chemical & Engineering News,* February 20, 1995, p. 6.
Stern, M. E., *The Carborundum Company: The First 100 Years, 1891–1991,* New York: The Carborundum Company, 1991.

—M. L. Cohen

CARLTON

Carlton Communications plc

15 St. George Street
Hanover Square
London W1R 0LU
United Kingdom
171 499 8050
Fax: 171 895 9575

Public Company
Incorporated: 1983
Employees: 10,000
Sales: £1.6 billion ($2.5 billion) (1995)
Stock Exchanges: London Toronto
SICs: 7812 Motion Picture & Video Production; 4833
   Television Broadcasting Stations; 7819 Services
   Allied to Motion Pictures; 3663 Radio & TV
   Communications Equipment

Carlton Communications plc thrived for more than a decade in the cramped, highly regulated waters of the British market. In the 1990s it began buying companies, both smaller and larger than itself. Besides owning UK television networks, the company provides production facilities, tape duplicating services, and electronic video equipment, which are marketed primarily in Europe and the United States.

Michael Green, the man who brought Carlton from obscurity to the leagues of $1 billion companies, grew up in a business family. Rather than relying on higher education (he left public school at 17), he benefitted from contacts through the family of his wife, Janet Wolfson, whom he married in 1972. Those contacts included brother David, with whom Green established a printing and photo-processing company dubbed Tangent Industries; and Lord Wolfson, Green's father-in-law, who owned Great Universal Stores, which hired Tangent to reproduce its catalogs.

After 15 years with Tangent, Green bought Transvideo (Carlton Television Studios) in 1982. Fleet Street Letter soon became part of the fold, and the group of companies went public

as Carlton Communications. The Moving Picture Company (MPC), Europe's largest video facilities provider, joined Carlton in a joint venture soon thereafter, acquiring the UK subsidiary of California's International Video Corporation for £400,000. Carlton acquired MPC itself in July 1983 for £13 million. MPC's Mike Luckwell remained as managing director in the new company and became Carlton's largest single shareholder.

Carlton acquired more than a dozen companies (at a cost of over £600 million) in the remainder of the decade, all related to either television and film or electronics. Importantly, Green valued cashflow and strict financial controls. When companies were acquired, existing managers were trained to practice strict accounting practices. The result was profits and success. By 1985, Carlton was producing projects as diverse as commercials, rock music clips, and corporate videos. The purchase (potentially worth £30 million) of Abekas Video Systems in 1985 made Carlton a manufacturer of video editing gadgets (the division was sold ten years later to Scitex Corporation for $52 million). Carlton grossed £38.1 million in 1985.

The goal of acquiring a broadcasting station took several years to develop to fruition and divided the partnership of Green and Luckwell. The two had different strategies for acquiring Thames after Britain's Independent Broadcasting Authority thwarted attempts to gain a controlling interest (Luckwell preferred to defy the IBA), and Luckwell left the company in 1986, selling his shares for £25 million. The IBA interfered with Green's bid for his next target, London Weekend Television, allowing him only a 10 percent share. In response, Green sold his existing 5 percent share for £1 million.

After failing in a group bid for a direct satellite broadcasting service, Green finally succeeded in acquiring a stake in a broadcast network, gaining 20 percent of Central Television in exchange for £18 million and stock. D.C. Thomson and Pergamon Holdings owned equal 20 percent shares. Green had previously hired Bob Phillis away from Central Television to replace Luckwell as Carlton's managing director; Phillis was able to return to his seat on the Central board of directors after the deal. Soon afterward, Carlton moved into film production with the £7.3

million acquisition of Zenith Productions; Carlton later had to sell much of Zenith so the company could stay independent.

Sometimes Carlton seemed a bit ahead of its time, as in the 1986 purchase of satellite dish manufacturer Skyscan, which was sold in 1988 due to poor sales. Carlton's biggest buy of the decade proved more fortuitous. The company paid $780 million for Ronald Perleman's US-based Technicolor, the world market leader in video cassette duplication and motion picture film processing. Despite the 1987 stock market crash, Green was able to raise the necessary funds. In five brisk years Green transformed Carlton from a relatively obscure company into an international corporation that garnered half its revenues (since the Technicolor purchase) from US operations.

In 1989 Carlton's stock took a serious fall, from a high of £9.60 a share to a low of £2.98 in the course of a year. Pre-tax profits grew just 13 percent in 1990, a lackluster performance for Carlton, and the market shuddered. Carlton won a 1991 bid for a London weekday broadcasting license, in spite of competition from Thames and a David Frost/Richard Branson coalition (CPV-TV), which outbid Carlton by £2 million but were denied the license as the ITC were unconvinced about the quality of their programming (Branson's Virgin Group later did outbid Carlton for MGM's British cinemas). The deal signaled a recovery for Carlton.

Besides the annual license fee, Carlton agreed to pay 15 percent of advertising revenue (estimated to be approximately £50 million per year) to the British government for the ten year duration of the contract. *The Daily Telegraph* and Italian publishers Rizzoli Corriere della Sera each bought five percent of Carlton's stock prior to the bid, worth £43.2 million. The Daybreak consortium, in which Carlton held a 20 percent share, lost the bid for the breakfast television license to the Sunrise consortium of LWT, Scottish Television, The Guardian newspaper company, and Walt Disney. Carlton, optimistic about the future of morning television, promptly bought a 20 percent share in Sunrise for £5.4 million.

At the end of 1993, Carlton announced it would buy Central Independent Television for £624 million ($925 million), thereby combining the first and third largest independent television companies in Britain. The timing could have helped both of them escape being consumed by European companies when ownership restrictions were relaxed in 1994. In 1995, Carlton was Britain's largest broadcaster, controlling 30 percent of ITV advertising revenues through its London and Midlands stations. *The Economist* reported Carlton's biggest challenge would be expanding into foreign broadcasting markets, in which Green expressed interest, as well as into newspapers and other types of media.

Although Carlton aborted a venture with the German station Vox, it invested in two other overseas ventures in 1995. France Télé Films, a cable channel launched in cooperation with France Télévision, would rely on programming from Carlton's CTE library (stocked with 4,000 hours as of 1995, including 200 films) as well as that of France Télévision. Carlton also entered a partnership with Singapore's Channel KTV, also cable-based, which prepared to add two karaoke channels to its existing services.

Almost half of Carlton's profits came from broadcast television in 1995. In spite of the growth of satellite and cable services, Carlton remained optimistic about the importance of free-to-air broadcasting. Nigel Walmsley, Carlton's Director for Broadcasting, told shareholders in a 1995 annual report that only terrestrial broadcasting reached mass audiences since cable and satellite channels "tend to take audience share from existing minority channels, thus fragmenting the total cable and satellite audience."

Technicolor benefitted in the 1990s as Hollywood studios issued large-scale releases (for example, *Batman Forever* opened simultaneously on 4,500 screens), which required many duplicates. Declining currency values brought Film and Television Services turnover down to £251.8 million in 1995, although operating profit increased nine percent to £41.6 million. Beside Technicolor, the division boasted some of the largest post-production facilities in the world, such as The Moving Picture Company in London and Complete Post in Los Angeles. In 1995, when sales for the Video Production and Duplication division (including Technicolor and Carlton Home Entertainment) were £474.2 million, (profits down 9 percent to £60.7 million), a new one-million-unit-per-day videocassette facility was under construction in Michigan. Digital video discs offered Technicolor a newly format to master beginning in 1996. It also produced CDs and CD-ROMs through Technicolor Optical Media Services.

A one percent increase in turnover (to £169.1 million) boosted operating profits for the Video and Sound Products division by 43 percent in 1995 to £32.5 million. Its primary components, Quantel and Solid State Logic, produced equipment for making special effects. Both companies were market leaders based on such state-of-the-art technologies as Quantel's digital visual effects editing systems ("Henry" for television and "Domino" for film) and Solid State Logic's "Axiom" and "9000-J Series" digital audio consoles. Quantel supplied the printing industry with its *Graphics Paintbox* system.

Increasing sales and profits supported observations that the company, in spite of (or because of) its enormous growth, was still on the way up. Pending British legislation, which would allow Carlton to control more of the UK broadcast television market, made Carlton's future outlook bright.

Principal Subsidiaries

Carlton Television Limited; Carlton UK Television Limited; Carlton Home Entertainment; Central Broadcasting; CTE; Carlton 021 Limited; The Television House; Meridian Broadcasting Limited (20%); GMTV Limited (20%); Independent Television News Limited (36%); London News Network Limited (50%); France Télé Films (France; 28%); Channel KTV (Singapore; 31%); Technicolor; Technicolor Optical Media Services; Euphon Technicolor S.p.A. (Italy; 50%); Technicolor Videocassette B.V. (Holland); Carlton Home Entertainment Limited; The Moving Picture Company Limited; Complete Post, Inc. (USA); TVI; Quantel Limited; Solid State Logic Limited; Carlton Cabletime Limited; Carlton Books Limited; Carlton Cromelim Circuits Limited; Westport Group plc (27.1%).

Principal Divisions

Broadcast Television; Video Production and Distribution; Film and Television Services; Video and Sound Products

Further Reading

Amdur, Meredith, "Battle Lines Drawn in Asian Satellite TV," *Broadcasting & Cable*, June 28, 1993, p. 21.

Baldo, Anthony, "Bonanza: American Reruns Dominate European Television, but Changes Are Coming," *Financial World*, April 16, 1991, pp. 44–45.

Baldo, Anthony, "Media: The Enemy Within," *Financial World*, April 16, 1991, pp. 24–32.

"Britain: And the Winners Are . . . ," *The Economist*, October 19, 1991, pp. 67–68.

Burton, Patrick, "C5 and the Threat of London TV Monopoly," *Marketing*, January 14, 1993, p. 15.

"Carlton Links with LWT Sales," *Marketing*, January 21, 1993, p. 10.

"Carlton Rev Ups Motor Show 'Advertorial'," *Marketing*, July 15, 1993, p. 5.

Carter, Meg, "ITV Takes Seats for the Big Fight," *Marketing Week*, July 9, 1993, pp. 20–21.

Carter, Meg, "Keeping and MAI on the Big Time," *Marketing Week*, January 28, 1994, pp. 16–17.

Douglas, Torin, "Big Bills in the New Year," *Marketing Week*, January 8, 1993, p. 15.

DuBois, Peter C, "Worth the Trip," *Barron's*, February 20, 1995.

Fisher, Liz, "Set on Broadcasting Its Ambitions," *Accountancy*, January, 1992, pp. 17–19.

Foster, Anna, "Behind the Carlton Screen," *Management Today*, April 1989, pp. 52–56.

Fry, Andy, "TV Franchises: Who Loses Out?" *Marketing*, April 4, 1991, pp. 18–19.

"Greenland," *The Economist*, December 4, 1993, pp. 68–69.

Guyon, Janet, "UK Broadcaster Carlton Makes Bid for Rest of Central," *The Wall Street Journal*, November 30, 1993, p. 12.

Higham, Nick, "Green Shoots of Discovery?" *Marketing Week*, April 29, 1994, p. 19.

Hudson, Richard L, "British Telecommunications Stirs Rush to Test Europe's Multimedia Market," *The Wall Street Journal*, November 18, 1994, p. 7D.

Lipin, Steven, "Bankers Trust Woes Spread to Money Unit," *The Wall Street Journal*, December 8, 1993, p. 3.

"London Cable Hitch," *Marketing*, May 20, 1993, p. 10.

Marcom, John, Jr, "Is This One for Real?" *Forbes*, July 24, 1994, p. 252.

Mistry, Tina, "Shock as Unilever Dumps Carlton TV," *Campaign-London*, January 7, 1994, p. 1.

Pratt, Tom, "Merrill Limps to Market with Two Big UK Preferred Deals," *Investment Dealers Digest*, October 4, 1993, pp. 14–15.

Robinson, Jeffrey, "The Modest Media Magnate," *Business-London*, October, 1990, pp. 100–104.

"The Wearing of the Green," *The Economist*, July 8, 1995, p. 68.

—Frederick C. Ingram

BERGNER'S   BOSTON STORE   CARSON PIRIE SCOTT

Carson Pirie Scott & Company

331 West Wisconsin Avenue
Milwaukee, Wisconsin 53203
U.S.A.
(414) 347-4141
Fax: (414) 278-5748

Public Company
Founded: 1854 as Carson, Pirie & Company
Employees: 12,000
Sales: $1.16 billion (1994)
Stock Exchange: New York
SICs: 5311 Department Stores

Carson Pirie Scott & Company is a regional department store chain, operating 51 stores in Illinois, Indiana, Minnesota, and Wisconsin. The company is a combination of several smaller department store chains, all with long ties to midwestern cities. Its key markets are Chicago, Milwaukee, and central Illinois, and in these three areas it is either the leading or number two department store. Carson Pirie Scott & Co. operates department stores under the name Carson Pirie Scott in Chicago, Bergner's in central Illinois, and Boston Store in Wisconsin. Its department stores are targeted primarily toward middle-income shoppers. Carson also operates two furniture stores.

Carson Pirie Scott & Company was founded by Irish immigrants Samuel Carson and John T. Pirie. The two men started from northern Ireland together aboard *The Philadelphia*, which shipwrecked off Newfoundland. Undeterred, Carson and Pirie found another ship to take them all the way to New York. From there, they went west to the railroad town of Amboy, Illinois, where they opened a dry goods store in 1854. This first store was housed modestly in a remodeled saloon, but in only four years, Carson & Pirie had branch stores in four nearby towns, making it one of the first chain stores in the United States. By 1864 Carson & Pirie had entered the Chicago market with a wholesale operation on downtown Lake Street. This early wholesale business was quite profitable, and the company soon built new quarters on State Street. This building perished in the great Chicago fire of 1871, which also destroyed 60 percent of the firm's goods. The remainder was saved only because one of Carson's partners flagged down teamsters as the building burned, and promised them 50 silver dollars for every wagonload they could haul from the flames.

The company moved into new quarters after the fire. In 1890 Carson and Pirie took on a new partner, Robert Scott, son of another Irish immigrant who had worked at the Amboy store. The company was then called Carson, Pirie Scott & Company. In 1904 the firm moved into a 12-story building on State Street, a beautiful tower designed by the renowned American architect Louis Sullivan. This distinctive building was named a Chicago Historical Landmark in 1959, and it still housed the Chicago flagship Carson Pirie Scott store in the mid-1990s.

Carson Pirie Scott operated in the shadow of another venerable department store, Chicago's Marshall Field & Company. The two chains had flagship stores only a few doors apart in downtown Chicago. Carson Pirie Scott aimed to sell to middle-income customers, and it was not as large or well-known as the more upscale Field's. But Carson supplemented its department store business with other ventures. In 1953 it became the first department store chain to sell insurance policies to its customers. And the company branched out further, operating two hotels near Chicago's O'Hare airport, running a chain of cheese shops, and operating subsidiary companies that made and distributed carpeting and floor coverings. By 1971 annual sales stood at around $250 million. About two-thirds of its sales were from its department stores, and the rest came from other activities.

But the company experienced slow growth in the 1970s, for reasons that affected other department stores in the area as well. The Chicago area lost population, as close to 300,000 people moved out of the city in the 1970s. And new department stores opened up in Chicago, including Neiman-Marcus, I. Magnin, and Lord & Taylor. This made competition for the dwindling retail market even more intense. Carson's sales and profits grew only about six percent per year in the late 1970s, and its profit margin was slight. In 1980 the company made a major acquisition to further diversify its business away from retailing. Carson borrowed $108 million to buy Dobbs Houses Inc., an airline caterer and operator of restaurant chains.

This acquisition marked a significant change for Carson. Carson Pirie Scott & Co. had done 80 percent of its business in northern Illinois and Indiana prior to the Dobbs acquisition. With its new business, the company actually had a worldwide operation. Dobbs Houses operated 234 restaurants, the Toddle House and Steak N Egg Kitchen chains, with outlets across the United States. But the bulk of its business came from in-flight airline catering and running airport restaurants, gift shops, and newsstands. It held the number two market share in these two areas, behind only Marriott Corp. for in-flight catering and Host International for airport shops and restaurants. Dobbs profit margin was substantially higher than Carson's, and its profits had been growing at close to 20 percent annually since the mid-1970s. Carson's chief executive, Harold Spurway, saw little growth possible in retailing, and he was willing to take a lot of debt to get the lucrative Dobbs. The acquisition left Carson with a debt of over 65 percent of capital.

Carson's new food service division did well. While earnings from department stores fell, airline catering and restaurants contributed over 50 percent of the company's operating earnings by 1982. Carson's found a new chief executive in 1983; former Federal Express Corporation president Peter Wilmott. Wilmott moved rapidly to shore up the retail division. His explicit goal was to move Carson Pirie Scott from a regional store to a national presence. The first step in this direction was the acquisition of County Seat in 1984. County Seat was a chain of casual-wear stores with 269 units in 33 states. Its sales for 1984 were close to $200 million, and its acquisition put Carson's revenues over $1 billion. The company spent $71 million to get Country Seat, increasing its debt. But the company for the first time had retail outlets outside the Chicago and northern Indiana area. Later that year, Carson's also acquired MacDonald Companies, a mail-order catalog and direct-marketing merchandiser, and Ridgewell's Inc., a Washington, D.C. caterer.

The company made other changes in its retail division as well. The company's department store division got a new head, Dennis Bookshester, three months after Wilmott took the presidency. Bookshester ordered more expensive and fashionable merchandise, in an effort to shake Carson's image as the store for the price-conscious shopper. The new merchandise was touted with heavy television advertising. This strategy seemed to pay off quickly. Sales per square foot went from $84 in fiscal 1982 to $133 the next year. Bookshester also initiated a new store-within-a-store, to lure big-spending women executives. Carson's new Corporate Level was a posh, mirrored space featuring designer outfits, shoes, and accessories all conveniently at hand. The Corporate Level also had a shoe repair service, a dry cleaner, a place to make photocopies, and a restaurant. Shoppers could pay also pay a $50 annual fee for extra services, including check cashing, use of meeting rooms, and use of a fashion consultant. The Corporate Level was open two hours earlier and closed two hours later than the rest of the store, and had a separate entrance guarded by a doorman. Sales at the Corporate Level in its first year ran 40 percent higher than in the rest of the store.

Carson Pirie Scott's sales rose to $1.3 billion in 1985. About half of this came from retail operations. Retailing contributed to just under 50 percent of the company's profits of $18.4 million. Carson still held the number two spot in the Chicago market, with 21 department stores in the area. Chicago's number three department store chain, Wieboldt's, had been bought by an investor group called Baytree Investors Inc. in 1985, and shortly after, Baytree set its sights on Carson.

Baytree specialized in leveraged buyouts. Except for its recent acquisition of Wieboldt's, Baytree's principals had no retailing experience. Its head, Gilbert Granet, had made unsuccessful bids for a slew of retailers, including Gimbels and B. Altman, only to land the ailing Weiboldts, which had not shown a profit since 1979. Another associate in Baytree had his commodity broker's registration revoked for falsifying data, and Granet himself had been fired from a company he headed in the 1970s after a buying spree led the company to bankruptcy. Baytree offered $347.2 million for Carson. The investor group claimed it would operate Carson Pirie Scott as a sister store to the Wieboldt chain, and that it would sell off the Dobbs Houses airline catering business. Carson's board retaliated by rejecting the offer and declaring a "poison pill" dividend to preferred share-holders. Baytree then upped its offer. Carson's chief executive Peter Wilmott described Baytree as a "corporate pirate," and after a third offer of $473 million, Baytree withdrew.

Department stores across the country were bought and sold in the 1980s, as some chains consolidated and others sold off assets. Carson Pirie Scott merged with Donaldson's department stores in 1987, acquiring a chain of 12 stores around Minneapolis. Then, in 1989, Carson Pirie Scott was itself acquired by P.A. Bergner & Company. Bergner had a chain of department stores in Illinois, and it also ran the Boston Store chain in Wisconsin. It was one of the largest regional chains in the country, and its stores had histories almost as long as Carson's. The first Bergner's, for example, opened in Peoria, Illinois in 1889, and the first Boston Store opened in Milwaukee in 1897. P.A. Bergner & Company had been owned by the Swiss firm Maus Freres since 1938. Bergner paid $343 million for Carson Pirie Scott, and also took on $300 million of Carson's debt. Bergner saw the purchase as an opportunity to get into the big city market, as most of its 28 Bergner's and Boston Stores were in small and mid-sized towns.

But the debt burden Bergner took on to get Carson Pirie Scott was apparently too much for the company. Bergner had expected to sell off Carson's unprofitable catalog operation to raise cash, but the company had to settle for far less than anticipated to liquidate the unit. Refinancing for Carson's flagship State Street store also fell through. Bergner's chairman, Alan Anderson, who had initiated the Carson acquisition, resigned in April 1991. There were reports from industry executives that Bergner's Swiss parent was unhappy with Anderson, because it had to shell out $150 million to help keep the newly merged company afloat. Just two years after the acquisition, Bergner was unable to get enough credit from its bank to pay its vendors. Vendors halted shipments, and the company was forced to file for bankruptcy. Plans to open a new Carson Pirie Scott store in Chicago's Merchandise Mart were put on hold, and Bergner put various assets up for sale. Maus Freres, Bergner's Swiss parent, raised money for the company through a sale of its stake in a French store, and paid off $300 million of Bergner's $900 million debt.

Bergner's bankruptcy was not surprising. Deep recession in the department store industry had sent several other chains into bankruptcy around the same time, including Federated Department Stores, Ames, and Carter Hawley Hale. The growth of discount chains such as Wal-Mart, Target, and Kmart had eaten into the department stores' market share all across the country, and competition was unusually fierce. But Bergner's creditors seemed to agree that the company's business was essentially good. It was the debt, rather than Bergner's operations, that was the problem. Bergner submitted a reorganization plan in bankruptcy court in early 1992, and at the same time announced an operating profit of $2.2 million from its third quarter 1991, and then a $35 million profit from its Christmas season sales. Retail operations seemed to be on the rebound. The company was taken over in bankruptcy court by a New York investment firm, Dickstein Partners LP. Its president, Mark Dickstein, became the new chairman. In October, 1993, the company emerged from bankruptcy, and changed its name from P.A. Bergner & Co. to Carson Pirie Scott & Co.

The company had safely come through Chapter 11, but the retail industry was just as perilous. Large department store chains were becoming larger to stay competitive. Carson Pirie Scott now had 59 stores spread across Illinois, Indiana, Minnesota and Wisconsin. May Department Stores, the biggest chain, had 300 stores. Carson made plans to expand. In late 1994, Carson's initiated an acquisition bid for another midwestern department store chain, the Des Moines-based Younkers.

Younkers had 53 stores operating in seven states; South Dakota, Nebraska, Minnesota, Iowa, Wisconsin, Illinois, and Michigan. Younkers itself had bought a Wisconsin chain, Prange's, in 1992. And Younkers, like Carson, had emerged from bankruptcy in 1993. The company had experienced several bad years in a row, and was reducing its debt and making its own expansion plans when it received the unsolicited bid from Carson. The combination of Younkers with Carson Pirie Scott would create a chain of 113 stores in eight contiguous states, with sales of around $1.7 billion. Both Younkers and Carson aimed at the middle-income consumer, and the stores would presumably be able to operate more efficiently with a combined distribution network. For Carson Pirie Scott, the Younkers acquisition seemed like a sensible strategy. The problem was that Younkers did not want to be bought. Carson's initial offer of $152 million set off a protracted boardroom battle.

After Younkers' board unanimously rejected Carson's bid, Carson used proceeds from the sale of eight Minnesota stores to offer a $17-a-share cash tender directly to Younkers' shareholders. Carson was able to buy about 40 percent of Younkers' common stock. The shareholders then voted at the May 1995 meeting to put the company up for sale, and three directors nominated by Carson were elected to Younkers' board. Younkers Chairman W. Thomas Gould lost his seat on the board. But the company came up with legal maneuvers that gave Gould and the other ousted directors their seats back, and the board voted again in June not to sell the company. Carson then took its battle to court, suing Younkers for ignoring its shareholders' wish to sell. As the proceedings dragged on, Carson raised its bid to $20 per share and promised to reseat its board candidates at the May, 1996 shareholder meeting.

While the merger remained undecided, Carson Pirie Scott concentrated on renovating stores. Six stores, including the flagship State Street store in Chicago, were renovated in 1994, and five more were improved in 1995. Sales were sluggish for most of 1995, but the recently renovated stores showed improved performance. Going into 1996, Carson remained committed to its acquisition strategy.

Principal Subsidiaries

CPS Holding Co.; P.A. Bergner & Co. Holding Company.

Further Reading

''Baytree Withdraws Its Bid to Buy Carson Pirie Scott,'' *Wall Street Journal,* April 23, 1986, p. 40.

Burns, Greg, ''This Takeover Goes Way Past Hostile,'' *Business Week,* July 3, 1995, pp. 72–73.

Carey, Susan, ''Carson Pirie Lets Younkers Offer Run Out,'' *Wall Street Journal,* July 5, 1995, p. B8.

''Carson Pirie Head Sees 1972 'Good' for Retailers,'' *Wall Street Journal,* January 10, 1972, p. 6.

''Carson Pirie Scott: Hoping to Get Fat on Food Services,'' *Business Week,* March 23, 1981, pp. 124–125.

''Carson Will Buy Casual-Wear Unit From Super Valu,'' *Wall Street Journal,* March 14, 1984, p. 5.

''Carson's Takes First Step National.'' *Advertising Age,* March 26, 1984, p. 36.

Daily, Jo Ellen, ''One-Stop Shopping For the Woman on the Go,'' *Business Week,* March 18, 1985, p. 116.

Dreyfack, Kenneth, ''The Man Who's After Gimbel's—and a Lot More,'' *Business Week,* April 14, 1986, pp. 40–41.

Fauber, John, ''Branching Out: Carson Looks to Extend Reach,'' *Milwaukee Journal,* October 30, 1994, p. B1.

Hendrickson, Robert, *The Grand Emporiums,* New York: Stein & Day, 1979, pp. 368–370.

Kilman, Scott, ''Carson Pirie Acquisition Bid by Baytree Lifted to $36 a share, or $362.9 Million,'' *Wall Street Journal,* April 3, 1986, p. 5.

''Rocking the Boat Starts to Pay Off at Carson Pirie,'' *Business Week,* April 9, 1984, p. 53.

Schwadel, Francine, ''P.A. Bergner Becomes Latest Retailer to Seek Bankruptcy-Court Protection,'' *Wall Street Journal,* August 26, 1991, p. A3.

Sharma-Jensen, Geeta, ''For Bergner, Swapping Debt for Equity Is a Likely Option,'' *Milwaukee Journal,* February 16, 1992, p.1.

Siler, Julia Flynn, ''The Wrong Way to Hit the Big Time,'' *Business Week,* September 9, 1991, p. 44.

Weiner, Steve, ''Carson Pirie Scott Rejects Takeover Bid of $347.2 Million From Investment Bank,'' *Wall Street Journal,* March 31, 1986, p. 6.

—A. Woodward

Caterpillar Inc.

100 Northeast Adams Street
Peoria, Illinois 61629
U.S.A.
(309) 675-1000
Fax: (309) 675-6155

Public Company
Incorporated: 1925 as Caterpillar Tractor Company
Employees: 54,352
Sales: $16.07 billion (1995)
Stock Exchanges: New York Midwest Pacific London
    Paris Brussels Frankfurt Zürich
SICs: 3052 Rubber & Plastics Hose & Belting; 3321
    Gray & Ductile Iron Foundries; 3511 Steam, Gas &
    Hydraulic Turbines; 3519 Internal Combustion
    Engines, Not Elsewhere Classified; 3531 Construction
    Machinery & Equipment; 3537 Industrial Trucks,
    Tractors, Trailers & Stackers; 3621 Motors &
    Generators; 5082 Construction & Mining Machinery
    & Equipment, Except Petroleum, Wholesale; 5084
    Industrial Machinery & Equipment; 6159
    Miscellaneous Business Credit Institutions; 7374
    Computer Processing & Processing & Data
    Preparation Services

Caterpillar Inc. is the world's largest manufacturer of earth-moving machinery. In addition to its tractors, trucks, graders, excavators, scrapers, and other heavy machinery used in the construction, mining, and agriculture industries, Caterpillar also makes diesel and gas engines used in medium- and heavy-duty trucks, electric power generation equipment, locomotives, and other industrial equipment. With 45 major production facilities worldwide and 187 dealers in 128 countries, Caterpillar does about half of its business within the United States and half abroad.

In 1859 Daniel Best left his Iowa home for California. After about ten years of working at various jobs, Best observed that many farmers transported their grain to special cleaning stations to make it suitable for market. Best thought there was a way to clean grain by machine at the same time as it was being harvested to avoid the costly step of transporting to another site. By 1871 Best had patented his first grain cleaner, which he manufactured and sold with great success. By the 1880s Best owned manufacturing centers in Oregon and Oakland, California.

Charles Holt arrived in California in 1863, and would found the firm that would put together what is today's Caterpillar. Intending to further the family business of selling hardwood products, Holt founded C.W. Holt & Company with his savings and operated it with his brothers, who came west from New Hampshire. The Holt brothers then set up the Stockton Wheel Company, in 1883, to season woods in a way that would prepare them for use in the arid midlands of California and deserts of the West. The Holts poured $65,000 into their venture, equipping their factory with the best machinery available. The new subsidiary manufactured wooden wheels, and marked the firm's first experience with the vehicular products that would be the company's strength in the years to come.

In the 1880s the combined harvester and thresher, known as the combine, revolutionized the farming industry because of its ability to cut and thresh, and later to clean and sack grain, in vast quantities, using far less time than previously needed for these individual operations. The Holt brothers' Link Belt Combined Harvester, developed in 1886, advanced agricultural technology further by using flexible chain belts rather than gears to transmit power from the ground wheels to the working parts of the machine. This innovation cut down on machine breakage.

Near the end of the 19th century, the major drawback in large-scale agriculture was the need for animal power. The combine had made large farms profitable, but the cost of housing and feeding large horse teams and the men who drove them cut into earnings. Both the Holts and Daniel Best were interested in solving this problem by using steam-driven engines to supply tractive power.

The Holts built a steam-driven tractor that could haul 50 tons of freight at three miles per hour. The Stockton Wheel Company was then incorporated as Holt Manufacturing Company in 1892. Almost concurrently, Daniel Best refined his steam-engine tractor into one of the finest available during this period, and throughout the 1890s steam-powered tractors were used for hauling freight and plowing fields, as well as for harvesting grain.

In the early 1900s the Holt brothers turned their ingenuity to another farming problem. The land around Stockton, California, where the Holt Company was headquartered, was boggy and became impassable when wet. To overcome this limitation the Holts produced the first caterpillar-style tractor, or crawler. It was built on tracks instead of wheels, and the "Cat" could negotiate any terrain short of a swamp. It soon allowed planters to reclaim thousands of acres of land previously thought useless. In 1906 a steam-powered crawler was perfected, and caught on quickly because of its ability to work on ground that all but swallowed other machines.

In 1908 the engineers who were building the 230-mile Los Angeles Aqueduct used a gas-powered crawler to transport materials across the Mojave Desert. The machine worked so well that 25 more tractors were purchased for further work on the aqueduct, thus giving the Holt tractor credibility with the public and a substantial boost to sales.

In 1908 Daniel Best sold out to the Holts, after decades of individual success. Best's son, C. W. Best, was taken on as company superintendent, but after two years, formed his own company and advanced the state of tractor technology even further on his own.

In 1909 Charles Holt, who had been looking for a new manufacturing plant in the eastern half of the United States, bought the abandoned but relatively new plant of a tractor company that had failed. The new Peoria, Illinois, location offered Holt everything he needed in a manufacturing center, and despite the need to pour capital into retooling the plant, it proved so profitable that by 1911 the factory employed 625 people. At that time Holt began to export his tractors to Argentina, Mexico, and Canada.

After the Peoria plant opened, Holt continued to improve his tractor and expand its range of applications. He experimented with several different materials for the body design to achieve a heavy-duty tractor that was not excessively heavy. Holt knew that his tractors could be used for even more rugged chores than agriculture or freighting, and fitted adjustable blades onto his tractors. He then hired them out to grade roads or move soil and rocks at construction sites.

Soon after World War I broke out in 1914, thousands of troops were caught in trench warfare. Observing such repeated attacks, a British lieutenant colonel, Ernest Swinton, sought an armored machine to resist automatic weapons, that also would be able to negotiate the war-scarred terrain of the battlefield. His requirements resulted in the invention in 1916 of an experimental tank, based on the track-laying tractors designed by Holt and others. A year later the tank was used to such telling effect that it is credited with winning the Battle of Cambrai, in France, for the Allies. Some historians point to this battle as the turning point of the war. Germany had investigated the military applications of the track-laying vehicle well before anyone else and concluded that tractors were without military significance.

Holt tractors themselves served the war effort by hauling artillery and supplies. In all, more than 10,000 Holt vehicles served the Allied forces, and the international exposure that the Holt tractor received during the war did much to popularize the tracked vehicle.

In the early 1920s the Holt company faced the problem of going from wartime boom to peacetime bust. Almost overnight the military orders that kept the factories working at capacity seemed to vanish. Holt used this down period to increase efficiency, both mechanical and human; for example, studies were made to determine how to use space and personnel to the best advantage.

In 1925 Holt and C. W. Best's company merged, this time to form the Caterpillar Tractor Company (Cat). Its first problem was to choose the outlets that would represent the new concern from among the many solid dealerships that Best and Holt had established under their respective names. Caterpillar picked only the most successful sites and quickly began to expand by opening dealerships in Australia, the Netherlands, east Africa, and Tunisia. Caterpillar dealerships developed a reputation for keeping their machines running. The firm insisted that the dealers keep a large supply of spare parts available and employ a large service force.

In 1929 Caterpillar's sales were $52 million, and the Peoria plant alone employed more than 4,000 workers. The crash of 1929, however, hit Caterpillar hard, but not as hard as it might have, thanks to an increase in sales to the Soviet Union in the early 1930s. In the aftermath of the financial world's collapse, Caterpillar went from sales of $45 million in 1930 to $13 million in 1932. Salaries were cut, including those of executives, and many factories went on a four-day workweek or were consolidated with other plants. Yet the company stayed profitable and rebounded in the late 1930s, primarily, again, because of Soviet purchases. The Soviets at that time were forming vast collective farms, some of which approached 400,000 acres in size. Caterpillar products helped make such farms manageable, and the Soviets ordered millions of dollars worth of tractors and combines from Caterpillar. In the early 1930s Caterpillar moved its main office to Peoria, for a more geographically central location.

By 1931, the diesel tractor engine, which had been used before but not widely, was finally perfected for common use by Caterpillar. Previously diesels had been too heavy and undependable for commercial use. The Diesel-60 tractor, however, made the diesel the staple engine for heavy-duty vehicles, as it is to this day. In 1933 Caterpillar's diesel production was double that of all other U.S. firms combined. This boon gave Cat the impetus to redesign many of its old models, making them more efficient and economical. Sales began to rise and continued to do so throughout the late 1930s, as Caterpillar benefited from the huge road-building projects of President Franklin D. Roosevelt's public-works programs. Caterpillar's many innovations in rubber-tired tractors and diesel engines for trucks clearly contributed to revitalizing the firm.

Caterpillar's contributions to World War II were many and varied. Of substantial importance was the conversion of a gasoline airplane engine into a dependable diesel engine. In 1942 Caterpillar unveiled the new RD-1820 radial diesel engine, which was used to power the M-4 tank. The company manufactured other engines, as well, and even artillery shells for the war effort. It set up an aluminum foundry in Decatur, Illinois, to help ease the shortage of this vital material. Caterpillar engineers found that they could make a stronger metal with cheaper, more plentiful raw materials if they used high-frequency electrical induction to harden the steel used in tanks and personnel carriers.

Caterpillar tractors worked in battle zones repairing damaged roads, building new ones, bulldozing tank traps and, constructing pillboxes. Because the Cat was usually seen doing such roadwork with a bulldozer blade attached, the term ''bulldozer'' came to be used for Caterpillar products. Caterpillar tractors and road-building equipment were used to build the Burma Road. The makeshift repair shop that was set up to service the machines working on that road by the 497th Heavy Shop Company was dubbed Little Peoria.

In the postwar period, Caterpillar experienced enormous growth rather than recession, because of the massive rebuilding campaigns begun both in Europe and Japan, with the use of Marshall Plan and other funds. In the United States itself, demand seemed limitless. Caterpillar could not get its products to its customers fast enough. It launched, therefore, an expansion program in 1949 that was the first step toward becoming a truly international firm with a major impact on world industry.

The new plant built in 1949 in Joliet, Illinois, was only the beginning of a program to establish manufacturing centers and subsidiaries around the globe. In 1950 Caterpillar announced the formation of its first overseas subsidiary, Caterpillar Tractor Company Ltd. of Great Britain. To further accommodate the postwar need for construction and road-building equipment, Caterpillar opened up subsidiaries in Brazil in 1954, in Australia in 1955, and in Scotland in 1956. In the 1950s, within the United States, Cat built new factories in Davenport, Iowa; York, Pennsylvania; and Milwaukee, Wisconsin, and parts distribution centers in Morton, Illinois; and Denver, Colorado.

In the 1960s the continuing boom in the construction of highways, dams, and mines kept sales increasing rapidly. By 1970 employment at Caterpillar was twice that of ten years prior. Caterpillar increased its exports, gaining a rival in the heavy-construction industry, Komatsu of Japan.

In 1961 Cat suffered the first of many labor conflicts with the United Auto Workers (UAW), when 12,600 workers in Peoria walked off their jobs in a wage dispute. An agreement was reached after only eight days, but this strike was the beginning of a series of increasingly bitter and complex battles between labor and management. Recognizing that industry works abroad by rules that differ from those of the United States, in 1962 Caterpillar announced the formation of a jointly owned venture in Japan. Caterpillar and Mitsubishi Heavy Industries built Cat-designed vehicles in a factory just outside of Tokyo.

After the three-year contract extension signed in 1961 was terminated, another strike began in Peoria. Announced as settled as early as February 1964, the strike was off and on until late October. In 1965 Caterpillar exceeded $1 billion in sales for the first time, announced that its stock would be sold on most of the major European stock exchanges, and started Caterpillar Belgium S.A. to build front-loading tractors there.

The year 1966 brought another confrontation with the UAW, this time in the form of a two-month walkout in Decatur. The lawsuit that Cat filed against the union, claiming an illegal strike, was settled out of court, in exchange for an agreement

that stipulated that the union would settle all conflicts not relating to contract specifications before going out on strike. During this year Caterpillar of Canada Ltd. announced the construction of a 64,000-square-foot addition to its distribution warehouse.

In March 1968 the Justice Department moved to block a proposed merger between Cat and Chicago Pneumatic Tool Company, and the merger did not take place. In the same year, Caterpillar was the first company located outside of a major city to enlist in a government-sponsored program to hire and train people considered to be unemployable. This program was directed to persons who had been out of work for extended periods. The hirees would work half of the day at entry-level positions and spend the other half of the day learning job skills for better-paying jobs.

A contract with Ford in 1970 to supply small V-8 truck engines convinced Cat that manufacturing smaller diesels could make money, and the firm spent millions of dollars redesigning and retooling existing plants to build the new engines. Profits earned from an increase in state construction programs helped pay the cost of these investments. By 1972 Cat had announced plans to build a 900,000-square-foot plant in Belgium and a 1.25 million-square-foot production facility in Mossville, Illinois. Sales to the Soviet Union increased during this year.

In 1974 Caterpillar embarked on another dramatic expansion program, announcing plans to build a 650,000-square-foot addition to its Aurora, Illinois plant, a 1.3 million-square-foot addition to its diesel engine shop in Mossville, a 720,000-square-foot addition to its Peoria plant, and a new 670,000-square-foot manufacturing center in Brazil. In 1975 Caterpillar allocated more funds than ever before for expansion and product development. The company expanded its foreign market at this time by selling pipe-laying equipment to China, cashing in on the thaw in relations between China and the United States.

By 1978 the Cat expansion program was paying off. Sales approached $6 billion and the new manufacturing plants were able to turn out thousands of vehicles. The product line had expanded to the point where Cat offered more heavy-duty agricultural, construction, and material-hauling machines than any other company. In 1978 plans were revealed to build more new plants in York, Pennsylvania; Lafayette, Indiana; and Pontiac, Illinois.

The longest UAW strike against Caterpillar (to that date) occurred in 1979. More than 23,000 workers in Illinois walked out of six of the company's major manufacturing plants. More than 3,500 workers were laid off because of the parts shortages that resulted from the strike. After almost three months of negotiations, a new three-year contract was forged, which offered better wages and a profit-sharing concession.

Caterpillar settled an involved lawsuit with Goodyear Tire & Rubber Company in 1981. Three years previously Goodyear had begun selling a radial earthmoving tire that infringed on Caterpillar's beadless-tire technology. The beadless tire lacked the beads, or edges, that attach the tire to wheel rims, and was more durable and economical than previous designs. In the out-of-court settlement Goodyear agreed to pay Caterpillar an amount mutually agreed upon, and become a licensee of Cat, paying the firm royalties for the use of beadless technology in the further manufacture of the tire.

In 1981 the firm won a political battle to be granted the right to sell $90 million in pipe-laying equipment to the Soviet Union, despite stiff opposition from the administration of President Ronald Reagan. That year the firm sold more machines than ever before, with sales of more than $9 billion for the year.

The recession of 1982 hit Caterpillar especially hard. The economic downturn caused sales to drop to $6.5 billion that year. Caterpillar laid off almost 12,000 employees at this time, and closed its plant in Mentor, Ohio. Trying to cut overhead, Cat proposed pay freezes and a cut in benefits, prompting a seven-month UAW strike, the firm's longest strike yet. To add to the company's problems, barely six weeks after the 37,500 UAW workers left their jobs, a jury awarded Kast Metals a $9.2 million settlement for Caterpillar's failure to live up to an oral agreement to buy steel castings from Kast if Kast were to build a new plant to make the castings.

Caterpillar began 1983 by announcing the first annual loss in earnings in half a century. Cat started laying off workers, and closed a plant in Newcastle-on-Tyne, England. Sales slumped to a recent-history low of $5.4 billion. Yet after the new contract was signed with UAW, Caterpillar acquired a new direction and strategy that made things look better. Despite the concession of a profit-sharing plan, the wage freeze that the firm won in the contract dispute helped stem rising costs. The anticipation of the bottled-up demand that would create a larger market after the recession made investors think that Cat stock might be a good buy. By committing itself to less expansion, more creative marketing techniques, and reduced costs, Caterpillar intended in late 1983 to ride out the economic slump and position itself to return to profitability in 1984.

Caterpillar's problems continued, however, in 1984. Despite this being the expected comeback year for the firm, the plant closings and layoffs continued. The Burlington, Iowa, parts plant locked its doors to workers and, despite optimistic projections of recalling around 3,200 workers in 1985, Cat actually laid off about 3,000 other workers during that year. Caterpillar continued to cut back operations at its factories, then eliminated cost-of-living allowances in wages, and delayed the completion of its Morton, Illinois, distribution center. The firm blamed its second straight losing year on high interest rates and stiff price competition from other companies.

In February 1985 George A. Schaefer was named chairman and CEO of Caterpillar, and Donald V. Fites was named president. Despite a net loss of almost $430 million the year before, Schaefer confidently predicted that Cat would make a profit during his first year as company head. During this year Caterpillar made two key strategic moves, which, despite their controversial nature, would be credited with making the firm once again profitable. Caterpillar first shifted some of its production and purchasing functions overseas. This meant that jobs previously performed in Peoria were moved to Scotland or Japan. The high value of the dollar overseas made such a change necessary for company survival, management argued. Secondly, Caterpillar embarked on a $600 million factory-modernization program. It would reduce permanently the labor force

needed to make tractors by automating as many manufacturing processes as possible. Approximately 2,300 workers were cut from the Caterpillar payroll during 1985. Company executives argued that the firm needed to compete with Komatsu, which had a much greater manufacturing efficiency than Cat because of its highly automated plants.

In 1986 Caterpillar Tractor Company became Caterpillar Inc. and announced that it had made a profit of almost $200 million in the previous year. The firm bounced back from its problems by marketing a new automated lift truck, which had the potential to secure part of a multibillion dollar market for Caterpillar. The firm even directly challenged Komatsu by expanding Cat's partnership with Mitsubishi Heavy Industries to include the production of hydraulic equipment.

Caterpillar faced, however, another strike during this year. Workers in Joliet walked out for four weeks, but were brought back to work under terms much like those previously rejected. Caterpillar again won a wage freeze, but cash bonuses as well as the firm's promise to lay off other workers as long as the strike continued were enough to get the Joliet workers to settle their grievances.

The weakening of the dollar abroad raised production costs and cut into profits for Caterpillar in 1987. Though the firm improved its sales and earnings over 1986, Caterpillar was still forced to close three factories. Nevertheless, in 1988 Caterpillar again made the kind of large profits it had made in the past, reaping $616 million for the year. In early 1989 Caterpillar's stock took a sharp downturn. The modernization campaign had swelled to a cost of more than $1.8 billion and flattened profits for the year. The cost of the program continued to affect company profits through 1992, while the company also suffered from the effects of the recession of the early 1990s.

A decline in sales in 1991 contributed to Cat's first loss since 1984, $404 million. Sales increased only marginally in 1992, while the firm suffered another loss, this time $218 million. Meanwhile, newly appointed CEO Fites initiated a corporate reorganization in 1990 which moved Cat away from a function-oriented structure to one revolving around product lines and geographic areas.

Labor strife returned to Peoria in late 1991 when Caterpillar tried to alter a pattern agreement that had been agreed to in October at John Deere. When the UAW and Cat workers refused to accept that contract, they struck two Cat plants with 2,400 workers in early November. Caterpillar responded by locking out 5,650 more workers. Over the next five months, Caterpillar used managers to fill in at the affected plants, then threatened to permanently replace 15,000 UAW workers. In April 1992 the workers returned to their jobs without a contract and eventually accepted a company-imposed contract. However, the striking workers returned to what they believed was a hostile environment, where they faced suspension or dismissal for wearing union-supporting T-shirts or buttons. By mid-1994, more than 80 complaints against Caterpillar for such tactics were issued by the National Labor Relations Board.

In 1993 Caterpillar completed the factory-modernization program and at the same time began to benefit from its results.

The time to process a part from start to finish was reduced by 75 percent and in-process inventories were reduced by 60 percent. Coupled with an overhaul of the new product development process, vast improvements were made in new product introductions. Only 24 new or improved products were introduced in 1991; that figure doubled in 1992 and reached 53 in 1994. Such gains led to record sales of $11.62 billion in 1993 and record profits of $652 million. The next year brought more records: $955 million in profits on sales of $14.33 billion.

In the early 1990s Caterpillar looked to the east and south for its future growth. The company strongly supported both the North American Free Trade Agreement (NAFTA) and the General Agreement on Tariffs and Trade (GATT), concluding that the elimination of trade barriers could add $350 million in Cat sales a year by 2000. By 1994 Caterpillar had already reaped the benefits of NAFTA when it posted $239 million in sales in Mexico, an increase of 59 percent over 1993. Outside North America, Caterpillar formed several joint ventures in Japan (with Mitsubishi), Russia (with AMO-ZiL and with Kirovsky), and China (with Shanghai Diesel and with Xuzhou Construction Machinery Group). New dealerships were also established in Vietnam and the Shanghai region of China in 1994.

On the heels of the firm's improving results came the longest and most bitter strike to hit Caterpillar yet. After sporadic wildcat walkouts following the 1991–92 strike, a full-scale strike began in June 1994 with 10,500 UAW workers honoring picket lines while about 4,000 workers stayed on the job. The issue that precipitated the walkout was Caterpillar's firing of union workers, but the dispute quickly evolved into one concerning a new contract. As with the 1991–92 strike, Caterpillar again shifted managers onto the assembly lines but it also hired temporary workers to fill in. As the strike dragged on into 1995, it was beginning to affect Cat's inventories and operating efficiencies, but its impact was mitigated by the decreasing number of union workers at the company. Caterpillar had been locating its new plants in right-to-work states and foreign countries, and had shifted some production to other manufacturers through outsourcing. While UAW workers made up 45 percent of Cat's workforce in 1980, by 1995 UAW workers numbered only 28 percent.

In early 1995 the two sides agreed to federal mediation for a new round of contract talks. As Caterpillar continued to post record profits and revenues, the company clearly had the upper hand. Even though workers voted to reject a contract offer in early December, the UAW promptly called off the strike and sent the workers back to their jobs without a contract. The rejected contract terms began to be implemented by the company unilaterally, including a two-tier wage system and no overtime pay for days longer than eight hours. Similar to the aftermath of the 1991–92 strike, Cat placed restrictions on what workers could say or display and by early 1996 at least 50 workers had been suspended or fired for violating what the company called its "standards of conduct." Meanwhile, Caterpillar's board voted to reward Fites for his handling of the strike and for the company's performance with a 1995 compensation package of $3.09 million, an increase of 75 percent over the $1.76 million he received in 1994.

The bitter strike behind it, Caterpillar announced more record results for 1995, with profits exceeding $1 billion for the first time ($1.14 billion) on sales of $16.07 billion. The firm planned to continue to grow internationally and aggressively pursue emerging markets in Asia, Latin America, Africa, the Middle East, and Eastern Europe. Caterpillar appeared likely to continue to maintain its industry-leading position for the foreseeable future.

Principal Subsidiaries

Advanced Filtration Systems, Inc. (50%); Advanced Technology Services Inc. (91.29%); Anchor Coupling Inc.; Balderson Inc. (82.5%); Carter Machinery Company, Inc.; Caterpillar Americas Co.; Caterpillar Asia Pacific Holding Inc.; Caterpillar Capital Company, Inc.; Caterpillar of Delaware, Inc.; Caterpillar Financial Services Corporation; Caterpillar Industrial Inc.; Caterpillar Insurance Services, Inc.; Caterpillar Investment Management Ltd.; Caterpillar Logistics Services, Inc.; Caterpillar Paving Products Inc.; Caterpillar Risk Management Services Inc.; Caterpillar Services Limited; Caterpillar World Trading Corporation; Engine Service Specialists, Inc.; Solar Turbines Incorporated.; Caterpillar of Australia Ltd.; Caterpillar Commercial N.V. (Belgium); Caterpillar Insurance Co., Ltd. (Bermuda); Caterpillar Brasil S.A. (Brazil); Caterpillar of Canada Ltd.; Caterpillar Commercial Services Ltd. (Canada); CONEK S.A. de C.V. (Mexico); Tecnologia Modificado S.A. de C.V. (Mexico); Caterpillar Financial Services N.V. (Netherlands Antilles); Caterpillar Commercial A/O (Russia); Caterpillar Asia Pte. Ltd. (Singapore); Caterpillar Overseas S.A. (Switzerland); Caterpillar Export Limited (Virgin Islands).

Principal Divisions

Asia/Pacific Division; Building Construction Products Division; Caterpillar Overseas; Component Products Division; Construction & Mining Products Division; Corporate Auditing and Compliance Division; Diversified Products Division; Engine Division; Financial Products Division; Human Services Division; Latin America Division; Logistics and Product Services Division; North American Commercial Division; Parts & Service Support Division; Technical Services Division.

Further Reading

Bremner, Brian, "Can Caterpillar Inch Its Way Back into Heftier Profits?," *Business Week,* September 25, 1989.

Century of Change: Caterpillar Special World Historical Edition, Peoria, Ill.: Caterpillar Inc., 1984.

Dubashi, Jagannath, "Cat-apult: The Cheap Dollar Helped, but Caterpillar's Turnaround Was Engineered in Peoria," *Financial World,* November 23, 1993, p. 34.

Elstrom, J. W., "Cat, Union Crawl toward Settlement: Weary Workers, Pressed Managers Tire of the Fight," *Crain's Chicago Business,* January 16, 1995.

Franklin, Stephen, "Questions Linger as Vote Nears on Caterpillar Pact: Was Strike Worth It? Will Anger Fade?," *Chicago Tribune,* November 27, 1995.

Kelly, Kevin, "Cat Is Purring, but They're Hissing on the Floor," *Business Week,* May 16, 1994.

Slutsker, Gary, "What's Good for Caterpillar . . . ," *Forbes,* December 7, 1992, p. 108.

—Wallace Ross
—updated by David E. Salamie

Catherines Stores Corporation

3742 Lamar Avenue
Memphis, Tennessee 38118
U.S.A.
(901) 363-3900
Fax: (901) 794-9726

Public Company
Incorporated: 1987 as Catherines Holding Corporation
Employees: 2,200
Sales: $256.43 million
Stock Exchanges: NASDAQ
SICs: 5621 Women's Clothing Stores; 6719 Holding
    Companies, Not Elsewhere Classified

Catherines Stores Corporation is a leading specialty retailer of women's large-size clothing and accessories. The holding company operates through four separate retail divisions: Catherine's; PS . . . Plus Sizes, Plus Savings; Added Dimensions; and The Answer. Each division's chain of stores has a distinct merchandise format and marketing strategy. At the end of October 1995, the company operated 443 stores in 40 states and the District of Columbia.

The oldest and largest of the divisions, Catherine's, was started in Memphis in 1960 when Catherine Weaver sold her Catherine's Stout Shop to Ralph Levy. Levy soon closed his own family business, Ralph Levy and Associates, and concentrated on growing the Catherine's company. Over the next 17 years Levy opened an average of 4.5 stores a year, in medium-sized cities, primarily in the Southeast, Southwest, and Midwest. The stores offered lower middle to middle income customers a broad assortment of moderately-priced apparel ranging from business suits to sportswear.

In 1977 Levy sold his 78-store chain to Garfinckel, Brooks Brothers, Miller & Rhodes, Inc. Garfinckel's continued to open new Catherine's stores, and in 1980, created the Plus Sizes division of Catherine's. The new division focused on major metropolitan areas such as Chicago, Washington, D.C., Dallas, and Los Angeles. It offered budget- to moderate-priced merchandise to the same customer group served by Catherines.

Just as the new division got underway, Garfinckel's was bought out by Allied Stores Corporation in an unexpected takeover bid. Initially, Garfinckel's had been negotiating with Allied to sell its 22 Miller & Rhoads department stores. Then Allied made a bid for the entire 272-store chain and purchased it, in August 1981, for an estimated $228 million.

For the next five years, Allied supported the expansion of both Catherine's and Plus Sizes. Then, in 1986, Allied in turn was bought by Canada's Campeau Corporation.

In October 1987, Catherine's management, along with affiliates of Investcorp S.A. (a Bahrain-based investment bank) and Citicorp Venture Capital, acquired the Catherine's division from Allied Stores for $42.3 million as part of Allied's divestitures, and formed Catherines Holding Corporation.

Bernard J. Wein, who had been with Catherine's and Allied, was named chairperson, president, and CEO of the holding company as well as of Catherine's. Stanley H. Grossman, formerly general manager of the Plus Sizes division, became executive vice-president of the company and executive vice-president and general manager of Plus Sizes. In 1989, the company was recapitalized with an additional $3.9 million in equity and Investcorp acquired controlling interest.

Investcorp, short for Arabian Investment Banking Corp., was a major conduit for Arab investment in the United States and Europe. Chase Manhattan banker Nemir A. Kirdar, an Iraqi national with an master of business administration from Fordham University, founded the investment bank in 1982. Investors in the firm included members of the Saudi royal family and wealthy Middle Eastern businessmen. As Kirdar told *Forbes* in a 1987 interview, ''We wanted to be a bridge between Middle Eastern investors and those companies in the West that needed new capital.''

The firm's philosophy was to make large, friendly investments to finance the buyouts of old-line companies with brand-name products and market share. Unlike other leveraged-buyout firms, Investcorp did not rely on debt to finance its purchases. Instead, it put its own equity capital into those companies and generally left the running of the companies to the management. ''We are owners, not managers,'' a top official told *Time*.

Investcorp's first big deal was buying Tiffany & Co. in 1984 and taking it public in 1987 at a profit of more than $100 million. Within ten years, the firm had put together a huge retail empire. Holdings in the U.S. included Saks Fifth Avenue, Color Tile (a carpet and tile chain), Circle K (convenience stores), Carvel (ice cream chain), and Camelot Music. Other than Tiffany's, Investcorp had taken just two other units public by 1994: the Sports & Recreation Inc. chain and Catherines.

In 1991, Investcorp changed the name of Catherines Holding Corporation to Catherines Stores Corporation and took the company public for $8 a share. At the time, Catherines Stores operated 217 stores in 35 states, a 278 percent increase in stores since its purchase by Garfinckel's.

The company's growth reflected a significant change in the demand for clothing for larger-sized women. Between 1982 and 1992, sales of large-size apparel increased from $6 billion to $10 billion. Name-brand designers recognized the trend and responded accordingly. Liz Claiborne introduced Elizabeth, designed specifically for larger women. Harvé Benard's Pour La Femme line offered chic designs with elastic waistbands. Designers' high-priced, large-size items accounted for $2 billion in sales during 1991 alone. Ellen Tracy, Evan Picone, and Jones New York also began offering bigger sizes, as did hosiery and lingerie manufacturers.

With more to offer this market than muumuus and polyester dresses, up-scale retailers began courting big women. Saks Fifth Avenue opened its Salon Z, a 6,000 square foot boutique for women size 14W and above; Bloomingdale's expanded the footage of its Shop for Women.

In the discount and off-price retail area, designers and retailers also began providing styles that paralleled regular-size fashions. Dress Barn, an off-price chain, opened more than 100 Dress Barn for Women stores in five years. Leslie Fay began manufacturing a plus-size category of dresses and sportswear for Wal-Mart, Kmart, and other mass merchandisers.

Retailers and designers were addressing a long-neglected but growing market, which by 1993 was worth $13.6 billion. Analysts that year estimated that more than 20 million American women wore large sizes. Among women over the age of 40, some 40 percent wore a size 14, 16, or 18. ''Unfortunately, as you get older, you also tend to get heavier,'' Paine Webber analyst Anita Wager told *Money* magazine. And the market continued to grow as women in the baby boom generation aged. Analysts predicted that between 1990 and 2000, the number of women ages 45 to 55 would increase by 35 percent.

When Catherines Stores went public, the company was still organized into two divisions—Catherine's and PS . . . Plus Sizes, Plus Savings—as it had been when part of Garfinckel's. The company also still competed in three price ranges: main floor (budget), moderate, and better. Both divisions carried a large selection of apparel in the moderate and lower moderate

price range. Catherine's, located in medium-size and small cities, emphasized moderately priced clothes and offered some higher priced goods. Its prices were generally competitive with department stores and other specialty stores offering similar merchandise.

PS . . . Plus Sizes, Plus Savings, with stores in major cities, concentrated on the more budget-conscious customer, with dresses, sportswear, and other apparel priced in the lower moderate and main floor range. Its prices were generally ten to 20 percent below those of its department and specialty store competitors.

Most of the company's merchandise consisted of brand name product lines, including Top Notch, Donkenny (DKGold), Koret, Baron-Abramson, Young Stuff, Cimy, Sharon Anthony, Damon, Chez of California, and Katherine Lindsay. Between 15 and 20 percent of this merchandise was made exclusively for Catherines Stores. The company also carried private label goods, in categories such as sweaters, blouses, shirts, coats, suits, activewear, and hosiery.

Catherines Stores grew much faster than originally anticipated. The 1991 stock prospectus announced plans to add 120 new stores by 1995, which would have brought the number to 337 units. By the end of the company's 1994 fiscal year, the actual number of stores was 404.

Catherines Stores' expansion strategy focused on adding new stores in communities in which it already operated and moving into selected geographical areas adjoining existing markets. Expansion was assisted by the purchase of existing companies. In 1992, the year after it went public, Catherines Stores gained more than additional stores when it bought the 108-unit Virginia Specialty Stores, Inc. for a total of $24.4 million. The two Virginia divisions, Added Dimensions and The Answer, gave Catherines Stores access to a more upscale, career-oriented segment of the large-size market. Virginia Specialty operated as a wholly owned subsidiary until 1995 when it was merged with Catherine's. In 1993, the company acquired 14 stores from direct competitors (Cramer's Half-Size Shops and Siefert's Plus), expanding its presence in the Northeast. That same year, Catherines Stores, which until then had been leasing facilities, bought land in Memphis and built a new corporate office and a distribution center with the capacity to serve up to 1,000 stores.

The company opened stores primarily in strip shopping centers, believing its customers preferred the convenience of being able to park directly outside the store. By 1995, 78 percent of the stores in the four chains were located in strip centers. Such locations were also less expensive than mall stores. The stores themselves tended to be small, averaging between 3,000 and 4,500 gross square feet.

During 1995, the company planned to open 40 new stores, and had 39 of these operating by November of that year. The new stores included the company's entry into Washington State (in Seattle and Olympia), Oregon, and North Dakota. The November total brought the number of stores to 443 in 40 states and the District of Columbia. Geographically, the company's stores were concentrated in the South (50 percent) and Midwest (30 percent).

The company employed multiple merchandise concepts to serve the broadest segment of the market. The Catherine's division (198 stores in 1995) concentrated its stores in medium-size cities, including Memphis, Atlanta, Tampa, and Indianapolis. Under the slogan, "Fashion independence for today's large size women," it provided lower middle to middle income women with full service and clothes at regular prices. Its moderately priced merchandise offered broad assortments of career and casual clothes, especially in the sportswear category. Approximately two-thirds of the items were brand name merchandise, with one-third of the remaining private label component designed and sourced directly by the company. By 1995, super-sized merchandise represented one-third of the dollar sales in this division, with size 34 apparel being offered. Catherine's represented 45 percent of the company's stores.

The PS . . . Plus Sizes, Plus Savings division (112 stores) offered similar merchandise at budget-to-moderate prices to this same demographic group in major metropolitan areas. It carried both career and casual apparel, with more emphasis on the latter. The percentage of brand-name clothes was slightly higher than Catherine's with narrower assortments. The prices at Plus Sizes were typically ten to 25 percent below those of department store competitors. Plus Sizes represented 25 percent of the company's stores, and operated in cities such as Chicago, Washington, D.C., Dallas, and Los Angeles.

Added Dimension (99 stores) targeted a slightly more upscale customer in medium-size cities. The Added Dimension concept ("Beautiful fashions in sizes 16W to 28W") emphasized career merchandise at moderate and upper moderate prices using many of its own private label brands. Growth centered on cities with successful Catherine's locations. As with the Catherine's concept, Added Dimension stores were full-service, regular price formats. Twenty-two percent of the company's stores were Added Dimension.

The Answer, the smallest division, focused on the urban off-price market ("Large sizes for less"). This concept targeted the slightly more upscale woman in major cities who wanted quality and fashion but was most concerned about value. It offered moderate to better-priced career-oriented merchandise at 20 percent below competitive prices. Eight percent of the stores (34) used this concept.

According to J.C. Bradford & Co., Catherines Stores corporate structure focused on controlled, efficient store expansion and operation. Two examples show how the company used that focus to reduce costs and please customers. First, the company used direct mail as its primary advertising approach. After the merger with Virginia Specialty, the company wanted to improve its management information system to provide updated background and purchasing information about its customers. The STS Customer Profile System information database software it installed led the company to refine its direct-mailing campaigns. Before the new system, each mailer generated $3.67 in sales. After using the software to narrow the scope and tastes of its customer base, sales per mailer jumped 67 percent in 1993 to $6.13. The ability to narrowly categorize the customer base also helped Catherines Stores reduce advertising expenses by $58,000 in one year, according to David C. Forell, executive vice-president and chief financial officer.

Second, concern about the customer as well as the bottom line was also evident in Catherines Stores' handling of its check recovery effort. With about 30 percent of its business done in checks, the company wanted both to collect the funds and keep the customer. It had been dealing with returned checks internally, sending a letter and making a phone call before turning the check over to a collection agency. In 1992, Catherines Stores signed on with a start-up company called Revenue Assurance Professionals in Memphis. Their ProCheck system operated under the assumption that if customers were treated with respect and dignity, they would not only redeem their returned check and pay an appropriate returned check fee, they would also continue to shop with the company. The company's success rate of collection efforts improved 25 percent.

With regard to staff, turnover at the store and district manager level was well below the industry average. And J.C. Bradford & Co. reported the company had a history of treating employees well, particularly regarding family leave issues. In 1992, shareholders approved an employee stock purchase plan, allowing full-time employees with at least one year of service to contribute from one to ten percent of their pay towards the purchase of the company's common stock.

With sales below expectations in 1994, the company focused on controlling and reducing expenses wherever possible. For example, it reduced training costs by using video tapes during the in-store training of its associates and reduced franchise taxes by reincorporating the company from Delaware to Tennessee. They also began experimenting with a program to take mail and phone orders and tested two frequent shopper programs. One program, which gave discounts as rewards whenever a customer shopped at the store, resulted in more frequent store visits with higher average sales. In the second program, a customer buying a frequent shopper card received a ten percent discount on all purchases for 12 months. Over 20,000 such cards were sold in August 1995 at $25 apiece, yielding half a million dollars.

In 1995, the company introduced a narrow assortment of shoes in hard-to-find sizes in 40 stores and planned to add shoes in another 40 locations if the pilot tests proved successful. Additionally, large-size petite departments, offering clothes for women under 5'4", were opened in nearly half the stores.

Catherines Stores competed primarily with department stores, specialty retailers, discount stores, and mail order companies. During the mid-1990s, the large-size market saw a rapid consolidation of specialty stores. Audrey Jones went out of business, as did Conston Corp. Other competitors, such as Women's World, closed stores. This resulted in a thinning out of Catherines Stores' competition. Despite a continuing softness in women's retail apparel overall and a rough 1994, the company's earnings were up in 1995 and expansion plans were on target. Analysts at both J.C. Bradford & Co. and Morgan Keegan gave the company a buy rating, indicating it appeared well positioned to take advantage of the reduced competition and the anticipated increase of its target population.

Principal Subsidiaries

Catherine's, Inc.; Catherine's Partners, L.P.; Catherine's of California, Inc.; Catherine's of Pennsylvania, Inc.

Further Reading

Abend, Jules, "More Makers Taking the Plus Size Plunge," *Bobbin,* August 1993, pp. 80–84.

Corwin, Pat, "Tailoring the Plus-Size Mix," *Discount Merchandising,* February 1993. pp. 28–32.

Feldman, Amy, "Hello, Oprah, Good-bye, Iman," *Forbes,* March 16, 1992, pp. 116–17.

Hoffman, Thomas, "Customer Data a Top Concern of Retailers," *Computerworld,* February 7, 1994, p. 53.

Morais, Richard, "The Boys from Bahrain," *Forbes,* October 5, 1987, p. 181.

"Recover the Check, Keep the Customer," *Chain Store Age Executive,* June 1993, p. 84.

"Retailing: Garfinckel Sheds a Profit Problem," *Business Week,* August 17, 1981, pp. 32, 37.

"Retailing: Garfinckel Struggles to Foil Allied's Bid," *Business Week,* August 31, 1981.

"This Specialty Retailer Sees Big Things Ahead," *Money,* September 1993, p. 66.

"Why Garfinckel Had to Give In to Allied," *Business Week,* September 14, 1981, p. 33.

Zinn, Laura, and Charles Hoots, "Tiffany's Sparkle May Have Blinded Investcorp," *Business Week,* August 29, 1994, pp. 86–87.

—Ellen D. Wernick

CHRISTIE'S

Christie's International plc

8 King Street, St. James's
London SW1Y 6QT
United Kingdom
(0171) 839 9060
Fax: (0171) 839 1611

Public Company
Incorporated: 1766
Employees: 1,700
Sales: £819.8 million (1994)
Stock Exchanges: London
SICs: 7389 Business Services, Not Elsewhere Classified

Christie's International plc oversees the operations of one of the world's premier art auction houses. While the company holds regular auctions worldwide, its principal selling centers are represented by subsidiaries Christie, Manson & Woods Ltd. in London and Christie, Manson & Woods, International Inc. in New York City. Dubbed ''the oldest fine arts auctioneers in the world'' (rival Sotheby's is 22 years older, but began by selling books), Christie's has been in the business over 200 years and has set record prices not only for works of art but also wine, scientific instruments, carpet, photographs, cameras, and teddy bears. In 1994, the firm garnered a turnover of £167.9 million on auction sales worth £820 million; profits were £13.4 million.

Eighteenth Century Origins

Although documentation on his early life story is somewhat sketchy, it is generally held that James Christie was born in Perth, Scotland, in 1730 to a Scottish mother and English father. After serving briefly as a midshipman in the Royal Navy, he worked for an auctioneer named Annesley as an apprentice in fashionable Covent Garden, London. After a few years, Christie opened his own auction house at Dalton's Print Rooms in the Pall Mall district. These premises also housed what was to become the Royal Academy of Arts. His first auction, on December 5, 1766, which included wine, netted £176, 16 shillings,

and six pence. This sale was the first recorded in a bound log of sales that has survived over 200 years.

James Christie excelled at auctioneering. In the early years, he sold many things besides works of art, including chamber pots, loads of hay, and even someone's suddenly unneeded coffin. All of these were proffered with mellifluous and verbose charm, earning Christie the nickname ''The Specious Orator'' from satirical cartoonists of the day.

Within only a few years, Christie was handling truly valuable paintings, such as those by Europe's ''Old Masters,'' which he picked up on the fashionable Grand Tour, as well as several by promising American artists. Christie eventually moved his offices (and residence) to 125 Pall Mall, becoming next door neighbors with Thomas Gainsborough, the great British painter, who later (like Sir Joshua Reynolds) painted Christie's portrait. (After changing hands several times, Gainsborough's *Portrait of James Christie* was bought by J. Paul Getty for $26,500 in 1938, Getty's first major painting purchase.)

Moreover, Christie was influential in the promotion of art, displaying the works of new artists at a time when, save the Royal Academy's annual show, there were no other public places to display contemporary works. Many esteemed artists, including Landseer, Rossetti, and Sargent, saw their work pass through the auction house. Increasingly, when an artist who had been helped by a Christie auction passed away, the executors of his estate naturally turned to Christie to sell pictures remaining in the studio.

Christie's reputation as a connoisseur was so esteemed that in 1778 he was called on to sell Sir Robert Walpole's magnificent art collection, which Catherine the Great eventually acquired for £40,000, then a colossal figure. (These pictures were eventually displayed at the Hermitage in St. Petersburg; a few bought by Andrew Mellon made their way to the National Gallery of Art in Washington, D.C.)

Christie's and the London art business as a whole benefited from the emigration of Huguenots from France. After the French Revolution destroyed Paris as the leading art market, the revolutionary government turned to the nation of shopkeepers, and to Christie's specifically, to dispose of La Comtesse Dubarry's "most superlative" collection of jewels after she was guillotined. However, the Reign of Terror both removed buyers and flooded the market with paintings, making jewelry sales still more important.

Industrial Era Transitions

American tycoons, newly rich from the Industrial Revolution, such as Mellon, Pierpoint-Morgan, Vanderbilt, and Kress, began to dominate buying activity in the 19th century. At the same time, Christie's became known as a clearinghouse for country estates, a tradition that has continued for two centuries. Such a sale in 1848, for the Duke of Buckingham's Stowe House, lasted 40 days and realized £77,562. It also brought in a new employee and a future partner, the gatekeeper's son, Thomas Woods, who thoroughly impressed the firm with his knowledge of the house's paintings.

James Christie died in 1803, whereupon management of the company was taken up by his son, James Christie II, and later his two grandsons. In 1823, Christie's moved its headquarters to 8 King Street, where it would remain for over 170 years. The auction room there—known as the "Big Room"—is said to have been designed by James Christie in the form of a hexagon in order to maximize wall space; paintings were hung on these walls all the way up to the ceiling.

In 1831 William Manson joined the firm. Thomas Woods became a partner in 1859, and the firm's name changed to Christie, Manson and Woods. The year 1889 saw the retirement of the last of the Christie's to be associated with the company: James Christie IV. Christie's held the first auction of Impressionist paintings in Britain in the same year.

The Modern Era

After 50 years of passing picture sales on to Christie's in favor of auctioning book collections, Sotheby's management decided to begin auctioning paintings. By 1917, the company was holding regular art auctions. In response, Christie's stopped referring books to Sotheby's, opting to auction such collections themselves. Thus began a competition and rivalry between the two auction houses that would continue into the 1990s.

Although it had begun to broaden its offerings to include books and even fine wines, Christie's focus remained primarily in the picture market. Among its more notable sales during this time was that of the *Portrait of Mrs. Davenport,* by British painter George Romney. The portrait was sold by Christie's for £360,900 in 1926. Other significant sales in the interwar period included the Russian crown jewels, which realized nearly £250,000 in 1927.

Global economic depression and the world wars were devastating to the art market, and in the 1930s talk began to surface of merger between Christie's and Sotheby's. Nothing came of the discussions, however, and in the race for the top auction house spot, Sotheby's began to gain ground, having been early to establish a presence in the United States.

In 1940, R. W. Lloyd bought a substantial share of Christie's stock and thus became chairman of the company. Under Lloyd, Christie's became a private limited company, and Sir Alec Martin, who had begun working for Christie's at the age of 12 as an office boy, was named managing director. New management faced several challenges. In addition to its financial concerns, Christie's suffered a terrible blow on April 16, 1941, when an incendiary bomb totally destroyed the firm's building on King Street; the premises would not be completely rebuilt until well after the war, in 1953. Another wartime inconvenience was the suspension of wine sales, which did not resume until 1966.

Postwar Crisis and Opportunity

Christie's market grew broader yet again after World War II, as art auctions, previously the domain of the upper classes, gained a more widespread appeal. Television cameras began to crowd into auction rooms, and the public began to hear news reports of important art sales and the money they fetched.

In 1958, Christie's was reorganized as Christie, Manson and Woods Ltd; the new company issued £60,000 worth of capital. Ivan O. "Peter" Chance was selected to lead the new company. In order to buy shares owned by Martin and Lloyd (who died in April 1958), the Crown Lease of 8 King Street was sold to the Commercial Union Assurance Co., and leased back to Christie's.

A process of professionalization had begun at Christie's. First, Peter Chance promptly hired consultants to set up a press office at Christie's. Then, the company began focusing on establishing a presence in Europe, becoming the first British auction house to hire a European representative, whom it situated in Rome. Soon offices in other European countries were established, and an American representative was hired. Christie's also began to appoint more specialists in areas such as collectible coins and porcelain. Finally, as competition between Christie's and Sotheby's intensified in the late 1950s, both houses began requiring their managers to read the obituaries daily, looking for estates that might need auctioning. Later, social intelligence gathering would become more sophisticated, all with the end of determining who would control known valuable art collections. Christie's had approximately 150 sales a year in this period.

In 1960 Christie's reported sales of £2.7 million, and the following year that figure had risen to £3.1 million. However, the company was trailing by significant margin behind Sotheby's, a trend that some analysts attributed to a lack of confidence in Christie's picture department. Nevertheless, Christie's continued to set sales records, recording the highest price paid until then ($27,950) for a Pre-Raphaelite painting, *The Lady of Shalott* by Holman Hunt.

In 1962, as the Cuban missile crisis was simmering, Peter Chance reportedly made a secret trip to Cuba to consider auctioning property seized when Castro had risen to power in 1959. Although a valuation team arrived to catalog the valuables in what was in many ways a febrile environment, no sales materialized from their efforts. In spite of the bold efforts, Christie's lost £6,000 that year, although it sold only slightly less art than the year before. Five years later, Christie's did succeed in establishing a business relationship with the Soviet Union, selling for £65,751 ($193,308) a 1,700-piece porcelain banqueting service made for Tsar Nicholas I in 1830.

A couple of notable staff additions helped bolster Christie's ailing reputation in its picture department, as did initial moves to divide the company's departments into areas of specialty. Moreover, the sale of the Cook collection of Old Masters in 1965 proved Christie's was a force to be reckoned with; Rembrandt's *Portrait of Titus* (his son) sold for $2.2 million, a price that surpassed all expectations.

In 1965, Christie's acquired White Bros. Printers for £38,000, a purchase that helped the company to produce its considerable volume of catalogs more efficiently. Interestingly, the company used an old-fashioned letter press system until 1979, when it converted to offset lithography (which also required using union labor for the first time). In 1980 White Bros. began printing all of Christie's Park Avenue catalogs as well.

To celebrate its 200-year anniversary, Christie's held a tremendous Bicentenary Exhibition in January 1967. About 60 important drawings and paintings that had passed through Christie's rooms over the years were lent back for the display, which raised about £3,000 for the National Art Collections Fund. Together, the works, which included Gainsborough's *Portrait of James Christie,* were valued at approximately £5 million.

During this time, Christie's European operations, based in Rome, were being hindered by Italy's strict art export laws. In response, Christie's established a new subsidiary, Christie's International S.A., which was incorporated in Geneva in 1967 to oversee European business. Switzerland, moreover, did not have the import taxes of Great Britain. A program of international expansion included a host of new Christie's auction houses in Australia, Japan, and Canada, as well as an American headquarters move to a new facility on Madison Avenue in New York.

New Leadership for a New Era

Christie's went public in 1973, strengthened by three years of good results and expansion. Pre-tax profits had grown tremendously in the prior five years: from £139,000 in 1968 to £1.1 million in 1972. In two years, after practically doubling 1972's profits, Peter Chance announced his retirement as chair of Christie, Manson and Woods, although he would remain chairman of Christie's International plc for two more years.

Jo Floyd took up Chance's former duties just in time to be met by a worldwide economic recession. In order to cope with dwindling profits in London, both Christie's and Sotheby's introduced a ten percent buyer's premium in the early 1970s. This new policy was not met with enthusiasm on the part of London's art dealers, several of whom began litigation against the auction houses.

In autumn 1974, Christie's acquired Debenham and Coe in South Kensington, for the purpose of handling lower value lots more efficiently than was possible at its King Street facility. At the end of the decade, Christie's bought Edmiston's, a Glasgow auction firm.

In 1977, Christie's opened a New York salesroom in the Delmonico Hotel, a 1920s era skyscraper at 502 Park Avenue. American sales were becoming increasingly important to the British-based firm; by 1983, New York sales had surpassed those from London. In 1978, a second New York showroom, dubbed Christie's East, was opened in a six-story East 67th Street garage. Christie's reputation in America seemed to be cemented when in 1980 Henry Ford II chose the firm to sell ten of his excellent Modern and Impressionist paintings. A painting that had performed so impressively for Sotheby's in 1958, Van Gogh's *Le Jardin du Poète, Arles,* was sold by Christie's for a record $5.2 million (£2.2 million) in London. Overall, the paintings brought in $18.3 million in one evening. Other great sales during this time included that of Coco Chanel's wardrobe, a huge production that earned £43,250 pounds for 40 dresses and brought in an even more impressive amount of good publicity.

In 1987 several records were set at Christie's, for paintings ($39.9 million for Van Gogh's *Sunflowers*), jewels ($6.4 million for a 65-carat pear-shaped diamond), and automobiles ($9.8 million for a 1931 Bugati Type 41 Royale). Christie's marketing efforts, aimed at broader audiences, helped sell large collections, such as the Nanking Cargo, consisting of gold bars and porcelain from a freighter sunk off the coast of Java in 1751. Human interest helped elevate the price to £10 million. Such valuable collections attracted interest from all walks of life, and in 1984 a group of armed robbers stormed into a jewelry auction at King Street, wielding a shotgun and a sledgehammer. Fortunately, the truly valuable pieces were overlooked.

In 1990 Christie's set a record for furniture; $15.1 million was offered for the Duke of Beaufort's Badminton cabinet. Then, the record for all works of art was broken with Christie's sale of Van Gogh's *Portrait of Dr. Gachet,* which went for $82.5 million. These records represented only the cream of many Modern and Impressionist paintings that Christie's handled during the late 1980s and early 1990s. Christie's was holding approximately 1,400 sales per year in the late 1980s.

Before resigning in 1989, Jo Floyd had secured a new 125-year lease for expanded premises on King Street. Christopher Davidge, whose grandfather had worked as a clerk at the firm, assumed the role of Christie's CEO after becoming managing director four years earlier. Davidge had previously worked his way up the ranks at White Brothers, Christie's printing company. He made effective communications and standardization throughout the organization two of his top priorities. He also streamlined the staff and aggressively cut commissions in order to gain sales. However, in 1995, the commission-cutting stopped, as profits did not rise with sales. Under Davidge, Christie's market share began to approach that of rival Sotheby's.

In 1994, Christie's sold £22 million worth of art works from the collection of the Marquess of Cholmondeley, a direct descendant of Robert Walpole, whose collection had been sold by Christie's more than two centuries earlier. Although Christie's has transformed into a forward-looking international firm, such links to the past seem vital to its enduring role as one of the only two truly world-class auction houses.

Principal Subsidiaries

Christie, Manson & Woods Ltd.; Christie's South Kensington Ltd.; Christie's Scotland Ltd.; Christie, Manson & Woods International (USA); Christie's (International) S.A. (Switzerland); Christie's Amsterdam B.V. (Netherlands); Christie's (Monaco) S.A.M. (Monaco); Christie's Swire (Hong Kong) Ltd. (Hong Kong); Christie's Australia Pty. Ltd. (Australia); Spink & Son Ltd; Christie's Education Ltd.; White Brothers (Printers) Ltd. (66⅔%); Woods of Perth (Printers) Ltd. (66⅔%); C.I. Property & Investments Ltd.; Christie's Fine Art Security Services Ltd.; Watmoughs Holdings plc (20%); Studio SMK; Christie's Images; Topsail Insurance; Christie's Great Estates.

Further Reading

"Artful Auctioneering," *Economist*, March 11, 1995.
"Blockage Discount at Issue in Andy Warhol's Estate," *Tax Management: Estates Gifts & Trusts Journal*, January 13, 1994, pp. 55–56.
Brough, James, *Auction!*, Indianapolis: Bobbs-Merrill, 1963.
DuBois, Peter C., "African Icon Brings $1.2 Million," *Barron's*, May 8, 1995, p. 16.
DuBois, Peter C., "Art Fix," *Barron's*, October 31, 1994, p. 20.
——, "The Art of the Sale," *Barron's*, May 15, 1995, p. 13.
——, "High Contrast," *Barron's*, November 21, 1994, pp. 24–25.
——, "Pretty Picture?" *Barron's*, May 8, 1995, pp. 15–16.
Grey, Sarah, "When the Sky's Not the Limit," *Accountancy*, March, 1995, p. 58.
"Hammering Asia," *Economist*, September 17, 1994.
Herbert, John, *Inside Christie's*, New York: St. Martin's Press, 1990.
The History of Christie's, company document, London: Christie's International plc.
Huus, Kari, "Art Market: Do I Hear Three?" *Far Eastern Economic Review*, May 12, 1994, pp. 69–70.
——, "Jewellery: East Buys West," *Far Eastern Economic Review*, May 12, 1994, p. 69.
Jaffe, Thomas, "10 C's, How Many G's?" *Forbes*, May 8, 1995, p. 20.
Jarrett, Ian, "A Gentler Kind of Bear Market," *Asian Business*, March, 1995, p. 61.
——, "Zoom In On a Good Buy," *Asian Business*, August, 1994, p. 56.
Lacey, Robert, "A Grand Old Rivalry," *Vanity Fair*, January, 1996, pp. 104–118.
Morais, R.C., "Blood and Monet," *Forbes*, November 25, 1991, p. 149.
"The Older the Better," *Economist*, March 5, 1994.
Raslan, Karim, "Art Market: Price Propping," *Far Eastern Economic Review*, March 17, 1994, pp. 44–45.
Richmond, Susannah, "Butterfield Day Founder Swaps Ads for Artefacts," *Campaign London*, January 28, 1994, 10.
Rozhon, Tracie, "Fighting for Turf: Sotheby's vs. Christie's, *New York Times*, April 14, 1996, Sec. 9, p. 1, 10.
Serwer, Andrew E., "Art Dealers Trade Screams for Smiles," *Fortune*, April 17, 1995.
Siobhan, Quin, "An Ethnical Investment," *Resident Abroad*, June, 1995, pp. 65–66.

—Frederick C. Ingram

Chromcraft Revington, Inc.

1100 N. Washington Street
Delphi, Indiana 46923
U.S.A.
(317) 564-3500
Fax: (317) 564-3722

Public Company
Incorporated: 1992
Employees: 1,400
Sales: $134.1 million
Stock Exchanges: New York
SICs: 2511 Wood Household Furniture; 2512
  Upholstered Household Furniture; 2514 Metal
  Furniture; 2522 Office Furniture Except Wood; 2531
  Public Building & Related Furniture

Chromcraft Revington, Inc., through its subsidiaries, designs, manufactures, and sells furniture for home and commercial use throughout the United States. Under the Chromcraft, Peters-Revington, and Silver brand names, its product lines compete in three market segments: casual dining furniture, occasional furniture, and commercial furniture. The company is among the lowest-cost producers in the furniture industry and regards itself as the second largest manufacturer of casual dining furniture.

Chromcraft Revington was formed in February 1992, when Mohasco Corporation announced it wanted to take two of its divisions, Chromcraft Corporation and Peters-Revington Corporation, public as one company. Within a month Chromcraft and Peters-Revington became wholly owned subsidiaries of the new company. At the same time, Chromcraft Revington completed its initial public offering of 2.5 million shares of its common stock at $11 per share on the NASDAQ exchange and restructured its long-term debt. Three years later, in April 1995, the company acquired the Silver Furniture Co., Inc., and in October 1995, Chromcraft Revington transferred its common stock to the New York Stock Exchange and changed its ticker symbol to CRC.

Although the company was relatively young, both Chromcraft and Peters-Revington had been making furniture since 1946. Chromcraft was founded in Mississippi and was credited with pioneering the casual dining market segment during the 1950s. It was the first company to make a tilt-swivel dining room chair, to introduce molded fire-retardant foam in upholstered products, and to plate with real brass. Peters-Revington was established in Delphi, Indiana, and used American hardwoods such as cherry, oak, and maple in the manufacture of coffee tables, end tables, and other occasional tables.

During the 1960s, after more than 15 years as independent companies, the two furniture makers would become involved in some of the major changes beginning to occur in the furniture industry. Before that time, the majority of the approximately 5,350 American furniture companies were still small, inefficient, and generally opposed to technological change. Few of the companies spent money on consumer research, development, or marketing. "This industry has always believed that there are only two ways to stimulate business. Bring out something new or cut prices," David Brunn, president of Drexel Furniture Co., was quoted as saying in the February 1967 *Forbes.*

Most furniture companies were controlled or managed by their founders or the founders' families. Only 18 companies were publicly owned in 1967 and two-thirds of the companies employed fewer than 20 people. Even the largest company, Kroehler Manufacturing Company, accounted for less than three percent of the industry's sales. Most companies were based in the South and turned out lower-priced wood furniture, since southern forests provided inexpensive lumber and the lack of unions assured a cheap labor force. But while the furniture was inexpensive, its quality often left much to be desired. Companies in the North, with higher wages and material costs, tended to specialize in well-designed, high-quality furniture.

The furniture market was largely untapped. People needed beds, tables, chairs, bookcases, and dressers as they married, bought homes, and had children. But according to the Bureau of

Labor Statistics, in 1967 people in urban areas spent an average of only $281 per year on furniture, less than the price of a color television. Attracted by the potential of an industry with an annual growth rate of over six percent, several major corporations began buying furniture companies, bringing a transfusion of capital, professional management, and national marketing to the industry. Magnavox, Massey-Ferguson, and confection maker Dolley Madison each bought furniture manufacturing concerns, and Litton Industries acquired wood, metal, and upholstery companies.

The Mohasco Corporation, which was then the maker of Mohawk Carpets and the largest carpet manufacturer in the country, was one of several corporations that saw furniture as the core of a new retail home-furnishings industry. Such an industry would offer consumers a coordinated package of furniture, carpet, textile, and home accessories. In 1963, Mohasco purchased Chromcraft, and Peters-Revington, along with Super Sagless Spring Corp., which made the mechanisms for reclining chairs and sleep sofas. Its buying spree continued with Barcolo Manufacturing, the maker of the Barcolounger reclining chair, and the Stratford Corporation, which manufactured the Stratoliner recliner. For a total cash outlay of $18.5 million, Mohasco assembled a multi-product furniture division with sales of over $60 million.

Mohasco's furniture companies became separate divisions of the corporation. A few years later, Mohasco expanded its home-furnishings activities with the purchase of Cort Furniture Rental operations, and the initiation of an interior furnishings distribution business.

While the furniture divisions regularly made money, the carpet division was a continual earnings troublemaker. In 1980, Mohasco lost $2.2 million, its poorest performance in a decade, according to a 1984 *Forbes* article. In response, the company named Herbert Broner president and CEO. Broner, who had come to Mohasco in 1972, closed plants and cut 500 headquarter jobs. He also moved carpet staff to Atlanta and rental furniture staff to Washington, D.C., closer to the company's major markets, and sold the interior furnishings distribution business. The $70 million proceeds from that sale helped cut corporate debt by half.

Broner's efforts appeared to work, as earnings for 1981 rose to a record $15 million, but in 1982 Mohasco posted a $9 million loss. In 1983, the company earned $13 million but had slipped from third to fourth place in the carpet industry, as Burlington Industries, World Carpets, and Shaw Industries had increasingly automated their carpet mills.

Chromcraft and Peters-Revington continued to grow, however. Chromcraft added more lines of commercial furniture, including office chairs and conference tables, as well as airport and lounge seating. Chromcraft held patented design features on its chairs and continued to obtain patents on new designs. In 1985 Peters-Revington began expanding its line by adding sets of shelves, often with cabinets or bureaus, that could be arranged along a wall in various combinations. These wall systems were followed in 1987 by entertainment systems, which combined in single pieces of furniture storage spaces for a television set, a stereo and related components, and video com-

ponents. In 1989 the company began producing bookcases and library systems, and in 1991, curio stands.

In 1988, Mohasco received takeover bids from 17 companies. To avoid a hostile takeover, the company merged with MHS Holdings Corp., an affiliate of Citicorp Investments Inc., in a $516 million leveraged buyout, and went private. As a result of the buyout, Mohasco became a wholly-owned subsidiary of Fairwood Corporation.

During the year it took to complete that transaction, Broner stepped down as CEO, and Mohasco sold both Mohawk Carpets and Cort Furniture Rental to finance the takeover defense. The company also moved from Amsterdam, New York, where it had been headquartered since 1878, to Fairfax, Virginia, a suburb of Washington, D.C.

In September 1989, Robert W. Hatch, previously with General Mills' furniture division and Interstate Bakeries, was named CEO of the scaled-down organization, which had annual sales of $400 million and 6,000 employees. In addition to Chromcraft and Peters-Revington, Mohasco's remaining divisions were Barcolounger Corp., Stratford, and Super Sagless Corp. In a 1989 *Washington Post* article, Hatch indicated that the most marketable aspect of the firm's production were the recliners and sofa beds, which were more economical because of their dual functions.

The late 1980s and early 1990s were a terrible time for the entire furniture industry. High interest rates slowed housing sales. Foreign competition increased until it accounted for one-third of the domestic furniture market, and prices for most wood doubled. The value of furniture industry shipments declined by 2.3 percent between 1989–1991, with metal furniture shipments, Chromcraft's specialty, falling by over six percent in value. 1990 was the worst year for Chromcraft and Peters-Revington, with sales dropping from $117.1 million to $114.7 million and net earnings falling from $2.5 million to $229,000. Operations improved somewhat in 1991, with combined net earnings of the two subsidiaries of $1.9 million on sales of $117.7 million.

In February 1992, Mohasco decided to concentrate on its mechanized furniture products and announced it was seeking SEC permission to take Chromcraft and Peters-Revington public as one company. Chromcraft Revington, to be based in Delphi, Indiana, would continue to sell residential and commercial furniture under the Chromcraft and Peters-Revington trade names through its two wholly owned subsidiaries.

The president and CEO of the new company was Michael E. Thomas, who had served as president of Peters-Revington since 1981. H. Martin Michael, president of Chromcraft Corporation, was named executive vice-president, while Frank T. Kane became vice-president of finance and CFO. Before joining the company in 1992, Kane was employed by Amalgamated Investment Corp. and its wholly-owned subsidiary, Papercraft Corporation.

The Chromcraft subsidiary continued to manufacture mid-to-higher priced casual dining furniture and medium-priced commercial furniture and had 35 percent of the high-priced dining-room market. Its dining room furniture was designed for use in family rooms, recreation rooms, country kitchens, and apartments without formal dining rooms. Coordinated dining suites in contemporary or traditional styles included tables manufactured from metal, wood, glass, faux marble, and other materials, along with stationary and tilt-swivel chairs, pedestal chairs, or barstools. Chairs were upholstered in a variety of fabrics, leathers, and vinyls. In 1994 Chromcraft expanded its wrought iron offerings and introduced wicker and rattan products as well.

An employee sales force and independent representatives sold the Chromcraft furniture nationwide to specialty retailers of casual furniture, general furniture retailers, and departments stores, including J.C. Penney Inc., Harverty Furniture Inc., and Nebraska Furniture Mart.

Commercial furniture made up one-third of Chromcraft business. The commercial furniture products included stationary and tilt-swivel office chairs, conference tables, and lounge-area seating products for airports, hospitals, and other public waiting areas. Chromcraft's STAXX line, for example, provided stackable metal-frame chairs for auditoriums, classrooms, cafeterias, and meeting rooms. Office chairs were offered in both contemporary and traditional styles and were upholstered in various grades and colors of fabric or leather. They included executive models with high backs, management models, ergonomic computer task chairs, and secretarial models with no arm rests. A separate employee sales force and independent representatives sold the commercial furniture to a dealer network throughout the United States. These dealers in turn marketed the furniture to architects, specifiers, and designers, as well as to businesses.

Chromcraft manufactured its furniture in Senatobia, Mississippi. Operations at its 530,000 square foot plant included metal fabricating, plating, painting, wood finishing, and chair foam production. Except for certain lines, most products were made to customer specifications within five weeks of the order and, therefore, were not carried in stock.

Peters-Revington manufactured moderately priced occasional furniture made of cherry, oak, and maple in traditional, contemporary, and country styles. Products included tables, bookcases, entertainment centers, library and modular wall units, and curio cabinets. Many table collections included 12 or more pieces in matching styles. In addition, different products incorporated the same design and styling themes, so that customers could furnish an entire room with coordinated pieces. In 1994, the company introduced a line of home office wood furniture and received strong orders for computer desks, all-wood filing cabinets, and barrister bookcases. The Chromcraft Revington 1994 Annual Report indicated plans to add non-occasional furniture, such as bedroom and dining room furniture, to the Peters-Revington line sometime in the future.

Peters-Revington sold its products through independent sales agents to a broad customer base of primarily smaller furniture retailers. At the end of 1994, that base numbered approximately 2,900 active accounts. The furniture was manufactured at a 380,000 square foot facility in Delphi, Indiana. Operations there included cutting, shaping, sanding, lacquering, finishing, and final assembly of wood furniture. In 1994, the

company announced plans for a new, larger plant which was expected to be operational in the first quarter of 1996.

In its first full year operating as a corporation, company sales for 1993 increased 5.6 percent, to $126.3 million. The increase was due to higher unit volume and, to a lesser degree, price increases. All product lines—occasional furniture, dining furniture, and commercial furniture—had higher sales in 1993 than in 1992.

Sales in 1994 continued to increase, by 6.2 percent, with both divisions reporting higher sales than in 1993. While sales for all Peters-Revington's occasional furniture lines were higher, its entertainment furniture sold particularly well. Chromcraft's dining sales also grew, in part due to its new lines of wrought iron, wicker, and rattan furniture. A drop in airport gate seating offset higher sales of office chairs, leaving commercial furniture unchanged for 1994.

Remarking on the new company's leadership, President Michael Thomas was "recognized in the industry as a cost-cutter who has streamlined manufacturing and dramatically improved profit margins," according to Kathleen Berry of *Investor's Business Daily*. In fact, Chromcraft and Peters-Revington were among the lowest-cost producers in the furniture industry. When wood prices jumped in 1993, Thomas cut back on labor and overhead costs to avoid passing price increases on to retailers. Between 1990 and 1994, earnings grew at a 70 percent rate as lower interest rates and a healthy housing market helped furniture sales skyrocket. Between 1992 and 1994, net earnings increased from $6.1 million to $11.2 million, and earnings per share from $1.07 to $1.91

Nevertheless, some analysts felt the company needed to be more aggressive in its marketing. "There is a limit to how much Mike can increase margins. Their growth rate could be higher with more marketing," Kevin Duyches of George K. Baum & Co. asserted in a December 27, 1994 *Investor's Business Daily* article. Sales distribution was concentrated in the Midwest and the East Coast, although some new products, such as the wicker and rattan pieces, helped sales in California, the Southwest, and Florida. According to *Investor's Business Daily*, the company's customer base increased about five percent between 1992 and 1994.

Duyches noted that the company had about $8 million to $9 million of excess cash a year, which was used to fund internal expansion. At the end of 1994, the company had no long-term debt. In April 1995, Chromcraft Revington acquired Silver Furniture Co., Inc., a manufacturer and importer of occasional tables, for a total price of $11.15 million. The Knoxville, Tennessee, company, which had 1994 sales of $30 million, merged with Chromcraft Revington as a wholly owned subsidiary. With the purchase of Silver Furniture, Chromcraft Revington's long-term debt stood at $6.6 million at the end of the third quarter of 1995.

Sales for that same quarter were $39.1 million, an increase of 18.6 percent over the same period in 1994. For the nine-month period ending September 30, sales had increased 11.4 percent to $112.4, with net earnings of $1.51 per share. These increases reflected the operations of the newest subsidiary, Silver Furniture. Excluding Silver, sales were lower for the quarter and nine months by three percent and 2.2 percent, respectively, as compared to the same periods in 1994. President Thomas blamed those numbers on the sluggishness of retail furniture sales overall.

As the first half of the 1990s ended, the residential furniture industry in the United States was still highly fragmented, with over 1,000 manufacturers. However, many of these companies did not compete directly with Chromcraft Revington. The commercial furniture segment of the industry was more concentrated and was dominated by a few very large companies, all of which had greater resources than Chromcraft. Within this environment, Chromcraft Revington was financially healthy and looking forward to using its new facility to add bedroom furniture to its product line. As an efficient, low-cost producer of brands associated with quality and design innovation, the company appeared well-positioned for continued expansion in its markets.

Principal Subsidiaries

Chromcraft Corporation; Peters-Revington Corporation; Silver Furniture Co., Inc.

Further Reading

Berry, Kathleen. "Cutting Costs in Furniture's Middle Market." *Investor's Business Daily*, December 27, 1994.

Blyskal, Jeff. "No Magic Carpet." *Forbes*, April 23, 1984, p. 84.

Budiansky, Stephen. "On The Cutting Edge: Sharp New Technology Helps the Woodworking Industry Compete." *U.S. News & World Report*, May 30, 1994, pp. 48–50.

Casper, Jennifer. "Mohasco's New CEO Charts Revitalization." *The Washington Post*, October 16, 1989.

Cuff, Daniel F., "Mohasco Chief Mixes Furniture and Buyouts," *New York Times*, October 2, 1989, p. D5.

O'Hanlon, Thomas, "5,350 Companies = A Mixed-Up Furniture Industry," *Forbes*, February, 1967, pp. 145–49.

—Ellen D. Wernick

Cincom Systems Inc.

2300 Montana Avenue
Cincinnati, Ohio 45211
U.S.A.
(513) 662-2300
Fax: (513) 481-8332

Private Company
Incorporated: 1968 as United Computer Systems, Inc.
Employees: 1,000
Sales: $152 million (1995 est.)
SICs: 7372 Prepackaged Software

Cincom Systems, Inc. ranks among the world's largest privately held commercial software companies. Although it wasn't the world's first independent producer of software, it has outlasted all its predecessors to become the oldest company of its kind. A long history of industry firsts fueled two decades of dynamic growth. From its foundation in database management systems and consulting, the firm has expanded to offer a full line of multi-platform business applications. After concentrating for most of its history on creating software for large corporate mainframe systems, Cincom sought ways to profitably target the fast-growing small business market as sales stagnated in the early 1990s. By the mid-1990s, Cincom had 60 offices in 20 countries worldwide and offered a roster of software products including: database managers, CASE tools, business control applications, network and systems management, office automation products, and information resource management applications.

The company was founded in 1968 as United Computer Systems by three expatriates from International Business Machines (IBM). Tom Nies, Tom Richley, and Claude Bogardus had all enjoyed successful careers at IBM; Nies as one of the company's most successful salesmen, and Richley and Bogardus as system engineers. But by the late 1960s, all three began to perceive a need for client-oriented software to complement IBM's hardware. At this time, IBM's computers were sold with only the most basic operating system; it was left to customers to program specific functions. Unable to convince others at IBM

of the efficacy of designing and selling more useful software, Nies, Richley, and Bogardus struck out on their own.

During its first decade in business, the trio established a foundation of innovative products, inventive marketing schemes, and a unique corporate culture. With a meager $600 and a card table in Nies' basement as its first office, United Computer Systems devised its first software application, the TOTAL database management system. When a potential client commented that TOTAL's unimpressive package—a series of punch cards in a cardboard box—didn't appear to justify its $20,000 price tag, Nies and company transferred it to a more impressive spool of tape. TOTAL helped such early clients as Hillenbrand Industries, American Tool, Champion Paper, and U.S. Shoe perform basic business tasks more efficiently and accurately.

Prodded in part by a lawsuit alleging trademark infringement (which was eventually thwarted), United Computer Systems changed its name to Cincom, a contraction of Cincinnati and computer. In spite of getting burned on a fixed-price contract, Cincom made a $1000 profit on $155,000 in revenues during its first year. It was a feat not many startup businesses achieve and was especially impressive in light of the young company's powerful competitors.

Upstart Cincom and its rivals in the fledgling software industry got a break in 1969 when IBM "unbundled" its software, technical support, installation, maintenance, and training services from the costs of its computer hardware. This let clients in on the actual cost of IBM's software, thereby giving Cincom and its competitors a price with which to compare their software and support services. Even so, marketing software separately remained a difficult proposition. In order to ease the high initial costs of software, Nies offered rental agreements, thereby reducing up-front expenses and simultaneously providing the young company with a reliable cash flow.

Nies introduced several other marketing techniques to the young software industry as well. Instead of fighting for America's largest metropolitan markets, the company established sales offices in secondary markets with a view toward "owning" them, rather than "sharing" the major markets. Quarterly user group meetings garnered feedback from, and provided support to, Cincom's clientele and would later become a software industry standard.

Cincom established its emphasis on research and development early on, adapting its software to multiple hardware platforms, including RCA, Honeywell, Univac Siemens, NCR, and more. The company also made all its products compatible with each other, thereby developing an entire proprietary business system. Thus, flexibility and intercompatibility became Cincom hallmarks.

In 1971, the company bought ENVIRON/1, a teleprocessing communication system, adding data communications capability to its database software. ENVIRON/1 had been created by Kent Salmond, another ex-IBM employee frustrated by Big Blue's lack of software initiative. He had quit IBM in 1966 and connected with a California company called ISS. Although it was essentially a manufacturer of hardware, ISS supported Salmond's concept of an on-line database and gave him the funds necessary to begin its development. But when ISS was acquired by Itel Corporation, the new parent sold ENVIRON/1 and its nine-member staff to Cincom for $100,000. After its completion under Cincom ownership, ENVIRON/1 became the first on-line operating system to be released independently of a hardware package. Although computer users were initially reluctant to use an operating system other than the one that came with the computer, the unique capabilities of its integrated ENVIRON/1 and TOTAL soon attracted a loyal following. Cincom became the first software company to merge database management, report writing, and data extraction with the 1972 addition of SOCRATES, an information retrieval and report-writing system, to the its application lineup in 1972.

Cincom achieved another industry first in 1971, when it became America's premier software company to export. The three-year-old company opened offices in Canada, Great Britain, and Brazil the following year, added a branch in Brussels in 1973, and established an International Licensee Department in 1974. Before the decade was out, the company had added subsidiaries in France, Australia, Japan, and New Zealand. Cincom's efforts in this arena earned it the software industry's first Presidential "E" award for exporting excellence.

After four years of working in Nies' basement, the founding trio rented office space and began to hire employees in 1972. As president, Nies strove to cultivate a "family atmosphere" at the growing company by emphasizing such values as entrepreneurial spirit, ethical integrity, creativity, and responsibility, among a long list of other standards. Nies expected employees, known as Cincomers, to embrace a demanding work ethic exemplified by a company fight song: "Work all day, fly all night, Cincom, Cincom fight, fight, fight!" He nurtured his employees' hard work and dedication with group social events such as the annual Cincom Prom and overseas trips; when the roster of employees grew too large for such gatherings, gifts of jewelry and dinners commemorated significant employee anniversaries and accomplishments. In 1974, the company established the Quixote Club, an honorary clique of the company's top performers, whether administrators, marketers, salesmen, engineers, or support staff. Quixote represented the visionary "tilting at windmills" of Cincom's formative years.

Cincom's annual revenues had increased to $7 million by 1974 and to $28 million by 1979. Operating profits grew from about $500,000 to $10 million during that same period, in spite of (some would argue because of) Cincom's industry-leading investments in research and development. By 1980, over two-thirds of Fortune 100 companies and half of Fortune 500 companies used Cincom's database/data communication software.

During the 1980s, Cincom encountered intense competition from rivals old and new, invested heavily in research and development, made alliances where necessary and profitable, and survived a software industry shake-out. Cincom opened its second decade in business with the 1979 launch of the MANTIS interactive application development system. MANTIS marked Cincom's transition from batch data processing to the practically instantaneous, on-line applications that would become the norm. MANTIS also incorporated basic functions (subroutines), thereby allowing people with less programming experience to create or customize their own software applications. MANTIS also represented Cincom's first push for interoperability, meaning that it could be run on personal computers (PCs) as well as mainframe systems.

In 1984, Tom Nies tapped Dennis Yablonski to succeed him as Cincom's president and chief operation officer, while Nies retained the chairmanship and chief executive office. Yablonski had started at Cincom as a programmer in 1975 and advanced through the organization's sales division. He progressed to head of U.S. sales by 1979, added international sales duties the following year, and oversaw company-wide marketing, sales, and service by 1982.

Unfortunately for Yablonski, his rise to Cincom's highest executive ranks coincided with one of the company's most difficult periods. The trouble began with the 1984 acquisition of Net/Master from Software Development Pty., Ltd. on a "long-term perpetual type license." This network management system was the first application of its kind to hit the market. Cincom and Software Development had jointly effected the development of Net/Master for the IBM platform, but the partners' interests began to diverge when it came to creating versions for other platforms. At that point, Cincom began to pursue the alternatives on its own. Within a couple of years, Net/Master was accounting for nearly 20 percent of Cincom's annual revenues, but still hadn't started generating a profit. That's when Software Development decided to terminate its "perpetual" contract with Cincom, a move Cincom fought in court for 18 months.

In order to extricate itself from the dispute with Software Development without incurring further losses, Cincom orchestrated a third-party buyout of both its adversary and its license for Net/Master. In November 1989, Cincom sold its right to market the application to Systems Center for $43.5 million. At the same time, Systems Center bought Software Development for about $42 million. Cincom continued to market Net/Master into the early 1990s, but although it was critically acknowledged to be a superior product to the segment-leading program from IBM, Net/Master's sales never took off.

Cincom used the proceeds of the divestment to retire debt, which had ballooned during this crisis. Although Cincom's revenues had multiplied from less than $30 million in 1979 to

$84.8 million in 1984 and $161 million in 1988, high research and development outlays and burgeoning operating expenses combined with the legal costs to result in back-to-back annual losses in 1985 and 1986 that negated all Cincom's previous 16 years' profits. The company's admittedly slow reaction to this deepening fiscal quagmire forced it to borrow in order to stay afloat, and rising interest rates in the last half of the decade further exacerbated its difficulties.

Throughout this demanding period, Cincom also found itself increasingly beset by competitors large and small. Having awakened from its dreamy disregard for the software market, IBM's launch of DB2 captured sales from Cincom's own applications. Digital Equipment Corporation (DEC), Cullinet Software Corporation, Ameritech's Applied Data Research, and Software AG also turned up the competitive heat during this period.

Yablonski resigned Cincom's presidency in the midst of these difficulties in 1987, and Nies resumed day-to-day leadership. In an effort to rejuvenate the entrepreneurial spirit of Cincom's early years, Nies directed the company's 1989 reorganization into product-oriented, rather than industry-oriented, divisions. The painful aspects of Cincom's concurrent downsizing effort were shared among all its employees, who each accepted a month of unpaid leave and deferred five percent to 15 percent of his or her annual salary. In stark contrast to the wholesale layoffs that characterized many companies' reorganizations during this period, Cincom reduced its staffing levels through attrition.

The 1989 reorganization signaled the advent of Cincom's third decade and the beginning of its transition to products for smaller customers. The company especially targeted the aerospace, health care, education, and science markets. Rosemary Hamilton of *Computerworld* characterized Cincom as a "consistent force in the software industry" that sought to become a "key player" in the 1990s. A new advertising tagline, "What we used to call competition, we're now calling prey," exemplified the company's aggressive new stance. It featured a bald eagle with wings spread and talons grasping for an unseen (but presumed) victim.

Cincom's ongoing investments in research and development, double the average software industry rate during the 1980s, resulted in spending of more than $100 million from 1979 to 1987. This massive investment culminated in the 1988 introduction of Cincom's most extensive roster of new products and strategic affiliations to date. New applications included the MANAGE series of office automation applications; the Comprehensive Planning and Control System (CPCS); computer aided software engineering (CASE) tools; and the SUPRA family of relational databases.

Although fiscal, legal, and competitive matters undoubtedly dominated the roster of concerns during the 1980s, Cincom did not allow those issues to halt its geographic expansion. By the early 1990s, the company had established agencies in India, the Middle East, Latin America, and on the continent of Africa. By 1991, international sales contributed over 60 percent of Cincom's annual revenues. The company's early and strong emphasis on overseas markets proved to be one of the elements that sustained it through the 1980s shake-out in the American software industry.

In fact, whereas many of Cincom's competitors experienced declining revenues during this period—and at least one slipped into bankruptcy—Cincom's annual sales continued to increase on the strength of international growth throughout the decade.

Cincom has flirted with going public since the mid-1980s. In 1987, in fact, Nies had announced that the company would float a $30 million to $50 million offering, but was thwarted by the October 1987 stock market crash. The leader reiterated plans to go public at some point during the 1990s, but the plan was contingent on several factors. The most important prerequisite was that Cincom employees retain a controlling interest in the firm. Nies had been providing for this eventuality by offering stock options as part of the company's incentive program beginning in 1981. In the mid-1990s, however, lackluster fiscal performance appeared to be the primary obstacle to Cincom's long-heralded initial public offering.

The explosive revenue growth Cincom experienced in its first two decades flattened in the early 1990s, ranging from $170 million in 1992 to $152 million in 1995. Herb Gepner, an industry observer with Datapro Information Services Group, noted that Cincom's heritage became a two-edged sword in the early 1990s. On one hand, Gepner told Mike Ricciuti of *Datamation* in 1992, Cincom's "mainframe heritage" contributed to its "technological lead." But at the same time, Cincom's "reputation as a big-iron vendor" branded it as an "old-line mainframe software vendor." Stalling sales growth seemed to indicate that Cincom's standing with customers as well as analysts was stuck in the mainframe market. However, more aggressive marketing and more timely software introductions, combined with the company's acknowledged technological foresight, could well spur the company to greater growth in the mid- and late-1990s.

Principal Divisions

Application Development Technologies Division; Manufacturing Solutions Division; System Software Division.

Further Reading

Bonfield, Tim, "Nies Is Still Chasing Dreams, and He's Catching a Few, Too," *Cincinnati Business Courier,* June 10, 1991, pp. 4, 35.

Cincom Systems, Inc. Courage, Creativity and Commitment: 25 Years in the Pursuit of Excellence. Cincinnati: Cincom Systems, Inc., 1993.

Gibson, Stanley, "Software Industry Born With IBM's Unbundling," *Computerworld,* June 19, 1989, p. 6.

Hamilton, Rosemary, "Steady Cincom Seeks Out the Spotlight," *Computerworld,* August 19, 1991, p. 65.

Harvey, Robert E., "Cincom Regroups as '88 Revenue Gain Evaporates," *Metalworking News,* September 4, 1989, p. 5.

Modic, Stanley J., "Cincom Bets Big on People Power: How Tom Nies Defines His CEO Title," *Industry Week,* August 21, 1989, p. 23.

Ricciuti, Mike, "Mainframe DBMS Power Unleashed!," *Datamation,* October 15, 1992, p. 26.

Verespej, Michael A., "Tom Nies Uses a Family Approach," *Industry Week,* April 28, 1986, p. 62.

Weinstein, Marc, "Cincom Defends Computer Turf," *Cincinnati Business Courier,* July 15, 1985, pp. 1, 2.

Weiss, Barbara, "Cincom Tightening Its Belt as Rival IBM Turns Up Heat," *Metalworking News,* March 27, 1989, p. 5.

—April Dougal Gasbarre

Coles Express Inc.

P.O. Box 918
Bangor, Maine 04401
U.S.A.
(207) 942-7311
Fax: (207) 942-8970

Wholly Owned Division of Roadway Services, Inc.
Incorporated: 1917
Employees: 400
Sales: $41 million
SICs: 4213 Trucking Except Local; 6719 Holding
      Companies, Not Elsewhere Classified; 5012
      Automobiles & Other Motor Vehicles; 7538 General
      Automotive Repair Shops

Coles Express Inc. is a comprehensive motor transportation and trucking service operating in the New England region of the United States. The company was purchased by Roadway Services in 1993, as a part of that company's efforts at geographic and service expansion through acquisition. In 1995, Coles Express was providing trucking services throughout Massachusetts, Connecticut, Rhode Island, Maine, Vermont, New Hampshire, New Jersey, New York, Pennsylvania, Maryland, Delaware, and along the Atlantic Coast of Canada.

The company was founded in 1917 by Allie Cole. Cole had left his home in Lowell, Maine, at the age of ten, realizing that his widowed mother could not support him and his several sisters and brothers on her washer-woman salary. Cole found employment as a farm hand, a stable boy, and, in 1910 when he was 17, as a baggage and freight handler at the Enfield, Maine, railroad station. According to Galen Cole's *Allie Cole: A Maine Pioneer,* one day Cole found himself helping a businessman lower a 600-pound load from the dock of the railroad to a horse-drawn wagon. Since this was against the normal operating rules of the railroad, the young man was harshly reprimanded. Bristling at the rebuke, and especially irritated at the railroad's attitude of not encouraging good customer treatment, Cole decided to quit his job and start his own company.

An opportunity presented itself when the U.S. Mail contract offered a bid for delivery between the railroad station at Enfield and the adjacent towns of Burlington, Lowell, Saponac, and Grand Falls. Cole won the contract and established his own firm, Coles Express. The new business venture blossomed, and by 1919 Cole had made enough money to purchase a Model T Ford for the delivery of mail and other packages. This modernization greatly impressed his customers since the delivery time was reduced to a fraction of what it took using horse transportation.

Soon Cole began to augment his mail route income by transporting lumbermen to and from the railroad station. Not long afterwards, Cole started a trucking and passenger service from Enfield to Bangor, Maine, about 30 miles away. After returning from an express run to and from Bangor, Cole decided that his business would benefit by moving to the larger city, so in 1925 he packed up his wife and four children and relocated to what would become the headquarters of Coles Express for many years.

An adventurous and determined businessman, Allie Cole expanded his services to Lincoln, and soon afterward, to Houlton. At the time, roads north of Lincoln weren't plowed during the wintertime by the Maine State Highway Commission, and people grew dependent upon Cole's overnight freight and passenger service. Most residents in the area stored their automobiles at Thanksgiving and brought them out again in May. The herculean effort by Cole to plow the roads with his freight trucks and also make deliveries finally convinced the state legislature to appropriate funds not only for plowing the roads north of Lincoln but for a comprehensive program to improve them for road traffic all year long.

By the time the Great Depression struck during the early 1930s, Coles Express was the largest trucking business in the region. Yet the company was on the verge of bankruptcy in just a few years. Luckily, one of Allie Cole's friends, Harold Russ, a vice-president at Merrill Trust Company, loaned him $2,000 in order to continue operations. In 1935, with the worst years of the Depression behind him, Cole was still in business with 13 worn out trucks and 20 employees. Besides hauling freight, the company was also repairing freight trucks, selling and hauling fertilizer, and building truck bodies. On the second and third floors of the firm's new headquarters, Cole raised and fed

10,000 chickens. At approximately the same time, the company packed and hauled thousands of pounds of potatoes to A&P grocery stores across the entire state of Maine.

World War II brought with it both opportunities and challenges for the company. U.S. Air Force bases located in Bangor, Houlton, and Presque Isle soon developed into major departure points for troops and war materials destined for Europe. Coles Express was contracted by the federal government to haul steel, pipes, foodstuffs, and a variety of construction equipment and general freight to the new bases. Soon all the firm's trucks were operating 24 hours a day, and Cole struck on the idea that if he could convert his trucks to tractors, more freight could be hauled. During the middle of the war, Cole made ten of these tractors with extended trailers for additional freight. As the intensity of fighting increased in all the theaters of war, and more men were called up for active duty, the company began to experience a shortage of drivers. Cole brought one of his sons, 16-year-old Galen Cole, into the company as a driver at this time, but Galen was also drafted during the latter part of the war, and served in Europe until the end of 1946.

When Galen Cole returned after the war, he joined his father and his brothers at Coles Express as terminal and operations supervisor, and later assumed the responsibility for the entire over-the-road driving fleet operation. Showing promise and talent, Galen began to participate in the general management of the company. As the health of his father deteriorated during the late 1940s and early 1950s, Galen become indispensable as the day-to-day administrator of the company's operations. In 1955, when Allie Cole died, Galen was chosen by the trustees of his father's estate and by his four brothers to assume the position of president of the company.

The late 1950s and 1960s were growth years for Coles Express. The firm was the first business to have been granted authority by the Interstate Commerce Commission to conduct full general freight service throughout the state of Maine and on the Atlantic coast of Canada, including New Brunswick, Prince Edward Island, and Nova Scotia. New terminals were opened and expanded service was offered in Portland, Sidney, Bangor, Woodland, Houlton, Fort Kent, and Presque Isle. The company also grew by means of an aggressive acquisitions strategy. Allie Cole had purchased Cliffs & Griffith's Express during the 1940s, and now Galen Cole built upon that foundation, acquiring several more trucking operations, such as Blaisdell, Sargents, McGary, Bemis, Houlton Truck Express, Grahams, Higgens, W.J. Foley, Fred's Hunnewell, Ayer's, Law Trucking, and Peerless. In addition, the company's truck and trailer repair operation had developed into one of the most successful parts of the business. The most comprehensive truck and trailer service in the entire New England region, A.J. Cole & Sons repaired thousands of trucks and trailers. With over 100 mechanics, the company had garnered a reputation as the best truck and trailer repair shop in the state of Maine.

Coles Express continued to expand during the 1970s. Freight service was extended to Boston, and the company soon developed into one of the largest carriers between Maine and Massachusetts. Yet deregulation of the carrier industry was on the horizon and, with the prospect of trouble from the Teamsters union, many freight companies began to shut down. In fact, the company's most important competitor, Fox & Ginn Motor Freight, went out of business at this time. After its departure, Coles Express was the undisputed leader in intrastate general freight service. The company was, in fact, doing more business in the state of Maine than all the other freight companies combined.

When the deregulation of the trucking industry arrived in the early 1980s, Galen Cole was well aware of the fact that his company could not compete with other non-union carriers that were jumping into the business. Management at Coles Express paid its employees above the average rates in Maine, but did not meet the Teamster demand for increases that companies in cities such as New York or Boston were able to pay. In 1982, the Teamsters union called for a strike against Coles Express, leaving approximately 20,000 pieces of freight undelivered. With a significant number of employees crossing the picket line, Coles Express was eventually able to deliver all the packages.

The strike lasted for 18 months. During this time, the Teamsters had called for strikes against dozens of carriers in the New England region, forcing them to pay higher wages or close their doors. Many firms decided to cease operations. Hours after the strike was initiated against Coles Express, the company lost its single largest customer. In order to cut costs, management decided to close all company terminals south of the state of Maine. After the first day of the strike, Coles Express had shrunk to barely one-third of its former size. But offers of assistance to provide extra trucks and drivers poured in from loyal customers and other carrier companies. With this help, the company was able to continue operations and bring in needed revenue. By the end of the strike, Coles Express had regained approximately 75 percent of its business and had become a non-union shop.

Still under the direction of Galen Cole, the company created Cole Transportation systems, a highly innovative computer software development service. This unit began to successfully sell software for delivery companies nationwide. In 1988, the firm established Cole Training Institute, a training school for individuals to learn how to operate a tractor/trailer and forklift. Management at Coles Express regarded the formation of this school as part of its duty to the state of Maine in order to help alleviate the shortage of freight carrier drivers at the time. By the late 1980s, the Cole family business was made up of Cole Express, A.J. Cole & Sons, Cole Properties, A.J. Cole Tire, Cole Warehouse and Distribution, Cole Computer Services, and Cole Training Institute. The company had developed into the one of the most successful, and provided the most extensive trucking services, throughout the entire New England region.

Under Cole family management, the company became known for commitment to its employees and to the people of the state of Maine. In 1958, management set up a company-financed profit sharing plan whose value, by the end of the 1980s, actually approached the net worth of the company. During the mid-1970s, Galen Cole purchased a farm near Bangor and established a setting where orphans and troubled youth could develop their skills in farming. Company employees were also one of the first organized corporate groups in Maine to become involved with the Literacy Volunteers of America in order to help reduce adult illiteracy in the state. In addition, the company funded a not-for-profit museum, the Cole Transportation Museum, to educate the populace about the more primitive automobiles and construction methods employed in the transportation industry during the early years of the 20th century.

During the late 1980s and early 1990s, the trucking industry suffered from the effects of a recession. When this economic downturn was combined with the deregulation of the trucking industry, all of the truckers and freight companies were dramatically affected. The easing of regulations within the industry encouraged the formation of companies in order to take advantage of the market, but this quickly led to widespread overcapacity and rate battles where profit margins became precariously thin. Many small regional trucking firms, like Coles Express, were threatened by the low rates of national carrier companies that could rely on economies of scale to help them through difficult financial periods. Still, thousands of both large and small truck carriers went out of business, while many of those remaining turned to acquisitions and mergers in order to remain competitive and survive.

During this period of upheaval within the entire trucking industry, Coles Express was purchased by Roadway Services Inc., a long-distance trucking firm that had implemented a strategy of acquisition and expansion into related shipping areas to offset the harmful effects of the recession and deregulation. Acquired through lengthy negotiations during 1992 and 1993, Coles Express was brought under the larger national umbrella of Roadway Services. The acquisition was beneficial for both companies. Coles Express was provided with the funds it needed to stabilize and expand its services throughout the New England region, while Roadway Services benefitted by extending its growing network into new regions.

As a division of Roadway Services, Coles Express nevertheless sought to distinguish itself as an industry leader in its niche. The company continued to open new terminals, establishing facilities in Pittsburgh and Altoona, Pennsylvania, as well as in Newburgh, New York, in the 1990s. Moreover, in 1995, the company initiated a "small shipment express" service, which featured, in the words of *Traffic Management*'s Ray Bohman, "a new pricing scheme to compete with the less-than-truckload services being offered by trucking companies."

Further Reading

Bohman, Ray, "The Battle for LTL Freight Heats Up," *Traffic Management*, June 1995, p. 68.
——, "Truckers in Small Shipment Press," *Gifts & Decorative Accessories*, July 1995, p. 46.
Bradley, Peter, "Making The Grade," *Purchasing*, July 16, 1992, p. 54.
Cole, Galen, *Allie Cole: A Maine Pioneer*. Portland, Maine: Casco Printing Company: 1980.
Cole, Galen, *The Cole Family of Businesses*, New York: Newcomen Society, 1989.
Graves, Jacqueline, "Truck Sales Keep On Trucking," *Fortune*, October 17, 1994, p. 19.
Hamilton, Dana, "Only The Fittest Survive," *Journal of Commerce*, January 10, 1994, p. S55.
Mehta, Stephanie, "Keep On Trucking? That Will Be Tough With Deregulation Small Firms Say," *The Wall Street Journal*, December 30, 1994, p. B2.
"Truckers Face A Hard Road," *Purchasing*, December 16, 1993, p. 39.

—Thomas Derdak

Columbia/HCA Healthcare Corporation

One Park Plaza
P.O. Box 550
Nashville, Tennessee 37202-0550
U.S.A.
(615) 327-9551
Fax: (615) 320-2331

Public Company
Incorporated: 1987 as Columbia Hospital Corp.
Employees: 220,000
Sales: $17 billion (1995 est.)
Stock Exchanges: New York
SICs: 8062 General Medical & Surgical Hospitals; 8063
   Psychiatric Hospitals

From a $250,000 investment in 1987, Columbia/HCA Healthcare Corporation has grown to become the largest healthcare services provider in the United States, owning and operating 340 hospitals, 125 outpatient centers, and 182 home health agencies, for revenues topping $17 billion in 1996. Led from the beginning by Richard L. Scott, Columbia/HCA combines past industry leaders Galen Health Care—the hospital network spin-off of Humana—acquired by Columbia in 1993; Hospital Corporation of America (HCA), merged in 1994; Medical Care America, acquired in 1994; and Healthtrust, merged in 1995. Columbia/HCA operates hospitals in 36 states, and in England and Switzerland, with principal holdings focused in Texas, Florida, Louisiana, Tennessee, Kentucky, Virginia, and Georgia, and plans to add 30 to 40 hospitals each year through the end of the century. Joining Scott, who functions as president and chief executive officer, are former HCA head Thomas Frist, Jr. and former Healthtrust chief R. Clayton McWhorter, who serve as vice-chairman and chairman, respectively.

Birth of a Healthcare Giant

Richard Scott, a Kansas City, Missouri, native and graduate of the University of Missouri and Southern Methodist Univer-

sity Law School, was 34 years old when he teamed up with Richard Rainwater, a Fort Worth financier, to form the Columbia Healthcare Corporation in 1987. Scott had been trying to start up a hospital operation, with a goal of creating a national healthcare provider network, but his initial approaches to hospital executives, including HCA's Frist, were rebuffed. Then Scott teamed up with Rainwater, whose credentials included acting as the Bass family financial advisor, and who also served as a director on HCA's board. Operating out of Rainwater's investment company, their first move was to purchase two El Paso, Texas hospitals for $60 million. Scott and Rainwater each put up $125,000 and financed the purchase with $65 million from Citicorp.

Both hospitals were poorly managed and in need of repair. Scott and Rainwater set out to reform operations, complete renovations, and along the way earned the goodwill of the hospitals' physicians. Next, Columbia and a group of physician investors formed El Paso Healthcare System, Ltd. (EPHS) as a limited partnership, which acquired the hospitals from Columbia, along with two physician-owned diagnostic centers, in exchange for partnership shares. The physician partnership would eventually gain a 40 percent share in EPHS, setting a pattern for much of Columbia's future dealings.

Five months after its formation, Columbia moved aggressively to consolidate its El Paso operations. EPHS purchased two new facilities, the general medical/surgical Landmark Medical Center and the adjacent Stanton Medical Building. Landmark, operating in the overbedded El Paso market, had 355 beds but only a 54-bed average daily census. EPHS's response was to close Landmark and transfer its patients and equipment to EPHS's existing hospitals. Landmark and the adjacent building were then sold to a local real estate developer. From this move, EPHS increased the average daily census at its other facilities by 35 patients, bringing an earnings (EBDIT) increase of $3.5 million, to $8.9 million EBDIT on 1988 revenues of $43 million.

In December 1988, Columbia and EPHS moved closer to its goal of becoming a full-service system, when EPHS opened its Sun Towers Behavioral Health Center, an 80-bed free-standing psychiatric facility. The behavioral health program from Sun Towers Hospital was transferred to the new facility, expanding the hospital's bed count. In its first year of operation, the psychiatric facility recorded a $2.5 million EBDIT; within two years, its average daily census increased from 11 patients to 45 patients. EPHS continued to expand its system, opening its Lifecare Center, which combined a cardiopulmonary rehabilitation facility with an outpatient wellness center. In 1989, EPHS introduced its One Source medical services program, marketing to major area employers, which provided discounts at EPHS system facilities. Within a year, One Source grew to nearly 15,000 members, generating $6.5 million in revenues.

Between 1988 and 1990, EPHS's systemwide average daily census grew from 174 patients to 303 patients. Revenues jumped to $113 million in 1989 and to nearly $135 million in 1990. EBDIT for 1990 was $27.7 million.

In 1990, EPHS continued to consolidate its El Paso position, acquiring two diagnostic imaging centers, beginning construction on a 296,000-square-foot medical office building, and initiating plans for a 29,000-square-foot oncology center. Both new facilities were connected to Sun Towers Hospital by glass-enclosed skywalks.

By 1990, however, EPHS formed only part of Columbia's growing empire. Scott had already begun to conquer new markets, purchasing the nearly bankrupt 300-bed Victoria Hospital in Miami in 1988 and expanding this new operation to four Miami hospitals by 1990. In that year, Columbia moved into the Corpus Christi, Texas market as well. In these new markets, Scott continued his successful El Paso strategy of creating a full-service healthcare network of facilities, while creating limited partnerships with physician investors.

These partnerships would generate the most criticism for Columbia's strategy. Such partnerships risked the danger of physician-partners overtreating their patients in an effort to drive up their own profits. Yet, these partnerships instead seemed to predict the rise of HMOs that would sweep the U.S. health insurance industry by the mid-1990s, by encouraging physicians toward greater efficiency and lower costs of treatment.

Columbia's total revenues were already approaching the half-billion mark by 1990. Scott next engineered two important deals. The first, the merger acquisition of Smith Laboratories and its subsidiary, Sutter Corp., in a stock swap of 3.3 million shares, led Columbia to go public. The second was a landmark joint venture with Medical Care America of Dallas, then the largest surgery center network in the country, in building a $50 million hospital in Corpus Christi.

Scott was on the acquisition trail. In 1990 Columbia made a $22 million cash purchase of HEI Corporation, Inc. (which it sold off again the following year), bringing the company into the Houston market. In September 1990 the company, through a limited partnership, acquired Coral Reef Hospital for nearly $18 million in cash and notes, and one month later acquired Southside Community Hospital for nearly $4.5 million, bringing Columbia's network to 11 hospitals. Its emphasis on full-service systems proved successful, and revenues grew not only by adding new hospitals to the chain, but also by attracting higher numbers of patients. More acquisitions followed over the next

two years, including the $185 million acquisition of Indianapolis-based Basic American Medical, with four hospitals in the Ft. Lauderdale market. By the end of 1992, Columbia's network had grown to 24 hospitals and over $1 billion in assets. Revenues passed $800 million, with EBITDA of $136 million.

The Mega-Mergers

By 1993, Scott, known to keep a paperweight on his desk reading "If you are not the lead dog, the view never changes," was ready to launch Columbia as a national healthcare provider. In June of that year, Columbia announced its intention to merge with Galen Health Care, raising its number of hospitals four times and catapulting its revenues past $5 billion. Scott remained in control of the newly renamed Columbia Healthcare Corporation.

Galen, with 74 hospitals in 1993, had formerly been part of Humana. Founded in 1968, Humana had been an earlier success story in the hospital network field, building the second largest hospital chain operation in the United States by 1979. During the 1980s, Humana entered the health insurance business, and by the late 1980s, was forced to divide its operations, as its hospitals and insurance business began competing with each other, especially as rival insurance agencies began directing their customers to other providers. By the early 1990s, Humana's hospital network was faltering, and in early 1993 the hospitals were spun off as Galen Health Care.

Under the terms of the merger, a stock swap worth $3.2 billion, Galen's stockholders received 0.775 shares of Columbia stock for each Galen share they held. Galen brought the number of Columbia hospitals to 94, adding 15 new markets—primarily metropolitan areas—to the chain, and bringing Columbia a presence in 19 states, as well as England and Switzerland. With 22,000 licensed beds, Columbia became the largest non-governmental hospital chain in the U.S., and second only to the Veteran's Affairs Department's 64,700-bed system.

In October 1993, one month after the Galen merger was consummated, Scott shook up the industry again by announcing an agreement to merge Columbia with Hospital Corp. of America. HCA had been formed by Frist family and Kentucky Fried Chicken founder Jack Massey in 1968 and grew steadily, reaching 50 hospitals by 1973 and 376 hospitals, including holdings in seven countries, by 1983. When changes in Medicare payments and the rise of HMOs began to depress its per-bed census rates, HCA moved to trim its hospital count, spinning off 102 hospitals to physician investors—which became Healthtrust, Inc.—in the late 1980s. In 1989, Frist, Jr. took control of the company in a leveraged buyout, and continued to sell off hospitals for the next three years before taking the company public again in 1992. By the time of the Columbia merger, HCA added 96 hospitals to Columbia's 94, creating the largest hospital chain in the United States.

Renamed Columbia/HCA Healthcare Corporation, the company formally merged in February 1994 in a stock swap worth $5.7 billion, creating a $10 billion company with operations in 26 states. Scott was named chief executive officer, while Frist became chairman. As HMOs, already notorious for their emphasis on tight cost control, achieved dominance in the private insurance industry, and government agencies too were beginning to tighten their reimbursement policies, Columbia/HCA moved to consolidate its formerly regional and local operations—including payroll, marketing, and purchasing—into its Louisville, Kentucky, corporate headquarters, creating in effect a national organization. Scott's initial $125,000 investment was by then worth $200 million.

Scott continued to eye new acquisitions and joint ventures, turning now to the non-profit hospital market, including the 585-bed Cedars Medical Center of Miami, and joint ventures with university medical schools and teaching hospitals, including the University of Miami, the University of Louisville, Tulane University, Emory University, the Medical College of Virginia, and the Medical University of South Carolina. Scott's next step was the $860 million purchase of Medical Care America, Inc., the largest provider of outpatient surgery services, in May 1994.

Scott was not yet finished, however. In September 1994, news broke that National Medical Enterprises planned to purchase Healthtrust and American Medical International, in a deal reported to be worth $10 billion that would have given NME a strong second place behind Columbia/HCA. However, in October 1994, Healthtrust instead agreed to be acquired by Columbia for $5.6 billion. Healthtrust's 116 hospitals brought the Columbia chain to 311 facilities, making it the 12th-largest employer in the United States and the 45th-largest in revenues—$14.5 billion for the 1994 fiscal year. Importantly, the Healthtrust acquisition expanded Columbia beyond its traditionally urban base, with Healthtrust's concentration of rural hospitals.

The Healthtrust merger was completed in April 1995, with Healthtrust stockholders receiving 0.88 Columbia shares for each share of Healthtrust stock. By then, Columbia had already completed several more acquisitions, including Colorado-based Rose Healthcare System, St. Francis Hospital of Charleston, West Virginia, and Angelo Community Hospital of San Angelo, Texas. Following the Healthtrust acquisition, Columbia announced acquisitions of The Family Clinic Ltd. of Little Rock, Arkansas, and a number of hospitals, including three in metropolitan Chicago.

By the beginning of 1996, Columbia/HCA had grown to 340 hospitals, 125 outpatient surgery centers, and a range of other healthcare facilities, including 182 home health agencies, with 70,000 licensed beds in 36 states, and England and Switzerland. Revenues had topped $17 billion, and the company held more than $18 billion in assets. In early 1996, the next step for Columbia seemed to be entering the insurance market, when the company was reported to be in negotiations with Blue Cross & Blue Shield of Ohio to enter a joint venture taking over that company's managed care business. Since Humana's failed attempt in the 1980s, the $700 billion healthcare market was seen to have changed enough to signal a slowdown to growth through acquisition, in favor of vertical integration of the business. With Richard Scott's record of the last decade, it seemed certain that he would lead Columbia to become a powerhouse in this area as well.

Principal Subsidiaries

Birmingham Outpatient Surgical Center, Inc.; Columbia/HCA Montgomery Healthcare System, Inc.; Galen Medical Corporation; Montgomery Regional Medical Center, Inc.; Surgicenters of America, Inc.; HCA Health Services of California, Inc.; Kingsbury Capital Partners, Inc.; MCA Management Partnership, Ltd.; Psychiatric Company of California Inc.; Sugical Centers of Sourthern California, Inc.; Sutter Corporation; Colorado Healthcare Management Inc.; HCA Health Services of Colorado, Inc.; Health Care Indemnity, Inc.; MOVCO, Inc.; AlternaCare Corp.; Amedicorp, Inc.; CHC Holdings, Inc.; Critical Care America, Inc.; Galen Health Care, Inc.; HCA Invesments, Inc.; HCA International.

Further Reading

Sandy Lutz. "Columbia on the Fast Track," *Modern Healthcare*, September 6, 1993, p. 10.
——, "Industry Follows, Fears the Leader," *Modern Healthcare*, February 14, 1994, p. 23.
——, "Columbia/HCA Nabs Healthtrust," *Modern Healthcare*, October 10, 1994, p. 2.
——, "Columbia Keeps on Growing," *Modern Healthcare*, March 6, 1995, p. 2.
Matt Walsh. "More Patients, Please," *Forbes*, October 10, 1994, p. 72.

—M.L. Cohen

Commercial Metals Company

7800 Stemmons Freeway
Dallas, Texas 75247
U.S.A.
(214) 689-4300
Fax: (214) 689-4320

Public Company
Incorporated: 1946
Employees: 6,272
Sales: $2.10 billion (1995)
Stock Exchanges: New York
SICs: 3341 Secondary Nonferrous Metals; 3351 Copper
Rolling & Drawing; 5093 Scrap & Waste Materials

One of the largest scrap processors in the United States, Commercial Metals Company recycles, manufactures, trades, and markets steel and metal products through more than 90 worldwide locations. During the mid-1990s, Commercial Metals operated more than 30 scrap yards and processing plants in the southern and southwestern United States, where the company began collecting and selling scrap metal in 1915. During the 1960s, Commercial Metals entered the manufacturing side of the scrap metal business, amassing four steel mini-mills by the 1990s. In addition to its domestic processing and manufacturing operations, the company was supported by a network of worldwide trading operations.

The resurgence of the U. S. economy following the conclusion of the Second World War obliterated any lingering affects of the country's decade-long, financial free fall during the 1930s, invigorating businesses and industries across the nation. For the decades to follow, a general and wide-sweeping era of prosperity reigned, increasing the magnitude of the country's major industries and engendering the rise of subsidiary, or minor, industries to levels of importance and worth substantially higher than during the first half of the 20th century.

Among other major industries in the United States, the metals industry achieved robust growth during the post-war era,

strengthened by an increasing demand for metals as manufacturers labored to produce larger quantities of consumer and industrial products. As the country's metals needs mounted, the metals industry was propelled forward, recording growth that closely paralleled the growth of the U.S. population following the war, but as the need for metals increased, the primary reserves of metallic ores dwindled, a natural effect of ravenous demand that dramatically altered the stature of the country's scrap metals industry. For decades, scrap metals companies had represented a largely insignificant segment of the broad-based metals industry, earning little compared to the manufacturers of virgin metal and suffering from the opprobrious image as junkyard peddlers. All this changed when soaring metals demand threatened to deplete ore reserves and technological advancements lowered the processing costs associated with converting scrap metals into "new" metals. Long the shunned stepchildren of the metals industry, scrap metals companies underwent a significant transformation, becoming integral contributors to annual production volume and, along the way, garnering a greater share of the revenues generated by the metals industry as a whole. By purchasing scrap metals from small individual dealers, salvage firms, manufacturing facilities, refineries, automobile wreckers, and other sources, and then processing the materials through giant presses, power shears, or shredders, scrap metal companies became essential suppliers of recycled metals to primary metals processors, carving a lasting position for themselves within the metals industry.

Such was the case for Commercial Metals, a scrap metals company that struggled to survive during its early years, then blossomed into one of the largest companies of its kind during the halcyon years following the Second World War. The company's historical roots stretch back to 1915, when Moses Feldman started a scrap metals company named American Iron & Metal Company. Feldman, who emigrated from Russia and settled in Houston ten years before he founded American Iron & Metal, superintended his company's growth during its early years, then was joined by son, Jacob Feldman, who eventually would take control of the company. The younger Feldman joined the family business after he graduated from Southern Methodist University and in 1932, with the help of family members, formed a brokerage house in Dallas named Commercial Metals Company to buttress the family's scrap operations. In 1946, the two family-owned operations were incorporated, just as the scrap metals industry as a whole began to burgeon, with the combined company's first acquisition occurring seven years later, when Jacob Feldman negotiated the purchase of the Charles Harley Company, a California-based scrap metals processor founded in 1856.

By the beginning of the 1960s, nearly five decades of operation had built a roughly $50 million company, one that was ready to take on the trappings characterizing Commercial Metals during the 1990s. In 1960, ownership of Commercial Metals changed from private to public hands when the company became the first independent metals firm to be listed on the American Stock Exchange. The switch to public ownership ushered in a period of diversification and expansion, touching off the first definitive surge of growth recorded by the company.

Entering the decade, Commercial Metals' scrap business was thriving, educing Jacob Feldman to diversify the company's interests and branch into manufacturing. During the 1960s, Feldman orchestrated the acquisition of a small steel manufacturer, a copper fabricator, and then later he started another steel mini-mill, making Commercial Metals one of the few scrap metals companies to operate its own steel mills. The broadening of the company's interests began in 1963, when Commercial Metals acquired 74 percent interest in Structural Metals, Inc. Located in Seguin, Texas, near San Antonio, Structural Metals operated an electric furnace steel mill that provided Commercial Metals with a new source of sales and increased the company's market for its own processed raw materials. The remaining percentage of Structural Metals, which constituted Commercial Metals' largest operating division during the 1990s, was purchased between 1963 and 1969, pushing the company's sales upward as more and more of the electric furnace steel mill came under Commercial Metals' ownership. Annual sales swelled from slightly less than $60 million in 1963 to nearly $150 million four years later, while the company's net income leaped from just under $600,000 to $1.85 million during the four-year period.

The acquisition of Structural Metals provided a significant boost to Commercial Metals' standing in the scrap metals industry, distinguishing it as a model for other scrap metals companies to emulate as they too diversified into the manufacturing side of the business, but the financial growth recorded during the 1960s was also fueled by the company's accomplishments overseas. During the years bridging the conclusion of the Second World War and the completion of the Structural Metals acquisition, Commercial Metals had extended its corporate reach overseas, establishing metals trading offices in key foreign markets. By the late 1960s, Commercial Metals ranked as the largest single exporter of ferrous scrap metals in the United States and one of the largest competitors in the metals industry in the world, deriving nearly half of its annual sales from abroad, particularly from Japan and Mexico, the company's two largest export markets. Its sixth international office was opened at the end of 1967 in Zug, Switzerland, complementing the company's other trading offices in Amsterdam, Tokyo, Taipei, Montreal, and Mexico City. In total, the growing Commercial Metals empire comprised 32 plants and offices in the United States and abroad by the late 1960s, positioning it as a major competitor in what was becoming an increasingly important and lucrative global industry.

The company continued to expand its international network as it entered the 1970s, recording financial growth as its foreign offices solidified their position in respective overseas markets. In 1970, three years into its program to foster trade in Central and Latin American countries, Commercial Metals generated nearly $290 million in sales and earned nearly $6.5 million in net income, the product of the company's resolute expansion during the 1960s. As the decade began, Commercial Metals was obtaining half of its annual sales and 40 percent of its profits from direct trading operations, while, comparatively, the company was deriving a third of it sales volume from the processing of secondary metals, nine percent from manufacturing operations, and the balance from the production of semi-finished products and other metals-related businesses.

By virtue of its success as a broker, manufacturer, and processor of scrap metals, Commercial Metals soared to the top of its industry, ranking as one of the largest independent companies on the country, but after the encouraging results of 1970, Jacob Feldman suffered a coronary and the company's financial health likewise deteriorated. Though Feldman remained titular head of the company following his coronary in 1971, Charlie Merritt, who joined Commercial Metals in 1937 as a stenographer, essentially assumed control of the company, taking responsibility for its day-to-day operation. Under Merritt's stewardship, Commercial Metals' financial growth came to an abrupt halt, but the blame did not rest on Merritt's shoulders. A nationwide recession and laggard demand overseas combined to hamper Commercial Metals' growth, curtailing production volume at its 22 scrap processing plants and diminishing its scrap metals trading activities. Annual sales declined as a result, plunging from $287 million in 1970 to $207 million in 1971, then slipped again the following year, falling to $200 million.

Despite the retrogressive financial slide, Commercial Metals continued to be regarded as one of the largest independent worldwide processors and brokers of secondary metals, so when national economic conditions rallied and ferrous scrap prices rose to as high as $100 a ton, the company benefitted commensurately. Annual sales eclipsed $320 million in 1973, then nearly doubled the following year, reaching $643 million, while earnings nearly quadrupled, soaring to more than $19 million.

Once the company's financial health was restored, it diversified into new areas and into new metals. Commercial Metals expanded its vital trading business into commodities such as coal, then bolstered its core businesses when it acquired part interest in two companies in 1976, Corpus Christi, Texas-based General Export Iron and Metals Company and Mobile, Alabama-based Pinto Island Metals Company.

Entering the 1980s, the company was once again subjected to recessionary economic conditions, its financial health drained by the pernicious affects of an anemic economy. Like a decade earlier, however, the passing of time healed all wounds. When the economy recovered, Commercial Metals resumed its strategy of controlled growth and strengthening its core businesses. In 1984, the company acquired Connors Steel Co.'s mini-mill in Birmingham, Alabama. Next, the company acquired Galveston,

Texas-based Island City Iron & Supply Inc. in January 1984, then purchased two additional companies, Newell Recycling Co. and Richelson Iron and Metal, later in 1984.

The following year, 1985, marked Commercial Metals' 70th year of business, a milestone that marked the passing of two world wars and numerous economic hills and valleys since Moses Feldman had arrived in Galveston and founded American Iron & Metals Company. Over the course of seven decades, Commercial Metals had evolved into an internationally recognized firm, involved in three main metals-related businesses through the manufacturing and fabrication of steel products and copper tubing, the recycling of ferrous and non-ferrous scrap metals, and the marketing and trading of metals products and raw materials. As the company moved past its anniversary year, it endeavored to augment its core businesses, acquiring Industrial Salvage in Corpus Christi in 1988, two scrap metal yards in Victoria, Texas in 1989, and the processing operations belonging to three Florida-based and one Tennessee-based companies in 1990.

The new decade brought the familiar refrain of economic malaise in the United States, but Commercial Metals emerged from the recessive early 1990s with dynamic vigor, its recovery engendered by the gradual recovery of the economy and the strides gained by steel mini-mills. Mini-mills such as Nucor Corporation and Birmingham Steel Corporation relied heavily on scrap steel to feed their manufacturing facilities, a dependence that buoyed the price of scrap and fueled Commercial Metals' resurgence. During the 1980s, mini-mills began to wrest away market share from large steel corporations, increasing their share of total steel production in the country from 25 percent to 35 percent. As mini-mills grew in stature, producing increasingly greater amounts of the nation's steel output, the price of scrap rose as demand increased, providing Commercial Metals with a much needed boost to its business. Once economic conditions regained their pre-recessionary vitality, Commercial Metals began to realize the financial benefits accrued from the burgeoning mini-mill industry. During the first nine months of 1993, the company's revenues increased 44 percent, while its profits exploded exponentially, jumping a prodigious 135 percent.

With scrap prices remaining at enviable levels, Commercial Metals moved to expand its operations in 1994. In August, the company acquired Jacksonville, Florida-based Tri-State Recycling Corporation, then at the end of the year completed its acquisition of Columbia, South Carolina-based Owen Steel Co. Inc. for $50 million. The addition of Owen Steel, which was renamed SMI-Owen Steel Co. Inc. and absorbed by Commercial Metals' largest manufacturing division, Commercial Metals Steel Group, increased annual steel production capacity to more than 1.7 million tons and raised steel fabrication capacity to more than 500,000 tons.

As Commercial Metals entered the mid-1990s and prepared for the remainder of the 1990s, its expectations for future growth were optimistic, predicated on the anticipated increasing demand for scrap metals and its own stalwart position within the industry as a diversified secondary metals processor, broker, and manufacturer. Lending credence to the company's confidence in achieving sustained growth, sales increased strongly in

1995, climbing from $1.65 billion to $2.10 billion. More encouraging, the company's earnings ballooned between 1994 and 1995, soaring 44 percent to $38.2 million. As these financial records were being achieved, the company strengthened its processing capabilities further, acquiring the assets of three Texas scrap processing facilities, Atlas Iron & Metal, Federal Iron & Metal, and Laredo Scrap Metals, in September 1995, then began charting plans for the future, intent on building the business first developed by Moses Feldman in 1915.

Principal Operating Units

CMC Steel Group; Steel Fabrication and Warehousing; Concrete Related Products Warehousing; Industrial Products; Scrap Processing; Copper Tube Manufacturing; Secondary Metals Processing; Railroad Salvage

Principal Subsidiaries

CMC (Australia) Pty. Ltd.; CMC Commercio de Metias, Ltda. (Brazil); CMC Concrete Accessories, Inc. (90%); CMC Fareast Ltd. (Hong Kong); CMC Finanz A.G. (Switzerland); CMC Information Systems, Inc.; CMC International (S.E. Asia) Pte. Ltd. (Singapore); CMC Oil Co.; CMC Process Products. Inc.; CMC Steel Holding Co.; CMC Steel Fabricators, Inc.; CMC Trading AG (Switzerland); CSC Engineering, Inc.; Cometals (Canada), Ltee.; Cometals China, Inc.; Cometals Far East, Inc.; Cometals, Inc.; Cometals International, S.A. (Belgium); Commercial Metals - Austin Inc.; Commercial Metals Company, Holding A.G. (Switzerland); Commercial Metals Overseas Export Co.; Commercial Metals Overseas Export (FSC) Corp.; Commercial Metals Railroad Salvage Co.; Commercial Metals SF/JV Co.; Commonwealth Metal Corp.; Daltrading Ltd. (Switzerland); Enterprise Metal Corp.; Howell Metal Co.; Mini-Mill Consultants, Inc.; Regency Advertising Agency, Inc.; SMI Steel Inc.; Structural Metals, Inc.; Zenith Finance & Construction Co.

Further Reading

"Commercial Metals Sees Sales Increase as Economy Improves," *American Metal Market,* June 30, 1993, p. 3.
"Commercial, Owen Deal Complete," *American Metal Market,* December 2, 1994, p. 3.
Goodfriend, Martin I., "Commercial Metals Co.," *Wall Street Transcript,* December 18, 1972, p. 31,190.
Goodwin, Morgan E., "CMC Acquires Three Scrap Yards in Texas," *American Metal Market,* September 4, 1995, p. 8.
Haflich, Frank, "CMC Expands Global Market," *American Metal Market,* August 30, 1990, p. 2.
Lawton, Clark, "Commercial Metals Expands and Diversifies to Process Scrap Metals for World Markets," *Investment Dealers' Digest,* August 5, 1968, p. 51.
Lubove, Seth, "Golden Grunge," *Forbes,* August 2, 1993, p. 103.
Rabin, Stanley, "Commercial Metals Looks Ahead," *American Metal Market,* May 18, 1988, p. 19.
"Scrap Is Beautiful," *Forbes,* May 1, 1975, p.26.
Sherman, Joseph V., "Sophisticated Scrap," *Barron's,* December 4, 1967, p. 3.
Willat, Norris, "More Than Warehouses," *Barron's,* April 27, 1964, p. 5.
Worden, Edward, "CMC Zeroing in on Steel Market," *American Metal Market,* April 15, 1988, p. 4.

—Jeffrey L. Covell

Community Psychiatric Centers

6600 West Charleston Boulevard
Suite 118
Las Vegas, Nevada 89102
U.S.A.
(702) 259-3600
Fax: (702) 259-3650

Public Company
Incorporated: 1969
Employees: 9,775
Sales: $427.7 million
Stock Exchanges: New York Boston Chicago Pacific
SICs: 8063 Psychiatric Hospitals; 8069 Specialty
Hospitals Except Psychiatric; 8082 Home Health Care
Services

Community Psychiatric Centers was one of the largest chains of investor-owned psychiatric hospitals in the United States and Britain, as well as a provider of long-term critical care in the early 1990s. At the end of 1995, however, it announced plans to sell its U.S. psychiatric operations.

CPC was founded in California in 1968 by Robert L. Green and James W. Conte. The two had already been working together when they founded CPC as part of an effort to link two private neighborhood hospitals; Alhambra Psychiatric Hospital in Rosemead, California, and Belmont Hills Psychiatric Hospital near San Francisco. In so doing they founded the concept of creating a multi-hospital system by joining community-based psychiatric centers.

The development of psychotropic drugs in the 1960s to fight mental illness made it possible for psychiatric patients to stay in the hospital for much a shorter time. With psychiatric expenses no longer potentially unlimited, many insurers began to cover mental illness. Hospitals like Alhambra and Belmont were founded partly to treat patients who had to be treated in state mental institutions until the development of psychotropic drugs. When CPC linked these hospitals it reduced operating and administrative costs by centralizing functions like finance, purchasing, construction, and design. Because community hospitals (compared to state facilities) usually offered convenient locations, a good environment, and specialized treatment, CPC's founders believed that demand for their concept would increase.

In June 1969 CPC went public, with Robert Green as its first president. Its headquarters was located in San Francisco. In 1970 newly constructed facilities opened in Santa Ana and Pomona, California. The firm also bought a hospital in West Los Angeles, bringing it into a huge new market. In 1971 it expanded further, buying Fairfax Hospital in Seattle. The firm diversified beyond psychiatric care in 1973 when it bought a Los Angeles-area dialysis company that operated three units. CPC also expanded to the East, opening St. John's River Hospital in Jacksonville, Florida.

In 1975, a new federal law (the Certificate of Need law) caused a nationwide slowdown in hospital expansion, making it harder for CPC to grow. Still, by 1975 the firm operated ten hospitals with 747 beds in five states. CPC had five dialysis centers in California, and by 1977 it had become the second-largest dialysis provider in the United States. Many competitors sprang up during the firm's first 15 years, but many of them spent heavily on advertising and other overhead, leaving them indebted and inefficient.

CPC joined the New York Stock Exchange in 1978. It then bought Priory Hospital, London's largest, oldest private psychiatry hospital. CPC used it to start the Priory Hospitals Group, which became the second-largest British provider of private acute psychiatric care (only the state-run National Health Service was larger).

Investor-owned psychiatric hospital chains boomed in the 1980s. A large part of this growth was fueled by generous employee benefit packages that paid for employees to pursue in-patient care for mental health problems, as well as drug and alcohol abuse. These plans were lucrative for psychiatric hospitals, which billed an average of $500 per patient day. Hospitals had operating profits of 35 to 45 percent from such patients. In

1983 CPC diversified into home healthcare through the purchase of Personal Care Health Services Corporation.

In 1985 the Certificate of Need law was nullified in several states, and CPC began a major construction program to beef up its hospital division. It added seven new hospitals in 1986, seven more in 1987, and another four in 1988, including one in Puerto Rico. In 1989 CPC's dialysis and home health business was spun off as a separate public company called Vivra Incorporated. Chairman Robert Green left the firm to head Vivra, and James Conte took his place. Richard L. Conte, formerly general counsel, became president and chief financial officer and oversaw the United Kingdom hospital division. CPC moved its headquarters downstate, from San Francisco to Laguna Hills.

In 1990, CPC bought two more psychiatric hospitals, while in 1991 the firm built its last new psychiatric hospital to date. The firm had grown at an impressive rate, always meeting its goal of annual earnings-per-share growth of 15 to 20 percent. Its operating margins were around 35 percent and its return on equity averaged more than 20 percent. On the basis of that strength, *Forbes* magazine labelled the firm ''the class act of the country's psychiatric hospital chains.'' But in the early 1990s the psychiatric market changed dramatically and CPC's growth stalled.

Corporations were rebelling against the rising cost of these mental health benefits, which were rising between 30 percent and 50 percent a year (more than twice the rise in other segments of the healthcare market). Critics charged that most plans gave hospitals no reason to release patients before their insurance benefits were exhausted. The industry was hurt by allegations that some psychiatric hospitals held patients against their will, then kicked them out when their benefits expired.

Because of the rising costs, many employers began using insurers and managed care companies to help reduce their costs. As a result, hospital admission standards were toughened and more employees were treated as outpatients. Insurers demanded shorter hospital stays and large discounts. Managed care became an important component of the psychiatry business, and it hurt revenues of psychiatric hospitals across the United States. Managed care and negotiated group discounts resulted in profit margin reduction to around 22 percent by 1991, and sometimes as low as ten percent. Since the late 1980s, moreover, the average length of patient hospitalization had shrunk from four weeks to three, then to less than two. Psychiatric hospitals across the United States were hit by these changes, and many closed.

Between 1988 and 1990, the percentage of managed rates in CPC's patient population climbed to 33 percent from only 12 percent. In the early 1990s CPC decided to adapt to this changed environment. It negotiated with managed care providers trying to increase its patient volume enough to offset the lower profits from each patient. Even so, the firm experienced its first loss in 1991. Upset about a plunge in the CPC's stock price, angry investors filed a class action suit against CPC. That same year Texas, Florida, and New Jersey launched investigations into for-profit psychiatric hospitals, causing a public relations disaster for the industry.

In the midst of these troubles, CPC head James Conte retired in 1992 and was replaced by Richard Conte, his son. CDC decided to switch gears, reformulating itself from a psychiatric hospital company into what it termed ''an integrated behavioral health delivery system.'' The firm diversified into the growing market for long-term critical care, hoping to escape the tightening psychiatric market. CPC launched a new subsidiary, Transitional Hospitals Corp., to develop and operate long-term critical care units with CPC hospitals, as well as to acquire or lease critical care units outside of CPC. The subsidiary offered long-term hospitalization for patients who required intensive nursing care as they recovered from a catastrophic illness or accident. Such patients needed services including life-support systems, post-surgical stabilization, intravenous therapy, and wound care. When opening hospitals, Transitional looked for large markets with a large proportion of elderly residents. Many of its patients were dependent on ventilators.

In 1993 CDC decided to reduce costs of its U.S. psychiatric division, and announced it would close as many as ten of its 44 hospitals. In 1994, CDC moved its headquarters again, this time to Las Vegas. By this point, the average hospital stay of a CPC patient had dropped to less than 11 days for an adult, down from four weeks about ten years earlier. In contrast to the troubles besetting the firm in the United States, its British division experienced its best year ever in 1994, with net operating revenues of $46.2 million. The Priory Hospital Group expanded its bed capacity by a third, and bought hospitals in Bristol, Reifate, and North West Surrey, giving the group a total of 13, including one joint-venture hospital.

CPC made $10.2 million in 1994 on revenues of $427.7 million. Its Psychiatric Care Operations offered five major services and programs. Inpatient treatment was geared toward patients who needed constant supervision. Residential treatment was offered to adolescents requiring more structured care than they could get in outpatient care. The firm had 21 residential treatment centers, each with a psychiatrist and 24-hour nursing. Partial hospitalization was designed for patients not requiring constant supervision. Patients were treated for six to 12 hours a day, up to seven days a week, around other requirements like work or school. Intensive outpatient programs were offered to patients requiring routine observation. Treatment was given three to four hours a day, usually three or four days a week. Outpatient treatment was the least intensive. It generally involved 45 to 90 minutes of individual, family, or group therapy on a scheduled basis.

By early 1995 the Transitional Hospitals subsidiary operated 14 facilities from Massachusetts to California. It relocated its headquarters from Atlanta to the CPC corporate offices in Las Vegas. The firm needed to expand its headquarters anyway, and decided it would be less expensive to construct a new building that consolidated the main corporate office with the office of Transitional Hospitals Corporation, formerly located in Atlanta. The Priory Hospitals Group continued to expand, reaching 13 facilities. Two-thirds of CPC's record 1994 revenues of $428 million still came from its U.S. psychiatric division's 36 facilities, but it seemed likely that the percentage would shrink.

CPC experienced a flurry of change in 1995, a year when the revenue of the Transitional Hospital subsidiary and United

Kingdom division grew larger than that of the U.S. psychiatric division. In November 1995 it announced that it would close six of its psychiatric hospitals that were losing money. The hospitals were located in Milwaukee, Laguna Hills, Fontana and Santa Ana, California, New Orleans and Skokie, Illinois. The operations of the last two were transferred to other CPC hospitals nearby. The New Orleans and Milwaukee hospitals shared space with the Transitional Hospitals subsidiary, which then expanded to take over the entire hospital.

CPC then reorganized the management of the U.S. psychiatric division, promoting William E. Hale to president. It consolidated regional operations, closing offices in Jacksonville, Sacramento and Seattle, and terminating more than 40 regional and corporate positions. In December 1995, CPC announced plans to spin-off its domestic psychiatric business to its shareholders, splitting the company into two publicly held corporations. CPC would hold onto the Priory Hospitals group and Transitional Hospitals Corp. Management felt that they were much better bets for future growth, and that dealing with the problems of the shrinking U.S. market for psychiatric care was sapping the CPC's resources. A management team lead by William Hale would remain to lead the new company.

Transitional Hospitals had grown to 14 hospitals in ten states, while Priory Hospitals Group had 15 hospitals in Britain.

The two combined had a 1995 gross income of about $258 million. The mid-1990s found CPC in the midst of an important transition. Only time would show if the firm had made the correct decision in abandoning the U.S. psychiatric market in favor of the British psychiatric market and long-term critical care.

Principal Subsidiaries

Priory Hospital Group, Ltd (United Kingdom); Transitional Hospitals Corp.; Community Psychiatric Centers

Further Reading

"Community Psychiatric Says Authorities Study Records from Hospital," *Wall Street Journal,* August 18, 1995, p. C11.
Lutz, Sandy, "Troubled Times For Psych Hospitals," *Modern Healthcare,* December 16, 1991, pp. 26–33.
——, "Bad News, Falling Profits Hamper Psych Providers," *Modern Healthcare,* May 24, 1993, pp. 54–57.
Taylor, John H., "Tranquilizers, Anyone?," *Forbes,* December 10, 1990, pp. 214, 216.
Wallace, Cynthia, "Psychiatric Chains Fuel Growth Through Debt and Internal Funds," *Modern Healthcare,* March 13, 1987, pp. 142. 144.

—Scott M. Lewis

CompCare

Comprehensive Care Corporation

4350 Von Karman Avenue, Suite 280
Newport Beach California 92660
U.S.A.
(714) 798-0460

Public Company
Incorporated: 1969
Employees: 448
Sales: $29.28 million (1995)
Stock Exchanges: New York
SICs: 8049 Offices of Health Practitioners, Not
Elsewhere Classified; 8063 Psychiatric Hospitals

Comprehensive Care Corporation (CompCare) specializes in managed care and drug detoxification programs. It dominated the market for treatment of alcoholism in the late 1970s and early 1980s, but suffered enormous setbacks when the market changed in the late 1980s. Between 1990 and 1995, the company's annual revenues decreased from around $84 million to just over $29 million. However, under the leadership of Chairman, President, and CEO Chriss W. Street, the company was optimistic about its ability to reverse its fortunes, and Street maintained that in 1995, CompCare was "repositioned to potentially grow rapidly as it strives to achieve profitability."

CompCare was founded in Newport Beach, California, in 1969 with the goal of creating a chain of acute-care psychiatric hospitals and nursing homes. The company was undercapitalized, however, and other companies already had the same idea. Startup costs proved higher than expected, and one hospital was damaged by an earthquake. By 1972 the firm faced bankruptcy as it lost $2.8 million on revenue of $3 million.

Hoping to turn things around, the firm named B. Lee Karns, a 42-year-old hospital management consultant, president in 1973. He looked for a market niche that required no further capital outlay and decided on treatment for alcoholism. CompCare set up treatment units in existing hospitals that had empty beds. It used hospital personnel for its staff and made its income from a share of each patient's bill. As additional incentive for the hospitals to join the plan, hospitals were not required to pay CompCare any fee until the alcoholism unit was in full operation. For many hospitals with beds to fill, the arrangement was attractive.

Alcoholism—and the awareness of it as a treatable disease—was growing in the United States, and Karns' plan quickly proved successful. To assist hospitals, which had been unwilling to make such treatment a specialty, CompCare's CareUnits combined medical treatment with psychiatric care and social workers, all supervised by an on-site CompCare employee. Patients were detoxified in the first few days of the three-to-four week program. Then patients attended individual and group therapy sessions geared toward changing their attitudes and behavior patterns.

The recruitment, training, and advertising for an average 20-bed CareUnit cost CompCare between $20,000 and $25,000. Ads in newspapers and on television brought in 30 percent of patients. Another 20 percent of the clientele came from corporate alcoholism programs, while the remainder were a result of personal referrals. Once set up, hospitals set their own patient fees and paid CompCare $55 per patient each day.

Seeking to expand its markets, in 1978 CompCare bought a money-losing Los Angeles surgical hospital, hoping to turn it around. The firm had $28.7 million in revenues in 1979, of which 35 percent came from its alcoholism rehabilitation program. By 1980 CompCare had 55 of its CareUnits in 17 states and was waiting regulatory approval for 18 more. In fact, its rehab program had become the second-largest in the United States, after that of the Veterans Administration. Sixty percent of CompCare's patients stopped drinking, while the other 40 percent of its patients reduced their drinking by two-thirds, a success rate well above the industry average. With this success, CompCare had 104 hospitals in its system by 1982. It therefore decided to sell its long-term care business. Its three nursing homes only accounted for three percent of the firm's 1982 revenues of $73.5 million, and CompCare chose to concentrate on its alcoholism and psychiatric services instead.

Profits reached $17.2 million in 1985, on revenues of $153 million. And then some problems began to occur, although it would take several years for the extent of the firm's change in fortune to become apparent. Specifically, the insurers and corporations that had been the major funding source behind the growth of the firm's treatment business became far more cost conscious. They began demanding lower rates and shorter hospital stays. At the same time, the treatment business became more competitive. Though CompCare's revenues continued to grow for several years, its earnings began to slowly decline. Moreover, the company also lost some key management personnel.

In 1987, CompCare proposed spinning off its subsidiary RehabCare Corp. as a separate public company. It backed away from the plan when the stock failed to attract sufficient interest and the stock market crashed in October 1987. Despite its earnings slowdown, the firm kept spending money on advertising. One particularly striking 1987 television ad showed a woman and her children looking into the open grave of a drug user. The ad prompted consumer complaints, however, and soon thereafter the firm began using softer-focus ads, most often on radio. The ads often employed treatment counselors talking about the dangers of abusing drugs.

CompCare earned $502,000 in 1988 on revenues of $211.6 million. In April 1989 the firm agreed in principle to merge with First Hospital Corp., which operated psychiatric hospitals and substance abuse centers. As First Hospital tried to work out financing, CompCare's financial condition deteriorated. The merger finally collapsed in November when First Hospital claimed that it could not obtain the necessary financing.

CompCare then announced that it would restructure itself and sell most of its California hospitals, including its Brea Hospital-Neuropsychiatric Center, with 142 beds; its CareUnit Hospital of San Diego, with 92 beds; and its Crossroads Hospital, Los Angeles, with 43 beds. It also sold its CareUnit Hospital in St. Louis for $2 million to Bethesda Eye Institute, and sold undeveloped property in Florida. The firm worked out new agreements with its creditors for its $43 million in secured debt, moved its headquarters to St. Louis, and sold its old headquarters for $9 million. Most of its management was already located in St. Louis, and the sale of the California facilities removed the need to have staff there to oversee them. Karns resigned, though he remained on the board of directors. W. James Nichol, who had managed the firm's CareUnit subsidiary and its RehabCare rehabilitation services subsidiary, became the new president.

Despite the restructuring, the firm's fortunes continued to sink. It lost $61.3 million in 1990 on revenues of $143.7 million. By 1990, a group of major shareholders had had enough. They seized control of the company and unseated six of the seven members on the board of directors. The board then brought in James P. Carmany to serve as the company's new chief executive. Carmany had been a CompCare manager from 1978 to 1989, when he was dismissed over his resistance to the merger with First Hospital Corp.

In May 1990 the firm's long-term debt stood at $87 million. But through debt-for-equity trades that raised $36.5 million, and the spinning off of RehabCare as a public company, which

raised $20.2 million, CompCare cut long-term debt to $30 million by October. But its debt schedule remained tough and some industry observers—as well as its auditor KPMG Peat Marwick—expressed doubt about its ability to survive as an independent company. Still, the company announced that it was moving toward a new strategy of growth. It began seeking federal and state contracts for psychiatric as well as chemical dependency services. It also offered managed care services and management information services, in addition to its traditional chemical dependency services.

In early 1992 CompCare announced plans to further cut its debt by spinning off its CMP Properties Inc., which managed hospital properties. CMP would then buy up to $31 million worth of CC hospitals and lease them back to the firm. The plan failed to get off the ground, however. Meanwhile CompCare continued to try and cut costs. It laid off 125 employees, about ten percent of its work force, in April 1992. In August CEO James Carmany and COO Donald G. Simpson resigned; the firm then went through several top executives in quick succession.

Despite its debt, CompCare found the money to buy Mental Health Programs Inc., located in Tampa, Florida. Mental Health cost $700,000 in stock, cash, and the assumption of debts. CompCare lost $4.5 million in 1992 on revenues of $59.9 million. At the time, the company was converting most of its substance-abuse treatment locations into psychiatric care facilities. In 1993, the still-struggling firm decided to give up on the inpatient hospital business entirely. It announced plans to sell or close most of its nine hospitals and shift to managed care. By October 1993, Comprehensive Care had closed six hospitals in a year, but five of them were still for sale. It still owned six hospitals, most of which were operating at far under capacity. The firm had 365 total hospital beds, with an average occupancy rate of 28 percent.

In May 1994 turnaround specialist and investment banker Chriss W. Street was named company chairperson. Street faced a formidable task. In addition to the declining revenues and increasing debt load that had characterized the past five years, a new snag arose: in 1994 the Internal Revenue Service refused CompCare's classification of some doctors and psychologists as independent contractors rather than employees, a decision that added about $5.7 million to the firm's debts.

In early 1995 the Lindner Funds mutual-funds group invested $2 million in CompCare, which the firm used to complete another restructuring. Thereafter the firm had four hospitals left, and its work force had been pared to 550 people, a drop from 2,800 in 1990. As part of the restructuring, CompCare moved its headquarters to Newport Beach, California, nearer the homes of Street and several other top executives.

Recognizing that the fee-for-service market whose growth it had ridden in the 1970s and 1980s had now shrunk severely, CompCare began to remake itself into a managed-care organization. The firm organized networks of medical specialists to contract with health care payers to assume the risk for chronic and catastrophic care. CompCare referred to its strategy as Disease State Management and signed contracts with HMOs, workman's compensation insurers and governmental organizations. Under the Disease State Management plan, doctors were professionally and financially responsible for managing a patient's care, a practice the company called 'reverse gatekeeping.'

The number of patients under the plan grew rapidly, from 360,000 in June 1995 to 593,000 in September 1995. CompCare announced it would seek to form networks specializing in orthopedics, nephrology, spina bifida, and AIDS. The firm also restructured and expanded CareUnit to 17 programs, its first expansion in five years.

Despite some successes, the firm's revenue came to only $29.3 million in 1995, and it lost $11.5 million. Moreover, it was in default on $9.5 million of debentures. In its 1995 annual report, CompCare admitted that its financial condition raised "substantial doubt about the company's ability to continue as a going concern." Nevertheless, the company had made some progress toward settling some of its federal tax debts, and management remained hopeful that the recent restructuring and new focus on managed care would help restore investor confidence. In November 1995 the firm won a $1.2 million contract to develop a drug treatment center for juveniles in conjunction with a hospital in Cincinnati.

Principal Subsidiaries

CareUnit, Inc.; Comprehensive Behavioral Care, Inc. (86.5%).

Further Reading

"CompCare Plans to Add 37 Psychiatric, Alcohol Centers," *Modern Healthcare,* October 1982, p. 9.

"CompCare Shareholders Target Board," *Modern Healthcare,* November 24, 1989, p. 7.

"CompCare: The Business of Treating Alcoholism," *Dun's Review,* August 1980, pp. 20–21.

Flannery, William, "Health-Care Firm Moves HQ," *St. Louis Post-Dispatch,* January 25, 1995, p. 3C.

Goodman, Adam, "Comprehensive Care Gets Needed Cash," *St. Louis Post-Dispatch,* January 10, 1995, p. 7C.

Lutz, Sandy, "CompCare's Woes Continue," *Modern Healthcare,* October 4, 1993.

Nemes, Judith, "CompCare to Sell off Facilities," *Modern Healthcare,* November 10, 1989.

"Sober Growth: Comprehensive Care Proves that Successful Rehabilitation of Alcoholics is a Growth Industry," *Financial World,* June 1, 1980, pp. 34–35.

Steyer, Robert, "Care Firm Moving to St. Louis," *St. Louis Post-Dispatch,* November 21, 1989, p. C1.

——, "Health Firm Tries to Regain Health," *St. Louis Post-Dispatch,* August 26, 1990, pp. C1, C8.

——, "Hospital Company to Spin off Unit," *St. Louis Post-Dispatch,* March 11, 1992, p. C1.

—Scott M. Lewis

Comverse Technology, Inc.

170 Crossways Park Drive
Woodbury, New York 11797
U.S.A.
(516) 677-7200
Fax: (516) 677-7355

Public Company
Incorporated: 1984
Employees: 840
Sales: $98.84 million (1994)
Stock Exchanges: NASDAQ
SICs: 3577 Computer Peripheral Equipment, Not
    Elsewhere Classified; 3669 Communications
    Equipment, Not Elsewhere Classified; 7373 Computer
    Integrated Systems Design

Comverse Technology, Inc. designs, develops, manufactures, and markets computer and telecommunications systems for specialty multimedia communications and information processing applications. The company sells its products through an international sales force and had installed its gear in more than 30 countries by 1995. Comverse was growing rapidly in the mid-1990s by expanding internationally and by introducing new technology to the marketplace.

Kobi Alexander founded Comverse Technology in 1984. A native of Israel, Alexander had studied economics in Tel Aviv before moving to New York in the early 1980s. He enrolled at New York University but also found a job as an investment banker at Shearson Lehman. Alexander worked full-time at Shearson and earned his Masters of Business Administration at night. Alexander had always wanted to run his own business, but he didn't expect an opportunity to arise so early. In 1982, Alexander met Boaz Misholi, an Israeli engineer who had an idea for a business venture. "The week after I met him, I resigned from Shearson," Alexander recalled in the June 18, 1990, *Newsday*. "I always knew I wanted to have my own company."

Misholi's idea was to develop a voice and fax messaging system that would allow customers to store, process, access, and transmit information from any telephone or fax machine. The system would offer a far more comprehensive alternative to answering machines and other rudimentary gear available at the time. Misholi and Alexander recruited some engineers to help them develop the system. They also moved to their native Israel, where the national government was awarding subsidies to high-technology start-up companies.

In Israel, Alexander and Misholi operated their venture as Efrat Future Technology Ltd. It took the company just a few years to design and develop a marketable messaging system. Alexander and Misholi worked with the development team in Israel for two years. Joining them was Alexander's brother-in-law, Yechiam Yemini, who served as the company's chief scientist. In 1984, Alexander, Yemini, and Misholi moved back to New York to begin laying the groundwork for an infrastructure through which they could market their product once it was ready to sell.

The three partners set up a company in Woodbury, New York, called Comverse (a fusion of "communication" and "versatility"). In fact, that enterprise became the parent company of Israel-based Efrat Future Technology, Ltd. Comverse was incorporated in New York in 1984. The company generated sales of a few million dollars annually during its first three full years of operations. Net losses during the period were only slightly less than the company's sales volume because of expenses related to marketing and ongoing research and development. To raise additional investment capital, Comverse went public on the New York Stock Exchange in 1986.

The product that Comverse began marketing in the late 1980s looked like a simple box. Inside the case, though, was a complex multimicroprocessor computer. The computer, when hooked to a customer's telephone line, was capable of performing a number of information-management functions related to voice and fax messaging, as well as call processing. For example, it could store incoming and outgoing messages for different people in personal "mailboxes." Although similar products were on the market at the time, Comverse claimed to be the first company to integrate voice, fax, and call processing functions into a single system.

Misholi served as president and chief executive of Comverse in 1986 and 1987. In 1988 he resigned to pursue other interests and later became a professor of computer science at Columbia University. Alexander stepped up to assume the helm, still aided by Yemini. Alexander realized that, because his tiny company was participating in an industry dominated by such telecommunications technology giants as AT&T , he would have to devise a savvy marketing strategy if he wanted to compete successfully. To that end, he decided early to target the international market, particularly in Europe. With the European economic unification scheduled for 1992, Alexander reasoned, Comverse could benefit by developing an early lead in its niche on that continent.

Specifically, Alexander and fellow executives succeeded during the late 1980s in securing exclusive relationships with several of the top equipment distributors in Europe. Between 1987 and 1990, Comverse signed marketing agreements with six large European distributors who had already established cozy relationships with governments and major equipment buyers. Those agreements gave Comverse an edge over larger rivals, because the distributors often learned of potential deals before Comverse or its rivals. That allowed Comverse to begin pushing its product early in the decision-making process. Among the companies that had agreed to distribute Comverse systems were Ascom (Switzerland), GPT (United Kingdom and Australia), Voice Data Systems (Holland), and Oki (Japan).

For example, the sixth major distributor that latched onto Comverse in the late 1980s was Nokia Data Systems, an electronics products distributor based in Helsinki, Finland. Nokia Data was a member of the $5-billion Nokia Group, the world's largest manufacturer of mobile phones and cable machines. The agreement was important for Comverse because it made the company Nokia's exclusive provider of messaging equipment. Nokia enjoyed a close relationship with the Finnish national telephone company and provided Comverse with a strong link to parts of Europe and the Soviet Bloc that were relatively inaccessible through other marketing channels. Indeed, Comverse was banking on such emerging regions as the former Eastern Bloc to drive industry growth in the long-term.

An example of the wisdom of Comverse's European marketing strategy was a contract worth up to $10 million awarded to Comverse in 1990 by the German government. The German post office, or Deutsch Bundespost, was accepting bids to supply messaging systems for German cellular telephone users. Competing for the contract were such telecommunications and computer giants as AT&T, Hewlett-Packard, the Netherlands' Alcatel, and Germany-based Siemens. Comverse was aided in the bidding process by Ascom Gfeller, a large Swiss distributor with which it had signed an agreement in the late 1980s. The giant contract—by far the largest ever captured by Comverse—gave the company instant recognition as a contender in the market for messaging systems.

The system that Comverse had developed during the 1980s and agreed to supply to the Deutsch Bundespost was dubbed the ''Trilogue.'' The German government was going to use the Trilogue Message Management System to store messages for cellular telephone users. When callers failed to connect with a cellular phone user, they could leave a message in the user's ''mailbox'' for later voice or fax retrieval, or remote paging. By the time it landed the big contract, Comverse had sold only about 300 Trilogue systems, mostly in the United States. It was also licensing some European telecommunications companies to sell Comverse gear under their brand names. The German government, though, planned to install enough Trilogue systems to create 100,000 mailboxes for cellular phone customers.

Before Comverse landed the $10 million German contract, it was employing about 150 people, roughly 40 of whom were located at the U.S. Comverse headquarters and the rest in Israel. The company performed most of its research, development, and manufacturing in Israel, then assembled, marketed, and distributed the systems from its New York headquarters. Most of the equipment was shipped to Europe. In fact, the percentage of its products shipped overseas had grown from ten percent in 1987 to about 80 percent by 1990. Comverse's U.S. sales were mostly to domestic telephone companies, particularly the wireless divisions of the Regional Bell Operating Companies and independent cellular companies like PacTel and McCaw.

Largely in response to the German deal, but also to subsequent contracts, Comverse began adding staff and beefing up operations in the early 1990s. Sales increased to nearly $16 million in 1990 and then to more than $21 million in 1991. After posting its first positive net income in 1989 (of $380,000), Comverse's profit rose to nearly $3 million in 1991. Augmenting growth in sales of its proven Trilogue systems were other technologies being developed and marketed by Comverse. In 1990, for instance, it started selling a product called Fax-Logue, a Trilogue add-on system that provided a wide range of options for sending, receiving, and storing facsimile messages. The technology was first implemented by US West Communications, a Regional Bell Operating Company.

A series of developments during the early 1990s combined to rapidly boost Comverse's revenue and profit. In 1991, for example, Comverse agreed to purchase (in 1992) the assets of Startel Corp., which became a subsidiary of Comverse. Based in Irvine, California, Startel was a leading supplier of transaction processing systems used mostly by the telephone answering service industry, hospitals, and corporate message centers. The acquisition brought important new technology to Comverse's research and development lab and gave it access to a new segment of the market.

Likewise, Comverse scored a big victory late in 1992 when it reached an agreement with global communications giant AT&T for that company to offer Comverse's multilingual voice-processing system to corporate customers and telecommunications providers outside of the United States. The deal was a huge boon for Comverse because it represented an endorsement of its technology by the communications industry leader. The agreement gave AT&T the right to market Comverse's Trilogue and newer Trilogue Infinity products. Among the systems' newer features was a ''virtual telephone'' feature that allowed residents in developing countries to have a telephone number without actually owning a telephone or paying for a separate line. AT&T planned to market the technology in 60 countries by 1996.

In addition to marketing successes, Comverse continued to profit from the development and introduction of cutting-edge technology. Going into the mid-1990s, its Trilogue systems featured a number of sophisticated features. For example, newer Trilogue units incorporated multilingual speech recognition that allowed users to control their messaging functions by speaking commands in their native language. Other complex functions allowed Comverse's gear to support a variety of protocols and equipment and to minimize communication costs and maximize the efficiency of information flow.

As important as advances in its core Trilogue product division was the success of a completely different line of technology called AudioDisk. Comverse had developed AudioDisk in the late 1980s and started marketing it in the early 1990s. It assumed a much lower public profile than Trilogue, however, because the AudioDisk systems were marketed primarily to police and intelligence organizations. Therefore, the company was comparatively discreet about sales of the units. AudioDisk systems enabled police and intelligence gatherers—but also public health, safety, and financial institutions, for example—a much-improved alternative to wire-tapping, which traditionally relied on reel-to-reel tape. AudioDisk used digital technology to simultaneously monitor hundreds of telephone and fax lines and retrieve data instantly.

Although it had received much less public attention than the Trilogue line, AudioDisk systems were accounting for about 50 percent of Comverse's total revenue base in 1993. Furthermore, growth prospects for that market were extremely favorable. Sales gains in the AudioDisk division amplified hefty gains in Trilogue shipments, which were driven largely by rapid international growth from Asia to Europe. The end result for Comverse was rapid expansion into the mid-1990s. Sales rose to $37.5 million in 1992 before more than doubling in 1993, while net income increased to nearly $15 million. In 1994, moreover, Comverse managed to boost revenues more than 40 percent to $98.84 million. Comverse continued to benefit in 1995 by increasing its share of the rapidly growing niche markets that it served.

Principal Subsidiaries

Efrat Future Technology, Ltd.; Startel Corp.; Applied Silicon Inc. (Canada); Telemesser Ltd.; DGM&S, Inc.

Principal Divisions

Trilogue Product Family; AudioDisk Product Family.

Further Reading

"$2 Million Order for Comverse," *Israel Business Today*, April 7, 1995, p. 12.

"AT&T Using Comverse Technology System," *LI Business News*, May 30, 1994, p. 43.

Alexander, Kobi, "Comverse Technology Announces 1994 Results," *Business Wire*, March 22, 1995.

Bernstein, James, "Big Catch for Small Fry," *Newsday*, May 18, 1990, p. 47.

——, "High-Tech David Beats out Goliaths," *Newsday*, June 18, 1990, Section 3, p. 5.

Berry, Don M., Alexander, Kobi, et al., "Comverse Technology Inc. Enters into Definitive Agreement to Acquire Startel Corp.," *Business Wire*, October 18, 1991.

"Best Comverse Profits Ever," *Israel Business Today*, May 21, 1993, p. 5.

Citrano, Virginia, "Telecom Contracts Spur N.Y. Exporters," *Crain's New York Business*, March 8, 1993, p. 17.

"Contract Signed by Comverse, US West," *Business News*, March 12, 1990, p. 13.

Demery, Paul, "Sales Calls Ringing for Telecom Exports," *Business News*, January 22, 1990, p. 3(2).

Labate, John, "Comverse Technology," *Fortune*, May 17, 1993, p. 102.

"Record Quarter at Comverse," *LI Business News*, December 4, 1989, p. 6.

Wax, Alan J., "Comverse, AT&T Connect," *Newsday*, October 7, 1992, p. A37.

—Dave Mote

Continental Can Co., Inc.

One Aerial Way
Syosset, New York 11791
U.S.A.
(516) 822-4940
Fax: (516) 931-6344

Public Company
Incorporated: prior to 1913
Sales: $537.2 million (1994)
Employees: 3,729
Stock Exchanges: New York
SICs: 2821 Plastic Materials, Synthetic Resins &
  Nonvulcanizable Elastomers; 3081 Unsupported
  Plastics Film & Sheet; 3083 Laminated Plastics Plate
  Sheet & Profile Shapes; 3411 Metal Cans; 6719
  Offices of Holding Companies, Not Elsewhere
  Classified; 8711 Engineering Services

Once the world's largest packaging firm, Continental Can Co., Inc. became a diversified company renamed Continental Group in the 1970s and was sold off, piece by piece, in the 1980s. A former Continental Can president bought the name and logo in 1992 and renamed his own company Continental Can. This holding company was, in 1995, producing a variety of packaging materials through several subsidiaries in the United States and Europe. Another subsidiary was providing engineering services, primarily in the northeastern United States.

Continental Can's beginnings actually date back to the creation in 1901 of its great rival—the American Can Co.—when a few men bought the companies producing about 90 percent of the tin cans in the United States. (These cans were actually 98.5 percent steel, with an outer coating of tin plate to avoid rusting.) The canmakers who sold out had to agree not to reenter the business for 15 years. But one of these canmakers, Edward Norton of the Norton Tin Can & Plate Co., noted that the agreement did not preclude his son from going into the business. Through Norton's son and T. G. Cranwell, who is regarded as the company's founder and was its first president,

several former canmakers who had sold out to American Can established the Continental Can Co. in 1904.

The new company, armed with $500,000 in start-up capital, purchased the patents of one of the few companies producing canmaking machinery that had not been acquired by American Can, United Machinery Co. of Rochester, New York. It opened factories in Chicago and Syracuse, New York, and began shipping cans in April 1905. A Baltimore plant was soon added. To assure a steady supply of tin, Continental Can bought the Standard Tin Plate Co. of Canonsburg, Pennsylvania, in 1909. At first production consisted of only packers' cans for fruits and vegetables. Because this business was seasonal, with a long slack period, the company entered the general-line canning field in 1912 in Chicago.

Continental Can was incorporated in the state of New York in 1913, having by then acquired all of the interests of a New Jersey corporation of the same name, plus the Export & Domestic Can Co. and the Standard Tin Plate Co. By 1921 it operated plants in Jersey City, Syracuse, Baltimore, Chicago, and Canonsburg, Pennsylvania, and the tin-plate mill in Canonsburg. It also owned a machine shop in Syracuse for special machinery and employed more than 6,000 persons. Headquarters were in Syracuse. Net income had risen from $1,325,839 in 1915 to $2,624,963 in 1919 before falling to $1,548,620 in 1920. At that point the company was about one-fourth the size of American Can.

During the 1920s Continental Can moved its headquarters to New York City and expanded rapidly, buying almost 20 competing firms. The first West Coast plant, in Los Angeles, was acquired in 1926, and a second one opened in Seattle the following year. In 1928 Continental Can purchased the United States Can Co., the nation's third-largest can company. O. C. Huffman, who had founded that firm in 1903 as the Virginia Can Co., became president of Continental Can, and Carle Cotter Conway, its president, moved up to chairman of the board.

By 1934 American and Continental were estimated to be making about two-thirds of the 10 million cans being produced annually in the United States. Continental at this time had 38 plants in the United States and Cuba. Although net income had fallen from a pre-Depression high of $9 million in 1929 to $4.8 million in 1932, Continental Can never had a money-losing year. Net income reached a new high of $10.7 million in 1934, when employment averaged 11,857.

By 1940 Continental Can had added plants in Canada as well. The greater part of its output consisted of cans for various food products, with the remainder for a variety of industrial uses, such as oil, paint, varnish, lard, beer, and drugs. Gross sales and operating revenue had increased to $120.7 million from $80.9 million in 1935 and had brought Continental Can up to about half the size of American Can. Net income, however, had fallen from $11.2 million to less than $9 million.

Continental Can's extensive acquisition program continued in the 1940s as it entered the fields of paper and fiber containers, bottle caps, and synthetic resins. By 1950 the company had 65 plants, including 8 plants producing fiber and paper containers, 4 plants producing crown caps, and 1 plant producing plastics. Gross sales rose from $174.3 million in 1944 to $397.9 million in 1950, with cans accounting for 83 percent, while net income rose from $6 million to $14.9 million over the same period. In 1950 gross sales reached 71 percent of American Can's level.

Conway, who had presided over Continental Can's growth as its chief executive officer since 1926, retired in 1950. His hand-picked successor was General Lucius Clay, military governor of the U.S.-occupied zone of Germany in the years immediately following World War II and chief organizer of the airlift that supplied West Berlin during the Soviet land blockade. Continental Can grew even more rapidly under Clay's direction. In 1954 gross sales reached $616 million—94 percent of American Can's total—and net income rose to a record of almost $21 million. The number of its plants had grown to 81, of which 45 were canmaking plants.

Acquisition and diversification were largely responsible for Continental Can's growth. In its first 50 years the company purchased and absorbed 28 independent can companies. Acquisition of concerns producing fiber drums, paper containers, and bottle tops in the 1940s broadened its range of products beyond metal containers. And the firm's campaign to pass American Can in sales drew impetus in 1950 from a federal judge's ruling that the practice by both companies of giving long-term discounts to quantity customers was a violation of antitrust law. This decision benefited Continental Can by allowing it to pick off some of its rival's big clients, although it also encouraged some large packers to begin manufacturing their own cans.

In 1956 Continental Can acquired Hazel-Atlas Glass Co., third-largest U.S. manufacturer of glass containers, and thus became the first company with a full line of containers in metal, paper, and glass. It also bought Robert Gair Co., a leading producer of paperboard products. In the same year it purchased Cochrane Foil Co. to manufacture and distribute aluminum plates and rigid foil packages for the frozen-food industry and other food suppliers. These acquisitions temporarily pushed Continental Can ahead of American Can in annual sales, which passed $1 billion in 1957. The Hazel-Atlas purchase, however, was challenged in federal court by the Department of Justice as a violation of antitrust law. When the Supreme Court voided the purchase in 1964, Continental Can was already in the process of

selling eight of Hazel-Atlas Glass's ten plants to Brockway Glass Co.

Continental Can operated 155 plant facilities in 1960. In that year its net sales fell for the first time since 1942, in part due to the aftermath of a steelworkers' strike, but the total still came to more than $1.1 billion. Net income dropped from $40 million to $27.8 million that year. During the early 1960s there was little growth in annual net sales, but net income reached a record $48.9 million in 1964 on sales of $1.2 billion. Of the sales total that year, about 55 percent came from cans.

The introduction of the easy-to-open metal can top in 1963 led to an increase in the use of metal cans rather than glass bottles for beverages. By the end of 1966 more than 45 percent of U.S. beer and more than 15 percent of U.S. soft drinks were being packaged in metal cans. In that year Continental Can announced the development of the first commercially practical welded can. T. C. Fogarty, chairman of the board, called the accomplishment "a giant step closer to freedom from dependence upon tin."

Continental Can's net sales passed the $2 billion market in 1970, and its net income was $76.4 million (down from a record $90.4 million in 1969). About 60 percent of its sales came from cans, 30 percent from paper products, and 10 percent from plastics, chemicals, and assorted lesser items. Aggressive expansion abroad, including the 1969 acquisition of West Germany's Schmalbach-Lubeca-Werke A.G. (which was merged into the Europemballage Corp.), the largest packaging producer in the European community, brought international sales to 24 percent of the company total. Continental Can had 228 manufacturing plants and employed 72,000 people in 1970.

By 1973 investment analysts deemed the metal can industry to be in a state of crisis because of oversupply and tough competition. Both Continental Can and American Can were said to have made the wrong decision in the 1960s by adding capacity for both tin plate and tin-free steel production while the aluminum can was rapidly gaining ground (although Continental Can converted its four Florida plants to aluminum in 1960 for fruit juice concentrates.) Another problem was increasing public opposition to throwaway cans. Continental Can's profits from domestic canmaking dropped from $115 million in 1969 to $52 million in 1973. Its response was to close many old-style integrated manufacturing plants in favor of large automated metal-processing centers and separate can-assembly operations situated near its customers' plants.

For future growth Continental Can also had been looking to 1.5 million acres of timberland in the South acquired in the 1950s. In 1973 forest products contributed 30 percent of the company's $96.8 million in net income—more than the metal (domestic container) group, even though Continental Can had definitively outstripped American Can to become the world's biggest canmaker. All four of Continental Can's paper mills ran at or near full capacity during the year. International operations also contributed 30 percent to company profit in 1973. The company had packaging licensees in 133 countries that year and, of its eight foreign subsidiaries, the European and Canadian ones dominated their markets. By 1975 Continental Can was making more than half of its capital expenditures overseas.

Continental Can indicated it would carry diversification even farther when it changed its name to Continental Group in 1976. The following year it acquired Richmond Corp., a life- and title-insurance holding company for cash and stock valued at $92.5 million. In 1979 the company's new Continental Financial Services Co. subsidiary, which included Richmond, accounted for 19 percent of corporate profits. Also in 1979, the company acquired Florida Gas Co. for $350 million in cash and stock and renamed it Continental Resources Co. It contributed 6 percent of corporate profits that year. In 1980 Continental Group's net sales and revenues came to $5.66 billion, of which the can company accounted for 46 percent (compared to 70 percent in 1969), forest industries for 19 percent, diversified businesses for 16 percent, financial services for 10 percent, and the resources company for 9 percent. Net income totaled a record $224.8 million.

Continental Group dipped farther into the energy resources field in 1981 by purchasing a half-interest in Supron Energy Corp., a natural-gas producer, for $830 million. Renamed Unicon, the acquisition proved a mistake when fuel prices began falling from record levels the following year. In 1983 Continental Group reversed direction, selling off two of its components. Its Canadian packaging subsidiary was acquired by CCL Industries, Ltd. for $130 million (in Canadian dollars), and the containerboard and brown-paper operations were sold to Stone Container Corp. for $510 million. Other divestitures brought the total inflow in assets to nearly $1 billion and made the company an attractive takeover target.

Continental Group was acquired in mid-1984 for $2.75 billion by Peter Kiewit Sons' Inc. and financier David Murdock, with the former allotted 80 percent of the shares and the latter the remaining fifth in the newly formed Kiewit-Murdock Investment Corp. To repay $2 billion in loans from a group of 16 banks, Kiewit-Murdock began selling parts of their acquisition. By mid-1985 the new owners had sold $1.6 billion worth of insurance and paper-products businesses, gas pipelines, and oil and gas reserves. The packaging business, Continental Can Co., remained a unit of Peter Kiewit.

Between 1983 and 1986 Continental Can invested heavily in the two-piece can-manufacturing process, spending nearly $500 million to meet the growing demand for aluminum containers. With Alumax Inc., the company built an aluminum plant in Texarkana, Texas, which began recycling used cans provided by Continental Resource Recovery, a subsidiary. But Continental Can's general-packaging division, a major producer of aerosol and metal general-line cans, was sold to United States Can Co. in 1987. Continental Can's future became even more problematic in March 1990, when Crown Cork & Seal Co. bought two units for $336 million. One, with 1989 revenue of about $1.3 billion, made metal cans for the domestic food and beverage industry. Three months later, Ball Corp. paid $1.03 billion in cash and stock for Continental Can's European operations, which had sales of $1.47 billion in 1989.

A white knight was coming to the rescue, however, in the form of Donald J. Bainton. Once president of Continental Can, Bainton had been fired in 1983 for disagreeing with Continental Group's divestiture policy. Taking on a small engineering company called Viatech, Inc., Bainton turned it into a $500-million-

a-year international packaging company. In 1991 he bought, with Merrywood, Inc., Continental Can's Plastic Containers and Caribbean Containers units from Kiewit for $153 million. A year later he bought the Continental Can name and corporate logo from Kiewit and renamed his company Continental Can. As a sentimental touch, he also bought the original 1904 boardroom table.

Meanwhile, Kiewit had assumed a $415 million liability payment to thousands of former workers who, it was found in federal court, had been wrongfully denied Continental Group pension benefits accumulated since the 1970s. As early as 1974, an article in *Barron's* had warned of the company's unfunded pension liability of about $100 million and the prospect of another $100 million in costs as the result of a labor settlement with the United Steel Workers.

Continental Plastic Containers and Continental Caribbean Containers consisted of 15 plants in the United States and 1,400 employees. The rest of the new Continental Can included three European packaging firms: Perembal S.A., France's second-largest manufacturer of food cans, acquired in 1989 for about $56 million; Dixie Union Verpackingen GmbH, a deficit-ridden German maker of plastic bags used to package foods, purchased in 1984 for $1.9 million; and Onena Bolsas de Papel S.A., a Spanish printer and laminator of plastic films, bought in 1989 for one peseta.

A passionate believer in keeping overhead and bureaucracy under control, Bainton was running Continental Can from its Long Island headquarters with a staff of only five in late 1992. The chief financial officer was also in charge of human resources and, according to Bainton, "any other staff function we need." "Most large companies," he told an *Industry Week* reporter, "give people responsibility, but they don't give them authority. Everything is done by committees. . . . I give my managers both responsibility and authority . . . they can earn more than anyone else would in a similar position in the packaging industry—if they get results. If they don't get results, they get replaced."

Viatech/Continental Can definitely got results from 1989 through 1993. During this five-year period it was the most profitable public packaging company by return on equity, averaging 18.1 percent a year. It was the fourth fastest-growing company in the New York metropolitan area of 50 surveyed during 1991–1993, increasing 62.2 percent in revenue growth.

In early 1994 Bainton was charged in a lawsuit by the Securities and Exchange Commission (SEC) with violating insider trading laws by disclosing to a close friend in March 1992 that Viatech was about to report poor profits. Bainton denied the accusation but in December 1995 agreed in federal court to pay a $30,000 fine and consented to an order preventing him from further violating SEC laws.

At the end of 1994 Continental Can was making extrusion blow-molded plastic containers, metal cans, and plastic films for the packaging industry, and it was laminating flexible packaging for the food and snack industries. Its main U.S. holding was Plastic Containers, Inc. (PCI), a subsidiary jointly owned with Merrywood. This subsidiary owned two other subsidiaries, Continental Plastic Containers and Continental Caribbean Containers (collectively CPC). CPC's customers included some of the largest U.S. consumer products companies, including Coca-Cola Foods, Colgate-Palmolive Co., and Procter & Gamble Co. Another subsidiary, Lockwood, Kessler & Bartlett, Inc., was providing engineering consulting services.

Continental Can wholly owned Dixie Union and owned 85 percent of Perembal, which in turn owned 64 percent of Obalex, a packaging firm in the Czech Republic. Continental Can also owned 57 percent of Onena. PCI had 16 plants in the United States (including one in Puerto Rico), of which 5 were owned by Continental Can. Continental Can headquarters were in Syosset, New York; PCI headquarters were in Norwalk, Connecticut.

Net sales fell in 1993 to $481.8 million from $511.2 million, and net income fell from $2.1 million to $988,000. In 1994, net sales rose to $537.2 million and net income rose to $4.4 million. Of the 1994 sales total, European sales accounted for 53 percent. Long-term debt was $143.4 million in March 1995. No dividends had been paid since 1960.

Principal Subsidiaries

Continental Caribbean Containers, Inc.; Continental Plastic Containers, Inc.; Dixie Union Verpackungen GmbH (Germany); Perembal S.A. (France; 85%); Lockwood, Kessler & Bartlett, Inc.; Obalex, A.S. (Czech Republic; 64%); Onena Bolsas de Papel S.A. (Spain; 57%); Plastic Containers, Inc. (50%).

Further Reading

''Canners Profit from Price War,'' *Business Week,* February 14, 1959, pp. 54, 56, 58, 61.

''Challenge & Response,'' *Forbes,* February 15, 1967, pp. 56, 58.

''Continental Group Inc. Approves Offer of $2.75 Billion from Kiewit, Murdock,'' *Wall Street Journal,* July 2, 1984, p. 3.

Dorfman, John R., ''Uncanny,'' *Forbes,* December 20, 1982, pp. 56–57.

Frank, Allan Dodds, ''More Takeover Carnage?,'' *Forbes,* August 12, 1985, pp. 40–41.

Guzzardi, Walter, Jr., ''The Fight for ⁹⁄₁₀ of a Cent,'' *Fortune,* April 1961, pp. 149, 151–155, 157, 222, 224, 229.

Hayes, Thomas C., ''Recruiting Via Acquisitions,'' *New York Times,* November 30, 1979, pp. D1, D4.

''How Continental Can Is Packaging Growth,'' *Business Week,* March 3, 1975, pp. 40–41.

Kapp, Sue, ''Continental Can's 'Golden Boy' Battles for Basics,'' *Business Marketing,* September 1985, pp. 16–17.

Khalaf, Roula, ''Field of Dreams,'' *Forbes,* November 9, 1992, pp. 58–59.

Pound, Arthur, ''Pouring Ideas into Tin Cans,'' *Atlantic Monthly,* May 1935, pp. 635–642.

Sheehan, Robert, ''Continental Can's Big Push,'' *Fortune,* April 1955, pp. 119–124, 145, 192–193, 212.

Sheridan, John H., ''On the Resurrection Trail,'' *Industry Week,* November 14, 1992, pp. 20–24.

Troxell, Thomas N., Jr., ''More Than Cans,'' *Barron's,* April 14, 980, pp. 61, 67.

Wilke, Gerd, ''Can Makers Grope Back Toward Solid Ground,'' *New York Times,* December 10, 1972, Sec. III, p. 3.

—Robert Halasz

Corel Corporation

1600 Carling Avenue
Ottawa, Ontario K1Z 8R7
Canada
(613) 728-8200
Fax: (613) 761-9350

Public Company
Incorporated: 1985
Employees: 390
Sales: US$196 million (1995)
Stock Exchanges: NASDAQ Toronto
SICs: 7372 Prepackaged Software

Corel Corporation is a leading global developer of graphics software and small computer system interface (SCSI) software, and a top seller of word processing software. The company's signature product is CorelDRAW, a graphics software package with more than a million users. In 1995, after ten years in business, Corel was selling its products through a network of 160 distributors in 60 countries worldwide and in 15 different languages. With the purchase of Novell Inc.'s WordPerfect division in early 1996, Corel instantly became a world leader in word processing software, as well.

Corel is the offspring of Michael Cowpland, a high-energy entrepreneur and Ottawa celebrity who is credited with founding two of Canada's most successful high-technology ventures: Corel and the earlier Mitel. Cowpland was born in Sussex, England, in 1943 and received his bachelor of engineering degree from Imperial College in London. In 1964 he emigrated to Canada. There, he earned a master's degree and finally a Ph.D. at Carleton University while working as a research and development engineer at the respected Bell-Northern Research Ltd.

Cowpland worked at Bell-Northern with Terry Matthews, a friend who had also emigrated from the United Kingdom. In 1973 the pair left Bell to form a new venture dubbed Mitel (an abbreviation for Mike and Terry Electronics). They launched the tiny company with the hope of creating a device that could translate the pulses generated by rotary dial telephones into the tones created by touch-tone phones. Laboring in Cowpland's garage in Ottawa, the pair achieved their goal and went on to build one of Canada's most successful private telecommunications products companies.

Cowpland and Matthews realized stunning success with Mitel during the 1970s and early 1980s, doubling sales of its advanced telephone switching equipment every year for ten straight years. The darlings of the Canadian investment community, Cowpland and Matthews grew rich. In the early 1980s they began to chase new markets by diversifying into various digital technologies, and the pair seemed to have the Midas touch when most of those projects took off.

All seemed to be going well until the mid-1980s. Mitel posted revenues of C$343 million in 1984, in fact, by which time the company was employing more than 5,000 workers in ten plants around the world. It was in 1984, though, that Mitel's diversification effort suddenly began to look like a miscalculation. Importantly, Cowpland and Matthews fell behind schedule on the development of a state-of-the-art phone switch called the SX-2000. When computer giant IBM tired of the delay and shopped elsewhere for the technology, Mitel was faced with plant overcapacity, cost overruns, and a C$50 million research-and-development tab. Mitel began losing money, and Cowpland and Matthews were compelled to sell the enterprise to British Telecom. Still, both founders walked away with millions in cash.

Undeterred, Cowpland viewed the sale of Mitel as an opportunity to pursue the development of technology that was of greater interest to him at the time and to escape a job that had become an administrative burden. In 1985 he dumped C$7 million of his own money into a new venture that he named Corel. His initial goal was to develop a better laser printer that could be used with personal computers. He found that it was too difficult to compete in that market with low-cost Asian manufacturers, however, and quickly shifted his strategy. Corel soon became a value-added reseller of computers, selling complete systems geared for desktop publishing tasks.

Cowpland scrambled during his first few years to find a role for Corel in the marketplace. He eventually added optical disk-drives to his desktop publishing system lineup and then started marketing local area networks. Considering the hefty start-up investment, sales grew tepidly—to about C$6.6 million during 1988—and for a few years, Cowpland seemed the consummate fallen star. ''The first couple of years were the most challenging as we were trying to find the right niche, but I think that is typical of any new company,'' Cowpland recalled in the June 1992 *Profit.* ''It's almost impossible to come up with the ideal concept right out of the starting gate.''

While he pushed his value-added hardware, Cowpland labored behind the scenes on what became a pet project: the creation of software that offered better design and layout capabilities than were offered by leading applications of the time. To that end, he hired a crack software development team that he allowed to work relatively autonomously. Before the end of the decade, the team had developed a graphic-arts software package that would become the standard for the PC-based desktop publishing industry. In 1989 Corel unveiled its cutting-edge Corel-DRAW software program. CorelDRAW, importantly, was the first graphics application to incorporate into one package all of the major graphics functions: illustration, charting, editing, painting, and presentation.

CorelDRAW was an instant success, which was surprising given the fact that Corel had never mass-marketed anything, much less a software application. However, Cowpland's savvy marketing strategy eventually earned him almost as much respect in the software community as did CorelDRAW. Cowpland plowed millions of dollars into an aggressive sales campaign. Specifically, he bucked the industry norm by marketing CorelDRAW heavily in Europe and Japan. Most software companies at the time started out focusing almost solely on English-speaking consumers. Furthermore, as CorelDRAW became more popular, Cowpland refused to adhere to the convention of selling different versions of the program one-after-the-other. Instead, Corel developed and simultaneously sold multiple versions of CorelDRAW, each of which was tailored for a select market niche.

Corel's rapid-fire product development and marketing effort quickly boosted its bottom line. Indeed, sales (roughly 80 percent of which were attributable to CorelDRAW) rose to C$36 million in 1990 and then to C$52 million in 1991, while net income increased to a solid C$7 million. Going into 1992, Corel was employing about 250 workers and had shipped nearly 300,000 of its CorelDRAW packages to more than 40 countries. CorelDRAW was becoming increasingly popular with such customer groups as children, artists, architects, and business owners, among others. In short, CorelDRAW allowed users to create anything from T-shirt designs to corporate logos and technical drawings. Using a computerized pencil, or drawing from 12,000 programmed images, they could create an endless array of color illustrations, designs, and drawings.

As Mitel had, Corel reflected the insatiable drive of its founder. Cowpland had established his name in the Canadian business scene with Mitel, but his remarkable success with Corel revived his fame in his home town, where he ''replaced Pierre Trudeau as Ottawa's most-watched celebrity,'' according to *Canadian Business Magazine.* In Ottawa, Cowpland was known as much for his persona as his business success. He

raced around the city in flashy sports cars and generally made no apologies for his wealth. He and his wife built a massive new home that included a ten-car underground garage and two squash courts and was designed to mimic the look of Corel's gold-colored headquarters.

Cowpland's no-holds-barred, unemotional business style was mirrored more clearly on the tennis court, where he was known as an aggressive contender driven to win at any cost. Evidencing that drive was Cowpland's relationship with long-time tennis partner Ed Hladkowicz, the tennis pro at a club that Cowpland bought during his Mitel days. Cowpland hired Hladkowicz to work for Corel, and Hladkowicz became a manager in the company's systems division. Meanwhile, the two friends continued what became a 20-year run of regular tennis matches. Then, one day in 1992, Cowpland coldly and abruptly eliminated the systems division and sent Hladkowicz packing. A week later he phoned the stunned Hladkowicz to arrange a time to play tennis (the two eventually did resume their association).

Although Cowpland was criticized for his callous treatment of employees, few could dispute the success of his philosophy in the business arena. Cowpland prided himself on making quick decisions and moving briskly to capitalize on new opportunities. During the early 1990s Corel introduced a string of CorelDRAW programs geared for entry-level users, intermediates, and advanced buyers. Those introductions helped Corel to capture a hefty 55 percent share of the global market for drawing and illustration software products. The resulting revenues rose to C$90 million in 1992, C$140 million in 1993, and then to C$226 million in 1994, while net income increased to nearly C$45 million.

Corel's success in 1993 and 1994 blasted critics, who claimed that Cowpland's downfall was imminent. Based on what they believed was a saturated market as well as Cowpland's history at Mitel, a number of investors began shortselling (betting against) Corel stock in 1992 in anticipation of an earnings slide. Instead, the company's earnings climbed rapidly in the wake of new product introductions and an improved balance sheet. Impressively, Cowpland had managed to grow Corel without taking on any debt. By 1994, in fact, Corel had virtually no long-term debt. Furthermore, Cowpland still owned an equity stake in the company of about 20 percent by 1995, giving him an estimated net worth of $200 million.

By 1994, though, it could be argued that Corel was relying too heavily on a single product line geared for a market niche that was becoming saturated. So, after shipping nearly one million CorelDRAW programs in 15 different languages, Cowpland began looking for a new avenue to growth. In 1994 the company launched an ambitious initiative to branch into four new markets: consumer CD-ROMs, office suites (or ''bundles'' of productivity software), video-conferencing, and computer-aided design (CAD). Production of CD-ROM games and educational products was a top priority—Corel planned to launch 30 titles in 1995 and an additional 50 each following year. Corel planned to tap its established network of distributors in 60 countries to vie with venerable Microsoft in the $1-billion CD-ROM consumer market.

Creating its CD-ROM products in cooperation with Artech Digital Entertainments, Inc., Corel launched several CD-ROM products in 1995, including an electronic coloring book called "Blue Tortoise," a Marilyn Monroe photo compilation, a movie database, and collections of card and board games. At the same time, it continued to enhance its CorelDRAW line and to chase the other market categories it had targeted in 1994. For example, it announced plans to begin shipping a CAD software application called CorelCAD, which was designed to help homebuilders and people doing home renovations. Cowpland expected that effort to generate sales of $50 million annually by 1998. Likewise, Corel introduced a video-conferencing system early in 1996 called CorelVideo that was designed to operate efficiently on local area network systems.

Critics wondered why Cowpland would take on so much risk by simultaneously jumping into industries in which he had little or no prior experience. Their concern was no doubt heightened early in 1996, when Corel stunned the software community by agreeing to purchase Novell Inc.'s vaunted WordPerfect division in a transaction valued at $124 million. WordPerfect word processing software was a leader in the massive word processing market. The deal also included Quattro Pro, a leading spreadsheet software, and the PerfectOffice application suite of productivity software. The surprising purchase was expected to more than triple Corel's annual revenue base.

The WordPerfect purchase vaulted Corel from a major niche player to a software industry contender in a business dominated by operating-system powerhouse MicroSoft: "Corel Feels Bold with WordPerfect Deal; CEO Has Glass House, but He Throws the First Stone at Microsoft," read the headline in the February 11, 1996, *Wall Street Journal*. With sales expected to rise to more than US$500 million in 1996, Corel (given its 52-year-old chief executive's competitive nature) appeared to have the potential to exert significant influence in the global software and multimedia industry.

Principal Subsidiaries

Corel Corporate Limited (Ireland).

Further Reading

Aragon, Lawrence, "Caution: Stories Graphic in Nature: CEO Mike Cowpland's Plan to Diversify into Publishing and Video-Conferencing Could Lead His Corel to the Heart of Palookaville," *PC Week*, September 4, 1995, p. A10(2).

Bagnall, James, "Corel Good Example of New Wave of Business," *Ottawa Citizen*, January 10, 1994, p. A9.

——, "Corel Marketing Machine Goes Formal; Software Star Offers Big Reward for Top Artist," *Ottawa Citizen*, August 10, 1995, p. C6.

Hatter, David, "The Fastest Finalists: Drawing on Innovation," *Profit*, June 1992, p. 32.

Hladkowicz, John, "Corel Establishes International Headquarters in Dublin," *PR Newswire*, June 11, 1993.

Kainz, Alana, "Corel's No. 2 Executive Abruptly Quits on High Note," *Ottawa Citizen*, December 21, 1993, p. C8.

——, "Corel Decides to Spread Its Software Bets Around; Company Moves Aggressively into New Markets," *Ottawa Citizen*, October 8, 1994, p. E1.

——, "Corel Up, Up and Away; Firm to Unseat Cognos as No. 1 in Software," *Ottawa Citizen*, December 24, 1994, p. H12.

Oberbeck, Steven, "Novell Finally Gets Monkey off Back," *Knight-Ridder/Tribune Business News*, February 1, 1996.

Scott, Cindy, "Corel Ships Wild Board Games," *PR Newswire*, August 31, 1995.

"Stitch in Time," *PC Week*, September 11, 1995, p. A5.

Sutcliffe, Mark, "Racquet Scientist," *Canadian Business*, June 1995, p. 62(5).

Tamburri, Rosanna, "Corel Feels Bold with WordPerfect Deal; CEO Has Glass House, but He Throws the First Stone at Microsoft," *Wall Street Journal*, Section 2, p. 2.

Urlocker, Michael, "Corel Has Last Laugh," *Financial Post*, July 11, 1992, p. 10.

—Dave Mote

CROWN

lift trucks

Crown Equipment Corporation

40 South Washington Street
New Bremen, Ohio 45869
U.S.A.
(419) 629-2311
Fax: (419) 629-3762

Private Company
Incorporated: 1945 as Crown Controls Corp.
Employees: 5,000
Sales: $610 million (1994 est.)
SICs: 3537 Industrial Trucks, Tractors, & Trailers; 5084
Material Handling Equipment; 3663 Radio & TV
Broadcasting Equipment

Crown Equipment Corporation is one of the world's top ten manufacturers of industrial lift trucks and ranks as America's top manufacturer of electric narrow-aisle lift trucks. Commonly known as forklifts, these material handlers are critical to virtually every industry. Although Crown wasn't an originator of the industry, the company's award-winning designs have helped drive the evolution of the lift truck from "warehouse workhorse" to "mobile workstation." Crown has emphasized production of electrically-powered materials handlers since the late 1950s, but also continues to manufacture the directional television antennas it has made since the late 1940s. The closely-held company has been owned and led by the Dicke family since its foundation. James F. Dicke II represented the clan's third generation of leadership, guiding Crown into its 50th year in 1995. By the early 1990s, the firm also boasted manufacturing plants and marketing operations in Australia, Ireland, Germany, and Mexico, as well as maintaining two factories in the United States.

Crown was formally organized in 1945, but its roots stretch back to the 1920s, when Carl Dicke founded the Pioneer Heat Regulator Company with his brothers, Oscar and Allen. The three Dicke siblings made quite a team: Oscar invented a thermostat for coal-fired home furnaces; Allen, an attorney, patented the concept; and Carl marketed it. When new home construction went bust during the Great Depression, the brothers sold Pioneer to Master Electric, a manufacturer in nearby Dayton. Carl Dicke continued to work as the Pioneer subsidiary's general manager through World War II.

Following a two-year, health-related hiatus, Carl, his son Jim, and brother Allen founded Crown Controls Company to market thermostats manufactured by Master Electric Company in 1945. In 1947, Master Electric sold the manufacturing operation back to the family team for $85,000. Unfortunately for the Dickes, however, coal was quickly losing favor as a home heating fuel, giving way to electric heaters and natural gas furnaces.

With this core business slipping away, the Dickes sought a new business interest on which to build Crown's future. On a hint from a business associate, they began producing and marketing television antenna rotators in 1949. These devices, also known as directional antennas, turned television antennas so that they would get the best possible reception. In 1950, Allen Dicke traded his stake in Crown to Carl in exchange for Carl's share of a local farm.

Crown Controls reached a tragic turning point in 1952, when 50-year-old founder Carl Dicke died, leaving his 31-year-old son to manage the business on his own. Jim Dicke's company continued to manufacture television antennas throughout the 1950s (and into the 1990s, in fact), turning marketing responsibilities over to the world's largest manufacturer of television antennas, New York's Channel Master Corporation, in 1957. Channel Master's superior distribution generated increased sales of Crown's TV antennas, but left a void in the Ohio company's marketing program. Crown cast about for new product ideas, dabbling in a variety of novelty products including "ice stoppers to keep the ice in your glass from bumping you in the nose;" "fishing arrowheads;" and a combination saw and drill. Of course, none of these products had the staying power to sustain a growing business.

Then, Jim Dicke's father-in-law, Warren Webster, suggested that Crown develop a "hydraulic lift table" that would make lifting and moving heavy objects easier and safer. Webster wasn't the first to come up with this concept; the lift truck was initially invented in 1918 by Lester Sears of Cleveland, Ohio. His "Towmotor" launched an industry that was crowded with competitors by the time Crown entered the fray in the 1950s.

But Webster and Dicke thought they had discovered an underexploited and potentially profitable segment of the forklift market. They would build small, walk-behind hand trucks for light industry. Crown had manufactured a hydraulic auto jack called a "bumper upper" for the Joyce-Cridland company in the postwar era, but didn't find a market for the device. Tom Bidwell, an engineer at Crown, adapted the concept to the LT-500 (500-pound capacity lift truck), a "walkie lifter" he designed in 1957. This initial entry featured a hand-pumped hydraulic lift and was pushed by hand like a cart.

Crown's E-Z Lift trucks entered a market that was already choked with well-entrenched competitors: Hyster, Clark, Yale, and Caterpillar, to name a few. The company needed an advantage that would differentiate its products from these rivals and win over both distributors and customers. In the early 1960s, Crown hired two young industrial designers, David Smith and Deane Richardson, in the hopes of gaining market leverage through superior design. In 1963, the Industrial Designers Institute awarded the resulting hand-controlled pallet truck Crown's first national Design Excellence Award. It was the beginning of a relationship that would last through the early 1990s. Although the design firm remained a separate business entity, it would continue to participate in the development of virtually every materials handler in Crown's continuously expanding line. By 1994, these products had accumulated 25 major design awards.

Those honors, and the features and benefits they recognized, helped Crown garner a growing roster of customers. The company's own distribution and service network grew to include more than 20 locations in the United States and over 100 independent dealerships.

Throughout the 1960s and 1970s, Crown continuously expanded the power, capacity, and capabilities of its materials handlers. Although internal combustion engines dominated the lift truck industry from its inception, Crown concentrated exclusively on production of electric vehicles. The company added rider trucks—including the industry's first side-stance model—during the 1970s, and earned its first national account with the development of a stockpicking truck.

During the 1980s, Crown introduced narrow-aisle reach trucks designed by Richardson/Smith that reduced the distance these handlers needed to maneuver between shelves in warehouses by at least one-third. The company extended this line with the launch of the TSP series of turret stockpickers, combining narrow-aisle capabilities with reaches as high as 45 feet. Narrower aisles meant customers could squeeze more rows of shelves in their storage facilities, and higher reaches meant those shelves could tower ever higher, effecting more efficient use of space and cost savings for Crown clients. The innovation won a Design Excellence Award from the Industrial Designers Society in 1981 and was selected as the Design of the Decade by that group in 1989.

Like so many other industries, from autos to electronics, the lift truck market was assaulted by competition from Japanese companies in the 1980s. American firms' controlling stake in the domestic market began to melt away under the onslaught. From 1980 to 1983 alone, Japanese imports priced up to 25 percent less than domestic trucks seized one-third of the U.S. market. By mid-decade, America was a net importer of forklifts. Although the U.S. government later determined that many of these foreign rivals were guilty of dumping—selling goods below fair market value in order to capture market share—the damage was already done.

While many domestic manufacturers met the competition by moving production capacity (and with it thousands of U.S. jobs) overseas, Crown continued to manufacture about 85 percent of its components domestically. More than national pride was behind this policy. According to a 1992 *Design News* article, Crown considered vertical integration vital to maintain fidelity to its designs and manufacturing quality. Instead of outsourcing, the company accomplished virtually everything, from forming sheet metal and plastic parts to designing and manufacturing circuit boards for electronic controls, in its own plants. Crown even built a factory in New Knoxville, Ohio, to produce electric motors. The company also avoided the merger and acquisition trend that swept the forklift industry in the late 1980s and early 1990s.

Just as it had in the late 1950s and early 1960s, Crown's design prowess helped it break into another segment of the intensely competitive lift truck industry, counter-balanced lift trucks. Launched in 1990, Crown's FC line of vehicles offered advanced ergonomics that improved comfort and efficiency, including tilt steering; adjustable seating; fingertip controls; onboard diagnostics; and more. Called "Crown's most ambitious development effort in 35 years," the FC series won three important design awards and, more importantly, captured market share.

Crown's concentration on development and production of electrically-powered lift trucks also proved providential. Electric forklifts overtook internal combustion engined models in 1979, and continued to hold a slight lead through the early 1990s. Advantages such as quieter operation, cheaper maintenance and repair, and longer working life helped draw customers from the internal combustion segment. Increasingly stringent emission regulations and general environmental concerns also helped drive the shift toward electric-powered lift trucks.

To offset the notoriously cyclical—one analyst even characterized it as "rollercoaster-like"—nature of the lift truck market, Crown established overseas manufacturing, distribution, and sales operations in Australia, England, Ireland, Germany, and Mexico. Increased housing starts, low interest rates, and pent-up demand were cited as the impetus behind rising sales in 1992, 1993 and 1994, when the industry recovered from downturns in 1990 and 1991. Industry analyst The Freedonia Group (Cleveland) forecast that the United States lift truck industry's rally would continue, growing to $1.8 billion by 1997. While Crown remained privately and closely held in the mid-1990s, it seemed apparent that the company's emphasis on forward-looking design, vertical integration, and globalization would enable it to remain independent indefinitely.

Further Reading

Avery, Susan, "Lift Trucks: The Competition Heats Up," *Purchasing,* February 7, 1991, p. 58.

——, "Design Updates Lift Trucks to New Heights," *Purchasing,* August 19, 1993, p. 85.

"Basic Handlers: Pallet Trucks, Walkie Stacker and Reach Trucks," *Modern Materials Handling,* February 1994, p. 54.

"Bigger, Better, Faster, More!," *Beverage World,* August 1993, p. 85.

Dicke, James F., II, *Crown Equipment Corporation: A Story of People and Growth,* New York: Newcomen Society, 1995.

"Lift Truck Market Picks Up Speed," *Purchasing,* September 8, 1994, pp. 34–39.

Maloney, Lawrence D., "Crown Puts Design on a Pedestal," *Design News,* July 20, 1992, p. 46.

Martin, James D., "One-Stop Shopping," *Chilton's Distribution,* March 1988, p. 90.

McGaffigan, James, "What Narrow Aisle Lift Trucks Can Do for You," *Handling & Shipping Management,* March 1984, p. 50.

Petreycik, Richard M., "Forklift Report: Changing Gears," *U.S. Distribution Journal,* September 15, 1993, p. 47.

Rohan, M. Thomas, "Making 'Em Overseas," *Industry Week,* December 12, 1983, p. 28.

Sears, Warren, "Our Friend the Forklift," *Beverage World,* April 1995, p. S24.

Weiss, Barbara, "Crown Controls to Build New $6M Forklift Plant," *American Metal Market,* June 9, 1986, p. 12.

Yengst, Charles R., "Where Have We Seen This Before?" *Diesel Progress Engines & Drives,* January 1991, p. 4.

—April Dougal Gasbarre

Culbro Corporation

387 Park Avenue South
New York, New York 10016-8899
U.S.A.
(212) 561-8700
Fax: (212) 561-8979

Public Company
Incorporated: 1906 as United Cigar Manufacturers
　　Company
Employees: 2,695
Sales: $185.42 million (1994)
Stock Exchanges: New York
SICs: 2121 Cigars; 6552 Subdividers & Developers, Not
　　Elsewhere Classified; 6719 Holding Companies, Not
　　Elsewhere Classified

Culbro Corporation is a diversified consumer and industrial products company operating in four principal areas: the manufacture and marketing of cigars and related tobacco products; the growing and sale of nursery products, including the owning and operating of field and container plant nurseries, and of wholesale sales centers; the manufacture and sale of packaging, labeling and other industrial products machinery, systems, and products such as shrink film labels and tamper-evident seals; and owning, managing, constructing, and developing commercial, industrial, and residential real estate. Culbro's 1994 sales—down from nearly $1.4 billion in 1993—reflect the deconsolidation of its Eli Witt Company subsidiary and the reduction of Culbro's ownership in Eli Witt from 85 percent to 50.1 percent. Culbro is led by chairman and CEO Edgar M. Cullman, brother to former Philip Morris CEO Joseph F. Cullman III. Cullman's son, Edgar M. Cullman Jr., functions as Culbro's president and chief operating officer. The Cullman family currently controls 52 percent of Culbro's stock.

Tobacco and the Cullman family have been intertwined since the late 19th century, when Ferdinand Kullmann worked as a tobacco merchant in Germany. His sons, Joseph and Jacob, founded Cullman Bros. in New York in 1892. Initially, Cullman Bros. was chiefly involved in purchasing tobacco at U.S. and international auctions and reselling the tobacco to cigar manufacturers, but this activity soon led the brothers into other areas of the tobacco industry, including making their own cigars.

In 1906, the Cullmans formed their cigar-making operations into the United Cigar Manufacturers Company, which was first listed on the New York Stock Exchange that year. Joseph Cullman remained with Cullman Bros. while aiding the new company as a tobacco appraiser. Cullman Bros. next turned to growing tobacco, purchasing land in Connecticut already in use for growing binder and wrapper tobacco. In 1928, Joseph Cullman's sons, Joseph Jr. and Howard, organized the Tobacco & Allied Stocks, Inc. tobacco trust, which would lead to control of Benson & Hedges by 1938, and, in a $22.4 million deal in 1954, would bring Joseph Jr. and Joseph III into Philip Morris's top management.

United Cigar Manufacturers grew quickly in its first decade—paying its first dividends in 1909—aided by a series of acquisitions of other cigar makers, during a time when the cigar industry itself was undergoing a rapid consolidation, especially among the largest tobacco companies, including American Tobacco and Consolidated Cigar Corp. In 1917, United Cigar Manufacturers changed its name to General Cigar Co., Inc., to reflect its growing holdings. The following year, General Cigar moved to change the face—and structure—of the U.S. cigar industry.

Until the early 1920s, cigars were primarily sold as local brands or under private labels, so that, across the United States, there were hundreds of small-volume cigar names. General Cigar alone represented about 150 different brands. However, in 1918, the company moved to establish the first national cigar brands. It dropped nearly all of its brands and instead concentrated its manufacturing, sales, and advertising on five core brand names. Each of General Cigar's brands—which included White Owl, Van Dyck, Wm. Penn, and Robt. Burns—hit a different price point. General Cigar was among the first companies to recognize the potential of radio and the developing radio networks, soon advertising and sponsoring programs on a nationwide scale. The company's net profits rose from $1.5 million in 1914 to $2.7 million in 1919. Cigar sales were on the rise throughout the country, reaching a high of 8.5 billion cigars sold in 1920.

During the 1920s, the cigar industry suffered, however, from image problems. The rise of organized crime during Prohibition and the image of the stogie-chomping gangster—developed in part by Hollywood and personified by Edward G. Robinson—gave the cigar an aura of unrespectability among the public. The cigar industry faced a second crisis later in that decade, when American Tobacco, promoting its new machine-rolled cigars, rolled out advertising that asked: "Why run the risk of cigars made by dirty yellowed fingers and tipped in spit?"

The image provoked by that campaign proved disastrous for the cigar industry as a whole. Even as cigar makers rushed to convert their manufacturing from hand-rolled to machine-rolled products, cigar sales plunged through the 1930s, down to 5.5 billion in 1939. The cigar industry was also hurt by the rise in cigarette usage across the United States during this same period, and cigar consumption would never recover to its early 1920s peak. General Cigar, which had posted a net income of $3.4 million in 1927, saw its own sales fall steadily throughout the 1930s. In 1924, General Cigar posted sales of $23.7 million and a profit of $2.3 million. By 1939, General Cigar's fortunes had dropped to less than $19 million in sales, with a slight $880,000 profit.

The cigar industry fought to improve its image, organizing the Cigar Institute of America in 1940. The cigar's image was helped, as the United States prepared to enter the Second World War, by Winston Churchill's everpresent cigar. Hollywood was coaxed to take cigars away from its movie villains and give them instead to the heroes. More and more, cigars became props for the film industry's romantic leads, softening the public's—and especially women's—resistance to cigars. General Cigar's sales climbed again, to $22 million in 1941, and $27 million in 1943. The following year, General Cigar again jolted the industry, with the rollout of its Robt. Burns Cigarillo.

The Cigarillo was a scaled-down panatela cigar, resembling more closely a cigarette than the old-style stogie, and wrapped in a lighter-shade wrapper tobacco. With a milder taste than the traditional cigar, the Cigarillo helped pull General Cigar's revenues up to $35.6 million by 1947. General Cigar turned its efforts to research, developing new tobacco products and manufacturing techniques. In the 1950s, General Cigar introduced Homogenized Tobacco Leaf (HTL), a blended, continuous band of binder tobacco, which not only allowed for a more uniform product and a milder taste, but also enabled the high-speed manufacture of the smaller-shaped cigars at significant cost-savings. General Cigar soon formed a separate department for its automated machinery and equipment research and development efforts, selling its machines to other manufacturers. However, General Cigar had neglected the marketing of its own cigars, and sales remained flat, hovering around $35 million into the mid-1950s.

General Cigar's R&D efforts began to pay off in the late 1950s, and its sales began a steady climb, to $45.2 million in 1956 and to $62 million in 1960. Licensing of its HTL systems and other equipment brought in growing income from royalty and licensing fees, from $680,000 in 1958 to $1.1 million in

1960. With about 37 percent of its common stock controlled by Bush Terminal Company, General Cigar gained a reputation as the industry's technological leader, while analysts noted the company's unbroken record of paying dividends in each year since 1909. Per capita consumption of cigars had risen steadily through the 1950s, to 134 cigars per adult male per year, up from 116. By 1961, General Cigar was firmly entrenched in its second-place industry position, behind leader Consolidated Cigar Corp. Most of General Cigar's sales were in the low and medium price segments, with the Cigarillo dominating the five-cent segment, and its White Owl brand competing for leadership of the ten-cent segment. By then, General Cigar operated eight manufacturing facilities, four processing plants, and about 50 warehouses. While the Cuban revolution placed a burden across the cigar industry, General Cigar controlled some 800 acres of tobacco-growing land in Connecticut, supplying more than half of its wrapper leaf needs. Nevertheless, the company was forced to write off its Cuban operations, and sales sagged.

Late in 1961, Edgar Cullman led an investment group in the purchase of 37 percent of General Cigar's stock, raising that stake to 45 percent by the following year. Cullman, who had joined Cullman Bros. in the late 1940s, taking over its 600 acres of tobacco growing and sales, soon assumed the presidency of General Cigar and began to revitalize its operations. Among General Cigar's innovations was the introduction of a new Robt. Burns cigar, a Cigarillo with a plastic tip. The Tiparillo was launched with a heavy promotional campaign—estimated at around $5.5 million in 1962—featuring the slogans "Cigars, Cigarettes, Tiparillos?" and the soon-to-be famous "Should a gentleman offer a Tiparillo to a lady?" Sales began slowly, but by 1963 had taken off, raising General Cigar's revenues to $69 million and giving the company the dominant position in the small cigar market.

The Surgeon General's report on smoking of January 1964 proved a new—if short-lived—boon to the cigar industry. Throughout the following year, millions of cigarette smokers switched to cigars, and especially the smaller cigars. General Cigar reaped the benefits of this movement, particularly with its Tiparillo brand; the company also introduced its Ultra homogenized wrapper tobacco, which, like HTL, produced substantial cost savings in cigar production, adding more royalties and licensing fees to the company's income. In order to meet the surge in demand, General Cigar expanded its production capacity. It also began a series of acquisitions, including Gradiaz, Annis & Co. and its premium cigar labels, and the Cullman Bros. Farms. In 1964, General Cigar expanded beyond cigars, with the acquisition of Metropolitan Tobacco Co. and New Jersey Tobacco Co., into wholesale distribution, with activities focused on cigars, cigarettes, candy, tobacco, drugs, and other items. Year-end revenues for 1964 jumped to $193 million. By the end of the decade, after the 1967 acquisition of the Connecticut wrapper tobacco and nursery operation of American Sumatra Tobacco Corp., followed by the 1969 purchase of Ex-Lax Inc. for $33 million, revenues climbed to $246 million. The 1971 introduction of a new line of cigars, Tijuana Smalls, designed for the growing baby-boomer youth market, brought General Cigar's revenues to $265 million, at a time when cigar sales overall continued their long decline. During this period, General Cigar also initiated its real estate development operations, converting portions of its 6,300-acre holdings into industrial and warehouse sites.

By the end of the 1970s, however, the company's fortunes had dwindled. The mid-1960s boom in cigar sales lasted less than a year, leaving General Cigar with production capacity far outreaching demand. The Ex-Lax acquisition gave the company a relatively stagnant product; to worsen matters, General Cigar almost immediately sold off that company's Feminine Hygiene division, its one division with growth potential. Next, General Cigar moved to enter the growing salted snack foods market, with the purchase for $26 million of Helme Products, Inc. and its smokeless tobacco and Bachman Foods subsidiaries. To emphasize its newly diversified operations, General Cigar changed its name to Culbro Corporation in 1976.

The Bachman brands of pretzels and potatoes were largely regional—marketed in Pennsylvania and in some northeastern states. Culbro attempted to take the Bachman label national, to the extent that the Bachman brand name was given to all of the company's snack products—which included the products of newly acquired Cains Marcelle Potato Chips Inc. and the potato/corn snack division of Fairmont Foods Co.—most of which had been local, yet successful brands. The Bachman brand failed to inspire consumer interest, and ran into distribution difficulties, so that, despite steady rises in the salted snack food market, Bachman began losing money, including $9 million on 1978 sales of $80 million. At the beginning of 1980, Culbro sold off its Bachman division, taking a substantial loss. Meanwhile, cigar sales slumped as new and stiffer tobacco taxes, and growing levels of smoking restrictions, were added across the country. Despite revenues of $430 million in 1979, Culbro followed its $4.5 million loss in 1978 with a loss of $21 million in 1979. The following year, Culbro left the proprietary drug market as well, selling that division, including Ex-Lax, to Sandoz Ltd. of Switzerland for $94 million, returning Culbro to profitability. By 1987, Culbro had sold off its Helme Tobacco smokeless tobacco operations, and its Metropolitan Distribution Services, as well as the remains of its snack food business.

Despite these difficulties, Culbro still retained more than 6,000 acres of land, worth about $6 million at purchase price value, but many more times that if converted to industrial or residential use. Then, in 1983, Culbro acquired all of the outstanding shares of Eli Witt Company. Culbro's revenues began a steady climb through the rest of the decade, from $626 million in 1983 to $1.1 billion in 1991. Through Eli Witt, Culbro began a new string of acquisitions, including those of Certified Grocers of Florida, Inc., and Trinity Distributors in 1993, and of the southern divisions of NCC L.P.'s wholesale distribution business. As part of that last transaction, Culbro sold part of its Eli Witt common stock to MD Distribution Inc., reducing Culbro's share—and unilateral control—of Eli Witt to 50.1 percent. In April 1994, Culbro deconsolidated Eli Witt from its financial statement.

Nearly half of Culbro's 1994 sales of $185 million came from its General Cigar consumer products division, which by then included the distribution of the strong-selling Djeep lighters, sold primarily through Wal-Mart. During the mid-1990s, the cigar industry saw a slight reversal in the long-time decline of cigar sales, primarily from a renewed interest in high-end and hand-rolled cigars. Despite this, the long-term future of the cigar industry continued to be bleak. In May 1995, Culbro announced its intention, as part of an overall plan toward international expansion, to sell 51 percent of its interest in its cigar business to Tabacalera SA of Madrid, Spain, for $100 million. Talks between the two companies fell through by September 1995. However, it seemed likely that Culbro would continue to seek to divest its core cigar line.

Principal Subsidiaries

General Cigar Co., Inc.; CMS Gilbreth Packaging Systems, Inc.; Imperial Nurseries, Inc.; Culbro Land Resources, Inc.; Culbro Machine Systems, Inc.; 387 PAS Corporation; Trine Manufacturing Company; The Eli Witt Company (50.1%).

Further Reading

"General Cigar Smokes a Sleeker Stogie," *Business Week*, December 14, 1968, p. 72.
Ginsburg, Stanley, "Everything Went Wrong for Edgar Cullman," *Forbes*, March 3, 1980, p. 90.

—M. L. Cohen

DaimlerBenz

Daimler-Benz AG

IR
70546 Stuttgart
Germany
(49) 711-1792287
Fax: (49) 711-1794109

Public Company
Incorporated: 1926
Employees: 330,551
Sales: DM 104.1 billion (US$74.0 billion)
Stock Exchanges: London New York Paris Singapore
    Tokyo Vienna Berlin Düsseldorf Frankfurt Hamburg
    Munich Stuttgart Basel Geneva Zurich
SICs: 6719 Holding Companies, Not Elsewhere
    Classified; 3711 Motor Vehicles & Car Bodies; 3714
    Motor Vehicle Parts & Accessories; 3721 Aircraft;
    3699 Electrical Equipment & Supplies, Not Elsewhere
    Classified; 5012 Automobiles & Other Motor
    Vehicles; 5013 Motor Vehicle Supplies & New Parts;
    6159 Miscellaneous Business Credit Institutions; 7389
    Business Services, Not Elsewhere Classified

Best known as the manufacturer of the luxurious Mercedes-Benz, Daimler-Benz AG is Europe's largest commercial truck producer and makes more heavy (over six-ton) trucks than any manufacturer in the world. As the owner of three huge conglomerates, purchased in the mid-1980s, the company also produces everything from fighter bombers to vacuum cleaners. Acquisition of the conglomerates made Daimler-Benz the largest industrial company in Germany and the nation's second-largest defense contractor.

The roots of this company go back to the mid-1880s and two engineers, Carl Benz and Gottlieb Daimler, who are cited by most authorities as the most important contributors to the development of the internal combustion engine. Despite the fact that they were both concerned with the same idea at virtually the same time, and they lived within 60 miles of each other, the two

apparently never even met. They certainly never envisioned the 1926 merger of their two companies.

Although Benz drove his first car in 1885 and Daimler ran his in 1886, neither was actually the first to create gasoline-powered vehicles. However, they were the first to persist long enough to make them viable as transportation. At this time the obstacles to motorized vehicles were enormous: gasoline was considered dangerously explosive; roads were poor; and few people could afford an automobile in any case. Nevertheless, Benz dedicated himself to revolutionizing the world's transportation with the internal combustion engine.

Early in 1885 Benz sat in a car and circled a track next to his small factory, while his workers and his wife stood nearby. The car had three wheels and a top speed of ten m.p.h. This engineering triumph was only slightly marred by Benz's first public demonstration, which took place shortly afterward, in which he forgot to steer the car and smashed into the brick wall around his own home. Despite this inauspicious debut, Benz's cars quickly became known for their quality of materials and construction. By 1888 Benz had 50 employees building his three-wheeled car. Two years later, he began making a four-wheeled vehicle.

Daimler's convictions about the internal combustion engine were as intense as Benz's. Originally a gunsmith, Daimler later trained as an engineer, studying in Germany, England, Belgium, and France. After working for a number of German and British firms, he became technical director for the Gasmotorenfabrik Deutz. Disillusioned by the company's limited vision, he and researcher Wilhelm Maybach resigned in 1882 to set up their own experimental workshop. They tested their first engine on a wooden bicycle. Later, they put engines into a four-wheeled vehicle and a boat. Daimler sold the French rights to his engines to Panhard-Levassor (which later fought him for the use of his name). In 1896 he granted a patent license to the British Daimler company, which eventually became independent of the German Daimler-Motoren-Gesellschaft.

The story of how Daimler found a new brand name for its cars has become legendary. In 1900 Austro-Hungarian Consul-General and businessman Emil Jellinek approached the company with a suggestion. He offered to underwrite the production of a new high performance car. In return, he asked that the vehicle be named after his daughter—Mercedes. Daimler's Mercedes continued to make automotive history. In 1906 the young engineer Ferdinand Porsche took the place of Daimler's oldest son, Paul, as chief engineer at the company's Austrian factory. (Paul Daimler returned to the main plant in Stuttgart.) In the five years Porsche was with Daimler, he produced 65 designs, which made him one of the most influential and prolific automotive designers ever. Approximately the same time, in 1909, the Mercedes star emblem was registered; it has embellished the radiators of all the company's cars since 1921.

In 1924 the Daimler and Benz companies began coordinating designs and production, but maintained their own brand names. They merged completely in 1926 to produce cars under the name Mercedes-Benz. The merger undoubtedly saved the two companies from bankruptcy in the poverty and inflation of post-World War I Germany.

The company continued to grow throughout the 1930s. The most consistently successful participant in automobile racing history, Mercedes-Benz scored international victories that added to its reputation. The company's racing success was also used as propaganda by the Third Reich in the years before World War II. The Mercedes-Benz became Adolph Hitler's parade transportation. Whenever he was photographed in a vehicle, it was a Mercedes. In 1939 the state took over the German auto industry, and during the war Daimler-Benz developed and produced trucks, tanks, and aircraft engines for the Luftwaffe. The company's importance to the German war machine made Daimler-Benz a primary target for Allied bombing raids. Two weeks of air strikes in September 1944 destroyed 70 percent or more of the company's plants. Although little was left of the company, workers returned to resume their old jobs after the war. To the surprise of many people, the factories recovered and the company again became one of the most successful auto manufacturers in the world.

Much of Daimler-Benz's growth in the 1950s occurred under the direction of stockholder Friedrich Flick. A convicted war criminal, Flick lost 80 percent of his steel fortune at the end of World War II. Yet he still had enough money to purchase just over 37 percent interest in Daimler-Benz between 1954 and 1957. By 1959 his $20 million investment was worth $200 million, and he had become Germany's second ranking industrialist. Flick's holdings allowed him to push the company to buy 80 percent of competitor Auto Union, in order to gain a smaller car for the Daimler product line. The acquisition made Daimler-Benz the fifth-largest automobile manufacturer in the world and the largest outside the United States.

The acquisition probably lessened the competitive impact of the new U.S. compact cars introduced in the 1950s; moreover, Daimler-Benz faced a lesser threat than other European automakers because the Mercedes appealed to the market segment made up of wealthy, status-conscious customers, and its appeal grew steadily. By 1960 Daimler-Benz already had 83,000 employees in seven West German plants. Additional plants were located in Argentina, Brazil, and India, and the company had established assembly lines in Mexico, South Africa, Belgium, and Ireland.

Daimler-Benz's conservative outlook was evident in its strategy of gradual growth, concentration on areas of expertise, foresight, and willingness to sacrifice short-term sales and earnings for long-term benefits. This conservatism helped soften the effect of the recession and gasoline shortages that had severely affected other automakers the 1970s. While many manufacturers were closing facilities and cutting workers' hours, Daimler-Benz registered record sales gains. Chairman Joachim Zahn, a lawyer, said the company had foreseen "the difficult phase" the auto industry was about to confront. Between 1973 and 1975, Zahn had set aside some $250 million as "preparation" for bad times. And while other automakers spent time and money on model changes, Daimler-Benz had invested in engines powered by inexpensive diesel fuel. These vehicles comprised 45 percent of its output by the mid-1970s. The company was not without problems during these years, as high labor costs and the increasing value of the deutsche mark were making Mercedes-Benz automobiles more expensive than ever. Rather than reducing costs or cutting corners, however, the company began to speak of its cars as "investments."

Although primarily known for its passenger cars, Daimler-Benz's commercial truck line was its largest source of profits for many years. The company profited from the oil price increase of the late 1970s, when demand for its commercial vehicles rose dramatically in the Middle East. Most of the company's trucks were made outside of Germany, unlike its cars. Later, the commercial line led the company into one risk that was stalled by unfortunate timing. In 1981 Daimler-Benz purchased the U.S.-based Freightliner Corp., a manufacturer of heavy trucks, just as sales ground to a halt in the face of a U.S. recession.

Some risk-taking was inevitable, of course; usually it paid off. Daimler-Benz increased its car production from 350,000 to 540,000 units a year between 1975 and 1983. Most of the increase was due to the introduction in 1983 of its "190" model, a smaller version of its saloon car. Despite some concern that the 190 would cannibalize sales of its larger cars, the 190 expanded Daimler-Benz's customer base, and the updated image of the new model attracted younger customers, lowering the average age of a Mercedes owner from 45 to 40.

As a manufacturer of luxury automobiles, Daimler-Benz was less vulnerable than most automakers to shifts in demand during the early 1980s. Most Mercedes-Benz customers were wealthy enough to rise above concerns about finance rates, inflation, recession, gasoline prices, or tax breaks. In early 1985, for example, German lawmakers vacillated over tax breaks for buyers of cars with lower exhaust emissions, and many Germans delayed purchasing a car until they could see which way the balance would swing. While other auto manufacturers suffered through the falling sales that resulted, Daimler-Benz was unaffected. Not only were its diesel-powered cars producing fewer fumes, but most Mercedes drivers were unconcerned about tax perks.

Another traditional safeguard for Daimler-Benz was its long-standing policy of making only as many cars as it could expect to sell, especially during a recession. The result was usually a backlog of demand when a recession ended. Additionally, since the company's sales were good even when the market was poor, Daimler-Benz never had to cater to demands from dealers. Although the United States comprised Daimler-Benz's largest export market, its 500 American dealers unsuccessfully requested more cars in 1985. Why wouldn't Daimler-Benz increase shipments? One reason was that sharp upswings in supply tended to lower the value of used Mercedes, which meant that owners were less likely to sell and buy a new one. And resales were vital to the company's success: 90 percent of West German owners bought another Mercedes when they changed cars. In foreign markets, the repurchase rate was often as high as 80 percent.

Due to limitations that the company placed on production and exports, a "grey market" in Mercedes-Benz cars operated in the United States. Dealers imported recent models from other countries without Daimler-Benz's authority, often illegally, and modified them to meet U.S. safety and emission standards; they then sold the cars at a lower price than regular dealer franchises. Daimler-Benz often tried to protect its carefully controlled market against these "grey market" dealers, but with little success. During the mid-1980s Daimler-Benz was confronted with a dramatic increase in competition for the luxury car market, the fastest-growing segment of the automobile business. Along with this market competition was the increasing speed and sophistication of competitors' automotive research. For example, pioneering Daimler-Benz engineers spent 18 years developing anti-skid brakes to enable drivers to keep control of their vehicles during sudden stops. A few months after the company introduced the breakthrough in the United States, Lincoln brought out a similar system as standard equipment.

Competition and the high price of research and development were two of the factors precipitating the sudden moves Daimler-Benz made in the year between February 1985 and February 1986. Industry analysts were surprised when the company acquired, in quick succession, three large conglomerates. This was a departure from Daimler-Benz's tradition of gradual growth. In February 1985 Daimler-Benz acquired Motoren-und-Turbinen-Union, which made aircraft engines and diesel motors for tanks and ships. Daimler already had a 50 percent interest in the company, and when MAN (a Daimler-Benz partner and manufacturer of heavy trucks and buses) wanted to acquire some cash, the company bought MAN's share for $160 million (Motoren-und-Turbinen-Union sales were $768 million in 1984).

The second acquisition followed in May 1985. Daimler-Benz spent $130 million for 65.6 percent of Dornier, a privately held manufacturer of spacecraft systems, commuter planes, and medical equipment with 1984 sales of $530 million. In early 1986 Daimler-Benz made its third acquisition, paying $820 million for control of AEG, a high-technology manufacturer of electronic equipment such as turbines, robotics, and data processing, as well as household appliances. Although the company's annual sales in 1984 were an impressive $3.7 billion, the company had just emerged from bankruptcy after losing $904 million in nine years building nuclear power plants. Many industry watchers were dubious about the diversification of a company that was already doing so well. Profits had increased every year but one between 1970 and 1985, and increased more than 50 percent in 1985 alone. Some analysts also questioned the speed of Daimler-Benz's purchases, as well as management's ability to hold such a large and diverse enterprise together.

Yet Werner Breitschwerdt, chairman of Daimler-Benz's management board, maintained full confidence in the moves. Breitschwerdt, an electrical engineer, joined the passenger car division of the company in 1953 and served as head of styling and product development. He became a member of the managing board in 1977 and chairman in 1983 after the death of his predecessor, Dr. Gerhard Prinz. Breitschwerdt was the first engineer to head the company in decades, and the only research and development expert to hold that position. By bringing the technical and research expertise of the new subsidiaries to Daimler-Benz, Breitschwerdt hoped to significantly expand the company's research base. The prospects were highly promising for the automotive division, whose engineers were already interested in developing "intelligent" cars. In this area, the radar technology of AEG and the materials expertise of Dornier would be extremely useful.

However, the Deutsche Bank (which owned 28 percent of Daimler-Benz) became increasingly troubled by Breitschwerdt's apparent lack of a clear program for integrating the company's $5.5 billion in recent acquisitions, and in July 1987 Breitschwerdt announced his resignation. Despite the major reservations of several board members, but with Deutsche Bank's full approval, Edzard Reuter, the company's chief strategic planner, was appointed to succeed Breitschwerdt. These recent upheavals seemed to have little impact on Daimler-Benz's performance; it still emerged as the largest industrial concern in Germany. And notwithstanding its recent diversification, the company remained closely identified with its line of expensive automobiles.

In 1989 Daimler-Benz InterServices AG (Debis) was created to handle data processing, financial and insurance services, and real estate management for the Daimler group. Modeling Debis after similar internal service divisions at Eastman Kodak, General Motors, and IBM, Debis's primary function was to trim much of the company's corporate fat. The following year the dismantling of the Berlin Wall had both positive and negative repercussions for Daimler-Benz: while the recently acquired aeronautical and defense businesses were hurt, the resulting unification provided a welcome jump in demand for Daimler-Benz's automotive division.

By the early 1990s the German economy took a turn for the worse, and the consequences of Daimler-Benz's mid-1980s spending spree began to take their toll. For the first time in its history, Daimler-Benz was forced to eliminate 14,000 jobs (through early retirement and attrition) in its automotive division as Mercedes sales plunged and Daimler's overall profit dropped 25 percent in 1992. Hoping to bolster sales by expansion, Mercedes-Benz bought a five percent stake in Korea's Ssangyong Motor Company in December to build four-wheel-drive vehicles, vans, and later passenger cars using Mercedes engines and technology.

First-quarter figures for 1993 reflected Germany's widening recession, with Daimler-Benz's net income plummeting by 96 percent to $12.4 million on sales of $13.1 billion, while Mercedes's sales (65 percent of the group's) fell 24 percent for the period. Yet with long-term goals in mind, Daimler-Benz announced hidden reserves of $2.45 billion in an effort to become the first German firm listed on the New York Stock

Exchange. The disclosure by Daimler-Benz, which had been prevented from admittance in the past by discrepancies between German and U.S. accounting procedures, was the first of several compliances offered to satisfy U.S. regulators. By mid-year, using stringent U.S. accounting procedures, Daimler-Benz reported sales of $69.6 billion and its first loss since the end of World War II. Yet the company's financial maneuvering earlier in the year had paid off: in October 1993, Daimler-Benz triumphantly listed its stock on the Big Board of the NYSE.

Mercedes-Benz, meanwhile, was busy with both internal and external expansion. A new lower-priced C-Class Mercedes (known as the "Baby-Benz") was introduced to appeal to younger buyers in the United States and Europe, while plans were announced to build a $300 million manufacturing facility in Tuscaloosa, Alabama, in return for massive tax breaks, investments from Jefferson County and the city of Birmingham, and a host of other incentives many labeled extravagant. Other big moves in 1993 included Debis's construction of new headquarters in Berlin, rewarded by $5.1 billion in sales, nearly double those of 1990. Daimler-Benz finished 1993 with overall revenue of $70 billion, with sales constrained by higher interest rates, an increase in value-added taxes, and a sluggish European market. The year's losses amounted to $1.3 billion, including an $88.3 million deficit from Deutsche Aerospace AG (DASA), which continued to hemorrhage for the next several years.

In 1994 Mercedes-Benz initiated a sweeping reorganization that included manufacturing more car parts outside Germany, appealing to younger buyers through radically different U.S. advertising, and developing more of the smaller, C-Class Mercedes or Baby-Benz models, as well as sport-utility vehicles and minivans built at the new Alabama plant. Near the end of the year Mercedes announced plans for a micro-Mercedes, a four-seat, four-door version of its luxurious A-Class car to be marketed to Americans as a "city" car for under $20,000, while an even tinier compact called the "Swatchmobile" would be built in France and sold through a partnership with Swiss businessman Nicolas Hayek (the driving force behind Swatch wristwatches). Also on the drawing board was a new model in Mercedes's E-Class full-size cars.

While Mercedes streamlined operations, Daimler-Benz's workforce reductions from 1992 to 1994 now totaled 20 percent of its 350,000 worldwide employees (bringing with it a $2.5 billion restructuring charge). Believing it had weathered the worst of its recessionary storms, Daimler-Benz climbed back to profitability in 1994 with earnings of $750 million, due in part to a sharp increase in both buying and selling outside Germany. Yet 1995 proved a series of highs and lows beginning with a changing of the guard: Edzard Reuter stepped down as CEO and was succeeded by former protege Jurgen E. Schrempp, former chairman of DASA.

Among Schrempp's first moves was to stem the flow of red ink at Daimler-Benz Industrie. Arranging a 50/50 merger with the Swedish-Swiss ABB Asea Brown Boveri Ltd. in exchange for $900 million in cash from Daimler-Benz, the new venture, ABB Daimler-Benz Transportation, would become the world's largest international rail systems provider, generating sales in the neighborhood of $4.5 billion annually. Yet the troubled DASA and Daimler-Benz Industrie, where losses were expec-

ted to reach $2 billion in 1995, still faced possible workforce reductions of 20,000 or more. On the positive side, Daimler-Benz signed up with China and Korea in May to develop a new $2.4 billion commercial jet (holding around 120 passengers) for Asian markets.

With the climb of the mark in 1995, Daimler-Benz was saddled with higher labor costs and serious setbacks as the dollar remained weak. Annointed as the Daimler-Benz group's savior, Mercedes-Benz, which earned $1.3 billion in 1994 and was expected to do at least the same in 1995, was held up as a model to its ailing parent. Always Daimler-Benz's cash cow, Mercedes had just agreed to a $1.2 billion joint venture with Nanfang South China Motor Corp. to build minivans and engines in China, as well as a second $50 million venture with Yangzhou Motor Coach Manufacturing Co. to build touring buses and commercial undercarriages.

Determined to keep Daimler-Benz on course, Schrempp vowed to fortify the "integrated transportation company" by eliminating 200 upper management positions at the Stuttgart headquarters. The embattled conglomerate still faced high production costs and hoped further global outsourcing would alleviate the problem. Additionally, Schrempp ordered shaky subsidiaries like DASA and Daimler-Benz Industrie to either shape up and stem losses or face the consequences. Yet despite cyclical slumps in its varied enterprises, Daimler-Benz endured as not only the parent of the perennially popular Mercedes-Benz, but as an example of German industry at its best.

Principal Operating Units

Mercedes-Benz; AEG Daimler-Benz Industrie; Daimler-Benz Aerospace; Daimler-Benz InterServices; Holding-und-Finanzgesellschaften.

Further Reading

Aeppel, Timothy, "Daimler-Benz Discloses Hidden Reserves of $2.45 Billion, Seeks Big Board Listing," *Wall Street Journal*, March 25, 1993, p. A10.

"Backbiting at Daimler," *Business Week*, August 7, 1995, p. 45.

Browning, E. S., and Helene Cooper, "States' Bidding War Over Mercedes Plant Made for Costly Chase," *Wall Street Journal*, November 24, 1993, pp. A1, A6.

Choi, Audrey, "Mercedes to Cut German Force by 14,000 Jobs," *Wall Street Journal*, August 25, 1993, p. A6.

——, "Mercedes-Benz Sets Restructuring Plans in Wake of Vehicle Units' Difficulties," *Wall Street Journal*, January 27, 1994, p. A10.

——, "Head of Deutsche Aerospace Expected to Succeed Reuter as Daimler Chairman," *Wall Street Journal*, June 28, 1994, p. A15.

——, "Daimler-Benz Plans Job Cuts of 13,500 in '95," *Wall Street Journal*, April 13, 1995, pp. A3–4.

——, "For Mercedes, Going Global Means Being Less German," *Wall Street Journal*, April 27, 1995, p. B4.

Cole, Jeff, "Boeing Faces European Competition in Effort to Build Small Plane for Asia," *Wall Street Journal*, May 8, 1995, p. B2.

Cooper, Helene, and Glenn Ruffenbach, "Alabama's Winning of Mercedes Plant Will Be Costly, with Major Tax Breaks," *Wall Street Journal*, September 30, 1993, pp. A2, 12.

Gumbel, Peter, "Daimler to Pay $900 Million to ABB as They Merge Railroad Operations," *Wall Street Journal*, March 17, 1995, p. A6.

——, and Choi, Audrey, "Germany Making Comeback, with Daimler in the Lead," *Wall Street Journal*, April 7, 1995, p. A10.

Kimes, Beverly Rae, *The Star and the Laurel: The Centennial History of Daimler, Mercedes, and Benz, 1886–1986,* Montvale, N.J.: Mercedes Benz of North America, 1986.

Marshall, Matt, and Joseph Kahn, "Mercedes Wins China Minivan Project," *Wall Street Journal,* July 13, 1995, p. A2.

Nelson, Mark M., "Daimler-Benz AG Makes Way In-House," *Wall Street Journal,* September 24, 1993, p. B11.

Raghavan, Anita, and Christi Harlan, "Daimler's SEC Pact to List in U.S. May Spur Other Foreign Firms to Follow," *Wall Street Journal,* March 31, 1993, p. B12.

Reed, Stanley, "Backbiting at Daimler," *Business Week,* August 7, 1995, p. 45.

Roth, Terence, "Daimler-Benz's 1st-Period Net Fell 96% as German Recession Hurt Auto Sales," *Wall Street Journal,* May 14, 1993, p. A8.

Schmid, John, "Daimler-Benz Reports First-Ever Loss, Reflecting New Accounting, Lower Sales," *Wall Street Journal,* September 20, 1993, p. A10.

Simison, Robert L., "Love Your Big, Luxurious Mercedes? German Car Maker Is Thinking Small," *Wall Street Journal,* December 12, 1994, p. B8.

Soo-Mi, Kim, "Ssangyong Places Hopes on Accord with Mercedes AG," *Wall Street Journal,* December 18, 1992, p. A5.

Steinmetz, Gene, "BellSouth and Thyssen Join to Compete in German Telecommunications Market," *Wall Street Journal,* May 9, 1995, p. A14.

Templeman, John, "The Shocks for Daimler's New Driver," *Business Week,* August 21, 1995, pp. 38–39.

Warner, Fara, "Mercedes Goes Hollywood and High-Tech," *Wall Street Journal,* January 24, 1995, p. B6.

Whitney, Glenn, and Timothy Roth, "Daimler's U.S. Listing May Be Sign of Change in German Equities Market," *Wall Street Journal,* March 29, 1993, p. B6.

—updated by Taryn Benbow Pfalzgraf

Donna Karan Company

550 Seventh Avenue
New York, New York 10018
U.S.A.
(212) 789-1627
Fax: (212) 354-5215

Private Company
Incorporated: 1984
Employees: 1,600
Sales: $550 million (1995)
SICs: 2311 Men's & Boys' Suits, Coats, & Overcoats;
2329 Men's & Boys' Clothing, Not Elsewhere
Classified; 2331 Women's/Misses' Blouses & Shirts;
2337 Women's/Misses' Suits & Coats; 2339
Women's/Misses' Outerwear, Not Elsewhere
Classified; 2844 Perfumes, Cosmetics & Other Toilet
Preparations

Donna Karan Company is a leading American clothing designer and a powerhouse in the international women's fashion industry. The company, run by the woman whose name it bears, also designs men's clothing, operates a beauty company, supports several retail stores, sells its own perfume, and designs various fashion accessories, among other endeavors. Popular company brand names include DKNY. Donna Karan Co. was growing rapidly in the mid-1990s by penetrating new product markets and expanding overseas.

Donna Karan Co. was created by designer and entrepreneur Donna Karan, who started the company in 1984. With help from outside investors, she and her husband developed the company into a half-billion-dollar fashion force in little more than a decade. Karan's quick success, though, was the result of a youth spent in and around the design and fashion industries. Her father, who died when Karan was three years old, was a custom tailor, and her mother was a showroom model and sales representative. Karan's stepfather, moreover, sold women's apparel.

Inspired by her parents and endowed with an innate knack for design, Karan enrolled in New York City's Parsons School of Design. At the age of 20, she took a job with fashion industry legend Anne Klein. Karan's rise at Anne Klein was phenomenal. She instantly found her niche and was able to thrive in the Klein organization. "Her hair was blowing, the fabrics were flying . . . ," recalled Burt Wayne, head of the Anne Klein design studio, in the December 21, 1992, *Time*, of the first time he met Karan. "You could instantly see Donna's enthusiasm—and her tenacity." Karan's energy, determination, and perfectionism helped her to succeed at Klein and later to prosper in her own design business, despite the fact that the design field was dominated by men. Anne Klein, who became a sort of idol to Karan, was known as extremely demanding and a perfectionist. It was those common qualities that drew Karan and Klein together. Indeed, after only four years at the company, Karan became Anne Klein's successor.

While at Klein, Karan married Mark Karan, a clothing-boutique owner. In 1974, at the age of 26, she gave birth to her first child, Gabby. Tragically, just one week after the baby was born, Anne Klein died. Karan, Klein's respected protege, was the natural successor. She was elevated to head of design and has been credited with preserving the Klein name and helping to build the company during the next ten years. During that time Karan worked with a friend from Parsons School of Design, Louis dell-Olio, to sustain the Anne Klein legacy and branch into new markets. In 1982, for example, they launched a successful line of clothes for working women (dubbed "Anne Klein II") targeted at the lower-priced market.

For the first time in her career, with the Anne Klein II line, Karan had designed an entire new collection of clothing. This success, along with the desire to have more creative control, influenced her decision to start her own company. Anne Klein was owned at the time by Japanese textile conglomerate Takihyo. Takihyo's executives were open to the idea of Karan branching out on her own, but Karan was hesitant to leave the security of Klein. So, in 1984, Karan's boss, Frank Mori, effectively fired her. Simultaneously, Takihyo offered to front $3 million in start-up capital to help Karan launch her own venture. Karan was offered a 50 percent equity stake. "It was like, 'The bad news is you're fired. And the good news is you have your own company'," Mori recalled in *Time*.

By 1984 Karan was married to her second husband, sculptor Stephan Weiss, and he teamed up with Karan—they shared the chief executive slot—to start the new design company. Karan showed her first collection at her own fashion show in 1985, just six months after leaving her post at Klein. The crowd greeted the line with wild applause, whistles, and a standing ovation. The market reacted similarly, generating a huge early demand for Karan's apparel. The chief appeal of the clothing was that it offered working women an elegant, classic alternative to the often quixotic, fanciful designs of the day.

Throughout the mid- and late 1980s Donna Karan was known as a savvy risk-taker: breaking new ground by designing practical, comfortable, refined clothing that made women look good, and shying away from bizarre, jaw-dropping fashions and tacky frills. Signature designs included easy-fitting jackets, wrap skirts, and one-piece silk bodysuits. Importantly, Karan (herself a size 12) became known for her ability to create skirts, pants, and other clothing that complemented a woman's figure, even if she wasn't as thin as a model. The down-to-earth approach was well received in the market, where Karan's style was considered refreshing. "I am accessible," Karan said in a 1989 *Time* article. "I see myself as a person who stays up all night and worries about her daughter and her husband, and would like to get the carpeting ordered."

During the late 1980s Karan relied primarily on her Donna Karan New York collection of upscale clothing. That apparel included blazers and blouses, for example, that ranged from $500 to $1000 or more in price. At the same time, she pursued other avenues that piggy-backed on the success of the Donna Karan line. In 1987, for example, Karan jumped into the hyper-competitive hosiery business. Karan was convinced, despite critics' protests, that women would be willing to spend more money to get thicker hosiery that would hide sags and other unattractive features. Karan, in partnership with Hanes, developed a hose that was twice as thick and twice as expensive as normal hosiery. Customers were willing to pay for the quality, and the product was well received. Within five years the company was selling more than $30 million worth of the hose to wholesalers.

In 1989 Karan drew on the recognition of her Donna Karan New York collection to launch a second line dubbed 'DKNY.' The DKNY line was designed to provide stylish, casual, and affordable clothing that would appeal to a less elite market segment. The apparel was still relatively expensive—a school blazer sold for about $450, a pair of jeans was priced at $85, and a plaid wool jacket went for $350—but it brought an entirely new and much broader group of buyers to Donna Karan Co. The line, which was craftily marketed on a background of black-and-white cityscapes that enhanced its urban nature, was one of the most successful launches in fashion history. Begun in early 1989, DKNY helped Donna Karan Co. generate about $115 million in sales for the year.

Karan's increasing influence on the fashion scene had earned her the title "The Queen of Seventh Avenue" with the press, and the Donna Karan name was considered 'red hot' in

the apparel retailing industry. Encouraged by gains, Karan and Weiss pushed ahead with new products ranging from perfume and accessories to children's clothing. In addition, Karan was hoping to expand overseas. The company was already selling clothes in a chic London boutique in 1989 and had started selling clothes to stores in Germany and Japan as early as 1986, but Karan wanted to aggressively market throughout Europe and Asia.

To help the company make the transition from a sort of family-owned business to a more conventional corporate entity, Karan brought in apparel industry pro Stephen Ruzow, a former Warnaco executive. Among other tasks, Ruzow was hired to eliminate production problems that were causing some quality control glitches in the company's clothing lines. Meanwhile, Karan continued to extend the company's reach. Among her boldest moves was her 1991 introduction of men's clothing under the DKNY label. Critics chastised the move, claiming that men would never wear the label of a woman designer, yet the effort was ultimately a success. Popular items in the men's line included a $475 leather vest and $600 cashmere crewneck sweaters.

Besides moving into men's and children's clothing, Karan began licensing its name for products ranging from intimate apparel and furs to shoes and eyeglasses. The company also launched a more aggressive international expansion initiative, started a beauty business, and tried to market its own perfume. The perfume effort was a big risk for the company because of the expense typically required to fund a perfume start-up. Most companies hired an outside company to market their perfume in exchange for a small percentage of royalties. Karan Co., in contrast, tried to market the perfume itself. Early results from the sales campaign were disappointing.

The slow start for Karan's perfume venture was just a precursor to a spate of setbacks that plagued the company beginning in 1992. The problems showed up on Karan Co.'s bottom line as financial losses and in the organization as late deliveries and insufficient cash flow. Part of the problem could be traced to Karan's 1992 addition of the men's lines and the start-up of the beauty business. Those expensive efforts, combined with other initiatives, loaded the company with debt that sapped cash flow and profits. Furthermore, Karan and Weiss were criticized for their unconventional licensing program, particularly related to the perfume endeavor. Although sales continued to rise rapidly, to $260 million in 1992 and well over $300 million in 1993, Donna Karan Co. was bleeding losses and buckling under its debt load.

Confident of Karan's core business strategy, investors stepped in to buoy the enterprise. Importantly, a group of banks led by Citicorp injected $125 million into the company. Likewise, a Singapore-based company invested $21 million in Donna Karan Japan, the company's Japanese subsidiary. Meanwhile, Donna Karan Co. scrambled to restructure its debt, cut unnecessary costs, and shuffle its management team. To that end, Karan's husband eventually announced his intent to relinquish his co-CEO position and return to sculpting, although he continued to be active as a legal adviser and in various product development initiatives.

As Donna Karan Co.'s finances stabilized, sales growth continued at a rampant pace. Annual revenues rose to more than $450 million in 1992, and then to $550 million in 1995. The gains came from several of Karan's operations. The DKNY line continued to excel, for example, and even the lagging beauty business began posting profits for the first time in 1995. In addition, the company had revised its licensing strategy. Karan's international business, moreover, was taking off. With distribution centers in Hong Kong, Amsterdam, and Japan, as well as 15 freestanding stores in Europe, Asia, and the Middle East, the company was generating about $140 million in overseas revenue by 1995.

For the late 1990s, Karan was planning aggressive growth overseas. The company's portion of overseas revenues, in fact, was scheduled to rise to at least 50 percent before the turn of the century, and Karan expected to be generating $300 million in sales in Asia, alone. Karan projected sales of $1 billion annually by the year 2000. Among new ventures, early in 1996 Karan launched a home page on the World Wide Web. "Fashion-savvy, conscious women around the world are responding to what I'm saying," Karan said in the December 18, 1995, *U.S. News & World Report*. "The totality of it just keeps growing and growing."

Principal Subsidiaries

Donna Karan New York; Donna Karan Japan; The Donna Karan Beauty Company; Donna Karan Hosiery; The Donna Karan Shoe Company; Donna Karan Menswear; DKNY Men.

Further Reading

"Donna Karan: Empress of Seventh Avenue," *Gala,* December 29, 1994, pp. 69–74.
Foley, Bridget, "Donna's Joint Venture," *WWD,* June 22, 1992, p. 4.
——, "Donna's Quest," *W,* August 1995, p. 96.
Gault, Ylonda, "Donna Karan Sells Her New York Style," *Crain's New York Business,* May 1, 1995, p. 24.
Rudolph, Barbara, "High Style for the 9–5 Set: Donna Karan Sells Working Women a Look of Their Own," *Time,* October 23, 1989, p. 70.
——, "Donna Inc.," *Time,* December 21, 1992, p. 54.
Seider, Jill Jordan, "Donna Karan's Chic Design for Success," *U.S. News & World Report,* December 18, 1995, pp. 59–60.

—Dave Mote

Electronics for Imaging, Inc.

2855 Campus Drive
San Mateo, California 94403
U.S.A.
(415) 286-8600
Fax: (415) 286-8686

Public Company
Incorporated: 1988
Employees: 249
Sales: $190.5 million (1995)
Stock Exchanges: NASDAQ
SICs: 7372 Prepackaged Software

Electronics for Imaging, Inc. designs and sells systems and software that support high-quality color printing in an office environment. The company has established itself as a global technological leader in its niche since its start in 1988. Through overseas expansion and the introduction of new technology, Electronics for Imaging was achieving explosive growth in the mid-1990s.

Electronics for Imaging (EFI) was founded in 1988 by Efraim Arazi, a native of Israel who was 51 years old at the time. Within a few years, that company would become a force in its niche. But even before his success with EFI, Arazi had developed a venerable reputation as a pioneer and visionary in the computer graphics equipment industry. Arazi earned an engineering degree in the 1960s at the Massachusetts Institute of Technology (MIT), where he was also exposed to computer science. After graduating, he remained in the United States for a few years and helped NASA develop a digital camera. He then returned to Israel and, in 1968, started a company that became known as Scitex Corp. Ltd.

During the 1970s and 1980s Arazi built Scitex into a leading developer and manufacturer of graphic-design and publishing hardware. Importantly, Scitex is credited with pioneering the electronic color imaging process in 1968, as well as with numerous related breakthroughs in the succeeding two decades. By the late 1980s, Scitex, with Arazi at the helm, was known as

a world leader in computerized color printing. The company's products were used to generate high-quality, pre-press, computerized color images that were printed using conventional 'long-run' printing techniques. Before Arazi left Scitex, the company was generating revenues approaching $500 million annually and had sold more than $1.5 billion worth of equipment since Arazi founded it.

By the late 1980s Arazi's inventive and entrepreneurial spirit was making him restless. So, in 1988 he simply walked away from his chief executive post at Scitex, despite the company's surging sales and profits. He decided to start a new company from scratch that he dubbed Electronics for Imaging, or 'Efi' as he nicknamed it. (By no coincidence, the 'Efi' moniker was a universal nickname of his own first name, Efraim.) Arazi's plan was to branch out into a new sphere of the color imaging industry that had been mostly unexplored up until that time. ''While CEO of Scitex, I began to see an opening for color software, but discovered there was no way to do it within a $600 million company,'' he said in the August 20, 1993 *San Francisco Business Times.* ''You don't use a Boeing 747 to go shooting at flies,'' Arazi wryly observed.

Arazi's specific plan was to develop a relatively low-cost, easy-to-use system that would allow users to process and print high-quality graphics, including photo images, in a low-technology environment. Prior to the late 1980s, high-quality color processing and printing was done only on expensive equipment, like that developed by Scitex, and typically by graphics professionals. The potential for a major shift in computerized color graphics printing technology began to emerge in the mid-1980s. During that time, such major copier manufacturers as Canon, Kodak, and Minolta began developing and introducing machines that were capable of generating extremely high-quality color copies for the mass market. The price of that technology declined rapidly in the late 1980s, putting it within reach of many smaller and mid-size companies.

Arazi wanted to initiate a revolution in color desktop publishing similar to the one caused by the black-and-white desktop laser printer. Those systems, introduced in the 1980s, made it possible for individuals to generate black-and-white text and graphics that could have been created just a few years earlier only on expensive, professional, 'offset' printing equipment. Rather than develop separate color imaging and printing machines that were the color equivalents of desktop laser printers, however, he realized that all that he needed to do was develop software that would allow a desktop computer or workstation to communicate with advanced color copiers. Users could then use their desktop computers and peripherals to print professional-looking color images on their copiers.

Arazi's new enterprise hardly resembled the classic shoe-string-budget, entrepreneurial start-up venture. Aside from his personal hoard of cash, Arazi had access to numerous capital sources. Scitex became a major investor in the company, for example, and EFI was able to get $10.1 million in startup cash in the form of advances on products and sublicenses from copier manufacturers. Indeed, the copier manufacturers eagerly supported Arazi's effort because they realized that his planned system could vastly increase the market for their products. Support from outside sources allowed EFI to show revenues of $3.7 million during its first two years, despite the lack of a salable product.

EFI also differed from the typical startup in that its management ranks were packed with heavy-hitting talent. Experienced veterans on EFI's team included principal scientist Dr. Yigal Accad and director of research Dr. Jacob Aizikowitz, both of whom had worked for Arazi at Scitex. Among other members were: Liz Bond, a former director at Adobe Systems; Donald McKinney, a former vice-president at Silicon Graphics; and David Izuka, a previous WordStar International executive and software industry veteran. In addition its own staff, EFI benefitted from links with researchers at MIT.

The association with MIT was important, because it provided the technological foundation upon which EFI would build its first product. EFI became the exclusive licensee of the W.F. Schreiber U.S. Patent 4,500,919. Issued in 1989 and effective for seven years, that patent was the result of eight years and $4 million worth of research conducted at MIT. The outcome of that research and development effort was the first layman-oriented, color preprinting, device-independent technology. A total of four Ph.D. and 12 masters degrees were awarded to researchers who contributed to the project. The chief advantage of the technology was that it brought under control the multiple variables that made it difficult to reproduce color images: lighting, inks, paper, and computer input devices, among others.

EFI's development team scrambled during 1989 and 1990 to build marketable products based on technology related to the patent. It started out focusing on four products: The Eport Color Server, a system that would move color between different desktop publishing and printing devices; the Fiery Controller, a device that would allow color copiers to function as color computer printers; Cachet, a software product that would allow desktop publishers to preview and manipulate color images; and the Color Receiver, which would effectively link desktop publishing and commercial printing systems. EFI planned to license and sell its technology and products to various software, hardware, and copier manufacturer companies.

EFI introduced its first product in 1991: the Fiery color server, the controller described above. The Fiery server was a box that housed hardware and software. The box could be used

to link a personal computer—Macintosh or IBM-compatible—and a high-grade color copier to generate four-color, offset-quality reproductions. As intimated earlier, users could create or manipulate the images using their computers. A major technological advantage of the product was that it offered, for the first time on a nonprofessional system, WYSIWYG (what-you-see-is-what-you-get, meaning that the printer produced a true reproduction of the computerized image).

The Fiery system was a landmark device, and represented the start of a pivotal transformation in color printing. The chief breakthrough was that, for the first time, users could print short runs of color images at reasonable prices (traditional offset-color printers, in contrast, had to produce hundreds or thousands of images to achieve price efficiency). The Fiery system was capable of producing a document or image for roughly 35 cents, whereas the first page printed by a conventional offset system effectively cost $2,000 to set up and print. Furthermore, because the technology was new, that price differential was expected to increase throughout the mid- and late 1990s.

With its licensing and distribution programs already in place, EFI was able to capitalize quickly on demand for its Fiery system. The company generated sales of $16.43 million and net income of $618,000 in 1991, its first year of product sales. Those figures rose to $53.7 million and $2.18 million, respectively, in 1992. In an effort to sustain that momentum, Arazi decided to generate investment capital in 1992 by taking EFI public. He had considered going public very early, in 1990, but the Persian Gulf War had thwarted the offering. Even as late as 1992, though, his plan was criticized, because some analysts believed that the company's short profit history would minimize the cashflow from any stock sale. Nevertheless, the successful October 1992 offering brought nearly $40 million into EFI's war chest.

1993 greeted EFI with a deluge of orders for its Fiery systems. EFI sold the systems primarily to Canon, Xerox, Kodak, and Agfa (of Belgium), which put the systems in the hands of companies that owned or leased their color copying equipment. The Fiery units were priced between $20,000 and $38,000, depending on printing speed and other features. In addition, by 1993 EFI was beginning to introduce other products from its development pipeline. Early in the year it began selling its Cachet software, which allowed a computer user to scan a photograph into the computer and manipulate the image for printing. That shrink-wrapped product sold for $500 to $600.

Strong demand allowed EFI to boost revenues to $89.5 million in 1993 and net income to nearly $8 million. The company's stock price jumped to $24 going into 1994 and then to nearly $30 later in the year. It fell into the mid-$20s later in the year, however, on speculation that the company's sales would slide early in 1995. That speculation was caused partly by EFI's intent to introduce a new, less expensive line of Fiery controller systems in 1995. Some observers believed that the company was trying to dump its inventory before it brought out the new line, thereby artificially raising its stock price. Those critics were undoubtedly surprised when EFI sales and profits continued to surge.

EFI's sales rose more than 40 percent in 1994 to $130 million, and net income increased to a record $21.3 million. Management seemed determined to repeat those impressive gains in 1995. Importantly, the company began selling its new Fiery XJ product line, which was a line of three color controller products, each shaped like a different-sized rectangular box and offering progressively advanced features. EFI executed a pivotal agreement with Canon for that company to market, sell, and service EFI's Fiery XJ products under the respected Canon brand name. That announcement and other positive developments pushed EFI's stock price past $50 by mid-1995.

By 1995 EFI had shipped more than 20,000 Fiery systems. That figure would rise to more than 30,000 in 1996. Sales surpassed $190 million for the 1995 year, and were growing rapidly early in 1996 with units being shipped throughout the United States, Europe, and Japan. EFI's founder, Arazi, relinquished the chief executive and presidency slots in 1995, but remained chairman of the board. He was succeeded by 32-year-old Dan Avida, a talented computer engineer who had joined EFI in 1989. Under Avida's and Arazi's direction, EFI planned to sustain its drive to make cost-efficient, high-quality color printing available to anyone with a personal computer.

Principal Subsidiaries

EFI Sales Corp., Inc.; Electronics for Imaging (Europe) Ltd.; Electronics for Imaging (Ireland) Ltd.; Electronics for Imaging (Israel) Ltd.

Further Reading

Abelson, Reed, ''Leapfrogger,'' *Forbes,* October 28, 1991, p. 203.

Carlsen, Clifford, ''EFI-vescence: Success Bubbles for 'Computer King of Color','' *San Francisco Business Times,* August 20, 1993, Sec. 2, p. 8A.

Carlsen, Clifford, ''Firm Pushes Color-Image Revolution,'' *San Francisco Business Times,* September 3, 1990, p. 1.

Davis, Gil, and Liz Bond, ''Profile of Electronics for Imaging,'' *Business Wire,* June 1, 1990.

''E.F.I. Opens Center in Israel,'' *Israel Business Today,* January 1, 1993, p. 4.

Labate, John, ''Electronics for Imaging,'' *Fortune,* June 28, 1993, p. 107.

Levy, Lawrence, ''Scitex Executive Named President of Electronics for Imaging Europe,'' *Business Wire,* April 7, 1994.

''Mr. Color; Dan Avia, Head of Electronics for Imaging, Hopes the Company's Fiery Product Will Help Make Black and White Printing Obsolete,'' *Forbes,* December 4, 1995, p. 270.

''Record Revenues for EFI,'' *Israel Business Today,* October 23, 1992, p. 11.

Serwer, Andrew E., ''America's Fastest Growing Companies,'' *Fortune,* August 8, 1994.

Weber, Merril, ''EFT the 'If Only' Story of the Year,'' *Israel Business Today,* April 21, 1995, p. 14.

—Dave Mote

English China Clays plc

1015 Arlington Business Park
Theale
Reading RG7 4SA
United Kingdom
(1734) 304010
Fax: (1734) 309501

Public Company
Incorporated: 1919 as English China Clays Ltd.
Employees: 8,788
Sales: £1.04 billion (1994)
Stock Exchanges: London NASDAQ
SICs: 1455 Kaolin and Ball Clay; 2865 Cyclic Crudes
   and Intermediates; 2899 Chemical Preparations, Not
   Elsewhere Classified; 6531 Real Estate Agents and
   Managers

English China Clays plc (formerly known as ECC Group plc) is perhaps best known as the world's largest producer of kaolin, a fine white clay used primarily for finishing glossy paper. This product as well as other specialty mineral pigments and chemicals produced by the company are used in the manufacture of high-quality printing and writing paper as well as in the manufacture of ceramics, paints, and polymers. While the company had also been active in the construction materials business, that division was spun off as CAMAS plc, an independent company, in 1994. More than half of the group's turnover now derives from its overseas operations, and the company continues to focus on enhancing its geographic influence. Sales outside the United Kingdom accounted for 87 percent of the company's revenue in 1995.

Kaolin (literally "white hill") takes its name from the mountain in China from which European manufacturers of ceramics originally obtained their supplies of the raw material. The increasing demand for ceramics in Europe stimulated a search for raw materials nearer home, and by the early 18th century, china clay deposits had been located in Bohemia, Thur-

ingia, Saxony, and near Limoges in France. In the United Kingdom china clay deposits that were found to be of a finer quality than elsewhere in Europe were discovered in Cornwall in the middle of the 18th century; their exploitation created the United Kingdom's china clay industry. Its development in the 19th century was economically most important to Cornwall, since its growth took place at a time when the industry upon which Cornwall had previously depended for employment and wealth creation, tin mining, was being forced into decline by foreign competition. Changes in the papermaking industry and its expansion in the second half of the 19th century created a new and growing market for china clay.

Twentieth century processes of extracting, refining, and drying china clay remained in essence the same as they were in the 19th century, although the application of technology transferred to machines much of the work done by manual labor in the early days, improved the purity of the final product, and made it possible to extract other minerals that formerly went to waste. Even so, waste remained a formidable problem for the English China Clays; despite the use of sand and the application of much research, the production of one ton of clay still created seven tons of waste. The first process, the pit operation, involved exposing china clay deposits by removing the overburden. Some deposits may be as close to the surface as three feet while others may be hundreds of feet below ground. Hydraulic mining, by firing water jets from a cannon at the clay deposits, freed the deposits and created a slurry which also contained sand and mica. The slurry was then pumped out and the coarser sand removed before the refining process proceeded. This process took out unwanted minerals such as quartz, mica, and feldspar.

Geologically, china clay is formed in granite rocks by the decomposition of feldspar. At this stage chemical bleaching to remove the stains in the clay caused by mineral salts, particularly iron oxide, can add value to the final product, a technological advance not available until after World War II. ECCI operated six refining plants in Devon and Cornwall that took clay from a number of pits and mixed it in the quantities required for finished products of varying characteristics. The final drying process, which usually took place in natural gas-fired driers, was originally done in coal-fired kilns and even, at some pits, wind and sun dried.

In the first half of the 19th century, production of china clay was in the hands of many small proprietors, some of whom owned the land on which the mine lay and some of whom leased it. Although some consolidation took place later in the century, in 1914 there were still some 70 individual producers. At that time the industry was characterized by low wages, overproduction, and price-cutting. These problems were exacerbated by the outbreak of World War I, particularly for an industry that depended on exporting, to the extent, in 1914, of 70 percent of its output. During the war, shipping capacity for goods such as china clay, which had little or no military purpose, was severely limited. By 1917 many china clay producers were making losses and few, if any, were making profits. A trade association, Associated China Clays, was established in that year, and in its seven-year existence—it terminated in 1924—had some success in stabilizing the industry by setting prices and sales quotas. In 1919, the three largest producers in Cornwall—Martin Brothers Ltd., established 1837; the West of England and Great Beam Company, established 1849; and the North Cornwall China Clay Company, established 1908—merged to form English China Clays Ltd. (ECC).

Reginald Martin of Martin Brothers was chairman of the new company but the most influential figure, until his premature death in 1931, was T. Medland Stocker of the West of England Company. A qualified mining engineer, anxious to see technical improvements and investment in an industry whose development was inhibited by fragmentation and a lack of capital, Stocker's company had before 1919 absorbed a number of smaller china clay companies. Stocker was very much the architect of the 1919 merger. Two more acquisitions, the Melbur China Clay Company and John Nicholls & Company, made shortly after the incorporation of English China Clays, gave English China Clays 21 pits to operate. With an annual output three times the tonnage of its nearest competitor, Lovering China Clays, ECC was the largest company in the industry. It was not, however, the only company involved in restructuring in the industry; in 1919 H.D. Pochin & Company acquired one of Cornwall's oldest china clay companies, J. W. Higman & Company, and their combined output made Pochin the third-largest producer.

Through the 1920s ECC faced the difficulties caused by the slump that followed the immediate postwar boom. Excess capacity in the china clay industry internationally, as world demand remained below prewar levels, engendered fierce price-cutting competition which became even worse after the failure of the trade association in 1924. The success of a new association, formed in 1927, was short-lived—it lasted only until 1929—although it was reflected in ECC's improved profits in 1929. Over the decade ECC increased its dominance of the industry by further acquisitions. Four companies were acquired in 1927, the North Goonbarrow, the Great Halviggan, the Imperial Goonbarrow, and the Rosevear, and in 1928 the Hallivet China Clay Company was purchased. There were four more smaller acquisitions in 1929, Burthy China Clays, New Halwyn China Clays, the Carbis China Clay & Brick Company, and the Trethowal China Clay Company, and, more importantly because of its consistent refusal to join any trade association,

William Varcoe & Sons was acquired in two stages by ECC in 1929 and 1930.

During the Great Depression, the china clay industry was severely affected. Production fell in the United Kingdom by 34 percent between 1929 and 1931, and remained below the 1929 level throughout the 1930s. Although the effect of the Great Depression was not as severe in the United Kingdom as it was in the United States, it was enough to provide a powerful stimulus to consolidation and amalgamation among the china clay producers, as in many other industries. In the interwar years rationalization, largely taken to mean the merger of small-scale manufacturing units in order to gain the benefit of economies of scale, became as widely practiced as diversification was to become in the 1950s and 1960s.

In these circumstances the merger of English China Clays with its two major, though smaller, competitors, Lovering China Clays and H. D. Pochin & Company, in 1932 was the next logical step towards rationalizing the industry. ECC became a holding company, owning 63 percent of its new operating subsidiary, English Clays Lovering Pochin & Company (ECLP). The remaining shares were held by members of the Pochin and Lovering families. The first chairman of ECLP was the Honorable Henry D. McLaren, who in 1935 succeeded his father as Lord Aberconway. Reginald Martin, who remained chairman of ECC until 1948, when he was over 70, was managing director of ECLP in 1932 to 1937. Martin's assistant managing director in 1932, who was to succeed him in 1937 and to exercise a major influence over the company until 1963, was John Keay—Sir John Keay from 1950, when he was knighted. An accountant by profession, Keay had joined ECC in 1929 and was responsible, with Reginald Martin, for the success of the negotiations leading to the 1932 merger.

The integration of so many diverse companies—another 12 china clay producers were acquired during the 1930s—would not have been easy at the best of times. In the 1930s when falling demand, surplus capacity, and low prices meant there was little spare cash for investment, it was even more difficult. However, some progress was made in modernizing, mechanizing, and making the industry more efficient. The engineering facilities at the company's 42 pits were reorganized and with the acquisition in 1935 of the Charlestown Foundry, despite its poor condition, the company had a nucleus for engineering. Electrification was extended to more of the company's pits and processes, and in 1936 a new central power station was commissioned at Drinnick, to supply all the company's operations. The company developed brickmaking using the high-temperature-resistant substance molochite, and looked for other uses for this material. A research department was established, initially to work on fractionating clay particles to produce the more highly refined selected particle size (SPS) clay required by paper manufacturers, especially in the United States.

World War II offered ECLP little hope of improving trading conditions. With home demand expected to fall and no hope of maintaining the export trade that, through the 1930s, had taken up nearly 65 percent of output, a 50 percent reduction of capacity was enforced by the Board of Trade under its war-time powers. For ECLP, the only bright spot was the Charlestown Foundry, which was able to undertake armaments contracts and, re-equipped with machinery and tools that were to prove of immense benefit to the company in the immediate postwar years, worked to full capacity throughout the war.

When the war ended, it soon became clear that the demand for china clay would expand rapidly. Although ECLP had formulated plans for postwar development, shortages of men, building materials, and fuel precluded any immediate expansion, nor was it an easy task to reopen pits that had been closed for the duration of the war. After representations had been made to the government, a Board of Trade working committee was appointed to look for ways of increasing production. Its report, published in March 1946, recommended short-term measures to alleviate the labor, materials, and fuel problems and suggested a wider ranging enquiry. A Board of Trade committee was therefore appointed, with John Keay from ECLP as its vice-chairman. Its report, delivered two years later, condemned the industry, but not ECLP, for among other things, its failure to innovate, poor research, and lack of welfare facilities for its workers. In 1950 an advisory council, on which sat representatives of all parts of the industry, was established. For ECLP, the immediate postwar years meant steady growth and recovery. One innovation for which it was responsible in those years made a major alleviation in the United Kingdom's postwar housing shortage. Cornish Unit houses, jointly designed and developed by ECC's subsidiaries Selleck Nicholls and John Williams, were bungalows built from concrete using china clay sand. In the ten years immediately after the war, 40,000 were built. ECC's building subsidiaries went on to extend the range of prefabricated building components for both housing and industrial use.

In the early 1950s, restructuring and reorganization paved the way for the emergence of what would be known as the ECC group. In 1951 and 1954 ECC was able to buy the shares in ECLP previously held by the Lovering and Pochin families and, with a financial reorganization in 1956, ECLP became a wholly owned subsidiary. The activities of the group's subsidiaries were then reorganized into four trading divisions, each one covering one of ECC's main operations: china clay, building, quarrying, and transport. The changing nature of the business since 1956 later resulted in transport being moved to the ECCI division, and the new IDF division being created.

ECC International (ECCI) was the operation concerned predominantly with the production and sale of china clay, a raw material used by a number of industries. In the late 1980s, some 80 percent of china clay output was used by the paper industry, 12 percent by the ceramic industry, and eight percent by miscellaneous industries, mainly in the manufacture of paint, rubber, and plastics. ECCI also produced and sold calcium carbonate and other industrial minerals. In 1989 the division's sales of industrial minerals exceeded six million tons for the first time. It also had plant hire and transport operations and a small waste-disposal business. Production facilities were located in the United Kingdom in Devon and Cornwall, as well as in the United States, Brazil, and Australia. In 1994, this business was split; ECCI Europe's sales contributed nearly half of the group's operating business turnover of £877.6 million; ECCI Americas/Pacific accounted for 29 percent.

The operations of the ECC Construction Materials (ECCM) division included the production and sale of quarry material, macadam, concrete products, and industrial sand in the United Kingdom and the United States, and a U.K. waste-disposal business. ECCCM contributed 34 percent of group turnover in 1989.

Two smaller divisions also operated under the ECC Group. ECC Construction (ECCC) was concerned with the construction, development, and refurbishment of private housing and, trading as SNW Homes and Bradley Homes, was responsible for building houses in the United Kingdom. This division accounted for approximately four percent of group turnover in 1989, and by the mid-1990s, the English China Clays was preparing to discontinue these operations entirely. The other division, IDF International, supplied drilling fluids to the oil and gas exploration industry, and accounted for six percent of group turnover in 1989.

The 1950s and 1960s saw considerable growth and profitability for ECC. Large amounts of capital were invested during this time in modernizing all parts of the china clay production process, and as research and technological developments offered scope for further improvements, the process continued in the 1970s and 1980s. Oil-fired driers replaced the coal-fired kilns in the 1960s to be replaced, in turn, with natural gas-fired driers in the 1980s. From the 1960s onward increasing quantities of china clay were transported as slurry.

ECC continued to acquire steadily the remaining independent china clay producers as well as allied quarrying, stone, building and building materials, and concrete companies, and extended its transport interests. It expanded its activities overseas. A sales presence in the United States that dated back to 1920 became, with the addition of clay manufacturing facilities in Georgia acquired in 1942, the Anglo-American Clays Corporation in 1956. The plant at Sandersville, Georgia, was expanded in the 1980s and specialized in the production of high-brightness hydrous clays and calcined clays. Southern Clay Products in Texas produced ball clay products, and in 1986 ECC acquired the Sylacauga Calcium Products Division of Moretti-Harrah Marble Company, which produced high-quality ground marble. In 1987 the U.S. construction aggregate producer J.L. Shiely was acquired.

In the 1980s ECC, like other United Kingdom companies, started to look at the Pacific region and the Far East as possible areas for development. In 1986, Fuji Kaolin Company, in which ECC had already a 50 percent interest, became a wholly owned subsidiary of the group, as did the Kaolin Australia Pty Ltd. in the same year. It entered a technology transfer agreement with the People's Republic of China in 1987. International expansion would remain a priority into the 1990s as ECC opened offices in Singapore and a calcium carbonate plant in South Korea.

Under the leadership of Andrew Teare, who was appointed chief executive in 1990, ECC entered a new era. It redefined itself as a specialty chemicals manufacturer as well as a supplier of industrial pigments and minerals. English China Clays relocated its headquarters to Reading, England, in 1991, after occupying the John Keay House, at St. Austell, Cornwall, for over 25 years. Wary of remaining, in Teare's words, ''almost a conglomerate,'' the company divested itself of a dozen businesses, including the company's construction materials division, which was sold in June 1994 and began trading under the name CAMAS.

The company also made acquisitions to strengthen its core product line. After selling a number of smaller companies worth together around $160 million, ECC bought Pittsburgh-based Calgon Water Management in 1993 from Merck and Co. for $307.5 million. The entry into the specialty chemicals market permanently changed ECC's outlook. Teare pointed out numerous ways Calgon would strengthen ECC, for example, in research and development and global marketing, particularly to the paper industry. The results were immediately apparent; sales of paper chemicals increased 35 percent in 1994, when turnover for Calgon was £158.5 million.

Kaolin remained vitally important to the English China Clays of the 1990s, although by 1995 specialty chemicals already accounted for 21 percent of the company's sales. Kaolin, worth 43 percent of sales ($620 million) in 1992, was predicted to account for 57 percent ($901 million) in 1996, partly on the strength of a recovery in the international paper industry. Calcium carbonate was also important, worth 15 percent ($217 million) of the company's sales in 1992. In 1995, ECC sought to strengthen these businesses by negotiating with Redland Plc for the fine-ground calcium carbonate operations of Genstar Stone Products Co. of Hunt Valley, Maryland. The company also had plans to invest £34 million on these types of operations in Sweden and the United States.

Principal Subsidiaries

ECC International Ltd (U.K.); ECC International Inc. (U.S.); Anglo-American Clays Corporation (U.S.); Calgon Corporation (U.S.); ECC Construction Ltd. (U.K.); ECC Overseas Investments Ltd (U.K.); English China Clays, Inc. (U.S.).

Further Reading

Bruce, Robert, ''The Down to Earth Approach to People,'' *CA Magazine*, November 1994, p. 6.
Byrne, Harlan S., ''English China Clays, Renamed, Geared for 'Nineties Expansion,'' *Barron's*, February 19, 1990, pp. 39–40.
ECC in Focus, company document, Cornwall: ECC Group, 1989.
Harrington, Maura J., ''ECC Returns to Start for System Building,'' *Computerworld*, June 18, 1990, p. 36.
Hudson, Kenneth, *The History of English China Clays*, Cornwall: ECC Ltd., 1969.
Kay, Helen, ''Dividing the Spoils,'' *Director*, April 1995, pp. 26–32.
Kiesche, Elizabeth S., ''English China Clays Dives Into Specialty Chemicals with Calgon Buy,'' *Chemical Week*, June 23, 1993, p. 9.
Kindel, Stephen, ''English China Clays: Old Product, New Markets,'' *FW*, May 11, 1993, p. 21.
Layman, Patricia L., ''Specialty Chemicals Signal New Era for English China Clays,'' *Chemical & Engineering News*, July 31, 1995, pp. 12–15.
Oates, David, ''English China's World Ambitions,'' *Director*, September 1987, pp. 56–60.
There Is More to ECC than China Clay, Cornwall: ECC Group, 1989.

—Judy Slinn
—updated by Frederick C. Ingram

Esterline Technologies Corp.

10800 Northeast 8th Street
Bellevue, Washington 98004
U.S.A.
(206) 453-9400
Fax: (206) 453-2916

Public Company
Incorporated: 1967 as Boyar-Schultz, Inc.
Employees: 2,800
Sales: $351.9 million (1995)
Stock Exchanges: New York
SICs: 3559 Special Industry Machinery, Not Elsewhere Classified; 3569 General Industrial Machinery, Not Elsewhere Classified; 3483 Ammunition, Except for Small Arms, Not Elsewhere Classified; 3823 Process Control Instruments; 3679 Electronic Components, Not Elsewhere Classified; 3824 Fluid Meters and Counting Devices; 3829 Measuring and Controlling Devices, Not Elsewhere Classified

A diversified manufacturing company divided into three business groups—Automation, Aerospace and Defense, and Instrumentation—Esterline Technologies Corp. serves several major markets, including electronic equipment manufacturers, metal fabricators, commercial aerospace companies, and the defense industry. During the mid-1990s, Esterline comprised 13 individual companies located in California, Ohio, Indiana, Washington, Missouri, Rhode Island, and Illinois, as well as abroad. Esterline's presence in international markets, where the company made roughly a third of its total annual sales, was sustained by manufacturing facilities in Dietzenbach, Germany; Rustington, England; Guadalajara, Mexico; Torino, Italy; and Torrejon de Ardoz, Spain.

When Gerhard R. Andlinger, a former chairman of Esterline, stood before the New York Society of Security Analysts on July 9, 1970, he informed his audience that it was his intention ''to create a new major industrial company based on the technology

of measurement sciences and automation.'' Although less than three years old at the time of Andlinger's pronouncement, Esterline was already well on its way toward achieving such an objective, having assembled through acquisitions a solid collection of properties and technological expertise that positioned the company as a rising contender in the measurement sciences field and the factory automation market. The company had been organized during the late summer and early fall of 1967: in August, Boyar-Schultz, Inc., was incorporated to acquire the assets of Boyar-Schultz Corp., a manufacturer of surface grinding machines, and two months later, Esterline Angus Instrument Company was merged into Boyar-Schultz Inc., with the resultant corporate entity adopting Esterline Corp. as its title. The company moved quickly to acquire additional assets that would deepen and broaden its interests, much of which were divested several years after Andlinger's presentation to the New York Society of Security Analysts. Those acquisitions that remained formed the foundation for the Esterline of the 1990s.

In the summer of 1968, the newly formed Esterline acquired Costa Mesa, California-based Babcock Electronics Corp., a manufacturer of sophisticated electronic devices used for defense-related applications. Although Babcock Electronics would later be sold, remaining in the Esterline fold until 1984, the addition of the company's connections to the aerospace and missile markets provided one of the three pillars that would support Esterline throughout the 1970s and 1980s, and into the 1990s. The same could not be said of the acquisitions made by Esterline in the wake of its purchase of Babcock Electronics. Beginning in 1969, Esterline acquired a handful of hospital equipment and medical supply distributors in a bid to develop a presence in the U.S. medical market, creating a medical products distribution network that encompassed 19 Eastern and Midwestern states by the beginning of the 1970s. The company's foray into the health care market was intensified further with the acquisition of several optical manufacturers and a hearing aid company, including the 1969 purchases of Titmus Optical Company, the fifth-largest manufacturer of ophthalmic goods in the United States, and Radioear Corporation, a company with 40 years of experience manufacturing hearing aids.

Combined, Esterline's medical products distribution system and its ophthalmic goods and hearing aid manufacturing businesses made up the company's medical group, part of which remained an aspect of Esterline's business throughout the first half of the 1970s. By the late 1970s, however, Esterline's attempt to build a lasting presence in the U.S. health care market was abandoned, and the entire medical group had been sold, beginning with the divestiture of the company's ophthalmic goods business in 1971. Next to go was Esterline's medical supply distribution business, which was completely divested by 1977, followed by the sale of the company's hearing aid business in 1978. The core of what remained after the divestiture of the medical group formed the basis of Esterline's business for the next two decades: production facilities geared toward the development of measurement sciences products and factory automation machinery.

Two acquisitions in particular bolstered Esterline's business early on, both of which were purchased in 1969. In the summer of 1969, as plans were being formulated to carve a presence in the medical products distribution market, Esterline acquired Providence, Rhode Island-based Federal Products Corporation, a manufacturer of precision instruments, then later in the fall the company purchased Rockford, Illinois-based W.A. Whitney Corporation, a producer of automatic steel-fabrication equipment. Both companies, once organized as subsidiaries, represented integral contributors to Esterline's business for the ensuing three decades. Esterline's automation segment served as the company's chief engine for growth, generating the majority of the company's annual sales through the manufacture of metal fabrication machinery, numerically controlled production equipment, and custom automation equipment used to produce a wide array of products, ranging from beer cans to hypodermic needles. With the manufacture of highly engineered, precision measurement instruments and factory automation equipment propelling the company forward, Esterline grew through both internal and external means during the 1970s, using company-funded research to spur technological developments that spawned new products and benefiting from a host of acquisitions that solidified the company's position in its two primary businesses.

By the mid-1970s, Esterline was generating roughly $125 million in annual sales, fast on its way toward becoming a leading manufacturer of "machines that make machines," as industry pundits referred to the factory automation industry. Largely dependent on the expansion of production capacity in the electronics industry, Esterline grew as the industry it served grew, more than doubling its annual sales volume between the mid-1970s and the beginning of the 1980s. In 1980 the company's annual sales hovered around $250 million, representing a prodigious increase from five years earlier, but the financial health of the company quickly turned anemic during the early 1980s.

From 1980 forward Esterline's financial growth stagnated, its annual sales volume remaining checked at approximately $250 million. Nearly half of Esterline's annual volume of business during the company's extended stretch of lackluster performance was derived from its printed-circuit automation group, which produced equipment for everything from printing to the automated drilling of printed-circuit boards. This equip-

ment was in high demand when electronics companies were increasing their production capacity, but during the sluggish early and mid-1980s, such facility expansion was slow. After six years of hobbled growth, Esterline at last reeled from the affects of stunted capital-goods demand, recording a $29.3 million loss in 1987 on $260 million in sales. Other financial statistics reflected the pallid performance: in 1980, Esterline's peak year, earnings stood at $2.51 a share; by 1987 earnings per share had plummeted to a $3.47 deficit, while the company's stock price had plunged from a high of $40 in 1980 to $8 in 1987.

A cost-cutting program had been in place for several years by the time 1987's financial figures were announced, but beginning in 1987 more drastic and pervasive changes were implemented. In November 1987, following the dismissal of the company's executive staff by Esterline's board of directors, the company relocated its corporate headquarters from Darien, Connecticut, to Bellevue, Washington, a suburb of Seattle. For a new management team Esterline's directors selected Carroll Martenson and his executive team, who had orchestrated a revival of floundering Criton Technologies, a company that had flourished during the 1960s as a manufacturer of airplane parts, electronic equipment, and building exteriors then fallen on hard times during the 1970s. Martenson had come to the attention of Esterline's directors through a New York investment group named Dyson-Kissner-Moran (DKM), Esterline's largest shareholder and Criton Technologies' parent company. In fact, a former chairman of Esterline and one of the company's founders, Charles Dyson, was a DKM principal, so news of Martenson's success at Criton Technologies did not have to travel far to reach Esterline's directors, who now looked to Martenson to resuscitate Esterline.

Martenson and six Criton officers took charge of Esterline under a management-services contract just after the disastrous financial figures of 1987 were reported, with their tenure beginning on the sourest of notes. To restore Esterline's lost luster, the management team quickly assessed the company's condition by visiting each of Esterline's 10 principal manufacturing sites, which were spread across seven states from California to New Hampshire, including one in Asnieres, France. Sweeping cost-containment measures were then implemented, followed by the liquidation of underperforming assets, stripping the company of properties that had been stifling profit growth. Those properties deemed to be performing well and capable of generating strong sales and profits in the future were revitalized with an infusion of cash to strengthen marketing efforts and to accelerate research and development work, creating a leaner and more strategically focused company.

By the end of 1988, the efforts of Martenson and Criton Technologies officials had realized great gains, enabling Esterline to put its decline behind it and face a more promising future. In fiscal 1988, the company generated a profit of $8.4 million on $284.4 million in sales. The relationship between Criton Technologies and Esterline soon grew beyond their identical executive management teams. In September 1989, Esterline finalized the buyout of its largest shareholder—DKM—and acquired six of eight subsidiaries from privately held Criton Technologies, creating a $400 million conglomerate that greatly increased the prospects of a bright future for Esterline as the company prepared to enter the 1990s.

With the addition of Criton Technologies' six subsidiaries, the number of Esterline's operating divisions increased from 11 to 17 and the company realized instant sales and profit growth, gaining $110 million in annual sales and $15 million in annual profits. Most importantly, however, the merger broadened Esterline's operations beyond the depressed capital goods manufacturing market and into specialized niches of the defense industry and the aerospace industry. Bolstered by the addition of Criton Technologies subsidiaries such as Korry Electronics Co., which manufactured lighted panels for airplane cockpits, and Hytek Finishes Co., an aerospace concern involved in finishing metal, Esterline entered the 1990s confident that the newly constituted company could look forward to considerably more robust growth than had been achieved during the previous decade.

For several years, such confidence was validated by Esterline's steady annual profit totals. But by 1993, when sales amounted to $285 million, earnings had slipped to a laggard $1.6 million after averaging $7 million a year between 1988 and 1991. By the following year, 1994, improvements were again evident, as internal efficiencies effected by the company and a revamped product line buoyed Esterline's financial performance. The company's net income increased to $7.6 million by the end of 1994, while sales inched up to $294 million, then rose more resolutely by the end of 1995, when net earnings more than doubled on a 20 percent gain in sales.

As Esterline moved into the late 1990s, the company was registering modest increases in its aerospace and defense and instrumentation businesses, but its greatest growth was being achieved by its automation group, which was benefiting from strong demand for automated manufacturing equipment. The company's Excellon subsidiary, the world's leading manufacturer of printed-circuit board drilling systems, was performing particularly well, fueling hopes that the company could look forward to stable earnings in the future.

Principal Subsidiaries

Angus Electronics Co.; Armtec Defense Products Co.; Auxitrol Co.; Equipment Sales Co.; Esterline International Finance N.V. (Netherlands Antilles); Excellon Automation Co.; Tulon Co. Excellon U.K. (England); Excellon Europe GmbH (Germany); Amtech; Federal Products Co.; Federal Products U.K. Ltd. (England); Hytek Finishes Co.; Scientific Columbus Co.; Korry Electronics Co.; Midcon Cables Co.; TA Mfg. Co.; W.A. Whitney Co. Auxitrol Technologies S.A. (France).

Principal Operating Units

Automation Group; Aerospace and Defense Group; Instrumentation Group.

Further Reading

Acohido, Byron, ''. . . And the Two Became One,'' *Seattle Times*, October 2, 1989, p. E1.
Cochran, Thomas N., ''In Line for a Rebound,'' *Barron's*, June 27, 1988, p. 56.
''Esterline Buys 4 Firms in Medical-Supply Field,'' *Wall Street Journal*, December 11, 1969, p. 4.
''Esterline Reports Year-End EPS. of $2.53 on $352 Million Sales,'' *PR Newswire*, December 12, 1995, p. 12.
Wilhelm, Steve, ''Esterline's Prospects Improve after 2-Year Slump,'' *Puget Sound Business Journal*, October 28, 1994, p. 19.
——, ''Life with Burgeoning Esterline Anything but Simple,'' *Puget Sound Business Journal*, March 5, 1990, p. 10.

—Jeffrey L. Covell

Farrar, Straus and Giroux Inc.

19 Union Square West
New York, New York 10003
U.S.A.
(212) 741-6900

Wholly Owned Subsidiary
Founded: 1946 as Farrar, Straus and Company
Sales: $20 million (1992 est.)
Employees: 100
SICs: 2731 Book Publishing

Farrar, Straus and Giroux Inc. is one of the premier literary publishing houses in the United States. A feisty independent for most of its existence, it became a wholly owned subsidiary of German publishing group Verlagsgruppe Georg von Holtzbrinck GmbH in 1995.

Farrar, Straus and Giroux was founded when John Farrar and Roger W. Straus, Jr., came together in 1945 to form Farrar, Straus and Company. Farrar had been involved with publishing for over two decades. Born in 1896, he began writing for the New York World after World War I, then moved on to George H. Doran Company, a publisher, where he became editor in chief in 1921. Farrar started the Breadloaf Writers' Conference at Middlebury College in Vermont in 1926, and became a director of Doubleday, Doran, after those two firms merged in 1927. He left in 1929 to found Farrar and Rinehart with Stanley Rinehart. Farrar left that firm during World War II, and when the war ended, he formed a new company with Roger Straus.

Straus was from a successful New York family. His father was a high-ranking corporate executive, and his grandfather had served as ambassador to Turkey and President Theodore Roosevelt's Secretary of Commerce. At 28 he was considerably younger than Farrar. He had been a journalist and had edited *Current History* and *Forum* magazines, before founding Book Ideas, a firm that packaged books. Straus served in the Navy's public relations department during World War II, and afterward decided to start a publishing house. Family friend Charles Merz,

the editorial page editor of the *New York Times,* introduced him to Farrar, and they agreed to go into business together.

Straus supplied $30,000 from his inheritance to fund the venture, and the two raised another $120,000 from various friends and acquaintances. The Navy rented Straus his old office for $1 a year, and Farrar, Straus opened for business in 1946. Margaret Petherbridge, Farrar's wife, served as associate and advisory editor. She had worked on medical and children's books at Farrar & Rinehart, overseen its list of mystery books, and edited the crossword puzzle in the *New York Times Sunday Magazine* for five years. James Van Alen, the firm's largest financial backer, had experience on the business end of publishing and served as vice-president. Stanley Young, a well-known author and playwright with extensive experience in publishing, joined the company's board. Other members of the firm's board had extensive experience in publishing or business as well.

Its staff was considered impressive for that of a new publishing firm, but the company almost didn't make it. Its first book was *Yank: The G.I. Story of the War,* which was compiled from articles that appeared in *Yank,* a weekly publication of the U.S. Army. This was followed by *There Were Two Pirates,* a novel by James Branch Cabell, and other books that were literary but not financial successes, including Carlo Levi's *Christ Stopped at Eboli,* and *The Lottery,* by Shirley Jackson. Despite its developing reputation for quality publications, by 1950 Farrar, Straus was barely solvent.

Farrar may have been far more widely known in literary circles, but Straus's persuasive skills proved vital to the company's success. In 1950 Straus enticed popular health writer Gaylord Hauser away from another publishing house. His first book for Farrar, Straus, *Look Younger, Live Longer,* sold 300,000 copies by year end, reversing the firm's fortunes. That same year, Farrar won over respected fiction writer Edmund Wilson, and the firm eventually published over 20 of his books. The firm's reputation as a literary publishing house grew stronger.

In 1951 Farrar, Straus bought the Creative Age Press's book list, which included books by Robert Graves, James Reynolds, and Gerald Sykes. Stanley Young had been playing an increasing role in the firm, and in 1951 it renamed itself Farrar, Straus and Young. In 1952 the company joined in a Ballantine Books plan under which Ballantine simultaneously published the paperback version of Farrar, Straus and Young's hardcover books.

In 1953 the company bought publisher Pellegrini and Cudahy, an eight-year-old Chicago firm. Sheila Cudahy joined the firm, which became Farrar, Straus and Cudahy when Young resigned. The purchase brought Farrar, Straus a line of children's books called Ariel Books, bringing it into this market for the first time. Cudahy also brought several Catholic writers, adding further strength to Farrar, Straus's list of religious books. In 1955 the firm started Vision Books, a series of books for younger readers which focused on the lives of saints and martyrs.

Robert Giroux, the respected editor-in-chief of publisher Harcourt, Brace & Co., also arrived in 1955. Literary tastes had become more conservative at Harcourt, Brace, and Giroux had been finding it hard to work there. After he left, Harcourt, Brace rejected Bernard Malamud's *The Assistant.* Giroux, who had worked with Malamud at Harcourt, Brace, landed the new work for Farrar, Straus. The novel went on to win the National Book Award. By similar means Giroux brought 17 authors with him during the next few years, including Flannery O'Connor and T. S. Eliot. He also found new talent, like Jack Kerouac, whose first novel, *The Town and the City,* was published by Farrar, Straus.

Giroux's contribution was the final push the firm needed to cement its reputation as a publishing house for quality literature, a reputation which grew during the 1960s and 1970s as it added more authors. When editor Henry Robbins joined, for example, authors Tom Wolfe and Joan Didion came with him. The firm also began publishing Philip Roth, Isaac Bashevis Singer, Susan Sontag, John McPhee, Donald Barthelme, and Alexander Solzhenitsyn. The firm bought Octagon Books in 1968 and Hill and Wang in 1971.

The firm changed its name to Farrar, Straus and Giroux in 1965. Giroux became chairman of the board, though Straus was making more and more of the decisions. Meanwhile, Farrar was becoming ill with arteriosclerosis. He retired in 1972, but continued reading manuscripts at home until his death in 1974.

The firm's reputation for literary excellence continued to grow; at the same time it was becoming one of the few publishing houses remaining independent as others were snapped up in corporate buyouts. Straus became increasingly outspoken about the state of publishing, resigning from the Association of American Publishers in the late 1970s because he felt that it sided with corporations over the independents.

In the late 1970s a number of the firm's authors began achieving a more widespread popularity that brought much-needed capital. John McPhee's 13th book, *Coming into the Country,* finally propelled him onto the bestseller lists. In 1979 the firm had books on the fiction and nonfiction bestseller lists of the *New York Times* simultaneously: Philip Roth's *The Ghost Writer* and Tom Wolfe's *The Right Stuff.*

Revenues for 1979 came to about $10 million, with profits of about $1 million. The firm published about 100 trade books a year. Farrar, Straus and Giroux was owned by about 35 shareholders, none owning more than 10 percent, save for Straus, who owned 62 percent.

As a result of the firm's high-profile authors and small size, corporations frequently tried to buy it. The company refused all offers, however, maintaining a hostile attitude toward large publishers, book store chains, and corporate ownership. "I think that a lot of publishing houses are being run by accountants, businessmen and lawyers who have very little concern for the book," Straus told the *New York Times* in 1980. "They could just as well be selling string, spaghetti or rugs." While Straus denigrated larger, more commercial publishers, some of them responded that his firm did not know how to promote books, and that Farrar, Straus and Giroux's authors suffered as a result.

To maintain its independence, Farrar, Straus and Giroux stuck to a strict budget and kept its overhead low. It had a reputation for underpaying its staff, and its cramped offices, located in the less-than-tony area around Union Square in Manhattan, were on the fourth and tenth floors of a dilapidated 12-story office building. Nevertheless, the firm enjoyed such a good reputation that Scott Turow accepted a $200,000 advance at Farrar, Straus and Giroux rather than take $275,000 elsewhere.

The firm thrived in the mid to late 1980s. Tom Wolfe's *Bonfire of the Vanities* reached number one on the bestseller lists, while Scott Turow's *Presumed Innocent* reached number three. Around the same time Walker Percy's *The Thanatos Syndrome* and Philip Roth's *The Counterlife* also made it onto the bestseller lists. *The Counterlife* was named the best novel of 1987 by The National Book Critics Circle. The firm picked up two more NBCC awards when the group gave its poetry award to C. K. Williams's *Flesh and Blood,* and another award to Larry Heinemann's *Paco's Story.* Another Farrar, Straus and Giroux author, Joseph Brodsky, won the Nobel Prize for Literature, giving the firm a total of seven living Nobel laureates on its lists. The others included Elias Canetti, William Golding, Isaac Bashevis Singer, Alexander Solzhenitsyn, Wole Soyinka, and Czeslaw Milosz.

These critical successes and bestsellers translated to a 50 percent increase in Farrar, Straus and Giroux's sales during a two-year period. As a result, the firm expanded, also increasing its staff 50 percent by 1992. In 1991 it started an imprint for Spanish-language children's books. In 1993 Farrar, Straus and Giroux gave the New York Public Library its 1946–80 editorial records. In 1992 the company bought the backlist of North Point Press, which had stopped putting out new books in 1990.

The firm's expansion came to an end in early 1992, when, in the midst of a recession, it was forced to lay off about 15 percent of its staff of about 100 people. Those laid off included Linda Healey, a vice-president and associate publisher, who had joined in 1988 to concentrate on journalistic nonfiction. Most others were junior staffers, including some from the children's division, which was the firm's most profitable at the time.

In February 1993, Elizabeth Sifton became vice-president of the firm and publisher of its Hill and Wang division. By this time, Straus essentially ran the company, while grooming his son Roger Straus 3d to take over. Roger Straus 3d began his career at the firm, then left in 1985 to work for Avon Books and Times Books, although it was understood that he would eventually return to Farrar, Straus and Giroux. He returned in the late 1980s when the firm was experiencing commercial success. The company's decision to increase its share of the market for serious nonfiction and hire several employees was largely due to pressure from Roger Straus 3d. After the recession forced cutbacks, father and son continued to have disagreements, with the younger Straus wanting to push growth and an emphasis on marketing and promotion.

Finally, in September 1993, Roger Straus 3d resigned as managing director of the company. The elder Straus was 76 years old, and wanted to protect the firm's authors even after he died, but the company's future seemed uncertain. Finally, in late 1994, he sold Farrar, Straus and Giroux to the German publishing group Verlagsgruppe Georg von Holtzbrinck GmbH, based in Stuttgart. The German company already owned publisher Henry Holt and Company, and published the periodical *Scientific American*. More importantly, it had a reputation for hands-off management. Straus remained president of Farrar, Straus and Giroux. The rest of the company's management also stayed in place, including Jonathan Galassi as vice-president and edi-tor-in-chief. As a result of the sale, Farrar, Straus and Giroux said it would put out about ten percent more books per year.

In 1995 Frances Foster became publisher of Frances Foster Books, part of Farrar, Straus and Giroux's children's books division; at the same time, the firm announced that North Point would begin to publish new titles again.

Further Reading

Fraser, Gerald, ''John C. Farrar, Publisher, Editor and Writer, Is Dead,'' *New York Times*, November 7, 1974.

Hall, Donald, ''Robert Giroux: Looking for Masterpieces,'' *New York Times Book Review*, January 6, 1980, pp. 3, 22–23.

Kleinfield, N. R., ''Roger Straus: Making It as an Independent,'' *New York Times Book Review*, March 23, 1980, pp. 3, 28–29.

Lyall, Sarah, ''Farrar Straus Heir Apparent Quits in a Genteel Family Tiff,'' *New York Times*, September 23, 1993, pp. D1–D2.

——, ''Sale of Farrar, Straus is Near, Its President Says, *New York Times*, October 20, 1994, p. D21.

''Publisher in Germany Agrees to Buy Farrar,'' *Wall Street Journal*, November 1, 1994, p. B8.

Shephard, R. Z., ''Winning the Old-Fashioned Way: Farrar, Straus Reaps Prizes and Profits on a Shoestring,'' *Time*, February 8, 1995, p. 76.

—Scott M. Lewis

✺FIRST COMMERCE

First Commerce Bancshares, Inc.

NBC Center
1248 O Streets
Lincoln, Nebraska 68508
U.S.A.
(402) 434-4110
Fax: (402) 434-4181

Public Company
Incorporated: May 2, 1985
Total Assets: $2.3 billion (est. 1995)
Employees: 950
Stock Exchanges: NASDAQ
SICs: 6712 Bank Holding Companies; 6021 National
   Commercial Banks

First Commerce Bancshares, Inc. is the holding company for National Bank of Commerce Trust & Savings Association, a bank with a long and distinguished history in the state of Nebraska. First Commerce holds over 99 percent interest in National Bank of Commerce and six other banks in the state, including First National Bank & Trust, Overland National Bank, North Platte National Bank, City National Bank, First National Bank of West Point, and First National Bank of McCook. First Commerce also manages a growing mortgage company, and an asset management firm. While providing a full range of financial services to its customers, through its subsidiary, NBC/Computer Services Corporation, the bank also supplies highly sophisticated computer technology services to banks throughout Nebraska and surrounding states.

The founder of the bank, Morris Weil, arrived in the United States from France at the tender age of 17 in 1875. He traveled to Kansas where he married and began to raise a family. An ambitious man working in the mercantile business, Weil opened his own store, the Lincoln Paint and Color Company in 1892. Turning the business over to his son Julius, Weil then decided to create a banking operation in Lincoln, Nebraska, as his other son, Carl, was working there in one of the local financial establishments. The Bank of Commerce was opened in 1902 with a state charter and $50,000 in capital.

Even though Weil had formed the bank for his son Carl, the father remained in control of all banking operations and served as president. During the early years of the bank's activities, the economy seemed like a roller-coaster ride for anyone involved in the financial services industry. The panic of 1907 drove many banks out of business throughout the United States, and severe drought in the plains states led to a series of agricultural crises. Yet under Weil's leadership, the Bank of Commerce not only survived these obstacles but thrived during the early part of the twentieth century. Weil recognized that the key to success in his situation was in becoming a banker's bank. As a result, Weil applied for a national charter, and the bank was renamed the National Bank of Commerce of Lincoln.

During the early years of the bank's existence, Weil traveled throughout the state of Nebraska and called on many regional and community banks. In return for counseling them on matters such as loans and investments, these banks opened accounts with National Bank of Commerce. In a few years, Weil had solicited over 100 new accounts from banks, resulting in approximately 50 percent of National Bank's total deposits. Although Weil concentrated on correspondent banking, at the same time he also cultivated the business of ordinary consumers and local merchants who had opened stores in Lincoln, Nebraska.

In 1911, National Bank of Commerce opened a savings department, one of the first in the entire state. As the bank grew during the First World War and into the 1920s, its burgeoning operations necessitated new offices. In 1924, the bank moved to a new location on the corner of 13th and O streets, and built a modern six-story building to house its administrative offices. When the Great Depression came, and America was thrown into social and economic chaos, National Bank remained a pillar of stability in the city of Lincoln. One of the few banks to survive the bank holiday of President Franklin Delano Roosevelt's New Deal policies, National Commerce served both its customers and the community of Lincoln, Nebraska well during the height of the Depression. For Morris Weil, the most significant loss that he experienced during these years was not brought on by the economic upheaval. When Carl Weil died in 1934, the son for whom he started the bank, Morris Weil was emotionally devastated. Yet the elderly man conducted himself with quiet dignity, and continued on as president of the bank. Although Weil managed the bank's operations through the tumultuous years of World War II, his once energetic spirit began to slowly diminish. Morris Weil died in July 1945, having served as president of the bank for 43 years.

Weil was replaced by Byron Dunn as president of the National Bank of Commerce. Dunn had started working in the bank in 1905 at the age of 17 and had gained invaluable experience first watching and later working closely with Morris Weil. During the 1920s, Weil sent Dunn to Colorado in order to collect cattle loans. National Bank of Commerce had gone into the business of arranging cattle loans through a bank in Denver, Colorado. Unfortunately, the bank in Denver collapsed. To collect on the loans, Dunn hired cowboys and rode over a good deal of range country rounding up cattle. At the same time, other banks that had made cattle loans disputed National Bank of Commerce's claiming the cattle as collateral. Dunn, however, was undeterred. He possessed more cowboys and guns than any other claimant, and thus National Bank of Commerce was able to round up the majority of the cattle to cover the bank's loans.

When Dunn took over leadership of the bank, he exhibited the same determination as he had in the 1920s at the time of the Colorado roundup. A confident and affable man, Dunn initiated an aggressive campaign to develop the bank into a full-service financial services facility. While keeping the correspondent banking business as the cornerstone of the bank's operations, Dunn created a marketing department to promote the bank's new services, increased the advertising budget for newspaper and radio spots, remodeled the interior of the bank to enhance its new emphasis on individual customer service, inaugurated a new charge account service, and printed checks in Braille for those people who were blind. Personally approved by Dunn, the slogan of the bank became: National Bank of Commerce, "The Family Bank."

During the 1950s, Dunn became well know both for his civic leadership and community involvement, and for the concern that he showed his employees. Dunn was also well-known as an amateur photographer and traveled across the United States snapping pictures of business executives whom he had met. He encouraged his employees to call him Byron and garnered a reputation for listening to and helping them with personal problems. Dunn was instrumental in creating an employee newspaper, the *Commerce Newsgram,* and built a lodge for the use and enjoyment of the bank's staff. Located in South Bend, Nebraska, the lodge become one of the most popular getaways for bank employees. All of these activities helped National Bank of Commerce grow. In 1952, deposits at the bank had grown to surpass $50 million. By the time Byron Dunn retired from his position as president in 1961, the bank's deposits had surpassed the $80 million mark.

In May 1961, Glenn Max Yaussi replaced Dunn as president of the bank. Yaussi started working at the bank in 1934, at the height of the Depression, when he walked in the front door and asked for a job. With an initial salary of only $55 per month,

Yaussi worked his way steadily up the executive and administrative ladder. By the time he became president, Yaussi realized that the banking industry was on the verge of enormous changes. Determined not be to left behind, the new president hired a management consulting firm to help the bank develop up-to-date planning, accounting, budgeting, and management procedures.

Less than two months after Yaussi took office, a merger had been arranged between National Commerce Bank and First Trust Company, located in Lincoln, Nebraska. The merger resulted in increased assets and experienced staff for National Bank of Commerce. First Trust brought with it one of the largest and most successful trust departments in the state of Nebraska, a sophisticated farm management department, and mortgage loan operation. In 1964, Yaussi and his chief executives had the foresight to see a credit problem on the horizon and arranged for the bank to offer expanded savings deposits. The bank offered four percent interest on regular savings accounts, at that time one of the highest rates in the nation. This strategy led to an impressive 21 percent jump for time deposits, a $5 million increase.

One of the most important developments at the bank also occurred during 1964. National Bank of Commerce bought a computer system, and converted its entire accounting operation to that system. The bank developed a highly sophisticated computer proof and transit operation, the first of its kind in the plains states. Armed with this technology, National Bank of Commerce soon started marketing and selling its computer services to financial institutions and corresponding banks throughout Nebraska and neighboring states.

The late 1960s were years full of activity at the bank. In 1967, Paul Amen was appointed the fourth president of National Bank of Commerce, while Yaussi moved up to chairman and chief executive officer. Under the direction of Amen and Yaussi, in 1968 the bank combined with other banks from surrounding states in order to issue a Master Charge card under the auspices of the MidAmerica Bankcard Association. Also that year, National Bank of Commerce created a travel service, Travel Unlimited, in order to provide travel services to bank customers. Moreover, a third generation system for the bank's computers was installed, thus allowing for faster and more efficient customer services.

During the early 1970s, National Bank of Commerce pursued an aggressive expansion program. In 1972, the bank acquired the Mutual Savings Company of Lincoln, Nebraska. The assets of this bank were relatively small, just less than $1 million, but management at National Bank of Commerce recognized the potential of its location and financial services. By 1977, Mutual Savings Company had increased its assets to over $23 million, vindicating the acquisition. In 1973, the bank acquired Nebraska Savings Company, located in Scottsbluff, Nebraska. This firm's assets were also small, but by 1977 had grown to over $10 million. At approximately the same time, the bank purchased the Robert E. Schweser Company, Inc., a successful bond underwriting company that had a long and illustrious history in Nebraska, and the bank also created the NBC Leasing Company, a subsidiary formed to provide the bank's customers with the opportunity to arrange financing by means of leases. And finally, by the end of the decade, the bank had constructed a new, 12-story modern office complex to house all its banking and financial services operations.

During the 1980s, National Bank of Commerce continued its expansion program. With a new president, James Stuart, Jr., a graduate of the University of Nebraska with extensive experience in the banking industry, most notably at Citibank in New York, the bank was thoroughly committed to developing an affiliate system that was part of its expansion strategy. In addition to National Bank of Commerce and Lincoln Bank South, the bank's affiliate network grew to include First National Bank, Fremont; First State Bank, Fremont, First National Bank, Kearney; Overland National Bank, Grand Island; City National Bank, Hastings; First National Bank, West Point; First Westroads Bank, Omaha; Lincoln Bank East; and North Platte State Bank. In 1985, a bank holding company was incorporated to form First Commerce Bancshares. The holding company was created specifically to manage, administer, and supervise all of the affiliates within the bank's growing network of financial services.

The early 1990s were devoted to developing the many subsidiaries and affiliates of First Commerce Bancshares. The NBC/Computer Software Services continued to develop highly sophisticated software programs for the financial services industry, and provided many new services to its banking customers. Over 20 new customers were contracted, thus bringing the total customer base of NBC/Computer Software Services to 284 banks. The weekly volume of new mortgage loans administered by First Commerce Mortgage Company shot up to over $10 million in 1993. And the BankCard Services division of National Commerce Bank grew to include over 90,000 active credit cards, with the average outstanding credit amounting to $78 million.

One of the outstanding regional bank holding companies, First Commerce Bancshares had an excellent reputation in Nebraska and the surrounding states. Management of the company was committed to providing its customers with high-quality, efficient banking services. And with the company's NBC/Computer Software Services riding the crest of banking technology, First Commerce Bancshares was well situated to grow larger and larger in the coming years.

Principal Subsidiaries

National Bank of Commerce Trust and Saving Association; First National Bank & Trust Company; Overland National Bank of Grand Island; North Platte National Bank; City National Bank and Trust Company; First National Bank of West Point; First National Bank of McCook; Commerce Affiliated Life Insurance Company; NBC/Computer Services Corporation; First Commerce Savings, Inc.; and First Commerce Investors, Inc.

Further Reading

Bank, Howard, "Early Signs That The Credit Crunch May Ease," *Forbes,* October 14, 1991, p. 37.

Burns, Greg, and Kelly Holland, "Plastic Talks," *Business Week,* February 14, 1994, pp. 105–7.

Foust, Dean, "Bank Reform: Be Careful What You Wish For," *Business Week,* November 22, 1993, p. 55.

Lenzner, Robert, and Philippe Mao, "Banking Pops Up In The Strangest Places," *Forbes,* April 10, 1995, pp. 72–76.

"Special Report: Bank Cards," *Banking,* September 1977, pp. 42–129.

Yaussi, Glenn, *National Bank of Commerce Trust and Savings Association,* Newcomen Society: New York, 1977.

—Thomas Derdak

Fisher Companies, Inc.

600 University Street, Suite 1525
Seattle, Washington 98101
U.S.A.
(206) 624-2752
Fax: (206) 682-7733

Private Company
Incorporated: 1971
Employees: 900
Sales: $250 million (1995 est.)
SICs: 6719 Holding Companies Not Elsewhere
    Classified; 2041 Flour & Other Grain Mill Products;
    4833 Television Broadcasting Stations; 6531 Real
    Estate Agents & Managers

The owner of an unusual combination of businesses, Fisher Companies Inc. operates as the holding company for three distinct businesses—Fisher Mills Inc., Fisher Broadcasting Co., and Fisher Properties Inc.—involved in flour milling, radio and television broadcasting, and real estate, respectively. Majority owned by members of the Fisher family, Fisher Companies originated as a flour milling company in 1911, then went on to diversify into a host of other business, including radio broadcasting in the mid-1920s, television broadcasting in the early 1950s, and real estate in the early 1970s. For a half century the Fisher family businesses were stewarded by O.D. Fisher, who founded the Fisher family's catalytic business concern, Fisher Flouring Mills, then developed the Fisher family fortune for the ensuing five decades. By the mid-1990s, Fisher Companies, through its subsidiaries, owned flour mills and flour distribution centers, television and radio stations, and various real estate properties.

When Oliver David (O.D.) Fisher arrived in Seattle in 1906, the 31-year old Missouri native had found his new home, deciding immediately that the entrepreneurial prospects in the region provided him with the opportunity to fulfill his ambitious business plans for the future. The decision to stay and build a business in Seattle came to O.D Fisher through an epiphany of sorts, prompted by a visit to the harbor abutting burgeoning downtown Seattle, where Fisher stood one day in 1906 and surveyed the bustling activity surrounding him. From his vantage point, Fisher could imagine more than he could see. Surrounding him was evidence of a thriving community abundant in natural resources and what promised to be an important commercial shipping waypoint. But Fisher, as was his custom, took in what he saw and thought on a grander scale, extrapolating the scene before him in terms of much larger issues concerning world trade and commerce. O.D. Fisher's epiphany would arrive shortly, and when it did, the single most defining moment in the history of Fisher Companies would occur as well, marking the genesis of a family business that would evolve into a family empire, employing generations of O.D. Fisher's descendants and thousands of others for decades to come.

According to business chroniclers of the era, as O.D. Fisher stood before Seattle's harbor he thought of the underdeveloped markets in the Far East, considered the rapidly growing population and trade along the Pacific Coast, and factored in the construction of the Panama Canal, then reportedly declared to his father, his brothers, and presumably anyone else in earshot, "The markets of the entire world are before you." Fisher's proclamation was a sweeping, somewhat vague and detached statement to make, but considering what became of his fateful utterance, the words and the actions to follow fit together perfectly. Fisher had decided to organize a flour milling and marketing company that, once established, would become one of the largest of its kind in the country. From flour milling and marketing, the Fisher family business would diversify into lumber, radio, television, real estate, and candy manufacture, among other businesses, assembling an eclectic array of interests that at first blush appeared as sweeping and as detached as the words of the man who had been instrumental in starting it all.

In the years bridging his birth and his arrival in Seattle in 1906, O.D. Fisher had established himself as an industrious worker with considerable experience in a broad assortment of businesses that would hold him in good stead once he organized his company in Seattle. Born in 1875 in Orleans, Missouri, Fisher began working at age ten, spending his hours away from school by helping to keep records at his father's bank. By age 13, Fisher was farming corn and herding cattle. By age 16 he was working as a transit and compass man on a logging-railroad construction project. Then he worked as a bookkeeper and lumber camp store manager, before being put in charge of all merchandising and purchasing for a lumber company in Birch Tree, Missouri at age 19. Seven years later, in 1902, Fisher organized a livestock and mining firm, then the following year, along with his father and brothers, he acquired a flour mill in Belgrade, Montana, where he served as secretary and manager of the company until he came to Seattle in 1906.

When Fisher left Belgrade and headed for Seattle, he was preparing once again to change occupations and industries. His brother Will P. Fisher had made the trek to the Puget Sound area before him, establishing a flour brokerage business named The Fisher Trading Co. But O.D. Fisher was more interested in the vast timber stands surrounding Puget Sound, so he followed his brother west to acquire timber lands for himself and business associates of his father. With the help of these wealthy investors, Fisher acquired options on large areas of standing timber in the region, forming, along with his financial backers, Grandin-Coast Lumber Co. But Fisher's vision of a flour mill along the shores of Puget Sound steered the never-idle businessman back into the flour industry and led to his organization of Fisher Flouring Mills Company.

Fisher Flouring Mills was formed in 1910, the same year construction of the company's mill was begun. By the spring of 1911, the mill was completed, a $400,000 facility equipped to grind 10,000 bushels of wheat per day for a production capacity of 2,000 barrels of flour every 24 hours. The first wheat was ground on April 11 of that year, with the sale of flour to the public beginning in June. Once up and running, the flour mill operated 24 hours a day, six days a week, grinding wheat into flour for retail sale. Six years after the mill began operating it was expanded, with a new unit added to the existing two at a cost of $600,000. The addition increased the mill's capacity from 2,000 barrels of flour per day to 5,000 barrels of flour per day, ranking the mill as the largest in the West, and moved Fisher Flouring Mills more heavily into poultry food production, which the company had previously produced in only negligible amounts.

Serving as general manager and active head of the company, Fisher had created a flourishing and dominant company in the Seattle business community by the time of the plant expansion in 1917, with family members—his brothers and father in particular—helping to operate one of the region's largest family-owned and -operated enterprises. In establishing the company's vertically integrated operations, Fisher had succeeded in winning a campaign to defeat an exclusive rail-service franchise on Harbor Island, where the mill was located, enabling him to establish company-owned railroad tracks to transport flour on land, while company-owned ships ferried flour on water. Fisher had also acquired a number of warehouses in Seattle and roughly 30 grain elevators in Montana, giving the company a solid foundation upon which to build in the decades ahead.

When the patriarch of the Fisher family, Oliver Williams (O.W.) Fisher died in 1922, O.D. Fisher became president of the family's numerous interests, including Fisher Flouring Mills,

Grandin-Coast Lumber, Louisiana Long Leaf Lumber, National Livestock and Mining Co., the Fisher-White-Henry Co., and Gallatin Valley Milling Company. From atop this already prodigious business empire, O.D. Fisher guided the family's interests into still other business arenas, making a pivotal, pioneering foray into a fledgling industry four years after his father's death that would represent one of the three pillars supporting the Fisher fortune in the 1990s. In 1926, Fisher was approached by man named Burt Fisher (not a member of the Fisher family) who was looking for financial help in founding a radio station. Already a radio aficionado known to stay up late listening to distant radio stations on a rudimentary receiver, Fisher was greatly interested on a personal level and on a business level, since the addition of a radio station would provide an invaluable advertising tool for the Fisher businesses. Accordingly, Fisher, in 1926, co-founded a radio station known as "the Fisher Blend Station" and by its call letters KOMO, establishing one of the first broadcasting companies in the Pacific Northwest region.

Roughly 30 years later, in 1953, a television station was added to the Fisher family's business, KOMO-TV, by which time the Fisher flour milling operations ranked as the fifth-largest in the nation and the biggest in size and capacity west of the Mississippi River, producing more kinds of flour than any other mill in the world. Years of expansion had increased the Fisher mill's 24-hour daily capacity to 15,000 hundredweights of flour, equivalent to 300,000 five-pound bags of flour. With this prodigious total, Fisher Flouring Mills served markets in Alaska, Hawaii, Central and South America, and the Far East, in addition to domestic markets.

O.D. Fisher, by now in his late 70s, still stood at the helm of the company, holding sway as chairman of the Fisher family enterprises and serving on the board of directors of 27 companies based in the Pacific Northwest and as far east as Louisiana. In 1958 another television station was added to the Fisher fold, KATU-TV in Portland, Oregon, strengthening the Fisher family's involvement in broadcasting and representing one of the last major acquisitions completed under O.D. Fisher's half century of leadership. By the beginning of the 1960s, O.D. Fisher had begun to cut back his heavy involvement in the affairs of non-Fisher companies and in the operation of the sprawling roster of companies he had assembled under the Fisher corporate umbrella. Instead of serving on the board of directors of 27 companies, Fisher, now in his mid-80s, pared back his extra-curricular business activities to serve on a mere 19 boards of directors, continuing to demonstrate the prolific energy that had characterized his working career since he was ten years old. Meanwhile, leadership of the Fisher family enterprises was assumed by third- and fourth-generation family members, who named O.D. Fisher honorary chairman in 1965. Two years later, at age 91, O.D. Fisher died after a short illness, his death marking the end of an era in the history of the Fisher family's rise to dynastic prominence in the Pacific Northwest business community.

After Fisher's death, his family reorganized the diverse collection of interests it owned, adding cohesion and structure to the variegated businesses that had become part of the Fisher empire during the previous six decades. In 1971, Fisher Companies, Inc. was formed to serve as the holding company for

Fisher Flouring Mills and the numerous other businesses owned by the Fisher family, which, aside from broadcasting, included a candy-making business, real estate holdings, and computer businesses. After 60 years of development, the businesses owned by the Fisher family had changed complexion, with each forming their own subsidiaries over the years, creating a sprawling labyrinth of business interests that had grown difficult to manage. The formation of a holding company resolved the difficulties in managing the Fisher family's business interests, lending more parity to the eclectic array of the family's enterprises and restructuring them into nine separate companies. Three of these companies would form the core of the Fisher family's business in the 1990s: Fisher Mills, Inc., comprising the family's flour milling and grain elevator properties; Fisher Blend Stations, Inc., constituting KOMO radio, KOMO-TV, and KATU-TV; and Fisher Properties, Inc., the Fisher family's burgeoning real estate business.

Fisher Properties represented one of the Fisher family's newest and most promising business pursuits as it moved forward from the 1970s into the 1980s and 1990s. From the outset, O.D. Fisher had acquired various real estate properties, which formed the core of Fisher Properties in the early 1970s. But by the early 1980s the company was fast-becoming a major competitor in the real estate development market, adopting the role as a developer of office and industrial properties in the Puget Sound region. By 1982, Fisher properties had purchased and developed two large warehouse and office complexes in and near Seattle, as well as ten acres of unimproved land in Lynnwood, Washington, a suburb of Seattle. On the land purchased in Lynnwood, Fisher Properties completed construction of a multi-storied, 195,000-square-foot office building named Fisher Business Center in 1986. Later that year, Fisher Properties began construction of the four-building Fisher Industrial Park at Kent, Washington, then took on similar office development projects as the 1990s neared.

During the 1990s, Fisher Companies was enjoying enviable stability, its business supported by its primary triumvirate of companies: Fisher Mills, Inc., Fisher Broadcasting, Inc., and Fisher Properties, Inc. The company's flour milling operations, the nucleus of the Fisher family fortune, were producing more than 450 million pounds of flour each year, with the Seattle plant, the vestige to O.D. Fisher's half-century of leadership, ranking as one of the largest flour mills in the Western United States. Supported by another large flour mill in Portland, and flour distributions centers in Seattle, Portland, San Francisco, and Los Angeles, the company was positioned firmly in the global flour industry. Yet, as there had been for decades, there were two other important contributors to the Fisher family's business. Fisher Broadcasting and Fisher Properties stood as integral components of Fisher Companies, lending a diversity to the company's operations that provided its greatest strength. As the company moved resolutely toward the completion of its first century of business, strength through diversity fueled hope that the future would bring success equal to the legacy left by the Fisher family's most notable figure, O.D. Fisher.

Principal Subsidiaries

Fisher Broadcasting Inc.; Fisher Mills, Inc.; Fisher Properties Inc.

Further Reading

"Fisher Broadcasting Tests Info Highway," *Puget Sound Business Journal,* March 3, 1995, p. 20.

"Fisher Mills Now Largest in West," *The Seattle Times,* September 16, 1917, p. 23.

"The Fisher Story: Saga of Free Enterprise," *The Seattle Times,* November 15, 1953, p. F3.

Fryer, Alexander, "Flour, Broadcasting, Real Estate: Fisher's Three Legs to Stand on," *Puget Sound Business Journal,* June 18, 1993, p. 33.

Mantz, Warren J., "New Holding Company for Fisher Mills," *The Seattle Times,* July 26, 1971, p. B14.

"O.D. Fisher," *Puget Sound Business Journal,* April 2, 1993, p. 3A.

Wolcott, John, "Fisher: From a 'Mealy' Start to Media, Real Estate Glamour," *Puget Sound Business Journal,* June 24, 1991, p. 10.

—Jeffrey L. Covell

Fleer Corporation

1120 Route 73
Mount Laurel, New Jersey 08054
U.S.A.
(609) 231-6200
Fax: (609) 727-9460

Private Subsidiary of Marvel Entertainment Group, Inc.
Incorporated: 1913
Employees: 500
Sales: $300 million (1994 est.)
SICs: 2675 Die-Cut Paper & Board; 2067 Chewing Gum;
2064 Candy & Other Confectionery Products

The Fleer Corporation holds a special position in the history and development of two quintessentially American activities: bubble gum and trading cards. After nearly seventy years, Fleer continues to manufacture more than four million pieces of its Dubble Bubble—the original bubble gum—each day. As one of the top three trading card companies, along with Topps and Donruss, Fleer sells about $300 million per year in sports and entertainment cards. Sports, including baseball, basketball, and football, account for roughly $225 million of these sales. Fleer also manufactures a line of cards tied in with parent company Marvel's comic book heroes. Other card series bearing the Fleer name are Fleer Ultra MTV Animation, featuring the 1990s cultural icons Beavis and Butthead, and television and film tie-ins such as the Mighty Morphin Power Rangers, Casper, and Batman. In 1995 Marvel purchased SkyBox, merging its established line of basketball cards with Fleer. Fleer also manufactures candy canes through its Asher Candy subsidiary, a New York-based candy manufacturer purchased by Fleer in 1990.

Frank Henry Fleer was involved with chewing gum long before his company made history with the invention of bubble gum. The first incarnation of the Fleer family business was founded in 1849 by Otto Holstein, a German Quaker who built a flavoring extracts factory in Philadelphia. Fleer, born in 1860, joined the business after marrying Holstein's daughter and took

over operations in the 1880s. Around 1885, Fleer's company began making chewing gum, adding its flavorings to the chicle gum base popular at the time.

Chicle, the dried sap from the South and Central American sapodilla tree, was first brought to the United States by the former Mexican president, dictator, and general Antonio Lopez de Santa Anna, whose exploits included the attack on the Alamo. In 1869 Santa Anna, who was living in exile in Staten Island, brought chicle to the attention of Thomas Adams. Adams agreed to try to invent a useful product with Santa Anna's chicle, eventually producing a chicle-based chewing gum. Sales of Adams's "New York No. 1" gum were slow at first, but helped by the inclusion in each box of gum of a "prize package" of tickets redeemable for prizes. Adams's business boomed, and soon chicle became the most widely used chewing gum base. The chewing gum habit quickly spread across the United States. Adams later became the first chairman of the American Chicle chewing gum trust, formed in 1899 from the country's five largest chewing gum producers.

In the late 1880s, trading cards made their debut. The honor for the first such insert is generally given to James Buchanan Duke, the tobacco magnate and popularizer of pre-rolled cigarettes. When Duke first began to produce packages of his cigarettes, he needed a way to keep the packages from being crushed during shipment. He added a strip of cardboard into the package and shortly after began to feature advertisements on the cardboard strips. Duke's first ads included graphics of popular actors and actresses of the time; by the late 1880s, however, other tobacco companies were adding cards to their packages featuring baseball players. By 1890, some twenty-five sets, or series, of baseball cards had been issued. The inclusion of trading cards would do much to popularize the use of tobacco, and especially cigarettes.

The Fleer family business continued making chewing gum, adding cola flavor to the chicle gum by 1897. During the 1880s, Fleer became one of the first companies to sell its gum in coin-operated vending machines. As related in *The Great American Chewing Gum Book*, Frank Fleer had been approached by a vending machine salesman with a proposal to sell Fleer's gum in the machines. Fleer was skeptical, but when the salesman asserted that the machines were such a novelty that people would be willing to use them even if they received nothing for their penny, Fleer agreed to put the machines to the test. A vending machine was placed at New York City's Flatiron Building, where people were told to ''drop a penny in the slot and listen to the wind blow.'' People did just that, by the hundreds, until the machine was taken away by the police. Fleer ordered several of the vending machines.

Fleer's company developed two more significant products around the turn of the century. The first was created by Fleer's brother, Henry Fleer. At the time, candy-coated almonds were a popular treat, and Henry Fleer hit on the idea of coating small pieces of chicle gum with candy. Showing the initial results to his brother, Henry Fleer purportedly referred to his new candy as ''little chiclets.'' Frank Fleer liked the name. ''Chiclets'' became a huge success, and would remain one of the best-known brand names for chewing gum throughout the next century.

By the turn of the century, gum chewing was firmly entrenched in the United States and spreading throughout the world. The companies that would dominate the chewing gum industry through the Twentieth century—American Chicle, Wrigley, and Beech Nut—were already established as the big three of the industry. Yet, while chewing gum could be stretched and pulled and chewed, it could not blow a bubble. Frank Fleer set to work. Instead of chicle, he experimented with other bases, moving toward a synthetic compound most likely based on natural rubber latex. In 1906 Fleer introduced the world's first bubble gum, called ''Blibber-Blubber.'' The gum, while able to blow bubbles, had its drawbacks: it was hard to chew, it fell apart too easily, and it was difficult to blow bubbles with. Worse, the gum was nearly impossible to remove from the face or whatever surface the bubble burst upon. In 1909 Fleer sold his chicle chewing gum company to the Sen-Sen Company, which, renamed as the Sen Sen Chiclet Company, was later merged into American Chicle.

Fleer was not yet finished with gum, however. In 1913 he went back into business, forming the Frank H. Fleer Corporation, still in Philadelphia. Terms of the sale of his former company prevented him from returning to chicle-based chewing gums. Instead, the new company manufactured other confectionery products, including Fleer's Bobs and Fruit Hearts. This may have been the first Fleer product to include trading cards—a set of 120 cards featuring entertainers and athletes, including Babe Ruth, Gloria Swanson, and Mary Pickford, issued in 1923. Fleer had not yet given up the pursuit of bubble gum, even after Frank Fleer retired and the company was taken over by his son-in-law Gilbert Mustin. Frank H. Fleer died in 1921.

The search for bubble gum continued until August 1928, when, after a year of trial-and-error experiments, Walter Diemer, a 23-year-old Fleer cost accountant with no background in chemistry, hit upon the right combination of ingredients. Not only did the batch produce a large bubble, but the gum didn't stick when the bubble burst. The first batch had its problems, however: after sitting overnight, it would not blow bubbles. Diemer worked on the problem for another four months, finally preparing a 300-pound batch that proved successful. The next day, while preparing a second batch of the new formula, Diemer

realized he had forgotten to add coloring. The only food coloring at hand was pink, so Diemer added that. Bubble gum has been predominately pink ever since.

The new gum, composed of natural ingredients, was dubbed Dubble Bubble and first tested at a small Philadelphia candy store on December 26, 1928. Fleer developed the market further by offering free samples of its product to candy, drug, and grocery stores. The product proved wildly successful. Diemer did not, however, patent his formula—he did not want to reveal its secret—and soon imitations rushed on the market. Dubble Bubble nonetheless dominated the market, far surpassing any other bubble gum in sales. Its biggest competitors were the Bowman Company's Balony bubble gum and, shortly before World War II, the Topps Company's Bazooka bubble gum. Fleer also produced trading cards in the years leading to the war, including a Cops and Robbers set in 1935, but these were packaged with its other confectionery products, not with its bubble gum, which were small balls wrapped like taffy and sold for a penny a piece. Novelties were nonetheless an important element of the bubble gum business from the beginning; early on Fleer added a comic strip—starring Pud—to the inside of the Dubble Bubble wrapper.

By the beginning of the war, bubble gum had grown to a $4.5 million industry. However, shortages of jelutong, a Asian gum essential to the manufacture of bubble gum, forced Fleer and many other bubble gum makers to halt production during the war. After the war, the bubble gum shortages continued, so much so that a ''pink'' market developed that saw a penny piece of Dubble Bubble often sell for as much as $1. The bubble gum craze boomed, and by the mid-1950s accounted for ten percent of all chewing gum sales. By then, Gilbert Mustin had passed leadership of Fleer to his sons Gilbert Jr. and Frank Mustin.

Chewing gum makers had long included trading cards, and especially baseball cards, with their products, but the success of Dubble Bubble made it unnecessary for Fleer to resort to this type of marketing. Instead, by the 1950s, the bubble gum trading card market was owned by Bowman, which would be challenged and later bought up by Topps. By the time Fleer made its first attempt at baseball cards—with an 80-card Ted Williams commemorative set in 1959—Topps had exclusive contracts with nearly every player in the major leagues, and much of the minor leagues as well. Fleer produced two more sets of commemorative cards in the first two years of the 1960s. But Topps, with its trading cards, promotional offers and tie-ins, and gifts for its retailers, soon pushed Fleer to the margins of the industry.

Fleer next attempted to produce sets featuring contemporary ballplayers. Topps, however, had already signed practically all of Major League Baseball to exclusive contracts, which were signed with individual players and set to expire at varying times. Fleer began signing up minor league players, hoping to be able to produce a full set of cards. With over 3,000 players signed, Fleer released a 66-card set in 1963. Topps quickly won an injunction again Fleer from producing more baseball cards. Topps' contracts gave Topps not only a monopoly on major league baseball, but also the exclusive right to market their cards with any gum, candy, or confectionery product. The courts upheld Topps' exclusivity, and Fleer stopped producing baseball cards. Fleer sold its players' contract to Topps for $395,000 in 1966. Fleer could, however, market other types of cards, and through the 1960s, it produced sets of commemorative baseball, American Football League, and National Basketball Association cards; entertainment sets such as Casper, Indians, Three Stooges, Gomer Pyle, Hogan's Heroes, McHale's Navy, Drag Strip racers; and novelty cards like "Baseball Wierdohs." Baseball cards, however, remained the most important trading card market. Fleer's annual sales in the late 1960s and early 1970s ranged from $8 million to $12 million per year. Net income reached a high of $382,300 in 1973. The following year, however, Fleer posted a loss of $309,000, its second losing year since 1969.

In the late 1960s, baseball's newly formed Players Association approached Fleer with a trading card contract offer: for $600,000, Fleer would gain exclusive rights to market baseball cards with gum, once Topps' contracts ran out in 1973. Fleer did not want to wait that long, however, and turned down the offer. Through the 1970s, Fleer remained a small, family owned business. Its president, Don Peck, who had been with the company since 1952 and named president in 1966, introduced new products to increase Fleer's market share, but still wanted to bring Fleer into the baseball card market. Realizing that he had made a mistake when he turned down the association's offer, Peck once again faced Topps' lock on the market.

This time, Fleer took Topps to court, filing an antitrust suit against Topps and the Players Association in Philadelphia in 1975. Meanwhile, the bubble gum market was growing, reaching $100 million in sales and a 20 percent share of the entire chewing gum market by the mid-1970s. Fleer was turning out more than five million pieces of Dubble Bubble each day. More and more companies were making bubble gum. But in 1976, a new entry created Fleer's biggest challenge—a new type of soft bubble gum created by Lifesavers Inc. called Bubble Yum. Other companies, including Fleer, brought out their own soft bubble gum products, which helped the bubble gum market reach new heights—Bubble Yum alone sold $100 million in 1979. Fleer's sales, which now included its Gatorgum, flavored with Gatorade, alongside its Dubble Bubble gum, grew to $15.6 million in 1978 and to $20 million in 1979. In that year, its suit against Topps finally came to trial. Fleer was granted the right to produce baseball cards (although, in a later court action, Topps retained the exclusive right to package its cards with gum). Fleer was also awarded $1 in damages. The baseball card market was then worth about $10 million per year.

Fleer's first Major League Baseball set appeared in 1981. Subsequent sets included team logo stickers instead of gum. Through the 1980s, Fleer added basketball cards and, by the end of the decade, football cards to its line. Sales rose to $51 million by 1988, with a net income of nearly $11 million. By then, the Mustin brothers were aging, and it was apparent that their children were unlikely to succeed them in the family business. In 1989 Paul Mullan, a former executive with another Fleer competitor, Donruss, approached Fleer with a $75 million leveraged buyout offer. The Mustins agreed. The following year, Mullan's Charterhouse Equity Partners took Fleer public, selling 1.9 million shares to raise $30 million. A secondary offering in 1990 raised an additional $12.2 million. Revenues in that year rose to $144 million, with a net income of $21.5 million. As the 1990s began, Charterhouse acquired the Asher Candy Company of New York and its line of candy canes, with the intention of expanding further into the candy and confectionery market. In 1991 Charterhouse sold its equity interest in the company; Mullan remained chairman and chief executive officer. That year, Fleer began to segment its products, introducing a premium series, the Fleer Ultra card.

In 1992 Fleer agreed to be acquired by Marvel Entertainment Group for 28 cents per share, or $265 million, a figure that analysts considered low. The Fleer-Marvel pairing nonetheless seemed a perfect match, combining the passions—baseball cards and comic books—of both companies' target market, which comprised boys between the ages of six and sixteen. Under Marvel, Fleer, which was reorganized as the Fleer Entertainment Group, introduced the new Fleer Flair premium trading card line, while adding new lines featuring Marvel comic book heroes, such as the X-Men. Fleer also issued its first National Hockey League cards in 1992.

In 1994 Fleer acquired the Panini company to expand its European presence. After the baseball strike of 1994, Fleer stepped up its production of entertainment cards, including television and movie tie-ins, and in 1995 also acquired Sky-Box—for $150 million—allowing it to increase its position in basketball and entertainment cards, and to lessen its reliance on the volatile sports market. By then, Fleer's sales had topped $300 million. And in the booming trading card market—which topped $2 billion by 1995—Fleer, which still makes more than five million pieces of Dubble Bubble each day, had not yet seen just how big a bubble it could blow.

Further Reading

Ambrosius, Greg, "The History of Fleer," company document, Mt. Laurel, N.J.: Fleer, 1995.

Hendrickson, Robert, *The Great American Chewing Gum Book*, Radnor, Penn.: Chilton Book Company, 1976.

Seideman, David, "RBIs and LBOs," *Philadelphia*, May 1990, p. 87.

Smith, Geoffrey, "The Dangers of Playing It Safe," *Forbes*, October 29, 1979, p. 95.

Williams, Pete, *Card Sharks*, New York: Macmillan, 1995.

Wyatt, Edward A., "Big-League Performance: Can Fleer Extend Its Torrid Growth?" *Barron's*, November 19, 1990, pp. 16, 18.

—M. L. Cohen

FLEXSTEEL
FINE UPHOLSTERED FURNITURE

SINCE 1893

Flexsteel Industries Inc.

P.O. Box 877
Dubuque, Iowa 52004-0877
U.S.A.
(319) 556-7730
Fax: (319) 556-8345

Public Company
Incorporated: 1918 as Sanitas Spring Company
Employees: 2,375
Sales: $208.43 million (1995)
Stock Exchanges: NASDAQ
SICs: 2512 Upholstered Household Furniture; 2531
   Public Building & Related Furniture; 2599 Furniture
   & Fixtures, Not Elsewhere Classified

Flexsteel Industries Inc. is a leading manufacturer of furniture seating for the home, commercial, and recreational vehicle markets. Under the slogan ''Quality To Last a Lifetime,'' Flexsteel's line—which ranges from upholstered chairs, recliners, sofas, and convertible sofa beds to seating and sofa bed units for vans, mobile homes, and other recreational vehicles—features the company's patented Flexsteel spring, a uniquely flexible and durable design backed by a lifetime guarantee. Traditional styling makes up the bulk of Flexsteel's business, although the company is strong in contemporary and modular designs, and leather seating is a quickly growing segment of Flexsteel's sales. The Flexsteel line is available in over 1,000 fabrics, colors, and patterns, much of which is kept in inventory, allowing the company a fast order-to-delivery turnaround. In 1995, Flexsteel's eight manufacturing plants, four permanent showrooms, and 161 retailer-positioned gallery showrooms combined to produce more than $208 million in revenues for a net income of $5.2 million. During 1995, Flexsteel spent nearly $10 million on capital improvements—including a $3.5 million expansion of its Starkville, Mississippi, plant.

Flexsteel's origins may be traced to Frank Bertsch, an upholstery apprentice born in Wurttenberg, Germany, who emigrated to the United States in 1881. Arriving with just 50 cents in his pocket, Bertsch traveled first to Dubuque, Iowa, then to Chicago, and finally to Minneapolis in search of work. By 1893, Bertsch had found employment with the McCloud & Smith Furniture Company. In that same year, a new company was founded in Minneapolis, called the Rolph & Ball Furniture Co., which manufactured upholstery. In 1901, Bertsch, together with three employees from McCloud & Smith, bought Rolph & Ball, and renamed it Grau & Curtis Co., after two of the partners. Bertsch initially functioned as the company's director of upholstery. The company's first catalog was sent out in 1902; by the following year the catalog's 64 pages offered furniture not only for the home but also for commercial use in hotels, lounges, and churches. Already, however, the company's focus was on seating. By the end of its first decade, the company employed 22 people, who crafted and assembled its furniture by hand.

Frank Bertsch bought out his partners in 1917 and brought his son, Herbert T. Bertsch, into the company. The Grau & Curtis Co. next attempted to move into other areas of the furniture industry, purchasing a dining room and bedroom furniture maker during the 1920s. Although the company lost that plant during the 1929 stock market crash, the rest of the Bertsch business survived, however, and, under the new name of Northome Furniture Industries in 1929, actually grew during the Great Depression. Part of the reason for this was its introduction of the ''flexsteel'' spring in its furniture designs.

The flexsteel spring was initially conceived by E. Werner Schlaprittzi while studying at the University of Zurich early in the 20th century. Schlaprittzi modeled it after the springs found in clocks, while also incorporating the springlike action of tree branches. He was able to sell the spring design for use in the seats of European railroad cars, and upon immigrating to the United States in 1918, he founded the Sanitas Spring Company in Minneapolis.

Nearby manufacturer Northome added the spring to its furniture designs in 1927, and soon purchased a 50 percent stake in Sanitas Spring, which was renamed the Flexsteel Spring Corporation in 1934. From the beginning, Northome products featuring the Flexsteel spring carried an extended guarantee, initially for 25 years, and later for the lifetime of the product. In the 1990s, the company could boast that they still received trade-ins of furniture from this era.

Northome furniture continued to be built by hand until 1936. In that year, attempts at unionizing the company's workers led the Bertsches to relocate their operations to Dubuque, Iowa, where they purchased the former Brunswick Victrola plant, a 480,000 square-foot facility. For the new plant, the Bertsches decided to incorporate the line production techniques developed by the Ford Motor Company. Northome, which had to replace and retrain its entire production staff, was among the first in the furniture industry to incorporate the moving assembly line in their manufacturing process. Over the next decade, production jumped from one million to four million units per year. In 1946, the first company-owned trucks began delivering its furniture; by the 1990s, the Flexsteel fleet would grow to 350 trucks traveling ten million miles per year. In 1948, Frank Bertsch died, and Herbert Bertsch took over the company.

Northome moved toward national distribution and greater expansion during the 1950s. The company built a second, 220,000 square-foot plant in Lancaster, Pennsylvania, in 1955. During that decade, Northome also initiated separate departments for design and development and for central engineering, and rolled out its first national advertising campaign. By 1958 the Flexsteel spring had become so well known that the company renamed itself as Flexsteel Industries Inc.

The company also kept up with the changes in furniture styles of the era. Through the 1920s and 1930s, mass market furniture styles had seen little change from the standard overstuffed Victorian design, but, as the country emerged from the second world war, furniture styles underwent dramatic—and more frequent—changes, from the simple look of the 1940s to the more dramatic styles of the 1950s.

By the mid-1960s, Flexsteel's revenues had topped $15 million per year. That decade saw the rise of the recliner, and Flexsteel began producing its own "Flex-o-Lounger" recliners and reclining mechanisms. During this time, the company also bought its first aircraft—turboprops, which it used to fly dealers to the company's factories. In 1965, Flexsteel created the Brunswick Converting Division for production and printing of its own "space age" nylon fabrics. The company also opened several more manufacturing plants and by the end of the decade expanded its line to include seating for the growing recreational vehicle (RV) market. The company went public in 1969, after posting a net income of $1.17 million on revenues of $25 million.

The company made a cash purchase of the National Furniture Manufacturing Co. in Evansville, Indiana, in 1970, and entered the exposed-wood furniture market with the introduction of its Charisma chair division. Flexsteel moved forward in RV seating, developing its own line of sofa sleepers specially scaled for the limited space requirements of mobile homes and other vehicles. By the end of the decade, the company had gained the entire seating and sleeping business for General Motors RVs. Flexsteel also brought in computerized automation to its production line, beginning in 1974 with the introduction of Gerber fabric cutting machines. These machines allowed

far more precise cutting of fabrics, reducing waste while allowing more precise pattern matching. Sales climbed steadily through the decade, from $38.5 million in 1972 to over $96 million in 1979. In that year, Flexsteel's net income reached nearly $4.5 million.

By then the third generation of Flexsteel's founders was leading the company, and the fourth generation was entering the business. The company opened a new plant in New Paris, Indiana, in 1982, moving part of its RV seating capacity closer to the van conversion center of Indiana. Flexsteel also opened showrooms, called Flexsteel Total Concept Galleries, the first of which was called Furniture Manor in Osseo, Minnesota; the company also opened two factory showrooms. Recliner sales became a more important part of the business, particularly with Flexsteel's invention of an adjustable lumbar support mechanism. Then the company moved into a new market in 1984, creating its commercial seating division with a separate salesforce and a product line for health care and other institutional settings. Sales increased throughout the 1980s, reaching $130 million in 1984, and $173 million in 1990.

The onset of the recession of the early 1990s saw Flexsteel's revenues drop in 1991, to $145 million, and the company was forced to write off some $1.6 million in uncollectible accounts receivable, while downsizing reduced its employee rolls by more than 300 people. The following year, the company also took restructuring charges of approximately $2.6 million in connection with the closing of its Evansville plant, and the consolidation of its recliner and motion furniture production at its Dublin, Georgia, plant. By 1992, however, Flexsteel was growing again, outpacing the furniture industry as a whole. Motion—or modular—furniture was helped by the company's newly designed latching mechanism. And in 1992, Flexsteel rolled out its moderate-price Grand Haven line of sofas, which hit the mid-range price point of $599–$699, compared to the typical Flexsteel sofa range of $799–$999. Costs were trimmed for the new line not by skimping on scale, but rather by limiting the range; the Grand Haven line featured only two sofa styles available in 14 fabrics, compared to the 1,000 fabric choices available for the Flexsteel line.

Leather furniture was another growing part of Flexsteel's business, doubling in size through the early 1990s and accounting for more than 10 percent of its revenues. RV products were particularly strong, growing at ten to 18 percent through 1994, and making up as much as 35 percent of total revenues. By 1993, these had climbed again to $177 million, and reached $195 million in 1994. And, from a low of $1.2 million in 1991, net income rose to $6.8 million in 1994. International sales also began to play a stronger role for the company.

By 1995, Flexsteel had rebuilt its employee levels to nearly 2,400 workers. Revenues grew a modest 6.7 percent, however, to $208 million, as RV sales suffered from an economic slowdown. Flexsteel closed its Sweetwater, Tennessee, plant, and consolidated its Charisma contract line at the Starkville plant. Yet Flexsteel continued to invest in new technologies, including dealer-friendly video cataloguing and automated sales inquiry systems, and computer-assisted design manufacturing techniques. And with a $3.5 million expansion of its Starkville plant and a 20,000 square-foot addition to its Dubuque facility completed in 1995, Flexsteel continued to show its commitment toward future growth.

Principal Divisions

Metal Division; Wood Products Division; Charisma Chairs; Commercial Seating Division.

Further Reading

Brin, Geri, ''Flexible Flexsteel,'' *HFD-The Weekly Home Furnishings Newspaper,* April 6, 1992, p. 28.
A Century of Seating Craftsmanship, Dubuque, Iowa: Flexsteel Industries, Inc., 1993.
Levine, Charlotte, ''Flexsteel Celebrates 100th Anniversary,'' *Central Penn Business Journal,* May 5, 1993, p. 12.

—M.L. Cohen

Fluke Corporation

P.O. Box 9090
Everett, Washington 98206-9090
U.S.A.
(206) 347-6100
Fax: (206) 356-5116

Public Company
Incorporated: 1953 as John Fluke Manufacturing
    Company, Inc.
Employees: 2500
Sales: $382.1 million (1994)
Stock Exchanges: New York
SICs: 3670 Electronic Components & Accessories; 3679
    Electronic Components, Not Elsewhere Classified;
    3820 Measuring & Controlling Devices; 3823
    Industrial Instruments for Measurement, Display &
    Control of Process Variables & Related Products;
    3825 Instruments for Measuring & Testing of
    Electricity & Electronic Signals

Fluke Corporation is a leading designer, developer, manufacturer, and seller of commercial electronic test and measurement instruments for scientific, service, educational, industrial, and government applications. Its products include oscilloscopes, voltmeters, ammeters, LANmeters, and other devices. With operations in the United States and the Netherlands, Fluke sells its products in more than 100 different countries.

Fluke Corporation was founded in 1948 by John Fluke to manufacture electronics testing equipment like power meters and Ohmmeters. Even in the late 1940s the electronics testing and measuring industry was relatively young, as measurement standards and truly reliable tube-type and electromechanical instruments had been introduced around the turn of the century. A highly accurate Ohmmeter (used to measure electrical resistance in a circuit), for example, was among the first of the new generation of testing equipment developed in the early 1900s. It was followed by more accurate power meters (for measuring voltage), ammeters (used to measure current), and other apparatus.

But the industry was entering an entirely new era when Fluke started his company, because Bell Laboratories had just introduced the transistor in 1947. The transistor was very important to the electronics field because it made it possible for scientists to develop testing and measuring devices that were accurate to within one-millionth of a unit of measurement, or less. Throughout the 1950s and 1960s, therefore, demand growth for testing and measuring equipment tracked the surge in the production of solid-state electronics products and equipment. The testing and measuring devices were used to help in the design, manufacture, testing, and servicing of electrical and electronic products. Fluke, with its technological expertise, benefited from market growth and was able to parlay engineering excellence into steady sales and profit growth.

John Fluke incorporated his company in the State of Washington on October 7, 1953 as the John Fluke Manufacturing Company, Inc. That move reflected healthy demand for Fluke's power meters and other measuring devices during the 1950s and 1960s. During those years, Fluke prospered by designing and manufacturing contraptions that were used by research and development lab scientists at high-technology companies like Hewlett-Packard, which was an important customer for Fluke. In fact, while studying at the Massachusetts Institute of Technology, John Fluke had been roommates with Hewlett-Packard cofounder David Packard. Fluke's equipment earned his company a solid reputation with buyers like Hewlett-Packard as a producer of cutting-edge technology. Some of those early inventions and devices would decorate the lobby of the $300-million-plus Fluke Corp. in the mid-1990s.

Fluke continued to profit from healthy markets and its technological expertise going into the 1970s. Market growth slowed beginning in the early 1970s, but Fluke was able to sustain profitability by introducing new products and maintaining its dominance of a few key product categories. By the end of the decade the total market for testing and measuring equipment had grown to $6 billion. Fluke's share of that figure was a healthy $150 million annually by the end of the 1970s. And industry sales continued to increase in the 1980s (between 1975 and 1985, industry sales rose at an average of nearly 20 percent annually). While Fluke benefited from general industry trends, however, it also was forced to confront major internal and external changes.

The external changes started in the late 1970s and intensified during the 1980s. That's when the complexion of Fluke's customer base began to change. Buyers of Fluke's equipment in the 1980s were less likely to be design engineers in labs, but were more likely to be one of the new breed of service technicians out in the field, working on fax machines, computerized cars, and computers. At the same time, Fluke and its U.S. competitors were facing a new threat from foreign companies vying for a share of a global market that the U.S. had traditionally dominated along with a few European manufacturers. Furthermore, as more electronics products were developed and manufactured overseas, Fluke would have to broaden its distribution and marketing channels to remain competitive.

The evolution of the testing and measuring device industry underscored the need for changes in the Fluke organization. Fluke managed to increase sales steadily during the early 1980s, to more than $200 million annually by the mid-1980s. And it continued to dominate key niches, even leading industry giants like Hewlett-Packard and Tektronix. In fact, Fluke Manufacturing was known as one of the three top players in the testing and measuring device industry. But the company had achieved that growth mostly by tweaking its existing line of about 150 products. Thus, by the mid-1980s Fluke's offerings had becoming staid and risked obsolescence in the rapidly changing technological environment of the 1980s.

John Fluke, still at the helm going into the 1980s, had started making changes in his company in the early 1980s. Importantly, he stepped aside and let other managers assume more responsibility. In 1982 he named George Winn president of Fluke. Winn had started with Fluke in 1968 and worked his way through the ranks. Then in 1983, just one year before his death, Fluke made his son, John Fluke Jr., chief executive. Under new management, Fluke began to whip its operations into shape, improve its products, and generally get its financial house in order.

When he assumed the presidency, Winn had also promised to concentrate on the introduction of new, breakthrough products. Fluke did introduce a few key products, such as its low-cost, pocket-sized multimeter. But it was falling behind changes in the marketplace, as evidenced by its sagging stock price in the mid-1980s. Importantly, Fluke had been slow to move into the market for computer-aided circuit design and modeling equipment, which was rapidly supplanting the use of traditional test equipment for the design of circuits. Augmenting the company's problems was an ugly downturn in its large defense-related business. Although Fluke remained profitable, its sales stagnated around $225 million annually during the mid- and late 1980s.

Fluke posted sales of about $240 million in 1990, and a net income of about $12 million. Despite the surplus, though, many analysts questioned the long-term viability of the company given its slowness to respond to new needs in the marketplace. Fluke *had* been successful at, for example, thwarting foreign competitors in its home market, and at penetrating new markets overseas. But some critics blamed the junior Fluke for failing to keep the company on the cutting edge of technology. They argued that he was too involved in outside interests, including the family's investment firm, Fluke Capital and Management Services Co. With sales stagnant and earnings sporadic, Fluke Jr. finally decided to step down in 1991. He and his brother David remained directors of the company, though, and the Fluke family still owned 28 percent of the enterprise.

Fluke's board hired former Hewlett-Packard veteran Bill Parzybok Jr. to turn the company around. Winn remained president, retaining control of day-to-day operations while Parzybok focused on long-term gains. Parzybok brought a mix of technical and marketing savvy to Fluke. He had shown his technical bent early in life, when, growing up in Kansas City, he spent his free time building radio kits and other electronic mechanisms. He started college at Colorado Rocky Mountain School and went on to major in electrical engineering at Colorado State University (CSU). At Colorado State, Parzybok was the goalie and captain for the varsity soccer team, the president of his fraternity, and president of the engineering society. After also tagging a business-related masters degree to his resume at CSU, Parzybok was recruited by Hewlett-Packard, where he spent 16 years involved in the test and measurement instrumentation business.

By 1984 Parzybok had worked his way up at Hewlett-Packard to vice-president, in charge of a staff of about 10,000 workers. Throughout the late 1980s he managed various groups in the company both in the United States and abroad. When Fluke approached him about the possibility of taking the helm early in 1991, he initially rejected the offer. "Then I started thinking about it," Parzybok recalled in the April 8, 1991 *Seattle Times,* noting "It was a smaller company, smaller environment. Hewlett-Packard was a $12 billion-a-year company. Frankly, in that kind of company, you wonder whether you can make a significant difference."

Parzybok spent his first several months at Fluke working with existing managers in an effort to build some sort of consensus about Fluke's future. What he found was a sort of rudderless ship, occupied by people that wanted to go somewhere but didn't know where they were going or how to get there. One of Parzybok's first moves was to issue a concise mission statement to all of the company's employees: "Fluke's mission is to be the leader in compact, professional electronic test tools." That statement reflected Parzybok's intent to refocus Fluke's operations on the development and manufacture of a new breed of testing and measuring devices that, compared to traditional equipment, were smaller, less expensive, more technologically advanced, and offered higher profit margins.

In addition to emphasizing products like Fluke's successful handheld meters (particularly a handheld oscilloscope dubbed the ScopeMeter), Parzybok went to work reorganizing and streamlining the company. For example, he jettisoned Fluke's touch-control screen product line, controller line, and printing and metal fabrication business because they didn't complement the company's new mission. He also laid off 150 workers and released several of Fluke's existing products in markets in which they had never been sold. In 1993, moreover, Parzybok shortened the company's name to Fluke Corp. The net effect of the effort, initially, was a reduction in both sales and profits. But the company was better positioned to compete in the long term.

Among Parzybok's most prolific moves was the 1993 purchase of the testing and measuring device division of N.V. Philips, the Netherlands-based electronics giant. Fluke had entered a partnership with Philips in 1987. The alliance gave Fluke new products to sell in its U.S. market, and also allowed it to begin selling its own gear through Philips distribution channels in Europe. The partnership was also responsible for the development of the ScopeMeter, which became a big seller for Fluke. Fluke finally decided to end the partnership by paying $41.8 million to simply buy the Philips division, which added about 900 employees to its payroll and roughly $125 million in annual revenues.

Fluke's restructuring and new product focus seemed to be paying off by the mid-1990s. Largely as a result of the Philips acquisition, revenues climbed to about $362.5 million (year ended April 29, 1994), about $8.8 million of which was net income. That figure climbed to about $389.8 million in 1995 as net income rose to a healthier $14.9 million. Meanwhile, management continued to engineer the overhaul of the once-moribund Fluke. To that end, the company was intensifying its effort to develop new high-tech testing and measuring devices for growth markets like computer networks, automobile computer systems, and office machines and equipment.

Principal Subsidiaries

Fluke International Corporation

Principal Divisions

Verification Tools Division; Service Tools Division; Worldwide Sales & Service; Philips T&M Group

Further Reading

Baker, M. Sharon, "Fluke Looks Past A Slow Year to A Promising Future," *Puget Sound Business Journal,* September 24, 1993, p. 5.
Fryer, Alex P., "Fluke Gains Momentum With New Testing Device," *Puget Sound Business Journal,* October 21, 1994, p. 18.
Heberlein, Greg, "New Duke of Fluke," *Seattle Times,* April 8, 1991, p. B1.
Jalonen, Wendy, "Analyst Wondering If John Fluke Is Gearing Up for an Acquisition," *Puget Sound Business Journal,* July 7, 1986, p. 6.
Lane, Polly, "New Products Boost Fluke: Despite Slow Economy, Orders Up 19 Percent," *Seattle Times,* September 29, 1993, p. D1.
Lim, Paul J., "Fluke is Rebounding," *Seattle Times,* March 13, 1995, p. C1.
Lim, Paul J., "New Devices Underscore Fluke's Success," *Seattle Times,* September 14, 1995, p. E1.
Saporito, Bill, "How to Revive a Fading Firm," *Fortune,* March 22, 1993, p. 80.
Sullivan, R. Lee, "School for Cheerleaders," *Forbes,* October 25, 1993, pp. 118–119.
Wilhelm, Steve, "Fluke Seeks New Markets to Bolster Profits," *Puget Sound Business Journal,* February 11, 1991, p. 1.
——, "Outsider Gives Fluke New Sense of Mission," *Puget Sound Business Journal,* April 17, 1992, p. 1.
——, "Parzybok: New Blood for Fluke's Invention Factory," *Puget Sound Business Journal,* December 25, 1992, p. 14.
Woodward, Liane M., "Fluke Elects New Vice President, Reorganizes Operations," *PR Newswire,* August 27, 1992.
Woodward, Liane M., "Fluke, Philips Intend to Merge Allied Test & Measurement Businesses," *PR Newswire,* August 26, 1992.

—Dave Mote

Food Lion, Inc.

2110 Executive Drive
Post Office Box 1330
Salisbury, North Carolina 28145-1330
U.S.A.
(704) 633-8250
Fax: (704) 636-5024

Public Company
Incorporated: 1957 as Food Town Inc.
Employees: 65,000
Sales: $8.21 billion (1995)
Stock Exchanges: New York
SICs: 5411 Grocery Stores

Food Lion, Inc. is the seventh-largest supermarket chain in the United States. The company operates more than 1,070 stores in 14 states, primarily in the Southeast but also extending to the mid-Atlantic region as far north as Pennsylvania and to the Southwest as far as Texas. Food Lion enjoyed rapid growth averaging 20 percent per year from the late 1960s through the 1980s based on its low-price, high-volume strategy. The chain sells many items at cost or even below cost to lure customers through its doors. By cutting its overhead dramatically, Food Lion has been able to offer "everyday low prices" to consumers and still manage to reap some of the highest profits in the supermarket industry. Starting in 1992, however, growth slowed dramatically and profits fell as the company had to deal with some negative media coverage, labor conflicts, and stiff competition in some of the new markets it had targeted for growth.

In December 1957 Ralph W. Ketner, Brown Ketner, and Wilson Smith opened a Food Town supermarket in Salisbury, North Carolina. The three men had worked together in the grocery business for some time at a small chain that was owned by the Ketners' father but had recently been sold to Winn-Dixie. Dissatisfied with their new employer, the Ketners and Smith set out to open their own chain of supermarkets. By calling on everyone they knew in Salisbury for a small investment, the trio slowly raised enough capital to begin operations. Although growth was sluggish for the first ten years or so, those early investors made out very well in the long run. After numerous stock splits, an initial investment of 100 shares, originally valued at $1,000, was worth more than $16 million by the end of 1987.

During Food Town's first decade, the company tried every kind of gimmick available to entice customers into its stores. Contests, free pancake breakfasts, trading stamps, beauty pageants, and other promotions captured shoppers' attention, but not their sustained business. By 1967, after a full decade of operations, Food Town had only seven stores, and earned less than $6 million that year.

In 1967 Ralph Ketner formulated the strategy that would launch Food Town's dramatic rise in the retail food industry. Ketner, the story goes, locked himself up in a Charlotte, North Carolina, motel room with six months worth of invoices and an adding machine. When he emerged three days later, he had determined that prices could be slashed on 3,000 items, and, if sales volume increased by 50 percent, the company would still show a profit. Gambling that the reduced-price strategy would adequately expand its repeat-customer base, Food Town implemented his plan. Ketner later remarked, "One thing about taking a gamble: when you're already broke you can't do much damage." Soon the company adopted an unusual new slogan: "LFPINC," which stood for "Lowest Food Prices In North Carolina," and shifted its advertising emphasis from print to television. Ketner's gamble was a winner; increased volume soon more than made up for the price reductions.

The 1970s were a period of tremendous growth for the company. By 1971, sales were nearly $37 million. Although it occasionally snapped up a particularly appealing acquisition, Food Town preferred to build its chain from within. The company tended to construct more smaller stores rather than fewer larger ones in order to provide greater convenience. In 1974 the second-largest Belgian supermarket chain, Delhaize Freres & Cie, "Le Lion," purchased a majority of Food Town's shares. Delhaize "Le Lion" signed an agreement to vote with Chairman Ralph Ketner for ten years on all policy issues. The company's growth accelerated dramatically in the late 1970s and the 1980s. Food Town opened stores in Virginia in 1978 and in Georgia in 1981. In 1977 the chain operated 55 stores; by 1987, it ran 475.

In 1982, Food Town was sued by the owner of several supermarkets in Virginia which operated under the name Food-town. The court restricted the use of Food Town's name in certain markets due to the similarity. As a result of this action and in anticipation of similar problems with another group of stores in Tennessee, the chain decided to change its name. The new name, Food Lion, was selected partly because the Belgian chain Delhaize had a lion logo, but also because the chain could save money in changing the signs on its stores: only two new letters, an "L" and an "I," needed to be purchased since the "O" and the "N" could be shifted over. This type of frugality was characteristic of the chain. In 1983, Food Lion carried its new banner into Tennessee as sales surpassed the $1 billion mark.

In the summer of 1984, the National Association for the Advancement of Colored People (NAACP) organized a boycott of Food Lion stores because the chain had declined to sign a "fair share" agreement. The agreement called for raising the number of African Americans in management, increasing minority employment, and pledging to do business with minority-owned vendors and construction firms. The NAACP moved its annual board meeting from New York to Charlotte, North Carolina, to attract attention to its protest. The boycott ended in September when Food Lion signed an agreement with the NAACP to increase minority opportunities with the company.

Food Lion branched into Maryland in 1984. Early the following year, the company acquired Giant Food Markets Inc. of Kingport, Tennessee. It soon sold the 22 Jiffy Convenience Stores that came with the Giant deal, sticking to what it did best—the conventional supermarket trade.

In January 1986, Tom Smith became CEO of Food Lion, replacing Ralph Ketner, who remained chairman. Smith, who had once worked as a bagger for a Food Town store, returned to the company in 1971 as a buyer and became president and chief operating officer in 1980. Smith steered Food Lion on the same course as Ketner had, stressing low prices and efficient service. The company topped the $2 billion sales mark at the end of Smith's first year as CEO.

By the late 1980s, Food Lion had become the dominant force in the regions in which it did business. Stunning earnings and market share encouraged the chain's further expansion. In 1987 Food Lion prepared to extend its territory into Florida. Food Lion saw Florida's increasing population and the relatively high prices of chains already in the area, such as Winn-Dixie and Publix, as an excellent opportunity for expansion. The chain planned to double its number of outlets by first tapping Florida's shoppers, then possibly moving westward through Alabama, Mississippi, and Louisiana. After nine months of market-softening advertising proclaiming "when we save, you save," three Food Lion stores opened in Jacksonville, Florida. The response was phenomenal; security guards had to be hired to help people form orderly lines at cash registers. By the end of the year, Food Lion had plans for 20 more stores and

a distribution center of 1,000,000 square-feet to be built in nearby Green Cove Springs. That facility positioned Food Lion for eventual entry into other Florida markets such as Tallahassee, Tampa, and Melbourne.

Since Ralph Ketner formulated Food Lion's everyday low-price strategy in 1967, the company stressed doing "1,000 things 1% better," an attitude that was responsible for Food Lion's operating expenses of only 13 percent of sales, compared to a 19 percent average in the industry. Food Lion cut costs in a variety of inventive ways: recycling banana boxes to ship cosmetics and health products and using exhaust from freezer motors to help heat the store in the winter, for example. Food Lion also used aggressive inventory strategies, ordering enormous quantities of products in order to save through volume buying.

By the end of the 1980s, Food Lion was the fastest-growing and one of the most profitable supermarket chains in the country. In 1990 alone, Food Lion opened 20 more stores, while sales hit $5.6 billion (beating Smith's goal of $5 billion set five years earlier). Earnings of $172.6 million for the year equated to a 3.1 percent margin, besting the industry average of one percent. Smith set a new goal of reaching $14 billion in sales by 1995. He also became chairman of Food Lion in 1990, replacing Ketner who remained on the board of directors.

To keep the company growing, Smith broke with tradition by targeting a state noncontiguous to the ones Food Lion already operated in: Texas. That market appeared vulnerable to a low-price operator since food prices there averaged 15 percent higher than Food Lion's. By the fall of 1991, Food Lion had opened 41 stores in the Dallas-Fort Worth area. Sales for 1991 increased 14.3 percent to $6.4 billion, and the firm's margin remained steady and healthy at 3.2 percent.

The following year, however, Food Lion faced several challenges. In November, toward the end of a year in which Food Lion opened 131 new stores and expanded to Oklahoma and Louisiana, ABC's *PrimeTime Live* news magazine television show aired a story claiming that Food Lion stores had knowingly sold spoiled meat, fish, and poultry to its customers. The report included hidden-camera videotape appearing to show Food Lion employees masking the spoiled states of the products by rewrapping products whose sell-by dates had passed. Through the power of television, the effect of this negative publicity was immediate and significant. Chainwide same-store sales plunged 9.5 percent in November.

Particularly hard hit were stores in the states into which Food Lion had only recently expanded: Florida, Texas, Oklahoma, and Louisiana. Compounding Food Lion's difficulties were its less than robust sales in these new markets, especially Texas. Some analysts contended that Food Lion had misread the Texas grocery market. In any case, 1992 ended with a disappointing sales increase of 12.5 percent and a decreased margin of 2.5 percent. The full brunt of the *PrimeTime* story was felt in 1993 when sales increased only 5.7 percent and the firm barely broke even, posting net income of only $3.9 million due in large part to a $170.5 million charge incurred in order to close 88 stores, about 50 of them in the poorly performing Texas and Oklahoma markets. Ketner announced early in 1993 that he would not seek reelection to the Food Lion board, citing his frustration with constantly being outvoted on key board matters. Ketner had reportedly opposed some of Smith's expansion plans.

Food Lion sued ABC for fraud and racketeering, claiming that ABC had concocted the story. Smith also fought back on several other fronts. He moved to quickly boost customer confidence in the quality of Food Lion products by offering money-back guarantees. Moreover, the number of planned new stores was scaled back in favor of the expansion and remodeling of existing stores. This was seen as particularly important in markets such as Dallas-Fort Worth, where customers who might be attracted by low prices were turned off by the smaller size, smaller selection, and no frills of most Food Lion stores. Many of the remodeled stores featured the addition of a deli/bakery. In 1994, 65 stores were remodeled, with the number of renovations increasing to 121 in 1995. By contrast, Food Lion opened only 47 new stores in 1995.

Finally, Smith moved to address an ongoing conflict with the United Food and Commercial Workers Union (UFCW), which had been attempting to organize Food Lion for years. The UFCW had brought to the attention of the U.S. Department of Labor claims that Food Lion had violated child-labor laws and had forced some of its workers to work extra hours without receiving overtime pay. Rather than continuing to fight, Food Lion agreed to a $16.2 million settlement in 1993. Two years later, however, the matter had not been completely resolved since as many as a thousand Food Lion employees opted out of the 1993 settlement in order to pursue independent claims. Food Lion began to settle these suits in 1995 (without any admission of wrongdoing), adding hundreds of thousands if not millions of dollars to the amount it agreed to pay in 1993.

During 1995—a year in which sales growth continued to slow (a 3.5 percent increase to $8.21 billion, well below Smith's $14 billion goal of five years earlier) and the company's margin fell further to 2.1 percent—Food Lion's lawyers and public relations staff remained busy. New reports from the consumer watchdog group Consumers United with Employees (CUE) claimed that Food Lion had a "chronic problem" with selling out-of-date infant formula and over-the-counter drugs. Food Lion maintained that CUE was biased because of its connections to labor unions and cited an inspection by the U.S. Food and Drug Administration of 63 Food Lion stores which resulted in an overall "excellent" rating. Food Lion even conducted its own investigation of some of its competitors' stores to show that they too were selling a certain percentage of out-of-date items, thus implying that Food Lion was being unfairly singled out for an industry-wide problem. The firm did, however, agree to refund CUE for 1,088 cans of outdated infant formula CUE had purchased from Food Lion stores. In mid-1995 it also filed a $100 million lawsuit against the UFCW, former employees, and others alleging a conspiracy to destroy the company through the continuing attacks.

The company also remained embroiled in a lawsuit against ABC, alleging fraud, trespassing, and breach of fiduciary duty in the way that ABC had conducted its investigation and in its use of hidden cameras. The company was seeking $100 million from ABC in damages, profits made by ABC from the *Prime-Time* broadcast, and attorneys' fees.

While the outcomes of its various lawsuits were sure to have a profound impact on Food Lion, some analysts suggested that regaining its niche in the market was perhaps more crucial to Food Lion's future, as, during this time, low-price competitors such as Albertson's and Winn-Dixie appeared to be gaining ground on Food Lion. Nevertheless, as it moved toward the 21st century, Food Lion management remained optimistic. According to one company publication, Food Lion looked forward "with confidence to a future of continued innovation, continued growth, continued price leadership, and continued service to its customers and communities."

Further Reading

Ketner, Ralph W., *Five Fast Pennies*, Salisbury, N.C.: R.W. Ketner, 1994, 227 p.

Konrad, Walecia, "Food Lion: Still Stalking in Tough Times," *Business Week*, June 22, 1992, p. 70.

"The Lion in Winter: Tom Smith Tells How He Plans for Food Lion to Come Roaring Back," *Business North Carolina*, June 1994, p. 28.

Mathews, Ryan, "Can Five Wrongs Make One Right?," *Progressive Grocer*, June 1995, pp. 53–61.

Napoli, Lisa, "In the Media Jungle, the Lion Weeps Tonight," *Business North Carolina*, March 1993, p. 16.

Poole, Claire, "Stalking Bigger Game," *Forbes*, April 1, 1991, pp. 73–74.

Tosh, Mark, "Can Food Lion Recover?," *Supermarket News*, December 21, 1992, p. 1.

Weinstein, Steve, "Food Lion on the Prowl," *Progressive Grocer*, October 1990, p. 78.

Wineka, Mark, and Jason Lesley, *Lion's Share: How Three Small-Town Grocers Created America's Fastest-Growing Supermarket Chain and Made Millionaires of Scores of Their North Carolina Friends and Neighbors*, Asheboro, N.C.: Down Home Press, 1991, 265 p.

Zwiebach, Elliot, "Food Lion Struggles Back," *Supermarket News*, November 8, 1993, p. 1.

—updated by David E. Salamie

Fortis, Inc.

The Fortis Building, Suite 1201
139 Water Street, P.O. Box 8837
St. John's, Newfoundland A1B 3T2
Canada
(709) 737-5862
Fax: (709) 737-5307

Public Company
Incorporated: 1987
Employees: 869
Stock Exchanges: Toronto Montreal
Sales: C$381.94 million (1994)
SICs: 4911 Electric Services; 6162 Mortgage Bankers
and Loan Correspondents; 6512 Operators of
Nonresidential Buildings; 6719 Holding Company

Fortis Inc., through its subsidiaries, is the leading distributor of electricity in the Province of Newfoundland and the Province of Prince Edward Island. Fortis was created in 1987 as a holding company, with Newfoundland Light and Power Co. as its chief subsidiary. Since then it has branched out into other power industry segments and diversified into the financial services, real estate, and telecommunications industries. The company was posting steady growth in the mid-1990s.

Although Fortis is a relatively new company, its core subsidiary and predecessor, Newfoundland Light & Power Co., boasts a rich history dating back to the 1880s. By that time, Edison's breakthrough electric lamp had been introduced as had his design for an entire electrical supply system. Demand for Edison's system was immediate and overwhelming. Not exempt from the clamber to develop an electric system were Edison's northern neighbors in Newfoundland (which did not actually join the Canadian confederation until 1949). In fact, it was on October 19, 1885, that residents of Newfoundland's port city of St. John's saw an electric light demonstrated for the first time. That event sparked a concerted drive to bring electricity to

St. John's and throughout the rugged, sparsely populated Newfoundland region.

Among the first communities along the North American coast to develop an electric system was St. John's, a relatively wealthy town of about 31,000 people who were mostly of English or Irish descent. In May 1885, five men—Alexander McLellan Mackay, John Steer, Walter Baine Grieve, Edwin John Duder, and Moses Monroe—incorporated themselves as Newfoundland Electric Light Company Limited. Through that venture, the investors planned to develop "an electric light station or stations in St. John's and elsewhere in Newfoundland."

Spearheading the effort were Monroe and Mackay. Mackay served as the company's first president until 1892, at which time he was succeeded by Monroe. Mackay had moved to Newfoundland in 1857 to head the local division of the New York, London, and Newfoundland Telegraph Company. He became a Newfoundland citizen and achieved notable success as a politician there. Monroe was a successful businessman and was operating a successful wholesale venture at the time.

The fledgling electricity company, which became known as St. John's Electric Light Company, strung electric wires and converted an old warehouse into a power station. By October 1885 the company was already burning electric street and store lamps. Despite initial glitches—one telephone office employee was blown six feet away from the switchboard when electric lines came into contact with the phone lines—the company was an early success. Several companies signed up for electric lighting service and, importantly, St. John's Electric secured a lucrative street lighting contract with the city. By 1887 St. John's Electric was supplying electric lighting to about 50 companies and by 1888 was fueling about 25 street lamps that replaced antiquated gas lamps.

Once the company had proven the viability of electric lighting, growth was rapid. In 1889 the company installed a new plant near to its first generation building to produce power for incandescent lamps. The advanced system consisted of two horizontal steam engines that drove a shaft connected to two dynamos. The contraption was capable of producing a total of about 330 amps at 125 volts (a very small amount of power by modern standards). Demand for electricity surged and within a few years generation capacity was again increased. In addition to lighting, St. John's Electric began producing power for other uses, including an electric street car in the early 1890s. The company also realized demand growth as a result of an unfortunate 1892 fire, which burned much of the city and severely damaged the competing gas company's infrastructure.

St. John's Electric and most of Newfoundland were rocked by financial turbulence during the mid-1890s. One result was that ownership and control of the electric company changed hands before the turn of the century. Simultaneously, other events were transpiring that would have an impact on the future of St. John's Electric Light Co. Among them was the creation of a street railway company by entrepreneur and statesman Sir Robert Gillespie Reid.

Reid had moved to Newfoundland in 1890, by which time the 48-year-old was already a multimillionaire. He took on the construction of a regional rail system as a new challenge beginning in 1890 and by the early 1890s had effectively built a rail network in and around St. John's. The importance of the development of St. John's Street Railway Company was that the venture entailed the development of a hydro electric station and other infrastructure that was eventually integrated with the original operations of St. John's Electric Light Co.

Electric power was supplied to the St. John's region during the early 1900s primarily through a company named Reid Newfoundland, which was headed by the Reid family and had effectively absorbed St. John's Light Electric Light Co. As the number of applications for electricity increased, demand rose and Reid Newfoundland expanded capacity. Despite that growth, Reid Newfoundland enjoyed only spotty profitability from its electric power operations. In fact, the Reids tried to jettison the division in the 1910s. By the 1920s, moreover, the electric infrastructure was becoming outdated and needed an overhaul. Reid Newfoundland incorporated a subsidiary named St. John's Light and Power Company that consisted of its electricity-related assets. It sold that company, by means of a relatively complex transaction, in 1924 to Montreal Engineering. The company was reincorporated as Newfoundland Light and Power Co.

New ownership of the power company was welcomed by many, because it was assumed that the new owners would inject the capital needed to update the aging system. Indeed, Montreal Engineering boasted wide experience in the North American light and power industry. Its expertise became evident at Newfoundland Light and Power as the company invested heavily and upgraded the system during the 1920s and 1930s. It boosted capacity, renovated the street car system, and launched a drive to increase consumption of electricity in St. John's and outlying areas. The company's main power generation station, for example, was upgraded during the mid-1920s to produce more than twice as much power as it had delivered prior to 1924. Customers were given incentives to use electricity, for example, to heat their homes, and electricity prices dropped as the aggregate volume of consumption rose.

Also boosting consumption for Newfoundland Light and Power was increased use of electricity by the company's major consumer outside of St. John's: the Bell Island iron works. Expansions at that facility during the late 1920s and 1930s, combined with other growth in the region, significantly boosted electricity output. Furthermore, during World War II electricity demand increased and the company expanded with additional hydro generation plants. After the war, the street car service was terminated to make way for the increasingly popular automobile. Despite that loss of power use, demand for Newfoundland Light and Power's electricity would rise as the postwar economy boomed; immediately following the war, though, consumption declined as use by local military installations diminished.

Just as important to the company as evolving power needs during the late 1940s and 1950s were striking political changes. In 1949, shortly after the tram service was stopped, Newfoundland became a Canadian Province. For Newfoundland Light and Power and its 135-member work force, that meant that the company was suddenly subject to regulatory control by the national government. Furthermore, it played a part in the formation of a labor union at the company, Local 1620 of the International Brotherhood of Electrical Workers (IBEW). It was with those changes that the company met the challenges of the 1950s and 1960s, most paramount of which were population growth and increased consumption of electricity per capita.

Indeed, the population of St. John's increased from about 50,000 in 1950 to 80,000 by the mid-1960s. Similarly, the company's power output grew more than three-fold between 1947 and 1957. Power output during the late 1950s and 1960s, moreover, increased rapidly as Newfoundland Light and Power labored to extend its services outside of St. John's and throughout Newfoundland. The company constructed several new generation facilities and updated infrastructure throughout the period. New infrastructure included an innovative steam plant during the mid-1950s and replacement of incandescent street lights with high-efficiency mercury-vapor lamps during the early 1960s. Meanwhile, the company overcame memorable obstacles to progress, including a devastating sleet storm that wreaked havoc on the electricity delivery systems.

It was during the 1950s and 1960s, when Newfoundland Light and Power began reaching outside of its traditional boundaries near St. John's, that its potential service offerings began to overlap with those of other power companies. Since the early 1900s, in fact, several smaller electric companies had emerged in more rural areas of Newfoundland. United Towns Electric (UTE), for example, had supplied power to areas outside of St. John's since the early 1900s. UTE had grown partly by purchasing other rural power companies, such as the Conception Bay Electric Company (which it bought in 1914), the Wabana Light and Power Company (acquired in 1931), and Public Service Electric Company (1932). As UTE grew, so did another regional power provider named Union Electric Light and Power Company (UELP). UELP had started in 1916 and, like UTE, had merged with or purchased several other power suppliers to become a major rural power company. By the 1960s both UTE and UELP had become major Newfoundland power suppliers.

During the early 1960s, UTE, UELP, and Newfoundland Light and Power—the three established private utility companies in Newfoundland—became physically joined when they linked power lines in various projects. The linking of the three companies started the ball rolling toward the inevitable merger of a province-wide utility company. Other factors driving the union included pubic pressure for uniform electric rates, territorial disputes between the three companies, and the need for an integrated provincial power grid system. That merger finally occurred in 1966, when executives at the three companies, with permission from regulators, agreed to become a single entity called Newfoundland Light & Power Company, Limited. The Newfoundland Light and Power moniker carried over primarily because that predecessor company was far and away the largest energy producer with about 95,000 kilowatts of capacity, compared to 25,000 and 4,662 for UTE and UELP, respectively. The newly amalgamated company enjoyed a customer base of more than 80,000.

Executives spent the next few years consolidating operations and streamlining the 77 different rate categories into just three. Management and administrative operations were combined and the systems were updated to create a uniform, Province-wide company. Meanwhile, electricity consumption in the region soared, particularly during the 1970s when the company encouraged customers to heat their homes with electricity. In 1974 alone, Newfoundland's electricity use surged more then 20 percent. To keep up with increased demand Newfoundland Light and Power added capacity and updated infrastructure. During the early 1980s rampant growth was squelched by the energy crises that pushed up electricity prices. Still, Newfoundland Light managed to post five percent annual consumption gains throughout the period and into the mid-1980s.

By the mid-1980s Newfoundland Light was generating about C$200 million in annual sales and capturing roughly C$16 million in net income. Its growth was predictably stable during most of the decade and into the 1990s because of its status as a government-regulated and protected utility. Revenues increased quickly to C$244 million in 1985 but then rose steadily to C$250 million in 1987 and then to about C$308 million in 1990, about C$24 million of which was netted as income. During the same period, the company's customer base increased from about 170,000 to 184,000, and then to 192,000. By 1990 the company was operating about 30 generating plants and serving roughly 85 percent of the province's electricity consumers. It purchased most of the electricity it sold from the Newfoundland and Labrador Hydro Electric Corporation. After years of operating purely as a government-regulated utility, however, Newfoundland Light and Power embarked on a new course in the late 1980s and early 1990s.

The change was partially the result of a new president. In 1985 Angus Bruneau was hired to run the company. Bruneau differed from his immediate predecessors in that his background was not in the utility or government sector. Among other initiatives, Bruneau created an advisory council designed to improve the company's customer relations. More importantly, it was under Bruneau's leadership that Newfoundland Light and Power began the transformation from a regulated public utility to a private-sector company engaged in nonregu-lated business. In 1987 the company created a holding company—Fortis, Inc.—to purchase the assets of Newfoundland Light and Power Co. The move was designed to allow the company, through Fortis, to participate in non-utility ventures.

Thus, Newfoundland Light and Power Co. had suddenly become a subsidiary of a larger company named Fortis, Inc. The change was somewhat superficial, as existing management remained entrenched. It was important, though, because it allowed the company to diversify and invest its resources in potentially higher-profit businesses. To that end, in 1989 Fortis established Fortis Properties as a real estate arm. During the early 1990s that division began purchasing shopping malls, retail and office buildings, and other commercial properties. That effort was viewed as a way to benefit from depressed real estate prices caused by an ugly commercial real estate downturn. Between 1989 and 1994, Fortis Properties' assets increased from C$6 million to C$87 million.

Also in 1989, Fortis purchased Newfoundland Building Savings and Loan. It used that bargain buy to form the foundation for a new subsidiary called Fortis Trust. Fortis Trust, a mortgage company, started out with C$5 million in mortgage assets but grew to C$60 million within four years. In 1990 Fortis bolstered its utility holdings when it acquired Maritime Electric, the power generation company that served approximately 90 percent of the population of nearby Prince Edward Island. During the early 1990s, Fortis used its expertise and deep pockets to whip the utility into shape. Rates were cut on the island by about nine percent and customer service was improved. Maritime was unique in that it was a private company almost exempt from government regulation, and therefore complemented Fortis' goal of private-sector diversification.

In 1991 Fortis made its foray into the telecommunications business when Fortis Properties joined in a partnership with Unitel Communications to provide wireless and other alternative telecommunications services to Newfoundland. Unitel quickly built a C$30 million system in Newfoundland, which became the most successful Unitel operation in Canada. Fortis also attempted a venture into the gas pipeline industry when it made a bid for a Saskatchewan gas pipeline company. The effort failed but signaled the company's intent to diversify broadly. "I jokingly say that at Fortis we have two rules," said Stanley Marshall, vice-president of corporate affairs, in a *Trade and Commerce Magazine* special supplement in 1994, "one, we invest in nothing that grows, i.e. cucumbers, fish, anything like that; and two, where government invests our taxes, no further investment by Fortis is warranted."

The impact of Fortis' diversification on sales was negligible during the early 1990s, given the immense size of its core Newfoundland Light and Power Co. operations. Revenues rose to about C$380 million in 1994, about C$31.3 million of which was netted as income. Each of its new divisions was posting steady gains though, and its core utility company continued to show profits. Net income at Fortis Trust, for example, grew from about C$50,000 to nearly C$500,000 between 1990 and 1994, while profits at Fortis Properties increased from almost nothing in 1991 to more than C$1.2 million. Its core utility operations, meanwhile, supplied power to more than a quarter of a million customers in 1994. The company's long-term goal was increased efficiency in its utility operations and ongoing diversification into growth industries.

Principal Subsidiaries

Fortis Properties Corporation; Fortis Trust Corporation; Maritime Electric Company, Limited; Newfoundland Light & Power Co. Limited.

Further Reading

Baker, Melvin, with Robert D. Pitt and Janet Miller Pitt, *The Illustrated History of Newfoundland Light & Power*, St. John's, Newfoundland: Creative Publishers, 1990.

Hebbard, Gary J., "Fortis Inc. Focused On Service," *Trade and Commerce Magazine*, special supplement, 1994.

Redmond, Michael, "Fortis 'Not in a Hurry'," *Financial Post*, January 19, 1991, p. 23.

—Dave Mote

G.S. Blodgett Corporation

P.O. Box 5669
Burlington, Vermont 05402
U.S.A.
(802) 658-6600
Fax: (802) 864-0183

Private Company
Incorporated: 1854 as G.S. Blodgett & Company
Employees: 600
Sales: $150 million (1995 est.)
SICs: 3556 Food Products Machinery; 3631 Household
Cooking Equipment

G.S. Blodgett Corporation is one of the world's leaders in manufacturing highly specialized commercial cooking materials and equipment. The company's convection oven holds the largest share of the market in the United States, and its premium charbroilers, conveyor ovens, and commercial fryers have also captured significant portions of their respective markets. Blodgett has manufacturing facilities spread over three states, including Vermont, New Hampshire, and Pennsylvania, and has organized an effective domestic dealership and international network which distributes the company's products throughout the United States and in over 50 foreign countries.

The company was started by Gardner S. Blodgett, an ambitious and imaginative plumber who ran his own store at 191 College Street in Burlington, Vermont. In 1848, when Blodgett was only 29 years old, he was approached by the owner of a nearby tavern, who told him that his oven wasn't heating food properly. Specifically, customers were complaining that the meat from the tavern was cooked on one side but not on the other. In response, Blodgett and his partner built a wood burning stove that solved the tavern owner's problems. The success of Blodgett's creation spread quickly and soon tavern owners from the surrounding areas were requesting new and improved ovens. By 1854, the young entrepreneur patented his improved baking oven and incorporated his business as G.S. Blodgett and Company.

The company thrived during the mid- and late 1850s, but with the onset of the American Civil War in 1860, Blodgett joined the Union Army and his business came to a standstill. Blodgett attained the rank of assistant quartermaster of volunteers, helping to outfit all the members of the First Vermont Cavalry. He was also instrumental in acquiring and planning the United States National Cemetery in Arlington, Virginia.

When Blodgett returned to civilian life, he began to rebuild his company. In just a few years, Blodgett was again providing high-quality commercial ovens to tavern owners in Burlington, Vermont, and was also experimenting with other types of ovens as well. Blodgett was convinced that newer, more efficient types of ovens were needed by the commercial cooking and baking industry, and he began producing convection ovens, deck ovens, and conveyor ovens. With the addition of these products, the company's revenues climbed rapidly. Blodgett became a wealthy man by the 1880s.

During the 1890s, the company continued to increase its revenues and expand its customer base. More and more employees were hired, including a young man named John S. Patrick. Patrick, hired as the company's secretary and treasurer, soon became an indispensable part of Blodgett's management team. He learned quickly about the company's affairs, even the intricate details surrounding the manufacture of convection ovens. After several years, Patrick decided to purchase Blodgett's interest in the company and assume control of the firm's operations. The new owner's acquisition signaled the beginning of three generations of Patrick family control and management over the company.

Like his predecessor, John Patrick was determined to develop and expand the company's product line. Following years of increasing sales and profits, Patrick decided to establish a new operating division outside Vermont. Located in Bow, New Hampshire, the new division was founded as Pitco Frialator in 1918. Specializing in the manufacture of commercial frying equipment, the new division was an immediate success. Restaurants from all over the country, especially on the eastern seaboard, began ordering Blodgett equipment, and sales continued to rise.

During the 1920s, the company took advantage of the expanding American economy and the plethora of new restaurants opening in major cities, including New York, Boston, Philadelphia, and Chicago. However, with the crash of the stock market in the fall of 1929 and the start of the Great Depression, people were forced to conserve their financial resources and, as a result, many restaurants were forced out of business due to a loss of customers. Although Blodgett felt the effects of the Depression, the company was able to remain competitive. In 1931, the firm was being managed so competently by the Patrick family that a new operating division was established in Quakertown, Pennsylvania. This division, called MagiKitch'n, a manufacturer of charbroilers and frying equipment for the commercial market, was another success story.

Having survived the depression, Blodgett entered the 1940s poised to expand its market share in the burgeoning commercial food service industry. With America's entry into World War II, the U.S. government placed numerous contracts with Blodgett to supply ovens for cooking food near the frontlines of battlefields. Former employees who were now soldiers would write back to company management describing how Blodgett ovens were able to cook food evenly in the most terrible weather conditions. When these same former employees were served food that was improperly cooked, they suggested to their quartermaster sergeants that Blodgett would be able to provide an efficient oven that would satisfy the battle-weary soldiers who needed a good hot meal. Surprisingly, it was in this way that Blodgett sold numerous ovens to the U.S. Army and Navy throughout the war years.

After World War II, and continuing through the 1950s, Blodgett built upon its previous success. Each passing year brought increased revenues, with more benefits accruing to the company's employees all the time. The Patrick family, still in control of the company's entire operations, built a tradition of excellent management-employee relations over the years. Not only rewarding its long-term workers with profit sharing and generous pension plans, the Patrick family never laid off a single worker during the time it ran the company. By 1958, Blodgett had grown large enough for management to consider expanding company operations overseas. Consequently, Blodgett International contracted its first foreign distributor in the same year.

Growth continued apace from the 1960s into the 1980s. The company sold ovens to the entire spectrum of the food services industry, from such large fast food restaurant chains as Pizza Hut and Taco Bell, to such small chains of three or four units as Zachary's Pizza in Burlington, Vermont. Blodgett also sold ovens to grade schools, high schools, universities, hospitals, bakeries, U.S. Army and Navy installations, sports complexes, gourmet restaurants, taverns, large volume food manufacturers, and hotels. In the foreign arena, Blodgett contracted numerous distributors throughout Europe. In 1985, the company purchased the intellectual property rights from a German manufacturer of multifunction steamer ovens. One year later, management created Blodgett Combi, a new division of the firm that produced both the multi-function steamer oven and the company's famous brand name Mastertherm conveyor ovens. Together, these two items quickly became the most popular of all Blodgett products.

During the mid-1980s, the Patrick family, who had remained in control of Blodgett over the years, began to contemplate how to raise liquidity for their shareholders. The three options the family considered included a merger with another company, a public offering of stock in the firm, and the sale of the company. Doug Johnson, hired as the president of Blodgett in 1985, reportedly contacted some of his friends on Wall Street and began to arrange for a leveraged buyout of Blodgett by the company's management. Along with Sam Hartwell, who joined Blodgett in 1988, the two men reached a deal with The First Boston Corporation and Metropolitan Life Insurance Company that accounted for approximately 85 percent of the capital needed for the buyout.

Johnson and Hartwell, acting as co-chairmen of the company, immediately analyzed Blodgett's financial condition and operational structure, and determined that certain changes were necessary. One year after the management buyout of Blodgett, Johnson and Hartwell either closed or sold three company divisions that were losing money or just breaking even. They relocated the conveyor oven business, which had previously been operating out of Chicago, to Burlington, Vermont. This relocation also signaled a more aggressive strategy for marketing the company's conveyor ovens, both domestically and internationally. Three production facilities were sold, including sites at Burlington and Philadelphia, and then leased back to Blodgett in order to raise more working capital. During these changes, Johnson and Hartwell also implemented strict cost control measures, while at the same time reducing expenses and working capital.

In the early 1990s, under the new management, Blodgett made an aggressive move to expand its international image. The company began to exhibit its products at trade shows in London, Prague, Singapore, and Sydney, Australia. As the firm 's international revenues grew, management decided to open sales offices in Prague, Amsterdam, Singapore, and Toronto. Slowly, Blodgett began to successfully compete with other top companies in the highly specialized field of commercial cooking equipment, including Cidelcem of France, Fujimak of Japan, Zanussi of Italy, and Rational of Germany.

The reorganization of Blodgett after the leveraged management buy-out started to reap rewards by the end of 1993. The term "de-leveraging," used by Wall Street analysts to describe the paying off of debts after a leveraged buy-out, was worked on assiduously by Johnson and Hartwell. Approximately 60 percent of all the company's senior debt was paid off during that year. At the same time, since 1988 Blodgett was able to increase its sales by an impressive 67 percent, up from $67 million to $110 million in just five years. More importantly, Blodgett snared nearly 12 percent of the entire market for products manufactured in the commercial cooking equipment industry, which has annual domestic sales greater than $1 billion. Of the 650 members that belonged to the National Association of Food Equipment Manufacturers, Blodgett was one of the top 50 companies with sales over the $25 million mark.

Blodgett management also made a commitment to research and development. Since the late 1980s, over $3 million per year was being devoted to developing new products, and by the mid-1990s over 50 percent of the company's offerings were new.

The company manufactured ovens that could bake 300 to 400 pizzas in one hour; combined microwave and radio frequency technology with traditional methods of hot air and atmospheric steam; and was in the process of developing products that used voice activation to control oven temperatures, magnetic induction, and automatically programmed cooking cycles. In the early 1990s, the company's products cost anywhere from $500 to $20,000, and Blodgett engineers traveled as far away as Sao Paulo, Brazil, to investigate new ideas and search for new technology in order to improve and develop its products.

In the mid-1990s, Blodgett operated as a decentralized, multi-company organization, with each of its divisions working as a stand alone business. This enabled the management in each division, such as Blodgett International, to respond to customer needs in the fast-paced food services industry. Management's goals for the late 1990s were to raise more capital, possibly through a public stock offering, and to initiate an acquisitions campaign in order to expand the company's holdings and increase its revenues.

Principal Divisions

Pitco Frialator, MagiKitch'n, Blodgett Ovens, Blodgett Combi, Blodgett International.

Further Reading

Johnson, J. Douglas, and Hartwell, Samuel A., The Story of G.S. Blodgett Corporation: 145 Years of Success and Still Growing. Newcomen Society: New York, 1993.

—Thomas Derdak

Greif Bros. Corporation

621 Pennsylvania Avenue
Delaware, Ohio 43015
U.S.A.
(614) 363-1271
Fax: (614) 363-1090

Public Company
Incorporated: 1926 as Greif Bros. Cooperage Corp.
Employees: 4,500
Revenues: $583.5 million (1994)
Stock Exchanges: Chicago
SICs: 2655 Fiber Cans, Tubes, and Drums; 3412 Metal
  Barrels, Drums and Pails; 2431 Millwork; 2499 Wood
  Products, Not Elsewhere Classified; 3089 Plastics
  Products, Not Elsewhere Classified; 2631 Paperboard
  Mills

Greif Bros. Corporation has been involved in the bulk packaging industry since its foundation and has evolved from the world's largest manufacturer of wooden barrels into a relatively small, yet highly profitable manufacturer of shipping containers. In the mid-1990s, Greif's sales were fairly evenly split between its two primary product groups: shipping containers and containerboard. The firm, which boasts that it is ''the only manufacturer that offers a complete line encompassing fibre, steel, plastic, multiwall bags and cartons,'' ranked as one of Ohio's 100 largest companies in the early 1990s. Greif had operations in 30 American states and three Canadian provinces in 1995. While one class of Greif Bros.' stock is publicly traded, the voting class of stock is held, directly or indirectly, by Chairman Emeritus John C. Dempsey, his wife Naomi, and the closely-associated Macauley & Co. After guiding the company for nearly half a century, John Dempsey retired from active leadership in 1994. He was succeeded as chairman and chief executive officer by Michael J. Gasser, who had served as Greif Bros.' chief operating officer since 1988. At 43, Gasser was the youngest member of the board.

The company, founded in Cleveland, was initially a manufacturer of wooden staves, headings, barrels, and kegs. By 1926, Greif owned 216 manufacturing plants and eight divisional offices, as well as timberlands, logging equipment, sawmills, and cooperages.

John Raible (later characterized by William Baldwin of *Forbes* as ''a wealthy investor with enough other interests to make cooperage only a sideline,'') took over from the founding Greif brothers in 1913. It was perhaps the worst time in the history of the cooperage industry for less than interested management. Wooden packaging, although buoyed during the first two decades of the 20th century by the rise of the petroleum industry, was devastated by the one-two-punch of prohibition and the development and introduction of 55-gallon steel drums. While Greif Bros. sales more than tripled from $11.4 million in 1940 to $36.1 million in 1946, its profitability decreased; net income only increased by 67 percent from $720,000 to $1.2 million during the same period. It was increasingly clear to some observers that traditional cooperage companies would have to diversify or die.

In 1946, John Dempsey, a 33-year-old accountant, mounted a challenge to Raible's corporate control. Dempsey's wife and mother-in-law had held stakes in the company, and he accumulated enough other shares to garner a controlling interest in 1946. While the new leader continued to buttress the cooperage business with the acquisition of timber acreage in the postwar era, he also tried to develop a proprietary machine to make the lightweight, disposable kraft-paper drums that were replacing old-fashioned wooden barrels in shipping.

Dempsey assigned a team of Greif mechanics the task of designing a proprietary fibre drum machine, but their attempts were unsuccessful. Faced with the imminent demise of his company, Dempsey acquired the rights to a drum winder from an outside inventor. Throughout the postwar era, he purchased the equipment necessary to manufacture steel, plastic and paper packaging and containers. The company also boosted its container capabilities with the acquisition of an interest in Brooklyn's Carpenter Container Corp. in 1948. By the mid-1950s, revenues from the new operations had drawn about even with the original cooperage business.

Dempsey's reorganization was costly. Sales declined by 15 percent from $31.7 million in 1946 to $26.9 million in 1949, and profits dropped by 40 percent, from $2 million to $1.2 million. In fact, it took the company more than a decade to regain the annual revenue and net income records established in the late 1940s; it wasn't until 1959, that Greif Bros. recovered its record fiscal levels of $40 million sales and $2 million profit.

Though Dempsey eliminated half of the company's 240 factories by 1963, he parlayed Greif Bros.' relatively small, but widespread plants, into a competitive advantage. Having production facilities near its clients' plants helped the company forge close ties with those customers, as well as to save on Greif's own shipping costs. By the early 1960s, Greif's product line had expanded to include steel drums, plywood drums, fibre drums, corrugated cartons, wire products and multiwall bags. In 1964, the company's headquarters was moved south from Cleveland to Delaware, a suburb of Columbus, Ohio.

Greif's sales more than doubled over the course of the decade, from $45 million in 1961 to $103 million in 1971. Net income followed suit, growing from $2.1 million to $5.5 million as the company grew accustomed to its new emphasis. The company formally recognized its exit from the barrel-making business by dropping "cooperage" from its name in 1969.

Unlike some of its larger, more diversified rivals like Continental Group, International Paper, and Mobil's Container Corp. of America, Greif Bros. didn't buy or build any paper mills, even though the company had hundreds of thousands of acres of timberland. Instead, the company acquired 50 percent of Macauley & Co. and its Virginia Fibre Corp. when they were created in 1974. Company namesake Robert Macauley was a "longtime Dempsey associate" and Greif Bros. board member. Dempsey believed that by limiting the parent company's investment in this capital-intensive business he would limit its exposure to risk and debt. By the early 1990s, however, Greif had increased its stake in Virginia Fibre to 100 percent.

Greif expanded via acquisition during the 1970s, acquiring Chipboard, Inc. and Narad, Inc. Although the disposition of these purchases is unclear, it appears that they developed into Greif's Michigan Packaging Company and Down River International, Inc. subsidiaries. Michigan Packaging was founded in 1967 and grew into a corrugated sheet board company with three plants in the eastern United States. Established in 1963, Down River started out manufacturing corrugated boxes, and evolved into a specialty producer of corrugated honeycomb filler for packaging and other applications. Acquisitions helped fuel a dramatic decade of growth. Sales nearly tripled from $103 million in 1971 to $307 million in 1981, and net income more than quadrupled, from $5.5 million to $25.2 million. This high level of profitability, combined with the stable majority ownership of the Dempsey family, allowed Greif to fund plant expansions and modernizations internally without incurring debt.

According to William Baldwin of *Forbes,* Greif ranked second only to Continental in the American fibre drum industry into the early 1980s. At five percent, Greif's average annual sales increases slowed significantly from the double-digit rate of the 1970s, but outpaced the fibre can industry's overall annual growth rate of 3.5 percent from 1982 to 1988. Annual profits increased at an average of three percent each year to a peak of $30.3 million in 1988.

But while sales continued to increase fairly steadily in the waning years of the decade and into the early 1990s, Greif's net income declined by more than one-fourth to $22.1 million in 1990. The reduced profitability was attributed to high capital investments ($66 million in 1989 alone), raw materials price increases, customers' price sensitivity, and increased global competition in Greif's primary markets. The company combated these trends by concentrating more intensely than ever on customer service. In the early 1990s, for example, Greif designed an ingeniously simple new shipping drum for Kraft General Foods. The custom-made containers revised the traditional cylindrical drum shape into a cube with rounded corners, allowing vastly more efficient transportation and storage. Whereas Kraft's trucks could hold 500 of the traditional cans, they could pack in 640 of the new drums.

Greif's 1990s-era environmental efforts included production of recycled and reusable packaging. As of 1995, the company's Greif Board subsidiary had been producing recycled-content corrugated board and kraft paper for nearly 30 years, and was working to incorporate more post-consumer corrugated into its products. And in 1993, Greif's Canadian container subsidiary worked with Ingersoll-Dresser Pump Co. to develop an award-winning reusable container for chemicals and hazardous materials. Progressive efforts such as these reflected Greif's heritage of meeting market challenges and helped ensure its place in the packaging industry.

By the mid-1980s, John C. Dempsey's over $300 million personal fortune ranked him as one of America's richest individuals, according to *Forbes* magazine. Dempsey was known among his colleagues and friends as "a deeply righteous person who gave of himself." His strongly-held religious beliefs were reflected in an illustration that graced the back cover of Greif Bros.' annual report virtually every year he was CEO. It was a photo of the corporate board room featuring Warner Sallman's famous "Head of Christ" painting. Dempsey served as Greif's chairman and CEO for 47 years, until 1994, when the 80-year-old's failing health forced his retirement from day-to-day leadership to the honorary post of chairman emeritus. Dempsey was succeeded by Greif Bros.' vice-president and controller, Michael J. Gasser.

The advent of new leadership for the first time in nearly half a century ushered in what the new CEO called "an era of great anticipation and virtually unlimited potential" in his first annual letter to shareholders. Gasser vowed to evaluate and reorganize Greif Bros.' operations, and even suggested the possibility of diversification and acquisition in pursuit of "aggressive growth." In 1995 the company applied to have both its classes of stock listed on the National Association of Securities Dealers Automated Quotes, suggesting the possibility of an equity floatation to fund expansion. The new leader noted that the moral principles embraced by his predecessor would "continue to play an integral part in the Company's operating policy."

Principal Subsidiaries

Barzon Corporation; Down River International, Inc.; Greif Board Corporation; Michigan Packaging Company; Soterra, Inc.; Contenants Greif Inc. (Canada); Virginia Fibre Corporation.

Principal Divisions

Raible Division; Seymour & Peck Division; Norco Division; West Coast Division; Corrugated Products Division; East Coast Division; The Cooperage; Plastics Division; Greif Division; International Division; Corrugated Products Division.

Further Reading

Allen, Michael Patrick, *The Founding Fortunes: A New Anatomy of the Super-Rich in America,* Truman Talley Books, 1987.

Baldwin, William, "Homely Virtues," *Forbes,* July 19, 1982, p. 54.

Eckhouse, Kimberly, "Shaped-up Shippers More Space- and Cost-Efficient," *Food Processing,* May 1993, p. 134.

"18-Year Veteran Named Greif Bros. President," *Columbus (Ohio) Dispatch,* November 2, 1995, p. 2B.

"They're in the Money," *The Cleveland Plain Dealer,* October 14, 1986, p. 1A.

—April Dougal Gasbarre

Grist Mill Company

21340 Hayes Avenue
P.O. Box 430
Lakeville, Minnesota 55044
U.S.A.
(612) 469-4981
Fax: (612) 469-5550

Public Company
Incorporated: 1917
Employees: 646
Sales: $78.92 million (1995)
Stock Exchanges: NASDAQ
SICs: 2048 Prepared Feeds, Not Elsewhere Classified;
2043 Cereal Breakfast Foods; 2041 Flour & Other
Grain Mill Products; 2064 Candy & Other
Confectionery Products

Minnesota-based Grist Mill Company manufactures cereal, cereal snacks, and confectionery products, such as ready-to-eat (RTE) cereals, granola bars, fruit-filled cereal bars, and pie crusts. Most of Grist Mill's products are sold under private supermarket labels, including 13 private labels of the 50 largest supermarket chains in the United States. Many of Grist Mill's private label cereals are meant to imitate well-known branded cereals of industry giants Kellogg's and General Mills. However, in 1995, Grist Mill rolled out a line of six premium private label cereals—Honey Glazed Corn Flakes; Extra Fruit Muesli; Extra-Raisin Raisin Bran; Apple Cinnamon Corn Flakes; Honey Glazed Bran Flakes; and Extra Fruit Low-Fat Granola—to be sold as original products. In addition to its 18 RTE products, Grist Mill manufactures a limited line of its own name-brand products and contract manufactures several products for other companies. The RTE cereal market was worth about $8 billion in 1995, with approximately $500 million of those sales going to private-label cereals. Grist Mill's $14 million in 1995 RTE sales, representing about four percent of the private-label market, placed it a distant third behind the Ralston Purina Group spinoff Ralcorp Holdings of St. Louis, with

nearly 60 percent, and Minneapolis's Malt-O-Meal Company, with approximately 25 percent. Private-label RTE cereals, however, had captured only about six percent of total cereal sales—compared to the 20 percent share private labels held in the $175 billion total grocery industry—leaving room for expansion. With its new and future product introductions, Grist Mill expected to increase its market share to about ten percent by the turn of the century. The bulk of Grist Mill's $80 million 1995 sales remained in the wholesome snack (granola bars, etc.) category, which Grist Mill continued to dominate in the United States.

Grist Mill's origins may be traced to a grain mill in Los Angeles established in 1917. By the 1930s, that business had evolved into one of the country's first natural foods stores. During the 1960s and 1970s, interest in natural foods began to spread throughout the country. In 1971, the assets of several companies, including the former Grist Mill store, were combined and moved to Lakeville, Minnesota. Operating as Grist Mill, the new company's original facilities were a modest 20,000 square feet. Production of its first granola cereal began that same year.

In 1973 Ronald Zuckerman and two partners bought a 65 percent share in Grist Mill for $85,000. In that year, Grist Mill began to supply its first private label product, known as "100% Natural Cereal." Contract manufacturing began the following year, with production of Enrights Natural Cereal. Grist Mill added another product in 1975, supplying the granola for the first of the granola bars, the Crunchola, marketed by Sunmark. Three years later, Grist Mill's sales had reached $1.3 million. Zuckerman, together with other members of the company's management, bought controlling interest in Grist Mill in 1981.

Zuckerman changed the focus of the company, taking an entrepreneurial direction that would see revenues jump to $23 million by 1985. The company began to expand its facilities beyond its original 20,000 square feet and brought in personnel "from more sophisticated environments to help the company become more sophisticated," as Glen Bolander, who would become the company's president and CEO, told *Candy Industry*. Bolander himself, a former independent food distributor, joined Grist Mill in 1982 in charge of sales. In 1982, Grist Mill also began production of private label graham cracker pie crusts. For the time being, the company's focus was on its private label business, and on expanding its sales and distribution networks to stimulate demand. Sales more than tripled over the previous year, to $4.2 million.

Production facilities were expanded to 50,000 square feet in 1983, including the addition of the company's first granola bar production line. Sales rose to $6.6 million, with a net loss of $3,000, but the company returned to profitability in 1984 with a $350,000 net on $12 million in revenues. Production of Grist Mill's private label granola bars began that year, and by 1984, two more granola bar lines were added. With a contract from Ralston Purina to manufacture that company's ''S'mores'' granola bars, Grist Mill added another 40,000 square feet of production space.

Zuckerman and Bolander took Grist Mill public in 1985, selling 24 percent of the company for $7 million. The company added chocolate-coated granola bars to its product line and moved into confectionery with the first of its real fruit snacks, Fruit Bits. The company also began production of RJR Nabisco's ''Goodstuff'' chocolate candy bar, then purchased the rights to that product when RJR Nabisco dropped it after its test marketing. While Grist Mill's private-label and contract manufacturing business grew, Zuckerman and Bolander made plans to take the company in a new direction. Using some of the cash raised in its initial public offering, Grist Mill entered the name-brand business, selling its Fruit Bits, and soon its RTE cereals as well, under the Grist Mill label. The company's strategy was to market low-end products priced between the private label and larger name brands. In 1986, name-brand products accounted for five percent of Grist Mill's grocery product line. By the end of the decade, name-brand products made up 35 percent of its grocery division.

Sales slipped as the company refocused itself. Its contract and industrial manufacturing business, which contributed over $6 million in revenue in 1986, suffered when Grist Mill's primary granola bar company left that market. However, the rollout of its fruit snacks led to more than $5.5 million in sales in 1987. Grist Mill added another 50,000 square feet to its plant in 1987–89. In 1988, the company expanded its fruit snacks line and established a self-standing Confections Division, with a separate sales and distribution network. Sales, which for three years were stuck at around $23 million, climbed to $31.7 million in 1988 and to $44 million in 1989. Profits were also up, increasing to $2.9 million, and now accounting for nearly seven percent of revenues.

In 1990 Grist Mill bought Tempo Confections, of Danville, Illinois, for $125,000. Tempo, formerly Chuckles Company, had been manufacturing much of Grist Mill's fruit snacks candies since their rollout. Renamed Grist Mill Confections, Inc., the new subsidiary added 125,000 square feet of production capacity, 125 employees, and annual production of 12–20 million pounds to Grist Mill's own 20 to 25 million pounds per year. Confectionery rose to account for 19 percent of Grist Mill's sales, while the bulk of its business remained in grocery, at 74 percent. Contract and industrial, which had been the core of Grist Mill's business, was by then scaled back to seven percent of sales.

Driven by its name brand products, sales jumped again to $60 million in 1990. By 1993, private label sales would account for less than 25 percent of Grist Mill's grocery business. However, consumer preferences were shifting as well. Private label products had begun to lose their reputation for lower quality, and, aided by the recession of the early 1990s, began to take more and more market share from the name brands. As it built its name brand business, Grist Mill all but neglected its cereal line, which evolved little beyond its core granola base. Competitors, especially Ralcorp and Malt-O-Meal, moved into the private label business, gaining dominant positions. At the same time, Grist Mill's confections divisions faced its own problems. The company's core candy bar, Goodstuff, had been less than successful, and was eventually dropped as unprofitable in 1993. That year brought more trouble to the confections division when the Farley Candy Co. introduced a private-label fruit snacks line. Modeled after Grist Mill's own fruit snacks, Farley's products sold for as much as 20 percent less. Grist Mill, however, lacked the money needed to counter with strong promotion campaign, and instead was forced to lower its prices. While Grist Mill managed to retain its market share—as much as 80 percent—the lower profit margins resulted in a 70 percent earnings drop for fruit snacks through 1994. Overall, Grist Mill's revenues fell from $67 million in 1993 to $55 million in 1994.

Zuckerman retired from Grist Mill in 1993, and Bolander took over as president and CEO. Zuckerman remained as chairman of the board. After discontinuing the Goodstuff bar, Bolander moved to scale back on fruit snack production, returning the company's focus to private label granola bars and cereals. Prior to 1993, Grist Mill's cereals had featured only granola and bran cereals. Grist Mill now moved to become a full-line cereal provider. The company stepped up the introduction of new private label products—such as corn flakes, frosted flakes, crispy rice, raisin bran, and bran flakes, as well as cereals modelled after such popular name-brand cereals as Kix, Cheerios, and Fruity Pebbles, adding 16 new products through 1995. With revenues rising to nearly $80 million that year, and earnings climbing to $4.6 million after the low of $1.2 million in 1994, the company also broadened its distribution, adding more customers and increasing its presence on existing customers' shelves.

In 1995, Grist Mill rolled out a new line of six premium cereals. Unlike its other cereals, which were meant to imitate existing brand name cereals, the new cereals were to be sold as original private label products. Yet the company's strongest sales and growth was with its granola and cereal snack bars; in 1994 Grist Mill added to its contract manufacturing business with production of Nabisco's brand-name granola bars. By the end of 1995, with six-month sales outpacing the previous year by 27 percent, Bolander was forecasting fiscal year 1996 revenues reaching to the low $90 million range. While it still trailed private-label competitors Ralcorp and Malt-O-Meal, the refocused Grist Mill appeared poised to make up for lost time.

Principal Subsidiaries

Grist Mill Confections, Inc.

Further Reading

DeSilver, Drew, "Grist Mill Rolls Out Premium Cereal Line," *Minneapolis-St. Paul CityBusiness,* June 23, 1995, p. 6.

Gibson, Richard, "Grist Mill Forecasts Big Rise in Sales Based on Acceptance of Cereal Line," *Wall Street Journal,* November 14, 1995, p. B18.

Moukheiber, Zina, "Eye Off the Ball," *Forbes,* December 5, 1994, p. 76.

Tiffany, Susan, "Grist Mill Rolls Out Bars, Jellies and Sales," *Candy Industry,* November 1991, p. 22.

—M.L. Cohen

GTE Corporation

One Stamford Forum
Stamford, Connecticut 06904
U.S.A.
(203) 965-2000
Fax: (203) 965-2277

Public Company
Incorporated: 1920 as Commonwealth Telephone
    Company
Employees: 111,000
Sales: $19.9 billion (1994)
Stock Exchanges: New York Midwest Pacific London
    Amsterdam Basel Geneva Lausanne Paris Zürich
    Tokyo
SICs: 4813 Telephone Communications Except
    Radiotelephone; 3661 Telephone & Telegraph
    Apparatus; 3663 Radio & T.V. Communications
    Equipment; 3641 Electric Lamps

GTE Corporation ranked as the world's third-largest publicly owned telecommunications company in 1996. With over 20 million telephone access lines in 40 states, the communications conglomerate was America's leading provider of local telephone services. The $6.6 billion acquisition of Contel Corporation in 1990 nearly doubled GTE's Mobilnet cellular operations, making it the second-largest provider of cellular telephone services in the United States, with over two million customers. GTE's strategy for the mid- to late 1990s focused on technological enhancement of wireline and wireless systems, expansion of data services, global expansion, and diversification into video services.

In March 1990 the largest merger in the history of the telecommunications industry united two former U.S. competitors, GTE Corporation and Contel Corporation, under the GTE name. With a market value of $28 billion, the merged company became a telecommunications powerhouse. Designed to take advantage of the two companies' complementary businesses, the merger strengthened GTE's assets in two of its three major areas of operations: telephone service and telecommunications products. While the two companies were united under one name, each has a rich history of its own.

GTE Corporation

GTE's heritage can be traced to 1918, when three Wisconsin public utility accountants pooled $33,500 to purchase the Richland Center Telephone Company, serving 1,466 telephones in the dairy belt of southern Wisconsin. From the outset, John F. O'Connell, Sigurd L. Odegard, and John A. Pratt worked under the guiding principle that better telephone service could be rendered to small communities if a number of exchanges were operated under one managing body.

In 1920 that principle was put into action, and the three accountants formed a corporation, Commonwealth Telephone Company, with Odegard as president, Pratt as vice-president, and O'Connell as secretary. Richland Center Telephone became part of Commonwealth Telephone, which quickly purchased telephone companies in three nearby communities. In 1922 Pratt resigned as vice-president and was replaced by Clarence R. Brown, a former Bell System employee.

By the mid-1920s Commonwealth had extended beyond Wisconsin borders and purchased the Belvidere Telephone Company in Illinois. It also diversified into other utilities by acquiring two small Wisconsin electrical companies. Expansion was stepped up in 1926, when Odegard secured an option to purchase Associated Telephone Company of Long Beach, California. Odegard, with the assistance of Marshall E. Sampsell, president of Wisconsin Power and Light Company, and Morris F. LaCroix, a partner in Paine, Webber & Company in Boston, proceeded to devise a plan for a holding company, to be named Associated Telephone Utilities Company.

That company was formed in 1926 to acquire Associated Telephone Company and assume the assets of Commonwealth Telephone. Sampsell was elected president of the new company, and Odegard and LaCroix were named vice-presidents. An aggressive acquisition program was quickly launched in eastern, midwestern, and western states, with the company using its own common stock to complete transactions.

During its first six years, Associated Telephone Utilities acquired 340 telephone companies, which were consolidated into 45 companies operating more than 437,000 telephones in 25 states. By the time the stock market bottomed out in October 1929, Associated Telephone Utilities was operating about 500,000 telephones with revenues approaching $17 million.

In January 1930 a new subsidiary, Associated Telephone Investment Company, was established. Designed to support its parent's acquisition program, the new company's primary business was buying company stock in order to bolster its market value. Within two years the investment company had incurred major losses, and a $1 million loan had to be negotiated. Associated Telephone Investment was dissolved but not before its parent's financial plight had become irreversible, and in 1933 Associated Telephone Utilities went into receivership.

The company was reorganized that same year and resurfaced in 1935 as General Telephone Corporation, operating 12 newly consolidated companies. John Winn, a 26-year veteran of the Bell System, was named president. In 1936 General Telephone created a new subsidiary, General Telephone Directory Company, to publish directories for the parent's entire service area.

In 1940 LaCroix was elected General Telephone's first chairman, and Harold Bozell, a former banker for Associated Telephone Utilities, was named president. Like other businesses, the telephone industry was under government restrictions during World War II, and General Telephone was called upon to increase services at military bases and war-production factories.

Following the war, General Telephone reactivated an acquisitions program that had been dormant for more than a decade and purchased 118,000 telephone lines between 1946 and 1950. In 1950 General Telephone purchased its first telephone-equipment manufacturing subsidiary, Leich Electric Company, along with the related Leich Sales Corporation.

Bozell retired in 1951 and Donald Power, a former executive secretary for Ohio Governor John Bricker, was named president. By the time Power took over, General Telephone's assets included 15 telephone companies operating in 20 states. During the 1950s Power guided the company in a steady, aggressive acquisition campaign punctuated by two major mergers.

In 1955 Theodore Gary & Company, the second-largest independent telephone company, which had 600,000 telephone lines, was merged into General Telephone, which had grown into the largest independent outside the Bell System. The merger gave the company 2.5 million lines. Theodore Gary's assets included telephone operations in the Dominican Republic, British Columbia, and the Philippines, as well as Automatic Electric, the second-largest telephone equipment manufacturer in the U.S. LaCroix and Power were to retain their positions in the merged company, but a month before the deal was closed, LaCroix died, and Power assumed the additional title of chairman.

In 1959 General Telephone and Sylvania Electric Products merged, and the parent's name was changed to General Telephone & Electronics Corporation (GT&E). The merger gave Sylvania—a leader in such industries as lighting, television and radio, and chemistry and metallurgy—the needed capital to expand. For General Telephone, the merger meant the added benefit of Sylvania's extensive research and development capabilities in the field of electronics. Power also orchestrated other acquisitions in the late 1950s, including Peninsular Telephone Company in Florida, with 300,000 lines, and Lenkurt Electric Company, Inc., a leading producer of microwave and data transmissions system.

In 1960 the subsidiary GT&E International Incorporated was formed to consolidate manufacturing and marketing activities of Sylvania, Automatic Electric, and Lenkurt, outside the United States. The following year, Leslie H. Warner, a former Theodore Gary executive, was named president. Another former Theodore Gary executive, Don Mitchell, was named to the new position of vice-chairman, while Power remained chief executive officer and chairman.

During the early 1960s the scope of GT&E's research, development, and marketing activities was broadened. In 1963 Sylvania began full-scale production of color television picture tubes, and within two years it was supplying color tubes for 18 of the 23 domestic U.S. television manufacturers. About the same time, Automatic Electric began supplying electronic switching equipment for the U.S. defense department's global communications systems, and GT&E International began producing earth-based stations for both foreign and domestic markets. GT&E's telephone subsidiaries, meanwhile, began acquiring community-antenna television systems (CATV) franchises in their operating areas.

In 1964 Warner orchestrated a deal that merged Western Utilities Corporation, the nation's second-largest independent telephone company, with 635,000 telephones, into GT&E. The following year Sylvania introduced the revolutionary four-sided flashcube, enhancing its position as the world's largest flashbulb producer.

Warner assumed the additional title of chief executive officer in 1966, while Power remained chairman. Acquisitions in telephone service continued under Warner during the mid-1960s. Purchases included Quebec Telephone in Canada, Hawaiian Telephone Company, and Northern Ohio Telephone Company and added a total of 622,000 telephone lines to GT&E operations. By 1969 GT&E was serving ten million telephones.

In March 1970 GT&E's New York City headquarters was bombed by a radical antiwar group in protest of the company's participation in defense work. In December of that year the GT&E board agreed to move the company's headquarters to Stamford, Connecticut. Power retired in 1971, and Warner was named chairman and chief executive officer. The following year Theodore F. Brophy was named president.

After initially proposing to build separate satellite systems, GT&E and its telecommunications rival, American Telephone & Telegraph Co., announced in 1974 joint venture plans for the construction and operation of seven earth-based stations interconnected by two satellites. That same year Sylvania acquired name and distribution rights for Philco television and stereo products. GTE International expanded its activities during the same period, acquiring television manufacturers in Canada and Israel and a telephone manufacturer in Germany.

Warner retired in 1976 and Brophy was named to the additional post of chairman. Brophy, soon after assuming his new position, reorganized the company along five global product lines: communications, lighting, consumer electronics, precision materials, and electrical equipment. GTE International was phased out during the reorganization, and GTE Products Corporation was formed to encompass both domestic and foreign manufacturing and marketing operations. At the same time, GTE Communications Products was formed to oversee operations of Automatic Electric, Lenkurt, Sylvania, and GTE Information Systems.

Thomas A. Vanderslice was elected president and chief operating officer in 1979, and another reorganization soon followed. GTE Products Group was eliminated as an organizational unit and GTE Electrical Products, consisting of lighting, precision materials, and electrical equipment, was formed. Vanderslice also revitalized the GT&E Telephone Operating Group in order to develop competitive strategies for anticipated regulatory changes in the telecommunications industry.

GT&E sold its consumer electronics businesses, including the accompanying brand names of Philco and Sylvania in 1980, after watching revenues from television and radio operations decrease precipitously with the success of foreign manufacturers. Following AT&T's 1982 announcement that it would divest 22 telephone operating companies, GT&E made a number of reorganizational and consolidation moves.

In 1982 the company adopted the name GTE Corporation and formed GTE Mobilnet Incorporated, to handle the company's entrance into the new cellular telephone business. In 1983 GTE sold its electrical equipment, brokerage information services, and cable television equipment businesses. That same year, Automatic Electric and Lenkurt were combined as GTE Network Systems.

GTE became the third-largest long-distance telephone company in 1983 through the acquisition of Southern Pacific Communications Company. At the same time, Southern Pacific Satellite Company was acquired, and the two firms were renamed GTE Sprint Communications Corporation and GTE Spacenet Corporation, respectively. Through an agreement with the Department of Justice, GTE conceded to keep Sprint Communications separate from its other telephone companies and limit other GTE telephone subsidiaries in certain markets. In December 1983 Vanderslice resigned as president and chief operating officer.

In 1984 GTE formalized its decision to concentrate on three core businesses: telecommunications, lighting, and precision metals. That same year, the company's first satellite was launched, and GTE's cellular telephone service went into operation; GTE's earnings exceeded $1 billion for the first time.

James (Rocky) L. Johnson, a former senior vice-president, was named president and chief operating officer in 1986. That same year, GTE acquired Airfone Inc., a telephone service

provider for commercial aircraft and railroads, and Rotaflex plc, a United Kingdom-based manufacturer of lighting fixtures.

Beginning in 1986 GTE spun off several operations to form joint ventures. In 1986 GTE Sprint and United Telecommunication's long-distance subsidiary, U.S. Telecom, agreed to merge and form US Sprint Communications Company, with each parent retaining a 50 percent interest in the new firm. That same year, GTE transferred its international transmission, overseas central office switching, and business systems operations to a joint venture with Siemens AG of Germany, which took 80 percent ownership of the new firm. The following year, GTE transferred its business systems operations in the United States to a new joint venture, Fujitsu GTE Business Systems, Inc., formed with Fujitsu Limited, which retained 80 percent ownership.

Johnson succeeded Brophy as chairman and chief executive officer in 1987 and then relinquished his president's title the following year to Charles R. Lee, a former senior vice-president. Johnson continued to streamline and consolidate operations, organizing telephone companies around a single national organization headquartered in the Dallas, Texas, area.

In 1988 GTE divested its consumer communications products unit as part of a telecommunications strategy to place increasing emphasis on the services sector. The following year GTE sold the majority of its interest in US Sprint to United Telecommunications and its interest in Fujitsu GTE Business Systems to Fujitsu.

In 1989 GTE and AT&T formed the joint venture company AG Communication Systems Corporation, designed to bring advanced digital technology to GTE's switching systems. GTE retained 51 percent control over the joint venture, with AT&T pledging to take complete control of the new firm in 15 years.

With an increasing emphasis on telecommunications, in 1989 GTE launched a program to become the first cellular provider offering nationwide service and introduced the nation's first rural service area, providing cellular service on the Hawaiian island of Kauai. The following year GTE acquired the Providence Journal Company's cellular properties in five southern states for $710 million and became the second largest cellular-service provider in the United States.

In 1990 GTE reorganized its activities around three business groups: telecommunications products and services, telephone operations, and electrical products. That same year, GTE and Contel Corporation announced merger plans that would strengthen GTE's telecommunications and telephone sectors.

Following action or review by more than 20 governmental bodies, in March 1991 the merger of GTE and Contel was approved. Johnson and Lee maintained their positions as chairman and president, respectively, while Contel's Chairman Charles Wohlstetter became vice-chairman of GTE. Contel's former president, Donald Weber, agreed to remain with the company during a six-month transition period, before leaving the merged company.

Contel Corporation

Contel Corporation's earliest predecessor, Telephone Communications Corporation, was founded by Charles Wohlstetter. After working as a Wall Street runner in the 1920s and as a Hollywood screenwriter in the 1930s, Wohlstetter returned to Wall Street in the 1940s and became a financier. In 1960 he made what he would later call a bad investment in an Alaskan oil company that would become the impetus for Contel.

To help turn that investment around, Wohlstetter recruited the services of Jack Maguire and Phillip Lucier from a telephone supply company and then raised $1.5 million to form a holding company, Telephone Communications Corporation. Wohlstetter was named chairman of the new corporation, Lucier was named president, and Maguire was named vice-president. Some 30 years later, Wohlstetter's $1.5 million investment had grown into a company that had acquired and consolidated more than 750 smaller companies with total corporate assets hovering around $6 billion.

One of the company's first acquisitions was Central Western Company, which merged with Telephone Communications in 1961 to form the new parent Continental Telephone Company. The acquisition of Central Western, along with Harfil, Inc., provided the company with customer billing, general accounting, and toll separation services.

Continental based its early acquisition strategy on Kreigspiel, a historical war game German generals played at Prussian war colleges. Wohlstetter applied the tenets of the game to telephone company operations and amassed detailed information on each independent telephone company in the United States. When those companies came up for sale, Wohlstetter and Maguire, who were pilots, and Lucier, whose wife was a pilot, would promptly fly off to meet the owners and negotiate purchase agreements.

Many of the early acquisitions were made through exchanges of stock, including the 1964 merger with Independent Telephone Company that doubled the company's size and changed its name in the process to Continental Independent Telephone Corporation. By the close of 1964, Continental had acquired more than 100 companies operating in 30 states.

The company adopted another new name, Continental Telephone Corporation, in 1965. Also during 1965 Continental acquired 65 more telephone companies and again doubled its size. By 1966 Continental had acquired more than 500 independent companies, had become the third-largest independent telephone company in the United States, and was one of the youngest companies ever listed on the New York Stock Exchange.

By 1970 Continental's assets had topped $1 billion, and sales volume had risen to $120 million. Lucier died that year and was succeeded as president by Maguire, who moved up from a vice-presidency. Aside from its dominating telephone business, the company's activities by that time had grown to include cable television systems, directory publishing, equipment leasing, and data services.

With the number of small independents having diminished considerably by 1970, Continental's pace in acquiring telephone operating companies was reduced. Continental sold its cable television business in 1971, and after a sluggish economy had taken its toll on Continental's manufacturing and supply subsidiaries, those, too, were sold in 1976. Maguire resigned in 1976 because of health problems and was succeeded as president by James V. Napier, a former executive vice-president. That same year, Continental became the first telephone company outside the Bell system to install a digital telephone switching system, a move that provided improved network operating efficiency, allowed the introduction of new calling features, and started the transition away from operations dominated by rural service areas.

In response to the changing regulatory climate of the telephone industry, in 1978 Continental mapped out a diversification strategy into nonregulated businesses. Continental's first diversification move came in 1979, with the acquisition of Executone, Inc., a New York-based communications equipment maker.

By 1980 Continental had two million telephone access lines in service and had established its first fiber-optic cable, a high-speed, high-capacity telecommunications transmission mode. While Continental continued the process of upgrading its telephone operations, during the early 1980s the company's focus turned to greater diversification.

In July 1980 Continental entered the satellite business through a joint venture with Fairchild Industries, and a communications partnership firm, American Satellite Company, was formed to operate a network of earth-based stations that provided voice and data services. To provide technology services to accommodate its expanding needs, Continental then acquired two consulting and research firms, Network Analysis Corporation and International Computing Company.

In 1981 Continental acquired Page Communications Engineers Inc., later renamed Contel Page, which gave Continental expertise in the engineering, installation, and maintenance of satellite-to-earth stations. One year later, Continental hooked up with Fairchild Industries in a second joint venture called Space Communications Company, a provider of tracking and relay data services for such clients as the National Aeronautics and Space Administration.

After the Federal Communications Commission opened the door to licenses for 30 cellular phone markets in 1981, Continental plunged into that field as well, acquiring sizable shares of cellular markets in Los Angeles, California; Washington, D.C.; and Minneapolis, Minnesota. Continental also entered the credit card authorization business in 1981, with the purchase of National Bancard Corporation. Two years later, Continental bolstered its interest in that business segment with the purchase of the Chase Merchants Services division of Chase Manhattan Bank.

In 1982 the corporation changed its name to Continental Telecom Incorporated, adopted a new corporate logo, and inaugurated an advertising campaign around the theme "architects of telecommunications." Continental's expansion into the information services sector continued in 1982 with the purchase of STSC Inc., a computer services supplier; and Cado Systems Corporation, a maker of small business computers. That same year company revenues surpassed the $2 billion mark for the first time.

In 1984 Continental formed the subsidiary Contel Cellular Inc. to handle the corporation's growing cellular operations. A year later, Continental culminated its diversification moves and reorganized into four business sectors: telephone and cellular operations; business systems, offering voice and data processing products and services; federal systems, handling various facets of communication and information systems for government agencies; and information systems, offering telecommunications systems and services to large corporations, institutions, and government entities.

As a result of the company's growing interest in the information services marketplace, in 1985 Continental acquired several computer system and software companies, including Northern Data Systems, Data Equipment Systems Corporation, and Sooner Enterprises, Inc. Continental also purchased Fairchild Industries's interests in American Satellite Co., later renamed Contel ASC, and Space Communications Company.

That same year, Continental sold its directory publishing division, its time-share services business, and its credit card authorization business. In the midst of reorganization in 1985, Napier resigned, and John N. Lemasters, former American Satellite Company president, was named president and chief executive officer.

Continental's telephone operations were repositioned during the mid-1980s through numerous sales and exchanges. Subsidiaries in Nebraska, Colorado, Alaska, the Bahamas, and Barbados were sold, and operations in Michigan were exchanged for similar operations in Indiana and three southern states.

The name Contel Corporation was adopted in 1986. That same year, Contel's new tenant services division set the stage for future growth by acquiring tenant service operations in Atlanta and Seattle. The tenant services division installed and managed customized communications systems in commercial buildings and marketed those systems to the buildings' tenants. Contel also enhanced its information services division with the acquisition of IPC Communications, Inc., a supplier of a special-purpose telephone system used by financial traders, and expanded its federal systems operations with the purchase of Western Union Corporation's government systems division, a provider of information handling systems.

In September 1986 Contel announced it had agreed to merge with Communications Satellite Corporation (Comsat), but by mid-1987 Contel had called off the deal, citing Comsat's unstable financial picture. The failed merger sparked the resignation of Lemasters. Donald W. Weber, former executive vice-president and head of telephone operations, was named Lemasters's successor as president and chief executive officer.

Contel acquired Comsat's international private-line business and its very-small-aperture terminal (VSAT) satellite business in 1987, as well as Equatorial Communications Company, a provider of private satellite data networks. That same year, Contel agreed to sell Executone, its troubled telephone inter-connect business, and Texocom, Contel's equipment supply business.

In the late 1980s Contel continued to narrow its focus in the information systems sectors. In 1988 it sold its computer-based business, Contel Business Systems, and a year later disposed of Contel Credit Corporation. Contel Federal Systems continued to grow during that same period, and in 1988 it acquired two Eaton Corporation subsidiaries: Information Management Systems and Data Systems Services. Two years later Contel purchased Telos Corporation, with expertise in government-preferred computer software. Contel's tenant services and cellular businesses also got a boost in 1988 with the acquisition of RealCom Communications Corporation, an IBM tenant services subsidiary, and Southland Mobilcom Inc.'s interests in the Mobile, Alabama, and the Pensacola, Florida, cellular markets.

In 1990 Contel completed the biggest acquisition in its history, a $1.3 billion purchase of McCaw Cellular Communications, Inc.'s controlling interests in 13 cellular markets, which added more than six million potential customers and doubled Contel's cellular potential population market (known in the industry as POPs). While important, that move was eclipsed by the merger with GTE announced later that same year. Through that transition, the two former competitors were expected to integrate telephone and mobile-cellular operations and capitalize on business unit similarities in the field of satellite-communications as well as in communications systems and services targeting government entities.

Over half of Contel's $6.6 billion purchase price, $3.9 billion, was assumed debt. When Charles Lee succeeded James (Rocky) L. Johnson to become CEO in 1992, his first order of business was reduction of that obligation. He sold GTE's North American Lighting business to a Siemens affiliate for over $1 billion, shaved off local exchange properties in Idaho, Tennessee, Utah, and West Virginia to generate another $1 billion, divested its interest in Sprint in 1992, and sold its GTE Spacenet satellite operations to General Electric in 1994.

The long-heralded telecommunications bill, expected to go into effect in 1996, promised to encourage competition among local phone providers, long distance services, and cable television companies. Many leading telecoms prepared for the new competitive realities by aligning themselves with entertainment and information providers. GTE, on the other hand, continued to focus on its core operations, seeking to make them as efficient as possible. In 1992, Lee launched a sweeping reorganization that was characterized by Telephony magazine as "easily one of the nation's largest re-engineering processes."

Among other goals, his plan sought to double revenues and slash costs by $1 billion per year by focusing on five key areas of operation: technological enhancement of wireline and wireless systems, expansion of data services, global expansion, and diversification into video services. GTE hoped to cross-sell its large base of wireline customers on wireless, data and video services, launching Tele-Go, a user-friendly service that combined cordless and cellular phone features. The company bought broadband spectrum cellular licenses in Atlanta, Seattle, Cincinnati and Denver, and formed a joint venture with SBC Communications to enhance its cellular capabilities in Texas. In

1995, the company undertook a 15-state test of video conferencing services, as well as a video dialtone (VDT) experiment that proposed to offer cable television programming to 900,000 homes by 1997. GTE also formed a video programming and interservices joint venture with Ameritech Corporation, BellSouth Corporation, SBC, and The Walt Disney Company in the fall of 1995. Foreign efforts included affiliations with phone companies in Argentina, Mexico, Germany, Japan, Canada, the Dominican Republic, Venezuela and China. The early 1990s reorganization included a 37.5 percent workforce reduction, from 177,500 in 1991 to 111,000 by 1994. Lee's five-fold strategy had begun to bear fruit by the mid-1990s. While the communication conglomerate's sales remained rather flat, at about $19.8 billion, from 1992 through 1994, its net income increased by 43.7 percent, from $1.74 billion to a record $2.5 billion, during the same period.

Principal Subsidiaries

Contel Corporation; GTE Products of Connecticut Corporation; GTE Leasing Corporation; Anglo-Canadian Telephone Company; GTE Holdings (Canada) Limited; GTE International Telecommunications Incorporated; GTE California Incorporated; GTE Florida Incorporated; GTE Midwest Incorporated; GTE North Incorporated; GTE Northwest Incorporated; GTE South Incorporated; GTE Southwest Incorporated; GTE Hawaiian Telephone Company Incorporated; GTE Data Services Incorporated; GTE Finance Corporation; GTE Information Services Incorporated; GTE Intelligent Network Services Incorporated; GTE Investment Management Corporation; GTE main Street Incorporated; GTE Mobile Communications Incorporated; GTE Mobilnet Incorporated; GTE Realty Corporation; GTE REinsurance Company Limited (Bermuda); GTE Service Corporation; GTE Telecom Marketing Corporation; GTE Vantage Incorporated.

Further Reading

Byrne, Harlan S., "Sleepy No More," *Barron's*, January 16, 1995, p. 15.
Bernier, Paula, "AT&T, GI Win Round 1 of GTE's Video Rollout," *Telephony*, March 13, 1995, p. 6.
Gold, Jacqueline S., "GTE: Poor Connection," *Financial World*, October 26, 1993, p. 19.
"GTE's New Twist on Cellular," *Electronics*, April 25, 1994, p. 1.
Klebnikov, Paul, "Techno-Skeptic," *Forbes*, February 26, 1996, p. 42.
Mason, Charles, "Sculpting a New Industry Structure," *Telephony*, April 19, 1993, p. 88.
McCarthy, Thomas E., *The History of GTE: The Evolution of One of America's Great Corporations*, Stamford, Conn.: GTE Corporation, 1990.
Mikolas, Mark, "What Makes Charles Run," *TE&M*, April 1, 1987.
Meeks, Fleming, " 'Fail' Is Not a Four-Letter Word," *Forbes*, April 30, 1990.
Welti, Patty, "Dream Job for GTE, IBM," *America's Network*, January 1, 1996, p. 18.

—Roger W. Rouland
—updated by April D. Gasbarre

Guccio Gucci, S.p.A.

Piazza San Fedele
20100 Milan
Italy
(2) 76013050
Telex: 571468 GUCCIFI
or
Gucci America, Inc.
2 East 54th Street
11th Floor
New York, New York 10022
U.S.A.
(212) 826-2600
Fax: (212) 486-4739

Wholly Owned Subsidiary of InvestCorp International
Incorporated: 1923
Employees: 900
Revenues: $450 million
SICs: 5632 Women's Accessories & Specialty Stores;
    5661 Shoe Stores

Gucci designs and clothing have become one of the most recognized labels in the retail industry. Along with Karl Lagerfeld, Cartier, Alfred Dunhill, and Ralph Lauren, Gucci offers wealthier clientele from around the world an acknowledged badge, the "GG" on its leather products that symbolizes membership in an elite club. During the late 1920s and throughout the 1930s, Gucci was the first company to establish a label in the retail industry that was regarded by the general public as synonymous with wealth, status, power, and luxury. Recently, however, the company has had major financial difficulties, and the Gucci family has been traumatized by the murder of Maurizio Gucci, the driving force behind the success of the company in the 1980s. Purchased by InvestCorp International in 1992, Gucci is managed by a group of individual investors from Bahrain.

The founder of the famous retail empire was Guccio Gucci. Born in Florence, Italy, in 1881, Gucci was forced to leave the country when his father's hatmaking company went bankrupt. Driven out of the house by his embittered father, Gucci traveled to London and got a job as a dishwasher at the Savoy Hotel. The Savoy Hotel was quickly becoming one of the most notable gathering places for the American and European upper classes. The reason for its popularity was Cezar Ritz, the most famous chef in the world at the time. Ritz knew how to lure the wealthy elite by appealing to the sensibilities of their taste buds, and Gucci soon learned that the key to attracting moneyed customers was the perception of quality and exclusiveness.

Gucci worked his way up from dishwasher to waiter, all the while observing the lifestyles and habits of the highest levels of international society. One of his most important lessons involved the way the hotel's affluent guests transported their personal possessions from one grand luxury palace to another. Gucci noticed that all the dwellers in the Savoy Hotel used quality leather luggage, made by craftsmen from all over Europe. Gucci also discovered that it was the notion of "quality" that obsessed people like Lilly Langtry and Sir Henry Irving. Items that were most fashionable and of the best quality had to be possessed, and people with good taste cared little about the cost. For three years, Gucci worked and learned about what was needed to secure the patronage of the gilded class. After saving enough money, Gucci returned home to Florence to begin a new life.

Gucci married a young seamstress, Aida Calvelli, and had four sons and one daughter; he also adopted a boy that Aida bore out of wedlock. He first worked in an antique store and then at a leather firm. With so many mouths to feed, money was always in short supply. When World War I started, Gucci was drafted to fight for the Italian army, and he served as a transport driver. After the war ended, he returned home to a city with an economy that had been destroyed. But Gucci recognized an opportunity to use the experience he had gained in London, and so he started working at a leather firm that specialized in quality leather products. The owner of the firm, a man named Franzi, taught him all the elements of leatherwork, including the selection of hides, the tanning processes, and how to work with different types of leather. An ambitious and able man, Gucci was chosen to open Franzi's new store in Rome.

By 1922, Guccio Gucci had dreams of opening his own shop, and, encouraged by his wife Aida (who also helped find an investor by the name of Calzoni), a Gucci leather business started operations in Florence one year later. The little store made leather goods for the wealthy tourists who visited Florence in record numbers during the 1920s. Soon he had made enough money to buy out his partner, Calzoni. As the business grew, reputation of Gucci's sturdy, quality luggage began to spread in European social circles. During this time, he also began a repair operation for luggage. This unexpected source of work helped increase the reputation of Gucci's store for quick, careful, first-class workmanship. The sense of quality he had learned from his time at the Savoy Hotel, and the perception that expensive products were more valued than inexpensive ones, convinced him to raise his prices. By the end of 1923, the Gucci store had become widely known for its distinctive craftsmanship, and it was frequented not only by wealthy tourists but by the local elite as well.

During the 1920s, Benito Mussolini rose to power as Italy's dictator, and many nations imposed harsh sanctions on the country. As a result, Gucci was no longer able to purchase all the leather needed for his shop. This apparent misfortune, however, turned to Gucci's favor. Without the needed leather, Gucci was forced to design and make handbags and luggage of both canvas and leather. Leather was employed only on the most-used parts of the luggage, such as corners, clasps, and straps. In addition, new items including belts, wallets, and various ornamental designs were becoming more fashionable, and Gucci capitalized on their popularity. By the end of the decade, the Gucci store had become one of the most important shopping places for wealthy customers from Italy and abroad. Flocking to his business in order to buy beautiful and highly innovative leather creations, people were willing to pay premium prices for quality goods made by expert craftsmen. The Gucci mystique had been born. Some of these early Gucci creations are displayed at the Museum of Modern Art in New York City.

The war clouds that grew over Europe during the 1930s did not affect the Gucci store. Tourists from around the world, especially the United States, traveled to Florence not only to view famous works of art such as Michelangelo's *David* but to purchase a piece of Gucci luggage. Business boomed and the family grew in wealth and prominence. With the onset of World War II in 1939, however, life changed suddenly for everyone in Italy, including the Gucci family. The war between Gucci's customers—British, German, French, American, Italian— almost destroyed the company. Sales dropped precipitously, and plans for expanding into other major Italian cities were indefinitely delayed. The family shop that already had been opened in Rome kept the family in business since the ancient metropolis had been declared an "open city" by the Allies and was not bombed during the early part of the war.

Unfortunately, by the end of the war Italy was in ruins as a result of the fighting between German and Allied forces, and the tumult and chaos left behind did not contribute to the sale of Gucci's premium-priced leather goods. Almost every person in Italy suffered from deprivation and impoverishment, and the Gucci family was not immune from the postwar hardships. Yet Gucci was able to arrange loan money from a number of Italian banks, and immediately he began to revitalize his shops in Florence and Rome. Guccio Gucci's son, Aldo, was in charge of the shop in Rome and achieved new heights of success during the occupation by Allied soldiers. American soldiers thronged the shop and purchased anything that Gucci had made to send to mothers, wives, and girlfriends back home. Within one year after the end of the war, both Gucci shops in Florence and Rome had achieved sales figures near prewar levels.

During the postwar period, Guccio Gucci and oldest son Aldo began to create a myth to surround the company's products. An exclusive design—back-to-back linked stirrups in the founder's initials "GG"—was printed on all the firm's luggage and handbags, and hunting and stableyard colors were used to give the Gucci shops an aristocratic air. The legend that the Gucci family had been saddlemakers to the great Florentine families also started at this time. All of this history was contrived, of course, but it helped place the Gucci family on a level more equal to the people who bought their wares.

The early 1950s brought many celebrities to Gucci's store in Florence, including Princess Elizabeth of England, Eleanor Roosevelt, Elizabeth Taylor, and Grace Kelly. Grace Kelly once appeared at the store in a panic, explaining that she was in desperate need of a gift for a friend's wedding. When she asked if the store had a floral scarf, Gucci replied that he did not but that he would be happy to make her one. This incident gave rise to the Gucci floral scarf that soon thereafter became world famous. In spite of the worldwide interest in the purchase of his products, Guccio Gucci was reluctant to expand his operations. However, when Guccio died in the summer of 1953, son Aldo immediately arranged for a Gucci company to open stores in the United States.

After the death of the founder, three of Guccio Gucci's sons, Rodolfo, Vasco, and Aldo, became equal shareholders in the company. Rodolfo acted as the general manager, Vasco as the supervisor of operations at the manufacturing plant in Florence, and Aldo as the director of foreign operations. Under Aldo's direction, new Gucci stores were opened in Philadelphia, San Francisco, Beverly Hills, Palm Beach, and Chicago. The factory in Florence located on the via Caldaie was expanded, and land was purchased in the Sandicci area outside the city for a new production plant. Demand for luxury items was growing by leaps and bounds in the late 1950s, and Gucci was at the forefront of companies that were frequented by the rich and famous.

The Gucci stores were most successful during the 1960s. Anyone who had the money sought the Gucci name on shoes, luggage, handbags, and scarfs. The Gucci moccasin was worn by John Wayne and Jerry Lewis. Princess Margaret of England, Audrey Hepburn, and Imelda Marcos purchased Gucci shoes— lots of them. Revenues were at an all-time high, and profits were pouring in. Although there were minor disagreements, the Gucci brothers and indeed the entire family lived and worked in peace and harmony.

When Vasco Gucci died in 1975, everything at the company began to change. Over 9,000 customers per day were buying products from the Gucci stores in America, over 600 employees were on payroll, and the business had increased 25 times over the previous decade. Gucci shoes were "the" item to buy and wear, along with Gucci belts, luggage, and accessories. Gucci products had achieved world status. Yet employees in the New York store, as well as in the other U.S. stores, developed a reputation for rude behavior toward customers. Discourteous treatment, icy stares, and put-downs were widely known to occur at Gucci, and rumor had it that Aldo did nothing to discourage the way his employees treated customers. Although this report was tolerated by Rodolfo, a more important problem had arisen. In 1978, Gucci Shops Incorporated, Aldo's U.S. branch of the family firm, had recorded revenues of over $48 million—but no profits. According to Aldo, the costs of opening up new stores across the United States had soaked up the firm's hefty profit margin.

As the company grew during the early 1980s, family feuds and disgruntled employees marred the aristocratic image the Guccis had carefully nurtured since the 1920s. Paolo, the son of Aldo, was bitter since he had been left out of the major decisions made during the board of directors meetings. He began to inquire into his father's record-keeping procedures and informed the Internal Revenue Service about certain discrepancies. Rodolfo died in May 1983, and his son, Maurizio, also began to take a keener interest in the company since he was now one of the major shareholders. A consummate businessman with a charming personality and ruthless disposition, Maurizio arranged for his cousin Paolo to sign over his shares in the company and forced his uncle Aldo to relinquish the position of president.

By 1985, despite what the world press had termed the "Gucci Wars," the company itself was still growing. The family squabbles and power plays had hurt the firm's reputation, but its long history and its pervasive trademark contributed to Gucci's continuing financial success. In the United States, Gucci Shops Incorporated reported profits of over $5 million on revenues of $62 million. In Italy, company shops reported revenues of over $200 million and profits approximating 8 percent of the total. The Gucci operation in London made over £10 million, with profits running at 10 percent. By 1986, 153 Gucci stores around the globe were selling over $500 million worth of merchandise.

The late 1980s were terrible times for the Gucci family and their luxury retail empire. In the United States, Aldo Gucci was charged with tax evasion and misappropriate use of company funds. Over $7 million worth of taxes had been evaded while Aldo was head of Gucci's U.S. operation, with approximately $11 million spirited out of the country. Aldo was sentenced to a year and a day in jail and was fined $30,000. He had already paid back over $1 million to the U.S. Treasury. At the age of 81, Aldo began serving his prison time in the "country club," the Eglin Penitentiary in Florida, where many of the convicted Watergate defendants had been incarcerated.

The conviction of Aldo was just the tip of the iceberg; by the early 1990s the Gucci operation was in disarray. Sales dropped precipitously, and debts began to accumulate. Now in complete control of the organization, Maurizio brought in an outside investor group from Bahrain, InvestCorp International, to help revive the firm. Yet even the influx of cash from InvestCorp did not help. In 1992, the renamed Gucci America Inc. had lost over $30 million, not counting past debts of over $100 million. As a result, InvestCorp brought suit against Maurizio for withholding information about the state of Gucci's U.S. operation. In attempting to force Maurizio to sell his remaining 50 percent ownership to InvestCorp, the Bahrain group said that additional money would be forthcoming only if Maurizio left the company. Maurizio fought back with countersuits, but finally he gave in and sold his remaining interest to InvestCorp in September of 1993. This transaction marked the first time that control of the firm was not in family hands.

During the mid-1990s, InvestCorp appointed its own management team and began the arduous task of rebuilding the company. Sales increased dramatically in both Europe and the United States during 1994, and figures for early 1995 were very promising. As the fortunes for Guccio Gucci S.p.A. and the firm's U.S. operation improved, the Gucci family was still reeling from the chaos it had created. An unknown assassin shot Maurizio Gucci on a street in Milan on March 27, 1995; Maurizio was dead at the age of 46. Italian investigators speculated that he had been killed because of personal debts that remained unpaid.

InvestCorp International, in firm control of the Gucci operation, lost no time in revitalizing the company. Sales continued to increase, and the atmosphere in Gucci shops grew more relaxed and comfortable as management encouraged employees to treat customers respectfully. As long as the Gucci symbol retained its appeal (and there can be no doubt that it shall) there will always be a clientele to purchase some of the most recognizable merchandise in the world.

Principal Subsidiaries

Gucci America Inc.

Further Reading

Auerbach, Jonathan, "Gucci Sues U.S. Unit for $63.9 Million," *Women's Wear Daily,* June 23, 1993, p. 2.
Bachrach, Judy, "A Gucci Knockoff," *Vanity Fair,* July 1995, p. 86.
Forden, Sara Gay, "Banks Putting Big Squeeze On Gucci Chief," *Women's Wear Daily,* April 26, 1993, p. 1.
——. "Bringing Back Gucci," *Women's Wear Daily,* December 12, 1994, p. 24.
——. "InvestCorp Buys All of Gucci," *Daily News Record,* September 28, 1993, p. 2.
——. "Maurizio Gucci and InvestCorp: A Total Buyout," *Women's Wear Daily,* September 28, 1993, p. 1.
——. "Maurizio Gucci Asks Court Help on InvestCorp," *Women's Wear Daily,* July 30, 1993, p. 2.
——. "Maurizio Gucci Slain Outside Milan Office by Unknown Assailant," *Women's Wear Daily,* March 28, 1995, p. 1.
McKnight, Gerald, *Gucci: A House Divided,* New York: Donald I. Fine, 1987.

—Thomas Derdak

Guess, Inc.

1444 S. Alameda Street
Los Angeles, California 90021
U.S.A.
(213) 765-3100
Fax: (213) 765-5915

Private Company
Incorporated: 1981
Employees: 2200
Sales: $600 million (1994)
SICs: 2339 Women's & Misses' Outerwear, Not
Elsewhere Classified; 2325 Men's & Boys' Trousers
& Slacks

Guess, Inc., designs, manufacture, and licenses an expanding line of women's and men's apparel centered around their popular Guess jeanswear. Guess owns and operates a chain of 61 retail clothing stores in the United States, and a flagship European retail store in Florence, Italy. The company also licenses Guess retail stores in Argentina, Australia, Brazil, Canada, Columbia, Costa Rica, Guatemala, Hong Kong, Italy, Kuwait, Lebanon, Malaysia, Monaco, Panama, Saudi Arabia, Singapore, Spain, and Venezuela, as well as more than 30 stores in Mexico. Guess wholesale sales reached over $600 million in 1994, with sales of licensed Guess merchandise, including footwear, perfume, and wristwatches, adding another $500 million in wholesale volume.

In 1981, Georges Marciano and his brother Maurice arrived in Los Angeles and opened a clothing store in Beverly Hills. Born in Morocco and raised in Marseilles, the Marcianos—who would be joined the following year by brothers Armand and Paul—had previously owned and operated a chain of twelve retail stores in France, but had left that country in order to avoid a tax bill of approximately FF 9 million. (The bill was finally settled in 1986.) Among the merchandise sold in the Marcianos' store were jeans designed by Georges Marciano. These jeans—named Guess, because it was easy for the brothers to pronounce—were meant to fit tightly and featured zippers at the ankles. Innovative for the time, the jeans were stone-washed, giving them a softer feel and lighter colors than typical denim jeans. They also featured what would soon become the distinctive Guess triangle on the back pocket. By then, however, the 1970s' boom in designer jeans had faded. It seemed unlikely that a new entry into this tapped-out market could be successful.

Georges Marciano flew to New York in December 1981. Despite his limited English, he convinced Bloomingdale's to display on consignment 30 pairs of his European-style jeans in Bloomingdale's flagship New York store. Within three hours, Bloomingdale's sold out of every pair, despite a $60 sales tag. Guess jeans sales took off spectacularly the following year when Paul Marciano arrived in California to direct the company's advertising campaign. Although he had no previous advertising experience, Paul Marciano devised a campaign that revolutionized the way jeans—and clothing—were sold. Instead of adopting the typical studio design, Paul brought his brother's jeans, and the models wearing them, outdoors, using grainy black-and-white photography and provocative poses described by *Forbes* as "catering to teenage cravings for sex, power, attention and self-love . . . electric not only with sexuality but with an implicit brutality and exhibitionism as well." The controversial ads and their sexy Western look swiftly created household names not only of the Guess brand, but also of its models, in effect starting the supermodel trend that would make many of the "Guess Girls"—including Carre Otis, Claudia Schiffer, Naomi Campbell, Eva Herzigova, and Anna Nicole Smith—international stars. By the end of 1982, the Marcianos had sold some $12 million dollars of their jeans.

Demand for their product soon overwhelmed the Marcianos. Searching for the capital to expand and access to cheaper foreign labor, the Marcianos signed a deal in July 1983 with the Nakash brothers of the company Jordache, giving Jordache 50 percent ownership of Guess in exchange for $4.8 million and use of Jordache's Hong Kong manufacturing plants. Under the deal, Jordache was also licensed to set up a new line of jeans, called Gasoline, to use parts of Guess designs in a lower-priced line. The Guess-Jordache deal neglected, however, to provide for written assurances against copying each others' designs, a common garment industry practice called ''knockoffs.'' Instead, the Marcianos relied on the Nakashes' assurances that, given the success of their own clothing designs, they had no need to knock off Georges Marciano's designs. This lack of written agreement would soon come to haunt the company.

Like the Marcianos, the Israeli-born Nakashes manufactured designer jeans, starting their company in 1977 from a single store in Brooklyn, New York and building a $280 million business by 1983. Jordache's fortunes, however, had already begun to slip, as the designer jean market fizzled and the Jordache name increasingly became known as a mass merchandise label. The Marcianos, on the other hand, sought to establish the Guess name as exclusively high-end. Throughout the company's growth, distribution of Guess clothing was limited largely to upscale department stores and the Marciano's own growing chain of MGA (for Maurice, Georges, and Armand) retail stores.

By the time of the Jordache deal, the Marcianos had already begun to expand their line beyond jeans. In 1982 they entered the menswear market through a licensing agreement with Jeff Hamilton, Inc., which marketed a line of men's clothing under the Guess name in exchange for a seven percent royalty fee. Between 1983 and 1984, sales of Guess menswear rose from $2.5 million to $27 million. However, Guess soon sought to terminate the Hamilton license agreement and bring the menswear line in-house, maintaining that Hamilton's Guess line was oriented too strongly toward the young men's market, and that Hamilton's ''dumping'' (according to Maurice Marcian in the *Daily News Report)* of Guess merchandise in Kmart and other discount stores was hurting the label's high-end image. This led to a legal battle with Hamilton that slowed growth in menswear, which Guess brought in-house in 1986.

The Marciano's largest legal battle, however, was with Jordache. By 1984, sales at Guess had reached $150 million, with the price of Guess jeans climbing as high as $85 per pair, but the partnership between the two sets of brothers had already soured. The Marcianos sued the Nakash brothers and Jordache in 1984, charging that company with unfair competition and claiming that the Nakash brothers were using their position on the Guess board of directors and their access to Guess designs in the Hong Kong plant to produce knockoffs of Guess clothing in their Jordache line. The Marcianos' suit asked the court to undo the 1983 agreement that had given the Nakashes control of half of Guess.

The battle for control of Guess continued for the next five years. Along the way, both sides leveled charges of corporate espionage and document shredding; the Nakashes weathered an investigation by the Internal Revenue Service into Marciano-alleged tax evasion and customs quota fraud, and the Marcianos faced allegations of improper dealings with the IRS. At one point, the Marcianos hired Israeli commandoes to patrol their offices; the Nakashes, for their part, hired security experts to sweep their offices for bugging devices. Meanwhile, the judge overseeing the suit ordered the Marcianos to repay more than $1.5 million of an alleged $1.8 million in unauthorized fees taken out of the company (including the Marcianos paying themselves double their salaries). Estimated attorney fees ran as

high as $10 million per year for each side. As one attorney involved in the case told *Forbes:* ''This is not just war, this is total war. Take no prisoners. There is not an issue that has not been filed. This is litigation at its worst.''

Despite Guess's legal distractions, sales continued to grow, reaching $350 million in 1987, with profits of $100 million. While much of its sales continued to be in jeans, Guess had successfully entered the women's market, with its upscale Georges Marciano label, as well as children's, leatherwear, and footwear. Relaunching its menswear line in 1986, Guess began to make inroads in that market as well, placing its products in men's departments of most major department stores. Licensed products, including Guess watches, eyewear, and a Guess women's fragrance line produced by Revlon, also contributed to overall sales: in 1990, Guess watches alone sold an estimated $60 million. Meanwhile, Guess's chain of retail stores, renamed Guess and averaging 2,000 square feet, grew to 19 locations. The company also moved its Los Angeles operations to a 14-acre site encompassing six buildings, where it manufactured 93 percent of its products. By 1990 sales reached an estimated $575 million.

The legal battle between the Marcianos and the Nakashes finally ended in early 1990, when a jury agreed with the Marcianos and returned 100 percent control of Guess to them. A second trial was set for May 1990 to determine damages. However, as the jury in that case was deliberating, the Marcianos announced that they had reached a settlement with the Nakashes for an undisclosed amount. This development occurred over the objections of their attorney, who pushed them to continue the case to full victory. The Marcianos stated, however, that they feared seeing the case continue through the appeals process and still more years of litigation. The Marcianos' attorney then sued them for $17 million in damages.

But with the battle with Jordache over, the Marcianos set about expanding their business. The years of litigation and the enormous attorneys' fees had limited their growth: the company believed that it would have topped $1 billion in sales by its tenth anniversary had it not been for the court case. With their resources freed up, the Marcianos increased their advertising budget to $22 million in 1991. The company also expanded its retail chain, to 33 stores by the end of 1991, including its European flagship store in Florence, Italy. While the recession of the early 1990s slowed growth somewhat, to seven percent in 1991 compared to double-digits throughout the 1980s, Guess menswear took off, with a 41 percent sales growth in 1991 alone. By the end of that year, menswear accounted for just under 40 percent of company sales. International sales were also becoming more important to overall revenues. Licensing arrangements brought Guess clothing to more than a dozen countries, with sales particularly strong in Canada and Japan.

In 1993 Guess and its licensees registered an estimated $700 million in sales. In that year, Georges Marciano stepped down as the company's chairman, chief executive officer, and designer, citing differences of opinion with his brothers over the direction of the company. Georges, who had left the company briefly in 1988, sold his 40 percent share of the company to his brothers for an estimated $200 million. The year before, Maurice Marciano had also left the company, but he returned shortly before Georges Marciano's departure. Maurice was named chairman and chief executive officer and took over direction of design; Paul Marciano remained president and chief operating officer, and Armand continued to act as senior executive vice-president. After leaving Guess, Georges Marciano sued Guess and his brothers for allegedly infringing on the Georges Marciano trademark. Meanwhile, Georges opened a new company, Go USA Surfwear, and purchased 80 percent of Yes Clothing Company.

With Guess ads now featuring Maurice's name instead of Georges Marciano, Guess looked to its overhauled junior's line and international distribution, along with a stepped up promotional campaign, to fuel its further growth. Advertising spending reached $28 million in 1993; international sales were expected to reach 25 percent of total sales by the end of 1995. Licensing also continued to be an important source of revenue, with products now including home furnishings, infant wear, and junior knitwear. Sales of Guess watches topped $100 million in 1994, and Guess footwear sold more than $60 million. Mean-while, Guess stores had also been growing, to an average of 3,500 square feet, and to 61 stores by the end of 1995, including a 7,000 square-foot store in Hawaii's Ala Moana Center and an 8,400 square-foot store in the Woodfield Mall in Schaumburg, Illinois. In less than fifteen years, the Guess label had grown from 30 pairs of jeans to a diversified, billion-dollar branded empire.

Further Reading

Behar, Richard, "Does Guess Have a Friend in the IRS?" *Forbes*, November 16, 1987, p. 147.

Marlow, Michael, "Guess Back on Track with Ambitious Plans for Global Expansion," *Women's Wear Daily*, February 16, 1995, p. 1.

——, "Guess Who's 10?" *Daily New Report*, December 20, 1991, p. 4.

Slutsker, Gary, "The Smoking Bun," *Forbes*, March 25, 1985, p. 210.

——"Marcianos Go Full Time Now at Guess," *Women's Wear Daily*, July 16, 1990, p. 1.

—M. L. Cohen

GYMBOREE

Gymboree Corporation

700 Airport Boulevard
Burlingame, California 94010-1912
U.S.A.
(415) 579-0600
Fax: (415) 696-7502

Public Company
Incorporated: 1979
Employees: 5,900
Sales: $259.4 million (fiscal year ended January 31,
    1996)
Stock Exchanges: NASDAQ
SICs: 2329 Men's & Boys' Clothing, Not Elsewhere
    Classified; 2361 Girls', Children's & Infants' Dresses,
    Blouses, & Shirts; 2369 Girls', Children's & Infants'
    Outerwear, Not Elsewhere Classified; 5641 Children's
    & Infants' Wear Stores

Based in Burlingame, California, Gymboree Corporation designs, manufactures, and retails unique, high-quality apparel and accessories for children from birth through seven years of age. In the mid-1990s the company was operating more than 279 retail stores throughout the United States and was planning to expand globally throughout the late 1990s. Gymboree also operates parent-child developmental play programs for children through the age of five years old. In 1995 it had franchised roughly 400 such centers internationally. The company grew rapidly during the late 1980s and into the mid-1990s by focusing on its retail operations.

Gymboree's children's recreation and exercise operation represented a relatively meager portion of its income by the 1990s, but it was that business that launched the venture in the 1970s and established a foundation for its future success in the retail industry. The concept of a commercial children's exercise program was inspired by Joan Barnes. Barnes, in her early 20s, had taught modern dance to children in New York City before organizing a children's recreation program for the Jewish Com-

munity Center in San Rafael, California. She was serving as the recreation administrator at that center when, in 1975, she came up with the notion of offering exercise classes for babies with their parents. The idea stemmed partly from her personal desire to share physical fitness playtime with her own daughter.

The baby exercise classes were an instant hit. Parents lined up to bring their babies and toddlers to Barnes's exercise sessions. Recognizing the commercial potential of her idea, Barnes left her job with the Jewish Community Center and opened her first commercial children's workout center in 1976. She had little trouble filling her classes with enthusiastic parents. She knew that she was dealing with a viable business concept, moreover, when some of those parents started asking her about opening their own children's exercise centers. After polishing her concept, Barnes did start opening other centers in the late 1970s.

Barnes recognized that her expertise was working with parents and children, not in building a sprawling franchise business. To help her take the concept cross-country, she hired franchise specialist Robert Jacob, who was best known for developing the hugely successful Midas International car-service franchise system. Jacob helped Barnes set up a successful licensing program for Gymboree centers that focused on low start-up costs. Franchisees typically paid Barnes a $20,000 start-up fee, which included about $8,000 worth of equipment and enough money to get the center moving. The franchisees also agreed to pay Barnes six percent of their revenue. To help fund the expansion effort, Barnes turned to venture-capital firm Venture Partners, of Menlo, California.

The Gymboree franchise effort was a triumph. By 1984, 125 Gymboree franchises were operating in 20 states and were bringing in more than $1 million in revenue annually. The franchises were typically operated by women, many of whom had training in occupational therapy or education. Classes were usually held in church halls and community buildings, and parents were charged only $4 to $8 per 45-minute session. Classes varied to accommodate children ranging from three months to four years in age, but a typical session included the children hanging from bars to build up arm muscles, popping soap bubbles to develop eye-hand coordination, or walking on inflated logs to improve balance. In addition, the tots could exercise on brightly colored tunnels, slides, and other apparatus, and no class was complete without a visit from a clown-puppet named "Gymbo."

By 1985 Barnes's net worth had sailed past $1 million. As important to her as the financial gain, though, was the success of her idea: "It's a neat feeling to know the same scene is going on in scores of centers at the same time," she said in the May 1984 *Money*. "It feels like I've given birth to a new experience." Barnes had, indeed, given birth to a viable concept, as evidenced by Gymboree's rapid expansion during the mid-1980s. By 1987, in fact, the Gymboree chain had grown to include more than 350 centers throughout the United States and in ten foreign countries. Those units were generating over $10 million in annual sales. Importantly, the Gymboree name had become known and respected by parents.

Barnes decided in 1986 to start capitalizing on the goodwill that Gymboree had accrued since she had opened the first exercise center in 1976. To that end, she opened the first few Gymboree retail stores: "... because we recognized that we have a unique marketing platform," she said in the November 1987 *Chain Store Age Executive*. "No one could approach our authenticity, no one could knock off what we do because of the number of children already participating in our Gymboree programs." The first Gymboree stores piggy-backed off of the original Gymboree concept. Approximately 1,000-square-feet in size, they were designed similar to a children's gym, incorporated displays that looked like bleachers, had video screens showing tapes of Gymboree exercise classes, and had pictures of Gymbo the clown throughout.

The first Gymboree store, opened in 1986, was a success. With financial backing from Venture Partners, Barnes opened an additional 15 stores by the end of 1987. The initial idea was to open the stores in areas where Gymboree centers were established (although the company eventually determined that the concept could work in areas without an established customer base). The outlets stocked about 60 percent apparel and 40 percent hard goods and targeted a price range that attracted buyers between the upscale and middle-income markets. Gymboree sustained its unique image and increased profit margins by designing and manufacturing many of its own products, which couldn't be found in other stores.

By 1989 Gymboree was operating 32 retail stores, mostly in malls, in addition to its base of 350 Gymboree franchises. Sales rose to nearly $17 million, although the company posted a net loss of nearly $1 million. It was clear that Gymboree's future was in retailing, rather than in children's fitness. Barnes's influence in operations had steadily declined in proportion to the amount of money infused by her investment partner, U.S. Venture Partners. U.S. Venture Partners believed that the company was failing to reach its potential, so the investment company began installing a new management team that it hoped would take Gymboree to new heights.

In 1989 U.S. Venture Partners brought in Don Cohn to serve as chairman and chief executive of Gymboree. Cohn was the founder of the successful New England Clothing Co. and had served stints with such venerable retailers as Mervyn's, Laura Ashley, I. Magnin, and Ross Stores. Among other moves, Cohn adopted an incentive-based approach to sales by allocating work hours to store employees based on a sliding scale influenced by their performance. He also fired several managers and brought in more experienced retail executives. Cohn also received much of the credit for the company's successful initial public offering in March 1993 that brought $43 million into Gymboree's coffers.

Partly as a result of Cohn's efforts, Gymboree's sales increased to $48.5 million in 1991 and then to a lofty $68 million in 1992 (fiscal year ended January 31, 1993), while net income rose to a healthy $6.9 million. The total number of retail outlets increased to 120 in late 1993, by which time Gymboree was employing more than 2,100 workers. Despite impressive gains, however, Cohn was forced to resign in 1993 to make way for a new chief executive: Nancy Pedot. In fact, it was Pedot, as the manager of Gymboree's merchandising strategy, who had been largely responsible for the chain's rapid rise during the early 1990s.

Pedot had been hired by Gymboree in 1989 to serve as a general merchandise manager. Previously, she had worked at Mervyn's Inc. as a division merchandise manager. She was effectively handed Gymboree's 32 retail stores and told to fill them with products. She quickly revamped the stores' entire product line and introduced brightly colored, high-quality jumpers, dresses, pants, and tops for newborns to six-year-olds. The Gymboree-brand apparel was a hit and per-store sales surged. She augmented that effort by reducing the number of toys in the product mix and shifting the focus to high-margin clothing items. The change moved Gymboree into a higher price bracket, which paid off in some of the highest profit margins in the industry.

Pedot's appointment as the president and chief executive cemented a near matriarchy at Gymboree, where the six vice-presidents for production, real estate, human resources, stores, merchandising, and franchise operations were all women—only the chief financial officer of the company, James Curley, was male. Under the direction of that management team, Gymboree sustained the aggressive growth it had achieved in the early 1990s, opening a stream of new Gymboree retail outlets and pushing both sales and profits to record levels. Indeed, revenues in 1993 rose to $130 million and net income doubled to $14.1 million. By late 1994 the Gymboree chain had grown to more than 200 stores throughout the United States.

Gymboree continued to expand during 1995, adding more than 50 new outlets to its chain. At the same time, management began intensifying efforts to whip the sprawling distribution and inventory operations into line. To that end, new purchasing, planning, and distribution managers were hired, and new information systems were implemented. In addition, the company launched a Gymboree mail-order catalog and introduced larger goods like furniture into many of its stores. After posting an average annual growth rate of 63 percent over five years, Gymboree increased revenues in 1994 (fiscal year ended January 31, 1995) to $188 million, about $22.2 million of which was netted as income.

To sustain future growth, in 1995 Gymboree began exploring the possibility of overseas retail expansion—its exercise franchises were already operating in Taiwan, Mexico, and eight other countries. Pedot identified potential areas for expansion in Europe and announced plans to open overseas retail units in late 1995 or 1996. In addition, the company planned to increase the size of new stores in the United States and to add more merchandise, in keeping with the superstore concept sweeping the retail industry in the mid-1990s. Gymboree was also working to develop its own educational toys and products and to extend its targeted age range to seven-year-olds. The company hoped to have as many as 500 Gymboree retail outlets operating by 1998.

Further Reading

Barber, Melissa, ''Corporate Profile for The Gymboree Corp.,'' *Business Wire*, August 11, 1995.

Bary, Andrew, ''Kid Stuff,'' *Barron's*, July 18, 1994, p. 17.

Burstiner, Marcy, ''Retailing's Child Prodigy,'' *San Francisco Business Times*, August 20, 1993, p. 4A.

Carlsen, Clifford, ''Shakeup Time in Gymboree's Executive Suite,'' *San Francisco Business Times*, January 21, 1994, p. 3.

———, ''Gymboree Toys with Catalog Sales, Overseas Expansion,'' *San Francisco Business Times*, October 21, 1994, p. 1.

Eng, Sherri, ''Market Share of California's Gymboree Rises on Merchandising Strategy,'' *Knight-Ridder/Tribune Business News*, February 13, 1994.

''Gymboree,'' *Fortune*, February 7, 1994, p. 137.

''Gymboree Is More Than Just Child's Play; Toddler Activity Classes Grow into Lifestyle Concept Retail Stores,'' *Chain Store Age Executive*, November 1987, p. 115.

Martin, Michael B. and Leslie Laurence, ''Joan Barnes's Workout Centers Help 12-Pound Weaklings Pump Iron,'' *Money*, May 1984, p. 21.

Mitchell, Russell, ''A Children's Retailer That's Growing Up Fast,'' *Business Week*, May 23, 1994, p. 95.

—Dave Mote

Hancock Holding Company

One Hancock Plaza
Gulfport, Mississippi 39501
U.S.A.
(601) 868-4000
Fax: (601) 868-4675

Public Company
Incorporated: 1984
Employees: 1,202
Total Assets: $3 billion
Stock Exchanges: NASDAQ
SICs: 6022 State Commercial Banks

Hancock Holding Company was incorporated in 1984 to acquire the Hancock Bank of Gulfport, Mississippi. Through its primary subsidiary of Hancock Bank, the fifth largest bank in Mississippi, as well as Hancock Bank of Louisiana and other financial service firms, the company offers a wide variety of products, such as commercial, mortgage, and consumer loans, savings and checking accounts, and safe deposit facilities. The company also manages real estate property, provides general insurance and consumer financing services, runs over 50 branch offices, and operates 85 automated teller machines.

Throughout its history, Hancock Bank has been closely tied to the events and natural resources of the Mississippi Gulf Coast. In 1898, the town of Gulfport was incorporated to reflect the growing population and commerce in the area. Sawmills and lumberyards operated up and down the Pearl and Jourdan Rivers, and Bay St. Louis became the county seat. Recognizing the essential need for a bank, a number of prominent citizens gathered together in order to establish and organize a bank to serve the growing needs of the county. On October 9, 1899, Hancock County Bank opened its doors for business. Located in a tiny wood-frame building, the bank began its operations with $10,000 in capital and $8,277 in deposits.

The first president of the bank, Peter Hellwege, was one of the original organizers and stockholders. Hellwege was the president of a highly successful brokerage house in New Orleans and had significant experience in financial matters. The new president's first task was to arrange for a permanent building for the bank. In 1900, he contracted a firm to construct a two-story brick building in Bay St. Louis that would serve as the headquarters of all Hancock County Bank operations. In September of the same year, the bank moved into its new location.

Determined to take advantage of the economic activity within the region, Hellwege opened a branch bank at Pearlington, Mississippi, the first branch bank to operate on the Mississippi Gulf Coast. Not long afterward, Hellwege opened another branch bank in Pass Christian, Mississippi, a thriving community with shipping and resort businesses. During this time, the Bay St. Louis office began to sell casualty insurance. By the time of Hellwege's death in 1907, the total assets of the Hancock Bank had increased to $382,508. The bank was now 33 times larger than when it first opened in 1899.

The second president of Hancock County Bank was Eugene H. Roberts. Like Hellwege, he was also one of the bank's founders and had also served as the bank's first cashier as well. Under Roberts' leadership, the Hancock County Bank made one of its first acquisitions, a local insurance company, for the purpose of establishing an insurance department within the bank. Roberts also supervised one of the earliest and most memorable of the bank's advertising campaigns. He purchased a number of highly prized rams to lend to sheep farmers to improve their herds and upgrade the quality of their wool. When Roberts resigned in 1918, assets of Hancock County Bank were nearing $800,000.

The next president was not a founder, but had served on the bank's board of directors since 1900. Horatio S. Weston, the owner of the world's biggest sawmill at the time, continued in the tradition of his predecessors. He expanded and improved all the bank's facilities, including relocating the Pearlington branch office to Logtown, building a new facility in Long Beach, and adding a two-story building in Pass Christian. As the bank grew, so did its activities. Hancock County Bank provided low interest loans to farmers in order to encourage strawberry growing and the improvement of radish crops. One of the bank's major investments during the 1920s included the purchase of all the county bonds in order to guarantee the construction of a gravel road through Mississippi that was to become U.S. 90, which would run all the way from Florida to California. In 1927, Hancock County Bank reported its assets at $3.5 million.

When Weston was incapacitated by a stroke in 1929, an employee named Leo W. Seal, Sr.—one of the workers Weston had brought with him when he left Weston Lumber Company—took over operational control of the bank. When Weston died in 1932, Seal had his hands full with the worst years of the Great Depression. From 1929 to 1932, over 160 banks in the state of Mississippi failed to remain open. But Hancock, under the astute management of Seal, never closed its doors.

Although the bank went through difficult years, its assets dropping to $1.7 million by 1932, it was the Depression itself that spurred the future growth of the company. When Gulfport's three banks were unable to open at the end of November 1931, and the city was left without a bank, Hancock County Bank was given permission to open a branch office in the municipality. Most importantly, after Franklin Delano Roosevelt's Bank Holiday proclamation in 1933, Hancock County Bank was one of the banks allowed to reopen. Making himself available during the holiday to assuage the fears of jittery customers, Seal was rewarded by seeing deposits at his bank increase when it reopened.

Not long afterward, Hancock County Bank became a member of the Federal Deposit Insurance Company, which guaranteed customer savings up to a certain amount. In a restructuring move designed to increase the bank's working capital, Seal closed the branch offices in Long Beach and Logtown, and chartered and divested the Hancock Insurance Agency from the bank's operations.

By 1938, the bank had done so well that the deposits in the Harrison County branches surpassed those of the main office. As a result, Seal had the bank's charter amended in order to relocate its headquarters to Gulfport and also changed the name from Hancock County Bank to the Hancock Bank.

The bank continued to grow during the war years. In fact, Hancock implemented a very unusual service during this time. While most banks across the United States were only paying interest on the first $1,000 in an individual's savings account, and sometimes paying no interest whatsoever, Hancock Bank assured its customers of a one percent interest rate on their entire balance. As an additional service to its customers, the bank opened a branch office on the Gulfport Army Air Base, so that soldiers, shipyard employees, and construction personnel were able to cash their paychecks and complete other banking business.

The postwar years and the entire decade of the 1950s were marked by increasing assets and significant expansion activities. A branch office was reopened in Long Beach, becoming one of the first facilities to include drive-in banking services in the country. Not long afterwards, the bank opened another branch on Pass Road in Gulfport, and still another branch in Mississippi City-Handsboro. In addition, Seal approved of a new four-story annex to the company's headquarters in Gulfport.

During the early 1960s, the U.S. government and NASA, under the direction of President John F. Kennedy, announced plans for a rocket test facility in order to land a man on the moon by the end of the decade; one of the sites under consideration was located in southern Mississippi. By 1962, the government had decided to acquire 140,000 acres of land in the Hancock and Pearl River County areas and planned to begin construction on the rocket test facility as soon as possible. This meant that all of the people in the area would have to be relocated which, not surprisingly, caused an uproar, prompting Senator John Stennis to call on Leo Seal for help. Seal not only advised the senator on financial matters surrounding construction of the test site, but also convinced the people affected that by relocating they were helping the government of the United States.

When Leo Seal, Sr. passed away in 1963, the Hancock Bank's assets had grown from $1.7 million to $41.8 million. His son, Leo W. Seal, Jr., a graduate of Harvard Business School who had worked at Continental Illinois Bank in Chicago, was named the fifth president in the bank's history. Leo Seal, Jr., immediately took advantage of the opportunities offered by the development of the Mississippi Gulf Coast region. The new president established a branch office on the NASA installation site, the first bank to do so in the nation. Additional branch offices were opened in Orange Grove, Edgewater Park, the U.S. Naval "Seebee" Center, Bayou View, West Bay St. Louis, Diamondhead, Pearlington, and Pineville. The company's impressive One Hancock Plaza building was also constructed during this time, occupied by the administrative offices of the bank. Expanded banking services were also initiated by the younger Seal, including the Hancock Travel Agency, the Hancock Mortgage Company, the Harrison Finance Company, a manufacturing joint venture, an electronic processing facility, and a credit life insurance company.

Moreover, during the 1970s the bank initiated a merger and acquisition campaign in order to expand its presence and services throughout the state. In 1973, Hancock Bank merged with the Bank of Commerce in Poplarville, and in 1975 with the Bank of Picayune. Negotiations were also underway to merge with Pascagoula-Moss Point Bank, located in Jackson County. This merger would bring 11 additional branches to Hancock Bank's growing network, including offices in Moss Point, Kreole, Escatawpa, St. Martin, Gautier, Pascagoula, and Ocean Springs.

The 1980s were marked by the participation of Leo Seal, Jr., in many public and social activities that were highly beneficial to the state. Seal was instrumental in lobbying for a four-lane highway that gave greater access to the NASA test facility and the surrounding area. From 1961 to 1985, shipping activity in the Port of Gulfport increased, due in part to the tireless efforts of Seal, who had successfully lobbied to transfer the Gulf of Gulfport from municipal to state ownership. Perhaps one of the most important of Seal's efforts involved his support for local business. When national companies were close to finalizing plans to build or expand facilities in either Hancock or Harrison Counties, only to have the primary financial underwriter back out, Seal was able to arrange for financing through the Hancock Bank, thereby improving the region's business activity. Seal was also instrumental in rebuilding the surrounding community in the wake of the destruction caused by Hurricane Camille. Seal called together a meeting of all the mayors, company presidents, and CEOs of the counties hit hardest by the hurricane, and formed a group to present a unified and comprehensive redevelopment plan to the Mississippi state legislature and federal government.

The Hancock Holding Company was formed in 1984 for the purpose of acquiring Hancock Bank, and during the late 1980s and early 1990s continued its expansion through mergers and acquisitions. The company also began to exhibit a major presence in Louisiana by merging with the First State Bank, located in Baker, Louisiana. This merger provided Hancock with four more branches in East Baton Rouge Parish. Washington Bank and Trust Company, situated in Franklinton, Louisiana, was also purchased, adding another six branches in Washington Parish. Another major acquisition included the First National Bank of Denham Springs, Louisiana, bringing a total of seven branch offices in Livingston Parish under the wing of Hancock.

Hancock Holding Company has continued the tradition established by Leo Seal, Jr., to improve the welfare of the communities that its banks serve. The company was involved in many community development and education programs in the 1990s, the most important of which included educational loans and grants to Mississippi Gulf Coast Community College, University of Southern Mississippi-Gulf Coast, Pearl River Community College, Louisiana State University, the University of Southern Mississippi, Southern University, and William Carey College on the Coast.

As it neared the turn of the 21st century, Hancock Holding Company was confident about its future. Assets continued to grow steadily, and the company's campaign to provide better services throughout the Mississippi and Louisiana gulf regions continued to improve. The company listed a total of 58 offices and 85 automatic teller machines in Mississippi and Louisiana in 1995. Although competition within the financial services industry was intense, by doing business primarily along the Gulf Coast of two states, Hancock Holding Company was well situated for the new millennium.

Principal Subsidiaries

Hancock Bank of Louisiana, Gulfport Building, Inc. of Mississippi, Hancock Insurance Agency, Hancock Bank Securities Corporation, Harrison Life Insurance Company (79%), Hancock Mortgage Corporation, Town Properties, Inc., Harrison Financial Services, Inc.

Further Reading

"Hancock Holding In A Louisiana Acquisition," *American Banker*, July 11, 1994, p. 6.
"Locally Owned Banks Offer Small Business Owners Superior Service," *Bank Marketing*, April 1993, pp. 43–45.
Marjanovic, Steven, "Major Investments Expected In New Product Development," *American Banker*, September 21, 1994, p. 12.
Meredith, Robyn, "FDIC Lets State Banks Do What National Banks Can't," *American Banker*, August 18, 1994, p. 2.
Seal, Leo., Jr., *The Hancock Bank*, Newcomen Society: New York, 1988.
"Supreme Court Allows State-Chartered Banking Subsidiaries To Sell Insurance," *The New York Times*, January 14, 1992, p. C8.

—Thomas Derdak

Handleman Company

500 Kirts Boulevard
Troy, Michigan 48084-4142
U.S.A.
(810) 362-4400
Fax: (810) 362-3415

Public Company
Incorporated: 1937
Employees: 4,147
Sales: $1.22 billion (1995)
Stock Exchanges: New York
SICs: 7386 Business Services; 7822 Motion Picture and
Tape Distribution; 5192 Books, Periodicals and
Newspapers; 5045 Computers, Peripherals and
Software

Handleman Company is one of the largest U.S. distributors of prerecorded videotapes and music, as well as computer software and books. It stocks the shelves of large retail chains, a task called rack jobbing. Handleman also licenses the right to exclusive manufacture of some video and audio products.

Handleman was founded in 1937 as partnership in distributing pharmaceuticals by Philip Handleman and his sons Joseph, Paul, and Moe. The firm soon shifted to selling health aids. By World War II, the company was being run by the sons. In 1946 another brother, David, joined the business.

During the 1950s the company made a decision that proved to be crucial to its future growth: it began wholesaling records. When Joe Handleman, then president of the company, wanted to buy a friend a gift, he was shocked at the poor quality of the record store's display and selection. He sensed an opportunity for a record distributor. With record sales already expanding and poised for far greater growth in the future, this was a fortunate move.

With record sales fluctuating wildly as trends came and went, Handleman became an expert in inventory control. Even-

tually stocking the racks for major retailers like Kmart, Wal-Mart, and Woolworth, Handleman became better at managing record displays than a large store could be. Record sales generally consisted of releases by many different artists. Some records had a short lifespan, others might become best-sellers overnight. Overstocking or understocking a record might prove to be a big mistake. As a result, major retailers handed over Handleman responsibility for supplying selections, deciding how many of each to stock, advertising records and setting up promotional displays.

David Handleman took charge of the company in 1967. In 1974 he became chairman and CEO. The following year, under his leadership, the firm moved into book distribution with the purchase of Sieberts, a record and book marketer.

By 1980 the firm stocked records at over 8,000 retail stores. It was a tough year for record sales, with sales across the entire industry declining. The U.S. economy was in recession, the usual crop of yearly recording hits failed to materialize, and Handleman's sales dropped to $199 million, down from $224 million in 1979. With those sales in 1979, Handleman built a large inventory in anticipation of another great year. When the sales slump hit, the firm was stuck with excess inventory, and many record companies restricted returns to 20 to 30 percent. As a result, the firm's suppliers forced it to lessen its future inventories. So, for example, in late 1980 the firm bought only 65,000 copies of a new Barbra Streisand, less than half of what it might have bought a few years earlier. Despite these troubles, in 1980 the company became the largest record and tape wholesaler in the United States, moving past the Pickwick division of American Can.

About half of the firm's sales were coming from Kmart. Handleman used optical scanners there, and at its other major accounts, to track customer inventory and send the information to a central computer. The firm used the information to examine trends and decide what to carry at its distribution centers and at individual stores. Handleman's gross profit margins averages about 27.7 percent for these services. The company had 21 distribution sites throughout the United States and Canada. It picked up a major new account when it began stocking records

210

at the Zayre chain's 250 stores in the Northeast United States. This gave it a total of about 5,000 record and tape departments.

Handleman was also expanding its book distribution business. The firm ran the book departments in 2,000 retail stores across the United States. It would only take customers for whom it already stocked records. This allowed the same sales representative to handle music and books for the same store, keeping costs down and simplifying the sales process. About 40 percent of book sales came from romance novels geared toward female customers. Books and magazines accounted for about nine percent of Handleman's 1980 revenues.

Handleman accounted for about nine percent of all sales in the record industry in 1980, but because so much of what the firm handled were major releases, it accounted for 20 percent of total hit sales. As a result, nearly 90 percent of the firm's revenues came from handling recorded music. This reliance on the products of one industry gave the firm a narrow base, however. And with the total number of records and tapes sold declining by 18 percent over a four-year period, the company wanted to broaden its product lines.

In 1983 Handleman began a major push into stocking home computer software. The company moved entertainment and education software into about 250 retail stores, hoping that the anticipated growth of the market for home computer software would make it a major new area of growth. Entertainment software made up over 50 percent of software sales in the large retail outlets Handleman served. Handleman also stocked word-processing software and software designed to help users with home and personal finance. In addition, the firm stocked accessories like computer discs and joy sticks for games, as well as some computer books. With its national distribution and inventory management systems already in place, the move into software seemed logical, and the company hoped to stock it at 4,500 stores by 1986. In 1984, Handleman won a contract to rack all software sold at Kmart.

To offset the decline in overall music sales, the firm also carried more lower-priced selections, and paid close attention to local taste preferences, for example, stocking more ethnic music in stores located where it was popular. It also pushed specialty items like exercise records and children's music, which made up 20 percent of music sales by 1983. The firm now had 22 distribution sites and over 500 field representatives, giving it a great deal of flexibility in transferring inventory around the country. In the meantime, music sales began to look up again. MTV, the cable music video channel, began to grow in the early 1980s, as did sales of high-margin compact discs.

In the mid-1980s a new medium came along for Handleman: videocassettes. In 1984 Handleman's clients had video sales of $1.5 million. Though videos were expensive at the time and most consumers rented them, Handleman believed that people would buy them if the price was low enough. The firm began by selling copies of movies that were in the public domain. With no royalties to pay, Handleman could duplicate them and sell them for $15 a piece, in comparison to the going rate of $70 for a copyright-controlled Hollywood movie. As a result, videotape revenues reached $43 million in 1985. Videos brought in twice the revenue per square foot of other merchandise and retailers began giving them more shelf space.

With video sales strong, the firm decided it would make more money if it actually owned some of the video products it sold. In 1988 Handleman bought Viking Entertainment, a southern California-based rack jobber of pre-recorded video and audio. Viking brought Handleman the master recordings for 500 public domain movies. Though Viking only had sales of about $16 million, it stocked supermarkets and drugstores, areas where Handleman was weak. The firm hoped to use this base to expand into the supermarket and drugstore sector. Soon thereafter, Handleman acquired a group of four companies that acquired licenses to copy and distribute taped versions of movies. The group had total sales of $10 million and were acquired in a stock exchange.

In the late 1980s Handleman was still making most of its sales through huge retailers, with Kmart accounting for 41 percent of sales and Wal-Mart for 15 percent. Despite a huge boom in software sales throughout the United States, software only accounted for two percent of Handleman's sales, partly because few people bought software through huge retailers. The firm was doing better with videotapes, however. By 1989 the firm was the largest U.S. tape distributor controlling about 15 percent of the market. In early 1989 Handleman spent $10 million for Video Treasures, which owned licenses and sub-licenses to duplicate and sell more than 400 films.

Recorded music still accounted for a large percentage of Handleman's sales—58 percent of its 1989 revenues of $646.7 million—but the market was changing. Sales of LPs were declining rapidly, replaced by fewer but higher-margin sales of compact discs. Consumers were buying compact disc players rapidly, promising more CD sales in the future. The firm also began a limited foray into becoming a retailer itself, operating Entertainment Zone, the video and audio department of a hyperstore opened in Georgia.

In 1991 the firm bought the entertainment software rack-jobbing business of Live Entertainment Company. Handleman had sales of $702.7 million that year, which increased to $1.2 billion the following year. In 1992 Handleman began stocking products by Lotus Software. In 1994 it completed a 42,000-square-foot addition to its headquarters building. Realizing that it was overly dependent on large retail chains, the firm began a push into Mexico and Canada. At the same time, it added 239 Woolworth stores to its customer list.

The company restructured in 1995, forming three business groups. The Core Business Group comprised Handleman's traditional rack jobbing in the United States in Canada for music, video, books and software. The firm formed North Coast Entertainment to focus on efforts to expand retail operations and proprietary products. The International business unit was designed to pave the way for future international expansion. While Handleman's only foreign rack jobbing took place in Mexico, plans were underway to move into Argentina and Brazil. Since rack jobbing was such a mature market in the United States, future company growth depended on moving into new territory, and the firm announced that it hoped to garner one-third of sales from International and North Coast by 1999. Handleman named

Peter J. Cline president of Core Business Group and Louis A. Kircos president of North Coast.

In 1995 the firm acquired Starmaker Entertainment, Inc., a budget video company with about $15 million in annual sales. It also bought a majority interest in Montreal-based Madacy Music Group for $22.7 million, and music and video rack jobber Levy Music and Video. Madacy's former owner, Amos Alter, remained as president. Madacy, which created specialty music products, had revenues of over $40 million. It owned Mediaphon GmbH, a German music supplier that owned over 2,000 classical music master recordings. To increase its presence in the computer and multimedia market, Handleman increased its ownership of Sofsource, a software development and licensing company. Handleman had already owned 27 percent, and increased its stake to above 50 percent.

To increase its book sales outside of the United States, Handleman began two joint ventures. One, with the Canada Publishing Corporation, Toronto, expanded its presence in Canada. The other, with Grupo Video Visa, created two new companies: one for sellthrough video and music products, the other for rack-jobbing services. Handleman expected to invest $20 million in Mexico over a two-year period. The firm also planned to move into Argentina and Brazil.

The number of music retail departments serviced by Handleman had grown to 6,500. Music accounted for $653.4 million of the firm's $1.23 billion total 1995 sales. The firm serviced even more video departments—7,400, and video sales had reached $461.6 million. The firm made $57.6 million from book sales in 2,600 retail departments, a drop of 13 percent. Meanwhile, software sales were showing signs of taking off, growing 36 percent to $53.3 million. The firm now serviced 4,700 software retail departments. Handleman remained heavily dependent on its two largest customers. Kmart, which was experiencing financial trouble, accounted for 40 percent of Handleman's sales, while Wal-Mart accounted for 25 percent.

Handleman also worked to decrease its costs. In September 1994 the firm opened an automated distribution center in Sparks, Nevada. The 324,000-square-foot center used automation to cut distribution costs on the West Coast. The center also separated sales and merchandising from the firm's other operations, leaving its 1,300 field representatives free to focus on customer sales and service. Handleman expected to open an automated distribution center in the Midwest in late 1995.

Principal Subsidiaries

Handleman Co. of Canada; Entertainment Zone, Inc.; Scorpio Productions, Inc.; Hanley Advertising Co.; Softprime, Inc.; Rackjobbing, S. A. de C. V.; Rackjobbing Services, S. A. de C. V.; Michigan Property and Risk Management Co. North Coast Entertainment, Inc.; Anchor Bay Entertainment, Inc.; Sellthrough Entertainment, Inc.; North Coast Entertainment, Ltd. (Canada); Sofsource, Inc.; Madacy Music Group, Inc.; Mediaphon, GmbH; Madacy Music Group, Ltd. (Canada); American Sterling Corp.

Principal Operating Units

Core Business Group; North Coast Entertainment; International.

Further Reading

Cochran, Thomas N., "Handleman Co.: Building Tomorrow's Business Today," *Barron's,* January 23, 1989, pp. 55–56.
Gubernick, Lisa, "We Are a Society of Collectors," *Forbes,* July 24, 1989, p. 80.
"The Middleman's Dilemma," *Financial World,* October 15, 1980, p. 30, 32.
Taub, Stephen, "The Sweet Music of Computer Software," *Financial World,* October 15, 1983, pp. 28–29.

—Scott M. Lewis

H

Harman International

Harman International Industries Inc.

1101 Pennsylvania Avenue N.W.
Suite 1010
Washington, D.C. 20004
U.S.A.
(202) 393-1101
Fax: (202) 393-2402

Public Company
Incorporated: 1980
Employees: 7,929
Sales: $1.17 billion (1995)
Stock Exchanges: New York
SICs: 3651 Household Audio & Video Equipment; 5064
Electrical Appliances, TV & Radio Sets; 5065
Electronic Parts and Equipment, Not Elsewhere
Classified

Harman International Industries, Inc. manufactures and markets a wide range of high-end, high-fidelity audio and video system components for consumer and professional markets. Well-known brands sold by the company include JBL, Infinity, and Harman Kardon. Harman was expanding rapidly in the early and mid-1990s, mostly through the acquisition of subsidiaries in Europe, Japan, and the United States.

Harman International was incorporated in 1980 by Dr. Sidney Harman, a politician, philosopher, entrepreneur, and one of the founding fathers of the stereo industry. He formed the enterprise to purchase the JBL loudspeaker unit operated by the mammoth Beatrice Companies, Inc. conglomerate. The roots of the company that Harman created in 1980, though, reach back to a venture that Harman himself launched in the 1950s. Indeed, Harman purchased the JBL division as part of a plan to regain control of the company that he had started and, over the course of nearly three decades, built into a respected developer and manufacturer of cutting-edge, high-fidelity stereo gear.

The predecessor to Harman International was founded in 1953 by Sidney Harman and Bernard Kardon. Both Harman and Kardon were engineers by training—the "Dr." in Harman's title, interestingly, refers to a PhD in social psychology that he earned at the Union Institute of New York. The two friends were working together during the early 1950s as engineers at the Bogen Company, which was then the top manufacturer of public address systems. High-fidelity technology that was emerging at the time had caught Harman's interest, and he tried to persuade his superiors at Bogen to become more involved in the burgeoning field.

Bogen showed little interest in Harman's desire to pioneer high-fidelity equipment for the home. So, in 1953, Harman and Kardon left the company to form their own enterprise: Harman-Kardon Inc. Drawing from their $10,000 in funds, the pair developed an advanced stereo system that could be used to play records at home. When their friends heard the system, they were amazed. "We knocked the hell out of them; they were trembling with Shostakovich's Fifth," Harman recalled in the September 1989 *Regardies—The Business of Washington*. "Nobody had heard anything like that in his living room," Harman added.

Harman and Kardon weren't alone in their quest for the ultimate home sound system. Several European companies—H. H. Scott and Fisher, for example—were both selling amplified home sound systems at the time. But the systems developed by Harman-Kardon differed from the competition in that they were designed with aesthetic appeal, as well as cutting-edge sound. Importantly, Harman-Kardon was the first company to put an amplifier, preamp, and radio tuner in a single unit that actually looked like a piece of furniture, rather than a commercial amplifier. That innovation is credited with bringing high-fidelity to the masses. And it gave the entrepreneurs an edge in the marketplace that would allow them to pursue their goal of developing continually better home stereo equipment.

Kardon retired in 1956 and Harman bought his share of the blossoming enterprise. Harman sold part of his company in 1962. For several years thereafter, Harman-Kardon, under Sidney Harman's control, operated as the flagship division of an enterprise that owned other high-fidelity products interests. During the next several years, Harman built the stereo company into a leading contender in the high-fidelity industry. At the same time, the innovative and intriguing Harman was involved in a number of other pursuits.

Among the most notable sidelines was his interest in higher education. Beginning in the early 1970s Harman became president of Friends World College, an experimental Quaker school in Long Island that was a sort of school-without-walls. Harman had also been heavily involved in the civil rights movement, and even cofounded and taught at a highly respected "free school" in Virginia (officials in the county had shuttered the local public schools and opened all-white academies to circumvent Supreme Court integration rulings).

Among Harman's top business ventures during the 1970s was a manufacturing plant in Tennessee that produced automobile side-view mirrors. Harman's management of that plant demonstrated how effectively he was able to mix his interests in education and business. In an effort that became known as the "Bolivar Experiment," Harman applied the principles that he taught at the Friends World College to the manufacturing plant. His attempt to enhance worker satisfaction and productivity by creating an employee-oriented work environment earned him recognition as a pioneer in the field of participatory management. Furthermore, his management strategies were considered a driving force in the success of Harman-Kardon during the 1960s and 1970s.

By the mid-1970s Harman-Kardon was a powerhouse in the U.S. stereo industry. Importantly, the company profited by pioneering the concept of separate components; instead of selling stereo systems as integrated units, Harman-Kardon began selling separate receivers, speakers, amplifiers, and other pieces that buyers could purchase separately and wire together to tailor their own home sound system. By 1976 the company was generating a whopping $136.5 million in annual sales and churning out a healthy $9.1 million in annual profits.

Meanwhile, Harman continued to pursue additional interests, including politics. Indeed, in 1976 newly elected president Jimmy Carter appointed Sidney Harman to the post of Undersecretary of Commerce. Harman accepted the job and in 1977 sold his 25 percent stake in Harman-Kardon to Chicago-based corporate behemoth Beatrice Foods. Harman pocketed $100 million from the sale and went on to achieve notable successes in the Carter administration. Beatrice, in contrast, mismanaged its Harman-Kardon subsidiary (one of 200 under the Beatrice umbrella) and promptly ran it into the ground.

Beatrice effectively butchered the company, selling off some chunks of the business and mismanaging what remained. By 1980 only about 60 percent of the organization of which Harman-Kardon had been a part before Sidney Harman exited remained. The original Harman-Kardon division, in fact, had been sold to a Japanese company named Shin Shirasuna, which was later absorbed by the giant Hitachi group of companies. Basically, all that was left of Harman's original company was JBL (a loudspeaker business) and some international distribution companies. Although Beatrice had damaged it, JBL remained a respected manufacturer of high-end professional speaker systems; JBL, founded in 1946, had helped to pioneer the loudspeaker industry.

Sidney Harman, from his station in Washington, D.C., watched from the corporate sidelines as Beatrice drove his company toward ruin. When Carter was ousted from office in 1980, Harman became determined to regain control of the enterprise and restore its former glory. In 1980 Sidney Harman and a group of investors paid $55 million for what amounted to about 60 percent of the assets of the company that Harman had sold in 1977. Harman established a bare-bones headquarters in Washington, D.C., and began streamlining and organizing the newly created Harman International Industries to compete in the 1980s.

Many electronics industry insiders doubted the wisdom of Harman's decision to jump back into the now-hyper-competitive stereo equipment industry. Aside from his age—Harman was 61 at the time, and some critics wondered if he lacked the vision to compete in the rapidly evolving, increasingly global electronics industry—the U.S. electronic components industry was experiencing global upheaval. The primary culprit in the downfall of many U.S. electronics and related equipment manufacturers was intense overseas competition, particularly in Japan. U.S. companies had ceded the bulk of their domestic market share to the Japanese, and pressure on companies like Harman International was intensifying.

Despite gloomy predictions, Harman proceeded during the 1980s and early 1990s to build Harman International Industries into a powerhouse in the niche for high-end consumer and professional audio equipment. He achieved that growth largely by acquiring smaller companies, reorganizing their management and operations, and allowing them to run relatively autonomously using his style of management. The strategy eventually proved to be hugely successful, and Harman International became known as one of the few large U.S. audio-equipment producers to prosper during the 1980s and 1990s.

Harman credited the prosperity of his companies to the success of a strategy that emphasized three tactics: 1) all of the company's products were built in factories that it owned, rather than purchased from companies that contracted to manufacture the goods for Harman; 2) Harman International vigorously marketed all of its products globally; and 3) the company honored its employees and treated them with respect. The success of that three-pronged strategy was evidenced by one of Harman's first acquisitions, a car stereo company that he purchased in 1982 and dubbed Harman Motive. When Harman bought the small company it was generating sales of about $8 million per year. Before the end of the decade, however, the division was churning out a big $100 million in annual revenues.

Just as important as management strategy was a string of acquisitions throughout the 1980s that pushed Harman International's sales from about $80 million in 1981 to more than $200 million by 1986, and then to more than $500 million by 1989. Notable among Harman's early acquisitions was UREI, a manufacturer of professional amplifiers. Of greater significance was the purchase in 1985 of the original Harman-Kardon operation from Shin Shirasuna. That buyout represented one of the few acquisitions of a Japanese electronics company by a U.S. firm during the 1980s. Harman International went public in 1986 with a stock offering on the New York Stock Exchange. Cash from that sale was used to, among many other purchases, buy

Soundcraft, a U.K. producer of professional mixing boards, in 1988, and Salt Lake City digital electronics producer DOD Electronics Corp. in 1990.

By 1990 the Harman organization had grown into a loose conglomeration of several autonomous companies, each of which catered to a specific niche in the high-end audio equipment industry—most of Harman's goods, though, were marketed under the venerable JBL, Infinity, or other top brand names. Harman's sales topped $550 million in 1990 and net income was shy of $15 million. Although Harman International achieved growth and much success during the 1980s, it became clear to Sidney Harman that major changes had to be initiated if the company was going to compete successfully in the 1990s. That concern was reflected in a disappointing $19.8 million loss experienced by Harman International in 1991, during the recession.

Harman moved away from his family in Washington—interestingly, Harman's wife (a Democrat from California) was elected to Congress in 1992—and moved to California to get closer to his operations. He sent the president of the company packing and, at the age of 70, took control of Harman's day-to-day operations. He merged the 21 scattered divisions into five units and eliminated duplicate departments and operations. He used the cash saved by that effort to intensify marketing efforts. Harman also adopted a new strategy of marketing the company's products through mass retail channels like Circuit City, because he believed that the consumer market was shifting away from ultra-high-end, "audiophile" products to more mainstream, value-oriented audio devices.

Harman didn't give his age a second thought. "[I'm] flat out uninterested in being retired," he said in the March 1, 1993 *Los Angeles Times,* adding, "I don't give a damn how old I am. I can run the pants off everybody working in this place." He was also unfazed by critics who believed the company would be unable to compete in the mainstream audio markets, which were dominated by low-cost giants in Asia.

Harman International bucked criticism with its performance during the early and mid-1990s. The company focused on growing existing operations, but also continued its aggressive acquisition drive. Sales jumped from $604 million in 1992 to $862 million in 1994, while net income rose from $3.5 million to $25.6 million. Harman also continued to streamline and consolidate, reducing its entire operation to just three divisions: professional, automotive, and consumer.

Harman sustained the pursuit of its assertive growth agenda in late 1994 and early 1995. It purchased Becker (a leading German maker of automotive radios and electronics), for exam-

ple, and took over the respected Mark Levinson and Proceed lines of U.S. electronics. The company also established Harman China (a new unit charged with marketing and distributing Harman products to that massive market), and opened an "Advanced Technology Center" that was designed to focus on developing critical digital audio technologies. Those and other efforts contributed to a rise in sales to $1.17 billion in 1995 (fiscal year ending in June), about $41.16 million of which was netted as income.

Principal Subsidiaries

AKG (Germany); Allen & Heath Limited (United Kingdom); Audax Industries, S.A. (France); BSS Audio (United Kingdom); DOD Electronics Corporation; Harman Belgium NV; Harman Consumer Europe A/S (Denmark); Harman Deutschland GmbH (Germany); Harman France, S.N.C.; Harman International Industries, Limited (United Kingdom); Harman International Japan Co., Limited; Harman-Kardon, Incorporated; Harman-Motive, Inc.; Harman Motive Limited (United Kingdom); Infinity Systems, Inc.; JBL Incorporated; Lexicon Incorporated; Lydig of Scandinavia A/S (Denmark); Soundcraft Electronics, Limited; Studer Professional Audio AG (Switzerland); Turbosound Ltd. (U.K.).

Principal Operating Units

Professional Group; Consumer Group; Automotive OEM Group

Further Reading

Abrahms, Doug, "Big Quake Didn't Shake Great Year for Harman," *Washington Times,* August 20, 1994, p. D5.

Burgess, John, "Harman Profits in Electronics Market Abroad," *Washington Post,* June 6, 1988, p. E5.

Kaplan, Fred, "Sidney Harman," *Regardies: The Business of Washington,* September 1989, p. 94.

Koehler, Ron, "Sidney Harman Talks Success," *Grand Rapids Business Journal,* November 10, 1986, p. 5.

Peltz, James F., "HII Founder Seeks to Pump Up Volume," *Los Angeles Times,* March 1, 1993, p. D2.

Segal, David, "The Hi-Fi Manufacturer That Listens Well; D.C.'s Harman International Stays Close to the Customer," *Washington Post,* September 4, 1995, Bus. Sec., p. 10.

Skopp, Roberta, "Christopher Stevens Appointed Harman Kardon President; Harman International Industries, Inc., Acquires Audio-Access, Phoenix Systems," *PR Newswire,* June 3, 1993.

"Top 100: #18 Harman International Industries Inc.," *Washington Post,* April 9, 1990, p. E28.

—Dave Mote

HarperCollins Publishers

10 East 53rd Street
New York, New York 10022
U.S.A.
(212) 207-2000
Fax: (212) 207-7065

Private Company
Founded: 1817
Employees: 2800 (1994)
Sales: $1.09 billion (1995)
SICs: 2731 Book Publishing & Printing

For nearly 170 years the Harper name has been synonymous with the printed word, having cradled American publishing from its infancy to world dominance in the 20th century. A variation of ''Harper'' has adorned the pages of a wide selection of materials, from hand-bound editions of the classics to textbooks for all ages, and from today's hardcover and paperback bestsellers to the firm's popular magazines launched in the second half of the 19th century (*Harper's Magazine, Harper's Weekly,* and *Harper's Bazar*). Harper publishing not only served as the backbone of the printed word's emergence in the United States—making Conan Doyle, Thackeray, the Bronte sisters, Melville, Henry James, and Mark Twain household names—but shaped the minds of generations of readers with the Harper brothers' precision and prescience in selecting books of abiding value. As the 1990s came to a close, HarperCollins had become one of the largest English-language publishers in the world as part of the vast News Corporation Limited.

In 1817, 22-year-old James Harper and his brother John, then age 20, founded the printing firm of J. & J. Harper in New York City. With a burgeoning population of 120,000, New York was the perfect backdrop for the brothers' ambition, which was to produce and market books of a quality derived from expert printing practices and exceptional writing, as ''no works will be published by J. & J. Harper but such as are interesting, instructive, and moral.'' The brothers' first job was to print 2,000 copies of *Seneca's Morals* for a bookseller named

Evert Duyckinck. After completing the project (with the help of their two younger brothers, Wesley and Fletcher), the elder Harpers filled a second order for Duyckinck. They then decided to print their own edition of Locke's *An Essay Concerning Human Understanding,* and Harper publishing was born. Promising to print booksellers' names on the title page, the Harpers acquired enough commissions to buy more equipment, expand operations and relocate twice (both suffered damages by fire) before settling at 82 Cliff Street in 1825.

Moving to Cliff Street signified a new era for the Harpers, as all four brothers were now involved in the firm. Wesley had bought into the business in 1823 and Fletcher in 1825, for $500 apiece. In the preceding years, the brothers had learned several important lessons: to keep books both in print and in stock; to produce better quality yet less expensive editions than the competition; and to be the first ones on the dock when ships came into harbor. Since there were no international copyright laws at the time, aspiring publishers haunted the docks for the latest proofs from Great Britain to rush them into print before competing firms. The Harpers became so adept at the practice, they often had a new American edition on the streets within 24 hours.

By the 1830s the Harpers' reputation for excellence made them the largest printing firm in the country, and the brothers continued to bring new and important authors into America both in general and textbook form. In 1832, *Swiss Family Robinson* by Johann Rudolf Wyss was issued as part of Harper's Boy's and Girl's Library, an offshoot of the firm's popular Family Library. The following year, 1833, a revolutionary steam printing press was installed and the company changed its name to Harper & Brothers to recognize the efforts of Wesley and Fletcher. Two years later, Fletcher drafted one of the earliest known contracts between an American publisher and British author Lord Bulwer-Lytton, whose *The Last Days of Pompeii, Rienzi,* and *The Last of the Barons* were Harper bestsellers, and the firm launched a textbook series by Charles Anthon of Columbia College.

The next decade brought more bestsellers for the Harper imprint, including Dana's *Two Years Before the Mast,* the abridged *Webster's Dictionary,* and a contract to supply the

N.Y. state school system. It also brought greater competition, with rivals even breaking into the firm's bindery to steal copies of forthcoming titles. In April 1844, while the firm's largest project, *Harper's Illustrated and New Pictorial Bible*, was readied for publication, James Harper was elected Mayor of New York City. The late 1840s brought the publication of Thackeray's *Vanity Fair*, as well as *Jane Eyre* and *Wuthering Heights* by the Bronte sisters. The latter title caused a considerable stir because of its "obscene" language. One Boston bookseller even returned copies, refusing to stock such profane writing.

The debut of a new publishing venue arrived with *Harper's New Monthly Magazine* in June 1850, created by James and then run by Fletcher. A chapter from Herman Melville's new book appeared in the October 1851 issue of *Harper's* to publicize the November issuance of *Moby Dick*, which gained neither the critical respect nor the popularity it deserved until well into the next century. By December 1853 the Harpers ran 41 presses ten hours a day, six days a week, averaging 25 volumes per minute, producing an income of about $2 million from sales. But on December tenth, 1853, the Harpers faced their third battle with fire. Everything in the Cliff Street operation was destroyed, save a few piles of papers and some printing plates worth $400,000 that were locked in an underground vault. Damages were in excess of $1 million, with only 20 percent covered by insurance. By the end of the day the Harpers announced they would rebuild. Telegrams and contributions poured in from around the country. The result was two new buildings constructed from wrought-iron beams and trusses (deemed fireproof) opening onto Franklin Square, completed by mid-1855.

Harper's Weekly, Fletcher's "Journal of Civilization," began publication in 1857 with top notch illustrations and a wide range of subjects, which became increasingly political in nature. In the 1860s and 1870s publishers dipped to new lows in competitive pricing, forcing many to go under. While Harpers lost money on many of its titles, the company survived and even launched its third periodical, *Harper's Bazar* (later *Bazaar*), in November of 1867. On Easter Sunday in 1869, after injuries suffered when he was thrown from his carriage, James Harper died. Less than a year later, Wesley died on Valentine's Day, 1870. His fate was followed by the deaths of John (April, 1875) and Fletcher (May 1877). As if in tribute, a Latin edition of *Seneca's Morals*, the first book printed by the optimistic James and John, was issued just days before Fletcher's death. It marked the end of an era. While the four brothers had remained involved in the family business, however, five second-generation sons and many third-generation Harpers had been running the firm for many years.

The last 20 years of the 19th century were marked with several highs and devastating lows. High points included the publication of Lew Wallace's *Ben-Hur* (1880) and the signing of an exclusive contract with Samuel Clemens for his Twain books (1895). The lowest point was Harper's fall into receivership in December 1899. Though Harper & Brothers had been reorganized as a stock company in 1896 with the financial help of J.P. Morgan, profits hadn't rallied and debts mounted. Unable to meet interest payments, Harper was first taken over by S.S. McClure, part of Doubleday & McClure, then by Colonel

George Harvey, who initiated a complete reorganization of the firm on February 17, 1900. Harvey installed himself as president with the blessing of Morgan, other creditors, and the few Harpers still left.

Within 15 years Colonel Harvey had restored Harper's tattered image with lavish banquets attended by statesmen (President Taft attended one in 1912), distinguished authors, and New York City's illuminate. Though *Harper's Bazar* had been sold to William Randolph Hearst in 1913, little of Harper's debt had been alleviated. In May of 1915 Harvey resigned and C.T. Brainard took control with the help of two vice-presidents; Thomas Wells and Henry Hoyns (who began as a clerk with the firm in 1884). Yet Brainard's style was the opposite of the flashy Harvey, and though debt was slashed, many important authors (including Joseph Conrad, Theodore Dreiser, and Sinclair Lewis) abandoned the firm. In 1916 the second of the firm's periodicals, *Harper's Weekly*, was bought out by the *Independent*. To celebrate Harper's centennial in 1917, gold-embossed cards were sent to publishers and authors worldwide, and the 118-page *The Harper Centennial 1817–1917* was compiled, with President Woodrow Wilson's letter of congratulations given prime space.

Publishing from the onset of World War I provided many milestones for the venerable firm. In 1923, the Franklin Square operations were deeded to the Morgan Company for $400,000 and Harper moved to 49 East 33rd Street (another building was added in 1930). The company then issued preferred stock to Morgan and an additional 25,000 shares of common stock to raise capital. In 1925 a book editor named Eugene F. Saxon joined Harper and set a new precedent for quality literature. Among the writers he signed were E.M. Delafield, Lloyd Douglas, Julian Green, Richard Hughes, Aldous Huxley, Anne Parrish, J.B. Priestly, James Thurber, and E.B. White. Despite the Depression and low sales, the 1930s brought several unknown authors to Harper with spectacular results. Those writers included Louis Bromfield, John Gunther (*Inside Europe* and subsequent series), Betty Smith (*A Tree Grows in Brooklyn*), Thornton Wilder, and Thomas Wolfe.

By 1937 the book selling industry had recovered. As WWII wound down, Harper had lost Henry Hoyns (then Chairman of the Board) after 61 years of unflagging service. Wilder's *The Ides of March* was a sensation, as were Gwendolyn Brooks' *Annie Allen* (which won the Pulitzer Prize in 1950), and Kennedy's *Profiles in Courage* (which first appeared in *Harper's Magazine* in 1956 and went on to win the Pulitzer Prize in 1957). In April of 1962, Harper & Brothers merged with Row, Peterson & Company, an Illinois textbook firm, and became Harper & Row Publishers, Inc. The next year President Kennedy was assassinated and several months later, at the request of Robert Kennedy, Harper agreed to publish William Manchester's *Death of a President* with the bulk of the profits going to the Kennedy Library. Unfortunately, a series of problems arose over certain passages in the book. After a protracted legal battle, the book finally appeared in April, 1967.

For the next two decades, Harper & Row broadened its scope considerably through the acquisition of T.Y Crowell (1977), J.B. Lippincott (1978), Zondervan Books (1988) and Scott, Foresman (1989). In the midst of this expansion, Harper listed with the New York Stock Exchange in 1983. Then, Harper itself was acquired in March of 1987 by the Rupert Murdoch's conglomerate, the News Corporation Limited, for $300 million. The next several years were marked by transition under the direction of George Craig, chief executive of all the News Corp.'s publishing enterprises. In 1990, Harper began a new line of paperbacks, then was merged with the U.K.'s William Collins & Sons to form HarperCollins, an international publishing firm that the News Corporation hoped to make the largest English-language publisher in the world. Then came the sale of J.B. Lippincott, followed by the merger of the Edinburgh-based Bartholomew with Times Books, and the reorganization of Harper's six West Coast operations into the Harper-Collins San Francisco Group.

By fiscal year 1994 (ending June 30), HarperCollins had reached worldwide revenue of $1.059 billion. That figure climbed over ten percent to $1.097 billion in 1995, helped in part by the acquisition of Westview Press, an academic and trade publisher in Colorado, and the launch of two Spanish-language imprints; Harper Arco Iris for children and Harper Libros for adults. While sales remained flat for HarperCollins U.K., Zondervan's evangelical book sales finished the year up 21 percent, Harper Audio climbed 26 percent, adult trade was up 11 percent, and the children's division increased revenue by 25 percent with new releases of C.S. Lewis' *Chronicles of Narnia* and the ever-popular *Little House on the Prairie* series.

Early 1996 brought more change when HarperCollins announced the sale of its elementary and high school publisher, Scott, Foresman, and its college division, which accounted for combined revenues of $317 million in fiscal year 1995. Proceeds from the March sale were slated to augment Zondervan's general books line. Another transition was the departure of George Craig and the appointment of Anthea Disney, a News Corp. executive, as president and chief executive, effective in April.

Principal Subsidiaries

HarperCollins Publishers Limited (U.K.); Zondervan Corporation

Principal Divisions

HarperCollins Adult Trade; Harper Business; Harper Paperbacks; Harper Audio; HarperCollins Children's Books; HarperCollins Interactive; HarperCollins San Francisco

Further Reading

Baker, John F., "HarperCollins Reports 10% Sales gain in 1995; Profits Up Slightly," *Publishers Weekly,* August 28, 1995, p. 24.
"Craig to Head All Murdoch Book Business," *Publishers Weekly,* February 3, 1989, pp. 10–11.
Exman, Eugene, *The Brothers Harper,* New York: Harper & Row Publishers, 1965.
——, *House of Harper: One Hundred and Fifty Years of Publishing,* New York: Harper & Row, 1967.
"HarperCollins Combines West Coast Companies," *Publishers Weekly,* November 2, 1992, p. 9.
"HarperCollins Launches Spanish Imprint," *Publishers Weekly,* March 6, 1995, p. 28.
Milliot, James, "HarperCollins to Acquire Westview," *Publishers Weekly,* January 2, 1995, p. 28.
——, "HarperCollins to Sell U.S. Education Units," *Publishers Weekly,* December 4, 1995, p. 10.
"Murdoch Makes it to a New League," *Fortune,* April 27, 1987, p. 8.

—Taryn Benbow Pfalzgraf

 **Hershey Foods**

Hershey Foods Corporation

100 Crystal A Drive
Hershey, Pennsylvania 17033
U.S.A.
(717) 534-6799
Fax: (717) 534-4078

Public Company
Incorporated: 1927 as Hershey Chocolate Corporation
Employees: 14,000
Sales: $3.61 billion (1994)
Stock Exchanges: New York
SICs: 2052 Cookies & Crackers; 2064 Candy &
   Confectionery Products; 2066 Chocolate & Cocoa
   Products; 2098 Macaroni, Spaghetti, Vermicelli &
   Noodles; 5145 Confectionery Wholesale Trade

The name Hershey is synonymous with chocolate, yet the company's founder made his first fortune by manufacturing caramel. Today, Hershey Foods Corporation holds the top position in the U.S. confectionery market and makes several of the top 20 candy brands in the country. Hershey makes and markets chocolate and nonchocolate candies; grocery products such as cocoa, unsweetened chocolate, and peanut butter; and several regional pasta brands that comprise the Hershey Pasta Group and leads the U.S. market for retail dry pasta. In addition to its operations in Canada and Mexico through the Hershey Chocolate North America division, Hershey's Hershey International division exports to more than 60 countries and manufactures and/or markets confectionery products in Italy, Germany, Belgium, the Netherlands, and Japan.

Milton S. Hershey was born in 1857 in central Pennsylvania. As a young boy Hershey was apprenticed to a Lancaster, Pennsylvania candymaker for four years. When he finished this apprenticeship in 1876, at age 19, Hershey went to Philadelphia to open his own candy shop. After six years, however, the shop failed, and Hershey moved to Denver, Colorado. There he went to work for a caramel manufacturer, where he discovered that caramel made with fresh milk was a decided improvement on the standard recipe. In 1883 Hershey left Denver for Chicago, then New Orleans and New York, until in 1886 he finally returned to Lancaster. There he established the Lancaster Caramel Company to produce "Hershey's Crystal A" caramels that would "melt in your mouth." Hershey had a successful business at last.

In 1893 Hershey went to the Chicago International Exposition, where he was fascinated by some German chocolate-making machinery on display. He soon installed the chocolate equipment in Lancaster and in 1895 began to sell chocolate-covered caramels and other chocolate novelties. At that time, Hershey also began to develop the chocolate bars and other cocoa products that were to make him famous.

In 1900 Hershey decided to concentrate on chocolate, which he felt sure would become a big business. That year he sold his caramel company for $1 million, retaining the chocolate equipment and the rights to manufacture chocolate. He decided to locate his new company in Derry Church, the central Pennsylvania village where he had been born, and where there would be a plentiful milk supply. In 1903 Hershey broke ground for the Hershey chocolate factory, which today is still the largest chocolate-manufacturing plant in the world.

Before this factory was completed, in 1905, Hershey produced a variety of fancy chocolates. But with the new factory, Hershey decided to mass-produce a limited number of products that he could sell at a low price. The famous Hershey's Milk Chocolate Bar, the first mass-produced chocolate product, was born.

In 1906 the village of Derry Church was renamed Hershey. The town was not simply named after the man or the company: it was Milton Hershey's creation, the beneficiary of and heir to his energy and his fortune. Hershey had begun planning a whole community that would fulfill all the needs of its inhabitants at the same time that he planned his factory. A bank, school, recreational park, churches, trolley system, and even a zoo soon followed, and the town was firmly established by its tenth anniversary. One of Hershey's most enduring contributions was the Hershey Industrial School for orphans, which he established in 1909 with his wife Catherine. After Catherine's death in

1915, the childless Hershey in 1918 gave the school Hershey company stock valued at about $60 million. In 1996, the school, which became the Milton Hershey School in 1951, still owned 42 percent of Hershey Foods Corporation's stock and controled 77 percent of the company's voting stock.

In 1907 Hershey's Kisses were first produced, and the next year, in 1908, the Hershey Chocolate Company was formally chartered. In 1911, its sales of $5 million were more than eight times the $600,000 made ten years earlier at the company's start.

The Hershey company continued to prosper, producing its milk chocolate bars (with and without almonds), Kisses, cocoa, and baking chocolate. In 1921 sales reached $20 million, and in 1925 Hershey introduced the Mr. Goodbar Chocolate Bar, a chocolate bar with peanuts. In 1927 the company was incorporated as the Hershey Chocolate Company and its stock was listed on the New York Stock Exchange.

By 1931, 30 years after the company was established, Hershey was selling $30 million worth of chocolate a year. As the Great Depression cast its shadow on the town of Hershey, Milton Hershey initiated a "grand building campaign" in the 1930s to provide employment in the area. Between 1933 and 1940, Hershey's projects included a 150-room resort hotel, a museum, a cultural center, a sports arena (where the Ice Capades was founded), a stadium, an exotic rose garden, and a modern, windowless, air-conditioned factory and office building. Hershey liked to boast that no one was laid off from the company during the Depression.

Though Hershey's intentions seem to have been wholly sincere, there was always some suspicion about his "company town." Labor strife came to the company in 1937, when it suffered its first strike. Though bitter, the strike was soon settled, and by 1940 the chocolate plant was unionized.

In 1938, another famous chocolate product was introduced: the Krackel Chocolate Bar, a chocolate bar with crisped rice. The next year Hershey's Miniatures, bite-sized chocolate bars in several varieties, were introduced.

During World War II, Hershey helped by creating the Field Ration D—a four-ounce bar that provided 600 calories and would not melt—for soldiers to carry to sustain them when no other food was available. The chocolate factory was turned over to the war effort and produced 500,000 bars a day. Hershey received the Army-Navy E award from the quartermaster general at the war's end. Hershey died soon after, on October 13, 1945.

After Milton Hershey's death, the chocolate company continued to prosper and maintain its strong position in the chocolate market. By the 1960s, Hershey was recognized as the number-one chocolate producer in America.

With the growth came expansion. In 1963 Hershey broke ground for the construction of two new chocolate factories, in Oakdale, California, and Smiths Falls, Ontario. Expansion for Hershey also meant looking for acquisitions, the first of which was the H.B. Reese Candy Company that same year. Also in 1963, the company's president and chairman, Samuel Hinkle,

arranged for the founding of the Milton S. Hershey Medical Center of the Pennsylvania State University in Hershey, Pennsylvania.

While the company played a hand in many developments within Pennsylvania, its main endeavor continued to be the food industry—and for the first time nonconfectionery food. Among its acquisitions were two pasta manufacturers, San Giorgio Macaroni Inc., in Lebanon, Pennsylvania, and Delmonico Foods Inc., in Louisville, Kentucky, in 1966. In 1967 the Cory Corporation, a Chicago-based food-service company, was acquired. Due to its expansions beyond chocolate, the company changed its name in 1968 to the Hershey Foods Corporation. The name change also marked the passing of an era when in 1969 it raised the price of Hershey's candy bars, which had been 5¢ since 1921, to 10¢.

As the 1970s unfolded, changes in American culture forced Hershey Foods Corporation to change also. Before the 1970s the company, heeding the words of its founder that a quality product was the best advertisement, had refused to advertise. Thousands of people who came to tour the chocolate factory each year had spread the world about Milton Hershey and his chocolate—a visitors bureau had been established as early as 1915 to handle tours of the facilities, and by 1970 almost a million people a year visited Hershey.

Word of mouth had served as a valuable source of advertising for Hershey during most of its existence. But as people became more health conscious and the consumption of candy declined, the influence of advertising became a greater factor in the candy business. By 1970, Mars had deposed Hershey as the leader in candy sales, provoking Hershey to launch a national advertising campaign. On July 19, 1970, Hershey's first consumer advertisement, a full-page ad for Hershey's Syrup, appeared in 114 newspapers. Within months, the corporation was running ads on radio and television as well. Also that year, under an agreement with British candymaker Rowntree Mackintosh, Hershey became the American distributor of the Kit Kat Wafer Bar. Hershey introduced a second Rowntree candy, Rolo Caramels, the next year.

In 1973, Hershey's Chocolate World Visitors Center, was opened to educate people about chocolate-making, with exhibits about tropical cocoa-tree plantations, Pennsylvania Dutch milk farms, and the various stages of the manufacturing process. The facility was established to replace tours of the actual plant, which were discontinued in 1973 due to an overload of traffic.

Under the direction of its chief executive officer, William E. Dearden, Hershey adopted an aggressive marketing plan in 1976 to offset its shrinking market share. Dearden, who had grown up in Milton Hershey's orphanage, joined forces with his chief operating officer, Richard A. Zimmerman, to implement a campaign aimed at customers in grocery stores, where half of all candy is sold. Specialty items such as a wide line of miniatures, holiday assortments, and family packs were marketed. A national ad campaign promoting Hershey's Kisses, and the introduction of the Giant Hershey's Kiss in 1978, tripled sales of the product between 1977 and 1984. The Big Block line of 2.2-ounce bars and premium candies such as the Golden Almond

Chocolate Bar were also introduced, as were Reese's Pieces Candy and Whatchamacallit and Skor Candy Bars.

Hershey also made plans to diversify, to lessen the company's vulnerability to unstable cocoa-bean and sugar prices. In 1977, Hershey acquired a 16 percent interest in A.B. Marabou, a Swedish confectionery company, and bought Y&S Candies Inc., the nation's leading manufacturer of licorice. The following year, it bought the Procino-Rossi Corporation (P&R), and in 1979, it acquired the Skinner Macaroni Company to add to its stable of brand-name pastas. In 1984, Hershey purchased American Beauty, another pasta brand, from Pillsbury and formed the Hershey Pasta Group.

Another 1979 acquisition, the Friendly Ice Cream Corporation, a 750-restaurant chain based in New England, tripled the number of employees on Hershey's payroll. After experiencing major structural changes owing to its 1970s expansion, the company implemented an intensive values study to pinpoint and communicate the principles inherent in its corporate culture and history.

In 1982 Hershey opened another plant, in Stuarts Draft, Virginia. The next year it introduced its own brand of chocolate milk, and in 1984 it introduced Golden Almond Solitaires (chocolate-covered almonds). In 1986, in addition to introducing two new products, the Golden III Chocolate Bar and the Bar None Wafer Bar, Hershey acquired the Dietrich Corporation, the maker of the 5th Avenue Candy Bar, Luden's throat drops, and Mello Mints. Not content with such a year—the first to top $2 billion in sales—in December Hershey purchased G&R Pasta Company, Inc., whose Pastamania brand became the eighth in Hershey's pasta group.

But the acquisitions did not stop there. In June 1987 Hershey acquired the Canadian candy and nut operations of Nabisco Brands for its subsidiary Hershey Canada Inc. The three main businesses Hershey acquired were Lowney/Moirs, a Canadian chocolate-manufacturing concern; the Canadian chocolate manufacturer of Life Savers and Breath Savers hard candy; and the Planters snack nut business in Canada.

The biggest acquisition of all came in August 1988, however, when Hershey made a $300 million deal for Peter Paul/Cadbury, an American subsidiary of the British candy and beverage company Cadbury Schweppes PLC. Hershey purchased the operating assets of the company and the rights to manufacture the company's brands, including Peter Paul Mounds and Almond Joy Candy Bars and York Peppermint Patties, and Cadbury products including Cadbury chocolate bars and Cadbury's Creme Eggs, an Easter specialty candy. Observers predicted that Hershey's economies of scale and clout with retailers would bring increased profitability to the newly acquired Cadbury lines. This purchase pushed Hershey's share of the candy market from 35 percent to 44 percent, and helped Hershey back to the top of the American candy business. At the same time, Hershey decided to sell the Friendly Ice Cream Corporation to concentrate on its core confectionery businesses. The company was sold to Tennessee Restaurant in September for $374 million.

The decline in candy consumption that began after World War II, as a prosperous America found its waistline expanding uncomfortably, accelerated during the 1970s as the fitness craze began. But in the 1980s, this trend reversed. Candy consump-

tion reportedly increased from 16 pounds per capita in 1980 to 19.5 pounds in 1988, coincidentally the same period during which Hershey regained the top spot in U.S. candy through its acquisitions of Dietrich Corporation and Peter Paul/Cadbury. In the early 1990s, Hershey maintained its confectionery position in the United States through several successful introductions: Hershey's Kisses with Almonds chocolates in 1990; Hershey's Cookies 'n' Mint chocolate bars in 1992; Hershey Hugs white chocolate-covered kisses in 1993 (which had become a $100 million brand by 1995); and Reese's NutRageous bar in 1994, which quickly moved into the top 20 candy-bar list.

Outside of its chocolate realm, Hershey continued to bolster its pasta business while also attempting to capture more of the nonchocolate confectionery market. In 1990 it acquired the Ronzoni Foods Corp., yet another regional pasta brand, and in 1993 the Hershey Pasta Group opened a new plant in Winchester, Virginia. Through such moves, Hershey became the leader in dry pasta in the United States by 1995. Meanwhile, continuing fierce competition with Mars and the low inflation of the period—both of which made increasing prices untenable—put pressure on Hershey's chocolate earnings. One of the company's responses to this pressure was to increase its offerings in nonchocolate confections. Among the 1990s introductions were Amazin' Fruit gummy bears in 1992, Twizzlers Pull-n-Peel candy in 1994, and Amazin' Fruit Super Fruits in 1995. By going after the nonchocolate confectionery business, Hershey aimed to capture more market share among youthful shoppers, who generally prefer nonchocolate candy. It also made sense in the overall U.S. market, where nonchocolate candy sales were increasing faster than chocolate candy sales.

In the early 1990s, Hershey attempted to lessen its dependence on the North American market by cautiously moving into overseas markets. In 1990 the company introduced the Hershey brand to the Japanese market through a joint venture with Fujiya. The European market, a difficult market for foreign firms to penetrate given differing European tastes and such entrenched firms as Nestlé, was targeted next although less than successfully, at least at first. In 1991 Hershey acquired the German chocolate maker Gubor Schokoladen, which in the first few years after the takeover failed to meet Hershey's expectations. In 1992 the firm purchased an 18.6 percent interest in the Norwegian confectionery firm Freia Marabou, but then promptly sold the stake the following year after it was outbid for majority control by Philip Morris. Later in 1993 Hershey acquired the Italian confectionery business of Heinz Italia S.p.A. for $130 million, which primarily gave it the Sperlari brand, a leader in nonchocolate confectionery products in Italy. Shortly thereafter, Hershey acquired the Dutch confectionery firm Oversprecht B.V. for $20.2 million, which under the Jamin brand manufactured confectionery products, cookies, and ice cream. Although primarily distributed in the Netherlands and Belgium, Jamin gave Hershey its first penetration of the potentially lucrative Russian market when it began to distribute chocolate there after the Hershey takeover.

Meanwhile, back in North America, Hershey was being hurt by results in Canada, where too many competitors were chasing too few customers, and in Mexico, where political and economic turmoil slowed Hershey's growth. In response, Hershey announced a restructuring in late 1994, taking a $106.1 million aftertax charge. Over the next 15 months, the company cut its staff by more than 400 and consolidated its operations in the United States, Canada, and Mexico into a Hershey Chocolate North America division. Earlier in 1994, Hershey had formed a Hershey Grocery division to give special attention to the company's various baking and grocery products. These two divisions, along with Hershey International and Hershey Pasta Group, comprised the four main areas in which Hershey operated.

In the mid-1990s, Hershey added partnering to its arsenal of corporate strategies. In 1994 Hershey partnered with General Mills to introduce Reese's Peanut Butter Puff's Cereal. In 1995 a partnership with Good Humor-Breyers resulted in Reese's Peanut Butter Ice Cream Cups. That same year a cross-marketing deal with MCI offered free long-distance telephone calls to purchasers of selected Hershey's chocolate products.

Having celebrated its 100th anniversary in 1994, Hershey looked forward to a bright future in its second century. By 1994 Hershey had increased its share of the U.S. confectionery market to 34.5 percent, while Mars had seen its share fall to 26 percent. Hershey's nonchocolate confectionery and pasta operations were growing. Hershey's biggest challenge remained to transfer its North American successes to other markets; Latin America and the Pacific Rim were seen as the regions Hershey was most likely to target.

Principal Subsidiaries

Cadbury Beverage Inc.; Luden's Inc.; Queen Anne Candy Co.; H.B. Reese Candy Co.; Hershey Canada Inc.; Ideal/Mrs. Weiss Noodle Co; Spelari, S.R.L. (Italy); Hershey Japan Co., Ltd.; Hershey Mexico, S.A. de C.V.; Overspecht B.V. (Netherlands).

Principal Divisions

Hershey Chocolate North America, comprised of Hershey Chocolate U.S.A., Hershey Mexico, and Hershey Canada groups; Hershey Grocery; Hershey International; Hershey Pasta Group.

Further Reading

Byrne, Harlan S., "Hershey Foods Corp.: It Aims to Sweeten Its Prospects with Acquisitions," *Barron's,* May 6, 1991, p. 41.

Castner, Charles Schuyler, *One of a Kind: Milton Snavely Hershey, 1857–1945,* Hershey, Penn.: Dairy Literary Guild, 1983, 356 p.

Gold, Jackey, "How Sweet It Is," *Financial World,* November 13, 1990, p. 17.

Halpert, Hedy, "Face to Face: Hershey's Next Century," *U.S. Distribution Journal,* September 15, 1993, p. 43.

Hershey's 100 Years: The Ingredients of Our Success, Hershey, Penn.: Hershey Chocolate Corporation, 1994, 24 p.

Koselka, Rita, "Candy Wars," *Forbes,* August 17, 1992, p. 76.

Kuhn, Mary Ellen, "Sweet Times in the Hershey Candy Kingdom," *Food Processing,* January 1995, p. 22.

A Profile of Hershey Foods Corporation, Hershey, Penn.: Hershey Chocolate Corporation, 1995, 24 p.

The Story of Chocolate and Cocoa, Hershey, Penn.: Hershey Chocolate Corporation, 1926, 30 p.

—updated by David E. Salamie

Ingersoll-Rand Company

200 Chestnut Ridge Road
Woodcliff Lake, New Jersey 07675
U.S.A.
(201) 573-0123
Fax: (201) 573-3448

Public Company
Incorporated: 1905
Employees: 35,932
Sales: $4.51 billion (1994)
Stock Exchanges: New York London Amsterdam
SICs: 3429 Hardware, Not Elsewhere Classified; 3492 Fluid Power Valves & Hose Fittings; 3519 Internal Combustion Engines, Not Elsewhere Classified; 3531 Construction Machinery & Equipment; 3533 Oil & Gas Field Machinery & Equipment; 3532 Mining Machinery & Equipment, Except Oil & Gas Field Machinery Equipment; 3536 Overhead Traveling Cranes, Hoists & Monorail Systems; 3546 Power Driven Hand Tools; 3549 Metalworking Machinery, Not Elsewhere Classified; 3554 Paper Industries Machinery; 3556 Food Products Machinery; 3561 Pumps & Pumping Equipment; 3562 Ball & Roller Bearings; 3563 Air & Gas Compressors; 3568 Mechanical Power Transmission Equipment, Not Elsewhere Classified; 3714 Motor Vehicle Parts & Accessories

Utilizing plants located throughout the world, Ingersoll-Rand Company manufactures a wide array of machinery and equipment for the automotive, construction, and energy markets and for general industry. The firm is a leader in air compressors, bearings, door locks and hardware, golf cars, pumps, road construction machinery, and skid-steer loaders, among other areas.

Ingersoll-Rand grew out of the efforts of four late 19th-century inventors. Simon Ingersoll, a farmer and inventor, patented a rock drill in 1871, then sold the rights to his patent;

Henry Clark Sergeant improved upon Ingersoll's drill and persuaded businessman José F. de Navarro to invest in the idea; William Lawrence Saunders developed many diversified forms of the rock drill; and Addison Crittenden Rand also improved rock drills. Rand also was successful in persuading mining companies to substitute the new technology for the traditional hammer and chisel.

In 1870 inventor Simon Ingersoll, who worked at truck farming to support his family, accepted a contractor's commission to develop a drill that would work on rock. Ingersoll worked on the invention in a New York machine shop owned by entrepreneur José F. de Navarro. Ingersoll received a patent on the rock drill in 1871, but the new tool did not stand up to New York's rocky streets.

Henry Clark Sergeant, one of the partners in the machine shop, made an important change in the drill design. He separated the front head from the cylinder, since a drill in two pieces could better resist breakage. Sergeant then persuaded de Navarro to buy Ingersoll's patent, and de Navarro organized the Ingersoll Rock Drill Company in 1874, with Sergeant as its first president. Ingersoll, who was forced to sell most of his patents and work halfheartedly at farming to feed his family, died nearly destitute in 1894.

Henry Clark Sergeant, however, was able to turn ideas into profitable businesses. Sergeant had been inventing since he was a teenager, and had secured his first patent when he was 20. In 1868, at the age of 34, he had arrived in New York City where he started a machine shop that specialized in developing the ideas of other inventors. As the business grew, he took a partner and moved into de Navarro's shop. After de Navarro formed the Ingersoll Rock Drill Company, Sergeant worked for several years to improve Ingersoll's drill by using compressed air rather than steam to operate it.

In 1885 Sergeant developed a completely different rock drill and formed the Sergeant Drill Company to manufacture it. In 1888 he merged the two companies, becoming president of the Ingersoll-Sergeant Rock Drill Company. After several years he became a director and devoted himself to inventing.

At the same time Ingersoll was patenting his rock drill in 1871, Addison Crittenden Rand moved to New York City from Massachusetts. Rand's brother, Alfred T. Rand, had been instrumental in founding the Laflin & Rand Powder Company, a mining firm. Addison Rand had formed the Rand Drill Company to develop a rock drill and air-compressing machinery for his brother's company. Rand's firm developed the Little Giant tappet drill and the Rand Slugger drill and marketed them effectively, convincing mining companies to switch from hammer and chisel to rock drills with air compressors.

Rand was known for his paternalistic approach to business. He carefully selected his employees and trained them for skilled positions. Rand avoided unions, and was personally affronted when employees at his Tarrytown, New York, plant struck in 1886. The plant was shut down for a year before Rand would agree to a settlement.

In 1905 Michael P. Grace—a brother of William R. Grace, who founded W. R. Grace & Company—brought Ingersoll-Sergeant Drill Company and the Rand Drill Company together. The two companies had specialized in slightly different segments of the drill market—Ingersoll-Sergeant specialized in construction work while Rand focused on underground mining—and their interests were complementary. The new company was incorporated as the Ingersoll-Rand Company (I-R) in June 1905 and billed itself as "the largest builder of air power machinery in the world." The Grace family owned the largest single block of stock, and a Grace has served on the I-R board ever since.

William Lawrence Saunders became the first president of the company. Saunders, an engineer, had developed a compressed-air drilling apparatus for subaqueous use while in his 20s. The widely used invention made development of Russia's Baku oil fields possible. Saunders had inspected an underwater rock drilling and blasting project himself, diving down to it so he could design a subaqueous drill appropriate for the job. He was active in engineering societies, and established an award given by the American Institute of Mining and Metallurgical Engineers to recognize achievements in mining methods. He also established *Compressed Air*, the company's industrial trade journal, in 1896 and served as its editor. In addition, Saunders was a two-time mayor of North Plainfield, New Jersey.

As president of Ingersoll-Rand, Saunders expanded upon the company's original line of rock drills and air compressors. He promoted development of diverse types of these machines. He also led Ingersoll-Rand into related areas of the tool business. I-R expanded into pneumatic tools in 1907 by acquiring the Imperial Pneumatic Tool Company of Athens, Pennsylvania. In 1909 the company bought the A.S. Cameron Steam Pump Works and entered the industrial pump business. In 1913 he added centrifugal pumps to I-R's product list. Under Saunders I-R also acquired the J. George Leyner Engineering Works Company. This firm had developed a small, hammer-type drill that could be operated by one man. I-R began to produce the jackhammer in 1913, and it quickly became a popular item.

Saunders moved to the board of directors in 1913 and was replaced as president by George Doubleday. Doubleday was determined to make Ingersoll-Rand the leader in its product areas—drills, air compressors, jackhammers, pneumatic tools, and industrial pumps. Doubleday led Ingersoll-Rand for 42 years.

Doubleday carefully adhered to the principles that Saunders had used to guide the company, using Ingersoll-Rand's four major plants in Phillipsburg, New Jersey; Easton and Athens, Pennsylvania; and Painted Post, New York, to handle increasing business. In these locations, I-R was the major employer. Community life centered on the firm: many workers lived in company-owned houses, and community and school events were held in company buildings. Doubleday hired boys off the farm and trained them to become skilled machinists through a seven-year apprenticeship. These artisans accepted the company's credo of pride in personal work, and only a handful of quality-control specialists were needed. Doubleday charged a premium price for the high-quality machinery this system produced.

Little is known about the company itself under Doubleday or about Doubleday's personal life—he refused even to release a photograph of himself to the press—and he provided a bare minimum of information about Ingersoll-Rand. Under Doubleday the company never released a quarterly report and its annual report was a single folded sheet of paper containing only the figures the New York Stock Exchange required.

Advances were made in the firm's products during the Doubleday years, however. In 1933 I-R introduced a new portable-compressor line, which was improved during the 1950s with the introduction of the revolutionary sliding-vane rotary portable unit. Ingersoll-Rand began to compete in the "big drill" field in 1947, when it introduced the Quarrymaster, which was used in quarrying, open-pit mining, and excavation. A self-propelled jumbo drill, the Drillmaster, was introduced in 1953, followed by the Downhole drill in 1955. Doubleday also purchased General Electric's centrifugal-compressor business in 1933, to become the leader in that sector of the business. In 1948 the company designed the first natural gas transmission centrifugal compressors.

When Doubleday retired in 1955 Ingersoll-Rand was indeed on sound financial footing. The company had more than $100 million in cash and no debt. With an operating profit margin of 37 percent and a net profit margin of 19 percent, it had paid a dividend every year since 1910, and return on stockholders' equity was 23 percent.

Doubleday had reached those impressive numbers, however, by abandoning the marketing orientation that he had originally brought to the job. By the end of his tenure he was 89 years old, and had become too conservative. The company's capital was the result of Doubleday's unwillingness to upgrade the company's plants to keep manufacturing costs low; to promote research and development to retain I-R's technological edge; or to maintain sufficient foreign parts inventory to keep equipment running overseas. He also eschewed diversification outside of I-R's basic product lines.

Doubleday died in 1955, and an interim management team followed his policies for another four years. Robert H. Johnson was named chairman of the company in 1959. At 58, Johnson had spent 35 years with the company he had joined as a salesman.

Johnson cut the company's premium prices to remain competitive. He also spent $25 million to increase parts inventories abroad, and thereby doubled sales overseas in five years; invested in research to promote a return to technological leadership; and increased spending for plant and equipment from an approximate average of $2 million a year to $15 million in 1965. Johnson put the company's excess cash—more than 65 percent of I-R's total assets in 1966—to work through a policy of careful acquisitions. He invested, for example, in Lawrence Manufacturing Company, which specialized in producing mechanical moles for urban underground utility tunneling.

Johnson's successor as CEO, 52-year-old William L. Wearly, gave those policies new momentum. Wearly, who took the top position in 1967, was the first leader at Ingersoll-Rand who had not grown up with the company, another sign that it was leaving its conservative past behind. Wearly came to I-R as a consultant in 1962 after leaving the presidency at Joy Manufacturing. With Wearly came a new generation of managers: President D. Wayne Hallstein was 49, while the four newest vice presidents were under 44. The youth of the new management team was no accident; Johnson had decided that managers who were over 55 had been too thoroughly indoctrinated in the Doubleday method of doing business and bypassed them completely.

Wearly reaped the advantages of Johnson's investment in plant and equipment, which allowed Ingersoll-Rand to increase sales—especially abroad—because of increased manufacturing capacity. Wearly also increased capacity through overseas acquisitions in England, Italy, Canada, South Africa, and Australia.

Wearly then took Ingersoll-Rand into new, diversified areas to help offset the cyclical nature of the capital-goods market. The acquisition of The Torrington Company in 1968, which brought needle and roller bearings, knitting needles, metal-forming machines, universal joints, and roller clutches to the company catalog, was especially important. So was Wearly's 1974 acquisition of the Schlage Lock Company, which produced locks, door hardware, and home and business security devices. Both acquisitions became consistent moneymakers for I-R.

Wearly had clearly moved away from the company's tradition of operating paternalistic plants in small towns. By the early 1960s Ingersoll-Rand operated 36 plants in the United States and 17 abroad. One of them, its Roanoke, Virginia, plant, became the first factory in the country to use computerized direct numerical control of a production line. The plant used a computer to run machine tools and to automatically move parts from one tool to another on conveyer belts without human assistance. The new Roanoke facility took over much of the capacity of the old Athens, Pennsylvania, plant, which had been crippled by strikes and rising labor costs. In 1959 the company had threatened to leave Athens if the union did not make significant concessions on work methods, and Ingersoll-Rand had won the new five-year contract it wanted. A decade later those union concessions were not forthcoming, and the Athens plant was substantially bypassed—by a mechanized system instead of by other workers.

Wearly's policies seemed destined to pay off in the early 1970s, when factors such as the search for new energy sources, Mideastern oil money, growing East-West trade, and Third

World industrialization led to increased demand for almost all Ingersoll-Rand products. Five years later, the boom turned into a bust. Capital spending had slowed after the energy crisis of 1973. Coal and railroad strikes hurt the company because it was still a major supplier of coal-mining machinery. Wearly said that President Jimmy Carter's human rights emphasis hurt business in the Soviet Union and Brazil. All of these factors left Ingersoll-Rand with too much capacity and too much inventory.

Wearly retired in 1980 and Thomas Holmes, a 30-year employee, took over as CEO. Holmes convinced Clyde Folley, a member of Price Waterhouse's governing board who had worked on the Ingersoll-Rand account, to become chief financial officer. The two executives faced the global recession and resulting fall in earnings and sales, especially of oil-drilling and construction equipment. Overall in 1993 Ingersoll-Rand lost $112 million, the first loss it had suffered since the 1930s.

As a result, the company closed 30 production plants and cut staff by one-third. The company's tight cash supply was spent only in the areas where returns were highest—bearings, locks, and tools—rather than on the traditional focus areas of the company—engineered equipment, coal-mining equipment, and air compressors. Holmes and Folley tied management compensation to return on assets instead of sales to promote more efficient asset use, and centralized inventory controls.

Holmes, Folley, and Theodore Black then initiated joint ventures with competitors. One of the most important of these ventures was Dresser-Rand, a 50–50 partnership formed in 1986 with Dresser Industries, another major mining- and oil-equipment company. Almost immediately successful, Dresser-Rand turned a profit in only its second year of operation. In 1987 I-R formed another joint venture in mining with B.R. Simmons. Folley said the joint ventures allowed the company to cut staff and losses while competing more effectively with Japanese and West German companies. Pooling talent also helped the firms stay current technologically.

Ingersoll-Rand had once again weathered recession by the time Holmes stepped down in 1988. His successor, Theodore Black, was able to focus on significant positive aspects of the company. Ingersoll-Rand continued to emphasize new product development, introducing improved home air compressors, new papermaking technology, and a new type of camshaft in 1988. Ingersoll-Rand also continued to make appropriate acquisitions, including a Swedish company that designs waterjet cutting systems, a Canadian manufacturer of paving equipment, and a German maker of special-purpose hydraulic rock drills, in 1988. In 1990, the company purchased The Aro Corporation, one of its larger acquisitions of the period. Ingersoll-Rand continued to utilize state-of-the-art computerized production and design techniques. New techniques that utilize manufacturing cells to produce a product from start to finish with much less labor than a production line were able to produce more, higher-quality goods.

Another recession during the early 1990s barely registered on Ingersoll-Rand's balance sheet; 1991 profits fell 19 percent to $150.6 million, while the company's competitors posted losses—$404 million for Caterpillar Inc. and $36 million for Timken Co. Part of the credit for Ingersoll-Rand's success was attributed to its geographical diversity. In the early 1980s only 30 percent of the company's sales were attributable to products manufactured outside the United States, but through a variety of acquisitions thereafter that percent had increased to 70 percent by 1992. The Dresser-Rand partnership was also paying off huge dividends on the home front. The joint venture's sales exceeded $1.2 billion by 1991 and more than one-quarter (or $40 million) of Ingersoll-Rand's 1991 profits were generated from Dresser-Rand.

Dresser Industries and Ingersoll-Rand recognized another possible area of cooperation in 1991 within their then-competitive industrial-pump manufacturing operations. The companies agreed in May of that year to combine their pump divisions into one organization that could better compete against competitors in Japan and Germany. The new firm would have annual sales of $800 million and 8,000 employees worldwide, and would dominate the pump manufacturing industry in the United States. The U.S. Justice Department initially opposed the joint venture under the Sherman Antitrust Act. Dresser and Ingersoll-Rand countered by contending that the Justice Department had to take the impact of foreign competition into account. After lengthy negotiations, in August 1992 the Justice Department agreed to let the merger go through provided that the two companies divest about $10 million of their pump operations to mitigate its impact on domestic competition. The newly formed company was called Ingersoll-Dresser Pump Company and Ingersoll-Rand owned 51 percent of it.

In September 1993, Black retired as chairman and CEO and was replaced by James E. Perrella, a 16-year veteran of the firm. Perrella continued to invest heavily in research and development, shelling out a record $154.6 million in 1994 alone, as well as to make strategic and significant acquisitions. Several smaller acquisitions in 1993 and 1994 served to increase Ingersoll-Rand's presence in the European market and brought additional complementary businesses into the company fold. These moves included the 1994 acquisitions of the France-based Montabert S.A., a manufacturer of hydraulic rock-breaking and drilling equipment, for $18.4 million and the Ecoair air compressor operation from MAN Gutehoffnungshütte AG for $10.6 million. In 1994 Ingersoll-Rand also invested $17.6 million in a joint venture with MAN to manufacture airends, an important component in certain industrial air compressors.

Ingersoll-Rand's most important acquisition of this period, and perhaps in its history, came the following year when it purchased Clark Equipment Co., the South Bend, Indiana, manufacturer of small and medium-sized construction machines. Perrella was seeking a major acquisition—a firm that was first or second in its market with sales of $500 million to $1.5 billion—and Clark became a prime candidate. A Clark acquisition was seen as a particularly complementary one, given Clark's focus on construction and Ingersoll-Rand's construction-related lines, which comprised only about 18 percent of company sales prior to the takeover. Clark became an even more attractive target in early March 1995 when it sold its half-interest in VME Group N.V., an earthmoving equipment manufacturer, to its partner, Volvo AB, for $573 million.

Before the acquisition was completed, however, Ingersoll-Rand had to fend off Clark's management which did not wish to relinquish control. After Clark's board rejected the first offer, Ingersoll-Rand made a hostile bid of $1.3 billion late in March.

Clark then brought suit against Ingersoll-Rand claiming that the takeover would violate antitrust laws; Ingersoll-Rand countered by taking steps to oust Clark's board at the annual meeting to be held in early May. In early April, Clark reluctantly accepted an increased offer of $1.5 billion, which many analysts viewed as fair. Through the acquisition, Ingersoll-Rand gained such Clark operations as Blaw-Knox, the world's leading manufacturer of asphalt road paving equipment; Melroe, the world leader in skid-steer loaders; and Club Car, the second largest golf car manufacturer in the world.

Ingersoll-Rand has changed dramatically since its early days when it emphasized staying on top of a few product lines in a centralized, paternalistic working environment. With its carefully diversified line of products and its worldwide operations, it appears that this strong company will continue to withstand international economic fluctuations to provide what the world needs to grow and develop.

Principal Subsidiaries

The Aro Corporation; California Pellet Mill Company; Clark Equipment Co; Dresser-Rand Co. (49%); Ingersoll-Dresser Pump Company (51%); Ingersoll-Rand China Limited; Ingersoll-Rand International, Inc.; Ingersoll-Rand International Sales, Inc.; Ingersoll-Rand International Holding Corporation; Ingersoll-Rand Sales Company Limited; Ingersoll-Rand Worldwide, Inc.; Schlage Lock Company; Silver Engineering Works, Inc.; Simmons-Rand Company; The Torrington Company; Ingersoll-Rand (Australia) Ltd.; Ingersoll-Rand Benelux (Belgium); Ingersoll-Rand Canada, Inc.; Compagnie Ingersoll-Rand (France); Ingersoll-Rand Beteiligungs GmbH (Germany); Ingersoll-Rand (India) Ltd. (74%); Ingersoll-Rand Italiana S.p.A. (Italy); Ingersoll-Rand Japan Ltd.; Tokyo Ryuki Seizo Kabushiki Kaisha (Japan); Ingersoll-Rand Philippines, Inc.; Ingersoll-Rand AB (Sweden); Ingersoll-Rand Services & Engineering Company (Switzerland).

Principal Operating Units

Standard Machinery, composed of Air Compressor, Construction and Mining, and Mining Machinery groups; Engineered Equipment, composed of Pump and Process Systems groups; Bearings, Locks and Tools, composed of Bearings and Components, Production Equipment, and Door Hardware group.

Further Reading

Byrne, Harlan S., "Ingersoll-Rand: Leaner and Poised to Build Stronger Profits," *Barron's*, June 8, 1992, pp. 39–40.

Johnson, James P., *New Jersey: A History of Ingenuity and Industry*, Northridge, Calif.: Windsor Publications, 1987.

Klebnikov, Paul, "A Traumatic Experience: Ingersoll-Rand Prospers Today Because It Stumbled So Badly a Few Years Ago," *Forbes*, January 18, 1993, pp. 83–84.

Koether, George, *The Building of Men, Machines, and a Company*, Woodcliff Lake, N.J., 1971, 107 p.

Lipin, Steven, "Clark Accepts Ingersoll Bid of $1.5 Billion for Takeover," *Wall Street Journal*, April 10, 1995, pp. A3, A5.

—Ginger G. Rodriguez
—updated by David E. Salamie

INTERNATIONAL (A) PAPER

International Paper Company

Two Manhattanville Road
Purchase, New York 10577
U.S.A.
(914) 397-1500
Fax: (914) 397-1596

Public Company
Incorporated: 1898
Employees: 88,000
Sales: $22 billion (1995 est.)
Stock Exchanges: New York Montreal Basel Geneva
Lausanne Zürich Amsterdam
SICs: 0811 Timer Tracts; 0831 Forest Nurseries & Forest
Products; 2421 Sawmills & Planing Mills, General;
2611 Pulp Mills; 2621 Paper Mills; 2631 Paperboard
Mills; 2657 Folding Paperboard Boxes, Including
Sanitary; 2761 Manifold Business Forms

International Paper Company (IP) is the world's largest producer of paper, packaging, and forest products. The firm also operates a distribution unit which transports its own products and those of other companies and various related specialty product businesses ranging from imaging products to nonwoven fabrics. The company began as a major player in its core industry and expanded through mergers, acquisitions, and product development. IP's manufacturing operations span 28 countries, and the company exports to more than 130 nations.

Established on January 31, 1898, the firm resulted from a merger of 18 paper and power companies, with 20 mills throughout five northeastern states and timberlands ranging as far north as Canada. The new company had one million acres of woodlands, and streams running through the properties were used to run the mills with hydroelectric power. At the turn of the century, the mills provided 60 percent of U.S. newsprint. In 1903, in order to enhance its research and development efforts, the company opened the Central Test Bureau in Glens Falls, New York.

The company's power interests played a dominant role in its early years. As household electricity demand grew in the 1920s, the firm established large hydroelectric plants and power companies. At one time, it produced enough electricity to light all of New England, and most of Quebec and Ontario. In 1928 International Paper & Power Company was organized in Massachusetts to acquire International Paper. IP continued to operate as a subsidiary of International Paper & Power. In 1935 the United States passed the Public Utility Holding Act, making it illegal for an organization to run both an industrial firm and a power company. The law signified the end of International Paper's involvement in the energy and power business. Instead, the company began to focus on key areas such as paper and packaging.

The company expanded into the southern United States in the 1920s and 1930s, primarily because trees could be grown more quickly and in greater volume than they could in the North. It also maximized its use of the trees through the kraft process, which involved use of a very strong pulp to manufacture packaging materials.

In June 1941 a new company was incorporated to acquire the assets of International Paper & Power Company. The new parent company was named International Paper Company to reflect the change from a paper and power company to a manufacturer devoted solely to paper. During World War II, International Paper did what it could to support the war effort. Its contributions included the development of nitrate pulp for use in explosives and the development of a waterproof board called V-board—victory board—which was used to make boxes to send food and other supplies to the troops. The new technology, along with the wartime inventions of other manufacturers, led to increased competition after the war. As a result, IP began to invest more capital in research and development. Shortly after the war, it established the Erling Riis Research Laboratory in Mobile, Alabama.

An emphasis on packaging products also characterized the firm's progress in the 1940s. In December 1940 it acquired the Agor Manufacturing Company, which included three subsidiaries and four container plants in Illinois, Kansas, Massachusetts, and New Jersey. In June 1941 IP merged the Southern Kraft Corporation with its main business. Previously a subsidiary,

Southern Kraft owned eight kraft board and paper mills in the southern United States. IP also bought the assets of a shipping-container maker, the Scharff-Koken Manufacturing Company.

In 1947 IP merged with Single Service Containers Inc., a manufacturer of milk containers, and in 1952 it founded the International Paper Company Foundation, a nonprofit organization developed to support charitable, educational, and scientific efforts. IP acquired the capital stock of a specialty coated paper manufacturer, A.M. Collins Manufacturing Company, of Philadelphia, in 1955. In 1957 the latter merged with IP. In 1958 IP bought Lord Baltimore Press, Inc., a Maryland manufacturer of cartons and labels.

IP's Canadian subsidiary, Canadian International Paper Company, also made its share of acquisitions in the 1950s. These included Brown Corporation in 1954; Hygrade Containers Ltd. in 1955; and Anglo American Paper Company, Mid-West Paper Ltd., Vancouver Pacific Paper Company, and Victoria Paper Company in 1959.

During the following decade, new technology improved both product design and manufacturing processes. In 1962, for example, IP began using computers to control paper machines at its mill in Georgetown, South Carolina. A year later, it introduced polyethylene-coated milk cartons. In addition to new products, the 1960s presented IP with challenges, including development of new production and management techniques. Since 1943 IP had been headed by the Hinman family; John Hinman was chief executive from 1943 to 1962, and his son, Edward B. Hinman, held the post from 1966 to 1969. Various associates appointed by the elder Hinman ran the company from 1962 to 1966.

During the 1960s IP continued to grow internally and took giant leaps toward diversification—many of them in haste—and learned that bigger is not always better. IP had emphasized production efficiency as a means of increasing output for most of the century. IP's production muscle came at the expense of marketing expertise, which lagged. The production emphasis led to overexpansion of paper plants, which in turn resulted in low profit margins. To increase profitability, IP diversified, with little success, into areas as far-ranging as residential construction, prefabricated housing, nonwoven fabrics, consumer facial tissue, and disposable diapers. It also moved into lumber and plywood, but found equally little success in those areas. White paper, paperboard, and pulp still accounted for more than half of the company's sales during the early 1970s; converted paper products comprised one-third; lumber, plywood, and other building products totaled nine percent; and the remaining sales came from real estate, packaging systems, and nonwoven fabrics.

By 1971 IP's long-term debt, which had been almost nonexistent in 1965, reached $564 million. When Edward Hinman took over, the company's greatest asset was its large share of real estate, including 8 million acres that it owned and 15.5 million that it leased. In 1968 Hinman sought the help of Frederick Kappel, formerly chairman of AT&T. The two ran the company together, but after earnings declined by 30 percent in 1970, Kappel and a team of outside directors replaced Hinman the following year with Paul A. Gorman, another AT&T executive. Gorman faced the challenge of returning the company to profitability.

Gorman started the long-term task by setting up a $78 million reserve to cover write-offs of inefficient facilities; closing a specialty mill in York Haven, Pennsylvania; and closing various plants in Ecuador, Italy, Puerto Rico, and West Germany. In 1972 he also sold most of Donald L. Bren Co., a southern California house builder acquired in 1970, and Spacemakers Inc., a prefabricated-housing subsidiary. The company also sold its interest in C.R. Bard, Inc. a medical-equipment manufacturer.

From 1966 to 1972, IP had spent $1 billion to increase its paper-making and -converting capacity by 25 percent. During the early 1970s the paper industry headed toward cyclical recession. IP laid off seven percent of its employees. Gorman felt that the firm needed more financial control, and saw to it that decisions made by the company's manufacturing groups were reviewed from a financial, marketing, and manufacturing perspective. In addition, all projects had to show a minimum after-tax profit of 10 percent. Ailing plants were improved, sold, or shut down. Gorman also reorganized international operations on a product line basis. His efforts were successful. Earnings of $69 million in 1971 were the lowest in ten years, despite record earnings just two years earlier, but they jumped 30 percent the first six months of 1972.

In 1973, J. Stanford Smith joined IP as vice-chairman. Previously a senior vice-president with General Electric, Smith eventually would replace Gorman as chairman. Smith felt that one way to increase profitability was to develop natural resources on the company's land. He devised a plan to purchase General Crude Oil Company, which IP did in 1974 for $489 million. The business was unsuccessful, however, in locating major oil or gas deposits on IP's land. Five years later, in order to raise capital for acquisitions and internal growth, the company sold General Crude Oil's oil and natural gas operations to Gulf Oil Corporation for $650 million. In addition, IP sold a Panama City, Florida, pulp and linerboard mill to Southwest Forest Industries for $220 million.

Between 1975 and 1980, IP's operating profits were mediocre. Again it turned to new management for help, and in 1978 Edwin Gee stepped in as chairman. A chemical engineer, Gee recognized that many of the company's 16 pulp and paper mills—all built in the 1920s and 1930s—were wasting labor and energy. Immediately, he instituted a $6 billion program to modernize the plants. Gee's goal was to turn the world's largest paper company into one of the lowest-cost producers of white paper and packaging materials, thus making it one of the most profitable papermakers as well.

To raise money for Gee's plan IP sold its remaining interest in General Crude Oil Company for $763 million and used the profits to buy Bodcaw Company of Dallas in 1979. Bodcaw added a highly efficient linerboard mill in Pineville, Louisiana, and 420,000 acres of prime timberland. In 1981 IP sold Canadian International Paper for US$900 million. In addition, Gee increased the research-and-development budget and reduced IP's labor force by 20 percent. By 1982 he had raised US$2 billion, aided by sales of land, timber, and other subsidiaries.

After determining that only two of the six major packaging mills were operating efficiently, Gee sold one mill, shut down three others, and invested $600 million in the Mansfield, Louisiana, mill. In April 1981 IP unveiled a new southern pine plywood and lumber manufacturing plant in Springhill, Louisiana. The $60 million facility, the brainchild of Gee, featured the latest computerized process controls and supplied the container board mill in Mansfield plus paper and pulp mills at Camden, Arkansas, and in Bastrop, Louisiana.

In the same year, John Georges became chief operating officer. His solution to IP's production problems was not to build new plants but to remodel existing facilities. The company also spent $500 million on remodeling a Georgetown, South Carolina, mill, changing its product focus in the process. Instead of brown linerboard, a cyclical product, part of the plant was set up to make white papers. The white paper business was to offer a faster-growing and more stable market.

In addition, Georges began a $350 million project to convert another mill in Mobile, Alabama. The 60-year-old facility, which housed the company's last remaining newsprint machine, was also remodeled to produce white papers in 1985, thus marking the end of the company's long-standing newsprint business. In 1987, newsprint prices began a steady decline.

A recession in the early 1980s meant further delays but the investments began to bear fruit in the mid-1980s. As a result of new automation, IP's production costs decreased 11 percent between 1981 and 1987 and its mills were able to use 25 percent less energy. Georges was named chairman in 1985, succeeding Gee.

The appointment had been preceded in 1984 by a decline in linerboard and pulp prices and a 14-year low in earnings. The white-paper market seemed to be one of the few that was profitable, so Georges hired a team of scientists and technicians to promote business in that area. Their work led to a major acquisition in 1986: Hammermill Paper Company. The $1.1 billion purchase increased IP's white-paper capacity by 750,000 tons and provided the technology to produce premium paper lines. Georges also reduced the number of salaried employees from 12,000 in 1981 to 9,200 in 1988, and streamlined management. Under his leadership, the firm also acquired Anitec Image Technology Corporation, maker of photographic film, papers, and darkroom chemicals; Avery Corporation, a Chicago-based envelope manufacturer; and Kendall Company's nonwoven fabrics division. As a result, profits improved in 1988 and set a record in 1989.

In addition to the company's recovery, however, it also weathered several crises. These included a 1984 fire that destroyed its Nacogdoches, Texas, plywood-manufacturing plant, causing $32.5 million in damages. The facility reopened in 1986 after being equipped to produce oriented-strand board. In 1987, to protest inadequate wages and benefits, 2,200 workers went on strike at paper mills in Alabama, Maine, Mississippi, and Wisconsin.

Under Georges's leadership, the watchword at IP in the late 1980s and early 1990s was diversity, both in geography and product mix. His aim was to lessen the firm's vulnerability to the cyclical nature of its core paper, packaging, and forestry operations. Many of the international acquisitions that Georges

pursued were aimed at expanding IP further into the area of specialty products, which generally produce higher margins. These products included photographic paper and films, specialty industrial papers, molded-wood products, laminated products, and nonwoven fabrics such as disposable diapers. Although similar in some ways to the firm's diversification of the 1960s, this round of expansion proved more successful.

Heading into its overseas spending spree, International Paper already owned box-manufacturing facilities in Italy, the Netherlands, Spain, Sweden, and the United Kingdom. In 1989 it acquired two major European manufacturers, Aussedat-Rey, the second-largest paper company in France, and the Ilford photographic-products division of Ciba-Geigy. In 1990 IP bought Germany's Zanders Feinpapiere AG, a high-quality coated-paper company, and the French operations of Georgia-Pacific Corporation.

The following year, in addition to bolstering its domestic base with the purchase of two U.S. paper companies—Dillon Paper and Leslie Paper—and its European holdings with the acquisition of Scaldia Paper BV of the Netherlands and the packaging equipment business of Dominion Industries Ltd., IP gained a presence in the Pacific Rim through a $258 million purchase of a 16 percent interest in the leading New Zealand forest-products company, Carter Holt Harvey Ltd. (CHH). IP increased its stake in CHH in 1992 to 24 percent by investing an additional $298 million. In addition to its dominance of its home market, CHH was a major exporter of forest products to Australia and Asia. Also in 1992, IP paid $209 million for an 11 percent stake in Israel's Scitex Corporation Ltd., a world leader in color electronic-imaging equipment. The stake was increased to 12 percent the following year. The company also purchased Kwidzyn from the government of Poland for $150 million and the promise to invest $75 million more in the firm, the country's largest white-paper manufacturer and operator of one of the most modern paper mills in Eastern Europe.

IP's diversification program appeared to pay off in the early 1990s when the paper industry encountered one of its worst cyclical downturns in 50 years. While competitors Boise Cascade Corp. and Champion International Corp. posted huge losses, IP continued to report profits, albeit smaller than those of 1988–90. Sales in 1992 hit a record $13.6 billion, although earnings were reduced substantially by a $263 million restructuring charge for the closure and consolidation of 20 underperforming mills and sales offices worldwide.

IP continued to expand aggressively in the mid-1990s. In 1994 its distribution unit picked up two paper-distributing companies in Mexico, while in the area of liquid packaging, a new plant was built in Brazil and a joint venture was formed in China to build and operate a plant near Shanghai. IP made its biggest purchases yet in 1995, however. The firm spent $1.15 billion to attain majority control of New Zealand-based Carter Holt Harvey Ltd. and $64 million to acquire DSM, a producer of ink and adhesive resin based in the Netherlands. IP attempted to acquire Holvis AG, a Swiss fiber and paper company, for $422 million but was rebuffed by the Holvis board. Late in 1995 IP announced a $3.6 billion purchase of Federal Paper Board Co., based in Montvale, New Jersey, and the 15th-largest paper company in the United States. Federal Paper specialized in bleached paperboard used for cigarette cartons, laundry detergent, and other consumer products, and added to IP's packaging operations would give IP about one-third of the bleached board market.

Fittingly, the Federal Paper acquisition was consummated nearly simultaneously with the announcement of Georges's retirement as chairman and CEO, both of which occurred in early 1996. Georges's diversification program had increased non-U.S. sales to 30 percent of total sales by 1994. And while IP's core paper, pulp, and paperboard businesses accounted for 78 percent of sales in 1988, they accounted for only 52 percent of sales by 1994. During the same period, IP's specialty products' share of sales increased from just 3.7 percent to 17.3 percent.

John T. Dillon, previously president and COO, succeeded Georges as chairman and CEO of International Paper. Although Dillon inherited a company in an enviably strong position, some observers felt that he might make some moves to refocus IP on its core businesses. IP had already exited the envelope business late in 1995 and divestments of additional specialty businesses were seen as possible, in particular given the $816 million in long-term debt IP took on as part of the Federal Paper deal.

Principal Subsidiaries

Anchor/Lith-Kem-Ko, Inc.; Federal Paper Board Co.; Ingram Paper Company; International Paper Realty Corp.; International Pulp Sales Company; IP Forest Resources Company; IP Timberlands, Ltd.; Ilford Inc.; Masonite Corporation; International Paper Company Pty. Limited (Australia); Anitec Image International B.V. (Belgium); International Paper (Europe) S.A. (Belgium); Veratec S.A. (Belgium); International Paper Canada, Inc.; Productora de Papeles S.A. (Colombia; 36.16%); Societe Mediterraneenne d'Emballages (France); Societe Normande de Carton Ondule (France); Hammermill Paper GmbH (Germany); Societe Guadeloupeene de Carton Ondule (Guadeloupe); International Paper (Asia) Limited (Hong Kong); International Paper USA Ltd. (Israel); Scitex Corporation Ltd. (Israel; 12%); International Paper Italia S.p.A. (Italy); International Paper Company (Japan) Ltd.; IPI Corporation (Japan; 51%); Veratec Japan, Ltd.; International Paper Korea Ltd. (80%); Societe Martiniquaise de Carton Ondule (Martinique); Akrosil Europe B.V. (Netherlands); Carter Holt Harvey Ltd. (New Zealand;

50.1%); Zaklady Celulozowa-Papierniecze S.A. w Kwidzynie (Poland); Cartonajes International, S.A. (Spain); Industrias De Tableros Y Derivados De La Madera, S.A. (Spain); International Paper (Espana), S.L. (Spain); International Paper Company (Europe) Limited (Switzerland); International Paper Taiwan Ltd; Envases Internacional S.A. (Venezuela; 51%).

Principal Divisions

Akrosil; Arizona Chemical; Bagpak; Building Materials Distribution; Bulkley Dunton JB Papers; Coated Papers Division; Containerboard Division; Dillard Paper Company; Dixon Paper Co.; Folding Carton Division; GCO Minerals Co.; Hammermill Papers; Imaging Products; International Paper-Bleached Board; International Paper-Distribution Group; Label Division; Masonite; Nevamar; Nicolet; Kraft Paper; Leslie Paper; Liquid Packaging; Springhill Papers; U.S. Container; Uniwood; Wood Products.

Principal Operating Units

Distribution; Forest Products; Printing Papers; Packaging; Specialty Products.

Further Reading

International Paper: Your Decision, Purchase: N.Y.: International Paper Company.

Killian, Linda, "A Walk in the Woods," *Forbes,* September 30, 1991, pp. 78–79.

Kimelman, John, "Slash and Build: While Restructuring at Home, International Paper Is Investing Overseas," *Financial World,* April 13, 1993, p. 28.

Loeffelholz, Suzanne, "Putting It on Paper," *Financial World,* July 25, 1989, p. 26.

Osborne, Richard, "An Unpretentious Giant: John Georges Has Quietly Built International Paper into a Diversified $15 Billion Corporation," *Industry Week,* June 19, 1995, pp. 73–76.

Palmer, Jay, "No Lumbering Giant: International Paper Races to New Peaks in Earnings," *Barron's,* January 2, 1989, p. 13.

"Pulp Friction," *Economist,* November 11, 1995, p. 66.

Young, Jim, "International Paper Co.: Worldwide Expansions Gear for Economic Recovery," *Pulp & Paper,* May 1994, pp. 32, 35.

—Kim M. Magon
—updated by David E. Salamie

Inter-Regional Financial Group, Inc.

Dain Bosworth Plaza
60 South Sixth Street
Minneapolis, Minnesota 55402-4422
U.S.A.
(612) 371-7750
Fax: (612) 371-7933

Public Company
Incorporated: 1909 as Kalman & Co.
Employees: 3,340
Sales: $542 million (1995)
Stock Exchanges: New York
SICs: 6211 Security Brokers & Dealers; 6289 Security &
Commodity Services, Not Elsewhere Classified

Inter-Regional Financial Group, Inc. (IFG) is one of the nation's ten largest full-service regional brokerage and investment banking companies. It operates through two subsidiaries that serve clients primarily in the western half of the United States: Dain Bosworth Incorporated, based in Minneapolis, and Rauscher Pierce Refsnes, Inc., which is headquartered in Dallas. IFG also supports smaller investment and asset management units as well as an operations and technology group.

IFG's roots reach back to 1909, when Oscar Kalman started a small brokerage shop in St. Paul, Minnesota. The venture, dubbed Kalman & Co., began selling stocks and municipal bonds to local customers. Kalman's shop was just one of many brokerage businesses that opened in the United States during the early part of the century. In fact, a surging industrial base generated huge markets for stocks and bonds, particularly during the 1920s. Several of the companies created to serve those markets would eventually be consolidated into the company that would become Inter-Regional Financial Group.

Kalman was the earliest of those companies. It was followed in 1916 by a Denver, Colorado, venture named Bosworth, Chanute, Loughridge & Co. That firm was formed by Arthur Bosworth, Octave Chanute, and Paul Loughridge. They created the company to take advantage of, and facilitate, municipal growth during a boom in Denver's economy. Other companies that would later join to form IFG included Quail & Co., which was founded in Iowa in 1922, and Sullivan & Co., another Denver firm that opened in 1927. But the enterprise that would later be credited with engineering the amalgamation of a brokerage network in the western United States was started by J.M. Dain in 1929, right before the infamous stock market crash that kicked off the Great Depression.

J.M. Dain had moved to Minneapolis in 1922 to represent a Chicago investment firm. In 1929 he decided to branch out on his own with J.M. Dain & Co., a municipal bond trading house. He hired a secretary, Mary Donohue, and opened a small office in Minneapolis. His timing couldn't have been worse. The stock market crash and ensuing depression devastated financial markets. Despite tough times, Dain persevered and, unlike many of the more established trading houses, managed to survive. Another company that started and managed to survive during the Depression was an enterprise that would become Rauscher Pierce Refsnes. That venture would become Dain's sister firm in the 1970s.

Merrill Cohen took control of Dain & Co. in 1933 and helped steer it through the crises and into the 1940s. Dain & Co.'s growth was relatively slow, but by the late 1950s the organization was employing 75 workers in eight offices. Dain began to expand much more quickly in the 1960s. That progress was largely the result of the efforts of Wheelock Whitney, who became chief executive of Dain in 1963. It was under his direction that Dain launched an aggressive growth and diversification drive. To that end, J.M. Dain & Co. merged with Kalman & Co. in 1967. Shortly thereafter the company purchased Quail & Co. The resultant organization became Dain, Kalman & Quail, Inc.

In addition to the mergers, Dain launched a new real estate affiliate in 1968 (later called Dain Corporation). By the late 1960s Dain, Kalman, & Quail, Inc. was sporting 17 offices in six upper-midwestern and western states including the Dakotas and Wyoming. Its headquarter offices swelled to house 400 employees and the name of its office building, the Rand Tower, was changed to Dain Tower to reflect the prominence of its major tenant. Dain acquired two other firms in the late 1960s before going public in 1972 with the sale of 250,000 shares on the New York Stock Exchange. A year later the company bought out Bosworth, Sullivan & Co., which was the successor to Bosworth, Chanute, Loughridge & Co.

It was in 1973 that Inter-Regional Financial Group, Inc. was formed. IFG was created by Dain as a holding company that effectively existed to own the assets of two separate companies; Dain, Kalman, & Quail, Inc. and Bosworth, Sullivan & Co. Those two organizations would operate as separate entities until 1979, when they were fused into Dain Bosworth Incorporated. Thus, Inter-Regional had become a major regional broker with offices in the Midwest and western United States through Dain Bosworth. Furthermore, its Dallas-based Rauscher Pierce Refsnes brokerage subsidiary gave it a powerful presence in the Southwest.

As it labored to expand its sprawling brokerage network in the western half of the United States during the 1970s and early 1980s, IFG simultaneously stepped up its effort to diversify into new markets. To that end, the company launched a number of new ventures and initiatives. Besides its Dain Corporation real estate affiliate, IFG started an investment consulting business (Investment Advisers) and even purchased a life insurance company (Midwest Life), among other ventures. In the early 1980s it also laid plans to open up its own savings and loan business, although that effort was ultimately thwarted by federal regulators.

Among IFG's most successful endeavors during the 1970s was IFG Leasing, a subsidiary that derived most of its income from leasing farm and office equipment. The business took off during the mid-1970s and, at its peak, was accounting for roughly 50 percent of IFG's entire earnings base. Unfortunately, IFG Leasing's prosperity began to wane in the late 1970s, signaling a period of misfortune for Inter-Regional Financial Group. Indeed, IFG Leasing's profits started tumbling in the late 1970s and continued to fall into the early 1980s. IFG Leasing finally became such a drag on IFG's bottom line that it almost forced its parent into bankruptcy.

IFG Leasing's problems began with the recession of the late 1970s and early 1980s. During the mid-1970s, the company profited from heavy leverage; it borrowed money to purchase equipment, which it leased to customers. The profit margin consisted of the spread between the lease rate charged to customers and the interest rate charged by IFG Leasing's lenders. The strategy failed when interest rates exploded under the Carter administration. Furthermore, because of the recession, many customers simply couldn't pay their bills. The net result was that IFG Leasing began hemorrhaging cash, paying high interest rates and generating insufficient cash flow from its troubled customer base.

By the mid-1980s IFG was teetering on the edge of bankruptcy. Augmenting problems with the leasing division was the disappointing performance of the Rauscher Pierce subsidiary and the Midwest Life unit. IFG managed to obscure problems with its leasing division until 1983, when the dilemma began to climax and IFG decided to shutter the subsidiary. As its troubles

became more obvious, IFG's stock price plummeted; from about $25 in 1983 to less than $10 in late 1985. By 1985, in fact, the company's long-term debt had climbed to $73 million (from just $10 million in 1981). Furthermore, IFG had lost $60 million between 1983 and 1985. Investors feared that the company was barreling toward bankruptcy.

Rising to the chief executive post during IFG's management shakeout in the mid-1980s was Richard D. McFarland, who succeeded Thomas Holloran in June of 1985. McFarland had started with Dain as a salesman in the 1960s and had progressed through the ranks before he became president of IFG in 1982. He was moved to the top slot in 1985 by a board of directors that was eager for a turnaround. Among IFG's first moves under McFarland's direction was to put Investment Advisers and Midwest Life on the auction block. Both subsidiaries were profitable at the time. The sale of the money management unit helped to reduce IFG's debt and allowed management to begin refocusing its attention on its core brokerage businesses.

Management's streamlining efforts were augmented by rebounding trading markets in 1986 and early 1987, when surging stock markets allowed IFG's core trading business to post record revenue and income figures. Meanwhile, new management continued to chip away at past problems. Among other moves, executives fired and successfully sued IFG's auditors, and managed to sell the life insurance business. During the late 1980s, moreover, the company began to reduce its brokerage staff and to improve the average commissions earned per broker. Although IFG posted a net loss in 1988, it appeared as though it had emerged from its crises by the end of the decade.

Inter-Regional's rebound during the late 1980s and early 1990s was largely attributable to the efforts of Iring Weiser, the man that McFarland had hired to serve as president of IFG. Weiser had served as an attorney for IFG's outside counsel before McFarland lured him away in 1985. The 38-year-old Weiser, a Polish Jewish immigrant, had experience in the industry, although he had never made a trade. His problem-fixing skills became valuable to IFG. Among other moves, for example, he helped to reorganize the real estate division after that industry collapsed in the late 1980s.

IFG continued to draw on Weiser's management skills during the early 1990s, during which he was promoted to chairman of the company. During that period, IFG emphasized its securities trading businesses, cut costs, and managed to boost revenue and profits. To that end, Weiser eliminated some poorly performing offices and continued to shrink the company's total work force. Healthy markets helped IFG to grow its revenue from about $312 million in 1990 to more than $500 million in 1993, about $47.6 million of which was netted as income. In 1993, in fact, the company started to expand again.

In late 1993 and 1994 IFG opened 14 new offices for a total of 93 in 23 states. It also started hiring new brokers, bringing the total brokerage staff at its two firms to a record 1,250 by year's end. Furthermore, IFG expanded eastward with the acquisitions of Clayton Brown Holding Company, a privately held, Chicago-based firm specializing in fixed-income securities. By late 1995 IFG was the tenth-largest full-service regional brokerage house in the nation and the leading broker in its region. The company posted record revenue of $542 million for 1995. About one-third of that amount came from Rauscher Pierce and most of the remainder was attributable to Dain Bosworth.

Principal Subsidiaries

Dain Bosworth Inc.; Dain Equity Partners, Inc.; Dain Kalman & Quail Municipal-Nebraska, Inc.; Clayton Brown Capital Corp.; Regional Operations Group, Inc.; Rauscher Pierce Refsnes, Inc.; Rauscher Pierce Refsnes Leasing, Inc.; RP Transportation Corp.; RPR Mortgage Finance Corp.; IFG Asset Management Services, Inc.

Principal Divisions

Dain Bosworth Retail Sales Group; Dain Bosworth Corporate Capital Group; Dain Bosworth Fixed Income Group; Rauscher Pierce Refsnes Retail Sales Group; Rauscher Pierce Refsnes Fixed Income Group; Rauscher Pierce Refsnes Corporate Capital Group; Rauscher Pierce Refsnes RPR Clearing Services.

Further Reading

Allen, James C., "School Finance Guru Jumps From First Southwest Ship," *Dallas Business Journal,* December 24, 1993, p. 1.

"A Commitment To Service, A Tradition of Trust," company document. Minneapolis: Inter-Regional Financial Group, Inc., 1994.

Foran, Pat, "Dain Bosworth's Local Foray Was Capital Idea, Observers Say," *Business Journal-Milwaukee,* February 6, 1989, Sec. 2, p. 1.

French, B. J., "David A. Smith to Step down as CEO of Rauscher Pierce Refsnes Inc.," *PR Newswire,* September 27, 1995.

Hayes, John R., "All's Fair," *Forbes,* November 21, 1994, p. 46.

Lowe, Sandra, "Rauscher Pierce Expands Locally," *San Antonio Business Journal,* May 20, 1994, p. 4.

Rich, Andrew, "IPO Emerges Out of a Deep Hole," *Minneapolis-St. Paul City Business,* July 15, 1987, p. 1.

Schafer, Lee, "Inter-Regional Financial Group," *Corporate Report Minnesota,* February 1990, p. 21.

St. Anthony, Neal, "New IFG Exec's Initial Challenge: Brokerage Merger," *Star Tribune,* May 18, 1992, Bus. Sec.

Tosto, Paul, "Inter-Regional Financial Executives Reap Bonus Bonanza," *Minneapolis-St. Paul City Business,* April 8, 1991, p. 1.

Walden, Gene, "IFG Finds Diversifications a Dangerous Game," *Minneapolis-St. Paul City Business,* October 9, 1985, p. 1.

—Dave Mote

INTRAWEST

The Intrawest Corporation

200 Burrard Street, Suite 800
Vancouver, British Columbia V6C 3L6
Canada
(604) 669-9777
Fax: (604) 669-0605

Public Company
Incorporated: 1979
Employees: 1,500
Revenues: C$194.7 million (1995)
Stock Exchanges: Toronto Montreal Vancouver
SICs: 7011 Ski Lodges and Resorts

The Intrawest Corporation, based in Vancouver, British Columbia, Canada, is the fourth largest operator of ski resorts in North America. Its ski resorts, with a combined two million skier days (one skier paying for one day of skiing), include Blackcomb Mountain and Panorama Resort in British Columbia, Mont Tremblant in Quebec Province, Snowshoe Mountain Resort in West Virginia, and the Stratton Ski Resort in Vermont. In 1996, the company also purchased a 33 percent share of the Mammoth Mountain Ski Area, which included Mammoth Mountain and June Mountain, in Mammoth Lake, California. Intrawest also developed several major residential and commercial projects in Canada and Seattle, including the Gateway Urban Centre in Surrey, British Columbia; Park Plaza in Edmonton, Alberta; the Pacific Reach Business Park in Vancouver, British Columbia; and Arbor Place in Seattle. However, the company began divesting itself of non-resort-related properties in the mid-1990s. Its stated corporate strategy in 1996 was to become North America's leading operator of mountain resorts, primarily through acquisitions in the United States.

Early History

Intrawest Properties Ltd. was formed in 1973 as a Vancouver real estate development firm by Joe Houssian, a native of Regina, Saskatchewan, with a master's degree in business administration from the University of British Columbia. He was joined in this venture by a Lebanese cousin, Mo Faris, who had financial contacts in Europe and the Middle East. Faris would leave the company when it went public in 1991.

For the first six years, the company concentrated on residential real estate, developing 26 projects encompassing about 1,800 apartments, townhouses, and single-family homes in Vancouver, as well as in Edmonton and Calgary, Alberta. In 1979, Intrawest Properties Ltd. and Intrawest Equities Ltd. were merged to create the Intrawest Development Corporation.

Intrawest expanded into commercial real estate in 1981 when it acquired the Cedarbrae Shopping Centre, then under construction in Calgary. That was followed by development of the Glenmore Landing Shopping Centre in Calgary, completed in 1985, and the Lonsdale Quay Public Market and Hotel, a mixed-use development in North Vancouver completed in 1986. In the mid-1980s, Intrawest also expanded into the United States, completing its first major U.S. project, Arbor Place, a $28 million residential and office complex in Seattle, in 1989.

The First Resorts: Blackcomb Mountain and Mont Tremblant

In 1986, Intrawest acquired half interest in Blackcomb Skiing Enterprises, which operated a ski resort on Blackcomb Mountain at Whistler Village, British Columbia, from the Aspen Skiing Company. That entrée into the resort business would eventually change the company's strategic focus.

Aspen Skiing, originally a partnership between 20th Century Fox and Alberta businessman Alan Graham, had formed Blackcomb Skiing Enterprises and begun developing Blackcomb in conjunction with the British Columbia provincial government in 1978. The resort opened in 1980, and after a new T-bar lift was installed in 1985, boasted the greatest vertical drop in North America: 5,280 feet.

Blackcomb quickly gained popularity among skiers. But by 1986, 20th Century Fox, then owned by U.S. billionaire Marvin Davis, had decided to sell its ski operations. Hugh Smythe, a Canadian from New Westminster, British Columbia, who had been managing Blackcomb, met Joe Houssian at a Young

Presidents Association dinner in Vancouver, and talked to him about purchasing the resort. Houssian, then 36, who admitted knowing practically nothing about the ski-resort business, negotiated to buy 50 percent of Blackcomb Skiing Enterprises for about $3.7 million, with an option to acquire the other 50 percent in five years for $5.8 million.

Intrawest then launched a $112 million expansion and upgrading of skiing and resort facilities at Blackcomb Mountain, adding a mountain-top restaurant and ultimately increasing resort capacity from 4,000 to 14,000 skiers per day. As a result, skier visits increased from 278,000 in 1986 to 972,000 in 1995. Blackcomb Skiing Enterprises had a management lease with the provincial government of British Columbia, which owned the mountain property, to operate the ski resort until 2029.

As part of its purchase of Blackcomb Skiing Enterprises, Intrawest also gained development rights to 118 acres at the base of the mountain, along with 8,000 "bed units" under Whistler Village's land-use regulations. Intrawest sold several parcels of land and assigned bed units to other developers to promote immediate use of the ski resort. In 1989, Intrawest also began developing residential projects of its own on the remaining land. By 1993, the company had completed more than 1,400 "resort units."

Intrawest went public in 1991, raising $26 million for 27 percent of the company's equity. Later that year, the company paid an estimated $22 million to acquire Mont Tremblant Resort, Inc., which managed a four-season resort and Canada's oldest operating ski area in the Laurentian Mountains north of Montreal, Quebec. The Mont Tremblant Resort, which had opened in 1939, included a summer beach and tennis club and 16,500 acres of mountain terrain leased from the Quebec provincial government. The lease ran through 2051.

As it did at Blackcomb, Intrawest expanded and upgraded resort facilities at Mont Tremblant, investing $48 million between 1991 and 1995, and increasing capacity from 8,500 skiers per day to 14,500. Included in the expansion were a 1,000-seat mountain top restaurant, an 18-hole golf course, and The Edge, the first new peak opened for skiing at Mont Tremblant since 1943. To help finance the expansion, Intrawest sold 23 percent of Blackcomb Skiing Enterprises to the Nippon Cable Company in Japan for $18 million.

Along with Mont Tremblant Resort, Inc., Intrawest also acquired 1,800 acres at the base of the mountain, which the company intended to develop as a $400 million, master-planned community, much like Whistler Village, including retail shops, several condominium and townhouse developments, and a full-service hotel projected to be completed by 1997. Intrawest was to have a 49 percent share of the proposed 308-room Chateau Mont Tremblant. Also in the works was Vieux Tremblant, a recreation of "old Mont Tremblant" with several renovated buildings from the 1940s. In 1994, Tremblant received Quebec's Grand Prize for the Development of Tourism.

In 1993, the Intrawest Development Corporation officially changed its name to the Intrawest Corporation. The company also acquired its third ski resort, Panorama Resort, near Invermere, British Columbia, for about $7.1 million. Panorama, a family-oriented resort at the edge of the Bugaboo mountains,

included a 107-room hotel, a tennis complex, and about 300 acres of land for development.

Intrawest also entered into a joint real-estate venture with Ralcorp Holdings, Inc., which owned the Keystone Resort in Keystone, Colorado, to develop a resort village called The Village at River Run. Ralcorp Holdings, a subsidiary of the Ralston Purina Company, also owned the nearby Breckenridge Ski Resort.

Intrawest entered the $4 billion vacation-club industry in 1993 by forming the Intrawest Resort Ownership Corporation, with Intrawest Resort Club members receiving an annual allotment of points that entitled them to stay at various club properties. The first Intrawest Resort Club, a 45-unit condominium development at Blackcomb Mountain, opened in 1994, and the company sold 500 memberships in the first six months. By 1996, Intrawest also had resort club facilities at Tremblant and had plans for club resorts in southern California, Hawaii, the Caribbean, Costa Rica, Mexico, and Florida.

Focusing on Resort Properties in the 1990s

Intrawest, which had retained an ownership interest in many of its larger residential and commercial developments, began divesting itself of all non-resort-related real estate in 1994, selling nearly half of its non-resort properties, including The Newmark and Belltown Court residential and retail developments in Seattle, and Station Tower, a high-rise office complex in Surrey, British Columbia, for $158 million. In 1996, Intrawest's remaining non-resort properties consisted primarily of undeveloped land and residential projects under construction. Emphasizing its decision to become "a pure resort company," Intrawest also reorganized into three operating divisions: the Resort Operations Group (with Smythe as president), the Resort Development Group, and the Resort Club Group.

Intrawest expanded its interest in the U.S. resort market in 1994 by acquiring the Stratton Ski Corporation, owner of the four-season Stratton Mountain Resort in southern Vermont, which included a 27-hole golf course, golf school, and sports and tennis complexes. Stratton was purchased from Victoria U.S.A., which had owned the resort since 1988.

The company followed up in 1995 by acquiring the Snowshoe Mountain Resort and the neighboring four-season Silver Creek Mountain Resort in West Virginia, which included an 18-hole golf course and 10,000 acres of land. Snowshoe, which opened in 1973, averaged 400,000 skier visits per year, making it the largest ski resort in the midatlantic and southeastern regions of the United States.

In January 1996, Intrawest announced that it had purchased a 33 percent interest in the Mammoth Mountain Ski Area, which included Mammoth Mountain and June Mountain, in Mammoth Lake, California, east of San Francisco in the Sierra Nevada mountains. With more than one million skiers annually, Mammoth was the official training center for the U.S. Olympic Ski Team, and ranked second only to the facilities at Vail, Colorado, in popularity and size.

Intrawest also acquired all the developable real estate owned by Mammoth Mountain including 92 acres at June Mountain and 14 acres in the town of Mammoth Lakes, and negotiated right of first refusal if Dave McCoy, founder, president and controlling shareholder of Mammoth Mountain, or his family decided to sell his remaining interest in the ski area. McCoy had reportedly opened Mammoth Mountain in 1938 with a portable rope tow he bought by selling his Harley Davidson motorcycle. He purchased June Mountain in 1986.

Future Growth

Intrawest was basing its strategy for growth on the aging Baby Boomers. In the company's 1993 annual report, founder Joe Houssian, then president and chief executive officer, wrote, "The largest group of buyers of vacation homes is between the ages of 45 and 64. The baby boom generation, which over the past 40 years has fueled so many industries, is now emerging as a catalyst in the leisure and resort industry." In 1994, Houssian said Intrawest's goal was to become "the dominant player in the North American mountain resort industry of the 21st century." Houssian, who became chairman in 1994, was the largest

individual shareholder in 1996 with four percent of the company's stock.

Principal Subsidiaries

Mont Tremblant Resort, Inc.; 2742241 Canada Inc.; Intrawest U.S. Holdings, Inc.; Intrawest U.S.A., Inc.; Intrawest Resort Ownership Corporation; The Stratton Corporation; Blackcomb Skiing Enterprises Ltd. (96.6%); Blackcomb Skiing Enterprises Limited Partnership (77%).

Further Reading

"Intrawest And Its Drive To Be The Best," *Ski Magazine,* October 1995.
Leidl, David, "Joe Houssian on Intrawest," *BC Business,* December 1992, p. 33.
Munk, Nina, "Perfect Partners," *Forbes,* May 23, 1994, p. 90.

—Dean Boyer

Irvin Feld & Kenneth Feld Productions, Inc.

8607 Westwood Center Drive
Vienna, Virginia 22182-7506
U.S.A.
(703) 448-4000
Fax: (703) 448-4100

Private Company
Incorporated: 1932 as Ringling Bros. and Barnum &
    Bailey Combined Shows, Inc.
Sales: $494 million (1993 estimated)
Employees: 2,500
SICs: 3999 Manufacturing Industries, Not Elsewhere
    Classified; 7999 Amusement & Recreation Services,
    Not Elsewhere Classified

Irvin Feld & Kenneth Feld Productions, Inc. is believed to be the largest live-entertainment company in the world. It is best known for mounting the Ringling Bros. and Barnum & Bailey Circus, but it also produces Walt Disney's *World on Ice,* the Siegfried & Roy magic show, and other attractions. Concessions account for about 40 percent of the company's income.

The circus was introduced to the United States in the late 1700s. But it reached unprecedented size and importance when the impresario P.T. Barnum joined W.C. Coup (a former sideshow manager) and Dan Castello (an ex-clown) in forming a tented show in Brooklyn in 1871 under three acres of canvas. The following year a second ring was added so that more customers could be seated, and the circus went on tour, traveling by rail. Founded under the name "Barnum's Great Traveling Museum, Menagerie, Caravan, Hippodrome and Circus," it was soon dubbed by Barnum, with characteristic modesty, "The Greatest Show on Earth." His show traveled successfully for many years.

Barnum formed a partnership with three other circus owners in 1881 to create the Barnum & London Circus. This enterprise introduced the American-style circus of three rings in order to accommodate even more ticketholders. In 1882 Barnum bought

Jumbo, the largest elephant in captivity, from the London Zoo for $10,000. He exhibiting the animal until it was killed in a railway accident in 1885.

James A. Bailey joined Barnum to establish the renamed Barnum & Bailey Circus in the late 1880s. He assumed sole control of the enterprise when Barnum died in 1891. The circus toured Europe from 1897 through 1902. Meanwhile the Ringling Bros. Circus, founded in 1884, had grown into a powerful competitor. A year after Bailey died in 1906, the five Ringling brothers bought a majority interest in the Barnum & Bailey Circus for $410,000. The two circuses continued to travel separately until 1919, when they were combined to form the Ringling Bros. and Barnum & Bailey Circus.

During the golden years between 1910 and 1930, annual earnings often totaled $1 million or more. The company eliminated its only serious competitor in 1929 when it purchased the American Circus Corp., a consortium of five circuses, for $1.7 million. Unfortunately, during the Great Depression John Ringling, the sole surviving founding brother after 1926, lost most of the fortune of $100 million he had accumulated. He subsequently lost control of the circus to a mortgage company in 1932. When he died in 1936, more than 100 lawsuits contested his remaining assets.

John Ringling North, a nephew, borrowed almost $1 million in 1937, paid off the outstanding debts, and was elected president of the enterprise. Under his leadership the Ringling circus installed air conditioning and added Gargantua, a large gorilla billed as "the world's most terrifying living creature." The circus made a steady profit in the following years (visiting 136 cities in 1941) and paid off the bank loan. After North's five-year contract expired, he was replaced in 1943 by Robert Ringling, a cousin. In 1944, the Ringling show suffered the most disastrous fire in circus history; 168 people, two-thirds of them children, died during a matinee performance in Hartford, Connecticut. Only a fraction of the claims for death and injury was covered by insurance and other assets, and Ringling Bros. eventually paid about $4 million in damages. Furthermore, five men went to jail for involuntary manslaughter.

Lingering recriminations concerning the tragedy and its aftermath enabled North to buy majority control of the family enterprise in 1947 and resume direction of the circus. It was under his direction that Ringling Bros., in a renowned effort, hired Igor Stravinsky to compose a ballet for elephants, and George Balanchine to arrange the choreography. By the mid-1950s, however, rising costs and antiquated practices had placed the Ringling circus into deficit. Its manager acknowledged in early 1956 that the enterprise had not been making money on the road for several years. That spring, moreover, the opening was marred by union picket lines, rail delays, and the use of inexperienced nonunion roustabouts. By July, when North closed the show, it had lost $1 million on top of another $1 million deficit in 1955.

The circus reopened for the 1957 season completely transformed. It was a tented show no longer, appearing only in indoor arenas and open-air venues like state fairgrounds. It also began traveling almost completely in trucks rather than railroad cars. The circus band was eliminated, as was (except in New York and Boston) the sideshow and menagerie of animals. These changes enabled Ringling Bros. to reduce its payroll from 1,300 to 300. The remaining employees received pay raises averaging 30 percent but were no longer provided with free room, board, and transportation.

The steady increase in the number of indoor arenas in North America also enabled the circus to extend its season. Instead of, as in the past, returning to winter quarters in Sarasota, Florida, in the first week of November, the 1957 circus continued into the following March before reopening at its traditional April home, New York City's Madison Square Garden. In later years the season extended from the first week in January to the third or last week in November.

Despite changes, Ringling Bros. and Barnum & Bailey Combined Shows, Inc. ran a deficit seven times between 1955 and 1966. In 1967, North, who had been living in Switzerland since 1962, sold the company for $8 million. Some 95 percent of the stock went to the families of Irvin and Israel Feld and the family of Roy Hofheinz, president of the association owning the Houston Astros baseball team and the lease on the Astrodome stadium. In 1963 the circus had drawn a record 162,819 visitors to a four-door Astrodome stay, including a single-performance record of 41,266.

The Feld brothers put up only $100,000 to buy their share of Ringling Bros. and were able to obtain the rest of the cash from other investors and bank loans. They had started in show business as children selling snake oil at carnivals and had long been partners in a number of entertainment ventures, including producing and promoting many of the early rock 'n' roll acts. Irvin, the new president of Ringling Bros., had been a consultant to North and was credited with the changes that modernized the circus in the 1950s.

Soon after taking charge of the company, Irvin Feld established a second touring Ringling circus unit in order to fill more dates. The circus began operating unchanged for two years instead of one, as the units switched circuits in the second year. While the "Blue Unit" was playing Madison Square Garden in the spring of 1970, for example, the "Red Unit," in Birmingham, Alabama, featured a cast including Gunther Gebel-Williams, a German animal trainer whose services Feld had secured in 1968 for $2 million by purchasing an entire European circus. Another addition, in 1973, was Michu, a 33-inch-tall, 25-pound Hungarian billed as the world's smallest man. To improve living conditions for the performers, the number of (double-length) railroad cars used by the circus was increased from 16 cars to 82 by 1983.

Feld also established ancillary sources of revenue, including income from television shows, licensing agreements, and commercial ventures like books and records designed to promote the Ringling name. The company also began to handle its own advertising as part of an effort to cut costs and strengthen profit margins. Among other changes, a clown college was founded at Ringling's winter quarters. Revenues increased from $8.5 million in 1967 to $15.7 million in 1969. The net profit of $125,318 in 1967 grew to $638,935 in 1968 and $832,414 in 1969, while company debt dropped from $5.5 million to $1.8 million in the same period.

Ringling Bros. became a public company in 1969. Sale of stock enabled Feld to finance his ambitious plans for expansion, even though the company was acquired by Mattel Inc. in 1971 for about $47 million in stock. Feld remained president of Ringling Bros. and continued to own its lucrative concessions business, Sells-Floto. The following year Ringling Bros. announced that it would spend $50 million to build "Living World," a circus-like complex on 600 acres near Orlando, Florida. The ill-fated attempt to draw visitors from nearby Disney World ended in a multimillion-dollar loss for Mattel.

Mattel's entertainment division earned $5.3 million in 1978 and just $2.3 million in 1980 before it lost $1.4 million in 1981. For $22.8 million, the company in 1982 sold Ringling Bros. back to Feld and his son, Kenneth, who had joined the circus in 1970 and had been serving as its president while his father was chairman and chief executive officer. The sale included the Ice Follies division and two Holiday on Ice shows that Feld had purchased from Wirtz Productions Ltd. for Mattel in 1979 for $12 million, as well as the Siegfried & Roy *Beyond Belief* illusionist act, acquired the same year. Irvin Feld said the following year that reported Ringling Bros. earnings of $5 million on $70 million in revenues were "approximately correct."

Irvin Feld died in 1984, leaving his 35-year-old son in full charge of Ringling Bros. As his father had done in the late 1960s, he quickly replaced almost all the existing circus performers with the notable exceptions of Gebel-Williams and Satin, an aerial act. By 1987 he had doubled the company's annual revenues to $250 million. During this period Siegfried & Roy played for six-and-a-half years at the Frontier Hotel in Las Vegas, making their act the longest-running hit in the history of the Strip. Subsequently, they were signed by the Mirage Hotel to a record five-year, $57.5-million contract. By 1989 the company name had been changed from Ringling Bros. and Barnum & Bailey Combined Shows to Irvin Feld & Kenneth Feld Productions, reflecting Kenneth Feld's widening interests.

The focus of the ice shows changed in the 1980s from star skaters, who were demanding more money than the Felds wanted to pay, to mostly anonymous skaters portraying licensed Walt Disney characters. Circus performances were placed on videotape, and ''food and taste'' festivals—short-term musical and food celebrations similar to small versions of county fairs—were launched in 1986. At the same time, ''Ringling Readers'' circus-theme publications were developed to help children learn to read. Ringling Bros. Barnum & Bailey Circus retail stores were opened in four cities in 1990, but all except one closed in 1992.

The Ringling Bros. circus was by far the nation's largest in the mid-1990s. In 1995 it visited 95 cities in 48 states, playing to more than 11 million people and giving over 1,200 performances. Each troupe, complete with equipment, was transported from city to city on a train about a mile-and-a-quarter in length.

Feld told *Variety* in 1995 that the circus would add two new touring units during 1996–97; one in Latin America and the other in the Pacific. That year he created a new company, Pachyderm Entertainment, to develop and produce movies, television, and alternative media based upon the circus. Pachyderm also was charged with producing a musical adaptation of the 1988 film *Big*.

Walt Disney's *World on Ice* started traveling abroad in 1986, touring Japan, South America, Southeast Asia, and Australia. There were six units in 1995 playing to about 15 million people a year. Feld Productions' *Super Live Adventure*, created in collaboration with Hollywood producer-director George Lucas, played Japan in 1993. The company also was presenting various theatrical productions and the world's only life-sized replica of the U.S. space shuttle, which toured South Korea in 1995. In all, Feld Production shows were being seen by an estimated 28 million people per year.

Feld Productions' Sells-Floto subsidiary was estimated to account for no less than 40 percent of the parent company's sales in 1993. Income from its concessions included the company's programs, souvenirs, and edibles like cotton candy, which sold for $6 a bucket but cost less than ten cents to produce. It also included a cut of the host arena's own sales from hot dogs, popcorn, and other items. Half of Sells-Floto's take was estimated to be profit, before taxes. Feld Productions also owned Hagenbeck-Wallace, a manufacturer of circus equipment.

Industry sources described Feld as a shrewd and tough manager who was able to extract top dollar from arena managers because of the high quality of his shows. He was also credited

with negotiating desirable booking dates in multiyear contracts that often specified there would be no competing family-oriented attraction for periods as long as 90 days each year before or after a Feld show. Former employees contended that circus people were paid poorly and suffered miserable conditions on circus trains. Indeed, the tight-fisted Feld charged circus performers, who commonly made only about $20 a show, $10 a week to stay on the circus train and 25 cents to ride the company shuttle bus from the train to the arena.

Kenneth Feld owned 82 percent of Irvin Feld & Kenneth Feld Productions in 1994. Three company executives owned the rest. Its headquarters were in Vienna, Virginia (a suburb of Washington, D.C.). A *Forbes* article estimated Feld's worth at more than $300 million in 1994.

Principal Subsidiaries

Feld Brothers Management; Hagenback-Wallace; Klowns Publishing Co.; Pachyderm Entertainment; Sells-Floto.

Further Reading

Berke, Lisa, and Hindes, Andrew, ''Big Top, Big Business,'' *Variety*, July 24–30, 1995, pp. 31, 34, 36, 40.

Galle, William, ''Ringling Bros. Celebrates Centennial with High-Flying Profits,'' *Investment Dealers' Digest*, September 22, 1970, pp. 21–22.

Kobler, John, ''John Ringling North,'' *Life*, August 8, 1949, pp. 86, 90–92, 94, 96, 101.

Langdon, Dorothy, '' 'Lord of the Rings' Irvin Feld Has Made a Fading Circus the Greatest Show on Earth Again,'' *People*, May 12, 1980, pp. 49–50, 53–54, 57.

Le Franco, Robert, ''The Tightest Man in Show Business?'' *Forbes*, November 8, 1993, pp. 67–68, 72–75.

Ogden, Tom. *Two Hundred Years of the American Circus*. New York: Facts on File, 1993.

O'Toole, Thomas and Joanne, ''The Remarkable Ringling Brothers,'' *American History Illustrated*, April 1984, pp. 19–21.

Powers, William F., ''Business Under the Big Tent,'' *Washington Post*, July 11, 1994, Washington Business section, pp. 1, 16–19.

Recio, Maria E., ''Ladies and Gentlemen, Presenting—Kenneth Feld,'' *Business Week*, June 8, 1987, pp. 76–77.

''Ringling Wrangling,'' *Fortune*, July 1947, pp. 114–115, 161–164, 167.

Schwab, Priscilla, ''The Greatest Showman on Earth,'' *Nation's Business*, October 1978, pp. 52, 55–60.

Solomon, Abby, ''Lord of the Rings,'' *Inc.*, February 1983, pp. 101–103, 106, 108.

—Robert Halasz

JG Industries, Inc.

1615 W. Chicago Avenue
Chicago, Illinois 60622
U.S.A.
(312) 850-8000
Fax: (312) 787-5625

Public Company
Incorporated: 1928 as Goldblatt Brothers., Inc.
Employees: 2,061
Sales: $196.2 million (1994)
Stock Exchanges: Chicago NASDAQ
SICs: 5712 Furniture Stores; 5661 Shoe Stores

JG Industries, Inc., is the holding company for Goldblatt's Department Stores, one of Chicago's oldest discount retailers. Under the slogan "The Incredible Bargain Centers," Goldlatt's 14 stores primarily operate in inner city neighborhoods and cater to poor and immigrant populations by offering goods at deeply discounted prices. Twelve stores are located in Chicago, with the two remaining stores in Homewood, Illinois, and Hammond, Indiana. Approximately 50 percent of sales are in apparel, which are often name-brand factory seconds or purchased through diverters, while the stores also sell linens and domestics and everything from shoes to small radios to kitchen and other household supplies. After declaring bankruptcy in 1981, Goldblatt's has returned to profitability. Its holding company, JG Industries, is partly owned by Jupiter Industries, Inc., a private Chicago-based corporation headed by real estate magnate Jerrold Wexler, which controlled approximately 55 percent of JG in 1995. A series of divestitures, most recently of JG's 58 percent interest in Huffman-Koos Inc., a New Jersey-based furniture retailer, signals JG's intention to focus its future growth strategy on its Goldblatt's store chain.

At its height, Goldblatt Brothers Inc. operated 47 stores, including its 11-story flagship store on Chicago's State Street, and accounted for fully 15 percent of the Chicago area's retail sales. From the beginning, Goldblatt's was a family operation, founded in 1914 by brothers Nate and Maurice Goldblatt, who were assisted by their two younger brothers, Joel and Louis. The Goldblatt family immigrated to the United States from the village of Stachev, Poland. Father Simon Goldblatt, a former chief rabbi, and oldest sons Nate and Maurice arrived in 1904. Two years later, they had saved enough money to send for the rest of the family, which included mother Hannah, son Louis, and four daughters. Joel Goldblatt was born in the United States the following year.

The family operated a grocery store and butcher shop on Chicago's West Side, living in an apartment behind the store. As was common with immigrant families, all of the children were expected to work and to contribute their earnings to the family pot. Family financial decisions were generally made by consensus, under the direction of Hannah Goldblatt. In 1914 oldest sons Maurice and Nate, then 21 and 19 years old, opened a small store near the corner of Chicago and Ashland Avenues, using $1,500 from the family pot. Administrative duties were handled by Maurice, while Nate acted as the store's merchandiser. Louis swept the floors, and Joel worked as cashier. The store catered to a largely poor, Polish-Ukrainian immigrant population, who traditionally shopped in their own neighborhood, walking to stores.

By 1922, the Goldblatt brothers recorded sales of over $800,000; five years later, sales had more than quadrupled, to $3.7 million, and a second store was added. The following year, the brothers incorporated as Goldblatt Brothers, Inc., with Maurice serving as president. Goldblatt's continued its successful discount formula; as a result, the stock market crash and resulting depression of 1929 presented an opportunity for the company to grow at a time when most businesses were failing. In that year, Goldblatt's acquired Lederer Company Department Stores, the H. C. Struve Company, and the Fields Furniture Company, all of Chicago. Two years later, the company bought up the department store operations of Loren Miller & Co. in Chicago and Kaufman S. Wolf, Inc., of Hammond, Indiana. In 1933, Nate Goldblatt brought the company's buyers to New York, together with $300,000 in cash, buying up goods from suppliers desperate to unload their inventories, a move that would have a significant impact on the company's success. In that year the company also opened a new store in Joliet, Illinois, in the former L. F. Beach department store building.

Sales jumped to $28 million in 1934, with a net income of over $1 million. The company operated seven stores, including five in Chicago, one in Joliet, and one in Hammond. Property was purchased for a store on Chicago's Southwest Side, and in 1936, Goldblatt's opened its flagship State Street store, purchased from the Chicago retail giant Marshall Fields Co. With that purchase, Goldblatt's ventured into more upscale products, with an inventory that included everything from appliances and apparel to delicatessen and confectionery products. Ten years later, with the acquisition of Chicago-based Logan Department Stores, there were fifteen Goldblatt's stores and a central distribution center, employing more than 2,500 people, and bringing in more than $62 million in annual sales, with net income of $1.25 million.

The Goldblatt Brothers developed lavish lifestyles. Younger brothers Louis and Joel took up residence in Chicago's exclusive Drake Hotel, or sailed on Joel's 150-foot yacht, while Nate's mansion in a Chicago suburb featured an indoor pool and Egyptian mummy. The company also supported many other family members, including two brothers-in-law who joined the company after their own businesses failed. Major decisions continued to be made by consensus. Quarrels erupted frequently among the brothers, but were usually settled by Hannah Goldblatt's influence.

Hannah Goldblatt's death in 1941, followed by Nate Goldblatt's death in 1944, marked the beginning of Goldblatt's decline. The quarrels among the remaining brothers grew more frequent and bitter without their mother's guidance. Joel Goldblatt took over as the company's president, handling its merchandising and administration. Sales continued to climb, to $95 million in 1949, but income did not keep the same pace, reaching only $1.5 million in that year. The company's attempt to expand into Buffalo, New York, opening one store in that city, met with limited success. The pace of new store openings and acquisitions slowed; until 1944, the company had averaged four new stores each year. By the end of the 1950s, however, the company still operated only 20 stores. Sales were flat through the decade, hovering at just over $100 million per year, while income saw a slow decline, down to $600,000 on revenues of $116 million in 1962.

Under Joel's leadership, the company attempted to expand into Chicago's suburbs, where Goldblatt's discount inventory failed to move the middle-class market. Joel was forced out of the presidency by Maurice after a bitter struggle in 1960. Thereafter, the company's leadership changed often, as the family members began to feud. New store openings stepped up, however, and by 1964 Goldblatt's operated 30 stores, including its central distribution facility, with 12 stores in Chicago, 13 throughout Illinois, two in Indiana, and one each in Michigan and Wisconsin. Sales climbed to $153 million in 1965, with a net income of $1.5 million.

After 1964, however, Goldblatt's stopped its expansion, building no new stores for more than a decade. The only new additions to the chain came through the company's 1967 acquisition of H. P. Wasson & Co., Inc., and its seven Indiana-based

department stores. During this time, many retailers, including Sears Roebuck & Co., were expanding rapidly, and new discounters such as Kmart and Venture were moving into the Chicago market, siphoning off many of Goldblatt's traditional customers. Sales continued to grow, however, from $190 million in 1967 to $214 million in 1970. Net income for those years, however, dropped from $3.2 million to $627,000.

The family's squabbles continued into the 1970s. By the end of that decade, the leadership of the company had changed many times, passing among various members of the family, including Louis, who served twice, and Maurice's son Stanford Goldblatt. Investment of earnings back into the company was minimal; instead, the company paid out profits in stock dividends, with the majority of stock being controlled by the Goldblatt family. Stanford Goldblatt took over as president and chief executive officer from Louis Goldblatt in May 1976. Stanford attempted to change the Goldblatt's image, introducing upscale and designer merchandise, a move that failed and forced the company to take a dramatic markdown on its inventory. Added difficulties for the company came from its policy of carrying its own receivables, with 300,000 outstanding accounts worth $50 million. An extra burden came from the many members of the Goldblatt family included on the corporate payroll. By 1977, despite posting its highest sales ever of $290 million, the company's net income dropped to $77,600 from $1.9 million the previous year. Despite this, the company paid out a 28 cents per share dividend in that year. Again, the following year, despite posting a loss, the company paid out a 13-cent dividend.

By December 1977, Stanford was ousted by Louis Goldblatt. An offer by the French Agache-Willot company the following year to buy out a majority interest in Goldblatt's was rejected; nevertheless, the company lacked the capital to upgrade its existing stores or to expand the chain. Analysts at the time attributed much of the company's difficulties to the Goldblatt family's dominance. The banks agreed, and, as conditions for a three-year, $10 million revolving credit agreement, forced the company to bring in management from outside the Goldblatt family, while also demanding that the company cease paying out dividends. Harrold Smith, formerly of Robert Hall and Wal-Mart, was named president in 1978 and chief executive officer in April 1979, but left four months later, citing the Goldblatt family's continued interference as a reason. Smith was replaced by Louis Duncan, who had been vice-chairman of Household Finance Corp., but Duncan lasted less than a year. Lionel Goldblatt, son of Nate Goldblatt, who had worked for the company as a buyer for men's shoes, took over the chairmanship in 1980 and led the company to its bankruptcy declaration in 1981.

By the time it filed for bankruptcy, the company reported liabilities of $52.5 million opposed to assets of $53.3 million, with $30 million owed to creditors. The chain was down to 22 department stores, and accounted for less than five percent of the Chicago area's retail sales. Eight more stores were sold off by the end of that year. Goldblatt's brought in William Hellman, former head of Bond's clothing stores in New York, who had also spent 17 years with Goldblatt's, to head the company during its reorganization. Under the terms of its reorganization, the company sold off eight more of its remaining stores, paying

52.5 cents to the dollar to its creditors. Among the stores to be sold was its State Street location, which was originally intended to become Chicago's new public library, but eventually was purchased by DePaul University. The company kept six stores, which were reopened in the spring of 1982 and included its original Chicago Avenue location, to which it moved its corporate headquarters. Under Hellman, Goldblatt's returned to its original sales concept. Stores were reduced in size to two floors, and inventory and pricing targeted the poor and immigrant populations of the stores' neighborhoods. The six stores—all in depressed Chicago neighborhoods—opened with less than $2 million in inventory, half of which sold out on the day of their reopening.

The reorganization effort faced a major obstacle when real-estate prices plunged during the recession of the early 1980s, leaving Goldblatt's $3 million short of the capital it needed in order to fulfill its creditors' liens. In 1983, however, the company was rescued from liquidation by Jupiter Industries. Headed by Jerrold Wexler, Jupiter was a multi-billion-dollar company with real estate holdings that included the Playboy Building, the Lake Point Towers residential apartment complex, much of Michigan Avenue, and some two dozen Chicago hotels, as well as properties in New York and Los Angeles. Jupiter arranged for a $3 million loan, borrowed against Goldblatt's assets, in exchange for 46 percent of the company. Jupiter also received approximately $60 million in tax-loss carryforwards. These were put to use the following year, with the $9.8 million purchase of Milgram-Kagan Corp., which operated a chain of 131 Florsheim, Naturalizer, and Cobbie shoe stores in seven states. In 1985, the company purchased, for $38 million, the Sussex Group furniture division of Household Merchandise Corp., including four furniture store chains. One of these chains, American Stores based in Texas, was sold off immediately, while the company retained the chains Huffman-Koos, Colby's Home Furnishings, and Barker Brothers.

By 1985, Goldblatt's had pulled out of bankruptcy and was once again profitable. In order to protect its acquisitions from its continued liabilities, the company was restructured, with the parent, JG Industries, Inc., acting as a holding company for Goldblatt's, Milgram-Kagan, and its Sussex Group of furniture stores. William Hellman was named president and CEO of the new company, while Jerrold Wexler functioned as chairman of the board. Lionel Goldblatt remained as chairman of Goldblatt's, and served as vice-president on JG's board of directors. In 1985, JG recorded sales of nearly $229 million, with net income of $2.4 million. The following year, Huffman-Koos was taken public, selling 43 percent of its shares. The company divested its Colby's Furniture Stores in 1987, dropping its net sales from $250 million in 1986 to $231 million in 1987.

Goldblatt's opened four new stores by 1988; three of these were essentially reopenings of former Goldblatt stores. Its strategy, as Hellman told the *Daily News Record,* was "to appeal to customers from the welfare level to just under the middle class." Its inventory consisted primarily of closeouts, irregulars, and "opportunistic purchases," including those from diverters of national, name-brand and private-label products. As the country entered the recession of the early 1990s, however, JG's other properties were less profitable. As early as 1991, the company sought to sell off its Milgram-Kagan division, and the remains of its Sussex Group division. Barker Brothers had been sold in 1990 for $12.6 million. The company purchased the Charles Kushins, Inc., shoe store chain for $9 million in 1988, but was forced to close the chain less than two years later, taking a charge of $6 million. JG recorded a loss of $10 million in its 1990 fiscal year, and net sales continued to drop, down to $137.7 million in 1991, with a net income of $510,000. Only Goldblatt's—which had opened two more stores—showed signs of success, with sales rising to more than $58 million, accounting for roughly one-third of JG's total sales.

The company's attempt to restructure its Milgram-Kagan division toward profitability failed, and in 1993 Milgram-Kagan filed a Chapter 11 liquidation plan and ceased operations. By then, JG had been pared down to two remaining divisions: Goldblatt's and Huffman-Koos, which was slowly climbing out of the crippling effects of the national recession. In 1993 Huffman-Koos' 13 stores contributed $91 million to JG's sales of $169 million. However, JG posted losses in each year from 1992 to 1994, including a loss of $7.6 million in 1992. In September 1995, the company sold Huffman-Koos to Breuner's Home Furnishings Corp., a holding company which also included 12 "Breuner's" and "Arnold's" furniture stores operating in California and Nevada.

As JG neared the end of 1995, its sole remaining subsidiary was its Goldblatt's Department Store chain, which then included 14 stores posting approximately $77 million in sales. Despite remaining profitable, Goldblatt's has faced increasing pressure from competitors such as Venture and Target, as well as from continued decreases in spending among its core customer base. With no new store openings planned through 1996, it remained to be seen whether "The Incredible Bargain Centers" could retain their position as leading inner city retailers.

Principal Subsidiaries

Goldblatt's Department Stores, Inc.

Further Reading

Buck, Genevieve, "Neighborly Tack Revives Goldblatt's," *Chicago Tribune,* October 1, 1995, p. C1.

Key, Janet, "Goldblatt's: Bravado to Bankruptcy," *Chicago Tribune,* December 27, 1981, Section 5, p. 1.

Sharoff, Robert, "The Midwest Closeout King," *Daily News Record,* March 2, 1988, p. 24

—M. L. Cohen

JAY JACOBS

Jay Jacobs, Inc.

1530 Fifth Avenue
Seattle, Washington 98101
U.S.A.
(206) 622-5400
Fax: (206) 621-9830

Public Company
Incorporated: 1941
Employees: 680
Sales: $90.4 million (1995)
Stock Exchanges: NASDAQ
SICs: 5621 Women's Clothing Stores; 5611 Men's &
Boy's Clothing Stores; 5136 Men & Boys' Clothing;
5137 Women & Children's Clothing

Jay Jacobs, Inc. operates a chain of fashion stores that sell contemporary men's and women's sportswear and outerwear, including fashion denim, dress and casual pants and tops, dresses, coats and jackets, and related accessories. In 1995, when the company emerged from Chapter 11 bankruptcy protection, there were 145 Jay Jacobs stores spread across 21 western and northwestern states, the majority of which were located in regional shopping malls. Although the company recorded meteoric growth during the 1980s, its fortunes soured during the early and mid-1990s, reducing the number of stores it operated roughly by half.

When 28-year old Jay Jacobs opened his first retail women's clothing store in downtown Seattle in 1941, the first link to what would become the Jay Jacobs chain of retail clothing stores was established. Although the company later would operate nearly 300 stores in more than 20 states, decades would pass before anyone would refer to Jay Jacobs' enterprise as a chain. The company did not open its second store until a decade after the first, and the third store did not open its doors until the second had already celebrated its tenth anniversary of existence. It was not until the mid-1970s—more than 30 years into the company's history—that Jay Jacobs, Inc. could rightly be referred to as a chain. With ten stores in operation in 1974, the company represented a discernible yet modest force in the Pacific North-

west retail fashion industry, but by the end of the decade the chain would begin to expand with decided aggression, increasing exponentially the number of stores it operated throughout the western United States.

During this formative period, the company established its reputation as a local retailer of women's sportswear in the Seattle area and led a purposefully quiet existence. Though the company's merchandise would mimic the vagaries of the fashion world, changing with the times and trends, Jay Jacobs management remained steadfast in its pursuit of young female customers, a type of customer Jay Jacobs stores would cater to from the 1940s to the 1990s. Inside the company's first store, which constituted a 40 feet by 60 feet main room with two balconies and a basement, moderately priced young women's clothing graced the shelves and racks, including dresses, sportswear, coats, and suits. Other Jay Jacob stores, as they slowly emerged onto the Pacific Northwest retail clothing scene, targeted the same type of customer with like merchandise, until men's clothing was added to the company's stores in 1970. Despite Jay Jacobs, Inc.'s foray into men's fashion, the company would continue to derive the overwhelming majority of its sales from young women's clothing after 1970, carving a niche for itself in the region's retail clothing industry and lending an easily recognizable identity to Jay Jacobs stores.

Chiefly responsible for creating and implementing Jay Jacobs, Inc.'s successful retail concept was its founder, Jay Jacobs, whose control over the company was resolute. Together with his wife Rose, who helped with selecting merchandise and served as the company's comptroller, Jay Jacobs closely watched over the operation of his original store and others to follow, orchestrating the development of Jay Jacobs, Inc. into a retail chain. In so doing, Jay Jacobs' name, which was emblazoned across his stores, became known throughout the Seattle area, but the founder of one of the region's most thriving retail operations kept largely to himself, distancing himself from other business leaders in Seattle's fashion community. Known for being a fierce handball competitor, Jay Jacobs was a fixture on Seattle handball courts for more than 30 years, but outside the court he fraternized little with other retailers or business people, exhibiting a personality that earned him a reputation as being a hard-working, private man.

As much as Jacobs avoided the public spotlight, so did his company eschew any unnecessary outside attention. During the company's first four decades of existence, it operated as an intensely private organization, never announcing or confirming annual sales figures. As an example of its commitment to privacy, the company operated a 3,500-account wholesale division for five years before more than a handful of outside observers learned of the company's diversification.

This secrecy would eventually be lifted somewhat as the number of Jay Jacobs stores proliferated during the 1980s. By that time, the reins of command had been passed to Jay Jacobs' son-in-law Doug Swerland, who earlier had married his boss's daughter Shelley. Swerland was named president of Jay Jacobs, Inc. in the late 1970s, inheriting a company that had been profitable every year since 1941. During Swerland's tenure, the number of Jay Jacobs stores increased exponentially, as the founder's son-in-law blanketed regions where the company already maintained a presence with additional stores and extended the company's geographic reach into virgin territories, transforming Jay Jacobs, Inc. into a genuine western United States retailing force.

In describing the corporate strategy that shaped Jay Jacobs' growth during the first half of the 1980s, Swerland told the *Puget Sound Business Journal* that the company would "open up a new market, saturate it, and dominate it." It was a succinct and apt description of Jay Jacobs, Inc.'s actions during Swerland's first half-decade of leadership, for the company expanded quickly, establishing a host of new stores in previously unoccupied territory and, as a result, held a firm grip on a wide-ranging area of operation. By the mid-1980s, the company had tripled in size over the previous five years, operating, in 1986, 103 stores scattered throughout Washington, Oregon, California, Idaho, Montana, Utah, Wyoming, Alaska, and Hawaii. In contrast to the sedate pace of expansion recorded during the previous four decades, the explosive growth of the 1980s represented a glaring aberration, with the company at one point in 1985 opening a new store an average of every 11 days.

Much of Jay Jacobs, Inc.'s growth had occurred in California, where the company first entered the northern half of the state, then began receiving inquiries by southern California shopping mall developers interested in having the rapidly growing chain expand in their direction. When the company purchased 24 Marsi's stores in 1984, the door south was opened and Jay Jacobs stores began popping up quickly. Elsewhere, the company's stores also appeared in rapid succession, and scored enviable success, leading industry observers to refer to the Jay Jacobs chain as one of the most successful and profitable retailers in the country. Moreover, the company began touting itself as the largest independent fashion retailer on the West Coast. With the company's retail business booming, Swerland branched into the wholesale side of the fashion business and quietly organized a separate division within Jay Jacobs, Inc.'s corporate structure that by the mid-1980s sold two lines of women's clothing, D.D. Sloane and J. Jordan, to stalwart retailers such as Bloomingdale's I. Magnin, and fellow Seattle-based Nordstrom's. Combined, the retail and wholesale businesses belonging to Jay Jacobs, Inc. helped push annual sales upward as the company's expansion progressed, jumping from an estimated $35 million in 1983 to between $60 and $75 million in 1985.

The 1980s were heady years for Jacobs (who continued to serve as his company's chairman), Doug Swerland, and the 1,400 employees who worked for the company. Confidence ran so high that the company opened an experimental store called Concepts in the mid-1980s that focused on more upscale customers than the traditional Jay Jacobs 15- to 25-year old target customer and loomed as a potential new chain for the company. Perhaps most encouraging, the company's prodigious expansion did not appear to tarnish its coveted reputation. In a survey sponsored by *Women's Wear Daily,* a leading fashion trade publication, Jay Jacobs, Inc. was found to be "most in tune with consumer preference, most aware of how each resource operates, and having the most professional buying and merchandising executives," attributes frequently lost during rapid expansion.

As Jacobs and Swerland looked back on the expansion that had swelled the unit size of their company to more than 100, they could also take heart in the fact that all of the expansion had been financed internally, with the successful operation of existing stores breeding the addition of new stores. The company had relied on short-term bank loans only to build inventory.

However, 1986 was the last year the pair could proclaim their independence, for further expansion lay ahead. Jay Jacobs, Inc. would establish roughly as many new stores during the latter half of the 1980s as it had during the first half of the decade, which meant the company needed capital from sources other than itself. In 1986, anticipating its future financial needs, Jay Jacobs, Inc. began the process of converting to public ownership, then made its initial public offering in mid-1987, thereby putting to an end its staunchly-held privacy.

By the end of the decade, there were 179 Jay Jacobs stores spread across 13 states, as the momentum built up during the first half of the 1980s carried over into the second half of the decade. About the only negative development suffered by the company as it entered the 1990s was its floundering wholesale division, which recorded an operating loss of $314,000 during the first fiscal quarter of 1990. Jay Jacobs, Inc. closed the division later in the year, but even the company's failure in the wholesale fashion business elicited praise from analysts, who were pleased by the company's abrupt exit since it meant greater attention could be paid to the nearly 200 Jay Jacobs retail stores. In the wake of the company's decision to desist marketing wholesale clothing, the price of its stock rose steadily, while sales for the year eclipsed $100 million, reaching $111.7 million, from which the company recorded $3.1 million in net income.

Flush with success, the company added eight stores in the Chicago and Milwaukee areas in March and April 1990—the first Jay Jacobs stores located east of the Rocky Mountains—then mapped out ambitious plans to saturate the region with additional stores. In the summer months of 1990, company officials announced plans to establish 30 new stores in the Midwest, intent on shoring up its position in and around Chicago and Milwaukee and following the strategy articulated by Swerland during the early 1980s. For everyone associated with the company, including employees, management, and stockholders, the future appeared to hold the coming of great developments for the company. Within two years, however, everything would change, as Jay Jacobs, Inc. began a deleterious financial slide. Less than two years after that, the company would file for bankruptcy, dashing the hopes of those who had much to look forward to in 1990.

Store expansion continued during the early 1990s, despite a recessionary economic climate, bringing the total number of Jay Jacobs stores in operation to 288 by the beginning of 1993. The total was an all-time high for the company and one it would not eclipse anytime in the near future. During the ensuing months, the number of Jay Jacobs stores fell sharply, as the company began to close unprofitable stores, particularly in southern California where the Jay Jacobs chain was recording its most serious losses.

The sudden unprofitability of Jay Jacobs, Inc., which began in 1992, was a complete turnaround from the robust years of the 1980s, and the cause was difficult to pinpoint. A recession during the early 1990s crippled many businesses, particularly retailers like Jay Jacobs, Inc. Exacerbating the effects of the harsh economic climate was the company's more than decade-long expansion program, which some critics regarded as too rapid and therefore the root of its financial woes. Others charged that founder Jay Jacobs had never given his son-in-law sufficient control over the company and had lost touch with the ever-changing trends of fashion. Whatever the cause, the company was reeling from declining business, forcing all those involved to search for a solution forthwith.

Swerland attempted to broaden the age of range of Jay Jacobs, Inc.'s target customer, hoping to attract older customers with more career-oriented clothing. However, by November 1993 Swerland was gone, opting to resign from the company as its losses mounted. In Swerland's place, Craig Bohman followed as president, capping off a 17-year career with the company during which he served as a treasurer, executive vice-president, chief financial officer, and director before securing his final promotion. Like Swerland, Bohman sought to attract slightly older customers to the dwindling number of Jay Jacobs stores, and like Swerland, Bohman's tenure as president ended with his resignation from Jay Jacobs, Inc., though Bohman served as president for a much shorter duration.

By the time Bohman vacated his post in May 1994, the number of Jay Jacobs stores in operation had dropped to 257. Concurrent with Bohman's departure, Jay Jacobs, Inc. filed for relief under Chapter 11 of the U.S. Bankruptcy Code, ushering in a difficult period of transition and reorganization for the company that would serve as a test of management's mettle. As a consequence of its financial slide, the company had lost the trade support of its vendors, making it difficult for the company's stores to get merchandise. Filing for Chapter 11 provided a solution for this pernicious problem, helping the company to get out of leases at unprofitable store sites. So Jay Jacobs, Inc. attempted to move forward under court protection, with a familiar figure to lead the company through its first several months under Chapter 11. Jay Jacobs, 81 years old at the time, took back the titles of president and chief executive officer in July 1994, then sought to reverse the damage caused, as he perceived it, by overambitious expansion.

Jacobs controlled two-thirds of the company's stock when he filled the void created by Bohman's departure, giving the octogenarian founder tremendous control over the nominally public company. But after two months he relinquished his posts to yet another new president and chief executive, the company's fourth leader in less than a year. Rex Steffey joined the company in September 1994, bringing hope that Jay Jacobs, Inc. could emerge successfully from bankruptcy. With Rex Steffey at the helm, such hope was justified primarily because the company's new president and chief executive had helped Indianapolis-based retail chain Paul Harris Stores Inc. wrest free from bankruptcy in 1992, accruing experience he brought to bear on Jay Jacobs, Inc. beginning in the fall of 1994.

Like his predecessors, Steffey decided to abandon the market niche Jay Jacobs, Inc. had occupied for decades, opting to steer away from junior-sized women's clothing for teenagers and young women and instead attract older clientele with private-label casual wear and career clothing. The objective was to lure customers in their 20s rather than high school-age customers. As management strove to bring about this change, it also labored at developing a reorganization plan to bring Jay Jacobs, Inc. out of bankruptcy. Many stores were closed, while others were converted to off-price units, leaving the company with 145 stores by November 1995, when Jay Jacobs, Inc. announced the U.S. Bankruptcy Court had approved the company's plan of reorganization.

As Jay Jacobs, Inc. plotted its course for the future, the company planned to open 25 new stores in 1996 and focus those openings on its most profitable concept during the mid-1990s: a combination men's and women's clothing format. Though the early 1990s had proven to be an exceedingly turbulent period for the company, it was determined to move forward, supported by a marketing strategy that emphasized increased private label merchandise, the development of its own products, and staying attuned to prevailing fashion trends.

Principal Subsidiaries

Green Light Fashions, Inc.; J.J. Distribution Company.

Further Reading

"Downtown Retailers on the Move," *Seattle Business,* October 1975, p. 25.

Fryer, Alex P., "Jay Jacobs Tries on a New Look to Woo Customers," *Puget Sound Business Journal,* June 9, 1995, p. 7.

"Jacobs Store at Northgate Has Anniversary," *The Seattle Times,* February 20, 1961, p. 16.

Jalonen, Wendy, "Jay Jacobs Is About to Go Public," *Puget Sound Business Journal,* July 14, 1986, p. 1.

"Jay Jacobs, Inc. Receives Court Approval of Reorganization Plan; Retailer Set to Emerge from Chapter 11 Prior to Holiday Selling Season," *PR Newswire,* November 17, 1995, p. 11.

"Jay Jacobs Re-Emerging?," *Washington CEO,* October 1995, p. 11.

Palmieri, Jean E., "New Jay Jacobs Set to Emerge from Bankruptcy; New CEO Rex Steffey Putting More Emphasis on Private Labels," *Daily News Record,* March 14, 1995, p. 12.

Prinzing, Debra, "When Business Sags, Change—and Jay Jacobs Did," *Puget Sound Business Journal,* July 23, 1990, p. 15.

Sather, Jeanne, "Jay Jacobs Struggles to Refashion His Chain," *Puget Sound Business Journal,* August 19, 1994, p. 1.

Staples, Alice, "Women's Fashion Firm Will Move," *The Seattle Times,* February 14, 1961, p. 4.

—Jeffrey L. Covell

Johnston Industries, Inc.

105 13th Street
Columbus, Georgia 31901
U.S.A.
(706) 641-3140
Fax: (706) 641-3158

Public Company
Incorporated: 1948 as Geon Trading Corp.
Sales: $263.3 million (fiscal 1995)
Employees: 1,470
Stock Exchanges: New York
SICs: 2211 Broadwoven Fabric Mills, Cotton; 2221
    Broadwoven Fabric Mills, Manmade Fiber and Silk;
    2231 Broadwoven Fabric Mills, Wool (Including
    Dyeing and Finishing)

Although it got its start selling auto replacement parts, Johnston Industries, Inc. is a diversified manufacturer of textile fabrics for home furnishings, basic apparel, industrial use, and the automotive industry. The company became a favorite on Wall Street and received honors in the 1990s for innovation and management. More than half of its output was for use in home furnishings—especially upholstery—in 1995, with the majority of the rest intended for industrial operations. Virtually every product in the textile spectrum was being produced by one or more of its divisions.

Johnston Industries traces its beginnings to the incorporation in 1948 of Geon Trading Corp. The company name became Geon International Corp. in 1951 and Geon Industries, Inc. in 1969. Established in the state of New York, Geon had executive offices in Woodbury, New York, when it went public in 1969, with its founder, George O. Neuwirth, as president and treasurer. At that time Geon was an importer, distributor, and exporter of auto replacement parts. It also exported tractor, industrial, aircraft, and marine parts. The company had established facilities in Los Angeles and two other southern California cities; San Francisco; Fairfax and Richmond in Virginia;

Hartford and New Haven in Connecticut; Dayton and Columbus in Ohio; Indianapolis, Indiana; Springfield, Massachusetts; and Manchester, New Hampshire. It had net sales of $13.3 million in 1968, net income of $421,374, and total assets of $6.5 million.

Geon grew rapidly in the 1970s, partly by acquisition. It purchased Imported Auto Parts, Inc. and BAP of New York, Inc. in 1970, AJS Auto Parts Inc. and Eatco, Inc. in 1971, and American Aviation Manufacturing Corp. in 1972. Net sales for 1972, including those of American Aviation, came to $40.6 million and net income to nearly $1.7 million. In 1971 Geon made a second public offering of stock at $21 a share, compared to $6 a share for the initial offering. Half of the sum raised was allotted to finance an increase in inventories.

In late 1973 Geon announced it had accepted in principle a cash offer of $36 million from Burmah Oil Co. to take over the company. The deal unraveled the following February, after Geon revealed that estimated net income for 1973 was $1.4 million to $1.5 million, lower than the level projected in negotiating the sale. The final figures for 1973 showed net sales of $47.9 million, net income of $1.4 million, and a burgeoning long-term debt of $16.6 million. A federal district court later ruled that Neuwirth had violated various provisions of the Securities Exchange Act of 1934 by disclosing information about Geon's negotiations with Burmah Oil to a friend and a broker. He was succeeded as chairman and president of Geon in 1974 by Robert L. Barbanell.

American Aviation, which had become a subsidiary of Geon, was sold in 1976 to its president for $1.5 million plus notes worth perhaps an additional $1 million. The following year Geon sold the bulk of its business, that which sold replacement parts for foreign cars, to a new U.S. unit of an Australian auto-parts company, Repco Ltd., for an estimated $6 million. This business had brought Geon $30.4 million in sales during 1976 but had resulted in a loss of $6.5 million. The rest of the company had sales of $8.8 million in 1976 and net operating profit of $1.1 million. The reduced company, which was renamed GI Export Corp. in 1977, had $13.5 million in debts.

Otto Hays succeeded Barbanell as president and chief executive officer of GI Export. Net sales increased to $11.3 million in 1978 and $13.9 million in 1980, while net income rose from $791,000 to $1.8 million during this period. In 1981 Founders of American Investment Corp. of Springfield, Missouri, purchased a 43-percent interest in GI Export for about $4.8 million. Redlaw Industries Inc., a manufacturer of auto parts and foundry products, held a controlling interest in the acquiring company through its GRM Industries Inc. unit. David L. Chandler, chairman of Redlaw's board, became chairman and chief executive officer of GI Export.

GI Export acquired Johnston Industries, Inc. in 1984 for $15 million cash and a note of $18.2 million. Johnston Industries was founded in 1972 by Paul A. Johnston of Chapel Hill, North Carolina. Formerly president of Glen Alden Corp., a conglomerate, Johnston initiated his company by purchasing Glen Alden's textile division. He later added Swift Textiles of Columbus, Georgia, and Opp and Micolas Mills of Opp, Alabama. The latter two mills dated back to 1921 and 1924, respectively.

Privately held Johnston Industries was based in New York City. The company soon sold Swift Textiles but kept one of its plants, Southern Phenix Textiles Inc. of Phenix City, Alabama. Built in 1968, this was one of the first mills to make woven goods from 100 percent polyester. In 1983, its last independent year, Johnston Industries had sales in excess of $100 million and what was said to be "significant profits." The amalgamated company, which had facilities in Gastonia, North Carolina, as well as Phenix City, took the Johnston Industries name as its own in 1985. The Gastonia facility was subsequently shed, as was GI Exports' business of exporting automotive and industrial parts.

Johnston Industries had net sales of $117.9 million in fiscal 1985 (ended August 31, 1985) and net income of $5.6 million. Its sales level remained flat in the late 1980s, but its profits reached $9.5 million in fiscal 1988 (ended June 30, 1987) and $7.8 million in fiscal 1989. Its shares moved up from the American Stock Exchange to the New York Stock Exchange in 1987. The company earned only $1.9 million, however, on sales of $118.9 million for fiscal 1990. In the following fiscal year, a recessionary period for the textile industry, Johnston Industries lost $1 million on just about the same volume of sales because cotton prices soared, and the company was unable to pass on higher costs to its customers.

Investors, however, expressed confidence in Johnston Industries and in Chandler, who in 1990 also assumed the title of president. By not hiking prices the company picked up business from firms that had been buying fabric from rival manufacturers. Placing its bets on the future, Johnston Industries spent $20 million in 1990 alone on new, faster yarn machines that enabled it to cut its work force. By November 1990 its stock was trading at a year-long high, especially pleasing to Chandler, who owned some 40 percent of the shares through GRM Industries. The firm rewarded investor confidence by earning $6.8 million on net sales of $138.3 million in fiscal 1992.

Johnston Industries' diversified sales, in 1991, consisted of 42 percent in home furnishings, 20 percent in coating and laminating, 12 percent in automotive, 11 percent in specialty-market industrial textiles, ten percent in apparel, and five percent in tufting and needle punch. It also earned a tidy sum from a 37-percent stake in Jupiter Industries, a publicly traded venture-capital investment company acquired in 1990. Johnston Industries invested $46 million in textile machinery from 1989 through 1991. All the company mills but one were running three shifts a day, seven days a week, at the end of 1991.

Johnston Industries moved to integrate its holdings in 1992, when Jupiter Industries acquired WestPoint Pepperell's custom-fabrics division, producer of industrial textiles. This division was renamed the Wellington Sears Co. for the venerable firm that traced its origins to a Boston outfitter of sailing ships in 1845 but whose name had been dropped by WestPoint in 1965. Also in 1992, Johnston Industries, in partnership with an English firm, formed Tech Textiles, USA to produce and sell sophisticated high-strength reinforced fabrics used in aircraft and autos.

Textile World devoted most of its June 1994 issue to Johnston Industries, which the magazine cited as its 22nd annual Model Mill "for its outstanding performance record, aggressive management approach to product and market innovation and strategic commitment to capital spending and high-tech operations." The company had enjoyed a record 1993 in net sales, which reached $154.1 million, and net income of $8.9 million. Adding the operating sales of Jupiter (which had been renamed Jupiter National) brought that figure over $275 million. Between 1983 and 1993 Johnston Industries returned stockholders an almost twelvefold total return on their investment.

"Name a product in the textile spectrum," *Textile World* declared, "and one of Johnston's divisions likely manufactures it. From filaments to spuns, from wovens and nonwovens to weft-insertion warp knits, it's all done somewhere in the Johnston realm. Company divisions process a wide array of fiber, including cotton, linen, polyester, rayon, acrylic, polyolefin, nylon, glass fiber, carbon, aramids and various fiber blends."

Johnston Industries struggled through some difficulties during fiscal 1994, when net income dropped to $6.5 million on sales volume of $159.9 million. Sharply rising raw-material costs, especially for cotton and polyester, were blamed. That year corporate headquarters were moved to Columbus, Georgia, consolidating its offices in New York and Phenix City. In fiscal 1995 Johnston and Jupiter National sales came to a total of $263.3 million, of which the latter accounted for about one-third. Net income was $7.9 million. Johnston Industries purchased full control of Tech Textiles, USA in 1995. Bean Fiberglass Inc. of Jaffrey, New Hampshire, had been purchased by and consolidated with Tech Textiles, USA earlier in the year. Tech Textiles, USA was renamed Johnston Industries Composite Reinforcements Inc. in 1996.

Textile World again honored Johnston Industries in October 1995 by selecting its president and chief operating officer, Gerald B. Andrews, as the magazine's leader of the year. Interviewed by magazine staffer Mac Isaacs, Andrews emphasized the importance of investing in capital improvements, disclosing that 35 percent of the company's products had not been produced three years earlier. He said its goal was to be the premier niche-market manufacturer in North America and added that he would be ''really disappointed'' if in three years annual sales had not reached $500 million, and the company was not much more profitable.

Another trade magazine, *ATI,* joined in the chorus of praise for Johnston Industries by selecting the company for its inaugural award for innovation in February 1996. ''Through its aggressive capital spending plan and mastery of product innovation,'' declared *ATI,* ''Johnston now looks at 1996 sales in the $350-million range.... The company is a waking dream of what the U.S. textile industry can and should be.''

Jupiter National was merged into Johnston Industries in March 1996, but not without a struggle. Although Johnston Industries owned about 55 percent of Jupiter in July 1995, Jupiter's board opposed Chandler's offer of $26 million ($29.50 a share) for the rest of the common stock and ousted him as the company's chairman and chief executive officer. The following month, however, the board agreed to accept a sweetened offer to minority stockholders of $35 million to $40 million. This payment was subsequently fixed at $33.97 a share.

Johnston Industries owned, through its subsidiaries and Jupiter National's Wellington Sears subsidiary, four textile mills in 1995. In all, the mills had an annual capacity of about 215 million linear yards of fabric (about 110 million pounds), about 21 million pounds of sales yarn, and about 93 million pounds in nonwoven operations. Some 55 percent of its production was for home furnishings; 25 percent for industrial use; nine percent for specialty markets; six percent for automotive use; four percent for apparel; and one percent miscellaneous. Its long-term debt was about $102 million. GRM Industries owned about 41 percent of Johnston Industries' common stock.

Southern Phenix Textiles was manufacturing fabrics from polyester fiber for use in home furnishings, the automotive industry, the coating and laminating trades, and by various other fabricators. Its operations included spinning, weaving, and stitch bonding and finishings, and its products were being used for foam car-seat cushions, tufted upholstery, marine coated products, mattress ticking for popularly priced mattresses, and products for soft furniture. Its lining fabric was being used for all National Football League footballs and 90 percent of the footballs used in the college game.

Opp and Micolas Mills was manufacturing more than 122 different styles of cotton fabrics and cotton/polyester blended fabrics for the coating, home-furnishings, and apparel markets. These were greige goods: that is, unbleached and undyed, as taken from the loom. This subsidiary also was producing fabrics for the footwear and building-supplies industry and for various industrial operations for use in a broad range of coated products, including apparel, wall coverings, coated fabrics for autos, such as convertible tops, cloth roof coverings, and felt window liners, rubber-coated products such as automotive V-belts and other belts for industrial machinery, industrial protective clothing, and specialty items such as tote bags, handbags, and shoes.

Wellington Sears was a diversified manufacturer of cotton and polyester fabrics for the home-furnishings and industrial markets. Its products were being used in outdoor furniture, wiper cloths, napery, furniture upholstery, mattress pads, bed linens, and other industrial applications. Tech Textiles, USA, Johnston Industries' smallest division, was producing noncrimp fabrics for composite-manufacturing uses. Its largest market was in the marine industry.

Jupiter National was also active in the venture-capital field through a wholly owned subsidiary named Greater Washington Investments, Inc. In mid-1995 Greater Washington held $29.6 million in investments and had $14.5 million of debt in subordinated debentures.

Johnston Industries' properties in 1995 included Southern Phenix's two mills and Tech Textiles, USA's mill in Phenix City, and Opp and Micolas' two mills in Opp. Wellington Sears had a large installation just off Interstate 85 between Valley, Alabama, and West Point, Georgia. It consisted of three manufacturing facilities, a finishing operation, a fabric-design center, a testing laboratory, a retail outlet, and a corporate facility. Wellington Sears also had four additional manufacturing facilities: a mill and finishing plant in Columbus, Georgia, and one each in Dewitt, Iowa, and Tarboro, North Carolina. A leased plant in Lanett, Alabama, was making nonwoven mattress pads.

Principal Subsidiaries

JI International, Inc.; Johnston Industries Composite Reinforcements Inc.; Jupiter National, Inc.; Opp and Micolas Mills, Inc.; Southern Phenix Textiles, Inc.; Wellington Sears Co.

Further Reading

Agovino, Theresa, ''A Profitable Web Woven in Reverse,'' *Crain's New York Business,* October 28, 1991, p. 4.

''Geon Holders Approve Selling Bulk of Business and Change in Name,'' *Wall Street Journal,* May 23, 1977, p. 4.

''Geon Says It Overstated Interim '73 Profits, Clouding Planned Take-Over by Burmah Oil,'' *Wall Street Journal,* February 26, 1974, p. 3.

''Johnston: Ahead of Its Time,'' *Textile World,* June 1994, pp. 30, 32, 35–36, 39–40, 43, 45–46, 49–50, 61, 63–64, 67, 69–70, 73, 75–76.

Kalogeridis, Carla, ''Watch Johnston Thrive with Flexible Drive,'' *Textile World,* December 1991, pp. 29, 31.

——,''New Ideas Fuel Johnston's Engine,'' *ATI,* February 1996, pp. 25–26, 28, 32, 34, 36, 38, 40, 42, 44.

Marcial, Gene G., ''A Strong Thread Runs through This Textile Maker,'' *Business Week,* October 12, 1992, p. 154.

''Redlaw Industries Unit Acquires 43% Stake in GI Export Corp.,'' *Wall Street Journal,* August 14, 1981, p. 61.

''The Rest of Jupiter National, Inc.,'' *Wall Street Journal,* August 17, 1995, p. B6.

''TW's 1995 Leader of the Year: Gerald B. Andrews,'' *Textile World,* October 1995, pp. 35–36, 39–40, 43–44, 46, 49–50.

—Robert Halasz

Joseph T. Ryerson & Son, Inc.

16th & Rockwell Streets
Box 8000
Chicago, Illinois 60680
U.S.A.
(312) 762-2121
Fax: (312) 762-0437

Wholly Owned Subsidiary of Inland Steel Industries, Inc.
Founded: 1842
Employees: 4,100
Sales: $1.24 billion
SICs: 5051 Metals Service Centers & Offices; 5169
    Chemicals & Allied Products, Not Elsewhere
    Classified; 3316 Cold-Finishing of Steel Shapes

Under the parentage of Inland Steel since 1935, Joseph T. Ryerson & Son, Inc. is a Chicago-based steel concern, with plants in 29 U.S. cities. As a part of Inland's Materials Distribution Group, the company processes and distributes carbon, stainless and alloy steels through its "service centers."

Joseph T. Ryerson, the founder of the company, arrived in Chicago in the early 1840s. Working as an agent for a firm of Pennsylvania iron masters, he leased a shop along the Chicago River and advertised for sale such wares as sheet iron, English and German steel, buggy springs, axles, nails, and wrought iron spikes, among other products. Two years later, with his inventory expanding, Ryerson acquired property and built an iron store in the city's downtown business district. By 1852, Ryerson's operation had again outgrown its space and moved to larger and more convenient facilities alongside the river, where a new dock allowed lake ships to deliver iron right to the Ryerson store.

In 1871, the company experienced a setback as the Great Chicago Fire devastated Ryerson's warehouse. The founder reopened in temporary quarters, however, and rebuilt his iron store on the same site. In a notice to his customers, Ryerson expressed his determination: "I shall do everything in my power to serve my customers as usual, in my line of goods. I still live, and intend to do business, not withstanding the awful calamity that has befallen our city, and the citizens generally. I am ready for the fight against misfortune, and I trust my old friends and customers will stand by me."

Ryerson remained owner and head of the company until 1883, when another family member, Edward L. Ryerson, Sr., took over as owner, president, and chairperson. The founder's son, Joseph T. Ryerson, II, was also an active part of the operation. During this time, the company had pared its offerings to focus on serving boilermakers, which, at the time, were Chicago's primary users of iron and steel. Ryerson also was offering corrugated furnaces for boilers and a variety of boilermaker tools. Indeed, the company would later name its newsletter, established in 1892, *The Boilermaker*. By the end of the decade, as railroads rapidly carved their paths throughout the country, the boiler shops and flue shops that serviced steam locomotives became increasingly important customers to Ryerson. To make room for an increasing demand and inventory, the Ryerson plant expanded several times during this period.

In the early 1900s increasing industrialization allowed Ryerson to expand its product lines in serving Chicago's metal users. Specifically, the company supplied rails to a large number of steel consumers in the railroad industry, iron and steel products for farm implement makers, and the steel used in the construction of skyscrapers. In 1908 the entire operation of Ryerson moved to facilities at 16th and Rockwell in Chicago, a plant that would continue in use into the 1990s. In 1909, Ryerson moved for the first time outside of Chicago, opening a plant in New York.

As steel became more popular, so did its derivative "alloy steel" materials. The research and applications of alloy had begun in the late 18th century, and as the Industrial Revolution spread throughout America, the demand for the stronger, more resilient alloy steels increased. Experiments with chromium and nickel brought the realization that a combination of elements produced a metal superior in many respects to steels alloyed with only one. The toughness and strength of nickel lengthened the service and dependability of gears, crank shafts, and other vital parts of machines used in transportation. Vanadium steel was introduced in 1907 to the U.S. automotive industry by Henry Ford. It was also used for structural steel and high-speed tool steels. Ryerson was a part of this growing trend, and in 1911 made its first offering of alloy stocks, including four grades of nickel, chrome, and vanadium steels, which were well suited for railroad, automotive and machinery needs.

Another industry development that Ryerson was able to take advantage of was that of stainless steel. In fact, in 1926 Ryerson's stocks of the new stainless steel were among the first available anywhere. The use of stainless steel spread throughout the chemical and drug industries and to other industrial applications because of its ability to stand up against corrosive properties. In 1929 stainless steel trim first appeared on cars and became increasingly popular in the auto industry for its beautiful finish and non-tarnishing quality. Stainless also proved remarkably strong, suggesting structural possibilities and weight saving economy. In 1934, for instance, the first streamlined train using stainless steel made its appearance in the United States; it was lighter in weight, and thus, capable of greater speeds. Other product introductions by Ryerson at this time included a line of Ryertex thermosetting plastic laminates.

The acquisition of Joseph T. Ryerson & Son by Inland Steel began a relationship that would remain in effect into the 1990s. In 1935 it was announced that Inland Steel Company and Ryerson had approved a plan to merge. Inland Steel was a well-established Chicago-based steel producer, engaged in the manufacture of bars, shapes, plates, sheets, strips, rails, track accessories, and tin plate. In fact, the company ranked seventh in size in the steel industry at the time. The acquisition of Ryerson gave Inland an outlet for its products milled at Indiana Harbor and Chicago Heights. Ryerson, with ten plants in midwestern and eastern cities including Detroit, Cleveland, Buffalo, Cincinnati, Boston, New York, and Philadelphia, continued to operate as a wholly owned subsidiary. The combined assets of the two companies at the time of the merger totalled over $116 million. Edward L. Ryerson, Jr., who had taken over the reins of the company in 1929, continued to lead Ryerson under the parentage of Inland Steel, until his retirement in 1953.

While war time was a period of significant expansion for most steel companies, Ryerson, being a distributor, did not initially share such growth during World War II. The War Production Board gave low priority to shipments for service centers, reasoning that channelling steel through middlemen was unnecessary and costly. However, as government contractors began to complain when their materials were not delivered in a timely manner, Ryerson soon proved that its services were essential, and the War Production Board agreed.

The postwar period was marked by expansion, both of the Ryerson product line and of its geographic scope. By 1946 Ryerson had established its first West Coast plant in Los Angeles, bringing the company's total number of service centers to 12. By 1955 the company was offering full stocks of aluminum and polyvinyl chloride (PVC) sheets, pipe, and fittings. The company's new plastics division was further supplemented by the addition of fiberglass structural shapes, pipe, tubing, bars, and sheet in 1963. During the 1970s Ryerson began converting stainless and aluminum coils into flat sheets to service special customer orders. Later, a stainless plate center and new plate processing facility were established in Chicago. Also during this time, Ryerson went through a period of acquisitions to increase its geographic presence, acquiring the Federal Steel Corp. in April 1967; the Vance Iron & Steel Co. in June 1975.

However, the country's steel industry began to experience serious problems in the 1960s and 1970s. Factors such as high labor costs, slowing growth in domestic markets, and declining world market share contributed to this downturn. Moreover, foreign competition intensified as did the popularity of such steel substitutes as plastic and aluminum. The decline continued, and between 1982 and 1986, the steel industry suffered a severe depression. Although certainly affected by the adverse conditions, Ryerson seemed to survive these years better than many in the industry. While other service center companies were forced to cut back during this time, Ryerson even experienced some moderate expansion, opening new facilities in Nebraska and Iowa while upgrading its headquarters and plants in Houston, Kansas City, and Milwaukee. According to an April 1984 article in *American Metal Market,* Ryerson reported a 1983 operating profit of $22.5 million, triple that of the previous year, while sales had increased 11.6 percent to $792.5 million. Moreover, in 1984 the company achieved its first billion dollar sales year.

However, to offset the declining U.S. steel market, parent company Inland Steel was forced to restructure. In its service center division, Inland combined subsidiary J.M. Tull Metals with Ryerson's service center networks to create four regional distribution units: Joseph T. Ryerson East, Joseph T. Ryerson West, Joseph T. Ryerson Central, and J.M. Tull Metals. The reorganization called for a ten percent cut in salaried work force, but was estimated to save the company about $10 million in 1991. Moreover, according to company officials, the reorganization allowed the units to operate closer to their markets, respond better to the needs of their customers, and be more acutely aware of competition.

In the mid-1990s Ryerson went through additional restructuring actions, seeking to consolidate some of its far-flung operations. The company announced in May 1994 that it would close its Boston outlet and move all inventory and processing to its more modern facility in Wallingford, Connecticut. According to company officials, the closing occurred because the Boston facility was inefficient and additional investment in the unit was not justified. In addition, current business volume and projected market growth did not support two Ryerson service centers in the New England market. Further analysis of business volume and projected growth prompted the 1995 closing of Ryerson's Jersey City service center, the operations of which were consolidated in the Philadelphia plant.

Despite necessary closings and the consolidation of operations, Ryerson did witness a growth in demand at its Minneapolis service center. In response the company called for an addition to that plant in 1995, resulting in a 300,000-square-foot facility with new metal processing and distribution equipment. The Minneapolis center received a laser cutting machine and another multi-torch flame-cutting machine, as well as a new overhead crane and an increase in its truck fleet.

The future of the steel industry remained uncertain. In Inland Steel's 1994 annual report, management addressed the issue of whether superior steel and a thriving distribution business would enable the company to remain profitable in a recession. Suggesting that the answer was perhaps ''no,'' management looked toward redefining their business by diversification. As Joseph T. Ryerson & Son also faced such challenges, its reputation for sound leadership and service would no doubt be a valuable asset.

Further Reading

Beirne, Mike, ''Joseph T. Ryerson closing another East Coast Location,'' *American Metal Market*, July 7, 1995, p. 4.

Beirne, Mike, ''Ryerson Eyeing New Niche?,'' *American Metal Market*, July 16, 1991, p. 5.

——, ''Ryerson Revamp Seen Clashing with Its Computers,'' *American Metal Market*, November 13, 1990, p. 4.

——, ''Ryerson to Quit Boston,'' *American Metal Market*, May 9, 1994, p. 2.

Bettner, Jill, ''Who's Done Better Diversifying?,'' *Forbes*, June 4, 1984.

Burgert, Philip, ''Ryerson to Continue Service Expansion,'' *American Metal Market*, March 17, 1983, p. 1.

Fisher, Douglas Alan, *The Epic of Steel*, New York: Harper & Row Publishers, 1963, 344 p.

Hohl, Paul, ''Ryerson and Tull Buoy Inland's Net,'' *American Metal Market*, January 26, 1988, p. 3.

Keefe, Lisa M., ''Reassembling Ryerson,'' *Crain's Chicago Buisness*, September 3, 1990, p. 1.

Ryerson: Celebrating the First 150 Years, Chicago: Joseph T. Ryerson & Sons, Inc., 1992.

—Beth Watson Highman

Kay-Bee Toy Stores

100 West St.
Pittsfield, Massachusetts 01201-5761
U.S.A.
(413) 499-0086
Fax: (413) 499-3739

Wholly Owned Subsidiary of Melville Corporation
Incorporated: 1922
Sales: $1,012 million
Employees: 13,000
SICs: 5945 Hobby, Toy & Game Shops

Kay-Bee Toy Stores is the fifth-largest retailer of toys in the United States and second only to Toys ''R'' Us among retailers that specialize in toys alone. Unlike the giant free-standing outlets run by its major competitor, Kay-Bee operates approximately 1,000 smaller mall-based toy stores. Kay-Bee stores carry brand name products along with stock from discontinued lines which are sold at bargain prices. Due to their smaller retail space Kay-Bee does not carry sporting goods, choosing instead to focus on video products, which account for 25 percent of overall sales. The company was purchased in 1981 by the multibillion-dollar retail conglomerate Melville Corporation. Melville also owns Marshalls, Wilson's, Linens 'n Things, Footaction USA, and CVS, among others. Ten years after becoming a part of the Melville family, Kay-Bee Toys reached the $1 billion mark in sales in 1990.

Kay-Bee began as Kaufman Brothers when two brothers in Pittsfield, Massachusetts, opened a wholesale candy business in 1922. Kaufman Brothers provided retailers with candy and soda fountain supplies. The Kaufman brothers got into the toy business by accident. During the 1940s they acquired a wholesale toy company from a previous client as payment for outstanding debts owed to Kaufman Brothers for purchased candy. It was an opportune moment for Kaufman Brothers to diversify, because the cost of producing candy was prohibitive during World War II due to shortages of important ingredients, especially sugar. Kaufman Brothers assumed operation of the toy company,

changing its name to K-B Toy & Hobby Stores. By 1948 the toy business was so much more successful than the confectionary business that the Kaufman brothers decided to focus their energies entirely on toys. Kaufman Brothers opened its first retail toy store in Connecticut in 1959.

It wasn't until 1973 that the Kaufman brothers, who still owned and operated the company, decided to move once and for all from wholesaling to retailing. They discontinued their wholesale business altogether and concentrated on their 26 retail stores. Suburban malls were popping up across the country, and the Kaufmans wanted to take advantage of the boom. By 1976, only three years after making the decision to focus solely on retail, K-B Toy & Hobby had more than doubled its number of stores from 26 to 65 across New England, New York, and New Jersey. One year later, in 1977, the company changed its name from K-B Toy & Hobby to Kay-Bee Toy and Hobby Shops, Inc., primarily to distinguish itself from competitors with initials in their names or logos. In 1981, when the company was operating 210 stores, it changed its name again, this time to Kay-Bee Toy Stores, reflecting a de-emphasis on hobby products. The company was purchased in 1981 by Melville Corporation. As a subsidiary of Melville, Kay-Bee acquired Toy World, with 52 stores, in 1982; Circus World, with 330 stores, in 1990; and K&K Toys, with 133 stores, in 1991. These three acquisitions moved Kay-Bee into the upper echelon of U.S. toy retailers.

Although Melville Corporation already had an impressive list of retail names as part of its corporate family before buying Kay-Bee Toys, the purchase price of $64.2 million represented the greatest expenditure that Melville had ever made. After the sale Howard Kaufman remained president of Kay-Bee Toys, and the company's strategy remained essentially the same, exploiting the niche it had developed in malls.

The toy business itself went through enormous structural changes during the period of Kay-Bee's rise to prominence. The relationship between manufacturers and retailers became much closer, to the detriment of wholesalers, distributors, and smaller retailers. Many small retailers were driven out of business during the 1970s and 1980s; however, Kay-Bee was large enough and could buy in enough volume to compete with its major competitors. Kay-Bee could also take advantage of its long-standing policy of buying discontinued stock from manufacturers at a favorable rate and selling it at extremely reduced prices. Kay-Bee's strategy was to pack the entrance of its locations with these bargains to entice shoppers into the store. Once inside, managers reasoned, shoppers would be likely to purchase higher-end products that were priced more conservatively. In this way Kay-Bee developed a very different strategy from most of its competitors. Kay-Bee's main competitors, Toys ''R'' Us and Wal-Mart, were developed as free-standing stores that customers would make a conscious decision to visit with the intention of making purchases. Kay-Bee, on the other hand, realized that having its stores inside large malls meant that most of its customers probably came to the mall for some other reason, and that Kay-Bee needed to draw this mall traffic in. An important part of this plan was store design. All Kay-Bee outlets were designed with bright, eye-catching colors at the front of the store along with neatly arranged stacks of toys at bargain prices.

Kay-Bee's corporate image was just as bright and wholesome as the look of its stores, with the company's public relations philosophy emphasizing family values as much as value for dollars. In 1994 Kay-Bee developed the program Prescribe Reading Early to Kids (Pre-K) to help foster literacy in disadvantaged families, providing grants and free books to the program, which was organized in conjunction with local health care and community organizations. Kay-Bee was also sensitive to issues of violence in children's toys. In 1993 Kay-Bee withdrew the Sega product Night Trap, which was controversial for its violence, despite the fact that Kay-Bee had a close relationship with Sega of America and that video sales were one of Kay-Bee's most important sectors.

Kay-Bee Chairman and CEO Ann Iverson took a strong stand against violence when she removed all realistic toy guns from Kay-Bee's stores in 1994. This decision was prompted by an incident earlier that year in New York City in which a 13-year-old boy was shot and killed by a policeman who mistook his toy weapon for the real thing. Almost 300,000 toy weapons were incinerated as a result of Iverson's decision, constituting an undetermined loss in revenue for Kay-Bee Toys. The company also participated in New York's ''Goods for Guns'' program. Although Ann Iverson left as chairman in 1994, her policy of not selling look-alike guns was continued by her successor, Alan Fine, who had been senior vice-president before becoming president and CEO.

In the early 1990s Kay-Bee began a major restructuring process that paralleled that of many other subsidiaries in the Melville Corporation group. Kay-Bee closed nearly 250 less-profitable stores from 1993 to 1994 in what the company described as a strategic realignment program. While Kay-Bee also opened some new stores during the same period, they nevertheless suffered somewhat in overall sales due to the dramatic number of store closings. After having reached the $1 billion mark in 1990, the company fell below that level for the year 1993 with $919,054. The realignment was well managed, however, because by 1994 the company was back to $1,012,164 in net sales, which was almost on par with their pre-alignment numbers despite continued store closings. One reason that Kay-Bee rebounded so quickly was that the company began to open new, bigger stores while it was closing older, mall-based stores.

Although Kay-Bee had been extremely successful in mall-based outlets, mall construction in the United States had slowed during the early 1990s, and Kay-Bee was finding no attractive new malls in need of a Kay-Bee outlet. For this reason, Kay-Bee decided to launch a new string of free-standing stores in 1994, under the name Toy Works. Each of the approximately 75 Toy Works stores had a race course design with colorful markings and category signage to guide shoppers through the wide aisles of stores averaging 15,000 square feet. Kay-Bee hoped to differentiate itself from competitor Toy ''R'' Us with this distinctive store design as well as by focusing on customer service. At the same time, Kay-Bee began expanding the floor space of some of its mall-based stores from an average of 3,500 square feet to 5,000 square feet. The bigger stores sold an expanded product line, including sporting goods and toys for adults.

The decision to move into free-standing stores, enlarge floorspace, and broaden the product line brought with it some potential risks, putting Kay-Bee in direct competition with Toys ''R'' Us for the first time. However, if Kay-Bee continues to dominate the market in nearly 1,000 malls while competing successfully in free-standing superstores, Kay-Bee could have a shot at becoming the number one toy retailer in the United States.

Further Reading

Blanton, Kimberly, ''Kay-Bee Stores Buy Southern Toy Retailer,'' *Boston Globe,* September 5, 1991, p. 52.

Daly, Christopher B., ''Toy Weapons Will Be Incinerated to Make Electricity, Retailer Says,'' *Washington Post,* November 9, 1994, p. A5.

Mehegan, David, ''A Berkshire Toy Empire,'' *Boston Globe,* October 9, 1990, p. 41.

Neuborn, Ellen, ''Melville to Close, Change Some Stores,'' *USA Today,* December 12, 1992, p. B1.

Stern, Sydney Ladensohn, and Schoenhaus, Ted, *Toyland: The High Stakes Game of the Toy Industry,* Chicago: Contemporary Books, 1990, pp. 280–81.

Walters, Donna K. H., ''Masters of the Toy Universe,'' *Los Angeles Times,* September 2, 1993, p. D1.

—Hilary Gopnik and Donald McManus

Kemper Corporation

1 Kemper Drive
Long Grove, Illinois 60049
U.S.A.
(708) 320-4700
Fax: (708) 320-4535

Wholly Owned Subsidiary of Zurich Insurance Group
(80%) and Insurance Partners L.P. (20%)
Incorporated: 1967 as Kemperco Inc.
Employees: 6,059
Total Assets: $13.15 billion (1994)
Stock Exchanges: New York
SICs: 6311 Life Insurance; 6719 Offices of Holding
Companies, Not Elsewhere Classified

Kemper Corporation is a holding company consisting of life insurance and real estate investment operations. Until a recent string of divestments, spinoffs, and mergers, Kemper consisted of a much broader array of insurance and investment services units, including property-casualty insurance, reinsurance, brokerage services, and asset management services. After a lengthy two-year period in which the sale of the company preoccupied company management, Kemper was sold in early 1996 to a partnership consisting of Zurich Insurance Group and Insurance Partners L.P.

Kemper Corporation's origins are tied directly to the general business climate of the early 20th century. In 1912, a new Illinois state law requiring compensation for industrial accidents, which were common for the industry at the time, was passed.

Sensing opportunity, a 25-year-old insurance salesman named James S. Kemper proposed to a group of Chicago lumber-industry leaders that they take control of the situation by organizing their own mutual insurance firm. Kemper pointed out that the group could also contain rising premium costs by making workshops safer.

Kemper was rewarded for his plan by being named manager of the new Lumbermens Mutual Casualty Company, incorporated in Illinois on November 18, 1912. Lumbermens issued its first policy, to the Rittenhouse and Embree lumberyard, seven days after the firm was incorporated.

In 1913 James Kemper founded National Underwriters insurance exchange to provide supplementary fire insurance for lumbermen. Slow growth continued through World War I. In 1919 Lumbermens opened offices in Philadelphia, Boston, and Syracuse, New York. By this time the company was providing auto insurance as well as workers' compensation and liability insurance. The company's product line continued to grow steadily.

By 1923 Lumbermens had organized or acquired two subsidiaries and had begun operating in Canada. Around this time, Lumbermens and National Underwriters informally adopted the name Kemper Insurance to refer collectively to the interests James Kemper had organized. Although the two companies were independent, they shared office space. According to company lore, a receptionist coined the name in order to shorten her phone salutation to callers.

James Kemper incorporated American Motorists Insurance Company (AMICO) in 1926. Organized as a stock company, AMICO became part of the Kemper Insurance group but had no financial relationship to Lumbermens. During the Great Depression, Glen Cove Mutual Insurance Company, a New York mutual company, joined Kemper Insurance and, after a reorganization, reemerged as American Manufacturers Mutual Insurance Company.

During World War II Lumbermens continued to grow. The company placed patriotic advertisements and employed more women, as men went off to fight. In the years after the war, Lumbermens continued to organize subsidiaries, and—in 1948—the company moved to a larger building on Chicago's Wacker Drive.

In 1954 James Kemper became U.S. ambassador to Brazil, but his group of companies continued to grow. The Fidelity Life Association was organized in 1954. Kemper Insurance's first move into life insurance, Fidelity Life, was a mutual company that, again, had no financial ties to Lumbermens. Also in 1954, the Kemper companies invested in an automatic billing machine that helped cut office expenses. This system got a boost in 1957, when the group installed computers to process the vast amounts of data Kemper Insurance collected.

As the company grew, Kemper management, which as of 1959 included James S. Kemper Jr., decided to establish a nonoperating holding company in order to give the group greater diversification flexibility. In October 1967, Kemperco Inc. was incorporated in Delaware as a holding company for the property and casualty and life insurance operations of Kemper Insurance. Kemperco was owned primarily by Lumbermens, but its stock was also publicly traded. The holding company began operations in June 1968, with 11 operating subsidiaries. Management established objectives for the new company, including annual average earnings growth of no less than 15 percent and continuation of diversification into related businesses.

Kemperco's internal development included the organization of National Loss Control Service Corporation in July 1968. The division, known as NATLSCO, offered consulting services in the areas of fire protection, safety, industrial hygiene, air pollution, and boiler and mechanical inspection services. Diversification through external integration included the acquisition of a 40 percent stake in Extel Corporation, a maker of telecommunications devices, including printers and stock-quotation equipment.

In 1969 Kemperco added a reinsurance division, Kemper Reinsurance Company, and in 1970 Kemperco purchased Supervised Investors Services, later known as Kemper Financial Services, to manage the firm's investment portfolio. The company's assets also included Bank of Chicago, which owned a local commercial banking operation. In 1972, the company acquired Kemper Investors Life Insurance Company, National Automobile and Casualty Insurance Company, and Sequoia Insurance.

The Kemper organization had outgrown the three buildings it then occupied in Chicago, and in 1971 it had moved to a 1,000-acre campus in Long Grove, Illinois, northwest of Chicago. In 1971 assets managed by the financial-services operation reached more than $2 billion, and investment income totaled $14 million—more than double the investment income four years earlier. In 1972 the firm reported a 13 percent volume increase compared to 1971, to $329 million. Much of this growth resulted from acquisitions.

When the 1973 Arab oil embargo sparked runaway inflation in the United States, Kemper suffered. Net income for the fiscal year plunged more than 19 percent, to $18.9 million, as a slump in Kemper's automobile, workers' compensation, and general liability insurance units offset the steady growth posted in the first three quarters of the year by the other divisions.

Kemper launched a corporate-identity program, and established one-year and five-year internal performance objectives in order to maintain the goal of 15 percent annual earnings growth set in 1968. As part of its corporate-identity program, Kemperco changed its name to Kemper Corporation, on January 15, 1974. Companywide, profits continued to plunge nearly 37 percent from the disappointing showing in 1973, with net income dipping to $12.6 million.

This two-year slump prompted Kemper management to reevaluate its operations. In 1974, insurance-premium income contributed about 90 percent of the company's gross revenues, while investment income contributed about 6.5 percent. Despite modest diversification, Kemper was still dependent on the maturing insurance industry for the lion's share of its income. Kemper Corporation suffered its worst performance ever in 1975, when net income slid 26 percent from 1974, to $9.3 million. Repositioning proved to be a wise tactic. In mid-1975 Kemper Corporation launched a new market-sensitive approach, and in 1986 the holding company enjoyed the highest earnings in its nine-year history. Net income soared more than 238 percent, to $31.4 million, while total assets topped $1 billion for the first time. In 1977 Kemper Corporation posted profits of more than $57 million on sales of $808 million. The company's assets by 1977 topped $1.3 billion.

James S. Kemper Jr. announced his intention to resign as chief executive officer on April 1, 1979. Around this time, the company hit another round of financial bumps after three years of steady growth in revenues and profits. Joseph E. Luecke, Kemper Corporation's new chief executive officer, blamed an annual inflation rate of 13.3 percent for hurting the company's auto and commercial property insurance rates. Also during 1979, Kemper Corporation adopted the umbrella designation Kemper Group to refer to what had been called the Kemper Insurance and Financial Companies.

In 1979 Kemper's catastrophe losses passed $1 billion for the first time in the history of the insurance industry. Kemper's share of these losses amounted to about $25 million. A catastrophic loss is defined by the Insurance Services Offices as a total insured loss to the industry of $1 million or more. A record 50 such losses were recorded in 1979.

In 1980 Kemper once again reevaluated its dependence on property and casualty operations. Continued diversification into reinsurance and financial services lowered the contribution of insurance operations to earnings by nearly 18 percent between 1970 and 1980. Kemper management, led by chairman and CEO Luecke, responded by launching an expansion that would carry the firm far beyond property and casualty insurance. One aspect of the diversification program was the purchase of a 24.9 percent stake in Gibraltar Financial Corporation of California, a savings and loan holding company. Kemper sold some of its other assets, such as its LaBow, Haynes Company insurance brokerage in Seattle, Washington, and its 95 percent stake in the Bank of Chicago. Combined with the sale of Kemper's 33 percent stake in Extel Corporation, a manufacturer of communications equipment, Kemper realized a capital gain of about $12 million.

In 1981, Kemper reported a slide in property and casualty insurance business as a result of high interest rates, and while sales climbed 40 percent over the previous year, operating income suffered. The high interest rates that had helped the investment operations post significant gains in the fiscal year also caused inadequate pricing throughout the insurance industry, resulting in a decline in underwriting results. The diversification program launched in the previous year was expected to cover losses as uncertainty about interest rates continued.

James S. Kemper, founder of Lumbermens, died September 17, 1981. Late in 1981, Kemper announced its intention to acquire Loewi Financial Companies, widening the company's involvement in the financial-services industry. The Milwaukee, Wisconsin-based company owned Blunt Ellis & Loewi, a regional brokerage firm with offices in six midwestern states. Loewi had been a distributor of Kemper Financial Services financial products for several years before the purchase, which was completed in 1982 at a cost of $64 million in cash and stock. It was the first of several acquisitions that expanded Kemper's financial-services division over the next three years.

The timing of the brokerage acquisitions coincided with the decline of the performance of Kemper's investment in Gibraltar Financial savings and loan operation in California. Kemper had lost almost $10 million in 1980 and almost $30 million in 1981 as a result of its investment in Gibralter. The long-term diversification program was meant to help soften the blow that Kemper's property and casualty insurance business would see in 1982 and beyond.

During 1981, Kemper's property and casualty insurance units contributed just 49 percent of the firm's operating income, compared to 60 percent in 1980. Rate competition and inflation were blamed for sharp declines in the industry, and Kemper responded by committing $20 million for expansion of its life insurance business, which continued to grow, along with Kemper's annuity products.

In 1982 operating earnings for Kemper's property-casualty operations fell more than 51 percent compared to the previous year, although life insurance, reinsurance, investment services, and other operations rose by nearly 38 percent. The expansion of the financial-services business continued with the purchase of Bateman Eichler Hill Richards of Los Angeles for $50 million. Kemper acquired its third brokerage firm in two years with the purchase of an 80 percent equity stake in Cleveland-based Prescott Ball & Turben in a deal valued at $64 million. The acquisitions made Kemper the 11th-largest brokerage operator in the nation.

The slump in Kemper's property and casualty division continued in 1983, although the firm remained optimistic about long-range prospects. Operating earnings fell 11.7 percent compared to the previous year, although Kemper's life insurance division posted a 6.1 percent gain in earnings. In the boardroom, James W. Harding retired as president of the corporation and chief financial officer of the Kemper Group. Kemper Corporation chairman and chief executive Luecke assumed the additional post of president.

Early in 1984, the investment-services division again broadened its operations with the acquisition of Burton J. Vincent, Chesley & Company, a Chicago-based regional securities firm. Kemper's life insurance unit, which saw earnings improve by 43 percent, continued to offset disappointing showings by the property and casualty business for the fourth straight year. CEO Luecke labeled 1984 the worst year in Kemper Corporation's relatively short history.

In 1985 operating earnings in the property and casualty division rebounded significantly. The company also instituted cost-cutting programs which contributed to improved results. The financial division continued its expansion when Kemper acquired an 80 percent stake in Boettcher & Company, a Denver, Colorado-based regional brokerage firm, for $16 million. Also in 1985, Kemper began selling its stake in Gibralter Financial. The savings and loan had been losing money consistently since 1980. The sale of its Gibralter stock was completed in May 1986.

James S. Kemper Jr. announced his retirement as chairman of Kemper Corporation in the spring of 1986. Having joined the Kemper organization in 1959, the son of the founder was instrumental in the decision to form Kemper Corporation in 1967.

Improving market conditions helped Kemper's property and casualty operations continue to recover in 1986. Organizational changes and further cost-cutting measures also helped improve bottom-line results, although operating results at the firm's life insurance segment declined by 32 percent. In an effort to maximize earnings, the company placed its financial-services business in an independent holding company, Kemper Financial Companies, in December 1986. Kemper Corporation then sold 12 percent of the unit to 1,100 employees in a deal worth about $88 million and retained the remaining 88 percent.

The stock market crash in October 1987 caused a shakeout in the financial-services industry and also at Kemper Financial Companies, especially at the company's securities brokerage units. Overall, the financial-services arm ended 1987 relatively unscathed by the stock market crash, posting earnings 25 percent higher than those in 1986.

Kemper's property and casualty insurance operations continued to improve as the firm launched a reorganization of the business. Kemper sold most of its accident and health business and established separate profit centers for its national personal and commercial insurance lines.

By 1988, the company was finally beginning to see the fruit of the ongoing diversification program launched nearly ten years earlier. Net income reached $220 million on revenues of $2.4 billion as the firm's life insurance, reinsurance, and investment-services operations all posted significant gains. Kemper also sought to further control expenses by establishing Kemper Clearing Corporation, a joint operation that clears securities trades for all of the company's securities brokerage operations. Kemper's property and casualty business suffered a decline in earnings, despite improved underwriting results. The division also exited the troubled Massachusetts auto insurance market, a move that cost the firm $21 million.

As the 1980s came to a close, Kemper Corporation plotted yet another major restructuring, one that would take the company further away from its sister company, Lumbermens, in an effort to spur profits. The first step was the reduction of Lumbermens Mutual Casualty Company's ownership of Kemper stock from 48.8 percent to 38.3 percent, effective April 1, 1989. This was accomplished through the sale of Kemper's American Motorists Insurance Company unit to Lumbermens in exchange for 9.6 million Kemper shares. The move boosted earnings per share by reducing the number of shares outstanding by nearly 15 percent.

In late 1989 Banco Santander, Spain's fourth-largest bank, acquired a three percent stake in Kemper Corporation for $60 million. The companies teamed up to offer investment and management services to clients in the United States, Europe, and South America and also began offering insurance services to customers in Chile.

In March 1990 the three members of the Kemper Group that were not also members of Kemper Corporation—Lumbermens Mutual Casualty Company, American Motorists Insurance Company, and American Manufacturers Mutual Insurance Company—became known as the Kemper National Insurance Companies, and the Kemper organizations ceased to be referred to as the Kemper Group. Luecke remained chairman of the boards of Kemper Corporation and of the three Kemper National Insurance Companies and David B. Mathis, a Kemper Corporation vice-president, became president and chief operating officer of Kemper Corporation. Gerald L. Maatman became president and CEO of the Kemper National Insurance Companies.

Also in 1990 Kemper's five regional brokerage operations were consolidated under Kemper Securities, Inc., which was made a subsidiary of Kemper Financial Services. The move was intended to establish better control over a group of operations beset by mounting lawsuits. Two years later, however, Kemper's Prescott Ball & Turbin brokerage lost a fraud and racketeering suit filed by ContiCommodity and was assessed $137 million in damages.

Revenues declined drastically in 1992 to $1.5 billion (21.3 percent lower than 1991) and, thanks in part to the brokerage suit, Kemper posted a net loss of $203.4 million. An even larger contributor to the dismal results were the continued difficulties with Kemper's real estate investments, which posted net losses of $209.1 million in 1992. Only the ongoing strength of Kemper's asset management unit—the only Kemper unit to post a profit for the year, $88.3 million—kept 1992 from being a complete disaster.

In 1992 Mathis became CEO of Kemper Corporation and early the following year moved to turn the company's fortunes around through a major restructuring. Economy Fire & Casualty Co. was sold to the St. Paul Companies, while Federal Kemper Insurance Co. was sold to Anthem P&C Holdings, part of the Associated Group (in the process Kemper exited from property-casualty insurance, the business upon which it was founded). The risk management and reinsurance businesses were sold to Lumbermans in return for most of the Kemper stock owned by Lumbermans, which thereafter held less than four percent of Kemper. The Lumbermans purchases became part of the separately operated Kemper National Insurance Companies. Kemper also took a $180 million charge to write off real estate investments and set up additional reserves. Following these moves, Kemper Corporation's remaining businesses were the asset management operations of Kemper Financial Services, the life insurance subsidiaries Federal Kemper Life Assurance Company and Kemper Investors Life Insurance Company, the securities brokerage operations of Kemper Securities, and a much-reduced real estate investment unit.

Year-end results for 1993 boded well for the restructuring's long-term chances of success as sales increased slightly to $1.55 billion and Kemper was profitable again with $235.5 million in net income. The time needed to render a judgment was never allowed, however, since early in 1994 corporate-control events became the overriding focus of company management for the next two years.

In January 1994, General Electric Capital Corporation (GECC), the financial services arm of General Electric, made a takeover proposal of $45 per share to Kemper's board. The following month the board turned down the offer, stating that the company was not for sale and wished to give the restructuring more time to bear fruit. In March GECC increased its offer to $55 per share (or $2.2 billion); when the board again refused to sell, GECC initiated a proxy fight. Kemper and GECC continued to talk and tentatively agreed in May on a $60/share bid, all in cash, although Kemper management indicated it would consider other offers as well.

In June Conseco, Inc., a life-insurance holding company much smaller than Kemper ($5.9 billion in assets compared to Kemper's $14 billion), made a $67/share bid (or $2.96 billion), with $56/share in cash and the remainder in Conseco stock. GECC immediately withdrew its offer. A definitive merger agreement between Conseco and Kemper was signed, with the deal to be largely financed with debt given the companies' relative sizes. Following the proposed merger, in fact, Conseco planned to adopt the Kemper name.

Over the next few months, Conseco attempted to secure the financing needed to bring the deal off. Unable to sell enough assets to raise significant cash and having to take into account the impact of rising interest rates, Conseco was forced to lower its bid to $60 per share in November. Shortly thereafter the deal fell apart completely, as both sides agreed to terminate the agreement. In December Mathis told stockholders at an annual meeting that Kemper was still for sale despite its battered stock, which had fallen from a high of $62 in June to $38, a sure sign that any new offers would not be as attractive as those of 1994.

Predictions that Kemper would now be sold piecemeal turned out to be true. In a deal announced in early April 1995 and completed in September, the brokerage unit of Kemper Securities was first to go in a spinoff to be 100 percent-owned by the new firm's employees. Renamed Everan Capital Corp., the spinoff forced Kemper to take an $88 million loss from discontinued operations in 1995.

Shortly after the spinoff was announced, in mid-April, a tentative agreement for the sale of the remaining Kemper operations was reached between Kemper, Zurich Insurance Group, and Insurance Partners L.P. Following the consummation of the deal in early 1996, Zurich—Switzerland's second-largest insurance company—took sole control of the asset management unit Kemper Financial Services, which was renamed Zurich Kemper Investments Inc. What remained of Kemper Corporation—the life insurance and real estate units—became 80 percent owned by Zurich and 20 percent owned by Insurance Partners, a New York-based investment partnership specializing in the property-casualty and life insurance industries. In the final deal, Zurich and Insurance Partners paid $49.50 per share to Kemper shareholders, or a total of $2.064 billion, all in cash.

The issue of corporate control finally resolved, the much smaller Kemper Corporation could now concentrate on rebuilding its shaky business backed by the wealth of Zurich. The Swiss insurance giant saw Kemper as an attractive target because of the Kemper name and because of the opportunity the acquisition afforded to increase Zurich's life-insurance business and decrease its dependence on property-casualty premiums, two of Zurich's main goals. Many questions still remained about Kemper's future as it headed into the end of the century, but its prospects seemed much brighter than they had in many years.

Principal Subsidiaries

Federal Kemper Life Assurance Company; Kemper Investors Life Insurance Company.

Further Reading

Burns, Greg, "A Suitor Blinded by Love?," *Business Week,* October 31, 1994, p. 46.
——, "Is Kemper Trying to Give Away the Store?," *Business Week,* January 23, 1995, p. 94.
——, "Now It's on a Swiss Watch," *Business Week,* January 22, 1996.
"Conseco Caves," *Economist,* July 2, 1994, pp. 71, 74.
Fritz, Michael, "Zurich's U.S. Boss Faces Kemper Challenge," *Crain's Chicago Business,* April 17, 1995.
Kahn, Virginia Munger, "Swiss Cheese: Can Zurich Insurance Plug the Holes in Kemper?," *Financial World,* May 9, 1995, p. 64.
Pouschine, Tatiana, "Getting Out from Under," *Forbes,* March 1, 1993, p. 54.
Smart, Tim, and Greg Burns, "Does GE Have Kemper Cornered?," *Business Week,* March 28, 1994, p. 30.

—Christopher A. Scott
—updated by David E. Salamie

King Kullen Grocery Co., Inc.

1194 Prospect Avenue
Westbury, New York 11590
U.S.A.
(516) 333-7100
Fax: (516) 333-7929

Private Company
Incorporated: 1930
Sales: $720 million (1993)
Employees: 4,500
SICs: 5411 Grocery Stores; 5912 Drug Stores &
   Proprietary Stores

King Kullen Grocery Co., Inc. is a regional supermarket chain centered on Long Island, with 45 stores in 1995. Often described as the world's first supermarket chain (and recognized by the Smithsonian Institution as America's first supermarket), it was founded by Michael J. Cullen in 1930 and, in the mid-1990s, was still owned and operated by his descendants. King Kullen, through affiliated companies, entered nonfood lines of business in the early 1990s, including real estate and data processing.

Michael Cullen joined the Great Atlantic & Pacific Tea Co. (A&P) grocery chain as a clerk at the age of 18 and remained with the company for 17 years. Ten years later, in 1929, he was general sales manager of a Kroger Stores branch in Herrin, Illinois, when he presented to the company's store a plan for five prototype self-service, cash-and-carry supermarkets "monstrous in size." Because of a high volume of business and low overhead, he asserted, such stores could earn profits with much lower markups than had previously been thought possible. His proposal, never seen by the president, was rejected by a subordinate.

Cullen resigned his position and moved to New York City. With a partner, he leased an abandoned garage in the borough of Queens and in August 1930 opened the first King Kullen store. It occupied 6,000 square feet and stocked about 1,000 items, including hardware and automotive accessories. As Cullen had proposed to Kroger, he offered well-advertised price discounts on a wide range of merchandise and, as he had predicted, the public flocked to the store. Aided by a parking lot, it attracted customers from as far away as 30 miles and averaged 20 times the volume of its average competitor. By the time he died in 1936 there were 17 King Kullen stores doing a combined total of $6 million worth of business per year.

Following Cullen's death his widow, Nan, assumed control of the company. She remained its chairman into the 1960s, when her son John A. Cullen was president. By the end of 1952 King Kullen had 30 stores ranging from 10,000 to 15,000 square feet of space and about 1,000 employees. It was the first supermarket chain in its area to offer trading stamps, in 1956. Between fiscal 1956 and 1960 sales grew from $30.9 million to $48.4 million, and net income rose from $329,374 to $712,507.

King Kullen was operating 41 stores on Long Island (including the New York City boroughs of Brooklyn and Queens) in 1962, all of them leased premises, and had 971 employees. It built a 95,000-square-foot warehouse on a 10-acre plot in Westbury, Long Island, in 1961. Total assets came to $10.6 million in that fiscal year. The company went public in 1961, offering shares over the counter, but the Cullen family reserved enough stock for itself to retain a controlling interest. During the 1960s the Cullens considered buyout offers from Gristede Bros., Inc. and First National Stores Inc., but ultimately rejected them.

The King Kullen operation of the 1960s was centered around the meat operation, because the company believed that meals were designed around the meat entree and that housewives would buy groceries where they bought meat. The company warehouse offered "naturally aged beef," which, it believed, made up for slightly higher cost by attracting more customers. Almost one-fourth of revenue came from the meat department in this period. The company also offered private-label merchandise under the King Kullen, High Chief, and Lady Nan labels. In 1966 King Kullen acquired the nine-store Blue Jay chain in Suffolk County, Long Island, for $1.3 million in cash. It purchased Hinsch Produce Co., Inc. in 1969.

With the full endorsement of President James A. Cullen, a management team of "young turks" led by Walter H. Miller, the executive vice-president, determined to rejuvenate King Kullen in the late 1960s. Miller told *Progressive Grocer* in 1969, "We had our heads in the sand for so long, we weren't really merchants anymore. We were going no place. Our methods were antiquated. We had lots of money, but we weren't spending it." That year King Kullen dropped trading stamps but softened the blow and retained sales volume by selling certain staple items at 1931 prices for three weeks.

During fiscal 1970 King Kullen passed the $100-million mark in sales, reaching $114.5 million. Net income rose to $1.1 million. During fiscal 1975 sales grew to $192.2 million and net income to $2.7 million. King Kullen had 45 stores in that year and was listed as 43rd in annual sales among publicly owned food chains in the United States. By the end of fiscal 1978 King Kullen leased 49 retail outlets, ranging from 10,000 to 30,000 square feet in size, and a 33,000-square-foot produce warehouse in Jamaica, a Queens neighborhood. The company-owned Westbury warehouse had grown to 240,000 square feet, and it owned three parking lots adjacent to retail outlets.

Miller became president of King Kullen in 1971 and chairman of the board as well in 1974. In 1980—the company's 50th anniversary—it had 53 stores, of which 31 were in Suffolk County. "We've got a loyal following," Miller told a *Progressive Grocer* interviewer. "Our customers kind of grew up with us, and their children have grown with us. That's why we stick to our basic operation. We're not heavy in general merchandise." He indicated that King Kullen, which had only reluctantly accepted Sunday openings, would avoid 24-hour-a-day operation and would not stock generic brands.

By the end of fiscal 1983 King Kullen owned, rather than leased, the trucks it used to distribute grocery and meat items to its 55 stores, which ranged in size between 10,000 and 44,000 square feet. At that time the Westbury facility was providing about 45 percent of the groceries and 95 percent of the meats sold by the retail outlets. Non-warehouse goods were being delivered directly to the stores by various other suppliers. In-store bakeries were introduced in 1982. Net sales grew from $318.4 million in fiscal 1979 to $439.2 million in 1983, and net income increased from $1.8 million to $2.5 million during this period. Total assets rose from $40.7 million to $63.4 million.

In addition to food items, King Kullen was selling a variety of housewares and health and beauty aids, amounting to 4.5 percent of sales volume in fiscal 1981. These items included automotive accessories, kitchen products, personal-care appliances, and sewing notions and were mostly being purchased from merchandisers like Star Drugs, Supermarket Services, Fishman, and Supro. Best-selling merchandise included brooms and mops, disposable foilware, greeting cards, and soft goods like socks, underwear, slippers, pillows, and hand towels.

Records for fiscal 1983, the last year King Kullen was required to file an annual statement with the federal Securities and Exchange Commission, reported about 285 stockholders. An employee stock-ownership plan held one-third of the shares and family trusts held another one-fifth. Other major shareholders included the Mutual Shares Corp., James A. Cullen, Jr., John B. Cullen (son of James A. Cullen), and Walter H. Miller. After 1983 King Kullen stock ceased to be traded on the NAS-

DAQ exchange, and the company subsequently came to be listed as private.

By the end of fiscal 1990 John B. Cullen had become chairman and chief executive officer of King Kullen. Bernard D. Kennedy, another grandson of Michael and Nan Cullen, had become president and chief operating officer. The company held 49 stores and was Long Island's second-largest private employer, with 4,200 employees (up from 3,600 in 1983). Virtually all of its stores were in Nassau and Suffolk Counties, but one had been opened in the Queens neighborhood of Astoria in 1985, and the company also had entered the New York City borough of Staten Island. A store in Suffern, New York, 20 miles north of New York City, was closed in 1989. Sales came to an estimated $650 million in fiscal 1990. The company was slowly replacing stores in the range of 20,000 square feet with units of 40,000 to 50,000 square feet. King Kullen ranked third on Long Island in market share in its field behind Waldbaum's and Pathmark, with an estimated 15 percent.

Interviewed for *Supermarket Business* in 1990, Thomas K. Cullen, a vice-president and another third-generation member of the family business, acknowledged that "some of our competitors are way ahead of us" in perishables, seafood, and bakery items. A remodeling program was intended to shore up these departments, enlarge salad bars, introduce stand-up snack bars, and add such services as automatic teller machines, fax machines, pharmacies, photo developing, and postage stamps. The delis were expanded with more international gourmet foods and catering services, and self-service cheese counters were introduced.

Faced with a shortage of warehouse capacity at this time, King Kullen was building a 55,000-square-foot produce warehouse on the grounds of its 38-acre Westbury corporate headquarters to replace the antiquated Jamaica operation. The company also was using supplementary space provided by White Rose Foods, which was supplying King Kullen with its dairy items. By the mid-1990s King Kullen also was operating a 40,000-square-foot meat, deli, and seafood warehouse on its Westbury grounds.

In January 1991 King Kullen announced a diversification program, with the authorization of five new businesses, in addition to a real estate firm already disclosed. Two of these affiliated companies were founded in 1991 at King Kullen Westbury offices. The Realty Development Co. was a multifaceted construction firm, with the ability to work on projects ranging from interior renovations to complete site development. Transking Inc. operated King Kullen's fleet of 36 tractors, 108 dry trailers, 36 refrigeration trailers, and several sleeper-trailers and also served outside customers.

Shelf Life Inc., Crown Advertising Agency, and Royal Data, Inc. were established in 1992. Shelf Life acted as an independent jobber, supplying both King Kullen and outside markets with housewares, soft goods, and sundries. Crown, a full-service advertising agency, handled all of King Kullen's print, broadcast, and promotional needs and also took on outside clients in a number of commercial areas. Royal Data dealt with data processing, consulting, personnel, and related services for King Kullen and other clients. Prospect Provisions, Inc. was founded in 1993 as a wholesale distributor of dry goods and perishables. All of the above had their headquarters on King Kullen's Westbury property except Shelf Life, which had its offices in Hauppauge, Long Island.

King Kullen installed a new communications network called Kingnet between 1989 and 1991. The use of packet switching on this network allowed every application—including scanning, inventory, security, energy management, and automatic teller machines—without new telephone lines or manual switching from modem to modem. The system also included data/voice multiplexers, making the company the first retailer in New York to use data-over-voice technology.

King Kullen opened its second store on Staten Island and its largest store to date, 53,000 square feet, in November 1992. By then all of its 47 stores—33 in Suffolk County and 11 in Nassau County, as well as the Astoria and Staten Island stores—were operating around the clock except on Sundays, when they closed at 9:00 in the evening. King Kullen ranked eighth in gross sales in 1993 among grocery chains in the New York metropolitan area.

In 1995 the company added Wild by Nature, a new division, at the initiative of Dana Conklin, daughter of the chairman of the board. King Kullen opened an 18,000-square-foot Wild by Nature store dedicated to organic and natural foods to replace a former company supermarket in East Setauket, Long Island. It was the first store by a mainstream supermarket chain given to this use. Ms. Conklin said at least 80 percent of the produce and the majority of the other items would be organic and that nothing in the store, including cosmetics, would contain artifi-

cial colors, preservatives, or flavors. A second Wild by Nature was expected to open in Huntington, Long Island, in 1996.

Principal Subsidiaries

Crown Advertising Agency; Prospect Provisions, Inc.; The Realty Development Co.; Royal Data, Inc.; Shelf Life, Inc.; Transking Inc.

Further Reading

Daykin, Leonard E., "How King Kullen Went Stampless . . . and Loved It," *Progressive Grocer,* September 1969, pp. 132, 134–136, 139.

Fabricant, Florence, "Organic Foods Go Mainstream," *New York Times,* November 8, 1995, p. C3.

Fox, Bruce, "Network Reaps Big Savings for King Kullen," *Chain Store Age Executive,* November 1992, pp. 79, 83.

"King Kullen Grocery Seems Likely To Ring Up Record High Sales, Net," *Barron's,* December 23, 1967, p. 24.

Klepacki, Laura, "King Kullen's Enduring Reign," *Supermarket News,* December 28, 1992, pp. 31–32, 28.

MacFadyen, J. Tevere, "The Rise of the Supermarket," *American Heritage,* October/November 1985, pp. 23–30.

Partch, Kenneth P., "Long Island's King Kullen Keeps Its Crown Shined," *Progressive Grocer,* August 1980, p. 27.

Riell, Howard, "King Kullen: Remodeling for a New Era," *Supermarket Business,* October 1990, pp. 65–68.

Turcsik, Richard, "King Kullen To Form New Businesses," *Supermarket News,* January 21, 1991, p. 12.

Turcsik, Richard, and Merrefield, David, "King Kullen Grows Aggressive," *Supermarket News,* October 1, 1990, pp. 1, 8, 10.

—Robert Halasz

Knight-Ridder, Inc.

One Herald Plaza
Miami, Florida 33132-1693
U.S.A.
(305) 376-3800
Fax: (305) 376-3875

Public Company
Incorporated: 1974 as Knight-Ridder Newspapers, Inc.
Employees: 21,000
Sales: $2.8 billion (1995)
Stock Exchanges: New York Frankfurt Tokyo
SICs: 2711 Newspapers: Publishing, or Publishing &
Printing; 4212 Local Trucking Without Storage; 4213
Trucking, Except Local; 4899 Communication
Services, Not Elsewhere Classified; 6719 Offices of
Holding Companies, Not Elsewhere Classified; 7313
Radio, Television & Publishers' Advertising
Representatives; 7383 News Syndicates

Knight-Ridder, Inc. is the second largest newspaper publisher in the United States, with 31 daily newspapers in 16
states, including the *Detroit Free Press, Miami Herald, Philadelphia Inquirer,* and the *San Jose Mercury News.* The company's newspapers are well regarded in terms of editorial quality, and have won numerous Pulitzer Prizes. The company also
is an international telecommunications company providing
business information services, electronic retrieval services, and
other media services that reach more than 100 million people in
more than 150 countries. Knight-Ridder generates 80 percent of
its revenue from its newspaper operations.

The company began as two separate newspaper groups,
which merged in 1974. The Ridder group originated in 1892,
when Herman Ridder purchased the *Staats-Zeitung,* a New
York German-language paper. The Knight group began in 1903
when Charles Landon (C. L.) Knight bought the *Akron Beacon
Journal,* in Ohio, which the company still owns. He soon
bought two smaller Ohio newspapers, the *Springfield Sun* and
the *Massillon Independent.*

C. L. Knight, a brilliant writer, began training his son John at
an early age to replace him. John S. Knight worked as copy boy
and reporter, then went to college and fought in World War I. In
1919, at age 25, he joined the *Beacon Journal*'s staff, and
became managing editor in 1925. He carefully observed the
operations of better newspapers and applied his insights to the
Beacon Journal. C. L. Knight died in 1933, in the depths of
the Great Depression, leaving an estate of $515,000 and debts of
$800,000 to his sons, John S. and James L. Knight. The *Beacon
Journal* was facing stiff competition from another Akron paper,
the *Times-Press,* owned by Scripps-Howard, and the Great
Depression was at its most severe. John Knight froze family
earnings and took on the *Times-Press,* running more news and
features than his competitor to win over readers. He paid off the
Beacon Journal's debts within four years, and made it Akron's
leading newspaper.

John Knight's first major test as publisher came during a
1936 Akron rubber strike. Rubber was the city's major industry,
and as the strike dragged on, money and advertising dried up.
The *Times-Press* cut back on editorial pages, but Knight increased local news coverage and won readers from the *Times-
Press.* When the strike ended, he kept the readers and won new
advertising.

On October 15, 1937, John Knight became president and
publisher of *The Miami Herald,* after purchasing it for $2.25
million. The business side of the paper had been run poorly before
the Knights bought it, so James Knight, who had studied the
business and production side of newspaper publishing, became
operations manager. The Knights' first move was to distance the
paper from the Miami political establishment, with which it had
previously had close ties. The *Herald* had two competitors. The
Knights soon bought one, the *Miami Tribune,* which had been
losing money. For a cost of $600,000 plus the *Massillon Indepen-
dent,* the Knights bought the *Tribune,* eliminating a competitor
and acquiring the *Tribune*'s building, new printing press, and
other equipment. Knight closed the *Tribune* on December 1,
1937, taking six of the *Tribune*'s best people with him.

The Knights added more photographs, comics, and new columnists to the *Herald*. In the next two years two local stories—a kidnapping case and a controversy over pasteurized milk—received national attention and won 14,000 new readers for the *Herald*. Having turned the *Miami Herald* around, the Knights bought another paper, the *Detroit Free Press,* in 1940.

In 1941 Knight Newspapers, Inc. was incorporated in Ohio. World War II found German submarines off the Florida coast driving away tourists and the business that had supported the *Herald*. The paper lost much of its staff to the army, but several large military bases were set up in the Miami area, and the soldiers boosted the *Herald*'s circulation again. Lee Hills was brought in as news editor. He immediately recruited talented journalists from other Florida papers to make up for the staff the *Herald* had lost to the war effort. When a serious newsprint shortage created problems toward the end of the war, Hills and James Knight decided to cut advertising and circulation outside the Miami metropolitan area rather than editorial content, which wrested a large number of readers from its remaining competitor, *The Miami News.*

In 1944 the Knights bought the *Chicago Daily News* for $3 million, and took on the paper's $12 million debt. The *Daily News* had won a reputation for having the most thorough foreign news section of any Chicago paper, but John Knight found the stories too long and poorly written. He ordered the stories to be made more succinct, creating a brief storm of protest among some writers and readers.

The population of Dade County, Florida, nearly doubled in the years 1940 to 1950, and the *Herald*'s circulation grew apace, from 86,313 in 1941 to 175,985 in 1951. In 1946 Lee Hills began the *Clipper Edition,* a streamlined version of the *Herald* that was distributed in 23 Latin American countries. The paper won prestige and readership in Latin America, while the *Herald*'s Miami edition began to specialize in coverage of Latin America. Because of these early efforts, the paper is considered by many to have the best Latin American coverage of any U.S. newspaper.

In 1948 the *Herald*'s printers began a lengthy, sometimes violent strike over wages and the length of their work week. They were among the best paid printers in the country, but wanted to receive the same wages for working 35 hours as they were getting for working 40. The strike dragged on, and on October 1, 1949, the paper's newsprint warehouse burned down in a mysterious fire. Because of the strike, the *Herald* experimented with alternative production methods, and ended up with production methods years ahead of those at most other papers. In 1950 the paper won its first Pulitzer Prize for fighting government corruption in southern Florida. The next year Hills became executive editor of the *Herald* and the *Detroit Free Press*. He encouraged individual style and quality writing and drew a large number of excellent reporters and columnists from other papers.

In 1960 Knight took a gamble and built a $30 million building, containing offices and printing presses, for *The Miami Herald*. At the time it was the biggest building in Florida, and the biggest newspaper printing plant ever built. It reflected the Knights's belief that the *Herald*—and Miami—would continue to grow, which they did.

In 1955 Knight bought *The Charlotte Observer,* in North Carolina, purchasing its rival, *The Charlotte News,* in 1959. In the same year, the Knights sold the *Chicago Daily News* to Marshall Field for $17 million.

As the group grew larger, the Knights wanted to increase financial coordination among the newspapers. At the suggestion of Lee Hills, the Knights formed an executive committee in 1960 to undertake quarterly reviews of the operations of Knight Newspapers. They also hired finance man Alvah H. Chapman Jr. as James Knight's assistant; he rose within ten years to be president of the *Herald* and executive vice-president of Knight Newspapers. He introduced computers for administration, layout, typesetting, and production; and for improving the operation of the circulation, advertising, and business departments. Chapman mandated budgeting at all Knight newspapers, which was rarely done at small and medium-sized newspapers up to that time.

Knight Newspapers began an aggressive acquisition campaign during the same period, looking for newspapers in growing cities with at least 50,000 inhabitants. In 1969 the son of Moses Annenberg (the former *Miami Tribune* owner who sold that paper to the Knights), Walter Annenberg, sold *The Philadelphia News* and *The Philadelphia Inquirer* to Knight Newspapers for $55 million. Knight Newspapers added the *Tallahassee Democrat,* in Florida, to the group in 1965. The five papers Knight bought in 1969 continued the company's strategy of owning more than one newspaper in a market, thereby eliminating competition. In 1969 Knight's combined daily circulation was 2.2 million, and it made $12.7 million in profits on revenue of $162.8 million, largely on rising advertising revenues. It had come to be regarded as a well-managed, highly profitable, and very aggressive group, although its editorial content was not top quality. In 1969 Knight Newspapers, Inc. went public, the first offering immediately selling out at $30 a share.

Knight acquired five more dailies in 1973: the *Lexington Herald* and the *Lexington Leader,* both in Kentucky; the *Columbus Ledger* and the *Columbus Enquirer,* both in Georgia; and *The Bradenton Herald* in Florida.

Herman Ridder, founder of the Ridder group, worked his way up through the ranks at the *Staats-Zeitung,* purchasing that New York newspaper in 1892. He was a founder and president of the Associated Press and an early supporter of the American Newspaper Publishers Association, becoming its president in 1907. His sons Bernard, Joseph, and Victor bought the *New York Journal of Commerce* and the *St. Paul Dispatch-Pioneer Press* in 1927. Ridder Publications was incorporated in Delaware in 1942.

After World War II the company expanded westward in search of well-priced properties in growing markets. They bought the *Long Beach Press-Telegram, Long Beach Independent, San Jose Mercury News,* and the *Pasadena Star News,* all in California, as well as some smaller California papers; a 65 percent stake in the *Seattle Times,* in Washington; the Gary *Post Tribune* in Indiana; and radio and television station WCCO, in Minneapolis, Minnesota. The *San Jose Mercury News* was the most profitable Ridder publication. The company bought the Boulder *Daily Camera* in Colorado in 1969 and the *Wichita Eagle* and Beacon Publishing Company of Kansas in 1973.

Ridder's 1973 earnings were $14.3 million on revenue of $166 million. Knight's 1973 earnings were $22.1 million on revenue of $341.9 million. Their merger grew out of talks between friends Lee Hills and Bernard Ridder Jr., grandson of Herman Ridder, who were interested in expansion. Influenced by the success of the rival Gannett group, both the Knight and the Ridder groups had gone public in 1969 to raise capital for acquisitions. The groups described the potential benefits of a merger to their stockholders as "a broader and more diversified income base, greater newspaper size, mix and geographical distribution, and a stronger balance sheet." The merger was accomplished through an exchange of stock, and five Ridder representatives joined ten from Knight Newspapers, to form Knight-Ridder's board of directors.

The Knight group had focused on the South and East, while Ridder had focused on the West and Midwest. At the time of the merger, Knight owned 16 dailies in seven states, while Ridder owned or had a substantial interest in 19 dailies in ten states. The Ridder dailies were all in exclusive markets, while the Knight's three largest revenue yielders—in Miami, Detroit, and Philadelphia—all faced competition. At the time of the merger, *Time*, July 22, 1974, reported that in general, "the Ridder papers do not have the heft and influence of the Knight dailies."

When the groups merged on November 30, 1974, Ridder became a wholly owned subsidiary of Knight, and the renamed Knight-Ridder Newspapers, Inc. became the largest newspaper company in the United States, with newspapers from coast to coast. The new company had 35 newspapers in 25 cities, with combined circulation averaging 3.8 million daily and 4.2 million on Sunday, total assets of $465 million, and profits of $36 million. Other large companies published newspapers, but they were diversified, while Knight-Ridder Newspapers focused on newspapers alone—Knight and Ridder had agreed to sell their radio and television holdings as part of the Federal Communications Commission's conditions for merging. The new company continued to give its newspapers editorial autonomy while maintaining strict central control of business operations. It organized its new papers into three groups along geographical lines.

In 1976 Knight-Ridder Newspapers, Inc. became Knight-Ridder, Inc. Alvah H. Chapman Jr. was elected chief executive officer, succeeding Lee Hills, and Bernard H. Ridder Jr. was elected chairman of the executive committee, succeeding James L. Knight, who resigned. James L. Knight died in 1991 at the age of 81. John Knight also retired as editorial chairman in 1976. He died in 1981 at the age of 81. Lee Hills took his place until 1979 when he retired and Bernard H. Ridder Jr. succeeded him.

Beginning in the late 1970s, many media companies went on newspaper-buying binges, snapping up what turned out to be bargains while Knight-Ridder watched from the sidelines. The company had concluded that newspapers were a mature market and moved into other areas. It bought radio stations; entered cable television in 1981 with TKR Cable Co., a 50–50 joint venture with Tele-Communications Inc.; and started Viewdata Corporation, which offered news and financial services on home computers. Viewdata never did well, and was closed in 1986 after losing $50 million. By that time Knight-Ridder recognized that it had made a mistake, and that profit gains might come from newspapers. Knight-Ridder finally acquired more newspapers that year when it bought the six-paper State-Record Company, based in Columbia, South Carolina, for $311 million.

By the mid-1980s, Knight-Ridder had a stable of Pulitzer Prize-winning reporters and 34 newspapers. Yet its largest four newspapers—Miami, Detroit, Philadelphia, and San Jose—which accounted for 55 percent of company revenues, had problems at various times in 1980s, including a 46-day strike in Philadelphia in 1985. The company's net profits fell 5.7 percent in 1985. They rose 5.5 percent in 1986, but competitors were doing far better in those years—Gannett's profits rose 23 percent, while the Times Mirror Company's rose 75 percent.

Part of the reason for the company's declining profits was that it had lost touch with its readers. Hispanics accounted for half the population of the Miami area, but only 20 percent of them read *The Miami Herald*. In 1986 several of the *Herald*'s offices were closed. In 1987, it redesigned the Spanish version of the paper, *El Nuevo Herald*, to win Hispanic readership. The *Detroit Free Press*, locked in a cutthroat price war with the rival *Detroit News*, lost $74 million between 1981 and 1987, prompting the company to request a joint operating agreement (JOA) from the U.S. Department of Justice allowing the *Free Press* and *News* to share advertising and production operations. Citizens' groups challenged the request on the grounds that the measure was anticompetitive and that both papers could coexist healthily if they raised their prices. The opposition created long delays and several more years of losses. The joint operating agreement was finally granted in 1989, when the Supreme Court approved the agreement.

By 1988 Knight-Ridder's business information services division was growing three times as fast as its newspapers. The company had also moved into computer-based graphics services. The Knight-Ridder Graphics Network went on line in October 1985, at first servicing only newspapers in the group. It began to offer a full-scale daily service to papers outside Knight-Ridder in 1986. Within a year it was used by 28 of the chain's newspapers and had 110 outside subscribers in North America and Europe. Subscribing newspapers paid $50 to $300 a month, depending on their circulation, for the privilege of using the system.

Beginning in 1987, Knight-Ridder undertook a cost-cutting campaign headed by P. Anthony Ridder, president of the newspaper division. By 1989, however, the company's debt approached $1 billion, fed by the 1988 purchase of Dialog Information Services, Inc., a leading online information service, for $353 million. In 1988 James Batten was appointed chief executive officer, replacing Alvah Chapman, and Anthony Ridder was named president of the company. To reduce debt, Batten sold the company's broadcasting group and the *Pasadena Morning Star News* netting $425 million. Still, the company was sufficiently wary of a takeover for its shareholders to vote a "quality of journalism" amendment to prevent a buyout by a media baron such as Rupert Murdoch.

Under Batten and Ridder, Knight-Ridder in the early through mid-1990s gradually tightened its focus to newspapers and business information services by making additional divestments. The company stayed away from costly bleeding-edge gambles similar to Viewdata, instead working to extend its core businesses in new ways and making strategic acquisitions complementary to those same core businesses.

Within Knight-Ridder's newspaper division, the *San Jose Mercury News*, through a partnership with online service provider America Online in 1993, became the first newspaper in the country to offer its readers an online extension of its paper. The flat-rate service offered news and features from the paper, advertising, and bulletin boards for messaging. That same year a similar venture began to be developed for the *Detroit Free Press*, this time in partnership with America Online competitor CompuServe. By 1995, Knight-Ridder had committed to putting all of its papers online by 1997.

In its business information services division, Knight-Ridder was disappointed with the lackluster growth of ten percent a year that Dialog had been achieving since it was acquired. To remedy this, the company adopted two strategies—geographic growth and user growth. In 1993 it acquired Data-Star, a European online service, from the Swiss engineering company Motor-Columbus. In its first year under Knight-Ridder, Data-Star helped boost Dialog's revenue 19 percent over 1992. In 1994, the company moved into the Canadian market with a joint venture with Southam, Inc. called Infomart DIALOG. The company's three online services—DIALOG, Data-Star, and Infomart DIALOG—were then grouped within the newly named Knight-Ridder Information, Inc. (KRII), the former Dialog Information Services. With regard to the second strategy, KRII's services were traditionally used primarily by librarians and other information specialists who had mastered the complex and powerful software the services ran on. In order to expand the potential user base, in 1993 KRII began to develop interfaces for the services that were easier for end-users— businesspeople and academics—to use themselves.

In late 1993, Batten was critically injured in a car crash, neared death, and finally recovered after spending 17 days in the hospital. Less than two months later, he was back on the job part-time and eventually returned on a full-time basis. In mid-1994, however, Batten was diagnosed with brain cancer, and in March 1995 stepped down as CEO although he remained chairman. Anthony Ridder took over as CEO, then also took over the chairmanship upon Batten's death three months later.

The revamping of the business information services division continued in the mid-1990s. In early 1994 Knight-Ridder acquired Technimetrics, a provider of investor relations information. The following year, the *Journal of Commerce* was sold to the Economist Group, the British publisher of the *Economist* magazine, for $115 million. The move was part of the company's strategy to move away from specialized markets. Early in 1996, the Knight-Ridder Financial news wire was put up for sale after the company failed in a years-long effort to make inroads against the top three business wires, Reuters, Dow Jones's Telerate, and Bloomberg Financial News. It was sold later that spring for $275 million. Two months later, Knight-Ridder made another significant divestment—this one outside

the business information sector—when it sold its stake in TKR Cable to its partner Tele-Communications Inc. for about $420 million in cash and stock. Knight-Ridder decided to leave the cable business because of the industry's increasing consolidation, which made it impossible for small players such as Knight-Ridder to compete.

With the newspaper division looming more important than ever to Knight-Ridder's future, the company made substantial investments there in the mid-1990s. In 1995, a $120 million, two-year modernization of the *Miami Herald*'s main plant was announced and $360 million was spent to acquire four daily newspapers in the San Francisco Bay area from Lehser Communications, Inc. The acquired papers had a combined circulation of 190,000 daily and 206,000 Sunday.

Unfortunately, 1995 was also the year in which a long, bitter, and sometimes violent strike began in Detroit and affected the two daily papers operating under the JOA, including the *Detroit Free Press*. Started in July, the strike hit Knight-Ridder hard, contributing greatly to an 82 percent decline in 1995's third-quarter profits. The company appeared to be banking on making up the losses in the long run by forcing the unions to accept lower wages.

With the strike in Detroit stretching well into 1996, Knight-Ridder faced an uncertain future. Having slimmed down to newspapers and business information services and cutting costs substantially in the process, the company now had to find ways to increase revenues from its core businesses (revenue in 1995 had increased only 3.9 percent). This had long proved difficult in the mature newspaper business, so Knight-Ridder's various electronic ventures were more important than ever to the company's future.

Principal Subsidiaries

Aberdeen News Company; Boca Raton News, Inc.; Boulder Publishing, Inc.; The Bradenton Herald, Inc.; Detroit Newspaper Agency (50%); Drinnon, Inc.; Grand Forks Herald, Incorporated; Gulf Publishing Company, Inc.; Keynoter Publishing Company, Inc.; Macon Telegraph Publishing Company; News Publishing Company; Newspapers First (33.33%); Nittany Printing & Publishing Co.; San Jose Mercury News, Inc.; The State-Record Company; Sun Publishing Company, Inc.; Tallahassee Democrat, Inc.; The Union-Recorder; Vu/TEXT Information Services; Wichita Eagle and Beacon Publishing Co., Inc.; Unicom, Inc. (U.K.).

Principal Divisions

Business Information Services Division; Newspaper Division.

Principal Operating Units

The Beacon Journal Publishing Company; The Charlotte Observer; Centre Daily Times, Inc.; The Columbus Ledger & Enquirer; Commodity News Services, Inc.; Duluth News-Tribune; Fort Wayne Newspapers, Inc.; The Knight Publishing Co.; Long Beach Press-Telegram Division; The Miami Herald; The R.W. Page Corp.; Philadelphia Newspapers, Inc.; Saint Paul Pioneer Press Division; Sun Herald; The Sun News.

Further Reading

DeGeorge, Gail, ''Knight-Ridder: Running Hard, but Staying in Place,'' *Business Week,* February 26, 1996.

DeGeorge, Gail, and Veronica N. Byrd, ''Knight-Ridder: Once Burned, and the Memory Lingers,'' *Business Week,* April 11, 1994.

'' 'Dynastic' Ridder Clan Gathers—40 Strong,'' *Editor & Publisher,* April 19, 1969.

Jones, Tim, ''For Newspapers, a Bundle of Woes,'' *Chicago Tribune,* October 29, 1995, p. 1.

''Knight-Ridder Will Become Largest All-Newspaper Firm,'' *Editor & Publisher,* November 16, 1974.

Sandoval, Ricardo, ''Knight-Ridder Buys Four Lesher Papers in San Francisco Bay Area,'' *San Jose Mercury News,* August 29, 1995.

Smiley, Nixon, *Knights of the Fourth Estate: The Story of the Miami Herald.* Miami: E.A. Seemann Publishing, 1974, 340 p.

Whited, Charles, *Knight: A Publisher in the Tumultuous Century,* New York: E.P. Dutton, 1988, 405 p.

—Scott M. Lewis
—updated by David E. Salamie

The Kroger Company

1014 Vine Street
Cincinnati, Ohio 45201
U.S.A.
(513) 762-4000
Fax: (513) 762-4454

Public Company
Incorporated: 1902 as The Kroger Grocery and Baking
    Company
Employees: 200,000
Sales: $23.94 billion (1995)
Stock Exchanges: New York Cincinnati Midwest
SICs: 2022 Natural, Processed & Imitation Cheese; 2045
    Prepared Flour Mixes & Doughs; 2086 Bottled &
    Canned Soft Drinks & Carbonated Waters; 2099 Food
    Preparations, Not Elsewhere Classified; 5411 Grocery
    Stores

The Kroger Company is the leading grocery retailer in the United States. It operates more than 1,300 supermarkets in 24 states across the country, primarily in the Midwest, South, Southeast, and Southwest. More than 1,050 of these are under the Kroger name, with the remainder operating under such names as Dillon Stores, King Soopers, and Fry's through its Dillon Companies, Inc. subsidiary. More than 93 percent of the company's sales come from its grocery operations, with most of the remainder coming from the more than 800 convenience stores Dillon operates under various names in 15 states. Kroger also operates 37 food processing facilities that produce dairy products, bakery goods, deli items, and other grocery products.

The Kroger Company traces its roots back to 1883, when Bernard H. Kroger began the Great Western Tea Company, one of the first chain store operations in America. Kroger left school to go to work at age 13 when his father lost the family dry goods store in the panic of 1873. At 16, he sold coffee and tea door-to-door. At 20, he managed a Cincinnati grocery store, and at 24, he became the sole owner of the Great Western Tea Company,

which by the summer of 1885 had four stores. Kroger's shrewd buying during the panic of 1893 raised the number to 17, and by 1902, with 40 stores and a factory in Cincinnati, Kroger incorporated and changed the company's name to The Kroger Grocery and Baking Company.

Kroger Company historians characterize B. H. Kroger as somewhat of a "crank," fanatically insistent upon quality and service. Profanity was called his second language; he often advised his managers to "run the price down as far as you can go so the other fellow won't slice your throat."

Part of Kroger's success came from the elimination of middlemen between the store and the customer. In 1901, Kroger's company became the first to bake its own bread for its stores, and in 1904, Kroger bought Nagel Meat Markets and Packing House and made Kroger grocery stores the first to include meat departments.

This important innovation, however, was not easy. It was common practice at that time for butchers to shortweigh and take sample cuts home with them, practices that did not coincide with B. H. Kroger's strict accounting policies. When Kroger installed cash registers in the meat departments, every one of them inexplicably broke. When Kroger hired female cashiers, the butchers opened all the windows to "freeze out" the women and then let loose with such obscene language that the women quit in a matter of days. When Kroger hired young men instead as cashiers, the butchers threatened them with physical force. But Kroger was stubborn, and in the long run his money-saving, efficient procedures won out.

From the beginning, Kroger was interested in both manufacturing and retail. His mother's homemade sauerkraut and pickles sold well to the German immigrants in Cincinnati. And in the back of his store, Kroger himself experimented to invent a "French brand" of coffee, which is still sold in Kroger stores.

The Kroger Grocery and Baking Company soon began to expand outside of Cincinnati; by 1920, the chain had stores in Hamilton, Dayton, and Columbus, Ohio. In 1912, Kroger made his first long-distance expansion, buying 25 stores in St. Louis, Missouri. At a time when most chains only hired trucks as needed, Kroger bought a fleet of them, enabling him to move the company into Detroit; Indianapolis, Indiana; and Springfield and Toledo, Ohio.

When America entered World War I in 1917, B. H. Kroger served on the president's national war food board and on the governor of Ohio's food board. His dynamic plain speech raised substantial amounts of money for the Red Cross and Liberty Bonds.

After the war, The Kroger Grocery and Baking Company continued to expand, following Kroger's preference for buying smaller, financially unsteady chains in areas adjacent to established Kroger territories. In 1928, one year before the stock market crashed, Kroger sold his shares in the company for more than $28 million. One of his executives, William Albers, became president. In 1929, Kroger had 5,575 stores, the most there have ever been in the chain.

Since the turn of the century, chain stores had been accused of driving small merchants out of business by using unfair business practices and radically changing the commerce of communities. In the 1920s, an anti-chain store movement began to gain momentum. Politicians, radio announcers, and newspapers talked about "the chain store menace." People feared the rapid growth of chains and their consequent power over their industries. Because the grocery industry was so much a part of most people's lives, food chains such as Kroger bore the brunt of public complaints.

Chain store company executives soon realized they would have to organize in order to prevent anti-chain legislation. In 1927, the National Chain Stores Association was founded and William Albers was elected president.

When Albers resigned as president of Kroger in 1930, he also resigned as president of the organization. Albert H. Morrill, an attorney who had served as Kroger's general counsel, was elected president of both in his stead. Morrill faced not only the economic challenges of the Great Depression, but also the political challenges of the growing public distrust of chain stores.

With the limited transportation and communication systems of the time, the company had to decentralize in order to grow. Morrill established 23 branches with a manager for each branch, and hired a real estate manager to close unprofitable stores. He also implemented policies that guarded against anti-chain accusations, while encouraging customers to shop at Kroger stores.

Instead of going through the usual channels for buying produce, The Kroger Grocery and Baking Company began to send its buyers to produce farms so they could inspect crops to ensure the quality of the food their stores sold. This counteracted the frequent complaint that chain stores sold low-quality foods. This policy eventually resulted in the formation of Wesco Food Company, the Kroger Company's own produce procurement organization.

Morrill also began the Kroger Food Foundation in 1930, making it the first grocery company to test food scientifically in order to monitor the quality of products. The foundation also established the Homemakers Reference Committee, a group of 750 homemakers who tested food samples in their own homes.

In 1930, one of the company's southern managers, Michael Cullen, proposed a revolutionary plan to his superiors: a bigger self-service grocery store that would make a profit by selling large quantities of food at low prices that competitors could not beat. But at this stage, Kroger executives were wary of the idea, and Cullen went on alone to begin the first supermarket, King Kullen, in Queens, New York.

Throughout the Depression, Kroger maintained its business; by 1935, Kroger had 50 supermarkets of its own. During the 1930s, frozen foods and shopping carts were introduced, and the Kroger Food Foundation invented a way of processing beef without chemicals so that it remained tender, calling the process "Tenderay" beef.

Morrill and Colonel Sherrill, vice-president of Kroger, became involved with the organization of the American Retail Association in 1935. A report of the organization's publicity release on the front page of *The New York Times* prompted controversy, because the headline stated that the organization would work as a "unified voice" in economic matters, which suggested a kind of "super lobby" to some people. This led to a congressional investigation and in 1938, a bill was introduced imposing a punitive tax against chain stores that would almost certainly force them out of business. Only after much controversy and public debate was the punitive tax bill defeated that year.

In 1942, Morrill died. Charles Robertson, formerly vice-president and treasurer, became president. The company's plans for growth were shelved during World War II, with about 40 percent of its employees serving in the armed forces. The Army Quartermaster Corps commissioned the Kroger Food Foundation to create rations that would boost the morale of soldiers, and the company produced individual cans of date pudding, plum pudding, and fruit cake. Other rations that came from Kroger included cheese bars, preserves, and "C-ration crackers."

After the war, in 1946, Joseph Hall, who had been hired in 1931 to close unprofitable stores, became president. He changed the company name from The Kroger Grocery and Baking Company to The Kroger Company, in keeping with indications that the company was moving into a new period of growth. In 1947, Kroger opened its first egg-processing plant in Wabash, Indiana, in order to further ensure egg quality. Hall also saw that 45 private-label brands were merged into one Kroger brand, and introduced the blue-and-white logo with the name change.

Hall's new policy of consumer research was an important change for the company. Decisions about products and methods of selling were to come from the "votes" shoppers left at the cash register. During his years as president, the company moved into Texas, Minnesota, and California. Annual sales grew as small neighborhood stores were replaced with larger supermarkets. In 1952, Kroger sales topped $1 billion.

This was a time of rapid growth for supermarkets. Between 1948 and 1963, the number of supermarkets in the country nearly tripled. Kroger was already testing the specialty shops that would later be integral to its "superstores." As competition in the industry grew more fierce, Kroger joined with six other firms to found the Top Value Stamp Company, which tried to bring customers into the stores with stamp collecting promotions.

In 1960 the company began its expansion into the drugstore business, with an eye on the potential for drugstores built next to grocery stores. The company bought a small drugstore chain and made its owner, James Herring, the head of the drugstore division. The first SupeRx drugstore opened in 1961 next to a Kroger food store in Milford, Ohio.

Discount stores—strategically located stores that aggressively merchandised goods on a low margin basis with minimum service—were the retailing trend of the 1960s. By 1962, Kroger had also gone into discounting.

In 1963 Kroger's sales reached $2 billion. In 1964, Jacob Davis, a former congressman and judge and a vice-president of Kroger, replaced Hall as president and CEO. Davis concentrated on the manufacturing branch of Kroger. With the construction of the interstate highway system in the 1950s and 1960s, central manufacturing facilities could now serve larger territories, allowing Kroger to combine small facilities into larger regional ones.

Davis's experience in both retail and law became important to the company as the government began to clamp down on the food industry. During hearings for the 1967 Meat Inspection Act, several chains were exposed for selling adulterated processed meats. The United States Department of Agriculture revealed that Kroger was selling franks and bolognas with two to four times the legal amount of water or extender and pork sausage treated with artificial colors to make it look fresh.

With the rapid growth of food chain stores, the government also began to concentrate on enforcing antitrust laws. Kroger was one of the companies the Federal Trade Commission challenged on its mergers. In 1971, the FTC proposed a consent order that required the company to divest itself of three discount food departments, charging that Kroger stores would "substantially lessen" competition in food retailing in the Dayton, Ohio, area. Kroger settled without admitting any violation of antitrust laws, and sold the three food departments. The order also prohibited Kroger from buying any food store or department in nonfood stores in which the number of stores or sales accrued would indicate a lessening of competition in that city or county.

James Herring became president of The Kroger Company in 1970 and began to take Kroger into the superstore age, closing hundreds of small supermarkets and building much larger ones with more specialty departments.

The 1970s were a turbulent time for the grocery industry in general, but both turbulent and productive for Kroger. The company perfected its "scientific methods" of consumer research, using the results in planning and advertising. In the early 1970s, at the request of consumer groups, Kroger led the industry in marking its perishable products with a "sell by" date. Kroger began to bake only with enriched flour to add nutrition to its bread products. Two years later, nutritional labels were put on Kroger private-brand products. And food and nonfood prod-

ucts were stocked in twice the variety they had been in the previous two decades.

To increase the accuracy and speed of checkout systems, Kroger, in partnership with RCA, became the first grocery company to test electronic scanners under actual working conditions, in 1972. An invention borrowed from the railroad industry, the scanner was originally used as the electric eye that read symbols on the side of railcars. Kroger and other grocery chains decided to try to use it to read prices on products.

While the government controlled prices between 1971 and 1974, grocery stores suffered depressed profits, but by 1974, the net profits of the top food chains were up 57 percent. As food chains grew into ever larger and more powerful businesses and gained increasing control over the agricultural economy through their enormous wholesalers, there was another round of Federal Trade Commission hearings that revealed the illegal business practices of several chains. In 1974, Kroger settled out of court on an antitrust claim against Kroger and two other chains for fixing beef prices. In 1974 the Federal Trade Commission also sued Kroger for violations of its 1973 trade rule that all stores must stock a sufficient supply of specials to meet anticipated demand and must give rainchecks if the supplies ran out. In 1977 Kroger consented to the FTC order.

But the biggest battle Kroger faced in its tangles with the Federal Trade Commission concerned the company's use of "Price Patrol," an advertising promotion used in certain markets at different times between 1972 and 1978, in which Kroger advertisements compared Kroger prices with the prices of its competitors on 150 products a week. The figures were based upon surveys conducted among housewives. The Federal Trade Commission ruled that slogans such as "Documented Proof: Kroger leads in lower prices" were unfair and deceptive because the items surveyed excluded meat, produce, and house brands. A controversy ensued when the Council on Wage and Price Stability expressed concern that tougher standards for Kroger might prevent the dissemination of food price information in the future, but the Federal Trade Commission decided that surveys must be conducted fairly and reliably and that their limitations should be made clear. Kroger appealed; the "Price Patrol" issue was not decided until 1983, when Kroger settled out of court with the Federal Trade Commission.

In 1978, Lyle Everingham, who began his career as a Kroger clerk, became CEO. The company sold Top Value Enterprises and opened Tara Foods, a peanut butter processing plant, in Albany, Georgia. As Kroger moved more towards the "superstore" concept of one-stop shopping, it began to test even more in-store specialty departments such as beauty salons, financial services, cheese shops, and cosmetic counters.

The 1980s were a period of significant expansion for Kroger. In 1981, Kroger began marketing its Cost Cutter brand products. In 1983, Kroger merged with the Dillon Companies and began operating stores coast to coast. That same year, the company acquired the Kwik Shop convenience store chain. A year later, Kroger formed a nonunion grocery wholesaler for Michigan called FoodLand Distributors with Wetterau. In 1987, however, Kroger reduced its involvement in stand-alone drug stores when it sold most of interests in the Hook and SupeRx chains.

In 1988, Kroger received several takeover bids, mainly from the Dart Group Corporation and from Kohlberg Kravis Roberts, whose highest bid topped $5 billion. Kroger rejected the bids and restructured, expecting that recapitalization would enhance its competitiveness. The reorganization expanded employee ownership to more than 30 percent of the company's shares. Kroger also awarded its shareholders with a dividend of cash and debentures worth $48.69 per share. Kroger financed the restructuring by selling $333 million worth of unprofitable assets and by assuming $3.6 billion in loan debt. Among the divested properties were 95 grocery stores, 29 liquor stores, its Fry's stores located in California, and the majority of its stake in Price Saver Membership Wholesale Clubs.

Following the restructuring, Kroger's debt load totaled $5.3 billion. For the next several years, the firm focused on paying down this debt and stayed away from major acquisitions and from significant expansion. Kroger did, however, purchase 29 Great Scott! supermarkets in Michigan in 1990 and add them to the Kroger chain.

During the recession of the early 1990s, Kroger felt the pressure of increasing competition in several of the markets it served. The geographic diversity of the firm's holdings, however, insulated it from serious trouble. Under the leadership of Joseph A. Pilcher, who became CEO in 1990, Kroger adopted a strategy of protecting market share at all costs, including sacrificing margins for the more important cash flow needed to pay off the debt. When faced with increased competition in a particular market—for example when Food Lion, Inc. expanded into Texas in 1991—Kroger would simply lower prices and accept the resulting reduced margins. In fact, Kroger lost money for a period in the early 1990s in Texas as well as in Cincinnati and Dayton, Ohio. The company was able to offset such losses to some degree by relying more heavily on higher margin markets, although such markets were becoming rarer thanks to the expansion of low-price competitors.

Kroger has also had to face the consequences of its unionized work force and had to compete with nonunion chains. In addition to the increasing competitive pressures, Kroger's sales and earnings were affected in 1992 by a ten-week strike in Michigan and another work stoppage in Tennessee. Although the Michigan strike ended with the workers essentially accepting the package initially offered them, 1992 sales increased only 3.7 percent over 1991 and the company margin remained in the 0.5 percent range where it had resided since 1990. Consequently, Kroger embarked on a major program to improve its efficiency through technological improvements. From 1992 to 1994, $120 million was spent to make checkout operations more efficient and accurate, to install a new management information system, and to improve direct-store delivery accounting.

By 1994 Kroger's debt load had been reduced significantly, to $3.89 billion. Kroger enjoyed savings of almost $23 million in 1994 alone from its technology investments. The company also benefited from the economic recovery during which interest rates fell, thus reducing the amount needed to spend servicing its debt whenever it could refinance its loans. Enough money could now be freed up for Kroger to shift its focus from debt maintenance to expansion. The timing of this expansion was critical in that Kroger now faced yet another and significant threat, this time from supercenters—such as those operated by Wal-Mart, Kmart, and Meijer's—which were combination food, pharmacy, and general merchandise stores. By 1994 more than one quarter of Kroger's sales base competed directly with a supercenter. Kroger's plan was to continue using its combination food and drug store format—facilities that were about one-third the size of the supercenters—but to increase their number dramatically.

During 1994, Kroger spent $534 million on the expansion, which included 45 new stores, 17 expanded stores, 66 remodelings, and the acquisition of 20 stores. From 1995 to 1997, $600 million was to be spent each year on expansion projects. Overall, this would be the largest capital expansion in Kroger history.

To free up additional money for the program and further reduce the company debt, Kroger in early 1995 sold Time Saver Stores, a division of Dillon which included 116 convenience stores in the New Orleans area, to E-Z Serve Convenience Stores, Inc. of Houston, Texas. Later that year, David B. Dillon, CEO of the Dillon subsidiary, became president and COO of Kroger.

Early returns from the company's mid-1990s expansion were positive. Kroger's 1994 margin of 1.2 percent was its best in several years, and 1995 saw a healthy sales increase of 4.3 percent. Kroger seemed solidly in position to maintain its number one position in the grocery market into the next century.

Principal Subsidiaries

Dillon Companies, Inc.

Principal Divisions

Garland Beverage Co.; Kenlake Foods; Pace Dairy Foods; Tara Foods.

Further Reading

Berss, Marcia, "Cash Flow Joe," *Forbes,* June 6, 1994, p. 47.

Cross, Jennifer, *The Supermarket Trap: The Consumer and the Food Industry,* Bloomington, Ind.: Indiana University Press, rev. ed., 1976, 306 p.

Hackney, Holt, "Kroger Co.: Price Check," *Financial World,* June 7, 1994, p. 18.

The Kroger Story: A Century of Innovation, Cincinnati: The Kroger Company, 1983.

Lebhar, Godfrey M., *Chain Stores in America,* New York: Chain Store Publishing Corporation, 1963.

Orgel, David, "Kroger Co. to Step up Expansion," *Supermarket News,* May 23, 1994, p. 1.

Tosh, Mark, "Kroger: Under Pressure," *Supermarket News,* January 18, 1993, p. 1.

—updated by David E. Salamie

Laclede Steel Company

One Metropolitan Square
St. Louis, Missouri 63102
U.S.A.
(314) 425-1400
Fax: (314) 425-1561

Public Company
Incorporated: 1911 as Laclede Steel Company
Employees: 1,900
Sales: $341.2 million (1994)
Stock Exchanges: NASDAQ
SICs: 3312 Blast Furnaces & Steel Mills; 6748 Business
Consulting Services, Not Elsewhere Classified

A leading scrap steel manufacturer, Laclede Steel Company manufactures carbon and alloy steel products, including pipe and tubular products, wire products, and welded chain. During the mid-1990s, Laclede's facilities included a steel-making plant in Alton, Illinois, a pipe finishing plant in Vandalia, Illinois, a chain manufacturing plant in Maryville, Missouri, a wire mill in Memphis, Tennessee, a wire oil tempering facility in Fremont, Indiana, and an electric resistance weld tubing mill in Benwood, West Virginia.

Organized in 1911, Laclede spent its formative decades recording only modest growth, at least compared to the pace of growth achieved by the company in its later years. For a scrap steel company, prosaic growth during the first half of the 20th century was common; Laclede was not alone in beginning its rise slowly within the steel industry. Though the steel industry as a whole represented one of the chief industries in the United States during the first half of the 20th century, its magnitude reflected the strength and enormous revenue volumes of the nation's primary steel manufacturers, the massive conglomerate corporations that dwarfed scrap steel companies like Laclede. It was not until roughly three decades after Laclede's formation that the demand for steel in the United States reached sufficient levels to transform scrap companies from anonymity to prominence, a phenomenon that provided the necessary impetus to at

last propel Laclede's growth at a robust pace. Once through this period of maturation, Laclede blossomed, sharing in the explosive years of steel consumption following the Second World War.

Beginning with its first public sale of stock in 1911, an initial public offering that raised $100,000, Laclede embarked on the slow trek toward the prominence it would later achieve, operating as a small scrap metal manufacturer in Missouri. By turning scrap steel into finished products, the company established itself during its inaugural year as a regional manufacturing concern, small in size and scope yet resilient enough to withstand the pernicious pressures every fledgling business venture faces. The conclusion of the company's second year of business brought investors their first dividend payment, marking the beginning of one of the best dividend records in the steel industry. From 1912, through the economically cataclysmic 1930s and into the 1960s, Laclede maintained sufficient profitability to pay dividends to its investors each year, demonstrating a consistency within the notoriously cyclical steel industry that firmly established the company as a solid competitor. Annual sales, however, were held in check by the subsidiary position occupied by scrap steel manufacturers within the steel industry.

From Laclede's founding year in 1911 to the outbreak of the Second World War, annual sales rose only modestly, falling short of $10 million by the time the company concluded its thirtieth year of business. The less-than-prolific growth of the company's annual sales would not have been worthy of note without the resolute rise in sales recorded after the conclusion of the Second World War, the two periods dividing Laclede's development into two chapters: one being the steady but slow growth of the company during its first 30 years of business and the second comprising a 15-year period of contrastingly different, energetic sales growth.

Annual sales by 1944 reached the $10 million mark as hostilities overseas neared their conclusion. In the next six years, Laclede quadrupled its revenue volume during the incipient stages of America's economic rebirth. Crippled during the decade-long Great Depression, then artificially bolstered by the country's involvement in the Second World War, the U.S. economy demonstrated vibrancy during the postwar years, buoyed and invigorated by pervasive manufacturing activity in nearly every U.S. industry. Infused with business by the soaring demand for steel and steel products, Laclede rode the crest of the wave, more than doubling its annual sales volume as the steel industry in general enjoyed a decade of vast growth. The $40 million generated in sales by 1950 had grown to nearly $90 million by the end of the decade, enlarged by the growing prominence of and dependency on scrap steel companies.

Entering the 1960s, Laclede served the Mississippi Valley and the Southwest with a range of products that included semi-finished and finished steel strip, wire, pipe, tubing, slabs, blooms, wire rods, and fabricated reinforcing bars. These products, among others, were manufactured at the company's two steel works at Alton, Illinois, and Madison, Illinois, and its five fabricating plants in Beaumont and Dallas, Texas, New Orleans, Louisiana, Tampa, Florida, and Memphis, Tennessee. Employing more than 4,000 workers, the company had benefited from the steel boom years during the 1950s, expanding its ingot capacity 50 percent during the decade. As it faced the decade ahead, Laclede was focusing on the continued modernization of its plants to reduce costs and to expand finishing capacity where market conditions warranted.

By the mid-1960s, Laclede's investment in its facilities had earned it a reputation as one of the nation's most modern and efficient steel producers, traits that would define success for scrap steel companies of Laclede's ilk in the decades ahead. Part of this ongoing program to modernize its manufacturing capabilities included the replacement of its four open-hearth furnaces with two 225-ton electric arc furnaces in late 1965. Within one year, the two modern furnaces enabled Laclede to reduce production costs by $2 per ton, yielding the company appreciable results for the $16 million it spent on capital expenditures between 1963 and 1966.

Despite the gains realized through extensive capital expenditure programs, the 1960s were frustrating years for Laclede and the steel industry as a whole, marking the end of the prosperous years following the conclusion of the Second World War. During the prolific growth of the U.S. steel industry in the 1950s, the steel industries in Europe and Japan were on the mend, struggling mightily to recover from the deleterious years of war that had laid waste to their manufacturing facilities. Their absence represented a boon to U.S. steel companies, which flourished without the pressures of any substantial competition, but after more than a decade of reconstructive work and government subsidization, European and Japanese steel companies were reemerging during the 1960s as formidable competitors, invigorated and intent on establishing themselves as leaders in the global steel market.

Foreign competition plagued U.S. steel companies in the 1960s and 1970s, leading to charges by many domestic steel concerns that foreign steel manufacturers, particularly Japanese steel manufacturers, were selling steel in the United States at prices below the cost of production in the U.S. market. Against the backdrop of this rancorous debate and against the backdrop of lobbying efforts by the U.S. steel industry to restrict the flow of foreign made steel crossing U.S. borders, Laclede did what it could to remain profitable. Profitability, however, had a price, and the price was an unflagging commitment to facility modern-

ization. In order to remain profitable, Laclede invested heavily in revamping its production techniques and equipment, as the push toward higher efficiency became the only means of survival for scrap steel companies of Laclede's size.

Aside from the mounting pressures engendered by the rebirth of European and Japanese steel companies, Laclede also faced other challenges as it moved forward from the 1960s, most notably the cyclical nature of the steel market, which could fluctuate wildly, sending small steel manufacturers like Laclede quickly into ruin. In this respect, Laclede stood well-positioned to withstand the vagaries of its business. By the early 1970s, no other steel producer as small as Laclede could claim a more diversified distribution of product lines or a more diversified mix within its product lines. The wide variety of steel products produced on its rolling mills and in its finishing facilities fit the requirements of nearly every steel-consuming market, insulating the company from market fluctuations exhibited by one market segment.

Laclede, by this point, was serving nearly 4,000 customers ranging in size from the country's largest corporations to small, local job shops. Shipments were made throughout a geographical area that stretched from the Gulf of Mexico to Canada and from the Appalachians to the Rockies. In total, 24 states were included within Laclede's territory, an area serviced by the company's 13 sales offices.

By the mid-1970s, the affects of foreign competition and a flagging U.S. steel market were wearing on Laclede, forcing the company during the latter half of the decade to narrow the scope of its operations. After the demand for fabricated reinforcing bars sagged, Laclede exited the business, then closed seven of its plants, a move that reduced its work force of 3,400 by 500 and left only its plant in Alton in operation. Announced in 1977 at the company's annual meeting, the plant closings and the decision to withdraw from the fabricated reinforcing business cut Laclede's sales volume by roughly 25 percent, stripping it of the majority of sales generated by its construction product group, and augured further changes that would be implemented in the coming years, as competitive pressures mounted.

By the beginning of the 1980s, the U.S. steel industry was occupying tenuous ground. The problems arising from the steady flow of foreign steel into the United States coupled with recessive economic conditions crippled the nation's steel companies. Over a two-year period, large U.S. steel companies lost nearly $6 billion, their position weakened by outdated facilities and inefficient production processes. For years, the upper tier companies within the steel industry had looked toward raising prices rather than improving their productivity as a means to ameliorate their profits, but such an approach no longer worked. Smaller companies like Laclede had invested enormously in improving their facilities and their production efficiency for decades, compensating for their diminutive size by conducting business more efficiently than the industry stalwarts. Nevertheless, Laclede stumbled during the early 1980s, losing $8.1 million in 1982. On the heels of this severe loss, Laclede effected sweeping changes throughout its operations, changes that positioned the company for a quick recovery and left it strengthened for the future ahead.

After 1982's debilitating loss, Laclede installed a computer-based financial system for corporate planning, operating, and marketing analysis, then over the next three years, trimmed overhead by nearly 25 percent, eliminating 380 of the company's 750 salaried positions. Increases in production efficiency were recorded as well, enabling the company to quickly climb out of the red and into the black. Laclede earned $5 million in 1983, then between 1983 and 1984 achieved a 22 percent improvement in revenues and an astounding 130 percent gain in net income. Equally as encouraging as the robust financial statistics were the signs of flourishing business activity. Laclede, by 1984, was operating its facilities at 90 percent capacity compared to 70 percent averaged by the rest of the steel industry, instilling confidence that the early 1980s downturn was a temporary lapse and not the beginning of a long-term retrogressive slide.

In 1985, after cost-cutting measures first implemented three years earlier had saved Laclede $30 million, the company paid its first dividend in eight years, having racked up 14 profitable quarters in a row while many of the country's larger steel companies continued to record staggering losses. The return to prosperity put Laclede in a position to bolster its operations, which the company did in mid-1984 when it acquired the chain manufacturing division of Nixdorf-Krein Industries Inc. The assets acquired were then organized as Laclede Chain Manufacturing Company, one of the primary subsidiaries that would support Laclede for the remainder of the decade and into the 1990s, providing the company with a major vehicle of growth for the future.

With the acquisition of Nixdorf-Krein's chain manufacturing operations and the addition of Presidents Island Steel & Wire Company in late 1985, Laclede entered the late 1980s occupying a solid position within the steel industry. Its products were sold to a wide variety of end-users, including automobile manufacturers, rail car manufacturers, heavy construction equipment manufacturers, bedding and furniture manufacturers, and metal-building manufacturers, with no single customer accounting for more than three percent of the company's total sales.

The early 1990s witnessed another economic recession in the United States, the severity of which caused the demand for steel to plunge precipitously. Hobbled by burdensome inventories that caused steel prices to tumble below selling prices of a decade before, steel companies, Laclede included, were hit hard, their business once again devastated by the vagaries of the steel market. In response to the adverse economic climate, Laclede shrank its work force and reduced costs wherever possible, striving to persevere through the downturn. By the mid-1990s, recovery was on its way, restoring the company's financial health as it prepared to enter the 21st century.

Annual sales by 1994 amounted to $341 million, up from $287 million at the beginning of the decade, while net earnings had emerged from the red, rising to $4.4 million. With the economy moving forward, Laclede was moving forward as well, its management confident that the future prospects for the company would remain strong provided the national economy continued its steady growth. Given Laclede's long tradition of survival and profitability within the capricious steel industry and its focus on production efficiency, such optimism appeared justified, infusing hope that Laclede's long-established resiliency would continue to characterize the company in the future.

Principal Subsidiaries

Laclede Chain Manufacturing Company; Laclede Pipe Company; Laclede Mid America, Inc.; Laclede Consulting Services, Ltd.

Further Reading

Abelson, Reed, "Laclede Steel," *Fortune*, July 3, 1989, p. 112.

Akin, Paul B., "Laclede Steel Company," *Wall Street Transcript*, February 10, 1969, p. 15,760.

——, "Laclede Steel Company," *Wall Street Transcript*, December 2, 1974, p. 38,880.

Beirne, Mike, "Laclede's Net Nearly Triples," *American Metal Market*, November 22, 1994, p. 4.

Brown, Anthony D., "Laclede Steel Co.," *Investment Dealers' Digest*, September 16, 1963, p. 22.

Burgert, Philip, "Laclede Keeps Accent on Diversification; Company on Acquisition Trail Eyeing Steel-Related Targets," *American Metal Market*, February 10, 1984, p. 1.

Edwards, A. G., "Laclede Steel Co.," *Wall Street Transcript*, June 13, 1977, p. 47,355.

Hohl, Paul, "Laclede's Income Increases Fourfold," *American Metal Market*, July 15, 1988, p. 3.

Houser, Douglas, "Laclede Steel Keeps High Volume, Has Sound Product Diversification," *Investment Dealers' Digest*, June 5, 1973, p. 26.

Lautenschlager, Scott, "Laclede, Bechtel Get 40% of Steel Project in Trinidad-Tobago," *American Metal Market*, April 9, 1985, p. 2.

Maturi, Richard J., "Efficiency Pays," *Barron's*, June 24, 1985, p. 48.

——, "Scrappy Laclede," *Barron's*, September 1, 1986, p. 49.

"Modernization Is the Keynote at Laclede," *Investment Dealers' Digest*, December 26, 1966, p. 28.

Petry, Corinna C., "Laclede to Shut Blooming, Rod Mills," *American Metal Market*, January 22, 1996, p. 1.

—Jeffrey L. Covell

Lamonts Apparel, Inc.

3650 131st Ave. S.E.
Bellevue, Washington 98006
U.S.A.
(206) 644-5700
Fax: (206) 746-3172

Public Company
Incorporated: 1985
Employees: 2,000
Sales: $237.92 million (1994)
Stock Exchanges: NASDAQ
SICs: 5611 Men's & Boys' Clothing and Accessory
 Stores; 5632 Women's Accessory & Specialty Stores;
 5651 Family Clothing Stores; 5661 Shoe Stores

Lamonts Apparel, Inc. retails brand-name family apparel and accessories through a chain of about 40 stores in the northwestern United States and Alaska. The company attracts middle-income, suburban consumers with its brand-name apparel and value pricing, filling the gap between discount merchandisers and traditional department stores. After experiencing financial difficulties for several years, Lamonts filed for Chapter 11 bankruptcy in January 1995 and was trying to reemerge going into 1996.

Lamonts Apparel started out in 1967 as a division of the M. Lamont Bean Co., a diversified holding company that was founded in 1923. Other enterprises in the holding company at the time included Earnst Hardware and Pay 'n Save drug stores. The apparel division that would later become Lamonts Apparel, Inc., began with three stores in Seattle, Washington. The stores carried an array of family apparel, including children's clothing. The success of the first three clothing shops prompted the company to expand with a fourth store in Spokane, Washington, in 1970. In 1975 Lamonts expanded into Alaska before opening its first outlet in Idaho in 1976 and then in Oregon in 1978.

Lamonts succeeded during the 1970s and early 1980s by offering a range of clothing—including many popular brand names—and a value orientation. Service and displays were scaled down in comparison to large department stores, for example, as part of an effort to minimize overhead and keep prices relatively low. In a way, therefore, Lamonts was a forerunner to the discount retailers that proliferated during the 1970s and 1980s. Lamonts particularly made a name for itself in its local markets with a broad selection of children's clothing. Children's apparel eventually became the core of the Lamonts stores and represented more than 25 percent of total annual sales in some units.

By the early 1980s Lamonts was a small but successful chain of family apparel stores operating in four states. The chain operated as a small division of the sprawling Pay 'n Save Corp. retail empire. By then, Pay 'n Save was operating more than 300 stores through various subsidiaries in ten western states. Believing that some of Pay 'n Save's companies were performing below their potential, brothers Julius and Eddie Trump (no relation to New York mogul Donald Trump) purchased a controlling interest in the corporation in 1984. One year later, the Trumps formed a new company dubbed Northern Pacific Corp. That New York-based group was created to purchase, for roughly $200 million, almost all of the assets of three Pay 'n Save subsidiaries: Schuck's Auto Supply, BiMart, and Lamonts. The Trumps created Northern Pacific because they wanted to have more direct control over those entities.

Lamonts operated as a subsidiary of Northern Pacific that was known as the LH Group, Inc. Under the direction of the Trump brothers, Lamonts initiated an aggressive expansion campaign designed to boost its exposure throughout the Northwest and Alaska. To that end, Lamont's poured millions of dollars into the company to add new stores throughout the late 1980s. The company achieved much of that growth under the direction of Leonard M. Snyder, the chief executive who the Trumps brought in to run Lamonts in 1987. Snyder was a retail veteran with more than 20 years in the industry. He had previously served as vice-president and executive group manager at Allied Stores Corp. and as president and chief executive of Donaldson's Department Stores. Snyder was joined at the helm by Frank E. Kulp, who served as president and later director of the company. Kulp had served 17 years with Federated and Allied Department Stores.

By the time Snyder joined Lamonts, the company had expanded its network to include 31 stores in four states. Between 1987 and 1989, though, the organization would add about 20 additional outlets and expand into Montana and Utah. Indeed, by late 1989 Lamonts was operating 50 stores in six states and was planning to expand at a rate of about 20 percent annually during the early 1990s. In addition to increasing the size of the chain, new management went to work restructuring and improving operations. Snyder believed that the stores had lost their focus and were trying to serve too many niches in the market. So he eliminated most of the chain's nonapparel items and jettisoned poorly performing categories like maternity wear and mens' big and tall clothing. Furthermore, Snyder had every store in the chain remodeled and updated with nicer displays.

Management's goal during the late 1980s was to narrow its target market, improve per-store profitability, and capitalize on the recognized Lamonts name by expanding in existing, as well as new, markets. Lamonts' target market was professionals aged 25 to 55 who earned $35,000 to $40,000 annually. Its stores were located in suburban shopping malls and in retail centers near middle-income neighborhoods, often in smaller towns. The stores averaged about 40,000 square feet in size, but ranged from 20,000 to more than 60,000 square feet. The goal was to offer many of the brand-name fashions sold at traditional department stores, but at lower prices. Key brands included Levi's, Osh-Kosh, Claiborne, and Arrow, as well as merchandise marketed under the Lamonts house brands of Cascade Classics, Traditions, Studio Age, and Cues.

As a result of Lamonts' chain expansion and improvement in per-store sales, revenues surged from about $150 million when the Trumps purchased the chain to about $170 million by 1987. By 1990, moreover, the enterprise was generating annual revenues of about $250 million from 49 stores. Unfortunately, the company's bottom line had failed to keep pace with sales gains. In fact, Lamonts profits had been sporadic throughout the mid- and late 1980s, and by the early 1990s the company was posting successive quarterly losses. Management attributed the deficits to short-term growth, which required heavy investments. Indeed, records showed that the Trumps injected about $122 million into the company between 1984 and 1989. One result of that investment, however, was that Lamonts accrued substantial debt, particularly following the rapid expansion drive launched in 1987.

After posting a painful loss of $1.8 million for the quarter, the Trump brothers sold Lamonts in September 1989 to Aris, Inc. Aris had started out in 1985 as Texstyrene Corporation. The corporation was formed to purchase the assets of Texstyrene Plastics Inc., a manufacturer of expandable polystyrene beads, foam cups and containers, and packaging materials. The new company divested the assets of the styrene business and changed its name to Aris Corporation late in 1988. Aris purchased Lamonts, its sole operating unit, from Northern Pacific and in 1991 changed its name from Aris to Lamonts Corp. (and in 1992 to Lamonts Apparel, Inc.). The purchase helped to buoy Lamonts because it brought a fresh injection of investment capital into the retail chain. Aris paid $135 million for the chain, but Northern Pacific financed part of the purchase and the Trumps retained about 20-percent ownership in the company.

Lamonts continued to lose money in the early 1990s. But the new owners weren't concerned about the losses, because the company seemed to have plenty of cash to meet its operating expenses. In fact, at the time of the purchase they had planned to lose money for a few years as they continued to invest money to grow the chain and to pay down the company's giant debt load. Lamonts opened its 50th Lamonts Apparel store in 1991. More importantly, it introduced a new apparel concept called Lamonts for Kids. Lamonts for Kids represented management's effort to capitalize on the retailer's traditional strength; children's apparel. The outlets were smaller—about 10,000 to 13,000 square feet—than normal Lamonts stores, and carried a complete selection of the most popular branded merchandise as well as the company's own 'Lamonster' brand for infants. Lamonts opened two Kids stores in 1991—one in Idaho and another in Utah—and three more in 1992.

As Lamonts continued to expand, its financial performance deteriorated. The problems were multifaceted. Chief among the setbacks was a general downturn in the retail industry that had severely battered many of Lamonts' competitors. At the same time, however, Lamonts was facing increasing pressure from other sectors of the retailing industry. Since the early 1980s, in fact, Lamonts had been operating in a rapidly changing industry. Importantly, discount retailers like Target and Wal-Mart had been increasing their share of the market while larger department store operators had been diversifying away from their traditional niches and treading on some of Lamonts' territory. Critics claimed that Lamonts had failed to keep pace with market changes and was operating with an obsolete strategy. The company's big losses did little to quell that criticism; Lamonts lost $8.5 million in 1990, $11.7 million in 1991, and then a whopping $19.3 million in 1992, despite a steady increase in sales.

Lamonts restructured its financing in 1992 in an effort to reduce the hemorrhage of cash related to its debt service. The move did little to stem the deficit. After posting a net loss of $10.8 million in 1993, the company began scrambling to reorganize and slow its move toward insolvency. The number of stores in the Lamonts chain peaked at 57 early in 1994. Before the end of the year, though, Lamonts shuttered four Lamonts Apparel shops and the five Lamonts for Kids outlets, which had failed to perform as expected. The failure of the Lamonts for Kids venture contributed to a net loss for 1994 of about $44.5 million from decreased sales of $238 million. Shortly before the end of the year Lamonts brought in a new chief executive to try to turn the company around. Snyder and Kulp vacated their posts to pursue other business interests.

To whip the floundering retail chain into shape, Lamonts hired Alan Schlesinger. Schlesinger had worked in retailing for 33 years. Most recently he had worked as a senior vice-president for retail giant May Co. Department Stores. Prior to that he had helped to turn around Ross Stores Inc. That company had lost $41 million in 1986. Schlesinger arrived in 1987 and helped the company post more than $100 million in net income during his three-year stay. He accomplished the feat by implementing a new operating strategy and refocusing the company on key market niches. He hoped to implement similar changes at Lamonts. "We've got to set ourselves apart," Schlesinger said in the November 23, 1994, *Journal American*, adding, "We can't be all things to all people in less than 50,000 square feet. . . . We need to change.''

Under Schlesinger's command, Lamonts began a concerted effort to cut costs throughout the organization and to change its inventory. The company dumped several product lines, such as cosmetics, that didn't complement its core strengths. Schlesinger planned to emphasize children's clothing and moderately priced brand name apparel for the entire family. Partly because of a continued lag in sales late in 1994, Lamonts filed for Chapter 11 bankruptcy in January 1995. Lamonts was able to use the bankruptcy to get out of some costly store leases and to reduce its debt service payments with rearranged financing. It also announced plans to close some of the approximately 48 stores that it was operating in early 1995, about half of which were located in Washington. The company hoped to emerge from bankruptcy within 12 to 18 months.

Principal Subsidiaries

Texstyrene Plastics, Inc.

Further Reading

Aaron, Peter, "Lamonts to Acquire Frederick & Nelson's Northtown Store," *Business Wire,* December 4, 1992.

Enbysk, Monte, " 'We Need to Change': Lamonts' New Boss Sent Here to Save Ailing Retailer," *Journal American,* November 23, 1994, p. B1.

Gauntt, Tom, "Clothing Retailer Ponders Portland," *Business Journal-Portland,* July 27, 1987, p. 10.

Giordano, Andrew, "Lamonts' Stockholders Approve Restructuring, Eight New Directors Named," *Business Wire,* October 28, 1992.

Giordano, Andrew, and Debbie Brownfield, "Lamonts Apparel, the Sole Operating Subsidiary of Aris Corp., Announces Strong Second Quarter Revenue Results," *Business Wire,* June 19, 1990.

Giordano, Andrew, and Susan McAllister. "First Two Lamonts for Kids Stores Open, Third Store Announced," *Business Wire,* August 1, 1991.

——, "Lamonts Launches New Retail Concept, Changes Corporate Name, Appoints Snyder Chairman," *Business Wire,* April 4, 1991.

Gupta, Himanee, "Lamonts Fashions Niche in Sluggish Retail Industry," *Seattle Times,* October 1, 1990, p. B2.

Lane, Polly, "Changes at Lamonts: Top Two Executives Resign; New President-CEO Named," *Seattle Times,* November 17, 1994, p. D1.

Lim, Paul J., "Lamont's Bankruptcy Comes As No Surprise," *Seattle Times,* January 7, 1995, p. D1.

Prinzing, Debra, "Fast Growth Drains Earnings at Lamonts," *Puget Sound Business Journal,* October 23, 1989, p. 1.

——, "To Refinance Lamonts, Investor Gets a Big Chunk," *Puget Sound Business Journal,* November 12, 1990, p. 3.

Sather, Jeanne, "Lamonts Wins Approval for $32-M Line of Credit," *Puget Sound Business Journal,* February 24, 1995, p. 8.

Tucker, Rob, and Debbie Cafazzo, "KRTB: Lamonts Apparel Corp. Files for Bankruptcy," *Knight-Ridder/Tribune Business News,* January 8, 1995.

—Dave Mote

Landry's Seafood Restaurants, Inc.

1400 Post Oak Boulevard
Houston, Texas 77056
U.S.A.
(713) 850-1010
Fax: (713) 623-4702

Private Company
Incorporated: 1993
Employees: 2,500
Sales: $84 million (1995)
Stock Exchanges: NASDAQ
SICs: 5812 Eating Places

Landry's Seafood Restaurants, Inc. operates a chain of full-service, casual-dining seafood restaurants. In mid-1995 the chain consisted of about 25 units in nine states. In addition, the company operated three eateries under the Joe's Crab Shack banner. Landry's was planning to expand its profitable chain rapidly during the mid-1990s.

The first Landry's restaurant, called Landry's Seafood Inn and Oyster Bar, was opened in 1980 in Katy, Texas, by brothers Bill and Floyd Landry. Bill and Floyd were sustaining a decades-old Landry family legacy of success in the restaurant business. In fact, Landry's was just one of several of the brothers' restaurant interests. They had started out working in Cajun-style restaurants that their father and two uncles operated. In 1976, when Bill was 38 and Floyd was 36, they opened their own restaurant, a seafood place dubbed ''Don's.'' By the mid-1980s they would be hands-on investors in five different restaurants, including The Magnolia Bar, Jimmy G's, Don's, and Willie G's. All of the outlets were located in East Texas and Louisiana, and sported seafood and Cajun fare. Furthermore, other Landry family members were operating more than 15 additional restaurants throughout the Southwest.

The Landry brothers profited from their restaurants primarily by offering excellent food, but also through economies of scale created by owning five seafood digs. They conducted most of the initial food preparation—cleaning, fileting, and shelling, for example—for all five establishments at a company-owned commissary operation called Creole Foods. Work at that center started at midnight and ended at eight in the morning, at which time the food was loaded onto trucks and delivered fresh to each kitchen. The brothers and other principal investors in the restaurant consortium kept food quality high by taking turns cooking at the different eateries.

Landry's Seafood Inn and Oyster Bar was among the smaller of the Landry restaurants by sales volume. Still, it was profitable. The average check was $12 to $16 per person, the 4,400-square-foot restaurant seated a maximum of 190, and the rent was only $3,500 monthly. The Landrys had created the eatery by purchasing an existing Cajun restaurant with only 85 seats, expanding it, and improving the menu. Landrys Seafood Inn offered a very casual dining atmosphere with a horseshoe bar, country-and-western music jukebox, and crayons for the kids. But it sported a somewhat upscale 101-item, dinner-only menu. Featured were catches from the Gulf of Mexico and the Louisiana coastal region, including various appetizers and seafood salads and soups. Main entrees, which ranged in price from about $5 to $15, included specialties like snapper, broiled speckled trout, frog legs, and crab. The menu also featured steaks, chicken, sandwiches, and desserts like ice cream and fresh fruit.

The most successful Landry operation was Willie G's, which had opened in 1981 and was bringing in a whopping $5 million annually by 1985. By that time, Landry's Seafood Inn was generating about $1.4 million in sales annually, while the family's other units were capturing about $3 million to $4 million per year. It was about that time that Tilman J. Fertitta became involved as one of several investors in the Landry brothers' restaurants. Fertitta was in his late twenties at the time, but had already made his mark as a successful developer during the Houston commercial real estate boom of the early 1980s. When real estate foundered in the mid-1980s, Fertitta began looking elsewhere for a challenge.

Fertitta had grown up in his father's seafood restaurant in Galveston, Texas, so he wasn't a complete newcomer to the industry. He was impressed with Landry's Seafood and believed that it had a lot of potential. A good restaurant concept coupled with his dealmaking skills, Fertitta reasoned, could be a powerful combination. "The original Landry's was a hole in the wall but it had great food," Fertitta recalled in the August 1994 issue of *Restaurant Hospitality*. "The basics were there, though, and I knew I could tweak it into a concept." In 1988 Fertitta purchased both Landry's and Houston-based Willie G's from the Landry brothers and several other investment partners.

Fertitta's goal from the start was to transform the Landry's and Willie G's restaurants into regional, and eventually national, chains. That strategy sprang from observations that he had made about trends in the national restaurant industry. He noticed that the mom-and-pop restaurants were being phased out and that well-capitalized chains were increasingly dominating the business. He also saw that within the chain restaurant industry, seafood was poorly represented in comparison to burger, chicken, steak, and ethnic fare. With the exception of Red Lobster and a handful of regional operators, there weren't any major seafood restaurant operators. Furthermore, Americans' consumption of seafood was rising faster than for any other food segment.

To ply the full potential of Landry's and Willie G's, Fertitta scrutinized every aspect of the operations and hired a crack management team to help him start building a chain. Throughout the late 1980s and the early 1990s he added a few new outlets to the chain each year. The restaurants were geared for relatively casual dining, although the atmosphere was more polished than the original Landry's; for example, the waiters and waitresses wore white shirts, ties, and formal black pants. The menu offered similar fare with the average check running between $12 and $14. Fertitta wanted his restaurants to convey the feel of an old seafood house from the 1930s and 1940s, but with a more festive, brighter atmosphere. He also positioned most of the restaurants close to water to project a fresh seafood image, and typically shunned the overbuilt suburban sites pursued by other big chains.

Fertitta wanted to keep his outlets distinctive in order to avoid a repetitive, commercial look. So each restaurant was given a unique feel by the company's design team. And some of the units were converted from old family-owned seafood places that Fertitta's purchased and made into a Landry's. For example, Landry's put one of its restaurants in an old barge that had formerly housed a family-owned seafood place. The previous place had generated sales of more than $1 million per year, but still went belly-up. Landry's moved in and was able to make a healthy profit with its superior concept and operating strategy. Although each restaurant had its own unique flair, all of the outlets were similar in that they wore the same neon, movie-like marquee, which was designed to let people know that the restaurants were fun and entertaining.

By boosting per-unit sales and adding a few new units, Fertitta's venture managed to squeak out about $11.5 million in sales in both 1988 and 1989. The company posted losses in both years, however, as management invested for growth. Despite ongoing investments, Landry's managed to post a positive net income in 1990 of $419,000 from sales of about $15.5 million. Revenues bobbed up to $19.5 million in 1991 and then to roughly $22.5 million in 1992, as net income surged to a healthy

$3 million. Improved profitability reflected the wisdom of Fertitta's operating strategy. Indeed, the Landry's restaurants were among the top in the industry with profit margins averaging more than 20 percent. High-margin menu items boosted that percentage. For example, more than 30 percent of the chain's orders were shrimp, which generated fat profits in comparison to most of the fare pushed in non-seafood restaurants.

By late 1993 Landry's Seafood Restaurants were operating 11 units in Texas and Louisiana. The company was focusing on developing family-oriented Landry's Seafood Grill restaurants, but was still operating a few Willie G's, which were targeted more toward business patrons. Until 1993, Fertitta had been satisfied to grow slowly by funding expansion largely out of earnings. "I had the chance to go public several years ago," Fertitta explained in the November 8, 1993, *Nation's Restaurant News,* "but I wanted to get my management team in place before I did that." Fertitta finally decided to go public with a September 1993 initial public offering of stock that brought $24 million into the company's war chest. The success of the offering was not surprising, given that Landry's sales per unit ($3.2 million in 1993) and cash flow were among the highest in the restaurant industry. Within two months the stock was trading at nearly one-and-one-half the initial offering price.

A second stock offering captured $37 million more for Landry's, which Fertitta used to intensify expansion efforts. Rather than build new establishments, he preferred to purchase independent seafood places and convert them into Landry's. For instance, early in 1994 Landry's purchased two units operating under the Atchafalaya River Cafe banner in Dallas, and another in Memphis, Tennessee, named Captain Bilbo's. The basic goal was to purchase independents that were operating below their potential and convert them into 215-seat, 8,000-square-foot Landry's Seafood Grills. By mid-1994 the company was running 18 restaurants in Texas, Arkansas, Florida, and Louisiana, and was planning to expand into several other states including Tennessee, Georgia, Mississippi, North Carolina, Nevada, Arizona, and Colorado.

By the end of 1994 Landry's was operating about 25 restaurants. *Forbes* ranked the chain fifth on its list of the 200 best small companies in America in that year. Landry's store number increased to 35 units in 12 states by August of 1995, helping to earn it a spot on *Business Week's* Top 100 Growth Companies list for the second consecutive year. Landry's sales rose to $34 million in 1993 and then to $66 million in 1994. Net income, moreover, surged nearly 100 percent between 1992 and 1994 to about $5.8 million. Fueling profit growth was an increased emphasis on a trend sweeping the restaurant business in the early and mid-1990s: value. As Jeff Price, senior director of the National Restaurant Association, said in reference to Landry's in the August 22, 1995, Knight-*Ridder/Tribune Business News,* "When you have a meal sold at a good price and add a theme, you get traffic."

Landry's continued to rapidly expand its chain during 1995. Furthermore, the company was moving ahead with plans to diversify into the more casual spectrum of the seafood restaurant market. Early in 1994 Landry's had purchased Joe's Crab Shack, a Houston-based chain of three seafood restaurants. Fertitta had planned to convert them into Landry's Seafood

Grills. Instead, Landry's managers tweaked the Joe's Crab Shack concept and came up with what they hoped would be a successful entry into the low-priced seafood eatery market. After the makeover, sales at the three units jumped 30 percent to average a big $3.2 million per unit. In 1995 Landry's opened a fourth Joe's in Dallas that achieved similar results.

Landry's planned to sustain the rapid growth of both its Landry's and Joe's Crab Shack restaurants into the mid- and late 1990s. The company still operated two Willie G's stores, as well. Fertitta believed that the Landry's chain alone could grow to as many as 150 or more restaurants. "There's no shortage of potential locations," he said in the May 16, 1994, *Nation's Restaurant News*. "We're the only ones who can screw things up and stop the momentum. It's just a matter of keeping that consistency and continuing to open in the right locations."

Principal Divisions

Landry's Seafood Grill; Joe's Crab Shack; Willie G's.

Further Reading

Carlino, Bill, "Landry's Seafood: Not Just Another Fish in the Sea," *Nation's Restaurant News*, May 16, 1994, p. 74.

Davis-Diaz, Pamela, "Landry's Seafood House to Open Restaurant in Rocky Point," *Knight-Ridder/Tribune Business News*, August 22, 1995.

Prewit, Milford, "Casual Dinner-House Chains Tap Secondary-brand Expansion (NRN Top 100)," *Nation's Restaurant News*, August 7, 1995, p. 120.

Reill, Howard, "Landry's Eyes Expansion of Cajun Food Restaurants; May Head for California, Chicago, New York," *Nation's Restaurant News*, February 17, 1986, p. 3.

Ruggless, Ron, "Landry's Eyes Joe's Crab Shack as Possible 2nd Growth Concept," *Nation's Restaurant News*, June 12, 1995, p. 3.

——, "Landry's in Swim after Stock Sale," *Nation's Restaurant News*, November 8, 1993, p. 3.

Sanson, Michael, "The Man Who Would Be King Fish," *Restaurant Hospitality*, August 1994, p. 74.

—Dave Mote

Levitz Furniture Inc.

6111 Broken Sound Parkway, N.W.
Boca Raton, Florida 33487-2799
U.S.A.
(407) 994-6006
Fax: (407) 998-5615

Public Company
Incorporated: 1965 as Levitz Furniture Corp.
Employees: 6,757
Sales: $1.05 billion (1995)
Stock Exchanges: New York
SICs: 5712 Furniture Stores; 6719 Offices of Holding
    Companies, Not Elsewhere Classified

A pioneer of the warehouse-showroom concept, in which both facilities are within a single building, Levitz Furniture Inc. is one of the largest furniture retailers in the United States. Because Levitz buys in bulk, customers can get good value, and because the warehouse is on the premises, they can take merchandise home immediately instead of waiting for delivery. In May 1995 Levitz operated 72 warehouse-showrooms and 62 satellite stores located in 26 states and 22 of the 25 largest metropolitan areas in the United States. A holding company with headquarters in Boca Raton, Florida, its only material asset in the mid 1990s was the common stock of Levitz Furniture Corp.

The origins of Levitz lay in the opening by Richard Levitz of a furniture store in Lebanon, Pennsylvania, in 1910. With $20,000 borrowed from their father, his sons Ralph and Leon opened a store of their own in Pottstown, Pennsylvania, in 1936. According to one account, it was not until 1963 that the Levitz brothers hit upon the idea that turned their business into a financial bonanza. In that year Ralph went to Tucson, Arizona, to help Sam Levitz—another brother—try to save his own struggling furniture business. To raise quick cash and save on costs, they organized a giant warehouse sale that required the customer to carry away the merchandise. (According to another account, Ralph and Leon helped Sam establish the Tucson store in 1956 and began experimenting there with selling low-cost discount-type furniture the following year.) In either event, Ralph and Leon Levitz decided to try warehouse sales on a permanent basis because it seemed likely to bring in many new customers while reducing operating costs. Although the warehouse-showroom concept was not new, the Levitz brothers put it into operation on a grander scale than ever before.

The first Levitz warehouse-showroom store opened in Allentown, Pennsylvania, in September 1963. A second one opened in Phoenix the following month and a third in Miami in October 1965. Sales reached $12.2 million in the fiscal year ending January 31, 1966, and increased to $18.7 million and $26.5 million, respectively, in the following two years. The business, previously a partnership, was incorporated in 1965 as the Levitz Furniture Corp. Another store, in Dallas, opened in 1967, and two more, in Tempe, Arizona, and Santa Clara, California, during 1968, the year Levitz went public. In the fiscal year covering 1968, sales reached $39.5 million, and in the following year, during which five more stores were opened, to $67 million.

The Levitz concept of supermarket furniture shopping called for a gross markup of 50 percent on brand-name furniture instead of the normal 100 percent. Increased volume would enable it to save money in purchasing, selling, handling, and transporting merchandise because of economy of scale. By 1970 Levitz was averaging more than $120 in sales per square foot of selling space, compared to the industry average of $26.54 in medium-sized stores and $54 in large stores. As a result, Levitz was able to earn, in net income, nearly $1.7 million in fiscal 1968 and $2.8 million in fiscal 1969.

By the end of 1971 Levitz was operating a chain of 27 stores, each one generally with a warehouse the size of several football fields and a showroom with 260 model-room "vignettes," both incorporated into a single building. The stores were located in population centers of at least 750,000, along expressways where land was cheap and railroad sidings were available. Free parking was generally available. Sixty percent of sales were pickup, with almost all the remainder including, in a day or two, delivery and set up, which each cost the buyer an additional four percent. Each store was expected to yield a profit margin of 4.5 percent on sales. Ralph supervised the eastern stores from Miami, and Leon oversaw the western ones from Phoenix.

Levitz was receiving its merchandise from about 300 suppliers, but the top 10 furniture makers provided about half the stock. The stores typically opened with well-advertised fanfare, including prizes and loss leaders. Other companies complained that Levitz's advertising campaigns included misleading comparisons between its prices and those of its rivals. The Federal Trade Commission ordered Levitz in 1976 to cease several deceptive advertising practices, including exaggeration of price reductions and misrepresentation of furniture materials.

During fiscal 1971 the 34 Levitz stores had sales of $183.8 million and a net profit of $9.2 million. The company had accumulated at least $47 million from retained earnings and stock issues by August 1971. Its stock had moved up from the American Stock Exchange to the Big Board, the New York Stock Exchange. Between the original 1968 offering and May 1972, the price of Levitz shares rose almost fifty-fold, when adjusted for three stock splits. Members of the Levitz family realized an estimated $33 million from publicly reported sales of Levitz common stock during the period from 1968 through 1971.

Despite Levitz's success, continued rapid growth could be sustained only by substantial infusions of outside capital. However, it was beginning to encounter opposition from rivals like Wickes Corp. and Unicapital, Inc., thereby putting pressure on its profit margins. The bubble burst on September 29, 1972, the day after Ralph Levitz announced that the latest quarterly earnings report would be disappointing after a long string of quarterly gains on an annual basis of 50 percent or more. In 23 minutes of frantic trading on the New York Stock Exchange, Levitz stock plummeted from about $47 to $33 a share before further business was suspended because of too many sellers and too few buyers.

Compounding Levitz's problems were charges by the federal Securities and Exchange Commission in June 1972 that the company had broken the law by agreeing to allow the United Brotherhood of Teamsters to organize its employees on condition that the union drive would not be announced or commenced until a 1972 stock issue had been completed. The SEC suspended trading in Levitz stock for 10 days. Leon Levitz immediately resigned as president, but Ralph remained as the company's chairman.

In spite of these problems Levitz's expansion continued through fiscal 1972, when sales from 49 stores reached $326.8 million, and fiscal 1973, when sales reached $380.4 million from 55 stores. Net profits reached a new high of $12.1 million in 1972 but fell to $8.6 million in 1973. With its stock falling below $5 a share in 1973, Levitz not only lacked the means to finance further growth but developed a cash-flow problem. Saddled with expensive leases, the company had a net profit of only $3.9 million in 1974. In 1975, a recession year during which the housing market was hard hit, it lost $142,000 on sales of $326.3 million.

Robert M. Elliott, a Montgomery Ward & Co. executive, was brought in as president and chief executive officer of Levitz in 1974. He immediately imposed stringent economies, reducing inventory by 25 percent and employment by 38 percent, and also brought the stores, which had been operating autonomously, under central command. Sales rebounded in 1976, and the company returned to the black. In 1977 Levitz announced it would place its primary expansion emphasis on gaining deeper penetration in its existing markets rather than venturing into new ones. Accordingly, in that year it acquired six furniture warehouse-showrooms from R.H. Macy & Co. operating under the J. Homestock name in New York, New Jersey, Connecticut, and Boston.

For fiscal 1979 Levitz had record sales of $546.6 million and record net income of $20.6 million, but high interest rates and a consequent recession in the early 1980s dealt a severe blow to the housing industry. Company sales and profits dropped in 1980, 1981, and 1982; in the last year sales came to only $485.7 million and net income to only $8.8 million. Elliott's continued tenure was opposed during this period by the Levitz family, which charged that he had abandoned the company's founding philosophy: deep discounting and rapid expansion. He had the crucial support, however, of Chicago's wealthy Pritzker family, which in 1979 acquired about 23 percent of the company stock. The holdings of Levitz family members fell from 22.5 percent to only 5.5 percent by 1983, the year Ralph Levitz retired as chairman.

Levitz remained the nation's top independent furniture retailer and kept its basic strategy of warehouse selling but increased its store total only to 80. Furniture manufacturers who once saw the company as a destructive force now, with obvious relief, regarded it as unlikely to initiate new price wars. One manufacturing executive, for example, told *Business Week*: "It's not the cheap discount anymore. The stores are clean, have a broad range of goods, tasteful accessories, and well-trained salespeople." Future Levitz stores were scheduled to be smaller ones in smaller markets, and some would be satellite units for display only, within a 25-mile radius of an existing store.

Sales jumped to $644.4 million in 1983 and $761.8 million in 1984, while profits soared to $27.4 million and $34.4 million, respectively. In 1984 Levitz was operating a nationwide chain of 84 retail facilities located in clusters of 10 to 14 each in primary metropolitan areas within six regional areas covering 26 states. Store size ranged from 64,000 to 155,000 square feet. Late that year the company went private by means of a leveraged buy out. A group that included members of the board and of management, Citicorp Capital Investors Ltd., and Drexel Burnham Lambert Inc. paid $318 million, or $39 a share, in cash to stockholders. A bid in cash and securities by Dalfort Corp., a company controlled by the Pritzkers, had been rejected earlier. The new private company, which had no participation from Levitz family members, took the name of LFC Holdings Corp.

The investors who initiated LFC rewarded themselves with cash payments of about $215 million from $257 million obtained in new financing during late 1986. Burdened by debt payments, the private company never reached the prior earnings level enjoyed by Levitz. After fiscal 1989 (the fiscal year ended March 31, 1989), in which sales came to $929.8 million, the sales volume dropped for three consecutive years. Net income hit an LFC high of $17.9 million in fiscal 1989. In the next year net income fell by half, and the company then lost money for four consecutive years. No dividends were paid on common stock after 1987.

LFC went public in mid-1993 under the new corporate name of Levitz Furniture Inc., with 13 million shares of common stock sold at $14 each in its initial public offering. By then the company held 67 warehouse-showrooms and 51 satellite stores in 25 states. Although it was highly leveraged, with $284 million in long-term debt, and had sustained a string of consecutive losses under the LFC banner, it found one big buyer in the government of Singapore, which paid $23.3 million at prices between $11.50 and $14 a share for 6.5 percent of the company.

For fiscal 1994 (ended March 31, 1994), net sales increased to $983.6 million from $922.4 million the previous year. Net income came to $17.4 million, but this turned into a loss of $27.8 million with a payment of $37.7 million for early retirement of debt. During 1994 the company bought John M. Smyth Co., a retailer with six Chicago-area Homemakers Furniture stores, for about $47 million. It also opened eight new satellite showrooms and five warehouse showrooms.

In fiscal 1995 (ended March 31, 1995) Levitz passed the $1-billion mark in net sales and had net income of nearly $4 million. Long-term debt increased, however, from $286.6 million to $348.9 million, which did not include $89 million in lease obligations. Figures for the first three quarters of fiscal 1996 indicated that the company would lose money for the completed year.

Levitz's stock turned sour after reaching a peak of $20.25 a share in early 1994, and it traded as low as $2.50 a share in 1995. The work force was reduced by 10.5 percent in the first six months of the year, and a reorganization consolidated the company's six geographic regions into only two, east and west. A 1995 *Financial World* article calculated the company's long-term debt at $430 million, more than its equity. Elliott, who had been chairman and chief executive officer of the company since 1985, retired in 1995. He was succeeded by Michael Bozic in November 1995.

In 1995 Levitz was offering a wide selection of brand-name furniture and accessories, including living-room, bedroom, dining-room, kitchen, and occasional furniture and bedding. It was purchasing merchandise from more than 350 independent manufacturers and was not manufacturing any of the merchandise sold in its stores. Its 72 warehouse-showrooms ranged in size

from 62,000 to 250,000 square feet within a single building. Merchandise was typically displayed in 175 to 260 model-room settings occupying 50,000 to 83,000 square feet within the building. The 62 satellite stores were free-standing showrooms ranging in size from 25,000 to 60,000 square feet, although one store had about 100,000 square feet of space. These stores were utilizing the warehouse and delivery functions of nearby warehouse-showrooms.

Levitz was selling merchandise for cash or under customer installment purchase or revolving charge plans but generally did not accept credit cards. During fiscal 1995, 38.4 percent of all sales were for cash and 61.6 percent under customer credit plans. Customer credit obligations were being sold to General Electric Capital Corp. The company's properties at the end of May 1995 included 25 owned warehouse-showrooms and eight owned satellite stores. Another 47 warehouse-showrooms and 54 satellite stores were being leased. Levitz also owned its 94,000-square-foot corporate headquarters in Boca Raton, Florida, and a 35,000-square-foot facility in Pottstown, Pennsylvania, used for accounting offices.

Principal Subsidiaries

Levitz Furniture Corp.

Further Reading

Anreder, Steven S., "All in the Family," *Barron's,* January 24, 1972, pp. 5, 16, 18.

"Death Valley Days," *Forbes,* February 1, 1975, pp. 36–37.

Fruhan, William E., Jr., "Levitz Furniture: A Case History in the Creation and Destruction of Shareholder Value," *Financial Analysts' Journal,* March–April 1980, pp. 26–44.

"Levitz Board Clears Proposal for Buyout of $318 Million," *Wall Street Journal,* November 7, 1984, p. 8.

"Levitz Furniture: Sitting Pretty As It Waits for the Recovery," *Business Week,* February 7, 1983, p. 76.

"Levitz: The Hot Name in 'Instant' Furniture," *Business Week,* December 4, 1971, pp. 90–91, 93.

Paul, Bill, "Levitz Thinks Internal Flaws That Spurred Investors' Sell-Off Are Getting Corrected," *Wall Street Journal,* October 19, 1972, p. 42.

Ritz, Robert, "Has Levitz Furniture Lost Its Glamour on Wall Street?" *New York Times,* June 6, 1972, pp. 49, 52.

"The Sad Saga of Levitz," *Financial World,* July 11, 1973, p. 10.

Sparks, Debra, "Levitz Furniture: Sell on the Rumor," *Financial World,* June 20, 1995, p. 20.

—Robert Halasz

Lockheed Martin Corporation

6801 Rockledge Drive
Bethesda, Maryland 20817
U.S.A.
(301) 897-6000
Fax: (301) 897-6252

Public Company
Incorporated: 1961
Employees: 69,000
Sales: $22.85 billion (1995)
Stock Exchanges: New York
SICs: 3761 Guided Missiles And Space Vehicles; 3812
   Search And Navigation Equipment; 3764 Space
   Propulsion Units And Parts; 7370 Computer And Data
   Processing Services; 3579 Office Machines, Not
   Elsewhere Classified; 1442 Construction Sand and
   Gravel

Formed in 1995 via the union of the nation's second- and third-ranking defense contractors, Lockheed Corporation and Martin Marietta Corporation, Lockheed Martin Corporation is the world's largest defense contractor. Lockheed Martin further broadened its lead over second ranking McDonnell Douglas with the January 1996 acquisition of Loral Corporation's Defense Electronics and Systems Integration for $9.1 billion and $2.1 billion of assumed debt. Both Lockheed and Martin Marietta had evolved from relatively small aerospace manufacturers into titans of the global defense industry. A thorough treatment of Lockheed's history appears elsewhere in this series, while the Martin Marietta saga is recounted here.

In 1905 a youthful Glenn Martin moved with his family to California. In the hills of Santa Ana, Martin built and flew his first experimental gliders. Not long afterwards Martin started a small airplane factory while working as a salesman for Ford and Maxwell cars. Martin applied his earnings from the auto sales, as well as money from barnstorming performances, to finance an airplane business. During this time he hired a man named Donald Douglas to help him develop new airplanes. Soon thereafter, Douglas and Martin collaborated to produce a small flight trainer called a Model TT which was sold to the U.S. Army and the Dutch government.

On the eve of World War I, Douglas was summoned to Washington to help the Army develop its aerial capabilities. Less than a year later, he became frustrated with the slow moving bureaucracy in Washington and returned to work for Martin, who had relocated to Cleveland. While there, Douglas directed the development of Martin's unnamed twin-engine bomber. Neither he nor Martin was willing to compromise or shorten the period of time needed for the development of their airplane. For that reason the "Martin" bomber, arrived too late to see action in World War I. When Martin moved to Baltimore in 1929, Douglas left the company to start his own aircraft company in California.

Martin continued to impress the military with his aircraft demonstrations even after the war. In July of 1921, off the Virginia Capes, seven Martin MB-2 bombers under the command of General Billy Mitchell sank the captured German battleship Ostfreisland. Continued interest from the War Department led Martin's company to develop its next generation of airplanes, culminating with the B-10 bomber. The B-10 was a durable bomber, able to carry heavy payloads and cruise 100 miles per hour faster than conventional bombers of the day. Martin's work on the B-10 bomber earned him the Collier Trophy in 1932.

Although Martin continued to manufacture bombers throughout the 1930s, he also began to branch out into commercial passenger aircraft. With substantial financial backing from Pan Am's Juan Trippe, Martin developed the M-130 "China Clipper," the first of which was delivered in 1932. The clipper weighed 26 tons, carried up to 32 passengers and was capable of flying the entire 2,500 miles between San Francisco and Honolulu. Pan Am flew Martin's planes to a variety of Asian destinations, including Manila and Hong Kong.

But Martin's consistent development of military aircraft through the decade prepared it well for the start of World War II. The company produced thousands of airplanes for the Allied war effort, including the A-30 Baltimore, the B-26 and B-29 bombers, the PBM Mariner flying boat, and the 70-ton amphibious Mars air freighter. Martin invited some criticism in 1942 when he suggested that the United States could dispense with its costly two-ocean navy and defense of the Panama Canal if it had enough airplanes like the Mars.

After the war ended Martin continued to manufacture what few airplanes the Army and Navy were still ordering. In 1947 the company re-entered the highly competitive commercial airliner market with a model called the M-202. The development of later aircraft, the M-303 (which was never built) and the M-404, was a severe drain on company finances. Despite loans from the Reconstruction Finance Corporation, the Mellon Bank of Pittsburgh, and a number of other sources, the Martin Company was unable to generate an operating profit.

In July 1949 Chester C. Pearson was hired as president and general manager of the company. Glenn Martin, at the age of 63, was moved up to the position of chairman. Despite the new management and an increase in orders as a result of the Korean War, the Martin Company was still losing money. There were two reasons: first, production of the 404 was interrupted which, in turn, halted delivery and therefore payment for the aircraft. Second, the company hired hundreds of new but unskilled workers, which lowered productivity.

By the end of 1951 George M. Bunker and J. Bradford Wharton, Jr. were asked to take over the management of the company. As part of a refinancing plan Glenn Martin was given the title of honorary chairman and his 275,000 shares in the company were placed in a voting trust. Glenn Martin resigned his position in the company in May of 1953, but remained as a company director until his death. George Bunker succeeded Martin as president and chairman and directed the company for the next 20 years. Pearson, who was demoted to vice-president, later resigned. Bunker and Wharton were successful in arresting the company's losses and by the end of 1954 declared the company out of debt. Martin, who never married, died of a stroke in 1955 at the age of 69.

Under its new leadership, Martin substantially reengineered a version of the English Electric Canberra bomber for the United States Air Force. Known as the M-272, the bomber was given the Air Force designation B-57. Martin built a number of scout and patrol planes, including the P5-M and P6-M flying boats, and expanded its interest in the development of rockets and missiles. One of Martin's first projects in this area was the Viking high-altitude research rocket, followed by the Vanguard missile. By the 1960s the company was a leader in the manufacture of second generation rockets like the Titan II.

Despite the company's return to profitability after the Korean War, the larger airplane manufacturers such as Boeing, Douglas and Lockheed had the advantage of size, which allowed them to compete more effectively with smaller companies like Martin, Vought and Grumman. These smaller companies, however, retained very different kinds of engineering teams which allowed them to continue developing unique aeronautic equipment and weapons systems.

The company was largely unsuccessful in achieving diversification in anything but its number of government customers. Martin aircraft was subject to the whims of the Department of Defense with its unstable pattern of purchases. By December of 1960 Martin's last airplane, a Navy P5M-2 antisubmarine patrol plane, rolled off the production line. From this point forward the company produced only missiles, including the Bullpup, Matador, Titan and Pershing among them.

The Martin Company diversified through a merger with the American-Marietta Corporation, a manufacturer of chemical products, paints, inks, household products and construction materials, in 1961. After convincing the government that the merger would not reduce competition in any of either company's industries, the two companies formed Martin Marietta. The diversification continued in 1968 with the purchase of Harvey Aluminum. The name of the subsidiary was changed to Martin Marietta Aluminum in 1971.

Martin Marietta became known for its space projects, but remained a major producer of aluminum and construction materials, during the late 1960s and early 1970s. In 1969 the company's aerospace unit was selected to lead construction of the two Viking capsules which landed on Mars in 1976. In 1973 the company was awarded a contract to build the external fuel tank for NASA's space shuttles.

Thomas G. Pownall advanced to the presidency of Martin Marietta in 1977 and chief executive officer in 1982, succeeding J. Donald Rauth. The same year Martin Marietta faced the most significant challenge to its existence in its history—a hostile takeover bid from the Bendix Corporation. Bendix, which had earlier abandoned an attempt to take over RCA, was led at the time by Bill Agee. For several years Agee had been divesting Bendix of its residual businesses, accumulating a $500 million "war chest" in the process. In 1982, he leveraged that fund into a $1.5 billion bid for Martin Marietta.

Martin Marietta responded with a surprising turnabout. CEO Pownall invited a friend, Harry Gray of United Technologies, to assist with a takeover strategy of their own. Pownall and Gray agreed to divide Bendix among them in the event that either Martin Marietta or United Technologies was successful in taking over Bendix. The takeover was stalemated until a three-way deal was arranged wherein the Allied Corporation agreed to purchase Martin Marietta's holdings in Bendix on the condition that Bendix abandon its bid for Martin Marietta. The deal left Allied with a 39 percent ownership of Martin Marietta, but it was agreed that Allied's voting share would be directed by Martin's board until such time that Allied could sell its interest in Martin. Bill Agee joined Allied's board of directors but later left the company. In the meantime, Martin Marietta went $1.34 billion into debt as a result of its takeover defense.

In order to reduce the company's debt load, Pownall divested its cement, chemical and aluminum operations, and accelerated a reorganization begun before the takeover crisis. By 1986 debt was down to $220 million, giving Martin Marietta a comfortable debt-to-total capitalization ratio of 24 percent. In retrospect, Tom Pownall acknowledged that his company had emerged from Bendix's takeover attempt as a more tightly managed and efficient business.

In the late 1980s, the company became active in the design, manufacture, and management of energy, electronics communication, and information systems, including the highly sophisticated level of computer technology known as artificial intelligence. Even with this diversification, 80 percent of Martin Marietta's revenues continued to be generated via U.S. government contracts. The company supplies the Pentagon with a number of weapons systems, including the Pershing II missile, a major part of the MX missile; the Patriot missile, designed for air defense of field armies; and the Copperhead, a "smart," or guided, cannon shell. Martin Marietta also developed a series of night vision devices for combat aircraft.

The company continued to build external fuel tanks for NASA's space shuttle program, despite the temporary suspension of that program following the Challenger tragedy. Martin Marietta was also a major contractor for the American space station scheduled to be built in 1993. In another public project, the company was working on a new air traffic management system for the Federal Aviation Administration.

Norman R. Augustine, Tom Pownall's hand-picked successor, succeeded his mentor as chairman and CEO upon the latter's mid-1980s retirement. Augustine proved an auspicious choice. Anticipating the impending reductions in the U.S. defense budget, which slid from a high of $96 billion in 1987 down to $75 billion by 1992, the new leader and his executive team developed a three-pronged plan to survive the shakeout. Dubbed the "Peace Dividend Strategy," the blueprint called for growth through acquisition, diversification into civil and commercial infrastructure markets, and maintaining financial health. Under Augustine, Martin Marietta dove into the wave of consolidation that swept over the American defense industry in the early 1990s. He guided the $3 billion acquisition of General Electric Co.'s aerospace operations in 1992. The merger, which added about $6 billion in annual sales, boosted Martin Marietta's capabilities in digital processing, artificial intelligence, and electronics. Two years later, Martin Marietta expanded its capabilities in the wireless communications and commercial aviation markets with the acquisition of Grumman Corp. for $1.9 billion.

However, Augustine's most dramatic move came in 1994, when Martin Marietta and Lockheed announced a "merger of equals." It took the Federal Trade Commission several months to approve the union, which created the world's largest defense company. While the federal government typically discouraged such massive combinations within the same business area, it regarded this consolidation in the defense industry with favor, since, according to one statement, it "boosts the industry's efficiency and lowers costs for the government, which in turn benefits taxpayers, shareholders and employees."

The spring 1995 exchange of stock created an advanced technology conglomerate with interests in the defense, space, energy, and government sectors serving the commercial, civil, and international markets. Daniel M. Tellep, chairman and CEO of Lockheed, held those same positions at the new company. Martin Marietta leader Augustine stepped into the office of president with the promise that he would advance into the top spots upon Tellep's retirement.

Headquartered in Bethesda, Maryland, Lockheed Martin began a process of consolidation and reorganization even before the merger was completed in March 1995. An organizational consolidation grouped operations around four major business sectors: space and strategic missiles, aeronautics, electronics, and information technology services. The plan merged and eliminated dozens of offices and functions, rendering thousands of jobs redundant in the process. In fact, Lockheed Martin slashed its work force from a combined total of 170,000 people to 130,000 by mid-1995 and expected to furlough another 12,000 by 1999.

The unified company was involved in a number of well-publicized projects, including the Hubble Space Telescope, Motorola's Iridium satellite telecommunications system, the F-22 Stealth fighter, Titan and Atlas space launch vehicles, the Space Shuttle program, and the space station Freedom.

The January 1996 acquisition of Loral Corp.'s Defense Electronics and Systems Integration business made it clear that Lockheed Martin would not soon relinquish its number-one status. Established in 1948, the Loral division was a $6.8 billion operation and a global leader in defense electronics, communications, space and systems integration. The acquisition was initially categorized as a sixth division, Tactical Systems, at Lockheed Martin. Anthony L. Velocci Jr., an analyst with *Aviation Week and Space Technology,* predicted that Lockheed Martin would encounter difficulty in consolidating the Loral operations into its own recently-reorganized divisions, but that the acquisition would bring economies of scale and boost electronics, tactical systems, and information technology.

Loral Chairman and CEO Bernard Schwartz held those same positions at the newly-formed Lockheed Martin subsidiary and was invited to join the latter company's board of directors. Schwartz, Tellep, and Augustine became the first members of Lockheed Martin's three-man office of the chairman as a result of the acquisition.

Principal Subsidiaries

Lockheed Foreign Sales Corp.; Lockheed Leadership Fund; Lockheed Missiles & Space Co.; Lockheed Support Systems Inc.; Lockheed Aircraft Service International; Lockheed Fort Worth International Corp.; Lockheed International Service & Investment Corp.; Lockheed Space Operations Co.; Lockheed Information Management Services Co.; Lockheed Aeronautical Systems Support Co.; Tri Star Parts Ltd.; Lockheed Boeing ATF Partnership; Murdock Engineering Co.; Lockheed Employment Services Co. Inc.; Lockheed Aeronautical Systems Employment Services Co., Inc.; Lockheed Finance Corp.; Lockheed Systems Co. Inc.; Lockheed Engineering & Sciences Co.; Lockheed Aeromod Center, Inc.; Lockheed Materials Processing Co.; Lockheed Aeroparts, Inc.; Formtek, Inc.; Lockheed Commercial Aircraft Center, Inc.; Lockheed International Services Inc.; Lockheed-Hellas, S.A.; Lockheed of Turkey, Inc.; Lockheed Ho-Chin, Inc.; Lockheed Information Technology Co.; Lockheed Commercial Electronics Co.; Lockheed Idaho Technologies Co.; Lockheed Transport Systems Inc.; Lockheed Mercartor Information Co. Inc.; Lockheed Aircraft Ltd. (Australia); Lockheed Canada; Lockheed International (Germany); Lockheed Corporation S.A. (Switzerland); Hellenic

Business Development & Investment Co. S.A. (Greece); Lockheed B.V. (Netherlands); Lockheed Investment Holding Co. (Turkey); Lockheed Aircraft Argentina; Lockheed Information Mgmt Service Co.; Mountaingate Data Systems; Lockheed Sanders Inc.; G.E. CFTS (U.S.); G.E. CFTS II (U.S.); EOSAT (U.S.) (50%); GETAC (Taiwan) (50%); KAPL, Inc.; Management Technical Services Co. (MATSCO); Martin Marietta International, Inc.; Martin Marietta International Commercial Sales, Inc.; Martin Marietta Overseas Corp.; Martin Marietta Overseas Services Corp.; MMC Acquisition Corp.; Lockheed Martin Integrated Systems, Inc.; Samdia Corp.; Technology Ventures Corp.; Martin Marietta Technologies, Inc.; Export Products Foreign Sales Corp.; Gamma Monolithics (75%); Innovative Ventures Corp.; International Launch Services, Inc.; International Light Metals Sales Corp.; TI/Javelin Joint Venture (50%); The Martin Co., Martin Marietta Australia Pty. Ltd.; Martin Marietta Canada, Ltd.; Martin Marietta Carbon Inc.; Martin Marietta Commercial Launch Services, Inc.; Martin Marietta Diversified Technologies, Inc.; Lockheed Martin Marietta Energy Systems, Inc.; Martin Marietta Environmental Holdings, Inc.; MMGE Martin Marietta-Gama Electronik ve Enformasyon (60%); Martin Marietta Information Tech., Inc.; Martin Marietta Millimeter Technologies, Inc.; Martin Marietta Ordnance Systems, Inc.; Martin Marietta Services, Inc.; Martin Marietta Spec. Components, Inc.; Martin Marietta Technical Services, Inc.; Martin Marietta Turkish Holdings, Inc.; Lockheed martin Utility Services, Inc.; Martin Metals Co.; Mathematica Pol. Res. Hold. Corp.; Tennessee Innovation Center; Torrance Advanced Metals Corp.

Principal Divisions

Aeronautics, Electronics, Energy & Environment, Information and Technology Services, Space & Strategic Missiles, Tactical Systems.

Further Reading

Banks, Howard, "Aerospace & Defense," *Forbes,* January 4, 1993, p. 96.

Biddle, Wayne, *Barons of the Sky,* Simon & Schuster, 1991.

Borrus, Amy, "This is Going to be the Biggest Kahuna Around," *Business Week,* September 12, 1994, p. 32.

Foust, Dean, "Guns, No Butter at Martin Marietta," *Business Week,* March 21, 1994, p. 39.

Haber, Carol, "Lockheed Martin to Buy Loral Defense," *Electronic News,* January 15, 1996, p. 6.

"Lockheed Martin Setting $1.7 billion Consolidation," *Electronic News,* July 3, 1995, p. 12.

"Lockheed to Buy Most of Loral Corp.," *The Cleveland Plain Dealer,* January 9, 1996, p. 1C.

Rich, Ben R., *Skunk Works: A Personal Memoir of My Years at Lockheed,* Boston: Little, Brown, 1994.

Solberg, Carl, *Conquest of the Skies,* Boston: Little Brown, 1979.

Vander Meulen, Jacob A., *The Politics of Aircraft: Building an American Military Industry,* University Press of Kansas, 1991.

Velocci, Anthony L., Jr., "Loral Buy Challenges Lockheed Martin Skills," *Aviation Week & Space Technology,* January 15, 1996, p. 22.

——, "Merger Now Must Meet Lofty Expectations," *Aviation Week & Space Technology,* November 30, 1992, pp. 23–24.

——, "Merger Partners Poised to Fulfill Strategic Plan," *Aviation Week & Space Technology,* November 14, 1994, pp. 40–42.

Whitehouse, Arthur, *The Sky's the Limit,* London: Macmillan, 1979.

—updated by April Dougal Gasbarre

MagneTek, Inc.

26 Century Boulevard
Nashville, Tennessee 37229
U.S.A.
(615) 316-5100
Fax: (615) 316-5181

Public Company
Incorporated: 1984
Employees: 14,300
Sales: $1.22 billion (1995)
Stock Exchanges: New York Philadelphia Chicago
SICs: 3612 Power, Distribution, and Specialty
    Transformers; 3621 Motors and Generators; 3625
    Relays and Industrial Controls; 3629 Electrical
    Industrial Apparatus, Not Elsewhere Classified; 3677
    Electronic Coils, Transformers, and Other Inductors

MagneTek, Inc., manufactures and markets electrical equipment products including lighting products, motors and generators, motor controls and drives, power supplies, and transformers. The company is distinguished as the largest U.S. manufacturer of fluorescent lighting ballasts, which are its primary product. The debt-heavy MagneTek was divesting noncore businesses in the mid-1990s following an aggressive acquisition campaign in the late 1980s and early 1990s.

MagneTek was created when Litton Industries, Inc. spun off its Magnetics Group in July 1984. Litton Industries was a diversified conglomerate with an emphasis on high-tech industries. Founded in 1954 by Charles "Tex" Thornton, Litton had expanded rapidly during the 1960s and 1970s by developing its own technologies and by acquiring numerous companies. Among the ventures in which it became involved were various electric equipment businesses. For example, in 1967 Litton purchased Louis Allis, a leading manufacturer of specialty electrical motors, condensers, and generators. Litton assembled several of its electric products companies into the Magnetics Group.

Litton fostered growth and success at many of its subsidiaries by providing investment capital and allowing them to cooperate with other Litton companies. In fact, engineers in Litton's electric products companies achieved a number of notable technological breakthroughs. In the mid-1970s, for example, they developed the first high-efficiency electric motor. Dubbed the E-plus, the device set the energy-saving standard in the industry for the next decade. Despite successes in the Magnetics Group, by the early 1980s Litton was ready to jettison the division as part of its ongoing effort to streamline operations and focus on key industries and technologies. Litton sold its Magnetics Group by way of a leveraged buyout, and MagneTek was incorporated on June 1, 1984 to purchase the assets of the Magnetics Group in July of that year.

At the time of the purchase, the Magnetics Group was generating close to $200 million in annual sales from four primary product lines: integral horsepower motors; drives and controls; lighting ballasts; and small transformers. Integral horsepower motors are used to power commercial mechanisms like heating and air-conditioning systems, mining and petrochemical equipment, and commercial laundry machines. Integral horsepower drives and drive systems are mechanisms used to adjust and control the speed and output of electric motors. They typically drive motors in applications like air conditioning systems, elevators, and machine tools. Lighting ballasts are used in both residential and commercial fluorescent lighting fixtures. The ballast controls the power going to the light bulbs and can have a significant impact on the amount of energy consumed by the lighting fixture. Finally, MagneTek's small transformers were used as power conversion devices in a range of electronic equipment.

MagneTek posted a net loss of $501,000 in 1985 from sales of $195 million. After reorganizing the former Magnetics Group during that first full year of business, however, MagneTek began posting consistently rising profits and sales. Indeed, revenues bolted to $273 million in 1986, $608 million in 1987, and then to more than $900 million in 1988. Those gains were primarily the result of an aggressive acquisition strategy adopted by MagneTek's management team. In February 1986 MagneTek purchased Universal Manufacturing Corp. for $71 million, the first in a string of buyouts. In October the company bought motor manufacturer Century Electric, Inc. for $76 million, and in December of that year MagneTek paid $108 million for Cooper Service, Inc., Cooper Controls, Inc., and Universal Electric Co. Six months later, MagneTek also snared ALS Corp. for about $50 million.

MagneTek's expansion strategy during the late 1980s and into the early 1990s was devised by Frank Perna, Jr., the chief executive hired in 1985 to head MagneTek. Perna was a veteran of the electric products industry. He had earned a master's degree in management from the Massachusetts Institute of Technology, as well as a master's degree in electrical engineering from Wayne State University. Perna spent 17 years with General Motors, after which he served as president of Sun Electric and as head of the Instrumentation Group at the venerable Bell & Howell Co. Prior to joining MagneTek, he was serving as the chief executive of a subsidiary of Whittaker Corp.

Perna had witnessed, first-hand, the evolution of the electrical equipment industry during the late 1970s and 1980s. Among the dominant trends were increasing foreign competition and a rising emphasis on advanced technology, particularly related to energy efficiency. Perna believed that for MagneTek to compete in the widely diverse electric products industry, the company would have to become big enough to overcome barriers such as low-cost foreign manufacturers and high capital requirements for product development and manufacturing. His plan was to purchase other companies and integrate them into a cohesive whole, thus achieving economies of scales related to product development, production, marketing, and distribution. To that end, during the late 1980s and early 1990s MagneTek made the six major acquisitions described above, added numerous product lines, and purchased various manufacturing operations including several in Europe.

By 1990 MagneTek was operating 50 manufacturing and service facilities throughout North America and overseas and employing roughly 15,000 workers. Revenues had risen to $961 million in 1989 before cruising past the $1 billion mark in 1990. Furthermore, the company had managed to post steady profit growth, culminating in a $33 million net income for 1990. MagneTek then ceased its acquisition efforts during the early 1990s, concentrating instead on whipping its existing operations into shape. Sales rose about eight percent in 1991 to $1.13 billion and then to $1.23 billion in 1992. Those sales gains were achieved despite an economic recession that reduced orders from many market segments, particularly those related to defense and new construction.

MagneTek had started out as a private venture. The leveraged buyout was funded heavily by two investment partnerships, Magtek Partners and Champlain Associates, which provided seed money for MagneTek's start-up and acquisition drive. The partnerships were created by colleagues of the infamous Michael Milken at investment firm Drexel Burnham Lambert. In 1989 the owners of MagneTek decided to take the venture public to help pay down the company's debt and to provide more growth capital. MagneTek made its initial public stock offering in July 1989 at a price of $12 per share. Unfortunately, the stock price languished during the early 1990s and

provided little opportunity for the company to benefit greatly from subsequent stock sales.

Part of the reason that MagneTek's stock stagnated was that investors were concerned about the Milken-related investment groups, which still owned about one-third of the company by the early 1990s. More importantly, Wall Street was concerned about the massive liabilities that MagneTek had assumed when it was created and during its buyout blitz of the late 1980s. Indeed, by the end of the 1980s MagneTek was staggering under a hefty debt load that was eating into profits and cash flow. The stock sale had helped to reduce that debt, and MagneTek went a long way toward improving its equity position between 1990 and 1992. But weak sales gains during the recession pressured the company and began to take a toll. Although sales rose to a peak of $1.5 million in 1993, profits slipped for the first time in the company's short history in 1992 and stood still in 1993.

Although MagneTek's financial performance waned, the company claimed victories in other arenas. For example, in 1992 MagneTek introduced an ultra-efficient light bulb designed to operate for 20,000 hours (compared to about 750 hours for the typical incandescent light bulb). The new bulb, dubbed the E-Lamp and priced at $10 to $20, operated without a filament. Instead, a signal generated by an electronic circuit excited a phosphor coating inside the bulb that produced a glow similar in intensity to a traditional filament bulb. The breakthrough device reflected MagneTek's marketing strategy of emphasizing energy-efficient products. "We've been pursuing this energy-engineered strategy for three and one-half years," Perna said in the June 8, 1992 *Los Angeles Business Journal.* "And I think it was finally recognized as a good strategy," he added.

Despite some engineering and marketing successes, MagneTek's balance sheet at the end of 1993 demanded that the company adopt a new strategy. Perna exited his post and was replaced as chief executive by Andrew G. Galef. The 60-year-old Galef had served as chairman of the company since its inception and had broad experience in investment and management consulting. Galef steered MagneTek on a new course. Rather than try to compete in the increasingly diverse electrical equipment industry, the company would eliminate non-core business and focus on product segments in which it was most competitive: ballasts, transformers, motors, and generators. Importantly, the move would allow MagneTek to sell off many of the assets that it had accrued during the late 1980s and early 1990s. The company hoped to use that cash to reduce its $530-million debt burden.

By the end of 1993 the sprawling MagneTek organization had grown to encompass 79 production and support facilities in North America, Europe, Japan, and the Far East. Early in 1994 MagneTek announced a restructuring plan that entailed the divestment of six business groups that accounted for roughly 30 percent of the company's annual revenues. Those groups encompassed certain non-core product lines related to electrical services, utility and power products, component transformers and converters, and controls. Among the businesses sold, for example, was the Louis Allis subsidiary, which by 1994 had become a relatively meager part of MagneTek's holdings. (Louis Allis was sold to managers at the subsidiary, making it independent for the first time since Litton bought it in 1967.) Also part of the restructuring was a move of the company headquarters from Los Angeles to Nashville, Tennessee.

MagneTek completed its restructuring and divestment plan by mid-1995. The effort reduced the number of production and support facilities by more than half, to 38, and generated about $200 million in cash. Similarly, MagneTek's 42 business units were consolidated into three groups: lighting products, motors and controls, and power electronics. Company revenues dipped to $1.13 billion in 1994 but rose to $1.2 billion in 1995, and net income recovered to $21.5 million. Meanwhile, MagneTek sustained its energy-engineering strategy, as evidenced by its introduction of the E-plus III in 1995. That motor, a successor to the E-plus motor that Litton had introduced in the 1970s, set a new standard for efficiency in the industry.

Principal Subsidiaries

MagneTek Century Electronics, Inc.; MagneTek Controls, Inc.; MagneTek Defense Systems; MagneTek Electric Inc.; MagneTek National Electric Coil, Inc.; MagneTek Europe, N.V.

Further Reading

Deady, Tim, "Restructuring Plan to Create Slimmer MagneTek," *Los Angeles Business Journal*, January 17, 1994, p. 28.

Kirchen, Rich, "MagneTek Future Upbeat As It Awaits New Owner," *Business Journal-Milwaukee*, July 1, 1995, p. 7.

"MagneTek, Inc.," *Machine Design*, November 26, 1992, p. 119.

Mullins, Robert, "From 'Round Error' to "The Whole Enchilada'," *Business Journal-Milwaukee*, August 27, 1994, p. A2.

Murray, Robert, "MagneTek Announces Fiscal 1994 Results," *Business Wire*, August 22, 1994.

——, "MagneTek Announces Restructuring Plan," *Business Wire*, January 6, 1994.

——, "Ronald W. Mathewson Named President of MagneTek's Lighting Group," *Business Wire*, May 18, 1994.

Stoll, Otto G., "Perna Elected Chief Executive Officer of MangeTek," *Business Wire*, September 17, 1990.

Vrana, Debora, and Todd White, "MagneTek Stock Jumps on News of Product Sales Rise," *Los Angeles Business Journal*, January 18, 1993, p. 31.

White, Todd, "MagneTek Lights Up Over Electronic Lamp," *Los Angeles Business Journal*, June 8, 1992, p. 5.

—Dave Mote

$\mathcal{MC}$ | *Marisa Christina Inc.*

Marisa Christina, Inc.

1410 Broadway, 20th Floor
New York, New York 10018
U.S.A.
(212) 221-5770
Fax: (212) 921-7632

Public Company
Incorporated: 1971
Employees: 45
Sales: $86.5 million (1995)
Stock Exchanges: NASDAQ
SICs: 5137 Women's, Children's, and Infants' Clothing
      and Accessories—Wholesale; 2339 Women's,
      Misses', and Juniors' Outerwear, Not Elsewhere
      Classified

Marisa Christina, Inc. is a popular designer, manufacturer, and marketer of clothing for women and children. The company has two major operating divisions, Marisa Christina and Flapdoodles, and also owns the well-known Adrienne Vittadini designer brand, acquired in early 1996. Under the Marisa Christina banner, the company designs and produces a broad line of ''better'' women's clothing. The classic Marisa Christina look includes sweaters with elaborate embroidered patterns, often combined with complementary skirts. The company is particularly known for the seasonal and holiday motifs it introduces into its line each year. In addition to its Marisa Christina Classics, the Marisa Christina division includes Marisa Christina Studio for more fashion-conscious consumers; a line of knit suits for professionals, marketed under the name Marisa Christina Knits; and Lisa Nichols, a line of ornamented knit sweaters with its own artistic look. The company's Flapdoodles division designs and makes a broad range of children's clothing under both the Flapdoodles and Marisa Christina brand names. Marisa Christina products are distributed to over 3,500 establishments, and can be found at many top department store and specialty chains, including Bloomingdale's, Lord & Taylor, and Saks Fifth Avenue.

Marisa Christina was founded in 1971 by David Seiniger. Seiniger named the company after two important women in his life: his favorite company model, Marisa, and his sister, Christina. The first generation of Marisa Christina sweaters were knitted from a wool, cotton, and silk blend by nuns in the Italian village of Lucca, Tuscany. Early on, the company established its name with a classic look featuring matching wool top and skirt sets. As the line developed a following, Seiniger moved the knitting operation from Italy to Hong Kong, where he could pay workers less than the rates charged by the Tuscan nuns.

In 1976, Seiniger and co-owner Irwin Turner—Marisa Christina's vice-president and treasure—sold the company to soap and detergent giant Colgate-Palmolive Company. Under its new ownership, Marisa Christina was operated as a separate subsidiary, with Seiniger and Turner both retaining their positions at the company. By 1981, Marisa Christina annual sales had grown to $32 million. The company changed hands again that year. Carl Marks & Co., a New York firm specializing in leveraged buyouts, acquired a 50 percent stake in Marisa Christina as a result of that transaction.

As the 1980s continued, however, the company began to lose steam. Sales plummeted to $10 million by 1986, as the Marisa Christina brand name fell out of favor with buyers in the fickle world of fashion. Meanwhile, Seiniger's failing health began to interfere with his ability to run the company. With Seiniger no longer able to devote the energy necessary to run a struggling company, Marisa Christina found itself in need of a new president. David Zalaznick, a Carl Marks & Co. partner, offered the job to Michael Lerner, an old acquaintance with a strong background in the apparel business. Lerner had recently quit his family's sportswear apparel company. As an incentive, the Marisa Christina ownership group offered to sell Lerner a 25 percent stake in the company for a mere $75,000. Lerner, convinced that the name Marisa Christina still carried some weight, accepted the stock and the job.

As the guiding force at Marisa Christina, Lerner orchestrated a turnaround that was no less than remarkable. Under Lerner, the company began bringing out five new collections of sweaters a year. He also added pants to the traditional sweaters and skirts line. Most importantly, Lerner introduced the elaborately embroidered sweaters that would become the signature Marisa Christina look. With ornate motifs that changed with the season, these sweaters made the Marisa Christina line instantly recognizable on store racks. They quickly became fixtures on the floors of many of the nation's top department stores.

These changes were made without tampering with the casual-but-traditional image the company had cultivated over the years. Lerner also cut costs by using a cotton-ramie blend, far less expensive than the wool used in Marisa Christina clothing up to that time. While economizing on materials, Lerner managed at the same time to inflate the value of the Marisa Christina name. This was necessary in order to justify the premium prices being charged for Marisa Christina apparel, since there was no way the company could compete on price with the likes of the Ann Taylor or Limited chains.

By the early 1990s, Marisa Christina was generating impressive profits on a regular basis, largely thanks to the inspired marketing ability of Lerner and his staff. In addition to its seasonal designs and holiday specialties, the company was constantly on the lookout for themes that were popular but traditional, while avoiding trendy fashions for the most part. In 1991, for example, Marisa Christina signed a licensing deal for the right to put out a line of Snoopy sweaters. That kind of market savvy helped the company grow its sales to $39 million by 1992, with earnings reaching $4.4 million.

In 1993, Marisa Christina thrust itself into the children's apparel market with the purchase of Flapdoodles. Although Flapdoodles were found mainly in children's boutiques, Lerner's hope was that the line could also be sold through Marisa Christina department store channels. By 1995, Flapdoodles accounted for about a third of Marisa Christina's total sales.

The year 1993 also marked the introduction of a line of ornamented knit sweaters designed by Lisa Nichols. The Lisa Nichols collection, brought out for that year's holiday season, featured bold colors in artistic designs concocted for customers with a youthful, independent self-image. The addition of the Flapdoodles and Lisa Nichols lines helped boost the company's earnings to $4.8 million in 1993, on sales of $56.9 million.

In spite of these big-time numbers, much of Marisa Christina's success was based on its ability to connect with smaller outlets. As much as 40 percent of company output was sold to small suburban stores, where managers are well-acquainted with the personal tastes of their customers. In June 1994, Marisa Christina went public, with the sale of 30 percent of the company's stock—worth $32.5 million—by Lerner and the leveraged buyout team that had brought him in. For that year, the company reported sales of over $76 million, nearly double its 1992 figure. The company also saw its net earnings jump to $8.5 million.

As the 1990s moved along, Marisa Christina continued to launch new products. Marisa Christina Kids was introduced for the 1994 holiday season. This line featured children's sweaters of classic design, as well as some matching mother-daughter outfits. Targeted primarily at mothers desiring to extend their own taste for the Marisa Christina novelty look to their children, the Kids line enabled the company to exploit the marketing and distribution network already in place for its Flapdoodles collection. For the Fall 1995 season, the company introduced Marisa Christina Knits, a line of two-piece knit suits with a tailored, professional look. Like Marisa Christina's existing products, these additions to the company's apparel output consisted of practical clothing, and were not designed to turn the heads of those interested in high fashion. Lerner makes this point in a 1995 article in *Forbes,* in which he is quoted describing a recent conversation: "Someone at a cocktail party said to me: 'Well, how do you like the fashion industry?' and my answer was, 'I wouldn't know. We make clothing'."

By 1995 Marisa Christina was no longer a secret to anybody, particularly to anybody on Wall Street. With profit margins more than twice as high as the average in the apparel manufacturing industry, the company checked in at number six on *Forbes* magazine's list of Best Small Companies. In November of 1995, the stock Lerner had bought for $75,000 was worth a cool $24 million. By that time, the company had built up a $20 million cash pool, and appeared to be poised to make another big acquisition, its first since picking up Flapdoodles in 1993.

The expected acquisition took place in early 1996, when Marisa Christina purchased designer knitwear brand Adrienne Vittadini, a label regularly found on the racks of high-end department stores. Vittadini, whose sales had fallen from a peak of $115 million in 1990 to $37 million in 1995, represented an aggressive attempt on the part of Lerner and Marisa Christina to go head-to-head against the best-known brands in the better clothing category, including such major names as Liz Claiborne and Jones New York. Company officials hoped that access to Marisa Christina's successful and growing marketing and distribution channels could breathe some much-needed life into the tiring Vittadini line, although the two companies were to be operated as separate entities with distinct stylistic identities.

A number of industry analysts viewed the addition of Adrienne Vittadini as the move that brought Marisa Christina into the big leagues of the apparel world. Bringing an upper-end designer brand into the fold gave the company its first access to a number of important specialty outlets, including Neiman Marcus and Saks Fifth Avenue. Prior to the acquisition, Marisa Christina was known among Wall Street types as the apparel industry's "little jewel" (in the words of analyst Marie J. de Lucia as quoted in *Crain's New York Business*). With its new, higher-profile status within the industry, Marisa Christina hoped to sustain an annual growth rate of 20 percent during the second half of the 1990s. Regardless of whether the company is more interested in making clothing or making fashion, the one thing it has certainly shown an aptitude for making is money.

Principal Divisions

Marisa Christina; Flapdoodles; Adrienne Vittadini.

Further Reading

Gault, Ylonda, ''Low-Key Marisa Christina Now Hot-Growth Possibility,'' *Crain's New York Business*, February 12, 1996, p. 23.

Moukheiber, Zina, ''Pumpkins and Stars,'' *Forbes*, November 6, 1995, pp. 254–255.

Ozzard, Janet, and Valerie Seckler, ''Expansion Strategy for Marisa Christina: Revitalizing Vittadini,'' *Women's Wear Daily*, January 22, 1996, p. 1.

Shonfeld, Erick, ''A Bright Spot in Apparel,'' *Fortune*, September 18, 1995, p. 245.

—Robert R. Jacobson

Matra-Hachette S.A.

4, Rue de Presbourg
75116 Paris
France
(33) 1 40 69 16 00
Fax: (33) 1 47 23 01 92

Public Company
Incorporated: 1826 as Librairie Louis Hachette
Employees: 40,314
Sales: FFr53.00 billion (US$9.9 billion) (1994)
Stock Exchanges: Paris
SICs: 5994 News Dealers and Newsstands; 2721
  Periodicals; 2731 Book Publishing; 3663 Radio & TV
  Communications Equipment; 3661 Telephone and
  Telegraph Apparatus

Matra-Hachette S.A. ranks as France's top communications enterprise and one of the country's top 15 industrial companies. The conglomerate was formed through the 1992 merger of longtime affiliates Matra S.A., a defense electronics and transportation company, with Hachette S.A., one of the world's top 20 media groups. The union was precipitated by Hachette's 1990 acquisition of the troubled French television station La Cinq. When La Cinq failed in 1991, Hachette recorded a loss of FFr1.9 billion (US$350 million) and its debt rose to more than Ffr8 billion (US$1.53 million). Jean-Luc Lagardère, whose Groupe Lagardère owned over 93 percent of Matra Hachette, oversaw the 1992 recapitalization and merger. The new company operated through nine divisions in 1995: distribution, press, book publishing, audio-visual production, telecommunications, defense, space, cars and transport equipment. Known in some circles as "the Green Octopus," Hachette used its dominant, 30 percent share of the French book market as a springboard to expansion throughout Europe and overseas. By the early 1990s the conglomerate ranked as top magazine publisher in the world, with over 100 magazines, including the globally circulated Elle. International sales surpassed domestic sales for the first time in 1994.

In 1821, when Monsignor Denis Frayssinous, whom Louis XVIII had put in charge of the French universities, ordered the suppression and closure of the Ecole Normale Supérieure, one of the most prestigious educational establishments in France, he could not have known that he was participating indirectly in the foundation of what is now France's largest publisher. In that very year Louis Hachette, a brilliant pupil of the ecole, was finishing his third year of studies there, and found himself thrown back upon his own resources; no longer a student, he decided to become a publisher. In 1826, after more than three years of planning and searching for financial backing, Hachette acquired the publishing house Librairie de Jacques-Francois Brétif, which he soon renamed after himself: Librairie Louis Hachette. He retained Brétif's list and began to publish educational journals and textbooks for primary schools. However, by 1831 he was already publishing the famous romantic historian Jules Michelet. His first catalog, which appeared in 1832, already reflected the diversity that lies at the roots of Hachette's success: it included a classical division, journals, and by 1836 two dictionary projects. Eight years after its creation, the Librairie Hachette's sales volume had tripled.

Louis Hachette soon realized the need for a partner in the business, and in 1840 Louis Breton filled this post. Together, Hachette and Breton launched numerous periodicals and both made known English-language literature: William Makepeace Thackeray, Henry Wadsworth Longfellow, and, most notably Charles Dickens, eleven of whose novels were published by Hachette. In 1851, Hachette returned from travels in England, where he had observed the parallel development of public transportation and public information technology. He followed the example of English news agent W.H. Smith, and in 1852 began to establish a network of bookstores and newspaper stands in French railroad stations. These emphasized interesting reading at a moderate price and offered tourist guides, general interest reading, and children's books published by Hachette. Louis Hachette went on to diversify into newspaper and magazine publishing. In 1859 his company expanded overseas, opening a foreign language bookstore in London.

Louis Hachette took a keen interest in French literature. Having acquired the publisher Librairie Victor Lecou in 1855, he became publisher of such well-known writers as George Sand, Victor Hugo, Gérard de Nerval, and Gustave Doré. Later he became editor of the Emile Littré dictionary, known as the Littré, which is still the most respected reference dictionary used in universities and schools. At his death in 1864, Louis Hachette left his heirs a considerable fortune, and a company with 165 employees and sales which reached FFr18 million in 1878. His son George took over the bookselling license, but the Librairie continued to be managed by Louis Breton, until the latter's death in 1883, and by a small group of partners who worked in close collaboration and sought rapid growth. This group included Emile Templier. He took the initiative of publishing the work of the Comtesse de Ségur, who wrote several classics of children's literature. The Franco-Prussian War of 1870 slowed down the activities of the Librairie considerably, but the company's recovery was as rapid as its decline had been. Tourist guides were particularly successful, but a major breakthrough came in 1897 with the creation of Messageries Hachette, a book and press distribution organization, which soon served the entire country and in 1914 employed more than 700 people. In 1900 Hachette opened the first newsstand in the Paris subway system.

World War I caused difficulties for the Librairie; the company's greatest problem was the loss of personnel. The men sent to the front were often replaced by women, many of whom had no experience in the business. However, this change did not seem to prevent the Librairie from further expansion, and in 1916, in the midst of war, the Librairie Hachette bought the company Pierre Lafitte, which included several newspapers, bestsellers, a bookshop, and a photographic studio.

After World War I, the Librairie Hachette underwent significant restructuring. Despite the reluctance of the employees and the fact that the company was essentially a family business, the Librairie became a "société anonyme"—a public company—in 1919. This change was prompted by a growing need to increase its registered capital and to issue redeemable stock. The new public limited company had five active partners and 24 sleeping partners, all relatives by marriage or direct descendants of Louis Hachette or Louis Breton. An increase of capital took place, which would be multiplied again in 1939, by nine times. Hachette also expanded overseas. The Librairie took over AGLP, a book and newspaper wholesaler that also operated retail bookshops throughout South America and in several European countries. From 1932, Hachette began to secure exclusive distribution rights for other publishers and in particular for the prestigious N.R.F. Gallimard, for Fasquelle, which would soon become a subsidiary of the group. In the 20 years between the two world wars, the Librairie's volume of business tripled. World War II slowed down this growth considerably, as it did for other publishers.

The occupying Germans began by requisitioning Hachette's offices in rue Réaumur and boulevard Saint-Germain, and by forcing out the company's directors. Finally the Germans tried to take over the Librairie, but were unsuccessful. During the four years of German occupation, Hachette's funds were nil. Little by little, however, a passive resistance was organized so effectively that as early as 1944 the directors returned to the company. Messageries d'Hachette was the most affected, the distribution system and transport system having changed considerably during the war. In 1947, after several fruitless attempts at recovery and the failure of the Messageries Françaises de la Presse, created in 1944, Hachette created the Nouvelles Messageries de la Presse Parisienne (N.M.P.P.). This organization, which continued to enjoy a worldwide influence throughout the postwar era, worked on a cooperative basis, and Hachette merely gave it its structure, only accepting a fee in compensation. In 1963, the N.M.P.P. achieved sales of FFr1.5 billion, half the sales of Hachette. In 1991, Hachette owned 49 percent of N.M.P.P., the remaining 51 percent being owned by nine other newspaper and magazine publishers.

Meanwhile, and after World War II, Hachette's book division expanded through a large number of acquisitions and through an original and important creation in literary publication, the Livre de Poche. The latter joined the four publishing divisions already in existence: the educational division, the young reader's division, the general literature division, and the tourist guide division. The new publishers that Hachette acquired retained their individual company styles and character. The first of these was the Editions Bernard Grasset, publisher of Marcel Proust—at the author's own expense—of Paul Morand, and of Montherland. Hachette had come to the aid of this company as early as 1938, but it was not until 1954 that the Librairie acquired a major holding in Grasset, which had been founded in 1907. Grasset then merged rapidly with Fasquelle, in which Hachette had held a majority stake since 1931. The process was similar in the case of the Librairie Fayard, founded in 1955. Hachette acquired an initial stake, which became a majority shareholding in 1958. Next came Stock, a publisher specializing in translations, in 1961. Livre de Poche was the creation in 1960 of the Librairie Générale Française—a subsidiary of Hachette created in 1922—and was largely inspired by publishing in Britain, where good literature in very cheap editions was becoming increasingly popular. Livre de Poche, a series including the best writers since the beginning of the century and a large number of classics at unrivaled prices, achieved considerable success. One year after the creation of the series, 15 million books had already been sold, and two years later, 24 million. Livre de Poche achieved such fame that, from being the proper name of a series, it has become a common name in French, designating paperback editions. In later years, when other paperback editions appeared in France, bookshops were obliged to distinguish a paperback of the Livre de Poche series by the name "poche-Poche."

By 1963 the Hachette group had become a complex of public limited companies or of limited-liability companies, and achieved sales of FFr1.5 billion, not including N.M.P.P. The publishing division accounted for FFr700 million. Of the total sales figure, FFr200 million came from Hachette's 36 subsidiaries and branch offices scattered around the whole world.

Between 1964 and 1980, the date of Matra's takeover of Hachette, the Librairie grew under the leadership of Robert Meunier de Houssoy, and after 1976 under that of Jacques Marchandise. The company's growth included a number of significant events. The break—made final in 1970—between Hachette and Gallimard, whereby Hachette lost the right to distribute Gallimard's books, was a blow to business. Five years later Hachette brought out the Encyclopédie Générale d'Hachette and thereby entered the highly competitive field of dictionaries. The encyclopedia, which covered 100,000 words in 12 volumes, was a success. In the newspaper and magazine publishing sector, Hachette acquired in 1976 the company Jean Prouvost, which owned most notably the weekly Tele 7 Jours, with the greatest circulation of any French newspaper or magazine, and Paris Match. In 1977 Jean Marchandise decided to change the group's name from the slightly old-fashioned Librairie Hachette to, simply, Hachette. A year later, armed with its new modern image, Hachette opened an immense distribution center, which was almost entirely operated by robots, and which won worldwide admiration. The Centre National de Distribution du Livre (CDL), soon renamed "the Cathedral of Books," consisted of 50,000 square meters dedicated to the storage and distribution of books.

Nevertheless, faced with increasing competition, Hachette was still vulnerable. Its middle-class, family-business management was not successfully meeting competition. Hachette's share price had fallen low enough for a takeover attempt to be made without excessive risk. As Jacques Sauvageot explained in Le Monde, December 10, 1990, "the real problem is that Hachette no longer presents to the powers that be the guarantees considered necessary." Giscard d'Estaing's government supported Matra, its principal arms supplier. After a takeover bid by the head of Matra, Jean-Luc Lagardère, Matra became the controlling owner of Hachette stock; by means of holding companies, Matra took control of the capital without holding a majority stake. This operation aroused varied and extreme reactions from the French press. Jérome Carcin expressed his fears in Les Nouvelles Litteraires: "The publishing industry is gradually losing its financial and intellectual independence," while Guy Sitbon of the Nouvel Observateur admitted to a belief that Jean-Luc Lagardère was "perfect" for the role of "proud and flamboyant servant" required by Giscard d'Estaing.

As the country's Manager of the Year for 1979, Lagardère has been called "France's most successful entrepreneur." Born in 1928, the budding media mogul had started his career in engineering, moving up through the ranks at Matra to eventually become its chief executive officer. By the early 1980s, his empire included racing cars, a professional soccer team, a stud farm, Matra, Hachette, and investment bank Arjil. With a view to making it the world's biggest publisher, Lagardère began restructuring Hachette, making more than 400 employees redundant as early as June 1981. Lagardère, who seemed to be nurturing his political connections, nevertheless managed, in October 1981, to ensure that Hachette escaped the tidal wave of nationalizations, which caught Matra head on. Indeed, while Matra was state-owned until a new administration reprivatized it in 1987, Hachette remained in the private sector.

Meanwhile the restructuring continued. Immediately after the takeover of the publisher Jean-Claude Lattès, Lattès himself, against all expectations, became managing director of the book division of the new multimedia group. The latter launched itself into an intensive period of acquisition in France and especially abroad. This began in 1985 with the purchase of a 50 percent stake in the publisher Harlequin, specialists in low-priced romantic novels. Shortly afterward came the creation of four new series in the Hachette Jeunesse division, which became one of Hachette's most promising divisions. In 1988, in its expansion in the United States, Hachette launched a successful,

$450 million takeover bid for Grolier, one of America's leading publishing companies specializing in encyclopedias and information publishing. Although Grolier ranked third among the U.S.'s top encyclopedia publishers, it led the pack in such new delivery technologies as CD-ROM and on-line database access. The Grolier acquisition also gave Hachette entreé into the high-potential Asian market. At the beginning of 1989, Hachette set its sights on Spain, buying Salvat, Spain's fifth-largest publisher of encyclopedias and dictionaries.

Gradually the book division's performance improved. By 1983 its balance sheet showed positive results in spite of two disappointing setbacks. The first concerned the opening of the Hachette multi-store in Paris in the Opéra district, which failed rapidly. The second, concerned the creation of the series Succès du Livre in 1987. Jean-Claude Lattès tried to emulate the France-Loisirs club and launched a series of reprinted bestsellers at a 30 percent discount. FFr15 million were spent on publicizing this project and some nine months later, in December 1987, Hachette sold the ill-named series to a clearance dealer in Lyons.

Nevertheless Lagardère remained essentially a communications man. The recovery of the book division owed a great deal to the intensive growth of the newspaper and magazine publishing division. As early as 1984, Hachette acquired the U.K. Seymour Press which, together with Cordon & Gotch, became Seymour International Press Distributor Ltd. In 1986, it was the turn of the Curtis Circulation Company, the second-largest distributor of magazines in the United States. The U.S. offensive continued with the 1988 acquisition of Diamandis Communications Inc., the seventh largest U.S. press group, for $712 million. Diamandis' stable of 12 magazines included Woman's Day, Car and Driver, and Stereo Review. Finally, after the arrival of Lagardère, the magazine Elle extended its distribution worldwide to 17 editions, including Japanese and Chinese editions. By 1988, Elle's global circulation reached 2.5 million.

Under Lagardère, Hachette's revenues multiplied from US$1.3 billion in 1981 to US$3.5 billion by 1988 and Lagardère's MMB S.A. grew into France's third-largest holding company. With this string of successes under his belt, the mogul began expanding his publishing empire into other media in 1986 with the acquisition of one of France's largest radio stations, Europe I. His first foray into television was thwarted in 1988, when he was unable to take over TFI, the leading French television network. In 1990 he acquired a 25 percent stake in the struggling French television station La Cinq and thus became its largest shareholder. It was an opportunity that soon turned into a disaster.

Lagardère was so confident that he could make La Cinq profitable that he promised his fellow shareholders that Hachette would make good on virtually all the channel's debts and losses, even though the publisher was only due one-fourth of the station's profits. His high-stakes gamble began to unravel in 1991, when La Cinq failed, Hachette recorded a loss of FFr1.9 billion (US$350 million) and its debt rose to more than Ffr8 billion (US$1.53 million). Jean-Luc Lagardère, whose Groupe Lagardère by then owned over 93 percent of Hachette, engineered a 1992 recapitalization and merger with the then-profitable and virtually debt-free Matra.

Although the union was financed by at least US$506 million in loans from some of France's largest state-owned financial institutions—Crédit Lyonnais and Banque Nationale de Paris—some analysts criticized the merger as an illogical attempt to save face. In 1992 Regis Lefort of Didier Philippe told *Advertising Age* that "This is simply a rescue of Hachette by Matra. . . . The bottom line on this was that Hachette could no longer continue alone. It has no more money." An analyst with *The Economist* implied that the French banks saved Hachette to keep it from being bought out by foreigners.

Matra-Hachette sold an estimated FFr1.6 billion (US$290 million) in assets for debt reduction and was able to generate a US$64 million profit for 1992. The new company's annual revenues remained flat, at around Ffr54 billion (US$10 billion), from 1992 through 1994, but its net income rebounded to Ffr615 million (US$152 million) during that same period.

Principal Subsidiaries

Matra Marconi Space BV (Netherlands) (51%); Matra Marconi Space France (51%); Matra Espace Holding BV (Netherlands) (51%); Matra Espace Participations (51%); Matra Marconi Space Systems Ltd (UK) (51%); Matra Marconi Space UK Holdings (51%); Matra Marconi Space UK Ltd; Matra Space Systems Participations BV (Netherlands) (51%); M.C.N. SAT Holding; M.C.N. SAT Service (99.8%); M.C.N. SAT US; S.C.I. Matra Toulouse (99.89%); Sofimades; Fairchild Controls (USA); Germantown (USA); M.A.I. (USA); Manhattan Beach (USA); Matec (99.77); Matra Défense; Matra Défense-Espace; Matra Électronique; Matrel; M.P. 65 (99.3%); M.P. 98 (99.3%); Intecom Inc. (USA); Matra Communication USA Inc.; Matra Nortel Communication; Matra Nortel Holding; Matra Systèmes de Sécurité (M2S) (50%); Stratcom; Matra Datavision (73.94%); M.P. 13; SFMRA (Société Financiére Matra Renault Automation) (65%); c.R.L.F. (73.94%); DTB International (70.25 %); Matra Datavision Ben (Belgium) (73.9%); Matra Datavision GmbH (Germany) (73.94%); Matra Datavision SPA (Italy) (73.94%); Matra Datavision Kk (Japan) (73.94%); Matra Datavision Ltd. (UK) (73.93%); Matra Datavision Inc. (USA) (73.93%); Matra Transport; Matra Transfinex; Matra Transit Inc. (USA); Matra Transport International; Matra Automobile; Hachette Libre; Alpha Éditions (93.31%); Brodard et Taupin; Calmann-Lévy (52.28%); Celiv; Diffulivre (Switzerland); Édition N° 1; Éditions Classiques d'Expression Française (EDICEF); Éditions Gérard de Villiers (80.2%); Éditions Grasset et Fasquelle (84.78%); Éditions Jean-Claude Lattés; Éditions Rombaldi; Éditions Stock; Grolier Hachette International (Italy); Grolier Hachette Gestione Clienti SRL (Italy); H.L. 93; Le Libre de Paris; Librarie Arthème Fayard (99.84%); Librairie des Champs-Élysées (99.37); Librairie Générale Française (L.G.F.); Nouvelles Éditions Marabout (Belgium); Sylemma Andrieu; Salvat Editores SA (SESA) (Spain); Difedi SA (Panama); EPFSA (Spain); Hachette Latino America (Mexico); PAGSA (Spain); Salvat Editores Argentina SA (Argentina); Salvat SA de Distribucion (Spain); Hachette Filipacchi Presse (65.96%); Affichage Centre Ville (A.C.V.) (65.96%); B.I.P. (61.8%); Brodard Graphique SNC (65.96%); Distriservice (63.33%); Echo Communication (63.32%); EDI 7 (65.96%); Elle Hong Kong (65.96%); Elle Publishing (USA) (65.96%); Exploitation Commerciale d'Editions de Presse (E.C.E.P.) (65.96%); F.E.P. U.K. Limited (65.96%); Gestao e Publicidade (Portugal) (65.29%); Hachette Filipacchi Australia (65.96%); Hachette Filipacchi Japan (65.96%); Hachette Filipacchi Magazines Inc. (USA) (65.96%); Hachette Filipacchi Publicacoes (Portugal) (65.89%); Hachette Filipacchi SA (Spain) (65.20%); Hachette Filipacchi USA (65.96%); Hachette Interdeco SA (Spain) (54.49%); Hachette Magazine House H.K. Ltd. (Hong Kong) (65.96%); Hachette Sverige HB (Sweden) (65.96%); H.C.B. Graphic (65.96%); Imprimerie Hélio Corbeil (I.H.C.) (65.96%); Inter-Hebdo (63.3%); International Media Holding BV (Netherlands) (65.96%); International Publications Holding (Netherlands) (65.96%); Interquot (57.07%); Inter Régies Centre Ouest (I.R.C.O.) (63.31%); Iota (65.96%); Média Informatique Service (M.I.S.) (65.96%); Publications France Monde (65.96%); Publications France Monde (65.96%); Publications Groupe Loisirs (P.G.L.) (65.96%); Publiprox (65.96%); Quillet S.A. (65.96%); Société d'Étude et de Développement de la Presse Périodique (S.E.D.P.P.) (65.96%); Sograph (62.18%); Hachette Distribution Services; Aéroboutiques France; Agence et Messageries de la Presse (A.M.P.) (Belgium) (92.3%); A.M.P. Transports (Belgium) (92.3%); Centre de Coordination Hachette Distribution Services (Belgium) (92.3%); Chaussem (Belgium) (92.3%); Curtis Circulation Company (USA) (90%); Diffusion Payot (Switzerland) (62.22%); Distrisud (Belgium) 92.06%); Dynapresse (Switzerland) (62.24%); Eastern Lobby Shops (USA); Hachette distribution Inc. (USA); H.D.H. Ltd. (UK); H.D.S. UK Ltd.; I.B.D. (Belgium) (75.69%); International Press Distributors Ltd. (UK); Les Messageries de Presse Internationales (Canada); Naville; Navistar; Payot Naville Distribution (Switzerland) (62.24%); Payot SA (Switzerland) (62.22%); Press-Shop Alg. (Belgium) (71.04%); Relais H SNC; Saarbach GmbH (Germany) (75.1%); Santino (Switzerland) (62.24%); Sigma (Spain) (50%); Sociedad General Española de Libreria (S.G.E.L.); Sodipress (Switzerland) 62.24%); Matra Hachette Multimédia; Armisse; Matra Hachette Multimédia On Line; Matra Hachette Multimédia Voyager (50%); Grolier Inc. (USA); Caribe Grolier (Puerto Rico); Children Press Inc. (USA); Federated Credit Corp. (USA); Grolier Australia PTY Limited (Australia); Grolier Education Corporation (USA); Grolier Electronic Publishing Inc. (USA); Grolier Enterprises Corporation (USA); Grolier Enterprises Inc. (USA); Grolier International Inc.(USA); Grolier International Limited (UK) (99.9%); Grolier Limited (UK) (99.9%); Grolier Limited Canada; Grolier Limited New Zealand (Australia) (99.9%); Grolier Overseas (USA); Grolier Publishing Inc. (USA); Grolier Reading Program Inc. (USA); Grolier Telemarketing Inc. (USA); Grolier Yearbook Inc.; Latco II Inc. (USA); Lexicon Publications (USA); Publishers World Trade Corporation; Scarecrow Press Inc. (USA); Waverly House Limited (UK) (99.9%); Legion UK Ltd; (UK) (99.78%); Legion International SA (99.78%); Fabian Holdings BV (Netherlands) (99.78%); Legion AG (Switzerland) (99.78%); Legion Ltd (UK) (99.78%); Legion Telecall PTY Ltd (Australia) (50.89%); Legion Telekommunikation GmbH (Germany) (99.78%); Telecom Scandinavia A/S (Denmark) (99.78%); Aberly; Abianne; Compagnie Versaillaise de Transports; Fradis France Distributique (98.37%); Hachette 5; Holpa; Lagardère Groupe North America (USA); Matra Hachette Général; Matra Participations; M.P. 55; SNC Sofrimat 4; Sofrimo; Sogemat Participations; Sopredis (89.2%).

Principal Divisions

Space; Defense; Telecommunications and CAD/CAM; Matra Datavision Group; Transit Systems; Automobile; Book Publishing; Salvat Group; Print Media; Distribution Services; Broadcasting, Film and Display; Multimedia.

Further Reading

Alderman, Bruce, "Hachette Big Loser in La Cinq Fiasco," *Variety*, March 30, 1992, p. 39.

——, "Lagardère Loses La Cinq Dare," *Variety*, April 6, 1992, p. 1.

Crumley, Bruce, "Hachette Woes = Filipacchi Gain," *Advertising Age*, May 10, 1992, p. 10.

"Edition: La Tournée des Pages," *Les Dossiers du Canard*, June–July, 1989.

Gibson, Paul, "Consolation Prize," *Financial World*, December 13, 1988, p. 26.

Lalanne, Bernard, and Nathalie Villard, "Le Grand Ecart d'Hachette," *L'Expansion*, February 7–20, 1991.

Lepape, Pierre, "Hachette-Groupe de la Cité: Le Face a Face de L'Edition," *Le Monde Affaires*, February 20, 1988.

Lottman, Herbert R., "The World of Hachette," *Publishers Weekly*, September 9, 1988, p. 102.

Misler, Jean, *La Librairie Hachette de 1826 à Nos Jours*, Paris: Hachette Editeur, 1964.

"The Odd Couple," *The Economist*, May 9, 1992, p. 89.

Sasseen, Jane, "Family Dynasty," *International Management*, February 1990, p. 24.

Sauvageot, Jacques, "Dans la Presse Hebdornadaire. Hachette: La Nouvelle Arme de Matra," *Le Monde*, December 1980.

——, "L'Etau," *Le Monde*, December 10, 1980.

Selinger, Iris Cohen, " 'Match': A European Magazine in 5 Languages," *ADWEEK Eastern Edition*, January 16, 1989, p. 4.

Smith, Evan, "Hachette lands $2M Ad Sale, Mulls Buying 1,001 Home Ideas," *MEDIAWEEK*, February 4, 1991, p. 5.

Wilson, Claire, " 'Green Octopus' Reaches Across the Sea," *Advertising Age*, October 24, 1988, p. S22.

—Sonia Kronlund. Translated from the French by Jessica Griffin.
—updated by April Dougal Gasbarre

Mike-Sell's Inc.

333 Leo Street
Dayton, Ohio 45404
U.S.A.
(513) 228-9400
Fax: (513) 461-5707

Private Company
Incorporated: 1910 as D.W. Mikesell & Company
Employees: 290
Sales: $34 million (1992 est.)
SICs: 5145 Confectionery; 6719 Holding Companies, Not Elsewhere Classified

Mike-Sell's Inc. manufactures and markets potato chips and snack foods in a five-state midwest region that includes parts of Kentucky, Ohio, West Virginia, Indiana, and Illinois. Its strongest market is Dayton, Ohio, where it controls about 75 percent of the potato chip market. The company was processing more than 100 tons of potatoes daily going into the 1990s and was growing its operations slowly. The private company releases little information about its operations or financial status.

Mike-Sell's was founded in 1910 by Ohio native Daniel W. Mikesell. Mikesell was born in Miami County, Ohio, in 1883. In 1906, when he was 23, Mikesell moved to Dayton with the desire to start his own business. He started out working for a wholesale and retail dry goods store before serving a short stint as a collector for the Home Telephone Company. Finally, in 1910, he started his own venture. He saw advertised in the newspaper a used dried-beef slicing machine. He bought the contraption and set up a makeshift meat shop in two rooms next to his home. He started selling dried beef and sausage snack foods that he processed with his machine. He delivered his products to customers via bicycle.

Mikesell upgraded his delivery system to a horse and buggy after a few years. At about this time, Mikesell became engaged in the potato chip business when he took advantage of an opportunity to purchase equipment designed to manufacture chips, which were relatively unknown in Dayton at the time. According to legend, a chef named George Crum invented the fried food at an upscale resort in Saratoga Springs, New York, when railroad baron Commodore Cornelius Vanderbilt sent his french fries back to the kitchen, complaining that they had been sliced too thick. Disgusted, Crum sliced thin shavings from a potato and threw them into hot oil. After they had fried to a crisp he sent them back to the table, to Vanderbilt's delight. "Saratoga chips," as they were first called, became popular throughout the eastern United States. With help from his wife Mikesell began producing the chips with a few cooking kettles, baskets, and stirrers. The operation was truly vertically integrated, with Mikesell and his wife peeling, slicing, frying, packaging, and then delivering the tasty potato chips to customers.

Customers who tried Mikesell's unique fried potato chips loved them. Mikesell continued to deliver snack food products other than potato chips, because most people considered the chips a seasonal picnic item, but it was clear that the chips were a big hit for the fledgling venture. Indeed, the Mikesells eventually employed their four children peeling potatoes to keep up with demand. Mikesell marketed the chips through county and state fairs, and the entire family traveled during the summers to operate the D.W. Mikesell Co. booth at such events. The Mikesells lived in a tent while traveling and sold the chips out of a glass case, scooping them into nickel bags. In 1913 Mikesell purchased a Ford delivery truck. Evidencing Mikesell's penchant for innovation, his was the first delivery panel truck in Dayton. The side of the truck was embossed with a new, more descriptive moniker: D.W. Mikesell Co. Food Specialties.

After an encouraging three year start-up, Mikesell encountered disaster. In March 1913 a great flood swept the Dayton area. The region was devastated when a levee gave way. Businesses and homes were destroyed. Mikesell and many other business owners were forced to rebuild and effectively start over. Mikesell did rebuild—only to be waylaid by another misfortune. In 1915 a fire destroyed the company's facilities. Again, Mikesell found investment capital and was able to rebuild his snack food company. The company recovered and managed to post solid gains throughout the late 1910s and into the 1920s. As potato chips began to catch on as a year-round food, new equipment was purchased, facilities were enlarged, workers were hired, and new delivery routes were established. Importantly, Mikesell's chips found their niche on local grocery store shelves.

For many U.S. businesses, the Great Depression meant failure or at least diminished profits. Mikesell's was one of the few exceptions. Through savvy marketing, shrewd management, and an emphasis on quality, the company recorded healthy growth throughout the 1920s and 1930s. It was in 1925 that Mikesell realized the need for a catchy logo that would stick in customers' minds. The company settled on the ''Mike-Sell's'' trademark that stuck with the company for more than 70 years. Mike-Sell's began to market its products under that name outside of Dayton for the first time in the 1930s. That effort augmented success in Dayton. Mikesell tore down his house and his potato chip factory and enlarged both. Always on the cutting edge, Mikesell purchased one of the first automated potato chip fryers in 1939. That event, according to company annals, marked a sort of turning point for Mike-Sell's.

Mike-Sell's continued to expand during the 1940s, 1950s, and 1960s. It retained its grip on the Dayton market but also established a venerable presence in surrounding Ohio regions and later in parts of Indiana and Kentucky. The success of its simple potato chips was no great secret. Mike-Sell's prospered with a simple strategy that revolved around quality. Mikesell used only the highest quality potatoes. He eventually discovered when and where to buy the best potatoes. As the seasons changed, the company would purchase its spuds from the best suppliers in different regions—it bought from Florida in May and gradually moved northward through Alabama, the Carolinas, Ohio, and then up into Michigan and the Dakotas.

Similarly, Mike-Sell's was the only manufacturer that fried its potato slivers in 100 percent premium peanut oil. Mikesell believed that it was the peanut oil that gave his chips a rich and distinctive flavor. A leader in manufacturing, Mike-Sell's installed the latest manufacturing equipment, and machinery suppliers frequently visited the Mike-Sell's factory to experiment with new ideas that might improve their latest equipment. Among other firsts, Mike-Sell's was one of the first companies to use automatic packaging machines that formed a bag, filled it with chips, sealed it, and then placed twin bags in an outer covering.

In 1955 Mike-Sell's finally moved its manufacturing operations away from the facilities that had been built on the site of the original chip factory. Mikesell built a larger facility, where a series of expansions and additions were made during the next several decades. All the while, the company enjoyed steady growth and financial stability. Dan Mikesell continued to lead his company into the 1960s and up until his death in 1965. Assuming the president and chief executive slot in that year was Leslie C. Mapp. Under Mapp's direction during the next 30 years, Mike-Sell's expanded geographically, retained its quality focus, and continued to be an industry innovator.

Les Mapp's rise to the presidency of Mike-Sell's was the embodiment of the American dream. His parents had immigrated to the United States in the early 1900s with the dream of owning farmland. They achieved that dream in Ohio, where the elder Mapp became a successful dairy farmer. Mapp received his education in a one-room schoolhouse near Springfield, Ohio, and then attended Bliss College in Columbus for two years before completing his degree at the Dayton Young Men's Christian Association night school (later named Sinclair College).

Early in his career Mapp was an administrative officer of the Miami Valley Milk Producers Association in Dayton. He helped that organization multiply several times in size during his tenure. It was also through that job that he became involved in numerous trade associations. Mapp, with a broad food industry background, eventually joined Mike-Sell's and in 1952 was named chief administrative officer. He oversaw the construction of a new manufacturing plant in 1955 and was integral to the implementation of modern manufacturing and marketing techniques during the 1960s and 1970s. In the early 1970s, for instance, Mapp oversaw Mike-Sell's introduction of the first packaging equipment that would handle aluminum foil. Other producers followed the company's lead, but throughout the 1970s and 1980s Mike-Sell's packaged more of its products in foil than any other potato chip maker. The cost of foil was higher, but it was a price the company was willing to pay for fresher, better tasting chips.

In addition to updating and expanding production facilities during the 1970s and 1980s, Mike-Sell's reached out into new geographic markets on the perimeter of its established customer base. Under Mapp's direction, the company extended distribution into Columbus in 1971 and then into Cincinnati in 1977. In 1978 Mike-Sell's started selling its chips in Lexington and Huntington, Kentucky, before adding Louisville to its territory in 1983. Shortly thereafter it moved into its fourth state with distribution in Charleston, West Virginia. In addition to his success at Mike-Sells, Mapp was a leader in the snack food industry. In 1977, for example, he was elected head of the Potato Chip/Snack Food Association, International, for which he established several new programs including key legislative initiatives in Washington, D.C.

For about ten years beginning in 1972, Mike-Sell's and the Dayton Coca-Cola Bottling Company were joined through a holding company. The idea was to bring together two respected local companies whose products were complementary. The union was successful but was terminated in 1982, when the bottling company was sold off during a period of general consolidation at Coca-Cola. Throughout the mid- and late 1980s Mike-Sell's sustained its steady growth. In 1986 it opened a major new distribution center adjacent to its Dayton manufacturing plant and offices. Then, in 1987, a second plant was opened in Indianapolis. The Indiana plant featured the most modern equipment used in the industry at the time. The plant was initially used to manufacture a new product dubbed ''Mike-Sell's Old Fashioned Potato Chips,'' which was introduced the same year the plant opened.

The new Indianapolis plant made it easier for Mike-Sell's to expand into Indiana, Kentucky, and eastern Illinois. By the late 1980s, in fact, Mike-Sell's was supporting more than 25 distribution centers that served more than 15,000 retail outlets. The core of its product line remained its foil bags of chips from ''all natural ingredients'' and its ''groovy,'' or ridged, potato chips, both of which were also sold in twin pack bags and in various flavors including barbecue, green onion, sour cream and onion, and mesquite bacon. In the 1990s, the company was planning to sustain its drive to expand geographically, and to focus on quality, customer satisfaction, and technological innovation.

Principal Subsidiaries

Mike-Sell's Potato Chip Co.; Mike-Sell's Indiana Inc.

Further Reading

Mapp, Leslie C., *A Common Thing Done Uncommonly Well: The Story of the 'Mike-Sell's' Potato Chip Company.* New York: The Newcomen Society of the United States, 1985.
Mitchell, Dennis P., "Computers, Expansion, Quality Give Mike-Sells 'Uncommon' Advantage," *Snack Food,* September 1988, pp. 37–40.

—Dave Mote

Moran Towing Corporation, Inc.

2 Greenwich Plaza
Greenwich, Connecticut 06830
U.S.A.
(203) 625-7857
Fax: (203) 625-7857

Private Company
Incorporated: 1905
Employees: 630
Sales: $89 million (1992)
SICs: 4492 Towing & Tugboat Services; 4449 Water
   Transportation of Freight, Not Elsewhere

The Moran Towing Corporation, Inc. is the largest privately owned tugboat company operating on the East Coast of the United States and a leader in oil and dry-bulk barge transportation. A family-owned business for more than a century, the company was purchased in 1994 by a group of investors headed by Paul R. Tregurtha and James R. Baker, who were also principals in the Mormac Marine Group and the Interlake Steamship Company.

Although it was incorporated in 1905, Moran Towing traces its origins to 1855, when Michael Moran, a 22-year-old immigrant from Ireland, used money he saved as a muleskinner on the Erie Canal to buy a barge. Five years later, after acquiring several more barges, Moran headed to New York City, where he set himself up as a tugboat agent. In 1863, he paid $2,700 for half interest in the *Ida Miller*, a 42-ton, steam-driven harbor towboat.

By the 1880s, Moran Towing was an established company serving the busy New York Harbor, and in 1883, Michael Moran was asked to serve as commodore of the tugboat division for the 1883 ship parade celebrating the centennial of the British evacuation during the Revolutionary War. After the parade, Michael Moran continued to use the title "Commodore." His son, Eugene F. Moran Sr., then 11 years old, recalled in *Tugboat: The Moran Story,* "Nothing, since he established himself

in New York, gave him a greater sense of accomplishment than the name of commodore. . . . He had become a personality among seafaring men." Almost 70 years later, *The New Yorker* would describe Michael Moran as a "bold but pious" man who "often found it necessary to use a fleshly approach in refining the general spirit. Upon finding a couple of his subordinates drunk and brawling, he would seize them and start banging their heads together, meanwhile crying out admonitions mixed with Scripture."

Michael Moran also started the company tradition of naming tugboats after family members in 1881, when he christened the *Maggie Moran,* the first tug built for Moran Towing, for his first wife, Margaret. About the same time, he began the tradition of painting a block letter "M" in white on the black smokestacks of his tugboats.

When Moran Towing was incorporated in 1905, Michael Moran, then 73, was president of the company, and Eugene Sr., then 33, was vice-president. That same year, Moran Towing set a record for long-distance hauls when it towed a barge from New York to San Francisco, 13,220 miles around Cape Horn. Michael Moran died a year later and was succeeded as president by his son, who quickly developed a reputation of his own.

Again according to *The New Yorker,* "The complaint was often made . . . that [Eugene Sr.] seemed to think that he had bought New York Harbor and was merely letting the public use it out of politeness." He also used the title commodore, "a rank he feels he inherited from his father." In fact, Eugene Sr. received a legitimate naval rank in March 1917, less than a month before the United States entered World War I, when he was commissioned a lieutenant in the Naval Reserve at the direction of Franklin D. Roosevelt, then Assistant Secretary of the Navy. Eugene Sr. was appointed to a three-man commission whose mission was to provide the French and English with boats for submarine patrols as quickly as possible.

After the war, *The New Yorker* noted that Eugene Sr. "tackled the job with his customary energy and before very long the rest of the board more or less gave up and let him proceed largely on his own." Under his direction, the commission purchased 50 yachts, tugs, and fishing boats from private owners, had them armed and painted gray, and sent overseas. Eugene Sr. was also responsible for securing and equipping 16 tugboats, including three from Moran Towing, as minesweepers to patrol the U.S. coast off New York City. He was later assigned to the Shipping Control Committee as a consultant to inspect vessels used to carry troops to France.

When the war ended, Eugene Sr. returned to running Moran Towing. One of his first decisions was to buy back the *M. Moran,* a tugboat that had been sold to the British Admiralty in 1916. Moran Towing also purchased five 100-foot, steam-powered tugboats built by the U.S. government during the war. He later wrote, ''With the introduction of the 100-foot tug the transport business in the Port of New York was revolutionized. The 100-foot tug, despite its faulty design and poor construction . . . furnished a force equal to two or three of the low-power tugs dispersed at random.''

In the mid-1930s, Moran Towing began to replace its steam-powered tugs with diesel-powered vessels, which allowed the company to expand its coastal and ocean-going operations. By 1940, the company had 11 diesel-powered tugs built at a cost of $2.5 million. One of these, the *Edmond J. Moran,* named for Eugene Sr.'s nephew, was designed to cross the Atlantic and back without refueling.

Eugene Sr. stepped down as president of Moran Towing in 1941, continuing as chairman of the board, and was succeeded by his nephew, Edmond. But his semi-retirement was short-lived. When the United States entered World War II the following January, Edmond resigned from the company and went on active duty as a lieutenant commander in the U.S. Naval Reserve. Eugene Sr. re-assumed the responsibilities of president.

Following in his uncle's footsteps, Edmond was appointed to the War Shipping Administration, a branch of the U.S. Maritime Commission, where he assembled a merchant marine fleet of 2,000 small boats. Later, he was assigned to the Eastern Sea Frontier where he was responsible for dispatching tugs to the aid of torpedoed ships. During the Allied invasion of Normandy in 1944, Edmond commanded an armada of tugs and barges that spent ten days ferrying concrete caissons and steel piers across the English Channel to establish man-made harbors. For his role in the D-Day invasion, Edmond was promoted to rear admiral and awarded the Legion of Merit by the United States and the Croix de Guerre by the French government. He was also named Honorary Commander, Military Division, Order of the British Empire. He resumed the presidency of Moran Towing in 1946.

During the war, Moran Towing had operated 112 towboats, including 49 195-foot V-4 tugs built by the U.S. government. The company completed 1,153 assignments for the military, losing two tugs and sinking a German submarine off the coast of Florida. Soon after the war ended, *The New York Times* reported that Moran Towing planned to spend $1 million to ''insure the most modern harbor fleet in the world in the post-war period.'' The Levingston Shipbuilding Company of Orange, Texas, was contracted to build five steel-hulled, diesel-electric tugs for Moran that were completed in 1949.

Moran Towing also began acquiring other tugboat companies, starting with E.E. Barrett & Co. in 1949, the Olsen Water

and Towing Co. in 1950, and the Meseck Towing Co. in 1954. By 1955, when Moran Towing acquired the Dauntless Towing Line, the company had become the largest commercial fleet in the world with 50 tugs and 19 scows and barges. At the time, Moran Towing had only two major competitors left in New York, the Dalzell Towing Company and McAllister Brothers.

Moran Towing and the Seaboard Shipping Co, also announced a joint venture in 1955 to haul petroleum products on the Ohio River between Mount Vernon, Indiana, and Pittsburgh, Pennsylvania. The Moran Inland Waterways Corporation lasted just four years before the company sold its assets to the National Marine Service.

In 1958, Moran Towing acquired Curtis Bay Towing, which extended the company's operations from Maryland to Texas. Divisions of Curtis Bay Towing would eventually become Moran Towing of Maryland, Moran Towing of Pennsylvania, Moran Towing of Virginia and Moran Towing of Texas.

When Eugene Sr. died in 1961, Edmond became chairman as well as president. Three years later, Edmond turned over the presidency to his son, Thomas E. Moran, who had spent 18 years with Marine Transport Lines, Inc., before joining the family business. Moran Towing also launched another expansion in the early 1960s, contracting for 13 new tugs to be delivered by 1967, including four 4,290-horsepower towboats designed to handle large tankers and container ships. That was followed in 1971 with an order for five 3,300 horsepower tugs and in 1974 with an order for four 4,750 horsepower tugs designed for long-haul ocean towing.

By 1976, when Moran Towing acquired the Florida Towing Company in Jacksonville, it was operating 30 tugs in New York Harbor and 80 worldwide. *The New York Times* noted that Thomas Moran was ''pushing Moran more heavily into transportation of bulk cargo by tug and barge.'' Indeed, revenues from docking activities would fall from 75 percent of the company's business in 1964 to just 25 percent in 1976.

There was further diversification in the late 1970s and early 1980s, including establishment of salvage, oil pollution clean-up, and ocean engineering services. In 1984, Thomas Moran, then president, CEO and chairman, consolidated ownership of the company, which had become dispersed among dozens of Moran family members, by acquiring 75 percent of the stock. The other 25 percent was held by a group of senior managers.

Thomas Moran stepped down as president of Moran Towing in 1987, but remained chairman and CEO. Malcolm MacLeod, a graduate of the Massachusetts Maritime Academy who went to work for the company as a mess boy in 1954, became the first person from outside the Moran family to be named president of the company. When MacLeod was named CEO three years later, *The New York Times* noted, ''In the tight-knit, tradition-bound world of tugboats and barges, big changes do not come often. But last week, one industry leader, the Moran Towing Corporation, for the first time in its 130-year history went outside the Moran family in naming a chief executive.''

In 1994, Paul R. Tregurtha and James R. Baker, principals in the Mormac Marine Group and The Interlake Steamship Company, formed the Moran Transportation Company, which acquired Thomas Moran's 75 percent stake in Moran Towing for an estimated $75 million. Mormac Marine and The Interlake Steam Ship Co. operated several oceangoing tankers and Great Lakes dry-bulk barges.

Principal Subsidiaries

Moran Towing and Transportation Co., Inc.; Moran Towing of New Hampshire, Inc.; Moran Mid-Atlantic Corporation; Moran Towing of Florida, Inc.; Moran Towing of Miami, Inc.; Moran Towing of Texas, Inc.

Further Reading

"Admiral Edmond J. Moran," *Tow Line* (company publication), Winter 1993/1994, p. 4.

"For Moran Towing, A Presidential First," *The New York Times,* March 26, 1987.

Horne, George, "Moran 'Too Busy' to Mark Birthday," *The New York Times,* March 23, 1950, p. V9.

Moran, Edmond J., "An Editorial," *Tow Line* (company publication), Summer 1968, p. 4.

Moran, Edmond J., *The Moran Story,* New York: The Newcomen Society, 1965.

Moran, Eugene F., and Louis Reid, *Tugboat: The Moran Story,* New York: Charles Scribner's Sons, 1956, 364 p.

"Moran Has First Chief Who Isn't a Moran," *The New York Times,* December 25, 1990, p. 45.

"Moran's Florida Towing Company Grows With Port of Jacksonville," *Tow Line* (company publication), Fall 1978, p. 4.

"National Marine Buys Barge Fleet," *The New York Times,* May 5, 1962, p. 54.

"A New Chapter in Moran's History," *Tow Line* (company publication), No. 1, 1985, p. 4.

"News of Interest in Shipping Field," *The New York Times,* March 30, 1955, p. 59.

"Oil Tank Barge Venture," *The New York Times,* June 22, 1955, p. 58.

Peet, Creighton, "The Man from Moran," *Popular Mechanics,* November 1967, pp. 136–139.

"Post-War Service in Towing Planned," *The New York Times,* September 10, 1945, p. 25.

"Power for the Port," *Tow Line* (company publication), Fall 1968, p. 3.

Taylor, Robert Lewis, "Profiles: The Elegant Tugboater I," *The New Yorker,* November 3, 1945, pp. 32–38.

——, "Profiles: The Elegant Tugboater II," *The New Yorker,* November 10, 1945, pp. 33–41.

"Tugboats: Brawn—and Brain," *Newsweek,* August 7, 1961, p. 58.

"Welcoming the Queen," *Tow Line* (company publication), Summer 1969, p. 4.

White, David F., "A Seagoing Tug-of-War: Morans vs. McAllisters," *The New York Times,* October 7, 1976, p. 49.

—R. Dean Boyer

Mosinee Paper Corporation

1244 Kronenwetter Drive
Mosinee, Wisconsin 54455-9099
U.S.A.
(715) 693-4470
Fax: (715) 693-4803

Public Company
Incorporated: 1910 as Wausau Sulphate Fibre Co.
Employees: 1,300
Sales: $267 million (1994)
Stock Exchanges: NASDAQ
SICs: 2672 Coated & Laminated Paper, Not Elsewhere
    Classified; 2676 Sanitary Paper Products

Mosinee Paper Corporation is a major producer of specialty papers for industrial, commercial, and consumer use. The company's Pulp and Paper Division makes specialty kraft paper used in a variety of industries. This division produces much of its own raw material at its kraft pulp mill, using wood from the company's 90,000-acre industrial forest. Through its Sorg Paper Company subsidiary, Mosinee also produces specialty tissue papers used by high-tech companies, as well as laminates used for decorating. Mosinee's Towel and Tissue Division, which includes its Bay West Paper Corporation subsidiary, manufactures paper towels and tissues found, among other places, in commercial and institutional rest rooms. Bay West also makes dispensers for some of its paper products. In addition to its facilities in Mosinee, Wisconsin, the company has manufacturing operations in Ohio, Mississippi, Kentucky, and two other Wisconsin towns, Columbus and Solon Springs.

The mill that eventually became Mosinee Paper Corporation was built in 1910, 64 years after the first commercial production of wood pulp in America. First called Wausau Sulphate Fibre Co., the mill was built toward the end of a period that saw the formation of dozens of paper companies along Wisconsin's largest rivers. Located on the Wisconsin River, the Mosinee mill was the first in the state—and one of the first in the country—built specifically to produce sulphate, or kraft, pulp and

paper. Among the company's founders were Olai Bache-Wiig, Louis Dessert, Karl Mathie, B. F. McMillan, and F. P. Stone, all of whom were from Wausau, Wisconsin, a well-known center of paper-manufacturing activity.

The Mosinee mill began operating in 1911, employing about 150 workers. From the start, Wausau Sulphate's core product was kraft wrapping paper. For its first several years of existence, in fact, that was its only product. In 1914 the company first began to guarantee the quality of its wrapping and packaging papers. As new uses of specialty papers began to evolve, the company found a niche as a maker of custom papers to order. With new industries appearing every year, Wausau Sulphate was able to position itself as a supplier of papers to meet the precise specifications of these emerging industries.

Two major changes took place at Mosinee in 1928. First the company changed its name to Mosinee Paper Mills Co., allowing its name to match its location for the first time. Later that year, the company purchased the Bay West Paper Company, a paper towel and tissue manufacturer based in Green Bay, Wisconsin. Bay West has remained a major part of the Mosinee operation since that time and has focused on essentially the same products throughout its history as a subsidiary of Mosinee—namely "away-from-home" paper towels and tissue paper for restaurants, hospitals, factories, and other institutions. Other early Bay West products included windshield wipe for use at gas stations—a product pioneered by Bay West—and the dispensers to go with a number of its paper goods.

Over the next several decades, Mosinee's growth ran parallel to the overall advance of technology. As industries became more automated, their paper needs became more exacting. Mosinee continued to find a growing market for its made-to-order sulphate papers in these increasingly high-tech industries. By the middle of the 1960s, the company was producing about 40 grades of industrial papers to meet roughly 5000 different specifications. Every order required something different, and Mosinee was equipped to make the necessary adjustments. Among the multitude of papers the company was putting out by that time were flameproof papers, moldproof papers, and creped papers. In 1964 Mosinee completed a new executive headquarters building. A new warehouse, a new water treatment plant, and at least one new machine for customizing specialty papers were also put into operation at about that time.

In 1971 the company changed its name to Mosinee Paper Corporation. After turning back an attempt that year by one of its stockholders—cheese merchant Francis Rondeau—to seize control of the company, Mosinee continued to expand its operations. Work was begun in 1972 on a $1.25 million water treatment facility for its Pulp and Paper Division. In 1974 Mosinee purchased J.U. Dickson Sawmill Inc., in Sturgis, South Dakota, a mill that employed about 50 people. Renamed Dickson Forest Products, Inc., the $1.5 million purchase was integrated into the company as a subsidiary. Mosinee also launched a $325,000 expansion program at its Converted Products Division in Columbus, Wisconsin, that year.

By 1976 Mosinee had 900 employees and annual sales of more than $60 million. With the help of over $2 million in tax credits for making large capital investments, the company turned a profit of $5.3 million that year. In 1981 James Kemerling, a 20-year Mosinee employee, was named company president. The company added another major division in 1983, when it purchased Sorg Paper Co. of Middletown, Ohio, for $18 million. Initially a producer of printing and writing papers and specialty papers like deep-color tissue, Sorg's operations were restructured after a few years to produce tissue and towels for Mosinee's Bay West division. The idea was that Bay West could be made more profitable if less of its raw material had to be purchased from outside companies.

Kemerling was given the additional title of chief executive officer in 1984. The following year Mosinee set up a new wholly owned subsidiary, Mosinee Paper International, Inc., based in the Virgin Islands. The Dickson Forest Products unit was sold off in 1986. Meanwhile, the integration of Sorg into the Mosinee process was not going as smoothly as company officials had hoped. Part of the problem was the 400-mile distance between Sorg and Bay West, resulting in higher than ideal transportation costs. While the rest of Mosinee's operating units remained profitable, Sorg lost money from 1986 to 1988.

When Kemerling resigned abruptly in May 1988, Mosinee was able to lure Richard Radt, the former head of Wausau Paper Mills, out of early retirement as his replacement. As CEO of Wausau from 1977 to 1987, Radt had overseen several successive years of record earnings. Even more impressive was the fact that those gains in income were made on fairly modest increases in sales. Radt's strategy at Wausau was to find profitable niche markets that were too small to interest the bigger companies. Shareholders at Mosinee hoped that he would be able to duplicate that plan with his new company and to yield similar results.

One of Radt's first moves as president and CEO of Mosinee was to shut down two of Sorg's paper machines and lay off 128 of its employees. Those and other cost-cutting measures enabled him to return Sorg to the break-even point by the fourth quarter of his first year at Mosinee. Radt also examined each product made by the other divisions as well, eliminating the unprofitable ones and seeking new outlets for the profitable ones. By 1989 Mosinee controlled about 20 percent of the

market for roll-wrap, a wax-laminated product used by manufacturers to protect paper rolls against moisture and other kinds of damage. Another important product was the creped paper used as backing on masking tape, a big seller to such customers as 3M Corporation. By exploiting niche markets overlooked by other companies, Mosinee reached number 14 on *Consolidated Paper*'s annual financial ranking of paper companies in 1989.

For 1989 Mosinee reported sales of $233 million. Under Radt, the company continued to cut costs wherever possible, while at the same time investing lavishly in keeping its facilities up to date. Although company sales dipped to $202 million for 1990, company officials insisted that Radt's restructuring measures would pay off soon. In 1991 alone, the company sank $100 million into capital expenditures. By that time, the Sorg subsidiary was focusing on such specialty products as vacuum cleaner bag filter paper and decorative laminate papers, and the unit was no longer losing money.

The Bay West operation was moved to Harrodsburg, Kentucky, at about the same time. That move put Bay West closer to both its customers and to its new source of raw materials—100 percent recycled tissue and toweling—in Middletown, Ohio, where it had taken over and refurbished part of the facility abandoned by Sorg during its downsizing process. Part of the new arrangement at the Middletown site involved an agreement by Bay West to hire some of the employees that Sorg had previously laid off. In addition, a new wholly owned subsidiary, Mosinee Holdings, Inc., was formed as a mechanism by which Bay West and Sorg could receive electricity and steam from a single shared coal-fired powerhouse at Middletown.

By the end of 1991, Mosinee had 1,200 employees, and although sales dropped slightly again (to $197 million for the year), the company's Radt-engineered overhaul was still considered promising by many investment analysts. In 1992, however, Mosinee experienced a handful of setbacks that saw its stock price plummet by 50 percent between March and October of that year. During the summer, the company lost about $2 million when a supply of waste paper it had purchased was found to be contaminated by bits of glass. To make matters worse, the paper had already been de-inked and recycled into raw material for paper towels by the time the contamination was discovered.

Another nagging problem was a steep drop in prices. The U.S. economy was so weak during 1992 that Mosinee was unable to sell some of its products at profitable prices. This problem was compounded by the actions of Fort Howard Corporation, a competitor based in Green Bay, Wisconsin. As Fort Howard cut prices on its tissue and towel products in order to keep control of its share of the market, Mosinee was forced to adjust its own prices accordingly. When the economy began to improve in 1993, Mosinee's profits began to stage a comeback as well. That year, the company reported net income of $9.6 million on sales of $244 million.

Citing health reasons, Richard Radt stepped down as president and chief executive officer of Mosinee in 1993. His successor was Daniel Olvey, formerly the company's executive vice-president and chief operating officer. Under Olvey's leadership additional gains were recorded by Mosinee in 1994, when the company earned a record $12.3 million on sales of $267 million.

Demand for Mosinee's products remained strong during the mid-1990s. Even sharp increases in raw materials, which would have been disastrous just a few years earlier, did not hurt the company, since most of this additional cost could be passed on to customers. Officials at Mosinee were confident that demand for the company's products—particularly the tissue and towels that make up 40 percent of its business—would remain strong during the near future.

Principal Subsidiaries

Bay West Paper Corporation; The Sorg Paper Company; Mosinee Paper International, Inc. (U.S. Virgin Islands); Mosinee Holdings, Inc.

Principal Divisions

Pulp and Paper Division; Mosinee Converted Products; Mosinee Industrial Forest.

Further Reading

Barrett, Amy, "Mosinee Paper: If You Missed the Ride at Wausau Paper . . . ," *Financial World,* December 10, 1991, pp. 18–19.

Bowman, Francis F., Jr., *Ninety-Two Years of Industrial Progress,* Mosinee, Wis.: Francis F. Bowman, Jr., 1940, p. 13.

Byrne, Harlan, "Riding a Boom," *Barron's,* March 20, 1995, p. 17.

Harrison, Andy, "Bay West Adds Papermaking Facility to Bolster Its Converting Operation," *Pulp and Paper,* July 1992, pp. 73–76.

Keane, Stephen, "Mosinee Targets Market," *Wisconsin Business,* February 1986.

Loeffelholz, Suzanne, "Encore, Encore," *Financial World,* August 22, 1989, pp. 62–65.

Martin, Chuck, "Frustrations Add Up for Mosinee Paper," *Milwaukee Journal,* October 11, 1992.

The Story of Paper at Mosinee, Mosinee, Wis.: Mosinee Paper Mills Co., 1965.

—Robert R. Jacobson

MR. C☀FFEE

Mr. Coffee, Inc.

24700 Miles Road
Bedford Heights, Ohio 44146-1399
U.S.A.
(216) 464-4000
Fax: (216) 464-5629

*Wholly Owned Subsidiary of Health O Meter Products,
Inc.*
Incorporated: 1968 as North American Systems, Inc.
Employees: 993
Sales: $174.13 million (1995)
SICs: 3639 Household Appliances, Not Elsewhere
Classified

Best known for its pioneering and market-leading automatic
drip coffeemakers, Mr. Coffee, Inc. also manufactures iced and
hot teamakers, coffee filters, and other small household appliances. In the late 1980s and early 1990s, the company hoped to
capitalize on its well-known brand name through new product
introductions. In 1992, Mr. Coffee launched the Potato Perfect
potato baker, a countertop appliance that gave two potatoes
oven-baked flavor and texture in half the time of conventional
baking. Other new product introductions followed in rapid
succession: the Mr. Coffee Juicer (1992); The Food Dehydrator
by Mr. Coffee (1993); and The Breadmaker by Mr. Coffee
(1994), and the Mrs. Tea hot teamaker (1995). By 1995, new
products contributed about one-third of Mr. Coffee's total annual sales of $174 million. Privately held from its inception
until 1987, the company thrived in the late 1970s and experienced agonizing losses in the late 1980s. Mr. Coffee endured a
leveraged buyout and two significant changes in ownership
before being acquired by Health O Meter Products, Inc. in 1994.
Notwithstanding its difficulties, Mr. Coffee brought two important, yet intangible, assets to the table: its extremely well-
recognized brand name and its highly praised distributor network. The new parent hoped to parlay those strengths to the
benefit of its Health O Meter and Pelouze brand scales.

Mr. Coffee's odyssey began in 1968, when Vincent G.
Marotta, Sr., and Samuel Glazer founded North American Systems, Inc. Friends since high school, the two had owned and
operated a real estate development company since 1949.
Launched with a $500 loan from Marotta's father, the pair's
Glazer-Marotta Co. had started out as a lumberyard, then began
building garages in the car-crazed post-war era and moved on to
residential and commercial construction in the 1960s. But when
the lending climate went sour in the late 1960s, the partners
sought a new business interest.

Glazer and Marotta started North American Systems (NAS)
as a coffee delivery service. According to a December 1983
biography in *Cleveland Magazine,* Marotta came up with the
idea for the Mr. Coffee automatic drip coffeemaker "in 1970
while recuperating from an operation on a benign brain tumor."
The key to his appliance was the water: it percolated through the
coffee grounds at 200° Fahrenheit, as opposed to the boiling
water that roiled through grounds in the traditional percolator.
Marotta enlisted the talents of two former Westinghouse engineers, Edward Able and Erwin Schulze, to handle the technological aspects of the product's development. Although Marotta
would later bill himself as the inventor of the automatic drip
coffeemaker (and even compared his creativity to that of Michelangelo in a 1979 *Forbes* piece), Able held the patent on the
original device. Able signed over his commission rights to
NAS, and the company began production of the coffeemaker
in 1972.

The Mr. Coffee machine was an instant hit; NAS sold one
million units by April 1974 and seized ten percent of the American coffee-making business. Investment house Bear, Stearns &
Co., Inc. later called the device "one of the first convenience
appliances that revolutionized food preparation in the 1970s and
1980s." NAS acquired the Fairfield Coffee Filter Division of
Tomlinson Industries, Inc., moved into that firm's suburban
headquarters that summer, and established a factory in California in 1975. Growth continued throughout the decade, as
evinced by employment that more than tripled from 300 in 1974
to 1,000 in 1975 and 2,300 in 1977.

Aside from its revolutionary brewing method, several factors contributed to Mr. Coffee's spectacular success. In the

mid-1970s, Marotta hired baseball hero "Joltin' Joe" DiMaggio as the Mr. Coffee spokesman. The brand's close, enduring association with this widely-recognized sports figure helped establish an astounding 82 percent rate of brand recognition. Bear, Stearns analogized that "Mr. Coffee is to ADCs [automatic drip coffeemakers] what Gillette is to razors and Black & Decker is to power tools" in a 1990 report. The company's nationally-televised commercials helped establish the product as a textbook case of "forced distribution," where nationwide customer demand drove retail orders. In order to fulfill these requests, NAS developed a widely-praised national retail distribution system of commissioned sales representatives. It didn't hurt that potential rivals like General Electric, Proctor-Silex, Norelco, and Sunbeam didn't enter the ADC market until 1973 and 1974.

NAS and its star product peaked in 1979, when annual sales topped $150 million and Mr. Coffee mastered over half of the automatic drip coffeemaker market it had pioneered. According to an October 1979 *Forbes* article, NAS was producing 40,000 units each day.

Mr. Coffee's prosperity drew increased competition and market maturity in the early 1980s. Under pressure from competitors like Norelco, General Electric, Proctor-Silex, and at least 20 others, coffeemaker prices eroded while corporate expenses continued to climb. Introduced at a retail price of about $40, by 1982 the basic (and most popular) Mr. Coffee model sold for $16. Marotta was willing to launch brand extensions like coffee filters, Mr. Coffee Jr. (which made only two cups), and a water filter, but was reluctant to stretch his brand beyond coffeemaking. In October 1979 he told Geoffrey Smith of *Forbes* that "Coffeemakers are the main show. How can we go to other things when the coffee thing was so good to us?" But Marotta had changed his tune by the time *Forbes* reporter Anne Field caught up with him again in 1982, when Mr. Coffee was readying the $150 "Mr. Pasta" pasta-making machine for market. While this appliance would have been a hot product in the early 1990s, it was a flop in the early 1980s. The rebuff sent Marotta back to his core interest, but his attempt to extend the Mr. Coffee brand to a line of gourmet, decaffeinated, and premeasured ground coffees was thwarted by intense competition and declining coffee consumption. The company continued to offer its branded coffees through the mid-1980s, but began to phase them out late in the decade.

As if competition and market maturity were not enough, Mr. Coffee was also beset with myriad legal problems in the early 1980s. The company showed vigilance against subtle trademark infringers who tried to sell "Mr. Automatic" and "Mrs. Coffee" coffeemakers and "Mr. Replacement" substitute carafes. But Marotta soon learned that the biggest threat to his company's success—and his hard-earned personal reputation— would come from within its own ranks.

Although Samuel Glazer continued to hold a half-interest in NAS, Marotta had taken center stage at the company. Having made his fortune, Marotta began to seek fame in the late 1970s and early 1980s. His "rags to riches" story won him a Horatio Alger Award in 1975, and his philanthropic endeavors earned tributes from several groups. But these accolades apparently didn't satiate what Edward Whelan of *Cleveland Magazine* called "a consuming drive . . . to seek honor and tribute at nearly any cost." By the early 1980s, this aspiration had manifested itself in a campaign to be appointed U.S. Ambassador to Italy.

Marotta found a willing aide in his quest for notoriety in Vincent J. Menier, head of NAS's Fairfield Filter Division. Menier orchestrated award dinners, organized fundraisers for the election campaigns of such influential national politicians as President Jimmy Carter and John Glenn, and ostensibly made appropriate contacts in support of Marotta's pursuit.

According to Whelan's December 1983 article, it seemed to Marotta that they were making all the right moves: Menier had apparently even garnered contacts with New Mexico Senator Pete Domenici and Presidential Appointments Secretary E. Pendleton James. But in 1982, Marotta discovered that Menier had enlisted at least two individuals to pose as those influential officials and convince Marotta that his appointment was forthcoming. This personal betrayal was only the tip of the iceberg. A subsequent investigation showed from 1979 to 1982, Menier had siphoned off $1.3 million from NAS, and spent about $900,000 of that "slush fund." Menier was found guilty of embezzlement in 1983 and sentenced to ten concurrent five-year prison terms. Although Menier contended that Marotta condoned the "slush fund," NAS's president was never proven guilty of anything more than a certain level of gullibility.

North American System's sales declined from about $150 million to less than $105 million during the early 1980s, as its share of the automatic drip coffeemaker market slid from over one-third to about one-fourth. During the latter years of the decade, industrywide unit sales of coffeemakers declined from about 13 million to less than 11.5 million. A 1988 article in *Crain's Cleveland Business* noted that the company was "lagging behind its competitors in product innovation and in trying new marketing campaigns." Even international expansions into Europe and Asia failed to turn the company around.

In 1987 Marotta and Glazer sold NAS to John "Jack" Eikenberg and McKinley Allsopp Inc., who kept the company private. A Connecticut native, Eikenberg had spent his entire 28-year career in the housewares industry, most of them at RevereWare Group, manufacturer of copper-bottomed cookware. The 15 percent stakeholder was quickly elected president and chief operating officer. The leveraged buyout piled $80 million in debt on the company and ushered in several years of turmoil. Before the year was out, Eikenberg renamed NAS for its most famous product, hired a new advertising agency (Meldrum & Fewsmith Communications, Inc. of Cleveland), and focused the company's efforts on product diversification with an emphasis on upscale markets.

In January 1989, Mr. Coffee launched its "first-of-a-kind" Iced Tea Pot. This appliance, which could brew and chill tea in less than ten minutes, helped the company achieve its first annual profit since 1986. The Iced Tea Pot also helped even out seasonal cycles by adding a summer-oriented product to the company's coffeemakers, which traditionally sold well during the holiday gift-giving season. It constituted about $19 million of Mr. Coffee's 1989 sales and was generating $52 million annually by 1990. Other products launched during Eikenberg's reign included: coffeemakers in a range of colors, espresso/cappuccino machines, coffee bean grinders, and the Mr. & Mrs. Coffee, an automatic drip coffeemaker that could brew two different kinds of coffee, decaffeinated and regular, for example, at the same time. In 1989, *Crain's Cleveland Business* reported that "The innovations at Mr. Coffee under Mr. Eikenberg, after many years in which the company made few new product introductions, impressed industry observers."

In the meantime, however, Eikenberg's emphasis on new product development combined with Mr. Coffee's heavy debt service to produce two consecutive annual losses totaling about $8 million and forcing the company to default on its debt obligations. Thus, while some of his ideas helped Mr. Coffee return to profitability, Eikenberg was ousted in early 1989.

He was succeeded by Peter C. McC. Howell, a 39-year-old British native who had served as Mr. Coffee's chief financial officer since 1988. Howell's advancement came just two months after McKinley Allsopp sold its majority stake in the company to a diverse group of investors. Building on Eikenberg's new product introductions, Howell increased sales by 60 percent, from $128 million in 1989 to $173 million in 1990; made an initial public offering of 59 percent of the company's stock to pay down high-cost debt; and quadrupled profits from $1.1 million to $5.7 million in the process.

Mr. Coffee slid back into the red in 1991 under pressure from mass marketers like Wal-Mart and KMart. These powerful retailers forced Mr. Coffee and other housewares manufacturers to make price concessions in exchange for their volume purchasing. Sales declined to $158.8 million in 1991, and the company suffered a $1.4 million loss.

Demand for coffee and coffeemaking products began to rebound in 1992 and reached its highest level in nearly a decade by 1994. By 1994, Mr. Coffee's market share had risen from a low of around 20 percent to 34 percent. The company's retention of 75 percent of the profitable iced teamaker market also contributed to its steadily rising sales and profits, which reached $175 million and $5.5 million, respectively, in 1993.

After two years of speculation that Mr. Coffee was ripe for takeover, the housewares company was acquired by Health O Meter Products for $186.5 million in June 1994. The purchase price included $134.3 million ($15.50 per share) for outstanding stock, $27.5 million to retire existing Mr. Coffee obligations, $12.5 million to retire Health O Meter debt, and $12.2 million in fees and expenses. According to *HFD—The Weekly Home Furnishings Newspaper*, one industry observer characterized the deal as "more of a LBO considering how the debt was restructured." In fact, the pricetag more than doubled Health O Meter's fiscal 1993 revenues of $67.6 million. The financing, which was coordinated by Health O Meter's largest shareholder, the Thomas Lee Co., included a $97.5 million loan from Banque Nationale de Paris, a $70 million bond offering, and a $19 million stock sale.

Howell assumed Health O Meter's chairmanship and chief executive office, while former Health O Meter leader S. Donald McCullough became president and chief operation officer.

Health O Meter hoped the union would effect the distribution and marketing efficiencies necessary to compete in the hotly-contested small appliance industry of the 1990s. The combination consolidated the two companies' headquarters at Mr. Coffee's Bedford plant and reduced their work force by 14 percent, from a combined, pre-merger total of 1,159 down to 993 in fiscal 1995. Health O Meter appeared to be "getting its bearings" that year, considering its rather meager $712,000 net income on post-merger revenues of $267.89 million.

Further Reading

Appelbaum, Cara, "A Tea in Mr. Coffee's Future," *Adweek's Marketing Week*, May 28, 1990, p. 1.

Ashyk, Loretta, "Mr. Coffee's Fresh Cup," *Crain's Cleveland Business*, December 7, 1987, p. 12.

"A Brief History of Brewing," *Consumer Reports*, January 1991, p. 42.

"Buyer of Mr. Coffee Outlines How It Will Finance the Deal," *Cleveland Plain Dealer*, June 12, 1994, p. 3I.

"Carafe Name Banned Until Court Hearing," *Cleveland Plain Dealer*, August 25, 1983, p. 1E.

Colodny, Mark M., "Mister Mr. Coffee," *Fortune*, March 25, 1991, p. 132.

Cook, Dan, "Can Mr. Coffee's Own Brew Jolt the Java Giants?," *Business Week*, March 4, 1985, p. 76.

Datzman, Cynthia, "Mr. Coffee Brewing Up New Marketing Plan," *Crain's Cleveland Business*, September 21, 1987, p. 2.

Freeh, John, "Maker of Mr. Coffee Sold to Partnership," *Cleveland Plain Dealer*, July 7, 1987, p. 1D.

Field, Anne, "Will Mr. Pasta Help?" *Forbes*, April 12, 1982, p. 186.

French, Janet Beighle, "Mr. Coffee Goes Into Details," *Cleveland Plain Dealer*, January 19, 1994, p. 11E.

Gerdel, Thomas W., "Mr. Coffee to Sell Stock, Pay Off Debt," *Cleveland Plain Dealer*, April 17, 1990, p. 1D.

Gleisser, Marcus, "A Hot Potato," *Cleveland Plain Dealer*, March 10, 1993, p. 1G.

——, "Innovative Products Stir Mr. Coffee's Success," *Cleveland Plain Dealer*, February 7, 1991, p. 1D.

——, "Mr. Coffee Stock Percolating," *Cleveland Plain Dealer*, January 22, 1994, p. 1F.

Griffith, John, "Menier is Sentenced to Five Years," *Cleveland Plain Dealer*, December 10, 1983, p. 13A.

Jaffe, Thomas, "Something Brewing?" *Forbes*, September 28, 1992, p. 175.

Levin, Gary, "DiMaggio Leads Off for Mr. Coffee's Bean Ballgame," *Crain's Cleveland Business*, October 29, 1984, p. 6.

Lewine, Peter, "Mr. Coffee Sets New Course: Howell Aims to be Number-One in Drip Coffeemakers," *HFD—The Weekly Home Furnishings Newspaper*, June 19, 1989, p. 55.

Liebecik, Laura, "New Mr. Coffee Chief Brews Plans for Products, Markets," *Discount Store News*, August 24, 1987, p. 34.

Mooney, Barbara, "Mr. Coffee's New President Likely to Watch Bottom Line," *Crain's Cleveland Business*, May 8, 1989, p. 1A.

"Mr. Coffee Shareholders Sues Firm," *Cleveland Plain Dealer*, May 28, 1994, 2C.

"New Mr. Coffee Owner Has Dream Come True," *New York Times*, July 7, 1987, p. D2.

Saul, Stephanie, "Mr. Coffee Ex-VP's Trial Based on Secret Fund Use," *Cleveland Plain Dealer*, September 4, 1983, p. 1A.

Smith, Geoffrey, "Like Michelangelo . . . ," *Forbes*, October 29, 1979, pp. 93–95.

Whelan, Edward P., "Bitter Grounds: Mr. Coffee, A Legend in His Own Mind," *Cleveland Magazine*, December 1983, p. 81.

—April Dougal Gasbarre

Mr. Gasket Inc.

8700 Brookpark Road
Brooklyn, Ohio 44129-6899
U.S.A.
(216) 398-8300
Fax: (216) 398-8910

Wholly Owned Subsidiary of Echlin Inc.
Incorporated: 1967
Employees: 250
Sales: $73 million (1995 est.)
SICs: 3714 Motor Vehicle Parts and Accessories

Throughout its more than 30 years in business, Mr. Gasket Inc. has catered to a specific market: the automotive enthusiast looking for a part or accessory that will boost his car's performance or give it a unique appearance. In 1993, after being founded and run for the better part of three decades by Joseph F. "Joe" Hrudka, the company emerged from a two-year bankruptcy reorganization in two parts. The independent Performance Industries Inc. was headquartered in Tempe, Arizona, and operated by Hrudka until 1995. Mr. Gasket continued on as a Brooklyn, Ohio-based subsidiary of Connecticut's Echlin Inc. In the mid-1990s, Mr. Gasket's product line included UltraSeal high-performance gaskets, Hurst shifters and linkage, Daytona accessories, Lakewood traction bars and bell housings; Hayes clutches, Black Magic II louvers, Rodware chrome accessories, and Bandit lug nuts and wheel accessories.

The company was founded in 1964 by 24-year-old hot rodder Joe Hrudka. Called "the epitome of the blue-collar hero" in a 1984 *Cleveland Magazine* profile, Hrudka had taken courses at Ohio's Bowling Green State University for a semester, then dropped out to drag race with his brother, Tom. In the course of winning back-to-back National Hot Rod Championships in 1961 and 1962, Hrudka realized that faulty exhaust gaskets were a major stumbling block to many racers. Upon investigating the problem, the young man created the durable asbestos gasket that launched his company. He started selling the parts under the Speed Specialties name in the early 1960s

and incorporated his company as Mr. Gasket in 1965 in a suburb of Cleveland, Ohio.

Characterized as an obsessive workaholic, Hrudka expanded from this base into the performance niche of the replacement auto parts industry. This market segment originally targeted the professional and amateur racing crowd, but over the years it expanded its appeal to motorists interested in improving the gas mileage, handling, and styling of their vehicles. Mr. Gasket grew exponentially in its early years by catering to brand-loyal, non-price-sensitive performance enthusiasts.

Mr. Gasket's sales quintupled, from $600,000 in 1967 to $3 million in 1969, the year Hrudka sold one-third of the company's equity to the public for $2.7 million. Two years later, the founder's remaining stake earned him $6 million when Mr. Gasket was acquired by W.R. Grace & Company for a total of $17 million. Hrudka stayed with Mr. Gasket for five years after the sale, but left in 1976. Then one of the world's largest international conglomerates, Grace tried to impose modern corporate controls that had successfully been operated on a more seat-of-the-pants basis. Hrudka stayed on as the subsidiary's leader until 1976, then resigned. When his non-compete contract expired in 1981, he and some other Mr. Gasket expatriates considered starting up a competing venture. To Hrudka's surprise, Grace offered to sell most of the faltering Mr. Gasket back to its founder. The price, a bargain at $4 million, sealed the deal, and Hrudka took the company private again in 1981.

During the 1980s, Hrudka directed an acquisition spree that more than tripled Mr. Gasket's product line from 4,500 to 14,000 items. Hrudka's primary goal was to accumulate a comprehensive line of brand names well-known to performance enthusiasts. Trends that seemed to endorse this strategy included the growth of the number of performance motorists and broader channels of distribution, including auto supply chains and general merchandisers.

Before the end of 1981, Hrudka had established a subsidiary in Mexico. He funded the 1980s-era investment program that followed with a 1983 offering of 40 percent of Mr. Gasket's stock, maintaining the remaining 60 percent as his personal stake. Key acquisitions during this period included the 1984 purchase of Cal Custom and Hollywood Accessories from Allen Group Inc. for $25 million. Two years later, Mr. Gasket bought Hurst Performance, the venerable manufacturer of shifters, for $3.3 million. Other acquisitions added Cyclone, Thrush Performance, Eagle brand exhaust products; Seal-Tite, Hawk, and Interpart accessories; Rough-Country and Super Tube off-road and four-wheel-drive accessories; and Pro-Trac, Cragar, Weldwheels, and Tru Spoke tires and wheels. The company moved its growing operations to Brooklyn, Ohio, in 1985.

But the company's rapid series of acquisitions slowed dramatically that year, when Mr. Gasket experienced the first quarterly shortfalls in its history. While annual sales had grown from about $74 million in 1984 to $119.3 million by 1987, net income shrunk from $7.7 million to $2.7 million over the same period. At first, the firm blamed its stumble on a group of unprofitable products that came with the Allen Group purchase, but late in 1988, Executive Vice President Howard B. Gardner admitted to the *Plain Dealer*'s Donald Sabath that "our problems began because we grew too fast."

Then, in 1988, Mr. Gasket experienced a $14.7 million annual loss. The company blamed the dip into the red on write-offs for excess inventory and product discontinuations (it would write off a total of $20.8 million from 1988 through 1991), but other analysts saw larger forces at work. Arthur G. Davis, an analyst with Prescott, Ball & Turben, Inc., noted that "the [auto] enthusiast today requires a computer chip to increase the horsepower of their cars. It's all high-tech and electronics today, and you can't work under a hood in the do-it-yourself market." Another commentator observed that "Detroit is adding its own accessories on new performance cars at the factory," thereby reducing the need for aftermarket parts. McDonald & Co. Securities analyst Harry W. Millis pointed out a fundamental weakness of the market, that the company's core customers, young males, "may be the first individuals to be laid off in a slow-down." Wall Street's anxiety raised another red flag; Mr. Gasket's stock slid from its 1985 peak of $18 down to $2.25 by 1988 and $1.63 by March 1991.

Things went from bad to worse in the ensuing years, as fire struck a Mexican warehouse in 1990 and rival Rally Manufacturing Inc. won a $10 million patent infringement suit against Mr. Gasket in 1991. The verdict ordered Mr. Gasket to remit $298,000 worth of Mr. Gasket profits on the products in question, $5.7 million for Rally's (estimated) lost profits and $4 million in punitive damages. The court decision coincided with the revelation that Mr. Gasket recorded its third consecutive annual loss in 1990.

In April 1991, when Mr. Gasket's lead lenders indicated that they would not extend the company's credit in order to pay the court award, the firm filed to reorganize under protection of Chapter 11 of the U.S. Bankruptcy Code. Sales continued to decline in 1991 and Mr. Gasket's losses deepened to $23 million that year. The company divested its Crager Wheel division (in 1992) and Mexican production facility (in 1993) to two separate investment groups for a total of about $13 million, applying the proceeds to debt reduction and reorganization.

The bankruptcy stretched out over two years, as two successive reorganization plans fell through. In December 1992, Mr. Gasket announced that it was selling its largest and most profitable operation, the Performance Group, to St. Louis' Harbour Group Industries Inc. for $45 million. But when Harbour cut off the talks early the following year, Mr. Gasket organized a limited partnership called Performance Parts Co. L.P. to purchase the assets for about $30 million. Mr. Gasket hoped to retain a 30 percent interest in the "new" company. Just a week later another party, Echlin Inc., made a sweeter bid, offering to pay $35 million cash and assume $1.5 million in debt in exchange for the right to assume control of Performance Parts. Echlin, of Branford, Connecticut, was a 70-year-old global manufacturer and distributor of aftermarket parts with annual sales of $1.8 billion. Echlin had proven immune to the difficulties that had plagued Mr. Gasket; despite the recession, it had recorded double-digit annual sales increases, while the rest of the industry eked out about seven percent annual growth.

The $20 million (sales) worth of businesses that remained— primarily exhaust parts interests—emerged from bankruptcy in May 1993, were renamed Performance Industries, Inc. and moved to Tempe, Arizona, where Hrudka had lived for several years. (This segment of the company was later sold to Racine, Wisconsin-based Walker Manufacturing.) The businesses purchased by Echlin retained the valuable Mr. Gasket name and suburban Cleveland headquarters. Echlin merged its ACCEL and DFI performance brands with Mr. Gasket's remaining products, and installed Bob Romanelli as president of the subsidiary.

Under the management of its new parent, Mr. Gasket's sales increased from about $40 million in 1993 to about $73 million by 1995. John "Jack" McGrath assumed Mr. Gasket's presidency in October 1995. McGrath brought two decades of experience in the automotive aftermarket, having been hired away from Allied Signal's Automotive Aftermarket division. McGrath revealed his two-part plan for Mr. Gasket in a February 1996 *SEMA* (Specialty Equipment Market Association) *News* interview. He said he hoped to increase the company's penetration of the high-tech end of the market through the creation of a Custom Racing Products Group, while building on the firm's core accessory market. Improvements in marketing and distribution were keys to the program's success. McGrath boosted retail and mail-order distribution, and increased Mr. Gasket's dozen or so brands' television exposure via sponsorships of segments and spot tv ads on "Motor Trend," "Shadetree Mechanic," "Road Test Magazine," and "Inside Drag Racing." The company even started cruising the "information superhighway" with a presence on the "Motorville Online" Web site.

With the theme "Now more than ever, our name means excitement," Mr. Gasket moved into the late 1990s hoping to parlay its strong brand recognition among performance enthusiasts into consistently profitable growth.

Principal Divisions

Ultra-Seal; Mr. Gasket; Hays; Lakewood; Daytona; Hamburger's Oil Pans; Hurst; TruckWare; Rodware; ACCEL.

Further Reading

"Driving Toward the Winner's Circle," *Cleveland Plain Dealer*, February 1, 1996, p. 1C.

''Face to Face with Jack McGrath,'' *SEMA News*, February 1996, p. 12.

Fish, Randy, ''Mr. Gasket Company: The Best Known Name in High Performance,'' *Street Rodder*, May 1995.

Gerdel, Thomas W., ''Mr. Gasket Getting out of Uncustomary Loss Rut,'' *Cleveland Plain Dealer*, August 3, 1987, p. 3B.

Gleisser, Marcus, ''Mr. Gasket Plans to Appeal $10 Million Damage Award,'' *Cleveland Plain Dealer*, March 29, 1991, p. 1E.

''Lender Cuts off Credit to Mr. Gasket,'' *Cleveland Plain Dealer*, April 12, 1991, p. 3F.

''Mr. Gasket Aims to Restore Its Shine with New Products,'' *Cleveland Plain Dealer*, December 13, 1989, p. 10E.

''Mr. Gasket: Brand Collector,'' *Mergers & Acquisitions*, July-August 1986, p. 150.

''Mr. Gasket Co. to Sell Division in Brooklyn,'' *Cleveland Plain Dealer*, October 24, 1992, p. 1F.

''Mr. Gasket Emerges From Bankruptcy,'' *Cleveland Plain Dealer*, May 6, 1993, p. 2F.

''Mr. Gasket Executive Joe Hrudka Profiled,'' *Cleveland Magazine*, February 1984, p. 52.

''Mr. Gasket Files to Go Public Again,'' *Cleveland Plain Dealer*, August 9, 1983, p. 2D.

''Mr. Gasket Jobs Safe So Far, New Owner Says,'' *Cleveland Plain Dealer*, May 7, 1993, p. 1E.

''Mr. Gasket's Market Apparently Stalling Out,'' *Cleveland Plain Dealer*, November 21, 1988, p. 1F.

''Mr. Gasket Plans to File Alternative Reorganization Plan,'' *Cleveland Plain Dealer*, July 29, 1992, p. 2F.

''Mr. Gasket Set To Reorganize,'' *Cleveland Plain Dealer*, April 24, 1993, p. 2E.

''Mr. Gasket to Sell Parts Business,'' *Cleveland Plain Dealer*, April 16, 1993, p. 1E.

Pettit, Dave, ''Mr. Coffee, Friends Recently Departed, Is Now Mr. Lonely,'' *Wall Street Journal*, June 21, 1993, p. A7.

Sabath, Donald, ''Riding High: Hrudka, Mr. Gasket Back in the Driver's Seat,'' *Cleveland Plain Dealer*, December 4, 1984, p. 1E.

—April Dougal Gasbarre

National City.

National City Corp.

1900 East 9th Street
Cleveland, Ohio 44114-3484
U.S.A.
(216) 575-2000
Fax: (216) 575-2509

Public Company
Incorporated: 1845 as City Bank of Cleveland
Employees: 20,306
Total Assets: $2.91 billion (1994)
Stock Exchanges: New York
SICs: 6712 Bank Holding Companies; 6021 National
   Commercial Banks; 6022 State Commercial Banks;
   6035 Savings Institutions Federal Chartered

With more than $32 billion in assets and over 600 branch offices in Ohio, Kentucky, and Indiana, National City Corp. is the third-largest bank holding company headquartered in Ohio and ranks among the top twenty banks in the United States in terms of assets. While the 150-year-old institution grew rapidly in the late twentieth century era of bank consolidation, its leaders professed no urge to build National City into a nationwide entity. Acquisitions have therefore focused on garnering "super-regional" status and maintaining independence. Reflecting its long-term, ongoing shift from commercial to retail banking, National City hoped to boost market share within its Ohio, Kentucky, Indiana, and (beginning in 1995) Pennsylvania markets by expanding its auto leasing and credit card businesses and boosting phone, computer, and video banking technology.

The company was founded in 1845, shortly after the Ohio Bank Act of that year brought a measure of stability to the state's banking system. Cleveland had endured three years without a bank of any kind and the City Bank of Cleveland, as National City Bank was initially known, was the first to be chartered under the new law. Ruben Sheldon and Theodoric C. Severance, both of the Fireman's Insurance Company, led the new institution. Formerly president of Fireman's Insurance,

Sheldon assumed those same duties at City Bank. Severance, formerly secretary at the insurance company, started his career in banking as a teller.

City Bank opened for business in July, providing its clients with secured paper money, a safe place to deposit savings, and a source of funds for commercial loans. Its function as a lender supported the oil, iron, steel, shipping, and railroad industries that would be vital to Cleveland's development as an important Midwestern city. During its first five years in operation, the City Bank's capital stock tripled from $50,000 to $150,000. Lemuel B. Wick served as president in the 1850s, during which time the bank's growth propelled two moves to successively larger headquarters.

Rampant inflation during the Civil War crystallized formerly divided opinions on a unified currency structure, prompting the 1863 ratification of the National Banking Act. The new law created a national currency secured by United States bonds, as well as a new system of federally regulated banks. These "national" banks were required to purchase bonds worth up to one-third of their capital stock and to deposit those bonds with the U.S. treasury as security for a new system for national currency. City Bank waited until its original state charter expired in 1865 before complying with the new law and becoming National City Bank that year.

W. P. Southworth succeeded Lemuel Wick as president upon the latter's death in 1873. In 1889 long-time employee John F. Whitelaw became president. A 1995 company history credited Whitelaw with establishing the conservative character that would continue to distinguish National City Bank throughout its history.

National City Bank grew and profited throughout the late nineteenth century, but remained one of the smaller commercial banks. Assets rose steadily, passing the $1 million mark in 1881, $1.5 million in 1890, and $2 million in 1901. This consistent rate of growth would have been admirable during a normal period, but was especially extraordinary given the severe panic (or national recession) of the mid-1890s, when almost 500 banks failed nationwide.

313

Whitelaw died in 1912 after serving the bank for more than half a century. His abrupt departure opened the door to a takeover by James M. Hoyt, who purchased a total of 1,000 shares (including Whitelaw's 842) to gain control of National City. The new stockholder moved the business, increased its capital stock to $500,000, expanded the board of directors from 5 to 25, and got Charles A. Paine elected president by the end of the year. National City opened an imposing new headquarters in 1913, replete with tile floors, marble, and luxurious fixtures. Rapid asset growth during this period seemed to reflect the bank's new image, doubling from $2.5 million in 1912 to $5.7 million in 1914. By that time, National City Bank ranked fourth among Cleveland's banks in terms of combined capital and surplus, and sixth in deposits and total assets. Nevertheless, a centennial history characterized the institution at this juncture as "plodding along nicely, but down among the minors," having not participated in the wave of mergers and acquisitions that characterized this period in banking history.

In an effort to decentralize and stabilize the nation's monetary system (which was then concentrated in New York City) the U.S. government ratified the Federal Reserve Act in 1913, creating a system of 12 regional banks. This new organization bolstered the public's confidence in national banks by requiring all, including National City, to deposit three percent of their capital and surplus with the regional Reserve bank for safekeeping. Although many bankers initially opposed the creation of the Federal Reserve, the agency helped prevent panics and runs on banks, gave the federal government more control over the country's money supply, made commercial credit more available, and inhibited venturesome banking practices.

National City grew quickly during World War I, and shared its good fortune by purchasing $100 million in U.S. bonds in support of the country's war effort. Assets increased from $4.5 million in 1913 to $15.5 million in 1919. Bank President Paine was elected to the newly created title of CEO and Chairman in 1918, and Hoyt V. Shulters, formerly of East Ohio Gas Co., advanced to the presidency.

Assets nearly doubled to $30.6 million by 1925 and totaled about $40 million by the end of this prosperous decade, when National City ranked second among Cleveland's national banks and fifth overall. The institution's conservative management sheltered it from the financial crisis of October 1929 and the devastating depression that followed. While over 30 percent of America's banks failed from 1929 to 1933, National City fared considerably better: its assets only declined 25 percent, to $29 million. In fact, National City was Cleveland's only major bank to maintain full access to accounts and was first to reopen after the March 1933 bank holiday.

The company also endured an unexpected management shakeup during this period. In 1932 President Hoyt Shulters died, and was replaced on an interim basis by Charles B. Reynolds. Sidney B. Congdon, who had served as a national bank examiner for the Cleveland, Pittsburgh, and Cincinnati region throughout the fiscal crisis, was elected president of National City in 1933. His long list of credentials, including Chief Examiner of the Reconstruction Finance Corporation, further bolstered National City's reputation for stability. The bank quickly resumed its rapid growth pattern, with assets ballooning from $35 million in 1932 to $475.5 million by 1944.

Like many other national commercial banks, National City began to move decisively into full-service retail banking in the post-World War II era, adding a trust department, personalized checks and check sorting, home service representatives, and 24-hour depository services at each branch. The company also began investing in automation, purchasing its first computer in 1959. By the 1960s, National City had 24 branch offices and had crossed the $1 billion asset mark.

The bank took its first step toward becoming a major regional player in 1973, when it created National City Corp. as a holding company and made National City Bank its primary subsidiary. This new corporate structure enabled the company to bypass some of the most stringent banking regulations and begin what it called a "cautious, well-planned strategy of acquiring affiliate banks." The charge was led by Julian McCall, who had begun his banking career at First National Bank of New York (later Citibank) in 1948 and joined National City as a first vice-president in 1971. He advanced to president and was elected to the board of directors within five months, and became chief executive in 1978 and chairman a year later. McCall guided National City Corp. through an intense series of in-state acquisitions. From 1974 to 1984, National City acquired eleven relatively small ($300 million to $750 million asset) banks, thereby increasing its asset level to about $6.5 billion. Unlike many of its competitors, National City maintained its affiliates' historical names and autonomous marketing programs, forming a federation of banks with unified back office operations.

Throughout this period of expansion, however, the Cleveland bank remained unable to break into Ohio's vital Columbus and Cincinnati markets. Then, in 1984, National City burst onto the state capital scene through the $315 million purchase of Columbus's BancOhio Corp. This union of Ohio's second- and third-largest banks created a $12.5 billion asset powerhouse that was 30 percent bigger than its next largest rival, BancOne. BancOhio also gave National City a leading 35 percent share of Columbus's deposits. The combination of National City's strength in commercial banking with BancOhio's retail forte more than doubled the resulting entity's number of branches and expanded its geographic reach to 53 of Ohio's 88 counties, or over 80 percent of the state's population. While McCall acknowledged that these increases were important, he characterized the union as an anticipation of the industrywide shift to interstate banking that occurred throughout the late 1980s. By 1990, federal strictures against interstate banking became practically irrelevant. The merger with BancOhio not only shielded National City from acquisition by an out-of-state bank, but also set the Cleveland institution up as a regional leader.

Aside from these positives, however, Forbes pointed out a few drawbacks to the union, including BancOhio's marginal profitability in the early 1980s (.32 percent, compared to a peer group average of .8 percent), and the fact that National City's long-term debt doubled to $200 million with the acquisition. The new parent addressed these problems quickly, closing 70 branches and furloughing 700 full-time employees in an effort to cut costs by reconciling overlapping operations. By 1985, BancOhio contributed $30 million of National City's $108 million in earnings, and helped it become Ohio's second bank to be listed on the New York Stock Exchange in 1986. During this period, cautious Midwestern banks like National City began to attract analysts' attention because many did not buy into the risky lending and investment strategies that ruined so many financial institutions in the 1980s.

In the meantime, National City had shored up its internal operations through joint ventures in electronic banking, including charter membership in Money Station, Ohio's largest system of automatic teller machines, as well as point-of-sale debit cards. The company forged strong ties with its locales by creating National City Community Development Corp., a for-profit development corporation that infused low and moderate income neighborhoods in the bank's key metropolitan markets with almost $50 million from 1982 through 1995. This and other community-conscious efforts earned the bank an outstanding rating from the Office of the Comptroller of the Currency for complying with the Community Reinvestment Act.

J. Robert Killpack, National City Corp. president since 1980, succeeded Julian McCall upon his 1986 retirement. Killpack only served in that capacity until the fall of 1987, when he retired and was succeeded by Edward B. Brandon. Called "the most popular executive at National City Corp." in an August 1986 article in the *Plain Dealer,* Brandon had earned his undergraduate degree in economics at Northwestern University and an MBA from the Wharton School of Banking and Finance. He moved up through National City Bank's ranks, becoming president of National City Corp.'s largest affiliate in 1984 and CEO one year later. He advanced to the parent company's presidency in 1986, and had a brief wait in the wings until Killpack's retirement. According to an October 1987 article in the *Plain Dealer,* Brandon's "one overriding priority" was "an interstate bank merger to get back into the running for status as a super-regional bank."

In pursuit of that goal, Brandon engineered several major acquisitions, both within and across Ohio's borders, in the late 1980s and early 1990s. One of the most significant of these came in 1988, when National City beat out four other bidders to win the hand of $6 billion (asset) First Kentucky National Corp. of Louisville. Like the BancOhio acquisition, the addition of First Kentucky boosted National City's size (making it America's eleventh-largest bank, according to market capitalization) and helped it remain independent of the even larger national banks then moving into the Midwest.

Nevertheless, the acquisition drew criticism from some industry analysts and stockholders because it diluted National City's stock by 11 percent during a "banking bust" that Fortune magazine characterized as the industry's most difficult period since the Great Depression. Over one thousand American banks failed from 1985 to 1992. Non-performing loans and correspondingly high loan loss provisions during this period battered National City's net. Earnings flattened, then started to erode in 1989, as non-performing assets rose to peak at $468 million in 1991.

Brandon incurred more criticism that year when, after eight months of behind-the-scenes negotiations, National City pursued a hostile, highly publicized takeover of Ameritrust

Corp., another Cleveland bank. National City was soon joined by Society Corporation, NBD, and BancOne in competition for Ameritrust. Society won the rivalry in September, and the rebuffed National City acquired Merchants National Corp. of Indianapolis in October. In the two months that followed, Wall Street registered its disapproval, driving the bank's stock down by 20 percent.

While Brandon continued to defend his acquisition strategy, he acknowledged some of the criticism, telling Brian Hellauer of American Banker that "We had acquired an awful lot of banks in a ten-year period, and in the process had gone from one of the most efficient banks in the industry to where we were at best mediocre." National City hired top consulting firm McKinsey & Co. to help guide a two-year reorganization dubbed the "Vision" plan. Economizations—especially at BancOhio, where costs ran up to 20 percent higher than National City's other subsidiaries—helped cut from $65 million to $120 million in annual operating costs. Between 1992 and 1994, all of the holding company's major affiliates took on the National City name, presenting a unified marketing front. National City also continued to decrease its dependence on interest income (already battered by loan losses) and focus more strongly on fee income. Interest income declined 24 percent from 1990 to 1993, while non-interest income increased by 48 percent. During this same period, National City's overall net grew by over 72 percent, from $249 million to $430 million. By early 1993, the company's stock price reflected these improvements, having recovered 71 percent from its late 1991 low. Brandon had repudiated his detractors by mid-1995, having boosted National City's stock 178 percent from 1985 to 1995 and increased assets from $14 billion to $35 billion.

David A. Daberko succeeded Brandon as president of National City Corp. in 1993 and CEO in 1995. The Phi Beta Kappa graduate of Denison University with an MBA from Case Western Reserve University had made his entire professional career at National City, advancing through the investment and corporate banking ranks of National City Bank. Upon his ascension to the presidency in 1993, Daberko asserted that "There will always be strong regional banks, and we will be one of them."

Although Daberko had previously maintained that market share gains would fuel National City's growth in the mid-1990s, the $2.1 billion acquisition of Pittsburgh's Integra Financial Corp. announced in August 1995 pushed the Cleveland bank over the $50 billion asset mark and into the list of the nation's top twenty banks. Faced with a new chorus of criticism, Daberko quickly announced a 29 percent cut in Integra's staff and rationalization of its 260 western Pennsylvania branches. If the new CEO continued to follow in his predecessors' footsteps throughout the late 1990s, National City could be expected to enjoy the double-digit earnings increases forecast for Midwest banks in the years leading up to the turn of the twenty-first century.

Principal Subsidiaries

Buckeye Service Corp.; Circle Equity Leasing Corporation of Michigan; Circle Leasing Corp.; Gem America Realty & Investment Corp.; Madison Bank & Trust Co.; Merchants Capital Management, Inc.; Merchants Mortgage Corp.; Merchants Service Corp.; Money Station, Inc.; Mortgage Company of Indiana, Inc.; National Asset Management Corp.; National City Bank; National City Bank, Ashland (99.5%); National City Bank, Columbus; National City Bank, Dayton; National City Bank, Indiana; National City Bank, Kentucky; National City Bank, Northeast; National City Bank, Northwest; National City Bank, Southern Indiana; National City Capital Corp.; National City Community Development Corp.; National City Credit Corp.; National City Financial Corp.; National City Holding Co.; National City Investments Capital, Inc.; National City Life Insurance Co.; National City Mortgage Co.; National City Processing Co.; National City Trust Co.; National City Venture Corp.; NC Acquisition, Inc.; NCC Services, Inc.; Ohio National Corporation of Columbus; Second Premises Corp.

Further Reading

Andrews, Greg, "Merchants Deal 'a Blockbuster'," *Indianapolis Business Journal,* November 4, 1991, p. 1.
Bennett, Robert A., "Brandon Dreams Expansion," *United States Banker,* March 1992, p. 27.
Benton, Elbert J., *A Century of Progress: Being a History of the National City Bank of Cleveland from 1845 to 1945,* Cleveland: National City Bank, 1945.
"Buckeye Banker," *Barron's,* November 24, 1986, p. 54.
Byrne, Harlan S., "National City Corp.," *Barron's,* September 17, 1990, p. 56.
Foster, Pamela E., "National City Sharpens Ax," *Business First Columbus,* August 12, 1991, pp. 1, 9.
Fuller, John, "BancOhio, National City Wed," *Cleveland Plain Dealer,* September 29, 1984, p. 3B.
——, "A Tale of Two Bankers," *Cleveland Plain Dealer,* September 30, 1984, p. 1E.
——, "Banks Map Big Future with Merger," *Cleveland Plain Dealer,* October 2, 1984, p. 1E.
Hellauer, Brian, "National City's Vision: A Strong, Independent Regional Bank," *American Banker,* November 8, 1993, p. 1A.
Hill, Miriam, "National City Chief Pushes Bid," *Cleveland Plain Dealer,* May 16, 1991, p. 1A.
——, "Mergers Help Bank Industry," *Cleveland Plain Dealer,* May 22, 1991, p. 1G.
——, "National City to Slash Costs, Jobs," *Cleveland Plain Dealer,* August 14, 1991, p. 1H.
——, "National City to Buy Ohio Bancorp," *Cleveland Plain Dealer,* April 3, 1993, p. 1C.
——, "National City CEO Passes the Baton," *Cleveland Plain Dealer,* July 25, 1995, p. 1C.
——, "National City Becomes 17th Largest Bank with Purchase," *Cleveland Plain Dealer,* August 28, 1995, p. 1A.
Klinkerman, Steve, "National City's Brandon Is Winning Bet in Indiana," *American Banker,* March 23, 1993, pp. 1, 13.
——, "It's Back to Basics for National City Chief," *American Banker,* November 29, 1993, p. 4.
Mahoney, Mike, "Brandon Is Contender," *Cleveland Plain Dealer,* August 5, 1986, p. 1D.
——, "Deregulation Will Test New Leaders of Banks Here," *Cleveland Plain Dealer,* October 13, 1987, p. 1E.
"National City Bank 150th Anniversary," *Cleveland Plain Dealer,* May 17, 1995, p. S1.
Serwer, Andrew E., "Banking Boom in the Heartland," *Fortune,* July 18, 1988, p. 21.
Shingler, Dan, "Same Bank, Two Views," *Crain's Cleveland Business,* p. 11.
Tippett, Karen, "National City: Noallrills Banking," *FW,* August 21, 1990, p. 19.
Weberman, Ben, and John Heins, "The Doughnut or the Hole," *Forbes,* December 17, 1984, p. 94.

—April Dougal Gasbarre

Nature's Sunshine Products, Inc.

75 East 1700 South
Provo, Utah 84605
U.S.A.
(801) 342-4407
Fax: (801) 798-2730

Public Company
Incorporated: 1972 as Hughes Development Corporation
Employees: 720
Sales: $160.9 million (1994)
Stock Exchanges: NASDAQ
SICs: 2833 Medicinals & Botanicals; 2834
    Pharmaceutical Preparations; 3589 Service Industry
    Machinery Not Elsewhere Classified

A leading alternative health care company, Nature's Sunshine Products, Inc. manufactures and sells tableted and encapsulated herbal products, natural vitamins, food supplements, and skin care products. During the mid-1990s Nature's Sunshine relied on nearly 300,000 independent sales representatives to sell the company's 450 products door-to-door and to small groups of potential customers. The company's international presence was supported by marketing operations in Mexico, Canada, Columbia, the United Kingdom, Venezuela, Japan, Brazil, Costa Rica, and Malaysia.

The historical roots of the largest U.S. producer of encapsulated herbs stretch back to Provo, Utah, to the four-bedroom home of Eugene and Kristine Hughes and, specifically, to the couples' kitchen table, which was the first manufacturing site of their fledgling business venture. It was a modest start, to be sure, particularly given what the company later would become. Over the course of roughly two decades, the Hugheses watched their enterprise develop into a $160-million-a-year business that eventually would employ, either on a part-time or full-time basis, more than a quarter million people. Nature's Sunshine's geographic presence expanded robustly as well between the 1970s and 1990s, extending throughout the United States and into nine foreign countries. In two decades, Nature's Sunshine developed into a vast organization, recording growth on an exponential scale while enriching the Hugheses, their original investors, and those prescient enough to purchase stock in the company.

None of those fortunes would have been created without the misfortune suffered by Eugene Hughes and the helpful suggestion of a neighbor. In 1972 Eugene Hughes was suffering from a bleeding stomach ulcer. Neither Kristine, whose days were amply filled by raising seven children, nor Eugene, who was employed as a fourth-grade school teacher, were intent on launching an entrepreneurial career during the early 1970s. But when a neighbor suggested a remedy for Eugene's ulcer, the seeds for Nature's Sunshine were planted.

Eugene, who developed his ulcer in the mid-1960s, had tried the conventional cures for stomach ulcers yet enjoyed little relief. He finally heeded his neighbor's advice and began swallowing spoonfuls of cayenne pepper; the Hugheses' neighbor had informed the couple that capsicum, which existed in abundant amounts in cayenne pepper, helped suppress the digestive acids that caused ulcers. For Eugene, the intimidating prospect of swallowing spicy red pepper powder to relieve the pain of an ulcer was exacerbated by its disagreeable taste, but he dutifully swallowed cayenne pepper and noticed an improvement in his condition.

Kristine Hughes then made her own fateful suggestion, one that was nearly as integral to the formation of Nature's Sunshine as her neighbor's. To eliminate its unappealing taste, Kristine suggested the pepper powder be put in gelatin capsules. Those gelatin capsules were the Hugheses' first products. Indeed, Eugene and Kristine Hughes spent their nights and weekends sitting at their kitchen table packing capsules full of red pepper. They convinced the owner of a tiny local health food store owner in Provo to sell the capsules. For capital to launch their start-up business, the Hugheses put their persuasive powers to work once again to convince five of Eugene's six siblings to invest $150 each into Hughes Development Corporation (incorporated in 1972).

During the Hugheses' first decade of business, the foundation was established for the massive organization that would hold a dominant place in the market for vitamins, minerals, and herbal supplements in the 1990s. Once the pursuit of health and fitness became a pervasive American trend, the Hugheses' business would enjoy accelerated growth, propelled by widespread consumer demand for salubrious, natural products. But the Hugheses also made pivotal moves that enabled their company to ride the crest of market demand for medicinal herbs and vitamins. Other natural products were added, such as chaparral for digestive problems and golden seal, which acted as a natural antibiotic, thus broadening the scope of the Hugheses' product line with each passing year.

In addition, salespeople, who sold the company's products door-to-door, were aggressively recruited and indoctrinated into an almost evangelical corporate culture that placed a premium on achieving sales records. These full-time and part-time independent sales representatives represented the backbone of the Hugheses' business. As their numbers grew, so did the geographic reach of the company. Enthusiasm for the company's products and effective sales techniques were imparted to aspirant salespeople at large sales conventions, where the engine that drove the company was fine-tuned.

As the company's success gained momentum, the Hugheses' business underwent several name changes before settling on the corporate title and brand name that would become familiar to hundreds of thousands of domestic and international customers during the late 1980s and 1990s. In 1973, one year after the Hugheses founded their business, National Multi Corporation was organized as a holding company for Hughes Development Corporation. Two years later, Amtec Industries Incorporated was formed for the primary purpose of holding the stock of National Multi Corporation, and in 1982 the Nature's Sunshine Products, Inc. moniker was adopted.

Meanwhile, the Hugheses had taken their company public in 1978, enabling others to share in the profits of their enterprise and generating an infusion of capital to sustain the company's expansion. In addition to a host of herbal supplements and other naturally medicinal products, the Hugheses added water purifiers and personal care products to their ever-expanding roster of products, the aggregate demand for which pushed Nature's Sunshine's annual sales above $25 million by the end of the company's first decade of operation. Ten years of existence had resulted in ten years of success for the Hugheses and their thriving business, with annual sales increasing each year and the ranks of faithful and determined salespeople swelling annually.

The first blemish on Nature's Sunshine's enviable record of growth occurred three years after the company celebrated its tenth anniversary, when a new marketing incentive plan was announced that quickly hobbled previously unbridled growth, awakening management to the vagaries of the business world and its dependence on the company's all-important sales force. A substantial portion of Nature's Sunshine's distributors, who composed the core of the company's direct sales network, disliked the new compensation program and demonstrated their disfavor by cutting their ties to Nature's Sunshine and the nearly 200 products produced by the company. Once the exodus of distributors shuddered to a halt, Kristine Hughes, who served as the company's chairwoman, and Eugene Hughes, the company's senior vice-president, found themselves without 28 percent of their distributors. Annual sales, for the first time in the company's history, declined in 1985, slipping from $33.3 million to $29.4 million, while earnings per share plummeted from 65 cents to 15 cents.

It was the first time Nature's Sunshine had recorded a decline in its number of distributors, an occurrence the Hugheses and the rest of the company's management did not want to repeat. In mid-1985, Nature's Sunshine's compensation program was replaced with a more acceptable plan that stopped the flow of distributors from the company's ranks. Management then began recruiting for additional distributors in earnest, hoping to replenish the company's sales force and invigorate sales. A bonus program for Nature's Sunshine distributors was reestablished and medical benefits were added to the list of perquisites offered to salespeople, enabling the company to score considerable success in attracting new and old distributors.

Nature's Sunshine's sales corps swelled 50 percent in the wake of 1985's losses, increasing to 25,000 distributors and roughly three times as many individual agents, while the number of products rose to more than 300 by the end of 1986. Buoyed by the increase in products and distributors, Nature's Sunshine's annual sales rebounded to $31 million in 1986 to $38 million in 1987. Once the recovery was complete, Nature's Sunshine stood solidly positioned as the nation's largest producer of encapsulated herbs, occupying a coveted place in a market that was experiencing strong growth as increasing numbers of Americans sought alternative, natural ways of improving their health and fitness.

As the company exited the mid-1980s, there was justifiable cause for celebration. Its firm grasp on the U.S. market augured well for the company's future, but in international markets Nature's Sunshine was registering perhaps its most encouraging success. By the end of 1986, in fact, the company's foray into foreign markets had developed into a meaningful and burgeoning portion of its business, contributing 20 percent toward Nature's Sunshine's annual sales volume. Roughly half of the company's foreign sales were derived from Canada, while the balance was plucked from the wallets of customers in Australia and New Zealand, with a small sales network in Japan contributing to annual sales as well. In the years ahead, Nature's Sunshine would greatly increase its international presence, particularly in Latin America. Before such expansion occurred, though, the company needed to fix some problems at home, the resolution of which would invigorate the company's growth.

The company's annual sales continued to register successive gains after 1985's decline, jumping to $44.5 million in 1988 and to $52.1 million in 1989, while net income rose 56 percent in 1988, soaring to $3.3 million. Though the increase in net income pointed to an undoubtedly flourishing company, the 16 percent sales growth achieved in 1988 only mirrored the pace of growth recorded by the industry, which induced the Hugheses to begin looking for a way to accelerate their company's financial growth. The couple decided that Nature's Sunshine had grown too large to be operated as a family business and, instead, needed the experience of a professional direct-marketing leader.

In 1989 the Hugheses hired Alan Kennedy, the person who would invigorate Nature's Sunshine's growth.

In Kennedy the Hugheses gained a leader with a proven record of success. Kennedy had earned the reputation that would make him Nature's Sunshine's president in 1989 by helping Shaklee Corporation quadruple its sales during the late 1970s. Serving as Shaklee's chief marketing officer, Kennedy pushed the company toward the top tier of direct marketing companies to rank among giants such as Mary Kay Cosmetics and Amway. To be counted among these pioneering leaders in door-to-door sales was what the Hugheses hoped Kennedy could achieve. Kennedy knew, as did the Hugheses, that the size of Nature's Sunshine's sales force directly dictated the magnitude of the company's sales volume, so he focused his initial efforts on recruiting additional salespeople.

In his first four years at Nature's Sunshine, Kennedy more than doubled the company's largely part-time sales army by boosting commissions paid to high production salespeople and creating a more inspirational atmosphere at sales conventions. Attendance at the company's sales meetings quadrupled as a consequence, and by the early 1990s more than 100,000 independent sales representatives were selling Nature's Sunshine products. Annual sales, which had begun to record prosaic increases before Kennedy's arrival, nearly tripled during his first four years of leadership, eclipsing $127 million in 1993, the bulk of which came from the company's strong presence in western and southern states.

As these gains in annual sales were being recorded, Kennedy also turned his attention to bolstering the company's involvement in foreign markets. A pivotal move in strengthening the company's international business was the establishment of a Mexican subsidiary, Nature's Sunshine de Mexico, in 1991. Once established in Mexico, the company moved into Central and South America, establishing operations in Costa Rica, Venezuela, Columbia, and Brazil, where the belief in medicinal herbs was considerably stronger than in the United States.

In late 1992, Nature's Sunshine sold its Australian and New Zealand marketing subsidiaries (Nature's Sunshine Products of Australia and Nature's Sunshine Products Ltd.) to local management, creating two independently owned and operated companies. A similar arrangement was made with Sunshine Scandinavia, AS, an independently owned-and-operated company located in Norway, as Nature's Sunshine built a small export network which also included China, the Philippines, and Hong Kong.

By 1993, annual sales had risen to $127 million, nearly 30 percent of which was derived from sales in foreign markets. Of the more than 350 products produced and sold by the company, 61 percent were herb-related products, while vitamins ac-counted for 23 percent. The balance of Nature's Sunshine's product mix comprised homeopathic medicine, skin care products, and diet-related products.

In 1994, Kennedy continued to carve a deeper presence for Nature's Sunshine in foreign markets, forming a joint venture during the year with Tokyo Tanabe Company, a leading pharmaceutical company in Japan, to sell herbs and nutritional products. The market for vitamins, minerals, and herb supplements by this time had grown dramatically since the Hugheses first entered the fray in 1972. An estimated $4.6 billion was spent on vitamins, minerals, and herbal supplements in 1994, with the market for herbal supplements alone increasing 20 percent. With the bulk of its business dependent on herbal supplement sales, Nature's Sunshine stood poised for robust growth as it entered the mid-1990s and charted its plans for the future.

By the end of 1995, Nature's Sunshine was expected to announce sales of more than $200 million, as the 450 products sold by the company continued to meet widespread demand. The company was supported by its 291,000 independent sales representatives, who knocked on doors and held sway over small groups in all 50 states and in nine foreign countries. With business growing briskly, particularly in Mexico and Latin America, Kennedy appeared to favor further international expansion as he prepared to meet the challenges of the late 1990s and beyond.

Principal Subsidiaries

Nature's Sunshine de Mexico; Nature's Sunshine Products of Canada, Ltd.; Nature's Sunshine de Columbia; Nature's Sunshine K.K. (Japan); Nature's Sunshine Produtos Naturais Ltda. (Brazil); Nature's Sunshine Products de Venezuela; Nature's Sunshine Products, Inc. (England); NSSP Malaysia Sdn. Bhd.; NSP de Centroamerica (Costa Rica).

Further Reading

Byrne, Harlan S., "Nature's Sunshine Products Inc.," *Barron's,* April 19, 1993, p. 45.
"Company Expects to Meet or Top Profit Estimates," *Wall Street Journal,* October 11, 1995, p. A4.
Gilbert, Nick, "Nature's Sunshine: Hope for Hype," *Financial World,* October 10, 1995, p. 26.
"Healthy Trend," *Barron's,* May 18, 1987, p. 104.
Lewis, Kate Bohner Lewis, "Ulcers? Try Hot Pepper," *Forbes,* November 6, 1995, p. 242.
Slovak, Julianne Slovak, "Nature's Sunshine," *Fortune,* December 5, 1988, p. 140.
Stovall, Robert, "Lesser-Known Consumer Stocks," *Financial World,* July 22, 1986, p. 72.

—Jeffrey L. Covell

NETSCAPE

Netscape Communications Corporation

501 E. Middlefield Road
Mountain View, California 94043
U.S.A.
(415) 254-1900
Fax: (415) 528-4124

Public Company
Incorporated: 1994 as Mosaic Communications Corp.
Employees: 260
Sales: $80.7 million (1995)
Stock Exchanges: NASDAQ
SICs: 7372 Computer Software Publishers, Prepackaged;
    7373 Computer Integrated Systems Design

Netscape Communications Corporation is one of the fastest growing software companies in the United States; in 1995, at least 70 percent of the World Wide Web's ten million visitors used the company's graphic interface to make exploring the Internet easier and more fruitful. The brain child of a computer industry veteran and a talented young programmer, Netscape has staked a considerable claim to a large part of one of the fastest-growing areas of consumer interest.

Genesis of the Enterprise

James H. Clark, one of Netscape's founders, was born into poverty in 1944 in Plainview, Texas. Although prone to mischief such as smuggling whiskey on high school band trips, he eventually earned a Ph.D. in computer science from the University of Utah, after first studying physics. Clark had discovered computers in the Navy, which he joined after dropping out of high school. His first teaching job, at the University of Santa Cruz, soured him on academia, so he began freelancing as a consultant, which seemed even more dismal to him.

Clark turned down an offer from Hewlett-Packard, having developed a disklike for big corporate culture during an earlier stint with Boeing. In 1979 Clark went to work as a professor at Stanford University, where he made three-dimensional graphics

the focus of his research for three years. Finding it difficult to sell his ideas to existing computer companies, Clark founded Silicon Graphics Inc. (SGI), a computer workstation manufacturer, in 1982. That company went public four years later and later garnered popular fame for animating the dinosaurs of the blockbuster movie *Jurassic Park*. Eventually Clark became frustrated at being unable to guide the company into low-cost, network-friendly hardware, and he resigned in February 1994, passing up $10 million worth of stock options. In 1995, SGI's annual revenues were $2.2 billion.

Netscape's co-founder, Mark Andreessen, was born in 1972 in New Lisbon, Wisconsin, to a salesman and his wife, who worked for Land's End. As Andreessen grew up, the personal computer was also coming of age, and he wrote his first BASIC programs—video games—at the precocious age of eight. While a 21-year-old undergraduate who had first leaned toward electrical engineering, Andreessen was assigned to work on three-dimensional visualization software for the prestigious National Center for Supercomputing Applications at the University of Illinois at Champaign-Urbana. While working there for $6.85 per hour, he and six other peers created Mosaic, a graphical interface program for finding interesting Internet sites without the need for specialized programming knowledge. Within its first 18 months, Mosaic was credited with sparking a threefold increase in the number of Internet users; the number of web sites grew by a factor of 100. After graduation, Andreessen began to work in Silicon Valley for Enterprise Integration Technologies, which produced Internet security products. Appropriately, his first connection with James Clark was electronic.

The future of the "information superhighway"—the theoretical network for carrying interactive video, e-mail, and all types of data—was subject of much speculation in 1993. Existing telephone lines and cable television seemed possible means. Clark had been considering the Internet as a possible carrier for interactive video, so he sent Andreessen an e-mail message the same day he resigned from Silicon Graphics.

After two months of introductions, discussion, and debate about potential products, Clark and Andreessen formed Mosaic

Communications in April 1994. Instead of working on 3-D video games or interactive television, Andreessen proposed making Mosaic even better, creating a "killer" program to be known as "Mozilla." Clark supplied $4 million to set up the company's headquarters in Mountain View, California, while Andreessen led the development effort.

In November, the company was renamed Netscape, as the University of Illinois objected to the company's use of the name "Mosaic." Spyglass Inc., started by another U.I. alumnus, Tim Krauskopf, had licensed the name along with the software from the school. Later, Microsoft paid Spyglass for the rights to bundle Mosaic with its Windows 95 operating systems.

Early Growth

To say the Netscape grew exponentially in its first two years would be an understatement. Beginning with the two founders and an assistant, employment grew to over 250. Not surprisingly, the first new hires were five of Andreessen's programming colleagues from the University of Illinois, as well as other programmers, software developers, and cryptographers. Clark also assembled the best management team he could find. In January 1995, the company hired Jim Barksdale away from AT&T's McCaw Cellular division—a $2.3 billion a year business—to be Netscape's CEO. Barksdale had earlier helped organize Federal Express into the state-of-the-art shipping dynamo it was to become. Andreessen served as vice-president of technology, in charge of overseeing product development, while Clark gave himself the job of "Head of PR."

Like the University of Illinois had done with the original Mosaic, Netscape gave away most of its Netscape Navigator browsing software free of charge, which generated goodwill from the community of Internet users. Nevertheless, it was an extremely controversial move for such a new company. Netscape did manage to avoid packaging costs—interested parties simply downloaded the software via modem. It also established an ultimate base of virtual shoppers.

In order to make money, the company charged from $1,500 to $50,000 to supply companies with web servers, the means to establish web sites on the Internet. The most expensive systems could create "virtual" stores in which customers could examine photographs and descriptions of products, order and pay for them with credit cards. This market had plenty of room for growth: in the mid-1990s, less than ten percent of Internet users participated in electronic commerce. By late 1996, it was estimated that more than 24 million North Americans used the Internet.

In December 1994, the company began selling improved versions of its browsing software for $40 per package. Resale partners included Apple, AT&T, Hewlett-Packard, Digital, IBM, Novell, to name only a few. By 1996, Netscape was selling its products in 29 countries. It also brokered arrangements with more than 100 Internet service providers to distribute Navigator to their customers. One of the keys to the system's acceptance was its ability to work with all kinds of computers and operating systems; i.e., its "open" architecture—the concept, in the form of TCP/IP (Transmission Control Protocol/Internet Protocol), that made the Internet itself possible.

The openness of the company's servers made them attractive for establishing internal corporate networks, dubbed "Intranets," that could also communicate easily with outside networks. Soon, Netscape approached a similar market share in this lucrative arena as it had on the Internet, gaining 70 percent of the Global *Fortune* 100 companies as customers, including AT&T, Hewlett-Packard, Lockheed Martin, McDonnell-Douglas, Silicon Graphics Inc., CNN, Dow Jones, National Semiconductor, Motorola, and Eli Lilly. MCI was Netscape's first major client.

Preparations for a Secure Future

In April 1995, a consortium of Adobe Systems, International Data Group, Knight Ridder, TCI, and Times Mirror bought an 11 percent share in the company. Netscape's initial public offering came in August, 1995. The first day market capitalization was worth $2.2 billion. The stock originally sold for $28 a share; after a day of trading, it was worth $75. On December 5, it peaked at $171. Clark owned 32 percent of the company, which made him, according to press reports, the first Internet billionaire. As *Time* noted, the year was a record one for high-tech IPOs in the United States: $8.5 billion in capital was created for these new ventures. IPOs in all industries raised $29 billion. The success of the initial public offering came in spite of the fact that Netscape had not yet posted a significant profit.

Although Bill Gates dryly characterized the excitement over new Internet stocks as "frothy," Microsoft, too, entered the market. Late in 1995, Microsoft offered a version of its own browser, called Internet Explorer 2.0, free for downloading, as well as including a browser with the new Windows 95 operating system. Numerous strategic alliances were subsequently formed. While Netscape teamed with Mastercard to develop Secure Courier encryption standards, Microsoft and Visa announced the development of Secure Transaction Technology. In January 1996, Netscape and VeriFone, the largest credit card transaction processor, announced their plans to develop credit card payment systems for use over the Internet that would use the new Secure Courier technology. Soon afterward, Netscape teamed up with America On-Line, the USA's largest provider of on-line services. The deal allowed AOL to offer improved Internet access through the Navigator browser (even though it had earlier spent $41 million to acquire similar technology) and strengthened Netscape's market share. GTE and MCI had earlier agreed to use Navigator in their networks.

In spite of the competition, both Netscape and Microsoft worked with Hewlett-Packard to develop a Hypertext Markup Language (HTML) that could be printed as seen on screen. HTML displays graphics and highlighted words that can be selected with a mouse to access other pages of information. At the same time, however, twenty-eight companies, including IBM and Apple, announced their support for the JavaScript language, a means of imbedding programs within web pages, developed by Sun Microsystems Inc. and Netscape.

Understandably, Netscape put a great deal of effort into making Internet transmissions secure. Nevertheless, in September 1995, two hackers at the University of California at Berkeley managed to undermine the Navigator security code. The company corrected the problem and posted warnings to users on the Internet. Damage to the company's image appeared to be mitigated by the newness of the field, the newness of companies specializing in this area of technology, and the lack of reliable and easy-to-use web software elsewhere.

Netscape's innovative way of attacking the security problem mirrored its marketing strategy; both involved giveaways. To strengthen its new browser software, the company distributed beta versions—test copies disseminated before the product's commercial release. To spur the testers, Netscape, in its "Bugs Bounty" program, offered prizes ranging from coffee mugs to $1,000 for the first people to identify flaws, particularly security lapses.

In January 1996, Netscape purchased its neighbor Collabra Software Inc. for $108.7 million. One of Collabra's main products was Share, a system enabling simultaneous e-mail discussions and document sharing among network users. Subsequent releases of Share combined these facilities with Navigator's Internet access capabilities. In February, Netscape acquired Paper Software, Inc., which had recently developed 3-D programs for the Internet.

Estimates of growth in the number of Internet users in the mid-1990s ranged from ten percent per month to one percent per day. The products of Netscape Communications, probably the fastest-growing company dedicated to developing Internet-related products, seemed likely to remain a preferred means for work, leisure, and commerce on the Internet.

Principal Subsidiaries

Netscape Communications Limited (U.K.); Netscape Communications Corp. Japan; Netscape Communications Corp. France; Netscape Communications Corp. Germany; Netscape Communications Corp. Canada.

Further Reading

Baker, Molly, "Stargazers Abound While Internet Stocks Skyrocket," *The Wall Street Journal*, December 7, 1995, p. C1.

Bottoms, David, "Jim Clark: The Shooting Star @ Netscape," *IW: The Management Magazine*, December 18, 1995, pp. 12–16.

Collins, James, "High Stakes Winners," *Time*, February 19, 1996, pp. 42–47.

Egan, Jack, "The Net-Net On Netscape," *US News & World Report*, August 14, 1995, p. 75.

Elmer-DeWitt, Philip, "Bugs Bounty," *Time*, October 23, 1995, p. 86.

Epper, Karen, "MasterCard Forms Link to Ensure Security of Transactions on Internet," *American Banker*, January 12, 1995, p. 19.

Hadjian, Ani, "Hackers Find a Chink In Netscape's Armor," *Fortune*, October 30, 1995, pp. 20–21.

Hof, Robert D., "Nothing But Net," *Business Week*, December 18, 1995, p. 69.

Holzinger, Albert G., "Netscape Founder Points, and It Clicks," *Nation's Business*, January, 1996, p. 32.

Johnson, Bradley, "Microsoft, Netscape Vie For 'Net," *Advertising Age*, December 11, 1995, p. 4.

Krantz, Michael, ".Com Before the storm: Microsoft and a Netscape-Sun Alliance Prepare to Battle Over the Spoils of the Web," *MEDIAWEEK*, September 4, 1995, p. 20.

Lewis, Jamie, "Netscape, Share Make Good Partners," *PC Week*, October 23, 1995, p. N20.

Lewis, Peter H., "Will Netscape Be the Next Microsoft, Or the Next Victim of Microsoft?" *The New York Times*, October 16, 1995.

Miller, Michael J., "Warfare on the World Wide Web," *PC Magazine*, November 7, 1995, p. 75.

Moeller, Michael, "Netscape's Andreessen Surfs Into Computing's Next Wave," *PC Week*, September 25, 1995, p. 18.

Moeller, Michael, and Talila Baron, "Online Players Vow JavaScript Support," *PC Week*, December 11, 1995, p. 8.

"A New Electronic Messiah," *The Economist*, August 5, 1995, p. 62.

Quittner, Joshua, "Browser Madness: Crazy for Internet Companies, Wall Street Investors Drove Netscape to the Sky. But Will the Bubble Burst?" *Time*, August 21, 1995, p. 56.

Rigdon, Joan E., "VeriFone and Netscape Plan Software To Ease Internet Credit Card Payments," *The Wall Street Journal*, January 22, 1996, p. B8.

Sandberg, Jared, "AOL, Netscape Are Discussing an Alliance," *The Wall Street Journal*, January 22, 1996, p. A3.

Serwer, Andrew, "Internet-Worth: Why the Frenzy Won't Stop Soon," *Fortune*, December 11, 1995, p. 26.

Sprout, Alison L., "The Rise of Netscape," *Fortune*, July 10, 1995, p. 140.

Sullivan, Ed, "Security On Web Not Quite Ready," *PC Week*, October 30, 1995, p. 73.

—Frederick C. Ingram

New England Confectionery Co.

254 Massachusetts Avenue
Cambridge, Massachusetts 012139-4285
U.S.A.
(617) 876-4700
Fax: (617) 876-2356

Wholly Owned Subsidiary of UIS Co.
Incorporated: 1847 as Chase and Company
Employees: 475
Sales: $60 million (1994 est.)
SICs: 2064 Candy & Other Confectionery Products

New England Confectionery Co. is the oldest candy company in the United States. The company manufacturers such time-tested delights as Mary Janes, Canada Mints, Sky Bars, and its core product the venerable NECCO Wafer. Necco (as the company became popularly known for the word formed by its initials) expanded during the early and mid-1990s by acquiring confectioners Stark and Haviland, which more than tripled the organization's revenue base.

American Oliver B. Chase, with help from his brother, founded New England Confectionery Co. in 1847. Chase immigrated from England to the United States, where, among other pursuits, he invented a lozenge-cutting machine. Chase discovered that he could use the device to cut wafers of crunchy candy made with a relatively simple recipe of sugar, gelatin, and flavorings. His machine is now distinguished as the first American candy machine. Chase used his machine to set up a small factory in South Boston. He began manufacturing 'Chase Lozenges,' which were the forerunner to the renowned NECCO Wafers and other of Chase's lozenge-like candies. Two other local candy companies launched at the time were Daniel Fobes' Hayward and Company, founded in 1848, and Bird, Wright and Company (later called Wright and Moody), which was started in 1856. The three companies would join forces in 1901 under the New England Confectionery Company (Necco) banner.

The Chase brothers' first big hit was Necco Wafers, which were about the size of a quarter and came in rolls wrapped in glassine paper that resembled stiff wax paper. The wafers, the first candies ever to be sold in multipiece rolls, became hugely popular. Not only did they taste good, but they were surprisingly durable and had a long shelf life, which gave them an advantage over many other treats of the period. Even in warm weather the wafers could be manufactured and then transported over long distances without negatively affecting their flavor or texture.

Chase managed to build a successful company around his NECCO Wafers. Indeed, throughout the late 1800s and early 1900s Necco manufactured and shipped millions of wafers and the candies assumed their place in American history. The wafers, in fact, widely predated such other American candy icons as Hershey bars (1880s) and Tootsie Rolls (1890s). "[NECCO Wafers] were probably at least 30 years before any other American product that's still sold today in essentially unchanged form," noted Susan Strasser in the February 21, 1995 *Wall Street Journal.*

Fat-free and offered in eight flavors—the coveted chocolate NECCOs developed something of a cult following in the 1900s—NECCO Wafers held their own for 150 years in an often hyper-competitive candy industry. The treats were a favorite during economic depressions, for example, because a few pennies bought a roll of wafers that a frugal person could savor for days or dole out to children one or two at a time. In the 1930s Admiral Richard Byrd took two tons of NECCO wafers on a 1930s polar expedition, and, during World War II, the U.S. Government requisitioned Necco's entire output of the rugged NECCO Wafers for its soldiers. Still a favorite with many sweet tooths, the wafers proved versatile into the 1990s as well. Necco was selling wafers accidentally dropped on the floor for hog feed, for example, while another buyer used the discs on rifle range targets. Moreover, homemaking guru Martha Stewart trailblazed the use of wafers to build roofs for gingerbread houses. Other uses included poker chips, checkers, and tollbooth tokens.

NECCO Wafers remained the centerpiece of Necco's offerings throughout its long history and into the mid-1990s. Since the late 1800s, however, the company introduced a number of different candies, many of which achieved notable success. Necco is credited with the invention of Boston Baked Beans candy in 1875, for example, as well as with the introduction of the first rolled lozenges in 1866. Other successful inventions included Canada Mints, Mary Jane peanut-butter chew candies, and Sky Bars. Unveiled in 1938, the Sky Bar was the first multicenter candy bar. Necco introduced the candy with a sky-writing campaign to capitalize on the aviation craze of the time. Necco entries that didn't stand the test of time included Hoarhound Ovals, Jujube Monoplanes, Whangbees, Chocolate Need-Ums, Montevideos, and Climax Mint Patties.

Among the most successful and endearing Necco products during the 20th century was the renowned candy Valentines Day 'conversation hearts' that Oliver Chase's brother invented in the 1860s. It's probable that almost every American living in the mid-1990s had at least seen the tiny candy hearts. Inscribed with such short messages as 'Kiss Me,' 'Will You,' 'Buzz Off,' or 'Be Mine,' the hearts were a crunchy, chalky candy similar to NECCO Wafers and offered in an assortment of pastels. Necco introduced the hugely successful conversation hearts in 1902 and proceeded to sell billions of them. In the early 1990s, in fact, the company estimated that it was churning out a whopping eight billion hearts (including larger 'motto hearts') annually, accounting for roughly one-quarter of total sales. In the mid-1990s Necco was printing 32 different heart messages, many of which had been used since the early 1900s.

Necco profited for about 100 years with its mainstay wafers and variety of candy innovations. But by the mid-1900s the confectionery industry was beginning to change, and Necco was failing to keep pace. One trend was increasing consolidation in the industry. Necco itself had merged with two other Boston confectioners in 1901, as described above, and in 1933 the company had acquired Lovell & Covel Co., a small manufacturer of packaged chocolate goods. In 1961, moreover, Necco bought out Daggett Chocolate Company, a well-known candy maker that was started in 1888. But major candy companies in the mid-1900s were gobbling up their competitors and amassing huge manufacturing and distribution operations that allowed them to benefit from economies of scale. At the same time, the Necco organization had become somewhat stagnant, relying on existing products and paying little attention to the need to improve or update its aging production facilities. Necco even phased out production of its candy hearts during the 1950s and 1960s.

By the early 1960s Necco was losing money and careening toward bankruptcy. Recognizing the potential of some of Necco's brands was UIS Co., a New York holding company. UIS was founded by Harry Lebensfeld, who liked to purchase poorly performing companies and turn them around. He had started in 1945 by acquiring a desk manufacturer and had purchased some other companies—UIS would eventually become focused on the auto parts industry—before snagging Necco in 1963. Immediately after purchasing Necco, Lebensfeld eliminated unprofitable brands and raised prices. Then, in 1968 he installed a new management team headed by former auto industry engineer Domenic Antonellis. Antonellis spearheaded a turnaround that had Necco generating profits by the early 1970s and would keep the company healthy for the next three decades.

Antonellis achieved the renewal at Necco by upgrading production and investing heavily in what he viewed as high-potential brands and divisions. At the same time, he initiated an aggressive drive to control costs. Toward that end, Antonellis upgraded Necco's operations by spending as little money as necessary to maximize profits. Indeed, much of the company's equipment had been built early in the century and some furnishings even dated back to the 1800s. Antonellis jettisoned antique leather conveyor systems and old wooden troughs in favor of more current gear. But he kept much of the equipment that had been installed after the turn of the century, such as the giant cooking kettles and cast iron wafer-stamping equipment. Necco updated those old machines with electronic controls and other modern accessories.

Necco's old-fashioned offices and production operations make for an interesting sidebar to the Necco story. Its facilities in 1995 were somewhat of a candy-making museum. To make its wafers, Necco used four giant wafer-cutting machines estimated to have been made around the turn of the century, although nobody really knew for sure. The wafers were wrapped by hand and placed on old, dependable conveyor belts. Other Necco candies were made similarly, with decades-old equipment that the company updated with electronic controls under Antonellis' direction. Some of the company's historic fixtures were employees, such as 55-year Necco veteran Joe Wicks, also known as 'Mr. Candy Cupboard.' ''We built this building in 1927, and it's a mausoleum. Look at those century-old walnut filing cabinets. Look at that doorknob,'' said Walter J. Marshall, Necco manager, in the Fall 1995 *Invention & Technology*. ''We make four and a half billion Necco Wafers a year, and we make them on the equipment we brought with us when we moved here in 1927,'' Wicks observed.

Although Necco retained its old-fashioned appeal under Antonellis, it also made important changes. Evidencing Necco's new management strategy, for example, was its resurrection of the conversation hearts that Oliver Chase's brother had invented in the 1860s and Necco had discontinued in the 1950s. Necco started making the hearts in the 1970s under Antonellis' direction. When they decided to resume production, managers were able to find the old hand-forged brass cutters used to shape the hearts, but they couldn't locate the printing attachments. Necco managers, including Antonellis himself, worked on weekends for four years to get the line up-and-running. The effort paid off when the little hearts became a major source of revenue for Necco. Managers achieved similar savings by purchasing machines that other companies sold or discarded. A chocolate enrobing machine and metal detectors (to detect metal objects that fell into the candy) used in the 1990s, for instance, were bought from competing candy manufacturers.

Even Necco's corporate offices and facilities reflected the low-cost approach. Necco's offices and plant in Cambridge were still served by an old elevator system that opened out onto several floors filled with old copper and brass candymaking machines. Most of the executive offices sported bare concrete floors, although Antonellis enjoyed vintage linoleum in his suite. The company was also known for discarding very little, a policy that was demonstrated to have value in an amusing incident involving Massachusetts' then-governor Michael Dukakis. Olympia Dukakis, the Governor's cousin, claimed in a speech that she had worked for Necco for six months in 1959 and had been exposed to ''awful'' working conditions. An outraged Necco manager pulled her work file and sent it to the Governor. The file showed that Olympia had only worked at Necco for two weeks. ''The company may not be in the fast lane,'' the manager wrote, as quoted in a *Wall Street Journal* article, ''but we do provide jobs and benefits. . . . Please do not belittle [it].''

Necco profited during the 1970s and 1980s with its savvy manufacturing and operating strategy and proven line of traditional candies. By the end of the 1980s the company, which was still operating as a subsidiary of UIS Co., was generating about $25 million annually. After years of relatively stable gains, however, Necco surged during the early and mid-1990s. Importantly, in 1990 Necco acquired the Howard B. Stark Candy Co. for $11 million. Stark was a family-owned candy manufacturer founded in 1939. It produced the well-known Sweetheart Valentine hearts, 'Gummi' candies, caramel goods, and other confectionery products.

Stark was generating sales of about $22 million annually going into the 1990s, but a management switch in 1988 had failed to bring profits. Antonellis had been familiar with the company for years and had watched from the sidelines as it tailspinned into financial decay. Stark brought three factories—in Louisiana, Massachusetts, and Milwaukee—to Necco, as well as about 140 employees. During the early 1990s Necco worked to whip Stark's operations into shape. It updated some of its production facilities and tweaked its product lines. At the same time, Necco invested to modernize some of its own operations. In 1993, for example, Necco installed an advanced new packaging system designed to speed up production and provide faster changeover to meet different packaging demands.

Necco posted sales of about $60 million in 1994. Revenue for 1995, though, was expected to surge toward the $100 million mark. That gain was primarily the result of a second major acquisition that Necco conducted late in 1994. In June of that year, creditors forced the shutdown of the Great American Brands candy factory in East Cambridge, not far from Necco's main plant. Three months later New England Confectionery Co. purchased the plant and reopened it as the Haviland Candy Co., which traced its origins to the 1929 formation of the Deran Confectionery Co. Antonellis rehired about 150 of the original 200-plus employees. ''I hired no one outside of the people who were part of that (shut down) organization,'' he said in the July 10, 1995, *Boston Herald*. ''They were an excellent group of people. It was a case of making them believe that they had a viable candy company and they had jobs,'' he added. Besides boosting Necco's revenue base, Haviland's boxed chocolates line diversified Necco's offerings.

Going into 1996, Necco was working to consolidate its recent acquisitions and streamline the overall company into an efficient, diversified candy manufacturer. 1997 would mark the 150th anniversary of one of the oldest companies in the United States. As they had been for nearly 150 years, Necco Wafers continued to be the company's centerpiece product.

Principal Subsidiaries

DMA Acquisition Corp.

Principal Operating Units

Necco; Stark Candy Co.; Haviland Candy Co.

Further Reading

Disckson, Harvey, ''One Sweet-Talkin' Biz,'' *Boston Herald*, February 14, 1993, p. 1.
Furman, Phyllis, ''Auto Part Firm,'' *Crain's New York Business*, October 12, 1987, p. 3.
Healy, Beth, ''How Sweet It Is: Candy Maker is Back,'' *Boston Business Journal*, September 23, 1994, p. 1.
Kass, Mark, ''Candy Connubium: NECCO Buys Stark,'' *The Business Journal-Milwaukee*, July 9, 1990, p. 1.
''Necco Aims to Boost Output and Flexibility,'' *Candy Industry*, February 1993, p. 35.
Primack, Phil, ''Candy Workers' Sweet Comeback,'' *Boston Herald*, July 10, 1995, Sec. BUS, p. 24.
Stipp, David, ''Initially Rolled Out in 1847, Necco Wafers Are a Profitable Relic,'' *The Wall Street Journal*, February 21, 1995, A1.

—Dave Mote

Oakwood Homes Corporation

2225 South Holden Road
P.O. Box 7386
Greensboro, North Carolina 27417-0386
U.S.A.
(910) 855-2400
Fax: (910) 852-1537

Public Company
Incorporated: 1946 as Oakwood Trailer Sales
   Corporation
Employees: 3,600
Sales: $579.1 million (1994)
Stock Exchanges: New York
SICs: 2451 Mobile Homes; 5271 Mobile Home Dealers;
   6141 Personal Credit Institutions; 6351 Surety Insurance

With about six percent of the highly fragmented $9.4 billion (retail) market, Oakwood Homes Corporation is America's largest mobile home dealer and ranks seventh among the leading mobile home manufacturers. Generally regarded as one of the industry's best-managed firms, Oakwood has targeted the middle and upper ranks of the manufactured housing market. The company has evolved from a postwar trailer park into a fully-integrated mobile home company with ten factories in four states, over 150 dealerships in 18 states, and financing and insurance services. Nicholas St. George, who led the company from 1978 into the mid-1990s, planned to more than double annual sales by the turn of the 21st century.

The mobile home industry is uniquely American. Although its roots can be traced to the 1920s, when early models were used as temporary shelter for farm and construction workers, mobile home living took hold during the post-World War II love affair with the automobile. Wartime defense contracts for temporary barracks had helped raise awareness and acceptance of mobile homes, which were more accurately called "trailers."

Oakwood was established on the cusp of the industry's postwar boom in 1946 as Oakwood Trailer Sales Corporation.

Founder Jack Jones named the trailer camp for the Greensboro, North Carolina, oak grove in which it was located. Since all the industry's production went to the war effort during this period, Jones started out selling renovated models. From 1946 until 1966, the company operated as essentially a dealer, marketing trailers manufactured by other firms.

Ralph L. Darling assumed control of Oakwood in 1952. He established a second sales outlet in Danville, Virginia, in 1955 and changed the company's name to Oakwood Mobile Homes in the early 1960s. The name change reflected more than an image makeover; it belied a significant industry shift from travel trailers to mobile homes. In the mid-1950s, manufacturers recognized that industry sales were driven more by affordability than portability, and they introduced ten-foot-wide models, which were two feet broader than their road-going predecessors. Furnished with carpeting, appliances, and furniture, these pre-fabricated abodes often found permanent locations in what used to be called "trailer camps" and came to be known as "trailer parks." Newlyweds and retirees constituted a significant proportion of the market's clientele.

Jim LaVasque took over Oakwood in the early 1960s. Described as "seat of the pants smart" by employees, LaVasque began a program of vertical consolidation and geographic expansion that reflected an industry-wide consolidation trend. Over the course of the decade, the company opened eight new sales outlets and acquired the heretofore independent Oakwood Land Operation. Oakwood made a bold move at the end of the decade, adding manufacturing to its growing slate of interests. The firm launched its first model, the "Richfield," in 1969. The company's sales division continued to offer many other manufacturers' models through the 1970s. By the early 1970s, Oakwood had established itself in the high-end of the mobile home market, offering large, well-equipped models. In order to depict the home's sturdiness, each sales lot featured a model with a car parked on its roof. The strategy apparently helped; Oakwood's revenues more than doubled, from nearly $4 million in 1967 to $10.9 million in 1970.

It was a heady period for the mobile home industry overall. Architects and bureaucrats as well as industry representatives praised mobiles as the flexible, low-cost housing of the future. Mobiles became the preferred mode of low-cost housing, offering low down payments and manageable monthly payments.

LaVasque seized the opportunity, floating a $3.1 million initial public offering of stock in Oakwood Homes Corporation in 1971. A concurrent corporate reorganization merged the retail operation, Oakwood Mobile Homes Inc. (established 1952); manufacturing operations, Homes by Fisher Inc. (established 1969); and the original mobile home park and sales operation. The infusion of cash, combined with the unparalleled expansion of the mobile home industry as a whole, fueled dramatic growth in the early 1970s. Oakwood opened 23 new retail sales centers, built a new headquarters, and doubled production capacity with a new factory, as annual sales blossomed to over $20 million. The mobile home industry grew at an annual rate of 20 percent from 1967 to $4.4 billion in 1972, and its share of single-family housing increased to 33 percent in 1973.

However, the bubble burst in mid-decade, when industry-wide unit shipments dropped by 63 percent from over 575,000 in 1972 to 212,700, and sales volume plunged by more than 40 percent to $2.4 billion. More than one-third of America's mobile home dealers went bankrupt, overall production capacity dipped 43 percent from 1973 to 1974, over 100,000 housing units were repossessed, and tight lending conditions limited new sales.

Although Oakwood was affected by this steep market downturn, it survived in much better condition than many of its rivals. Annual sales actually increased in 1974, then declined by 19 percent the following year. Nevertheless, the company opened eight new sales outlets during these difficult years, launched a finance department, and its stock was listed on the American Stock Exchange.

One key to Oakwood's success during this crisis and beyond was its marriage of homes and sites on which to put them. In a virtual abandonment of the concept of mobility, Oakwood packaged its homes with sites, creating "mobile home subdivisions." During the early 1970s, the company developed six separate locations, totaling nearly 700 acres and over 600 homesites. These planned communities more closely resembled their conventional counterparts, featuring larger-than-normal lots, landscaping, and other amenities, and were more accepted both by potential buyers and owners of neighboring real estate. Oakwood was also located propitiously. A 1979 article in *Financial World* observed that "buying a mobile home happen[ed] to be viewed with greater acceptance, and less stigma, in the Southeast than in other regions of the country." In fact, North Carolina remained Oakwood's largest market into the mid-1990s.

The mobile home industry overall continued to evolve during the late 1970s. Federal building codes and warranty standards were enacted and lending policies were relaxed to encourage mobile homeownership. Within the industry, manufacturers launched larger, 14-foot and "double-wide" models, and also placed a greater emphasis on quality control. Oakwood's strength through the early 1970s proved telling in the later years of the decade. While total mobile home shipments declined from 1976 to 1980, Oakwood returned to the growth trail in 1976 and chalked up new annual sales records throughout the remainder of the decade.

By 1979, Oakwood had expanded its reach into South Carolina, Virginia, Tennessee, and West Virginia. Upon the 1978 death of Jim LaVasque in a plane crash, Chairman Ralph Darling returned to the post of president until 1979, when Nicholas J. St. George was elected to lead on a permanent basis. A former investment banker, St. George had been asked to serve on Oakwood's board after helping to organize the 1971 initial public offering. Darling continued in the post of chairman through the mid-1990s.

Unit production in the mobile home industry never recovered to the levels of the 1972 boom, but sales volume rose to a record $4.78 million in 1983 on unit price increases. Oakwood's vertical integration helped balance out the vagaries of the retail mobile home market. The company manufactured, sold, financed, and leased homes and the land on which they were parked, rendering a bit of profit at each step in the transaction and insulating itself from the industry's violent cycles.

In fact, Oakwood's real estate development operation proved vital in the 1980s and 1990s, as potential sites for mobile home parks dwindled in the face of a wave of anti-mobile home zoning. From 1981 to 1985, the company added a net total of 22 new sales offices and expanded its geographic reach to Florida and New Mexico. The firm also continued to expand its financial services operations throughout the early 1980s, adding Oakwood Acceptance Corporation in 1983 and life insurance arm Oakwood Life, Ltd. in 1985. Financing, in fact, proved an important service; conventional lenders were prone to reject mobile home loan applications since mobile homes, unlike most conventional housing, tended to depreciate.

These various activities enabled Oakwood to record the industry's longest string of consecutive sales and production increases, a ten-year streak from 1975 to 1985. Eleanor Johnson Tracy of *Fortune* called it "a stunning achievement in the highly cyclical industry."

Unfortunately, this extraordinary rise was followed by a spectacular decline that *Business North Carolina* described as a "near-death experience." The late 1980s brought an attenuated industry shakeout, during which half of the 200 mobile home companies operating in 1978 went bankrupt as unit sales slid to 170,000 and sales volume flattened at about $4.25 billion per year. One of Oakwood's primary competitors, Conner Corp., succumbed in 1987. This North Carolina-based company's Chapter 11 "fire sales" flooded the market with bargains that Oakwood simply couldn't meet.

Mid-decade, the "oil bust" thwarted Oakwood's fledgling efforts in Texas, leaving the company with costly repossessions. Oakwood had counted on the fast-growing Texas market to provide one-fifth of annual revenues, but instead took a $93 million charge in 1987 to close operations there. Sales dropped by over 20 percent from 1987 to 1988, and earnings declined 94 percent from $6.5 million in 1986 to $400,000 in 1987 and 1988.

The crisis drew some negative attention from analysts. Wounded by bad press and determined to refute it, St. George undertook a drastic turnaround plan in 1988. A ''reorganization of management'' sacked 40 percent of Oakwood's top managers. The CEO also cut selling, general, and administrative costs from 29.4 percent of sales in 1989 to 21.8 percent by 1993 by enlisting employees to come up with economizations and rewarding them with up to $1000 for their ideas. Oakwood also expanded from its base in single-wide models into double-wides or ''multi-sectionals,'' which by this time constituted nearly half of the market. The late 1994 acquisition of California-based Golden West Homes helped boost Oakwood's revenues from double-wides to one-third of annual revenues.

Earnings rebounded to $9 million and sales were up over $106 million by 1991. Industry observers and colleagues alike credited St. George with the turnaround, but the leader may have taken even more satisfaction from the fact that Oakwood was one of only 90 mobile home manufacturers remaining after the late 1980s shakeout. From 1989 to 1994, Oakwood chalked up the New York Stock Exchange's seventh-best record of financial growth, as sales rose two-and-a-half times from $223.1 million in 1990 to $579.1 million in 1994. Net income quadrupled during that same period, from $7.2 million to $33.9 million. Nicholas St. George capped his early 1990s achievements with *The Wall Street Transcript*'s 1994 gold medal for ''best chief executive in the manufactured housing.'' Buoyed by the renewed success, St. George predicted that Oakwood would break the $1 billion sales mark by the year 2000.

Principal Subsidiaries

Oakwood Mobile Homes, Inc.; Homes By Oakwood, Inc.; Homes By Fisher, Inc.; Oakwood Land Development Corp.; Oakwood Acceptance Corp.; Oakwood Realty Services, Inc.; Oakwood Agency, Inc.; Oakwood Funding Corp.; Oakwood Financial Corp. (North Carolina); Oakwood Financial Corp. (Delaware); Acorn Acquisition Corp.; Acorn Financial Corp.; Pin Oak Financial Corp.; Oakwood Life, Ltd.; Oakwood Mortgage Investors, Inc.; Golden West Homes; Golden Circle Financial Services.

Further Reading

Aiken, Eric, ''For the Long Haul,'' *Barron's,* October 29, 1973, p. 3.
''Bucking the Mobile Home Recession,'' *Financial World,* June 15, 1979, p. 35.
''Deal on Wheels,'' *Business North Carolina,* November 1991, p. 63.
''Expanded Output Enhances Outlook for Operations of Oakwood Homes,'' *Barron's,* June 26, 1972, p. 29.
Giltenan, Edward, ''Standing Out,'' *Forbes,* December 23, 1991, p. 132.
The History of Oakwood Homes: A Tribute to 40 Years of Pride and Integrity, Greensboro, N.C.: Oakwood Homes Corporation, 1986.
''An Idea Whose Time Has Come?'' *Forbes,* May 15, 1976, p. 53.
Lurz, William H., ''Oakwood Seeks to Delight the Home Buyer,'' *Professional Builder,* October 1995, p. S40.
Mahon, Gigi, ''Painful Turnaround,'' *Barron's,* January 12, 1976, p. 11.
''New Chance for Mobile Homes,'' *Business Week,* June 28, 1976, p. 96.
Scheer, Lisa, ''Pump Up the Volume,'' *Business North Carolina,* March 1995, p. 24.
Schmuckler, Eric, ''The Gods Must be Angry,'' *Forbes,* May 2, 1988, p. 64.
Tracy, Eleanor Johnson, ''Oakwood Homes Has the Key to Profits,'' *Fortune,* March 18, 1985, p. 49.
''Where Housing Market Has Lots of Life,'' *Business Week,* September 3, 1966, p. 148.
Wynn, Jack, ''The $17,000 Single-Family Home,'' *Forbes,* April 9, 1984. p. 68.

—April Dougal Gasbarre

OfficeMax Inc.

P.O. Box 22500
Cleveland, Ohio 44122-0500
U.S.A.
(216) 921-6900
Fax: (216) 349-4220

Public Company
Incorporated: 1988
Employees: 17,133
Sales: $1.84 billion (1995)
Stock Exchanges: New York
SICs: 5712 Furniture Stores; 5734 Computer &
Computer Software Stores; 5943 Stationery Stores;
5999 Miscellaneous Retail Stores Not Elsewhere
Classified

OfficeMax, Inc. is the second largest operator of high-volume, deep-discount office products superstores in the United States. In mid-1995, the company was operating more than 400 superstores in 41 states and Puerto Rico and was planning to open more than 150 additional stores within two years. The company was also experimenting with related business concepts, including a chain of furniture stores and a string of copy-service centers.

OfficeMax started in 1988 as a simple idea. In little more than five years the company bolted to the forefront of the American business supplies industry, posting more than $2 billion in annual sales by 1995 and generating sound profits by 1993. The company achieved that stunning success despite intense competition and an economic recession that began in the late 1980s and lingered throughout the early 1990s. The company's savvy marketing, distribution, management, and financial systems and strategies became models for other superstore retailers in the 1990s.

The OfficeMax idea was hatched by entrepreneurs Michael Feuer and Robert Hurwitz. Feuer, who became the driving force behind the chain's growth, had been nurturing the idea during more than 17 years of service with Fabri-Centers of America, a 600-store, Cleveland-based retailer. By his early 40s, Feuer had risen to the executive ranks. Still, he was frustrated by his inability to run the company as he believed it should be operated. "At age 42 . . . I was bored, and like many executives, I also suffered from the Frank Sinatra syndrome—I wanted to do it my way," Feuer recalled in the September 1993 *Corporate Cleveland.* "I had always claimed that if we could just cut through all the nonsense—for example, the 20 to 25 percent of time most executives spend on CYB (covering your butt)—and do it my way, we could make millions," Feuer observed.

Feuer finally jumped ship and, despite other excellent corporate job offers, decided to start his own enterprise. He and Hurwitz decided that they didn't want to fund the start-up with bank debt or venture capital, because they didn't want to forfeit control of the operation. So they scrambled to raise capital from friends and family. They eventually found 50 investors, including several doctors and lawyers, who were willing to contribute a total of $3 million. The sum was paltry compared to other retail start-up businesses at the time, but the pair thought that they could parlay the cash into a winning enterprise.

Feuer and Hurwitz launched their enterprise on April Fool's Day in 1988. On that day, they laid out on a blank sheet of paper their concept for a new type of office products store. Their goal was to create a large business supplies discount store that was an exciting place to shop, proffered professional and friendly service, and offered prices between ten percent and 30 percent less that those found in more traditional office supply retailer shops. The main goal was to bypass all of the middlemen, such as wholesalers and distributors. Achieving that goal, they reasoned, would allow them to effectively replace mom-and-pop office supply stores, much as supermarkets had replaced small grocers years earlier.

OfficeMax was fighting an uphill battle from the start. In May, an office supplies industry trade paper published a list of 15 start-up companies that were trying to crack into the business; OfficeMax was 14th on the list by asset size. The start-up team knew that it had to keep expenditures at an absolute minimum to compete. So Feuer and Hurwitz rented office space in a 500-square-foot brick warehouse that had barely any heat or air-conditioning. The space was equipped with a few pieces of cheap office furniture, a coffee machine, and a copier (the copier and coffee machine couldn't be operated at the same time, however, because the fuse would blow). They decided not to invest in a fax machine until it became absolutely necessary.

OfficeMax started out with a skeletal staff of seven people, not including the founders. Their requirements for potential employees were simple: they had to be hard workers with open minds, big hearts, and plenty of enthusiasm. They also had to be willing to work for very little money. Feuer and Hurwitz attracted the workers by promising them part ownership in the company if they stuck with it and by offering them the chance to go farther, faster, and to have more fun than they had ever had in another job. From the beginning, Feuer made it clear that Office-Max would be operated differently from the bureaucracies from which most of the team members had come. There would be no secrets, criticism and praise would be swift and frank, and everyone would cooperate as a team.

Thus, OfficeMax was up-and-running without a single store or any other operation that could bring in any money. The founders hoped that they would be able to get manufacturers to fund their inventory, but they soon found that few big companies were eager to do business with a meager upstart. To overcome such hurdles, the team got together every morning and created a game plan for the day on a blackboard. They flew by the seat of their pants and used every trick they could conjure to get what they needed. Importantly, the company was able to get an unsecured line of credit from a local Cleveland bank. The bank granted the line of credit under one condition: that the founders agree never to use it.

Feuer and Hurwitz were able to take their "line of credit" to big suppliers like Xerox and convince them to fund their inventory on credit, sometimes for a full year or more. Indeed, the OfficeMax team learned early that the only way to get the cooperation of potential suppliers was to act as though Office-Max was much bigger than it really was. They dealt with suppliers as though OfficeMax was a soon-to-be major chain with 20, 50, or even 300 stores going up in the near future, suggesting that if those suppliers wanted to secure a place with OfficeMax tomorrow, they would have to cooperate today. To the founders' surprise, most companies played along. Those that didn't often regretted it, as OfficeMax quickly became the leading customer for many major office equipment and supplies manufacturers.

Incredibly, OfficeMax opened its first store just 90 days after the founders had created their business blueprint on April Fool's Day. Observers were surprised that the team had managed to find space, hire and train a store staff, and hone a store concept in just three months. But to them it was a simple matter of survival; they had to start generating cash flow so that they could pay their bills. The first OfficeMax was opened on July 5, 1988, at the Golden Gate Shopping Center in the Cleveland area. The only advertising for the grand opening was a newspaper ad two days prior to the store's opening. Nevertheless, the mart had sales of $6,400 on its first day.

After only six months in operation, the store was breaking even (before corporate overhead). That feat was accomplished partly as a result of the grueling hours put in by the team. Feuer, for instance, worked at the corporate office from seven a.m. to seven p.m. He would then race home, shower, put on casual clothes, and drive out to the store to observe the customers and employees. When a customer left the store without purchasing anything, Feuer was known to chase him down in the parking lot and ask him if OfficeMax had failed in any way. That type of thinking was later reflected in OfficeMax's intensive customer-satisfaction orientation. For example, the company began requiring that all customer complaints be resolved to the customer's satisfaction within 24 hours.

Enthused by the quick success of the first store, Feuer and Hurwitz hurried back to the original investment group and raised additional capital for expansion. They dumped the cash into an aggressive growth program that, amazingly, had Office-Max operating 13 stores in Ohio and Michigan less than 12 months after opening the first outlet. Sales had climbed to an impressive rate of $13 million annually and, more importantly, the stores were operating at a profit. The success was so quick that it worried Feuer, who was convinced that the company's accounting system was messed up and that OfficeMax could easily be teetering on the edge of bankruptcy.

Shortly before OfficeMax had fired up its first store, a similar office superstore venture called Office World had started in Chicago. The business was funded heavily by retailer Montgomery Ward, but despite hefty financial backing, the effort had lost a big $10 million in the span of a few years. Thus, when Montgomery Ward approached OfficeMax about the possibility of a merger between OfficeMax and Office World, Feuer and Hurwitz were hesitant. They eventually warmed up to the idea, however, and the resulting agreement brought seven new stores to their chain as well as the resources of several deep-pocketed venture capital firms. OfficeMax, for its part, only had to give up two of the ten seats on its board.

By the summer of 1990, following the Office World merger, OfficeMax was operating a total of 30 stores. After once again going back to its investment group, the company was banking an impressive $33 million in cash. The cost-conscious founders finally decided that it was time to move into a better headquarters facility, one that featured separate men's and women's bathrooms, for example. The rest of the money was put to use funding an aggressive expansion plan that would, the company hoped, tag 20 more stores onto the chain within a year. Despite healthy gains and a bright future, however, a development in 1990 threatened to quash OfficeMax and its competitors.

Feuer and Hurwitz had perceived the threat years earlier. Finally, their fears were being realized when mass discount merchant Kmart announced plans to roll out an office supplies superstore dubbed Office Square. OfficeMax executives realized that the new venture, backed by Kmart's massive bank account and retailing savvy, could literally crush start-ups like OfficeMax. Feuer and Hurwitz, refusing to ignore the threat, began trying to initiate talks with Kmart. The talks initially centered around an outright purchase of OfficeMax by Kmart. But Feuer and Hurwitz were hesitant to give up control of their company. The two companies finally agreed to a plan whereby Kmart invested $40 million in OfficeMax in return for a 22 percent ownership share.

Fortunately for the founders, Kmart turned out to be OfficeMax's greatest ally, rather than its worst enemy. Feuer and Hurwitz were allowed to maintain total control of the company, and Kmart smartly became a silent financial partner. With its new bankroll, OfficeMax intensified its expansion efforts and quickly met the goals that it had set with Kmart executives. Both companies were so pleased with the arrangement that Kmart decided to up the ante in 1991. It purchased 92 percent of the outstanding shares from the original investors and became the owner of OfficeMax. The net result was the OfficeMax was sitting on a mountain of cash and had virtually no long-term debt. Furthermore, Feuer and Hurwitz were still firmly in control of the company.

The deal couldn't have been sweeter for OfficeMax, which was suddenly positioned to launch a bid to dominate the national business supplies superstore segment. That's exactly what the company did. During the next 18 months the company began opening new OfficeMax outlets at a feverish pitch. More importantly, the company purchased the 46-store Office Warehouse chain and the 105-outlet Bizmart chain, and eventually integrated those stores into the OfficeMax organization. As a result of store additions and acquisitions, OfficeMax was operating 328 stores, coast-to-coast, in 38 states by the end of 1993. Sales for that year climbed to $1.41 billion from just $245 million in 1991, while net income increased to $1.08 billion (OfficeMax's first positive annual net income).

Although cash was a major ingredient in the company's recipe for growth, its shrewd operating strategy was just as important for success. Indeed, throughout its expansion OfficeMax maintained its customer focus. It also adapted the format of its stores to capitalize on the huge growth in the small and home-based business markets, which became the dominant industry trend during the early 1990s. In addition, OfficeMax managed to implement cutting-edge information and distribution systems that allowed the top mega-discounters like Kmart and Walmart to thrive. By the mid-1990s, OfficeMax was efficiently operating nearly 400 stores and several distribution centers, and stocking more than 6,000 brand name office products, business machines, computers and related electronic devices, software, and other goods.

With Kmart's financial backing and the OfficeMax team's successful operating strategy, the company sustained its blistering growth rate in 1994. By the end of the year the company was operating 388 stores in 40 states and Puerto Rico. Importantly, the end of 1994 marked a huge change for the company. Late in that year, its well-heeled parent, Kmart, sold out. Kmart's investors had been pressuring Kmart to sell off its side interests and refocus its resources on the hyper-competitive general merchandise discount industry. Kmart's directors stooped to the pressure and decided to bail out of the OfficeMax venture. OfficeMax completed the largest initial public offering in the history of the retail chain industry when it sold 35.7 million shares at a price of $19, bringing in $678 million that allowed Kmart to reduce its ownership interest. A subsequent offering in July 1995 entirely eliminated Kmart's ownership share.

Thus, after growing by leaps and bounds with the help of Kmart, OfficeMax was suddenly on its own again as a publicly held enterprise. For the 1994 year, OfficeMax posted $1.81 billion in sales, $30.4 million of which was netted as income. As Hurwitz had removed himself from day-to-day operations at OfficeMax following the stock sale, Feuer stepped up expansion plans in 1995, hoping to boost OfficeMax's 11-percent share of the U.S. office supplies superstore market. By 1995, in fact, OfficeMax had become the second largest business superstore in the nation (behind Office Depot), and was gunning for the number one slot.

To that end, Feuer hoped to add about 200 new stores to the chain by January 1997. Meanwhile OfficeMax launched related ventures beginning in 1994, including FurnitureMax, a chain of discount office furniture stores, and CopyMax, a chain of copy-service centers. Both of the new store concepts were designed to be connected to existing OfficeMax stores and to serve as add-on profit centers. The company also initiated a computer service called OfficeMax Online, which was designed to enable customers to purchase OfficeMax products online from their home or office computers. OfficeMax expected to post sales of about $2.5 billion for the fiscal year ending January 31, 1996.

Principal Subsidiaries

Bizmart, Inc.

Principal Operating Units

FurnitureMax; CopyMax; OfficeMax Online.

Further Reading

Baird, Kristen, ''OfficeMax Plan May Supply 900 More Local Jobs,'' *Crain's Cleveland Business,* July 31, 1995, p. 1.

Brandt, John R., and Michael Feuer, ''. . . Taking It to the MAX: How Did Michael Feuer Take a Start-up Company to $1.5 Billion in Revenue in Just Five Years?,'' *Corporate Cleveland,* September 1993, p. 16.

Harrison, Kimberly P., ''OfficeMax to Launch New Unit: Company to Test Concept of Furniture Showroom,'' *Crain's Cleveland Business,* November 14, 1994, p. 1.

Howes, Daniel, ''Kmart Plans to Sell Rest of Stake in OfficeMax,'' *Detroit News,* June 27, 1995, p. E1.

King, Angela G., ''OfficeMax Stock Shines for Openers,'' *Detroit News,* November 3, 1994, p. E1.

Nottingham, Nancy, ''Office Superstore Opens Today on West End,'' *Billings (Montana) Gazette,* June 15, 1995, p. D5.

Russell, John M., ''OfficeMax Breaks Loose,'' *Small Business News-Cleveland,* September 1994, p. 16.

Shingler, Dan, ''Hurwitz Trading Paper for Pillows,'' *Crain's Cleveland Business,* April 11, 1994, p. 1.

Thompson, Chris, ''OfficeMax Sees Profits Stack Up for Pending IPO,'' *Crain's Cleveland Business,* September 12, 1994, p. 3.

—Dave Mote

Old National Bancorp

420 Main Street
P.O. Box 718
Evansville, Indiana 47705-0718
U.S.A.
(812) 464-1434
Fax: (812) 464-1567

Public Company
Incorporated: 1834
Employees: 1,948
Total Assets: $4.82 billion
Stock Exchanges: NASDAQ
SICs: 6712 Bank Holding Companies; 6021 National
    Commercial Banks

Old National Bancorp (ONB) is the largest bank holding company in Indiana, providing a variety of general banking and banking-related services through its 24 affiliates, which comprise nearly 100 branch outlets in southern and central Indiana, western Kentucky, and southern Illinois. The bank holding company was formed in 1983 by ONB's board of directors in anticipation of the impending reform of banking regulations at the state and federal levels in the late 1980s and early 1990s. In 1995, ONB was ranked number one in earnings momentum by banking journal *Financial World.* Acknowledging ONB's relatively small size among world-class banks, analysts nevertheless expressed admiration for the corporation's financial performance and conservative management; according to *Financial World,* "relative anonymity is just fine with Old National. Unlike its better-known rivals, it has not been stung by derivatives losses, wrong bets on currency movements, or soured real estate investments."

The company traces its roots to the founding of the Branch Bank at Evansville of the State Bank of Indiana in 1834. Evansville, a city in southwestern Indiana along the Ohio River, was at that time a loose gathering of pioneers who sorely needed a bank to provide capital, security, and cash flow for the local river-based economy. The new bank was granted a 20-year charter and John Mitchell was named the bank's first president; Mitchell would have the unenviable job of transporting the bank's money with him to New York City to make transactions, until rail and telegraph lines were later established. The bank's first cashier, John Douglas, had the combined responsibilities of bookkeeper, teller, and janitor. At the end of its first year in business, the Evansville bank reported total deposits of over $29,000 and gross profits of almost $4,000.

The bank's entrance into major financing was well-intentioned, but rather inauspicious. Specifically, in 1836, it loaned $30,000 toward the completion of the Wabash-Erie Canal, which was to have eventually linked Evansville with Lake Erie, over 400 miles away. Because of high construction and maintenance costs, however, the canal project was abandoned in 1837, and the "loan" was never repaid. One of the reasons for the failure of the canal project was the nationwide financial panic of 1837. Many banks ceased operations during this economic crisis, but the Branch Bank at Evansville remained open. Moreover, the State Bank of Indiana, of which the bank was then a branch, redeemed its notes from the federal government in gold coins, thereby becoming the only bank offering to pay off its debt in hard currency.

In the decades that followed, the bank experienced steady growth, becoming an integral part of Indiana's, and Evansville's, economic development. In 1846, it loaned the state government $10,000 for clothing Indiana's volunteers during the Mexican War, and in 1850, it provided a $20,000 loan to help establish the city's first railroad. Another nationwide financial panic, in 1857, gained national attention for the ONB predecessor, when once again it was able to redeem all notes with cash, while other banks were closing their doors.

In 1855, the bank received a new charter and became known as the Evansville Branch Bank of the State Bank of Indiana, which would be shortened to Evansville National Bank 11 years later. The Civil War was a severe blow to Evansville's economy, since much of the trade that took place there was with river captains of the South. When those states seceded, much of the river trade ceased. In addition, the war caused great hardship on banks because of the unreliability of currency. Most of the "money" in circulation was printed with nothing more backing it than a promise—and sometimes a fairly flimsy promise, at that. By a combination of sound fiscal policy and strong leadership, the Evansville National Bank was not only able to keep operating (although it did hire armed militiamen to keep the deposits safe) but was also able to lend money to the government of the Union to aid in the war effort.

National history had local repercussions once again in 1873 with a Congressional Act that actually had the effect of demonetarizing silver. Adding to the upheaval caused by that controversial act, the closing of a large banking firm in New York City actually set off a "domino effect," which caused yet another nationwide depression. Although many other banks and industries closed permanently, ONB's predecessor never missed a day of operation. By 1884, the bank had been granted its fourth charter and, as was traditional by this time, changed its name once again, this time settling on Old National Bank of Evansville.

By this time, Old National was enjoying a reputation as one of the strongest, most reliable banks in its area of the country. A journalist for *Once a Month* magazine, published in St. Louis, reported in 1896: "In the proud record accompanying the Old National Bank of Evansville, we find exemplified a model banking history and the highest qualities displayed by those who have formed and now form its directorate and officiary." The turn of the century also marked the reception of Old National's fifth charter and fifth name—Old State National Bank.

In 1913, Congress passed the Federal Reserve Act. The law divided the country into 12 districts, each of which had its own Federal Reserve Bank. Participation was optional, but the incentives to join the Federal Reserve System were great, and Old National naturally joined. Coinciding with Old National's entrance to the Federal Reserve banking system was the election of Henry Reis to the presidency of the bank. Reis's biography, printed in *The Bankers Magazine* in 1914, characterized Old National as "a direct successor of one of the members of the very best examples of good banking this country has ever afforded.... Students of American banking who wish to find a practical exemplification of sound management, and especially of a sound and safe credit bank note, can find it in the history of the State Bank of Indiana."

Reis, who had begun his career at Old National as a teller in 1872 would see Old National through the boom years of 1914 through 1916, as the wartime economy boosted production everywhere, as well as the hardships of 1917 and 1918, when wartime rationing and sacrificing took their toll on the local economy. In 1922, Old National's sixth and final (permanent) charter was granted, the bank's name officially changed once more to The Old National Bank in Evansville, and a new president, William H. McCurdy, was installed.

At the time the stock market crashed in 1929, there were 11 banks operating in Evansville; by 1935, seven of those banks had been forced to close their doors. Old National was one of the four that continued to operate throughout this most difficult financial time in the history of the United States. Just as the country was headed toward economic recovery, severe flooding

in much of the Ohio and Mississippi River valleys in 1937 proved catastrophic for Evansville residents. Most of the city was under water for weeks, including the "skyscraper" which housed Old National. A temporary building was found so that operations could continue.

At about this time, a series of visionary, innovative men would take over the presidency of Old National. The banking industry to this time had been fairly stable, with few innovations either of process or technology. Starting with Robert Mathias in 1940, and extending through William Carson and Walter A. Schlechte, who finished his term as president of the bank in 1966, the presidents of Old National were responsible for changing the way bank business was done in that region of the country.

Mathias's major achievement was a thorough review and reform of the personnel policy of the bank. He told a meeting of the American Bankers Association "creation of sound personnel programs is the number one objective of Indiana banks... We are attempting to prevail upon our banks to rank personnel management as a major function the same as deposit and loan development." Mathias also presided over the establishment of the first Old National "drive-up" teller window in 1941, and he found much favor with employee groups by instituting the first group hospitalization, life insurance, and pension plans for bank employees in 1946.

William Carson's tenure as president lasted only from 1948 to 1953, but he developed and oversaw the beginnings of the branch banking system. Moreover, he set new standards for community philanthropy and service and also recruited to Old National the man who would guide the bank for the next 30 years as president and then chief executive officer: Walter Schlechte.

Schlechte was bank president from 1953–1966, and remained as CEO until 1982. According to one writer for *The Evansville Press*, "During Schlechte's career in Evansville, Old National Bank grew from a $50 million business into a $460 million institution and along the way became one of the soundest, most profitable banks in the country. In 1976, Old National was sixth highest in return on assets (a standard measure of profitability) among the nation's major banks, according to a national survey." Schlechte also presided over a six-fold growth in number of bank employees, establishment of credit card business (Old National was one of the first three banks in the nation to do so), the addition of three more branch banks to the fold, and the addition of services such as mortgage financing, data processing, and industrial development.

In the 1960s, Old National began to diversify its offerings through a careful acquisitions program. In 1961, the bank purchased the Carter Mortgage Company, and three years later it acquired the Tabco Corp., a data processing operation. (Indeed, the technology and information revolution of the 1960s and 1970s forced banks across the country to move quickly to benefit from the increased possibilities.) In 1969, Old National moved into its new $5 million, 18-story headquarters, the tallest office building in Evansville. At that time, the bank was comprised of several operations, including marketing, auditing, accounting, purchasing, consumer lending, and credit card departments, among others.

By the early 1980s, Old National Bank was still a relatively small banking business, with ten branches in southern Indiana. By 1982, however, management was ready to step up its expansion efforts, announcing the formation of the Old National Bancorp holding company. Anticipating the legalization of interstate banking by the state government, the officers of Old National Bank decided to form a corporation that would allow them to expand operations into other states when the opportunity presented itself. By the end of the year, Old National Bancorp was incorporated, and in 1985, when Indiana began permitting such corporations to go beyond the state's borders, Old National began acquiring other banks in nearby Kentucky and Illinois.

Throughout the late 1980s and early 1990s, Old National experienced rapid growth. ONB steadily expanded its asset base, and in 1994 it was ranked among the *Forbes* 500 in terms of total assets, which were reported at $4.15 billion. The following year, ONB was ranked 984th on the *Business Week* 1000, as assets increased an impressive 16 percent to reach $4.82 billion.

This steady growth showed no signs of abating in the mid-1990s. With a favorable banking environment characterized by low interest rates and low inflation, ONB was averaging three mergers per year, acquiring banks as well as affiliates that dealt exclusively with trusts, insurance, and investment services. Nevertheless, the company continued to emphasize its conservatism and stability, valuing safe, long-term gains for shareholders in its 1995 annual report.

Principal Subsidiaries

Old National Bank (Evansville, Ind.); ONB Bank (Bloomington, Ind.); Bank of Western Indiana (Covington, Ind.); First Citizens Bank and Trust Co. (Greencastle, Ind.); Dubois County Bank (Jasper, Ind.); People's Bank & Trust Co. (Mt. Vernon, Ind.); Orange County Bank (Paoli, Ind.); Gibson County Bank (Princeton, Ind.); Palmer-American National Bank (Danville, Ill.); First National Bank (Harrisburg, Ill.); Peoples National Bank (Lawrenceville, Ill.); Security Bank and Trust Co. (Mt. Carmel, Ill.); Citizens National Bank (Tell City, Ind.); Indiana State Bank (Terre Haute, Ind.); Merchants National Bank (Terre Haute, Ind.); First State Bank (Greenville, Ky.); Farmers Bank & Trust Co. (Madisonville, Ky.); Old National Trust Company; Old National Service Corporation; ONB Insurance; Indiana Old National Insurance Co.

Further Reading

Bronstein, Barbara F., ''In Evansville, All the Top Players are Local,'' *American Banker,* March 10, 1995, p. 7.

Meschi, Robert L., and Kurt Badenhausen, ''The Big Mo: FW Grades America's 100 Largest Banks on Their Earnings Momentum,'' *Financial World,* February 21, 1995.

Old National Bank 150th Anniversary, 1834–1984: From Evansville's First to Evansville's Largest, Evansville, Ind.: Old National Bank, 1984.

Perrone, Ellen, ''Old National to Increase Its Out-Of-State Influence,'' *Indianapolis Business Journal,* May 22, 1995, p. 9B.

—Michael Kelley

Ottaway Newspapers, Inc.

Route 416, P.O. Box 401
Campbell Hall, New York 10916
U.S.A.
(914) 294-8181

Wholly Owned Subsidiary of Dow Jones & Co., Inc.
Incorporated: 1946 as Empire Newspapers-Radio
Employees: 3,500
Sales: $252 million (1994)
SICs: 2711 Newspapers

Ottaway Newspapers, Inc. is the community newspapers subsidiary of the publishing giant Dow Jones & Co., Inc. With 20 newspapers scattered throughout the nation, the company has averaged around 550,000 total circulation during the 1990s. The company's largest circulation base is in the East, where its largest paper, New York's *Times Herald-Record,* has an average daily circulation of 87,000. Such papers as the Massachusetts-based *Peabody Times,* however, serve readerships of just over 3,000. Founded during the Great Depression by newspaper legend James Ottaway, Sr., the company has maintained a reputation throughout its history for adhering to the highest standards of editorial quality and reporting objectivity.

The story of one of the nation's most respected newspaper groups dates back to the fall of 1936 and the ambitions of a 25-year-old aspiring newspaper publisher, James H. Ottaway. Having grown up in the newspaper business—his father co-founded the *Port Huron (Michigan) Times-Herald* in 1900—Ottaway set out with his wife Ruth, with whom he had worked as editor of their college newspaper, to purchase a small newspaper and enter the publishing arena. When *Endicott Bulletin* of New York went on the market, the Ottaways, undaunted by their own limited financial resources, left their home in Port Huron to negotiate the purchase of their first paper. The owners of the *Bulletin,* however, were asking $50,000—in cash or certified check—for their modestly profitable paper, a sum the Ottaways did not have readily available. Showing a skill for bargaining that would serve him well throughout his career,

Ottaway convinced the stubborn proprietor of the *Bulletin* to accept a down payment of $22,500 and $4,500 a year at six percent interest. The Ottaways' publishing odyssey had begun.

Ottaway had selected the Endicott location largely because of the proximity of two large employers: Endicott Johnson, a long-time giant in the footwear manufacturing industry, and the rapidly expanding International Business Machines Corp. (IBM). Despite being in the midst of the Great Depression, which brought many local industries down to a four-day work week, Ottaway set his sights on transforming the *Bulletin* from a semi-weekly to a daily newspaper—a change that would require expanding the customer base of 4,000 by at least 3,000 to justify a higher advertising rate commensurate with a six-day operation.

Ottaway's strategy for expansion was simple: market a better editorial product. In the 1930s commercial radio was in its infancy and television was only in the early stages of development; newspapers were the main source of news and information. Having learned his craft by serving as the vice-president and assistant general manager of a Florida paper owned by his father, the young publisher stressed concise writing, thorough local coverage, and a strong editorial page covering local, state, national, and world issues. Assisting Ottaway in his bid to bolster sales was Barney French, a holdover from the previous owners' staff, whose selling strategies and business savvy were instrumental in the newspaper's rise to profitability. In 1939, two years after becoming a daily paper, the *Bulletin* recorded its first profits and would continue to operate in the black for almost two decades before perishing in 1960.

As evidence of Ottaway's emphasis on the editorial rather than the business end of publishing, the *Bulletin* introduced several innovations to the newspaper industry. Its typographical design, for instance, featured dropped column rules; lower case, flush left headlines; and bullets to indicate the important developments in a packaged story. Underlying this surface-level improvement was Ottaway's commitment to the quality of the content of his paper and the well-being of his employees. "I've always figured that if we put out a good editorial product, the business end would take care of itself," said Ottaway in Charles King's history of the company, *Ottaway Newspapers: The First*

50 Years. Indeed, while Ottaway focused on producing a good paper, he lived off his savings and investments and borrowed money from his mother, who served as his chief banker during the early years. Despite the difficult economic times, the *Bulletin* never missed a payroll.

Although World War II took Ottaway away from direct involvement in his growing newspaper business, it did not prevent him from planning for the future of his company. In mid-1944, while serving as a lieutenant at his Navy post in Philadelphia, he learned that the *Oneonta Star,* with its 9,000 New York subscribers, had been put up for sale. Although Ottaway was not mustered out of the military until March 1946, he made his first acquisition, purchasing the *Star* for a down payment of $50,000—most of which was advanced by his mother—and notes payable over 20 years at four percent. The purchase of the *Star* brought Ottaway his first Associated Press membership, an organization for which he would one day serve as chairman of the board.

Although Ottaway's purchase brought his company's long-term debt to $193,000, he continued to expand his operations through the 1940s. "Jim Ottaway," one veteran executive told King, "never worried about all the loans floating around. His mother told him he would die owing money." In 1946, after a profitable year for both of his papers, he formed a new corporation, Empire Newspapers-Radio, Inc., which, as its name suggested, ushered the company into the first of its 23 years in the radio business, applying for its first FCC license that same year. In keeping with his philosophy of plowing profits back into the operation, Ottaway purchased his third paper, the *Stroudsburg (Pennsylvania) Daily Record.* Having already earned a solid reputation for the editorial quality of his newspapers, Ottaway was able to make up for his financial weaknesses at the negotiation table by convincing publishers that he would improve the quality of the papers he took over.

In his first 15 years of business, Ottaway managed to acquire three newspapers, build two newspaper plants, and start three radio stations. While such accomplishments were made largely through complicated and creative financial negotiations, Ottaway continued to build his reputation for producing newspapers of only the highest quality. As circulation and profits increased, Ottaway invariably reinvested the money into the corporation, improving the technology of his existing papers and purchasing new ones. This would be the key to continued expansion: borrow money to generate more cash, and reinvest in the operation to make a better product.

Ottaway's aggressive growth strategy found a new ally in the 1950s and the free-market economic policies of the Eisenhower administration. With minimum government interference, he was able to add four more newspapers—three in Connecticut and one in New York—to his stable and bring the company into an era that would no longer be characterized by the huge financial risks of the early years. Chief among the major developments that signalled the company's stability was the restructuring plan carried out in 1953. Having obtained a favorable ruling from the Internal Revenue Service in a bid for tax-free reorganization, the company divided itself into five separate corporations: Empire, which served as the operating-holding company, and four wholly owned subsidiaries. The new orga-

nizing strategy was designed to give the company better control over borrowing, centralize purchasing, enhance corporate prestige, and provide more power for acquisitions. Perhaps more importantly, though, as Ottaway explained in a letter to the IRS reprinted by King, the strategy facilitated the "formation of a closely-knit organization."

With the new decade, came the addition of what would remain Ottaway's largest paper into the 1990s, the *Daily Record.* The first daily paper in the United States to be assembled by photo-composition and printed by the offset process, the *Record* was founded in 1956 and had gained a respectable circulation of 19,000 in its first three years of operation. But it was losing money fast. And when its proprietor, Jacob Kaplan, met the Ottaways at an airport on their way to a vacation in St. Thomas, informal negotiations began. Several months of negotiations later, Ottaway made his most costly acquisition to date, paying an estimated $1.5 million for the paper and its pioneering brand of "community journalism." As one of the paper's early editors explained, the paper's aim was to cover "mainstream issues at the local level" with editorial standards of in-depth and objective reporting not usually found in other papers in the category. Moreover, the paper would strive to avoid becoming "a mirror image of the community" and vowed not to succumb to the special interests represented by politicians or advertisers.

Two more multi-million-dollar expansions and the continued financial drain from expensive quality-improvement programs brought the company to a crossroads by the end of the decade. For the company to expand—and keep pace with the revolutionary era of electronic newspaper production on the horizon—the company had two options: merge or go public. The company had previously explored merger possibilities, but it had yet to find a party that it believed shared the Ottaway commitment to editorial quality. Not encumbered by any immediate financial trouble, the Ottaways could afford to wait for an offer that suited their high standards. And in the summer of 1969 that offer came: the publishing giant Dow Jones was interested in a deal. Once they were assured that they would lose neither their independence nor their editorial freedom, the Ottaways agreed to the terms of the agreement, receiving 914,038 shares of Dow Jones stock valued at approximately $36 million. Ottaway Newspapers, operating as a wholly owned subsidiary of Dow Jones, would benefit from the immense financial resources of its parent and would retain its autonomy and editorial freedom.

The merger with Dow Jones, to be sure, benefitted Ottaway's expansionary vision. During the first 15 years of its alliance with Dow Jones, Ottaway International Newspapers invested more than $88 million in adding to and improving its operations. The parent company did not turn down a single project. The 1970s, for instance, saw the company make 14 acquisitions, increasing total circulation to more than 500,000 by 1977. One of the papers purchased during this period of rapid expansion made national headlines with its groundbreaking story on a child pornography ring. The efforts of the Traverse City, Michigan *Eagle-Record* exemplified the traditional Ottaway commitment to getting the story—whatever the costs. What started as a tip that a boy's camp on an island in Lake Michigan was the setting for a child pornography ring evolved, after several weeks of tenacious reporting work, into the discovery of a nation-wide film and magazine distribution operation. With the help of other Ottaway reporters and police agencies throughout the country, the *Eagle-Record* gathered enough information to publish a series of articles that directly resulted in the passage of a landmark child pornography law. The governor, to honor the paper's efforts, signed the bill right in the *Eagle-Record* newsroom.

The 1980s brought a changing of the guard for Ottaway Newspapers: the retirement of the company founder and the passage of the corporate reins to his son, Jim Ottaway, Jr., who had worked in the family business since he began delivering papers as an 11-year-old. Although his father's 48 years of success in the business was difficult to follow, the younger Ottaway was well prepared to take over the company, having played an instrumental role in numerous acquisitions and other company decisions, such as the Dow Jones merger. Shortly after the 1984 transition, the new chief negotiated the purchase of the *Sun City (Arizona) News-Sun,* a six-day per week afternoon paper serving what the city's developers tabbed the "world's premier adult resort community." The fast-growing 15,000-circulation paper became the 22nd under the Ottaway banner.

Having helped the company stay abreast of the latest in technology during his career, Jim Ottaway, Jr., made sure that he would keep Ottaway at the forefront of the computer revolution. By 1985, the company had begun to standardize its business systems at group papers throughout the company while centralizing its operations in a New York-based computer center. Although such a move went against the general trend of corporate decentralization, the strategy actually enabled the company to lead the industry in using the very latest computer hardware and software. With the financial support of the technologically-minded Dow Jones, the company was able to outfit its diverse publishing sites with world-class equipment, without compromising local autonomy. Freed of the responsibility of system selection, installation, and maintenance, individual papers were able to devote more time to editorial and business decisions. Fueled by such technological improvements, Ottaway Newspapers followed a pattern of steady growth through-

out the 1980s, largely on the strength of operating improvements and increases in classified advertising. By 1988, total revenue had jumped to $231.7 million, a steady seven percent increase from the previous year typical of this period.

The early and mid-1990s saw the company's rate of growth slow. Although revenue and profits increased modestly, total circulation stayed around the 550,000 mark. Industry-wide weaknesses in retail and classified advertising, resulting from the recessionary conditions of the period, were largely responsible for the flattening of revenue and income. Increases in advertising rates and higher sales of preprinted advertisements, however, enabled the company to record modest gains. In 1994, for instance, revenue rose three percent to $252 million.

As Ottaway Newspapers entered the late 1990s, it was expected to benefit from an improved domestic economy and continued acquisitions, such as the March 1995 purchase of the *Salem (Massachusetts) Evening News,* which boasted a circulation of 30,000. In keeping with the vision of its founder, however, the company has maintained its principal emphasis on the editorial quality of its product. And in 1994 the company continued its award-winning tradition. Among the many Ottaway papers recognized for excellence were the *Middletown Times Herald-Record,* which was named "Newspaper of the Year" in the 30,000 to 100,000 category, by the New York State Society of Newspaper Editors, and the *Gloucester (Massachusetts) Daily Times,* which received the National Commission Against Drunk Driving's print media awareness award for its year-long series of articles on alcohol abuse within the community.

Further Reading

Giobbe, Dorothy, "Staffers at New York Paper Concerned About High-Level Departures," *Editor & Publisher,* September 23, 1995, p. 19.
King, Charles A., *Ottaway Newspapers: The First 50 Years,* Ottaway Newspapers, Inc., 1986.
Rosenberg, Jim, "Ottaway MIS Creates 'Living System,'" *Editor & Publisher,* November 16, 1991, p. 32.

—Jason Gallman

OTTO

Otto-Versand (GmbH & Co.)

Wandsbecker Strasse, 3-7
22179 Hamburg
D-2000
Germany
(49) 40 6461-0
Fax: (49) 40 6461 8571

Private Company
Incorporated: 1949
Employees: 37,700
Sales: DM19.25 billion (US$13.18 billion) (1994)
SICs: 5961 Catalog and Mail-Order Houses

While Otto-Versand (GmbH & Co.) is the world's largest mail-order company with subsidiaries and affiliates in Europe, Asia, and the United States, it remains very much a family concern, being majority-owned and operated by the Otto family. Based in Hamburg, Otto-Versand's three dozen catalog businesses in 16 countries included America's Spiegel and Eddie Bauer, France's 3 Suisses, Britain's Grattan, and Italy's Postalmarket. Founded in 1949, the same year as the West German nation, it has followed the country's rising fortunes from occupied state to reunification. In March 1990, after 40 years of steady growth, Otto-Versand became the first mail-order company to open an order center in the former East Germany.

The company was founded in Hamburg by Werner Otto, a refugee from Communist East Germany. Otto was one of a generation of extremely successful German entrepreneurs after World War II that included such famous names as Max Grundig, Axel Springer, and Heinx Nixdorf. These men seemed to appear from nowhere after the currency reforms of June of 1948 that restored confidence to consumers in the U.S., British, and French zones of occupied Germany. After three years of severe shortages, Germans had no faith in the money issued by the occupation powers. Cigarettes were a more popular parallel currency and the black market ruled supreme. However, Ludwig Erhard, director of the economic council for the joint Anglo-U.S. occupation zone, persuaded the Western Allies to accept his currency reform plan, which required the population

to exchange a limited amount of the old currency for the new Deutsche Mark. Goods suddenly appeared as if by magic and Germans went on a buying spree, first for food, then household goods, and finally clothes, which were to become the mainstay of the Otto-Versand mail-order empire. In this new market, Otto's formula was to offer low-cost fashion garments and cheap credit. For the first time, German customers were invoiced, rather than required to pay upon delivery. Later, Otto-Versand acquired its own Hanseatic Bank and offered three-, six-, and nine-month payment plans.

In retrospect, the mail-order market was ripe for development when 300 hand-bound copies of Otto's first, 14-page shoe catalog were distributed in 1950. In the then-new West Germany, retail distribution was still badly dislocated by World War II. Rationing and shortages meant that many goods had been unavailable for years in local shops and the range of choice was poor. City commercial centers had been heavily bombed, and the absence of Jews left a noticeable gap in retail distribution, as in many other fields where Jews had been successful and innovative before the rise of the Nazis. By 1950, however, West Germany had restored most of its postal and telephone systems, which were a relatively low-cost way to facilitate the distribution of goods in a country in which many store locations were still in ruins. German shop hours were restrictive, giving working people little opportunity to shop. Even in the early 1990s, all shops closed at 6:30 PM on weekdays. Retailers closed at 2 PM on Saturday afternoons, except on the first Saturday of the month, and were closed all day on Sundays. These hours were zealously protected by the shopworkers' union. In fact, the only way Otto-Versand was able to offer 24-hour ordering was to establish its telephone bank in Denmark and hire German-speaking operators.

In 1949 Ludwig Erhard became economics minister of the new Federal Republic of Germany and pushed through further reforms that, along with Marshall Plan aid, helped create the famous Wirtschaftswunder, or German economic miracle. Rationing and price controls were ended, duties on imports were lowered, and tax on overtime work was abolished. Erhard encouraged production of consumer goods to stimulate employment and economic revival. The boom lasted into the early 1990s and the wealth spread downward to lower-paid workers.

By 1953 living standards were higher than in 1938 and by 1961 Germany was one of the world's largest industrial powers. German incomes tripled between 1950 and 1965. In this rising tide of prosperity, mail order bridged gaps between supply and demand. Today, Germany remains by far Europe's largest annual per capita spender on mail order with 40 percent of the total European Community market. Seventy percent of all German households receive at least one catalog, and mail order accounts for five percent of all retail sales.

By 1951, Otto's sales had already reached DM1 million, generated by 1,500 catalogues of 20 pages each. In 1952, Werner Otto's next major innovation was to introduce a system whereby customers ordered through agents or representatives who forwarded the orders to the company's main office in Hamburg.

Werner Otto believes that his company owes its early success to this form of personal contact. It also enabled the company to keep costs and prices low through lower catalog numbers. By 1953, Otto-Versand had more than 100 employees, and the company's catalog had grown to 82 pages. A total of 37,000 copies were distributed, and sales reached DM5 million.

Unlike Werner Otto's archrival, Quelle, whose market strategy included a safety net of retail stores as well as a mail-order empire, Werner Otto concentrated on mail-order catalogs and representatives throughout the 1950s. From the 1960s telephone ordering to Otto's regional centers began to replace representatives. In the early 1990s, three-quarters of Otto's orders were placed by telephone.

In the United States, the United Kingdom, and a number of other countries, mail order has in the past suffered from a very downmarket image as many of its customers have been low-income bargain hunters or people living in remote rural areas, far from centers of population. By the mid-1950s, however, German consumers began to demand higher-quality goods, and Otto-Versand discovered that all kinds of potential customer groups could be successfully targeted. The company became most successful by going against the grain of conventional mail-order wisdom. Otto-Versand developed a methodical, computerized approach and gained knowledge of preferred customers in highly concentrated urban areas. Catalogs such as "Otto Heimwerker" targeted specific groups such as home enthusiasts, while "Post Shop" offered the latest styles to fashion-oriented youth. When the company later began its overseas expansion, areas such as Scandinavia, with its widely dispersed population, were ignored in favor of more urbanized, densely populated countries such as Holland and Belgium.

By the end of Otto's first decade in business, the company had more than 1,000 employees and sales of DM150 million. In the early 1960s, Otto-Versand became one of the first German companies to install integrated data-processing equipment. Otto-Versand used this equipment to become the first mail-order company to offer telephone ordering.

The 1966 Otto-Versand catalog had 828 pages and was now the largest in Germany. It had moved upmarket, featuring designers like Pierre Balmain, Jean Patou, Nina Ricci, and Christian Dior. In 1972 Otto-Versand launched Hermes Paketschnelldienst, a proprietary delivery service named for the mythic Greek messenger. Stores magazine called this operation

"a significant competitive edge, since it can offer domestic deliveries within 24 hours and free pick up of returned items." By the end of 1972, only 50 percent of all Otto-Versand shipments were being handled by the German Federal Post Office.

By 1974, the year of the company's 25th anniversary, Otto-Versand felt strong enough to begin a period of international expansion, which intensified in the 1980s. The company's first move was into France, where it acquired 50 percent of 3 Suisses, the second largest mail-order firm in France. In 1979, Otto-Versand founded Otto BV, which has grown to become one of the largest mail-order companies in the Netherlands. Otto-Versand formed partnerships with Venca, the largest Spanish mail-order company, and Austria's 3 Pagen. In 1974 Otto-Versand acquired an interest in Heine, a company specializing in luxury clothing and household goods. At the same time Otto-Versand continued to expand within Germany, acquiring Schwab in 1976, Alba Moda in 1982, the linen and home textiles company Witt Weiden in 1987, and a holding in Sport-Scheck in 1988.

Michael Otto succeeded his father as chairman in 1981. Having set up his own financial and real estate business, the second-generation leader joined his father's company in 1971, advancing from textile purchasing through the corporate ranks. Michael Otto pushed his family's company to undertake its riskiest venture to date when it seized an opportunity to buy the Spiegel catalog sales company in the United States. Although Spiegel was still a U.S. household name, its fortunes had been declining for years. Like the early Otto-Versand company, it had concentrated on low-cost women's fashions. Otto-Versand realized that the U.S. mail-order market had changed and gambled by taking the entire operation upmarket. The image makeover was accompanied by a thorough fiscal reorganization and productivity enhancements.

Spiegel's sales quadrupled within its first two years under its new management, and it had become the United States' biggest mail-order company by the end of the decade. The Spiegel venture was so successful that in 1988 Otto-Versand extended its interests in the United States by buying Eddie Bauer Ltd. This company had started as an Alaska expedition outfitter based in Seattle, Washington, but had grown into a national network of stores and mail order. Less well known than the famous Maine outdoor clothing company L.L. Bean, it rode some similar trends to prosperity in the 1970s and 1980s, such as the desire of many affluent young Americans to participate in outdoor activities or, at least, to affect a healthy outdoor image.

The Otto-Versand company bought Eddie Bauer, with its predominantly male market, ostensibly to complement Spiegel, which specialized in women's clothing. Through those two companies and also Honeybee, a high-fashion catalog and retail store chain, Otto-Versand appealed to the upwardly mobile young, thought to be an easy target because they had high incomes and little time to shop in retail outlets.

Otto-Versand did not want to be outdone by its rivals in the former East Germany. By March 1990, three months before formal economic unification, Otto-Versand had opened mail-order centers in Leipzig, Dresden, and the former East Berlin. By July of that year, Otto-Versand was the only mail-order house to boast a comprehensive distribution network in all five of the new federal states, the result of an earlier agreement with an East German association of consumer cooperatives. Sales in these new states exceeded DM1.1 billion, more than double the company's original forecast, and more than 1,000 order centers were soon established throughout the former East Germany.

Initially the company was less interested in the other former communist countries in Eastern Europe, but moves by Quelle and other competitors rapidly changed Otto's outlook. With the formation of Otto-Epoka mbH, Warsaw, a joint venture, Otto-Versand entered the Polish market in May 1990. Order centers were established in Czechoslovakia, Hungary, and the Soviet Union. At the same time, Otto-Versand worked to strengthen its presence in Western Europe in anticipation of the unified European market. In 1988 Otto-Versand acquired a 75 percent stake in Euronova S.R.L., the third-largest Italian mail-order house.

Otto-Versand had wanted to expand into the United Kingdom for many years before its well publicized £165 million bid for Grattan, the mail-order arm of the troubled Next retailer, finally succeeded in March of 1991. In 1986, it had been outbid by Next, which paid £300 million, but in 1991 it was prepared to pay a premium of £15 million above a rival £150 million bid by Sears plc, which controls the Freemans mail-order house, to secure this U.K. base. Grattan had a computerized warehouse system, a huge customer base, and 13 percent of the U.K. mail-order market, but it had been devastated by the recession of the early 1990s and a postal strike. Its parent company, Next, desperately needed to refinance a convertible bond issue. Otto-Versand had already begun to enter the U.K. market in a joint venture with Fine Art Developments Ltd., a greeting card company. In December 1988 Otto-Versand launched Rainbow Home Shopping Ltd., a Bradford mail-order firm, and announced that Rainbow would join forces with Grattan, also Bradford-based.

Otto-Versand also made significant inroads into largely untapped Asia, forming a joint venture with Sumitomo Corporation, Otto Sumisho Inc., in 1986. The German company hoped to develop this market, which boasted many of the characteristics of markets in which it had been successful elsewhere, namely urban concentrations of the newly affluent and fashion-conscious. Otto-Versand took Eddie Bauer to Japan in 1993. From the Japanese base, the company developed similar markets on the Pacific Rim, including a 1994 strategic alliance with Burlingtons' in India known as Otto-Burlington's Mail Order Pt. Ltd. Initial results were encouraging.

The company did not shy away from new technology or new business opportunities in the early 1990s, becoming Germany's first mail-order firm to offer an interactive CD-ROM catalog in 1994, for example. Having dabbled in the travel industry since the early 1980s, Otto-Versand stepped up its efforts in this segment with the 1993 acquisition of a controlling interest in Reisland GmbH's 60 travel agencies. The company also bought two British collection agencies in 1994.

Retail industry analysts remained divided about the impact of the single European market on the prospects for mail-order firms. Companies like Otto-Versand were expected to achieve economies of scale with pan-European operations, and the development of satellite networks increased opportunities for home shopping, but mail-order firms still had to cope with problems of distance and national distribution networks. Proposed European Community directives also threatened the use of mailing lists. With 25 percent of the European Community market, Otto-Versand was also concerned not to breach competition laws. In recognition of this situation, Otto-Versand announced that it would continue its policy of operating through national subsidiaries and allowing a degree of freedom to local subsidiaries familiar with local customs and markets.

In his 14 years at Otto-Versand's helm, Michael Otto built his father's company into an international retail colossus and garnered high praise from analysts and competitors alike in the process. His "green" side was evinced by environment-friendly business policies like reducing energy consumption and selecting environmentally-sensitive products. He was named Environment Manager of the Year in 1991 and created the Michael Otto Foundation for the Environment in 1993. In 1988, Otto-Versand introduced employee equity ownership through participation rights. By 1990 participation rights capital increased by DM4 million to DM10 million, and one-third of employees were participating in the profit-sharing scheme. Michael Otto's combination of business sense and social awareness helped win him 1995's National Retail Federation International Award.

These progressive strategies did not preclude growth or profitability. Annual sales increased 17.2 percent from DM16.42 in 1992 to DM19.25 in 1994, and net income increased 32 percent from DM369.83 million to DM488.07 million during the same period. By the mid-1990s Otto-Versand was represented by 36 mail-order firms on three continents and in a total of 16 countries.

Principal Subsidiaries

SCHWAB VERSAND Aktiengesellschaft (94%); Handelsgesellschaft Heinrich Heine GmbH & Co., Karlsrue; Bon Prix Handelsgesellschaft A.G. (Switzerland); Corso Handelsgesellschaft mbH; Oktavia Gesellschaft fuer Bekleidung m.b.H.; Media Handelsgesellschaft mbH; Reiseland GmbH (51%); OTTO-SUMISHO Inc. (Japan; 51%); Grattan Plc (United Kingdom; 84%); Together Production Ltd. (Hong Kong; 60%); Otto-Versand International GmbH; 3 Suisses France S.A. (France); KG Hermes Versand Service G.m.b.H. & Co.; Hermes Versand Service Berlan G.m.b.H.; Hermes Technischer Kundendienst GmbH & Co.; Deutschlier Inkasso-Dienst B.V. (Netherlands); COLLECTION AGENCIES PLC (United Kingdom); Hanseatic Versicherungedienst GmbH; Hanseatic Bank GmbH & Co.; OHG FEGRO-SELGROS Gesellschaft fuer Grosshandel mbH & Co. (50%); FCB Fureizeit-Club Betreuings-GmbH & Co. (50%); 3 Suisse International S.A. (France; 50%); Beaute Createurs S.A. (France; 50%); OEID Inkasso-ienst Gesellschaft mbH (Austria; 50%).

Further Reading

Krienke, Mary, "Michael Otto," *Stores*, January 1995, p.150.
Miller, Karen L., "Otto the Great Rules in Germany," *Business Week*, January 31, 1994, p. 70J.
Paine, Mandi, and Suzanne Bidlake, "Catalogues Face a New Order, *Marketing*, January 31, 1991, p. 2.

—Clark Siewert
—updated by April Dougal Gasbarre

Pamida Holdings Corporation

8800 F Street
Omaha, Nebraska 68127
U.S.A.
(402) 339-2400
Fax: (402) 596-7326

Public Company
Incorporated: 1963 as Pamida, Inc.
Employees: 7,200
Sales: $712.7 million (1995)
Stock Exchanges: American
SICs: 5331 Variety Stores; 6719 Holding Companies,
   Not Elsewhere Classified

Owner of a leading discount general merchandise chain, Pamida Holdings Corporation operates 181 stores in 15 midwestern, north central, and Rocky Mountain states. From its inception, Pamida targeted small, rural communities as the preferred location for its discount stores, quickly expanding into trading areas with populations below 15,000. Able to expand with virtually no local discount competition, Pamida flourished during its inaugural decade, establishing a foundation that would support the company during the 1970s, 1980s, and into the 1990s. By the mid-1990s, the company operated 40 in-store pharmacies as a complementary money-earner to its mainstay business of selling apparel, toys, home furnishings, housewares, stationery, and other merchandise.

Much of what defined Pamida during the 1990s was established during the 1960s, when the company's founders devised a strategic plan that would underpin the success and proliferation of their discount, general merchandise stores for decades to come. From its origination, Pamida established itself as a regional chain focused exclusively on small, rural markets, targeting trading areas and towns too small to support stores operated by large, national chains. By establishing a presence in a host of small communities with populations ranging between 5,000 and 15,000, Pamida avoided the pernicious pressures of competition and quickly secured a solid position in what previously had been largely untapped markets.

For the implementation and refinement of the winning strategy, the company was indebted to its founders, D.J. Witherspoon and Lee Wegener, two men of divergent business philosophies and contrasting personalities who, despite their differences, orchestrated the development of Pamida during its make-or-break formative years. One referred to himself as a "cotton picker from Texas," while the other was a self-described "corn picker from Nebraska." Chiefly responsible for creating the Pamida empire that dominated rural America during the 1990s was Witherspoon, the "cotton picker from Texas," whose magnetic charm, energetic spirit, and sanguine business perspective pervaded Pamida's operation for nearly 20 years. Witherspoon's effusive and infective optimism would carry Pamida through its most crucial decade of existence, enabling the son of a West Texas migrant farmer to realize riches and success that belied his humble origins.

Born in 1912, Witherspoon graduated from Southwestern State Teachers College in 1936. He taught mathematics and coached football at Leveland, Texas' high school before moving to Omaha, Nebraska in 1938, ready to start a new career. After his arrival in Omaha, Witherspoon, along with his father-in-law Lewis Turner, founded Gibson Products Company, which warehoused and sold novelties to "wagon jobbers," or people who travelled across the country selling merchandise from trucks. By the late 1940s, after roughly a decade of stewarding the fortunes of Gibson Products, Witherspoon began selling cosmetics, medicines, and similar products to grocery stores, operating as a "rack-jobber" during the post-war years.

After more than a decade in the rack-jobbing business, Witherspoon unwittingly made a pivotal move in 1962 toward the establishment of Pamida by acquiring Marks Distributing Company, a wholesaler of rack-jobbing items such as socks, housewares, and underwear. Though Witherspoon's connection to the rack-jobbing business would play a substantial role in the founding of Pamida, more important was the beginning of a business relationship engendered by the purchase of Marks Distributing. One of the employees of Marks Distributing was "a corn picker from Nebraska," Lee Wegener, a two-year employee with more than 20 years experience in the retail industry. Together, Witherspoon and Wegener would create one of the fastest-growing chains of discount stores in the United States during the 1960s, employing a business philosophy that represented a fusion of their distinct personalities.

Witherspoon was compulsive, inspirational, and irrepressibly ambitious. Wegener, in contrast, was cautious, reserved, and conservative in his approach to business. As Wegener explained to *Fortune* magazine after Pamida had developed into a 170-unit chain spread across an 11-state area, "If it wouldn't have been for me, we'd have gone broke, and if it wouldn't have been for him [Witherspoon] we'd have only about 20 stores." The two men were opposites, but with Witherspoon providing the motivational drive to propel the company forward and with Wegener prudently checking and redirecting Pamida's expansion, their differences synthesized into an enormously successful business enterprise that was predicated on their one common bond: familial roots imbedded in rural America.

After their introduction following Witherspoon's 1962 acquisition of Marks Distributing, the two soon-to-be founders of Pamida worked together traveling the countryside as rack-jobbers until a disheartening day in the fall of 1963. A sales presentation the two had made to a potential customer in Chariton, Iowa had yielded disappointing results, shaking Witherspoon's and Wegener's confidence in the rack-jobbing business. They felt their sales pitch had been strong, but the customer was not convinced. Discouraged, the pair mused about their future prospects as they drove through Iowa after their failure. When they passed through Knoxville, Iowa and noticed an empty furniture store abutting the town's courthouse square, however, their future became clear; Witherspoon and Wegener decided to enter the discount business. The empty furniture store would serve as the proving ground for their new venture.

Foreshadowing the rapid expansion that would unfold, Witherspoon and Wegener rented another store 25 miles away in Oskaloosa, then hurriedly set about preparing the Knoxville store for its grand opening. Shelves were constructed, walls were painted, and suppliers were located for items like work clothes and auto accessories that were not available through Witherspoon's and Wegener's rack-jobbing business. In November 1963, the doors to the Knoxville store were opened to the public, creating a remarkable surge of excitement among the town's residents. Sales after the first day hovered around $5,000, or six times the amount Witherspoon and Wegener had calculated as the weekly break-even point for their fledgling store. Crowds during the day were nearly uncontrollable, forcing Witherspoon and Wegener to bar entry into the store, letting shoppers enter one by one as customers exited the store. The opening was a tremendous success, exceeding even Witherspoon's most optimistic expectations. When the Oskaloosa store opened three weeks later, it recorded similar success, attracting crowds of patrons who were lured by Witherspoon's and Wegener's unique format.

At the time of the Knoxville and Oskaloosa store openings, rural America had been largely ignored by the country's national discount chains. For the residents of the nation's smaller communities, the opportunity to purchase merchandise at bargain prices generally required taking a long trip to the bigger cities, a trek that farm families would endure to realize the advantages of bargain shopping. Beginning with the openings of Witherspoon's and Wegener's discount stores in Knoxville and Oskaloosa, however, such journeys became unnecessary, enabling the residents of the two small towns to shop for bargains at home. Inside the stores were popular items usually found in drugstores and hardware stores, plus clothing and automotive accessories, all under one roof. It was a winning combination—low prices, one-stop shopping convenience, and an inventory tailored to the needs and tastes of farming communities—that enjoyed resounding success, educing Witherspoon and Wegener to open additional stores in small, rural communities.

Expansion came quickly following the initial success of the two stores in Knoxville and Oskaloosa. By the end of 1964, Pamida's first full year of operation, sales amounted to $8.5 million. Four years later, annual sales had climbed to $28 million, with 45 stores in Iowa, Minnesota, Kansas, Missouri, Wisconsin, and Nebraska composing the Pamida chain. Although the stores were owned and operated by Pamida, a name derived from the first two letters of Witherspoon's three sons, Pat, Mike, and David, individually they operated under the names "Gibson Discount Center," "Super D Discount Center," and "Top Brands Discount Center." By 1969, the year Pamida, Inc. became a publicly owned company, there were 72 stores operating under various names, all of which contributed to Pamida's nearly $44 million in annual sales at the time.

As Pamida entered the 1970s, expansion continued at a robust clip, outpacing the rate of growth recorded by the national discount chains. The strategy of targeting small, rural midwestern towns with populations ranging between 5,000 and 15,000 was proving to be highly effective, positioning the company as perhaps the most successful regional discount-store chain in the country. With cost-conscious Wegener assiduously monitoring the company's daily operation and Witherspoon exhorting employees and management forward, uninterrupted, energetic growth had been achieved without sacrificing profitability. By the early 1970s, when annual sales had eclipsed $100 million, Pamida was consistently ranking as the largest moneymaker per dollar of sales in the country, with its 169 stores enjoying a near-monopoly position in an 11-state region from Kansas and Missouri to the Canadian border and into Wyoming and Idaho.

Like the first two stores in Knoxville and Oskaloosa, nearly all of Pamida's units were acquired from existing businesses. Of the 169 stores in operation in 1972, only 18 were new structures. The rest were converted garages, skating rinks, theaters, and grocery stores, creating an eclectic assortment of stores that matched the motley group of store managers employed by the company, many of whom came from working backgrounds far afield from discount store management. Witherspoon's management style, described by colleagues as "inspirational," had created a loyal, hard-working retinue of Pamida employees, nearly all of whom shared Witherspoon's and Wegener's rural roots. Among the store managers who presided over the operation of individual Pamida units were former welders, gas station attendants, mental hospital attendants, bartenders, policemen, mechanics, and used-car dealers, each lured to make the leap into discount store management by the infectious enthusiasm generated by Witherspoon.

No two Pamida-owned stores were alike, but all shared one characteristic: enviable success. By the early 1970s, the Pamida chain was roughly as large as it was during the mid-1990s, at least in terms of the number of units operated by the company. In the years ahead, the number of stores operated by the company would increase only marginally. Its sales volume and the size of its stores, however, would continue to grow. Slowly, yet inexorably, large, national chains such as Wal-Mart Stores and Super Valu Stores began to encroach upon increasingly smaller markets, threatening to invade the small towns dominated by Pamida.

Although the population of the towns in which Pamida operated averaged 8,700 (too small for a national discount chain to survive), Witherspoon and Wegener responded to the potential incursion by their much larger competition by increasing the size of their stores. Beginning in the early 1970s, Pamida began replacing its existing stores, which averaged 8,500 square feet in selling space, with new stores three to four times as large. As the decade unfolded and Pamida's sales volume steadily swelled, the emphasis moved to converting existing stores into larger stores rather than on increasing the number of units operated by the company.

By the beginning of the 1980s, after shoring up its market presence during the 1970s, Pamida stood well-positioned for the new decade, its grip still firm on rural, midwestern America. Sweeping changes in the ownership of Pamida and in its management lay ahead, though, beginning in 1981, when the nearly 20-year era of Witherspoon and Wegener leadership came to an end. The two founders had spent nearly two decades orchestrating the growth of their entrepreneurial venture, creating an impressive and highly successful business. But by the beginning of the 1980s they were ready to end their association with the company. In 1981, Witherspoon, who owned the majority of Pamida's stock, sold the company to its employees through an employee stock ownership plan financed with borrowed money. The $55 million transaction ranked Pamida as the largest company on the New York Stock Exchange ever to be purchased by its employees.

Pamida operated as an employee-owned company for the first half of the 1980s, until another switch in ownership occurred in 1986. In July, top management and CitiCorp Capital Investors, Ltd. acquired a principal financial interest in Pamida, paying $168 million for control over the 164-unit chain. By this point, annual sales hovered around $500 million, up from $333 million three years earlier. Despite the signs of vitality, however, the company began to reel from mounting debt in the wake of the management-led leveraged buyout.

The financing involved in the two ownership changes had saddled Pamida with sizeable bills as the company entered the late 1980s, exacerbating the deleterious effect of competition from large, national chains. Although Pamida had always avoided direct competition with the Wal-Marts of the discount world, decades of expansion by regional and national chains had left only the smallest markets without at least one general merchandiser of Pamida's ilk. Consequently, debt and increasing competitive pressures forced Pamida to take action during the late 1980s. Merchandising layouts were revamped, with a greater emphasis placed on higher profit apparel items, and inventory and sales performance data were computerized and centralized. After these changes were effected, Pamida once again became a publicly owned company in 1990, enabling it to raise much needed cash.

More intensive efforts to relieve the nagging problems associated with Pamida's debt were taken in March 1993, when the company restructured its debt, ceding it greater financial stability and providing it with sufficient means to continue expansion. Once the restructuring was complete and management was reorganized, Pamida moved forward, striving to reduce its involvement in saturated markets and to increase the square footage of its stores. Prototype stores in 1994 were in excess of 40,000 square feet (considerably larger than the existing average store size of 28,000), and for the past several years had been outfitted with in-store pharmacies.

As Pamida entered the mid-1990s, management was seeking to reduce the company's exposure to large, national discount chains. In 1992 Pamida competed against Wal-Mart stores in 45 percent of its markets, but by late 1995, after closing several stores, the percentage had declined to 34 percent and was expected to continue its decline into the late 1990s. Future plans called for bolstering apparel, jewelry, and accessories sales, which accounted for 22 percent of sales in 1995, with a long-term objective set at increasing the apparel mix to 28 percent of total sales. By placing a greater emphasis on apparel and apparel-related items and continuing to increase the number of Pamida units, the company hoped to build upon the $712.7 million generated in sales in 1995, and to boost revenues past $1 billion by 1997.

Principal Subsidiaries

Pamida, Inc.; Seaway Importing Company; Pamida Transportation Company

Further Reading

Conley, John H., ''Pamida, Inc.,'' *Wall Street Transcript,* October 10, 1977, p. 48,383.
Greene, Joan, ''Off the Shelf,'' *Barron's,* November 10, 1975, p. 5.
Halverson, Richard, ''Market Woes Force Pamida to Postpone Sale of Stock,'' *Discount Store News,* September 3, 1990, p. 1.
Kelly, Mary Ellen, ''Pamida Holds Its Ground Against Big Shot Chains,'' *Discount Store News,* January 6, 1992, p. 7.
Malanga, Steve, ''Top Management, Investors Offer to Purchase Pamida from ESOP,'' *Discount Store News,* May 12, 1986, p. 1.
''Pamida Inc. Considers Plan to Sell Its Assets to Firm to Be Formed,'' *Wall Street Journal,* June 23, 1980, p. 29.
''Pamida's Plan to Sell Most Assets, Operations to New Firm Cleared,'' *Wall Street Journal,* January 14, 1981, p. 43.
''Pamida Will Alter Plan to Sell Assets, Business,'' *Wall Street Journal,* October 13, 1980, p. 11.
Robertson, Wyndham, ''Pamida Doesn't Know What It's Doing, But It Sure makes a Lot of Money,'' *Fortune,* August 1972, p. 143.
''Staying in Smaller Markets,'' *Chain Store Age Executive,* February 1995, p. 38.

—Jeffrey L. Covell

Papa John's International, Inc.

11492 Bluegrass Parkway
Louisville, Kentucky 40299
U.S.A.
(502) 266-5200
Fax: (502) 266-2925

Public Company
Incorporated: 1993
Employees: 4,000
Sales: $161.5 million (1994)
Stock Exchanges: NASDAQ
SICs: 5812 Eating places; 6794 Patent Owners & Lessors

Papa John's International, Inc. is widely recognized as the fastest-growing pizza chain in the United States. The company operates and franchises pizza delivery and carry-out restaurants under the trademark "Papa John's" in 21 states primarily in the Midwest, Mideast, South, and Southeast. Papa John's expanded to more than 750 stores after the opening of its first store in 1985, roughly doubling its size every year well into the 1990s. Although Papa John's competes in a market dominated by such giants as Pizza Hut, Domino's, and Little Caesar's, it has managed to carve out a highly profitable niche by concentrating on four menu items: pizza (which is accompanied by a container of the company's special garlic sauce and two pepperoncinis); breadsticks; cheese sticks; and canned soft drinks. The company devotes its energy and resources to improving delivery time and product quality.

Papa John's was born in what was once a broom closet in the back of a southern Indiana tavern. The idea for the company ranked number one on *Business Week*'s 1994 list of "Hot Growth Companies" originated in the mind of a 23-year-old entrepreneur who felt that he knew how to make a better pizza. In September 1983, shortly after attaining a business degree from Ball State University in just three years, John Schnatter returned to his hometown of Jeffersonville, Indiana to take over the management of Mick's Lounge, a bar co-owned by his father. The tavern, noted for its fist fights and biker clientele, was physically and financially decrepit; beer dealers and other vendors even refused to give the establishment credit. In his first week, Schnatter, $64,000 in debt with a long list of angry creditors, cleaned and repainted the bar, determined to make the most of his opportunity. He lowered and simplified beer prices, while adding more pool tables and video games. And he began to market the bar through promotions that resulted in word-of-mouth advertising. In just three months, he had paid off half of his debt.

Although Schnatter quickly succeeded in resurrecting the bar to profitability a month later, his ambitions extended far beyond the walls of a smoke-filled beer joint. In March of 1984, he sold his business partner, Bob Ehringer, who had purchased the elder Schnatter's stake in the business, on the idea of supplementing revenues by serving pizza out of the bar's broom closet. With $1,600 worth of equipment and ingredients, Papa John's was born. Schnatter tore down a wall with a sledge hammer to make room for an eight-by-ten-foot kitchen. During those early days Schnatter and his partner worked from 9 a.m. to 1:30 a.m., sleeping in the bar so they would not miss any calls. For the first six months, the pizza business generated only $1,000 to $1,500 a week and was financially dependent on the bar. But as the fledgling establishment became better known, sales increased. By March 1985, the two partners, along with a few helpers, were making 3,000 to 4,000 pizzas a week.

With Mick's Lounge financially sound and not enough room in the "broom closet" kitchen to keep up with the growing demand for pizzas, Schnatter and Ehringer set their eyes on an empty retail space next door where they could open their first restaurant. Having gained valuable experience working in several restaurants in high school and in college preparing himself for such an opportunity, Schnatter was eager to put his ideas into practice. "One day he sat at his desk in the dorm and had a menu laid out, along with a company logo," recalled Schnatter's college roommate in *Business First*. "Papa John's was on his mind even on campus."

But before the 23-year-old entrepreneur could launch his new venture, his father and top supporter died. "You're supposed to feel sorry for yourself, and I could have sat at the bar and moped," he said in *Business First*. "But I'm pretty tough on myself, and I got on with it." Having inherited his father's unwavering determination, Schnatter acquired the site for his restaurant through sweat equity. With the help of his uncle, Bill Schnatter, who became a partner in charge of store layout and construction, and Ehringer, who took over operations and maintenance, Schnatter, the firm's president and chief marketer, opened his first restaurant.

In January 1986 the company was incorporated and able to stand on its own. A year later Schnatter and Ehringer sold Mick's Lounge so they could devote more time to Papa John's. The strategy that brought them such rapid success was simple: make the best pizza and sell it at a competitive price. What Schnatter had learned while working in pizza joints as a teenager and a college student was to keep his product line focused. While other restaurants offered salad bars and chicken wings, he devoted his energy to producing the "Perfect Pizza" (a slogan that would later become a registered company trademark) and delivering it to customers in a timely fashion. Behind the focused strength of this strategy, Papa John's generated revenues of $500,000 in its first year and opened two more restaurants in the "Kentuckiana" region.

To prepare the company for more serious expansion, the visionary Schnatter built a commissary near corporate headquarters in Louisville's Bluegrass Industrial Park to supply his stores with fresh pizza dough and spices. In the commissary, giant mixers turn bags of flour mix and warm water into dough balls of several sizes. The dough is then chilled until it is firm enough to be shipped to individual stores twice a week and shaped into pizza crusts or breadsticks. The commissary system has frequently been cited by industry analysts and company officials as a key factor in the success of Papa John's. The system not only reduces labor costs and reduces wastes because the dough is pre-measured; it, perhaps more importantly, maintains control over the consistency of the product. In many other restaurants, for instance, the least-experienced employees are responsible for making the dough because it is such a messy job.

Not only did this centralized production facility furnish all of the Papa John's stores with the same high-quality ingredients for their pizzas, but it lowered start-up costs for new restaurants by saving them the cost of expensive equipment. From this early stage in the company's history, Schnatter made sure that he expanded the production capacity of his commissary system before he added new restaurants. Accordingly, four additions were made to the company's first commissary by the end of the decade and the opening of the 23rd Papa John's.

In 1989 Schnatter enlisted the services of pizza industry veteran Dan Holland to help the company strengthen its financial base and fashion a strategy for further growth. A former executive with Mr. Gatti's and Pizza Hut, Holland, who took over as company president in 1990, brought more than a decade of experience in the pizza business to Papa John's. That same year, which brought in $15 million in revenue, Ehringer, who did not share his partner's expansionary vision, sold his 40 percent share in the company to Schnatter.

During the early 1990s the company embarked on a phenomenal pattern of growth, expanding to 200 restaurants and $82

million in sales. At least part of the success was due to a surge in the overall pizza market, which grew at the fastest rate of any major segment of the restaurant industry during the mid-1980s and early 1990s. Pizza sales also benefited from the larger trend toward more off-premise food consumption; pizza was, to some extent, viewed as one of the leading replacements for the home-cooked meal and realized a greater increase in sales than other large quick-service segments, such as hamburgers and chicken. Having established itself from the beginning as primarily a delivery and carry-out restaurant, Papa John's was poised to take full advantage of this growing demand.

Another contributing factor to the company's success during this period was its ability to keep start-up costs low for new franchises during the recession of the early 1990s. Whereas some restaurant franchises cost upwards of $1 million, a Papa John's could be purchased during this period for less than $100,000. This bargain price, combined with the company's profitable history, attracted a number of high-profile franchisees into the Papa John's stable. Such restauranteurs as Rick Sherman, former president of Rally's and Church's Fried Chicken chains; Frank Carney, one of the founders of Pizza Hut; Ed Johnson, founder of Grandy's; and Jack Laughery, former chairman and CEO of Hardee's, all opened several stores.

After recording total revenues of close to $50 million in 1992, having roughly doubled its size every year since 1986, the company looked to raise money to pay off debts and finance continued expansion. In June 1993, Papa John's went public with an initial offering of 1.45 million shares at $13 a share. As evidence of the strong faith of the financial community in the company, the stock closed at $20, generating proceeds of about $12 million after costs. The stock sale helped to strengthen the company's financial base while providing capital for entrance into three new markets: Atlanta, Georgia; Orlando, Florida; and Charlotte, North Carolina.

Geographic expansion required the building of two more commissaries to supply the new stores during the early 1990s; one in Orlando and one in Raleigh, North Carolina. The commissaries, which were designed to serve a 400-mile radius, enabled the company to open its 400th store in 1993, nearly doubling the size of the company from the previous year. Total revenue, likewise, increased more than 80 percent, surpassing the $89-million mark.

Just as Papa John's was nearing the 500-store milestone in mid-1994, it was named by *Business Week* as the nation's best-run small business, based on three-year results in sales growth, earnings growth, and return on invested capital. The attention the company received from this report, as well as from other reports by business and industry publications ranging from *Forbes* to *Nation's Restaurant News*, helped the company to attract management talent and gain momentum in the investment community. Taking advantage of this energy, Papa John's completed two common stock offerings during the year, raising an additional $35 million and preparing the way for further expansion.

In keeping with the company's strategy of ensuring that the commissary system is developed to support the growth and geographical expansion of restaurants, Papa John's constructed its fourth commissary in Jackson, Mississippi during 1994. The company also finalized plans to build a full-service commissary in Orlando to replace the existing dough-producing facility. The additional production capacity provided the infrastructure to serve up to 1,200 restaurants in 20 states. The timely expansion of this system, according to many industry experts, enabled the company to continue its ability to monitor and control product quality and consistency, while lowering food costs.

Papa John's, having set quality standards for all products used in its restaurants, required all of its franchises to purchase dough and spices from the commissary. What is more, virtually all of the franchises, although they were not required to do so, purchased their other supplies from the commissary as well, taking advantage of the lower prices offered. While the commissaries helped to improve quality control and efficiency by providing each individual franchise with the same products, they also facilitated the growth of the company by lowering start-up costs. With the commissary system, there was no need for franchises to purchase expensive dough-making equipment and train their employees how to use it.

Throughout Papa John's tremendous growth during its first ten years of operation, its marketing programs targeted the delivery area of each restaurant, primarily through print materials in direct mail and store-to-door couponing. In 1994, for instance, approximately 80 percent of all purchases were made using a coupon, at a savings of about 17 percent. As the company has become more affluent and attempted to serve a larger geographic area, it has increasingly supplemented local marketing efforts with radio and television advertising. To maximize the resources of its individual restaurants, the company has also created the Papa John's Marketing Fund, Inc., a non-profit corporation that oversees market-wide marketing programs, such as radio, television, and billboards. The Marketing Fund, which is supported by required contributions from each store, also provides company-owned and franchised restaurants with catalogs and toll-free numbers for uniforms and promotional items.

As Papa John's entered the late 1990s, it had no plans to change the simple formula that has placed it in position to become the nation's fourth-largest pizza chain. Schnatter has promised to keep what Bill McDowell of *Restaurants and Institutions* magazine has called "an almost obsessive focus on the core product." No additions to the four core menu items—pizza, breadsticks, cheesesticks, and canned soft drinks—had

been planned. As Schnatter stated in a 1995 letter to stockholders, Papa John's does not intend to follow the lead of its competitors who "clutter their menus with chicken wings, salads, pasta and subs." Rather, the company will direct its energy and resources towards "delivering the Perfect Pizza" to more people and in a larger geographical region.

With more than 250 restaurants projected to open by the close of 1995, the company planned to open a new distribution center in Dallas in early 1996 and a full-service commissary in Denver during the latter part of 1996 to facilitate western expansion. The ambitious Schnatter hoped to eventually control a 3,000- to 4,000-store empire that would rival the likes of Pizza Hut, Domino's, and Little Caesar's. This broadened vision of the future may also entail a greater emphasis on television spots and other forms of electronic media. According to Schnatter's estimates, 50 percent of those who have not tried Papa John's have never heard of Papa John's. "Once they've tried us, though," he says. "Nine out of ten come back."

Principal Subsidiaries

PJFood Service, Inc.; Papa John's USA, Inc.; Printing & Promotions, Inc.; PJFS of Mississippi, Inc.

Further Reading

Cooper, Ron, "Focus Was Key Ingredient in Schnatter's Success," *Business First-Louisville*, June 12, 1995.
——, "Papa John's Rolls Out the Dough," *Business First-Louisville*, December 16, 1991, p. 1.
Egerton, Judith, "Papa John's at 10: The Growth is Spectacular," *Courier-Journal (Louisville)*, April 17, 1995.
George, Eric, "Putting Pop in Papa John's," *Louisville*, January 1994, p. 26.
Henderson, Angelo B., "Out of the Broom Closet and Into the Oven," *Courier-Journal (Louisville)*, September 5, 1988, p. E1.
McDowell, Bill, "Papa John's Slice of Success," *Restaurants and Institutions*, February 15, 1995.
"Nobody's Growing Like Papa John's," *Pizza Today*, July 1994, p. 50.
Papiernik, Richard L., "Papa John's 'Simple' Policy Pays Off: Profits up 77%," *Nation's Restaurant News*, March 6, 1995.
Reichert, Walt, "Pizza on the Move," *Louisville*, September 1991, p. 31.
Schiller, Zachary, "From a Broom Closet in a Bar to 485 Pizza Restaurants," *Business Week*, May 23, 1994, p. 94.

—Jason Gallman

PAYCHEX

Paychex, Inc.

911 Panorama Trail South
Rochester, New York 14625
U.S.A.
(716) 385-6666

Public Company
Incorporated: 1979
Employees: 3,500
Sales: $267.2 million (1995)
Stock Exchanges: NASDAQ
SICs: 8721 Accounting, Auditing and Bookkeeping

Paychex, Inc. is the second-largest payroll accounting service in the United States. The company processes payrolls for over 200,000 businesses nationwide. Paychex finds its clients mostly among small businesses with fewer than 100 employees. Its typical client has just 14 employees. Though payroll processing is its main service, Paychex also provides payroll tax calculation, payment, and filing of tax forms for about half its clients. It also offers a direct deposit service, sending employees' pay directly to their bank accounts. Paychex also handles human resources recordkeeping for some of its clients, keeping track of employee benefit plans. The company operates out of close to 100 offices across the United States.

Paychex was founded by B. Thomas Golisano, who still heads the company. In 1971, Golisano worked as a sales manager at Electronic Accounting Systems (EAS), a payroll processing company based in Rochester, New York. EAS aimed its services at large companies with at least 50 employees. Its minimum charges were generally too much for smaller companies to afford, and EAS did not pursue the small-company market. But Golisano, then 29 years old, speculated that small companies had as much need for a payroll accounting service as large companies. A little research at the library confirmed Golisano's suspicions that the potential market was enormous—in 1971, 95 percent of the nation's 3.5 million businesses had fewer than 50 employees. Golisano's father ran his own small heating contracting firm, and Golisano knew first-hand that making out payroll checks was a big headache for the small businessman. Golisano decided to market a payroll service that would be cheap enough for small businesses like his father's to afford.

Golisano first took his idea to EAS, but the company was not interested in pursuing small clients. But EAS did agree to rent Golisano an office for his venture. So in 1971 Golisano started his own company, then called PayMaster. His service was offered to companies for only a $5 minimum charge per pay period, and the total fee was proportional to the number of employees. Not only was the price reasonable, but Golisano made his service extremely convenient. Whereas clients of EAS had to fill out forms each pay period and turn them in to the company, Golisano's clients only had to make one phone call. The client simply called in the hours each employee worked, and any changes, and the company did the rest. The process only took about four minutes.

It took Golisano a year to attract 42 clients, and Paychex did not break even for three more years. During that time, Golisano kept the business afloat, somewhat precariously, with borrowed money and credit card loans. Because Paychex clients were small, the company needed a lot of accounts to keep going. Golisano marketed to CPAs, and increasingly got referrals from satisfied customers. After five years, Paychex had attracted about 300 clients in Rochester, and the business was relatively stable.

The impetus to expand the company came from two friends of Golisano, who approached him independently in 1974. One suggested opening a branch office in Syracuse, and he and Golisano would be co-owners. The second asked Golisano to sell him a franchise, and he started up a branch in Miami. Then Golisano began to recruit people to open branches in other cities. By 1979, he had 17 partners, 11 of them joint ventures, and six franchises. These operated in 22 cities, spread across the country. Golisano's partners came from various backgrounds. They were teachers, salesmen and engineers. Some were high school friends or friends of the family; some were his softball buddies. One partner, Golisano met on a trip to Florida—the doorman of the Boca Raton Hotel. Golisano trained them at his Rochester base, and then helped them set up business elsewhere.

By 1979, it began to be apparent that there were problems with the looseness of the organization. Paychex had 200 employees, 5,700 clients, and 18 principals. Different partners had different skills and different aims. Some locations offered different services than others, so that the Paychex product was not consistent. There was little central planning, and little input from one office to another. Golisano decided he wanted to consolidate Paychex into one company. For this he needed the acquiescence of his partners. It was difficult to persuade people who had headed their own branches that they would be better off as part of a more traditional company organization. Golisano came up with an equitable stock distribution formula, and presented a five-year plan for the future of the company, which included taking it public. After a tense two-day meeting in the Bahamas, all the principals agreed to the consolidation. In 1979, the company incorporated as Paychex, Inc.

The company began to change quickly. People who had been president of their own branches became vice-president of the new corporation. The company immediately began hiring and training a crew of sales professionals. The branches, which had previously operated more or less independently, were now subjected to management controls such as location-by-location comparisons of productivity. The company also strove to standardize its services. This was extremely important as the company grew. Most of its new business came from referrals from satisfied clients. It was crucial that if one company praised the way its account was handled by, for example, the Syracuse office, a company in New York could also expect the very same service. Golisano himself kept careful track of his growing organization, lugging around a three-ring notebook with hundreds of pages of relevant figures wherever he went.

Paychex initially experienced financial difficulties as a result of the reorganization, and at one point in 1980 cash-flow problems caused the company to suspend salaries. But this crisis was quickly resolved, and Paychex did grow as expected. With its new professional sales team in place, Paychex began to attract clients in numbers much higher than anticipated. By 1982, the average salesperson was bringing in 100 clients a year. This figure rose steadily. In August 1983, Paychex made its initial public offering. The company raised $7.7 million, which was used to fuel further expansion. By 1986, Paychex had close to 60,000 clients. The company had 58 offices in 32 states. Sales doubled in the three years since the public offering, to $51 million. The company was far bigger than Golisano's former employer, EAS. In fact, Paychex was the second-largest firm in the payroll accounting industry, behind only giant Automatic Data Processing Inc. (ADP).

Revenues close to doubled again in the next three years. In 1989, the company brought in $101 million, from its client base of 115,000 accounts. Some of the growth came from acquisitions, such as the 900 clients acquired when Paychex bought a Minneapolis company, Purchase Payroll, in 1987. Paychex also began to expand its services. In 1987, Paychex opened a division of Benefit Services, to keep track of clients' employee benefit plans. The next year, the company opened a Personnel Services division. The new services under this rubric included preparation of employee handbooks, providing information on new laws affecting the workplace, and updating clients on equal-employment regulations. And Paychex began offering a new service called Taxpay in 1989. For clients selecting Taxpay, Paychex prepared payroll tax returns, made the payments, and actually filed the returns with the government. Taxpay provided a real revenue boost to Paychex, for two reasons. For each client who selected Taxpay, Paychex gained about a 45 percent increase in revenue on that account. Salespeople who were soliciting regular payroll accounts could also try to enroll customers in Taxpay, with only a little additional work. Paychex also benefited from Taxpay because it accepted money in advance to pay the taxes. Before the taxes came due, Paychex could collect interest on this so-called "float" money. Paychex invested the "float" money, an average daily balance of $4,000 per customer, in tax-free municipal securities, and earned an average annual return of three to four percent. Taxpay proved very successful. In just a few years, almost half of Paychex payroll clients were also using Taxpay, and Paychex experienced a vital boost in revenue.

Paychex had experienced growth of around 20 percent annually in the 1980s, and the company was consistently featured on lists such as *Forbes*' "Best Small Companies in America" and the *OTC Review* list of "100 Most Profitable NASDAQ Companies." The company's success did not go unnoticed, and Paychex began to have competition from the leading payroll accounting service firm, ADP. ADP began a separate sales division to try to hook small business accounts. By 1989, ADP had 400 sales representatives in this division, versus Paychex's 310. In that year, companies with fewer than 50 employees made up 60 percent of ADP's accounts, and brought in about twice as much revenue as did Paychex. Even so, the small business market was enormous, and there was still room for growth. And about 80 percent of Paychex's clients renewed every year. Most of the clients the company lost did not turn to another provider. The rate of failure among small businesses is very high, and most lost clients simply went out of business. But to keep up with this turnover, Paychex sales representatives had to bring in an average of 160 new clients a year, or over three a week.

To train salespeople to keep up with this demanding quota, Paychex opened its own school at its Rochester branch. In 1991, Paychex spent approximately $3,500 per trainee to put its new salespeople through a seven-week course in tax law, accounting principles, and selling skills, and to send them on rounds with experienced sales representatives. The expense of the school, which had 11 full-time instructors, was far less than it cost Paychex to recruit a replacement for sales reps who quit or were fired. And new hires who had come through the training school started making money for the company twice as fast as before. Paychex had started in the 1970s with people with little or no background in either selling or payroll accounting, and had come full circle in the 1990s, with a highly professional and well-prepared staff.

By 1990, Paychex had 335 sales representatives and around 125,000 clients. But a recession in the autumn set back the number of paychecks the company was processing, and sales representatives found it hard to meet their ambitious quota. Nevertheless, the Taxpay service was increasingly successful. At the end of fiscal 1991, Paychex estimated it had lost several million dollars due to recessionary cutbacks, but it more than made up the difference with revenue from Taxpay. 1991 saw record sales of $137 million, as well as record earnings of $9.6 million. And Taxpay continued to add clients. In 1991, there were around 26,000 Taxpay customers. That number rose to over 50,000 by 1993.

Paychex added other services as well. In 1991, the company formed a Human Resource Services division, offering clients a package of employee evaluation and testing tools, employee handbooks, insurance services, customized job descriptions, and other benefits. Paychex used its expertise to help its Human Resource clients keep abreast of government regulations affecting the workplace, and took over time-consuming administrative procedures. The company then introduced Paylink in 1993. Paylink appealed to businesses that used personal computers, allowing clients to send payroll information in to the Paychex database via computer modem. In 1994, Paychex added a similar service, Reportlink. After a client's payroll was computed, Reportlink sent the figures back to the client's computers, for use in internal reports and accounting.

Paychex continued to roll out new services, though in 1994 over 80 percent of its revenue still came from its basic payroll accounting service. And enrolling new payroll clients was still the key to the company's growth. According to CEO Golisano in a June 13, 1994 *Barron's* article, Paychex aimed to expand its client base by 11 to 12 percent a year, to keep revenue growing at close to 20 percent annually. This actually meant bringing in even more new clients than it seemed, because Paychex always had to make up the 20 percent of clients it lost each year. And though there were still in 1994 more than 4.6 million businesses with fewer than 100 employees, more than 60 percent of these had only one to four employees, and so were too small to be likely potential clients. Paychex also had to contend with increasing competition from software manufacturers. Business owners with personal computers had an array of cheap software packages to choose from that made doing their own payroll relatively cheap and convenient.

But Golisano was confident the company could meet its goal. He took time off in 1994 to run for governor of New York, as an independent party candidate. Golisano had become increasingly interested in trying to solve Rochester's urban problems, working with city youths on running their own businesses and heading a city campaign to lower the rate of teen pregnancies. Golisano also had an in-depth knowledge of government regulations and tax codes that he believed harassed small businesses. Though Paychex had made its living dealing with government red tape for its clients, Golisano claimed he would work for tax reform and simplification if elected. A long shot at best, Golisano did not win the governorship, but Paychex flourished. In 1995, the company increased its client base by 11.8 percent, exactly as Golisano had wished. Paychex had over 200,000 clients, and half of these were using the lucrative Taxpay service. Earnings were up almost 40 percent, with net income of $39 million. The company increased its penetration in the California market with three acquisitions—Pay-Fone, Precision Payroll, and Payday. The Human Services division introduced a 401(k) recordkeeping service, and other human resources services, as well as Paylink and Taxpay, continued to grow significantly.

Paychex aimed to expand even more through the remainder of the 1990s. Its market penetration was still low enough to leave room for growth. The company also committed to make use of blossoming technologies in computer networking and digital communications to enhance its service and capabilities.

Further Reading

Barrier, Michael, "The Power of a Good Idea," *Nation's Business,* November 1990, pp. 34–36.

Burlingham, Bo, and Michael S. Hopkins, "How to Build an Inc. 500 Company," *Inc.,* December 1988, pp. 41–56.

Cowan, Alison Leigh, "Getting Rich on Other People's Paychecks," *Business Week,* November 17, 1986, pp. 148–49.

Gold, Howard R., "Lofty Paychex," *Barron's,* October 24, 1994, p. 13.

"An In-House Sales School," *Inc.,* May 1991, pp. 85–86.

Golisano, B. Thomas, and Robert J. Warth, "Managing After Startup," *Management Accounting,* February 1989, pp. 27–30.

Martin, Douglas, "New York's Answer to Ross Perot," *New York Times,* October 2, 1994, Sec. 3, p. 7.

Meeks, Fleming, "Tom Golisano and the Red Tape Factory," *Forbes,* May 15, 1989, pp. 80–82.

Meeks, Fleming, with Jean Sherman Chetzky, "Hear, Watch, and Sell the Customer," *Forbes,* November 11, 1991, pp. 218–20.

Montgomery, Leland, "Business Services," *Financial World,* January 5, 1993, pp. 53–54.

"Newer Services Promise Sharp Gains in Growth," *Barron's,* March 12, 1990, pp. 52–53.

"Paychex Inc. to Post 3% Increase in Profit for Fiscal 4th Quarter," *Wall Street Journal,* July 7, 1987, p. 36.

Welles, Edward O., "Tom Golisano Goes Public," *Inc.,* November 1992, pp. 126–30.

Zipser, Andy, "Burning Bright," *Barron's,* April 6, 1992, pp. 18, 40–41.

—A. Woodward

PETROLITE

Petrolite Corporation

369 Marshall Avenue
St. Louis, Missouri 63119
U.S.A.
(314) 961-3500
Fax: (314) 241-1833

Public Company
Incorporated: 1930 as Petrolite Corporation, Ltd.
Employees: 1,800
Sales: $364.8 million (1995)
Stock Exchanges: NASDAQ
SICs: 2899 Chemical Preparations, Not Elsewhere
   Classified; 3569 General Industrial Machinery, Not
   Elsewhere Classified

A leader and a pioneer in the oil field chemical industry, Petrolite Corporation manufactures specialty chemicals, equipment, polymers, and waxes that enable its customers to realize maximum performance for their products and processes. From its founding in the 1930s on into the mid-1990s, Petrolite has culled a tradition of innovation, developing proprietary products, processes, and equipment to serve a variety of industries. However, throughout its existence the company has relied on sales to the petroleum industry for the bulk of its revenues. During the mid-1990s, Petrolite derived the majority of its annual sales from the production of specialty chemicals formulated to assist oil drillers and refiners in eliminating or separating the sundry contaminants impinging upon optimum production.

Founded in 1930, Petrolite entered the business world at a running start, having already established itself as an integral supplier to the petroleum industry before its inaugural year of business was concluded. For this early momentum, the company was indebted to the work of two scientists, William S. Barnickel and Frederick G. Cottrell, whose pioneering efforts during the early 20th century ceded Petrolite the technological expertise that would enable it to distinguish itself early on as a highly respected and innovative competitor within its industry.

When they began their experimentations, Barnickel and Cottrell were separated by nearly 2,000 miles, their respective scientific work conducted independently of one another, but the formation of Petrolite united the groundbreaking discoveries of each man, creating a flourishing concern that would function as an important supplier to the petroleum industry and other industries for the remainder of the century.

William S. Barnickel was a 29-year-old St. Louis chemist working in Sapulpa, Oklahoma, as a consultant in 1907 when he began investigating a problem that was confounding oil drillers in the area. At night, while looking across the oil fields surrounding Sapulpa, Barnickel watched bright plumes of fire spewing from the ground, their intensity fueled by earthen pits of oil. During the day, the apocalyptic nighttime display gave way to billowing clouds of black smoke belching from the pits. Though spectacular, the fire and the smoke were representative of the futile effort to dispose of crude oil mixed with water, a worthless substance known by oil workers as "roily oil." For years, oil drilling companies had endeavored in vain to find a way to dispose of the wet crude. Channels were dug in the ground to guide the oil into earthen pits, where it was hoped the water would settle out, but the results were only negligibly successful. Heating the oil with steam coils had also been tried, but the process had proved to be prohibitively expensive, leaving oil drillers saddled with mounting levels of roily oil.

Prodded by the sight of flames and smoke to find a solution to the problem, Barnickel took to the oil fields in 1907, hoping to discover a chemical process that would separate water from oil. After four years of putting his training as a chemist to practical use in the fields, Barnickel developed a chemical process in 1911 that economically and efficiently recovered crude oil from emulsified oil, a discovery that yielded Barnickel the first of several U.S. patents in 1914. Once he had discovered the chemical process that would rid oil fields of environmentally harmful roily oil, Barnickel contended with his next formidable task: gaining the ability to prepare large quantities of his treating chemical in the field. In 1916, he achieved his objective by modifying a small factory in St. Louis to suit his needs; then, in the fall, Barnickel sold the first two drums of his product, which was marketed under the name "Tret-O-Lite."

Tret-O-Lite, manufactured by the Tretolite Company, was an instant success. Within a few short years, oil companies in Oklahoma, Texas, and Louisiana were using the Tret-O-Lite process to recover hundreds of thousands of barrels of wet crude, gaining marketable oil from what previously had been a worthless substance.

At roughly the same time Barnickel was surveying the burning and smoking pools of roily oil in Sapulpa and about to launch his scientific investigation, another scientist, nearly 2,000 miles to the west, was completing a scientific discovery of his own. Dr. Frederick G. Cottrell, while working at the University of California, had developed a method of separating solid particles from flue gases by using electricity. When he learned of the vast amounts of California crude oil being discarded because of its water content, Cottrell's mind turned to the same problem riddling Barnickel in Sapulpa.

Cottrell and Barnickel were pursuing the same objective, but their approaches were different. Barnickel found his answer through chemistry; Cottrell, on the other hand, hoped to apply his newly discovered method of precipitating solid particles from flue gases to the roily oil tainting California's oil fields. By 1908, Cottrell had done just that when he used electricity to separate water from oil four years before Barnickel would achieve the same result with his chemical process. In 1909, the first commercial application of Cottrell's technology was performed successfully; then two years later, the same year Barnickel developed his Tret-O-Lite process, Cottrell's pioneering work in reclaiming crude oil from roily oil through electricity gave birth to a new company, the Petroleum Rectifying Company of California.

Such were the origins of Petrolite, formed in 1930 when the Tretolite Company merged with the Petroleum Rectifying Company of California and linked the technologies first developed by Barnickel and Cottrell. From these two demulsification techniques, the company's expertise grew to embrace a wide range of demulsification processes for a number of different industries, each of which benefited from Petrolite's ability to isolate and remove unwanted contaminants.

Though the contributions of Barnickel and Cottrell predicated Petrolite's formation and reputation during its formative years, providing the foundation upon which the company was built, nearly all of the company's success after 1930 was attributable to the pioneering tradition established by wave after wave of Petrolite inventors, scientists, and engineers. The consistent development of sophisticated technologies and their applicability to other industries enabled Petrolite to move past the historic discoveries of Barnickel and Cottrell and establish a presence in other markets that would support its existence for decades to come.

One such diversifying move came shortly after Petrolite's formation in 1930, when company employees developed a process for recovering microcrystalline waxes from crude oil tank bottoms. Once recovered, the refined microwaxes were sold by Petrolite to polish manufacturers and other companies engaged in a variety of businesses, ranging from food packaging to cosmetics. Other innovative discoveries followed, each one resolving a difficulty that plagued a particular industry.

Petrolite scientists and engineers pioneered technologies that prevented the corrosive effects of sour gases deep inside oil wells, developed electrostatic desalting technology to remove salt and other contaminants from crude oil streams inside refineries, and created the first turbine fuel treatment system, which was used by the power generation industry to purify low-grade fuels used in gas turbine engines.

By the beginning of the 1960s, after the company's legacy of innovation had driven its growth for three decades, Petrolite was generating roughly $30 million a year in sales, half of which came from sales to the petroleum industry. Although diversification had engendered a more well-rounded company, leading Petrolite into several key markets, the company was dependent to a large degree on the sale of its processing equipment, chemical formulations, and services to the petroleum industry to sustain its operation. During the late 1960s, after profits stagnated for several years, management restructured Petrolite's global marketing operations and its prolific research activities, transferring full control over both domestic and international operations to the company's headquarters. After this change, Petrolite entered the 1970s and ushered in the decade by eclipsing the $50 million mark in annual sales, recording its 40th consecutive year of dividend payments.

The company's operations by this point were organized into three divisions, each representing a pillar that would support Petrolite's existence in the decades to come. With manufacturing plants in St. Louis, Missouri; Brea, California; and Kirby, England, the company's Tretolite division ranked as the market leader in the oil field chemical industry, supported by its traditional product line of oil heating and water treating specialty chemicals. The production of oil field and refining equipment, industrial gas turbines, and a turbine fuel treating system used by the utility industry was assigned to Petrolite's Petreco division and its manufacturing facility in Houston. In Barnsdall, Oklahoma, and Kilgore, Texas, Petrolite operated its commercial wax production business through its Bareco division, which ranked as the world's leading producer of microcrystalline waxes, accounting for nearly 30 percent of worldwide production. Supported by these three divisions, along with foreign subsidiaries in Canada, England, France, and Germany, Petrolite stood well-positioned for the growth it would record in the coming years, growth that would greatly outpace what had been achieved during the previous 40 years.

By the mid-1970s, Petrolite was manufacturing nearly all of its products at unprecedented levels, with its Petreco division recording particularly vigorous growth abroad, as the international demand for oil field and refining equipment rose substantially. Annual sales halfway through the decade approached $100 million, having nearly doubled in five years. As it had from the outset, the company relied on extensive research and development to fuel its growth, with the internal generation of new proprietary products boosting sales as they entered worldwide industrial markets. This emphasis, combined with the growing wealth and importance of the petroleum industry, propelled Petrolite forward, positioning the company as a vital resource for oil companies in pursuit of maximum production.

By looking inward to Petrolite research specialists to develop products, chemicals, and processes that enabled the petroleum industry to clear previously insurmountable hurdles, the company maintained a technological lead over its competition, consistently developing new products to fuel its growth. One Petrolite employee, Dr. Melvin DeGroote, was named inventor or co-inventor in 963 U.S. patents, the greatest number of chemical-related patents ever issued to one individual, a record that epitomized Petrolite's commitment to innovation. The intensity of this commitment continued to move Petrolite into new businesses as the company moved past the 1970s, including the entry into a new field that would develop into an integral component of the company's overall business scope during the mid-1990s. When the supply of raw materials required to sustain Petrolite's various manufacturing activities began to wane, company scientists developed a family of unique synthetic polymers. The production of these polymers, which proved to be more desirable than the natural materials they replaced, became one of the primary business segments supporting Petrolite and one of the highlights of the company's business during the 1990s.

During the 1990s, Petrolite increasingly looked to alliance agreements with customers and other manufacturers to enhance the development of new products. In 1992, one such agreement was struck with Houston, Texas-based Energy Biosystems Corp. to develop and bring to market a biodesulfurization process for use in the refining industry. The following year another alliance agreement was reached with Chevron U.K. Ltd., which designated Petrolite as the sole supplier of specialty chemicals and related services to Chevron's North Sea oil platform.

As Petrolite entered the mid-1990s, it was looking to increase the number of its alliances within the petroleum industry. In late 1994, the company's polymer division and Penzoil Products Company agreed to form a 50-50 partnership called Bareco Products, which was created to provide a broad line of wax products to domestic and international wax users. As the company prepared for the late 1990s, a weak North American petroleum market was educing Petrolite to increase its involvement in foreign markets. Toward this objective, the company opened a $6 million, 40,000-square-foot laboratory and office facility in Liverpool, England, in the mid-1990s. As the only technical facility of its kind outside North America, Petrolite's

International Technology Center promised to strengthen the company's position in overseas markets, providing vast new areas of growth for the future.

Principal Subsidiaries

Ecuatoriana de Petroquimicos-Petrolite S.A. (Ecuador); Luzzatto & Figlio S.A. (France); Petrolite Canada Inc.; Petrolite France, S.A.; Petrolite GmbH (Germany); Petrolite Handelsgesellschaft m.b.H. (Austria); Petrolite Iberica, S.A.; Petrolite International Sales Corporation; Petrolite Italiana S.p.A. (Italy); Petrolite Limited (England); Petrolite de Mexico S.A. de C.V.; Petrolite Nederland B.V.; Petrolite Norge A/S (Norway); Petrolite Pacific Pte. Ltd. (Singapore); Petrolite Saudi Arabia Ltd.; Petrolite Suramericana, S.A. (Venezuela); Petrolite Wax Partner Company; P.T. Petrolite Indonesia Pratama; South America Petrolite Corporation; Petrolite Trinidad, Inc.; A.B. Engineering.

Principal Divisions

Industrial Chemicals Division; International Division; Tetrolite Division; EuroChem Division; Petreco Division; Polymers Division.

Further Reading

Houser, Douglas, "Petrolite Holds Favorable Position with Oil, Gas Industry Products," *Investment Dealers' Digest,* December 17, 1974, p. 24.
Kobusch, R. B., "Petrolite Corporation," *Wall Street Transcript,* May 20, 1968, p. 13,298.
Langenberg, Oliver M., "Petrolite Corporation," *Wall Street Transcript,* October 7, 1974, p. 38,360.
Miller, Patricia, "Petrolite Talks Buyout of Largest Shareholder; Barnickel's Stake Worth $170 Million," *St. Louis Business Journal,* August 1, 1994, p. 16.
"Petrolite Builds Base for Continued Growth with Products, Plants," *Investment Dealers' Digest,* April 13, 1971, p. 29.
Santos, William, "Penzoil, Petrolite to Join in Wax products Partnership," *Chemical Marketing Reporter,* September 12, 1994, p. 10.
Sherman, Joseph V., "Shine and Rise," *Barron's,* February 22, 1965, p. 5.

—Jeffrey L. Covell

Pirelli S.p.A.

Viale Sarca, 222
20126 Milan
Italy
2 85351
Fax: 2 64423300

Public Company
Incorporated: 1872 as Pirelli & C.
Employees: 38,485
Sales: L19.79 trillion (US$6 billion) (1994)
Stock Exchanges: Milan Amsterdam Antwerp Brussels
    Frankfurt Paris
SICs: 3357 Drawing & Insulating of Nonferrous Wire;
    3011 Tires & Inner Tubes; 3315 Steel Wiredrawing,
    Steel Nails, & Spikes; 5051 Metals Service Centers &
    Offices

Pirelli S.p.A. is among the world's leaders in both tire and cable manufacturing, and is one of the largest companies in Italy. Its founder, Giovanni Battista Pirelli, a 24-year-old engineering graduate from the Milano Politecnico, formed the company Pirelli & C. with an initial share capital of L215,000. Annual sales neared L20 trillion by the mid-1990s, with core operations producing and distributing tires for cars, motorcycles, and farm and industrial vehicles, and cables for power transmission and telecommunications.

Pirelli had astutely realized that rubber was to become one of the most important commodities in the rapidly industrializing Italy. Less than a year after its inception in 1872, Pirelli's company built its first factory in Milan. There were 45 people employed in the small, 1,000-square-meter building as demand for the company's rubber sheets, belts, slabs, and vulcanized products increased. The rapid growth in the popularity of the motor car, which was now seen as more than a fashionable plaything for the rich, led to contracts to supply pneumatic tubes and transmission belts.

From its earliest years Pirelli demonstrated a willingness to diversify its product range and to produce overseas in order to satisfy its desire for ambitious, yet controlled, expansion. The company began the manufacture of insulated telegraph cables in 1879 and within seven years had developed the technology to produce underwater telegraph cables. In 1890 pneumatic bicycle tires rolled off the production line and were followed in 1900 by the company's first car tires.

Pirelli established a trend that many Italian companies were to follow when it began to expand abroad as early as 1902. The new cable and electrical lead factory set up near Barcelona in Spain was followed by a similar venture in Britain in 1914, and by 1920 factories had also been set up in Brazil, Greece, Argentina, Turkey, and Germany. Product diversification at home was encouraged by the firm's long-term commitment to investing in research and development. Giovanni brought his two sons into the business and they helped to run the new motorcycle tire production plant built at Bicocca in 1908. Forever at the forefront of new technology, the company began to produce rubberized fabrics as early as 1909.

Two major factors were to account for Pirelli's growth in the years immediately preceding World War I. First, between 1900 and 1914, Italy saw increased social reforms and political stability, which created more favorable conditions for trade and industry. Pirelli, which derived much of its demand from newly established ventures, was well placed to benefit from these changes by producing fluid control devices, transmission belts, and fuel distribution machinery. Second, the invention of the internal combustion engine in 1910 made the mass production of cars economically viable. The so-called "rubber boom" of 1911 marked the acceptance of the material as a worldwide commodity and ensured the continued success of the company.

New factories were opened in Spain in 1917 and Argentina in 1919, but the first major event to affect the company after the end of the war was a change in its organizational structure, implemented in 1920. Pirelli & C., the original company founded by Giovanni Pirelli, changed its status and became an investment rather than a production company. Società Italiana Pirelli, later to become Pirelli S.p.A., was incorporated to act as a holding company to control the group's varied industrial operations based in Italy. Compagnie Internationale Pirelli S.A., incorporated in Brussels, was set up to manage the group's rapidly increasing overseas operations.

In 1924 Luigi Emanueli, an employee of the company, developed the first commercially viable oil-filled cable. The world's first crossply tire—the Superflex Stella Bianca—was successfully launched in 1927 and within two years a new cable production unit was opened in Brazil and a new tire factory was opened at Burton-on-Trent in England. Initiatives were also made in India and Malaysia to guarantee the supply of natural rubber to Milan and Pirelli's overseas subsidiaries.

This was a period when Pirelli's products, fitted to the Ferraris and Alfa Romeos of Nuvolari and Ascari, became synonymous with success in international Grand Prix racing. Nevertheless, the rise of Mussolini's fascists and Italy's increasingly disastrous foreign policy in the mid-1930s led to a further period of economic and political turbulence. To counteract the impending threat of international boycotts, Compagnie Internationale Pirelli S.A. was transferred into Pirelli Holdings S.A., a holding company incorporated in neutral Switzerland.

World War II left Italy politically and economically crippled. A weak leadership was unable to cope with the severe poverty, rampant inflation, and high unemployment that affected the whole country. But Alcide de Gasperi, the Christian Democrat leader, was able to bring both inflation and the budget deficit under some degree of control and by 1948 a large-scale public investment program was instigated.

Italian industry had been situated in the north of the country for a number of reasons. Milan, Turin, and Genoa became business centers because of the availability of both capital and raw materials—steel for machinery and railways, coal for power—and again Pirelli, which derived much of its success from the success of others, was well placed to take advantage of the new boom in the north. Pirelli responded to this opportunity by producing the first fabric-belted tire, the Cinturato CF67, which revolutionized the tire industry.

In the 1950s and 1960s Italy enjoyed the same kind of economic miracle experienced by many European countries as postwar depression gave way to years of growth and prosperity. An influx of new talent, often from comparatively humble backgrounds, suffused the established upper crust of Italian society and led to an improvement in the quality of management. Pirelli set new records for expansion overseas, opening a further cable factory in Canada in 1953, a latex foam plant in France in 1957, and new tire plants in Greece and Turkey in 1960. The company reinforced its position in both South America and Australasia when it opened further cable manufacturing operations in Peru in 1968 and Australia in 1975. Pirelli was also involved in establishing several turnkey plants during the 1960s to provide tires for Eastern European companies.

Throughout this period of expansion Pirelli followed the strategy, common to most of the Italian multinationals, of eschewing joint ventures and the purchase of minority and majority shares in established companies. Instead, product ranges that had already proved successful in the Italian domestic market were transferred for production and sale overseas. In this way the company has been able to retain complete control over its operations abroad while being able to overcome barriers preventing Italian exports.

In the late 1960s Pirelli's reputation for being at the forefront of innovation was usurped by Michelin when the latter introduced steel-belted radial tires. Michelin also entered the U.S. cable market seven years before Pirelli. Some commentators suggested that Pirelli's management was more concerned with producing glossy calendars than tires. The company responded by embarking on a long-term research and development agreement with the British Dunlop group. This surprising move did not lead to a full merger and neither party seemed to be too disappointed when the agreement was terminated in 1981. Despite successes in the development of low-profile tires and in revolutionary fiber optics, the joint venture now appears, with the benefit of hindsight, to have been too much of a defensive measure designed to counter the perceived threat of Michelin.

A personal tragedy hit the firm in the early 1970s when Giovanni Pirelli, a direct descendant of the original founder, was killed in a car crash. This natural leader of the firm was replaced by his younger brother, Leopoldo, who was also severely injured in the accident. Leopoldo led the company through a period of protracted change.

The oil crises of the 1970s brought about a change in attitude towards the role of the motor car. Sales of new cars slumped as the price of gasoline soared, and as a consequence the worldwide demand for tires fell dramatically. Italy, far more dependent on imported sources of energy than most of its European partners, was particularly badly hit by the 1974 crisis, which saw the return of rampant inflation and a massive drop in the value of the lire. The second oil crisis of 1979 followed the withdrawal of the Communists from the "historic compromise" coalition government that had done so much to stabilize Italian political life. The Naples earthquake of November 1980 and the public exposure of P2, the secret Masonic lodge, six months later further damaged the morale of the country.

After the ending of the agreement with Dunlop, Pirelli benefited from the upturn in the European economy of the early 1980s. The Italian and Swiss parent companies were responsible for an extensive reorganization of the group in 1982, which saw an equalization of the shares each company held in the group's many and varied subsidiary companies. A new management company, Pirelli Société Générale S.A., was created in Basel to ensure that unified policies and centralized objectives were put in place in Pirelli companies throughout the world.

In 1985 Pirelli acquired the share capital of Metzeler Kautschuk, a German company with many interests in the rubber industry. The acquisition of Metzeler led to a 13 percent increase in consolidated turnover and reinforced Pirelli's position in the market for motorcycle tires and automobile components. Just as important, the move provided Pirelli with a well-established distribution chain that dealt with manufacturing activities. This apparent change in strategy—favoring growth through acquisition at the expense of traditional organic growth—was also demonstrated in 1988 when the group acquired Armstrong Tire Co., the sixth-largest U.S. tire manufacturer. In the same year Pirelli bought Filergie S.A., a cable manufacturer with 13 plants in France and Portugal. Although the pace of technical development appeared to be slowing down and no further radically different tires were introduced, the company did benefit from the increased margins offered by a shift in demand in favor of low-profile and premium radial tires.

A further share restructuring was undertaken in 1988 when Pirelli S.p.A. acquired Société Internationale Pirelli S.A.'s holding in Pirelli Société Générale S.A., thereby accepting direct responsibility for the day-to-day management of the operating companies. In turn, these operating companies were restructured into self-contained divisions in order to facilitate faster responses to financial, production, and employment problems. The three divisions—Pirelli Tire, Pirelli Cavi, and Pirelli Prodotti Diversificati—were each given separate holding companies.

The worldwide tire industry was badly hit by the recession of the late 1980s and early 1990s as any other manufacturing sector. Worldwide sales of tires stagnated, and producers were unable to pass on increases in the cost of raw materials—especially oil—to the final consumer. Car makers, suffering from reduced demand, cut their costs by forcing tire manufacturers to accept lower prices. A spate of ill-conceived takeovers in the early 1980s and an increasing market dominance by a decreasing number of companies led to pressure on margins in the struggle to gain market share. Excess capacity and oversupply exacerbated the situation.

Pirelli's reaction to these market forces was to engage in two major merger and acquisition exercises. First, the company became involved in an acrimonious battle with Bridgestone to take control of the U.S. company Firestone in 1988 and 1989. With the benefit of hindsight, Pirelli should be content to have lost the battle and thereby have avoided what has proved to be a costly and largely unsuccessful acquisition for Bridgestone.

Pirelli's second attempt to increase its market share by entering the world of mergers and acquisitions led to a long series of merger discussions with the German company Continental AG and ultimately, near-disaster. The plan to merge the fourth- and fifth-largest tire producers in the world was designed to produce a force powerful enough to achieve critical mass in a fairly stagnant market. Damaging price competition would be avoided and overcapacity would be reduced. This deal seemed a far more attractive proposition than the opportunity to acquire Firestone two years earlier. The proposed merger, however, proved to be problematic from the very first time the two parties met. The board of Continental, led by chief executive Horst Urban, angered the Pirelli leadership by publicly revealing details of secret meetings. Pirelli believed that its attempts to follow traditional German merger practice, in which friendly approaches are made to willing partners in order to achieve mutual benefit, was the best way to act in the early stages of the deal. Continental's belligerent defensive strategy, inspired by the aggressive tactics employed by the City of London and Wall Street in the mid-1980s, led Pirelli to hire an investor group to buy up Continental stock. While talks between the two firms dragged on into 1991, Pirelli's financial condition weakened

under the strain of the stagnant economy to the point where Continental pulled out of the merger discussions.

It was subsequently revealed that Pirelli lost almost $300 million on the Continental stock its investor group had purchased, further damaging the company's fortunes and instigating a shareholder revolt (after an earnings gain of 11¢ per share in 1990, the company posted a loss of 48¢ per share in 1991). In 1992 Leopoldo Pirelli was pushed aside of day-to-day management (he remained chairman of the board) in favor of his son-in-law Marco Tronchetti Provera, who had opposed the Continental takeover attempt. Tronchetti instigated a massive restructuring effort to forestall threatened bankruptcy. Many of the businesses his predecessors had acquired in preceding decades were sold off, eventually reducing Pirelli to two core divisions—tires and cables—out of the nine it had operated at its peak of diversification. In addition to the sale of such operations as conveyor belt and apparel manufacturing, much of Pirelli's downtown Milan real estate was sold, bringing in $563 million which contributed to cutting the firm's $2.5 billion debt load in half. The company's workforce was cut from 53,500 in 1990 to 38,500 in 1994, or about 25 percent, and the number of factories Pirelli operated was reduced from 103 in 1990 to 74 in 1994.

After its near-disastrous loss of L657 billion in 1991, Pirelli's newfound concentration on its core tire and cable businesses slowly turned the company around. After smaller losses of L69 billion in 1992 and L41 billion in 1993, Pirelli returned to profitability in 1994 with a gain of L72 billion. Its tire operation was boosted by a resurgence in European sales based primarily on Pirelli's emphasis on increasingly popular high-performance tires. By 1995, Pirelli had captured 12 percent of the European tire market, behind only Michelin. The North American market lagged behind, however, because of the poor performance of Armstrong. Pirelli replaced Armstrong's management team in early 1995, giving the new team until 1997 to break even.

On the cable side of its business, Pirelli had built itself into one of the world's top two manufacturers of fiber optic cables. It aimed to increasingly emphasize telecommunications cables over those used for power. Pirelli had expressed interest in broadening its telecommunications business by purchasing a stake in the state-owned Telecom Italia, which the Italian government had considered privatizing. But threats to block any such Pirelli move to further enhance its position in the Italian telecommunications sector were immediately raised by Italian legislators.

As it neared the end of the 20th century, Pirelli appeared stronger and more stable than it had in the early 1990s. As it consolidated its positions in the tire and cable industries and pushed into new markets through such moves as expanding its tire business into East Asia, observers wondered what was next for a company that had undergone such remarkable changes over the previous 30 years. Some speculated that a further divestment was to come, with Pirelli choosing to concentrate solely on telecommunications, an industry predicted for more growth than that of tires. Ironically, then, a company that had aggressively sought to expand its tire business through two failed acquisitions and one successful one was rumored to be considering selling off that same core business.

Principal Subsidiaries

F.O.S. Fibre Ottiche Sud S.p.A.; Holdim S.p.A.; Innex—Fili Isolati Speciali S.p.A.; Pirelli Cavi S.p.A.; Pirelli Coordinamento Pneumatici S.p.A.; Pirelli Pneumatici Holding Italia S.r.l.; Pirelli Prodotti Diversificati S.p.A.; Pirelli Servizi Finanziari S.p.A.; Pirelli Servocavi S.p.A.; Società Pneumatici Pirelli S.p.A.; Pirelli Gesellschaft mbH (Austria); Pirelli Tyres Benelux S.A. (Belgium); Cables Pirelli S.A. (France); Pneus Pirelli S.A. (France); Deutsche Pirelli Reifen Holding GmbH (Germany); Pirelli Deutschland A.G. (Germany); Elastika Pirelli S.A. (Greece); Pirelli Cable Holding N.V. (Netherlands); Pirelli Finance (Holding) N.V. (Netherlands); Pirelli Tyre Holding N.V. (Netherlands); Sipir Finance N.V. (Netherlands); Pirelli Polska Sp.zo.o. (Poland); Desco Fabrica Portuguesa de Material Electrico e Electronico Ltda (Portugal; 70.91%); Pirelli Neumaticos S.A. (Spain); Productos Pirelli S.A. (Spain); Pirelli Scandanavia AB (Sweden); Lunares S.A. (Switzerland); Pirelli Société Générale S.A. (Switzerland); Çelikord A.S. (Turkey; 50.98%); Türk-Pirelli Lastikleri A.S. (Turkey; 62.21%); Pirelli General plc (U.K.); Pirelli UK plc; Pirelli UK Tyres Ltd.; Pirelli Canada Inc. (Canada); Pirelli Armstrong Tire Corporation (U.S.A.); Pirelli Cable Corporation (U.S.A.); Pirelli Argentina de Mandatos S.A.; Muriaè S.A. (Brazil); Pirelli Cabos S.A. (Brazil; 85.17%); Pirelli Pneus S.A. (Brazil; 86.35%); Pirelli Instalaciones Chile S.A.; Neumaticos de Venezuela C.A. (75%); Pirelli Cables Australia Ltd (51%); Pirelli Tyres Australia Pty Ltd; Pirelli K.K. (Japan); Materials Purchasing Private Ltd (Singapore); Pirelli Cable Systems Pte Ltd.

Further Reading

King, Russel, *Italy,* London: Harper & Row, 1987.

Kline, Maureen, "Pirelli Says It's Poised for a Recovery Following Painful Restructuring Moves," *Wall Street Journal,* April 8, 1994, p. B6B.

La Pirelli: Vita di una azienda industriale, Milan: Industrie Grafiche A. Nicola, 1946.

Onida, Fabrizio, and Gianfranco Viesti, *The Italian Multinationals,* Beckenham: Croom Helm, 1988.

Perulli, Paolo, *Pirelli, 1980–1985: Le relazioni industriali: Negoziando l'incertezza,* Milan: F. Angeli, 1986.

Pirelli, Alberto, *Economia e guerra,* Milan: Istituto per gli Studi di Politica Internazionale, 1940.

Rossant, John, "How Pirelli Pulled Off a 180-Degree Turn," *Business Week* (International Edition), October 16, 1995.

"Still Spinning Its Wheels," *Financial World,* April 13, 1993, p. 64.

Tagliabue, John, "Pirelli Tires Rolling Again in Italy," *International Herald Tribune,* July 23, 1994, p. 11.

—Andreas Loizou
—updated by David E. Salamie

Playtex Products, Inc.

300 Nyala Farms Road
Westport, Connecticut 06880
U.S.A.
(203) 341-4000
Fax: (203) 341-4260

Public Company
Incorporated: 1988
Employees: 1,600
Sales: $482 million (1995 est.)
Stock Exchanges: New York
SICs: 2676 Sanitary Paper Products; 3089 Plastics
    Products, Not Elsewhere Classified; 3069 Fabricated
    Rubber Products, Not Elsewhere Classified; 6719
    Holding Companies, Not Elsewhere Classified

Playtex Products, Inc. is a leading manufacturer and distributor of household and personal care products. Its brand name products include Playtex and Ultimates Silk Glide tampons; Playtex Nurser disposable feeding systems for infants; Cherubs and Smile Tote cups and bottles for babies and toddlers; Playtex Living, Handsaver, and Wearshield household and industrial gloves; Banana Boat sun and skin care products; Jhirmack shampoo, conditioner, and styling products; Woolite rug and upholstery cleaning products; and Tek toothbrushes. In the mid-1990s, a 40-percent share of Playtex was sold to Haas Wheat & Partners, an investment firm based in Dallas, for $180 million, in an effort on the part of Chief Financial Officer Michael Goss and others to help pare down interest expenses and to secure for Playtex better funding for its research and development and acquisition programs.

The origins of Playtex Products may be traced to the 1932 founding of the International Laytex Company, which later became known as International Playtex Inc. The company's primary focus during its early years was in the production of ladies' undergarments, specifically girdles, for which the company pioneered the development of latex. In 1954, International Playtex applied the latex technology it had developed in making its girdles to a new line of household latex gloves, the first of their kind. Since that time, Playtex gloves have been the top product in this market in the United States.

With this expansion, the company added a Family Products division to its existing Apparel division. In the 1960s the new Family Products division also introduced Playtex disposable nipples and bottles for infant feeding to its product line and acquired a tampon manufacturing business. However, the company was still known primarily for its undergarments.

In 1969, Joel Smilow was named president of International Playtex, which was by then a subsidiary of Glen Alden Corporation, part of Rapid American Corporation. At that time, Playtex had annual sales of $183 million and 12,000 employees. Smilow, a graduate of Yale and a Harvard MBA, had been a brand manager at Procter and Gamble. When passed over there for a promotion, he joined some former P&G colleagues in the formation of Glendinning Cos., a marketing consulting firm. There, one of Smilow's clients was Playtex; he was eventually recruited by Playtex to fill the presidency.

Smilow brought to Playtex his marketing know-how from the packaged goods industry. Under his direction, the company began marketing bras, girdles, and rubber gloves in individual boxes and running coupon promotions. He also modified the company's sales approach, encouraging the sales force to make more frequent calls on customers, stocking their inventories as needed rather than just in bulk at the beginning of each season.

In 1975, International Playtex was acquired from Rapid American by Esmark Inc. Esmark allowed Playtex management to operate in relative autonomy, and Smilow was encouraged to diversify the company's products. He did this mainly by securing the rights to market promising new products at cheap prices, beginning with the expansion of the company's tampon business.

Tampons were invented in 1936 by Tambrands (long known as Tampax) as an alternative to sanitary napkins. Tambrands had a near-monopoly in this category until the mid-1970s, by which time International Playtex, Procter & Gamble, Johnson & Johnson, and Kimberly-Clark had each introduced its own line of tampons under the brand names of Playtex, Rely, o.b., and

Kotex, respectively. By 1980, Tambrands' share of the U.S. market had fallen from 100 to 42 percent.

The intense competition in this market led companies to strive to offer a better product; for tampons, this meant higher absorbencies, which were achieved by using different chemical compositions. Such new develpments, however, had serious drawbacks. Toxic Shock Syndrome (TSS), first identified in 1977, was a disease caused by a poison produced by a common and usually harmless bacterium, *staphylococcus aureus.* The majority of victims were menstruating women who used tampons, and in 1980, the Centers for Disease Control reported 890 cases of TSS, the most ever recorded. Tampon absorbency was suspected to be a factor, and Proctor & Gamble voluntarily withdrew their Rely products from the market that fall.

Five years later, researchers from Harvard proved that certain tampon fibers, including polyacrylate rayon, soaked up large amounts of magnesium, and that without that magnesium, *staphylococcus aureus* produced as much as 20 times the usual amount of the poison. The findings led International Playtex and Tambrands to replace products containing polyacrylate rayon with the safer, although less absorbent, surgical cotton. Product sales declined nationwide, as women were made aware of TSS and were encouraged to curtail their use of tampons in favor of sanitary napkins.

During this time, Esmark chairman Donald P. Kelly had named Smilow president of Esmark's Consumer Products group, and Smilow had hired Walter Bregman as president of International Playtex. Together, Smilow and Bregman had increased their diversification efforts and International Playtex had moved into marketing cosmetics, hair care, and sportswear.

In 1979, the company secured the rights (for free, according to a 1986 *Business Week* article) to distribute Jhirmack, a brand of hair care products then sold only in beauty salons. Five years after the first Jhirmack products were marketed in drugstores as an upscale product, the line was reporting annual sales of $70 million. Then, in 1983, International Playtex bought Almay cosmetics, which had been $5 million in the red the year before on sales of $19 million. After one year under Playtex's control, Almay made $3 million on sales of $33 million.

Smilow and Bregman's only mistake was with Danskin, acquired by Playtex in 1980 for $40 million. Under Playtex's parentage, Danskin's line of fashion swimwear was dropped and the product line was refocused on its rather plain nylon leotards for dancers, just as the fitness craze had women demanding more colors, styles, and cotton fibers in their exercise clothes. Management also decided to drop the company's sales commission policy, and 60 percent of the sales force left. Within five years Danskin had shrunk from $104 million in revenues and a command of 80 percent of the bodywear market to $54 million in sales and a 35 percent share. A group of investors, headed by Byron Hero, Jr., would later acquire Danskin for $20 million and help return the company to its position as a leading bodywear manufacturer.

By 1984, International Playtex was a $1.4 billion business, with 40 locations and 24,000 employees. That year, Donald P. Kelly tried to take Esmark private in a $2.4 billion leveraged buyout. He was outbid (by $300 million) by Beatrice Cos., Inc., the food and consumer products conglomerate. Smilow, by then chairman of the International Playtex division, was named executive vice-president and president of Beatrice's Consumer Products division. However, after four months he left the company and, in February 1985, Walter Bregman was fired from his position as president of International Playtex.

Within 18 months, Kelly, Smilow, and other former Esmark managers had bought out Beatrice and had taken it private in a giant leveraged buyout, borrowing $6.9 billion to do so. Smilow resumed his position as the head of Playtex, However, according to several articles, Smilow wanted his own company. When the lenders wanted a large part of their money back quickly, Kelly had to put parts of Beatrice up for sale.

In August 1986, Smilow and a group of executives formed Playtex Holdings, Inc. and bought International Playtex for $1.25 billion from BCI Holdings Corp., the owner of Beatrice Cos. At the same time, Playtex announced it was selling its cosmetic division to the Revlon Group for $375 million. International Playtex began its transition from being a subsidiary of a large, wealthy corporation to being a smaller, private company. Playtex Holdings created certain wholly owned subsidiaries: Playtex Family Products Corp., Jhirmack, and Playtex Apparel, Inc.

Early in 1988, Johnson & Johnson was poised to acquire Playtex Family Products for $726 million, a deal that eventually fell through. Jhirmack was also for sale during this time, and, according to an *Advertising Age* article, Smilow was hinting that Playtex Holdings would keep only its Playtex Apparel subsidiary. Then, later that year, an investor group, which included Smilow and other senior executives of Playtex Holdings, formed Playtex FP Group Inc. and bought Playtex Family Products and Jhirmack from Playtex Holdings. When the buyout was complete in December, Smilow became chairman and chief executive officer of the new company, with its wholly owned subsidiary, Playtex Family Group Corporation.

Throughout the buyout morass, Playtex management was making lots of money. Because of a stock option plan that "wasn't exactly stock-related," according to Smilow in a 1995 *Chief Executive* article, every hourly worker at Playtex got a small windfall when management sold the company and bought it back.

At the same time, after the repayment of $340 million of intercompany indebtedness, Playtex Holdings divested Playtex Apparel, Inc. to Playtex Apparel Partnership, L.P., a limited partnership owned by Smilow and the operating management of Playtex Apparel, Inc., for a $40 million subordinated debt. Smilow was named chairman and chief executive officer of Playtex Apparel Partnership, L.P., which focused solely on manufacturing and marketing women's undergarments.

Smilow was also in control of Playtex FP Group Inc., a heavily indebted manufacturer and/or distributor of tampons, gloves, hair care products (shampoo, conditioner, spray, and styling lotion), and disposable bottles, nipples, and nursing kits for infants. In line with his strategy of building Playtex brands and buying other companies, Playtex acquired the Cherubs collection of hard baby bottles for $9.3 million in 1989. This gained the company an entry into that segment of the infant care market.

Playtex FP's products operated in highly competitive markets, characterized by the frequent introduction of new products accompanied by major advertising and promotional campaigns. During the early 1990s, this was especially true of the hair care and tampon markets. By 1991, lower-priced shampoos and conditioners with the same up-scale attraction had cut Jhirmack's share to 2.4 percent of the $1.4 billion market. The company responded by reformulating the Jhirmack product line and positioning it as a fortifying product. Marketing did away with the outer carton, introduced a new bottle, and dropped Victoria Principal, Jhirmack's celebrity endorser, from its ad campaign. The relaunch of the line was backed by a $23 million ad and promotion campaign with the themes ''Bounce back beautiful hair'' and ''New Jhirmack gives your hair the strength to be beautiful.''

In late 1991, a major advertising and promotion ''war'' between Playtex FP and Tambrands began over plastic versus cardboard tampon applicators. Playtex FP had been a leader in the plastic applicator field, while Tambrands, Inc. was just about the only producer in the cardboard category. That year, Tambrands introduced its first plastic applicator. Playtex FP responded with Ultimates, a new line of cardboard applicator tampons. Playtex FP's share of the tampon market increased from 29 to 30 percent for 1992, and its introduction of Ultimates proved timely, as several states began proposing legislation to ban nondegradable plastic tampon applicators for environmental reasons.

Also during 1991, Playtex FP's senior management approached the Sara Lee Corporation to discern whether that company might be interested in acquiring Playtex FP or in making a large equity investment. In December, Sara Lee acquired 25 percent of the company and an option to purchase all remaining outstanding share of common stock. The proceeds of the $40 million transaction were used to refinance the company's debt. In November 1991, in a separate action, Smilow's other company, Playtex Apparel Partnership L.P., became a wholly owned subsidiary of Sara Lee; from that time on, there would be no corporate connection between Playtex undergarments and Playtex tampons.

However, Sara Lee's stock option placed certain restrictions on Playtex FP. Playtex was not allowed to issue any common stock through the end of December 1993, and all securities issued after that time were subject to the option. Furthermore, the company could not sell assets other than non-Playtex branded businesses.

In 1992, Playtex FP moved into the suntan lotion business when, for $5 million, it bought 22 percent interest in Banana Boat Holding Corp. The Banana Boat line was started by Robert Bell who, at age 13, developed a suntan lotion of baby oil, oranges, and bananas, which he mixed in coconut shells. He sold his concoction to tourists in Miami and Miami Beach for 50 cents to one dollar, including the shell.

Twenty years later, Bell's company, Sun Pharmaceuticals, marketed 54 tanning and sun-protection products worldwide under the Banana Boat brand and had sales of nearly $80 million. Playtex's investment allowed Sun, the wholly owned subsidiary of Banana Boat Holding, to acquire the assets of Sun Pharmaceuticals. In 1993, Playtex began distributing Banana Boat sun and skin care products for Sun in the United States and Canada.

By 1993, it was evident that the Sara Lee Corporation was unlikely to exercise its option on Playtex FP stock. Since Playtex management had limited alternatives for reducing its debt, they approached Sara Lee during the summer about terminating the option early and recapitalizing the debt. In December, Sara Lee agreed, for a consent fee of $15 million.

Freed from the option restrictions and attempting to raise much-needed cash, the company changed its name to Playtex Products, Inc. and went public, issuing 20 million shares of common stock in January 1994 at $13 per share. The company also merged its subsidiary, Playtex Family Products Corporation, into Playtex Products, Inc.

At the time, Thomas Cochran noted in a *Barron's* article: ''Playtex is a fine brand name, but it will carry so much debt [$927 million] that many investors will decide it lacks the resources to survive a business reversal, and additionally, lacks attraction because there is scant evidence to suggest sharp earnings improvement.'' The company used the net proceeds of the stock offering and other borrowing under the recapitalization to retire most of its outstanding debt and preferred stock.

The rest of 1994 was a busy year for Playtex. Following the recapitalization, the company completed the purchase of the Smile Tote line of baby products for $7 million. Smile Tote manufactured leak proof cups and bottles for infants and toddlers, using a patented snap top closure. In less than three years it had won 20 percent of the market. In 1991, its toddler juice cup was judged one of the most innovative new products launched that year, earning the Great Expectations award of the Juvenile Products Manufacturing Association. During 1994, Playtex also introduced several improvements in the Playtex disposable nurser line and updated colors, designs, and packaging. The Spill-Proof cup, introduced in October 1993, was the fastest-growing cup in the toddler market category, gaining almost a seven percent dollar market share in its first year.

Playtex also took over the sales and marketing responsibilities for Banana Boat from 17 independent distributors and sponsored a five-event volleyball series with the U.S. Volleyball Association to promote the brand. Rather than conducting large, nationwide advertising campaigns, the company concentrated on local radio. As a result, 50 radio stations, whose listeners were largely women in the 15-37 age group, conducted their own Banana Boat promotions. The promotions consisted of on-the-air contests for event tickets and day-long beach parties, at which Banana Boat products were given away. The marketing had its effect. Banana Boat's share of the market increased from 9.9 percent in 1993 to 13.7 percent in 1994, second only to Coppertone.

New products introduced at Playtex in 1994 included Dura Mitt, a cleaning tool which combined a latex mitt with a scouring pad or sponge. AcuPoll, a product idea screening company, identified Dura Mitt as one of the year's best new products, based on initial interest by surveyed consumers. Playtex also brought out several new tampon products, including Ultimates Silk Glide and Multi-Pack.

At the end of the year, the company announced a joint venture with Johnson & Johnson to export tampons abroad. The U.S. tampon market, which accounted for 54 percent of the company's net sales during this time, was regarded as a mature market, with little expansion likely. Therefore, it was hoped that the joint venture with Johnson & Johnson for overseas exports would help offset U.S. market trends.

Acquisitions continued apace in the mid-1990s. In February 1995, Playtex bought the assets of the Woolite rug and upholstery cleaning business for $20 million from Reckitt & Coleman. While Reckitt & Coleman, a London-based consumer products giant, retained the Woolite trademark, Playtex received a royalty-free trademark license. Woolite generated about $35 million in sales annually.

A major management change occurred later that year when Playtex sold 40 percent of its stock to Haas Wheat & Harrison Investment Partners for $180 million. Seven increases in short-term interest rates and increased promotional spending, particularly in the tampon market, had left the company with limited financial flexibility for new product development or further acquisitions. Management and various investment banks approached, directly or indirectly, 20 companies in the personal care industry, three companies in the paper products industry, and four pharmaceutical companies regarding the sale of Playtex Products. There were no takers until Haas Wheat, a Dallas investment firm, indicated its interest.

Joel Smilow, then 62 years old, resigned as chairman and CEO at this time. Robert Haas, chairman of Haas Wheat, replaced him as company chair, while Michael R. Gallagher, formerly of Reckitt & Coleman, was named CEO. When Playtex president and chief operating officer Calvin Gauss resigned in September 1995, Gallagher assumed his duties as well. Executive vice-president and chief financial officer positions were awarded to Michael F. Goss, formerly of Oak Industries. The new management team had its work cut out for them as Playtex Products faced depressed earnings and increased competition.

During the year the company completed acquisition of the remaining 78 percent of Banana Boat Holding Corp. it did not already own for a purchase price of $40.4 million plus the assumption of $27.1 million of long-term debt. "Sun care will now join our tampon, infant care, and glove businesses as a core part of Playtex's future," Gallagher stated in announcing the action.

By the end of 1995, Playtex had reduced its debt and its brands had strong, stable positions in their domestic markets. Earnings for 1995 and 1996 were expected to be low, however, because of the competitiveness of Playtex's markets and the need to spend so much for marketing. The company was still highly dependent on the tampon market, which represented 54 percent of its $473.3 million in sales in 1994 and more than two-thirds of its profits. Moreover, the company and its rival Tambrands were facing several lawsuits implicating their roles in cases of Toxic Shock Syndrome. In order to reduce the company's dependence on its line of tampons, new leadership at Playtex Products appeared to be following the company's long-term strategy of adding new products to its existing lines and buying up smaller businesses.

Principal Subsidiaries

Playtex Investment Corp.

Further Reading

Behar, Richard, "Faces Behind the Figures: Our Hero," *Forbes*, October 20, 1986, p. 156.

Byrne, John A., "The Anatomy of a Sacking," *Forbes*, August 12, 1985, pp. 100–102, 106.

Cochran, Thomas N., "Offerings in the Offing: Playtex Products," *Barron's*, January 10, 1994, p. 42.

Dreyfack, Kenneth, "Donald Kelly Just Can't Keep His Hands Off Beatrice," *Business Week*, November 4, 1985, p. 27.

Freeman, Laurie, and Pat Sloan, "Extra Prodtection: J&J Buys Playtex Tampons," *Advertising Age*, February 22, 1988, p. 70.

Harris, Marilyn, "Joel Smilow Finds The End Of His Rainbow," *Business Week*, August 25, 1986, pp. 67, 71.

McQuillen, Daniel, "Corporate Spotlight: Banana Boat," *Incentive*, July 1995, pp. 30–31.

"Playtex Products," *Morningstar Stock Reports*, Chicago: Morningstar, Inc., 1996.

"Playtex Products to Sell Haas Wheat 40% Stake for $180 Million," *New York Times*, March 20, 1995.

Resnick, Rosalind, "A Florida Businessman's Sunscreens Turn Out To Be As Golden As His Suntan," *Nation's Business*, March 1992.

Rotenier, Nancy, ed., "Faces Behind the Figures: Mr Fixit?," *Forbes*, February 12, 1996, p. 104.

Rudolph, Barbara, "Situation Wanted," *Forbes*, December 3, 1984, p. 246.

Sloan, Pat, "New UV Index May Help Make It A 'Banana Boat Kind of Day'," *Advertising Age*, May 2, 1994, p. 12.

Sparks, Barbara, "Mission Possible," *FW*, January 31, 1995, pp. 42–44.

Worthy, Ford S., "Beatrice's Sell-Off Strategy," *Fortune*, June 23, 1986, pp. 44–49.

—Ellen D. Wernick

Ponderosa Steakhouse

P.O. Box 578
Dayton, Ohio 45401
U.S.A.
(513) 454-2400
Fax: (513) 454-2525

Wholly Owned Subsidiary of Metromedia Company
Founded: 1968
Employees: 18,000
Sales: $450 million (1994)
SICs: 5812 Eating Places

Under the parentage of the Metromedia Company, Ponderosa Steakhouse is one of America's leading budget steak house chains. After 20 years of sometimes heated competition, Ponderosa was brought together with rival Bonanza under the corporate umbrella of John Warner Kluge's Metromedia Company. Each chains' profitability has historically been subject to the vagaries of fluctuating beef prices and a highly price-sensitive clientele. Moreover, when the United States dipped into recession in the late 1980s, Metromedia's budget steak chains went into a persistent decline. While Ponderosa had more locations than any other U.S. steak house chain in the early 1990s, it faced some challenges in the form of declining profits and management shakeups, and its sales lagged segment leader Sizzler by more than $100 million.

The first Ponderosa Steak House was established in 1968 in Kokomo, Indiana, by Dan Lasater and Norm Wiese. Barely out of his teens, Lasater had a high school education and a couple of years' experience managing McDonald's restaurants. Wiese was an auto dealer who held a key piece of real estate near a highway interchange. The two had joined forces to launch their own hamburger chain, Scotty's, but were inspired to enter the budget steak arena after learning of Bonanza's success in the South.

Bonanza International had been founded in Dallas by the Wyly brothers, Sam and Charles, in 1963 and was beginning to develop a national presence. But instead of buying a Bonanza franchise, Wiese and Lasater worked with their own, albeit similar, concept, which they called Ponderosa. Both Ponderosa and Bonanza menus featured a limited selection of steaks served with baked potato, salad, and a dinner roll. Cafeteria-style service kept labor costs low, and the use of lower-grade meat tenderized with enzymes helped keep food costs low. Much of the savings was passed on to the customer; Ponderosa's basic dinner cost just $1.39. The Indiana chain later bought its own beef processing subsidiary, ESI Meats, to further cut costs.

In keeping with the restaurants' shared western theme, competition between Bonanza and Ponderosa was wild. When the Wylys discovered the threat from the North, they looked for ways to trip up their new rival. Lasater related one of their "skirmishes" in an interview with Lawrence A. Armour excerpted in *Dun's*: "When the Bonanza International people saw that [we were starting a steak house] they hot-footed down and trademarked the Ponderosa name, which we had forgotten to do. We were pretty upset, but I got to wondering how smart they really were.... They hadn't [trademarked their own name]. So I went down and trademarked Bonanza, and we swapped off with them."

Lasater and Wiese were soon joined by Jack Roshman, a Dayton, Ohio, restaurateur who had been the largest franchisee in the now-defunct Burger Chef chain. Roshman took the Ponderosa concept to Ohio, while the original partners licensed expansions into Illinois and Kentucky. From 1968 to 1969 alone, Ponderosa System's sales multiplied from less than $1 million to $3.5 million. But the chain soon encountered a problem endemic to the fast food industry during this period: uncontrolled growth. Lasater pinpointed the difficulties in his interview with Armour: "We didn't have any controls, and we were having management problems. Money was going into unproductive investments like land, and legitimate creditors like equipment manufacturers weren't being paid." Lasater's expertise was in operations, and Wiese was little more than an investor; neither was particularly interested in fiscal administration. The company was insolvent by December 1969, and some creditors made moves to foreclose. The chain's credit was so bad that Wiese and Lasater were forced to take out personal loans to keep it afloat.

At that time, they promoted 28-year-old Gerald S. Office, Jr., from general counsel to chairman and chief executive officer. Office helped turn Ponderosa around. By mid-1971, the company had recovered enough to warrant a new stock offering. Annual sales increased from $42 million in 1972 to $73.54 million in 1973 and $114.76 million in 1974 Net grew from $6.05 million in 1973 to $9.47 million in 1974. Ponderosa's stock soared from $3 per share in 1970 to $84 per share in 1972, when it surpassed Bonanza to become the country's largest steak house chain. At that point Lasater, a 30-year-old multimillionaire, retired.

Ponderosa's managers got their first inkling of the beef industry's cyclical nature when a mid-1970s recession saw earnings tumble by more than 80 percent. But the chain recovered along with the nation in the late 1970s. Ponderosa's best year of the decade came in 1978, when the company chalked up $13.8 million in profits on an estimated $272 million in sales.

The roller coaster ride continued in the 1980s, however. Annual revenues increased to about $490 million by 1985, but earnings plummeted to $4.8 million. From 1980 to 1985, Ponderosa's return on equity averaged 9.9 percent, compared to 15 percent for Los Angeles-based Sizzler International, an up-and-comer that appealed to a more upscale clientele. Ponderosa's poor results were blamed on a variety of problems. Over half of the chain's restaurants were located in the Midwest's "rust belt," which was then enduring a major transition from its traditional manufacturing base to a more service-oriented economic base. Moreover, due to a lack of reinvestment, Ponderosa restaurants were becoming run-down and dated. The company also failed to quickly change its menus to accommodate American dietary trends that were increasingly calling for healthier fare, such as fish and chicken.

In an effort to balance out its changeable returns, Ponderosa attempted an early 1980s diversification within the restaurant industry. In 1982, CEO Office directed the acquisition of the five-unit Casa Lupita Mexican dinner chain. He hoped that the chain's high meal tabs, low food costs, and fatter profit margins would be the formula for more consistent earnings at Ponderosa Systems.

Ponderosa became a target of several takeover attempts during this period. The first came in 1980, when General Host Corp., the Stamford, Connecticut, parent of Hickory Farms, made its play for the steak houses. Then, in 1984, third-ranking Bonanza (U.S.A. Cafes) tendered a $154.8 million takeover bid for Ponderosa. Although the Wylys offered a ten percent premium over their rival's prevailing stock price, the leading chain's board rejected the offer as inadequate. Ponderosa's takeover defense cost it hundreds of thousands, but the company did manage to repel the threat.

In 1985, Ponderosa hired Thomas J. Russo as president. Russo had enjoyed a long career with Howard Johnson Restaurants, and had been credited with engineering a successful two-year turnaround at the struggling chain. He hoped to build Ponderosa into a 1,000-location chain by 1991. Instead, the mid-to-late 1980s deteriorated into a "baffling and demoralizing" time for Ponderosa and especially its franchisees, who operated over 40 percent of the chain's more than 650 locations.

Increased competition within the budget steak segment combined with management and ownership instability to create an extremely difficult operating environment. A Ponderosa franchisee recalled in a 1991 article by Bill Carlino of *Nation's Restaurant News*: "I don't care how good you are; you can't operate successfully with three leaders in three years."

In 1986, takeover artist Asher Edelman made his play for Ponderosa with the purchase of 18.5 percent of the chain's shares, a larger stake than that of the entire board of directors. Later that year, Edelman offered a generous $27.50 per share for the remainder of the company's stock, finally sealing the deal with a $29.95 bid that valued the chain at $235 million. The takeover shocked many restaurant industry observers. Charles Bernstein of *Nation's Restaurant News* editorialized that Ponderosa was "just a financial toy in Edelman's growing network of unrelated companies" and mourned "the loss of [the restaurant industry's] entrepreneurial spirit" in a March 1988 commentary.

His characterization of Edelman's approach proved accurate. Edelman installed himself as chairman, as Gerald Office ended his career at Ponderosa with a $12 million "golden parachute" severance package, and went on to purchase Empire Family Restaurants Inc. In classic fashion, Edelman tried to squeeze as much cash from Ponderosa as possible in as short a time as possible. He cut $7 million in expenses, eliminated 30 percent of the corporate staff, and terminated quality programs.

The newly-appointed management team was led by CEO Frank Holdraker. Formerly an executive with Pizza Hut, Holdraker instituted the Grand Buffet concept, an 80-item "all-you-can-eat" food bar. Although the Grand Buffet would become a popular feature at Ponderosa, it initially infuriated franchisees. Specifically, franchisees believed that the Grand Buffet raised their costs, while discounts and couponing intended to increase traffic (and thereby raise cash flow) only squeezed profits. Holdraker's unilateral decisions also engendered franchisee criticism. For example, the new leadership upgraded meats at company restaurants to USDA choice, while franchisees kept lesser cuts on their menus. When the chain tried to pass its higher costs onto customers, it only drove the notoriously price-sensitive clientele away.

In spite of all his efforts, Edelman found himself unable to reduce his heavy takeover-related debt, let alone turn the quick profit he had hoped for. In 1988, he sold out to John Warner Kluge's privately-held Metromedia Co. It was later revealed that Kluge had paid $8.6 million cash and assumed $290 million in debt to take control of the chain. Ponderosa formed the cornerstone of Metromedia's second incarnation. The new parent had operated a group of largely independent television stations from the 1950s to the early 1980s, when Kluge took it private. The six TV stations he sold to Rupert Murdoch in 1985 had formed the core of the Fox television network. At that time, Kluge liquidated virtually all of Metromedia's holdings, thereby generating a multi-billion-dollar personal fortune. Not content to sit back and count his billions, the venture capitalist saw in Ponderosa an opportunity to build a second empire, this time in steak houses.

Ponderosa's second ownership change in as many years brought a corresponding management transition. Holdraker resigned in 1989 and was replaced by J. Michael Jenkins. Jenkins had left S&A Restaurant Corp., operator of the Steak & Ale chain, in 1986 to assume the presidency of T.G.I. Friday's. He had tried to acquire S&A in the intervening years, but apparently gave up to join Ponderosa. Jenkins boosted his standing with Ponderosa's franchisees with the prompt ouster of Senior Marketing Vice-President Darrough B. Diamond. Many of the chain's affiliates had blamed Diamond for the costly Grand Buffet and what they perceived as Ponderosa's general lack of marketing focus.

In the midst of this management upheaval, Metromedia had purchased two of Ponderosa's competitors, S&A Restaurant (which operated both the previously mentioned Steak & Ale chain, as well as the Bennigan's chain) and Bonanza. Many analysts suggested, in fact, that Bonanza co-founders Sam and Charles Wyly, who had owned about 47 percent of the master limited partnership's stock, were behind the $83 million transaction. Immediately following its acquisition, the Bonanza chain was affiliated with Ponderosa under the aegis of Metromedia Steak Houses L.P.

This rapid succession of acquisitions and corporate shuffles sent another rumble through the restaurant industry, as well as Bonanza franchisees. Roger Lipton, an industry analyst with Ladenburg Thalman (New York) told *Nation's Restaurant News*'s Bill Carlino that Ponderosa "had been mismanaged for years," while Bonanza had "a good management team in addition to profitable stores."

Jeff Rogers, who had come up through marketing and became CEO of Bonanza in 1983, was the leader of that highly-praised team. He had guided Bonanza to its best year ever, in 1987, when net income rose to $8.6 million on about $500 million sales. Bonanza franchisees were chagrined to hear that Rogers was included in a 1989 management purge. His ouster was just one complication in what Carlino called a "bumpy transition process."

In spite of their apparent similarities, Ponderosa and Bonanza had evolved into two very different enterprises. Ponderosa's mostly company-owned units were concentrated in the Midwest. Bonanza had developed into a "pure franchiser," with only two company-owned locations. Most of its restaurants were located in the Southwest. As the "acquirees," Bonanza franchisees feared that the Bonanza name would be phased out and that they would have less input in the new organizational scheme. Several "area developers" (regional franchisee managers) joined forces and wrote an angry letter to Kluge noting that they had "retained independent counsel." Another group of "Bonanzans" incorporated their own franchise association. After an initial period of criticism—both from Bonanza franchisees and restaurant industry observers—several major Bonanza franchise owners converted to the Ponderosa format. It did not appear, however, that Metromedia would compel a wholesale changeover.

It seemed that Kluge had accumulated a critical mass in the steak house segment. The acquisitions gave Metromedia a stronghold of 1,300 units and over one-third of the $4 billion (1989) steak segment of the restaurant market. But this stronghold in no way ensured the type of success to which Kluge (and Kluge-watchers) had become accustomed.

In fact, Metromedia Steak Houses was regarded by many as a disappointment. Although Kluge was said to have poured over $1 billion into the steak house affiliate, it lost more than $190 million from 1989 to 1994. To top it off, by 1993 Ponderosa had slipped from number one to number two, and Bonanza dropped to sixth place in annual sales. These problems may have contributed to the reorganization that split Ponderosa (and Casa Lupita) off as the Ponderosa Steakhouse subsidiary and combined Bonanza with the more upscale S&A under the METSA, Inc. umbrella. Industry analysts blamed the difficulties on everything from high competition to scanty capital improvements and lingering takeover debt, but no one seemed to know how to turn them around. Continuing management purges could not have helped. In 1992, Kluge replaced Michael Jenkins with Michael Kaufman, an acquisitions specialist.

Although some observers speculated that Kluge would dispose of Metromedia Steak Houses, "the man with the Midas touch" wasn't known to sell at a loss. In 1993, Ponderosa franchisees attended an annual convention at which they learned of a new plan for the chain's success. Specifically, management was committed to updating and modernizing its restaurants and providing better training programs for employees. Moreover, the company proposed a "quality, service, and cleanliness program" (QSC) under which each restaurant would be analyzed and employee feedback would be sought in order to ensure efficient operations. With such reforms underway, Ponderosa hoped to realize improved sales figures in the mid-1990s.

Principal Subsidiaries

Casa Lupita Restaurants, Inc.; ESI Meats, Inc.; Ponderosa Financial Corporation; Ponderosa International Development, Inc.; Ponlupa Restaurant Financing, Inc.

Further Reading

Armour, Lawrence A., "Dan Lasater: How to Make $30 Million in Twelve Years," *Dun's*, May 1973, p. 14.

Bernstein, Charles, "Chains Play Pawns in Acquisition Game," *Nation's Restaurant News*, March 21, 1988, p. F3.

——, "Conglomerate Menace Stalks Chains," *Nation's Restaurant News*, August 14, 1989, p. F3.

——, "Edelman Group Wins Ponderosa," *Nation's Restaurant News*, January 1, 1987, p. 1.

Biderman, Charles, "A Bit Overdone?," *Barron's*, May 8, 1972, p. 11.

Brooks, Steve, "Round Up: Can an East Coast Billionaire Corral a Herd of Restaurants into One Rugged Team?," *Restaurant Business*, October 10, 1992, p. 86.

Carlino, Bill, "Ponderosa Franchisees Find New Optimism, *Nation's Restaurant News*, May 10, 1993, p. 1.

——, "Ponderosa Ropes Bonanza," *Nation's Restaurant News*, September 11, 1989, p. 1.

——, "Rogers Ousted From Bonanza," *Nation's Restaurant News*, November 20, 1989, p. 1.

——, "Wild Ride May Not Be Over for Metromedia and Its Steak Chains," *Nation's Restaurant News*, February 25, 1991, p. 8.

Cohen, Laurie P., "The Man With the Midas Touch Meets His Match in the Nation's Steakhouses," *The Wall Street Journal*, January 3, 1994, p. 9.

Kearns, R. L., "Ponderosa Systems: Trouble Around the Bend," *Commercial & Financial Chronicle*, January 6, 1975, p. 64.

Marshall, Christy, "Steak Chains Revamp Image and Ad Thrust," *Advertising Age*, October 3, 1977, p. 26.

Pillsbury, Richard, *From Boarding House to Bistro: The American Restaurant Then and Now*, Boston: Unwin Hyman, 1990.

"Ponderosa: A Steakhouse Tries to Fatten Profits by Going Mexican," *Business Week*, April 25, 1983, p. 98.

Romeo, Peter, "Steakhouses Check In at the Hotel," *Restaurant Business*, April 10, 1994, p. 24.

Sawaya, Zina, "Overcooked?," *Forbes*, June 8, 1992, p. 46.

Scarpa, James, "U.S.A. Cafes: Building a Better Bonanza," *Restaurant Business*, March 1, 1989, p. 146.

Simon, Ruth, "Charred Meat," *Forbes*, April 21, 1986, p. 93.

—April Dougal Gasbarre

Precision Castparts Corp.

4600 Southeast Harney Drive
Portland, Oregon 97206
U.S.A.
(503) 777-3881
Fax: (503) 653-4665

Public Company
Incorporated: 1956 as Precision Castparts Corp.
Employees: 5,166
Sales: $436.4 million (1995)
Stock Exchanges: New York
SICs: 3369 Nonferrous Foundries, Not Elsewhere
Classified; 3324 Steel Investment Foundries; 3724
Aircraft Engines and Engine Parts

A leading manufacturer of large, complex structural investment castings for the aerospace industry, Precision Castparts Corp. also manufactures blades and vanes used in commercial and military aircraft jet engines, as well as castings for use in industrial, automotive, medical, and other commercial applications. During the mid-1990s, Precision Castparts controlled 80 percent of the market for large investment castings, operating as a globally recognized force in a technologically advanced industry. With manufacturing facilities in Oregon, Ohio, Georgia, North Carolina, Colorado, Pennsylvania, and France, the company derived roughly half of its sales from Pratt & Whitney and General Electric, relying on its dominant position in the aerospace market to support its existence.

By the time Precision Castparts had entered into the business world on its own, the company had already established a national reputation as a manufacturer able to produce aircraft castings that the rest of the country's aircraft manufacturers were not capable of supplying. It was a remarkable distinction to have earned, particularly considering that Precision Castparts' formative years were spent within the corporate structure of another company, Oregon Saw Company, which was involved in a different line of business. Despite the success achieved by the casting operations that later became Precision

Castparts, when Oregon Saw Company was sold in 1953, four years after it was founded, the buyer did not want the casting operations. Occupying a singular position within its field, the future Precision Castparts was left aside and organized along with another company, Powder Power Tools, into a company called Omark Industries Inc. Three years later, in 1956, the casting operations were again passed over when Omark Industries was sold to Oregon Saw, which at the time was only interested in acquiring Powder Power Tools. As a result, the casting operations were spun off and incorporated as Precision Castparts Corp. in October 1956, marking the beginning of the company's rise to the top of its industry.

While these transactions were being negotiated and concluded, Precision Castparts was busy creating a unique identity for itself in the aerospace castings industry, developing technology that would give it a running start in business once it was spun off as a separate company. The genesis of the company occurred under the supervision of Oregon Saw, when during the early 1950s a group of workers developed a metals casting process for which the parent company had no use. In order to find a use for their process, the team of workers left Portland, Oregon, and headed south to the Los Angeles area, where a rapidly growing aerospace industry offered the greatest opportunity for finding customers interested in their casting process. After two years of doggedly canvassing the region's aerospace manufacturers, the clique of Precision Castparts workers finally secured their first order when AirResearch Corp. hired the company to make a part no one else could manufacture.

Beginning with the AirResearch order, which the company fulfilled to the customer's exacting specifications and complete satisfaction, Precision Castparts established itself as a respected manufacturer of structural castings, eventually becoming a world leader in the field largely through its use of the investment casting process. Investment casting involved using a wax replica of a part, then surrounding it with a ceramic shell—the investment—to create a mold. After heating the mold, which melted the wax, molten alloy, generally a combination of titanium, nickel, and other metals, was poured into the mold, creating a final product that rivaled the strength of forged and machined parts, at less than 50 percent of the cost of forging and fabrication. The investment casting process, also known as the "lost wax process," had originated during the Shang Dynasty (1766–1122 B.C.) in China before becoming a technique widely used by jewelers and dentists. For companies like Precision Castparts, however, investment casting could not produce parts big enough for their customers. Precision Castparts changed that with its proprietary process technology, transforming the casting method into one suitable for large-scale manufacturing purposes and etching a lasting position for itself in the casting industry.

By developing special mold materials and casting techniques, Precision Castparts was able to produce casting pieces as large as 60 inches. Soon Precision Castparts was inundated with orders, its initial success with the AirResearch contract spawning a host of others and providing the fuel to carry the company through the 1950s. At the end of the decade, the company added another casting method to its capabilities when it purchased a vacuum furnace in 1959 to prepare for the anticipated demand for structural aircraft parts that could withstand increasingly higher temperatures.

Vacuum casting soon became a pervasive trend within the industry and Precision Castparts benefited from the foresightedness of its management, as aircraft engine temperatures marched upward from 1,400 to 1,500 degrees Fahrenheit, then to 2,100 degrees Fahrenheit. Two more vacuum furnaces were added to the company's operations within the next ten years, helping sales increase fourfold between 1963 and 1967 to reach $9.5 million. On the heels of this first consequential surge in annual sales, Precision Castparts went public, making its initial public offering of stock in early 1968 as its prospects became increasingly brighter with each passing year. The company's greatest growth, however, would be recorded during the next two decades, a span during which Precision Castparts would evolve from a $10 million-a-year company into a $500-million-a-year market leader.

From its founding to the year the company went public, all of Precision Castparts' growth had been achieved by internal means, but its greatest growth was achieved once management jumped into the acquisitions fray and realized instant growth with the addition of established metals casting companies. Precision Castparts completed its first acquisition in 1976 with the purchase of Centaur Cast Alloys Ltd., based in Sheffield, England. Acquired to manufacture small investment castings for the British and European aerospace markets, Centaur Alloys was organized as a Precision Castparts subsidiary and renamed Precision Castparts, U.K. Ltd. (PCC-UK), bolstering the company's presence across the Atlantic, where Precision Castparts already sold castings to every major jet engine manufacturer in Europe, including Rolls Royce in Germany, SNECMA in France, and Fiat in Italy.

Domestically, General Electric and Pratt & Whitney ranked as Precision Castparts' two largest customers, accounting for the bulk of the company's annual sales, which by 1978 amounted to slightly less than $40 million. Over the next two years, annual sales more than doubled, reaching $97 million by 1980, providing part of the impetus for the next definitive development in Precision Castparts' history. With sales increasing exponentially, Edward H. Cooley, who had orchestrated

Precision Castparts' development since the company's incorporation, invested heavily in expanding the company's facilities and in developing new technology, spending $23 million to double production capacity just as the recessive early 1980s sent the airline industry into a pernicious tailspin.

Cooley's strategy might have ruined the company, but he was convinced that the airline industry would recover and orders would eventually come pouring in, with his investment enabling the company to take full advantage of the upswing. In the short term, however, aircraft deliveries in 1982 plummeted to less than 60 percent of 1980 levels. As a consequence, Precision Castparts' annual sales stalled at roughly $90 million, leading Cooley to hopefully confide to *Forbes*, "We've got plenty of capacity, we're just waiting for the orders."

Any anxiety created by the costly expansion of the company's operations on the eve of a downturn in the airline industry was obliterated when Cooley's predictions became true and the orders for structural airplane parts came rushing in. Sales began to climb upward, enabling the company to complete its second acquisition in 1984, when it purchased two small titanium foundries in Arudy, France. By the following year, annual sales had risen to $145 million, restoring the company's former vitality and setting the stage for the single most important acquisition in the company's history.

In the summer of 1986, Precision Castparts paid $66 million for Cleveland, Ohio-based TRW Inc.'s airfoils division, a producer of cast airfoils for aircraft and industrial gas turbine engines. The acquisition nearly doubled Precision Castparts' U.S. employment from 2,500 to 4,900, adding eight manufacturing facilities to the company's three manufacturing plants in Oregon, and other facilities in Ohio, Georgia, and North Carolina, and increasing its annual sales volume 80 percent to $180 million. Aside from providing an enormous boost to Precision Castparts' payroll, manufacturing scope, and annual sales, the addition of TRW's airfoils division lessened Precision Castparts' dependence on new aircraft production. Since two-thirds of the airfoils division's business was derived from the production of replacement parts; its business also moved Precision Castparts inside the aircraft engine for the first time, opening up a new market that complemented the company's world-renowned expertise in producing structural aircraft parts.

The acquisition of TRW's airfoils division represented a considerable boon to Precision Castparts' business, but while under TRW's management the division had been losing $15 million a year, prompting industry observers to qualify their approval of the company's acquisition. Although the airfoils division was reporting more than $1 million in monthly losses prior to its purchase by Precision Castparts, the company's new management moved quickly to find a solution and achieved astounding results before the new division crimped the company's overall profits. By the end of its first quarter of ownership, Precision Castparts' management had transformed the airfoils division, renamed PCC Airfoils, Inc., into a money-earner, creating a vibrant new facet to the company's business. At the end of PCC Airfoils' first full year, its effect on the company's finances was clearly evident: net income in 1987 totaled $21.2 million, up substantially from the $9.3 million posted in 1986, while sales during the year had leaped from $192.3 million to $326.2 million.

Recognized as the world leader in large investment casting, Precision Castparts entered the late 1980s buoyed by its acquisition and quick rejuvenation of TRW's airfoils division and propelled by a strong surge in business. Cooley's decision to double the company's manufacturing capacity at the beginning of the 1980s was paying enviable dividends by the end of the decade, as airline companies furiously expanded their fleets, replacing aging aircraft and installing new engines on old planes at a pace that lifted Precision Castparts' sales upward. Since Cooley's gamble, sales had more than quadrupled, climbing to $443 million by 1989, while profits had increased sevenfold, reaching almost $30 million.

With an order backlog standing at a record high of $445 million, spirits were high at Precision Castparts as the company prepared to enter the 1990s. In 1991 the company purchased Advanced Forming Technology Inc., a $7 million-a-year company that manufactured metal-injection molded parts for companies involved in the production of military ordnance, business machines, electronics, firearms, and medical instruments. The addition of Advanced Forming Technology's capabilities to produce small, complex metal parts for numerous industries strengthened Precision Castparts' involvement in non-aerospace business, which would become increasingly important in the coming years as economic recession once again affected the airline industry. The company's business grew steadily, with annual sales eclipsing the $500 million mark in 1991, rising to $538 million. In 1992, when PCC-U.K. was sold as part of the company's consolidation of its European operations in France at its subsidiary Precision Castparts Corp.—France SA, sales climbed to $583 million, from which a prodigious $47.3 million was recorded in net income. But by the following year the airline industry's slump had affected the company's financial health. Net income dropped to $1.8 million and sales slipped to $461 million in 1993, stalling the company's robust growth.

As Precision Castparts entered the mid-1990s, it continued to record stagnant sales growth, although its net income had climbed to $25.1 million by 1994. In April 1994 Precision Castparts acquired ACC Electronics Inc., a small manufacturer of advanced-technology metal matrix composite parts that was renamed PCC Composites, Inc., and organized as a subsidiary.

In early 1995 the company acquired Quamco, Inc., a manufacturer of a wide range of tools and equipment for industrial applications. Renamed PCC Specialty Products, Inc., the acquisition illustrated Precision Castparts' desire to increase its involvement in non-aerospace markets to lessen its dependence on the capricious industry. As Precision Castparts was preparing for the late 1990s and beyond, it was anxiously awaiting the return of a steady flow of aircraft parts orders to restore the pace of growth recorded during the 1980s, with its future growth dependent in large part on the vitality of its primary industry.

Principal Subsidiaries

PCC Airfoils, Inc.; PCC Specialty Products, Inc.; Advanced Forming Technology, Inc.; Precision Castparts Corp.—France, SA; PCC Composites, Inc.

Further Reading

Balcerek, Tom, ''Vacuum Casters Invest in Growth Industry; Costly Equipment, Experienced Operators Are Two Keys to Success,'' *American Metal Market*, June 10, 1986, p. 10.

''Castparts Buys Metal Matrix Composite Firm,'' *American Metal Market*, April 20, 1994, p. 5.

Cieply, Michael, ''Double or Nothing,'' *Forbes*, October 25, 1982, p. 54.

Furukawa, Tsukasa, ''Precision, Hitachi Units in Venture,'' *American Metal Market*, January 27, 1992, p. 4.

Jaffe, Thomas, ''Investment Investment,'' *Forbes*, October 3, 1988, p. 210.

''Precision Castparts Corp., *Wall Street Journal*, January 23, 1995, p. A13.

''Precision Castparts Corp.,'' *Wall Street Transcript*, August 6, 1974, p. 37, 790.

Reingold, Jennifer, ''Precision Castparts: What's Going On?,'' *Financial World*, March 2, 1993, p. 14.

Sherman, Joseph V., ''Investment Casting,'' *Barron's*, April 1, 1968, p. 11.

Velocci, Anthony L., ''Precision Castparts Dominates Its Market through Technology, Textbook Management,'' *Aviation Week & Space Technology*, May 27, 1991, p. 72.

Weiss, Barbara, ''Precision Castparts Has Turned Ailing Airfoils Div. Around in Vital Areas,'' *Metalworking News*, October 26, 1987, p. 14.

—Jeffrey L. Covell

Prince Sports Group, Inc.

One Tennis Court
Bordentown, New Jersey 08505-9630
U.S.A.
(609) 291-5800
Fax: (609) 895-7092

Wholly Owned Subsidiary of Benetton Sportsystem SpA
Incorporated: 1970 as Prince Manufacturing Co.
Employees: 300
Sales: $200 (1994)
SICs: 2329 Men's/Boy's Clothing Not Elsewhere
    Classified; 3021 Rubber & Plastics Footwear; 3949
    Sporting & Athletic Goods, Not Elsewhere Classified;
    6719 Holding Companies, Not Elsewhere Classified

Prince Sports Group, Inc. is the leading global manufacturer of tennis rackets. Renowned for its innovations in the tennis equipment industry, Prince also manufacturers Ektelon racquetball gear, footwear and sports apparel, ball-stringing machines, sports bags, tennis balls, and other goods. The company has retained its dominance of the tennis racket industry through innovation and savvy marketing.

The growth and success of Prince Sports Group is primarily attributable to the efforts of American inventor, sportsman, and entrepreneur Howard Head. Head, a consummate tinkerer and inventor, was an aeronautical engineer by trade during the 1940s. It was in the workshop of his Baltimore home that he staked his claim to fame. In 1950 Head invented the aluminum ski. Light and flexible, the innovation took the ski industry by storm and virtually revolutionized the sport during the 1950s and 1960s. In 1964 a pair of skis built by Head's ski company were used to capture a gold medal in the Olympics; the Head name was instantly imprinted on the minds of skiers around the world. Head capitalized on the popularity of his name by forming Head Sportswear International in 1966. The clothing line was an instant hit with the big-spending baby-boom generation,

and Head Sportwear was quickly thrust to the forefront of the surging sports apparel industry.

In 1971 Head, then a 60-year-old multi-millionaire, was ready to retire from his business, and he sold the company to AMF, a maker of sports equipment. Thereafter, Head decided to take up, among other pursuits, the game of tennis. Head found the game of tennis frustrating, partly because he found it difficult to hit the ball squarely with the small rackets that were used at the time. True to his nature, he went back to the drawing board and designed a better racket. Head spent two years perfecting the first all-metal, oversized tennis racket to replace the traditional small, wooden tennis racket. He patented the racket in 1975 and decided to try manufacturing and selling the invention himself, as he had his aluminum skis.

In 1976 Head purchased Prince Sports Manufacturing Co. Prince had been founded in 1970 as a small manufacturer of tennis ball throwing machines and had enjoyed some degree of success in its niche. Head planned to use the company to make and market his new design. Critics were initially amused with Head's new racket. Big, metal, and apparently unwieldy, the racket looked silly and out of place among tennis traditionalists. Just as Head's aluminum skis had changed the sport of skiing, however, the new racket was destined to change forever the game of tennis. Importantly, 16-year-old Baltimore native Pam Shriver used Head's unusual racket to become one of the youngest players ever to advance to the U.S. Open Tennis finals. That achievement renewed Head's international fame and established the credibility of the oversized racket.

Sales of Head rackets exploded during the late 1970s. Amazingly, by 1980—less than four years after introducing the new design—Prince was in control of a whopping 30 percent of the entire tennis racket market. Leading racket manufacturers gasped as they watched Prince rocket to the top of the global tennis racket industry. Suddenly, the key to Prince's success seemed incredibly obvious: a larger racket head made it easier to hit and control the tennis ball. Indeed, the face of the racket that Head sold during the late 1970s proffered 108 square inches of surface area, which was a full 30 square inches larger than standard racket faces. Its larger 'sweet spot,' or prime hitting surface, gave both recreational and professional players more control, power, and flexibility. The result was that the game of tennis was forever changed as more players adopted the oversized weapon and adjusted their playing strategies.

Prince captured its 30 percent U.S. market share and nearly 25 percent global market share during the late 1970s and early 1980s by selling its line of 108-inch rackets. Besides generating more sales from rackets than any other manufacturer in the world, Prince was able to generate some of the highest profit margins in the industry because its rackets were protected by a patent. In addition to its aluminum racket, Prince was able to boost profit margins by introducing 108-inch rackets made of exotic materials like magnesium (selling for $115 in the early 1980s), graphite ($250), and high-strength boron ($450). By 1980 Prince was generating revenues at a rate of more than $30 million annually. Sales for 1981 topped $35 million before vaulting 60 percent to nearly $57 million in 1982. In 1983, Prince's revenues stabilized some, rising 13 percent to about $64 million.

The slowdown in Prince's sales growth in 1983 reflected general deterioration of the tennis equipment market. Indeed, encouraged by Prince's market share gains, Chesebrough-Pond's, a massive consumer products conglomerate, had purchased Prince Sports in 1982. Chesebrough hoped to use its deep pockets to finance Prince's rapid expansion. The downturn in the tennis industry turned out to be worse than expected, however, as evidenced by Prince's sluggish sales gains in comparison to the increase in 1982 (Nevertheless, Prince's performance during the mid-1980s was impressive when contrasted with that of its peers). Prince had hopped into the tennis industry just as it was hitting its peak. 8.6 million rackets were sold in the United States in 1976. But that number began to decline substantially. By 1983 Americans were buying only three million rackets annually valued at about $170 million.

To make matters worse, U.S. tennis equipment manufacturers came under pressure during the early 1980s from foreign competitors. Specifically, low-cost Taiwanese manufacturers invaded the U.S. market with inexpensive knock-offs of popular rackets. To combat the market downturn and evade the onslaught of low-priced imports, Head began to expand its product line to take full advantage of Howard Head's original patent. The patent had covered racket head sizes ranging from 85 to 130 square inches, while the standard face was roughly 70 square inches. Late in 1984, Prince, for the first time, introduced two new racket head sizes: a 90-inch head and a giant 125-square-incher. The 90-inch head was tailored for long, hard shots more typical of singles play and was thus designed to compete in the burgeoning market for 'mid-size' rackets that had become popular with veteran pros like John McEnroe and Jimmy Connors. That segment was expected to offer the most growth through the mid-1980s.

Prince's supersized magnesium 125-square-inch racket was designed for doubles players, and was specifically intended for players who liked to plant themselves at the net and block the ball. Even Prince admitted that the racket was less than ideal for ground strokes from the baseline. Described as a "garbage can cover" by one sporting goods salesman, the racket pushed the limits of the International Tennis Federation rules.

In addition to the two new racket sizes, Prince tried to beef up sales beginning in 1985 with a new line of tennis apparel. Spearheading the entrance into the apparel market was a tennis suit lined with polypropylene, a material used in paper diapers that was designed to carry perspiration away from the skin to the outer layer of the garment.

Prince's new product introductions were integral to its survival during the malaise that continued into the mid-1980s. The number of rackets sold in the United States plunged to 2.5 million in 1985 for a total of only $160 million in receipts. Many racket manufacturers left the business or were absorbed by their struggling competitors. Prince, by contrast, managed to sustain moderate growth by snapping up market share. During the first six months of 1986, for example, U.S. racket sales slumped six percent while Prince's racket sales jumped ten percent. Aside from new sizes and new composite materials, Prince sustained growth through savvy and efficient marketing. Prince had chosen not to hire big-name tennis players to promote its products. Instead, it had invested heavily in collegiate and recreational marketing channels. It had also emphasized advertising to hard-core club players, because they tended to stick with the game and therefore were more reliable than more leisurely tennis players.

In 1987, Prince Sports Manufacturing Co. was purchased by members of its senior management team along with Brentwood Associates, a Los Angeles-based management buyout firm that would later be credited with engineering buyouts of Mobile Technology, Graphic Controls, Educational Publishing Co., and Acme Rents, among other companies. Under management ownership, Prince continued to boost sales and profits during the late 1980s, despite lackluster growth in the tennis industry. To augment tennis racket sales during the period, Prince diversified its offerings to include footwear, various apparel lines, racket strings, sport bags, ball stringing machines, and other racket-related gear that could be marketed under the respected Prince name. Most notable was Prince's entrance into the racquetball equipment industry with its Ektelon line of rackets and related gear. Likewise, Prince penetrated the golf market with golf shafts sold under the Grafalloy brand name.

Although the private company released only selected financial data, it claimed increases in both revenues and profits during the late 1980s. In 1990, however, management elected to sell the company "to allow Prince to continue its growth and development as the world's premier racquet sports company and, equally important, allow Prince to enter other sporting goods categories," according to John M. Sullivan, chairman of Prince Holdings Inc., in the September 6, 1990, *Business Wire*. Management sold the enterprise to Edizione Holding SpA, the Italian company that controlled, among other companies, Benetton Group. Prince was set up to operate as a subsidiary of Benetton Sportsystem, itself a subsidiary of Benetton. Sullivan acted as president and chief executive of Prince until 1993, when Arthur Bylin was named as his successor.

Also in 1993, the company's name was changed to Prince Sports Group, Inc. The name change reflected Prince's increasing product diversity during the early 1990s. Indeed, erratic tennis equipment markets required that Prince expand into more prosperous arenas to sustain growth. To that end, Prince aggressively chased the global sports apparel market, drawing on Benetton's proven track record in the apparel industry to make its mark. By 1992 Prince had elevated itself to the fifth largest global manufacture of tennis apparel and the sixth leading producer of tennis sneakers. In addition, it was posting gains with its racquetball and golf equipment operations. Going into 1993, in fact, tennis rackets were contributing only about 60 percent of total company sales.

Prince expanded production capacity to keep pace with growth, and added distribution facilities in Holland and Singapore. All the while, it continued to lead the tennis racket industry. Prince controlled about 25 percent of the global tennis racket market in 1993 and about 35 percent of what was considered the high-end racket market. To help make up for an early 1990s downturn in the tennis industry, Prince introduced new products and initiated new marketing schemes. Early in 1993, for instance, Prince introduced the Synergy Extender, a monster racket with a head of 116 square inches and an extra-wide body for added power. It also brought out rackets composed of new ceramic, alloy, and synthetic materials. Also in 1993, Prince organized the first Prince Cup, an amateur tennis tournament sponsored by Prince. The event drew about 6,500 participants in the United States, and the company planned to follow up with a world tournament beginning in the mid-1990s.

Estimated sales for Benetton's Prince subsidiary were $200 million in 1994, representing marked gains since Benetton assumed ownership of the company in 1990. Going into 1995, the company retained its position as the leading global tennis racket manufacturer and remained active in golf, racquetball, and sports apparel industries. It served those markets through three divisions that were created in 1993: Prince Golf International, Prince Sports Footwear, and Prince Racquet Sports.

Principal Subsidiaries

Ektelon-Prince; Langert Golf Co., Inc.

Principal Divisions

Prince Golf International; Prince Sports Footwear; Prince Racquet Sports

Further Reading

Bolger, Ray, "Inventor Howard's HEAD: Activewear Company of Late Sports Inventor Changes Hands, Seeks to Reinvigorate," *Warfield's Business Record,* October 16, 1992, p. 1.

Dumaine, Brian, "Prince Gets Into Some New Rackets," *Fortune,* October 19, 1984, p. 78.

Gallagher, Patricia, "After Bad Run, Can Wilson 'Just Do It'? The Latest CEO Hustles to Put Pep in its Step," *Crain's Chicago Business,* August 15, 1994, p. 1.

Jarman, Max, "Tennis Innovator Faces Patent Fight," *Arizona Business Gazette,* March 29, 1991, p. 3.

Reilly, Patrick, "Tennis Anyone? Dwindling Interest Hurts an Industry," *Crain's New York Business,* December 1, 1986, p. 1.

Siegel, Ralph, "Top Tennis Racket Firm Relocating in County," *Burlington County Times,* October 28, 1992, Bus. Sec.

Teitelbaum, Larry, "Prince Serves Up Corporate HQ in Burlington County," *Philadelphia Business Journal,* September 24, 1993, p. 5B.

Winskie, Julie, "Leading Tennis Manufacturer Prince Holdings Acquired by Edizione," *Business Wire,* September 6, 1990.

—Dave Mote

Progress Software Corporation

14 Oak Park
Bedford, Massachusetts 01730
U.S.A.
(617) 280-4000
Fax: (617) 280-4095

Public Company
Incorporated: 1981 as Data Language Corp.
Employees: 1,200
Sales: $180.13 million (1995)
Stock Exchanges: NASDAQ
SICs: 7372 Prepackaged Software

Progress Software Corporation is a global supplier of application-development and database software products and services for information-service organizations in business, industry, and government. The company's Enterprise Division markets the company's PROGRESS product line which includes a software application development environment (ADE) that consists of the PROGRESS fourth generation language (4GL), the PROGRESS relational database management system (RDBMS), and related application development tools. PROGRESS products enable developers to quickly and cost-effectively create and deploy enterprise-class client/server software applications for PROGRESS, Oracle, Sybase, SQL Server, ODBC, and DB2/400 databases. The company's Crescent Division is a leading supplier of software tools and add-on components, services, and support programs for corporate users developing business-critical applications with Microsoft Corporation's Visual Basic application development environment. The products of Progress are sold directly to organizations and through more than 2,300 resellers offering thousands of applications and serving a wide range of industries. The company markets and supports its products in more than 60 countries through a network of more than 20 subsidiaries and more than 30 distributors operating in Europe, Australia, Latin America, and Asia.

Progress Software Corporation was founded in Bedford, Massachusetts, in 1981 by three veterans of the mainframe computer application development market—Joseph Alsop (nephew of the political columnist Joseph Alsop and older brother of future computer industry commentator Stewart Alsop II), Charles Clyde, and Ziering Kessel—and incorporated that same year as Data Language Corporation. Alsop went on to become president of the company, while Clyde became director of development and Kessel became chief technical officer.

Targeting the need for comprehensive and high-level application development products able to enhance information processing productivity in a growing midrange computer systems market, Data Language Corporation was launched after its founders developed the PROGRESS Application Development Environment (ADE), designed to enable development and deployment of software applications that were scalable, portable, and reconfigurable across client/server, host-based and mixed computer environments. Opting to avoid head-on competition with established mainframe computer software companies and choosing not to develop software for the then-young IBM personal computer (with limited memory), the company's founders initially developed the PROGRESS ADE for only the Unix operating system, closely associated with the third generation Cobol or language C, a programming language then popular only within academic and scientific communities.

In 1984 Data Language released its first commercial version of the PROGRESS ADE for Unix and the following year unveiled a version for MS-DOS. In 1985, the company's first full year of product shipments, Data Language recorded its first profitable year. By 1987 the company had released PROGRESS software for computer networks and the VAX/VMS (a Digital Equipment platform) and CTOS/BTOS operating systems and was gaining increasing marketplace attention and brand name recognition; as a result, the company changed its name to Progress Software Corporation to reflect the name of its software.

By the end of the decade Progress's growth was being recognized by business periodicals. In 1989 the company was ranked 38 on *Inc.* magazine's list of the 500 fastest-growing private American companies and was first among that list's $10-million software companies as well as the largest supplier of database and application development software on *Inc.*'s list. In 1989 Progress was also ranked seventh on the *New England*

Business list of the 100 fastest-growing private and public companies in that region.

During the late 1980s about half of Progress's revenues were being generated annually from international business which stemmed from a network of wholly owned subsidiaries in Europe and Australia that had grown in number to ten and a distribution system spanning Europe, Asia, and Latin America. By 1990 Progress sales had mushroomed sevenfold since 1987, from $6.1 to $40 million.

Between 1989 and 1990 Progress released PROGRESS Version 5 and Version 6, both enhanced versions of its 4GL language and RDBMS. New features of Version 5 included support for ANSI-standard Structured Query Language (SQL) and a DOS memory saver. Applications developed with Version 5 could run unaltered on multiple operating systems—such as microcomputers and minicomputers and diverse and dissimilar networks of different hardware, operating systems and network protocols—including VAX/VMS, MS-DOS, UNIX, XENIX, ULTRIX, AIX, A/UX and CTOS/BTOS and also networks using NetBIOS, TCP/IP, DECnet, OpeNET, and SPX/IPX protocols. Version 6 allowed users to access, modify and integrate data in and among databases made by Progress, Oracle, and Digital Equipment Corp. (DEC), and the updated RDBMS additionally allowed users to access third generation language (3GL) and as many as 240 databases simultaneously.

By 1990 Unix had become a commercially popular operating system because it was not restricted to particular computer brands and functioned on a multiple-user network. Unix was as a result popular with Progress's customers: large corporation computer programmers writing custom-designed software for in-house use, representing about one-third of the company's business, and resellers, typically selling deployment versions to clients in retailing, medical accounting, manufacturing and trucking. Entering the 1990s the company's marketing focus was directed towards these "value-added" resellers that utilized Progress products to develop their own commercially sold software applications. The middleman resellers of PROGRESS products purchased program development software from Progress and then in turn spawned business as their clients purchased dozens of scaled-down program versions, each requiring a deployment license from Progress and thereby generating substantial follow-on revenues (represented by more than 60 percent of the company's 1990 North American revenues).

In 1991 Progress expanded its cross-platform reach after agreeing with Micro Decisionware Inc. to develop and market a link from the PROGRESS 4GL and RDBMS to IBM host environments that could connect to Micro Decisionware's database. That same year the PROGRESS ADE was chosen over competing systems made by Oracle, Ingres, Informix and Sybase to support the new second-generation library automation system made by CLSI Inc., a leader in the library-automation industry.

In July 1991—with the popularity of the Progress's computer development language and database growing—Progress went public, selling 1.2 million shares of stock (half by the company and half by certain stockholders) at an initial offering price of $25 as the company's stock debuted as one of the most active stocks in over-the-counter trading on the New York Stock Exchange. Proceeds were used to cover working capital needs through the 1992 fiscal year. With technology stocks a hot commodity on Wall Street, within a week of the initial public offering Progress's stock had climbed to 28 and three-quarters and by November of that same year risen to $44. For its 1991 fiscal year, Progress's earnings rose 58 percent to $6 million on revenues that jumped 46 percent to $58.3 million.

After broadening its focus in 1991 to include IBM platforms, in February 1992 Progress released PROGRESS/400, an updated version of its application development software for the IBM AS/400 operating environment. The new software allowed AS/400 developers and users to create and run client/server applications in the AS/400 environment and for the first time to support development and implementation of distributed applications that allowed users to access data across a network of MS-Windows, OS/2 and RS/6000-AIX that was linked to IBM AS/400 database servers. The release of PROGRESS/400 not only brought the capabilities of PROGRESS to the IBM AS/400 mid-range computer family; it also marked a formalization of a marketing and sales agreement that named Progress an IBM "industry applications specialist" and helped spawn an agreement for Progress to develop cooperative applications for J.D. Edwards & Company, a leading supplier of AS/400 environment software.

In 1992 Progress and Object Design, Inc. agreed to jointly develop and market software linking the PROGRESS 4GL to Object Design's ObjectStore object-oriented database management system. That same year Progress linked up with Avis Inc. to develop a new transaction-processing system for rental car tracking based on the PROGRESS system.

By the close of 1992 the global operations of Progress had been expanded to 12 subsidiaries and 34 distributors operating in more than 50 countries. For fiscal 1992 Progress's earnings mushroomed 58 percent to $9.61 million on revenues which leaped 46 percent to $85 million.

Progress entered 1993 fifth in the $1.2 billion Unix market for application development tools (controlling about 4 percent of the market), with its shares trading at $57, down from a 52-week high that peaked in December 1992 at $61.50 but substantially higher than its 1992 low in the mid-20s. Progress's business strategy had evolved by this time to include competing with major application-development forces such as Oracle in the open database system market by producing application development tools which could run on both PROGRESS and Oracle databases. And while larger competitors often targeted a customer base that focused on central corporate offices such as accounting, Progress's products targeted individual lines of business within corporations that tended to require customized applications and thereby offered a marketing niche for Progress.

In order to broaden the ability of PROGRESS to support other operating systems, in 1993 Progress expanded its strategic alliances and was named an "independent software vendor" for Unisys, making the PROGRESS ADE the first to be jointly marketed under the Unisys developer relations program. That same year Progress also signed a cooperative software marketing agreement with IBM, becoming one of the first application development tool vendors chosen by IBM to join its market development program designed to increase the number of AS/400 application development tools available. In 1993 Progress additionally signed an agreement to support Novell Inc.'s network operating systems (which in turn could be connected to IBM's AS/400 midrange platform) and an agreement with Santa Cruz Operation, an international leader in open systems software, for joint engineering, training and support.

Delays in the delivery of PROGRESS Version 7 pushed the company's stock into the mid-30s range in 1993 before the new operating system was released late that year in Progress's first worldwide marketing initiative and global positioning of its product line. Version 7, a cross-platform ADE featuring new capabilities for client/server environments, expanded Progress's stake in the server and application development market to include Windows and Motif graphical user interface (GUI) platforms, with versions released for Windows, SCO Unix, HP/UX, AIX and SPARC operating systems. Version 7's cross-platform ADE allowed users to create both character-based and GUI applications and move applications to Windows or Motif without any code changes, making it easier for developers to create new Windows and Motiff applications.

In 1993 Progress continued expanding its marketing reach, adding three new wholly owned subsidiaries—in Spain, Mexico, and Singapore—aimed at strengthening the company's position in Asian/Pacific, Latin American and European markets. By the end of the year Progress had 15 international subsidiaries and the company was ranked 82nd on *Fortune* magazine's list of America's 100 fastest-growing companies and 86th on *Forbes* 1993 list of the 200 best small publicly traded companies. Progress also had a network of more than 2,000 resellers using the company's application tools to develop custom applications, with 60 percent of the company's revenues in 1993 coming from these activities and add-on sales of deployment software versions. For 1993, the company's earnings rose 34 percent to $12.8 million on revenues that broke the nine-figure plateau for the first time and rose 31 percent to $111.64 million. Despite the company's move into the IBM AS/400, more than two-thirds of the company's revenues came from Unix products in 1993.

By 1994 Progress had a range of products that could work in a variety of development and deployment environments and support graphical, character mode and block mode application deployment using either the PROGRESS RDBMS or other high performance dataservers to work across networked, client/server designs. In 1994 Progress began focusing on speeding up the process of application development and providing greater access to various operating systems, resulting in the release of PROGRESS Dataserver, a Windows-based program enabling users to access information in databases of two competitors, Oracle and Sybase. That same year Progress entered into a cross-platform support agreement with Novell.

In June 1994 Progress formed a joint venture subsidiary with Nissho Iwai Corporation, one of Japan's largest diversified general trading companies. The new 50 percent-owned subsidiary, designed to market PROGRESS products and expand the company's presence in the Pacific Rim, was later incorporated as Progress Software KK.

With more 250,000 product licenses worldwide and a network of 18 international subsidiaries and 33 distributors operating in 60 countries, Progress entered 1995 by substantially expanding its product line through a signficant acquisition. In January 1995 Progress acquired Crescent Software Inc., a Connecticut-based leading developer of add-on components for users of Microsoft's Visual Basic (VB), for $3 million (including about $2.5 million of in-process software development). At the same time Progress created two divisions within the company: the Enterprise Division, to develop and market all PROGRESS products; and the Crescent Division, to market existing Crescent add-on components and develop an integrated suite of high-performance products to enhance and make application development within Visual Basic easier. The acquisition of Crescent targeted Progress's growing interest in serving an estimated one million Visual Basic users and giving those developers of client/server applications more options when working with the Microsoft application development program. With Visual Basic growing in popularity as a client/server tool for personal and workgroup market segments, the acquisition resulted in several strategic benefits: it legitimized the market for VB add-ons (which previously were often of low quality and developed by smaller software firms); it expanded Progress's product line into low-end software; and it provided the company with a means to turn around a two-year slide in sales growth by capitalizing on the growing popularity of Visual Basic and offering developers tools and components to build more complex applications.

At the time of the acquisition Crescent developed and sold VB tools and components and had its own communications add-on code; in addition, Progress set its new division on a course to create development tools for faster VB applications and announced the planned development of new VB add-ons that could translate VB code into C++ (a modified version of language C). Two months after Progress acquired Crescent, the company unveiled the division's first new product: PowerPak Pro, a suite of VB development tools and components designed to provide users with more efficient development and deployment of workgroup and departmental applications for businesses.

Progress continued expanding its international operations in 1995. In February the company opened its first Central European subsidiary (and its 13th European subsidiary) in Prague, Czech Republic. The new subsidiary, Progress Software SPOL, S.R.O., was formed to market and support the company's PROGRESS ADE in the rapidly growing republic and serve governmental and industrial customers, including those in banking, finance, healthcare and manufacturing. In June 1995 Progress opened a centralized technical support facility in Rotterdam, The Netherlands to serve its operations in Europe, the Middle East and Africa. The new EMEA Technical Service Centre—offering a laboratory, training capabilities and engineers fluent in local languages—initiated service for The Netherlands with support for other countries expected to be phased in through 1996.

In November 1995 Progress released its PROGRESS Version 8 ADE, making client/server application development easier and faster by capitalizing on the power of Object-Oriented (OO) programming, a component-based visual programming development environment. Features of Version 8 included the new PROGRESS SmartObjects that capitalized on the advanced OO technology and provided reusable application components (or pre-programmed components) that could be assembled into applications. The Version 8 RDBMS was expected to be released in early 1996.

In late 1995 Progress announced it would support Digital Equipment's Alpha systems running on Microsoft Windows operating system, and the Crescent Division released its new VB4 Jump Start Kit which could assist corporate developers with their transition to the Microsoft Windows 95 operation system and VB 4.0. Crescent also introduced OLE Custom Controls (OCX) versions of its entire product line, enabling corporate developers to create more sophisticated VB business applications using custom controls.

In 1995 Progress was listed 116th on *Forbes* 1995 200 Best Companies in America. And while Progress's sales growth began declining during the early 1990s—falling from 46 percent in 1992 to 25 percent in 1994 as resellers were slow to convert from the company's older character-driven versions of PROGRESS to the more graphical, event-driven programs beginning with Version 7—that conversion was nearly complete by the close of 1995. For the year Progress's sales growth climbed to 29 percent, and earnings rose 16 percent to $16.68 million on revenues of $180.13 million (compared to 1994 when the company's stock fluctuated from a high of $56.50 to a low of $27.25 and Progress earned $16.9 million on revenues of $139.2 million).

In early 1996 Progress began initial steps to become a major World Wide Web supplier of products by using the Web to market its products, offering buyers the opportunity to secure and order delivery of products. The company also announced that by mid-year its Enterprise Division would sell Smart-Objects products through a Web site storefront. In early 1996 the Crescent Division also took initial steps to use the Internet for marketing purposes and launched Code Depot, a on-line storefront designed to serve the needs of VB application programmers.

Progress moved towards the close of 1996 with its principal competition comprised of larger companies: Oracle, Sybase (which in 1995 acquired another competitor, PowerSoft Corp.) and Informix. Nonetheless, Progress had a distinct competitive advantage in its RDBMS which could work on most types of computer hardware, including that made by competitors. The company also expected to profit from the growing Visual Basic add-on tools market by introducing new products and capitalizing on the strong relationship Crescent has had with Microsoft Corporation, allowing Progress to take advantage of the release of new Microsoft desktop standards. Progress additionally hoped to benefit from two business trends: the growth in corporate client/server-based networks and the decentraliza-

tion of large corporations, making more important the departmental market for application development software.

Principal Subsidiaries

Progress Security Corp.; Progress Software International Sales Corp. (Barbados); Progress Software Corporation of Canada Ltd.; Progress Software GesmbH (Austria); Progress Software Ltd. (Hong Kong); Progress Software NV (Belgium); Progress Software A/S (Denmark); Progress Software Corp. Ltd. (China); Progress Software Oy (Finland); Progress Software GmbH (Germany); Progress Software B.V. (The Netherlands); Progress Software Svenska AB (Sweden); Progress Software AG (Switzerland); Progress Software de Argentina S.A.; Progress Software KK (50%) (Japan); Progress Software Ltd. (United Kingdom); Progress Software Pty., Ltd. (Australia); Progress Software S.A. (France); Progress Software SPOL, S.R.O. (Czech Republic); Progress Software A/S (Norway); Progress Software International Corporation; Progress Software Europe BV; Progress Spain S.A.; Progress Software de Mexico S.A. de C.V. (Mexico); Progress Software Ptc. Ltd. (Singapore).

Principal Divisions

Enterprise Division; Crescent Division.

Further Reading

Bozman, Jean S., "First Links Between Object, Relational Databases Forged: Vendors Announce Partnerships, Tools to Bridge Architectural Gaps," *Computerworld*, July 27, 1992, p. 12.

Churbuck, David, "Speaking the Language," *Forbes*, November 25, 1991, p. 192.

Derringer, Pam, "Progress Plugs on with Steady Growth," *MASS HIGH TECH*, October 2, 1995, p. 9.

Gambon, Jill, "Progress Software Reaps Profits, Wants Visibility," *Boston Business Journal*, January 25, 1993, p. 7.

Heichler, Elizabeth, "High-End Updates Target Visual Basic: Vendors Address Trend with Expanded Capabilities," *Computerworld*, January 30, 1995, p. 63.

Leach, Norvin, "Progress Looks to Low-End Tools for Higher Growth," *PC Week*, February 6, 1995, p. 116.

Kingoff, Elaine, "Progress Marches On," *VarBusiness*, April 15, 1995.

McLaughlin, Mark, "Progress Software: Developing the Strategic Gain," *Boston Globe*, October 27, 1991, p. 74.

Ricciuti, Mike, "Progress Cross-Object Framework on the Way: Will Mask Object Difference," *InfoWorld*, May 22, 1995, p. 6.

Scheier, Robert, "Progress Pledges VB Tools: Extensions to Simplify SQL Queries," *PC Week*, January 16, 1995, p. 21.

Slater, Derek, "Progress Strategy Paying Off," *Computerworld*, May 17, 1993, p. 115.

Wilson, Jayne, and Scott Mace, "Progress Marches into Graphical Environment," *InfoWorld*, July 12, 1993, p. 13.

—Roger W. Rouland

Pulitzer Publishing Company

900 N. Tucker Boulevard
St. Louis, Missouri 63101
U.S.A.
(314) 340-8000
Fax: (314) 340-3050

Public Company
Incorporated: 1878
Employees: 2,400
Operating Revenues: $485.6 million
SICs: 2711 Newspapers; 4833 Television Broadcasting
    Stations; 4832 Radio Broadcasting Stations

Pulitzer Publishing Co. is one of the oldest media companies in the United States. It owns two newspapers, nine television stations and two radio stations.

Joseph Pulitzer, born into an educated Hungarian family, left his home in Mako, near Budapest, in 1864. He was 17, and used a chance to serve in the Union Army as his ticket to emigrate to the United States. After serving in the Army for eight months, he moved to St. Louis.

Virtually destitute, he took odd jobs and sometimes slept in a park. Because he was fluent in German (though not yet in English), Pulitzer got a job at the German-language newspaper *Westliche Post.* He proved to be a remarkable reporter, frequently scooping reporters at rival English-language papers. By 1871 he was able to buy part of the *Westliche Post,* and in the next few years he bought and sold several area newspapers. In 1878 he bought the bankrupt *St. Louis Evening Dispatch* for $2,500, and merged it with John A. Dillon's struggling *St. Louis Evening Post.* In 1879 Pulitzer bought out Dillon's share for $40,000.

The *St. Louis Post-Dispatch* combined tales of crime and scandal with respect for the working class and advocacy of democracy and civil rights. The newspaper also exposed government corruption and other problems, becoming one of the first practitioners of crusading journalism. It investigated gambling, prostitution, and a railroad monopoly that some felt was

hurting business in St. Louis. Few other newspapers were as aggressive in their reporting. This mixture proved to be a successful formula. As Pulitzer's newspaper grew in popularity, he dreamed of becoming a press baron. In 1883 he bought the *New York World* for $346,000 from railroad magnate Jay Gould. It quickly became a success: in two years its circulation climbed from 15,000 to 150,000, making it the biggest newspaper in the United States, and in 1886 it earned over $500,000. In 1887 Pulitzer established the *Evening World.* He built a modern headquarters for his newspaper holdings in New York in 1889 and 1890, at a cost of $2.5 million.

In 1893 the *World* published the first color supplement in a newspaper, composed of reprints from humor magazines. It increased the newspaper's circulation, partly because so many newspaper readers were immigrants trying to learn English. Two years later, the World published what became the world's first comic strip, "Hogan's Alley," starring the Yellow Kid. In late 1896 Pulitzer's rival William Randolph Hearst began using a color press. He lured away Richard F. Outcault, the strip's creator, and a huge circulation war broke out in New York, punctuated by raids on newspaper staffs, promotion contests, and price reductions.

At the same time, Joseph Pulitzer's health was declining. He suffered from asthma and diabetes, and had to have newspapers read to him because his sight had grown so poor. He also suffered from intense mood swings that made him difficult to work with. The elder Pulitzer gradually turned over operations in St. Louis and New York to his sons and officially retired in 1907. Upon his death in 1911, Ralph and Herbert Pulitzer directed the *New York World,* while Joseph Pulitzer II, whom his father had thought less promising, took over the *Post-Dispatch.* The elder Pulitzer's will stipulated that Pulitzer Publishing be set up as a trust with equal votes for each of his three sons. They elected Joseph the president of Pulitzer Publishing in 1912.

Joseph Pulitzer II focused on the editorial side of the *Post-Dispatch,* but he did make occasional business decisions. One of his first moves was to ban the advertising of dubious medical products, turning away millions of dollars of advertising. He had often fought with his father over this, but the elder Pulitzer had refused to give up the revenue brought by such ads.

Pulitzer became interested in radio earlier than most other newspapers, joining in a 1904 demonstration of what was then called "wireless telegraphy." The firm's serious involvement with broadcasting began in 1922 with radio station KSD. In 1926 the station joined with others to form the NBC Radio Network.

The *Post-Dispatch* continued to investigate and expose corruption, playing a leading role in reporting the corruption that became the Teapot Dome oil scandal in the 1920s, for example, and leading a crusade against the Ku Klux Klan.

In 1931 the *New York World* folded, done in by a combination of bad management and the Great Depression. It was bought by the *New York Telegram*. The *Post-Dispatch*, in contrast, remained financially and journalistically healthy. In 1936 it received a Pulitzer Prize for uncovering St. Louis voter registration fraud, and another for a 1941 crusade against air pollution.

Post-Dispatch managing editor Oliver K. Bovard, one of the most senior figures at the newspaper, left in 1938 over differences with Joseph Pulitzer II. Bovard wanted complete control over the editorial section and wanted the *Post-Dispatch* to advocate socialism, which he saw as a remedy for the social toll taken by the Great Depression. Pulitzer refused, and after Bovard's departure he became a more dominating editor-in-chief. The editorial page was in flux for years after this as Joseph Pulitzer II had trouble finding editorialists who were neither too liberal nor too sedate for his taste.

During World War II the *Post-Dispatch* had its own correspondents covering the war. The paper received another Pulitzer Prize in 1948 for an investigation of a mine disaster in nearby Centralia, Illinois, and in 1950 the newspaper won its fourth Pulitzer Prize under Joseph Pulitzer II for revelations that some Illinois journalists were on the State of Illinois payroll.

Pulitzer took an early interest in television. The firm bought television equipment from the RCA Company in the early 1940s. In 1947 KSD-TV became the first television station in St. Louis. Television dramatically changed the newspaper marketplace. With afternoon and evening newspapers being hurt by the emergence of television, the firm bought the afternoon *St. Louis Star-Times* in 1951 and folded it into the *Post-Dispatch*. Joseph Pulitzer II died in 1955, and was replaced by his son, Joseph Pulitzer III, who had already been working for the company for many years.

In St. Louis the *Globe-Democrat* competed with the *Post-Dispatch*. Under a 1961 agency agreement, which allows competing newspaper to share printing and other facilities so that both can stay in business, the *Post-Dispatch* was St. Louis's afternoon and Sunday newspaper, while the *Globe-Democrat* was the morning paper and produced a weekend edition. Pulitzer managed the production and printing of both newspapers, while their news, editorial, advertising, circulation, accounting, and promotion departments remained separate. In the late 1960s the *Post-Dispatch* became one of the first major U.S. newspapers to oppose the Vietnam war.

Joseph Pulitzer III wanted the company to expand. In 1968 the firm bought part of KVOA-TV in Tucson, Arizona. Under U.S. Department of Justice rules it had to sell that interest in

1971 when it bought the *Tucson Daily Star* for $10 million. Michael Pulitzer, at that point assistant managing editor of the *Post-Dispatch*, moved to Tucson to take control of the *Daily Star*. In 1974 Pulitzer bought WOW-TV in Nebraska from the Meredith Corporation.

In 1979 the Pulitzer Company took over the advertising, circulation, accounting, and promotion of the *St. Louis Globe-Democrat* under their agency agreement. By the early 1980s, some industry observers felt that the Pulitzer editorial philosophy, as embodied in the *Post-Dispatch*, was out of touch with an increasingly conservative country. The newspaper also received criticism in some quarters for placing more emphasis on covering national news than St. Louis news. The newspaper's daily circulation declined to 241,000 in 1982, down from 326,000 in 1972.

In 1979 the firm sold KSD-AM to Combined Communications. In 1981 it traded KSDK-TV St. Louis to Multimedia for stations in Greenville, South Carolina, and Winston-Salem, North Carolina.

The *Post-Dispatch* became the first U.S. newspaper to switch to offset cold-type printing from the letterpress printing process. The switch allowed the newspaper to use high-quality color printing—a move pushed by Joseph Pulitzer III.

In 1983 Pulitzer bought UHF television stations in Louisville and Fort Wayne, Indiana, from Gannett. In 1984 the *Globe-Democrat* folded. The *Post-Dispatch* became a morning newspaper, and the *Herald Company*, which had owned the *Globe-Democrat*, received half the profits, but also had to share half the losses, of the *Post-Dispatch*.

Seeking to expand, in 1985 Pulitzer bought the Lerner Newspapers chain of 52 small local Chicago weeklies for $9.1 million. The firm hoped to win readers and advertising dollars from the large metropolitan dailies, the *Chicago Tribune* and *Sun-Times*, in the same way that the *Suburban Journal* chain of suburban weeklies was weakening the *Post-Dispatch*. The Lerner papers had a combined circulation of about 300,000, and Pulitzer planned to increase that to compete in the Chicago newspaper market.

In April 1986 the firm bought the *Southtown Economist*, a small newspaper focusing on the south side of Chicago, for $40 million. The far larger *Chicago Tribune* and *Chicago Sun-Times* quickly counterattacked by beefing up their coverage and distribution. The *Southtown* also made money by printing the Midwest editions of national newspapers like the *New York Times*, *USA Today*, and *Investor's Business Daily*.

In 1986 an ugly takeover battle erupted when Detroit real estate investor A. Alfred Taubman offered first $500 million and then $625 million to buy Pulitzer. Taubman was encouraged by a group of Joseph Pulitzer descendants who had large blocks of stock in the company, but no control over it. Under the rules of the Pulitzer trust established in 1950, the firm's stock could only be sold for the amount it was acquired for, not the current market value. A group of 10 relatives controlling about 43 percent of the firm's stock wanted to sell out, and they were frustrated by these rules. Communications companies were valuable at the time, and the relatives wanted to sell while prices were high.

The group of ten sued, claiming that the Pulitzers who controlled the company were enriching themselves at the cost of other shareholders; the Pulitzers who controlled the company countersued. By mid 1986, Pulitzer Publishing agreed to buy the 22 percent stake held by four family members for $95 million. A later, similar agreement covered 21 percent owned by another family group. The move consolidated control of the company, but left it with $180 million in debt. The firm subsequently made its first public stock offering to help pay for the buyout.

After the buyout, Joseph Pulitzer III gave up his posts with the *Post-Dispatch* to concentrate on the now-public Pulitzer Publishing Co. In 1988 Pulitzer invested millions in machinery to automatically handle rolls of paper and on computer layout and composition equipment. The firm made $19.6 million that year, on sales of $391 million.

In the fall of 1989 Pulitzer faced its first real challenge in years on its home turf in St. Louis. Ingersoll Publications launched the *St. Louis Sun*, a daily tabloid. Ingersoll already owned a chain of weeklies in the St. Louis area that had been cutting into the suburban circulation of the *Post-Dispatch*. Although the *Post-Dispatch* had an impressive lead, with a circulation of 375,000 daily and 550,000 on Sunday, it scrambled to improve its local coverage. In the end the challenge from Ingersoll only lasted about seven months before the *Sun* folded. Sales for 1989 came to $402.2 million.

This did not mean all was well at Pulitzer. The firm's plans for the Lerner chain ran into repeated problems. Lerner was hurt badly by the recession of the early 1990s, which severely eroded its narrow advertising base. Over half of the chain's advertising revenue came from help-wanted classified ads, and with widespread layoffs, this market shriveled. Lerner tried to win automotive ads away from the *Chicago Sun-Times* and real estate ads from the *Tribune*, but it failed in both areas. Pulitzer closed and combined many of its weekly Lerner newspapers, until only 15 were left of the original 52. Circulation had plummeted from 300,000 in 1985 to 100,000 in 1992. The moves were not enough, however, and in mid-1992, Pulitzer announced it would shut down Lerner if it did not find a buyer by October 1992. At the last minute, a group of investors bought Lerner. The Associated Press reported that the price was $4 million, though Pulitzer officials disputed that figure.

Pulitzer cut costs elsewhere by eliminating 113 production jobs at the *Post-Dispatch* and additional jobs elsewhere. The cuts were made easier by changes in union contracts, and cost about $4.5 million in severance fees. Pulitzer also formed a company that delivered advertising, catalogs, and magazines in the St. Louis area.

Joseph Pulitzer III died in 1993, and Michael Pulitzer became chairman of Pulitzer Publishing. That same year Pulitzer bought two television stations from H&C Communications Inc. for $165 million. One station was WESH-TV, an NBC affiliate reaching Orlando, Daytona Beach, and Melbourne, Florida. The Orlando area was the 23rd largest television market in the United States, and its population was growing. The other station was KCCI-TV, a CBS affiliate in Des Moines, Iowa, the most popular station in the 70th largest television market in the United States. With broadcast revenue nationwide growing faster than revenue from printed publications, the move seemed logical.

With these purchases Pulitzer owned nine television stations. The others were WLKY in Louisville, Kentucky; WDSU in New Orleans; WYFF in Greenville, South Carolina; WGAL in Lancaster, Pennsylvania; WXII in Winston-Salem, North Carolina; KOAT in Albuquerque, New Mexico; and KETV in Omaha. The firm also owned two radio stations in Phoenix. Pulitzer announced that it would not make any further acquisitions in the near future, and made a second stock offering to help offset the cost of the two television stations.

In 1993 Pulitzer changed the name of the *Southtown Economist* to the *Daily Southtown*, and switched it from an afternoon to a morning paper. Its daily circulation stood at 53,000, while it sold 61,000 copies on Sundays. Despite these changes, the firm sold the newspaper in December 1994, to American Publishing Co., owner of the *Chicago Sun-Times*, for $31.9 million. The sale ended Pulitzer's attempts to expand into the Chicago market, and left the firm with only two newspapers, but nine television stations. The *Daily Southtown* contributed $46.5 million to Pulitzer's total 1993 revenue of $427 million. Despite its apparent move away from print and into broadcast media, Pulitzer officials told the *Post-Dispatch* that the firm was interested in buying paid-circulation daily newspapers outside of suburbs and major metropolitan areas.

Principal Subsidiaries

St. Louis Post-Dispatch; The Arizona Daily Star; KETV-TV; KOAT-TV; KCCI-TV; WLKY-TV; WGAL-TV; WDSU-TV; WYFF-TV; WXII-TV; WESH-TV; KTAR-AM; KKLT-FM.

Further Reading

Byrne, Harlan S., "Pulitzer Publishing Co.: A Prized Newspaper Name Girds to Fight New Rival," *Barron's*, June 26, 1989, pp. 45–46.
——, "Pulitzer Publishing: Extra! Extra! After Years of Strife, It's Turned the Corner," *Barron's*, November 22, 1993, pp. 51–52.
Carey, Christopher, "Pulitzer to Purchase 2 More TV Stations," *St. Louis Post-Dispatch*, February 19, 1993, pp. 1, 8.
Fabrikant, Geraldine, "Pulitzer to Buy Back Stock," *New York Times*, May 15, 1986, p. D4.
Fitzgerald, Mark, "Pulitzer to Fold Lerner Papers," *Editor and Publisher*, August 15, 1992, p. 9.
Goodman, Adam, "Pulitzer Selling Its Newspapers in Chicago," *St. Louis Post-Dispatch*, December 24, 1994.
Hevesi, Dennis, "Joseph Pulitzer Jr. Is Dead at 80," *New York Times*, May 27, 1993.
"Joseph Pulitzer, Publisher, Dead," *New York Times*, April 1, 1955.
Jones, Alex, S., "And Now the Pulitzers Go to War," *New York Times*, April 13, 1986.
Manor, Robert, "Pulitzer Sells Lerner Papers," *St. Louis Post-Dispatch*, October 8, 1992.
Pulitzer, Joseph, Jr., and Michael E. Pulitzer, *Pulitzer Publishing Company, Newspapers and Broadcasting in the Public Interest*, New York: Newcomen Society, 1988.

—Scott M. Lewis

Quixote Corporation

One East Wacker Drive
Chicago, Illinois 60601
U.S.A.
(312) 467-6755
Fax: (312) 467-1356

Public Company
Incorporated: 1969 as Energy Absorption Systems, Inc.
Employees: 1,599
Sales: $185.4 million (1995)
Stock Exchanges: NASDAQ
SICs: 3089 Plastic Products Not Elsewhere Classified

Quixote Corporation operates as a holding company for leading manufacturers in two specialized technology areas. Quixote's Energy Absorption Systems, Inc. (EAS) subsidiary is the world's leading manufacturer of energy-absorbing highway crash cushions, guardrails, and related highway safety devices. EAS and its subsidiaries, Spin-Cast Plastics, Inc. and Safe-Hit Corporation, design and manufacture crash-cushion components, flexible guide posts, portable sign systems, and other plastic products at four company-owned plants in California, Alabama, and Indiana. Quixote's Disc Manufacturing, Inc. (DMI) is the United States' largest independent designer and supplier of compact discs for the audio and CD-ROM markets. DMI's two production facilities in Anaheim, California, and Huntsville, Alabama, combine for a production capacity of 200 million units per year. DMI accounted for 47 percent of Quixote's $185 million sales in 1995. EAS provided 25 percent of sales. In February 1996, Quixote sold off the remaining principal units of its failing third subsidiary, Legal Technologies, Inc., including Stenograph Corporation and Integrated Information Services, Inc., which together had produced $40.6 million of the Quixote's 1995 sales. Founder Philip E. Rollhaus, Jr., continues to function as chairman and chief executive officer. Leslie J. Jezuit was named president and chief operating officer in January 1996.

Making an Impact in the 1970s

Philip Rollhaus, together with group of fellow entrepreneurs, formed Energy Absorption Systems, Inc. in Chicago in 1969. Rollhaus' road to entrepreneurship was as diverse as his company's growth would prove to be. Raised near New York City, Rollhaus graduated from Wesleyan University with a degree in English Literature. Rollhaus then joined the Navy's Officers Candidate School, where a misreading of the E-N-G of his degree led him to a four-year stint as an engineering officer at sea. That exposure to technology would become pivotal to Rollhaus' later career.

Upon his discharge from the Navy, Rollhaus entered Oxford University to continue his English studies. He soon left the university, traveling to Paris, where he attempted to write a novel. During his time in Paris, Rollhaus began developing his entrepreneurial skills, starting up a literary magazine, selling cars, and eventually opening Paris' first coin-operated laundry. After five years in Paris, however, Rollhaus returned to the United States, joining an investment banking firm in Chicago.

As Rollhaus would later say, it was at the investment banking firm that he developed "an affinity for inventors and their ideas, and a passion for them to succeed." In 1969, Rollhaus left his position with the investment firm and with his associates set out to acquire and develop a series of patents for a product that had come to Rollhaus' attention: a bumper for automobiles called the Hi-Dro Cell Cushion Bumper. The Hi-Dro bumper was molded from plastic bumper and filled with water, and later foam, providing greater impact protection than the standard chrome bumpers of the time. In exchange for stock in EAS, Rollhaus acquired certain of the rights to the Hi-Dro bumper, providing marketing services to the Sacramento, California company that manufactured them.

The new company quickly hit a snag. While their bumper sold to a number of taxicab companies and bus lines, the automobile manufacturers and automotive aftermarket displayed little interest in the product, believing that their consumers would not easily give up the traditional chrome bumper. EAS struggled to remain profitable.

Facing the reluctance of the automobile industry to convert its bumper systems, EAS turned to a related product being developed by the Sacramento company. This product, call the Hi-Dro Cell Barrier, was a highway attenuater guardrail system based on the same energy absorption and dissipation principles as the Hi-Dro bumper. EAS submitted the Cell Barrier to the Federal Highway Administration, which approved it for experimental use. The company also developed a foamed urethane bumper system for transit bus use, called the Transafe bumper. EAS continued to market the Hi-Dro bumper, but the automobile manufacturers remained intransigent.

Public concern for highway safety, however, was starting to build during the early 1970s. Rollhaus next recognized a potential market for designing, developing, and manufacturing another product related to the Cell Barrier, that of highway crash cushions. In 1972, the FHA removed the Cell Barrier and EAS's crash cushions from its experimental list, approving them for highway use. Acceptance of these new systems, while applauded by the motoring public, was slow at first. But by 1973, EAS's sales had topped $2 million, and the company turned a profit of $470,000. In 1976, as a settlement for a patent infringement lawsuit filed against the company, EAS made a cash purchase to acquire the basic patent to the highway crash cushion field.

Sales climbed slowly but steadily through the 1970s, reaching $4.2 million in 1977. By then, the federal government had begun to mandate the use of energy-absorbing bumper systems on all newly manufactured automobiles. EAS, however, faced strong competition for this market as the automobile manufacturers and their suppliers began producing their own impact absorption systems. Its Transafe bus bumper was also under attack by traditional suppliers to the bus industry. The competition in the vehicle bumper market, which formed 12 percent of EAS's sales, forced down EAS's profit margins, and quickly its profits as well. In 1977, EAS made the decision to exit the vehicle bumper market, licensing its patents, and turned its impact absorption focus entirely on its highway barrier systems.

Acceptance of these highway barriers continued to grow, but remained dependent on government funding initiatives, making growth unstable and unpredictable. Faced with becoming a one-product company with an uncertain market, EAS made its first attempt to diversify, with the $1.6 million purchase of Melley Energy Systems, Inc. of Pompano Beach, Florida, in October 1976. Melley was a producer of mobile power generating systems, chiefly for the foreign market. Despite an early $9 million order from Saudi Arabia, EAS found itself under pressure to repay the loans needed to finance its Melley purchase while expanding that company's production and marketing efforts. As its Melley operation began to cut into its Energy Absorption capital, EAS saw its profits drop from a net of $253,000 in 1976 to $72,000 in 1977. By June of that year, EAS sold Melley for $1.67 million.

EAS continued in its efforts to diversify its business. Rollhaus and company identified two areas that they wanted to pursue, those of vapor capture and solar energy. Two new divisions were formed, the Clean Air Division, later called the QualAir Division, and the Solarstor Division. Through the Clean Air Division, EAS purchased the rights to equipment designed to recapture the vapors escaping when gasoline was pumped into automobiles at service stations, converting the vapors back into gasoline. Encouraged by the California Air Resources Board and other agencies, EAS turned its R & D efforts toward perfecting the vapor capture device. The device, however, met resistance from the oil companies, which pushed through their own vapor capture design. EAS's solar energy efforts under its Solarstor division included developing fiberglass solar collector panels and water heating tanks. But in the late 1970s, the rush was on to develop solar-energy based products, and, faced with a market overburdened by manufacturers, EAS soon shut down its solar energy activities.

Despite these difficulties, Rollhaus's interest in high-technology and his willingness to pursue and develop new markets were already beginning to shape the future of EAS. Meanwhile, sales of its highway impact absorption products were rising steadily, to $7.3 million by 1979, providing a cushion for the company's continued desire for diversification.

The Technology of the 1980s

With its crash cushion profits, EAS next purchased Stenograph Corporation of Skokie, Illinois. Stenograph was by then a fading, 40-year-old company serving the country's court reporter market. The Stenograph machine allowed a court reporter to type as fast as people spoke, producing transcripts in phonetic code which then had to be translated and retyped into plain English. Under EAS, Stenograph moved to incorporating the new developments in computer technology, which by then were producing the first small-scale personal computers. By 1980, after acquiring and merging Cimarron Systems, Inc. of Greenville, Texas, into Stenograph, the company was ready with its first computer-aided transcription system, using computers to translate the phonetic code into plain English. Success for the new product was immediate, and Stenograph's revenues quickly grew five-fold and its market share grew to 90 percent of the country's court reporters.

In 1980, the company went public, restructuring its EAS and Stenograph subsidiaries under a holding company named Quixote Corporation. Taking a venture capital strategy, nicknamed "Long Shots Incorporated" within Quixote, the company next established a new subsidiary, LaserVideo, Inc. Begun by giving an inventor "$60,000 a year, a white coat and a laboratory," as Rollhaus told *Financial World,* LaserVideo developed a proprietary process for manufacturing laser discs for the newly developing compact disc technology.

Buoyed by EAS and Stenograph, which together produced nearly $27 million in sales and a $1.36 million net profit by 1983, Quixote poured some $13 million into developing its disc production capacity, positioning itself as one of only two U.S.-based compact disc manufacturers when the market broke open in the mid-1980s. Its production capacity at its Anaheim, California, plant would grow to three million units per year; the addition of a new plant in Huntsville, Alabama, would bring total production capacity to 60 million units per year, more than the entire compact disc market in the United States at the time. However, the compact disc market was growing at a phenomenal rate, from under six million units in 1984 to nearly 23 million in 1985, with predictions of over 300 million units by the end of the decade. Focused on the small-label market, LaserVideo would have the U.S. production to themselves for most of the 1980s. Nevertheless, LaserVideo operated at a loss for much of the decade, posting a $3.6 million operating loss on only $1.9 million in revenues in 1985. The surging position of EAS—which now provided its barrier systems to seven countries and throughout the United States—and Stenograph continued to cushion the development of LaserVideo and Quixote's new technology ventures.

Quixote's and Rollhaus's interest in "taking ideas and making them work against all odds" led the company into several new areas during the 1980s. The first was the acquisition of Amtel Systems Corp. in 1984 and the development of an inter-office messaging system, a simplified type of local area network, with early clients featuring such giants as Citicorp, PepsiCo, and Goldman, Sachs, as well as General Electric. Quixote's next formed a joint venture with Allstate Insurance called Synthetic Blood Corp. after scientists had contacted Rollhaus with their design for producing a synthetic, whole-blood substitute. Development of this venture too would be supported by Quixote's EAS and Stenograph earnings, which combined to provide sales of $4 million and a net profit of nearly $2 million in 1986. In that year, Quixote also acquired an 80 percent interest in Ocean Scientific, Inc., a manufacturer of instruments for medical diagnostics testing, an area which, with the rise of AIDS and other infectious diseases, was showing promise during the 1980s. By then LaserVideo had begun to branch out into the newly developing CD-ROM market.

Quixote's heavy investments in such long-term projects—at the time, testing for its synthetic blood, for example, was expected to require three to five years; ten years later, there were still no synthetic bloods approved for use—cut into the company's earnings, at a time when its Stenograph and EAS subsidiaries were experiencing their own troubles. The failure of the Federal government to approve funding for its highway crash systems in 1987 crippled EAS's sales. The launch of Stenograph's newest computer-aided transcription systems failed, forcing Stenograph to withdraw the new line. 1987 sales barely passed those of 1986, and the company posted a net loss of nearly $2.2 million. The following year, despite a rise in revenues to $56 million, the company posted a loss of $107,000.

With competition in the compact disc market heating up, Quixote sold off its LaserVideo subsidiary to Disctronics, Ltd., for $55.5 million, with $29 million in cash, in 1988. The next year, with federal funding assured for five years, EAS rebounded, the company's revenues neared $65 million, and profits again climbed past $2 million.

Streamlined for the 1990s

Quixote's troubles were not behind them. As the country entered the recession of the early 1990s, Quixote posted two more losing years, with a loss of nearly $3.7 million in 1990 followed by a $3.1 million loss in 1991. During the first half of the decade, the company would exit its unprofitable ventures,

retaining its still-profitable subsidiaries, EAS and Stenograph, which would be reorganized as Legal Technologies, Inc. to reflect Quixote's new pursuit of a position in software and other products and services for the legal community. These subsidiaries were again joined by LaserVideo, renamed by Disctronics as Disc Manufacturing Inc. (DMI), after Disctronics defaulted on its remaining $26.5 million obligation in 1990. By then, demand for compact discs had grown beyond expectations, and the market for laser discs and especially CD-ROMs was just beginning to explode. Meanwhile, Disctronics' capital improvements had increased DMI's capacity to 3.2 million units per month, making DMI the largest independent supplier of compact discs in the United States. Its largest customer was BMG Music, which accounted for 38-40 percent of its sales. Quixote made plans to boost capacity still higher, to 4.5 million units per month. By 1992, the company posted net earnings of nearly $8 million on $129 million in sales.

The rise of multimedia personal computers in the mid-1990s boosted revenues still higher. From 1993 to 1994, DMI's sales of CD-ROMs increased 155 percent. Sales climbed to $145 million in 1993 and nearly $177 million in 1994. Earnings rose as well, to $11.6 million in 1994. In response to falling compact disc prices, Quixote stepped up production, opening a new manufacturing facility in Anaheim and expanding its Huntsville, Alabama, plant. By 1995, DMI accounted for 47 percent of Quixote's total sales of $185 million.

In that year, Quixote announced its intention to discontinue its Legal Technologies subsidiary, beginning with its Litigation Sciences, Inc. unit acquired in 1993. In February 1996, Quixote completed the sale of Integrated Information Services, Inc., also acquired in 1993, as well as Stenograph Corporation to Chicago-based The Heico Companies.

At the end of 1995, BMG Music ended its supply account with DMI. However, Rollhaus, who stepped down from Quixote's presidency in January 1996, announced the streamlined company's intention to step up DMI's activity in the fast-growing CD-ROM market, while maintaining its commitment to its steady-selling, original namesake, Energy Absorption Systems.

Principal Subsidiaries

Energy Absorption Systems, Inc.; Disc Manufacturing, Inc.

Further Reading

Goodman, JoEllen, "Betting on CDs, Quixote's Rollhaus Tilts at Big Time," *Crain's Chicago Business*, November 24, 1986, p. 3.

Rollhaus, Philip E., "Travels Along the Entrepreneurial Road," an address delivered the Building the High Technology Business seminar, September 1986.

Stevens, Catherine, "Working Against the Odds," *Financial World*, January 8–21, 1986, p. 90.

—M.L. Cohen

RECOTON®

Recoton Corp.

145 East 57th Street
New York, New York 10022
U.S.A.
(212) 644-0220
Fax: (212) 644-8205

Public Company
Incorporated: 1936 as Record Town
Employees: 850
Stock Exchanges: NASDAQ
Sales: $164 (1994)
SICs: 5064 Electrical Appliances, Television & Radio
   Sets; 5065 Electronic Parts & Equipment, Not
   Elsewhere Classified

Recoton Corp. is a leading U.S. manufacturer and distributor of consumer electronics products and accessories. Under various brand names, the company markets wireless stereo speaker systems, audio/video editing equipment, and thousands of accessories for car and home stereos, home office equipment, televisions, camcorders, and other electronic products. The enterprise expanded rapidly in the 1980s and 1990s, primarily by acquiring other companies.

The roots of the company that would become Recoton can be traced back to two companies: Record Town, whose name was later abbreviated to Recoton, and a pre-World War II German concern named Polydor Records. Polydor was run by Herbert Borchardt. Borchardt, who was in his twenties at the time, was the scion of a wealthy German industrialist: "Before Hitler, my uncle was one of the richest men in Germany," Borchardt said in the December 4, 1995, *Forbes*. By the 1940s, though, the political situation in Germany had become intolerable. Borchardt and his family fled the country in 1941. They arrived at Ellis Island, New York, with a $500 nest egg.

In Germany, Borchardt had made the first and some of the best recordings of the internationally renowned singer Edith Piaf. Piaf, the daughter of an impoverished Parisian acrobat, had been discovered in 1935 and quickly achieved international fame with her sentimental ballads. Although he had lost his successful recording business in Germany, Borchardt hoped to build a new record company from scratch in America. He started out by recording two fellow refugees, Kurt Weill and Lotte Lenya. Unfortunately, the shellac that he needed to make their records was unavailable because of the U.S. war effort. After only three years Borchardt was forced to shutter his fledgling recording venture.

Borchardt found a job running a tiny manufacturing company called Record Town. The company had been founded in 1936 to manufacture long-lasting steel phonograph needles—its high-tech 'cactus needle stylus' could be used for a whopping 10 record plays. Borchardt eventually purchased the business and ran it throughout the 1950s and 1960s. He kept the company small but profitable, and assumed little debt. In 1969 Borchardt took the company public with a stock offering that helped to raise growth capital. He gradually added other record-related products like brushes, cloths, and record-care items. When eight-track tapes were introduced in the 1960s, Recoton began selling carrying cases for the cartridges. Then, in the 1970s, Recoton started offering cassette storage and maintenance products as well as accessories for the then-red-hot citizens band (CB) radio market.

Borchardt had brought his 23-year-old son, Robert, into the business in 1961, and fifteen years later he handed over to Robert control of day-to-day operations. When Robert Borchardt was named president in 1976, he began to slowly add new accessories to Recoton's product lines. Indeed, Robert Borchardt recognized that over the years Recoton had developed a very fluid distribution network that wasn't being utilized to its fullest potential. Most of Recoton's products, such as the inserts that kept 45-rpm records from sliding on the carousel, brought measly profit margins of two percent or less. Thus, Recoton was competing in what was essentially a commodity industry. Robert Borchardt wanted to expand the company's product offerings and add items that gleaned higher profit margins.

Not all of the new goods that Recoton added to its line-up during the late 1970s and early 1980s brought profits to the company. For instance, the CB radio market eventually went bust and Recoton was left sitting on a pile of devalued inventory. Similarly, Recoton tried to get in on the home video game boom when Atari and Intellivision computer games were introduced. That market also bombed, leaving Recoton's warehouse full of unwanted joysticks, dust covers, and other accessories. At the same time, Robert Borchardt enjoyed a number of major successes from the myriad items added to Recoton's product portfolio. By the early 1980s, in fact, the company was selling hundreds of different accessories for consumer electronics ranging from telephones and personal computers to stereos and televisions.

Of import was Recoton's move into the video cassette recorder (VCR) market in the early 1980s. The VCR market exploded, and Recoton was able to profit handsomely from a full line of accessories. "We were the first to come out with a comprehensive line," Robert Borchardt said in the August 27, 1995, *Newsday.* Among its best-selling product introductions was a gold-plated connector cable, which was touted as a seamless link between a television and a VCR. That and other products helped Recoton to establish a reputation as a dependable and innovative supplier within its niche. In fact, by the mid-1980s Recoton had become the clear leader in the consumer electronics accessories industry.

Besides diversifying and increasing Recoton's offerings, Robert Borchardt improved returns by tweaking marketing and manufacturing strategies. For example, he began contracting out much of the company's manufacturing activities to low-cost foreign producers; by 1985, about 75 percent of the company's goods were being made overseas. He also cut costs by simplifying the company's sales approach. Salespeople had previously sold individual items to buyers. Because most of the goods were priced at less than $10 each, that practice was tedious and labor intensive. Under Robert Borchardt's direction, salespeople began bartering for space in retailer's stores. Recoton would find out how much space the retailer could devote to its products, and then design a display to fit the space.

The result of Recoton's overall efforts during the late 1970s and early 1980s showed up on its bottom line. Indeed, profits spiraled as sales surged. Annual revenues bulged more than five-fold between 1981 and 1984 to nearly $25 million. Average profit margins on individual products more than tripled during the same period, pushing Recoton's annual net income to $1.6 million. Hoping to push margins even higher, Robert Borchardt launched a product development initiative that he hoped would allow Recoton to begin marketing high-tech proprietary products. In 1985, for example, Recoton unveiled its Friendly Recoton Entertainment Decoder (FRED), a device designed to decode television stereo signals and synthesize stereo from regular signals. Priced at $150, the decoder was the only one on the market that could operate with any brand of television—other decoders were designed to work only with the manufacturer's own television brand.

Despite a dip in profitability, Recoton continued to post steady sales gains throughout the late 1980s as it bolstered its product line and broadened its distribution network. Sales rose to $30.9 million in 1987, $39.7 million in 1988, and then to more than $41 million in 1989. The rapid rise in the late 1980s reflected Recoton's new growth strategy, which was implemented under the direction of Robert Borchardt (Robert was serving as president, but sharing the chief executive and chairman posts with his father). Borchardt recognized that the consumer electronics accessories industry was becoming increasingly consolidated. Only the most efficient and best-financed companies, he reasoned, stood a chance of surviving in the long term. Armed with that philosophy, Borchardt initiated a strategy of aggressive growth through acquisition.

In 1988 Recoton issued $15 million in debt, which it used to begin purchasing competing accessories manufacturers. The strategy was well timed because the economic recession of the early 1990s allowed Recoton to purchase companies at relatively low prices. Recoton's first acquisition was Transcriber, a small manufacturer of record needles and accessories. Armed with its $15 million war chest, the company then bought a manufacturer of stereo headphones named Calibron. Importantly, that 1989 purchase gave Recoton an 80,000-square-foot warehouse and a factory in central Florida that eventually became a major manufacturing and storage hub for Recoton. Borchardt followed the Calibron purchase with the buyout of Rembrandt, a television antenna manufacturer. Those takeovers pushed Recoton's 1990 sales to $46.6 million.

In 1991 Recoton acquired Discwasher, the well-known manufacturer of album, tape, and CD cleaning kits. It also purchased Parsec, a maker of television and AM/FM antennas. After buying the companies, Borchardt consolidated most of their manufacturing and warehousing operations in the Florida unit, which was expanded to meet increased production requirements. The result was lower operating costs and higher profit margins. In 1992 Borchardt added Ambico Inc. and Proturn Inc. Ambico, an audio/video editing company, cost Recoton about $6 million. Proturn, a Canadian company that manufactured carrying cases and storage units for audio and video products, was converted into a wholly owned subsidiary called Recoton Canada. Sales grew to $76.7 million in 1992, $3.66 million of which was netted as income.

Recoton sustained its acquisition drive in 1993 and 1994, first with the purchase of SoleControl, a producer of universal remote controls. It next picked up Sound Quest, a car audio components and accessories maker, and Ampersand, a manufacturer of equipment used by car audio installers. As Recoton found new additions for its growing portfolio, it maintained its efforts to develop and patent its own proprietary products. In the late 1980s, for example, the company's 12-person research and development team invented a device that allowed consumers to play portable CD players through the tape decks on their car stereos. More importantly, during the early 1990s Recoton developed advanced wireless technology similar to that used to operate cordless phones. Recoton invented wireless speakers that could be connected to stereo and television units by miniature transmitters, thus eliminating the need for wiring. The breakthrough proved to be a major boon for Recoton, as sales of the company's wireless products surged in the mid-1990s.

Indeed, revenues grew to $121 million in 1993 and then to $164 million in 1994, largely as a result of increased sales of its patented wireless audio devices. Sales gains were also achieved in international markets, where Recoton managed to boost revenues more than 100 percent to about $28 million. More importantly, Recoton's net income for 1994 ascended to a record $11.84 million and the price of its stock soared. Recoton had managed to post that growth while accruing very little debt; in fact, during the mid-1990s the company repurchased much of its stock in order to increase its equity stake in the company. Recoton cashed in on the buyback in April 1994 when it raised $46.5 million in growth capital with a stock offering.

By 1995, Recoton had become a global leader in the consumer electronics accessories industry. Sales and profits continued to rise, and the company was planning for continued expansion. Toward that end, Recoton was setting its sites on global markets where it could funnel its venerable product line into new distribution channels. "We want to maximize our return without making major investments," Borchardt explained in the September 1995 *International Business*. "We get faster returns by building distribution in markets that are less mature." Those markets included Western Europe, South Africa, Russia, and South America. In 1995 Recoton acquired STD Holdings Ltd. (Interact/STD), a Hong Kong-based international manufacturer and marketer of multimedia and computer accessories, including video game joysticks, controllers, and computer speakers.

Going into 1996, Recoton was marketing about 3,500 different products through several divisions and subsidiaries. Its latest addition was The Audio Group, an audio speaker company in Chatsworth, California, which was headed by loudspeaker designer Cary Christie. Borchardt planned for the unit to design and produce speakers for Recoton, as well as for other manufacturers. Company-wide sales were expected to top $215 million for 1995. With its aggressive move into international markets, new products, and efforts to penetrate new marketing channels like the discount superstore chains, Borchardt hoped to achieve $1 billion in annual revenues by the year 2000.

Principal Subsidiaries

Recoton Canada Ltd; Recoton (Far East) Ltd.; The Audio Group.

Principal Operating Units

Ambico; Ampersand; Calibron; Discwasher; Parsec; Recoton; Rembrandt; Solecontrol; Soundquest.

Further Reading

Brown, Paul B., "Right Place, Right Time," *Forbes,* January 18, 1984, p. 109.

Calem, Robert E., "They're Big in the Little Things," *Newsday,* August 27, 1995.

Davies, Barbara, "Recoton Accessorizing with New Companies," *Billboard,* November 7, 1992, p. 50.

Gault, Ylonda, "Accessories Firm Turns up Volume," *Crains New York Business,* November 18, 1991, Section 1, p. 31.

"Hitachi, Recoton in Deal," *Television Digest,* June 12, 1995, p. 17.

Jeffrey, Don, "Recoton Spring Profits on the Rise," *Billboard,* August 21, 1993, p. 45.

Meeks, Fleming, "Falling through the Cracks," *Forbes,* December 4, 1995, pp. 116–17.

Mirabella, Alan, "Electronic Gadget Firm Getting Hazy Reception," *Crains New York Business,* January 30, 1995, Section 1, p. 39.

Moss, Linda, "Recoton's Decoder Tunes into Stereo TV and Increased Sales," *Crains New York Business,* January 6, 1986, Section 1, p. 3.

Olenick, Doug, "Recoton Growing, Diversifying," *HFN The Weekly Newspaper for the Home Furnishing Network,* August 14, 1995, p. 81.

"Recoton Plans to Acquire STD," *HFN The Weekly Newspaper for the Home Furnishing Network,* May 15, 1995, p. 79.

Savona, Dave, "Buying into China," *International Business,* September 1995.

Teitelbaum, Richard S., "Recoton," *Fortune,* July 27, 1992, p. 97.

Weiner, Daniel P., "Recoton Corp.," *Fortune,* September 16, 1985, p. 62.

—Dave Mote

Rexel, Inc.

150 Alhambra Circle
Coral Gables, Florida 33134
U.S.A.
(305) 446-8000
Fax: (305) 446-8128

Public Company
Incorporated: 1866 was Willcox & Gibbs Sewing
    Machine Co.
Employees: 2,800
Sales: $1.12 billion (1995)
Stock Exchanges: New York
SICs: 5063 Electronic Apparatus and Equipment, Wiring
    Supplies and Construction Materials; 5065 Electronic
    Parts and Equipment, Not Elsewhere Classified; 5085
    Industrial Supplies

Rexel, Inc. is the fifth largest distributor of electric parts and supplies in the United States, with most of its business in the South and Southwest. For more than a century Rexel was a manufacturer and distributor of industrial sewing machines named Willcox & Gibbs. It began to diversify in 1958 and eventually came to concentrate its efforts on the wholesale distribution of electrical parts and supplies. During the early 1990s the world's largest company in this field, a French firm named Rexel, S.A., bought a controlling interest in Willcox & Gibbs, disposed of its remaining links to the apparel industry, and renamed the company Rexel, Inc.

A Century in the Sewing-Machine Trade

Established in 1859, Willcox & Gibbs Sewing Machine Co. was incorporated in New York seven years later. It was engaged in the sale of sewing machines and accessories for industrial applications, manufactured by others under contract. The company had assets of $2.6 million in 1923, of which $1.4 million consisted of inventories. There were 128 employees in 1930 and 218 stockholders in 1931. Dividends were paid consistently for

many years, dating back to at least 1927. During the Great Depression, however, inventories were reduced and no dividends were paid during much of that time.

Willcox & Gibbs purchased Metropolitan Sewing Machine Corp. in 1935 and opened an English subsidiary in 1937. The company did not disclose annual income until 1939, when it reported net income of only $28,960, followed by $12,466 in 1940. In 1941 Willcox & Gibbs opened its first manufacturing plant, in Nyack, New York. Its net income varied during the decade from $74,125 in 1945 to $286,867 in 1948. In 1950 the company had 545 employees, 299 holders of its common stock, and net income of $259,748.

Willcox & Gibbs first reported its sales total in 1952, when it earned $149,709 on net sales of $4,861,135, a figure not surpassed until 1957. It ran a deficit in 1953 and ceased, except during 1956-57, to pay dividends on common stock until 1985. Seeking to end its dependence on the low-profit sewing-machine business, it acquired, in 1958, Thermatron Co., which produced and sold electronic equipment for heat sealing and welding of soft plastic products. In 1960 Willcox & Gibbs opened a plant in Orangeburg, New York, and also added a Swiss subsidiary. That year it earned $161,036 on sales of more than $8.4 million and had 548 employees and 526 stockholders.

Diversified Manufacturers in the 1960s

Willcox & Gibbs grew by acquisition and diversification during the 1960s. In 1960 it acquired the European and U.S. rights to the automatic doffing machine, developed to supplant the manual operation of removing full bobbins of yarn and replacing them with empty plastic or paper tubes on the spindles of the spinning frame. It sold the North American rights to this machine to the Draper Corp. in 1961 for a share of the receipts from its sale or lease. The company acquired Raybond Electronics, a manufacturer and distributor of high-frequency wood-gluing and laminating equipment, in 1966. During the same year it acquired Faratron, a manufacturer of high-frequency sealing and curing equipment, the manufacturing and distributing rights to a sealing machine used to package such items as phonograph records, toys, and candy, and the U.S. manufacturing and distributing rights to a British technique electronically joining the uppers of shoes.

Willcox & Gibbs dropped "sewing machine" from its name in 1967, the year its net sales reached $17 million and its net income $675,000. Also in 1967, the company acquired Stanelco Industrial Services, manufacturer and distributor of high-frequency plastic-welding and induction-heating equipment, and Tele-Sonic, designer and manufacturer of bag-opening and -filling machinery, bag sealers, and overwrap machinery. In January 1968 the company acquired the rights to a new moldless process of fusing polystyrene beads directly inside a shipping container.

In 1968 sewing machines for industrial use accounted for about half of company income. This included not only the machines manufactured by Willcox & Gibbs and its U.K. subsidiary, but also distribution of the machines manufactured by G.M. Pfaff A.G. of West Germany. The Thermatron division was manufacturing equipment joining soft plastic products and other materials through the dielectric-heating process. Stanelco-Thermatron Ltd., a U.K. subsidiary, was producing induction-heating equipment for metals and plastic welding equipment. Raybond, also a subsidiary, was making equipment for the bonding of wood, such as furniture or flooring. Tele-Sonic and other divisions were engaged in making packaging equipment. Four divisions were involved in the manufacture of high-frequency heat-sealing, curing, and drying machinery, making the company the nation's foremost producer in this field.

In 1969, the first year Willcox & Gibbs stock was listed on the American Stock Exchange, it acquired two companies making swatch cards and sample books for the wall-covering, textile, garment, carpeting, upholstery, and drapery industries, making this division the largest operation of its kind in the United States. A third acquired company manufactured and imported trimmings and decorative buttons. The following year Willcox & Gibbs acquired Sunbrand Corp., which became a subsidiary selling some 50,000 items for the apparel industry. After losing $1.7 million in 1969, Willcox & Gibbs recovered the following year, earning $338,912 on net sales of $26.7 million. The company had four plants in New York, two in California, one in Atlanta, and two in England.

Bankruptcy in the 1970s

Willcox & Gibbs continued to acquire small companies in related businesses through the early 1970s while, in 1972, selling its Dielectric Division, which included Stanelco-Thermatron, for cash, notes, and stock. Sales rose each year, but in 1974 the company lost $1.5 million on net income of $40.5 million. The following January, John K. Ziegler, the company's vice-president for finance, moved up to president and chief executive officer, but that year Willcox & Gibbs lost $11.4 million on net income of $48.8 million. This outcome was attributed mainly to abnormally low profit margins on sales of industrial sewing equipment.

In June 1976, soon after the American Stock Exchange suspended trading in its shares, Willcox & Gibbs borrowed $28.2 million to consolidate its debts. When the company's creditors refused to accept a delay in payments, however, it filed

for reorganization in November 1976 under Chapter 11 of the federal bankruptcy act. A new $10 million loan allowed the company to continue business without interruption, but it owed $38 million and had negative net worth of $27 million.

During the following years Willcox & Gibbs persuaded its creditors to settle for what turned out to be only 20 cents on the dollar, paid in cash, preferred stock, and warrants. Trading of the company's stock on the American Stock Exchange resumed in June 1979. For 1978 Willcox & Gibbs reported net income (after an extraordinary credit) of $1.3 million on net sales of $63.8 million, followed in 1979 by net income of $2.1 million on net sales of $69.7 million. In 1980 its properties included plants in Atlanta, Brooklyn, Dallas, El Paso, Los Angeles, Miami, and Pittsburgh, as well as in Fall River, Massachusetts, and Inwood, New York. Overseas, the company had properties in Paris, London, and High Wycombe, England.

Electrical Parts Distribution in the 1980s

In 1982 Willcox & Gibbs sold its domestic sewing-machine operations to a new Japanese-owned company, Pfaff-Pegasus of U.S.A. Inc., for about $2.5 million and a 29 percent interest. It also sold, in the same year, almost all of its operations in England and France to G.M. Pfaff of West Germany for $2.1 million in cash and notes. These divestitures reduced its debt by $8.3 million. However, in 1983 the firm purchased Regal Manufacturing Co., the leading producer of covered elastic yarn, chiefly for pantyhose, for $3.2 million in cash and a promise of added payments over seven years. Later that year it paid $20 million in cash and notes, plus payments contingent on profits, for Consolidated Electric Supply Inc. and its affiliates, a major wholesale distributor of electrical components and supplies to building contractors in southern California and southern Florida.

The addition of Regal, and especially Consolidated, which had annual sales larger than the prior Willcox & Gibbs, hiked the revenues of the amalgamated company from $74.9 million in 1983 to $207.8 million in 1984 at a total cost of only $29 million. Net income, excluding extraordinary credits, rose from $1.3 million to $5.1 million. In addition to its acquisitions and its manufacture of cards and books for the textile, apparel, and wall-covering industries by the Reliance Sample Card division, the company now consisted of its Sunbrand division, which continued to distribute sewing machines and parts, serving as exclusive U.S. distributor for Pfaff and Pfaff-Pegasus and also marketing a wide range of other products to the apparel and related industries, including pressing and cutting equipment; the Unity Sewing Supply division, a wholesale distributor of sewing-equipment replacement parts; and the Montrose Supply & Equipment division, distributing parts and equipment to the textile and apparel industries, mainly to companies engaged in knitting operations.

Willcox & Gibbs continued to expand in 1984 by acquiring Inter-City Wholesale Electric Inc., another distributor in the thriving housing market of southern California, and Eildon Electronics Ltd., a Scottish company producing hardware and software for automated apparel manufacturing. In 1985 it acquired Leadtec Systems, Inc., another supplier of computer-based automation equipment for the apparel industry, and its stock moved up to the New York Stock Exchange. For the year net income, excluding an extraordinary credit, came to $6 million on net sales of $224.7 million. Of this total, distributing electrical products accounted for about 60 percent, distributing apparel equipment for about 20 percent, and manufacturing for about 20 percent.

In 1986 Willcox & Gibbs acquired Rubyco, Inc., the largest Canadian manufacturer of covered yarn, for about $6.4 million and thus became the world's largest manufacturer of this product. The following year it purchased three electrical-supply companies in the South. Clark Consolidated Industries, Inc., a big Ohio electrical-parts distributor, was bought in January 1989 for about $17.3 million. Willcox & Gibbs introduced Satellite Plus, its automated system for monitoring employee productivity in the apparel industry, in 1987. For the seventh straight year, sales rose, in 1989, to a record level, $547.7 million; net income came to a record $17.9 million.

Electrical Supplies Focus in the 1990s

In the company's most expensive acquisition yet, Willcox & Gibbs purchased Filiz Lastex, S.A. of Troyes, France, a producer of covered yarn, in 1990 for $44.9 million. In 1992, however, the company spun off its covered-yarn subsidiary, Worldtex Inc., into a separate company. Willcox & Gibbs shareholders received one share of Worldtex for each share of the parent company's stock in a tax-free transaction. That year, following a meager 1991 in which the company earned only $248,000, Willcox & Gibbs lost $4.9 million on net sales of $359 million.

Willcox & Gibbs returned to the black in 1993, reporting net income of $9.1 million on net sales of $521.5 million. In April 1993 it paid $13.6 million for Sacks Electrical Supply Co., and in December acquired another distributor of electrical parts and supplies, Summers Group Inc., for $91 million in cash and notes. To finance the purchase, Willcox & Gibbs sold 3.5 million shares of newly issued common stock to a French firm, Rexel, S.A., for $31.4 million in cash and agreed to allow Rexel to appoint five of the company's nine directors. In March 1994 Ziegler resigned as chairman, president, and chief executive officer, turning over the presidency to Alain Viry, a former Rexel executive.

By acquiring a controlling interest in Willcox & Gibbs, Rexel, the world's largest distributor of electrical parts, was taking dead aim at the $40-billion U.S. market. (It had first bought 27 percent of the company in 1992, paying with $9.9 million in cash and all its stock in Southern Electric Supply Co.) Viry told *International Business* in 1994 that his goal was to free Willcox & Gibbs's assets by reducing the receivables cycle to a maximum of 45 days and decreasing inventory. He also said he planned to improve the purchasing system and to find better ways to invest the additional cash he expected to generate.

Since Rexel was not interested in serving the apparel industry, it sold this segment of Willcox & Gibbs's business to WG, Inc. for about $44 million in cash, stock, and warrants and moved the company's headquarters from Manhattan's garment district to Coral Gables, Florida. In 1995 Rexel, S.A. raised its stake in Willcox & Gibbs to 44 percent and changed the name of

the company to Rexel Inc. Net sales rose to $1.07 billion and $1.12 billion in 1994 and 1995, respectively. Net income jumped from $8.9 million in 1994 to a record $19.8 million in 1995. The company's long-term debt was reduced from $112 million to $50 million during the year. By October 1995 Rexel, S.A. had raised its stake in Rexel, Inc. to about 47 percent. Rexel, S.A. was a subsidiary of France's Pinault-Printemps-Redoute group.

By the end of 1994 the company, renamed Rexel, Inc., was engaged only in the wholesale distribution of electrical parts and supplies, operating 171 electrical-distribution locations in 19 states and the Bahamas. During that year substantially all of the company's operating subsidiaries were merged into Southern Electric Supply Co., a unit in the eastern region, and Summers Group Inc., a unit in the western region.

Each of the company's locations served an average of 400 customers in an area of approximately 50 miles in radius and carried about 15,000 items. Its clientele consisted of electrical contractors engaged in construction work and industrial customers who needed materials for the manufacture of equipment and for maintenance and repairs. The product line included electrical fixtures, cable, cords, boxes, covers, wiring devices, conduit, raceway duct, safety switches, motor controls, breakers, panels, lamps, fuses, and related supplies and accessories. It also included materials and special cables for computers and advanced communications systems.

In addition, the company had two divisions focused on specialty markets. The DataCom division distributed products used to interconnect voice, data, and video systems. The Cummins division distributed supplies to the utility industry. These two divisions were responsible for about eight percent of the company's sales in 1994.

Principal Subsidiaries

Calcon Electric Supply, Inc.; C.E.S. Industries, Inc.; Clark Consolidated Industries, Inc.; Consolidated Electric Supply, Inc.; Consolidated Electric Supply (Bahamas) Ltd.; Duellman Electric Supply Co.; Elgee Electric Supply Co.; Engineered Apparel Concepts, Inc.; Rawlinson Electric Co.; Robin Service Corp.; Rogers Lighting Co.; Seaco Electrical Supplies, Inc.; Southern Electric Supply Co., Inc.; Spindletop Electrical Distributing Co.; Summers Electric Co.; Summers Group, Inc.; The Sacks Electrical Supply Co.; W & G Export Corp.; Willcox & Gibbs of Alabama, Inc.; Willcox & Gibbs DN, Inc.; Willcox & Gibbs DS, Inc.

Principal Divisions

Consolidated Electric Supply; DataCom; Midwest Division; Southern Electric Supply; Cummins Utility Supply; Summers Group.

Further Reading

Byrne, Harlan S., ''Willcox & Gibbs Inc.,'' *Barron's*, November 6, 1989, pp. 54–55.

Colgate, Anne Imperato, ''Glamour Stock, Industry Rock,'' *Bobbin*, July 1988, pp. 104–106, 108.

''A Conglomerate That Wall Street Likes,'' *Fortune,* January 6, 1986, pp. 108–109.

Marcial, Gene G., ''Sparks Fly at Rexel,'' *Business Week,* November 3, 1995, p. 128.

Silverman, Suzann D., ''The Waiting Game,'' *International Business,* June 1994, pp. 102, 104.

Slutsker, Gary, ''The Joys of Bankruptcy,'' *Forbes,* July 28, 1986, pp. 136, 139.

Troxell, Thomas N., Jr., ''New Chapter,'' *Barron's,* April 16, 1982, pp. 72–73.

——, ''New Direction,'' *Barron's,* June 24, 1985, pp. 49, 51.

——, ''Skein of Profits,'' *Barron's,* September 15, 1986, p. 47.

''Willcox & Gibbs, Inc.,'' *Wall Street Transcript,* November 18, 1968, p. 14, 941.

—Robert Halasz

Robbins & Myers Inc.

1400 Kettering Tower
Dayton, Ohio 45423
U.S.A.
(513) 222-2610
Fax: (513) 225-3355

Public Company
Incorporated: 1889 as The Robbins & Myers Co.
Employees: 2,230
Operating Revenues: $121.65 million (1994)
Stock Exchanges: NASDAQ
SICs: 3561 Pumps & Pumping Equipment; 3577
   Computer Peripheral Equipment, Not Elsewhere
   Classified

With operations in North and South America, Europe and Asia, Robbins & Myers Inc. (commonly known as R&M) is a leading manufacturer of fluid control devices, or industrial pumps and pumping equipment. The company underwent a significant overhaul of its operations in the early 1990s, shedding its electric motor and other businesses in order to focus on the industrial pump business that it had first entered in the mid-1930s. Augmented by an unprecedented era of acquisition, R&M's annual sales volume nearly quadrupled to over $300 million by 1995. At that time, Pfaudler glass-lined vessels contributed 42 percent of annual sales, Moyno pumps—Robbins & Myers's core fluid process business—brought in 36 percent of sales, and Chemineer and Prochem industrial mixers generated about 22 percent of revenues. R&M's Pfaudler and Moyno products led their respective markets, while Chemineer ranked a distant number two to its top competitor.

The company was originally established in 1878 by Chandler Robbins and James Myers in Springfield, Ohio, near Dayton. The founders brought varied experiences to the business. Robbins had worked as an astronomer and surveyor, while Myers had been a teacher and grocer. Robbins had invested $500 in a gray-iron foundry in 1876, and was joined two years later by Myers. The new owners changed the company name from Lever Wringer Company to The Robbins & Myers Company. The company namesakes initially manufactured castings for agricultural tools and machines, then broadened into bicycle parts when that industry boomed at the turn of the century.

The late Nineteenth-century development of direct-current generators freed electric motors from the big, heavy batteries to which they had been bound and opened up a new universe of electric appliances. Robbins & Myers entered this burgeoning new market in 1897, when the company began manufacturing electric desk, ceiling, oscillating and ventilating fans. Over the course of its history, Robbins & Myers developed into a full-line producer of electric fans, and later acquired the well-known Hunter brand of overhead fans.

The company concurrently developed and began production of a series of small (under 15 horsepower) motors known in the industry as fractional motors. These motors were widely applied in household appliances like sewing machines, vacuums, washing machines, and refrigerators in the early Twentieth century.

Robbins & Myers quickly earned a reputation for precision engineering and manufacturing that won it contracts with several important inventors. For example, R&M's motor generator sets helped Guglielmo Marconi take the wireless telegraph from concept to commercial feasibility. In 1910 Charles Kettering called on Robbins & Myers to help him design and manufacture a very efficient armature for his revolutionary DELCO (Dayton Engineering Laboratories Company) automobile starter motor. R&M went to produce starters for both General Motors and Ford Motor Company throughout the 1910s and 1920s.

In fact, Henry Ford's development of mass production techniques indirectly influenced R&M's expansion into a new market in the late 1920s. That's when the company began manufacturing labor-saving electric hoists, winches and cranes that quickly and efficiently moved goods down the assembly line.

While Robbins & Myers had manufactured rotary and force pumps as well as air compressors since the 1910s, this business segment reached a critical turning point in the 1930s, when then-president Walter S. Quinlan met with Rene Joseph Louis

Moineau. Moineau had devised and patented an innovative new concept in pumping technology called the "progressing cavity pump." This versatile device could be slanted in any way and would pump in either direction. It was durable enough to withstand such exacting functions as waste water treatment, pulp and paper production, and food and beverage processing. According to a 1978 centennial history of Robbins & Myers, Moineau's machine "revolutionized that portion of the pump industry wherever thick, viscous, abrasive and corrosive substances needed to be handled." R&M became one of the first companies to license the design, and in 1936 began producing the "Moyno" brand pump that would later become the core of its business.

But throughout the late 1930s and early 1940s, Robbins & Myers was involved in a more pressing project. In 1938 Carl Norden, inventor of the "Norden bombsight," asked R&M to build the motors used in these strategic devices. Since each sight required several motors, this sideline grew to consume 80 percent of R&M's production capacity by the end of World War II.

At war's end, Robbins & Myers resumed its traditionally diverse product line. With its standing in both motors and materials handling, R&M was well positioned to benefit from the postwar boom in consumer consumption. But in spite of continuously growing demand, the market for electric motors began to mature in the 1960s, plagued by the twin demons of intensifying competition and rapidly rising raw material costs. Imports from the United Kingdom and Japan exacerbated competitive pressures in the 1960s, during which time the unit rate of imports more than quintupled.

Inflation intensified the industry's difficulties in the early 1970s, and the dollar volume of shipments in the electric motor industry actually declined during this period. R&M reacted by reorganizing its operations into four autonomous, product-oriented divisions: electric motors, material handling devices, comfort conditioners (i.e. fans), and fluids handlers (i.e. pumps). By the end of the decade, Robbins & Myers annual sales volume had grown to about $90 million in accord with double-digit increases in the electric motor market overall.

The advent of the 1980s brought a new wave of inflation, retarded market growth, and intensified import competition that had a devastating effect on Robbins & Myers. The company recorded annual losses in four of the decade's first five years, a string of negatives that culminated in the departure of company President Fred Walls in 1986.

Walls was succeeded by an outsider, Daniel W. Duval, who had previously served as president and chief operating officer of Midland-Ross Corporation. The new CEO lead Robbins & Myers to its first profit in two years in 1987, in part by divesting unprofitable divisions. While the company's profitability continued to rebound in the late 1980s, its ability to generate cash made it more an acquisition target than an influential player in any of its historical businesses. Realizing that their company had become, to a certain degree, a "jack-of-all-trades and master-of-none," R&M's managers made a revolutionary proposal for reorganization of the company around its fast-growing fluids management division.

By the early 1990s, in fact, pumps and related equipment (known collectively as the fluids process controls) industry had grown into the second-most-common machine used in industry and a $40 billion worldwide market. (Electric motors, ironically, ranked as the most prevalent device.) R&M already had a foothold in the fluids management business. Its manufacture of Moyno pumps had broadened to include industrial pumps for the food and beverage, pulp and paper, pharmaceutical, chemical, and waste water treatment markets, as well as an entire line of pumps for oil and gas recovery. R&M divested its motion control and electric motor operations in 1991.

Building on the foundation laid by Moyno, the unprecedented era of acquisition that followed gave R&M capabilities in virtually every segment of the fluid control industry. The $125 million-plus in purchases from 1991 to 1995 built R&M into a full-line designer, manufacturer and servicer of fluid process equipment. The additions of Prochem in 1992, JWI in 1993, and Chemineer Limited in 1994 positioned R&M with the second-largest share of the worldwide industrial mixing and agitation market. These subsidiaries, which began to be merged in 1995, designed and manufactured mixing equipment for virtually all the industries already served by Moyno, from food manufacturing to waste water treatment and from chemicals to polymer makers. The acquisitions of Pfaudler, Inc., and Edlon, Inc., in 1994 gave R&M a leading position in the global market for glass-lined storage and reactor vessels. Pfaudler had pioneered the fusion of glass to steel to combine strength and durability while maintaining the integrity of the substances stored and/or combined in its containers. Purchased in 1995, Pharaoh Corp. and Cannon Process Equipment augmented this business. In all, acquisitions from 1991 to 1995 cost R&M over $125 million—more than double its 1988 sales of $53 million.

By 1995, Robbins & Myers's acquisitions was able to service virtually all the equipment needs of its target markets, from the pumps that moved the fluids, to the containers in which they were mixed, to the software that controlled the entire process, and more. The company's concentration on equipment for hard-wearing applications like oil fields, foods, and chemicals opened the door to a thriving (and recession-resistant) service and replacement parts business. In fact, replacement parts generated up to 50 percent of some divisions' sales. The acquisitions also expanded R&M's geographic reach into South America, continental Europe, Asia and the Far East. By 1995, international sales contributed more than 45 percent of annual revenues. And in 1995, R&M formed a strategic alliance with Universal Process equipment, a global distributor of reconditioned industrial equipment. Thus, while the company was focused on a single market, its diversification (in terms of product, target market, and geography) within that business was expected to shield it from economic cycles.

Robbins & Myers's strategy appeared to be succeeding by the mid-1990s. The parent company's annual sales volume nearly quadrupled during the first half of the decade, from $78.66 million in 1991 to $302.95 million in 1995. Debt also ballooned, from zero to more than $80 million by September 1994, but R&M immediately began to whittle that burden, reducing it to about $62 million by the end of fiscal 1995 (August 31). That December, the company announced an offering of over one million new shares, the proceeds of which would be used to further reduce debt. Growing pains (and an accounting change) resulted in a loss of $1.84 million in 1993, but annual profits more than doubled from $5.01 million in 1991 to $13.12 million by 1995. In 1995 analysts Wertheim Schroder & Co., Inc., forecast that Robbins & Myers "should outperform the market" through 1997.

Principal Subsidiaries

Robbins & Myers Canada, Ltd.; Robbins & Myers Ltd. (England); Robbins & Myers International Sales Company, Inc.; Robbins & Myers NRO Ltd. (Canada); R & M Environmental Strategies, Inc.; Chemineer, Inc.; Chemineer Ltd. (England); Edlon Inc.; Pfaudler, Inc.; Pfaudler Equipamentos Industrias Ltda. (Brazil); Chemical Reactor Services Ltd.; Pfaudler-Werke GmbH (Germany); Pfaudler Balfour Holdings, Ltd.; Pfaudler S.A. de C.V. (Mexico); Pfaudler Balfour Ltd.

Further Reading

"Fred Wall Quits Robbins & Myers after Reporting Fourth Loss for Last Five Years," *Journal Herald,* December 4, 1986, p. 57.

"Robbins & Myers Triples Size; Buys Three Businesses from Eagle Industries," *Dayton Daily News,* July 1, 1994, p. 5B.

Wall, Fred G., *The Standard of the Industry: The Story of Robbins & Myers, Inc.,* New York: Newcomen Society, 1978.

Wertheim Schroder & Co., Inc., *Robbins & Myers, Inc.,* March 24, 1995.

—April Dougal Gasbarre

Robert Mondavi Corporation

P.O. Box 106
7801 St. Helena Highway
Oakville, California 94562
U.S.A.
(707) 963-9611
Fax: (707) 963-1077

Public Company
Incorporated: 1966
Employees: 783
Sales: $199.47 million (1995)
Stock Exchanges: NASDAQ
SICs: 2084 Wines, Brandy & Brandy Spirits; 0172
    Grapes; 6719 Holding Companies, Not Elsewhere
    Classified

Robert Mondavi Corporation, with its family of Robert Mondavi wineries, is one of the United States' premier winemakers and has done much to bring the Napa Valley region to the forefront of international winemaking. Dedicated to producing only premium wines, the Mondavi wine family includes the brands Robert Mondavi, Woodbridge by Robert Mondavi, Vichon, Byron, Robert Mondavi Coastal, and the more recently introduced La Famiglia di Robert Mondavi. Since 1979 Mondavi has also produced, in a joint partnership with the Baron Phillippe de Rothschild wine family, the ultrapremium Opus One label. Together, these wines accounted for sales of more than 4.5 million cases and nearly $200 million in revenues in 1995. In that year, Mondavi owned more than 1,500 acres of vineyards in the Napa Valley and surrounding regions. Founded by Robert Mondavi in 1966, Mondavi went public in 1993, although the Mondavi family retains control of 92 percent of voting stock. Robert Mondavi is chairman of Robert Mondavi Corporation. His oldest son, Michael, is president and CEO, and his youngest son, Tim, is managing director and winemaker.

The Mondavi family's involvement in winemaking began in the early 1920s. Cesare Mondavi emigrated to the United States from Marches, Italy, in 1906, finding work in the iron mines of Minnesota. Two years later he returned to Italy to marry; returning to Minnesota with his bride, he opened a saloon and boarding house. Robert Mondavi was born in 1913 in the town of Virginia, Minnesota.

Prohibition brought the Mondavi family to California. A provision of the Prohibition laws allowed families to make up to two hundred gallons of fruit juice per year. A member of the local Italian Club, Cesare Mondavi was sent to California to buy grapes, which could be processed into wine. Soon after, Mondavi settled in Lodi, California with his family, and set up a business shipping grapes from the Napa Valley and Central Valley regions. At thirteen, Robert Mondavi began working for his father, including acting as the family's chauffeur, while attending high school. After high school, Robert Mondavi went on to study at Stanford University.

When the Prohibition laws were repealed, Cesare Mondavi moved from shipping grapes to pressing wine. In 1936 he bought a small winery in Napa Valley, the Sunny St. Helena, which produced bulk wines. Robert Mondavi, then in his last year of college, began taking chemistry courses in order to prepare to join his father's new business. After graduating, Robert Mondavi moved to St. Helena, and began learning to make bulk wines. His younger brother, Peter, then a student at the University of California at Berkeley, also turned his studies toward the making of wines, including cold fermentation techniques. The Mondavis incorporated cold fermentation into the making of their wine, producing a lighter, fruitier taste than the predominately sweet California wines available at the time. Before long, St. Helena's production reached more than a million gallons per year.

At the time, the bulk-wine market was dominated by a few large wineries, such as the Gallo Brothers, and bulk-wine making was made still less lucrative by a government imposed price-freeze that held the price of bulk wine at 27 cents per gallon. Robert Mondavi's interest began to lean more and more toward producing the more sophisticated dry wines. In 1943 Robert learned that the Charles Krug Winery, one of the region's oldest, was up for sale. Robert planned to produce higher quality dry wines under the Krug label, while financing the purchase with the continued sale of St. Helena bulk wine. After Cesare Mondavi's initial reluctance, the family bought the Krug winery and its 160 acres of vines for $87,000. Robert and Peter Mondavi were each given 12 percent of the new business. Peter, then still in the Army, would join the business as its winemaker. Robert Mondavi became general manager, handling the development and marketing of their wines. The new company was called C. Mondavi & Sons.

The old Krug vines were torn out and replaced by Cabernet Sauvignon, Sauvignon Blanc, Riesling, and Chardonnay vines. The winery itself—which, in its later years, had served as bulk wine factory—needed extensive renovations. Sales of the Mondavi's bulk wine, selling in half-gallon and gallon jugs, financed the new Krug operation. The bulk wine was renamed CK Mondavi, marking the first appearance of the Mondavi name on a label. The premium wine to be produced would be sold under the Krug label.

By then, Robert Mondavi had spent many years consulting wine-growing experts and experimenting with wine production techniques. In an effort to improve the quality of the Krug wines, he bought a number of used brandy barrels. By aging the wine in smaller barrels, in contrast to the giant aging vats common in the American wine industry at the time, Mondavi hoped to produce a finer wine. It wasn't long before the Krug wines began to win its first prizes at state fair competitions. Still more important to Krug's growth were Robert Mondavi's tireless promotional efforts. Mondavi was convinced that the Napa Valley region could produce a grape—and wines—equal to those of the renowned French and Italian wine-growing regions. He also insisted on blind tastings, which allowed his wines to stand on their own merits, uncompromised by the stigma still attached to Californian wine. Soon, the Napa Valley name—and Krug's—appeared on more and more wine lists and store shelves across the country.

Unfortunately, tensions arose between Robert and Peter Mondavi. Peter Mondavi resented Robert's interference in the winemaking, and Robert's salesmanship also placed continuous pressure on the winery's production capacity. By 1946 the brothers faced a crisis: Robert had placed large orders for grapes from the local growers, but a bumper crop that year cut the price of grapes in half and the Mondavis faced a loss of nearly half a million dollars. Nevertheless, the family made good on its contracts with the growers, and the Krug winery went into debt. Robert Mondavi continued to promote the Krug wines, and continued to push his brother to expand the winery's production.

In order to meet the demand that Robert was creating, however, Peter was forced to release their wines before they were properly aged. Quality declined, followed shortly thereafter by sales. Robert appealed to Cesare Mondavi, who still controlled the majority of the company, and was placed in full control of the winery's production. When Cesare Mondavi died, however, Rosa Mondavi, inheriting the majority of the company, made herself president, and Rosa favored Peter's vision of running the Mondavi wineries. Meanwhile, both Peter and Robert were trying to establish their sons in the family business. Nonethe-

less, largely due to Robert Mondavi's abilities as a salesman, the Mondavis were showing pretax profits of $200,000 by 1965.

The tensions between Peter and Robert reached a head in that year and ended in a fistfight. Robert was dismissed as general manager and given a six-month leave from the company. At the same time, Robert's eldest son, Michael, then 23, who had grown up at the Krug winery and recently graduated from the University of Santa Clara, was barred from working at the company for ten years. It was then that Robert Mondavi decided to open his own winery.

Together with two partners, Mondavi raised $200,000 and purchased property in Oakville, California. Financing for construction was arranged through an insurance firm, while a glass company funded a bottling line. In September 1966, the Robert Mondavi Winery was ready for its first crushing. It was the first new winery to appear in Napa Valley since Prohibition. From the outset, the Mondavi Winery was dedicated to producing premium wines. It was Robert Mondavi's ambition to one day produce wines that could compete with Europe's best.

The Krug side of the Mondavi family responded to the new winery by dismissing Robert Mondavi from the company altogether. This set the stage for a legal battle that would not be resolved until 1979. Robert Mondavi still controlled 24 percent of the C. Mondavi & Sons, and remained on its board until 1973. The feud between the brothers extended to include the pronunciation of the family name. Peter called himself "mon-*day*-vi," the Americanized pronunciation first adopted by Cesare Mondavi. Robert Mondavi began calling himself "mon-*dah*-vi," the traditional Italian pronunciation.

The new winery featured many of the innovations Robert Mondavi had introduced to California winemaking, including cold fermentation. On a trip through Europe in 1962, visiting the great *chateaux* and tasting their wines, Mondavi discovered what he considered a key element to the quality of French wines: they were aged in small barrels. Over the next several years, Mondavi experimented with a variety of wood types and barrel sizes, finally choosing small French oak barrels for his wines. At the new Mondavi winery, all wines were to be aged in French oak barrels.

Joined by Michael Mondavi and, later, by Tim Mondavi, the Robert Mondavi Winery produced its first wine for sale—a $3 Chenin Blanc—in 1967. By the following year, sales of this wine, previously known as White Pinot, increased fivefold. In that year, Mondavi also introduced a new wine, Fumé Blanc. This wine was, in fact, a Sauvignon Blanc, not a highly regarded wine variety. Mondavi changed the fermentation, blended the wine with Semillion, and aged it in French oak barrels, producing a drier wine. In order to distinguish his new wine, Mondavi coined the new name. The Americanized structure of the name—with the adjective first—connected it to California, while achieving a link to the renown of the French Blanc Fumé wines. Fumé Blanc was an immediate success, and did much to put Mondavi on the winemaking map.

The success of Robert Mondavi's wines was not enough, however. By 1969, Mondavi had run out of capital he would need to increase production beyond 25,000 cases per year, and he was forced to look for a fresh source of financial backing. Mondavi advertised for investors in the *Wall Street Journal* and received more than 250 responses. Both Suntory of Japan and Nestlé approached Mondavi with partnership offers, but Mondavi turned them down. Then Mondavi's two partners sold their share of the winery and vineyards to the Rainier Companies, a Seattle-based brewer, 48 percent of which was owned by the Molson Companies of Canada. The Mondavi Winery now had the capital to expand: over the next decade, Rainier poured more than $6 million into expanding the winery. At the same time, Rainier had also gained 100 percent of the vineyards and 75 percent of the winery, with Robert Mondavi retaining only 25 percent of the winery. Importantly, however, he remained its president, still in control of its winemaking operations.

The feud over the C. Mondavi & Sons winery—which enjoyed considerable success through the 1960s and 1970s—gave way to a series of lawsuits and trials in the mid-1970s. Robert Mondavi emerged victorious in 1976, and by the following year, the courts ordered C. Mondavi & Sons to be sold in order to pay Robert Mondavi fair market value for his 24 percent interest. Eventually, the brothers reached an out-of-court settlement. Robert Mondavi received more the $5 million, which included five million gallons of wine and 430 acres of vineyards.

The settlement enabled Mondavi to take back financial control of his winery. After Rainier sold its brewing operations to G. Heileman Brewing Co. in 1977, Molson agreed to sell its interest in Rainier to Robert Mondavi, at $9.40 for each of its one million shares. At the same time, Rainier, now little more than a holding company for the winery, began liquidation procedures, including buying back its stock from its shareholders. In the end, Robert Mondavi and his family regained full control of the Robert Mondavi Winery.

Despite several years of losses and nearly $10 million in debt by 1978, Mondavi's wine enjoyed considerable success during the 1970s. In 1972 the *Los Angeles Times* named the Mondavis' 1969 Cabernet Sauvignon as its top wine. Production expanded to include red, rosé, and white wines by 1974, and by 1975, Mondavi wines were distributed nationwide. Two years later, Mondavi began exporting. In 1976 Napa Valley wines gained international renown when a 1973 Cabernet Sauvignon from the Stag's Leap winery won in a blind tasting of Californian and French wines that became known as the Paris Tasting.

Napa Valley's reputation was further enhanced when Baron Phillippe de Rothschild, of the famed Chateau Mouton Rothschild, announced plans to collaborate with Robert Mondavi on a new ultrapremium wine, to be called Opus One and to be produced in the United States. Importantly, the U.S. market for premium wines was beginning an explosion: by the end of the 1970s, U.S. wine consumption had grown to more than 450 million gallons per year. Robert Mondavi, with its commitment to quality, became one of the most powerful brand names in the U.S. wine industry. This, despite the fact that the company spent almost no money on advertising, relying instead on the salesmanship—and showmanship—of Robert Mondavi himself.

Through the 1980s, Mondavi continued to expand its product line. Its purchase of the Woodbridge Winery in 1979 allowed it to expand into California varietal wines, selling premium wines in the important $3-$7 per bottle market. In 1980 the first Mondavi vintage-dated wines were introduced, selling in the super premium, $14-per-bottle-and-over category. Mondavi purchased the Vichon Winery, in Napa Valley, in 1985, giving it greater vineyards and research capacity. Five years later, the company bought the Byron Vineyard & Winery in Santa Maria Valley in Santa Barbara County. Exports continued to grow, from one percent of the company's sales in 1980 to six percent in the 1990s, reaching more than 75 countries. By 1988 its revenues had reached $95 million, with earnings of $7.2 million.

In 1990, at age 76, Robert Mondavi turned over active management of the company to sons Michael and Tim. Michael was named managing director and chief executive officer; Tim became managing director, and continued his role as head winemaker. Robert Mondavi remained chairman of the company, and continued his role as promoter of California wines. By the following year, production had reached 500,000 cases per year. However, despite growing revenues—reaching $145 million in 1992—income had dropped, struggling to $7.1 million that year. By then the company was carrying more than $126 million in debt.

A greater problem threatened the Mondavis, and the whole of Napa Valley, in the late 1980s and early 1990s. Grape phylloxera, a species of lice that attacks the roots and leaves of grape vines, had attacked much of the Napa and Sonoma valleys. With no cure for the disease, growers were forced to tear out their old vines and replace them with phylloxera-resistant varieties. Grape production throughout the Napa and Sonoma valleys, which accounted for some 80 percent of grapes used in the making of premium wines, was expected to drop by more than a third over the coming years. The majority of the Mondavis' grapes came from outside growers; however, they were largely shielded from rising grape prices because most of their grape purchases were done through long-term contracts. Nevertheless, some 15 percent of their grapes were grown in their own vineyards, and the Mondavis were faced with spending $20 million or more to replace their damaged vines with new stock, which would take five years or more before they were ready to produce commercial quantities of grapes—which would require still more years of aging before they could be released as Mondavi wine. Meanwhile, growing competition from such countries as Chile and Australia, as well as increasing exports from Europe, forced American wineries to keep their prices low despite rising grape costs. More and more wineries were being bought up by large, cash-rich corporations.

Intent on maintaining control of their company, the Mondavis went public to raise funds. Despite misgivings from some industry analysts, the initial public offering of Mondavi stock, made in 1993, raised $32.3 million. A secondary offering two years later raised an additional $35.5 million. Yet the Mondavis still retained control of 92 percent of the voting stock. Production rose, to 3.9 million cases in 1993 to 4.5 million in 1995. Revenues had grown to nearly $200 million in 1995, while net income more than doubled from $8.6 million in 1993 to $17.8

million in 1995. The company also discovered a hidden benefit of the phylloxera plague: the new disease-resistant vines could be planted closer together, allowing up to four times more vines per acre. In keeping with the Mondavi tradition, the company intended to grow fewer grapes per vine, producing a more intense flavor; nonetheless, it expected a 50-70 percent increase in yields.

In 1995 the company planned to spend $2.5 million on its first print advertising campaign, while Robert Mondavi continued to be the company's chief spokesman, salesman, and ambassador. With both Michael and Tim Mondavi raised in the art of winemaking, the company expected to double its production by the end of the century without sacrificing its hard-won reputation for quality.

Principal Subsidiaries

Robert Mondavi Winery; Woodbridge by Robert Mondavi; Vichon Winery; Bryon Vineyard & Winery; Opus One Winery (50%).

Further Reading

Conaway, James, *Napa: The Story of an American Eden,* Boston: Houghton Mifflin Company, 1990.
Erdman, Andrew, ''Robert Mondavi,'' *Fortune,* March 11, 1991, p. 99.
Ferguson, Tim W., ''Mondavi Bucks the Tide,'' *Forbes,* October 23, 1995, p. 203.
Koselka, Rita, ''A Pox on the Stox,'' *Forbes,* June 7, 1993, p. 46.

—M. L. Cohen

Rollerblade, Inc.

5101 Shady Oak Road
Minnetonka, Minnesota 55343
U.S.A.
(612) 930-7000
Fax: (612) 930-7030

Private Company, Wholly Owned by Nordica, which is
part of Benetton Sportsystem of Italy, a division of
Edizione Holdings
Incorporated: 1982 as Ole's Innovative Sports, later
renamed North American Training Corporation
Employees: 280
Sales: $265.0 million (1994 est.)
SICs: 3949 Sporting & Athletic Goods Manufacturer

Rollerblade, Inc., founder of the sport of in-line skating, is the leading manufacturer in the estimated $700 million in-line skate market. Through product innovation and aggressive marketing Rollerblade established a sport which became synonymous with its name and, according to the National Sporting Goods Association (NSGA), is close to becoming one of the top ten participant sports in the United States. Kevin Krajick wrote in the September 1995 issue of *Smithsonian*, ''No one thought it would go this far. Every year of the 1990s as the number of in-line skaters doubled, triple, quadrupled, pundits said the 'fad' would peak.''

Rollerblade started the in-line skating phenomenon by improving and rejuvenating an existing product. In-line skates were invented in Netherlands in the early 1700s: a Dutchman looking for a way to skate in the summer months nailed wooden spools to strips of wood and attached them to shoe bottoms. The first patent for skates with wheels in a single line was issued in Paris in 1819 to M. Petitbled. Models of the skate were made in both Europe and America, but all were unstable and difficult to turn. Skates with side-by-side wheels, or ''quad'' skates, were developed by an American, James L. Plimpton, in 1863. The new skates were easier to control, and they quickly became popular. Versions of the single-line skates continued to be produced, but rollerskating dominated that segment of recreational sports. A young semi-pro hockey player and his brothers changed everything with innovations that made the single-line skates faster and more maneuverable than roller skates.

Thousands of new sport and recreation products are introduced to the market every year, but few have the success and name recognition of the Rollerblade skate developed by Scott Olson and his brothers. Olson, after a successful high school hockey career in Minnesota, went north to play junior level hockey in Brandon, Manitoba. He advanced to the National Hockey League (NHL) system and played with the Winnipeg Jets' minor league teams. In 1978 Olson came upon a pair of ice skates with wheels. He loved the idea of being able to skate all year round and believed that other hockey players would also want the skates for off-season training. Olson obtained the distribution rights for Canada and the Upper Midwest from the Los Angeles-based company that sold the skates. In 1980 Olson left professional hockey and began selling the skates full time. He pitched the skates by wearing them—everywhere. He even skated from Minneapolis to Grand Rapids, Minnesota, a distance of about 200 miles, in order to promote the skates in Minnesota's hockey towns.

Because Olson was constantly on the skates he knew they could use some improvement. He devised a way to make the blade length adjustable and, therefore, more maneuverable and developed a dual-bearing wheel which made the skate faster. However, the manufacturer was not interested in the innovations. Through a patent search Olson found that Chicago Rollerskate, the largest U.S. manufacturer of roller skates, had an inactive single-line skate which was similar to his design. The twenty-year-old Olson went to Chicago to negotiate to buy the patent, which he finally obtained in 1981.

Olson incorporated Ole's Innovative Sports in 1982. The company started out small, with Olson, his brothers Brennan and Jim, and a few others assembling skates in the Olson family basement. First year sales on Rollerblade skates, which were equipped with a molded polyurethane boot shell for ankle support and a heel brake for stopping, exceeded $300,000. In 1983 the company moved to a facility in Eden Prairie, Minnesota, near the Minnesota Vikings Training Center. By then Olson had a growing company to manage. He also was busy seeking NHL player endorsements, promoting the skates to the media, and convincing sporting goods dealers to carry the skates. He needed more help and brought on a friend to handle the finances, but by the next year the growing business was in financial trouble which Olson attributed to his friend.

Help came from a Twin Cities automobile dealer, who first put $75,000 into the company to keep it afloat and later offered $300,000 for 50 percent of the business. Robert L. Sturgis, a Minneapolis entrepreneur, was also interested in the company. According to Terry Fiedler in the September 1989 *Corporate Report Minnesota*, ''Sturgis told Olson he could raise $1.5 million in a limited partnership for that same half of the company's stock.'' Olson agreed to the deal, and Sturgis, and Robert O. Naegele, president of an investment company, Naegele Communications, and former owner of his family's billboard concern, extended Olson $100,000 in the form of a note. Sturgis was named chief executive officer of Ole's Innovative Sports, and Scott Olson continued with sales and promotion of the skates. A few months later Sturgis told Olson he was having difficulty raising the $1.5 million and cut the offer in half. By late 1985 the money still had not been raised, and Sturgis and Naegele finally offered to buy out Olson. Unable to pay back the money the investors had put into the company Olson settled for $96,000 over two years and a royalty package. Olson's brothers stayed with the company.

Once out of the company Olson fought for the rights to his product designs, and when his royalties were reduced from two to one percent he filed a suit against Naegele and began a legal battle that lasted six years. Two disparate views of the high-profile Scott Olson were circulated. In one he was portrayed as a business owner without management skills or capital, and that he was fortunate to get as much as he did from the sale of the company. In the other he was cast as too honest and trusting and was forced out of the company he had founded. Dick Youngblood, in April 1993, wrote, ''There's no need to mourn for Scott Olson, whose creative genius produced a gold mine called Rollerblade Inc. in 1979—but whose dearth of capital and management expertise cost him control of the company six years later.'' In addition to pulling in Rollerblade royalties (which were expected to total about $10 million over the 10-year deal), Olson went into competition with the company he founded. He produced his Switch-it brand skates through Innovative Sports Systems, Inc. (ISS), and then through O.S. Designs Inc., he developed the Nuskate, which he sold in 1993 to CCM Sport Maska, Inc. of Canada. The company Olson first founded went on without him under a new name—as North American Training Corporation before becoming Rollerblade, Inc.—and under new leadership.

In 1986, the year financial expert John Sundet and sports marketing veteran Mary Horwath joined Rollerblade Inc., the company was still losing money. The next year Sturgis sold his share of the company to Naegele, and Sundet succeeded him as president. Sundet, along with Horwath, repositioned the company in the marketplace. Rollerblade skates were trimmed down, painted neon colors, and given to beach-side, skate-rental shops on popular California beaches. The skate took off. ''Instead of trying to market in-line skates as an adjunct to ice hockey, we focused on selling the product as a leisure sport in

and of itself,'' said Sundet in a February 1995 Minneapolis *Star Tribune* article. Rollerblade sales doubled in 1988, and the company claimed to have 70 to 75 percent of the estimated $10 to $12 million market. Another Minnesota-based company, First Team Sports, Inc., was a distant second in the in-line skate market.

Top sales for Rollerblade were in the ice skating strongholds of Minneapolis/St. Paul and Boston, but sales in Southern California were rising rapidly. By 1990 nearly one-quarter of Rollerblade's business was in California, and the total in-line market had grown to about $60 million. The sagging sporting goods industry was getting a boost from sales on in-line skates priced from $100 for basic skates up to $330 for five-wheel racing models. No longer only a cross-training sport for hockey players and cross-country skiers, one-third of the skaters were female. Demand for Rollerblade skates started to outstrip production. The number of retail outlets selling the skates had grown from 31 in 1984 to 3,000 in 1990. The skates were sold in Canada, Europe, Australia, New Zealand, and Korea, as well as, the United States.

In January 1991, Rollerblade doubled its space with a move to new headquarters in Minnetonka, Minnesota. Three months later the world's leading ski-boot manufacturer, Nordica, purchased 50 percent of Rollerblade, Inc. from Naegele for an undisclosed amount. Naegele continued in his position as chairman of the newly formed board. Competitors, Scott Olson, then president of ISS, and David G. Soderquist, president of First Team Sports, Inc., saw the purchase as a positive development for the in-line skate industry. Nordica, with consolidated revenues of $450 million, had money available to promote the sport and establish it as more than just a fad.

Fad or not, Rollerblade sales had at least doubled every year from 1987 to 1991, and the competition was heating up. Number two manufacturer First Team Sports brought NHL hockey superstar Wayne Gretzky aboard to promote its Ultra-Wheels line. Canstar Sports, Inc. was gaining market share with its Bauer Precision In-Line Skates. The low end of the market was being tapped by Taiwanese-made skates selling for under $50, but because all but First Team Sports were privately held, market figures for the rapidly growing industry remained sketchy, and claims by the leading manufacturers conflicted with each other.

Competition was not the only threat to Rollerblade's market domination. Because Rollerblade was so successful in establishing the sport of in-line skating its trademark was in danger of becoming a generic name—aspirin, linoleum, and cellophane were all once brand names that lost their trademarks to general use. The brand name Rollerblade was being used as a noun (rollerblades or blades) and as a verb (rollerblading or blading). In 1990 the company launched a campaign to protect its identity. Its market strategy shifted from promoting the sport of in-line skating to developing brand identification. Print advertising and national TV ads were added to their less traditional promotional tool box. Concept shops, which highlighted their skates, brightly-colored Blade Gear sportswear, accessories, and protective gear, were opened in sporting goods stores, but the company continued to use the unorthodox promotions that brought them early success.

When Mary Horwath joined Rollerblade in 1986, she relied on "guerilla marketing" tactics that equated in-line skating with a fun, active, and sexy lifestyle. With only a $200,000 budget she depended on aggressive and unorthodox, yet inexpensive, methods to get the skate into the public eye. Rollerblade skates were given to high profile celebrities and athletes who were seen and often photographed wearing the skates. Cross promotional ties-ins paired Rollerblade with large, well-known companies that sought to be identified with youthful, athletic activities. Team Rollerblade, a group of elite stunt skaters, traveled around the country on "Rock 'N' Rollerblade Tours," appeared in commercials, and performed at the Super Bowl and at the Olympic games. Perhaps most important, the company took the skates out on the streets and gave the public opportunities to try them. Wherever people gathered—fairs, festivals, theme parks, and college campuses—Rollerblade demonstration vans arrived.

The year 1992 was a time of transition for Rollerblade as it moved further away from its entrepreneurial roots. The in-line market and the in-line leader were maturing. In an executive overhaul, former Tonka executive, John F. Hetterick, assumed the roles of president and chief operating officer, and other top level positions were filled by people with experience in major corporations. John Sundet resigned as CEO in May 1992 and was succeeded by Hetterick. (Mary Horwath, who in 1992 was ranked as one of the nation's 100 top marketing executives by the trade journal *Advertising Age*, left Rollerblade the next year.) Rollerblade began to place more emphasis on the efficiency of operations, especially striving to meet shipping dates: late orders had been an ongoing headache for distributors. Twenty-four jobs were cut, mostly in marketing, sales, and finance, and more emphasis was placed on customer service. By the end of 1992 the company was again looking for more space to accommodate its rapid growth. *Corporate Report Minnesota* estimated Rollerblade's average annual growth rate to be 115.5 percent between the years 1987 and 1992.

Rollerblade's growth rate was propelled by a tripling of the number of in-line skaters in the United States. However, *The Wall Street Journal* (WSJ) predicted in November 1993 that the industry was headed for a fall: sales growth had slowed, big ski industry concerns had entered the high-end market ($150-$300 range), and low-end skates accounted for 44 percent of total in-line sales. Michael Selz, of the WSJ wrote, "To cope with competition, skate makers are fighting harder. Rollerblade mounted one of the most aggressive responses, partly because it has the most to lose." In February 1993, Rollerblade filed a patent law suit against 33 competitors. Later that year, Rollerblade settled out-of-court with seven of the manufacturers, including the number two maker. First Team Sports, which was ranked 15th on *Business Week*'s 1993 Hot Growth list, had experienced depressed earnings due to the suit.

Rollerblade remained the big name in recreational in-line skates, but Bauer and Cooper brands, owned by the largest hockey equipment maker in the world, Canstar Sports, Inc., were the skates of choice for in-line hockey. Sunbelt in-line hockey leagues were becoming as popular as Little League, and Canstar banked on brand name recognition and status as official sponsor of a professional league to help them overtake Rollerblade and First Team. Canstar's 1993 in-line sales grew to $26

million. Second place First Team had sales of $38.2 million, and Rollerblade planned to challenge Canstar with its own in-line hockey skate.

Safety was an ongoing concern for all the manufacturers. As the number of in-line skating injuries rose, the Consumer Product Safety Commission issued warnings about the dangers of the sport. The June 1994 issue of the *Journal of the American Medical Association* (JAMA) cited key factors that contributed to in-line injuries: cruising speeds of 10-17 miles per hour; sharing the roadways with motor vehicles, bicyclists, pedestrians, and pets; and falling on hard surfaces. Rollerblade encouraged use of safety equipment and lessons for beginners through its "Skate Smart" safety education program and its "Asphalt Bites" campaign. In 1994 Rollerblade introduced Active Brake Technology (ABT), an award-winning innovation which made stopping easier for beginners and improved speed control.

Rollerblade's 1994 sales were estimated by *Newsweek* to be about $260 million or about 40 percent of the $650 million in-line market, and its competitors appeared poised to capture more of Rollerblade's market share. In late 1994 Canstar was purchased by Nike Inc., the athletic footwear and clothing giant. Already benefiting from the resurgence of hockey, Canstar received an added boost from Nike's marketing and sales mastery. First Team Sports also was capitalizing on the in-line hockey boom and reported sales revenues of $86 million in fiscal year 1995. Rollerblade was still relying on its grassroots activities and promotional tie-ins to sell its skates. The company's advertising budget remained modest—$4 million in 1995—and was limited to spot markets.

In November 1995—following months of speculation about the company's future—Naegele sold his stake in Rollerblade to Nordica. *The New York Times* said that Naegele received at least $150 million for his 50 percent share of the company. Nordica, in turn, had sold a minority interest of Rollerblade to G.S. Capital Partners II L.P. , an affiliate of Goldman, Sachs & Company. No longer under a dual ownership Rollerblade appeared to be in a better position to capitalize on the financial strength, research and development support, manufacturing capacity, and international distribution capabilities that Nordica offered.

Rollerblade, Inc. and in-line skating have moved into the mainstream of recreational sports, yet there is still room for growth with only 14 percent of U.S. households owning in-line skates in 1995 as compared with 51 percent owning bicycles. In-line makers were optimistic about growth in the international marketplace in which Rollerblade had a foothold by way of Nordica. According to industry and company estimates Rollerblade still held nearly half of the market in 1995, but it remained to be seen if in-line skating would continue to grow or would follow the path of the roller skate industry and slip into a cycle of boom and bust.

Further Reading

Alexander, Steve, "Rollerblade, Inc. Settles Out-of-Court with Seven Competitors over Patents," *Star Tribune* (Minneapolis), September 15, 1993, p. 1D.

Benezra, Karen, ''Rollerblade Taps Disney, Gatorade,'' *Brandweek*, October 10, 1994, p. 3.

Beran, George, ''Rollerblade, Inc. on a Roll,'' *Pioneer Press Dispatch* (St. Paul, Minn.), June 19, 1988.

Brumback, Nancy, ''Mega-Deals on Wheels,'' *Daily News Record*, August 11, 1995, p. 22.

Comte, Elizabeth, ''Blade Runner,'' *Forbes*, October 12, 1992, pp. 114–117.

Duchschere, Kevin, ''Rolling into Peril,'' *Star Tribune* (Minneapolis), June 10, 1994, p. 1A.

Feyder, Susan, ''Nordica Buys 50 Percent of Rollerblade,'' *Star Tribune* (Minneapolis), March 22, 1991, p. 1D.

Fiedler, Terry, ''Rolling with the Punches,'' *Corporate Report Minnesota*, September 1989, pp. 47–52.

Gill, Penny, ''In-Line Skating: Rolling Along!'' *Stores*, December 1990, pp. 6–12.

Goerne, Carrie, ''Rollerblade Reminds Everyone That Its Success Is Not Generic,'' *Marketing News*, March 2, 1992, pp. 1–2.

Greising, David, ''A Fleet No. 2 in the Rollerblade Derby,'' *Business Week*, May 24, 1993, pp. 67–68.

Gross, David M., ''Zipping along in Asphalt Heaven,'' *Time*, August 13, 1990, p. 56.

Horwath, Mary, ''Guerrilla Marketing 101,'' *Working Women*, December 1991, pp. 23–24.

Jones, Jim, ''Rollerblade Scored at Vikes Game,'' *Star Tribune* (Minneapolis), December 16, 1988, p. 1D.

——, ''At First He Didn't Succeed, But Sturgis Did Try Again,'' *Star Tribune* (Minneapolis), December 19, 1988, p. 1D.

——, ''Rollerblade Trims Jobs in Minor Restructuring,'' *Star Tribune* (Minneapolis), April 17, 1992, p. 3D.

Kaszuba, Mike, ''Rollerblade's Success Hasn't Brought Happiness,'' *Star Tribune* (Minneapolis), March 6, 1991, p. 1D.

Krajick, Kevin, ''Don't Look Now, But Here Come the Bladerunners,'' *Smithsonian*, September 1995, pp. 60–69.

Maler, Kevin, ''SnowRunner Glides to IPO,'' *CityBusiness* (Minneapolis/St. Paul), January 28, 1994.

Marin, Rick, with T. Trent Gegax, ''Blading on Thin Ice,'' *Newsweek*, December 12, 1994, pp. 64–65.

Matzer, Marla, ''A Nice One for the Great One,'' *Forbes*, May 8, 1995, p. 88.

Merrill, Ann, ''Italian Investors Want Piece of Skate Maker Rollerblade,'' *CityBusiness* (Minneapolis/St. Paul), March 18-24, 1991, pp. 1, 19.

——, ''Growing Pains Afflict In-Line Skate Firms,'' *CityBusiness* (Minneapolis/St. Paul), May 29, 1992, p. 2.

——,''Rollerblade Chairman Sells His 50 Percent Stake to Partner Nordica,'' *Star Tribune* (Minneapolis), November 14, 1995, p. 1D.

Munk, Nina, ''Hockey in the Sun,'' *Forbes*, August 15, 1994, pp. 95–96.

Pesky, Greg, ''Sharpening the Blade,'' *Sporting Goods News*, August 1992, pp. 56–57.

Peterson, Susan E., ''Sundet Resigns as Rollerblade CEO,'' *Star Tribune* (Minneapolis), May 9, 1992, p. 3D.

Selz, Michael, ''Once-Rolling In-Line Skate Makers Skid Amid Rivalry,'' *The Wall Street Journal*, November 30, 1993, p. 2B.

Schafer, Lee, ''It's Not A Fad,'' *Corporate Report Minnesota*, April 1992, pp. 31–39.

Schieber, M.D., Richard A.; Christine M. Branche-Dorsey, Ph.D., MSPH; and George W. Ryan, Ph.D., ''Comparison of In-Line Skating Injuries with Rollerskating and Skateboarding Injuries,'' *JAMA*, June 15, 1994, pp. 1856–1858.

Schott, Susan, ''In-Line Skating Boom Breaks the Ice,'' *Reuter Business Report*, February 8, 1995.

Smith, Tom, ''When Gravity Fails: The State's Fastest Growing Companies,'' *Corporate Report Minnesota*, May 1993, p. 88.

Therrien, Lois, ''Rollerblade Is Skating in Heavier Traffic,'' *Business Week*, June 24, 1991, pp. 114–115.

Waters, Jennifer, ''Racing Sales Cause Rollerblade to Expand Its Space,'' *CityBusiness* (Minneapolis/St. Paul), October 9, 1992, p. 2.

——, ''Rollerblade Sale Rumors Gain Fuel,'' *CityBusiness* (Minneapolis/St. Paul), May 12, 1995.

Youngblood, Dick, ''Scott Olson Still Developing Plenty of Capital Ideas,'' *Star Tribune* (Minneapolis), April 11, 1993, p. 2D.

——, ''From In-Line Skates to Penguins That Waddle in the Wind,'' *Star Tribune* (Minneapolis), September 26, 1993, p. 2D.

——, ''Two Rollerblade Alums Running with the Sled Dogs,'' *Star Tribune* (Minneapolis), February 26, 1995, p. 2D.

''A Business That's On a Roll,'' *Star Tribune* (Minneapolis), November 17, 1985.

''How Can I Be In-Line Skating If There's No One Else Around?'' *Corporate Report Minnesota*, April 1991, p. 18.

''Nike to Acquire Canadian Hockey Gear Firm,'' *Star Tribune*, (Minneapolis), December 15, 1994, p. 7D.

''Rollerblade Rolls Out Store Concept Shops,'' *Sporting Goods Business*, July 1991, p. 26.

''Rollerblade Complaint Rocks In-Line Market,'' *Sporting Goods Business*, March 1993, p. 8.

''Rollerblade Co-Owner Sells Stake to Nordica,'' *The New York Times*, November 14, 1995, p. C3.

—Kathleen Peippo

Ronco, Inc.

5308 Derry Avenue
Agoura Hills, California 91301
U.S.A.
(818) 775-4680
Fax: (818) 775-4664

Private Company
Incorporated: 1964 as Ronco Teleproducts, Inc.
Employees: 100
Sales: $75 million (1994 est.)
SICs: 5961 Mail Order Houses

Best-known for its fast-paced, late-night commercials and pioneering informercials, Ronco Inc. has manufactured and distributed an astonishing array of well-known gadgets and goodies since its inception in the early 1960s. From the Veg-O-Matic and the Pocket Fisherman of the early days to GLH Formula #9 and the Electric Food Dehydrator of the 1990s, Ronco has chalked-up a series of well-promoted hits.

In the process, company founder Ron Popeil has garnered quite a bit of media attention. In 1993 friend and fellow Mirage Hotel board member Steve Wynn told *People* magazine that "Ron has a knack for convincing you that you need something." A July 1981 article in *People* magazine dubbed him "the Horatio Alger of the TV age." The "CBS Evening News" called Popeil "a master, a pioneer, the king of the infomercial, a gadget savant," while television newsmagazine "20/20" dubbed him a "television visionary, the man who turned the hard sell into a blunt instrument, [and] the granddaddy of TV hucksters."

Many successes and a popular leader notwithstanding, Ronco's history has included some challenges as well. After its foundation near Chicago in 1964, the firm went public in 1969. Sales and profits increased erratically throughout the 1970s, but the early 1980s brought intense competition and eventual bankruptcy. Ron Popeil revived his firm in the late 1980s with such products as GLH "Great Looking Hair" Formula #9 (a "spray-on toupee"), the Popeil Automatic Pasta Maker, and the Ronco Electric Dehydrator. Headquartered in southern Califor-

nia, the reincarnated Ronco remained privately and closely held into the mid-1990s. Although company representatives declined to release annual sales estimates, Popeil's 1995 autobiography entitled *Salesman of the Century* boasted that his firm had generated more than $1 billion in retail sales over the course of its more than 30 years in business.

The Ronco saga is as much the story of Ron Popeil as it is a company history. The hyperbolic pitchman was born to Sam and Julia Popeil in 1935 in the Bronx. Sam Popeil was trained by his uncles to demonstrate and sell kitchen gadgets, and he and his sibling Raymond launched Popeil Brothers, Inc. in Chicago in 1947. A 1989 article about the Popeil family businesses noted that their postwar television commercials were among the first to bring live demonstration to the new media, foreshadowing the infomercials and home shopping channels that would emerge decades later. Although Ron Popeil would later downplay his father's influence, a writer for the *Journal of Popular Film and Television* asserted that Ron "rode to success on the coattails of Popeil Brothers." Ron Popeil's career brought two generations of selling to its ultimate fruition.

He got an early education in the housewares market working weekends in his father's Chicago factory making kitchen products. At 16, Ron began selling Popeil Brothers' "Spiral Slicers" and "Slice-A-Way" gadgets in street markets. Within a year, the teenager had moved out on his own, hawking Popeil Brothers' products on a flat commission basis at the Woolworth's store in downtown Chicago.

There's little doubt that Popeil was a natural salesman. He claims to have made $1,000 each week in the early 1950s—four times an average monthly salary. He earned enough to pay for a year of classes at the University of Illinois, where he met future business partner Mel Korey. But it was hard for Popeil to justify paying for college classes when he was making money hand over fist without an advanced education. So while Korey earned his undergraduate degree, Popeil continued to sell at Woolworth's during the winter and hit the Midwest "fair circuit" in the summer. The fair circuit included county and state fairs, as well as auto, home, and garden shows. Korey joined Popeil upon graduation, selling knives, kitchen gadgets, spray shoe polish, and hobbycraft kits throughout the Midwest.

Their long, hard days of live demonstrations came to an end in 1964, when Popeil and Korey launched a joint partnership called Ronco Inc. in Elk Grove Village, Illinois. Their first product—and the demonstrative television commercial that promoted it—set the standard for the dozens of Ronco offerings that would follow. The Ronco Spray Gun was manufactured on contract by another company; Ronco acted essentially as a promoter and distributor. The product, a hose nozzle, was a fairly basic, inexpensive household item with a twist: the high-pressure sprayer featured water-soluble tablets of soap, wax, insecticide, or herbicide, and so the nozzle could be used to wash and wax the car, fertilize the lawn, kill weeds or insects, and wash windows. The tablets were a key consideration: they would continue to generate high-profit-margin sales long after the initial purchase of the spray nozzle.

Popeil wrote a script, traveled to a Florida television station to tape the advertisement, and starred in the spot using the motor-mouthed style that had brought him success on the fair circuit. The production cost a total of $550. Korey spent another $400 to place the ad in cheap, late-night timeslots on television stations in Illinois and Wisconsin. They sold the goods on a "guaranteed-sale" basis through local retailers. Popeil defined guaranteed-sale as the direct sale of product to the retailer with the provision that any unsold merchandise would be repurchased by Ronco. Korey eventually placed the Ronco Spray Gun in 100 cities. The campaign featured "trade support marketing"—a mention of the retail outlets that carried the product—a technique pioneered by Popeil Brothers. The spray gun was an undeniable success. Within four years, Ronco had sold almost one million units.

Several elements of Ronco's strategy emerged over the course of the next two decades, some of which were reflected in that initial offering. First, the vast majority of Ronco's products were inexpensive. Until the late 1970s, the company didn't float a single item over $20 and most were priced under $10. Also, Ronco avoided manufacturing in the early days, thereby side-stepping the hefty capital outlays and risks involved in mass production. Contrary to popular belief, only a few of the company's products were invented by Ron Popeil. While he often had a hand in "refining" the gadgets, most of the products were purchased from the manufacturer or developer and sold on an exclusive contract. Therefore, Ronco vacillated between retail and mail order distribution.

Finally, one of the most important factors in the long-term Ronco scheme was the continuous introduction of new products to replace those that had lost their novelty. Toward that end, the company considered a reported 400-plus potential products every year. In order to whittle that daunting list down to the dozen or so annual offerings, the company evaluated each one's potential for demonstration on television, whether it could be positioned as a problem-solving device, its novelty, mass appeal, and profit margin.

But, as Popeil reiterated throughout his book, television marketing was the engine that drove demand. In a rare moment of modesty in his 1995 autobiography, Popeil admitted that "In those [early] days you could advertise empty boxes on TV and sell them. It was hard not to be successful." The salesman's on-screen technique mixed old-fashioned demonstration with breathless hyperbole to convince millions of viewers that his gadgets solved everyday "problems" they didn't even know they suffered until that very moment. Such Popeilesque phrases as "as seen on TV," "the perfect Christmas gift," "miracle (add product name here)," and "and that's not all!" would trigger millions of people to reach for wallets and pocketbooks in the coming decades.

Ronco refined its marketing and distribution techniques with its second televised product, the "Chop-O-Matic." Produced by Popeil Brothers, this "food chopper with rotating blades" had been peddled by Ron Popeil on the fair circuit since the late 1950s. Not only was the commercial for this device longer, at five minutes, but Ronco also made this its first mail-order product. Delighted with the Chop-O-Matic's success, Sam Popeil invented and manufactured the Dial-O-Matic and what would become Ronco's first blockbuster, the Veg-O-Matic. Ron Popeil's television ad fueled the sale of over nine million units for $50 million worth of these rather primitive food processors.

But while the Veg-O-Matic was Ronco's best-known product of the era, it was pantyhose that generated over half of the company's annual sales in the late 1960s. Ronco's ads for London Aire Hosiery, the pantyhose "guaranteed in writing not to run," featured Ron Popeil abusing the double-locked-stitch nylons with such outrageous tools as a scissors, a nail file, a scouring pad, and a lit cigarette, all to show that the fabric would not run.

Ronco's sales increased from about $89,000 in 1964 to over $14 million in 1969. Net income multiplied from $4,400 to over $1.25 million during the same period. The company went public as Ronco Teleproducts, Inc. in 1969, selling a $5 million, 22 percent stake.

The 1970s were Ronco Teleproduct's heyday. Over the course of the decade, the company broadened its product line from its base in housewares to personal care products, record albums, and hobbycrafts, while expanding its geographic reach internationally to include Canada, Great Britain, and Australia. In the early 1970s, Ronco ranked among America's top 25 television advertisers. The new offerings formed a panoply of gadgets. Housewares included the Miracle Broom, the Roller Measure, the Salad Spinner, the Glass Froster, the Cookie Machine, and the Miracle Brush. In 1974, Ron Popeil brought out his first invention, the "Smokeless Ashtray." This device filtered cigarette smoke from the air at its source and was offered in both home and car models. Ronco's Egg Scrambler featured a battery-powered needle that whisked yolk and white together while still in the shell.

Craft and hobby products included the Mr. Microphone, the Ronco Bottle and Jar Cutter, the Ronco Rhinestone and Stud Setter, a Candle-Making Kit, a Pottery Wheel, and a Flower Loom. The Pocket Fisherman, developed by Sam Popeil, featured a telescoping rod which was so compact that it could fit into a car's glove compartment. The gadget was one of the company's best-selling (at 35 million units) and best-remembered products. Ronco also started offering record album compilations of popular music during this period, promoting four to six discs each year.

Ronco's line of personal care products included the Trim-Comb hair groomer, the Tidie Drier hair/clothes dryer, the

Steam Away clothing steamer, and the Mr. Dentist. The Button-eer had originally been something of a flop for manufacturer Dennison Manufacturing, but Popeil reduced the price by more than 25 percent and produced one of his typical problem-solving television spots. Buttoneer sales multiplied ten times within just one year.

This rapid series of product launches helped fuel steady sales growth throughout the 1970s, from $16 million in 1970 to $22.2 million in 1975 and $36.9 million by 1980. But Ronco's profit-ability vacillated erratically throughout this period, from a net loss of $796,000 in 1973 to a net income of $1.4 million in 1978.

In an effort to raise its profit margins, Ronco Teleproducts introduced its best-quality, highest-priced product, the Clean-Aire Machine, in the late 1970s. Essentially a larger version of the "Smokeless Ashtray," the CleanAire Machine featured a charcoal filter that could clean a whole room's worth of air. But the CleanAire machine would also help contribute to Ronco's early 1980s demise. Ronco overbought the device for the 1983 Christmas season and wasn't up to competition from the likes of Norelco, Remington, and other leading housewares manufac-turers, who initiated a price war in the category. Ronco also got burned on its guaranteed sales policy; retailers returned well over two-thirds of the CleanAire machines that year. The re-duced cash flow lowered Ronco's all-important advertising budget at a time when TV advertising costs were rising quickly. Without his hallmark television ads to keep products in front of the consumer, revenues dropped by one-third from 1982 to 1983. To make matters worse, Ronco's bank called in the company's $15 million revolving line of credit.

The company tried to reorganize under Chapter 11 of the federal bankruptcy code, but was soon forced into Chapter 7 and out of business. Popeil, who did not declare personal bank-ruptcy, was able to purchase much of Ronco's inventory at auction. He entered into a new partnership with former Ronco salesman Malcolm Sherman shortly thereafter. (Mel Korey had resigned from Ronco's executive team early in 1983.) From 1984 to 1987, Popeil and Sherman concentrated on selling the CleanAire Machine and the Ronco Electric Food Dehydrator. But as the end of the 1980s loomed, Popeil and Sherman parted ways. Sherman got the rights to the CleanAir Machine, while Popeil assumed sole control of the food dehydrator and the partnership.

Popeil went into a period of what he called "semi-retire-ment" following the demise of his namesake company. He returned to his old hunting grounds on the fair circuit from 1987 to 1990 and emerged from his self-imposed exile from televi-sion in 1989. That's when a friend suggested that Popeil team up with mail order powerhouse Fingerhut, which was testing a home shopping television channel. Although Fingerhut closed down its home shopping operation not long thereafter, Popeil was reinfected with the television bug. In 1991, he produced his first half-hour infomercial.

Entitled Incredible Inventions, the long-form ad essentially reproduced Popeil's fair demonstration and offered direct sales via a toll-free phone bank. Production and airing of the ad cost $33,000—a far cry from the $550 that Popeil had spent on his first one-minute spot. But the dehydrator sold for around $60,

whereas the Chop-O-Matic had sold from $3.98. The infomercial generated a total of $80 million in food dehydrator sales by 1993.

Popeil followed up the dehydrator success with GLH For-mula #9 and the Popeil Automatic Pasta Maker. He bought the first product, a spray-on "toupee" called Great Looking Hair, from its Australian inventors. The fibrous aerosol came in nine colors and cost $39.92 per can. Ronco sold 900,000 cans of the formula within just one year.

In 1993, he launched the Popeil Automatic Pasta Maker, a device that one observer called "the most substantial product Popeil's bizarrely successful company . . . has ever produced." While promotions via infomercials and the QVC (Quality Value Convenience) home shopping network generated unit sales of over 500,000, the introduction was not without its stumbling blocks. In 1994, Creative Technologies Corp. sued Popeil and the retailers affiliated with his pasta maker for patent infringe-ment, false advertising, and unfair competition. State and fed-eral courts, however, found Popeil and his company not guilty on all counts. While both parties continued to file suits and countersuits through 1995, Popeil was able to continue promo-tion of his device. In 1994, he forged a contract giving Salton-Maxim the right to distribute the pasta machine in retail outlets. Popeil also hoped to derive additional sales with the introduc-tion of branded pasta mixes.

The 60-year-old Popeil showed no signs of slowing down in 1995. Fresh from the release of his autobiography, he toured the United States promoting the book, himself, and his products old and new. Salesman of the Century hinted that future Ronco of-ferings could include a revival of the Pocket Fisherman and a new-fangled spatula called the Popeil Gripper. And no matter what the company introduces, it's liable to be pitched as "amazing."

Further Reading

Abdeddaim, Michelle N., "CTC, Popeil Swap Tacks for Marketing Pasta Makers," HFN—The Weekly Newspaper for the Home Fur-nishing Network, April 10, 1995, p. 107.

Bailey, Doug, "Still Selling After All These Years," Boston Globe, November 7, 1993, p. 77.

Gliatto, Tom, "He Yells! He Sells! Amazing! Pitchman Ron Popeil Strikes Gold with His Spray-on Toupee," People, May 3, 1993, p. 154.

"It Slices! It Dices! It Goes Belly Up!" Newsweek, February 13, 1984, p. 74.

Koris, Sally, "In the Wee Small Hours, Pitchman Ron Popeil is Never at a Loss for a Miracle," People, July 13, 1981.

Popeil, Ron, The Salesman of the Century: Inventing, Marketing, and Selling on TV: How I Did it and How You Can Too!, New York: Delacorte Press, 1995.

"Popeil Wins an Appeal, and Countersues CTC," HFN, June 12, 1995, p. 82.

Rivenburg, Roy, "Still Slicing & Dicing," Los Angeles Times, Decem-ber 15, 1995, p. 1E.

Serwer, Andrew E., "Ron Popeil: The King of Thingamabobs," For-tune, June 12, 1995, p. 124.

Thomas, Clarence W., "It Chops, It Slices, It Dices: Television Market-ing and the Rise and Fall of the Popeil Family Businesses," Journal of Popular Film and Television, Summer 1989, pp. 67-73.

—April Dougal Gasbarre

Roper Industries Inc.

160 Ben Burton Road
Bogart, Georgia 30622
U.S.A.
(706) 369-7170
Fax: (706) 353-6496

Public Company
Incorporated: 1981
Employees: 961
Sales: $147.6 million (1994)
Stock Exchanges: NASDAQ
SICs: 3561 Pumps & Pumping Equipment; 3824 Fluid
    Meters & Counting Devices; 3563 Air & Gas
    Compressors; 3714 Motor Vehicle Parts & Accessories

A rising competitor in the fluid handling and industrial controls industry, Roper Industries Inc. manufactures and distributes highly engineered, application-specific products for a broad range of industries, including the oil and gas, chemical and petrochemical processing, and power generation industries. During the mid-1990s, Roper Industries operated in two business segments: industrial controls, which manufactured microprocessor-based turbomachinery control systems, pressure sensors, and thermostatic valves; and fluid handling, which manufactured rotary gear pumps, air-operated diaphragm pumps, and centrifugal pumps. With slightly more than half of its sales derived from overseas, the company recorded resolute growth during the early 1990s by expanding internationally through several key acquisitions.

Stoves and Pumps: Early History

Roper Industries' historical roots reach back to its founder, George D. Roper, and the company he started in 1919, the Geo. D. Roper Corporation. Founded in Rockford, Illinois, as a manufacturer of gas stoves and gear pumps, Geo. D. Roper Corp. became best known for its production stoves, developing into a flourishing concern that eventually manufactured electric

and gas kitchen ranges, power gardening tools, and a host of other home-related goods. The company's smaller business segment, the manufacture of pumps, which constituted the origins of Roper Industries, remained overshadowed by the association of the Roper name with kitchen appliances, existing for decades as a little known enterprise, while the appliance segment garnered the bulk of Geo. D. Roper Corp.'s total sales and, consequently, nearly all of its publicity.

For much of the first half of the 20th century, the two businesses—gear pumps and kitchen stoves—operated together within the same corporate structure, but in the late 1950s the two segments were split into two different companies that 30 years later existed as Roper Corporation, a large kitchen appliance manufacturer with more than $700 million in annual sales, and Roper Industries, a manufacturer of an assortment of pumps and controls with an annual sales volume roughly 25 times smaller than Roper Corporation.

The Postwar Years: Two Distinct Companies Emerge

The two distinct business segments embarked on their separate paths of development when the Florence Stove Company, founded in the early 1870s as a maker of wood-burning stoves, set its acquisitive sights on the Geo. D. Roper Corp. In 1957, Florence Stove sold its manufacturing facility in Florence, Massachusetts, and transferred production to Illinois, then purchased the inventories of finished products, receivables, and all capital stock of Geo. D. Roper Corp. The entire new operation took the name Geo. D. Roper Corp. in 1958. Meanwhile, the pump manufacturing operations belonging to Geo. D. Roper Corp. were moved to Georgia, as the newly assembled corporation flourished under the beneficent corporate umbrella of retailing giant Sears, Roebuck & Co.

Sears not only was Geo. D. Roper Corp.'s largest customer but also owned nearly half of the Illinois-based appliance manufacturer. This relationship between Sears and Geo D. Roper Corp. was strengthened when Geo D. Roper Corp. merged with a wholly owned Sears subsidiary, Newark Ohio Co., in 1964. Newark Ohio, which manufactured electric ranges, lawn mowers, and other products for Sears, sold nearly all of its products to its parent company prior to the merger, while Geo D. Roper Corp. derived 55 percent of its annual revenue from sales to Sears before the merger. Once combined, the merged entity relied on its relationship with Sears to generate more than three-quarters of total sales, ranking as Sears' largest supplier of gas and electric ranges, rotary mowers, and a major supplier of drapery hardware.

When Geo. D. Roper and Newark Ohio merged, the Geo. D. Roper Corporation corporate title was retained for several years until Roper Corporation was adopted as the company's new name in April 1968, by which time the gas stove manufacturing business originally founded by George Roper was rapidly approaching the $200-million-a-year sales mark. Over the ensuing two decades, Roper Corporation broadened its product line and grew as Sears grew, developing into a more than $500 million a year concern by the mid-1980s, when the company implemented a major restructuring program. Nonessential businesses, such as the company's involvement in luggage and window blind production, were spun off; manufacturing facilities were relocated from the Midwest to Georgia and South Carolina; and 60 percent of its shares were bought back from Sears, making Roper Corporation a more cost-efficient maker of electric kitchen ranges than other major producers. The changes effected during the mid-1980s also made Roper Corporation a much more attractive acquisition target, and in 1988 a bidding war between Whirlpool Corporation and the General Electric Company was touched off, as the two giant appliance makers battled for the rights to acquire one of the few U.S. electric appliance manufacturers still in existence. In the end, General Electric emerged the victor, and acquired Roper Corporation's manufacturing capacity for stoves and lawn equipment, the core of its more than $700-million-a-year business at the time.

1980s and Beyond: New Leadership and Expansion at Roper Industries

As Roper Corporation slowly disappeared from the business press spotlight, existing in relative anonymity deep within the sundry organizational layers comprising behemoth General Electric, the other half of the former Geo. D. Roper Corporation—the pump manufacturing facilities that were relocated to Georgia in the late 1950s—was beginning to etch a new identity for the Roper name as Roper Industries Inc. During Roper Corporation's rise as a major supplier to Sears, the Georgia-based pump works—Roper Pump Company—operated as a public company until 1981, when a leveraged buyout transferred ownership of the company to private hands. The following year, the person chiefly responsible for Roper Industries' growing stature during the 1980s and 1990s arrived, marking the beginning of a new era in the company's history that would punctuate its decades of quiet existence with resolute, international growth.

This pivotal figure in the company's ascension was British-born Derrick N. Key, who was named vice-president of Roper Industries in June 1982. A former consultant for Johnson & Johnson, Key put his experience in marketing consumer products to work at Roper Industries, introducing a management system that had achieved considerable success at numerous consumer products companies, but rarely had been used at manufacturing companies like Roper Industries. Key's importation of the prod-

uct manager system, which was adopted by Roper Industries following Key's arrival, pushed the decision-making process down the company's management ladder, ceding substantial control to company managers. Within Roper Industries, each major product was assigned its own manager, who was then put in charge of overseeing the full development of the product, wielding control over production, sales, and advertising.

As the success engendered by the implementation of the product manager system grew, Key moved up Roper Industries' corporate ladder, becoming president of Roper Industries' primary revenue-generating engine, Roper Pump Company, in November 1985. Less than four years later, in February 1989, Key was named president of Roper Industries, assuming the company's presidential post at a time when annual sales hovered around $35 million and earnings stood at $2 million. Under Key's direction, these modest financial totals would rise strongly, propelled by an aggressive acquisition and expansion program orchestrated by Key that would position Roper Industries as a considerably larger international competitor in the specialty controls industry. In the first five years of Key's leadership, annual sales more than quadrupled, while earnings recorded a more prodigious gain, increasing ten-fold, as Roper Industries began to attract the attention long-accorded to Roper Corporation's appliance business.

The first pivotal move in Roper Industries bid to become a larger, more globally-oriented competitor was executed a year after Key's promotion to president, when the company acquired Amot Controls Corporation and its U.K. and Switzerland subsidiaries in July 1990 for approximately $28 million. Amot Controls, which manufactured valves, switches, and sensors for the oil and gas, power generation, and transportation industries, represented an important addition to Roper Industries, giving the company one of the primary pillars supporting its existence during the 1990s. After its first full year as a Roper Industries' company, Amot Controls helped push company-wide annual sales to $75 million, or more than twice as much as Roper Industries generated two years earlier, setting the tone for the rapid growth to follow during the early 1990s.

Another important acquisition, one that would play a leading role in Roper Industries' most publicized event in its history, was completed two years after the purchase of Amot Controls. In September 1992, Roper Industries acquired Compressor Controls Corporation, the world's leading turbocompressor control manufacturer, for an estimated $35 million. Together, Amot Controls and Compressor Controls composed Roper Industries' industrial controls business segment, the smaller of the company's two business segments in 1992, but the segment that would provide the bulk of the company's growth between 1992 and the mid-1990s.

After an 11-year hiatus, Roper Industries once again became a publicly-owned company in 1992, giving it the necessary capital to continue its acquisition and expansion campaign, which became increasingly international in focus following the purchase of Compressor Controls. Relying on the global connections it had realized through its two international acquisitions, Roper Industries made the headlines in the business press the year after its public offering by striking a deal with the massive Russian natural gas conglomerate, GAZPROM, to supply computerized control systems for Russia's enormous pipeline system. The agreement between Compressor Controls and GAZPROM led to a seven-year contract worth $350 million, the announcement of which drew enough praise from certain sectors of the financial community to push Roper Industries' stock from a low of $5.75 a share to $78 a share before splitting two-for-one.

Although Roper Industries' Russian deal represented a potential boon to the company's business, it also represented a potential tinderbox, given the economic and political instability pervading Russia during the early and mid-1990s and the confounding vagaries of Russian bureaucracy. When shipments to GAZPROM began in April 1993, however, expectations were high and largely substantiated by year's end. By the end of 1993, in an abbreviated year as far as the company's contract with GAZPROM was concerned, Roper Industries shipped $42 million worth of high-technology, high-speed controls to GAZPROM, but in 1994, the difficulties inherent in doing business in Russia led to lackluster financial results. Installation delays and problems with financing in Russia hindered Roper Industries' GAZPROM-related activities during the year, reducing the amount of the company's shipments to $35 million for the year.

Elsewhere in the family of Roper Industries companies, more promising results were being achieved. In September 1993, Roper Industries acquired Integrated Designs Inc. (IDI) for $12 million, adding IDI's semiconductor-manufacturing equipment capabilities and its high profitability to the company's fluid handling business segment. The following year, as the company contended with the difficulties associated with GAZPROM, it continued to focus on building other facets of its business by looking for industrial equipment companies to acquire, seeking to strengthen its involvement in the production of highly engineered, high-margin products. Roper Industries found such a company in August 1994 when it acquired Instrumentation Scientifique de Laboratoire, S.A. (ISL) for approximately $10.5 million. Headquartered in Verson, France with sales and service offices in the United States, the United Kingdom, Brazil, and Russia, ISL was one of the leading competitors in the world for oil refinery laboratory testing equipment, bolstering Roper Industries' position in an industry—oil and refined petroleum products—it already served and increasing its international presence.

By the end of 1994, Roper Industries was deriving more than half its annual sales from outside the United States, largely through the foreign business developed by Key, who had been named chief executive officer in 1991, then finally chairman of Roper Industries in December 1994. Annual sales, which had reached $75 million in 1991, had climbed to $147 million by the end of 1994, thanks primarily to the development of the company's industrial controls segment, made up entirely of companies acquired since 1990. ISL, Compressor Controls Corporation, and Amot Controls Corporation composed Roper Industries' industrial controls segment, with Richmond, California-based Amot U.S. and Bury St. Edmunds, England-based Amot U.K. functioning as the two operating companies of Amot Controls Corporation. Combined, these companies generated $91 million of Roper Industries' 1994 sales total, with the company's fluid handling business segment, comprising Roger Pump Company, Cornell Pump Company and IDI, accounting for the balance.

As Roper Industries entered the mid-1990s hoping to resolve the difficulties hobbling its business activities with GAZPROM, the company began mapping plans for the future, which included the strengthening of its U.S. businesses to offset any further problems with its contract to supply compressor controls to Russia. Toward this objective, the company announced the completion of its acquisition of Houston, Texas-based Metrix Instrument Company in October 1995. A manufacturer of vibration detection and analysis equipment for the rotating machinery industry, Metrix Instrument was expected to be incorporated into Roper Industries' burgeoning industrial controls segment as the company prepared to meet the challenges of the late 1990s, supported in large part by newly acquired companies, but with historical roots stretching back to 1919 and the formative efforts of George D. Roper.

Principal Subsidiaries

Amot Controls Corp.; Compressor Controls Corp.; Cornell Pump Co.; Roper Pump Co.; ISL Holdings, S.A.

Principal Operating Units

Fluid Handling; Industrial Controls

Further Reading

Byrne, Harlan S., "Russian Roulette," *Barron's*, July 31, 1995, p. 21.
Du Bois, Peter C., "On the Front Burner," *Barron's*, August 14, 1961, p. 11.
——, "Made-to-Order Profits: Companies Which Supply Sears Are Sharing in the Giant Retailer's Prosperity," *Barron's*, July 22, 1963, p. 3.
Eichenwald, Kurt, "G.E. in Deal to Acquire Roper," *New York Times*, April 1, 1988, p. D1.
"George D. Roper—Special Situation," June 5, 1963, p. 9.
Gordon, Mitchell, "Roper Recovery," *Barron's*, October 20, 1986, p. 60.
Gottschalk, Arthur, "Russian Deal 'Blessing and Curse' for Roper," *Journal of Commerce*, June 21, 1994, p. 5B.
Husted, Bill, "With Georgia's Roper Industries, Only Thing Flashy Is Profit Line," *Knight-Ridder/Tribune Business News*, June 19, 1994, p. 6.
Karp, Richard, "The Home-Run Hitters," *Institutional Investor*, March 1989, p. 73.
Lacroix, Edmond H., "Roper Corp.," *Wall Street Transcript*, November 4, 1968, p. 14, 800.
"Net at Geo. D. Roper Cooking on All Burners," *Barron's*, March 21, 1968, p. 23.
"Roper Corp. Discloses It Is Talking Merger with Unit of Sears," *Wall Street Journal*, April 13, 1964, p. 20.
"Roper Corp. to Make Gas Ranges for Whirlpool," *Wall Street Journal*, March 14, 1962, p. 31.
"Roper Industries, Inc. Announces Acquisition of Metrix Instrument Company and a Fifty Percent Increase in Dividend Rates," *PR Newswire*, October 2, 1995, p.10.
"Roper: Turncoat in a Takeover War," *Business Week*, April 11, 1988, p. 68.
"Sears' Unit and Roper Agree on Merger Plan," *Wall Street Journal*, April 20, 1994, p. 32.
Solomon, Goody L., "Nation of Magic Chefs?," *Barron's*, March 8, 1965, p. 11.
"Whirlpool Moves into the Kitchen," *Business Week*, March 14, 1988, p. 44.

—Jeffrey L. Covell

Rosemount Inc.

12001 Technology Drive
Eden Prairie, Minnesota 55344
U.S.A.
(612) 941-5560
Fax: (612) 828-7777

Wholly Owned Division of Emerson Electric Co.
Incorporated: 1956
Employees:
Sales: $600 million (1995 est.)
SICs: 3823 Process Control Instruments; 5049
   Professional Equipment & Supplies

Rosemount Inc., which began as a space-age engineering company, designs and produces measurement instrumentation for industrial applications. The complex sensors and transmitters the company manufacturers are critical components of sophisticated energy, process, and manufacturing facilities. Purchased by Emerson Electric Co. in 1976, Rosemount proved to be a top performer for the century-old company. Rosemount was integrated with another Emerson acquisition, Fisher Controls International, in 1992. The combined operations of Fisher and Rosemount represent the largest supplier of process control equipment in the world.

Rosemount's history is linked to the development of supersonic jet aircraft and the United States-Soviet Union space race. Dr. Frank D. Werner, a scientist and inventor, was involved in temperature and pressure sensor research at The Rosemount Research Center at the University of Minnesota when the U.S. Air Force asked him to manufacture the total temperature sensors he had developed for their high-performance aircraft. Werner asked Robert E. Keppel, an engineer at the aeronautical lab, and Vernon H. Heath, the business manager, to join him in the part-time project. With $8,000 in seed money the men incorporated Rosemount Engineering Company in 1956. They produced their first product in a building that had once been a chicken hatchery.

The total temperature sensors they produced could measure the air compression-caused heat which was generated during high speed flights. The technological breakthrough allowed test pilots to get precise readings on the speed of their prototype jets for the first time. The start-up company sold $30,000 worth of the sensors in their first year. The next year they had a full-time operation with 20 employees and sales of $196,000. In 1957 the Soviet Union launched the first artificial satellite, Sputnik I. The United States responded by accelerating the pace of their own space program, and Rosemount's sensors were soon in demand for deep space exploration applications.

Rosemount Engineering was a custom business in those early days. The government supplied the company with sensor specifications, and Rosemount would fabricate them. Nearly all its sensors were used in aircraft and missiles. Its products were technologically advanced and produced at low volumes and high labor costs; in 1960, 24 of the company's 144 employees were engineers. Sales reached $1.5 million in 1960, but the owners still needed a $300,00 bank loan to keep going. Expansion costs associated with new products, such as low-pressure sensors, were outpacing sales.

But revenues continued to rise steadily and reached $5.6 million by 1963 with earnings of $240,000. "By then we were also getting a little smug about our success," said Vernon Heath in a March 1984 *Star Tribune* article. "We were innovative, we were growing, and we thought we could make anything happen if it involved technology." The company made a stab at a consumer product line. It developed the first engineered, molded-plastic ski boot—which eventually found its way to a place in the Smithsonian Institution—but plagued the company with manufacturing problems and high costs.

High performance aircraft and the space program continued to be the forces propelling the company forward in the 1960s. McDonnell's Gemini, North American's Saturn and Apollo, Martin's Titan Series, General Dynamics F111, Lockheed's C-141, Douglas' DC9, Boeings's 707, 720, and 727, and the European Supersonic Concorde all depended on Rosemount sensors. Rosemount celebrated the end of its first decade with sales of $8.5 million and a 19 percent increase in profits. By 1965 they had developed a British subsidiary, Rosemount Engineering Company Limited, which served the aircraft manufacturing market in England. Applications for temperature and pressure sensors were being expanded and associated equipment, such as airplane stall warning and ice detection systems, were added to the product line. But only seven percent of Rosemount sales were coming from the industrial market.

When Vernon Heath succeeded Werner as president of Rosemount Engineering Company in mid-1968, he faced changes in the industries it depended on for the vast majority of its sales. Heath attributed a 7.15 percent decrease in sales in 1969 to a shift in the defense industry. Net income had risen but only due to the sale of a manufacturing plant and the ski boot division. The ski boot line, which was sold to G. H. Bass & Co., had cost the company more than $2 million in losses. Undaunted, Rosemount rolled another high-tech project out and into a wholly owned subsidiary named Unifol Systems Co.

Unifol was a computer controlled, air pressure levitated and propelled personal rapid transit (PRT) system. A Honeywell researcher, who had worked on and then purchased the rights for the project, interested Frank Werner in pursuing its development. Rosemount had hoped to fund the project with public financing or equity participation by another firm, but even with renewed federal interest in public transportation Rosemount had trouble funding Uniflo. A joint effort with Northrup Corp. to win a Department of Transportation (DOT) contract for a demonstration mass transit system at Dulles International Airport failed. The DOT passed over the Uniflo project for more conventional mass transit systems. Uniflo later received two other federal research grants but made no sales. The project, which was abandoned in 1973, cost Rosemount about $1 million.

Rosemount did have one successful spin-off from its main concern in those early days. The company's rapid growth had left it with a space crunch, but the owners could not afford to buy themselves office cubicles. So Frank Werner assembled panels from lumberyard hollow-core doors and molded casings. The office partitions worked so well the company decided to begin selling them. In 1966 Rosemount created a subsidiary, Rosemount Partitions Inc., to manufacture the movable office partitions called "Rotopanels." They later expanded into desks, storage areas, and other office furniture.

But Rosemount's other efforts to reduce its dependency on the U.S. space and defense programs proved to be the most profitable. In the late 1960s it had devised a plan to move temperature and pressure measurement instruments into areas of the industrial market which had a need for high accuracy measurement. It got off to a good start increasing industrial sales by 33 percent from 1969 to 1970. Heath said in a December 1972 *Corporate Report Minnesota* article, "We feel the financial results for fiscal 1972 are good indicators of the progress we are making in our carefully planned program of applying proven Rosemount technology to new markets."

The basic research which Rosemount used to develop space and defense technology was applied to products for commercial aviation, synthetic fiber, petrochemical, and nuclear and conventional power production needs. The company opened five new sales offices in Europe and three in the United States. New marketing efforts commenced in South America and Canada.

Rosemount Engineering Company changed its name to Rosemount Inc. The company wanted to declare that it had expanded beyond its instrument engineering roots to become a producer and seller of engineering instruments on multi-industry and multi-national level. To cap things off, 1972 was the company's first million-dollar profit year.

During the ten years from 1963 to 1973, Rosemount's sales rose at a compound annual rate of 16 percent with earnings rising at a rate of 19 percent. It also expanded its facilities four times during that time period. By the end of its second decade, in 1975, sales were more evenly distributed between the defense, space, and commercial aviation market and the energy, process, and manufacturing market. In spite of an economic recession, Rosemount sales for fiscal year 1975 increased 26 percent to $41 million, and earnings per share were $3.30, up from $1.66 the previous year. International and export sales grew 42 percent and comprised over 25 percent of total sales. The company had more than 1,300 employees in the United States, Switzerland, West Germany, England, France, Denmark, Canada, and Japan.

Rosemount's earnings nearly doubled from 1974 to 1975, and its success cost the company its independence. In a March 1984 *Star Tribune* article Dick Youngblood wrote, "The response on Wall Street—down on small companies in general and wary of Rosemount's tendency to veer into off-the-wall business—was to value the company's stock at a peak of eight times earnings per share." Takeover threats by billion-dollar corporations moved Heath to accept a friendly merger. Emerson Electric Co., a St. Louis-based $4 billion conglomerate with a reputation for giving autonomy to the companies it acquired, bought Rosemount Inc. in 1976 for $54 per share, double its trading level. Stockholders received $54 million in Emerson stock. Heath was named head of the consolidated aerospace and industrial control operations.

Rosemount, which was once referred to by Youngblood as "a small company with an impressive talent for making space-age sensing instruments—and an absolute genius for diluting that effort with unrelated, unprofitable ventures," had a new image by the early 1980s. Rosemount was no longer small nor diverted by technological challenges like PRT systems and ski boots. Aerospace know-how had been balanced by industrial acumen. Rosemount's 1983 revenues, which had been consolidated with Emerson's, were estimated to exceed $250 million. Operating profits were about $50 million, and return on assets was between 18 and 20 percent. By 1985 government contracts had been reduced to 20 percent of sales.

Although Rosemount clearly had moved the majority of its business into the industrial segment its products still had an important presence in the U.S. space effort. The first "reusable-returnable" space craft, the space shuttle, relied on Rosemount instruments. A pair of Rosemount sensors assisted pilots with determining the shuttles's angle of re-entry into the earth's atmosphere. Other sensors in the shuttle's rocket motor had a matter of seconds to response to temperatures changes of 2000 degrees Fahrenheit that occurred during the crucial launch phase. For Rosemount Inc. testing devises such as wind tunnels and environmental chambers were just tools of the trade.

While Rosemount strived to apply the rigorous standards of the highly technical aerospace industry to the industrial market, Heath seemed equally committed to creating a atmosphere that fostered a committed and involved work force. Heath said in a 1985 *Corporate Report Minnesota* article, "For us, success is a matter of identifying common goals and establishing a culture that feeds itself and builds upon its." People as well as profit were important to him, and that philosophy elevated Rosemount to a position among the world's largest manufacturers of precision measurement and control instruments.

Rosemount revenues doubled over the five year period from 1983 to 1988 and reached the $500 million mark. Likewise, the employment figure nearly doubled in that time period to about 4,500 workers. Then in 1987 four Emerson instrument divisions were consolidated as the Rosemount Measurement and Control Instrumentation Group. The new group, which was managed by Heath, had 9,000 employees world wide and an estimated $1 billion in sales. Rosemount not only grew larger but continued improving its products. The company earned a place on the *Fortune* magazine "100 Products That America Makes Best" list in 1988—and again in 1991—for its "pressure transmitters for industrial power plants."

Rosemount, like many other international businesses, had its share of problems in the 1980s. United States trade sanctions short circuited a sales agreement with a French company for pressure transmitters. The Reagan administration had banned sales destined for a Soviet natural gas pipeline to Europe. Rosemount was concerned not only with the broken contract but with losing in market share and good will it had built up in Europe. Rosemount was also struggling in the Far Eastern markets. Rosemount-designed pressure transmitters were already being used in nuclear power plants in China, but Chinese government regulations and shortage of capital were inhibiting sales in that huge market. And in Japan a joint venture begun in 1975 was stalled by the company's inability to crack through the Japanese distribution system. Despite roadblocks the consolidated Rosemount group entered the 1990s accounting for about one-sixth of Emerson's total sales volume.

In 1991 Heath left his position as CEO but remained on as chairman. Rosemount revenues were about $1.1 billion at the time. Instrumentation-related acquisitions which were rolled into the company and the steady development and improvement of products facilitated Rosemount's rapid growth. Rosemount consistently was its parent company's greatest generator of stockholder value. In a move to further enhance its position in the process control market, Emerson purchased Fisher Controls International in 1992 for $1.25 billion. According to Emerson, the combined Fisher and Rosemount businesses created, "with one move, a marketing and technology leadership position in a $15 billion global industry." Fisher's strength was in control valve products and Rosemount's in measurement instrumentation. Emerson expected the new division to make half its sales outside the United States.

In 1993 Rosemount Inc. came under the scrutiny of the Nuclear Regulatory Commission (NRC). A utility company engineer implicated Rosemount in a 1988 coverup of faulty transmitters in a Connecticut nuclear power plant. According to the engineer, Rosemount corrected the transmitter failure warn-

ing problem but pressured the utility to keep the problem quiet. Nuclear industry vendors are required to report problems with products. At the time, both Rosemount and Emerson officials declined to comment on the investigation, and the company was seeking to have the suit dismissed. Rosemount held more than 40 percent of the worldwide market for pressure transmitters. That same year a Rosemount facility was named one of "America's 10 Best Plants" by *Industry Week*. The pressure transmitters produced in the plant, which was opened in 1990, were used to measure pressure in everything from oil pipelines and power plants to beer vats. Honeywell Incorporated, one of Rosemount's largest competitors, also had a plant on the list.

Rosemount's long-time relationship with the aerospace industry ended in 1993. Emerson sold the Rosemount Aerospace unit to B. F. Goodrich Company for $300 million in cash. The division, which manufactured aircraft temperature and pressure sensors, had sales of $130 million in fiscal year 1993, with 60 percent of that revenue from commercial and 40 percent from military aircraft. More employee layoffs, in addition to those related to the integration with Fisher, followed the elimination of the aerospace division. Another of Rosemount's earliest divisions was sold in 1995. Vernon Heath, who had retired from his chairmanship position with Rosemount in 1994, bought Office Systems Inc. The office furniture business's 1994 revenues were $20 million; the company had been profitable for nearly its entire existence.

Rosemount Inc.'s history was one of transformations. From its aerospace roots, through misguided attempts at diversification, and finally success in the industrial marketplace Rosemount seemed like a classic American success story. In spite of ups and downs the company gravitated back to what it did best. Emerson had brought in money for research and capital equipment and improved asset management, but the company had remained much the same. But in the 1990s Emerson was moving towards consolidating its operations, and Rosemount Inc. went under another transformation. The company faced the 21st century identified as part of a process control system division, rather than as an independent manufacturer. Whether this would have an impact on its future remained to be seen.

Further Reading

Alexander, Steve, "B.F. Goodrich Agrees to Buy Rosemount Aerospace," *Star Tribune* (Minneapolis), November 11, 1993, p. 1D.

Beal, Dave, "Rosemount Loses Independence, Finds Growth," *St. Paul Pioneer Press*, March 1, 1991.

Bree, Marlin, "Managing the Space Age," *Corporate Report Minnesota*, March 1977, p. 20.

"Eden Prairie Firm Could Lose $8 Million in Pipeline Contracts," *Star Tribune* (Minneapolis), August 30, 1982.

Gross, Steve, "Rosemount to Cut 90 Jobs in Burnsville," *Star Tribune* (Minneapolis), March 24, 1993, p. 3D.

Kiser, Kim, "Starting Again," *Twin Cities Business Monthly*, July 1995, pp. 39–41.

Lubove, Seth, "It Ain't Broke, But Fix It Anyway," *Forbes*, August 1, 1994, pp. 56–60.

Peterson, Susan E., "Measure of Success: Industry Week Magazine Names Rosemount Plant to Top 10 in U.S.," *Star Tribune* (Minneapolis), October 15, 1993, pp. 1D, 4D.

——, "Rosemount Inc. Lays Off 43 Workers," *Star Tribune* (Minneapolis), April 30, 1994, p. 3D.

''Rosemount's Five-year Struggle to Get Uniflo Off the Ground,'' *Corporate Report Minnesota*, May 1972, pp. 11, 15.

Sell, Julie, ''Technology-Transfer Pact Gives Rosemount, Inc. a China Toehold, *Star Tribune* (Minneapolis), December 14, 1986, p. 1D.

Strand, Phil, ''Tenacity Beats Talk,'' *Corporate Report Minnesota*, April 1985, pp. 70–74.

Weinberger, Betsy, ''Feds Probe Rosemount on Coverup Charges,'' *CityBusiness* (Minneapolis/St. Paul), May 7, 1993, p. 1.

Youngblood, Dick, ''Rosemount Saga Has Happy Ending,'' *Star Tribune* (Minneapolis), March 18, 1984, pp. 1D, 12D.

——, ''Who Could Forget Rags-to-Riches Rosemount?'' *Star Tribune* (Minneapolis), May 4, 1988, p. 1D.

——, ''Vernon Heath Working Hard in Retirement,'' *Star Tribune* (Minneapolis), January 16, 1995, p. 2D.

—Kathleen Peippo

Roto-Rooter Corp.

255 East 5th Street
Cincinnati, Ohio 45202
U.S.A.
(513) 762-6690
Fax: (513) 762-6590

Subsidiary of Chemed Corp.
Incorporated: 1935 as Roto-Rooter Inc.
Employees: 1,550
Sales: $171.9 million (1994)
Stock Exchanges: NASDAQ
SICs: 7699 Repair Services, Not Elsewhere Classified

With 17 percent of the market for drain and sewer cleaning service, Roto-Rooter Corp. is this industry's indisputable leader. Richard Phalon of *Forbes* magazine called the business "one of the U.S.'s most successful small companies" in 1989, and his assessment continued to ring true through 1994, when Roto-Rooter chalked up its tenth successive year of record results. Family-owned and operated from its inception until 1980, the Iowa firm was sold that year to Cincinnati-based Chemed Corporation. Chemed transformed the company from a loose amalgamation of independent operators into a modern franchisee system, then proceeded to buy out many of the largest licensees. By the early 1990s, Roto-Rooter had purchased so many of its franchisees in major metropolitan areas that franchise fees constituted less than ten percent of annual revenues. With the support of its new parent, Roto-Rooter expanded into plumbing and general maintenance service in the mid-1980s. Although general maintenance had grown to contribute over one-third of annual revenues by 1994, Roto-Rooter announced in 1995 that it would divest that business. Although Roto-Rooter was counted among Chemed's subsidiaries in the early 1990s, about 40 percent of its stock was publicly traded.

Roto-Rooter was founded in 1935 by Samuel Oscar Blanc in West Des Moines, Iowa. Born in Wisconsin in 1883, Blanc had been forced to quit school in the fifth grade, when his father committed suicide. He traveled throughout the Pacific North-west working as a lumberman and telephone linesman during the first decade of the Twentieth century, returning to Wisconsin in 1906 to marry. Blanc had taken a variety of sales jobs over the course of the ensuing two decades, but like so many others in Depression-era America, was limited to odd jobs by the early 1930s. Little did he know that a backed-up toilet would lead to a permanent career.

In 1934, Blanc's son, Milton, asked for help unclogging a sewer system blocked with potato peelings. Together they used a length of flexible metal cable to free the clog, prompting the father to seek "a better way" to do the job. Having taken correspondence courses in electrical and mechanical engineering, S. O. Blanc spent the next few months developing an electrically-powered drain cleaner that featured a rotating steel coil with blades at one end to cut through virtually any blockage, even tree roots. Blanc knew he had a great idea on his hands; the alternative was to dig a trench along the pipes, find the clog, and clear it. Before the year was out, he had started advertising his service and applied for a patent on his device. Wife Lettie came up with the name that would become the company's most valuable asset: Roto-Rooter. The firm was incorporated in 1936, the same year Blanc registered his trademark.

The foundation of the company's nationwide franchise system was laid early in 1935, when C. W. Crawford wrote asking to "rent" a Roto-Rooter and start his own business. That first contract, for $400, bought an exclusive, four-county territory for "the life of the patent," but the agreement was soon revised to five cents per sewer in a given region. Within two years of its first lease agreement, Roto-Rooter had licensed more than 100 territories from Florida to Washington, with a concentration in the Midwest. The central organization manufactured drain cleaning machines and replacement parts and provided a minimal amount of technical and managerial support to licensees.

But franchising fees alone were not enough to support ongoing patent and trademark registration and defense of those intellectual properties. In 1936, Blanc set up a separate operation, Roto-Rooter Service Company, with an entirely new modus operandi. Instead of licensing territories, this business essentially employed individual contractors in New York City,

Boston, Baltimore, and other east coast cities. Headquartered in Iowa, the central organization supervised advertising (but little else) in exchange for a percentage of each contractor's receipts.

By 1938, when Blanc received a patent on his original design, company machinists had developed an industrial-sized drain cleaner called the Royal Street Sewer Cleaning Machine as well as a kitchen-sized model dubbed the "Niard"—drain spelled backwards.

Blanc realized that the Roto-Rooter concept was terribly easy to reproduce. Although he continued to defend the physical design throughout the life of the patent, he began in the early 1940s to put more support behind the Roto-Rooter trademark through advertising in such nationally circulated publications as *Better Homes & Gardens*. Up to this point, the vast majority of advertising had been underwritten by individual operators.

Although World War II's raw material shortages stunted Roto-Rooter's expansion, postwar rural electrification and water works projects furnished seemingly endless growth potential. Eric Peterson, grandson of S. O. Blanc and author of a 1988 company history, characterized this period as "a time of unimaginable prosperity." By the mid-1950s, Roto-Rooter had operations in virtually every city with more than 100,000 people. The company established its first international franchise, in Mexico City, in 1945, and shipped machines to Brazil in 1952. In spite of these early efforts, international operations remained negligible until the 1970s.

Roto-Rooter reached a critical juncture in 1955, when the patent on the original device expired and the company was reorganized around the Roto-Rooter trademark. The central organization decided at this time to charge a higher franchise fee based on the number of people served in a given region. In spite of the upheaval, the firm lost less than ten percent of its 300 franchisees. Roto-Rooter followed up the reorganization with a new national advertising campaign featuring the ditty that would help establish the brand as America's most recognizable sewer cleaning service. Recorded by Captain Stubby and the Buccaneers, the snappy jingle, "Roto-Rooter, that's the name, and away go troubles down the drain," became one of U.S. advertising's most memorable and enduring taglines.

Notwithstanding the outward appearance of success, several endemic problems began to manifest themselves during the 1960s. Perhaps the most fundamental of these was what Eric Peterson called a "management vacuum"; Roto-Rooter's founding executives had never really provided much guidance to franchisees or expected much more than fees from them, and, by the 1960s, many top leaders were reaching retirement age. At the same time, a growing body of antitrust law endangered the company's loose franchise system, the threat of takeover loomed large, and corruption in some operations (especially those in the Service Co. segment) endangered Roto-Rooter's future.

When founder S. O. Blanc died in 1964, his son-in-law, Russell Young, was elected to succeed him. (Blanc's own son, Milton, had not been significantly involved in the company.) The change in leadership, however, did not necessarily herald new management practices. The company moved into a new

West Des Moines headquarters and built a new factory, but little else about Roto-Rooter changed in the late 1960s.

Roto-Rooter's corporate lethargy ended in 1970, when another of S. O. Blanc's sons-in-law, Henry Peterson, advanced from secretary to president. Unlike most of the company's aging executives, Peterson brought varied outside experience in law and banking to the business. He hired new managers, instituted modern inventory controls and production schedules, automated the company's antiquated manufacturing methods, and spurred new product introductions.

Peterson also began to investigate lagging returns from the Roto-Rooter Service Company, which had been presided over (but not closely supervised by) Russ Young since its inception. The subsequent examination uncovered an organization rife with corruption; individual contractors were not reporting their gross sales accurately, sometimes keeping 90 percent of their receipts instead of the 50 percent they were contractually allowed to retain. Peterson oversaw a reorganization of the Service Company, converting it from a contractor basis to a more traditional service company with regional managers and local employees. At some point, he also changed the affiliated firm's name to Nurotoco Inc. ("new roto co"). The cleanup helped quintuple Nurotoco's profits within seven years and make it Roto-Rooter's primary revenue generator. In the meantime, the number of traditional franchisees had nearly doubled from 425 in 1969 to more than 700 by 1979.

Peterson had snatched Roto-Rooter from imminent decline, and by the end of the 1970s he was ready to retire. But no one in the next generation of the Blanc family had shown interest in accepting the mantle of leadership. Peterson had actually begun researching the sale of the company in 1975, but was impeded by litigation and reorganization concerns from concentrating on the issue. In 1980, Peterson was able to negotiate a $23 million cash/stock deal with Cincinnati's Chemed Corporation, a manufacturer of specialty materials for the chemical and medical industries.

Chemed moved Roto-Rooter's headquarters from West Des Moines to Cincinnati and imposed modern standards of franchise management on the corporate system. A revised franchise contract proposed by newly appointed president and chief executive officer William Griffin opened franchisee books to corporate review, reserved right of first refusal for Roto-Rooter, and prohibited interfranchise competition. New across-the-board standards included 24-hour service, employee training in customer service, uniforms, and logo-emblazoned vehicles. Chemed also began to buy back licenses in the largest metropolitan areas, transforming them into employer-employee operations much like those of the east coast's Nurotoco. By the end of the decade, Roto-Rooter Inc. had purchased 39 such territories. Despite initial resistance from operators, these changes brought a higher level of standardization to the organization, benefiting the parent company, the franchisees, and their customers.

Chemed made a private placement of 15 percent of Roto-Rooter's stock in 1984 and raised $12.5 million in an initial public offering of another 23 percent stake the following year. (Chemed had been spun off to the public by its own parent, W. R. Grace Co., in 1982.) The proceeds of these sales were used to expand Roto-Rooter's roster of services through internal growth as well as acquisition. Roto-Rooter had made its first reach into plumbing services in 1981; by mid-decade this sideline was contributing about ten percent of annual sales. Chemed also expanded the subsidiary's industrial and municipal drain cleaning services. But an initial venture into heating, ventilation, and air conditioning (HVAC) was not as successful. Roto-Rooter acquired Apollo Heating & Air Conditioning Inc., an Ohio service company, in 1986, but when the division did not pan out, it was sold to its management team.

Roto-Rooter experienced phenomenal growth under the guidance of its new parent. Sales multiplied from a mere $4.7 million in 1980 to $66.8 million by 1989, and net income grew to more than $5.5 million.

Roto-Rooter's growth strategy for the early 1990s included expansion of service to restaurants and motels, a reentry into the HVAC segment, and addition of general maintenance services to the roster. From 1991 to 1993, the company acquired three businesses in Florida and Arizona that offered residential customers annual maintenance contracts for many major repairs, ranging from heating and air conditioning systems to major appliances and plumbing. These operations were combined in 1994 under the Service America trademark. But as the middle of the decade approached, the future of this business segment was uncertain. Roto-Rooter's 1994 annual report noted a "plan to offer HVAC services under the name PEAK in 10 company-owned markets." A 1995 report by William Blair & Co., however, stated that Roto-Rooter had "decided to exit the [general maintenance service] which had grown to contribute over 35 percent of revenues by 1994." Although the company had captured only two percent of the U.S. plumbing service market, this was its fastest-growing business segment, increasing by 20 percent from 1993 to 1994.

By the mid-1990s, Roto-Rooter had purchased 80 of its largest franchisees. The company still had 550 independent franchisees, but these businesses only contributed $6 million of 1994's $171 million in revenues. Whereas annual turnover had more than doubled from 1990's $75.2 million to 1994, net income expanded about half as fast, from $5.7 million to $8.8 million during the same period.

Principal Subsidiaries

Service America Systems, Inc. (70%); Roto-Rooter Services Co.; Roto-Rooter Corp.; Roto-Rooter Management Co.

Further Reading

Jaffe, Thomas, "Two for the Stocking," *Forbes,* January 11, 1988, p. 266.
Labate, John, "Companies To Watch: Roto-Rooter," *Fortune,* June 27, 1994, p. 103.
Paton, Huntley, "Roto-Rooter Sells Apollo to Management Group," *Cincinnati Business Courier,* March 13, 1989, p. 11.
Peterson, Eric Gregory, *Roto-Rooter, 1935–1988,* Michigan State University: M.A. Thesis, 1988.
Phalon, Richard, "Roto-Rooter's New Drill," *Forbes,* December 11, 1989, p. 176.
"Roto-Rooter Boosts Net 20%, Completes Encore Acquisition," *Contractor,* August 1993, p. 16.
"Roto-Rooter Continues Growth as Residential Service Giant," *Contractor,* April 1995, p. 8.
Sheets, Ken, "When Boring Stocks Are Beautiful," *Kiplinger's Personal Finance Magazine,* February 1995, p. 81.
Sword, Doug, "Roto-Rooter Plumbing Services To Boost '86 Sales," *Cincinnati Business Courier,* August 18, 1986, p. 1.
Weinstein, Marc, "Roto-Rooter Stock Flying High," *Cincinnati Business Courier,* June 24, 1985, p. 1.

—April Dougal Gasbarre

The Rouse Company

Rouse Company Building
10275 Little Patuxent Parkway
Columbia, Maryland 21044-3456
U.S.A.
(410) 992-6000
Fax: (410) 992-6363

Public Company
Incorporated: 1954 as James W. Rouse Company, Inc.
Employees: 5,000
Sales: $646.81 million
Stock Exchanges: NASDAQ
SICs: 6512 Nonresidential Building Operators; 7011
   Hotels and Motels; 6519 Real Property Lessors, Not
   Elsewhere Classified

One of America's largest publicly held real estate development and management firms, The Rouse Company has a reputation for innovation. Under the direction of founder and "industry prophet" James W. Rouse, the company was in the vanguard of suburban enclosed-mall construction in the 1950s, the planned community movement in the 1960s, and the proliferation of urban "festival marketplaces" in the 1970s and early 1980s. The saturation of the retail development market in the early 1990s led the company into the construction and management of more office and mixed-use projects. By 1995, The Rouse Company owned and/or operated 78 retail centers and 115 office and industrial properties, having also developed the community of Columbia, Maryland, from which it operated its headquarters.

The Rouse Company traces its roots to the Moss-Rouse Company, a Baltimore mortgage banking firm owned by James W. Rouse and Hunter Moss in 1939. The partners, who had borrowed $20,000 to start their business, originated Federal Housing Administration loans for several years. When World War II drew Rouse and other key employees into military service the firm lapsed. But the company flourished in the postwar era when there was a boom in government-funded veterans' housing.

Hunter Moss left the partnership in 1954, when it was renamed James W. Rouse & Company, Inc. Rouse expanded the scope of his financing activities to commercial real estate projects, including the new strip shopping centers that were springing up on the outskirts of cities. After conducting pre-construction market research, arranging financing, leasing space to merchants, and directing construction for the owners of the Mondawmin Shopping Center in Baltimore, Rouse decided to enter the real estate development business. To conduct these endeavors, he created Community Research and Development (CRD), a real estate development subsidiary, in 1956. CRD opened Rouse's first enclosed large shopping center, Harundale Mall, two years later. By the early 1960s, James Rouse was one of the United States' busiest and most prosperous mortgage bankers and shopping center executives. His company acted as a mortgage correspondent for 50 lenders, had a loan portfolio of over $500 million, and was famous for uniting esthetics and profitability in retail centers.

The Rouse Company experimented with community development through the creation of The Village of Cross Keys, a Baltimore townhouse development. Then, in 1963, Rouse formed a partnership with Connecticut General Life Insurance Company to create Howard Research and Development Corporation. The lofty goal of this new venture was to plan and create the entire city of Columbia, Maryland. Rouse set his "total city concept" in motion by anonymously accumulating more than 14,000 acres in Howard County, Maryland, between Baltimore and Washington, D. C. The 165 separate parcels cost less than $1,500 per acre, in compliance with a stipulation of Connecticut General, which provided the majority of the funding for the project. Rouse surprised Howard County's commissioners when he revealed in a meeting that he owned ten percent of the region they governed and requested rezoning of the area. Although the commissioners had a mandate to keep the county rural, Rouse's ensuing public relations campaign convinced them and their electorate that they would be better off planning for (and exercising some control over) the inevitable urbanization of the strategic corridor between two of the East Coast's most vital cities.

Rouse assembled a coterie of planners, sociologists, educators, religious groups, and cultural and medical institutions to advise and support the creation of the new city. When it was launched in 1967, Columbia featured 11,000 residences (including low-cost housing jointly sponsored by the three primary religions); schools within walking distance of elementary and junior high schoolers; Howard County's first hospital; public transportation; and a shopping center. By 1975, when the city boasted 38,000 residents, it had become "suburban Baltimore," and within a decade it would be, according to *Financial World* (1986), "one of the hottest developing territories in the country."

Rouse's stock soared from $2 per share in the early 1960s to $30 by 1972. But during the 1974–1975 real estate slowdown, the company lost Housing and Urban Development funding for a major low-income housing project. This, in turn, effected a $7 million loss and compelled Rouse to pull out of two engineered communities in Tennessee and Maryland, resulting in additional losses of $4.2 million. Connecticut General even had to purchase most of Rouse's share of the Columbia project during this difficult time. Short-term debt stood at $80 million, while equity was at $6 million. From 1974 to 1976, the company retrenched by selling 50 percent stakes in seven of 24 retail centers, reaping a total of $24 million cash. It also eliminated half the headquarters staff and wrote off $30 million in bad investments.

During the company's difficult years, Rouse invented his own method of accounting. He pioneered a new accounting figure dubbed "current value." During this decade of economic uncertainty, Rouse claimed that current value gave a more fair and accurate estimation of the company's assets than depreciation under generally accepted accounting standards. At the time, both *Business Week* and the Securities and Exchange Commission praised the outside-auditor-certified figures as "more realistic." The use of such estimates would come under fire in the early 1990s, however.

Rouse did not rely on number-crunching alone to improve his company's financial prospects. After leading the postwar exodus to suburbia in the 1940s and 1950s, Rouse defied conventional wisdom by starting urban development projects in the late 1970s and early 1980s. His first, and definitive, undertaking transformed three virtually abandoned 150-year-old, block-long Greek revival buildings in Boston's warehouse district into an enticing complex of food markets, restaurants, offices and retail shops. Rouse was approached by architect Benjamin Thompson with his idea for the project. After overcoming his own initial skepticism, the developer convinced the city of Boston to join him in a 99-year partnership wherein the city received 25 percent of the project's gross rentals. Rouse added funding from local and regional financiers to the municipal contributions.

Named for Mayor Josiah Quincy and opened August 26, 1976 (150 years after its namesake had originally dedicated it), the retail center attracted 100,000 shoppers on its first day. By the end of its first year, Quincy Market had attracted as many consumers as Disneyland had attracted tourists, and its average per-square foot sales more than doubled comparable department store figures. In 1978, it won an Honor Award from the American Institute of Architects. Rouse hoped that his revival of the "spirit of festival" embodied in this project would satisfy the "yearning for life at the heart of the city," according to *Fortune*.

The developer applied his festival marketplace concept, with appropriate adaptations, in Philadelphia, Santa Monica, New York City, Milwaukee, St. Louis, and San Francisco. By the end of the decade, Rouse managed about thirty shopping centers in ten states and two Canadian provinces, claiming $479 million in assets. The company's mortgage banking subsidiary ranked among the largest in the United States, with a $1.4 billion loan portfolio. Columbia's population had risen to 50,000 and had bounced back from recession-related indebtedness. With his company back on track, Rouse retired the presidency and chief executive office in 1979 (but retained the chairmanship) to devote himself more fully to the social welfare activities he had long espoused.

Unlike other real estate mavens who had trouble engineering the transfer of power, Rouse had groomed a successor. He convinced Mathias DeVito to relinquish his partnership in the prestigious Baltimore law firm of Piper & Marbury and create an in-house legal department for Rouse in 1968. DeVito advanced from general counsel to vice-president and chief operations officer later that year. He also played a vital role in the company's survival of the 1974-1975 recession, and gradually assumed Rouse's responsibilities over the ensuing five years.

With many traditional suburban markets saturated with malls by the 1980s, DeVito took a more conservative tack than his intrepid predecessor. He eschewed the middle markets that many developers targeted to concentrate on what he described as "expensive, high-amenity urban projects," according to *Forbes*. He continued to pursue Rouse's one-of-a-kind renovations, however, leveraging the company's talent and reputation with relatively small capital investments. In Milwaukee, for example, municipal and federal governments combined with two major department stores, local businesses, and a large insurance company to invest $70 million in the Grand Avenue Mall, while Rouse's cash contribution was only $500,000. In spite of its comparatively small cash outlay, Rouse was able to command half the excess cash flow and a share of residual values as its share of the profits. The new CEO also made strategic alliances with investment groups to renovate and manage older malls. Institutional investors contributed the capital necessary to purchase 21 malls from 1979 to 1983, while Rouse brought its esthetic and managerial expertise to the joint ventures.

James Rouse retired from the company's chair in 1984 to give his full attention to the Enterprise Foundation, a non-profit organization he began in 1981 to improve housing, health care, and job programs in America's poorest neighborhoods. Rouse's social sensitivity was evidenced early in his career. In the late 1940s, he led an attempt to rehabilitate Baltimore slums without gentrifying them. In 1953 Rouse was appointed to President Eisenhower's Task Force on Housing, which crafted the Urban Renewal Administration. But as the developer began to believe that "government programs . . . tend to be costly in relation to their benefits," he increasingly employed his own resources for societal improvement.

A subsidiary of the Foundation, Enterprise Development Company, was formed to build festival marketplaces for smaller cities. Its profits were intended to fuel the charity's endeavors, a tangible product of Rouse's belief that "the free enterprise system should have the capability to produce profits for the poor as well as for the rich.'' The nonprofit also accepted donations from corporations, foundations, and individuals, with $1 million donated from Rouse. By the time he fully retired, the Enterprise Foundation had formed relationships with 22 neighborhood groups in 12 cities.

In the meantime, DeVito sold the company's founding business, Rouse Real Estate Finance, to PaineWebber for $50.5 million in 1984. The 45-year-old, mid-sized mortgage company was getting squeezed out in an industry increasingly dominated by giants. The following year, however, Rouse regained one of its most celebrated projects. After a decade of minority ownership, Rouse re-acquired the planned community of Columbia, Maryland, by adding CIGNA's 80 percent stake of Howard Research and Development Corporation to its 20 percent. The purchase increased Rouse's debt to $120 million, but DeVito hoped that income from mixed-use projects, combining hotel, office, and retail spaces, would provide new sources of cash flow. By 1986, the company's holdings were valued at $1.6 billion.

But in the absence of headline-grabbing new development projects that had characterized James Rouse's tenure, Mathias DeVito's term came under increasing scrutiny. In October 1989, *Forbes* reporter Tatiana Pouschine characterized Rouse's future as "cloudy" and its $29 shares as "overvalued." She also criticized the company's current value statistics (used virtually unchallenged since 1976) as particularly high when compared to traditional valuations, which were 22 times lower. In addition, she noted that Rouse had negative cash flows that were declining.

In the early 1990s, Rouse has been embroiled in a debate pitting its "current value" asset estimates against generally accepted accounting principles (GAAP). In 1991, for example, GAAP figures set its assets at $2.4 billion, compared to the company's current value calculation of $4 billion. It has not been merely an academic dispute, however. Based on conventional data, Rouse's stock was trading around $14 per share, but based on its own figures, the company thought it should be selling closer to $26 per share. That year, DeVito commissioned the highly respected firm of Landauer Associates Real Estate Counselors to corroborate its current valuation. As a result, Rouse acknowledged the early 1990s real estate slump by lowering its current value in 1990, 1991, and 1992.

From 1990 to 1993, Rouse recorded a cumulative net loss of $11.56 million (according to GAAP). The company's only year of profitability was 1991 during the period. Rouse contended that, since it is not valid to depreciate its earnings in a conventional way, it is more telling to examine the company's earnings before depreciation and deferred taxes from operations (EBDT). Rouse reported that its EBDT rose from $50.29 million in 1990 to $78.28 million in 1993. Rouse also increased its current value in 1993.

Even Adrienne Linsenmeyer-Hardman, an analyst with *Financial World* who was critical of Rouse's accounting methods, conceded that Rouse was "a powerhouse in its industry" in 1992. She cautioned, however, that as retail sales shifted from department stores and regional malls to discounters, specialty shops and strip malls, Rouse would be forced to adapt its

holdings and construction plans. James Rouse had met such a challenge in the 1970s with his pioneering festival marketplaces. Whether DeVito could meet the challenges of the 1990s in the same way would determine the company's future.

Principal Subsidiaries

American City Corp.; Baltimore Center, Inc.; Charlottetown, Inc.; Charlottetown North, Inc.; Clover Square of Pennsylvania, Inc.; Community Research & Development, Inc.; Cross Keys Management Services, Inc.; Exton Square, Inc.; Four Owing Mills Corporate Center, Inc.; Gallery Maintenance, Inc.; Harbor Funding, Inc.; Harbor Overlook Investments, Inc.; Harborplace, Inc.; Harborplace Management Corp.; Harundale Mall, Inc.; Hermes Inc.; Howard Research and Development Corp.; It's Showtime of Maryland, Inc.; Louisville Shopping Center, Inc.; Kalimba Marketplace, Inc.; Midfield Airport Retail Management, Inc.; Mondawmin Corp.; O.M. Guaranty, Inc.; O.M. Land Development, Inc.; O.M. Management Company, Inc.; One Owings Mills Corporate Center, Inc.; Plymouth Meeting Mall, Inc.; PT Funding, Inc.; Rouse-Brandywood, Inc.; Rouse-Columbus, Inc.; Rouse-Commerce, Inc.; Rouse Communications Company, Inc.; Rouse Company at Owings Mills; Rouse Company Financial Services, Inc.; Rouse Company of Alabama, Inc.; Rouse Company of Arkansas, Inc.; Rouse Company of California, Inc.; Rouse Company of Colorado, Inc.; Rouse Company of Connecticut, Inc.; Rouse Company of Florida, Inc.; Rouse Company of Georgia, Inc.; Rouse Company of Illinois, Inc.; Rouse Company of Iowa, Inc.; Rouse Company of Louisiana; The Rouse Company of Massachusetts, Inc.; Rouse Company of Michigan, Inc.; Rouse Company of Minnesota, Inc.; Rouse Company of New Jersey, Inc.; Rouse Company of New York, Inc.; Rouse Company of North Carolina, Inc.; Rouse Company of Ohio, Inc.; Rouse Company of Oklahoma, Inc.; Rouse Company of Oregon, Inc.; Rouse Company of Pennsylvania, Inc.; Rouse Company of South Carolina, Inc.; Rouse Company of Tennessee, Inc.; Rouse Company of Texas, Inc.; Rouse Company of the District of Columbia; Rouse Company of Virginia, Inc.; Rouse Company of Washington, Inc.; Rouse Company of Wisconsin, Inc.; Rouse Credit Corp.; Rouse Development Company of California, Inc.; Rouse Event Marketing, Inc.; Rouse-Farwood Development Corp.; Rouse Fashion Island Management Company, Inc.; Rouse Holding Co.; Rouse Holding Company of Arizona, Inc.; Rouse-Huntington, Inc.; Rouse-Inglewood, Inc.; Rouse Investing Co.; Rouse Management, Inc.; Rouse Management Services Corp.; Rouse Management Services Corporation of Arkansas, Inc.; Rouse Management Services Corporation of Louisiana, Inc.; Rouse Metro Plaza, Inc.; Rouse-Metro Shopping Center, Inc.; Rouse-Milwaukee, Inc.; Rouse-Milwaukee Garage Maintenance, Inc.; Rouse Missouri Holding Co.; Rouse-Oakwood Shopping Center, Inc.; Rouse-Oakwood Two, Inc.; Rouse Office Management, Inc.; Rouse Office Management of Pennsylvania, Inc.; Rouse Philadelphia, Inc.; Rouse Philadelphia Two, Inc.; Rouse Philadelphia Three, Inc.; Rouse-Pontiac, Inc.; Rouse-Randhurst Shopping Center, Inc.; Rouse Service Co.; Rouse Shopping Center, Inc.; Rouse Tristate Venture, Inc.; Rouse Venture Capital, Inc.; RREF Holding, Inc.; Salem Mall, Inc.; Saratoga Equipment Corp.; Six Owings Mills Corporate Center, Inc.; SMPL Management, Inc.; Three Owings Mills Corporate Center, Inc.; TRC Central, Inc.; TRCD, Inc.; TRC Holding Company of Washington, D.C.; TRC Property Management, Inc.; Two Owings Mills Corporate Center, Inc.; Village of Cross Keys, Inc.; White Marsh Equities Corp.; White Marsh Mall, Inc.

Further Reading

"Back to Earth," *Forbes*, October 1, 1974, p. 26.

Bivins, Jacquelyn, "James Rouse: Enterprise for the Public Good," *Chain Store Age Executive*, September 1986, pp. 45–51.

Breckenfeld, Gurney, "The Rouse Show Goes National," *Fortune*, July 27, 1981, pp. 49–54.

"An Equitable Distribution," *Financial World*, May 2-15, 1984, p. 93.

James, Ellen L., "The Sure Touch of the Rouse Co.," *Financial World*, July 10-23, 1985, pp. 44–46.

Linsenmeyer-Hardman, Adrienne, "Value Judgment," *Financial World*, July 21, 1992, pp. 34–35.

Luebke, Cathy, "The Rouse Co.," *The Business Journal—Serving Phoenix & the Valley of the Sun*, June 25, 1993, p. 107.

"Master Builder with a New Concept," *Business Week*, August 20, 1966, pp. 106–110.

Pouschine, Tatiana, "Malled," *Forbes*, October 30, 1989, pp. 46, 49.

"Rouse," *Financial World*, July 22, 1986, pp. 50–51.

Rudnitsky, Howard, "Make Room, Disney World, Federated and Gimbels," *Forbes*, May 9, 1983, pp. 100–104.

—April Dougal Gasbarre

Royal Appliance Manufacturing Company

650 Alpha Drive
Cleveland, Ohio 44143-2123
U.S.A.
(216) 449-6150
Fax: (216) 449-7806

Public Company
Incorporated: 1905 as P. A. Geier Company
Employees: 685
Sales: $280.12 million (1994)
Stock Exchanges: New York
SICs: 3635 Household Vacuum Cleaners; 3589 Service
Industry Machinery, Not Elsewhere Classified

Best known for its Dirt Devil brand vacuum cleaners, Royal Appliance Manufacturing Company is one of the world's oldest vacuum makers. After languishing for decades, a new management team and a redesigned product line took the firm to the top of the hand-vacuum heap in the late 1980s. Fueled by sales of its devil-red hand-vacuums, Royal rose to the number-three spot among vacuum companies, behind Hoover and Eureka. But Royal's sales and profits declined precipitously in the early 1990s, as the hand-held segment matured and Royal encountered intense competition in the hotly contested upright vacuum market. The company suffered a net loss in 1993 and CEO John A. Balch resigned in mid-1995. He was succeeded by Michael Merriman, the 38-year-old chief financial officer who had come to Royal just three years before. Merriman and his team of "young turks" hoped to parlay the Dirt Devil brand's 90 percent awareness level into consistent sales and profitability in the mid-to-late 1990s.

Early History

Royal was founded as the P. A. Geier Company in 1905. Company namesake Philip Geier established the business in his garage, where he made some of the earliest vacuum cleaners by hand. Geier diversified into washing machines, hair dryers, mixers, and other small electric appliances, and was soon able to move his growing company into a four-story headquarters. In 1937, the company introduced what it called "the industry's first hand-held vac," known either as "the Princess" or the "Royal Prince."

Geier's appliance production continued unabated until World War II, when the company's facility was drafted to make military goods like aircraft fittings, tank transmissions, and even some incendiary devices. Geier continued to make vacuums in the postwar era, expanding his product line to include such eclectic devices as peanut roasters and hydraulic devices.

Postwar Reorganizations

The company experienced the first of many management shakeups in 1953, when it went bankrupt, was acquired by the Walter E. Schott Organization, and was renamed Royal Appliance Mfg. Co. Widely known as the owners of the Cincinnati Reds professional baseball club, the Schotts were more interested in what would now be called Royal's "breakup value" than in its viability as a manufacturer. In 1954, Stanley E. Erbor led an employee buyout and became president of the rejuvenated company. According to a company history, Royal "thrived under Erbor's leadership," moving to a modernized, suburban headquarters in 1969. Nevertheless, by the late 1970s Royal was little more than a niche player in the national vacuum industry, having eschewed the plastics revolution for its traditionally durable, but costly and awkward metal machines. When Erbor died (reportedly at the company water fountain) in 1979 at the age of 82, the company's fate once again came into question.

Royal had been on the market two years when John A. Balch led a $4.5 million leveraged buyout of the venerable vacuum manufacturer. Raised in rural Coshocton, Ohio, Balch had graduated from that state's Miami University in 1953 with a degree in accounting and had gone to work for the Arthur Andersen accounting firm. He entered the Navy's officers candidate school in 1958 and returned to Arthur Andersen in 1961 after completing a tour of duty in the Mediterranean. Balch lost his job as an information manager with a medical equipment manufacturer in a 1978 takeover. When the opportunity to purchase Royal arose, Balch borrowed $40,000, rounded up 12 other investors, and bought Royal from Erbor's estate in 1981.

CEO Balch and his new management team overhauled the company from top to bottom. They started by making slight revisions to the Princess/Prince, but failed to change its metal construction or its high price. Balch quickly changed gears, reserving the heavy-duty Royal brand for the industrial market and creating an entirely new product for the consumer market. His company's second stab at the design resulted in the eye-catching, lightweight, red plastic model dubbed the "Dirt Devil" by Wyse Advertising agency. Although it was a late-comer to the hand vac segment (which was created with Black & Decker's 1979 DustBuster launch), the Dirt Devil's 1984 launch caught a swelling wave of replacement sales. Customers were drawn by the model's low price (about $30), its old-fashioned styling, deep-cleaning revolving brush, and large capacity.

The transformation of Royal included operational changes in manufacturing, distribution, and marketing techniques. The company outsourced parts manufacture, maintaining assembly plants instead. This strategy enabled Royal to stay fast on its feet in the rapidly changing, highly competitive vacuum market, and greatly reduced its overhead. The company moved its distribution from independent "mom and pop" vacuum shops to mass retailers like Wal-Mart, KMart, and Target. New marketing strategies included point-of-sale displays, cooperative advertising, a toll-free customer service number, and a 30-day return policy. Chairman John Balch appeared in a new television advertising campaign with Sam, the Dirt Devil dog. Advertising became a keystone of Royal's program; the company's ad budget burgeoned from less than $6 million to $40 million by 1991.

The Balch-led revitalization was wildly successful: Royal sold 50,000 Dirt Devils in 1984 alone and had captured a whopping two-thirds share of the hand-held vacuum segment by 1986. Sales increased from less than $5 million in 1981 to more than $120 million by 1990 and profits grew to $11.7 million during that period. Royal worked to capitalize on the Dirt Devil success with product line and geographic expansions in the late 1980s. Although the brand dominated the hand-held segment, hand vacs constituted only less than one-third of the overall vacuum market. The real sales potential resided with uprights, which made up 70 percent of U.S. vacuum sales. Royal launched the Dirt Devil Broom Vac, a lightweight upright, in 1987 and began offering a canister model the following year.

1991 Initial Public Offering

Balch and his fellow executives took Royal public in 1991 with one of the year's most successful offerings, a $100 million stock floatation. *Business Week* reported that the stock opened at $15.50, climbed to $35 within a month, and peaked at $59 in February 1992, shortly after sales and profits for 1991 were reported at $273.3 million and $32.8 million, respectively. But after this exhilarating performance, the stock began to slide, dropping to $37 by the middle of May 1992. The decline was precipitated by a combination of rumors and disappointing reports. Some analysts believed that the stock had risen unrealis-

tically high and fast and that it was going through a predictable correction. Others blamed Wall Street's rumor mill for the drop.

Royal's guaranteed sales policy was a major bone of contention. Guaranteed sale can be defined as the direct sale of product to the retailer with the provision that any unsold merchandise will be repurchased. The company reported that a strong 1991 holiday season had fueled a 128 percent year-over-year increase in sales. But some analysts and shareholders began to question that robust figure early in 1992, when they found that Wal-Mart, a retailer that accounted for more than 10 percent of Royal's sales, had returned $5 million to $10 million worth of Dirt Devil vacuums under the guaranteed sales policy.

Although Dan Carasso, a pro-Royal analyst with Goldman Sachs & Company (not coincidentally the lead underwriter for Royal's initial stock offering), noted in a June 1992 *Business Week* article that the company had accounted for the returns in the fourth quarter of 1991, some shareholders were not reassured, and with good reason. Two consecutive quarterly earnings declines went over like lead balloons: Royal's stock market value dropped by $309 million in one day in July 1992 as shareholders left in droves. The ones who stuck with the stock filed a dozen class action lawsuits, charging that Royal executives used guaranteed sales to inflate earnings figures, did not maintain a reserve against returns, and mischaracterized the company's financial health.

Richard Ringer of *The New York Times* blamed the company's stock problems more on CEO Balch's apparent disdain for stockholders than deliberate deception. In the years after Royal went public, Balch was quoted more than once as saying, "I'm not in the business of selling stock, I'm in the business of selling vacuums." In fact, Balch had no qualms about telling Ringer that "he did not want to take Royal public in the first place but was persuaded to by his partners." The CEO subsequently cut off communication with the media, leading several investment firms, including Goldman Sachs, to drop their coverage of Royal.

Although the stockholder suits were dismissed in 1994, Royal's problems continued throughout the early 1990s. Royal's low stock price, which had shrunk to about $5, attracted unwanted investors. Richmont Capital Partners I, the Dallas partnership that had previously acquired Mary Kay Corporation, bought 7.2 percent of Royal for more than $10 million in September 1993 and increased its stake to 9.4 percent by the end of the year. Richmont was thwarted in its attempt to gain a seat on Royal's board of directors, but increased its investment in the vacuum company to 12.5 percent in 1995.

The fourth quarter 1992 merchandise returns came back to haunt Royal during 1993's holiday selling season, when retailers cut back their orders by 50 percent to avoid a repeat performance. Royal's sales declined from $395 million in 1992 to $313.9 million in 1993 and net dropped from $20.2 million to a loss of $8.3 million. The company blamed its poor performance on high European advertising expenses and competitive pressure to lower prices.

Royal was also stung by losses in market share on both its hand vac and upright fronts—its share of the upright market declined from 24.3 percent to 17.2 percent during 1992 and its share of the hand-held segment slid from more than 60 percent to about 50 percent by 1995. In 1993, the company moved its battle with primary competitor Hoover to the courtroom, challenging the latter's "Cleaning Efficiency Rating" as "misleading advertising." Hoover countersued mid-year, with charges of false advertising and defamation. Royal and Hoover continued to wage this part of their "floor war" through 1995.

Analysts agreed that the company needed a hot new product to resume profitability and growth. In the early 1990s, Royal introduced the Dirt Devil Cyclone carpet shampooer, a wet/dry vacuum, a cordless rechargeable hand vacuum, and a car vacuum, and even strayed from its signature red color to make green and black models. On the operations side, Royal cut 125 jobs, closed a plant, and shaved 30 percent from the domestic advertising budget. The company appeared to have effected a tentative turnaround by 1994. Although sales declined to $280.1 million, Royal chalked up a $1.6 million profit; it was less than 1988's net, but a profit nonetheless.

New Leadership for the Late 1990s and Beyond

The company dipped back into the red in 1995. In July, after two consecutive quarterly losses, Royal's board of directors asked for and received John Balch's resignation. Balch and company had promoted CEO Michael Merriman to president and the new position of chief operating officer earlier that year, and the 38–year-old executive advanced to the top position after just three years at Royal. Merriman had spent his entire career at Arthur Andersen, and had been senior auditor of Royal's account there since 1981. Louis Schneeberger, an outside director, was elected chairman.

Merriman publicly revealed his strategy to revitalize Royal during his first month at the helm, thereby taking a first step toward one goal, "re-establishing ties to Wall Street." He decided to place Royal's European subsidiary, which had racked up $30 million in cumulative operating losses in its brief five-year history, on the auction block. The new CEO continued the new product rollout, focusing on high margin appliances like the Dirt Devil Impulse, "a light upright retailing for $79," and the Dust Devil, a cordless rechargeable challenge to Black & Decker's DustBuster. Late in 1995, Royal used its first-ever infomercial to promote the new cordless Dirt Devil Broom Vac, which combined features of a broom for hard surfaces and a vacuum for carpets in an appliance that retailed for less than $50. The company added an ingenious on-board tool, a leaf blower, to its Dirt Devil Wet Dry vacuum. Merriman also hoped to continuously raise product quality and improve productivity.

Royal continued to struggle through the second half of 1995, eventually recording a $13.8 million loss on the year. The company blamed much of the loss on charges related to the pending sale of its European operations, but some of the shortcoming was also due to sliding gross margins. In spite of its persistent difficulties, Royal had at least one undeniable strength: its widely known Dirt Devil brand. Merriman and company hoped to use that valuable tool to return to profitability and growth in the late 1990s.

Principal Subsidiaries

Royal Appliance International Co.; Dirt Devil, Inc.; Royal Appliance FSC Inc.

Further Reading

Abdeddaim, Michelle Nellet, "The Reign at Royal Now Cleft in Twain," *HFN—The Weekly Newspaper for the Home Furnishings Network,* January 2, 1995, p. 58.

Canedy, Dana, "CPA Moving to New Realm as CEO of Royal Appliance," *Cleveland Plain Dealer,* April 21, 1992, p. 4F.

——, "Group Buys $10 billion Worth of Royal Stock," *Cleveland Plain Dealer,* October 1, 1993, p. 1E.

——, "Lawsuits Against Royal Dismissed," *Cleveland Plain Dealer,* February 10, 1994, p. 1C.

——, "Royal Appliance Earnings Drop," *Cleveland Plain Dealer,* February 22, 1994, p. 1C.

——, "Thanks, But No Thanks, Royal Tells Its Suitor," *Cleveland Plain Dealer,* May 19, 1994, p. 1C.

——, "New Floor Plan," *Cleveland Plain Dealer,* December 20, 1994, p. 1C.

——, "Royal Appliance Manufacturing Returns to Profitability," *Cleveland Plain Dealer,* February 18, 1995, p. 3C.

"Company Backgrounder," Cleveland: Royal Appliance Manufacturing Co., 1996.

Frinton, Sandra, "Hand Vac Faceoff," *HFN,* May 22, 1995, p. 35.

Mallory, Maria, "The Dirt Devil Made Royal Do It," *Business Week,* August 26, 1991, pp. 30–31.

McLoughlin, Bill, "Turning Royal Around: New CEO Draws Up His List of Tasks," *HFN,* July 31, 1995, p. 27.

——, "Dust Devil, MVP Star in Royal Ads," *HFN,* September 4, 1995, p. 52.

——, "A Royal Revamp: Vac Maker Aims for a Turnaround," *HFN,* November 13, 1995, 45.

——, "Infomercial for Royal's Broom Vac," *HFN,* December 25, 1995, p. 33.

Narisetti, Raju, "Royal Appliance To Study Plan of Investor Group," *Wall Street Journal,* May 16, 1994, p. A11D.

Phillips, Stephen, "Royal Investor Increases Share," *Cleveland Plain Dealer,* February 21, 1996, p. 1C.

Pledger, Marcia, "Royal Appliance Co. Hoping Its New Broom Will Clean Up," *Cleveland Plain Dealer,* January 16, 1996, p. 1C.

Ringer, Richard, "Dirt Devil Disappoints Investors," *New York Times,* August 12, 1993, pp. D1, D20.

——, "Investor Group Purchases 7.2 Percent Royal Appliance Stake," *New York Times,* September 22, 1993, p. D4.

"Royal Incorporates Dirt Devil," *Cleveland Plain Dealer,* January 30, 1996, p. 4C.

"Royal's Colorful History," *Dirt Devil News!,* November/December 1994.

Sabath, Donald, "Royal Puts European Unit Up for Sale," *Cleveland Plain Dealer,* October 31, 1995, p. 1C.

——, "Three Experts Join Royal Appliance Team," *Cleveland Plain Dealer,* December 2, 1995, p. 2C.

Thompson, Lynne, "The Royal King," *Cleveland Magazine,* November 1993, pp. 36–37.

Yerak, Becky, "Royal Appliance CEO Resigns as Company's Financial Losses Grow," *Cleveland Plain Dealer,* July 25, 1995, p. 1C.

—April Dougal Gasbarre

Ryan's

Ryan's Family Steak Houses, Inc.

Post Office Box 100
Greer, South Carolina 29652
U.S.A.
(803) 879-1000

Public Company
Incorporated: 1977
Employees: 15,000
Sales: $513.17 million (1995)
Stock Exchanges: NASDAQ
SICs: 5812 Eating Places; 6794 Patent Owners and
Lessors

Ryan's Family Steak Houses, Inc., one of two successful restaurant chains founded by Alvin McCall, competes by selling high-quality food at modest prices. Ryan's, which operates over 225 restaurants in the southern and midwestern United States, has been consistently recognized as one of the best small companies in America by *Forbes* and *Business Week* magazines.

Ryan's founder, Alvin A. McCall, Jr., was born in 1927, ninth in a family of 11. His parents worked at a mill in Pelzer, South Carolina, and he and his siblings grew up poor. His entrepreneurial bent showed itself at an early age as he recruited his sister Martha to help him raise chickens, peppers, and tomatoes for sale. As a teenager McCall delivered newspapers and also cleaned a movie theater and worked in a couple of grocery stores, including a Dixie Home Store, one of the forerunners of the Winn-Dixie chain.

After graduating high school, McCall served a stint at a mortuary owned by the father of a friend. After serving a year in the Navy at the end of World War II, he studied business and accounting at schools in Greenville, South Carolina, and Johnson City, Tennessee. He also moonlighted as a bookkeeper for a restaurant and a gas station, both of which provided practical perks. When he returned to Greenville, he joined an accounting firm and married. He continued his habit of moonlighting, which earned him more than his regular salary.

The restless McCall next began to build houses. His initial success prompted him to quit his accounting job to form McCall Construction Co., which, according to McCall, showed a $43,000 profit its first year, 1958. This led to property development; eventually he built and ran a Volkswagen dealership in Sumter, South Carolina.

McCall's search for interesting businesses to run brought him to restaurants. In 1970, inspired by the successful Ponderosa chain, he started his own, Western Family Steak House, most of which took the name Quincy's in 1976. The first restaurant was on Wade Hampton Boulevard in Greenville, built by employees from his contracting business. After the hired manager lost $50,000 in three months, McCall took the reins and developed a formula based on principles of quality he had learned as a contractor. Quality at his steak house began with using fresh meat, not frozen.

In 1977, McCall sold his interest in Quincy's to what would become Trans World Corp., but he retained the freedom to compete. He started Ryan's the same year and the first restaurant opened in 1978 on Laurens Road in Greenville. Sales for the first year were $568,000. Although the restaurants, which numbered seven by 1981 (including one franchisee), were successful, growth was limited by the structure of the company, which put profits back in the hands of the partners, not into the business. At the end of 1981 (when sales were $8.1 million) the partnerships were consolidated; Ryan's first public stock offering raised $4 million.

Unfortunately, there was initially a small obstacle to expansion and the stock offering. The name "Ryan's" had been chosen because it was short and recognizable, with a wholesome and frugal Irish ring to it. However, the registration of the trademark was opposed by John Rian, owner, through Rian's Inc., of ten restaurants in the metropolitan Portland area of Oregon. In order to speed its 1982 initial public offering, McCall agreed not to use the name "Ryan's" west of the Mississippi except for in Texas, Oklahoma, and Louisiana. In 1987, to clear the way for westward expansion, Ryan's paid Rian $150,000 for use of the name in the remaining United States.

Once these hurdles were cleared, Ryan's growth was impressive. A share of stock, worth $9.25 originally, rose to over $30 at its peak. Ryan's never paid dividends and was thus able to use all of its profits for expansion. Fred Grant, a finance officer, explained in 1991 that issuing a 25-cent dividend would cost $13 million, enough to start six restaurants. The company maintained that its policy helped secure stock prices in a highly leveraged industry. In the 1990s, Ryan's opened approximately 20 new restaurants each year, peaking at 30 in 1993. This performance flew in the face of emerging concerns over the health risks related to the animal fat and cholesterol in beef, or the "beef scare" of the 1980s. The variety found in the Mega Bar helped satisfy wider crowds; the restaurants also sold a few à la carte fish and poultry dishes.

McCall relied on conservative methods to maintain control of the restaurant's destiny. Although he tinkered with franchising in the beginning, McCall found it left him unable to ensure consistent quality from store to store. However, franchises did come to contribute a significant portion of company revenues, though not without some difficulties. When Family Steak Houses of Florida, Inc., Ryan's largest franchisee, fell behind in royalty payments in 1993, Ryan's restructured its agreement. Family Steak Houses, based in Neptune Beach, lost $2.1 million in 1993, largely due to the closure of unprofitable stores. The company, which went public in 1986, was founded by Eddie Ervin, Alvin McCall's brother-in-law, owner of Margate, Florida's Rustic Inn Crabhouse. The first Ryan's in a foreign country was a franchised restaurant, which opened in Ballarat, Australia, in 1994.

Borrowing also surrendered control of the company, and Ryan's developed a habit of relying on cash, not credit. In fact, it gained a reputation for extraordinary promptness in paying its vendors. In the late 1980s the company did begin to borrow to fund expansion. Inside the restaurants, Ryan's did not accept credit cards until 1991.

In some ways, the company took an unconventional approach. Besides its lukewarm embrace of franchising, at least in the early days, it also disdained advertising, even for store openings. The company did not run a significant advertising campaign until 1994, when it bought television and radio spots in Charleston. By 1996 the company planned to support one-third of its stores with $1.7 million of advertising, a great deal for a chain that for years relied exclusively on word of mouth.

While most restaurants invested three to four percent of sales in advertising, Ryan's, according to company officials, preferred to apply the money towards what it stated were the highest food costs in the business, hoping that would bring back customers. The high costs made high volumes critical to the success of the restaurants. Ryan's stores also boasted twice the volume of others in its segment, about $2 million each in the 1980s.

In May 1986, McCall's son T. Mark McCall was named president of the company, after shepherding the introduction of the "Mega Bar." These offered salads, entrees and vegetables, and desserts. After just one year, the buffet bars accounted for nearly half of Ryan's total sales, and pushed same-store sales up 50 percent to 2.5 times the industry average. At the same time,

bread-baking ovens were installed, allowing the chain to offer fresh rolls made from scratch (the recipe was developed with help from General Mills). In 1986, annual sales were up 99 percent to $103.3 million; profits rose 92 percent over the previous year.

Mark McCall faced difficult times in his tenure as president. In October 1987, the company's stock fell, as did the stock of just about every other company in the wake of the stock market crash. The average restaurant stock fell 42 percent during this time. This prompted company officials to think about the possibility of a takeover for the first time. The success of the Mega Bars drew many imitators, which flattened sales.

In June 1988 Alvin McCall resumed his role as CEO as his son Mark left the post to start a restaurant chain in Texas. Greenville accountant Charles Way took over as CEO in 1989 after serving as controller since the company was only two years old. Way, whom Alvin McCall described as his protégé, had already been serving as president. In 1992 he became board chairman as well.

In 1990, a *Restaurants & Institutions* survey named Ryan's the best steak house in the United States. Nevertheless, the company slowed its expansion temporarily around this time and hired more staff to improve service. It also made retention of managers (who typically worked 14-hour days) a top priority, feeling that consistency in management helped reduce employee turnover. The pay of managers and supervisors was heavily tied to performance, and generally exceeded the industry average, although high volumes made payroll consume a lower portion of sales.

In 1991, "Bakery Bars" were added to Ryan's restaurants, offering desserts baked in the store. They were successful in boosting sales, but start-up costs and a poor economy prevented them, at least initially, from increasing earnings. The Mega Bar concept was revitalized in 1993, when it was changed from one central station to five buffet stations, known as "scatter bars," which reduced traffic congestion and increased variety. Expanded installation of the scatter bars in 1995 helped Ryan's turn around sales declines. In 1993, the company experimented with a higher priced weekend buffet bar, which featured seafood, prime rib, and Virginia ham. The new bar, which cost $11 per plate—nearly double the usual check average—was an attempt to increase declining same-store sales.

In order to create tax savings and in preparation for more growth, Ryan's created three subsidiaries in 1993. Ryan's Properties would manage Ryan's trademarks and service marks. Ryan's Family Steak House East operated the restaurants. Ryan's Capital Holding Corp. would deal with debt financing. Another subsidiary, Big R Procurement Co., had already been created in 1992 to purchase supplies.

In the mid-1990s Ryan's searched for ways to diversify in light of fierce competition in the family dining segment. In 1994, it began talks with Frankie's Food, Sports, and Spirits, an Atlanta sports bar. The company also built its own Caliente Grill, a Tex-Mex restaurant, in Greenville and operated it on a test basis. Another casual dining concept being tested in 1994 was an upscale Western-style steak house, the Laredo Grille, which opened in Plano, Texas, at the site of an existing Ryan's. Both of these casual dining restaurants offered alcoholic beverages, unlike Ryan's steak houses, and featured full service dining as opposed to Ryan's order line and buffet tables. Observers cited these forays into casual dining as evidence of Ryan's mature management team.

Principal Subsidiaries

Big R Procurement Co.; Ryan's Properties; Ryan's Family Steak Houses East; Ryan's Capital Holding Corp.

Further Reading

Brammer, Rhonda, "What's the Beef?" *Barron's,* January 2, 1995, 23–24.

Carlino, Bill, "Despite Rebound, Ryan's Still Feels January Chill," *Nation's Restaurant News,* May 9, 1994.

——, "Ryan's Explores Upscale All-You-Can-Eat Format," *Nation's Restaurant News,* January 4, 1993.

——, "Ryan's to Test Tex-Mex with Caliente Grille," *Nation's Restaurant News,* July 11, 1994.

Feldman, Rona, "Steak: Nutritional Concerns Have Not Hurt Segment Profits," *Restaurant Business,* June 10, 1992, p. 176.

Festa, Gail, "Ryan's Express," *Restaurant Hospitality,* August 1987.

Fleet, Lee Ann, "Cutting No Corners: Alvin McCall Built Ryan's His Way," *Greenville News,* August 31, 1992.

——, "Ryan's Officials See Business Rebounding," *Greenville News,* April 25, 1991.

Hayes, Jack, "Christman Takes Helm at Family Steak Houses," *Nation's Restaurant News,* May 2, 1994, pp. 3, 123.

——, "Ryan's Making a Pitch for High-Volume Sports Bar," *Nation's Restaurant News,* March 7, 1994, p. 4.

——, "Steak Rivals Sell Sizzle of Image Upgrades," *Nation's Restaurant News,* August 1, 1994, pp. 140, 148.

Little, Loyd, "Alvin McCall Had Hunger to Succeed," *Upstate Business.* May 23, 1993.

——, "McCall's Successor Charting Way for Ryan's Family Steak Houses," *Upstate Business,* May 23, 1993.

Mamis, Robert A., "Meat and Potatoes," *Inc.,* July, 1986, pp. 53–63.

Marcial, Gene G., "Steak Houses That May Soon Sizzle," *Business Week,* July 22, 1991, p. 62.

Mehegan, Sarah, "Ryan's Hope," *Restaurant Business,* September 1, 1995.

Netzer, Baie, "Regional Brokers Pick Them from Their Own Backyards," *Money,* November, 1991, p. 84.

Palmeri, Christopher, "The Two Hundred Best Small Companies," *Forbes,* November 9, 1992, p. 210.

Patterson, Pat, "Southern Steak-House Chain Finds Flexibility Spells Success," *Nation's Restaurant News,* January 15, 1990, p. 47.

Person, Sarah, "Ryan's Stake in Budget Beef Segment," *Restaurant Business,* October 10, 1995.

Rogers, Monica, "Steakhouses Looking to Add Sizzle," *Restaurants & Institutions,* July 15, 1994, pp. 144–46.

——, "Steakhouses Say Adios to Big-Menu Strategies," *Restaurants & Institutions,* July 15, 1993, pp. 124–34.

—Frederick C. Ingram

S&C Electric Company

6601 North Ridge Boulevard
Chicago, Illinois 60626
U.S.A.
(312) 338-1000
Fax: (312) 338-3657

Private Company
Founded: 1911 as Schweitzer & Conrad Inc.
Sales: $130 million
Employees: 1,500
SICs: 3613 Switchgear and Switchboard Apparatus

S&C Electric Company develops and manufactures products for the highly competitive electric power industry. The company primarily focuses on high-voltage switching and protection products, including such items as trademarked SMD Power Fuses, Pad-Mounted Gear, Fault Filter Electronic Power Fuses, and Scada-Mate Switching Systems. These products help ensure the delivery of electrical power and the continuity of service under the most severe weather conditions by minimizing damage to circuits and high-voltage equipment.

The company was founded by Nicholas J. Conrad and Edmund O. Schweitzer. Around the turn of the century, Conrad worked as a electrical engineer for a man named Schweitzer, an electrical engineer and chief testing engineer for Commonwealth Edison in Chicago, Illinois. Both men were involved in the construction of central power stations, of which Commonwealth Edison was a leader in the field. In the early part of the 20th century, numerous breakdowns of electrical power stations were a regular occurrence. During one of these breakdowns at the Fisk Street station on Chicago's north side, Schweitzer and Conrad discovered that the cause was a fuse failure. Immediately both men recognized the need for a new fuse design.

Joining together, Conrad and Schweitzer developed the S&C Electric Fuse, a highly innovative fuse unlike anything manufactured up to that time. In 1911, the two men formed a partnership and began to market their invention. The fuse became hugely popular, especially since it was developed with enough protection that it could be used outdoors, and led to the construction of outdoor distribution substations by electrical utility companies. Soon the S&C Electric Fuse was sold in Australia, Germany, Canada, Japan, Italy, and England. In the United States, Conrad and Schweitzer's fuse dominated the high-voltage fuse market with a 75 percent share.

By 1916, the company was growing at such a fast pace that Conrad decided to leave Commonwealth Edison and concentrate on developing new products at S&C while Schweitzer remained at the utility firm. One year later, S&C relocated to Wilson and Ravenswood Avenues on Chicago's far north side. To augment their production of the liquid fuse, the two men began to develop fuse mountings, disconnect switches, lightning arresters, voltage detectors and choke coils. Throughout the 1920s, the company improved upon its development of innovative fuse designs. Operating voltages of this second generation of liquid fuse designs increased from 15,000 volts to 138,000 volts by the end of the decade. Conrad, the driving force behind the firm, had applied for and was granted 49 patents for developing liquid fuse and switching apparatuses by 1930.

Yet by the end of 1930, Conrad had withdrawn from managing the daily operations of the firm due to ill health. With Schweitzer still committed to working at Commonwealth Edison, as he always had done, the controlling interests in the firm were sold to Cutler-Hammer, a larger midwestern manufacturer of motor control parts for the automobile industry. Yet the onset of the Great Depression during the 1930s seriously affected S&C, and sales of liquid fuses declined dramatically. Nonetheless, the men who were Conrad's earlier associates were committed to developing new products for the company. One of the most important product developments during this time was the SM Power Fuse, one of the first solid-material fuses which significantly expanded the use of power fuses for the electrical utility industry. From 1930 to 1940, these men were granted patents for 111 new products.

The advent of World War II brought new challenges to the company, and S&C retooled its facility in Chicago to meet the requirements of a war-time industry. Products such as high-voltage channel selectors were developed and manufactured for radars used by ships in the U.S. Navy, and fused load interrupters were designed for use by companies engaged in war-related production. Due to the increased demand and new areas of application for power fuses at this time, S&C was able to pursue its specialty in electrical fuses and high-voltage protection even though construction within the electrical utility industry had virtually come to a complete standstill during the war.

The postwar years for S&C signaled great changes. S&C reviewed and reorganized its product line, dropping items that were incompatible with the company's growing list of highly specialized products for high-voltage circuit interruption. Most important, however, was the return of Nicholas Conrad. Having fully recovered from his illness, he acquired all of Cutler-Hammer's controlling interest, purchased all of Edmund Schweitzer's minority interest, and assumed complete control of the company's operations. His first decision was to keep S&C Electric as the company's name, while his second decision involved a complete overhaul and re-equipment of the plant in Chicago. From 1945 to 1949, Conrad implemented measures that doubled the company's production capacity.

S&C Electric Company grew by leaps and bounds during the 1950s. Under the new leadership of John Conrad, Nicholas Conrad's son who had been working for the firm since 1945, the company remained committed to developing better uses for its specialty power fuses and interrupter switches. With electrical consumption within the United States nearly doubling every 10 years, the continuity of electrical service had to be assured with the least possibility of power shortages. This development required substantially improved switching flexibility, and S&C responding by developing its Alduti Interrupter Switch. But management recognized that there was an entirely new, and rapidly growing, group of large electrical power consumers. The demand for more power brought on by such new products as air-conditioning, space heating, automation, and more lighting, compelled companies and owners of office buildings to distribute electrical power at higher voltages than ever used before. S&C discovered that an entirely new market for their fuses and interrupter switches was being created by the demand for ever-increasing electrical power.

The company started developing a brand-new product line of switchgear, fuses, and fuse interrupters, and soon innovative new designs and expanded versions of older products began to multiply. The company's revenues increased astronomically and, as a reward, S&C's research and development department was given greater autonomy than ever before. A new marketing strategy was put into place, along with a larger staff and additional sales offices throughout the country. An S&C testing site was added in Arnhem, The Netherlands, one of the first instances of an American company arranging to test its products overseas on a regular basis. The company's manufacturing facilities in north Chicago were also expanded during the years 1951 to 1957. In the midst of all the growth and increasing profitability, Nicholas Conrad gradually withdrew from his daily supervisory activities at the firm. He eventually died in 1956 after an extended illness.

During the late 1950s, company sales continued to increase. Although S&C had sold and even manufactured its products primarily through licensing agreements started in the 1920s, management thought it more cost-effective to eliminate this process by making and marketing all of its own product line. As a result, the company established S&C Canada, Ltd., to manufacture its products. Originally located in Toronto, the factory grew rapidly until a new factory was built in Rexdale, adjacent to Toronto International Airport. By the end of the decade, the Rexdale plant and the Chicago factory were producing some of the most important, and also the most innovative, items for the electrical power industry, including SMD-2D Power Fuses, SM Power Fuses with interrupting capacities, SM Metal-Enclosed Fuses, Switch Operators, Potential Devices, Control Panels, Fusistor Fuses, Loadbuster Disconnects, XS Open Cutouts, Pad-Mounted Gear, New Heavy-Duty Indoor Alduti Interrupter Switches, and many more. The company also used its technical expertise to introduce new models of old products, such as High Voltage Detectors, various Handling Tools, and Liquid Fuses with Resistors.

In 1961, S&C Electric developed one of the most innovative products in the electric power industry: the Circuit Switcher. A combination of circuit breaker and interrupter, the name described a new product line of switchgears for transmission breakers. With the invention of this product, utility companies were able to adopt entirely new methods for protecting transmission systems. Along with this new development in switchgears, the company celebrated its Golden Jubilee Anniversary by dedicating the brand new Nicholas J. Conrad Laboratory. At a cost of $2 million, the laboratory was the largest building heated by electricity in the city of Chicago.

When first built, the Nicholas J. Conrad Laboratory was a state-of-the-art experimental and research facility, one of the best in the country for developing products for the electric power industry. The laboratory included high-voltage rooms for flashover testing, an indoor short-circuit test cell, an experimental arcing room, a generator room with two motor-generated machines, an outdoor substation used for load-switching and short-circuit testing, and an environmental test chamber where various weather conditions such as icing, salt spray, and humidity could be controlled and maintained with precision in order to test switchgear. The laboratory's control room was the company's showcase, with its master test consoles, cathode-ray oscillography machine, recording instruments, automatic programmer, and various other kinds of monitoring equipment. By the end of the 1960s, S&C's Conrad Laboratory had developed high-voltage circuit interruption into an art form.

During the 1970s, S&C concentrated on developing its Conrad Laboratory, and devoted large sums of money to hiring personnel in technical fields such as electrical, mechanical, chemical, electronic, and metallurgical engineering. The company also spent generously on updating its state-of-the-art facilities, from design and prototype development equipment to experimentation and testing mechanisms. Management was convinced, and their judgement was vindicated, that the future of development and research in the electrical power industry was largely dependent upon a company's ability to reproduce field conditions in the laboratory setting to test and rate various products such as circuit breakers and fuses. By the end of the decade, S&C's Conrad Laboratory had garnered the reputation as the most sophisticated, comprehensive, and reliable research and development facility in the entire electrical power industry.

The 1980s mirrored the 1970s in many way for S&C Electric. Company revenues continued to increase and profitability also rose. The firm's reputation as the undisputed leader in the development, design, and manufacture of products for the electrical power industry was known throughout the United States. Management remained committed to providing adequate funding for the Conrad Laboratory, evident in its installation of a 1.6 million-volt impulse testing generator which reproduces voltage surges similar to lightning strikes, a test generator designed to bear extreme electrical, mechanical, and thermal stresses, a high-speed video system that is able to record 12,000 frames per second, a robotic welding system, and modern manufacturing operations such as four-axis turning centers. Perhaps the most important addition to the Conrad Laboratory's research and development capabilities during this time was the inclusion of a Computer Aided Design System (CAD). This system allows engineers to employ computer-aided modeling and analysis to explore the various alternatives in designing a product, and minimizes the time between development and product introduction.

By the mid-1990s, S&C Electric Company was still known as the pre-eminent firm in the development and manufacture of high-voltage switching and protection products. The company was selling more power fuses, fuse cutouts, regulator bypass switches, recloser bypass connectors, interrupter switches pad-mounted gear, and metal-enclosed switchgear than any other firm within the electrical power industry. Sales for S&C Electric were reported to approach the $150 million mark.

Principal Subsidiaries

S&C Electric Canada, Ltd.

Further Reading

The Hidden Energy of S&C, company document, Chicago: S&C Electric, 1995.

S&C Electric Company: High-Voltage Switching and Protection Products, Information Bulletin 102, company document, 1994.

The S&C Story . . . Its First Fifty Years as a Specialist in High-Voltage Circuit Interruption, Chicago: S&C Electric, 1961.

—Thomas Derdak

Sanderson Farms, Inc.

225 North 13th Avenue
P.O. Box 988
Laurel, Mississippi 39441-0988
U.S.A.
(601) 649-4030
Fax: (601) 426-1461

Public Company
Incorporated: 1955 as Sanderson Brothers Farms
Employees: 4,854
Sales: $371.50 million (1994)
Stock Exchanges: NASDAQ
SICs: 0251 Broiler, Fryer & Roaster Chickens; 2013
   Sausages & Other Prepared Meats; 2015 Poultry
   Slaughtering & Processing; 2038 Frozen Specialties,
   Not Elsewhere Classified

Sanderson Farms, Inc., produces, processes, markets, and distributes fresh and frozen chicken and other prepared food items. It sells whole and cut chicken primarily under the Miss Goldy brand name in the southeastern, southwestern, and western United States. More than 100 other food items, including frozen foods, are distributed nationally and even internationally under the Sanderson Farms brand name. The company was growing rapidly and posting healthy profits in the mid-1990s.

The chicken business that would become Sanderson Farms was founded in the 1940s by D. R. Sanderson and his sons. D. R. Sanderson, better known as Mr. Bob, and his brother had operated a grocery business in Hazlehurst, Mississippi, for several years before going into the chicken business. D. R. had brought sons Dewey and Joe Frank to work in the store as soon as they were old enough ''to make change,'' according to Joe. It was primarily through the boys' experience at the store that Mr. Bob instilled in them a hardy Protestant work ethic. ''Our father taught us honesty, he taught us industry, he taught us to treat people fairly, taught us to work,'' Dewey recalled in company annals. Joe added, ''He had a very strong work ethic, and he saw to it that everybody who surrounded him, all his family and all his children, had that work ethic instilled into them.''

The Sandersons also opened a vegetable business in Hazlehurst, through which they shipped cabbage, beans, and other vegetables throughout the region. After World War II Dewey opened a Purina franchise feed and seed business in Laurel, Mississippi, a city about 80 miles east of Hazlehurst and 80 miles southeast of Jackson. Joe was working in a hatchery in Meridian, Mississippi, but he moved to Laurel in 1951 to help the family expand into the growing poultry business. The Sandersons' chicken business thrived and the brothers decided to simply exit their Purina franchise and devote all of their energy to the poultry operation. Joe and Dewey built the first feed mill and hatchery in the area and incorporated their business in 1955 as Sanderson Brothers Farms.

Shortly after Joe and Dewey opened their feed mill and hatchery, Mr. Bob and his brother Tom constructed a broiler processing plant in Hazlehurst. They opened the operation, in partnership with Durr Wise, as Miss Goldy, Inc. In 1961 Miss Goldy and Sanderson Brothers Farms merged, forming a company with both poultry production and processing capabilities. Demand for the company's chicken products spiraled, and within a few years the Sandersons began looking for a way to expand. The avenue to growth was provided by a bond issue passed by the citizens of the City of Laurel in 1964. The issue provided $3 million that Sanderson Farms used to construct a poultry complex. The facility, which became a major employer in the area, opened its doors in 1965. The joint effort began a close relationship that the City of Laurel and Sanderson Farms would share for years to come.

Sanderson Farms' poultry operation prospered during the late 1960s and early 1970s. In 1969 Joe Frank, as his father had done years earlier, brought his son, Joe Sanderson, Jr., into the business. Joe, Jr. watched Sanderson Farms grow from a local chicken producer and processor to a major regional poultry supplier in the southern and western United States. That growth was achieved partly through the acquisition of other companies.

Sanderson Farms purchased a processing plant in 1974, for instance, and in 1978 built a new feed mill. Then, in 1981, the company acquired Collins Chill Pack Division, which had been part of a company called MFC Services. That move reflected the company's strategy of vertical integration, which allowed it to reduce costs and eventually gain control over most phases of the production, processing, and distribution processes.

Aside from savvy operational tactics, Sanderson succeeded by following conservative fiscal, managerial, and personnel practices. Such principles had been the foundation of the company's success since Mr. Bob had started his grocery operation. The elder Sanderson was known for keeping a tight rein on expenses, for example, and for incurring little debt. Long-time employee Walter Washington related the following incident: "... going down Old Highway 51 there was a long, steep hill and then valleys. He would get to the top of the hill, cut the motor off and cruise down the hill. I said, 'Why do you do that, Mr. Bob?' and he said, 'I'm saving gas. You never can be a success unless you cut the cost.' " Similarly, Odell Johnson, a long-time employee and president of the company between 1984 and 1989, recalled the Sanderson family's emphasis on integrity: "One of the things that Joe Frank told me the day he hired me was that at any point if I felt like the company was doing anything that was not right and that would affect my conscience, that I ought to leave. I never had to leave. They've always believed in treating other people like they want to be treated."

Joe Frank assumed the presidency of Sanderson Farms in 1982. By that time the company was generating roughly $100 million in annual sales and enjoying healthy profits. Sanderson Farms continued to post steady gains under the leadership of Joe, Jr. Indeed, sales shot up to more than $130 million in 1985 and then to $150 million in 1986, by which time Odell Johnson was acting as president. Sanderson took a big step forward in 1986 when it purchased National Prepared Foods, based in Jackson, Mississippi, giving Sanderson an entry into the beef, pork, and seafood segments. Sanderson also diversified by moving into the market for further-processed, or value-added, poultry products. Sadly, Mr. Bob died in 1985. He was credited with developing the company from a small feed and chicken operation to one of the larger poultry companies in the United States.

Sanderson Farms grew rapidly during the late 1980s and early 1990s. Family owned, the company had traditionally funded growth internally. In 1987, though, the Sandersons took the company public with a stock offering that raised more than $16 million. During the next several years Sanderson Farms used capital generated from the sale of stock to finance growth. The company invested heavily, expanding with projects at plants in Hazlehurst, Jackson, Laurel, Collins, and in Hammond, Louisiana—between 1991 and 1994, Sanderson invested more than $125 million to grow its operations. In addition to increasing production and distribution capacity, the company diversified into new product lines. Most notable was Sanderson's 1990 introduction of a line of frozen entrees that included chicken primavera, lasagna, seafood gumbo, and Mexican casserole.

Expansion and diversification pushed sales and profits to new highs. Annual revenues climbed to $166 million in 1988 before leveling out around $186 million during the early 1990s, while operating profits averaged about $18 million per year between 1988 and 1991. Joe Sanderson, Jr., followed Odell Johnson as president in 1990. Johnson had started working at Sanderson when the company was processing 30,000 chickens a week; by the time he retired, Sanderson was processing nearly two million chickens weekly. Joe, Jr., became the third generation of Sandersons to lead the enterprise, bringing 20 years of experience at Sanderson Farms with him to the helm. As noted above, the company invested heavily to expand, diversify, and update facilities after Joe, Jr., became president. In 1992, for example, Sanderson Farms began constructing a new $40 million processing plant, hatchery, and feed mill.

Besides expanding Sanderson Farms, Joe, Jr., achieved growth by maintaining the company's long-time strategy of vertical integration. To that end, Sanderson Farms' management worked to become involved in all aspects of the marketing process with a broad product mix that appealed to retail, food service, discount, export, and other markets. Integral to that effort was the company's emphasis on value-added products, such as boneless, cut, frozen, marinated, or cooked chicken; "When my grandmother wanted to serve chicken, she caught a chicken, wrung its neck, plucked it, cut it up, and cooked it," Joe, Jr. explains in company literature. "... when my wife wants to serve chicken, she goes to the supermarket, buys chicken already cut into pieces, often boneless or skinless, takes it home and cooks it. When my daughter wants to serve chicken, she buys it already cooked, takes it home and serves it." By the early 1990s, more than 95 percent of all chicken products that Sanderson Farms sold were considered value-added.

By 1992 Sanderson Farms employed a work force of 2,500 people. Revenues jumped to $210 million in 1992 and then to a whopping $269 million in 1993, while operating profits bulged from $16 million in 1992 to more than $32 million in 1993. The company rapidly boosted sales to $372 million in 1994, a record $43.8 million of which was operating profit. Augmenting an aggressive expansion strategy were general trends in the marketplace that complemented Sanderson Farms' offerings. Consumption of chicken in the United States continued to rise, for example—per capita chicken consumption had already climbed from 30 pounds in the 1960s to about 80 pounds in the early 1990s. Furthermore, Sanderson was realizing healthy growth in demand for its various frozen entrees and foods sold to wholesale accounts and for the retail market under the Sanderson Farms label.

In 1995 Sanderson Farms was operating four hatcheries, three feed mills, five processing plants, and a byproducts plant, and employing more than 4,000 workers. Furthermore, it was contracting with more than 600 growers and breeders that supplied its chicken. In 1994 Sanderson Farms processed more than 160 million chickens to create about 522 million pounds of dressed meat. In addition to various chicken products, which made up about 80 percent of the company's revenues in the mid-1990s, Sanderson sold various processed beef, pork, and seafood items. A complete line of fresh and frozen chicken was marketed under the Miss Goldy brand name, primarily to retailers and distributors in the southeastern, southwestern, and western United States. Under the Sanderson Farms label, the company was shipping more than 100 different processed and prepared frozen entrees and specialty food products to wholesalers and retailers throughout the United States.

In the long term, Sanderson Farms planned to boost its share of the U.S. poultry market by focusing on value-added products and by diversifying its product and market mixes. As it had since the Sandersons started it, the company prided itself on keeping a low level of debt and advocating a conservative management philosophy.

Further Reading

McCann, Nita Chilton, ''Sanderson Farms Sees 1995 as Year for Strategic Planning,'' *Mississippi Business Journal,* December 12, 1994, Section 1, p. 21.

Sanderson, Joe Frank, Jr., *Family Matters: The Story of Sanderson Farms, Inc.,* Laurel, Miss.: Sanderson Farms, Inc., November 1992.

Thorp, Susan A., ''Morgan Keegan Emerges as Leader in Initial Public Offering Arena,'' *Memphis Business Journal,* June 8, 1987, Section 1, p. 8.

——, ''Sanderson Farms Is Well-Kept Poultry Industry Secret,'' *Memphis Business Journal,* November 7, 1988, Section 1, p. 14.

—Dave Mote

San Miguel Corporation

40 San Miguel Avenue
Mandaluyong City
1501 Metropolitan Manila
Philippines
(63) 2 632 3000
Fax: (63) 2 632 3099

Public Company
Incorporated: 1913
Employees: 32,832
Sales: P68.4 billion (1994)
Stock Exchanges: Philippine
SICs: 2080 Beverages; 2010 Meat Products; 2020 Dairy
Products; 3221 Glass Containers; 2671 Paper Coated
& Laminated Packaging

Best known for its internationally distributed beer, San Miguel Corporation can only be described in superlatives. It is Southeast Asia's oldest and largest brewer. With nearly 33,000 employees, the company also ranks among the Philippines' largest, most consistently profitable, and most admired manufacturers. San Miguel's flagship beer utterly dominates both the Filipino and Hong Kong markets, with 90 percent and 60 percent respective shares. A 1988 brief in *The Economist* noted that Filipinos order ''beer'' at bars and restaurants, knowing that they'll receive a San Miguel. But San Miguel didn't make it to the top of the regional heap on good beer alone. It also makes agricultural feeds, processed and fresh meats, ready-to-eat foods, packaging, and non-alcoholic beverages. By the early 1990s, beer constituted about half of San Miguel's annual turnover. In fact, the conglomerate has grown over the course of its more than 105 years in business to generate four percent of its home country's gross national product and six percent of tax revenues.

San Miguel grew to its commanding position in the Southeast Asian market in spite of political upheaval, infrastructure glitches, and high taxes. It achieved its status through aggres-

sive competitive strategies and shrewd long-range planning over the decades. Having diversified into agribusiness, foods, and packaging in the mid-20th century, the conglomerate dominated its domestic markets by the early 1980s. At that time, San Miguel undertook an aggressive program of international expansion that came to fruition in the mid-to-late 1990s.

Early History

Don Enrique Ma Barretto de Ycaza established the brewery, Southeast Asia's first, in 1890 as La Fabrica de Cerveza de San Miguel. He named the company after the section of Manila in which he lived and worked. He was soon joined by Don Pedro Pablo Roxas, who brought with him a German brewmaster. San Miguel's brew won its first major award at 1895's Philippines Regional Exposition, and led its imported competitors by a five-to-one margin by the turn of the 20th century. The company was incorporated in 1913 following the death of Don Pedro Roxas.

By that time, San Miguel was exporting its namesake brew to Hong Kong, Shanghai, and Guam. Andrés Soriano y Roxas joined San Miguel in 1918, beginning a multi-generation (albeit interrupted) reign of Sorianos. In 1990, San Miguel's Beer Bulletin noted that ''Beer was the heart of San Miguel's business, and the soul from which emanated all its other businesses.'' Andrés Soriano initiated the company's diversification, which proceeded rather logically via vertical integration. The experience cultivating barley naturally evolved into other agricultural businesses, for example. San Miguel gathered steam in the 1920s, when the company expanded into nonalcoholic beverages with the creation of the Royal Soft Drinks Plant in 1922. San Miguel entered the frozen foods market in 1925 with the creation of the Magnolia Ice Cream Plant. By the early 1990s, Magnolia held four-fifths of the frozen dessert market. Soriano created the first national Coca-Cola bottling and distribution franchise in 1927. The Philippine company owned 70 percent of the joint venture, which grew to become Coke's sixth-largest operation. By the early 1990s, San Miguel had captured over two-thirds of the domestic soft drink market.

Although World War II interrupted San Miguel's brewing business, the company got back on the growth track in the postwar era, acquiring production facilities in Hong Kong in 1948. The company also resumed its program of vertical integration, even building its own power plant so that it would not be dependent on the Philippines' notoriously poor infrastructure. San Miguel also built a liquid carbon dioxide plant, glass bottle manufacturing facilities, and a carton plant during the postwar period.

The company shortened its name to San Miguel Corporation in the early 1960s, and Andrés Soriano, Jr. advanced to the company's presidency upon his father's 1964 death. He has been credited with instituting modern management theory, including decentralization along product lines. Soriano Jr. continued to diversify the food business during the early 1980s, expanding into poultry production in 1982, building an ice cream plant in 1983, adding shrimp processing and freezing in 1984, and adding beef and pork production in 1988.

Over the decades, San Miguel earned a formidable reputation as a fierce competitor. The company used all the tools at its disposal. When it could not beat a rival through traditional means, it acquired and intimidated upstarts into submission. The Filipino government's complicity didn't hurt, either. Long protected by high tariffs, San Miguel encountered its first major competitor in the beer market in the late 1970s. That's when Asia Brewery entered the segment. The rivalry between Asia Brewery and San Miguel came to a head in 1988, when Asia Brewery cannily introduced a bargain-priced "brand" called, simply, "Beer." The imported product looked and tasted like its primary competitor, playing upon the fact that in the Philippines, the San Miguel brand was synonymous with "beer." It was a creative counter to San Miguel's notoriously aggressive and sometimes cutthroat competitive strategy, which had reportedly included "attempts to sabotage [Asia Brewery's] sales network and smash its empty bottles." Asia Brewery, whose owner was reputedly connected to Marcos sympathizers, even hired away San Miguel's brewmaster.

Although San Miguel enjoyed virtual monopolies in its markets, that status did not shield it from the political machinations of the Philippines. The reign of Ferdinand Marcos brought this element into sharp focus in the 1980s, when an intra-familial proxy fight at San Miguel turned political. The dispute was instigated in 1983 by Enrique Zobel, a wealthy cousin of the Sorianos who owned the Ayala banking and real estate group and sided with the Marcos government. Unable to execute a takeover on his own, Zobel sold his 19.5 percent stake to Eduardo Cojuanco, Jr. (known in some circles as "the coconut king"). Although Cojuanco was a cousin of Marcos opponent Corazon Aquino, he too sided with Marcos. Cojuanco's Coconut Industry Investment Fund (a.k.a. United Coconut Planters Bank) accumulated an additional 31 percent of San Miguel, giving him effective control of the conglomerate and leaving the Soriano family with a mere three percent. Cojuanco scooped up the chairmanship in 1984, when Andrés Soriano Jr. died of cancer. But his reign over San Miguel lasted only two years. When Marcos lost the 1986 election to Aquino, Cojuanco and many other Marcos backers fled the country.

Andrés Soriano III resumed San Miguel's chairmanship and launched a campaign to reclaim the family legacy that year. But when the new chairman tried to buy back the abandoned shares,

he was blocked by an unexpected agency; the Aquino administration's Presidential Commission on Good Government (PCGG) assumed control (but not legal ownership) of the 51.4-percent stake and refused to relinquish it. The controlling interest carried nine of San Miguel's 15 directors seats with it. The PCGG continued to tend its San Miguel stake into the early 1990s, but it acceded de facto control of the conglomerate to Andrés Soriano III via a management contract with his A. Soriano Corp.

Soriano III was characterized by *Business Week*'s Maria Shao as an "introverted, almost reclusive" leader. Schooled at the University of Pennsylvania's prestigious Wharton School, Soriano III had dabbled in investment banking in New York City before returning to the Philippines. Soriano tried everything from legal machinations to joint-venture buyout schemes to wrest control of San Miguel from the PCGG, but to no avail.

In 1990, San Miguel threw a five-month party to celebrate its centenary. President Corazon Aquino called San Miguel "the best showcase of a Filipino company, a shining example of creative management and commitment to its public." *The Economist* contrastingly called San Miguel "a showcase for much that is wrong with business in the Philippines." The latter assertion was substantiated that same year, when Cojuanco returned to the Philippines (the *Journal of Commerce* noted that he "sneaked back into the country [in 1990] despite a ban on his return") to lay claim to his holdings. Notwithstanding the circumstances of his repatriation, a November 1992 article in *Asian Business* noted that "Cojuanco [was] expected to win eventually." All the same, Soriano III continued to hold the chairmanship through 1995.

International Expansion in the 1980s and 1990s

Soriano III led the company to a new era of dramatic growth based on internationalization. This move was motivated by a number of factors. First, San Miguel had developed its core Philippine and Hong Kong markets to maturity and was faced with relatively slow growth there. Soriano hoped to expand into other countries and thereby mitigate the effects of the Philippines' unstable economy. Finally, the leader wanted to head off encroaching competition from the world's biggest breweries, namely Anheuser-Busch and Miller of the United States, Kirin of Japan, and BSN of France. In an interview with *Asian Business*' Michael Selwyn, San Miguel President Francisco C. Eizmendi Jr. said that "what we are aiming to do is be a David among the Goliaths of international business, without losing our grip on the local market."

Having determined that overseas growth was imperative, Soriano allocated US$1 billion to a five-year strategic internationalization program that focused on shaping up domestic operations, then progressing to licensing and exporting, overseas production, and finally to distribution of non-beer products. San Miguel's plant modernization plan involved sweeping improvements, from computerization to quality circles. These efforts laid the groundwork that would enable the company to compete with the world's food and beverage multinationals. A subsequent decentralization created a holding company structure with the 18 non-beer operations positioned as subsidiaries. This corporate reorganization freed the spun-off businesses from the bureaucratic shackles of a large conglomerate. In the course of this multifaceted effort to attain optimum efficiency, San Miguel reduced its work force by more than 16 percent, from a 1989 high of 39,138 to 32,832 by 1993. *Asian Business* noted that these programs helped increase profit per employee by 56 percent in 1991 alone.

With its domestic "ducks in a row," San Miguel turned to the next stage in its internationalization, beer licensing, and exporting initiative. Although the company had exported beer for most of its history, this effort was intensified dramatically in the late 1980s. San Miguel's beer exports grew by 150 percent from 1985 to 1989 alone, and the brand was soon exported to 24 countries, including all of Asia's key markets as well as the United States, Australia, and the Middle East. Once the core brand was established in a particular market, San Miguel would begin to create production facilities, sometimes on an independent basis and sometimes in concert with an indigenous joint-venture partner. By 1995, San Miguel had manufacturing plants in Hong Kong, China, Indonesia, Vietnam, Taiwan, and Guam.

Thus, in spite of the overarching quarrel regarding San Miguel's ownership (not to mention other problems endemic to operating in the Philippines), the company's sales quintupled from P12.23 billion in 1986 to P68.43 billion by 1994. The conglomerate's heavy investment in the internationalization program paid off handsomely; net income increased twice as fast, from P1.11 billion to P11.86 billion over the same period. Under the continuing direction of its 44-year-old leader in 1996, San Miguel was well-positioned to take advantage of the dramatic growth forecast for the Asia-Pacific region in the 1990s and beyond.

Principal Subsidiaries

San Miguel International Limited; San Miguel Foods, Inc.; SMC Stock Transfer Service Corporation; Premium Packaging International, Inc.; Packaging Products Corporation; Rightpak International Corporation; Pacific Warehouse Company; SMC Juice, Inc.; Tagbita Silica Industries Corporation; San Miguel Properties Philippines, Inc. (99%); Philippine Breweries Corporation (99%); Monterey Farms Corporation (93%); Coca-Cola Bottlers Philippines, Inc. (70%); La Tondeña Distillers, Inc. (70%); Philippine Dairy Products Corporation (70%); San Miguel Campofrio Corporation (60%); San Miguel Yamamura Asia Corporation (60%); Rizalag Land Company, Inc.; Mindanao Corrugated Fibreboard Inc. (60%); SMC Yamamura Fuso Molds Corporation (60%); San Miguel Yamamura Ball Corporation (60%); Anchor Insurance Brokerage Corporation (58%).

Further Reading

Abueg, Jose Marte, "Soriano Adjusts to Aquino," *Asian Business,* September 1989, p. 6.

Alley, Lindsey, and Thomas Stanley, "San Miguel's Expansion Into Southeast Asia," *Journal of Asian Business,* Summer 1993, pp. 71–92.

Caplen, Brian, "San Miguel Brewery: Brewing Up New Business," *Asian Business,* April 1991, pp. 9–12.

Furukawa, Tsukasa, "Ball Joins Philippine Can Venture," *American Metal Market,* October 20, 1994, p. 5.

Jones, Arthur, "The Philippines," *Forbes,* December 19, 1983, p. 128.

"Mine's a Beer (Patent Pending, All Rights Reserved)," *The Economist,* October 29, 1988, p. 74.

Moore, Hannah, "Battle for San Miguel Brewing in Philippines," *The Journal of Commerce,* March 6, 1991, p. 3A.

"Opéra Bouffe," *The Economist,* April 28, 1990, pp. 72–73.

"The Philippines," *Asiamoney,* July/August 1995, p. 26.

"Returning the Empties," *The Economist,* April 5, 1986, pp. 78–79.

"San Miguel Corporation: A Tradition of Leadership," *Scientific American,* February 1996, p. P22.

Selwyn, Michael, "The Secrets of San Miguel's Sparkle," *Asian Business,* November 1992, pp. 28–30.

——, "Honour Is the Watchword," *Asian Business,* November 1992, pp. 36–37.

Shao, Maria, "Andrés Soriano's Battle for San Miguel," *Business Week,* September 28, 1987, p. 54.

—April Dougal Gasbarre

The Sanwa Bank, Ltd.

1-1 Otemachi, 1-chome
Chiyoda-ku
Tokyo, 100
Japan
(03) 52-52-1111

Public Company
Incorporated: 1933
Employees: 20,480
Total Assets: US$521.31 billion (1994)
Stock Exchanges: Osaka Tokyo Kyoto Frankfurt London
SICs: 6036 Savings Institutions, Not Federally Chartered;
    6081 Branches & Agencies of Foreign Banks; 6159
    Miscellaneous Business Credit Institutions; 6211
    Security Brokers, Dealers & Flotation Companies; 6712
    Offices of Bank Holding Companies; 7359 Equipment
    Rental & Leasing, Not Elsewhere Classified

The Sanwa Bank, Ltd. is the world's most profitable bank and second only to Bank of Tokyo-Mitsubishi Ltd. in terms of total assets. Its surge to the top of the banking world during the mid-1990s has been based on the serious efforts it has made in Japan to contain costs and expand its retail base; expansion into North America in the 1980s; and an early entry into and continued growth of its operations in the nascent economies of Asia. The company's long-term goal is to become the leading universal bank in the world.

Few other companies in the world have histories as long as Sanwa's. The product of a merger in 1933, Sanwa's principal predecessor was the Konoike Bank. The Konoike family enterprise began in 1656 and built a considerable fortune brewing sake. This fortune financed a number of other ventures, most notably a shipping operation. Additional capital generated by these businesses was later used to start a money exchange whose principal business was lending.

Although Japan remained isolated from the world for the next two centuries and commerce there remained limited by traditional practices, the Konoike money exchange gained prominence in the Osaka region. After Japan's opening to the world in 1868, the government sponsored an ambitious industrialization campaign that brought about a modernization of the banking industry. The Konoike money exchange was awarded a national banking charter in 1877. Over the next several decades, Konoike profited from an expansion in personal income and from the growth of small and medium-sized companies.

Konoike was a small city bank, especially compared to banks affiliated with the *zaibatsu* conglomerates. It did not engage in foreign activities, even when Japanese commercial interests were extended to Taiwan, Korea, and Manchuria. And although the bank benefited indirectly from Japan's modernization, it suffered indirectly from financial shocks and recessions caused by government economic mismanagement and uneven industrial development.

In the early 1930s, the bank began to lose ground to the *zaibatsu* banks, which were closely linked to the rapidly expanding heavy-industry sector. In order to remain competitive, the Konoike Bank merged with the Yamaguchi Bank and the Sanjushi Bank in 1933. After the merger the new entity, based in Osaka and tied to textile production and other light industries, took the name Sanwa (*san* meaning "three," *wa* meaning "harmony").

The Sanwa Bank had the largest deposits of any Japanese commercial bank. Still, since it was not directly involved in large-scale industrial finance or overseas investments, Sanwa avoided direct confrontation with the militarists who rose to power in the early 1930s. Only after Japan went to war with the United States in 1941 did Sanwa become part of the government's centralization plan: between 1942 and 1945 Sanwa absorbed an affiliated trust company and several more local banks. When the war ended, however, Sanwa was forced to sell many of its operations under terms established by the occupation authority. Several operations were spun off, leaving the original "harmonious three."

Most of the largest Japanese banks after the war were former *zaibatsu* affiliates (although the *zaibatsu* were officially outlawed, the independent companies they were divided into continued to maintain close relationships with each other). These banks provided much of the financing for large industries. Sanwa, however, was never affiliated with any one industrial group, and in many cases was seen as a competitor not just of the *zaibatsu* banks, but also of the large industrial companies they were affiliated with. As a result, the bank continued to concentrate on individual banking and the financing of small businesses, most of which were not involved in war production, and so survived the war relatively undamaged.

In 1953 Sanwa adopted a green clover-like symbol as its logo and opened its first overseas office, in San Francisco, in anticipation of the needs of Japanese exporters.

As a growing city bank with a solid account base, Sanwa had greater success winning large corporate accounts. With loans to companies in steel production, shipbuilding, automobile manufacture, and petrochemicals, Sanwa became directly linked to Japanese heavy industry. Japan's first period of export-led growth, from 1955 to 1965, depended heavily on the development of basic industries. As these industries grew, Sanwa not only recovered its loans, but won further business and, as an investment partner, grew with its clients.

Sanwa redoubled its effort to expand in international banking and, studying the Bank of America as a model, mapped out a strategy for growth in the retail sector. It also moved its center of activity from Osaka to the more dynamic Tokyo. Of the three "Osaka banks" (the others being Sumitomo and Daiwa), Sanwa was most successful in exploiting the growth of the Tokyo market.

In 1959 Sanwa sold its trust operations to the Toyo Trust and Banking Company. The sale was not required by industrial decentralization laws, but was made simply to permit Sanwa to focus its attention on two new financial products: credit cards and leases. It founded the Japan Credit Bureau, or JCB, in 1961, and established Orient Leasing in 1964. Both of these subsidiaries later became the leaders in their markets in Japan.

The bank's growth during the 1960s was characterized by conservative management and avoidance of high-risk investments. It also benefited early from computerization and "near-banking" activities. Its one notable loss came from its involvement with financially troubled Maruzen Oil, an industry in which Sanwa had little experience. Overall, Sanwa's expansion paralleled the rapid growth of the Japanese economy.

Sanwa turned its attention to building an international network during the 1970s. With offices in London, Sydney, Singapore, and Hong Kong, the bank served its clients' needs in a new way. Japanese industry had evolved to a position from which it not only traded in goods, but exported production capacity to less expensive operating environments—particularly in textiles.

The bank entered a new phase of development in the United States in 1972 when it established the Sanwa Bank of California. This subsidiary later acquired the Charter Bank and the Golden State Bank, both in southern California, and in 1978 changed its name to Golden State Sanwa Bank. Continuing its expansion in California—the world's sixth-largest economy— the bank acquired the First City Bank of Rosemead in 1981.

Sanwa's 1980s activities in the United States peaked in 1986 with the acquisition of Lloyds Bank California for US$263 million. With the deal, Sanwa became the first Japanese bank to acquire a major U.S. bank. Sanwa, meanwhile, opened offices in New York, Chicago, Atlanta, Dallas, Boston, Los Angeles, Toronto, and Vancouver.

As lending and other traditional banking operations became less profitable during the 1980s, Sanwa moved even further into predominantly fee-based near-banking services, notably leasing. In 1984 it acquired a leasing subsidiary from Continental Illinois Bank for US$500 million, one of the largest Japanese takeovers to that date. Within the first four years following the takeover, the renamed Sanwa Business Credit Corporation— which was involved in vendor leasing and corporate, commercial, and direct finance—doubled its business volume to US$1.2 billion. Also in 1984, Sanwa entered into a joint venture with Germany's Dresdner Bank and the Bank of China to form China Universal Leasing Co., Ltd., which became the largest bank-affiliated leasing company in China. Additional leasing operations were subsequently established in Jakarta, Bangkok, Singapore, Kuala Lumpur, and other Asian cities.

The year 1984 was also a key one for Sanwa in terms of its overall management philosophy. That year the bank shifted its primary emphasis from asset growth to increased profits, in fact setting a goal of becoming the world's most profitable bank. In addition to tightening controls on costs, through cuts in the work force and other strategies, Sanwa shifted its lending practices even more in the favor of small and medium-sized businesses, generally considered less risky than large corporations. By 1988, 73 percent of the bank's loans went to smaller corporations.

In 1988 Sanwa's president, Hiroshi Watanabe, initiated another major philosophical change when he scrapped what he considered the wishy-washy aim of becoming known as "the people's bank" of Japan. Rather, Watanabe preferred a more concrete goal and settled on becoming "the global leader in universal banking."

In Sanwa's initial efforts at reaching this lofty goal, its most important actions occurred in Japan and elsewhere in Asia. In its home market, Sanwa had a relatively weak standing in retail banking, with, for example, only 79 branches and subbranches in Tokyo in 1988 compared with at least 140 each for its major rivals. Rather than acquiring smaller banks—as some of Sanwa's competitors did to their later regret after purchasing troubled banks—Sanwa concentrated on setting up an extensive automated teller machine (ATM) network, which grew to number 653 by 1994. At the same time that this filled the bank's need for retail banking outlets, it also meshed nicely with Sanwa's emphasis on profits since 20 ATMs could be set up for the same cost as just one branch, and the employeeless ATMs were much cheaper to operate. Sanwa also pioneered in such profit-smart areas as electronic banking. And, although its desire to expand into financial services was frustrated by the slow pace of deregulation in Japan, Sanwa established a securities operation there in 1994 and a trust business in 1995.

Perhaps even more important for Sanwa in the long run was the bank's aggressive moves into other Asian markets during the late 1980s and early 1990s. Always the innovator, Sanwa established a branch in Shenzhen in 1986, becoming the first Japanese commercial bank to enter China. True to its roots, Sanwa's overall strategy in China and elsewhere in Asia was to focus on banking services for small and medium-sized companies, which proved particularly successful in Hong Kong. By 1994, Sanwa's Asian operations included 18 offices in China and Hong Kong; 18 more elsewhere in Asia; the Shanghai International Finance Company Limited, a joint venture in merchant banking; and its various leasing operations.

Sanwa's aggressive international expansion had decreased its dependence on the domestic market to a level below that of any of its rivals. In 1994, 32 percent of its revenues and 27 percent of its profits originated outside Japan. Sanwa also weathered Japan's lending crisis and economic recession of the early 1990s much better than other Japanese banks, and moved briefly to the top spot in worldwide banking in 1995 in terms of assets (the 1996 merger of Bank of Tokyo and Mitsubishi Bank pushed Sanwa down to number two). More important to Sanwa's overall goal, however, the bank was also able to achieve the top spot in banking profitability in 1995, posting pretax profits of US$572 million.

Heading into the end of the 1990s, Sanwa was not yet the world leader in universal banking, and observers noted weaknesses particularly in Europe. Still, with rapid growth projected throughout Asia for the foreseeable future and Sanwa far ahead of its rivals in these markets, Sanwa was well-positioned to maintain a position near the top of world banking into the 21st century.

Principal Subsidiaries

JCB Co., Ltd.; Sanwa Business Finance Co., Ltd.; Sanwa Capital Co., Ltd.; Sanwa Capital Management Co., Ltd.; Sanwa Card Services Co., Ltd.; The Sanwa Credit Co., Ltd.; Sanwa Factors Ltd.; Sanwa Network Services Corp.; Sanwa Research Institute Corp.; Sanwa Systems Development Co., Ltd.; Sanwa Australia Finance Limited; Sanwa Australia Limited; Banco Bradesco S.A. (Brazil); Sanwa Bank Canada; Sanwa McCarthy Securities Limited (Canada); China Universal Leasing Co., Ltd.; Shanghai International Finance Company Limited (China); Sanwa Bank (Deutschland) AG (Germany); Sanwa Leasing (Deutschland) GmbH (Germany); Sanwa-DSP Credit Limited (Hong Kong); Sanwa Financial Products Co., L.P. Hong Kong; Sanwa International Finance Limited (Hong Kong); P.T. Inter-Pacific Bank (Indonesia); P.T. Inter-Pacific Securities (Indonesia); P.T. Sanwa-BRI Finance (Indonesia); P.T. Sanwa Indonesia Bank; Sanwa International (Ireland) PLC; Korea Development Leasing Corporation; Commerce International Merchant Bankers Berhad (Malaysia); Rizal Commercial Banking Corporation (Philippines); Banco Portugues de Investimento, S.A. (Portugal); Sanwa Futures (Singapore) PTE Limited; Sanwa Singapore Limited; Sanwa Bank (Schweiz) AG (Switzerland); Bangkok International Banking Facility (Thailand); The Siam Sanwa Industrial Credit Co., Ltd. (Thailand); The Siam Sanwa Trilease Co., Ltd. (Thailand); Sanwa Business Credit (UK) Limited; Sanwa Financial Products (UK) Co. Ltd.; Sanwa Financial Services Limited (U.K.); Sanwa International plc (U.K.); Liberty Bank (U.S.); Sanwa Bank California (U.S.); Sanwa Bank Trust Company of New York (U.S.); Sanwa Financial Products Co., L.P. (U.S.); Sanwa Futures L.L.C. (U.S.); Sanwa General Equipment Leasing (U.S.); Sanwa Leasing Corp. (U.S.); Sanwa Securities (USA) Co., L.P.

Further Reading

Eisenstodt, Gale, "Good News for U.S. Banks," *Forbes*, December 10, 1990, pp. 84, 88.
Hirsh, Michael, "Why Sanwa Leads the Pack," *Institutional Investor*, February 1994, pp. 155–58.
Holyoke, Larry, and William Glasgall, "The Japanese Bank that Knows How to Hustle," *Business Week*, May 30, 1994, p. 117.
Kraus, James R., "Sanwa Bank Revving Up for Growth in U.S. Market," *American Banker*, January 27, 1995, p. 5.
"More Pain," *Economist*, May 9, 1992, pp. 105–06.
Read, Richard, "Crossing the Tracks to Success," *Euromoney*, June 1988, pp. 177–80.
"Sanwa Avoids the Japanese Sickness," *Asian Business*, October 1993, p. 64.
Sender, Henny, "Japan's California Comeuppance," *Institutional Investor*, December 1991, p. 125.
Sunahara, Kazuo, *Za banku: saisentan o hiraku Sanwa-man*, Tokyo: Sankei Shuppan, 1983, 245 p.

—updated by David E. Salamie

Sara Lee Corporation

**Three First National Plaza
Chicago, Illinois 60602-4260
U.S.A.
(312) 726-2600
Fax: (312) 726-3712**

Public Company
Incorporated: 1941 as C.D. Kenny Company
Employees: 149,000
Sales: $17.72 billion (1995)
Stock Exchanges: New York Midwest Pacific London
    Amsterdam Paris Zurich Geneva Basel
SICs: 2011 Meat Packing Plants; 2013 Sausage & Other
    Prepared Meats; 2053 Frozen Baking Products,
    Except Bread; 2095 Roasted Coffee; 2251 Women's
    Full-Length & Knee-Length Hosiery; 2253 Knit
    Outerwear Mills; 2842 Specialty Cleaning, Polishing
    & Sanitation Preparations; 2844 Perfumes, Cosmetics
    & Other Toilet Preparations; 5142 Packaged Frozen
    Foods; 5147 Meats & Meat Products

Sara Lee Corporation is a leading global manufacturer and marketer of brand-name consumer packaged goods within four major business areas: packaged meats and bakery, coffee and grocery, household and personal care, and personal products. Within packaged meats and bakery, a predominantly U.S.-oriented operation, Sara Lee holds a leading position in the U.S. retail packaged meat market through such brands as Hillshire Farm, Ball Park, and Jimmy Dean; is number one in U.S. retail frozen baked goods (the flagship Sara Lee brand); and operates the third-largest full-line foodservice company in the country. The primarily European coffee and grocery operations are led by the Douwe Egberts coffee brand and Pickwick tea, and enjoy number one or number two positions in retail roasted coffee in several European countries. The household and personal care area includes shoe care and body care products and insecticides and is Sara Lee's most global business. Active mainly in Europe and North America, Sara Lee's personal products businesses include leading brands of hosiery, bras, panties, activewear, and underwear under such brands as Bali, Champion, Dim, Hanes, Hanes Her Way, L'eggs, Playtex undergarments, and the Wonderbra. Although seemingly disparate, most Sara Lee products would be considered staples, helping insulate the company from the effects of economic cycles. Sara Lee has manufacturing operations in nearly 40 countries and sells its products in more than 140 countries.

Formally organized in 1939, what is now the Sara Lee Corporation spent the next three decades under the direction of founder Nathan Cummings. Although he retired from active management of the company in 1968, Cummings remained the largest stockholder until his death in 1985, when Sara Lee bought back 1.8 million common shares from his estate.

Born in Canada in 1896, Cummings began his career in his father's shoe store. By 1917 he had built his own shoe manufacturing firm. Cummings's enterprise eventually expanded into a successful importer of general merchandise. This venture allowed him to purchase a small biscuit and candy company, which he later sold at a profit.

In 1939, at the age of 43, Cummings borrowed $5.2 million to buy the C.D. Kenny Company, a wholesale distributor of sugar, coffee, and tea established in 1870. The Baltimore-based company represented Cummings's first entry into U.S. markets, and he sought to increase the number of Kenny-label products.

Cummings broadened his geographic scope in 1942 with the purchase of Sprague, Warner & Company, a distributor of canned and packaged food nationwide. Under the established Richelieu label, sales came to $19 million that year, allowing Cummings to begin a significant expansion through acquisition, a strategy the company has consistently pursued.

After several smaller acquisitions, in 1945 Cummings acquired Reid, Murdoch and Company, the producer of the nationally recognized Monarch label. After this acquisition, the C.D. Kenny Company changed its name to the Consolidated Grocers Corporation, and in 1946 Consolidated made its first public stock offering. The Monarch purchase boosted sales to $123 million in 1946.

Smaller food companies struggled through a difficult period in the late 1950s and early 1960s as operational expenses and competition increased—continual development of new products and large promotional budgets were typically the only way to keep shelf space in supermarkets. But small companies offered their already-established brands to a large company like Consolidated, saving the cost of internal development. By 1970, Cummings had supervised the purchase of more than 90 companies by pursuing family-owned businesses who consented to mergers.

In 1951 Consolidated consisted of more than a dozen companies, and in 1953 sales passed $200 million. They did not remain that high for very long, however. Sales in 1954, the year Consolidated Grocers changed its name to Consolidated Foods, dropped to $133 million. Sales fell another $15 million the following year, when after-tax profits were only slightly above $1 million and earnings per common share fell almost 40 percent.

Cummings met these losses with further diversification. The Kitchens of Sara Lee, a five-year-old maker of frozen baked goods with annual sales of $9 million, was acquired in 1956 for 164,890 shares—not Consolidated's biggest purchase to date, but eventually a significant one. A slightly larger purchase of 34 Piggly Wiggly supermarkets marked Consolidated's first venture into food retailing. An even larger purchase, of the Omaha Cold Store Company, demonstrated Consolidated's preference for distribution and marketing operations rather than direct-to-consumer sales.

Consolidated continued a rapid acquisition pace into the 1960s with Shasta beverages and the Eagle Supermarket chain in 1961. L.H. Parke Company, Michigan Fruit Canners, and Monarch Food Ltd. of Toronto together added $35 million in sales for 1962. The corporation first went international in 1960 by buying a controlling interest in a Venezuelan vinegar company; a second foreign investment came in 1962, with the purchase of Jonker Fris, a Dutch canner. Although growth was rapid, analysts considered Consolidated stock a risk since dividend increases depended on purchases.

During the 1960s recently acquired Booth Fisheries reported a 16 percent rise in sales volume for 1962, up to $56.6 million. By following the industry trend toward packaging seafood for the convenience market, Booth Fisheries fought off fish shortages and normally unstable prices, raising division earnings from $2.35 per share to $3.22.

In 1966 Consolidated agreed to a Federal Trade Commission (FTC) order to spin off its supermarket division within three years, principally its Piggly Wiggly and Eagle supermarket chains. This agreement came as a surprise to analysts, because the industry expected leniency from the FTC due to the high cost of small-scale food production and distribution. But Consolidated Foods President William Howlett publicly welcomed the agreement, stating that Consolidated no longer wished to compete at the retail level with its other customers. And Consolidated still kept its convenience retail outlets such as Lawson Milk, purchased in 1960.

As Cummings prepared for retirement, Consolidated searched for a larger share of European and American markets.

New production facilities were planned for Shasta and Sara Lee in 1964, tripling the latter's output, and sales that year topped $600 million. In 1966, Consolidated made two more important food purchases: Kahn's Meats and Idaho Frozen Foods.

Between 1964 and 1967, Consolidated made eight of its first nonfood acquisitions, including Oxford Chemical Corporation, a maker of cleaning products; Abbey Rents, a home furnishings company; Electrolux vacuum cleaners; and the Fuller Brush Company. Consolidated also entered the apparel industry when it purchased Gant shirts and several other clothing makers during this period. Within five years, nonfood businesses comprised 50 percent of the company's profits. William Howlett became Cummings's successor in 1968, but Cummings remained a director, and the largest shareholder, until his death. Howlett left two years later due to disagreements with the founding director. Despite the turbulence of the decade, sales tripled and after-tax earnings increased fivefold.

William A. Buzick Jr. became president in 1970, beginning a difficult decade for the corporation; by 1980, the selling price for a common share was almost 40 percent lower than 1970's purchase price. Although sales continued to rise, as the leader in the trend toward diversification, Consolidated soon discovered the drawbacks of the strategy as well. Consolidated's profits rose only 4 percent from 1972 to 1973—the year sales hit $2 billion—compared to an industry average of 17 percent. Sales continued to rise in 1974, but earnings dropped for the first time in 19 years as nonfood business did poorly.

During Buzick's five-year reign, Consolidated sold many of its food distribution businesses and production facilities. Buzick also increased the company's commitment to nonfood products with the purchase of Max Klein, Inc., a Philadelphia-based clothing company and Erdal (later Intradal), a Dutch personal care products company.

Nonfood activity peaked in 1975 as durable goods provided almost two-thirds of corporate profits. The diversification was prompted in part by the company's belief that federal restraints on the food industry would continue. In addition, economic constraints made Consolidated's growth goals difficult to achieve as only a food company. Under President Richard Nixon's economic-stabilization program of 1973, for instance, Sara Lee was allowed to raise prices on frozen baked goods only 6.35 percent; Consolidated had requested a 7.52 percent hike. Moving into nonfood businesses would make the corporation less dependent on federal decisions and less vulnerable to the antitrust suits that had impeded competitors.

Buzick left in 1975 and John H. Bryan became president. Bryan's family-owned business, Bryan Brothers Packing, was a 1968 Consolidated purchase. Bryan quickly sold more than 50 companies, most of which were smaller acquisitions made in the early 1970s. Fuller Brush and four furniture companies were singled out as problem units and divested. Earnings recovered the following year to $77.5 million, and Consolidated's operating margin returned to 7.6 percent.

Bryan continued to value nonfood sales, however. For the next ten years, nonfood products continued to make up more than 50 percent of corporate income but only 30 percent of total sales. Purchases during the 1980s continued the trend toward solidifying durable goods production.

Bryan's acquisition portfolio represented a more aggressive stance in all of its markets. Before the 1978 purchase of Douwe Egberts, a Dutch coffee, tea, and tobacco producer, only 11 percent of Consolidated's income came from abroad; by 1989 it made up nearly 30 percent. In 1979 Consolidated completed a hostile takeover of the Hanes Corporation, a family-owned undergarment manufacturer.

Despite difficulties—poor performance of some nonfood companies led to earnings losses in 1974 and 1975—Consolidated's performance excelled by the end of the 1970s. Between 1967 and 1973, sales doubled to $2 billion and total assets topped $1 billion. These figures allowed the company to set a goal of doubling sales volume by 1980; the actual amount achieved exceeded $5 billion.

Bryan's initial management goals were to keep the company diversified and decentralized, while keeping the corporate office responsible for financial control and strategic planning. Acquisition targets would be brands with leading market shares in new areas and "integrating acquisitions"—large companies with established brands in Consolidated's markets. Hillshire Farm meats and Chef Pierre pies fell into the latter category, and were purchased in the late 1970s, building on Consolidated's meat and pastry market shares.

In 1985 Consolidated announced that it would change its name to Sara Lee Corporation. The name was chosen because it was the corporation's most prominent brand name, and as a corporate name would give the company higher visibility and make advertising efforts more cost effective.

The first of two major foreign acquisitions came in 1985 when Nicholas Kiwi Ltd.'s foreign subsidiaries were purchased for $330 million, in addition to 14 percent of its Australian domestic operations. Kiwi—seller of a variety of shoe care products, medicines, cleaners, and cosmetics—complemented Intradal, Sara Lee's Dutch subsidiary. Akzo, a Dutch conglomerate with annual sales of $720 million, was acquired in 1987 for approximately $600 million, the company's largest purchase ever. Another producer of household goods, Akzo was absorbed into Douwe Egberts and Kiwi. By mid-1987, just nine years since its first international venture, Sara Lee was among the largest U.S. multinationals, with foreign revenue reaching almost $2 billion, making up 24.1 percent of total sales, 26.8 percent of profits, and 40.5 percent of total corporate assets.

Although still very active in acquisitions, Bryan also drew praise for stressing internal product development. Return on total investment typically decreases in the wake of large purchases, but Bryan kept return on equity above 20 percent in nearly every year since 1985. This was especially unusual for a company whose growth was almost entirely through acquisition—96 percent of Sara Lee's 141 entries into new businesses were through acquisition between 1950 and 1986.

Bryan was responsible for easing the uncertainty of the 1970s, shifting the company's focus to the marketing of consumer products only. He also improved manufacturing efficiency and product development. In 1986 sales dropped from $8.1 billion to $7.9 billion, yet income increased $17 million. Domestic consumer and institutional food divisions reported the largest sales drop, as Shasta, Idaho Frozen Foods, and Union Sugar were divested and Popsicle was restructured and eventually divested. Bryan also introduced lower-priced items to complement the corporation's premium Sara Lee and Hanes labels. Bryan hoped, with this tactic, to improve total sales volume as successfully as the meat division had done in the past. In 1989 the company began the divestiture of its food-service operations, then its poorest-performing division.

During the early 1990s Sara Lee continued to grow through acquisition and increased its market presence abroad. During the first three years of the decade, it spent more than $1.7 billion in adding a variety of properties to the Sara Lee stable, including Playtex undergarments; Brylcreem; Mark Cross leather goods; hosiery companies in France (Dim S.A.), Spain (Sans, S.A.), Italy (Filodoro) and the United Kingdom (Pretty Polly Limited); the consumer food group of BP Nutrition; and Smith-Kline Beecham's European bath and body care business.

Perhaps most significant among these purchases was Playtex. Coupled with such existing holdings as Bali, the acquisition of Playtex gave Sara Lee a commanding presence in the intimate apparel market in the United States, with overall market share of more than 31 percent and market share in some niche areas surpassing 65 percent. Although some competitors expressed concerns about the monopolistic nature of the combination, they made little headway with the free marketers of the Bush administration.

Ironically, Sara Lee's spending spree within another area—hosiery—quickly came back to haunt the company. A combination of several factors converged to lead to declining hosiery sales starting in late 1992. In the midst of a recession in Europe, the newly acquired hosiery units in France, Spain, and the United Kingdom experienced increasing competitive pressure. Sara Lee also erred in replacing the managers of the firms with U.S. personnel not as familiar with the local markets. Most importantly, both in Europe and the United States, the company failed to recognize quickly enough the trend toward more casual attire both at the office and for social events, and, therefore, the resultant decreased demand for formal hosiery. Since hosiery comprised 25 percent of overall apparel sales, the decrease in hosiery sales presented a significant challenge. In response, Sara Lee quickly moved to decrease hosiery capacity by closing two U.S. plants, cutting capacity at a third, and closing a plant in France. Sara Lee's apparel division was also realigned into a more flattened organizational structure.

Leading the way in these efforts was newly appointed president Cornelius Boonstra. A 20-year Sara Lee veteran with a strong background in operations, Boonstra provoked some disenchantment with his aggressive cost-cutting measures, which included reducing staff in the Chicago headquarters by ten percent. Although praised by Wall Street for the cuts, several senior managers left Sara Lee soon after his appointment and continuing friction with other executives led to his resignation in early 1994 after only six months in the job. No one was immediately appointed to succeed him.

In another irony, in June 1994 Sara Lee announced a major restructuring of its European personal products operations, which included cuts much more severe than those imposed by Boonstra. The company took a $732 million charge mainly to reduce capacity in its hosiery operations. Several more plants were closed and more than 8,000 jobs were cut.

Rebounding from the difficult restructuring year of 1994, Sara Lee enjoyed record sales of $17.71 billion (a 14 percent increase over 1994) and record operating income of $1.6 billion in fiscal 1995, with 12 Sara Lee brands racking up sales in excess of $250 million. For the year, 40 percent of Sara Lee's sales and 45 percent of its operating income were generated from its operations abroad.

Under Bryan's leadership, Sara Lee had enjoyed tremendous growth fueled by aggressive and targeted acquisitions, which were integrated into a highly decentralized organizational structure. When faced with difficulties, the company was able to respond quickly enough to prevent lasting damage to the firm's reputation or financial health. The potential for growth of this well-managed company into the next century seemed promising, and Bryan intended to base it on five strategies: building brands; lowering production costs and keeping them low; making further strategic and complementary acquisitions; investing in high-margin, value-added products; and increasing non-U.S. operations, particularly those in developing countries.

Principal Subsidiaries

Sara Lee Holdings (Australia); Canadelle, Inc. (Canada); Giltex Hosiery (Canada); Merrild Kaffe (Denmark); Dim S.A. (France); Sara Lee Personal Products Europe (France); Vatter (Germany); Sara Lee Corp.-Asia (Hong Kong); Compack Douwe Egberts RT (Hungary); Filodoro (Italy); Maglificio Bellia S.p.A. (Italy); Playtex - Europe (Italy); Nihon Sara Lee K.K. (Japan); Upxon, Inc. (Japan); Estelar SA de CV (Mexico); House of Fuller, S.A. de C.V. (Mexico); Kir Alimentos, S.A. de C.V. (Mexico; joint venture); Manufacturas Mallorca S.A. (Mexico); Rinbros, S.A. (Mexico); Sara Lee Knit Products-Mexico; Kortman Intradal (Netherlands); Sara Lee/DE (Netherlands); Sara Lee Processed Meats-Europe (Netherlands); Intercon Garments, Inc. (Philippines); Sara Lee/DA Asia (Singapore); Avroy Shlain Cosmetics (Pty.) Ltd. (South Africa); Kiwi Brands South Africa Playtex - South Africa; South African Hosiery Company Ltd.; Cruz Verde-Legrain (Spain); Sans, S.A. (Spain); Kitchens

of Sara Lee - U.K.; Pretty Polly Limited (U.K.); Sara Lee Household & Personal Care-U.K.; Nuvo (Uruguay).

Principal Divisions

Adams-Millis; Aris Isotoner; Bali Company; Bessin; Bil Mar Foods; Bryan Foods; Champion Products; Coach; Douwe Egberts Coffee Systems Americas; Gallo/Galileo Salame; Hanes Hosiery; Hillshire Farm & Kahn's; Hygrade Food Products; International Baking Co.; Jimmy Dean Foods; Jogbra, Inc.; King Cotten Foods; Kiwi Brands North America; L'eggs Products; Mark Cross; Playtex Apparel; PYA/Monarch; Sara Lee Bakery North America; Sara Lee Bakery Worldwide; Sara Lee Direct; Sara Lee Hosiery; Sara Lee Intimates; Sara Lee Knit Products; Sara Lee Meats; Sara Lee Personal Products; Scotch Maid; Seitz Foods; Spring City Knitting; State Fair Foods; Superior Coffee and Foods; Sweet Sue Kitchens; Wolferman's, Inc.

Principal Operating Units

Sara Lee Packaged Meats and Bakery; Sara Lee Coffee and Grocery; Sara Lee Household and Personal Care; Sara Lee Personal Products.

Further Reading

Byrne, Harlan S., "Sara Lee Corp.," *Barron's*, October 12, 1992, p. 51.

Crown, Judith, "He Didn't Do Things Like Sara Lee: Cost-Cutting, Style Led to Boonstra's Quick Exit," *Crain's Chicago Business*, January 10, 1994, p. 3.

"Designs on Europe's Knickers: Sara Lee," *Economist*, November 14, 1992, p. 86.

Gallagher, Patricia, "Sara Lee's Track Record Has a $732-Mil. Run in It," *Crain's Chicago Business*, June 13, 1994.

Melcher, Richard A., "Sara Lee Isn't Exactly Cooking," *Business Week*, January 24, 1994.

Morgello, Clem, "John Bryan of Sara Lee Corp.: A Winning Global Strategy," *Institutional Investor*, May 1992, p. 17.

Our Corporate History, Chicago: Sara Lee Corporation, 1986.

Weiner, Steve, "How Do You Say L'eggs in French?," *Forbes*, November 27, 1989, p. 73.

Weiner, Steve, "On the Road to Eastern Europe," *Forbes*, December 10, 1990, p. 193.

Zweig, Phillip L., "Aris Doesn't Fit Sara Lee Like a Glove Anymore," *Business Week*, September 18, 1995.

—updated by David E. Salamie

Science Applications
International Corporation

An Employee-Owned Company

Science Applications International Corporation

10260 Campus Point Drive
San Diego, California 92121
U.S.A.
(619) 546-6000
Fax: (619) 546-6634

Private Company
Incorporated: 1969
Employees: 19,000
Sales: $1.9 billion (1995)
SICs: 7374 Computer Processing & Data Preparation &
Processing Services; 8731 Commercial Physical
Research; 8732 Commercial Economic, Sociological,
& Educational Research

Science Applications International Corporation is a leading U.S. specialty technology company. Its activities have traditionally been related primarily to the defense industry, but the organization also develops technology and provides research for a wide range of environmental, security, data processing, transportation, and other applications. The unique enterprise boasts a long track record of success as a high-tech hothouse and brain trust. Science Applications has played a pivotal role in the development of many of the technologies that have made the U.S. defense complex the most advanced in the world. From atomic weapons systems designed in the 1970s to the Strategic Defense Initiative (SDI or ''Star Wars'') launched in the 1980s, the company has supplied important brain power. Largely because of its focus on defense, but also because it is has always been privately owned, Science Applications has traditionally operated as a very secretive, low-profile company that shunned publicity and diffused little information about its operations or activities. Only since the late 1980s, when it began to diversify away from the defense sector, did the organization gradually allow greater public exposure.

Science Applications was founded in 1969 by Dr. J. Robert Beyster, a nuclear physicist. Beyster was working at General Atomic Co. (later called GA Technologies Inc.) before he jumped ship to establish his own venture. He and a team of about 20 employees managed to generate revenues from research and development contracts during their first year of about $250,000. Beyster and his associates would parlay that early success into a $1 billion-plus company with thousands of employees around the world by the 1980s. Although little is known about the specifics of the company's early projects, it is clear that its technological expertise was sought by U.S. defense and energy establishments. For two decades after the startup, in fact, Science Applications' stock price rose at an impressive compound annual rate of 27 percent.

Beyster attributed his company's stunning growth during the 1970s and 1980s to a simple set of management principles to which he adhered: hire the smartest people; give employees authority and a voice in company operations; build business in areas where the company is most capable; and get out of areas where the company is weak. That guiding philosophy had evolved over time, as Beyster observed his competitors and labored to avoid the pitfalls that brought them down. Specifically, Beyster noted that many companies in high-tech industries languished after following the traditional route of attracting venture capital and then taking the company public by selling stock in the market.

Beyster saw that those companies, after going public, typically suffered a loss of talent, because the entrepreneurial atmosphere that had attracted that talent was effectively obliterated by the oppressive influence of outside investors. Thus, he decided early to resist the temptation of outside investment. Beyster was able to get financial backing during the startup from a local lending manager at Bank of America in La Jolla, California. In addition, Science Application raised about $200,000 in capital through a private placement of stock, a move that Beyster later regretted. He learned from the experience and later bought back all of the shares for a pricey $2 million. ''I began to learn, if you don't need the money, it's much better to have the equity stand in the hands of the people of the company,'' Beyster remarked.

Thus, an important element of Science Application's strategy became its compensation system, whereby employees were granted ownership in the company, in addition to salaries and benefits. Beyster started out using the compensation system to reward people who brought in new business. He soon realized that he could also use the system to motivate engineers, technicians, secretaries, and others. Every quarter, employees were rewarded, according to their performance, with the opportunity to buy more stock in the company. The net result was that all of the company's employees had a vested interested in the performance of the overall organization and were therefore willing to work to ensure its success.

In addition to giving talented employees a reason to stay at the company (they had to sell their stock if they quit), Beyster profited by adhering to a philosophy of employee empowerment that would become the hallmark of the top management gurus beginning in the mid-1980s. Science Applications became a company made up almost entirely of engineers and technicians, having no marketing department or outside sales force, and only a thin top layer of management. The lack of a traditional management structure forced employees to become their own bosses and create their own profit centers. They basically had to find and bring jobs into the company, and then organize and complete the projects. One employee described the company as "a farmers market with central heat," meaning that Science Applications supplied the financial, administrative, and management support, while individuals and groups within the company autonomously operated their own ventures.

By the early 1980s Science Applications was generating about $300 million in annual sales and capturing healthy profits. Sales jumped to $420 million in 1985—a 19 percent gain over the previous year—and net income grew to $14.5 million. Those gains were partly the result of increased spending by the Federal Government, particularly on defense. Indeed, in 1985 Science Applications was garnering nearly 90 percent of its total revenue from federal contracts and about two-thirds just from the Department of Defense. By category, the company's projects were roughly broken down into national security (65 percent of company sales), energy (15 percent), and environmental protection (ten percent), with miscellaneous projects accounting for the remainder of sales.

Science Applications' growth by the mid-1980s was impressive, particularly given the fact that it was primarily a service company that developed, rather than manufactured, technology. The company did produce a few products. It built some high-tech military items like a personal computer adapted for battlefield use, and even tried to sell shrink-wrapped software products in the consumer market (the effort failed partly because of a weak marketing and distribution system). But its emphasis was on the research, design, and development of cutting-edge systems and software for clients ranging from the Central Intelligence Agency to the Department of Energy.

Examples of projects for which Science Applications had been hired included the design of nuclear submarines and subsystems, research into artificial intelligence, nuclear energy systems, and the locating and construction of toxic waste disposal sites. Among the company's biggest contracts by the mid-1980s was the $191 million job of packaging an electronic warfare

system for an undisclosed foreign navy. Illustrating the wide scope of the organization's activities was its contract to design the yacht that American Dennis Connor sailed to victory to recapture the America's Cup. Science Applications designed and tested more than 40 scale models of 12-meter ship hulls before settling on the design for the famed *Stars & Stripes.*

Among the more intriguing projects with which Science Applications was involved were a bevy of high-tech, futuristic undertakings reminiscent of James Bond techno-frills. For example, the company operated a Soviet studies institute in Denver, Colorado, that was designed to aid the Pentagon in developing war strategies and plans. Various endeavors at the center included the research of military uses for the Arctic, designing a flight simulator for the B-1B bomber, and developing a space/air craft (the transatmospheric vehicle) that could fly along the fringes of space and reach any point on the globe within 90 minutes.

While Beyster's simple operating strategy was still producing stellar results in the mid-1980s, he realized that the organization was going to have to adapt if it was going to succeed in the late 1980s and 1990s. Part of the change was being forced by the evolving nature of some federal contracts, which were becoming larger in scope. For example, the massive Star Wars project, for which Science Applications was hired, required that the company suspend its entrepreneurial team approach and bring together several groups to work in a more structured environment. To that end, Beyster felt the need to add a new chief financial officer and a controller to the executive ranks, and to focus on developing more skilled managers that could oversee huge projects.

Furthermore, Beyster realized that the company's system of marketing was becoming obsolete. In the past, the company had secured most of its projects directly from government officials. It didn't have to bid on the jobs because it was often the only company that possessed the technology necessary to complete a particular project. That situation began to change in the 1980s when more companies started vying for lucrative government contracts, and when the Federal Government started clamping down on the contracting process and requiring companies like Science Applications to submit fixed-price, competitive bids for jobs.

While Beyster tweaked operating and management systems, he left the proven compensation system intact. Furthermore, he continued to evade publicity; even by the late 1980s the company's main offices (in La Jolla, California, and McLean, Virginia) bore no outside mark or reference disclosing the company's name or purpose. The overall strategy seemed to work, as Science Application's sales rose to 43 percent in 1986 to $600 million. Revenues continued to rise rapidly in 1987, by which time the company was employing 7,000 workers in 17 cities around the United States. Those workers owned about 90 percent of Science Applications' stock.

The defense contracting industry was stifled beginning in the late 1980s and throughout the early 1990s by marked reductions in federal spending, particularly on defense. It was that slowdown that proved the value of Science Applications' flexible and entrepreneurial management system. When the defense contracts began drying up, the large but nimble Science Applications organization quickly adapted. To sustain its federal contracts, the company began emphasizing technologies that complemented the governments new cost-cutting and efficiency approach. At the same time, it began to aggressively market its services to the private sector, often drawing on technology developed for the government.

Among the new contracts secured during the early 1990s, was a $200 million contract to develop a hospital information system for the Veteran's Administration, and a $150 million agreement with NASA to study natural and human-induced changes (including global warming) in the global environment. It also won a job to provide a workstation-based score-reporting system for the 1992 Summer Olympics in Barcelona. Ballard Power Systems, of Canada, hired Science Applications to develop the world's first fuel-cell-powered transit bus. And IBM and J.B. Hunt Transport Inc. contracted the company to help design a system that communicated, via satellite and hand-held bar code readers, the status of freight on the road. At the same time, Science Applications was able to land a few of the major military contracts that were still available, such as a $200 million deal to help design a system for the U.S. Army's Missile Command (MICOM).

Science Applications' spate of new civilian and military contracts allowed it to increase sales substantially to $1.29 billion in 1992, about $33 million of which was netted as income. Its work force by that time had grown to 14,500 worldwide. While it made impressive advances in the marketplace, the company was less successful in court. The year 1992, in particular, brought a string of temporary legal setbacks. First, a former executive filed a bias suit against the firm. Then, a former rocket scientist was sentenced to two-and-a-half years in prison for illegally exporting "Star Wars" technology to Japan and South Africa. Finally, another Science Applications ex-employee won a $3.17 million wrongful termination and gender-bias suit against the company.

Despite those hurdles, Science Applications achieved strong growth going into the mid-1990s. Sales rose to a record $1.7 billion in 1994 (fiscal year ended January 31, 1994) and profits hit $41.5 million, as the company's work force increased to 17,000. In 1995, moreover, revenues grew to $1.9 billion and net income increased to $49 million. Those figures represented 26 successive years of revenue and profit growth, thus solidifying Science Applications' status as one of the most successful employee-owned companies in the United States.

A diversity of new projects at Science Applications in the mid-1990s included: the development of combat simulators that integrated virtual reality technology for the U.S. Army; the creation of a new office in Mexico to provide environmental protection services; the creation of an inspection systems designed to detect smuggled explosives and drugs; and a $1 billion contract to computerize military health records. Beyster, the company's founder, was still chairman of the board going into 1996.

Further Reading

"Corporate Profiles '93: Science Applications," *San Diego Daily Transcript*, January 11, 1993, p. D9.

Fikes, Bradley J., "Can-do Attitude Spurs Rapid Growth of SAIC," *San Diego Business Journal*, November 7, 1994, p. 1.

O'Reiley, Tim, "Beyster Pushes Changes at Science Applications," *San Diego Business Journal*, June 24, 1985, p. 1.

Perry, Nancy J., "Talk About Pay For Performance! (Employee Ownership of Science Applications International Corp.)," *Fortune*, May 4, 1992, p. 77.

Rowe, Bruce, "Big Orders Are Routine For Science Applications," *San Diego Business Journal*, June 22, 1987, p. 11.

Semich, J. William, "Science Applications International Corp.," *Datamation*, June 15, 1992, p. 160.

——, "Science Applications International Corp.," *Datamation*, June 15, 1993, p. 102.

Wells, Ken R., "SAIC, GA Get Contracts Totaling $163.5 million," *San Diego Business Journal*, October 23, 1995, p. 7.

—Dave Mote

Scottish & Newcastle plc

Abbey Brewery
111 Holyrood Road
Edinburgh EH8 8YS
Scotland
0131 556 2591
Fax: 0131 556 2807

Public Company
Incorporated: 1931 as Scottish Brewers Ltd.
Employees: 44,256
Sales: £2.022 billion (1995)
Stock Exchanges: London
SICs: 2082 Malt Beverages; 5813 Drinking Places; 5180
   Beer, Wine, and Distilled Beverages; 5921 Liquor
   Stores; 7011 Hotels and Motels

Although Scottish & Newcastle plc operates two successful lines of hotels, its name and history are most strongly associated with beer. In 1994, almost half of the group's revenues came from making and marketing beer. In 1995, having acquired the second largest U.K. brewer, Courage, from Foster's of Australia, the brewing division of Scottish & Newcastle (S&N) became known as Scottish Courage Ltd. and the company became Great Britain's largest brewer, displacing Bass Brewers Ltd. Moreover, following the Courage merger, S&N moved into the ranks of Europe's top six breweries. (Before the merger, only about 15 percent of S&N's turnover came from Europe excluding the United Kingdom.) Scottish Courage markets such foreign brands as Holsten, Kronenbourg, Miller, and Anheuser-Busch in the United Kingdom.

Since the days of seafaring British colonialism, English beer has traditionally been marketed worldwide. More than 30 countries, including China, were supplied with Scottish Courage products in the mid-1990s. However, the home market has resisted foreign domination due to the strength of its own distinctive traditions. While most of the world switched to the lager style of beer developed in Continental Europe in the 19th century (particularly the pale Pilsner lager of Bohemia), the British remained largely loyal to ale. (The yeast used to ferment ales rises in foam; that in lagers, brewed at colder temperatures, sinks.) Several distinctive styles are associated with various regions in the British Isles: brown ales near Newcastle, for example, and milder ales and porter to the south.

Scottish & Newcastle's roots begin with the establishment of the William Younger Brewery in Leith in 1749. Its founder left management of the brewery to his wife, Grizell, in 1753 when he became an exciseman. Grizell continued to operate it, and another brewery he had purchased in the late 1760s, after her husband died in 1770. Grizell Younger married the original owner of the second brewery, Robert Anderson, in the 1780s; by then her sons had apprenticed under her and the elder, Archibald Campbell Younger, had set up a brewery at Holyrood Abbey. This generation of Youngers established several other breweries in this area, and sold the Leith Brewery in 1801. In 1821, William Younger II, the youngest son, combined the various family interests into William Younger & Co., which prospered in the 1830s and beyond. William Younger II took on his son, William Younger III, and Alexander Smith and his son Andrew as partners in 1836. Smith's son Andrew and several Younger heirs served as partners until 1887, when the company was registered as a limited liability company, two years before its stocks were traded publicly. The previous year, William Younger IV and Andrew Smith had built the Holyrood Brewery after purchasing an additional site next to the company's existing property. This brewery continued to operate for 100 years, and was rebuilt by Scottish & Newcastle (partially financed by Guinness for the Harp Lager consortium) in 1971.

In 1931 William Younger & Co. merged with William McEwan & Co. Ltd., another Edinburgh brewer, forming Scottish Brewers Ltd. Later, Scottish & Newcastle would locate its headquarters in William Younger's Holyrood Abbey Brewery and their production facilities in McEwan's, each on opposite sides of Edinburgh, a brewing center since the monastic breweries of the 12th century.

McEwan's was started by William McEwan, a shipowner's son who established the Fountain Brewery in 1856 at Fountainbridge, Edinburgh, after serving an apprenticeship. McEwan's nephew, James Younger, managed the operation after 1886, when William McEwan entered political life. Three years later the firm was registered as William McEwan & Co. Ltd. Before the merger with Younger, McEwan's acquired the trade of yet another Edinburgh brewer, Alexander Melvin & Co., in 1907. Scottish and Newcastle continued to brew at the Fountain Brewery into the 1990s. McEwan's Export (sometimes identified as ''MacEwan's'' in foreign markets), a light ale, led canned ale sales for Britain in the 1990s.

Scottish Brewers acquired several more operations after World War II, including Manchester's Red Tower Lager Brewery Ltd. in 1956 and Edinburgh's Thomas & James Bernard Ltd., J & J Morison Ltd., and Robert Younger Ltd. in 1960. In April of that year, Scottish Brewers and Newcastle Breweries merged to form Scottish & Newcastle Breweries Ltd. After the merger, the wines and spirits businesses were combined and the two brewing centers essentially carried on business as before.

Newcastle Breweries Ltd. had incorporated in 1890. Proud of its urban origins, the brewery's logo featured the city's skyline in silhouette against its trademark blue star. The city of Newcastle itself claimed, somewhat tenuously, to be England's first brewing town. Newcastle Breweries was most strongly identified with its Newcastle Brown Ale (in the 1990s, the largest selling bottled ale in Britain), which continued to be produced in the city of its namesake throughout changes in ownership. Nicknamed ''The (Brown) Dog,'' the beer won a top award for bottled beer in London in 1928, a year after it was introduced.

Like Scottish Brewers, Newcastle Breweries was an amalgamation of regional brewers, all family-controlled: John Barras & Co. Ltd. (which dated back to 1770), William Henry Allison & Co., James, John & William Henry Allison, and Carr Brothers & Carr. The Barras company operated the Tyne Brewery, which became the center of the Newcastle Breweries' production and, like the Fountain Brewery, remained operational under Scottish and Newcastle. In Newcastle Breweries' first thirty years other brewers and pubs were acquired, such as John Sanderson & Sons (1898), Fosters' Bishop Middleham Brewery Ltd. (1910), Addison, Potter & Son (1918), and Matthew Wood & Son Ltd. (1919). Between the end of World War II and the creation of Scottish & Newcastle, Newcastle picked up the Northern Corporation (1955), the Duddingston Brewery (from Steel, Coulson & Co. Ltd. in 1954), James Deuchar Ltd. (1956), and John Rowell & Son Ltd. (1959).

In the 1950s and 1960s, many breweries were scrambling to form alliances of one type or another. Some brewers, including Courage, Barclay, and Newcastle, received some protection from hostile mergers in the form of the Whitbread ''Umbrella,'' investments by the giant brewer in the late 1950s. In return, these associations offered Whitbread certain marketing advantages. Another type of alliance was formed in 1961, when Courage, Barclay & Simonds, Scottish & Newcastle, and Bass, Mitchells, & Butlers all joined Ireland's Guinness firm in the Harp Lager Ltd. consortium, which produced a very successful draught lager, quickly leading its category in sales. The Harp lineup changed considerably over the years, with Courage and

Scottish & Newcastle leaving in 1979 but becoming franchisees.

S&N produced and marketed wine and spirits through Mackinlay-McPherson Ltd., formed in 1962. This division was later known as Waverly Vinters. It sold the products of Glenallchie Distillery Co. Ltd. and Isle of Jura Distillery Co. Ltd. County Hotels & Wine Co. Ltd. was acquired in the 1962; Christopher & Co. Ltd. was added in 1972, and wine and spirit distributors Gough Brothers Ltd. were owned from 1979 to 1984.

In 1965, the company entered the leisure industry with Thistle Hotels Ltd., which was expanded in 1979 with the purchase of Thorn EMI's hotel group. In 1989, S&N acquired a majority interest (65 percent) in the Dutch hotelier Center Parcs (founded in 1967) while it sold Thistle Hotels for £645 million. It bought Pontin's Ltd. the same year. In 1991, the rest of Center Parcs was obtained. The Leisure Division achieved turnover of £406.6 million in 1995, when it operated 14 resorts under the Center Parc name in five countries and 17 Holiday Club Pontin's hotels in the British Isles. By that time, Center Parcs attracted over three million guests a year to its recreation-oriented, natural settings.

S&N attempted to buy Cameron in 1984, but the bid was scuttled by government regulators. In 1985, Moray Firth Maltings was acquired. In 1986, when company turnover was £828 million, it acquired Nottingham's Home Brewery (including 450 pubs), and the next year (in its second attempt) Matthew Brown. These purchases gave S&N the Theakston line of ales and three breweries that continued to operate in the 1990s. The cost for the Home, Brown, and Theakston breweries was £272 million.

In 1990, a retail division, headquartered in Northampton, was formed to manage pubs and restaurants. Although ownership of bars by brewers was forbidden in the United States, this market could not be ignored, since it accounted for most of the beer sales in Britain. S&N became the fourth largest pub operator in the U.K. after acquiring Chef & Brewer from Grand Metropolitan plc in 1993 for £628 million. Operating over 2,600 sites in 1995, including those of Inntrepreneur Estates Ltd. acquired in the Courage merger, the division earned operating profits of £142.7 million in 1995 on turnover of £722.7 million. Brands included Chef & Brewer, T&J Bernard, Barras & Co., and Rat 'N' Parrot ale houses; Homespreads and Country Carvery & Grill restaurants; and Vino Veritas bistros. Big Hand Mo, a line of pubs featuring video games, was designed to attract 18- to 24-year olds.

The forerunners of these establishments were the revived, multi-use pubs introduced by brewers such as Courage and Newcastle in the 1920s and 1930s to meet the demands of competition and public responsibility. The brewers sought to attract middle-class customers with elaborate architecture and restaurants. Barclay Perkins opened one of the most grand, the Downham Tavern, near Bromley in 1930. In order to promote food sales, it had no bars, but it did have a huge hall where Shakespeare was eventually performed. Nevertheless, the take-home market eroded pub sales so that by 1980 pubs only supplied 63 percent of the beer market, down from 80 percent in

1955. In 1963, Courage, Barclay & Simonds owned 4,800 establishments; Scottish & Newcastle 1,700. S&N's holdings remained between 1,400 and 1,700 houses for the next two decades, but by 1970 Courage owned 6,000, which fell to about 5,000 by 1986. John Smith's owned 1,536 in 1967. Amusement With Prize machines helped brewers dependent on tied estate survive through hard times. In the mid-1970s, Courage received about £2.5 million per year from them. S&N owned 2300 pubs in 1990, when it employed 20,000.

The name of Scottish & Newcastle's beer division was changed to Scottish Courage Limited in 1995 after taking over Courage Ltd., a wholly-owned subsidiary of Foster's Brewing Group of Australia in a transaction worth the equivalent of £858 million. Based in Bristol and Plymouth, Courage had been traditionally strongest in the southwest of England. John Courage, a shipping agent and a Scot of French Huguenot extraction, founded Courage at a brewhouse he bought in London for £615 in 1787. After his death in 1793, his wife Harriet took over the firm's operation; she was succeeded by John Donaldson, the senior clerk, upon her death in 1797. Within a few years Donaldson had become a partner. Around mid-century John Courage, Jr. and his sons began to run the business as the Donaldsons assumed a less active role.

Although the company specialized in mild ale, Courage brewed porter (which from the 1700s to the 1830s had been London's main brew) in a London brewery acquired in the late Eighteenth Century; production there ceased in 1980. In the late 1800s Courage bought fashionable pale ale from Burton brewers to meet demand in London; in 1903 it bought Hall's Hampshire brewery, rebuilding it.

Courage produced an estimated 10,000 barrels in 1830 and 250,000 in 1880. The company, typical of London brewers, continued to use draught horses to distribute their products locally throughout the 19th century. Courage owned about eighty horses in this period, a larger brewer like Barclay Perkins, perhaps two to three times as many. After World War I they were eventually displaced.

At the turn of the century, Courage sought ownership of more pubs, and bought several brewers: Alton Brewery Co. (1903), Camden Brewery Co. Ltd. (1923), Farnham United Breweries Ltd. (1927), Noakes & Co. Ltd. (1930), C. N. Kidd & Sons Ltd. (1937), and Kingston Brewery Co. Ltd. (1943). In the Edwardian period, Courage was one of the top twenty brewers in Britain, and one of the top fifty industrial concerns. William McEwan, William Younger, John Smith, and Newcastle Breweries occupied a lower tier.

In 1957, Courage & Barclay Ltd., a limited liability company registered in 1955, took over the brewing rights of both Courage & Co. and Barclay, Perkins & Co. In the post war years, Courage & Barclay was the country's fourth largest brewer, based on its capital of £15.8 million. A new wave of acquisitions followed: Reffell's Bexley Brewery Ltd. (1956), wine and spirit merchant Charles Kinloch & Co. Ltd. (1957), Nicholsons & Sons Ltd. (1959), and Yardley's London & Provincial Stores (1959). In 1960, H. & G. Simonds Ltd., a brewing concern which itself had expanded rapidly in the 1930s, was

bought, whereupon Courage & Barclay Ltd. was renamed Courage, Barclay & Simonds Ltd. and its brewing rights were sold back to Barclay, Perkins & Co. Ltd., which then became known as Courage & Barclay Ltd. The company acquired a league of other breweries after these ownership shuffles, including Bristol Brewery Georges & Co. Ltd. (1961), Clinchy & Co. Ltd. and Uxbridge Brewery Ltd. (1962), Charles Beasley Ltd. (1963), Star Brewery Co. (1965), Plymouth Breweries Ltd. (1969), and John Smith's Tadcaster Brewery Co. Ltd. (1970). Again, in 1970, the company changed its name, to Courage Ltd.

The 1961 takeover of Bristol Brewery Georges came in response to a United Breweries takeover attempt, and outbidding United proved quite expensive: Courage & Barclay paid about £19 million for share capital previously valued at £12 million. However, it denied United access to Courage's home territory, the South. The same year, a merger with Bass was discussed.

John Smith's brewery in Yorkshire, next door to the Samuel Smith brewery, merged with Courage in 1970. John Smith's dated back to 1847. A new brewery, housing Courage's headquarters, was built in 1883, and another brewhouse was added in 1976; yet another replaced the original in 1984.

In 1972, Imperial Tobacco Group Ltd., continuing a diversification into less controversial products, bought Courage for £320 million, whereupon it became known as Imperial Brewing & Leisure Ltd. Ironically, S&N had also made a bid for Courage, and observers saw the northern and southern firms as complementary. However, Courage's wary directors believed the company would be significantly restructured in such a deal, beginning with a relocation of its headquarters to Edinburgh. In 1986, when Courage's turnover was £839 million, Hanson Trust plc acquired the Imperial Group and sold Courage to Elders IXL (owners of the Foster's brand) for £1.4 billion. Courage held 9 per cent of the British beer market in 1988. Scottish & Newcastle finally bought it in 1995.

Scottish and Newcastle's considerable success from 1960 to 1980 was powered by a few brands—such as Newcastle Brown Ale and McEwan's Export—that led the free trade sector. From 1965 to 1975 its U.K. sales nearly doubled; its free trade sales increased by about 150 percent. Besides participating in the Harp consortium, S&N developed its own lager brands—McEwan's and Kestrel—in the mid-1970s. The acquisition of Courage strengthened its brand lineup overall, to the point of possibly overstocking its import lager category.

The title of largest brewer in the United Kingdom has shifted several times throughout the centuries. With virtually all of its units posting sales gains in the mid-1990s and overall profits up 19 percent in 1995, Scottish & Newcastle plc seemed assured of a reasonably long tenure at its unique position in the world of brewing.

Principal Subsidiaries

Center Parcs N.V. (Netherlands); Cleveland Place Holdings plc; The Chef & Brewer Group Limited; Huggins & Company Limited; Waverly Vinters; Canongate Technology; Moray Firth Maltings; Public House Company Limited (50%).

Principal Divisions

Scottish Courage Limited; Scottish & Newcastle (Retail); Leisure Division.

Further Reading

Foster, Geoffrey. "How Thistle Was Grasped," *Management Today*, June, 1987, pp. 68–69.

Gilbert, David C., and Rachel Smith, "The UK Brewing Industry: Past, Present, and Future," *International Journal of Wine Marketing*, 1992, Vol. 4, No. 1, pp. 19–27.

Gourvish, Terence R., and R.G. Wilson. *The British Brewing Industry, 1830–1980*, Cambridge, Eng.: Cambridge University Press, 1994.

Mathias, Peter, *The Brewing Industry in England, 1700–1830*, Cambridge, Eng.: Cambridge University Press, 1959.

Pitcher, George, "A Beerage Made in Heaven?" *Marketing Week*, March 31, 1995, p. 25.

Richmond, Lesley, and Alison Turton, eds., *The Brewing Industry: A Guide to Historical Records*, Manchester, Eng.: Manchester University Press, 1990.

Rock, Stuart, "Scottish & Newcastle: A Brewery on the Hop," *Chief Executive*, June 1986, pp. 34–36.

Slingsby, Helen, "Last Chance Saloon," *Marketing Week*, February 17, 1995, pp. 35–36.

Sigsworth, Eric M. *The Brewing Trade During the Industrial Revolution: The Case of Yorkshire*, York: St. Anthony's Press, 1967.

Snowdon, Ros. "S&N Overhauls Pub Strategies," *Marketing*, July 27, 1995, p. 3.

——, "Takeover is No Small Beer," *Marketing*, May 25, 1995, p. 12.

Wombwell, David, "Newcastle Brown," *Marketing*, May 18, 1995, p. 10.

—Frederick C. Ingram

Seattle Times Company

1120 John Street
Seattle, Washington 98109
U.S.A.
(206) 464-2111
Fax: (206) 464-2905

Private Company
Incorporated: 1896
Employees: 2,524
Sales: $250 million (1995 est.)
SICs: 2711 Newspapers

Owner and operator of one of the last independent and locally owned metropolitan newspapers in the United States, the Seattle Times Company publishes *The Seattle Times* and controls the production, advertising, and circulation of the *Seattle Post-Intelligencer,* the two largest newspapers in Washington. In addition, the company owns the *Yakima Herald-Republic,* the *Walla Walla Union-Bulletin,* and several regional weekly newspapers in Washington state.

When Colonel Alden J. Blethen stepped off the steamship *Walla Walla* in 1896, the city of Seattle gained its newest and most vocal newspaper publisher, a man who reportedly walked with a defiant strut and carried a heavy, gold-headed cane for protection against those riled by his decided and purposeful invectiveness. Blethen would impart his unhesitatingly frank and unabashedly bold personality to *The Seattle Times,* transforming the struggling evening newspaper into the largest daily in Washington State and creating a newspaper publishing dynasty that would employ generations of Blethens to follow. The ownership stability established by Colonel Blethen—the fifth generation of Blethens were being groomed during the mid-1990s to guide the family business in the 21st century—stood in sharp contrast to the newspaper's early years, a 15-year span before Blethen's arrival when ownership of *The Seattle Times'* direct predecessor, *The Seattle Chronicle,* changed hands frequently. Shortly after Blethen's arrival in Seattle,

however, the shaky and fitful beginnings of *The Seattle Times* gave way to a century of ownership stability, as the paper flourished under the stewardship of it most colorful leader.

When Blethen acquired *The Seattle Times,* ownership of the newspaper had devolved into the hands of C.A. Hughes and T.A. Davies, who had no intention of continuing its publication, hoping only to sell the paper to the first interested party able to pay a price that would yield the two businessmen a profit. The newspaper Hughes and Davies had purchased represented a combination of several Seattle daily papers that descended from *The Seattle Chronicle,* the newspaper from which *The Seattle Times* inherited its Associated Press franchise. *The Seattle Chronicle,* an evening paper issued every day except Sunday, had been founded by Kirk C. Ward, who published the first copy on October 10, 1881. The following year, *The Seattle Chronicle* changed from an evening to a morning paper and began printing Associated Press dispatches, then in 1884 resumed evening publication, concurrent with its securement of the Associated Press franchise for the day report. Two years later, *The Seattle Chronicle* was sold and consolidated with another daily newspaper, *The Daily Call,* forming *The Daily and Weekly Press.* When the former owners of *The Daily Call* were given positions at the newly formed newspaper, displacing a group of *Chronicle* employees, another Seattle daily newspaper was organized, *The Times,* published by The Times Publishing Company, founded by the *Chronicle* employees who had lost their jobs in the consolidation of *The Chronicle* and *The Daily Call.*

Change had been rampant during five years following the founding of *The Chronicle,* the pace of which would not slacken by much in the years leading up to Blethen's arrival in Seattle. Ownership of *The Daily and Weekly Press* changed twice in the three years following its formation, the second of which, in 1889, touched off a bitter feud between Seattle's two evening papers, *The Times* and *The Daily and Weekly Press.* The cloud of acrimony pervading the battle between the two evening newspapers was cleared away by the most ameliorative means possible in the business world when *The Daily and Weekly Press* acquired *The Times* in 1891 and began publishing the newspaper as *The Seattle Press-Times.*

Ownership of *The Seattle Press-Times* passed through several receiverships during the ensuing years, as the newspaper's financial woes mounted. In March 1895, Hughes and Davies purchased the floundering evening newspaper, representing perhaps the most uninterested of all the newspaper's owners. As Colonel Blethen would write of the 17-month Hughes-Davies ownership, the pair operated *The Seattle-Press Times* "as a mere incident to [their] job—a printing business which had already been established," demonstrating a carelessness that would require, once again, a name change for the newspaper. Under the management of Hughes and Davies, an incorrect circulation figure was reported to the George P. Rowell Newspaper Directory, resulting in the newspaper being blacklisted from the directory. Consequently, "Press" was dropped from the newspaper's official name to obscure its identity and the newspaper continued on as *The Seattle Times*, less than a year before Blethen's arrival.

Blethen disembarked from the steamship *Walla Walla* on July 26, 1896, having already lost two businesses by the age of 40. Born in Knox, Maine, Blethen had previously published a newspaper, but lost the business to a fire, then founded a bank, which collapsed as well in the bank panic of 1893. His business failures, neither of which were attributable to his mismanagement, did not dilute Blethen's willingness to assume the mantle of responsibility once again, something he promptly did 15 days after arriving in Seattle when he purchased *The Seattle Times* from Hughes and Davies on August 10, 1896.

Decisive leadership, a trait critics would contend was lacking in the decades following Colonel Blethen's tenure, was apparent from the outset, as Blethen strategically positioned the newspaper as a working man's alternative to the larger, more successful, and entrenched *Seattle Post-Intelligencer* (*P-I*), a morning newspaper founded in 1863. By consistently baiting the *P-I* into controversies and adopting an editorial position that distinguished his newspaper from the *P-I*, Blethen increased the circulation of *The Seattle Times*. Through his newspaper, Blethen was bitingly blunt about his views, particularly if they butted against the perspective espoused in the *P-I*. As a result, Blethen exposed himself to wave after wave of criticism, but enemies and friends alike were readers of *The Seattle Times*, enabling the outspoken publisher to establish a solid base of readership that would serve as the newspaper's foundation for the remainder of the century.

Growth came quickly to *The Seattle Times* under the leadership of Blethen, securing the newspaper's financial future, which for several years before Blethen assumed control had threatened to cause the newspaper's collapse. From a circulation of less than 8,000 copies in 1896, *The Seattle Times* had increased its circulation to 25,000 by 1901, eclipsing the circulation of the rival *P-I*, then reached 40,000 by 1906, by which time the newspaper's annual revenues had jumped to roughly $580,000 from the $60,000 it generated at the beginning of Blethen's ownership. Revenue growth had enabled the construction of a new printing plant in 1898 and supported the newspaper's expansion from four pages in 1896 to more than 20 pages by 1906. Encouraged by his success, Blethen had launched a Sunday version of *The Seattle Times* in February 1902, which in four years' time recorded more robust growth than the daily version, exceeding 51,000 in circulation, making it the largest published west of Chicago and north of Los Angeles.

Blethen died in 1915, having completed the transformation of *The Seattle Times* from an upstart newspaper to a market leader that ranked as the largest daily newspaper in Washington. As it would for decades to come, leadership of *The Seattle Times* was handed down to the next generation, Blethen's sons, Joseph Blethen and Clarence Brettun (C.B.) Blethen, who assumed the titles of president and managing editor, respectively. Six years later, in 1921, when William Randolph Hearst acquired the *P-I*, C.B. Blethen bought out his brother's share in the family company, grabbing a firm hold on *The Seattle Times* and wielding his authority with a style entirely distinct from his father. It was C.B.'s intent, insiders noted, to make *The Seattle Times* a mass-circulation newspaper, an objective he pursued by running the newspaper like a business, taking particular care, unlike his father, to avoid controversy in order to increase circulation. Wishing to produce a newspaper that no person would be ashamed to have around the house at night, C.B. sanitized *The Seattle Times'* editorial posture, eliminating crime news from the front page and prohibiting reporters from using words such as "gun" and "blood" in their published accounts of the daily news. Meanwhile, the newspaper's orientation was altered, moving away from the upper-class audience drawn by Alden Blethen to embrace the more cautious middle-class members of Seattle's society.

Under C.B.'s leadership, heart-warming local news stories filled *The Seattle Times'* front page, creating a newspaper that could offend no one. But despite C.B.'s solicitous approach to running the company he came close to losing the family business in the early 1930s when the cost of constructing new corporate offices for the newspaper raised debt to a dangerous level. C.B saved the company from potential failure by selling a 49.5 percent interest in the company to a hostile minority partner that later became known as Knight-Ridder Inc. It was a necessary but regrettable move on C.B.'s part, leading to periodic takeover attempts by Knight Ridder that continued until after C.B.'s death in 1941, with the last formal challenge mounted in 1949 and ending in a victory for the Blethen family.

Despite his uncharacteristic slip in the early 1930s, no one was more responsible for *The Seattle Times'* financial success than C.B. Blethen, whose business-first approach to running the newspaper fueled two decades of steady growth. His years in charge left a lasting impression for the generations of Blethen leaders to follow, setting a conservative journalistic tone at the newspaper that would predicate its growth, yet prompt critics to accuse *The Seattle Times* of being overly cautious and bland in its reporting. In the decades after C.B.'s death, his legacy lived on, leading one former reporter to characterize *The Seattle Times* in the late 1960s as "the good, gray place," a newspaper that lacked the stinging editorial stance prevalent in Alden Blethen's day, yet one that had grown enormously successful, ranking as the largest newspaper in the Washington.

After C.B.'s death in 1941, Elmer Todd, his best friend and attorney, took control of running the newspaper, the first non-family member to steward *The Seattle Times*. Todd was succeeded after an eight-year stint by two of C.B.'s sons, William K. Blethen, Sr., who was named publisher, and Frank A.

Blethen, Sr., who became president. The two Blethen brothers were then succeeded by their younger brother John Blethen, who was named publisher in 1968, by which time the daily version of the newspaper had a circulation of slightly more than 250,000, or nearly 50,000 more than the *P-I*, while the Sunday edition had a circulation of 310,000, 52,000 more than the *P-I* could claim. Carrying roughly 60 percent of the advertising appearing in both papers, *The Seattle Times* had established a solid lead over its morning rival, a lead that would widen during the 1970s and into the early 1980s. For years, the two newspapers had competed fiercely against each other, at times opposing each other as bitter foes, with each closely monitoring how the other was reporting the news. By the early 1980s, however, intense competition had created the need for the two newspapers to seek each other's help, particularly the *P-I*, which was beginning to succumb to the financial pressures resulting from the stronger market position enjoyed by *The Seattle Times*. In 1983, the two newspapers ended their sometimes contentious battle not by a shake of their figurative hands, but by fully embracing each other.

On May 23, 1983, after narrowly surviving legal challenges to defeat it, a 50-year joint operating agreement between *The Seattle Times* and the *P-I* took effect, enabling the two newspapers to legally cooperate in order to ensure their mutual survival in the marketplace. Editorially, the two newspapers remained separate, but the Seattle Times Company took control of all *P-I*-related production, advertising, and circulation matters, removing the costly expense of waging a circulation war. Under the joint operating agreement, *The Seattle Times* ceased publication of its daily morning edition, begun in 1980, and was awarded the lion's share of the profits generated by both newspapers. In addition to taking a management fee equal to six percent of any profits earned by both newspapers in a year, *The Seattle Times* also took 66 percent of the remaining profits, leaving the balance for the *P-I*.

Buoyed by the financial boost provided by the joint operating agreement, *The Seattle Times* faced a brighter economic outlook as it moved toward the future and its greatest period of financial growth. Leading the company during this stretch of energetic growth was Frank Blethen, Jr., great-grandson of Colonel Alden Blethen. Frank Blethen, Jr. took the reins at *The Seattle Times* when his predecessor, W.J. Pennington, a non-family member who succeeded John Blethen in 1983, died unexpectedly in 1985. When Frank Blethen, Jr. was thrust into the leadership of *The Seattle Times* in 1985, he became the newspaper's sixth publisher and chief executive officer, gaining authority he would use to steer the newspaper toward what company officials described as unprecedented financial growth.

To realize this financial growth, Frank Blethen, Jr. launched several spin-off niche publications, acquired three regional weeklies, and in 1989, acquired the *Yakima Herald-Republic*, a daily newspaper with a circulation of more than 40,000. Three years after the purchase of the *Yakima Herald-Republic*, the Seattle Times company opened a $175 million, state-of-the-art satellite printing plant, then began operating its Infoline service, a telephone reader-information line supported financially through advertisers.

As *The Seattle Times* entered the mid-1990s, it represented one of the last independent and locally owned metropolitan newspapers in the country, one of the few newspapers to avoid absorption by large publishing chains. Operating as Washington's largest newspaper, with a circulation of 232,616 for its daily editions and 505,604 for its Sunday edition in 1995, the newspaper occupied solid ground as it prepared to enter the late 1990s and its second century of existence. As the newspaper prepared to celebrate its 100th anniversary in 1996, steps were being taken to ensure the legal transfer of company ownership to the fifth generation of Blethens, who could look forward to inheriting a newspaper and a company enjoying a decade of especially strong financial growth. Revenues nearly doubled between 1984 and 1994, driven upwards primarily by the acquisitions completed in the late 1980s, providing the generations of Blethens to come with a model of success to emulate.

Principal Subsidiaries

Walla Walla Union Bulletin.

Further Reading

Brewster, David, "Behind the Times," *Seattle Magazine*, November 1969, pp. 33–8.
"The First Fifty Years," *The Seattle Times*, August 11, 1946, pp. 1–3.
"Labor Disputes Which Closed Times for 95 Days Are Detailed," *The Seattle Times*, October 19, 1953, p. 1.
Lucan, Eric, "Times Walking the Fine Line between Smug and Confident," *Puget Sound Business Journal*, July 3, 1989, p. 19A.
Park, Clayton, "Times Hangs onto Its Roots as Family-Owned Paper," *Puget Sound Business Journal*, November 17, 1995, p. 7A.
"The Times Observes Its Sixtieth Birthday," *The Seattle Times*, August 5, 1956, p. 21.

—Jeffrey L. Covell

Seaway Food Town, Inc.

1020 Ford Street
Maumee, Ohio 43537
U.S.A.
(419) 893-9401
Fax: (419) 891-4214

Public Company
Incorporated: 1957
Employees: 4,551
Revenues: $559.24 million (1995)
Stock Exchanges: NASDAQ
SICs: 5410 Grocery Stores; 5910 Drug Stores and
Proprietary Stores

In spite of intense competition from powerful regional and national chains, Seaway Food Town, Inc. was maintaining its leading share of the metropolitan Toledo food market in the mid-1990s. The local supermarketer has held its own against regional giants by anticipating major trends, acquiring less fortunate competitors, and maintaining a consistent reputation as a low-price leader. Initially established as a cooperative and a public company since the early 1960s, Seaway has been guided from its inception into the mid-1990s by the Iott family. It appeared likely that octogenarian co-founder Wallace D. "Wally" Iott would eventually be succeeded as chairman and CEO by his son, Seaway Food Town President Richard B. Iott.

The impetus behind the creation of Seaway Food Town originated with Joseph A. Altschuller. According to a 1972 article in the *Toledo Blade*, Altschuller had come from a family of grocers and reluctantly entered the industry in 1940. Upon his return from World War II military service, the young entrepreneur found his small business under increasing competition from increasingly powerful national chains. In order to combat this threat, Altschuller and his wife put in long hours printing and hand-addressing advertising flyers.

Tired of the physical effort involved in this promotional process and hoping to reach greater numbers of potential customers, the independent grocer began advertising in the local newspaper. But print advertising was expensive, and Altschuller began looking for other independent grocers to form an advertising cooperative.

Wallace Iott was one of the first of Altschuller's independent competitors to sign on with the program. Iott had purchased his first grocery store, Wally's Inc., in 1939 for $3,000. His wife, Jeanette, ran the store while he served in the military during the war. Upon his return, they closed the corner grocery in favor of a new 7,500 square-foot supermarket called "Wally's Food Town."

Together, Iott and Altschuller recruited four other northwest Ohio grocers: Frank A. Ulrich, Thomas E. Swinghammer, Oscar Joseph, Sr., and Paul Pope. In 1948, the six founded a buying and advertising cooperative and named it for Iott's Food Town. Altschuller later ascribed the young co-op's early success to Wally Iott's "strength and diplomacy," and the other members' dedication to their mutual interests.

The association grew closer and stronger during the 1950s as the group inaugurated a full-time advertising and promotion staff and opened jointly-owned stores. By the mid-1950s, the members had begun to investigate their incorporation as a full-fledged chain. But the individual affiliates encountered difficulty in appraising their separate contributions to the venture. Then, in 1956, an outside entity—a Detroit supermarket chain—helped make the valuations for the members. The partners entertained the bid from the Michigan group, given that the acquirer bargained on an individual basis with each Food Town affiliate and that it buy all the Food Town units or none.

Although the Detroit company was able to reach agreements with each of the co-op members, it was unable to achieve the terms of payment. Armed with the impartial appraisals, the partners incorporated as Seaway Food Town, Inc. in 1957 with Iott as president.

Over the course of its first five years of incorporation, Seaway Food Town developed the everyday low price strategy that became its hallmark and would be adopted by supermarket chains across the country in the late 1980s and early 1990s. A

1972 *Toledo Blade* article by Seymour Rothman characterized the move as "the firm's greatest gamble." Food Town became its own perishables supplier with the acquisition of West Toledo Wholesale Produce Distributors and joined Staff Supermarket Associates, a cooperative distributor of private label groceries. Food Town's combination of wholesaling and warehousing generated enough cost savings to allow it to lower retail prices. Rothman characterized Food Town as "a penny-pinching operation with its success based entirely on volume."

This strategy proved so successful that Altschuller was ready to retire in 1958, at the age of 43. He asked his fellow Food Town affiliates to buy out his stock five years later, but the remaining members weren't liquid enough to purchase his whole stake. Nevertheless, Altschuller's proposition sowed the seed of an idea—an initial public offering—in the minds of his partners. In 1962, the company offered Altschuller's stake "and a small amount of the others' holdings" to the public in a $1.4 million flotation. By this time, Seaway Food Town had opened nine company stores.

The chain used the proceeds of its initial public offering to finance a period of growth and diversification through acquisition that would continue through the mid-1980s. Seaway supplemented its retail operations with the purchase of four stores from National Tea in 1963 and seven Gruber's Food Stores in southeastern Michigan in 1968. The company boosted the wholesale side of its business with the acquisition of Portion Control Meats, Inc. in 1966 and the purchase of Vlasic Foods of Ohio and Snow Maid Frozen Food, Inc. in 1968. Seaway also formed Toledo Milk Processing, Inc. as a joint venture with Driggs Dairy. By 1971, when annual sales volume topped $100 million, the company boasted a wide array of businesses, including 42 retail outlets, a dairy, a bakery, a portion meat control firm, a restaurant and institutional supply business, a produce firm, a frozen food firm, and various other businesses.

Food Town continued to grow via acquisition in the 1970s and 1980s. The company bought Buckeye Specialties Co., a non-food wholesaler that had been established in 1922 and boasted sales of $5.5 million by 1977. By the end of the decade, Seaway acquired six Toledo-area Joseph's Supermarkets, six Columbus, Ohio, Fisher Foods stores, and ten T&A Thrif-T-Marts in north central Ohio. Food Town also established northwest Ohio's first warehouse-style supermarket, dubbed the Kash 'n' Karry Warehouse Market. This move presaged the incursion of alternative format retailers on supermarketers, and to a certain degree insulated Seaway Food Town from that trend.

Acquisitions helped fuel dramatic increases in sales and profits. Annual revenues more than doubled from $128 million in 1972 to $325.8 million and net income grew even faster, from $1.5 million to $4.7 million, during the same period.

The late 1970s and early 1980s brought an unprecedented level of competition to the low-growth, store-saturated, Toledo-area food market. The primary aggressor during this period was Cincinnati-based Kroger Co., which invested $50 million in the construction of several full-service, multi-department, "Sav-On" stores over the course of the 1980s. Seaway countered the threat with a variety of strategies, perhaps the most

fundamental of which was the discontinuation of the company's wholesaling operations in order to shift managerial concentration to the retail side. The company invested more than $20 million in store remodels from 1978 to 1983 and developed the Food Town Plus store concept in the later years of the 1980s. These large format (48,000 to 60,000 square feet) units featured video rental areas, diverse general merchandise departments, prepared foods, photofinishing, and other one-stop shopping elements.

Seaway also covered more of its competitive bases with a foray into deep discounting. In 1988, the company transformed a supermarket into a W.D.'s Deep Discount store, with a heavy concentration on health and beauty aids, over-the-counter drugs, and general merchandise. Before the year was out, Seaway added several Pharm Deep Discount Drugstores to the roster. These had operated as the Westhaven Drug Stores until 1982, when President Bill Fox changed to the deep discount warehouse format. The Pharm model would become the linchpin of Seaway Food Town's continuing strategy. By 1994, nearly one-third of its stores operated under the deep discount banner. Seaway also acquired four traditional supermarkets in the metro Toledo area before the end of the decade.

Kroger's northwest Ohio push helped it nearly double its share of the metropolitan Toledo market, from 15.5 percent in 1983 to about 32 percent by the early 1990s. Food Town was able to retain its near-30 percent share of the area's supermarket sales, as its annual revenues increased from $428.5 million in 1981 to $512.4 million in 1989. But price wars and other competitive factors squeezed its net income from $5.2 million to $3.8 million during the same period.

In the midst of this competitive environment, Seaway also withstood a takeover threat from Sun Equities Corporation and the Sussex Group. These two companies acquired over five percent of Seaway Food Town's common stock before the company tendered an offer to repurchase it for more than $1 million.

The 1990s brought a new competitive push, this time from Grand Rapids, Michigan-based Meijer, Inc. The non-union Meijer entered the market with its supercenters and promptly launched a price war. The encroachment of Super Kmarts, Cub Foods, and other combination grocery/general merchandise discounters added fuel to the intense rivalries. While Food Town's annual sales continued to rise, albeit erratically, from $512.4 million in 1989 to $566.9 million in 1993, competitive pressures reduced the company's yearly profits from $3.8 million to $1.1 million during the same period. The retailer continued to hold onto its leading share of the Toledo area market through 1994, but its 29.8 percent share was closely shadowed by Kroger's 27.2 percent. Moreover, Meijer had become more than just an irritant, with 11.5 percent of the market.

Under the continuing leadership of Wally Iott into the mid-1990s, Food Town began to rebound. Sales stayed relatively flat, around $555 million, but net income quadrupled from $1.1 million in 1993 to $4.5 million in 1995. The company's 1995 annual report credited ongoing capital investment programs, the introduction of debit card capabilities, productivity enhancements, and new products and services with the improving results. But Seaway Food Town's status as one of Toledo's few remaining hometown chains cannot be discounted. The company maintained a strong commitment to the community through sponsorship of charity, social, educational, and cultural events and efforts. While Seaway gave no indication that Wally Iott was prepared to step aside, it seemed clear that his son, 43-year-old company President Richard Iott, was poised to assume the duties of chairman and chief executive officer. No matter which Iott was to lead Seaway Food Town into the 20th century, the company had its work cut out for it, with net income lagging around the level of the early 1980s and no respite from competition in sight.

Principal Subsidiaries

Northern Distributing Co.; Gruber's Food Town, Inc.; Tracy & Avery Food Town, Inc.; Fjord Properties, Inc.; Second Fjord Properties, Inc.; Third Fjord Properties, Inc.; Third Fjord Properties Community Urban Redevelopment Corp.; Fifth Fjord Properties, Inc.; Fifth Fjord Properties Of Ohio, Inc.; Seaway Properties, Inc.; Custer Pharmacy, Inc. (75 percent); Buckeye Discount, Inc.; Toledo Milk Processing, Inc.; Monroe Acquisition Corp.

Further Reading

Baessler, Jack, "Employees Could Kill Centre Sale," *The Toledo Blade*, April 14, 1989.

——, "Food Town Sets Sales Record, But its Profits Drop," *The Toledo Blade*, January 7, 1994.
Barger, Melvin D., *Toledo: Focused For the Future: A Contemporary Portrait*, Windsor Publications, 1991, pp. 118–119.
"Beat 'Em By Joining 'Em," *Progressive Grocer*, February 1994, p. 82.
Bell, Ned, "Back in Black, Chain Planning Expansion," *The Toledo Blade*, January 6, 1995.
Braknis, Greg, "Seaway Food Town Reports Increase in Profits, Drop in Sales for Fiscal Year," *The Toledo Blade*, October 21, 1994.
DeSanta, Richard, "Unusual Drawing Cards: Never Say Never," *Progressive Grocer*, February 1987, p. 20.
Kisiel, Ralph, "Food Town Pact Approved 2-1; Strike Averted," *The Toledo Blade*, November 23, 1994, p. 21.
——, "Food Town Workers Reject New Contract, But Head Off Strike," *The Toledo Blade*, November 11, 1994.
Linsen, Mary Ann, "Following a Low Price Leader," *Progressive Grocer*, July 1988, p. 35.
McLauglin, Mary-Beth, and Ralph Kisiel, "Food Town Talks Delayed; Union Head to Attend Conference," *The Toledo Blade*, November 12, 1994.
Rothman, Seymour, "How a Little Co-Op Grew Up to $100 Million Gross," *The Toledo Blade*, January 23, 1972, p. B6.
Weber, Ann, "Supermarkets Battling For Market Share," *The Toledo Blade*, October 9, 1983.

—April Dougal Gasbarre

Sierra Health Services, Inc.

2724 North Tenaya Way
Las Vegas, Nevada 89128
U.S.A.
(702) 242-7000
Fax: (702) 242-1531

Public Company
Incorporated: 1984
Employees: 1,700
Sales: $295.8 million (1994)
Stock Exchanges: New York
SICs: 6324 Hospital & Medical Service Plans; 6311 Life
    Insurance; 8082 Home Health Care Services; 6719
    Holding Companies, Not Elsewhere Classified

Overseeing the largest and oldest health maintenance organization (HMO) in Nevada, Sierra Health Services, Inc. is the parent company for a collection of subsidiaries that provide comprehensive managed health care and administrative services. Sierra Health's subsidiaries during the mid-1990s included: Health Plan of Nevada, Inc., an HMO based in Las Vegas; Sierra Health and Life Insurance Company, Inc., a subsidiary licensed to provide health and life insurance in 23 states; Sierra Healthcare Options, Inc., an administrative services company specializing in workers compensation services; Southwest Medical Associates, Inc., Nevada's largest multi-specialty medical group practice; Family Healthcare Services, Inc., a home health care agency; Family Home Hospice, Inc., a hospice available to all terminally ill members of Sierra Health's plans and to the general public; and Behavioral Healthcare Options, Inc., which arranged for and managed the delivery of mental health and substance abuse services. Supported by these primary subsidiaries, Sierra Health occupied a dominant market position in Nevada, with its full range of managed care plans and facilities ranking it as one of the leading companies of its kind in the nation.

During the 1980s, the number of individuals enrolled in HMOs in the United States increased fourfold, rising from less than ten million to more than 35 million, constituting by the end of the decade roughly 15 percent of the nation's population. Although HMOs had been in existence for more than three decades by time their membership ranks began to swell, their share of the medical care market had always been negligible, dwarfed by the conventional "fee-for-service" approach in which patients submit insurance claims to pay for their medical care. HMOs and other managed-care programs did not begin to rise in popularity until health care spending began to spiral uncontrollably upward, forcing those who bore the brunt of escalating health care costs—business and government—to search for more economical alternatives to fee-for-service medicine. One cost-containment alternative was directing employees toward HMOs, which realized savings by limiting a patient's choice of physicians, purchasing medical care wholesale, and eliminating unnecessary procedures. As a result, the number of HMOs in the country increased considerably during the 1980s, jumping from slightly more than 200 in 1980 to more than 600 midway through the decade. Though their increased presence in the health care industry did not arrest mushrooming health care spending in the country—the United States in 1990 spent 40 percent more per capita on health care than Canada, the second biggest spender, and 70 percent more than the third biggest, Switzerland—the emergence of HMOs and managed-care plans gave birth to a new niche within the health care industry: companies whose twin goals were to provide quality medical care and to make a profit.

Early 1980s Incorporation

One of the numerous managed-care companies to begin business during the 1980s was Sierra Health, incorporated as a holding company in 1984 for the express purpose of acquiring Health Plan of Nevada, Ltd., a Nevada partnership, and four affiliated Nevada corporations, Southwest Medical Associates, HPN, Inc., Rancho Surgical Plaza, Inc., and HPN Pharmacy, Inc. The two primary components of the Sierra Health system at its outset were Health Plan of Nevada, an HMO that had been established in 1981, then began enrolling members in October 1982, and Southwest Medical Associates, a group medical practice headed by Anthony M. Marlon, M.D., the founder of Sierra Health.

With Marlon serving as president and chief executive officer, Sierra Health entered the HMO arena at what appeared to be an auspicious time, its formation occurring just as the movement toward increased usage of HMOs was beginning to gain momentum. Conditions within the HMO industry were not, however, as they appeared at first blush. Though the 1980s witnessed the rise to prominence of HMOs within the U.S. health care industry, many of the companies that competed in the burgeoning market during the decade suffered through difficult years, Sierra Health included, as operators struggled to market their new brand of medical care.

Providing quality care and maintaining profitability were formidable and, to some, contrary objectives to pursue, a corporate mission made more difficult by the inferior image of HMOs as second-rate medical care programs. To succeed Sierra Health would need to convince potential customers that managed-care plans, with their restricted lists of physicians, were not impersonal, substandard health care plans, but instead were plans designed to contain medical costs without sacrificing the quality of medical care offered. In pursuing this objective, Sierra Health had a head start of sorts, at least in terms of already having a core customer base when it began operating in 1984. Health Plan of Nevada had been operating in the Las Vegas area for roughly two years by the time Sierra Health began its corporate life, drawing its initial membership from the gaming casinos in the gambling mecca of the United States. Using the business relationships with casino employers in Las Vegas cultivated by Health Plan of Nevada, Sierra Health expanded into other gambling locales in Nevada during its inaugural year, establishing offices in Reno and Carson City, where it secured the bulk of its business from casino employers in search of more inexpensive health care for their employees.

Expansion and Retreat during the Mid-1980s

From there, Sierra Health entered into other, out-of-state markets, establishing managed-care plans in New Mexico, Colorado, and Arizona. During this expansion into states neighboring its headquarters in Las Vegas, Sierra Health became a publicly owned corporation, selling common shares for the first time on the American Stock Exchange in 1985, but those investors who tied their investments to the Nevada-based company were soon disappointed. Sierra Health recorded a net loss of nearly $9 million for the year following its public offering, then barely eked out a small profit the following year, in 1987. Changes were in the offing, as the company was reeling in its third year of business from a debilitative drain on its profits.

Following the disastrous $8.8 million loss in 1986, Marlon and the rest of Sierra Health's management reassessed their company's position and initiated sweeping changes, deciding to narrow the focus of their operations. In 1987, the HMOs in New Mexico, Colorado, and Arizona were divested, leaving the company with only its medical care plans in Nevada. By the end of 1987, the first signs of an encouraging recovery were evident. The company climbed out of the red in 1987, posting $218,000 in profit on $140.3 million in revenue, a promising return to profitability that would have been more remarkable without the money-losing, out-of-state HMOs. Together, the HMOs in New Mexico, Colorado, and Arizona lost $3.7 million in 1987, checking what otherwise would have been a more resolute rise

in profits, but once the company had retreated from its presence outside of Nevada, it occupied more tenable ground, supported by its strong position in its home state.

The sale of the three floundering, out-of-state HMOs were not the only changes effected in the wake of 1986's substantial financial loss, as Sierra Health took further steps to ensure that another precipitous drop in net income would not occur again. The company instituted controls and incentives to contain costs, revised its multi-option health insurance plan to include financial incentives for enrollees to use selected hospitals and physicians, and purchased Family Health Care Services in 1988, a provider of home health care services. Despite the improvements, divestments, and the acquisition of Family Health Care, which provided services to the company's HMO and insurance plans in southern Nevada, Sierra Health once again saw it profits plummet, recording a $3.4 million loss in 1988 on a modest gain in annual revenue. Consistent financial growth was eluding the company, but aside from its fluctuating net income and lackluster revenue growth there were several positive aspects of Sierra Health's business that fueled hopes for future financial growth. The company's medical loss ratio, the percentage of revenues spent on medical expenses, hovered in the low 70s, appreciably less than the mid-80 percent figure that was typical in the HMO industry, and its presence in Nevada was encouragingly strong. Though the company marketed a health insurance plan through its Sierra Health and Life Insurance Co. subsidiary in New Mexico, Arizona, and Colorado, the bulk of its business was conducted in Nevada, where the company ranked as the largest and oldest HMO in the state.

At the heart of its operations in Nevada was the company's Southwest Medical Associates subsidiary, the largest specialty group practice in the state with seven full-service medical centers, each of which provided care for Sierra Health's HMO and insurance enrollees. In total, Sierra Health had roughly 123,000 HMO enrollees and approximately 1,600 HMO enrolled employer groups by the end of the 1980s, relatively small figures when compared against larger HMOs in the nation, but in Nevada Sierra Health's magnitude was virtually unrivalled.

Superior Financial Growth in the 1990s

Entering the 1990s, Sierra Health's management hoped to bring to an end what one *Barron's* reporter referred to as the company's "abysmal earnings history." Sierra Health's annual net income had dipped and dived during the 1980s, demonstrating an unpredictability that left potential investors wary of the company's stock, but the 1990s would be entirely different. Consistent sales and profit growth, which had eluded the company throughout the 1980s, would arrive during the first half of the 1990s, marking the beginning of a more promising era in Sierra Health's history and a period during which rapidly mounting U.S. health care spending captured headlines across the nation. As the debate over health care spending intensified during the early years of the decade, becoming an integral issue in the 1992 presidential election and casting HMOs as a possible solution for spiraling medical costs, Sierra Health recorded an impressive string of annual profit increases, beginning with the $3.2 million in net income it posted in 1990. Over the course of the ensuing four years, the company's annual net income increased each year, rising to $10.8 million in 1991, $13.6

million in 1992, $17.5 million in 1993, and reaching $22.2 million in 1994, while annual revenue climbed from the $158.6 million generated in 1990 to $269.3 million by 1994.

The financial results in 1994 were records for the company, underscoring what had been a highly successful and productive year. Nearly without exception, the subsidiary companies owned by Sierra Health had performed remarkably well, with each expanding in different directions as its parent company prepared for the late 1990s. Health Plan of Nevada Inc., part of Sierra Health's HMO and insurance operations, ranked as the largest HMO in Nevada, covering roughly 60 percent of all HMO members in Nevada, and was expected to increase its lead over competing HMOs by marketing its services in the northern section of the state in 1995. Sierra Health and Life Insurance Company, Inc., a health and life insurance company licensed in 23 states, was aggressively extending its service territory at the end of 1994, attempting to add to the more than 33,000 insurees it covered by expanding into northern Nevada, Texas, Mississippi, Louisiana, Missouri, and California. Southwest Medical Associates, Inc., Nevada's largest multi-specialty medical group practice, opened its tenth medical facility in the Las Vegas area in 1994, and, as the subsidiary was entering 1995, was beginning construction of a new outpatient surgery center.

The success achieved by these and other subsidiaries enabled Sierra Health to conclude 1994 on a high note. The company's stock price reached an all-time high during the year, highlighted by the completion of a stock offering that netted $45 million for the express purpose of funding the company's expansion and new business development. Toward this end, Sierra Health signed a joint venture agreement with The Galtney Group, Inc. in 1994 to begin marketing an HMO plan in Houston in 1995, and reorganized its management structure, readying itself for anticipated growth in the future. Though any future changes to the nation's health care system remained uncertain as Sierra Health entered the mid-1990s, the steady growth of the company during the first half of the decade augured a continuation of financial growth during the latter half of the decade, fueling hope that consistent growth throughout the 1990s would erase the memory of erratic growth during the 1980s.

Principal Subsidiaries

Health Plan of Nevada, Inc.; Sierra Health and Life Insurance Company, Inc.; Southwest Medical Associates, Inc.; Family Healthcare Services, Inc.; Family Home Hospice, Inc.; Sierra Healthcare Options, Inc.; Behavioral Healthcare Options, Inc.; Southwest Realty, Inc.; HMO Texas, L.C. (50%)

Further Reading

"The Best of 1989 So Far," *Business Week,* June 26, 1989, p. 112.
"Nevada-Based Firm Pulls Back, Builds on Home Turf," *Modern Healthcare,* January 13, 1989, p. 38.
Payne, Chris, "Top Nevada HMO Expanding into Houston," *Houston Business Journal,* May 27, 1994, p. 1.
Savitz, Eric J., "No Miracle Cure: HMOs Are Not the Rx for Spiraling Health-Care Costs," *Barron's,* August 5, 1991, p. 8.
"Sierra Health Services Seeks to Become Involved in Department of Defense Tricare Program," *PR Newswire,* March 20, 1996, p. 32.
Zipser, Andy, "HMO Operator Shapes Up," *Barron's,* August 26, 1991, p. 32.

—Jeffrey L. Covell

Sierra On-Line Inc.

3380 146th Place SE, Suite 300
Bellevue, Washington 98007
U.S.A.
(206) 649-9800
Fax: (206) 641-7617

Public Company
Incorporated: 1979 as On-Line Systems
Employees: 629
Sales: $83.4 million (1995)
Stock Exchanges: NASDAQ
SICs: 7372 Prepackaged Software

Sierra On-Line Inc. thrills computer users with interactive educational software and games such as *Phantasmagoria,* one of the best-selling CD-ROM games of the 1990s. Sierra has been acknowledged as one of the most creative companies in a progressive industry, retaining market leadership in personal computer (PC) entertainment software in spite of continuous challenges by large and small competitors.

Sierra's story began when personal computers were a novelty. In 1979, Los Angeles computer programmer Ken Williams bought an Apple for Christmas. His wife Roberta, a real estate speculator, soon found herself hooked on an early text-only, interactive game called *Colossal Cave.* She was intrigued by the possibilities of incorporating graphics into such a narrative adventure game. Ken Williams had himself previously stumbled upon these games while logged onto a remote mainframe computer during a tax software programming session. In 1980, Roberta Williams wrote a murder mystery and her husband wrote the computer code for the game in less than a month. *Mystery House,* the resulting product, immediately sparked incredible demand as the first computer adventure game to combine text and graphics. In the first six months, more than 3,000 copies were sold, worth a retail value of $75,000. These impressive sales came in spite of low-tech packaging involving Ziploc bags and text clipped from magazines.

The company, first known as On-Line Systems, moved in 1980 to Oakhurst, California, at the foot of the Sierra Mountains and was renamed Sierra On-Line. Its second product, also authored by Roberta Williams, was *The Wizard and the Princess;* it sold more than 60,000 copies and offered color graphics. Within three years the company's sales reached $10 million. Roberta Williams's attention to story made her games stand out among the industry's first games, which had been developed by programmers, students, and hackers. This was ironic, since the innovation in her first adventure game was the graphics.

Although Ken and Roberta Williams believed their venture to have lucrative possibilities from the beginning, her success was limited by the growth of the personal computer industry. At first, computers were simply too expensive for the mass market. At the urging of investors, in 1983 the company began producing cartridges for the early Atari video game machines, which were about to fall out of fashion. The resulting disaster forced Sierra to cut its number of employees from 120 to 30. Sierra later agreed to produce a version of its *Red Baron* game, to be released in 1996, for Nintendo's cartridge-based video game system.

A major break for the company came in 1987, when IBM hired the company to develop a game to highlight its XT line of PCs. *King's Quest,* conceived by Roberta Williams, proved Sierra could continue to ride the crest of innovation and lead a new generation of video games. Besides garnering international awards, *King's Quest* spawned as many sequels as a Hollywood blockbuster. By the mid-1990s, series sales had reached 3 million copies, with each sequel selling better than its predecessor.

Sierra On-Line featured female heroines in later versions of *King's Quest* and in the 1995 release *Phantasmagoria,* a development in which Roberta Williams took pride. Realizing that most buyers of computer software were male, she dared to make a female character, Princess Rosella, the protagonist for *King's Quest IV.* The gambit worked, and the game sold twice as well as its predecessors. In 1994 Roberta Williams estimated that women made up 15 percent (growing two percent yearly) of Sierra On-Line's customers.

In 1989, the company started its own games-only network, another first, which fared poorly out of the gate in spite of a $1 million investment. The ImagiNation Network, originally known as the Sierra Network, formed an alliance with Prodigy in 1993, and added CUC International's Shopper's Advantage on-line shopping service. Although the network reached 45,000 subscribers, high development costs consumed its increasing revenues ($20 million in 1994). The company's poor performance at this time prompted lay-offs of 60 employees. The network was taken over by American Telephone & Telegraph in 1994, which agreed to pay royalties to Sierra for its software used on the network, as well as certain development costs.

In 1990, Sierra acquired Eugene, Oregon-based Dynamix, a specialist in flight simulation games founded in 1984 by Jeff Tunnell and Damon Slye. Bright Star Technologies, an educational software firm founded by programmer Elon Gasper, was added in 1992 just as the educational software market was becoming the fastest-growing segment of the software industry. The timing was perfect for Sierra: according to Software Publishers of America, annual home educational software sales rose from $146 million to $243 million in 1993. Bright Star benefited from improved distribution and marketing, and Sierra was able to build on Bright Star's HyperAnimation, Talking Tiles, and Alphabet Blocks offerings. The success of this enterprise resulted in 19 new employees being hired at Bright Star in the first year, quadrupling the work force.

The company went public in 1989, and a second offering followed in 1992, when sales were $41.7 million. The year 1993 proved to be a bleak one; losses were also reported in 1994. Sierra relocated its headquarters to Seattle in 1993. Ken Williams cited difficulties convincing senior executives to move to rural Oakhurst, California as the prime reason for the move. In the same year, Sierra bought Coktel Vision, headquartered in Paris, which published both education and entertainment software. Ken Williams stated that Sierra's goal was to become the leader in educational software. Further to this end, Sierra and Western Publishing Group Inc., a leading publisher of children's books, joined in developing interactive software for children aged three to eight under Western's "Golden Step Ahead" brand. Children's Television Workshop, producers of "Sesame Street," announced plans to create a show based on Sierra's Dr. Brain math and science series. Sierra Education also marketed and developed such titles as Berlitz Live! and Talking Tutors. A 1995 joint venture with Pioneer Electronic Corp. established a presence in Japan through Sierra Pioneer, Inc. European sales were worth $15.7 million in 1995 and American sales hit $60.7 million. Other exports, including Canada and Asia, were worth $5.0 million.

With $90 million in cash available in 1995, Sierra shopped for underdeveloped companies in fields beyond the highly seasonal entertainment and educational software markets. To round out its strategy games, Sierra bought Cambridge, Massachusetts-based Impressions Software. Sports, auto racing, and flight simulation offerings were beefed up with the purchase of Papyrus Design Group (Watertown, Massachusetts) and SubLogic (Champaign, Illinois), respectively. Home productivity, however, was the focus of Sierra's 1995 acquisitions. The rights to Print Artist, a desktop publishing program for produc-

ing greeting cards and banners, were acquired from The Pixellite Group, a group of 10 California developers. Green Thumb Software and Arion added gardening and cooking titles to the Sierra line. P. F. Collier embarked on a joint venture with Sierra to produce a multimedia encyclopedia. Sierra breezed into the kitchen with its 1995 purchase of Arion Software's MasterCook series. The series offered a way to manage a database of recipes, as well as scale down the ingredients to produce differing numbers of servings. Although the adventure category's share of Sierra's sales fell to 36 percent in 1995 from 47.4 percent the previous year, education sales hovered around 14 percent. Most of the growth came in the simulation category, nearly doubling from 15.2 percent to 27.9 percent.

With the coursing growth of computer technology, Sierra On-Line came into its own. Multimedia systems and the compact disc added the capacity for full-motion video and high fidelity audio to the gaming scene. Mixed-Up Mother Goose, touted as the first true PC multimedia game, was released in 1990. Sierra On-Line spent lavishly to make the game-playing experience live up to its potential; development efforts occupied more than 75 percent of its staff, and scores of writers, musicians, and actors were employed. The company developed a special computer language, Sierra Creative Interpreter, to allow artists and musicians to contribute without being mired in programming details.

After months of delays, *Phantasmagoria* was finally released in 1995. A true multimedia product, the game was contained on seven CD-ROMs and featured live actors, three-dimensional backgrounds, and high fidelity sound effects. CD-ROM products, with their capacity to hold tremendous amounts of sound and picture data, grew increasingly important to Sierra, accounting for 36 percent of game sales in 1994 and 65 percent in 1995. *Phantasmagoria* was too violent for retailer CompUSA Inc., which refused to carry it. The company included a password protection option with the game to let concerned parents limit their children's access to explicit scenes. The *Leisure Suit Larry* series had earlier made certain critics groan because of suggestive themes. Nevertheless, by 1995 it had sold more than 1 million copies.

Sierra pushed the envelope of gaming again in 1995 when it applied IBM VoiceType speech recognition technology to its *Command* U-boat simulation. Allowing players to merely speak commands rather than enter them through a keyboard or mouse, the CD-ROM included a video orientation featuring historical footage of World War II U-boat commanders. To operate, the game required up-to-date hardware and Windows 95.

The company's products were distributed in at least 50 countries in the mid-1990s. Massive investments in the most advanced technologies, world class talent, and the uncanny instincts of Ken and Roberta Williams have virtually ensured Sierra's presence at the top of the programming heap into the new century.

Principal Subsidiaries

Coktel Vision S.A. (France); Bright Star Technology, Inc.; Dynamix, Inc.; Sierra Pioneer, Inc. (Japan; 51%).

Further Reading

Baker. M. Sharon. "CFO's Sharp Pencil Puts Sierra On-Line on Track." *Puget Sound Business Journal,* November 18, 1994, p. 9.

——. "Sierra On-Line Goes Shopping for Smaller Software Firms." *Puget Sound Business Journal,* June 9, 1995, p. 4.

——. "Sierra On-Line Moving HQ to Seattle Area," *Puget Sound Business Journal,* May 21, 1993, pp. 1, 39.

——. "'Visionary' Workaholic Leads Game-Maker Sierra," *Puget Sound Business Journal,* October 22, 1993, pp. 1, 49.

"A Brief History of Sierra On-Line. . ." Bellevue, Wash.: Sierra On-Line, Inc., n.d.

Brandt, Richard, "Serious Money from the Games PCs Play," *Business Week,* May 21, 1990, p. 112.

Brenesal, Barry, "Journey to the Dark Side with Gabriel Knight," *PC Magazine,* May 31, 1994.

Champion, Jill, "Redesigning the Classics," *Compute,* January, 1992, p. 8.

Eng, Paul M., and Evan I. Schwartz, "The Games People Play in the Office," *Business Week,* October 11, 1993, p. 40.

Greenman, Catherine, "The Teaching Game: Big Bucks Lure Software Makers To Mix Education and Entertainment," *HFD: The Weekly Home Furnishings Newspaper,* June 20, 1994, p. C14.

——, "Phantasmagoria Retailers Wait," *HFN: The Weekly Newspaper for the Home Furnishing Network,* July 10, 1995, p. 85.

Khalaf, Roula, "Accounting Adventure," *Forbes,* September 28, 1992, pp. 116–118.

Khermouch, Gerry, "IBM, Sierra Set Campus Disk Drive," *Brandweek,* August 30, 1993, p. 3.

Kramer, Farrell, "Game Designer Touts Story: Woman Has Seen Some Controversy With Career Choice," *The State* (Columbia, S. Car.), November 5, 1995, p. H3.

LaPlante, Alice. "The Other Half," *PC Week,* March 21, 1994, p. A1.

Losee, Stephanie. "*Fortune* Visits 25 Cool Companies: Sierra On-Line," *Fortune,* Autumn, 1993, p. 82.

Manly, Lorne, "Titles Try Hybrid Online Options," *Folio: The Magazine for Magazine Management,* May 1, 1994, p. 22.

"Next He Does Robo-Cop?," *Time,* October 4, 1993, p. 93.

Nicholls, Paul, "Multimedia Personal Computing: A Guide to the New MPC," *CD-ROM Professional,* September 1992, pp. 113–117.

Rubenking, Neil J., "Leisure Suit Larry Shapes Up," *PC Magazine,* March 29, 1994, p. 408.

Sandberg, Jared, "AT&T Corp. Agrees To Pay $40 Million for Remaining 80% of ImagiNation," *The Wall Street Journal,* November 16, 1994, p. 6.

Schiff, David, "The Dangers of Creative Accounting," *Worth,* March 1993.

Schwartz, Steven A., "Space Quest 1: Roger Wilco in the Sarien Encounter," *Macworld,* April 1993, p. 171.

Shaw, Simon, "Games War," *Management Today,* December 1994, pp. 76–80.

"Sierra Intros Voice-Controlled Game," *Newsbytes,* September 18, 1995.

"Sierra On-Line Inc.," *Television Digest,* February 13, 1995, p. 14.

Spector, Lincoln, "Recipe Software—It Isn't All Out to Lunch," *PC World,* January 1996.

Trivette, Donald B., "The Top 100 CD-ROMs: Entertainment," *PC Magazine,* September 13, 1994.

—Frederick C. Ingram

S·K·I

LIMITED

S-K-I Limited

Airport Executive Plaza #5
P.O. Box 5494
West Lebanon, New Hampshire 03784
U.S.A.
(603) 298-1111
Fax: (603) 298-1144

Public Company
Incorporated: 1956 as Sherburne Corporation
Employees: 2,500
Revenues: $114 million (1995)
Stock Exchange: NASDAQ
SICs: 6719 Holding Companies, Not Elsewhere
   Classified; 7011 Hotels & Motels; 7999 Amusement
   & Recreation, Not Elsewhere Classified

A holding company of several ski resorts, S-K-I Limited is best known for founding the Killington ski area, located in the Green Mountains of Vermont. Killington is the most popular ski resort in the eastern United States. Other ski resorts owned by S-K-I include Mount Snow (Vermont), Haystack (Vermont), Sugarloaf (Maine), and Waterville Valley (New Hampshire). The resorts also provide summer recreation, including tennis, hiking, mountain biking, and golf. S-K-I's corporate address is in New Hampshire, where it handles accounting, auditing, and payroll for all its resorts. S-K-I also maintains corporate offices at the Killington resort.

Vermont was an area of early ski development in the United States. The first known rope tow in the United States was installed in 1934 at Gilbert's Hill, near Woodstock, Vermont. Six years later, in 1940, the country's first T-bar lift opened at Pico Ski Area, also in Vermont and close to the future Killington resort. Downhill ski areas would sprout up in great numbers after World War II, in part because the postwar economic boom provided Americans with more disposable income for recreation. Also helpful was government support. Access roads, for example, were built with government funds, and the U.S. mili-

tary, which provided skis and ski equipment for its ski troopers, flooded the market after the war with inexpensive skis.

S-K-I's founder, Preston Leete Smith, was himself caught up in the new sport. Born in New York in 1930, Smith grew up in Connecticut and attended Earlham College, a Quaker school in Indiana. After graduating in 1952, he returned to Connecticut, settling in Guilford, where he became the manager of a silk-screen shop. At this point Smith could hardly ski, but he joined the New Haven and Waterbury ski clubs, which sponsored trips to Vermont ski resorts, including Mount Snow, which S-K-I would eventually own. Smith recalled, "I had a terrible time skiing every weekend because I didn't earn very much money. I used to drive 12 hours in a snowstorm in an old convertible, wearing a moth-eaten raccoon coat and eating peanut butter and crackers."

After marrying Susanne Hahn in 1954, Smith began to look for a career. He considered setting up a ski lodge at Stowe, an existing resort in Vermont, but only briefly. He explained, "I had no money and few people would be interested in financing a ski lodge. But there were a lot of people interested in a ski area, and I thought the financial support would be there."

Another man, Perry Merrill, Vermont's commissioner of forests and parks, also had an interest in establishing ski resorts. As early as 1941 he had tried to encourage someone to develop Killington Peak, which at 4,241 feet was the second-highest in the state, but there were a number of drawbacks, such as the lack of a suitable access road. Killington had been used for recreation as far back as 1859, when there were organized horseback excursions. The Killington Summit House, moreover, open from about 1880 to 1915, attracted numerous visitors, including Oscar Wilde.

Smith initially considered purchasing Mount Ascutney, a small, existing ski area. He decided to approach Merrill with his idea. Reportedly, Merrill said, "Come back and see me after you've seen Killington." Smith did, but "It wasn't until I got into a methodological review of potentialities of various locations that I began to understand the value of Killington, with [the towns of] Rutland and Woodstock already built up on either side and roads coming in to Sherburne from several directions."

Though he had no experience in the ski industry, Smith began contacting New York and Boston investors, providing them with a plan to develop the Killington area. These early attempts came to nothing. A friend, Tom Bodine, set up a meeting with insurance executives in Hartford, Connecticut. That effort also failed to raise money, but it was there that Smith met Joseph Sargent, who was representing Conning and Company, an investment research firm that advised insurance companies. Sargent, himself just 26 and a long-time skier, found Smith's plan for a "million dollar ski area" that would have spread across three mountain peaks interesting but too extravagant. At the meeting he told Smith only a scaled-down version would be possible.

In October 1955 Smith and Sargent again met, and several months later the two men, along with fellow Yale graduate Joseph Van Vleck, traveled to Killington to survey the area. Sargent and Van Vleck were impressed with Killington, and the short distance to metropolitan areas was seen as especially important. Sargent also felt a kindred spirit with Smith. They soon decided to form a corporation of stockholders to raise money. The first five investors were Preston and Susanne Smith, Sargent and his wife, Mary, and Van Vleck, each of whom put up $250 for a total capital of $1,250. Called Sherburne Corporation (Sherburne was the nearest town to Killington), the company was registered in Vermont on April 6, 1956.

Although the new corporation would be successful in raising money ($127,500 by 1958), the project was heavily dependent upon cooperation with the state government, which owned the Killington area. Before constructing buildings, cutting trees, or installing lifts, the company needed approval from the state. Most important, perhaps, the resort needed a new access road, which the state agreed to build at a cost of $254,512 (though delays on building the road would put the Killington project behind schedule).

The first trails were cut in 1957, and work on the access road began the following April. Two "poma" surface lifts were installed in late 1958. Smith and Sargent oversaw the construction themselves and took part in the physical work, putting together lift poles, for example, and cutting trees. Sargent explained, "We could simply not afford to take the risk of someone else doing it wrong with what little stockholder capital we had."

Initially called Killington Basin Ski Area, the resort opened for business on December 13, 1958. Although there was significant coverage in the local press, no special events were held at the beginning. Tickets were sold from a converted chicken coop. Two more poma lifts were installed in January, making Killington the first U.S. resort to have as many as four lifts in its first season. Sales were slow at first; $113.35 in gross receipts in the first week, and in January monthly receipts reached only $2,860.15. But Sargent remembers waking up one February morning to the sound "zoom, zoom, zoom," as cars flew by on the way to the resort. Killington had been discovered, and in February monthly lift receipts jumped to more than $10,000. The season ended with gross receipts of $42,847. Although Sherburne Corporation lost $21,045 its first year, it proved to its stockholders that Killington would likely be a profitable operation. In fact, from 1958 to 1995, that would be its only year without a profit.

In the 1960s Sherburne would oversee a growing Killington that was destined to become Vermont's largest ski resort. "Skier visits" reached 118,000 in the 1961–1962 year. More trails were cut, additional lifts were installed (the first chair lift came in 1960), and the state again supported the resort by constructing a large day lodge and expanding the parking lot. The company's success was attributable to many factors, including a growing population of skiers throughout the United States. But it also had the advantage of being run by two men with complimentary strengths; Smith had a remarkable ability to guess what skiers wanted, and Sargent possessed financial and business expertise.

One of Smith's most significant early decisions, in 1963, was to install a snowmaking system, which was unheard of in Vermont, where there was much natural snow. But conditions varied, bringing occasional warm weather and rain, and Sherburne wanted to extend the ski season as long as possible to boost revenues. Instead of running from mid-December to mid-April, as was customary for resorts, Killington would eventually be able to open in October and close in early June. Smith also decided to develop an all-novice area, Snowshed, complete with its own chair lift, which was looked upon with suspicion by competing resorts. It was a huge success.

Other Killington innovations included the "ticket wicket," developed in 1963, which was a piece of shaped wire threaded through a zipper talon; a lift ticket was stapled over it (adhesive would later be used). This not only prevented skiers from sharing tickets but allowed them to attach the ticket to a jacket without damaging the material. The wicket was patented and sold to resorts around the country. It was also at Killington that the famous GLM (Graduated Length Method) of ski instruction was started. Beginners were given lessons on short skis, which were easy to turn, and as they improved they were given increasingly longer skis (longer skis were optimal because they provided more stability). The GLM technique spread across the country, becoming for a while a dominant method of instruction. Beginning in the 1967–68 season, skiers could also ski the first hour at Killington without a charge, allowing them to test conditions before buying a ticket.

By 1968 the resort was recording more than 300,000 annual skier visits, providing $2 million in revenue. 30 trails, nine lifts, and three base lodges spilled off Killington Peak and three other mountain areas. That year Killington also began to install a gondola. Stretching three-and-a-half miles up the mountain, the gondola was the world's longest ski lift. The gondola brought prestige and increased publicity to Killington, and its great length boosted the vertical drop (the difference in elevation between the resort's top and bottom) to 3,000 feet, making Killington, in that respect comparable to famous Western ski areas.

In the early 1970s the state of Vermont passed new environmental laws, a reaction in part to reckless resort development (near Willington, Vermont, for example, developers built vacation homes without proper sewage disposal). The new laws made all development, including the construction of trails, lifts, and buildings, more difficult. For Killington, which hoped to build a resort village (as many Western resorts had already done), it meant delays in and an eventual scaling back of its plans. Rather than grow Killington, Sherburne began looking for an existing resort to buy. In 1972 the company purchased a 52 percent share of Sunday River, a ski resort in western Maine, which had many weaknesses, including a poor marketing program and a shortage of indoor space. Sherburne immediately built a new base lodge, revamped the marketing program, and improved the snowmaking system, and by the next season Sunday River recorded a 13 percent increase in revenues.

Sherburne raised its share of ownership in Sunday River to 67 percent in 1973. Although the resort continued to improve, growth was less than hoped for, and in 1980 Sherburne sold its interest in Sunday River to the resort's general manager, Les Otten (who would go on to found LBO Holdings, a ski resort holding company in the East and a major competitor to Sherburne). More successful would be Sherburne's 1977 acquisition of Mount Snow, a resort in southern Vermont. Though suffering from poor management, outmoded equipment, and declining skier visits, Mount Snow had the advantage of being near the Massachusetts border and thus close to major day markets. Over the next decade Sherburne would dump some $26 million in Mount Snow, making it the second most popular ski area in the East (second only to Killington).

By 1980 Sherburne, with its two successful resorts, had revenues of $17.8 million (684,000 skier visits). That figure rose to $31.8 million (1.1 million visits) in 1982 and $43.3 million (1.3 million visits) in 1984. Despite this growth, its shares were available only on the ''pink sheets'' (a service for stocks not listed on an exchange), which made it difficult to raise capital. Partly as a way to get its stock on an exchange, the company decided to undergo a major restructuring. In November 1984 it formed a new holding company, S-K-I Limited, in the state of Delaware; the initials S-K-I stood for ''Sherburne-Killington-Investments.'' Delaware was chosen, Smith said, because ''its business laws were as good or better than anywhere else and known to be more progressive in regard to corporate law.'' Sherburne Corporation (renamed Killington Limited in 1985) subsequently became a subsidiary of S-K-I, and management of Mount Snow was reorganized in 1986 into its own subsidiary, Mount Snow Limited. S-K-I's stock was listed on the NASDAQ system.

By the late 1980s S-K-I was one of the largest and most profitable ski companies in the United States. In 1987 it recorded some 1.6 million skier visits, bringing in revenues of $66.1 million. The company also continued to make large investments, including the installation of ''high-speed quads'' (introduced at Killington in 1988), which were faster, four-person chair lifts. At a cost of more than $1 million, a high-speed quad had the advantages of moving skiers quickly up the mountain and providing exceptionally easy loading and unloading. The Killington village, too, was growing, though at a slow pace because of environmental concerns about new development.

S-K-I also continued to buy existing ski areas. In 1986 Mount Snow acquired adjacent Carinthia Ski Area, giving it an additional 18 trails, three lifts, and a lodge (compared to Mount Snow, which in 1988 had 75 trails, 16 lifts, and four base lodges). Next, in 1988, S-K-I purchased Goldmine Ski Area in California for $10 million and invested another $12 million in better snowmaking, more trails, a new lodge, and other improvements. Renamed Bear Mountain, the resort would increase its revenues, though not as much as anticipated. S-K-I sold the resort in 1995. This sale, however, came just a year after S-K-I had acquired three other resorts: Waterville Valley in New Hampshire; Sugarloaf (51 percent share) in Maine; and Haystack (adjacent to Mount Snow) in Vermont. With these resorts S-K-I raised revenues to $114 million in 1995 and total skier visits to more than 2 million. By this time its Killington resort had grown to 165 trails, seven base lodges, and 20 lifts, including an eight-passenger lift with heated cabins.

By the mid-1990s a new corporate age of ski resorts had emerged. Small and midsize resorts were struggling to stay in business, and large corporations were buying up existing ski areas. In the East, S-K-I's largest competitor was LBO Holdings, controlled by Les Otten, which owned not only Sunday River but also Attitash (New Hampshire) and Sugarbush (Vermont). Purchasing nearby resorts had many advantages—notably savings in management costs, public relations, and purchasing—that freed up money for additional improvements, such as high-speed quads. Acquisitions also allowed companies to sell multi-area season passes and ticket books, giving skiers more choices. In 1994–95, for example, S-K-I sold a $990 season pass good at Killington, Sugarloaf, Waterville, Haystack, and Mount Snow. Perhaps most impressive, however, was S-K-I's ability to run a profit in the face of seemingly any obstacle, from recessions and years of poor snowfall to environmental challenges. In 1995 it completed its 36th year of consecutive profitability. By February of the following year, plans were underway for S-K-I to be acquired by rival American Skiing Co., headed by Leslie Otten, for an estimated $105 million. The move was reportedly part of a general shakeout in the ski industry, in which players in a flat resort market faced either downsizing or aligning themselves with large hotel and entertainment companies. S-K-I appeared positioned to benefit from the deep pockets of Otten's ski empire.

Principal Subsidiaries

Killington Limited; Mount Snow Limited; Sugarloaf Mountain Corporation (51%); Waterville Valley Ski Area Limited; Ski Insurance Company

Further Reading

Carlson, Lee, ''Resorts Enter New, Corporate Age,'' *Skiing Trade News,* November 1994, p. 22.

Kanter, Evelyn, ''Eastern Areas in Buying Frenzy, *Skiing Trade News,* October 1993, p. 14.

Lane, Randall, ''Shakeout in Skiing,'' *Forbes,* May 6, 1996, pp. 56, 58.

Lorenz, Karen D., *Killington: A Story of Mountains and Men,* Shrewsbury, Vt.: Mountain Publishing, Inc, 1990.

Sneyd, Ross, ''Killington's Mogul Smith Drives SKI Ltd. Expansion,'' *Burlington Free Press,* September 18, 1994. pp. 1E, 3E.

——, ''Rival Companies Fight for New England Skiers, *Burlington Free Press,* September 18, 1994, p. 1E.

—Thomas Riggs

Skis Rossignol S.A.

38500 Voiron
France
(76) 66-65-65
Fax: (76) 65-67-51

Public Company
Incorporated: 1972
Employees: 2,330
Sales: $340 million
Stock Exchanges: Paris
SICs: 3949 Sporting and Athletic Goods, Not Elsewhere
     Classified

Skis Rossignol S.A. is one of the world's premier manufacturers of ski equipment. Headquartered in Voiron, a small town in southeastern France, the company was among the first to make skis in France and was an early leader in ski technology and design. Its skis, for example, were used in the 1936 Winter Olympics, the very first to include alpine ski events, and have in later years been worn by numerous Olympic and World Cup champions. In the 1990s some one-third of all downhill skis sold throughout the world were manufactured by Rossignol. The company's major markets are in Europe, Japan, and the United States. Since the 1970s the company has diversified into new areas of ski equipment, first cross-country skis and later ski boots, poles, snowboards, bindings, and accessories. Rossignol also manufactures tennis rackets and golf clubs. While most of its products are sold under the Rossignol brand name, the company has also expanded through the purchase of existing brands, such as Lange (boots) and Dynastar (skis).

For thousands of years skiing was a practical activity, forming an important means of transportation in snowbound regions. Skiing was particularly popular in Scandinavia, and hunters and soldiers wore skis during the winter months. But it was not until the 19th century that skiing began to develop into a sport. Early events focused on cross-country skiing. Downhill events were begun after skiers had developed new techniques, most notably the telemark turn, and competitors would race down the moun-

tain at speeds as fast as 80 miles an hour. Compared with modern equipment, skis of this era were heavy and long; made of solid wood, they measured between eight and 14 feet.

In France an interest in sport skiing took hold in the vicinity of Grenoble, a town in the French Alps not far from the Italian border. Skiers initially wore equipment manufactured in Scandinavia, though these skis were not designed for the conditions of the French Alps, which tended to be steeper and more icy. The military ski school in Briançon, southeast of Grenoble, produced the first French-made downhill skis, introduced in 1906. By the next year the popularity of sport skiing had boomed in France. Numerous ski events were held in the Alps, and French artisans joined in the production of skis to meet the new demand. These new skis were generally made of ash, pine, or larch, woods that were chosen for their flexibility and resilience.

Early in the 19th century, Abel Rossignol, a skiing enthusiast and craftsman, was the head of a wood turnery in Voiron, a town just northeast of Grenoble. The turnery, founded in 1901, was producing wooden articles for the textile industry. In 1907 Abel decided to introduce his own pair of downhill skis, which were made of solid wood protected with a light-colored varnish. No ordinary skis, they were awarded first prize at a contest sponsored by the Touring Club of France, and in 1911, bolstered by his success, Rossignol established a new "skis and sleds" division of his company. Rossignol would continue to make solid-wood skis for the next three decades, and production would reach several hundred per year.

In the 1930s France emerged as a skiing power, led by Emile Allais. At the 1936 Winter Olympics held at Garmisch-Partenkirchen, Germany, Allais won the bronze medal in the alpine combined, and the following year, at the world championships, he won the gold medal in all three alpine events, earning the title "champion of the world." All his medals were won on Rossignol skis. During this time Allais was also codifying his own method of ski instruction, published in the book *Ski Français*.

In 1936 Rossignol hired Allais as its technical adviser and official tester, a position Allais used to help the company design some of the world's most advanced skis. The primary weakness of the company's skis was their solid-wood construction. Unless the wood had a uniform grain, for example, the ski would tend to warp during production, and even good solid wood skis would begin to lose their shape with age. Some of Rossignol's competitors had already found a solution—a laminated, or layered, construction similar to plywood, with wood grains running in different directions—which made a lighter, more durable wooden ski. By using different types of wood and various patterns of lamination, manufacturers could also choose the ski's specific flexibility and resilience. Although Rossignol was not the originator of this idea, the company's first laminated ski, the Olympic 41, was an advance in design. Developed in 1941, the ski found great success after World War II, carrying such racers as Henri Oreiller (1948) and Ottmar Schneider (1952) to Olympic victories. The ski's success was also seen at Rossignol's Voiron factory, where production would jump to several thousand by 1951.

Laminated skis also had problems with maintenance and durability. Like all wooden skis, they absorbed water and were easily damaged, and to slide smoothly across the snow, they needed to be regularly waxed. Some manufacturers began to experiment with other materials, especially metal. Metal skis would prove to be more durable, more resilient, and faster than wooden skis. The first successful metal ski was made by American aviation engineer Howard Head. Using the "sandwich"-type design found on aircraft, Head placed two strips of aluminum (the top and bottom of the ski) around a plywood core, added a plastic bottom, and then attached an exceptionally hard metal edge to improve control. Introduced in the early 1950s, Head skis were an immediate hit, especially among recreational skiers.

Allais, who tested an early pair of Head skis in the United States, was impressed with their handling in soft snow and powder, but he found them "totally unsuited" for the hard-packed snow of competitive skiing. Even so, he brought several pairs of Head skis back to France and began with Rossignol to come up with his own design. One of Rossignol's first metal skis, the Allais 60, would quickly get the world's attention. At the 1960 Winter Olympics, held at Squaw Valley, California, Frenchman Jean Vuarnet won the men's downhill event using the Allais 60, making it the first metal ski to win an Olympic gold medal. According to Emile Allais, the ski's "characteristics, notably its ability to grip [the snow], were much superior to the wooden skis still used during this time." Despite their success, the Allais 60 and other metal skis would prove to be merely a transition from wooden skis to those made from fiberglass and other synthetic materials, which were both lighter and more resilient than metal.

While Rossignol was embarking on a program of new technology, the company itself was undergoing significant change. In the mid-1950s Rossignol was still organized into two main activities—ski manufacture and the production of wooden articles for the textile industry. The textile industry, however, was in decline, a trend that was putting a severe financial strain on Rossignol. Thus, in order to save itself, Allais approached his friend Laurent Boix-Vives, a 29-year-old French businessman, who was the owner of Société des Téléskis de Moriond, a small ski-lift company in Courchevel, a town northeast of Grenoble. Boix-Vives agreed to purchase Rossignol for a mere $50,000.

One of his first decisions, in 1956, was to drop the company's textile operations (Rossignol's original line of business) and to have it focus solely on ski production. Under Boix-Vives's guidance, first as *gérant* (managing director, 1956–1960) and then as *président-directeur général* (from 1960), the company would be transformed from a small factory producing several thousand skis per year to a multinational corporation with subsidiaries in several countries. By 1972, when the company was incorporated as Skis Rossignol S.A., Rossignol had become the world's best-selling brand of ski, a position it would continue to hold into the 1990s, when the company's production reached some two million pairs of skis per year.

This phenomenal growth would be aided by several external factors, including the increased popularity of skiing in the 1960s and 1970s, especially in the United States, an important export market. In 1973 Rossignol established a subsidiary in the United States, Rossignol Ski Company, Inc., in Williston, Vermont, and manufactured skis in that state from 1973 to 1984. More skiers meant greater sales for all companies, but Rossignol also gained market share through its investment in research and development, which allowed it to manufacture some of the world's most advanced ski equipment.

Rossignol's first truly successful fiberglass ski was the Strato, introduced in the mid-1960s, which was actually made of a complex layering of various materials, including a plastic called acrylonitrile butadien styrene, or simply ABS, which formed the top layer and the side walls of the ski. The Strato, like previous Rossignol skis, proved popular among world-class racers. At the 1968 Winter Olympics, held in Grenoble (near the Voiron factory), the Strato was worn by five medalists, including Canadian Nancy Greene, winner of the giant slalom. By this time the company was also producing skis under the name Dynastar, a brand bought by Rossignol in 1967.

In the early 1970s Rossignol introduced its first skis made without any wood at all. These featured a light density, polyurethane core, which not only was cheaper than wood but also made the ski more comfortable. Rossignol's racing skis, including the ROC and the ST, were filled with this polyurethane plastic and, as expected, performed exceptionally well in international competition. For example, at the 1976 Olympic games at Innsbruck, Austria, Rossignol's plastic-core skis were worn by six medalists, twice as many as the nearest competing brand.

Over the next two decades Rossignol spent millions of dollars refining the design of its plastic-based skis. Performance and comfort were enhanced, for example, by Rossignol's patented Vibration Absorbing System (VAS), introduced in 1981. Made with an inner layer of steel wire and other materials, VAS was designed to reduce only harmful vibration, while preserving vibration that actually improved ski performance and speed. Complementing this system beginning in 1984 was an "external" VAS—a light-alloy stress plate attached with "viscoelastic" material to the top of Rossignol skis. Another notable improvement was the "Rossitop," introduced in 1992, which was an eight-millimeter-thick layer of transparent plastic that protected the ski's cosmetics.

Also important to the company's success was its decision to produce other types of ski equipment. Its first major diversification was in 1971, when the company introduced a Rossignol brand of cross-country skis. Manufactured in Sweden, these skis were still made entirely of wood, as were many cross-country skis at the time, but in 1974 the Voiron factory began making a fiberglass model. Cross-country skiing grew increasingly popular during the 1970s, and thus, in 1976, Rossignol established a separate cross-country division to oversee the product. This commitment to the sport was seen ten years later, in 1987, when it introduced its ''System Concept'' line of cross-country skis, boots, and bindings, which were specifically designed to work together. That year Rossignol also developed an air-injection method that produced exceptionally lightweight, durable cross-country skis.

Though Rossignol was the world's largest manufacturer of downhill skis, the company did not have its own line of downhill ski boots until 1989, when it purchased Lange, a brand of ski boots since 1965. Rossignol would gain much from Lange's existing research and development program. In the 1980s Lange had been working on a compromise between the two most popular types of ski boots. The first—pioneered by Lange's founder, Bob Lange of Dubuque, Iowa—was an all-plastic boot fitted with a series of buckles across the front. Exceptionally stiff, this boot efficiently translated body movement to the ski and was especially popular among competitive racers. The second, introduced in the early 1970s, was an all-plastic rear-entry model, in which the back of the boot hinged off to provide easy access for the foot. The rear-entry boot was more convenient and comfortable than front-buckle models, though its performance was generally regarded as inferior. The eventual compromise, introduced in 1989 under both the Lange and Rossignol brand names, was the MID line of ski boots. Although these were, in fact, front-buckle boots, a unique hinge system allowed the top to open wider, thus making them easier to put on. The traditional front-buckle design, however, continued to be used for many Rossignol and Lange boots, especially for high-performance models.

By the early 1990s Rossignol was also making a variety of other ski equipment, including ski poles, monoskis, snowboards, and accessories, such as bags, gloves, socks, shirts, sweaters, and hats. By this time the company had also diversified outside the ski industry. In 1977 it had introduced a line of Rossignol tennis rackets, and in 1990 Rossignol Ski Company purchased Roger Cleveland Golf Company of Paramount, California.

As early as 1991 Rossignol was testing prototypes of a new downhill ski binding, which was the only major piece of ski equipment it did not yet manufacture. It soon became clear, however, that development and marketing of an entirely new binding would be more expensive than simply buying an existing brand. Thus, in 1994 Rossignol purchased two well-known brands of ski bindings, Look and Geze, and plans were begun to sell bindings under the Rossignol brand name as well.

In the mid-1990s Skis Rossignol S.A. was the world's dominant manufacturer of ski equipment. The company each year sold some two million pairs of Rossignol and Dynastar skis, or about 30 percent of the world's ski category, putting them far ahead of their numerous competitors, such as Head, K2, Elan, Atomic, Salomon, and Pre. The company also had yearly sales of some 800,000 boots (Rossignol and Lange), 80,000 cross-country skis (Rossignol), and 900,000 ski poles (Rossignol, Dynastar, and Kerma).

There were, however, a number of sales variables beyond the company's control. Perhaps most important were changes in worldwide snow conditions. From 1987 to 1989, for example, poor snowfall in Europe brought declining sales there for Rossignol and other ski brands. Revenues from Rossignol's products were also heavily affected by exchange rate fluctuations between the French franc and the currencies of its major markets, as more than 80 percent of all Rossignol's sales were outside of France.

Meanwhile, Skis Rossignol S.A. was also benefiting from a number of advantages. As the world's leading producer of skis, Rossignol has enjoyed almost universal name recognition among skiers. The Rossignol name, prominently marked on skis and other ski equipment, could be seen on almost any ski slope around the world. Many ski shops rented out the company's products, thus introducing a large number of potential customers to the Rossignol brands. Its reputation for quality was also maintained through the sponsorship of top skiers, many of whom have won Olympic and World Cup races on Rossignol equipment.

Principal Subsidiaries

Skis Dynastar S.A. (France); Lange International S.A. (Switzerland); Rossignol SC S.P.A. (Italy); Rossignol Ski AG (Switzerland); Rossignol Ski Deutschland GmbH (Germany); Skis Rossignol de Espana S.A. (Spain); Rossignol Ski Company, Inc. (U.S.); Roger Cleveland Golf Company (U.S.).

Further Reading

Bays, Ted, *Nine Thousand Years of Skis: Norwegian Wood to French Plastic,* Ishpeming, Mich.: National Ski Hall of Fame, 1990.

Beilinson, Jerry, ''Rossignol: Race Support Pays Off in Olympics,'' *Skiing Trade News,* April 1992, p. 6.

''Going Downhill: Rossignol's Image Takes a Spill,'' *Time,* February 23, 1987, p. 68.

Meader, Cliff, ''In 95: Look to Dynastar, Geze to Rossi,'' *Skiing Trade News,* October 1994, p. 12.

——, ''Second Year Is First Year for Full Rossi Boot Line,'' *Skiing Trade News,* March 1990, p. 40.

''France's Ski Industry: No Business like Snow Business,'' *The Economist,* March 3, 1990, p. 65.

Pachod, Patrick, ''Laurent Boix-Vives Discloses Rossignol's Future Path,'' *Skiing Trade News,* February 1991, p. 19.

Regard sur 50 ans d'innovation dans le ski, Voiron, France: Skis Rossignol S.A., 1993.

''Skis Rossignol—Company Report,'' *FT Analysis Report,* Thomson Financial Networks Inc., 1993.

Tanler, Bill, ''Ski Production Turns to the Fewer, the Bigger,'' *Skiing Trade News,* October 1993, p. 30.

—Thomas Riggs

SMITHBARNEY

A Member of *TravelersGroup*

Smith Barney Inc.

388 Greenwich Street
New York, New York 10013
U.S.A.
(212) 891–8900
Fax: (212) 816–6308

Wholly Owned Subsidiary of Travelers Group Inc.
Incorporated: 1964 as Smith, Barney & Co., Inc.
Sales: $5.53 billion (1994)
Employees: 28,000
SICs: 6211 Security Brokers, Dealers and Flotation
Companies; 6221 Commodity Contracts Brokers and
Dealers; 6282 Investment Advice

From its unprepossessing beginnings in Philadelphia more than a century ago, Smith Barney has grown into a financial powerhouse. The acquisition in 1993 of Shearson Lehman Brothers Holdings' retail brokerage and asset management businesses made the amalgamated firm, with an army of 11,000 financial consultants (brokers) and 495 branch offices, second only in the brokerage field to mighty Merrill Lynch. It also embarked on an effort to become a world-class investment bank. In 1995 Smith Barney Inc. was a subsidiary of the Investment Services division of Travelers Group Inc.

Charles D. Barney was a son-in-law of Jay Cooke, a banker who sold Treasury bonds to finance the Union cause during the Civil War but who later went bankrupt, precipitating the panic of 1873. He started his own brokerage and banking house, Charles D. Barney & Co., in Philadelphia in December 1873. Another Philadelphian, Edward B. Smith, founded an investment banking firm bearing his name in 1892.

Responding to the shifting of the nation's financial center from Philadelphia to New York City, Barney's firm purchased a seat on the New York Stock Exchange in 1898 and later opened a New York office. Among his clients were E.H. Harriman, Henry Frick, and William Rockefeller. Barney retired in 1907 and was succeeded as senior partner of the firm by J. Horace

Harding, who was married to one of Barney's six daughters. Harding believed the company should maintain close ties with its corporate clients; accordingly, he served as director of almost 40 companies.

Although Edward B. Smith & Co. quickly bought a seat on the New York Stock Exchange, it did not move the center of its activities to New York City until the 1920s. During this decade the number of its employees grew from 114 to 671. By the 1930s Smith had been doing an extensive commission business for many years on the New York, Philadelphia, and Boston stock exchanges and had been engaged in the underwriting of new issues as well as in the financing of municipal and other issues.

For both Barney and Smith, the Great Depression proved an opportunity as well as a challenge. The failure of the Wall Street firm of Farnum, Winter & Co. in 1932 led Barney to open branch offices in Chicago, Milwaukee, Minneapolis, and St. Paul under the supervision of Wallace C. Winter. Smith benefited from a New Deal act that forced the Guaranty Trust Co. to divest itself of its securities affiliate, Guaranty Co., in 1934. Most of Guaranty's officers, employees, and clientele then joined Smith, which also added Guaranty's offices in Chicago, Pittsburgh, and London.

Smith ran short of cash during a 1937 Wall Street slump and, in order to remain in the underwriting business, merged with Barney at the end of the year to form Smith, Barney & Co. Each brought to the consolidated business distinct strengths: Smith in underwriting and investment banking; Barney in brokering stocks and bonds. The merged firm had 27 general partners, four limited partners, and a staff of 730. It closed several branches to concentrate on large institutional and individual investors rather than the general public.

One of Barney's grandsons, Charles Barney Harding, succeeded Joseph R. Swan as senior partner of Smith, Barney in 1944. In the ensuing years the firm was active in developing financing for emerging companies and mergers and acquisitions as well as for municipalities. By the early 1950s private placements accounted for nearly half of all its debt and preferred-stock issues. In 1963 Smith, Barney ranked 16th among major underwriters of corporate securities and eighth in sales of new municipal bond issues. The company also opened offices in London, Paris, and Geneva. Previously a private partnership, Smith, Barney became a corporation in 1964.

During the late 1960s, Smith, Barney became one of the most aggressive financiers in pursuing corporate mergers and tender offers. It played a part in 1968 in the merger of Bunker Hill Co. into Gulf Resources & Chemical Corp., Fairchild Publications into Capital Cities Broadcasting Corp., and MCA, Inc. into Spencer Gifts, Inc. Also that year, the company introduced the Smith, Barney Equity Fund, a no-load diversified mutual fund aimed at achieving long-term capital growth. By mid 1972 this fund had consistently outperformed the various market indicators and had total net assets of $89.2 million. Also in 1968, the company established the Smith, Barney Income & Growth Fund and Smith Barney Real Estate Corp., its real-estate arm, which was later sold to Security Capital Corp. in 1984 for $40 million.

In October 1975 Barney merged with another old-line investment firm, Harris, Upham & Co. By then Smith, Barney had 18 offices in the United States and abroad and employed a work force of 1,200. It was considered strongest in the financing of corporate and municipal bonds, institutional brokerage, block trading, asset management, and research but was not highly active in retail operations, where Harris, Upham was strong. Retail banking had become more important when mandatory commission rates ended in 1975, allowing institutional buyers to negotiate deep discounts. The combined firm became Smith Barney, Harris Upham & Co., which in turn became the principal unit of SBHU Holdings, a closely-held holding company, in 1977. SBHU Holdings was renamed Smith Barney Inc. in 1982.

According to most analysts, as Smith Barney began concentrating on retail business, it neglected what had been its strong suit: investment banking. Several big clients, such as Eastern Airlines, Atlantic Richfield, and G.D. Searle, took their business to other companies. In 1979 the firm decided to beef up its staff in mergers and acquisitions, project finance, and private placement. Smith Barney became one of five foreign investment banks accorded full-branch status in Japan in 1980 and expanded its European trading operation, which it moved from Paris to London. During the early 1980s it rose to 15th place among U.S. securities firms.

Smith Barney raised its public profile higher by means of a highly successful advertising campaign on television, begun in 1979 and continuing until 1986, that starred John Houseman, who had played a crusty law professor in the television network series "The Paper Chase." These spots exploited the company's long tradition; after touting Smith Barney's services to its clients, Houseman closed by growling, "They make money the old-fashioned way. They EARN it." The firm's retail sales force reached 1,450 registered representatives, one of the highest numbers in the securities industry, in 1983.

In 1982, 34 individuals and institutions from Saudi Arabia, Kuwait, and Bahrain bought (at an estimated cost of $40 million) almost a quarter of Smith Barney through a specially formed holding company. Four men received seats on the board of directors, and they used their influence to urge expansion,

having found the company "supercautious and too conservative." The firm also entered the government-securities market for the first time.

Smith Barney's success continued through the mid-1980s. By 1987, despite a poor 1984, earnings had grown by an average of 25 percent a year for a decade, with an average annual return of 20 to 25 percent on equity. Its capital had grown to $413 million, compared to $175 million in early 1983, and its number of sales representatives to 2,250. However, it became clear that the firm would need even more capital in order to continue to expand. In June 1987 Smith Barney was sold to Primerica Corp., a diversified financial-service company, for $750 million. The deal turned sour for Primerica, however, when the stock markets crashed in October 1987 and Smith Barney lost $93 million before taxes, including $43 million trading in the previously hot arbitrage market.

The year 1988 brought more bad news. By August the firm had dropped from second to fifth place among underwriters of tax-exempt bonds, even though many competitors, including Salomon Brothers and L.F. Rothschild, had dropped out because they were losing money. The company's share of the taxable municipal market had also fallen, and it had missed out on renewed arbitrage profitmaking by disbanding its department in that field. In August Smith Barney fired five of its top public-finance officials in an attempt both to reduce costs and to cut losses in trading and underwriting. Smith Barney lost $53 million before taxes in 1988.

Primerica agreed in August 1988 to be acquired by Commercial Credit Group, Inc., whose president, Sanford I. Weill, immediately replaced Smith Barney's president with a close associate of his, Frank G. Zarb. (Commercial Credit was renamed Primerica in early 1989.) During the first nine months of 1989 the company had revenue of $1.1 billion, sixth among retail brokers. It reentered arbitrage trading in this period and also acquired 16 prime retail offices from troubled Drexel Burnham Lambert Inc., yet cut costs by $50 million. The company had net profit of $63 million in 1989 and had operating earnings of $51.7 million in 1990. In 1991 Smith Barney, now the nation's seventh-largest securities firm, posted a record $152.1 million in operating earnings. It topped this record with net income of $157 million in 1992, on revenues of $1.82 billion.

In March 1993 Primerica acquired the domestic retail-brokerage and asset-management businesses of Shearson Lehman Brothers Holdings Inc. for about $2.1 billion and combined it with Smith Barney, Harris Upham & Co. to form a new firm named Smith Barney Shearson Inc., a subsidiary of Smith Barney Holdings Inc. The amalgamated company, whose name was shortened to Smith Barney Inc. in 1994, became the second-largest brokerage firm in the United States. (Primerica Corp. merged with Travelers Corp. at the end of 1993 and, still under Weill's direction, changed its name to Travelers Inc. It became Travelers Group Inc. in 1995.)

The amalgamated company's new chief executive officer, Robert F. Greenhill, formerly president of Morgan Stanley & Co., vowed to offer corporate clients a full range of worldwide financial services. To do so he hired 22 former Morgan Stanley executives and investment bankers, offering them top dollar. Advisory services in the fields of credit cards, mortgage banking, and bank technology won the firm an impressive clientele among financial institutions. It became a leader in underwriting subordinated bank debt and as a dealmaker in over-the-counter bank stocks, and it rose from 22nd in 1992 to eighth in 1994 in mergers and acquisitions.

Smith Barney Shearson had net income of $306 million in 1993 on revenues of $3.37 billion and (as Smith Barney) $390 million on revenues of $5.53 billion in 1994, when its return on equity of 16.4 percent outperformed every other major firm in its field except Merrill Lynch. At the end of the year the company's equity capital totaled $2.3 billion, and assets under its management came to $74.1 billion. Of its net revenues of $4.8 billion, commissions constituted 41 percent; principal trading, 19 percent; asset management fees, 15 percent; investment banking, 14 percent; net interest-income, seven percent; and other income, four percent.

The company, however, seemed to be failing to meet its professed expectations. A *Wall Street Journal* article concluded in March 1995 that "Despite a two-year drive to build an investment-banking powerhouse, Smith Barney isn't quite ready for prime time.... Today, Smith Barney stands about where it was two years ago, a minor presence in the global rankings of stock and bond underwriters." It also noted that the firm had decided to close its unprofitable investment-banking operations in Hong Kong.

Subsequent news stories indicated that Smith Barney faced a considerable degree of internal dissatisfaction as well. The president of Smith Barney's Consulting Group resigned in August, raising concern over possible loss of the company's dominance over wrap accounts (investment programs sponsored by brokerage firms that wrap money management, financial planning, and brokerage services into a single package for one annual fee). The Consulting Group reportedly held 58 percent of the wrap-account market and more than $70 billion in client assets. Moreover, the head of Smith Barney's government-bond trading desk quit in May of that year, after his group lost $10 million in trades, infuriating his boss. Finally, the head of the firm's research department departed in October after that area fell from fifth to eighth place in a ranking by *Institutional Investor.*

Nevertheless, during 1995 Smith Barney rose from eighth to fifth in equity underwriting (excluding closed-end funds). And it was enjoying a spectacular year at the bottom line. For the first nine months of 1995, the company had net operating earnings of about $560 million, with a return on equity of 23 percent. Its profits were particularly impressive because its risk profile was lower than that of almost any other Wall Street firm. This happy state of affairs—high profits and low risk—was attributed to tight-fisted management; one securities analyst observed that Smith Barney's noncompensation costs were about one-third less than that of rival Merrill Lynch.

Further Reading

Allan, John H., "A Young Chief Heads Old-Line Smith, Barney," *New York Times,* August 11, 1968, Sec. III, p. 3.

Carroll, Michael, "Don't Look Back," *Institutional Investor,* January 1994, pp. 36–42, 44, 47.

Cole, Robert J., "Merger Weighed by Smith, Barney," *New York Times,* October 24, 1975, p. 51.

Cooper, Ron, "Talking Shop at Smith Barney," *Investment Dealers' Digest,* February 17, 1992, pp. 20–26.

Friedman, John, "Sandy Weill Roars Back," *Business Week,* December 4, 1989, pp. 89–90.

Mitchell, Russell, and Anthony Bianco, "For Smith, Barney, the Go-Go Years Have Just Begun," *Business Week,* June 8, 1987, pp. 39–40.

Pratt, Tom, "Smith Barney's Unfinished Business," *Investment Dealers' Digest,* November 27, 1995, pp. 14–19.

Quint, Michael, "His Formula: Smith Barney + Shearson = Powerhouse," *New York Times,* March 28, 1993, Sec. III, p. 10.

Retkwa, Rosalyn, "Full of Eastern Promise," *Euromoney,* May 1983, pp. 172–173, 176, 179.

Sigonolfi, Michael, and Anita Raghavan, "Smith Barney Fails to Crack Big Leagues of Investment Banking," *Wall Street Journal,* March 23, 1995, pp. A1, A6.

"Smith Barney: The Early Years," "Ten Decades of Continuity and Change," and "An Original, Not a Reprint," in *Smith Barney Forum,* May–June 1973.

—Robert Halasz

SMITH INTERNATIONAL, INC.

Smith International, Inc.

16740 Hardy Street
Houston, Texas 77032
U.S.A.
(713) 443-3370
Fax: (713) 233-5259

Public Company
Incorporated: 1937 as H.C. Smith Oil Tool Company
Employees: 4,100
Sales: $653.9 million (1994)
Stock Exchanges: New York Pacific
SICs: 3533 Oil & Gas Field Machinery; 3544 Special Dies, Tools, Jigs & Fixtures; 3545 Machine Tool Accessories

A leading supplier of equipment and services used in the drilling of oil and gas wells, Smith International, Inc. manufactures and markets drilling fluids and systems, highly-engineered drill bits, and drilling and completion products and services. During the mid-1990s, Smith International derived 97 percent of its revenues from sales to the oil and gas industry, with international sales accounting for more than half of the company's total sales. The company filed for protection under Chapter 11 of the U.S. Bankruptcy Code in early 1986, then emerged out of bankruptcy reorganized and restructured in late 1987. By the mid-1990s, after several years of consolidating its businesses, Smith International had begun to restore much of its lost luster and stood positioned as the second-largest drill bit manufacturer in the world, poised to take advantage of gains recorded by the market for high-technology drill bits.

The historical roots of Houston, Texas-based Smith International originate in southern California, where the founder of the company, Herman C. Smith, resided and where the company maintained its corporate offices for most the 20th century. The chain of events that led up to the creation of Smith International began in 1902, when Herman Smith opened a blacksmith shop in Whittier, California. Later that same year, oil was discovered

in the area, a defining and auspicious discovery for Smith International and an event to be heralded by the 20-year-old Smith and his infant blacksmith shop. The arrival of oil rigs and attendant oil workers provided a welcomed infusion of business for Smith's shop, keeping the young blacksmith busy sharpening the oilmen's drill bits and providing a steady source of cash for the newly opened shop. For years, Smith kept the area's drill bits sharp and repaired other tools used in drilling for oil, developing a relationship with the oil drillers who frequented his shop that gradually led Smith in a new business direction and formed the foundation for Smith International.

By listening to oil drillers discuss the shortcomings of the tools of their trade and by eliciting their suggestions for improvements, Smith developed an expertise that set him apart from the typical blacksmith and, over time, distinguished his shop as a haven for oil drillers and their equipment. Using the information he had gleaned from oil drillers, Smith began making unique adjustments to the tools brought into his shop and he began developing new tools. By the 1920s, Smith's business, which had been named H.C. Smith Manufacturing Company, subsisted on re-working fishtail bits and modifying oil tools as its mainstay business, having secured a place for itself in the California oil and gas industry by staying attuned to the peculiar needs of its customers. The business of H.C. Smith Manufacturing Company, however, would not be inherited by Smith International, despite logical inferences to the contrary. In the history of Smith International, the three decades Smith spent in building H.C. Smith Manufacturing Company represented a proving ground for the establishment of the company that would eventually become one of the world's largest suppliers of drill bits and other oilfield products to the global oil and gas industry. For Smith International, the history of H.C. Smith Manufacturing Company was merely the prelude to its distinct genesis and the decades of development to follow.

The cause for the interruption was attributable solely to Herman Smith, who, by the late 1920s, had decided it was time to retire. In 1929, at age 47, Smith sold the business he had created over the previous 27 years to Globe Oil Tools, then settled into retirement and ended his working days in the oil and gas industry. As it turned out, however, Smith's departure from the oil and gas industry did not mark the beginning of his retirement, but rather the start of a seven-year hiatus. Unable to enjoy the vicissitudes of retirement, Smith returned to action in the business world in 1936 when he purchased Allen Brothers Oil Tools and renamed the company H.C. Smith Oil Tool Company, the earliest predecessor to Smith International.

Once back in business, Smith set to work building an enterprise that would make his name internationally recognized decades after his death, leaving a lasting vestige to his efforts in creating H.C. Smith Manufacturing Company and H.C. Smith Oil Tool Company. The H.C. Smith Oil Tool Company corporate title was retained until 1959, when the company went public and changed its name to Smith Tool Co. The following year a parent organization, Smith Industries International, Inc. was formed to facilitate expansion both domestically and abroad in the coming decade, which the company accomplished at a 15 percent rate during the 1960s. By the end of the 1960s, yet another name change was in the offing, occurring in 1969 when "Industries" was dropped from the corporate title and Smith International, Inc. was adopted as the company's official name. As Smith International, Inc., the company would record its most prolific growth, rising to become an international giant in the oil and gas equipment industry, and, under the same corporate banner, the company also would struggle through its most tortuous years, teetering on the brink of failure.

By the beginning of the 1970s, Smith International had established itself as a leading manufacturer of drilling equipment for natural resource development, its broad line of drilling equipment used by companies involved in developing oil, gas, minerals, and water. Supported by a well-established overseas business, which generated nearly 40 percent of the company's total annual sales, Smith International had grown to become a roughly $100-million-a-year concern by the early 1970s, deriving three-quarters of its sales from its involvement in oil and gas markets. In the decade ahead, Smith International would register its most prodigious success, outdistancing its competitors to leap to the top tier of its industry, ranking, by the beginning of the 1980s, as the second-largest drill-bit manufacturer in the world, trailing only Hughes Tool Co. Through internal growth, astute acquisitions, and international and domestic expansion, annual sales for the company soared exponentially, swelling to $1.2 billion by the beginning of the 1980s, while earnings followed suit, jumping to $133 million, more than the company had collected in sales a decade earlier.

Despite the impressive financial figures posted by the company, the early 1980s marked the beginning of what could have been the end for Smith International, as the demand for oil rigs shuddered to a halt in the face of declining oil prices. Heavily dependent on the fortunes of the oil and gas industry, Smith International began to suffer from the repercussive affects of anemic drilling activity, not the first time the company's business had faltered in its nearly 50 years of existence in the frequently capricious oil market. Periods of market stagnation had pocked Smith International's financial performance throughout its history, but the affects of widespread depressed oil activity were exacerbated by other negative developments peculiar to Smith International, which, once their deleterious power reached full force, left the company perilously close to complete collapse.

The first of the negative developments to compound the severity of pervasive depressed oil drilling activities was Smith International's ill-conceived, ill-timed attempt to take control of Gearhart Industries Inc., an oilfield services company that specialized in sophisticated wireline, measurement-while-drilling services. In November 1983, as the oil industry continued its retrogressive slide, Smith International paid more than $100 million for General Electric company's 23 percent stake in Gearhart, a move welcomed by Gearhart's founder, Marvin Gearhart, since it staved off General Electric's attempt to purchase his company. Marvin Gearhart's ire was raised, however, when Smith International increased its holding in Gearhart Industries to 33 percent, then announced it intended to acquire 56 percent of the wireline services firm. Marvin Gearhart vehemently opposed Smith International's tender offer and did everything in his power to thwart such a transaction from being completed, touching off a squabble between the two companies that, in the end, left Marvin Gearhart victorious in his attempt keep his unwanted suitor at arm's length and saddled Smith International with enormous debt.

When the dust had settled from Smith International's failed attempt to acquire control of Gearhart Industries' sophisticated "downhole" measuring technology, the losses amounted to nearly $200 million. Smith International withdrew its bid in March 1985, by which time the company had spent $165 million in trying to buy Gearhart Industries. The stock Smith International had acquired was sold for $80 million, but the company took an $85 million charge against working capital after selling its Gearhart Industries holdings, giving it a cumbersome burden to carry in the depressed economic times within the oil industry. By mid-1985, the combined affects of a laggard economic climate and the losses incurred from the failed Gearhart Industries acquisition had thrust Smith International into a precarious position, forcing it to close plants, lay off more than half of its 14,000 employees, and cease production of certain products. Annuals sales, which had stood at $1.2 billion in 1981, plummeted to $747 million in 1984. Earnings took a more precipitous plunge, dropping from $133 million in 1981 to a loss of $65 million in 1984. By all accounts, the early 1980s had been disastrous years for the company, but the worse was yet to come. The "St. Valentine's Day Massacre," as a Smith International chief financial officer dubbed it, was looming ahead, and its arrival would deliver a near fatal blow to Smith International.

The company was still contending with the difficulties caused by its declining business and the Gearhart Industries imbroglio when, on February 14, 1986, the Federal District Court for the Central District of California issued a ruling that rocked all those at Smith International. The judgment by the court marked the culmination of a lawsuit originally filed by Smith International against Hughes Tool in 1974, a lawsuit Smith International would later regret having filed. By the end of the protracted legal dispute over patents, Smith International was found to be the culprit and was ordered to pay what ended up being $205.4 million for its infringement upon Hughes Tool's patent for an "O-ring seal" rock bit. Combined with Smith International's other losses, the ruling handed down by the court represented the third devastating strike incurred by the company, the meting of a "triple whammy" as one industry observer phrased it, and Smith International reeled from the successive blows, leading a host of bankers and analysts to predict that Smith International would either be sold or forced into Chapter 11 bankruptcy.

On the heels of the judgment against Smith International, immediate steps were taken to salvage the company, leading to what one analyst referred to as the company's "weekend blood-bath." Smith International laid off 32 vice-presidents, consolidated several divisions, and announced it would lay off as many as 2,000 employees, but by the first week of March 1986 there was nothing left to do but seek protection under Chapter 11 of the U.S. Bankruptcy Code.

While under Chapter 11, Smith International divested its non-core businesses, retaining only its tool manufacturing and drilling divisions to carry the company forward. Its corporate office building in Newport Beach, California was sold as well as a plant in Irvine, California, giving the company $46 million to go along with the $200 million raised through its divestiture of non-core businesses. Smith International's headquarter offices were then relocated to a one-story industrial building next to its primary plant in Irvine, as consolidation and cost-cutting reigned during the company's nearly two-year-long battle to reorganize while in bankruptcy.

In December 1987, Smith International emerged from under the protective umbrella of bankruptcy, coming out of a year in which the company recorded $264.4 million in sales and registered a $26.1 million loss in earnings. Smith International was a shadow of its former self, but what remained was lean and, despite the profit loss recorded in 1987, capable of generating positive gains for the company. Over the course of the following year, a vibrant company began to emerge, buoyed by its continued investment in research that provided Smith International with a range of new, high-technology drilling products. Net productivity per employee during 1988 stood at $126,000, an all-time high, fueling hopes that the company had begun to wrest free from the debilitating first half of the decade.

In 1989, Smith International closed its sprawling 638,000-square-foot Irvine, California production facility, then consolidated all petroleum and mining-bit operations into its 169,000 square-foot manufacturing plant in Ponca City, Oklahoma. The company's headquarters moved as well, relocating from Irvine to Houston, Texas, where Smith International's management could superintend a company that had dramatically ameliorated its ability to compete as an oil and gas equipment and services firm.

Smith International entered the 1990s as a company well-positioned in the high-technology drilling market, where demand was high for its heavy investment in products such as "steerable systems," or devices patterned after aerospace guidance systems that allowed oil workers to drill in different directions from a single site. In 1990, a proposed merger between Dresser Industries Inc. and Smith International fell through when Dresser

Industries backed out of the deal citing potential antitrust problems with the U.S. Justice Department, but in early 1994 the two would-be partners announced a transaction that ranked as Smith International's largest acquisition in its history, restoring some of the magnitude lost during the previous decade.

On February 28, 1994, eight years and two weeks after the bleakest day in Smith International's history, the company acquired a 64 percent interest in M-I Drilling Fluids Co. from Dresser Industries, an acquisition that provided a tremendous boost to Smith International's stature as a competitor in the oil and gas equipment and services industry. Concurrent with the acquisition, Smith International reorganized into three operating divisions: Smith Drill Bits, Smith Drilling and Completion Services, and M-I Drilling Fluids. In the wake of the purchase of M-I Drilling Fluids, Smith International's revenues leaped to $653.9 million from the $220 million generated in 1993, while gross earnings doubled, spawning hope that the company's future could eradicate the staggering developments of the 1980s.

Principal Subsidiaries

Smith International, S.A. de C.V. (Mexico); Omega II Insurance Ltd. (Bermuda); S.I. Nederland B.V. (Netherlands); Smith International Acquisition Corp.; Smith International Australia (Pty) Ltd.; Smith International Canada Ltd.; Smith International do Brasil Ltda. (Brazil); Smith International Deutschland GmbH (Germany); Smith International France, S.A.R. L.; Smith International Italia S.p.A. (Italy); Smith International (North Sea) Ltd. (Scotland); Smith International de Venezuela, C.A.

Principal Operating Units

Smith Drill Bits; Smith Drilling and Completion Services; M-I Drilling Fluids

Further Reading

"Another Setback for Smith," *Business Week*, March 3, 1986, p. 46.
Carson, Teresa, "Smith International: When a Takeover Try Goes Bust," *Business Week*, April 1, 1985, p. 65.
Francis, Robert, "Smith Int'l Lays Off 32 VPs, Consolidates Some Divisions," *American Metal Market*, March 3, 1986, p. 4.
Jaffe, Thomas, "Someone's Knocking," *Forbes*, May 7, 1984, p. 213.
Kindel, Stephen. "Mission Mistaken," *Financial World*, May 31, 1988, p. 16.
Klinkerman, Steve, "Marvin Gearhart Has Won His Independence—But Not Much Else," *Business Week*, April 1, 1985, p. 64.
Koprowski, Gene, "New Zealand Financier Wants Control of Smith," *Metalworking News*, June 5, 1989, p. 6.
Pybus, Kenneth R., "Revenues Rise after Largest Buy in Smith International's History," *Houston Business Journal*, June 9, 1995, p. 22B.

—Jeffrey L. Covell

Sportmart, Inc.

1400 South Wolf Road
Suite 200
Wheeling, Illinois 60090
U.S.A.
(708) 520–0100
Fax: (708) 520–1570

Public Company
Incorporated: 1970
Employees: 4000
Sales: $424.18 million (1994)
Stock Exchanges: NASDAQ
SICs: 5941 Sporting Goods & Bicycle Shops

The Sportmart, Inc. chain of sporting goods superstores is the original (and still one of the largest) "category killer" sporting goods retailers in the United States. At year-end 1995, there were 63 Sportmarts operating in the United States, Canada, and Japan, with a total of 16 to 18 new stores expected to open before the company's fiscal year end in January 1996. Sportmart also operates a growing chain of smaller No Contest! athletic footwear specialty stores. After two decades of modest growth focused on the Chicago and Los Angeles markets, Sportmart went public in 1992 and launched an aggressive expansion campaign, more than doubling the number of stores in three years and establishing a presence in Minneapolis, Columbus, Ohio, Milwaukee, San Francisco, San Diego, Seattle, Portland, and Toronto.

In 1957, Larry J. Hochberg co-founded Children's Bargain Town USA, a small chain of toy stores that operated in Chicago, Milwaukee, and Detroit through the 1960s. The Hochberg family were pioneers of the superstore concept, offering large stores stocked with a broad array of brand-name merchandise. At the same time, a similar chain of stores started up on the East Coast. It was named Toys R Us. In the early 1960s, Children's Bargain Town and Toys R Us formed a cooperative purchasing agreement, allowing the two chains to buy in larger quantities and to offer their merchandise at deep discounts. Toys R Us was bought up by the retail giant Interstate Stores, Inc. in 1967. Two years later, Interstate purchased Children's Bargain Town USA, merging the toy store operations. In the early 1970s, however, Interstate went bankrupt. The chain of toy stores continued under the name Toys R Us, and eventually won over 25 percent of the huge U.S. toy market.

Hochberg remained with Interstate for about a year after the merger. However, he left Interstate in 1970 to found a new company. Together with Sanford Cantor, who had worked with him through the 1960s at Children's Bargain Town, Hochberg decided to try the superstore concept in the sporting goods market. As he told *Crain's Chicago Business,* "It seemed like the sporting goods concept ought to be all right. That's about as scientific as we got."

The first Sportmart opened in 1971 in Niles, Illinois. It was the first category killer to enter the sporting goods market, which was then a relatively minor category of the retail marketplace. Hochberg remained close to his toy store strategy, offering a broad range of first-run, name-brand merchandise at prices kept low by volume purchasing and quick inventory turnover. Hochberg's timing was perfect; the sporting goods market, spurred by the increasing presence of televised sporting events and a turn in the national mood toward a new awareness of health and fitness, exploded in the early 1970s. Joggers became fixtures on more and more streets, sparking demand for more sophisticated footwear and apparel.

Likewise, aerobics, merging with the suddenly popular disco sound, emerged by the late 1970s, while skiing moved from an elite pursuit to an affordable sport. The 1970s also saw the appearance of lightweight, multi-speed bicycles, as well as sturdier and swifter rollerskate designs, and more sophisticated weight-training apparatus. Environmental concerns swept the nation at the same time, as more medical studies described the importance of physical and cardiovascular fitness in overall health. Before long, exercise became an American way of life. Despite a loss in its first year of operations, Sportmart was posting profits by 1972 and would continue to blossom throughout the decade.

Sportmart's growth was steady, but slow. A second Sportmart opened in Lombard, Illinois in 1973. By 1983 there were seven Sportmarts operating in the Chicago suburban area. In that year, Sportmart expanded to the West Coast, opening its first Los Angeles-area store. Throughout the 1980s, Sportmart continued to expand in these two areas, reaching 13 Chicago-area stores and 11 Los Angeles-area outlets by the end of 1989. In that year, the company generated annual revenues of $187 million in a market that had grown to approximately $12 billion per year, while dominating two of the most important U.S. markets. Sportsmart's original four-person corporate staff had grown to over 100, and the company's payroll totalled more than 2,000 employees. Despite overtures from the investment industry to go public, Hochberg retained private control of the company, funding expansion through working capital and bank debts. In 1987, Hochberg's son Andrew joined the company, followed a year later by Hochberg's son-in-law, John Lowenstein. It seemed certain that the company would remain under the Hochberg family's control.

For much of its history, Sportmart had been the sole superstore in the sporting goods industry, competing against smaller-store concepts such as Morrie Mages and Herman's World of Sporting Goods, as well as department stores like Sears and Montgomery Ward. However, in the 1980s other competitors emerged to contend in Sportmart's niche. Chief among these was the Sports Authority chain, founded in 1987 by former Herman's COO Jack Smith. By then, the retail warehouse concept, begun by the Price Company and joined by such chains as Sam's Clubs and Costco, was nearly a decade old. Smith adapted the warehouse formula to sporting goods, and by 1990 operated eight Sports Authority stores, primarily on the southern East Coast.

Smith dropped plans to take his company public and instead accepted an offer from Kmart to buy out his chain. He remained in place as chairman and president of the new Kmart subsidiary. With massive cash backing from Kmart, the Sports Authority chain jumped to 19 stores in 1991. Four years later, there were 110 Sports Authority stores, including entries into both the Chicago and Los Angeles markets. In 1994, the increasingly troubled Kmart spun off the Sports Authority chain and Smith took the company public. In its five years under Kmart, Sports Authority's yearly revenues skyrocketed from $53 million in 1990 to nearly $840 million in 1995, with forecasts of over $1 billion in sales by 1996.

At the same time, Sportmart faced competition from two other growing superstore chains. Sportstown, Inc., a Georgia-based chain of 14 stores, went public in the spring of 1992, followed by the August 1992 initial public offering of Sports & Recreation, Inc., a 20-store chain based in Florida that announced plans to double in size within two years. Up until that year, the sporting goods superstores had grown in largely separated markets. Beginning in 1992, however, the superstore chains started to compete head-to-head.

In response, Sportmart had no choice but to expand more aggressively than before. By the time Sports Authority announced plans to enter the Chicago market in 1992, that chain had grown to nearly 50 stores, compared to Sportmart's 25 stores, which by then included one store in San Diego. Between

1991 and 1992, Sportmart opened eight new stores, including one in the Minneapolis/St. Paul region and three in the San Francisco Bay area. Sportmart also began an extensive remodeling of its older stores. By 1992, its sales had risen to over $250 million, though net income was down slightly from 1991 to $5.36 million. Sportmart was the fourth-largest sporting goods retailer in the country, with its approximately 0.5 percent of the market equivalent to Sports Authority's, and behind the 1.4 percent of the industry leader, Herman's (Herman's would soon go bankrupt).

Sportmart became the third sporting goods superstore to go public in 1992, with an initial public offering at $15 per share raising $46.9 million. Sportmart sold three million shares, which represented about one-third of the company. Hochberg, who together with his family controlled 89 percent of the company before the IPO, took approximately $21 million raised by the offering as unpaid profits. Another $13.5 million went to pay down debt, and the remainder went to fund Sportmart's further expansion, doubling the number of its stores with three years. By the end of 1992, Sportmart operated 31 superstores. The following year, that number rose to 42, including entries into Seattle and Portland. Sportmart then added units in Minneapolis, San Francisco, Los Angeles, San Diego, and Chicago. In Chicago, Sportmart expanded its distribution center to 142,000 square feet to serve its midwestern stores, and added a 40,000-square-foot distribution center to the 61,000-square-foot facility already operating in Los Angeles. In-store changes included the addition of its ''Training Room for Women'' boutique to its successful ''Cheering Section'' boutique, which sold licensed sports team apparel and goods.

In 1992, Sportmart also began development of its No Contest! specialty stores, opening two stores in the St. Louis area. These smaller stores (11,000–15,000 square feet) operated as category killers in the athletic footwear and apparel market, targeting the aged 12 to 25 consumer bracket. Sportmart's 1993 revenues were over $338 million, and net income jumped to about $7.9 million.

Eleven more Sportmarts appeared in 1994, boosting revenues to nearly $425 million. In 1994, Sportmart became the first of the superstores to enter the foreign market, opening in Toronto. Sportmart also became the first sporting goods category killer to enter Japan, with a store in Kagogawa, outside of Osaka. Eight more Japanese stores followed, with an average size of 12,000 square feet. Sportmart's Japanese presence was supported by an agreement with Japanese retailing giant Nichii Company, which posted 1993 sales of about $16 billion. The company also announced a joint-venture agreement with Dovrat Shrem in Israel to open as many as five stores in that country. To fund its growth, Sportmart issued a second stock offering, reducing the Hochberg family's control to just under 60 percent, with Sanford Cantor possessing an added 6.5 percent. By the end of 1994, Sportmart had grown to a 53-store chain, including its newest market of Columbus, Ohio.

Yet Sportmart's expansion seemed to come too late to regain the momentum lost to Sports Authority in the first half of the 1990s. By 1995, Sports Authority had stores in 22 states. It had all but locked up the crucial Northeastern market, and, with deeper pockets than Sportmart, had successfully established itself in the Chicago and Los Angeles areas. When Sportstown filed for Chapter 11 bankruptcy protection in 1995, Sports Authority bought up seven of its southeastern stores. With twice the number of Sportmart stores and twice its revenues, Sports Authority made plans to enter Canada, Japan, and England. Consumer acceptance of the no-frills warehouse store concept, spurred in part by the recession of the early 1990s, also aided Sports Authority's growth. Meanwhile, the mild winter of 1994 cut into Sportmart's crucial winter sales, and the company was further hurt by flooding in California, with about half of its stores still concentrated in that state. Sportmart's policy of saturating its market had led to some of its California stores cannibalizing each other, while some of its older stores were criticized for their tired appearance. Nevertheless, Sportmart received praise for its defense of its territory, and continued to dominate the Chicago market.

In August 1995 Sportmart opened a 26,000-square-foot store in Utazu, Japan, the largest among its nine Japanese stores. In 1996, moreover, Sportmart expected to add to its five-store Canadian presence with ten new stores, including stores in Calgary and Edmonton. The company was still developing its No Contest! concept, as well, which remained at four stores through 1995. Preparations for the future began with the March 1995 appointment of Andrew Hochberg as Sportmart president. John Lowenstein was named to the newly created position of executive vice-president of operations the following month. Larry Hochberg remained as chief executive officer and chairman, and together with co-founder, long-time partner, and vice-chairman Sanford Cantor, continued to control the majority of Sportmart's stock.

Further Reading

Crown, Judith, "Suffering at Sportmart: Competition, Calif. Floods Crimp Sales," *Crain's Chicago Business,* February 20, 1995.

Elliot, Christopher, "Sportmart's Offer Heats Up Rivalry in Sports-Equipment Retailing Market," *Wall Street Journal,* September 9, 1992.

Lettich, Jill, "Sportmart Fine Tunes Stores To Defend Its Turf," *Discount Store News,* March 2, 1992, p. 3.

Waldstein, Peter D., "How Sportmart KO's Foes," *Crain's Chicago Business,* September 11, 1989, p. 1.

—M. L. Cohen

Standard Register Co.

600 Albany Street
Dayton, Ohio 45401
U.S.A.
(513) 443–1000
Fax: (513) 443–1263

Public Company
Incorporated: 1912
Employees: 6,201
Sales: $767.42 million (1994)
Stock Exchanges: NASDAQ
SICs: 2761 Manifold Business Forms; 2672 Coated &
    Laminated Paper, Not Elsewhere Classified; 3579
    Office Machines, Not Elsewhere Classified

With about ten percent of the $7.3 billion domestic market, the Standard Register Co. is America's second-largest manufacturer of business forms and form-handling devices. The company's emphasis on service has enabled it to carve out a profitable niche in an industry fraught with change, and the company has become as much a service business as a manufacturer. Throughout its more than 80 years in operation, Standard Register's strategy of adopting, adapting, and originating information management processes and products has enabled it to grow and prosper in the face of such challenging technological innovations as automation, computerization, and electronic communication. By the mid-1990s, forms management services generated more than one-third of Standard Register's annual revenues—nearly as much as its traditional lines, including custom continuous forms, unit sets (multi-copy sets of individual forms with or without carbon) and stock forms. The segment upon which the company was founded, document processing equipment, chipped in just over 11 percent.

The Standard Register Co. was founded upon an invention dreamt up by Theodore Schirmer. It was a fairly simple, yet revolutionary adaptation of the autographic register, which had been devised in 1883 by James C. Shoup. Shoup's machine featured two separate rolls of paper—one printed with lines, the other blank—interlayered with carbon paper. When a user wrote on the top document, for example a sales receipt, the machine made a copy for record-keeping. The user turned a crank, thereby propelling the finished set of handwritten records out of the machine and advancing a fresh set to the frame. Although a significant advance over the alternative—writing out copies in longhand—the autographic register's primary drawback was that the layers of carbon and forms often slipped, becoming misaligned.

Schirmer applied the concept of the chain and sprocket to the autographic register. His "standard register" featured a wooden cylinder with sprocket wheels at either end. The pins corresponded to holes punched down the margins of a continuous roll of paper. His idea earned a patent, but Schirmer could not attract enough start-up capital to begin production. In a last-ditch effort to get his idea off the ground, he contacted John Q. Sherman's real estate brokerage in the hopes that Sherman would lend him the necessary funds.

After initially rejecting the idea, Sherman asked Schirmer to build a prototype. Together they refined the machine so that it would produce up to eight copies of a document at a single writing. Keeping the multiple documents aligned allowed all the layers of paper to be pre-printed with lines, check blocks and other organizational formats, thereby vastly increasing their utility.

Convinced that the idea was feasible, John Sherman liquidated his real estate firm and called on business associates, including his brother William C. ("W. C.") Sherman, to contribute the necessary start-up capital. The Standard Register Company was incorporated in 1912 with Thomas Schirmer as president and John Sherman as a director. They founded the business in rented space with some machining equipment and two printing presses bought on credit. Sherman traveled to the west coast to set up sales operations there.

Although the fledgling company's second floor office saved it from the Great Dayton Flood of 1913, the firm nearly went under in a flood of debt and backlogged orders. With Standard Register slipping into receivership, W. C. Sherman began to take an active role in its management. He summoned John back from California, and together they devised a plan to save the business. They borrowed against their own life insurance policies in order to raise enough money to buy out Standard Register's primary investors, including Thomas Schirmer. John assumed the duties of the office of president, and William became vice-president and treasurer. In order to fill past-due orders and revive cash flow, the brothers borrowed to create their own power source, doubled production, and freed the company from receivership within seven months.

Standard Register had entered a market dominated by Moore Corporation, the Canadian company that had founded the business forms industry in the 1880s. Moore and other well-entrenched competitors derided Standard Register's documents as "mutilated," "ventilated," and even "smallpox" forms. Nevertheless, Standard Register's innovative machines and documents gained a following. By 1916, the company had generated enough capital to erect a purpose-built factory.

In the early 1930s, it occurred to John Sherman to apply the pin-feed concept to machine-written documents in order to speed up the process with continuous forms. He designed a cylindrical rubber platen equipped with sprockets at either end that could replace the friction feeder in virtually any business machine. Called a "registrator platen," the invention helped broaden the potential market for Standard Register's specialized forms.

In spite of the Great Depression, Standard Register's annual sales reached about $1 million in 1933 and quintupled to over $5 million by 1938. This rapid growth was fueled in part by international licensing agreements. The company authorized R. L. Crain Limited, a Canadian firm, to produce its patented forms in 1934, and affiliated with W.H. Smith & Son (Alacra) Ltd. in England a year later. William Sherman succeeded his brother John as president upon the latter's death in 1939.

At the outset of America's entry into World War II, Standard Register was stunned to learn that it had been pronounced "nonessential" by the federal government and was slated to be shut down for the duration of the war. However, the government and the military soon discovered that the business forms that Standard Register provided were vital to many operations. In fact, an arsenal actually shut down because of a lack of forms and documents. Standard Register wound up winning awards for its efforts on the home front.

William Sherman served as Standard Register's president until his death in 1944. At that time Milferd A. Spayd, who had joined the company in 1933, advanced to Standard Register's presidency. His ascension coincided with a period of rapid growth for the business forms industry overall and Standard Register in particular. Sales volume nearly quadrupled, from $11.4 million in 1946 to over $43 million in 1956. Postwar growth was fueled by the company's "Paperwork Simplification Program." Developed during World War II, the program emphasized the creation of more efficient record-keeping systems. Paperwork Simplification was a harbinger of the evolution of the business forms industry from strictly manufacturing and marketing forms to selling custom-made information gathering and retrieval systems. It became vital to Standard Regis-

ter's continued success in the computer age as threats to paper business forms compelled the transformation of the industry.

Standard Register grew rapidly during the 1950s, adding factories in Pennsylvania, California and Arkansas; licensing new overseas affiliates in Cuba, Venezuela and Sweden; and creating distributorships in Peru, Nicaragua, Guatemala and Haiti during this period. The company went public in 1956, but the Sherman family (and by marriage, the Clarks) continued to hold a controlling stake in the company through the early 1990s.

Automation drove the business forms industry's growth in the 1960s. The boom in computers and optical scanners helped make business forms one of America's fastest-growing industries, expanding at twice the rate of the gross national product, from $530 million in 1962 to $1.4 billion in 1972. Standard Register's sales more than quadrupled, from $24.4 million to $107.9 million, during that same period. By 1966, the company had added international affiliates in Australia, Brazil, Finland, France, Ireland, Japan and South Africa. On the domestic front, new factories in Pennsylvania and Vermont added production capacity and increased distribution flexibility. Under the direction of President Kenneth P. Morse beginning in 1966, the Paperwork Simplification Program evolved into a forms management program that not only helped clients slim their record keeping systems, but also helped manage clients' inventory of forms. David Henwood of Prescott, Ball & Turben (Cleveland) would later call Standard's forms management program "the Cadillac of the industry."

The business forms business started to show signs of maturity in the 1970s, when its annual growth rate slowed from double-digit percentages to nine percent and down to four percent by the early 1980s. After having solidly held the number-two spot in the industry for decades, Standard Register slipped to number three in 1973, when rival UARCO Inc. slid past it. Under the leadership of D. F. Whitehead during the 1970s, Standard Register refocused its customer base from the large, but cyclical companies it had traditionally targeted— automotive, steel, and tire companies, for example—to more stable markets like financial, health care, direct mail and service industries. Revenues from health care clients increased from $5 million in 1970 to more than $60 million by 1982. Printing personalized letters and contest forms for the rapidly-growing direct mail segment multiplied from $1 million in 1970 to $32 million by 1982. Serving these new target markets helped Standard Register regain the number-two standing in the business forms industry, as its annual sales nearly tripled from $107 million in 1972 to $319.6 million in 1981.

Its emphasis on service enabled Standard Register to maintain profit margins in spite of an early 1980s recession that shaved competitors' profits. In fact, from 1981 to 1985, the company's profits doubled from $15.4 million to $31.8 million, while revenues only increased by about 27.5 percent, from $319.6 million to $441.05 million. That trend reversed in the latter years of the decade, however, as Standard Register's sales increased by over 60 percent to $708.9 million, while its net income grew at less than half that rate to $40.4 million by 1989. The recessionary period of the late 1980s and early 1990s took its toll on the forms industry, which found itself burdened with over capacity, rising paper prices, weakening demand and intensifying competition.

When its profits were nearly halved from 1989 to $21.8 million in 1990, Standard Register was forced to close plants and furlough five percent of its work force.

Notwithstanding the economic slowdown, the company continued to adapt to new technologies, both within its own operations and in its customer-oriented services and products. Internally, Standard Register adopted automated manufacturing resource planning (MRP) software that helped it decrease waste, manage its inventory of over 13,000 items, and generally become more productive. Externally, Standard Register surprised some analysts by adopting electronic data interchange (EDI), an electronic ordering system that was proclaimed an important factor in the long-heralded "paperless office." The company subscribed to an outside EDI network in addition to its own proprietary service, AccuServ. It was a classic example of the firm's adoptive strategy: Brent Rawlins, a specialist at Standard Register, pointed out that the EDI terminals installed at client sites served as "constant reminder[s] to do business with Standard Register." Instead of allowing the new technology to reduce its markets, the company used innovation to its advantage.

Standard Register furthered its efforts in this area through strategic alliances with electronic forms imaging and software firms, combining their longstanding customer relationships with the software companies' document management applications. Partners included Computer Sciences Corp., Saros Corp., and F3 Software Corp. in systems that coordinated ordering, pricing, and design of business forms.

The company also boosted its direct mail operations through the acquisition of rival UARCO Inc.'s 22-year-old direct mail division, Promotional Graphics. Combined with Standard Register's own COMMUNICOLOR Division, the Kansas-based entity expanded the firm's geographic reach westward, added $20 million in annual revenue, and broadened its product offerings.

These various activities helped increase Standard Register's revenues by an aggregate of about seven percent from $716.4 million in 1990 to $767.4 million in 1994. Net income more than doubled from its recession-battered low of $21.8 million to $43.9 million during that same period. While this result established a new record for earnings, it was only eight percent more than 1987's net, when annual revenues stood at only $666.7 million.

John Darragh retired as president and chief executive officer after just over a decade of leading Standard Register and was succeeded by Peter S. Redding. Paul H. Granzow, who had served as chairman since 1984, continued in that capacity through the mid-1990s.

Principal Divisions

Forms Division; Business Equipment and Systems Division; COMMUNICOLOR Division; Advanced Medical Systems (AMS) Division.

Further Reading

Breakey, James, "New Directions for the Forms Industry," *The Office,* January 1979, p. 169.

"Business-Form Makers Return to Form," *Financial World,* November 12, 1975, p. 14.

"Business Forms: Riding Computer Boom," *Financial World,* November 26, 1969, p. 20.

"Electronics: Threat to Paper?" *Pulp & Paper,* August 1976, p. 17.

Flax, Steven, "Win on Price, Lose on Price," *Forbes,* November 8, 1982, p. 108.

"Forms Meeting Functions," *InformationWeek,* 7 August 1995, p. 28.

Gubser, Jay, "Paper Will Not Be the Way of the Future," *The Office,* January 1979, p. 162.

"Mounting Demand Puts Operations of Standard Register in Top Form," *Barron's,* November 7, 1966, p. 28.

Olson, Thomas, "Families Fight While Standard Hopes," *Cincinnati Business Courier,* February 25, 1991, p. 1.

Robbins, Susan, "Business Form Makers Grow at Record Pace," *The Commercial and Financial Chronicle,* March 10, 1975, p. 1.

Schied, John P., "A Brief History of the Forms Industry," *The Office,* May 1973, p. 57.

Skolnik, Rayna, "Standard Register Sells in Top Form," *Sales & Marketing Management,* October 11, 1982, p. 49.

Spayd, M. A., *A Business Built on Holes! The Standard Register Company.* New York: Newcomen Society in North America, 1957.

——, "A Business Built on Holes in Paper," *Industrial Development and Manufacturing Record,* April 1960, p. 12.

"Standard Register Acquires UARCO Direct Mail Division," *Printing-Impressions,* August 1994, p. 5.

Tanzillo, Kevin. "EDI Becomes Standard," *Communications News,* November 1990, p. 22.

"Watch Out for Big Brother," *Forbes,* May 1, 1967, p. 44.

—April Dougal Gasbarre

Stanhome Inc.

333 Western Avenue
Westfield, Massachusetts 01085
U.S.A.
(413) 562–3631
Fax: (413) 568–2820

Public Company
Incorporated: 1931 as Stanley Home Products, Inc.
Employees: 4,940
Sales: $790 million (1994)
Stock Exchanges: New York Pacific
SICs: 5947 Gift, Novelty & Souvenir Shops; 5961
    Catalog & Mail-Order Houses; 5912 Drug Stores &
    Proprietary Stores

A pioneer in the direct-sales industry, Stanhome Inc. markets a wide range of consumer products, including giftware, collectibles, cosmetics, and home care and personal care products, through a variety of distribution channels. For decades, Stanhome sold its home care and personal care products through its "Famous Stanley Hostess Plan," a marketing innovation in the direct-sales industry that produced remarkable results for the company and prompted other direct-sales marketers to follow suit. By the 1990s, however, the company made the bulk of its money through its Enesco subsidiary, which imported porcelain figurines and roughly 7,000 other products from the Far East and sold them through more than 50,000 retail outlets.

The origins of Stanhome can be traced to the birth of the company's founder, Frank Stanley Beveridge, the Nova Scotian native whose contributions to the art of direct sales created the nearly $800 million Stanhome empire and helped spawn the formation of direct-sales stalwarts Mary Kay Cosmetics, Tupperware, Jafra Cosmetics, and Home Interiors. Born in 1879, Beveridge was raised in the small Nova Scotia town of Pembroke Shores, where, as a youth, he developed an interest in horticulture. His interest in horticulture played an auspicious role in the formation of Stanhome, leading the would-be founder of the company away from the secluded confines of Pembroke Shores and to Northfield, Massachusetts. There the young aspiring horticulturist gained admittance to Mt. Hermon School, a highly regarded private academy. At Mt. Hermon, Beveridge intended to pursue a career in horticulture, but he was forced to find a job to defray the cost of Mt. Hermon's tuition. Beveridge's search for a part-time job introduced him to the world of sales and forever changed the door-to-door sales industry in the United States and abroad.

While at Mt. Hermon, Beveridge landed a sales job with a local company named Underwood & Underwood selling home entertainment stereoscopes and viewgraphs during his time away from studies at Mt. Hermon. Beveridge's career aspirations had been reshaped by his experiences at Underwood & Underwood, and after leaving school he shelved his dreams of a career in horticulture and instead chose to pursue a path in sales. In 1913, at age 34, Beveridge joined the Fuller Brush Company, beginning his tenure there as a manager of college sales charged with visiting campuses and recruiting prospective sales representatives for Fuller Brush. Beveridge distinguished himself as a successful recruiter for the company, achieving sufficient success to be named vice-president in charge of sales in 1919, the same year he hired Catherine O'Brien as his secretary. It was a pivotal moment in the history of Stanhome and in the lives of Beveridge and O'Brien. Together, Beveridge and O'Brien would build a pioneering force in the direct-sales industry and develop a working partnership that would span nearly 40 years.

Before Beveridge and O'Brien went on to launch the business venture that would help create a multibillion dollar industry, boss and secretary worked together at Fuller Brush for ten years, until 1929 when Beveridge decided to resign from the company and work as a consultant for Real Silk Hosiery. Catherine O'Brien remained at Fuller Brush for a short time, then she left as well, becoming the manager of an insurance agency in Hartford. The two long-time working associates each pursued their respective professional careers separately for roughly two years until Beveridge decided to use the savings he had accumulated over the years to start his own door-to-door sales company with the help of O'Brien. On August 15, 1931,

Stanley Home Products, Incorporated, the predecessor to Stanhome Inc., commenced business. At age 52, Beveridge had decided to test his entrepreneurial skills; the success of his efforts would create a new type of direct-sales industry and induce other entrepreneurs to put the selling techniques learned while working for Stanley Home Products to work for themselves.

Initially headquartered on the first floor of a tobacco shed in Westfield, Massachusetts, the company's beginnings were quintessentially humble, established in the humblest of economic times. Beveridge started Stanley Home Products as the country was plunging into the most precipitous economic free-fall in its history, a decade-long financial slide that would put millions of Americans out of work and force thousands of companies out of business. Looking forward from 1931, economic conditions would worsen before they would improve, offering little help to fledgling business ventures like Stanley Home Products, which found itself thrust in the crucible of the Great Depression during its most vulnerable years. Expectations were particularly bleak for a company that relied on door-to-door sales to stay alive, although with more than 12 million people unemployed, the odds of finding idle, prospective customers at home were unusually good; their ability to pay for household products was another matter entirely.

Times were tough and sales were hard to come by, but the Depression, if it had any positive effect on Stanley Home Products, honed the sales techniques of the company's sales force. To sell products to customers with exceedingly tight grips on their wallets, sales pitches needed to be highly persuasive and thematically more diverse. Cost had to be downplayed, while service, quality, and educating the prospective customer about a product's invaluable uses had to be stressed. By developing this skill, Stanley Home Products salespeople recorded enough success to beat back the debilitating pressures of the Depression, giving Beveridge, O'Brien, and the generations of company dealers to come the opportunity to share in the riches that came pouring in as the intensity of the Depression began to ebb.

From the outset, Catherine O'Brien had taken responsibility for organizing Stanley Home Products' office in the Westfield tobacco shed and developing the company's initial product line of household cleaners, mops, and brushes. Frank Stanley Beveridge, meanwhile, took charge of recruiting salespeople for the company, assuming much the same duties as he had while employed as a manager of college sales for Fuller Brush nearly 20 years earlier. Business commenced in mid-August, and the first order arrived one month later. Shortly thereafter a sales manager in New York sent in the first $1,000 order for the company. As the company began to build momentum in spite of the general inertia that prevailed in the 1930s, Beveridge rallied his troops forward, reportedly telling his dealers, "There is something of real value in the home. You're not simply selling brushes and chemicals, you are also selling what they do. You are selling clean walls, clean ceilings, clean teeth. You are selling health and sanitation."

Beveridge's attempts to encourage his all-important sales corps steered the company through the most difficult years of the 1930s and perhaps instilled the motivating force in a particu-lar Stanley Home Products dealer for the sales approach that would exponentially accelerate the company's growth. The first signal that triggered Stanley Home Products' rise to the role of pioneer in the sales industry and then ushered in decades of abounding annual revenues was vigilantly received in 1937 by one of the company's sales managers. The sales manager, who superintended a northeastern region of the United States, noticed that the sales orders sent in by a dealer in Maine were unusually high. The sales manager decided to investigate and talked to the surprisingly successful dealer. What the sales manager discovered set a spark beneath the entire organization of Stanley Home Products that blazed for decades.

As the sales manager discovered, the dealer in Maine had by chance knocked on the door of a minister's wife who had guests assembled inside and was attempting to raise money for her husband's church. Too busy for a home demonstration, the woman asked the Stanley Home Products dealer to return another day, which he agreed to do. As he was turning away, however, the woman stopped the dealer and made a suggestion that would dramatically alter the future of Stanley Home Products. She proposed that if the dealer would contribute a percentage of his sales to the church, she would allow him to demonstrate his products in front of the group gathered inside. The dealer agreed, and from that point forward Stanley Home Products' sales volume began to rise steadily. Word of the new marketing approach spread from the dealer in Maine to his sales manager and finally to corporate headquarters in Westfield, and soon Stanley Home Products dealers everywhere were approaching local clubs and meetings to ask if they could demonstrate their products in front of those in attendance.

By demonstrating in front of a captive group audience, a Stanley Home Products dealer could achieve results in one sales call that otherwise would have taken a day-and-a-half of knocking on individual doors, making everyone within the company appreciably more successful. When the company's dealers ran out of organizations to approach, they began organizing their own parties by asking a housewife to invite a small group of friends to her house for a demonstration of the company's products. As compensation for hosting the party, the hostess at first was given a percentage of the sales in Stanley Home Products merchandise. Later, after the company's compensation program was revamped, the hostess was rewarded with a collectible gift, such as a portion of a silverware set. It was the birth of the "Famous Stanley Hostess Plan," as the company called it, the success of which fueled the growth of Stanley Home Products and extended the company's geographic reach into an array of foreign markets.

By 1937, the company had moved out of its tobacco shed and into a new manufacturing facility. With the Stanley Home Products party plan propelling the company forward, growth came quickly in the next few decades, and the company's corporate staff and manufacturing personnel struggled to keep pace with the orders for products that came pouring in. Annual sales reached a record high of $3 million in 1940, then swelled exponentially to $50 million in 1950. During this decade of prodigious growth, the volume of business conducted by Stanley Home Products required continual expansion of the company's facilities. By the end of the Second World War, the company operated out of 16 separate buildings in the Westfield area. Even this sprawling collection of facilities soon proved inadequate, however, so Stanley Home Products acquired a large textile mill in Southhampton, Massachusetts and tailored it to the company's needs.

With manufacturing and shipping facilities stretching nearly one quarter of a mile, Stanley Home Products stood poised for the aggressive expansion that characterized its development during the latter half of the 20th century. Much of Stanley Home Products' growth was achieved overseas, as the company's party plan marketing concept crossed international borders and thrived in diverse cultures. The expansion into foreign markets began in Canada, where Stanley Home Products established operations in 1948. Next, the company entered Puerto Rico in 1955, with operations in Mexico and Venezuela established soon afterward.

By the beginning of the 1960s, the company was supported by 20,000 dealers, whose efforts to sell products through the Famous Stanley Hostess Plan pushed annual sales to the $100 million mark just in time for Stanley Home Products' 30th anniversary in 1961. In the following decade, the company continued to extend its geographic presence into foreign countries, as the network of Stanley Home Products dealers expanded to embrace a host of lucrative markets. The company's entry into Europe began with the formation of a wholly owned Italian subsidiary, Stanhome S.p.A., in 1964, followed by the establishment of operations in Spain in 1968 and entry into the French market in 1972. Brazil and the Caribbean became part of Stanley Home Products' growing global empire during the decade as well. With the company's entry into the Far East during the late 1970s its worldwide presence was spread in four directions from its home state of Massachusetts.

In the first 40 years of the company's existence, Stanley Home Products became a massive direct-sales marketer, both in the United States and throughout its extensive international sales territories. The company's party plan merchandising approach spurred its growth, attracting dealers into the Stanley Home Products' fold and fueling revenue growth, while carving a new niche in the sales industry. Other companies aped the sales techniques employed at Stanley Home Products, creating a host of direct-sales firms that relied on sales to organized groups rather than the time-consuming, less effective drudgery of walking through a neighborhood and knocking on doors. Not surprisingly, several companies that distinguished themselves as highly successful direct-sales marketers were founded by individuals who had learned the nuances of the party plan approach while employed by Stanley Home Products. Among the list of people who spent the early years of their careers under the employ of Stanley Home Products were Mary Kay Ash of Mary Kay Cosmetics, Brownie Wise of Tupperware, Jan and Frank Day of Jafra Cosmetics, and Mary Crowley of Home Interiors. Stanley Home Products originated the marketing technique used by these direct-sales concerns in their rise to success and served as a learning center for the founders of the companies. Despite the company's pioneering role in the direct-sales industry and the enormous success derived from the use of its party plan approach, however, the effectiveness of the Famous Stanley Hostess Plan began to wane by the end of the 1970s. In the years following, Stanley Home Products needed new sales strategies to ensure the company's continued success. America's social structure had changed; the structure of Stanley Home Products' business had to change as well.

By the late 1970s, the housewife had become an increasingly less ubiquitous fixture of American society, and her departure from the home and into the workplace signaled the beginning of the end for Stanley Home Products' Famous Stanley Hostess Plan in the United States. Elsewhere, particularly in parts of Europe and in Latin America where the traditional role of wife remained largely unchanged, Stanley Home Products' party plan continued to record encouraging success, but in the United States the performance of the company's direct-sales operations was beginning to suffer from the exodus of women from home to office.

A nationwide economic recession plagued Americans during the early 1980s and exacerbated the company's domestic woes. In 1983, however, Stanley Home Products made a move to relieve the pressures exerted both by the lackluster economic climate and the poor growth recorded by the company's domestic direct-sales operations. At the time of this significant redirection of the company's priorities, Stanley Home Products was stewarded by H. L. Tower, who joined the company in 1978 as chief executive officer. In explaining the decision behind the company's defining 1983 acquisition Tower later confided to *Fortune* magazine, "My strategy was to turn around our U.S. business and search for the right acquisition. We offer Stanley representatives free gifts if they host a party, so I decided a great gift company would be a synergistic move."

In July 1983, exactly one year after Stanley Home Products, Inc. changed its name to Stanhome Inc., the company acquired Chicago-based Enesco Imports Corporation, a giftware designer that imported a wide range of giftware and collectible items from Asia and sold the products through card shops and other U.S. retail outlets. Founded in 1959 as a division of Chicago retailer N. Shure Company, Enesco had become a leading giftware company in the United States by the time Stanhome acquired the company, recording much of its success through a line of porcelain figurines marketed under the name "Precious Moments." The ever-expanding line of porcelain figurines, each inscribed with a scriptural message, catapulted Enesco to the top tier of the U.S. giftware industry, attracting legions of customers who purchased the Precious Moments statuettes, treating them as a series of collectible items. At one point, more than 300,000 people counted themselves as members of a Precious Moments collectors club. The most faithful followers made pilgrimages to a Precious Moments chapel in Missouri.

Five years after the acquisition of Enesco, Stanhome's annual sales had risen sharply, jumping from $277 million in 1983 to $480 million in 1988. The porcelain and metalware figurines, music boxes, and other imported products—more than 7,000 in total—composing Enesco's giftware line accounted for nearly half of Stanhome's revenues in 1988 and generated more than half of the company's total profit. Conversely, Stanhome's direct-sales business, though doing well in parts of Europe and in Latin America, had become a barely break-even enterprise in the United States, accounting for a meager 9 percent of the company's total revenues in 1988.

The dwindling number of women who spent their days at home and the proliferation of discount retail chains that offered essentially the same mops, brooms, brushes, and cosmetics as Stanhome, but at much cheaper prices, had rendered the Famous Stanley Hostess Plan passé and largely ineffective. Stanhome management perceived Enesco as a source of hope for the future, in that it could compensate for the decline in Stanhome's U.S. direct-sales business, particularly after the subsidiary began retailing its giftware in Europe and Japan in 1989. From 1989 forward, Stanhome management also pinned its hopes on newly acquired Hamilton Group Limited, which sold collectible plates, dolls, and figurines through advertising and direct mail, as well as a line of giftware sold through traditional retail channels. The purchase of Jacksonville, Florida-based Hamilton in May 1989 gave the company a third selling strategy—direct-response—to spur its growth into the 1990s, helping Stanhome record $571 million in sales in 1989 as it prepared to face the challenges of the coming decade.

In 1991, Enesco for the first time overtook Stanhome's direct-sales business segment in contribution toward overall sales and profits, accounting for 46 percent of operating revenues and 56 percent of earnings. The Precious Moments line of figurines alone accounted for one quarter of the company's total revenues, sending a clear signal to Stanhome's management that the future growth of the company hinged on the growth of Enesco's business.

One of the company's board members, G. William Seawright, was one who believed that the company's future growth depended on the continued success of Enesco. A 25-year veteran of Heublein, Inc., where he eventually took charge of overseas sales of brands such as Smirnoff vodka, J&B scotch, and Bailey's Irish Cream liqueur, Seawright joined Stanhome's board of directors in mid-1990 and almost immediately began railing against the company's seemingly sluggish development of its Enesco subsidiary, particularly management's slow progress in Europe and other foreign markets. After years of urging the company to accelerate Enesco's expansion, Seawright eventually was rewarded with the chance to effect the foreign expansion he wanted when Stanhome's board of directors named him chief executive officer in November 1993.

With Seawright at the helm, Stanhome moved toward the mid-1990s supported in large part by its Enesco subsidiary. In 1994, when the company acquired Lilliput Group plc, a maker of miniature replicas of English cottages, Stanhome's line of giftware and collectibles generated roughly $550 million of its $790 million in total sales and accounted for $73 million of its $81 million in operating profit. With Enesco performing as the primary earner for the company and instilling hope for future growth, Stanhome severed its ties with its floundering direct-sales business in the United States in 1995, marking the termination of the company's former mainstay business established 64 years earlier by Frank Stanley Beveridge. In an ironic twist, the domestic operations of Stanley Home Products were licensed to Leicester, New York-based CPAC Inc., a specialty chemicals manufacturer that prior to acquiring the licensing rights for Stanhome's U.S. direct-sales business had entered into the direct-sales business by purchasing the Fuller Brush Company. With the product of Beveridge's entrepreneurial efforts indirectly in the hands of his former employer, Stanhome charted its plans for the remainder of the 1990s and beyond, supported by the Famous Stanley Hostess Plan, continuing to thrive in international markets, and its Enesco and Hamilton subsidiaries.

Principal Subsidiaries

Border Fine Arts Company Limited (Scotland); Border Fine Arts Ltd. (N. Ireland); Collector Appreciation, Inc.; Consumer Products Group, Inc.; Cosmhogar, S.A. (Spain); Enesco Corporation; Enesco European Giftware Group Limited (England); Enesco Import GmbH (Germany); Enesco International Ltd.; Enesco International Limited (Hong Kong); Enesco Limited (United Kingdom); Enesco Worldwide Holdings, Inc.; Heinz Deichert GmbH (Germany); Lilliput Lane Limited (England); Lilliput Incorporated; N.C. Cameron & Sons Limited (Canada); Sports Impressions, Inc.; Stanhome Capital, Inc.; Stanhome de Mexico, S.A. de C.V.; Stanhome European Development Center, S.A. (Spain); Stanhome Iberia, S.A. (Spain); Stanhome Inter-American Corporation; Stanhome Panamericana, C.A. (Venezuela); Stanhome plc (England); Stanhome S.A. (France); Stanhome S.A. (Spain); Stanhome S.p.A. (Italy); Stanhome Trading Company Ltd. (Slovenia); Stanhome West Germany Limited; The Hamilton Group Limited, Inc.; The Hamilton Collection, Inc.; Via Vermont Ltd.; Via Vermont, S.A. de C.V. (Mexico).

Principal Operating Units

Enesco Corporation; Hamilton Collection; Stanhome Direct Selling Group.

Further Reading

Byrne, Harlan S., "Stanhome Inc.," *Barron's,* May 21, 1990, p. 45.
Cochran, Thomas N., "Cleaning Up," *Barron's,* November 20, 1989, p. 52.
"Collectible Stock," *Forbes,* June 22, 1992, p. 245.
Schifrin, Matthew, "Okay, Big Mouth," *Forbes,* October 9, 1995, p. 47.
Slovak, Julianne, "Stanhome," *Fortune,* May 8, 1989, p. 85.
Stanhome, Inc., *Our Edge Is Quality,* Westfield: Stanhome, Inc., 1991.
"Stanhome To Quit Direct Sales Business in U.S.," *The New York Times,* January 19, 1995, p. D4.
Wyatt, Edward A., "No Party Pooper," *Barron's,* February 24, 1992, p. 14.

—Jeffrey L. Covell

SUPER FOOD SERVICES, INC.

Super Food Services, Inc.

3233 Newmark Drive
Miamisburg, Ohio 45342
U.S.A.
(513) 439–7500
Fax: (513) 439–7514

Public Company
Incorporated: 1957
Employees: 1,451
Sales: $1.13 billion (1995)
Stock Exchanges: New York
SICs: 5141 Groceries, General Line

Although its operations were limited to six midwestern states, Super Food Services Inc. ranked as one of the largest food distributors in the United States in the mid-1990s. In addition to its core wholesale services, the company offered its retailing customers advertising and promotions, private label products, data processing, accounting and data processing services, and even store development advice. The wholesaler's clients were fairly evenly split among Independent Grocers Alliance Distribution Co. (IGA) stores (284), contract stores (326), and convenience marts (265). Under the leadership of Chairman and CEO Jack Twyman since the early 1970s, the company struggled in the mid-1990s to maintain both its profitability and its independence in an increasingly competitive environment.

Super Food Service was founded in Chicago in 1957 as a distributor for the Independent Grocers Alliance Distributing Co.'s New York City franchise area, serving about 41 IGA affiliates in the metropolitan region. Chicago-based IGA had pioneered the wholesale industry when it was founded by J. Frank Grimes in 1926 to buttress independent supermarketers against the rise of chain groceries. In 1958, Super Food acquired virtually all the stock of Dayton, Ohio, wholesaler F.N. Johnson Co. and began providing management, planning, warehousing and delivery to the area's fast-growing group of independents. Super Food helped IGA associates expand their share of the

Dayton-area market from nothing in 1950 to over 25 percent by the end of the decade. In the face of well-entrenched competition from established chain stores, this performance was considered a major achievement for IGA and Super Food. This success probably influenced Super Food's 1963 move from Chicago to Dayton.

A combination of internal growth and acquisitions propelled Super Food's rapid sales increase and geographic expansion in the late 1950s and 1960s. Over the course of its first decade, the company purchased wholesaling operations in Orlando, Detroit, and Syracuse. By 1963, the company served about 1,000 IGA and unaffiliated stores in Ohio, Florida, New York, and Michigan. Annual sales multiplied from $25.4 million in 1957 to $236.9 million in 1967, and net income blossomed from $206,000 to $1.2 million over the same period.

W.H. Tegtmeyer led Super Food Service from its inception in 1957 to 1968, when D.L. Fox succeeded him. But Fox only held his office for a few years. In 1972 John "Jack" Twyman, the hand-picked designate of top shareholder Loren M. Berry, supplanted Fox as the wholesaler's top executive. During Super Food's formative years, Twyman had been a standout player on the NBA's now-defunct Cincinnati Royals. (Although the team didn't last, Twyman was elected to the NBA Hall of Fame in 1982.) After retiring from professional sports, Twyman became a sportscaster and insurance agent. The insurance business brought him into close contact with Loren Berry, who was quickly impressed with Twyman and advocated the 35-year-old as a candidate for leadership in Super Food. Berry's son, John, later told *Forbes* that "There were others with more experience in the food business, but my father was struck by Jack's determination." Twyman was elected to the board of directors in 1970 and advanced to chairman and CEO in 1972 at the age of 36.

In spite of his lack of experience in the grocery industry, Twyman proved himself up to the challenge during the difficult 1970s. High inflation, intense competition, and consolidation distinguished the wholesale grocery industry during this decade. Consolidation alone shrunk Super Food's roster of 1,000 grocery customers down to 560 supermarkets. A major industry shakeout reduced the number of supermarket wholesalers in the United States from 1,000 in 1974 to 400 in 1984. Twyman met the challenges of the era in part by broadening Super Food's product line. In 1973, for example, he formed General Merchandise Services, Inc. to add high-margin non-food items to the wholesale offerings. Super Food not only survived, but thrived during this period. From 1972 to 1982, sales and profits nearly tripled, from $289.9 million to over $1 billion and from $1.2 million to $3.6 million, respectively.

This period of phenomenal growth hit a major snag in 1981. That year, Super Food's net profit margin dipped to what William Cahill of *Barron's* called "an embarrassing .22 percent," compared to an industry average of about .8 percent. Difficulties continued in 1982, when L.M. Berry's estate sold its controlling 24 percent stake in Super Food back to the company. The sale precipitated an unexpected shareholder mutiny led by American Pacific, a California-based real estate company. Twyman guided a difficult, but ultimately successful fight for the company's independence, before launching a multi-year growth program.

The CEO would later ascribe his company's progress in the 1980s to three primary factors: capital investment in a consolidation of the company's distribution centers; adoption of productivity standards; and perhaps most significantly, computerization. Twyman later told *U.S. Distribution Journal* that "We are moving from the archaic manual conduct of our business to dependency and utilization of technology, which has resulted in efficiencies that were inconceivable ten years ago." The company's use of electronic data interchange helped streamline customer ordering and internal inventory control, while simultaneously reinforcing its relationships with both producers and retailers.

While Super Food had been minimally involved in retailing in the early 1970s, Twyman made it clear that the company would concentrate exclusively on wholesaling under his administration. This policy did not preclude diversification within wholesaling, however. Over the course of the 1980s, Super Food broadened its product offerings to include a wider variety of perishable foods, branched out into photo finishing and video rental, and expanded its client base from independents to include convenience stores and even some chain supermarkets. By 1990, the wholesaler had close to 900 clients.

Super Food's sales increased by 90 percent from $891 million to $1.69 billion and net income quadrupled from $3.4 million to $15.9 million from 1979 to 1989. In 1990, *Forbes* ranked Super Food as the most productive of the United States' eight largest publicly-held food wholesalers. The company rounded out the 1980s by moving its stock from the American Stock Exchange to the New York Stock Exchange in December 1989. Twyman said that Super Food's strong financial performance would enable it to begin growing through acquisition in the early 1990s, but cautioned that "Our criteria is not to be the biggest, it's to be the best." He hoped to connect the "corridor" between the company's Midwest locus and its Florida operations. In 1991 the company made its first move toward that goal with the acquisition of Affiliated Foods of Kentucky for $150 million. Affiliated Foods serviced 100 clients in its namesake state as well as Virginia and Tennessee.

But several underlying problems, some endemic to the wholesale industry and others specific to Super Food, converged in 1992 to thwart Twyman's plans for expansion. The wholesale food industry in general was impacted by the difficulties of its retail customers, including anemic growth and competition from nationwide chains and deep discounters. The decline of Super Food's core constituency of independent grocers also had a negative impact. In 1992, *Progressive Grocer* reported that the independents' share of U.S. retail supermarket revenues had declined from 65 percent in 1952 to 42 percent by 1972 and to less than 30 percent in 1992. Traditional wholesalers also felt the squeeze from food producers, many of whom eliminated deals and promotions in favor of "everyday low prices" (EDLP).

Many of Super Food Service's wholesaling competitors had combated these trends by acquiring retail operations and expanding nationwide, but Twyman remained staunchly dedicated to wholesaling. He felt that avoiding direct competition with Super Food's retailing clients would engender their loyalty. But a major customer in Florida debunked that theory in 1992. By the early 1990s, Albertson's, a leading grocery retailer headquartered in Idaho, constituted about 85 percent of Super Food's Florida division's sales and over one-third of the company's total annual revenues. Albertson's had been developing its own regional wholesale operations and methodically phasing out its traditional suppliers in an industry trend known as "self-distribution." Twyman's strong personal relationship with Albertson's Chairman and CEO Warren McCain had cemented the two companies' 18-year relationship. But when McCain retired in 1991, his successor, Gary Michael, wasn't bound by those personal ties.

The two parties started negotiating the sale of Super Food's Florida distribution center to Albertson's in 1991, but the retailer backed out of the deal in January 1992, forcing Super Food to close its 800,000 square foot facility, and take a $23 million charge against earnings as well as a $5.5 million loss on the year. Super Foods brought charges of breach of contract against its longtime customer and sued for restitution, but its lawsuit and subsequent appeals were repeatedly dismissed.

In the aftermath of the loss of Albertson's, several industry observers questioned Super Food's continuing viability as an independent player in the wholesale industry. In mid-1992, Gary Vinceberg, an analyst with Dean Witter (New York) told *U.S. Distribution Journal* that the loss of Albertson's would be "very devastating to Super Foods." In February 1993 Toddi Gutner of *Forbes* agreed, writing that the company was "threatened with extinction." Others suggested consolidation. George A. Niemond, an analyst with Value Line, for example, predicted that Super Foods would acquire or be acquired in the consolidation trend that continued to distinguish the wholesale industry of the mid-1990s. David Katz of Matrix Asset Advisors (New York) concurred, telling Jim Bohman of the *Dayton Daily News* that a merger "makes strategic sense." But these forecasts of imminent doom had not yet materialized by early 1996. Annual sales, which had risen to $1.77 billion in 1990, dropped by 28 percent and flattened out at $1.2 billion from 1993 to 1995. Net income declined 47 percent during that same period, from $17.2 million to around $9 million. Twyman told shareholders at the company's 1995 annual meeting that "Our sales are considerably stronger as we go into 1996, [and] any incremental increase in sales will flow right to the bottom line."

Principal Subsidiaries

General Merchandise Services Inc.; Kentucky Food Stores Inc.

Principal Divisions

General Merchandise Services Division; Bellefontaine, Ohio Division; Cincinnati, Ohio Division; Bridgeport, Michigan Division.

Further Reading

Bohman, Jim, "Super Food Services Rolls Uninterestingly Along," *Dayton Daily News,* August 28, 1995, p. 4.

——, "Super Food Still Facing Questions: Profits, Stock Prices Irk Shareholders," *Dayton Daily News,* December 13, 1995, p. 7B.

Cahill, William R., "No Laggard: Super Food Services Now on a Path Toward Industry Leadership," *Barron's,* April 27, 1987, p. 55.

"Following Albertson's Showdown, Super Food Looks for Comeback," *U.S. Distribution Journal,* May 15, 1992, p. 11.

Fucini, Suzy, "Jack Twyman, Super Food Services Inc.: 'We're Totally Focused on Wholesaling'," *U.S. Distribution Journal,* March 15, 1990, p. 26.

Greene, Richard, "Wholesaling," *Forbes,* January 2, 1984, p. 226.

Gutner, Toddi, "Dinosaur?," *Forbes,* February 15, 1993, p. 156.

"Inside Warehousing & Distribution," *Transportation & Distribution,* January 1988, p. 59.

Jaffe, Thomas, "Super Food For Thought," *Forbes,* February 3, 1992, p. 129.

Rosenberg, Hilary, "Wholesale Gains: Food Distributors Are Racking Up Healthy Profits," *Barron's,* October 14, 1985, p. 32.

Rudolph, Barbara, "The Education of Jack Twyman," *Forbes,* March 11, 1985, p. 75.

"60th Annual Report of the Grocery Industry," *Progressive Grocer,* April 1992.

"Sprawling IGA Achieves Flexibility With FourGen's Solutions," *Chain Store Age Executive with Shopping Center Age,* September 1995, p. 16B.

"Super Food Links Midwest, Florida," *U.S. Distribution Journal,* June 15, 1991, p. 4.

"Super Food Sees Sunshine in Sale of Florida Unit," *U.S. Distribution Journal,* January 15, 1992, p. 8.

Tanner, Ronald, "60 Years With IGA; A Saga of American Independence," *Progressive Grocer,* June 1986, p. 25.

Valero, Greg, "Slot Machine," *U.S. Distribution Journal,* December 15, 1994, p. 30.

"The Who's Who of IGA Wholesalers," *Progressive Grocer,* June 1986, p. 72.

—April Dougal Gasbarre

Symbol Technologies, Inc.

116 Wilbur Place
Bohemia, New York 11716
U.S.A.
(516) 563–2400
Fax: (516) 244–4645

Public Company
Founded: 1973
Employees: 2,600
Revenues: $540 million (1995 est.)
Stock Exchanges: New York Chicago Pacific
SICs: 3577 Computer Peripheral Equipment, Not
    Elsewhere Classified; 3578 Calculating Machines
    Except Computers

Symbol Technologies, Inc. is the world's leading manufacturer of bar code technology and related products and the only one of its growing competition with in-house design and development services to carry products from ideation to point of sale and beyond. From its bar code reading equipment and remarkable hand-held portable data collectors to radio frequency (RF) data communication systems, Symbol's innovations have allowed health care, postal, retail, and transportation companies worldwide to revolutionize their order and inventory management systems.

Symbol was founded in New York in 1973 by Dr. Jerome Swartz and a venture partner named Sheldon Harrison. A physicist with a keen interest in laser applications, Swartz was a graduate of the Brooklyn Polytechnic Institute and had been working as a consultant in optical and electronic systems and instruments. Building and experimenting out of his garage in Stony Brook, New York, Swartz invented a laser scanning device for use with bar codes. His new invention drastically changed the grocery and retail industries over the next decade, and Swartz's newly formed Symbol Technologies, Inc. rode the wave. Throughout the next several years, Swartz's technical skill and innovative thinking earned him dozens of technical

U.S. patents, many of which were basic patents for Symbol's growing line of sophisticated hand-held scanning devices.

Early in its evolution, Symbol formed a reciprocal relationship with the State University of New York (SUNY). Dr. Swartz served as a part-time professor of electrical engineering at SUNY Stony Brook, while Symbol contributed funds for grants and research and recruited students for internships and part-time positions. This was a somewhat unusual arrangement, since Symbol was a very small company and not in a position to spend what little money it had on charitable contributions. Yet Swartz believed in supporting higher learning, and the relationship proved fruitful for both. By the end of the decade, a young graduate named Rich Bravman, who had received a computer science degree from SUNY, was recommended by the chairman of the electrical engineering department to Symbol's management. Bravman was hired and would eventually served in a variety of top management positions with the company.

In June 1979, Symbol went public with an initial offering of 456,500 shares on the NASDAQ exchange. (The company later switched over to the New York Stock Exchange in 1988). Four years later, at the end of 1983, Raymond Martino joined Symbol as president and COO, leaving his position as vice-president of marketing and sales at Mars Electronics (a division of M&M/Mars Inc.) of Folcroft, Pennsylvania. The president of M&M/Mars Inc., Dr. Fred Heiman, also had a connection with Symbol—he was a member of Symbol's board, played a pivotal role in the fledgling company's development, and eventually came aboard full-time. During these years, Symbol was bringing in only around $5 million per year, but Martino, Heiman, and the rest of Symbol's employees and board believed in Dr. Swartz's abilities and the expanding product line.

Between 1983 and 1985, Symbol's revenues leapt to $13.9 million and its work forced swelled to 152. As sales increased, Symbol continued to add to its team of engineers and by 1987 the company's size required a move to new, spacious corporate headquarters. Due in part to the company's 1988 acquisition of the MSI Data Corp. of Costa Mesa, California, originators of a portable data terminal, Symbol became the sole contractor to the U.S. Department of Defense for hand-held laser scanners.

With technology from MSI and its own research and product development, Symbol built a very lightweight (20 ounces) hand-held scanner and then provided a radio frequency to link it to computer terminals. The concept was revolutionary; the applications almost limitless. Though the purchase of MSI wasn't without complications, the combined technologies allowed Symbol to both break unprecedented new ground with its products and enhance the company's marketing capabilities in the U.S and especially in Europe.

By 1989 the company's sales had reached $222.3 million, increasing by a phenomenal 1,498 percent over the previous four years. Rich Bravman, the SUNY graduate who joined the company fresh out of school, was now vice-president of marketing. Symbol's employee roster, which had grown to 1,800 worldwide, was cited by Bravman as representing the company's "number one principle" of maintaining a motivated, happy work force, which in turn kept productivity and sales high.

Around mid-year 1989 the bar code industry slipped into a recession and holding its own despite a weakening industry, Symbol captured 40 percent of the market by 1990 and whittled competitors from nearly a dozen down to three by stringent protection of its patents, forcing those who survived to pay royalties (which amounted to nearly ten percent of the year's revenues). Though sales weren't up dramatically from the previous year's, Symbol's $231.5 million was impressive under the circumstances.

In 1991 the company made a major move in developing its prospects in the Far East. Previously unable to secure a footing in the vast Asian market, Symbol successfully defended itself against a lawsuit brought by the Japan-based Opto-Electronics Corp., which had sought to challenge Symbol's laser scanning technology patents. With the lawsuit out of the way, Symbol announced a joint venture with Olympus Optical Company, Ltd. of Tokyo to design and manufacture bar code data collection products under the name of Olympus Symbol, Inc. (Symbol owned 50.10 percent), which also became Symbol's worldwide distributor. In other international news, European sales (with the help of the MSI Data Corp., purchased the previous year) accounted for 30 percent of Symbol's overall revenue, and Japanese sales were expected to boost the figure substantially (by as much as $75 million) in time.

The year 1991 also marked the bar code industry's climb out of its recessionary trough, helped by what some analysts deemed Phase Two of the bar coding and data collection business. Phase One had included introducing the technology and convincing clients of its value. During Phase Two, bar coding products gained wider acceptance and use within the retail sector and other businesses. Moreover, clients began ordering the next generation of scanners in even greater quantities than before. This momentum was borne out by Symbol's year-end results with sales hitting $317 million, a wholesome leap of 37 percent over 1990's revenues.

In August 1992, Symbol reduced its 1,100 work force by 140 to control costs and improve efficiency. Four months later, the company initiated a restructuring program to consolidate engineering and manufacturing operations and to trim sales, marketing, finance, and administrative costs. The company took a pre-tax charge of $40.9 million for both actions. Despite a loss of $3.4 million in the third quarter from a domestic sales fall-off and the work force reduction, Symbol finished the year with net revenues of $344.9 million and a loss of $16.2 million.

Thanks to a sizeable jump in research and development funding from 1992's $13.6 million to $16.3 million in 1993, Symbol stunned the industry with several major innovations. Among them was the PDF417 Symbology, which encoded 100 times more data than traditional bar code labels, all in the same amount of space. Using a two-dimensional format, data was compressed into a denser code with multiple rows of encoded information that could be read both horizontally and vertically. Additional payoffs came in the forms of two new licensing agreements and an alliance with Microsoft. This year also saw a shift in focus away from Symbol's traditional laser scanning devices as the bulk of its earnings, to its newer products and applications. Bar code scanners had long dominated Symbol's sales, but went from representing 50 percent of sales in 1992, to 45 and 40 percent in 1993 and 1994, respectively. Symbol had also begun construction of a new $50 million headquarters in nearby Holbrook, New York, to house its growing work force, which had now reached 2,000 employees.

After 11 years with the company, Ray Martino retired as president and COO in 1994 and was named vice-chairman of Symbol's board of directors. Succeeding him was Jan Lindelow, formerly president of Swiss conglomerate Asea Brown Boveri, and a 25-year veteran of the information technology industry. Major boons for the company came in the form of contracts with the Arizona Department of Transportation Motor Vehicle Division; the American Association of Motor Vehicle Administrations' selection of the Symbol's PDF417 (2-D symbology and portable data file system) as its standard equipment; the installation on three continents of the Spectrum One wireless networks for retailer Toys 'R' Us; and a sales surge to $465.3 million (a 29 percent increase from 1993's $359.9 million), with international sales growing by over 48 percent to a record $141.1 million.

By 1995 Symbol dominated the worldwide bar code scanner industry, holding what analysts projected as 75 percent of the market, having installed more than three million scanners and portable data terminals and handling such heavy-hitting customers as the federal government (the U.S. Postal Service, the U.S. Army, and the Department of Defense), as well as American Freightways, Eckerd Drug Stores, Home Depot, Kmart, Target, UPS, Volvo, and others. By the end of the year, change was afoot when Lindelow resigned and longtime senior vice-president and Tomo Razmilovic was named president and COO.

Headed toward the 21st century, Symbol's future seemed secure, with more and more products and applications being introduced to a world increasingly needful of its technology. With portable data collection equipment ranging from $400 to $4,400 per unit, depending upon the level of technical configuration, Symbol's handiwork was accessible to companies of all sizes throughout the world, with customer support operations in 11 U.S. states and foreign offices in Australia, Austria, Belgium, Canada, France, Germany, Italy, Norway, Singapore, Spain, and the United Kingdom.

Principal Subsidiaries

Symbol Australia Pty. Ltd.; SymboLease, Inc.; SymboLease Canada, Inc.; Symbol Technologies Asia, Inc.; Symbol Technologies Canada, Inc.; Symbol Technologies GmbH (Austria); Symbol Technologies GmbH (Germany); Symbol Technologies International, Inc. (Delaware); Symbol Technologies International, Inc. (New York); Symbol Technologies Limited (United Kingdom); Symbol Technologies, S.A. (France); Symbol Technologies S.A. (Spain); Symbol Technologies, S.R.L. (Italy); Symbol Technologies Texas, Inc.; True Data Corporation.

Principal Divisions

Laser Scanning Division.

Further Reading

Biesada, Alexandra, "Symbol Technologies: Buy on the Short Frenzy?" *Financial World,* April 28, 1992, p. 18.

Demery, Paul, "Symbol, Olympus Target Far East," *LI (Long Island) Business News,* March 25, 1991, pp. 1,16.

"Fastest Growing Companies in N.Y. Area," *Crain's New York Business,* October 21, 1991, p. 20.

Frankland, Christine, "Close Up: Martino and Symbol on the Fast Track," *LI Business News,* December 2, 1991, p. 3.

———, "Motivated Workforce Helps Symbol Grow," *LI Business News,* November 13, 1989, p. 3.

Hord, Christine, "LI's Symbol of High Tech Change," *LI Business News,* February 7, 1994, pp. 17, 19.

Jochum, Glenn, "Close Up: Symbol's Chief Scans New Markets," *LI Business News,* January 2, 1995, p. 9.

Mamis, Robert A., "The *Inc.* 100: The 12th Annual Ranking of America's Fatest Growing Small Public Companies," *Inc.,* May 1990, pp. 40–41.

Needle, David, "10 Hot Companies," *Information Week,* January 30, 1995.

Schonfeld, Erick, "Bar Codes: The Latest Industry Scan," *Fortune,* June 12, 1995, p. 141.

"Symbol Names Lindelow President," *LI Business News,* June 20, 1994, p. 16.

Talley, Karen, "Symbol is Stymied by Failed Bond Act," *LI Business News,* November 16, 1992, pp. 1, 13.

Zipser, Andy, "Attractive Symbol," *Barron's,* January 14, 1991, p. 32.

—Taryn Benbow-Pfalzgraf

TACO JOHN'S.

Taco John's International Inc.

P.O. Box 1589
Cheyenne, Wyoming 82003
U.S.A.
(307) 635-0101
Fax: (307) 638-0603

Private Company
Incorporated: 1969 as Taco John's
Employees: 350
Sales: $146 million (1994 est.)
SICs: 5812 Eating Places; 6794 Patent Owners & Lessors

Taco John's International Inc. franchises and supports a chain of Mexican-style fast-food restaurants. In the mid-1990s the company was supporting more than 400 outlets in 30 states, and was centered in the upper Midwest and West. Through an emphasis on food seasonings, good service, and fair prices, the company has become the second-largest Mexican quick service chain in the United States. In the 1990s, Taco John's was expanding through alternative distribution systems and by updating the image of its existing stores.

The sprawling restaurant chain dubbed Taco John's was born as a single, tiny taco stand. The "Taco House" as it was called, opened in 1968 in Cheyenne, Wyoming. It was started by a high-plains cowboy rancher named John ("Taco John") Turner and his wife. The Taco House was a big hit with the locals in Cheyenne because it offered good-tasting Mexican food, fast. An important ingredient in the taco stand's success was the spice that the Turners used in the food. They ground various spices and prepared all of the seasonings in their basement and garage. They used the seasonings to flavor traditional Mexican fare, including tacos and burritos.

Intrigued by the success of the bustling taco stand, Cheyenne businessmen Harold Holmes and Jim Woodson purchased the franchise rights to the fledgling venture in 1969. They believed that they could transport the concept to other cities in the region and, if the new restaurants were as popular as the first Taco

House, profit handsomely. They realized that the special seasonings developed by the Turners were important to the chain's success. In fact, the Turners' seasonings became a closely guarded trade secret that continued to be used by Taco John's restaurants throughout the 1980s and into the 1990s.

Holmes and Woodson immediately began franchising restaurants based on the Taco House concept. They changed the name of the outlets to "Taco John's," but left many other elements the same, including much of the menu. They opened their first franchised stores in Rapid City, South Dakota; Scottsbluff, Nebraska; and Torrington, Wyoming. Like the first Taco House, the new Taco John's outlets were a big success. Holmes and Woodson knew that they were onto something. Throughout the 1970s, then, they expanded throughout the upper Midwest and West, franchising Taco John's outlets primarily in small towns.

The decision to target small towns evidenced a new strategy that became characteristic of the Taco John's organization. The franchising concept was relatively new at the time, and most companies up to that period had focused on opening franchise outlets solely in larger urban areas. In contrast, Holmes and Woodson decided to open their stores in small towns, which were often devoid of competition. Their goal was to bring to those small towns a unique eating experience, including good-tasting Mexican food, served fast, at reasonable prices. The overall strategy was ultimately a big success. Each Taco John's eatery developed a loyal customer base in its town, and also managed to attract regular patrons from outlying regions that would become desperate for a Taco John's "fix."

In fact, Taco John's loyal fans played an important role in the company's growth during the 1970s and 1980s. Many customers in outlying areas would write to the Cheyenne headquarters, begging the company to open an outlet closer to them. In some cases, those same customers became franchisees, owning and operating their own store. Likewise, some Taco John's fans that relocated to other regions, realizing that no Taco John's existed in their area, would open their own Taco John's franchise. The result was that the company gradually blanketed many parts of the upper Midwest—South Dakota, Minnesota, Nebraska, Wisconsin, Iowa, Wyoming—with Taco John's outlets.

485

Taco John's prospered during the 1970s and 1980s by culti-vating a win-win partnership with its franchisees. Franchisees paid Taco John's a franchise fee, plus royalties on income from their stores. In return, they got complete support from Taco John's. In the early years, Taco John's would ship a prefabri-cated 12-by-30-foot taco stand from Wyoming; the stand was complete with kitchen appliances and other necessary fixtures. Later, the company built or outfitted larger structures with seating, rather than shipping prebuilt units. (One of the original prefabricated units was still operating in 1995 in Des Moines, where it had been a lunchtime favorite with high school students since 1973.) Taco John's would then work to ensure that its franchisees were given the training and support they needed to make their stores prosper. When the franchisees profited, so did Taco John's. As the word got out that a Taco John's franchise was a good investment, the company found a steady supply of franchisee candidates.

Thus, it was the enterprising franchisees that became the engine for Taco John's growth. Those entrepreneurs typically toiled long hours to make their restaurants successful, and often opened other Taco John's outlets in their areas. Representative of the franchisees who helped to grow Taco John's during the 1970s and 1980s were Bill Byrne and Dean Neese, owners of one of Taco John's largest franchise groups. Byrne, who was in his late 20s when he opened his first Taco John's, was working as a branch manager of a Dain Bosworth Inc. stock brokerage in the early 1970s. He became interested in the emerging Taco John's concept, and convinced 38-year-old Neese to join him in investing $39,500 to open the first Taco John's outlet in Des Moines, Iowa (one of the first Taco John's opened in a larger urban area).

Byrne and Neese labored to make their first Taco John's a success. Once the store was up-and-running and the Taco John's name began to catch on in Des Moines, they added a second outlet. They added one restaurant at a time, making sure that each store was a success before they opened another unit. In 1978 they opened the first Taco John's that sported both a drive-up window and indoor seating. The unit became a model for the next generation of Taco John's stores. They also helped to pioneer Taco John's mall stores. Over time, Byrne gravitated toward the finance and operations end of the business, while Neese focused on real estate and site location. Both partners also became involved with Taco John's International in Chey-enne, helping to formulate and implement corporate strategy. By the late 1980s, Byrne and Neese were operating ten Taco John's outlets in Des Moines, compared to six units operated by their nearest competitor. Those ten outlets consumed ten tons of beef and two tons of cheese each month.

Also demonstrating the importance of Taco John's fran-chisees were husband-and-wife team Charles and DeMaris Mathison, the owners and operators of one of Taco John's International's most successful stores. Charles grew up in Rapid City, South Dakota, where his parents operated a diner. After getting a degree in engineering and working in sales for a few years, he and DeMaris purchased a Taco John's franchise in 1976 for the city of Marshalltown, a small city in Iowa. They set up shop in an A-frame building and went to work. The first three years were "tough, real tough," DeMaris recalled in the March 14, 1994 *Des Moines Register*. "We were both exhausted for three years. One of us was there all the time. He would close one night, and I would close the next."

Despite various setbacks, the Mathisons managed to get the store off the ground by focusing on quality food and good service. They also worked to develop a loyal customer base, and were known for being able to greet more than half of their customers by name. Over time, the Mathison's Taco John's developed a regular clientele that spanned all socio-economic groups, from businessmen to laborers whose ethnic heritage ranged from German and Swedish to Hispanic. The couple moved their store to a larger space in 1985, and in 1988 added an atrium that boosted seating capacity to 114. With help from a professional restaurant manager, they were able to grow their Taco John's into one of the most successful units in the history of the company. In 1994, in fact, the Marshalltown Taco John's, after leading all other units in sales volume for four straight years, became the first unit to generate more than $1 million in receipts during a single year.

The efforts of franchisees, with support from headquarters staff in Cheyenne, allowed Taco John's to post big gains. By the end of the 1980s, in fact, Taco John's comprised a network of approximately 400 units, most of which were located in the upper Midwest and West. Those stores were generating annual sales approaching $150 million. States with the greatest number of restaurants included Minnesota, Wisconsin, Iowa, the Dako-tas, Nebraska, and Wyoming. But the chain had also extended into both large and small towns in Missouri, Montana, Illinois, and other states in those regions. At the same time, Taco John's was branching out with units in other parts of the nation, including (by the early 1990s) Tennessee, Florida, Arkansas, and New York.

Taco John's managed to sustain its growth during the 1980s, despite an onslaught of competition that knocked many of its competitors out of the industry. Notable was the threat posed beginning in the 1980s by Mexican-style fast-food behemoth Taco Bell, which was a subsidiary of the giant Pepsico. Taco Bell used its parent's deep pockets to fund an aggressive expan-sion drive, often penetrating markets where Taco John's had long been established. Taco John's executives realized that its franchisees couldn't compete with Taco Bell on price. Instead, they chose to buck the industry trend toward "value pricing" and stick with Taco John's proven strategy of offering larger portions of high-quality food in an attractive, friendly setting. Taco John's nacho chips, for example, were made fresh in each store, daily. "We'll leave it to the other guys to sell the bite-sized items," said Taco John's president, Pieter Roelofs, in the March 14, 1994 *Des Moines Register*.

Taco John's also retained its long-time philosophy of estab-lishing win-win relationships with its franchisees. For example, to confront increased competition, the company stepped up its advertising efforts and began working more closely with fran-chisees to develop multimedia campaigns. Taco John's reputa-tion for treating its franchisees fairly was rewarded in 1994, when Taco John's received the first-ever "Fair Franchising Seal of Approval" from the America Association of Franchisees and Dealers. At the same time, Taco John's was named by Dow Jones' National Business Employment Weekly as one of the best franchise buys in the country.

By 1994, Taco John's was operating 430 units in 30 states. It was still privately owned, and the original founders remained active in the company, although they had handed control of day-to-day operations to restaurant industry veteran Roelofs. Under Roelofs' direction, Taco John's initiated a number of changes in the early 1990s. For example, its menu was broadened to incorporate a variety of new items, including several "Heart Smart" items that proffered low-fat ingredients. In addition to those newer items were Taco John's more traditional, popular features, like the Beef Burrito, Taco, Taco Burger, Mexican Style Rice, and various platters and combos. Taco John's was also moving to grow through new distribution channels, such as "Mexpress" kiosks and small food court units.

Going into the mid-1990s, Taco John's was updating its image. Among other moves, the company replaced its long-time logo and character, Juan, a cartoon-like Mexican with a big hat. The new character, dubbed John, was less representative of the stereotypical Mexican image, and "more of a contemporary person who probably has a broader agenda, if you will,"

according to Byrne. The logo change was part of Taco John's "Image 2000" program, which also included updating the chain's stores with new, brighter colors and completely remodeling the stores. The first franchisee to completely renovate his stores under the new program was Byrne, who by 1994 was operating 12 units in Des Moines.

Further Reading

Backgrounder: About Taco John's International, Inc. Cheyenne, Wyo.: Taco John's International, 1996.

Elbert, David, "Big Success in a Small Town," *Des Moines Register,* March 14, 1994, p. 1B.

Jost, Rick, "Welcome to the New Taco John, A New Age, '90s Fellow," *Des Moines Register,* September 26, 1994, Sec. B.

Lacher, Lisa, "Franchise Partners Make a Hot Combo," *Business Record,* February 22, 1988, p. 12.

Taco John's: Working Together for Quality. Cheyenne, Wyo.: Taco John's International, 1994.

—Dave Mote

Tillotson Corp.

59 Water Avenue
Everett, Massachusetts 02149
U.S.A.
(617) 387–9400
Fax: (617) 389–9639

Private Company
Incorporated: 1931 as Gardner Rubber Co.
Employees: 2,800
Sales: $114 million (1994 est.)
SICs: 3069 Fabricated Rubber Products, Not Elsewhere
Classified; 3842 Surgical Appliances & Supplies

Tillotson Corp. is probably best known for its manufacture of synthetic gloves used by surgeons, doctors, and industrial workers. While the company also produces fiberglass products, including sailboats, and various wholesale industrial chemicals and latex compounds, it was engaged in divesting some of these businesses in order to streamline operations in the mid-1990s. The privately held Tillotson releases little financial or operating data.

Tillotson Rubber Company was founded in 1931 by entrepreneur Neil Tillotson, or "Mr. T," as he was affectionately called. Synthetic rubber had been invented only 20 years earlier by Russian scientist S. V. Lebedev, and latex (rubber in its liquid form) had just been introduced in the 1920s. Those breakthroughs, combined with processing and vulcanizing technologies developed earlier and improved during the 1910s and 1920s, initiated a new era for the rubber industry. During World War I, particularly, demand for rubber surged as warring nations sought substitutes for limited traditional rubber supplies.

Tillotson got into the latex and synthetic rubber industry just as it was dawning. The 16-year-old Tillotson left a commercial trade school early, forgoing a probable future as an accountant to pursue his interest in technology and engineering. He answered an ad for a position in Singapore with the United States Rubber Company, but a concerned uncle arranged for him to take a job closer to home with the Hood Rubber Company laboratory in nearby Watertown, Massachusetts. His experiences at Hood, a processor of natural rubber, eventually led him to become interested in emerging synthetic rubber technologies and to form his own company.

From the start, the adventurous, ambitious, and forward-thinking Tillotson was destined to run his own unique and successful enterprise. And his background had prepared him well for the challenges he would face. His ancestors had thrived in the Northeastern United States before the French and Indian Wars, and Tillotson was raised by frugal, independent Yankees in northern Vermont. His upbringing taught him that "the simple solution was often the best one and that an open mind was the seed bed of successful solutions," and that "if you own things at the 'right price' you never have to worry about being able to make a profit."

Tillotson had shown his entrepreneurial bent at the age of ten. He saved enough money to buy a 1,000-mile book of commuter railroad tickets, for which he paid only two cents per mile. The cost of a single ticket was three cents per mile. The enterprising Tillotson was able to rent the books to other travelers at a rate of two-and-one-half cents per mile and turn a quick profit. According to his son Tom (in a 1990 speech to the Newcomen Society), that "fifty-fifty sharing of the benefits between the participants in a transaction became the cornerstone of his business philosophy."

By the time he was in high school Tillotson was anxious to be on his own. He left home and high school early, in his early teens, and managed to find work on a chicken farm for room and board in Lowell, Massachusetts. He began attending the commercial trade school to prepare for a career in accounting. Shortly thereafter he left to take the job with Hood Rubber. He would work for Hood Rubber for several years before starting his own business, but not continuously. Shortly after taking the job at Hood, he quenched his desire for adventure by enlisting in the cavalry during World War I. The underaged recruit—Tillotson lied about his age to get in—expected to go to Europe, but was sent to Texas instead. Interestingly, Tillotson served as a cavalry trooper under General Pershing, chasing the infamous Pancho Villa through the hills of northern Mexico.

In 1918 Tillotson returned to Boston, and to his job at Hood Rubber. He studied engineering at night school, but his boss at Hood quickly realized that Tillotson's problem-solving abilities and lab skills were largely innate. Tillotson, a high school dropout, in many ways was outperforming graduate engineers from the Massachusetts Institute of Technology. In fact, Tillotson's lack of formal training was a plus in that he often reached solutions based on intuition—Tillotson later adopted a lab technique championed by rubber industry guru Harvey Firestone of not taking any lab notes and minimizing formality in an effort to enhance creativity and problem solving.

After latex was invented in the 1920s in Germany, Hood Rubber assigned Tillotson to a team of researchers that investigated uses for the natural liquid rubber. Tillotson quickly realized that a big advantage that latex had over hardened natural rubber was that it could be used to create products without heavy machinery. Although Tillotson was fascinated by latex, Hood Rubber showed little interest in the material because it had already invested heavily in hardened rubber technologies. So Tillotson worked in his attic lab at home, along with his unemployed brother and father-in-law, to develop a product that they could produce with latex and sell.

True inspiration to develop a product came to the threesome early in 1931, when fallout from the Great Depression forced Hood to shut down its Watertown plant for a few weeks and to furlough its workers. The entire Tillotson family worked almost endlessly during the downtime to perfect their first marketable product: a balloon made with ears and painted with a cat's face. A Boston novelty company named C. Decieco & Son was Tillotson's first customer. Decieco purchased more than 2,000 of the balloons and was able to sell them the next day at a parade in Lexington.

The Tillotson family went to the parade to see how their product was received. Neil Tillotson was sure that they had a hot product on their hands when he saw a little girl pull her balloon down and kiss the cat's face. The next day he sunk his entire savings of $720 into his new venture. He rented a factory for $25 per month and started what was first called Gardner Rubber Co. and soon dubbed Tillotson Rubber Co. Incredibly, the fledgling business churned out a whopping 5 million balloons during its first year of business. The company generated sales of $85,000 that year and turned a tidy profit of $5,000, which was an impressive sum for a business started with only $720 in the midst of the Depression.

Tillotson left his job at Hood in 1932 to devote all of his time to the new company. He paid $8 for a Greyhound bus ticket that would allow him unlimited stops on a trip from Boston to St. Louis. For five weeks he jockeyed from town to town. When he would get to a new city he would get the names of wholesale novelty dealers out of the phone book at the bus station and then visit and try to sell his cat-faced balloons to them. True to his frugal upbringing, he cut costs by sleeping on the bus, washing in men's rooms, and eating sparingly in small-town cafeterias. He returned from the five-week trip with a bounty of orders for the upcoming year.

Tillotson managed to grow his company throughout the early and mid-1930s, despite the rough economy of the period.

In 1937 he moved to a larger manufacturing facility. He also began developing and manufacturing a few other latex products, including latex-coated gloves and aprons for chemical workers. During World War II, when demand for latex and other rubber products soared, Neil Tillotson served as a consultant to the War Production Board, identifying sources of rubber to replace depleted natural supplies.

It was not until after the Second World War that Tillotson's sales soared. Balloons continued to be the company's mainstay, but Tillotson began experimenting with other products. Among other successful offerings, the company developed and manufactured latex girdles, baby pants, and latex-coated ink sacks. Tillotson Rubber secured its niche by staying on the cutting edge of technology. The company built the first high-volume automated dipping conveyor, which allowed a single operator to produce large volumes of balloons and other goods at a rapid pace. The high-tech machine was a major advancement, as most companies at the time still performed latex dipping by hand using racks. The conveyor was still in use in the early 1990s, producing boots that kept windshield wipers from freezing in the winter.

Tillotson Rubber's big breakthrough came in the early 1960s, although the company would not fully capitalize on the breakthrough until the 1970s. Neil had hired a part-time lab technician named Bud Consolie. Consolie, who was a full-time fireman, became known in the company as a development genius. He was instrumental in helping Tillotson Rubber to develop the first latex medical glove. The chief advantage of the glove was that it was elastic, so one size easily fit all hands. With gloves and balloons as its core products, Tillotson Rubber managed to post average annual sales of about $1 million throughout the late 1960s and into the 1970s.

Neil's sons, Rick and Tom, became involved in the business in the 1960s and in 1971 the family restructured the company as a partnership composed of all three men. Rick took charge of plant operations and Tom assumed responsibility for sales. The brothers started moving the company's manufacturing operation to Dixville Notch, New Hampshire, where their father had purchased a hotel called The Balsams. The hotel had been a successful resort near Neil Tillotson's grandparents' home when he was a boy. It went bankrupt in the 1960s and Neil purchased it with the intent of running it as a hotel, or even as a factory for his company. It eventually became both; the Balsams became a premier ski resort in the 1970s and was also used to house part of the company's manufacturing operations.

Tillotson Rubber flourished during the 1970s and much of the 1980s under the direct guidance of Tom and Rick. Rick took control of the balloon business, diversifying from conventional novelties into new markets for balloon bouquets, balloon sculptures, and mylar foil balloons. The company was eventually churning out more than 100 million balloons per year, and it was still producing the original cat-faced balloons. Tom oversaw the medical glove business, which grew rapidly. By the mid-1980s Tillotson was operating the largest examination glove plant in the world. A subsequent plant expansion gave the company a production capacity of more than 1 billion gloves annually.

Meanwhile, Neil Tillotson remained active in the business and pursued related interests. In 1972 he engineered the purchase of the former Firestone Tire & Rubber facility in Fall River, Massachusetts. It became the foundation of the company's manufacturing expansion in the Northeast. In the late 1970s Neil pursued a goal he had set during World War II of developing a commercially viable source of natural rubber latex in the Americas. He bought 35,000 acres on the east coast of Nicaragua on which he planned to build a plantation, but the property was seized a few years later by the rebel Sandinista government. In 1979 Neil purchased an experimental plantation in Guatemala from Firestone. He nurtured the plantation and by the late 1980s all of Tillotson's latex glove operations were being supplied by the local source. Neil even bought a freighter and built a latex processing plant as part of an effort that resulted in full vertical integration for the company.

Aside from innovative products and manufacturing technology, Tillotson Rubber Co.'s success throughout the mid-1900s and through the 1980s was largely attributable to Neil Tillotson's partnership philosophy. Tillotson believed that any time the right people were brought together with the right products, success was imminent. Thus Tillotson's organization was essentially composed of a number of partnerships that gave responsibility for different aspects of the business to different people or entities.

For example, Tillotson marketed its latex examination gloves by forming numerous partnerships with medical products distributors. To set up that marketing stratagem, the company formed a partnership with a respected Tillotson employee named Cal Robinson. The Tillotsons helped Robinson set up his own company, which ultimately assumed responsibility for all aspects related to marketing the gloves. Meanwhile, Tillotson handled all manufacturing-related duties. As with all of the company's partnerships, the arrangement created a win-win situation in which all parties benefited.

Tillotson's partnership strategy eventually resulted in a network of companies centered around Tillotson Rubber Co. Those companies, by the early 1990s, included the following: Best Manufacturing, a top producer of industrial gloves; Tillotson-Pearson, a maker of fiberglass sail and power boats and industrial fiberglass products; Textile Rubber and Chemical Company, the largest independent supplier of backing compounds used by the carpet industry; and Borden and Remington Chemical, which was a leading New England manufacturer and distributor of industrial chemicals.

Among the most prosperous of Tillotson's segments during the late 1980s was latex gloves. The fear of contracting and transmitting AIDS in the medical community, and in other markets, spawned massive demand growth for latex gloves. Tillotson benefited from demand growth. At the same time, though, FDA regulations and a flurry of new entrants into the industry created extreme turbulence in the market—for example, more than 200 new companies entered the latex glove industry, which had formerly been served almost entirely by only 5 manufacturers.

Tillotson changed its name to Tillotson Corp. in the early 1990s and focused its efforts on its core latex products businesses. Early in the decade, the company was generating more than $300 million in annual sales. After jettisoning less profitable operations and focusing on key growth segments, that figure was more than halved. Going into the mid-1990s, Tillotson Corp. was capturing an estimated $115 million in annual revenues. Remarkably, the company's 97-year-old founder, Neil Tillotson, was still active in the company in 1995 after nearly 65 years of service.

Principal Subsidiaries

Best Manufacturing.

Further Reading

Carlson, Barbara, "The Wizard of Dixville Notch," *New England Business,* January 1989, p. 30(5).
Tillotson Rubber Co., Inc.: The Power of Partnership, New York: The Newcomen Society of the United States, 1993.

—Dave Mote

Timberline Software Corporation

9600 S.W. Nimbus Avenue
Beaverton, Oregon 97008–7163
U.S.A.
(503) 626–6775
Fax: (503) 641–7498

Public Company
Incorporated: 1979 as Timberline Systems, Inc.
Employees: 300
Revenues: $24.82 million (1995)
Stock Exchanges: NASDAQ
SICs: 7372 Prepackaged Software

Timberline Software Corporation develops, markets, and supports accounting and management software for construction, estimating, property management, and architect/engineering industries. With roughly $25 million in annual sales, more than $1.7 million in annual earnings, and more than 25,000 design and construction companies as customers, Timberline is the leading national supplier of accounting and estimating software for the construction industry. It is also a developer of accounting and management information software for the property management, architecture, and engineering sectors.

Timberline was founded in Oregon in 1971 by John Gorman. It began operations that year with a staff of four people. In 1975 the company released one of its first industry-specific products, a construction accounting software package for minicomputers. It was the first of several operating environments for which Timberline would design software during its first 25 years (in succeeding years, Timberline would produce software for personal computers, including DOS, OS/2, and Microsoft Windows environments). In 1977 Timberline followed up on its accounting software for the construction industry with the release of a similar accounting package for property managers. In 1979 the company was incorporated as Timberline Systems, Inc. Gorman became president and Leslie F. Clarke, II was named executive vice-president.

During the first half of the 1980s Timberline entered the estimating and architect/engineer markets with software for mini- and micro-computers. In 1980, two years after joining Timberline as a construction consultant, Curtis Peltz designed Timberline's first construction cost-estimating software, AccuBid, for minicomputers. In 1984 Timberline released its first software for personal computers (PCs), the Medallion Collection, a line of accounting and project management software. The PC-based Medallion family operated in the DOS environment and specifically targeted home builders/remodelers and small to mid-sized contractors. Along with the Medallion Collection, Timberline introduced its first accounting system for architects and engineers.

With five products and revenues that had grown from $3.3 million in 1977 to $10.4 million seven years later, Timberline went public in 1984. That same year, Timberline began reducing its national sales force to focus on its two key distribution channels—value-added resellers and direct dealerships—which had grown into a network of 250 dealers. In 1985 the company secured a contract with IBM, in which the computer maker agreed to use its product centers to market Timberline's construction industry software.

For 1985 Timberline's sales remained flat, although the company did reduce its loss of $153,000 a year earlier by more than half. In 1986 Timberline sold its tax preparation software product, deemed incompatible with the company's strategy to serve construction and property-related markets, and sales fell to $7.2 million as losses deepened to $152,000. During the last half of the decade, however, Timberline stepped up its development efforts and increased its number of product releases, resulting in consistently rising revenues and positive income figures between 1986 and 1989.

In 1986 the company changed its name to Timberline Software Corporation and named John M. Meek vice-president of research and development and Curtis L. Peltz vice-president of the company's Estimating Division. Peltz became responsible for leading the development of Timberline's first PC-based family of software for the estimating industry, the Precision Collection, which in 1987 debuted its first core product, Precision Estimating (it replaced the earlier minicomputer estimating system, ACCUBID, that Peltz had developed).

The Precision Collection was well-received. It was an integrated family of estimating software applications that allowed construction estimators to devise project bids based on such variables as architectural design, required building materials, and labor costs. In 1987 Timberline released an accounting and management program for architects and engineers dubbed AEasy. Designed by an outside developer, AEasy provided architects and engineers with basic accounting information. It also generated billing information for design projects. Timberline's distribution network received a boost in 1987 when Businessland Inc. joined the company's network of retailers. Earnings for the year pulled back into the black to $413,000 on revenues of $7.6 million.

In November 1988, following the debut of IBM's OS/2 system, Timberline released the first property management system designed specifically for the OS/2 operating environment: Property Management Gold. This software package, targeting midsized to large companies using the OS/2 system, provided property managers with multi-tasking and advanced networking capabilities. The following year Timberline debuted On-Site Residential Gold, a property management and accounting software package for on-site property managers.

Meanwhile, Timberline's accounting software for the construction industry continued to expand during the late 1980s, growing to include Medallion General for general contractors, Medallion Builder for large home builders, Medallion Specialty for speciality contractors, and Medallion HomeBuilder for small home builders. Medallion HomeBuilder, which was favorably received by its target base of small, growth-oriented homebuilders, became available in single and multi-user versions and featured applications to manage job costs, subcontractor schedules, cash flow, and profitability.

During the late 1980s Timberline also expanded its Precision Collection to include Precision Estimating Plus (an advanced version of Precision Estimating), Bid Analysis, Pricer, and several specialized databases. Timberline also released the Precision CADLink interface system that allowed estimators using Precision Estimating Plus to, for the first time, interface with AutoCAD (computer-aided drafting) programs and compile an estimate directly from Autodesk's computer-aided design software/system. The program was later developed to interface with other systems, including those of Primavera and Microsoft. Precision CADLink, targeting estimators and contractors seeking more detailed and accurate construction schedules, provided estimators with the ability to electronically remove dimension and building specifications from any AutoCAD file when compiling estimates. It represented a cutting-edge trend to improve construction productivity by giving access to information used in various building phases.

Between 1988 and 1989 Timberline expanded its distribution reach beyond the United States by signing agreements with a Vancouver, British Columbia-based distribution firm and Tactical Computer Services Pty. Ltd. of Australia, the latter of which began selling and servicing Timberline's construction-industry estimating software in Australia and New Zealand. Timberline closed the decade with earnings of $446,000 on revenues that climbed to nearly $9 million in 1988, and with 1989 earnings of $769,000 on sales that jumped to $10.7 million.

In June 1990 Timberline, after teaming up with ASG, a leading developer of AutoCAD applications, released Precision CAD Integrator. It provided a link between Precision Estimating Plus and ASG Architectural software and joined the contractor information used in design and building phases. Timberline also introduced Precision Estimating Extended, featuring greater capabilities than Precision Estimating and Precision Estimating Plus. By the end of 1990 Timberline had grown into a company with 170 employees and $12.7 million in revenues.

During the early 1990s growth was hampered and the company was affected by a weak construction market and economic uncertainty created by tensions in the Middle East. Earnings slipped to $429,000 in 1990 and revenues remained flat in 1991, as income plummeted to $15,587. The following year revenues climbed to $14.9 million and earnings rebounded, though far from record territory, to $328,000. In response to the weakened market, Timberline adopted a strategy designed to distance itself from competitors and siphon market share by developing products for future OS/2 and Windows-based applications. This move was specifically aimed at capitalizing on the advent of graphical user interface (GUI) technology that was revolutionizing the software industry with on-screen graphics and multiple windows that provided users with quicker and easier access to information.

In 1992 Timberline released its first GUI product for Windows, Construction Gold, a construction accounting and management program for use with Microsoft Windows or OS/2 platforms. Construction Gold streamlined information searches by allowing users to move through a series of computer-screen windows to find precise bits of data. The construction accounting program became Timberline's biggest selling software. Following on the heels of Construction Gold, Timberline released an updated version of Property Management Gold for GUI environments.

In 1992 Timberline also released the DOS-based SitePro, a program for managers of residential properties. It also offered a database estimation package, ASG Estimator (compatible with the Precision Estimating series and created for the System ASG product line); and an estimating software add-on, Precision Buyout, designed to automatically create purchase orders and subcontracts from a project estimate. In 1992 Timberline also released AEasy Plus, which replaced a high-end time and billing program and incorporated the design of Timberline's low-end forerunner, AEasy.

In 1993 Timberline joined with other software developers and computer makers, including Microsoft, IBM, Lotus, Novell, Oracle, Borland, Sybase and Gupta, to support Open Database Connectivity (ODBC), an industry standard for sharing data between proprietary and mainframe database products of different vendors developed by Microsoft Corporation. That same year Timberline joined with PageAhead Software to develop an ODBC driver for Timberline's Construction Gold 2.0 version software. The new version allowed Timberline customers to directly access data stored in Construction Gold that used any other OBDC-based spreadsheet, word processing, or database application.

For 1993 Timberline's revenues increased 22 percent to $18.2 million while income nearly doubled to $620,000. Contributing to the rise in profitability was the success of Construction Gold, as well as the growing revenues generated from support services, which increased from 23 percent of all revenues in 1988 to 40 percent in 1993. In 1994 Timberline upgraded its entire product line to comply with OBDC standards. That same year the company released a new feature called "Modeling" for its estimating product line. The feature enabled users to make more accurate preliminary estimates while reducing the time required to refine estimates as a project was modified. Timberline also released an architect/engineer application called TimeTrax that enhanced and streamlined the process of tracking billable time and labor costs.

For 1994 Timberline increased revenues 19 percent to $21.6 million and boosted earnings 93 percent to $1.19 million. Support services accounted for revenues of $8.8 million, and constructing and estimating represented nearly 80 percent of all software sales. In October 1995 Timberline released Construction Gold 3.0, a significant update providing increased performance, improved controls, and additional enhancements for construction accounting. Construction Gold's accounting applications signaled Timberline's intent to enter the highway/heavy construction market. To that end, the following month the company released Equipment Costing, an accounting and information application (which interfaced with Construction Gold 3.0) for equipment-intensive construction companies involved in the heavy/highway construction market segment.

Timberline was ranked 139th on *Forbes* magazine's list of "200 Best Small Companies in America" in 1995, the first time the company was ranked by *Forbes*. The company's attributes that led to inclusion on the list included a five-year average return on equity of 16.5 percent and five-year average earnings growth rate of 119 percent. Timberline was the only software firm of its type featured on the list and one of only five Pacific Northwest companies. The company's leading product line, Construction Gold, was the best-selling software package for the construction accounting market and the only one available for Windows or OS/2 operating environments.

In January 1996 Timberline restructured its operations to focus on applications rather than targeted industries. The company reorganized into two divisions; the Estimating Division was the only one left untouched, and the areas that had previously been represented by three divisions—property management, construction, and architects/engineers—became the Accounting Division.

Timberline entered 1996 in a heavy developmental mode, with its entire product line being retooled for Microsoft's Windows and Windows 95 (an operating system which was released in 1995 and offered significant new features). The company's construction and estimating product divisions were expected to release their first Windows 95 products by July of that year, while the first Windows 95 products for architect/engineer and property management industries were also under development by the beginning of 1996, although no release dates had been scheduled.

Further Reading

Barnett, Jim, "Timberline's New Software Program for Contractors Leads to Sales Jump," *Oregonian,* June 5, 1994, p. N11.
Black, Pamela, "Customers Aid Vendors," *Venture,* January 1986, pp. 88–89.
Frankel, Gerald, "How a Software Firm Teamed Up with Big Blue," *Business Marketing,* October 1985, p. 37.
Girardi, Jim, "Timberline Estimating System (Precision Extended)," *Builder,* September 1994, p. 162.
"Project Accounting Package Bridges a Gap," *ENR,* December 13, 1993, p. 34.
"Timberline Software Corporation Company Profile," Beaverton, Ore.: Timberline Software Corporation, 1995.

—Roger W. Rouland

The Tokai Bank, Limited

21–24, Nishiki 3-chome
Naka-ku
Nagoya, 460
Japan
(052) 211–1111
Fax: (03) 3245–1487

Public Company
Incorporated: 1941
Employees: 12,319
Total Assets: ¥30.86 trillion (US$345.39 billion) (1995)
Stock Exchanges: Tokyo Osaka Nagoya London Paris
    Zurich Geneva Basel
SICs: 6081 Branches & Agencies of Foreign Banks

The Tokai Bank, Limited is one of the leading city banks in Japan. Based in Nagoya, it is the dominant bank in Japan's industrial region of Chubu, where Toyota, among other companies, is based. The product of a wartime amalgamation, Tokai offers retail, commercial, and investment banking services in its home market through 285 retail branches and more than 21 subsidiaries and affiliates. Active overseas throughout Asia and Oceania, the Americas, Europe, and the Middle East, Tokai is represented in 42 cities in 26 countries and regions, offering banking, securities, leasing, fund management, and trust services.

Tokai Bank was established in 1941, approximately six months before Japan entered World War II but in the midst of Japan's war with China. At that time the Japanese government was dominated by a military group which had ordered the concentration of several industries in an effort to increase economic efficiency. As part of that initiative, three small banks in Nagoya—the Aichi Bank, the Nagoya Bank, and the Ito Bank—were merged. Each had been in existence for many years. The oldest, the Aichi Bank, was founded in 1877 as the Eleventh National Bank.

The three banks were roughly equal in size. Because they all wanted to make a break with their troubled pasts as small local banks, they adopted a different name for the new bank: *Tokai,* Japanese for "East Sea." The East Sea, or Sea of Japan, was at the time a rich source of food and the main conduit between Japan and its colonies and conquests on the Asian mainland. Tokai Bank never got an opportunity to participate in any large wartime development projects, however, but instead was forced into defensive measures and spent much of the war issuing debt.

When the war ended in 1945, the occupation authority laid plans for the postwar banking industry and initiated purges of managers suspected of aiding the war effort. The Tokai Bank was deemed the appropriate size for a regional bank, and, because it had not contributed significantly to the war effort, was permitted to keep its management and to retain its name. In 1947 Tokai was awarded a foreign exchange license, greatly improving its clout. The following year, under the Reconstruction and Reorganization Act, it was permitted to increase its capitalization to ¥435 million—a substantial increase in size.

During the 1950s, Tokai was given de facto responsibility for aiding recovery in Chukyo prefecture. Because Japan's Ministry of International Trade and Industry had set broad and ambitious goals, the bank had a great deal of work to do. The completion of large plants required tremendous amounts of capital and long lead times that often exceeded the bank's capacity. Nagoya, however, grew steadily during this period and savings rates remained high. By the mid-1950s, as some of the bank's client projects came on line, margins were greatly improved.

Dedicated to offering the highest degree of service in a relatively unsophisticated market, Tokai inaugurated checking accounts in 1960. The bank had also developed a successful trust business. In 1962, however, Tokai became obligated under financial regulations to separate this business from its regular operations and in the process founded the Chuo Trust & Banking Company. Tokai began loan services in 1963, started the country's first online money-order system in 1965, and in 1968 opened a foreign trade information center, whose aim was to assist in marketing financial opportunities overseas.

Once it had successfully expanded its offices in Tokyo and Osaka, Tokai began to look overseas. The bank opened its first overseas branch, in London, in 1963, partially in an effort to assist Japanese export firms in European markets but mostly to gain representation in a major world capital. A New York office, established in 1954, was upgraded to a branch in 1965.

As Japan entered its second period of industrial growth in the mid-1960s, Tokai's location gained greater significance. Situated midway between Tokyo and Osaka, Nagoya had grown into a major industrial region, and Tokai was the only major bank with its head office there. It naturally had the strongest relationships with local government and businesses, and therefore became the most important economic intermediary in the region.

Tokai gained even greater significance in the early 1970s as domestic demand in basic industries began to show the first signs of saturation. Equally important were preparations for an ambitious export drive being made by leading manufacturers and trading companies. In order to maintain its position in the region, Tokai started to emphasize international expansion. Additional offices were opened in Los Angeles, Amsterdam, Hong Kong, Zurich, Sydney, and Singapore, while the foreign-trade information center was upgraded to include investment activities.

Tokai's most important customer during this period was undoubtedly the Toyota Motor Corporation, which became Tokai's largest shareholder. Toyota's tremendous sales, particularly in the United States, created numerous expansion opportunities for both the company and the bank. But, although both companies were closely associated with other firms, they fell short of creating an industrial group similar to the Dai-Ichi Kangyo, Sumitomo, or Mitsubishi groups. Tokai had cultivated important relationships with many companies associated with otherwise rival industrial groups, but it was simply not in its interest to become involved in such an industrial group.

Tokai pursued its expansion in international markets into the 1980s by opening a branch in Chicago and offices in Atlanta, Dallas, and Lexington, Kentucky, among other locations. As part of its expansion, Tokai established subsidiaries in North America, including Tokai Bank of California (1974), Tokai Trust Company of New York (1986), and Tokai Bank Canada (1987).

The trust operation in New York allowed Tokai to begin building its expertise in trust banking, an activity it was not chartered to perform in Japan. The liberalization of financial regulations in Japan, however, ensured that eventually institutions such as Tokai will be permitted to engage in trust banking, insurance, and securities underwriting.

Tokai undertook a reorganization in 1987 that resulted in the creation of a treasury and capital market group and a corporate planning group. These new groups were intended to enhance the bank's ability to manage information in bond and other securities markets and assist client corporations in developing sound business strategies. In 1988 three regional headquarters were established for the Americas, Europe and the Middle East, and Asia and Oceania.

While working to develop capabilities in a broader range of activities, Tokai in the late 1980s concentrated on consolidating its position with middle-market corporations, offering these companies services that were once available only to large corporations. As a result, the bank became exceedingly popular in that sector, which made up a growing share of Tokai's business.

In foreign markets, Tokai seized an opportunity to work with non-Japanese clients in such areas as leveraged buyouts, corporate restructuring, and large-scale real estate development projects. While these were higher-risk activities than Tokai had been accustomed to undertaking in Japan, they were also normally fee-based, and therefore somewhat more stable.

Tokai's expansion in the United States continued in the late 1980s, with this growth period broadening the services it offered there. In 1989 Tokai acquired the leasing firm Master Lease Corporation, which was renamed Tokai Financial Services, Inc. in 1991. Also in 1989 a securities firm, Tokai Securities, Inc., was established in the United States, and Tokai became the first foreign bank to sell commercial paper in the United States.

Back on the home front, Tokai reconfigured its retail banking network. Like other banks, it started to rely more heavily on automated teller machines (ATMs), which were more cost-effective than branches. Tokai increased the number of ATMs in its network from 349 in 1992 to 508 in 1995. During this same period, the bank combined branches in some areas so that the number of branches fell from 294 to 285.

The early 1990s were difficult years for all Japanese banks, as unsound lending practices of the late 1980s came back to haunt the banking industry at the same time that the Japanese economy entered into a prolonged recession. During this period, Tokai was involved both in rescuing other troubled banks and in cleaning up its own house. In 1992, Tokai and three other Japanese banks helped to bail out Taiheiyo Bank by granting it low-interest loans. In late 1995, Tokai took over operations of Osaka Shinyo Kumiai, a credit union that had compiled some US$1.5 billion in unrecoverable loans, out of the thrift's total loan portfolio of US$2.7 billion. Tokai only absorbed the credit union's deposits and recoverable loans, with the Japanese government taking on the bad loans. Two years earlier, Tokai was itself forced to write off ¥70 billion (US$654 million) in loans. The difficult times showed clearly in Tokai's declining asset base, which fell from ¥37.49 trillion in 1991 to ¥30.86 trillion in 1995.

With such difficulties at home, it is little wonder that Tokai sought to increase its presence overseas during this period. Asia became the region of highest interest both because of the rapidly growing economies there and because middle-market corporations in Japan—Tokai's prime customers—were increasingly looking overseas for expansion and usually targeting Asia first. In 1993 alone, Tokai set up operations in Taipei, Labuan, Kuala Lumpur, and Ho Chi Minh City. In 1994 the bank established an Asia Department and a China Department, which were designed to provide Japan's small and medium-sized companies information on and assistance with doing business elsewhere in Asia. The departments also offered their clients financial services.

Although deregulation of Japan's financial markets had been proceeding slower than expected, Tokai was able in 1995 to enter the Japanese securities market for the first time through its Tokai International Securities Co., Ltd. subsidiary, which was primarily involved in corporate bond underwriting. Tokai had, of course, years earlier already established securities businesses in Europe, the United States, and Hong Kong. As Japan's markets become increasingly liberalized, then, Tokai seemed well-positioned to transfer the expertise it had gained overseas back to its home market.

Principal Subsidiaries

Asahi Tokai Building Kanri Co., Ltd. (33.3%); Tokai Banking Software Co., Ltd.; Tokai Building Maintenance Co., Ltd.; Tokai Business Service Co., Ltd.; Tokai Career Service Co., Ltd.; Tokai International Securities Co., Ltd.; Tokai Mortgage Service Co., Ltd.; Tokai Real Estate Management, Ltd.; Tokai Sogo Service Co., Ltd.; Tosho Co., Ltd.; Tokai Australia Finance Corporation Limited; Tokai Bank Canada; Tokai Bank (Deutschland) GmbH (Germany); Tokai Asia Limited (Hong Kong); P.T. Tokai Lippo Bank (Indonesia; 75%); Tokai Bank Nederland N.V (Netherlands); Tokai Finance (Curaçao) N.V. (Netherlands Antilles); Tokai Bank (Switzerland) Ltd.; Tokai Airfinance Europe Limited (U.K.); Tokai Bank Europe plc (U.K.); Tokai Capital Markets Limited (U.K.; 91.8%); Tokai Derivative Products Limited (U.K.); Tokai Bank of California (U.S.); Tokai Credit Corporation (U.S.); Tokai Financial Services, Inc. (U.S.); Tokai Securities, Inc. (U.S.); Tokai Trust Company of New York (U.S.).

Principal Divisions

Personnel Division; Audit Division; Legal Division; Corporation Planning Division; ALM Division; Public Relations Division; Quality Management Division; Affiliated Business Division; Premises & General Affairs Division; Economic Research Division; Operations & Administration Division; Systems Development Division; Data Processing Division; Credit Division I; Credit Division II; Credit Division III; Credit Division IV; Corporate Research Division; Financial Institutions Division; Business Information Development Division; Business Planning Division; Business Development Division; Chubu Banking Division; Public Institutions Division, Head Office; Tokyo Banking Division; Public Institutions Division, Tokyo; Kansal Banking Division; Foreign Business Promotion Division; International Finance Division; International Credit Division; Capital Markets Planning Division; Treasury & Securities Division; Capital Markets & Derivatives Marketing Division; International Treasury Division.

Further Reading

"Bank Chief Quits in Japan," *New York Times,* April 30, 1992, p. C8.
Dawkins, William, "Tokai Bank to Rescue Failed Credit Union," *The Financial Times,* December 8, 1995, p. 26.
Friedland, Jonathan, "Don't Bank on It: Troubles Ahead for Lenders as They Try to Recover from the Late 1980s," *Far Eastern Economic Review,* December 9, 1993, pp. 50–54.
Sapsford, Jathon, "Japanese Takeover May Be New Model for Bank Rescues," *Wall Street Journal,* December 8, 1995, p. A6.
"Tough Times for Tokai," *Economist,* March 25, 1995, p. 81.

—updated by David E. Salamie

Toll Brothers

Quality Homes by Design®

Toll Brothers Inc.

3103 Philmont Avenue
Huntington Valley, Pennsylvania 19006
U.S.A.
(215) 938–8000
Fax: (215) 938–8010

Public Company
Incorporated: 1986
Employees: 935
Sales: $504.06 million (1994)
Stock Exchanges: New York Philadelphia Pacific
   Chicago
SICs: 1521 Single-Family Housing Construction; 1531
   Operative Builders; 6552 Land Subdividers &
   Developers, Except Cemeteries

Toll Brothers Inc. is a leading U.S. builder of single-family homes. In 1995 the company was the 12th-largest home builder in the nation by sales, and the biggest company involved primarily in the construction of luxury dwellings. Toll, a family-owned and operated company, is distinguished in its industry by a long record of profitability and revenue growth.

Toll Brothers was founded in 1967 by brothers Robert I. (Bob) and Bruce E. Toll. Bob Toll was only 26 years old at the time and had received his B.A. from Cornell University as well as a law degree from the University of Pennsylvania. Bob served a brief stint as an attorney at a firm called Wolf, Block, Shorr and Solis before determining that his future didn't lie in the legal profession. Both Bob and Bruce had been exposed to the construction business by their father, Albert, who built homes, and Bob believed that industry had more to offer.

In 1967 Bob teamed up with his brother to start building homes. Bruce, who had an accounting degree from the University of Miami, was 24 years old at the time. Their educational backgrounds were a comfortable fit; Bob had a good foundation in principles related to buying land and conducting legal transactions, while Bruce held a firm grip on the basics of the financial side of the business. They started out buying land and building homes in southeastern Pennsylvania—their first deal was the sale of two colonial-style houses—and would continue to build solely in that territory for more than a decade. The brothers built about 30 homes annually during the start-up years, and gradually increased that number throughout the 1970s to become a dominant homebuilder in Pennsylvania.

The Toll brothers' success during the 1970s was the result of several factors. From the start, they emphasized quality construction and customer satisfaction. Their efforts would eventually earn them a reputation as the ''dream house'' builder in their markets. Just as importantly, the brothers determined early on that they were going to pursue a conservative financial strategy that would allow them to evade the homebuilding cycles that so commonly wreaked havoc on the industry. To that end, they tried to keep construction costs to a minimum and were careful not to invest heavily in land that might become overpriced when the economy soured.

By the end of the 1970s the Toll brothers' annual home sales were approaching the $50-million mark. After spending nearly 15 years constructing houses only in southern Pennsylvania, they decided that it was time to branch out geographically. In 1982 they began building homes in central New Jersey. Success in that region augmented ongoing gains in their core Pennsylvania market. Revenues climbed rapidly, growing nearly 300 percent between 1982 and 1987 to more than $137 million. By the mid-1980s Toll Brothers had become a respected builder in the upscale central New Jersey housing market.

The Toll brothers' gains during the mid-1980s resulted from factors other than geographic expansion. Indeed, a serious decline in earnings in 1984 convinced the pair that they were going to have to make some radical changes in their management style if they were going to succeed in the evolving and increasingly competitive homebuilding industry. They instituted tighter operating and financial controls and began hiring top-flight managers to handle individual projects. Each development was run by a manager who operated largely autonomously. Most of the recruits were quite young and often sported advanced degrees in law, engineering, or business.

Besides top-flight management and strict controls, Toll benefited from a savvy marketing strategy during the mid-1980s. Toll billed itself as a designer of luxury homes, but it did not build custom homes. Instead, it offered customers a variety of floor plans with customized options. Thus, Toll effectively brought the efficiencies of the mass homebuilding sector to the luxury segment. Toll was able to build the luxury homes for less money than custom builders because of its high-volume purchasing power and computerized construction cost controls. To cut costs further and to ensure quality, Toll also operated its own lumber and panel plant that supplied trusses and other prefabricated units for its homes. The company also maintained a separate mortgage affiliate to serve its clients.

In 1986 the Tolls incorporated their company as Toll Brothers, Inc., and went public for the first time with an offering on the New York Stock Exchange that raised about $40 million. They used that money to begin branching into other regions of the Northeast. In 1987 they expanded into northern Delaware and Massachusetts and in 1988 tapped the Maryland market. They typically entered new markets by building their mid-range homes, called "Executive" models. The Executive homes were priced from $170,000 to about $300,000, sported 2,400 to 3,000 square feet, and were located on lots ranging from one-quarter to three-quarters of an acre in size.

Once the brothers established the Toll Brothers name in an area with their Executive homes, the company would start building its lower-end and high-end models. Its low-end line of houses, which were also considered move-up homes, had 1,700 to 2,000 square feet of space and were usually situated on lots of about 10,000 square feet or less. Dubbed the Glen line, they were priced from $120,000 to $170,000. In contrast, the high-end, or Estate, line of homes were often priced around half a million dollars and ranged in size from 3,000 to 4,500 square feet. They were located on three-quarters to three acres of land and offered such features as two-story foyer entries, curved staircases, walk-in closets, and whirlpool master baths.

As a result of geographic expansion and some of the highest profit margins in the industry, Toll Brothers managed to boost sales from about $76 million in 1985 to more than $200 million in 1988, while net income climbed from less than $4 million to more than $24 million during the same period. Toll Brothers even received *Professional Builder* magazine's coveted "Builder of the Year" award in 1988. Going into 1989 the company was in the process of building hundreds of homes throughout much of the Northeast. Unfortunately, the housing boom of the mid-1980s went bust in 1989. Many homebuilders were forced out of business, while even the most financially conservative companies experienced severe slumps. Toll Brothers was not exempt from the shakeout. For the first time in its 22-year history the company failed to show a rise in net income. In fact, profits slumped to about $13 million for the year as sales slipped to $177 million.

Although Toll was hurt by the downturn, it was recognized as one of the healthiest survivors. It continued to post a profit and even managed to secure several new building contracts. In fact, Toll used the slump as an opportunity to invest its excess cash in land that stressed developers and banks were trying to unload at significantly depressed prices. Toll would later be praised for this savvy strategy; it loaded up on land when other companies were trying to get rid of it at low prices, and it developed and sold the properties at inflated prices when housing markets recovered. The company was able to execute the tactic because, unlike many other builders, it only built homes after they were sold and it refused to pay too much for a property.

Indeed, following the late 1980s and early 1990s housing slump, Toll further tightened its controls and became even more conservative in its building strategy. The company's land buyers perused literally hundreds of properties and purchased only a small fraction of them. Its pursuit of devalued properties allowed it to expand into other regions in the Northeast and Mid-Atlantic. In 1992 Toll began building in Connecticut and Virginia before cracking into New York in 1993. In addition to its land and building interests, Toll began operating a subsidiary called Toll Advisors in 1990. That company was set up as a consulting firm to help other financiers and developers work out their problem development projects.

Toll's ability to profit throughout the recession was partly attributable to the health of its market niche. By the early 1990s Toll had become the largest homebuilder in the nation that specialized in luxury homes. During the slump in homebuilding, the segment least fazed was the upscale housing market. Toll geared its homes to high-income move-up buyers between the ages of 35 and 55. That segment of the population continued to post household income gains and was increasing its proportion of the national wealth going into the mid-1990s. Furthermore, those buyers were less affected by interest rate volatility because they typically had large amounts of money to put down on a new home (from equity in their previous home). That cash also made it easier for them to qualify for a new mortgage loan.

The overall result was that demand for upscale housing stayed strong, and Toll was positioned to benefit. Furthermore, housing markets strengthened going into the mid-1990s and Toll Brothers started developing many of the properties it had purchased a few years earlier. Revenues bounced up to a record $281 million in 1992 before jumping to $395 million in 1993 and then to $504 million in 1994. Meanwhile, net income rose from a low of $5 million in 1991 to more than $36 million in 1994.

Encouraged by gains in its core markets, Toll made plans in 1994 to expand out of the Northeast and into Orange County, California, and Raleigh, North Carolina. In early 1995, moreover, Toll announced its intent to expand into Palm Beach County, Florida; Charlotte, North Carolina; and Dallas, Texas. Furthermore, Toll Brothers reached an agreement to acquire its first company in 1995, announcing plans to purchase Geoffrey H. Edmunds & Associates, Inc., a Scottsdale, Arizona-based builder of luxury homes.

Despite a decline in housing starts, Toll managed to boost construction activity during 1995 and increase sales and profits. It accomplished that feat by pursuing the same basic strategy that it had followed for several years: build large numbers of high-quality, upscale homes at the lowest prices, and keep a close eye on costs. By 1995 the average cost of Toll's move-up home line had increased to a range of $175,000 to about $400,000, while its mid-range Executive homes were going from about $230,000 to $425,000. Its high-end Estate homes sold for as much as $665,000, or more in some instances. The company was also constructing some attached homes, including townhouses, "carriage homes," and "villas" priced from $100,000 to more than $400,000.

Threatening Toll Brothers' dominance of the upscale housing segment in several regions in the mid-1990s were several other national and regional home builders that were mimicking its operating and marketing strategy. Furthermore, industry insiders wondered whether Toll would be able to recreate in other regions the success it had achieved in the Northeast, where the company's inventory of land and low cost structure provided a benefit less attainable in some other regions. Despite critics' doubts, Bruce and Bob Toll, who were still running the company and remained the primary stockholders, expected to expand successfully in their existing markets and to branch out into new regions in the late 1990s.

Principal Subsidiaries

First Brandywine Investment Corp. II; Polekoff Farm, Inc.; Eastern States Engineering, Inc.; Fairway Valley, Inc.; Chersterbrooke, Inc.; Fairway Valley Golf Club, Inc.; First Huntington Finance Corp.; Green Spring Hunt, Inc.; Heather Ridge, Inc.; Maryland Ltd. Land Corp.; Shrewsbury Hills, Inc.; Uwchlan Hunt, Inc.; Warren Chase, Inc.; Washington Greene, Inc.; Westminster Mortgage Corp.; Windsor Development Corp.; Mountain View Real Estate, Inc.; Dover General, Inc.; Buckingham Chase, Inc.; MA Ltd. Land Corp.; Franklin Farms G.P., Inc.; Anwell Chase, Inc.; Bunker Hill Estates, Inc.; Connecticut Land Corp.; Corner Ketch, Inc.; Daylesford Development Corp.; Doylestown Ridge, Inc.; First Brandywine Investment Corp.; Mansfield Development Corp.; Palmer Hunt, Inc.; Springfield Chase, Inc.; Stewarts Crossing, Inc.; TB Proprietary Corp.; Maple Point, Inc.; Bennington Hunt, Inc.; Montgomery Development, Inc.; Tenby Hunt, Inc.; VA Land Corp.; Westminster Abstract Co.

Further Reading

Covaleski, John, "Toll Brothers Jumps in on the Business of S&L Crisis," *Philadelphia Business Journal*, September 10, 1990, Sec. 2, p. 7B.

——, "Toll Takes Some Lumps, Looks for Opportunity," *Philadelphia Business Journal*, May 28, 1990, Sec. 2, p. 17B.

Croghan, Lore, "The Careful Carpenter: Why Home Builder Toll Brothers Thrives when Most Others Don't," *Financial World*, August 29, 1995, p. 36.

Goodspeed, Linda, "New England Tastes Mean a Tough Market for Homebuilders," *Boston Business Journal*, September 22, 1995, Sec. 2, p. 4.

Lelen, Kenneth, "Looking for Profits in the Old Pumpkin Patch," *Business for Central New Jersey*, June 12, 1989, p. 10.

Moore, Paula, "Pa. Home Builder Scouts Denver Market," *Denver Business Journal*, October 7, 1994, p. 17.

Orrin, Spellman, "Toll Brothers Broadens Market in Northeast," *Focus*, March 2, 1988, p. 38.

Phillipidis, Alex, "Toll Brothers on Building Spree," *Westchester County Business Journal*, August 21, 1995, p. 1.

"Toll Brothers Announces Record Sales Level," *Delaware Business Review*, May 25, 1992, p. 18.

"Toll Brothers Emerges as Luxury Builder," *Mercer Business*, May 1988, p. 72.

—Dave Mote

The Tranzonic Cos.

30195 Chagrin Boulevard
Pepper Pike, Ohio 44124
U.S.A.
(216) 831-5757
Fax: (216) 831-5647

Public Company
Incorporated: 1946 as Ace Cigarette Service Co.
Employees: 1,201
Sales: $148.9 million (1995)
Stock Exchanges: American
SICs: 2676 Sanitary Paper Products; 3581 Automatic Vending Machines; 2211 Broad Woven Fabric Mills, Cotton; 2297 Nonwoven Fabrics; 2392 House Furnishings Except Curtains; 2655 Fiber Cans Tubes Drums; 3089 Plastics Products, Not Elsewhere Classified; 2511 Wood Household Furniture; 2542 Office and Store Fixtures Except Wood; 2541 Wood Office and Store Fixtures and Shelves

The Tranzonic Cos. manufactures products in four highly fragmented business segments: personal care products (Maxi-thins and private-label feminine napkins, as well as diapers), industrial textiles (disposable wiping cloths and work clothes), housewares (travel, storage and laundry accessories), and industrial packaging (paper tubes and sleeves). First established as a vending and distributing company, the firm underwent a series of acquisitions and divestments in the early 1980s that transformed it into a manufacturing enterprise. Although Tranzonic stock is publicly traded, descendants of the founding Golden family continued to control over 80 percent of the company's stock through the mid-1990s. In light of the slow growth projected for its core businesses, Tranzonic CEO Robert S. Reitman planned for future growth to come from acquisitions, both within and without the company's four primary operating areas.

The business was founded in 1933 by Louis B. Golden, who had emigrated to Cleveland, Ohio, from Russia in 1892 at the age of 17. Golden earned a bachelors degree from Case Western Reserve University and a law degree from the John Marshall Law School, but eschewed a legal career to found the Golden Tobacco Co. in 1931. With the help of wife Miriam and an $800 initial investment, Golden ran the business—renamed Ace Cigarette Service Co. in 1933—from his kitchen table.

Ace Cigarette was incorporated in 1946, by which time it was already one of America's largest cigarette vendors. From this early foundation the company expanded into candy and soft drinks. A registered dietitian and longtime company executive, Miriam probably influenced the firm's move into automatic food service. In the late 1950s, the company acquired a half-interest in the Industrial Vending Co., and began to sell food prepared at its Cleveland headquarters through vending machines in local factories. Annual sales surpassed $6.5 million by 1957, when profits totaled about $83,750. While sales remained flat through the remainder of the 1950s, profits multiplied to $174,500 by 1959. The family took the company public and changed its name to Ace Vending Co. to reflect its broadened activities in 1961. A 1962 name change, to American Automatic Vending Corp., anticipated an acquisitive push that took the firm nationwide.

American Automatic Vending (AAV) used the proceeds of its initial public offering to fund a decade-long spate of acquisitions that expanded its business interests beyond vending into personal care products and manual food service. Before its first fiscal year was out, the company had purchased Cincinnati's American Vending Service Inc. and Detroit's Market Vending Co. In 1962, the company acquired Consumers Cigarette Service Co., Seaway Vending Co., and Hospital Specialty Co., a business that would prove key to AAV's long-term growth. At the time it was purchased, Hospital Specialty had over 80,000 vending machines in all fifty states and brought with it valuable contracts to vend leading Kotex and Tampax brands of feminine napkins and tampons, as well as its own Gards, She, and Soft n' Thin labels. Hospital Specialty had been founded by the Ensheimer family, called "pioneers in the vending industry" by a 1962 *Plain Dealer* article. Swifty Food Commissaries, Inc., a Cleveland catering company, was acquired in 1963, by which time AAV ranked as "Ohio's largest operator of vending equipment."

The ensuing years brought a relative lull in the pace of acquisitions. AAV bought Deegan-Denham Candy and Tobacco Co., a distributor of tobacco, candy and over-the-counter drugs, in 1965, and expanded its vending reach into Kentucky and Indiana with the acquisitions of Southern Automatic Music Co., Wagg Vending Co., and Toledo Music and Novelty Co. in 1968. AAV rounded out the busy 1960s with the purchases of Nursing Homes Council, Budd, Inc., and Catering Management Inc. Renamed American Nursing Home Consulting Company, Nursing Homes Council formed the core of AAV's institutional food service division, which also catered to schools and factories.

Fueled by the growth of the overall vending industry, which doubled from $3 billion in 1963 to $6 billion in 1970, as well as its string of acquisitions, AAV's sales nearly doubled from $14.3 million in 1962 to $37.67 million in 1969. During that same period, net income nearly tripled, from $392,000 to $1.2 million. By 1971, American Automatic Vending boasted over 20,000 vending machines in Ohio, Michigan, Indiana, Kentucky, and Florida, and ranked among the top ten players in the industry. In 1972, the company formally abbreviated its name to AAV Cos. to reflect its expansion beyond vending. Having surpassed many of his growth goals, Golden moved to Florida in 1970 and was succeeded by his son-in-law, Robert S. Reitman, that same year. Golden continued as chairman until 1973, when Reitman assumed that title as well.

Reitman continued his father-in-law's acquisition strategy into the early 1970s, purchasing Scan-O-Vision, a closed-circuit television security service, in 1971; Standard Cigar & Tobacco Co., a Washington, D.C. distributor, in 1972; and Beaver Falls Candy and Tobacco Co., a Pennsylvania distributor, in 1974. AAV's sales burgeoned over the course of the decade, from $40 million in 1970 to $73.8 million in 1979. But while the company's profits grew steadily to $1.8 million in 1976, AAV endured three consecutive annual earnings declines from that point through 1979, by which time net income had halved to $834,000. Mitchell Gordon, an analyst for *Barron's* magazine, blamed the erosion of AAV's profits on "the deteriorating industrial economy in the upper Midwest region, where its vending and distribution activities were located."

CEO Reitman must have concurred. In 1981, he began to execute a reorganization strategy that shed two-thirds of his company's operations and created an entirely new corporate focus. That year's $9.5 million acquisition of Cleveland Cotton Products Co. was a pivotal factor in the new corporate scheme. Founded in 1921, this family-owned firm had grown to lead the industrial wiping cloth business by the late 1970s. Industrial wiping cloths, which Reitman called "new rags" in a 1988 *Crain's Cleveland Business* article, are tailored to customers' requirements for strength, absorbency and texture. The disposable cloths are used in health care, food service, auto repair and auto body, oil-drilling, and electronics. When Cleveland Cotton Products' second-generation company leaders died within six months of one another in 1979, the private firm became an asset of their estate, and executor Larry L. Wymor sold Cleveland Cotton Products to AAV in 1981. Wymor went on to become president of Cleveland Cotton Products, which formed the core of the parent company's Industrial Wiping Division, contributing over half of total annual revenues by 1983.

In 1982, Chairman and CEO Robert S. Reitman decided to sell off AAV's traditional vending machine business, as well as its tobacco and candy wholesaling and food service operations. *Crain's Cleveland Business* called the spun-off businesses "regional cash cows that in recent years drained each other." Reitman's original deal with Edwin M. Roth's Electronic Theatre Restaurants Corp. fell through, but before the year was out, AAV sold the businesses to Crescott, Inc., a New York firm, for $5.6 million in cash and $6.3 million in notes. In order to keep its bond payments coming, Reitman's firm continued to provide Crescott with support such as public and shareholder relations and financial services through the ensuing few years.

Reitman retained the Personal Care Division and expanded its product line from the core feminine hygiene goods into elastic-leg disposable diapers, sterile obstetrical pads for hospitals and nursing homes, and an adult incontinent diaper. While AAV's share of the disposable diaper market stood at less than one percent, CEO Reitman told *Crain's Cleveland Business* that he expected the company's own-label diapers under the "Best Buy," "Precious," and "Happy Bottom" names to "come into their own" in the 1980s. Indeed, the $1.9 billion private-label disposable diaper market was advancing at about eight percent each year during the early 1980s, and this became "one of AAV's fastest-growing segments" mid-decade.

Reitman changed his company's moniker to Tranzonic Cos. in 1983. Flush with cash from the divestment, the CEO started aggressively seeking out acquisition candidates, eyeing at least six companies from 1983 to 1985. Left with two core businesses, industrial textiles and personal care, the company hoped to focus its future efforts on other "low-cost, repeatable goods." In 1987, Reitman told *Barron's* reporter Richard J. Maturi that Tranzonic was "looking for a complementary firm with growth opportunities and a reasonable price." Although the firm had trouble finding a good takeover target, its stock was one of *Forbes* magazine's 100 best-performing stocks for 1987, ranking 66th on that year's list.

After suffering a net loss during the transition from vending to industrial wiping, Tranzonic's sales increased steadily from $43 million in 1983 to $58.6 million in 1987. Profits grew erratically, from $1.2 million in 1983 to a high of $4.1 million in 1986, then declined to $2.4 million in 1987.

Tranzonic made its first post-reorganization acquisition the following year, a transaction that heralded a rash of corporate purchases in the late 1980s and early 1990s. American Homeware Inc. was a Dallas company whose line of personal travel organizers, garment bags, sweater drying racks, clothes hampers, and other storage items were made overseas and shipped directly to retailers, thereby eliminating warehousing expenses. American Homeware became the nucleus of Tranzonic's Housewares Division. The 1989 purchase of J.C. Baxter Co. formed the core of Tranzonic's industrial packaging division, which made spiral-wound paper tubes and cores for industrial and consumer markets.

In 1992, Tranzonic bought Tambrands Inc.'s Maxithins sanitary pad business, giving the company a nationally-recognized addition to its line of feminine hygiene products. The parent increased its holdings in the household goods business with the purchase of Ever-Ready Appliance Manufacturing Co., a top producer of ironing boards and step stools, the following year. The 1995 acquisition of Plezall Wipers, Inc., complemented Tranzonic's Industrial Textiles Division.

These acquisitions fueled a 113 percent increase in sales, from $69.7 million in 1988 to a record $149 million in 1995. Profits slid from $3.9 million in 1988 to $2.8 million in 1994, then reached a record $5.3 million in 1995. Tranzonic's fiscal 1995 annual report laid out CEO Reitman's plan to more than triple annual sales to $500 million by fiscal 2001. While the corporate leader expected internal growth to contribute to the realization of this "admittedly ambitious" objective, his 1995 letter to shareholders acknowledged that the firm "will not achieve [its] growth goal without acquisitions, given the slow-growth nature of our existing markets."

Principal Subsidiaries

Hospital Specialty Co.; CCP Industries Inc.; Cleveland Cotton Products Co.; Design Trend, Inc.; Ever-Ready Appliance Mfg. Co.; Plezall Wipers Inc.; Tranzonic Cos.; Pressing Supply Co.; Baxter Tube Co.; American Homeware Inc.

Principal Divisions

Personal Care Division; Industrial Textiles Division; Housewares Division; Industrial Packaging Division.

Further Reading

Barnes, Jon, "More Good Changes are Tranzonic's Goal," *Crain's Cleveland Business,* May 9, 1988.

Bryan, John E., "Vending Firm Buys Hospital Specialty," *Cleveland Plain Dealer,* August 2, 1962.

Datzman, Cynthia, "Brothers Let Family Heritage Set Firm's Course," *Crain's Cleveland Business,* September 1, 1986, p. 2.

Gleisser, Marcus, "Tranzonic Buys Maxithins Business," *Cleveland Plain Dealer,* June 26, 1992, p. 2G.

——, "Tranzonic to Hike Prices to Improve Earnings," *Cleveland Plain Dealer,* June 13, 1995, p. 5C.

Golden, Louis B., and George Golden, *American Automatic Vending Corporation: Profits for Progress in a Growth Industry,* 1963.

Gordon, Mitchell, "Well-Disposed: Tranzonic, Formerly AAV, Narrows Focus After Sale of Big Operations," *Barron's,* January 9, 1984, p. 52.

Kapner, Bill, "Tranzonic is Looking for An Opportunity to Unload Some Cash," *Crain's Cleveland Business,* May 27, 1985, p. 14.

"Louis Golden, Founded Food Service Firm," *Cleveland Plain Dealer,* December 27, 1981, p. 22A.

Maturi, Richard J., "Clean Shot: That's What Tranzonic Cos. Has at Record Earnings," *Barron's,* June 8, 1987, p. 51.

Pergler, Dick, "Automatic Vending Firm Grows Fast," *Cleveland Press,* May 31, 1967.

Sabath, Donald, "Small But Mighty Tranzonic Set to Grow," *Cleveland Plain Dealer,* July 19, 1988, p. 1D.

Ward, Leah, "AAV: 'Detoured But Not Derailed'," *Crain's Cleveland Business,* July 11, 1983, p. 2.

——, "AAV Now Disposed to National Market," *Crain's Cleveland Business,* May 30, 1983, p. 1.

Wyatt, Edward A., "Smiles on Chagrin Boulevard: Tranzonic Shrugs Off Cyclical Dips," *Barron's,* April 13, 1992, p. 15.

—April Dougal Gasbarre

Trico Products Corporation

817 Washington Street
Buffalo, New York 14203
U.S.A.
(716) 852–5700
Fax: (716) 857–3459

Wholly Owned Subsidiary of Stant Corporation
Incorporated: 1920
Employees: 4,300
Sales: $366 million (1994)
SICs: 3714 Motor Vehicle Parts & Accessories; 3451
　　Screw Machine Products; 3069 Fabricated Rubber
　　Products; 3082 Unsupported Plastics & Shapes

Trico Products Corporation, a subsidiary of the Stant Corporation, is the world's largest manufacturer of automobile windshield-wiper systems, with 1994 sales in excess of $366 million. In the mid-1990s, seven out of every ten cars manufactured in North America were outfitted with Trico windshield wiper-systems as original equipment. Trico was also a leading brand of original-equipment windshield wiper systems in Europe, Japan, and Australia. Trico's share of the replacement market for windshield wipers was considerably less, but in 1995, the company introduced a new line of after-market wiper blades designed to be easier for consumers to install. The 1994 Stant annual report called the replacement wiper blades "possibly Trico Products' most significant product breakthrough since it commercialized the windshield wiper blade in 1917." Based in Buffalo, New York, the company also had plants in Brownsville, Texas; Matamoros, Mexico; Springvale, Australia; and Pontypool, Wales. In addition to wiper blades and wiper-blade systems, Trico manufactured hose clamps, grease guns, specialty tools and automobile flashers, and remanufactured power-steering units.

Trico was incorporated in 1920, but the origins of the company go back to 1916, when John R. Oishei, a theater manager in Buffalo, reached agreement with John W. Jepson, a retired electrical engineer, to market a hand-operated squeegee for cleaning automobile windshields. Jepson's invention, marketed as the Rain Rubber, consisted of a rubber blade attached to a handle. Carried in the automobile's tool box during good weather, the handle of the Rain Rubber fit through the opening between the upper and lower sections of the two-part windshields of the day. By pushing the handle back and forth, the driver could clear rain from the windshield.

Oishei's interest in the device apparently stemmed from an automobile accident in which he struck a man on a bicycle. The man was not seriously injured, but Oishei later described the mishap as a "harrowing experience which imprinted on my mind the definite need for maintaining vision while driving in the rain." Soon after the accident, Oishei saw a small card in a store window advertising Jepson's squeegee, which the inventor was marketing himself locally. Oishei arranged to set up a company to manufacture and market the Rain Rubber and formed a partnership with another Buffalo theater manager, Dr. Peter C. Cornell.

Before long, Oishei, who received a patent on Jepson's squeegee, was distributing the Rain Rubber nationally. However, when the United States entered World War I in 1917, automobile production came to a standstill and Oishei's company, then with 35 employees, turned its attention to making locks and hinges for ammunition boxes.

After the war, Oishei expanded wiper distribution to Europe and Australia, as well as North America, and the company took the name Tri-Continental Corporation. The name was later shortened to Trico, which was the company's telegraph and cable-code designation. By 1921, automobile makers were installing a rubber strip between the upper and lower windshields and Trico introduced the Crescent Cleaner, a manual wiper that mounted above the upper windshield. That same year, Trico also introduced the first automatic wiper system, powered by a vacuum pump, which Cadillac adopted as standard equipment a year later.

But, as Oishei would recall, "It wasn't all clear sailing in the early days, not by a long shot. In 1921, we were pressed very definitely by our creditors. It looked as if we couldn't go much farther." Oishei also realized that real success would come when other manufacturers began installing wipers as standard equipment, and in 1924, Trico hired Carl Larson to sell wipers in Detroit.

"What you have to remember," Larson recalled for the Automotive Hall of Fame, "is that cars didn't come in as complete a package as they do today. Certain things, such as bumpers, locks, chains, stop signals, were optional. And that's what windshield wipers were until Trico pushed them as original equipment." Larson went on to explain, "I installed the first hand-wiper on Henry Ford's car. I knew that if I were to sell to the company, I had to convince him first. So I kept after the people over at Ford and they finally let me put one on Mr. Ford's car. We got our order from them shortly after that."

A year later, Trico was able to pay $1 million to buy the Folberth Auto Specialty Co., a competitor in Cleveland. The companies were merged in 1928. Trico also took over Folberth's English subsidiary, which became known as Trico-Folberth in 1930 and was reorganized as Trico Limited in 1946. (Trico Limited later organized Trico Pty. Limited in Australia in 1955.)

The late 1920s and 1930s saw several new product introductions. Trico introduced a five-ply rubber blade designed to channel water away in 1928. The company began marketing the first dual-wiper system in 1929 and the first "two little squirts" windshield-washer system in 1936.

The company again turned its attention to manufacturing munitions during World War II, but returned to developing better wiper-systems soon afterwards. In 1948, Trico introduced the Rainbow wiper blade with a flexible backing strip and a triple-yoke arm, designed to follow the curve of modern windshields. In later years, Trico would introduce the first combination wiper/washer system (1949), the first air pressure motor (1956), the first vacuum-driven, rear-window wiper system (1959), the first intermittent wiper system (1963), plastic wiper blades (1980), and the first modular wiper system (1985).

In 1968 Oishei, then in his late 70s, died after 50 years at the helm of Trico. In a lengthy obituary, *The Buffalo Evening News* reported, "The internationally known industrialist, who harnessed a vacuum to wipe the windshields of the world, had—by his creative imagination and ability to 'think at least two years' ahead—made Trico known wherever motor vehicles are used." Oishei was succeeded as chairman and chief executive officer by his son, R. John Oishei, who changed the spelling of the family name.

Under the younger Oishei's leadership, Trico, which had concentrated on the original-equipment market since the mid-1920s, began putting more effort into aftermarket sales. Much later, President Richard L. Wolf would recall that Oishei "took the replacement parts business from practically no business to a very important part of our strategy and sales." In addition to Trico-branded products, which were marketed through discount stores, parts stores and repair shops, the company produced private-label products for NAPA, Carquest, Atlas, and Canadian Tire.

Unfortunately, it also eventually fell to Oishei to renege on a promise to Buffalo made by his father. In 1929, when an

automobile maker tried to persuade Oishei to move Trico to Detroit, the Buffalo native answered, "Buffalo is where we operate and Buffalo is where we stay." But in the mid-1980s, Oshei decided that Trico had to move its manufacturing operations, not to Detroit, but to Mexico where labor costs were significantly less.

Cutting costs became increasingly important as, despite strong sales, Trico's manufacturing operations lost more than $27 million between 1980 and 1984. The company posted a profit of $781,000 in 1985 on then-record sales of $145.9 million, but the die was cast. In the company's 1985 annual report, newly named Trico President Richard Wolf and Oshei announced jointly, "The advent of economic change in the automotive industry and the emergence of worldwide competition have combined to deny us any realistic opportunity to carry on our Buffalo manufacturing operations on a profitable basis over a sustained period. . . . Our plan of restructuring represents a bold move to assure the future of Trico."

At the company's annual meeting in 1986, Oshei explained, "Today we have an inability to find individuals who will work for wages that would allow us to keep all our operations here. We're surely not going to stand by and watch our profits drop until we had to go bankrupt." Over the next two years, Trico closed two of its three plants in Buffalo and shifted most of its assembly work to a new facility in Matamoros, Mexico. The company also built a technology center and warehouse in Brownsville, Texas, seven miles away, to handle product development and distribution in the United States.

Close to 3,000 jobs were eventually eliminated in Buffalo where Trico employees had been paid an average of $15 an hour, including benefits. At the time, Trico paid workers in Mexico between $1.20 and $1.30 an hour, including benefits, while those in Texas received $4.50 to $6 an hour. The restructuring appeared to work and after posting an operating loss of $16 million in 1987, Trico reported net income of $5.6 million on sales of $232.7 million in 1988.

By 1991, however, Trico was again losing money, posting a $14.6 million loss on sales of $228.7 million. The company, and particularly Wolf, who presided over the plant closings, began to come under increasing criticism from the United Auto Workers, which represented Trico workers in Buffalo. In 1992, James A. Kaczmarek, then president of the UAW local in Buffalo, told *The Washington Post* that Wolf had "respect for the people who make the product."

Trico celebrated its 75th anniversary in 1992. The company posted modest earnings of $2.4 million and $3.3 million in 1992 and 1993, respectively, on rising sales of $265.4 million and $311.9 million. However, the company would have posted losses in both years if it hadn't liquidated almost $20 million in securities. In Trico's annual report for 1993, Wolf admitted the year "was a major disappointment for us. Expected improvements in profitability in our North American and United Kingdom manufacturing operations did not develop."

In 1994, Peter Cundill & Associates Ltd., a Vancouver-based investment firm that owned 13 percent of Trico's stock, began pressing for the company to be sold. In a filing with the

Securities Exchange Commission, Cundill & Associates said that selling the company was the best way for shareholders to maximize the value of their investment. At the time, Trico had voted dividends on its stock just three times in the last 15 years, paying $1 in 1981 and 75 cents in 1986 and 1992. Moreover, the investment firm also asked the Charities Bureau in the New York attorney general's office to require the Oishei Family Charitable Foundation and other family trusts, which then owned 33 percent of Trico, to sell their shares if a buyer could be found. The Charities Bureau regulated charitable foundations to ensure they were administered properly, and Cundill & Associates maintained that the shares had depreciated "very materially" in recent years.

At least in part because of the pressure applied by Cundill & Associates, Trico put itself up for sale in the summer of 1994. In November 1994, the Stant Corporation, a Richmond, Indiana-based manufacturer of hose clamps, engine thermostats, radiator caps, car heaters, and other automotive equipment, including motors for windshield-wiper systems, offered $85 a share for 1.9 million outstanding shares of Trico stock, which was then trading for $61.50 on the NASDAQ exchange. The offer was accepted and Stant, itself a subsidiary of Bessemer Capital Partners L.P., acquired 93.5 percent of Trico's stock for $160 million in December.

Wolf retired with the acquisition. He was replaced by Christopher T. Dunstan, who became executive vice-president and general manager, reporting to Stant President and CEO David R. Paridy. In a press release, Stant explained Trico's decision to seek a buyer: "As the automobile manufacturers increasingly look to suppliers having an ability to provide complete wiper systems rather than portions thereof, (Trico) deemed it to be important to the company's position in the original equipment market to have a long-term source of motors."

In Stant's 1994 annual report, Paridy was cautiously optimistic, writing, "Our near term challenges are clear. Trico Products, our largest and most recent acquisition, has made enormous progress in revitalizing its manufacturing base and competitive position, but its profitability in recent years has not been adequate. He added, "We believe that through a carefully implemented plan, its profitability can improve substantially. It will take time and great effort, but we believe the payoff will be significant." The parent company was also expected to use Trico's international presence to market other Stant automotive products outside North America.

Principal Subsidiaries

Trico Technologies Corp.; Wiper Check, Inc.; Trico Componentes, S.A de C.V. (Mexico); Trico Limited (Wales); Trico Pty. Limited (Australia).

Further Reading

Auerbach, Stuart, and Edward Cody, "Trico Products: A Firm's Move Means Some Shattered Lives," *The Washington Post,* May 17, 1992, p. A29.

Buckham, Tom, "Trico Workers to Get U.S. Aid Quickly," *The Buffalo News,* September 26, 1987.

Fairbanks, Phil, "Trico Products Sells Off Stock To Finance Move to Southwest," *The Buffalo News,* August 20, 1986, p. C7.

Hartley, Tom, "Stant Corp.'s $85-A-Share Offer Makes Trico Products a Big Gainer," *Business First of Buffalo,* November 14, 1994, p. 27.

Ritz, Joseph P., "Trico, Union Pursue Talks Aimed At Easing Pain of Mexico Move," *The Buffalo News,* December 5, 1986, p. B10.

Robinson, David, "Wolf retires as Trico Completes Merger with Stant," *The Buffalo News,* December 14, 1994.

Schroeder, Richard, "Stant First Sought to Buy Trico Back in January," *The Buffalo News,* November 20, 1994, p. B17.

Summers, Robert J., "Trico Products Remains in Red Despite Sales Gain," *The Buffalo News,* May 23, 1983.

——, "Trico Profits Rise, But Local Plants Just Break Even," *The Buffalo News,* August 16, 1984, p. B8.

Zremski, Jerry, "Employment Up at Trico Plants—But Not for Long," *The Buffalo News,* June 5, 1986, p. C11.

——, "Trico Begins Construction, Production in Mexico," *The Buffalo News,* April 2, 1986, p. C5.

—R. Dean Boyer

Turtle Wax, Inc.

5655 W. 73rd Street
Chicago, Illinois 60638
U.S.A.
(708) 563–3600
Fax: (708) 563–4302

Private Company
Incorporated: 1941
Employees: 600
Sales: $145 million (1994 est.)
SICs: 2842 Polishes & Sanitation Goods

Turtle Wax, Inc. is the world's largest manufacturer of car-care products. The Chicago-based company controls over 60 percent of the U.S. car wax market and sells its products in Europe, the Pacific Basin, and Central and South America. It also markets chemicals for commercial car washes, owns and operates the largest chain of full-service car washes in the Chicago market, and manufactures shoe polishes and household cleaners. The family-owned business had estimated revenues of $145 million in 1994, according to *Crain's Chicago Business*.

Benjamin Hirsch, the founder of Turtle Wax, wanted to be a chemist, but had to drop out of college during the Great Depression. Instead, he became a magician, supporting his family with his silks and wand. But he never lost his interest in chemistry nor his fascination with cars. In the late 1930s he developed a car wax and mixed up batches at night in the bathtub. His wife, Marie, filled the bottles by hand. During the day, Hirsch traveled by street car to gas stations around Chicago, selling the wax he named Plastone. In 1941, he invested $500 and opened the Plastone Co., which operated out of a series of storefronts.

To promote his wax, Hirsch would go into a parking lot and shine one fender of each car. He then waited for the owners to arrive and hope to convince them to buy his wax to finish the job. Plastone was a couple of years old when, according to company lore, Hirsch made a sales call in Turtle Creek, Wisconsin. The name of the town clicked in his mind with the hard

shell of a turtle and the protection his wax offered. Thus was born a new name for the company and for the wax, Turtle Wax Super Hard Shell.

In the early years, Hirsch nearly went bankrupt several times. "It was an arduous period," remembered Turtle Wax chairman Sondra Hirsch Healy in a 1993 *Chicago Tribune* article. "We moved around a lot in the Chicago area. I can remember we, my brother and I, slept on the countertop of this storefront on Clark Street." Her father kept the company going by borrowing money from his employees and giving them stock in repayment. Some of those employees, or their children, relatives, and friends, still worked for Turtle Wax in the mid-1990s.

As the popularity of the wax grew, Hirsch wanted to diversify. To appeal to a larger group of customers, he saw the need to sell products through grocery stores, not just to gas stations and hardware stores. In the mid-1950s Hirsch branched out, developing shoe polish, rug shampoo, and floor wax. The company even produced a line of dessert toppings called Party Day.

By 1966, the company boasted huge factory facilities. Its brand-name products, for auto care and household cleaning, had established a foothold in the market, and the firm had just opened a factory in England. Then Hirsch died. As was the case with many fledgling family companies, there was no plan for succession, and Hirsch's widow took over control of the firm. His daughter Sondra, a graduate of the Goodman School of Drama, left her job teaching drama in the Wilmette schools and joined the company as vice-president of public relations. "I felt I had to hold the company together," she told the *Chicago Tribune* in 1993.

Hirsch had been the developer and marketer of the company. With his death, the family followed the conservative advice of those who believed the company had to concentrate on the company's automotive products to survive. Products not related to car care were eliminated, and the company was 99 percent automotive by 1971, the year in which Mrs. Hirsch died. That year, Sondra Hirsch married Denis Healy, a chemist and product developer whom she had met at a trade show in Miami Beach in 1970. Healy joined Turtle Wax as general vice-president. In 1972, Sondra Healy was named chairman of the board, and, in 1977, Denis Healy became president of the company.

Denis Healy had spent most of his career developing new products. He started with Colgate-Palmolive, then moved to the Mennan Co., and finally to the Barr Co., a packager of aerosol and liquid products. With this background, he began rebuilding Turtle Wax's marketing and development efforts, in both the automotive and broader consumer markets.

In 1982, the company introduced several new car-care products. Minute Wax, a silicone-based spray wax, was aimed at the increasing numbers of women who drove and maintained their own cars. For the growing number of older cars on the road, Color Back, a finish restorer, was developed to revive dull finishes. Another introduction, Clear Coat, was a non-abrasive wax and polish designed for new cars.

The Healys also reinstituted Ben Hirsh's efforts to move more strongly into supermarkets and consumer products. John Dellert, then vice-president of marketing, explained the company's strategy for moving into new markets in a 1985 *Advertising Age* article: "We had to come up with what we felt was a unique product that could command a much higher price and then could support advertising to educate the consumer on our presence in the category."

They began with shoe polish. In 1983, the company introduced a six-color line of Turtle Wax Shoe Polish. After success in test markets, the line went national, representing the first phase of the supermarket assault. At the time, the $125 million retail shoe polish and paste business was dominated by Kiwi. Marketed in the U.S. by Sara Lee Corp.'s Kiwi Polish Co., Kiwi accounted for nearly 80 percent of the market. To convince grocery store buyers to stock its polish, Turtle Wax priced its 3.5 oz. bottles at $2.49, with a built-in margin of $1.12 for retailers, compared to a 95¢ price and 50¢ margin for Kiwi.

Once the polish was on the shelves, Turtle Wax launched a $2 million television advertising campaign, larger than any previous introduction for a shoe polish. During 1984, the company spent $1.9 million (58 percent of all the advertising dollars for shoe care products for the year) advertising Turtle Wax Shoe Polish. Within a year, Turtle Wax ranked second, above American Home Product Corp.'s Griffin and Knomark's Esquire polishes, with nearly ten percent of the market. The campaign also gained the company valuable shelf space at many mass merchandiser and retail outlets.

Turtle Wax used the same strategy to take on Armor All, which introduced the first vinyl protectant/beautifier in 1974, and, within 11 years, had 80 percent or more of the estimated $175 million vinyl protectant retail business. Turtle Wax developed Clear Guard and introduced it in 1985, pricing it higher to give retailers a larger margin and unleashing an advertising blitz and rebate offer to lure customers away from Armor All. Unlike other brands on the market, Clear Guard contained no water. A spray, it was packaged in a unique, beaker-type bottle, in five-, ten-, and 16-ounce sizes, all premium priced. The ad campaign compared the new product's clear spray with Armor All's cloudy spray, with the tagline, "Introducing new Clear Guard from Turtle Wax . . . a clear new challenge to Armor All."

In 1985, Turtle Wax introduced a disposable wax-coated cloth and wax-filled sponge, which offered convenience and less mess. During this time, the company also undertook its first licensing agreement. Together with American Greetings Corp., Turtle Wax introduced a line of air fresheners for children's bedrooms. Turtle Wax took the technology it had been using for years to make air fresheners in the shapes of playing cards and dice and packaged them to resemble the Strawberry Shortcake and Care Bears characters. "That's a sort of test for us," Denis Healy told *Advertising Age* at the time. "We're looking to license our name and we're looking to license other people's names."

With its consumer products division well underway, Turtle Wax created an industrial products division in 1985. The new division reflected the company's decision to place more emphasis on the potential business in the industrial market and not to focus only on the retail arena. "Because of our name, we've grown by osmosis into developing bulk chemicals [soaps and waxes] for the car wash business. It was treated as kind of a weak sister, but the business still grew a respectable 5 percent to 10 percent each year," Charles Abate, vice-president of operations and industrial products, told the *Chicago Tribune* in 1986. "The key is to remember that we are a surface treatment company," said Turtle Wax President Denis Healy in the same article.

The new division first concentrated on the car wash industry, which in 1986 had an estimated 9,000 firms across the country, ranging from large chains to small neighborhood operations. Although the technology of the car wash business had changed dramatically in the previous decade, little attention had been given by most manufacturers to developing soaps and waxes appropriate for the new equipment and the lightweight plastics used in cars. Turtle Wax saw an opportunity—and had the financial resources—to develop a national distributor network for its industrial products.

By 1995, the company was the name brand marketer of chemicals for the commercial car wash industry. It marketed a full line of products to all types of car washes through Sam's Club stores and through distributors of car wash chemicals and equipment. The industrial division manufactured six Turtle products: car wash pre-soak, two types of foaming detergent, sealer wax, foaming brush detergent, and high pressure powder detergent. Users in 1995 included 12,000 self-service car wash operations, 9,000 exterior car washes, 9,000 full-service operations, as well as pressure wash operators cleaning trucks, buses, and trains.

Throughout the last half of the 1980s and into the 1990s, Turtle Wax continued to develop new products. 1986 saw the introduction of household cleaning products. "Every bit of research we've done shows not only a high consumer awareness of our name but a perception that we've been selling household products for some time," Charles A. "Chuck" Tornabene, vice-president of marketing, explained in a May 5, 1986 *Chicago Tribune* article.

That year, six new products came on the market from the consumer products division. Rust Eater, designed to "convert rust to a primed surface that will never re-rust," was introduced with a big television ad campaign and customer rebate program.

Three new aerosol products, under the Turtle Wax name, included a spot remover, an upholstery cleaner, and a carpet cleaner. Graphics of pets adorned the packages of the new cleaners, highlighting the special formulation of the products to get rid of pet stains and odors. Repel fabric protector and the Brillante brand of metal polishes were also marketed under the Turtle Wax umbrella.

The company also faced some challenges during this time. In 1986, for example, Turtle Wax agreed to pay nearly $100,000 in civil penalties and to discontinue its use of "potentially deceptive containers," which were not, according to allegations, filled to capacity. The payment settled a lawsuit filed by the district attorney's office in Los Angeles.

In the mid-1980s, Turtle Wax's automotive division responded to changing trends in the car care industry by adding new automotive products. 1987 saw the introduction of Zip Wax Hydro-System Spray Wash. A person needed only to attach a garden hose to the fitting on top of the plastic bottle and he or she could wash and wax a car. The product came in three formulations: wash, wax and wash, and wax. That same year the company also introduced a non-abrasive car wax, aimed at new cars, and a Clean Machine Car Detailer for cleaning all car surfaces, inside and out. At the time, Turtle Wax had an impressive 40 percent share of the $120 million-a-year car wax and polish market. Top-selling Super Hard Shell alone reached a 29 percent share of the overall market, a new high.

In 1988, the company entered the premium segment of the car wax market with Turtle Wax Plus with Teflon. This put the company head to head with Rain Dance, which had been the dominant brand among premium car waxes. Premium waxes accounted for about 20 percent of retail car wax sales. The company worked on the new product for 16 months, during which time it had to convince Du Pont that its Teflon could be functionally used in a mass-market car wax. Until this product, the only Teflon car waxes available were for the professional market. The new wax sold for about $2 more than mid-priced or premium-priced car waxes, including Turtle Wax Super Hard Shell, which had increased its market share to 30 percent.

Determined to reach into every segment of the market, the company introduced Liquid Crystal into the super-premium segment of the car wax market in 1989. For the first time in the company's history, the name Turtle Wax was not associated in any way with the product. Aimed at car buffs, the suggested retail price for Liquid Crystal was $15 to $16, while Super Hard Turtle Wax sold for $4 to $5.

Demographic and consumer research by Turtle Wax showed that about half of all automobile owners regularly washed and waxed their vehicles, and 90 percent would give their cars a basic cleaning "from time to time." The heaviest users were people, primarily 18- to 40-year-old males, who regarded their car as an extension of themselves. But women were a growing segment of the market, representing about 40 percent of the car care product market in 1991, up from about 25 percent ten years earlier.

In 1993, Turtle Wax expanded its overseas operations, increasing its presence in Europe and entering into a deal with one of Japan's largest auto retail chains. New products during this period included Formula 2001, to protect new tires; Instant Foam 'n Shine, the first no-wait car wax; and Color Wax, a car wax that came in different colors to match a car's paint job. Phil Katcher, products editor at *Automotive Marketing*, a trade publication, told the *Chicago Tribune*: "That product breathed a lot of life into what was a pretty stagnant market. The car wax market had been hurt by automakers switching to no-wax car finishes."

Continuing to go after the top segments of the market, in 1995 Turtle Wax took aim at classic car owners. The company teamed up with Chuck Bennett, maker of Zymol Natural Liquid Auto Polish, to offer the pricey polish ($20 a bottle) to the mass market. The polish contained coconut and banana oils, almond paste and aloe, and a touch of vitamin E. Turtle Wax also announced it would use informercials to introduce two new products in 1996: Lubricator 2001 is a new engine treatment and Sudden Shine is an auto polish.

In addition to its three products divisions, Turtle Wax also owned and operated the largest chain of full-service car washes in the Chicago area through its auto appearance division. Turtle Wax's Car Wash and Auto Appearance Centers provided a wide-ranging menu of detailing services as well as car washes. The centers also served as a testing ground for Industrial Division products. The first ten centers were located in buildings converted from other uses. In 1990, Turtle Wax hired the Chicago architectural firm of Perkins & Will to design two state-of-the-art facilities, in Bloomingdale and Aurora, Illinois. To attract and keep customers, the centers offered yearly wash plans. For $199 (in 1994), a plan member received unlimited car washes on weekdays; for $259, the car could be washed on weekends as well.

As the company entered the last half of the 1990s, Turtle Wax car waxes had over a 60 percent share of the market, with a 95 percent brand awareness. Products from the automotive division were being marketed in Europe (the United Kingdom, Germany, Scandinavia), Central and South America (Mexico, Venezuela, Panama), Australia, and the Far East (Japan, South Korea). Through its industrial division, the company was the name brand marketer of chemicals for the commercial car wash industry. Items from the consumer products division including shoe polish, furniture polish, and other polishes and cleaners were sold through food, drug, and mass merchandise chains. The Healys and their family-owned firm appeared to be successfully carrying on Benjamin Hirsch's dreams.

Further Reading

Buursma, Bruce, "Rise in Shine Rich or Not, Motorists Find What a Difference a Wax Job Makes," *Chicago Tribune*, August 11, 1991, Trans. Sec.

Gruber, William, "Car Wash a Stretch for High-Rise Firm," *Chicago Tribune*, May 4, 1990, Sec. 3, p. 2.

"The High Priced Spread," *Chicago Tribune*, April 30, 1995, Trans. Sec.

Hodge, Sally Saville, "Turtle Wax Hoping Its Drive for Industrial Sales Will Wash," *Chicago Tribune*, February 14, 1986, Bus. Sec.

Lazarus, George, "Info Shine For Turtle Wax," *Chicago Tribune*, November 20, 1995, Bus. Sec.

——, "Turtle Puts On High-Priced Shine," *Chicago Tribune*, August 29, 1989, Bus. Sec.

——, "Turtle Wax Back Out of its Shell," *Chicago Tribune*, February 11, 1985, Bus. Sec.

——, "Turtle Wax Did It, But It Took A While," *Chicago Tribune*, August 24, 1987, Bus. Sec.

——, "Turtle Wax Takes on a Teflon Shine," *Chicago Tribune*, October 10, 1988, Bus. Sec.

——, "Turtle Wax Ventures Out of Its Shell Into Household Cleaning Products," *Chicago Tribune*, May 5, 1986, Bus. Sec.

Liesse, Julie, "Chuck Tornabene: Exec Gives New Polish to Turtle Wax," *Advertising Age*, January 14, 1991, p. 28.

Malham, Howell J., Jr., "Soap Opera," *Chicago Tribune*, April 14, 1994, Sec. 5, pp. 1, 13.

McGeehan, Pat, "Turtle Wax Emerges From Car-Market Shell," *Advertising Age*, August 26, 1985, pp. 4, 51.

Randle, Wilma, "Strong Family Histories Help Turtle Wax Shine," *Chicago Tribune*, April 11, 1993, Sec. 7, p. 5.

"Turtle Wax Agrees to Penalty," *Chicago Tribune*, August 22, 1986.

"Whipped Wax," *Home Mechanix*, October 1994, p.

—Ellen D. Wernick

TVI, Inc.

1400 S.E. 6th Street
Bellevue, Washington 98004
U.S.A.
(206) 462–1515
Fax: (206) 451–2250

Private Company
Incorporated: 1972
Employees: 3,000
Sales: $152 million (1995)
SICs: 5311 Department Stores

TVI, Inc. was the largest for-profit chain of thrift stores in the United States in 1995. At the beginning of 1996, TVI, based in Bellevue, Washington, had 110 "Value Village" and "Savers" stores in 17 states and eight Canadian provinces. The company planned to open 90 more stores by the year 2000.

TVI was started by William Ellison, whose father, Benjamin, managed a chain of thrift stores in Sacramento, California. Benjamin enticed his son to join the business by offering to bankroll a store in San Francisco. That was in 1954, when William, a graduate of the University of Washington, was selling advertising for a radio station in Seattle. But it was almost inevitable that William would wind up in the thrift-store business.

Benjamin and his brother, Orlo, joined the Salvation Army as career officers during the Depression and managed the charitable organization's secondhand clothing stores for more than two decades. Orlo's wife, Stella, was credited in family lore with coining the term "thrift store." Orlo left the Salvation Army in 1949 and opened his own thrift store. Benjamin left in 1951 and also went into business for himself. They were later joined by three younger brothers, and by the mid-1990s there were at least 100 members of the Ellison clan operating secondhand-clothing stores throughout the United States.

When William Ellison, then 24, opened The Thrift Shop in San Francisco's Mission District in 1954, he followed a successful business plan established by his father. He financed and managed the business, but the store was actually owned by a local charity. Six years later, Ellison had management contracts with several charities. He incorporated his business as the Salvage Management Corporation. Within a few years, however, Ellison decided to become the store owner as well the manager. As he later explained, "Each time we got a store going well, the charity would terminate our contract because they figured they didn't need us anymore. When we lost six stores in one year, that's when we decided we needed to own our own stores."

In 1966 Ellison opened his first company-owned store in Renton, Washington, using the name Value Village. The next year, he opened a store in Redwood City, California, that used the name Thrift Village. Within five years Ellison had stores in several more cities, including Los Angeles, Portland, and Seattle. In 1972 he incorporated the business as Thrift Village Inc. and moved his company's headquarters to Renton.

By the mid-1970s, with the nation in recession, Thrift Village was operating nine stores. But only five were profitable. Thomas Ellison, William's son, later recalled a ski trip with his father in 1975 when they discussed "how to slice up" the company if it went under. "Contrary to what most people believe, the thrift business is not better in rough times," Thomas Ellison recalled. "In 1975, it was a matter of survival." Although Thrift Village Inc. was turned down for loans by several banks, the company managed to hang on and began to grow again in the late 1970s. The company opened its first Canadian store in Vancouver in 1980.

By 1983, Thrift Village Inc. was doing business in Canada as Value Village Stores and was operating 23 secondhand clothing outlets. However, as the for-profit company grew, its financial association with local charities came under scrutiny. When Orlo Ellison opened his first thrift store soon after World War II, he negotiated with veterans' organizations to supply secondhand merchandise. William Ellison had adopted the same practice. In a straightforward arrangement, Thrift Village Inc. contracted with nonprofit organizations to provide used clothing and other items for specific stores. The company absorbed all the nonprofit organization's costs of soliciting and picking up the items, and then split the profits evenly at the end of the year. Thomas Ellison later defended the arrangement, explaining, "It would have been hard in the early days for nonprofits to function as a business. They didn't operate that way philosophically."

But in 1979 a nonprofit organization that supplied a Thrift Village store in San Jose, California, suggested a more formal arrangement, with Thrift Village Inc. contracting to buy used clothing directly from the nonprofit group. In the early 1980s the company began changing the way it treated nonprofit organizations. Ellison explained, "We also decided it was good to be totally at arm's length. We were spending too much time running [the nonprofit organization's] business and not enough time running ours." By the mid-1980s, Thrift Village Inc. (which changed its name to TVI, Inc. when it became a Washington corporation in 1984) had signed all its nonprofit suppliers to bulk-purchase agreements.

In 1996 the company paid its suppliers per "OK" (an industry measurement of 2.7 cubic feet that approximated two grocery bags, or one box, of used goods). TVI paid nonprofit organizations $37 million for almost 7.5 million OKs in 1995, which amounted to more than 50,000 tons of secondhand clothing and merchandise. Jim McClurg, executive director of the Northwest Center for the Retarded in Seattle, which started supplying TVI in 1966, told *The Journal American* that "TVI is one of the lesser known companies in our community, but it has a greater impact on the success of nonprofits nationwide than any other I know of. I know it's a business, but the net result is that TVI finances social services across the United States and Canada." For example, the Northwest Center for the Retarded, which supplied eight Value Village stores in Washington, expected to receive $4 million from TVI in 1996, netting $1.5 million after expenses. In 1995, TVI estimated that it had paid more than $264 million to charitable organizations.

Thomas Ellison, who had gone to work for his father in 1974, became president of TVI in 1984, by which time he was 27 years old. Under the younger Ellison, the company nearly doubled the number of secondhand shops to 45 by 1990, expanding into Texas, Alaska, Arizona, Minnesota, Idaho, Utah, Hawaii, and three more Canadian provinces. TVI stores used the name Value Village in Canada and the Pacific Northwest, but adopted the name Savers for other areas of the country. The Savers name was trademarked nationally.

In the late 1980s, TVI also introduced the concept of the "thrift department store," which proffered bright lights, wide aisles, neatly arranged displays, and clothing racks. In 1995, Thomas Ellison told *The Voice,* TVI's employee newsletter, "The goal was to take our stores mainstream. Back then, many people wouldn't admit to shopping in thrift stores. We wanted to create a store that would appeal to a broader segment of the population."

Forbes magazine, in 1993, noted, "TVI's outlets look more like Wal-Mart's than the dingy, cluttered Goodwills of years past." Likewise, in 1995, *The Toronto Star*'s fashion editor wrote, "Not every garment is a prize. You may find the perfect handknit sweater, but not necessarily in your size. And time and energy are required to rifle through the jam-packed racks. But that's half the fun."

One of the company's first "thrift department stores" was a Value Village in Redmond, Washington, which was an upscale suburb of Seattle and the home of Microsoft Corp. TVI had started moving its stores out of low-income neighborhoods (where secondhand stores were traditionally located) into blue-collar communities in the early 1980s. Market research, however, showed that the stores were also attracting shoppers from more affluent neighborhoods looking for bargains. Indeed, the Redmond store, which opened in 1984, was TVI's best performing store for many years.

As the idea of the thrift department store caught on, Value Village and Savers stores became "anchor tenants" in retail strip malls. TVI, which had never before done any marketing, also began advertising its stores on television, starting in the Seattle market. Scott Blomquist, then a TVI vice-president, told *The Voice* in 1995, "We started seeing middle-income customers who were excited about our stores and had discovered them through hearsay or driving by. We wanted to speed up the process of 'hearsay' and get more of those people in." The company started by advertising sales, but soon introduced everyday advertising as well.

Under Thomas Ellison in the late 1980s, TVI also began selling over-stocked or discontinued items, referred to as "Labels," from major department stores including Bon Marche, Nordstroms, Neiman Marcus, and Bloomingdales. But TVI eliminated its Labels department in 1996. "A lot of us at TVI liked to say we had new merchandise as well as used," Ellison said. "It made us feel good about ourselves. We had upscale people coming into our stores." But the new merchandise cut into the sales of used clothing, which ultimately hurt the bottom line. "We actually got good at marketing Labels," Ellison said. "But we agree to buy all the secondhand clothing the nonprofits can give us, and if it doesn't sell, we lose money."

The decision to eliminate Labels wasn't without risk. Forbes magazine had noted in 1993, "The new merchandise makes up only about 20 percent of TVI stores' sales, but it serves a more important marketing purpose by upgrading the entire store's image, bringing in customers that might otherwise never go into a secondhand store." But when TVI eliminated Labels in it's Canadian stores in 1995, overall sales went up, which convinced TVI to eliminate new merchandise in all its stores.

TVI also abandoned two other efforts to expand beyond used clothing and household goods. In the early 1980s the company became a national distributor for Buck Stoves and Hunter Fans, and also opened secondhand furniture stores in Seattle and Spokane. Neither venture lasted long. "They were distractions," Ellison said in 1996. "My commitment now, as long as there is room for growth, is to stick with what we know."

The company doubled in size again between 1990 and 1995, opening its 100th store in Mount Vernon, Washington, and solidifying its place as the third-largest thrift-store chain in the United States, behind only the nonprofit groups Salvation Army and Goodwill. In 1995 the company formally adopted a business plan that called for 200 stores by the end of the century. Thomas Ellison predicted, "We will probably top out at 80 to

90 stores in Canada, but we could go as high as 600 in the United States, so we have lots of room for growth.''

Further Reading

Boyer, Dean, ''Secondhand Is First-Rate: Eastside-Based Chain Has 110 Stores, Still Growing,'' *The Journal American,* January 21, 1996, p. D1.

''The Early Years,'' *The Voice,* February 1995, p. 1.

''The Canadian Cousins,'' *The Voice,* June 1995, p. 1.

''The Early Years: The Extended Family,'' *The Voice,* May 1995, p. 1.

''The Early Years: The Next Generation,'' *The Voice,* April 1995, p. 1.

''The Early Years: TVI Arrives in Washington State,'' *The Voice,* March 1995, p. 1.

Fox, Bruce, ''The New Momentum in Used Merchandise,'' *Chain Store Age,* August 1995, pp. 23–32.

Gubernick, Lisa, ''Secondhand Chic,'' *Forbes,* April 26, 1993, pp. 172–173.

Morra, Bernadette, ''True Value: The Deals Are Real at the Value Village Thrift Store Chain,'' *The Toronto Star,* October 26, 1995, p. C1.

''Quarter of a Billion Paid to Charities,'' *The Voice,* September 1995, p. 1.

—R. Dean Boyer

United Technologies Automotive Inc.

5200 Auto Club Drive
Dearborn, Michigan 48126
U.S.A.
(313) 593–9600
Fax: (313) 593–9580

Wholly Owned Subsidiary of United Technologies Corp.
Incorporated: 1930
Employees: 37,000
Sales: $2,683 million
SICs: 3714 Motor Vehicle Parts & Accessories; 3694
    Engine Electrical Equipment

United Technologies Automotive is a global designer and supplier of components and systems for automotive manufacturers. Its products include a broad array of automobile components ranging from sun shades to electrical distribution systems. UTA, a subsidiary of the giant United Technologies Corporation, was formed in 1979 when the Essex Group was merged with Ambac Industries. The Sheller-Globe Corporation, in addition to a number of smaller producers of automotive products, were later absorbed.

The Essex Wire Corporation was founded in Detroit in 1930 when Addison E. Holton acquired the wire and cable division of the Ford Motor Company. Ford had been producing internal wire assemblies for its cars since the early 1920s but had begun to farm out secondary production. The large automaker reached an agreement with Holton whereby it leased a portion of its sprawling Highland Park plant to the new firm, and Essex met Ford's wire needs in addition to manufacturing for the general market.

As the demand for auto wire grew, Holton found that the small corner of the Highland Park plant was no longer sufficient to meet the company's manufacturing needs. So, during the early 1930s Essex acquired the Chicago Transformer Company (an Indiana automotive switch manufacturer) and the Indiana Rubber and Insulated Wire Company. But Essex's most signifi-

cant acquisition was made in 1936 with the purchase of the wire manufacturing facilities of the Dudlo Manufacturing Company in Fort Wayne, Indiana. Holton was searching for facilities in which to manufacture the enamelled magnet wire that was in great demand by electric motor manufacturers. Dudlo had been a pioneer in the production of this wire, but its 38,000-square-foot plant had fallen victim to the Great Depression and had been idle for three years. The revived plant became Essex's largest manufacturing facility and would eventually become the company's corporate headquarters.

By the early 1940s Essex was an established independent manufacturing firm with 12 plants in several states. The company's diverse line of products included electrical wire assemblies for cars, small transformers, magnet wire, power cords for electrical equipment manufacturers, and cable wire for the construction industry. Like many American companies, Essex's focus during the mid-1940s was on wartime needs. The organization quickly adapted its facilities to produce the field wire and airplane wire assemblies needed for the war effort.

The postwar boom of the 1950s was a period of further diversification and growth for Essex. Essex's expertise in electric wiring systems was in great demand by the growing electric appliance industry. Automobile manufacturers were also calling on Essex to produce the increasingly sophisticated wire assemblies demanded by new car designs. In response to these growing markets, the company, which was still controlled by its founder Addison Holton, expanded its product line to include electrical insulating materials and electrical and electro-magnetic controls and systems. New plants were added to accommodate increased demand. By 1959, Essex's earnings had grown to over $8 million, an almost fourfold increase in just two years.

The early 1960s was a period of tremendous growth for Essex. The decade saw the company transform itself from a moderate-sized manufacturing firm to an international competitor in the automotive equipment industry. This transition, however, was not accomplished without growing pains. In 1959 Walter Probst succeeded company founder Holton as president of Essex. He began a reorganization of the 30-year-old firm.

The head office was moved to Fort Wayne and the business was consolidated into six divisions.

In spite of its rapid post war expansion, Essex had remained a very tightly held private corporation. Probst's vision for a multi-national corporation, however, could not succeed without a new influx of capital. In 1965 Essex shares were offered on the New York Stock Exchange. Although the offering was successful, the Chapin family, which had owned six percent of Essex through the 1950s, sued the company for $12 million, claiming that management had misrepresented the company's financial position in order to repurchase shares at a reduced cost before the initial public offering. The suit was settled in 1967, but not without damage to the Essex's reputation. Labor relations also became a serious problem for Essex during that period. An unusually violent strike closed the company's Hillsdale, Michigan magnet wire plant for four months in the spring of 1964, and a series of labor disputes followed during the next few years.

With the new capital provided by the sale of shares to the public, Essex was in a position to begin serious expansion. From 1967 to 1972 Essex acquired 16 manufacturing companies with a diverse range of products. In addition to its long-standing automotive wire assemblies and electrical components, Essex now also produced extruded aluminum products, plumbing and hydraulic fittings, and plastic moldings. It also operated a copper mining and exploration division. To reflect this diversification, in 1968 Essex Wire Corp. changed its name to Essex International. By 1974 Essex had lived up to its new name by opening plants in Spain, The United Kingdom, Canada, and Mexico, in addition to its nearly 100 American manufacturing plants. Essex's 1973 earnings had reached $40 million on sales of $845 million, attracting the attention of United Aircraft Corporation's president and CEO Harry Gray.

Harry Gray had been appointed president of the United Aircraft Corporation in 1971. United Aircraft was at that time one of the largest companies in the country and had a long history of manufacturing airplanes and helicopters for the American military. Gray was determined to diversify United Aircraft in order to diminish the company's reliance on defense contracts. Flourishing Essex International became his first acquisition. Under United Aircraft, soon to be renamed United Technologies, Essex operated as the Essex Group but continued to produce essentially the same range of products as it had before the change in ownership.

Through the 1970s, Gray continued his program of growing and diversifying United Technologies through acquisitions. Among his many new purchases was Ambac Industries. Ambac, founded in 1906 as the American Bosch Magneto Corp, had begun life as a manufacturer of small magnet-powered generators for early internal combustion engines. By the 1950s the company was a leading producer of automobile voltage regulators and ignition equipment for commercial stationary engines. When Gray became interested in Ambac in 1978, the company was manufacturing medical, scientific, and environmental equipment in addition to its traditional fuel injection systems. At the time of its acquisition by United Technologies, Ambac's annual profits were about $16 million on sales of $225 million. Gray surprised the business community by paying $220

million for Ambac even though the company's underlying net assets were worth only about $130 million. The outstanding $90 million was written off as ''goodwill'' in a move that raised eyebrows among some analysts.

In 1979, as part of an attempt to reorganize the growing number of companies entering the United Technologies stable, the electrical and electronics operations of the Essex Group and the operations of Ambac Industries were merged to form United Technologies Automotive, which became a unit of the United Technologies Industrial Products Division. The newly formed unit established its headquarters in Dearborn, Michigan, strategically placed in the heart of the automotive industry. The principal products of UTA remained Essex's wire assemblies and electrical components, and Ambac's fuel injection systems. But in 1985 UTA acquired Alma Plastics, which added interior plastic trim and moldings to the product line. By 1987 sales to the automotive industry had reached about $155 million and were accounting for more than half of the Industrial Products Division of United Technologies.

Although Harry Gray's aggressive policy of growth through acquisitions had built United Technologies into one of the 20 largest industrial corporations in the United States, in the mid-1980s a number of Gray's riskier ventures turned sour. Indeed, net income dropped by about $600 million between 1985 and 1986. After a great deal of internal turmoil amongst UTC management, Gray stepped down as CEO of the troubled firm in 1986. Robert Daniell was appointed in his place. Daniell immediately undertook a major restructuring of UTC, streamlining the unwieldy company by selling off divisions that did not fit into United Technologies' main product lines. In 1988, as part of this reorganization, the wire manufacturing operations of Essex were spun off as an independent company, although the new enterprise continued to produce the wire for the automotive wire assemblies and electronic devices manufactured by United Technologies Automotive. Daniell's reorganization of UTC also included the dissolution of The Industrial Products Division, thus making United Technologies Automotive an independent business unit within UTC.

By the late 1980s, with the major building blocks of the restructuring in place, UTC began to look once again towards strategic expansion, although this time only businesses that would mesh with their major product lines would be considered. The Sheller-Globe Corporation was acquired in 1989 and merged into the operations of UTA. Sheller-Globe was formed in 1966 when the Sheller Manufacturing Corp. was merged into Globe-Wernicke Industries. Sheller had been the primary producer of independently manufactured steering wheels for some 30 years, and Globe was a leading producer of automotive replacement parts. By the time of the UTC acquisition, the company had largely abandoned replacement part sales in favor of original equipment interior automotive products. UTA was seeking to expand its line of interior trim products, and Sheller-Globe's steering wheels and other interior components were ideally suited to these goals.

Throughout the 1980s and 1990s UTA made extensive efforts to expand its international sales. During the mid-1980s the company entered into joint agreements with Renault, Grundig, and Furukawa Electric to produce wiring systems in Europe and

Asia. UTA was also quick to respond to the emergence of new foreign markets created by the changing political climate of the 1990s. The company opened a plant in Godollo, Hungary in 1991 and entered into joint manufacturing agreements with Dongfeng-Citroen of China for production of electrical distribution systems in 1994. By 1994 UTA had manufacturing facilities in 14 countries worldwide in addition to a dozen international sales and engineering offices. In the same year, UTA's international sales had reached $939 million, which was approximately 35 percent of total revenues.

Back at home, UTA increased sales to domestic automakers by expanding their product line. By the mid-1990s, UTA was producing a huge variety of automotive products, ranging from electrical components like junction boxes and DC motors to interior trim including mirrors, visors, and door trim. It was also still producing the wire assemblies and steering wheels that had been the mainstay of Essex and Sheller-Globe. As American automobile manufacturers began increasingly to look towards suppliers to provide not only individual components but overall design and engineering capabilities, UTA expanded its engineering and product development programs. Ford Motor Company, which had long been UTA's major domestic customer, granted the company full-service supplier status in 1995, reaffirming the strong relationship between the two companies.

In 1994, with sales of $2.6 billion, United Technologies decided that UTA's performance was strong enough to warrant a public offering of UTA stock and thereby unlock some of the parent company's investment in the automotive subsidiary. UTC was to remain in control of the company, however, by retaining 60 percent of the equity interest and by electing 80 percent of UTA's directors. The offering, however, was not favorably received by the investment community, which was generally unwilling to meet the targeted stock price. The IPO was postponed indefinitely. In spite of this setback, United Technologies Automotive remained a significant contributor to UTC revenues into the mid-1990s.

Further Reading

Ankenbruck, John, "Essex Group of United Technologies," *The Fort Wayne Story: A Pictorial History,* Woodland Hills, Calif.: Windsor Publications, 1980, pp. 178–179.

Fernandez, Ronald, *Excess Profits: The Rise of United Technologies,* Reading, Mass.: Addison-Wesley, 1983.

Naj, Amal Kumar, "Offerings of Stock Planned for United Technologies Unit," *Wall Street Journal,* January 20, 1994, p. A6.

"Roy D. Chapin Heirs Sue Essex Wire Charging Erroneous Information," *Wall Street Journal,* December 16, 1966, p. 4.

—Hilary Gopnik

Varsity Spirit Corp.

2525 Horizon Lake Drive, Suite 1
Memphis, Tennessee 38133
U.S.A.
(901) 387–4300
Fax: (901) 387–4356

Public Company
Incorporated: 1983
Employees: 500
Sales: $62.60 million
Stock Exchanges: NASDAQ
SICs: 2329 Men's & Boys' Clothing, Not Elsewhere
   Classified; 2339 Women's, Misses' & Juniors'
   Outerwear, Not Elsewhere Classified; 2389 Apparel &
   Accessories, Not Elsewhere Classified; 7032 Sporting
   & Recreational Camps

Varsity Spirit Corp. sells products and services to the school spirit industry throughout the United States and in Japan. It designs and markets cheerleader, dance team, and booster club uniforms and accessories, including sweatshirts, jumpers, vests, sweaters, pompons, jackets, pins, and other paraphernalia. The company also operates, and markets its products through high school and college cheerleader and dance team camps in the United States and Japan.

Varsity Spirit is a leader in a business niche that it helped to create, the school spirit industry. When the company was launched in 1974, there was only one other significant player in the industry: National Cheerleaders Association (later dubbed National Spirit Group), a privately owned Dallas-based venture. National Cheerleaders had been founded by Lawrence Herkimer in 1948. The company had grown and profited chiefly through the operation of cheerleading camps, where high school and college kids could learn cheerleading routines and hone related athletic and gymnastic skills. Among the company's employees in the early 1970s was Jeffrey Webb, the soon-to-be

entrepreneur destined to pose the first serious challenge to Herkimer's enterprise.

Webb, a self-described sports nut, had become absorbed in cheerleading during a one-year stint as a cheerleader for the University of Oklahoma's football team. While he was a student at Oklahoma he began teaching at, and directing, cheerleading training camps for National Cheerleaders Association. It was that experience that prompted him to launch a similar venture. Although Webb enjoyed cheerleading, he believed that the activity had become stagnant and, more specifically, that National Cheerleaders was missing opportunities to advance the sport. He wanted to breathe new life into cheerleading and take it in a new, more dynamic direction that incorporated athleticism and entertainment. "I wanted to modernize cheerleading," Webb recalled in the June 1994 issue of *Nation's Business.*

Webb left National Cheerleaders in 1974 and, at the age of 23, started a company that he called Universal Cheerleaders Association. With no business experience and a relatively unconventional business plan, Webb was unable to secure institutional financing. Instead, he raised $80,000 by establishing a limited partnership and selling $5,000 shares in his company to his family and friends. He also invested $5,000 from his own savings. At the time, the burgeoning cheerleading business was gravitating toward Texas. Webb bucked the trend by setting up his office in Memphis because it was in the middle of the region where he had developed most of his contacts.

Webb's original goal was to provide high-quality, innovative instructional programs for young people on a national basis. He would attract young people to his camps by promising to shun the staid, monotonous routines taught year after year at National Cheerleaders Association, and instead teach new routines that emphasized more athletic and gymnastic stunts. "From the very beginning, he had a good vision of what cheerleading fashions and the whole school spirit industry would look like ten years down the road with the athletics and national television exposure," said Greg Webb, Jeffrey's younger brother and vice-president, in the February 22, 1993 issue of *Memphis Business Journal.* "We knew we were working with a changing environment for school spirit efforts, while some of our competitors were still holding to the traditional role and look.''

After setting up his base in Memphis, Webb started scouting out and reserving college and university dormitories and athletic facilities that were empty during the summer, in anticipation of enrolling high school students interested in attending his camps. Then he mailed letters announcing the training camps, with registration forms, to every high school within 100 miles of each of the campuses where he had reserved space. The effort sapped all of the company's start-up capital, so Webb was relieved when the return mail brought a sack of registration forms. ''If the registration forms didn't come in, we were out of business,'' he recalled in an article printed in the October 25, 1993 issue of *Forbes*. ''I was yelling and screaming, throwing letters into the air. I knew we were going to survive.''

With a rapidly expanding registry, Webb knew that he would be able to find the talent to teach at his camps because several of his associate instructors at National Cheerleaders had promised to join him once he got his venture ''up and running.'' Webb hired 24 instructors during his first summer and operated a total of 20 of his high-energy clinics throughout the Midwest and Southeast. A total of 4,000 students attended. He sometimes slept in his car during that summer as he traveled from clinic to clinic. The venture was an immediate success. Universal Cheerleaders posted a profit in its first year and continued to do so every year thereafter into the mid-1990s.

Once the word spread, Universal's rosters were filled with eager students. By 1979 the company was generating $2 million from its training camps. Encouraged by the success, Webb decided that it was time to branch into a new segment of the market: fashions and supplies. Webb realized that most of the clothing being marketed by the competition at the time did not suit the style of cheerleading taught at his camps. The clothing was restrictive and often tore under the stress of more athletic cheerleading routines. Furthermore, it was outdated. Webb wanted to introduce an updated line of clothing that was durable and stylish.

In 1979 Universal Cheerleaders started a division named Varsity Spirit Fashions and Supplies. Through that unit, Webb began offering updated outfits that were less constrictive and that featured, for example, sleeveless tops, jumpers, and a variety of necklines. The uniforms contrasted with the traditional sweaters and skirts that had been worn for years. The clothing line was an instant hit, and Webb found that it was relatively easy to market through his clinics. During its first year, the Varsity Spirit division chalked up $200,000 in sales. That early gain signaled the success of a venture that soon overcame Universal's core cheerleading clinic business and vaulted the company to multimillion-dollar corporate status.

Webb realized the potential of the clothing and equipment business and quickly moved to emphasize its growth. Throughout the 1980s and early 1990s he was able to boost sales rapidly through a large sales force, promotional videotapes, and full-color catalogs. At the same time, he was able to increase profits steadily from the cheerleading clinics. Despite steady sales and profit growth, however, Webb was still unable to find a financial institution that was willing to back his company during the first seven years. So, he was forced to rely on savvy, cost-effective marketing funded directly from the company's profits.

Among his most successful efforts was the creation of several special events, many of which were televised, sponsored by Universal Cheerleaders Association. Universal's nationally televised events included the National High School Cheerleading Championship, the National Dance Team Championship, the National College Cheerleading and Dance Team Championship, as well as various parade exhibitions and college football bowl half-time shows. The events became a profitable advertising channel for Universal because they established goodwill toward the company and often gave national exposure to its Varsity Spirit products.

Buoyed by external financing, Universal Cheerleaders Association was able to increase its annual revenue base from barely more than $2 million in 1980 to about $10 million going into the late 1980s. Of import was the 1985 purchase of a Winona, Minnesota-based concern called Varsity Spirit Fashions. Strengthened by that addition, Universal's Varsity Spirit division and cheerleading camp unit were each capturing sales of about $5 million per year by 1987. The company was employing about 40 full-time workers as well as 350 cheerleading camp instructors who trained 60,000 cheerleaders annually.

Furthermore, Webb was beginning to expand overseas. In 1987 Universal signed an agreement to consult with the Japan Drill & Cheer Association. The agreement led to the creation of a separate licensed venture called UCA-Japan. Universal developed the firm's teaching staff and began supplying it with uniforms and equipment. The partnership was a perfect fit with Universal's U.S. operations because Japan's cheerleading camp season occurred between November and March, whereas U.S. clinics were offered between April and October. By the early 1990s, the joint venture was sponsoring more than 20 clinics in Japan annually.

By 1989 Universal was bringing in more than $20 million in annual sales. It was late in that year that the original limited partners, who had each fronted $5,000, chose to cash out. They effectively sold two-thirds of the company to a group of investors by way of a leveraged buyout. The deal loaded Universal with debt until the investment group took the company public in 1992. It sold shares in the company and used the cash to pay off all of the company's debt. Webb pocketed about $7.7 million in the deal and also managed to hold on to about 13 percent of the company. The company went public with a name change to Varsity Spirit Corp.

The name change reflected the increasing influence of the organization's clothing and supplies division. Indeed, by the early 1990s the company's uniforms and equipment were contributing more than 60 percent of total sales and more than 70 percent of profits. In fact, the cheerleading and dance clinics had become a marketing tool for the organization's products. In 1993 Varsity Spirit trained 116,000 cheerleaders at 600 camps held on campuses throughout the United States. For a four-day session, students paid only $155, which barely covered Varsity Spirit's costs. Varsity was able to profit, though, by having its instructors pass out product catalogs to the students. Because the average cheerleader spent $200 on clothes, pompons, duffel bags, megaphones, and other various items, Varsity was able to generate hefty product sales from clinic patrons.

As a result of its savvy marketing strategy and innovative clinics and products, Varsity Spirit was able to sustain steady sales and profit growth throughout the early and mid-1990s. Sales increased to $28.1 million in 1991, $33.8 million in 1992, and then to $41.6 million in 1993. Likewise, net income rose from about $623,000 in 1991 to about $2.4 million in 1993. In 1993, Varsity Spirit hosted its first international cheerleading championship in Tokyo. A total of 31 U.S. and Japanese teams participated in the event, which was televised nationally in Japan. That effort helped Webb to win the *Memphis Business Journal*'s Small Business Executive of the Year award, among other honors.

During the 1994 summer camp season, Varsity Spirit trained 137,000 coaches and students at more than 700 camps in 50 states. It employed a staff of about 250 full-time workers, although its work force could grow to as many as 1,000 or more during the summers. In addition to marketing goods at those camps, Varsity employed a 100-member sales force that called on 15,000 schools and colleges to sell Varsity Spirit's products and services. For the late 1990s, Webb considered expanding in foreign nations other than Japan and hoped to continue pushing the growing dance-team market segment (the dance teams performed at half-time shows and contests). Having surpassed Webb's former employer (National Cheerleaders Association)

in sales during the early 1990s, the company planned to sustain its position as the leading school spirit company in the nation.

Principal Subsidiaries

Varsity Spirit Fashions & Supplies, Inc.; Varsity/Intropa Tours, Inc.

Principal Divisions

Universal Cheerleaders Association.

Further Reading

Becker, Susan, "Cheerleading Company Will Begin Exporting Its Universal Message to Japan," *Memphis Business Journal,* February 9, 1987, p. 1.

Lacey, Nicole, "'93 Executive of the Year Winner Knows Value of Team Spirit," *Memphis Business Journal,* January 10, 1994, p. 1(2).

Rodgers, Cheryl, "Spirit! Let's Hear It!," *Nation's Business,* June 1994, p. 16.

Sullivan, R. Lee, "School for Cheerleaders," *Forbes,* October 25, 1993, p. 118(2).

"Universal Cheerleaders Buys Minnesota Uniform Plant," *Memphis Business Journal,* December 9, 1985, p. 17.

Yawn, David, "Webb's Vision Guiding Varsity Spirit Along Route to New Markets," *Memphis Business Journal,* February 22, 1993, p. 1.

—Dave Mote

VEBA A.G.

Karl-Arnold-Platz 3
D–4000 Dusseldorf 30
Federal Republic of Germany
(49) 0211 457 9367
Fax: (49) 0211 457 9532

Public Company
Incorporated: 1929
Employees: 126,875
Sales: DM71.04 billion (US$47.78 billion) (1994)
Stock Exchanges: Berlin Hanover Munich Hamburg
    Dusseldorf Frankfurt
SICs: 4911 Electric Services; 1200 Coal Mining; 1241
    Coal Mining Services; 2992 Lubricating Oils and
    Greases; 5171 Petroleum Bulk Stations and
    Terminals; 5169 Chemicals and Allied Products, Not
    Elsewhere Classified; 4412 Deep Sea Foreign
    Transportation of Freight; 4449 Water Transportation
    of Freight, Not Elsewhere Classified; 4931 Electric
    and Other Services Combined

With interests in electricity, oil, chemicals and transportation, VEBA A.G. is Germany's fourth-largest conglomerate. While over two-thirds of its annual revenues are generated in the European Community, the business also has operations in North America, Latin America, the Asia/Pacific region, and Africa. VEBA was state-owned for most of its history, from its creation by the Prussian government in 1929 as an amalgamation of private and public companies, through the era of Nazism and postwar partition to the reunification in the late 1980s. The Federal Republic of Germany sold 60 percent of VEBA's shares to the public in 1965, but remained the company's largest shareholder (with a 25 percent stake) until 1987, when privatization was completed.

Founded as Vereinigte Elektrizitäts und Bergwerke A.G. (VEBA) in 1929, the company traces its roots to the mid-nineteenth century, when William Thomas Mulvaney emigrated from London to Germany. Mulvaney was born in Northern Ireland in 1806 and began his working life as a surveyor in London. When the British Civil Service was restructured in the 1850s, Mulvaney was among the many who were made redundant. Upon moving to Germany in 1855, he used his surveying skills to select for purchase a number of coal fields in Westphalia. He employed new procedures for the construction of extremely efficient mine shafts, which put his mines ahead of others in production. By 1865 his 1230 miners were mining 330,000 tons of coal per year, much more than others with the same number of miners. After the war of 1870–72, coal prices fell and Mulvaney's Irish shareholders sold out. In 1873 he formed, with two German banks, the Hibernia & Shamrock-Bergwerksgesellschaft zu Berlin, with 5.6 million marks as capital. Mulvaney served as the chairman of the board until his death in 1885.

Leo Gräff succeeded the founder and led the company through the depression of the 1880's and a strike in May 1889 when 80,000 miners walked out. Gräff died shortly after the end of the strike and was replaced by Carl Behrens, who led the company through a period of expansion. The company's growth attracted the unwanted attention of the Prussian government, which accumulated a 46 percent stake in the energy company by 1904. In spite of opposition from privately-held banks and mining companies, the state acquired full control of Hibernia in 1917.

Hibernia formed the core of a state-owned energy cartel created through the 1929 amalgamation of the coal company with Preussischen Elektrizitäts-G.G. (PreussenElektra), the federal electric utility formed in 1927, and Preussichen Bergwerks- und Hütten AG (Preussag). The purpose of the formation of VEBA was to entice international financing for the companies. No foreign capital was invested, though some internal investments were obtained.

In the meantime, a businessman named Hugo Stinnes was creating what would become the biggest business concern in German history. His namesake company, Hugo Stinnes A.G., would become part of the VEBA group in 1965, while another affiliate, Rheinisch-Westfälische Elektrizitätswerk A.G. (RWE), developed into one of VEBA's key competitors. Born in 1870,

Stinnes was the grandson of the successful coal merchant Mathias Stinnes. Hugo learned business in Coblenz, and the trade in the mines of Wiethe, where he worked for a few months, and then in Berlin's School of Mines. He was taken into his grandfather's firm upon graduating, but left at the age of 23 with a capital of 50,000 marks to found his own firm, Hugo Stinnes A.G.

Initially, Hugo Stinnes followed his grandfather's formula for success, acquiring mines, building ships, and setting up coal depots throughout the North, Baltic, and Mediterranean seas. In partnership with August Thyssen, he founded a holding company, Mülheimer Bergwerksvereins in order to acquire more mines. He bought into the huge Deutsch-Luxemburgische Bergwerks-und Hütten A.G., a company which had grown via acquisition from one million marks at its founding in 1901 to over 100 million in 1910. Stinnes was also involved in the massive expansion by amalgamation of the gas and electricity supplier Rheinisch-Westfälische Elektrizitätswerk A.G. In 1909 he began to build up a trading center for his businesses in Hamburg, and it was here that he was most active during World War I.

Under the guise of the patriotic industrialist helping his country's cause, Stinnes took over every business he could during the Great War. He was a welcome guest at official functions and served as an advisor and supplier to the government. Thus given free rein, he bought out, in 1916, Eduard Woermann and acquired the Hamburg-Amerika and the Norddeutscher-Lloyd, as well as shares in the Woermann and German East African lines. The following year he bought the entire business of coal merchants H.W. Heidmann, and threw in a couple of hotels, one of which he turned into offices for his empire. After wiping out his competitors at home, he moved toward those in the occupied countries of Belgium and France, amalgamating and incorporating at will, and encouraging the German government to deport Belgian workers.

Unperturbed by the damage done to his business by the peace terms, Stinnes continued after the war as he had done before. His Deutsch-Luxemburg concern had been most seriously damaged, so in 1920 Stinnes arranged for its merger with the Gelsenkirchener Bergwerks A.G., founded in 1873 by Emil and Adolf Kirdorf, to form the Rheinelbe Union. He linked this with the Siemens-Konzern, which dealt in electrical appliances, instruments, automobiles, and trucks. The huge Siemens-Rheinelbe-Schuckert-Union now had absolute control of both supply and market. With a capital of 615 million marks, it was bigger than even the Klöchner group, and made Stinnes the most powerful businessman in Germany, if not in Europe.

Stinnes may have sensed his lack of popularity, particularly with the press. He tried to earn their favor by purchasing book publishers, paper mills, book binders, printers, and, finally, a few newspapers. For variety, he bought an automobile factory, the Esplanade Hotel in Berlin, and a few other hotels in Thüringen. Lastly, he began to move into banking, where he met his greatest opposition.

Stinnes once said that he had worked hard in order to make money for his children. If so, his efforts were in vain. Within a year after his death in 1924, his sons had argued with the directors of the empire and with the banks their father had

offended, and the whole concern collapsed. Hugo Stinnes Jr. did get some American backing to form a couple of new companies, the Hugo Stinnes Corporation in New York, and Hugo Stinnes Industries. The last remains of his father's empire can be found in Rheinisch-Westfälische Elektrizitätswerk A.G., Essen (RWE).

While VEBA did not profit so much from the First World War as did Stinnes's business, it survived, as a stateowned business, very well in the 1930s. In 1933 the company was politicized, and in 1935 Wilhelm Tengelmann was appointed chairman of the board. VEBA was a major participant in the Third Reich's Four Year Plan, and converted some of its works into armaments factories. VEBA expanded into the petroleum industry in 1935, when it created a chemical refinery called Hüls. Intense wartime research led to the development of coal-derived gasoline and synthetic rubber. The company managed to avoid bombing by the Allies until 1944, and by the end of 1945 the works were all repaired and in full operation again. After the War, most of the members of the board were arrested; one managed to disappear.

The Allies turned VEBA over to the Federal Republic of Germany (West Germany) at the war's end. The government formed a new 21-member board of directors in 1952 and inaugurated a period of expansion. There were major extensions to chemical works and power plants. In 1956, because of the high cost of coal production, VEBA turned to oil production. Initially, share prices were high, but when they dropped VEBA bought quite a few of its own shares. This led to an investigation, which was dropped. The court was satisfied not only that VEBA needed to buy its own shares, but that it had committed no crime in failing to mention its purchases in the annual report for that year. Soon afterward, another VEBA subsidiary built the first nuclear power plant in West Germany. By the early 1990s, nuclear generators would provide nearly half of VEBA's power.

Rudolf von Benningsen-Foerder was appointed chairman of the board in 1971. He immediately tried to improve VEBA's image, and embarked upon a grand reorganization scheme. One part of this plan involved the disbanding of Hibernia, and of putting nearly all of its shares into VEBA Chemie A.G. VEBA was restructured along four main lines of operation: the supply of energy, chemicals, glass, and trade-transport services. The concern seems to have inherited some of Hugo Stinnes's talents, for twice, in 1973 and then in 1979, the Federal Antitrust Commission ruled against VEBA's share dealings. In both cases, the Commission's ruling was ignored and the deals permitted by means of "ministerial permission." By this time, VEBA had some 900,000 shareholders, and was the biggest joint stock company in Europe.

VEBA encountered difficulties in the 1970s, when overcapacity and the global oil shortage combined to put the squeeze on the energy company's oil business. In 1981, VEBA added the United States-based exploration firm Mark Producing to its oil-seeking arms in Libya and Syria. When oil prices started to decline, VEBA again found itself on the wrong end of the energy industry's cycle. While the purchase and eventual divestment of Mark Producing was judged a "disaster" by Sharon Reier of *Financial World*, VEBA's subsequent affiliation with the state-owned Petroleos de Venezuela (PDVSA) helped build VEBA Oel into the largest German-owned oil company, supplying 60 percent of its own petroleum needs.

Rudolf von Benningsen-Foerder remained at the helm of VEBA through 1989, occasionally selling off a company or two or buying a few others. In 1987 the government's last 25.55 percent was sold and VEBA became a public company. Two years later, 53-year-old Klaus Piltz succeeded Benningsen-Foerder as managing director of VEBA. Piltz had joined the conglomerate in 1961, advancing to chief financial officer in 1976. But Piltz's administration was tragically short, ending in April 1993 when he, his son, his daughter, and an associate died in an avalanche in the Austrian Alps. Chief Financial Officer Ulrich Hartmann advanced to CEO and led the company through the mid-1990s.

VEBA's sales fell by 6.8 percent from 1992 to 1993 as declining chemical prices contributed to a 47.3 percent drop in net income. In 1991, when British investment bank S.G. Warburg's report that VEBA's constituent parts were more valuable than the whole, the company instituted a reorganization, selling several divisions and restructuring those that remained. The program included the elimination of 10,000 jobs. Hüls was the hardest hit, with 27 percent work force reduction by the end of 1994. According to The Economist, Hartmann hinted that VEBA could possibly shed its petrochemical core in the years to come.

The criticism, combined with a general downturn in the petrochemicals market, helped prompt an early 1990s diversification. In 1991, VEBA formed Baltic Cable, a joint venture with Swedish utility Sydkraft, to provide cable services in the two countries. The impending opening of Germany's telephone market in 1998 propelled VEBA's 1995 strategic alliance with Britain's second-largest telephone company, Cable & Wireless. VEBA also acquired Lion, a small software company, in the early 1990s. At the same time, VEBA faced wider competition in the energy business, as Germany opened that industry to international competition.

These measures helped fuel a seven percent rise in sales, from DM66.3 billion in 1993 to DM 71.0 billion in 1994, and a healthy 51 percent rebound in profits, from DM 1.01 billion to DM 1.53 billion over the same period. Morgan Stanley predicted that VEBA's earnings per share would increase 16 percent a year.

Principal Subsidiaries

PreussenElektra A.G.; Hüls A.G. (99.6%); VEBA OEL A.G.; STINNES A.G.; RAAB KARCHER A.G.; VEBA IMMO-BILIEN A.G.; Chemcinschaftskernkraftwerk Grohnde GmbH (50%); Karnkraftwerk Kruemmel GmbH (50%); Energie und Umwelttechnik GmbH (50%); Gemeinschaftsckraftwerk Kiel GmbH (50%); Badische Gas- und Elektrizitatsversorgung A.G. (59.7%); Kraftwerk Mehrum GmbH (50%); Kraftwerk EV 3 IS (50%); CYRO Industries (United States) (50%); GAF Hüls Chemie GmbH (50%); Daicel-Hüls Ltd. (Japan) (50%); RUHR OEL GmbH (50%); ARAL A.G. (55.9%); Induboden GmbH (50%).

Further Reading

Breskin, Ira, "VEBA to Streamline Chemical Operations after 'Marked' Loss," Journal of Commerce and Commercial, December 11, 1992, p. 7A.

"Die Doppelganger: German Utilities," The Economist, July 8, 1995, p. 64.

"Falling Chemical Prices Tip VEBA Into the Red," ECN-European Chemical News, August 23, 1993, p. 15.

"German Company VEBA A.G. to Lay Off 10,000 by 1995," The Oil and Gas Journal, September 13, 1993, p. 40.

"Klaus Pilts, VEBA Director, Dies in Avalanche," Journal of Commerce and Commercial, April 16, 1993, p. 7A.

Reier, Sharon, "At the Crossroads," Financial World, July 7, 1992, p. 27.

"VEBA Results Held Back by Chemical Prospects," ECN-European Chemical News, April 4, 1994, p. 21.

"Why West Germany is Selling Two Gems in the Crown Jewels," The Economist, July 5, 1986, p. 57.

—updated by April Dougal Gasbarre

Pharmacy Services

Vitalink Pharmacy Services, Inc.

1250 E. Diehl Road, Suite 208
Naperville, Illinois 60563
U.S.A.
(708) 505-1320
Fax: (708) 505-1319

Public Company
Incorporated: 1967 as TotalCare Pharmacy Services
Employees: 700
Sales: $112 million (1995)
Stock Exchanges: NASDAQ
SICs: 5912 Drug Stores and Proprietary Stores; 8099
 Health & Allied Services, Not Elsewhere Classified

Vitalink Pharmacy Services, Inc., provides institutional pharmacy services to nursing facilities and other institutions. Those services include dispensing medications, furnishing infusion therapy products and services, and providing medical supplies and pharmacy consulting. In 1995 Vitalink was the sixth largest institutional pharmacy company in the United States, with 18 pharmacies serving more than 42,000 long-term care beds in 18 states. Vitalink is majority-owned by Manor Care Inc., the company that spun off Vitalink in 1992.

Vitalink Pharmacy Services was the new name given in 1992 to an enterprise known as TotalCare Pharmacy Services. TotalCare had previously operated as the pharmacy services division of two different healthcare companies: Americana Healthcare Corp. and Manor Care Corp. Americana Healthcare, which owned and operated nursing homes, had launched TotalCare in 1967 to serve as its pharmacy services subsidiary. Totalcare effectively provided drugs and related products to patients and residents. During the next several years, Americana slowly grew TotalCare in sync with its other operations. By the early 1980s the TotalCare subsidiary consisted of three pharmacies serving Americana's chain of 90 nursing homes.

In 1981 Americana Healthcare Corp., along with its Total-Care subsidiary, was purchased by rival Manor Care Inc. Manor

Care was incorporated in 1968, about the same time that Americana initiated the TotalCare division. Stewart Bainum, a Marylander and Republican who was active in state politics, had started the company several years earlier when he began investing in real estate, including apartments, hotels, and nursing homes. During his travels, he had become intrigued by Quality Courts, a chain of motels that were known for being extremely clean and neat. He bought a stake in the company and eventually took control of it in 1968. Bainum incorporated Manor Care in the same year to organize his property holdings.

During the 1970s Bainum added several other properties to the Manor Care portfolio. Not until the 1980s, however, did the company's growth rate surge. Indeed, the 1981 TotalCare buyout reflected a general trend toward consolidation in the healthcare industry that intensified throughout the 1980s. The consolidation was driven by increasing pressures to reduce costs and eliminate waste and overlap. In the case of Manor Care and Americana, for example, operating costs were reduced through various economies of scale. Thus, Manor Care went on to purchase a number of other companies during the decade to become one of the largest hospital and nursing home chains in the world.

Riding on the wave of that growth and benefiting from general industry trends during the decade was the TotalCare Pharmacy subsidiary, which remained intact under Manor Care's ownership. By the end of the 1980s, TotalCare was generating about $15 million in sales annually. Still, TotalCare remained a relatively meager part of Manor Care's overall operations. It effectively operated in a protected environment, selling pharmaceutical products to its captive base of Manor Care nursing homes and facilities, and providing related recordkeeping services. About 90 percent of its total revenue by the late 1980s, in fact, was derived from its parent company's operations.

Although TotalCare's parent, Manor Care, managed to become one of the largest nursing home companies in the country during the 1980s, it wasn't the most profitable or financially sound. Between 1981 and 1988, Manor Care invested heavily to acquire other businesses and build new facilities. It purchased land at peak prices when interest rates were high and borrowed heavily to fund expansion. The effort allowed Bainum to more than double the company's size to more than $1 billion in revenues by the late 1980s. When the real estate market crashed in the 1980s, though, Manor Care was hurt. The company became so highly leveraged that its debt became classified as junk.

Stewart Bainum's son, Stewart Bainum, Jr., had taken over as chief executive of Manor Care shortly before the real estate industry collapse. Like his father, he was active in state politics—but as a Democrat—and had even served two terms in the Maryland General Assembly. During the late 1980s the junior Bainum scrambled to bring Manor Care's balance sheet under control. He cut costs, brought in new managers, and reorganized and redirected the company's wide array of holdings (including Totalcare) in an effort to improve profitability and ease the organization's debt burden. The result was that during the 1990s Manor Care's return on equity far exceeded the industry norm.

TotalCare Pharmacy was among the many operations that was transformed during the shakeup at Manor Care during the late 1980s and early 1990s. Specifically, Bainum realized that TotalCare was not living up to its potential. Rather than primarily serving Manor Care facilities, he reasoned, the subsidiary could be bringing additional cash flow and profit to the company by using its resources to tap the massive U.S. market for institutional pharmaceutical products and related record keeping services. Importantly, that market was growing rapidly as institutional pharmacies were devouring market share that had previously belonged to retail pharmacists. The retail pharmacists were unable to provide increasingly important consulting and recordkeeping services.

To whip TotalCare into shape and expand it, Manor Care put Donna DeNardo in charge of the unit. DeNardo was a college dropout who had learned bookkeeping skills from her grandmother. She had worked as a nursing home bookkeeper for several years before ending up at Manor Care in 1981. Her performance there earned her a top slot in the reorganized TotalCare unit in December 1989, by which time she was only 37 years old. DeNardo and fellow executives would invest nearly $50 million in the company during the next five years, boosting sales from less than $20 million in the late 1980s to more than $110 million by 1995.

To break out of its comfortable but limiting relationship with Manor Care, TotalCare management knew that it had to aggressively market its services to other institutions. The company hoped to boost the percentage of revenue from outside companies from about ten percent in 1989 to more than 50 percent by the mid-1990s. To that end, it began drawing on Manor Care's financial resources to acquire other pharmaceutical companies and to develop new locations. That initiative gave it nine branches in six states—Illinois, Indiana, Ohio, Wisconsin, Pennsylvania, and Maryland—by 1991, and boosted the number of nursing home beds under its service from about 7,000 to nearly 12,000.

During 1990 and 1991, TotalCare managed to increase annual sales 48 percent (from $18.4 million to $27.3 million), while net income rose 41 percent to about $3.8 million. The

subsidiary, while still a relatively small part of its parent's operations, was one of Manor Care's top performers during the two-year period. In 1991, therefore, Manor Care executives decided to capitalize on the subsidiary's potential by spinning the company off. In March 1992, Manor Care took TotalCare public, incorporating the newly-independent company as Vitalink Pharmacy Services, Inc. DeNardo was named president of Vitalink, while Manor Care's chief executive, Stewart Bainum Jr., became the company's chairman.

Manor Care sold 18 percent of its stock in the venture, which brought about $37 million into its coffers. Manor Care used some of the money to pare its heavy debt load. The remaining cash was retained by Vitalink as a war chest for new acquisitions and development. Indeed, at the time of the public offering Vitalink was still garnering well over 75 percent of its sales from facilities owned and operated by Manor Care. DeNardo hoped to quickly reduce that portion using the cash gleaned from the spin-off.

To that end, Vitalink completed a succession of acquisitions during the next several months. In August 1992, Vitalink acquired the assets of Northern Nursing Home Pharmacy, Inc. In December of that year it completed a much larger deal when it paid $25.7 million for the institutional pharmacy and medical supply business of West End Family Pharmacy, Inc. Then, in August 1993, Vitalink acquired White, Mack and Wart, Inc., a Portland, Oregon-based pharmacy company, in a deal valued at roughly $6 million. The important result of those acquisitions, combined with internal growth, was that the number of beds serviced by Vitalink's operations rose to well over 30,000. Furthermore, more than half of those beds were in institutions not owned by Manor Care.

Vitalink's sales increased to $40.16 million in 1992 and then to $65.7 million in 1993, while net income rose to $7.34 million (from $2.66 million in 1990 and $5.5 million in 1992). Although the growth seemed impressive, the company's stock price failed to keep pace. In fact, Vitalink's stock tumbled as its sales and profits gained. Investor apathy reflected the reality of Vitalink's situation. Under the Manor Care umbrella, Vitalink had found it relatively easy to secure high profit margins from captive customers. The more it sought outside business, however, the more it was subject to the competitive pressures of the marketplace.

"Unfortunately, our profit margins were probably the highest they'll ever be a year ago," said Vitalink's chief financial officer in the August 13, 1993, *Warfield's Business Record*. "The industry average is less than what our experience historically has been, and as we acquire more outside business, our margins will tend to mirror the industry average." Also squelching profitability for Vitalink in the early 1990s were mounting cost and price pressures inherent to the healthcare industry of the early and mid-1990s. For example, the Clinton administration was pressuring the pharmaceutical industry to ease prices, and managed care organizations were striving to eliminate unnecessary drug-related expenses.

Despite some obstacles, Vitalink continued to aggressively pursue growth going into the mid-1990s and to try capitalizing on marketplace changes. Increasing government regulation, for example, meant that demand for some of its consulting services would likely rise. Similarly, cost pressures were creating a greater demand from Vitalink's customers for intravenous therapies, which were increasingly being furnished in non-hospital settings. Vitalink was also shifting its focus to the proliferating generic drug segment. It was with those growing markets in mind that Vitalink's managers continued to acquire competitors and develop new facilities.

In January 1994 Vitalink purchased the institutional pharmacy business of Apothecary Services of Colorado. Similarly, in April 1995 Vitalink acquired the institutional pharmacy business of San Antonio, Texas-based Parker's Pharmacy, Inc. Shortly thereafter, it bought out Home Intravenous Care Co., a Colorado-based infusion-therapy concern. Those acquisitions helped Vitalink boost sales to $98.57 million in 1994 and then to $112.26 million in 1995. More notably, net income rose to a record high of $11.68 million in 1995, causing the company's stock price to rally.

By mid-1995, Vitalink was operating 18 pharmacies that were serving a customer network encompassing more than 42,000 beds in 18 states. About 75 percent of its revenue was gleaned from its traditional prescription-management activities, while 16 percent and seven percent, respectively, were garnered from infusion-therapy and medical-supplies operations. Roughly three percent of sales were attributable to consulting services. Vitalink's dependence on Manor Care had decreased markedly since the early 1990s, although its alliance with the company (which still owned 82 percent of Vitalink) gave it a competitive edge over several of its competitors. With virtually no long-term debt and access to Manor Care's deep pockets, Vitalink was hoping to boost its rank from the sixth-largest institutional pharmacy operation in the country.

Principal Subsidiaries

Vitalink Infusion Services, Inc.

Further Reading

"Drug Runner," *Forbes,* October 23, 1995, p. 332.

Escobar, Louisa Shepard, "Manor Care Inc. to Go Public With Total-Care Pharmacies," *Washington Business Journal,* October 21, 1991, p. 4.

Hinden, Stan, "Manor Care Gets a Shot in the Arm From Vitalink Spinoff," *Washington Post,* March 16, 1992, p. E35.

Hinebaugh, Cathy, "Manor Care Posts Healthy Growth in Second Fiscal Quarter Earnings," *Daily Record,* December 15, 1992, p. 5.

Meisol, Patricia, "Taking Care of Business: Healthy Manor Care Poised to Expand in Growing Long-term Nursing Market," *Baltimore Sun,* February 20, 1994, Bus. Sec.

Murphy, H. Lee, "Nursing Home Drug Distributor Expands Niche Via Acquisitions," *Crain's Chicago Business,* October 30, 1995, p. 40.

Myers, Randy, "Vitalink Makes a Play for Larger Markets," *Warfield's Business Record,* August 13, 1993, p. 1.

—Dave Mote

W.R. Berkley Corp.

P.O. Box 2518
Greenwich, Connecticut 06836-2518
U.S.A.
(203) 629-2880
Fax: (203) 629-3492

Public Company
Incorporated: 1967 as Fine-Vest Services, Inc.
Employees: 2,607
Total Assets: $3.58 billion
Stock Exchanges: NASDAQ
SICs: 6331 Fire, Marine, and Casualty Insurance; 6411
  Insurance Agents, Brokers, & Services; 8742
  Management Consulting Services

W.R. Berkley Corp. is an insurance holding company active in four segments of the industry: regional property casualty; specialty lines; insurance services; and reinsurance. The company operates through numerous specialty and regional subsidiaries located primarily in the midwestern, southwestern, and northeastern United States.

W.R. Berkley Corp. is the creation of entrepreneur and investor William R. Berkley. Berkley got his start as an investor at the age of 12, when he began using spare money from his lawn-mowing business to buy stocks. Among his top picks at the time was Decca Record Co., which signed many of the most promising British rock artists of the 1960s. Decca's stock jumped in price from $13 to $42, helping Berkley to become hooked on investing. In the late 1960s, the brilliant Berkley attended Harvard's business school, where he and a classmate ran a $2-million mutual fund out of their four-bedroom apartment. The fund, which formed the foundation for W.R. Berkley's predecessor (Berkley Dean & Co.), was a smashing success. Its assets ballooned to $10 million by the time Berkley was out of college, and it turned out to be one of the hottest mutual funds of the period.

Berkley earned a reputation at Harvard as brilliant, arrogant, and boastful. "This guy was very confident, there's no doubt," recalled Dennis Duggan, a reporter that profiled Berkley in the 1960s for *New York Newsday*. Duggan added, "He said he'd be rich. He wanted to be one of the richest people in America. He was arrogant; he exuded it." Berkley's swaggering style earned him a cream pie in the face from his contemptuous Harvard classmates, but it apparently also helped to make him very wealthy. By the time Berkley was 23 years old, in fact, Berkley Dean & Co. was managing $10 million in mutual fund assets, as well as $15 million in other investments, and generating nearly $1 billion in annual revenues. Berkley would later attribute his cockiness to youth and simplistic views of the world, but not before building the multi-million-dollar insurance holding company that became W.R. Berkley Corp.

Berkley succeeded in the stock market during the 1960s and early 1970s by purchasing the stocks of companies with earnings that were growing faster than the economy. He was widely publicized at the time as an investment 'genius' for his ability to sniff out undervalued stocks. In reality, much of his success at the time was the result of a strong bull market that complemented his investment strategy. When the market stalled in the early 1970s, Berkley's investment performance waned. Berkley bailed out of the stock-picking business and decided to jump into the insurance business with the purchase of Houston General Insurance Co. He bought the company because the sale price was low. But it represented the first of a large portfolio of companies, rather than stocks, that Berkley would accrue during the next twenty years.

Berkley took his company public in 1973 as W.R. Berkley Corp. He invested proceeds from the offering in Houston General. Like many of his stock picks, the Houston General investment soared. Berkley sold the company 14 months later for nearly twice the purchase price. He used profits from the sale to buy other insurers. Berkley's strategy in the insurance business during the 1970s was multi-faceted. Importantly, Berkley recognized an pivotal emerging industry trend; changing financial controls for property-casualty insurers were rapidly increasing the number of investment dollars available per each dollar of capital held by the companies. The additional investment pool meant that insurers could invest more conservatively in government bonds and other low-risk instruments and still rack up healthy profits. Markets were slow to realize the significance of the changing financial controls, so Berkley was able to buy insurance companies at very low prices in relation to their future worth.

Aside from the investment dynamics of the insurance industry during the 1970s and 1980s, Berkley planned to profit from a unique operating strategy. He believed that many insurance companies, in an effort to impress competitors and customers, had grown too large. They had succeeded in setting up giant, nationwide networks that allowed them to benefit from economies of scale related to marketing, investing, and data processing. In doing so, however, they had forfeited benefits associated with operating intimately with local and regional markets. Thus, Berkley's plan was to purchase a network of independent, regional insurance companies. He would reduce expenses by, for example, centralizing data processing tasks. But he would allow each of his companies to operate autonomously in their respective regions. That way, managers of the subsidiaries could respond to the intricacies of their local markets and provide more personalized service to customers.

Throughout the 1970s and early 1980s Berkley purchased a string of insurance companies, most of which he whipped into high-profit performers. In addition to regional insurers, Berkley utilized his strategy to break into the specialty insurance business. Berkley subsidiaries were eventually offering several types of unique coverage. For example, W.R. Berkley was one of only a handful of American insurance organizations that offered collision insurance on Rolls-Royces. Another of its exotic policies protected sports tournament directors from having to pay big prizes to lucky winners—In a hole-in-one contest at a golf tournament, for instance, or for a record-size catch at a fishing contest. "The laws of probability are in our favor," Berkley explained in the March 1987 *Money*, adding that "Because we insure 100 sports tournaments, for example, it is unlikely we will have to pay off on very many."

Berkley achieved above average returns from his insurance companies during the 1970s and early 1980s. And he managed to do so without incurring excessive debt or jeopardizing the financial stability of his companies. The fiscal strength of W.R. Grace became apparent during the property-casualty industry blowout of the early 1980s. Indeed, many property-casualty insurers suffered huge losses during the downturn because returns from investments soured and claim payments outstripped investment income. Berkley, by contrast, had sacked away large cash reserves in preparation for the downturn. Furthermore, he had wisely invested most of the assets from his companies in conservative, low-risk instruments that were less impacted by stagnant stock markets.

Besides surviving the industry shakeout relatively unscathed, Berkley took advantage of market conditions during the early and mid-1980s. For example, in his typical nonconformist style, Berkley jumped into the commercial truck insurance business during the mid-1980s while most of his competitors were trying to get out. Most commercial truck insurers at the time were suffering heavy losses for a variety of economic and regulatory reasons. Berkley, sensing an upturn in

that niche, purchased Carolina Casualty Insurance Co. The market rebounded and the company was able to increase its premium volume by more than 50 percent over a five-year period.

It eventually became clear to investors that, despite Berkley's investment background and skills, the key ingredient to W.R. Berkley's success during the 1970s and 1980s was sound management and operating strategies. While other companies enjoyed temporary bursts of success by making risky boom-and-bust investments, sound management allowed Berkley to enjoy moderate returns when investment markets were down and big gains when markets were strong. Providing evidence of the company's value-added strategy were a number of innovations that W.R. Berkley had pioneered. For example, W.R. Berkley was one of the first insurers to market a captive risk-retention group to businesses; the 'self-insurance' groups effectively enabled companies to handle insurance needs without traditional policies. Berkley was also a pioneer in the field of environmental insurance, which protects companies against liability from accidents like oil and chemical spills.

By 1986 the sprawling W.R. Berkley Corp. was generating about $400 million in annual revenue—an increase of nearly 100 percent over 1985. Throughout the late 1980s and early 1990s the company's annual revenue fluctuated between $415 million and $450 million. Profits, however, grew from $7 million in 1985 to $30 million in 1986, before leveling out around a healthy $50 million annually through the late 1980s and into the mid-1990s. Those sales and profit figures reflected Berkley's emphasis on steady profitability rather than growth. "Profit is sanity. Volume is vanity," Berkley quipped in the July 26, 1993 *Business Insurance.*

Besides capturing fat profits from his portfolio of more than 20 insurance companies, Berkley became engaged in a number of other businesses that interested him. In 1981, for example, he started National Guardian Corporation, a company that installed and serviced alarm systems. Berkley got the idea to launch the venture after he had an alarm installed in his own home. After trying to start the company from scratch, he decided instead to build it by acquiring his competitors. Between 1983 and 1987 he purchased nearly 100 companies at a cost of about $130 million. By 1987, in fact, the company was employing 6,000 workers, generating income of $5.5 million annually, and providing alarm and security guard services throughout the northeastern United States.

In addition to National Guardian, Berkley launched Finevest Services Inc. in 1987. The venture stemmed from Berkley's chance purchase of a dairy company, which got him interested in the food business. Finevest was established as an investment and consulting firm with interests in the food and food distribution industry. Finevest Foods was created in 1987 as a holding company for four food companies that Berkley had purchased since January 1986. By 1988 Finevest Foods was distributing more than 2,200 frozen food products to 18 states. Also during the late 1980s, Berkley fired up Strategic Information Inc. to get in on the booming computer/communications industry. The firm was created to specialize in market research, and Berkley hoped to use the company to support his insurance and food holdings.

Although Berkley tinkered with other business ventures, the W.R. Berkley insurance operations remained the core of his personal empire. In fact, some of his other investments soured during the recession of the late 1980s and early 1990s. Finevest, for example, finally went bankrupt in 1991 and ended up costing Berkley a whopping $20 million. "Financially, it was a great deal of money," Berkley acknowledged in the September 21, 1992, *Business Week,* adding "but that's life." In contrast, W.R. Berkley continued to flourish, despite an ugly industry shakeout in the property-casualty insurance business. Indeed, as they had in the late 1970s and early 1980s, many of Berkley's competitors loaded up on risky investments like real estate and junk bonds in an effort to boost returns. When the bottom fell out of the market, those companies got burned. Berkley, with its conservative investment portfolio and profitable operating strategy, sustained steady revenues and even managed to steadily boost investment income. The result was healthy, relatively constant profitability.

Going into the mid-1990s, W.R. Berkley Corp. was following a strategy of creating new insurance companies and divisions, rather than purchasing existing companies. The strategy was designed to, among other benefits, reduce tax liabilities. Berkley was also increasing its emphasis on managed care in the mid-1990s, and expanding overseas with planned investments in Central and South America and Asia. Finally, Berkley was stepping up its investments in the reinsurance business. Although net income dipped in 1994, W.R. Berkley continued to outperform the industry average in terms of profitability (excluding investment income). Furthermore, the company boasted a capital surplus far above the government-required minimum and above the industry average, which reflected W.R. Berkley's excellent financial condition. With an estimated net worth approaching $500 million in 1995, Berkley had achieved his youthful goal of becoming one of the wealthiest men in the United States.

Principal Subsidiaries

Acadia Insurance Company; American West Insurance Company; Continental Western Insurance Company; Firemen's Insurance Company of Washington, D.C.; Habitational Insurance Division; Chesapeake Insurance Division; Great River Insurance Company; Tri-State Insurance Company of Minnesota; Union Insurance Company; Union Standard Insurance Company; Admiral Insurance Company; Monitor Liability Managers, Inc.; Nautilus Insurance Company; Great Divide Insurance Company; Carolina Casualty Insurance Company; Berkley Administrators; Berkley Risk Services, Inc.; Key Risk Management Services, Inc.; Rasmussen Administrators; Berkley Risk Managers, Inc.; All American Agency Facilities, Inc.; Berkley Dean & Company, Inc.; Berkley Information Services; Signet Star Holdings, Inc.; Signet Star Reinsurance Company; Fidelity and Surety Division; Facultative ReSources, Inc.

Further Reading

Berkley, William R., "W.R. Berkley Corp. Names John J. Kinsella President and CEO of Admiral Insurance Co.," *PR Newswire,* May 26, 1994.

Bryant, Adam, "Greenwich-Based Firm Hopes Market's Not Cold to Public Stock Offering," *Southern Connecticut Business Journal,* March 7, 1988, p. 1.

Cone, Edward F., "Boy Wonder Grows Up," *Forbes,* February 20, 1989, p. 49.

Goodman, Jordan E., and Walter L. Updegrave, "Earnings from Insuring Against a Big Fish," *Money,* March 1987, p. 8.

Montgomery, Shep, "Great River Forms New Insurance Company," *Mississippi Business Journal,* March 7, 1994, p. 1.

Porter, John W., "National Guardian Grows at Alarming Rate," *Intercorp,* November 13, 1987, p. 11.

Schachner, Michael, "Berkley's Strategy Proves a Winner for His Collection of P/C Insurers," *Business Insurance,* July 26, 1993, p. 1.

Smart, Tim, "William Berkley Had a Hard Act to Follow: Himself," *Business Week,* September 21, 1992, p. 80.

—Dave Mote

Watkins-Johnson Company

Stanford Research Park
3333 Hillview Avenue
Palo Alto, California 94304
U.S.A.
(415) 493-4141
Fax: (415) 813-2402

Public Company
Incorporated: 1957
Employees: 2,220
Sales: $332.6 million (1994)
Stock Exchanges: New York Pacific Boston
SICs: 3663 Radio & T.V. Communications Equipment;
  3825 Instruments to Measure Electricity; 3674
  Semiconductors & Related Devices

A leading high-technology competitor, Watkins-Johnson Company is a producer of semiconductor-manufacturing equipment and electronic products for the wireless-telecommunications and defense industries. Founded in 1957, Watkins-Johnson emerged as a developer and manufacturer of surveillance, communications, and electronic countermeasure equipment used in covert operations, selling the bulk of its equipment for decades to the U.S. Department of Defense. During the late 1980s, as defense spending began to ebb, the company gradually placed a greater emphasis on the production of semiconductor equipment to lessen its heavy reliance on military contracts. By the mid-1990s, Watkins-Johnson had etched a new identity for itself as a producer of chemical-vapor-deposition (CVD) equipment, which deposits layers of nonconducting dielectrics onto silicon wafers. The company's semiconductor equipment group, which was enjoying robust growth during the mid-1990s, accounted for 60 percent of total sales in 1995, roughly equivalent to the percentage of sales formerly contributed by Watkins-Johnson's military-related business. Of the remaining percentage of the company's sales in 1995, 30 percent was derived from defense-related work, while telecommunications and wireless communications accounted for ten percent.

Company Origins

When Dean A. Watkins and H. Richard Johnson decided to start a new business in 1957, their objectives were clear, their strategy precise. The two men, both established professionals within their field, entered the entrepreneurial fray in December 1957, then spent the ensuing 30 years pursuing the objectives and following the strategy they embraced before their company's first day of business. Both Watkins and Johnson would still superintend over the operation of their company when it began to diversify during the late 1980s, their tenure as leaders encompassing two eras in the history of their company. In each era, the company was regarded as a formidable competitor, its market position underpinned by the technological foundation established by its founders.

Watkins, in the years leading up to the formation of Watkins-Johnson, was working as a professor of electrical engineering at Stanford University, while Johnson was working at Hughes Aircraft Company, where he was head of the company's microwave laboratory in southern California. Together, Watkins and Johnson had the capacity to enter the business world at the highest technological level; their plan was to enter the electronic components field, then the electronic systems field. Specifically, the two founders decided in 1957 to develop and manufacture microwave tubes and microwave solid-state devices, then use those products as a foundation from which to diversify into related electronic systems and equipment devices areas.

After receiving financial assistance from Kern County Land Company, the pair incorporated Watkins-Johnson Company on December 6, 1957, then set themselves to their predetermined task of developing and manufacturing sophisticated electronic devices, principally backward-wave tubes and forward-wave tubes. Backward-wave tubes, which functioned as sources of microwave power, were used in a variety of settings, including electronic test equipment, frequency agile radar missile control systems, and other areas where the generation of an electrically tunable microwave signal was required. Forward-wave tubes, physically similar to backward-wave tubes, were used primarily in microwave reconnaissance and surveillance receiving equipment and in electronic jamming equipment, as well as part of radar systems. Not surprisingly, considering the applications for the company's products, Watkins-Johnson's largest customer was the U.S. Department of Defense, which would purchase the majority of the company's products for decades to come, as Watkins and Johnson transformed their business venture into a leading competitor in the electronic warfare market.

Consistent Growth During the 1960s

Adhering to their original strategy of first penetrating the electronic components field and then branching out into related business activities, Watkins and Johnson recorded an encouragingly successful first decade of business. Watkins-Johnson was a profitable enterprise in its first year of business, collecting $80,000 in net income from nearly $500,000 in sales. Profits and revenues increased each year thereafter, rising to $3.2 million and $31.1 million, respectively, by the end of 1967, Watkins-Johnson's 10th anniversary of existence. The following year, when stock in the company was traded for the first time on the New York Stock Exchange in June, Watkins-Johnson formed a subsidiary named Watkins-Johnson International to handle its nascent yet fast-growing international business.

Annual sales and profits increased each year during Watkins-Johnson's first decade of business, recording a 31 percent and 38 percent compounded average annual rise, respectively, realizing growth fueled in part by the two acquisitions completed during the 1960s. In 1963, Watkins-Johnson made its first acquisitive move, purchasing Santa Cruz, California-based Stewart Engineering Company, a manufacturer of backward-wave oscillators, devices used primarily in electronic test equipment, and a maker of a line of controlled atmosphere furnaces for the semiconductor industry. Four years later, as annual sales eclipsed $30 million, the company completed the second acquisition in its history, absorbing Rockville, Maryland-based Communication Electronics Inc., a manufacturer of lower frequency reconnaissance and surveillance equipment used principally for monitoring radio communications.

Watkins-Johnson's record of consecutive annual increases in earnings and revenues ended in 1969, when sales slipped 18 percent and profits fell 43 percent. The losses, however, were largely the result of delays in Defense Department funding and not indicative of any debilitative weakness within Watkins-Johnson's operations. The company by this point employed more than 1,250 workers, with its business divided evenly between the production of electronic components and the production of electronic systems and equipment, the business areas Watkins and Johnson had targeted a decade earlier. From a total of three plant locations—one in Palo Alto, California, another in Santa Cruz, California, and a third in Rockville, Maryland—the company developed and manufactured its surveillance, communications, and electronic countermeasure products, the overwhelming majority of which were purchased either directly or indirectly by the U.S. Department of Defense. As Watkins-Johnson entered the 1970s, government contracts would continue to propel the company forward, driving its growth and funding the development of its highly sophisticated equipment.

By the mid-1970s, Watkins-Johnson was generating roughly $75 million a year in sales and controlled between four and five percent of the $1.5 billion electronic warfare market. Earlier in the decade, the company completed its third acquisition, purchasing in 1970 Mountain View, California-based RELCOM, a closely-held manufacturer of precision components such as mixers, frequency converters, transformers, and switches. In the wake of this acquisition, the company fell victim to rising inflation, problems arising from production difficulties, and parts shortages. Its financial health suffered as a result, particularly in 1974, but by the mid-1970s Watkins-Johnson had recovered completely, with its international business demonstrating encouraging growth. Sales outside the United States accounted for 30 percent of the company's total sales by the mid-1970s, up from approximately ten percent during the late 1960s.

By the end of the 1970s, Watkins-Johnson had completed another decade of strong growth. The company, profitable in every year since its founding, was supported by approximately 3,000 employees, four manufacturing facilities, and 15 sales offices in the United States and in Europe. Annual sales were approaching $130 million, driven upwards by the continued patronage of the Department of Defense. Since the company's inception, when tensions between the Soviet Union and the United States were, perhaps, at their most strained level, the Cold War and the specter of global conflict had fueled spiraling defense spending, buoying Watkins-Johnson's business considerably. More than half of the company's business was dependent on the continued rise in military spending, which, as the company prepared to enter the 1980s, appeared threatened under the last years of the Carter Administration. Addressing a gathering of the New York Society of Security Analysts in 1980, Dean Watkins conveyed as much with his closing remarks, stating "we are pleased at the President's perception, albeit belated, of the dangerous and rapidly growing strength of the Soviet Union."

Redirection of Business in the 1980s

Watkins would find a greater ally in Ronald Reagan, who assumed the presidential post in 1981, then presided over the country during a two-term presidency that included major increases in defense spending. The 1980s were robust years of growth for defense-oriented companies, Watkins-Johnson included, as the pressing need to outmatch the Soviet Union in military might fostered widespread growth throughout the company's key markets. Despite the vitality of the defense industry during the Reagan Administration, Watkins-Johnson initiated a significant shift in its business mix during the decade that would begin to steer the company away from its heavy involvement in the electronic warfare market, marking the beginning of a new era of business for a firm long-reliant on the vagaries of defense spending.

The diversification away from military markets, subtle at first, began when W. Keith Kennedy, a Watkins-Johnson employee since 1968, took over management of the company in 1988. With Kennedy at the helm and Watkins and Johnson occupying the posts of chairman and vice-chairman, respectively, the company gradually began to shift its emphasis away from defense electronics to systems for making semiconductor wafers. In the years ahead, Watkins-Johnson would become a leading supplier of chemical-vapor-deposition (CVD) systems to semiconductor manufacturers, developing equipment that deposited layers of nonconducting dielectrics onto silicon wafers.

However, the road toward becoming a leading supplier of CVD systems was a difficult one, draining Watkins-Johnson's sales volume. When Kennedy was named president in 1988, the company derived 90 percent of its $280 million in revenues from defense-related products, a percentage that would decline as the company slowly shifted its focus toward the computer chip market and defense spending began declining. Exacerbating Watkins-Johnson's woes during its signal transition was the onset of a nationwide economic recession during the early 1990s, forcing the company to reduce its work force from 3,200 to 2,400 and to close a plant in North Carolina in 1991.

Recovery was on the way by 1993, however, bolstering the company's position as it intensified its efforts to shed its image as a defense contractor. In April 1993, as part of its plan to more aggressively pursue commercial business, Watkins-Johnson renamed its two divisions, giving its Defense Group the new title Electronics Group and changing the name of its Commercial Group to Semiconductor Equipment Group.

By the mid-1990s, the efforts invested in developing new markets for the company were beginning to pay large dividends. The demand for CVD equipment was skyrocketing, propelled by the enormous growth of the computer industry since Kennedy began deepening the company's involvement in the chip market in 1988. Watkins-Johnson's semiconductor equipment sales were up 50 percent in 1995, contributing $220 million in annual sales, or 60 percent of the company total volume. Although the company's semiconductor equipment group represented its main business during the mid-1990s, ranking as the third-largest producer of CVD systems in the world, Watkins-Johnson was not abandoning defense electronics entirely. Instead, the company was adapting its military signal-processing expertise to wireless communications equipment and still taking on defense work, including a $16 million Hughes Aircraft Co. contract awarded in October 1995 for part of the Advanced Medium Range Air-to-Air Missile's radar system.

As Watkins-Johnson charted its course for the late 1990s and the 21st century, the company was constructing many of its future plans around its fast-growing semiconductor equipment business. In May 1995, the company sold its microwave elec-

tronics unit to Condor Systems Inc., freeing up manufacturing space at its San Jose facility for semiconductor equipment production. Further strengthening of its involvement in the computer ship business was expected during the late 1990s, as Watkins-Johnson focused its efforts on developing a dominant position in a market that promised substantial growth for the company in the future.

Principal Subsidiaries

Watkins-Johnson Associates; Watkins-Johnson FSC; Watkins-Johnson International; Watkins-Johnson International Japan, K.K.; Watkins-Johnson International Korea, Ltd.; Watkins-Johnson International Singapore Pte., Ltd.; Watkins-Johnson International Taiwan; Watkins-Johnson Italiana, S.p.A.; Watkins-Johnson Limited; Watkins-Johnson (UK) Limited.

Principal Operating Units

Semiconductor Equipment Group; Electronic Group.

Further Reading

"Chipmaker's Maker," *Forbes*, February 27, 1995, p. 162.

"A Defense Stock with Firepower," *Business Week*, January 11, 1988, p. 64.

Hayes, Mary, "No More Checks for Namesake Founders of Watkins-Johnson," *San Francisco Business Times*, April 8, 1994, p. 8.

Jaffe, Thomas, "Surviving the Crunch," *Forbes*, May 27, 1991, p. 379.

Jones, John A., "Watkins-Johnson Shifts to Hot Semiconductor Equipment," *Investor's Business Daily*, October 2, 1995, p. 12.

Matsumoto, Craig, "Chip Equipment Group Powering Growth at Watkins-Johnson Co." *The Business Journal*, January 15, 1996, p. 3.

McFadden, Michael, "Betting on the Military's Hot Weapon: Electronics," *Fortune*, April 28, 1986, p. 248.

Rejent, Cass, "Watkins-Johnson Company," *Wall Street Transcript*, September 16, 1968, p. 14,347.

Watkins, Dean A., "Watkins-Johnson Company," *Wall Street Transcript*," January 31, 1980, p. 57,090.

——, "Watkins-Johnson Company," *Wall Street Transcript*, March 1, 1976, p. 43,030.

——, "Watkins-Johnson Company," *Wall Street Transcript*, December 1, 1969, p. 18,752.

Wrubel, Robert, "Buyout Candidate Watkins-Johnson," *Financial World*, November 3, 1987, p. 12.

—Jeffrey L. Covell

weis*Markets*

Weis Markets, Inc.

1000 South Second Street
Sunbury, Pennsylvania 17108
U.S.A.
(717) 286-4571
Fax: (717) 286-3692

Public Company
Incorporated: 1924
Employees: 16,500
Sales: $1.56 billion
Stock Exchanges: New York
SICs: 5411 Grocery Store Chain

Weis Markets, Inc. is one of the oldest and most profitable supermarket companies in the eastern United States. Based in Sunbury, Pennsylvania, the company operates 150 stores in six states. Widely diversified, Weis owns and operates its own dairy, ice cream, and meat processing plants, its own fleet of trucks, and much of its own real estate, as well as Weis Food Service, a restaurant and institutional food supplier based in Northumberland, Pennsylvania. In addition, in 1993 Weis purchased an 80 percent share of SuperPetz, a pet supply company with 14 stores, with the expectation that the number would double by 1997. Fiscally conservative, yet innovative, and with a reputation for creatively exploiting new market trends, Weis Markets prospered, often ranking number one in profitability among U.S. supermarket chains in the mid-1990s.

The 122-year-old Weis dynasty began with a German immigrant named Sigfried Weis, who arrived in New York on March 16, 1867. Records show that Sigfried filed a petition for naturalization in 1874. Although it is not certain how this Weis patriarch supported himself during his first years in America, he eventually settled in Selinsgrove, Pennsylvania, where, according to an obituary citation in the Snyder County *Tribune,* he opened a small "notions and fancy goods" store that would eventually grow into the largest "mercantile emporium" in the county.

Sigfried Weis had two sons—Harry and Sigmund—both of whom attended Susquehanna University. In 1904, Sigfried's sons became his business partners. However, Harry and Sigmund were not as enchanted with the general store business and soon became interested in branching into other areas. In 1912, they opened their first grocery store—Weis Pure Foods—in Sunbury. By the time they opened a second store in 1915, their father's general store business had ceased operations. During the prosperous decade of the 1920s, the brothers opened more and more stores until, by 1933, they were operating 115 stores in 15 mid-state counties.

Grocery stores all over the country had by this time transformed from largely credit-based operations into cash-and-carry stores. This change, and others, were not always welcome. Initially, self-service supermarkets were not popular with American customers who were accustomed to corner groceries where they were waited on by clerks. But by the Depression, patrons were anxious for ways to save money, and self-service markets began to gain momentum. As the business changed, the brothers' roles became more proscribed, with Harry doing much of the work of setting up new stores, while Sigmund handled the grocery purchasing.

The two brothers in turn had sons—Sigfried and Robert—who each worked part-time in the Sunbury stores during the 1920s and 1930s. The cousins were both graduated from Yale University and served as officers in the armed forces during World War II. Upon returning to Sunbury, Sigfried and Robert Weis joined the family business. In the 1950s and 1960s, Weis Markets moved out of its traditional territory with new market regions in York and Lancaster. By 1965, when the company went public, the business was profitable enough to make millionaires of the Weis family. Expansion continued in the 1970s and 1980s with new targeted growth areas in Maryland, New York, Virginia, West Virginia, and New Jersey.

Fiscally conservative, the company had the remarkable advantage of being able to finance its growth internally, while remaining debt-free. But Weis received some criticism from outside investors who were discouraged by the slow rate of growth, which in turn contributed to the lack of progress in the company's stock price. The tendency of the company to only make acquisitions that paid for themselves in three to five years was considered by some an impediment to Weis' growth progress. The company was also criticized by some for its resistance to unions and for hiring mostly part-time workers.

In January 1995, Sigfried Weis retired as co-chairman due to health problems but remained as chairman emeritus until his death in June 1995. Robert F. Weis took on the positions of chairman and treasurer, while Norman S. Rich, formerly director of the company's quality control division, was named president. In September 1995, Les Knox was named vice-president of merchandising, a newly created position. Jonathan Weis, son of Robert, also began working at the company in the early 1990s. Groomed to eventually take over the business, Jonathan started out working in the real-estate end of the business.

In the early 1990s, Weis embarked on the most ambitious growth program in its 83-year history. This growth revolved around four major areas: acquisitions, expansion, merchandising/marketing strategies, and new technology. In December 1993, Weis purchased 14 Mr. Z's stores (IGAs at the time), eventually adding five more. This acquisition greatly expanded Weis' market in the northeastern region of Pennsylvania, including the popular Pocono Mountain area, and provided a strong base for expansion into New Jersey. Market analysts estimated that the former IGA stores would bring in an additional $100 million annually. In August 1994, Weis purchased King's Supermarkets, a six-unit operator based in Hamburg, Pennsylvania, with stores in the Allentown/Lehigh Valley region. In addition, Weis opened three Scott's Low-Cost outlets. The impulse behind this acquisition was to protect market share. Regarded by Weis as a good test format for the EDLP ("Everyday-Low-Price") strategy, these stores had a different configuration with less service than traditional retail stores, and were evaluated on an as-needed basis. Finally, at the end of 1993, Weis obtained 80 percent ownership of SuperPetz, a four-unit pet supply store. This acquisition in particular revealed Weis' pattern of taking an emerging trend and making it profitable. Under Weis ownership, the pet superstore format thrived, growing to 30 stores, with an expectation of doubling its units by 1997.

This program was in part a response to company performance during this time. After many years of uninterrupted growth, earnings had begun to dip in the early 1990s, with sales down in 1991 and 1992. Causes cited for this decline included deflationary market conditions, the rise in Pennsylvania's corporate net income tax, and increasing outside competition, which caused the company to lower prices and increase advertising expenditures. But by 1993, however, sales were up by 11.8 percent for the year, due in large part to Weis' purchase of 14 IGA Food Mart stores in the Pocono mountains. These 14 stores added an estimated $42 million to Weis' annual volume.

Same-store sales for 1993 remained low, however, due to strong competition, the absence of price increases at the retail level, and growing pains resulting from the added volume of 14 new stores and store opening expenses. Weis had also opened its first New Jersey store on the first day of the third quarter in 1993. In 1994, Weis had a record $1.55 billion in sales, an increase of eight percent over the year before. Earnings increased by 4.5 percent to $76.2 million. After the first three quarters of 1995, the company was reporting a sales increase of 8.2 percent and a net earnings increase of five percent. Three existing stores were remodeled and seven new stores were under construction. In addition, SuperPetz opened six new stores during the second quarter of 1995. Weis increased its supermarket expansion efforts as well, with 21 new stores and 16 major remodels.

Due to increased competition and encouraging preliminary feedback from initial expansion and enlargement efforts, Weis Markets began a deliberate effort to expand into new market territories, especially in Pennsylvania, Maryland, and New Jersey, where it already operated 150 stores. An April 17, 1995 article in *Supermarket News* indicated that Weis Markets had pledged $105 million in capital expenditure to cover opening eight or nine new stores and remodeling or enlarging an additional ten. These new stores were built in Weis' new "superstore" format, which emphasized customer service, prepared foods, and in many cases utilized Weis' EDLP approach. Later that same year, *Supermarket News* described Weis' plans to open stores in Laurel and Havre de Grace, Maryland, as well as in Lebanon, Mechanicsburg, Wellsboro, Gap, Altoona, and East Stroudsburg, Pennsylvania. Plans for another four to six undisclosed new locations and eight to 12 expansions were also under way. Although financing for the capital expenditures came from company funds, Weis maintained its "no-debt" status. (In 1995, it was estimated that Weis had nearly $457 million in cash and marketable securities, more than half of its $892 million in total assets.)

Primarily interested in growth contiguous to existing markets, Weis traditionally located stores within a day's round-trip time of its distribution facilities. To pave the way for expansion, the company often bought store sites where residential development was slated to occur, then held onto those sites, for as long as five years in some cases, in order to see what transpired in the area demographically.

In Pennsylvania, Weis considered itself a market leader, although it faced heavy competition from Giant Food Stores, a Carlisle-based chain. A June 25, 1995 *Harrisburg Patriot-News* article reported that Giant had another strong year, putting it within one percentage point and spitting distance of Weis. On a per-store basis, Giant had outpaced Weis by $18.4 million per store compared to Weis' $12.1 million per store. Together, Giant and Weis accounted for more than half of central Pennsylvania's supermarket business. While Giant's strategy seemed to emphasize new or replacement sites, Weis focused instead on modernization and remodeling of what it already owned. The slow pace of Weis' expansion, especially relative to its incredible cash reserves, stemmed in part from the fact that the population in many of the company's markets wasn't growing and that each new grocery store required a lot of time and effort to launch successfully. In addition, it took longer to obtain construction approvals. Giant's momentum in 1995 seemed to indicate, however, that it would surpass Weis in sales volume in central Pennsylvania for that year.

Through the years, the Weis family demonstrated a knack for monopolizing on emerging trends, from cash-only stores in the early 1900s to self-service shopping during the Depression. One old, but consistently viable, profit-building strategy they exploited to good end was private labeling. Sigmund and Harry Weis first started selling private-label products in the 1920s. They roasted their own coffee, produced their own mayonnaise and salad dressings, and started a line of canned goods. By the mid-1990s, Weis was offering more than 2,000 products, ranging from frozen vegetables to breakfast cereals, and accounting for nearly 25 percent of its total sales volume. Paper tags were posted beside the items, noting the price differences between Weis brands and brand-name items. Private labeling accomplished three things for Weis: it created a low-price image for the chain without hurting its margins; it convinced customers that they could buy products at Weis that they couldn't get anywhere else; and it ultimately bolstered the bottom line. The company had a premium brand (Weis Choice); a national brand equivalent (Weis Quality); and an economy brand (Big Top). This cornerstone of Weis' merchandising program was integral to maintaining its competitive edge, but the company made a deliberate effort not to compromise on quality, establishing a quality-control lab in 1964 to test products manufactured for them.

In the mid-1990s, Weis became much more aggressive in its price-comparison advertising, responding to the increasingly heated regional competition with lower prices and strong promotional activity. Whereas before Weis had confined price comparison to internal merchandising, in 1995, partly in response to an aggressive television and radio campaign initiated by Giant Food Stores that targeted Wal-mart, Weis began directing its price comparison advertising outside the store in hopes of remaining competitive in the tough central Pennsylvania region and to pump up its northeastern market.

A second Weis strategy was to shore up its one-stop shopping program. In addition to the traditional bakery, deli, and pharmacy, Weis made a concerted effort to get more and more banks into the stores, and introduced floral shops and natural food centers to its units. Non-traditional items such as greeting cards, books, and take-out foods, ranging from rotisserie chicken to cappuccino, were introduced with the goal of capturing a much greater percentage of customer business.

In 1995, Weis introduced a direct store delivery program that was implemented chain-wide. This meant that 25 to 30 percent of all grocery products were delivered directly to individual units, leading to significant cost savings. Other technological additions included the installation of VISION, an electronic marketing and financial services program, in 1992. Eventually phased out, VISION was replaced with ACT-MEDIA, an in-store coupon dispenser located where products were sold, and the CATALINA system, a coupon dispensing system that provided coupons at point-of-sale.

Weis' Lewisburg, Pennsylvania, store, which opened in 1995, could serve as the blueprint for Weis' new store format, which included some 3,000 additional stock-keeping units. New store features included a bakery showcasing Weis' first bagel program, capable of producing 12 different kinds of bagels. The new deli, three times larger than traditional Weis delis, included a hot pizza program and cappuccino/espresso service. The produce section offered organic fruits and vegetables, and all departments were enlarged to allow for greater selection and variety.

A sizable health foods area, an ethnic foods area, and an extensive ice cream department, much of the ice cream manufactured by Weis itself, lent the store a distinctive, more promotionally savvy look. The new format reflects the overriding philosophy that has characterized Weis Markets over the years—conservative adaptability. In the words of Jonathan Weis, the fourth generation of Weises to lead the company, as quoted in the *Harrisburg Patriot News*: "I think our fundamentals would do well to stay the same. But we're always changing."

Principal Subsidiaries

Albany Public Markets, Inc.; Dutch Valley Food Co., Inc.; Martin's Farm Market, Inc.; Shamrock Wholesale Distributors Inc.; Weis Food Service; Mr. Z's Supermarkets, Inc.; King's Supermarkets, Inc.; SuperPetz (80%).

Further Reading

Beres, Glen A., "Growing Weis," *Supermarket News*, November 6, 1995, p. 1.

Croghan, Lore, "What the Hare Told the Tortoise," *Financial World*, April 25, 1995, p. 33.

DeKok, David, "The Weis Dynasty," *Harrisburg Patriot-News*, February 20, 1994, p. F1.

Elson, Joel, "Weis Markets to Open 4th Scott's Low Cost," *Supermarket News*, May 10, 1993, p. 48.

Nayyar, Seema, "Ralston Unit Alienates Retailers," *Brandweek*, August 10, 1992, p. 1.

"Net Income, Volume Rise at Weis Markets," *Supermarket News*, August 14, 1995, p. 9.

Redman, Russell, "ShopRite, Insalaco Targeted By Weis' Price Comparisons," *Supermarket News*, September 18, 1995, p. 36.

"Sales, Net Rise at Weis in Quarter," *Supermarket News*, April 25, 1994, p. 4.

Saxton, Lisa, "Weis, Superpetz Link Stirs Industry Interest," *Supermarket News*, May 30, 1994, p. 29.

Southall, Brooke, "Giant and Weis Together Dominate Local Market, *Central Penn Business Journal*, June 23, 1995, p. 3.

Tibbitts, Lisa A., "Weis Sets $105 Million Outlay," *Supermarket News*, April 17, 1995, p. 5.

Tosh, Mark, "Weis Buys 14 Pennsylvania IGAs," *Supermarket News*, January 11, 1993, p. 4.

Weigel, George, "Supermarket Sweepstakes: Giant Poised to Take Over No. 1 Spot," *Harrisburg Patriot-News*, June 25, 1995, p. D1.

"Weis Earnings Decline 7% in 1991," *Supermarket News*, March 2, 1992, p. 13.

"Weis Markets Adds VP Slot," *Supermarket News*, September 11, 1995, p. 6.

"Weis Markets Profits, Sales Up," *Supermarket News*, March 20, 1995, p. 12.

"Weis Profit, Sales Increase," *Supermarket News*, May 15, 1995, p. 8.

"Weis to Install Vision Terminal, *Supermarket News*, November 2, 1992, p. 17.

"Weis to Purchase Independent," *Supermarket News*, June 27, 1994, p. 50.

Zwiebach, Elliot, "Weis Sales, Earnings Down in Quarter, Year," *Supermarket News*, February 15, 1993, p.8.

——, "Weis to Construct 10 New Stores," *Supermarket News*, April 25, 1994, p. 4.

—Lynda D. Schrecengost

Western Company of North America

P.O. Box 56006
Houston, Texas 77256
U.S.A.
(713) 629-2600
Fax: (713) 629-2720

Wholly Owned Subsidiary of BJ Services, Inc.
Incorporated: 1939
Employees: 2,616
Sales: $350 million
Stock Exchanges: New York
SICs: 1389 Oil & Gas Field Services; 1381 Drilling Oil
& Gas Wells

The Western Company of North America is one of the most prominent and innovative companies in the oil and gas services industry. During the late 1930s and throughout the 1940s, the firm was one of the pioneers of the "acidizing process," a method of improving the flow from gas and oil wells. The company is divided into three separate divisions: Western Petroleum Services, which provides gas and oil well acidizing, fracturing, and cementing services; Petroleum Services International Company, which provides equipment, construction, and management and engineering services to natural resource companies around the globe; and Western Oceanic, Inc., which provides offshore drilling services to oil companies on a contractual basis. Although Western Company of North America has always been in financial good health, its acquisition by BJ Services, another prominent firm in oil and gas services, indicates a growing tend toward consolidation within the industry.

Western Company of North America was founded by Eddie Chiles. Born in Itasca, Oklahoma, Chiles graduated from the University of Oklahoma School of Engineering in 1934 and went to work for the Reed Roller Bit Company located in Houston, Texas. Chiles sold rotary bits to companies that drilled for oil. After a five-year stint at Reed, however, Chiles had amassed enough information to start his own company, so he traveled to the Permian Basin in West Texas and, with his partner, Bob Wood, established a new firm. Chiles and Wood were convinced their company would be successful for four important reasons: 1) the nascent conservation movement in the 1930s, strongly supported by the federal government, emphasized the recovery of oil and gas by acidizing, gas injection, and water flooding, new and highly experimental methods which were the center of research at many engineering schools across the U.S.; 2) from his previous work experience Chiles believed that he knew exactly where oil and gas services were needed; 3) the new method of acidizing was rapidly replacing nitroglycerine as the preferred way to improve the gas and oil flow of wells; and 4) the most important oil boom since the one located in East Texas was just beginning.

Situating their business in Seagraves, Gaines County, Texas, the two partners owned one automobile, purchased an acid pump truck, rented office space in an old building and an acid storage tank near the Santa Fe railroad yards, and had run up a debt of approximately $10,000. Chiles served as salesman, district manager, and service engineer while Wood took care of all the company's administrative and financial responsibilities. The first contract was arranged with the Aloco Oil Company in 1939, and soon the new venture was servicing numerous oil and gas wells in the Permian Basin.

Chiles and Wood were pacesetters within the oil and gas services industry through their use of engineered acidizing. The acidizing process is one in which hydrochloric acid is used to dissolve limestone and dolomite rock with extremely low permeability. The fields throughout the Permian Basin in Southeast New Mexico and West Texas were crowded with these hard rock formations, and the acidizing process was more effective than the old method of using nitroglycerine to improve the flow of oil and gas wells. In addition, the acidizing process was much less expensive than purchasing nitroglycerine. By 1948, the company had zoned and treated over 4,500 liquid petroleum and natural gas wells in the Permian Basin region. In order to develop even more efficient acidizing processes, Western Company constructed a geological, engineering and chemical research facility in Midland, Texas. By the end of the 1940s, the firm was garnering a well-deserved reputation for setting records in providing services for its customers in the Permian

Basin. One such record was the 30,000-gallon treatment of the Ellenburger formation at a depth of approximately 9,000 feet. From a small local operation in 1939, Western Company of North America had developed into one of the leaders in the gas and oil services industry.

Beginning with the 1950s, the firm implemented an expansion policy that lasted for nearly three decades. At first Western Company expanded its services to companies working in the Anadarko Basin of Kansas, Oklahoma, and Texas, and also started providing its services to firms operating in the Texas-Louisiana Gulf Coast as well as other Mid-Continental regions. These services included such new methods as hydraulic fracturing and cementing. By 1959, the company had grown so large that a new headquarters building was constructed in Fort Worth, Texas. To Chiles and Wood, this move signified Western Company's growth from a regional firm to a national business. However, the boom days of the East Texas and West Texas oilfields were almost at an end. Although there were still significant amounts of fossil fuel to be recovered in those areas, oil and gas were getting harder to find and harder to extricate. Consequently, the exploration and drilling processes were growing more and more expensive. The major oil companies in the United States began to shift their operations to fields in the Middle East, where crude oil was cheaper. Both Chiles and Wood had foreseen the coming of declining markets in America, and began searching for new areas of growth and development.

Along with the search for new markets, the company also implemented a new management system that Chiles and Wood dubbed "Management By Objectives." This new style of management included a goal-oriented management strategy that demanded the participation of executives at all levels of the firm's operations. The most important part of the management by objectives approach was the concentration on providing services exclusively for gas and oil well drilling. Chiles and Wood both hoped that their new management philosophy would form the cornerstone for future expansion and for the acquisition and development of capital resources.

By the mid-1960s, the new management style was beginning to pay huge dividends. Western Company had developed a reputation as the leader in acid stimulation design for oil and gas wells deeper than 20,000 feet. During this period of time, the company enhanced its image through a unique advertising campaign combining both wit and credibility. One of the television advertisements for the company included the tagline, "If you don't have an oil well, get one—you'll love doing business with Western." The new management style and advertising campaign resulted in additional expansion, especially in the areas of offshore contract drilling. In order to continue funding their expansion activities, Chiles and Wood decided to take the Western Company public in 1968, and made its initial offering on the New York Stock Exchange.

With the coming of the OPEC oil embargo in 1973, the entire situation within the American oil industry changed dramatically overnight. As the price of crude oil skyrocketed from an all-time low of $4.00 per barrel to a high of $40.00 per barrel, the American federal government, including both the White House and Congress, called for reducing the country's dependence on foreign-produced crude oil. Immediately, the domestic oil producing industry began a process of rebuilding. Western Company was well prepared for this opportunity, and offered more extensive services than most of the other American oil and gas companies. In 1974, the company built the *Western Pacesetter III*, a oil drilling rig in the gulf of Mexico. This was followed by two more drilling rigs, the *Western Triton III* and the *Alaskan Star*, also in the Gulf of Mexico, in 1976 and 1979 respectively. The *Western Pacesetter IV*, another oil drilling rig, was built in the North Sea.

By 1981, the United States had increased the number of oil rigs from a low of 975 when the oil embargo began to a high of 4,530 in December of that year. Western Company was one of the American firms that contributed significantly to that increased figure. In New Mexico, Texas, Louisiana, Mississippi, Oklahoma, and Wyoming, the company was providing improved services to ever-deeper oil and gas wells. Soon Western Company had grown to over $1 billion worth of assets, with operations in twenty states across America, and with 17 offshore drilling rigs located around the world.

The technical achievements of Western Company during this time were impressive. The company set numerous records in many areas, including: cementing 15,500 sacks, of 20-inch casings, at 8,930 feet for a well in Atchafalaya, Louisiana; hydraulic fracturing of 3.39 million pounds of sand at 11,000 feet for a well located in Harrison County, Texas; and acidizing 330,000 gallons at pumping pressures of 10,000 pounds pressure per square inch at 22,112 feet for a well situated in the Ellenburger formation in Terrell County, Texas. With its fleet of five semi-submersible oil drilling rigs and 12 jack-up oil rigs, the company was well prepared to operate wells at depths of 25,000 feet in more than 300 feet of water.

The resurgence of the oil drilling industry did not last long, however. By 1985, oil and gas drilling service companies across the United States were virtually in tatters. The bottom fell out of the market with the perception that the OPEC oil embargo had spent its course, and drilling for oil soon afterwards hit its lowest level of domestic activity in almost 40 years. There was an oil glut, and profits across the entire industry began to plummet. Western Company, still under the direction of Eddie Chiles, began to sell its assets and close down operations. In 1986, the company closed 7 out of a total of 41 on-shore service locations, and by the end of the year only 6 out of a total of 17 offshore drilling rigs remained in operation. During the same year, Western Company, short of cash and without the prospect of a rosy future, defaulted on over $550 million of its debts.

The attempted liquidation of Western Company of North America wasn't entirely successful, and the company muddled through the late 1980s. Morgan Guaranty Trust Company, one of the firm's bankers, put three of Western Company's rigs up for sale. Located in the North Sea, they seemed ideal for a larger, more financially stable company in the oil and gas servicing industry to snatch up. But Morgan only received one offer, and that only amounted to two-thirds of the $120 million Western Company owed on the rigs. Other attempts to sell the company's assets, including such items as trucks, fared no better. At one auction the trucks only garnered 20 to 30 cents on the dollar. Although it was no consolation, bigger companies like Schlumberger Ltd. and Haliburton Co. were also experiencing tough times.

Adding to Chiles' problems was his ownership of the Texas Rangers baseball team. In 1986, the Rangers had already posted a consecutive losing streak of 13 seasons, and trying to rebuild the team was beginning to drain the Chiles family coffers. In 1985, the team lost $4 million, and it was projected to lose even more over the next season since Chiles didn't have the money to make the team a winner. In fact, Chiles' own stake in Western Company's stock had dropped enormously. From a high of over $350 million in 1981, when Western Company was at the peak of its success, the worth of Chiles' holdings declined to just $12 million by the end of 1986. Each share of Western Company stock was worth only one dollar.

By the early 1990s, Chiles was gone and Western Company of North America had new management. No longer a family enterprise, the new leadership was concerned solely with whether or not the firm could remain a financially viable enterprise in the depressed oil and gas services industry. Based on the potential for new customers in the North Sea, the company made a huge financial commitment to design and built a number of stimulation vessels, high-technology boats that provide services such as acidizing and fracturing. Although there were construction delays and cost overruns for the stimulation vessels, once they were fully operational they began to bring in significant numbers of customers in the North Sea region. Soon the company reported that approximately 75 percent of all its revenues were due to the activities of its stimulation vessels.

Having stabilized the financial condition of the company, management then decided to build upon its services. As a result, Betz Energy Chemicals was purchased from Betz Laboratories in 1994. The sale included everything from technology to product inventory in the field of specialty chemicals for oil and gas production. With the oil and gas services industry still plagued by a glutted market and too many companies in competition with each other, Western Company was caught up in the consolidation trend that hit during the mid-1990s. BJ Services Company, a leading supplier of pressure pumping services in the oil and gas industry, offered to purchase and merge its operations with Western Company. At first, management at Western Company rejected the offer, but finally accepted a sweetened deal for $500 million. BJ Services and Western Company planned to combine all their oil and gas service operations, and by the middle of 1995 the restructuring was well under way.

The combined resources of Western Company of North America and BJ Services should create a potent and strong oil and gas services firm. Both companies have created their niche within the industry and hope to develop new services to customers around the world. Once the oil and gas services market revives, which many Wall Street analysts expect in the not-too-distant future, Western Company and BJ Services will be prepared to take advantage of the opportunities.

Principal Subsidiaries

Western Oceanic Inc.; Western Oceanic Service, Inc.; Western Petroleum Services International Co.

Further Reading

Alger, Alexandra, "Back In The Game," *Forbes,* November 21, 1994, p. 21.

"An Oil-Services Gamble That Isn't Paying Off," *Business Week,* November 29, 1982, p. 40.

"Betz Laboratories Completes Sale Of Oil-Field Chemicals," *Chemical & Engineering News,* July 11, 1994, p. 18.

"BJ Services In Merger Deal," *New York Times,* November 18, 1994, p.D5.

Chiles, Eddie, *The Western Company Of North America,* Newcomen Society: New York, 1984.

"Icahn Group Raises Stake In Western To 8.1%," *New York Times,* November 17, 1994, p. D4.

Mason, Todd, "For Eddie Chiles, Oil And Baseball No Longer Mix," *Business Week,* July 21, 1986, p. 72.

Ritter, Scott, "U.S. Energy Sector Has Hit A Gusher Of Consolidations," *The Wall Street Journal,* December 29, 1994, p. B4.

Walsh, Campion, "Activity In Gulf Lures Stimulation Vessel From U.K. North Seas," *The Oil Daily,* July 7, 1994, p. 3.

"Western Buys Betz Chemicals," *The Oil Daily,* July 5, 1994, p. 5.

—Thomas Derdak

ШmS GAMING INC.

WMS Industries, Inc.

3401 N. California Avenue
Chicago, Illinois 60618
U.S.A.
(312) 728-2300
Fax: (312) 267-3747

Public Company
Incorporated: 1946 as Williams Manufacturing Company
Employees: 3,000
Sales: $385.37 million (1995)
Stock Exchanges: New York
SICs: 3999 Manufacturing Industries, Not Elsewhere Classified; 3944 Games, Toys & Children's Vehicles; 7011 Hotels & Motels

WMS Industries, Inc. is a worldwide leader in the design and manufacture of coin-operated entertainment machines. In addition to its line of pinball machines under the Williams, Midway, and Bally brand names, which together account for 70 percent of the world's pinball machine market, WMS produces video lottery terminal (VLT) machines, casino machines, and shuffle alley and other novelty games. Williams also maintains a strong presence in the video arcade and home video game markets, particularly with its best-selling Mortal Kombat series. Since 1994, WMS has held a long-term, worldwide license to produce and distribute arcade and home video games for Nintendo's 64-bit video system under a joint venture called Williams/Nintendo Inc. Headed by Louis and Neil Nicastro, who together hold more than 53 percent of the company's stock, WMS is also active in hotel and casino management, primarily in Puerto Rico. Sumner Redstone, head of Viacom, is a long-time stockholder, owning 24.6 percent of WMS through National Amusements, Inc. In its fiscal year ended June 1995, WMS reported revenues of more than $385 million, the largest part of which—$314.5 million—came through sales of its gaming machines and related products.

The modern pinball industry took off during the Depression era, and Harry Williams was one of the industry's first great game designers. In 1929, Williams graduated from Stanford University; five years later, his name was important enough to

be a selling point in advertisements. Working for Los Angeles-based Pacific Amusements Company, Williams designed the first electromechanical pinball machine in 1933. That game, called "Contact," featured two solenoid-powered contact holes, which gave points when the pinball landed in them. The solenoid quickly became an industry standard, used to operate a variety of features on the pinball playing field. "Contact" was also the first pinball machine to feature electrically generated sound when Williams attached a doorbell to the machine. These innovations created boom years for the entire industry through the Depression.

While working for Pacific Amusements, Williams also designed games for other pinball makers, including Bally and Rock-Ola in Chicago. Williams was responsible for several more important innovations, including the kicker, the pedestal tilt, and pendulum tilt mechanisms. For years, pinball had been largely a game of chance, as the player had little influence over the course the ball took. Williams' designs were among the first to introduce skill elements to the game. He was also instrumental in introducing the first replay feature, allowing the player to compete for extra balls and free games, rather than prizes. This would be important for the entire industry, as more and more communities and states outlawed pinball as a game of chance.

Williams moved to Chicago, the center of the coin-operated amusements industry, in 1936, and for the next several years designed games for Bally, Rock-Ola, and other pinball manufacturers. The Second World War came close to shutting down the pinball industry, however, as raw materials made it impossible to build new machines. The war would later prove important to the industry in another way, as American GIs brought pinball machines to other countries, opening an international market that at times rivaled the market in the United States. In 1941, Williams joined with Lyn Durant, a designer who had also worked for Bally and Exhibit, to form the United Manufacturing Company. Their business was almost wholly in reconditioning and redesigning old machines.

Williams left United at the end of the war and in 1946 founded the Williams Manufacturing Company in Chicago. The most significant moment of the pinball industry's history occurred the following year, when another company, Gottlieb, introduced the first pinball machines featuring flippers. This innovation allowed the player greater control of the ball, transforming the game at last from a game of chance to one of skill. Through its early history, pinball had been banned at various times virtually everywhere in the United States. (San Francisco was the only community that had never banned the game; pinball prohibitions remained in force until the late 1970s in many other communities, including New York City.) As a game of chance that offered prizes and cash rewards, early pinball also suffered from its link to gambling and organized crime.

Williams, joined by Sam Stern, a former operator and distributor of coin-op amusement machines, brought out his first flipper pinball machine—called "Sunny"—in 1947. The postwar boom in the American economy created a huge demand for new pinball machines, and with raw materials once again in ready supply, manufacturers were soon making and selling thousands of units of each model they created. During the 1950s and 1960s, pinball boomed, dominated by Gottlieb. For most of this time, Williams and Bally would vie for second place. This era also saw the rise of another Chicago company, soon to become important for the Williams company. In 1948, the Seeburg Corporation, begun in 1903 as a piano maker and through the 1930s and 1940s a competitor with Wurlitzer for the jukebox market, brought out the first jukebox offering 100 selections. By the end of the next decade, Seeburg's jukeboxes captured 70 percent of the jukebox market. Seeburg would retain its leading position for the next two decades.

Harry Williams retired back to California in 1959 and Sam Stern took over Williams Manufacturing. In the following year, Stern retooled the company's manufacturing facilities. By then, Seeburg, which had revenues of nearly $30 million in 1960, had started an aggressive expansion campaign beyond the jukebox market. In 1958, it entered the vending machine business, selling cigarettes, and in the early 1960s expanded its vending machine business to include cigars, soft drinks, hot coffee, soup, candy, milk, and laundry products. Seeburg also went into the home music field, selling transistorized musical equipment and home stereo equipment. Meanwhile, Seeburg continued to sell its 100- and now 200-selection jukeboxes, retaining its market lead. A series of acquisitions, coupled with new product development, helped raise Seeburg's revenues to $76 million by 1964. In May of that year, Seeburg acquired Williams Manufacturing, reorganizing it as the Williams Electronics Manufacturing division. Late in 1964, Williams Electronics acquired United Manufacturing, which, led by Lyn Durant, who did not like flippered pinball, manufactured other types of coin-op amusement games, such as shuffle alleys. Williams paid $1.2 million for United and Sam Stern remained as president of the Williams division.

Seeburg consolidated its six manufacturing facilities into a new one million-square-foot facility in Chicago in 1965. With its Qualitone division, Seeburg manufactured hearing aids, and the company also moved into background music systems, including extensive copyright holdings used in its own recordings. In addition to making electronic organs through its 1963 Kinsman Manufacturing Co. acquisition, in 1965 and 1966 Seeburg acquired three more companies to make it one of the largest musical instrument manufacturers in the country. These three were Kay Musical Instrument Co., which made guitars, basses, and cellos; Gulbransen Co., which made quality pianos and organs and featured a 1,100-dealer distribution network;

and N.H. White Co., which made band instruments under the King brand name. Revenues for 1965 reached $89 million, although profits dropped to absorb the costs of consolidating its manufacturing facilities. The following year, revenues jumped again to nearly $115 million. During this time, Louis Nicastro joined Seeburg as vice-president. By 1968, Nicastro had risen to become Seeburg's president. In that year, Seeburg was acquired by Commonwealth United Corp. of New York for $12 million.

Commonwealth, which produced films and television programs, had started up in 1967 with $6 million in revenues. From the start, Commonwealth launched a series of acquisitions, including Seeburg, that would raise its revenues to $155 million in its second year of operations. One year later, however, Commonwealth was in trouble, coming up short on cash for another acquisition. In 1969, Commonwealth lost some $60 million. Nicastro, who had joined Commonwealth's board but then returned to run Seeburg, became president and CEO of Commonwealth in 1970.

One year later, Nicastro spun off Commonwealth's main subsidiary, Seeburg, as Seeburg Industries, Inc. In that year, Commonwealth had posted a $1.6 million loss on sales of $54 million, while its Seeburg subsidiary had seen a $3.3 million profit on $53 million in sales. Under the reorganization plan, Nicastro, together with several partners, purchased Seeburg for $2.75 million, while assuming $9 million of Consolidated's debts of about $13 million. As Nicastro told *Business Week* at the time, "Nobody's delighted to accept any deal we propose. It's only the realization that the alternatives are worse." The spin-off was completed by 1973.

Nicastro moved Seeburg's headquarters to New York, where it would remain until 1990. By 1976, the new Seeburg's revenues had once again risen to more than $125 million. In 1977, Seeburg was renamed Xcor International. At this time, the pinball industry was undergoing a revolution of sorts with the introduction of the first solid-state pinball machines. Featuring far more exciting play than electromechanical machines, solid state quickly became the industry standard, and by 1977, Williams Electronics followed industry-leader Bally—which grabbed 70 percent of the then-$75-million market—and converted all of its machines to the new technology. By 1980, Williams was selling more than 60,000 pinball machines per year. However, while Williams remained profitable, it was not enough to prevent Xcor losses of $1.5 million in 1977. Revenues dropped through the next year, although Xcor managed to record a $5 million profit. But in 1979, Xcor once again posted a loss, now of $2.5 million. In that year, Xcor faced a $33 million debt with only $1.8 million in shareholder equity. Meanwhile, a new revolution was looming: the video arcade.

Begun with "Pong" in the early 1970s, video arcade games grew to a $70 million market by 1977. Its boom years, however, were shortly to follow. In 1979, Bally brought out the industry's first great hit, "Space Invaders," which was soon followed by Atari's "Asteroids." By 1981, the video arcade market would grow to $650 million. The boom would be too late to salvage Xcor, however. The Seeburg division declared Chapter 11 bankruptcy in 1979. And in 1980, Nicastro moved again to spin off his most profitable subsidiary, now Williams Electronics, which acquired about $18 million of Xcor's debt. Nicastro remained as chairman and CEO of both Williams and Xcor.

Williams went public, selling 5 million shares at $12.25 per share; its shareholders, including Gulf & Western, kept 4 million shares. Nicastro also attempted to enter the burgeoning Atlantic City casino business by buying the Sands Hotel, but was rebuffed. Instead, Williams looked to Puerto Rico, purchasing a controlling interest in a new hotel-casino complex there. Xcor quickly faded from view, posting losses of $3.9 million on revenues of nearly $24 million in 1982.

Meanwhile, business boomed for Williams. While the video arcade business hurt pinball sales for most manufacturers, Williams' pinball sales actually grew, to $80 million in 1981, giving it the industry lead for the first time. But most important to Williams was its first entry into the video arcade. Its game, "Defender," introduced in 1981, was a smash success, becoming one of the top-selling arcade games of the time, with 50,000 machines ordered in its first year alone. Williams revenues soared to $150 million in 1981—some $110 million of which came from sales of Defender. By then the coin-op industry had grown to a $4 billion market. To accommodate demand for its video arcade machines, Williams scaled back pinball production, to as low as 2,300 machines in 1983. Nevertheless, Williams machines continued to top pinball sales, with five of the top nine selling machines in the early 1980s.

By the summer of 1982, however, the video market slowed. Despite the successes of such games as "Pac Man," "Galaxian," "Space Invaders," "Defender," and "Asteroids," the industry was unable to come up with strong followup games. The recession of the early 1990s also contributed to the slowing sales of video arcade machines. Williams attempted to introduce a pinball-video hybrid, called "Hyperball," which largely failed. Its sales began to dry up, dropping to $136 million in 1982. But the following year, the bottom fell out of the video market. Revenues from its amusement games fell by $65 million. Williams was unable to take up the slack with pinball sales. Despite about $39 million in revenues added by its hotel-casinos, Williams lost $14 million on revenues of $57.5 million in 1984. Williams stock, which had risen to $29 per share three years earlier, fell to $2 per share.

Losses continued through the next year. But by 1986, Williams' fortunes had turned again. Renewed interest in pinball, and successes with new pinball machines such as "Comet" and "Space Shuttle," set up the Williams 1986 introduction of one of the great pinball machines of all time, "High Speed," which posted initial orders of more than 7,500 machines. Williams casino holdings continued to do well, with its Condado Plaza in San Juan, Puerto Rico adding $11 million in revenues and operating profits of almost $4 million, bringing Williams a 1986 net profit of $3 million on revenues of $105 million.

Williams acquired Bally Manufacturing Co.'s pinball and video arcade game unit in 1988 for $8 million, giving Williams an 80 percent share of the pinball market, which in turn had grown to account for more than 20 percent of the $5 billion coin-op game industry. Under the Williams, Bally, and Midway names, Williams pinball production grew to about 35,000 by the turn of the decade; approximately 48 percent of its machines were now being shipped overseas. The company was renamed WMS in 1988, as its casino holdings grew to provide more than 40 percent of company revenues. Two years later, the company

moved back to Chicago to be closer to its core gaming division. It also doubled its research and development (R&D) spending, to about $1.5 million per game, a move that would prove crucial to its success in the coming years.

In the 1990s, WMS moved into the home video game market, granting an exclusive licensing contract to Acclaim. Despite the success of WMS-designed titles such as "Mortal Kombat" and "NBA Jam," WMS licensing fees were meager compared to the earnings enjoyed by Acclaim. When that contract ended in 1995, WMS—which had acquired Tradewest Inc. and related companies for $15 million in 1994—began to market its video games through its newly formed Williams Entertainment Inc. subsidiary. In 1995, WMS also entered a joint venture with Nintendo of America Inc. as the exclusive creator and distributor of games for that company's new 64-bit video game system. The 1995 release of "Mortal Kombat 3" sold 250,000 copies in its first three days, bringing in around $15 million in just one weekend.

WMS next entered the VLT market in 1992, and soon after began producing casino gaming machines for the exploding casino industry. By 1995, WMS was licensed to manufacture and distribute its casino machines in 12 states, including Nevada and New Jersey, as well as in Australia and Canada, and its casino games had grown to an estimated $26 million in revenues. In that year, overall revenues jumped to $385 million, with sales in 1996 projected to reach $550 million. WMS faced a setback in late 1995 when it failed in an attempt to acquire Bally Gaming International, losing out to Las Vegas-based Alliance Gaming Corp.'s hostile takeover bid. Nevertheless, the company's troubled past seemed far behind it, and WMS's future in casino gaming machines appeared strong. As Neil Nicastro, company president and son of Louis Nicastro, told the *Chicago Tribune*: "[There] is not much we haven't ended up leading after entering."

Principal Subsidiaries

Williams Electronics Games, Inc.; Midway Manufacturing Company; Williams Innovative Technologies, Inc.; Lenc-Smith Inc.; WMS Games Parts & Service, Inc.; Williams Entertainment Inc.; WMS Gaming Inc.; Posadas de Puerto Rico Associates, Incorporated (Hotel and Casino operations); Williams Hospitality Group, Inc.

Further Reading

Barnfather, Maurice, "Tilt?" *Forbes*, March 2, 1981, p. 42.
Byrne, Harlan S., "The Mystery of Williams Electronics," *Barron's*, April 7, 1986, p. 30.
Franklin, Stephen, "Pinball Power Puts Money into the Slots," *Chicago Tribune*, May 9, 1994, p. B9.
Mehlman, William, "Williams Seen Benefiting From Video Game Shakeout," *The Insiders' Chronicle*, February 21, 1983, p. 1.
Natkin, Bobbye Claire, and Steve Kirk, *All About Pinball*, New York: Grosset & Dunlap, 1977.
—— "A Spinoff to Break a Fall," *Business Week*, September 25, 1971, p. 38.
—— "New Player in the Video Game," *Financial World*, August 15, 1981, p. 22.

—M.L. Cohen

WYSE

Wyse Technology, Inc.

3471 North First Street
San Jose, California 95134
U.S.A.
(408) 473-1960
Fax: (408) 473-2401

Private Company
Incorporated: 1981
Employees: 1,802
Sales: $480 million (1993)
SICs: 3575 Computer Terminals

Wyse Technology, Inc. is a designer and manufacturer of computer monitors and terminals for mainframe, mini, and desktop computing markets. It is the worldwide leader in the video display terminal market, with over seven million units shipped by 1995. Taiwanese investors purchased Wyse in 1989, but the company maintains headquarters offices in the United States and sales offices throughout the world.

Wyse was launched in 1981 by husband-and-wife team Bernard and Grace Tse. Bernard was a native of Hong Kong and Grace was Taiwanese. They met in the United States while studying engineering at the University of Illinois. While still in school, the couple became convinced that they could design a computer terminal that was better and less expensive to produce than terminals that were already being sold. They persuaded two colleagues to join them in a business venture that would eventually become the largest terminal manufacturer in the world.

The Tses were unlikely candidates for such an achievement. Indeed, by the time they decided to launch their company the computer terminal market was already glutted with well over 100 manufacturers. Furthermore, the industry was about to enter a period of consolidation; as terminal producers began competing fiercely on price, economies of scale became paramount. The Tses, undeterred by the increasingly competitive business environment, marched ahead with plans to launch a

manufacturing operation and began looking for investment capital. They first approached venture capital firms, which at the time were the most likely sources of cash for a technology start-up. But those groups realized that the Tse's chance of success was slim, and refused to front any money.

Undaunted, the Tses mortgaged their house for startup cash. That show of good faith helped them to convince David Jackson, the founder of nearby Altos Computers Systems, to supply $1.6 million in additional funding. With cash in hand, the Tses scrambled during the next few years to design a low-cost, high-performance computer terminal that could beat the competition. They achieved their goal in 1983, when they introduced the company's first big hit: the WY50. Offering a larger screen and higher resolution, the WY50 was priced a stunning 44 percent lower than its nearest competitors. "People thought we were giving away $50 with every shipment," Grace Tse recalled in the November 16, 1987, *Forbes*. The WY50 was an immediate success. Within a few years Wyse had sprinted past its competitors to become one of the largest manufacturers of terminals in the world, second only to computer leviathan International Business Machines (IBM).

Wyse posted an impressive $4 million sales figure in 1983. More importantly, the company showed a profit for the first time, and would continue to record surpluses for more than four straight years. Indeed, between 1983 and 1987 Wyse managed to increase annual sales to more than $250 million. The Tses achieved that success using a relatively straight-forward operating and sales strategy. Importantly, they tapped Grace's Taiwan roots and set up low-cost manufacturing operations in that country. In addition to inexpensive labor, Wyse's production facilities benefited from close proximity to low-cost parts suppliers. Wyse kept marketing costs low by selling through established distributors and resellers, rather than through a more expensive direct sales force or retail channel.

Complementing Wyse's operations and distribution savvy was a shrewd product strategy. Rather than spend heavily to research and develop cutting-edge technology, Wyse focused on its core competencies of manufacturing and distribution. It waited for its competitors to establish a new technology. Once demand for the new technology reached a high volume, Wyse would jump in with its own low-cost version. The notable wrinkle in that tactic was that Wyse would also tag on neat, low-tech features that gave its terminals an edge in the marketplace other than a low price. Such gimmicks included European styling, larger screens, and tilt-and-swivel bases. The end result was surging demand for Wyse's products and its stock. After going public with a stock sale in 1984, Wyse's stock climbed from $7 to $39 per share by 1987 in the wake of investor excitement.

Wyse's gains during the mid-1980s were primarily the result of the explosive success of Wyse's WY50 and subsequent terminal models. But Wyse bolstered that core product line with its venture into personal computers. The Tses recognized that most future growth in the computer industry would be in personal computers, rather than in terminals that were connected to mainframes. To meet that demand, Wyse began developing and selling low-cost personal computers using roughly the same strategy it had used with its terminals. It utilized existing technology to mass produce low-cost, attractive computers. And instead of selling the units through traditional retail or direct sales channels, it sold the computers to other companies that simply attached their name to the units and resold them.

By 1985 Wyse was still generating more than 90 percent of its revenues from sales of terminals, of which it was shipping about 300,000 annually. As it moved to emphasize its personal computer business, however, that share dropped to about 75 percent by 1987. Among other initiatives, Wyse inked a deal in 1986 to supply personal computers as house-brand products to Businessland, which at the time was the top computer retailer in the United States. That helped boost Wyse's 1987 net income 44 percent to $18 million. Wyse management boldly predicted that sales in 1988 would balloon to about $400 million.

Wyse's optimistic sales target for 1988 reflected management's intent to aggressively pursue the booming market for personal computers. To that end, in 1986 Wyse had purchased a computer equipment manufacturer named Amdek. Amdek was a leader in the market for computer monitors. Shortly after the buyout, Wyse announced a plan to begin marketing its computers under the Amdek name, launching Wyse to the status of computer retailer. Wyse quickly developed new lines of personal computers based on the then-popular 80286 and 80386 Intel microprocessors. To give its units an advantage, Wyse designed them to be easily upgradable, meaning that the owners could adapt the systems to changing technology instead of having to replace the entire unit when it became obsolete.

The jump into personal computer retailing marked a divergence from the route Wyse had taken during the mid-1980s. By becoming a retailer, the company was trying to establish itself as a full-line supplier of computer systems. It hoped to use its traditional competencies to prosper in the retail marketplace and steal market share from venerable competitors like IBM, Apple, and Compaq. To spearhead the effort, Wyse hired H.L. "Sparky" Sparks, the personal computer industry veteran who had developed IBM's successful distribution strategy earlier in the decade. Sparks was intrigued by the opportunity, because he thought he could parlay Wyse's inexpensive systems into retail success. Wyse's newest computer in 1987 (the WY3216), for example, sold for about $1,500 to $2,000 less than comparable systems offered by IBM and Compaq.

Some analysts were skeptical of Wyse's retail strategy, with good reason. By the late 1980s the personal computer market was becoming glutted with competition. Just a few years earlier, in fact, one of Wyse's competitors in the terminal market, TeleVideo Systems, had ventured into the personal computer retailing market with disastrous results. But the Tses had faced intense competition before, and were confident that they could profit by retailing their PCs. Most observers were optimistic, as well. The company's stock price shot up during 1987 (before the stock crash), and *Inc.* magazine predicted that Wyse would be the third fastest-growing small public company in 1987.

Wyse began shipping the first Amdek personal computers late in 1987. As a result, Wyse's sales rose rapidly, surpassing $400 million by 1989. That growth belied profit setbacks, however. Indeed, a number of factors combined to put an end to the 23 consecutive quarters of profit growth Wyse had enjoyed since the early 1980s. Among other problems, Wyse's Amdek computer line was slow to win the approval of top-tier PC dealers, largely as a result of aggressive price slashing throughout the industry. To make matters worse, sales of Wyse's PCs through nonretail channels slowed after the company raised prices on the units during the height of the memory chip shortage of 1988. Then, after posting a miserable fourth quarter loss of $15 million in 1988, Wyse was dumped by one its largest PC buyers, Tandem Computers Inc.

To try and stem the tide of red ink flowing from its balance sheet, Tse hired Larry Lummis to take control of the Amdek subsidiary. Lummis had been one of the original cofounders of Wyse back in 1981, and agreed to come out of retirement to help his old business partner. But Amdek continued to bleed cash, and Wyse was forced to announce big quarterly losses throughout 1988 and into 1989. That's when Tse began looking for a deep-pocketed partner to help pull it out of its slump. Wyse found its savior in 1989, when the Taiwan-based Mitac Group agreed to buy the company for $262 million. The Mitac Group was itself a division of Chanel International Corp., a Taiwanese government-supported consortium that was pushing to boost Taiwan's presence in the global computer industry.

Moving to the chairman and chief executive posts at Wyse following the December 1989 buyout was Morris Chang, the head of Chanel International. Chang received an engineering degree at Massachusetts Institute of Technology before earning his doctorate in electrical engineering at Stanford. Among other management posts in Taiwan and the United States, he had served as president at General Instruments Corp. before agreeing to head Taiwan's Industrial Technology Research Institute (ITRI) in 1985. It was through ITRI that Chang helped to construct the consortium of technology companies that, going into 1990, included Wyse. "The acquisition [of Wyse] was perceived as a step toward globalization for Taiwan industry. . . ," Chang explained in the June 25, 1990 *Electronic Business.*

Under new management, Wyse began to back off of its drive into personal computer retailing, focus on its traditional core strengths, and develop new products that would help it succeed in the more competitive and rapidly evolving computer industry. Wyse was aided in that effort by the other companies in the Taiwanese consortium, all of which worked together, exchanging technology, partnering manufacturing, and sharing marketing and distribution channels. Wyse introduced a full range of 386- and 486-based PCs during the early 1990s, and even jumped into the market for multiprocessor servers with a full family of systems. Meanwhile, it continued to bolster its lines of terminals. The result was that the company regained profitability in 1991 and doubled profits in 1992, when sales jumped to $480 million.

Wyse eventually decided to completely exit the systems side of the hyper-competitive computer business. Under the direction of president and chief executive Douglas Chance, whom Chang hired in 1994 (Chang remained as chairman of the board), Wyse shifted its focus to its traditional strengths in terminals and monitors. Indeed, restructuring during 1993 and 1994 left Wyse Technology Inc. a company focused entirely on video display terminals and monitors. In that niche, Wyse had become the leader after surpassing IBM in 1992. By 1995, in fact, its Qume, Link, and Wyse brand terminals controlled 37 percent of the general purpose computer terminal market (which included terminals connected to mainframes and minicomputers). Augmenting those products were its low-cost, high-performance desktop computer monitors, which proffered such features as digital panel controls and low-radiant emissions.

In November 1995, Wyse introduced the Winterm product line, the world's first Microsoft Windows terminal. The terminal was designed to run the popular Windows interface, thus providing a low-cost alternative to networking several complete personal computer systems; for example, a company could purchase several Winterm terminals for $500 to $750 each and connect them to a server, allowing multiple users to get the look, feel, and approximate performance of a PC, but at a much lower cost. For the remainder of the decade, the privately-held Wyse planned to remain focused on markets for terminals and PC video displays.

Principal Operating Units

Wyse Technology Ltd. U.K.; Wyse Technology GmbH Germany; Wyse Technology Spol Czech Republic; Wyse Technology France; Wyse Technology Italy.

Further Reading

"Executive Profile," *San Francisco Business Times*, January 5, 1996, p. 7.

Jones, Stephen, "A Foray Into PC Retailing," *Business Journal-San Jose*, April 27, 1987, p. 10.

Krey, Michael, "Taiwan Takes Giant Stride With Wyse Purchase," *Business Journal-San Jose*, December 18, 1989, p. 42.

——, "Wyse Arrives at 'Turning Point' as It Enters UNIX," *Business Journal-San Jose*, January 29, 1990, p. 29.

——, "Wyse Buyout Puts 2 Taiwanese Firms in Close Competition," *Business Journal-San Jose*, February 5, 1990, p. 17.

Pinella, Paul, "Wyse Technology Inc.," *Datamation*, June 15, 1992, p. 129(2).

Pitta, Julie, "Once Buoyant Wyse Adjusts to Choppy Waters," *Computerworld*, April 17, 1989, p. 100.

Snell, Ned, "Wyse Technology Inc.," *Datamation*, June 15, 1993, p. 108.

Wiegner, Kathleen K., "And the Last Shall Be First," *Forbes*, November 16, 1987, p. 100(2).

Wieman, Earl, "Morris Chang: Taiwan's Emperor of Electronics?" *Electronic Business*, June 25, 1990, p. 77(2).

Wyse Technology Inc. Company Profile. San Jose, Calif.: Wyse Technology, Inc.

—Dave Mote

Doing It Right

Zilog, Inc.

210 E. Hacienda Avenue
Campbell, California 95008
U.S.A.
(408) 370-8000
Fax: (408) 370-8056

Public Company
Incorporated: 1974
Employees: 1,500
Stock Exchanges: NASDAQ
Sales: $223.23 million
SICs: 3674 Semiconductors & Related Devices

Zilog, Inc., designs, develops, manufactures, and markets application-specific standard integrated circuit products for the data communications, intelligent peripheral controller, and consumer product controller markets. The company was a pioneer of the computer chip industry in the mid-1970s, stumbled during the 1980s, and was making a comeback in the early and mid-1990s.

Formed in the mid-1970s, Zilog was a trailblazer in the semiconductor industry and a pioneer of the California high-tech hotbed known as Silicon Valley. The company was founded by electrical engineer and entrepreneur Ralph Ungermann. Ungermann grew up in California. His parents, both educators, encouraged active learning, and Ralph proved to be a quick study and hard worker. In high school, Ungermann was fascinated by an event that would change the course of his life: the Soviet Union launched Sputnik, the world's first satellite. "I was leaning toward a career in law or medicine when the Russians launched the space race," Ungermann recalled in the December 17, 1990, *Business Journal-San Jose.* "I was absolutely enthralled. I would be an engineer."

Ungermann won a Navy scholarship that allowed him to eventually complete his electrical engineering degree at the University of California, Berkeley, and then a masters degree in computer architecture from the University of California, Irvine.

After college, Ungermann took a job with Collins Radio, which was one of the leading technology firms of its day. During his stint at Collins, Ungermann became fascinated with semiconductors. Semiconductor breakthroughs during the 1960s by Bell Labs and other companies were just beginning to open the door to a commercial chip industry. When Rockwell International purchased Collins in 1969, Ungermann decided to leave the company for Silicon Valley pioneer Intel.

Ungermann gained valuable experience working for Intel between 1971 and 1974. He also invested heavily in Intel stock options and learned a tough lesson in personal debt accumulation. While looking for a better-paying job to help him pay off some of his debts, he developed a plan to start his own company. Ungermann teamed up with another Intel engineer, Federico Faggin, to co-found Zilog. They planned to develop an 8-bit microprocessor (a computer's central processing unit on a silicon chip) that could drive desktop computers, which were a relatively new concept at the time. Shortly after starting the company, the two engineers scored a major victory when they managed to convince the giant Exxon Corp. to write a $1.5 million check to launch their research and development effort.

In less than a year Ungermann's team had created a breakthrough 8-bit microprocessor, beating the well-heeled Intel and Motorola to the punch. Dubbed the Z80, Zilog's chip was an immediate hit. The Z80 became the heart of many of the earliest personal computers and the processor of choice for electronic game manufacturers like Coleco in the emerging video game industry. Within a few years Zilog was generating $50 million in sales annually. Exxon, delighted with Zilog's success, began investing heavily in the company. With Exxon's financial backing, Zilog began drafting plans to start manufacturing computer systems and semiconductor components to complement its cutting-edge chips.

At the same time, Zilog tried to maintain its lead in the race to build faster, more powerful microprocessor chips. To that end, in 1979 Zilog introduced its second-generation, 16-bit chip, called the Z8000. The chip was a dynamo, but it appeared about a year after Intel's 16-bit chip, the 8086. Zilog was also slow to bring out the complementary software that potential users of the chip needed to incorporate the microprocessors into their electronics products, and as a result the company was unable to capitalize on its established market presence to counter its late start. The result was a pounding by the competition.

The hardest blow to Zilog was delivered by IBM, which selected Intel's easier-to-program 8086 to drive its first personal computer, and Intel went on to become the multi-billion-dollar leader of the global chip industry. Besides losing its command of the chip industry, Zilog was also forced to deal with the displeasure of Exxon. After investing millions of dollars into research and development at Zilog, Exxon began to lose patience.

Throughout the late 1970s Exxon had allowed Zilog to operate autonomously. Critics charged that Zilog, free from constraints placed on other companies by financial markets, wasted millions of dollars developing technologies without a solid business plan. When it became clear that Zilog was losing the chip race, Exxon began to assert more control and started to steer Zilog toward the field of computerized manufacturing. Zilog's management resisted Exxon's direction, and in 1979 Ungermann left to start a new company. Faggin remained for another year in a diminished managerial role before leaving to start his own venture.

After peaking at more than $100 million in annual sales, Zilog's revenues started to slip and the company began to lose money, posting an embarrassing deficit of more than $30 million in 1981 and 1982, combined, as Exxon scrambled to fill the leadership void left by Ungermann. Manny Fernandez, a rising star that Exxon lured away from Fairchild, filled in as chief executive for several months. But he too fled to start his own computer company after becoming disillusioned with Zilog.

In May 1982 Exxon hired Franc deWeeger to head the limping Zilog. 50-year-old deWeeger was a seasoned semiconductor manager with more than 15 years at Motorola and two years with a small technology company called Signetics. DeWeeger moved quickly to change the situation at Zilog. "When I joined the company," he said in the June 20, 1983 *Forbes,* "everybody was moaning and groaning about Exxon. I said, stop pointing the finger at Exxon . . . the responsibility lies with the management team." Aside from shaking up management, deWeeger scored a few encouraging victories. Importantly, he succeeded in getting Commodore to adopt Zilog's Z8000 chip as the microprocessor for its next-generation home and business computers. He also won an $18 million contract to supply the Internal Revenue Service with computers from Zilog's struggling systems division.

Despite deWeeger's best efforts, Zilog posted successive losses throughout the early 1980s and into the mid-1980s, and, were it not for the deep-pocketed Exxon, would likely have gone out of business. By 1985 the end seemed near. "It did not seem as if there were any way to recover," William Walker, senior vice-president and chief financial officer of Exxon Corp., recalled in the June, 1989, *Electronics.* As a last-ditch effort, Walker brought in 55-year-old E. A. Sack to try his hand at revitalizing the chip company. "Turn it around or shut it down," was the mandate given to Sack.

Sack was born and raised in Pittsburgh and had worked as an underaged employee in the local steel mills during World War

II. Older G.I.s got him interested in the field of electronics at Carnegie Mellon University, where Sack was a top student. One of his professors was Gaylord Penney, the inventor of many early cutting-edge electronics products. Sack and Penney struck up a relationship and continued to talk regularly on the telephone into the early 1990s, by which time Penney was 95 years old. Sack graduated at the top of his class and went on to get master's and doctorate degrees in electrical engineering. He worked at various technology leaders including Bell Labs, General Electric Co., and Westinghouse, where he was a rising star in research and development. Sack also had a knack for sales, which allowed him to work his way into the executive ranks first at Westinghouse and then at General Instruments Corp. He boosted sales from $10 million to $180 million over a 10-year period at General Instruments before accepting Exxon's Zilog challenge.

By the time Sack took over, sales had fallen to $50 million, the organization was losing $5 million per month, employee morale was at an all-time low, and the company's prospects were dismal. In Sack's estimation, Zilog was still trying to be a contender in an industry niche that it had long ago forfeited. Sack quickly took drastic steps, laying off most of the 1,000 employees at Zilog's Campbell, California, headquarters, and moving manufacturing activities to lower-cost regions in the United States and overseas. He jettisoned unremarkable managers and junked many of Zilog's poorly performing operations. His actions earned him little favor within the ranks of Zilog's work force. One disgruntled former employee, in fact, returned with a rifle and fired shots into windows at the headquarters building.

Zilog's financial performance quickly began to improve, with the company posting its first profit in 1986 after several years of consecutive losses and continuing to record surpluses throughout the late 1980s and early 1990s. Much of the key to Zilog's turnaround was Sack's innovative product strategy. Rather than chase the hyper-competitive market for cutting-edge microprocessors, he decided to tailor Zilog's existing and proven technologies for specific niche markets that were less competitive, but also less risky. "The whole company was trying to relive the Z80 thing," Walker explained in the October 12, 1992, *Business Journal-San Jose.* "He was quick and decisive in making the fundamental changes that clearly saved the company."

Recognizing Zilog's limited ability to compete in 16-bit and emerging 32-bit technologies, Sack decided to draw on Zilog's old Z80 8-bit chip to manufacture new application-specific standard circuits (ASSCs), which are essentially chips tailored for specific applications. For example, Zilog was able to create special versions of its Z80 chip for use in telephone answering machines and to control closed-caption television systems. The strategy was effective, as evidenced by sales and profit gains beginning in 1986. To augment its 8-bit ASSCs, Sack initiated the development of a new family of 8-bit microcontroller chips called the Z8. Sales of those controllers, combined with demand growth for Z80 processors, allowed Zilog to double its revenues between 1985 and 1989 to more than $100 million annually. Furthermore, Zilog was aggressively developing technology for cell-based application-specific integrated circuits, or ciruits designed for a specific customer, rather than a standard application.

In addition to his savvy product strategy, Sack was able to realize impressive gains at Zilog with a management strategy he had created at General Instrument Corp. called "forward controllership." Forward controllership was a closed-loop system used to manage revenue, variable costs, fixed costs, and cash. The advantage of the system was that it helped managers to focus on current and future growth and costs, rather than on past performance. The system involved relatively advanced computer modeling techniques and information management systems. Sack had found it extremely helpful in minimizing expenses and maximizing the return from limited resources.

Having achieved profitability with the subsidiary, Exxon decided early in 1989 that it was time to sell off Zilog and get out of the semiconductor business. With the backing of venture capital firm Warburg Pincus, Sack and a group of executives spearheaded a leveraged buyout that included Zilog's employees. The purchase made Zilog independent, but it also saddled the company with $33 million in debt. Fortunately for Zilog, Sack's new operating strategy proved more successful than most observers had suspected it would. The company was soon generating more than enough cash to cover its debt service and was even able to begin reducing its liabilities. Zilog capitalized on its success in 1991 by taking the company public. The initial public offering virtually eliminated Zilog's long-term debt and positioned it to capitalize on overall semiconductor market growth throughout the early 1990s and into the mid-1990s.

Zilog topped its remarkable late 1980s recovery with impressive revenue and profit gains in the 1990s. Sales grew 10 percent to $110 million in 1991 before jumping to $146 million in 1992, $203 million in 1993, and $223 million in 1994. Likewise, net income grew from $6.8 million in 1990 to $15.8 million in 1992, and $34.9 million in 1994. Zilog managed to achieve that growth without assuming any long-term debt, and invested heavily to continually upgrade its state-of-the-art production facilities and to sustain its research and development pipeline of new circuits. By the mid-1990s, Zilog was manufacturing and marketing circuits for a wide range of applications, including interactive television controllers, computer modems, electronic musical instruments, garage door openers, and a digital video-image enhancement system that converted standard television pictures to much sharper images.

Zilog entered the mid-1990s with its sights set on the sprawling information highway. Still drawing on Z80 and Z8 ASSP technology, as well as other proprietary technologies, it was manufacturing and developing a wide range of semiconductor products aimed at computer networks, interactive multimedia, and wireless communications. In 1995 Zilog employed about 1,500 workers, operated manufacturing facilities in the United States and the Philippines, and supported 26 direct sales offices and 120 distributors throughout the world.

Principal Subsidiaries

Zilog Electronics Philippines, Inc.; Zilog Philippines, Inc.; Zilog TOA; Zilog Asia; Zilog Japan; Zilog Philippines; Zilog Europe; Zilog U.K.

Further Reading

Bradley, Chris, "Key Zilog Executives Recognized," *Business Wire*, January 12, 1993.
——, "Zilog Opens New Wafer Facility on Their Idaho Campus," *Business Wire*, June 14, 1995.
Bursky, Dave, "The Secret's Out: Zilog's in the Black," *Electronics*, January 1989, p. 159.
Cole, Bernard C., "How Zilog Managed to Turn Itself Around: The Key Is a Concept Called Forward Controllership," *Electronics*, June 1989, p. 117.
Krey, Michael, "Edgar Stack: Strong Leadership Helped Save Zilog from Total Failure," *Business Journal-San Jose*, October 12, 1992, p. 12.
——, "Ralph Ungermann: Former Dean of Zilog U. Now in Networking," *Business Journal-San Jose*, December 17, 1990, p. 12.
Pitta, Julie, "Back to Basics," *Forbes*, July 8, 1991, p. 95.
Poletti, Therese, "Manny Fernandez: Resilient Entrepreneur, Thoughtful Leader Rides Career Roller Coaster to Sweeping Heights," *Business Journal-San Jose*, December 12, 1988, p. 12.
Rose, Deborah, "New Ownership for Zilog," *Business Wire*, June 14, 1989.
Walker, William R., "Zilog Announces Second Quarter Record Revenue—Record Profits," *Business Wire*, July 13, 1992.
Weigner, Kathleen, "Remember 'Spare the Rod' . . . ? (Zilog and Exxon)," *Forbes*, June 20, 1983, p. 36.

—Dave Mote

INDEX TO COMPANIES

Index to Companies

Listings in this index are arranged in alphabetical order under the company name. Company names beginning with a letter or proper name such as Eli Lilly & Co. will be found under the first letter of the company name. Definite articles (The, Le, La) are ignored for alphabetical purposes as are forms of incorporation that precede the company name (AB, NV). Company names printed in bold type have full, historical essays on the page numbers appearing in bold. Updates to entries that appeared in earlier volumes are signified by the notation (**upd.**). Company names in light type are references within an essay to that company, not full historical essays. This index is cumulative with volume numbers printed in bold type.

A.A. Housman & Co., **II** 424; **13** 340
A.A. Mathews. *See* CRSS Inc.
A & C Black Ltd., **7** 165
A&E Plastics, **12** 377
A. Ahlström Oy, **IV** 276–77
A. & J. McKenna, **13** 295
A&K Petroleum Co., **IV** 445
A & M Instrument Co., **9** 323
A&N Foods Co., **II** 553
A. and T. McKenna Brass and Copper Works, **13** 295
A&P. *See* Great Atlantic & Pacific Tea Company, Inc.
A&P Water and Sewer Supplies, Inc., **6** 487
A&W Root Beer Co., **II** 595
A.B. Chance Co., **II** 20
A.B. Hemmings, Ltd., **13** 51
A.B. Leasing Corp., **13** 111–12
A-B Nippondenso, **III** 593
A-BEC Mobility, **11** 487
A.C. Nielsen Company, **IV** 605; **13 3–5**
A.C. Wickman, **13** 296
A.D. International (Australia) Pty. Ltd., **10** 272
A. Dager & Co., **I** 404
A. Dunkelsbuhler & Co., **IV** 20–21, 65; **7** 122
A.E. Fitkin & Company, **6** 592–93
A.E. LePage, **II** 457
A.G. Becker, **II** 259–60; **11** 318
A.G. Edwards, Inc., **8 3–5**
A.G. Industries, Inc., **7** 24
A.G. Morris, **12** 427
A.G. Spalding & Bros., **I** 428–29
A.G. Stanley Ltd., **V** 17, 19
A. Gettelman, Co., **I** 269
A. Goertz and Co., **IV** 91
A.H. Belo Corporation, **IV** 605; **10 3–5**
A.H. Robins Co., **I** 366; **9** 356; **10** 70; **12** 188
A.I. Credit Corp., **III** 196
A.J. Caley and Son. Ltd., **II** 569
A.J. Oster Co., **III** 681

A. Johnson & Co. *See* Axel Johnson Group.
A.L. Laboratories Inc., **12** 3
A.L. Pharma Inc., **12 3–5**
A.M. Collins Manufacturing Co., **IV** 286
A.O. Smith Corporation, **11 3–6**
A.O. Smith Data Systems, **7** 139
A-1 Steak Sauce Co., **I** 259
A-1 Supply, **10** 375
A.R. Pechiney, **IV** 173
A. Roger Perretti, **II** 484
A.S. Abell Co., **IV** 678
A.S. Aloe, **III** 443
A.S. Cameron Steam Pump Works, **III** 525
A/S Titan, **III** 418
A.S. Yakovlev Design Bureau, **15 3–6**
A. Schulman, Inc., **8 6–8**
A.V. Roe & Co., **I** 50; **III** 508
A.W. Bain Holdings, **III** 523
A.W. Shaw Co., **IV** 635
A.W. Sijthoff, **14** 555
A-Z International Cos., **III** 569
AA Development Corp., **I** 91
AA Energy Corp., **I** 91
Aachener und Münchener Feuer-Versicherungs-Gesellschaft, **III** 376
Aachener und Münchener Gruppe, **III** 349–50
Aachener Union, **II** 385
Aalborg, **6** 367
Aansworth Shirt Makers, **8** 406
AAR Ltd., **III** 687; **IV** 60
Aargauische Portlandcement-Fabrik Holderbank-Wildegg, **III** 701
Aaron Rents, Inc., **14 3–5**
Aastrom Biosciences, Inc., **13** 161
AAV Cos., **13** 48
Aavant Health Management Group, Inc., **11** 394
AB Dick Co., **II** 25
AB-PT. *See* American Broadcasting-Paramount Theatres, Inc.
ABA. *See* Aktiebolaget Aerotransport.
Abacus Fund, **II** 445

ABB ASEA Brown Boveri Ltd., **II 1–4**; **IV** 109; **15** 483
Abbatoir St.-Valerien Inc., **II** 652
Abbey Business Consultants, **14** 36
Abbey Life Group PLC, **II** 309
Abbey Medical, Inc., **11** 486; **13** 366–67
Abbey National PLC, **10 6–8**
Abbey Rents, **II** 572
Abbey Road Building Society, **10** 6–7
Abbott Laboratories, **I 619–21**, 686, 690, 705; **II** 539; **10** 70, 78, 126; **11 7–9 (upd.)**, 91, 494; **12** 4; **14** 98, 389
Abbott, Proctor & Paine, **II** 445
ABC. *See* American Broadcasting Co. *and* Capital Cities/ABC Inc.
ABC Appliance, Inc., **10 9–11**
ABC Records, **II** 144
ABD Securities Corp., **II** 239, 283
ABECOR. *See* Associated Banks of Europe Corp.
Abercom Holdings, **IV** 92
Abercrombie & Fitch Co., **V** 116; **15 7–9**
Aberthaw Cement, **III** 671
Abex Aerospace, **III** 512
Abex Corp., **I** 456; **10** 553
Abex Friction Products, **III** 512
ABF. *See* Associated British Foods PLC.
ABI, **I** 289
Abington Shoe Company. *See* The Timberland Company.
Abitibi-Price Inc., **IV 245–47**, 721; **9** 391
Abko Realty Inc., **IV** 449
ABN. *See* Algemene Bank Nederland N.V.
ABR Foods, **II** 466
Abraham & Straus, **V** 168; **8** 443; **9** 209
Abraham Schaaffhausenscher Bankverein, **IV** 104
Abri Bank Bern, **II** 378
Abu Dhabi National Oil Company, **IV 363–64**, 476
Abu Qir Fertilizer and Chemical Industries Co., **IV** 413
Academic Press, **IV** 622–23
Access Graphics Technology Inc., **13** 128
Access Technology, **6** 225

Accessory Network Group, Inc., **8** 219
Accident and Casualty Insurance Co., **III** 230–31
Acclaim Entertainment, **13** 115
ACCO World Corporation, **7** 3–5; **12** 264
Accor SA, **10** 12–14; **13** 364
Accountants on Call, **6** 10
Accounting and Tabulating Corporation of Great Britain, **6** 240
Accuralite Company, **10** 492
Accurate Forming Co., **III** 643
Accuride Corp., **IV** 179
Accuscan, Inc., **14** 380
Ace Comb Company, **12** 216
Ace Electric Co., **I** 156
Ace Hardware Corporation, **12** 6–8
Ace Refrigeration Ltd., **I** 315
Acer America Corporation, **10** 257
Acer Group, **6** 244
Aceros Fortuna S.A. de C.V., **13** 141
Acheson Graphite Corp, **I** 399; **9** 517
ACI Holding Inc., **I** 91
Aciéries et Minières de la Sambre, **IV** 52
Aciéries Réunies de Burbach-Eich-Dudelange S.A., **IV** 24–26
Ackerley Communications, Inc., **9** 3–5
Acklin Stamping Company, **8** 515
ACLC. *See* Allegheny County Light Company.
ACLI Government Securities Inc., **II** 422
Acme Boot, **I** 440–41
Acme Can Co., **I** 601; **13** 188
Acme Carton Co., **IV** 333
Acme Corrugated Cases, **IV** 258
Acme Cotton Products, **13** 366
Acme Quality Paint Co., **III** 744
Acme Screw Products, **14** 181
Acme-Cleveland Corp., **13** 6–8
Acme-Delta Company, **11** 411
Acorn Computer, **III** 145
Acorn Financial Corp., **15** 328
Acoustics Development Corporation, **6** 313
Actava Group, **14** 332
Action, **6** 393
Acton Bolt Ltd., **IV** 658
Acumos, **11** 57
Acuson Corporation, **9** 7; **10** 15–17
ACX Technologies, **13** 11
Acxiom, **6** 14
Ad Astra Aero, **I** 121
AD-AM Gas Company, **11** 28
Adam Opel AG, **7** 6–8; **11** 549
Adams Childrenswear, **V** 177
Adams Express Co., **II** 380–81, 395–96; **10** 59–60; **12** 533
Adanac General Insurance Company, **13** 63
Adaptec, **11** 56
Adar Associates, Inc. *See* Scientific-Atlanta, Inc.
ADC Telecommunications, Inc., **10** 18–21
Adco Products, **I** 374
Addison Wesley, **IV** 659
Addressograph-Multigraph, **11** 494
Adelphi Pharmaceutical Manufacturing Co., **I** 496
Ademco. *See* Alarm Device Manufacturing Company.
Adger Assuranceselskab, **III** 310
Adhere Paper Co., **IV** 252
Adia S.A., **6** 9–11; **9** 327
Adiainvest S.A., **6** 9, 11
Adidas AG, **8** 392–93; **13** 513; **14** 6–9

Adler and Shaykin, **III** 56; **11** 556–57
Adler Line. *See* Transatlantische Dampfschiffahrts Gesellschaft.
Adley Express, **14** 567
ADM. *See* Archer-Daniels-Midland Co.
Admiral Co., **II** 86; **III** 573
Admiral Cruise Lines, **6** 368
Adnan Dabbagh, **6** 115
ADNOC. *See* Abu Dhabi National Oil Company.
Adobe Systems Incorporated, **10** 22–24; **15** 149
Adolph Coors Company, **I** 236–38, 255, 273; **13** 9–11 (upd.)
Adonis Radio Corp., **9** 320
Adria Produtos Alimenticios, Ltda., **12** 411
Adria Steamship Company, **6** 425
Adrian Hope and Company, **14** 46
Adriatico Banco d'Assicurazione, **III** 206, 345–46
Adrienne Vittadini, **15** 291
Adsega, **II** 677
ADT Security Systems, Inc., **12** 9–11
Adtel, Inc., **10** 358
Advance Foundry, **14** 42
Advance Publications Inc., **IV** 581–84; **13** 178, 180, 429
Advance Transformer Co., **13** 397
Advance-Rumely Thresher Co., **13** 16
Advanced Communications Engineering. *See* Scientific-Atlanta, Inc.
Advanced Entertainment Group, **10** 286
Advanced Medical Technologies, **III** 512
Advanced Micro Devices, Inc., **6** 215–17; **9** 115; **10** 367; **11** 308
Advanced MobilComm, **10** 432
Advanced System Applications, **11** 395
Advanced Technology Laboratories, Inc., **9** 6–8
Advanced Telecommunications Corporation, **8** 311
ADVANTA Corp., **8** 9–11; **11** 123
Advantage Company, **8** 311
Advantage Health Plans, Inc., **11** 379
Advertising Unlimited, Inc., **10** 461
Advo, Inc., **6** 12–14
AEA. *See* United Kingdom Atomic Energy Authority.
AEA Investors Inc., **II** 628; **13** 97
AEG A.G., **I** 151, 409–11; **II** 12, 279; **III** 466, 479; **IV** 167; **6** 489; **14** 169; **15** 142
AEG Kabel A.G., **9** 11
AEG-Daimler, **I** 193
AEG-Telefunken, **II** 119
Aegis Group plc, **6** 15–16
Aegis Insurance Co., **III** 273
AEGON N.V., **III** 177–79, 201, 273
AEL Ventures Ltd., **9** 512
AEON, **V** 96–99; **11** 498–99
AEP. *See* American Electric Power Company.
AEP-Span, **8** 546
Aer Lingus, **6** 59; **12** 367–68
Aeritalia, **I** 51, 74–75, 467
Aero Engines, **9** 418
Aero International Inc., **14** 43
Aero Mayflower Transit Company. *See* Mayflower Group Inc.
Aero O/Y, **6** 87–88
Aero-Coupling Corp., **III** 641
Aero-Portuguesa, **6** 125
Aeroflot Soviet Airlines, **I** 105, 110, 118; **6** 57–59; **14** 73

Aerojet, **8** 206, 208
Aerojet-General Corp., **9** 266
Aerolíneas Argentinas, **I** 107; **6** 97
Aeroquip Corp., **III** 640–42; **V** 255
Aerospace Avionics, **III** 509
Aérospatiale, **I** 41–42, 46, 50, 74, 94; **7** 9–12; **12** 190–91; **14** 72
The AES Corporation, **10** 25–27; **13** 12–15 (upd.)
Aetna Life and Casualty Company, **II** 170–71, 319; **III** 78, **180–82**, 209, 223, 226, 236, 254, 296, 298, 305, 313, 329, 389; **IV** 123, 703; **10** 75–76; **12** 367; **15** 26
Aetna National Bank, **13** 466
Aetna Oil Co., **IV** 373
AFC. *See* America's Favorite Chicken Company, Inc.
AFCO Industries, Inc., **III** 241; **IV** 341
Afcol, **I** 289
AFE Ltd., **IV** 241
Affiliated Enterprises Inc., **I** 114
Affiliated Products Inc., **I** 622
Affiliated Publications, Inc., **6** 323; **7** 13–16
Affordable Inns, **13** 364
AFG Industries Inc., **I** 483; **9** 248
AFLAC Inc., **10** 28–30 (upd.). *See also* American Family Corporation.
AFP. *See* Australian Forest Products.
African and European Investment, **IV** 96
African Coasters, **IV** 91
African Explosive and Chemical Industries, **IV** 22
AG Communication Systems Corporation, **15** 194
AG&E. *See* American Electric Power Company.
AGA, **I** 358
Agar Manufacturing Company, **8** 267
AGCO Corp., **13** 16–18
AGEL&P. *See* Albuquerque Gas, Electric Light and Power Company.
Agence France Presse, **IV** 670
Agency, **6** 393
AGF, **III** 185
AGFA, **I** 310–11
Agfa-Ansco Corp., **I** 337–38
AGFA-Gevaert, **III** 487
Agiba Petroleum, **IV** 414
Agip SpA, **IV** 420–21, 454, 466, 472–74, 498; **12** 153. *See also* Azienda Generale Italiana Petroli.
AGLP, **IV** 618
AGO, **III** 177, 179, 273, 310
Agor Manufacturing Co., **IV** 286
AGRAN, **IV** 505
AgriBank FCB, **8** 489
Agrico Chemical Company, **IV** 82, 84, 576; **7** 188
Agricultural Insurance Co., **III** 191
Agricultural Minerals and Chemicals Inc., **IV** 84; **13** 504
Agrifan, **II** 355
Agrigenetics Corp., **I** 361
Agrippina Versicherungs AG, **III** 403, 412
Agroferm Hungarian Japanese Fermentation Industry, **III** 43
AGTL. *See* Alberta Gas Trunk Line Company, Ltd.
Aguila (Mexican Eagle) Oil Co. Ltd., **IV** 657
Agway, Inc., **7** 17–18

Ahmanson. *See* H.F. Ahmanson & Company.
Ahold's Ostara, **II** 641
AHP. *See* American Home Products.
AHSC Holdings Corp., **III** 9–10
Ahtna AGA Security, Inc., **14** 541
AIC. *See* Allied Import Company.
Aichi Bank, **II** 373
Aichi Kogyo Co., **III** 415
Aichi Steel Works, **III** 637
Aida Corporation, **11** 504
AIG. *See* American International Group, Inc.
AIGlobal, **III** 197
Aiken Stores, Inc., **14** 92
Aikoku Sekiyu, **IV** 554
AIM Create Co., Ltd., **V** 127
Ainsworth National, **14** 528
Air & Water Technologies Corporation, 6 441–42
Air Afrique, **9** 233
Air BP, **7** 141
Air Brasil, **6** 134
Air Canada, 6 60–62, 101; **12** 192
Air Co., **I** 298
Air Compak, **12** 182
Air Express International Corporation, 13 19–20
Air France, **I** 93–94, 104, 110, 120; **II** 163; **6** 69, 95–96, 373; **8** 313; **12** 190. *See also* Groupe Air France.
Air Inter, **6** 92–93; **9** 233
Air La Carte Inc., **13** 48
Air Lanka Catering Services Ltd., **6** 123–24
Air Liberté, **6** 208
Air Micronesia, **I** 97
Air Midwest, Inc., **11** 299
Air New Zealand Limited, 14 10–12
Air Nippon Co., Ltd., **6** 70
Air Products and Chemicals, Inc., I 297–99, 315, 358, 674; **10 31–33** (upd.); **11** 403; **14** 125
Air Reduction Co., **I** 297–98; **10** 31–32
Air Southwest Co. *See* Southwest Airlines Co.
Air Spec, Inc., **III** 643
Air-India, 6 63–64
Airborne Accessories, **II** 81
Airborne Freight Corp., 6 345–47 345; **13** 19; **14** 517
Airbus Industrie, **6** 74; **7** 9–11, 504; **9** 418; **10** 164; **13** 356. *See also* G.I.E. Airbus Industrie.
AirCal, **I** 91
Aircraft Marine Products, **II** 7; **14** 26
Aircraft Services International, **I** 449
Aircraft Transport & Travel Ltd., **I** 92
Airlease International, **II** 422
Airmec-AEI Ltd., **II** 81
Airpax Electronics, Inc., **13** 398
Airport Ground Service Co., **I** 104, 106
Airstream, **II** 468
Airtel, **IV** 640
AirTouch Communications, 10 118; **11 10–12**
Airtours International GmbH. and Co. K.G., **II** 164
Airways Housing Trust Ltd., **I** 95
Airwick, **II** 567
Aisin Seiki Co., Ltd., III 415–16; **14** 64
AITS. *See* American International Travel Service.
Ajax, **6** 349

Ajax Iron Works, **II** 16
Ajinomoto Co., Inc., II 463–64, 475; **III** 705
Ajman Cement, **III** 760
AJS Auto Parts Inc., **15** 246
Akane Securities Co. Ltd., **II** 443
Akashic Memories, **11** 234
AKO Bank, **II** 378
Akron Brass Manufacturing Co., **9** 419
Akron Corp., **IV** 290
Akroyd & Smithers, **14** 419
Akseli Gallen-Kallela, **IV** 314
Aktiebolaget Aerotransport, **I** 119
Aktiebolaget Electrolux, **III** 478–81
Aktiebolaget SKF, III 622–25; **IV** 203
Aktiengesellschaft für Berg- und Hüttenbetriebe, **IV** 201
Aktiengesellschaft für Maschinenpapier-Zellstoff-Fabrikation, **IV** 323
Aktiv Placering A.B., **II** 352
AKU. *See* Akzo Nobel N.V.
Akzo Nobel N.V., I 674; **II** 572; **III** 44; **13 21–23**, 545; **14** 27; **15** 436
Al Copeland Enterprises, Inc., **7** 26–28
Alaadin Middle East-Ersan, **IV** 564
Alabaster Co., **III** 762
Aladdin's Castle, **III** 430, 431
Alais et Camargue, **IV** 173
Alamito Company, **6** 590
Alamo Engine Company, **8** 514
Alamo Rent A Car, Inc., 6 348–50
Alarm Device Manufacturing Company, **9** 413–15
Alascom, **6** 325–28
Alaska Air Group, Inc., 6 65–67; **11** 50
Alaska Co., **III** 439
Alaska Commercial Company, **12** 363
Alaska Hydro-Train, **6** 382; **9** 510
Alaska Natural Gas Transportation System, **V** 673, 683
Alaska Pulp Co., **IV** 284, 297, 321
Alba, **III** 619–20
Albany and Susquehanna Railroad, **II** 329
Albany Assurance Co., Ltd., **III** 293
Albany Felt Company. *See* Albany International Corp.
Albany International Corp., 8 12–14
Albemarle Paper Co., **I** 334–35; **10** 289
Albers Brothers Milling Co., **II** 487
Albert E. Reed & Co. Ltd., **7** 343
Albert Heijn NV, **II** 641–42
Albert Nipon, Inc., **8** 323
Albert Willcox & Co., **14** 278
Alberta Distillers, **I** 377
Alberta Gas Trunk Line Company, Ltd., **V** 673–74
Alberta Sulphate Ltd., **IV** 165
Alberto, **II** 641–42
Alberto-Culver Company, 8 15–17
Albertson's Inc., II 601–03, 604–05, 637; **7 19–22 (upd.)**; **8** 474; **15** 178, 480
Albi Enterprises, **III** 24
Albion Reid Proprietary, **III** 673
Albright & Friel, **I** 313; **10** 154
Albright & Wilson Ltd., **I** 527; **IV** 165; **12** 351
Albuquerque Gas & Electric Company. *See* Public Service Company of New Mexico.
Albuquerque Gas, Electric Light and Power Company, **6** 561–62
Albury Brickworks, **III** 673
Alcan Aluminium Limited, II 415; **IV** 9–13, 14, 59, 154–55; **9** 512; **14** 35

Alcantara and Sores, **II** 582
Alcatel Alsthom Compagnie Générale d'Electricité, II 13, 69; **7** 9; **9 9–11**, 32; **11** 59, 198; **15** 125
Alcatel Bell, **6** 304
Alchem Capital Corp., **8** 141, 143
Alco Cab Co., **I** 64
Alco Health Services Corporation, III 9–10
Alco Hydro-Aeroplane, **I** 64
Alco Standard Corporation, I 412–13; **III** 9; **9** 261
Alcoa. *See* Aluminum Company of America.
Alcon Laboratories, **II** 547; **7** 382; **10** 46, 48
Alcudia, **IV** 528
Aldermac Mines Ltd., **IV** 164
Aldi Group, 11 240; **13 24–26**
Aldine Press, **10** 34
Aldrich Chemical Co., **I** 690
Aldus Corporation, 10 34–36
Aldwarke Main & Car House Collieries, **I** 573
Alenia, **7** 9, 11
Alert Management Systems Inc., **12** 380
Alessio Tubi, **IV** 228
Alex & Ivy, **10** 166–68
Alexander & Alexander Services Inc., III 280; **10 37–39**; **13** 476
Alexander & Baldwin, Inc., I 417; **10 40–42**
Alexander and Lord, **13** 482
Alexander Grant & Co., **I** 481, 656
Alexander Hamilton Life Insurance Co., **II** 420
Alexander Howden Group, **III** 280; **10** 38–39
Alexander Martin Co., **I** 374
Alexander's Inc., **10** 282; **12** 221
Alexis Lichine, **III** 43
Alfa Romeo, I 163, 167; **11** 102, 104, 139, 205; **13 27–29**, 218–19
Alfa-Laval AB, III 417–21; **IV** 203; **8** 376
Alfinal, **III** 420
Alfred A. Knopf, Inc., **13** 428, 429
Alfred Hickman Ltd., **III** 751
Alfred Marks Bureau, Ltd., **6** 9–10
Alfred Nobel & Co., **III** 693
Alfred Teves, **I** 193
Alfried Krupp von Bohlen und Halbach Foundation, **IV** 89
ALG. *See* Arkla, Inc.
Algemeene Bankvereeniging en Volksbank van Leuven, **II** 304
Algemeene Friesche, **III** 177–79
N.V. Algemeene Maatschappij tot Exploitatie van Verzekeringsmaatschappijen, **III** 199
Algemeene Maatschappij van Levensverzekering en Lijfrente, **III** 178
Algemeene Maatschappij voor Nijverheidskrediet, **II** 304–05
Algemeene Nederlandsche Maatschappij ter begunstiging van de Volksvlijt, **II** 294
Algemene Bank Nederland N.V., II 183–84, 185, 239, 527; **III** 200
Algoma Steel Corp., **IV** 74; **8** 544–45
Algonquin Energy, Inc., **6** 487
Algonquin Gas Transmission Company, **6** 486; **14** 124–26
Alidata, **6** 69
Aligro Inc., **II** 664

Alimentana S.A., **II** 547
Alitalia—Linee Aeree Italiana, SpA, **I** 110, 466–67; **6** 96, **68–69**
Alken, **II** 474
Oy Alkoholiliike Ab, **IV** 469
Alkor-Oerlikon Plastic GmbH, **7** 141
All American Airways, **I** 131. *See also* USAir Group, Inc.
All American Gourmet Co., **12** 178, 199
All Nippon Airways Company Limited, **I** 106, 493; **6 70–71** 118, 427; **9** 233
Allami Biztosito, **III** 209; **15** 30
Allders International, **III** 502
Alleanza & Unione Mediterranea, **III** 208
Alleanza-Securitas-Esperia, **III** 208
Alleghany Corporation, **II** 398; **IV** 180–81; **10 43–45**
Allegheny Airlines, **I** 131. *See also* USAir Group, Inc.
Allegheny Beverage Corp., **7** 472–73
Allegheny County Light Company, **6** 483–84
Allegheny International, Inc., **III** 732; **8** 545; **9** 484
Allegheny Ludlum Corporation, **I** 307; **II** 402; **8 18–20**; **9** 484
Allegheny Power System, Inc., **V 543–45**
Allegheny Steel and Iron Company, **9** 484
Allegis, Inc., **6** 129; **9** 283; **10** 301. *See also* UAL, Inc.
Allegmeine Transpotmittel Aktiengesellschaft, **6** 394
Allen & Co., **I** 512, 701; **II** 136; **12** 496; **13** 366
Allen & Ginter, **12** 108
Allen & Hanbury's, **I** 640
Allen-Bradley Co., **I** 80; **II** 110; **III** 593; **11** 429–30
Allen-Leversidge Ltd., **I** 315
Allergan, Inc., **10 46–49**
Allforms Packaging Corp., **13** 442
Allgemeine Deutsche Creditanstalt, **II** 211, 238, 383; **12** 536
Allgemeine Eisenbahn-Versicherungs-Gesellschaft, **III** 399
Allgemeine Elektricitäts-Gesellschaft. *See* AEG A.G.
Allgemeine Rentenstalt Lebens- und Rentenversicherung, **II** 258
Allgemeine Versicherungs-Gesellschaft Helvetia, **III** 375
Alliance Agro-Alimentaires S.A., **II** 577
Alliance Amusement Company, **10** 319
Alliance Assurance Co., **III** 369–73
Alliance Brothers, **V** 356
Alliance Gaming Corp., **15** 539
Alliance Insurance Co., **III** 224
Alliance Manufacturing Co., **13** 397
Alliance Marine, **III** 373
Alliance Mortgage Co., **I** 610
Alliance Packaging, **13** 443
Alliance Paper Group, **IV** 316
Alliance Tire and Rubber Co., **II** 47
Alliant Techsystems, Inc., **8 21–23**
Allianz AG Holding, **I** 411, 426; **II** 239, 257, 279–80; **III 183–86**, 200, 250, 252, 299–301, 347–48, 373, 377, 393; **IV** 222; **14** 169–70; **15 10–14 (upd.)**
Allibert, **III** 614
Allied Bakeries Ltd., **II** 465–66; **13 52–53**
Allied Breweries Ltd., **I** 215; **III** 105; **IV** 712
Allied Chemical, **I** 310, 332, 351–52; **8** 526; **9** 521–22; **13** 76

Allied Chemical & Dye Corp., **I** 414; **7** 262; **9** 154
Allied Color Industries, **8** 347
Allied Container Corp., **IV** 345
Allied Corp., **I** 68, 141, 143, 414, 534; **III** 118, 511; **6** 599; **7** 356; **9** 134; **11** 435
Allied Crude Vegetable Oil Refining Co., **II** 398; **10** 62
Allied Distributing Co., **12** 106
Allied Dunbar, **I** 427
Allied Engineering Co., **8** 177
Allied Food Markets, **II** 662
Allied Gas Company, **6** 529
Allied Grape Growers, **I** 261
Allied Health and Scientific Products Company, **8** 215
Allied Import Company, **V** 96
Allied Maintenance Corp., **I** 514
Allied Mills, Inc., **10** 249; **13** 186
Allied Oil Co., **IV** 373
Allied Overseas Trading Ltd., **I** 216
Allied Plywood Corporation, **12** 397
Allied Polymer Group, **I** 429
Allied Safety, Inc., **V** 215
Allied Signal Engines, **9 12–15**
Allied Steel and Wire Ltd., **III** 495
Allied Stores Corporation, **II** 350, 611–12; **V** 25–28; **9** 211; **10** 282; **13** 43; **15** 94, 274
Allied Structural Steel Company, **10** 44
Allied Supermarkets, Inc., **7** 570
Allied Suppliers, **II** 609
Allied Telephone Company. *See* Alltel Corporation.
Allied Tin Box Makers Ltd., **I** 604
Allied Towers Merchants Ltd., **II** 649
Allied Van Lines Inc., **6** 412, 414; **14** 37
Allied Vintners, **I** 215
Allied-Lyons plc, **I** 215–16, 258, 264, 438; **IV** 721; **9** 100, 391; **10** 170; **13** 258
Allied-Signal Corp., **I** 141, 143, **414–16**; **III** 511; **V** 605; **6** 599–600; **9** 519; **11** 444; **13** 227
Allis-Chalmers Corp., **I** 163; **II** 98, 121; **III** 543–44; **9** 17; **11** 104; **12** 545; **13** 16–17, 563; **14** 446
Allis-Gleaner Corp. *See* AGCO Corp.
Allison Gas Turbine Division, **9 16–19**, 417; **10** 537; **11** 473
Allmanna Svenska Elektriska Aktiebolaget, **II** 1; **IV** 66
Allmänna Telefonaktiebolaget L.M. Ericsson, **V** 334
Allnatt London & Guildhall Properties, **IV** 724
Allnet, **10** 19
Allo Pro, **III** 633
Allor Leasing Corp., **9** 323
Alloy & Stainless, Inc., **IV** 228
Alloys Unlimited, **II** 82
The Allstate Corporation, **I** 23; **III** 231–32, 259, 294; **V** 180, 182; **6** 12; **10 50–52**; **13** 539
Alltel Corporation, **6 299–301**
Almac Electronics Corporation, **10** 113
Almaden Vineyards, **I** 377–78; **13** 134
Almanij. *See* Algemeene Maatschappij voor Nijverheidskrediet.
Almay, Inc., **III** 54
Almeida Banking House. *See* Banco Bradesco S.A.
Almours Security Co., **IV** 311
Aloha Airlines, **I** 97; **9** 271–72

Alpen-Elektrowerke Aktiengesellschaft, **IV** 230
Alpex Computer Corp., **III** 157
Alpha Beta Co., **II** 605, 625, 653
Alphonse Allard Inc., **II** 652
Alpina Versicherungs-Aktiengesellschaft, **III** 412
Alpine, **IV** 234
Alpine Electronics, Inc., **II** 5; **13 30–31**
Alps Electric Co., Ltd., **II** 5–6; **13** 30
Alric Packing, **II** 466
Alsen-Breitenbury, **III** 702
Alsons Corp., **III** 571
Alsthom, **II** 12
Alsthom-Atlantique, **9** 9
Alta Gold Co., **IV** 76
ALTA Health Strategies, Inc., **11** 113
Alta Holidays Ltd., **I** 95
Altamil Corp., **IV** 137
Alte Leipziger, **III** 242
Altec Electronics, **I** 489–90
Alternate Postal Delivery, **6** 14
Althoff KG, **V** 101
Althouse Chemical Company, **9** 153
Althus Corp, **I** 361
Alton & Eastern Railroad Company, **6** 504
Alton Box Board Co., **IV** 295
Altos Computer Systems, **6** 279; **10** 362
Altos Hornos de Mexico SA de CV, **13** 144
Aluma Systems Corp., **9** 512
Alumax, Inc., **I** 508; **III** 758; **IV** 18–19; **8** 505–06
Alumina Partners of Jamaica, **IV** 123
Aluminate Sales Corp, **IV** 373
Aluminio de Galicia, **IV** 174
Aluminium Co. of London, **IV** 69
L'Aluminium Francais, **IV** 173
Aluminium Ltd., **IV** 9–11, 14, 153
Aluminium Plant and Vessel Co., **III** 419
Aluminium-Oxid Stade GmbH, **IV** 231
Aluminum Can Co., **I** 607
Aluminum Co. of Canada Ltd., **II** 345; **IV** 10–12, 154
Aluminum Company of America, **I** 373, 599; **II** 315, 402, 422; **III** 490–91, 613; **IV** 9–12, **14–16**, 56, 59, 121–22, 131, 173, 703; **6** 39; **12** 346
Aluminum Cooking Utensil Co., **IV** 14
Aluminum Forge Co., **IV** 137
Aluminum Norf GmbH, **IV** 231
Aluminum of Korea, **III** 516
Aluminum Sales Corporation, **12** 346
Aluminum Seating Corp., **I** 201
Alun Cathcart, **6** 357
Alup-Kompressoren Pressorun, **III** 570
Alupak, A.G., **12** 377
Alusaf, **IV** 92
Alusuisse, **IV** 12
Alva Jams Pty., **I** 437
Alyeska Pipeline Service Co., **IV** 522, 571; **14** 542
Alyeska Seafoods Co., **II** 578
ALZA Corporation, **10 53–55**
Alzwerke GmbH, **IV** 230
AM Acquisition Inc., **8** 559–60
Am-Par Records, **II** 129
AM-TEX Corp., Inc., **12** 443
Amagasaki Co., **I** 492
Amagasaki Spinners Ltd., **V** 387
Amagasaki Steel Co., Ltd., **IV** 130
Amalgamaize Co., **14** 18
Amalgamated Chemicals, Ltd., **IV** 401

Amalgamated Dental International, **10** 271–72
Amalgamated Distilled Products, **II** 609
Amalgamated Press, **IV** 666; **7** 244, 342
Amalgamated Roadstone Corp., **III** 752
Amalgamated Sugar Co., **14** 18
Amalgamated Weatherware, **IV** 696
Amana Refrigeration, **II** 86; **11** 413
Amaray International Corporation, **12** 264
Amarillo Railcar Services, **6** 580
Amarin Plastics, **IV** 290
AMAX Inc., **I** 508; **IV 17–19**, 171, 239, 387; **6** 148; **12** 244
Amazôna Mineracao SA, **IV** 56
Ambac Industries, **I** 85
AmBase Corp., **III** 264
Ambrose Shardlow, **III** 494
AMC Entertainment Inc., **12 12–14**; **14** 87
AMCA International Finance Corporation, **7** 513
AMCA International, Ltd., **8** 545; **10** 329
Amchem Products Inc., **I** 666
AMCO, Inc., **13** 159
Amcor Limited, **IV 248–50**
AMD. *See* Advanced Micro Devices, Inc.
Amdahl Corporation, **III 109–11**, 140; **6** 272; **12** 238; **13** 202; **14 13–16 (upd.)**
AME Finanziaria, **IV** 587
AMEC, **I** 568
Amedco, **6** 295
Amerada Hess Corporation, **IV 365–67**, 400, 454, 522, 571, 658; **11** 353
Amerco, **6 351–52**
America Japan Sheet Glass Co., **III** 714
America Latina Companhia de Seguros, **III** 289
America Online, Inc., **10 56–58**, 237; **13** 147; **15** 54, 265, 321
America Today, **13** 545
America West Airlines, **6 72–74**, 121
American & Efird Inc., **12** 501
American Agricultural Chemical Co., **IV** 401
American Airlines, **I** 30–31, 48, 71, **89–91**, 97, 106, 115, 118, 124–26, 130, 132, 512, 530; **III** 102; **6** 60, 81, **75–77 (upd.)**, 121, 129–31; **9** 271–72; **10** 163; **11** 279; **12** 190, 192, 379, 381, 487, 13 173; **14** 73
American Alliance Co., **III** 191
American Allsafe Co., **8** 386
American Amusements, Inc., **III** 430
American Appliance Co., **II** 85; **11** 411
American Arithmometer Company, **III** 165. *See also* Burroughs Corporation.
American Asiatic Underwriters, **III** 195
American Association of Retired Persons, **9** 348
American Automar Inc., **12** 29
American Automated, **11** 111
American Automobile Insurance Co., **III** 251
American Aviation and General Insurance Co., **III** 230
American Aviation Manufacturing Corp., **15** 246
American Avitron Inc., **I** 481
American Bakeries Company, **12** 275–76
American Bancorp, **11** 295
American Bancshares, Inc., **11** 457
American Bank, **9** 474–75
American Bank Note, **IV** 599
American Bank of Vicksburg, **14** 41

American Bankcorp, Inc., **8** 188
American Banker/Bond Buyer, **8** 526
American Barge and Towing Company, **11** 194
American Beauty Cover Company, **12** 472
American Beet Sugar Company, **11** 13–14
American Bell Telephone Company, **V** 259; **14** 336
American Beryllium Co., Inc., **9** 323
American Beverage Corp., **II** 528
American Biodyne Inc., **9** 348
American Biomedical Corporation, **11** 333
American Biscuit Co., **II** 542
American Box Board Company, **12** 376
American Box Co., **IV** 137
American Brake Shoe and Foundry, **I** 456
American Brands, Inc., **II** 468, 477; **IV** 251; **V 395–97**, 398–99, 405; **7** 3–4; **9** 408; **12** 87, 344; **14** 95, 271–72
American Bridge Co., **II** 330; **IV** 572; **7** 549
American Broadcasting Co., **I** 463–64; **II** 89, 129–33, 151, 156, 170, 173; **III** 188, 214, 251–52; **6** 157–59, 164; **11** 197–98. *See also* Capital Cities/ABC Inc.
American Broadcasting-Paramount Theatres, Inc., **II** 129
American Builders, Inc., **8** 436
American Building Maintenance Industries, Inc., **6 17–19**
American Cable Systems, Inc. *See* Comcast Corporation.
American Cablesystems, **7** 99
American Cafe, **I** 547
American Can Co., **IV** 36, 290; **8** 476; **10** 130; **11** 29, 197; **12** 408; **13** 255; **15** 127–28. *See also* Primerica Corp.
American Carbide Corporation, **7** 584
American Cash Register Co., **III** 150; **6** 264
American Casualty Co., **III** 230–31, 404
American Casualty Co. of Dallas, **III** 203
American Cellular Network, **7** 91
American Cellulose and Chemical Manufacturing Co., **I** 317
American Central Insurance Co., **III** 241
American Cereal Co., **II** 558; **12** 409
American Chicle, **I** 711
American Chocolate & Citrus Co., **IV** 409
American Chrome, **III** 699
American Clay Forming Company, **8** 178
American Clip Company, **7** 3
American Colloid Co., **13 32–35**
American Commercial Bank, **II** 336
American Commonwealths Power Corporation, **6** 579
American Community Grocers, **II** 670
American Continental Insurance Co., **III** 191–92
American Cotton Oil Co., **II** 497
American Council on Education, **12** 141
American Crayon Company, **12** 115
American Credit Corp., **II** 236
American Crystal Sugar Company, **7** 377; **11 13–15**
American Cyanamid, **I 300–02**, 619; **III** 22; **IV** 345, 552; **8 24–26 (upd.)**; **10** 269; **11** 494; **13** 231–32; **14** 254, 256
American Dairy Queen Corporation, **10** 373
American Data Technology, Inc., **11** 111
American Distilling Co., **I** 226; **10** 180–81

American District Telegraph Co., **III** 644; **12** 9
American Diversified Foods, Inc., **14** 351
American Drew, Inc., **12** 301
American Drug Company, **13** 367
American Eagle Fire Insurance Co., **III** 240–41
American Eagle Outfitters Inc., **14** 427
American Education Press, **10** 479
American Electric Co., **II** 27; **12** 193
American Electric Power Company, **II** 3; **IV** 181; **V 546–49**; **6** 449, 524; **11** 516
American Empire Insurance Co., **III** 191
American Emulsions Co., **8** 455
American Envelope Co., **III** 40
American Equipment Co., **I** 571
American Export Steamship Lines, **I** 89
American Express Company, **I** 26–27, 480, 614; **II** 108, 176, 309, 380–82, **395–99**, 450–52, 544; **III** 251–52, 319, 340, 389; **IV** 637, 721; **6** 206–07, 409; **8** 118; **9** 335, 343, 391, 468–69, 538; **10** 44–45, **59–64 (upd.)**; **11** 41, 416–17, 532; **12** 533; **14** 106; **15** 50
American Factors Ltd., **I** 417, 566
American Family Corporation, **III 187–89**. *See also* AFLAC Inc.
American Feldmühle Corp., **II** 51
American Filtrona Corp., **IV** 260–61
American Finance Systems, **II** 349
American Financial Corporation, **II** 596; **III 190–92**, 221; **8** 537; **9** 452
American Flavor & Fragrance Company, **9** 154
American Food Management, **6** 45
American Fore Group, **III** 241–42
American Foreign Insurance Assoc., **III** 223, 226
American Forest Products Co., **IV** 282; **9** 260
American Fructose Corp., **14** 18–19
American Furniture Co. of Martinsville, **12** 300
American Gage Co., **I** 472
American Gas & Electric. *See* American Electric Power Company.
American Gasoline Co., **IV** 540
American General Capital Corp., **I** 614
American General Corporation, **III 193–94**; **10 65–67 (upd.)**; **11** 16
American General Finance Corp., **11 16–17**
American General Life Insurance Company, **6** 294
American Greetings Corporation, **7 23–25**; **12** 207–08; **15** 507
American Grinder and Manufacturing Company, **9** 26
American Harvester, **II** 262
American Heritage Savings, **II** 420
American Hoechst Corporation. *See* Hoechst Celanese Corporation.
American Hoist & Derrick Co., **8** 544
American Home Assurance Co., **III** 196–97
American Home Assurance Co. of New York, **III** 203
American Home Products, **I** 527, **622–24**, 631, 676–77, 696, 700; **III** 18, 36, 444; **8** 282–83; **10 68–70 (upd.)**, 528; **11** 35; **15** 64–65
American Home Publishing Co., Inc., **14** 460
American Home Shield, **6** 46

American Home Video, **9** 186
American Homeware Inc., **15** 501
American Honda Motor Co., **I** 174; **10** 352
American Hospital Association, **10** 159
American Hospital Supply Corp., **I** 627, 629; **III** 80; **10** 141–43; **11** 459, 486
American Hydron, **13** 366
American I.G. Chemical Corp., **I** 337
American Impacts Corporation, **8** 464
American Independent Oil Co., **IV** 522, 537. *See also* Aminoil, Inc.
American Industrial Manufacturing Co., **I** 481
American Information Services, Inc., **11** 111
American Instrument Co., **I** 628; **13** 233
American Insurance Agency, **III** 191, 352
American Insurance Co., **III** 251
American International Group, Inc., **II** 422; **III** 195–98, 200; **6** 349; **10** 39; **11** 532–33; **15** 15–19 **(upd.)**
American International Travel Service, **6** 367
American Iron and Steel Manufacturing Co., **IV** 35; **7** 48
American Jet Industries, **7** 205
American Ka-Ro, **8** 476
American La-France, **10** 296
American Laboratories, **III** 73
American Learning Corporation, **7** 168
American Life Insurance Co., **III** 195–96
American Light and Traction. *See* MCN Corporation.
American Lightwave Systems, Inc., **10** 19
American Limestone Co., **IV** 33
American Linseed Co, **II** 497
American Machine and Foundry Co., **II** 7; **III** 443; **7** 211–13; **11** 397
American Machine and Metals, **9** 23
American Machinist Press, **IV** 634
American Magnesium Products Co., **I** 404
American Maize-Products Co., **14** 17–20
American Management Systems, Inc., **11** 18–20
American Manufacturers Mutual Insurance Co., **III** 269, 271; **15** 257
American Medical International, Inc., **III** 73–75, 79; **14** 232
American Medical Services, **II** 679–80; **14** 209
American Medicorp., **III** 81; **6** 191; **14** 432
American Merchandising Associates Inc., **14** 411
American Merchants Union Express Co., **II** 396
American Metal Climax, Inc., **III** 687; **IV** 18, 46
American Metal Co. Ltd., **IV** 17–19, 139
American Metal Products Corp., **I** 481
American Metals Corp., **III** 569
American Microsystems, **I** 193
American Milk Products Corp., **II** 487
The American Mineral Spirits Company, **8** 99–100
American Motorists Insurance Co., **III** 269, 271; **15** 257
American Motors Corp., **I** 135–37, 145, 152, 190; **II** 60, 313; **III** 543; **6** 27, 50; **8** 373; **10** 262, 264
American Movie Classics Co., **II** 161
American National Bank, **13** 221–22
American National Bank and Trust Co., **II** 286

American National Can Co., **III** 536; **IV** 173, 175
American National Corp., **II** 286
American National Fire Insurance Co., **III** 191
American National General Agencies Inc., **III** 221; **14** 109
American National Insurance Company, **8** 27–29
American Natural Resources Co., **I** 678; **IV** 395; **13** 416
American Newspaper Publishers Association, **6** 13
American of Philadelphia, **III** 234
American Oil Co., **IV** 369–70; **7** 101; **14** 22
American Olean Tile Co., **III** 424
American Optical Co., **I** 711–12; **III** 607; **7** 436
American Overseas Airlines, **12** 380
American Overseas Holdings, **III** 350
American Paging, **9** 494–96
American Paper Box Company, **12** 376
American Petrofina, Inc., **IV** 498; **7** 179–80
American Photographic Group, **III** 475; **7** 161
American Physicians Service Group, Inc., **6** 45
American Platinum Works, **IV** 78
American Postage Meter Co., **III** 156
American Potash and Chemical Corp., **IV** 95, 446
American Power & Light Co., **6** 545, 596–97; **12** 542
American Premier Underwriters, Inc., **10** 71–74
American President Companies Ltd., **III** 512; **6** 353–55
American Protective Mutual Insurance Co. Against Burglary, **III** 230
American Publishing Co., **IV** 597
American Pure Oil Co., **IV** 497
American Radiator & Standard Sanitary Corp., **III** 663–64
American Railway Express Co., **II** 382, 397; **10** 61
American Railway Publishing Co., **IV** 634
American Re Corporation, **III** 182; **10** 75–77
American Record Corp., **II** 132
American Ref-Fuel, **V** 751
American Refrigeration Products S.A. **7** 429
American Republic Assurance Co., **III** 332
American Research and Development Corp., **II** 85; **III** 132; **6** 233
American Residential Mortgage Corporation, **8** 30–31
American Resorts Group, **III** 103
American River Transportation Co., **I** 421; **11** 23
American Robot Corp., **III** 461
American Rolling Mill Co., **IV** 28; **8** 176–77
American Royalty Trust Co., **IV** 84; **7** 188
American RX Pharmacy, **III** 73
American Safety Equipment Corp., **IV** 136
American Safety Razor Co., **III** 27–29
American Sales Book Co., Ltd., **IV** 644
American Salt Co., **12** 199
American Satellite Co., **6** 279; **15** 195
American Savings & Loan, **10** 117
American Savings Bank, **9** 276

American Sealants Company. *See* Loctite Corporation.
American Seating Co., **I** 447
American Seaway Foods, Inc, **9** 451
American Sheet Steel Co., **IV** 572; **7** 549
American Smelting and Refining Co., **IV** 31–33
American Standard Inc., **III** 437, 663–65
American States Insurance Co., **III** 276
American Steamship Company, **6** 394–95
American Steel & Wire Co., **I** 355; **IV** 572; **7** 549; **13** 97–98
American Steel Foundries, **7** 29–30
American Stock Exchange, **10** 416–17
American Stores Company, **II** 604–06; **12** 63, 333; **13** 395
American Sumatra Tobacco Corp., **15** 138
American Technical Services Company. *See* American Building Maintenance Industries, Inc.
American Telephone and Telegraph Company, **I** 462; **II** 13, 54, 61, 66, 80, 88, 120, 252, 403, 430–31, 448; **III** 99, 110–11, 130, 145, 149, 160, 162, 167, 246, 282; **IV** 95, 287; **V** 259–64, 265–68, 269, 272–75, 302–04, 308–12, 318–19, 326–30, 334–36, 339, 341–342, 344–346; **6** 267, 299, 306–07, 326–27, 338–40; **7** 88, 118–19, 146, 288–89, 333; **8** 310–11; **9** 32, 43, 106–07, 138, 320, 321, 344, 478–80, 495, 514; **10** 19, 58, 87, 97, 175, 202–03, 277–78, 286, 431, 433, 455–57; **11** 10, 59, 91, 183, 185, 196, 198, 302, 500–01; **12** 9, 135–36, 162, 544; **13** 57, 212–13, 326, 402, 448; **14** 15, 35–36, 95, 251–53, 257–61, 318, 336–37, 345, 347, 354, 363–64; **15** 125–26, 228, 455
American Television and Communications Corp., **I** 534–35; **II** 161; **IV** 596, 675; **7** 528–30
American Textile Co., **III** 571
American Tin Plate Co., **IV** 572; **7** 549
American Title Insurance, **III** 242
American Tobacco Co., **I** 12–14, 28, 37, 425; **V** 395–97, 399, 408–09, 417–18, 600; **14** 77, 79; **15** 137–38. *See also* American Brands Inc.
American Tool & Machinery, **III** 420
American Tool Company, **13** 563
American Totalisator Corporation, **10** 319–20
American Tourister, Inc., **10** 350; **13** 451, 453
American Tractor Corporation, **10** 379
American Trading and Production Corporation, **7** 101
American Transport Lines, **6** 384
American Trust and Savings Bank, **II** 261
American Trust Co., **II** 336, 382; **12** 535
American Ultramar Ltd., **IV** 567
American Viscose Corp. *See* Avisco.
American Water Works Company, **V** 543–44; **6** 443–45
American Wood Reduction Company, **14** 174
American Woolen, **I** 529
American Yearbook Company, **7** 255
American-Marietta Corp., **I** 68, 405
American-Palestine Trading Corp., **II** 205–06
American-South African Investment Co. Ltd., **IV** 79

American-Strevell Inc., **II** 625
Americana Healthcare Corp., **15** 522
Americana Hotel, **12** 316
America's Favorite Chicken Company, Inc., 7 26–28
AmeriFirst Bank, **11** 258
Amerifirst Federal Savings, **10** 340
AmeriGas Partners, L.P., **12** 498
AmeriGas Propane, Inc., **12** 500
Amerimark Inc., **II** 682
Amerisystems, **8** 328
Ameritech Corporation, V 265–68; **6** 248; **7** 118; **10** 431; **11** 382; **12** 137; **14** 252–53, 257, 259–61, 364; **15** 197
Ameritech Illinois. *See* Illinois Bell Telephone Company.
Ameritrust Corporation, **9** 476
Amerock Corp., **13** 41
Amerotron, **I** 529
Amersil Co., **IV** 78
Ames Department Stores, Inc., V 197–98; **9** 20–22; **10** 497; **15** 88
AMETEK, Inc., 9 23–25; **12** 88
N.V. Amev, III 199–202
Amey Roadstone Corp., **III** 503; **7** 209
Amfac Inc., I 417–18, 566; **IV** 703; **10** 42
Amfas, **III** 310
Amgen, Inc., I 266; **8** 216–17; **10** 78–81; **13** 240; **14** 255
Amherst Coal Co., **IV** 410; **7** 309
Amiga Corporation, **7** 96
Aminoil, Inc., **IV** 523. *See also* American Independent Oil Co.
AMISA, **IV** 136
Amitron S.A., **10** 113
AMK Corporation, **II** 595; **7** 85
Ammirati, **14** 316
Ammo-Phos, **I** 300; **8** 24
L'Ammoniac Sarro-Lorrain S.a.r.l., **IV** 197
Amoco Corporation, I 516, 202; **II** 376; **III** 611; **IV** 368–71, 412, 424–25, 453, 525; **7** 107, 443; **10** 83–84; **11** 441; **12** 18; **14** 21–25 (upd.), 494
Amoseas, **IV** 453–54
Amoskeag Company, 6 356; **8** 32–33; **9** 213–14, 217
Amot Controls Corporation, **15** 404
AMP, Inc., II 7–8; **11** 319; **13** 344; **14** 26–28 (upd.)
AMPAL. *See* American-Palestine Trading Corp.
AMPCO Auto Parks, Inc. *See* American Building Maintenance Industries, Inc.
AMPEP, **III** 625
Ampex Corp., **III** 549; **6** 272
Ampol Ltd., **III** 729
AMR Corp., **I** 90–91; **6** 76; **8** 315
AMR Information Services, **9** 95
Amram's Distributing Limited, **12** 425
AMRE, **III** 211
Amrep S.A., **I** 563
Amro. *See* Amsterdam-Rotterdam Bank N.V.
AMS Trading Co., **III** 112
AmSouth Bancorporation, 12 15–17
Amstar Corp., **14** 18
Amstar Sugar, **II** 582; **7** 466–67
Amsted Industries Incorporated, 7 29–31
Amstel Brewery, **I** 257
Amsterdam-Rotterdam Bank N.V., II 184, **185–86**, 279, 295, 319; **III** 200; **14** 169
Amstrad plc, III 112–14
Amtec Systems Corp., **11** 65

Amtech. *See* American Building Maintenance Industries, Inc.
Amtel, Inc., **8** 545; **10** 136
Amtliches Bayerisches Reisebüro, **II** 163
Amtorg, **13** 365
Amtrak, **II** 2; **10** 73
AmTrans. *See* American Transport Lines.
Amway Corporation, III 11–14; **13** 36–39 (upd.)
Amylum, **II** 582
ANA Enterprises, Ltd., **6** 70
Anacomp, Inc., **11** 19
Anaconda Aluminum, **11** 38
Anaconda Co., **III** 644; **IV** 33, 376; **7** 261–63
Anaconda-Jurden Associates, **8** 415
Anadarko Petroleum Corporation, 10 82–84
Analog Devices, Inc., 10 85–87
Analytic Sciences Corporation, 10 88–90; **13** 417
Anamax Mining Co., **IV** 33
AnAmo Co., **IV** 458
ANB Bank, **I** 55
Anchor Bancorp, Inc., 10 91–93
Anchor Cable, **III** 433
Anchor Corporation, **12** 525
Anchor Hocking Glassware, I 609–10; **13** 40–42; **14** 483
Anchor Motor Freight, Inc., **12** 309–10
Anchor National Financial Services, Inc., **11** 482
Anchor National Life Insurance Company, **11** 482
Anchor Oil and Gas Co., **IV** 521
Anchor Records, **II** 130
Ancienne Mutuelle, **III** 210
Andersen Consulting, **9** 344; **11** 305
Andersen Corporation, 10 94–95
Anderson & Kerr Drilling Co., **IV** 445
Anderson and Campbell, **II** 479
Anderson Box Co., **IV** 342; **8** 267
Anderson Clayton & Co., **II** 560; **12** 411
Anderson, Greenwood & Co., **11** 225–26
Anderson Testing Company, Inc., **6** 441
Anderton, **III** 624
Andes Candies, **II** 520–21
Andian National Corp. Ltd., **IV** 415–16
André Courrèges, **III** 47; **8** 342–43
Andrew Corporation, 10 96–98
Andrew Jergens Co., **III** 38
Andrew Weir & Co., **III** 273
Andrews, Clark & Company, **IV** 426; **7** 169
Andrews Group, Inc., **10** 402
Anfor, **IV** 249–50
Angele Ghigi, **II** 475
Angelica Corporation, 15 20–22
Angelo's Supermarkets, Inc., **II** 674
ANGI Ltd., **11** 28
Anglo American Corporation of South Africa Limited, I 289, 423; **IV** 20–23, 56–57, 64–68, 79–80, 90, 92, 94–96, 118–20, 191, 239–40; **7** 121–23, 125
Anglo American Paper Co., **IV** 286
Anglo Company, Ltd., **9** 363
Anglo Energy, Ltd., **9** 364
Anglo Mexican Petroleum Co. Ltd., **IV** 657
Anglo-American Chewing Gum Ltd., **II** 569
Anglo-American Clays Corp., **III** 691; **IV** 346

Anglo-American Oil Company Limited, **IV** 427; **7** 170
Anglo-American Telegraph Co., **IV** 668
Anglo-Belge, **II** 474
Anglo-Canadian, **III** 704
Anglo-Canadian Mining & Refining, **IV** 110
Anglo-Canadian Telephone Company of Montreal. *See* British Columbia Telephone Company.
Anglo-Dutch Unilever group, **9** 317
Anglo-Egyptian D.C.O., **II** 236
Anglo-Egyptian Oilfields, **IV** 412, 414
Anglo-Elementar-Versicherungs-AG, **III** 185
Anglo-Huronian Ltd., **IV** 164
Anglo-Iranian Oil Co., **IV** 379, 419, 435, 450, 466, 559; **7** 57, 141
Anglo-Lautaro Nitrate Corporation, **9** 363
Anglo-Palestine Co., **II** 204
Anglo-Persian Oil Co., **IV** 363, 378–79, 381, 429, 450, 466, 515, 524, 531, 557–59; **7** 56–57, 140
Anglo-Swiss Condensed Milk Co., **II** 545
Anglo-Thai Corp., **III** 523
Anglo-Transvaal Consolidated, **IV** 534
Angus Hill Holdings, **IV** 249
Anheuser-Busch Company, Inc., I 32, **217–19**, 236–37, 254–55, 258, 265, 269–70, 290–91, 598; **IV** 624; **6** 20–21, 48; **9** 100; **10** 99–101 (upd.), 130; **11** 421; **12** 337–38; **13** 5, 10, 258, 366; **15** 429
ANIC Gela, **IV** 421
Anikem, **I** 374
Anitec Image Technology Corp., **IV** 287; **15** 229
Ann Taylor Stores Corporation, V 26–27; **13** 43–45; **15** 9
Annabelle's, **II** 480–81
Anne Klein, **15** 145–46
Annuaries Marcotte Ltd., **10** 461
Anonima Infortunia, **III** 208
Ansa Software, **9** 81
Ansaldo, **II** 191
Ansbacher-Siegle Corp., **13** 460
Anschütz & Co. GmbH, **III** 446
Anschutz Corp., 12 18–20
Anschütz-Kaempfe, **III** 446
Ansell, **I** 215
Ansell Rubber Company, **10** 445
Ansett Airlines, **6** 73; **14** 11
Ansett Transport Industries Limited, **V** 523–25
Ansonia Brass and Battery Co., **IV** 176–77
Ansonia Manufacturing Co., **IV** 176
Ant Nachrichtentechnik GmbH., **I** 411
Anta Corporation, **6** 188
Antar group, **IV** 544, 546
Antares Alliance Group, **14** 15
Antares Electronics, Inc., **10** 257
ANTEX. *See* American National Life Insurance Company of Texas.
Anthem Electronics, Inc., 13 46–47
Anthem P&C Holdings, **15** 257
Anthes Imperial Ltd., **I** 274
Anthes Industries Inc., **9** 512
Anthony Stumpf Publishing Company, **10** 460
Anthropologie, **14** 524–25
Antillaase Bank-Unie N.V., **II** 184
Antoine Saladin, **III** 675
Antwerp Co., **IV** 497

ANZ. *See* Australia and New Zealand Banking Group Ltd.
Anzon Ltd., **III** 681
AOE Plastic GmbH, **7** 141
Aoki Corporation, **9** 547, 549
AON Corporation, III 203–05
AP. *See* The Associated Press.
AP Bank, Ltd., **13** 439
AP&L. *See* American Power & Light Co.
AP-Dow Jones/Telerate Company, **10** 277
APAC, Inc., **IV** 374
Apache Corp., 10 102–04; 11 28
Apex Financial Corp., **8** 10
Apex Smelting Co., **IV** 18
Apita, **V** 210
APL. *See* American President Companies Ltd.
APL Corporation, **9** 346
Apline Guild, **12** 173
APM Ltd., **IV** 248–49
Apogee Enterprises, Inc., 8 34–36
Apollo Apparel Partners, L.P., **12** 431
Apollo Computer, **III** 143; **6** 238; **9** 471; **11** 284
Apollo Heating & Air Conditioning Inc., **15** 411
Apollo Ski Partners LP of New York, **11** 543, 545
Apollo Technologies, **I** 332
Apotekarnes Droghandel A.B., **I** 664–65
Apothekernes Laboratorium A.S., **12** 3–5
Appalachian Computer Services, **11** 112
Apple Computer, Inc., II 6, 62, 103, 107, 124; **III** 114, **115–16**, 121, 125, 149, 172; **6 218–20 (upd.)**, 222, 225, 231, 244, 248, 254–58, 260, 289; **8** 138; **9** 166, 170–71, 368, 464; **10** 22–23, 34, 57, 233, 235, 404, 458–59, 518–19; **11** 45, 50, 57, 62, 490; **12** 139, 183, 335, 449, 455, 470; **13** 90, 388, 482
Apple Container Corp., **III** 536
Applebee's International Inc., 14 29–31
Appleton & Cox, **III** 242
Appleton Papers, **I** 426
Appleton Wire Works Corp., **8** 13
Appliance Buyers Credit Corp., **III** 653
Les Applications du Roulement, **III** 623
Applied Bioscience International, Inc., 10 105–07
Applied Color Systems, **III** 424
Applied Communications, Inc., **6** 280; **11** 151
Applied Data Research, Inc., **6** 225
Applied Digital Data Systems Inc., **II** 83; **9** 514
Applied Engineering Services, Inc. *See* The AES Corporation.
Applied Films Laboratory Inc., **12** 121
Applied Komatsu Technology, Inc., **10** 109
Applied Learning International, **IV** 680
Applied Materials, Inc., 10 108–09
Applied Power, Inc., 9 26–28
Applied Programming Technologies, Inc., **12** 61
Applied Solar Energy, **8** 26
Applied Technology Corp., **11** 87
Approvisionnement Atlantique, **II** 652
Appryl, **I** 303
APS. *See* Arizona Public Service Company.
Apura GmbH, **IV** 325
APUTCO, **6** 383
Aqua Glass, **III** 570
Aqua Pure Water Co., **III** 21

Aqua-Chem, Inc., **I** 234; **10** 227
Aquafin N.V., **12** 443
Aquarium Supply Co., **12** 230
Aquarius Group, **6** 207
Aquila, **IV** 486
Aquila Energy Corp., **6** 593
Aquitaine. *See* Société Nationale des Petroles d'Aquitaine.
AR-TIK Systems, Inc., **10** 372
ARA Services, II 607–08
Arab Contractors, **III** 753
Arab Japanese Insurance Co., **III** 296
Arab Petroleum Pipeline Co., **IV** 412
Arabian American Oil Co., **I** 570; **IV** 386, 429, 464–65, 512, 536–39, 552, 553, 559; **7** 172, 352; **14** 492–93. *See also* Saudi Arabian Oil Co.
Arabian Gulf Oil Co., **IV** 454
Arabian Investment Banking Corp., **15** 94
Arabian Oil Co., **IV** 451
Aral, **IV** 487
Aramark Corporation, 13 48–50
Aramco. *See* Arabian American Oil Co. *and* Saudi Arabian Oil Company.
Aratex Inc., **13** 49
Aratsu Sekiyu, **IV** 554
ARBED Finance S.A., **IV** 26
ARBED S.A., **IV 24–27**, 53
ARBED-Felten & Guilleaume Tréfileries Réunies, **IV** 26
Arbitron Corp., **III** 128; **10** 255, 359; **13** 5
Arbor Acres, **13** 103
Arbor Drugs Inc., 12 21–23
Arbor Living Centers Inc., **6** 478
Arbuthnot & Co., **III** 522
Arby's Inc., II 614; **8 536–37; 14 32–34**, 351
ARC Ltd., **III** 501
ARC Materials Corp., **III** 688
ARC Propulsion, **13** 462
Arcadia Company, **14** 138
Arcadian Marine Service, Inc., **6** 530
Arcata Corporation, **12** 413
Arcata National Corp., **9** 305
Arcelik, **I** 478
Arch Mineral Corporation, IV 374; **7 32–34**
Archbold Ladder Co., **12** 433
Archer Drug, **III** 10
Archer-Daniels-Midland Co., I 419–21; IV 373; **7** 432–33;, 241 **8** 53; **11 21–23 (upd.)**
Archers Gilles & Co., **II** 187
ARCO. *See* Atlantic Richfield Company.
ARCO Chemical Company, IV 376–77, 456–57; **10 110–11**
Arco Electronics, **9** 323
Arco Societa Per L'Industria Elettrotecnica, **II** 82
Arctco, Inc., **12** 400–01
Arctic, **III** 479
Arctic Alaska Fisheries Corporation, **14** 515
ARD. *See* American Research & Development.
Ardal og Sunndal Verk AS, **10** 439
Ardent Computer Corp., **III** 553
Areal Technologies, **III** 715
Argbeit-Gemeinschaft Lurgi und Ruhrchemie, **IV** 534
Argentine National Bank, **14** 46
Argo Communications Corporation, **6** 300
Argon Medical, **12** 327
Argonaut, **I** 523–24; **10** 520–22

Argos, **I** 426
Argus Chemical Co., **I** 405
Argus Corp., **IV** 22, 272, 611
Argus Energy, **7** 538
Argyll Group PLC, I 241; **II 609–10**, 656; **12** 152–53
Aris, Inc., **15** 275
Aristech Chemical Corp., **12** 342
Arizona Copper Co., **IV** 177
Arizona Edison Co., **6** 545
Arizona Public Service Company, **6** 545–47
Arizona Refrigeration Supplies, **14** 297–98
Arjo Wiggins Appleton, **13** 458
Ark Securities Co., **II** 233
Arkady Co., Ltd., **I** 421; **11** 23
Arkansas Breeders, **II** 585
Arkansas Chemicals Inc., **I** 341
Arkansas Louisiana Gas Company. *See* Arkla, Inc.
Arkansas Power & Light, **V** 618
Arkay Computer, **6** 224
ARKE, **II** 164
Arkla, Inc., V 550–51; 11 441
Arlesey Lime and Portland Cement Co., **III** 669
Arlington Corporation, **6** 295
Arlington Motor Holdings, **II** 587
Armaturindistri, **III** 569
Armco Inc., III 259, 721; **IV 28–30**, 125, 171; **10** 448; **11** 5, 255; **12** 353
Armin Corp., **III** 645
Armin Poly Film Corp., **III** 645
Armitage Shanks, **III** 671
Armor All Products Corp., **12** 333; **15** 507
Armor Elevator, **11** 5
Armour & Company, **8** 144; **12** 198; **13** 21, 506
Armour Food Co., **I** 449–50, 452; **II** 494, 518; **12** 81, 370; **13** 270
Armour Pharmaceutical Co., **III** 56
Armour-Dial, **I** 14; **8** 144
Armstrong Advertising Co., **I** 36
Armstrong Air Conditioning Inc., **8** 320–22
Armstrong Autoparts, **III** 495
Armstrong Communications, **IV** 640
Armstrong Nurseries, **I** 272
Armstrong Rees Ederer Inc., **IV** 290
Armstrong Tire Co., **15** 355
Armstrong, Whitworth & Co. Ltd., **I** 50; **III** 508; **IV** 257
Armstrong World Industries, Inc., III 422–24; 9 466; **12** 474–75
Armstrong-Siddeley Co., **III** 508
Armtek, **7** 297
Army Cooperative Fire Insurance Company, **10** 541
Army Signal Corps Laboratories, **10** 96
Arndale, **IV** 696
Arno Press, **IV** 648
Arnold Foods Co., **II** 498
Arnold Thomas Co., **9** 411
Arnoldo Mondadori Editore S.p.A., IV 585–88, 675
Arnotts Ltd., **II** 481
Aro Corp., **III** 527; **14** 477, 508; **15** 225
Aromat Corporation, **III** 710; **7** 303
Arpet Petroleum, **III** 740; **IV** 550
Arpic, **III** 426
Arrow Electronics, Inc., 10 112–14; 13 47
Arrow Food Distributor, **II** 675
Arrow Oil Co., **IV** 401

Arrow Oil Tools, **III** 570
Arrow Pump Co., **I** 185
Arrow Specialty Co., **III** 570
Arrowsmith & Silver, **I** 428
A.B. Arsenalen, **II** 352
Artec, **III** 420; **12** 297
Artech Digital Entertainments, Inc., **15** 133
Artek Systems Corporation, **13** 194
Artesian Manufacturing and Bottling
  Company, **9** 177
Artex Enterprises, **7** 256
Arthur Andersen & Company, Société
  Coopérative, **III** 143; **6** 244; **10**
  115–17, 174
Arthur D. Little, **IV** 494; **10** 139, 174–75
Arthur Ovens Motor Freight Co., **6** 371
Arthur Tappan & Co., **IV** 604
Arthur Young & Company, **IV** 119; **10**
  386. *See also* Ernst & Young.
Artists & Writers Press, Inc., **13** 560
Arts & Entertainment Network, **IV** 627
Arvey Corp., **IV** 287
Arvida Corp., **IV** 703
Arvin Industries, Inc., 8 37–40
ASAB, **III** 480
Asahi Breweries Ltd., I 220–21, 282,
  520; **13** 454
Asahi Chemical Industry Co., **I** 221; **III**
  760; **IV** 326
Asahi Glass Company, Limited, **I** 363;
  III 666–68; **11** 234–35
Asahi Kasei Industry Co. Ltd., **IV** 476
Asahi Komag Co., Ltd., **11** 234
Asahi Kyoei Co., **I** 221
Asahi Manufacturing, **III** 592
Asahi Milk Products, **II** 538
Asahi National Broadcasting Company,
  Ltd., 9 29–31
Asahi Oil, **IV** 542
Asahi Real Estate Facilities Co., Ltd., **6**
  427
Asahi Seiko, **III** 595
Asahi Shimbun, **9** 29–30
Asahi Trust & Banking, **II** 323
Asano Group, **III** 718
ASARCO Incorporated, **I** 142; **IV 31–34**
ASB Agency, Inc., **10** 92
Aschaffenburger Zellstoffwerke AG, **IV**
  323–24
Ascom AG, 9 32–34
Ascom Gfeller, **15** 125
Ascometal, **IV** 227
ASD, **IV** 228
ASDA, **11** 240
Asda Group PLC, **II 611–12**, 513, 629
ASEA A.B., **II** 1–4; **III** 427; **IV** 204, 300
Asea Brown Boveri. *See* ABB ASEA
  Brown Boveri Ltd.
ASEA-ATOM, **II** 2
Asean Bintulu Fertilizer, **IV** 518
A.B. Asesores Bursatiles, **III** 197–98; **15**
  18
ASF. *See* American Steel Foundries.
Asgrow Florida Company, **13** 503
Ash Company, **10** 271
Ashitaka Rinsan Kogyo, **IV** 269
Ashland Iron and Mining Co., **IV** 28
Ashland Oil, Inc., **I** 420; **IV** 71, 198, 366,
  372–74, 472, 658; **7** 32–33; **8** 99; **9**
  108; **11** 22
Ashton Joint Venture, **IV** 60, 67
Ashton Mining, **IV** 60
Ashton-Tate Corporation, **9** 81–82; **10**
  504–05

Asia Life Insurance Co., **III** 195–96
Asia Oil Co., Ltd., **IV** 404, 476
Asia Television, **IV** 718
Asia Terminals Ltd., **IV** 718
Asiana Airlines, **9** 233
Asiatic Petroleum Co., **IV** 434, 530
Asil çelik, **I** 479
ASK Group, Inc., 9 35–37. *See also*
  Software Dimensions, Inc.
Asland SA, **III** 705, 740
Aso Cement, **III** 705
Aspen Mountain Gas Co., **6** 568
Aspen Skiing Company, **II** 170; **15**
  23–26, 234
Aspen Systems, **14** 555
Assam Co. Ltd., **III** 522–23
Assam Oil Co., **IV** 441, 483–84
L'Assicuratrice Italiana, **III** 346–47
Assicurazioni Generali SpA, **II** 192; **III**
  206–09, 211, 296, 298; **14** 85; **15 27–31**
  (upd.)
Associated Anglo-Atlantic Corp., **III** 670
Associated Aviation Underwriters, **III** 220
Associated Banks of Europe Corp., **II** 184,
  239
Associated Biscuit Co., **II** 631
Associated Book Publishers, **8** 527
Associated Bowater Industries, **IV** 258
Associated Brewing Co., **I** 254
Associated British Foods PLC, **II**
  465–66, 565, 609; **11** 526; **13 51–53**
  (upd.)
Associated British Maltsters, **II** 500
Associated British Picture Corp., **I** 531; **II**
  157
Associated City Investment Trust, **IV** 696
Associated Communications Corporation, **7**
  78
Associated Cooperative Investment Trust
  Ltd., **IV** 696
Associated Dairies Ltd., **II** 611
Associated Dry Goods, **V** 134; **12** 54–55
Associated Electrical Industries, Ltd., **II**
  25; **III** 502
Associated Employers General Agency, **III**
  248
Associated Food Holdings Ltd., **II** 628
Associated Fresh Foods, **II** 611–12
Associated Fuel Pump Systems Corp., **III**
  593
Associated Gas & Electric Company, **V**
  621, 629–30; **6** 534; **14** 124
Associated Gas Services, Inc., **11** 28
Associated Grocers, Incorporated, **9**
  38–40
Associated Grocers of Arizona, **II** 625
Associated Grocers of Colorado, **II** 670
The Associated Group, **10** 45
Associated Hospital Service of New York,
  III 245–46
Associated Iliffe Press, **IV** 666
Associated Indemnity Co., **III** 251
Associated Inns and Restaurants Company
  of America, **14** 106
Associated Insurance Cos., **III** 194
Associated Lead Manufacturers Ltd., **III**
  679, 680–81
Associated London Properties, **IV** 705
Associated Madison Insurance, **I** 614
Associated Milk Producers, Inc., 11
  24–26
Associated National Insurance of Australia,
  III 309

Associated Natural Gas Corporation, **11**
  27–28
Associated Newspapers, **IV** 686
Associated Octel Company Limited, **10**
  290
Associated Oil Co., **IV** 460
Associated Pipeline Contractors, **III** 559
Associated Piping & Engineering Corp.,
  III 535
Associated Portland Cement Manufacturers
  (1900) Ltd., **III** 669–71
The Associated Press, **IV** 629, 669–70; **7**
  158; **10** 277; **13 54–56**
Associated Pulp & Paper Mills, **IV** 328
Associated Spring Co., **III** 581; **13** 73
Associated Stationers, **14** 521, 523
Associated Television, **7** 78
Associated Timber Exporters of British
  Columbia Ltd., **IV** 307
Associated TV, **IV** 666
Associates Investment Co., **I** 452
Assubel, **III** 273
Assurances du Groupe de Paris, **III** 211
Assurances Generales de France, **III** 351
AST Holding Corp., **III** 663, 665
AST Research, Inc., **9 41–43**; **10** 459,
  518–19; **12** 470
Asta Pharma AG, **IV** 71
Asta Werke AG, **IV** 71
Asteroid, **IV** 97
Astley & Pearce, **10** 277
Aston Brooke Software, **14** 392
Astor Trust Co., **II** 229
Astra A.B., **I 625–26**, 635, 651; **11** 290
Astra Resources, **12** 543
Astrolac, **IV** 498
Astrotech, **11** 429
Astrum International Corp., **12** 88; **13** 453
Asylum Life Assurance Co., **III** 371
Asymetrix, **6** 259
AT&T. *See also* American Telephone and
  Telegraph Company.
AT&T Bell Laboratories, Inc., 13 57–59
AT&T Communications, **V** 262–63
AT&T Global Information Solutions, **11**
  395
AT&T Information Systems, **13** 58
AT&T Istel Ltd., 14 35–36
AT&T Microelectronics, **II** 125
AT&T Network Systems International, **V**
  262–63
AT&T Ricoh Co., **III** 160
Ataka & Co., **I** 433; **II** 361
Atari Corporation, **II** 176; **III** 587; **IV**
  676; **6** 244; **7** 395–96; **9 44–47**; **10** 284,
  482, 485; **13** 472
ATC, **III** 760; **13** 280
Atchison, Topeka and Santa Fe Railroad, **V**
  507–08; **12** 19–20
ATCO Ltd., **13** 132
ATD Group, **10** 113
ATE Investment, **6** 449
Atelier de Construction Electrique de
  Delle, **9** 9
ATEQ Corp., **III** 533
Atex, **III** 476; **7** 162; **10** 34
ATH AG, **IV** 221
Atha Tool Co., **III** 627
Athalon Products, Ltd., **10** 181; **12** 313
Athenia Steel Co., **13** 369
Athens National Bank, **III** 190
Athens Piraeus Electricity Co., **IV** 658
Athletic Textile Company, Inc., **13** 532
Athletic X-Press, **14** 293

Athol Machine Co., **13** 301
ATI, **IV** 651; **7** 390
Atlanta Braves, **II** 166
Atlanta Gas Light Company, 6 446–48
Atlanta Hawks, **II** 166
Atlanta Paper Co., **IV** 311
Atlantic Acceptance Corporation, **7** 95
Atlantic Aircraft Corp., **I** 34
Atlantic and Pacific Telegraph Company, **6** 338
Atlantic Cement Co., **III** 671
Atlantic Computers, **14** 35
Atlantic Energy, Inc., 6 449–50
Atlantic Gulf and Caribbean Airways, **I** 115
Atlantic Import, **I** 285
Atlantic Precision Instrument Company, **13** 234
Atlantic Precision Works, **9** 72
Atlantic Records, **II** 176
Atlantic Refining Co., **III** 497; **III** 498; **IV** 375–76, 456, 504, 566, 570
Atlantic Research Corp., **13** 462
Atlantic Richfield Company, I 452; **II** 90, 425; **III** 740; **IV** 375–77, 379, 435, 454, 456–57, 467, 494, 522, 536, 571; **7** 57, 108, 537–38, 558–59; **8** 184, 416; **10** 110; **13** 13, 341
Atlantic Sea Products, **13** 103
The Atlantic Seaboard Dispatch. *See* GATX.
Atlantic Securities Ltd., **II** 223; **III** 98
Atlantic Southern Properties, Inc., **6** 449–50
Atlantic Surety Co., **III** 396
Atlantic Wholesalers, **II** 631
Atlantic-Union Oil, **IV** 570
Atlantis Ltd., **II** 566
Atlas Assurance Co., **III** 370
Atlas Chemical Industries, **I** 353
Atlas Copco AB, III 425–27, 480; **IV** 203
Atlas Corp., **I** 58, 512; **10** 316
Atlas Hotels, Inc., **V** 164
Atlas Petroleum Ltd., **IV** 449
Atlas Powder Co., **I** 343–44
Atlas Shipping, **I** 285
Atlas Steel Works, **I** 572
Atlas Steels, **IV** 191
Atlas Supply Co., **IV** 369
Atlas Tag & Label, **9** 72
Atlas Van Lines, Inc., 14 37–39
Atlas Works, **I** 531
Atlas-Werke AG, **IV** 88
Atle Byrnestad, **6** 368
Atmos Lebensmitteltechnik, **III** 420
ATO Chimie, **I** 303; **IV** 560
Atochem S.A., I 303–04, 676; **IV** 525, 547; **7** 484–85
Atom-Energi, **II** 2
ATR, **7** 9, 11
ATS. *See* Magasins Armand Thiéry et Sigrand.
ATT Microelectrica España, **V** 339
Attachmate Corp., **11** 520
Au Printemps S.A., V 9–11
Aubrey G. Lanston Co., **II** 301
Auchan, **10** 205
Audi, **I** 202; **IV** 570
Audio Development Company, **10** 18
Audio/Video Affiliates, Inc., **10** 468–69
Audiotronic Holdings, **III** 112
Aufina Bank, **II** 378
Aug. Stenman A.B., **III** 493
Aughton Group, **II** 466

Augsburger Aktienbank, **III** 377
Auguri Mondadori S.p.A., **IV** 586
August Max Woman, **V** 207–08
August Thyssen-Hütte AG, **IV** 221–22
Auguste Metz et Cie, **IV** 24
Aunor Gold Mines, Ltd., **IV** 164
Aunt Fanny's Bakery, **7** 429
Aurora Products, **II** 543
Ausilio Generale di Sicurezza, **III** 206
Ausimont N.V., **8** 271
Ausplay, **13** 319
AUSSAT Ltd., **6** 341
Aussedat-Rey, **IV** 288
The Austin Company, 8 41–44
Austin Motor Company, **I** 183; **III** 554; **7** 458
Austin Nichols, **I** 248, 261, 280–81
Austin Rover, **14** 321
Austin-Morris, **III** 494
Austral Waste Products, **IV** 248
Australasian Paper and Pulp Co. Ltd., **IV** 248
Australasian Sugar Co., **III** 686
Australasian United Steam Navigation Co., **III** 522
Australia and New Zealand Banking Group Ltd., II 187–90
Australia Gilt Co. Group, **II** 422
Australia National Bank, Limited, **10** 170
Australian Airlines, **6** 91, 112
Australian and Kandos Cement (Holdings) Ltd., **III** 687, 728
Australian and Overseas Telecommunications Corporation, **6** 341–42
Australian Associated Press, **IV** 669
Australian Automotive Air, Pty. Ltd., **III** 593
Australian Bank of Commerce, **II** 188
Australian Blue Asbestos, **III** 687
Australian Consolidated Investments, Limited, **10** 170
Australian Forest Products, **I** 438–39
Australian Guarantee Corp. Ltd., **II** 389–90
Australian Gypsum Industries, **III** 673
Australian Iron & Steel Co., **IV** 45
Australian Metal Co., **IV** 139
Australian Mutual Provident Society, **IV** 61, 697
Australian Paper Co., **IV** 248
Australian Telecommunications Corporation, **6** 342
Australian United Corp., **II** 389
Australian Window Glass, **III** 726
Austrian Industries, **IV** 485, 486
Austrian National Bank, **IV** 230
Austro-Americana, **6** 425
Austro-Daimler, **I** 138, 206; **11** 31
Auto Avio Costruzione, **13** 219
Auto Coil Springs, **III** 581
Auto Shack. *See* AutoZone, Inc.
Auto Strop Safety Razor Co., **III** 27–28
Auto Union, **I** 150
Auto-Flo Corp., **III** 569
Auto-Trol Technology, **14** 15
Autodesk, Inc., 10 118–20
Autolite, **I** 29, 142; **III** 555
Automat, **II** 614
Automated Building Components, **III** 735
Automated Communications, Inc., **8** 311
Automated Loss Prevention Systems, **11** 445
Automated Security (Holdings) PLC, **11** 444

Automated Wagering Systems, **III** 128
Automatic Data Processing, Inc., III 117–19; 9 48–51 (upd.), 125, 173
Automatic Fire Alarm Co., **III** 644
Automatic Manufacturing Corporation, **10** 319
Automatic Payrolls, Inc., **III** 117
Automatic Retailers of America, Inc., **II** 607; **13** 48
Automatic Sprinkler Corp. of America, **7** 176–77
Automatic Telephone & Electric, **II** 81
Automatic Vaudeville Arcades Co., **II** 154
Automobile Insurance Co., **III** 181–82
Automobiles Citroen, I 162, 188; **III** 676; **IV** 722; **V** 237; **7** 35–38; **11** 103
Automobili Lamborghini S.p.A., 13 60–62, 219
Automotive Components Group Worldwide, **10** 325
Automotive Diagnostics, **10** 492
Autonet, **6** 435
Autophon AG, **9** 32
AutoTrol Technology, **III** 111
AutoZone, Inc., 9 52–54
Avana Group, **II** 565
Avco. *See* Aviation Corp. of the Americas.
Avco Financial Services Inc., 13 63–65
Avco National Bank, **II** 420
Avecor, **8** 347
Avendt Group, Inc., **IV** 137
Avenir, **III** 393
Avery Dennison Corporation, IV 251–54; 15 229
Avesta Steel Works Co., **I** 553–54
Avfuel, **11** 538
Avgain Marine A/S, **7** 40
Avia Group International, Inc., **V** 376–77
Aviacion y Comercio, **6** 95–96
AVIACO. *See* Aviacion y Comercio.
Aviation Corp. of the Americas, **I** 48, 78, 89, 115, 530; **III** 66; **6** 75; **9** 497–99; **10** 163; **11** 261, 427; **12** 379, 383; **13** 64
Aviation Power Supply, **II** 16
Avion Coach Corp., **I** 76; **III** 484; **11** 363
Avions Marcel Dassault-Breguet Aviation, I 44–46; 7 11; **7** 205; **8** 314
Avis, Inc., I 30, 446, 463; **II** 468; **III** 502; **IV** 370; **6** 348–49, **356–58,** 392–93; **8** 33; **9** 284; **10** 419; **11** 198
Avisco, **I** 317, 365, 442–43; **V** 359
Avisun Corp., **IV** 371
Avnet Inc., 9 55–57; 10 112–13; **13** 47
Avon Products Inc., III 13, **15–16,** 62; **8** 329; **9** 331; **11** 282, 366; **12** 314, 435; **13** 38; **14** 501–02
Avon Publications, Inc., **IV** 627
Avoncraft Construction Co., **I** 512
Avondale Industries, Inc., I 512–14; **7 39–41**
Avondale Mills, Inc., **8** 558–60; **9** 466
Avondown Properties Ltd., **IV** 711
Avro, **I** 81
AVS, **III** 200
Avtex Fibers Inc., **I** 443; **11** 134
Award Foods, **II** 528
AXA, III 209, **210–12**
Axa Group, **15** 30
Axel Johnson Group, I 553–55
Axel Springer Verlag AG, IV 589–91
Axelrod Foods, **II** 528
Axon Systems Inc., **7** 336
Ayco Corp., **II** 398; **10** 62
Ayerst, **I** 623

Ayshire Collieries, **IV** 18
Azienda Generale Italiana Petroli, **IV** 419–21. *See also* Agip SpA.
Azienda Nazionale Idrogenazione Combustibili, **IV** 419–22
AZL Resources, **7** 538
Aznar International, **14** 225
AZP Group Inc., **6** 546
Aztar Corporation, 13 66–68
Azuma Leather Co. Ltd., **V** 380
Azuma Shiki Manufacturing, **IV** 326
Azusa Valley Savings Bank, **II** 382

B & O. *See* Baltimore and Ohio Railroad.
B.A.T. Industries PLC, **14** 77
B&Q, **V** 106, 108
B&W Diesel, **III** 513
B. B. & R. Knight Brothers, **8** 200
B.B. Foods, **13** 244
B.C. Rail Telecommunications, **6** 311
B.C. Sugar, **II** 664
B. Dalton Bookseller, **10** 136; **13** 545
B.F. Ehlers, **I** 417
B.F. Goodrich Co. *See* BFGoodrich Company.
B.F. Walker, Inc., **11** 354
B.J.'s Wholesale, **12** 335
B. Perini & Sons, Inc., **8** 418
B.R. Simmons, **III** 527
B.S. Bull & Co., **II** 668
B. Stroh Brewing Co., **I** 290
B.T.I. Chemicals Ltd., **I** 313; **10** 154
B.V. Tabak Export & Import Compagnie, **12** 109
BA. *See* British Airways.
BAA plc, 10 121–23
Babbage's, Inc., 10 124–25
Babcock & Wilcox Co., **III** 465–66, 516, 559–60; **V** 621
Baby Furniture and Toy Supermarket, **V** 203
Baby Superstore, Inc., 15 32–34
Babybird Co., Ltd., **V** 150
BAC. *See* Barclays American Corp.
Bache, **III** 340
Bache & Company, **8** 349
Bachman Foods, **15** 139
Bachman Holdings, Inc., **14** 165
Bachrach Advertising, **6** 40
Backer & Spielvogel, **I** 33; **12** 168; **14** 48–49
Backroom Systems Group, **II** 317
Bacon & Matheson Drop Forge Co., **I** 185
Badger Co., **II** 86
Badger Illuminating Company, **6** 601
Badger Paint and Hardware Stores, **II** 419
Badger Paper Mills, Inc., 15 35–37
Badische Analin & Soda Fabrik A.G., **I** 305
BAFS. *See* Bangkok Aviation Fuel Services Ltd.
Bahia de San Francisco Television, **IV** 621
Bailey Controls, **III** 560
Bain & Co., **III** 429; **9** 343
Bain Capital, **14** 244–45
Baird, **7** 235, 237
Bakelite Corp., **I** 399; **9** 517; **13** 231
Baker & Co., **IV** 78
Baker & Crane, **II** 318
Baker & McKenzie, 10 126–28
Baker & Taylor, **I** 548
Baker Casing Shoe Co., **III** 429
Baker Cummins Pharmaceuticals Inc., **11** 208

Baker Hughes Incorporated, III 428–29; **11** 513
Baker Industries, Inc., **III** 440; **8** 476; **13** 124
Baker International Corp., **III** 428–29
Baker Oil Tools, **III** 428–29
Baker-Raulang Co., **13** 385
Bakers Square, **12** 510. *See also* VICORP Restaurants, Inc.
Bakersfield Savings and Loan, **10** 339
Bakery Products Inc., **IV** 410
Balair Ltd., **I** 122
Balco, Inc., **7** 479–80
Balcor Co., **II** 398; **IV** 703
Balcor, Inc., **10** 62
Baldwin Hardware Manufacturing Co., **III** 570
Baldwin Rubber Industries, **13** 79
Baldwin-United Corp., **III** 254, 293
Baldwins Ltd., **III** 494
Bålforsens Kraft AB, **IV** 339–40
Balfour Beatty Construction Ltd., **III** 433–34; **13** 206
Balikpapan Forest Industries, **I** 504
Ball & Young Adhesives, **9** 92
Ball Corporation, I 597–98; 10 129–31 (upd.); 13 254, 256; **15** 129
Ball Stalker Inc., **14** 4
Ball-Bartoe Aircraft Corp., **I** 598; **10** 130
Ballantine & Sons Ltd., **I** 263
Ballantine Beer, **6** 27
Ballantine Books, **13** 429
Ballard & Ballard Co., **II** 555
Bally Gaming International, **15** 539
Bally Manufacturing Corporation, III 430–32; **6** 210; **10** 375, 482; **12** 107; **15** 538–39
AB Baltic, **III** 418–19
Baltic Cable, **15** 521
Baltimore & Ohio Railroad, **I** 584; **II** 329; **V** 438–40
Baltimore Aircoil Company, **7** 30–31
Baltimore Gas and Electric Company, V 552–54; 11 388
Baltimore Paper Box Company, **8** 102
Baltino Foods, **13** 383
Balzaretti-Modigliani, **III** 676
Bamberger's of New Jersey, **V** 169; **8** 443
Banana Boat Holding Corp., **15** 359
Banana Republic, **V** 61–62
Banc One Corporation, 9 475; 10 132–34; 11 181
Banca Brasiliana Italo-Belga, **II** 270
Banca Coloniale di Credito, **II** 271
Banca Commerciale Italiana SpA, I 368, 465, 467; II 191–93, 242, 271, 278, 295, 319; **III** 207–08, 347
BancA Corp., **11** 305
Banca d'America e d'Italia, **II** 280
Banca Dalmata di Sconto, **II** 271
Banca de Gottardo, **II** 361
Banca di Genova, **II** 270
Banca Internazionale Lombarda, **II** 192
Banca Italiana di Sconto, **II** 191
Banca Italo-Cinese, **II** 270
Banca Italo-Viennese, **II** 270
Banca Jacquet e Hijos, **II** 196
Banca Luis Roy Sobrino, **II** 196
Banca Nazionale de Lavoro, **II** 239
Banca Nazionale dell'Agricoltura, **II** 272
Banca Nazionale di Credito, **II** 271
Banca Unione di Credito, **II** 270
BancItaly Corp., **II** 226–27, 288, 536; **13** 528

Banco Aleman-Panameno, **II** 521
Banco Bilbao Vizcaya, S.A., II 194–96
Banco Bradesco S.A., 13 69–71
Banco Central, II 197–98; III 394; **IV** 397
Banco Chemical (Portugal) S.A. *See* Chemical Banking Corp.
Banco de Barcelona, **II** 194
Banco di Roma, **I** 465, 467; **II** 191, 257, 271
Banco di Santo Spirito, **I** 467
Banco do Brasil S.A., II 199–200
Banco Español de Credito, **II** 195, 198; **IV** 160
Banco Espírito Santo e Comercial de Lisboa S.A., 15 38–40
Banco Industrial de Bilbao, **II** 195
Banco Italo-Belga, **II** 270, 271
Banco Italo-Egiziano, **II** 271
Banco Nacional de Cuba, **II** 345
Banco Nacional de Mexico, **9** 333
Banco Popolar, **III** 348; **6** 97
Banco Santander, **III** 271, 294; **15** 257
Banco Trento & Bolanzo, **II** 240
Banco Vascongado, **II** 196
BancOhio National Bank in Columbus, **9** 475
Bancorp Leasing, Inc., **14** 529
BancorpSouth, Inc., **14** 40–41
Bancroft Racket Co., **III** 24
BancSystems Association Inc., **9** 475, 476
Banesto. *See* Banco Español de Credito.
Banexi, **II** 233
Bangkok Airport Hotel, **6** 123–24
Bangkok Aviation Fuel Services Ltd., **6** 123–24
Bangor and Aroostook Railroad Company, **8** 33
Bangor Mills, **13** 169
Bangor Punta Corp., **I** 452, 482; **II** 403
Bank Brussels Lambert, II 201–03, 295, 407
Bank Bumiputra, **IV** 519
Bank CIC-Union Européenne A.G., **II** 272
Bank Européene de Credità Moyen Terme, **II** 319
Bank for International Settlements, **II** 368
Bank für Elektrische Unternehmungen. *See* Elektrowatt AG.
Bank für Gemeinwirtschaft, **II** 239
Bank Hapoalim B.M., II 204–06
Bank Leu, **I** 252
Bank of Adelaide, **II** 189
Bank of America, **I** 536–37; **II** 226–28, 252–55, 280, 288–89, 347, 382; **III** 218; **6** 385; **8** 94–95; **9** 50, 123–24, 333, 536; **12** 106, 466; **13** 69; **14** 170. *See also* BankAmerica Corporation.
Bank of America National Trust and Savings Assoc. (NT & SA), **I** 536; **II** 227, 288; **13** 528. *See also* BankAmerica Corporation.
Bank of Antwerp, **IV** 497
Bank of Asheville, **II** 336
Bank of Australasia, **II** 187–89
The Bank of Bishop and Co., Ltd., **11** 114
Bank of Boston Corporation, II 207–09; **7** 114; **12** 31; **13** 467; **14** 90
Bank of Britain, **14** 46–47
Bank of British Columbia, **II** 244, 298
Bank of British Honduras, **II** 344
Bank of British North America, **II** 220
Bank of California, **II** 322, 490
Bank of Canada, **II** 210, 376

Bank of Central and South America, **II** 344
Bank of Chicago, **III** 270
Bank of China, **II** 298
Bank of Chosen, **II** 338
Bank of Commerce, **II** 331
Bank of England, **II** 217, 235–36, 306–07, 318–19, 333–34, 357, 421–22, 427–28; **III** 234, 280; **IV** 119, 366, 382, 705, 711; **10** 8, 336; **14** 45–46
Bank of Finland, **III** 648
Bank of France, **II** 232, 264–65, 354; **III** 391
Bank of Hamilton, **II** 244
Bank of Hindustan, **IV** 699
Bank of Israel, **II** 206
Bank of Italy, **I** 536; **II** 192, 226, 271–72, 288; **III** 209, 347; **8** 45
The Bank of Jacksonville, **9** 58
Bank of Japan, **I** 519; **II** 291, 325
Bank of Kobe, **II** 371
Bank of Lee County, **14** 40
Bank of Liverpool, **II** 236
Bank of London and South America, **II** 308
Bank of Manhattan Co., **II** 247–48
The Bank of Milwaukee, **14** 529
Bank of Mississippi, Inc., 14 40–41
Bank of Montreal, II 210–12, 231, 375
Bank of Nettleton, **14** 40
Bank of New Brunswick, **II** 221
Bank of New England Corporation, II 213–15; 9 229
Bank of New Orleans, **11** 106
Bank of New Queensland, **II** 188
Bank of New South Wales, **II** 188–89, 388–90
Bank of New York Company, Inc., II 192, **216–19**, 247
Bank of North Mississippi, **14** 41
Bank of Nova Scotia, II 220–23, 345; **IV** 644
Bank of Ontario, **II** 210
Bank of Osaka, **II** 360
Bank of Ottawa, **II** 221
Bank of Pasadena, **II** 382
Bank of Queensland, **II** 188
The Bank of Scotland. *See* The Governor and Company of the Bank of Scotland.
Bank of Sherman, **14** 40
Bank of Spain, **II** 194, 197
Bank of the Ohio Valley, **13** 221
Bank of the People, **II** 210
Bank of the United States, **II** 207, 216, 247
Bank of the West, **II** 233
Bank of Tokyo, Ltd., II 224–25, 276, 301, 341, 358; **IV** 151; **12** 138; **15** 41–42
Bank of Tokyo-Mitsubishi Ltd., 15 41–43 (upd.), 431
Bank of Toronto, **II** 375–76
Bank of Tupelo, **14** 40
Bank of Upper Canada, **II** 210
Bank of Wales, **10** 336, 338
Bank of Western Australia, **II** 187
Bank of Winterthur, **II** 378
Bank Powszechny Depozytowy, **IV** 119
Bank voor Handel en Nijverheid, **II** 304
BankAmerica Corporation, II 226–28, 436; **8 45–48 (upd.)**, 295, 469, 471; **13** 69. *See also* Bank of America *and* Bank of America National Trust and Savings Assoc.
Bankers and Shippers Insurance Co., **III** 389

Bankers Co., **II** 230
Bankers Corporation, **14** 473
Bankers Investment, **II** 349
Bankers Life and Casualty Co., **10** 247
Bankers Life Co., **III** 328–30
Bankers National Bank, **II** 261
Bankers National Life Insurance Co., **II** 182; **10** 246
Bankers Trust New York Corporation, I 601; **II** 211, **229–31**, 330, 339; **III** 84–86; **10** 425; **11** 416; **12** 165, 209; **13** 188, 466
Bankhaus IG Herstatt, **II** 242
BankVermont Corp., **II** 208
Banner Aerospace, Inc., 14 42–44
Banner International, **13** 20
Banner Life, **III** 273
Banque Belge et Internationale en Egypte, **II** 295
Banque Belge pour l'Etranger, **II** 294
Banque Belgo-Zairoise, **II** 294
Banque Bruxelles Lambert. *See* Bank Brussels Lambert.
Banque Commerciale du Maroc, **II** 272
Banque Commerciale-Basle, **II** 270
Banque d'Anvers/Bank van Antwerpen, **II** 294–95
Banque de Bruxelles, **II** 201–02, 239
Banque de Credit et de Depot des Pays Bas, **II** 259
Banque de France, **14** 45–46
Banque de l'Indochine et de Suez, **II** 259
Banque de l'Union Européenne, **IV** 94
Banque de l'Union Parisienne, **II** 270; **IV** 497, 557
Banque de la Construction et les Travaux Public, **II** 319
Banque de la Société Générale de Belgique, **II** 294–95
Banque de Louvain, **II** 202
Banque de Paris et des Pays-Bas, **II** 136, 259; **10** 346
Banque de Reports et de Depots, **II** 201
Banque du Congo Belge, **II** 294
Banque Européenne pour l'Amerique Latine, **II** 294
Banque Française et Espagnol en Paris, **II** 196
Banque Française pour le Commerce et l'Industrie, **II** 232, 270
Banque Générale des Pays Roumains, **II** 270
Banque Générale du Luxembourg, **II** 294
Banque Indosuez, **II** 429
Banque Internationale à Luxembourg, **II** 239
Banque Internationale de Bruxelles, **II** 201–02
Banque Italo-Belge, **II** 294
Banque Italo-Francaise de Credit, **II** 271
Banque Lambert, **II** 201–02
Banque Nationale de Paris S.A., II 232–34, 239; **III** 201, 392–94; **9** 148; **13** 203; **15** 309
Banque Nationale Pour le Commerce et l'Industrie, **II** 232–33
Banque Nordique du Commerce, **II** 366
Banque Orea, **II** 378
Banque Paribas, **II** 192, 260; **IV** 295
Banque Rothschild, **IV** 107
Banque Sino-Belge, **II** 294
Banque Stern, **II** 369
Banque Transatlantique, **II** 271
Banque Worms, **III** 393

Banquet Foods Corp., **II** 90, 494; **12** 81
Banta Corporation, 12 24–26
Bantam Ball Bearing Company, **13** 522
Bantam Books, Inc., **III** 190–91
Bantam Doubleday Dell Publishing Group, **IV** 594; **13** 429; **15** 51
Banyu Pharmaceutical Co., **I** 651; **11** 290
BAP of New York, Inc., **15** 246
BAPCO, **III** 745
Barat. *See* Barclays National Bank.
Barberet & Blanc, **I** 677
Barclay Furniture Co., **12** 300
Barclay Group, **I** 335; **10** 290
Barclays Business Credit, **13** 468
Barclays PLC, I 604–05; **II** 202, 204, **235–37**, 239, 244, 308, 319, 333, 383, 422, 429; **III** 516; **IV** 23, 722; **7** 332–33; **8** 118; **11** 29–30
BarclaysAmerican Mortgage Corporation, 11 29–30
Barcolo Manufacturing, **15** 103
Barden Cablevision, **IV** 640
Bareco Products, **15** 352
Barings PLC, III 699; **14 45–47**
Barker & Dobson, **II** 629
Barker and Company, Ltd., **13** 286
Barlow Rand Ltd., I 288–89, **422–24; IV** 22, 96
Barmer Bankverein, **II** 238, 241
Barnato Brothers, **IV** 21, 65; **7** 122
Barnes & Noble, Inc., 10 135–37; 12 172; **13** 494, 545; **14** 61–62; **15** 62
Barnes Group, **III** 581
Barnes-Hind, **III** 56, 727
Barnett Banks, Inc., 9 58–60
Barnett Brass & Copper Inc., **9** 543
Barnetts, Hoares, Hanbury and Lloyds, **II** 306
Barnstead/Thermolyne Corporation, **14** 479–80
Barr & Stroud Ltd., **III** 727
Barranquilla Investments, **II** 138
Barratt Developments plc, I 556–57
Barret Fitch North, **II** 445
Barrett Burston, **I** 437
Barrett Co., **I** 414–15
Barry & Co., **III** 522
Barry Wright Corporation, **9** 27
Barsab, **I** 288–89
Barsotti's, Inc., **6** 146
Bart Starr, **12** 284
Barth Smelting Corp., **I** 513
Barton Brands, **I** 227; **II** 609; **10** 181
Barton, Duer & Koch, **IV** 282; **9** 261
Barton Incorporated, **13** 134
BASF A.G., I 275, **305–08**, 309, 319, 346–47, 632, 638; **II** 554; **IV** 70–71; **13** 75; **14** 308
Basic American Retirement Communities, **III** 103
Basic Resources, Inc., **V** 725
Basics, **14** 295
BASIS Information Technologies, Inc., **11** 112–13, 132
Baskin-Robbins Ice Cream Co., **I** 215; **7** 128, 372
Basle A.G., **I** 632–33, 671–72; **8** 108–09
Basle Air Transport, **I** 121
Basler Bankverein, **II** 368
Bass & Co., **I** 142
Bass Brewers Ltd., **15** 441
Bass PLC, I 222–24; III 94–95; **9** 99, 425–26; **15 44–47 (upd.)**
Bassett Foods, **II** 478

Bassett-Walker Inc., **V** 390–91
Bassins Food Chain, **II** 649
BAT. *See* British-American Tobacco Co., Ltd.
BAT Industries plc, **I** 425–27, 605; **II** 628; **III** 66, 185, 522; **9** 312
Bataafsche Petroleum Maatschappij, **V** 658
Batavia Wine Company, **13** 134
Batchelors Ltd., **I** 315
Bateman Eichler Hill Richards, **III** 270
Bates & Robins, **II** 318
Bates Chemical Company, **9** 154
Bates Manufacturing Company, **10** 314
Bates Worldwide, Inc., **14** 48–51
Batesville Casket Company, **10** 349–50
Bath & Body Works, **11** 41
Bath Iron Works Corporation, **12** 27–29
Bathurst Bank, **II** 187
Baton Rouge Gas Light Company. *See* Gulf States Utilities Company.
Battelle Memorial Institute, Inc., **6** 288; **10** 138–40
Batten Barton Durstine & Osborn, **I** 25, 28–31, 33
Battle Creek Food Company, **14** 557–58
Battle Creek Toasted Corn Flake Co., **II** 523; **13** 291
Battle Mountain Gold Co., **IV** 490
BATUS Inc., **9** 312
Bauborg, **I** 560–61
Baudhuin-Anderson Company, **8** 553
Bauer Publishing Group, **7** 42–43
Bausch & Lomb Inc., **III** 446; **7** 44–47; **10** 46–47; **13** 365–66
Bavarian Railway, **II** 241
Bavarian Specialty Foods, **13** 383
Baxter Estates, **II** 649
Baxter International Inc., **I** 627–29; **9** 346; **10 141–43 (upd.)**; **11** 198–99; **11** 459–60; **12** 325
Bay Area Review Course, Inc., **IV** 623
Bay Cities Transportation Company, **6** 382
Bay City Cash Way Company, **V** 222
Bay Colony Life Insurance Co., **III** 254
Bay Petroleum, **I** 526
Bay Ridge Savings Bank, **10** 91
Bay State Glass Co., **III** 683
Bay State Iron Manufacturing Co., **13** 16
Bay State Tap and Die Company, **13** 7
Bay West Paper Corporation. *See* Mosinee Paper Corporation.
BayBanks, Inc., **12** 30–32
Bayer A.G., **I** 305–06, **309–11**, 319, 346–47, 350; **II** 279; **12** 364; **13 75–77 (upd.)**; **14** 169
Bayer S.p.A., **8** 179
Bayerische Aluminium AG, **IV** 230
Bayerische Hypotheken- und Wechsel-Bank AG, **II** 238–40, 241–42; **IV** 323
Bayerische Kraftwerke AG, **IV** 229–30
Bayerische Landesbank, **II** 257–58, 280; **14** 170
Bayerische Motoren Werke A.G., **I** 73, 75, **138–40**, 198; **II** 5; **III** 543, 556, 591; **11 31–33 (upd.)**; **13** 30
Bayerische Rückversicherung AG, **III** 377
Bayerische Rumpler Werke, **I** 73
Bayerische Stickstoff-Werke AG, **IV** 229–30
Bayerische Vereinsbank A.G., **II** 239–40, **241–43**; **III** 401
Bayerische Versicherungsbank, **II** 238; **III** 377

Bayerische Wasserkraftwerke Aktiengesellschaft, **IV** 231
Bayerische Zellstoff, **IV** 325
Bayernwerk AG, **IV** 231–32, 323; **V** 555–58, 698–700
Bayon Steel Corp., **IV** 234
Bayou Boeuf Fabricators, **III** 559
Bayside National Bank, **II** 230
Baystate Corporation, **12** 30
Baytree Investors Inc., **15** 87
Bayview, **III** 673
BBC. *See* British Broadcasting Corp.
BBC Brown, Boveri Ltd., **II** 1, 3–4, 13; **III** 466, 631–32
BBDO. *See* Batten Barton Durstine & Osborn.
BBME. *See* British Bank of the Middle East.
BBO & Co., **14** 433
BC TEL. *See* British Columbia Telephone Company.
BCal. *See* British Caledonian Airways.
BCE, Inc., **V** 269–71; **6** 307; **7** 333; **12** 413
BCI. *See* Banca Commerciale Italiana SpA.
BDB Corp., **10** 136
BDDP. *See* Wells Rich Greene BDDP.
BeachviLime Ltd., **IV** 74
Beacon Manufacturing, **I** 377
Beacon Oil, **IV** 566
Beacon Participations, **III** 98
Beacon Publishing Co., **IV** 629
Bean Fiberglass Inc., **15** 247
Bear Automotive Service Equipment Company, **10** 494
Bear Creek Corporation, **12** 444–45
Bear Stearns Companies, Inc., **II** 400–01, 450; **10 144–45 (upd.)**, 382
Beard & Stone Electric Co., **I** 451
Bearings, Inc., **I** 158–59; **13 78–80**
Beatrice Company, **I** 353, 440–41; **II** 467–69, 475; **III** 118, 437; **6** 357; **9** 318; **12** 82, 87, 93; **13** 162–63, 452; **14** 149–50; **15** 213–14, 358
Beauharnois Power Company, **6** 502
Beaulieu Winery, **I** 260
Beaumont-Bennett Group, **6** 27
Beaver Lumber Co., **I** 274
Beazer Plc., **7** 209
Bechtel Group Inc., **I** 558–59, 563; **III** 248; **IV** 171, 576; **6** 148–49, 556; **13** 13
Beck & Gregg Hardware Co., **9** 253
Becker Paribas Futures, **II** 445
Becker Warburg Paribas, **II** 259
Beckley-Cardy Co., **IV** 623–24
Beckman Instruments, Inc., **I** 694; **14** 52–54
Becton, Dickinson & Company, **I** 630–31; **IV** 550; **9** 96; **11 34–36 (upd.)**
Bed Bath & Beyond Inc., **13 81–83**; **14** 61
Beddor Companies, **12** 25
Bedford Chemical, **8** 177
Bedford-Stuyvesant Restoration Corp., **II** 673
Bee Chemicals, **I** 372
Bee Gee Shoe Corporation, **10** 281
Bee Gee Shrimp, **I** 473
Beech Aircraft Corporation, **II** 87; **8** 49–52, 313; **11** 411, 413
Beech Holdings Corp., **9** 94
Beech-Nut Corp., **I** 695; **II** 489
Beecham Group PLC, **I** 626, 640, 668; **II** 331, 543; **III** 18, 65–66; **9** 264; **14** 53

Beechwood Insurance Agency, Inc., **14** 472
Beerman Stores, Inc., **10** 281
Beghin Say S.A., **II** 540
Behr-Manning Company, **8** 396
Behringwerke AG, **14** 255
Beijerinvest Group, **I** 210
Beijing Machinery and Equipment Corp., **II** 442
Beirao, Pinto, Silva and Co. *See* Banco Espírito Santo e Comercial de Lisboa S.A.
Bejam Group PLC, **II** 678
Beker Industries, **IV** 84
Bekins Company, **15 48–50**
Bel Air Markets, **14** 397
Belairbus, **I** 42; **12** 191
Belcher New England, Inc., **IV** 394
Belcher Oil Co., **IV** 394
Belden Corp., **II** 16
Belfast Banking Co., **II** 318
Belgacom, **6 302–04**
Belgian De Vaderlandsche, **III** 309
Belgian Rapid Access to Information Network Services, **6** 304
Belgian Société Internationale Forestière et Minière, **IV** 65
Belgochim, **IV** 499
Belize Sugar Industries, **II** 582
Belk Stores Services, **V** 12–13
Bell (Quarry and Concrete), **III** 674
Bell Aerospace, **I** 530
Bell Aircraft Company, **I** 529; **11** 267; **13** 267
Bell and Howell Company, **I** 463; **IV** 642; **9** 33, **61–64**; **11** 197; **14** 569; **15** 71
Bell Atlantic Corporation, **V** 272–74; **9** 171; **10** 232, 456; **11** 59, 87, 274; **12** 137; **13** 399
Bell Canada, **V** 269, 308–09; **6 305–08**; **12** 413
Bell Canada Enterprises Inc. *See* BCE, Inc.
Bell Communications Research (Bellcore), **13** 58
Bell Fibre Products, **12** 377
Bell Industries, **13** 47
Bell Laboratories, **II** 33, 60–61, 101, 112; **V** 259–64; **8** 157; **9** 171; **10** 108; **11** 327, 500–01; **12** 61; **14** 52, 281–82. *See also* AT&T Bell Labroaties, Inc.
Bell Mountain Partnership, Ltd., **15** 26
Bell Pharmacal Labs, **12** 387
Bell Resources, **I** 437–38; **III** 729; **10** 170
Bell System, **II** 72, 230; **6** 338–40; **7** 99, 333; **11** 500
Bell Telephone Company, **I** 409; **6** 332, 334
Bell Telephone Company of Pennsylvania, **I** 585
Bell Telephone Manufacturing, **II** 13
Bell's Asbestos and Engineering, **I** 428
Bell-Northern Research, Ltd., **V** 269–71; **15** 131
Belle Alkali Co., **IV** 409; **7** 308
Belledune Fertilizer Ltd., **IV** 165
Bellefonte Insurance Co., **IV** 29
Bellemead Development Corp., **III** 220; **14** 108
Bellofram Corp., **14** 43
BellSouth Corporation, **V** 276–78; **9** 171, 321; **10** 431, 501; **15** 197
Belmin Systems, **14** 36
Belmont Electronics, **II** 85–86; **11** 412
Belmont Plaza, **12** 316

Belmont Savings and Loan, **10** 339
Belmont Springs Water Company, Inc., **I** 234; **10** 227
Belo Productions, Inc., **10** 3, 5
Beloit Corporation, 8 243; **14 55–57**
Beloit Woodlands, **10** 380
Belridge Oil Co., **IV** 541
Belzer Group, **IV** 198–99
Bemis Company, Inc., 8 53–55
Bemrose group, **IV** 650
Ben & Jerry's Homemade, Inc., 10 146–48
Ben Franklin, **V** 152–53; **8** 555
Ben Franklin Savings & Trust, **10** 117
Ben Hill Griffin, **III** 53
Ben Johnson & Co. Ltd., **IV** 661
Ben Line, **6** 398
Bendicks, **I** 592
Bendix Corp., I 68, **141–43**, 154, 166, 192, 416; **III** 33; **III** 166, 555; **7** 356; **8** 545; **9** 16–17; **10** 260, 279; **11** 138; **13** 356–57; **15** 284
Beneficial Corporation, II 236; **8 56–58**, 117; **10** 490
Beneficial National Bank USA, **II** 286
Beneficial Standard Life, **10** 247
Benesse Corporation, **13** 91, 93
Benetton Group S.p.A., 8 171; **10 149–52; 15** 369
Bengal Iron and Steel Co., **IV** 205–06
Benjamin Allen & Co., **IV** 660
Benjamin Moore and Co., 13 84–87
Benn Bros. plc, **IV** 687
Bennett Biscuit Co., **II** 543
Bennigan's, **II** 556–57; **7** 336; **12** 373; **13** 408
Benson & Hedges, **V** 398–99; **15** 137
Benson Wholesale Co., **II** 624
Bentley Mills, Inc., **8** 272
Bentley Motor Ltd., **I** 194
Bentley Systems, **6** 247
Benton & Bowles, **I** 33; **6** 20, 22
Benxi Iron and Steel Corp., **IV** 167
Benzina, **IV** 487
Benzinol, **IV** 487
N.V. Benzit. *See* N.V. Gemeenschappelijk Benzit van Aandeelen Philips Gloeilampenfabriken.
Berec Group, **III** 502; **7** 208
Berg Manufacturing Sales Co., **I** 156
Berg- und Metallbank, **IV** 139–40
Bergdorf Goodman, **I** 246; **V** 30–31
Bergedorfer Eisenwerk, **III** 417–20
Bergen Bank, **II** 352
Bergen Brunswig Corporation, I 413; **V 14–16,** 152; **13 88–90 (upd.)**
Berger Jenson and Nicholson, **I** 347
Bergische-Markische Bank, **II** 278
Berglen, **III** 570
Bergmann & Co., **II** 27
Bergstrom Paper Company, **8** 413
Bergswerksgesellschaft Hibernia, **I** 349; **IV** 194
Bergvik & Ala, **IV** 336, 338–39
Berkeley Computers, **III** 109; **14** 13
Berkey Photo Inc., **I** 447; **III** 475
Berkley Dean & Co., **15** 525
Berkshire Hathaway Inc., III 29, **213–15; 12** 435–36, 554–55
Berkshire International, **V** 390–91
Berkshire Partners, **10** 393
Berleca Ltd., **9** 395
Berlex Laboratories, **I** 682; **10** 214
Berlin Exchange, **I** 409

Berlin Göring-Werke, **IV** 233
Berliner Bank, **II** 256
Berliner Bankverein, **II** 278
Berliner Handels- und Frankfurter Bank, **II** 242
Berliner Union, **I** 409
Berlinische Bodengesellschaft, **I** 560
Berlitz International, Inc., IV 643; **7** 286, 312; **13 91–93**
Berni Inns, **I** 247
Bernie Schulman's, **12** 132
Bernstein Macauley, Inc., **II** 450
Berrios Enterprises, **14** 236
Berry Bearing Company, **9** 254
Berry Industries, **III** 628
Bert L. Smokler & Company, **11** 257
Bertea Corp., **III** 603
Bertelsmann AG, IV 592–94, 614–15; **10** 196; **15 51–54 (upd.)**
Bertron Griscom & Company, **V** 641
Berwind Corp., **14** 18
Beryllium Resources, **14** 80
Berzelius Metallhütten Gesellschaft, **IV** 141
Berzelius Umwelt-Service, **III** 625; **IV** 141
Bess Mfg., **8** 510
Bessemer Capital Partners L.P., **15** 505
Bessemer Gas Engine Co., **II** 15
Bessemer Limestone & Cement Co., **IV** 409
Bessemer Steamship, **IV** 572; **7** 549
Besser Vibrapac, **III** 673
Best Apparel, **V** 156
Best Buy Co., Inc., 9 65–66; 10 305
Best Foods, Inc., **II** 496–97
Best Manufacturing, **15** 490
Best Western, **14** 106
Bestwall Gypsum Co., **IV** 281; **9** 259
Bestway Transportation, **14** 505
Beswick, **II** 17
Bethesda Research Labs, **I** 321
Bethlehem Steel Corporation, IV 35–37, 228, 572–73; **6** 540; **7 48–51 (upd.),** 447, 549–50; **11** 65; **12** 354; **13** 97, 157
Beton Union, **III** 738
Better Communications, **IV** 597
Betz Laboratories, Inc., I 312–13; **10 153–55 (upd.); 15** 536
Bevan and Wedd Durlacher Morduant & Co., **II** 237
Beveridge-Marvellum Company, **8** 483
Beverly Enterprises, Inc., III 76–77, 80; **14** 242
Beverly Hills Savings, **II** 420
Bevis Custom Furniture, Inc., **12** 263
BFGoodrich Company, I 28, 428, 440; **II** 414; **III** 118, 443; **V 231–33; 8** 80–81, 290; **9** 12, 96, 133; **10** 438; **11** 158
BG&E. *See* Baltimore Gas and Electric Company.
BGC Finance, **II** 420
Bharat Coking Coal Ltd., **IV** 48–49
Bharat Petroleum Ltd., **IV** 441
BHC Communications, **9** 119
BHP. *See* Broken Hill Proprietary Company Ltd.
Bi-Lo Inc., **II** 641; **V** 35
Bianchi, **13** 27
BIC Corporation, 8 59–61
Bic Pen Corp., **III** 29
BICC PLC, III 433–34; 11 520
Bicoastal Corporation, II 9–11
Biederman & Company, **14** 160
Bienfaisance, **III** 391

Bierbrauerei Wilhelm Remmer, **9** 86
Biffa Waste Services Ltd. *See* Severn Trent PLC.
Big Bear Stores Co., 13 94–96
Big Boy, **III** 102–03
Big 5 Sporting Goods, **12** 477
Big Foot Cattle Co., **14** 537
Big Horn Mining Co., **8** 423
Big M, **8** 409–10
Big Rivers Electric Corporation, 11 37–39
Big Three Industries, **I** 358
Big-K, **13** 445
Bilfinger & Berger Bau A.G., I 560–61
Billboard Publications, Inc., **7** 15
Billerud, **IV** 336
Billiton Metals, **IV** 56, 532
Bill's Casino, **9** 426
Biltwell Company, **8** 249
Binder Hamlyn, **IV** 685
Bindley Western Industries, Inc., 9 67–69
Bing Crosby Productions, **IV** 595
Binghamton Container Company, **8** 102
Binney & Smith, **II** 525; **IV** 621; **13** 293
Binny & Co. Ltd., **III** 522
Binter Canarias, **6** 97
Bio/Dynamics, Inc., **10** 105, 107
Bio-Clinic, **11** 486–87
Bio-Toxicological Research Laboratories, **IV** 409
Biofermin Pharmaceutical, **I** 704
Biogen Inc., I 638, 685; **8** 210; **14 58–60**
Biokyowa, **III** 43
Biological Research, **III** 443
Biological Technology Corp., **IV** 252
Biomedical Reference Laboratories of North Carolina, **11** 424
Biomet, Inc., 10 156–58
BioSensor A.B., **I** 665
Biotechnica International, **I** 286
Bioteknik-Gruppen, **I** 665
Bioter S.A., **III** 420
Bioter-Biona, S.A., **II** 493
Biotherm, **III** 47
Birdsall, Inc., **6** 529, 531
Birfield Ltd., **III** 494
Birkbeck, **10** 6
Birkenstock Footprint Sandals, Inc., 12 33–35
Birmingham & Midland Bank, **II** 318
Birmingham Joint Stock Bank, **II** 307
Birmingham Screw Co., **III** 493
Birmingham Slag Company, **7** 572–73, 575
Birmingham Steel Corporation, 13 97–98
Birtman Electric Co., **III** 653; **12** 548
Biscayne Bank. *See* Banco Espírito Santo e Comercial de Lisboa S.A.
Biscayne Federal Savings and Loan Association, **11** 481
Biscuiterie Nantaise, **II** 502; **10** 323
Biscuits Belin, **II** 543
Biscuits Delacre, **II** 480
Biscuits Gondolo, **II** 543
Bishop & Babcock Manufacturing Co., **II** 41
Bishop & Co. Savings Bank, **11** 114
Bishop National Bank of Hawaii, **11** 114
Bishopsgate Insurance, **III** 200
BISSELL, Inc., 9 70–72
Bit Software, Inc., **12** 62

Bitumax Proprietary, **III** 672
Bitumen & Oil Refineries (Australia) Ltd., **III** 672–73
Bizmark, **13** 176
BizMart, **6** 244–45; **8** 404–05
BJ Services, Inc., **15** 534, 536
BJ's Wholesale Club, **12** 221; **13** 547–49
Björknäs Nya Sågverks, **IV** 338
BKW, **IV** 229
BL Ltd., **I** 175; **10** 354
BL Systems. *See* AT&T Istel Ltd.
Black & Decker Corporation, **I** 667; **III** 435–37, 628, 665; **8** 332, 349; **15** 417–18
Black Arrow Leasing, **II** 138
Black Flag Co., **I** 622
Black Hawk Broadcasting Group, **III** 188; **10** 29
Black Spread Eagle, **II** 235
Blackburn, **III** 508
Blackhawk, **9** 26
Blackhorse Agencies, **II** 309
Blackmer Pump Co., **III** 468
Blackstone Capital Partners L.P., **V** 223; **6** 378
The Blackstone Group, **II** 434; **IV** 718; **11** 177, 179
Blackstone Group and Wasserstein Perella, **13** 170
Blackstone National Bank, **II** 444
Blaine Construction Company, **8** 546
Blair and Co., **II** 227
Blair Paving, **III** 674
Blair Radio, **6** 33
Blakiston Co., **IV** 636
Blane Products, **I** 403
Blatz Breweries, **I** 254
Blaupunkt-Werke, **I** 192–93
BLC Insurance Co., **III** 330
Bleichröder, **II** 191
Blendax, **III** 53; **8** 434
Blessings Corporation, **14** 550
Blimpie International, Inc., **15** 55–57
Blochman Lawrence Goldfree, **I** 697
Block Drug Company, Inc., **6** 26; **8** 62–64
Block Medical, Inc., **10** 351
Blockbuster Entertainment Corporation, **II** 161; **IV** 597; **9** 73–75, 361; **11** 556–58; **12** 43, 515; **13** 494
Blockson Chemical, **I** 380; **13** 379
Bloedel, Stewart & Welch, **IV** 306–07
Blohm & Voss, **I** 74
Bloomingdale's Inc., **I** 90; **III** 63; **IV** 651, 703; **9** 209, 393; **10** 487; **12** 36–38, 307, 403–04
Blount, Inc., **I** 563; **12** 39–41
Blue Arrow PLC, **II** 334–35; **9** 327
Blue Bell, Inc., **V** 390–91; **12** 205
Blue Chip Stamps, **III** 213–14
Blue Circle Industries PLC, **III** 669–71, 702
Blue Cross and Blue Shield Association, **10** 159–61; **14** 84
Blue Cross and Blue Shield Mutual of Northern Ohio, **12** 176
Blue Cross and Blue Shield of Colorado, **11** 175
Blue Cross and Blue Shield of Greater New York, **III** 245, 246
Blue Cross and Blue Shield of Ohio, **15** 114
Blue Cross Blue Shield of Michigan, **12** 22

Blue Cross of Northeastern New York, **III** 245–46
Blue Funnel Line, **I** 521; **6** 415–17
Blue Line Distributing, **7** 278–79
Blue Metal Industries, **III** 687
Blue Mountain Arts, **IV** 621
Blue Ribbon Beef Pack, Inc., **II** 515–16
Blue Ribbon Sports, **V** 372. *See also* Nike, Inc.
Blue Ridge Grocery Co., **II** 625
Blue Water Food Service, **13** 244
Bluebird Inc., **10** 443
Bluffton Grocery Co., **II** 668
Blunt Ellis & Loewi, **III** 270
Blyth and Co., **I** 537; **13** 448, 529
Blyth Eastman Dillon & Co., **II** 445
Blyth Eastman Paine Webber, **II** 445
Blyth Merrill Lynch, **II** 448
Blythe Colours BV, **IV** 119
BMC Industries Inc., **6** 275
BMC Software Inc., **14** 391
BMG/Music, **IV** 594; **15** 51
BMI Ltd., **III** 673
BMI Systems Inc., **12** 174
BMO Corp., **III** 209
BMW. *See* Bayerische Motoren Werke.
BNA. *See* Banca Nazionale dell'Agricoltura.
BNCI. *See* Banque Nationale Pour le Commerce et l'Industrie.
BNE. *See* Bank of New England Corp.
BNP. *See* Banque Nationale de Paris S.A.
BOAC. *See* British Overseas Airways Corp.
Boardwalk Regency, **6** 201
Boart and Hard Metals, **IV** 22
Boase Massimi Pollitt, **6** 48
Boatmen's Bancshares Inc., **15** 58–60
Bob Evans Farms, Inc., **9** 76–79; **10** 259
Bobbs-Merrill, **11** 198
Bobingen A.G., **I** 347
BOC Group plc, **I** 314–16, 358; **11** 402; **12** 500
Bochumer Verein für Gusstahlfabrikation, **IV** 88
Bock Bearing Co., **8** 530
Bodcaw Co., **IV** 287; **15** 228
Bodegas, **8** 556
The Body Shop International PLC, **11** 40–42
The Boeing Company, **I** 41–43, **47–49**, 50, 55–56, 58, 61, 67–68, 70–72, 74, 77, 82, 84–85, 90, 92–93, 96–97, 100, 102, 104–05, 108, 111–13, 116, 121–22, 126, 128, 130, 195, 489–90, 511, 530; **II** 7, 32–33, 62, 442; **III** 512, 539; **IV** 171, 576; **6** 68, 96, 130, 327; **7** 11, 456, 504; **8** 81, 313, 315; **9** 12, 18, 128, 194, 206, 232, 396, 416–17, 458–60, 498; **10** 162–65 **(upd.)**, 262, 316, 369, 536; **11** 164, 267, 277–79, 363, 427; **12** 180, 190–91, 380; **13** 356–58
Boeke & Huidekooper, **III** 417
Boerenbond, **II** 304
Boettcher & Co., **III** 271
Bofors Nobel Inc., **9** 380–81; **13** 22
Bogen Company, **15** 213
Bohemia, Inc., **13** 99–101
Bohm-Allen Jewelry, **12** 112
Böhme-Fettchemie, Chenmitz, **III** 32
Bohn Aluminum & Brass, **10** 439

Boise Cascade Corporation, **I** 142; **III** 499, 648, 664; **IV** 255–56, 333; **6** 577; **7** 356; **8** 65–67 **(upd.)**, 477; **15** 229
Bokaro Steel Ltd., **IV** 206
Bolands Ltd., **II** 649
Boliden Mining, **II** 366
Bolinder-Munktell, **I** 209; **II** 366
Bolitho Bank, **II** 235
Bölkow GmbH, **I** 74
Bolles & Houghton, **10** 355
The Bolsa Chica Company, **8** 300
BOMAG, **8** 544, 546
Bombardier, Inc., **12** 400–01
The Bombay Company, Inc., **III** 581; **10** 166–68
Bon Appetit, **II** 656
The Bon Marche, **V** 25; **9** 209
Bonanza, **7** 336; **10** 331; **15** 361–63
Bonaventura, **IV** 611
Bonaventure Liquor Store Co., **I** 284
Bond Corporation Holdings Limited, **I** 253, 255; **10** 169–71
Bondex International, **8** 456
Boni & Liveright, **13** 428
Bonifiche Siele, **II** 272
Bonimart, **II** 649
Bonwit Teller, **13** 43
Book-of-the-Month Club, Inc., **IV** 661, 675; **7** 529; **13** 105–07
Booker PLC, **13** 102–04
Booker Tate, **13** 102
Bookmasters, **10** 136
Books-A-Million, Inc., **14** 61–62
Bookstop, **10** 136
Booth Fisheries, **II** 571
Booth, Inc., **II** 420
Booth Leasing, **I** 449
Booth-Kelly Lumber Co., **IV** 281; **9** 259
Boots Company PLC, **I** 640, 668, 708; **II** 650; **V** 17–19; **8** 548
Booz Allen & Hamilton Inc., **10** 172–75
Boral Limited, **III** 672–74
Borax Holdings, **IV** 191
Bordas, **IV** 615
Borden and Remington Chemical, **15** 490
Borden Cabinet Corporation, **12** 296
Borden, Inc., **II** 470–73, 486, 498, 538, 545; **IV** 569; **7** 127, 129, 380; **11** 173
Border Fine Arts, **11** 95
Borders Group, Inc., **15** 61–62
Borders Inc., **9** 361; **10** 137
Borg-Warner Automotive, Inc., **14** 63–66
Borg-Warner Corporation, **I** 193, 339, 393; **III** 428, **438–41**; **14** 63, 357
Borg-Warner Security Corporation, **13** 123–25; **14** 63, 65, 541
Borland International, Inc., **6** 255–56; **9** 80–82; **10** 237, 509, 519, 558; **15** 492
Borman's, **II** 638
Borneo Airways. *See* Malaysian Airlines System BHD.
Borneo Co., **III** 523
Borsheim's, **III** 215
Borun Bros., **12** 477
Bosanquet, Salt and Co., **II** 306
Bosch. *See* Robert Bosch GmbH.
Boschert, **III** 434
Bose Corporation, **II** 35; **13** 108–10
Bosendorfer, L., Klavierfabrik, A.G., **12** 297
Bosert Industrial Supply, Inc., **V** 215
Boso Condensed Milk, **II** 538
Bostich, **III** 628
Boston Casualty Co., **III** 203

Boston Celtics Limited Partnership, 14 67–69
Boston Chicken, Inc., 12 42–44
Boston Co., **II** 451–52
Boston Consulting Group, **I** 532; **9** 343
Boston Distributors, **9** 453
Boston Edison Company, 12 45–47
Boston Fruit Co., **II** 595
Boston Garden Arena Corporation, **14** 67
Boston Gas Company, **6** 486–88
Boston Globe, **7** 13–16
Boston Herald, **7** 15
Boston Industries Corp., **III** 735
Boston Marine Insurance Co., **III** 242
Boston National Bank, **13** 465
Boston News Bureau, **IV** 601
Boston Overseas Financial Corp., **II** 208
Boston Whaler, Inc., **V** 376–77; **10** 215–16
BOTAS, **IV** 563
Botsford Ketchum, Inc., **6** 40
Botto, Rossner, Horne & Messinger, **6** 40
Bottu, **II** 475
Bougainville Copper Pty., **IV** 60–61
Boulet Dru DuPuy Petit Group, **6** 48. See also Wells Rich Greene BDDP.
Boulevard Bancorp, **12** 165
Boundary Gas, **6** 457
Boundary Healthcare, **12** 327
Bouquet, **V** 114
Bourjois, **12** 57
Boussois Souchon Neuvesel, **II** 474; **III** 677
Bouygues SA, I 562–64; 13 206
Bouzan Mines Ltd., **IV** 164
Bovaird Seyfang Manufacturing Co., **III** 471
Bovis Ltd., **I** 588
Bowater PLC, III 501–02; **IV** 257–59; **7** 208; **8** 483–84
Bower Roller Bearing Co., **I** 158–59
Bowery and East River National Bank, **II** 226
Bowery Savings Bank, **II** 182; **9** 173
Bowes Co., **II** 631
Bowman Gum, Inc., **13** 520
Bowmar Instruments, **II** 113; **11** 506
Box Innards Inc., **13** 442
Box Office Attraction Co., **II** 169
BoxCrow Cement Company, **8** 259
Boyer Brothers, Inc., **14** 17–18
Boykin Enterprises, **IV** 136
Boz, **IV** 697–98
Bozel, Électrométallurgie, **IV** 174
Bozzuto's, Inc., 13 111–12
BP. See British Petroleum Company PLC.
BPB, **III** 736
BPD, **13** 356
BPI Communications, Inc., **7** 15
BR. See British Rail.
Braas, **III** 734, 736
Brabant, **III** 199, 201
Brabazon, **III** 555
Brach and Brock Confections, Inc., 15 63–65
Bradbury Agnew and Co., **IV** 686
Bradford District Bank, **II** 333
Bradford Insulation Group, **III** 687
Bradford Pennine, **III** 373
Bradlees Discount Department Store Company, II 666–67; **12 48–50**
Bradley Lumber Company, **8** 430
Bradley Producing Corp., **IV** 459
Bradstreet Co., **IV** 604–05

Braegen Corp., **13** 127
Bragussa, **IV** 71
BRAINS. See Belgian Rapid Access to Information Network Services.
Bramalea Ltd., 9 83–85; 10 530–31
Brambles Industries, **III** 494–95
Bramco, **III** 600
Bramwell Gates, **II** 586
Bran & Lübbe, **III** 420
Brand Companies, Inc., **9** 110; **11** 436
Branded Restaurant Group, Inc., **12** 372
Brandenburgische Motorenwerke, **I** 138
Brandywine Iron Works and Nail Factory, **14** 323
Brandywine Valley Railroad Co., **14** 324
Braniff Airlines, **I** 97, 489, 548; **II** 445; **6** 50, 119–20
Branigar Organization, Inc., **IV** 345
Brascade Resources, **IV** 308
Brascan, Ltd., **II** 456; **IV** 165, 330
Braspetro, **IV** 454, 501–02
Brass Craft Manufacturing Co., **III** 570
Brasseries Kronenbourg, **II** 474–75
Braswell Motor Freight, **14** 567
Brauerei Beck & Co., 9 86–87
Braun, **III** 29
Braunkohlenwerk Golpa-Jessnitz AG, **IV** 230
Brazilian Central Bank, **IV** 56
Brazos Gas Compressing, **7** 345
Breakstone Bros., Inc., **II** 533
Breakthrough Software, **10** 507
Bredel Exploitatie B.V., **8** 546
Bredell Paint Co., **III** 745
Bredero's Bouwbedrijf of Utrecht, **IV** 707–08, 724
Breedband NV, **IV** 133
Brega Petroleum Marketing Co., **IV** 453, 455
Breguet Aviation, **I** 44
Breitenburger Cementfabrik, **III** 701
Bremner Biscuit Co., **II** 562; **13** 426
Brenda Mines Ltd., **7** 399
Brennan College Services, **12** 173
Brenntag AG, 8 68–69, 496
Brentano's, **7** 286
Breslube Enterprises, **8** 464
Brewster Lines, **6** 410
Breyers Ice Cream Co. See Good Humor-Breyers.
BRI Bar Review Institute, Inc., **IV** 623; **12** 224
Brian Mills, **V** 118
Briarpatch, Inc., **12** 109
Brickwood Breweries, **I** 294
Bridge Oil Ltd., **I** 438
Bridge Technology, Inc., **10** 395
Bridgeman Creameries, **II** 536
Bridgeport Brass, **I** 377
Bridgestone Corporation, V 234–35; 15 355
Bridgestone Liquefied Gas, **IV** 364
Bridgeway Plan for Health, **6** 186
Bridgford Company, **13** 382
Brier Hill, **IV** 114
Briggs & Stratton Corporation, III 597; **8 70–73**
Briggs and Lundy Lumber Cos., **14** 18
Brigham's Inc., **15** 71
Bright of America Inc., **12** 426
Bright Star Technologies, **13** 92; **15** 455
Brighton Federal Savings and Loan Assoc., **II** 420
Brimsdown Lead Co., **III** 680

Brin's Oxygen Co., **I** 314
Brinco Ltd., **II** 211
Brink's, Inc., **IV** 180–82
Brinker International, Inc., 10 176–78
BRIntec, **III** 434
Brinton Carpets, **III** 423
Brisbane Gas Co., **III** 673
Bristol Aeroplane, **I** 50, 197; **10** 261
Bristol PLC, **IV** 83
Bristol-BTR, **I** 429
Bristol-Erickson, **13** 297
Bristol-Myers Squibb Company, I 26, 30, 37, 301, 696, 700, 703; **III 17–19,** 36, 67; **IV** 272; **6** 27; **7** 255; **8** 210, 282–83; **9 88–91 (upd.); 10** 70; **11** 289; **12** 126–27
Bristol-Siddeley Ltd., **I** 50
Britannia Airways, **8** 525–26
Britannia Security Group PLC, **12** 10
Britannica Software, **7** 168
Britches of Georgetowne, **10** 215–16
British & Commonwealth Shipping Company, **10** 277
British Aerospace plc, I 42, 46, **50–53,** 55, 74, 83, 132, 532; **III** 458, 507; **V** 339; **7** 9, 11, 458–59; **8** 315; **9** 499; **11** 413; **12** 191; **14** 36
British Airways plc, I 34, 83, **92–95,** 109; **IV** 658; **6** 60, 78–79, 118, 132; **14 70–74 (upd.)**
British Aluminium, Ltd., **II** 422; **IV** 15
British American Cosmetics, **I** 427
British American Insurance Co., **III** 350
British American Nickel, **IV** 110
British and Dominion Film Corp., **II** 157
British and Foreign Marine, **III** 350
British and French Bank, **II** 232–33
British Bank of North America, **II** 210
British Bank of the Middle East, **II** 298
British Borneo Timber Co., **III** 699
British Broadcasting Corporation, III 163; **IV** 651; **7 52–55**
British Caledonian Airways, **I** 94–95; **6** 79
British Can Co., **I** 604
British Car Auctions, **14** 321
British Celanese Ltd., **I** 317
British Cellulose and Chemical Manufacturing Co., **I** 317
British Chrome, **III** 699
British Coal Corporation, IV 38–40
British Columbia Forest Products Ltd., **IV** 279
British Columbia Packers, **II** 631–32
British Columbia Resources Investment Corp., **IV** 308
British Columbia Telephone Company, IV 308; **6 309–11**
British Commonwealth Insurance, **III** 273
British Commonwealth Pacific Airways, **6** 110
British Continental Airlines, **I** 92
British Credit Trust, **10** 443
British Dyestuffs Corp., **I** 351
British Dynamite Co., **I** 351
British Engine, **III** 350
British European Airways, **I** 93, 466
British Executive, **I** 50
British Fuels, **III** 735
British Gas plc, II 260; **V 559–63; 6** 478–79; **11** 97
British Gauge and Instrument Company, **13** 234
British General, **III** 234
British Goodrich Tyre Co., **I** 428

British Home Stores, **II** 658; **13** 284
British Hovercraft Corp., **I** 120
British India and Queensland Agency Co. Ltd., **III** 522
British India Steam Navigation Co., **III** 521–22
British Industrial Solvents Ltd., **IV** 70
British Industry, **III** 335
British Insulated and Helsby Cables Ltd., **III** 433–34
British Isles Transport Co. Ltd., **II** 564
British Land Company, **10** 6
British Leyland Motor Corporation, **I** 175, 186; **III** 516, 523; **13** 286–87; **14** 35–36
British Linen Bank, **10** 336
British Marine Air Navigation, **I** 92
British Metal Corp., **IV** 140, 164
British Motor Corporation, **III** 555; **7** 459; **13** 286
British Motor Holdings, **7** 459
British National Films Ltd., **II** 157
British National Oil Corp., **IV** 40
British Newfoundland Corporation, **6** 502
British Nuclear Fuels PLC, I 573; **6 451–54**; **13** 458
British Overseas Airways Corp., **I** 51, 93, 120–21; **III** 522; **6** 78–79, 100, 110, 112, 117; **14** 71
British Oxygen Co. *See* BOC Group.
British Petroleum Company PLC, I 241, 303; **II** 449, 563; **IV** 61, 280, 363–64, **378–80**, 381–82, 412–13, 450–54, 456, 466, 472, 486, 497–99, 505, 515, 524–25, 531–32, 557; **6** 304; **7 56–59 (upd.)**, 140–41, 332–33, 516, 559; **9** 490, 519; **11** 538; **13** 449; **14** 317
British Plasterboard, **III** 734
British Portland Cement Manufacturers, **III** 669–70
British Printing and Communications Corp., **IV** 623–24, 642; **7** 312; **12** 224
British Prudential Assurance Co., **III** 335
British Rail, **III** 509; **V** 421–24; **10** 122
British Railways, **6** 413
British Railways Board, V 421–24
British Road Services, **6** 413
British Royal Insurance Co., Ltd., **III** 242
British Satellite Broadcasting, **10** 170
British Shoe Corporation, **V** 178
British South Africa Co., **IV** 23, 94
British South American Airways, **I** 93
British South American Corporation, **6** 95
British Steel Brickworks, **III** 501; **7** 207
British Steel plc, III 494–95; **IV** 40, **41–43**, 128
British Sugar plc, **II** 514, 581–82; **13** 53
British Tabulating Machine Company, **6** 240
British Telecom, **8** 153; **11** 185, 547; **15** 131
British Telecommunications plc, I 83, 330; **II** 82; **V 279–82**; **6** 323; **7** 332–33; **9** 32; **11** 59; **15 66–70 (upd.)**
British Thermoplastics and Rubber. *See* BTR plc.
British Timken Ltd., **8** 530
British Tyre and Rubber Co., **I** 428
British United Airways, **I** 94
British Vita PLC, 9 92–93
British Zaire Diamond Distributors Ltd., **IV** 67
British-American Tobacco Co., Ltd., **V** 396, 401–02, 417; **9** 312
Britoil, **IV** 380

Britt Airways, **I** 118
Britt Lumber Co., Inc., **8** 348
Brittains Bricks, **III** 673
BRK Electronics, **9** 414
Broad, Inc., **11** 482
Broad River Power Company, **6** 575
Broadcast Technology Systems, Inc., **13** 398
Broadcom Eireann Research, **7** 510
Broadcort Capital Corp., **13** 342
BroadPark, **II** 415
Broadway-Hale Stores, Inc., **12** 356
Brock Candy Company. *See* Brach and Brock Confections, Inc.
Brock Hotel Corp., **13** 472–73
Brock Residence Inn, **9** 426
Brockway Glass Co., **I** 524; **15** 128
Broderbund Software, Inc., 10 285; **13 113–16**
Broederlijke Liefdebeurs, **III** 177
Broken Hill Proprietary Company Ltd., I 437–39; **II** 30; **III** 494; **IV 44–47**, 58, 61, 171, 484; **10** 170
The Bronfman Group, **6** 161, 163
Brooke Group Ltd., 15 71–73
Brooke Partners L.P., **11** 275
Brooklyn Flint Glass Co., **III** 683
Brooklyn Trust Co., **II** 312
Brooklyn Union Gas, 6 455–57
Brooks Brothers, **V** 26–27; **13** 43
Brooks, Harvey & Co., Inc., **II** 431
Brooks, Shoobridge and Co., **III** 669
Brooks-Scanlon Lumber Co., **IV** 306
Brookstone, **II** 560; **12** 411
Brookville Telephone Company, **6** 300
Brookwood Health Services, **III** 73
Brother Industries, Ltd., 13 478; **14 75–76**
Brown & Dureau Ltd., **IV** 248–49
Brown & Root, Inc., III 498–99, 559; **13 117–19**
Brown and Williamson Tobacco Corporation, I 426; **14 77–79**; **15** 72
Brown Bibby & Gregory, **I** 605
Brown Boveri. *See* BBC Brown Boveri.
Brown Co., **I** 452; **IV** 289
Brown Corp., **IV** 286
Brown Drug, **III** 9
Brown Foundation, **III** 498
Brown Group, Inc., V 351–53; **9** 192; **10** 282
Brown Instrument Co., **II** 41
Brown Jordan Co., **12** 301
Brown Oil Tools, **III** 428
Brown Paper Mill Co., **I** 380; **13** 379
Brown Shipbuilding Company. *See* Brown & Root, Inc.
Brown Shoe Co., **V** 351–52; **14** 294
Brown-Forman Corporation, I 225–27; **III** 286; **10 179–82 (upd.)**; **12** 313
Brown-Service Insurance Company, **9** 507
Brown-Shipley Ltd., **II** 425; **13** 341
Browne & Nolan Ltd., **IV** 294
Browning Manufacturing, **II** 19
Browning Telephone Corp., **14** 258
Browning-Ferris Industries, Inc., V 749–53; **8** 562; **10** 33
Broyhill Furniture Industries, Inc., III 528, 530; **10 183–85**; **12** 308
BRS Ltd., **6** 412–13
Bruce's Furniture Stores, **14** 235
Brufina, **II** 201–02
Brummer Seal Company, **14** 64
Brunner Mond and Co., **I** 351

Bruno's Inc., 7 60–62; **13** 404, 406
Brunswick Corporation, III 442–44, 599; **9** 67, 119; **10** 262
Brunswick Pulp & Paper Co., **IV** 282, 311, 329; **9** 260
The Brush Electric Light Company, **11** 387
Brush Electrical Machines, **III** 507–09
Brush Moore Newspaper, Inc., **8** 527
Brush Wellman Inc., 14 80–82
Bryan Bros. Packing, **II** 572
Bryant Heater Co., **III** 471
Bryce & Co., **I** 547
Bryce Brothers, **12** 313
Bryce Grace & Co., **I** 547
Brymbo Steel Works, **III** 494
Brynwood Partners, **13** 19
BSB, **IV** 653; **7** 392
BSC (Industry) Ltd., **IV** 42
BSkyB, **IV** 653; **7** 392
BSN Groupe S.A., II 474–75, 544
BSR, **II** 82
BT. *See* British Telecommunications, plc.
BTI Services, **9** 59
BTM. *See* British Tabulating Machine Company.
BTR plc, I 428–30; **III** 185, 727; **8** 397
Buchanan, **I** 239–40
Buchanan Electric Steel Company, **8** 114
Buckeye Union Casualty Co., **III** 242
Buckingham Corp., **I** 440, 468
Buckler Broadcast Group, **IV** 597
Bucyrus Blades, Inc., **14** 81
Bucyrus-Erie Company, **7** 513
The Budd Company, III 568; **IV** 222; **8 74–76**
Buderus AG, **III** 692, 694–95
Budget Rent a Car Corporation, I 537; **6** 348–49, 393; **9 94–95**; **13** 529
Buena Vista Distribution, **II** 172; **6** 174
Buffalo Forge Company, **7 70–71**
Buffalo Insurance Co., **III** 208
Buffalo Mining Co., **IV** 181
Buffets, Inc., 10 186–87
Buffett Partnership, Ltd., **III** 213
Bugatti Industries, **14** 321
Buick Motor Co., **I** 171; **III** 438; **8** 74; **10** 325
Builders Emporium, **13** 169
Builders Square, **V** 112; **9** 400; **12** 345, 385; **14** 61
Buitoni SpA, **II** 548
Bulgarian Oil Co., **IV** 454
Bull. *See* Compagnie des Machines Bull S.A.
Bull HN Information Systems, **III** 122–23
Bull Motors, **11** 5
Bull S.A., **III** 122–23
Bull Tractor Company, **7** 534
Bull-GE, **III** 123
Bulldog Computer Products, **10** 519
Bullock's, **III** 63
Bulolo Gold Dredging, **IV** 95
Bulova Corporation, I 488; **II** 101; **III** 454–55; **12** 316–17, 453; **13 120–22**; **14** 501
Bumble Bee Seafoods, Inc., **II** 491, 508, 557
Bumkor-Ramo Corp., **I** 539
Bunawerke Hüls GmbH., **I** 350
Bunker Ramo Info Systems, **III** 118
Bunte Candy, **12** 427
Bunzl PLC, IV 260–62; **12** 264
Burbank Aircraft Supply, Inc., **14** 42–43
Burberry's Ltd., **V** 68; **10** 122

Burdines, **9** 209
Bureau de Recherches de Pétrole, **IV** 544–46, 559–60; **7** 481–83
Burger Boy Food-A-Rama, **8** 564
Burger Chef, **II** 532
Burger King Corporation, **I** 21, 278; **II** 556–57, **613–15**, 647; **7** 316; **8** 564; **9** 178; **10** 122; **12** 43, 553; **13** 408–09; **14** 25, 32, 212, 214, 452
Burke Scaffolding Co., **9** 512
BURLE Industries Inc., **11** 444
Burlesdon Brick Co., **III** 734
Burlington Air Express, Inc., **IV** 182
Burlington Coat Factory Warehouse Corporation, **10 188–89**
Burlington Homes of New England, **14** 138
Burlington Industries, Inc., **V** 118, **354–55**; **8** 234; **9** 231; **12** 501
Burlington Mills Corporation, **12** 117–18
Burlington Northern Air Freight, **IV** 182
Burlington Northern, Inc., **V 425–28**; **10** 190–91; **12** 145, 278
Burlington Northern Railroad, **11** 315
Burlington Resources Inc., **10 190–92**; **11** 135; **12** 144
Burmah Castrol PLC, **IV** 378, **381–84**, 440–41, 483–84, 531; **7** 56
Burmah Oil Co., **15** 246
Burmeister & Wain, **III** 417–18
Burn & Co., **IV** 205
Burn Standard Co. Ltd., **IV** 484
Burnards, **II** 677
Burnham and Co., **II** 407–08; **6** 599; **8** 388
Burns & Wilcox Ltd., **6** 290
Burns Cos., **III** 569
Burns Fry Ltd., **II** 349
Burns International Security Services, **III** 440; **13 123–25**
Burpee Co. See W. Atlee Burpee Co.
Burr & Co., **II** 424; **13** 340
Burrill & Housman, **II** 424; **13** 340
Burris Industries, **14** 303
Burroughs Corp., **I** 142, 478; **III** 132, 148–49, 152, 165–66; **6** 233, 266, 281–83. See also Unisys Corporation.
Burroughs Wellcome & Co., **I** 713; **8** 216
Burrows, Marsh & McLennan, **III** 282
Burry, **II** 560; **12** 410
Bursley & Co., **II** 668
Burt Claster Enterprises, **III** 505
Burthy China Clays, **III** 690
Burton Group plc, **V 20–22**
Burton J. Vincent, Chesley & Co., **III** 271
Burton, Parsons and Co. Inc., **II** 547
Burton Retail, **V** 21
Burton Rubber Processing, **8** 347
Burton-Furber Co., **IV** 180
Burtons Gold Medal Biscuits Limited, **II** 466; **13** 53
Burwell Brick, **14** 248
Bury Group, **II** 581
Bush Boake Allen Ltd., **IV** 346
Bush Terminal Company, **15** 138
Business Depot, Limited, **10** 498
Business Expansion Capital Corp., **12** 42
Business Men's Assurance Company of America, **III** 209; **13** 476; **14 83–85**; **15** 30
Business Science Computing, **14** 36
Business Software Association, **10** 35
Business Software Technology, **10** 394
Businessland Inc., **III** 153; **6** 267; **10** 235; **13** 175–76, 277, 482
Busse Broadcasting, **7** 200

Büssing Automobilwerke AG, **IV** 201
Buster Brown, **V** 351–52
Butano, **IV** 528
Butler Cox PLC, **6** 229
Butler Manufacturing Co., **12 51–53**
Butterfield & Swire, **I** 469, 521–22; **6** 78
Butterfield Brothers, **I** 521
Butterfield, Wasson & Co., **II** 380, 395; **10** 59; **12** 533
Butterley Company, **III** 501; **7** 207
Butterworth & Co. (Publishers) Ltd., **IV** 641; **7** 311
Butz Thermo-Electric Regulator Co., **II** 40; **12** 246
Buxton, **III** 28
Buzzard Electrical & Plumbing Supply, **9** 399
BVA Investment Corp., **11** 447
BVA Mortgage Corporation, **11** 446
Byrnes Long Island Motor Cargo, Inc., **6** 370
Byron Jackson, **III** 428, 439
Bytrex, Inc., **III** 643

C & O. See Chesapeake and Ohio Railway.
C.&E. Cooper Co., **II** 14
C.&G. Cooper Co., **II** 14
C.A. Pillsbury and Co., **II** 555
C.A. Reed Co., **IV** 353
C.A. Swanson & Sons, **II** 479–80; **7** 66–67
C&A Brenninkmeyer KG, **V 23–24**
C&E Software, **10** 507
C&S Bank, **10** 425–26
C&S/Sovran Corporation, **10** 425–27
C. Bechstein, **III** 657
C. Brewer, **I** 417
C.D. Haupt, **IV** 296
C.D. Kenny Co., **II** 571
C.D. Magirus AG, **III** 541
C.E.T. See Club Européen du Tourisme.
C.F. Hathaway Company, **12** 522
C.F. Mueller Co., **I** 497–98; **12** 332
C. Francis, Son and Co., **III** 669
C.G. Conn, **7** 286
C.H. Dexter & Co., **I** 320
C.H. Knorr Co., **II** 497
C.H. Musselman Co., **7** 429
C.H. Robinson, Inc., **8** 379–80; **11 43–44**
C-I-L, Inc., **III** 745; **13** 470
C. Itoh & Co., **I 431–33**, 492, 510; **II** 273, 292, 361, 442, 679; **IV** 269, 326, 516, 543; **7** 529; **10** 500
C.J. Devine, **II** 425
C.J. Lawrence, Morgan Grenfell Inc., **II** 429
C.J. Smith and Sons, **11** 3
C.L. Bencard, **III** 66
C. Lee Cook Co., **III** 467
C.M. Aikman & Co., **13** 168
C.M. Armstrong, Inc., **14** 17
C.M. Barnes Company, **10** 135
C.M. Page, **14** 112
C.O. Lovette Company, **6** 370
C/P Utility Services Company, **14** 138
C.R. Bard Inc., **IV** 287; **9 96–98**
C. Reichenbach'sche Maschinenfabrik, **III** 561
C. Rowbotham & Sons, **III** 740
C.S. Rolls & Co., **I** 194
C.T. Bowring, **III** 280, 283
C.V. Buchan & Co., **I** 567
C.V. Gebroeders Pel, **7** 429
C.V. Mosby Co., **IV** 677–78

C.W. Holt & Co., **III** 450
C.W. Zumbiel Company, **11** 422
Cable & Wireless plc, **15** 69, 521
Cable and Wireless (Hong Kong). See Hongkong Telecommunications Ltd.
Cable and Wireless plc, **IV** 695; **V 283–86**; **7** 332–33; **11** 547
Cable Communications Operations, Inc., **6** 313
Cable News Network, **II** 166–68; **6** 171–73; **9** 30; **12** 546
Cablec Corp., **III** 433–34
Cableform, **I** 592
Cabletron Systems, Inc., **10 193–94**; **10** 511
Cablevision Systems Corporation, **7 63–65**
Cabot Corporation, **8 77–79**
Cadadia, **II** 641–42
Cadbury Schweppes PLC, **I** 25–26; **II 476–78**, 510, 512, 592; **III** 554; **6** 51–52; **9** 178; **15** 221
Caddell Construction Company, **12** 41
Cadence Design Systems, Inc., **6** 247; **10** 118; **11 45–48**, 285, 490–91
Cadence Industries Corporation, **10** 401–02
Cadillac Automobile Co., **I** 171; **10** 325
Cadillac Fairview Corp., **IV** 703
Cadillac Plastic, **8** 347
Cadisys Corporation, **10** 119
Cadoricin, **III** 47
CAE Systems Inc., **8** 519
Caesar-Wollheim-Gruppe, **IV** 197
Caesars World, Inc., **6 199–202**
Caf'Casino, **12** 152
Café Grand Mère, **II** 520
CAFO, **III** 241
Cahners Publishing, **IV** 667; **12** 561
CAI Corp., **12** 79
Cailler, **II** 546
Cain Chemical, **IV** 481
Cains Marcelle Potato Chips Inc., **15** 139
Caisse Commericale de Bruxelles, **II** 270
Caisse de dépôt et placement du Quebec, **II** 664
Caisse des Dépôts, **6** 206
Caisse National de Crédit Agricole, **II** 264–66
Caisse Nationale de Crédit Agricole, **15** 38–39
Caja General de Depositos, **II** 194
Cal Circuit Abco Inc., **13** 387
Cal/Ink, **13** 228
Calcined Coke Corp., **IV** 402
Calco, **I** 300–01
CalComp Inc., **13 126–29**
Calculating-Tabulating-Recording Company. See International Business Machines Corporation.
Calcutta & Burmah Steam Navigation Co., **III** 521
Caldbeck Macgregor & Co., **III** 523
Caldor Inc., **12 54–56**, 508
Caledonian Airways. See British Caledonian Airways.
Caledonian Bank, **10** 337
Caledonian Paper plc, **IV** 302
Calédonickel, **IV** 107
Calgary Power Company. See TransAlta Utilities Corporation.
Calgon Corporation, **6** 27
Calgon Water Management, **15** 154
California Arabian Standard Oil Co., **IV** 536, 552

California Automated Design, Inc., **11** 284
California Bank, **II** 289
California Computer Products, Inc. *See* CalComp Inc.
California Cooler Inc., **I** 227, 244; **10** 181
California First, **II** 358
California Ink Company, **13** 227
California Institute of Technology, **9** 367
California Insurance Co., **III** 234
California Oilfields, Ltd., **IV** 531, 540
California Perfume Co., **III** 15
California Petroleum Co., **IV** 551–52
California Pizza Kitchen Inc., 15 74–76
California Plant Protection, **9** 408
California Portland Cement Co., **III** 718
California Steel Industries, **IV** 125
California Telephone and Light, **II** 490
California Test Bureau, **IV** 636
California Texas Oil Co., **III** 672
California Tile, **III** 673
California Woodfiber Corp., **IV** 266
California-Western States Life Insurance Co., **III** 193–94
Caligen, **9** 92
Call-Chronicle Newspapers, Inc., **IV** 678
Callaghan & Company, **8** 526
Callard and Bowser, **II** 594
Callaway Golf Company, 15 77–79
Callaway Wines, **I** 264
Callebaut, **II** 520–21
Callender's Cable and Construction Co. Ltd., **III** 433–34
Calloway's Nursery Inc., **12** 200
Calma, **II** 30; **12** 196
Calmar Co., **12** 127
CalMat Co., **III** 718
Calmic Ltd., **I** 715
Calor Group, **IV** 383
Caloric Corp., **II** 86
Calpine Corp., **IV** 84
Calsil Ltd., **III** 674
Caltex Petroleum Corp., **II** 53; **III** 672; **IV** 397, 434, 440–41, 479, 484, 492, 519, 527, 536, 545–46, 552, 560, 562, 718; **7** 483
Calumet & Arizona Mining Co., **IV** 177
Calumet Electric Company, **6** 532
Calvert & Co., **I** 293
Calvin Bullock Ltd., **I** 472
Calvin Klein Cosmetics Corporation, **9** 203
Camargo Foods, **12** 531
Cambex, **12** 147–48
Cambria Steel Company, **IV** 35; **7** 48
Cambridge Applied Nutrition Toxicology and Biosciences Ltd., **10** 105
Cambridge Biotech Corp., **13** 241
Cambridge Electric Co., **14** 124, 126
Cambridge Gas Co., **14** 124
Cambridge Interactive Systems Ltd., **10** 241
Cambridge Steam Corp., **14** 124
Camco Inc., **IV** 658
Camden Wire Co., Inc., **7** 408
CAMECO, **IV** 436
Cameron & Barkley Co., **13** 79
Cameron Iron Works, **II** 17
Cameron Oil Co., **IV** 365
Cameron-Brown Company, **10** 298
CAMI Automotive, **III** 581
Camintonn, **9** 41–42
Camp Manufacturing Co., **IV** 345; **8** 102
Campbell Box & Tag Co., **IV** 333
Campbell Hausfeld. *See* Scott Fetzer Company.

Campbell Industries, Inc., **11** 534
Campbell Soup Company, I 21, 26, 31, 599, 601; **II 479–81**, 508, 684; **7 66–69 (upd.)**, 340; **10** 382; **11** 172
Campbell Taggart Inc., **I** 219
Campbell-Ewald Co., **I** 16–17
Campbell-Mithun Inc., **13** 516
Campeau Corporation, IV 721; **V 25–28**; **9** 209, 211, 391; **12** 36–37; **13** 43; **15** 94
CAMPSA. *See* Compañia Arrendataria del Monopolio de Petróleos Sociedad Anónima.
Campus Services, Inc., **12** 173
Canada & Dominion Sugar Co., **II** 581
Canada Cable & Wire Company, **9** 11
Canada Cement, **III** 704–05
Canada Cup, **IV** 290
Canada Development Corp., **IV** 252
Canada Dry, **I** 281
Canada Packers Inc., II 482–85
Canada Safeway Ltd., **II** 650, 654
Canada Trust. *See* CT Financial Services Inc.
Canada Tungsten Mining Corp., Ltd., **IV** 18
Canada Wire & Cable Company, Ltd., **IV** 164–65; **7** 397–99
Canadair, **I** 58; **7** 205; **13** 358
Canadian Airlines International Ltd., **6** 61–62, 101; **12** 192
Canadian Bank of Commerce, **II** 244–45
Canadian British Aluminum, **IV** 11
Canadian Cellucotton Products Ltd., **III** 40
Canadian Copper, **IV** 110
Canadian Copper Refiners, Ltd., **IV** 164
Canadian Dominion Steel and Coal Corp., **III** 508
Canadian Eastern Finance, **IV** 693
Canadian Fina Oil, **IV** 498
Canadian Football League, **12** 457
Canadian Forest Products, **IV** 270
Canadian Fuel Marketers, **IV** 566
Canadian General Electric Co., **8** 544–45
Canadian Government Merchant Marine, **6** 360–61
Canadian Gridoil Ltd., **IV** 373
Canadian Imperial Bank of Commerce, II 244–46; **IV** 693; **7** 26–28; **10** 8
Canadian Industrial Alcohol Company Limited, **14** 141
Canadian International Paper Co., **IV** 286–87; **15** 228
Canadian Keyes Fibre Company, Limited of Nova Scotia, **9** 305
Canadian National Railway System, 6 359–62; **12** 278–79
Canadian Northern Railway, **I** 284; **6** 359–60
Canadian Odeon Theatres, **6** 161
Canadian Pacific Enterprises, **III** 611
Canadian Pacific Limited, V 429–31; **8** 544–46
Canadian Pacific Railway, **I** 573; **II** 210, 220, 344; **III** 260; **IV** 272, 308, 437; **6** 359–60
Canadian Packing Co. Ltd., **II** 482
Canadian Petrofina, **IV** 498
Canadian Radio-Television and Telecommunications Commission, **6** 309
Canadian Telephones and Supplies, **6** 310
Canadian Transport Co., **IV** 308
Canadian Utilities Limited, 13 130–32
Canal Bank, **11** 105
Canal Electric Co., **14** 125–26

Canal Plus, III 48; **7** 392; **10 195–97**, 345, 347
CanAmera Foods, **7** 82
Canandaigua Wine Company, Inc., 13 133–35
Cananwill, **III** 344
Canfor Corp., **IV** 321
Cannon Assurance Ltd., **III** 276
Cannon Mills, Co., **9** 214–16
Canon Inc., I 494; **II** 103, 292; **III 120–21**, 143, 172, 575, 583–84; **6** 238, 289; **9** 251; **10** 23; **13** 482; **15** 150
Canpet Exploration Ltd., **IV** 566
Cans Inc., **I** 607
Canstar Sports, Inc., **15** 396–97
Canteen Corp., **I** 127; **II** 679–80; **12** 489; **13** 321
Cantel Corp., **11** 184
Canton Chemical, **I** 323; **8** 147
Canton Railway Corp., **IV** 718
Cantor Fitzgerald Securities Corporation, **10** 276–78
Cap Rock Electric Cooperative, **6** 580
CAPCO. *See* Central Area Power Coordination Group *or* Custom Academic Publishing Company.
Capcom Co., **7** 396
Cape and Vineyard Electric Co., **14** 124–25
Cape Cod-Cricket Lane, Inc., **8** 289
Cape Horn Methanol, **III** 512
Cape May Light and Power Company, **6** 449
Cape Wine and Distillers, **I** 289
Capehart-Farnsworth, **I** 463; **11** 197
Capex, **6** 224
AB Capital & Investment Corporation, **6** 108
Capital Airlines, **I** 128; **III** 102; **6** 128
Capital and Counties Bank, **II** 307; **IV** 91
Capital Cities/ABC Inc., II 129–31; **III** 214; **IV** 608–09, 613, 652; **11** 331; **15** 464. *See also* American Broadcasting Co.
Capital Concrete Pipe Company, **14** 250
Capital Controls Co., Inc. *See* Severn Trent PLC.
Capital Financial Services, **III** 242
Capital Holding Corporation, III 216–19
Capital Life Insurance Company, **11** 482–83
Capital-Gazette Communications, Inc., **12** 302
Capitol Film + TV International, **IV** 591
Capitol Pack, Inc., **13** 350
Capitol Printing Ink Company, **13** 227–28
Capitol Publishing, **13** 560
Capitol Radio Engineering Institute, **IV** 636
Capitol-EMI, **I** 531–32; **11** 557
Capper Pass, **IV** 191
Capseals, Ltd., **8** 476
Capsugel, **I** 712
Car-lac Electronic Industrial Sales Inc., **9** 420
Car-X, **10** 415
Caracas Petroleum Sociedad Anónima, **IV** 565–66
Carando Foods, **7** 174–75
Carat Group, **6** 15–16
Caravali, **13** 493–94
Carbide Router Co., **III** 436
Carbis China Clay & Brick Co., **III** 690
Carbocol, **IV** 417

Carboline Co., **8** 455
CarboMedics, **11** 458–60
Carbon Research Laboratories, **9** 517
Carborundum Company, **III** 610; **15 80–82**
Cardboard Containers, **IV** 249
Cardem Insurance Co., **III** 767
Cardiac Pacemakers, Inc., **I** 646; **11** 90; **11** 458
Cardinal Distributors Ltd., **II** 663
Caremark International Inc., **10** 143, **198–200**
Carenes, SA, **12** 377
CarePlus, **6** 42
CareUnit, Inc., **15** 123
Carey Canada Inc., **III** 766
Carey Straw Mill, **12** 376
Carey-McFall Corp., **V** 379
S.A. CARFUEL, **12** 152
Cargill, Inc., **II** 494, 517, **616–18**; **11** 92; **13 136–38 (upd.)**, 186, 351
Cargill Trust Co., **13** 467
CARGOSUR, **6** 96
Cariani Sausage Co., **II** 518
Caribair, **I** 102
Caribbean Chemicals S.A., **I** 512
Caribe Co., **II** 493
Caribe Shoe Corp., **III** 529
Cariboo Pulp & Paper Co., **IV** 269
Carintusa Inc., **8** 271
CARIPLO, **III** 347
Carita, **III** 63
Carl Byoir & Associates, **I** 14
Carl Marks & Co., **11** 260–61
Carl's Superstores, **9** 452
Carl-Zeiss-Stiftung, **III 445–47**, 583
Carlan, **III** 614
Carless Lubricants, **IV** 451
Carleton Financial Computations Inc., **II** 317
Carlin Gold Mining Company, **7** 386–87
Carling O'Keefe Ltd., **I** 218, 229, 254, 269, 438–39; **7** 183; **12** 337
Carlingford, **II** 298
Carlisle Companies Incorporated, **8 80–82**
Carlisle Memory Products, **14** 535
Carlo Erba S.p.A., **I** 635
Carlon, **13** 304–06
Carlsberg A/S, **I** 247; **9 99–101**
Carlson Companies, Inc., **6 363–66**
Carlton and United Breweries Ltd., **I 228–29**, 437–39; **7** 182–83
Carlton Communications plc, **15 83–85**
Carlyle Group, **11** 364; **14** 43
Carmeda AB, **10** 439
Carmike Cinemas, Inc., **14 86–88**
Carnation Company, **I** 269; **II 486–89**, 518, 548; **7** 339, 383, 429; **10** 382; **12** 337
Carnaud Basse-Indre, **IV** 228
CarnaudMetalbox, **13** 190
Carnegie Brothers & Co., Ltd., **9** 407
Carnegie Foundation for the Advancement of Teaching, **12** 141
Carnegie Steel Co., **II** 330; **IV** 572; **7** 549
Carnival Cruise Lines, Inc., **6 367–68**
Carol Moberg, Inc., **6** 40
Carol-Braugh-Robinson Co., **II** 624
Carolco Pictures Inc., **IV** 48; **10** 196
Carolina Biological Supply, **11** 424
Carolina Coach Co., **13** 397–98
Carolina Coin Caterers Corporation, **10** 222
Carolina Energies, Inc., **6** 576

Carolina First National, **II** 336
Carolina Freight Corporation, **6 369–72**
Carolina Power & Light Company, **V 564–66**
Carolina Telephone and Telegraph Company, **10 201–03**
Carpenter Paper Co., **IV** 282; **9** 261
Carpenter Technology Corporation, **13 139–41**
Carpets International Plc., **8** 270–71
Carr Fowler, **III** 673
Carr's of Carlisle, **I** 604; **II** 594
Carr-Lowrey Glass Co., **13** 40
Carr-Union Line, **6** 397
Carrabba's Italian Grill, **12** 373–75
Carrefour SA, **II** 628; **8** 404–05; **10 204–06**; **12** 153
Carreras, **V** 411–12
Carrier Corporation, **I** 85; **III** 329; **7 70–73**
Carrier Transicold Corporation, **13** 507
Carroll County Electric Company, **6** 511
Carroll Reed Ski Shops, Inc., **10** 215
Carroll's Foods, **7** 477
Carson Pirie Scott & Company, **II** 669; **9** 142; **15 86–88**
Carte Blanche, **9** 335
Carter & Co., **IV** 644
Carter Automotive Co., **I** 159
Carter, Berlind, Potoma & Weill, **II** 450
Carter Hawley Hale Stores, **I** 246; **V 29–32**; **8** 160; **12** 356; **15** 88
Carter Holt Harvey Ltd., **IV** 280; **15** 229
Carter Oil Company, **IV** 171; **11** 353
Carter-Wallace, Inc., **6** 27; **8 83–86**
Carteret Savings Bank, **III** 263–64; **10** 340
Cartier Monde, **IV** 93; **V** 411, 413
Cartier Refined Sugars Ltd., **II** 662–63
Cartiera F.A. Marsoni, **IV** 587
Cartiere Ascoli Piceno, **IV** 586
Cartiers Superfoods, **II** 678
Cartillon Importers, Ltd., **6** 48
Carworth Inc., **I** 630; **11** 34
Cary-Davis Tug and Barge Company. *See* Puget Sound Tug and Barge Company.
CASA, **7** 9
Casa Bancária Almeida e Companhia. *See* Banco Bradesco S.A.
Casa Bonita, **II** 587
Cascade Fiber, **13** 99
Cascade Lumber Co., **IV** 255; **8** 65
Cascade Natural Gas Corporation, **6** 568; **9 102–04**
Casco Northern Bank, **14 89–91**
Case Manufacturing Corp., **I** 512
Case, Pomeroy & Co., Inc., **IV** 76
Case Technologies, Inc., **11** 504
Casein Co. of America, **II** 471
Casino, **10** 205
Casino. *See* Etablissements Economiques de Casino Guichard, Perrachon et Cie, S.C.A.
Casio Computer Co., Ltd., **III 448–49**, 455; **IV** 599; **10** 57
Cassa Generale Ungherese di Risparmio, **III** 207
Cassady Broiler Co., **II** 585
Cassatt, **II** 424
Castex, **13** 501
Castle & Cooke, Inc., **I** 417; **II 490–92**; **9** 175–76; **10** 40
Castle Brewery, **I** 287
Castle Tretheway Mines Ltd., **IV** 164
Castlemaine Tooheys, **10** 169–70

Castrol Ltd., **IV** 382–83
Castrorama, **10** 205
Casual Corner, **V** 207–08
CATCO. *See* Crowley All Terrain Corporation.
Caterpillar Inc., **I** 147, 181, 186, 422; **III 450–53**, 458, 463, 545–46; **9** 310; **10** 274, 377, 381, 429; **11** 473; **12** 90; **13** 513; **15 89–93 (upd.)**, 225
Cathay Insurance Co., **III** 221; **14** 109
Cathay Pacific Airways Limited, **I** 522; **II** 298; **6** 71, **78–80**
Catherines Stores Corporation, **15 94–97**
Cathodic Protection Services Co., **14** 325
Cato Corporation, **14 92–94**
Cato Oil and Grease Co., **IV** 446
Cattybrook Brick Company, **14** 249
CATV, **10** 319
Caudill Rowlett Scott. *See* CRSS Inc.
Caudle Engraving, **12** 471
CAV, **III** 554–55
Cavallo Pipeline Company, **11** 441
Cavedon Chemical Co., **I** 341
Cavendish International Holdings, **IV** 695
Cavendish Land, **III** 273
Cavenham Ltd., **7** 202–03
Cawoods Holdings, **III** 735
Caxton Holdings, **IV** 641
CB&I, **7** 76–77
CB&Q. *See* Chicago, Burlington and Quincy Railroad Company.
CBC Film Sales Co., **II** 135
CBI Industries, Inc., **7 74–77**
CBM Realty Corp., **III** 643
CBN Cable Network, **13** 279–81
CBN Satellite Services, **13** 279
CBS Inc., **I** 29, 488; **II** 61, 89, 102–03, 129–31, **132–34**, 136, 152, 166–67; **III** 55, 188; **IV** 605, 623, 652, 675, 703; **6 157–60 (upd.)**; **11** 327; **12** 75, 561
CBS Records, **II** 103, 134, 177; **6** 159
CBT Corp., **II** 213–14
CBWL-Hayden Stone, **II** 450
CC Soft Drinks Ltd., **I** 248
CCAir Inc., **11** 300
CCG. *See* The Clark Construction Group, Inc.
CCH Computax, **7** 93–94
CCH Inc., **7** 93; **14 95–97**
CCI Electronique, **10** 113
CCL Industries, Ltd., **15** 129
CCM Sport Maska, Inc., **15** 396
CCP Insurance, Inc., **10** 248
CCS Automation Systems Inc., **I** 124
CCT. *See* Crowley Caribbean Transport.
CdF-Chimie, **I** 303; **IV** 174, 198, 525
CDI Corporation, **6 139–41**
CDMS. *See* Credit and Data Marketing Services.
CDR International, **13** 228
CE-Minerals, **IV** 109
Ceat Cavi, **III** 434
Ceco Doors, **8** 544–46
CECOS International, Inc., **V** 750
Cedar Engineering, **III** 126
Cedarapids, Inc., **11** 413
Cedec S.A., **14** 43
Cederroth International AB, **8** 17
CEDIS, **12** 153
Cegedur, **IV** 174
CEIR, **10** 255
Celanese Corp., **I 317–19**, 347. *See also* Hoechst Celanese Corporation.
Celestial Farms, **13** 383

Celestial Seasonings, **II** 534
Celfor Tool Company, **8** 114. *See also* Clark Equipment Company.
Celite Corporation, **III** 706; **7** 291; **10** 43, 45
Cella Italian Wines, **10** 181
Cellnet, **11** 547
Cellonit-Gesellschaft Dreyfus & Cie., **I** 317
Cellu-Products Co., **14** 430
Cellular America, **6** 300
Cellular One, **9** 321
CellularVision, **13** 399
Cellulosa d'Italia, **IV** 272
Cellulose & Chemical Manufacturing Co., **I** 317
Cellulose & Specialties, **8** 434
Cellulose du Pin, **III** 677, 704
Celotex Corp., **III** 766–67
Celsius Energy Company, **6** 569
CELTEX, **I** 388–89
Celtex. *See* Pricel.
Cementia, **III** 705
Cemij, **IV** 132
Cemsto, **13** 545
CenCall Communications, **10** 433
Cenco, Inc., **6** 188; **10** 262–63
Cenex Cooperative, **II** 536
Cengas, **6** 313
Centel Corporation, 6 312–15, 593; **9** 106, 480; **10** 203; **14** 258
Centerior Energy Corporation, V 567–68
Centex Corporation, 8 87–89, 461
Centex Telemanagement Inc., **11** 302
Centocor Inc., 14 98–100
CentraBank, **II** 337; **10** 426
Central and South West Corporation, V 569–70
Central Area Power Coordination Group, **V** 677
Central Arizona Light & Power Company, **6** 545
Central Bancorp of Cincinnati, **II** 342
Central Bank for Railway Securities, **II** 281
Central Bank of Italy, **II** 403
Central Bank of London, **II** 318
Central Bank of Oman, **IV** 516
Central Bank of Scotland, **10** 337
Central Coalfields Ltd., **IV** 48–49
Central Computer Systems Inc., **11** 65
Central Covenants, **II** 222
Central Detallista, **12** 154
Central Electric & Gas Company. *See* Centel Corporation.
Central Electric and Telephone Company, Inc. *See* Centel Corporation.
Central Fiber Products Company, **12** 376
Central Finance Corp. of Canada, **II** 418
Central Foam Corp., **I** 481, 563
Central Hankyu Ltd., **V** 71
Central Hardware, **III** 530
Central Hudson Gas And Electricity Corporation, 6 458–60
Central Illinois Public Service Company. *See* CIPSCO Inc.
Central Independent Television plc, 7 78–80; 15 84
Central India Spinning, Weaving and Manufacturing Co., **IV** 217
Central Indiana Power Company, **6** 556
Central Investment Corp., **12** 184
Central Japan Heavy Industries, **III** 578–79; **7** 348

Central Maine Power, 6 461–64; 14 126
Central Maloney Transformer, **I** 434
Central Mining and Investment Corp., **IV** 23, 79, 95–96, 524, 565
Central National Bank, **9** 475
Central National Bank & Trust Co., **13** 467
Central National Life Insurance Co., **III** 463
Central Nebraska Packing, **10** 250
Central Newspapers, Inc., 10 207–09
Central Pacific Railroad, **II** 381; **13** 372
Central Park Bank of Buffalo, **11** 108
Central Penn National Corp., **11** 295
Central Planning & Design Institute, **IV** 48
Central Point Software, **10** 509
Central Public Service Corporation, **6** 447
Central Public Utility Corp., **13** 397
Central Savings and Loan, **10** 339
Central Solvents & Chemicals Company, **8** 100
Central Soya Company, Inc., 7 81–83
Central Telephone & Utilities Corporation. *See* Centel Corporation.
Central Terminal Company, **6** 504
Central Transformer, **I** 434
Central Trust Co., **II** 313; **11** 110
Central Union Telephone Company, **14** 251, 257
Central Union Trust Co. of New York, **II** 313
Central West Public Service Company. *See* Centel Corporation.
Centralab Inc., **13** 398
Centrale Verzorgingsdienst Cotrans N.V., **12** 443
Centran Corp., **9** 475
Centre de Dechets Industriels Group, **IV** 296
Centre Lait, **II** 577
Centrum Communications Inc., **11** 520
CenTrust Federal Savings, **10** 340
Centura Software, **10** 244
Centurion Brick, **14** 250
Century Bank, **II** 312
Century Communications Corp., 10 210–12
Century Data Systems, Inc., **13** 127
Century Electric Company, **13** 273
Century Hutchinson, Ltd., **13** 429
Century Savings Assoc. of Kansas, **II** 420
Century Telephone Enterprises, Inc., 9 105–07
Century Tool Co., **III** 569
Century 21 Real Estate, **I** 127; **II** 679; **III** 293; **11** 292; **12** 489
CEPCO. *See* Chugoku Electric Power Company Inc.
CEPSA. *See* Compañia Española de Petroleos S.A.
Cera Trading Co., **III** 756
Ceramesh, **11** 361
Ceramic Art Company, **12** 312
Ceramic Supply Company, **8** 177
Cerberus Limited, **6** 490
Cereal Industries, **II** 466
Cereal Packaging, Ltd., **13** 294
Cereal Partners Worldwide, **10** 324; **13** 294
Cerebos, **II** 565
Cerex, **IV** 290
Ceridian Corporation, **10** 257
Cermalloy, **IV** 100
Cerro Corp., **IV** 11, 136
Cerro de Pasco Corp., **IV** 33
CertainTeed Corp., **III** 677–78, 621, 762

Certanium Alloys and Research Co., **9** 419
Certified Grocers of Florida, Inc., **15** 139
Certified Laboratories, **8** 385
Certified TV and Appliance Company, **9** 120
Certus International Corp., **10** 509
Cerveceria Polar, I 230–31
Cessna Aircraft Company, III 512; **8** 49–51, **90–93**, 313–14
Cetus Corp., **I** 637; **III** 53; **7** 427; **10** 78, 214
CF AirFreight, **6** 390
CF Braun, **13** 119
CF Holding Corporation, **12** 71
CF Industries, **IV** 576
CF&I Steel Corporation, **8** 135
CFM. *See* Compagnie Française du Méthane.
CFP. *See* Compagnie Française des Pétroles.
CFS Continental, **II** 675
CG&E. *See* Cincinnati Gas & Electric Company.
CGCT, **I** 563
CGE, **II** 117
CGM. *See* Compagnie Générale Maritime.
CGR-MeV, **III** 635
Chaco Energy Corporation, **V** 724–25
Chadwick's of Boston, **V** 197–98
Chalet Suisse International, Inc., **13** 362
Chalk's International Airlines, **12** 420
Challenge Corp. Ltd., **IV** 278–79
Challenger Minerals Inc., **9** 267
Chambers Corporation, **8** 298
Champion Engineering Co., **III** 582
Champion, Inc., **8** 459; **12** 457
Champion International Corporation, III 215; **IV** 263–65, 334; **12** 130; **15** 229
Champion Spark Plug Co., **II** 17; **III** 593
Champion Valley Farms, **II** 480
Champlin Petroleum Company, **10** 83
Champs Sports, **14** 293, 295
Chance Bros., **III** 724–27
Chance Vought Aircraft Co., **I** 67–68, 84–85, 489–91
Chanco Medical Industries, **III** 73
The Chandris Group, **11** 377
Chanel, 12 57–59
Channel Master Corporation, **II** 91; **15** 134
Channel Tunnel Group, **13** 206
Chantiers de l'Atlantique, **9** 9
Chaparral Steel Co., 8 522–24; 13 142–44
Chapman Valve Manufacturing Company, **8** 135
Chargeurs, 6 373–75, 379
Charise Charles Ltd., **9** 68
Charisma Communications, **6** 323
Charles A. Eaton Co., **III** 24
Charles B. Perkins Co., **II** 667
Charles D. Burnes Co., Inc. *See* The Holson Burnes Group, Inc.
Charles Hobson, **6** 27
Charles Huston & Sons, **14** 323
Charles Luckman Assoc., **I** 513
Charles of the Ritz Group Ltd., **I** 695–97; **III** 56
Charles Pfizer Co., **I** 96
Charles Phillips & Co. Ltd., **II** 677
Charles R. McCormick Lumber Company, **12** 407
Charles Schwab Corp., II 228; **8 94–96**
Charles Scribner's Sons, **7** 166

Charleston Consolidated Railway, Gas and Electric Company, **6** 574
Charlestown Foundry, **III** 690
Charley Brothers, **II** 669
Charmin Paper Co., **III** 52; **IV** 329; **8** 433
Charming Shoppes, Inc., 8 97–98
Charrington & Co., **I** 223
Chart House, **II** 556, 613–14
Charter Bank, **II** 348
Charter Club, **9** 315
Charter Consolidated, **IV** 23, 119–20
Charter Corp., **III** 254; **14** 460
Charter National Life Insurance Company, **11** 261
Charter Oil Co., **II** 620; **12** 240
Charter Security Life Insurance Cos., **III** 293
Chartered Bank, **II** 357
Chartered Co. of British New Guinea, **III** 698
Chartered Mercantile Bank of India, London and China, **II** 298
Charterhouse Petroleum, **IV** 499
Chartwell Associates, **III** 16; **9** 331
Chartwell Land, **V** 106
Chas. A. Stevens & Co., **IV** 660
Chase & Sanborn, **II** 544
Chase Corp., **II** 402
Chase Drier & Chemical Co., **8** 177
Chase, Harris, Forbes, **II** 402
The Chase Manhattan Bank Clients AC, **15** 38–39
The Chase Manhattan Corporation, **I** 123, 334, 451; **II** 202, 227, **247–49,** 256–57, 262, 286, 317, 385, 397, 402; **III** 104, 248; **IV** 33; **6** 52; **9** 124; **10** 61; **13 145–48 (upd.),** 476; **14** 48, 103
Chastain-Roberts, **II** 669
Chaston Medical & Surgical Products, **13** 366
Chateau Cheese Co. Ltd., **II** 471
Chateau Grower Winery Co., **II** 575
Chatfield & Woods Co., **IV** 311
Chatfield Paper Co., **IV** 282; **9** 261
Chatham and Phenix National Bank of New York, **II** 312
Chatham Bank, **II** 312
Chattanooga Gas Company, Inc., **6** 577
Chattanooga Gas Light Company, **6** 448
Chatto, Virago, Bodley Head & Jonathan Cape, Ltd., **13** 429
Chaux et Ciments de Lafarge et du Teil, **III** 703–04
Chaux et Ciments du Maroc, **III** 703
Checker Holding, **10** 370
Checker Motors Corp., **10** 369
Checkers, **14** 452
Chef Boyardee, **10** 70
Chef Francisco, **13** 383
Chef Pierre, **II** 572
Chef's Orchard Airline Caterers Inc., **I** 513
Chef-Boy-Ar-Dee Quality Foods Inc., **I** 622
Cheil Sugar Co., **I** 515
Cheil Wool Textile Co., **I** 515
Chelan Power Company, **6** 596
Chem-Nuclear Systems, Inc., **9** 109–10
Chemap, **III** 420
Chemcentral Corporation, 8 99–101
Chemcut, **I** 682
Chemdal Corp., **13** 34
Chemed Corporation, 13 149–50; 15 409–11
Chemetron Process Equipment, Inc., **8** 545

Chemex Pharmaceuticals, Inc., **8** 63
Chemical Banking Corporation, **II** 234, **250–52,** 254; **9** 124, 361; **12** 15, 31; **13** 49, 147, 411; **14 101–04 (upd.);** **15** 39
Chemical Coatings Co., **I** 321
Chemical Process Co., **IV** 409; **7** 308
Chemical Products Company, **13** 295
Chemical Specialties Inc., **I** 512
Chemical Waste Management, Inc., **V** 753; **9 108–10;** **11** 435–36
Chemins de fer de Paris à Lyon et à la Méditerranée, **6** 424
Chemins de fer du Midi, **6** 425
Chemins de Fer Fédéraux, **V** 519
Chemisch-Pharmazeutische AG, **IV** 70
Chemische Fabrik auf Actien, **I** 681
Chemische Fabrik Friesheim Elektron AG, **IV** 229
Chemische Fabrik vormals Sandoz, **I** 671
Chemische Fabrik Wesseling AG, **IV** 70–71
Chemische Werke Hüls GmbH. *See* Hüls A.G.
Chemise Lacoste, **9** 157
ChemLawn, **13** 199
Chemmar Associates, Inc., **8** 271
Chempump, **8** 135
Chemurgic Corporation, **6** 148
Chemway Corp., **III** 423
Cheney Bigelow Wire Works, **13** 370
Cheplin Laboratories, **III** 17
Cherokee Insurance Co., **I** 153; **10** 265
Cherry Co., **I** 266
Cherry Hill Cheese, **7** 429
Cherry-Burrell Process Equipment, **8** 544–45
Chesapeake and Ohio Railroad, **II** 329; **V** 438–40; **10** 43; **13** 372
Chesapeake Corporation, 8 102–04; 10 540
Chesebrough-Pond's USA, Inc., **II** 590; **7** 544; **8 105–07; 9** 319
Cheshire Wholefoods, **II** 528
Chester Engineers, **10** 412
Chester G. Luby, **I** 183
Chester Oil Co., **IV** 368
Cheung Kong (Holdings) Limited, **I** 470; **IV 693–95**
Chevrolet Motor Division, **V** 494; **9** 17
Chevron Corporation, **II** 143; **IV** 367, **385–87,** 452, 464, 466, 479, 484, 490, 523, 531, 536, 539, 563, 721; **9** 391; **10** 119; **12** 20
Chevron U.K. Ltd., **15** 352
Chevy Chase Savings Bank, **13** 439
Cheyenne Software, Inc., 12 60–62
CHF. *See* Chase, Harris, Forbes.
Chi-Chi's Inc., 13 151–53; 14 195
Chiat/Day Inc. Advertising, **9** 438; **11** 49–52
Chiba Riverment and Cement, **III** 760
Chibu Electric Power Company, Incorporated, V 571–73
Chicago & Calumet Terminal Railroad, **IV** 368
Chicago and Alton Railroad, **I** 456
Chicago and North Western Holdings Corporation, **I** 440; **6 376–78**
Chicago and Southern Airlines Inc., **I** 100; **6** 81
Chicago Bears, **IV** 703
Chicago Bridge & Iron Company, **7** 74–77
Chicago Burlington and Quincy Railroad, **III** 282; **V** 425–28

Chicago Chemical Co., **I** 373; **12** 346
Chicago Corp., **I** 526
Chicago Cubs, **IV** 682–83
Chicago Directory Co., **IV** 660–61
Chicago Edison, **IV** 169
Chicago Flexible Shaft Company, **9** 484
Chicago Heater Company, Inc., **8** 135
Chicago Magnet Wire Corp., **13** 397
Chicago Motor Club, **10** 126
Chicago Pacific Corp., **I** 530; **III** 573; **12** 251
Chicago Pneumatic Tool Co., **III** 427, 452; **7** 480
Chicago Radio Laboratory, **II** 123
Chicago Rawhide Manufacturing Company, **8** 462–63
Chicago Rock Island and Peoria Railway Co., **I** 558
Chicago Rollerskate, **15** 395
Chicago Screw Co., **12** 344
Chicago Steel Works, **IV** 113
Chicago Sun-Times Distribution Systems, **6** 14
Chicago Times, **11** 251
Chicago Title and Trust Co., **III** 276; **10** 43–45
Chicago Tribune. *See* Tribune Company.
Chicopee Manufacturing Corp., **III** 35
Chief Auto Parts, **II** 661
Chiers-Chatillon-Neuves Maisons, **IV** 227
Chilcott Laboratories Inc., **I** 710–11
Child World Inc., **13** 166
Children's Book-of-the-Month Club, **13** 105
Children's Palace, **13** 166
Children's Record Guild, **13** 105
Children's Television Workshop, **12** 495; **13** 560
Children's World Learning Centers, **II** 608; **V** 17, 19; **13** 48
Chiles Offshore Corporation, 9 111–13
Chili's, **10** 331; **12** 373–74
Chillicothe Co., **IV** 310
Chilton Corp., **III** 440
Chiminter, **III** 48
Chimio, **I** 669–70; **8** 451–52
China Airlines, **6** 71; **9** 233
China Borneo Co., **III** 698
China Canada Investment and Development Co., **II** 457
China Coast, **10** 322, 324
China Electric, **II** 67
China Foreign Transportation Corporation, **6** 386
China Industries Co., **II** 325
China International Trade and Investment Corporation, **II** 442; **IV** 695; **6** 80
China Light & Power, **6** 499
China Mutual Steam Navigation Company Ltd., **6** 416
China National Automotive Industry Import and Export Corp., **III** 581
China National Aviation Co., **I** 96
China National Chemicals Import and Export Corp., **IV** 395
China National Machinery Import and Export Corporation, **8** 279
China Navigation Co., **I** 521
China Orient Leasing Co., **II** 442
China Zhouyang Fishery Co. Ltd., **II** 578
Chinese Electronics Import and Export Corp., **I** 535
Chinese Metallurgical Import and Export Corp., **IV** 61

Chinese Petroleum Corporation, IV 388–90, 493, 519
Chinese Steel Corp., **IV** 184
Chino Mines Co., **IV** 179
Chinon Industries, **III** 477; **7** 163
CHIPS and Technologies, Inc., 6 217; **9 114–17**
Chiquita Brands International, Inc., II 595–96; **III** 28; **7 84–86**
Chiro Tool Manufacturing Corp., **III** 629
Chiron Corporation, 7 427; **10 213–14**
Chisso Chemical, **II** 301
Chiswick Products, **II** 566
Chita Oil Co., **IV** 476
Chivers, **II** 477
Chiyoda Bank, **I** 503; **II** 321
Chiyoda Chemical, **I** 433
Chiyoda Fire and Marine, **III** 404
Chiyoda Kogaku Seiko Kabushiki Kaisha, **III** 574–75
Chiyoda Konpo Kogyo Co. Ltd., **V** 536
Chiyoda Mutual, **II** 374
Chloé Chimie, **I** 303
Chloride S.A., **I** 423
Choay, **I** 676–77
Chocolat Ibled S.A., **II** 569
Chocolat Poulait, **II** 478
Chocolat-Menier S.A., **II** 569
Chogoku Kogyo, **II** 325
Choice Hotels International Inc., 6 187, 189; **14 105–07**
Chorlton Metal Co., **I** 531
Chosen Sekiyu, **IV** 554
Chotin Transportation Co., **6** 487
Chow Tai Fook Jewellery Co., **IV** 717
Chris-Craft Industries, Inc., II 176, 403; **III** 599–600; **9 118–19**
Christal Radio, **6** 33
Christensen Company, **8** 397
Christian Bourgois, **IV** 614–15
Christian Broadcasting Network, **13** 279
Christian Dior, **I** 272
Christie, Mitchell & Mitchell, **7** 344
Christie's International plc, 15 98–101
Chromalloy American Corp., **13** 461
Chromalloy Gas Turbine Corp., **13** 462
Chromatic Color, **13** 227–28
Chromcraft Revington, Inc., 15 102–05
Chrysler Corp., I 10, 17, 28, 38, 59, 79, 136, **144–45**, 152, 162–63, 172, 178, 182, 188, 190, 207, 420, 504, 516, 525, 540; **II** 5, 313, 403, 448; **III** 439, 517, 544, 568, 591, 607, 637–38; **IV** 22, 449, 676, 703; **7** 205, 233, 461; **8** 74–75, 315, 505–07; **9** 118, 349–51, 472; **10** 174, 198, 264–65, 290, 317, 353, 430; **11 53–55 (upd.)**, 103–04, 429; **13** 28–29, 61, 448, 501, 555; **14** 321, 367, 457
Chu Ito & Co., **IV** 476
Chubb Corporation, II 84; **III** 190, **220–22**, 368; **11** 481; **14 108–10 (upd.)**
Chubu Electric Power Co., **IV** 492
Chuck E. Cheese, **13** 472–74
Chugai Pharmaceutical Company, **8** 215–16; **10** 79
Chugai Shogyo Shimposha, **IV** 654–55
Chugoku Electric Power Company Inc., V 574–76
Chuo Trust & Banking Co., **II** 373, 391
Church, Goodman, and Donnelley, **IV** 660
Church's Fried Chicken, Inc., **I** 260; **7** 26–28; **15** 345
Churchill Insurance Co. Ltd., **III** 404

Churny Co. Inc., **II** 534
Cianbro Corporation, 14 111–13
Cianchette Brothers, Inc. *See* Cianbro Corporation.
Ciba-Geigy Ltd., I 625, **632–34**, 671, 690, 701; **III** 55; **IV** 288; **8** 63, **108–11 (upd.)**, 376–77; **9** 153, 441; **10** 53–54, 213; **15** 229
CIBC. *See* Canadian Imperial Bank of Commerce.
CICI, **11** 184
CIDLA, **IV** 504–06
Cie Continental d'Importation, **10** 249
Cie des Lampes, **9** 9
Cie Générale d'Electro-Ceramique, **9** 9
Cifra, S.A. de C.V., 8 556; **12 63–65**
CIGNA Corporation, III 197, **223–27**, 389; **10** 30; **11** 243
Cii-HB, **III** 123, 678
Cilag-Chemie, **III** 35–36; **8** 282
Cilbarco, **II** 25
Cilva Holdings PLC, **6** 358
Cima, **14** 224–25
Cimarron Utilities Company, **6** 580
Ciments d'Obourg, **III** 701
Ciments de Chalkis Portland Artificiels, **III** 701
Ciments de Champagnole, **III** 702
Ciments de l'Adour, **III** 702
Ciments Lafarge France, **III** 704
Ciments Lafarge Quebec, **III** 704
Cimos, **7** 37
Cincinnati Bell, Inc., 6 316–18
Cincinnati Chemical Works, **I** 633
Cincinnati Electronics Corp., **II** 25
Cincinnati Gas & Electric Company, 6 465–68, 481–82
Cincinnati Milacron Inc., 12 66–69
Cincom Systems Inc., 15 106–08
Cineamerica, **IV** 676
Cinecentrum, **IV** 591
Cinema International Corp., **II** 149
Cinemax, **IV** 675; **7** 222–24, 528–29
Cineplex Odeon Corporation, II 145, **6 161–63**; **14** 87
Cinnabon, **13** 435–37
Cintel, **II** 158
CIPSCO Inc., 6 469–72, 505–06
Circle A Ginger Ale Company, **9** 177
Circle K Corporation, II 619–20; **V** 210; **7** 113–14, 372, 374
Circle Plastics, **9** 323
Circuit City Stores, Inc., 9 65–66, **120–22**; **10** 235, 305–06, 334–35, 468–69; **12** 335; **14** 61; **15** 215
Circus Circus Enterprises, Inc., 6 201, **203–05**
Cirrus Logic, Incorporated, 9 334; **11 56–57**
Cisco Systems, Inc., 11 58–60, 520; **13** 482
CIT Alcatel, **9** 9–10
CIT Financial Corp., **II** 90, 313; **8** 117; **12** 207
CIT Group/Business Credit, Inc., **13** 446
CIT Group/Commercial Services, **13** 536
Citadel General, **III** 404
CITGO Petroleum Corporation, II 660–61; **IV 391–93**, 508; **7** 491
Citibanc Group, Inc., **11** 456
Citibank, **II** 227, 230, 248, 250–51, 253–55, 331, 350, 358, 415; **III** 243, 340; **6** 51; **9** 124; **10** 150; **11** 418; **13** 146; **14** 101

CITIC. *See* China International Trade and Investment Corporation.
Citicorp, II 214, **253–55**, 268, 275, 319, 331, 361, 398, 411, 445; **III** 10, 220, 397; **7** 212–13; **8** 196; **9 123–26 (upd.)**, 441; **10** 463, 469; **11** 140; **12** 30, 310, 334; **13** 535; **14** 103, 108, 235; **15** 94, 146, 281
Cities Service Co., **IV** 376, 391–92, 481, 575; **12** 542
Citinet. *See* Hongkong Telecommunications Ltd.
Citivision PLC, **9** 75
Citizen Watch Co., Ltd., III 454–56, 549; **13** 121–22
Citizen's Electric Light & Power Company, **V** 641
Citizen's Federal Savings Bank, **10** 93
Citizen's Fidelity Corp., **II** 342
Citizen's Industrial Bank, **14** 529
Citizens and Southern Bank, **II** 337; **10** 426
Citizens Bank, **11** 105
Citizens Bank of Hamilton, **9** 475
Citizens Bank of Savannah, **10** 426
Citizens Building & Loan Association, **14** 191
Citizens Federal Savings and Loan Association, **9** 476
Citizens Financial Group, **12** 422
Citizens Gas Co., **6** 529
Citizens Gas Fuel Company. *See* MCN Corporation.
Citizens Gas Light Co., **6** 455
Citizens Gas Supply Corporation, **6** 527
Citizens National Bank, **II** 251; **13** 466
Citizens National Gas Company, **6** 527
Citizens Savings & Loan Association, **9** 173
Citizens Telephone Company, **14** 257–58
Citizens Trust Co., **II** 312
Citizens Utilities Company, 7 87–89
Citizens' Savings and Loan, **10** 339
Citroën. *See* Automobiles Citroen.
City and St. James, **III** 501
City and Suburban Telegraph Association and Telephonic Exchange, **6** 316–17
City and Village Automobile Insurance Co., **III** 363
City Auto Stamping Co., **I** 201
City Bank Farmers' Trust Co., **II** 254; **9** 124
City Bank of New York, **II** 250, 253
City Brewery, **I** 253
City Centre Properties Ltd., **IV** 705–06
City Finance, **10** 340
City Finance Company, **11** 261
City Ice Delivery, Ltd., **II** 660
City Investing Co., **III** 263; **IV** 721; **9** 391; **13** 363
City Light and Traction Company, **6** 593
City Light and Water Company, **6** 579
City Market Inc., **12** 112
City Mutual Life Assurance Society, **III** 672–73
City National Bank of Baton Rouge, **11** 107
City National Leasing, **II** 457
City of London Real Property Co. Ltd., **IV** 706
City of Seattle Water Department, **12** 443
The City Post Publishing Corp., **12** 359
City Products Corp., **II** 419
City Public Service, 6 473–75

City Savings, **10** 340
Cityhome Corp., **III** 263
Civic Drugs, **12** 21
Civil & Civic Contractors, **IV** 707–08
Civil Service Employees Insurance Co., **III** 214
Clabir Corp., **12** 199
Clairol, **III** 17–18
Clairton Steel Co., **IV** 572; **7** 550
CLAM Petroleum, **7** 282
Clancy Paul Inc., **13** 276
Clara Candy, **15** 65
Clares Equipment Co., **I** 252
Clark & Co., **IV** 301
Clark & Rockefeller, **IV** 426
Clark Bros. Co., **III** 471
The Clark Construction Group, Inc., 8 112–13
Clark, Dietz & Associates-Engineers. *See* CRSS Inc.
Clark Equipment Company, I 153; **7** 513–14; **8 114–16; 10** 265; **13** 500; **15** 226
Clark Estates Inc., **8** 13
Clark Materials Handling Company, **7** 514
Clark Motor Co., **I** 158; **10** 292
Clarkson International Tools, **I** 531
CLASSA. *See* Compañia de Líneas Aéreas Subvencionadas S.A.
Claussen Pickle Co., **12** 371
Clayton & Dubilier, **III** 25
Clayton Brown Holding Company, **15** 232
Clayton Homes Incorporated, 13 154–55
Clayton-Marcus Co., **12** 300
Clean Window Remodelings Co., **III** 757
Cleanaway Ltd., **III** 495
Cleancoal Terminal, **7** 582, 584
Clearing Inc., **III** 514
Clearwater Tissue Mills, Inc., **8** 430
Clef, **IV** 125
Clements Energy, Inc., **7** 376
Cleo Inc., **12** 207–09
Cletrac Corp., **IV** 366
Cleveland and Western Coal Company, **7** 369
Cleveland Electric Illuminating Company. *See* Centerior Energy Theodor.
Cleveland Iron Mining Company, **13** 156
Cleveland Oil Co., **I** 341
Cleveland Paper Co., **IV** 311
Cleveland Pneumatic Co., **I** 457; **III** 512
Cleveland Twist Drill Company **I** 531. *See also* Acme-Cleveland Corp.
Cleveland-Cliffs Inc., 13 156–58
Clevepak Corporation, **8** 229; **13** 442
Clevite Corporation, **14** 207
Clifford & Wills, **12** 280–81
Cliffs Corporation, **13** 157
Climax Molybdenum Co., **IV** 17–19
Clinchfield Coal Corp., **IV** 180–81
Clinical Assays, **I** 628
Clinical Science Research Ltd., **10** 106
Clinton Pharmaceutical Co., **III** 17
Clipper Group, **12** 439
Clipper, Inc., **IV** 597
Clipper Manufacturing Company, **7** 3
Clipper Seafoods, **II** 587
Clorox Company, III 20–22, 52; **8** 433
Clouterie et Tréfilerie des Flandres, **IV** 25–26
Clover Leaf Creamery, **II** 528
Clover Milk Products Co., **II** 575
Clovis Water Co., **6** 580
CLSI Inc., **15** 372

Club Aurrera, **8** 556
Club Européen du Tourisme, **6** 207
Club Méditerranée SA, I 286; **6 206–08**
Clubhôtel, **6** 207
Cluett, Peabody & Co., Inc., **II** 414; **8** 567–68
Clyde Iron Works, **8** 545
Clydebank Engineering & Shipbuilding Co., **I** 573
Clyne Maxon Agency, **I** 29
CM Industries, **I** 676
CM&M Equilease, **7** 344
CMB Acier, **IV** 228
CMB Packaging, **8** 477
CML Group, Inc., 10 215–18
CMP Properties Inc., **15** 122
CMS Energy Corporation, IV 23; **V 577–79; 8** 466; **14 114–16 (upd.)**
CN. *See* Canadian National Railway System.
CNA Financial Corporation, I 488; **III 228–32,** 339; **12** 317
CNA Health Plans, **III** 84
CNC Holding Corp., **13** 166
CNCA. *See* Caisse National de Crédit Agricole.
CNEP. *See* Comptoir National d'Escompte de Paris.
CNG. *See* Consolidated Natural Gas Company.
CNN. *See* Cable News Network.
Co-Axial Systems Engineering Co., **IV** 677
Co. Luxembourgeoise de Banque S.A., **II** 282
Co. of London Insurers, **III** 369
Co-Steel International Ltd., **8** 523–24; **13** 142–43
Coach Leatherware, 10 219–21; 12 559
Coach Specialties Co., **III** 484
Coal India Limited, IV 48–50
Coalport, **12** 528
Coast American Corporation, **13** 216
Coast Consolidators, Inc., **14** 505
Coast-to-Coast Stores, **II** 419; **12** 8
Coastal Coca-Cola Bottling Co., **10** 223
Coastal Corporation, IV 366, **394–95; 7** 553–54
Coastal States Corporation, **11** 481
Coastal States Life Insurance Company, **11** 482
Coastal Valley Canning Co., **I** 260
CoastAmerica Corp., **13** 176
Coates/Lorilleux, **14** 308
Coating Products, Inc., **III** 643
Coats Viyella Plc, V 356–58
CoBank. *See* National Bank for Cooperatives.
Cobb & Branham, **14** 257
Cobb, Inc., **II** 585; **14** 515
COBE Laboratories, Inc., 13 159–61
Cobra Electronics Corporation, 14 117–19
Coburn Optical Industries, **III** 56
Coburn Vision Care, **III** 727
Coca-Cola Bottling Co. Consolidated, II 170, 468; **10 222–24; 15** 299
The Coca-Cola Company, I 17, **232–35,** 244, 248, 278–79, 286, 289, 440, 457; **II** 103, 136–37, 477–78; **III** 215; **IV** 297; **6** 20–21, 30; **7** 155, 383, 466; **8** 399; **9** 86, 177; **10** 130, 222–23, **225–28 (upd.); 11** 421, 450–51; **12** 74; **13** 284; **14** 18, 453; **15** 428

Coca-Cola Enterprises, Inc., 10 223; **13 162–64**
Cochrane Corporation, **8** 135
Cochrane Foil Co., **15** 128
Cockerill Sambre Group, IV 26–27, **51–53**
Coco's, **I** 547
Codex Corp., **II** 61
Codville Distributors Ltd., **II** 649
COFINA, **III** 347
COFIRED, **IV** 108
Cogéma, **IV** 108
COGEMA Canada, **IV** 436
Cogentrix Energy, Inc., 10 229–31
Cogetex, **14** 225
Cognos Corp., **11** 78
Cohasset Savings Bank, **13** 468
Cohn-Hall-Marx Co. *See* United Merchants & Manufacturers, Inc.
Coinamatic Laundry Equipment, **II** 650
Coktel Vision, **15** 455
Colbert Television Sales, **9** 306
Colchester Car Auctions, **II** 587
Coldwell, Banker & Company, **IV** 715; **V** 180, 182; **11** 292; **12** 97
Coldwell Banker Commercial Group, Inc., **IV** 727
Cole & Weber Inc., **I** 27
Cole National Corporation, 13 165–67, 391
Cole's Craft Showcase, **13** 166
Coleco Industries, **III** 506
Coleman & Co., **II** 230
The Coleman Company, Inc., III 485; **9 127–29**
Colemans Ltd., **11** 241
Coles Book Stores Ltd., **7** 486, 488–89
Coles Express Inc., 15 109–11
Coles Myer Ltd., V 33–35
Colex Data, **14** 556
Colgate-Palmolive Company, I 260; **II** 672; **III 23–26; IV** 285; **9** 291; **11** 219, 317; **14 120–23 (upd.),** 279
Collabra Software Inc., **15** 322
College Construction Loan Insurance Assoc., **II** 455
College Entrance Examination Board, **12** 141
College Survival, Inc., **10** 357
Collegiate Arlington Sports Inc., **II** 652
Collett Dickenson Pearce, **I** 33
Collins & Aikman Corporation, I 483; **13 168–70**
Collins Radio Co., **III** 136; **11** 429
Colo-Macco. *See* CRSS Inc.
Cologne Reinsurance Co., **III** 273, 299
Colonia, **III** 273, 394
Colonial & General, **III** 359–60
Colonial Air Transport, **I** 89, 115; **12** 379
Colonial Airlines, **I** 102
Colonial Bancorp, **II** 208
Colonial Bank, **II** 236
Colonial Container, **8** 359
Colonial Food Stores, **7** 373
Colonial Healthcare Supply Co., **13** 90
Colonial Insurance Co., **IV** 575–76
Colonial Life Assurance Co., **III** 359
Colonial Life Insurance Co. of America, **III** 220–21; **14** 108–09
Colonial Life Insurance Company, **11** 481
Colonial National Bank, **8** 9
Colonial National Leasing, Inc., **8** 9
Colonial Packaging Corporation, **12** 150

Colonial Penn Group Insurance Co., **11** 262

Colonial Penn Life Insurance Co., **V** 624

Colonial Rubber Works, **8** 347

Colonial Stores, **II** 397

Colonial Sugar Refining Co. Ltd., **III** 686–87

Colony Communications, **7** 99

Color Corporation of America, **8** 553

Color-Box, Inc., **8** 103

Colorado Belle Casino, **6** 204

Colorado Cooler Co., **I** 292

Colorado Electric Company. *See* Public Service Company of Colorado.

Colorado Fuel & Iron (CF&I), **14** 369

Colorado Gathering & Processing Corporation, **11** 27

Colorado Interstate Gas Co., **IV** 394

Colorado National Bank, **12** 165

Colorcraft, **I** 447

Colorfoto Inc., **I** 447

Colossal Pictures, **10** 286

Colson Co., **III** 96; **IV** 135–36

Colt Industries Inc., **I** 434–36, 482, 524; **III** 435

Colt Pistol Factory, **9** 416

Colt's Manufacturing Company, Inc., 12 70–72

Columbia Broadcasting System. *See* CBS Inc.

Columbia Chemical Co., **III** 731

Columbia Electric Street Railway, Light and Power Company, **6** 575

Columbia Forest Products, **IV** 358

Columbia Gas & Electric Company, **6** 466. *See also* Columbia Gas System, Inc.

Columbia Gas Light Company, **6** 574

Columbia Gas of New York, Inc., **6** 536

Columbia Gas System, Inc., **V** 580–82

Columbia Gas Transmission Corporation, **6** 467

Columbia General Life Insurance Company of Indiana, **11** 378

Columbia House, **IV** 676

Columbia Insurance Co., **III** 214

Columbia News Service, **II** 132

Columbia Paper Co., **IV** 311

Columbia Pictures Entertainment, Inc., **II** 103, 134, **135–37**, 170, 234, 619; **IV** 675; **10** 227; **12** 73, 455. *See also* Columbia TriStar Motion Pictures Companies.

Columbia Railroad, Gas and Electric Company, **6** 575

Columbia Recording Corp., **II** 132

Columbia River Packers, **II** 491

Columbia Savings & Loan, **II** 144

Columbia Steel Co., **IV** 28, 573; **7** 550

Columbia TriStar Motion Pictures Companies, 12 73–76 (upd.). *See also* Columbia Pictures Entertainment, Inc.

Columbia/HCA Healthcare Corporation, 13 90; **15 112–14**

Columbian Chemicals Co., **IV** 179

Columbian Peanut Co., **I** 421; **11** 23

Columbus & Southern Ohio Electric Company (CSO), **6** 467, 481–82

Columbus Bank and Trust, **12** 465

Columbus Savings and Loan Society, **I** 536; **13** 528

Columbus-Milpar, **I** 544

Com Ed. *See* Commonwealth Edison.

Com-Link 21, Inc., **8** 310

Comair Holdings Inc., 13 171–73

Comalco Fabricators (Hong Kong) Ltd., **III** 758

Comalco Ltd., **IV** 59–61, 191. *See also* Commonwealth Aluminium Corp.

Comat Services Pte. Ltd., **10** 514

Comau, **I** 163

Combined American Insurance Co. of Dallas, **III** 203

Combined Casualty Co. of Philadelphia, **III** 203

Combined Communications Corp., **II** 619; **IV** 612; **7** 191

Combined Insurance Co. of America, **III** 203–04

Combined International Corp., **III** 203–04

Combined Mutual Casualty Co. of Chicago, **III** 203

Combined Registry Co., **III** 203

Combustiveis Industriais e Domésticos. *See* CIDLA.

Comcast Corporation, 7 90–92; 9 428; **10** 432–33

Comdisco, Inc., 9 130–32; 11 47, 86, 484, 490

Comdor Flugdienst GmbH., **I** 111

Comer Motor Express, **6** 370

Comerco, **III** 21

Comet, **II** 139; **V** 106–09

Cometra Oil, **IV** 576

ComFed Bancorp, **11** 29

Comforto GmbH, **8** 252

Cominco Fertilizers Ltd., **IV** 75, 141; **13** 503

Comitato Interministrale per la Ricostruzione, **I** 465

Comm-Quip, **6** 313

CommAir. *See* American Building Maintenance Industries, Inc.

Commander Foods, **8** 409

Commander-Larabee Co., **I** 419

Commentry, **III** 676

Commerce and Industry Insurance Co., **III** 196, 203

Commerce Clearing House, Inc., 7 93–94. *See also* CCH Inc.

Commerce Group, **III** 393

Commerce Union, **10** 426

Commercial & General Life Assurance Co., **III** 371

Commercial Alliance Corp. of New York, **II** 289

Commercial Aseguradora Suizo Americana, S.A., **III** 243

Commercial Assurance, **III** 359

Commercial Bank of Australia Ltd., **II** 189, 319, 388–89

Commercial Bank of London, **II** 334

Commercial Bank of Tasmania, **II** 188

Commercial Banking Co. of Sydney, **II** 187–89

Commercial Bureau (Australia) Pty., **I** 438

Commercial Credit Company, III 127–28; **8 117–19; 10** 255–56; **15** 464

Commercial Exchange Bank, **II** 254; **9** 124

Commercial Federal Corporation, 12 77–79

Commercial Filters Corp., **I** 512

Commercial Insurance Co. of Newark, **III** 242

Commercial Life, **III** 243

Commercial Life Assurance Co. of Canada, **III** 309

Commercial Metals Company, 15 115–17

Commercial Motor Freight, Inc., **14** 42

Commercial National Bank, **II** 261; **10** 425

Commercial National Bank & Trust Co., **II** 230

Commercial National Bank of Charlotte, **II** 336

Commercial Ship Repair Co., **I** 185

Commercial Union plc, **II** 272, 308; **III** 185, **233–35**, 350, 373; **IV** 711

Commerzbank A.G., **II** 239, 242, **256–58**, 280, 282, 385; **IV** 222; **9** 283; **14** 170

Commerzfilm, **IV** 591

Commodity Credit Corp., **11** 24

Commodore Corporation, **8** 229

Commodore International, Ltd., **II** 6; **III** 112; **6** 243–44; **7 95–97**, 532; **9** 46; **10** 56, 284

Commonwealth & Southern Corporation, **V** 676

Commonwealth Aluminium Corp., Ltd., **IV** 122. *See also* Comalco Ltd.

Commonwealth Bank, **II** 188, 389

Commonwealth Board Mills, **IV** 248

Commonwealth Edison, **II** 28, 425; **III** 653; **IV** 169; **V 583–85; 6** 505, 529, 531; **12** 548; **13** 341; **15** 422

Commonwealth Energy System, 14 124–26

Commonwealth Hospitality Ltd., **III** 95

Commonwealth Industries, **III** 569; **11** 536

Commonwealth Insurance Co., **III** 264

Commonwealth Land Title Insurance Co., **III** 343

Commonwealth Life Insurance Co., **III** 216–19

Commonwealth Mortgage Assurance Co., **III** 344

Commonwealth National Financial Corp., **II** 316

Commonwealth Oil Refining Company, **II** 402; **7** 517

Commonwealth Power Railway and Light Company, **14** 134

Commonwealth Southern Corporation, **14** 134

Commtron, Inc., **V** 14, 16; **11** 195; **13** 90

Communication Services Ltd. *See* Hongkong Telecommunications Ltd.

Communications Data Services, Inc., **IV** 627

Communications Properties, Inc., **IV** 677

Communications Solutions Inc., **11** 520

Communications Technology Corp. (CTC), **13** 7–8

Communicorp, **III** 188; **10** 29

Community Direct, Inc., **7** 16

Community HealthCare Services, **6** 182

Community Hospital of San Gabriel, **6** 149

Community Medical Care, Inc., **III** 245

Community National Bank, **9** 474

Community Power & Light Company, **6** 579–80

Community Psychiatric Centers, 15 118–20

Community Public Service Company, **6** 514

Community Savings and Loan, **II** 317

Comnet Corporation, **9** 347

Compac Corp., **11** 535

Compactom, **I** 588

Compagnia di Assicurazioni, **III** 345

Compagnia di Genova, **III** 347

Compagnie Auxiliaire de Navigation, **IV** 558

Compagnie Bancaire, **II** 259

Compagnie Belge pour l'industrie, **II** 202

Compagnie Continentale, **I** 409–10

Compagnie d'Assurances Générales, **III** 391

Compagnie d'assurances Mutuelles contre l'incendie dans les départements de la Seine Inférieure et de l'Eure, **III** 210

Compagnie d'Investissements de Paris, **II** 233

Compagnie de Compteurs, **III** 617

Compagnie de Five-Lille, **IV** 469

Compagnie de Mokta, **IV** 107–08

Compagnie de Navigation Mixte, **III** 185

Compagnie de Reassurance Nord-Atlantique, **III** 276

Compagnie de Recherche et d'Exploitation du Pétrole du Sahara, **IV** 545

Compagnie de Saint-Gobain S.A., **II** 117, 474–75; **III 675–78**, 704; **8** 395, 397; **15** 80

Compagnie de Transport Aerien, **I** 122

Compagnie des Machines Bull S.A., **II** 40, 42, 70, 125; **III 122–23**, 154; **IV** 600; **12** 139; **13** 574. *See also* Groupe Bull.

Compagnie des Messageries Maritimes, **6** 379

Compagnie des Produits Chimiques et Électrométallurgiques d'Alais, Froges et Camargue, **IV** 173–74

Compagnie du Midi, **III** 209, 211

Compagnie du Nord, **IV** 108

Compagnie Européenne de Publication, **IV** 614–15

Compagnie Financiere Alcatel, **9** 10

Compagnie Financiere de Paribas, **II** 192, **259–60**; **III** 185

Compagnie Financière de Suez, **III** 394

Compagnie Française de Distribution en Afrique, **IV** 559

Compagnie Française de Raffinage, **IV** 558–60

Compagnie Française des Lubricants, **I** 341

Compagnie Française des Minerais d'Uranium, **IV** 108

Compagnie Française des Mines de Diamants du Cap, **IV** 64; **7** 121

Compagnie Française des Pétroles, **II** 259; **IV** 363–64, 423–24, 454, 466, 486, 504, 515, 544–46, 557–60; **7** 481–83

Compagnie Française des Produits d'Orangina, **I** 281

Compagnie Française du Méthane, **V** 626

Compagnie Française Thomson-Houston, **I** 357; **II** 116

Compagnie Générale d'Électricité, **I** 193; **II 12–13**, 25; **IV** 174, 615; **9** 9–10

Compagnie Generale de Cartons Ondules, **IV** 296

Compagnie Generale de Radiologie, **II** 117

Compagnie Generale de Telegraphie Sans Fils, **II** 116

Compagnie Générale des Eaux, **V** 632–33; **6** 441

Compagnie Générale des Établissements Michelin, **V 236–39**

Compagnie Générale Maritime et Financière, **6 379–81**

Compagnie Industriali Riunite S.p.A., **IV** 587–88

Compagnie Internationale de l'Informatique, **III** 123

Compagnie Internationale Pirelli S.A., **V** 249

Compagnie Luxembourgeoise de Télédiffusion, **15** 54

Compagnie Navale Des Pétroles, **IV** 558

Compagnie Parisienne de Garantie, **III** 211

Compagnie Pneumatique Commerciale, **III** 426

Compagnie Tunisienne de Ressorts a Lames, **III** 581

Companhia Brasileira de Aluminio, **IV** 55

Companhia Brasileira de Mineracão e Siderugica, **IV** 54

Companhia de Celulose do Caima, **14** 250

Companhia de Diamantes de Angola, **IV** 21

Companhia de Minerales y Metales, **IV** 139

Companhia de Pesquisas Mineras de Angola, **IV** 65; **7** 122

Companhia de Seguros Argos Fluminense, **III** 221

Companhia de Seguros Tranquilidade Vida, S.A. *See* Banco Espírito Santo e Comercial de Lisboa S.A.

Companhia Siderúrgica de Tubarao, **IV** 125

Companhia Siderúrgica Mannesmann S.A., **III** 565–66

Companhia Siderúrgica Nacional, **II** 199

Companhia Uniao Fabril, **IV** 505

Companhia Vale do Rio Doce, **IV 54–57**

Compañia Arrendataria del Monopolio de Petróleos Sociedad Anónima, **IV** 396–97, 527–29

Compañia de Investigacion y Exploitaciones Petrolifera, **IV** 397

Compañia de Líneas Aéreas Subvencionadas S.A., **6** 95

Compañia Española de Petroleos S.A., **IV 396–98**, 527

Compañia Minera La India, **IV** 164

Compañia Nacional Minera Petrólia del Táchira, **IV** 507

Compañia Telefónica Nacional de España S.A., **V** 337

Compaq Computer Corporation, **II** 45; **III** 114, **124–25**; **6** 217, **221–23 (upd.)**, 230–31, 235, 243–44; **9** 42–43, 166, 170–71, 472; **10** 87, 232–33, 366, 459, 518–19; **12** 61, 183, 335, 470; **13** 388, 483

Compass Group, plc, **6** 193

Compeda, Ltd., **10** 240

Competition Tire East/West, **V** 494

Compex, **II** 233

Components Agents Ltd., **10** 113

Composite Craft Inc., **I** 387

Comprehensive Care Corporation, **15 121–23**

Comprehensive Resources Corp., **IV** 83

Compressed Industrial Gases, **I** 297

Compression Labs, **10** 456

Compressor Controls Corporation, **15** 404

Comptoir d'Escompte de Mulhouse, **II** 232

Comptoir des Textiles Artificielles, **I** 122, 388–89

Comptoir Métallurgique Luxembourgeois, **IV** 25

Comptoir National d'Escompte de Paris, **II** 232–33, 270

Compton Communications, **I** 33

Compton Foods, **II** 675

Compton's MultiMedia Publishing Group, Inc., **7** 165

Compton's New Media, Inc., **7** 168

CompuAdd Computer Corporation, **11 61–63**

CompuChem Corporation, **11** 425

CompuCom Systems, Inc., **10 232–34**, 474; **13** 176

Compugraphic, **III** 168; **6** 284

Compumotor, **III** 603

CompuPharm, Inc., **14** 210

CompUSA, Inc., **10 235–36**; **11** 63

CompuServe Incorporated, **9** 268–70; **10 237–39**; **12** 562; **13** 147; **15** 265

Computax, **6** 227–28

Computer Associates International, Inc., **6** 224–26; **10** 394; **12** 62; **14** 392

Computer City, **12** 470

The Computer Company, **11** 112

Computer Consoles Inc., **III** 164

Computer Data Systems, Inc., **14 127–29**

The Computer Department, Ltd., **10** 89

Computer Depot, **6** 243

Computer Discount Corporation. *See* Comdisco, Inc.

Computer Dynamics, Inc., **6** 10

Computer Factory, Inc., **13** 176

Computer Peripheral Manufacturers Association, **13** 127

Computer Plaza K.K., **IV** 542–43

Computer Power, **6** 301

Computer Research Corp., **III** 151; **6** 265

Computer Sciences Corporation, **6** 25, **227–29**; **13** 462; **15** 474

Computer Shoppe, **V** 191–92

Computer Systems and Applications, **12** 442

Computer Systems Division (CDS), **13** 201

Computer Terminal Corporation, **11** 67–68

ComputerCity, **10** 235

Computerized Lodging Systems, Inc., **11** 275

ComputerLand Corp., **6** 243; **9** 116; **10** 233, 563; **12** 335; **13 174–76**, 277

Computervision Corporation, **6** 246–47; **7** 498; **10 240–42**; **11** 275; **13** 201

Computing Scale Company of America, **III** 147. *See also* International Business Machines Corporation.

Computing-Tabulating-Recording Co., **III** 147

Compuware Corporation, **10 243–45**

Comsat, **II** 425; **12** 19; **13** 341

Comstock Canada, **9** 301

Comte, **I** 121

Comverse Technology, Inc., **15 124–26**

Con Ed. *See* Consolidated Edison of New York, Inc.

Con-Ferro Paint and Varnish Company, **8** 553

ConAgra, Inc., **II 493–95**, 517, 585; **7** 432, 525; **8** 53, 499–500; **12 80–82 (upd.)**; **13** 138, 294, 350, 352; **14** 515

Conahay & Lyon, **6** 27

Concert Communications Company, **15** 69

Concord International, **II** 298

Concordia, **IV** 497

Concrete Industries (Monier) Ltd., **III** 735

The Condé Nast Publications Inc., **IV** 583–84; **13 177–81**

Condor Systems Inc., **15** 530

Cone Mills Corporation, **8 120–22**

Conelectron, **13** 398

Conestoga National Bank, **II** 316
Confederation of Engineering Industry, **IV** 484
Confidata Corporation, **11** 111
Confindustria, **I** 162
Congas Engineering Canada Ltd., **6** 478
Congoleum Corp., **12** 28
Congress Financial Corp., **13** 305–06
Congressional Information Services, **IV** 610
Conic, **9** 324
Conifer Group, **II** 214
Conill Corp., **II** 261
Coniston Partners, **I** 130; **II** 680; **III** 29; **6** 130; **10** 302
CONNA Corp., **7** 113
Connecticut Bank and Trust Co., **II** 213–14
Connecticut Light and Power Co., 13 182–84
Connecticut Mutual Life Insurance Company, III 225, **236–38**, 254, 285
Connecticut National Bank, **13** 467
Connecticut River Banking Company, **13** 467
Connecticut Telephone Company. *See* Southern New England Telecommunications Corporation.
Connecticut Trust and Safe Deposit Co., **II** 213
Connecting Point of America, **6** 244
Conner Corp., **15** 327
Conner Peripherals, Inc., 6 230–32; 10 403, 459, 463–64, 519; **11** 56, 234
Connie Lee. *See* College Construction Loan Insurance Assoc.
Connolly Data Systems, **11** 66
Connors Brothers, **II** 631–32
Connors Steel Co., **15** 116
Conoco Inc., I 286, 329, 346, 402–04; **II** 376; **IV** 365, 382, 389, **399–402**, 413, 429, 454, 476; **6** 539; **7** 346, 559; **8** 152, 154, 556; **11** 97, 400
Conorada Petroleum Corp., **IV** 365, 400
Conover Furniture Company, **10** 183
Conrad International Hotels, **III** 91–93
Conrail. *See* Consolidated Rail Corporation.
Conseco Inc., 10 246–48; 15 257
Consgold. *See* Consolidated Gold Fields of South Africa Ltd. *and* Consolidated Gold Fields PLC.
Consolidated Aircraft Corporation, **9** 16, 497
Consolidated Aluminum Corp., **IV** 178
Consolidated Brands Inc., **14** 18
Consolidated Cable Utilities, **6** 313
Consolidated Cement Corp., **III** 704
Consolidated Cigar Corp., **I** 452–53; **15** 137–38
Consolidated Coal Co., **IV** 82, 170–71
Consolidated Coin Caterers Corporation, **10** 222
Consolidated Controls, **I** 155
Consolidated Copper Corp., **13** 503
Consolidated Denison Mines Ltd., **8** 418
Consolidated Diamond Mines of South-West Africa Ltd., **IV** 21, 65–67; **7** 122–25
Consolidated Distillers Ltd., **I** 263
Consolidated Edison Company of New York, Inc., I 28; **V 586–89; 6** 456
Consolidated Electric & Gas, **6** 447
Consolidated Electric Supply Inc., **15** 385

Consolidated Electronics Industries Corp. (Conelco), **13** 397–98
Consolidated Foods Corp., **II** 571–73, 584; **III** 480; **12** 159, 494
Consolidated Freightways, Inc., V 432–34; 6 280, 388; **12** 278, 309; **13** 19; **14** 567
Consolidated Gold Fields of South Africa Ltd., **IV** 94, 96, 118, 565, 566
Consolidated Gold Fields PLC, **II** 422; **III** 501, 503; **IV** 23, 67, 94, 97, 171; **7** 125, 209, 387
Consolidated Grocers Corp., **II** 571
Consolidated Insurances of Australia, **III** 347
Consolidated Marketing, Inc., **IV** 282; **9** 261
Consolidated Mines Selection Co., **IV** 20, 23
Consolidated Mining and Smelting Co., **IV** 75
Consolidated National Life Insurance Co., **10** 246
Consolidated Natural Gas Company, V 590–91
Consolidated Oatmeal Co., **II** 558
Consolidated Papers, Inc., 8 123–25; 11 311
Consolidated Power & Light Company, **6** 580
Consolidated Power & Telephone Company, **11** 342
Consolidated Press Holdings, **8** 551
Consolidated Products, Inc., 14 130–32, 352
Consolidated Rail Corporation, II 449; **V 435–37**, 485; **10** 44; **12** 278; **13** 449; **14** 324
Consolidated Rand-Transvaal Mining Group, **IV** 90
Consolidated Specialty Restaurants, Inc., **14** 131–32
Consolidated Steel, **I** 558; **IV** 570
Consolidated Stores Corp., **13** 543
Consolidated Temperature Controlling Co., **II** 40; **12** 246
Consolidated Theaters, Inc., **14** 87
Consolidated Tyre Services Ltd., **IV** 241
Consolidated Vultee, **II** 7, 32
Consolidated Zinc Corp., **IV** 58–59, 122, 189, 191
Consolidated-Bathurst Inc., **IV** 246–47, 334
Consolidation Coal Co., **IV** 401; **8** 154, 346–47
Consoweld Corporation, **8** 124
Constar International Inc., **8** 562; **13** 190
Constellation, **III** 335
Constellation Insurance Co., **III** 191–92
Construcciones Aeronauticas S.A., **I** 41–42; **12** 190
Construcciones y Contratas, **II** 198
Construtora Moderna SARL, **IV** 505
Consul Restaurant Corp., **13** 152
Consumer Value Stores, **V** 136–37; **9** 67
Consumer's Gas Co., **I** 264
Consumers Cooperative Association, **7** 174
Consumers Distributing Co. Ltd., **II** 649, 652–53
Consumers Electric Light and Power, **6** 582
The Consumers Gas Company Ltd., 6 476–79

Consumers Power Co., V 577–79, 593–94; **14** 114–15, **133–36**
Consumers Water Company, 14 137–39
Contact Software International Inc., **10** 509
Contadina, **II** 488–89
Container Corp. of America, **IV** 295, 465; **V** 147; **7** 353; **8** 476
Container Transport International, **III** 344
Containers Packaging, **IV** 249
Conte S.A., **12** 262
Contech, **10** 493
Contel Corporation, **II** 117; **V** 294–98; **6** 323; **13** 212; **14** 259; **15** 192
Contempo Associates, **14** 105
Contherm Corp., **III** 420
ContiCommodity Services, Inc., **10** 250–51
Continental AG, **9** 248; **15** 355
Continental Airlines, I 96–98, 103, 118, 123–24, 129–30; **6** 52, 61, 105, 120–21, 129–30; **12** 381
Continental Aktiengesellschaft, V 240–43, 250–51, 256; **8** 212–14
Continental American Life Insurance Company, **7** 102
Continental Assurance Co., **III** 228–30
Continental Baking Co., **I** 463–64; **II** 562–63; **7** 320–21; **11** 198; **12** 276; **13** 427
Continental Bancor, **II** 248
Continental Bank and Trust Co., **II** 251; **14** 102
Continental Bank Corporation, II 261–63; IV 702. *See also* Continental Illinois Corp.
Continental Blacks Inc., **I** 403
Continental Cablevision, Inc., 7 98–100
Continental Can Co., Inc., I 597; **II** 34, 414; **III** 471; **10** 130; **13** 255; **15 127–30**
Continental Carbon Co., **I** 403–05; **II** 53; **IV** 401
Continental Care Group, **10** 252–53
Continental Casualty Co., **III** 196, 228–32
Continental Cities Corp., **III** 344
Continental Corporation, III 230, **239–44**, 273; **10** 561; **12** 318; **15** 30
Continental Cos., **III** 248
Continental Divide Insurance Co., **III** 214
Continental Equipment Company, **13** 225
Continental Express, **11** 299
Continental Fiber Drum, **8** 476
Continental Gas & Electric Corporation, **6** 511
Continental Grain Company, 10 249–51; 13 185–87 (upd.)
Continental Group Co., I 599–600, 601–02, 604–05, 607–09, 612–13, 615; **IV** 334; **8** 175, 424
Continental Gummi-Werke Aktiengesellschaft, **V** 241; **9** 248
Continental Illinois Corp., **I** 526; **II** 261–63, 285, 289, 348. *See also* Continental Bank Corporation.
Continental Illinois Venture Co., **IV** 702
Continental Insurance Co., **III** 239–42, 372–73, 386
Continental Insurance Cos. of New York, **III** 230
Continental Investment Corporation, **9** 507; **12** 463
Continental Life Insurance Co., **III** 225
Continental Medical Systems, Inc., 10 252–54; 11 282; **14** 233
Continental Milling Company, **10** 250

Continental Motors Corp., **I** 199, 524–25; **10** 521–22

Continental National American Group, **III** 230, 404

Continental National Bank, **II** 261; **11** 119

Continental Oil Co., **IV** 39, 365, 382, 399–401, 476, 517, 575–76

Continental Packaging Inc., **13** 255

Continental Radio, **IV** 607

Continental Reinsurance, **11** 533

Continental Restaurant Systems, **12** 510

Continental Risk Services, **III** 243

Continental Savouries, **II** 500

Continental Scale Works, **14** 229–30

Continental Securities Corp., **II** 444

Continental Telephone Company, **V** 296–97; **9** 494–95; **11** 500; **15** 195

Continental Wood Preservers, Inc., **12** 397

Continental-Caoutchouc und Gutta-Percha Compagnie, **V** 240

Continental-Emsco, **I** 490–91

Continental-National Group, **III** 230

Continentale Allgemeine, **III** 347

Contrans Acquisitions, Inc., **14** 38

Control Data Systems, Inc., **III** 118, **126–28**, 129, 131, 149, 152, 165; **6** 228, 252, 266; **8** 117–18, 467; **10** 255–57, 359, 458–59; **11** 469

Controlonics Corporation, **13** 195

Controls Company of America, **9** 67

Convair, **I** 82, 121, 123, 126, 131; **II** 33; **9** 18, 498; **13** 357

Convenient Food Mart Inc., **7** 114

Convergent Technologies, **III** 166; **6** 283; **11** 519

Converse Inc., **III** 528–29; **V** 376; **9** **133–36**, 234; **12** 308

Conycon. *See* Construcciones y Contratas.

Conzinc Riotinto of Australia. *See* CRA Limited.

Cook Data Services, Inc., **9** 73

Cook Industrial Coatings, **I** 307

Cook Standard Tool Co., **13** 369

Cook United, **V** 172

Cooke Engineering Company, **13** 194

Cooking and Crafts Club, **13** 106

Cookson Group plc, **III** **679–82**

Coolerator, **I** 463

Cooper Industries, Inc., **II** **14–17**; **14** 564

Cooper Laboratories, **I** 667, 682

Cooper LaserSonics Inc., **IV** 100

Cooper McDougall & Robertson Ltd., **I** 715

Cooper Tire & Rubber Company, **8** **126–28**

Cooper's, Inc., **12** 283

Cooper-Weymouth, **10** 412

Cooperative Grange League Federation Exchange, **7** 17

Coopers & Lybrand, **9** **137–38**; **12** 391

CooperVision, **7** 46

Coordinated Caribbean Transport. *See* Crowley Caribbean Transport.

Coors Company. *See* Adolph Coors Company.

Coorsh and Bittner, **7** 430

Coos Bay Lumber Co., **IV** 281; **9** 259

Coosa River Newsprint Co., **III** 40

Coote & Jurgenson, **14** 64

Cooymans, **I** 281

Copeland Corp., **II** 20

Copeman Ridley, **13** 103

Copland Brewing Co., **I** 268

Copley Pharmaceuticals Inc., **13** 264

Copley Real Estate Advisors, **III** 313

Copolymer Corporation, **9** 242

Copper Queen Consolidated Mining Co., **IV** 176–77

Copper Range Company, **IV** 76; **7** 281–82

Copperweld Steel Co., **IV** 108–09, 237

Copycat Ltd., **8** 383

Cora Verlag, **IV** 590

Coral Drilling, **I** 570

Coral Leisure Group, **I** 248

Coral Petroleum, **IV** 395

Corbett Enterprises Inc., **13** 270

Corby Distilleries Limited, **14** **140–42**

Corco. *See* Commonwealth Oil Refining Company.

Corcoran & Riggs. *See* Riggs National Corporation.

Cordiant plc. *See* Saatchi & Saatchi plc.

Cordon & Gotch, **IV** 619

Cordon Bleu, **IV** 609

Cordovan Corp., **IV** 608

Core Laboratories Inc., **I** 486; **11** 265

Corel Corporation, **15** **131–33**

Corimon, **12** 218

Corinthian Broadcast Corporation, **IV** 605; **10** 4

Cormetech, **III** 685

Corn Exchange Bank, **II** 316

Corn Exchange Bank Trust Co., **II** 251; **14** 102

Corn Exchange National Bank, **II** 261

Corn Products Refining Co., **II** 496–97

Corn Sweetners Inc., **I** 421; **11** 23

Cornerstone Direct Marketing, **8** 385–86

Cornerstone Title Company, **8** 461

Cornhill Insurance Co., **I** 429; **III** 185, 385

Cornhusker Casualty Co., **III** 213

Corning Asahi Video Products Co., **III** 667

Corning Incorporated, **I** 609; **III** 434, 667, **683–85**, 720–21; **8** 468; **11** 334; **13** 398

Coronado Corp., **II** 112

Coronet Industries, Inc., **II** 90; **14** 436

Corp. d'acquisition Socanav-Caisse Inc., **II** 664

Corp. of Lloyd's, **III** 278–79

Corporacion Estatal Petrolera Ecuatoriana, **IV** 510–11

Corporación Venezolana de Petroleo, **IV** 507

Corporate Microsystems, Inc., **10** 395

Corporate Partners, **12** 391

Corporate Software Inc., **9** **139–41**

Corporation for Public Broadcasting, **14** **143–45**

Corporation Trust Co. *See* CCH Inc.

Corpoven, **IV** 508

Corrado Passera, **IV** 588

Corral Midwest, Inc., **10** 333

Corrigan-McKinney Steel Company, **13** 157

Corroon & Black, **III** 280

Corrugated Paper, **IV** 249

Cortec Corporation, **14** 430

Corvallis Lumber Co., **IV** 358

Cory Corp., **II** 511

Cory Food Services, Inc., **II** 608

Cosden Petroleum Corp., **IV** 498

Cosgrove & Co., **III** 283

Cosmair Inc., **III** 47–48; **8** **129–32**, 342–44; **12** 404

Cosmo Oil Co., Ltd., **IV** **403–04**

Cosmopolitan Productions, **IV** 626

Cosorzio Interprovinciale Vini, **10** 181

Cost Plus, **12** 393

Costa Apple Products, **II** 480

Costa e Ribeiro Ltd., **IV** 504

Costco Wholesale Corporation, **V** 36; **10** 206; **11** 240; **XIV** 393–95; **15** 470

Costruzioni Meccaniche Nazionalia, **13** 218

Côte d'Or, **II** 521

Cott Beverage Corporation, **9** 291

Cottees General Foods, **II** 477

Cotter & Company, **V** **37–38**; **12** 8

Coty, **I** 662

Counselor Co., **14** 230

Country Kitchen Foods, **III** 21

Country Music Television, **11** 153

Country Poultry, Inc., **II** 494

Country Seat Stores, Inc., **15** 87

Country Store of Concord, Inc., **10** 216

County Bank, **II** 333

County Catering Co., **13** 103

County Fire Insurance Co., **III** 191

County Market, **II** 670

County NatWest, **II** 334–35

County Perfumery, **III** 65

County Seat Stores Inc., **II** 669; **9** **142–43**

County Trust Co., **II** 230

Cour des Comptes, **II** 233

Courage Brewing Group., **I** 229, 438–39; **III** 503

Courcoux-Bouvet, **II** 260

Courrèges Parfums, **III** 48; **8** 343

The Courseware Developers, **11** 19

Court House Square, **10** 44

Courtaulds PLC, **I** 321; **IV** 261, 670; **V** 356–57, **359–61**; **12** 103

Courtney Wines International, **II** 477

Courtot Investments, **II** 222

Courtyard by Marriott, **9** 427

Cousins Mortgage and Equity Investments, **12** 393

Coutts & Co., **II** 333–34

Couvrette & Provost Ltd., **II** 651

Covantage, **11** 379

Covenant Life Insurance, **III** 314

Coventry Climax Engines, Ltd., **13** 286

Coventry Co., **III** 213

Coventry Machinists Company, **7** 458

Coventry Ordnance Works, **I** 573

Coventry Union Banking Co., **II** 318

Covidea, **II** 252

Cow & Gate Ltd., **II** 586–87

Cowham Engineering, **III** 704

Cowles Communications Co., **IV** 648

Cowles Media, **IV** 613; **7** 191

Cox & Co., **II** 236, 307–08

Cox Enterprises, Inc., **IV** 595–97; **6** 32; **7** 327; **9** 74

Cox Newsprint, Inc., **IV** 246

Cox Woodlands Co., **IV** 246

CP. *See* Canadian Pacific Limited.

CP Air, **6** 60–61

CP National, **6** 300

CPC International Inc., **II** 463, **496–98**

CPL. *See* Carolina Power & Light Company.

CRA Limited, **IV** 58–61, 67, 192; **7** 124

Crabtree Electricals, **III** 503; **7** 210

Cracker Barrel Old Country Store, Inc., **9** 78; **10** **258–59**

Craft House Corp., **8** 456

Craig Bit Company, **13** 297

Crain Communications, Inc., **12** **83–86**

Cramer Electronics, **10** 112
Crane Co., 8 133–36, 179
Crane Supply Company, **8** 135
Cranston Mills, **13** 168
Crate and Barrel, 9 144–46
Craven Tasker Ltd., **I** 573–74
Crawford and Watson, **IV** 278
Crawford Gosho Co., Ltd., **IV** 442
Crawford Supply Company, **6** 392
Cray Research, Inc., III 126, 128,
  129–31; **10** 256
CRD Total France, **IV** 560
Cream City Railway Company, **6** 601
Cream of Wheat Corp., **II** 543
Creamola Food Products, **II** 569
Creasy Co., **II** 682
Creative Artists Agency, **10** 228
Creative Engineering Inc., **13** 472
Creative Food 'N Fun Co., **14** 29
Creative Forming, Inc., **8** 562
Creative Homes, Inc., **IV** 341
Creative Technologies Corp., **15** 401
Crédit Agricole, II 264–66, 355
Credit and Data Marketing Services, **V** 118
Credit Clearing House, **IV** 605
Credit du Nord, **II** 260
Crédit Foncier, **II** 264
Crédit Général de Belgique, **II** 304
Credit Immobilier, **7** 538
Crédit Liégiois, **II** 270
Crédit Lyonnais, II 242, 257, 354; **6** 396;
  7 12; **9 147–49**
Credit Mobilier, **II** 294
Crédit National S.A., 9 150–52
Credit Service Exchange, **6** 24
Crédit Suisse, II 267–69, 369–70,
  378–79, 402–04. See also
  Schweizerische Kreditanstalt.
Credit Suisse First Boston. See Financière
  Crédit Suisse-First Boston.
Creditanstalt-Bankverein, **II** 242, 295
CrediThrift Financial, **11** 16
Credithrift Financial of Indiana, **III** 194
Credito de la Union Minera, **II** 194
Credito Italiano, I 368, 465, 567; **II** 191,
  270–72; **III** 347
Cree Research, Inc., **13** 399
Crellin Holding, Inc., **8** 477
Crellin Plastics, **8** 13
Creole Petroleum Corporation, **IV** 428; **7**
  171
Crescendo Productions, **6** 27
Crescent Box & Printing Co., **13** 442
Crescent Chemical, **I** 374
Crescent Niagara Corp., **II** 16
Crescent Software Inc., **15** 373
Crescent Vert Co. Ltd., **II** 51
Crescent Washing Machine Company, **8**
  298
Crescott, Inc., **15** 501
Cressbrook Dairy Company, **II** 546
Cressey Dockham & Co., **II** 682
Crest Service Company, **9** 364
Crestbrook Forest Industries Ltd., **IV** 285
Crestmont Financial Corporation, **14** 472
Creusot-Loire, **II** 93–94
Crevettes du Cameroun, **13** 244
Criterion Casualty Company, **10** 312
Criterion Life Insurance Company, **10** 311
Critikon, Inc., **III** 36
Crocker National Bank, **II** 226, 317, 319,
  383; **13** 535
Crocker National Corporation, **12** 536
Crockett Container Corporation, **8** 268

Croda International Ltd., **IV** 383
Crompton & Knowles Corp., I 633; **9**
  153–55
Crop Production Services, Inc., **IV** 576
Croscill Home Fashions, **8** 510
Crosfield, Lampard & Co., **III** 696
Cross & Trecker Corporation, **10** 330
Crossair, **I** 121
Crosse and Blackwell, **II** 547
Crossett Lumber Co., **IV** 281; **9** 259
Crossland Capital Corp., **III** 293
Crossley Motors, Ltd., **13** 285
Crothall, **6** 44
Crouse-Hinds Co., **II** 16
Crow Catchpole, **III** 752
Crowell-Collier Publishing Company, **IV**
  310; **7** 286
Crowley Foods, Inc., **II** 528
Crowley Maritime Corporation, 6
  382–84; **9** 510–11
Crown Advertising Agency. See King
  Kullen Grocery Co., Inc.
Crown Aluminum, **I** 544
Crown America Corp., **13** 393
Crown Books, **14** 61
Crown Can Co., **I** 601
Crown Center Redevelopment Corp., **IV**
  621
Crown Central Petroleum Corporation,
  7 101–03
Crown, Cork & Seal Company, Inc., I
  601–03; **13 188–90 (upd.)**; **15** 129
Crown Drugs, **II** 673
Crown Equipment Corporation, 15
  134–36
Crown Forest Industries, **IV** 279
Crown Life Insurance Company, **III** 261; **6**
  181–82
Crown Oil and Refining Company, **7** 101
Crown Publishing Group, **IV** 584; **13** 429
Crown Zellerbach Corp., **IV** 290, 345; **8**
  261
Crownx Inc., **6** 181–82
CRSS Inc., 6 142–44
CRTC. See Canadian Radio-Television and
  Telecommunications Commission.
Crucible Steel, **I** 434–35
Crude Oil Pipe Line Co., **IV** 400
Cruden Investments Pty Ltd., **IV** 651; **7**
  390
Crum & Forster, **II** 448; **III** 172; **6** 290; **13**
  448
Crump E & S, **6** 290
Crump Inc., **I** 584
Crush International, **II** 478; **III** 53
Crushed Stone Sales Ltd., **IV** 241
Cruzeiro do Sul Airlines, **6** 133
Cryomedics Inc., **I** 667
Crystal Brands, Inc., 9 156–58; **12** 431
Crystal Oil Co., **IV** 180, 548
CS First Boston Inc., II 269, **402–04**; **III**
  289; **12** 209. See also First Boston Corp.
CSA Press, **IV** 661
CSC. See Computer Sciences Corporation.
CSC Industries, Inc., **IV** 63
CSE Corp., **III** 214
CSFB. See Financière Crédit Suisse-First
  Boston.
CSK, **10** 482
CSO. See Columbus & Southern Ohio
  Electric Company.
CSR Limited, III 686–88, 728, 735–36;
  IV 46
CST Office Products, **15** 36

CSX Corporation, V 438–40, 485; **6** 340;
  9 59; **13** 462
CSY Agri-Processing, **7** 81–82
CT Financial Services Inc., **V** 401–02
CT&T. See Carolina Telephone and
  Telegraph Company.
CTA. See Comptoir des Textiles
  Artificielles.
CTG, Inc., 11 64–66
CTNE, **I** 462
CTR. See International Business Machines
  Corporation.
CTX Mortgage Company, **8** 88
Cub Foods, **II** 669–70; **14** 411
Cuban American Nickel Co., **IV** 82; **7** 186
Cuban American Oil Company, **8** 348
Cuban Telephone Co., **I** 462–63
Cuban-American Manganese Corp., **IV** 81;
  7 186
Cubitts Nigeria, **III** 753
Cuckler Steel Span Co., **I** 481
Cudahy Corp., **12** 199
Culbro Corporation, 14 19; **15 137–39**
Culinary Foods, Inc., **14** 516
Culligan International Company, I 373;
  II 468; **12 87–88**, 346
Cullinet Software Corporation, **6** 225; **14**
  390; **15** 108
Cullman Bros. See Culbro Corporation.
Cullum Companies, **II** 670
Cumberland Federal Bancorporation, **13**
  223
Cumberland Newspapers, **IV** 650; **7** 389
Cumberland Paper Board Mills Ltd., **IV**
  248
Cumberland Pipeline Co., **IV** 372
Cumberland Property Investment Trust
  Ltd., **IV** 711
Cummins Engine Co. Inc., I 146–48,
  186; **III** 545; **IV** 252; **10 273–74**; **12**
  89–92 (upd.)
CUNA Mutual Insurance Group, **11** 495
Cunard Steamship Co., **I** 573
Cuno Kourten, **13** 353
Cupples Products Co., **IV** 15
Current, Inc., **7** 137, 139
Currys Group PLC, **V** 49
Cursenir, **I** 280
Curtice-Burns Foods, Inc., 7 17–18,
  104–06
Curtis Circulation Co., **IV** 619
Curtis Industries, **13** 165
Curtiss Candy Co., **II** 544
Curtiss-Wright Corporation, I 524; **III**
  464; **7** 263; **8** 49; **9** 14, 244, 341, 417;
  10 260–63; **11** 427
Curver Group, **III** 614
Curver-Rubbermaid, **III** 615
Cushman Motor Works, **III** 598
Custom Academic Publishing Company
  (CAPCO), **12** 174
Custom Electronics, Inc., **9** 120
Custom Expressions, Inc., **7** 24
Custom Metal Products, Inc., **III** 643
Custom Organics, **8** 464
Custom Products Inc., **III** 643
Cutler-Hammer Inc., **I** 155; **III** 644–45
Cutter Laboratories, **I** 310
CVL Inc., **II** 457
CVN Companies, **9** 218
CVS. See Consumer Value Stores.
CWM. See Chemical Waste Management,
  Inc.
CWT Farms International Inc., **13** 103

Cybernet Electronics Corp., **II** 51
Cybernex, **10** 463
CYBERTEK Corporation, **11** 395
CyberTel, **IV** 596–97
Cycle Video Inc., **7** 590
Cyclo Chemical Corp., **I** 627
Cyclo Getriebebau Lorenz Braren GmbH,
    III 634
Cyclone Co. of Australia, **III** 673
Cyclops Corporation, **10** 45; **13** 157
Cygna Energy Services, **13** 367
Cymbal Co., Ltd., **V** 150
Cynosure Inc., **11** 88
Cyphernetics Corp., **III** 118
Cypress Amax Minerals Co., **13** 158
Cypress Insurance Co., **III** 214
Cypress Semiconductor, **6** 216
Cyprus Minerals Company, **7 107–09**
Cyrix Corp., **10** 367

D & P Studios, **II** 157
D & W Food Stores, Inc., **8** 482
D'Arcy Masius Benton & Bowles, Inc., **I**
    233–34; **6 20–22**; **10** 226–27
D&K Wholesale Drug, Inc., **14 146–48**
D&N Systems, Inc., **10** 505
D&W Computer Stores, **13** 176
D.B. Marron & Co., **II** 445
D.C. Heath & Co., **II** 86; **11** 413
D.C. National Bancorp, **10** 426
D. Connelly Boiler Company, **6** 145
D.E. Makepeace Co., **IV** 78
D.E. Winebrenner Co., **7** 429
D.G. Calhoun, **12** 112
D. Hald & Co., **III** 417
D.M. Osborne Co., **III** 650
D.W. Mikesell Co. *See* Mike-Sell's Inc.
Dabney, Morgan & Co., **II** 329
Dade Wholesale Products, **6** 199
DADG. *See* Deutsch-Australische
    Dampfschiffs-Gesellschaft.
Dae Won Kang Up Co., **III** 581
Daejin Shipping Company, **6** 98
Daesung Heavy Industries, **I** 516
Daewoo Group, **I** 516; **II** 53; **III 457–59**,
    749; **12** 211
DAF, **I** 186; **III** 543; **7** 566–67
Dage-Bell, **II** 86
Dagincourt, **III** 675
Dagsbladunie, **IV** 611
Dahlgren, **I** 677
Dahlonega Equipment and Supply
    Company, **12** 377
Dai Nippon. *See also listings under*
    Dainippon.
Dai Nippon Brewery Co., **I** 220, 282
Dai Nippon Ink and Chemicals, **I** 303
Dai Nippon Mujin, **II** 371
Dai Nippon Printing Co., Ltd., **IV**
    598–600, 631, 679–80
Dai Nippon X-ray Inc., **II** 75
Dai Nippon Yuben Kai, **IV** 631–32
Dai-Ichi. *See also listings under* Daiichi.
Dai-Ichi Bank, **I** 507, 511; **IV** 148
Dai-Ichi Kangyo Bank Ltd., **II 273–75**,
    325–26, 360–61, 374; **III** 188
Dai-Ichi Mokko Co., **III** 758
Dai-Ichi Mutual Life Insurance Co., **II**
    118; **III** 277, 401
Daido Spring Co., **III** 580
Daido Steel Co., Ltd., **IV 62–63**
Daido Trading, **I** 432, 492
Daiei, **V** 11, **39–40**

Daihatsu Motor Company, Ltd., **7**
    110–12
Daiichi. *See also listings under* Dai-Ichi.
Daiichi Atomic Power Industry Group, **II**
    22
Daiichi Bussan Kaisha Ltd., **I** 505, 507
Daiichi Fire, **III** 405
Daijugo Bank, **I** 507
Daikin Industries, Ltd., **III 460–61**
Daikyo Oil Co., Ltd., **IV** 403–04, 476
Dailey & Associates, **I** 16
Daily Chronicle Investment Group, **IV** 685
Daily Mirror, **IV** 665–66
Daily Press Inc., **IV** 684
Daimaru, **V 41–42**, 130
Daimler Airway, **I** 92
Daimler-Benz A.G., **I** 27, 138, **149–51**,
    186–87, 192, 194, 198, 411, 549; **II**
    257, 279–80, 283; **III** 495, 523, 562,
    563, 695, 750; **7** 219; **10** 261, 274; **11**
    31; **12** 192, 342; **13** 30, 286, 414; **14**
    169; **15 140–44 (upd.)**
Dain Bosworth Inc., **15** 231–33, 486
Daina Seikosha, **III** 620
Daini-Denden Incorporated, **12** 136–37
Daini-Denden Kikaku Co. Ltd., **II** 51
Dainippon. *See also listings under* Dai-
    Nippon.
Dainippon Celluloid, **I** 509; **III** 486
Dainippon Ink & Chemicals, Inc., **IV** 397;
    10 466–67; **13** 308, 461
Dainippon Shurui, **III** 42
Dainippon Spinning Company, **V** 387
Daio Paper Corporation, **IV 266–67**,
    269. *See also* Taio Paper Manufacturing
    Co.
Dairy Farm, **I** 471
Dairy Farm Ice and Cold Storage Co., **IV**
    700
Dairy Maid Products Cooperative, **II** 536
Dairy Mart Convenience Stores, Inc., **7**
    113–15
Dairy Queen National Development
    Company, **10** 372
Dairy Supply Co., **II** 586; **III** 418, 420
Dairyland Food Laboratories, **I** 677
Dairymen, Inc., **11** 24
Daishowa Paper Manufacturing Co.,
    Ltd., **II** 361; **IV 268–70**, 326, 667
Daisy/Cadnetix Inc., **6** 248
Daisy Systems Corp., **11** 46, 284–85, 489
Daiwa Bank, Ltd., **II 276–77**, 347, 438
Daiwa Securities Company, Limited, **II**
    276, 300, **405–06**, 434; **9** 377
Dakota Power Company, **6** 580
Dakotah Mills, **8** 558–59
Dalberg Co., **II** 61
Daleville & Middletown Telephone
    Company, **14** 258
Dalfort Corp., **15** 281
Dalgety, PLC, **II 499–500**; **III** 21; **12** 411
Dalian, **14** 556
Dalian Cement Factory, **III** 718
Dallas Airmotive, **II** 16
Dallas Lumber and Supply Co., **IV** 358
Dallas Power & Light Company, **V** 724
Dallas Semiconductor Corp., **13 191–93**
Dallas Southland Ice Co., **II** 660
Dallas-Fort Worth Suburban Newspapers,
    Inc., **10** 3
Damar, **IV** 610
Dammann Asphalt, **III** 673
Damodar Valley Corp., **IV** 49
Damon Corporation, **11** 334

Dana Corporation, **I** 152–53; **10 264–66**
    (upd.)
Danaher Corporation, **7 116–17**
Danair A/S, **I** 120
Danapak Holding Ltd., **11** 422
Danat-Bank, **I** 138
Dancer Fitzgerald Sample, **I** 33
Daniel International Corp., **I** 570–71; **8**
    192
Daniel P. Creed Co., Inc., **8** 386
Danieli & C. Officine Meccaniche, **13** 98
Daniels Linseed Co., **I** 419
Daniels Packaging, **12** 25
Danish Almindelinge Brand-Assurance-
    Compagni, **III** 299
Danley Machine Corp., **I** 514
Dannon Co., Inc., **II** 468, 474–75; **14**
    149–51
Danray, **12** 135
Dansk Bioprotein, **IV** 406–07
Dansk International Designs Ltd., **10** 179,
    181; **12** 313
Dansk Metal, **III** 569
Dansk Rejsebureau, **I** 120
Danskin, Inc., **12 93–95**; **15** 358
Danville Resources, Inc., **13** 502
Danzas Group, **V 441–43**
DAP, Inc., **III** 66; **12** 7
Darigold, Inc., **9 159–61**
Darling and Hodgson, **IV** 91
Darmstadter, **II** 282
Darracq, **7** 6
Dart & Kraft Financial Corp., **II** 534; **III**
    610–11; **7** 276; **12** 310; **14** 547
Dart Group Corp., **II** 645, 656, 667, 674;
    12 49; **15** 270
Dart Industries, **II** 533–34; **III** 610; **9**
    179–80
Dart Transit Co., **13** 550
Dart Truck Co., **I** 185
Darvel Realty Trust, **14** 126
DASA. *See* Deutsche Aerospace Airbus.
Dassault-Breguet. *See* Avions Marcel
    Dassault-Breguet Aviation.
Dassler, **14** 6
Dastek Inc., **10** 464; **11** 234–35
DAT GmbH, **10** 514
Dat Jidosha Seizo Co., **I** 183
Data Architects, **14** 318
Data Base Management Inc., **11** 19
Data Business Forms, **IV** 640
Data Card Corp., **IV** 680
Data Corp., **IV** 311
Data Documents, **III** 157
Data Force Inc., **11** 65
Data General Corporation, **II** 208; **III**
    124, 133; **6** 221, 234; **8 137–40**; **9** 297;
    10 499; **12** 162; **13** 201
Data One Corporation, **11** 111
Data Preparation, Inc., **11** 112
Data Resources, Inc., **IV** 637
Data Specialties Inc. *See* Zebra
    Technologies Corporation.
Data Structures Inc., **11** 65
Data Systems Technology, **11** 57
Data 3 Systems, **9** 36
Datachecker Systems, **II** 64–65; **III** 164;
    11 150
Datacraft Corp., **II** 38
Datamatic Corp., **II** 41, 86; **12** 247
Datapoint Corporation, **11 67–70**
Datapro Research Corp., **IV** 637
Dataquest Inc., **10** 558
Datas Incorporated, **I** 99; **6** 81

Datastream International Ltd., **IV** 605; **10** 89; **13** 417

Datavision Inc., **11** 444

Datext, **IV** 596–97

Datran, **11** 468

Datsun. *See* Nissan Motor Company, Ltd.

Datteln, **IV** 141

Datura Corp., **14** 391

Dauphin Deposit Corporation, 14 152–54

Dauphin Distribution Services. *See* Exel Logistics Ltd.

Davenport & Walter, **III** 765

The Davey Tree Expert Company, 11 71–73

David B. Smith & Company, **13** 243

David Berg & Co., **14** 537

David Brown, Ltd., **10** 380

David Crystal, Inc., **II** 502; **9** 156; **10** 323

The David J. Joseph Company, 14 155–56

David Sandeman Group, **I** 592

David Sassoon & Co., **II** 296

David Williams and Partners, **6** 40

Davidson Automatic Merchandising Co. Inc., **II** 607

Davies, William Ltd., **II** 482

Davis & Henderson Ltd., **IV** 640

Davis and Geck, **I** 301

Davis Coal & Coke Co., **IV** 180

Davis Estates, **I** 592

Davis Manufacturing Company, **10** 380

Davis Wholesale Company, **9** 20

Davis-Standard Company, **9** 154

Davison Chemical Corp., **IV** 190

Davy Bamag GmbH, **IV** 142

Davy McKee AG, **IV** 142

Dawe's Laboratories, Inc., **12** 3

Dawnay Day, **III** 501

Dawson Mills, **II** 536

Day & Zimmermann Inc., 6 579; **9 162–64**

Day Brite Lighting, **II** 19

Day International, **8** 347

Day Runner, Inc., 14 157–58

Day-Glo Color Corp., **8** 456

Day-Lee Meats, **II** 550

Day-N-Nite, **II** 620

Daybridge Learning Centers, **13** 49

Daybridge/Children's World, **13** 299

Dayco Products, **7** 297

Days Inns of America, Inc., **III** 344; **11** 178; **13** 362, 364

Daystar International Inc., **11** 44

Daystrom, **III** 617

Daytex, Inc., **II** 669

Dayton Engineering Laboratories, **I** 171; **9** 416; **10** 325

Dayton Flexible Products Co., **I** 627

Dayton Hudson Corporation, V 43–44; **8** 35; **9** 360; **10** 136, 391–93, 409–10, 515–16; **13** 330; **14** 376

Dayton Power & Light Company, **6** 467, 480–82

Dayton Walther Corp., **III** 650, 652

Daytron Mortgage Systems, **11** 485

DB. *See* Deutsche Bundesbahn.

DBMS Inc., **14** 390

DCA Food Industries, **II** 554

DCL BioMedical, Inc., **11** 333

DCMS Holdings Inc., **7** 114

DDB Needham Worldwide, 14 159–61

DDI Corporation, 7 118–20; **13** 482

De Beers Consolidated Mines Limited / De Beers Centenary AG, I 107; **IV** 20–21, 23, 60, **64–68**, 79, 94; **7 121–26 (upd.)**

De Grenswisselkantoren NV, **III** 201

De Groote Bossche, **III** 200

de Havilland Aircraft Co., **I** 82, 92–93, 104, 195; **III** 507–08; **7** 11

De La Rue PLC, 10 267–69

De Laurentiis Entertainment Group, **III** 84

De Laval Turbine Company, **III** 418–20; **7** 236–37

De Leuw, Cather & Company, **8** 416

De Nederlandse Bank, **IV** 132

De Ster 1905 NV, **III** 200

De Tomaso Industries, **11** 104

De Trey Gesellchaft, **10** 271

De Walt, **III** 436

de Wendel, **IV** 226–27

De-sta-Co., **III** 468

Dealer Equipment and Services, **10** 492

Dean & Barry Co., **8** 455

Dean Foods Company, 7 127–29

Dean Witter, Discover & Co., II 445; **IV** 186; **V** 180, 182; **7** 213; **12 96–98**

Dean-Dempsy Corp., **IV** 334

Debenhams, **V** 20–22

Debron Investments Plc., **8** 271

DEC. *See* Digital Equipment Corp.

Decca Ltd., **II** 81, 83, 144

Decision Base Resources, **6** 14

Decoflex Ltd., **IV** 645

Decolletage S.A. St.-Maurice, **14** 27

Dee Corp., **I** 549; **II** 628–29, 642

Deeks McBride, **III** 704

Deep Oil Technology, **I** 570

Deep Rock Oil Corp., **IV** 446

Deep Rock Water Co., **III** 21

Deepsea Ventures, Inc., **IV** 152

Deepwater Light and Power Company, **6** 449

Deer Park Spring Water Co., **III** 21

Deere & Company, I 181, 527; **III** 462–64, 651; **10** 377–78, 380, 429; **11** 472; **13** 16–17, 267

Deering Co., **II** 330

Deering Harvester Co., **IV** 660

Deering Milliken, **V** 366–67; **8** 13

Defense Plant Corp., **IV** 10, 408

Deft Software, Inc., **10** 505

DEG. *See* Deutsche Edison Gesellschaft.

Degussa Group, I 303; **IV 69–72**, 118

Deinhard, **I** 281

DeKalb AgResearch Inc., **9** 411

Del Monte Corporation, II 595; **7 130–32**; **12** 439; **14** 287

Del Webb Corporation, 14 162–64

Del-Rey Petroleum, **I** 526

Delafield Industries, **12** 418

Delagrange, **I** 635

Delaware Charter Guarantee & Trust Co., **III** 330

Delaware Lackawanna & Western, **I** 584

Delaware Management Holdings, **III** 386

Delaware North Companies Incorporated, 7 133–36

Delbard, **I** 272

Delchamps, **II** 638

Delco Electronics, **II** 32–35; **III** 151; **6** 265

Delhaize Freres & Cie, **II** 626; **15** 176

Delhi Gas Pipeline Corporation, **7** 551

Delhi International Oil Corp., **III** 687

Deli Universal, **13** 545

Delicious Foods, **13** 383

Delimaatschappij, **13** 545

Dell Computer Corp., 9 165–66; **10** 309, 459; **11** 62

Dell Publishing Co., **13** 560

Dellwood Elevator Co., **I** 419

Delmar Chemicals Ltd., **II** 484

Delmar Paper Box Co., **IV** 333

Delmarva Properties, Inc., **8** 103

Delmonico Foods Inc., **II** 511

Delmonico International, **II** 101

Deloitte & Touche, 9 167–69, 423

DeLong Engineering Co., **III** 558

DeLorean Motor Co., **10** 117; **14** 321

Delphax, **IV** 252

Delprat, **IV** 58

Delta Acceptance Corporation Limited, **13** 63

Delta Air Lines Inc., I 29, 91, 97, **99–100**, 102, 106, 120, 132; **6** 61, **81–83 (upd.)**, 117, 131–32, 383; **12** 149, 381; **13** 171–72; **14** 73

Delta Biologicals S.r.l., **11** 208

Delta Communications, **IV** 610

Delta Faucet Co., **III** 568–69

Delta Lloyd, **III** 235

Delta Manufacturing, **II** 85

Delta Motors, **III** 580

Delta Savings Assoc. of Texas, **IV** 343

Delta Steamship Lines, **9** 425–26

Delta Woodside Industries, Inc., 8 141–43

Deluxe Corporation, 7 137–39

DeLuxe Laboratories, **IV** 652

Deluxe Upholstering Ltd., **14** 303

Delvag Luftürsicherungs A.G., **I** 111

Demag AG, **II** 22; **III** 566; **IV** 206

Demerara Company, **13** 102

Deminex, **IV** 413, 424

Deming Company, **8** 135

Demka, **IV** 132–33

Dempsey & Siders Agency, **III** 190

Den Fujita, **9** 74

Den norske Creditbank, **II** 366

Den Norske Stats Oljeselskap AS, IV 405–07, 486

Den-Tal-Ez, **I** 702

Denain-Nord-Est-Longwy, **IV** 227

Denault Ltd., **II** 651

Denison Corp., **III** 628

Denison Mines, Ltd., **12** 198

Denki Seikosho, **IV** 62

Denney-Reyburn, **8** 360

Dennison Manufacturing Co., **IV** 251–52, 254; **15** 401

Denny's Restaurants Inc., **II** 680; **III** 103; **V** 88–89; **12** 511; **13** 526

Denshi Media Services, **IV** 680

Dent & Co., **II** 296

Dentsply International Inc., 10 270–72

Dentsu Inc., I 9–11, 36, 38; **6** 29; **9** 30; **13** 204

Denver & Rio Grande Railroad, **12** 18–19

Denver Chemical Company, **8** 84

Denver Gas & Electric Company, **IV** 391; **6** 558. *See also* Public Service Company of Colorado.

Department 56, Inc., 14 165–67

Department Stores International, **I** 426

Deposito and Administratie Bank, **II** 185

Depositors National Bank of Durham, **II** 336

Depuy Inc., **10** 156–57

Der Anker, **III** 177

Derby Commerical Bank, **II** 318
Derbyshire Stone and William Briggs, **III** 752
Deritend Computers, **14** 36
Deruluft, **6** 57
Derwent Publications, **8** 526
Des Moines Electric Light Company, **6** 504
DESA Industries, **8** 545
Deseret National Bank, **11** 118
Desert Partners, **III** 763
Design Craft Ltd., **IV** 640
Desmarais Frères, **IV** 557, 559
DeSoto, Inc., **8** 553; **13** 471
Desoutter, **III** 427
Destec Energy, Inc., 12 99–101
Det Danske/Norske Luftartselskab, **I** 119
Detroit Aircraft Corp., **I** 64; **11** 266
Detroit Automobile Co., **I** 164
Detroit Ball Bearing Co., **13** 78
Detroit Chemical Coatings, **8** 553
Detroit City Gas Company. *See* MCN Corporation.
Detroit Copper Co., **IV** 176–77
Detroit Diesel Corporation, V 494–95; **9** 18; **10** 273–75; **11** 471; **12** 90–91
The Detroit Edison Company, I 164; **V** 592–95; **7** 377–78; **11** 136; **14** 135
Detroit Fire & Marine Insurance Co., **III** 191
Detroit Gear and Machine Co., **III** 439
Detroit Radiator Co., **III** 663
Detroit Red Wings, **7** 278–79
Detroit Steel, **13** 157
Detroit Steel Products Co. Inc., **IV** 136
Detroit Toledo & Ironton Railroad, **I** 165
Detroit Vapor Stove Co., **III** 439
Detroit-Graphite Company, **8** 553
Detrola, **II** 60
Deutsch Erdol A.G., **IV** 552
Deutsch Shea & Evans Inc., **I** 15
Deutsch-Australische Dampfschiffs-Gesellschaft, **6** 398
Deutsch-Luxembergische Bergwerks und Hütten AG, **I** 542; **IV** 105
Deutsch-Österreichische Mannesmannröhren-Werke Aktiengesellschaft, **III** 564–65
Deutsch-Skandinavische Bank, **II** 352
Deutsche Aerospace Airbus, **7** 9, 11
Deutsche Airbus, **I** 41–42; **12** 190–91
Deutsche Allgemeine Versicherungs-Aktiengesellschaft, **III** 412
Deutsche Anlagen Leasing GmbH, **II** 386
Deutsche BA, **14** 73
Deutsche Babcock AG, II 386; **III** 465–66
Deutsche Bank A.G., I 151, 409, 549; **II** 98, 191, 239, 241–42, 256–58, **278–80,** 281–82, 295, 319, 385, 427, 429; **III** 154–55, 692, 695; **IV** 91, 141, 229, 232, 378, 557; **V** 241–42; **14 168–71 (upd.);** **15** 13
Deutsche BP Aktiengesellschaft, 7 **140–43**
Deutsche Bundepost Telekom, V 287–90
Deutsche Bundesbahn, V 444–47; **6** 424–26
Deutsche Edelstahlwerke AG, **IV** 222
Deutsche Edison Gesellschaft, **I** 409–10
Deutsche Erdol Aktiengesellschaft, **7** 140
Deutsche Gold-und Silber-Scheideanstalt vormals Roessler, **IV** 69, 118, 139
Deutsche Hydrierwerke, **III** 32
Deutsche Industriewerke AG, **IV** 230

Deutsche Kreditbank, **14** 170
Deutsche Länderbank, **II** 379
Deutsche Lufthansa A.G., I 94, **110–11,** 120; **6** 59–60, 69, 95–96, 386; **12** 191
Deutsche Marathon Petroleum, **IV** 487
Deutsche Mineralöl-Explorationsgesellschaft mbH, **IV** 197
Deutsche Nippon Seiko, **III** 589
Deutsche Petroleum-Verkaufsgesellschaft mbH, **7** 140
Deutsche Reichsbahn, **V** 444. *See also* Deutsche Bundesbahn.
Deutsche Schiff-und Maschinenbau Aktiengesellschaft "Deschimag," **IV** 87
Deutsche Shell, **7** 140
Deutsche Spezialglas AG, **III** 446
Deutsche Strassen und Lokalbahn A.G., **I** 410
Deutsche Texaco, **V** 709
Deutsche Union, **III** 693–94
Deutsche Union-Bank, **II** 278
Deutsche Wagnisfinanzierung, **II** 258
Deutsche Werke AG, **IV** 230
Deutsche-Asiatische Bank, **II** 238, 256
Deutsche-Nalco-Chemie GmbH., **I** 373
Deutscher Aero Lloyd, **I** 110
Deutscher Automobil Schutz Allgemeine Rechtsschutz-Versicherung AG, **III** 400
Deutscher Kommunal-Verlag Dr. Naujoks & Behrendt, **14** 556
Deutsches Reisebüro DeR, **II** 163
Deutz AG, **III** 541
Deutz Farm Equipment, **13** 17
Deutz-Allis, **III** 544. *See also* AGCO Corp.
Devcon Corp., **III** 519
Development Finance Corp., **II** 189
DeVilbiss Company, **8** 230
DeVilbiss Health Care, Inc., **11** 488
Devoe & Raynolds Co., **12** 217
DeVry Technical Institute, Inc., **9** 63
Dewars Brothers, **I** 239–40
Dewey & Almy Chemical Co., **I** 548
The Dexter Corporation, I 320–22; **12** **102–04 (upd.)**
DFS Dorland Worldwide, **I** 35
DFW Printing Company, **10** 3
DG&E. *See* Denver Gas & Electric Company.
DH Compounding, **8** 347
DHI Corp., **II** 680
DHJ Industries, Inc., **12** 118
DHL Worldwide Express, 6 385–87
Di Giorgio Corp., II 602; **12 105–07**
Di-Rite Company, **11** 534
Dia Prosim, S.A., **IV** 409
Diagnostic Health Corporation, **14** 233
Diagnostics Pasteur, **I** 677
The Dial Corp., 8 144–46
Dialight Corp., **13** 397–98
Dialog Information Services, Inc., **IV** 630
Diamandis Communications Inc., **IV** 619, 678
Diamang, **IV** 65, 67
Diamedix, **11** 207
Diamond Communications, **10** 288
Diamond Corporation Ltd., **IV** 21, 66–67; **7** 123
Diamond International Corp., **IV** 290, 295; **13** 254–55
Diamond M Offshore Inc., **12** 318
Diamond Match Company, **14** 163
Diamond Oil Co., **IV** 548
Diamond Savings & Loan, **II** 420

Diamond Shamrock, Inc., IV 408–11, 481; **7** 34, 308–099, 345; **13** 118
Diamond Trading Company, **IV** 66–67; **7** 123
Diamond Walnut Growers, **7** 496–97
Diamond-Star Motors Corporation, **9** 349–51
Dibrell Brothers, Incorporated, 12 **108–10;** **13** 492
Dickerman, **8** 366
Dickson Forest Products, Inc., **15** 305
Dickstein Partners, L.P., **13** 261
Dictaphone Corp., **III** 157
Didier Werke AG, **IV** 232
Diebold, Inc., 7 144–46
Diehl Manufacturing Co., **II** 9
Diemakers Inc., **IV** 443
Diesel United Co., **III** 533
AB Diesels Motorer, **III** 425–26
Diet Center, **10** 383
Dieter Hein Co., **14** 537
Dieterich Standard Corp., **III** 468
Dietrich Corp., **II** 512; **15** 221
Dietrich's Bakeries, **II** 631
DiFranza Williamson, **6** 40
DIG Acquisition Corp., **12** 107
Digi International Inc., 9 170–72
Digital Audio Disk Corp., **II** 103
Digital Data Systems Company, **11** 408
Digital Devices, Inc., **III** 643
Digital Equipment Corporation, II 8, 62, 108; **III** 118, 128, **132–35,** 142, 149, 166; **6** 225, **233–36 (upd.),** 237–38, 242, 246–47, 279, 287; **8** 137–39, 519; **9** 35, 43, 57, 166, 170–71, 514; **10** 22–23, 34, 86, 242, 361, 463, 477; **11** 46, 86–88, 274, 491, 518–19; **12** 147, 162, 470; **13** 127, 202, 482; **14** 318; **15** 108
Diligent Engine Co., **III** 342
Dill & Collins, **IV** 311
Dill Enterprises, Inc., **14** 18
Dillard Department Stores, V 45–47; **10** 488; **11** 349; **12** 64; **13** 544–45
Dillard Paper Company, 11 74–76
Dillingham Corp., I 565–66
Dillingham Holdings Inc., **9** 511
Dillon Companies Inc., II 645; **12** **111–13;** **15** 267
Dillon Paper, **IV** 288
Dillon, Read and Co., Inc., **I** 144, 559; **III** 151, 389; **6** 265; **11** 53
Dime Banking and Loan Association of Rochester, **10** 91
Dime Savings Bank of New York, F.S.B., **9 173–74**
Dimeling, Schreiber & Park, **11** 63
Dimeric Development Corporation, **14** 392
DiMon Inc., **12** 110
Diners Club, **II** 397; **6** 62; **9** 335; **10** 61
Dinner Bell Foods, Inc., **11** 93
de Dion, **III** 523
Dirección General de Correos y Telecomunicaciónes, **V** 337
Dirección Nacional de los Yacimientos Petrolíferos Fiscales, **IV** 577–78
Direct Container Lines, **14** 505
Direct Line, **12** 422
Direct Mail Services Pty. Ltd., **10** 461
Direct Spanish Telegraph Co., **I** 428
Direction Générale des Télécommunications, **V** 471
Directorate General of **Telecommunications, 7 147–49**

Dirr's Gold Seal Meats, **6** 199
Disc Manufacturing, Inc., **15** 378
Disco SA, **V** 11
Discol SA, **V** 11
Disconto-Gesellschaft, **II** 238, 279
Discount Bank, **II** 205
Discount Corporation, **12** 565
Discount Drug Mart, Inc., 14 172–73
Discover, **9** 335; **12** 97
DiscoVision Associates, **III** 605
Disctronics, Ltd., **15** 380
Disney Channel, **6** 174–75; **13** 280
Disney Co. *See* Walt Disney Company.
Disney Studios, **II** 408; **6** 174, 176
Disneyland, **6** 175
Dispatch Communications, **10** 432
Display Components Inc., **II** 110
Displayco Midwest Inc., **8** 103
Disposable Hospital Products, **I** 627
Distillers and Cattle Feeders Trust, **I** 376
Distillers Co. plc, I 239–41, 252, 263,
  284–85; **II** 429, 609–10; **IV** 70
Distillers Securities, **I** 376
Distinctive Printing and Packaging Co., **8**
  103
Distinctive Software Inc., **10** 285
Distribution Centers Incorporated. *See* Exel
  Logistics Ltd.
Distribution Services, Inc., **10** 287
District Bank, **II** 333
District Cablevision, **II** 160
District News Co., **II** 607
Distrigas, **IV** 425
DITAS, **IV** 563
Ditzler Color Co., **III** 732
DIVAL, **III** 347
Diversey Corp., **I** 275, 333; **13** 150, 199
Diversified Agency Services, **I** 32
Diversified Retailing Co., **III** 214
Diversified Services, **9** 95
Diversifoods Inc., **II** 556; **13** 408
Dixie Bearings, Inc., **13** 78
Dixie Container Corporation, **12** 377
Dixie Hi-Fi, **9** 120–21
Dixie Home Stores, **II** 683
Dixie Paper, **I** 612–14
Dixie Power & Light Company, **6** 514
Dixie Yarns, Inc., **9** 466
Dixie-Narco, Inc., **III** 573
Dixieland Food Stores, **II** 624
Dixon Ticonderoga Company, 12 114–16
Dixons Group plc, II 139; **V** 48–50; **9** 65;
  10 45, 306
DKB. *See* Dai-Ichi Kangyo Bank Ltd.
DLC. *See* Duquesne Light Company.
DMB&B. *See* D'Arcy Masius Benton &
  Bowles.
DMP Mineralöl Petrochemie GmbH, **IV**
  487
DNAX Research Institute, **I** 685; **14** 424
DNEL-Usinor, **IV** 227
DNP DENMARK A/S, **IV** 600
Dobbs Houses Inc., **I** 696–97; **15** 87
Dobrolet, **6** 57
Doctors' Hospital, **6** 191
Documentation Resources, **11** 65
DOD Electronics Corp., **15** 215
Dodd, Mead & Co., **14** 498
Dodge Corp., **I** 144; **8** 74; **11** 53
The Dodge Group, **11** 78
Dodge Manufacturing Company, **9** 440
Dodwell & Co., **III** 523
Doe Run Company, **12** 244
Dofasco Inc., IV 73–74

Doherty Clifford Steers & Sherfield Inc., **I**
  31
Doherty, Mann & Olshan. *See* Wells Rich
  Greene BDDP.
Dole Food Company, Inc., I 565; **II**
  491–92; **9 175–76**
Dolland & Aitchison Group, **V** 399
Dollar Rent A Car, **6** 349
Dollar Steamship Lines, **6** 353
Dolphin Book Club, **13** 106
Domain Technology, **6** 231
Domaine Chandon, **I** 272
Dombrico, Inc., **8** 545
Dome Laboratories, **I** 654
Dome Petroleum, Ltd., **II** 222, 245, 262,
  376; **IV** 371, 401, 494; **12** 364
Domestic Electric Co., **III** 435
Domestic Operating Co., **III** 36
Dominick International Corp., **12** 131
Dominick's Finer Foods, **9** 451; **13** 25, 516
Dominion Bank, **II** 375–76
Dominion Bridge Company, Limited, **8**
  544
Dominion Cellular, **6** 322
Dominion Dairies, **7** 429
Dominion Engineering Works Ltd., **8** 544
Dominion Far East Line, **I** 469
Dominion Foundries and Steel, Ltd., **IV**
  73–74
Dominion Hoist & Shovel Co., **8** 544
Dominion Industries Ltd., **15** 229
Dominion Life Assurance Co., **III** 276
Dominion Mushroom Co., **II** 649–50
Dominion Ornamental, **III** 641
Dominion Paper Box Co. Ltd., **IV** 645
Dominion Resources, Inc., V 591, **596–99**
Dominion Securities, **II** 345
Dominion Stores Ltd., **II** 650, 652
Dominion Tar & Chemical Co. Ltd., **IV**
  271–72
Dominion Terminal Associates, **IV** 171; **7**
  582, 584
Dominion Textile Inc., V 355; **8** 559–60;
  12 117–19
Domino's Pizza, Inc., 7 150–53; 9 74; **12**
  123; **15** 344, 346
Domtar Inc., IV 271–73, 308
Don Baxter Intravenous Products Co., **I**
  627
Donac Company, **V** 681
Donald L. Bren Co., **IV** 287
Donaldson, Lufkin & Jenrette, **II** 422, 451;
  III 247–48; **9** 115, 142, 360–61
Donaldson's Department Stores, **15** 274
Doncaster Newspapers Ltd., **IV** 686
Dong-A Motor, **III** 749
Dong-Myung Industrial Co. Ltd., **II** 540
Dongbang Life Insurance Co., **I** 515
Dongil Frozen Foods Co., **II** 553
Dongsu Industrial Company, **III** 516; **7**
  232
Donna Karan Company, 15 145–47
Donnelley, Gassette & Loyd, **IV** 660
Donnellon McCarthy Inc., **12** 184
Donnelly Corporation, 12 120–22
Donohue Inc., **12** 412
Donzi Marine Corp., **III** 600
Dooner Laboratories, **I** 667
Door-to-Door, **6** 14
Dorado Beach Development Inc., **I** 103
Dordrecht, **III** 177–78
Dorman Long & Co. Ltd., **IV** 658
Dornier, **I** 46, 74, 151; **15** 142
Dornier-Merkur, **I** 121

Dorothy Hamill International, **13** 279, 281
Dorothy Perkins, **V** 21
Dortmunder Union, **II** 240; **IV** 103, 105
Doskocil Companies, Inc., 12 123–25
Doubleday Book Shops, **10** 136
Doubleday-Dell, **IV** 594, 636
Douglas Aircraft Co., **I** 48, 70, 76, 96, 104,
  195; **II** 32, 425; **III** 601; **9** 12, 18, 206;
  10 163; **13** 48, 341
Douglas Oil Co., **IV** 401
Douglas-Dahlin Co., **I** 158–59
Doulton Glass Industries Ltd., **IV** 659
Douwe Egberts, **II** 572
Dove International, **7** 299–300
Dover Corporation, III 467–69
Dovrat Shrem, **15** 470
Dow Chemical Co., I 323–25, 334,
  341–42, 360, 370–71, 708; **II** 440, 457;
  III 617, 760; **IV** 83, 417; **8 147–50**
  (upd.), 153, 261–62, 548; **9** 328–29,
  500-501; **10** 289; **11** 271; **12** 99–100,
  254, 364; **14** 114, 217
Dow Corning, **II** 54; **III** 683, 685
Dow Jones & Company, Inc., IV
  601–03, 654, 656, 670, 678; **7** 99; **10**
  276–78, 407; **13** 55; **15** 335–36
Dow Jones Telerate, Inc., 10 276–78
Dowdings Ltd., **IV** 349
Dowell Australia Ltd., **III** 674
Dowell Schlumberger, **III** 617
Dowidat GmbH, **IV** 197
Dowlais Iron Co., **III** 493
Down River International, Inc., **15** 188
Downe Communications, Inc., **14** 460
Downingtown Paper Company, **8** 476
Downyflake Foods, **7** 429
Doyle Dane Bernbach, **I** 9, 20, 28, 30–31,
  33, 37, 206; **11** 549; **14** 159
DP&L. *See* Dayton Power & Light
  Company.
DPCE, **II** 139
DPF, Inc., **12** 275
DPL Inc., 6 480–82
DQE, 6 483–85
DR Holdings, Inc., **10** 242
Dr Pepper/7Up Companies, Inc., I 245;
  II 477; **9 177–78**
Dr. Ing he F. Porsche GmbH, **13** 413–14
Dr. Miles' Medical Co., **I** 653
Dr. Richter & Co., **IV** 70
Dr. Tigges-Fahrten, **II** 163–64
Drackett Professional Products, III 17;
  12 126–28
Dragados y Construcciones S.A., **II** 198
Dragon, **III** 391
The Drake, **12** 316
Drake Bakeries, **II** 562
Drake Beam Morin, Inc., **IV** 623
Draper & Kramer, **IV** 724
Draper Corporation, **14** 219; **15** 384
Drathen Co., **I** 220
Dravo Corp., **6** 143
Draw-Tite, Inc., **11** 535
Drayton Corp., **II** 319
Dresdner Bank A.G., I 411; **II** 191,
  238–39, 241–42, 256–57, 279–80,
  281–83, 385; **III** 201, 289, 401; **IV** 141;
  14 169–70; **15** 13
Dresdner Feuer-Versicherungs-Gesellschaft,
  III 376
Dresser Industries, Inc., I 486; **III** 429,
  470–73; 499, 527, 545–46; **12** 539; **14**
  325; **15** 225–26, 468
Dresser Power, **6** 555

Drew Graphics, Inc., **13** 227–28
Drewry Photocolor, **I** 447
Drexel Burnham Lambert Incorporated,
II 167, 329–30, **407–09**, 482; **III** 10,
253, 254–55, 531, 721; **IV** 334; **6**
210–11; **7** 305; **8** 327, 349, 388–90,
568; **9** 346; **12** 229; **13** 169, 299, 449;
14 43; **15** 71, 281, 464. See also New
Street Capital Inc.
Drexel Heritage Furnishings Inc., **III**
571; **11** 534; **12** 129–31
Dreyer's Grand Ice Cream, Inc., **10**
147–48
Dreyfus Interstate Development Corp., **11**
257
DRI. See Dominion Resources, Inc.
Dribeck Importers Inc., **9** 87
Drott Manufacturing Company, **10** 379
Drouot Group, **III** 211
Drug City, **II** 649
Drug Emporium, Inc., **12 132–34**, 477
Drug House, **III** 9
Drug, Inc., **III** 17
Drummond Lighterage. See Puget Sound
Tug and Barge Company.
Drummonds' Bank, **12** 422
Druout, **I** 563
Dry Milks Inc., **I** 248
DryClean U.S.A., **14** 25
Dryden and Co., **III** 340
Drysdale Government Securities, **10** 117
DSC Communications Corporation, **9**
170; **12 135–37**
DSM N.V., **I 326–27**; **III** 614; **15** 229
DST Systems Inc., **6** 400–02
Du Bouzet, **II** 233
Du Mont Company, **8** 517
Du Pont. See E.I. du Pont de Nemours &
Co.
Du Pont Fabricators, **III** 559
Du Pont Glore Forgan, Inc., **III** 137
Du Pont Photomask, **IV** 600
Dublin and London Steam Packet
Company, **V** 490
DuBois Chemicals Division, **13** 149–50
Ducatel-Duval, **II** 369
Duck Head Apparel Company, Inc., **8**
141–43
Ducon Group, **II** 81
Duff Bros., **III** 9–10
Duffy-Mott, **II** 477
Duke Power Company, **V 600–02**
Dumes SA, **13** 206
Dumez, **V** 655–57
Dumont Broadcasting Corporation, **7** 335
Dun & Bradstreet Corporation, **I** 540;
IV 604–05, 643, 661; **8** 526; **9** 505; **10**
4, 358; **13** 3–4
**Dun & Bradstreet Software Services
Inc.**, **11 77–79**
Duncan Foods Corp., **I** 234; **10** 227
Duncan, Sherman & Co., **II** 329
Duncanson & Holt, Inc., **13** 539
Dundee Cement Co., **III** 702; **8** 258–59
Dunfey Brothers Capital Group, **12** 368
Dunfey Hotels Corporation, **12** 367
Dunhams Stores Corporation, **V** 111
Dunhill Holdings, **IV** 93; **V** 411
Dunkin' Donuts, **II** 619
Dunlop Holdings, **I** 429; **III** 697; **V** 250,
252–53
Dunn Paper Co., **IV** 290
Dunning Industries, **12** 109
Dunoyer, **III** 675

Duo-Bed Corp., **14** 435
Dupil-Color, Inc., **III** 745
Dupol, **III** 614
Dupont Chamber Works, **6** 449
Duquesne Light Company, **6** 483–84
Duquesne Systems, **10** 394
Dura Convertible Systems, **13** 170
Dura Corp., **I** 476
Dura-Vent, **III** 468
Duracell International Inc., **9 179–81**; **12**
559; **13** 433
Durand & Huguenin, **I** 672
Duray, Inc., **12** 215
Durban Breweries and Distillers, **I** 287
Durham Chemicals Distributors Ltd., **III**
699
Durham Raw Materials Ltd., **III** 699
Durkee Famous Foods, **II** 567; **7** 314; **8**
222
Durr-Fillauer Medical Inc., **13** 90
Dutch Boy, **II** 649; **III** 745; **10** 434–35
Dutch Crude Oil Company. See
Nederlandse Aardolie Maatschappij.
Dutch East Indies Post, Telegraph and
Telephone Service, **II** 67
Dutch Nuts Chocoladefabriek B.V., **II** 569
Dutch Pantry, **II** 497
Dutch State Mines. See DSM N.V.
Dutton Brewery, **I** 294
Duty Free International, Inc., **11 80–82**
Duval Corp., **IV** 489–90; **7** 280
DWG Corporation. See Triarc Companies,
Inc.
Dyckerhoff, **III** 738
Dynaco Inc., **III** 643
Dynamatic Corp., **I** 154
Dynamic Controls, **11** 202
Dynamic Microprocessor Associated Inc.,
10 508
Dynamit Nobel AG, **III** 692–95
Dynamix, **15** 455
Dynapar, **7** 116–17
Dynascan AK, **14** 118
Dynatech Corporation, **13 194–96**
Dynatron/Bondo Corporation, **8** 456
Dynell Electronics, **I** 85
Dyno Industrier AS, **13** 555
Dyonics Inc., **I** 667
DYR, **I** 38

E & H Utility Sales Inc., **6** 487
E & J Gallo, **15** 391
E & J Gallo Winery, **I** 27, **242–44**, 260;
7 154–56 (upd.)
E & S Retail Ltd. See Powerhouse.
E. & B. Carpet Mills, **III** 423
E.A. Miller, Inc., **II** 494
E.A. Pierce & Co., **II** 424; **13** 340
E.A. Stearns & Co., **III** 627
E&B Company, **9** 72
E.B. Badger Co., **11** 413
E.B. Eddy Forest Products, **II** 631
E.C. Snodgrass Company, **14** 112
E.C. Steed, **13** 103
E. de Trey & Sons, **10** 270–71
E.F. Hutton Group, **I** 402; **II** 399, 450–51;
8 139; **9** 469; **10** 63
E. Gluck Trading Co., **III** 645
E.H. Bindley & Company, **9** 67
E.I. du Pont de Nemours & Company, **I**
21, 28, 305, 317–19, 323, **328–30**, 334,
337–38, 343–44, 346–48, 351–53, 365,
377, 379, 383, 402–03, 545, 548, 675;
III 21; **IV** 69, 78, 263, 371, 399,

401–02, 409, 481, 599; **V** 360; **7** 546; **8**
151–54 (upd.), 485; **9** 154, 216, 352,
466; **10** 289; **11** 432; **12** 68, 365,
416–17; **13** 21, 124
E-II Holdings Inc., **II** 468; **9** 449; **12** 87;
13 453
E.J. Brach, **II** 521
E.J. Brach & Sons. See Brach and Brock
Confections, Inc.
E. Katz Special Advertising Agency. See
Katz Communications, Inc.
E.L. Phillips and Company, **V** 652–53
E.M. Warburg Pincus & Co., **7** 305; **13**
176
E.N.V. Engineering, **I** 154
E.R. Squibb, **I** 695
E. Rabinowe & Co., Inc., **13** 367
E.S. Friedman & Co., **II** 241
E.S. International Holding S.A. See Banco
Espírito Santo e Comercial de Lisboa
S.A.
E-Systems, Inc., **I** 490; **9 182–85**
E.W. Bliss, **I** 452
E.W. Oakes & Co. Ltd., **IV** 118
E.W. Scripps Company, **IV 606–09**; **7**
157–59 (upd.)
E.W.T. Mayer Ltd., **III** 681
E-Z Serve Convenience Stores, Inc., **15**
270
Eagle Credit Corp., **10** 248
Eagle Electric & Plumbing Supply, **9** 399
Eagle Floor Care, Inc., **13** 501
Eagle Industries, **8** 230
Eagle Oil Transport Co. Ltd., **IV** 657
Eagle Printing Co. Ltd., **IV** 295
Eagle Snacks Inc., **I** 219
Eagle Square Manufacturing Co., **III** 627
Eagle Star Insurance Co., **I** 426–27; **III**
185, 200
Eagle Supermarket, **II** 571
Eagle Thrifty Drug, **14** 397
Eagle Travel Ltd., **IV** 241
Eagle-Lion Films, **II** 147
Eagle-Picher Industries, Inc., **8 155–58**
Earth Resources Co., **IV** 459
Easco Hand Tools, Inc., **7** 117
Eason Oil Company, **6** 578; **11** 198
East Chicago Iron and Forge Co., **IV** 113
East Hartford Trust Co., **13** 467
East India Co., **I** 468; **III** 521, 696; **IV** 48
East Japan Heavy Industries, **III** 578–79; **7**
348
East Japan Railway Company, **V 448–50**
East Midlands Electricity, **V** 605
The East New York Savings Bank, **11**
108–09
East of Scotland, **III** 359
East Texas Pulp and Paper Co., **IV** 342,
674; **7** 528
Easter Enterprises, **8** 380
Eastern Airlines, **I** 41, 66, 78, 90, 98–99,
101–03, 116, 118, 123–25; **III** 102; **6**
73, 81–82, 104–05; **8** 416; **9** 17–18, 80;
11 268, 427; **12** 191, 487
Eastern Associated Coal Corp., **6** 487
Eastern Bank, **II** 357
Eastern Carolina Bottling Company, **10**
223
Eastern Coal Corp., **IV** 181
Eastern Coalfields Ltd., **IV** 48–49
Eastern Corp., **IV** 703
Eastern Electricity, **13** 485
Eastern Enterprises, **IV** 171; **6 486–88**

Eastern Gas and Fuel Associates, **I** 354; **IV** 171

Eastern Indiana Gas Corporation, **6** 466

Eastern Kansas Utilities, **6** 511

Eastern Machine Screw Products Co., **13** 7

Eastern Operating Co., **III** 23

Eastern Pine Sales Corporation, **13** 249

Eastern States Farmers Exchange, **7** 17

Eastern Telegraph, **V** 283–84

Eastern Texas Electric. *See* Gulf States Utilities Company.

Eastern Tool Co., **IV** 249

Eastern Wisconsin Power, **6** 604

Eastern Wisconsin Railway and Light Company, **6** 601

Eastex Pulp and Paper Co., **IV** 341–42

Eastman Chemical Company, 14 174–75

Eastman Kodak Company, I 19, 30, 90, 323, 337–38, 690; **II** 103; **III** 171–72, **474–77**, 486–88, 547–48, 550, 584, 607–09; **IV** 260–61; **6** 288–89; **7** **160–64 (upd.)**, 436–38; **8** 376–77; **9** 62, 231; **10** 24; **12** 342; **14** 174–75, 534

Eastman Radio, **6** 33

Eastmaque Gold Mines, Ltd., **7** 356

Eatco, Inc., **15** 246

Eaton Axle Co., **I** 154

Eaton, Cole & Burnham Company, **8** 134

Eaton Corporation, I 154–55, 186; **III** 645; **10 279–80 (upd.)**; **12** 547

Eavey Co., **II** 668

Ebamsa, **II** 474

EBASCO. *See* Electric Bond and Share Company.

Ebasco Services, **III** 499; **V** 612; **IV** 255–56

EBC Amro Ltd., **II** 186

Eberhard Faber, **12** 115

Eberhard Foods, **8** 482

EBIC. *See* European Banks' International Co.

EBS. *See* Electric Bond & Share Company.

EC Erdolchemie GmbH, **7** 141

ECC Group plc, III 689–91. *See also* English China Clays plc.

Echigoya Saburobei Shoten, **IV** 292

Echlin Inc., I 156–57; **11 83–85 (upd.)**; **15** 310

Echo Bay Mines Ltd., IV 75–77

Les Echos, **IV** 659

Eckerd Corporation, 9 186–87

Eckert-Mauchly Corp., **III** 166

Ecko Products, **I** 527

Ecko-Ensign Design, **I** 531

Eclipse Machine Co., **I** 141

Eco Hotels, **14** 107

Ecolab Inc., I 331–33; 13 197–200 (upd.)

Econo-Travel Corporation, **13** 362

Economist Group, **15** 265

Economy Book Store, **10** 135

Economy Grocery Stores Corp., **II** 666

Ecopetrol. *See* Empresa Colombiana de Petróleos.

EcoSystems Software, Inc., **10** 245

ECS S.A., 12 138–40

Ecusta Corporation, **8** 414

Edah, **13** 544–45

Eddie Bauer Inc., II 503; **V** 160; **9** **188–90**; **9** 316; **10** 324, 489, 491; **11** 498; **15** 339

Eddy Bakeries, Inc., **12** 198

Eddy Paper Co., **II** 631

Edeka Zentrale A.G., II 621–23

Edelstahlwerke Buderus AG, **III** 695

Edenhall Group, **III** 673

Edenton Cotton Mills, **12** 503

EDF. *See* Electricité de France.

Edgars, **I** 289

Edgcomb Metals, **IV** 576

Edgcomb Steel Co., **IV** 575

Edgell Communications Inc., **IV** 624

Edgewater Hotel and Casino, **6** 204–05

Edina Realty Inc., **13** 348

Edison Brothers Stores, Inc., 9 191–93

Edison Electric Appliance Co., **II** 28; **12** 194

Edison Electric Co., **I** 368; **II** 330; **III** 433; **6** 572

Edison Electric Illuminating Co., **II** 402; **6** 595, 601; **14** 124

Edison Electric Illuminating Company of Boston, **12** 45

Edison Electric Light & Power, **6** 510

Edison Electric Light Co., **II** 27; **6** 565, 595; **11** 387; **12** 193

Edison General Electric Co., **II** 27, 120, 278; **12** 193; **14** 168

Edison Machine Works, **II** 27

Edison Phonograph, **III** 443

Editions Albert Premier, **IV** 614

Editions Bernard Grasset, **IV** 618

Editions Dalloz, **IV** 615

Editions Nathan, **IV** 615

Editorial Centro de Estudios Ramón Areces, S.A., **V** 52

Editoriale L'Espresso, **IV** 586–87

Editoriale Le Gazzette, **IV** 587

EdK. *See* Edeka Zentrale A.G.

Edmark Corporation, 14 176–78

Edmonton City Bakery, **II** 631

Edogawa Oil Co., **IV** 403

EdoWater Systems, Inc., **IV** 137

Edper Equities, **II** 456

EDS. *See* Electronic Data Systems Corporation.

Education Funds, Inc., **II** 419

Education Systems Corporation, **7** 256

Educational & Recreational Services, Inc., **II** 607

Educational Credit Corporation, **8** 10

Educational Supply Company, **7** 255

Educational Testing Service, 12 141–43

EduQuest, **6** 245

Edward Ford Plate Glass Co., **III** 640–41, 731

Edward J. DeBartolo Corporation, V 116; **8 159–62**

Edward Lloyd Ltd., **IV** 258

Edward P. Allis Company, **13** 16

Edward Smith & Company, **8** 553

Edwards, **13** 445

Edwards & Jones, **11** 360

Edwards Dunlop & Co. Ltd., **IV** 249

Edwards Food Warehouse, **II** 642

Edwards George and Co., **III** 283

Edwards Industries, **IV** 256

Edwardstone Partners, **14** 377

Eerste Nederlandsche, **III** 177–79

Eff Laboratories, **I** 622

Effectenbank, **II** 268

Efnadruck GmbH, **IV** 325

Efrat Future Technology Ltd. *See* Comverse Technology, Inc.

EG&G Incorporated, 8 163–65

EGAM, **IV** 422

Egerton Hubbard & Co., **IV** 274

Egghead Inc., 9 194–95; **10** 284

EGPC. *See* Egyptian General Petroleum Corporation.

EGUZKIA-NHK, **III** 581

Egyptair, I 107; **6 84–86**

Egyptian General Petroleum Corporation, IV 412–14

EHAPE Einheitspreis Handels Gesellschaft mbH. *See* Kaufhalle AG.

Eidgenössische Bank, **II** 378

Eidgenössische Versicherungs-Aktien-Gesellschaft, **III** 403

84 Lumber Company, 9 196–97

Eildon Electronics Ltd., **15** 385

EIMCO, **I** 512

EIS Automotive Corp., **III** 603

Eisai Company, **13** 77

Eisen-und Stahlwerk Haspe AG, **IV** 126

Eisen-und Stahlwerk Hoesch, **IV** 103

Eisenhower Mining Co., **IV** 33

EKA AB, **I** 330; **8** 153

Eka Nobel AB, **9** 380

Ekco Products Inc., **12** 377

El Al Israel Airlines, **I** 30

El Camino Resources International, Inc., 11 86–88

El Corte Inglés, S.A., V 51–53

El Dorado Investment Company, **6** 546–47

El Paso & Southwestern Railroad, **IV** 177

El Paso Healthcare System, Ltd., **15** 112

El Paso Natural Gas Company, 10 190; **11** 28; **12 144–46**

El Pollo Loco, **II** 680

El Taco, **7** 505

ELAN, **IV** 486

Elan Corp. plc, **10** 54

Elano Corporation, 14 179–81

Elco Motor Yacht, **I** 57

Elda Trading Co., **II** 48

Elder Dempster Line, **6** 416–17

Elder's Insurance Co., **III** 370

Elder-Beerman Stores Corporation, 10 281–83

Elders IXL Ltd., I 216, 228–29, 264, **437–39**, 592–93; **7 182–83**

Elders Keep, **13** 440

Electra Corp., **III** 569

Electra/Midland Corp., **13** 398

Electralab Electronics Corp., **III** 643

Electric Boat Co., **I** 57–59, 527; **II** 7; **10** 315

Electric Bond & Share Company, **V** 564–65; **6** 596

Electric Energy, Inc., **6** 470, 505

Electric Fuels Corp., **V** 621

Electric Heat Regulator Co., **II** 40; **12** 246

Electric Iron and Steel, **IV** 162

Electric Light and Power Company, **6** 483

Electric Light Company of Atlantic City. *See* Atlantic Energy, Inc.

Electric Thermostat Co., **II** 40; **12** 246

Electrical Lamp Service Co., **I** 531

Electricité de France, I 303; **V 603–05**, 626–28

Electro Dynamics Corp., **I** 57, 484; **11** 263

Electro Metallurgical Co., **I** 400; **9** 517; **11** 402

Electro Refractories and Abrasives Company, **8** 178

Electro-Alkaline Co., **III** 20

Electro-Chemische Fabrik Natrium GmbH, **IV** 69–70

Electro-Flo, Inc., **9** 27

Electro-Mechanical Research, **III** 617

Electro-Motive Engineering Company, **10** 273
Electro-Nite International N.V., **IV** 100
Electro-Optical Systems, **III** 172; **6** 289
Electrobel, **II** 202
ElectroData Corp., **III** 165; **6** 281
Electrolux Group, **II** 69, 572; **III** 420, **478–81**; **IV** 338; **6** 69; **11** 439; **12** 158–59, 250; **13** 562, 564
Electromedics, **11** 460
Electronic Arts Inc., **10 284–86**; **13** 115
Electronic Banking Systems, **9** 173
Electronic Data Systems Corporation, **I** 172; **II** 65; **III 136–38**, 326; **6** 226; **9** 36; **10** 325, 327; **11** 62, 123, 131; **13** 482; **14** 15, 318
Electronic Rentals Group PLC, **II** 139
Electronics for Imaging, Inc., **15 148–50**
Electrorail, **II** 93
Electrowerke AG, **IV** 230
Elektra, **III** 480
Elektriska Aktiebolaget, **II** 1
Elektrizitäts-Gesellschaft Laufenburg, **6** 490
Elektrizitätswerk Westfalen AG, **V** 744
ElektroHelios, **III** 479
Elektromekaniska AB, **III** 478
Elektromekano, **II** 1
Elektrowatt AG, **6 489–91**
Eleme Petrochemicals Co., **IV** 473
Eletson Corp., **13** 374
Elettra Broadcasting Corporation, **14** 509
Elettrofinanziaria Spa, **9** 152
Eleventh National Bank, **II** 373
Elf. *See* Société Nationale Elf Aquitaine.
Elgin Blenders, Inc., **7** 128
Eli Lilly & Co., **I** 637, **645–47**, 666, 679, 687, 701; **III** 18–19, 60–61; **8** 168, 209; **9** 89–90; **10** 535; **11** 9, **89–91 (upd.)**, 458, 460; **12** 187, 278, 333; **14** 99–100, 259
Eli Witt Company, **15** 137, 139
Elias Brothers Restaurants, **III** 103
Elit Circuits Inc., **I** 330; **8** 153
Elite Microelectronics, **9** 116
Elite Sewing Machine Manufacturing Co., **III** 415
Elizabeth Arden Co., **I** 646, **III** 48; **8 166–68**, 344; **9** 201–02, 428, 449; **11** 90; **12** 314
Eljer Industries, **II** 420
Elk River Resources, Inc., **IV** 550
Elka, **III** 54
Elke Corporation, **10** 514
Elko-Lamoille Power Company, **11** 343
Ellenville Electric Company, **6** 459
Ellesse International, **V** 376
Ellington Recycling Center, **12** 377
Elliott Automation, **II** 25; **6** 241; **13** 225
Elliott Paint and Varnish, **8** 553
Ellis Adding-Typewriter Co., **III** 151; **6** 265
Ellis Banks, **II** 336
Ellis, Chafflin & Co., **IV** 310
Ellis Paperboard Products Inc., **13** 442
Ellos A.B., **II** 640
ELMA Electronic, **III** 632
Elmendorf Board, **IV** 343
Elrick & Lavidge, **6** 24
Elsevier NV, **IV 610–11**, 643, 659; **7** 244; **14** 555–56
Elsi, **II** 86
ELTO Outboard Motor Co., **III** 597
Eltra, **I** 416, 524

Elwerath, **IV** 485
Elyria Telephone Company, **6** 299
Email Ltd., **III** 672–73
Emballage, **III** 704
Embankment Trust Ltd., **IV** 659
Embassy Book Co., Ltd., **IV** 635
Embassy Hotel Group, **I** 216; **9** 426
Embassy Suites, **9** 425
Embry-Riddle, **I** 89
EMC Corporation, **12 147–49**
Emco, **III** 569
Emerald Coast Water Co., **III** 21
Emerald Technology, Inc., **10** 97
Emerson Drug, **I** 711
Emerson Electric Co., **II 18–21**, 92; **III** 625; **8** 298; **12** 248; **13** 225; **14** 357; **15** 405–06
Emerson-Brantingham Company, **10** 378
Emery Air Freight Corporation, **6** 345–46, 386, **388–91**
Emery Group, **I** 377; **III** 33
Emeryville Chemical Co., **IV** 408
Emge Packing Co., Inc., **11 92–93**
Emhart Corp., **III** 437; **8** 332
EMI Ltd., **I** 531; **6** 240
Empain-Schneider, **II** 93
Empire Blue Cross and Blue Shield, **III** **245–46**; **6** 195
Empire Brewery, **I** 253
Empire Co., **II** 653
Empire Cos., **IV** 391
Empire District Electric, **IV** 391
Empire Family Restaurants Inc., **15** 362
Empire Gas & Fuel, **IV** 391
Empire Hanna Coal Co., Ltd., **8** 346
Empire Inc., **II** 682
Empire Life and Accident Insurance Co., **III** 217
Empire National Bank, **II** 218
Empire of America, **11** 110
Empire Pencil, **III** 505
Empire Savings, Building & Loan Association, **8** 424
Empire State Group, **IV** 612
Empire State Petroleum, **IV** 374
Empire Trust Co., **II** 218
Employers Reinsurance Corp., **II** 31; **12** 197
Employers' Liability Assurance, **III** 235
Empresa Brasileira de Aeronautica, S.A., **15** 73
Empresa Colombiana de Petróleos, **IV** **415–18**
Empresa Nacional de Electridad, **I** 459
Empresa Nacional del Petroleo, **IV** 528
Empresa Nacional Electrica de Cordoba, **V** 607
Empresa Nacional Hidro-Electrica del Ribagorzana, **I** 459; **V** 607
Empresa Nacional Hulleras del Norte, **I** 460
Emprise Corporation, **7** 134–35
Ems-Chemi, **III** 760
Enagas, **IV** 528
ENCASO, **IV** 528
ENCI, **IV** 132
Encore Computer Corporation, **13** **201–02**
Encyclopedia Britannica, Inc., **7 165–68**; **12** 435, 554–55
Endata, Inc., **11** 112
ENDESA Group, **V 606–08**
Endevco Inc., **11** 28
Endiama, **IV** 67

Endicott Trust Company, **11** 110
Endo Vascular Technologies, Inc., **11** 460
ENECO. *See* Empresa Nacional Electrica de Cordoba.
ENEL. *See* Ente Nazionale per l'Energia Elettrica.
Enercon, Inc., **6** 25
Energen Corp., **6** 583
Energie-Verwaltungs-Gesellschaft, **V** 746
Energizer, **9** 180
Energy Absorption Systems, Inc., **15** 378
Energy Biosystems Corp., **15** 352
Energy Coatings Co., **14** 325
Energy Corp. of Louisiana, **V** 619
Energy Systems Group, Inc., **13** 489
Enesco Corporation, **11 94–96**; **15** 475, 477–78
Engelhard Corporation, **II** 54; **IV** 23, **78–80**
Engen, **IV** 93
Engineered Polymers Co., **I** 202
Engineering Co. of Nigeria, **IV** 473
Engineering Company, **9** 16
Engineering for the Petroleum and Process Industries, **IV** 414
Engineering Plastics, Ltd., **8** 377
Engineering Research Associates, **III** 126, 129
England Corsair Furniture, **14** 302
Englander Co., **I** 400
English China Clays plc, **III** 689–91; **15** **151–54 (upd.)**
English Condensed Milk Co., **II** 545
English Electric Co., **I** 50; **II** 25, 81; **6** 241
English Mercantile & General Insurance Co., **III** 376
English Property Corp., **IV** 712
English, Scottish and Australian Bank Ltd., **II** 187–89
Engraph, Inc., **12 150–51**
Enhance, **12** 445
ENHER. *See* Empresa Nacional Hidro-Electrica del Ribagorzana.
ENI. *See* Ente Nazionale Idrocarburi.
ENIEPSA, **IV** 528
Enimont, **IV** 422, 525
Ennia, **III** 177, 179, 310
Eno Proprietaries, **III** 65
Enocell Oy, **IV** 277
Enogex, Inc., **6** 539–40
Enpetrol, **IV** 528
Enquirer/Star Group, Inc., **10 287–88**; **12** 358
Enron Corp., **III** 197; **V 609–10**; **6** 457, 593
Enseco, **III** 684
Enserch Corp., **V 611–13**
Ensidesa, **I** 460
Ensign Oil Company, **9** 490
Enskilda S.A., **II** 352–53
Enso-Gutzeit Oy, **IV 274–77**
ENSTAR Corporation, **IV** 567; **11** 441
Enstar Group Inc., **13** 299
Ensys Environmental Products, Inc., **10** 107
ENTASA, **IV** 528
Ente Gestione Aziende Minerarie, **I** 466
Ente Nazionale di Energia Elettrica, **I** 466
Ente Nazionale Idrocarburi, **I** 369; **IV** 412, **419–22**, 424, 453, 466, 470, 486, 546; **V** 614–17
Ente Nazionale per l'Energia Elettrica, **V 614–17**
Entenmann's, **I** 246, 712; **10** 551

Entergy Corp., **V 618–20**; **6** 496–97
Enterprise Development Company, **15** 413
Enterprise Leasing, 6 392–93
Enterprise Metals Pty. Ltd., **IV** 61
Enterprise Oil plc, 11 97–99
Entertainment Zone, Inc., **15** 212
Entity Software, **11** 469
Entrada Industries Incorporated, **6** 568–69
Entré Computer Centers, **6** 243–44; **13** 175
Entremont, **I** 676
Entreprise de Recherches et d'Activités
    Pétrolières, **IV** 453, 467, 544, 560; **7**
    481, 483–84
Entreprise Nationale Sonatrach, IV
    423–25; **V** 626, 692; **10** 83–84
Entrex, Inc., **III** 154
Envirex, **11** 361
ENVIRON International Corporation, **10**
    106
Environmental Defense Fund, **9** 305
Environmental Planning & Research. *See*
    CRSS Inc.
Environmental Systems Corporation, **9** 109
Environmental Testing and Certification
    Corporation, **10** 106–07
Environmentals Incorporated. *See* Angelica
    Corporation.
Enwright Environmental Consulting
    Laboratories, **9** 110
Enzyme Technologies Corp., **I** 342; **14** 217
Eon Productions, **II** 147
Eon Systems, **III** 143; **6** 238
l'Epargne, **12** 152
Les Epiceries Presto Limitée, **II** 651
Epoch Systems Inc., **9** 140; **12** 149
Eppler, Guerin & Turner, Inc., **III** 330
Eppley, **III** 99
Epsilon Trading Corporation, **6** 81
Equator Bank, **II** 298
EQUICOR-Equitable HCA Corp., **III** 80,
    226
Equifax, Inc., 6 23–25
Equitable Bancorporation, **12** 329
Equitable Equipment Company, **7** 540
Equitable Life Assurance Society of the
    United States, II 330; **III** 80, 229, 237,
    247–49, 274, 289, 291, 305–06, 316,
    329, 359; **IV** 171, 576, 711; **6** 23; **13**
    539
Equitable Resources, Inc., 6 492–94
Equitable Trust Co., **II** 247, 397; **10** 61
Equitec Financial Group, **11** 483
Equity & Law, **III** 211
Equity Corp. Tasman, **III** 735
Equity Corporation, **6** 599
Equity Title Services Company, **13** 348
Equivalent Company, **12** 421
Eramet, **IV** 108
ERAP. *See* Entreprise de Recherches et
    d'Activités Pétrolières.
Erasco, **II** 556
Erdal, **II** 572
Erdölsproduktions-Gesellschaft AG, **IV** 485
Erftwerk AG, **IV** 229
Ericson Yachts, **10** 215
Ericssan, AB, **11** 501
Ericsson, **9** 32–33; **11** 196. *See also* L.M.
    Ericsson.
Eridania Beghin-Say, S.A., **14** 17, 19
Erie and Pennyslvania, **I** 584
Erie County Bank, **9** 474
Erie Railroad, **I** 584; **II** 329; **IV** 180
Erie Scientific Company, **14** 479–80
Eritsusha, **IV** 326

ERKA. *See* Reichs Kredit-Gesellschaft
    mbH.
Ernest Oppenheimer and Sons, **IV** 21, 79
Ernst & Young, I 412; **9 198–200**, 309,
    311; **10** 115
Erol's, **9** 74; **11** 556
ERPI, **7** 167
Erste Allgemeine, **III** 207–08
Erving Distributor Products Co., **IV** 282; **9**
    260
Erving Healthcare, **13** 150
Erwin Wasey & Co., **I** 17, 22
Erzbergbau Salzgitter AG, **IV** 201
ES&A. *See* English, Scottish and
    Australian Bank Ltd.
Esanda, **II** 189
ESB Inc., **IV** 112
Esbjerg Thermoplast, **9** 92
Escada AG, **14** 467
Escambia Chemicals, **I** 298
Escanaba Paper Co., **IV** 311
Escaut et Meuse, **IV** 227
Escher Wyss, **III** 539, 632
Eschweiler Bergwerks-Verein AG, **IV**
    25–26, 193
Esco Trading, **10** 482
Escoffier Ltd., **I** 259
Esdon de Castro, **8** 137
ESE Sports Co. Ltd., **V** 376
ESGM. *See* Elder Smith Goldsbrough
    Mort.
ESI Energy, Inc., **V** 623–24
Eskay Screw Corporation, **11** 536
Eskilstuna Separator, **III** 419
Esmark, Inc., **I** 441; **II** 448, 468–69; **6**
    357; **12** 93; **13** 448; **15** 357
Esperance-Longdoz, **IV** 51–52
Espírito Santo. *See* Banco Espírito Santo e
    Comercial de Lisboa S.A.
ESPN, **II** 131; **IV** 627
Esprit de Corp., 8 169–72
La Espuela Oil Company, Ltd., **IV** 81–82;
    7 186
Esquire Education Group, **12** 173
Esquire Inc., **I** 453; **IV** 672; **13** 178
Essantee Theatres, Inc., **14** 86
Esselte Pendaflex Corporation, 11
    100–01
Essener Reisebüro, **II** 164
Essex Outfitters Inc., **9** 394
Esso, **I** 52; **II** 628; **III** 673; **IV** 46, 276,
    397, 421, 423, 432–33, 439, 441, 454,
    470, 484, 486, 517–19, 531, 555, 563; **7**
    140, 171; **11** 97; **13** 558. *See also*
    Standard Oil Company of New Jersey.
Estée Lauder Inc., I 696; **III** 56; **8** 131; **9**
    201–04; **11** 41
Estel N.V., **IV** 105, 133
Esterline Technologies Corp., 15 155–57
Eston Chemical, **6** 148
ETA Systems, Inc., **10** 256–57
Etablissement Mesnel, **I** 202
Etablissement Poulenc-Frères, **I** 388
Etablissements Economiques du Casino
    Guichard, Perrachon et ie, S.C.A., 12
    152–54
Etablissements Pierre Lemonnier S.A., **II**
    532
Eteq Microsystems, **9** 116
Ethan Allen Interiors, Inc., III 530–31;
    10 184; **12** 307; **12 155–57**
Ethicon, Inc., **III** 35; **8** 281; **10** 213
Ethyl Corp., I 334–36, 342; **IV** 289; **10**
    289–91 (upd.); **14** 217

Etienne Aigner, **14** 224
Etimex Kunstoffwerke GmbH, **7** 141
L'Etoile, **II** 139
Etos, **II** 641
ETPM Entrêpose, **IV** 468
Euclid, **I** 147; **12** 90
Euclid Chemical Co., **8** 455–56
Euclid Crane & Hoist Co., **13** 385
Euralux, **III** 209
Eurasbank, **II** 279–80; **14** 169
The Eureka Company, III 478, 480; **12**
    158–60; **15** 416. *See also* White
    Consolidated Industries Inc.
Eureka Insurance Co., **III** 343
Eureka Specialty Printing, **IV** 253
Eureka Tent & Awning Co., **III** 59
Eureka X-Ray Tube, Inc., **10** 272
Euro Disney, **6** 174, 176
Euro RSCG Worldwide S.A., 10 345,
    347; **13 203–05**
Euro-Pacific Finance, **II** 389
Eurobel, **II** 139; **III** 200
Eurobrokers Investment Corp., **II** 457
Eurocan Pulp & Paper Co. Ltd., **III** 648;
    IV 276, 300
Eurocard France, **II** 265
Eurocom S.A. *See* Euro RSCG Worldwide
    S.A.
Eurocopter SA, **7** 9, 11
Eurogroup, **V** 65
Euromarché, **10** 205
Euromarket Designs Inc., **9** 144
Euromissile, **7** 9
Euronda, **IV** 296
Euronova S.R.L., **15** 340
Europa Metalli, **IV** 174
Europaischen Tanklager- und Transport
    AG, **7** 141
Europcar Interrent, **10** 419
Europe Computer Systems. *See* ECS S.A.
European and African Investments Ltd., **IV**
    21
European Banking Co., **II** 186
European Banks' International Co., **II**
    184–86, 295
European Coal and Steel, **II** 402
European Gas Turbines, **13** 356
European Investment Bank, **6** 97
European Periodicals, Publicity and
    Advertising Corp., **IV** 641; **7** 311
European Petroleum Co., **IV** 562
European Retail Alliance (ERA), **12**
    152–53
European-American Bank & Trust
    Company, **14** 169
European-American Banking Corp., **II** 279,
    295
Europeia, **III** 403
Europemballage, **I** 600
Europensiones, **III** 348
Eurotec, **IV** 128
Eurotechnique, **III** 678
Eurotunnel PLC, 13 206–08
Eurovida, **III** 348
Euthenics Systems Corp., **14** 334
EVA Airways Corporation, **13** 211
Evaluation Associates, Inc., **III** 306
Evan Picone, **III** 55
Evans, **V** 21
Evans Products Co., **13** 249–50, 550
Evans-Aristocrat Industries, **III** 570
Evansville Veneer and Lumber Co., **12** 296
Eve of Roma, **III** 28
Evelyn Haddon, **IV** 91

Evelyn Wood, Inc., **7** 165, 168
Evence Coppée, **III** 704–05
Evening News Association, **IV** 612; **7** 191
Ever Ready Label Corp., **IV** 253
Ever Ready Ltd., **7** 209; **9** 179–80
Everan Capital Corp., **15** 257
Everest & Jennings, **11** 200
Everex Systems, Inc., **12** 162
Evergenius, **13** 210
Evergreen Healthcare, Inc., **14** 210
Evergreen Marine Corporation Taiwan Ltd., 13 209–11
Evergreen Resources, Inc., **11** 28
Everlaurel, **13** 210
Everready Battery Co., **13** 433
Eversharp, **III** 28
Everything's A Dollar Inc. (EAD), **13** 541–43
Evian, **6** 47, 49
Evinrude Motor Co., **III** 597–99
Evinrude-ELTO, **III** 597
Ewell Industries, **III** 739
Ewo Breweries, **I** 469
Ex-Cell-O Corp., **IV** 297
Ex-Lax Inc., **15** 138–39
Exabyte Corporation, 12 161–63
Exacta, **III** 122
Exar Corp., 14 182–84
Exatec A/S, **10** 113
Excaliber, **6** 205
Excel Corporation, **11** 92–93; **13** 138, 351
Excel Mining Systems, Inc., **13** 98
Excelsior Life Insurance Co., **III** 182
Excerpta Medica International, **IV** 610
Exchange & Discount Bank, **II** 318
Exchange Bank of Yarmouth, **II** 210
Exchange Oil & Gas Corp., **IV** 282; **9** 260
Exco International, **10** 277
Execu-Fit Health Programs, **11** 379
Executive Gallery, Inc., **12** 264
Executive Income Life Insurance Co., **10** 246
Executive Life Insurance Co., **III** 253–55; **11** 483
Executive Systems, Inc., **11** 18
Executone Information Systems, Inc., 13 212–14; 15 195
Exel Logistics Ltd., **6** 412, 414
Exel Ltd., **13** 150
Exeter Oil Co., **IV** 550
Exide Electronics, **9** 10
Exors. of James Mills, **III** 493
Expercom, **6** 303
Experience, **III** 359
Exploitasi Tambang Minyak Sumatra Utara, **IV** 492
Explosive Fabricators Corp., **III** 643
Export & Domestic Can Co., **15** 127
Export-Import Bank, **IV** 33, 184
Express Foods Inc, **I** 247–48
Express Newspapers plc, **IV** 687
Extel Corp., **II** 142; **III** 269–70
Extel Financial Ltd., **IV** 687
Extendicare Health Services, Inc., III 81; **6 181–83**
Extracorporeal Medical Specialties, **III** 36
Exxon Corporation, I 16–17, 360, 364; **II** 16, 62, 431, 451; **IV** 171, 363, 365, 403, 406, **426–30**, 431–33, 437–38, 454, 466, 506, 508, 512, 515, 522, 537–39, 554; **V** 605; **7 169–73 (upd.)**, 230, 538, 559; **9** 440–41; **11** 353; **14** 24–25, 291, 494; **12** 348
Eyeful Home Co., **III** 758

Eyelab, **II** 560; **12** 411
EZ Paintr Corporation, **9** 374
EZPor Corporation, **12** 377

F. & F. Koenigkramer Company, **10** 272
F. & J. Heinz, **II** 507
F & M Distributors, **12** 132
F. & M. Schaefer Brewing Co., **I** 253, 291, **III** 137
F & M Scientific Corp., **III** 142; **6** 237
F & R Builders, Inc., **11** 257
F.A. Computer Technologies, Inc., **12** 60
F.A. Ensign Company, **6** 38
F.A.I. Insurances, **III** 729
F.A.O. Schwarz, **I** 548
F&G International Insurance, **III** 397
F. Atkins & Co., **I** 604
F.E. Compton Company, **7** 167
F.F. Dalley Co., **II** 497
F.F. Publishing and Broadsystem Ltd., **IV** 652; **7** 392
F.H. Tomkins Buckle Company Ltd., **11** 525
F. Hoffmann-La Roche & Co. A.G., I 637, 640, **642–44**, 657, 685, 693, 710; **7** 427; **9** 264; **10** 80, 549; **11** 424–25; **14** 406
F.J. Walker Ltd., **I** 438
F.K.I. Babcock, **III** 466
F. Kanematsu & Co., Ltd., **IV** 442
F.L. Industries Inc., **I** 481, 483
F.L. Moseley Co., **III** 142; **6** 237
F.N. Burt Co., **IV** 644
F. Perkins, **III** 651–52
F.S. Smithers, **II** 445
F.W. Dodge Corp., **IV** 636–37
F.W. Means & Company, **11** 337
F.W. Sickles Company, **10** 319
F.W. Williams Holdings, **III** 728
F.W. Woolworth Co., **II** 414; **IV** 344; **V** 225–26; **14** 294. *See also* Woolworth Corporation.
Fabergé, Inc., **II** 590; **III** 48; **8** 168, 344; **11** 90
Fabri-Centers of America, **15** 329
Fabrica de Cemento El Melan, **III** 671
Facchin Foods Co., **I** 457
Facit, **III** 480
Facts on File, Inc., **14** 96–97
Fafnir Bearing Company, **13** 523
FAG Kugelfischer, **11** 84
Fagersta, **II** 366; **IV** 203
Fahr AG, **III** 543
Fahrzeugwerke Eisenach, **I** 138
FAI, **III** 545–46
Failsafe, **14** 35
Fairbanks Morse Co., **I** 158, 434–35; **10** 292; **12** 71
Fairchild Aircraft, Inc., 9 205–08, 460; **11** 278
Fairchild Camera and Instrument Corp., **II** 50, 63; **III** 110, 141, 455, 618; **6** 261–62; **7** 531; **10** 108; **11** 503; **13** 323–24; **14** 14
Fairchild Communications Service, **8** 328
Fairchild Industries, **I** 71, 198; **11** 438; **14** 43; **15** 195
Fairchild Semiconductor Corporation, **II** 44–45, 63–65; **III** 115; **6** 215, 247; **10** 365–66
Fairclough Construction Group plc, I 567–68
Fairey Industries Ltd., **IV** 659
Fairfax, **IV** 650

Fairfield Manufacturing Co., **14** 43
Fairfield Publishing, **13** 165
Fairmont Foods Co., **7** 430; **15** 139
Fairmount Glass Company, **8** 267
Falcon Oil Co., **IV** 396
Falcon Seaboard Inc., **II** 86; **IV** 410; **7** 309
Falconbridge, Ltd., **IV** 165–66
Falconbridge Nickel Mines Ltd., **IV** 111
Falconet Corp., **I** 45
Falls Financial Inc., **13** 223
Falls National Bank of Niagara Falls, **11** 108
Falls Rubber Company, **8** 126
Family Channel. *See* International Family Entertainment Inc.
Family Dollar Stores, Inc., 13 215–17
Family Health Program, **6** 184
Family Life Insurance Co., **II** 425; **13** 341
Family Mart Company, **V** 188
Family Restaurants, Inc., **14** 194
Family Steak Houses of Florida, Inc., **15** 420
Famosa Bakery, **II** 543
Famous Players-Lasky Corp., **I** 451; **II** 154; **6** 161–62
FAN, **13** 370
Fannie Mae. *See* Federal National Mortgage Association.
Fantus Co., **IV** 605
Fanuc Ltd., III 482–83
Far East Airlines, **6** 70
Far East Machinery Co., **III** 581
Far West Restaurants, **I** 547
Faraday National Corporation, **10** 269
Farben. *See* I.G. Farbenindustrie AG.
Farbenfabriken Bayer A.G., **I** 309
Farbwerke Hoechst A.G., **I** 346–47; **IV** 486; **13** 262
Farine Lactée Henri Nestlé, **II** 545
Farinon Corp., **II** 38
Farley Candy Co., **15** 190
Farley Northwest Industries Inc., I 440–41
Farm Credit Bank of St. Louis, **8** 489
Farm Credit Bank of St. Paul, **8** 489–90
Farm Electric Services Ltd., **6** 586
Farm Power Laboratory, **6** 565
Farmers and Mechanics Bank of Georgetown, **13** 439
Farmers and Merchants Bank, **II** 349
Farmers Bank of Delaware, **II** 315–16
Farmers National Bank & Trust Co., **9** 474
Farmers Regional Cooperative, **II** 536
Farmers' Loan and Trust Co., **II** 254; **9** 124
Farmland Foods, Inc., IV 474; **7** 17, **7 174–75**
Farnam Cheshire Lime Co., **III** 763
Farrar, Straus and Giroux Inc., IV 622, 624; **12** 223, 225; **15 158–60**
Fasco Industries, **III** 509; **13** 369
Faserwerke Hüls GmbH., **I** 350
Fashion Bug, **8** 97
Fashion Co., **II** 503; **10** 324
Fasquelle, **IV** 618
Fasson, **IV** 253
Fasuel, **III** 308
Fast Fare, **7** 102
Fastenal Company, 14 185–87
Fata, **IV** 187
Fateco Förlag, **14** 556
Fatum, **III** 308
Faugere et Jutheau, **III** 283
Faulkner, Dawkins & Sullivan, **II** 450
Fawcett Books, **13** 429

Fayette Tubular Products, **7** 116–17
Fayva, **13** 359–61
Fazoli's, **13** 321
FB&T Corporation, **14** 154
FBC. *See* First Boston Corp.
FBO. *See* Film Booking Office of America.
FCBC, **IV** 174
FCC. *See* Federal Communications Commission.
FCC National Bank, **II** 286
FDIC. *See* Federal Deposit Insurance Corp.
Fearn International, **II** 525; **13** 293
Fechheimer Bros. Co., **III** 215
Federal Barge Lines, **6** 487
Federal Bearing and Bushing, **I** 158–59
Federal Bicycle Corporation of America, **11** 3
Federal Coca-Cola Bottling Co., **10** 222
Federal Communications Commission, **6** 164–65; **9** 321
Federal Deposit Insurance Corp., **II** 261–62, 285, 337; **12** 30, 79
Federal Electric, **I** 463; **III** 653
Federal Express Corporation, **II** 620; **V** **451–53**; **6** 345–46, 385–86, 389; **12** 180, 192; **13** 19; **14** 517
Federal Home Life Insurance Co., **III** 263; **IV** 623
Federal Home Loan Bank, **II** 182
Federal Insurance Co., **III** 220–21; **14** 108–109
Federal Lead Co., **IV** 32
Federal Light and Traction Company, **6** 561–62
Federal Mining and Smelting Co., **IV** 32
Federal National Mortgage Association, **II** **410–11**
Federal Pacific Electric, **II** 121; **9** 440
Federal Packaging and Partition Co., **8** 476
Federal Paper Board Company, Inc., **I** 524; **8** **173–75**; **15** 229
Federal Paper Mills, **IV** 248
Federal Signal Corp., **10** **295–97**
Federal Steel Co., **II** 330; **IV** 572; **7** 549
Federal Trade Commission, **6** 260; **9** 370
Federal Yeast Corp., **IV** 410
Federal-Mogul Corporation, **I** **158–60**; **III** 596; **10** **292–94 (upd.)**
Federale Mynbou, **IV** 90–93
Federated Department Stores Inc., **IV** 703; **V** 25–28; **9** 209–12; **10** 282; **11** 349; **12** 37, 523; **13** 43, 260; **15** 88
Federated Development Company, **8** 349
Federated Metals Corp., **IV** 32
Federated Publications, **IV** 612; **7** 191
Federated Timbers, **I** 422
Fedmart, **V** 162
Feikes & Sohn KG, **IV** 325
Feinblech-Contiglühe, **IV** 103
Felco. *See* Farmers Regional Cooperative.
Feldmühle Kyocera Elektronische Bauelemente GmbH, **II** 50
Feldmühle Nobel AG, **II** 51; **III** **692–95**; **IV** 142, 325, 337
Felten & Guilleaume, **IV** 25
Femtech, **8** 513
Fendel Schiffahrts-Aktiengesellschaft, **6** 426
Fenestra Inc., **IV** 136
Fenner & Beane, **II** 424
Fenwal Laboratories, **I** 627; **10** 141
Ferguson Machine Co., **8** 135
Ferguson Radio Corp., **I** 531–32
Ferienreise GmbH., **II** 164

Fermentaciones Mexicanas, **III** 43
Fernando Roqué, **6** 404
Ferngas, **IV** 486
Ferranti Ltd., **II** 81; **6** 240
Ferrari S.p.A., **I** 162; **11** 103; **13** **218–20**
Ferrier Hodgson, **10** 170
Ferro Corporation, **III** 536; **8** **176–79**; **9** 10
Ferroxcube Corp. of America, **13** 397
Ferruzzi, **I** 369
Ferruzzi Agricola Finanziario, **7** 81–83
Fesca, **III** 417–18
Fetzer Vineyards, **10** 182
FHP International Corporation, **6** **184–86**
Fiat S.p.A., **I** 154, 157, **161–63**, 459–60, 466, 479; **II** 280; **III** 206, 543, 591; **IV** 420; **9** 10; **11** **102–04 (upd.)**, 139; **13** 17, 27–29, 218–20
Fiber Chemical Corporation, **7** 308
Fiberglas Canada, **III** 722
Fibermux, **10** 19
Fibre Containers, **IV** 249
Fibreboard Corp., **IV** 304; **12** 318; **14** 110
FibreChem, Inc., **8** 347
Fibro Tambor, S.A. de C.V., **8** 476
Fichtel & Sachs AG, **III** 566; **14** 328
Fidata Corp., **II** 317
Fidelco Capital Group, **10** 420
Fidelity and Casualty Co. of New York, **III** 242
Fidelity and Guaranty Life Insurance Co., **III** 396–97
Fidelity Federal Savings and Loan, **II** 420
Fidelity Fire Insurance Co., **III** 240
Fidelity Insurance of Canada, **III** 396–97
Fidelity Investments Inc., **II** **412–13**; **III** 588; **8** 194; **9** 239; **14** **188–90 (upd.)**. *See also* FMR Corp.
Fidelity Life Association, **III** 269
Fidelity Mutual Insurance Co., **III** 231
Fidelity National Life Insurance Co., **III** 191
Fidelity Oil Group, **7** 324
Fidelity Title and Trust Co., **II** 315
Fidelity Trust Co., **II** 230
Fidelity Union Life Insurance Co., **III** 185
Fidelity-Phenix Fire Insurance Co., **III** 240–42
Field Enterprises, Inc., **IV** 672; **12** 554
Field Oy, **10** 113
Fieldcrest Cannon, Inc., **8** **32–33**; **9** **213–17**
Fieldstone Cabinetry, **III** 571
Fifteen Oil, **I** 526
Fifth Generation Systems Inc., **10** 509
Fifth Third Bancorp, **II** 291; **9** 475; **11** 466; **13** **221–23**
Figgie International Inc., **7** **176–78**
Figi's Inc., **9** 218, 220
Filene's, **V** 132, 134
Filergie S.A., **15** 355
Filiz Lastex, S.A., **15** 386
Filles S.A. de C.V., **7** 115
Film Booking Office of America, **II** 88
Filtrol Corp., **IV** 123
Fin. Comit SpA, **II** 192
FINA, Inc., **7** **179–81**
Financial Computer Services, Inc., **11** 111
Financial Corp. of Indonesia, **II** 257
Financial Data Services, Inc., **11** 111
Financial Investment Corp. of Asia, **III** 197

Financial Network Marketing Company, **11** 482
Financial News Ltd., **IV** 658
Financial Security Assurance, **III** 765
Financial Services Corp., **III** 306–07
Financial Services Corporation of Michigan, **11** 163
Financial Systems, Inc., **11** 111
Financière Crédit Suisse-First Boston, **II** 268, 402–04
Financiere de Suez, **II** 295
Financière Saint Dominique, **9** 151–52
FinansSkandic A.B., **II** 352–53
Finast. *See* First National Supermarkets, Inc.
Fincantieri, **I** 466–67
Findus, **II** 547
Fine Art Developments Ltd., **15** 340
Fine Fare, **II** 465, 609, 628–29
Finelettrica, **I** 465–66
Finevest Services Inc., **15** 526
Fingerhut Companies, Inc., **I** 613; **V** 148; **9** **218–20**; **15** 401
Fininvest Group, **IV** 587–88
Finland Wood Co., **IV** 275
Finlay Forest Industries, **IV** 297
Finmare, **I** 465, 467
Finmeccanica, **II** 86; **13** 28
Finnair Oy, **I** 120; **6** **87–89**
Finnforest Oy, **IV** 316
Finnigan Corporation, **11** 513
Finnish Cable Works, **II** 69
Finnish Fiberboard Ltd., **IV** 302
Oy Finnish Peroxides Ab, **IV** 300
Finnish Rubber Works, **II** 69
Oy Finnlines Ltd., **IV** 276
Finsa, **II** 196
Finservizi SpA, **II** 192
Finsider, **I** 465–66; **IV** 125
Fire Association of Philadelphia, **III** 342–43
Fireman's Fund Insurance Company, **I** 418; **II** 398, 457; **III** 214, **250–52**, 263; **10** 62
Firemen's Insurance Co. of Newark, **III** 241–42
Firestone Tire and Rubber Co., **III** 440, 697; **V** 234–35; **8** 80; **9** 247; **15** 355
The First, **10** 340
First Acadiana National Bank, **11** 107
First American Bank Corporation, **8** 188
First American National Bank-Eastern, **11** 111
First and Merchants, **10** 426
First Bancard, Inc., **11** 106
First BanCorporation, **13** 467
First Bank and Trust of Mechanicsburg, **II** 342
First Bank of the United States, **II** 213, 253
First Bank System Inc., **11** 130; **12** **164–66**; **13** 347–48
First Boston Corp., **II** 208, 257, 267–69, 402–04, 406–07, 426, 434, 441; **9** 378, 386; **12** 439; **13** 152, 342. *See also* CS First Boston Inc.
First Brands Corporation, **8** **180–82**
First Capital Financial, **8** 229
First Chicago Corporation, **II** **284–87**
First City Bank of Rosemead, **II** 348
First Colony Farms, **II** 584
First Colony Life Insurance, **I** 334–35; **10** 290

First Commerce Bancshares, Inc., 15 161–63
First Commerce Corporation, 11 105–07
First Commercial Savings and Loan, 10 340
First Consumers National Bank, 10 491
First Dallas, Ltd., II 415
First Data Corp., 10 63
First Data Management Company of Oklahoma City, 11 112
First Delaware Life Insurance Co., III 254
First Deposit Corp., III 218–19
First Empire State Corporation, 11 108–10
First Engine and Boiler Insurance Co. Ltd., III 406
First Executive Corporation, III 253–55
First Federal Savings & Loan Assoc., IV 343; 9 173
First Federal Savings and Loan Association of Crisp County, 10 92
First Federal Savings and Loan Association of Hamburg, 10 91
First Federal Savings and Loan Association of Fort Myers, 9 476
First Federal Savings and Loan Association of Kalamazoo, 9 482
First Federal Savings Bank of Brunswick, 10 92
First Fidelity Bank, N.A., New Jersey, 9 221–23
First Fidelity Bank of Rockville, 13 440
First Financial Management Corporation, 11 111–13
First Florida Banks, 9 59
First Hawaiian, Inc., 11 114–16
First Health, III 373
FIRST HEALTH Strategies, 11 113
First Healthcare, 14 242
First Heights, fsa, 8 437
First Hospital Corp., 15 122
First Industrial Corp., II 41
First Insurance Co. of Hawaii, III 191, 242
First International Trust, IV 91
First Interstate Bancorp, II 228, 288–90; 8 295; 9 334
First Investment Advisors, 11 106
First Investors Management Corp., 11 106
First Jersey National Bank, II 334
First Liberty Financial Corporation, 11 457
First Line Insurance Services, Inc., 8 436
First Madison Bank, 14 192
First Mid America, II 445
First Mississippi Corporation, 8 183–86
First Mississippi National, 14 41
First National Bank, 10 298; 13 467
First National Bank (Revere), II 208
First National Bank and Trust Company of Kalamazoo, 8 187–88
First National Bank and Trust of Oklahoma City, II 289
First National Bank in Albuquerque, 11 119
First National Bank of Akron, 9 475
First National Bank of Allentown, 11 296
First National Bank of Azusa, II 382
First National Bank of Boston, II 207–08, 402; 12 310; 13 446
First National Bank of Carrollton, 9 475
First National Bank of Chicago, II 242, 257, 284–87; III 96–97; IV 135–36
First National Bank of Commerce, 11 106

First National Bank of Harrington, Delaware. *See* J.C. Penny National Bank.
First National Bank of Hartford, 13 466
First National Bank of Hawaii, 11 114
First National Bank of Highland, 11 109
The First National Bank of Lafayette, 11 107
The First National Bank of Lake Charles, 11 107
First National Bank of Lake City, II 336; 10 425
First National Bank of Mexico, New York, II 231
First National Bank of New York, II 254, 330
First National Bank of Raleigh, II 336
First National Bank of Salt Lake, 11 118
First National Bank of Seattle, 8 469–70
First National Bank of York, II 317
First National Boston Corp., II 208
First National Casualty Co., III 203
First National City Bank, 9 124
First National City Bank of New York, II 254; 9 124
First National City Corp., III 220–21
First National Insurance Co., III 352
First National Life Insurance Co., III 218
First National Supermarkets, Inc., II 641–42; 9 452
First Nationwide Bank, 8 30; 14 191–93
First Nationwide Financial Corp., I 167; 11 139
First New England Bankshares Corp., 13 467
First Nitrogen, Inc., 8 184
First of America Bank Corporation, 8 187–89
First of America Bank-Monroe, 9 476
First of Boston, II 402–03
First Penn-Pacific Life Insurance Co., III 276
First Pick Stores, 12 458
First Railroad and Banking Company, 11 111
First Republic Bank of Texas, II 336
First Republic Corp., III 383; 14 483
First RepublicBank Corporation, II 337; 10 425–26
First Savings and Loan, 10 339
First Seattle Dexter Horton National Bank, 8 470
First Security Corporation, 11 117–19
First Signature Bank and Trust Co., III 268
1st State Bank & Trust, 9 474
First SunAmerican Life Insurance Company, 11 482
First Team Sports, Inc., 15 396–97
First Tennessee National Corporation, 11 120–21
First Texas Pharmaceuticals, I 678
First Trust and Savings Bank, II 284
First Union Corporation, 10 298–300
First Union Trust and Savings Bank, II 284–85; 11 126
First United Financial Services Inc., II 286
First USA, Inc., 11 122–24
First Virginia Banks, Inc., 11 125–26
First Westchester National Bank of New Rochelle, II 236
First Western Bank and Trust Co., II 289
Firstamerica Bancorporation, II 288–89
Firstar Corporation, 11 127–29

FirstBancorp., 13 467
FirstMiss, Inc., 8 185
Fischbach & Moore, III 535
Fischbach Corp., III 198; 8 536–37
FISCOT, 10 337
Fiserv Inc., 11 130–32
Fisher & Company, 9 16
Fisher Body Company, I 171; 10 325
Fisher Broadcasting Co., 15 164
Fisher Companies, Inc., 15 164–66
Fisher Controls International, Inc., 13 224–26; 15 405, 407
Fisher Corp., II 92
Fisher Foods, Inc., II 602; 9 451, 452; 13 237
Fisher Marine, III 444
Fisher Nut, 14 275
Fisher Scientific Group, III 511–12
Fisher-Camuto Corp., 14 441
Fisher-Price Inc., II 559–60; 12 167–69, 410–11; 13 317
Fishers Agricultural Holdings, II 466
Fishers Nutrition, II 466
Fishers Seed and Grain, II 466
Fishery Department of Tamura Kisen Co., II 552
Fisk Telephone Systems, 6 313
Fisons plc, 9 224–27
Fitch Lovell PLC, 13 103
Fitchburg Daily News Co., IV 581
Fitchell and Sachs, III 495
Fitel, III 491
Fitzwilton Public Limited Company, 12 529
FL Industries Holdings, Inc., 11 516
Flachglass A.G., II 474
Flagstar Companies, Inc., 10 301–03
Flanagan McAdam Resources Inc., IV 76
Flapdoodles, 15 291
Flatbush Gas Co., 6 455–56
Fleer Corporation, 10 402; 13 519; 15 167–69
Fleet Call, Inc., 10 431–32
Fleet Financial Group, Inc., IV 687; 9 228–30; 12 31; 13 468
Fleetway, 7 244
Fleetwood Enterprises, Inc., III 484–85; 13 155
Fleischmann Co., II 544; 7 367
Fleischmann Malting Co., I 420–21; 11 22
Fleming Companies, Inc., II 624–25, 671; 7 450; 12 107, 125; 13 335–37
Fleming Machine Co., III 435
Fleming-Wilson Co., II 624
Fletcher Challenge Ltd., III 687; IV 250, 278–80
Fleuve Noir, IV 614
Flex-O-Lite, 14 325
Flexi-Van Corp., II 492
Flexible Packaging, I 605
Flexsteel Industries Inc., 15 170–72
Flextronics Inc., 12 451
FLGI Holding Company, 10 321
Flick Industrial Group, II 280, 283; III 692–95
Flight Transportation Co., II 408
FlightSafety International, Inc., 9 231–33
Flint and Walling Water Systems, III 570
Flint Eaton & Co., I 627
Flint Ink Corporation, 13 227–29
Floral City Furniture Company, 14 302–03
Flori Roberts, Inc., 11 208
Florida Cypress Gardens, Inc., IV 623

Florida East Coast Railway Company, **8** 486–87; **12** 278
Florida Frozen Foods, **13** 244
Florida Gas Co., **15** 129
Florida Gas Transmission Company, **6** 578
Florida National Banks of Florida, Inc., **II** 252
Florida Presbyterian College, **9** 187
Florida Progress Corp., V 621–22
Florida Steel Corp., **14** 156
Florida Telephone Company, **6** 323
FloridaGulf Airlines, **11** 300
Florimex Verwaltungsgesellschaft mbH, **12** 109
Florsheim Shoe Company, **III** 528–29; **9** 135, **234–36**; **12** 308
Flow Laboratories, **14** 98
Flower Gate, **I** 266
Flower Time, Inc., **12** 179, 200
Flowers Industries, Inc., 12 170–71
Floyd West & Co., **6** 290
Fluf N'Stuf, Inc., **12** 425
Fluke Corporation, 15 173–75
Fluor Corporation, I 569–71, 586; **III** 248; **IV** 171, 533, 535, 576; **6** 148–49; **8 190–93 (upd.)**; **12** 244
Flushing National Bank, **II** 230
Flying Tiger Line, **V** 452; **6** 388
Flymo, **III** 478, 480
FMC Corp., I 442–44, 679; **II** 513; **11 133–35 (upd.)**; **14** 457
FMR Corp., II 412; **8 194–96**; **14** 188
FN Life Insurance Co., **III** 192
FN Manufacturing Co., **12** 71
FNC Comercio, **III** 221
FNCB. *See* First National City Bank of New York.
FNMA. *See* Federal National Mortgage Association.
Focke Wulf, **III** 641
Fodens Ltd., **I** 186
Fodor's Travel Guides, **13** 429
Fokker. *See* Koninklijke Nederlandse Vliegtuigenfabriek Fokker.
Fokker Aircraft Corporation of America, **9** 16
Fokker-VFW, **I** 41–42; **12** 191
Folgers, **III** 52
Folland Aircraft, **I** 50; **III** 508
Follett Corporation, 12 172–74
Fondiaria Group, **III** 351
Fonditalia Management, **III** 347
Font & Vaamonde, **6** 27
Font Vella, **II** 474
FONTAC, **II** 73
Fontana Asphalt, **III** 674
Food City, **II** 649–50
Food Giant, **II** 670
Food Investments Ltd., **II** 465
Food Lion, Inc., II 626–27; **7** 450; **15 176–78 (upd.)**, 270
Food Machinery Corp. *See* FMC Corp.
Food Marketing Corp., **II** 668
Food Town Inc., **II** 626–27
Food-4-Less, **II** 624
Foodbrands America, Inc. *See* Doskocil Companies, Inc.
FoodLand Distributors, **II** 625, 645, 682
Foodmaker, Inc., II 562; **13** 152, 426; **14 194–96**
Foodstuffs, **9** 144
Foodtown, **II** 626; **V** 35; **15** 177
Foodways National, Inc., **12** 531; **13** 383
Foot Locker, **V** 226; **14** 293–95

Foote Cone & Belding Communications Inc., I 12–15, 28, 34; **11** 51; **13** 517
Foote Mineral Company, **7** 386–87
Footquarters, **14** 293, 295
Forages et Exploitations Pétrolières, **III** 617
Ford Motor Co., **I** 10, 14, 20–21, 136, 142, 145, 152, 154–55, 162–63, **164–68**, 172, 183, 186, 201, 203–04, 280, 297, 337, 354, 423, 478, 484, 540, 693; **II** 7–8, 33, 60, 86, 143, 415; **III** 58, 259, 283, 439, 452, 495, 515, 555, 568, 591, 603, 637–38, 651, 725; **IV** 187, 597, 722; **6** 27, 51; **7** 377, 461, 520–21; **8** 70, 74–75, 117, 372–73, 375, 505–06; **9** 94, 118, 126, 190, 283–84, 325, 341–43; **10** 32, 241, 260, 264–65, 279–80, 290, 353, 407, 430, 460, 465; **11** 53–54, 103–04, **136–40 (upd.)**, 263, 326, 339, 350, 528–29; **12** 68, 91, 294, 311; **13** 28, 219, 285, 287, 345, 555; **14** 191–92; **15** 91, 171, 513, 515
Ford Transport Co., **I** 112; **6** 103
Fordyce Lumber Co., **IV** 281; **9** 259
Foreman State Banks, **II** 285
Foremost Dairy of California, **I** 496–97
Foremost Warehouse Corp., **14** 372
Foremost-McKesson Inc., **I** 496–97, **III** 10; **11** 211; **12** 332
Forenza, **V** 116
Forest Laboratories, Inc., 11 141–43
Forest Products, **III** 645
Forethought Group, Inc., **10** 350
Forex Chemical Corp., **I** 341; **14** 216
Forex-Neptune, **III** 617
Forges d'Eich–Le Gallais, Metz et Cie, **IV** 24
Forges de la Providence, **IV** 52
Formica Corporation, **10** 269; **13 230–32**
Forming Technology Co., **III** 569
Formosa Plastics Corporation, **11** 159; **14 197–99**
Formosa Springs, **I** 269; **12** 337
Formularios y Procedimientos Moore, **IV** 645
Formule 1, **13** 364
Forney Fiber Company, **8** 475
Forsakrings A.B. Volvia, **I** 20
Forstmann, Little & Co., **I** 446, 483; **II** 478, 544; **III** 56; **7** 206; **10** 321; **12** 344, 562; **14** 166
Fort Associates, **I** 418
Fort Bend Utilities Company, **12** 269
Fort Dummer Mills, **III** 213
Fort Howard Corporation, **8 197–99**; **15** 305
Fort Mill Manufacturing Co., **V** 378
Fort William Power Co., **IV** 246
Forte Plc, **15** 46
Forte's Holdings Ltd., **III** 104–05
Fortis, Inc., 15 179–82
Fortuna Coffee Co., **I** 451
Fortune Enterprises, **12** 60
Forum Hotels, **I** 248
Foseco plc, **IV** 383
Foss Maritime Co., **9** 509, 511
Foster & Kleiser, **7** 335; **14** 331
Foster & Marshall, **II** 398
Foster and Braithwaite, **III** 697
Foster Grant, **I** 670; **II** 595–96; **12** 214
Foster Management Co., **11** 366–67
Foster Medical Corp., **III** 16; **11** 282
Foster Sand & Gravel, **14** 112

Foster Wheeler Corporation, **I** 82; **6 145–47**
Foster's Brewing Group Ltd., 7 182–84
Fotomat Corp., **III** 549
Foundation Computer Systems, Inc., **13** 201
Foundation Health Corporation, **11** 174; **12 175–77**
Founders Equity Inc., **14** 235
Founders of American Investment Corp., **15** 247
Four Seasons Hotels Inc., II 531; **9 237–38**
Four Seasons Nursing Centers, Inc., **6** 188
Four Winns, **III** 600
Four-Phase Systems, Inc., **II** 61; **11** 327
Fournier Furniture, Inc., **12** 301
Fourth Financial Corporation, **11 144–46**; **15** 60
Foussard Associates, **I** 333
Fowler Road Construction Proprietary, **III** 672
Fowler-Waring Cables Co., **III** 162
Fox & Jacobs, **8** 87
Fox Broadcasting Co., **II** 156; **IV** 608, 652; **7** 391–92; **9** 428
Fox Film Corp., **II** 146–47, 154–55, 169
Fox, Fowler & Co., **II** 307
Fox Glacier Mints Ltd., **II** 569
Fox Grocery Co., **II** 682
Fox, Inc., **12** 359
Fox Paper Company, **8** 102
Fox Photo, **III** 475; **7** 161
Foxboro Company, **13 233–35**
Foxmeyer Corporation, **V** 152–53
FP&L. *See* Florida Power & Light Co.
FPL Group, Inc., V 623–25
Fram Corp., **I** 142, 567
Framatome, **9** 10
Framingham Electric Company, **12** 45
France Cables et Radio, **6** 303
France 5, **6** 374
France Quick, **12** 152
France Telecom Group, **V 291–93**, 471; **9** 32; **14** 489
France-Loisirs, **IV** 615–16, 619
Franco-American Food Co., **I** 428; **II** 479
Frank & Hirsch, **III** 608
Frank & Schulte GmbH, **8** 496
Frank Dry Goods Company, **9** 121
Frank H. Nott Inc., **14** 156
Frank J. Rooney, Inc., **8** 87
Frank's Nursery & Crafts, Inc., 12 178–79, 198–200
Fränkel & Selz, **II** 239
Frankenberry, Laughlin & Constable, **9** 393
Frankford-Quaker Grocery Co., **II** 625
Frankfort Oil Co., **I** 285
Frankfurter Allgemeine Versicherungs-AG, **III** 184
Franklin Assurances, **III** 211
Franklin Baker's Coconut, **II** 531
Franklin Container Corp., **IV** 312
Franklin Corp., **14** 130
Franklin Life Insurance Co., **III** 242–43; **V** 397
Franklin Mint, **IV** 676; **9** 428
Franklin National Bank, **9** 536
Franklin Quest Co., 11 147–49
Franklin Rayon Yarn Dyeing Corp., **I** 529
Franklin Research & Development, **11** 41
Franklin Resources, Inc., 9 239–40
Franklin Steamship Corp., **8** 346
Franks Chemical Products Inc., **I** 405

Frans Maas Beheer BV, **14** 568
Franz and Frieder Burda, **IV** 661
Franz Foods, Inc., **II** 584
Franz Ströher AG, **III** 68–69
Fraser & Chalmers, **13** 16
Fraser Cos. Ltd., **IV** 165
Fratelli Manzoli, **IV** 585
Fratelli Treves, **IV** 585
Fraternal Assurance Society of America, **III** 274
Fray Data International, **14** 319
Fre Kote Inc., **I** 321
Frears, **II** 543
Fred Harvey Hotels, **I** 417
Fred Meyer, Inc., **II** 669; **V 54–56**
Fred S. James and Co., **III** 280; **I** 537
Fred Sammons Co., **9** 72
Fred Sands Realtors, **IV** 727
Fred Schmid Appliance & T.V. Co., Inc., **10** 305
The Fred W. Albrecht Grocery Co., **13 236–38**
Fredelle, **14** 295
Frederick Miller Brewing Co., **I** 269
Freeborn Farms, **13** 244
Freedom Technology, **11** 486
Freedom-Valvoline Oil Co., **IV** 373
Freemans, **V** 177
Freeport-McMoRan Inc., **IV 81–84**; **7 185–89 (upd.)**
Freezer House, **II** 398; **10** 62
Freezer Shirt Corporation, **8** 406
Freiberger Papierfabrik, **IV** 323
Freightliner, **I** 150; **6** 413
FreightMaster, **III** 498
Frejlack Ice Cream Co., **II** 646; **7** 317
Fremlin Breweries, **I** 294
Fremont Butter and Egg Co., **II** 467
Fremont Canning Company, **7** 196
Fremont Savings Bank, **9** 474–75
French and Richards & Co., **I** 692
French Bank of California, **II** 233
French Kier, **I** 568
French Petrofina, **IV** 497
Frequency Sources Inc., **9** 324
Freshbake Foods Group PLC, **II** 481; **7** 68
Fretter, Inc., **9** 65; **10** 9–10, **304–06**, 502
Frialco, **IV** 165
Frictiontech Inc., **11** 84
Friden, Inc., **II** 10
Fridy-Gauker & Fridy, **I** 313; **10** 154
Fried. Krupp GmbH, **II** 257; **IV** 60, **85–89**, 104, 128, 203, 206, 222, 234
Friedrich Flick Industrial Corp., **I** 548; **III** 692
Friedrich Roessler Söhne, **IV** 69
Friedrichshütte, **III** 694
Friendly Hotels PLC, **14** 107
Friendly Ice Cream Corp., **II** 511–12; **15** 221
Friesch-Groningsche Hypotheekbank, **III** 179
Frigidaire Company, **III** 572; **13** 564
Frigo, **II** 587
Friguia, **IV** 165
Frisia Group, **IV** 197–98
Frito-Lay, **I** 219, 278–79; **III** 136
Fritz Companies, Inc., **12 180–82**
Fritz Thyssen Stiftung, **IV** 222
Fritz W. Glitsch and Sons, Inc. *See* Glitsch International, Inc.
Fritzsche Dodge and Ollcott, **I** 307
Froebel-Kan, **IV** 679
Fromageries Bel, **II** 518; **6** 47

Frome Broken Hill Co., **IV** 59
Fromm & Sichel, **I** 285
Frontec, **13** 132
Frontier Airlines Inc., **I** 97–98, 103, 118, 124, 129–30; **6** 129; **11** 298
Frontier Expeditors, Inc., **12** 363
Frontier Oil Co., **IV** 373
Fru-Con Corp., **I** 561
Fruehauf Corp., **I 169–70**, 480; **II** 425; **III** 652; **7** 259–60, 513–14; **13** 341
Fruit of the Loom, Inc., **8 200–02**
Fry's Diecastings, **III** 681
Fry's Food Stores, **12** 112
Fry's Metal Foundries, **III** 681
Frye Copy Systems, **6** 599
F3 Software Corp., **15** 474
Fuel Pipeline Transportation Ltd., **6** 123–24
Fuel Resources Development Co., **6** 558–59
Fuel Resources Inc., **6** 457
FuelMaker Corporation, **6** 569
Fuji Bank, Ltd., **I** 494; **II 291–93**, 360–61, 391, 422, 459, 554; **III** 405, 408–09
Fuji Electric Co., Ltd., **II 22–23**, 98, 103; **III** 139; **13** 356
Fuji Heavy Industries, **I** 207; **III** 581; **9** 294; **12** 400; **13** 499–501
Fuji Iron & Steel Co., Ltd., **I** 493; **II** 300; **IV** 130, 157, 212
Fuji Kaolin Co., **III** 691
Fuji Paper, **IV** 320
Fuji Photo Film Co., Ltd., **III** 172, 476, **486–89**, 549–50; **6** 289; **7** 162
Fuji Seito, **I** 511
Fuji Television, **7** 249; **9** 29
Fuji Xerox, **III** 172. *See also* Xerox Corporation.
Fuji Yoshiten Co., **IV** 292
Fujian Hualong Carburetor, **13** 555
Fujikoshi Kozai, **III** 595
Fujimoto Bill Broker & Securities Co., **II** 405
Fujisawa Pharmaceutical Co., **I 635–36**; **III** 47; **8** 343
Fujita Airways, **6** 70
Fujitsu Limited, **I** 455, 541; **II** 22–23, 56, 68, 73, 274; **III** 109–11, 130, **139–41**, 164, 482; **V** 339; **6** 217, 240–42; **10** 238; **11** 308, 542; **13** 482; **14** 13–15, 512
Fujitsu-ICL Systems Inc., **11 150–51**
Fujiyi Confectionery Co., **II** 569
Fukuin Electric Works, Ltd., **III** 604
Fukuin Shokai Denki Seisakusho, **III** 604
Fukuju Fire, **III** 384
Fukuoka Paper Co., Ltd., **IV** 285
Fukutake Publishing Co., Ltd., **13** 91, 93
Ful-O-Pep, **10** 250
Fulcrum Communications, **10** 19
Fulham Brothers, **13** 244
Fuller Brush Co., **II** 572; **15** 475–76, 78
Fuller Co., **6** 395–96
Fuller Manufacturing Company **I** 154. *See also* H.B. Fuller Company.
Fulton Bank, **14** 40
Fulton Co., **III** 569
Fulton Insurance Co., **III** 463
Fulton Manufacturing Co., **11** 535
Fulton Municipal Gas Company, **6** 455
Fulton Performance Products, Inc., **11** 535
Funai-Amstrad, **III** 113
Fund American Cos., **III** 251–52

Funk & Wagnalls, **IV** 605
Funk Software Inc., **6** 255
Fuqua Industries Inc., **I 445–47**, 452; **8** 545; **12** 251; **14** 86
Furalco, **IV** 15
The Furniture Center, Inc., **14** 236
Furr's Inc., **II** 601
Furukawa Electric Co., Ltd., **II** 22; **III** 139, **490–92**; **IV** 15, 26, 153
Fusi Denki, **II** 98
Fuso Marine Insurance Co., **III** 367
Fuso Metal Industries, **IV** 212
Futagi Co., Ltd., **V** 96
Future Now, Inc., **6** 245; **12 183–85**
Fuyo Group, **II** 274, 291–93, 391–92, 554
FWD Corporation, **7** 513

G & H Products, **III** 419
G.A.F., **I 337–40**, 524–25, 549; **II** 378; **III** 440; **8** 180; **9** 518
G.A. Serlachius Oy, **IV** 314–15
G&G Shops, Inc., **8** 425–26
G&L Albu, **IV** 90
G. and T. Earle, **III** 669, 670
G&R Pasta Co., Inc., **II** 512
G.B. Lewis Company, **8** 359
G.C.E. International Inc., **III** 96–97
G.C. Murphy Company, **9** 21
G.C. Smith, **I** 423
G.D. Searle & Company, **I** 365–66, **686–89**; **III** 47, 53; **8** 343, 398, 434; **9** 356–57; **10** 54; **12 186–89 (upd.)**
G.H. Bass & Co., **15** 406
G.H. Rinck, NV, **V** 49
G.H. Wetterau & Sons Grocery Co., **II** 681
G. Heileman Brewing Co., **I 253–55**, 270; **10** 169–70; **12** 338
G.I.E. Airbus Industrie, **I 41–43**, 49–52, 55–56, 70, 72, 74–76, 107, 111, 116, 121; **9** 458, 460; **11** 279, 363; **12 190–92 (upd.)**
G.L. Kelty & Co., **13** 168
G.L. Rexroth GmbH, **III** 566
G.P. Group, **12** 358
G.P. Putnam's Sons, **II** 144
G. R. Kinney Co., Inc., **V** 226, 352; **14** 293
G. Riedel Kälte- und Klimatechnik, **III** 420
G.S. Blodgett Corporation, **15 183–85**
G.S. Capital Partners II L.P. *See* Goldman, Sachs & Company.
G. Washington Coffee Refining Co., **I** 622
Gabelli Group, **13** 561
Gable House Properties, **II** 141
Gabriel Industries, **II** 532
GAC Corp., **II** 182; **III** 592
GAC Holdings L.P., **7** 204
Gagliardi Brothers, **13** 383
Gail Borden, Jr., and Co., **II** 470
Gain Technology, Inc., **10** 505
Gaines Dog Food Co., **II** 531
Gainsborough Craftsmen Ltd., **II** 569
Gair Paper Co., **I** 599
Galaxy Energies Inc., **11** 28
Gale Research Inc., **8** 526
Galen Health Care, **15** 112
Galen Laboratories, **13** 160
Galeries Lafayette S.A., **V 57–59**
Galesburg Coulter Disc Co., **III** 439–40
Gallaher Limited, **IV** 260; **V 398–400**
Gallatin Bank, **II** 312
Galletas, **II** 543
Gallimard, **IV** 618

Gallo. *See* E & J Gallo.
Galor, **I** 676
GALP, **IV** 505
Galvanizing Co., **IV** 159
Galveston *Daily News*, **10** 3
Galvin Manufacturing Corp., **II** 60; **11** 326
Gamble-Skogmo, **13** 169
Gambro Engstrom AB, **13** 159–61, 327–28
Gamesa, **II** 544
GAMI. *See* Great American Management and Investment, Inc.
Gamlestaden, **9** 381–82
Gamlestadens Fabriker, **III** 622
Gang-Nail Systems, **III** 735
Gannett Co., Inc., III 159; **IV 612–13**, 629–30; **7 190–92 (upd.)**; **9** 3
Gap, Inc., V 60–62; **9** 142, 360; **11** 499
Garden Botanika, **11** 41
Garden State BancShares, Inc., **14** 472
Garden State Life Insurance Company, **10** 312
Gardenia, **II** 587
Gardner & Harvey Container Corporation, **8** 267
Gardner Advertising. *See* Wells Rich Green BDDP.
Gardner Cryogenics, **13** 140
Gardner Merchant Ltd., **III** 104; **11** 325
Gardner Rubber Co. *See* Tillotson Corp.
Gardner-Denver Co., **II** 16
Garfield Weston, **13** 51
Garfinckel, Brooks Brothers, Miller & Rhodes, Inc., **15** 94
Garlock, **I** 435
Garnier, **III** 47
A.B. Garnisonen, **II** 352
Garrard Engineering, **II** 82
Garrett, **9** 18; **11** 472
Garrett AiResearch, **9** 18
Garrett Poultry Co., **II** 584; **14** 514
Garrett-Buchanan, **I** 412
Gartrell White, **II** 465
Garuda Indonesia, I 107; **6 90–91**
Gary Industries, **7** 4
Gary-Wheaton Corp., **II** 286
Gas Authority of India Ltd., **IV** 484
Gas Corp. of Queensland, **III** 673
Gas Energy Inc., **6** 457
Gas Group, **III** 673
Gas Light and Coke Company. *See* British Gas plc.
Gas Light Company. *See* Baltimore Gas and Electric Company.
Gas Machinery Co., **I** 412
Gas Service Company, **6** 593; **12** 542
Gas Supply Co., **III** 672
Gas Tech, Inc., **11** 513
Gas Utilities Company, **6** 471
Gaston Paper Stock Co., Inc., **8** 476
Gasunie. *See* N.V. Nederlandse Gasunie.
GATC. *See* General American Tank Car Company.
Gate City Company, **6** 446
The Gates Corporation, 9 241–43
Gates Distribution Company, **12** 60
Gates Radio Co., **II** 37
Gateway Books, **14** 61
Gateway Corporation Ltd., II 612, **628–30**, 638, 642; **10** 442
Gateway Foodmarkets Ltd., **II** 628; **13** 26
Gateway 2000, Inc., 10 307–09; **11** 240
Gatliff Coal Co., **6** 583
GATX, 6 394–96
Gaumont-British, **II** 157–58

Gauntlet Developments, **IV** 724
Gavilan Computer Corp., **III** 124; **6** 221
Gaylord Container Corporation, 8 203–05
Gaylord Entertainment Company, 11 152–54
Gaz de France, IV 425; **V 626–28**
GB Papers, **IV** 290
GB Stores, Inc., **14** 427
GB-Inno-BM, **II** 658; **V** 63
GBL, **IV** 499
GCFC. *See* General Cinema Finance Co.
GDF. *See* Gaz de France.
GE. *See* General Electric Company.
GE Aircraft Engines, 9 244–46
Geant Casino, **12** 152
Gearhart Industries Inc., **III** 499; **15** 467
Gearmatic, **I** 185
Gebrüder Kiessel GmbH, **IV** 197
Gebrüder Sulzer Aktiengesellschaft. *See* Sulzer Brothers Limited.
Gebrüder Volkart, **III** 402
Gebrueder Ahle GmbH, **III** 581
GEC. *See* General Electric Company, PLC.
GECO, **III** 618
Geco Mines Ltd., **IV** 165; **7** 398
Geer Drug, **III** 9–10
GEGC, **III** 434
GEICO Corporation, III 214, 248, 252, 273, 448; **10 310–12**
Gelatin Products Co., **I** 678
Gellatly, Hankey and Sewell, **III** 521
Gelsenberg AG, **IV** 454; **7** 141
Gelsenkirchener Bergwerks AG, **I** 542; **IV** 194
Gem State Utilities, **6** 325, 328
GEMA Gesellschaft für Maschinen- und Apparatebau mbH, **IV** 198
Gemcolite Company, **8** 178
N.V. Gemeenschappelijk Benzit van Aandeelen Philips Gloeilampenfabrieken, **II** 79; **13** 396
Gemey, **III** 47
Gemina, **I** 369
Gemini Computers, **III** 109; **14** 13
Genbel Investments Ltd., **IV** 92
Gencor Ltd., I 423; **IV 90–93**
GenCorp Inc., 8 206–08; **9 247–49**; **13** 381
Gendex Corp., **10** 270, 272
Gene Reid Drilling, **IV** 480
Gene Upton Co., **13** 166
Genentech Inc., I 628, **637–38**; **III** 43; **8 209–11 (upd.)**, 216–17; **10** 78, 80, 142, 199
General Accident plc, III 256–57, 350
General America Corp., **III** 352–53
General American Oil Co., **IV** 523
General American Tank Car Company, **6** 394–95
General Aniline Works Inc., **I** 337–39
General Artificial Silk Co., **IV** 310
General Automotive Parts Corp., **I** 62; **9** 254
General Aviation Corp., **I** 54; **9** 16
General Battery Corp., **I** 440–41
General Binding Corporation, 10 313–14
General Box Corp., **IV** 342
General Brewing Corp, **I** 269
General Bussan Kaisha, Ltd., **IV** 431–32, 555
General Cable Co., **IV** 32; **7** 288; **8** 367
General Casualty Co., **III** 258, 343, 352, 404

General Chemical Co., **I** 414
General Chocolate, **II** 521
General Cigar Co., Inc. *See* Culbro Corporation.
General Cinema Corporation, I 245–46; **II** 478; **IV** 624; **12** 12–13, 226, 356; **14** 87
General Cinema Finance Co., **II** 157–58
General Co. for Life Insurance and Superannuation, **III** 309
General Corporation, **9** 173
General Credit Ltd., **II** 389
General Crude Oil Co., **II** 403; **IV** 287; **15** 228
General DataComm Industries, Inc., 14 200–02
General Diaper Corporation, **14** 550
General Dynamics Corporation, I 55, **57–60**, 62, 71, 74, 77, 482, 525, 527, 597; **6** 79, 229; **7** 520; **8** 51, 92, 315, 338; **9** 206, 323, 417–18, 498; **10 315–18 (upd.)**, 522, 527; **11** 67, 165, 269, 278, 364; **13** 374
General Electric Capital Corp., **15** 257, 282
General Electric Company, I 41, 52, 82–85, 195, 321, 454, 478, 532, 534, 537; **II** 2, 16, 19, 22, 24, **27–31**, 38–39, 41, 56, 58–59, 66, 82, 86, 88–90, 98–99, 116–17, 119–21, 143, 151–52, 330, 349, 431, 604; **III** 16, 110, 122–23, 132, 149, 152, 154, 170–71, 340, 437, 440, 443, 475, 483, 502, 526, 572–73, 614, 655; **IV** 66, 203, 287, 596, 675; **V** 564; **6** 13, 27, 32, 164–66, 240, 261, 266, 288, 452, 517; **7** 123, 125, 161, 456, 520, 532; **8** 157, 262, 332, 377; **9** 14–18, 27, 128, 162, 244, 246, 352–53, 417–18, 439, 514; **10** 16, 241, 536–37; **11** 46, 313, 318, 422, 472, 490; **12** 68, 190, **193–97 (upd.)**, 237, 247, 250, 252, 484, 544–45, 550; **13** 30, 124, 326, 396, 398, 501, 529, 554, 563–64; **15** 196, 228, 285, 380, 403, 467
General Electric Company, PLC, I 411, 423; **II** 3, 12, **24–26**, 31, 58, 72, 80–83; **III** 509; **9** 9–10; **13** 356
General Electric Venture Capital Corporation, **9** 140; **10** 108
General Electronics Co., **III** 160
General Europea S.A., **V** 607
General Export Iron and Metals Company, **15** 116
General Felt Industries Inc., **I** 202; **14** 300
General Film Distributors Ltd., **II** 157
General Finance Corp., **II** 419; **III** 194, 232; **11** 16
General Finance Service Corp., **11** 447
General Fire and Casualty, **I** 449
General Fire Extinguisher Co., **III** 644. *See also* Grinnell Corp.
General Foods Corp., **I** 26, 36, 608, 712; **II** 414, 463, 477, 497, 502, 525, 530–34, 557, 569; **III** 66; **V** 407; **7** 272–74; **10** 323, 551; **12** 167, 372; **13** 293
General Foods, Ltd., **7** 577
General Furniture Leasing Co., **III** 200
General Gas Co., **IV** 432
General Glass Corporation, **13** 40
General Growth Properties, **III** 248
General Health Services, **III** 79
General Host Corporation, 7 372; **12** 178–79, **198–200**, 275; **15** 362
General Instrument Corporation, II 5, 112, 160; **10 319–21**

General Insurance Co. of America, **III** 352–53

General Jones Processed Food, **I** 438

General Learning Corp., **IV** 675; **7** 528

General Life Insurance Co. of America, **III** 353

General Merchandise Company, **V** 91

General Merchandise Services, Inc., **15** 480

General Milk Co., **II** 487; **7** 429

General Milk Products of Canada Ltd., **II** 586

General Mills, Inc., **II** 493, **501–03**, 525, 556, 576, 684; **III** 505; **7** 547; **8** 53–54; **9** 156, 189–90, 291; **10** 177, **322–24 (upd.)**; **11** 15, 497–98; **12** 80, 167–68, 275; **13** 244, 293–94, 408, 516; **15** 189

General Mining and Finance Corp. Ltd., **I** 423; **IV** 90–93, 95

General Mortgage and Credit Corp., **II** 256

General Motors Corp., **I** 10, 14, 16–17, 54, 58, 78–80, 85, 101–02, 125, 136, 141, 144–45, 147, 154–55, 162–63, 165–67, **171–73**, 181, 183, 186–87, 203, 205–06, 280, 328–29, 334–35, 360, 448, 464, 481–82, 529, 540; **II** 2, 5, 15, 32–35, 268, 431, 608; **III** 55, 136–38, 292, 442, 458, 482–83, 536, 555, 563, 581, 590–91, 637–38, 640–42, 760; **6** 140, 256, 336, 356, 358; **7** 6–8, 427, 461–64, 513, 565, 567, 599; **8** 151–52, 505–07; **9** 16–18, 36, 283, 293–95, 341, 343, 344, 439, 487–89; **10** 198, 232, 262, 264, 273–74, 279–80, 288–89, **325–27 (upd.)**, 419–20, 429, 460, 537; **11** 5, 29, 53, 103–04, 137–39, 339, 350, 427–29, 437–39, 471–72, 528, 530; **12** 90, 160, 309, 311, 487; **13** 109, 124, 179, 344–45, 357; **14** 321, 458; **15** 171

General Nucleonics Corp., **III** 643

General Nutrition Companies, Inc., **11 155–57**

General Petroleum and Mineral Organization of Saudi Arabia, **IV** 537–39

General Petroleum Corp., **IV** 412, 431, 464; **7** 352

General Physics Corporation, **13** 367

General Portland, **III** 704–05

General Precision Equipment Corp., **II** 10

General Printing and Paper, **II** 624–25

General Printing Ink Corp. See Sequa Corp.

General Property Trust, **IV** 708

General Public Utilities Corporation, **V 629–31**; **6** 484, 534, 579–80; **11** 388

General Railway Signal Company. See General Signal Corporation.

General Re Corporation, **III 258–59**, 276

General Rent A Car, **6** 349

General Research Corp., **14** 98

General Seafoods Corp., **II** 531

General Sekiyu K.K., **IV 431–33**, 555

General Signal Corporation, **III 645; 9 250–52; 11** 232

General Steel Industries Inc., **14** 324

General Supermarkets, **II** 673

General Telephone and Electronics Corp., **II** 47; **V** 295, 345–46; **13** 398

General Telephone Corporation, **V** 294–95; **9** 478, 494

General Tire, Inc., **8 206–08, 212–14; 9** 247–48

General Transistor Corporation, **10** 319

General Utilities Company, **6** 555

Generale Bank, **II 294–95**

Générale Biscuit S.A., **II** 475

Générale de Mécanique Aéronautique, **I** 46

Générale des Eaux Group, **V 632–34**

Générale Occidentale, **II** 475; **IV** 614–15

Generali. See Assicurazioni Generali.

GenerComit Gestione SpA, **II** 192

Genesco, Inc., **14** 501

Genesee Iron Works, **V** 221

Genesis, **II** 176–77

Genetic Systems Corp., **I** 654; **III** 18

Genetics Institute, Inc., **8 215–18; 10** 70, 78–80

Geneva Pharmaceuticals, Inc., **8** 549

Geneva Steel, **7 193–95**

Genex Corp., **I** 355–56

GENIX, **V** 152

Genix Group. See MCN Corporation.

Genossenschaftsbank Edeka, **II** 621–22

Genstar Gypsum Products Co., **IV** 273

Genstar Stone Products, **III** 735

Genstar Stone Products Co., **15** 154

Gentex Corporation, **12** 121–22

Gentry Associates, Inc., **14** 378

Gentry International, **I** 497

Genuine Parts Company, **9 253–55**

Genung's, **II** 673

Genzyme Corporation, **13 239–42**

Geo. W. Wheelwright Co., **IV** 311

Geodynamics Oil & Gas Inc., **IV** 83

Geomarine Systems, **11** 202

The Geon Company, **11 158–61**

Geon Industries, Inc. See Johnston Industries, Inc.

Geophysical Service, Inc., **II** 112; **III** 499–500; **IV** 365

George A. Hormel and Company, **II 504–06; 7** 547; **12** 123–24

George A. Touche & Co., **9** 167

George Batten Co., **I** 28

George Booker & Co., **13** 102

George Fischer, Ltd., **III** 638

George H. Dentler & Sons, **7** 429

The George Hyman Construction Company, **8** 112–13

George K. Smith & Co., **I** 692

George Kent, **II** 3

George Newnes Company, **IV** 641; **7** 244

George Peabody & Co., **II** 329, 427

George R. Newell Co., **II** 668

George R. Rich Manufacturing Company, **8** 114. See also Clark Equipment Company.

George W. Neare & Co., **III** 224

George Weston Limited, **II** 465, **631–32**, 649; **13** 51

George Wimpey PLC, **12 201–03**

Georges Renault, **III** 427

Georgetown Steel Corp., **IV** 228

Georgia Credit Exchange, **6** 24

Georgia Federal Bank, **I** 447; **11** 112–13

Georgia Gulf Corporation, **IV** 282; **9 256–58**, 260

Georgia Hardwood Lumber Co., **IV** 281; **9** 259

Georgia International Life Insurance Co., **III** 218

Georgia Kraft Co., **IV** 312, 342–43; **8** 267–68

Georgia Natural Gas Corporation, **6** 447–48

Georgia Power & Light Co., **V** 621; **6** 447, 537

Georgia Railway and Electric Company, **6** 446–47

Georgia-Pacific Corporation, **IV 281–83**, 288, 304, 345, 358; **9** 256–58, **259–62 (upd.)**; **12** 19, 377; **15** 229

Georgie Pie, **V** 35

Geosource Inc., **III** 182

Geothermal Resources International, **11** 271

Gerber Products Co., **II** 481; **III** 19; **7 196–98**, 547; **9** 90; **11** 173

Gerber Scientific, Inc., **12 204–06**

Gerbes Super Markets, Inc., **12** 112

Geren Associates. See CRSS Inc.

Geriatrics Inc., **13** 49

Gerling of Cologne, **III** 695

Germaine Monteil Cosmetiques Corp., **I** 426; **III** 56

German Cargo Service GmbH., **I** 111

German Mills American Oatmeal Factory, **II** 558; **12** 409

German-American Car Company. See GATX.

German-American Securities, **II** 283

Germania Refining Co., **IV** 488–89

Germplasm Resource Management, **III** 740

Gerresheimer Glas AG, **II** 386; **IV** 232

Gerrity Oil & Gas Corporation, **11** 28

Gervais Danone, **II** 474

GESA. See General Europea S.A.

Gesbancaya, **II** 196

Gesellschaft für Chemische Industrie im Basel, **I** 632

Gesellschaft für den Bau von Untergrundbahnen, **I** 410

Gesellschaft für Linde's Eisenmachinen, **I** 581

Gesellschaft für Markt- und Kühlhallen, **I** 581

Gesparal, **III** 47; **8** 342

Gestettner, **II** 159

Gestione Pubblicitaria Editoriale, **IV** 586

Getty Oil Co., **II** 448; **IV** 367, 423, 429, 461, 479, 488, 490, 551, 553; **6** 457; **8** 526; **11** 27; **13** 448

Getz Corp., **IV** 137

Geyser Peak Winery, **I** 291

Geysers Geothermal Co., **IV** 84, 523; **7** 188

GFS. See Gordon Food Service Inc.

GFS Realty Inc., **II** 633

GHH, **II** 257

GI Communications, **10** 321

GI Export Corp. See Johnston Industries, Inc.

Giant Eagle, Inc., **12** 390–91; **13** 237

Giant Food Inc., **II 633–35**, 656; **13** 282, 284; **15** 532

Giant Resources, **III** 729

Giant Stores, Inc., **7** 113

Giant Tire & Rubber Company, **8** 126

Giant Wholesale, **II** 625

GIB Group, **V 63–66**

Gibbons, Green, Van Amerongen Ltd., **II** 605; **9** 94; **12** 28

Gibbs Automatic Molding Co., **III** 569

GIBCO Corp., **I** 321

Gibraltar Casualty Co., **III** 340

Gibraltar Financial Corp., **III** 270–71

Gibson Greetings, Inc., **7** 24; **12 207–10**

Gibson McDonald Furniture Co., **14** 236

Giddings & Lewis, Inc., **8 545–46; 10 328–30**

Gilbert Lane Personnel, Inc., **9** 326

Gilbert-Ash Ltd., **I** 588
Gilde-Verlag, **IV** 590
Gilde-Versicherung AG, **III** 400
Gildon Metal Enterprises, **7** 96
Gilkey Bros. *See* Puget Sound Tug and Barge Company.
Gill and Duffus, **II** 500
Gill Industries, **II** 161
Gillett Holdings, Inc., **7 199–201**; **11** 543, 545
Gillette Company, **III 27–30**, 114, 215; **IV** 722; **8** 59–60; **9** 381, 413
Gilliam Furniture Inc., **12** 475
Gilliam Manufacturing Co., **8** 530
Gilman & Co., **III** 523
Gilman Fanfold Corp., Ltd., **IV** 644
Gilmore Brother's, **I** 707
Gilmore Steel Corporation. *See* Oregon Steel Mills, Inc.
Giltspur, **II** 587
Gimbel's Department Store, **I** 426–27; **8** 59
Gindick Productions, **6** 28
Ginn & Co., **IV** 672
Ginnie Mae. *See* Government National Mortgage Association.
Gino's, **III** 103
Ginsber Beer Group, **15** 47
Giorgio, Inc., **III** 16
Girard Bank, **II** 315–16
Girling, **III** 556
Gist-Brocades Co., **III** 53
The Gitano Group, Inc., **8 219–21**
GK Technologies Incorporated, **10** 547
GKN plc, **III 493–96**, 554, 556
Glaceries de Sain-Roch, **III** 677
Glaces de Boussois, **II** 474–75
Glacier Park Co., **10** 191
Gladieux Corp., **III** 103
Glamar Group plc, **14** 224
Glamor Shops, Inc., **14** 93
Glasrock Home Health Care, **I** 316
Glass Containers Corp., **I** 609–10
Glass Fibres Ltd., **III** 726
GlasTec, **II** 420
Glatfelter Wood Pulp Company, **8** 413
Glaverbel, **III** 667
Glaxo Holdings plc, **I 639–41**, 643, 668, 675, 693; **III** 66; **6** 346; **9 263–65 (upd.)**; **10** 551; **11** 173
Glen & Co, **I** 453
Glen Alden Corp., **15** 247
Glen Cove Mutual Insurance Co., **III** 269
Glen Iris Bricks, **III** 673
Glen Line, **6** 416
Glen-Gery Corporation, **14** 249
Glendale Federal Savings, **IV** 29
Glens Falls Insurance Co., **III** 242
GLF-Eastern States Association, **7** 17
The Glidden Company, **I** 353; **8 222–24**
Glitsch International, Inc., **6** 146
Global Energy Group, **II** 345
Global Engineering Company, **9** 266
Global Marine Inc., **9 266–67**; **11** 87
Global Natural Resources, **II** 401; **10** 145
Global Transport Organization, **6** 383
Globe & Rutgers Insurance Co., **III** 195–96
Globe Co. **I** 201
Globe Electric Co., **III** 536
Globe Files Co., **I** 201
Globe Grain and Milling Co., **II** 555
Globe Industries, **I** 540
Globe Insurance Co., **III** 350

Globe Life Insurance Co., **III** 187; **10** 28
Globe National Bank, **II** 261
Globe Newspaper Co., **7** 15
Globe Petroleum Ltd., **IV** 401
Globe-Union, **III** 536
Globe-Wernicke Co., **I** 201
Globetrotter Communications, **7** 199
La Gloria Oil and Gas Company, **7** 102
Gloria Separator GmbH Berlin, **III** 418
Glosser Brothers, **13** 394
Gloster Aircraft, **I** 50; **III** 508
Gloucester Cold Storage and Warehouse Company, **13** 243
Glovatorium, **III** 152; **6** 266
Glycomed Inc., **13** 241
Glyn, Mills and Co., **II** 308; **12** 422
GM Hughes Electronics Corporation, **II 32–36**; **10** 325
GMARA, **II** 608
GMFanuc Robotics, **III** 482–83
GNB International Battery Group, **10** 445
GND Holdings Corp., **7** 204
GNMA. *See* Government National Mortgage Association.
Goal Systems International Inc., **10** 394
Godfather's Pizza, **II** 556–57; **11** 50; **12** 123; **14** 351
Godfrey Co., **II** 625
Godfrey L. Cabot, Inc., **8** 77
Godiva Chocolatier, **II** 480
Godo Shusei, **III** 42
Godsell, **10** 277
Godtfred Kristiansen, **13** 310–11
Goebel & Wetterau Grocery Co., **II** 681
Goering Werke, **II** 282
Göhner AG, **6** 491
Gokey's, **10** 216
Gold Bond Stamp Co., **6** 363–64
Gold Crust Bakeries, **II** 465
Gold Dust Corp., **II** 497
Gold Exploration and Mining Co. Limited Partnership, **13** 503
Gold Fields of South Africa Ltd., **I** 423; **IV** 91, **94–97**
Gold Kist, **7** 432
Gold Seal, **II** 567
Gold Star Foods Co., **IV** 410
Goldblatt Bros., **IV** 135
Goldblatt's Department Stores, **15** 240–42
Golden, **III** 47
Golden Circle Financial Services, **15** 328
Golden Corral Corporation, **10 331–33**
Golden Eagle Exploration, **IV** 566–67
Golden Grain Macaroni Co., **II** 560; **12** 411
Golden Hope Rubber Estate, **III** 697, 699
Golden Nugget Company, **III** 92, 431. *See also* Mirage Resorts, Inc.
Golden Partners, **10** 333
Golden Press, Inc., **13** 559–61
Golden Sea Produce, **10** 439
Golden Skillet, **10** 373
Golden State Bank, **II** 348
Golden State Newsprint Co. Inc., **IV** 296
Golden State Sanwa Bank, **II** 348
Golden Tulip International, **I** 109
Golden West Homes, **15** 328
Golden Wonder, **II** 500; **III** 503
Goldenberg Group, Inc., **12** 396
Goldenlay Eggs, **II** 500
Goldfield Corp., **12** 198
Goldkuhl & Broström, **III** 419
Goldline Laboratories Inc., **11** 208

Goldman, Sachs & Co., **II** 11, 268, 326, 361, **414–16**, 432, 434, 448; **III** 80, 531; **IV** 611; **9** 378, 441; **10** 423; **12** 405; **13** 95, 448, 554; **15** 397
Goldome, **11** 110
Goldsbrough Mort & Co., **I** 437
Goldsmith's, **9** 209
Goldstar Co., Ltd., **II** 5, 53–54; **III** 517; **7** 233; **12 211–13**; **13** 213
Goldwell, **III** 38
Goldwyn Picture Corp., **II** 148
Gomoljak, **14** 250
Good Foods, Inc., **II** 497
The Good Guys!, Inc., **10 334–35**
The Good Humor-Breyers Ice Cream Company, **II** 533; **14 203–05**; **15** 222
Good Times, Inc., **8** 303
Good Weather International Inc., **III** 221; **14** 109
Goodbody & Co., **II** 425; **13** 341
Goodby, Berlin & Silverstein, **10** 484
Goodebodies, **11** 41
Gooderham and Worts, **I** 216, 263–64
Goodlass, Wall & Co., **III** 680–81
Goodman Bros. Mfg. Co., **14** 436
Goodman Fielder, Wattie's, Ltd., **II** 565; **7** 577
Goodrich, **V** 240–41
Goodrich Oil Co., **IV** 365
Goodrich, Tew and Company, **V** 231
Goodrich Tire Company, **6** 27
Goodwill, **15** 511
Goodwin & Co., **12** 108
Goody Products, Inc., **12 214–16**
Goodyear Tire & Rubber Company, **I** 21; **II** 304; **III** 452; **V 244–48**; **8** 81, 291–92, 339; **9** 324; **10** 445; **15** 91
Gordon A. Freisen, International, **III** 73
Gordon B. Miller & Co., **7** 256
Gordon Capital Corp., **II** 245
Gordon Food Service Inc., **8 225–27**
Gordon Investment Corp., **II** 245
Gordon Manufacturing Co., **11** 256
Gordon Publications, **IV** 610
Gordon-Van Cheese Company, **8** 225
Gore Newspapers Co., **IV** 683
Gorges Foodservice, Inc., **14** 516
Gorham Silver, **12** 313
Gormully & Jeffrey, **IV** 660
Gorton's, **II** 502; **10** 323; **13 243–44**
Gosho Co., Ltd., **IV** 442
Gotaas-Larsen Shipping Corp., **6** 368
Götabanken, **II** 303, 353
Göteborgs Handelsbank, **II** 351
Göteborgs Handelskompani, **III** 425
Gothenburg Light & Power Company, **6** 580
Gothenburg Tramways Co., **II** 1
Gott Corp., **III** 614
Goulard and Olena, **I** 412
Gould Electronics, Inc., **13** 201; **14 206–08**
Gould Inc., **III** 745; **11** 45; **13** 127
Goulding Industries Ltd., **IV** 295
Gourmet Foods, **II** 528
Government Bond Department, **9** 369
Government Employees Insurance Company. *See* GEICO Corporation.
Government National Mortgage Assoc., **II** 410
The Governor and Company of the Bank of Scotland, **II** 422; **III** 360; **V** 166; **10 336–38**

GP Group Acquisition Limited Partnership, **10** 288
GPT, **15** 125
GPU. *See* General Public Utilities Corporation.
Graber Industries, Inc., **V** 379
Grace. *See* W.R. Grace & Co.
Grace Drilling Company, **9** 365
Gradco Systems, Inc., **6** 290
Gradiaz, Annis & Co., **15** 138
Gradmann & Holler, **III** 283
Graef & Schmidt, **III** 54
Graf Bertel Dominique/New York, **6** 48
Graficas e Instrumentos S.A., **13** 234
Graham Container Corp., **8** 477
Graham Page, **III** 568
Grahams Builders Merchants, **I** 429
Gralla, **IV** 687
Grampian Electricity Supply Company, **13** 457
Gran Central Corporation, **8** 487
Granada Group PLC, II 70, **138–40**
Granada Royale Hometels, **9** 426
GranCare, Inc., 14 209–11
Grand Bazaar Innovations Bon Marché, **13** 284
Grand Metropolitan plc, I 247–49, 259, 261; **II** 555–57, 565, 608, 613–15; **9** 99; **13** 391, 407, 409; **14 212–15 (upd.)**; **15** 72
Grand Rapids Carpet Sweeper Company, **9** 70
Grand Rapids Gas Light Company. *See* MCN Corporation.
Grand Rapids Wholesale Grocery Company, **8** 481
Grand Trunk Corp., **6** 359–61
Grand Union Company, II 637, 662; **7 202–04**; **8** 410; **13** 394
Grand Valley Gas Company, **11** 28
Grandmet USA, **I** 248
Grands Magasins L. Tietz, **V** 103
Grandy's, **15** 345
Granger Associates, **12** 136
Gränges, **III** 480
Granite City Steel Company, **12** 353
Granite Furniture Co., **14** 235
Grant Oil Tool Co., **III** 569
Grant Street National Bank, **II** 317
GranTree, **14** 4
Graphic Controls Corp., **IV** 678
Graphic Research, Inc., **13** 344–45
Graphic Services, **III** 166; **6** 282
Graphics Systems Software, **III** 169; **6** 285; **8** 519
Graphite Oil Product Co., **I** 360
Grass Valley Group, **8** 518, 520
Grasselli Dyestuffs Corp., **I** 337
Grasset, **IV** 617–18
Grattan, **V** 160
Gray Dawes & Co., **III** 522–23
Gray Drug Stores, **III** 745
Gray Dunn and Co., **II** 569
Gray, Seifert and Co., **10** 44
Grayarc, **III** 157
Grayrock Capital, **I** 275
Greaseater, Ltd., **8** 463–64
Great American Entertainment Company, **13** 279
Great American First Savings Bank of San Diego, **II** 420
Great American Life Insurance Co., **III** 190–92
Great American Lines Inc., **12** 29

Great American Management and Investment, Inc., 8 228–31
Great American Reserve Insurance Co., **IV** 343; **10** 247
Great American Restaurants, **13** 321
Great Atlantic & Pacific Tea Company, Inc., II 636–38, 629, 655–56, 666; **13** 25, 127, 237; **15** 259
Great Beam Co., **III** 690
Great Eastern Railway, **6** 424
Great 5¢ Store, **V** 224
Great Halviggan, **III** 690
Great Lakes Bancorp, 8 232–33
Great Lakes Bankgroup, **II** 457
Great Lakes Carbon Corporation, **12** 99
Great Lakes Chemical Corp., I 341–42; **8** 262; **14 216–18 (upd.)**
Great Lakes Corp., **IV** 136
Great Lakes Pipe Line Co., **IV** 400, 575
Great Lakes Steel Corp., **IV** 236; **8** 346; **12** 352
Great Lakes Window, Inc., **12** 397
Great Land Seafoods, Inc., **II** 553
Great Northern, **III** 282
Great Northern Import Co., **I** 292
Great Northern Nekoosa Corp., **IV** 282–83, 300; **9** 260–61
Great Northern Railway Company, **6** 596
Great Shoshone & Twin Falls Water Power Company, **12** 265
Great Universal Stores P.L.C., V 67–69; **15** 83
Great Western Billiard Manufactory, **III** 442
Great Western Financial Corporation, 10 339–41
Great Western Railway, **III** 272
Great-West Lifeco Inc., III 260–61
Greatamerica Corp., **I** 489; **10** 419
Greater All American Markets, **II** 601; **7** 19
Greater New York Film Rental Co., **II** 169
Greater Washington Investments, Inc., **15** 248
Greeley Beef Plant, **13** 350
Green Bay Food Company, **7** 127
Green Cross K.K., **I** 665
Green Giant, **II** 556; **13** 408; **14** 212, 214
Green Island Cement (Holdings) Ltd. Group, **IV** 694–95
Green Power & Light Company. *See* UtiliCorp United Inc.
Green River Electric Corporation, **11** 37
Green Thumb, **II** 562
Green Tree Financial Corporation, 11 162–63
Greenfield Industries Inc., **13** 8
Greenleaf Corp., **IV** 203
Greensboro Life Insurance Company, **11** 213
Greenville Insulating Board Corp., **III** 763
Greenwell Montagu Gold-Edged, **II** 319
Greenwich Capital Markets, **II** 311
Greenwood Mills, Inc., 14 219–21
Greenwood Publishing Group, **IV** 610
Gregg Publishing Co., **IV** 636
Greif Bros. Corporation, 15 186–88
Grenfell and Colegrave Ltd., **II** 245
Gresham Life Assurance, **III** 200, 272–73
Grey Advertising, Inc., I 175, 623; **6 26–28**; **10** 69; **14** 150
Grey United Stores, **II** 666
Greyhound Corp., I 448–50; **II** 445; **6** 27; **8** 144–45; **10** 72; **12** 199

Greylock Mills, **III** 213
GRiD Systems Corp., **II** 107
Griesheim Elektron, **IV** 140
Grieveson, Grant and Co., **II** 422–23
Griffin and Sons, **II** 543
Griffin Pipe Products Co., **7** 30–31
Griffin Wheel Company, **7** 29–30
Griffon Cutlery Corp., **13** 166
Grigg, Elliot & Co., **14** 555
Grindlays Bank, **II** 189
Gringoir/Broussard, **II** 556
Grinnell Corp., III 643–45; **11** 198; **13 245–47**
Grip Printing & Publishing Co., **IV** 644
Grisewood & Dempsey, **IV** 616
Grist Mill Company, 15 189–91
GRM Industries Inc., **15** 247–48
Grocer Publishing Co., **IV** 638
Grocery Store Products Co., **III** 21
Grocery Warehouse, **II** 602
Groen Manufacturing, **III** 468
Grogan-Cochran Land Company, **7** 345
Grolier, **IV** 619
Groot-Noordhollandsche, **III** 177–79
Groovy Beverages, **II** 477
Gross Townsend Frank Hoffman, **6** 28
Grosset & Dunlap, Inc., **II** 144; **III** 190–91
Grossman's Inc., 13 248–50
Grossmith Agricultural Industries, **II** 500
Grosvenor Marketing Co., **II** 465
Groton Victory Yard, **I** 661
Ground Services Inc., **13** 49
Group Hospitalization and Medical Services, **10** 161
Group Lotus, **13** 357
Groupe AG, **III** 201–02
Groupe Air France, 6 92–94. *See also* Air France.
Groupe Ancienne Mutuelle, **III** 210–11
Groupe Barthelmey, **III** 373
Groupe Bull, **10** 563–64; **12** 246. *See also* Compagnie des Machines Bull.
Groupe Casino. *See* Etablissements Economiques de Casino Guichard, Perrachon et Cie, S.C.A.
Groupe Danone, **14** 150
Groupe de la Cité, IV 614–16, 617
Groupe de la Financière d'Angers, **IV** 108
Groupe Jean Didier, **12** 413
Groupe Lagadère, **15** 293
Groupe Salvat, **IV** 619
Groupe Victoire, **III** 394
Groupement des Exploitants Pétroliers, **IV** 545
Groux Beverage Corporation, **11** 451
Grove Manufacturing Co., **I** 476–77; **9** 393
Grow Group Inc., 12 217–19, 387–88
Growmark, **I** 421; **11** 23
Gruene Apotheke, **I** 681
Grumman Corp., I 58–59, **61–63**, 67–68, 78, 84, 490, 511; **7** 205; **8** 51; **9** 17, 206–07, 417, 460; **10** 316–17, 536; **11 164–67 (upd.)**, 363–65, 428; **15** 285
Grün & Bilfinger A.G., **I** 560–61
Grundig, **I** 411; **II** 80, 117; **13** 402–03; **15** 514
Grundig Data Scanner GmbH, **12** 162
Grunenthal, **I** 240
Gruner + Jahr AG & Co., **IV** 590, 593; **7** 245; **15** 51
Gruntal and Co., **III** 263
Gruntal Financial Corp., **III** 264
Grupo Carso, **14** 489

Grupo Corvi S.A. de C.V., **7** 115
Grupo Industrial Alfa, **II** 262; **11** 386
Grupo Televisa, S.A., **9** 429
Grupo Tudor, **IV** 471
Grupo Zeta, **IV** 652–53; **7** 392
Gruppo IRI, **V** 325–27
GSG&T, **6** 495
GSI. *See* Geophysical Service, Inc.
GSU. *See* Gulf States Utilities Company.
GTE Corporation, **II** 38, 47, 80; **III** 475;
    V 294–98; **9** 49, 171, 478–80; **10** 19,
    97, 431; **11** 500; **14** 259, 433; **15**
    192–97 (upd.). *See also* British
    Columbia Telephone Company.
GTO. *See* Global Transport Organization.
GTS Duratek, Inc., **13** 367–68
Guangzhou M. C. Packaging, **10** 130
Guaranty Bank & Trust Company, **13** 440
Guaranty Federal Savings & Loan Assoc.,
    IV 343
Guaranty Properties Ltd., **11** 258
Guaranty Savings and Loan, **10** 339
Guaranty Trust Co. of New York, **II**
    329–32, 428; **IV** 20
Guardian, **III** 721
Guardian Bank, **13** 468
Guardian Federal Savings and Loan
    Association, **10** 91
Guardian Mortgage Company, **8** 460
Guardian National Bank, **I** 165; **11** 137
Guardian Royal Exchange Plc, **III** 350;
    11 168–70
Gubor Schokoladen, **15** 221
Guccio Gucci, S.p.A., **12** 281; **15**
    198–200
Guelph Dolime, **IV** 74
Guernsey Banking Co., **II** 333
Guess, Inc., **15 201–03**
Guest, Keen and Nettlefolds plc. *See* GKN
    plc.
Gueyraud et Fils Cadet, **III** 703
Guild Press, Inc., **13** 559
Guild Wineries, **13** 134
Guilford Industries, **8** 270–72
Guilford Mills Inc., **8 234–36**
Guinness Peat, **10** 277
Guinness plc, **I** 239, 241, **250–52**, 268,
    272, 282; **II** 428–29, 610; **9** 100, 449;
    10 399; **13** 454
Gujarat State Fertilizer Co., **III** 513
Gulco Industries, Inc., **11** 194
Güldner Aschaffenburg, **I** 582
Gulf + Western Inc., **I** 418, **451–53**,
    540; **II** 147, 154–56, 177; **III** 642, 745;
    IV 289, 672; **7** 64; **10** 482; **13** 121, 169,
    470
Gulf Air, **6** 63
Gulf Canada Ltd., **I** 216, 262, 264; **IV** 495,
    721; **6** 478; **9** 391; **13** 557–58
Gulf Caribbean Marine Lines, **6** 383
Gulf Engineering Co. Ltd., **IV** 131
Gulf Exploration Co., **IV** 454
Gulf Mobile and Northern Railroad, **I** 456
Gulf Mobile and Ohio Railroad, **I** 456; **11**
    187
Gulf of Suez Petroleum Co., **IV** 412–14
Gulf Oil Chemical Co., **13** 502
Gulf Oil Corp., **I** 37, 584; **II** 315, 402,
    408, 448; **III** 225, 231, 259, 497; **IV**
    198, 287, 385–87, 392, 421, 450–51,
    466, 470, 472–73, 476, 484, 508, 510,
    512, 531, 538, 565, 570, 576
Gulf Plains Corp., **III** 471
Gulf Public Service Company, **6** 580

Gulf Resources & Chemical Corp., **15** 464
Gulf States Paper, **IV** 345
Gulf States Steel, **I** 491
Gulf States Utilities Company, **6 495–97**;
    12 99
Gulf United Corp., **III** 194
Gulfstream Aerospace Corp., **7 205–06**;
    13 358
Gulfstream Banks, **II** 336
Gulton Industries Inc., **7** 297
Gummi Werke, **I** 208
Gump's, **7** 286
Gunder & Associates, **12** 553
Gunfred Group, **I** 387
The Gunlocke Company, **12** 299; **13** 269
Gunns Ltd., **II** 482
Gunpowder Trust, **I** 379; **13** 379
Gunter Wulff Automaten, **III** 430
Gunther, S.A., **8** 477
Gupta, **15** 492
Gurneys, Birkbeck, Barclay & Buxton, **II**
    235
Gusswerk Paul Saalmann & Sohne, **I** 582
Gustav Schickendanz KG, **V** 165
Gustavus A. Pfeiffer & Co., **I** 710
Gutehoffnungshütte Aktienverein AG, **III**
    561, 563; **IV** 104, 201
Guthrie Balfour, **II** 499–500
Gutta Percha Co., **I** 428
Gutzeit. *See* W. Gutzeit & Co.
Guy Carpenter & Co., **III** 282
Guy Motors, **13** 286
Guy Salmon Service, Ltd., **6** 349
GW Utilities Ltd., **I** 264; **6** 478
Gwathmey & Co., **II** 424; **13** 340
Gymboree Corporation, **15 204–06**
Gypsum, Lime, & Alabastine Canada Ltd.,
    IV 271

H & R Block, Incorporated, **9 268–70**
H N Norton Co., **11** 208
H.A. Job, **II** 587
H.B. Claflin Company, **V** 139
H.B. Fuller Company, **8 237–40**
H.B. Nickerson & Sons Ltd., **14** 339
H.B. Reese Candy Co., **II** 511
H.B. Viney Company, Inc., **11** 211
H.C. Christians Co., **II** 536
H.C. Frick Coke Co., **IV** 573; **7** 550
H.C. Petersen & Co., **III** 417
H.D. Lee Company, Inc. *See* Lee Apparel
    Company, Inc.
H.D. Pochin & Co., **III** 690
H. Douglas Barclay, **8** 296
H.E. Butt Grocery Co., **13 251–53**
H.F. Ahmanson & Company, **II 181–82**;
    10 342–44 (upd.)
H. Fairweather and Co., **I** 592
H.G. Anderson Equipment Corporation, **6**
    441
H. Hackfeld & Co., **I** 417
H. Hamilton Pty, Ltd., **III** 420
H.I. Rowntree and Co., **II** 568
H.J. Green, **II** 556
H.J. Heinz Company, **I** 30–31, 605, 612;
    II 414, 480, 450, **507–09**, 547; **III** 21; **7**
    382, 448, 576, 578; **8** 499; **10** 151; **11**
    171–73 (upd.); **12** 411, 529, 531–32; **13**
    383
H.K. Ferguson Company, **7** 355
H.L. Green Company, Inc., **9** 448
H.L. Judd Co., **III** 628
H.L. Yoh Company, **9** 163
H. Lewis and Sons, **14** 294

H.M. Byllesby & Company, Inc., **6** 539
H.M. Goush Co., **IV** 677–78
H.M. Spalding Electric Light Plant, **6** 592
H. Miller & Sons, Inc., **11** 258
H.O. Houghton & Company, **10** 355
H.P. Foods, **II** 475
H.P. Hood, **7** 17–18
H.P. Smith Paper Co., **IV** 290
H.R. MacMillan Export Co., **IV** 306–08
H. Reeve Angel & Co., **IV** 300
H. Salt Fish and Chips, **13** 320
H.T. Cherry Company, **12** 376
H.V. McKay Proprietary, **III** 651
H.W. Heidmann, **I** 542
H.W. Johns Manufacturing Co., **III** 663,
    706–08; **7** 291
H.W. Madison Co., **11** 211
H. Williams and Co., Ltd., **II** 678
Häagen-Dazs, **II** 556–57, 631; **10** 147; **14**
    212, 214
Haake-Beck Brauerei AG, **9** 86
Haas Corp., **I** 481
Haas Wheat & Partners, **15** 357
Habirshaw Cable and Wire Corp., **IV** 177
Hach Co., **14** 309
Hachette S.A., **IV** 614–15, **617–19**, 675;
    10 288; **11** 293; **12** 359. *See also* Matra-
    Hachette S.A.
Hachmeister, Inc., **II** 508; **11** 172
Hacker-Pschorr Brau, **II** 242
Hadleigh-Crowther, **I** 715
Haemocell, **11** 476
Hafez Insurance Co., **III** 242
Haggie, **IV** 91
Haile Mines, Inc., **12** 253
Hain Pure Food Co., **I** 514
Hainaut-Sambre, **IV** 52
A.B. Hakon Swenson, **II** 639
Hakuhodo, Inc., **6 29–31**, 48–49
Hakunetsusha & Company, **12** 483
HAL Inc., **9 271–73**
Halcon International, **IV** 456
Halfords Ltd., **IV** 17, 19, 382–83
Halifax Banking Co., **II** 220
Halifax Timber, **I** 335
Hall & Levine Agency, **I** 14
Hall and Co., **III** 737
Hall and Ham River, **III** 739
Hall Bros. Co., **IV** 620–21; **7** 23
Hall Containers, **III** 739
Hallamore Manufacturing Co., **I** 481
Haller, Raymond & Brown, Inc., **II** 10
Halliburton Company, **II** 112; **III** 473,
    497–500, 617; **11** 505; **13 118–19**
Hallivet China Clay Co., **III** 690
Hallmark Cards, Inc., **IV 620–21**; **7**
    23–25; **12** 207, 209
Hallmark Chemical Corp., **8** 386
Haloid Company. *See* Xerox Corporation.
Halsey, Stuart & Co., **II** 431; **III** 276
Hamada Printing Press, **IV** 326
Hamashbir Lata'asiya, **II** 47
Hambrecht & Quist, **10** 463, 504
Hambro American Bank & Trust Co., **11**
    109
Hambro Life Assurance Ltd., **I** 426; **III**
    339
Hambros, **II** 422
Hamburg-Amerikanische-Packetfahrt-
    Actien-Gesellschaft, **6** 397–98
Hamburg Banco, **II** 351
Hamburg-Amerika, **I** 542
Hamburger Flugzeubau GmbH., **I** 74
Hamer Hammer Service, Inc., **11** 523

Hamersley Holdings, **IV** 59–61
Hamilton Aero Manufacturing, **I** 47, 84; **10** 162
Hamilton Beach/Proctor-Silex, Inc., **7** 369–70
Hamilton Blast Furnace Co., **IV** 208
Hamilton Brown Shoe Co., **III** 528
Hamilton Group Limited, **15** 478
Hamilton Malleable Iron Co., **IV** 73
Hamilton National Bank, **13** 465
Hamilton Oil Corp., **IV** 47
Hamilton Standard, **9** 417
Hamilton Steel and Iron Co., **IV** 208
Hamish Hamilton, **IV** 659; **8** 526
Hammamatsu Commerce Bank, **II** 291
Hammarplast, **13** 493
Hammarsforsens Kraft, **IV** 339
Hammerich & Lesser, **IV** 589
Hammermill Paper Co., **IV** 287; **15** 229
Hammers Plastic Recycling, **6** 441
Hammerson Property Investment and Development Corporation PLC, IV 696–98
Hammery Furniture Company, **14** 302–03
Hamming-Whitman Publishing Co., **13** 559
Hammond Corp., **IV** 136
Hammond Lumber Co., **IV** 281; **9** 259
Hammond's, **II** 556
Hammonton Electric Light Company, **6** 449
Hamomag AG, **III** 546
Hampton Inns, **9** 425–26
Han Kook Fertilizer Co., **I** 516
Hanbury, Taylor, Lloyd and Bowman, **II** 306
Hancock Holding Company, 15 207–09
Hancock Jaffe Laboratories, **11** 460
Hand in Hand, **III** 234
Handelsbank of Basel, **III** 375
Handelsfinanz Bank of Geneva, **II** 319
Handelsmaatschappij Montan N.V., **IV** 127
Handelsunion AG, **IV** 222
Handleman Company, 15 210–12
Handley Page Transport Ltd., **I** 50, 92–93
Handy Dan, **V** 75
Hanes Corp., **II** 572–73; **8** 202, 288; **15** 436
Hanes Holding Company, **11** 256
Hang Seng Bank, **II** 298; **IV** 717
Hanil Development Company, **6** 98
Hanjin Group, **6** 98
Hankook Tyre Manufacturing Company, **V** 255–56
Hankuk Glass Industry Co., **III** 715
Hankyu Corporation, V 454–56
Hankyu Department Stores, Inc., V 70–71
Hanley Brick, **14** 250
Hanmi Citizen Precision Industry, **III** 455
Hanna Iron Ore Co., **IV** 236
Hanna Mining Co., **8** 346–47
Hanna Ore Mining Company, **12** 352
Hanna-Barbera, **7** 306
Hannaford Bros. Co., 12 220–22
Hannen Brauerei GmbH, **9** 100
Hannifin Corp., **III** 602
Hannoversche Bank, **II** 278
Hanover Bank, **II** 312–13
Hanovia Co., **IV** 78
Hanrstoffe-und Düngemittelwerk Saar-Lothringen GmbH, **IV** 197
Hans Grohe, **III** 570
Hanseco Reinsurance Co., **III** 343

Hanson PLC, **I** 438, 475, 477; **II** 319; **III** 501–03, 506; **IV** 23, 94, 97, 169, 171, 173, 290; **7** 207–10 (upd.); **8** 224; **13** 478–79
Hapag-Lloyd Ag, 6 397–99
Happy Eater Ltd., **III** 106
Haralambos Beverage Corporation, **11** 451
Harald Quant Group, **III** 377
Harbert Corporation, **13** 98; **14** 222–23
Harbison-Walker, **III** 472
Harbor Tug and Barge Co., **6** 382
Harborlite Corporation, **10** 45
Harcourt Brace and Co., **IV** 622; **12** 223–26
Harcourt Brace Jovanovich, Inc., **II** 133–34; **III** 118; **IV** 622–24, 642, 672; **7** 312; **12** 224; **13** 106; **14** 177
Harcourt General, Inc., **12** 226
Harcros Chemical Group, **III** 699
Harcros Investment Trust Ltd., **III** 698–99
Hard Rock Cafe International, Inc., 12 227–29
Hardee's, **II** 679; **7** 430; **8** 564; **9** 178; **15** 345
Hardison & Stewart Oil, **IV** 569
Hardman Inc., **III** 699
Hardware Wholesalers Inc., **12** 8
Hardwick Stove Co., **III** 573
Hardy Spicer, **III** 595
Harima Shipbuilding & Engineering Co., Ltd., **I** 511, 534; **III** 513, 533; **12** 484
Harima Zosenjo, Ltd., **IV** 129
Harlem Globetrotters, **7** 199, 335
Harlequin Enterprises Ltd., **IV** 587, 590, 617, 619, 672
Harley-Davidson Inc., **III** 658; **7** 211–14; **13** 513
Harlow Metal Co. Ltd., **IV** 119
Harman International Industries Inc., 15 213–15
Harmon Publishing Company, **12** 231
Harnischfeger Industries, Inc., **I** 186; **8** 241–44; **14** 56
Harold A. Wilson & Co., **I** 405
Harp Lager Ltd., **15** 442
Harper Group, Inc., **12** 180; **13** 20
Harper House, Inc. *See* Day Runner, Inc.
HarperCollins Publishers, **IV** 652; **7** 389, 391; **14** 555–56; **15** 216–18
Harpers, Inc., **12** 298
Harpo Productions, **9** 307
Harrah's, **9** 425–27
Harrell International, **III** 21
Harriman Co., **IV** 310
Harriman, Ripley and Co., **II** 407
Harris Abattoir Co., **II** 482
Harris Bankcorp, **II** 211
Harris Corporation, **II** 37–39; **11** 46, 286, 490
Harris Daishowa (Australia) Pty., Ltd., **IV** 268
Harris Financial, Inc., **11** 482
Harris Laboratories, **II** 483; **14** 549
Harris Microwave Semiconductors, **14** 417
Harris Pharmaceuticals Ltd., **11** 208
Harris Publications, **13** 179
Harris Transducer Corporation, **10** 319
Harrisburg National Bank and Trust Co., **II** 315–16
Harrison & Sons (Hanley) Ltd., **III** 681
Harrisons & Crosfield plc, III 696–700
Harrow Stores Ltd., **II** 677
Harry F. Allsman Co., **III** 558
Harry Ferguson Co., **III** 651

Harry N. Abrams, Inc., **IV** 677
Harsco Corporation, **8** 245–47; **11** 135
Harshaw Chemical Company, **9** 154
Harshaw/Filtrol Partnership, **IV** 80
Hart Glass Manufacturing, **III** 423
Hart Press, **12** 25
Hart, Schaffner & Marx, **8** 248–49
Hart Son and Co., **I** 592
Harte & Co., **IV** 409; **7** 308
Harter Bank & Trust, **9** 474–75
Hartford Container Company, **8** 359
Hartford Electric Light Co., **13** 183
Hartford Fire Insurance, **11** 198
Hartford Insurance, **I** 463–64
Hartford Machine Screw Co., **12** 344
Hartford National Bank and Trust Co., **13** 396
Hartford National Corporation, **13** 464, 466–67
Hartford Trust Co., **II** 213
Hartley's, **II** 477
Hartmann & Braun, **III** 566
Hartmann Fibre, **12** 377
Hartmann Luggage, **12** 313
Hartmarx Corporation, **8** 248–50
The Hartstone Group plc, 14 224–26
The Hartz Mountain Corporation, **12** 230–32
Harvest International, **III** 201
Harvestore, **11** 5
Harvey Aluminum, **I** 68
Harvey Benjamin Fuller, **8** 237–38
Harvey Lumber and Supply Co., **III** 559
Harza Engineering Company, **14** 227–28
Hasbro, Inc., **III** 504–06; **IV** 676; **7** 305, 529; **12** 168–69, 495; **13** 561
Hasler Holding AG, **9** 32
Hassenfeld Brothers Inc., **III** 504
Hasten Bancorp, **11** 371
Hathaway Manfacturing Co., **III** 213
Hathaway Shirt Co., **I** 25–26
Hattori Seiko Co., Ltd., **III** 455, 619–21
Havas, SA, **IV** 616; **10** 195–96, **345–48**; **13** 203–04
Haven Automation International, **III** 420
Haviland Candy Co., **15** 325
Hawaii National Bank, **11** 114
Hawaiian Airlines Inc., **6** 104; **9** 271–73
Hawaiian Dredging & Construction Co., **I** 565–66
Hawaiian Electric Industries, Inc., 9 274–77
Hawaiian Fertilizer Co., **II** 490
Hawaiian Pineapple Co., **II** 491
Hawaiian Tug & Barge, **9** 276
Hawaiian Tuna Packers, **II** 491
Hawker Siddeley Group Public Limited Company, **I** 41–42, 50, 71, 470; **III** 507–10; **8** 51; **12** 190
Hawkeye Cablevision, **II** 161
Hawley & Hazel Chemical Co., **III** 25
Hawley Group Limited, **12** 10
Haworth Inc., 8 251–52
Hawthorn Company, **8** 287
Hawthorn-Mellody, **I** 446; **11** 25
Hawthorne Appliance and Electronics, **10** 9–11
Hay Group, **I** 33
Hayakawa Electrical Industries, **II** 95–96
Hayakawa Metal Industrial Laboratory, **II** 95; **12** 447
Hayaku Zenjiro, **III** 408
Hayama Oil, **IV** 542
Hayashi Kane Shoten, **II** 578

Hayashikane Shoten K.K., **II** 578
Hayden Clinton National Bank, **11** 180
Hayden Stone, **II** 450; **9** 468
Hayes Microcomputer Products, **9** 515
Hayes Wheel Company, **7** 258
Hays Petroleum Services, **IV** 451
Hazard, **I** 328
HAZCO International, Inc., **9** 110
Hazel Bishop, **III** 55
Hazel-Atlas Glass Co., **I** 599; **15** 128
Hazell Sun Ltd., **IV** 642; **7** 312
Hazeltine, Inc., **II** 20
Hazlenut Growers of Oregon, **7** 496–97
HBO. *See* Home Box Office Inc.
HCA Management Co., **III** 79
HCA Psychiatric Co., **III** 79
HCI Holdings, **I** 264
HCL America, **10** 505
HCL Sybase, **10** 505
HDM Worldwide Direct, **13** 204
HDR Inc., **I** 563
Head Sportswear International, **15** 368
Heads and Threads, **10** 43
Heal's, **13** 307
Heald Machine Co., **12** 67
Healey & Baker, **IV** 705
Health & Tennis Corp., **III** 431
Health Care Corp., **III** 79
Health Care International, **13** 328
Health Maintenance Organization of
  Pennsylvania. *See* U.S. Healthcare, Inc.
Health Maintenance Organizations, **I** 545
Health O Meter Products Inc., 14
  229–31; **15** 307
Health Plan of America, **11** 379
Health Plan of Virginia, **III** 389
Health Products Inc., **I** 387
Health Services, Inc., **10** 160
Health Systems International, Inc., 11
  174–76
Health Way, Inc., **II** 538
HealthAmerica Corp., **III** 84
HealthCare USA, **III** 84, 86
HealthSouth Rehabilitation Corporation,
  14 232–34
HealthTrust, **III** 80; **15** 112
Healthy Choice, **12** 531
Hearst Corporation, IV 582, 596, 608,
  625–27; **12** 358–59
Hearthstone Insurance Co. of
  Massachusetts, **III** 203
Heartland Building Products, **II** 582
Heartland Components, **III** 519
Heartland Express Inc., **13** 550–51
Heat Transfer Pty. Ltd., **III** 420
Heatcraft Inc., **8** 320–22
Heath Co., **II** 124; **13** 573
Heath Steele Mines Ltd., **IV** 18
Heatilator Inc., **13** 269
Hebrew National Kosher Foods, **III** 24
Hechinger Company, 12 233–36
Hecker-H-O Co., **II** 497
Heckett Technology Services Inc., **8**
  246–47
Heco Envelope Co., **IV** 282; **9** 261
Heekin Can Inc., 10 130; **13 254–56**
HEI Investment Corp., **9** 276
The Heico Companies, **15** 380
Heidelberg, **III** 701
Heidelburger Drueck, **III** 301
Heidi Bakery, **II** 633
Heidrick & Struggles, **14** 464
Heights of Texas, fsb, **8** 437
Heil-Quaker Corp., **III** 654

Heileman Brewing Co. *See* G. Heileman
  Brewing Co.
Heilig-Meyers Co., 14 235–37
Heimstatt Bauspar AG, **III** 401
Heineken N.V., I 219, **256–58**, 266, 288;
  II 642; **13 257–59 (upd.)**; **14** 35
Heinkel Co., **I** 74
Heinrich Bauer North America, **7** 42–43
Heinrich Koppers GmbH, **IV** 89
Heinrich Lanz, **III** 463
Heinz Co. *See* H.J. Heinz Company.
Heinz Deichert KG, **11** 95
Heinz Italia S.p.A., **15** 221
Heisers Inc., **I** 185
Heiwa Sogo Bank, **II** 326, 361
Heizer Corp., **III** 109–11; **14** 13–15
HEL&P. *See* Houston Electric Light &
  Power Company.
Helemano Co., **II** 491
Helena Rubenstein, Inc., **III** 24, 48; **8**
  343–44; **9** 201–02; **14** 121
Helene Curtis Industries, Inc., I 403; **8**
  253–54
Helix Biocore, **11** 458
Hellefors Jernverk, **III** 623
Heller Financial Corporation, **7** 213
Hellschreiber, **IV** 669
Helme Products, Inc., **15** 139
Helmsley Enterprises, Inc., 9 278–80
Helmut Delhey, **6** 428
Helmuth Hardekopf Bunker GmbH, **7** 141
Help-U-Sell, Inc., **III** 304
Helvetia General, **III** 376
Helvetia Milk Condensing Co., **II** 486; **7**
  428
Helvetia Schweizerische
  Feuerversicherungs-Gesellschaft St.
  Gallen, **III** 375
Hely Group, **IV** 294
Hemelinger Aktienbrauerei, **9** 86
Hemex, **11** 458
Hemlo Gold Mines Inc., 9 281–82
Hemma, **IV** 616
A.B. Hemmings, Ltd., **II** 465
Henderson's Industries, **III** 581
Henderson-Union Electric Cooperative, **11**
  37
Henijean & Cie, **III** 283
Henkel KGaA, III 21, **31–34**, 45; **IV** 70;
  9 382; **13** 197, 199
Henley Drilling Company, **9** 364
The Henley Group, Inc., I 416; **III**
  511–12; **6** 599–600; **9** 298; **11** 435; **12**
  325
Henney Motor Company, **12** 159
Henredon Furniture Industries, **III** 571; **11**
  534
Henry Grant & Co., **I** 604
Henry Holt & Co., **IV** 622–23; **13** 105
Henry J. Tully Corporation, **13** 531
The Henry Jones Co-op Ltd., **7** 577
Henry Jones Foods, **I** 437–38, 592; **7** 182;
  11 212
Henry L. Doherty & Company, **IV** 391; **12**
  542
Henry, Leonard & Thomas Inc., **9** 533
Henry Meadows, Ltd., **13** 286
Henry Pratt Company, **7** 30–31
Henry S. King & Co., **II** 307
Henry Tate & Sons, **II** 580
Henry Telfer, **II** 513
Henry Waugh Ltd., **I** 469
Henthy Realty Co., **III** 190

HEPCO. *See* Hokkaido Electric Power
  Company Inc.
Her Majesty's Stationery Office, 7
  215–18
Heraeus Holding GmbH, IV 98–100, 118
Herald and Weekly Times, **IV** 650, 652; **7**
  389, 391
Herald Publishing Company, **12** 150
Heralds of Liberty, **9** 506
Herbert W. Davis & Co., **III** 344
Herco Technology, **IV** 680
Hercofina, **IV** 499
Hercules Filter, **III** 419
Hercules Inc., I 343–45, 347; **III** 241
Hercules Nut Corp., **II** 593
Hereford Paper and Allied Products Ltd.,
  14 430
Herff Jones, **II** 488
Heritage Bankcorp, **9** 482
Heritage Communications, **II** 160–61
Heritage Federal Savings and Loan
  Association of Huntington, **10** 92
Heritage House of America Inc., **III** 81
Heritage Life Assurance, **III** 248
Heritage National Health Plan, **III** 464
Heritage Springfield, **14** 245
Herman Miller, Inc., 8 251–52, **255–57**
Herman's World of Sporting Goods, **I** 548;
  II 628–29; **15** 470
Hermannshütte, **IV** 103, 105
Hermes Kreditversicherungsbank, **III** 300
Hermès S.A., 14 238–40
Herrburger Brooks P.L.C., **12** 297
Herring-Hall-Marvin Safe Co. of Hamilton,
  Ohio, **7** 145
Hersey Products, Inc., **III** 645
Hershey Bank, **II** 342
Hershey Foods Corporation, I 26–27; **II**
  478, 508, **510–12**, 569; **7** 300; **11** 15; **12**
  480–81; **15** 63–64, **219–22 (upd.)**, 323
Hertel AG, **13** 297
Hertford Industrial Estates, **IV** 724
Hertie Waren- und Kaufhaus GmbH, V
  72–74
Herts & Beds Petroleum Co., **IV** 566
The Hertz Corporation, I 130; **II** 90; **6**
  52, 129, 348–50, 356–57, 392–93; **V**
  494; **9 283–85**; **10** 419; **11** 494
Hess Oil & Chemical Corp., **IV** 366
Hessische Berg- und Hüttenwerke AG, **III**
  695
Hessische Landesbank, **II** 385–86
Hessische Ludwigs-Eisenbahn-Gesellschaft,
  6 424
Hesston Corporation, **13** 17
Hetteen Hoist & Derrick. *See* Polaris
  Industries Inc.
Heublein Inc., I 226, 246, 249, **259–61**,
  281; **7** 266–67; **10** 180; **14** 214
Heuga Holdings B.V., **8** 271
Hewitt & Tuttle, **IV** 426
Hewitt Motor Co., **I** 177
Hewlett-Packard Company, II 62; **III**
  116, **142–43**; **6** 219–20, 225, **237–39**
  (upd.), 244, 248, 278–79, 304; **8** 139,
  467; **9** 7, 35–36, 57, 115, 471; **10** 15,
  34, 86, 232, 257, 363, 404, 459, 464,
  499, 501; **11** 46, 234, 274, 284, 382,
  491, 518; **12** 61, 147, 162, 183, 470; **13**
  128, 326, 501; **14** 354; **15** 125
Hexatec Polymers, **III** 742
Hexcel Medical Corporation, **11** 475
Heyden Newport Chemical Corp., **I** 526
HFC. *See* Household Finance Corporation.

HG Hawker Engineering Co. Ltd., **III** 508
HGCC. *See* Hysol Grafil Composite Components Co.
HI. *See* Houston Industries Incorporated.
Hi-Bred Corn Company, **9** 410
Hi-Mirror Co., **III** 715
Hi-Tek Polymers, Inc., **8** 554
Hibbing Transportation, **I** 448
Hibernia & Shamrock-Bergwerksgesellschaft zu Berlin, **I** 542–43
Hibernian Banking Assoc., **II** 261
Hickory Farms of Ohio, Inc., **12** 178, 199
Hickorycraft, **III** 571
Hicks & Greist, **6** 40
Hicks & Haas, **II** 478
Hicksgas Gifford, Inc., **6** 529
Higginson et Hanckar, **IV** 107
Higgs & Young Inc., **I** 412
High Point Chemical Corp., **III** 38
High Retail System Co., Ltd., **V** 195
Highland Container Co., **IV** 345
Highland Superstores, **9** 65–66; **10** 9–10, 304–05, 468
Highland Telephone Company, **6** 334
Highlands Insurance Co., **III** 498
Highmark International, **I** 109
Highveld Steel and Vanadium Corp., **IV** 22
Higo Bank, **II** 291
Hilbun Poultry, **10** 250
Hilco Technologies, **III** 143; **6** 238
Hilex Poly Co., Inc., **8** 477
Hill & Knowlton Inc., **I** 21; **6** 53. *See also* WPP Group PLC.
Hill Publishing Co., **IV** 634
Hill Stores, **II** 683
Hill's Pet Nutrition, **14** 123
Hill-Rom Company, **10** 349–50
Hillard Oil and Gas Company, Inc., **11** 523
Hillards, PLC, **II** 678
Hillenbrand Industries, Inc., 6 295; **10** **349–51**
Hiller Aircraft Company, **9** 205
Hiller Group, **14** 286
The Hillhaven Corporation, **III** 76, 87–88; **6** 188; **14 241–43**
Hillin Oil, **IV** 658
Hillman, **I** 183
Hills & Dales Railway Co. *See* Dayton Power & Light Company.
Hills Brothers Inc., **II** 548; **7** 383
Hills Pet Products, **III** 25
Hills Stores Company, **11** 228; **13** **260–61**, 445
Hillsborough Holdings Corp., **III** 765–67
Hillsdale Machine & Tool Company, **8** 514
Hillsdown Holdings, PLC, II 513–14
Hillshire Farm, **II** 572
Hilo Electric Light Company, **9** 276
Hilton, Anderson and Co., **III** 669
Hilton Gravel, **III** 670
Hilton Hotels Corporation, **II** 208; **III** **91–93**, 98–99, 102; **IV** 703; **6** 201, 210; **9** 95, 426
Hilton International Co., **6** 385; **12** 489
Himley Brick, **14** 248
Himolene, Inc., **8** 181
Hinde & Dauch Ltd., **IV** 272
Hindell's Dairy Farmers Ltd., **II** 611–12
Hinds, Hayden & Eldredge, **10** 135
Hindustan Petroleum Corp. Ltd., **IV** 441
Hindustan Shipyard, **IV** 484
Hindustan Steel Ltd., **IV** 205–07
Hino Motors, Ltd., 7 219–21

Hinode Life Insurance Co., Ltd., **II** 360; **III** 365
Hinomaru Truck Co., **6** 428
Hip Hing Construction, **IV** 717
Hipercor, S.A., **V** 52
Hiram Walker Resources Ltd., **I** 216, **262–64**; **IV** 721; **6** 478; **9** 391
Hiram Walker-Consumers' Home Ltd. *See* Consumers' Gas Company Ltd.
Hispanica de Petroleos, **IV** 424, 527, 546
Hispano Aviacion, **I** 74
HISPANOBRAS, **IV** 55
Hispanoil. *See* Hispanica de Petroleos.
Hispeed Tools, **I** 573
Hisshin-DCA foods, **II** 554
History Book Club, **13** 105–06
Hit, **II** 164
Hit or Miss, **V** 197–98
Hitachi Ltd., **I 454–55**, 494, 534; **II** 5, 30, 59, 64–65, 68, 70, 73, 75, 114, 273–74, 292–91; **III** 130, 140, 143, 464, 482; **IV** 101; **6** 238, 262; **7** 425; **9** 297; **11** 45, 308, 507; **12 237–39 (upd.)**, 484; **14** 201
Hitachi Metals, Ltd., **IV 101–02**
Hitachi Zosen Corporation, **III 513–14**; **8** 449
Hitco, **III** 721–22
Hjalmar Blomqvist A.B., **II** 639
HL&P. *See* Houston Lighting and Power Company.
HLH Products, **7** 229
HMO-PA. *See* U.S. Healthcare, Inc.
HMT Technology Corp., **IV** 102
HMV, **I** 531
Hoare Govett Ltd., **II** 349
Hobart Corp., **II** 534; **III** 610–11, 654; **7** 276; **12** 549
Hobart Manufacturing Company, **8** 298
Hobbes Manufacturing, **I** 169–70
Hobson, Bates & Partners, Ltd., **14** 48
Hochschild, Kohn Department Stores, **II** 673
Hochtief AG, **14** 298
Hocking Glass Company, **13** 40
Hoden Oil, **IV** 478
Hodenpyl-Walbridge & Company, **14** 134
Hodgkin, Barnett, Pease, Spence & Co., **II** 307
Hoechst A.G., **I** 305–06, 309, 317, **346–48**, 605, 632, 669–70; **IV** 451; **8** 262, 451–53; **13** 75, 262–64
Hoechst Celanese Corporation, **8** 562; **11** 436; **12** 118; **13** 118, **262–65**
Hoeganaes Corporation, **8** 274–75
Hoerner Waldorf Corp., **IV** 264
Hoesch AG, **IV 103–06**, 128, 133, 195, 228, 232, 323
Hoffmann-La Roche & Co. *See* F. Hoffmann-La Roche & Co.
Högbo Stål & Jernwerks, **IV** 202
Högforsin Tehdas Osakeyhtiö, **IV** 300
Hokkaido Butter Co., **II** 575
Hokkaido Colonial Bank, **II** 310
Hokkaido Dairy Cooperative, **II** 574
Hokkaido Dairy Farm Assoc., **II** 538
Hokkaido Electric Power Company Inc., **V 635–37**
Hokkaido Forwarding, **6** 428
Hokkaido Rakuno Kosha Co., **II** 574
Hokkaido Takushoku Bank, **II** 300
Hokoku Cement, **III** 713
Hokoku Fire, **III** 384
Hokuetsu Paper Manufacturing, **IV** 327

Hokuriku Electric Power Company, **V** **638–40**
Hokusin Kai, **IV** 475
Hokuyo Sangyo Co., Ltd., **IV** 285
Holbrook Grocery Co., **II** 682
Holcroft & Company, **7** 521
Holden Group, **II** 457
Holderbank Financière Glaris Ltd., **III** **701–02**; **8** 258–59, 456
Holdernam Inc., **8** 258–59
Holga, Inc., **13** 269
Holiday Inns, Inc., **I** 224; **III 94–95**, 99–100; **6** 383; **9** 425–26; **10** 12; **11** 178, 242; **13** 362; **14** 106; **15** 44, 46
Holiday Rambler Corporation, **7** 213
Holland & Barrett, **13** 103
Holland America Line, **6** 367–68
Holland Hannen and Cubitts, **III** 753
Holland House, **I** 377–78
Holland Motor Express, **14** 505
Holland van 1859, **III** 200
Hollandsche Bank-Unie, **II** 184–85
Hollandse Signaalapparaten, **13** 402
Holley Carburetor, **I** 434
Hollingsworth & Whitney Co., **IV** 329
Hollostone, **III** 673
Holly Corporation, **12 240–42**
Holly Farms Corp., **II** 585; **7** 422–24; **14** 515
Holly Sugar Company. *See* Imperial Holly Corporation.
Hollywood Pictures, **II** 174
Hollywood Records, **6** 176
Holmen Hygiene, **IV** 315
Holmen S.A., **IV** 325
Holmens Bruk, **IV** 317–18
Holmes Electric Protective Co., **III** 644
Holmsund & Kramfors, **IV** 338
Holnam Inc., **III** 702; **8 258–60**
Holson Burnes Group, Inc., **14 244–45**
Holt Manufacturing Co., **III** 450–51
Holt, Rinehart and Winston, Inc., **IV** 623–24; **12** 224
Holthouse Furniture Corp., **14** 236
Holvick Corp., **11** 65
Holvis AG, **15** 229
Holzer and Co., **III** 569
Holzverkohlungs-Industrie AG, **IV** 70
Homart Development, **V** 182
Home & Automobile Insurance Co., **III** 214
Home Box Office Inc., **II** 134, 136, 166–67, 176–77; **IV** 675; **7 222–24**, 528–29; **10** 196; **12** 75
Home Charm Group PLC, **II** 141
Home Depot, Inc., **V 75–76**; **9** 400; **10** 235; **11** 384–86; **12** 7, 235, 345, 385; **13** 250, 548
Home Furnace Co., **I** 481
Home Insurance Company, **I** 440; **III** **262–64**
Home Interiors, **15** 475, 477
Home Oil Company Ltd., **I** 264; **6** 477–78
Home Quarters Warehouse, Inc., **12** 233, 235
Home Savings of America, **II** 181–82; **10** 342–43
Home Shopping Network, Inc., **V 77–78**; **9** 428
Home Telephone and Telegraph Company, **10** 201
Home Telephone Company. *See* Rochester Telephone Corporation.
Homebase, **II** 658; **13** 547–48

HomeClub Inc., **13** 547–48
Homécourt, **IV** 226
HomeFed Bank, **10** 340
Homemade Ice Cream Company, **10** 371
Homemakers Furniture. *See* John M. Smyth Co.
Homer McKee Advertising, **I** 22
Homes By Oakwood, Inc., **15** 328
Homestake Mining Company, **IV** 18, 76; **12 243–45**
Homewood Stores Co., **IV** 573; **7** 550
Homewood Suites, **9** 425–26
Hominal Developments Inc., **9** 512
Hon Industries Inc., **13 266–69**
Honam Oil Refinery, **II** 53
Honcho Real Estate, **IV** 225
Honda Motor Company Limited (Honda Giken Kogyo Kabushiki Kaisha), **I** 9–10, 32, **174–76**, 184, 193; **II** 5; **III** 495, 517, 536, 603, 657–58, 667; **IV** 443; **7** 212–13, 459; **8** 71–72; **9** 294, 340–42; **10 352–54 (upd.)**; **11** 33, 49–50, 352; **12** 122, 401; **13** 30
Hondo Oil & Gas Co., **IV** 375–76
Honeywell Inc., **I** 63; **II** 30, **40–43**, 54, 68; **III** 122–23, 149, 152, 165, 535, 548–49, 732; **6** 266, 281, 283, 314; **8** 21; **9** 171, 324; **11** 198, 265; **12 246–49 (upd.)**; **13** 234, 499
Hong Kong Aircraft Engineering Co., **I** 522; **6** 79
Hong Kong Airways, **6** 78–79
Hong Kong and Kowloon Wharf and Godown Co., **I** 470; **IV** 699
Hong Kong Island Line Co., **IV** 718
Hong Kong Resort Co., **IV** 718
Hong Kong Telecommunications Ltd., **IV** 700; **V** 285–86; **6 319–21**
Hong Leong Corp., **III** 718
Hongkong and Shanghai Banking Corporation Limited, **II** 257, **296–99**, 320, 358; **III** 289
Hongkong Electric Company Ltd., **6 498–500**
Hongkong Land Holdings Ltd., **I** 470–71; **IV 699–701**; **6** 498–99
Honig-Copper & Harrington, **I** 14
Honjo Copper Smeltery, **III** 490
Honolulu Oil, **II** 491
Honolulu Sugar Refining Co., **II** 490
Honshu Paper Co., Ltd., **IV** 268, **284–85**, 292, 297, 321, 326
Hood Rubber Company, **15** 488–89
Hood Sailmakers, Inc., **10** 215
Hoogovens. *See* Koninklijke Nederlandsche Hoogovens en Staalfabricken NV.
Hooiberg, **I** 256
Hook's Drug Stores, **9** 67
Hooker Chemical, **IV** 481
Hooker Petroleum, **IV** 264
Hoover Ball and Bearing Co., **III** 589
The Hoover Company, **II** 7; **III** 478; **12** 158, **250–52**; **15** 416, 418
Hoover Industrial, **III** 536
Hoover Treated Wood Products, Inc., **12** 396
Hoover-NSK Bearings, **III** 589
Hopkinton LNG Corp., **14** 126
Hopper Soliday and Co. Inc., **14** 154
Horizon Bancorp, **II** 252; **14** 103
Horizon Corporation, **8** 348
Horizon Holidays, **14** 36
Horizon Travel Group, **8** 527

Hormel Co. *See* George A. Hormel and Company.
Horn & Hardart, **II** 614
Horn Silver Mines Co., **IV** 83; **7** 187
Hornblower & Co., **II** 450
Hornbrook, Inc., **14** 112
Horne's, **I** 449
Hornsberg Land Co., **I** 553
Horten, **II** 622
Hospital Corporation of America, **II** 331; **III 78–80**; **15** 112
Hospital Cost Consultants, **11** 113
Hospital Products, Inc., **10** 534
Hospital Service Association of Pittsburgh, **III** 325
Hospitality Franchise Systems, Inc., **11 177–79**; **14** 106
Host International, **III** 103
Hot Dog Construction Co., **12** 372
Hot Sam Co., **12** 179, 199
Hot Shoppes Inc., **III** 102
Hotchkiss-Brandt, **II** 116
Hoteiya, **V** 209–10
Hotel Scandinavia K/S, **I** 120
Houdry Chemicals, **I** 298
Houghton Mifflin Company, **10 355–57**
Housatonic Power Co., **13** 182
House and Land Syndicate, **IV** 710
House of Miniatures, **12** 264
House of Windsor, Inc., **9** 533
Household Finance Corp., **I** 31; **II** 417; **8** 117
Household International, Inc., **II 417–20**, 605; **7** 569–70; **10** 419
Household Products Inc., **I** 622; **10** 68
Houston, Effler & Partners Inc., **9** 135
Houston General Insurance, **III** 248
Houston Industries Incorporated, **V 641–44**; **7** 376
Houston International Teleport, Inc., **11** 184
Houston Natural Gas Corp., **IV** 395; **V** 610
Houston Oil & Minerals Corp., **11** 440–41
Houston Oil Co., **IV** 342, 674
Hoveringham Group, **III** 753
Hoving Corp., **14** 501
Hovis-McDougall Co., **II** 565
Howaldtswerke-Deutsche Werft AG, **IV** 201
Howard B. Stark Candy Co., **15** 325
Howard Flint Ink Company, **13** 227
Howard H. Sweet & Son, Inc., **14** 502
Howard Hughes Medical Institute, **II** 33, 35
Howard Humphreys, **13** 119
Howard Johnson Co., **III** 94, 102–03; **6** 27; **7** 266; **11** 177–78; **15** 36
Howard Printing Co., **III** 188; **10** 29
Howard Research and Development Corporation, **15** 412, 414
Howard Smith Paper Mills Ltd., **IV** 271–72
Howden. *See* Alexander Howden Group.
Howdy Company, **9** 177
Howe and Brainbridge Inc., **I** 321
Howe Sound Co., **12** 253
Howe Sound Inc., **IV** 174
Howe Sound Pulp and Paper Ltd., **IV** 321
Howmet Corp., **12 IV** 174; **253–55**
Hoya Corp., **III** 715
Hoyt Archery Company, **10** 216
HQ Office International, **8** 405
Hrubitz Oil Company, **12** 244
HSBC Holdings plc, **12 256–58**

HTH, **12** 464
H2O Plus, **11** 41
Huaneng Raw Material Corp., **III** 718
Hubbard Air Transport, **10** 162
Hubbard, Baker & Rice, **10** 126
Hubbard, Westervelt & Motteley, **II** 425; **13** 341
Hubbell Incorporated, **9 286–87**
Hubinger Co., **II** 508; **11** 172
Huddart Parker, **III** 672
Hudnut, **I** 710
The Hudson Bay Mining and Smelting Company, Limited, **12 259–61**; **13** 502–03
Hudson Engineering Corp., **III** 559
Hudson Foods Inc., **13 270–72**
Hudson Motor Car Co., **I** 135, 158; **III** 568; **10** 292
Hudson Packaging & Paper Co., **IV** 257
Hudson River Railroad, **II** 396
Hudson River Rubber Company, **V** 231
Hudson Scott & Sons, **I** 604
Hudson Software, **13** 481
Hudson Underground Telephone Company, **6** 299
Hudson's, **V** 43–44. *See also* Dayton Hudson Corporation.
Hudson's Bay Company, **I** 284; **IV** 400–01, 437; **V 79–81**; **6** 359; **8** 525; **12** 361
Hue International, **8** 324
Hueppe Duscha, **III** 571
Huff Daland Dusters, **I** 99; **6** 81
Huffco, **IV** 492
Huffman Manufacturing Company, **7** 225–26
Huffy Corporation, **7 225–27**
Hugh O'Neill Auto Co., **12** 309
Hughes Aircraft Co., **I** 172, 484, 539; **II** 32–35; **III** 428, 539; **7** 426–27; **9** 409; **10** 327; **11** 263, 540; **13** 356, 398; **15** 528, 530
Hughes Communications, Inc., **13** 398
Hughes Electric Heating Co., **II** 28; **12** 194
Hughes Supply, Inc., **14 246–47**
Hughes Television Network, **11** 184
Hughes Tool Co., **I** 126; **II** 32; **III** 428–29; **12** 488; **15** 467
Hugo Stinnes GmbH, **I** 542; **8** 69, 494–95
Huguenot Fenal, **IV** 108
Hüls A.G., **I 349–50**
Humana Inc., **III** 79, **81–83**; **6** 28, 191–92, 279; **15** 113
Humason Manufacturing Co., **III** 628
Humber, **I** 197
Humble Oil & Refining Company, **III** 497; **IV** 373, 428; **7** 171; **13** 118; **14** 291. *See also* Exxon.
Humboldt-Deutz-Motoren AG, **III** 541–42, 543; **IV** 126
Hummel, **II** 163–64
Humphrey Instruments, **I** 693
Humphrey's Estate and Finance, **IV** 700
Humphreys & Glasgow Ltd., **V** 612
Hunco Ltd., **IV** 640
Hungária Biztosító, **III** 185
Hungarotex, **V** 166
Hunt Lumber Co., **IV** 358
Hunt Manufacturing Company, **12 262–64**
Hunt Oil Company, **IV** 367, 453–54; **7 228–30**, 378
Hunter Engineering Co., **IV** 18
Hunter Fan Company, **13 273–75**

Hunter-Douglas, **8** 235
Hunter-Hayes Elevator Co., **III** 467
Hunters' Foods, **II** 500
Hunting Aircraft, **I** 50
Huntington Bancshares Inc., 11 180–82
Huntley and Palmer Foods, **II** 544
Huntley Boorne & Stevens, **I** 604
**Huntsman Chemical Corporation, 8
    261–63; 9** 305
Hupp Motor Car Company, **III** 601; **8** 74;
    10 261
Hurd & Houghton, **10** 355
Hurlburt Paper Co., **IV** 311
Huse Food Group, **14** 352
Husky Oil Ltd., **IV** 454, 695; **V** 673–75
Husqvarna Forest & Garden Company, **III**
    480; **13** 564
Hussmann Corp., **I** 457–58; **7** 429–30; **10**
    554; **13** 268
Hutchinson Wholesale Grocery Co., **II** 624
Hutchinson-Mapa, **IV** 560
Hutchison, **I** 470
Hutchison Microtel, **11** 548
Hutchison Whampoa, **IV** 694–95
Huth Manufacturing Corporation, **10** 414
Hüttenwerk Oberhausen AG, **IV** 222
Hüttenwerk Salzgitter AG, **IV** 201
Huttig Sash & Door Company, **8** 135
Hutton, E.F. *See* E.F. Hutton.
Huyck Corp., **I** 429
Hyatt Corporation, II 442; **III** 92, **96–97;**
    9 426
Hyatt Medical Enterprises, **III** 73
Hyatt Roller Bearing Co., **I** 171–72; **9** 17;
    10 326
Hybridtech, **III** 18
Hyde Company, A.L., **7** 116–17
Hydra Computer Systems, Inc., **13** 201
Hydraulic Brake Co., **I** 141
Hydro Med Sciences, **13** 367
Hydro-Aire Incorporated, **8** 135
Hydro-Carbon Light Company, **9** 127
Hydro-Electric Power Commission of
    Ontario, **6** 541; **9** 461
Hydro-Québec, 6 501–03
Hydrocarbon Services of Nigeria Co., **IV**
    473
Hydroponic Chemical Co., **III** 28
Hydrox Corp., **II** 533
Hygeia Sciences, Inc., **8** 85, 512
Hygienic Ice Co., **IV** 722
Hygrade Containers Ltd., **IV** 286
Hygrade Foods, **III** 502; **7** 208; **14** 536
Hyland Laboratories, **I** 627
Hyosung Group, **III** 749
Hyper Shoppes, Inc., **II** 670
Hyperion Press, **6** 176
Hypermart USA, **8** 555–56
Hyplains Beef, **7** 175
Hypo-Bank. *See* Bayerische Hypotheken-
    und Wechsel-Bank AG.
Hypobaruk, **III** 348
Hypro Engineering Inc., **I** 481
Hysol Corp., **I** 321; **12** 103
Hyster-Yale Materials Handling, Inc., **I**
    424; **7** 369–71
Hystron Fibers Inc., **I** 347
Hyundai Group, I 207, 516; **II** 53–54,
    122; **III** 457–59, **515–17; 7 231–34
    (upd.); 9** 350; **10** 404; **12** 211, 546; **13**
    280, 293–94

I.C.H. Corp., **I** 528
I.C. Johnson and Co., **III** 669

I.D. Systems, Inc., **11** 444
I-DIKA Milan SRL, **12** 182
I.G. Farbenindustrie AG, **I** 305–06,
    309–11, 337, 346–53, 619, 632–33,
    698–99; **II** 257; **III** 677, 694; **IV** 111,
    485; **8** 108–09; **11** 7; **13** 75–76, 262
I.J. Stokes Corp., **I** 383
I.M. Pei & Associates, **I** 580; **III** 267
I.M. Singer and Co., **II** 9
I. Magnin Inc., **8** 444; **15** 86
I/N Kote, **IV** 116
I/N Tek, **IV** 116
I.R. Maxwell & Co. Ltd., **IV** 641; **7** 311
I-T-E Circuit Breaker, **II** 121
IBC Holdings Corporation, **12** 276
Iberdrola, **V** 608
Iberia Líneas Aéreas De España S.A., I
    110; **6 95–97**
Ibero-Amerika Bank, **II** 521
Iberswiss Catering, **6** 96
Ibex Engineering Co., **III** 420
IBH Holding AG, **7** 513
IBJ. *See* The Industrial Bank of Japan Ltd.
IBM. *See* International Business Machines
    Corporation.
IBP, inc., II 515–17; 7 525
Ibstock plc, III 735; **14 248–50**
IC Industries Inc., I 456–58; III 512; **7**
    430; **10** 414, 553. *See also* Whitman
    Corporation.
ICA AB, II 639–40
ICA Mortgage Corporation, **8** 30
ICA Technologies, Ltd., **III** 533
ICE, **I** 333
ICI. *See* Imperial Chemical Industries plc.
ICL plc, II 65, 81; **III** 141, 164; **6
    240–42; 11** 150
ICM Mortgage Corporation, **8** 436
ICOA Life Insurance, **III** 253
ICS. *See* International Care Services.
ICX, **IV** 136
ID, Inc., **9** 193
Idaho Frozen Foods, **II** 572–73
Idaho Power Company, 12 265–67
**IDB Communications Group, Inc., 11
    183–85**
Ide Megumi, **III** 549
Ideal Basic Industries, **III** 701–02; **8**
    258–59; **12** 18
Ideal Corp., **III** 602
Idemitso Petrochemicals, **8** 153
Idemitsu Kosan K.K., II 361; **IV 434–36,**
    476, 519
IDG Communications, Inc, **7** 238
IDG World Expo Corporation, **7** 239
IDO. *See* Nippon Idou Tsushin.
IEL. *See* Industrial Equity Ltd.
IFI, **I** 161–62; **III** 347
IFS Industries, **6** 294
IG Farben. *See* I.G. Farbenindustrie AG.
IGA, **II** 624, 649, 668, 681–82; **7** 451; **15**
    479
Iggesund Bruk, **IV** 317–18
IGT-International, **10** 375–76
IGT-North America, **10** 375
IHI, **I** 534
IHI Granitech Corp., **III** 533
Iida & Co., **I** 493
IinteCom, **III** 169
IISCO-Ujjain Pipe and Foundry Co. Ltd.,
    IV 206
IKEA Group, V 82–84
Il Giornale, **13** 493
Illco Toy Co. USA, **12** 496

Illinois Bell Telephone Company, **IV**
    660; **14 251–53**
Illinois Central Corporation, **I** 456, 584;
    8 410; **10** 553; **11 186–89**
Illinois Glass Co., **I** 609
Illinois Merchants Trust Co., **II** 261
Illinois National Bank & Trust Co., **III**
    213–14
Illinois Power Company, 6 470, **504–07**
Illinois Steel Co., **IV** 572; **7** 549; **8** 114
Illinois Terminal Company, **6** 504
Illinois Tool Works Inc., III 518–20
Illinois Traction Company, **6** 504
Illinois Trust and Savings Bank, **II** 261
Ilmor Engineering of Great Britain, **V** 494
Ilse-Bergbau AG, **IV** 229–30
Ilsender Hütte, **IV** 201
Ilwaco Telephone and Telegraph Company.
    See Pacific Telecom, Inc.
IMA Holdings Corp., **III** 73–74
Image Business Systems Corp., **11** 66
Image Technologies Corporation, **12** 264
Imasa Group, **IV** 34
Imasco Limited, **I** 514; **II** 605; **V 401–02**
Imatran Voima Osakeyhtiö, **IV** 469
IMC Drilling Mud, **III** 499
IMC Fertilizer Group, Inc., 8 264–66
Imcera Group, Inc., **8** 264, 266
IMED Corp., **I** 712; **III** 511–12; **10** 551
Imetal S.A., IV 107–09
IMI plc, III 593; **9 288–89**
Imigest Fondo Imicapital, **III** 347
Immunex Corporation, 8 26; **14 254–56**
Immuno Serums, Inc., **V** 174–75
Imo Industries Inc., 7 235–37
IMO Ltd., **III** 539
Impala Platinum Holdings, **IV** 91–93
Imperial Airways, **I** 92; **6** 109–10, 117.
    See also AirEgypt.
Imperial Bank of Canada, **II** 244–45
Imperial Bank of Persia, **II** 298
Imperial British East Africa Co., **III** 522
Imperial Business Forms, **9** 72
Imperial Chemical Industries plc, I 303,
    351–53, 374, 605, 633; **II** 448, 565; **III**
    522, 667, 677, 680, 745; **IV** 38, 110,
    698; **7** 209; **8** 179, 222, 224; **9** 154, 288;
    10 436; **11** 97, 361; **12** 347; **13** 448, 470
Imperial Fire Co., **III** 373
Imperial Goonbarrow, **III** 690
Imperial Group, **II** 513; **III** 503; **7** 209
Imperial Holly Corporation, 12 268–70
Imperial Life Co., **III** 288, 373
Imperial Marine Insurance Co., **III** 384,
    405–06
Imperial Metal Industries Ltd. *See* IMI plc.
Imperial Oil Limited, IV 428, **437–39,**
    494
Imperial Paper, **13** 169
Imperial Pneumatic Tool Co., **III** 525
Imperial Premium Finance, **III** 264
Imperial Savings Association, **8** 30–31
Imperial Smelting Corp., **IV** 58
Imperial Sugar Company. *See* Imperial
    Holly Corporation.
Imperial Tobacco, **I** 425–26, 605; **IV** 260;
    V 401
Imported Auto Parts, Inc., **15** 246
Impressions Software, **15** 455
Imprimis, **8** 467
Impulse, **9** 122
Imreg, **10** 473–74
IMS International, Inc., **10** 105
In-Sink-Erator, **II** 19

INA Corp., **II** 403; **III** 79, 208, 223–25, 226; **11** 481
INA Wälzlager Schaeffler, **III** 595
INA-Naftaplin, **IV** 454
Inabata & Co., **I** 398
InaCom Corporation, **13** 176, **276–78**
Incasso Bank, **II** 185
Inchcape PLC, **II** 233; **III 521–24**
Incheon Iron & Steel Co., **III** 516
Inchon Heavy Industrial Corp., **IV** 183
Inco Limited, **IV** 75, 78, **110–12**
INCO-Banco Indústria e Comércio de Santa Catarina, **13** 70
Incola, S.A., **II** 471
InControl Inc., **11** 460
Incredible Universe, **12** 470
Ind Coope, **I** 215
Indemnité, **III** 391
Indemnity Insurance Co., **III** 224
Indentimat Corp., **14** 542
Independent Breweries Company, **9** 178
Independent Grocers Alliance. *See* IGA.
Independent Lock Co., **13** 166
Independent Metal Products Co., **I** 169
Independent Oil & Gas Co., **IV** 521
Independent Petrochemical, **14** 461
Independent Power Generators, **V** 605
Independent Warehouses, Inc., **IV** 180
India General Steam Navigation and Railway Co., **III** 522
India Life Assurance Co., **III** 359
India Rubber, Gutta Percha & Telegraph Works Co., **I** 428
Indian, **7** 211
Indian Airlines Corporation. *See* Air-India.
Indian Iron & Steel Co. Ltd., **IV** 49, 205–07
Indian Oil Corporation Ltd., **IV 440–41**, 483
Indian Point Farm Supply, Inc., **IV** 458–59
Indiana Bearings, Inc., **13** 78
Indiana Bell Telephone Company, Incorporated, **14 257–61**
Indiana Board and Filler Company, **12** 376
Indiana Electric Corporation, **6** 555
Indiana Gas & Water Company, **6** 556
Indiana Group, **I** 378
Indiana Oil Purchasing Co., **IV** 370
Indiana Power Company, **6** 555
Indiana Refining Co., **IV** 552
Indianapolis Air Pump Company, **8** 37
Indianapolis Brush Electric Light & Power Company, **6** 508
Indianapolis Cablevision, **6** 508–09
Indianapolis Light and Power Company, **6** 508
Indianapolis Motor Speedway Company, **9** 16
Indianapolis Power & Light Company, **6** 508–09
Indianapolis Pump and Tube Company, **8** 37
Indianhead Truck Lines, **6** 371
Indo-Asahi Glass Co., Ltd., **III** 667
Indo-China Steam Navigation Co., **I** 469
Indola Cosmetics B.V., **8** 16
Indonesia Petroleum Co., **IV** 516
Induban, **II** 196
Industria Gelati Sammontana, **II** 575
Industria Metalgrafica, **I** 231
Industria Raffinazione Oli Minerali, **IV** 419
Industrial & Trade Shows of Canada, **IV** 639
Industrial Acceptance Bank, **I** 337

Industrial Bancorp, **9** 229
Industrial Bank of Japan, Ltd., **II 300–01**, 310–11, 338, 369, 433, 459
Industrial Bank of Scotland, **10** 337
Industrial Bio-Test Laboratories, **I** 374, 702
Industrial Cartonera, **IV** 295
Industrial Circuits, **IV** 680
Industrial Computer Corp., **11** 78
Industrial Development Corp., **IV** 22, 92, 534
Industrial Development Corp. of Zambia Ltd., **IV** 239–41
Industrial Engineering, **III** 598
Industrial Engineering Associates, Inc., **II** 112
Industrial Equity Ltd., **I** 438
Industrial Fuel Supply Co., **I** 569
Industrial Gas Equipment Co., **I** 297
Industrial Instrument Company. *See* Foxboro Company.
Industrial Light & Magic, **12** 322
Industrial Mutual Insurance, **III** 264
Industrial National Bank, **9** 229
Industrial Publishing Company, **9** 413
Industrial Reorganization Corp., **III** 502, 556
Industrial Resources, **6** 144
Industrial Trade & Consumer Shows Inc., **IV** 639
Industrial Trust Company, **9** 228
Industrial Vehicles Corp. B.V., **III** 543–44
Industrias y Confecciones, S.A. **V** 51
Industrie Regionale du Bâtiment, **IV** 108
Industrie-Aktiengesellschaft, **IV** 201
Industriegas GmbH., **I** 581
Les Industries Ling, **13** 443
Industrionics Control, Inc., **III** 643
Industrivärden, **II** 366
Induyco. *See* Industrias y Confecciones, S.A.
Inelco Peripheriques, **10** 459
Inexco Oil Co., **7** 282
Infinity Broadcasting Corporation, **11 190–92**
INFLEX, S.A., **8** 247
Inflight Sales Group Limited, **11** 82
Infobase Services, **6** 14
Infonet Services Corporation, **6** 303
Infoplan, **14** 36
Informatics, **III** 248
Informatics General Corporation, **11** 468
Informatics Legal Systems, **III** 169; **6** 285
Information Access Company, **12** 560–62
Information and Communication Group, **14** 555
Information Associates Inc., **11** 78
Information Builders, Inc., **14** 16
Information Consulting Group, **9** 345
Information, Dissemination and Retrieval Inc., **IV** 670
Information Management Science Associates, Inc., **13** 174
Information Resources, Inc., **10 358–60**; **13** 4
Information Unlimited Software, **6** 224
Informix Corp., **10 361–64**, 505
Infrasud, **I** 466
ING, B.V., **14** 45, 47
Ing. C. Olivetti & C., S.p.A., **III** 122, **144–46**, 549, 678; **10** 499
Ingalls Quinn and Johnson, **9** 135
Ingalls Shipbuilding, Inc., **I** 485; **11** 264–65; **12** 28, **271–73**
Ingear, **10** 216

Ingersoll-Rand Company, **III** 473, **525–27**; **10** 262; **13** 27, 523; **15** 187, **223–26 (upd.)**
Inglenook Vineyards, **13** 134
Inglis Ltd., **III** 654; **12** 549
Ingram Corp. Ltd., **III** 559; **IV** 249
Ingram Industries, Inc., **10** 518–19; **11 193–95**; **13** 90, 482
AB Ingredients, **II** 466
Ingredients Technology Corp., **9** 154
Ingres Corporation, **9** 36–37
Ingwerson and Co., **II** 356
INH. *See* Instituto Nacional de Hidrocarboros.
Inhalation Therapy Services, **III** 73
INI. *See* Instituto Nacional de Industria.
Inland Container Corporation, **IV** 311, 341–42, 675; **7** 528; **8 267–69**
Inland Pollution Control, **9** 110
Inland Specialty Chemical Corp., **I** 342; **14** 217
Inland Steel Industries, Inc., **II** 403; **IV 113–16**, 158, 703; **7** 447; **13** 157; **15** 249–50
Inmos Ltd., **I** 532; **11** 307
Inno-France. *See* Societe des Grandes Entreprises de Distribution, Inno-France.
Innovative Pork Concepts, **7** 82
Innovative Products & Peripherals Corporation, **14** 379
Innovative Software Inc., **10** 362
Innovative Sports Systems, Inc., **15** 396
Inns and Co., **III** 734
Innwerk AG, **IV** 229
Inoue Electric Manufacturing Co., **II** 75–76
Input/Output, Inc., **11** 538
Insalaco Markets Inc., **13** 394
INSCO, **III** 242
Insilco Corp., **I** 473; **12** 472
Insley Manufacturing Co., **8** 545
Inspiration Resources Corporation, **12** 260; **13** 502–03
Insta-Care Pharmacy Services, **9** 186
Instant Milk Co., **II** 488
Instapak Corporation, **14** 429
Institut de Sérothérapie Hémopoiétique, **I** 669
Institut für Gemeinwohl, **IV** 139
Institut Merieux, **I** 389
Institut Ronchese, **I** 676
Institute for Scientific Information, **8** 525, 528
Instituto Nacional de Hidrocarboros, **IV** 528
Instituto Nacional de Industria, **I 459–61**; **V** 606–07; **6** 95–96
Instituto per la Ricostruzione Industriale, **V** 614
Instone Airline, **I** 92
Instrumentarium Corp., **13** 328
Instrumentation Laboratory Inc., **III** 511–12
Instrumentation Scientifique de Laboratoire, S.A., **15** 404
Insulite Co. of Finland, **IV** 275
Insurance Co. against Fire Damage, **III** 308
Insurance Co. of North America, **III** 190, 223–25, 367
Insurance Co. of Scotland, **III** 358
Insurance Co. of the State of Pennsylvania, **III** 196
Insurance Corp. of Ireland (Life), **III** 335

Insurance Partners L.P., **15** 257
Intalco Aluminum Corp., **12** 254
INTEC, **6** 428
InteCom Inc., **6** 285
Integon Corp., **IV** 374
Integra-A Hotel and Restaurant Company, **13** 473
Integral Corp., **14** 381
Integrated Business Information Services, **13** 5
Integrated Data Services Co., **IV** 473
Integrated Genetics, **I** 638; **8** 210; **13** 239
Integrated Health Services, Inc., **11** 282
Integrated Medical Systems Inc., **12** 333
Integrated Resources, Inc., **11** 483
Integrated Software Systems Corporation, **6** 224; **11** 469
Integrated Systems Operations. *See* Xerox Corporation.
Integrated Systems Solutions Corp., **9** 284; **11** 395
Integrated Technology, Inc., **6** 279
Integrated Telecom Technologies, **14** 417
Integrity Life Insurance, **III** 249
Intel Corporation, II 44–46, 62, 64; **III** 115, 125, 455; **6** 215–17, 222, 231, 233, 235, 257; **9** 42–43, 57, 114–15, 165–66; **10 365–67 (upd.)**, 477; **11** 62, 308, 328, 490, 503, 518, 520; **12** 61, 449; **13** 47
Intelcom Support Services, Inc., **14** 334
Intelicom Solutions Corp., **6** 229
IntelliCorp, **9** 310
Intelligent Electronics, Inc., 6 243–45; 12 184; **13** 176, 277
Inter IKEA Systems B.V., **V** 82
Inter Island Telephone, **6** 326, 328
Inter State Telephone, **6** 338
Inter-American Development Bank, **IV** 55
Inter-American Satellite Television Network, **7** 391
Inter-City Gas Corp., **III** 654
Inter-City Western Bakeries Ltd., **II** 631
Inter-City Wholesale Electric Inc., **15** 385
Inter-Comm Telephone, Inc., **8** 310
Inter-Mountain Telephone Co., **V** 344
Inter-Regional Financial Group, Inc., 15 231–33
Interactive Systems, **7** 500
Interamericana de Talleras SA de CV, **10** 415
Interbake Foods, **II** 631
InterBold, **7** 146; **11** 151
Interbrás, **IV** 503
Interchemical Corp., **13** 460
Intercity Food Services, Inc., **II** 663
Interco Incorporated, III 528–31; 9 133, 135, 192, 234–35; **10** 184; **12** 156, 306–08
Intercolonial, **6** 360
Intercomi, **II** 233
Intercontinental Apparel, **8** 249
Intercontinental Breweries, **I** 289
Intercontinental Hotels, **I** 248–49
Intercontinental Mortgage Company, **8** 436
Intercontinental Rubber Co., **II** 112
Intercontinentale, **III** 404
Intercostal Steel Corp., **13** 97
Interedi-Cosmopolitan, **III** 47
Interessen Gemeinschaft Farbenwerke. *See* I.G. Farbenindustrie AG.
Interface Group, **13** 483
Interface, Inc., 8 270–72
Interferon Sciences, Inc., **13** 366–67
Interfinancial, **III** 200

InterFirst Bankcorp, Inc., **9** 482
Interfood Ltd., **II** 520–21, 540
Intergraph Corporation, 6 246–49; 10 257
Interhandel, **I** 337–38; **II** 378
INTERIM Services, Inc., **9** 268, 270
The Interlake Corporation, 8 273–75
Interlake Steamship Company, **15** 302
Intermagnetics General Corp., **9** 10
Intermark, Inc., **12** 394
Intermed, **I** 429
Intermedics, **III** 633; **11** 458–59; **12** 325–26
Intermedics Intraocular Inc., **I** 665
Intermoda, **V** 166
Intermountain Broadcasting and Television Corp., **IV** 674
International Aero Engines, **9** 418
International Agricultural Corporation, **8** 264–65
International Assurance Co., **III** 195
International Bank, **II** 261
International Bank of Moscow, **II** 242
International Banking Corp., **II** 253; **9** 123
International Banking Technologies, Inc., **11** 113
International Basic Economy Corporation (IBEC), **13** 103
International Business Machines Corporation, I 26, 455, 523, 534, 541; **II** 6, 8, 10, 42, 44–45, 56, 62, 68, 70, 73, 86, 99, 107, 113, 134, 159, 211, 274, 326, 379, 397, 432, 440; **III** 9, 109–11, 113–18, 121–28, 130, 132–34, 136, 139–43, 145, **147–49**, 151–52, 154–55, 157, 165–72, 200, 246, 313, 319, 326, 458, 475, 549, 618, 685; **IV** 443, 711; **6** 51, 218–25, 233–35, 237, 240–42, 244–48, **250–53 (upd.)**, 254–60, 262, 265, 269–71, 275–77, 279, 281–89, 320, 324, 346, 390, 428; **7** 145–46, 161; **8** 138–39, 466–67; **9** 36, 41–42, 48, 50, 114–15, 131, 139, 165–66, 170–71, 184, 194, 284, 296–97, 310, 327, 463–64; **10** 19, 22–24, 58, 119, 125, 161, 194, 232, 237, 243–44, 255–56, 309, 361–62, 366–67, 394, 456, 463, 474, 500–01, 505, 510, 512–13, 518–19, 542; **11** 19, 45, 50, 59, 61–62, 64–65, 68, 86–88, 150, 273–74, 285, 364, 395, 469, 485, 491, 494, 506, 519; **12** 61, 138–39, 147–49, 161–62, 183, 204, 238, 278, 335, 442, 450, 469–70, 484; **13** 47, 127, 174, 214, 326, 345, 387–88, 403, 482; **14** 13–15, 106, 268–69, 318, 354, 391, 401, 432–33, 446, 533; **15** 106, 440, 454–55, 491–92
International Care Services, **6** 182
International Cellucotton Products Co., **III** 40
International Commercial Bank, **II** 257
International Computers. *See* ICL plc.
International Controls Corporation, 10 368–70
International Corona Corporation, **12** 244
International Credit Card Business Assoc., **II** 436
International Dairy Queen, Inc., 7 266; **10 371–74**
International Data Group, 7 238–40; 12 561
International Development Bank, **IV** 417
International Digital Communications, Inc., **6** 327

International Egyptian Oil Co., **IV** 412
International Engineering Company, Inc., **7** 355
International Epicure, **12** 280
International Equities Corp., **III** 98
International Factoring Corp., **II** 436
International Factors, Limited, **II** 208
International Family Entertainment Inc., 13 279–81
International Flavors & Fragrances Inc., 9 290–92
International Foods, **II** 468
International Game Technology, 10 375–76
International Graphics Corp., **IV** 645
International Group, **13** 277
International Harvester Co., **III** 473, 650, 651; **10** 264, 280, 378, 380, 528; **13** 16. *See also* Navistar International Corporation.
International Healthcare, **III** 197
International Hydron, **10** 47; **13** 367
International Income Property, **IV** 708
International Learning Systems Corp. Ltd., **IV** 641–42; **7** 311
International Lease Finance Corp., **III** 198; **6** 67
International Light Metals Corp., **IV** 163
International Marine Oil Co., **IV** 363
International Match, **12** 463
International Mercantile Marine Co., **II** 330
International Mineral & Chemical, Inc., **8** 265–66
International Multifoods Corporation, II 493; **7 241–43; 12** 80, 125; **14** 515
International News Service, **IV** 626–27
International Nickel Co. of Canada, Ltd., **III** 677; **IV** 78, 110–12
International Nutrition Laboratories, **14** 558
International Pacific Corp., **II** 389
International Paper Company, I 27; **II** 208, 403; **III** 693, 764; **IV** 16, 245, **286–88**, 289, 326; **8** 267; **11** 76, 311; **15 227–30 (upd.)**
International Parts Corporation, **10** 414
International Petroleum Co., Ltd., **IV** 415–16, 438, 478
International Petroleum Corp., **IV** 454, 484
International Playtex, Inc., **12** 93
International Publishing Corp., **IV** 641, 666–67; **7** 343
International Sealants Corporation, **8** 333
International Shoe Co., **III** 528–30
International Silver Company, **I** 30; **12** 472; **14** 482–83
International Standard Electric, **II** 66–68
International Stores, **I** 427
International Supply Consortium, **13** 79
International Telcell Group, **7** 336
International Telephone & Telegraph Corporation, I 434, 446, **462–64**, 544; **II** 13, 66, 68, 86, 130, 331; **III** 98–99, 162–64, 166, 644–45, 684; **V** 334–35, 337–38; **6** 356; **8** 157; **9** 10–11, 324; **10** 19, 44, 301; **11 196–99 (upd.)**, 337, 516; **12** 18; **13** 246; **14** 332, 488
International Terminal Operation Co., **I** 513
International Time Recording Company, **III** 147. *See also* International Business Machines Corporation.
International Trust and Investment Corp., **II** 577
International Trust Co., **II** 207

International Utilities Corp., **IV** 75–76; **6** 444

International Western Electric Co., **I** 462; **II** 66; **III** 162; **11** 196

International Wind Systems, **6** 581

International Wine & Spirits Ltd., **9** 533

International Wire Works Corp., **8** 13

Internationale Industriële Beleggung Maatschappij Amsterdam BV, **IV** 128

InterNorth, Inc., **II** 16; **V** 610

Interocean Management Corp., **9** 509–11

Interpac Belgium, **6** 303

Interprovincial Pipe Line Ltd., **I** 264; **IV** 439

Interpublic Group Inc., **I 16–18**, 31, 36; **6** 53; **14** 315

Intersil, **II** 30; **12** 196

Interstate & Ocean Transport, **6** 577

Interstate Bag, **I** 335

Interstate Bakeries Corporation, **7** 320; **12 274–76**

Interstate Brick Company, **6** 568–69

Interstate Electric Manufacturing Company. *See* McGraw Electric Company.

Interstate Finance Corp., **11** 16

Interstate Financial Corporation, **9** 475

Interstate Paint Distributors, Inc., **13** 367

Interstate Power Company, **6** 555, 605

Interstate Public Service Company, **6** 555

Interstate Stores Inc., **V** 203; **15** 469

Interstate Supply Company. *See* McGraw Electric Company.

Interstate United Corporation, **II** 679; **III** 502; **13** 435

Intertype Corp., **II** 37

Interunfall, **III** 346

Intervideo TV Productions-A.B., **II** 640

Interweb, **IV** 661

Intrac Handelsgesellschaft mbH, **7** 142

Intradal, **II** 572

Intraph South Africa Ltd., **6** 247

IntraWest Bank, **II** 289

The Intrawest Corporation, **15 234–36**

IntroGene B.V., **13** 241

Intuit Inc., **13** 147; **14 262–64**

Invacare Corporation, **11 200–02**, 486

Invep S.p.A., **10** 150

Inveresk Paper Co., **III** 693; **IV** 685

Invergordon Distillers, **III** 509

Inversale, **9** 92

InvestCorp International, **15** 200

Investcorp S.A. *See* Arabian Investment Banking Corp.

Investors Diversified Services, Inc., **II** 398; **6** 199; **8** 348–49; **10** 43–45, 59, 62

Investors Group, **III** 261

Investors Management Corp., **10** 331

Investors Overseas Services, **10** 368–69

Invista Capital Management, **III** 330

Iolab Corp., **III** 36

Ionpure Technologies Corporation, **6** 486–88

Iowa Beef Processors, **II** 516–17; **IV** 481–82; **13** 351

Iowa Manufacturing, **II** 86

Iowa Public Service Company, **6** 523–25

IP Gas Supply Company, **6** 506

IP Services, Inc., **IV** 597

IP Timberlands Ltd., **IV** 288

IP&L. *See* Illinois Power & Light Corporation.

Ipalco Enterprises, Inc., **6 508–09**

IPC Communications, Inc., **15** 196

IPC Magazines Limited, **IV** 650; **7 244–47**

Ipko-Amcor, **14** 225

IPSOA Editore, **14** 555

Iran Air, **6** 101

Iran Pan American Oil Co., **IV** 466

Iranian Oil Exploration and Producing Co., **IV** 466–67

Iraq Petroleum Co., **IV** 363, 386, 429, 450, 464, 558–60

Irby-Gilliland Company, **9** 127

IRI. *See* Instituto per la Ricostruzione Industriale.

IRIS Holding Co., **III** 347

Irish Paper Sacks Ltd., **IV** 295

Irish Sugar Co., **II** 508

Iron and Steel Corp., **IV** 22, 41, 92, 533–34

Iron Cliffs Mining Company, **13** 156

Iron Mountain Forge, **13** 319

Iron Ore Company of Canada, **8** 347

Iroquois Gas Corporation, **6** 526

Irvin Feld & Kenneth Feld Productions, Inc., **15 237–39**

Irving Bank Corp., **II** 192

Irving Trust Co., **II** 257

Irvington Smelting, **IV** 78

Irwin Lehrhoff Associates, **11** 366

Irwin Toy Limited, **14 265–67**

Isabela Shoe Corporation, **13** 360

Iscor. *See* Iron and Steel Corporation.

Isetan Company Limited, **V 85–87**

Iseya Tanji Drapery, **V** 85

Ishikawajima-Harima Heavy Industries Co., Ltd., **I** 508, 511, 534; **II** 274; **III 532–33**; **9** 293; **12** 484

Ishizaki Honten, **III** 715

Isis Distributed Systems, Inc., **10** 501

Island Holiday, **I** 417

Isolite Insulating Products Co., **III** 714

Isosceles PLC, **II** 628–29

Isotec Communications Incorporated, **13** 213

Isover, **III** 676

ISS International Service System, Inc., **8** 271

Istanbul Fertilizer Industry, **IV** 563

Istituto per la Ricostruzione Industriale S.p.A., **I** 207, 459, **465–67**; **II** 191–92, 270–71; **IV** 419; **11 203–06**; **13** 28, 218

Isuzu Motors, Ltd., **II** 274; **III** 581, 593; **7** 8, 219; **9** 293–95; **10** 354

IT International, **V** 255

Itabira Iron Ore Co. Ltd., **IV** 54

ITABRASCO, **IV** 55

Italcarta, **IV** 339

Italcementi, **IV** 420

Italiatour, **6** 69

Italmobiliare, **III** 347

Italstate. *See* Societa per la Infrastrutture e l'Assetto del Territorio.

Italtel, **V** 326–27

Itaú Winterthur Seguradura S.A., **III** 404

Itek Corp., **I** 486; **11** 265

Itel Corporation, **II** 64; **III** 512; **6** 262, 354; **9** 49, **296–99**; **15** 107

Ithaca Gas & Electric. *See* New York State Electric and Gas.

ITM International, **IV** 239

Ito Bank, **II** 373

Ito Food Processing Co., **II** 518

Ito Gofuku Co. Ltd., **V** 129

Ito Meat Processing Co., **II** 518

Ito Processed Food Co., **II** 518

Ito-Yokado Co., Ltd., **II** 661; **V 88–89**

Itochu and Renown, Inc., **12** 281

Itochu of Japan, **14** 550

Itoh. *See* C. Itoh & Co.

Itoham Foods Inc., **II 518–19**

Itokin, **III** 48

ITT. *See* International Telephone and Telegraph Corporation.

ITT Sheraton Corporation, **III 98–101**

ITW. *See* Illinois Tool Works Inc.

ITW Devcon, **12** 7

IURA Edition, **14** 556

IVAC Corp., **I** 646; **11** 90

IVACO Industries Inc., **11** 207

Ivanhoe, Inc., **II** 662, 664

IVAX Corporation, **11 207–09**

Iveco, **I** 148; **12** 91

Iwai & Co., **I** 492, 509–10; **IV** 151

Iwata Air Compressor, **III** 427

IYG Holding Company of Japan, **7** 492

Izod Lacoste, **II** 502–03; **9** 156–57; **10** 324

Izumi Fudosan, **IV** 726

Izumiya, **V** 477

J Bibby & Sons, **I** 424

J Sainsbury PLC, **II 657–59**, 677–78; **10** 442; **11** 239, 241; **13 282–84 (upd.)**

J&G Meakin, **12** 529

J&J Colman, **II** 566

J&J Corrugated Box Corp., **IV** 282; **9** 261

J&L Industrial Supply, **13** 297

J&L Steel. *See* Jones & Laughlin Steel Corp.

J. Aron & Co., **II** 415

J.B. Hunt Transport Services Inc., **12 277–79**; **15** 440

J.B. Lippincott & Company, **IV** 652; **14** 554–56

J.B. McLean Publishing Co., Ltd., **IV** 638

J.B. Williams Company, **III** 66; **8** 63

J.B. Wolters Publishing Company, **14** 554

J. Baker, Inc., **13** 361

J. Bulova Company. *See* Bulova Corporation.

J. Byrons, **9** 186

J.C. Baxter Co., **15** 501

J.C. Penney Company, Inc., **I** 516; **V 90–92**; **6** 336; **8** 288, 555; **9** 156, 210, 213, 219, 346–94; **10** 409, 490; **11** 349; **12** 111, 431, 522; **14** 62

J. Crew Group Inc., **12 280–82**

J.D. Edwards & Company, **14 268–70**

J.D. Powers & Associates, **9** 166

J.E. Baxter Co., **I** 429

J.E. Nolan, **11** 486

J.E. Sirrine. *See* CRSS Inc.

J.E. Smith Box & Printing Co., **13** 441

J. Evershed & Son, **13** 103

J.F. Corporation, **V** 87

J.F. Lauman and Co., **II** 681

J. Fielding & Co., **IV** 249

J.G. McMullen Dredging Co., **III** 558

J. Gadsden Paper Products, **IV** 249

J. George Leyner Engineering Works Co., **III** 525–26

J.H. Stone & Sons, **IV** 332

J.H. Whitney & Company, **9** 250

J. Homestock. *See* R.H. Macy & Co.

J.I. Case Company, **I** 148, 527; **III** 651; **10 377–81**; **13** 17

J.K. Armsby Co., **7** 130–31

J.K. Starley and Company Ltd, **7** 458

J.L. Kraft & Bros. Co., **II** 532

J.L. Shiely Co., **III** 691
J. Levin & Co., Inc., **13** 367
J. Lyons & Co., **I** 215
J.M. Brunswick & Brothers, **III** 442
J.M. Douglas & Company Limited, **14** 141
J.M. Horton Ice Cream Co., **II** 471
J.M. Jones Co., **II** 668
J.M. Kohler Sons Company, **7** 269
The J.M. Smucker Company, **11 210–12**
J.M. Tull Metals Co., Inc., **IV** 116; **15** 250
J-Mass, **IV** 289
J. Muirhead Ltd., **I** 315
J.P. Heilwell Industries, **II** 420
J.P. Morgan & Co. Incorporated, **II** 281,
  329–32, 407, 419, 427–28, 430–31,
  441; **III** 237, 245, 380; **IV** 20, 180, 400;
  9 386; **11** 421; **12** 165; **13** 13
J.P. Stevens Company, **8** 234; **12** 404
J.P. Wood, **II** 587
J.R. Geigy S.A., **I** 632–33, 635, 671; **8**
  108–10
J.R. Parkington Co., **I** 280
J.R. Wyllie & Sons, **I** 437
J. Ray McDermott & Co., **III** 558–59
J.S. Fry & Sons, **II** 476
J.S. Morgan & Co., **II** 329, 427
J. Sanders & Sons, **IV** 711
J. Sears & Company (True-Form Boot
  Company) Ltd., **V** 177
J.T. Wing and Co., **I** 158
J.U. Dickson Sawmill Inc. See Dickson
  Forest Products, Inc.
J.W. Bateson, **8** 87
J.W. Buderus and Sons, **III** 694
J.W. Higman & Co., **III** 690
J. Walter Thompson Co., **I** 9, 17, 25, 37,
  251, 354, 623; **10** 69; **11** 51; **12** 168
J. Weingarten Inc., **7** 203
J. Wiss & Sons Co., **II** 16
J. Zinmeister Co., **II** 682
Jacintoport Corporation, **7** 281
Jack Daniel Distillery, **10** 180
Jack Houston Exploration Company, **7** 345
Jack in the Box, Inc., **14** 194
Jackson & Curtis, **II** 444
Jackson Box Co., **IV** 311
Jackson Cushion Spring Co., **13** 397
Jackson Ice Cream Co., **12** 112
Jackson Marine Corp., **III** 499
**Jackson National Life Insurance
  Company**, **III** 335–36; **8 276–77**
Jackson Purchase Electric Cooperative
  Corporation, **11** 37
Jacksonville Shipyards, **I** 170
Jacob Leinenkeugle Brewing Company, **12**
  338
Jacobs Brake Manufacturing Company, **7**
  116–17
Jacobs Engineering Group Inc., **6
  148–50**
Jacobs Suchard (AG), **II 520–22**, 540,
  569; **15** 64
Jacor Communications, **6** 33
Jacques Borel International, **II** 641; **10** 12
Jacques Fath Perfumes, **III** 47
Jacuzzi, Inc., **7** 207, 209
Jade Accessories, **14** 224
JAF Pampryl, **I** 281
Jafra Cosmetics, **15** 475, 477
Jagenberg AG, **9** 445–46; **14** 57
Jaguar Cars, Ltd., **III** 439, 495; **11** 140;
  13 28, 219, **285–87**, 414
JAI Parabolic Spring Ltd., **III** 582

Ab Jakobstads Cellulosa-Pietarsaaren
  Selluloosa Oy, **IV** 302
Jamaica Gas Light Co., **6** 455
Jamaica Plain Trust Co., **II** 207
Jamaica Water Supply Company. See JWP
  Inc.
JAMCO, **III** 589
James A. Ryder Transportation (Jartran), **V**
  505
James Bay Development Corporation, **6**
  502
James Beam Distilling Co., **I** 226; **10** 180
James Ericson, **III** 324
James Fison and Sons. See Fisons plc.
James Fleming, **II** 500
James G. Fast Company. See Angelica
  Corporation.
James Gulliver Associates, **II** 609
James Hardie Containers, **IV** 249
James Hartley & Son, **III** 724
James Heekin and Company, **13** 254
James Lyne Hancock Ltd., **I** 428
James Magee & Sons Ltd., **IV** 294
James McNaughton Ltd., **IV** 325
James O. Welch Co., **II** 543
James R. Osgood & Company, **10** 356
James River Corporation of Virginia, **IV
  289–91**; **8** 483
James Stedman Ltd., **II** 569
James Talcott, Inc., **11** 260–61
James Thompson, **IV** 22
James Wrigley & Sons, **IV** 257
Jamesway Corporation, **IV** 136; **13** 261
Jamna Auto Industries Pvt. Ltd., **III** 581
Jämsänkoski Oy, **IV** 347
Jane's Information Group, **8** 525
Janesville Electric, **6** 604
Janet Frazer, **V** 118
Janssen Pharmaceutica, **III** 36; **8** 282
Janssen-Kyowa, **III** 43
JANT Pty. Ltd., **IV** 285
Jantzen Inc., **V** 391
Janus Capital Corporation, **6** 400–02
Japan Acoustics, **II** 118
Japan Air Filter Co., Ltd., **III** 634
Japan Air Lines Co., **I 104–06**; **6** 70–71,
  118, 123, 386, 427
Japan Brewery Co., **I** 220, 265
**Japan Broadcasting Corporation
  (Nippon Hoso Kyokai)**, **I** 586; **II** 66,
  101, 118; **7 248–50**; **9** 31
Japan Cable Television, **9** 31
Japan-California Bank, **II** 274
Japan Commerce Bank, **II** 291
Japan Copper Manufacturing Co., **II** 104;
  IV 211
Japan Cotton Co., **IV** 150
Japan Creative Tours Co., **I** 106
Japan Credit Bureau, **II** 348
Japan Dairy Products, **II** 538
Japan Day & Night Bank, **II** 292
Japan Development Bank, **II** 300, 403
Japan Dyestuff Manufacturing Co., **I** 397
Japan Electricity Generation and
  Transmission Company (JEGTCO), **V**
  574
Japan Energy Corporation, **13** 202; **14** 206,
  208
Japan Food Corporation, **14** 288
Japan International Bank, **II** 292
Japan International Liquor, **I** 220
Japan Iron & Steel Co., Ltd., **IV** 157
Japan Leasing Corporation, **8 278–80**;
  11 87

Japan National Oil Corp., **IV** 516
Japan National Railway, **V** 448–50; **6** 70
Japan Oil Development Co., **IV** 364
Japan Petroleum Development Corp., **IV**
  461
Japan Petroleum Exploration Co., **IV** 516
**Japan Pulp and Paper Company
  Limited**, **IV 292–93**, 680
Japan Reconstruction Finance Bank, **II** 300
Japan Special Steel Co., Ltd., **IV** 63
Japan Steel Manufacturing Co., **IV** 211
Japan Steel Works, **I** 508
Japan Telecom, **7** 118; **13** 482
Japan Tobacco Incorporated, **V 403–04**
Japan Trust Bank, **II** 292
Japan Try Co., **III** 758
Japanese and Asian Development Bank, **IV**
  518
Japanese Electronic Computer Co., **III** 140
Japanese Enterprise Co., **IV** 728
Japanese National Railway, **I** 579; **III** 491
Japanese Victor Co., **II** 118
Japex Oman Co., **IV** 516
Japonica Partners, **9** 485
Jarcho Brothers Inc., **I** 513
Jardine Matheson Holdings, **I 468–71**,
  521–22, 577, 592; **II** 296; **IV** 189,
  699–700
Jartran Inc., **V** 505
Järvenpään Kotelo Oy, **IV** 315
Jas, Hennessy & Co., **I** 272
Jas. I. Miller Co., **13** 491
JASCO Products, **III** 581
Jasper Corp., **III** 767. See also Kimball
  International, Inc.
Jato, **II** 652
Jauch & Hübener, **14** 279
Java-China-Japan Line, **6** 403–04
Javelin Software Corporation, **10** 359
Javex Co., **IV** 272
Jax, **9** 452
Jay Cooke and Co., **III** 237; **9** 370
Jay Jacobs, Inc., **15 243–45**
Jay's Washateria, Inc., **7** 372
Jay-Ro Services, **III** 419
Jayco Inc., **13 288–90**
Jaywoth Industries, **III** 673
JCB, **14** 321
JCJL. See Java-China-Japan Line.
Jean Lassale, **III** 619–20
Jean Nate, **I** 695
Jean Pagées et Fils, **III** 420
Jean Prouvost, **IV** 618
Jeanne Piaubert, **III** 47
Jefferson Chemical Co., **IV** 552
Jefferson Fire Insurance Co., **III** 239
Jefferson National Life Group, **10** 247
Jefferson Smurfit Group PLC, **IV
  294–96**
Jefferson Standard Life Insurance, **11**
  213–14
Jefferson Ward, **12** 48–49
Jefferson Warrior Railroad Co., **III** 767
Jefferson-Pilot Corporation, **11 213–15**
Jeffery Sons & Co. Ltd., **IV** 711
Jeffrey Galion, **III** 472
JEGTCO. See Japan Electricity Generation
  and Transmission Company (JEGTCO).
Jell-O Co., **II** 531
Jenaer Glaswerk Schott & Genossen, **III**
  445, 447
Jenn-Air Co., **III** 573
Jennie-O Foods, **II** 506
Jenny Craig, Inc., **10 382–84**; **12** 531

Jeno's, **13** 516
Jensen Salsbery, **I** 715
JEORA Co., **IV** 564
Jeppesen Sanderson, **IV** 677
Jepson Corporation, **8** 230
Jerome Increase Case Machinery Company.
    See J.I. Case Company.
Jerrold Corporation, **10** 319–20
Jerry's Restaurants, **13** 320
Jersey Paper, **IV** 261
Jersey Standard. *See* Standard Oil Co. of
    New Jersey.
Jesse L. Lasky Feature Play Co., **II** 154
Jessup & Moore Paper Co., **IV** 351
Jet America Airlines, **I** 100; **6** 67, 82
Jet Capital Corp., **I** 123
Jet Petroleum, Ltd., **IV** 401
Jet Research Center, **III** 498
Jetway Systems, **III** 512
Jeumont-Industrie, **II** 93
Jeumont-Schneider, **II** 93–94; **9** 10
Jewel Companies, **II** 605; **6** 531; **12** 63
Jewel Food Stores, **7** 127–28; **13** 25
Jewell Ridge Coal Corp., **IV** 181
JG Industries, Inc., 15 240–42
Jiffee Chemical Corp., **III** 21
Jiffy Convenience Stores, **II** 627
Jiffy Lube International, Inc., **IV** 490
Jiffy Packaging, **14** 430
Jim Beam Brands Co., 14 271–73
Jim Walter Corp., **III** 765–67
Jim Walter Papers, **IV** 282; **9** 261
Jitsugyo no Nihon-sha, **IV** 631
Jitsuyo Jidosha Seizo Co., **I** 183
JLA Credit, **8** 279
JMB Realty Corporation, IV 702–03
Jno. Swisher & Son, Inc., **14** 17
JNR. *See* Japan National Railway.
Jo-Gal Shoe Company, Inc., **13** 360
Joanna Cotton Mills, **14** 220
Joannes Brothers, **II** 668
Jockey International, Inc., 12 283–85
Joe Alexander Press, **12** 472
Joe B. Hughes, **III** 498
Joe's Crab Shack, **15** 279
Joh. Parviaisen Tehtaat Oy, **IV** 276
Johann Jakob Rieter & Co., **III** 402
Johannesburg Consolidated Investment Co.
    Ltd., **IV** 21–22, 118
John A. Frye Company, **V** 376; **8** 16
John Alden Life Insurance, **10** 340
**John B. Sanfilippo & Son, Inc., 14
    274–76**
John Bean Spray Pump Co., **I** 442
John Blair & Company, **6** 13
John Brown plc, I 572–74
John Bull, **II** 550
John Crosland Company, **8** 88
John de Kuyper and Son, **I** 377
John Deere. *See* Deere & Company.
John F. Jelke Company, **9** 318
John F. Murray Co., **I** 623; **10** 69
**John Fairfax Holdings Limited, 7
    251–54**
John Gardner Catering, **III** 104
John Govett & Co., **II** 349
John Gund Brewing Co., **I** 253
**John Hancock Mutual Life Insurance
    Company, III 265–68**, 291, 313, 332,
    400; **IV** 283; **13** 530
John Hill and Son, **II** 569
John Holroyd & Co. of Great Britain, **7**
    236
John L. Wortham & Son Agency, **III** 193

John Labatt Ltd., **I** 267; **II** 582; **8** 399
John Laing plc, I 575–76, 588
John Lewis Partnership plc, V 93–95; 13
    307
John Lucas Co., **III** 745
John Lysaght, **III** 493–95
John M. Hart Company, **9** 304
John M. Smyth Co., **15** 282
John Macfarlane and Sons, **II** 593
John Mackintosh and Sons, **II** 568–69
John McConnell & Co., **13** 102
John McLean and Sons Ltd., **III** 753
John Morrell and Co., **II** 595–96
John Nicholls & Co., **III** 690
John Nuveen & Co., **III** 356
John Oster Manufacturing Company, **9** 484
John Pew & Company, **13** 243
John R. Figg, Inc., **II** 681
John Rogers Co., **9** 253
John Strange Paper Company, **8** 358
John Swire & Sons Ltd., **I** 521–22; **6** 415
John Walker & Sons, **I** 239–40
John Williams, **III** 691
John Wyeth & Bro., **I** 713
John Yokley Company, **11** 194
Johns Perry, **III** 673
Johns-Manville Corp., **III** 708; **7** 293; **11**
    420
Johnsen, Jorgensen and Wettre, **14** 249
Johnson. *See* Axel Johnson Group.
Johnson & Higgins, 14 277–80
Johnson & Johnson, I 301; **II** 582; **III**
    18, **35–37**; **IV** 285, 722; **7** 45–46; **8**
    281–83 (upd.), 399, 511–12; **9** 89–90;
    10 47, 69, 78, 80, 534–35; **11** 200; **12**
    186; **15** 357–58, 360
Johnson and Patan, **III** 671
Johnson and Sons Smelting Works Ltd., **IV**
    119
Johnson Brothers, **12** 528
Johnson, Carruthers & Rand Shoe Co., **III**
    528
Johnson Controls, Inc., III 534–37; 13
    398
Johnson Diversified, Inc., **III** 59
Johnson Matthey PLC, II 390; **IV** 23,
    117–20
Johnson Motor Co., **III** 597–99
Johnson Products Co., Inc., **11** 208
Johnson Systems, **6** 224
Johnson Wax. *See* S.C. Johnson & Son,
    Inc.
Johnston Coca-Cola Bottling Company of
    Chattanooga, **13** 163–64
Johnston Evans & Co., **IV** 704
Johnston Foil Co., **IV** 18
Johnston Harvester Co., **III** 650
Johnston Industries, Inc., 15 246–48
Johnstown Sanitary Dairy, **13** 393
Jointless Rim Ltd., **I** 428
Jokisch, **II** 556
Jonathan Backhouse & Co., **II** 235
Jonathan Logan Inc., **13** 536
Jonell Shoe Manufacturing Corporation, **13**
    360
Jones & Babson, Inc., **14** 85
Jones & Johnson, **14** 277
Jones & Laughlin Steel Corp., **I** 463,
    489–91; **IV** 228; **11** 197
Jones Apparel Group, Inc., 11 216–18
Jones Brothers Tea Co., **7** 202
Jones Environmental, **11** 361
Jones Intercable, **14** 260
Jones Motor Co., **10** 44

Jonker Fris, **II** 571
Jonkoping & Vulcan, **12** 462
Jordache, **15** 201–02
The Jordan Company, **11** 261
Jordan Marsh, **III** 608; **V** 26; **9** 209
Jordan Valley Electric Cooperative, **12** 265
Jos. A. Bank Clothiers, **II** 560; **12** 411
Josef Meys, **III** 418
Joseph Bellamy and Sons Ltd., **II** 569
Joseph Campbell Co., **II** 479; **7** 66
Joseph Crosfield, **III** 31
Joseph E. Seagram & Sons, **I** 266, 285
Joseph Garneau Co., **I** 226; **10** 180
Joseph Leavitt Corporation, **9** 20
Joseph Lucas & Son, **III** 554–56
Joseph Magnin, **I** 417–18
Joseph Nathan & Co., **I** 629–40
Joseph Rank Limited, **II** 564
Joseph T. Ryerson & Son, Inc., IV 114;
    15 249–51
Joshin Denki, **13** 481
Joshu Railway Company, **6** 431
Josiah Wedgwood and Sons Limited, **12**
    527–29. *See also* Waterford Wedgewood
    Holdings PLC.
Jostens Inc., 7 255–57
Journey's End Corporation, **14** 107
Jovan, **III** 66
Jove Publications, Inc., **II** 144; **IV** 623; **12**
    224
Jovi, **II** 652
Joy Manufacturing, **III** 526
Joy Planning Co., **III** 533
Joy Technologies, **II** 17
JP Household Supply Co. Ltd., **IV** 293
JP Information Center Co., Ltd., **IV** 293
JP Planning Co. Ltd., **IV** 293
JPC Co., **IV** 155
JPT Publishing, **8** 528
JT Aquisitions, **II** 661
JTL Corporation, **13** 162–63
Jude Hanbury, **I** 294
Judel Glassware Co., Inc., **14** 502
Judson Dunaway Corp., **12** 127
Judson Steel Corp., **13** 97
Jugend & Volk, **14** 556
Jugo Bank, **II** 325
Juice Bowl Products, **II** 480–81
Jujo Paper Co., Ltd., IV 268, 284–85,
    292–93, **297–98**, 321, 326, 328, 356
Julius Berger-Bauboag A.G., **I** 560–61
Jung-Pumpen, **III** 570
Junghans Uhren, **10** 152
Junkers Luftverkehr, **I** 110, 197; **6** 87–88
Juovo Pignone, **13** 356
Jupiter National, **15** 247–48
Jurgens, **II** 588–89
Jurgovan & Blair, **III** 197
Juristförlaget, **14** 556
JUSCO Co., Ltd., V 96–99; 11 498
JVC. *See* Victor Company of Japan, Ltd.
JWP Inc., 9 300–02; 13 176
JWT Group Inc., I 9, **19–21**, 23; **6** 53.
    See also WPP Group plc.
Jylhävaara, **IV** 348

K Line. *See* Kawasaki Kisen Kaisha, Ltd.
K&B Inc., 12 286–88
K&L, **6** 48
K & R Warehouse Corporation, **9** 20
K-C Aviation, **III** 41
K.C.C. Holding Co., **III** 192
K.F. Kline Co., **7** 145
K-H Corporation, **7** 260

K. Hattori & Co., Ltd., **III** 454–55,
    619–20
k.k. Staatsbahnen, **6** 419
K-III Holdings, **7** 286; **12** 360
Ka Wah AMEV Insurance, **III** 200–01
Kable Printing Co., **13** 559
Kaduna Refining and Petrochemicals Co.,
    IV 473
Kaestner & Hecht Co., **II** 120
Kaga Forwarding Co., **6** 428
Kagami Crystal Works, **III** 714
Kagle Home Health Care, **11** 282
Kahan and Lessin, **II** 624–25
Kahn's Meats, **II** 572
Kai Tak Land Investment Co., **IV** 717
**Kaiser Aluminum & Chemical
    Corporation**, **IV** 11–12, 15, 59–60,
    121–23, 191; **6** 148; **12** 377; **8** 348, 350
Kaiser Cement, **III** 501, 760; **IV** 272
Kaiser Company, **6** 184
Kaiser Engineering, **IV** 218
Kaiser Industries, **III** 760
Kaiser Packaging, **12** 377
Kaiser Permanente Corp., **6** 279; **12** 175
Kaizosha, **IV** 632
Kajaani Oy, **II** 302; **IV** 350
Kajima Corp., **I 577–78**
Kalamazoo Paper Co., **IV** 281; **9** 259
Kalbfleish, **I** 300
Kaldveer & Associates, **14** 228
Kalua Koi Corporation, **7** 281
Kalumburu Joint Venture, **IV** 67
Kamaishi, **IV** 157
Kaman Corp., **12 289–92**
Kamioka Mining & Smelting Co., Ltd., **IV**
    145, 148
Kanagawa Bank, **II** 291
Kane Financial Corp., **III** 231
Kane Foods, **III** 43
Kane Freight Lines, **6** 370
Kane-Miller Corp., **12** 106
Kanebo Spinning Inc., **IV** 442
Kanegafuchi Shoji, **IV** 225
Kanematsu Corporation, **IV 442–44**
Kangaroo. *See* Seino Transportation
    Company, Ltd.
Kangol Ltd., **IV** 136
Kangyo Bank, **II** 300, 310, 361
Kanhym, **IV** 91–92
Kansai Electric Power Co., Inc., **IV** 492;
    V 645–48
Kansai Seiyu Ltd., **V** 188
Kansai Sogo Bank, **II** 361
Kansallis-Osake-Pankki, **II** 242, **302–03**,
    366; **IV** 349
Kansas City Power & Light Company, **6
    510–12**, 592; **12** 541–42
Kansas City Southern Industries, Inc., **6
    400–02**
Kansas City White Goods Company. *See*
    Angelica Corporation.
Kansas Fire & Casualty Co., **III** 214
Kansas Power Company, **6** 312
Kansas Public Service Company, **12** 541
Kansas Utilities Company, **6** 580
Kanto Steel Co., Ltd., **IV** 63
Kanzaki Paper Manufacturing Co., **IV** 285,
    293
Kao Corporation, **III 38–39**, 48
Kaohsiung Refinery, **IV** 388
Kaolin Australia Pty Ltd., **III** 691
Kaplan Educational Centers, **12** 143
Kapy, **II** 139
Karafuto Industry, **IV** 320

Karan Co. *See* Donna Karan Company.
Karg'sche Familienstiftung, **V** 73
Karmelkorn Shoppes, Inc., **10** 371, 373
Karstadt Aktiengesellschaft, **V 100–02**
Kasado Dockyard, **III** 760
Kasai Securities, **II** 434
Kaset Rojananil, **6** 123
Kasmarov, **9** 18
Kast Metals, **III** 452; **15** 92
Katalco, **I** 374
Kataoka Electric Co., **II** 5
Katelise Group, **III** 739–40
Kathleen Investment (Australia) Ltd., **III**
    729
Katies, **V** 35
Kativo Chemical Industries Ltd., **8** 239
Katy Industries Inc., **I 472–74**; **14**
    483–84
Katz Communications, Inc., **6 32–34**
Katz Drug, **II** 604
Kauffman-Lattimer, **III** 9–10
Kaufhalle AG, **V** 104
Kaufhof Holding AG, **II** 257; **V 103–05**
Kaufman and Broad Home Corporation,
    8 284–86; **11** 481–83
Kaufmann's Department Stores, **V** 132–33;
    6 243
Kaukaan Tehdas Osakeyhtiö, **IV** 301
Oy Kaukas Ab, **IV** 300–02
Kauppaosakeyhtiö Kymmene Aktiebolag,
    IV 299
Kauppiaitten Oy, **8** 293
Kautex Werke Reinold Hagen AG, **IV** 128
Kautex-Bayern GmbH, **IV** 128
Kautex-Ostfriedland GmbH, **IV** 128
Kawachi Bank, **II** 361
Kawamata, **11** 350
Kawasaki Denki Seizo, **II** 22
Kawasaki Heavy Industries, Ltd., **I** 75;
    II 273–74; **III** 482, 513, 516, **538–40**,
    756; **IV** 124; **7** 232; **8** 72
Kawasaki Kisen Kaisha, Ltd., **V 457–60**
Kawasaki Steel Corporation, **I** 432; **II**
    274; **III** 539, 760; **IV** 30, **124–25**, 154,
    212–13; **13** 324
Kawashimaya Shoten Inc. Ltd., **II** 433
Kawecki Berylco Industries, **8** 78
Kawneer GmbH., **IV** 18
Kawsmouth Electric Light Company. *See*
    Kansas City Power & Light Company.
Kay County Gas Co., **IV** 399
Kay's Drive-In Food Service, **II** 619
Kay-Bee Toy Stores, **V** 137; **15 252–53**
Kayex, **9** 251
Kaynar Manufacturing Company, **8** 366
Kayser Aluminum & Chemicals, **8** 229
Kayser-Roth, **8** 288
Kaysersberg, S.A., **IV** 290
KBLCOM Incorporated, **V** 644
KC Holdings, Inc., **11** 229–30
KCPL. *See* Kansas City Power & Light
    Company.
KCS Industries, **12** 25–26
KCSI. *See* Kansas City Southern
    Industries, Inc.
KCSR. *See* Kansas City Southern Railway.
KDT Industries, Inc., **9** 20
Keebler Co., **II** 594
Keefe Manufacturing Courtesy Coffee
    Company, **6** 392
Keen, Robinson and Co., **II** 566
KEG Productions Ltd., **IV** 640
Keihan JUSCO, **V** 96
Keil Chemical Company, **8** 178

Keio Teito Electric Railway Company, **V
    461–62**
Keisei Electric Railway, **II** 301
Keith-Albee-Orpheum, **II** 88
Kelley & Partners, Ltd., **14** 130
Kellock, **10** 336
Kellogg Company, **I** 22–23; **II** 463,
    502–03, **523–26**, 530, 560; **10** 323–24;
    12 411; **13** 3, **291–94 (upd.)**; **15** 189
Kellwood Company, **V** 181–82; **8 287–89**
Kelly & Associates, **III** 306
Kelly & Cohen, **10** 468
Kelly, Douglas and Co., **II** 631
Kelly Nason, Inc., **13** 203
Kelly Services, Inc., **6 35–37**, 140; **9** 326
The Kelly-Springfield Tire Company, **8
    290–92**
Kelsey-Hayes Group of Companies, **I**
    170; **III** 650, 652; **7 258–60**
Kelso & Co., **III** 663, 665; **12** 436
Kelty Pack, Inc., **10** 215
KemaNobel, **9** 380–81; **13** 22
Kemet Corp., **14 281–83**
Kemi Oy, **IV** 316
Kemira, Inc., **III** 760; **6** 152
Kemp's Biscuits Limited, **II** 594
Kemper Corporation, **III** 269–71, 339;
    15 254–58 (upd.)
Kemper Motorenfabrik, **I** 197
Kemperco Inc., **III** 269–70
Kempinski Group, **II** 258
Kemps Biscuits, **II** 594
Ken-L-Ration, **II** 559
Kendall International, Inc., **I** 529; **III**
    24–25; **IV** 288; **11 219–21**; **14** 121; **15**
    229
Kenetech Corporation, **11 222–24**
Kennametal, Inc., **IV** 203; **13 295–97**
Kennecott Corporation, **III** 248; **IV**
    33–34, 79, 170–71, 179, 192, 288, 576;
    7 261–64; **10** 262, 448; **12** 244
Kenner, **II** 502; **10** 323; **12** 168
Kenner Parker Toys, Inc., **II** 503; **9** 156;
    10 324; **14** 266
Kenroy International, Inc., **13** 274
Kent Drugs Ltd., **II** 640, 650
Kent Fire, **III** 350
Kent-Moore Corp., **I** 200; **10** 492–93
Kentland-Elkhorn Coal Corp., **IV** 181
Kentucky Bonded Funeral Co., **III** 217
Kentucky Fried Chicken, **I** 260–61; **II** 533;
    III 78, 104, 106; **6** 200; **7 26–28**, 433; **8**
    563; **12** 42; **13** 336. *See also* KFC
    Corporation.
Kentucky Utilities Company, **6 513–15**;
    11 37, 236–38
Kenway, **I** 155
Kenwood, **I** 532
Kenworth Motor Truck Corp., **I** 185–86
Kenyon Sons and Craven Ltd., **II** 593–94
Keo Cutters, Inc., **III** 569
KEPCO. *See* Kyushu Electric Power
    Company Inc.
Kerlick, Switzer & Johnson, **6** 48
Kerlyn Oil Co., **IV** 445–46
Kern County Land Co., **I** 527; **10** 379, 527
Kernite SA, **8** 386
Kernkraftwerke Lippe-Ems, **V** 747
Kernridge Oil Co., **IV** 541
Kerr Concrete Pipe Company, **14** 250
Kerr Corporation, **14** 481
Kerr Glass Manufacturing Co., **III** 423
Kerr Group Inc., **10** 130
Kerr-Addison Mines Ltd., **IV** 165

Kerr-McGee Corporation, IV 445–47; **13** 118
Keski-Suomen Tukkukauppa Oy, **8** 293
Kesko Ltd (Kesko Oy), **8** 293–94
Ketchikan International Sales Co., IV 304
Ketchikan Pulp Co., IV 304
Ketchum Communications Inc., **6** 38–40
Ketner and Milner Stores, II 683
Keumkang Co., III 515; **7** 231
Kewanee Public Service Company, **6** 505
Key Computer Laboratories, Inc., **14** 15
Key Markets, II 628
Key Pharmaceuticals, Inc., **11** 207
Key Tronic Corporation, **14** 284–86
KeyCorp, **8** 295–97; **11** 110; **14** 90
Keyes Fibre Company, **9** 303–05
Keystone Aircraft, I 61; **11** 164
Keystone Custodian Fund, IV 458
Keystone Foods Corporation, **10** 443
Keystone Franklin, Inc., III 570; **9** 543
Keystone Gas Co., IV 548
Keystone Insurance and Investment Co., **12** 564
Keystone International, Inc., **11** 225–27
Keystone Life Insurance Co., III 389
Keystone Paint and Varnish, **8** 553
Keystone Pipe and Supply Co., IV 136
Keystone Savings and Loan, II 420
KFC Corporation, **7** 265–68; **10** 450. *See also* Kentuckey Fried Chicken.
Khalda Petroleum Co., IV 413
KHD AG. *See* Klöckner-Humboldt-Deutz AG.
KHD Konzern, III 541–44
KHL. *See* Koninklijke Hollandsche Lloyd.
Kholberg, Kravis & Roberts, **13** 453
Kia Motors Corp., I 167; **12** 293–95
Kidde Inc., I 475–76; III 503; **7** 209
Kidder, Peabody & Co., II 31, 207, 430; IV 84; **7** 310; **12** 197; **13** 465–67, 534
Kidder Press Co., IV 644
Kids ''R'' Us, V 203–05; **9** 394
Kids Foot Locker, **14** 293, 295
Kidston Mines, I 438
Kiekhaefer Corp., III 443
Kien, **13** 545
Kienzle Apparate GmbH, III 566
Kierulff Electronics, **10** 113
Kieser Verlag, **14** 555
Kiewit Diversified Group Inc., **11** 301
Kiewit-Murdock Investment Corp., **15** 129
Kijkshop/Best-Sellers, **13** 545
Kikkoman Corporation, I 9; **14** 287–89
Kilburn & Co., III 522
Kilgo Motor Express, **6** 370
Kilgore Ceramics, III 671
Kilgore Federal Savings and Loan Assoc., IV 343
Kilsby Tubesupply, I 570
Kimball International, Inc., **12** 296–98
Kimbell Inc., II 684
Kimberley Central Mining Co., IV 64; **7** 121
Kimberly-Clark Corporation, I 14, 413; III 36, 40–41; IV 249, 254, 297–98, 329, 648, 665; **8** 282; **15** 357
Kimco Realty Corporation, **11** 228–30
Kincaid Furniture Company, **14** 302–03
Kinden Corporation, **7** 303
KinderCare Learning Centers, Inc., **13** 298–300
Kinear Moodie, III 753
King Bearing, Inc., **13** 79
King Cullen, II 644

King Features Syndicate, IV 626
King Folding Box Co., **13** 441
King Fook Gold and Jewellery Co., IV 717
King Kullen Grocery Co., Inc., **15** 259–61
King Ranch, Inc., **14** 290–92
King Soopers Inc., **12** 112–13
King World Productions, Inc., **9** 306–08
King's Lynn Glass, **12** 528
King-Seeley Thermos, II 419
Kingfisher plc, V 106–09; **10** 498
Kings County Lighting Company, **6** 456
Kings County Research Laboratories, **11** 424
Kings Mills, Inc., **13** 532
Kingsford Corp., III 21
Kingsin Line, **6** 397
Kingsport Pulp Corp., IV 310
Kinki Nippon Railway Company Ltd., V 463–65
Kinko's, **12** 174
Kinnevik, IV 203–04
Kinney National Service Inc., II 176; IV 672
Kinney Services, **6** 293
Kinney Shoe Corp., V 226; **11** 349; **14** 293–95
Kinney Tobacco Co., **12** 108
Kinoshita Sansho Steel Co., I 508
Kinross, IV 92
Kintec Corp., **10** 97
Kirby, III 214. *See also* Scott Fetzer Company.
Kirby Forest Industries, IV 305
Kirch Group, **10** 196
Kirchner, Moore, and Co., II 408
Kirin Brewery Co., I 258, 265–66, 282; **10** 78, 80; **13** 258, 454
Kirk Stieff Company, **10** 181; **12** 313
Kirkstall Forge Engineering, III 494
Kirsch Co., II 16
Kishimoto & Co., I 432, 492
Kishimoto Shoten Co., Ltd., IV 168
Kistler, Lesh & Co., III 528
Kita Karafunto Oil Co., IV 475
Kita Nippon Paper Co., IV 321
Kitagawa & Co. Ltd., IV 442
Kitchell Corporation, **14** 296–98
KitchenAid, III 611, 653–54; **8** 298–99
Kitchenbell, III 43
Kitchens of Sara Lee, II 571–73
Kittery Electric Light Co., **14** 124
Kittinger, **10** 324
Kiwi Packaging, IV 250
Kiwi Polish Co., **15** 507
Kjøbenhavns Bandelsbank, II 366
KJPCL. *See* Royal Interocean Lines.
KKK Shipping, II 274
KKR. *See* Kohlberg Kravis Roberts & Co.
KLA Instruments Corporation, **11** 231–33
Kleiner, Perkins, Caufield & Byers, I 637; **6** 278; **10** 15, 504; **14** 263
Kleinwort Benson Group PLC, II 379, 421–23; IV 191
Kline Manufacturing, II 16
KLM. *See* Koninklijke Luftvaart Maatschappij N.V.
Klöckner-Humboldt-Deutz AG, I 542; III 541–44; IV 126–27; **13** 16–17
Klöckner-Werke AG, IV 43, 60, 126–28, 201
Klondike, **14** 205
Klopman International, **12** 118

King Features Syndicate, IV 626
Kloth-Senking, IV 201
Kluwer Publishers, IV 611; **14** 555
Klynveld Main Goerdeler, **10** 387
Klynveld Peat Marwick Goerdeler. *See* KPMG Worldwide.
KM&G. *See* Ketchum Communications Inc.
Kmart Corporation, I 516; V 35, 110–12; **6** 13; **7** 61, 444; **9** 361, 400, 482; **10** 137, 410, 490, 497, 515–16; **12** 48, 54–55, 430, 477–78, 507–08; **13** 42, 260–61, 274, 317–18, 444, 446; **14** 192, 394; **15** 61–62, 210–11, 330–31, 470
KMP Holdings, I 531
KN. *See* Kühne & Nagel Group.
Kna-Shoe Manufacturing Company, **14** 302
Knapp & Tubbs, III 423
Knapp Communications, II 656; **13** 180
Knapp-Monarch, **12** 251
Knauf, **721**, 736
KNI Retail A/S, **12** 363
Knickerbocker Toy Co., III 505
Knickerbocker Trust Company, **13** 465
Knife River Coal Mining Company, **7** 322–25
Knight Paper Co., III 766
Knight-Ridder, Inc., III 190; IV 597, 613, **628–30**, 670; **6** 323; **7** 191, 327; **10** 407; **15** 262–66 **(upd.)**
Knoff-Bremse, I 138
Knogo Corp., **11** 444
Knoll Group Inc., I 202; **14** 299–301
Knoll Pharmaceutical, I 682
Knomark, III 55
Knorr Co. *See* C.H. Knorr Co.
Knorr-Bremse, **11** 31
Knott, III 98
Knowledge Systems Concepts, **11** 469
KnowledgeWare Inc., **9** 309–11
Knoxville Paper Box Co., Inc., **13** 442
KNSM. *See* Koninklijke Nederlandsche Stoomboot Maatschappij.
Knudsen & Sons, Inc., **11** 211
Knutange, IV 226
Kobayashi Tomijiro Shoten, III 44
Kobe Shipbuilding & Engine Works, II 57
Kobe Steel, Ltd., I 511; II 274; IV 16, 129–31, 212–13; **8** 242; **11** 234–35; **13** 297
Kobelco Middle East, IV 131
Koç Holdings A.S., I 167, 478–80; **11** 139
Koch Industries, Inc., IV 448–49
Koch-Light Laboratories, **13** 239
Kockos Brothers, Inc., II 624
Kodak. *See* Eastman Kodak Company.
Kodansha Ltd., IV 631–33
Ködel & Böhn GmbH, III 543
Koehring Company, **8** 545
Koehring Cranes & Excavators, **7** 513
Koei Real Estate Ltd., V 195
Kohl's Corporation, **9** 312–13
Kohl's Food Stores, I 426–27
Kohlberg, Kravis, Roberts & Co., I 566, 609–11; II 370, 452, 468, 544, 645, 654, 656, 667; III 263, 765–67; IV 642–43; V 55–56, 408, 410, 415; **6** 357; **7** 130, 132, 200; **9** 53, 180, 230, 469, 522; **10** 75–77, 302; **12** 559; **13** 163, 166, 363; **14** 42; **15** 270
Kohler Bros., IV 91
Kohler Company, **7** 269–71; **10** 119
Kohner Brothers, II 531
Koholyt AG, III 693
Koike Shoten, II 458

Kojiro Matsukata, **V** 457–58
Kokomo Gas and Fuel Company, **6** 533
Kokuei Paper Co., Ltd., **IV** 327
Kokura Sekiyu Co. Ltd., **IV** 554
Kokura Steel Manufacturing Co., Ltd., **IV** 212
Kokusai Kisen, **V** 457–58
Kokusaku Kiko Co., Ltd., **IV** 327
Kokusaku Pulp Co., **IV** 327
Kolbenschmidt, **IV** 141
Kolker Chemical Works, Inc., **IV** 409; **7** 308
The Koll Company, 8 300–02
Komag, Inc., 11 234–35
Komatsu Ltd., III 453, 473, **545–46; 15** 92
Kommanditgesellschaft S. Elkan & Co., **IV** 140
Kommunale Energie-Beteiligungsgesellschaft, **V** 746
Kompro Computer Leasing, **II** 457
Konan Camera Institute, **III** 487
Kongl. Elektriska Telegraf-Verket, **V** 331
Kongo Bearing Co., **III** 595
Konica Corporation, III 547–50
Koninklijke Ahold N.V., II 641–42; **12** 152–53
Koninklijke Distilleerderijen der Erven Lucas Böls, **I** 226
Koninklijke Java-China Paketvaart Lijnen. *See* Royal Interocean Lines.
Koninklijke Luchtvaart Maatschappij N.V., I 55, **107–09,** 119, 121; **6** 95, 105, 109–10; **14** 73
Koninklijke Nederlandsche Hoogovens en Staalfabrieken NV, IV 105, 123, **132–34**
Koninklijke Nederlandsche Maatschappig Tot Exploitatie van Petroleumbronnen in Nederlandsch-indie, **IV** 530
Koninklijke Nederlandsche Petroleum Maatschappij, **IV** 491
Koninklijke Nederlandse Vliegtuigenfabriek Fokker, I 46, **54–56,** 75, 82, 107, 115, 121–22
Koninklijke Nedlloyd Groep N.V., 6 403–05
Koninklijke PTT Nederland NV, V 299–301
Koninklijke Wessanen N.V., II 527–29
Koniphoto Corp., **III** 548
Konishi Honten, **III** 547
Konishi Pharmaceutical, **I** 704
Konishiroku Honten Co., Ltd., **III** 487, 547–49
Konoike Bank, **II** 347
Koopman & Co., **III** 419
Koor Industries Ltd., II 47–49
Koortrade, **II** 48
Kop-Coat, Inc., **8** 456
Kopin Corp., **13** 399
Koppens Machinenfabriek, **III** 420
Kopper United, **I** 354
Koppers Inc., I 199, **354–56;** III 645, 735; **6** 486
Korbel, **I** 226
Korea Automotive Fuel Systems Ltd., **13** 555
Korea Development Leasing Corp., **II** 442
Korea Steel Co., **III** 459
Korea Telecommunications Co, **I** 516
Korean Air Lines Co. Ltd., II 442; **6** **98–99**
Korean Development Bank, **III** 459

Korean Tungsten Mining Co., **IV** 183
KorrVu, **14** 430
Kortbetalning Servo A.B., **II** 353
Kortgruppen Eurocard-Köpkort A.B., **II** 353
Korvettes, E.J., **14** 426
Koryeo Industrial Development Co., **III** 516; **7** 232
Koryo Fire and Marine Insurance Co., **III** 747
Kosset Carpets, Ltd., **9** 467
Kotobukiya Co., Ltd., V 113–14
Kowa Metal Manufacturing Co., **III** 758
Koyo Seiko, **III** 595–96, 623–24
KPM. *See* Koninklijke Paketvaart Maatschappij.
KPMG Worldwide, 7 266; **10** 115, **385–87**
Kraft General Foods, Inc., II 129, **530–34,** 556; **V** 407; III 610; **7** 272–77 **(upd.),** 339, 433, 547; **8** 399, 499; **9** 180, 290, 318; **11** 15; **12** 372, 532; **13** 408, 515, 517; **14** 204
Kraft-Versicherungs-AG, **III** 183
Kraftwerk Union, **I** 411; **III** 466
Kramer, **III** 48
Krämer & Grebe, **III** 420
Krauss-Maffei AG, **I** 75; **II** 242; **III** 566, 695; **14** 328
Kravco, **III** 248
Kredietbank N.V., II 295, **304–05**
Kreditanstalt für Wiederaufbau, **IV** 231–32
Kreft, **III** 480
Krelitz Industries, Inc., **14** 147
Krema Hollywood Chewing Gum Co. S.A., **II** 532
Kremers-Urban, **I** 667
Kresge Foundation, **V** 110
Kreuger & Toll, **IV** 338; **12** 462–63
Kreymborg, **13** 544–45
Kriegschemikalien AG, **IV** 229
Kriegsmetall AG, **IV** 229
Kriegswollbedarfs AG, **IV** 229
Krislex Knits, Inc., **8** 235
Krispy Kitchens, Inc., **II** 584
The Kroger Company, II 605, 632, **643–45,** 682; III 218; **6** 364; **7** 61; **12** 111–13; **13** 25, 237, 395; **15** 259, **267–70 (upd.),** 449
Krohn-Fechheimer Shoe Company, **V** 207
Krones A.G., **I** 266
Krovtex, **8** 80
Krumbhaar Chemical Inc., **14** 308
Krupp. *See* Fried. Krupp GmbH.
Krupp Widia GmbH, **12** 66
KSSU Group, **I** 107–08, 120–21
KTR. *See* Keio Teito Electric Railway Company.
KU Energy Corporation, 6 513, 515; **11** **236–38**
Kubota Corporation, I 494; **III 551–53;** **10** 404; **12** 91, 161
Kubota, Gonshiro. *See* Gonshiro Oode.
Kuhara Mining Co., **IV** 475
Kuhlmann, **III** 677; **IV** 174
Kuhn Loeb, **II** 402–03
Kühne & Nagel International AG, V **466–69**
Kuitu Oy, **IV** 348
KUK, **III** 577, 712
Kukje Group, **III** 458
Kulka Smith Inc., **13** 398
Kulmobelwerk G.H. Walb and Co., **I** 581
Kum-Kleen Products, **IV** 252

Kumagai Gumi Co., I 579–80
Kumsung Companies, **III** 747–48
Kunst und Technik Verlag, **IV** 590
Kuo International Ltd., **I** 566
The Kuppenheimer Company, **8** 248–50
Kureha Chemical Industry, **I** 675
Kureha Textiles, **I** 432, 492
Kurosawa Construction Co., Ltd., **IV** 155
Kurose, **III** 420
Kurt Möller Verlag, **7** 42
Kurushima Dockyard, **II** 339
Kuusankoski Aktiebolag, **IV** 299
Kuwait Investment Office, **II** 198; **IV** 380, 452
Kuwait Petroleum Corporation, IV 364, **450–52,** 567
Kwaishinsha Motor Car Works, **I** 183
Kwik Save Group plc, 11 239–41; 13 26
Kwik Shop, Inc., **12** 112
KWIM. *See* Koninklijke West-Indische Maildienst.
KWV, **I** 289
Kygnus Sekiyu K.K., **IV** 555
Kymi Paper Mills Ltd., **IV** 302
Kymmene Corporation, IV 276–77, **299–303,** 337
Kyocera Corporation, II **50–52;** III 693; **7** 118
Kyodo Dieworks Thailand Co., **III** 758
Kyodo Gyogyo Kaisha, Limited, **II** 552
Kyodo Kako, **IV** 680
Kyodo Oil Co. Ltd., **IV** 476
Kyodo Securities Co., Ltd., **II** 433
Kyodo Unyu Kaisha, **I** 502–03, 506; **IV** 713; **V** 481
Kyoei Mutual Fire and Marine Insurance Co., **III** 273
Kyoritsu Pharmaceutical Industry Co., **I** 667
Kyosai Trust Co., **II** 391
Kyoto Bank, **II** 291
Kyoto Ceramic Co., **II** 50–51
Kyoto Ouchi Bank, **II** 292
Kyowa Hakko Kogyo Co., Ltd., III **42–43**
Kyusha Refining Co., **IV** 403
Kyushu Electric Power Company Inc., **IV** 492; **V 649–51**
Kyushu Oil Refinery Co. Ltd., **IV** 434
Kywan Petroleum Ltd., **13** 556
KYZ International, **9** 427
KZO, **13** 21

L'Air Liquide, **I** 303, **357–59; 11** 402
L'Escaut, **III** 335
L'Oréal, II 547; **III 46–49,** 62; **7** 382–83; **8** 129–31; **341–44 (upd.); 11** 41
L'Unite Hermetique S.A., **8** 515
L.A. Darling Co., **IV** 135–36
L.A. Gear, Inc., 8 303–06; 11 349
L&W Supply Corp., **III** 764
L.B. DeLong, **III** 558
L. Bamberger & Co., **V** 169; **8** 443
L. Bosendorfer Klavierfabrik, A.G., **12** 297
L.C. Bassford, **III** 653
The L.D. Caulk Company, **10** 271
L. Fish, **14** 236
L.G. Balfour Company, **12** 472
L. Grossman and Sons. *See* Grossman's Inc.
L.H. Parke Co., **II** 571
L.J. Knowles & Bros., **9** 153
L.L. Bean, Inc., 9 190, 316; **10 388–90;** **12** 280

L.M. Electronics, **I** 489
L.M. Ericsson, **I** 462; **II** 1, 70, 81–82, 365; **III** 479–80; **11** 46, 439; **14** 488
L-N Glass Co., **III** 715
L-N Safety Glass, **III** 715
L-O-F Glass Co. *See* Libbey-Owens–Ford Glass Co.
L. Prang & Co., **12** 207
L.S. DuBois Son and Co., **III** 10
L.S. Starrett Co., 13 301–03
L. Straus and Sons, **V** 168
L.W. Hammerson & Co., **IV** 696
L.W. Singer, **13** 429
La Barge Mirrors, **III** 571
La Cerus, **IV** 615
La Choy, **II** 467–68
La Cinq, **IV** 619
La Concorde, **III** 208
La Crosse Telephone Corporation, **9** 106
La Cruz del Campo S.A., **9** 100
La Favorita Bakery, **II** 543
La India Co., **II** 532
La Petite Academy, **13** 299
La Quinta Inns, Inc., 11 242–44
La Rinascente, **12** 153
La Ruche Meridionale, **12** 153
La Vie Claire, **13** 103
La-Z-Boy Chair Company, 14 302–04
Laakirchen, **IV** 339–40
LAB. *See* Lloyd Aereo de Bolivia.
LaBakelite S.A., **I** 387
Labatt Brewing Co., I 267–68
Labaz, **I** 676; **IV** 546
Labelcraft, Inc., **8** 360
LaBelle Iron Works, **7** 586
Labor für Impulstechnik, **III** 154
Laboratoire Michel Robilliard, **IV** 546
Laboratoire Roger Bellon, **I** 389
Laboratoires d'Anglas, **III** 47
Laboratoires Goupil, **III** 48
Laboratoires Roche Posay, **III** 48
Laboratoires Ruby d'Anglas, **III** 48
Laboratorios Grossman, **III** 55
Laboratory for Electronics, **III** 168; **6** 284
LaBour Pump, **I** 473
LaBow, Haynes Co., **III** 270
Lachine Rapids Hydraulic and Land Company, **6** 501
Lackawanna Steel & Ordnance Co., **IV** 35, 114; **7** 48
Laclede Steel Company, 15 271–73
Lacombe Electric. *See* Public Service Company of Colorado.
Lacquer Products Co., **I** 321
Ladbroke Group PLC, II 139, 141–42
Ladd and Tilton, **14** 527–28
LADD Furniture, Inc., 12 299–301
Ladd Petroleum Corp., **II** 30
LADECO, **6** 97
Ladenso, **IV** 277
Lady Foot Locker, **V** 226; **14** 293, 295
Lafarge Coppée S.A., III 702, 703–05, 736; 8 258; 10 422–23
Lafayette Manufacturing Co., **12** 296
Lafayette Radio Electronics Corporation, **9** 121–22
Laflin & Rand Powder Co., **I** 328; **III** 525
LAG&E. *See* Los Angeles Gas and Electric Company.
Lagoven, **IV** 508
Laidlaw Transportation, Inc., **6** 410
Laing, **IV** 696
Laing's Properties Ltd., **I** 575
Laitaatsillan Konepaja, **IV** 275

Lake Arrowhead Development Co., **IV** 255
Lake Central Airlines, **I** 131; **6** 131
Lake Erie Screw Corp., **11** 534, 536
Lake Superior Consolidated Iron Mines, **IV** 572; **7** 549
Lakeland Fire and Casualty Co., **III** 213
Läkemedels-Industri Föreningen, **I** 664
Laker Airways, **I** 94; **6** 79
Lakeside Laboratories, **III** 24
The Lakeside Publishing and Printing Co., **IV** 660
Lakestone Systems, Inc., **11** 469
Lam Research Corporation, IV 213; **11 245–47**
Lamb Technicon Corp., **I** 486
Lamb-Weston, **I** 417
Lambert Brothers, Inc., **7** 573
Lambert Brussels Financial Corporation, **II** 407; **11** 532
Lambert Kay Company, **8** 84
Lambert Pharmacal Co., **I** 710–11; **III** 28
Lamborghini. *See* Automobili Lamborghini S.p.A.
Lamkin Brothers, Inc., **8** 386
Lamons Metal Gasket Co., **III** 570; **11** 535
Lamontagne Ltd., **II** 651
Lamonts Apparel, Inc., 15 274–76
Lamson & Sessions Co., 13 304–06
Lamson Bros., **II** 451
Lamson Corporation, **7** 145
Lamson Industries Ltd., **IV** 645
Lamson Store Service Co., **IV** 644
Lanca, **14** 224
Lancashire, **III** 350
Lancaster Caramel Co., **II** 510
Lancaster Colony Corporation, 8 307–09
Lancaster Cork Works, **III** 422
Lancaster Financial Ltd., **14** 472
Lancaster National Bank, **9** 475
Lance, Inc., 14 305–07
Lanchester Motor Company, Ltd., **13** 286
Lancia, **I** 162; **11** 102
Lancôme, **III** 46–48; **8** 342
Land O'Lakes, Inc., II 535–37; 7 339; 13 351
Land Securities PLC, IV 704–06
Land-Wheelwright Laboratories, **III** 607; **7** 436
Lander Alarm Co., **III** 740
Länderbank, **II** 282
Landesbank für Westfalen Girozentrale, Münster, **II** 385
Landis International, Inc., **10** 105–06
Landmark Banks, **10** 426
Landmark Communications, Inc., 12 302–05
Landmark Financial Services Inc., **11** 447
Landmark Target Media, **IV** 597
Landor Associates, **I** 94
Landry's Seafood Restaurants, Inc., 15 277–79
Lands' End, Inc., 9 314–16; 12 280
Lane Bryant, **V** 115–16
The Lane Co., Inc., III 528, 530; 12 306–08
Lane Drug Company, **12** 132
Lane Processing Inc., **II** 585
Lane Publishing Co., **IV** 676; **7** 529
Lane Rossi, **IV** 421
Laneco, Inc., **II** 682
Lange International S.A., **15** 462
Lange, Maxwell & Springer, **IV** 641; **7** 311
Langford Labs, **8** 25

Lanier Business Products, Inc., **II** 39; **8** 407
Lano Corp., **I** 446
Lansi-Suomen Osake-Pankki, **II** 303
Lanson Pere et Fils, **II** 475
Lantic Industries, Inc., **II** 664
Lanvin, **I** 696; **III** 48; **8** 343
LAPE. *See* Líneas Aéreas Postales Españolas.
Lapine Technology, **II** 51
Laporte Industries Ltd., **I** 303; **IV** 300
Lapp, **8** 229
Larami Corp., **14** 486
Laroche Navarron, **I** 703
Larousse Group, **IV** 614–15
Larrowe Milling Co., **II** 501; **10** 322
Larsen & Toubro, **IV** 484
Larsen Company, **7** 128
Larson Lumber Co., **IV** 306
Larwin Group, **III** 231
LaSalle Machine Tool, Inc., **13** 7–8
LaSalle National Bank, **II** 184
LaSalles & Koch Co., **8** 443
Oy Läskelä Ab, **IV** 300
Lasky's, **II** 141
Lasmo, **IV** 455, 499
Latrobe Steel Company, **8** 529–31
Laura Ashley Holdings plc, 13 307–09
Laura Scudder's, **7** 429
Laurentien Hotel Co., **III** 99
LaVista Equipment Supply Co., **14** 545
Law Life Assurance Society, **III** 372
Lawn Boy Inc., **7** 535–36; **8** 72
Lawrence Manufacturing Co., **III** 526
Lawrence Warehouse Co., **II** 397–98; **10** 62
Lawrenceburg Gas Company, **6** 466
The Lawson Co., **7** 113
Lawson Milk, **II** 572
Lawter International Inc., 14 308–10
Lawyers Cooperative, **8** 527–28
Lawyers Trust Co., **II** 230
Layne & Bowler Pump, **11** 5
Lazard Freres & Co., **II** 268, 402, 422; **IV** 23, 79, 658–59; **6** 356; **7** 287, 446; **10** 399; **12** 165, 391, 547, 562
LBO Holdings, **15** 459
LBS Communications, **6** 28
LDDS-Metro Communications, Inc., 8 310–12
LDX NET, Inc., **IV** 576
Le Brun and Sons, **III** 291
Le Buffet System-Gastronomie, **V** 74
Le Courviour S.A., **10** 351
Le Rocher, Compagnie de Reassurance, **III** 340
Lea & Perrins, **II** 475
Lea County Gas Co., **6** 580
Lea Lumber & Plywood Co., **12** 300
Leach McMicking, **13** 274
Lead Industries Group Ltd., **III** 681; **IV** 108
Leadership Housing Inc., **IV** 136
Leaf River Forest Products Inc., **IV** 282, 300; **9** 261
Leamington Priors & Warwickshire Banking Co., **II** 318
Lean Cuisine, **12** 531
Lear Inc., **II** 61; **8** 49, 51
Lear Romec Corp., **8** 135
Lear Siegler Inc., I 481–83; III 581; 8 313; **13** 169, 358, 398
Learjet Inc., 8 313–16; 9 242

Leasco Data Processing Equipment Corp.,
  III 342–44; **IV** 641–42; **7** 311
Lease International SA, **6** 358
Leaseway Transportation Corp., V 494;
  12 309–11
Lechmere Inc., 10 391–93
Lechters, Inc., 11 248–50
Leclerc, **12** 153
Lederle Laboratories, **I** 300–02, 657, 684;
  8 24–25; **14** 254, 256, 423
Lee Apparel Company, Inc., 8 317–19
Lee Brands, **II** 500
Lee Company, **V** 390–92
Lee Enterprises, Incorporated, 11
  251–53
Lee Hecht Harrison, **6** 10
Lee Optical, **13** 390
Lee Telephone Company, **6** 313
Lee Way Holding Co., **14** 42
Lee Way Motor Freight, **I** 278
Leeds & County Bank, **II** 318
Leeds & Northrup Co., **III** 644–45
Lefeldt, **III** 417, 418
Lefrak Organization, **8** 357
Legal & General Group plc, III 272–73;
  IV 705, 712
Legal Technologies, Inc., **15** 378
Legault and Masse, **II** 664
Legent Corporation, 10 394–96; **14** 392
Legetojsfabrikken LEGO Billund A/S. *See*
  Lego A/S.
Legg, Mason & Co., **11** 493
Leggett & Platt, Incorporated, 9 93; **11**
  254–56
Lego A/S, 12 495; **13** 310–13
Lehigh Railroad, **III** 258
Lehman Brothers, **I** 78, 125, 484; **II** 192,
  259, 398, 448, 450–51; **6** 199; **10**
  62–63; **11** 263–64; **13** 448; **14** 145
Lehmer Company, **6** 312. *See also*
  McGraw Electric Company.
Lehn & Fink, **I** 699
Lehnkering AG, **IV** 140
Lehrman Bros., **III** 419
Lehser Communications, Inc., **15** 265
Leinenkugel, **I** 253
Leisure Lodges, **III** 76
Leisure System Inc., **12** 359
Leitz, **III** 583–84
LeMaster Litho Supply, **13** 228
Lempereur, **13** 297
Lena Goldfields Ltd., **IV** 94
Lenc-Smith, **III** 430
Lend Lease Corporation Limited, IV
  707–09
Lennar Corporation, 11 257–59
Lennon's, **II** 628
Lennox International Inc., 8 320–22
Lenoir Furniture Corporation, **10** 183
Lenox Awards, **7** 256
Lenox, Inc., I 227; **10** 179, 181; **12**
  312–13
LensCrafters, **V** 207–08; **13** 391
Lentheric, **I** 426
Leo, **I** 665
Leo Burnett Co., I 22–24, 25, 31, 37; **11**
  51, 212; **12** 439
Leonard Development Group, **10** 508
Leonard Express, Inc., **6** 371
Leonard Green & Partners, **12** 477–78
Leonard Silver, **14** 482
Leonardo Editore, **IV** 587
Leonberger Bausparkasse, **II** 258
Lepco Co., **III** 596

Lern, Inc., **II** 420
Lerner Plastics, **9** 323
Lerner Stores, **V** 116
Les Chantiers de l'Atlantique, **II** 13
Les Industries Ling, **13** 443
The Leslie Fay Companies, Inc., 8
  323–25
Leslie Paper, **IV** 288
Lesser-Goldman, **II** 18
Lester B. Knight & Associates, **II** 19
Lester Ink and Coatings Company, **13** 228
Lestrem Group, **IV** 296
Let op Uw Einde, **III** 199
Leucadia National Corporation, 6 396;
  11 260–62
Leuna-Werke AG, **7** 142
N.V. Levensverzekering Maatschappji
  Utrecht, **III** 199–200
Lever Brothers Company, I 17, 21, 26,
  30, 333; **II** 497, 588–89; **III** 31; **7**
  542–43, 545; **9** 291, **317–19**; **13** 199; **14**
  314
Levi Strauss & Co., I 15; **II** 634, 669; **V**
  60–61, **362–65**; **9** 142; **12** 430
Levine, Huntley, Vick & Beaver, **6** 28
Levitt & Sons, **IV** 728
Levitt Homes, **I** 464; **11** 198
Levitz Furniture Inc., 15 280–82
Levy Bakery Goods, **I** 30
Lewis and Marks, **IV** 21–22, 96
Lewis Batting Company, **11** 219
Lewis Construction, **IV** 22
Lewis Grocer Co., **II** 669
Lewis's, **V** 178
Lewis's Bank, **II** 308
Lewis-Howe Co., **III** 56
Lex Electronics, **10** 113
Lexington Broadcast Services, **6** 27
Lexington Furniture Industries, **III** 571
Lexington Ice Company, **6** 514
Lexington Insurance Co., **III** 197
Lexington Utilities Company, **6** 514; **11**
  237
Lexitron, **II** 87
Lexmark International, Inc., **9** 116; **10** 519
Leybold AG, **IV** 71
Leyland and Birmingham Rubber Co., **I**
  429
Leyland Motor Corporation, **7** 459
LFC Financial, **10** 339
LFC Holdings Corp. *See* Levitz Furniture
  Inc.
LFE Corp., **7** 297
LG Electronics Inc., **13** 572, 575
LG&E Energy Corp., 6 516–18
Lhomme S.A., **8** 477
Liaoyang Automotive Spring Factory, **III**
  581
Libbey-Owens-Ford Glass Co., **I** 609; **III**
  640–42, 707, 714–15, 725–26, 731; **IV**
  421; **7** 292
Libby, **II** 547; **7** 382
Libby McNeil & Libby Inc., **II** 489
Libeltex, **9** 92
Liber, **14** 556
Liberty Bank of Buffalo, **9** 229
Liberty Brokerage Investment Company,
  10 278
Liberty House, **I** 417–18
Liberty Life, **IV** 91, 97
Liberty Mexicana, **III** 415
Liberty Mutual Insurance Co., **I** 28
Liberty Mutual Insurance Group, **11** 379
Liberty National Bank, **II** 229

Liberty National Insurance Holding Co., **9**
  506, 508
Liberty National Life Insurance Co., **III**
  217; **9** 506–07
Liberty Natural Gas Co., **11** 441
Liberty's, **13** 307
Libra Bank Ltd., **II** 271
Librairie de Jacques-Francois Brétif, **IV**
  617
Librairie Fayard, **IV** 618
Librairie Générale Francaise, **IV** 618
Librairie Larousse, **IV** 614–16
Librairie Louis Hachette, **IV** 617–18
Librairie Nathan, **IV** 614, 616
Librairie Victor Lecou, **IV** 617
Libyan Arab Airline, **6** 85
Libyan Arab Foreign Bank, **IV** 454
Libyan National Oil Corporation, IV
  453–55
Libyan-Turkish Engineering and
  Consultancy Corp., **IV** 563
Lidköpings Mekaniska Verkstad AB, **III**
  623
Liebert Corp., **II** 20
Life and Casualty Insurance Co. of
  Tennessee, **III** 193
Life Assoc. of Scotland, **III** 310
Life Fitness Inc., **III** 431
Life Insurance Co. of Georgia, **III** 310
Life Insurance Co. of Scotland, **III** 358
Life Insurance Co. of Virginia, **III** 204
Life Insurance Securities, Ltd., **III** 288
Life Investors International Ltd., **III** 179;
  12 199
Life of Eire, **III** 273
Life Retail Stores. *See* Angelica
  Corporation.
Life Savers Co., **II** 129, 544; **7** 367
Life Science Research, Inc., **10** 105–07
Life Technologies, Inc., **I** 321; **12** 103
Life Uniform Shops. *See* Angelica
  Corporation.
Lifecycle, Inc., **III** 431
LifeLink, **11** 378
Lifemark Corp., **III** 74; **14** 232
LIFETIME, **IV** 627
Lifetime Foam Products, Inc., **12** 439
Lift Parts Manufacturing, **I** 157
Ligand Pharmaceutical, **10** 48
Liggett & Meyers, **V** 396, 405, 417–18
Liggett Group Inc., **I** 248; **7** 105; **14** 213;
  15 71
Light & Power Company, **12** 265
Light Corrugated Box Co., **IV** 332
Light-Servicos de Eletricidade S.A., **II** 456
Lightel Inc., **6** 311
Lighting Corp. of America, **I** 476
LIGHTNET, **IV** 576
Lightwell Co., **III** 634
Lignum Oil Co., **IV** 658
LILCO. *See* Long Island Lighting
  Company.
Lillian Vernon Corp., 12 314–15
Lilliput Group plc, **11** 95; **15** 478
Lilly & Co. *See* Eli Lilly & Co.
Lillybrook Coal Co., **IV** 180
Lillywhites Ltd., **III** 105
Lily Tulip Co., **I** 609, 611; **8** 198
Limburger Fabrik und Hüttenverein, **IV**
  103
The Limited, Inc., V 115–16; **9** 142; **12**
  280, 356; **15** 7, 9
Limmer and Trinidad Ltd., **III** 752

LIN Broadcasting Corp., II 331; **6** 323; **9** 320–22; **11** 330
Lin Data Corp., **11** 234
Lincoln American Life Insurance Co., **10** 246
Lincoln Benefit Life Company, **10** 51
Lincoln Electric Co., II 19; **13** 314–16
Lincoln Electric Motor Works, **9** 439
Lincoln First Bank, II 248
Lincoln Income Life Insurance Co., **10** 246
Lincoln Liberty Life Insurance Co., III 254
Lincoln Motor Co., I 165
Lincoln National Corporation, III 274–77; **6** 195; **10** 44
Lincoln Property Company, **8** 326–28
Lincoln Savings, **10** 340
Lincoln Savings & Loan, **9** 199
Lincoln Telephone & Telegraph Company, **14** 311–13
LinCom Corp., **8** 327
Linde A.G., I 297–98, 315, **581–83**; **9** 16, 516; **10** 31–32; **11** 402–03
Lindemann's, I 220
Lindex, II 640
Lindsay Parkinson & Co., I 567
Lindustries, III 502; **7** 208
Linear Corp., III 643
Líneas Aéreas Postales Españolas, **6** 95
Linens 'n Things, **13** 81–82
Linfood Cash & Carry, **13** 103
Linfood Holdings Ltd., II 628–29
Ling Products, **12** 25
Ling-Temco-Vought. See LTV Corporation.
Linjeflyg, I 120
Link House Publications PLC, IV 687
Link-Belt Corp., I 443; IV 660
Lintas: Worldwide, I 18; **6** 30; **14** 314–16
Lintott Engineering, Ltd., **10** 108
Lion Corporation, III 44–45
Lion Manufacturing, III 430
Lion Oil, I 365
Lion's Head Brewery, I 290
Lionel, **12** 494
Lionex Corporation, **13** 46
Lippincott & Margulies, III 283
Lippincott-Raven Publishers, **14** 556
Lipton. See Thomas J. Lipton Company.
Liquid Carbonic, **7** 74, 77
Liquor Barn, II 656
Liquorland, V 35
Liquorsave, II 609–10
LIRCA, III 48
Lisbon Coal and Oil Fuel Co., IV 504
Liscaya, II 196
Litco Bancorp., II 192
Litho-Krome Corp., IV 621
Litronix, III 455
Little, Brown & Company, IV 675; **7** 528; **10** 355
Little Caesar International, Inc., **7** 278–79; **7** 278–79; **15** 344, 346
Little Chef Ltd., III 105–06
Little General, II 620; **12** 179, 200
Little Giant Pump Company, **8** 515
Little Leather Library, **13** 105
Little, Royal, I 529–30; **8** 545; **13** 63
Little Tikes Co., III 614; **12** 169; **13** 317–19
Littlewoods Organisation PLB, V 117–19
Litton Industries Inc., I 85, 452, 476, **484–86**, 523–24; II 33; III 293, 473, 732; IV 253; **6** 599; **10** 520–21, 537; **11**

263–65 (upd.), 435; **12** 248, 271–72, 538–40; **15** 287
Litwin Engineers & Constructors, **8** 546
Livanos, III 516
Liverpool and London and Globe Insurance Co., III 234, 350
Liverpool and London Fire and Life Insurance Co., III 349
Liverpool Fire and Life Insurance Co., III 350
Livia, I 154; **10** 279
Living Centers of America, **13** 49
Living Videotext, **10** 508
Livingston Communications, **6** 313
Livingston, Fargo and Co., II 380, 395; **10** 59
LivingWell Inc., **12** 326
Liz Claiborne, Inc., **8** 329–31
LKB-Produkter AB, I 665
Lloyd A. Fry Roofing, III 721
Lloyd Adriatico S.p.A., III 377
Lloyd Aereo de Bolivia, **6** 97
Lloyd Italico, III 351
Lloyd's Electronics, **14** 118
Lloyd's of London, III 234, **278–81**; **9** 297; **10** 38; **11** 533
Lloyds Bank PLC, II **306–09** 319, 334, 358
Lloyds Life Assurance, III 351
LM Ericsson. See Telefonaktiebolaget LM Ericsson.
LME. See Telefonaktiebolaget LM Ericsson.
LNG Co., IV 473–74
Lo-Cost, II 609
Lo-Vaca Gathering Co., IV 394; **7** 553
Loadometer Co., III 435
Lobitos Oilfields Ltd., IV 381–82
Loblaw Companies., II 631–32
Local Data, Inc., **10** 97
Locations, Inc., IV 727
Locke, Lancaster and W.W.&R. Johnson & Sons, III 680
Lockhart Catering, III 104
Lockhart Corporation, **12** 564
Lockheed Corporation, I 13, 41, 48, 50, 52, 54, 61, 63, **64–66**, 67–68, 71–72, 74, 76–77, 82, 84, 90, 92–94, 100, 102, 107, 110, 113, 121, 126, 195, 493–94, 529; II 19, 32–33; III 84, 539, 601; IV 15; **6** 71; **9** 12, 17–18, 272, 417, 458–60, 501; **10** 163, 262–63, 317, 536; **11** 164, 166, **266–69 (upd.)**, 278–79, 363–65; **12** 190; **13** 126, 128
Lockheed Martin Corporation, **15** **283–86 (upd.).** See also Martin Marietta Corporation.
Lockwood Banc Group, Inc., **11** 306
Lockwoods Foods Ltd., II 513
Loctite Corporation, **8** 332–34
Lodding Engineering, **7** 521
Lodestar Group, **10** 19
Lodge-Cottrell, III 472
Lodging Group, **12** 297
Loeb Rhoades, Hornblower & Co., II 450–51; **9** 469
Loening Aeronautical, I 61; **11** 164
Loew's Consolidated Enterprises, II 154
Loewi Financial Cos., III 270
Loews Corporation, I 245, **487–88**; II 134, 148–49, 169; III 228, 231; **12** **316–18 (upd.)**, 418; **13** 120–21
LOF Plastics, Inc., III 642; **8** 124. See also Libbey-Owens-Ford.

Loffland Brothers Company, **9** 364
Loft Inc., I 276; **10** 451
Logged Off Land Co., IV 355–56
Logic Modeling, **11** 491
Logica plc, **14** 317–19
Logistics, III 431
Logistics Data Systems, **13** 4
Logistics Management Systems, Inc., **8** 33
Logitech, Inc., **9** 116
Logo 7, Inc., **13** 533
Logon, Inc., **14** 377
Loma Linda Foods, **14** 557–58
Lomas & Nettleton Financial Corporation, III 249; **11** 122
Lombard North Central, II 442
Lombard Orient Leasing Ltd., II 442
London & Hull, III 211
London & Leeds Development Corp., II 141
London & Midland Bank, II 318
London and County Bank, II 334
London and Hanseatic Bank, II 256
London and Lancashire Insurance Co., III 350
London and Scottish Marine Oil, **11** 98
London and Westminster Bank, II 333–34
London Asiastic, III 699
London Assurance Corp., III 278, 369–71, 373
London Brick Co., III 502; **7** 208; **14** 249
London Brokers Ltd., **6** 290
London Buses Limited, **6** 406
London Chartered Bank of Australia, II 188
London Clermont Club, III 431
London County and Westminster Bank, II 334
London County Freehold & Leasehold Properties, IV 711
London East India Company, **12** 421
London, Edinburgh and Dublin Insurance Co., III 350
London Electricity, **12** 443
London Film Productions Ltd., II 157; **14** 399
London General Omnibus Company, **6** 406
London Guarantee and Accident Co., III 372
London Insurance Co., III 373
London Joint Stock Bank, II 318, 388
London Life Assoc., IV 711
London Life Insurance Co., II 456–57
London, Provincial and South Western Bank, II 235
London Regional Transport, **6** 406–08
London Weekend Television, IV 650–51; **7** 389
Lone Star and Crescent Oil Co., IV 548
Lone Star Brewing Co., I 255
Lone Star Gas Corp., V 609, 611
Lone Star Industries, III 718, 729, 753; IV 304
Lone Star Steel, I 440–41
Long Distance Discount Services, Inc., **8** 310
Long Distance/USA, **9** 479
Long Island Airways, I 115; **12** 379
Long Island Cable Communication Development Company, **7** 63
Long Island Daily Press Publishing Co., IV 582–83
Long Island Lighting Company, V 652–54; **6** 456
Long Island Trust Co., II 192, 218

Long John Silver's Restaurants Inc., 13 **320–22**

Long Lac Mineral Exploration, **9** 282

Long Life Fish Food Products, **12** 230

Long Manufacturing Co., **III** 439; **14** 63

Long Valley Power Cooperative, **12** 265

Long-Airdox Co., **IV** 136

Long-Term Credit Bank of Japan, Ltd., **II** 301, **310–11**, 338, 369

The Longaberger Company, 12 319–21

Longines-Wittenauer Watch Co., **II** 121

Longman Group Ltd., **IV** 611, 658

Longmat Foods, **II** 494

Longs Drug Stores Corporation, V 120

Longview Fibre Company, 8 335–37

Longwy, **IV** 227

Lonrho Plc, **IV** 651–52; **10** 170

Lonsdale Investment Trust, **II** 421

Lonvest Corp., **II** 456–57

Loomis, Sayles & Co., **III** 313

Loose Leaf Metals Co., Inc., **10** 314

Loral Corporation, II 38; **7** 9; **8 338–40;** **9** 323–25; **13** 356; **15** 283, 285

Lord & Taylor, **13** 44; **14** 376; **15** 86

Lord & Thomas, **I** 12–14; **IV** 660

Lord Baltimore Press, Inc., **IV** 286

Lord Chetwynd's Insurance, **III** 370

Lord Onslow's Insurance, **III** 370

Lorenz, **I** 463

Lorillard Industries, **I** 488; **V** 396, 407, 417; **12** 317

Lorimar Telepictures, **II** 149, 177

Lorraine-Escaut, **IV** 227

Lorvic Corp., **I** 679

Los Angeles Can Co., **I** 599

Los Angeles Drug Co., **12** 106

Los Angeles Gas and Electric Company, **V** 682

Los Angeles Steamship Co., **II** 490

Los Lagos Corp., **12** 175

Los Nietos Co., **IV** 570

Lothringer Bergwerks- und Hüttenverein Aumetz-Friede AG, **IV** 126

Lothringer Hütten- und Bergwerksverein, **IV** 126

Lotus Cars Ltd., 14 320–22

Lotus Development Corp., IV 597; **6** 224–25, 227, **254–56**, 258–60, 270–71, 273; **9** 81, 140; **10** 24, 505; **12** 335

Lotus Publishing Corporation, **7** 239

Lotus Radio, **I** 531

Loucks, Hoffman & Company, **8** 412

Loughead Aircraft Manufacturing Co., **I** 64

Louis Allis, **15** 288

Louis B. Mayer Pictures, **II** 148

Louis C. Edwards, **II** 609

Louis Kemp Seafood Company, **14** 515

Louis Marx Toys, **II** 559; **12** 410

Louis Rich, Inc., **II** 532; **12** 372

Louis Vuitton, I 272; **III** 48; **8** 343; **10** **397–99**

Louisiana & Southern Life Insurance Co., **14** 460

Louisiana Bank & Trust, **11** 106

The Louisiana Land and Exploration Company, IV 76, 365, 367; **7 280–83**

Louisiana-Pacific Corporation, IV 282, **304–05; 9** 260

Louisville Cement Co., **IV** 409

Louisville Gas and Electric Company. *See* LG&E Energy Corporation.

Louisville Home Telephone Company, **14** 258

Louthan Manufacturing Company, **8** 178

Lovelace Truck Service, Inc., **14** 42

Lovering China Clays, **III** 690

Lowe Bros. Co., **III** 745

Lowe's Companies, Inc., V 122–23; 11 384; **12** 234, 345

Lowell Bearing Co., **IV** 136

Lowell Shoe, Inc., **13** 360

Löwenbräu, **I** 220, 257; **II** 240

Lowney/Moirs, **II** 512

Loyalty Group, **III** 241–43

LRL International, **II** 477

LSI. *See* Lear Siegler Inc.

LSI Logic Corporation, 13 323–25

LTA Ltd., **IV** 22

LTV Corporation, I 62–63, **489–91; 7** 107–08; **8** 157, 315; **10** 419; **11** 166, 364; **12** 124

Luberef, **IV** 538

Lubrizol Corp., I 360–62

Lucas Bols, **II** 642

Lucas Digital Ltd., **12** 322

Lucas Girling, **I** 157

Lucas Industries Plc, III 509, **554–57**

Lucasfilm Ltd., 9 368, 472; **12 322–24**

Lucchini, **IV** 228

Lucky Lager Brewing Co., **I** 268

Lucky Stores Inc., **II** 605, 653; **6** 355; **8** 474; **12** 48

Lucky Strike, **II** 143

Lucky-Goldstar, II 53–54; III 457; **13** 574. *See also* Goldstar Co., Ltd.

Ludlow Corp., **III** 645

Lufkin Rule Co., **II** 16

Luftag, **I** 110

Lufthansa. *See* Deutsche Lufthansa A.G.

The Luggage Company, **14** 224

Lukens Inc., 14 323–25

Lukey Mufflers, **IV** 249

Lum's, **6** 199–200

Lumac B.V., **I** 387

Lumbermen's Investment Corp., **IV** 341

Lumbermens Mutual Casualty Co., **III** 269–71; **15** 257

La Lumière Economique, **II** 79

Lummus Co., **IV** 469

Lumonics Inc., **III** 635

Lunenburg Sea Products Limited, **14** 339

Lunevale Products Ltd., **I** 341

Lunn Poly, **8** 525–26

Luotto-Pankki Oy, **II** 303

Lurgei, **6** 599

LURGI. *See* Metallurgische Gesellschaft Aktiengesellschaft.

Luria Bros. and Co., **I** 512–13; **6** 151

Luther's Bar-B-Q, **II** 556

Lux, **III** 478

Lux Mercantile Co., **II** 624

Luxor, **II** 69; **6** 205

Luxury Linens, **13** 81–82

LVMH, **I** 272

LVO Cable Inc., **IV** 596

Lydex, **I** 527

Lykes Corp., **I** 490–91

Lynx Express Delivery, **6** 412, 414

Lyon & Healy, **IV** 660

Lyon's Technological Products Ltd., **III** 745

Lyondell Petrochemical Company, IV 377, **456–57; 10** 110

Lyonnaise Communications, **10** 196

Lyonnaise des Eaux-Dumez, I 576; **V** **655–57**

Lyons. *See* J. Lyons & Co. Ltd.

Lypho-Med, **IV** 333

Oy Lypsyniemen Konepaja, **IV** 275–76

Lysaght's Canada, Ltd., **IV** 73

Lystads, **I** 333

M & S Computing. *See* Intergraph Corporation.

M and G Fund Management, **III** 699

M Stores Inc., **II** 664

M/A Com Inc., **6** 336; **14** 26–27

M.A. Hanna Company, 8 345–47; 12 352

M.A.N., **III** 561–63; **IV** 86

M&M Limited, **7** 299

M&M/Mars, **14** 48; **15** 63–64

M&T Capital Corporation, **11** 109

M.D.C., **11** 258

M.E.P.C. Ltd., **IV** 711

M. Guggenheim's Sons, **IV** 31

M.H. McLean Wholesaler Grocery Company, **8** 380

M. Hensoldt & Söhne Wetzlar Optische Werke AG, **III** 446

M-I Drilling Fluids Co., **III** 473; **15** 468

M.J. Brock Corporation, **8** 460

M. Loeb Ltd., **II** 652

M. Lowenstein Corp., **V** 379

M.M. Warburg. *See* SBC Warburg.

M.P. Burke PLC, **13** 485–86

M.P. Pumps, Inc., **8** 515

M. Polaner Inc., **10** 70

M. Samuel & Co., **II** 208

M.W. Carr, **14** 245

M.W. Kellogg Co., **III** 470; **IV** 408, 534

Ma. Ma-Macaroni Co., **II** 554

Maakauppiaitten Oy, **8** 293–94

Maakuntain Keskus-Pankki, **II** 303

MaasGlas, **III** 667

Maatschappij tot Exploitatie van Steenfabrieken Udenhout, voorheen Weyers, **14** 249

MABAG Maschinen- und Apparatebau GmbH, **IV** 198

Mabley & Carew, **10** 282

Mac Tools, **III** 628

MacAndrews & Forbes Holdings Inc., **II** 679; **III** 56; **9** 129; **11** 334

Maccabees Life Insurance Co., **III** 350

MacDonald Companies, **15** 87

MacDonald, Halsted, and Laybourne, **10** 127

Macdonald Hamilton & Co., **III** 522–23

Macey Furniture Co., **7** 493

Macfarlane Lang & Co., **II** 592–93

Macfield Inc., **12** 502

MacGregor Sporting Goods Inc., **III** 443

Machine Vision International Inc., **10** 232

Mack Trucks Inc., I 147, **177–79; 9** 416; **12** 90

MacKay-Shields Financial Corp., **III** 316

MacKenzie & Co., **II** 361

Mackenzie Hill, **IV** 724

Mackenzie Mann & Co. Limited, **6** 360

Mackey Airways, **I** 102

Mackinnon Mackenzie & Co., **III** 521–22

Maclaren Power and Paper Co., **IV** 165

Maclean Hunter Limited, IV 638–40

Macleans Ltd., **III** 65

Maclin Co., **12** 127

MacMarr Stores, **II** 654

MacMillan Bloedel Limited, IV 165, 272, **306–09**, 721; **9** 391

Macmillan, Inc., IV 637, 641–43; **7** **284–86**, 311–12, 343; **9** 63; **12** 226; **13** 91, 93

Macnaughton Blair, **III** 671

Macneill & Co., **III** 522
Macon Gas Company, **6** 447
Macon Kraft Co., **IV** 311; **11** 421
Maconochie Bros., **II** 569
Macy's. *See* R.H. Macy & Co., Inc.
Maddingley Brown Coal Pty Ltd., **IV** 249
Maddux Air Lines, **I** 125; **12** 487
Madison & Sullivan, Inc., **10** 215
Madison Foods, **14** 557
Madison Furniture Industries, **14** 436
Madison Gas & Electric Company, **6** 605–06
Madison Resources, Inc., **13** 502
Madison Square Garden, **I** 452
Maes Group Breweries, **II** 475
Maeva Group, **6** 206
Magasins Armand Thiéry et Sigrand, **V** 11
Magazine and Book Services, **13** 48
Magazins Réal Stores, **II** 651
Magcobar, **III** 472
Magdeburg Insurance Group, **III** 377
Magdeburger Versicherungsgruppe, **III** 377
Magic Chef Co., **III** 573; **8** 298
Magic Pan, **II** 559–60; **12** 410
Magic Pantry Foods, **10** 382
MagicSoft Inc., **10** 557
Magirus, **IV** 126
Maglificio di Ponzano Veneto dei Fratelli Benetton. *See* Benetton.
Magma Copper Company, 7 287–90, 385–87
Magma Power Company, 11 270–72
Magna Computer Corporation, **12** 149; **13** 97
Magnaflux, **III** 519
Magnavox Co., **13** 398
Magne Corp., **IV** 160
Magnesium Metal Co., **IV** 118
Magnet Cove Barium Corp., **III** 472
MagneTek, Inc., 15 287–89
Magnetic Controls Company, **10** 18
Magnolia Petroleum Co., **III** 497; **IV** 82, 464
Magnus Co., **I** 331; **13** 197
La Magona d'Italia, **IV** 228
Magor Railcar Co., **I** 170
MAGroup Inc., **11** 123
Maharam Fabric, **8** 455
Mahir, **I** 37
Mahou, **II** 474
Mai Nap Rt, **IV** 652; **7** 392
MAI Systems Corporation, 10 242; **11** 273–76
Mailson Ferreira da Nobrega, **II** 200
MAIN. *See* Mid-American Interpool Network.
Main Event Management Corp., **III** 194
Main Street Advertising USA, **IV** 597
Mainline Industrial Distributors, Inc., **13** 79
Mainline Travel, **I** 114
Maison Bouygues, **I** 563
Maizuru Heavy Industries, **III** 514
Majestic Contractors Ltd., **I** 8 419–20
Majestic Wine Warehouses Ltd., **II** 656
Major League Baseball, **12** 457
Major Video Concepts, **6** 410
Major Video, Inc., **9** 74
MaK Maschinenbau GmbH, **IV** 88
Mak van Waay, **11** 453
Makhteshim, **II** 47
Makita Electric Works, **III** 436
Makiyama, **I** 363
Makovsky & Company, **12** 394
Malama Pacific Corporation, **9** 276

Malapai Resources, **6** 546
Malayan Breweries, **I** 256
Malayan Motor and General Underwriters, **III** 201
Malaysia LNG, **IV** 518–19
Malaysian Airlines System BHD, 6 71, **100–02,** 117
Malaysian International Shipping Co., **IV** 518
Malaysian Sheet Glass, **III** 715
Malbak Ltd., **IV** 92–93
Malcolm's Diary & Time-Table, **III** 256
Malcus Industri, **III** 624
Malheur Cooperative Electric Association, **12** 265
Malleable Iron Works, **II** 34
Mallinckrodt Inc., **III** 16; **IV** 146; **8** 85
Malmö Flygindustri, **I** 198
Malmsten & Bergvalls, **I** 664
Malone & Hyde, Inc., **II** 625, 670–71; **9** 52–53; **14** 147
Malrite Communications Group, **IV** 596
Malt-A-Milk Co., **II** 487
Malt-O-Meal Company, **15** 189
Mameco International, **8** 455
Man Aktiengesellschaft, III 301, **561–63**
MAN Gutehoffnungshütte AG, **15** 226
Management Decision Systems, Inc., **10** 358
Management Engineering and Development Co., **IV** 310
Management Recruiters International, **6** 140
Management Science America, Inc., **11** 77
Manbré and Garton, **II** 582
Manchester and Liverpool District Banking Co., **II** 307, 333
Manchester Commercial Buildings Co., **IV** 711
Manco, Inc., **13** 166
Mandabach & Simms, **6** 40
Mandarin Oriental International Ltd., **I** 471; **IV** 700
Mandel Bros., **IV** 660
Manhattan Co., **II** 217, 247
Manhattan Electrical Supply Co., **9** 517
Manhattan Fund, **I** 614
Manhattan Trust Co., **II** 229
Manifatture Cotoniere Meridionali, **I** 466
Manistique Pulp and Paper Co., **IV** 311
Manitoba Bridge and Engineering Works Ltd., **8** 544
Manitoba Paper Co., **IV** 245–46
Manitoba Rolling Mill Ltd., **8** 544
Mann Egerton & Co., **III** 523
Mann Theatres Chain, **I** 245
Mann's Wine Company, Ltd., **14** 288
Manne Tossbergs Eftr., **II** 639
Mannesmann AG, I 411; **III** 564–67; **IV** 222, 469; **14** 326–29 **(upd.)**
Mannheimer Bank, **IV** 558
Manning, Selvage & Lee, **6** 22
Mannstaedt, **IV** 128
Manor Care, Inc., 6 187–90; **14** 105–07; **15** 522
Manorfield Investments, **II** 158
Manos Enterprises, **14** 87
Manpower, Inc., 6 10, 140; **9** 326–27
Mantua Metal Products. *See* Tyco Toys, Inc.
Manufacturers & Merchants Indemnity Co., **III** 191
Manufacturers and Traders Trust Company, **11** 108–09

Manufacturers Hanover Corporation, II 230, 254, **312–14,** 403; **III** 194; **9** 124; **11** 16, 54, 415; **13** 536; **14** 103
Manufacturers National Bank of Brooklyn, **II** 312
Manufacturers National Bank of Detroit, **I** 165; **11** 137
Manufacturers Railway, **I** 219
Manus Nu-Pulse, **III** 420
Manville Corporation, III 706–09, 721; **7** **291–95 (upd.);** **10** 43, 45; **11** 420–22
MAPCO Inc., IV 458–59
Mapelli Brothers Food Distribution Co., **13** 350
Maple Leaf Mills, **II** 513–14
MAPP. *See* Mid-Continent Area Power Planner.
Mar-O-Bar Company, **7** 299
A.B. Marabou, **II** 511
Marantha! Music, **14** 499
Marantz Co., **14** 118
Marathon Oil Co., **IV** 365, 454, 487, 572, 574; **7** 549, 551; **13** 458
Marathon Paper Products, **I** 612, 614
Maraven, **IV** 508
Marbodal, **12** 464
Marboro Books, Inc., **10** 136
Marbro Lamp Co., **III** 571
Marceau Investments, **II** 356
Marchand, **13** 27
Marchland Holdings Ltd., **II** 649
Marconi Wireless Telegraph Co. of America, **II** 25, 88
Marconiphone, **I** 531
Marcus Samuel & Co., **IV** 530
Mardon Packaging International, **I** 426–27
Mardorf, Peach and Co., **II** 466
Maremont Corporation, **8** 39–40
Margarine Unie N.V. *See* Unilever PLC (Unilever N.V.).
Marge Carson, Inc., **III** 571
Margo's La Mode, **10** 281–82
Marico Acquisition Corporation, **8** 448, 450
Marie Callender, **13** 66
Marie-Claire Album, **III** 47
Marigold Foods Inc., **II** 528
Marinduque Mining & Industrial Corp., **IV** 146
Marine Bank and Trust Co., **11** 105
Marine Bank of Erie, **II** 342
Marine Computer Systems, **6** 242
Marine Diamond Corp., **IV** 66; **7** 123
Marine Group, **III** 444
Marine Harvest International, **13** 103
Marine Midland Corp., **I** 548; **II** 298; **9** 475–76; **11** 108
Marine Office of America, **III** 220, 241–42
Marine-Firminy, **IV** 227
Marineland Amusements Corp., **IV** 623
Marion Brick, **14** 249
Marion Freight Lines, **6** 370
Marion Laboratories Inc., I 648–49; **8** 149; **9** 328–29
Marion Manufacturing, **9** 72
Marion Merrell Dow, Inc., 9 328–29 **(upd.)**
Marionet Corp., **IV** 680–81
Marisa Christina, Inc., 15 290–92
Maritime Electric Company, Limited, **15** 182
Mark Goldston, **8** 305
Mark Hopkins, **12** 316
Mark IV Industries, Inc., 7 296–98

Markborough Properties, **II** 222; **V** 81; **8** 525

Market Horizons, **6** 27

Market National Bank, **13** 465

Marketime, **V** 55

Marketing Information Services, **6** 24

Markham & Co., **I** 573–74

Marks and Spencer p.l.c., **I** 588; **II** 513, 678; **V** 124–26; **10** 442

Marks-Baer Inc., **11** 64

Marland Refining Co., **IV** 399–400

MarLennan Corp., **III** 283

Marley Tile, **III** 735

Marlin-Rockwell Corp., **I** 539; **14** 510

Marlow Foods, **II** 565

Marmon Group, **III** 97; **IV** 135–38

Marmon-Perry Light Company, **6** 508

Marquardt Aircraft, **I** 380; **13** 379

Marquette Electronics, Inc., 13 326–28

Marquette Paper Corp., **III** 766

Marriage Mailers, **6** 12

Marriner Group, **13** 175

Marriott Corporation, **II** 173, 608; **III** 92, 94, 99–100, **102–03**, 248; **7** 474–75; **9** 95, 426; **15** 87

Mars, Inc., **II** 510–11; **III** 114; **7** 299–301

Marschke Manufacturing Co., **III** 435

Marsene Corp., **III** 440

Marsh & McLennan Companies, Inc., **III** 280, **282–84**; **10** 39; **14** 279

Marshalk Co., **I** 16

Marshall Die Casting, **13** 225

Marshall Field & Co., **I** 13, 426; **III** 329; **IV** 660; **V** 43–44; **8** 33; **9** 213; **12** 283; **15** 86

Marshalls Incorporated, 13 329–31; 14 62

Marsin Medical Supply Co., **III** 9

Marstellar, **13** 204

The Mart, **9** 120

Martha, **IV** 486

Martin Bros. Ltd., **III** 690

Martin Bros. Tobacco Co., **14** 19

Martin Dennis Co., **IV** 409

Martin Electric Co., **III** 98

Martin Marietta Corporation, **I** 47, **67–69**, 71, 102, 112, 142–43, 184, 416; **II** 32, 67; **III** 671; **IV** 60, 163; **7** 356, 520; **8** 315; **9** 310; **10** 162, 199, 484; **11** 166, 277–78, 364; **12** 127, 290; **13** 327, 356; **15** 283. *See also* Lockheed Martin Corporation.

Martin Mathys, **8** 456

Martin Rooks & Co., **I** 95

Martin Sorrell, **6** 54

Martin Theaters, **14** 86

Martin's, **12** 221

Martin-Brower Corp., **II** 500; **III** 21

Martin-Senour Co., **III** 744

Martineau and Bland, **I** 293

Martins Bank, **II** 236, 308

Martinus Nijhoff, **14** 555

Marubeni K.K., **I** 432, **492–95**, 510; **II** 292, 391; **III** 760; **IV** 266, 525; **12** 147

Maruei & Co., **IV** 151

Marufuku Co., Ltd., **III** 586; **7** 394

Marui Co. Ltd., V 127

Marukuni Kogyo Co., Ltd., **IV** 327

Marutaka Kinitsu Store Ltd., **V** 194

Maruzen Oil Co., Ltd., **II** 348; **IV** 403–04, 476, 554

Marvel Entertainment Group, Inc., 10 400–02

Marvel Metal Products, **III** 570

Marvel-Schebler Carburetor Corp., **III** 438; **14** 63–64

Marvin & Leonard Advertising, **13** 511–12

Marvin Windows, **10** 95

Marwick, Mitchell & Company, **10** 385

Marwitz & Hauser, **III** 446

Marx, **12** 494

Mary Ann Co. Ltd., **V** 89

Mary Ann Restivo, Inc., **8** 323

Mary Ellen's, Inc., **11** 211

Mary Kathleen Uranium, **IV** 59–60

Mary Kay Corporation, **III** 16; **9** **330–32**; **12** 435

Mary Kay Cosmetics, **15** 475, 477

Maryland Casualty Co., **III** 193, 412

Maryland Cup Company, **8** 197

Maryland Distillers, **I** 285

Maryland National Corp., **11** 287

Maryland National Mortgage Corporation, **11** 121

Maryland Shipbuilding and Drydock Co., **I** 170

Maryland Steel Co., **IV** 35; **7** 48

Masayoshi Son, **13** 481–82

Mascan Corp., **IV** 697

Maschinenbauanstalt Humboldt AG, **III** 541

Maschinenfabrik Augsburg-Nürnberg. *See* M.A.N.

Maschinenfabrik Deutschland, **IV** 103

Maschinenfabrik für den Bergbau von Sievers & Co., **III** 541

Maschinenfabrik Gebr. Meer, **III** 565

Maschinenfabrik Sürth, **I** 581

Masco Corporation, **III** 568–71; **11** 385, 534–35; **12** 129, 131, 344; **13** 338

Masco Optical, **13** 165

Mascon Toy Co., **III** 569

MASCOR, **14** 13

Mase Westpac Limited, **11** 418

Maserati. *See* Officine Alfieri Maserati S.p.A.

Masinfabriks A.B. Scania, **I** 197

MASkargo Ltd., **6** 101

Mason & Hamlin, **III** 656

Mason Best Co., **IV** 343

Masonite Corp., **III** 764

Masonite Holdings, **III** 687

Massachusetts Bank, **II** 207

Massachusetts Capital Resources Corp., **III** 314

Massachusetts Mutual Life Insurance Company, **III** 110, **285–87**, 305; **14** 14

Massey-Ferguson, **II** 222, 245; **III** 439, 650–52; **13** 18

Mast Industries, **V** 115–16

Master Boot Polish Co., **II** 566

Master Builders, **I** 673

Master Electric Company, **15** 134

Master Pneumatic Tool Co., **III** 436

Master Products, **14** 162

Master Shield Inc., **7** 116

Master Tank and Welding Company, **7** 541

MasterBrand Industries Inc., **12** 344–45

MasterCard International, Inc., 9 333–35

Mastercraft Homes, Inc., **11** 257

Mastercraft Industries Corp., **III** 654

Matairco, **9** 27

Matchbox Toys Ltd., **12** 168

Matco Tools, **7** 116

Materials Service Corp., **I** 58

Mather & Crother Advertising Agency, **I** 25

Mather Co., **I** 159

Mather Metals, **III** 582

Matheson & Co., **IV** 189

Mathews Conveyor Co., **14** 43

Mathieson Chemical Corp., **I** 379–80, 695; **13** 379

Matra, **II** 38, 70; **IV** 617–19; **13** 356

Matra-Hachette S.A., 15 293–97 (upd.)

Matrix Science Corp., **II** 8; **14** 27

Matson Navigation Company, Inc., **II** 490–91; **10** 40

Matsumoto Medical Instruments, **11** 476

Matsushita Electric Industrial Co., Ltd., **II** 5, **55–56**, 58, 61, 91–92, 102, 117–19, 361, 455; **III** 476, 710; **6** 36; **7** 163, 302; **10** 286, 389, 403, 432; **11** 487; **12** 448; **13** 398

Matsushita Electric Works, Ltd., **III** **710–11**; **7** 302–03 (upd.); **12** 454

Matsushita Kotobuki Electronics Industries, Ltd., **10** 458–59

Matsuura Trading Co., Ltd., **IV** 327

Matsuzakaya Company, **V** 129–31

Mattatuck Bank & Trust Co., **13** 467

Mattel, Inc., **II** 136; **III** 506; **7** 304–07; **12** 74, 168–69, 495; **13** 560–61; **15** 238

Matthes & Weber, **III** 32

Matthew Bender & Company, Inc., **IV** 677; **7** 94; **14** 97

Maud Foster Mill, **II** 566

Maui Electric Company, **9** 276

Mauna Kea Properties, **6** 129

Maurice H. Needham Co., **I** 31

Maus-Nordmann, **V** 10

Max Factor & Co., **III** 54, 56; **6** 51; **12** 314

Max Klein, Inc., **II** 572

Maxcell Telecom Plus, **6** 323

Maxell Corp., **I** 500; **14** 534

Maxi Vac, Inc., **9** 72

MAXI-Papier, **10** 498

Maxicare Health Plans, Inc., III 84–86

Maxis Software, **13** 115

Maxoptix Corporation, **10** 404

Maxtor Corporation, **6** 230; **10** 403–05, 459, 463–64

Maxus Energy Corporation, **IV** 410; **7** **308–10**; **10** 191

Maxwell Communication Corporation plc, **IV** 605, 611, **641–43**; **7** 286, **311–13 (upd.)**, 343; **10** 288; **13** 91–93

Maxwell House Coffee, **II** 531

Maxwell Morton Corp, **I** 144, 414

MAXXAM Inc., **IV** 121, 123; **8** 348–50

Maxxim Medical Inc., 12 325–27

May and Baker, **I** 388

May Company Department Stores, **I** 540; **II** 414; **V** 132–35; **8** 288; **11** 349; **12** 55, 507–08; **13** 42, 361; **15** 275

Maybelline, **I** 684

Mayfair Foods, **I** 438

Mayfield Dairy Farms, Inc., **7** 128

Mayflower Group Inc., **6** 409–11; **15** 50

Mayne Nickless Ltd., **IV** 248

Mayo Foundation, **9** 336–39; **13** 326

Maytag Corporation, **III** 572–73; **12** 252, 300

Mayville Metal Products Co., **I** 513

Mazda Motor Corporation, **I** 520; **II** 4, 361; **III** 603; **9** 340–42; **11** 86; **13** 414

MBNA Corporation, **11** 123; **12** 328–30

MBPXL Corp., **II** 494

MCA Inc., II 143–45; 6 162–63; 10 286; 11 557

McArthur Glen Realty, 10 122

McCaffrey & McCall, I 33; 11 496

McCain Feeds Ltd., II 484

McCall Printing Co., 14 460

McCann-Erickson Hakuhodo, Ltd., I 10, 14, 16–17, 234; 6 30; 10 227

McCann-Erickson Worldwide, 14 315

McCarthy Milling, II 631

McCaughan Dyson and Co., II 189

McCaw Cellular Communications, Inc., II 331; 6 274, 322–24; 7 15; 9 320–21; 10 433; 15 125, 196

McClanahan Oil Co., I 341; 14 216

McClintic-Marshall, IV 36; 7 49

The McCloskey Corporation, 8 553

McColl-Frontenac Inc., IV 439

McComb Manufacturing Co., 8 287

McCormack & Dodge, IV 605; 11 77

McCormick & Company, Incorporated, 7 314–16

McCormick Harvesting Machine Co., I 180; II 330

McCrory Stores, II 424; 9 447–48; 13 340

McCulloch Corp., III 436; 8 348–49

McCullough Environmental Services, 12 443

McDermott International, Inc., III 558–60

McDonald Glass Grocery Co. Inc., II 669

McDonald's Company (Japan) Ltd., V 205

McDonald's Corporation, I 23, 31, 129; II 500, 613–15 646–48; III 63, 94, 103; 6 13; 7 128, 266–67, 316, 317–19 (upd.), 435, 505–06; 8 261–62, 564; 9 74, 178, 290, 292, 305; 10 122; 11 82, 308; 12 43, 180, 553; 13 494; 14 25, 32, 106, 195, 452–53

McDonnell Douglas Corporation, I 41–43, 45, 48, 50–52, 54–56, 58–59, 61–62, 67–68, 70–72, 76–77, 82, 84–85, 90, 105, 108, 111, 121–22, 321, 364, 490, 511; II 442; III 512, 654; 6 68; 7 456, 504; 8 49–51, 315; 9 18, 183, 206, 231, 233, 271–72, 418, 458, 460; 10 163–64, 317, 536; 11 164–65, 267, 277–80 (upd.), 285, 363–65; 12 190–91, 549; 13 356; 15 283

McDonough Co., II 16; III 502

McDougal, Littell & Company, 10 357

McDowell Energy Center, 6 543

McDowell Furniture Company, 10 183

McDuff, 10 305

McElligott Wright Morrison and White, 12 511

McFadden Industries, III 21

McFadden Publishing, 6 13

McGaughy, Marshall & McMillan, 6 142

McGaw Inc., 11 208

McGill Manufacturing, III 625

McGraw Electric Company, 6 312. See also Centel Corporation.

McGraw-Edison Co., II 17, 87

McGraw-Hill, Inc., II 398; IV 584, 634–37, 643, 656, 674; 10 62; 12 359; 13 417

McGregor Cory, 6 415

McGrew Color Graphics, 7 430

MCI Communications Corporation, II 408; III 13, 149, 684; V 302–04; 6 51–52, 300, 322; 7 118–19; 8 310; 9 171, 478–80; 10 19, 80, 89, 97, 433, 500; 11 59, 183, 185, 302, 409, 500; 12

135–37; 13 38; 14 252–53, 260, 364; 15 222

Mcjunkin Corp., 13 79

McKee Foods Corporation, 7 320–21

McKenna Metals Company, 13 295–96

McKesson Corporation, I 413, 496–98, 713; II 652; III 10; 6 279; 9 532; 11 91; 12 331–33 (upd.)

McKesson Envirosystems, 8 464

McKinsey & Company, Inc., I 108, 144, 437, 497; III 47, 85, 670; 9 343–45; 10 175; 13 138

McLain Grocery, II 625

McLane Company, Inc., V 217; 8 556; 13 332–34

McLaren Consolidated Cone Corp., II 543; 7 366

McLaughlin Motor Company of Canada, I 171; 10 325

McLean Clinic, 11 379

McLouth Steel Products, 13 158

MCM Electronics, 9 420

McMahan's Furniture Co., 14 236

McMan Oil and Gas Co., IV 369

McManus, John & Adams, Inc., 6 21

McMoCo, IV 82–83; 7 187

McMoRan, IV 81–83; V 739; 7 185, 187

McMurtry Manufacturing, 8 553

MCN Corporation, 6 519–22; 13 416

McNeil Laboratories, III 35–36; 8 282–83

McNellan Resources Inc., IV 76

MCO Holdings Inc., 8 348–49

MCorp, 10 134; 11 122

MCS, Inc., 10 412

McTeigue & Co., 14 502

McVitie & Price, II 592–93

McWhorter Inc., 8 553

MD Distribution Inc., 15 139

MD Pharmaceuticals, III 10

MDI Co., Ltd., IV 327

MDS/Bankmark, 10 247

MDU Resources Group, Inc., 7 322–25

Mead Corporation, IV 310–13, 327, 329, 342–43; 8 267; 9 261; 10 406; 11 421–22

Mead Cycle Co., IV 660

Mead Data Central, Inc., IV 312; 7 581; 10 406–08

Mead Johnson, III 17

Mead Packaging, 12 151

Meade County Rural Electric Cooperative Corporation, 11 37

Meadow Gold Dairies, Inc., II 473

Means Services, Inc., II 607

Mears & Phillips, II 237

Measurex Corporation, 8 243; 14 56

MEC - Hawaii, UK & USA, IV 714

Mecca Leisure PLC, I 248; 12 229

Mechanics Exchange Savings Bank, 9 173

Mechanics Machine Co., III 438; 14 63

Medal Distributing Co., 9 542

Medallion Pictures Corp., 9 320

Medco Containment Services Inc., 9 346–48; 11 291; 12 333

Medcom Inc., I 628

Medeco Security Locks, Inc., 10 350

Medfield Corp., III 87

Medi Mart Drug Store Co., II 667

Media General, Inc., III 214; 7 326–28

Media Play, 9 360–61

Medical Care America, Inc., 15 112, 114

Medical Expense Fund, III 245

Medical Indemnity of America, 10 160

Medical Marketing Group Inc., 9 348

Medical Service Assoc. of Pennsylvania, III 325–26

Medical Tribune Group, IV 591

Medicine Bow Coal Company, 7 33–34

Medicus Intercon International, 6 22

Mediobanca Banca di Credito Finanziario SpA, II 191, 271; III 208–09; 11 205

The Mediplex Group, Inc., III 16; 11 282

Medis Health and Pharmaceuticals Services Inc., II 653

Meditrust, 11 281–83

Medlabs Inc., III 73

Medtech, Ltd., 13 60–62

Medtronic, Inc., 8 351–54; 11 459

Medusa Corporation, 8 135

Mees & Hope, II 184

MEGA Natural Gas Company, 11 28

Megafoods Stores Inc., 13 335–37

Mei Foo Investments Ltd., IV 718

Meijer Incorporated, 7 329–31; 15 449

Meiji Commerce Bank, II 291

Meiji Fire Insurance Co., III 384–85

Meiji Milk Products Company, Limited, II 538–39

Meiji Mutual Life Insurance Company, II 323; III 288–89

Meiji Seika Kaisha, Ltd., I 676; II 540–41

Meikosha Co., II 72

Meinecke Muffler Company, III 495; 10 415

Meis of Illiana, 10 282

Meisei Electric, III 742

Meissner, Ackermann & Co., IV 463; 7 351

Meister, Lucious and Company, 13 262

Meiwa Manufacturing Co., III 758

N.V. Mekog, IV 531

Mel Klein and Partners, III 74

Melbur China Clay Co., III 690

Melco, II 58

Melkunie-Holland, II 575

Mellbank Security Co., II 316

Mellon Bank Corporation, I 67–68, 584; II 315–17, 342, 402; III 275; 9 470; 13 410–11

Mellon Indemnity Corp., III 258–59

Mellon-Stuart Co., I 584–85; 14 334

Mélotte, III 418

Meloy Laboratories, Inc., 11 333

Melroe Company, 8 115–16

Melville Corporation, V 136–38; 9 192; 13 82, 329–30; 14 426; 15 252–53

Melvin Simon and Associates, Inc., 8 355–57

Melwire Group, III 673

Memco, 12 48

Memorex Corp., III 110, 166; 6 282–83

Menasco Manufacturing Co., I 435; III 415

Menasha Corporation, 8 358–61

Menck, 8 544

Mendelssohn & Co., II 241

Meneven, IV 508

Menka Gesellschaft, IV 150

Mennen Company, I 19; 6 26; 14 122

Mental Health Programs Inc., 15 122

Mentholatum Co., IV 722

Mentor Graphics Corporation, III 143; 8 519; 11 46–47, 284–86, 490; 13 128

MEPC plc, IV 710–12

Mepco/Electra Inc., 13 398

MeraBank, 6 546

Mercantile Agency, IV 604

Mercantile and General Reinsurance Co., **III** 335, 377
Mercantile Bank, **II** 298
Mercantile Bankshares Corp., 11 287–88
Mercantile Estate and Property Corp. Ltd., **IV** 710
Mercantile Fire Insurance, **III** 234
Mercantile Mutual, **III** 310
Mercantile Property Corp. Ltd., **IV** 710
Mercantile Security Life, **III** 136
Mercantile Stores Company, Inc., V 139
Mercantile Trust Co., **II** 229, 247
Mercedes Benz. *See* Daimler-Benz A.G.
Merchant Co., **III** 104
Merchants & Farmers Bank of Ecru, **14** 40
Merchants Bank, **II** 213
Merchants Bank of Canada, **II** 210
Merchants Bank of Halifax, **II** 344
Merchants Dispatch, **II** 395–96; **10** 60
Merchants Fire Assurance Corp., **III** 396–97
Merchants Home Delivery Service, **6** 414
Merchants Indemnity Corp., **III** 396–97
Merchants Life Insurance Co., **III** 275
Merchants National Bank, **9** 228; **14** 528
Merchants National Bank of Boston, **II** 213
Merchants Union Express Co., **II** 396; **10** 60
Merchants' Assoc., **II** 261
Merchants' Loan and Trust, **II** 261; **III** 518
Merchants' Savings, Loan and Trust Co., **II** 261
Mercier, **I** 272
Merck & Co., Inc., I 640, 646, **650–52,** 683–84, 708; **II** 414; **III** 42, 60, 66, 299; **8** 154, 548; **10** 213; **11** 9, 90, **289–91 (upd.); 12** 325, 333; **14** 58, 422; **15** 154
Mercury Asset Management (MAM), **14** 420
Mercury Communications, Ltd., V 280–82; **7** 332–34; **10** 456; **11** 547–48
Mercury, Inc., **8** 311
Mercury Record Corp., **13** 397
Mercury Telecommunications Limited, **15** 67, 69
Meredith and Drew, **II** 593
Meredith Corporation, IV 661–62; **11 292–94**
Meridian Bancorp, Inc., 11 295–97
Meridian Insurance Co., **III** 332
Meridian Oil Inc., **10** 190–91
Merillat Industries Inc., III 570; **13 338–39**
Merisel, Inc., 10 518–19; **12 334–36; 13** 174, 176, 482
Merit Distribution Services, **13** 333
Merit Tank Testing, Inc., **IV** 411
Merivienti Oy, **IV** 276
Merla Manufacturing, **I** 524
Merlin Gerin, **II** 93–94
Merpati Nusantara Airlines, **6** 90–91
Merrell Drug, **I** 325
Merrell-Soule Co., **II** 471
Merriam and Morgan Paraffine Co., **IV** 548
Merriam-Webster, Inc., **7** 165, 167
Merrill Gas Company, **9** 554
Merrill Lynch & Co., Inc., I 26, 339, 681, 683, 697; **II** 149, 257, 260, 268, 403, 407–08, 412, **424–26,** 441, 445, 449, 451, 456, 654–55, 680; **III** 119, 253, 340, 440; **6** 244; **7** 130; **8** 94; **9** 125, 187, 239, 301, 386; **11** 29, 122,

348, 557; **13** 44, 125, **340–43 (upd.),** 448–49, 512; **14** 65; **15** 463
Merrill, Pickard, Anderson & Eyre IV, **11** 490
Merrill Publishing, **IV** 643; **7** 312; **9** 63
Merry Group, **III** 673
Merry Maids, **6** 46
Merry-Go-Round Enterprises, Inc., 8 362–64
Mersey Paper Co., **IV** 258
Mersey White Lead Co., **III** 680
Merv Griffin Enterprises, **II** 137; **12** 75
Mervyn's, V 43–44; **10 409–10; 13** 526
Mesa Airlines, Inc., 11 298–300
Mesa Limited Partnership, **IV** 410, 523; **11** 441
Mesa Petroleum, **IV** 392, 571
Mesaba Transportation Co., **I** 448
Messageries du Livre, **IV** 614
Messerschmitt-Bölkow-Blohm GmbH., I 41–42, 46, 51–52, 55, **73–75,** 111, 121; **II** 242; **III** 539; **11** 267
Messner, Vetere, Berger, Carey, Schmetterer, **13** 204
Mestek, Inc., 10 411–13
Metabio-Joullie, **III** 47
Metal Box plc, I 604–06
Metal Closures, **I** 615
Metal Industries, **I** 531–32
Metal Manufactures, **III** 433–34
Metal Office Furniture Company, **7** 493
Metal-Cal, **IV** 253
Metaleurop, **IV** 108–09
Metall Mining Corp., **IV** 141
Metallgesellschaft AG, IV 17, **139–42,** 229
MetalPro, Inc., **IV** 168
Metals and Controls Corp., **II** 113
Metals Exploration, **IV** 82
Metaphase Technology, Inc., **10** 257
Metcalf & Eddy Companies, Inc., **6** 143, 441
Methane Development Corporation, **6** 457
Methanex Corp., **12** 365
Methode Electronics, Inc., 13 344–46
Metinox Steel Ltd., **IV** 203
MetLife General Insurance Agency, **III** 293
MetMor Financial, Inc., **III** 293
MetPath, Inc., **III** 684
Metro Distributors Inc., **14** 545
Metro Drugs, **II** 649–50
Metro Glass, **II** 533
Metro Pictures, **II** 148
Metro Southwest Construction. *See* CRSS Inc.
Metro Vermögensverwaltung GmbH & Co. of Dusseldorf, **V** 104
Metro-Goldwyn-Mayer, **I** 286, 487; **II** 135, 146–47, 148–50, 155, 161, 167, 169, 174–75; **12** 73, 316. *See also* MGM/UA Communications Company.
Metro-Mark Integrated Systems Inc., **11** 469
Metro-Richelieu Inc., **II** 653
Metro-Verwegensverwaltung, **II** 257
Metromail Corp., **IV** 661
Metromedia Companies, II 171; **6** 33, 168–69; **7** 91, **335–37; 8** 311; **14** 107, **330–32 (upd.); 15** 362
Metromedia Steak Houses L.P., **15** 363
Metromont Materials, **III** 740
Metroplitan and Great Western Dairies, **II** 586

Metropolitan Accident Co., **III** 228
Metropolitan Bank, **II** 221, 318; **III** 239; **IV** 644
Metropolitan Broadcasting Corporation, **7** 335
Metropolitan Distributors, **9** 283
Metropolitan District Railway Company, **6** 406
Metropolitan Estate and Property Corp. Ltd., **IV** 710–11
Metropolitan Financial Corporation, 12 165; **13 347–49**
Metropolitan Furniture Leasing, **14** 4
Metropolitan Gas Light Co., **6** 455
Metropolitan Housing Corp. Ltd., **IV** 710
Metropolitan Life Insurance Company, II 679; **III** 265–66, 272, **290–94,** 313, 329, 337, 339–40, 706; **IV** 283; **6** 256; **8** 326–27; **11** 482
Metropolitan National Bank, **II** 284
Metropolitan Petroleum Corp., **IV** 180–81
Metropolitan Railway, **6** 407
Metropolitan Railways Surplus Lands Co., **IV** 711
Metropolitan Tobacco Co., **15** 138
Metropolitan Vickers, **III** 670
METSA, Inc., **15** 363
Metsä-Serla Oy, IV 314–16, 318, 350
Mettler United States Inc., **9** 441
Metzeler Kautschuk, **15** 354
Mexican Eagle Oil Co., **IV** 365, 531
Mexican Original Products, Inc., **II** 585; **14** 515
Mexofina, S.A. de C.V., **IV** 401
Meyer and Charlton, **IV** 90
Meyers & Muldoon, **6** 40
Meyers and Co., **III** 9
Meyrin, **I** 122
MFI, **II** 612
MFS Communications Company, Inc., 11 301–03; 14 253
MG Holdings. *See* Mayflower Group Inc.
MG Ltd., **IV** 141
MG&E. *See* Madison Gas & Electric.
MGM Grand Hotels, **III** 431; **6** 210
MGM/UA Communications Company, II 103, **146–50,** 161, 167, 408; **IV** 676; **6** 172–73; **12** 323, 455; **15** 84. *See also* Metro-Goldwyn-Mayer.
mh Bausparkasse AG, **III** 377
MHI, **13** 356
MHT. *See* Manufacturers Hanover Trust Co.
Miami Power Corporation, **6** 466
Micamold Electronics Manufacturing Corporation, **10** 319
Michael Baker Corp., 14 333–35
MICHAEL Business Systems Plc, **10** 257
Michael Joseph, **IV** 659
Michael Reese Health Plan Inc., **III** 82
MichCon. *See* MCN Corporation.
Michelin, **III** 697; **7** 36–37; **8** 74; **11** 158, 473
Michelin et Compagnie, **V** 236
Michiana Merchandising, **III** 10
Michie Co., **IV** 312
Michigan Automotive Compressor, Inc., **III** 593, 638–39
Michigan Bell Telephone Co., 14 336–38
Michigan Carpet Sweeper Company, **9** 70
Michigan Consolidated Gas Company. *See* MCN Corporation.
Michigan Fruit Canners, **II** 571
Michigan General, **II** 408

Michigan International Speedway, **V** 494
Michigan Motor Freight Lines, **14** 567
Michigan National Corporation, 11 304–06
Michigan Packaging Company, **15** 188
Michigan Plating and Stamping Co., **I** 451
Michigan Radiator & Iron Co., **III** 663
Michigan State Life Insurance Co., **III** 274
Michigan Steel Corporation, **12** 352
Michigan Tag Company, **9** 72
Mickey Shorr Mobile Electronics, **10** 9–11
Micro D, Inc., **11** 194
Micro Decisionware, Inc., **10** 506
Micro Power Systems Inc., **14** 183
Micro Switch, **14** 284
Micro-Circuit, Inc., **III** 645
Micro-Power Corp., **III** 643
Micro/Vest, **13** 175
Microamerica, **12** 334
MicroBilt Corporation, **11** 112
MicroComputer Accessories, **III** 614
Microcomputer Asset Management Services, **9** 168
Microdot Inc., I 440; **8 365–68**, 545
Microfal, **I** 341
Microform International Marketing Corp., **IV** 642; **7** 312
Microfral, **14** 216
Micron Technology, Inc., III 113; **11 307–09**
Micropolis Corp., **10** 403, 458, 463
MicroPro International, **10** 556
Microprocessor Systems, **13** 235
Microseal Corp., **I** 341
Microsoft Corporation, III 116; **6** 219–20, 224, 227, 231, 235, 254–56, **257–60**, 269–71; **9** 81, 140, 171, 195, 472; **10** 22, 34, 57, 87, 119, 237–38, 362–63, 408, 477, 484, 504, 557–58; **11** 59, 77–78, 306, 519–20; **12** 180, 335; **13** 115, 128, 147, 482, 509; **14** 262–64, 318; **15** 132–33, 321, 371, 483, 492, 511
Microtel Limited, **6** 309–10
Microware Surgical Instruments Corp., **IV** 137
Microwave Communications, Inc., **V** 302
Mid-America Capital Resources, Inc., **6** 508
Mid-America Dairymen, Inc., II 536; **7 338–40**; **11** 24
Mid-America Industries, **III** 495
Mid-America Interpool Network, **6** 506, 602
Mid-America Packaging, Inc., **8** 203
Mid-America Tag & Label, **8** 360
Mid-Central Fish and Frozen Foods Inc., **II** 675
Mid-Continent Area Power Planner, **V** 672
Mid-Continent Computer Services, **11** 111
Mid-Continent Telephone Corporation. *See* Alltel Corporation.
Mid-Georgia Gas Company, **6** 448
Mid-Illinois Gas Co., **6** 529
Mid-Pacific Airlines, **9** 271
Mid-South Towing, **6** 583
Mid-Texas Communications Systems, **6** 313
Mid-Valley Dairy, **14** 397
Mid-West Drive-In Theatres Inc., **I** 245
Mid-West Paper Ltd., **IV** 286
MidAmerican Communications Corporation, **8** 311

Midas International Corporation, I 457–58; **10 414–15**, 554
MIDCO, **III** 340
Midcon, **IV** 481
Middle South Utilities, **V** 618–19
Middle West Corporation, **6** 469–70
Middle West Utilities Company, **V** 583–84; **6** 555–56, 604–05; **14** 227
Middle Wisconsin Power, **6** 604
Middleburg Steel and Alloys Group, **I** 423
Middlesex Bank, **II** 334
Middleton Packaging, **12** 377
Middleton's Starch Works, **II** 566
Middletown National Bank, **13** 467
Midhurst Corp., **IV** 658
Midial, **II** 478
Midland Bank PLC, II 208, 236, 279, 295, 298, **318–20**, 334, 383; **9** 505; **12** 257; **14** 169
Midland Brick, **14** 250
Midland Cooperative, **II** 536
Midland Counties Dairies, **II** 587
Midland Electric Coal Co., **IV** 170
Midland Enterprises Inc., **6** 486–88
Midland Gravel Co., **III** 670
Midland Industrial Finishes Co., **I** 321
Midland Insurance, **I** 473
Midland International, **8** 56–57
Midland Investment Co., **II** 7
Midland Linseed Products Co., **I** 419
Midland National Bank, **11** 130
Midland Railway Co., **II** 306
Midland Southwest Corp., **8** 347
Midland Steel Products Co., **13** 305–06
Midland United, **6** 556
Midland Utilities Company, **6** 532
Midland-Ross Corporation, **14** 369
Midlands Electricity, **13** 485
Midlands Energy Co., **IV** 83; **7** 188
Midlantic Corp., **13** 411
Midrange Performance Group, **12** 149
Midrex Corp., **IV** 130
Midvale Steel and Ordnance Co., **IV** 35, 114; **7** 48
Midway Airlines, **6** 105, 120–21
Midway Manufacturing Company, **III** 430; **15** 539
Midwest Agri-Commodities, **11** 15
Midwest Air Charter, **6** 345
Midwest Biscuit Company, **14** 306
Midwest Com of Indiana, Inc., **11** 112
Midwest Dairy Products, **II** 661
Midwest Express Airlines, **III** 40–41; **11** 299
Midwest Federal Savings & Loan Association, **11** 162–63
Midwest Financial Group, Inc., **8** 188
Midwest Foundry Co., **IV** 137
Midwest Manufacturing Co., **12** 296
Midwest Refining Co., **IV** 368
Midwest Resources Inc., 6 523–25
Midwest Steel Corporation, **13** 157
Midwest Synthetics, **8** 553
Midwinter, **12** 529
Miele & Cie., **III** 418
Mike-Sell's Inc., 15 298–300
Mikko, **II** 70
Mikko Kaloinen Oy, **IV** 349
Mikon, Ltd., **13** 345
Milani, **II** 556
Milbank Insurance Co., **III** 350
Milbank, Tweed, Hope & Webb, **II** 471
Milcor Steel Co., **IV** 114
Miles Druce & Co., **III** 494

Miles Kimball Co., **9** 393
Miles Laboratories, I 310, **653–55**, 674, 678; **6** 50; **13** 76; **14** 558
Miles Redfern, **I** 429
Milgo Electronic Corp., **II** 83; **11** 408
Milgram Food Stores Inc., **II** 682
Milk Producers, Inc., **11** 24
Milk Specialties Co., **12** 199
Millbrook Press Inc., **IV** 616
Miller Brewing Company, I 218–19, 236–37, 254–55, 257–58, **269–70**, 283, 290–91, 548; **10** 100; **11** 421; **12 337–39 (upd.)**, 372; **13** 10, 258; **15** 429
Miller Chemical & Fertilizer Corp., **I** 412
Miller Container Corporation, **8** 102
Miller Freeman, **IV** 687
Miller, Mason and Dickenson, **III** 204–05
Miller, Tabak, Hirsch & Co., **13** 394
Millet's Leisure, **V** 177–78
Millicom, **11** 547
Milliken & Co., V 366–68; **8** 270–71
Milliken, Tomlinson Co., **II** 682
Millipore, **9** 396
Millstone Point Company, **V** 668–69
Millville Electric Light Company, **6** 449
Milner, **III** 98
Milton Bradley, **III** 504–06
Milton Light & Power Company, **12** 45
Milton Roy Co., **8** 135
Milwaukee Electric Manufacturing Co., **III** 534
Milwaukee Electric Railway and Light Company, **6** 601–02, 604–05
Milwaukee Insurance Co., **III** 242
Milwaukee Mutual Fire Insurance Co., **III** 321
Minatome, **IV** 560
Minemet Recherche, **IV** 108
Mineral Point Public Service Company, **6** 604
Minerals & Chemicals Philipp, **IV** 79–80
Minerals & Metals Trading Corporation of India Ltd., IV 143–44
Minerals and Resources Corporation Limited, **IV** 23; **13** 502
Minerals Technologies Inc., 11 310–12
Minerec Corporation, **9** 363
Minerva, **III** 359
Minerve, **6** 208
Mines et Usines du Nord et de l'Est, **IV** 226
Minet Holdings PLC, **III** 357
Mini Stop, **V** 97
Mining and Technical Services, **IV** 67
Mining Corp. of Canada Ltd., **IV** 164
Mining Development Corp., **IV** 239–40
Mining Trust Ltd., **IV** 32
MiniScribe, Inc., **6** 230; **10** 404
Minister of Finance Inc., **IV** 519
Minivator Ltd., **11** 486
Minneapolis General Electric of Minnesota, **V** 670
Minneapolis Heat Regulator Co., **II** 40–41; **12** 246
Minneapolis Millers Association, **10** 322
Minneapolis-Honeywell Regulator Co., **II** 40–41, 86; **8** 21; **12** 247
Minnesota Cooperative Creameries Assoc., Inc., **II** 535
Minnesota Linseed Oil Co., **8** 552
Minnesota Mining & Manufacturing Company (3M), I 28, 387, **499–501**; **II** 39; **III** 476, 487, 549; **IV** 251, 253–54;

6 231; **7** 162; **8** 35, **369–71 (upd.);** **11** 494; **13** 326

Minnesota Paints, **8** 552–53

Minnesota Power & Light Company, 11 313–16

Minnesota Sugar Company, **11** 13

Minnesota Valley Canning Co., **I** 22

Minnetonka Corp., **II** 590; **III** 25

Minolta Camera Co., Ltd., III 574–76, 583–84

Minorco, **III** 503; **IV** 67–68, 84, 97

Minstar Inc., **11** 397; **15** 49

Minute Maid Corp., **I** 234; **10** 227

Minute Tapioca, **II** 531

MIPS Computer Systems, **II** 45; **11** 491

Mirage Resorts, Inc., 6 209–12; 15 238

Miramar Hotel & Investment Co., **IV** 717

Mircali Asset Management, **III** 340

Mircor Inc., **12** 413

Mirrlees Blackstone, **III** 509

Mirror Group Newspapers plc, IV 641; **7** 244, 312, **341–43**

Mirror Printing and Binding House, **IV** 677

Misceramic Tile, Inc., **14** 42

Misr Airwork. *See* AirEgypt.

Misrair. *See* AirEgypt.

Miss Clairol, **6** 28

Miss Selfridge, **V** 177–78

Misset Publishers, **IV** 611

Mission Energy Company, **V** 715

Mission First Financial, **V** 715

Mission Group, **V** 715, 717

Mission Insurance Co., **III** 192

Mississippi Chemical Corporation, **8** 183; **IV** 367

Mississippi Drug, **III** 10

Mississippi Gas Company, **6** 577

Mississippi Power & Light, **V** 619

Mississippi River Corporation, **10** 44

Missouri Book Co., **10** 136

Missouri Gas & Electric Service Company, **6** 593

Missouri Pacific Railroad, **10** 43–44

Missouri Public Service Company. *See* UtiliCorp United Inc.

Missouri Utilities Company, **6** 580

Missouri-Kansas-Texas Railroad, **I** 472; **IV** 458

Mistral Plastics Pty Ltd., **IV** 295

Mitchell Construction, **III** 753

Mitchell Energy and Development Corporation, 7 344–46

Mitchell Home Savings and Loan, **13** 347

Mitchell Hutchins, **II** 445

Mitchell International, **8** 526

Mitchells & Butler, **I** 223

Mitchum Co., **III** 55

Mitchum, Jones & Templeton, **II** 445

MiTek Industries Inc., **IV** 259

MiTek Wood Products, **IV** 305

Mitel, **15** 131–32

MitNer Group, **7** 377

Mitsubishi, **V** 481–82; **7** 377

Mitsubishi Aircraft Co., **III** 578; **7** 348; **9** 349; **11** 164

Mitsubishi Bank, Ltd., II 57, 273–74, 276, **321–22,** 323, 392, 459; **III** 289, 577–78; **7** 348; **15** 41

Mitsubishi Chemical Industries Ltd., I 319, **363–64,** 398; **II** 57; **III** 666, 760; **11** 207

Mitsubishi Corporation, I 261, 431–32, 492, **502–04,** 505–06, 510, 515, 519–20; **II** 57, 59, 101, 118, 224, 292,

321–25, 374; **III** 577–78; **IV** 285, 518, 713; **6** 499; **7** 82, 233, 590; **9** 294; **12 340–43 (upd.)**

Mitsubishi Electric Corporation, II 53, **57–59,** 68, 73, 94, 122; **III** 577, 586; **7** 347, 394

Mitsubishi Estate Company, Limited, IV 713–14

Mitsubishi Gas Chemical Company, **I** 330; **8** 153

Mitsubishi Heavy Industries, Ltd., II 57, 75, 323, 440; **III** 452–53, 487, 532, 538, **577–79,** 685, 713; **IV** 184, 713; **7 347–50 (upd.); 8** 51; **9** 349–50; **10** 33; **13** 507; **15** 92

Mitsubishi Kasei Corp., **III** 47–48, 477; **8** 343; **14** 535

Mitsubishi Kasei Industry Co. Ltd., **IV** 476

Mitsubishi Marine, **III** 385

Mitsubishi Materials Corporation, III 712–13; IV 554

Mitsubishi Motors Corporation, III 516–17, 578–79; **6** 28; **7** 219, 348–49; **8** 72, 374; **9 349–51**

Mitsubishi Oil Co., Ltd., IV 460–62, 479, 492

Mitsubishi Paper Co., **III** 547

Mitsubishi Petrochemical Co., **I** 364; **III** 685

Mitsubishi Petroleum, **III** 760

Mitsubishi Pulp, **IV** 328

Mitsubishi Rayon Co. Ltd., I 330; **V 369–71; 8** 153

Mitsubishi Sha Holdings, **IV** 554

Mitsubishi Shipbuilding Co. Ltd., **II** 57; **III** 513, 577–78; **7** 348; **9** 349

Mitsubishi Shoji Trading, **IV** 554

Mitsubishi Shokai, **III** 577; **IV** 713; **7** 347

Mitsubishi Trading Co., **IV** 460

Mitsubishi Trust & Banking Corporation, II 323–24; III 289

Mitsui and Co., **I** 282; **IV** 18, 224, 432, 654–55; **V** 142; **6** 346; **7** 303; **13** 356

Mitsui Bank, Ltd., II 273–74, 291, **325–27,** 328, 372; **III** 295–97; **IV** 147, 320; **V** 142

Mitsui Bussan K.K., I 363, 431–32, 469, 492, 502–04, **505–08,** 510, 515, 519, 533; **II** 57, 66, 101, 224, 292, 323, 325–28, 392; **III** 295–96, 717–18; **IV** 147, 431; **9** 352–53

Mitsui Gomei Kaisha, **IV** 715

Mitsui Group, **9** 352

Mitsui House Code, **V** 142

Mitsui Light Metal Processing Co., **III** 758

Mitsui Marine and Fire Insurance Company, Limited, III 209, **295–96,** 297

Mitsui Mining & Smelting Co., Ltd., IV 145–46, 147–48

Mitsui Mining Company, Limited, IV 145, **147–49**

Mitsui Mutual Life Insurance Company, III 297–98

Mitsui O.S.K. Lines, Ltd., I 520; **IV** 383; **V 473–76; 6** 398

Mitsui Petrochemical Industries, Ltd., I 390, 516; **9 352–54**

Mitsui Real Estate Development Co., Ltd., IV 715–16

Mitsui Shipbuilding and Engineering Co., **III** 295, 513

Mitsui Toatsu, **9** 353–54

Mitsui Trading, **III** 636

Mitsui Trust & Banking Company, Ltd., II 328; III 297

Mitsui-no-Mori Co., Ltd., **IV** 716

Mitsukoshi Ltd., I 508; **V 142–44; 14** 502

Mitsuya Foods Co., **I** 221

Mitteldeutsche Creditbank, **II** 256

Mitteldeutsche Energieversorgung AG, **V** 747

Mitteldeutsche Privatbank, **II** 256

Mitteldeutsche Stickstoff-Werke Ag, **IV** 229–30

Mitteldeutsches Kraftwerk, **IV** 229

Mixconcrete (Holdings), **III** 729

Miyoshi Electrical Manufacturing Co., **II** 6

Mizushima Ethylene Co. Ltd., **IV** 476

MJB Coffee Co., **I** 28

MK-Ferguson Company, **7** 356

MLC Ltd., **IV** 709

MLH&P. *See* Montreal Light, Heat & Power Company.

MML Investors Services, **III** 286

MNC Financial. *See* MBNA Corporation.

MNC Financial Corp., **11** 447

MND Drilling, **7** 345

MNet, **11** 122

Mo och Domsjö AB, IV 315, **317–19,** 340

Moa Bay Mining Co., **IV** 82; **7** 186

Mobay, **I** 310–11; **13** 76

Mobil Communications, **6** 323

Mobil Corporation, I 30, 34, 403, 478; **II** 379; **IV** 93, 295, 363, 386, 401, 403, 406, 423, 428, 454, **463–65,** 466, 472–74, 486, 492, 504–05, 515, 517, 522, 531, 538–39, 545, 554–55, 564, 570–71; **V** 147–48; **6** 530; **7** 171, **351–54 (upd.); 8** 552–53; **9** 546; **10** 440; **12** 348

Mobile and Ohio Railroad, **I** 456

Mobile Communications Corp. of America, **V** 277–78

Mobira, **II** 69

Mobley Chemical, **I** 342

Mobu Company, **6** 431

Mobujidosha Bus Company, **6** 431

MOÇACOR, **IV** 505

Mocatta and Goldsmid Ltd., **II** 357

Mochida Pharaceutical Co. Ltd., **II** 553

Moctezuma Copper Co., **IV** 176–77

Modern Equipment Co., **I** 412

Modern Furniture Rental, **14** 4

Modern Maid Food Products, **II** 500

Modern Patterns and Plastics, **III** 641

Modernistic Industries Inc., **7** 589

Modine Manufacturing Company, 8 372–75

MoDo. *See* Mo och Domsjö AB.

Moen Incorporated, 12 344–45

Moët-Hennessy, I 271–72; **10** 397–98

Mogul Corp., **I** 321

Mogul Metal Co., **I** 158

Mohasco Corporation, **15** 102

Mohawk & Hudson Railroad, **9** 369

Mohawk Airlines, **I** 131; **6** 131

Mohawk Rubber Co. Ltd., **V** 256; **7** 116

Mohr-Value Stores, **8** 555

Moilliet and Sons, **II** 306

Moist O'Matic, **7** 535

Mojo MDA Group Ltd., **11** 50–51

Mokta. *See* Compagnie de Mokta.

MOL. *See* Mitsui O.S.K. Lines, Ltd.

Molecular Biosystems, **III** 61

Molex Incorporated, II 8; **11 317–19; 14** 27

Moline National Bank, **III** 463

Molinos de Puerto Rico, **II** 493
Molinos Nacionales C.A., **7** 242–43
Molins Co., **IV** 326
Molkerie-Zentrak Sud GmbH, **II** 575
Molloy Manufacturing Co., **III** 569
Mölnlycke, **IV** 338–39
Molson Companies Ltd., **I** 273–75, 333;
  II 210; **7** 183–84; **12** 338; **13** 150, 199
Molycorp, **IV** 571
Mon-Valley Transportation Company, **11**
  194
MONACA. *See* Molinos Nacionales C.A.
Monarch Food Ltd., **II** 571
Monarch Marking Systems, **III** 157
MonArk Boat, **III** 444
Mond Nickel Co., **IV** 110–11
Mondadori. *See* Arnoldo Monadori Editore
  S.p.A.
Mondi Paper Co., **IV** 22
Monet Jewelry, **II** 502–03; **9** 156–57; **10**
  323–24
Money Access Service Corp., **11** 467
Monfort, Inc., **13** 350–52
Monheim Group, **II** 521
Monier Roof Tile, **III** 687, 735
Monis Wineries, **I** 288
Monk-Austin Inc., **12** 110
Monochem, **II** 472
Monogram Aerospace Fasteners, Inc., **11**
  536
Monogramme Confections, **6** 392
Monolithic Memories, **6** 216
Monon Corp., **13** 550
Monon Railroad, **I** 472
Monoprix, **V** 57–59
Monroe Auto Equipment, **I** 527
Monroe Calculating Machine Co., **I** 476,
  484
Monroe Cheese Co., **II** 471
Monroe Savings Bank, **11** 109
Monrovia Aviation Corp., **I** 544
Monsanto Company, **I** 310, 363, 365–67,
  402, 631, 666, 686, 688; **III** 741; **IV**
  290, 379, 401; **8** 398; **9** 318, 355–57
  (upd.), 466; **12** 186; **13** 76, 225
Monsanto Oil Co., **IV** 367
Monsavon, **III** 46–47
Montabert S.A., **15** 226
Montan Transport GmbH, **IV** 140
Montana Enterprises Inc., **I** 114
Montana Power Company, **6** 566; **7** 322;
  11 320–22
Montana Refining Company, **12** 240–41
Montana Resources, Inc., **IV** 34
Montana-Dakota Utilities Co., **7** 322–23
Montaup Electric Co., **14** 125
Montecatini, **I** 368; **IV** 421, 470, 486
Montedison SpA, **I** 368–69; **IV** 413,
  421–22, 454, 499; **14** 17
Montefibre, **I** 369
Montefina, **IV** 499
Monterey Mfg. Co., **12** 439
Monterey's Tex-Mex Cafes, **13** 473
Montfort of Colorado, Inc., **II** 494
Montgomery Ward & Co., Incorporated,
  III 762; **IV** 465; **V** 145–48; **7** 353; **8**
  509; **9** 210; **10** 10, 116, 172, 305, 391,
  393, 490–91; **12** 48, 309, 315, 335, 430;
  13 165; **15** 330, 470
Montreal Bank, **II** 210
Montreal Engineering Company, **6** 585
Montreal Light, Heat & Power
  Consolidated, **6** 501–02
Montres Rolex S.A., **8** 477; **13** 353–55

Montrose Chemical Company, **9** 118, 119
Montrose Chrome, **IV** 92
Monument Property Trust Ltd., **IV** 710
Monumental Corp., **III** 179
MONYCo., **III** 306
Moody's Investors Service, **IV** 605
Moog Inc., **13** 356–58
Moon-Hopkins Billing Machine, **III** 165
Moore Corporation Limited, **IV** 644–46,
  679; **15** 473
Moore McCormack Resources Inc., **14** 455
Moore-Handley Inc., **IV** 345–46
Moorhouse, **II** 477
Moran Group Inc., **II** 682
MoRan Oil & Gas Co., **IV** 82–83
Moran Towing Corporation, Inc., **15**
  301–03
Morana, Inc., **9** 290
Moreland and Watson, **IV** 208
Moretti-Harrah Marble Co., **III** 691
Morgan & Cie International S.A., **II** 431
Morgan Construction Company, **8** 448
Morgan Edwards, **II** 609
Morgan Engineering Co., **8** 545
Morgan Grampian Group, **IV** 687
Morgan Grenfell Group PLC, **II** 280,
  329, 427–29; **IV** 21, 712
Morgan Guaranty International Banking
  Corp., **II** 331; **9** 124
Morgan Guaranty Trust Co. of New York,
  I 26; **II** 208, 254, 262, 329–32, 339,
  428, 431, 448; **III** 80; **10** 150
Morgan Guaranty Trust Company, **11** 421;
  13 49, 448; **14** 297
Morgan, Harjes & Co., **II** 329
Morgan, J.P. & Co. Inc. *See* J.P. Morgan
  & Co. Incorporated.
Morgan, Lewis, Githens & Ahn, Inc., **6**
  410
Morgan Mitsubishi Development, **IV** 714
Morgan Stanley Group, Inc., **I** 34; **II**
  211, 330, 403, 406–08, 422, 428,
  430–32, 441; **IV** 295, 447, 714; **9** 386;
  11 258; **12** 529
Morgan Yacht Corp., **II** 468
Morgan's Brewery, **I** 287
Mori Bank, **II** 291
Moria Informatique, **6** 229
Morino Associates, **10** 394
Morita & Co., **II** 103
Mormac Marine Group, **15** 302
Morris Motors, **III** 256; **7** 459
Morrison Industries Ltd., **IV** 278
Morrison Knudsen Corporation, **IV** 55;
  7 355–58; **11** 401, 553
Morrison Restaurants Inc., **11** 323–25
Morse Chain Co., **III** 439; **14** 63
Morse Equalizing Spring Company, **14** 63
Morse Industrial, **14** 64
Morse Shoe Inc., **13** 359–61
Morss and White, **III** 643
Morstan Development Co., Inc., **II** 432
Mortgage & Trust Co., **II** 251
Mortgage Associates, **9** 229
Mortgage Insurance Co. of Canada, **II** 222
Mortgage Resources, Inc., **10** 91
Morton Foods, Inc., **II** 502; **10** 323
Morton International Inc., **9** 358–59
  (upd.), 500–01
Morton Salt, **I** 371
Morton Thiokol Inc., **I** 325, 370–72
MOS Technology, **7** 95
Mosby-Year Book, **IV** 678

Moseley, Hallgarten, Estabrook, and
  Weeden, **III** 389
Mosher Steel Company, **7** 540
Mosinee Paper Corporation, **15** 304–06
Mosler Safe Co., **III** 664–65; **7** 144, 146
Moss-Rouse Company, **15** 412
Mossgas, **IV** 93
Mostek Corp., **I** 85; **II** 64; **11** 307–08; **13**
  191
Motel 6 Corporation, **10** 13; **13** 362–64
Mother Karen's, **10** 216
Mother's Oats, **II** 558–59; **12** 409
Motion Designs, **11** 486
Moto-Truc Co., **13** 385
Motor Haulage Co., **IV** 181
Motor Parts Industries, Inc., **9** 363
Motor Transit Corp., **I** 448; **10** 72
Motoren-und-Turbinen-Union, **I** 151; **III**
  563; **9** 418; **15** 142
Motoren-Werke Mannheim AG, **III** 544
Motorenfabrik Deutz AG, **III** 541
Motorenfabrik Oberursel, **III** 541
Motornetic Corp., **III** 590
Motorola, Inc., **I** 534; **II** 5, 34, 44–45, 56,
  60–62, 64; **III** 455; **6** 238; **7** 119, 494,
  533; **8** 139; **9** 515; **10** 87, 365, 367,
  431–33; **11** 45, 308, **326–29 (upd.)**,
  381–82; **12** 136–37, 162; **13** 30, 356,
  501
Motown Records, **II** 145
Mount. *See also* Mt.
Mount Hood Credit Life Insurance Agency,
  14 529
Mount Isa Mines, **IV** 61
Mount Vernon Group, **8** 14
Mountain Fuel Supply Company, **6** 568–69
Mountain Pass Canning Co., **7** 429
Mountain State Telephone Company, **6** 300
Mountain States Telephone & Telegraph
  Co., **V** 341
Mountain States Wholesale, **II** 602
Mounts Wire Industries, **III** 673
Mountsorrel Granite Co., **III** 734
Movado-Zenith-Mondia Holding, **II** 124
Movies To Go, Inc., **9** 74
Moving Co. Ltd., **V** 127
The Moving Picture Company, **15** 83
MPB Corporation, **8** 529, 531
MPM, **III** 735
Mr. Coffee, Inc., **14** 229–31; **15** 307–09
Mr. D's Food Centers, **12** 112
Mr. Gasket Inc., **11** 84; **15** 310–12
Mr. Gatti's, **15** 345
Mr. Goodbuys, **13** 545
Mr. How, **V** 191–92
Mr. M Food Stores, **7** 373
MRC Bearings, **III** 624
Mrs. Paul's Kitchens, **II** 480
Mrs. Smith's Frozen Foods, **II** 525; **13**
  293–94
MS-Relais GmbH, **III** 710; **7** 302–03
MSAS Cargo International, **6** 415, 417
MSI Data Corp., **10** 523; **15** 482
MSL Industries, **10** 44
MSU. *See* Middle South Utilities.
Mt. *See also* Mount.
Mt. Carmel Public Utility Company, **6** 506
Mt. Goldsworthy Mining Associates, **IV** 47
Mt. Lyell Investments, **III** 672–73
Mt. Summit Rural Telephone Company, **14**
  258
Mt. Vernon Iron Works, **II** 14
MTC Pharmaceuticals, **II** 483
MTM Entertainment Inc., **13** 279, 281

Mueller Co., **III** 645
Mueller Furniture Company, **8** 252
Mueller Industries, Inc., 7 359–61
Mujirushi Ryohin, **V** 188
Mukluk Freight Lines, **6** 383
Mule Battery Manufacturing Co., **III** 643
Mülheimer Bergwerksvereins, **I** 542
Mullen Advertising, **13** 513
Mullens & Co., **14** 419
Multi Restaurants, **II** 664
Multibank Inc., **11** 281
Multicom Publishing Inc., **11** 294
MultiMed, **11** 379
Multimedia, Inc., IV 591; **11 330–32**
Multiple Access Systems Corp., **III** 109
Multiple Properties, **I** 588
MultiScope Inc., **10** 508
Münchener Rückversicherungs-
   Gesellschaft. *See* Munich Re.
Mungana Mines, **I** 438
Munich Re, II 239; **III** 183–84, 202,
   299–301, 400–01, 747
Municipal Assistance Corp., **II** 448
Munising Paper Co., **III** 40; **13** 156
Munising Woodenware Company, **13** 156
Munksund, **IV** 338
Murfin Inc., **8** 360
Murmic, Inc., **9** 120
Murphy Farms, **7** 477
Murphy Oil Corporation, 7 362–64
Murphy-Phoenix Company, **14** 122
Murray Bay Paper Co., **IV** 246
Murray Corp. of America, **III** 443
Murray Goulburn Snow, **II** 575
Murrayfield, **IV** 696
Murtaugh Light & Power Company, **12**
   265
Musashino Railway Company, **V** 510
Muscatine Journal, **11** 251
Muscocho Explorations Ltd., **IV** 76
Muse Air Corporation, **6** 120
Music Corporation of America. *See* MCA
   Inc.
Music Plus, **9** 75
Music-Appreciation Records, **13** 105
**Musicland Stores Corporation, 9
   360–62**; **11** 558
Muskegon Gas Company. *See* MCN
   Corporation.
Musotte & Girard, **I** 553
Mutoh Industries, Ltd., **6** 247
**Mutual Benefit Life Insurance Company,
   III** 243, **302–04**
Mutual Gaslight Company. *See* MCN
   Corporation.
Mutual Life Insurance Co. of the State of
   Wisconsin, **III** 321
**Mutual Life Insurance Company of New
   York, II** 331; **III** 247, 290, **305–07**,
   316, 321, 380
Mutual Medical Aid and Accident
   Insurance Co., **III** 331
Mutual of Omaha, **III** 365
Mutual Oil Co., **IV** 399
Mutual Papers Co., **14** 522
Mutual Safety Insurance Co., **III** 305
Mutual Savings & Loan Assoc., **III** 215
Mutualité Générale, **III** 210
Mutuelle d'Orléans, **III** 210
Mutuelle de l'Quest, **III** 211
Mutuelle Vie, **III** 210
Mutuelles Unies, **III** 211
Muzak Corporation, **7** 90–91
Muzzy-Lyon Co., **I** 158–59

Mwinilunga Canneries Ltd., **IV** 241
MXL Industries, **13** 367
MY Holdings, **IV** 92
Myanmar Oil and Gas Enterprise, **IV** 519
MYCAL Group, **V** 154
Mycrom, **14** 36
Mygind International, **8** 477
Mylan Laboratories, I 656–57
Myllykoski Träsliperi AB, **IV** 347–48
Myokenya, **III** 757
Myson Group PLC, **III** 671
Mysore State Iron Works, **IV** 205

N M Electronics, **II** 44
N.A. Otto & Cie., **III** 541
N.A. Woodworth, **III** 519
N.C. Cameron & Sons, Ltd., **11** 95
N.C. Monroe Construction Company, **14**
   112
N.K. Fairbank Co., **II** 497
N.M. Rothschild & Sons, **IV** 64, 712
N.M.U. Transport Ltd., **II** 569
N.R.F. Gallimard, **IV** 618
N. Shure Company, **15** 477
N.V. Philips Gloeilampenfabriken. *See*
   Philips Electronics N.V.
N.W. Ayer & Son, **I** 36; **II** 542
N.Y.P. Holdings Inc., **12** 360
Nabisco Brands, Inc., II 475, 512,
   542–44; **7** 128, 365–67; **12** 167. *See
   also* RJR Nabisco.
Nabisco Foods Group, 7 365–68 (upd.);
   9 318; **14** 48
Nabors Industries, Inc., 9 363–65
NACCO Industries, Inc., 7 369–71
Nacional Financiera, **IV** 513
NAFI. *See* National Automotive Fibers,
   Inc.
Nagano Seiyu Ltd., **V** 188
Nagasaki Shipyard, **I** 502
Nagasakiya Co., Ltd., V 149–51
Nagase & Company, Ltd., 8 376–78
Nagase-Alfa, **III** 420
Nagel Meat Markets and Packing House, **II**
   643
Nagoya Bank, **II** 373
Nagoya Electric Light Co., **IV** 62
Naigai Tsushin Hakuhodo, **6** 29
Naikoku Tsu-un Kabushiki Kaisha, **V** 477
Nakai Shoten Ltd., **IV** 292
Nalco Chemical Corporation, I 373–75;
   12 346–48 (upd.)
Nalfloc, **I** 374
Nalge Co., **14** 479–80
NAM. *See* Nederlandse Aardolie
   Maatschappij.
Namco, **III** 431
Namkwang Engineering & Construction
   Co. Ltd., **III** 749
Nampack, **I** 423
Nan Ya Plastics Corp., **14** 197–98
NANA Regional Corporation, **7** 558
Nankai Kogyo, **IV** 225
Nansei Sekiyu, **IV** 432
Nantucket Corporation, **6** 226
Nantucket Mills, **12** 285
Nanyo Bussan, **I** 493
NAPC. *See* North American Philips Corp.
Napier, **I** 194
NAPP Systems, Inc., **11** 253
Narmco Industries, **I** 544
NASA. *See* National Aeronautics and
   Space Administration.
Nash Finch Company, 8 379–81; **11** 43

Nash Motors Co., **I** 135; **8** 75
Nash-Kelvinator Corp., **I** 135; **12** 158
Nashaming Valley Information Processing,
   III 204
Nashua Corporation, 8 382–84
The Nashville Network, **11** 153
Nassau Gas Light Co., **6** 455
NASTECH, **III** 590
Nasu Aluminium Manufacturing Co., **IV**
   153
Natal Brewery Syndicate, **I** 287
Natco Corp., **I** 445
NaTec Ltd. *See* CRSS Inc.
National, **10** 419
National Acme Company. *See* Acme-
   Cleveland Corp.
National Advanced Systems, **II** 64–65
National Aeronautics and Space
   Administration, **II** 139; **6** 227–29, 327;
   11 201, 408; **12** 489
National Air Transport Co., **I** 128; **6** 128; **9**
   416; **11** 427
National Airlines, **I** 97, 116; **6** 388
National Aluminate Corp., **I** 373; **12** 346
National Aluminum Company, **11** 38
National American Life Insurance Co. of
   California, **II** 181
National American Title Insurance Co., **II**
   181
National Aniline & Chemical Co., **I** 414
**National Association of Securities
   Dealers, Inc., 10 416–18**
National Australia Bank, **III** 673
National Automobile and Casualty
   Insurance Co., **III** 270
National Automotive Fibers, Inc., **9** 118
National Aviation, **I** 117
National Baby Shop, **V** 203
National Bancard Corporation, **11** 111–13
National Bancorp of Arizona, **12** 565
National Bank, **II** 312
National Bank for Cooperatives, **8** 489–90
National Bank für Deutschland, **II** 270
National Bank of Belgium, **II** 294
National Bank of Commerce, **II** 331; **9**
   536; **11** 105–06; **13** 467
National Bank of Commerce Trust &
   Savings Association, **15** 161
National Bank of Detroit, **I** 165. *See also*
   NBD Bancorp, Inc.
National Bank of Egypt, **II** 355
The National Bank of Jacksonville, **9** 58
National Bank of New Zealand, **II** 308
National Bank of North America, **II** 334
National Bank of South Africa Ltd., **II** 236
National Bank of the City of New York, **II**
   312
National Bank of Turkey, **IV** 557
National Bank of Washington, **13** 440
National BankAmericard Inc., **9** 536
National Bankers Express Co., **II** 396; **10**
   60
National Basketball Association, **12** 457
National Bell Telephone Company, **V** 259
National Benefit and Casualty Co., **III** 228
National Benefit Co., **III** 228
National Binding Company, **8** 382
National Biscuit Co., **II** 542–43; **IV** 152; **7**
   365
National Bridge Company of Canada, Ltd.,
   8 544
National Broach & Machine Co., **I** 481–82
National Broadcasting Company, Inc., II
   30, 88–90, 129–33, **151–53**, 170, 173,

487, 543; **III** 188, 329; **IV** 596, 608, 652; **6** 157–59, **164–66 (upd.)**; **10** 173
National Building Society, **10** 6–7
National Cable & Manufacturing Co., **13** 369
National Can Corp., **I** 601–02, **607–08**; **IV** 154; **13** 255
National Car Rental System, Inc., **I** 489; **II** 419–20, 445; **6** 348–49; **10** 373, **419–20**
National Carbon Co., Inc., **I** 400; **9** 516; **11** 402
National Carriers, **6** 413–14
National Cash Register Company. *See* NCR Corporation.
National Cheerleaders Association, **15** 516–18
National Chemsearch Corp. *See* NCH Corporation.
National Child Care Centers, Inc., **II** 607
National City Bank, **9** 475
National City Bank of New York, **I** 337, 462; **II** 253–54; **III** 380; **IV** 81
National City Co., **II** 254; **9** 124
National City Corp., **9** 475; **15 313–16**
National Cleaning Contractors, **II** 176
National Coal Board, **IV** 38–40
National Coal Development Corp., **IV** 48
National Commercial Bank, **11** 108; **12** 422; **13** 476
National Components Industries, Inc., **13** 398
National Container Corp., **I** 609
National Convenience Stores Incorporated, **7** 372–75
National Credit Office, **IV** 604
National CSS, **IV** 605
National Dairy Products Corp., **II** 533; **7** 275; **14** 204
National Demographics & Lifestyles Inc., **10** 461
National Development Bank, **IV** 56
National Disinfectant Company. *See* NCH Corporation.
National Distillers and Chemical Corporation, **I** 226, **376–78**; **IV** 11; **8** 439–41; **9** 231; **10** 181
National Drive-In Grocery Corporation, **7** 372
National Drug Ltd., **II** 652
National Economic Research Associates, **III** 283
National Education Association, **9** 367
National Electric Company, **11** 388
National Electric Instruments Co., **IV** 78
National Electric Products Corp., **IV** 177
National Employers Life Assurance Co. Ltd., **13** 539
National Enquirer, **10** 287–88
National Express Laboratories, Inc., **10** 107
National Fidelity Life Insurance Co., **10** 246
National Fidelity Life Insurance Co. of Kansas, **III** 194; **IV** 343
National Finance Corp., **IV** 22–23
National Fire & Marine Insurance Co., **III** 213–14
National Fire Insurance Co., **III** 229–30
National Football League, **12** 457
National Freight Corporation, **6** 412–13
National Fuel Gas Company, **6 526–28**
National Gateway Telecom, **6** 326–27
National General Corp., **III** 190–91
National Geographic Society, **9 366–68**

National Greyhound Racing Club, **II** 142
National Grid Company, **11** 399–400; **12** 349; **13** 484
National Grocers of Ontario, **II** 631
National Gypsum Company, **8** 43; **10** 421–24; **13** 169
National Health Enterprises, **III** 87
National Health Laboratories Incorporated, **11 333–35**
National Hockey League, **12** 457
National Hotel Co., **III** 91
National Hydrocarbon Corp., **IV** 543
National Import and Export Corp. Ltd., **IV** 240
National Indemnity Co., **III** 213–14
National India Rubber Company, **9** 228
National Industries, **I** 446
National Inking Appliance Company, **14** 52
National Integrity Life Insurance, **III** 249
National Intergroup, Inc., **IV** 237, 574; **V** 152–53; **12** 354
National Iranian Oil Company, **III** 748; **IV** 370, 374, **466–68**, 484, 512, 535
National Key Company. *See* Cole National Corporation.
National Kinney Corp., **IV** 720; **9** 391
National Lead Co., **III** 681; **IV** 32
National Liability and Fire Insurance Co., **III** 214
National Liberty Corp., **III** 218–19
National Life and Accident Insurance Co., **III** 194
National Life Insurance Co., **III** 290
National Life Insurance Co. of Canada, **III** 243
National Living Centers, **13** 49
National Loss Control Service Corp., **III** 269
National Manufacturing Co., **III** 150; **6** 264; **13** 6
National Marine Service, **6** 530
National Market System, **9** 369
National Medical Enterprises, Inc., **III** 79, **87–88**; **6** 188; **10** 252; **14** 233
National Minerals Development Corp., **IV** 143–44
National Mortgage Agency of New Zealand Ltd., **IV** 278
National Mortgage Assoc. of Washington, **II** 410
National Motor Bearing Co., **I** 159
National Mutual Life Assurance of Australasia, **III** 249
National Office Furniture, **12** 297
National Oil Corp. *See* Libyan National Oil Corporation.
National Oil Distribution Co., **IV** 524
National Old Line Insurance Co., **III** 179
National Packaging, **IV** 333
National Paper Co., **8** 476
National Patent Development Corporation, **7** 45; **13 365–68**
National Permanent Mutual Benefit Building Society, **10** 6
National Petrochemical Co., **IV** 467
National Petroleum Publishing Co., **IV** 636
National Pharmacies, **9** 346
National Postal Meter Company, **14** 52
National Potash Co., **IV** 82; **7** 186
National Power PLC, **11** 399–400; **12** 349–51; **13** 458, 484
National Propane Corporation, **8** 535–37
National Provident Institution for Mutual Life Assurance, **IV** 711

National Provincial Bank, **II** 319–20, 333–34; **IV** 722
National Quotation Bureau, Inc., **14** 96–97
National Railways of Mexico, **IV** 512
National Regulator Co., **II** 41
National Reinsurance Co., **III** 276–77
National Rent-A-Car, **6** 392–93
National Research Corporation, **8** 397
National Rubber Machinery Corporation, **8** 298
National Sanitary Supply Company, **13** 149–50
National School Studios, **7** 255
National Science Foundation, **9** 266
National Sea Products Ltd., **14 339–41**
National Seal, **I** 158
National Semiconductor Corporation, **II** 63–65; **III** 455, 618, 678; **6** 215, **261–63**; **9** 297; **11** 45–46, 308, 463
National Service Industries, Inc., **11 336–38**
National Stamping & Electric Works, **12** 159
National Standard Co., **IV** 137; **13 369–71**
National Star Brick & Tile Co., **III** 501; **7** 207
National Starch and Chemical Corp., **IV** 253
National Starch Manufacturing Co., **II** 496
National Steel and Shipbuilding Company, **7** 356
National Steel Car Corp., **IV** 73
National Steel Corporation, **I** 491; **IV** 74, 163, 236–37, 572; **V** 152–53; **7** 549; **8** 346, 479–80; **11** 315; **12 352–54**; **14** 191
National Student Marketing Corporation, **10** 385–86
National Supply Co., **IV** 29
National Surety Co. of New York, **III** 395
National System Company, **9** 41; **11** 469
National Tanker Fleet, **IV** 502
National Tea, **II** 631–32
National Technical Laboratories, **14** 52
National Telecommunications of Austin, **8** 311
National Telephone and Telegraph Corporation. *See* British Columbia Telephone Company.
National Telephone Co., **III** 162; **7** 332, 508
National Theatres, Inc., **III** 190
National Transcontinental, **6** 360
National Travelers' Insurance Co., **III** 290
National Trust Life Insurance Co., **III** 218
National Tube Co., **II** 330; **IV** 572; **7** 549
National Union Electric Corporation, **12** 159
National Union Fire Insurance Co. of Pittsburgh, Pa., **III** 195–97
National Union Life and Limb Insurance Co., **III** 290
National Utilities & Industries Corporation, **9** 363
National Westminster Bank PLC, **II** 237, **333–35**; **IV** 642; **13** 206
National-Ben Franklin Insurance Co., **III** 242
National-Southwire Aluminum Company, **11** 38; **12** 353
Nationalbank, **I** 409
Nationale Bank Vereeniging, **II** 185

Nationale-Nederlanden N.V., III 179, 200–01, **308–11**; IV 697
Nationar, **9** 174
NationsBank Corporation, **6** 357; **10 425–27**; **11** 126; **13** 147
Nationwide Credit, **11** 112
Nationwide Income Tax Service, **9** 326
Nationwide Logistics Corp., **14** 504
NATIOVIE, **II** 234
Native Plants, **III** 43
NATM Buying Corporation, **10** 9, 468
Natomas Co., **IV** 410; **6** 353–54; **7** 309; **11** 271
Natref, **IV** 535
Natronag, **IV** 325
Natronzellstoff-und Papierfabriken AG, **IV** 324
Natudryl Manufacturing Company, **10** 271
Natural Gas Clearinghouse, **11** 355
Natural Gas Pipeline Company, **6** 530, 543; **7** 344–45
Natural Wonders Inc., **14 342–44**
The Nature Company, **10** 215–16; **14** 343
Nature's Sunshine Products, Inc., **15 317–19**
NatWest. *See* National Westminster Bank PLC.
Naugles, **7** 506
Nautilus, **III** 315–16; **13** 532
Nautor Ab, **IV** 302
Navajo Refining Company, **12** 240
Navale, **III** 209
Naviera Vizcaina, **IV** 528
Navigation Mixte, **III** 348
Navistar International Corporation, **I** 152, 155, **180–82**, 186, 525, 527; **II** 330; **10** 280, **428–30 (upd.)**. *See also* International Harvester Co.
NBC. *See* National Broadcasting Company, Inc.
NBC/Computer Services Corporation, **15** 163
NBD Bancorp, Inc., **9** 476; **11 339–41**, 466
NCA Corporation, **9** 36, 57, 171
NCB. *See* National City Bank of New York.
NCB Brickworks, **III** 501; **7** 207
NCC L.P., **15** 139
NCH Corporation, **8 385–87**
Nchanga Consolidated Copper Mines, **IV** 239–40
NCNB Corporation, **II 336–37**; **12** 519
NCR Corporation, **I** 540–41; **III** 147–52, **150–53**, 157, 165–66; **IV** 298; **V** 263; **6** 250, **264–68 (upd.)**, 281–82; **9** 416; **11** 62, 151, 542; **12** 162, 148, 246, 484
nCube, **14** 15
ND Marston, **III** 593
NDL. *See* Norddeutscher Lloyd.
NEA. *See* Newspaper Enterprise Association.
NEAC Inc., **I** 201–02
Nebraska Bell Company, **14** 311
Nebraska Cellular Telephone Company, **14** 312
Nebraska Consolidated Mills Company, **II** 493; **III** 52; **8** 433
Nebraska Furniture Mart, **III** 214–15
Nebraska Light & Power Company, **6** 580
NEC Corporation, **I** 455, 520; **II** 40, 42, 45, 56–57, **66–68**, 73, 82, 91, 104, 361; **III** 122–23, 130, 140, 715; **6** 101, 231,

244, 287; **9** 42, 115; **10** 257, 366, 463, 500; **11** 46, 308, 490; **13** 482
Neches Butane Products Co., **IV** 552
Neckermann Versand AG, **V** 100–02
Nedbank, **IV** 23
Nederland Line. *See* Stoomvaart Maatschappij Nederland.
Nederlands Talen Institut, **13** 544
Nederlandsche Heide Maatschappij, **III** 199
Nederlandsche Kunstzijdebariek, **13** 21
Nederlandsche Nieuw Guinea Petroleum Maatschappij, **IV** 491
Nederlandsche Stoomvart Maatschappij Oceaan, **6** 416
Nederlandse Cement Industrie, **III** 701
Nederlandse Crediebank N.V., **II** 248
Nederlandse Dagbladunie NV, **IV** 610
N.V. Nederlandse Gasunie, **I** 326; **V** 627, **658–61**
Nederlandse Handel Maatschappij, **II** 183, 527; **IV** 132–33
Nederlandse Vliegtuigenfabriek, **I** 54
Nedsual, **IV** 23
Neeco, Inc., **9** 301
Needham Harper Worldwide, **I** 23, 28, 30–33; **13** 203; **14** 159
Needlecraft, **II** 560; **12** 410
Neenah Paper Co., **III** 40
Neenah Printing, **8** 360
NEES. *See* New England Electric System.
Neilson/Cadbury, **II** 631
Neiman Bearings Co., **13** 78
Neiman Marcus, **15** 50, 86, 291
Neiman Marcus Co., **I** 246; **II** 478; **V** 10, 31; **12 355–57**
Neisler Laboratories, **I** 400
Neisner Brothers, Inc., **9** 20
Nekoosa Edwards Paper Co., **IV** 282; **9** 261
NEL Equity Services Co., **III** 314
Nelio Chemicals, Inc., **IV** 345
Nelson Bros., **14** 236
Nemuro Bank, **II** 291
Nenuco, **II** 567
Neodata, **11** 293
Neoterics Inc., **11** 65
Neozyme I Corp., **13** 240
Nepera Chemical, **I** 682
NERCO, Inc., **V** 689, **7 376–79**
Nesbitt Thomson, **II** 211
Nesher Cement, **II** 47
Neste Oy, **IV** 435, **469–71**, 519
Nestlé S.A., **I** 15, 17, 251–52, 369, 605; **II** 379, 456, 478, 486–89, 521, **545–49**, 568–70; **III** 47–48; **6** 16; **7 380–84 (upd.)**; **8** 131, 342–44, 498–500; **10** 47, 324; **11** 15, 205; **12** 480–81; **13** 294; **14** 214; **15** 63
Netherland Bank for Russian Trade, **II** 183
Netherlands Fire Insurance Co. of Tiel, **III** 308, 310
Netherlands India Steam Navigation Co., **III** 521
Netherlands Insurance Co., **III** 179, 308–10
Netherlands Trading Co. *See* Nederlandse Handel Maatschappij.
Netron, **II** 390
Netscape Communications Corporation, **15 320–22**
Nettai Sangyo, **I** 507
Nettlefolds Ltd., **III** 493
Netto, **11** 240

Network Communications Associates, Inc., **11** 409
Neue Frankfurter Allgemeine Versicherungs-AG, **III** 184
Neue Holding AG, **III** 377
Neuenberger Versicherungs-Gruppe, **III** 404
Neuralgyline Co., **I** 698
Nevada Bell Telephone Company, **V** 318–20; **14 345–47**
Nevada Community Bank, **11** 119
Nevada National Bank, **II** 381; **12** 534
Nevada Power Company, **11 342–44**; **12** 265
Neversink Dyeing Company, **9** 153
New America Publishing Inc., **10** 288
New Asahi Co., **I** 221
New Bedford Gas & Edison Light Co., **14** 124–25
New Broken Hill Consolidated, **IV** 58–61
New Century Network, **13** 180
New Consolidated Canadian Exploration Co., **IV** 96
New Consolidated Gold Fields, **IV** 21, 95–96
New Daido Steel Co., Ltd., **IV** 62–63
New Departure, **9** 17
New Departure Hyatt, **III** 590
New England Confectionery Co., **15 323–25**
New England CRInc, **8** 562
New England Electric System, **V 662–64**
New England Gas & Electric Association, **14** 124–25
New England Glass Co., **III** 640
New England Life Insurance Co., **III** 261
New England Merchants National Bank, **II** 213–14; **III** 313
New England Mutual Life Insurance Co., **III 312–14**
New England National Bank of Boston, **II** 213
New England Network, Inc., **12** 31
New England Nuclear Corporation, **I** 329; **8** 152
New England Power Association, **V** 662
New England Trust Co., **II** 213
New Fire Office, **III** 371
New Found Industries, Inc., **9** 465
New Guinea Goldfields, **IV** 95
New Halwyn China Clays, **III** 690
New Hampshire Gas & Electric Co., **14** 124
New Hampshire Insurance Co., **III** 196–97
New Hampshire Oak, **III** 512
New Haven District Telephone Company. *See* Southern New England Telecommunications Corporation.
New Hokkai Hotel Co., Ltd., **IV** 327
New Ireland, **III** 393
New Jersey Bell, **9** 321
New Jersey Hot Water Heating Company, **6** 449
New Jersey Shale, **14** 250
New Jersey Tobacco Co., **15** 138
New Jersey Zinc, **I** 451
New London City National Bank, **13** 467
New London Ship & Engine, **I** 57
New Mather Metals, **III** 582
New Mitsui Bussan, **I** 507; **III** 296
New Nippon Electric Co., **II** 67
New Orleans Canal and Banking Company, **11** 105
New Orleans Refining Co., **IV** 540

New Plan Realty Trust, 11 345–47
New Process Cork Company Inc., I 601; 13 188
New Street Capital Inc., 8 388–90 (upd.). See also Drexel Burnham Lambert Incorporated.
New Sulzer Diesel, III 633
New Trading Company. See SBC Warburg.
New United Motor Manufacturing Inc., I 205
New World Development Company Ltd., IV 717–19; 8 500
New World Hotel (Holdings) Ltd., IV 717; 13 66
New York Air, I 90, 103, 118, 129; 6 129
New York Airways, I 123–24
New York and Richmond Gas Company, 6 456
New York and Suburban Savings and Loan Association, 10 91
New York Biscuit Co., II 542
New York Central Railroad Company, II 329, 369; IV 181; 9 228; 10 43–44, 71–73
New York Chemical Manufacturing Co., II 250
New York City Transit Authority, 8 75
New York Condensed Milk Co., II 470
New York Electric Corporation. See New York State Electric and Gas.
New York Evening Enquirer, 10 287
New York Gas Light Company. See Consolidated Edison Company of New York.
New York Glucose Co., II 496
New York Guaranty and Indemnity Co., II 331
New York Harlem Railroad Co., II 250
New York Improved Patents Corp., I 601; 13 188
New York, Lake Erie & Western Railroad, II 395; 10 59
New York Life Insurance Company, II 217–18, 330; III 291, 305, 315–17, 332; 10 382
New York Magazine Co., IV 651; 7 390; 12 359
New York Manufacturing Co., II 312
New York Marine Underwriters, III 220
New York Quinine and Chemical Works, I 496
New York Quotation Company, 9 370
New York, Rio and Buenos Aires Airlines, I 115
New York State Board of Tourism, 6 51
New York State Electric and Gas Corporation, 6 534–36
New York Stock Exchange, Inc., 9 369–72; 10 416–17
New York Telephone Co., 9 321
New York Times Company, III 40; IV 647–49; 6 13; 15 54
New York Trust Co., I 378; II 251
New York, West Shore and Buffalo Railroad, II 329
New York's Bankers Trust Co., 12 107
New York-Newport Air Service Co., I 61
New Zealand Aluminum Smelters, IV 59
New Zealand Co., II 187
New Zealand Countrywide Banking Corporation, 10 336
New Zealand Forest Products, IV 249–50
New Zealand Press Assoc., IV 669
New Zealand Sugar Co., III 686

New Zealand Wire Ltd., IV 279
Newark Electronics Co., 9 420
Newco Waste Systems, V 750
Newcrest Mining Ltd., IV 47
Newell and Harrison, II 668
Newell Co., 9 373–76; 12 216; 13 40–41
Newey and Eyre, I 429
Newfoundland Light & Power Co. See Fortis, Inc.
Newgateway PLC, II 629
Newhall Land and Farming Company, 14 348–50
Newhouse Broadcasting, 6 33
Newmont Mining Corporation, III 248; IV 17, 20, 33, 171, 576; 7 287–89, 385–88; 12 244
Newport News Shipbuilding and Dry Dock Co., I 58, 527; 13 372–75
News America Publishing Inc., 12 358–60
News and Westminster Ltd., IV 685
News Corporation Limited, II 169; IV 650–53; 7 389–93 (upd.); 8 551; 9 429; 12 358–60
Newsfoto Publishing Company, 12 472
Newspaper Co-op Couponing, 8 551
Newspaper Enterprise Association, 7 157–58
Newspaper Proprietors' Assoc., IV 669
Newspaper Supply Co., IV 607
Newsweek, Inc., IV 688
Newth-Morris Box Co. See Rock-Tenn Company.
Newtherm Oil Burners, Ltd., 13 286
Newtown Gas Co., 6 455
Next Inc., III 116, 121; 6 219
Next PLC, 6 25
Nextel Communications, Inc., 10 431–33
Neyveli Lignite Corp. Ltd., IV 49
NFC plc, 6 412–14; 14 547
NHK, 9 31. See also Japan Broadcasting Corporation.
NHK Spring Co., Ltd., III 580–82
Niagara Fire Insurance Co., III 241–42
Niagara First Savings and Loan Association, 10 91
Niagara Insurance Co. (Bermuda) Ltd., III 242
Niagara Mohawk Power Corporation, V 665–67; 6 535
Niagara Silver Co., IV 644
Niagara Sprayer and Chemical Co., I 442
NIBRASCO, IV 55
Nicaro Nickel Co., IV 82, 111; 7 186
Nice Day, Inc., II 539
Nice Systems, 11 520
NiceCom Ltd., 11 520
Nichi-Doku Shashinki Shoten, III 574
Nichia Steel, IV 159
Nichibo, V 387
Nichii Co., Ltd., V 154–55; 15 470
Nichimen Corporation, II 442; IV 150–52, 154; 10 439
Nichimo Sekiyu Co. Ltd., IV 555
Nicholas Kiwi Ltd., II 572; 15 436
Nicholas Turkey Breeding Farms, 13 103
Nicholas Ungar, V 156
Nichols & Company, 8 561
Nichols Copper Co., IV 164, 177
Nicholson File Co., II 16
Le Nickel. See Société Le Nickel.
Nicolai Pavdinsky Co., IV 118
Nicolet Instrument Company, 11 513
NICOR Inc., 6 529–31

Niederbayerische Celluloswerke, IV 324
Niederrheinische Hütte AG, IV 222
Niehler Maschinenfabrick, III 602
Nielsen, 10 358
Nielsen & Petersen, III 417
Nielsen Marketing Research. See A.C. Nielsen Company.
Niemann Chemie, 8 464
Niese & Coast Products Co., II 681
Nieuwe Eerste Nederlandsche, III 177–79
Nieuwe HAV-Bank of Schiedam, III 200
Nigeria Airways, I 107
Nigerian National Petroleum Corporation, IV 472–74
Nihol Repol Corp., III 757
Nihon Denko, II 118
Nihon Keizai Shimbun, Inc., IV 654–56
Nihon Kensetsu Sangyo Ltd., I 520
Nihon Kohden Corporation, 13 328
Nihon Lumber Land Co., III 758
Nihon Sangyo Co., I 183; II 118
Nihon Sugar, I 511
Nihon Synopsis, 11 491
Nihon Teppan, IV 159
Nihon Timken K.K., 8 530
Nihon Yusen Kaisha, I 503, 506; III 577, 712
Nihron Yupro Corp., III 756
NII. See National Intergroup, Inc.
Niitsu Oil, IV 542
Nike, Inc., V 372–74, 376; 8 303–04, 391–94 (upd.); 9 134–35, 437; 10 525; 11 50, 349; 13 513; 14 8; 15 397
Nikka Oil Co., IV 150
Nikka Whisky Distilling Co., I 220
Nikkei. See also Nihon Keizai Shimbun, Inc.
Nikkei Aluminium Co., IV 153–55
Nikkei Shimbun Toei, 9 29
Nikken Stainless Fittings Co., Ltd., IV 160
Nikko Copper Electrolyzing Refinery, III 490
Nikko International Hotels, I 106
Nikko Kido Company, 6 431
Nikko Petrochemical Co. Ltd., IV 476
The Nikko Securities Company Limited, II 300, 323, 383, 433–35; 9 377–79 (upd.); 12 536
Nikko Trading Co., I 106
Nikon Corporation, III 120–21, 575, 583–85; 9 251; 12 340
Nile Faucet Corp., III 569
Nillmij, III 177–79
Nimas Corp., III 570
Nine West Group Inc., 11 348–49; 14 441
Nineteen Hundred Washer Co., III 653; 12 548
Nintendo Co., Ltd., III 586–88; 7 394–96 (upd.); 10 124–25, 284–86, 483–84; 13 403; 15 539
NIOC. See National Iranian Oil Company.
Nippon ARC Co., III 715
Nippon Breweries Ltd., I 220, 282; 13 454
Nippon Broilers Co., II 550
Nippon Cable Company, 15 235
Nippon Cargo Airlines, 6 71
Nippon Chemical Industries, I 363
Nippon Credit Bank, II 310, 338–39
Nippon Educational Television (NET), 9 29. See also Asahi National Broadcasting Company, Ltd.
Nippon Electric Co., II 66–68

Nippon Express Co., Ltd., II 273; V **477–80**
Nippon Fruehauf Co., IV 154
Nippon Fukokin Kinyu Koku, II 300
Nippon Funtai Kogyo Co., III 714
Nippon Gakki Co., Ltd., III 656–58
Nippon Ginko, III 408
Nippon Gyomo Sengu Co. Ltd., IV 555
Nippon Hatsujo Kabushikikaisha. *See* NHK Spring Co., Ltd.
Nippon Helicopter & Aeroplane Transport Co., Ltd., **6** 70
Nippon Hoso Kyokai. *See* Japan Broadcasting Corporation.
Nippon Idou Tsushin, **7** 119–20
Nippon International Container Services, **8** 278
Nippon Interrent, **10** 419–20
Nippon K.K. *See* Nippon Kokan K.K.
Nippon Kairiku Insurance Co., III 384
Nippon Kakoh Seishi, IV 293
Nippon Kogaku K.K., III 583–84
Nippon Kogyo Co. Ltd. *See* Nippon Mining Co. Ltd.
Nippon Kokan K.K., IV 161–63, 184, 212; **8** 449; **12** 354
Nippon Life Insurance Company, II 374, 451; III 273, 288, **318–20**; IV 727; **9** 469
Nippon Light Metal Company, Ltd., IV **153–55**
Nippon Machinery Trading, I 507
Nippon Meat Packers, Inc., II **550–51**
Nippon Menka Kaisha, IV 150–51
Nippon Merck-Banyu, I 651; **11** 290
Nippon Mining Co., Ltd., III 759; IV **475–77**; **14** 207
Nippon Motorola Manufacturing Co., II 62
Nippon New Zealand Trading Co. Ltd., IV 327
Nippon Oil Company, Limited, IV 434, 475–76, **478–79**, 554
Nippon Onkyo, II 118
Nippon Paint Co., Ltd, **11** 252
Nippon Pelnox Corp., III 715
Nippon Polaroid Kabushiki Kaisha, III 608; **7** 437
Nippon Pulp Industries, IV 321
Nippon Rayon, V 387
Nippon Sangyo Co., Ltd., IV 475
Nippon Sanso, I 359
Nippon Seiko K.K., III **589–90**, 595
Nippon Sekiyu Co. *See* Nippon Oil Company, Limited.
Nippon Sheet Glass Company, Limited, III **714–16**
Nippon Shinpan Company, Ltd., II **436–37**, 442; **8** 118
Nippon Silica Kogyo Co., III 715
Nippon Soda, II 301
Nippon Soken, III 592
Nippon Steel Chemical Co., **10** 439
Nippon Steel Corporation, I 466, 493–94, 509; II 300, 391; IV 116, 130, **156–58**, 184, 212, 228, 298; **6** 274; **14** 369
Nippon Suisan Kaisha, Limited, II **552–53**
Nippon Tar, I 363
Nippon Telegraph and Telephone Corporation (NTT), II 51, 62; III 139–40; V **305–07**; **7** 118–20; **10** 119; **13** 482
Nippon Television, **7** 249; **9** 29

Nippon Tire Co., Ltd., V 234
Nippon Trust Bank Ltd., II 405; **15** 42
Nippon Typewriter, II 459
Nippon Victor (Europe) GmbH, II 119
Nippon Wiper Blade Co., Ltd., III 592
Nippon Yusen Kabushiki Kaisha, IV 713; V **481–83**; **6** 398
Nippon Yusoki Company, Ltd., **13** 501
Nippon-Fisher, **13** 225
Nippondenso Co., Ltd., III **591–94**, 637–38
NIPSCO Industries, Inc., **6** **532–33**
Nishi Taiyo Gyogyo Tosei K.K., II 578
Nishikawaya Co., Ltd., V 209
Nishimbo Industries Inc., IV 442
Nishizono Ironworks, III 595
Nissan Construction, V 154
Nissan Motor Company, Ltd., I 9–10, **183–84**, 207, 494; II 118, 292–93, 391; III 485, 517, 536, 579, 591, 742, 750; IV 63; **7** 111, 120, 219; **9** 243, 340–42; **10** 353; **11** 50–51, **350–52 (upd.)**
Nissan Trading Company, Ltd., **13** 533
Nisshin Chemical Industries, I 397
Nisshin Chemicals Co., II 554
Nisshin Flour Milling Company, Ltd., II **554**
Nisshin Pharaceutical Co., II 554
Nisshin Steel Co., Ltd., I 432; IV 130, **159–60**; **7** 588
Nissho Iwai K.K., I 432, **509–11**; IV 160, 383; **6** 386; **8** 75, 392; **15** 373
Nissho Kosan Co., III 715
Nissui. *See* Nippon Suisan Kaisha.
Nitratos de Portugal, IV 505
Nitroglycerin AB, **13** 22
Nitroglycerin Ltd., **9** 380
Nittetsu Curtainwall Corp., III 758
Nittetsu Sash Sales Corp., III 758
Nitto Warehousing Co., I 507
Nittoku Metal Industries, Ltd., III 635
Nittsu. *See* Nippon Express Co., Ltd.
Nixdorf Computer AG, I 193; II 279; III 109, **154–55**; **12** 162; **14** 13, 169
Nixdorf-Krein Industries Inc. *See* Laclede Steel Company.
NKK Corporation, IV 74, **161–63**, 212–13; V 152
NL Industries, Inc., III 681; **10** **434–36**
NLM City-Hopper, I 109
NLM Dutch Airlines, I 108
NLT Corp., II 122; III 194; **10** 66; **12** 546
NMC Laboratories Inc., **12** 4
NMH Stahlwerke GmbH, IV 128
NMT. *See* Nordic Mobile Telephone.
No-Leak-O Piston Ring Company, **10** 492
Noah's New York Bagels, **13** 494
Nobel Industries AB, I 351; **9** **380–82**. *See also* Akzo Nobel N.V.
Nobel-Bozel, I 669
Nobel-Hoechst Chimie, I 669
Noble Affiliates, Inc., **11** **353–55**
Noble Roman's Inc., **14** **351–53**
Nobles Industries, **13** 501
Noblesville Telephone Company, **14** 258
Noblitt-Sparks Industries, Inc., **8** 37–38
Noell, IV 201
Nokia Corporation, II **69–71**; IV 296
Nokia Group, **6** 242; **15** 125
Noma Industries, **11** 526
Nomura Securities Company, Limited, II 276, 326, 434, **438–41**; **9** 377, **383–86 (upd.)**
Non-Fiction Book Club, **13** 105

Non-Stop Fashions, Inc., **8** 323
Nonpareil Refining Co., IV 488
Noordwinning Group, IV 134
Nopco Chemical Co., IV 409; **7** 308
Nopri, V 63–65
Nor-Am Agricultural Products, I 682
NORAND, **9** 411
Noranda Inc., IV **164–66**; **7** **397–99 (upd.)**; **9** 282
Norcast Manufacturing Ltd., IV 165
Norcen Energy Resources, Ltd., **8** 347
Norcliff Thayer, III 66
Norco Plastics, **8** 553
Norcon, Inc., **7** 558–59
Nord-Aviation, I 45, 74, 82, 195; **7** 10
Nordarmatur, I 198
Nordbanken, **9** 382
Norddeutsche Affinerie, IV 141
Norddeutsche Bank A.G., II 279
Norddeutscher-Lloyd, I 542; **6** 397–98
Nordfinanzbank, II 366
Nordic Bank Ltd., II 366
Nordic Joint Stock Bank, II 302
Nordic Mobile Telephone, II 70
Nordica, **10** 151; **15** 396–97
NordicTrack, **10** 215–17
Nordland Papier GmbH, IV 300, 302
Nordson Corporation, **11** **356–58**
Nordstahl AG, IV 201
Nordstjernan, I 553–54
Nordstrom, Inc., V **156–58**; **11** 349; **13** 494; **14** 376
Nordwestdeutsche Kraftwerke AG, III 466; V **698–700**
Norelco Consumer Products Group, **12** 439
Norell, I 696
Norex Laboratories, I 699
Norfolk Carolina Telephone Company, **10** 202
Norfolk Southern Corporation, V **484–86**; **6** 436, 487; **12** 278
Norfolk Steel, **13** 97
Norge Co., III 439–40
Norinchukin Bank, II **340–41**
NORIS Bank GmbH, V 166
Norma Cie., III 622
Norman BV, **9** 93
Norman J. Hurll Group, III 673
Normond/CMS, **7** 117
Norrell Corporation, **6** 46
Norris Cylinder Company, **11** 535
Norris Grain Co., **14** 537
Norsk Hydro A.S., IV 405–06, 525; **10** **437–40**; **14** 494
Norstar Bancorp, **9** 229
Nortek Inc., I 482; **14** 482
Nortex Products, **7** 96
North & South Wales Bank, II 318
North Advertising, Inc., **6** 27
North African Petroleum Ltd., IV 455
North American Aviation, I 48, 71, 78, 81, 101; **7** 520; **9** 16; **10** 163; **11** 278, 427
North American Bancorp, II 192
North American Cellular Network, **9** 322
North American Coal Corporation, **7** 369–71
North American Company, **6** 443, 552–53, 601–02
North American Dräger, **13** 328
North American Insurance Co., II 181
North American InTeleCom, Inc., IV 411
North American Life and Casualty Co., III 185, 306

North American Light & Power Company, **V** 609; **6** 504–05; **12** 541
North American Managers, Inc., **III** 196
North American Philips Corp., **II** 79–80
North American Printed Circuit Corp., **III** 643
North American Printing Ink Company, **13** 228
North American Reinsurance Corp., **III** 377
North American Rockwell Corp., **10** 173
North American Systems, **14** 230
North American Training Corporation. *See* Rollerblade, Inc.
North American Van Lines, **I** 278; **14** 37
North Atlantic Packing, **13** 243
North British Insurance Co., **III** 234–35
North Broken Hill Peko, **IV** 61
North Carolina National Bank Corporation, **II** 336; **10** 425–27
North Carolina Natural Gas Corporation, **6** 578
North Carolina Shipbuilding Co., **13** 373
North Central Airlines, **I** 132
North Central Finance, **II** 333
North Central Financial Corp., **9** 475
North Cornwall China Clay Co., **III** 690
North Eastern Bricks, **14** 249
North Eastern Coalfields Ltd., **IV** 48
North Face, **8** 169
North Goonbarrow, **III** 690
North Holland Publishing Co., **IV** 610
North New York Savings Bank, **10** 91
North of Scotland Bank, **II** 318
North Pacific Paper Corp., **IV** 298
North Pacific Railroad, **II** 330
North Sea Oil and Gas, **10** 337
North Sea Sun Oil Co. Ltd., **IV** 550
North Shore Gas Company, **6** 543–44
North Shore Medical Centre Pty. Ltd., **IV** 708
North Star Egg Case Company, **12** 376
North Star Marketing Cooperative, **7** 338
North Star Mill, **12** 376
North Star Steel, **13** 138
The North West Company, Inc., 12 361–63
North West Water Group plc, 11 359–62
North-West Telecommunications, **6** 327
Northamptonshire Union Bank, **II** 333
Northcliffe Newspapers, **IV** 685
Northeast Airlines Inc., **I** 99–100; **6** 81
Northeast Federal Corp., **13** 468
Northeast Petroleum Industries, Inc., **11** 194; **14** 461
Northeast Savings Bank, **12** 31; **13** 467–68
Northeast Utilities, V 668–69; 13 182–84
Northeastern Bancorp of Scranton, **II** 342
Northeastern New York Medical Service, Inc., **III** 246
Northern Aluminum Co. Ltd., **IV** 9–10
Northern and Employers Assurance, **III** 235
Northern Arizona Light & Power Co., **6** 545
Northern Border Pipeline Co., **V** 609–10
Northern California Savings, **10** 340
Northern Crown Bank, **II** 344
Northern Dairies, **10** 441
Northern Development Co., **IV** 282
Northern Drug Company, **14** 147
Northern Electric Company. *See* Northern Telecom Limited.

Northern Energy Resources Company. *See* NERCO, Inc.
Northern Fibre Products Co., **I** 202
Northern Foods PLC, I 248; **II** 587; **10 441–43**
Northern Illinois Gas Co., **6** 529–31
Northern Indiana Power Company, **6** 556
Northern Indiana Public Service Company, **6** 532–33
Northern Joint Stock Bank, **II** 303
Northern National Bank, **14** 90
Northern Natural Gas Co., **V** 609–10
Northern Pacific Corp., **15** 274
Northern Pacific Railroad, **II** 278, 329; **III** 228, 282; **14** 168
Northern Paper, **I** 614
Northern States Life Insurance Co., **III** 275
Northern States Power Company, V 670–72
Northern Stores, Inc., **12** 362
Northern Sugar Company, **11** 13
Northern Telecom Limited, II 70; **III** 143, 164; **V** 271; **V 308–10**; **6** 242, 307, 310; **9** 479; **10** 19, 432; **11** 69; **12** 162; **14** 259
Northern Trust Company, III 518; **9 387–89**
Northfield Metal Products, **11** 256
Northland. *See* Scott Fetzer Company.
Northrop Corporation, I 47, 49, 55, 59, **76–77**, 80, 84, 197, 525; **III** 84; **9** 416, 418; **10** 162; **11** 164, 166, 266, 269, **363–65 (upd.)**
Northrup King Co., **I** 672
NorthStar Computers, **10** 313
Northwest Airlines Inc., I 42, 64, 91, 97, 100, 104, **112–14**, 125, 127; **6** 66, 74, 82 **103–05 (upd.)**, 123; **9** 273; **11** 266, 315; **12** 191, 487
Northwest Benefit Assoc., **III** 228
Northwest Engineering Co. *See* Terex Corporation.
Northwest Industries, **I** 342, 440; **II** 468 **8** 367. *See also* Chicago and North Western Holdings Corporation.
Northwest Instruments, **8** 519
Northwest Paper Company, **8** 430
Northwest Steel Rolling Mills Inc., **13** 97
Northwest Telecommunications Inc., **6** 598
Northwestern Bell Telephone Co., **V** 341
Northwestern Benevolent Society, **III** 228
Northwestern Engraving, **12** 25
Northwestern Expanded Metal Co., **III** 763
Northwestern Financial Corporation, **11** 29
Northwestern Industries, **III** 263
Northwestern Manufacturing Company, **8** 133
Northwestern Mutual Life Insurance Company, III 321–24, 352; **IV** 333
Northwestern National Insurance Co., **IV** 29
Northwestern National Life Insurance Co., **14** 233
Northwestern Public Service Company, **6** 524
Northwestern States Portland Cement Co., **III** 702
Northwestern Telephone Systems, **6** 325, 328
Norton Company, III 678; **8 395–97**
Norton Healthcare Ltd., **11** 208
Norton Opax PLC, **IV** 259
Norton Simon Inc., **I** 446; **IV** 672; **6** 356
Norwales Development Ltd., **11** 239

Norwalk Truck Lines, **14** 567
Norweb, **13** 458
Norwegian Assurance, **III** 258
Norwegian Globe, **III** 258
Norwegian Petroleum Consultants, **III** 499
Norweld Holding A.A., **13** 316
Norwest Mortgage Inc., **11** 29
Norwest Publishing, **IV** 661
Norwich Pharmaceuticals, **I** 370–71; **9** 358
Norwich Union Fire Insurance Society, Ltd., **III** 242, 273, 404; **IV** 705
Norwich Winterthur Group, **III** 404
Norwich-Eaton Pharmaceuticals, **III** 53; **8** 434
Norwood Company, **13** 168
Nostell Brick & Tile, **14** 249
Nottingham Manufacturing Co., **V** 357
Nouvelles Galeries, **10** 205
Nouvelles Messageries de la Presse Parisienne, **IV** 618
Nova Corporation of Alberta, V 673–75; **12** 364–66
Nova Pharmaceuticals, **14** 46
NovaCare, Inc., 11 366–68; **14** 233
Novacor Chemicals Ltd., 12 364–66
Novalta Resources Inc., **11** 441
Novell, Inc., 6 255–56, 260, **269–71**; **9** 170–71; **10** 232, 363, 473–74, 558, 565; **11** 59, 519–20; **12** 335; **13** 482; **15** 131, 133, 373, 492
Novello and Co., **II** 139
Novo Industri A/S, I 658–60, 697
Nowell Wholesale Grocery Co., **II** 681
Nox Ltd., **I** 588
Noxell Corporation, **III** 53; **8** 434
NPD Group, **13** 4
NPD Trading (USA), Inc., **13** 367
NPS Waste Technologies, **13** 366
NRG Energy, Inc., **11** 401
NS. *See* Norfolk Southern Corporation.
NS Petites Inc., **8** 323
NSG Information System Co., **III** 715
NSK. *See* Nippon Seiko K.K.
NSK-Warner, **14** 64
NSMO. *See* Nederlandsche Stoomvart Maatschappij Oceaan.
NSP. *See* Northern States Power Company.
NSU Werke, **10** 261
NTCL. *See* Northern Telecom Limited.
NTN Corporation, III 595–96, 623
NTRON, **11** 486
NTT. *See* Nippon Telegraph and Telephone Corp.
NTTPC. *See* Nippon Telegraph and Telephone Public Corporation.
NU. *See* Northeast Utilities.
Nuclear Electric, **6** 453; **11** 399–401; **12** 349; **13** 484
Nucoa Butter Co., **II** 497
Nucor Corporation, 7 400–02; **13** 143, 423; **14** 156
Nucorp Energy, **II** 262, 620
NUG Optimus Lebensmittel-Einzelhandelgesellschaft mbH, **V** 74
Nugget Polish Co. Ltd., **II** 566
Numerax, Inc., **IV** 637
Nuovo Pignone, **IV** 420–22
NUR Touristic GmbH, **V** 100–02
Nurad, **III** 468
Nurotoco Inc. *See* Roto-Rooter Service Company.
Nursefinders, **6** 10
NutraSweet Company, II 463, 582; **8 398–400**

Nutrena, **II** 617; **13** 137
Nutrilite Co., **III** 11–12
NutriSystem, **10** 383; **12** 531
Nu-Era Gear, **14** 64
NVR L.P., 8 401–03
NWA Aircraft, **I** 114
NWK. *See* Nordwestdeutsche Kraftwerke AG.
NWL Control Systems, **III** 512
NWS BANK plc, **10** 336–37
Nya AB Atlas, **III** 425–26
Nydqvist & Holm, **III** 426
Nyhamms Cellulosa, **IV** 338
NYK. *See* Nihon Yusen Kaisha, Nippon Yusen Kabushiki Kaisha *and* Nippon Yusen Kaisha.
Nylex Corp., **I** 429
Nyman & Schultz Affarsresbyraer A.B., **I** 120
NYNEX Corporation, **V** 311–13; **6** 340; **11** 19, 87; **13** 176
Nyrop, **I** 113
Nysco Laboratories, **III** 55
NYSEG. *See* New York State Electric and Gas Corporation.
NZI Corp., **III** 257

O&Y. *See* Olympia & York Developments Ltd.
O.B. McClintock Co., **7** 144–45
O. Kraft & Sons, **12** 363
O.S. Designs Inc., **15** 396
Oahu Railway & Land Co., **I** 565–66
Oak Farms Dairies, **II** 660
Oak Hill Investment Partners, **11** 490
Oak Industries, **III** 512
OakStone Financial Corporation, **11** 448
Oakwood Homes Corporation, **13** 155; **15 326–28**
OASIS, **IV** 454
Oasis Group P.L.C., **10** 506
ÖBB. *See* Österreichische Bundesbahnen GmbH.
Obbola Linerboard, **IV** 339
Oberrheinische Bank, **II** 278
Oberschlesische Stickstoff-Werge AG, **IV** 229
Oberusel AG, **III** 541
Object Design, Inc., **15** 372
Obunsha, **9** 29
Occidental Insurance Co., **III** 251
Occidental Life Insurance Company, **I** 536–37; **13** 529
Occidental Overseas Ltd., **11** 97
Occidental Petroleum Corporation, **I** 527; **II** 432, 516; **IV** 264, 312, 392, 410, 417, 453–54, 467, **480–82**, 486, 515–16; **7** 376; **8** 526; **12** 100
Ocean, **III** 234
Ocean Combustion Services, **9** 109
Ocean Drilling and Exploration Company. *See* ODECO.
Ocean Group plc, 6 415–17
Ocean Salvage and Towage Co., **I** 592
Ocean Scientific, Inc., **15** 380
Ocean Spray Cranberries, Inc., 7 403–05; 10 525
Ocean Steam Ship Company, **6** 117, 415. *See also* Malaysian Airlines System BHD.
Ocean Systems Inc., **I** 400
Ocean Transport & Trading Ltd., **6** 417
Oceanic Contractors, **III** 559

Oceanic Properties, **II** 491–92
OCL. *See* Overseas Containers Ltd.
Ocoma Foods, **II** 584
Octek, **13** 235
Octel Communications Corp., **III** 143; **14** 217, **354–56**
Octopus Publishing, **IV** 667
Oculinum, Inc., **10** 48
Odakyu Electric Railway Company Limited, V 487–89
Odam's and Plaistow Wharves, **II** 580–81
Odd Lot Trading Company, **V** 172–73
Odeco Drilling, Inc., **7** 362–64; **11** 522; **12** 318
Odeon Theatres Ltd., **II** 157–59
Odetics Inc., 14 357–59
Odhams Press Ltd., **IV** 259, 666–67; **7** 244, 342
O'Donnell-Usen Fisheries, **II** 494
Odyssey Partner L.P., **V** 135
Odyssey Partners, **II** 679; **12** 55; **13** 94
Odyssey Press, **13** 560
Oelwerken Julius Schindler GmbH, **7** 141
Oertel Brewing Co., **I** 226; **10** 180
Oësterreichischer Phönix in Wien, **III** 376
Oetker Group, **I** 219
Off the Rax, **II** 667
Office Depot Incorporated, **8 404–05**; **10** 235, 497; **12** 335; **13** 268; **15** 331
Office Mart Holdings Corporation, **10** 498
Office National du Crédit Agricole, **II** 264
Office Systems Inc., **15** 407
Office Works, Inc., **13** 277
OfficeMax Inc., **8** 404; **15 329–31**
Official Airline Guides, Inc., **IV** 605, 643; **7** 312, 343
Officine Alfieri Maserati S.p.A., **11** 104; **13** 28, **376–78**
Offset Gerhard Kaiser GmbH, **IV** 325
Offshore Co., **III** 558; **6** 577
Offshore Food Services Inc., **I** 514
Offshore Transportation Corporation, **11** 523
Ogden Corporation, **I** 512–14, 701; **6** **151–53**, 600; **7** 39
Ogden Food Products, **7** 430
Ogden Gas Co., **6** 568
Ogilvie Flour Mills Co., **I** 268; **IV** 245
Ogilvy Group Inc., **I** 20, **25–27**, 31, 37, 244; **6** 53; **9** 180. *See also* WPP Group.
Oglethorpe Power Corporation, **6** **537–38**
O'Gorman and Cozens-Hardy, **III** 725
Ogura Oil, **IV** 479
Oh la la!, **14** 107
Ohbayashi Corporation, **I** 586–87
The Ohio Art Company, 14 360–62
Ohio Ball Bearing. *See* Bearings Inc.
Ohio Barge Lines, Inc., **11** 194
Ohio Bell Telephone Company, 14 **363–65**
Ohio Boxboard Company, **12** 376
Ohio Brass Co., **II** 2
Ohio Casualty Corp., **III** 190; **11 369–70**
Ohio Edison Company, **V** 676–78
Ohio Electric Railway Co., **III** 388
Ohio Mattress Co., **12** 438–39
Ohio Oil Co., **IV** 365, 400, 574; **6** 568; **7** 551
Ohio Pizza Enterprises, Inc., **7** 152
Ohio Pure Foods Group, **II** 528
Ohio River Company, **6** 487
Ohio Valley Electric Corporation, **6** 517
Ohio Ware Basket Company, **12** 319

Ohio-Sealy Mattress Mfg. Co., **12** 438–39
Ohlmeyer Communications, **I** 275
Ohlsson's Cape Breweries, **I** 287–88
Ohmite Manufacturing Co., **13** 397
Ohrbach's Department Store, **I** 30
Ohta Keibin Railway Company, **6** 430
ÖIAG, **IV** 234
Oil Acquisition Corp., **I** 611
Oil and Natural Gas Commission, **IV** 440–41, **483–84**
Oil and Solvent Process Company, **9** 109
Oil City Oil and Grease Co., **IV** 489
Oil Co. of Australia, **III** 673
Oil Distribution Public Corp., **IV** 434
Oil Drilling, Incorporated, **7** 344
Oil India Ltd., **IV** 440, 483–84
Oil Shale Corp., **IV** 522; **7** 537
Oilfield Industrial Lines Inc., **I** 477
Oilfield Service Corp. of America, **I** 342
Oita Co., **III** 718
Oji Paper Co., Ltd., **I** 506, 508; **II** 326; **IV** 268, 284–85, 292–93, 297–98, **320–22**, 326–27
OK Bazaars, **I** 289
Okadaya Co. Ltd., **V** 96
Oki, **15** 125
Oki Electric Industry Company, Limited, **II** 68, **72–74**
Okidata, **9** 57
Okinoyama Coal Mine, **III** 759
Oklahoma Airmotive, **8** 349
Oklahoma Entertainment, Inc., **9** 74
Oklahoma Gas and Electric Company, **6** **539–40**; **7** 409–11
Oklahoma Oil Co., **I** 31
Oklahoma Publishing Company, **11** 152–53
Okonite, **I** 489
Okura & Co., Ltd., **I** 282; **IV** 167–68
OLC. *See* Orient Leasing Co., Ltd.
Olcott & McKesson, **I** 496
Old Colony Trust Co., **II** 207; **12** 30
Old Dominion Power Company, **6** 513, 515
Old El Paso, **I** 457; **14** 212
Old Kent Financial Corp., **11 371–72**
Old Line Life Insurance Co., **III** 275
Old Mutual, **IV** 23, 535
Old National Bancorp, **14** 529; **15** **332–34**
Old Quaker Paint Company, **13** 471
Old Republic International Corp., **11** **373–75**
Old Stone Trust Company, **13** 468
Oldham Estate, **IV** 712
Olds Motor Vehicle Co., **I** 171; **10** 325
Olds Oil Corp., **I** 341
Ole's Innovative Sports. *See* Rollerblade, Inc.
Oleochim, **IV** 498–99
OLEX. *See* Deutsche BP Aktiengesellschaft.
Olex Cables Ltd., **10** 445
Olin Corporation, **I** 318, 330, **379–81**, 434; **III** 667; **IV** 482; **8** 23, 153; **13** **379–81 (upd.)**
Olin Mathieson Chemical Corp., **I** 695; **11** 420
Olinkraft, Inc., **II** 432; **III** 708–09; **11** 420
Olins Rent-a-Car, **6** 348
Olinvest, **IV** 454
Olive Garden Italian Restaurants, **10** 322, 324
Olivetti. *See* Ing. C. Olivetti & C., S.p.A.

Olivine Industries, Inc., **II** 508; **11** 172
Olofsson, **I** 573
Olohana Corp., **I** 129; **6** 129
Olsen Dredging Co., **III** 558
Olson & Wright, **I** 120
Olsonite Corp., **I** 201
Olsten Corporation, **6 41–43**; **9** 327
Olveh, **III** 177–79
Olympia & York Developments Ltd., **IV**
    245, 247, 712, **720–21**; **6** 478; **8** 327; **9**
    390–92 (upd.)
Olympia Arenas, Inc., **7** 278–79
Olympia Brewing, **I** 260; **11** 50
Olympia Floor & Tile Co., **IV** 720
Olympiaki, **III** 401
Olympic Airways, **II** 442
Olympic Fastening Systems, **III** 722
Olympic Packaging, **13** 443
Olympus Optical Company, Ltd., **15** 483
Olympus Sport, **V** 177–78
Olympus Symbol, Inc., **15** 483
Omaha Cold Store Co., **II** 571
Oman Oil Refinery Co., **IV** 516
Omega Gas Company, **8** 349
Omega Gold Mines, **IV** 164
Omex Corporation, **6** 272
OMI International Corp., **IV** 34; **9** 111–12
Omlon, **II** 75
Ommium Française de Pétroles, **IV** 559
Omni Construction Company, Inc., **8**
    112–13
Omni Hearing Aid Systems, **I** 667
Omni Hotels Corp., **12 367–69**
Omni Products International, **II** 420
Omni-Pac, **12** 377
Omnibus Corporation, **9** 283
Omnicare, Inc., **13** 150
Omnicom Group, **I 28–32**, 33, 36; **14** 160
OmniSource Corporation, **14 366–67**
Omron Tateisi Electronics Company, **II**
    75–77; **III** 549
ÖMV Aktiengesellschaft, **IV** 234, 454,
    485–87
On Cue, **9** 360
On-Line Software International Inc., **6** 225
On-Line Systems. *See* Sierra On-Line Inc.
Onan Corporation, **8** 72
Onbancorp Inc., **11** 110
Oncogen, **III** 18
Ondal GmbH, **III** 69
Ondulato Imolese, **IV** 296
One Hundredth Bank, **II** 321
One-Hundred Thirtieth National Bank, **II**
    291
O'Neal, Jones & Feldman Inc., **11** 142
Oneida Bank & Trust Company, **9** 229
Oneida County Creameries Co., **7** 202
Oneida Gas Company, **9** 554
Oneida Ltd., **7 406–08**
ONEOK Inc., **7 409–12**
Onitsuka Tiger Co., **V** 372; **8** 391
Online Distributed Processing Corporation,
    6 201
Online Financial Communication Systems,
    11 112
Onoda Cement Co., Ltd., **I** 508; **III**
    717–19
Ontario Hydro, **6 541–42**; **9** 461
Ontel Corporation, **6** 201
Oode Casting Iron Works, **III** 551
O'okiep Copper Company, Ltd., **7** 385–86
Open Board of Brokers, **9** 369
Opp and Micolas Mills, **15** 247–48

Oppenheimer. *See* Ernest Oppenheimer and
    Sons.
Opryland USA, **11** 152–53
OPTi Computer, **9** 116
Opti-Ray, Inc., **12** 215
Optilink Corporation, **12** 137
Optimum Financial Services Ltd., **II** 457
Opto-Electronics Corp., **15** 483
Optronics, Inc., **6** 247
OPW, **III** 467–68
Oracle Systems Corporation, **6 272–74**;
    10 361, 363, 505; **11** 78; **13** 483; **14** 16;
    15 492
Orange Julius, **10** 371, 373
Orange Line Bus Company, **6** 604
Orcofi, **III** 48
Ore and Chemical Corp., **IV** 140
Ore-Ida Foods Incorporated, **II** 508; **11**
    172; **12** 531; **13 382–83**
Oregon Pacific and Eastern Railway, **13**
    100
Oregon Steel Mills, Inc., **14 368–70**
Orford Copper Co., **IV** 110
Organon, **I** 665
Oriel Foods, **II** 609
Orient Glass, **III** 715
Orient Leasing. *See* Orix Corporation.
Oriental Land Co., Ltd., **IV** 715
Oriental Precision Company, **13** 213
Origin Systems Inc., **10** 285
Origin Technology, **14** 183
Original Cookie Co., **13** 166
Original Wassertragers Hummel, **II** 163
Orinoco Oilfields, Ltd., **IV** 565
Orion, **III** 310
Orion Bank Ltd., **II** 271, 345, 385
Orion Healthcare Ltd., **11** 168
Orion Personal Insurances Ltd., **11** 168
Orion Pictures Corporation, **II** 147; **6**
    167–70; **7** 336; **14** 330, 332
Orit Corp., **8** 219–20
Orix Corporation, **II 442–43**, 259, 348
Orkem, **IV** 547, 560
Orkin Pest Control, **11** 431–32, 434
Orm Bergold Chemie, **8** 464
Ormco Corporation, **14** 481
ÖROP, **IV** 485–86
Orowheat Baking Company, **10** 250
Ortho Diagnostic Systems, Inc., **10** 213
Ortho Pharmaceutical Corporation, **III** 35;
    8 281; **10** 79–80
Orthopedic Services, Inc., **11** 366
Orval Kent Food Company, Inc., **7** 430
Oryx Energy Company, **IV** 550; **7**
    413–15
Osaka Aluminium Co., **IV** 153
Osaka Beer Brewing Co., **I** 220, 282
Osaka Electric Tramway, **V** 463
Osaka Gas Co., Ltd., **V 679–81**
Osaka General Bussan, **IV** 431
Osaka Iron Works, **III** 513
Osaka Marine and Fire Insurance Co., **III**
    367
Osaka Nomura Bank, **II** 276, 438–39
Osaka North Harbor Co. Ltd., **I** 518
Osaka Shinyo Kumiai, **15** 495
Osaka Shosen Kaisha, **I** 503; **V** 473–74,
    481–82
Osaka Spinning Company, **V** 387
Osaka Sumitomo Marine and Fire
    Insurance Co., Ltd., **III** 367
Osaka Textile Co., **I** 506
Osakeyhtiö Gustaf Cederberg & Co., **IV**
    301

Osakeyhtiö T. & J. Salvesen, **IV** 301
Osborne Books, **IV** 637
Oscar Mayer Foods Corp., **II** 532; **7** 274,
    276; **12** 123, **370–72**
Osco Drug, **II** 604–05
Oshawa Group Limited, **II 649–50**
OshKosh B'Gosh, Inc., **9 393–95**
Oshkosh Electric Power, **9** 553
Oshkosh Gas Light Company, **9** 553
Oshkosh Truck Corporation, **7 416–18**;
    14 458
OSK. *See* Osaka Shosen Kaisha.
Oster. *See* Sunbeam-Oster.
Österreichische Bundesbahnen GmbH, **6**
    418–20
Österreichische Creditanstalt-Wiener
    Bankverein, **IV** 230
Österreichische Elektrowerke, **IV** 230
Österreichische Industrieholding AG, **IV**
    486–87
Österreichische Industriekredit AG, **IV** 230
Österreichische Länderbank, **II** 239
Österreichische Mineralölverwaltung AG,
    IV 485
Österreichische Post- und
    Telegraphenverwaltung, **V 314–17**
Österreichische Stickstoffswerke, **IV** 486
Ostschweizer Zementwerke, **III** 701
Osuuskunta Metsäliito, **IV** 316
Oswald Tillotson Ltd., **III** 501; **7** 207
Otagiri Mercantile Co., **11** 95
Otake Paper Manufacturing Co., **IV** 327
OTC, **10** 492
Otis Company, **6** 579
Otis Elevator Company, Inc., **I** 85, **III**
    467, 663; **13 384–86**
Otis Engineering Corp., **III** 498
Otosan, **I** 167, 479–80
Otsego Falls Paper Company, **8** 358
Ott and Brewer Company, **12** 312
Ottawa Fruit Supply Ltd., **II** 662
Ottaway Newspapers, Inc., **15 335–37**
Otto Sumisho Inc., **V** 161
Otto-Epoka mbH, **15** 340
Otto-Versand (GmbH & Co.), **V 159–61**;
    10 489–90; **15 338–40 (upd.)**
Ottumwa Daily Courier, **11** 251
Outback Steakhouse, Inc., **12 373–75**
Outboard Marine Corporation, **III** 329,
    597–600; **8** 71
The Outdoorsman, Inc., **10** 216
Outlet, **6** 33
Outokumpu Oy, **IV** 276
Ovako Oy, **III** 624
OVC, Inc., **6** 313
Overhill Farms, **10** 382
Overland Energy Company, **14** 567
Overland Mail Co., **II** 380–81, 395; **10** 60;
    12 533
Overnite Transportation Co., **14 371–73**
Overseas Air Travel Ltd., **I** 95
Overseas Containers Ltd., **6** 398, 415–16
Overseas Petroleum and Investment Corp.,
    IV 389
Overseas Shipholding Group, Inc., **11**
    376–77
Overseas Telecommunications
    Commission, **6** 341–42
Owatonna Tool Co., **I** 200; **10** 493
Owen Steel Co. Inc., **15** 117
Owens & Minor Inc., **10** 143
Owens Yacht Co., **III** 443
Owens-Corning Fiberglas Corporation, **I**
    609; **III** 683, **720–23**; **8** 177; **13** 169

Owens-Illinois Inc., **I 609–11**, 615; **II** 386; **III** 640, 720–21; **IV** 282, 343; **9** 261
Owensboro Municipal Utilities, **11** 37
Oxdon Investments, **II** 664
Oxfam America, **13** 13
Oxford Biscuit Fabrik, **II** 543
Oxford Chemical Corp., **II** 572
Oxford Industries, Inc., **8 406–08**
Oxford Instruments, **III** 491
Oxford Paper Co., **I** 334–35; **10** 289
Oxford-AnsCo Development Co., **12** 18
Oxirane Chemical Co., **IV** 456
Oxy Petrochemicals Inc., **IV** 481
Oxy Process Chemicals, **III** 33
OxyChem, **11** 160
Ozalid Corp., **I** 337–38; **IV** 563
Ozark Airlines, **I** 127; **12** 489
Ozark Pipe Line Corp., **IV** 540
Ozark Utility Company, **6** 593

P & M Manufacturing Company, **8** 386
P & O. *See* Peninsular & Oriental Steam Navigation Company.
P.A. Bergner & Company, **9** 142; **15** 87–88
P.A. Geier Company. *See* Royal Appliance Manufacturing Company.
P.A.J.W. Corporation, **9** 111–12
P.A. Rentrop-Hubbert & Wagner Fahrzeugausstattungen GmbH, **III** 582
P&C Foods Inc., **8 409–11**; **13** 95, 394
P&O, **6** 79
P.C. Hanford Oil Co., **IV** 368
P. D'Aoust Ltd., **II** 651
P.D. Kadi International, **I** 580
P.D. Magnetics, **I** 330; **8** 153
P.G. Realty, **III** 340
P.H. Glatfelter Company, **8 412–14**
P.L. Porter Co., **III** 580
P.R. Mallory, **9** 179
P. Sharples, **III** 418
P.T. Dai Nippon Printing Indonesia, **IV** 599
P.T. Muaratewe Spring, **III** 581
P.T. Semen Nusantara, **III** 718
P.W. Huntington & Company, **11** 180
Pabst Beer, **I** 217, 255; **10** 99
PAC Insurance Services, **12** 175
Pac-Am Food Concepts, **10** 178
Paccar Inc., **I** 155, **185–86**; **10** 280
Pace Companies, **6** 149
Pace Express Pty. Ltd., **13** 20
PACE Membership Warehouse, Inc., **V** 112; **10** 107; **12** 50
Pace-Arrow, Inc., **III** 484
Pacemaker Plastics, Inc., **7** 296
Pachena Industries Ltd., **6** 310
Pacific Aero Products Co., **I** 47; **10** 162
Pacific Air Freight, Incorporated, **6** 345
Pacific Air Transport, **I** 47, 128; **6** 128; **9** 416
Pacific Alaska Fuel Services, **6** 383
Pacific Bell, **V** 318–20; **11** 59; **12** 137
Pacific Brick Proprietary, **III** 673
Pacific Car & Foundry Co., **I** 185
Pacific Cascade Land Co., **IV** 255
Pacific Coast Co., **IV** 165
Pacific Coast Condensed Milk Co., **II** 486
Pacific Coast Oil Co., **IV** 385
Pacific Communication Sciences, **11** 57
Pacific Dry Dock and Repair Co., **6** 382
Pacific Dunlop Limited, **10 444–46**
Pacific Electric Heating Co., **II** 28; **12** 194

Pacific Electric Light Company, **6** 565
Pacific Enterprises, **V 682–84**; **12** 477
Pacific Express Co., **II** 381
Pacific Finance Corp., **I** 537; **9** 536; **13** 529
Pacific Gamble Robinson, **9** 39
Pacific Gas and Electric Company, **I** 96; **V 685–87**; **11** 270; **12** 100, 106
Pacific Guardian Life Insurance Co., **III** 289
Pacific Health Beverage Co., **I** 292
Pacific Home Furnishings, **14** 436
Pacific Indemnity Corp., **III** 220; **14** 108, 110
Pacific Lighting, **12** 477
Pacific Lighting Company, **V** 682–84
Pacific Lighting Corp., **IV** 492
Pacific Linens, **13** 81–82
Pacific Lumber Company, **III** 254; **8** 348–50
Pacific Magazines and Printing, **7** 392
Pacific Mail Steamship Company, **6** 353
Pacific Manifolding Book/Box Co., **IV** 644
Pacific Metal Bearing Co., **I** 159
Pacific Monolithics Inc., **11** 520
Pacific National Bank, **II** 349
Pacific Natural Gas Corp., **9** 102
Pacific Northern, **6** 66
Pacific Northwest Bell Telephone Co., **V** 341
Pacific Northwest Laboratories, **10** 139
Pacific Northwest Pipeline Corporation, **9** 102–104, 540; **12** 144
Pacific Northwest Power Company, **6** 597
Pacific Pearl, **I** 417
Pacific Petroleum, **IV** 494
Pacific Petroleums Ltd., **9** 102
Pacific Platers Ltd., **IV** 100
Pacific Power & Light Company. *See* PacifiCorp.
Pacific Recycling Co. Inc., **IV** 296
Pacific Refining Co., **IV** 394–95
Pacific Resources Inc., **IV** 47
Pacific Silver Corp., **IV** 76
Pacific Southwest Airlines Inc., **I** 132; **6** 132
Pacific Steel Ltd., **IV** 279
Pacific Telecom, Inc., **V 689**; **6 325–28**
Pacific Telesis Group, **V 318–20**; **6** 324; **9** 321; **11** 10–11; **14** 345, 347; **15** 125
Pacific Teletronics, Inc., **7** 15
Pacific Towboat. *See* Puget Sound Tug and Barge Company.
Pacific Trading Co., Ltd., **IV** 442
Pacific Western Oil Co., **IV** 537
Pacific-Burt Co., Ltd., **IV** 644
Pacific-Sierra Research, **I** 155
PacifiCare Health Systems, Inc., **III** 85; **11 378–80**
PacifiCorp, **V 688–90**; **6** 325–26, 328; **7** 376–78
Package Products Company, Inc., **12** 150
Packaging Corporation of America, **I** 526; **12 376–78**, 397
Packard Bell Electronics, Inc., **I** 524; **II** 86; **10** 521, 564; **11** 413; **13 387–89**, 483
Packard Motor Co., **I** 81; **8** 74; **9** 17
Packer's Consolidated Press, **IV** 651
Packerland Packing Company, **7** 199, 201
PacTel. *See* Pacific Telesis Group.
Paddington Corp., **I** 248
PAFS. *See* Pacific Alaska Fuel Services.
Page, Bacon & Co., **II** 380; **12** 533

Page Boy Inc., **9** 320
PageAhead Software, **15** 492
Pageland Coca-Cola Bottling Works, **10** 222
Paging Network Inc., **11 381–83**
Pagoda Trading Co., **V** 351, 353
Paid Prescriptions, **9** 346
PaineWebber Group Inc., **I** 245; **II** **444–46**, 449; **III** 409; **13** 449
Painter Carpet Mills, **13** 169
Painton Co., **II** 81
La Paix, **III** 273
Pak Arab Fertilizers Ltd., **IV** 364
Pak-a-Sak, **II** 661
Pak-All Products, Inc., **IV** 345
Pak-Paino, **IV** 315
Pak-Well, **IV** 282; **9** 261
Pakhoed Holding, N.V., **9** 532
Pakkasakku Oy, **IV** 471
Paknet, **11** 548
PAL. *See* Philippine Airlines, Inc.
Pal Plywood Co., Ltd., **IV** 327
Palatine Insurance Co., **III** 234
Palestine Coca-Cola Bottling Co., **13** 163
Pall Corporation, **9 396–98**
Palm Beach Holdings, **9** 157
Palmafina, **IV** 498–99
Palmer G. Lewis Co., **8** 135
Palmer Tyre Ltd., **I** 428–29
Palmolive Co... *See* Colgate-Palmolive Company.
Palo Alto Research Center, **10** 510
Pamida Holdings Corporation, **15 341–43**
Pamour Porcupine Mines, Ltd., **IV** 164
Pamplemousse, **14** 225
Pan American Banks, **II** 336
Pan American Petroleum & Transport Co., **IV** 368–70
Pan American World Airways, Inc., **I** 20, 31, 44, 64, 67, 89–90, 92, 99, 103–04, 112–13, **115–16**, 121, 124, 126, 129, 132, 248, 452, 530, 547–48; **III** 536; **6** 51, 65–66, 71, 74–76, 81–82, 103–05, 110–11, 123, 129–30; **9** 231, 417; **10** 561; **11** 266; **12** 191, **379–81** **(upd.)**, 419; **13** 19; **14** 73
Pan European Publishing Co., **IV** 611
Pan Ocean, **IV** 473
Panacon Corp., **III** 766
Panagra, **I** 547–48
Panama Refining and Petrochemical Co., **IV** 566
Panarctic Oils, **IV** 494
Panasonic, **9** 180; **10** 125; **12** 470
Panatech Research & Development Corp., **III** 160
Panavia Consortium, **I** 74–75
Pandair, **13** 20
Pandel, Inc., **8** 271
Panhandle Eastern Corporation, **IV** 425; **V 691–92**; **10** 82–84; **11** 28
Panhandle Eastern Pipe Co., **I** 377
Panhandle Eastern Pipeline Co., **I** 569; **14** 135
Panhandle Oil Corp., **IV** 498
Panhandle Power & Light Company, **6** 580
Panhard, **I** 194
Panhard-Levassor, **I** 149
AB Pankakoski, **IV** 274
Panmure Gordon, **II** 337
Pannill Knitting Company, **13** 531
Panocean Storage & Transport, **6** 415, 417

Panola Pipeline Co., **7** 228
Panosh Place, **12** 168
Pansophic Systems Inc., **6** 225
Pantepec Oil Co., **IV** 559, 570
Pantera Energy Corporation, **11** 27
Pantheon Books, **13** 429
Panther, **III** 750
Panther Express International Company, **6** 346
Pantry Pride, **I** 668; **II** 670, 674; **III** 56
Pants Corral, **II** 634
Papa John's International, Inc., 15 344–46
Pape and Co., Ltd., **10** 441
Papelera Navarra, **IV** 295
Papeleria Calparsoro S.A., **IV** 325
The Paper Factory of Wisconsin, Inc., **12** 209
Paper Makers Chemical Corp., **I** 344
Paper Mate Co., **III** 28
Paper Recycling International, **V** 754
Paper Software, Inc., **15** 322
Paper Stock Dealers, Inc., **8** 476
Paperituote Oy, **IV** 347–48
Paperwork Data-Comm Services Inc., **11** 64
Papeterie de Pont Sainte Maxence, **IV** 318
Papeteries Aussedat, **III** 122
Papeteries Boucher S.A., **IV** 300
Les Papeteries de la Chapelle-Darblay, **IV** 258–59, 302, 337
Papeteries Navarre, **III** 677
Papierfabrik Salach, **IV** 324
Papierwaren Fleischer, **IV** 325
Papierwerke Waldhof-Aschaffenburg AG, **IV** 323–24
Papyrus Design Group, **IV** 336; **15** 455
Para-Med Health Services, **6** 181–82
Parade Gasoline Co., **7** 228
Paragon, **IV** 552
Paramax, **6** 281–83
Paramount Paper Products, **8** 383
Paramount Pictures Corporation, I 451–52; **II** 129, 135, 146–47, **154–56,** 171, 173, 175, 177; **IV** 671–72, 675; **7** 528; **9** 119, 428–29; **10** 175; **12** 73, 323
Paravision International, **III** 48; **8** 343
Parcelforce, **V** 498
PARCO, **V** 184–85
Parcor, **I** 676
Parfums Chanel, **12** 57
Parfums Christian Dior, **I** 272
Parfums Rochas, **I** 670; **III** 68; **8** 452
Parfums Stern, **III** 16
Pargas, **I** 378
Paribas. *See* Compagnie Financiere de Paribas.
Paridoc and Giant, **12** 153
Paris Playground Equipment, **13** 319
Parisian, Inc., 14 374–76
Park Consolidated Motels, Inc., **6** 187; **14** 105
Park Hall Leisure, **II** 140
Park Inn International, **11** 178
Park Ridge Corporation, **9** 284
Park View Hospital, Inc., **III** 78
Parkdale Wines, **I** 268
Parke, Davis & Co. *See* Warner-Lambert Co.
Parke-Bernet, **11** 453
Parker, **III** 33
Parker Appliance Co., **III** 601–02
Parker Bros., **II** 502; **III** 505; **10** 323
Parker Drilling Company of Canada, **9** 363

Parker Hannifin Corporation, III 601–03
Parker Pen Corp., **III** 218; **9** 326
Parker's Pharmacy, Inc., **15** 524
Parkinson Cowan, **I** 531
Parkmount Hospitality Corp., **II** 142
Parks Box & Printing Co., **13** 442
Parr's Bank, **II** 334; **III** 724
Parson and Hyman Co., Inc., **8** 112
The Parsons Corporation, III 749; **8 415–17**
Parsons Place Apparel Company, **8** 289
Partek Corporation, **11** 312
Partex, **IV** 515
Parthenon Insurance Co., **III** 79
Participating Annuity Life Insurance Co., **III** 182
La Participation, **III** 210
Partlow Corporation, **7** 116
Partnership Pacific Ltd., **II** 389
Parts Industries Corp., **III** 494–95
Pascale & Associates, **12** 476
Paschen Contractors Inc., **I** 585
Pasha Pillows, **12** 393
Pasminco, **IV** 61
Pataling Rubber Estates Syndicate, **III** 697, 699
Patchoque-Plymouth Co., **IV** 371
PATCO. *See* Philippine Aerial Taxi Company.
Patent Arms Manufacturing Company, **12** 70
Patent Nut & Bolt Co., **III** 493
Patent Slip and Dock Co., **I** 592
La Paternelle, **III** 210
Paternoster Stores plc, **V** 108
Paterson, Simons & Co., **I** 592
Path-Tek Laboratories, Inc., **6** 41
Pathé Cinéma, **6** 374
Pathe Communications Co., **IV** 676; **7** 529
Pathé Fréres, **IV** 626
Pathmark, **II** 672–74; **9** 173; **15** 260
Patience & Nicholson, **III** 674
Patient Care, Inc., **13** 150
Patil Systems, **11** 56
Patriot Co., **IV** 582
Patriot Life Insurance Co., **III** 193
Patterson Industries, Inc., **14** 42
Pattison & Bowns, Inc., **IV** 180
Patton Paint Co., **III** 731
Paul A. Brands, **11** 19
Paul C. Dodge Company, **6** 579
Paul H. Rose Corporation, **13** 445
Paul Harris Stores Inc., **15** 245
Paul Masson, **I** 285
The Paul Revere Corporation, 12 382–83
Paul Wahl & Co., **IV** 277
Paul Williams Copier Corp., **IV** 252
Paul Wurth, **IV** 25
Pauls Plc, **III** 699
Paxall, Inc., **8** 545
Pay 'n Save Corp., **12** 477; **15** 274
Pay 'N Pak Stores, Inc., 9 399–401
Pay Less, **II** 601, 604
Paychex, Inc., 15 347–49
Payless Cashways, Inc., 11 384–86; 13 274
Payless DIY, **V** 17, 19
PayLess Drug Stores, **12** 477–78
Payless ShoeSource, Inc., **V** 132, 135; **13** 361
PC Globe, Inc., **13** 114
PC Realty, Canada Ltd., **III** 340

PCA-Budafok Paperboard Ltd., **12** 377
PCI Acquisition, **11** 385
PCI/Mac-Pak Group, **IV** 261
PCL Industries Ltd., **IV** 296
PCO, **III** 685
PCS Health Systems Inc., **12** 333
PDO. *See* Petroleum Development Oman.
PDVSA. *See* Petróleos de Venezuela S.A.
Peabody Coal Company, I 559; **III** 248; **IV** 47, 169–71, 576; **7** 387–88; **10 447–49**
Peabody Holding Company, Inc., IV 19, **169–72; 6** 487; **7** 209
Peabody, Riggs & Co., **II** 427
Peachtree Doors, **10** 95
Peachtree Federal Savings and Loan Association of Atlanta, **10** 92
Peak Oilfield Service Company, **9** 364
The Peak Technologies Group, Inc., 14 377–80
Peakstone, **III** 740
Pearce-Uible Co., **14** 460
Pearl Health Services, **I** 249
Pearl Package Co., Ltd., **IV** 327
Pearle Vision, Inc., I 688; **12** 188; **13 390–92; 14** 214
Pearson plc, IV 611, 652, **657–59; 14** 414
Peat Marwick. *See* KPMG Peat Marwick.
Peaudouce, **IV** 339
Peavey Co., **II** 494; **12** 81
Pebble Beach Corp., **II** 170
PEC Plastics, **9** 92
Pechelbronn Oil Co., **III** 616
Pechiney, I 190, 341; **IV** 12, 59, 108, **173–75,** 560; **V** 605; **12** 253–54; **14** 216
Péchiney-Saint-Gobain, **I** 389; **III** 677
PECO Energy Company, 11 387–90
Peel-Conner Telephone Works, **II** 24
Peerless, **III** 467; **8** 74; **11** 534
Peerless Gear & Machine Company, **8** 515
Peerless Industries, **III** 569
Peerless Paper Co., **IV** 310
Peerless Pump Co., **I** 442
Peerless Spinning Corporation, **13** 532
Peet's Coffee, **13** 493
Pegulan, **I** 426–27
Peine, **IV** 201
Pekema Oy, **IV** 470–71
Peko-Wallsend Ltd., **13** 97
Pel-Tex Oil Co., **IV** 84; **7** 188
Pelican and British Empire Life Office, **III** 372
Pelican Homestead and Savings, **11** 107
Pelican Insurance Co., **III** 349
Pelican Life Assurance, **III** 371–72
Pella Corporation, 10 95; **12 384–86**
Pelto Oil Company, **14** 455
Pemex. *See* Petróleos Mexicanos.
Peñarroya, **IV** 107–08
Pendexcare Ltd., **6** 181
Penguin Publishing Co. Ltd., **IV** 585, 659
Peninsular and Oriental Steam Navigation Company, II 296; **III** 521–22, 712; **V 490–93**
Peninsular and Oriental Steam Navigation Company (Bovis Division), I 588–89
Peninsular Portland Cement, **III** 704
Peninsular Power, **6** 602
Penn Central Corp., **I** 435; **II** 255; **IV** 576; **10** 71, 73, 547
Penn Champ Co., **9** 72
Penn Controls, **III** 535–36
Penn Corp., **13** 561

Penn Cress Ice Cream, **13** 393
Penn Fuel Co., **IV** 548
Penn Health, **III** 85
Penn Square Bank, **II** 248, 262
Penn Traffic Company, **8** 409–10; **13** 95, 393–95
Penn-American Refining Co., **IV** 489
Penn-Texas Corporation, **I** 434; **12** 71
Penn-Western Gas and Electric, **6** 524
Pennaco Hosiery, Inc., **12** 93
Pennington Drug, **III** 10
Pennroad Corp., **IV** 458
Pennsalt Chemical Corp., **I** 383
Pennsylvania Blue Shield, **III** 325–27
Pennsylvania Coal & Coke Corp., **I** 434
Pennsylvania Coal Co., **IV** 180
Pennsylvania Electric Company, **6** 535
Pennsylvania Farm Bureau Cooperative Association, **7** 17–18
Pennsylvania General Fire Insurance Assoc., **III** 257
Pennsylvania Glass Sand Co., **I** 464; **11** 198
Pennsylvania House, Inc., **10** 324; **12** 301
Pennsylvania International Raceway, **V** 494
Pennsylvania Power & Light Company, **V** 676, 693–94; **11** 388
Pennsylvania Pump and Compressor Co., **II** 16
Pennsylvania Railroad, **I** 456, 472; **II** 329, 490; **6** 436; **10** 71–73
Pennsylvania Refining Co., **IV** 488–89
Pennsylvania Salt Manufacturing Co., **I** 383
Pennsylvania Steel Co., **IV** 35; **7** 48
Pennwalt Corporation, **I** 382–84; **IV** 547; **12** 18
Penny Curtiss Baking Co., Inc., **13** 395
Pennzoil Company, **IV** 488–90, 551, 553; **10** 190; **14** 491, 493
Penray, **I** 373
Penrod Drilling Corporation, **7** 228, 558
Pension Benefit Guaranty Corp., **III** 255; **12** 489
Penske Corporation, **V** 494–95
Pentair, Inc., **III** 715; **7** 419–21; **11** 315
Pental Insurance Company, Ltd., **11** 523
Pentane Partners, **7** 518
Pentaverken A.B., **I** 209
Pentech Corp., **14** 217
Pentland Industries, **V** 375
Penton, **9** 414
People Express Airlines Inc., **I** 90, 98, 103, 117–18, 123–24, 129–30; **6** 129
People That Love (PTL) Television, **13** 279
People's Bank of Halifax, **II** 210
People's Bank of New Brunswick, **II** 210
People's Drug Store, **II** 604–05
People's Ice and Refrigeration Company, **9** 274
People's Insurance Co., **III** 368
People's Natural Gas, **IV** 548; **6** 593
People's Trust Co. of Brooklyn, **II** 254; **9** 124
Peoples Bancorp, **14** 529
Peoples Bank, **13** 467
Peoples Bank of Youngstown, **9** 474
Peoples Energy Corporation, **6** 543–44
Peoples Finance Co., **II** 418
Peoples Gas Light & Coke Co., **IV** 169; **6** 529, 543–44
Peoples Gas Light Co., **6** 455
Peoples Life Insurance Co., **III** 218

Peoples Natural Gas Company of South Carolina, **6** 576
Peoples Savings of Monroe, **9** 482
Peoples Security Insurance Co., **III** 219
PeopleSoft Inc., **11** 78; **14** 381–83
The Pep Boys—Manny, Moe & Jack, **11** 391–93
PEPCO. *See* Portland Electric Power Company *and* Potomac Electric Power Company.
Pepperidge Farms, **I** 29; **II** 480–81; **7** 67–68
PepsiCo, Inc., **I** 234, 244–46, 257, 269, 276–79, 281, 291; **II** 103, 448, 477, 608; **III** 106, 116, 588; **7** 265, 267, 396, 404, 434–35, 466, 505–06; **8** 399; **9** 177, 343; **10** 130, 199, 227, 324, 450–54 (upd.); **11** 421, 450; **12** 337, 453; **13** 162, 284, 448, 494; **15** 72, 75, 380
Pepsodent Company, **I** 14; **9** 318
Perception Technology, **10** 500
Percy Bilton Investment Trust Ltd., **IV** 710
Percy Street Investments Ltd., **IV** 711
Perdue Farms Inc., **7** 422–24, 432
Perfect Circle Corp., **I** 152
Perfect-Ventil GmbH, **9** 413
Performance Contracting, Inc., **III** 722
Performance Technologies, Inc., **10** 395
Pergamon Holdings, **15** 83
Pergamon Press, **IV** 611, 641–43, 687; **7** 311–12
Perini Corporation, **8** 418–21
Perisem, **I** 281
The Perkin-Elmer Corporation, **III** 455, 727; **7** 425–27; **9** 514; **13** 326
Perkins, **I** 147; **12** 90
Perkins Bacon & Co., **10** 267
Perkins Cake & Steak, **9** 425
Perkins Engines Ltd., **III** 545, 652; **10** 274; **11** 472
Perkins Oil Well Cementing Co., **III** 497
Perkins Products Co., **II** 531
Perland Environmental Technologies Inc., **8** 420
Permaneer Corp., **IV** 281; **9** 259
Permanent General Companies, Inc., **11** 194
Permanente Cement Co., **I** 565
Permanente Metals Corp., **IV** 15, 121–22
Permian Corporation, **V** 152–53
PERMIGAN, **IV** 492
Permodalan, **III** 699
Pernod Ricard S.A., **I** 248, 280–81
Pernvo Inc., **I** 387
Perot Systems, **13** 482
Perret-Olivier, **III** 676
Perrigo Company, **12** 218, 387–89
Perrin, **IV** 614
Perrot Brake Co., **I** 141
Perrow Motor Freight Lines, **6** 370
Perry Drugs, **12** 21
Perry Sports, **13** 545; **13** 545
Perscombinatie, **IV** 611
Personal Performance Consultants, **9** 348
Personal Products Company, **III** 35; **8** 281, 511
Perstorp A.B., **I** 385–87
PERTAMINA, **IV** 383, 461, 491–93, 517, 567
Perusahaan Minyak Republik Indonesia, **IV** 491
Peruvian Corp., **I** 547
Pet Food & Supply, **14** 385

Pet Incorporated, **I** 457; **II** 486–87; **7** 428–31; **10** 554; **12** 124; **13** 409; **14** 214
Peter Bawden Drilling, **IV** 570
Peter, Cailler, Kohler, Chocolats Suisses S.A., **II** 546; **7** 381
Peter Cundill & Associates Ltd., **15** 504
Peter Gast Shipping GmbH, **7** 40
Peter J. Schmitt Co., **13** 394
Peter J. Schweitzer, Inc., **III** 40
Peter Jones, **V** 94
Peter Kiewit Sons' Inc., **I** 599–600; **III** 198; **8** 422–24; **15** 18
Peter Norton Computing Group, **10** 508–09
Peter Paul, **II** 477
Peter Paul/Cadbury, **II** 512; **15** 221
Peterbilt Motors Co., **I** 185–86
Peters Shoe Co., **III** 528
Peters-Revington Corporation. *See* Chromcraft Revington, Inc.
Peterson, Howell & Heather, **V** 496
Peterson Soybean Seed Co., **9** 411
La Petite Academy, **13** 299
Petite Sophisticate, **V** 207–08
Petrie Stores Corporation, **8** 425–27
Petrini's, **II** 653
Petro/Chem Environmental Services, Inc., **IV** 411
Petro-Canada Limited, **IV** 367, 494–96, 499; **13** 557
Petro-Coke Co. Ltd., **IV** 476
Petro-Lewis Corp., **IV** 84; **7** 188
Petroamazonas, **IV** 511
Petrobel, **IV** 412
Petrobrás. *See* Petróleo Brasileiro S.A.
Petrocarbona GmbH, **IV** 197–98
Petrochemical Industries Co., **IV** 451
Petrochemie Danubia GmbH, **IV** 486–87
Petrochim, **IV** 498
Petrocomercial, **IV** 511
Petroecuador. *See* Petróleos del Ecuador.
Petrofertil, **IV** 501
Petrofina, **IV** 455, 495, 497–500, 576; **7** 179
Petrogal. *See* Petróleos de Portugal.
Petroindustria, **IV** 511
Petrol, **IV** 487
Petrol Ofisi Anonim Sirketi, **IV** 564
Petróleo Brasileiro S.A., **IV** 424, 501–03
Petróleo Mecânica Alfa, **IV** 505
Petróleos de Portugal S.A., **IV** 504–06
Petróleos de Venezuela S.A., **II** 661; **IV** 391–93, 507–09, 571
Petróleos del Ecuador, **IV** 510–11
Petróleos Mexicanos, **IV** 512–14, 528
Petroleum and Chemical Corp., **III** 672
Petroleum Authority of Thailand, **IV** 519
Petroleum Co. of New Zealand, **IV** 279
Petroleum Development (Qatar) Ltd., **IV** 524
Petroleum Development (Trucial States) Ltd., **IV** 363
Petroleum Development Corp. of the Republic of Korea, **IV** 455
Petroleum Development Oman LLC, **IV** 515–16
Petroleum Projects Co., **IV** 414
Petroleum Research and Engineering Co. Ltd., **IV** 473
Petrolgroup, Inc., **6** 441
Petroliam Nasional Bhd. *See* Petronas.
Petrolite Corporation, **15** 350–52
Petrolube, **IV** 538
Petromex. *See* Petróleos de Mexico S.A.
Petronas, **IV** 517–20

Petronor, **IV** 514, 528
Petropeninsula, **IV** 511
Petroproduccion, **IV** 511
Petroquímica de Venezuela SA, **IV** 508
Petroquimica Española, **I** 402
Petroquisa, **IV** 501
PETROSUL, **IV** 504, 506
Petrotransporte, **IV** 511
PETsMART, Inc., 14 384–86
Petstuff, Inc., **14** 386
Petzazz, **14** 386
Peugeot S.A., I 163, **187–88; II** 13; **III** 508; **11** 104
Pfaff-Pegasus of U.S.A. Inc., **15** 385
The Pfaltzgraff Co. *See* Susquehanna Pfaltzgraff Company.
Pfaudler Vacuum Co., **I** 287
PFCI. *See* Pulte Financial Companies, Inc.
Pfizer, Hoechst Celanese Corp., **8** 399
Pfizer Inc., I 301, 367, **661–63**, 668; **9** 356, **402–05 (upd.); 10** 53–54; **11** 207, 310–11, 459; **12** 4
PGE. *See* Portland General Electric.
PGH Bricks and Pipes, **III** 735
Phar-Mor Inc., 12 209, **390–92**, 477
Pharma Plus Drugmarts, **II** 649–50
Pharmacia A.B., I 211, **664–65**
Pharmaco Dynamics Research, Inc., **10** 106–07
Pharmacom Systems Ltd., **II** 652
PharmaKinetics Laboratories, Inc., **10** 106
Pharmaprix Ltd., **II** 663
Pharmazell GmbH, **IV** 324
Pharmedix, **11** 207
Pharos, **9** 381
Phelan & Collender, **III** 442
Phelan Faust Paint, **8** 553
Phelps Dodge Corporation, IV 33, **176–79**, 216; **7** 261–63, 288
Phenix Bank, **II** 312
Phenix Cheese Corp., **II** 533
Phenix Insurance Co., **III** 240
Phenix Mills Ltd., **II** 662
PHF Life Insurance Co., **III** 263; **IV** 623
PHH Corporation, V 496–97
PHH Group, Incorporated, **6** 357
Phibro Corp., **II** 447–48; **IV** 80; **13** 447–48
Philadelphia and Reading Corp., **I** 440; **II** 329; **6** 377
Philadelphia Carpet Company, **9** 465
Philadelphia Coke Company, **6** 487
Philadelphia Company, **6** 484, 493
Philadelphia Drug Exchange, **I** 692
Philadelphia Electric Company, V 695–97; 6 450
Philadelphia Life, **I** 527
Philadelphia Smelting and Refining Co., **IV** 31
Philco Corp., **I** 167, 531; **II** 86; **III** 604; **13** 402
Philip Morris Companies Inc., I 23, 269; **II** 530–34; **V** 397, 404, **405–07**, 409, 417; **6** 52; **7** 272, 274, 276, 548; **8** 53; **9** 180; **12** 337, 372; **13** 138, 517; **15** 64, 72–73, 137
Philipp Abm. Cohen, **IV** 139
Philipp Bros., Inc., **II** 447; **IV** 79–0
Philipp Holzmann, **II** 279, 386; **14** 169
Philippine Airlines, Inc., I 107; **6 106–08**, 122–23
Philippine American Life Insurance Co., **III** 195
Philippine Sinter Corp., **IV** 125

Philips, **V** 339; **6** 101; **10** 269
Philips Electronics N.V., 8 153; **9** 75; **10** 16; **12** 475, 549; **13** 396, **400–03 (upd.); 14** 446
Philips Electronics North America Corp., 13 396–99
N.V. Philips Gloeilampenfabriken, **I** 107, 330; **II** 25, 56, 58, **78–80**, 99, 102, 117, 119; **III** 479, 654–55; **IV** 680; **12** 454. *See also* Philips Electronics N.V.
Phillip Hawkins, **III** 169; **6** 285
Phillippe of California, **8** 16
Phillips & Drew, **II** 379
Phillips & Jacobs, Inc., **14** 486
Phillips Cables, **III** 433
Phillips Carbon Black, **IV** 421
Phillips Manufacturing Company, **8** 464
Phillips Petroleum Company, I 377; **II** 15, 408; **III** 752; **IV** 71, 290, 366, 405, 412, 414, 445, 453, 498, **521–23**, 567, 570–71, 575; **10** 84, 440; **11** 522; **13** 356, 485
Phillips Sheet and Tin Plate Co., **IV** 236
PHLCorp., **11** 261
PHM Corp., **8** 461
Phoenix Assurance Co., **III** 242, 257, 369, 370–74
Phoenix Financial Services, **11** 115
Phoenix Fire Office, **III** 234
Phoenix Insurance Co., **III** 389; **IV** 711
Phoenix Microsystems Inc., **13** 8
Phoenix Oil and Transport Co., **IV** 90
Phoenix State Bank and Trust Co., **II** 213
Phoenix Technologies Ltd., **13** 482
Phoenix-Rheinrohr AG, **IV** 222
Phone America of Carolina, **8** 311
Phuket Air Catering Company Ltd., **6** 123–24
Physician Sales & Service, Inc., 14 387–89
Physician's Weight Loss Center, **10** 383
Physicians Formula Cosmetics, **8** 512
Physicians Placement, **13** 49
PIC Realty Corp., **III** 339
Pick, **III** 98
Pick-N-Pay, **II** 642; **9** 452
Pickands Mather, **13** 158
Picker International Corporation, **II** 25; **8** 352
Pickfords Ltd., **6** 412–14
Pickland Mather & Co., **IV** 409
PickOmatic Systems, **8** 135
Pickwick, **I** 613
Pickwick Dress Co., **III** 54
Pickwick International, **9** 360
Piclands Mather, **7** 308
Picture Classified Network, **IV** 597
PictureTel Corp., 10 455–57
Piedmont Airlines, **6** 132; **12** 490
Piedmont Coca-Cola Bottling Partnership, **10** 223
Piedmont Concrete, **III** 739
Piedmont Pulp and Paper Co., **IV** 351
Pier 1 Imports, Inc., 12 179, 200, **393–95**
Pierburg GmbH, **9** 445–46
Pierce, **IV** 478
Pierce Brothers, **6** 295
Pierce Steam Heating Co., **III** 663
Pierre Frozen Foods Inc., **13** 270–72
Pierson, Heldring, and Pierson, **II** 185
Pietro's Pizza Parlors, **II** 480–81
Pig Improvement Co., **II** 500
Piggly Wiggly Southern, Inc., II 571, 624; **13** 251–52, **404–06**

Pignone, **IV** 420
Pike Adding Machine, **III** 165
Pike Corporation of America, **I** 570; **8** 191
Pikrose and Co. Ltd., **IV** 136
Pilgrim Curtain Co., **III** 213
Pilgrim's Pride Corporation, 7 432–33
Pilkington plc, I 429; **II** 475; **III** 56, 641–42, 676–77, 714–15, **724–27**
Pillar Holdings, **IV** 191
Pilliod Furniture, Inc., **12** 300
Pillsbury Company, II 133, 414, 493–94, 511, **555–57**, 575, 613–15; **7** 106, 128, 277, 469, 547; **8** 53–54; **10** 147, 176; **11** 23; **12** 80, 510; **13 407–09 (upd.)**, 516; **14** 212, 214; **15** 64
Pilot, **I** 531
Pilot Insurance Agency, **III** 204
Pinal-Dome Oil, **IV** 569
Pinault-Printemps-Redoute, **15** 386
Pincus & Co., **7** 305
Pinecliff Publishing Company, **10** 357
Pinelands, Inc., **9** 119
Pineville Kraft Corp., **IV** 276
Pinewood Studios, **II** 157
Pininfarina, **I** 188
Pinkerton's Inc., 9 406–09; 13 124–25; **14** 541
Pinnacle West Capital Corporation, 6 545–47
Pinsetter Corp., **III** 443
Pinto Island Metals Company, **15** 116
Pioneer Airlines, **I** 96
Pioneer Asphalt Co., **I** 404
Pioneer Asphalts Pty. Ltd., **III** 728
Pioneer Concrete Services Ltd., **III** 728–29
Pioneer Cotton Mill, **12** 503
Pioneer Electronic Corporation, II 103; **III 604–06**
Pioneer Federal Savings Bank, **10** 340; **11** 115
Pioneer Financial Corp., **11** 447
Pioneer Hi-Bred International, Inc., 9 410–12
Pioneer International Limited, III 687, 728–30
Pioneer Life Insurance Co., **III** 274
Pioneer Natural Gas Company, **10** 82
Pioneer Readymixed Concrete and Mortar Proprietary Ltd., **III** 728
Pioneer Saws Ltd., **III** 598
Pioneer-Standard, **13** 47
Pipe Line Service Company. *See* Plexco.
Pipeline and Products Marketing Co., **IV** 473
Piper Aircraft Corp., **I** 482; **II** 403; **8** 49–50
Pirelli S.p.A., IV 174, 420; **V 249–51; 10** 319; **15 353–56 (upd.)**
Pisces Inc., **13** 321
Pispalan Werhoomo Oy, **I** 387
The Piston Ring Company, **I** 199; **10** 492
Pitcairn Aviation, **I** 101
Pitney Bowes Inc., III 156–58, 159
Pittsburgh & Lake Angeline Iron Company, **13** 156
Pittsburgh & Lake Erie Railroad, **I** 472
Pittsburgh Aluminum Alloys Inc., **12** 353
Pittsburgh Brewing, **10** 169–70
Pittsburgh Chemical Co., **IV** 573; **7** 551
Pittsburgh Consolidation Coal Co., **8** 346
Pittsburgh Corning Corp., **III** 683
Pittsburgh Life, **III** 274
Pittsburgh National Bank, **II** 317, 342
Pittsburgh National Corp., **II** 342

Pittsburgh Paint & Glass. *See* PPG Industries, Inc.
Pittsburgh Plate Glass Co., **III** 676, 725. *See also* PPG Industries, Inc.
Pittsburgh Railway Company, **9** 413
Pittsburgh Reduction Co., **II** 315; **IV** 9, 14
Pittsburgh Steel Company, **7** 587
Pittsburgh Trust and Savings, **II** 342
Pittston Company, **IV** 180–82, 566; **10** 44
Pittway Corporation, **9** 413–15
Pixel Semiconductor, **11** 57
Pizza Dispatch. *See* Dominos's Pizza, Inc.
Pizza Hut Inc., **I** 221, 278, 294; **II** 614; **7** 152–53, 267, **434–35**, 506; **10** 450; **11** 50; **12** 123; **13** 336, 516; **14** 107; **15** 344–46
PizzaCo, Inc., **7** 152
PKbanken, **II** 353
Place Two, **V** 156
Placer Cego Petroleum Ltd., **IV** 367
Placer Development Ltd., **IV** 19
Placer Dome, **IV** 571
Placid Oil Co., **7** 228
Plaid Holdings Corp., **9** 157
Plain Jane Dress Company, **8** 169
Plainwell Paper Co., Inc., **8** 103
Planet Insurance Co., **III** 343
Plank Road Brewery, **I** 269; **12** 337
Plankinton Packing Co., **III** 534
Plant Genetics Inc., **I** 266
Planters Lifesavers, **14** 274–75
Planters Nut & Chocolate Co., **I** 219; **II** 544
Plas-Techs, Inc., **15** 35
Plastic Coating Corporation, **IV** 330; **8** 483
Plastic Containers, Inc., **15** 129
Plasticos Metalgrafica, **I** 231
Plastics, Inc., **13** 41
Plastrier, **III** 675
Plateau Holdings, Inc., **12** 260; **13** 502
PLATINUM Technology, Inc., **14 390–92**
Platt & Co., **I** 506
Platt Bros., **III** 636
Platt's Price Service, Inc., **IV** 636–37
Playskool Mfg., **III** 504, 506; **12** 169; **13** 317
Playtex Products, Inc., **II** 448, 468; **8** 511; **13** 448; **15 357–60**
Plaza Coloso S.A. de C.V., **10** 189
Plaza Medical Group, **6** 184
Plaza Securities, **I** 170
Pleasurama PLC, **I** 248; **12** 228
Plessey Company, PLC, **II** 25, 39, **81–82**; **IV** 100; **6** 241
Plews Manufacturing Co., **III** 602
Plexco, **7** 30–31
Plezall Wipers, Inc., **15** 502
Plitt Theatres, **6** 162
Plon et Juillard, **IV** 614
Plough Inc., **I** 684
Plum Associates, **12** 270
Plumb Tool, **II** 16
Plus Development Corporation, **10** 458–59
Plus Mark, Inc., **7** 24
Plus System Inc., **9** 537
Plus-Ultra, **II** 196
Ply Gem Industries Inc., **12 396–98**
Plymouth County Electric Co., **14** 124
PMC Specialties Group, **III** 745
PMI Corporation, **6** 140
PMI Mortgage Insurance Company, **10** 50
PMS Consolidated, **8** 347

PN Pertambangan Minyak Dan Gas Bumi Negara, **IV** 492
PNC Bank Corp., **13 410–12 (upd.)**; **14** 103
PNC Financial Corporation, **II** 317, **342–43**; **9** 476
Pneumo Abex Corp., **I** 456–58; **III** 512; **10** 553–54
Pneumo Dynamics Corporation, **8** 409
PNL. *See* Pacific Northwest Laboratories.
PNM. *See* Public Service Company of New Mexico.
PNP. *See* Pacific Northwest Power Company.
POAS, **IV** 563
POB Polyolefine Burghausen GmbH, **IV** 487
Pocket Books, Inc., **10** 480; **13** 559–60
Poclain Company, **10** 380
Pogo Producing, **I** 441
Pohang Iron and Steel Company Ltd., **IV 183–85**
Pohjan Sellu Oy, **IV** 316
Pohjoisminen Osakepankki, **II** 302
Pohjola Voima Oy, **IV** 348
Pohjolan Osakepankki, **II** 303
Point Chehalis Packers, **13** 244
Polak & Schwarz Essencefabricken, **9** 290
Polar Star Milling Company, **7** 241
Polaris Industries Inc., **I** 530; **12 399–402**
Polaroid Corporation, **I** 30–31; **II** 412; **III** 475–77, 549, 584, **607–09**; **IV** 330; **7** 161–62, **436–39 (upd.)**; **12** 180
Polbeth Packaging Limited, **12** 377
Policy Management Systems Corporation, **11 394–95**
Polo Food Corporation, **10** 250
Polo/Ralph Lauren Corporation, **9** 157; **12 403–05**
Poly P, Inc., **IV** 458
Poly Version, Inc., **III** 645
Poly-Hi Corporation, **8** 359
Polyblend Corporation, **7** 4
Polycell Holdings, **IV** 666
Polydress Plastic GmbH, **7** 141
PolyGram International, **13** 402
Polyken Technologies, **11** 220
Polysar Energy & Chemical Corporation of Toronto, **V** 674
Polysius AG, **IV** 89
Pommersche Papierfabrik Hohenkrug, **III** 692
Pommery et Greno, **II** 475
Ponderosa Steakhouse, **7** 336; **12** 373; **14** 331; **15 361–64**
Ponderosa System Inc., **12** 199
Pont-à-Mousson, **III** 675, 677–78, 704
Pontiac, **III** 458; **10** 353
Pontificia, **III** 207
Pony Express, **II** 380–81, 395
Poorman-Douglas Corporation, **13** 468
Pope and Talbot, Inc., **12 406–08**
Pope Tin Plate Co., **IV** 236
Popeyes Famous Fried Chicken and Biscuits, Inc., **7** 26–28
Poppin' Fresh Pies, Inc., **12** 510
Popsicle, **II** 573; **14** 205
Popular Aviation Company, **12** 560
Popular Club Plan, **12** 280
Popular Merchandise, Inc., **12** 280
Pori, **IV** 350
Poron Diffusion, **9** 394
Porsche AG, **13** 28, 219, **413–15**

Port Harcourt Refining Co., **IV** 473
Portals Water Treatment, **11** 510
Porter Shoe Manufacturing Company, **13** 360
Portland General Corporation, **6 548–51**
Portland Heavy Industries, **10** 369
Portnet, **6** 435
Portways, **9** 92
Poseidon Exploration Ltd., **IV** 84; **7** 188
Posey, Quest, Genova, **6** 48
Post Office Counters, **V** 496
Post Office Group, **V 498–501**
PostBank, **II** 189
La Poste, **V 470–72**
Posti- Ja Telelaitos, **6 329–31**
Postum Cereal Company, **II** 497, 523, 530–31; **7** 272–73; **13** 291
Potlatch Corporation, **IV** 282; **8 428–30**; **9** 260
Potomac Electric Power Company, **6 552–54**
Potomac Insurance Co., **III** 257
Potomac Leasing, **III** 137
Potter & Brumfield Inc., **11 396–98**
Pottery Barn, **13** 42
Potts, **IV** 58
Poulan/Weed Eater. *See* White Consolidated Industries Inc.
Poulsen Wireless, **II** 490
Powell Duffryn, **III** 502; **IV** 38
Powell Energy Products, **8** 321
Powell River Co. Ltd., **IV** 306–07
Power Applications & Manufacturing Company, Inc., **6** 441
Power Financial Corp., **III** 260–61
Power Jets Ltd., **I** 81
Power Parts Co., **7** 358
Power Products, **8** 515
Power Specialty Company, **6** 145
Power Team, **10** 492
PowerFone Holdings, **10** 433
PowerGen PLC, **11 399–401**; **12** 349; **13** 458, 484
Powerhouse, **13** 485
Powers Accounting Machine Company, **6** 240
Powers Regulator, **III** 535
Powers-Samas, **6** 240
PowerSoft Corp., **11** 77; **15** 374
Pozzi-Renati Millwork Products, Inc., **8** 135
PP&L. *See* Pennsylvania Power & Light Company.
PPG Industries, Inc., **I** 330, 341–42; **III** 21, 641, 667, 722, **731–33**; **8** 153, 222, 224
PR Newswire, **IV** 687
Prac, **I** 281
Practical and Educational Books, **13** 105
Pragma Bio-Tech, Inc., **11** 424
Prairie Farmer Publishing Co., **II** 129
Prairie Holding Co., **IV** 571
Prairie Oil and Gas Co., **IV** 368
Prairielands Energy Marketing, Inc., **7** 322, 325
Pratt & Whitney, **I** 47, 78, 82–85, 128, 434; **II** 48; **III** 482; **6** 128; **7** 456; **9** 14, 16–18, 244–46, **416–18**; **10** 162; **11** 299, 427; **12** 71; **13** 386; **14** 564
Pratt Holding, Ltd., **IV** 312
Pratt Properties Inc., **8** 349
Praxair, Inc., **11 402–04**
Praxis Biologics, **8** 26
Pre-Fab Cushioning, **9** 93

Precious Metals Development, **IV** 79
Precision Castparts Corp.. 15 365–67
Precision Interconnect Corporation. **14** 27
Precision LensCrafters. **13** 391
Precision Optical Co., **III** 120, 575
Precision Software Corp., **14** 319
Precision Studios, **12** 529
Precor, **III** 610–11
Predica, **II** 266
Predicasts Inc., **12** 562
Preferred Products, Inc., **II** 669
PREINCO Holdings, Inc., **11** 532
PREL&P. *See* Portland Railway Electric
   Light & Power Company.
Prelude Corp., **III** 643
Premark International, Inc., **II** 534; **III**
   610–12; **14** 548
Premex A.G., **II** 369
Premier (Transvaal) Diamond Mining Co.,
   IV 65–66
Premier & Potter Printing Press Co., Inc.,
   II 37
Premier Brands Foods, **II** 514
Premier Consolidated Oilfields PLC, **IV**
   383
Premier Cruise Lines. **6** 368
Premier Diamond Mining Company, **7** 122
Premier Health Alliance Inc., **10** 143
Premier Industrial Corporation. 9
   419–21
Premier Milling Co., **II** 465
Premiere Products, **I** 403
Premisteres S.A., **II** 663
Prémontré, **III** 676
Prentice Hall Computer Publishing, **10** 24
Prentice-Hall Inc., **I** 453; **IV** 672
Prescott Ball & Turben, **III** 271; **12** 60
Prescott Investors, **14** 303
Prescription Learning Corporation, **7** 256
Présence, **III** 211
La Preservatrice, **III** 242
Preserves and Honey, Inc., **II** 497
Presidential Airlines, **I** 117
Presidents Island Steel & Wire Company.
   See Laclede Steel Company.
Presidio Oil Co., **III** 197; **IV** 123
Press Assoc., **IV** 669
Press Trust of India, **IV** 669
Presse Pocket, **IV** 614
Pressed Steel Car Co., **6** 395
Presses de la Cité, **IV** 614–15
Pressware International, **12** 377
Prest-O-Lite Co., Inc., **I** 399; **9** 16, 516; **11**
   402
Prestige et Collections, **III** 48
Presto, **II** 609–10
Presto Products, Inc., **IV** 187
Preston Corporation, 6 421–23; **14** 566,
   568
Pretty Neat Corp., **12** 216
Pretty Paper Inc., **14** 499
Pretty Polly, **I** 429
Preussag AG, **I** 542–43; **II** 386; **IV** 109,
   201, 231
Preussenelektra Aktiengesellschaft, I
   542; **V 698–700**
Priam Corporation, **10** 458
Price Club, **V** 162–64
Price Co. Ltd., **IV** 246–47
Price Company, II 664; **V 162–64**; **14**
   393–94
Price Enterprises, Inc., **14** 395
Price Waterhouse, III 84, 420, 527; **9**
   422–24; **14** 245

PriceCostco, Inc.. 14 393–95
Pricel, **6** 373
Prichard and Constance, **III** 65
Pride & Clarke. **III** 523
Priggen Steel Building Co., **8** 545
Primark Corp.. 10 89–90; **13 416–18**
Prime Computer, Inc. *See* Computervision
   Corporation.
Prime Motor Inns, **III** 103; **IV** 718; **11** 177
Prime Telecommunications Corporation, **8**
   311
The Prime-Mover Co., **13** 267
PrimeAmerica, **III** 340
Primerica Corporation, I 597, 599–602,
   604, 607–09, **612–14**, 615; **II** 422; **III**
   283 **8** 118; **9** 218–19, 360–61; **11** 29;
   15 464. *See also* American Can Co.
Primes Régal Inc., **II** 651
Primex Fibre Ltd., **IV** 328
Primo Foods Ltd., **I** 457; **7** 430
Prince Co., **II** 473
Prince Motor Co. Ltd., **I** 184
Prince of Wales Hotels, PLC, **14** 106
Prince Sports Group, Inc.. 15 368–70
Prince Street Technologies, Ltd., **8** 271
Prince William Bank, **II** 337; **10** 425
Princess Cruises, **IV** 256
Princess Dorothy Coal Co., **IV** 29
Princeton Gas Service Company, **6** 529
Princeton Laboratories Products Company,
   8 84
Princeton Review, **12** 142
**Principal Mutual Life Insurance
   Company. III 328–30**
Principles, **V** 21–22
Princor Financial Services Corp., **III** 329
Printex Corporation, **9** 363
Printronix, **14** 377–78
Prism Systems Inc., **6** 310
Prismo Universal, **III** 735
Prisunic SA, **V** 9–11
Pritzker & Pritzker, **III** 96–97
Privatbanken, **II** 352
Pro-Fac Cooperative Inc., **7** 104–06
Procino-Rossi Corp., **II** 511
Procordia, **II** 478
Procter & Gamble Company, I 34, 129,
   290, 331, 366; **II** 478, 493, 544, 590,
   684, 616; **III** 20–25, 36–38, 40–41, 44,
   50–53; **IV** 282, 290, 329–30; **6** 26–27,
   50–52, 129, 363; **7** 277, 300, 419; **8** 63,
   106–07, 253, 282, 344, 399, **431–35**
   (upd.), 477, 511–12; **9** 260, 291,
   317–19, 552; **10** 54, 288; **11** 41, 421; **12**
   80, 126–27, 439; **13** 39, 197, 199, 215;
   14 121–22, 262, 275; **15** 357
Proctor & Collier, **I** 19
Prodigy, Inc., **10** 237–38; **12** 562; **13** 92
Productos Ortiz, **II** 594
Produits Chimiques Ugine Kuhlmann, **I**
   303; **IV** 547
Professional Care Service, **6** 42
Professional Computer Resources, Inc., **10**
   513
Professional Health Care Management Inc.,
   14 209
Professional Research, **III** 73
Profimatics, Inc., **11** 66
PROFITCo.. **II** 231
Progil, **I** 389
Progress Development Organisation, **10**
   169
**Progress Software Corporation, 15
   371–74**

Progressive Corporation. 11 405–07
Progressive Distributors, **12** 220
Progressive Grocery Stores, **7** 202
Progresso, **I** 514; **14** 212
Projiis, **II** 356
Prolabo, **I** 388
Proland, **12** 139
Proler International Corp., **13** 98
Promigas, **IV** 418
Promotional Graphics, **15** 474
Promstroybank, **II** 242
Promus Companies, Inc.. III 95; **9**
   425–27; **15** 46
Pronto Pacific, **II** 488
Prontophot Holding Limited, **6** 490
Prontor-Werk Alfred Gauthier GmbH, **III**
   446
Prophet Foods, **I** 449
Propwix, **IV** 605
Prosim, S.A., **IV** 409
Prospect Farms, Inc., **II** 584; **14** 514
The Prospect Group, Inc., **11** 188
Prospect Provisions, Inc. *See* King Kullen
   Grocery Co., Inc.
Prospectors Airways, **IV** 165
Protective Closures, **7** 296–97
La Protectrice, **III** 346–47
Protek, **III** 633
Proto Industrial Tools, **III** 628
Proventus A.B., **II** 303
Provi-Soir, **II** 652
Provi-Viande, **II** 652
Provibec, **II** 652
La Providence, **III** 210–11
Providence National Bank, **9** 228
Providence Steam and Gas Pipe Co. *See*
   Grinnell Corp.
Providencia, **III** 208
Provident Bank, **III** 190
Provident Institution for Savings, **13** 467
**Provident Life and Accident Insurance
   Company of America, III 331–33**, 404
Provident National Bank, **II** 342
Provident Services, Inc., **6** 295
Provident Travelers Mortgage Securities
   Corp., **III** 389
Provigo Inc., II 651–53; **12** 413
Les Provinces Réunies, **III** 235
Provincetown-Boston Airlines, **I** 118
Provincial Engineering Ltd, **8** 544
Provincial Gas Company, **6** 526
Provincial Insurance Co., **III** 373
Provincial Newspapers Ltd., **IV** 685–86
Provincial Traders Holding Ltd., **I** 437
Provinzial-Hülfskasse, **II** 385
Provost & Provost, **II** 651
Prudential Bache Securities, **9** 441
Prudential Corporation plc, II 319; **III**
   334–36; **IV** 711; **8** 276–77
**Prudential Insurance Company of
   America, I** 19, 334, 402; **II** 103, 456;
   III 79, 92, 249, 259, 265–67, 273,
   291–93, 313, 329, **337–41**; **IV** 410, 458;
   10 199; **11** 243; **12** 28, 453, 500; **13**
   561; **14** 95, 561
Prudential Oil & Gas, Inc., **6** 495–96
Prudential Refining Co., **IV** 400
Prudential Steel, **IV** 74
Prudential-Bache Trade Corp., **II** 51
PSA. *See* Pacific Southwest Airlines.
PSA Peugeot-Citroen Group, **7** 35
PSCCo. *See* Public Service Company of
   Colorado.
PSE, Inc., **12** 100

PSI Resources, **6** 555–57
Psychiatric Institutes of America, **III** 87–88
Psychological Corp., **IV** 623; **12** 223
PT Components, **14** 43
PT PERMINA, **IV** 492, 517
PTI Communications, Inc. *See* Pacific Telecom, Inc.
PTT Telecom BV, **V** 299–301; **6** 303
PTV. *See* Österreichische Post- und Telegraphenverwaltung.
Public Home Trust Co., **III** 104
Public National Bank, **II** 230
Public Savings Insurance Co., **III** 219
Public Service Co., **14** 124
Public Service Company of Colorado, **6** 558–60
Public Service Company of Indiana. *See* PSI Energy.
Public Service Company of New Mexico, **6** 561–64
Public Service Electric and Gas Company, **IV** 366; **V** 701–03; **11** 388
Public Service Enterprise Group, **V** 701–03
Publicis FCB, **13** 204
Publicker Industries Inc., **I** 226; **10** 180
Publishers Paper Co., **IV** 295, 677–78
Publishers Press Assoc., **IV** 607
Publix Super Markets Inc., **II** 155, 627; **7** 440–42; **9** 186
Puente Oil, **IV** 385
Puerto Rican Aqueduct and Sewer Authority, **6** 441
Puerto Rican-American Insurance Co., **III** 242
Puget Mill Company, **12** 406–07
Puget Sound Alaska Van Lines. *See* Alaska Hydro-Train.
Puget Sound National Bank, **8** 469–70
Puget Sound Power And Light Company, **6** 565–67
Puget Sound Pulp and Timber Co., **IV** 281; **9** 259
Puget Sound Tug and Barge Company, **6** 382
Pulitzer Publishing Company, **15** 375–77
Pullman Co., **II** 403; **III** 94, 744
Pullman Standard, **7** 540
Pulte Corporation, **8** 436–38
Puma, **14** 6–7
AB Pump-Separator, **III** 418–19
Punchcraft, Inc., **III** 569
Purdue Fredrick Company, **13** 367
Pure Milk Products Cooperative, **11** 24
Pure Oil Co., **III** 497; **IV** 570
Pure Packed Foods, **II** 525; **13** 293
Purex Corp., **I** 450; **III** 21
Purex Pool Products, **I** 13, 342
Purfina, **IV** 497
Puris Inc., **14** 316
Puritan Chemical Co., **I** 321
Puritan-Bennett Corporation, **13** 419–21
Purity Stores, **I** 146
Purity Supreme, Inc., **II** 674
Purle Bros., **III** 735
Purnell & Sons Ltd., **IV** 642; **7** 312
Purodenso Co., **III** 593
Purolator Courier Corporation, **6** 345–46, 390
Purolator Products Co., **III** 593
Puss 'n Boots, **II** 559
Putnam Management Co., **III** 283
Putnam Reinsurance Co., **III** 198
PWA Group, **IV** 323–25

PWS Holding Corporation, **13** 406
PWT Worldwide, **11** 510
PYA Monarch, **II** 675
Pyramid Communications, Inc., **IV** 623
Pyramid Electric Company, **10** 319
Pyramid Technology Corporation, **10** 504
Pytchley Autocar Co. Ltd., **IV** 722
Pyxis Resources Co., **IV** 182

Qantas Airways Limited, **I** 92–93; **6** 79, 91, 100, 105, **109–13**, 117; **14** 70, 73
Qatar General Petroleum Corporation, **IV** 524–26
Qintex Australia Ltd., **II** 150
QO Chemicals, Inc., **14** 217
QSP, Inc., **IV** 664
Quaker Oats Company, **I** 30; **II** 558–60, 575, 684; **12** 167, 169, **409–12 (upd.)**; **13** 186
Quaker State Corporation, **7** 443–45
Qualicare, Inc., **6** 192
QualiTROL Corporation, **7** 116–17
Quality Bakers of America, **12** 170
Quality Care Inc., **I** 249
Quality Courts Motels, Inc., **14** 105
Quality Importers, **I** 226; **10** 180
Quality Inns International, **13** 363; **14** 105
Quality Markets, Inc., **13** 393
Quality Oil Co., **II** 624–25
Quality Paperback Book Club (QPB), **13** 105–07
Qualtec, Inc., **V** 623
Quanex Corporation, **13** 422–24
Quantum Chemical Corporation, **8** 439–41; **11** 441
Quantum Corporation, **6** 230–31; **10** 56, 403, **458–59**, 463
Quantum Overseas N.V., **7** 360
Quarrie Corporation, **12** 554
Quasi-Arc Co., **I** 315
Quebec Bank, **II** 344
Quebéc Hydro-Electric Commission. *See* Hydro-Quebéc.
Quebecor Inc., **12** 412–14
Queen Casuals, **III** 530
Queen Insurance Co., **III** 350
Queens Isetan Co., Ltd., **V** 87
Queensland Alumina, **IV** 59
Queensland and Northern Territories Air Service. *See* Qantas Airways Limited.
Queensland Mines Ltd., **III** 729
Queensland Oil Refineries, **III** 672
Queiroz Pereira, **IV** 504
Quelle Group, **V** 165–67
Quennessen, **IV** 118
Quesnel River Pulp Co., **IV** 269
Questar Corporation, **6** 568–70; **10** 432
Questor, **I** 332
QUICK Corp., **IV** 656
Quick-Shop, **II** 619
Quickie Designs, **11** 202, 487–88
Quik Stop Markets, Inc., **12** 112
QuikWok Inc., **II** 556; **13** 408
Quilter Goodison, **II** 260
Quimica Industrial Huels Do Brasil Ltda., **I** 350
Quincy Compressor Co., **I** 434–35
Quincy Family Steak House, **II** 679; **10** 331
Quinton Hazell Automotive, **III** 495; **IV** 382–83
Quintron, Inc., **11** 475
Quintus Computer Systems, **6** 248
Quixote Corporation, **15** 378–80

Quixx Corporation, **6** 580
Quotron, **III** 119; **IV** 670; **9** 49, 125
QVC Network Inc., **9** 428–29; **10** 175; **12** 315

R & B Manufacturing Co., **III** 569
R.A. Waller & Co., **III** 282
R-B. *See* Arby's, Inc.
R. Buckland & Son Ltd., **IV** 119
R-Byte, **12** 162
R-C Holding Inc. *See* Air & Water Technologies Corporation.
R. Cubed Composites Inc., **I** 387
R.E. Funsten Co., **7** 429
R.G. Dun-Bradstreet Corp., **IV** 604–05
R.H. Macy & Co., Inc., **I** 30; **V** 168–70; **8** 442–45 (upd.); **10** 282; **11** 349; **13** 42; **15** 281
R.H. Squire, **III** 283
R.H. Stengel & Company, **13** 479
R. Hoe & Co., **I** 602; **13** 189
R. Hornibrook (NSW), **I** 592
R.J. Brown Co., **IV** 373
R.J. Reynolds Industries Inc., **I** 259, 261, 363; **II** 542, 544; **III** 16; **IV** 523; **V** 396, 404–05, 407–10, 413, 415, 417–18; **7** 130, 132, 267, 365, 367; **9** 533; **13** 490; **14** 78; **15** 72–73. *See also* RJR Nabisco.
R.K. Brown, **14** 112
R.L. Crain Limited, **15** 473
R.L. Manning Company, **9** 363–64
R.L. Polk & Co., **10** 460–62
R.N. Coate, **I** 216
R.O. Hull Co., **I** 361
R.P. Scherer, **I** 678–80
R.R. Donnelley & Sons Company, **IV** 660–62, 673; **9** 430–32 (upd.); **11** 293; **12** 414, 557, 559
R.S. Stokvis Company, **13** 499
R. Scott Associates, **11** 57
R. Stock AG, **IV** 198
R.T. French USA, **II** 567
R.T. Securities, **II** 457
R.W. Harmon & Sons, Inc., **6** 410
R.W. Sears Watch Company, **V** 180
RABA PLC, **10** 274
Racal Electronics PLC, **II** 83–84; **11** 408, 547
Racal-Datacom Inc., **11** 408–10
Racine Hardware Co., **III** 58
Racine Threshing Machine Works, **10** 377
Rack Rite Distributors, **V** 174
Rada Corp., **IV** 250
Radiant Lamp Corp., **13** 398
Radiation Dynamics, **III** 634–35
Radiation, Inc., **II** 37–38
Radiation-Medical Products Corp., **I** 202
Radiator Specialty Co., **III** 570
Radio & Allied Industries, **II** 25
Radio Austria A.G., **V** 314–16
Radio Corporation of America. *See* RCA Corporation.
Radio Receptor Company, Inc., **10** 319
Radio Shack, **II** 106–08; **12** 470; **13** 174
Radio-Keith-Orpheum, **II** 32, 88, 135, 146–48, 175; **III** 428; **9** 247; **12** 73
Radiotelevision Española, **7** 511
Radium Pharmacy, **I** 704
Radix Group, Inc., **13** 20
Radnor Venture Partners, LP, **10** 474
Raf, Haarla Oy, **IV** 349
Raffineriegesellschaft Vohburg/Ingolstadt mbH, **7** 141

Ragazzi's, **10** 331
Ragnar Benson Inc., **8** 43–43
RAI, **I** 466
Railway Express Agency, **I** 456; **II** 382; **6** 388–89
Railway Maintenance Equipment Co., **14** 43
Railway Officials and Employees Accident Assoc., **III** 228
Railway Passengers Assurance Co., **III** 178, 410
Rainbow Crafts, **II** 502; **10** 323
Rainbow Home Shopping Ltd., **V** 160
Rainbow Production Corp., **I** 412
Rainbow Programming Holdings, **7** 63–64
Rainbow Resources, **IV** 576
Raky-Danubia, **IV** 485
Ralcorp Holdings Inc., **13** 293, 425, 427; **15** 189, 235
Raley's Inc., **14 396–98**
Ralli International, **III** 502; **IV** 259
Rally's, **14** 452; **15** 345
Rallye S.A., **12** 154
Ralph Lauren. *See* Polo/Ralph Lauren Corportion.
The Ralph M. Parsons Company. *See* The Parsons Corporation.
Ralph Wilson Plastics, **III** 610–11
Ralston Purina Company, **I** 608, **II** 544, 560, **561–63**, 617; **III** 588; **6** 50–52; **7** 209, 396, 547, 556; **8** 180; **9** 180; **12** 276, 411, 510; **13** 137, 270, 293, **425–27 (upd.)**; **14** 194–95, 558
Ram dis Ticaret, **I** 479
Ram Golf Corp., **III** 24
Ram's Insurance, **III** 370
Ramada International Hotels & Resorts, **II** 142; **III** 99; **IV** 718; **9** 426; **11** 177; **13** 66
Ramazotti, **I** 281
Ramo-Woolridge Corp., **I** 539; **14** 510
Ramón Areces Foundation, **V** 52
Rand American Investments Ltd., **IV** 79
Rand Drill Co., **III** 525
Rand Group, Inc., **6** 247
Rand Mines Ltd., **I** 422; **IV** 22, 79, 94
Rand Selection Corp. Ltd., **IV** 79
Random House, Inc., **II** 90; **IV** 583–84, 637, 648; **13** 113, 115, 178, **428–30**; **14** 260
Randsworth Trust P.L.C., **IV** 703
Rank Organisation PLC, **II** 139, 147, **157–59**; **III** 171; **IV** 698; **6** 288; **12** 229; **14 399–402 (upd.)**
Ranks Hovis McDougall PLC, **II** 157, **564–65**
Ransom and Randolph Company, **10** 271
Ransomes America Corp., **III** 600
Rapicom, **III** 159
Rapid American, **I** 440
Rapides Bank & Trust Company, **11** 107
Rapifax of Canada, **III** 160
RAS. *See* Riunione Adriatica di Sicurtà SpA.
Rassini Rheem, **III** 581
Rational Systems Inc., **6** 255
Rauland Corp., **II** 124; **13** 573
Rauma-Repola Oy, **II** 302; **IV** 316, 340, 349–50
Rauscher Pierce Refsnes, Inc., **15** 233
Raven Press, **14** 555
Ravenna Metal Products Corp., **12** 344
Ravenseft Properties Ltd., **IV** 696, 704–05
Rawlings Sporting Goods, **7** 177

Rawlplug Co. Ltd., **IV** 382–83
Rawls Brothers Co., **13** 369
Rawson, Holdsworth & Co., **I** 464
Ray's Printing of Topeka, **II** 624
Raychem Corporation, **III** 492; **8 446–47**
Raycom Sports, **6** 33
Raymar Book Corporation, **11** 194
Raymond, Jones & Co., **IV** 647
Raymond, Trice & Company, **14** 40
Raynet Corporation, **8** 447
Rayovac Corporation, **13 431–34**
Raytheon Company, **I** 463, 485, 544; **II** 41, 73, **85–87**; **III** 643; **8** 51, 157; **11** 197, **411–14 (upd.)**; **12** 46, 247; **14** 223
RCA Corporation, **I** 142, 454, 463; **II** 29–31, 34, 38, 56, 61, 85–86, **88–90**, 96, 102, 117–18, 120, 124, 129, 132–33, 151–52, 313, 609, 645; **III** 118, 122, 132, 149, 152, 165, 171, 569, 653–54; **IV** 252, 583, 594; **6** 164–66, 240, 266, 281, 288, 334; **7** 520; **8** 157; **9** 283; **10** 173; **11** 197, 318, 411; **12** 204, 208, 237, 454, 544, 548; **13** 106, 398, 429, 506, 573; **14** 357, 436
RCG International, Inc., **III** 344
REA. *See* Railway Express Agency.
Rea & Derick, **II** 605
Rea Magnet Wire Co., **IV** 15
React-Rite, Inc., **8** 271
Read, R.L., **II** 417
Read-Rite Corp., **10** 403–04, **463–64**
Reader's Digest Association, Inc., **IV 663–64**
Reading and Bates, **III** 559
Reading Railroad, **9** 407
Ready Mixed Concrete, **III** 687, 737–40
RealCom Communications Corporation, **15** 196
Reale Mutuale, **III** 273
Realty Development Co. *See* King Kullen Grocery Co., Inc.
Réassurances, **III** 392
Reckitt & Colman PLC, **II 566–67**; **15** 46, 360
Reconstruction Bank of Holland, **IV** 707
Reconstruction Finance Bank, **II** 292
Reconstruction Finance Corp., **I** 67, 203; **II** 261; **IV** 10, 333
Record Bar / Licorice Pizza, **9** 361
Record World Inc., **9** 361
Recoton Corp., **15 381–83**
Recoupe Recycling Technologies, **8** 104
Recovery Centers of America, **III** 88
Recticel S.A., **III** 581
Rectigraph Co., **III** 171
Red & White, **II** 682
Red Arrow, **II** 138
Red Kap, **V** 390–91
Red L Foods, **13** 244
Red Lobster Restaurants, **II** 502–03; **6** 28; **10** 322–24
Red Owl Stores Inc., **II** 670
Red Roof Inns, **13** 363
Red Rooster, **V** 35
Red Sea Insurance Co., **III** 251
Red Star Express, **14** 505
Red Star Milling Co., **II** 501; **6** 397; **10** 322
Red Wing Shoe Company, Inc., **9 433–35**
Redactron, **III** 166; **6** 282
Redbook Publishing Co., **14** 460
Reddy Elevator Co., **III** 467
Reddy Ice, **II** 661

Redentza, **IV** 504
Redhill Tile Co., **III** 734
Redi, **IV** 610
Rediffusion, **II** 139
Reditab S.p.A., **12** 109
Redken Laboratories, **8** 131
Redland plc, **III** 495, 688, **734–36**; **14** 249, 739; **15** 154
Redlaw Industries Inc., **15** 247
Redmond & Co., **I** 376
La Redoute, S.A, **V** 11
Redpath Industries, **II** 581–82
Redwood Design Automation, **11** 47
Redwood Fire & Casualty Insurance Co., **III** 214
Reebok International Ltd., **V 375–77**; **8** 171, 303–04, 393; **9** 134–35, **436–38 (upd.)**; **11** 50–51, 349; **13** 513; **14** 8
Reed & Gamage, **13** 243
Reed Corrugated Containers, **IV** 249
Reed International P.L.C., **I** 423; **IV** 270, 642, **665–67**, 711; **7** 244–45, 343; **10** 407; **12** 359
Reed Tool Co., **III** 429
Reeder Light, Ice & Fuel Company, **6** 592
Reedpack, **IV** 339–40, 667
Reese Finer Foods, Inc., **7** 429
Reese Products, **III** 569; **11** 535
Reeves Banking and Trust Company, **11** 181
Reeves Pulley Company, **9** 440
Refco, Inc., **10** 251
Reference Software International, **10** 558
Refined Sugars, **II** 582
Reform Rt, **IV** 652; **7** 392
Regal Drugs, **V** 171
Regal Inns, **13** 364
Regal Manufacturing Co., **15** 385
Regency, **12** 316
Regency Electronics, **II** 101
Regency International, **10** 196
Regenerative Environmental Equipment Company, Inc., **6** 441
Regeneron Pharmaceuticals Inc., **10** 80
Regent Canal Co., **III** 272
Regent Insurance Co., **III** 343
Regent International Hotels Limited, **9** 238
Régie Autonome des Pétroles, **IV** 544–46
Régie des Mines de la Sarre, **IV** 196
Régie des Télégraphes et Téléphones. *See* Belgacom.
Régie Nationale des Usines Renault, **I** 136, 145, 148, 178–79, 183, **189–91**, 207, 210; **II** 13; **III** 392, 523; **7** 566–67; **11** 104; **12** 91; **15** 514
Regina Verwaltungsgesellschaft, **II** 257
Regional Bell Operating Companies, **15** 125
Registered Vitamin Company, **V** 171
Regnecentralen AS, **III** 164
Rego Supermarkets and American Seaway Foods, Inc., **9** 451; **13** 237
Rehab Hospital Services Corp., **III** 88; **10** 252
RehabClinics Inc., **11** 367
Reichart Furniture Corp., **14** 236
Reichhold Chemicals, Inc., **I** 386, 524; **8** 554; **10 465–67**
Reichs-Kredit-Gesellschaft mbH, **IV** 230
Reichs-Kredit- und Krontrollstelle GmbH, **IV** 230
Reichswerke AG für Berg- und Hüttenbetriebe Hermann Göring, **IV** 200

Reichswerke AG für Erzbergbau und Eisenhütten, **IV** 200
Reichswerke Hermann Göring, **IV** 233
Reid Bros. & Carr Proprietary, **III** 672–73
Reid Dominion Packaging Ltd., **IV** 645
Reid Ice Cream Corp., **II** 471
Reid, Murdoch and Co., **II** 571
Reid Press Ltd., **IV** 645
Reidsville Fashions, Inc., **13** 532
Reigel Products Corp., **IV** 289
Reims Aviation, **8** 92
Rein Elektronik, **10** 459
Reinsurance Agency, **III** 204–05
Reisebüro Bangemann, **II** 164
Reisholz AG, **III** 693
Reisland GmbH, **15** 340
Reiue Nationale des Usines Renault, **7** 220
Relational Database Systems Inc., **10** 361–62
Relational Technology Inc., **10** 361
Release Technologies, **8** 484
Reliable Stores Inc., **14** 236
Reliable Tool, **II** 488
Reliance Electric Company, **IV** 429; **9** **439–42**
Reliance Group Holdings, Inc., **II** 173; **III 342–44**; **IV** 642
Reliance Life Insurance Co., **III** 275–76
ReLife Inc., **14** 233
Rembrandt Group, **I** 289; **IV** 91, 93, 97; **V** 411–13
Remgro, **IV** 97
Remington Arms Company, Inc., **I** 329; **8** 152; **12 415–17**
Remington Rand, **III** 122, 126, 148, 151, 165–66, 642; **6** 251, 265, 281–82; **10** 255; **12** 416
REN Corp. USA, Inc., **13** 161
Renault. *See* Régie Nationale des Usines Renault.
Rendeck International, **11** 66
Rendic International, **13** 228
René Garraud, **III** 68
Rengo Co., Ltd., **IV 326**
Rennies Consolidated Holdings, **I** 470
Reno Technologies, **12** 124
Repco Ltd., **15** 246
REPESA, **IV** 528
Repligen Inc., **13** 241
Repola Oy, **IV** 316, 347, 350
Repsol SA, **IV** 396–97, 506, 514, **527–29**
Repubblica, **IV** 587
Republic Aircraft Co., **I** 89
Republic Airlines, **I** 113, 132; **6** 104
Republic Aviation Corporation, **I** 55; **9** 205–07
Republic Corp., **I** 447
Republic Engineered Steels, Inc., **7** **446–47**
Republic Freight Systems, **14** 567
Republic Indemnity Co. of America, **III** 191
Republic Insurance, **III** 404
Republic New York Corporation, **11** **415–19**
Republic Pictures, **9** 75
Republic Powdered Metals, Inc., **8** 454
Republic Realty Mortgage Corp., **II** 289
Republic Rubber, **III** 641
Republic Steel Corp., **I** 491; **IV** 114; **7** 446; **12** 353; **13** 169, 157; **14** 155
Republic Supply Co. of California, **I** 570
Research Analysis Corporation, **7** 15
Research Cottrell, Inc., **6** 441

Research Polymers International, **I** 321; **12** 103
Research Publications, **8** 526
Resem SpA, **I** 387
Residence Inns, **III** 103; **9** 426
Residential Funding Corporation, **10** 92–93
Resinous Products, **I** 392
Resolution Systems, Inc., **13** 201
Resolution Trust Corp., **10** 117, 134; **11** 371; **12** 368
Resorts International, Inc., **I** 452; **12** **418–20**
Resource Associates of Alaska, Inc., **7** 376
Resource Electronics, **8** 385
Rest Assured, **I** 429
Restaurant Enterprises Group Inc., **14** 195
Restaurant Franchise Industries, **6** 200
Restaurants Les Pres Limitée, **II** 652
Restaurants Unlimited, Inc., **13 435–37**
Resurgens Communications Group, **7** 336; **8** 311
Retail Credit Company. *See* Equifax.
Retail Ventures Inc., **14** 427
Retailers Commercial Agency, Inc., **6** 24
Retirement Inns of America, Inc., **III** 16; **11** 282
Reuben H. Donnelley Corp., **IV** 605, 661
Reunion Properties, **I** 470
Reuters Holdings PLC, **IV** 259, 652, 654, 656, **668–70**; **10** 277, 407
Revco D.S., Inc., **II** 449; **III** 10; **V** **171–73**; **9** 67, 187; **12** 4; **13** 449
Revere Copper and Brass Co., **IV** 32. *See also* The Paul Revere Corporation.
Revere Foil Containers, Inc., **12** 377
Revere Furniture and Equipment, **14** 105
Revlon Group, Inc., **I** 29, 449, 620, 633, 668, 677, 693, 696; **II** 498, 679; **III** 29, 46, **54–57**, 727; **6** 27; **8** 131, 341; **9** 202–03, 291; **11** 8, 333–34; **12** 314
Revson Bros., **III** 54
Rex Pulp Products Company, **9** 304
REX Stores Corp., **10 468–69**
Rexall Drug & Chemical Co., **II** 533–34; **III** 610; **13** 525; **14** 547
Rexel, Inc., **15 384–87**
Rexene Products Co., **III** 760; **IV** 457
Rexham Inc., **IV** 259; **8** 483–84
Rexnord Corp., **I** 524; **14** 43
Reymer & Bros., Inc., **II** 508; **11** 172
Reymersholm, **II** 366
Reynolds Metals Company, **II** 421–22; **IV** 11–12, 15, 59, **186–88**; **IV** 122; **12** 278
RF Communications, **II** 38
RF Monolithics Inc., **13** 193
RHC Holding Corp., **10** 13; **13** 364
Rhee Syngman, **I** 516; **12** 293
Rhein-Elbe Gelsenkirchener Bergwerks A.G., **IV** 25
Rheinelbe Union, **I** 542
Rheinisch Kalksteinwerke Wulfrath, **III** 738
Rheinisch Oelfinwerke, **I** 306
Rheinisch-Westfalische Bank A.G., **II** 279
Rheinisch-Westfälischer Sprengstoff AG, **III** 694
Rheinisch-Westfälisches Elektrizatätswerke AG, **I** 542–43; **III** 154; **IV** 231; **V** 744
Rheinische Aktiengesellschaft für Braunkohlenbergbau, **V** 708
Rheinische Creditbank, **II** 278
Rheinische Metallwaaren- und Maschinenfabrik AG, **9** 443–44

Rheinische Wasserglasfabrik, **III** 31
Rheinmetall Berlin AG, 9 443–46
Rheinische Girozentrale und Provinzialbank, Düsseldorf, **II** 385
Rheinstahl AG, **IV** 222
Rheinstahl Union Brueckenbau, **8** 242
Rheintalische Zementfabrik, **III** 701
Rhenus-Weichelt AG, **6** 424, 426
RHM. *See* Ranks Hovis McDougall.
Rhodes & Co., **8** 345
Rhodesian Anglo American Ltd., **IV** 21, 23
Rhodesian Development Corp., **I** 422
Rhodesian Selection Trust, Ltd., **IV** 17–18, 21
Rhodesian Sugar Refineries, **II** 581
Rhodiaceta, **I** 388–89
Rhokana Corp., **IV** 191
Rhône-Poulenc S.A., **I** 303–04, 371, **388–90**, 670, 672, 692; **III** 677; **IV** 174, 487, 547; **8** 153, 452; **9** 358; **10 470–72** **(upd.)**
Rhymey Breweries, **I** 294
Rhythm Watch, **III** 454
La Riassicuratrice, **III** 346
Ricard, **I** 280
Rice Broadcasting Co., Inc., **II** 166
Rice-Stix Dry Goods, **II** 414
Rich Products Corporation, **7 448–49**
Rich's, **9** 209; **10** 515
Richard A. Shaw, Inc., **7** 128
Richard D. Irwin Inc., **IV** 602–03, 678
Richard Hellman Co., **II** 497
Richard Manufacturing Co., **I** 667
Richard P. Simmons, **8** 19
Richard Shops, **III** 502
Richard Thomas & Baldwins, **IV** 42
Richards Bay Minerals, **IV** 91
Richardson-Vicks Company, **III** 53; **8** 434
Richfood Holdings, Inc., **7 450–51**
Richland Co-op Creamery Company, **7** 592
Richland Gas Company, **8** 349
Richmon Hill & Queens County Gas Light Companies, **6** 455
Richmond American Homes of Florida, Inc., **11** 258
Richmond Carousel Corporation, **9** 120
Richmond Cedar Works Manufacturing Co., **12** 109
Richmond Corp., **I** 600; **15** 129
Richway, **10** 515
Richwood Building Products, Inc., **12** 397
Ricils, **III** 47
Rickel Home Centers, **II** 673
Ricoh Company, Ltd., **III** 121, 157, **159–61**, 172, 454; **6** 289; **8** 278
Ridder Publications, **IV** 612–13, 629; **7** 191
Ridge Tool Co., **II** 19
Ridgewell's Inc., **15** 87
Ridgewood Properties Inc., **12** 394
Ridgway Color, **13** 227–28
Rieck-McJunkin Dairy Co., **II** 533
Riegel Bag & Paper Co., **IV** 344
Rieke Corp., **III** 569; **11** 535
Rieter Machine Works, **III** 638
Rig Tenders Company, **6** 383
Riggin & Robbins, **13** 244
Riggs National Corporation, **13 438–40**
Rike's, **10** 282
Riken Corp., **IV** 160; **10** 493
Riken Kankoshi Co. Ltd., **III** 159
Riken Optical Co., **III** 159

Riklis Family Corp., **9** 447–50; **12** 87; **13** 453
Riku-un Moto Kaisha, **V** 477
La Rinascente, **12** 153
Ring King Visibles, Inc., **13** 269
Ringköpkedjan, **II** 640
Rini Supermarkets, **9** 451; **13** 237
Rini-Rego Supermarkets Inc., **13** 238
Rinker Materials Corp., **III** 688
Rio Grande Industries, Inc., **12** 18–19
Rio Grande Oil Co., **IV** 375, 456
Rio Grande Valley Gas Co., **IV** 394
Rio Sul Airlines, **6** 133
Rio Tinto-Zinc Corp., **II** 628; **IV** 56, 58–61, 189–91, 380
Rioblanco, **II** 477
Riordan Freeman & Spogli, **13** 406
Riordan Holdings Ltd., **I** 457; **10** 554
Riser Foods, Inc., **9** 451–54; **13** 237–38
Rising Sun Petroleum Co., **IV** 431, 460, 542
Risk Planners, **II** 669
Rit Dye Co., **II** 497
Rite Aid Corporation, **V** 174–76; **9** 187, 346; **12** 221, 333
Rite-Way Department Store, **II** 649
Rittenhouse and Embree, **III** 269
Ritz Firma, **13** 512
Ritz-Carlton Hotel Company, **9** 455–57
Riunione Adriatica di Sicurtà SpA, **III** 185, 206, **345–48**
River Boat Casino, **9** 425–26
River Steam Navigation Co., **III** 522
River-Raisin Paper Co., **IV** 345
Riverside Chemical Company, **13** 502
Riverside Iron Works, Ltd., **8** 544
Riverside National Bank of Buffalo, **11** 108
Riverside Press, **10** 355–56
Riverwood International Corporation, **7** 294; **11 420–23**
Riviana Foods, **III** 24, 25
Rizzoli Publishing, **IV** 586, 588
RJR Nabisco, **I** 249, 259, 261; **II** 370, 426, 477–78, 542–44; **7** 130, 132, 277, 596; **9** 469; **12** 559; **13** 342; **14** 214, 274. *See also* Nabisco Brands, Inc. *and* R.J. Reynolds Industries, Inc.
RJR Nabisco Holdings Corp., **V 408–10, 415; 12** 82
RKO. *See* Radio-Keith-Orpheum.
RKO Radio Sales, **6** 33
RKO-General, Inc., **8** 207
RLA Polymers, **9** 92
RM Marketing, **6** 14
RMC Group p.l.c., **III** 734, **737–40**
RMF Inc., **I** 412
RMP International, Limited, **8** 417
Roadline, **6** 413–14
Roadway Bodegas y Consolidación, **V** 503
Roadway Services, Inc., **V 502–03**; **12** 278, 309; **14** 567; **15** 111
Roaman's, **V** 115
Roan Selection Trust Ltd., **IV** 18, 239–40
Roanoke Fashions Group, **13** 532
Robb Engineering Works, **8** 544
Robbins & Myers Inc., **13** 273; **15 388–90**
Robbins Co., **III** 546
Robeco Group, **IV** 193
Roberk Co., **III** 603
Robert Allen Cos., **III** 571
Robert Benson, Lonsdale & Co. Ltd., **II** 232, 421–22; **IV** 191

Robert Bosch GmbH., **I 392–93**, 411; **III** 554, 555, 591, 593; **13** 398
Robert E. McKee Corporation, **6** 150
Robert Fleming Holdings Ltd., **I** 471; **IV** 79; **11** 495
Robert Gair Co., **15** 128
Robert Garrett & Sons, Inc., **9** 363
Robert Grace Contracting Co., **I** 584
Robert Hall Clothes, Inc., **13** 535
Robert Johnson, **8** 281–82
Robert McLane Company. *See* McLane Company, Inc.
Robert McNish & Company Limited, **14** 141
Robert Mondavi Corporation, **15 391–94**
Robert R. Mullen & Co., **I** 20
Robert W. Baird & Co., **III** 324; **7** 495
Robert Warschauer and Co., **II** 270
Robert Watson & Co. Ltd., **I** 568
Roberts Express, **V** 503
Roberts, Johnson & Rand Shoe Co., **III** 528–29
Robertson Building Products, **8** 546
Robertson-Ceco Corporation, **8** 546
Robin Hood Flour Mills, Ltd., **7** 241–43
Robinair, **10** 492, 494
Robinson Clubs, **II** 163–64
Robinson Radio Rentals, **I** 531
Robinson Smith & Robert Haas, Inc., **13** 428
Robinson's Japan Co. Ltd., **V** 89
Robinson-Danforth Commission Co., **II** 561
Robinson-Humphrey, **II** 398; **10** 62
Roc, **I** 272
Roche Biomedical Laboratories, Inc., **8** 209–10; **11 424–26**
Roche Bioscience, **14 403–06 (upd.)**
Roche Products Ltd., **I** 643
Rochester American Insurance Co., **III** 191
Rochester Gas And Electric Corporation, **6 571–73**
Rochester German Insurance Co., **III** 191
Rochester Telephone Corporation, **6 332–34**; **12** 136
Röchling Industrie Verwaltung GmbH, **9** 443
Rock Island Oil & Refining Co., **IV** 448–49
Rock Island Plow Company, **10** 378
Rock-Tenn Company, **IV** 312; **13 441–43**
Rockcor Inc., **I** 381; **13** 380
Rockcote Paint Company, **8** 552–53
Rockefeller & Andrews, **IV** 426; **7** 169
Rockefeller Group, **IV** 714
Rockford Drilling Co., **III** 439
Rockland Corp., **8** 271
Rockland React-Rite, Inc., **8** 270
Rockmoor Grocery, **II** 683
Rockower of Canada Ltd., **II** 649
Rockport Company, **V** 376–77
Rockwell International Corporation, **I** 71, **78–80**, 154–55, 186; **II** 3, 94, 379; **6** 263; **7** 420; **8** 165; **9** 10; **10** 279–80; **11** 268, 278, **427–30 (upd.)**, 473; **12** 135, 248, 506; **13** 228
Rocky Mountain Financial Corporation, **13** 348
Rocky Mountain Pipe Line Co., **IV** 400
Rocky River Power Co. *See* Connecticut Light and Power Co.
Rodamco, **IV** 698
Rodeway Inns of America, **II** 142; **III** 94; **11** 242

Roegelein Co., **13** 271
Roehr Products Co., **III** 443
Roermond, **IV** 276
Roessler & Hasslacher Chemical Co., **IV** 69
Roger Cleveland Golf Company, **15** 462
Roger Williams Foods, **II** 682
Rogers Bros., **I** 672
Rohe Scientific Corp., **13** 398
Röhm and Haas, **I 391–93**
Rohm Company Ltd., **14** 182–83
Rohölgewinnungs AG, **IV** 485
Rohr Incorporated, **I** 62; **9 458–60**; **11** 165
Roja, **III** 47
Rokuosha, **III** 547
Rol Oil, **IV** 451
Rola Group, **II** 81
Roland Murten A.G., **7 452–53**
Rolex. *See* Montres Rolex S.A.
Rollalong, **III** 502; **7** 208
Rollerblade, Inc., **15 395–98**
Rollins Burdick Hunter Co., **III** 204
Rollins Communications, **II** 161
Rollins, Inc., **11 431–34**
Rollins Specialty Group, **III** 204
Rolls-Royce Motors Ltd., **I** 25–26, 81–82, 166, **194–96**; **III** 652; **9** 16–18, 417–18; **11** 138, 403
Rolls-Royce plc, **I** 41, 55, 65, **81–83**, 481; **III** 507, 556; **7 454–57 (upd.)**; **9** 244; **11** 268; **12** 190; **13** 414
Rolm Systems, **II** 99; **III** 149
Rolscreen. *See* Pella Corporation.
Rombas, **IV** 226
Rome Cable and Wire Co., **IV** 15
Rompetrol, **IV** 454
Ron Nagle, **I** 247
Ronco, Inc., **15 399–401**
Rondel's, Inc., **8** 135
Ronel, **13** 274
Ronningen-Petter, **III** 468
Ronzoni Foods Corp., **15** 221
Roots-Connersville Blower Corp., **III** 472
Roper Industries Inc., **III** 655; **12** 550; **15 402–04**
Rorer Group, **I** 666–68; **12** 4
Rose Foundation, **9** 348
Rose's Stores, Inc., **13** 261, **444–46**
Rosefield Packing Co., **II** 497
RoseJohnson Incorporated, **14** 303
Rosemount Inc., **II** 20; **13** 226; **15 405–08**
Rosen Enterprises, Ltd., **10** 482
Rosenblads Patenter, **III** 419
Rosenbluth International Inc., **14 407–09**
Rosenthal, **I** 347
Rosevear, **III** 690
Ross Carrier Company, **8** 115
Ross Clouston, **13** 244
Ross Gear & Tool Co., **I** 539; **14** 510
Ross Hall Corp., **I** 417
Rossendale Combining Company, **9** 92
Rossignol Ski Company, Inc. *See* Skis Rossignol S.A.
Rössing Uranium Ltd., **IV** 191
Rossville Union Distillery, **I** 285
Rostocker Brauerei VEB, **9** 87
Roswell Public Service Company, **6** 579
Rota Bolt Ltd., **III** 581
Rotan Mosle Financial Corp., **II** 445
Rotary Lift, **III** 467–68
Rotax, **III** 555–56
Rotelcom Business Systems, **6** 334

Rotex, **IV** 253
Rothmans International p.l.c., **I** 438; **IV** 93; **V** 411–13
Rothschild Financial Corporation, **13** 347
Rothschild Group, **6** 206
Rothschild Investment Trust, **I** 248; **III** 699
Roto-Rooter Corp., **13** 149–50; **15** 409–11
Rotodiesel, **III** 556
Rotor Tool Co., **II** 16
Rotterdam Bank, **II** 183–85
Rotterdam Lloyd, **6** 403–04
Rouge et Or, **IV** 614
Rouge Steel Company, **8** 448–50
Roughdales Brickworks, **14** 249
Roundup Wholesale Grocery Company, **V** 55
Roundy's Inc., **14** 410–12
The Rouse Company, **15** 412–15
Rouse Real Estate Finance, **II** 445
Roussel Uclaf, **I** 669–70; **8** 451–53 (upd.)
Rousselot, **I** 677
Roux Séguéla Cayzac & Goudard. *See* Euro RSCG Worldwide S.A.
Rover Group Plc, **I** 186; **7** 458–60; **11** 31, 33; **14** 36
Rowe & Pitman, **14** 419
Rowe Bros. & Co., **III** 680
Rowe Price-Fleming International, Inc., **11** 495
Rowntree Mackintosh, **II** 476, 511, 521, 548, **568–70**; **7** 383
Roxana Petroleum Co., **IV** 531, 540
Roxoil Drilling, **7** 344
Roy Farrell Import-Export Company, **6** 78
Roy Rogers, **III** 102
Royal Aluminium Ltd., **IV** 9
Royal Appliance Manufacturing Company, **15** 416–18
Royal Baking Powder Co., **II** 544; **14** 17
Royal Bank of Australia, **II** 188
Royal Bank of Canada, **II** 344–46
Royal Bank of Queensland, **II** 188
The Royal Bank of Scotland Group plc, **II** 298, 358; **10** 336–37; **12** 421–23
Royal Brewing Co., **I** 269; **12** 337
Royal Business Machines, **I** 207, 485; **III** 549
Royal Canada, **III** 349
Royal Caribbean, **6** 368
Royal Copenhagen A/S, **9** 99
Royal Crown Cola, **II** 468; **6** 21, 50; **8** 536–37; **14** 32–33
Royal Data, Inc. *See* King Kullen Grocery Co., Inc.
Royal Doulton Plc, **IV** 659; **14** 413–15
Royal Dutch Harbour Co., **IV** 707
Royal Dutch Paper Co., **IV** 307
Royal Dutch Petroleum Company, **IV** **530–32**, 657. *See also* Shell Transport and Trading Company p.l.c.
Royal Dutch/Shell, **I** 368, 504; **III** 616; **IV** 132–33, 378, 406, 413, 429, 434, 453–54, 460, 491–92, 512, 515, 517–18, 530–32, 540–45, 557–58, 569; **7** 56–57, 172–73, 481–82
Royal Electric Company, **6** 501
Royal Exchange Assurance Corp., **III** 233–34, 278, 349, 369–71, 373
Royal Food Distributors, **II** 625
Royal General Insurance Co., **III** 242
Royal Hawaiian Macadamia Nut Co., **II** 491

Royal Insurance Holdings plc, **III** 349–51
Royal International, **II** 457; **III** 349
Royal Interocean Lines, **6** 404
Royal Jackson, **14** 236
Royal Jordanian, **6** 101
Royal London Mutual Insurance, **IV** 697
Royal Mail, **V** 498
Royal Mail Group, **6** 416
Royal Orchid Holidays, **6** 122–23
Royal Ordnance, **13** 356
Royal Packaging Industries Van Leer B.V., **9** 305
Royal Pakhoed N.V., **9** 532
Royal Re, **III** 349
Royal Sash Manufacturing Co., **III** 757
Royal Securities Company, **6** 585
Royal Securities Corp. of Canada, **II** 425
Royal Trust Co., **II** 456–57; **V** 25
Royal Union Life Insurance Co., **III** 275
Royal USA, **III** 349
Royal Wessanen, **II** 527
Royale Belge, **III** 177, 200, 394
Royalite, **I** 285
Royce Electronics, **III** 569
Royce Ltd., **I** 194
Royster-Clark, Inc., **13** 504
Rozes, **I** 272
RPC Industries, **III** 635
RPI. *See* Research Polymers International.
RPM Inc., **8** **III** 598; **454–57**
RSI Corp., **8** 141–42
RTE Corp., **II** 17
RTL-Véeronique, **IV** 611
RTZ Corporation PLC, **IV** **189–92**; **7** 261, 263
Rubber Latex Limited, **9** 92
Rubbermaid Incorporated, **III** 613–15; **12** 168–69; **13** 317–18
Ruberoid Corp., **I** 339
Rubloff Inc., **II** 442
Rubo Lederwaren, **14** 225
Rubry Owen, **I** 154
Ruby, **III** 47
Rubyco, Inc., **15** 386
La Ruche Meridionale, **12** 153
Rudisill Printing Co., **IV** 661
Rudolf Wolff & Co., **IV** 165
Rudolph Fluor & Brother, **I** 569
Rug Corporation of America, **12** 393
Ruhr-Zink, **IV** 141
Ruhrgas AG, **V** **704–06**; **7** 141
Ruhrkohle AG, **III** 566; **IV** 26, 89, 105, **193–95**
Ruinart Père et Fils, **I** 272
Rumbelows, **I** 532
Runcorn White Lead Co., **III** 680
Runnymede Construction Co., **8** 544
Runo-Everth Treibstoff und Ol AG, **7** 141
Rural Bank, **IV** 279
Rurhkohle AG, **V** 747
Rush Laboratories, Inc., **6** 41
Russ Berrie and Company, Inc., **12** **424–26**
Russell & Co., **II** 296
Russell Corporation, **8** 458–59; **12** 458
Russell Electric, **11** 412
Russell Electronics, **II** 85
Russell Kelly Office Services, Inc. *See* Kelly Services Inc.
Russell, Majors & Waddell, **II** 381
Russell Stover Candies Inc., **12** 427–29
Russwerke Dortmund GmbH, **IV** 70

Rust Craft Greeting Cards Incorporated, **12** 561
Rust International Inc., **V** 754; **6** 599–600; **11** 435–36
Rustenburg Platinum Co., **IV** 96, 118, 120
Rütgerswerke AG, **IV** 193; **8** 81
Ruti Machinery Works, **III** 638
Rutland Plastics, **I** 321; **12** 103
RWE Group, **V** 707–10
Ryan Aeronautical, **I** 525; **10** 522; **11** 428
Ryan Aircraft Company, **9** 458
Ryan Homes, Inc., **8** 401–02
Ryan Insurance Co., **III** 204
Ryan Milk Company of Kentucky, **7** 128
Ryan's Family Steak Houses, Inc., **15** 419–21
Rycade Corp., **IV** 365, 658
Rydelle-Lion, **III** 45
Ryder Systems, Inc., **V** 504–06; **13** 192
The Ryland Group, Inc., **8** 460–61
Ryobi Ltd., **I** 202
Ryukyu Cement, **III** 760
The Ryvita Company, **II** 466; **13** 52

S Pearson & Son Ltd., **IV** 657–59
S. & W. Berisford, **II** 514, 528
S.A. CARFUEL, **12** 152
S.A. Schonbrunn & Co., **14** 18
S&A Restaurant Corp., **7** 336; **10** 176; **14** 331; **15** 363
S&C Electric Company, **15** 422–24
S&H Diving Corporation, **6** 578
S&V Screen Inks, **13** 227–28
S&W Fine Foods, **12** 105
S.B. Irving Trust Bank Corp., **II** 218
S.B. Penick & Co., **I** 708; **8** 548
S.C. Johnson & Son, Inc., **I** 14; **III** 45, **58–59**; **8** 130; **10** 173; **12** 126–28
S-C-S Box Company, **8** 173
S.D. Cohn & Company, **10** 455
S.D. Warren Co., **IV** 329–30
S-E Bank Group, **II** 351–53
S.E. Massengill, **III** 66
S.F. Braun, **IV** 451
S.G. Warburg and Co., **II** 232, 259–60, 422, 629; **14** 419. *See also* SBC Warburg.
S.H. Benson Ltd., **I** 25–26
S.I.P., Co., **8** 416
S-K-I Limited, **15** 457–59
S.K. Wellman, **14** 81
S. Kuhn & Sons, **13** 221
S.M.A. Corp., **I** 622
S.R. Dresser Manufacturing Co., **III** 470–71
S.S. Kresge Company, **V** 110–12. *See also* Kmart Corporation.
S.S. White Dental Manufacturing Co., **I** 383
S. Smith & Sons, **III** 555
S.T. Cooper & Sons, **12** 283
S.T. Dupont, **III** 28
SAA. *See* South African Airways.
SAAB. *See* Svenska Aeroplan Aktiebolaget.
Saab-Scania A.B., **I** 197–98, 210; **III** 556; **V** 339; **10** 86; **11** 437–39 (upd.)
Saarberg-Konzern, **IV** 196–99
Saarstahl AG, **IV** 228
Saatchi & Saatchi plc, **I** 21, 28, **33–35**, 36; **6** 53, 229; **14** 49–50
SAB. *See* South African Breweries Ltd.
Sabah Timber Co., **III** 699
Sabena, **6** 96

Saber Energy, Inc., **7** 553–54
SABIM Sable, **12** 152
Sabine Corporation, **7** 229
Sabine Investment Co. of Texas, Inc., **IV** 341
Sachsgruppe, **IV** 201
Sacilor, **IV** 174, 226–27
Sackett Plasterboard Co., **III** 762
Sacks Industries, **8** 561
SACOR, **IV** 250, 504–06
Sacramento Savings & Loan Association, **10** 43, 45
Saeger Carbide Corp., **IV** 203
Saes, **III** 347
SAFECO Corporation, III 352–54; 10 44
Safeguard Scientifics, Inc., 10 232–34, **473–75**
Safety Fund Bank, **II** 207
Safety Rehab, **11** 486
Safety Savings and Loan, **10** 339
Safety-Kleen Corp., 8 462–65
Safeway Stores Incorporated, II 424, 601, 604–05, 609–10, 628, 632, 637, **654–56; 6** 364; **7** 61, 569; **9** 39; **10** 442; **11** 239, 241; **12** 113, 209, 559; **13** 90, 336, 340
Safmarine, **IV** 22
Safrap, **IV** 472
Saga Corp., **II** 608; **III** 103; **IV** 406
Sagebrush Sales, Inc., **12** 397
Sagittarius Productions Inc., **I** 286
Sai Baba, **12** 228
Saia Motor Freight Line, Inc., **6** 421–23
Saibu Gas, **IV** 518–19
SAIC, **12** 153
Saiccor, **IV** 92
Sainrapt et Brice, **9** 9
Sainsbury's. *See* J Sainsbury PLC.
St. Alban's Sand and Gravel, **III** 739
St. Andrews Insurance, **III** 397
St. Charles Manufacturing Co., **III** 654
St. Clair Industries Inc., **I** 482
St. Clair Press, **IV** 570
St. Croix Paper Co., **IV** 281; **9** 259
St. George Reinsurance, **III** 397
St. Helens Crown Glass Co., **III** 724
St. Joe Minerals Corp., **I** 569, 571; **8** 192
St. Joe Paper Company, 8 485–88
St. John Knits, Inc., 14 466–68
St. John's Wood Railway Company, **6** 406
St. Joseph Co., **I** 286, 684
St. Jude Medical, Inc., 6 345; **11 458–61**
St. Lawrence Cement Inc., **III** 702; **8** 258–59
St. Lawrence Corp. Ltd., **IV** 272
St. Lawrence Steamboat Co., **I** 273
St. Louis and Illinois Belt Railway, **6** 504
St. Louis Refrigerator Car Co., **I** 219
St. Louis Troy and Eastern Railroad Company, **6** 504
St. Paul (U.K.) Ltd., **III** 357
St. Paul Bank for Cooperatives, 8 489–90
St. Paul Companies, **15** 257
St. Paul Fire and Marine Insurance Co., **III** 355–56
St. Regis Corp., **I** 153; **IV** 264, 282; **9** 260; **10** 265
St. Regis Paper Co., **IV** 289, 339; **12** 377
Saint-Gobain. *See* Compagnie de Saint Gobain S.A.
Saint-Gobain Pont-à-Mousson, **IV** 227
Saint-Quirin, **III** 676
Sainte Anne Paper Co., **IV** 245–46

Saipem, **IV** 420–22, 453
Saison Group, **V** 184–85, 187–89
Saito Ltd., **IV** 268
Saiwa, **II** 543
Saks Fifth Avenue, **I** 426; **15** 291
Sakurai Co., **IV** 327
Salada Foods, **II** 525; **13** 293
Salant Corporation, 12 430–32
Sale Knitting Company, **12** 501. *See also* Tultex Corporation.
Salem Carpet Mills, Inc., **9** 467
Salen Energy A.B., **IV** 563
Sallie Mae. *See* Student Loan Marketing Association.
Sally Beauty Company, Inc., **8** 15–17
Salmon Carriers, **6** 383
Salmon River Power & Light Company, **12** 265
Salomon Inc., I 630–31; **II** 268, 400, 403, 406, 426, 432, 434, 441, **447–49; III** 221, 215, 721; **IV** 80, 137; **7** 114; **9** 378–79, 386; **11** 35, 371; **13** 331, **447–50 (upd.)** Inc.
Salora, **II** 69
Salsåkers Ångsågs, **IV** 338
Saltos del Sil, **II** 197
Salvation Army, **15** 510–11
Salzgitter AG, IV 128, 198, **200–01**
Sam Goody, **I** 613; **9** 360–61
Sam's Clubs, **V** 216–17; **8** 555–57; **12** 221, 335; **13** 548; **14** 393; **15** 470
Samancor Ltd., **IV** 92–93
Sambo's, **12** 510
Sambre-et-Moselle, **IV** 52
Samcor Glass, **III** 685
Samedan Oil Corporation, **11** 353
Samim, **IV** 422
Samkong Fat Ltd. Co., **III** 747
Samna Corp., **6** 256
Sampson's, **12** 220–21
Samsonite Corp., 6 50; **13** 311, **451–53**
Samsung Electronics Co., Ltd., 14 416–18
Samsung Group, I 515–17; II 53–54; **III** 143, 457–58, 517, 749; **IV** 519; **7** 233; **12** 211–12; **13** 387
Samuel Austin & Son Company, **8** 41
Samuel Meisel & Co., **11** 80–81
Samuel Montagu & Co., **II** 319
Samuel Moore & Co., **I** 155
Samuel Samuel & Co., **IV** 530, 542
Samwha Paper Co., **III** 748
San Antonio Public Service Company, **6** 473
San Diego Gas & Electric Company, V 711–14; 6 590; **11** 272
San Giorgio Macaroni Inc., **II** 511
San Miguel Corporation, I 221; **15 428–30**
SAN-MIC Trading Co., **IV** 327
Sanborn Co., **III** 142; **6** 237
Sanders Associates, Inc., **9** 324; **13** 127–28
Sanderson & Porter, **I** 376
Sanderson Computers, **10** 500
Sanderson Farms, Inc., 15 425–27
Sandoz Ltd., I 632–33, **671–73**, 675; **7** 315, 452; **8** 108–09, 215; **10** 48, 199; **11** 173; **12** 388; **15** 139
Sandpoint, **12** 562
Sandvik AB, III 426–27; **IV 202–04**
Sandwell, Inc., **6** 491
SANFLO Co., Ltd., **IV** 327
Sangu Express Company, **V** 463
Sanitary Farm Dairies, Inc., **7** 372

Sanitas Food Co., **II** 523
Sanjushi Bank, **II** 347
Sanka Coffee Corp., **II** 531
Sankin Kai Group, **II** 274
Sanko K.K., **I** 432, 492
Sanko Steamship Co., **I** 494; **II** 311
Sankyo Company Ltd., I 330, **674–75; III** 760; **8** 153
Sanlam, **IV** 91, 93, 535
Sano Railway Company, **6** 430
Sanofi Group, I 304, **676–77; III** 18; **IV** 546; **7** 484–85
Sanseisha Co., **IV** 326
Santa Ana Savings and Loan, **10** 339
Santa Cruz Operation, **6** 244
Santa Cruz Portland Cement, **II** 490
Santa Fe Industries, **II** 448; **12** 19; **13** 448
Santa Fe International, **IV** 451–52
Santa Fe Pacific Corporation (SFP), V 507–09
Santa Fe Railway, **12** 278
Santa Fe South Pacific Corporation, **6** 599
Santa Fe Southern Pacific Corp., **III** 512; **IV** 721; **6** 150; **9** 391
Santa Rosa Savings and Loan, **10** 339
Santiam Lumber Co., **IV** 358
Sanus Corp. Health Systems, **III** 317
Sanwa Bank, Ltd., II 276, 326, **347–48**, 442, 511; **III** 188, 759; **IV** 150–51; **7** 119; **15** 43, **431–33 (upd.)**
Sanyo Chemical Manufacturing Co., **III** 758
Sanyo Electric Company, Ltd., I 516; **II** 55–56, **91–92; III** 569, 654; **6** 101; **14** 535
Sanyo Ethylene Co. Ltd., **IV** 476
Sanyo Petrochemical Co. Ltd., **IV** 476
Sanyo Railway Co., **I** 506; **II** 325
Sanyo-Kokusaku Pulp Co., Ltd., IV 326, **327–28**
SAP AG, **11** 78
Sapac, **I** 643
Sapirstein Greeting Card Company, **7** 23
Sappi Ltd., IV 91–93
Sapporo Breweries, Ltd., I 9, 220, 270, **282–83**, 508, 615; **II** 326; **13 454–56 (upd.)**
Sara Lee Corporation, I 15, 30; **II** **571–73**, 675; **7** 113 **8** 262; **10** 219–20; **11** 15, 486; **12** 494, 502, 531; **15** 359, **434–37 (upd.),** 507
Sarawak Trading, **14** 448
Sargent & Lundy, **6** 556
Sarget S.A., **IV** 71
SARL, **12** 152
SARMA, **III** 623–24
Saros Corp., **15** 474
Sarotti A.G., **II** 546
Sarpe, **IV** 591
SAS. *See* Scandinavian Airlines System.
SAS Institute Inc., 10 476–78
Saseba Heavy Industries, **II** 274
Saskatchewan Oil and Gas Corporation, **13** 556–57
Sasol Limited, IV 533–35
Sason Corporation, **V** 187
SAT. *See* Stockholms Allmänna Telefonaktiebolag.
Satellite Business Systems, **III** 182
Satellite Information Services, **II** 141
Satellite Software International, **10** 556
Satellite Television PLC, **IV** 652; **7** 391
Satellite Transmission and Reception Specialist Company, **11** 184

Säteri Oy, **IV** 349
Sato Yasusaburo, **I** 266
Saturday Evening Post Co., **II** 208; **9** 320
Saturn Corporation, **III** 593, 760; **7** 461–64
SATV. *See* Satellite Television PLC.
Saucona Iron Co., **IV** 35; **7** 48
Sauder Woodworking Co., **12** 433–34
Saudi Arabian Airlines, **6** 84, 114–16
Saudi Arabian Oil Company, **IV** 536–39.
  See also Arabian American Oil Co.
Saudi Arabian Parsons Limited, **8** 416
Saudi British Bank, **II** 298
Saudi Consolidated Electric Co., **IV** 538
Saudi Refining Inc., **IV** 539
Saudia. *See* Saudi Arabian Airlines.
Sauer Motor Co., **I** 177
Saul Lerner & Co., **II** 450
Saunders-Roe Ltd., **IV** 658
Sav-on Drug, **II** 605; **12** 477
Sav-X, **9** 186
Savacentre Ltd., **II** 658; **13** 284
Savage Shoes, Ltd., **III** 529
Savannah Foods & Industries, Inc., **7** 465–67
Savannah Gas Company, **6** 448
Save & Prosper Group, **10** 277
Save Mart, **14** 397
Save-A-Lot, **II** 682; **11** 228
Saviem, **III** 543
Savin, **III** 159
Savings of America, **II** 182
Savio, **IV** 422
Oy Savo-Karjalan Tukkuliike, **8** 293
Savon Sellu Mills, **IV** 315
Savory Milln, **II** 369
Savoy Group, **I** 248; **IV** 705
Savoy Industries, **12** 495
Sawyer Electrical Manufacturing Company, **11** 4
Sawyer Industries, Inc., **13** 532
Sawyer Research Products, Inc., **14** 81
Saxby, S.A., **13** 385
Saxon and Norman Cement Co., **III** 670
Saxon Oil, **11** 97
Sayama Sekiyu, **IV** 554
SBC. *See* Southwestern Bell Corporation.
SBC, **15** 197
SBC Portfolio Management International, Inc., **II** 369
SBC Warburg, **14** 419–21
Sberbank, **II** 242
SCA. *See* Svenska Cellulosa Aktiebolaget.
SCA Services, Inc., **V** 754; **9** 109
Scaldia Paper BV, **15** 229
Scali, McCabe and Sloves Co., **I** 27
Scan Screen, **IV** 600
Scana Corporation, **6** 574–76
Scandinavian Airlines System, **I** 107, 119–20, 121; **6** 96, 122
Scandinavian Bank, **II** 352
Scandinavian Trading Co., **I** 210
ScanDust, **III** 625
Scania-Vabis, **I** 197–98. *See also* Saab-Scania AB.
Scarborough Public Utilities Commission, **9** 461–62
SCEcorp, **V** 713–14, **715–17**; **6** 590
Schaffhausenschor Bankverein, **II** 281
Schaper Mfg. Co., **12** 168
Scharff-Koken Manufacturing Co., **IV** 286
Scharnow, **II** 163–64
Schaum Publishing Co., **IV** 636
Schauman Wood Oy, **IV** 277, 302

Schein Pharmaceutical Inc., **13** 77
Schenker-Rhenus Ag, **6** 424–26
Schenley Industries Inc., **I** 226, 285; **9** 449; **10** 181
Scherer. *See* R.P. Scherer.
Schering A.G., **I** 681–82, 684, 701; **10** 214; **14** 60
Schering-Plough Corporation, **I** 682, **683–85**; **II** 590; **III** 45, 61; **11** 142, 207; **14** 58, 60, **422–25** (upd.)
Schiavi Homes, Inc., **14** 138
Schicht Co., **II** 588
Schick Shaving, **I** 711; **III** 55
Schieffelin & Co., **I** 272
Schindler Holdings, **II** 122; **12** 546
Schlage Lock Co., **III** 526
Schleppschiffahrtsgesellschaft Unterweser, **IV** 140
Schlesischer Bankverein, **II** 278
Schlitz Brewing Co., **I** 218, 255, 268, 270, 291, 600; **10** 100; **12** 338
Schlumberger Limited, **III** 429, 499, **616–18**; **13** 323
Schmalbach-Lubeca-Werke A.G., **15** 128
Schmidt, **I** 255
Schneider Co., **III** 113
Schneider et Cie, **IV** 25
Schneider National Inc., **13** 550–51
Schneider S.A., **II** 93–94
Schocken Books, **13** 429
Scholastic Corporation, **10** 479–81
Scholl Inc., **I** 685; **14** 424
Scholz Homes Inc., **IV** 115
Schott Glaswerke, **III** 445–47
Schottenstein Stores Corp., **14** 426–28
Schrader Bellows, **III** 603
Schrock Cabinet Company, **13** 564
Schroder Darling & Co., **II** 389
Schroeter, White and Johnson, **III** 204
Schuitema, **II** 642
Schuler Chocolates, **15** 65
Schuller International, Inc., **11** 421
Schumacher Co., **II** 624
Schuykill Energy Resources, **12** 41
Schwabe-Verlag, **7** 42
Schwan's Sales Enterprises, Inc., **7** 468–70
Schwartz Iron & Metal Co., **13** 142
Schweiz Allgemeine, **III** 377
Schweiz Transport-Vericherungs-Gesellschaft, **III** 410
Schweizer Rück Holding AG, **III** 377
Schweizerische Bankgesellschaft AG, **II** 379; **V** 104
Schweizerische Kreditanstalt, **III** 375, 410; **6** 489
Schweizerische Nordostbahn, **6** 424
Schweizerische Post-, Telefon- und Telegrafen-Betriebe, **V** 321–24
Schweizerische Ruckversicherungs-Gesellschaft. *See* Swiss Reinsurance Company.
Schweizerische Unfallversicherungs-Actiengesellschaft in Winterthur, **III** 402
Schweizerische Unionbank, **II** 368
Schweizerischer Bankverein, **II** 368
Schweppe, Paul & Gosse, **II** 476
Schweppes Ltd., **I** 220, 288; **II** 476–77.
  See also Cadbury Schweppes PLC.
Schwitzer, **II** 420
SCI. *See* Service Corporation International.
SCI Systems, Inc., **9** 463–64; **12** 451
Scicon, **14** 317

Science Applications International Corporation, **15** 438–40
Scientific Communications, Inc., **10** 97
Scientific Data Systems, **II** 44; **III** 172; **6** 289; **10** 365
Scientific Games, Inc., **III** 431
Scientific-Atlanta, Inc., **6** 335–37
SciMed Life Systems, **III** 18–19
Scioto Bank, **9** 475
Scitex Corp. Ltd., **15** 148, 229
SCM Corp., **I** 29; **III** 502; **IV** 330; **7** 208; **8** 223–24
SCOA Industries, Inc., **13** 260
Scor SA, **III** 394
Scot Bowyers, **II** 587
Scot Lad Foods, **14** 411
Scotia Securities, **II** 223
Scotiabank. *See* The Bank of Nova Scotia.
Scotsman Industries, **II** 420
Scott Communications, Inc., **10** 97
Scott Fetzer Company, **III** 214; **12** 435–37, 554–55
Scott, Foresman, **IV** 675
Scott Graphics, **IV** 289; **8** 483
Scott Lithgow, **III** 516; **7** 232
Scott Paper Company, **III** 749; **IV** 258, 289–90, 311, 325, 327, **329–31**; **8** 483
Scott-McDuff, **II** 107
Scottish & Newcastle plc, **13** 458; **15** 441–44
Scottish Aviation, **I** 50
Scottish Brick, **14** 250
Scottish Electric, **6** 453
Scottish General Fire Assurance Corp., **III** 256
Scottish Hydro-Electric PLC, **13** 457–59
Scottish Inns of America, Inc., **13** 362
Scottish Land Development, **III** 501; **7** 207
Scottish Malt Distillers, **I** 240
Scottish Union Co., **III** 358
Scotts Stores, **I** 289
Scotty's Inc., **12** 234
Scovill Mfg., **IV** 11
Scranton Corrugated Box Company, Inc., **8** 102
Scranton Plastics Laminating Corporation, **8** 359
Screen Gems, **II** 135–36; **12** 74
SCREG, **I** 563
Scribbans-Kemp Ltd., **II** 594
Scriha & Deyhle, **10** 196
Scripps-Howard, Inc., **IV** 607–09, 628; **7** 64, 157–59
Scudder, Stevens & Clark, **II** 448; **13** 448
Scurlock Oil Co., **IV** 374
SDC Coatings, **III** 715
SDGE. *See* San Diego Gas & Electric Company.
SDK Parks, **IV** 724
Sea Diamonds Ltd., **IV** 66; **7** 123
Sea Far of Norway, **II** 484
Sea Insurance Co. Ltd., **III** 220
Sea Life Centre Aquariums, **10** 439
Sea Ray, **III** 444
Sea World, Inc., **IV** 623–24; **12** 224
Sea-Alaska Products, **II** 494
Sea-Land Service Inc., **I** 476; **9** 510–11
Seaboard Finance Company, **13** 63
Seaboard Fire and Marine Insurance Co., **III** 242
Seaboard Life Insurance Co., **III** 193
Seaboard Lumber Sales, **IV** 307
Seaboard Oil Co., **IV** 552
Seaboard Surety Co., **III** 357

Seabourn Cruise Lines, **6** 368
Seabury & Smith, **III** 283
Seacoast Products, **III** 502
Seafield Estate and Consolidated
  Plantations Berhad, **14** 448
Seafirst. *See* Seattle First National Bank,
  Inc.
SeaFirst Corp., **II** 228
Seagate Technology, Inc., 6 230–31; **8**
  466–68; **9** 57; **10** 257, 403–04, 459; **11**
  56, 234; **13** 483
Seagram Company Ltd., I 26, 240, 244,
  284–86, 329, 403; **II** 456, 468; **IV** 401;
  7 155
Seagull Energy Corporation, 11 440–42
Seal Products, Inc., **12** 264
Sealand Petroleum Co., **IV** 400
Sealectro, **III** 434
Sealed Air Corporation, 14 429–31
Sealed Power Corporation, I 199–200;
  10 492–94
Sealtest, **14** 205
Sealy Inc., 12 438–40
Seamless Rubber Co., **III** 613
Seaquist Manufacturing Corporation, **9**
  413–14
Searle & Co. *See* G.D. Searle & Co.
Sears plc, V 177–79
Sears, Roebuck & Co., **I** 26, 146, 516,
  556; **II** 18, 60, 134, 331, 411, 414; **III**
  259, 265, 340, 536, 598, 653–55; **V**
  180–83; **6** 12–13; **7** 166, 479; **8** 224,
  287–89; **9** 44, 65–66 156, 210, 213,
  219, 235–36, 430–31, 538; **10** 10,
  50–52, 199, 236–37, 288, 304–05,
  490–91; **11** 62, 349, 393, 498; **12** 54,
  96–98, 309, 311, 315, 430–31, 439,
  522, 548, 557; **13** 165, 260, 268, 277,
  411, 545, 550, 562–63; **14** 62; **15** 402,
  470
Seashore Transportation Co., **13** 398
Season-all Industries, **III** 735
SEAT. *See* Sociedad Española de
  Automoviles de Turismo.
Seattle Electric Company, **6** 565
Seattle First National Bank Inc., 8
  469–71
Seattle Times Company, 15 445–47
Seaview Oil Co., **IV** 393
Seaway Express, **9** 510
Seaway Food Town, Inc., 9 452; **15**
  448–50
SEB-Fastigheter A.B., **II** 352
SECA, **IV** 401
SECDO, **III** 618
SECO Industries, **III** 614
Secon GmbH, **13** 160
Second Bank of the United States, **II** 213;
  9 369
Second National Bank, **II** 254
Second National Bank of Bucyrus, **9** 474
Second National Bank of Ravenna, **9** 474
Secoroc, **III** 427
Le Secours, **III** 211
SecPac. *See* Security Pacific Corporation.
Secure Horizons, **11** 378–79
Securicor, **11** 547
Securitas Esperia, **III** 208
Securities Industry Automation
  Corporation, **9** 370
Securities International, Inc., **II** 440–41
Security Connecticut Life Insurance Co.,
  III 276
Security Engineering, **III** 472

Security Express, **10** 269
Security First National Bank of Los
  Angeles, **II** 349
Security Life and Annuity Company, **11**
  213
Security Management Company, **8** 535–36
Security National Bank, **II** 251, 336
Security National Corp., **10** 246
Security Pacific Corporation, II 349–50,
  422; **III** 366; **8** 45, 48; **11** 447
Security Trust Company, **9** 229, 388
Security Union Title Insurance Co., **10**
  43–44
Sedat Eldem, **13** 475
Sedgwick Group PLC, **I** 427; **III** 280, 366;
  10 38
SEDTCO Pty., **13** 61
See's Candies, **III** 213
Seeburg Corporation, **II** 22; **III** 430; **15**
  538
Seed Restaurant Group Inc., **13** 321
Seed Solutions, Inc., **11** 491
Seeger Refrigerator Co., **III** 653; **12** 548
Seeger-Orbis, **III** 624
SEEQ Technology, Inc., **9** 114; **13** 47
SEG, **I** 463
Sega of America, Inc., 7 396; **10** 124–25,
  284–86, **482–85**
Segespar, **II** 265
Sego Milk Products Company, **7** 428
Seguros El Corte Inglés, **V** 52
Seibels, Bruce & Co., **11** 394–95
Seiberling Rubber Company, **V** 244
Seibu Department Stores, Ltd., II 273; **V**
  184–86
Seibu Railway Co. Ltd., V 187, **510–11**,
  526
Seibu Saison, **6** 207
Seijo Green Plaza Co., **I** 283
Seikatsu-Soko, **V** 210
Seiko Corporation, I 488; **III 619–21**; **11**
  46; **12** 317; **13** 122
Seikosha Co. Ltd., **III** 619
Seine, **III** 391
Seino Transportation Company, Ltd., 6
  427–29
Seismograph Service Corp., **II** 86; **11** 413
Seiwa Fudosan Co., **I** 283
Seiyu, Ltd., V 187–89; **10** 389
Seizo-sha, **12** 483
Sekisui Chemical Co., Ltd., III 741–43
SEL, **I** 193, 463
Selden, **I** 164, 300
Select-Line Industries, **9** 543
Selection Trust, **IV** 67, 380, 565
Selective Auto and Fire Insurance Co. of
  America, **III** 353
Selective Insurance Co., **III** 191
Selenia, **I** 467; **II** 86
Self Service Restaurants, **II** 613
The Self-Locking Carton Company, **14** 163
Selfridge (Department Store), **V** 94,
  177–78
Selleck Nicholls, **III** 691
Seltel, **6** 33
Semarca, **11** 523
Sembler Company, **11** 346
Seminole Electric Cooperative, **6** 583
Seminole Fertilizer, **7** 537–38
Semrau and Sons, **II** 601
SEN AG, **IV** 128
Senelle-Maubeuge, **IV** 227
Senior Corp., **11** 261
Senshusha, **I** 506

Sensormatic Electronics Corp., 11
  443–45
Sentinel Foam & Envelope Corporation, **14**
  430
Sentinel Group, **6** 295
Sentinel Savings and Loan, **10** 339
Sentinel Technologies, **III** 38
Sentinel-Star Co., **IV** 683
Sentrust, **IV** 92
Sentry, **II** 624
Sentry Insurance Company, **10** 210
Senyo Kosakuki Kenkyujo, **III** 595
Seohan Development Co., **III** 516; **7** 232
Sepa, **II** 594
AB Separator, **III** 417–19
SEPIC, **I** 330
Sept, **IV** 325
Sequa Corp., 13 460–63
Séquanaise, **III** 391–92
Sequent Computer Systems Inc., **10** 363
Sequoia Insurance, **III** 270
Sequoia Pharmacy Group, **13** 150
Sera-Tec, **V** 175–76
Seraco Group, **V** 182
Serck Group, **I** 429
SEREB, **I** 45; **7** 10
Serewatt AG, **6** 491
Sergeant Drill Co., **III** 525
Sero-Genics, Inc., **V** 174–75
Servam Corp., **7** 471–73
Servel, Inc., **III** 479
Service America Corp., 7 471–73
Service Bureau Corp., **III** 127
Service Control Corp. *See* Angelica
  Corporation.
Service Corporation International, 6
  293–95
Service Games Company, **10** 482
Service Merchandise Company, Inc., V
  190–92; **6** 287; **9** 400
Service Partner, **I** 120
Service Pipe Line Co., **IV** 370
Service Q. General Service Co., **I** 109
Service Systems, **III** 103
Servicemaster Limited Partnership, 6
  44–46; **13** 199
Services Maritimes des Messageries
  Impériales. *See* Compagnie des
  Messageries Maritimes.
Servicios Financieros Quadrum S.A., **14**
  156
Servisco, **II** 608
SERVISTAR, **12** 8
ServoChem A.B., **I** 387
Servomation Corporation, **7** 472–73
Servoplan, S.A., **8** 272
Sesame Street Book Club, **13** 560
Sespe Oil, **IV** 569
SET, **I** 466
SETCAR, **14** 458
Settsu Marine and Fire Insurance Co., **III**
  367
Seven Arts Productions, Ltd., **II** 147, 176
7-Eleven. *See* The Southland Corporation.
Seven-Up Bottling Co. of Los Angeles, **II**
  121
Seven-Up Co., **I** 245, 257; **II** 468, 477
Severn Trent PLC, 12 441–43
Seversky Aircraft Corporation, **9** 205
Sevin-Rosen Partners, **III** 124; **6** 221
Sewell Coal Co., **IV** 181
Sewell Plastics, Inc., **10** 222
Seybold Machine Co., **II** 37; **6** 602
Seymour Electric Light Co., **13** 182

Seymour International Press Distributor Ltd., **IV** 619
Seymour Press, **IV** 619
Seymour Trust Co., **13** 467
SGC. *See* Supermarkets General Corporation.
SGLG, Inc., **13** 367
SGS Corp., **II** 117; **11** 46
Shaffer Clarke, **II** 594
Shaklee Corporation, 12 444–46
Shalco Systems, **13** 7
Shamrock Advisors, Inc., **8** 305
Shamrock Capital L.P., **7** 81–82
Shamrock Holdings, **III** 609; **7** 438; **9** 75; **11** 556
Shamrock Oil & Gas Co., **I** 403–04; **IV** 409; **7** 308
Shanghai Crown Maling Packaging Co. Ltd., **13** 190
Shanghai Hotels Co., **IV** 717
Shanghai International Finance Company Limited, **15** 433
Shared Financial Systems, Inc., **10** 501
Shared Medical Systems Corporation, 14 432–34
Shared Technologies Inc., **12** 71
Shared Use Network Systems, Inc., **8** 311
Sharon Steel Corp., **I** 497; **7** 360–61; **8** 536; **13** 158, 249
Sharon Tank Car Corporation, **6** 394
Sharp & Dohme, Incorporated, **I** 650; **11** 289, 494
Sharp Corporation, I 476; **II 95–96; III** 14, 428, 455, 480; **6** 217, 231; **11** 45; **12 447–49 (upd.); 13** 481
The Sharper Image Corporation, 10 486–88
Sharples Co., **I** 383
Sharples Separator Co., **III** 418–20
Shasta, **II** 571–73
Shaw Industries, 9 465–67
Shaw's Supermarkets, **II** 658–59
Shawell Precast Products, **14** 248
Shawinigan Water and Power Company, **6** 501–02
Shawmut National Corporation, II 207; **12** 31; **13 464–68**
Shea's Winnipeg Brewery Ltd., **I** 268
Shearson Lehman Brothers Holdings Inc., I 202; **II** 398–99, 450, 478; **III** 319; **8** 118; **9 468–70 (upd.); 10** 62–63; **11** 418; **12** 459; **15** 124, 463–64
Shearson Lehman Hutton Holdings Inc., II 339, 445, **450–52; III** 119; **9** 125; **10** 59, 63
Shedd's Food Products Company, **9** 318
Sheepbridge Engineering, **III** 495
Sheffield Banking Co., **II** 333
Sheffield Motor Co., **I** 158; **10** 292
Sheffield Twist Drill & Steel Co., **III** 624
Shelby Insurance Company, **10** 44–45
Shelby Steel Tube Co., **IV** 572; **7** 550
Shelby Williams Industries, Inc., 14 435–37
Shelf Life Inc. *See* King Kullen Grocery Co., Inc.
Shell. *See* Shell Transport and Trading Company p.l.c. *and* Shell Oil Company.
Shell Australia Ltd., **III** 728
Shell BV, **IV** 518
Shell Chemical Corporation, **IV** 410, 481, 531–32, 540; **8** 415
Shell Coal International, **IV** 532
Shell France, **12** 153

Shell Nederland BV, **V** 658–59
Shell Oil Company, I 20, 26, 569; **III** 559; **IV** 392, 400, 531, **540–41; 6** 382, 457; **8** 261–62; **11** 522; **14** 25, **438–40 (upd.)**
Shell Transport and Trading Company p.l.c., I 605; **II** 436, 459; **III** 522, 735; **IV** 363, 378–79, 381–82, 403, 412, 423, 425, 429, 440, 454, 466, 470, 472, 474, 484–86, 491, 505, 508, **530–32**, 564. *See also* Royal Dutch Petroleum Company *and* Royal Dutch/Shell.
Shell Western E & P, **7** 323
Shell Winning, **IV** 413–14
Sheller-Globe Corporation, I 201–02
Shelly Brothers, Inc., **15** 65
Shenley Laboratories, **I** 699
Shepard Warner Elevator Co., **III** 467
Shepard's Citations, Inc., **IV** 636–37
Shepherd Plating and Finishing Company, **13** 233
Shepler Equipment Co., **9** 512
Sheraton Corp. of America, **I** 463–64, 487; **III** 98–99; **11** 198; **13** 362–63
Sheridan Bakery, **II** 633
Sheridan Catheter & Instrument Corp., **III** 443
Sherix Chemical, **I** 682
Sherritt Gordon Mines, **7** 386–87; **12** 260
The Sherwin-Williams Company, III 744–46; 8 222, 224; **11** 384; **12** 7; **13 469–71 (upd.)**
Sherwood Medical Group, **I** 624; **III** 443–44; **10** 70
SHI Resort Development Co., **III** 635
ShianFu Optical Fiber, **III** 491
Shibaura Seisakusho Works, **I** 533; **12** 483
Shields & Co., **9** 118
Shikoku Coca-Cola Bottling Co., **IV** 297
Shikoku Drinks Co., **IV** 297
Shikoku Electric Power Company, Inc., V 718–20
Shikoku Machinery Co., **III** 634
Shimotsuke Electric Railway Company, **6** 431
Shimura Kako, **IV** 63
Shin Nippon Machine Manufacturing, **III** 634
Shin-Nihon Glass Co., **I** 221
Shinano Bank, **II** 291
Shinko Electric Co., Ltd., **IV** 129
Shinko Rayon Ltd., **I** 363; **V** 369–70
Shinriken Kogyo, **IV** 63
Shintech, **11** 159–60
Shinwa Tsushinki Co., **III** 593
Shiomi Casting, **III** 551
Shionogi & Co., Ltd., I 646, 651; **III 60–61; 11** 90, 290
Ship 'n Shore, **II** 503; **9** 156–57; **10** 324
Shipowners and Merchants Tugboat Company, **6** 382
Shiro Co., Ltd., **V** 96
Shirokiya Co., Ltd., **V** 199
Shiseido Company, Limited, II 273–74, 436; **III** 46, 48, **62–64; 8** 341, 343
Shoe Carnival Inc., 14 441–43
Shoe Corp., **I** 289
Shohin Kaihatsu Kenkyusho, **III** 595
Shoman Milk Co., **II** 538
Shonac Corp., **14** 427
Shoney's, Inc., 7 474–76; 14 453
Shop 'n Bag, **II** 624
Shop 'n Save, **II** 669, 682; **12** 220–21
Shop & Go, **II** 620

Shop Rite Foods Inc., **II** 672–74; **7** 105
ShopKo Stores, Inc., **II** 669–70
Shopwell/Food Emporium, **II** 638
Shore Manufacturing, **13** 165
Short Aircraft Co., **I** 50, 55, 92
Shoshi-Gaisha, **IV** 320
Shotton Paper Co. Ltd., **IV** 350
Showa Aircraft Industry Co., **I** 507–08
Showa Aluminum Corporation, **8** 374
Showa Bank, **II** 291–92
Showa Bearing Manufacturing Co., **III** 595
Showa Cotton Co., Ltd., **IV** 442
Showa Denko, **I** 493–94; **II** 292; **IV** 61
Showa Marutsutsu Co. Ltd., **8** 477
Showa Paper Co., **IV** 268
Showa Photo Industry, **III** 548
Showa Products Company, **8** 476
Showa Shell Sekiyu K.K., II 459; **IV 542–43**
ShowBiz Pizza Time, Inc., 12 123; **13 472–74; 15** 73
Showerings, **I** 215
Showtime, **II** 173; **7** 222–23; **9** 74
Shredded Wheat Co., **II** 543; **7** 366
Shreve and Company, **12** 312
Shrewsbury and Welshpool Old Bank, **II** 307
Shu Uemura, **III** 43
Shubrooks International Ltd., **11** 65
Shueisha, **IV** 598
Shuford Mills, Inc., **14** 430
Shugart Associates, **6** 230; **8** 466
Shull Lumber & Shingle Co., **IV** 306
Shun Fung Ironworks, **IV** 717
Shunan Shigyo Co., Ltd., **IV** 160
SHV Holdings N.V., **IV** 383; **14** 156
SI Holdings Inc., **10** 481
SIAS-MPA, **I** 281
Sibco Universal, S.A., **14** 429
SIBV/MS Holdings, **IV** 295
Sicard Inc., **I** 185
Siddeley Autocar Co., **III** 508
Sidélor, **IV** 226
Siderbrás, **IV** 125
Sidermex, **III** 581
Sidérurgie Maritime, **IV** 26
SIDMAR NV, **IV** 128
Siebe P.L.C., **13** 235
Siebel Group, **13** 544–45
Siegas, **III** 480
Siegler Heater Corp., **I** 481
Siemens A.G., I 74, 192, 409–11, 462, 478, 542; **II** 22, 25, 38, 80–82, **97–100**, 122, 257, 279; **III** 139, 154–55, 466, 482, 516, 724; **6** 215–16; **7** 232; **9** 11, 32, 44; **10** 16, 363; **11** 59, 196, 235, 397–98, 460; **12** 546; **13** 402; **14** 169, **444–47 (upd.); 15** 125
Sierra Designs, Inc., **10** 215–16
Sierra Health Services, Inc., 15 451–53
Sierra Leone Selection Trust, **IV** 66
Sierra On-Line Inc., 13 92, 114; **14** 263; **15 454–56**
Sierrita Resources, Inc., **6** 590
Sigma Coatings, **IV** 499
Sigma Network Systems, **11** 464
Sigma-Aldrich, I 690–91
Sigmor Corp., **IV** 410
Signal Companies, I 85, 414, 416; **III** 511–12; **6** 599; **11** 435
Signal Galaxies, **13** 127
Signal Oil & Gas Inc., **I** 71, 178; **IV** 382; **7** 537; **11** 278
Signalite, Inc., **10** 319

Signature Group, **V** 145
Signet Banking Corporation, 11 446–48
Signetics, **III** 684; **11** 56
Signode Industries, **III** 519
SIKEL NV, **IV** 128
Sikes Corporation, **III** 612
Sikorsky Aerospace, **I** 47, 84, 115, 530; **III** 458, 602; **9** 416; **10** 162
SIL&P. *See* Southern Illinois Light & Power Company.
Silenka, **III** 733
Silicon Beach Software, **10** 35
Silicon Compiler Systems, **11** 285
Silicon Graphics Inc., 9 471–73; 10 119, 257; **12** 323; **15** 149, 320
Silicon Microstructures, Inc., **14** 183
Silicon Systems Inc., **II** 110
Silo Holdings, **9** 65
Silo Inc., **V** 50; **10** 306, 468
Silver & Co., **I** 428
Silver Burdett Co., **IV** 672, 675; **7** 528
Silver City Casino, **6** 204
Silver Furniture Co., Inc., **15** 102, 104
Silver King Mines, **IV** 76
Silver Screen Partners, **II** 174
Silver's India Rubber Works & Telegraph Cable Co., **I** 428
Silverado Banking, **9** 199
Silverstar Ltd. S.p.A., **10** 113
Silvertown Rubber Co., **I** 428
Silvey Corp., **III** 350
Simca, **I** 154, 162; **11** 103
Sime Darby Berhad, 14 448–50
SIMEL S.A., **14** 27
Simkins Industries, Inc., **8** 174–75
Simms, **III** 556
Simon & Schuster Inc., II 155; **IV** 671–72; **13** 559
Simon Adhesive Products, **IV** 253
Simon de Wit, **II** 641
Simon Engineering, **11** 510
Simonius'sche Cellulosefabriken AG, **IV** 324
Simonize, **I** 371
AB Simpele, **IV** 347
Simplex Wire and Cable Co., **III** 643–45
Simplicity Pattern Company, **I** 447; **8** 349
Simpson Marketing, **12** 553
Simpsons, **V** 80
Sims Telephone Company, **14** 258
SimuFlite, **II** 10
Sinai Kosher Foods, **14** 537
Sincat, **IV** 453
Sinclair Coal Co., **IV** 170; **10** 447–48
Sinclair Crude Oil Purchasing Co., **IV** 369
Sinclair Oil Corp., **I** 355, 569; **IV** 376, 394, 456–57, 512, 575
Sinclair Paint Company, **12** 219
Sinclair Petrochemicals Inc., **IV** 456
Sinclair Pipe Line Co., **IV** 368–69
Sinclair Research Ltd., **III** 113
Sindo Ricoh Co., **III** 160
Singapore Airlines Ltd., 6 100, **117–18,** 123; **12** 192
Singapore Alpine Electronics Asia Pte. Ltd., **13** 31
Singapore Candle Company, **12** 393
Singapore Cement, **III** 718
Singapore Petroleum Co., **IV** 452
Singapore Straits Steamship Company, **6** 117
Singapour, **II** 556
Singareni Collieries Ltd., **IV** 48–49
Singer and Friedlander, **I** 592

Singer Company, **I** 540; **II** 9–11; **6** 27, 241; **9** 232; **11** 150; **13** 521–22. *See also* Bicoastal Corp.
Singer Controls, **I** 155
Singer Hardware & Supply Co., **9** 542
Singer Sewing Machine Co., **12** 46
Single Service Containers Inc., **IV** 286
Singleton Seafood, **II** 494
Singular Software, **9** 80
Sioux City Gas and Electric Company, **6** 523–24
SIP. *See* Società Italiana per L'Esercizio delle Telecommunicazioni p.A.
SIRCOMA, **10** 375
Sirloin Stockade, **10** 331
Sirrine. *See* CRSS Inc.
Sirrine Environmental Consultants, **9** 110
Sirte Oil Co., **IV** 454
Sisters Chicken & Biscuits, **8** 564
SIT-Siemens. *See* Italtel.
Sitzmann & Heinlein GmbH, **IV** 198–99
Six Companies, Inc., **IV** 121; **7** 355
Six Flags Corp., **III** 431; **IV** 676
600 Fanuc Robotics, **III** 482–83
61 Going to the Game!, **14** 293
Sizes Unlimited, **V** 115
Sizzler International Inc., **15** 361–62
Skånes Enskilda Bank, **II** 351
Skånska Ättiksfabriken, **I** 385
Skadden, Arps, Slate, Meagher & Flom, **10** 126–27
Skaggs Drugs Centers, **II** 602–04; **7** 20
Skaggs-Albertson's Properties, **II** 604
Skagit Nuclear Power Plant, **6** 566
Skandinaviska Enskilda Banken, II 351–53, 365–66; **IV** 203
Skanska AB, **IV** 204
Skelly Oil Co., **IV** 575
SKF Industries Inc., **III** 623–24
Skidmore, Owings & Merrill, 13 475–76
Skil-Craft Playthings, Inc., **13** 560
Skillware, **9** 326
Skinner Macaroni Co., **II** 511
Skis Rossignol S.A., 15 460–62
Skönvik, **IV** 338
SKW-Trostberg AG, **IV** 232
Sky Channel, **IV** 652
Sky Climber Inc., **11** 436
Sky Courier, **6** 345
Sky Merchant, Inc., **V** 78
Sky Television, **IV** 652–53; **7** 391–92
Skyband, Inc., **IV** 652; **7** 391; **12** 359
SkyBox International Inc., **15** 72–73
Skywalker Sound, **12** 322
Skyway Airlines, **6** 78; **11** 299
Slade Gorton & Company, **13** 243
Slater Co. Foods, **II** 607
Slater Systems, Inc., **13** 48
Slick Airways, **6** 388
Slim Fast, **12** 531
Slip-X Safety Treads, **9** 72
SLN-Peñarroya, **IV** 108
Slots-A-Fun, **6** 204
Slough Estates plc, IV 722–25
AB Small Business Investment Co., Inc., **13** 111–12
SMALLCO, **III** 340
Smalley Transportation Company, **6** 421–23
SMAN. *See* Societe Mecanique Automobile du Nord.
Smart & Final Inc., **12** 153–54
Smart Shirts Ltd., **8** 288–89
Smedley's, **II** 513

Smethwick Drop Forgings, **III** 494
Smirnoff, **14** 212
Smith & Hawken, **10** 215, 217
Smith Barney Inc., I 614; **III** 569; **6** 410; **10** 63; **13** 328; **15 463–65**
Smith Bros., **I** 711
Smith Corona Corp., III 502; **7** 209; **13** 477–80; **14** 76
Smith International, Inc., III 429; **15** 466–68
Smith Mackenzie & Co., **III** 522
Smith McDonell Stone and Co., **14** 97
Smith Meter Co., **11** 4
Smith New Court PLC, **13** 342
Smith Packaging Ltd., **14** 429
Smith Parts Co., **11** 3
Smith Transfer Corp., **II** 607–08; **13** 49
Smith's Food & Drug Centers, Inc., 8 472–74
Smith's Stampings, **III** 494
Smith-Higgins, **III** 9–10
Smithfield Foods, Inc., 7 477–78, 524–25
SmithKline Beckman Corporation, I 389, 636, 640, 644, 646, 657, **692–94,** 696; **II** 331; **III** 65–66; **14** 46, 53
SmithKline Beecham PLC, III 65–67; 8 210; **9** 347; **10** 47, 471; **11** 9, 90, 337; **13** 77; **14** 58
Smiths Bank, **II** 333
Smiths Food Group, Ltd., **II** 502; **10** 323
Smiths Industries, **III** 555
Smitty's Super Valu Inc., **II** 663–64; **12** 391
SMS, **IV** 226; **7** 401
Smucker. *See* The J.M. Smucker Company.
Smurfit Companies, **IV** 295–96
SN Repal. *See* Société Nationale de Recherche de Pétrole en Algérie.
Snack Ventures Europe, **10** 324
Snam Montaggi, **IV** 420
Snam Progetti, **IV** 420, 422
Snap-on Tools Corporation, III 628; **7 479–80**
Snapper, **I** 447
Snapple Beverage Corporation, 11 449–51; 12 411
Snappy Car Rentals, **6** 393
SNE Enterprises, Inc., **12** 397
SNEA. *See* Société Nationale Elf Aquitaine.
SNET. *See* Southern New England Telecommunications Corporation.
SNMC Management Corporation, **11** 121
Snoqualmie Falls Plant, **6** 565
Snow Brand Milk Products Company, Limited, II 574–75
Snow King Frozen Foods, **II** 480
Snowy Mountains Hydroelectric Authority, **IV** 707; **13** 118
SNPA, **IV** 453
SnyderGeneral Corp., **8** 321
Soap Opera Magazine, **10** 287
Sobrom, **I** 341
Sobu Railway Company, **6** 431
Socal. *See* Standard Oil Company (California).
SOCAR, **IV** 505
Sochiku, **9** 30
Sociade Intercontinental de Compressores Hermeticos SICOM, S.A., **8** 515
La Sociale di A. Mondadori & C., **IV** 585
La Sociale, **IV** 585
Sociedad Alfa-Laval, **III** 419

Sociedad Bilbaina General de Credito, **II** 194

Sociedad Española de Automobiles del Turismo S.A. (SEAT), **I** 207, 459–60; **6** 47–48; **11** 550

Sociedade Anónima Concessionária de Refinacao em Portugal. *See* SACOR.

Sociedade de Lubrificantes e Combustiveis, **IV** 505

Sociedade Nacional de Petróleos, **IV** 504

Sociedade Portuguesa de Petroquimica, **IV** 505

Sociedade Portuguesa e Navios-Tanques. *See* SOPONATA.

Società Anonima Fabbrica Italiana di Automobili, **I** 161

Società Anonima Lombarda Fabbrica Automobili, **13** 27

Società Azionaria Imprese Perforazioni, **IV** 419–20

Società Concessioni e Costruzioni Autostrade, **I** 466

Società Edison, **II** 86

Societa Esercizio Fabbriche Automobili e Corse Ferrari, **13** 219

Società Finanziaria Idrocarburi, **IV** 421

Società Finanziaria Telefonica per Azioni, **I** 465–66; **V** 325–27

Società Generale di Credito Mobiliare, **II** 191

Società Idrolettrica Piemonte, **I** 465–66

Societa Italiana Gestione Sistemi Multi Accesso, **6** 69

Società Italiana per L'Esercizio delle Telecommunicazioni p.A., **I** 466–67; **V** 325–27

Società Italiana per la Infrastrutture e l'Assetto del Territoria, **I** 466

Società Italiana Pirelli, **V** 249

Società Italiana Vetro, **IV** 421

Società Nazionale Metanodotti, **IV** 419–21

Società Ravennate Metano, **IV** 420

Società Reale Mutua, **III** 207

Société Air France. *See* Groupe Air France.

Societe Anonima Italiana Ing. Nicola Romeo & Company, **13** 27

Societe Anonomie Alfa Romeo, **13** 28

Societe Anonyme Automobiles Citroen, **7** 35–36

Société Anonyme de la Manufactures des Glaces et Produits Chimiques de Saint-Gobain, Chauny et Cirey, **III** 676

Société Anonyme des Ciments Luxembourgeois, **IV** 25

Société Anonyme des Hauts Fourneaux et Aciéries de Differdange-St. Ingbert-Rumelange, **IV** 26

Société Anonyme des Mines du Luxembourg et des Forges de Sarrebruck, **IV** 24

Societe Anonyme Francaise Timken, **8** 530

Société Anonyme Telecommunications, **III** 164

Société, Auxiliaire d'Entrepreses SA, **13** 206

Société Belge de Banque, **II** 294–95

Societe BIC, S.A., **III** 29; **8** 60–61

Société Calédonia, **IV** 107

Société Centrale Union des Assurances de Paris, **III** 391, 393

Société Chimiques des Usines du Rhône, **I** 388

Societe Commerciale Citroen, **7** 36

Société d'Ougrée-Marihaye, **IV** 51

Societe de Construction des Batignolles, **II** 93

Société de Crédit Agricole, **II** 264

Société de Développements et d'Innovations des Marchés Agricoles et Alimentaires, **II** 576

Société de Diffusion de Marques, **II** 576

Société de Diffusion Internationale Agro-Alimentaire, **II** 577

Societé de garantie des Crédits à court terme, **II** 233

Société de l'Oléoduc de la Sarre a.r.l., **IV** 197

Société de Prospection Électrique, **III** 616

La Société de Traitement des Minerais de Nickel, Cobalt et Autres, **IV** 107

Société des Eaux d'Evian, **II** 474

Société des Forges d'Eich–Metz et Cie, **IV** 24

Société des Forges et Aciéries du Nord-Est, **IV** 226

Société des Forges et Fonderies de Montataire, **IV** 226

Société des Grandes Entreprises de Distribution, Inno-France, **V** 58

Société des Hauts Fourneaux et Forges de Denain-Anzin, **IV** 226

Société des Mines du Luxembourg et de Sarrebruck, **IV** 25

Société des Pétroles d'Afrique Equatoriale, **IV** 545; **7** 482

Société des Usines Chimiques des Laboratoires Français, **I** 669

Société des Vins de France, **I** 281

Société Électrométallurgique Francaise, **IV** 173

Société European de Semi-Remorques, **7** 513

Societé Européenne de Brasseries, **II** 474–75

Société Financiére Européenne, **II** 202–03, 233

Société Française des Cables Electriques Bertrand-Borel, **9** 9

Société Française des Teintures Inoffensives pour Cheveux, **III** 46

Société Française pour l'Exploitation du Pétrole, **IV** 557

Société Gélis-Poudenx-Sans, **IV** 108

Société Générale, **II** 233, 266, 295, **354–56**; **9** 148; **13** 203, 206

Société Générale de Banque, **II** 279, 295, 319; **14** 169

Société Générale de Belgique, **II** 270, 294–95; **IV** 26; **10** 13

Société Générale pour favoriser l'Industrie nationale, **II** 294

Société Industrielle Belge des Pétroles, **IV** 498–99

Société Internationale Pirelli S.A., **V** 250

Société Irano-Italienne des Pétroles, **IV** 466

Société Le Nickel, **IV** 107–08, 110

Societe Mecanique Automobile de l'Est/du Nord, **7** 37

Société Métallurgique, **IV** 25–26, 227

Société Minière de Bakwanga, **IV** 67

Société Minière des Terres Rouges, **IV** 25–26

Société Nationale de Recherche de Pétrole en Algérie, **IV** 545, 559; **7** 482

Société Nationale de Transport et de Commercialisation des Hydrocarbures, **IV** 423

Société Nationale des Chemins de Fer Français, **V** 512–15

Société Nationale Elf Aquitaine, **I** 303–04, 670, 676–77; **II** 260; **IV** 174, 397–98, 424, 451, 453–54, 472–74, 499, 506, 515–16, 518, 525, 535, **544–47**, 559–60; **V** 628; **7** 481–85 **(upd.)**; **8** 452; **11** 97; **12** 153

Société Nationale pour la Recherche, la Production, le Transport, la Transformation et la Commercialisation des Hydrocarbures, **IV** 423–24

Société Nord Africaine des Ciments Lafarge, **III** 703

Societe Parisienne pour l'Industrie Electrique, **II** 93

Société pour l'Eportation de Grandes Marques, **I** 281

Société pour l'Étude et la Realisation d'Engins Balistiques. *See* SEREB.

Société pour L'Exploitation de la Cinquième Chaîne, **6** 374

Societe Vendeenne des Emballages, **9** 305

Societe-Hydro-Air S.a.r.L., **9** 27

Society Corporation, **9** 474–77

Society of Lloyd's, **III** 278–79

SOCO Chemical Inc., **8** 69

Socombel, **IV** 497

Socony. *See* Standard Oil Co. (New York).

Socony Mobil Oil Co., Inc., **IV** 465; **7** 353

Sodak Gaming, Inc., **9** 427

Sodastream Holdings, **II** 477

SODIAAL, **II** 577

SODIMA, **II** 576–77

Sodyeco, **I** 673

Soekor, **IV** 93

Sofiran, **IV** 467

Sofrem, **IV** 174

Softbank Corp., **12** 562; **13** 481–83

Softsel Computer Products, **12** 334–35

SoftSolutions Technology Corporation, **10** 558

Software AG, **11** 18

Software Arts, **6** 254

Software Development Pty., Ltd., **15** 107

Software Dimensions, Inc., **9** 35

Software, Etc., **13** 545

Software International, **6** 224

Software Plus, Inc., **10** 514

Software Publishing Corp., **14** 262

Softwood Holdings Ltd., **III** 688

Sogebra S.A., **I** 257

Sogen International Corp., **II** 355

Sogexport, **II** 355

Soginnove, **II** 355–56

Sohio Chemical Company, **13** 502

Sohken Kako Co., Ltd., **IV** 327

Soinlahti Sawmill and Brick Works, **IV** 300

Sola Holdings, **III** 727

Solair Inc., **14** 43

La Solana Corp., **IV** 726

Solar, **IV** 614

Solar Electric Corp., **13** 398

Solectron Corp., **12** 161–62, **450–52**

Solel Boneh Construction, **II** 47

Soletanche Co., **I** 586

Solid Beheer B.V., **10** 514

Solid State Dielectrics, **I** 329; **8** 152

Sollac, **IV** 226–27

Solmer, **IV** 227

Solomon Valley Milling Company, **6** 592

Solon Automated Services, **II** 607

Solvay & Cie S.A., I 303, **394–96**, 414–15; III 677; IV 300
Solvay Animal Health Inc., **12** 5
Solvent Resource Recovery, Inc., **9** 109
Solvents Recovery Service of New Jersey, Inc., **8** 464
SOMABRI, **12** 152
SOMACA, **12** 152
Somerville Electric Light Company, **12** 45
Sommers Drug Stores, **9** 186
SONAP, IV 504–06
Sonat Coal Gas, Inc., **6** 578
Sonat, Inc., 6 577–78
Sonatrach, V 626; **12** 145. *See also* Entreprise Nationale Sonatrach.
Sonecor Systems, **6** 340
Sonesson, I 211
Sonic Corporation, 14 451–53
Sonneborn Chemical and Refinery Co., I 405
Sonnen Basserman, II 475
Sonoco Products Company, 8 475–77; 12 150–51
Sonoma Mortgage Corp., II 382
Sonometrics Inc., I 667
Sony Corporation, I 30, 534; II 56, 58, 91–92, **101–03**, 117–19, 124, 134, 137, 440; III 141, 143, 340, 658; **6** 30; **7** 118; **9** 385; **10** 86, 119, 403; **11** 46, 490–91, 557; **12** 75, 161, 448, **453–56 (upd.)**; **13** 399, 403, 482, 573; **14** 534
Sonzogno, IV 585
Soo Line, V 429–30
Soo Line Mills, II 631
SOPEAL, III 738
Sophia Jocoba GmbH, IV 193
SOPI, IV 401
Sopwith Aviation Co., III 507–08
Soravie, II 265
Sorbus, **6** 242
Sorcim, **6** 224
Soreal, **8** 344
Sorg Paper Company. *See* Mosinee Paper Corporation.
SOS Co., II 531
Sosa, Bromley, Aguilar & Associates, **6** 22
Soterra, Inc., **15** 188
Sotheby's Holdings, Inc., 11 452–54; 15 98–100
Sound of Music Inc. *See* Best Buy Co., Inc.
Sound Warehouse, **9** 75
Source One Mortgage Services Corp., **12** 79
Source Perrier, **7** 383
South African Airways Ltd. (SAA), **6** 84, 433, 435
South African Breweries Ltd., I 287–89, 422
South African Coal, Oil and Gas Corp., IV 533
South African Railways, **6** 434–35
South African Torbanite Mining and Refining Co., IV 534
South African Transport Services, **6** 433, 435
South American Cable Co., I 428
South Carolina Electric & Gas Company, **6** 574–76
South Carolina Industries, IV 333
South Central Bell Telephone Co. V 276–78
South Central Railroad Co., **14** 325

South China Morning Post (Holdings) Ltd., II 298; IV 652; **7** 392
South Coast Gas Compression Company, Inc., **11** 523
South Dakota Public Service Company, **6** 524
South Fulton Light & Power Company, **6** 514
South Improvement Co., IV 427
South Manchuria Railroad Co. Ltd., IV 434
South Penn Oil Co., IV 488–89
South Puerto Rico Sugar Co., I 452
South Puerto Rico Telephone Co., I 462
South Sea Textile, III 705
South Texas Stevedore Co., IV 81
South-Western Publishing Co., **8** 526–28
Southam Inc., 7 486–89; 15 265
Southco, II 602–03; **7** 20–21
Southdown, Inc., 14 454–56
Southeast Bank of Florida, **11** 112
Southeast Banking Corp., II 252; **14** 103
Southeast Public Service Company, **8** 536
Southeastern Power and Light Company, **6** 447
Southeastern Telephone Company, **6** 312
Southern and Phillips Gas Ltd., **13** 485
Southern Bank, **10** 426
Southern Bearings Co., **13** 78
Southern Bell, **10** 202
Southern Biscuit Co., II 631
Southern Box Corp., **13** 441
Southern California Edison Co., II 402; V 711, 713–15, 717; **11** 272; **12** 106
Southern California Gas Co., I 569
Southern Casualty Insurance Co., III 214
Southern Clay Products, III 691
Southern Clays Inc., IV 82
Southern Colorado Power Company, **6** 312
Southern Comfort Corp., I 227
Southern Connecticut Newspapers Inc., IV 677
Southern Cotton Co., IV 224
Southern Cotton Oil Co., I 421; **11** 23
Southern Discount Company of Atlanta, **9** 229
Southern Electric PLC, 13 484–86
Southern Electric Supply Co., **15** 386
Southern Extract Co., IV 310
Southern Forest Products, Inc., **6** 577
Southern Gage, III 519
Southern Graphic Arts, **13** 405
Southern Guaranty Cos., III 404
Southern Idaho Water Power Company, **12** 265
Southern Illinois Light & Power Company, **6** 504
Southern Indiana Gas and Electric Company, 13 487–89
Southern Japan Trust Bank, V 114
Southern Kraft Corp., IV 286
Southern Lumber Company, **8** 430
Southern Manufacturing Company, **8** 458
Southern National Bankshares of Atlanta, II 337; **10** 425
Southern Natural Gas Co., III 558; **6** 447–48, 577
Southern Nevada Power Company, **11** 343
Southern Nevada Telephone Company, **6** 313; **11** 343
Southern New England Telecommunications Corporation, 6 338–40
Southern Nitrogen Co., IV 123

Southern Oregon Broadcasting Co., **7** 15
Southern Pacific Communications Corporation, **9** 478–79
Southern Pacific Rail Corp., **12** 18–20
Southern Pacific Railroad, I 13; II 329, 381, 448; IV 625
Southern Pacific Transportation Company, V 516–18; 12 278
Southern Peru Copper Corp., IV 33
Southern Phenix Textiles Inc., **15** 247–48
Southern Pine Lumber Co., IV 341
Southern Railway Company, V 484–85
Southern States Trust Co., II 336
Southern Sun Hotel Corp., I 288
Southern Surety Co., III 332
Southern Telephone Company, **14** 257
Southern Television Corp., II 158; IV 650; **7** 389
Southern Union Company, **12** 542
Southern Utah Fuel Co., IV 394
Southern Video Partnership, **9** 74
The Southland Corporation, II 449, 620, 660–61; IV 392, 508; V 89; **7** 114, 374, **490–92 (upd.);** **9** 178; **13** 333, 449, 525
Southland Mobilcom Inc., **15** 196
Southland Paper, **13** 118
Southland Royalty Co., **10** 190
Southlife Holding Co., III 218
Southmark, **11** 483
Southtrust Corporation, 11 455–57
Southview Pulp Co., IV 329
Southwest Airlines Co., I 106; 6 72–74, 119–21
Southwest Airmotive Co., II 16
Southwest Enterprise Associates, **13** 191
Southwest Forest Industries, IV 287, 289, 334
Southwest Potash Corp., IV 18; **6** 148–49
Southwestern Bell Corporation, V 328–30; 6 324; **10** 431, 500; **14** 489
Southwestern Gas Pipeline, **7** 344
Southwestern Illinois Coal Company, **7** 33
Southwestern Life Insurance, I 527; III 136
Southwestern Pipe, III 498
Southwestern Public Service Company, 6 579–81
Southwestern Refining Co., Inc., IV 446
Southwestern Textile Company, **12** 393
Southwire Company, Inc., 8 478–80; 12 353
Souvall Brothers, **8** 473
Sovereign Corp., III 221; **14** 109
Sovran Financial, **10** 425–26
SovTransavto, **6** 410
Soyland Power Cooperative, **6** 506
SP Reifenwerke, V 253
SP Tyres, V 253
Space Craft Inc., **9** 463
Space Systems/Loral, **9** 325
Spacemakers Inc., IV 287
Spanish International Communication, IV 621
Spanish River Pulp and Paper Mills, IV 246
SPARC International, **7** 499
Spare Change, **10** 282
Sparklets Ltd., I 315
Sparks Family Hospital, **6** 191
Spartan Motors Inc., 14 457–59
Spartan Stores Inc., I 127; II 679–80; 8 481–82; 10 302; **12** 489; **14** 412
Spartech Corporation, **9** 92
SPCM, Inc., **14** 477

Spécia, **I** 388
Special Agent Investigators, Inc., **14** 541
Special Foods, **14** 557
Special Light Alloy Co., **IV** 153
Specialty Coatings Inc., 8 483–84
Specialty Papers Co., **IV** 290
Specialty Products Co., **8** 386
Spectra-Physics AB, **9** 380–81
Spectral Dynamics Corporation. *See*
  Scientific-Atlanta, Inc.
Spectrum Concepts, **10** 394–95
Spectrum Dyed Yarns of New York, **8** 559
Spectrum Health Care Services, **13** 48
Spectrum Technology, Inc., **7** 378
Speed-O-Lac Chemical, **8** 553
SpeeDee Marts, **II** 661
Speedy Muffler King, **10** 415
Speidel Newspaper Group, **IV** 612; **7** 191
Spelling Entertainment Group, Inc., 9
  75; 14 460–62
Spencer Beef, **II** 536
Spencer Gifts, Inc., **II** 144; **15** 464
Spencer Stuart and Associates, Inc., 14
  463–65
Spenco Medical Corp., **III** 41
Sperry & Hutchinson Co., **12** 299
Sperry Aerospace Group, **II** 40, 86; **6** 283;
  12 246, 248
Sperry Corporation, **I** 101, 167; **III** 165,
  642; **6** 281–82; **8** 92; **11** 139; **12** 39; **13**
  511. *See also* Unisys Corporation.
Sperry Milling Co., **II** 501; **10** 322
Sperry Rand Corp., **II** 63, 73; **III** 126, 129,
  149, 166, 329, 642; **6** 241, 261, 281–82.
Sphere Inc., **8** 526; **13** 92
Spicer Manufacturing Co., **I** 152; **III** 568
Spie Batignolles SA, **I** 563; **II** 93–94; **13**
  206
Spiegel, Inc., III 598; **V** 160; **8** 56–58; **10**
  168, **489–91**; **11** 498; **9** 190, 219; **13**
  179; **15** 339
Spillers, **II** 500
Spin Physics, **III** 475–76; **7** 163
SPIRE Corporation, **14** 477
Spirella Company of Great Britain Ltd., **V**
  356
Spoerle Electronic, **10** 113
Spokane Falls Electric Light and Power
  Company. *See* Edison Electric
  Illuminating Company.
Spokane Falls Water Power Company, **6**
  595
Spokane Gas and Fuel, **IV** 391
Spokane Natural Gas Company, **6** 597
Spokane Street Railway Company, **6** 595
Spokane Traction Company, **6** 596
Spom Japan, **IV** 600
Spoor Behrins Campbell and Young, **II**
  289
Spoornet, **6** 435
Sporloisirs S.A., **9** 157
Sporting Dog Specialties, Inc., **14** 386
Sporting News Publishing Co., **IV** 677–78
Sportmart, Inc., 15 469–71
Sports & Recreation, Inc., **15** 470
Sports Authority, **15** 470
Sports Experts Inc., **II** 652
Sports Inc., **14** 8
Sportservice Corporation, **7** 133–35
Sportstown, Inc., **15** 470
Sportsystems Corporation, **7** 133, 135
Sprague Co., **I** 410
Sprague Devices, Inc., **11** 84
Sprague Electric Company, **6** 261

Sprague Electric Railway and Motor Co.,
  II 27; **12** 193
Sprague, Warner & Co., **II** 571
Spray-Rite, **I** 366
Sprayon Products, **III** 745
Sprecher & Schub, **9** 10
Spring Forge Mill, **8** 412
Spring Industries, Inc., V 378–79
Spring Valley Brewery, **I** 265
Springbok Editions, **IV** 621
Springer Verlag GmbH & Co., **IV** 611,
  641
Springfield Bank, **9** 474
Springhouse Corp., **IV** 610
Springhouse Financial Corp., **III** 204
Sprint Communications Company, L.P.,
  9 478–80; 10 19, 57, 97, 201–03; **11**
  183, 185, 500–01. *See also* US Sprint
  Communications.
Spruce Falls Power and Paper Co., **III** 40;
  IV 648
Spun Yarns, Inc., **12** 503
Spur Oil Co., **7** 362
SPX Corporation, 10 492–95
SQ Software, Inc., **10** 505
SQL Solutions, Inc., **10** 505
Squibb Corporation, I 380–81, 631, 651,
  659, 675, **695–97**; **III** 17, 19, 67; **8** 166;
  9 6–7; **13** 379–80
SR Beteilgungen Aktiengesellschaft, **III**
  377
SRI International, **10** 139
SRI Strategic Resources Inc., **6** 310
SS Cars, Ltd. *See* Jaguar Cars, Ltd.
Ssangyong Cement Industrial Co., Ltd.,
  III 747–50; IV 536–37, 539
SSC&B-Lintas, **I** 16–17; **14** 315
SSI Medical Services, Inc., **10** 350
SSMC Inc., **II** 10
St. *See under* Saint
Staal Bankiers, **13** 544
Städtische Elecktricitäts-Werke A.G., **I** 410
Staefa Control System Limited, **6** 490
Stafford Old Bank, **II** 307
Stag Cañon Fuel Co., **IV** 177
Stahl-Urban Company, **8** 287–88
Stahlwerke Peine-Salzgitter AG, **IV** 201
Stahlwerke Röchling AG, **III** 694–95
Stahlwerke Südwestfalen AG, **IV** 89
Stal-Astra GmbH, **III** 420
Staley Continental, **II** 582
Stamford Drug Group, **9** 68
Stanadyne, Inc., **7** 336; **12** 344
Standard & Poor's Corp., **IV** 29, 482,
  636–37; **12** 310
Standard Accident Co., **III** 332
Standard Aero, **III** 509
Standard Aircraft Equipment, **II** 16
Standard Alaska, **7** 559
Standard Bank of Canada, **II** 244
Standard Brands, **I** 248; **II** 542, 544; **7**
  365, 367
Standard Chartered PLC, II 298, 309,
  319, 357–59, 386; **10** 170
Standard Chemical Products, **III** 33
Standard Commercial Corporation, 12
  110; **13 490–92**
Standard Drug Co., **V** 171
Standard Electric Lorenz A.G., **II** 13, 70
Standard Electric Time Company, **13** 233
Standard Electrica, **II** 13
Standard Equities Corp., **III** 98
Standard Federal Bank, 9 481–83
Standard Fire Insurance Co., **III** 181–82

Standard Fruit and Steamship Co. of New
  Orleans, **II** 491
Standard Gauge Manufacturing Company,
  13 233
Standard General Insurance, **III** 208
Standard Industrial Group Ltd., **IV** 658
Standard Insulation Co., **I** 321
Standard Insurance Co. of New York, **III**
  385
Standard Investing Corp., **III** 98
Standard Kollsman Industries Inc., **13** 461
Standard Life Assurance Company, III
  358–61; IV 696–98
Standard Life Insurance Company, **11** 481
Standard Magnesium & Chemical Co., **IV**
  123
Standard Metals Corp., **IV** 76
Standard Microsystems Corporation, 11
  462–64
Standard Milling Co., **II** 497
Standard Motor Co., **III** 651
Standard of America Life Insurance Co.,
  III 324
Standard of Georgia Insurance Agency,
  Inc., **10** 92
Standard Oil Co., **III** 470, 513; **IV** 46, 372,
  399, 426–29, 434, 463, 478, 488–89,
  530–31, 540, 542, 551, 574, 577–78,
  657; **V** 590, 601; **6** 455; **7** 169–72, 263,
  351, 414, 551; **8** 415; **10** 110, 289; **14**
  21, 491–92
Standard Oil Co. (California), **II** 448; **IV**
  18–19, 385–87, 403, 429, 464, 536–37,
  545, 552, 560, 578; **6** 353; **7** 172, 352,
  483; **13** 448
Standard Oil Co. (Illinois), **IV** 368
Standard Oil Co. (Indiana), **II** 262; **IV** 366,
  368–71, 466–67; **7** 443; **10** 86; **14** 222
Standard Oil Co. (Minnesota), **IV** 368
Standard Oil Co. (New York), **IV** 428–29,
  431, 460, 463–65, 485, 504, 537, 549,
  558; **7** 171, 351–52
Standard Oil Co. (Ohio), **IV** 373, 379, 427,
  452, 463, 522, 571; **7** 57, 171, 263; **12**
  309
Standard Oil Co. of Iowa, **IV** 385
Standard Oil Co. of Kentucky, **IV** 387
Standard Oil Co. of New Jersey, **I** 334,
  337, 370; **II** 16, 496; **IV** 378–79,
  385–86, 400, 415–16, 419, 426–29,
  431–33, 438, 460, 463–64, 488, 522,
  531, 537–38, 544, 558, 565, 571; **V**
  658–59; **7** 170–72, 253, 351; **13** 124
Standard Oil Development Co., **IV** 554
Standard Oil Trust, **IV** 31, 368, 375,
  385–86, 427, 463
Standard Rate & Data Service, **IV** 639; **7**
  286
Standard Register Co., 15 472–74
Standard Sanitary, **III** 663–64
Standard Screw Co., **12** 344
Standard Shares, **9** 413–14
Standard Steel Propeller, **I** 47, 84; **9** 416;
  10 162
Standard Telephone and Radio, **II** 13
Standard Telephones and Cables, Ltd., **III**
  162–63; **6** 242
Standard Tin Plate Co., **15** 127
Standard-Vacuum Oil Co., **IV** 431–32,
  440, 460, 464, 491–92, 554–55; **7** 352
Stanhome Inc., 9 330; **11** 94–96; **15**
  475–78
STANIC, **IV** 419, 421
Stanko Fanuc Service, **III** 483

Stanley Electric Manufacturing Co., **II** 28; **12** 194

Stanley Home Products, Incorporated. *See* Stanhome Inc.

Stanley Works, **III** 626–29; **7** 480; **9** 543; **13** 41

Stanolind Oil & Gas Co., **III** 498; **IV** 365, 369–70

Stant Corporation, **15** 503, 505

Staples, Inc., **8** 404–05; **10 496–98**

Star, **10** 287–88

Star Air Service. *See* Alaska Air Group, Inc.

Star Banc Corporation, **11** 465–67; **13** 222

Star Engraving, **12** 471

Star Enterprise, **IV** 536, 539, 553

Star Enterprises, Inc., **6** 457

Star Finishing Co., **9** 465

Star Paper Ltd., **IV** 300

Star Video, Inc., **6** 313

Starber International, **12** 181

Starbucks Corporation, **13 493–94**

StarCraft, **III** 444; **13** 113

Stardent, **III** 553

StarKist Foods, **II** 508; **11** 172

Starlawerken, **I** 527

StarMed Staffing Corporation, **6** 10

Starpointe Savings Bank, **9** 173

Startech Semiconductor Inc., **14** 183

Startel Corp., **15** 125

Starter Corp., **12 457–458**

State Bank of Albany, **9** 228

State Farm Mutual Automobile Insurance Company, **III 362–64**; **10** 50

State Finance and Thrift Company, **14** 529

State Leed, **13** 367

State Metal Works, **III** 647

State Savings Bank and Trust Co., **11** 180

State Street Boston Corporation, **8 491–93**

State Trading Corp. of India Ltd., **IV** 143

State-Record Co., **IV** 630

Staten Island Advance Corp., **IV** 581–82

Static, Inc., **14** 430

Stationers Distributing Company, **14** 523

Statler Hotel Co., **III** 92, 98

Statoil. *See* Den Norske Stats Oljeselskap AS.

Statter, Inc., **6** 27

Staubli International, **II** 122; **12** 546

Stauffer Chemical Company, **8** 105–07

Stauffer-Meiji, **II** 540

STC PLC, **III** 141, **162–64**

Stead & Miller, **13** 169

Steag AG, **IV** 193

Steak & Ale, **II** 556–57; **7** 336; **12** 373; **13** 408–09

Steak n Shake, **14** 130–31

Steam and Gas Pipe Co., **III** 644

Stearman, **I** 47, 84; **9** 416; **10** 162

Stearns & Foster, **12** 439

Stearns Catalytic World Corp., **II** 87; **11** 413

Stearns Coal & Lumber, **6** 514

Steaua-Romana, **IV** 557

Steel and Tube Co. of America, **IV** 114

Steel Authority of India Ltd., **IV 205–07**

Steel Ceilings and Aluminum Works, **IV** 22

Steel Co. of Canada Ltd., **IV** 208

Steel Mills Ltd., **III** 673

Steel Products Engineering Co., **I** 169

Steel Stamping Co., **III** 569

Steelcase Inc., **7 493–95**; **8** 251–52, 255, 405

Steelmade Inc., **I** 513

Steely, **IV** 109

Steenfabriek De Ruiterwaard, **14** 249

Steenkolen Handelsvereniging, **IV** 132

Steering Aluminum, **I** 159

Stefany, **12** 152

Steil, Inc., **8** 271

Steinbach Inc., **IV** 226; **14** 427

Steinberg Incorporated, **II** 652–53, **662–65**; **V** 163

Steinman & Grey, **6** 27

Steinmüller Verwaltungsgesellschaft, **V** 747

Stelco Inc., **IV 208–10**

Stella D'Oro Company, **7** 367

Stellar Systems, Inc., **III** 553; **14** 542

Stellenbosch Farmers Winery, **I** 288

Stelux Manufacturing Company, **13** 121

Stensmölla Kemiska Tekniska Industri, **I** 385

Stentor Canadian Network Management, **6** 310

Stephen F. Whitman & Son, Inc., **7** 429

Stephens, **IV** 76

Sterchi Bros. Co., **14** 236

Sterling Drug Inc., **I** 309–10, **698–700**; **III** 477; **7** 163; **13** 76–77

Sterling Engineered Products, **III** 640, 642

Sterling Forest Corp., **III** 264

Sterling Industries, **13** 166

Sterling Information Services, Ltd., **IV** 675; **7** 528

Sterling Manhattan, **7** 63

Sterling Oil, **I** 526

Sterling Oil & Development, **II** 490

Sterling Organics Ltd., **12** 351

Sterling Plastics, **III** 642

Sterling Products Inc., **I** 622; **10** 68

Sterling Remedy Co., **I** 698

Sterling Software, Inc., **11 468–70**

Sterling Winthrop, **7** 164

Stern & Stern Textiles, **11** 261

Stern Brothers, **V** 362–65

Stern's, **9** 209

Stern-Auer Shoe Company, **V** 207

Sternco Industries, **12** 230–31

STET. *See* Società Finanziaria Telefonica per Azioni.

Steuben Glass, **III** 683

Stevcoknit Fabrics Company, **8** 141–43

Stevens Linen Associates, Inc., **8** 272

Stevens Park Osteopathic Hospital, **6** 192

Stevens Sound Proofing Co., **III** 706; **7** 291

Stevens, Thompson & Runyan, Inc. *See* CRSS Inc.

Steward Esplen and Greenhough, **II** 569

Stewards Foundation, **6** 191

Stewart & Stevenson Services Inc., **11 471–73**

Stewart Bolling Co., **IV** 130

Stewart Cash Stores, **II** 465

Stewart P. Orr Associates, **6** 224

Steyr Walzlager, **III** 625

Stichting Continuïteit AMEV, **III** 202

Stieber Rollkupplung GmbH, **14** 63

Stimson & Valentine, **8** 552

Stinnes AG, **6** 424, 426; **8** 68–69, **494–97**

Stirling Readymix Concrete, **III** 737–38

STM Systems Corp., **11** 485

Stock, **IV** 617–18

Stock Clearing Corporation, **9** 370

Stockholder Systems Inc., **11** 485

Stockholm Southern Transportation Co., **I** 553

Stockholms Allmänna Telefonaktiebolag, **V** 334

Stockholms Enskilda Bank, **II** 1, 351, 365–66; **III** 419, 425–26

Stockholms Intecknings Garanti, **II** 366

Stockton and Hartlepool Railway, **III** 272

Stockton Wheel Co., **III** 450

Stoelting Brothers Company, **10** 371

Stokely-Van Camp, **II** 560, 575; **12** 411

Stokvis/De Nederlandsche Kroon Rijwiefabrieken, **13** 499

Stone & Webster, Inc., **13 495–98**

Stone and Kimball, **IV** 660

Stone Container Corporation, **IV 332–34**; **8** 203–04; **15** 129

Stone Exploration Corp., **IV** 83; **7** 187

Stone Manufacturing Company, **14 469–71**

Stonega Coke & Coal Co., **7** 583–84. *See also* Westmoreland Coal Company.

Stoner Associates. *See* Severn Trent PLC.

Stonewall Insurance Co., **III** 192

Stoomvaart Maatschappij Nederland, **6** 403–04

Stop & Shop Companies, Inc., **II 666–67**; **9** 451, 453; **12** 48–49

Stop N Go, **7** 373

Stora Kopparbergs Bergslags AB, **III** 693, 695; **IV 335–37**, 340; **12** 464

Storage Dimensions Inc., **10** 404

Storage Technology Corporation, **III** 110; **6 275–77**; **12** 148, 161

Storebrand Insurance Co., **III** 122

Storer Communications, **II** 161; **IV** 596; **7** 91–92, 200–01

Storer Leasing Inc., **I** 99; **6** 81

Storz Instruments Co., **I** 678

Stouffer Corp., **I** 485; **II** 489, 547; **6** 40; **7** 382; **8** **498–501**

Stout Air Services, **I** 128; **6** 128

Stout Airlines, **I** 47, 84; **9** 416; **10** 162

Stout Metal Airplane Co., **I** 165

Stowe Woodward, **I** 428–29

STRAAM Engineers. *See* CRSS Inc.

Straits Steamship Co. *See* Malaysian Airlines System.

Stran, **8** 546

Strata Energy, Inc., **IV** 29

StrataCom, **11** 59

Stratford Corporation, **15** 103

Strathmore Consolidated Investments, **IV** 90

Stratos Boat Co., Ltd., **III** 600

Stratton Ski Corporation, **15** 235

Stratus Computer, Inc., **6** 279; **10 499–501**

Strauss Turnbull and Co., **II** 355

Strawbridge & Clothier's, **6** 243

Street & Smith Publications, Inc., **IV** 583; **13** 178

Stride Rite Corporation, **8 502–04**; **9** 437

Stroehmann Bakeries, **II** 631

Stroh and Co., **IV** 486

Stroh Brewing Company, **I** 32, 255, **290–92**; **13** 10–11, 455

Strömberg, **IV** 300

Stromberg Carburetor Co., **I** 141

Stromberg-Carlson, **II** 82

Stromeyer GmbH, **7** 141

Strong Brewery, **I** 294

Strother Drug, **III** 9–10

Structural Dynamics Research Corporation, **10** 257
Strydel, Inc., **14** 361
Stryker Corporation, **10** 351; **11 474–76**
Stuart Co., **I** 584
Stuart Medical Inc., **10** 143
Stuart Perlman, **6** 200
Stuckey's, Inc., **7** 429
Studebaker Co., **I** 141–42, 451; **8** 74; **9** 27
Studebaker Wagon Co., **IV** 660
Studebaker-Packard, **9** 118; **10** 261
Student Loan Marketing Association, II 453–55
Studiengesellschaft, **I** 409
Studley Products Inc., **12** 396
Stuffit Co., **IV** 597
Sturbridge Yankee Workshop, Inc., **10** 216
Stuttgart Gas Works, **I** 391
Stuttgarter Verein Versicherungs-AG, **III** 184
Stuyvesant Insurance Group, **II** 182
Stymer Oy, **IV** 470–71
Subaru, **6** 28
SubLogic, **15** 455
Submarine Boat Co., **I** 57
Submarine Signal Co., **II** 85–86; **11** 412
Suburban Cablevision, **IV** 640
Suburban Coastal Corporation, **10** 92
Suburban Cos., **IV** 575–76
Suburban Light and Power Company, **12** 45
Suburban Propane, **I** 378
Suburban Savings and Loan Association, **10** 92
Subway, **15** 56–57
Suchard Co., **II** 520
Sud-Aviation, **I** 44–45; **7** 10; **8** 313
Suddeutsche Bank A.G., **II** 279
Süddeutsche Donau-Dampfschiffahrts-Gesellschaft, **6** 425
Süddeutsche Kalkstickstoffwerke AG, **IV** 229, 232
Sudler & Hennessey, **I** 37
Südpetrol, **IV** 421
Suez Bank, **IV** 108
Suez Canal Co., **IV** 530
Suez Oil Co., **IV** 413–14
Sugarland Industries. *See* Imperial Holly Corporation.
Suita Brewery, **I** 220
Suito Sangyo Co., Ltd. *See* Seino Transportation Company, Ltd.
Sullair Co., **I** 435
Sullivan, Stauffer, Colwell & Bayles, **14** 314
Sullivan Systems, **III** 420
Sulphide Corp., **IV** 58
Sulzbach, **I** 409
Sulzer Brothers Limited, **III** 402, 516, **630–33**, 638
Suminoe Textile Co., **8** 235
Sumisei Secpac Investment Advisors, **III** 366
Sumitomo Bank, Ltd., **I** 587; **II** 104, 224, 273–74, 347, **360–62**, 363, 392, 415; **IV** 269, 726; **9** 341–42
Sumitomo Chemical Company Ltd., **I** 363, **397–98**; **II** 361; **III** 715; **IV** 432
Sumitomo Corporation, **I** 431–32, 492, 502, 504–05, 510–11, 515, **518–20**; **III** 43, 365; **V** 161; **7** 357; **11 477–80 (upd.)**, 490; **15** 340
Sumitomo Electric Industries, **I** 105; **II 104–05**; **III** 490, 684; **IV** 179; **V** 252

Sumitomo Heavy Industries, Ltd., **III** 533, **634–35**; **10** 381
Sumitomo Life Insurance Co., **II** 104, 360, 422; **III** 288, **365–66**
Sumitomo Marine and Fire Insurance Company, Limited III 367–68
Sumitomo Metal Industries, Ltd., **I** 390; **II** 104, 361; **IV** 130, **211–13**, 216; **10** 463–64; **11** 246
Sumitomo Metal Mining Co., Ltd., **IV 214–16**; **9** 340
Sumitomo Realty & Development Co., Ltd., **IV 726–27**
Sumitomo Rubber Industries, Ltd., **V 252–53**
Sumitomo Trust & Banking Company, Ltd., **II** 104, **363–64**; **IV** 726
Summa Corporation, **9** 266
Summers Group Inc., **15** 386
The Summit Bancorporation, 14 472–74
Summit Constructors. *See* CRSS Inc.
Summit Engineering Corp., **I** 153
Summit Screen Inks, **13** 228
Sun Alliance Group PLC, **III** 296, **369–74**, 400
Sun Chemical Corp. *See* Sequa Corp.
Sun Company, Inc., **I** 286, 631; **IV** 449, **548–50**; **7** 114, 414; **11** 484; **12** 459
Sun Country Airlines, **I** 114
Sun Distributors L.P., 12 459–461
Sun Electric, **15** 288
Sun Electronics, **9** 116
Sun Equities Corporation, **15** 449
Sun Federal, **7** 498
Sun Federal Savings and Loan Association of Tallahassee, **10** 92
Sun Fire Coal Company, **7** 281
Sun Fire Office, **III** 349, 369–71
Sun Foods, **12** 220–21
Sun International Hotels, Limited, **12** 420
Sun Kyowa, **III** 43
Sun Life Assurance Co. of Canada, **IV** 165
Sun Life Group of America, **11** 482
Sun Men's Shop Co., Ltd., **V** 150
Sun Microsystems, Inc., **II** 45, 62; **III** 125; **6** 222, 235, 238, 244; **7 498–501**; **9** 36, 471; **10** 118, 242, 257, 504; **11** 45–46, 490–91, 507; **12** 162; **14** 15–16, 268; **15** 321
Sun Newspapers, **III** 213–14
Sun Oil Co., **III** 497; **IV** 371, 424, 548–50; **7** 413–14; **11** 35
Sun Optical Co., Ltd., **V** 150
Sun Ship, **IV** 549
Sun Techno Services Co., Ltd., **V** 150
Sun Technology Enterprises, **7** 500
Sun Television & Appliances Inc., 10 502–03
Sun-Diamond Growers of California, **7 496–98**
Sun-Fast Color, **13** 227
Sun-Maid Growers of California, **7** 496–97
Sun-Pat Products, **II** 569
SunAir, **11** 300
SunAmerica Inc., 11 481–83
Sunbeam-Oster Co., Inc., 9 484–86; **14** 230
Sunbelt Coca-Cola, **10** 223
Sunbelt Nursery Group, Inc., **12** 179, 200, 394
Sunbird, **III** 600; **V** 150
Sunburst Yarns, Inc., **13** 532
Sunciti Manufacturers, **III** 454
Sunclipse Inc., **IV** 250

Suncoast Motion Picture Company, **9** 360
SunCor Development Company, **6** 546–47
Sundance Publishing, **IV** 609; **12** 559
Sunday Pictorial, **IV** 665–66
Sundheim & Doetsch, **IV** 189
Sunds Defibrator AG, **IV** 338–40, 350
Sundstrand Corporation, 7 502–04
SunGard Data Systems Inc., 11 484–85
Sunglee Electronics Co. Ltd., **III** 748–49
Sunila Oy, **IV** 348–49
Sunkist Growers, **7** 496
Sunkist Soft Drinks Inc., **I** 13
Sunkus Co. Ltd., **V** 150
Sunray DX Oil Co., **IV** 550, 575; **7** 414
Sunrise Medical Inc., **11** 202, **486–88**
Sunrise Test Systems, **11** 491
SunSoft, **7** 500
Sunsweet Growers, **7** 496
Suntory Ltd., **13** 454
Sunward Technologies, Inc., **10** 464
Supasnaps, **V** 50
Super D Drugs, **9** 52
Super 8 Motels, Inc., **11** 178
Super Food Services, Inc., 15 479–81
Super Quick, Inc., **7** 372
Super Rite, **V** 176
Super Sagless Spring Corp., **15** 103
Super Store Industries, **14** 397
Super Valu Stores, Inc., **II** 632, **668–71**; **6** 364; **7** 450; **8** 380; **14** 411
Super-Power Company, **6** 505
SuperAmerica Group, Inc., **IV** 374
Superbrix, **14** 248
Supercomputer Systems, Inc., **III** 130
Superdrug PLC, **V** 175
Superenvases Envalic, **I** 231
Superior Bearings Co., **I** 159
Superior Healthcare Group, Inc., **11** 221
Superior Industries International, Inc., 8 505–07
Superior Oil Co., **III** 558; **IV** 400, 465, 524; **7** 353
Superior Transfer, **12** 309
Supermarchés Montréal, **II** 662–63
Supermarkets General Holdings Corporation, II 672–74
Supermart Books, **10** 136
Supersaver Wholesale Clubs, **8** 555
SuperStation WTBS, **6** 171
Supertest Petroleum Corporation, **9** 490
Supervalue Corp., **13** 393
Supervised Investors Services, **III** 270
SupeRx, **II** 644
Supreme Sugar Co., **I** 421; **11** 23
Supron Energy Corp., **15** 129
Surety Life Insurance Company, **10** 51
Surgical Health Corporation, **14** 233
Surgical Mechanical Research Inc., **I** 678
Surgikos, Inc., **III** 35
Surgitool, **I** 628
Surpass Software Systems, Inc., **9** 81
Survey Research Group, **10** 360
Susie's Casuals, **14** 294
Susquehanna Pfaltzgraff Company, 8 508–10
Sussex Group, **15** 449
Sutter Corp., **15** 113
Sutter Health, **12** 175–76
Suwa Seikosha, **III** 620
Suzaki Hajime, **V** 113–14
Suzannah Farms, **7** 524
Suze, **I** 280
Suzuki & Co., **I** 509–10; **IV** 129; **9** 341–42

Suzuki Motor Corporation, III 581. 657:
  7 110: 8 72: 9 487–89
Suzuki Shoten Co., V 380, 457–58
Svea Choklad A.G., II 640
Svensk Fastighetskredit A.B., II 352
Svenska A.B. Humber & Co., I 197
Svenska Aeroplan Aktiebolaget. See Saab-
  Scania AB.
Svenska Cellulosa Aktiebolaget, II
  365–66: IV 295–96, 325, 336, 338–40,
  667
Svenska Centrifug AB, III 418
Svenska Elektron, III 478
A.B. Svenska Flaktfabriken, II 2
Svenska Flygmotor A.B., I 209
Svenska Handelsbanken, II 353, 365–67:
  IV 338–39
Svenska Järnvagsverkstäderna A.B., I 197
Svenska Kullagerfabriken A.B., I 209: III
  622: 7 565
Svenska Oljeslageri AB, IV 318
Svenska Varv, 6 367
Svenskt Stål AB, IV 336
Sverdrup Corporation, 14 475–78
Sverker Martin-Löf, IV 339
SVF. See Société des Vins de France.
Sviluppo Iniziative Stradali Italiene, IV
  420
SVPW, I 215
Swallow Airplane Company, 8 49
Swallow Sidecar and Coach Building
  Company, 13 285
Swan, 10 170
Swan Electric Light Co., I 410
Swan's Down Cake Flour, II 531
Swann Corp., I 366
Swatch, 7 532–33
Swearingen Aircraft Company, 9 207
SwedeChrome, III 625
Swedish Furniture Research Institute, V 82
Swedish Intercontinental Airlines, I 119
Swedish Match S.A., IV 336–37: 9 381:
  12 462–64
Swedish Ordnance-FFV/Bofors AB, 9
  381–82
Swedish Telecom, V 331–33
Sweedor, 12 464
Sweeney Specialty Restaurants, 14 131
Sweet & Maxwell, 8 527
Swett & Crawford Group, III 357
Swift & Co., II 447, 550: 13 351, 448
Swift Adhesives, 10 467
Swift Independent Packing Co., II 494: 13
  350, 352
Swift Textiles, Inc., 12 118: 15 247
Swift-Armour S.A., II 480
Swift-Eckrich, II 467
Swingline, Inc., 7 3–5
Swire Pacific Ltd., I 470, 521–22
Swisher International, Inc., 14 17–19
Swiss Air Transport Company Ltd., I
  107, 119, 121–22: 9 233
Swiss Banca della Svizzera Italiano, II 192
Swiss Bank Corporation, II 267, 368–70,
  378–79: 14 419–20
Swiss Cement-Industrie-Gesellschaft, III
  701
Swiss Colony Wines, I 377
Swiss Drilling Co., IV 372
Swiss Federal Railways (Schweizerische
  Bundesbahnen), V 519–22
Swiss General Chocolate Co., II 545–46: 7
  380–81

Swiss Locomotive and Machine Works. III
  631–32
Swiss Oil Co., IV 372–73
Swiss Reinsurance Company. III 299,
  301, 335, 375–78: 15 13
Swiss-American Corp., II 267
Swissair Associated Co., I 122: 6 60, 96,
  117
Sybase, Inc., 6 255, 279: 10 361, 504–06:
  11 77–78: 15 492
SyberVision, 10 216
Sybron International Corp., 14 479–81
Sydney Electricity, 12 443
Sydney Paper Mills Ltd., IV 248
Sydney Ross Co., I 698–99
Syfrets Trust Co., IV 23
Sylacauga Calcium Products, III 691
Sylvan Lake Telephone Company, 6 334
Sylvan Learning Centers, 13 299
Sylvania Companies, I 463: II 63: III 165.
  475: V 295: 7 161: 8 157: 11 197: 13
  402
Sylvia Paperboard Co., IV 310
Symantec Corporation, 10 507–09
Symbiosis Corp., 10 70
Symbol Technologies, Inc., 10 363,
  523–24: 15 482–84
Symington-Wayne, III 472
Symphony International, 14 224
Syncordia Corp., 15 69
Syncrocom, Inc., 10 513
Synercom Technology Inc., 14 319
Synergen Inc., 13 241
Synergy Dataworks, Inc., 11 285
Synopsis, Inc., 11 489–92
SynOptics Communications, Inc., 10 194,
  510–12: 11 475
Synovus Financial Corp., 12 465–67
Syntax Ophthalmic Inc., III 727
Syntex Corporation, I 512, 701–03: III
  18, 53: 8 216–17, 434, 548: 10 53: 12
  322
Synthecolor S.A., 8 347
Synthélabo, III 47–48
Synthetic Blood Corp., 15 380
Syracuse China, 8 510
Syratech Corp., 14 482–84
Syrian Airways, 6 85
Syroco, 14 483–84
Sysco Corporation, II 675–76: 9 453
Sysorex Information Systems, 11 62
SysScan, V 339
System Development Co., III 166: 6 282
System Fuels, Inc., 11 194
System Integrators, Inc., 6 279
System Software Associates, Inc., 10
  513–14
Systematics Inc., 6 301: 11 131
Systems and Services Co., II 675
Systems Center, Inc., 6 279: 11 469
Systems Construction Ltd., II 649
Systems Engineering and Manufacturing
  Company, 11 225
Systems Engineering Labs (SEL), 11 45:
  13 201
Systems Exploration Inc., 10 547
Systems Magnetic Co., IV 101
Systems Marketing Inc., 12 78
Systronics, 13 235
Szabo, II 608

T/Maker, 9 81
T.J. Falgout, 11 523
T.J. Maxx, V 197–98: 13 329–30: 14 62

T. Kobayashi & Co., Ltd., III 44
T. Mellon & Sons, II 315
T. Rowe Price Associates, Inc., 10 89: 11
  493–96
T.S. Farley. Limited. 10 319
TA Associates, 10 382
TA Media AG, 15 31
Tabacalera, S.A., V 414–16: 15 139
Table Supply Stores, II 683
Tabulating Machine Company, III 147: 6
  240. See also International Business
  Machines Corporation.
Taco Bell, I 278: 7 267, 505–07: 9 178:
  10 450: 13 336, 494: 14 453: 15 486
Taco John's International Inc., 15
  485–87
Taco Kid, 7 506
Tadiran, II 47
Taehan Cement, III 748
TAG. See Techniques d'Avant Garde
  Group SA.
Taguchi Automobile. See Seino
  Transportation Company. Ltd.
Taiba Corporation, 8 250
Taiheiyo Bank, 15 495
Taikoo Dockyard Co., I 521
Taikoo Sugar Refinery, I 521
Taio Paper Mfg. Co., Ltd., IV 266, 269.
  See also Daio Paper Co., Ltd.
Taisho America, III 295
Taisho Marine and Fire Insurance Co.,
  Ltd., III 209, 295–96
Taisho Pharmaceutical, I 676: II 361
Taiwan Aerospace Corp., 11 279
Taiwan Auto Glass, III 715
Taiway, III 596
Taiyo Bussan, IV 225
Taiyo Fishery Company, Limited, II
  578–79
Taiyo Kobe Bank, Ltd., II 326, 371–72
Taiyo Metal Manufacturing Co., III 757
Takada & Co., IV 151
Takaro Shuzo, III 42
Takashimaya Co., Limited, V 193–96
Takeda Chemical Industries Ltd., I
  704–06: III 760
Takeda Riken, 11 504
Takeuchi Mining Co., III 545
Takihyo, 15 145
Takkyubin, V 537
Tako Oy, IV 314
The Talbots, Inc., II 503: 10 324: 11
  497–99: 12 280
Talcott National Corporation, 11 260–61
Taliq Corp., III 715
Talisman Energy, 9 490–93
Talley Industries, Inc., 10 386
TAM Ceramics, III 681
Tamar Bank, II 187
Tamarkin Co., 12 390
Tambrands Inc., 8 511–13: 12 439: 15
  359–60, 501
Tamco Distributors Co., 12 390
TAMET, IV 25
Tampa Electric Company, 6 582–83
Tampax Inc., III 40: 8 511–12. See also
  Tambrands Inc.
Oy Tampella Ab, II 47: III 648: IV 276
Tampere Paper Board and Roofing Felt
  Mill, IV 314
Tampereen Osake-Pankki, II 303
Tampimex Oil, 11 194
Tamura Kisan Co., II 552
Tanaka, 6 71

Tanaka Kikinzoku Kogyo KK, **IV** 119
Tanaka Matthey KK, **IV** 119
Tandem Computers, Inc., 6 278–80; **10** 499; **11** 18; **14** 318
Tandy Corporation, **II** 70, **106–08**; **6** 257–58; **9** 43, 115, 165; **10** 56–57, 166–67, 236; **12 468–70 (upd.)**; **13** 174; **14** 117
Tangent Industries, **15** 83
Tangent Systems, **6** 247–48
Tanjong Pagar Dock Co., **I** 592
Tanks Oil and Gas, **11** 97
Tanner-Brice Company, **13** 404
TAP Air Portugal. *See* Transportes Aereos Portugueses.
Tapiola Insurance, **IV** 316
Tappan. *See* White Consolidated Industries Inc.
Tara Exploration and Development Ltd., **IV** 165
Tara Foods, **II** 645
Target Stores, **V** 35, 43–44; **10** 284, **515–17**; **12** 508; **13** 261, 274, 446; **14** 398; **15** 275
Tarkett, **12** 464
Tarmac PLC, **III** 734, **751–54**; **14** 250
TarMacadam (Purnell Hooley's Patent) Syndicate Ltd., **III** 751
Tarslag, **III** 752
TASC. *See* Analytical Sciences Corp.
Tashima Shoten, **III** 574
Tasman Pulp and Paper Co. Ltd., **IV** 278–79
Tasman U.E.B., **IV** 249
Tasmanian Fibre Containers, **IV** 249
Tasty Baking Co., 14 485–87
TAT European Airlines, **14** 70, 73
Tata Airlines. *See* Air-India.
Tata Enterprises, **III** 43
Tata Iron and Steel Company Ltd., **IV** 48, 205–07, **217–19**
Tate & Lyle PLC, **II** 514, **580–83**; **7** 466–67; **13** 102
Tatebayashi Flour Milling Co., **II** 554
Tateisi Electric Manufacturing, **II** 75
Tateisi Medical Electronics Manufacturing Co., **II** 75
Tatham/RSCG, **13** 204
Tatung Co., **III** 482; **13** 387
Taurus Programming Services, **10** 196
Taylor Diving and Salvage Co., **III** 499
Taylor Material Handling, **13** 499
Taylor Medical, **14** 388
Taylor Publishing Company, **12 471–73**
Taylor Rental Corp., **III** 628
Taylor Wines Co., **I** 234; **10** 227
Taylor Woodrow plc, **I 590–91**; **13** 206
Taylor Woodrow-Anglian, **III** 739
Taylor-Evans Seed Co., **IV** 409
Taylors and Lloyds, **II** 306
Tazuke & Co., **IV** 151
TBS. *See* Turner Broadcasting System, Inc.
TBWA Advertising, Inc., 6 47–49
TCBC. *See* Todays Computers Business Centers.
TCF Holdings, Inc., **II** 170–71
TCH Corporation, **12** 477
TCI. *See* Tele-Communications, Inc.
TCPL. *See* TransCanada PipeLines Ltd.
TDK Corporation, **I** 500; **II 109–11**; **IV** 680
TDS. *See* Telephone and Data Systems, Inc.
Teaberry Electronics Corp., **III** 569

Teachers Insurance and Annuity Association, **III 379–82**
Teachers Service Organization, Inc., **8** 9–10
Team America, **9** 435
Team Penske, **V** 494
Teamsters Union, **13** 19
Tebel Maschinefabrieken, **III** 420
Tebel Pneumatiek, **III** 420
Tech Data Corporation, **10 518–19**
Tech Textiles, USA, **15** 247–48
Techalloy Co., **IV** 228
Technical Ceramics Laboratories, Inc., **13** 141
Technical Coatings Co., **13** 85
Technical Materials, Inc., **14** 81
Technical Publishing, **IV** 605
Technicare, **11** 200
Technicon Corp., **III** 56; **11** 333–34
Technifax, **8** 483
Techniques d'Avant Garde Group SA, **7** 554
Techno-Success Company, **V** 719
AB Technology, **II** 466
Technology Venture Investors, **11** 490; **14** 263
Teck Corporation, **9** 282
Tecnamotor S.p.A., **8** 72, 515
Tecneco, **IV** 422
Tecnifax Corp., **IV** 330
Tecnipublicaciones, **14** 555
TECO Energy, Inc., 6 582–84
Tecumseh Products Company, **8** 72, **514–16**
Ted Bates & Co., **I** 33, 623; **10** 69
Teddy's Shoe Store. *See* Morse Shoe Inc.
Tedelex, **IV** 91–92
TEIC. *See* B.V. Tabak Export & Import Compagnie.
Teijin Limited, **I** 511; **V 380–82**
Teikoku Bank, **I** 507; **II** 273, 325–26
Teikoku Hormone, **I** 704
Teikoku Jinken. *See* Teijin Limited.
Teikoku Sekiyu Co. Ltd., **IV** 475
Teikoku Shiki, **IV** 326
Teito Electric Railway, **V** 461
Teito Transport Co. Ltd., **V** 536
Tekrad, Inc., **8** 517. *See also* Tektronix, Inc.
Tekton Corp., **IV** 346
Tektronix, Inc., **II** 101; **8 517–21**; **10** 24; **11** 284–86; **12** 454
Tel-A-Data Limited, **11** 111
Tele Consulte, **14** 555
Tele-Communications, Inc., **II 160–62**, 167; **10** 484, 506; **11** 479; **13** 280; **15** 264—65
TeleCheck Services, Inc., **11** 113
Teleclub, **IV** 590
Teleco Oilfield Services, Inc., **6** 578
TeleColumbus, **11** 184
Telecom Australia, **6 341–42**
Telecom Canada. *See* Stentor Canadian Network Management.
Telecom Eireann, **7 508–10**
Telecom Italia, **15** 355
Telecomputing Corp., **I** 544
Telecredit, Inc., **6** 25
Telectronic Pacing Systems, **10** 445
Teledyne Inc., **I** 486, **523–25**; **II** 33, 44; **10** 262–63, 365, **520–22 (upd.)**; **11** 265; **13** 387
Telefonaktiebolaget LM Ericsson, **V** 331–32, **334–36**; **9** 381

Telefonbau und Normalzeit, **I** 193
Telefónica de España, S.A., **V 337–40**
Telefonos de Mexico S.A. de C.V., **14 488–90**
Telefunken Fernseh & Rundfunk GmbH., **I** 411; **II** 117
Teleglobe Inc., **14** 512
Telegraph Condenser Co., **II** 81
Telegraph Manufacturing Co., **III** 433
Telegraph Works, **III** 433
TeleMarketing Corporation of Louisiana, **8** 311
Telemarketing Investments, Ltd., **8** 311
Telemecanique, **II** 94
Telemundo Group, Inc., **III** 344
Telenorma, **I** 193
Telenova, **III** 169; **6** 285
Telephone and Data Systems, Inc., **9 494–96**, 527–529
Telephone Company of Ireland, **7** 508
Telephone Exchange Company of Indianapolis, **14** 257
Telephone Management Corporation, **8** 310
Telephone Utilities, Inc. *See* Pacific Telecom, Inc.
Telephone Utilities of Washington, **6** 325, 328
Telepictures, **II** 177
Teleport Communications Group, **14** 253
Teleprompter Corp., **II** 122; **7** 222; **10** 210
Telerate Systems Inc., **IV** 603, 670; **10** 276–77
Teleregister Corp., **I** 512
Telerent Europe, **II** 139
TeleRep, **IV** 596
Telesis Oil and Gas, **6** 478
Telesphere Network, Inc., **8** 310
Telesystems SLW Inc., **10** 524
Telettra S.p.A., **V** 326; **9** 10; **11** 205
Teletype Corp., **14** 569
Television Española, S.A., 7 511–12
Television Sales and Marketing Services Ltd., **7** 79–80
Teleway Japan, **7** 118–19; **13** 482
Telex Corporation, **II** 87; **13** 127
Telfin, **V** 339
Telia Mobitel, **11** 19
Telihoras Corporation, **10** 319
Telinfo, **6** 303
Telinq Inc., **10** 19
Telios Pharmaceuticals, Inc., **11** 460
Tellabs, Inc., **11 500–01**
Telpar, Inc., **14** 377
Telport, **14** 260
Telrad, **II** 48
Telxon Corporation, **10 523–25**
Tembec, Inc., **IV** 296
Temco Electronics and Missile Co., **I** 489
Temenggong of Jahore, **I** 592
Temp World, Inc., **6** 10
Temple, Barker & Sloan/Strategic Planning Associates, **III** 283
Temple Inks Company, **13** 227
Temple Press Ltd., **IV** 294–95
Temple-Inland Inc., **IV** 312, **341–43**, 675; **8** 267–69
Templeton, **II** 609
TEMPO Enterprises, **II** 162
Tempus Expeditions, **13** 358
TemTech Ltd., **13** 326
10 Sen Kinitsu Markets, **V** 194
Tengelmann Group, **II** 636–38
Tengen Inc., **III** 587; **7** 395
Tennant Company, **13 499–501**

Tenneco Inc., **I** 182, **526–28**; **IV** 76, 152, 283, 371, 499; **6** 531; **10** 379–80, 430, **526–28 (upd.)**; **11** 440; **12** 91, 376; **13** 372–73

Tennessee Book Company, **11** 193

Tennessee Coal, Iron and Railroad Co., **IV** 573; **7** 550

Tennessee Eastman Corporation, **III** 475; **7** 161. *See also* Eastman Chemical Company.

Tennessee Electric Power Co., **III** 332

Tennessee Gas Pipeline Co., **14** 126

Tennessee Gas Transmission Co., **I** 526; **13** 496; **14** 125

Tennessee Insurance Company, **11** 193–94

Tennessee Paper Mills Inc. *See* Rock-Tenn Company.

Tennessee Restaurant Company, **9** 426

Tennessee River Pulp & Paper Co., **12** 376–77

Tennessee Trifting, **13** 169

Tennessee Valley Authority, **II** 2–3, 121; **IV** 181

Tenngasco, **I** 527

Teollisuusosuuskunta Metsä-Saimaa, **IV** 315

TEP. *See* Tucson Electric Power Company.

Teradata Corporation, **6** 267

Teradyne, Inc., **11 502–04**

Terex Corporation, **7** 513–15; **8** 116

Terminal Transfer and Storage, Inc., **6** 371

Terminix International, **6** 45–46; **11** 433

Terra Industries, Inc., **13** 277, **502–04**

Terrace Park Dairies, **II** 536

Terracor, **11** 260–61

Terragrafics, **14** 245

Terre Haute Electric, **6** 555

Territorial Hotel Co., **II** 490

Territory Enterprises Ltd., **IV** 59

Terry Coach Industries, Inc., **III** 484

Terry's of York, **II** 594

Tesco PLC, **II** 513, **677–78**; **10** 442; **11** 239, 241

Tesoro Petroleum Corporation, **7 516–19**

Tesseract Corp., **11** 78

Testor Corporation, **8** 455

TETI, **I** 466

Tetley Inc., **I** 215; **14** 18

Tetra Plastics Inc., **V** 374; **8** 393

Teutonia National Bank, **IV** 310

Tex-Star Oil & Gas Corp., **IV** 574; **7** 551

Texaco Inc., **I** 21, 360; **II** 31, 313, 448; **III** 760; **IV** 386, 403, 418, 425, 429, 439, 461, 464, 466, 472–73, 479–80, 484, 488, 490, 510–11, 530–31, 536–39, 545, **551–53**, 560, 565–66, 570, 575; **7** 172, 280, 483; **9** 232; **10** 190; **12** 20; **13** 448; **14 491–94 (upd.)**

Texada Mines, Ltd., **IV** 123

Texas Air Corporation, **I** 97, 100, 103, 118, **123–24**, 127, 130; **6** 82, 129; **12** 489

Texas Almanac, **10** 3

Texas Butadiene and Chemical Corp., **IV** 456

Texas Co., **III** 497; **IV** 386, 400, 464, 536, 551–52; **7** 352

Texas Commerce Bankshares, **II** 252

Texas Eastern Corp., **6** 487; **11** 97, 354; **14** 126

Texas Eastern Transmission Company, **11** 28

Texas Eastman, **III** 475; **7** 161

Texas Electric Service Company, **V** 724

Texas Gas Resources, **IV** 395

Texas Gypsum, **IV** 341

Texas Industries, Inc., **8 522–24**; **13** 142–43

Texas Instruments Incorporated, **I** 315, 482, 523, 620; **II** 64, **112–15**; **III** 120, 124–25, 142, 499; **IV** 130, 365, 681; **6** 216, 221–22, 237, 241, 257, 259; **7** 531; **8** 157; **9** 43, 116, 310; **10** 22, 87, 307; **11** 61, 308, 490, 494, **505–08 (upd.)**; **12** 135, 238; **14** 42–43

Texas International Airlines, **I** 117, 123; **II** 408; **IV** 413

Texas Life Insurance Co., **III** 293

Texas Metal Fabricating Company, **7** 540

Texas Oil & Gas Corp., **IV** 499, 572, 574; **7** 549, 551

Texas Overseas Petroleum Co., **IV** 552

Texas Pacific Coal and Oil Co., **I** 285–86

Texas Pacific Oil Co., **IV** 550

Texas Pipe Line Co., **IV** 552

Texas Power & Light Company, **V** 724

Texas Public Utilities, **II** 660

Texas Super Duper Markets, Inc., **7** 372

Texas Trust Savings Bank, **8** 88

Texas United Insurance Co., **III** 214

Texas Utilities Company, **V 724–25**; **12** 99

Texas-New Mexico Utilities Company, **6** 580

Texasgulf Inc., **IV** 546–47; **13** 557

Texboard, **IV** 296

Texize, **I** 325, 371

Texkan Oil Co., **IV** 566

Texstar Petroleum Company, **7** 516

Texstyrene Corp., **IV** 331

Textile Paper Tube Company, Ltd., **8** 475

Textile Rubber and Chemical Company, **15** 490

Textron Inc., **I** 186, **529–30**; **II** 420; **III** 66, 628; **8** 93, 157, 315, 545; **9** 497, 499; **11** 261; **12** 251, 382–83, 400–01; **13** 63–64

Textron Lycoming Turbine Engine, **9 497–99**

TF-I, **I** 563

TFN Group Communications, Inc., **8** 311

TGEL&PCo. *See* Tucson Gas, Electric Light & Power Company.

TGI Friday's, **10** 331

Th. Pilter, **III** 417

TH:s Group, **10** 113

Thai Airways International Ltd., **I** 119; **II** 442; **6 122–24**

Thai Aluminium Co. Ltd., **IV** 155

Thalassa International, **10** 14

Thalhimer Brothers, **V** 31

Thames Board Ltd., **IV** 318

Thames Television Ltd., **I** 532

Thames Water plc, **11 509–11**

Tharsis Co., **IV** 189–90

Thatcher Glass, **I** 610

Thayer Laboratories, **III** 55

Theo H. Davies & Co., **I** 470

Theo Hamm Brewing Co., **I** 260

Théraplix, **I** 388

Therm-o-Disc, **II** 19

Therm-X Company, **8** 178

Thermacote Welco Company, **6** 146

Thermal Power Company, **11** 270

Thermal Transfer Ltd., **13** 485

Thermo Electron Corporation, **7 520–22**; **11** 512–13; **13** 421

Thermo Instrument Systems Inc., **11** 512–14

Thermo King Corporation, **13 505–07**

Thermodynamics Corp., **III** 645

Thermogas Co., **IV** 458–59

Thermoplast und Apparatebau GmbH, **IV** 198

Thies Companies, **13** 270

Thiess, **III** 687

Thiess Dampier Mitsui, **IV** 47

Things Remembered, **13** 165–66

Think Entertainment, **II** 161

Think Technologies, **10** 508

Thiokol Corporation, **I** 370; **8** 472; **9** 358–59, **500–02 (upd.)**; **12** 68

Third National Bank. *See* Fifth Third Bancorp.

Third National Bank of Dayton, **9** 475

Third National Bank of New York, **II** 253

Thistle Group, **9** 365

Thom McAn, **V** 136–37; **11** 349

Thomas & Betts Corp., **II** 8; **11 515–17**; **14** 27

Thomas & Howard Co., **II** 682

Thomas and Hochwalt, **I** 365

Thomas and Judith Pyle, **13** 433

Thomas Barlow & Sons Ltd., **I** 288, 422; **IV** 22

Thomas Cook Travel Inc., **6** 84; **9 503–05**

Thomas Firth & Sons, **I** 573

Thomas H. Lee Company, **11** 156, 450; **14** 230–31; **15** 309

Thomas J. Lipton Company, **II** 609, 657; **11** 450; **14 495–97**

Thomas Jefferson Life Insurance Co., **III** 397

Thomas Linnell & Co. Ltd., **II** 628

Thomas Nationwide Transport. *See* TNT.

Thomas Nelson Inc., **8** 526; **14 498–99**

Thomas Tilling plc, **I** 429

Thomas Y. Crowell, **IV** 605

Thomasville Furniture Industries, Inc., **III** 423; **12 474–76**

Thompson Aircraft Tire Corp., **14** 42

Thompson Products Co., **I** 539

Thompson-Hayward Chemical Co., **13** 397

Thompson-Ramo-Woolridge, **I** 539

Thompson-Werke, **III** 32

The Thomson Corporation, **IV** 651, 686; **7** 390; **8 525–28**; **12** 562

Thomson International, **10** 407; **12** 361

Thomson S.A., **I** 411; **II** 31, **116–17**; **7** 9; **13** 402

Thomson T-Line, **II** 142

Thomson-Bennett, **III** 554

Thomson-Brandt, **I** 411; **II** 13, 116–17; **9** 9

Thomson-CSF, **II** 116–17; **III** 556

Thomson-Houston Electric Co., **II** 27, 116, 330; **12** 193

Thomson-Jenson Energy Limited, **13** 558

Thomson-Lucas, **III** 556

Thomson-Ramo-Woolridge. *See* TRW Inc.

Thonet Industries Inc., **14** 435–36

Thorn Apple Valley, Inc., **7 523–25**; **12** 125

Thorn EMI plc, **I** 52, 411, **531–32**; **II** 117, 119; **III** 480

Thorndike, Doran, Paine and Lewis, Inc., **14** 530

Thornton, **III** 547

Thornton & Co., **II** 283

Thornton Stores, **14** 235

Thoroughgood, **II** 658

Thousand Trails, Inc., **13** 494

Thousands Springs Power Company, **12** 265

3 Guys, **II** 678, **V** 35

3 Suisses International, **12** 281

Three-Diamond Company. *See* Mitsubishi Shokai.

3-in-One Oil Co., **I** 622

3Com Corp., **III** 143; **6** 238, 269; **10** 237; **11 518–21**

3DO Inc., **10** 286

3M. *See* Minnesota Mining & Manufacturing Co.

3S Systems Support Services Ltd., **6** 310

Threlfall Breweries, **I** 294

Thrif D Discount Center, **V** 174

Thrift Drug, **V** 92

ThriftiCheck Service Corporation, **7** 145

Thriftimart Inc., **12** 153

Thriftway Foods, **II** 624

Thrifty Corporation, **V** 682, 684; **12** 477–78

Thrifty PayLess, Inc., **12 477–79**

Thrifty Rent-A-Car, **6** 349

Throwing Corporation of America, **12** 501

Thuringia Insurance Co., **III** 299

Thurston Motor Lines Inc., **12** 310

Thy-Marcinelle, **IV** 52

Thyssen AG, **II** 279; **III** 566; **IV** 195, **221–23**, 228; **8** 75–76; **14** 169, 328

TI. *See* Texas Instruments.

TI Corporation, **10** 44

Tianjin Agricultural Industry and Commerce Corp., **II** 577

Tibbals Floring Co., **III** 611

Ticino Societa d'Assicurazioni Sulla Vita, **III** 197

Ticketmaster Corp., **13 508–10**

Ticketron, **13** 508–09

Ticknor & Fields, **10** 356

Tickometer Co., **III** 157

Ticor Title Insurance Co., **10** 45

Tidel Systems, **II** 661

Tidewater Inc., **11 522–24**

Tidewater Oil Co., **IV** 434, 460, 489, 522

Tidi Wholesale, **13** 150

Tidy House Products Co., **II** 556

Tiel Utrecht Fire Insurance Co., **III** 309–10

Tien Wah Press (Pte.) Ltd., **IV** 600

Le Tierce S.A., **II** 141

Tiffany & Co., **III** 16; **12** 312; **14 500–03**; **15** 95

Tiger Management Associates, **13** 158, 256

Tiger Oats, **I** 424

Tigon Corporation, **V** 265–68

Tilcon, **I** 429

Tilden Interrent, **10** 419

Tile & Coal Company, **14** 248

Tilgate Pallets, **I** 592

Tillie Lewis Foods Inc., **I** 513–14

Tillotson Corp., **14** 64; **15 488–90**

Tim-Bar Corp., **IV** 312

Timber Realization Co., **IV** 305

The Timberland Company, **11** 349; **13 511–14**

Timberline Software Corporation, **15 491–93**

TIMCO. *See* Triad International Maintenance Corp.

Time Distribution Services, **13** 179

Time Industries, **IV** 294

Time Saver Stores, **12** 112

Time Warner Inc., **II** 155, 161, 168, 175–177, 252, 452; **III** 245; **IV** 341–42, 636, **673–76**; **6** 293; **7** 63, 222–24, 396, **526–30 (upd.)**; **8** 267–68, 527; **9** 119, 469, 472; **10** 168, 286, 484, 488, 491; **13** 105–06, 399; **14** 260; **15** 51, 54. *See also* Warner Communications Inc.

Time-Life Books, Inc., **IV** 674–75; **7** 528–29; **12** 531; **13** 106

Time-O-Stat Controls Corp., **II** 41; **12** 247

Time-Sharing Information, **10** 357

Timely Brands, **I** 259

Timeplex, **III** 166; **6** 283; **9** 32

Times Media Ltd., **IV** 22

Times Mirror Company, **I** 90; **IV** 583, 630, **677–78**; **14** 97

Times Newspapers, **8** 527

Times-Picayune Publishing Co., **IV** 583

Timex Enterprises Inc., **III** 455; **7 531–33**; **10** 152; **12** 317

The Timken Company, **III** 596; **7** 447; **8 529–31**; **15** 225

Timpte Industries, **II** 488

Tioxide Group PLC, **III** 680

Tip Corp., **I** 278

TIPC Network, **10** 307. *See also* Gateway 2000.

Tiphook PLC, **13** 530

Tipton Centers Inc., **V** 50

Tiroler Hauptbank, **II** 270

Tishman Realty and Construction, **III** 248

Tissue Papers Ltd., **IV** 260

Titanium Metals Corporation of America, **10** 434

Titanium Technology Corporation, **13** 140

Titianium Enterprises, **IV** 345

TITISA, **9** 109

Title Guarantee & Trust Co., **II** 230

Titmus Optical Inc., **III** 446

Tivoli Systems, Inc., **14** 392

TJX Companies, Inc., **V 197–98**; **13** 548; **14** 426

TKD Electronics Corp., **II** 109

TKM Foods, **II** 513

TKR Cable Co., **15** 264

TLC Associates, **11** 261

TLC Group, **II** 468

TML Information Services Inc., **9** 95

TMS, Inc., **7** 358

TMS Systems, Inc., **10** 18

TMT. *See* Trailer Marine Transport.

TNT Freightways Corporation, **IV** 651; **14 504–06**

TNT Limited, **V 523–25**; **6** 346

Toa Airlines, **I** 106; **6** 427

Toa Fire & Marine Reinsurance Co., **III** 385

Toa Kyoseki Co. Ltd., **IV** 476

Toa Nenryo Kogyo, **IV** 432

Toa Oil Co. Ltd., **IV** 476, 543

Toa Tanker Co. Ltd., **IV** 555

Toasted Corn Flake Co., **II** 523; **13** 291

Tobata Imaon Co., **I** 183

Tobler Co., **II** 520–21

Tobu Railway Co Ltd, **6 430–32**

Tocom, Inc., **10** 320

Todays Computers Business Centers, **6** 243–44

Todays Temporary, **6** 140

Todd Shipyards Corporation, **IV** 121; **7** 138; **14 507–09**

Todorovich Agency, **III** 204

Toei, **9** 29–30

Tofas, **I** 479–80

Toggenburger Bank, **II** 378

Toho Chemical Co., **I** 363

Toho Oil Co., **IV** 403

Tohoku Alps, **II** 5

Tohoku Pulp Co., **IV** 297

Tohuku Electric Power Company, Inc., **V** 724, 732

Tojo Railway Company, **6** 430

Tokai Aircraft Co., Ltd., **III** 415

The Tokai Bank, Limited, **II** 373–74; **15 494–96 (upd.)**

Tokai Paper Industries, **IV** 679

Tokan Kogyo, **I** 615

Tokio Marine and Fire Insurance Co., Ltd., **II** 323; **III** 248, 289, 295, **383–86**

Tokushima Ham Co., **II** 550

Tokushima Meat Processing Factory, **II** 550

Tokushu Seiko, Ltd., **IV** 63

Tokuyama Soda, **I** 509

Tokuyama Teppan Kabushikigaisha, **IV** 159

Tokyo Broadcasting, **7** 249; **9** 29

Tokyo Car Manufacturing Co., **I** 105

Tokyo Confectionery Co., **II** 538

Tokyo Corporation, **V** 199

Tokyo Dairy Industry, **II** 538

Tokyo Denki Kogaku Kogyo, **II** 109

Tokyo Dento Company, **6** 430

Tokyo Disneyland, **IV** 715; **6** 123, 176

Tokyo Electric Company, Ltd., **I** 533; **12** 483

Tokyo Electric Express Railway Co., **IV** 728

Tokyo Electric Light Co., **IV** 153

Tokyo Electric Power Company, **IV** 167, 518; **V 729–33**

Tokyo Electronic Corp., **11** 232

Tokyo Express Highway Co., Ltd., **IV** 713–14

Tokyo Express Railway Company, **V** 510, 526

Tokyo Fire Insurance Co. Ltd., **III** 405–06, 408

Tokyo Food Products, **I** 507

Tokyo Fuhansen Co., **I** 502, 506

Tokyo Gas and Electric Industrial Company, **9** 293

Tokyo Gas Co., Ltd., **IV** 518; **V 734–36**

Tokyo Ishikawajima Shipbuilding and Engineering Company, **III** 532; **9** 293

Tokyo Maritime Insurance Co., **III** 288

Tokyo Motors, **9** 293

Tokyo Sanyo Electric, **II** 91–92

Tokyo Shibaura Electric Company, Ltd., **I** 507, 533; **12** 483

Tokyo Steel Works Co., Ltd., **IV** 63

Tokyo Tanker Co., Ltd., **IV** 479

Tokyo Telecommunications Engineering Corp. *See* Tokyo Tsushin Kogyo K.K.

Tokyo Trust & Banking Co., **II** 328

Tokyo Tsushin Kogyo K.K., **II** 101, 103

Tokyo Yokohama Electric Railways Co., Ltd., **V** 199

Tokyu Corporation, **IV** 728; **V** 199, **526–28**

Tokyu Department Store Co., Ltd., **V 199–202**

Tokyu Electric Power Company, **V** 736

Tokyu Kyuko Electric Railway Company Ltd., **V** 526

Tokyu Land Corporation, **IV 728–29**

Tokyu Railway Company, **V** 461

Toledo Edison Company. *See* Centerior Energy Corporation.
Toledo Milk Processing, Inc., **15** 449
Toledo Scale Corp., **9** 441
Toledo Seed & Oil Co., **I** 419
Toll Brothers Inc., 15 497–99
Tom Bowling Lamp Works, **III** 554
Tom Huston Peanut Co., **II** 502; **10** 323
Tom Piper Ltd., **I** 437
Tomakomai Paper Co., Ltd., **IV** 321
Tombstone Pizza Corporation, 13 515–17
Tomei Fire and Marine Insurance Co., **III** 384–85
Tomen Corporation, IV 224–25
Tomen Transportgerate, **III** 638
Tomkins plc, 11 525–27
Tomlee Tool Company, **7** 535
Tomoe Trading Co., **III** 595
Tonami Transportation Company, **6** 346
Tone Coca-Cola Bottling Company, Ltd., **14** 288
Tonen Corporation, IV 554–56
Tong Yang Group, **III** 304
Toni Co., **III** 28; **9** 413
Tonka Corp., **12** 169; **14** 266
Toohey, **10** 170
Tootal Group, **V** 356–57
Tootsie Roll Industries Inc., 12 480–82; 15 323
Top End Wheelchair Sports, **11** 202
Top Man, **V** 21
Top Shop, **V** 21
Top Value Stamp Co., **II** 644–45; **6** 364
Toppan Printing Co., Ltd., IV 598–99, 679–81
Topps Company, Inc., 13 518–20
Topy Industries, Limited, **8** 506–07
Toray Industries, Inc., V 380, 383
Torbensen Gear & Axle Co., **I** 154
Torchmark Corporation, III 194; 9 506–08; 10 66; **11** 17
Torise Ham Co., **II** 550
Tornator Osakeyhtiö, **IV** 275–76
Toro Assicurazioni, **III** 347
The Toro Company, III 600; **7 534–36**
Toronto and Scarborough Electric Railway, **9** 461
Toronto Electric Light Company, **9** 461
Toronto-Dominion Bank, II 319, **375–77,** 456
Torpshammars, **IV** 338
Torrey Canyon Oil, **IV** 569
The Torrington Company, III 526, 589–90; **13 521–24**
Torrington National Bank & Trust Co., **13** 467
Torstar Corp., **IV** 672; **7** 488–89
Tosa Electric Railway Co., **II** 458
Toscany Co., **13** 42
Tosco Corporation, 7 537–39; 12 240
Toshiba Corporation, I 221, 507–08, **533–35; II** 5, 56, 59, 62, 68, 73, 99, 102, 118, 122, 326, 440; **III** 298, 461, 533, 604; **6** 101, 231, 244, 287; **7** 529; **9** 7, 181; **10** 518–19; **11** 46, 328; **12** 454, **483–86 (upd.),** 546; **13** 324, 399, 482; **14** 117, 446
Toshin Kaihatsu Ltd., **V** 195
Toshin Paper Co., Ltd., **IV** 285
Tostem. *See* Toyo Sash Co., Ltd.
Total Compagnie Française des Pétroles S.A., I 303; **III** 673; **IV** 425, 486, 498,

515, 525, 544, 547, **557–61; V** 628; **7** 481, 483–84; **13** 557
Total Exploration S.A., **11** 537
Total Global Sourcing, Inc., **10** 498
Total System Services, Inc., **12** 465–66
Totem Resources Corporation, 9 509–11
Totino's Finer Foods, **II** 556; **13** 516
Toto Bank, **II** 326
Toto, Ltd., III 755–56
Totsu Co., **I** 493
Touche Remnant Holdings Ltd., **II** 356
Touche Ross, **10** 529. *See also* Deloitte & Touche.
Touchstone Films, **II** 172–74; **6** 174–76
Tour d'Argent, **II** 518
Tourang Limited, **7** 253
Touristik Union International GmbH. and Company K.G., II 163–65
Touron y Cia, **III** 419
Touropa, **II** 163–64
Toval Japon, **IV** 680
Towa Nenryo Kogyo Co. Ltd., **IV** 554–55
Tower Records, **9** 361; **10** 335; **11** 558
Towers, **II** 649
Towle Manufacturing Co., **14** 482–83
Town & City, **IV** 696
Town & Country, **7** 372
Town Investments, **IV** 711
Townsend Hook, **IV** 296, 650, 652
Toy Biz, Inc., **10** 402
Toy Liquidators, **13** 541–43
Toyad Corp., **7** 296
Toyo Bearing Manufacturing, **III** 595
Toyo Cotton Co., **IV** 224–25
Toyo Kogyo, **I** 167; **II** 361; **11** 139
Toyo Marine and Fire, **III** 385
Toyo Menka Kaisha Ltd., **I** 508; **IV** 224–25
Toyo Microsystems Corporation, **11** 464
Toyo Oil Co., **IV** 403
Toyo Pulp Co., **IV** 322
Toyo Rayon, **V** 381, 383
Toyo Sash Co., Ltd., III 757–58
Toyo Seikan Kaisha Ltd., I 615–16
Toyo Soda, **II** 301
Toyo Tire & Rubber Co., **V** 255–56; **9** 248
Toyo Toki Co., Ltd., **III** 755
Toyo Tozo Co., **I** 265
Toyo Trust and Banking Co., **II** 347, 371
Toyoda Automatic Loom Works, Ltd., I 203; **III** 591, 593, 632, **636–39**
Toyokawa Works, **I** 579
Toyoko Co., Ltd., **V** 199
Toyoko Kogyo, **V** 199
Toyomenka (America) Inc., **IV** 224
Toyomenka (Australia) Pty., Ltd., **IV** 224
Toyota Gossei, **I** 321
Toyota Motor Corporation, I 9–10, 174, 184, **203–05,** 507–08, 587; **II** 373; **III** 415, 495, 521, 523, 536, 579, 581, 591–93, 624, 636–38, 667, 715, 742; **IV** 702; **6** 514; **7** 111, 118, 212, 219–21; **8** 315; **9** 294, 340–42; **10** 353, 407; **11** 351, 377, 487, **528–31 (upd.); 14** 321; **15** 495
Toyota Tsusho America, Inc., **13** 371
Toys "R" Us, Inc., III 588; **V 203–06; 7** 396; **10** 235, 284, 484; **12** 178; **13** 166; **14** 61; **15** 469
Tozer Kemsley & Milbourn, **II** 208
TPCR Corporation, **V** 163; **14** 394
Tracey Bros., **IV** 416
Tracey-Locke, **II** 660
Tracker Services, Inc., **9** 110

Traco International N.V., **8** 250
Tracor Inc., **10** 547
Tractor Supply Corp., **I** 446
Tradax, **II** 617; **13** 137
Trade Assoc. of Bilbao, **II** 194
Trade Development Bank, **11** 415–17
Trade Waste Incineration, Inc., **9** 109
Trade Winds Campers, **III** 599
TradeARBED, **IV** 25
Trader Joe's Co., 13 525–27
Trader Publications, Inc., **IV** 597
Trader Publishing Company, **12** 302
Traders & General Insurance, **III** 248
Traders Bank of Canada, **II** 344
Traders Group Ltd., **11** 258
Tradesmens National Bank of Philadelphia, **II** 342
The Trading Service, **10** 278
Traex Corporation, **8** 359
Trafalgar House, **I** 248–49, 572–74; **IV** 259, 711
Trailer Marine Transport, **6** 383
Trailways, **I** 450; **9** 425
Trammell Crow Company, IV 343; **8** 326–28, **532–34**
Tran Telecommunications Corp., **III** 110; **14** 14
Trane Co., **III** 663, 665; **10** 525
Trans Air System, **6** 367
Trans Colorado, **11** 299
Trans International Airlines, **I** 537; **13** 529
Trans Ocean Products, **II** 578; **8** 510
Trans Rent-A-Car, **6** 348
Trans Union Corp., **IV** 137; **6** 25
Trans World Airlines, Inc., I 58, 70, 90, 97, 99–100, 102, 113, 121, 123–24, **125–27,** 132, 466; **II** 32–33, 142, 425, 679; **III** 92, 428; **6** 50, 68, 71, 74, 76–77, 81–82, 114, 130; **9** 17, 232; **10** 301–03, 316; **11** 277, 427; **12** 381, **487–90 (upd.); 13** 341; **14** 73; **15** 419
Trans World Music, **9** 361
Trans World Seafood, Inc., **13** 244
Trans-Arabian Pipe Line Co., **IV** 537, 552
Trans-Australia Airlines, **6** 110–12
Trans-Continental Leaf Tobacco Company (TCLTC), **13** 491
Trans-Natal Coal Corp., **IV** 93
Trans-Resources Inc., **13** 299
Transaction Technology, **12** 334
TransAlta Utilities Corporation, 6 585–87
Transamerica Corporation, I 536–38; **II** 147–48, 227, 288–89, 422; **III** 332, 344; **7** 236–37; **8** 46; **11** 273, 533; **13 528–30 (upd.)**
Transat. *See* Compagnie Générale Transatlantique (Transat).
Transatlantic Holdings, Inc., III 198; **11 532–33; 15** 18
Transatlantische Dampfschiffahrts Gesellschaft, **6** 397
Transatlantische Gruppe, **III** 404
Transbrasil, **6** 134
TransCanada PipeLines Limited, I 264; **V** 270–71, **737–38**
Transco Energy Company, IV 367; **V** 739–40; **6** 143
Transcontinental Air Transport, **I** 125; **9** 17; **11** 427; **12** 487
Transcontinental and Western Air Lines, **9** 416; **12** 487
Transcontinental Gas Pipe Line Corporation, **V** 739; **6** 447

Transcontinental Pipeline Company, **6** 456–57
Transelco, Inc., **8** 178
TransEuropa, **II** 164
Transflash, **6** 404
Transfracht, **6** 426
Transinternational Life, **II** 422
Transit Mix Concrete and Materials Company, **7** 541
Transking Inc. *See* King Kullen Grocery Co., Inc.
Transkrit Corp., **IV** 640
Translite, **III** 495
Transmanche-Link, **13** 206–08
Transmitter Equipment Manufacturing Co., **13** 385
Transnet Ltd., 6 433–35
TransOcean Oil, **III** 559
Transpac, **IV** 325
Transport Management Co., **III** 192
Transport- und Unfall-Versicherungs-Aktiengesellschaft Zürich, **III** 411
Transportacion Maritima Mexican, **12** 279
Transportation Insurance Co., **III** 229
Transportes Aereos Portugueses, S.A., 6 125–27
Transtar, **6** 120–21
Transue & Williams Steel Forging Corp., **13** 302
Transvaal Silver and Base Metals, **IV** 90
Transway International Corp., **10** 369
Transworld Corp., **14** 209
Transworld Drilling Co. Ltd., **IV** 446
The Tranzonic Cos., 8 512; 15 500–02
Trasgo, S.A. de C.V., **14** 516
Trausch Baking Co., **I** 255
Trävaru Svartvik, **IV** 338
Travel Air Company, **8** 49
Travel Automation Services Ltd., **I** 95
Travelers Bank & Trust Company, **13** 467
Travelers Book Club, **13** 105
Travelers Corporation, I 37, 545; **III** 313, 329, **387–90**, 707–08; **6** 12; **15** 463
Traveller's Express, **I** 449
TraveLodge, **III** 94, 104–06
Travenol Laboratories, **I** 627–28; **10** 141–43
Trayco, **III** 570
Traylor Engineering & Manufacturing Company, **6** 395
Treatment Centers of America, **11** 379
Trechmann, Weekes and Co., **III** 669
Tredegar Industries, Inc., **10** 291
Tree of Life Inc., **II** 528
TreeSweet Products, **12** 105
TrefilARBED, **IV** 26
Tréfimétaux, **IV** 174
Trefoil Capital Investors, L.P., **8** 305
Trek, **IV** 90, 92–93
Trelleborg A.B., **III** 625; **IV** 166
Tremletts Ltd., **IV** 294
Trend International Ltd., **13** 502
TrendWest, **12** 439
Trent Tube, **I** 435
Trenton Foods, **II** 488
Tresco, **8** 514
Trethowal China Clay Co., **III** 690
Tri-City Federal Savings and Loan Association, **10** 92
Tri-City Utilities Company, **6** 514
Tri-County National Bank, **9** 474
Tri-Miller Packing Company, **7** 524
Tri-State Improvement Company, **6** 465–66

Tri-State Recycling Corporation, **15** 117
Tri-State Refining Co., **IV** 372
Triad, **14** 224
Triad International Maintenance Corp., **13** 417
Triangle Auto Springs Co., **IV** 136
Triangle Industries Inc., **I** 602, 607–08, 614; **II** 480–81; **14** 43
Triangle Portfolio Associates, **II** 317
Triangle Publications, Inc., **IV** 652; **7** 391; **12** 359–60
Triangle Refineries, **IV** 446
Triarc Companies, Inc. (formerly DWG Corporation), 8 535–37; 13 322; 14 32–33
Triathlon Leasing, **II** 457
Tribune Company, III 329; **IV 682–84**; **10** 56; **11** 331
Trical Resources, **IV** 84
Tricity Cookers, **I** 531–32
Trico Products Corporation, I 186; **15 503–05**
Tridel Enterprises Inc., 9 512–13
Trident Seafoods, **II** 494
Trifari, Krussman & Fishel, Inc., **9** 157
Trigen Energy Corp., **6** 512
Trigon Industries, **13** 195; **14** 431
Trilan Developments Ltd., **9** 512
Trilon Financial Corporation, II 456–57; **IV** 721; **9** 391
TriMas Corp., III 571; **11 534–36**
Trinidad Oil Co., **IV** 95, 552
Trinidad-Tesoro Petroleum Company Limited, **7** 516, 518
Trinity Beverage Corporation, **11** 451
Trinity Broadcasting, **13** 279
Trinity Distributors, **15** 139
Trinity Industries, Incorporated, 7 540–41
Trinkaus und Burkhardt, **II** 319
TRINOVA Corporation, III 640–42, 731; **13** 8
Trintex, **6** 158
Triology Corp., **III** 110
Triplex, **6** 279
Triplex (Northern) Ltd., **III** 725
Trippe Manufacturing Co., **10** 474
Triquet Paper Co., **IV** 282; **9** 261
TriStar Pictures, **I** 234; **II** 134, 136–37; **6** 158; **10** 227; **12** 75, 455
Triton Bioscience, **III** 53
Triton Energy Corporation, 11 537–39
Triton Group Ltd., **I** 447
Triton Oil, **IV** 519
Triumph American, Inc., **12** 199
Triumph, Finlay, and Philips Petroleum, **11** 28
Triumph-Adler, **I** 485; **III** 145; **11** 265
Trivest Insurance Network, **II** 457
Trizec Corporation Ltd., 9 84–85; 10 529–32
Trojan, **III** 674
Troll, **13** 561
Trona Corp., **IV** 95
Tropical Oil Co., **IV** 415–16
Tropical Shipping, Inc., **6** 529, 531
Tropicana Products, **II** 468, 525; **13** 293
Troy & Nichols, Inc., **13** 147
Troy Metal Products. *See* KitchenAid.
Troyfel Ltd., **III** 699
TRT Communications, Inc., **6** 327; **11** 185
Tru-Trac Therapy Products, **11** 486
True Form, **V** 177
True Value Hardware Stores, **V** 37–38

Trugg-Hansa Holding AB, **III** 264
Truitt Bros., **10** 382
Truman Dunham Co., **III** 744
Truman Hanburg, **I** 247
Trumball Asphalt, **III** 721
Trümmer-Verwertungs-Gesellschaft, **IV** 140
Trunkline Gas Company, **6** 544; **14** 135
Trunkline LNG Co., **IV** 425
Trustcorp, Inc., **9** 475–76
Trustees, Executors and Agency Co. Ltd., **II** 189
Trusthouse Forte PLC, I 215; **III 104–06**
TRW Inc., I 539–41; **II** 33; **6** 25; **8** 416; **9** 18, 359; **10** 293; **11** 68, **540–42 (upd.)**; **12** 238; **14 510–13 (upd.)**
Tryart Pty. Limited, **7** 253
Tsai Management & Research Corp., **III** 230–31
TSB Group plc, 12 491–93
TSO. *See* Teacher's Service Organization, Inc.
TSO Financial Corp., **II** 420; **8** 10
Tsuang Hine Co., **III** 582
Tsubakimoto-Morse, **14** 64
Tsukumo Shokai, **I** 502; **III** 712
Tsumeb Corp., **IV** 17–18
Tsurumi Steelmaking and Shipbuilding Co., **IV** 162
Tsurusaki Pulp Co., Ltd., **IV** 285
Tsutsunaka Plastic Industry Co., **III** 714; **8** 359
TTK. *See* Tokyo Tsushin Kogyo K.K.
TTX Company, 6 436–37
Tube Investments, **II** 422; **IV** 15
Tuborg, **9** 99
TUCO, Inc., **8** 78
Tucson Electric Power Company, V 713; **6 588–91**
TUI. *See* Touristik Union International GmbH. and Company K.G.
Tuileries et Briqueteries d'Hennuyeres et de Wanlin, **14** 249
Tultex Corporation, 13 531–33
Tunhems Industri A.B., **I** 387
Tupperware, **I** 29; **II** 534; **III** 610–12;, **15** 475, 477
Turbinbolaget, **III** 419
Turkish Engineering, Consultancy and Contracting Corp., **IV** 563
Turkish Petroleum Co. *See* Türkiye Petrolleri Anonim Ortakliği.
Türkiye Garanti Bankası, **I** 479
Türkiye Petrolleri Anonim Ortaklıği, IV 464, 557–58, **562–64**; **7** 352
Turnbull, **III** 468
Turner Broadcasting System, Inc., II 134, 149, 161 **166–68**; **IV** 676; **6 171–73 (upd.)**; **7** 64, 99, 306, 529
The Turner Corporation, 8 538–40
Turner Glass Company, **13** 40
Turner's Turkeys, **II** 587
TURPAS, **IV** 563
Turtle Wax, Inc., 15 506–09
Tussauds Group Ltd., **IV** 659
TV & Stereo Town, **10** 468
TV Asahi, **7** 249
TV Guide, **10** 287
TVE. *See* Television Española, S.A.
TVH Acquisition Corp., **III** 262, 264
TVI, Inc., 15 510–12
TVS Entertainment PLC, **13** 281
TVW Enterprises, **7** 78
TVX, **II** 449; **13** 449

TW Kutter, **III** 420
TW Services, Inc., II 679–80; **10** 301–03
TWA. *See* Trans World Airlines *and* Transcontinental & Western Airways.
Tweeds, **12** 280
Twen-Tours International, **II** 164
Twentieth Century Fox Film Corporation, **II** 133, 135, 146, 155–56, **169–71**, 175; **IV** 652; **7** 391–92; **12** 73, 322, 359; **15** 23, 25, 234
Twentsche Bank, **II** 183
Twenty-Second National Bank, **II** 291
21 Invest International Holdings Ltd., **14** 322
Twin City Wholesale Drug Company, **14** 147
Twining Crosfield Group, **II** 465; **13** 52
Twinings Tea, **II** 465; **III** 696
Twinings' Foods International, **II** 466
Twinpak, **IV** 250
Two Guys, **12** 49
2-in-1 Shinola Bixby Corp., **II** 497
TXL Oil Corp., **IV** 552
TXP Operation Co., **IV** 367
TxPort Inc., **13** 8
Ty-D-Bol, **III** 55
Tyco Laboratories, Inc., III 643–46; **13** 245–47
Tyco Toys, Inc., 12 494–97; **13** 312, 319
Tyndall Fund-Unit Assurance Co., **III** 273
Typhoo Tea, **II** 477
Typpi Oy, **IV** 469
Tyrolean Airways, **9** 233
Tyrväan Oy, **IV** 348
Tyson Foods, Inc., II 584–85; **7** 422–23, 432; **14 514–16 (upd.)**

U S West, Inc., V 341–43; **11** 12, 59, 547
U.C.L.A.F. *See* Roussel-Uclaf.
U-Haul International Inc. *See* Amerco.
U.K. Corrugated, **IV** 296
U.S. Bancorp, 12 165; **14 527–29**
U.S. Bank of Washington, **14** 527
U.S. Bearings Co., **I** 159
U.S. Electrical Motors, **II** 19
U.S. Food Products Co., **I** 376
U.S.G. Co., **III** 762
U.S. Geological Survey, **9** 367
U.S. Guarantee Co., **III** 220; **14** 108
U.S. Healthcare, Inc., 6 194–96
U.S. Home Corporation, 8 541–43
U.S. Industries, **7** 208
U.S. International Reinsurance, **III** 264
U.S. Land Co., **IV** 255
U.S. Life Insurance, **III** 194
U.S. Lines, **I** 476; **III** 459; **11** 194
U.S. Lock, **9** 543
U.S. Marine Corp., **III** 444
U.S. Overall Company, **14** 549
U.S. Plywood Corp. *See* United States Plywood Corp.
U.S. Realty and Improvement Co., **III** 98
U.S. RingBinder Corp., **10** 313–14
U.S. Robotics Inc., 9 514–15
U.S. Rubber Company, **I** 478; **10** 388
U.S. Satellite Systems, **III** 169; **6** 285
U.S. Smelting Refining and Mining, **7** 360
U.S. Steel Corp. *See* United States Steel Corp.
U.S. Telephone Communications, **9** 478
U.S. Tile Co., **III** 674
U.S. Time Corporation, **13** 120
U.S. Trust Co. of New York, **II** 274
U.S. Vanadium Co., **9** 517

U.S. Venture Partners, **15** 204–05
U.S. Vitamin & Pharmaceutical Corp., **III** 55
U.S. Windpower, **11** 222–23
U-Tote'M, **II** 620; **7** 372
UAA. *See* AirEgypt.
UAL, Inc., **II** 680; **IV** 23; **9** 283. *See also* United Airlines.
UAP. *See* Union des Assurances de Paris.
UARCO Inc., **15** 473–74
UAT. *See* UTA.
Ub Iwerks, **6** 174
Ube Industries, Ltd., III 759–61
Uberseebank A.G., **III** 197
UBS. *See* Union Bank of Switzerland.
Ucabail, **II** 265
UCC-Communications Systems, Inc., **II** 38
Uccel, **6** 224
Uchiyama, **V** 727
UCI, **IV** 92
UCPMI, **IV** 226
Uddeholm and Bohler, **IV** 234
Udet Flugzeugwerke, **I** 73
Udo Fischer Co., **8** 477
UE Automotive Manufacturing, **III** 580
UGI. *See* United Gas Improvement.
UGI Corporation, 12 498–500
Ugine, **IV** 174
Ugine Steels, **IV** 227
Ugine-Kuhlmann, **IV** 108, 174
UI International, **6** 444
UIB. *See* United Independent Broadcasters, Inc.
Uinta Co., **6** 568
Uintah National Corp., **11** 260
UIS Co., **13 554–55**; **15** 324
Uitgeversmaatschappij Elsevier, **IV** 610
UJB Financial Corp., **14** 473
UK Paper, **IV** 279
UKF. *See* Unie van Kunstmestfabrieken.
Ullrich Copper, Inc., **6** 146
Ullstein AV Produktions-und Vertriebsgesellschaft, **IV** 590
Ullstein Langen Müller, **IV** 591
Ullstein Tele Video, **IV** 590
ULPAC, **II** 576
Ulster Bank, **II** 334
Ultra Bancorp, **II** 334
Ultra High Pressure Units Ltd., **IV** 66; **7** 123
Ultra Radio & Television, **I** 531
Ultralar, **13** 544
Ultramar PLC, IV 565–68
Ultronic Systems Corp., **IV** 669
UM Technopolymer, **III** 760
Umacs of Canada Inc., **9** 513
Umm-al-Jawabi Oil Co., **IV** 454
Umpqua River Navigation Company, **13** 100
Unadulterated Food Products, Inc., **11** 449
UNAT, **III** 197–98
Uncas-Merchants National Bank, **13** 467
Under Sea Industries, **III** 59
Underground Group, **6** 407
Underwood, **III** 145
Underwriters Adjusting Co., **III** 242
Underwriters Reinsurance Co., **10** 45
UNELCO. *See* Union Electrica de Canarias S.A.
Unelec, Inc., **13** 398
Unfall, **III** 207
Ungermann-Bass, Inc., **6** 279
Uni Europe, **III** 211
Uni-Cardan AG, **III** 494

Uni-Charm, **III** 749
Uni-Sankyo, **I** 675
Unic, **V** 63
Unicapital, Inc., **15** 281
Unicare Health Facilities, **6** 182
Unicer, **9** 100
Unichema International, **13** 228
Unicoa, **I** 524
Unicomi, **II** 265
Unicon Producing Co., **10** 191
Unicorn Shipping Lines, **IV** 91
UniCorp, **8** 228
Unicorp Financial, **III** 248
Unicredit, **II** 265
Uniden, **14** 117
UniDynamics Corporation, **8** 135
Unie van Kunstmestfabrieken, **I** 326
Uniface Holding B.V., **10** 245
Unifi, Inc., 12 501–03
Unified Management Corp., **III** 306
Unigate PLC, II 586–87
Unigep Group, **III** 495
Unigesco Inc., **II** 653
Uniglory, **13** 211
Unigroup, **15** 50
UniHealth America, **11** 378–79
Unilac Inc., **II** 547
Unilever PLC / Unilever N.V., I 369, 590, 605; **II** 547, **588–91**; **III** 31–32, 46, 52, 495; **IV** 532; **7** 382, **542–45 (upd.)**, 577; **8** 105–07, 166, 168, 341, 344; **9** 449; **11** 205, 421; **13** 243–44; **14** 204–05
Unilife Assurance Group, **III** 273
UniMac Companies, **11** 413
Unimat, **II** 265
Unimation, **II** 122
Unimetal, **IV** 227
Uninsa, **I** 460
Union, **III** 391–93
Union & NHK Auto Parts, **III** 580
Union Acceptances Ltd., **IV** 23
Unión Aérea Española, **6** 95
Union Aéromaritime de Transport. *See* UTA.
Union Assurance, **III** 234
Union Bag–Camp Paper Corp., **IV** 344–45
Union Bancorp of California, **II** 358
Union Bank, **II** 207; **8** 491–92. *See also* State Street Boston Corporation.
Union Bank of Australia, **II** 187–89
Union Bank of Birmingham, **II** 318
Union Bank of Canada, **II** 344
Union Bank of England, **II** 188
Union Bank of Finland, **II** 302, 352
Union Bank of Halifax, **II** 344
Union Bank of London, **II** 235
Union Bank of New London, **II** 213
Union Bank of New York, **9** 229
Union Bank of Prince Edward Island, **II** 220
Union Bank of Scotland, **10** 337
Union Bank of Switzerland, **II** 257, 267, 334, 369, 370, **378–79**
Union Battery Co., **III** 536
Union Camp Corporation, IV 344–46; **8** 102
Union Carbide Corporation, I 334, 339, 347, 374, 390, **399–401**, 582, 666; **II** 103, 313, 562; **III** 742, 760; **IV** 92, 374, 379, 521; **7** 376; **8** 180, 182, 376; **9** 16, **516–20 (upd.)**; **10** 289, 472; **11** 402–03; **12** 46, 347; **13** 118; **14** 281–82
Union Cervecera, **9** 100

Union Colliery Company, **V** 741
Union Commerce Corporation, **11** 181
Union Corp., **I** 423; **IV** 90–92, 95, 565
Union d'Etudes et d'Investissements, **II** 265
Union des Assurances de Paris, **II** 234; **III** 201, **391–94**
Union des Transports Aériens. *See* UTA.
Union Electric Company, **V** 741–43; **6** 505–06
Union Electrica de Canarias S.A., **V** 607
Union Equity Co-Operative Exchange, **7** 175
Union et Prévoyance, **III** 403
Union Fertilizer, **I** 412
Union Fidelity Corp., **III** 204
Union Gas & Electric Co., **6** 529
Union Générale de Savonnerie, **III** 33
l'Union Générale des Pétroles, **IV** 545–46, 560; **7** 482–83
Union Glass Co., **III** 683
Union Hardware, **III** 443
Union Hop Growers, **I** 287
Union Levantina de Seguros, **III** 179
Union Light, Heat & Power Company, **6** 466
Union Marine, **III** 372
Union Mutual Life Insurance Company. *See* UNUM Corp.
Union National Bank, **II** 284; **10** 298
Union of Food Co-ops, **II** 622
Union of London, **II** 333
Union Oil Associates, **IV** 569
Union Oil Co., **9** 266
Union Oil Co. of California, **I** 13; **IV** 385, 400, 403, 434, 522, 531, 540, 569, 575; **11** 271
Union Pacific Corporation, **I** 473; **II** 381; **III** 229; **V** **529–32**; **12** 18–20, 278; **14** 371–72
Union Pacific Tea Co., **7** 202
Union Paper Bag Machine Co., **IV** 344
Union Petroleum Corp., **IV** 394
L'Union pour le Developement Régional, **II** 265
Union Power Company, **12** 541
Union Rückversicherungs-Gesellschaft, **III** 377
Union Savings, **II** 316
Union Savings Bank, **9** 173
Union Savings Bank and Trust Company, **13** 221
Union Steam Ship Co., **IV** 279
Union Steel Co., **IV** 22, 572; **7** 550
Union Sugar, **II** 573
Union Sulphur Co., **IV** 81; **7** 185
Union Supply Co., **IV** 573; **7** 550
Union Tank Car Co., **IV** 137
Union Telephone Company, **14** 258
Union Texas Petroleum Holdings, Inc., **I** 415; **7** 379; **9** **521–23**
Union Trust Co., **II** 284, 313, 315–16, 382; **9** 228; **13** 222
The Union Underwear Company, **I** 440–41; **8** 200–01
Union Wine, **I** 289
Union-Capitalisation, **III** 392
Union-Transport, **6** 404
Unionamerica Insurance Group, **III** 243
Uniroyal Corp., **I** 30–31; **II** 472; **V** 242; **8** 503; **11** 159
Unisource, **I** 413

Unisys Corporation, **II** 42; **III** **165–67**; **6** **281–83 (upd.)**; **8** 92; **9** 32, 59; **12** 149, 162
The Unit Companies, Inc., **6** 394, 396
Unit Group plc, **8** 477
United Acquisitions, **7** 114
United Advertising Periodicals, **12** 231
United Agri Products, **II** 494
United Air Lines Transportation Company. *See* United Airlines.
United Aircraft and Transportation Co., **I** 48, 76, 78, 85–86, 96, 441, 489; **9** 416, 418; **10** 162, 260; **12** 289
United Airlines, **I** 23, 47, 71, 84, 90, 97, 113, 116, 118, 124, **128–30**; **II** 142, 419, 680; **III** 225; **6** 71, 75–77, 104, 121, 123, **128–30 (upd.)**, 131, 388–89; **9** 271–72, 283, 416, 549; **10** 162, 199, 561; **11** 299; **12** 192, 381; **14** 73
United Alaska Drilling, Inc., **7** 558
United Alkalai Co., **I** 351
United American Insurance Company of Dallas, **9** 508
United American Lines, **6** 398
United Arab Airlines. *See* AirEgypt.
United Artists Corp., **I** 537; **II** 135, 146–48, 149, 157–58, 160, 167, 169; **III** 721; **IV** 676; **6** 167; **9** 74; **12** 13, 73; **13** 529; **14** 87, 399. *See also* MGM/UA Communications Company.
United Bank of Arizona, **II** 358
United Biscuits (Holdings) PLC, **II** 466, 540, **592–94**; **III** 503
United Brands Company, **II** **595–97**; **III** 28; **7** 84–85; **12** 215
United Breweries Ltd. **I** 221, 223, 288. *See also* Carlsberg A/S.
United Cable Television Corporation, **II** 160; **9** 74
United California Bank, **II** 289
United Car, **I** 540; **14** 511
United Carbon Co., **IV** 373
United Central Oil Corporation, **7** 101
United Cigar Manufacturers Company, **II** 414. *See also* Culbro Corporation.
United City Property Trust, **IV** 705
United Co., **I** 70
United Communications Systems, Inc. **V** 346
United Computer Services, Inc., **11** 111
United Corp., **10** 44
United County Banks, **II** 235
United Dairies, **II** 586–87
United Dairy Farmers, **III** 190
United Dominion Corp., **III** 200
United Dominion Industries Limited, **IV** 288; **8** **544–46**
United Drapery Stores, **III** 502; **7** 208
United Drug Co., **II** 533
United Electric Light and Water Co., **13** 182
United Engineering Steels, **III** 495
United Engineers & Constructors, **II** 86; **11** 413
United Express, **11** 299
United Factors Corp., **13** 534–35
United Features Syndicate, Inc., **IV** 607–08
United Federal Savings and Loan of Waycross, **10** 92
United Financial Corporation, **12** 353
United Financial Group, Inc., **8** 349
United 5 and 10 Cent Stores, **13** 444
United Fruit Co., **I** 529, 566; **II** 120, 595; **IV** 308; **7** 84–85

United Gas and Electric Company of New Albany, **6** 555
United Gas and Improvement Co., **13** 182
United Gas Corp., **IV** 488–90
United Gas Improvement Co., **IV** 549; **V** 696; **6** 446, 523; **11** 388
United Gas Industries, **III** 502; **7** 208
United Gas Pipe Line Co., **IV** 489–90
United Geophysical Corp., **I** 142
United Graphics, **12** 25
United Grocers, **II** 625
United Guaranty Corp., **III** 197
United Health Maintenance, Inc., **6** 181–82
United HealthCare Corporation, **9** **524–26**
United Independent Broadcasters, Inc., **II** 132
United Industrial Syndicate, **8** 545
United Information Systems, Inc., **V** 346
United Insurance Co., **I** 523
Oy United International, **IV** 349
United International Pictures, **II** 155
United Iron & Metal Co., **14** 156
United Kent Fire, **III** 350
United Kingdom Atomic Energy Authority, **6** 451–52
United Liberty Life Insurance Co., **III** 190–92
United Life & Accident Insurance Co., **III** 220–21; **14** 109
United Life Insurance Company, **12** 541
United Light & Railway Co., **V** 609
United Light and Power, **6** 511
United Machinery Co., **15** 127
United Match Factories, **12** 462
United Medical Service, Inc., **III** 245–46
United Merchandising Corp., **12** 477
United Merchants & Manufacturers, Inc., **13** **534–37**
United Meridian Corporation, **8** 350
United Metals Selling Co., **IV** 31
United Micronesia, **I** 97
United Molasses, **II** 582
United Natural Gas Company, **6** 526
United Netherlands Navigation Company. *See* Vereenigde Nederlandsche Scheepvaartmaatschappij.
United Newspapers plc, **IV** **685–87**
United of Omaha, **III** 365
United Office Products, **11** 64
United Oil Co., **IV** 399
United Optical, **10** 151
United Pacific Financial Services, **III** 344
United Pacific Insurance Co., **III** 343
United Pacific Life Insurance Co., **III** 343–44
United Pacific Reliance Life Insurance Co. of New York, **III** 343
United Packages, **IV** 249
United Paper Mills Ltd., **II** 302; **IV** 316, **347–50**
United Paramount Theatres, **II** 129
United Parcel Service of America Inc. (UPS), **V** **533–35**; **6** 345–46, 385–86, 390; **11** 11; **12** 309, 334; **13** 19, 416; **14** 517
United Pipeline Co., **IV** 394
United Power and Light Corporation, **6** 473; **12** 541
United Presidential Life Insurance Company, **12** 524, 526
United Press Assoc., **IV** 607, 627, 669; **7** 158

United Press International, **IV** 670; **7** 158–59

United Retail Merchants Stores Inc., **9** 39

United Roasters, **III** 24; **14** 121

United Satellite Television, **10** 320

United Savings of Texas, **8** 349

United Servomation, **7** 471–72

United Skates of America, **8** 303

United Software Consultants Inc., **11** 65

United States Baking Co., **II** 542

United States Can Co., **15** 127, 129

United States Cellular Corporation, **9** 494–96, **527–29**

United States Department of Defense, **6** 327

United States Distributing Corp., **IV** 180–82

United States Electric and Gas Company, **6** 447

The United States Electric Lighting Company, **11** 387

United States Export-Import Bank, **IV** 55

United States Express Co., **II** 381, 395–96; **10** 59–60; **12** 534

United States Fidelity and Guaranty Co., **III** 395

United States Filter Corp., **I** 429; **IV** 374

United States Foil Co., **IV** 186

United States Glucose Co., **II** 496

United States Graphite Company, **V** 221–22

United States Gypsum Co., **III** 762–64

United States Health Care Systems, Inc. *See* U.S. Healthcare, Inc.

United States Independent Telephone Company, **6** 332

United States Leasing Corp., **II** 442

United States Mortgage & Trust Company, **II** 251; **14** 102

United States National Bank of Oregon, **14** 527

The United States National Bank of Portland, **14** 527–28

United States National Bank of San Diego, **II** 355

United States Pipe and Foundry Co., **III** 766

United States Plywood Corp., **IV** 264, 282, 341; **9** 260; **13** 100

United States Postal Service, **10** 60; **14 517–20**

United States Realty-Sheraton Corp., **III** 98

United States Security Trust Co., **13** 466

United States Shoe Corporation, **V 207–08**

United States Steel Corp., **I** 298, 491; **II** 129, 330; **III** 282, 326, 379; **IV** 35, 56, 110, 158, 572–74; **6** 514; **7** 48, 70–73, 401–02, 549–51; **10** 32; **11** 194; **12** 353–54. *See also* USX Corporation.

United States Sugar Refining Co., **II** 496

United States Surgical Corporation, **10 533–35**; **13** 365

United States Tobacco Company, **9** 533

United States Trucking Corp., **IV** 180–81

United States Underseas Cable Corp., **IV** 178

United States Zinc Co., **IV** 32

United Stationers Inc., **14 521–23**

United Steel, **III** 494

United Supers, **II** 624

United Technologies Automotive Inc., **15 513–15**

United Technologies Corporation, **I** 68, **84–86**, 143, 411, 530, 559; **II** 64, 82; **III** 74; **9** 18, 418; **10 536–38 (upd.)**; **11** 308; **12** 289; **13** 191, 384–86

United Telecommunications, Inc., **V 344–47**; **8** 310; **9** 478–80; **10** 202; **12** 541

United Telephone Company, **7** 508; **14** 257

United Telephone Company of the Carolinas, **10** 202

United Telephone of Indiana, **14** 259

United Telephone System, Inc., **V** 346

United Telespectrum, **6** 314

United Television, Inc., **9** 119

United Television Programs, **II** 143

United Transportation Co., **6** 382

United Truck Lines, **14** 505

United Utilities, Inc., **V** 344; **10** 202

United Van Lines, **14** 37; **15** 50

United Verde Copper Co., **IV** 178

United Vintners, **I** 243, 260–61

United Westphalia Electricity Co., **IV** 127

United-American Car, **13** 305

Unitek Corp., **III** 18

Unitel Communications, **6** 311

Unitika Ltd., **V 387–89**

Unity Joint-Stock Bank, **II** 334

UNIVAC, **III** 133, 152, 313; **6** 233, 240, 266

Univar Corporation, **8** 99; **9 530–32**; **12** 333

Univas, **13** 203

Universal Adding Machine, **III** 165

Universal American, **I** 452

Universal Atlas Cement Co., **IV** 573–74; **7** 550–51

Universal Belo Productions, **10** 5

Universal Cheerleaders Association. *See* Varsity Spirit Corp.

Universal Cigar Corp., **14** 19

Universal Containers, **IV** 249

Universal Controls, Inc., **10** 319

Universal Cooler Corp., **8** 515

Universal Corporation, **V 417–18**

Universal Data Systems, **II** 61

Universal Foods Corporation, **7 546–48**

Universal Forest Products Inc., **10 539–40**

Universal Furniture, **III** 571

Universal Genève, **13** 121

Universal Guaranty Life Insurance Company, **11** 482

Universal Health Services, Inc., **6 191–93**

Universal Highways, **III** 735

Universal Industries, Inc., **10** 380; **13** 533

Universal Instruments Corp., **III** 468

Universal Leaf Tobacco Company. *See* Universal Corporation.

Universal Manufacturing, **I** 440–41

Universal Match, **12** 464

Universal Matchbox Group, **12** 495

Universal Matthey Products Ltd., **IV** 119

Universal Paper Bag Co., **IV** 345

Universal Pictures, **II** 102, 135, 144, 154–55, 157; **10** 196; **14** 399

Universal Press Syndicate, **10** 4

Universal Resources Corporation, **6** 569

Universal Stamping Machine Co., **III** 156

Universal Studios, **II** 143–44; **12** 73

Universal Studios Florida, **14** 399

Universal Telephone, **9** 106

Universal Television, **II** 144

Universal Textured Yarns, **12** 501

Universal Transfers Co. Ltd., **IV** 119

University Computing Co., **II** 38; **11** 468

University Microfilms, **III** 172; **6** 289

Univision Holdings Inc., **IV** 621

Unix, **6** 225

Uno-Ven, **IV** 571

Unocal Corporation, **IV** 508, **569–71**

UNUM Corp., **III** 236; **13 538–40**

Uny Co., Ltd., **II** 619; **V 209–10**, 154; **13** 545

UPI. *See* United Press International.

Upjohn Company, **I** 675, 684, 686, 700, **707–09**; **III** 18, 53; **6** 42; **8 547–49 (upd.)**; **10** 79; **12** 186; **13** 503; **14** 423

UPS. *See* United Parcel Service of America Inc.

Upton Machine Company, **12** 548

Uraga Dock Co., **II** 361; **III** 634

Uraga Heavy Industries, **III** 634

Urbaine, **III** 391–92

Urban Investment and Development Co., **IV** 703

Urban Outfitters, Inc., **14 524–26**

Urban Systems Development Corp., **II** 121

Urenco, **6** 452

Urwick Orr, **II** 609

US Industrial Chemicals, Inc., **I** 377; **8** 440

US Order, Inc., **10** 560, 562

US Sprint Communications Company, **V** 295–96, 346–47; **6** 314; **8** 310; **9** 32; **10** 543; **11** 302; **12** 136, 541; **14** 252–53; **15** 196. *See also* Sprint Communications Company, L.P.

US Telecom, **9** 478–79

US West Communications. *See* Regional Bell Operating Companies.

USA Cafes, **14** 331

USAA, **10 541–43**

USAir Group, Inc., **I** 55, **131–32**; **III** 215; **6** 121, **131–32 (upd.)**; **11** 300; **14** 70, 73

USCC. *See* United States Cellular Corporation.

USCP-WESCO Inc., **II** 682

USF&G Corporation, **III** 395–98; **11** 494–95

USG Corporation, **III** 762–64

Usines de l'Espérance, **IV** 226

Usines Métallurgiques de Hainaut, **IV** 52

Usinor Sacilor, **IV** 226–28

USLIFE, **III** 194

USM, **10** 44

USSC. *See* United States Surgical Corporation.

UST Inc., **9 533–35**

USV Pharmaceutical Corporation, **11** 333

USX Corporation, **I** 466; **IV** 130, 228, **572–74**; **7** 193–94, **549–52 (upd.)**

UTA, **I** 119, 121; **6** 373–74, 93; **9** 233

Utag, **11** 510

Utah Construction & Mining Co., **I** 570; **IV** 146; **14** 296

Utah Gas and Coke Company, **6** 568

Utah Group Health Plan, **6** 184

Utah International, **II** 30; **12** 196

Utah Mines Ltd., **IV** 47

Utah Oil Refining Co., **IV** 370

Utah Power & Light Company, **9** 536; **12** 266

UTI Energy Corp., **12** 500

Utilicom, **6** 572

Utilicorp United Inc., **6 592–94**

Utilities Power & Light Corporation, **I** 512; **6** 508

Utility Constructors Incorporated, **6** 527

Utility Engineering Corporation, **6** 580
Utility Fuels, **7** 377
Utility Supply Co. *See* United Stationers Inc.
AB Utra Wood Co., **IV** 274
Utrecht Allerlei Risico's, **III** 200
UV Industries, Inc., **7** 360; **9** 440

V & V Cos., **I** 412
V.A.W. of America Inc., **IV** 231
V&S Variety Stores, **V** 37
V.L. Churchill Group, **10** 493
Vabis, **I** 197
Vacuum Metallurgical Company, **11** 234
Vacuum Oil Co., **IV** 463–64, 504, 549; **7** 351–52
Vadic Corp., **II** 83
Vadoise Vie, **III** 273
Vagnfabriks A.B., **I** 197
Vail Associates, Inc., 11 543–46
Val Royal LaSalle, **II** 652
Valassis Communications, Inc., 8 550–51
Valcambi S.A., **II** 268
Valcom, **13** 176
ValCom Inc. *See* InaCom Corporation.
Valdi Foods Inc., **II** 663–64
Valdosta Drug Co., **III** 9–10
Vale Power Company, **12** 265
Valentine & Company, **8** 552–53
Valeo, **III** 593
Valero Energy Corporation, IV 394; **7 553–55**
Valhi, Inc., **10** 435–36
Valid Logic Systems Inc., **11** 46, 284
Valio-Finnish Co-operative Dairies' Assoc., **II** 575
Valke Oy, **IV** 348
Valley East Medical Center, **6** 185
Valley Falls Co., **III** 213
Valley Federal of California, **11** 163
Valley Fig Growers, **7** 496–97
Valley Forge Life Insurance Co., **III** 230
Valley National Bank, **II** 420
Valley Transport Co., **II** 569
Valley-Todeco, Inc., **13** 305–06
Vallourec, **IV** 227
Valmac Industries, **II** 585
Valmet Corporation, I 198; **III 647–49**; **IV** 276, 350, 471
Valmont Industries, Inc., **13** 276
The Valspar Corporation, 8 552–54
Valtec Industries, **III** 684
Valtur, **6** 207
Value Foods Ltd., **11** 239
Value Giant Stores, **12** 478
Value House, **II** 673
Value Investors, **III** 330
Value Merchants Inc., 13 541–43
Value Rent-A-Car, **9** 350
Valueland, **8** 482
Valvoline, Inc., **I** 291; **IV** 374
Valvtron, **11** 226
Van Ameringen-Haebler, Inc., **9** 290
Van Brunt Manufacturing Co., **III** 462
Van Camp Seafood Company, Inc., II 562–63; **7 556–57**; **13** 426
Van de Kamp, **II** 556–57; **7** 430
Van den Bergh Foods, **II** 588; **9** 319
Van der Horst Corp. of America, **III** 471
Van Dorn Company, **13** 190
Van Dorn Electric Tool Co., **III** 435
Van Gend and Loos, **6** 404
Van Houton, **II** 521
Van Kirk Chocolate, **7** 429

Van Kok-Ede, **II** 642
Van Leer Holding, Inc., **9** 303, 305
Van Munching & Company, Inc., **I** 256; **13** 257, 259
Van Nostrand Reinhold, **8** 526
Van Ryn Gold Mines Estate, **IV** 90
Van Schaardenburg, **II** 528
Van Sickle, **IV** 485
Van Waters & Rogers, **8** 99
Van Wijcks Waalsteenfabrieken, **14** 249
Vanadium Alloys Steel Company (VASCO), **13** 295–96
Vanant Packaging Corporation, **8** 359
Vance International Airways, **8** 349
Vancouver Pacific Paper Co., **IV** 286
Vanderbilt Mortgage and Finance, **13** 154
Vanderlip-Swenson-Tilghman Syndicate, **IV** 81; **7** 185
Vanessa and Biffi, **11** 226
The Vanguard Group of Investment Companies, 9 239; **14 530–32**
Vanity Fair Mills, Inc., **V** 390–91
Vanity Fair Paper Mills, **IV** 281; **9** 259
Vansickle Industries, **III** 603
Vanstar, **13** 176
Vantage Analysis Systems, Inc., **11** 490
Vantona Group Ltd., **V** 356
Vantress Pedigree, Inc., **II** 585
Vapor Corp., **III** 444
Varco-Pruden, Inc., **8** 544–46
Vare Corporation, **8** 366
Variable Annuity Life Insurance Co., **III** 193–94
Varian Associates Inc., 12 504–06
Varibus Corporation, **6** 495
Variform, Inc., **12** 397
VARIG, SA, 6 133–35
Varity Corporation, III 650–52; **7** 258, 260
Varney Air Lines, **I** 47, 128; **6** 128; **9** 416
Varney Speed Lines, **I** 96
Varo, **7** 235, 237
Varsity Spirit Corp., 15 516–18
Varta, **III** 536; **9** 180–81
Vasco Metals Corp., **I** 523; **10** 520, 522
Vascoloy-Ramet, **13** 295
VASP, **6** 134
VAW Leichtmetall GmbH, **IV** 231
VBB Viag-Bayernwerk-Beteiligungs-Gesellschaft mbH, **IV** 232
VDM Nickel-Technologie AG, **IV** 89
VEB Londa, **III** 69
VEBA A.G., I 349–50, **542–43**; **III** 695; **IV** 194–95, 199, 455, 508; **8** 69, 494–495; **15 519–21 (upd.)**
VECO International, Inc., 7 558–59
Vector Automotive Corporation, **13** 61
Vector Gas Ltd., **13** 458
Vector Video, Inc., **9** 74
Vedelectric, **13** 544
Vedior International, **13** 544–45
Veeder-Root Company, **7** 116–17
Vellumoid Co., **I** 159
VeloBind, Inc., **10** 314
Velsicol, **I** 342, 440
Vemar, **7** 558
Vencor, Inc., **IV** 402; **14** 243
Vendex International N.V., 10 136–37; **13 544–46**
Vendors Supply of America, Inc., **7** 241–42
Vennootschap Nederland, **III** 177–78
Venture Stores Inc., V 134; **12 507–09**
Venturi, Inc., **9** 72

Vepco. *See* Virginia Electric and Power Company.
Vera Cruz Electric Light, Power and Traction Co. Ltd., **IV** 658
Vera Imported Parts, **11** 84
Verafumos Ltd., **12** 109
Veratex Group, **13** 149–50
Verbatim Corporation, III 477; **7** 163; **14 533–35**
Verd-A-Fay, **13** 398
Vereenigde Nederlandsche Scheepvaartmaatschappij, **6** 404
Vereeniging Refractories, **IV** 22
Vereeniging Tiles, **III** 734
Verein für Chemische Industrie, **IV** 70
Vereinigte Aluminium Werke AG, **IV** 229–30, 232
Vereinigte Deutsche Metallwerke AG, **IV** 140
Vereinigte Elektrizitäts und Bergwerke A.G., **I** 542
Vereinigte Elektrizitätswerke Westfalen AG, IV 195; **V 744–47**
Vereinigte Energiewerke AG, **V** 709
Vereinigte Flugtechnische Werke GmbH., **I** 42, 55, 74–75
Vereinigte Glanzstoff-Fabriken, **13** 21
Vereinigte Industrie-Unternehmungen Aktiengesellschaft, **IV** 229–30
Vereinigte Leichtmetall-Werke GmbH, **IV** 231
Vereinigte Papierwarenfabriken GmbH, **IV** 323
Vereinigte Stahlwerke AG, **III** 565; **IV** 87, 104–05, 132, 221; **14** 327
Vereinigte Versicherungsgruppe, **III** 377
Vereinigten Westdeutsche Waggonfabriken AG, **III** 542–43
Vereinsbank Wismar, **II** 256
Vereinte Versicherungen, **III** 377
N.V. Verenigde Fabrieken Wessanen and Laan, **II** 527
Verenigde Spaarbank Groep. *See* VSB Groep.
Verienigte Schweizerbahnen, **6** 424
VeriFone, **15** 321
Verlagsgruppe Georg von Holtzbrinck GmbH, **15** 158, 160
Vernon and Nelson Telephone Company. *See* British Columbia Telephone Company.
Vernon Graphics, **III** 499
Vernon Paving, **III** 674
Vernon Savings & Loan, **9** 199
Vernons, **IV** 651
Vero, **III** 434
La Verrerie Souchon-Neuvesel, **II** 474
Verreries Champenoises, **II** 475
Versatec Inc., **13** 128
Versicherungs-Verein, **III** 402, 410–11
Vertical Technology Industries, **14** 571
Vestek Systems, Inc., **13** 417
Vesuvius Crucible Co., **III** 681
Vesuvius USA Corporation, **8** 179
Veterinary Cos. of America, **III** 25
VEW, **IV** 234
VF Corporation, V 390–92; **12** 205; **13** 512
VFW-Fokker B.V., **I** 41, 55, 74–75
VI-Jon Laboratories, Inc., **12** 388
VIA/Rhin et Moselle, **III** 185
Viacao Aerea Rio Grandense of South America. *See* VARIG, SA.
Viacom Enterprises, **6** 33; **7** 336

Viacom International Inc., **7** 222–24, 530, **560–62**; **9** 429; **10** 175
VIAG, **IV 229–32**, 323
VIASA, **I** 107; **6** 97
Vichy, **III** 46
Vickers Inc., **III** 640, 642; **13** 8
Vickers PLC, **I** 194–95; **II** 3; **III** 555, 652, 725
Vickers-Armstrong Ltd., **I** 50, 57, 82
Vicoreen Instrument Co., **I** 202
VICORP Restaurants, Inc., **12 510–12**
Vicra Sterile Products, **I** 628
Vicsodrive Japan, **III** 495
Victor Company, **10** 483
Victor Company of Japan, Ltd., **I** 411; **II** 55–56, 91, 102, **118–19**; **III** 605; **IV** 599; **12** 454
Victor Comptometer, **I** 676; **III** 154
Victor Manufacturing and Gasket Co., **I** 152
Victor Musical Industries Inc., **II** 119; **10** 285
Victor Talking Machine Co., **II** 88, 118
Victor Value, **II** 678
Victoria, **III** 308
Victoria & Legal & General, **III** 359
Victoria Coach Station, **6** 406
Victoria Creations Inc., **13** 536
VICTORIA Holding AG, **III 399–401**
Victoria Paper Co., **IV** 286
Victoria Sugar Co., **III** 686
Victoria Wine Co., **I** 216
Victoria's Secret, **V** 115–16; **11** 498; **12** 557, 559
Victory Fire Insurance Co., **III** 343
Victory Insurance, **III** 273
Victory Oil Co., **IV** 550
Victory Savings and Loan, **10** 339
Video Concepts, **9** 186
Video Independent Theatres, Inc., **14** 86
Video Library, Inc., **9** 74
Video Superstores Master Limited Partnership, **9** 74
Videoconcepts, **II** 107
Videotex Network Japan, **IV** 680
La Vie Claire, **13** 103
Vienna Sausage Manufacturing Co., **14 536–37**
View-Master/Ideal Group, **12** 496
Viewdata Corp., **IV** 630; **15** 264
Viewlogic, **11** 490
Viewtel, **14** 36
Vigilance-Vie, **III** 393
Vigilant Insurance Co., **III** 220; **14** 108
Vigortone, **II** 582
Viiala Oy, **IV** 302
Viking, **II** 10; **IV** 659
Viking Brush, **III** 614
Viking Computer Services, Inc., **14** 147
Viking Direct Limited, **10** 545
Viking Foods, Inc., **8** 482; **14** 411
Viking Office Products, Inc., **10 544–46**
Viking Penguin, **IV** 611
Viking Press, **12** 25
Viktor Achter, **9** 92
Village Inn. *See* VICORP Restaurants, Inc.
Village Super Market, Inc., **7 563–64**
Villager, Inc., **11** 216
Vine Products Ltd., **I** 215
Vingaarden A/S, **9** 100
Vingresor A.B., **I** 120
Vining Industries, **12** 128
Viniprix, **10** 205
Vinland Web-Print, **8** 360

Vinyl Maid, Inc., **IV** 401
Vipont Pharmaceutical, **III** 25; **14** 122
VIPS, **11** 113
Virgin Atlantic Airlines, **14** 73
Virgin Group PLC, **12 513–15**
Virgin Retail, **9** 75, 361
Virginia Electric and Power Company (Vepco), **V** 596–98
Virginia Fibre Corporation, **15** 188
Virginia Folding Box Co., **IV** 352
Virginia Laminating, **10** 313
Virginia National Bankshares, **10** 426
Virginia Railway and Power Company (VR&P), **V** 596
Virginia Trading Corp., **II** 422
Visa International, **II** 200; **9** 333–35, **536–38**
Visco Products Co., **I** 373; **12** 346
Viscodrive GmbH, **III** 495
Viscount Industries Limited, **6** 310
Vishay Intertechnology, Inc., **11** 516
VisiCorp, **6** 254
Vision Centers, **I** 688; **12** 188
Visionworks, **9** 186
Visking Co., **I** 400
Visnews Ltd., **IV** 668, 670
VisQueen, **I** 334
Vista Bakery Inc., **14** 306
Vista Chemical Company, **I 402–03**; **V** 709
Vista Concepts, Inc., **11** 19
Visual Information Technologies, **11** 57
Visual Technology, **6** 201
Vita Lebensversicherungs-Gesellschaft, **III** 412
Vita Liquid Polymers, **9** 92
Vita-Achter, **9** 92
Vitafoam Incorporated, **9** 93
Vital Health Corporation, **13** 150
Vitalink Communications Corp., **11** 520
Vitalink Pharmacy Services, Inc., **15 522–24**
Vitex Foods, **10** 382
Vitro Corp., **8** 178; **10 547–48**
Viva Home Co., **III** 757
Vivesvata Iron and Steel Ltd., **IV** 207
Viviane Woodard Cosmetic Corp., **II** 531
Vivra Incorporated, **15** 119
VK Mason Construction Ltd., **II** 222
Vlasic Foods, **II** 480–81; **7** 67–68
VLN Corp., **I** 201
VLSI Research Inc., **11** 246
VMX Inc., **14** 355
VND, **III** 593
Vnesheconobank, **II** 242
VNS. *See* Vereenigde Nederlandsche Scheepvaartmaatschappij.
VNU/Claritas, **6** 14
Vodac, **11** 548
Vodafone Group plc, **II** 84; **11 547–48**
Vodapage, **11** 548
Vodata, **11** 548
Vodavi Technology Corporation, **13** 213
Voest-Alpine Stahl AG, **IV 233–35**
Vogel Peterson Furniture Company, **7** 4–5
Vogoro Corp., **13** 503
Voice Data Systems, **15** 125
Voice Response, Inc., **11** 253
Voith, **II** 22
Vokes, **I** 429
Volkert Stampings, **III** 628
Volkswagen A.G., **I** 30, 32, 186, 192, **206–08**, 460; **II** 279; **IV** 231; **7** 8; **10**

14; **11** 104, **549–51 (upd.)**; **13** 413; **14** 169
Volta Aluminium Co., Ltd., **IV** 122
Volume Service Company. *See* Restaurants Unlimited, Inc.
Voluntary Hospitals of America, **6** 45
Volunteer State Life Insurance Co., **III** 221
AB Volvo, **I** 186, 192, 198, **209–11**; **II** 5, 366; **III** 543, 591, 623, 648; **IV** 336; **7** **565–68 (upd.)**; **9** 283–84, 350, 381; **10** 274; **12** 68, 342; **13** 30, 356; **14** 321; **15** 226
von Roll, **6** 599
von Weise Gear Co., **III** 509
Von's Grocery Co., **II** 419; **8** 474
The Vons Companies, Incorporated, **II** 655; **7 569–71**; **12** 209
VOP Acquisition Corporation, **10** 544
Votainer International, **13** 20
Vought Aircraft Co., **11** 364
Voxson, **I** 531
Voyage Conseil, **II** 265
Voyager Energy, **IV** 84
Voyager Ltd., **12** 514
Voyager Petroleum Ltd., **IV** 83; **7** 188
VR&P. *See* Virginia Railway and Power Company.
Vroom & Dreesmann, **13** 544–46
Vrumona B.V., **I** 257
VS Services, **13** 49
VSA. *See* Vendors Supply of America, Inc.
VSB Groep, **III** 199, 201
VSM. *See* Village Super Market, Inc.
Vtel Corporation, **10** 456
Vulcan Materials Company, **7 572–75**; **12** 39
Vulcraft, **7** 400–02
VVM, **III** 200
VW&R. *See* Van Waters & Rogers.
VWR Textiles & Supplies, Inc., **11** 256
VWR United Company, **9** 531

W H Smith Group PLC, **V 211–13**
W. & G. Turnbull & Co., **IV** 278
W. & M. Duncan, **II** 569
W.A. Bechtel Co., **I** 558
W.A. Harriman & Co., **III** 471
W&F Fish Products, **13** 103
W. Atlee Burpee Co., **II** 532; **11** 198
W.B. Constructions, **III** 672
W.B. Doner & Company, **10** 420; **12** 208
W.B. Saunders Co., **IV** 623–24
W.C. Heraeus GmbH, **IV** 100
W.C. Norris, **III** 467
W.C. Platt Co., **IV** 636
W.C. Ritchie & Co., **IV** 333
W.C. Smith & Company Limited, **14** 339
W. Duke & Sons, **V** 395, 600
W.F. Linton Company, **9** 373
W. Gunson & Co., **IV** 278
W. Gutzeit & Co., **IV** 274–77
W.H. McElwain Co., **III** 528
W.H. Morton & Co., **II** 398; **10** 62
W.H. Smith & Son (Alacra) Ltd., **15** 473
W.J. Noble and Sons, **IV** 294
W.L. Gore & Associates, Inc., **14 538–40**
W.M. Ritter Lumber Co., **IV** 281; **9** 259
W.O. Daley & Company, **10** 387
W.R. Berkley Corp., **III** 248; **15 525–27**
W.R. Breen Company, **11** 486
W.R. Grace & Company, **I** 547–50; **III** 525, 695; **IV** 454; **11** 216; **12** 337; **13** 149, 502, 544; **14** 29
W. Rosenlew, **IV** 350

W. S. Barstow & Company, **6** 575
W.T. Young Foods, **III** 52; **8** 433
W. Ullberg & Co., **I** 553
W.V. Bowater & Sons, Ltd., **IV** 257–58
W.W. Cargill and Brother, **II** 616; **13** 136
W.W. Grainger, Inc., V 214–15; **13** 297
W.W. Kimball Company, **12** 296
Waban Inc., V 198; **13 547–49**
Wabash National Corp., 13 550–52
Wabash Valley Power Association, **6** 556
Wabush Iron Co., **IV** 73
Wachovia Bank and Trust Company, **10** 425; **12** 16
Wachovia Corporation, II 336; **12 516–20**
The Wackenhut Corporation, 13 124–25; **14 541–43**
Wacker Oil Inc., **11** 441
Wadsworth Inc., **8** 526
Waffle House Inc., 14 544–45
The Wagner & Brown Investment Group, **9** 248
Wagner Litho Machinery Co., **13** 369–70
Wah Chang Corp., **I** 523–24; **10** 520–21
Waialua Agricultural Co., **II** 491
Waite Amulet Mines Ltd., **IV** 164
Waitrose, **V** 94–95
Wakefern Cooperative, **II** 672
Wakefern Food Corp., **7** 563–64
Wakodo Co., **I** 674
Wal-Mart Stores, Inc., II 108; **V** 216–17; **6** 287; **7** 61, 331; **8** 33, 295, **555–57 (upd.); 9** 187, 361; **10** 236, 284, 515–16, 524; **11** 292; **12** 48, 53–55, 63–64, 97, 208–09, 221, 277, 333, 477, 507–08; **13** 42, 215–17, 260–61, 274, 332–33, 444, 446; **14** 235; **15** 139, 275
Walbro Corporation, 13 553–55
Waldbaum, **II** 638
Waldbaum's, **15** 260
Waldenbooks, **V** 112; **10** 136–37
Waldes Truarc Inc., **III** 624
Oy Waldhof AB, **IV** 324
Wales & Company, **14** 257
Walgreen Co., V 218–20; **9** 346
Walker & Lee, **10** 340
Walker Cain, **I** 215
Walker Interactive Systems, **11** 78
Walker Manufacturing, **I** 527
Walker McDonald Manufacturing Co., **III** 569
Walkers Parker and Co., **III** 679–80
Walki GmbH, **IV** 349
AB Walkiakoski, **IV** 347
Walkins Manufacturing Corp., **III** 571
Wall Paper Manufacturers, **IV** 666
Wall Street Leasing, **III** 137
Wallace and Tiernan, **I** 383; **11** 361
Wallace International Silversmiths, **I** 473; **14** 482–83
Wallace Murray Corp., **II** 420
Wallbergs Fabriks A.B., **8** 14
Wallens Dairy Co., **II** 586
Wallin & Nordstrom, **V** 156
Wallingford Bank and Trust Co., **II** 213
Wallis, **V** 177
Wallis Tin Stamping Co., **I** 605
Walsin-Lihwa, **13** 141
Walston & Co., **II** 450; **III** 137
Walt Disney Company, II 102, 122, 129, 156, **172–74; III** 142, 504, 586; **IV** 585, 675, 703; **6** 15, **174–77 (upd.)**, 368; **7** 305; **8** 160; **10** 420; **12** 168, 208, 229, 323, 495–96; **13** 551; **14** 260; **15** 197

Walt Disney World, **6** 82, 175–76
Walter Baker's Chocolate, **II** 531
Walter Industries, Inc., III 765–67
Walter Kidde & Co., **I** 475, 524
Walter Pierce Oil Co., **IV** 657
Walton Manufacturing, **11** 486
Walton Monroe Mills, Inc., 8 558–60
Wander Ltd., **I** 672
Wang Laboratories, Inc., II 208; **III** 168–70; **6** 284–87 **(upd.); 8** 139; **9** 171; **10** 34; **11** 68, 274; **12** 183
Wanishi, **IV** 157
Waples-Platter Co., **II** 625
War Damage Corp., **III** 353, 356
War Emergency Tankers Inc., **IV** 552
War Production Board, **V** 676
Warburg, Pincus Capital Corp., **6** 13; **9** 524; **14** 42
Ward Manufacturing Inc., **IV** 101
Wardley Ltd., **II** 298
Wards. *See* Circuit City Stores, Inc.
Waring and LaRosa, **12** 167
The Warnaco Group Inc., 9 156; **12 521–23**
Warner & Swasey Co., **III** 168; **6** 284; **8** 545
Warner Communications Inc., II 88, 129, 135, 146–47, 154–55, 169–70, **175–77**, 208, 452; **III** 443, 505; **IV** 623, 673, 675–76; **7** 526, 528–30 **8** 527; **9** 44–45, 119, 469; **10** 196; **11** 557; **12** 73, 495–96. *See also* Time Warner Inc.
Warner Cosmetics, **III** 48; **8** 129
Warner Gear Co., **III** 438–39; **14** 63–64
Warner Records, **II** 177
Warner Sugar Refining Co., **II** 496
Warner-Lambert Co., I 643, 674, 679, 696, **710–12; 7** 596; **8** 62–63; **10 549–52 (upd.); 12** 480, 482; **13** 366
Warren Bank, **13** 464
Warren, Gorham & Lamont, **8** 526
Warren Oilfield Services, **9** 363
Warri Refining and Petrochemicals Co., **IV** 473
Warringah Brick, **III** 673
Warrior River Coal Company, **7** 281
Wartsila Marine Industries Inc., **III** 649
Warwick Chemicals, **13** 461
Warwick Electronics, **III** 654
Warwick International Ltd., **13** 462
Wasa, **I** 672–73
Wasag-Chemie AG, **III** 694
Wasatch Gas Co., **6** 568
Wascana Energy Inc., 13 556–58
Washburn Crosby Co., **II** 501, 555; **10** 322
Washington Duke Sons & Co., **12** 108
Washington Mills Company, **13** 532
Washington National Corporation, 11 482; **12 524–26**
Washington Natural Gas Company, 9 539–41
Washington Post Company, III 214; **IV 688–90; 6** 323; **11** 331
Washington Railway and Electric Company, **6** 552–53
Washington Specialty Metals Corp., **14** 323, 325
Washington Steel Corp., **14** 323, 325
Washington Water Power Company, 6 566, **595–98**
Washtenaw Gas Company. *See* MCN Corporation.

Wasserstein Perella & Co., **II** 629; **III** 512, 530–31; **V** 223
Waste Management, Inc., V 749–51, **752–54; 6** 46, 600; **9** 73, 108–09; **11** 435–36
Water Engineering, **11** 360
Water Pik, **I** 524–25
Water Products Group, **6** 487–88
Water Street Corporate Recovery Fund, **10** 423
Waterford Wedgwood Holdings PLC, IV 296; **12 527–29**
Waterloo Gasoline Engine Co., **III** 462
Waterlow and Sons, **10** 269
The Waterman Pen Company, **8** 59
WaterPro Supplies Corporation, **6** 486, 488
Watertown Insurance Co., **III** 370
Watkins Manufacturing Co., **I** 159
Watkins-Johnson Company, 15 528–30
Watkins-Strathmore Co., **13** 560
Watmough and Son Ltd., **II** 594
Watney Mann and Truman Brewers, **I** 228, 247; **9** 99
Watson-Wilson Transportation System, **V** 540; **14** 567
Watt AG, **6** 491
Watt Electronic Products, Limited, **10** 319
Wattie's Ltd., 7 576–78; 11 173
Waukesha Engine Servicenter, **6** 441
Waukesha Foundry Company, **11** 187
Waukesha Motor Co., **III** 472
Wausau Paper Mills, **15** 305
Wausau Sulphate Fibre Co. *See* Mosinee Paper Corporation.
Waverly Book Exchange, **10** 135
Waverly Oil Works, **I** 405
Waverly Pharmaceutical Limited, **11** 208
Waxman Industries, Inc., III 570; **9 542–44**
Wayco Foods, **14** 411
Waycross-Douglas Coca-Cola Bottling, **10** 222
Wayne Home Equipment. *See* Scott Fetzer Company.
Wayne Oakland Bank, **8** 188
WCI Holdings Corporation, **V** 223; **13** 170
WCK, Inc., **14** 236
WCRS Group plc, **6** 15
WearGuard, **13** 48
Wearne Brothers, **6** 117
The Weather Department, Ltd., **10** 89
Weather Guard, **IV** 305
Weathers-Lowin, Leeam, **11** 408
Weaver, **III** 468
Webb & Knapp, **10** 43
Webber Gage Co., **13** 302
Webers, **I** 409
Weblock, **I** 109
Webster Publishing Co., **IV** 636
Webtron Corp., **10** 313
Wedgwood. *See* Waterford Wedgewood Holdings PLC.
Week's Dairy, **II** 528
Wegmans Food Markets, Inc., 9 545–46
Weidemann Brewing Co., **I** 254
Weight Watchers International Inc., II 508; **10** 383; **11** 172; **12 530–32; 13** 383
Weirton Steel Corporation, I 297; **IV 236–38; 7** 447, 598; **8** 346, 450; **10** 31–32; **12** 352, 354
Weis Markets, Inc., 15 531–33
Welbecson, **III** 501
Welcome Wagon, **III** 28

Weldless Steel Company, **8** 530
Welex Jet Services, III 498–99
Wella Group, III **68–70**
Wellby Super Drug Stores, **12** 220
Wellcome Foundation Ltd., I 638, **713–15**; **8** 210, 452; **9** 265; **10** 551
Weller Electric Corp., II 16
Wellington, II 457
Wellington Management Company, **14** 530–31
Wellington Sears Co., **15** 247–48
Wellman, Inc., **8 561–62**
Wellmark, Inc., **10** 89
Wellness Co., Ltd., IV 716
Wells Aircraft, **12** 112
Wells Fargo & Company, II **380–84**, 319, 395; III 440; **10** 59–60; **12** 165, **533–37 (upd.)**
Wells Lamont, IV 136
Wells Rich Greene BDDP, **6 50–52**
Welsbach Mantle, **6** 446
Weltkunst Verlag GmbH, IV 590
Wendy's International, Inc., II **614–15**, 647; **7** 433; **8 563–65**; **9** 178; **12** 553; **13** 494; **14** 453
Wenger, III 419
Wenlock Brewery Co., I 223
Wenstroms & Granstoms Electriska Kraftbolag, II 1
Werkhof GmbH, **13** 491
Werner International, III 344; **14** 225
Wernicke Co., I 201
Wesco Financial Corp., III 213, 215
Wesco Food Co., II 644
Wescot Decisison Systems, **6** 25
Weserflug, I 74
Wesray Corporation, **6** 357; **13** 41
Wesray Holdings Corp., **13** 255
Wesray Transportation, Inc., **14** 38
Wessanen. *See* Koninklijke Wessanen N.V.
Wessanen and Laan, II 527
Wessanen Cacao, II 528
Wessanen USA, II 528
Wessanen's Koninklijke Fabrieken N.V., II 527
West Australia Land Holdings, Limited, **10** 169
West Bend Co., III **610–11**; **14 546–48**
West Coast Grocery Co., II 670
West Coast Machinery, **13** 385
West Coast of America Telegraph, I 428
West Coast Power Company, **12** 265
West Coast Savings and Loan, **10** 339
West Coast Telecom, III 38
West End Family Pharmacy, Inc., **15** 523
West Fraser Timber Co. Ltd., IV 276
West Georgia Coca-Cola Bottlers, Inc., **13** 163
West Ham Gutta Percha Co., I 428
West Harrison Electric & Water Company, **6** 466
West Harrison Gas & Electric Company, **6** 466
West India Oil Co., IV 416, 428
West Japan Heavy Industries, III 578–79; **7** 348
West Jersey Electric Company, **6** 449
West Missouri Power Company. *See* UtiliCorp United Inc.
West Newton Savings Bank, **13** 468
West Newton Telephone Company, **14** 258
West of England, III 690
West of England Sack Holdings, III 501; **7** 207

West One Bancorp, **11 552–55**
West Penn Electric. *See* Allegheny Power System, Inc.
West Point-Pepperell, Inc., **8 566–69**; **9** 466
West Publishing Co., IV 312; **7 579–81**; **10** 407
West Rand Consolidated Mines, IV 90
West Rand Investment Trust, IV 21
West Richfield Telephone Company, **6** 299
West Side Bank, II 312
West Side Printing Co., **13** 559
West Surrey Central Dairy Co. Ltd., II 586
West Texas Utilities Company, **6** 580
West Virginia Bearings, Inc., **13** 78
West Virginia Pulp and Paper Co., IV 351–53
West Witwatersrand Areas Ltd., IV 94–96
West Yorkshire Bank, II 307
West's Holderness Corn Mill, II 564
WestAir Holding Inc., **11** 300
Westburne Group of Companies, **9** 364
Westchester County Savings & Loan, **9** 173
Westdeutsche Landesbank Girozentrale, II 257–58, **385–87**
Western Aerospace Ltd., **14** 564
Western Air Express, I 125; III 225; **9** 17
Western Air Lines, I 98, 100, 106; **6** 82
Western Alaska Fisheries, II 578
Western American Bank, II 383
Western Assurance Co., III 350
Western Atlas Inc., III 473; **12 538–40**
Western Australian Specialty Alloys Proprietary Ltd., **14** 564
Western Auto Supply Co., **8** 56; **11** 392
Western Automatic Machine Screw Co., **12** 344
Western Bancorporation, I 536; II 288–89; **13** 529
Western California Canners Inc., I 513
Western Canada Airways, II 376
Western Coalfields Ltd., IV 48–49
Western Company of North America, **15 534–36**
Western Condensing Co., II 488
Western Copper Mills Ltd., IV 164
Western Corrugated Box Co., IV 358
Western Crude, **11** 27
Western Dairy Products, I 248
Western Digital, **10** 403, 463; **11** 56, 463
Western Edison, **6** 601
Western Electric Co., II 57, 66, 88, 101, 112; III 162–63, 440; IV 181, 660; V 259–64; VII 288; **11** 500–01; **12** 136; **13** 57
Western Empire Construction. *See* CRSS Inc.
Western Federal Savings & Loan, **9** 199
Western Fire Equipment Co., **9** 420
Western Geophysical, I 485; **11** 265; **12** 538–39
Western Glucose Co., **14** 17
Western Grocers, Inc., II 631, 670
Western Illinois Power Cooperative, **6** 506
Western Inland Lock Navigation Company, **9** 228
Western International Hotels, I 129; **6** 129
Western Kraft Corp., IV 358; **8** 476
Western Life Insurance Co., III 356
Western Light & Telephone Company. *See* Western Power & Gas Company.
Western Light and Power. *See* Public Service Company of Colorado.

Western Massachusetts Co., **13** 183
Western Merchandise, Inc., **8** 556
Western Mining Corp., IV 61, 95
Western National Life Company, **10** 246; **14** 473
Western Natural Gas Company, **7** 362
Western New York State Lines, Inc., **6** 370
Western Newell Manufacturing Company. *See* Newell Co.
Western Nuclear, Inc., IV 179
Western Offset Publishing, **6** 13
Western Offshore Drilling and Exploration Co., I 570
Western Pacific Industries, **10** 357
Western Paper Box Co., IV 333
Western Piping and Engineering Co., III 535
Western Playing Card Co., **13** 559
Western Powder Co., I 379; **13** 379
Western Power & Gas Company, **6** 312–13. *See also* Centel Corporation.
Western Public Service Corporation, **6** 568
Western Publishing Group, Inc., IV 671; **13** 114, **559–61**; **15** 455
Western Reserve Bank of Lake County, **9** 474
Western Reserve Telephone Company. *See* Alltel Corporation.
Western Reserves, **12** 442
Western Resources, Inc., **12 541–43**
Western Rosin Company, **8** 99
Western Sizzlin', **10** 331
Western Slope Gas, **6** 559
Western Steer, **10** 331
Western Sugar Co., II 582
Western Telephone Company, **14** 257
Western Union, I 512; III 644; **6** 227–28, 338, 386; **9** 536; **10** 263; **12** 9; **14** 363; **15** 72
Western Union Insurance Co., III 310
Western Vending, **13** 48
Western Veneer and Plywood Co., IV 358
Western-Mobile, III 735
Westfair Foods Ltd., II 649
Westfalenbank of Bochum, II 239
Westfalia AG, III 418–19
Westfalia Dinnendahl Gröppel AG, III 543
Westfälische Transport AG, **6** 426
Westfälische Verbands-Elektrizitätswerk, V 744
Westgate House Investments Ltd., IV 711
Westimex, II 594
Westin Hotel Co., I 129–30; **6** 129; **9** 283, **547–49**
Westinghouse Air Brake Co., III 664
Westinghouse Brake & Signal, III 509
Westinghouse Electric Corporation, I 4, 7, 19, 22, 28, 33, 82, 84–85, 524; II 57–58, 59, 80, 86, 88, 94, 98–99, **120–22**, 151; III 440, 467, 641; IV 59, 401; **6** 39, 164, 261, 452, 483, 556; **9** 12, 17, 128, 162, 245, 417, 439–40, 553; **10** 280, 536; **11** 318; **12** 194, **544–47 (upd.)**; **13** 230, 398, 402, 506–07; **14** 300–01
Westland Aircraft Ltd., I 50, 573; IV 658
WestLB. *See* Westdeutsche Landesbank Girozentrale.
Westmark Mortgage Corp., **13** 417
Westmill Foods, II 466
Westminster Bank Ltd., II 257, 319, 320, 333–34
Westminster Press Ltd., IV 658
Westminster Trust Ltd., IV 706

Westmoreland Coal Company, **7** 582–85
Westmount Enterprises, **I** 286
Weston and Mead, **IV** 310
Weston Bakeries, **II** 631
Weston Foods Ltd., **II** 631
Weston Pharmaceuticals, **V** 49
Weston Resources, **II** 631–32
Westpac Banking Corporation, **II** 388–90
Westphalian Provinzialbank-Hülfskasse, **II** 385
WestPoint Pepperell, **15** 247
Westvaco Corporation, **I** 442; **IV** 351–54
Westwood Pharmaceuticals, **III** 19
Westwools Holdings, **I** 438
Westwynn Theatres, **14** 87
Wetterau Incorporated, **II** 645, 681–82; **7** 450
Wexpro Company, **6** 568–69
Weyerhaeuser Company, **I** 26; **IV** 266, 289, 298, 304, 308, **355–56**, 358; **8** 428, 434; **9** 550–52 (upd.)
Weyman-Burton Co., **9** 533
Whalstrom & Co., **I** 14
Wharf Holdings Limited, **12** 367–68
Wheaton Industries, **8** 570–73
Wheel Horse, **7** 535
Wheel Restaurants Inc., **14** 131
Wheelabrator Technologies, Inc., **I** 298; **II** 403; **III** 511–12; **V** 754; **6** 599–600; **10** 32; **11** 435
Wheeler Condenser & Engineering Company, **6** 145
Wheeler, Fisher & Co., **IV** 344
Wheeling-Pittsburgh Corp., **7** 586–88
Wheelock Marden, **I** 470
Whemo Denko, **I** 359
Wherehouse Entertainment Incorporated, **9** 361; **11** 556–58
WHI Inc., **14** 545
Whippet Motor Lines Corporation, **6** 370
Whirl-A-Way Motors, **11** 4
Whirlpool Corporation, **I** 30; **II** 80; **III** 572, 573, **653–55**; **8** 298–99; **11** 318; **12** 252, 309, **548–50** (upd.); **13** 402–03, 563; **15** 403
Whirlwind, Inc., **6** 233; **7** 535
Whiskey Trust, **I** 376
Whistler Corporation, **13** 195
Whitaker Health Services, **III** 389
Whitaker-Glessner Company, **7** 586
Whitall Tatum, **III** 423
Whitbread & Company plc, **I** 288, **293–94**
Whitby Pharmaceuticals, Inc., **10** 289
White Automotive, **10** 9, 11
White Brand, **V** 97
White Bus Line, **I** 448
White Castle Systems, Inc., **12** 551–53
White Consolidated Industries Inc., **II** 122; **III** 480, 654, 573; **8** 298; **12** 252, 546; **13** 562–64
White Eagle Oil & Refining Co., **IV** 464; **7** 352
White Fuel Corp., **IV** 552
White Industrial Power, **II** 25
White Machine Tools, **III** 480
White Miller Construction Company, **14** 162
White Motor Co., **II** 16
White Oil Corporation, **7** 101
White Rock Corp., **I** 377
White Rose Corp., **12** 106
White Stores, **II** 419–20

White Swan Foodservice, **II** 625
White Tractor, **13** 17
White Weld, **II** 268
White-New Idea, **13** 18
White-Rodgers, **II** 19
White-Westinghouse. *See* White Consolidated Industries Inc.
Whiteaway Laidlaw, **V** 68
Whitehall Canadian Oils Ltd., **IV** 658
Whitehall Electric Investments Ltd., **IV** 658
Whitehall Labs, **8** 63
Whitehall Petroleum Corp. Ltd., **IV** 657–58
Whitehall Securities Corp., **IV** 658
Whitehall Trust Ltd., **IV** 658
Whitewater Group, **10** 508
Whitewear Manufacturing Company. *See* Angelica Corporation.
Whitman Corporation, **7** 430; **10** 414–15, **553–55** (upd.); **11** 188. *See also* IC Industries.
Whitman Publishing Co., **13** 559–60
Whitman's Chocolates, **I** 457; **7** 431; **12** 429
Whitney Communications Corp., **IV** 608
Whitney National Bank, **12** 16
Whittaker Corporation, **I** 544–46; **III** 389, 444
Whittar Steel Strip Co., **IV** 74
Whitteways, **I** 215
Whittle Communications, **IV** 675; **7** 528; **13** 403
The Wholesale Club, Inc., **8** 556
Wholesale Depot, **13** 547
Wholesale Food Supply, Inc., **13** 333
Whyte & Mackay Distillers Ltd., **V** 399
Wicat Systems, **7** 255–56
Wichita Industries, **11** 27
Wickes Companies, Inc., **I** 453, 483; **II** 262; **III** 580, 721; **V** 221–23; **10** 423; **13** 169–70; **15** 281
Wickman-Wimet, **IV** 203
Widows and Orphans Friendly Society, **III** 337
Wien Air Alaska, **II** 420
Wifstavarfs, **IV** 325
Wiggins Teape Ltd., **I** 426; **IV** 290
Wild by Nature. *See* King Cullen Grocery Co., Inc.
Wiles Group Ltd., **III** 501; **7** 207
Wiley Manufacturing Co., **8** 545
Oy Wilh. Schauman AB, **IV** 300–02
Wilhelm Fette GmbH, **IV** 198–99
Wilhelm Wilhelmsen Ltd., **7** 40
Wilkinson Sword Co., **III** 23, 28–29; **12** 464
Willamette Falls Electric Company. *See* Portland General Corporation.
Willamette Industries, Inc., **IV** 357–59; **13** 99, 101
Willcox & Gibbs Sewing Machine Co., **15** 384
Willetts Manufacturing Company, **12** 312
William A. Rogers Ltd., **IV** 644
William B. Tanner Co., **7** 327
William Barnet and Son, Inc., **III** 246
William Barry Co., **II** 566
William Benton Foundation, **7** 165, 167
William Bonnel Co., **I** 334; **10** 289
William Burdon, **III** 626
William Colgate and Co., **III** 23
William Collins & Sons, **II** 138; **IV** 651–52; **7** 390–91

William Cory & Son Ltd., **6** 417
William Crawford and Sons, **II** 593
William Douglas McAdams Inc., **I** 662; **9** 403
William Duff & Sons, **I** 509
William E. Pollack Government Securities, **II** 390
William E. Wright Company, **9** 375
William Gaymer and Son Ltd., **I** 216
William H. Rorer Inc., **I** 666
William Hancock & Co., **I** 223
William J. Hough Co., **8** 99–100
William Lyon Homes, **III** 664
William M. Mercer Inc., **III** 283
William Mackinnon & Co., **III** 522
William McDonald & Sons, **II** 593
William Morris, **III** 554
William Neilson, **II** 631
William Odhams Ltd., **7** 244
William Penn Cos., **III** 243, 273
William Press, **I** 568
William R. Warner & Co., **I** 710
William S. Kimball & Co., **12** 108
William Southam and Sons, **7** 487
William T. Blackwell & Company, **V** 395
William Underwood Co., **I** 246, 457; **7** 430
William Varcoe & Sons, **III** 690
William Zinsser & Co., **8** 456
Williams & Glyn's Bank Ltd., **12** 422
Williams Bros. Co., **IV** 575–76
Williams Brother Offshore Ltd., **I** 429
Williams Communications, **6** 340
Williams Companies, **III** 248; **IV** 84, 171, **575–76**
Williams Deacon's Bank, **12** 422
Williams, Donnelley and Co., **IV** 660
Williams Electronics, **III** 431; **12** 419
Williams Electronics Games, Inc., **15** 539
Williams Gold Refining Co., **14** 81
Williams Oil-O-Matic Heating Corporation, **12** 158
Williams/Nintendo Inc., **15** 537
Williams-Sonoma, **13** 42; **15** 50
Williamsburg Gas Light Co., **6** 455
Williamson-Dickie Manufacturing Company, **14** 549–50
Willie G's, **15** 279
Willis Faber, **III** 280, 747
Williston Basin Interstate Pipeline Company, **7** 322, 324
Willor Manufacturing Corp., **9** 323
Willys-Overland, **I** 183; **8** 74
Wilmington Coca-Cola Bottling Works, Inc., **10** 223
Wilsdorf & Davis, **13** 353–54
Wilshire Restaurant Group Inc., **13** 66
Wilson & Co., **I** 490
Wilson Brothers, **8** 536
Wilson Foods Corp., **I** 489, 513; **II** 584–85; **12** 124; **14** 515
Wilson Jones Company, **7** 4–5
Wilson Pharmaceuticals & Chemical, **I** 489
Wilson Sporting Goods, **I** 278, 489; **13** 317
Wilson's Motor Transit, **6** 370
Wilson's Supermarkets, **12** 220–21
Wilson-Maeulen Company, **13** 234
Wilts and Dorset Banking Co., **II** 307
Wiltshire United Dairies, **II** 586
Wimpey International Ltd., **13** 206
Wimpey's plc, **I** 315, 556
Win Schuler Foods, **II** 480
Win-Chance Foods, **II** 508
Wincanton Group, **II** 586–87
Winchell's Donut Shops, **II** 680

Winchester Arms, **I** 379–81, 434; **13** 379
Windsor Manufacturing Company, **13** 6
Windsor Trust Co., **13** 467
Windstar Sail Cruises, **6** 368
Wingate Partners, **14** 521, 523
Wings & Wheels, **13** 19
Wings Luggage, Inc., **10** 181
Winkelman Stores, Inc., **8** 425–26
Winkler-Grimm Wagon Co., **I** 141
Winmar Co., **III** 353
Winn-Dixie Stores, Inc., II 626–27, 670, **683–84**; **7** 61; **11** 228; **15** 178
Winnebago Industries Inc., 7 589–91
Winners Apparel Ltd., **V** 197
Winschermann group, **IV** 198
Winston & Newell Co., **II** 668–69
Winston Group, **10** 333
Winston, Harper, Fisher Co., **II** 668
Wintershall, **I** 306; **IV** 485
Winterthur Schweizerische Versicherungs-Gesellschaft, III 343, **402–04**
Winthrop Laboratories, **I** 698–99
Winton Engines, **10** 273
Winton Motor Car Company, **V** 231
Wire and Plastic Products PLC. *See* WPP Group PLC.
Wireless Hong Kong. *See* Hong Kong Telecommunications Ltd.
Wireless Management Company, **11** 12
Wireless Speciality Co., **II** 120
Wirtz Productions Ltd., **15** 238
Wisaforest Oy AB, **IV** 302
Wisconsin Bell, Inc., 14 551–53
Wisconsin Central, **12** 278
Wisconsin Dairies, 7 592–93
Wisconsin Energy Corporation, 6 601–03, 605
Wisconsin Knife Works, **III** 436
Wisconsin Public Service Corporation, 6 604–06; **9 553–54**
Wisconsin Steel, **10** 430
Wisconsin Tissue Mills Inc., **8** 103
Wisconsin Toy Company. *See* Value Merchants Inc.
Wiser's De Luxe Whiskey, **14** 141
Wishnick-Tumpeer Chemical Co., **I** 403–05
Wispark Corporation, **6** 601, 603
Wisvest Corporation, **6** 601, 603
Witco Corporation, I 403, **404–06**
Witech Corporation, **6** 601, 603
Wittington Investments Ltd., **13** 51
WLR Foods, Inc., **14** 516
Wm. Wrigley Jr. Company, 7 594–97
WMS Industries, Inc., III 431; **15 537–39**
WMX Technologies, Inc., **11** 435–36
Woermann and German East African Lines, **I** 542
Wöhlk, **III** 446
Wolf Furniture Enterprises, **14** 236
Wolff Printing Co., **13** 559
Wolters Kluwer NV, IV 611; **14 554–56**
Wolvercote Paper Mill, **IV** 300
Wolverine Die Cast Group, **IV** 165
Womack Development Company, **11** 257
Women's World, **15** 96
Wometco Coca-Cola Bottling Co., **10** 222
Wometco Coffee Time, **I** 514
Wometco Enterprises, **I** 246, 514
Wood Fiberboard Co., **IV** 358
Wood Gundy, **II** 345
Wood Hall Trust plc, I 438, **592–93**

Wood River Oil and Refining Company, **11** 193
Wood Shovel and Tool Company, **9** 71
Woodall Industries, **III** 641; **14** 303
Woodard-Walker Lumber Co., **IV** 358
Woodcock, Hess & Co., **9** 370
Woodfab, **IV** 295
Woodhaven Gas Light Co., **6** 455
Woodhill Chemical Sales Company, **8** 333
Woodlands, **7** 345–46
Woods and Co., **II** 235
Woodville Appliances, Inc., **9** 121
Woodward Corp., **IV** 311
Woodward Governor Co., 13 565–68
Woolco Department Stores, **II** 634; **7** 444; **V** 107, 225–26; **14** 294
Woolverton Motors, **I** 183
Woolworth Corporation, V 106–09, **224–27**; **8** 509; **14** 293–95
Woolworth Holdings, **II** 139; **V** 108
Woolworth's Ltd., **II** 656
Wooster Preserving Company, **11** 211
Wooster Rubber Co., **III** 613
Worcester City and County Bank, **II** 307
Worcester Gas Light Co., **14** 124
Worcester Wire Works, **13** 369
Word, Inc., **14** 499
Word Processors Personnel Service, **6** 10
WordPerfect Corporation, 6 256; **10** 519, **556–59**; **12** 335
WordStar International, **15** 149
Work Wear Corp., **II** 607
World Air Network, Ltd., **6** 71
World Airways, **10** 560–62
World Book Group. *See* Scott Fetzer Company.
World Book, Inc., IV 622; **12 554–56**
World Color Press Inc., 12 557–59
World Communications, Inc., **11** 184
World Financial Network National Bank, **V** 116
World Flight Crew Services, **10** 560
World Foot Locker, **14** 293
World Gift Company, **9** 330
World International Holdings Limited, **12** 368
World Journal Tribune Inc., **IV** 608
World Publishing Co., **8** 423
World Trade Corporation. *See* International Business Machines Corporation.
World-Wide Shipping Group, **II** 298; **III** 517
WorldCom Inc., **14** 330, 332
WorldCorp, Inc., 10 560–62
WorldGames, **10** 560
Worldwide Underwriters Insurance Co., **III** 218–19
Wormald International Ltd., **13** 245, 247
Wormser, **III** 760
Wortham, Gus Sessions, **III** 193; **10** 65
Worthen Banking Corporation, **15** 60
Worthington & Co., **I** 223
Worthington Corp., **I** 142
Worthington Foods, Inc., I 653; **14 557–59**
Worthington Industries, Inc., 7 598–600; **8** 450
Worthington Telephone Company, **6** 312
Woven Belting Co., **8** 13
WPL Holdings, 6 604–06
WPP Group plc, I 21; **6 53–54**
Wrenn Furniture Company, **10** 184
WRG. *See* Wells Rich Greene BDDP.
Wright Aeronautical, **9** 16

Wright Airplane Co., **III** 151; **6** 265
Wright and Son, **II** 593
Wright Company, **9** 416
Wright Engine Company, **11** 427
Wright Manufacturing Company, **8** 407
Wright, Robertson & Co., **IV** 278
Wright Stephenson & Co., **IV** 278
Write Right Manufacturing Co., **IV** 345
WSI Corporation, **10** 88–89
WSM Inc., **11** 152
WTC Airlines, Inc., **IV** 182
Wührer, **II** 474
Wunderlich Ltd., **III** 687
Wunderman, Ricotta & Kline, **I** 37
Württembergische Landes-Elektrizitäts AG, **IV** 230
Wyandotte Corp., **I** 306
Wyeth Laboratories, **I** 623; **10** 69
Wyle Electronics, 14 560–62
Wyly Corporation, **11** 468
Wyman-Gordon Company, 14 563–65
Wymore Oil Co., **IV** 394
Wynncor Ltd., **IV** 693
Wyoming Mineral Corp., **IV** 401
Wyse Technology, Inc., 10 362; **15 540–42**

X-Acto, **12** 263
X-Chem Oil Field Chemicals, **8** 385
XA Systems Corporation, **10** 244
Xaos Tools, Inc., **10** 119
Xcelite, **II** 16
Xcor International, **III** 431; **15** 538
Xenia National Bank, **9** 474
Xerox Corporation, I 31–32, 338, 490, 693; **II** 10, 117, 157, 159, 412, 448; **III** 110, 116, 120–21, 157, 159, **171–73**, 475; **IV** 252, 703; **6** 244, **288–90 (upd.)**, 390; **7** 45, 161; **8** 164; **10** 22, 139, 430, 510–11; **11** 68, 494, 518; **13** 127, 448; **14** 399
XRAL Storage and Terminaling Co., **IV** 411
XTX Corp., **13** 127
Xynetics, **9** 251
Xytek Corp., **13** 127

Y & S Candies Inc., **II** 511
Yacimientos Petrolíferos Fiscales Sociedad Anónima, **IV** 578
Yale & Towne Manufacturing Co., **I** 154–55; **10** 279
Yamabun Oil Co., **IV** 403
Yamaguchi Bank, **II** 347
Yamaha Corporation, III 366, 599, **656–59**; **11** 50; **12** 401
Yamaichi Securities Company, Limited, II 300, 323, 434, **458–59**; **9** 377
Yamanouchi Pharmaceutical, **12** 444–45
Yamatame Securities, **II** 326
Yamato Transport Co. Ltd., V 536–38
Yamazaki Baking Co., **II** 543; **IV** 152
Yanbian Industrial Technology Training Institute, **12** 294
Yankee Energy Gas System, Inc., **13** 184
Yankton Gas Company, **6** 524
Yaryan, **I** 343
Yashica Co., **II** 50–51
Yasuda Fire and Marine Insurance Company, Limited, II 292, 391; **III 405–07**, 408
Yasuda Mutual Life Insurance Company, II 292, 391, 446; **III** 288, 405, **408–09**

Yasuda Trust and Banking Company, Ltd., **II** 273, 291, **391–92**
Yates Circuit Foil, **IV** 26
Yawata Iron & Steel Co., Ltd., **I** 493, 509; **II** 300; **IV** 130, 157, 212
Year Book Medical Publishers, **IV** 677–78
Yearbooks, Inc., **12** 472
Yeargin Construction Co., **II** 87; **11** 413
Yellow Cab Co., **I** 125; **V** 539; **10** 370; **12** 487
Yellow Corporation, **14 566–68**
Yellow Freight System, Inc. of Deleware, **V** 503, **539–41**; **12** 278
Yeomans & Foote, **I** 13
Yeomans & Partners Ltd., **I** 588
YES!, **10** 306
Yeung Chi Shing Estates, **IV** 717
YGK Inc., **6** 465, 467
Yhtyneet Paperitehtaat Oy. *See* United Paper Mills Ltd.
Yili Food Co., **II** 544
YMOS A.G., **IV** 53
Yokado Clothing Store, **V** 88
Yokogawa Electric Corp., **III** 142–43, 536
Yokogawa Electric Works, Limited, **6** 237; **13** 234
Yokohama Cooperative Wharf Co., **IV** 728
Yokohama Electric Cable Manufacturing Co., **III** 490
Yokohama Rubber Co., Ltd., **V 254–56**
Yokohama Specie Bank, **I** 431; **II** 224
Yoplait S.A., **II** 576
York & London, **III** 359
York Corp., **III** 440
York Developments, **IV** 720
York International Corp., **13 569–71**
York Manufacturing Co., **13** 385
York Safe & Lock Company, **7** 144–45
York Wastewater Consultants, Inc., **6** 441
York-Benimaru, **V** 88
Yorkshire and Pacific Securities Ltd., **IV** 723
Yorkshire Insurance Co., **III** 241–42, 257
Yorkshire Paper Mills Ltd., **IV** 300
Yorkshire Post Newspapers, **IV** 686
Yorkshire Television Ltd., **IV** 659
Yorkville Group, **IV** 640
Yosemite Park & Curry Co., **II** 144
Yoshikazu Taguchi, **6** 428
Yoshitomi Pharmaceutical, **I** 704
Young & Selden, **7** 145
Young & Son, **II** 334
Young and Rubicam Inc., **I** 9–11, 25, **36–38**; **II** 129; **6** 14, 47; **9** 314; **13** 204
Young Readers of America, **13** 105
Young's Engineering Co., **IV** 717
Youngs Drug Products Corporation, **8** 85
Youngstown, **IV** 114
Youngstown Pressed Steel Co., **III** 763
Youngstown Sheet & Tube, **I** 490–91; **13** 157
Yount-Lee Oil Co., **IV** 369
Yoxall Instrument Company, **13** 234
Yoyoteiki Cargo Co., Ltd., **6** 428
YPF Sociedad Anónima, **IV 577–78**
Yuasa Battery Co., **III** 556
Yuba Heat Transfer Corp., **I** 514
Yurakucho Seibu Co., Ltd., **V** 185
Yutani Heavy Industries, Ltd., **IV** 130
Yves Rocher, **IV** 546
Yves Saint Laurent, **I** 697; **12** 37
Yves Soulié, **II** 266

Z.C. Mines, **IV** 61

Zaadunie B.V., **I** 672
Zahnfabrik Weinand Sohne & Co. G.m.b.H., **10** 271
Zahnradfabrik Friedrichshafen, **III** 415
Zambezi Saw Mills (1968) Ltd., **IV** 241
Zambia Industrial and Mining Corporation Ltd., **IV 239–41**
Zander & Ingeström, **III** 419
Zanders Feinpapiere AG, **IV** 288; **15** 229
Zanussi, **III** 480
Zapata Drilling Co., **IV** 489
Zapata Gulf Marine Corporation, **11** 524
Zapata Offshore Co., **IV** 489
Zapata Petroleum Corp., **IV** 489
Zayre Corp., **V** 197–98; **9** 20–21; **13** 445, 547–48
Zebra Technologies Corporation, **14** 378, **569–71**
Zecco, Inc., **III** 443; **6** 441
Zehrmart, **II** 631
Zeiss Ikon AG, **III** 446
Zell/Chilmark Fund Limited Partnership, **12** 439
Zellers, **V** 80
Zellstoff AG, **III** 400
Zellstoffabrik Waldhof AG, **IV** 323–24
Zellweger Telecommunications AG, **9** 32
Zenith Data Systems, Inc., **II** 124–25; **III** 123; **6** 231; **10 563–65**
Zenith Electronics Corporation, **II** 102, **123–25**; **10** 563; **11** 62, 318; **12** 183, 454; **13** 109, 398, **572–75 (upd.)**
Zentec Corp., **I** 482
Zeus Components, Inc., **10** 113
Zewawell AG, **IV** 324
Ziff Communications Company, **7** 239–40; **12 560–63**; **13** 483
Ziff-Davis Publishing Co., **12** 359
Zijlker, **IV** 491
Zilber Ltd., **13** 541
Zilkha & Company, **12** 72
Zilog, Inc., **15 543–45**
Zimbabwe Sugar Refineries, **II** 581
Zimmer AG, **IV** 142
Zimmer Inc., **10** 156–57; **11** 475
Zimmer Manufacturing Co., **III** 18
Zinc Corp., **IV** 58–59, 61
Zions Bancorporation, **12 564–66**
Zippy Mart, **7** 102
Zircotube, **IV** 174
Zivnostenska, **II** 282
Zody's Department Stores, **9** 120–22
Zoecon, **I** 673
Zondervan Publishing House, **14** 499
Zortech Inc., **10** 508
Zotos International, **III** 63
ZS Sun Limited Partnership, **10** 502
Zuid Nederlandsche Handelsbank, **II** 185
Zürcher Bankverein, **II** 368
Zurich Insurance Group, **15** 257
Zürich Versicherungs-Gesellschaft, **III** 194, 402–03, **410–12**
Zycad Corp., **11** 489–91
Zymaise, **II** 582
ZyMOS Corp., **III** 458

INDEX TO INDUSTRIES

Index to Industries

ACCOUNTING

Deloitte & Touche, 9
Ernst & Young, 9
L.S. Starrett Co., 13
McLane Company, Inc., 13
Price Waterhouse, 9

ADVERTISING & OTHER BUSINESS SERVICES

A. C. Nielsen Company, 13
Ackerley Communications, Inc., 9
Adia S.A., 6
Advo, Inc., 6
Aegis Group plc, 6
American Building Maintenance Industries, Inc., 6
The Associated Press, 13
Bates Worldwide, Inc., 14
Bearings, Inc., 13
Berlitz International, Inc., 13
Burns International Security Services, 13
Chiat/Day Inc. Advertising, 11
Christie's International plc, 15
D'Arcy Masius Benton & Bowles, Inc., 6
DDB Needham Worldwide, 14
Dentsu Inc., I
Equifax, Inc., 6
Euro RSCG Worldwide S.A., 13
Foote, Cone & Belding Communications, Inc., I
Grey Advertising, Inc., 6
Hakuhodo, Inc., 6
Handleman Company, 15
Interpublic Group Inc., I
Japan Leasing Corporation, 8
JWT Group Inc., I
Katz Communications, Inc., 6
Kelly Services Inc., 6
Ketchum Communications Inc., 6
Leo Burnett Company Inc., I
Lintas: Worldwide, 14
The Ogilvy Group, Inc., I
Olsten Corporation, 6
Omnicom Group, I
Paychex, Inc., 15
Pinkerton's Inc., 9
Ronco, Inc., 15
Saatchi & Saatchi PLC, I
ServiceMaster Limited Partnership, 6
Shared Medical Systems Corporation, 14
Skidmore, Owings & Merrill, 13
Sotheby's Holdings, Inc., 11
Spencer Stuart and Associates, Inc., 14
TBWA Advertising, Inc., 6
Ticketmaster Corp., 13
The Wackenhut Corporation, 14
Wells Rich Greene BDDP, 6
WPP Group plc, 6
Young & Rubicam, Inc., I

AEROSPACE

A.S. Yakovlev Design Bureau, 15
Aerospatiale, 7
Avions Marcel Dassault-Breguet Aviation, I
Banner Aerospace, Inc., 14
Beech Aircraft Corporation, 8
The Boeing Company, I; 10 (upd.)
British Aerospace PLC, I
Cessna Aircraft Company, 8
Fairchild Aircraft, Inc., 9
G.I.E. Airbus Industrie, I; 12 (upd.)
General Dynamics Corporation, I; 10 (upd.)
Grumman Corporation, I; 11 (upd.)
Gulfstream Aerospace Corp., 7
N.V. Koninklijke Nederlandse Vliegtuigenfabriek Fokker, I
Learjet Inc., 8
Lockheed Corporation, I; 11 (upd.)
Lockheed Martin Corporation, 15 (upd.)
Martin Marietta Corporation, I
McDonnell Douglas Corporation, I; 11 (upd.)
Messerschmitt-Bölkow-Blohm GmbH., I
Moog Inc., 13
Northrop Corporation, I; 11 (upd.)
Pratt & Whitney, 9
Rockwell International Corporation, I; 11 (upd.)
Rolls-Royce plc, I; 7 (upd.)
Sequa Corp., 13
Sundstrand Corporation, 7
Textron Lycoming Turbine Engine, 9
Thiokol Corporation, 9
United Technologies Corporation, I; 10 (upd.)

AIRLINES

Aeroflot Soviet Airlines, 6
Air Canada, 6
Air New Zealand Limited, 14
Air-India, 6
Alaska Air Group, Inc., 6
Alitalia—Linee Aeree Italiana, SPA, 6
All Nippon Airways Company Limited, 6
America West Airlines, 6
American Airlines, I; 6 (upd.)
British Airways PLC, I; 14 (upd.)
Cathay Pacific Airways Limited, 6
Comair Holdings Inc., 13
Continental Airlines, I
Delta Air Lines, Inc., I; 6 (upd.)
Deutsche Lufthansa A.G., I
Eastern Airlines, I
EgyptAir, 6
Finnair Oy, 6
Garuda Indonesia, 6
Groupe Air France, 6
HAL Inc., 9
Iberia Líneas Aéreas de España S.A., 6
Japan Air Lines Company Ltd., I
Koninklijke Luchtvaart Maatschappij, N.V., I
Korean Air Lines Co. Ltd., 6
Malaysian Airlines System BHD, 6
Mesa Airlines, Inc., 11
Northwest Airlines, Inc., I; 6 (upd.)
Pan American World Airways, Inc., I; 12 (upd.)
People Express Airlines, Inc., I
Philippine Airlines, Inc., 6
Qantas Airways Limited, 6
Saudi Arabian Airlines, 6
Scandinavian Airlines System, I
Singapore Airlines Ltd., 6
Southwest Airlines Co., 6
Swiss Air Transport Company, Ltd., I
Texas Air Corporation, I
Thai Airways International Ltd., 6
Trans World Airlines, Inc., I; 12 (upd.)
Transportes Aereos Portugueses, S.A., 6
United Airlines, I; 6 (upd.)
USAir Group, Inc., I; 6 (upd.)
VARIG, SA, 6

AUTOMOTIVE

Adam Opel AG, 7
Alfa Romeo, 13
American Motors Corporation, I
Arvin Industries, Inc., 8
Automobiles Citroen, 7
Automobili Lamborghini S.p.A., 13
Bayerische Motoren Werke A.G., I; 11 (upd.)
Bendix Corporation, I
Borg-Warner Automotive, Inc., 14
The Budd Company, 8
Chrysler Corporation, I; 11 (upd.)
Cummins Engine Co. Inc., I; 12 (upd.)
Daihatsu Motor Company, Ltd., 7
Daimler-Benz A.G., I; 15 (upd.)
Dana Corporation, I; 10 (upd.)
Eaton Corporation, I; 10 (upd.)
Echlin Inc., I; 11 (upd.)
Federal-Mogul Corporation, I; 10 (upd.)
Ferrari S.p.A., 13
Fiat S.p.A, I; 11 (upd.)
Ford Motor Company, I; 11 (upd.)
Fruehauf Corporation, I
General Motors Corporation, I; 10 (upd.)
Genuine Parts Company, 9
Harley-Davidson Inc., 7
Hino Motors, Ltd., 7
Honda Motor Company Limited (Honda Giken Kogyo Kabushiki Kaisha), I; 10 (upd.)
Isuzu Motors, Ltd., 9
Kelsey-Hayes Group of Companies, 7
Kia Motors Corp., 12
Lotus Cars Ltd., 14
Mack Trucks, Inc., I
Mazda Motor Corporation, 9
Midas International Corporation, 10
Mitsubishi Motors Corporation, 9
Navistar International Corporation, I; 10 (upd.)
Nissan Motor Company Ltd., I; 11 (upd.)
Officine Alfieri Maserati S.p.A., 13
Oshkosh Truck Corporation, 7
Paccar Inc., I

The Pep Boys—Manny, Moe & Jack, 11
Peugeot S.A., I
Porsche AG, 13
Regie Nationale des Usines Renault, I
Robert Bosch GmbH., I
Rolls-Royce Motors Ltd., I
Rover Group plc, 7
Saab-Scania A.B., I; 11 (upd.)
Saturn Corporation, 7
Sealed Power Corporation, I
Sheller-Globe Corporation, I
Spartan Motors Inc., 14
SPX Corporation, 10
Superior Industries International, Inc., 8
Suzuki Motor Corporation, 9
Toyota Motor Corporation, I; 11 (upd.)
TRW Inc., 14 (upd.)
United Technologies Automotive Inc., 15
Volkswagen A.G., I; 11 (upd.)
AB Volvo, I; 7 (upd.)
Winnebago Industries Inc., 7

BEVERAGES

Adolph Coors Company, I; 13 (upd.)
Allied-Lyons PLC, I
Anheuser-Busch Companies, Inc., I; 10
   (upd.)
Asahi Breweries, Ltd., I
Bass PLC, I; 15 (upd.)
Brauerei Beck & Co., 9
Brown-Forman Corporation, I; 10 (upd.)
Canandaigua Wine Company, Inc., 13
Carlsberg A/S, 9
Carlton and United Breweries Ltd., I
Cerveceria Polar, I
Coca Cola Bottling Co. Consolidated, 10
The Coca-Cola Company, I; 10 (upd.)
Corby Distilleries Limited, 14
Distillers Company PLC, I
Dr Pepper/7Up Companies, Inc., 9
E & J Gallo Winery, I; 7 (upd.)
Foster's Brewing Group Ltd., 7
G. Heileman Brewing Company Inc., I
General Cinema Corporation, I
Grand Metropolitan PLC, I
Guinness PLC, I
Heineken N.V, I; 13 (upd.)
Heublein, Inc., I
Hiram Walker Resources, Ltd., I
Kikkoman Corporation, 14
Kirin Brewery Company Ltd., I
Labatt Brewing Company Ltd., I
Miller Brewing Company, I; 12 (upd.)
Moët-Hennessy, I
Molson Companies Ltd., I
Pepsico, Inc., I; 10 (upd.)
Pernod Ricard S.A., I
Robert Mondavi Corporation, 15
Sapporo Breweries, Ltd., I; 13 (upd.)
Scottish & Newcastle plc, 15
The Seagram Company, Ltd., I
Snapple Beverage Corporation, 11
South African Breweries Ltd., I
Starbucks Corporation, 13
The Stroh Brewing Company, I
Whitbread and Company PLC, I

BIOTECHNOLOGY

Amgen, Inc., 10
Biogen Inc., 14
Centocor Inc., 14
Chiron Corporation, 10
Immunex Corporation, 14

CHEMICALS

A. Schulman, Inc., 8

Air Products and Chemicals, Inc., I; 10
   (upd.)
Akzo Nobel N.V., 13
American Cyanamid, I; 8 (upd.)
ARCO Chemical Company, 10
Atochem S.A., I
BASF A.G., I
Bayer A.G., I; 13 (upd.)
Betz Laboratories, Inc., I; 10 (upd.)
Boc Group PLC, I
Brenntag AG, 8
Cabot Corporation, 8
Celanese Corporation, I
Chemcentral Corporation, 8
Ciba-Geigy Ltd., I; 8 (upd.)
Crompton & Knowles, 9
The Dexter Corporation, I; 12 (upd.)
The Dow Chemical Company, I; 8 (upd.)
DSM, N.V, I
E.I. Du Pont de Nemours & Company, I; 8
   (upd.)
Eastman Chemical Company, 14
Ecolab, Inc., I; 13 (upd.)
English China Clays plc, 15 (upd.)
Ethyl Corporation, I; 10 (upd.)
Ferro Corporation, 8
First Mississippi Corporation, 8
Formosa Plastics Corporation, 14
G.A.F., I
Georgia Gulf Corporation, 9
Great Lakes Chemical Corporation, I; 14
   (upd.)
Hercules Inc., I
Hoechst A.G., I
Hoechst Celanese Corporation, 13
Huls A.G., I
Huntsman Chemical Corporation, 8
IMC Fertilizer Group, Inc., 8
Imperial Chemical Industries PLC, I
International Flavors & Fragrances Inc., 9
Koppers Inc., I
L'air Liquide, I
Lawter International Inc., 14
Lubrizol Corporation, I
M.A. Hanna Company, 8
Mitsubishi Chemical Industries, Ltd., I
Mitsui Petrochemical Industries, Ltd., 9
Monsanto Company, I; 9 (upd.)
Montedison SpA, I
Morton International Inc., 9 (upd.)
Morton Thiokol, Inc., I
Nagase & Company, Ltd., 8
Nalco Chemical Corporation, I; 12 (upd.)
National Distillers and Chemical
   Corporation, I
NCH Corporation, 8
NL Industries, Inc., 10
Nobel Industries AB, 9
Novacor Chemicals Ltd., 12
NutraSweet Company, 8
Olin Corporation, I; 13 (upd.)
Pennwalt Corporation, I
Perstorp A.B., I
Petrolite Corporation, 15
Praxair, Inc., 11
Quantum Chemical Corporation, 8
Reichhold Chemicals, Inc., 10
Rhône-Poulenc S.A., I; 10 (upd.)
Rohm and Haas, I
Roussel Uclaf, I; 8 (upd.)
Sequa Corp., 13
Solvay & Cie S.A., I
Sumitomo Chemical Company Ltd., I
Terra Industries, Inc., 13
Union Carbide Corporation, I; 9 (upd.)
Univar Corporation, 9
Vista Chemical Company, I
Witco Corporation, I

CONGLOMERATES

Accor SA, 10
AEG A.G., I
Alcatel Alsthom Compagnie Générale
   d'Electricité, 9
Alco Standard Corporation, I
Allied-Signal Inc., I
AMFAC Inc., I
Aramark Corporation, 13
Archer-Daniels-Midland Company, I; 11
   (upd.)
Barlow Rand Ltd., I
Bat Industries PLC, I
Bond Corporation Holdings Limited, 10
BTR PLC, I
C. Itoh & Company Ltd., I
Cargill Inc., 13 (upd.)
CBI Industries, Inc., 7
Chemed Corporation, 13
Chesebrough-Pond's USA, Inc., 8
Colt Industries Inc., I
Delaware North Companies Incorporated, 7
The Dial Corp., 8
Elders IXL Ltd., I
Farley Northwest Industries, Inc., I
Fisher Companies, Inc., 15
FMC Corporation, I; 11 (upd.)
Fuqua Industries, Inc., I
Gillett Holdings, Inc., 7
Grand Metropolitan PLC, 14 (upd.)
Great American Management and
   Investment, Inc., 8
Greyhound Corporation, I
Gulf & Western Inc., I
Hanson PLC, III; 7 (upd.)
Hitachi Ltd., I; 12 (upd.)
IC Industries, Inc., I
Ingram Industries, Inc., 11
Instituto Nacional de Industria, I
International Controls Corporation, 10
International Telephone & Telegraph
   Corporation, I; 11 (upd.)
Istituto per la Ricostruzione Industriale, I
Jardine Matheson Holdings Ltd., I
Katy Industries, Inc., I
Kesko Ltd (Kesko Oy), 8
Kidde, Inc., I
KOC Holding A.S., I
Lancaster Colony Corporation, 8
Lear Siegler, Inc., I
Leucadia National Corporation, 11
Litton Industries, Inc., I; 11 (upd.)
Loews Corporation, I; 12 (upd.)
Loral Corporation, 8
LTV Corporation, I
Marubeni K.K., I
MAXXAM Inc., 8
McKesson Corporation, I
Menasha Corporation, 8
Metromedia Co., 7
Minnesota Mining & Manufacturing
   Company, I; 8 (upd.)
Mitsubishi Corporation, I; 12 (upd.)
Mitsui Bussan K.K., I
NACCO Industries, Inc., 7
National Service Industries, Inc., 11
Nissho Iwai K.K., I
Norsk Hydro A.S., 10
Ogden Corporation, I
Pentair, Inc., 7
The Rank Organisation Plc, 14 (upd.)
Samsung Group, I
San Miguel Corporation, 15
Sara Lee Corporation, 15 (upd.)
Sime Darby Berhad, 14
Sumitomo Corporation, I; 11 (upd.)
Swire Pacific Ltd., I

Teledyne, Inc., I; 10 (upd.)
Tenneco Inc., I; 10 (upd.)
Textron Inc., I
Thorn Emi PLC, I
Time Warner Inc., IV; 7 (upd.)
Tomkins plc, 11
Toshiba Corporation, I; 12 (upd.)
Transamerica Corporation, I; 13 (upd.)
The Tranzonic Cos., 15
Triarc Companies, Inc., 8
TRW Inc., I; 11 (upd.)
Unilever PLC, II; 7 (upd.)
Veba A.G., I; 15 (upd.)
Virgin Group PLC, 12
W.R. Grace & Company, I
Wheaton Industries, 8
Whitman Corporation, 10 (upd.)
Whittaker Corporation, I
WorldCorp, Inc., 10

CONSTRUCTION

A. Johnson & Company H.B., I
The Austin Company, 8
Baratt Developments PLC, I
Bechtel Group Inc., I
Bilfinger & Berger Bau A.G., I
Bouygues, I
Brown & Root, Inc., 13
Centex Corporation, 8
Cianbro Corporation, 14
The Clark Construction Group, Inc., 8
Dillingham Corporation, I
Eurotunnel PLC, 13
Fairclough Construction Group PLC, I
Fluor Corporation, I; 8 (upd.)
George Wimpey PLC, 12
John Brown PLC, I
John Laing PLC, I
Kajima Corporation, I
Kaufman and Broad Home Corporation, 8
Kitchell Corporation, 14
The Koll Company, 8
Kumagai Gumi Company, Ltd., I
Lennar Corporation, 11
Lincoln Property Company, 8
Linde A.G., I
Mellon-Stuart Company, I
Michael Baker Corp., 14
Morrison Knudsen Corporation, 7
NVR L.P., 8
Ohbayashi Corporation, I
The Peninsular & Oriental Steam
   Navigation Company (Bovis Division), I
Perini Corporation, 8
Peter Kiewit Sons' Inc., 8
Pulte Corporation, 8
The Ryland Group, Inc., 8
Taylor Woodrow PLC, I
Toll Brothers Inc., 15
Trammell Crow Company, 8
Tridel Enterprises Inc., 9
The Turner Corporation, 8
U.S. Home Corporation, 8
Wood Hall Trust PLC, I

CONTAINERS

Ball Corporation, I; 10 (upd.)
Continental Can Co., Inc., 15
Continental Group Company, I
Crown, Cork & Seal Company, Inc., I, 13
Gaylord Container Corporation, 8
Greif Bros. Corporation, 15
Inland Container Corporation, 8
Keyes Fibre Company, 9
The Longaberger Company, 12
Longview Fibre Company, 8
Metal Box PLC, I

National Can Corporation, I
Owens-Illinois, Inc., I
Primerica Corporation, I
Sonoco Products Company, 8
Toyo Seikan Kaisha, Ltd., I

DRUGS

A.L. Pharma Inc., 12
Abbott Laboratories, I; 11 (upd.)
ALZA Corporation, 10
American Home Products, I; 10 (upd.)
Amgen, Inc., 10
A.B. Astra, I
Baxter International Inc., I; 10 (upd.)
Bayer A.G., I; 13 (upd.)
Becton, Dickinson & Company, I
Block Drug Company, Inc., 8
Carter-Wallace, Inc., 8
Chiron Corporation, 10
Ciba-Geigy Ltd., I; 8 (upd.)
D&K Wholesale Drug, Inc., 14
Eli Lilly & Company, I; 11 (upd.)
F. Hoffmann-Laroche & Company A.G., I
Fisons plc, 9
Fujisawa Pharmaceutical Company Ltd., I
G.D. Searle & Company, I; 12 (upd.)
Genentech, Inc., I; 8 (upd.)
Genetics Institute, Inc., 8
Genzyme Corporation, 13
Glaxo Holdings PLC, I; 9 (upd.)
Johnson & Johnson, III; 8 (upd.)
Marion Merrell Dow, Inc., I; 9 (upd.)
McKesson Corporation, 12
Merck & Co., Inc., I; 11 (upd.)
Miles Laboratories, I
Mylan Laboratories, I
National Patent Development Corporation,
   13
Novo Industri A/S, I
Pfizer Inc., I; 9 (upd.)
Pharmacia A.B., I
R.P. Scherer, I
Roche Bioscience, 14 (upd.)
Rorer Group, I
Roussel Uclaf, I; 8 (upd.)
Sandoz Ltd., I
Sankyo Company, Ltd., I
Sanofi Group, I
Schering A.G., I
Schering-Plough Corporation, I; 14 (upd.)
Sigma-Aldrich, I
SmithKline Beckman Corporation, I
Squibb Corporation, I
Sterling Drug, Inc., I
Syntex Corporation, I
Takeda Chemical Industries, Ltd., I
The Upjohn Company, I; 8 (upd.)
Vitalink Pharmacy Services, Inc., 15
Warner-Lambert Co., I; 10 (upd.)
The Wellcome Foundation Ltd., I

ELECTRICAL & ELECTRONICS

ABB ASEA Brown Boveri Ltd., II
Acuson Corporation, 10
Advanced Technology Laboratories, Inc., 9
Alpine Electronics, Inc., 9
Alps Electric Co., Ltd., II
AMP Incorporated, II; 14 (upd.)
Analog Devices, Inc., 10
Andrew Corporation, 10
Arrow Electronics, Inc., 10
Atari Corporation, 9
Autodesk, Inc., 10
Avnet Inc., 9
Bicoastal Corporation, II
Bose Corporation, 13
Cabletron Systems, Inc., 10

Cobra Electronics Corporation, 14
Compagnie Générale d'Électricité, II
Cooper Industries, Inc., II
Dallas Semiconductor Corp., 13
Digi International Inc., 9
Dynatech Corporation, 13
E-Systems, Inc., 9
Electronics for Imaging, Inc., 15
Emerson Electric Co., II
Exar Corp., 14
Fluke Corporation, 15
Foxboro Company, 13
Fuji Electric Co., Ltd., II
General Electric Company, II; 12 (upd.)
General Electric Company, PLC, II
General Instrument Corporation, 10
General Signal Corporation, 9
GM Hughes Electronics Corporation, II
Goldstar Co., Ltd., 12
Gould Electronics, Inc., 14
Harman International Industries Inc., 15
Harris Corporation, II
Honeywell Inc., II; 12 (upd.)
Hubbell Incorporated, 9
Hughes Supply, Inc., 14
Intel Corporation, II; 10 (upd.)
Itel Corporation, 9
Kemet Corp., 14
KitchenAid, 8
KnowledgeWare Inc., 9
Koor Industries Ltd., II
Kyocera Corporation, II
Loral Corporation, 9
LSI Logic Corporation, 13
Lucky-Goldstar, II
MagneTek, Inc., 15
Marquette Electronics, Inc., 13
Matsushita Electric Industrial Co., Ltd., II
Methode Electronics, Inc., 13
Mitsubishi Electric Corporation, II
Motorola, Inc., II; 11 (upd.)
National Semiconductor Corporation, II
NEC Corporation, II
Nokia Corporation, II
Oki Electric Industry Company, Limited, II
Omron Tateisi Electronics Company, II
The Peak Technologies Group, Inc., 14
Philips Electronics N.V., II; 13 (upd.)
Philips Electronics North America Corp.,
   13
Pittway Corporation, 9
The Plessey Company, PLC, II
Potter & Brumfield Inc., 11
Premier Industrial Corporation, 9
Racal Electronics PLC, II
Raychem Corporation, 8
Rayovac Corporation, 13
Raytheon Company, II; 11 (upd.)
RCA Corporation, II
Read-Rite Corp., 10
Reliance Electric Company, 9
Rexel, Inc., 15
S&C Electric Company, 15
Samsung Electronics Co., Ltd., 14
Sanyo Electric Company, Ltd., II
Schneider S.A., II
SCI Systems, Inc., 9
Sensormatic Electronics Corp., 11
Sharp Corporation, II; 12 (upd.)
Siemens A.G., II; 14 (upd.)
Silicon Graphics Incorporated, 9
Solectron Corp., 12
Sony Corporation, II; 12 (upd.)
Sumitomo Electric Industries, Ltd., II
Sunbeam-Oster Co., Inc., 9
Tandy Corporation, II; 12 (upd.)
TDK Corporation, II
Tektronix, Inc., 8

Telxon Corporation, 10
Teradyne, Inc., 11
Texas Instruments Incorporated, II; 11
  (upd.)
Thomson S.A., II
Varian Associates Inc., 12
Victor Company of Japan, Ltd., II
Vitro Corp., 10
Westinghouse Electric Corporation, II; 12
  (upd.)
Wyle Electronics, 14
Zenith Data Systems, Inc., 10
Zenith Electronics Corporation, II; 13
  (upd.)

ENGINEERING & MANAGEMENT SERVICES

Analytic Sciences Corporation, 10
The Austin Company, 8
Brown & Root, Inc., 13
CDI Corporation, 6
CRSS Inc., 6
Day & Zimmermann Inc., 9
EG&G Incorporated, 8
Foster Wheeler Corporation, 6
Harza Engineering Company, 14
Jacobs Engineering Group Inc., 6
JWP Inc., 9
McKinsey & Company, Inc., 9
Ogden Corporation, 6
The Parsons Corporation, 8
Rosemount Inc., 15
Rust International Inc., 11
Science Applications International
  Corporation, 15
Stone & Webster, Inc., 13
Susquehanna Pfaltzgraff Company, 8
Sverdrup Corporation, 14
United Dominion Industries Limited, 8
VECO International, Inc., 7

ENTERTAINMENT & LEISURE

AMC Entertainment Inc., 12
Asahi National Broadcasting Company,
  Ltd., 9
Aspen Skiing Company, 15
Aztar Corporation, 13
Bertelsmann AG, 15 (upd.)
Blockbuster Entertainment Corporation, 9
Boston Celtics Limited Partnership, 14
British Broadcasting Corporation, 7
Cablevision Systems Corporation, 7
Capital Cities/ABC Inc., II
Carmike Cinemas, Inc., 14
CBS Inc., II; 6 (upd.)
Central Independent Television plc, 7
Cineplex Odeon Corporation, 6
Columbia Pictures Entertainment, Inc., II
Columbia TriStar Motion Pictures
  Companies, 12 (upd.)
Comcast Corporation, 7
Continental Cablevision, Inc., 7
Corporation for Public Broadcasting, 14
Gaylord Entertainment Company, 11
Granada Group PLC, II
Home Box Office Inc., 7
International Family Entertainment Inc., 13
The Intrawest Corporation, 15
Irvin Feld & Kenneth Feld Productions,
  Inc., 15
Japan Broadcasting Corporation, 7
King World Productions, Inc., 9
Ladbroke Group PLC, II
Lego A/S, 13
Lucasfilm Ltd., 12
MCA Inc., II
Media General, Inc., 7

Metromedia Companies, 14
MGM/UA Communications Company, II
National Broadcasting Company, Inc., II; 6
  (upd.)
Orion Pictures Corporation, 6
Paramount Pictures Corporation, II
Promus Companies, Inc., 9
Rank Organisation PLC, II
S-K-I Limited, 15
Sega of America, Inc., 10
Spelling Entertainment Group, Inc., 14
Tele-Communications, Inc., II
Television Española, S.A., 7
Thomas Cook Travel Inc., 9
The Thomson Corporation, 8
Ticketmaster Corp., 13
Touristik Union International GmbH. and
  Company K.G., II
Turner Broadcasting System, Inc., II; 6
  (upd.)
Twentieth Century Fox Film Corporation,
  II
Vail Associates, Inc., 11
Viacom International Inc., 7
Walt Disney Company, II; 6 (upd.)
Warner Communications Inc., II

FINANCIAL SERVICES: BANKS

Abbey National PLC, 10
Algemene Bank Nederland N.V., II
American Residential Mortgage
  Corporation, 8
AmSouth Bancorporation, 12
Amsterdam-Rotterdam Bank N.V., II
Anchor Bancorp, Inc., 10
Australia and New Zealand Banking Group
  Ltd., II
Banc One Corporation, 10
Banca Commerciale Italiana SpA, II
Banco Bilbao Vizcaya, S.A., II
Banco Bradesco S.A., 13
Banco Central, II
Banco do Brasil S.A., II
Banco Espírito Santo e Comercial de
  Lisboa S.A., 15
Bank Brussels Lambert, II
Bank Hapoalim B.M., II
Bank of Boston Corporation, II
Bank of Mississippi, Inc., 14
Bank of Montreal, II
Bank of New England Corporation, II
The Bank of New York Company, Inc., II
The Bank of Nova Scotia, II
Bank of Tokyo, Ltd., II
Bank of Tokyo-Mitsubishi Ltd., 15 (upd.)
BankAmerica Corporation, II; 8 (upd.)
Bankers Trust New York Corporation, II
Banque Nationale de Paris S.A., II
Barclays PLC, II
BarclaysAmerican Mortgage Corporation,
  11
Barings PLC, 14
Barnett Banks, Inc., 9
BayBanks, Inc., 12
Bayerische Hypotheken- und Wechsel-
  Bank AG, II
Bayerische Vereinsbank A.G., II
Beneficial Corporation, 8
Boatmen's Bancshares Inc., 15
Canadian Imperial Bank of Commerce, II
Casco Northern Bank, 14
The Chase Manhattan Corporation, II; 13
  (upd.)
Chemical Banking Corporation, II; 14
  (upd.)
Citicorp, II; 9 (upd.)
Commercial Credit Company, 8

Commercial Federal Corporation, 12
Commerzbank A.G., II
Compagnie Financiere de Paribas, II
Continental Bank Corporation, II
Crédit Agricole, II
Crédit Lyonnais, 9
Crédit National S.A., 9
Crédit Suisse, II
Credito Italiano, II
The Dai-Ichi Kangyo Bank Ltd., II
The Daiwa Bank, Ltd., II
Dauphin Deposit Corporation, 14
Deutsche Bank A.G., II; 14 (upd.)
Dime Savings Bank of New York, F.S.B.,
  9
Dresdner Bank A.G., II
Fifth Third Bancorp, 13
First Bank System Inc., 12
First Chicago Corporation, II
First Commerce Bancshares, Inc., 15
First Commerce Corporation, 11
First Empire State Corporation, 11
First Fidelity Bank, N.A., New Jersey, 9
First Hawaiian, Inc., 11
First Interstate Bancorp, II
First Nationwide Bank, 14
First of America Bank Corporation, 8
First Security Corporation, 11
First Tennessee National Corporation, 11
First Union Corporation, 10
First Virginia Banks, Inc., 11
Firstar Corporation, 11
Fleet Financial Group, Inc., 9
Fourth Financial Corporation, 11
The Fuji Bank, Ltd., II
Generale Bank, II
The Governor and Company of the Bank
  of Scotland, 10
Great Lakes Bancorp, 8
Great Western Financial Corporation, 10
H.F. Ahmanson & Company, II; 10 (upd.)
Hancock Holding Company, 15
The Hongkong and Shanghai Banking
  Corporation Limited, II
HSBC Holdings plc, 12
Huntington Bancshares Inc., 11
The Industrial Bank of Japan, Ltd., II
J.P. Morgan & Co. Incorporated, II
Japan Leasing Corporation, 8
Kansallis-Osake-Pankki, II
KeyCorp, 8
Kredietbank N.V., II
Lloyds Bank PLC, II
Long-Term Credit Bank of Japan, Ltd., II
Manufacturers Hanover Corporation, II
MBNA Corporation, 12
Mellon Bank Corporation, II
Mercantile Bankshares Corp., 11
Meridian Bancorp, Inc., 11
Metropolitan Financial Corporation, 13
Michigan National Corporation, 11
Midland Bank PLC, II
The Mitsubishi Bank, Ltd., II
The Mitsubishi Trust & Banking
  Corporation, II
The Mitsui Bank, Ltd., II
The Mitsui Trust & Banking Company,
  Ltd., II
National City Corp., 15
National Westminster Bank PLC, II
NationsBank Corporation, 10
NBD Bancorp, Inc., 11
NCNB Corporation, II
Nippon Credit Bank, II
Norinchukin Bank, II
Northern Trust Company, 9
NVR L.P., 8
Old Kent Financial Corp., 11

Old National Bancorp, 15
PNC Bank Corp., 13 (upd.)
PNC Financial Corporation, II
Pulte Corporation, 8
Republic New York Corporation, 11
Riggs National Corporation, 13
The Royal Bank of Canada, II
The Royal Bank of Scotland Group plc, 12
The Ryland Group, Inc., 8
St. Paul Bank for Cooperatives, 8
The Sanwa Bank, Ltd., II; 15 (upd.)
SBC Warburg, 14
Seattle First National Bank Inc., 8
Security Pacific Corporation, II
Shawmut National Corporation, 13
Signet Banking Corporation, 11
Skandinaviska Enskilda Banken, II
Société Générale, II
Society Corporation, 9
Southtrust Corporation, 11
Standard Chartered PLC, II
Standard Federal Bank, 9
Star Banc Corporation, 11
State Street Boston Corporation, 8
The Sumitomo Bank, Ltd., II
The Sumitomo Trust & Banking Company,
   Ltd., II
The Summit Bancorporation, 14
Svenska Handelsbanken, II
Swiss Bank Corporation, II
Synovus Financial Corp., 12
The Taiyo Kobe Bank, Ltd., II
The Tokai Bank, Limited, II; 15 (upd.)
The Toronto-Dominion Bank, II
TSB Group plc, 12
U.S. Bancorp, 14
Union Bank of Switzerland, II
Wachovia Corporation, 12
Wells Fargo & Company, II; 12 (upd.)
West One Bancorp, 11
Westdeutsche Landesbank Girozentrale, II
Westpac Banking Corporation, II
The Yasuda Trust and Banking Company,
   Ltd., II
Zions Bancorporation, 12

FINANCIAL SERVICES: NON-BANKS

A.G. Edwards, Inc., 8
ADVANTA Corp., 8
American Express Company, II; 10 (upd.)
American General Finance Corp., 11
Arthur Andersen & Company, Société
   Coopérative, 10
Avco Financial Services Inc., 13
Bear Stearns Companies, Inc., II; 10 (upd.)
Bozzuto's, Inc., 13
Charles Schwab Corp., 8
Coopers & Lybrand, 9
CS First Boston Inc., II
Daiwa Securities Company, Limited, II
Dean Witter, Discover & Co., 12
Dow Jones Telerate, Inc., 10
Drexel Burnham Lambert Incorporated, II
Federal National Mortgage Association, II
Fidelity Investments Inc., II; 14 (upd.)
First USA, Inc., 11
FMR Corp., 8
Fortis, Inc., 15
Franklin Resources, Inc., 9
Goldman, Sachs & Co., II
Green Tree Financial Corporation, 11
H & R Block, Incorporated, 9
Household International, Inc., II
Inter-Regional Financial Group, Inc., 15
Istituto per la Ricostruzione Industriale
   S.p.A., 11

Kleinwort Benson Group PLC, II
KPMG Worldwide, 10
MasterCard International, Inc., 9
Merrill Lynch & Co., Inc., II; 13 (upd.)
Morgan Grenfell Group PLC, II
Morgan Stanley Group Inc., II
National Association of Securities Dealers,
   Inc., 10
New Street Capital Inc., 8
New York Stock Exchange, Inc., 9
The Nikko Securities Company Limited, II;
   9 (upd.)
Nippon Shinpan Company, Ltd., II
Nomura Securities Company, Limited, II; 9
   (upd.)
Orix Corporation, II
PaineWebber Group Inc., II
Safeguard Scientifics, Inc., 10
Salomon Inc., II; 13 (upd.)
SBC Warburg, 14
Shearson Lehman Brothers Holdings Inc.,
   II; 9 (upd.)
Smith Barney Inc., 15
State Street Boston Corporation, 8
Student Loan Marketing Association, II
T. Rowe Price Associates, Inc., 11
Trilon Financial Corporation, II
The Vanguard Group of Investment
   Companies, 14
Visa International, 9
Yamaichi Securities Company, Limited, II

FOOD PRODUCTS

Agway, Inc., 7
Ajinomoto Co., Inc., II
Alberto-Culver Company, 8
Aldi Group, 13
American Crystal Sugar Company, 11
American Maize-Products Co., 14
Associated British Foods PLC, II; 13
   (upd.)
Associated Milk Producers, Inc., 11
Beatrice Company, II
Ben & Jerry's Homemade, Inc., 10
Booker PLC, 13
Borden, Inc., II
Brach and Brock Confections, Inc., 15
BSN Groupe S.A., II
Cadbury Schweppes PLC, II
Campbell Soup Company, II; 7 (upd.)
Canada Packers Inc., II
Cargill Inc., 13 (upd.)
Carnation Company, II
Castle & Cook, Inc., II
Central Soya Company, Inc., 7
Chiquita Brands International, Inc., 7
Coca-Cola Enterprises, Inc., 13
Conagra, Inc., II; 12 (upd.)
Continental Grain Company, 10; 13 (upd.)
CPC International Inc., II
Curtice-Burns Foods, Inc., 7
Dalgety, PLC, II
Dannon Co., Inc., 14
Darigold, Inc., 9
Dean Foods Company, 7
Del Monte Corporation, 7
Di Giorgio Corp., 12
Dole Food Company, Inc., 9
Doskocil Companies, Inc., 12
Emge Packing Co., Inc., 11
Farmland Foods, Inc., 7
Fleer Corporation, 15
Flowers Industries, Inc., 12
General Mills, Inc., II; 10 (upd.)
George A. Hormel and Company, II
Gerber Products Company, 7

Good Humor-Breyers Ice Cream Company,
   14
Gorton's, 13
Grist Mill Company, 15
H. J. Heinz Company, II; 11 (upd.)
The Hartz Mountain Corporation, 12
Hershey Foods Corporation, II; 15 (upd.)
Hillsdown Holdings, PLC, II
Hudson Foods Inc., 13
IBP, Inc., II
Imperial Holly Corporation, 12
International Multifoods Corporation, 7
Interstate Bakeries Corporation, 12
Itoham Foods Inc., II
The J.M. Smucker Company, 11
Jacobs Suchard A.G., II
Jim Beam Brands Co., 14
John B. Sanfilippo & Son, Inc., 14
Kellogg Company, II; 13 (upd.)
Kikkoman Corporation, 14
King Ranch, Inc., 14
Koninklijke Wessanen N.V., II
Kraft General Foods Inc., II; 7 (upd.)
Lance, Inc., 14
Land O'Lakes, Inc., II
Mars, Inc., 7
McCormick & Company, Incorporated, 7
McKee Foods Corporation, 7
Meiji Milk Products Company, Limited, II
Meiji Seika Kaisha, Ltd., II
Mid-America Dairymen, Inc., 7
Mike-Sell's Inc., 15
Monfort, Inc., 13
Nabisco Foods Group, II; 7 (upd.)
National Sea Products Ltd., 14
Nestlé S.A., II; 7 (upd.)
New England Confectionery Co., 15
Newhall Land and Farming Company, 14
Nippon Meat Packers, Inc., II
Nippon Suisan Kaisha, Limited, II
Nisshin Flour Milling Company, Ltd., II
Northern Foods PLC, 10
NutraSweet Company, 8
Ocean Spray Cranberries, Inc., 7
Ore-Ida Foods Incorporated, 13
Oscar Mayer Foods Corp., 12
Perdue Farms Inc., 7
Pet Incorporated, 7
Pilgrim's Pride Corporation, 7
Pillsbury Company, II; 13 (upd.)
Pioneer Hi-Bred International, Inc., 9
The Procter & Gamble Company, III; 8
   (upd.)
Quaker Oats Company, II; 12 (upd.)
Ralston Purina Company, II; 13 (upd.)
Ranks Hovis McDougall PLC, II
Reckitt & Colman PLC, II
Rich Products Corporation, 7
Roland Murten A.G., 7
Rowntree Mackintosh, II
Russell Stover Candies Inc., 12
Sanderson Farms, Inc., 15
Sara Lee Corporation, II
Savannah Foods & Industries, Inc., 7
Schwan's Sales Enterprises, Inc., 7
Smithfield Foods, Inc., 7
Snow Brand Milk Products Company,
   Limited, II
SODIMA, II
Stouffer Corp., 8
Sun-Diamond Growers of California, 7
Taiyo Fishery Company, Limited, II
Tasty Baking Co., 14
Tate & Lyle PLC, II
Thomas J. Lipton Company, 14
Thorn Apple Valley, Inc., 7
Tombstone Pizza Corporation, 13
Tootsie Roll Industries Inc., 12

Tyson Foods, Incorporated, II; 14 (upd.)
Unigate PLC, II
United Biscuits (Holdings) PLC, II
United Brands Company, II
Universal Foods Corporation, 7
Van Camp Seafood Company, Inc., 7
Vienna Sausage Manufacturing Co., 14
Wattie's Ltd., 7
Wisconsin Dairies, 7
Wm. Wrigley Jr. Company, 7
Worthington Foods, Inc., 14

FOOD SERVICES & RETAILERS

Albertson's Inc., II; 7 (upd.)
Aldi Group, 13
America's Favorite Chicken Company,
  Inc., 7
American Stores Company, II
Applebee's International Inc., 14
ARA Services, II
Arby's Inc., 14
Argyll Group PLC, II
Asda Group PLC, II
Associated Grocers, Incorporated, 9
Big Bear Stores Co., 13
Blimpie International, Inc., 15
Bob Evans Farms, Inc., 9
Boston Chicken, Inc., 12
Brinker International, Inc., 10
Bruno's Inc., 7
Buffets, Inc., 10
Burger King Corporation, II
C. H. Robinson, Inc., 11
California Pizza Kitchen Inc., 15
Cargill, Inc., II
Chi-Chi's Inc., 13
The Circle K Corporation, II
Consolidated Products Inc., 14
Cracker Barrel Old Country Store, Inc., 10
Dairy Mart Convenience Stores, Inc., 7
Domino's Pizza, Inc., 7
Edeka Zentrale A.G., II
Etablissements Economiques du Casino
  Guichard, Perrachon et Cie, S.C.A., 12
Flagstar Companies, Inc., 10
Fleming Companies, Inc., II
Food Lion, Inc., II; 15 (upd.)
Foodmaker, Inc., 14
The Fred W. Albrecht Grocery Co., 13
The Gateway Corporation Ltd., II
George Weston Limited, II
Giant Food Inc., II
Golden Corral Corporation, 10
Gordon Food Service Inc., 8
Grand Union Company, 7
The Great Atlantic & Pacific Tea
  Company, Inc., II
H.E. Butt Grocery Co., 13
Hannaford Bros. Co., 12
Hard Rock Cafe International, Inc., 12
ICA AB, II
International Dairy Queen, Inc., 10
J Sainsbury PLC, II; 13 (upd.)
KFC Corporation, 7
King Kullen Grocery Co., Inc., 15
Koninklijke Ahold N. V., II
The Kroger Company, II; 15 (upd.)
Kwik Save Group plc, 11
Landry's Seafood Restaurants, Inc., 15
Little Caesars International, Inc., 7
Long John Silver's Restaurants Inc., 13
McDonald's Corporation, II; 7 (upd.)
Megafoods Stores Inc., 13
Meijer Incorporated, 7
Metromedia Companies, 14
Morrison Restaurants Inc., 11
Nash Finch Company, 8

National Convenience Stores Incorporated,
  7
Noble Roman's Inc., 14
The Oshawa Group Limited, II
Outback Steakhouse, Inc., 12
P&C Foods Inc., 8
Papa John's International, Inc., 15
Penn Traffic Company, 13
Piggly Wiggly Southern, Inc., 13
Pizza Hut Inc., 7
Ponderosa Steakhouse, 15
Provigo Inc., II
Publix Supermarkets Inc., 7
Restaurants Unlimited, Inc., 13
Richfood Holdings, Inc., 7
Riser Foods, Inc., 9
Ryan's Family Steak Houses, Inc., 15
Safeway Stores Incorporated, II
Seaway Food Town, Inc., 15
Service America Corp., 7
Shoney's, Inc., 7
ShowBiz Pizza Time, Inc., 13
Smith's Food & Drug Centers, Inc., 8
Sonic Corporation, 14
The Southland Corporation, II; 7 (upd.)
Spartan Stores Inc., 8
Steinberg Incorporated, II
The Stop & Shop Companies, Inc., II
Super Food Services, Inc., 15
Super Valu Stores, Inc., II
Supermarkets General Holdings
  Corporation, II
Sysco Corporation, II
Taco Bell, 7
Taco John's International Inc., 15
Tesco PLC, II
Trader Joe's Co., 13
TW Services, Inc., II
VICORP Restaurants, Inc., 12
Village Super Market, Inc., 7
The Vons Companies, Incorporated, 7
Waffle House Inc., 14
Wegmans Food Markets, Inc., 9
Weis Markets, Inc., 15
Wendy's International, Inc., 8
Wetterau Incorporated, II
White Castle Systems, Inc., 12
Winn-Dixie Stores, Inc., II

**HEALTH & PERSONAL CARE
PRODUCTS**

Alberto-Culver Company, 8
Alco Health Services Corporation, III
Allergan, Inc., 10
Amway Corporation, III; 13 (upd.)
Avon Products Inc., III
Bausch & Lomb Inc., 7
Becton, Dickinson & Company, 11 (upd.)
Bindley Western Industries, Inc., 9
Block Drug Company, Inc.
Bristol-Myers Squibb Company, III; 9
  (upd.)
C.R. Bard Inc., 9
Carter-Wallace, Inc., 8
Chesebrough-Pond's USA, Inc., 8
The Clorox Company, III
Colgate-Palmolive Company, III; 14 (upd.)
Cosmair, Inc., 8
Dentsply International Inc., 10
Drackett Professional Products, 12
Elizabeth Arden Co., 8
Estée Lauder Inc., 9
Forest Laboratories, Inc., 11
General Nutrition Companies, Inc., 11
Genzyme Corporation, 13
The Gillette Company, III
Helene Curtis Industries, Inc., 8

Henkel KGaA, III
Invacare Corporation, 11
IVAX Corporation, 11
Johnson & Johnson, III; 8 (upd.)
Kao Corporation, III
Kendall International, Inc., 11
Kimberly-Clark Corporation, III
Kyowa Hakko Kogyo Co., Ltd., III
L'Oreal, III; 8 (upd.)
Lever Brothers Company, 9
Lion Corporation, III
Mary Kay Corporation, 9
Maxxim Medical Inc., 12
Medco Containment Services Inc., 9
Medtronic, Inc., 8
Nature's Sunshine Products, Inc., 15
Perrigo Company, 12
Physician Sales & Service, Inc., 14
Playtex Products, Inc., 15
The Procter & Gamble Company, III; 8
  (upd.)
Revlon Group Inc., III
Roche Biomedical Laboratories, Inc., 11
S. C. Johnson & Son, Inc., III
Schering-Plough Corporation, 14 (upd.)
Shionogi & Co., Ltd., III
Shiseido Company, Limited, III
SmithKline Beecham PLC, III
Sunrise Medical Inc., 11
Tambrands Inc., 8
Turtle Wax, Inc., 15
United States Surgical Corporation, 10
Wella Group, III

HEALTH CARE SERVICES

American Medical International, Inc., III
Applied Bioscience International, Inc., 10
Beverly Enterprises, Inc., III
Caremark International Inc., 10
COBE Laboratories, Inc., 13
Columbia/HCA Healthcare Corporation, 15
Community Psychiatric Centers, 15
Comprehensive Care Corporation, 15
Continental Medical Systems, Inc., 10
Extendicare Health Services, Inc., 6
FHP International Corporation, 6
GranCare, Inc., 14
Health Systems International, Inc., 11
HealthSouth Rehabilitation Corporation, 14
The Hillhaven Corporation, 14
Hospital Corporation of America, III
Humana Inc., III
Jenny Craig, Inc., 10
Manor Care, Inc., 6
Maxicare Health Plans, Inc., III
Mayo Foundation, 9
National Health Laboratories Incorporated,
  11
National Medical Enterprises, Inc., III
NovaCare, Inc., 11
PacifiCare Health Systems, Inc., 11
St. Jude Medical, Inc., 11
Sierra Health Services, Inc., 15
U.S. Healthcare, Inc., 6
United HealthCare Corporation, 9
Universal Health Services, Inc., 6

HOTELS

Aztar Corporation, 13
Caesars World, Inc., 6
Choice Hotels International Inc., 14
Circus Circus Enterprises, Inc., 6
Club Méditerranée SA, 6
Four Seasons Hotels Inc., 9
Helmsley Enterprises, Inc., 9
Hilton Hotels Corporation, III
Holiday Inns, Inc., III

Hospitality Franchise Systems, Inc., 11
Hyatt Corporation, III
ITT Sheraton Corporation, III
La Quinta Inns, Inc., 11
Marriott Corporation, III
Mirage Resorts, Inc., 6
Motel 6 Corporation, 13
Omni Hotels Corp., 12
Promus Companies, Inc., 9
Resorts International, Inc., 12
Ritz-Carlton Hotel Company, 9
Trusthouse Forte PLC, III
Westin Hotel Co., 9

INFORMATION TECHNOLOGY

Adobe Systems Incorporated, 10
Advanced Micro Devices, Inc., 6
Aldus Corporation, 10
Amdahl Corporation, III; 14 (upd.)
America Online, Inc., 10
American Management Systems, Inc., 11
Amstrad PLC, III
Analytic Sciences Corporation, 10
Apple Computer, Inc., III; 6 (upd.)
ASK Group, Inc., 9
AST Research Inc., 9
AT&T Bell Laboratories, Inc., 13
AT&T Istel Ltd., 14
Automatic Data Processing, Inc., III; 9
  (upd.)
Battelle Memorial Institute, Inc., 10
Bell and Howell Company, 9
Booz Allen & Hamilton Inc., 10
Borland International, Inc., 9
Broderbund Software, Inc., 13
Cadence Design Systems, Inc., 11
CalComp Inc., 13
Canon Inc., III
Cheyenne Software, Inc., 12
CHIPS and Technologies, Inc., 9
Cincom Systems Inc., 15
Cirrus Logic, Incorporated, 11
Cisco Systems, Inc., 11
Commodore International Ltd., 7
Compagnie des Machines Bull S. A., III
Compaq Computer Corporation, III; 6
  (upd.)
CompuAdd Computer Corporation, 11
CompuCom Systems, Inc., 10
CompuServe Incorporated, 10
Computer Associates International, Inc., 6
Computer Data Systems, Inc., 14
Computer Sciences Corporation, 6
Computervision Corporation, 10
Compuware Corporation, 10
Conner Peripherals, Inc., 6
Control Data Corporation, III
Control Data Systems, Inc., 10
Corel Corporation, 15
Corporate Software Inc., 9
Cray Research, Inc., III
CTG, Inc., 11
Data General Corporation, 8
Datapoint Corporation, 11
Dell Computer Corp., 9
Digital Equipment Corporation, III; 6
  (upd.)
Dun & Bradstreet Software Services Inc.,
  11
ECS S.A, 12
Edmark Corporation, 14
Egghead Inc., 9
El Camino Resources International, Inc., 11
Electronic Arts Inc., 10
Electronic Data Systems Corporation, III
EMC Corporation, 12
Encore Computer Corporation, 13

Exabyte Corporation, 12
First Financial Management Corporation,
  11
Fiserv Inc., 11
FlightSafety International, Inc., 9
Fujitsu Limited, III
Fujitsu-ICL Systems Inc., 11
Future Now, Inc., 12
Gateway 2000, Inc., 10
Hewlett-Packard Company, III; 6 (upd.)
ICL plc, 6
Information Resources, Inc., 10
Informix Corp., 10
Ing. C. Olivetti & C., S.p.a., III
Intelligent Electronics, Inc., 6
Intergraph Corporation, 6
International Business Machines
  Corporation, III; 6 (upd.)
Intuit Inc., 14
J.D. Edwards & Company, 14
KLA Instruments Corporation, 11
Komag, Inc., 11
Lam Research Corporation, 11
Legent Corporation, 10
Logica plc, 14
Lotus Development Corporation, 6
MAI Systems Corporation, 11
Maxtor Corporation, 10
Mead Data Central, Inc., 10
Mentor Graphics Corporation, 11
Merisel, Inc., 12
Micron Technology, Inc., 11
Microsoft Corporation, 6
National Semiconductor Corporation, 6
NCR Corporation, III; 6 (upd.)
Netscape Communications Corporation, 15
Nextel Communications, Inc., 10
Nixdorf Computer AG, III
Novell, Inc., 6
Odetics Inc., 14
Oracle Systems Corporation, 6
Packard Bell Electronics, Inc., 13
PeopleSoft Inc., 14
Pitney Bowes Inc., III
PLATINUM Technology, Inc., 14
Policy Management Systems Corporation,
  11
Primark Corp., 13
Progress Software Corporation, 15
Quantum Corporation, 10
Racal-Datacom Inc., 11
Ricoh Company, Ltd., III
SAS Institute Inc., 10
Seagate Technology, Inc., 8
Sierra On-Line Inc., 15
Softbank Corp., 13
Standard Microsystems Corporation, 11
STC PLC, III
Sterling Software, Inc., 11
Storage Technology Corporation, 6
Stratus Computer, Inc., 10
Sun Microsystems, Inc., 7
SunGard Data Systems Inc., 11
Sybase, Inc., 10
Symantec Corporation, 10
Symbol Technologies, Inc., 15
Synopsis, Inc., 11
System Software Associates, Inc., 10
Tandem Computers, Inc., 6
3Com Corp., 11
Timberline Software Corporation, 15
Unisys Corporation, III; 6 (upd.)
Verbatim Corporation, 14
Wang Laboratories, Inc., III; 6 (upd.)
WordPerfect Corporation, 10
Wyse Technology, Inc., 15
Xerox Corporation, III; 6 (upd.)
Zilog, Inc., 15

INSURANCE

AEGON N.V., III
Aetna Life and Casualty Company, III
AFLAC Inc., 10 (upd.)
Alexander & Alexander Services Inc., 10
Alleghany Corporation, 10
Allianz AG Holding, III
Allianz Aktiengesellschaft Holding, 15
  (upd.)
The Allstate Corporation, 10
American Family Corporation, III
American Financial Corporation, III
American General Corporation, III; 10
  (upd.)
American International Group, Inc., III; 15
  (upd.)
American National Insurance Company, 8
American Premier Underwriters, Inc., 10
American Re Corporation, 10
N.V. AMEV, III
Aon Corporation, III
Assicurazioni Generali SpA, III; 15 (upd.)
Axa, III
Berkshire Hathaway Inc., III
Blue Cross and Blue Shield Association,
  10
Business Men's Assurance Company of
  America, 14
Capital Holding Corporation, III
The Chubb Corporation, III; 14 (upd.)
CIGNA Corporation, III
CNA Financial Corporation, III
Commercial Union PLC, III
Connecticut Mutual Life Insurance
  Company, III
Conseco Inc., 10
The Continental Corporation, III
Empire Blue Cross and Blue Shield, III
The Equitable Life Assurance Society of
  the United States Fireman's Fund
  Insurance Company, III
First Executive Corporation, III
Foundation Health Corporation, 12
GEICO Corporation, 10
General Accident PLC, III
General Re Corporation, III
Great-West Lifeco Inc., III
Guardian Royal Exchange Plc, 11
The Home Insurance Company, III
Jackson National Life Insurance Company,
  8
Jefferson-Pilot Corporation, 11
John Hancock Mutual Life Insurance
  Company, III
Johnson & Higgins, 14
Kemper Corporation, III; 15 (upd.)
Legal & General Group PLC, III
Lincoln National Corporation, III
Lloyd's of London, III
Marsh & McLennan Companies, Inc., III
Massachusetts Mutual Life Insurance
  Company, III
The Meiji Mutual Life Insurance Company,
  III
Metropolitan Life Insurance Company, III
Mitsui Marine and Fire Insurance
  Company, Limited, III
Mitsui Mutual Life Insurance Company, III
Munich Re (Münchener
  Rückversicherungs-Gesellschaft), III
The Mutual Benefit Life Insurance
  Company, III
The Mutual Life Insurance Company of
  New York, III
Nationale-Nederlanden N.V., III
New England Mutual Life Insurance
  Company, III

New York Life Insurance Company, III
Nippon Life Insurance Company, III
Northwestern Mutual Life Insurance Company, III
Ohio Casualty Corp., 11
Old Republic International Corp., 11
The Paul Revere Corporation, 12
Pennsylvania Blue Shield, III
Principal Mutual Life Insurance Company, III
Progressive Corporation, 11
Provident Life and Accident Insurance Company of America, III
Prudential Corporation PLC, III
The Prudential Insurance Company of America, III
Reliance Group Holdings, Inc., III
Riunione Adriatica di Sicurtà SpA, III
Royal Insurance Holdings PLC, III
SAFECO Corporaton, III
The St. Paul Companies, Inc., III
The Standard Life Assurance Company, III
State Farm Mutual Automobile Insurance Company, III
Sumitomo Life Insurance Company, III
The Sumitomo Marine and Fire Insurance Company, Limited, III
Sun Alliance Group PLC, III
SunAmerica Inc., 11
Swiss Reinsurance Company (Schweizerische Rückversicherungs-Gesellschaft), III
Teachers Insurance and Annuity Association, III
Texas Industries, Inc., 8
The Tokio Marine and Fire Insurance Co., Ltd., III
Torchmark Corporation, 9
Transatlantic Holdings, Inc., 11
The Travelers Corporation, III
Union des Assurances de Pans, III
UNUM Corp., 13
USAA, 10
USF&G Corporation, III
VICTORIA Holding AG, III
W.R. Berkley Corp., 15
Washington National Corporation, 12
''Winterthur'' Schweizerische Versicherungs-Gesellschaft, III
The Yasuda Fire and Marine Insurance Company, Limited, III
The Yasuda Mutual Life Insurance Company, Limited, III
''Zürich'' Versicherungs-Gesellschaft, III

LEGAL SERVICES

Baker & McKenzie, 10

MANUFACTURING

A. O. Smith Corporation, 11
ACCO World Corporation, 7
Acme-Cleveland Corp., 13
AGCO Corp., 13
Aisin Seiki Co., Ltd., III
Aktiebolaget SKF, III
Alfa-Laval AB, III
Alliant Techsystems, Inc., 8
Allied Signal Engines, 9
Allison Gas Turbine Division, 9
AMETEK, Inc., 9
Anchor Hocking Glassware, 13
Andersen Corporation, 10
Anthem Electronics, Inc., 13
Applied Materials, Inc., 10
Applied Power, Inc., 9
Armstrong World Industries, Inc., III
Atlas Copco AB, III

Avondale Industries, Inc., 7
Baker Hughes Incorporated, III
Bally Manufacturing Corporation, III
Barnes Group Inc., 13
Bath Iron Works Corporation, 12
Beckman Instruments, Inc., 14
Beloit Corporation, 14
Benjamin Moore and Co., 13
BIC Corporation, 8
BICC PLC, III
Biomet, Inc., 10
BISSELL, Inc., 9
The Black & Decker Corporation, III
Blount, Inc., 12
Borg-Warner Automotive, Inc., 14
Borg-Warner Corporation, III
Briggs & Stratton Corporation, 8
Brother Industries, Ltd., 14
Broyhill Furniture Industries, Inc., 10
Brunswick Corporation, III
Bulova Corporation, 13
Butler Manufacturing Co., 12
Callaway Golf Company, 15
Carl-Zeiss-Stiftung, III
Carrier Corporation, 7
Casio Computer Co., Ltd., III
Caterpillar Inc., III; 15 (upd.)
Chanel, 12
Chromcraft Revington, Inc., 15
Cincinnati Milacron Inc., 12
Citizen Watch Co., Ltd., III
Clark Equipment Company, 8
Clayton Homes Incorporated, 13
Colt's Manufacturing Company, Inc., 12
Converse Inc., 9
Crane Co., 8
Crown Equipment Corporation, 15
Culligan International Company, 12
Curtiss-Wright Corporation, 10
Daewoo Group, III
Daikin Industries, Ltd., III
Danaher Corporation, 7
Deere & Company, III
Department 56, Inc., 14
Detroit Diesel Corporation, 10
Deutsche Babcock A.G., III
Diebold, Inc., 7
Dixon Ticonderoga Company, 12
Donnelly Corporation, 12
Dover Corporation, III
Dresser Industries, Inc., III
Drexel Heritage Furnishings Inc., 12
Duracell International Inc., 9
Eagle-Picher Industries, Inc., 8
Eastman Kodak Company, III; 7 (upd.)
Eddie Bauer Inc., 9
Elano Corporation, 14
Electrolux Group, III
Enesco Corporation, 11
Esterline Technologies Corp., 15
Ethan Allen Interiors, Inc., 12
The Eureka Company, 12
Fanuc Ltd., III
Federal Signal Corp., 10
Figgie International Inc., 7
First Brands Corporation, 8
Fisher Controls International, Inc., 13
Fisher-Price Inc., 12
Fisons plc, 9
Fleetwood Enterprises, Inc., III
Flexsteel Industries Inc., 15
Florsheim Shoe Company, 9
Foxboro Company, 13
Fuji Photo Film Co., Ltd., III
The Furukawa Electric Co., Ltd., III
G.S. Blodgett Corporation, 15
The Gates Corporation, 9
GE Aircraft Engines, 9

GenCorp Inc., 8; 9
Gerber Scientific, Inc., 12
Giddings & Lewis, Inc., 10
GKN plc, III
The Glidden Company, 8
Goody Products, Inc., 12
Grinnell Corp., 13
Grow Group Inc., 12
H.B. Fuller Company, 8
Halliburton Company, III
Harnischfeger Industries, Inc., 8
Harsco Corporation, 8
Hasbro, Inc., III
Hawker Siddeley Group Public Limited Company, III
Haworth Inc., 8
Health O Meter Products Inc., 14
Heekin Can Inc., 13
The Henley Group, Inc., III
Herman Miller, Inc., 8
Hillenbrand Industries, Inc., 10
Hitachi Zosen Corporation, III
Holnam Inc., 8
Holson Burnes Group, Inc., 14
HON INDUSTRIES Inc., 13
The Hoover Company, 12
Huffy Corporation, 7
Hunt Manufacturing Company, 12
Hunter Fan Company, 13
Hyundai Group, III; 7 (upd.)
Illinois Tool Works Inc., III
IMI plc, 9
Imo Industries Inc., 7
Inchcape PLC, III
Ingalls Shipbuilding, Inc., 12
Ingersoll-Rand Company, III; 15 (upd.)
Interco Incorporated, III
Interface, Inc., 8
The Interlake Corporation, 8
International Controls Corporation, 10
International Game Technology, 10
Irwin Toy Limited, 14
Ishikawajima-Harima Heavy Industries Co., Ltd., III
J.I. Case Company, 10
Jayco Inc., 13
Johnson Controls, Inc., III
Jones Apparel Group, Inc., 11
Jostens Inc., 7
Kaman Corp., 12
Kawasaki Heavy Industries, Ltd., III
Key Tronic Corporation, 14
Keystone International, Inc., 11
KHD Konzern, III
Kimball International, Inc., 12
Knoll Group Inc., 14
Kohler Company, 7
Komatsu Ltd., III
Konica Corporation, III
Kubota Corporation, III
LADD Furniture, Inc., 12
Lamson & Sessions Co., 13
The Lane Co., Inc., 12
Leggett & Platt, Incorporated, 11
Lennox International Inc., 8
Lenox, Inc., 12
Lincoln Electric Co., 13
Little Tikes Co., 13
Loctite Corporation, 8
The Longaberger Company, 12
Louis Vuitton, 10
Lucas Industries PLC, III
MAN Aktiengesellschaft, III
Mannesmann AG, III; 14 (upd.)
Marisa Christina, Inc., 15
Mark IV Industries, Inc., 7
Masco Corporation, III
Mattel, Inc., 7

Maytag Corporation, III
McDermott International, Inc., III
Merillat Industries Inc., 13
Mestek Inc., 10
Microdot Inc., 8
Minolta Camera Co., Ltd., III
Mitsubishi Heavy Industries, Ltd., III; 7 (upd.)
Modine Manufacturing Company, 8
Moen Incorporated, 12
Molex Incorporated, 11
Montres Rolex S.A., 13
Mr. Coffee, Inc., 15
Mr. Gasket Inc., 15
Mueller Industries, Inc., 7
Nashua Corporation, 8
National Gypsum Company, 10
National Standard Co., 13
Newell Co., 9
Newport News Shipbuilding and Dry Dock Co., 13
NHK Spring Co., Ltd., III
Nikon Corporation, III
Nintendo Co., Ltd., III; 7 (upd.)
Nippon Seiko K.K., III
Nippondenso Co., Ltd., III
Nordson Corporation, 11
Norton Company, 8
NTN Corporation, III
Oakwood Homes Corporation, 15
The Ohio Art Company, 14
Oneida Ltd., 7
Otis Elevator Company, Inc., 13
Outboard Marine Corporation, III
Pacific Dunlop Limited, 10
Pall Corporation, 9
Parker Hannifin Corporation, III
Pella Corporation, 12
The Perkin-Elmer Corporation, 7
Pioneer Electronic Corporation, III
Ply Gem Industries Inc., 12
Polaris Industries Inc., 12
Polaroid Corporation, III; 7 (upd.)
Precision Castparts Corp., 15
Premark International, Inc., III
Prince Sports Group, Inc., 15
Puritan-Bennett Corporation, 13
Quixote Corporation, 15
Raychem Corporation, 8
Red Wing Shoe Company, Inc., 9
Reichhold Chemicals, Inc., 10
Remington Arms Company, Inc., 12
Rheinmetall Berlin AG, 9
Robbins & Myers Inc., 15
Rohr Incorporated, 9
Rollerblade, Inc., 15
Roper Industries Inc., 15
Royal Appliance Manufacturing Company, 15
Royal Doulton Plc, 14
RPM Inc., 8
Rubbermaid Incorporated, III
Russ Berrie and Company, Inc., 12
St. John Knits, Inc., 14
Salant Corporation, 12
Samsonite Corp., 13
Sauder Woodworking Co., 12
Schlumberger Limited, III
Scott Fetzer Company, 12
Sealed Air Corporation, 14
Sealy Inc., 12
Seiko Corporation, III
Sequa Corp., 13
Shelby Williams Industries, Inc., 14
Skis Rossignol S.A., 15
Smith Corona Corp., 13
Smith International, Inc., 15
Snap-on Tools Corporation, 7

The Stanley Works, III
Steelcase Inc., 7
Stewart & Stevenson Services Inc., 11
Stryker Corporation, 11
Sulzer Brothers Limited (Gebruder Sulzer Aktiengesellschaft), III
Sumitomo Heavy Industries, Ltd., III
Susquehanna Pfaltzgraff Company, 8
Swedish Match S.A., 12
Sybron International Corp., 14
Syratech Corp., 14
Tecumseh Products Company, 8
Tektronix, Inc., 8
Tennant Company, 13
Terex Corporation, 7
Thermo Electron Corporation, 7
Thermo Instrument Systems Inc., 11
Thermo King Corporation, 13
Thomas & Betts Corp., 11
Thomasville Furniture Industries, Inc., 12
Timex Enterprises Inc., 7
The Timken Company, 8
Todd Shipyards Corporation, 14
Topps Company, Inc., 13
The Toro Company, 7
The Torrington Company, 13
Toyoda Automatic Loom Works, Ltd., III
Trico Products Corporation, 15
TriMas Corp., 11
Trinity Industries, Incorporated, 7
TRINOVA Corporation, III
Tultex Corporation, 13
Tyco Laboratories, Inc., III
Tyco Toys, Inc., 12
U.S. Robotics Inc., 9
United Dominion Industries Limited, 8
Valmet Corporation (Valmet Oy), III
The Valspar Corporation, 8
Varity Corporation, III
W.L. Gore & Associates, Inc., 14
Wabash National Corp., 13
Walbro Corporation, 13
Waterford Wedgwood Holdings PLC, 12
Wellman, Inc., 8
West Bend Co., 14
Whirlpool Corporation, III; 12 (upd.)
White Consolidated Industries Inc., 13
WMS Industries, Inc., 15
Woodward Governor Co., 13
Wyman-Gordon Company, 14
Yamaha Corporation, III
York International Corp., 13

MATERIALS

American Colloid Co., 13
American Standard Inc., III
Apogee Enterprises, Inc., 8
Asahi Glass Company, Limited, III
Blue Circle Industries PLC, III
Boral Limited, III
British Vita PLC, 9
Carborundum Company, 15
Carlisle Companies Incorporated, 8
Compagnie de Saint-Gobain S. A., III
Cookson Group plc, III
Corning Incorporated, III
CSR Limited, III
The David J. Joseph Company, 14
The Dexter Corporation, 12 (upd.)
ECC Group plc, III
84 Lumber Company, 9
English China Clays plc, 15 (upd.)
Feldmuhle Nobel A.G., III
Formica Corporation, 13
The Geon Company, 11
Harrisons & Crosfield plc, III
"Holderbank" Financière Glaris Ltd., III

Howmet Corp., 12
Ibstock plc, 14
Joseph T. Ryerson & Son, Inc., 15
Lafarge Coppée S.A., III
Manville Corporation, III; 7 (upd.)
Matsushita Electric Works, Ltd., III; 7 (upd.)
Mitsubishi Materials Corporation, III
Nippon Sheet Glass Company, Limited, III
OmniSource Corporation, 14
Onoda Cement Co., Ltd., III
Owens-Corning Fiberglass Corporation, III
Pilkington plc, III
Pioneer International Limited, III
PPG Industries, Inc., III
Redland plc, III
RMC Group p.l.c., III
Sekisui Chemical Co., Ltd., III
Shaw Industries, 9
The Sherwin-Williams Company, III; 13 (upd.)
Southdown, Inc., 14
Ssangyong Cement Industrial Co., Ltd., III
Sun Distributors L.P., 12
Tarmac PLC, III
Toto, Ltd., III
Toyo Sash Co., Ltd., III
Ube Industries, Ltd., III
USG Corporation, III
Vulcan Materials Company, 7
Walter Industries, Inc., III
Waxman Industries, Inc., 9

MINING & METALS

Alcan Aluminium Limited, IV
Alleghany Corporation, 10
Allegheny Ludlum Corporation, 8
Aluminum Company of America, IV
AMAX Inc., IV
Amsted Industries Incorporated, 7
Anglo American Corporation of South Africa Limited, IV
ARBED S.A., IV
Arch Mineral Corporation, 7
Armco Inc., IV
ASARCO Incorporated, IV
Bethlehem Steel Corporation, IV; 7 (upd.)
Birmingham Steel Corporation, 13
British Coal Corporation, IV
British Steel plc, IV
Broken Hill Proprietary Company Ltd., IV
Brush Wellman Inc., 14
Carpenter Technology Corporation, 13
Chaparral Steel Co., 13
Cleveland-Cliffs Inc., 13
Coal India Limited, IV
Cockerill Sambre Group, IV
Commercial Metals Company, 15
Companhia Vale do Rio Duce, IV
CRA Limited, IV
Cyprus Minerals Company, 7
Daido Steel Co., Ltd., IV
De Beers Consolidated Mines Limited/De Beers Centenary AG, IV; 7 (upd.)
Degussa Group, IV
Dofasco Inc., IV
Echo Bay Mines Ltd., IV
Engelhard Corporation, IV
Freeport-McMoRan Inc., IV; 7 (upd.)
Fried. Krupp GmbH, IV
Gencor Ltd., IV
Geneva Steel, 7
Gold Fields of South Africa Ltd., IV
Hemlo Gold Mines Inc., 9
Heraeus Holding GmbH, IV
Hitachi Metals, Ltd., IV
Hoesch AG, IV

Homestake Mining Company, 12
The Hudson Bay Mining and Smelting
   Company, Limited, 12
Imetal S.A., IV
Inco Limited, IV
Inland Steel Industries, Inc., IV
Johnson Matthey PLC, IV
Kaiser Aluminum & Chemical Corporation,
   IV
Kawasaki Steel Corporation, IV
Kennecott Corporation, 7
Klockner-Werke AG, IV
Kobe Steel, Ltd., IV
Koninklijke Nederlandsche Hoogovens en
   Staalfabrieken NV, IV
Laclede Steel Company, 15
Lukens Inc., 14
Magma Copper Company, 7
The Marmon Group, IV
MAXXAM Inc., 8
Metallgesellschaft AG, IV
Minerals and Metals Trading Corporation
   of India Ltd., IV
Minerals Technologies Inc., 11
Mitsui Mining & Smelting Co., Ltd., IV
Mitsui Mining Company, Limited, IV
National Steel Corporation, 12
NERCO, Inc., 7
Newmont Mining Corporation, 7
Nichimen Corporation, IV
Nippon Light Metal Company, Ltd., IV
Nippon Steel Corporation, IV
Nisshin Steel Co., Ltd., IV
NKK Corporation, IV
Noranda Inc., IV; 7 (upd.)
Nucor Corporation, 7
Okura & Co., Ltd., IV
Oregon Steel Mills, Inc., 14
Peabody Coal Company, 10
Peabody Holding Company, Inc., IV
Pechiney, IV
Peter Kiewit Sons' Inc., 8
Phelps Dodge Corporation, IV
The Pittston Company, IV
Pohang Iron and Steel Company Ltd., IV
Quanex Corporation, 13
Republic Engineered Steels, Inc., 7
Reynolds Metals Company, IV
Rouge Steel Company, 8
The RTZ Corporation PLC, IV
Ruhrkohle AG, IV
Saarberg-Konzern, IV
Salzgitter AG, IV
Sandvik AB, IV
Southwire Company, Inc., 8
Steel Authority of India Ltd., IV
Stelco Inc., IV
Sumitomo Metal Industries, Ltd., IV
Sumitomo Metal Mining Co., Ltd., IV
Tata Iron and Steel Company Ltd., IV
Texas Industries, Inc., 8
Thyssen AG, IV
The Timken Company, 8
Tomen Corporation, IV
Usinor Sacilor, IV
VIAG Aktiengesellschaft, IV
Voest-Alpine Stahl AG, IV
Weirton Steel Corporation, IV
Westmoreland Coal Company, 7
Wheeling-Pittsburgh Corp., 7
Worthington Industries, Inc., 7
Zambia Industrial and Mining Corporation
   Ltd., IV

PAPER & FORESTRY

Abitibi-Price Inc., IV
Amcor Limited, IV

Avery Dennison Corporation, IV
Badger Paper Mills, Inc., 15
Bemis Company, Inc., 8
Bohemia, Inc., 13
Boise Cascade Corporation, IV; 8 (upd.)
Bowater PLC, IV
Bunzl plc, IV
Champion International Corporation, IV
Chesapeake Corporation, 8
Consolidated Papers, Inc., 8
Daio Paper Corporation, IV
Daishowa Paper Manufacturing Co., Ltd.,
   IV
Dillard Paper Company, 11
Domtar Inc., IV
Enso-Gutzeit Oy, IV
Esselte Pendaflex Corporation, 11
Federal Paper Board Company, Inc., 8
Fletcher Challenge Ltd., IV
Fort Howard Corporation, 8
Georgia-Pacific Corporation, IV; 9 (upd.)
Honshu Paper Co., Ltd., IV
International Paper Company, IV; 15 (upd.)
James River Corporation of Virginia, IV
Japan Pulp and Paper Company Limited,
   IV
Jefferson Smurfit Group plc, IV
Jujo Paper Co., Ltd., IV
Kymmene Corporation, IV
Longview Fibre Company, 8
Louisiana-Pacific Corporation, IV
MacMillan Bloedel Limited, IV
The Mead Corporation, IV
Metsa-Serla Oy, IV
Mo och Domsjö AB, IV
Mosinee Paper Corporation, 15
Nashua Corporation, 8
NCH Corporation, 8
Oji Paper Co., Ltd., IV
P. H. Glatfelter Company, 8
Packaging Corporation of America, 12
Pope and Talbot, Inc., 12
Potlatch Corporation, 8
PWA Group, IV
Rengo Co., Ltd., IV
Riverwood International Corporation, 11
Rock-Tenn Company, 13
St. Joe Paper Company, 8
Sanyo-Kokusaku Pulp Co., Ltd., IV
Scott Paper Company, IV
Sealed Air Corporation, 14
Specialty Coatings Inc., 8
Stone Container Corporation, IV
Stora Kopparbergs Bergslags AB, IV
Svenska Cellulosa Aktiebolaget, IV
Temple-Inland Inc., IV
Union Camp Corporation, IV
United Paper Mills Ltd. (Yhtyneet
   Paperitehtaat Oy), IV
Universal Forest Products Inc., 10
Westvaco Corporation, IV
Weyerhaeuser Company, IV; 9 (upd.)
Willamette Industries, Inc., IV

PERSONAL SERVICES

ADT Security Systems, Inc., 12
The Davey Tree Expert Company, 11
Educational Testing Service, 12
Franklin Quest Co., 11
KinderCare Learning Centers, Inc., 13
Manpower, Inc., 9
Rollins, Inc., 11
Rosenbluth International Inc., 14
Service Corporation International, 6
Weight Watchers International Inc., 12

PETROLEUM

Abu Dhabi National Oil Company, IV
Amerada Hess Corporation, IV
Amoco Corporation, IV; 14 (upd.)
Anadarko Petroleum Corporation, 10
Anschutz Corp., 12
Apache Corp., 10
Ashland Oil, Inc., IV
Atlantic Richfield Company, IV
British Petroleum Company PLC, IV; 7
   (upd.)
Burlington Resources Inc., 10
Burmah Castrol plc, IV
Chevron Corporation, IV
Chiles Offshore Corporation, 9
Chinese Petroleum Corporation, IV
CITGO Petroleum Corporation, IV
The Coastal Corporation, IV
Compañia Española de Petróleos S.A., IV
Conoco Inc., IV
Cosmo Oil Co., Ltd., IV
Crown Central Petroleum Corporation, 7
Den Norse Stats Oljeselskap AS, IV
Deutsche BP Aktiengesellschaft, 7
Diamond Shamrock, Inc., IV
Egyptian General Petroluem Corporation,
   IV
Empresa Colombiana de Petróleos, IV
Ente Nazionale Idrocarburi, IV
Enterprise Oil plc, 11
Entreprise Nationale Sonatrach, IV
Exxon Corporation, IV; 7 (upd.)
FINA, Inc., 7
General Sekiyu K.K., IV
Global Marine Inc., 9
Holly Corporation, 12
Hunt Oil Company, 7
Idemitsu Kosan K.K., IV
Imperial Oil Limited, IV
Indian Oil Corporation Ltd., IV
Kanematsu Corporation, IV
Kerr-McGee Corporation, IV
King Ranch, Inc., 14
Koch Industries, Inc., IV
Kuwait Petroleum Corporation, IV
Libyan National Oil Corporation, IV
The Louisiana Land and Exploration
   Company, 7
Lyondell Petrochemical Company, IV
MAPCO Inc., IV
Maxus Energy Corporation, 7
Mitchell Energy and Development
   Corporation, 7
Mitsubishi Oil Co., Ltd., IV
Mobil Corporation, IV; 7 (upd.)
Murphy Oil Corporation, 7
Nabors Industries, Inc., 9
National Iranian Oil Company, IV
Neste Oy, IV
Nigerian National Petroleum Corporation,
   IV
Nippon Mining Co. Ltd., IV
Nippon Oil Company, Limited, IV
Noble Affiliates, Inc., 11
Occidental Petroleum Corporation, IV
Oil and Natural Gas Commission, IV
ÖMV Aktiengesellschaft, IV
Oryx Energy Company, 7
Pennzoil Company, IV
PERTAMINA, IV
Petro-Canada Limited, IV
Petrofina, IV
Petróleo Brasileiro S.A., IV
Petróleos de Portugal S.A., IV
Petróleos de Venezuela S.A., IV
Petróleos del Ecuador, IV
Petróleos Mexicanos, IV

Petroleum Development Oman LLC, IV
Petronas, IV
Phillips Petroleum Company, IV
Qatar General Petroleum Corporation, IV
Quaker State Corporation, 7
Repsol S.A., IV
Royal Dutch Petroleum Company/ The
  ''Shell'' Transport and Trading Company
  p.l.c., IV
Sasol Limited, IV
Saudi Arabian Oil Company, IV
Seagull Energy Corporation, 11
Shell Oil Company, IV; 14 (upd.)
Showa Shell Sekiyu K.K., IV
Société Nationale Elf Aquitaine, IV; 7
  (upd.)
Sun Company, Inc., IV
Talisman Energy, 9
Tesoro Petroleum Corporation, 7
Texaco Inc., IV; 14 (upd.)
Tonen Corporation, IV
Tosco Corporation, 7
Total Compagnie Française des Pétroles
  S.A., IV
Triton Energy Corporation, 11
Türkiye Petrolleri Anonim Ortakliği, IV
Ultramar PLC, IV
Union Texas Petroleum Holdings, Inc., 9
Unocal Corporation, IV
USX Corporation, IV; 7 (upd.)
Valero Energy Corporation, 7
Wascana Energy Inc., 13
Western Atlas Inc., 12
Western Company of North America, 15
The Williams Companies, Inc., IV
YPF Sociedad Anonima, IV

PUBLISHING & PRINTING

A.H. Belo Corporation, 10
Advance Publications Inc., IV
Affiliated Publications, Inc., 7
American Greetings Corporation, 7
Arnoldo Mondadori Editore S.p.A., IV
Axel Springer Verlag A.G., IV
Banta Corporation, 12
Bauer Publishing Group, 7
Berlitz International, Inc., 13
Bertelsmann A.G., IV; 15 (upd.)
Book-of-the-Month Club, Inc., 13
CCH Inc., 14
Central Newspapers, Inc., 10
Commerce Clearing House, Inc., 7
The Condé Nast Publications Inc., 13
Cox Enterprises, Inc., IV
Crain Communications, Inc., 12
Dai Nippon Printing Co., Ltd., IV
Day Runner, Inc., 14
De La Rue PLC, 10
Deluxe Corporation, 7
Dow Jones & Company, Inc., IV
The Dun & Bradstreet Corporation, IV
The E.W. Scripps Company, IV; 7 (upd.)
Edmark Corporation, 14
Elsevier N.V., IV
Encyclopedia Britannica, Inc., 7
Engraph, Inc., 12
Enquirer/Star Group, Inc., 10
Farrar, Straus and Giroux Inc., 15
Flint Ink Corporation, 13
Follett Corporation, 12
Gannett Co., Inc., IV; 7 (upd.)
Gibson Greetings, Inc., 12
Groupe de la Cite, IV
Hachette, IV
Hallmark Cards, Inc., IV
Harcourt Brace and Co., 12
Harcourt Brace Jovanovich, Inc., IV

HarperCollins Publishers, 15
Havas, SA, 10
The Hearst Corporation, IV
Her Majesty's Stationery Office, 7
Houghton Mifflin Company, 10
International Data Group, 7
IPC Magazines Limited, 7
John Fairfax Holdings Limited, 7
Knight-Ridder, Inc., IV; 15 (upd.)
Kodansha Ltd., IV
Landmark Communications, Inc., 12
Lee Enterprises, Incorporated, 11
Maclean Hunter Limited, IV
Macmillan, Inc., 7
Marvel Entertainment Group, Inc., 10
Matra-Hachette S.A., 15 (upd.)
Maxwell Communication Corporation plc,
  IV; 7 (upd.)
McGraw-Hill, Inc., IV
Meredith Corporation, 11
Mirror Group Newspapers plc, 7
Moore Corporation Limited, IV
Multimedia, Inc., 11
National Geographic Society, 9
The New York Times Company, IV
News America Publishing Inc., 12
News Corporation Limited, IV; 7 (upd.)
Nihon Keizai Shimbun, Inc., IV
Ottaway Newspapers, Inc., 15
Pearson plc, IV
Pulitzer Publishing Company, 15
Quebecor Inc., 12
R.L. Polk & Co., 10
R.R. Donnelley & Sons Company, IV; 9
  (upd.)
Random House, Inc., 13
The Reader's Digest Association, Inc., IV
Reed International P.L.C., IV
Reuters Holdings PLC, IV
Scholastic Corporation, 10
Scott Fetzer Company, 12
Seattle Times Company, 15
Simon & Schuster Inc., IV
Softbank Corp., 13
Southam Inc., 7
Standard Register Co., 15
Taylor Publishing Company, 12
Thomas Nelson Inc., 14
The Thomson Corporation, 8
The Times Mirror Company, IV
Toppan Printing Co., Ltd., IV
Tribune Company, IV
United Newspapers plc, IV
Valassis Communications, Inc., 8
The Washington Post Company, IV
West Publishing Co., 7
Western Publishing Group, Inc., 13
Wolters Kluwer NV, 14
World Book, Inc., 12
World Color Press Inc., 12
Zebra Technologies Corporation, 14
Ziff Communications Company, 12

REAL ESTATE

Bramalea Ltd., 9
Cheung Kong (Holdings) Limited, IV
Del Webb Corporation, 14
The Edward J. DeBartolo Corporation, 8
The Haminerson Property Investment and
  Development Corporation plc, IV
Harbert Corporation, 14
Hongkong Land Holdings Limited, IV
JMB Realty Corporation, IV
Kaufman and Broad Home Corporation, 8
Kimco Realty Corporation, 11
The Koll Company, 8
Land Securities PLC, IV

Lend Lease Corporation Limited, IV
Lincoln Property Company, 8
Meditrust, 11
Melvin Simon and Associates, Inc., 8
MEPC plc, IV
Mitsubishi Estate Company, Limited, IV
Mitsui Real Estate Development Co., Ltd.,
  IV
New Plan Realty Trust, 11
New World Development Company Ltd.,
  IV
Newhall Land and Farming Company, 14
Olympia & York Developments Ltd., IV; 9
  (upd.)
Perini Corporation, 8
The Rouse Company, 15
Slough Estates PLC, IV
Sumitomo Realty & Development Co.,
  Ltd., IV
Tokyu Land Corporation, IV
Trammell Crow Company, 8
Tridel Enterprises Inc., 9
Trizec Corporation Ltd., 10

RETAIL & WHOLESALE

Aaron Rents, Inc., 14
ABC Appliance, Inc., 10
Abercrombie & Fitch Co., 15
Ace Hardware Corporation, 12
Ames Department Stores, Inc., 9
Amway Corporation, 13
Ann Taylor Stores Corporation, 13
Arbor Drugs Inc., 12
Au Printemps S.A., V
AutoZone, Inc., 9
Babbage's, Inc., 10
Baby Superstore, Inc., 15
Barnes & Noble, Inc., 10
Bearings, Inc., 13
Bed Bath & Beyond Inc., 13
Belk Stores Services, Inc., V
Bergen Brunswig Corporation, V; 13 (upd.)
Best Buy Co., Inc., 9
Bloomingdale's Inc., 12
The Body Shop International PLC, 11
The Bombay Company, Inc., 10
Book-of-the-Month Club, Inc., 13
Books-A-Million, Inc., 14
The Boots Company PLC, V
Borders Group, Inc., 15
Bozzuto's, Inc., 13
Bradlees Discount Department Store
  Company, 12
Burlington Coat Factory Warehouse
  Corporation, 10
The Burton Group plc, V
C&A Brenninkmeyer KG, V
Caldor Inc., 12
Campeau Corporation, V
Carrefour SA, 10
Carson Pirie Scott & Company, 15
Carter Hawley Hale Stores, Inc., V
Catherines Stores Corporation, 15
Cato Corporation, 14
Cifra, S.A. de C.V., 12
Circuit City Stores, Inc., 9
CML Group, Inc., 10
Cole National Corporation, 13
Coles Myer Ltd., V
Comdisco, Inc., 9
CompUSA, Inc., 10
Computerland Corp., 13
Corby Distilleries Limited, 14
Costco Wholesale Corporation, V
Cotter & Company, V
County Seat Stores Inc., 9
Crate and Barrel, 9

The Daiei, Inc., V
The Daimaru, Inc., V
Dayton Hudson Corporation, V
Dillard Department Stores, Inc., V
Dillon Companies Inc., 12
Discount Drug Mart, Inc., 14
Dixons Group plc, V
Drug Emporium, Inc., 12
Duty Free International, Inc., 11
Eckerd Corporation, 9
El Corte Inglés Group, V
Elder-Beerman Stores Corporation, 10
Family Dollar Stores, Inc., 13
Fastenal Company, 14
Federated Department Stores Inc., 9
Fingerhut Companies, Inc., 9
Florsheim Shoe Company, 9
Follett Corporation, 12
Frank's Nursery & Crafts, Inc., 12
Fred Meyer, Inc., V
Fretter, Inc., 10
Galeries Lafayette S.A., V
The Gap, Inc., V
General Binding Corporation, 10
General Host Corporation, 12
GIB Group, V
The Good Guys!, Inc., 10
The Great Universal Stores P.L.C., V
Grossman's Inc., 13
Guccio Gucci, S.p.A., 15
Hankyu Department Stores, Inc., V
Hechinger Company, 12
Heilig-Meyers Co., 14
Hertie Waren- und Kaufhaus GmbH, V
Hills Stores Company, 13
The Home Depot, Inc., V
Home Shopping Network, Inc., V
Hudson's Bay Company, V
The IKEA Group, V
InaCom Corporation, 13
Isetan Company Limited, V
Ito-Yokado Co., Ltd., V
J.C. Penney Company, Inc., V
Jay Jacobs, Inc., 15
JG Industries, Inc., 15
John Lewis Partnership PLC, V
JUSCO Co., Ltd., V
K & B Inc., 12
Karstadt Aktiengesellschaft, V
Kaufhof Holding AG, V
Kay-Bee Toy Stores, 15
Kingfisher plc, V
Kinney Shoe Corp., 14
Kmart Corporation, V
Knoll Group Inc., 14
Kohl's Corporation, 9
Kotobukiya Co., Ltd., V
La-Z-Boy Chair Company, 14
Lamonts Apparel, Inc., 15
Lands' End, Inc., 9
Lechmere Inc., 10
Lechters, Inc., 11
Levitz Furniture Inc., 15
Lillian Vernon Corp., 12
The Limited, Inc., V
The Littlewoods Organisation PLC, V
Longs Drug Stores Corporation, V
Lowe's Companies, Inc., V
Marks and Spencer p.l.c., V
Marshalls Incorporated, 13
Marui Co., Ltd., V
Matsuzakaya Company Limited, V
The May Department Stores Company, V
McLane Company, Inc., 13
Melville Corporation, V
Mercantile Stores Company, Inc., V
Merry-Go-Round Enterprises, Inc., 8
Mervyn's, 10

Mitsukoshi Ltd., V
Montgomery Ward & Co., Incorporated, V
Morse Shoe Inc., 13
Musicland Stores Corporation, 9
Nagasakiya Co., Ltd., V
National Intergroup, Inc., V
Natural Wonders Inc., 14
Neiman Marcus Co., 12
Nichii Co., Ltd., V
Nine West Group Inc., 11
Nordstrom, Inc., V
The North West Company, Inc., 12
Office Depot Incorporated, 8
OfficeMax Inc., 15
Otto-Versand (GmbH & Co.), V; 15 (upd.)
Pamida Holdings Corporation, 15
Parisian, Inc., 14
Pay 'N Pak Stores, Inc., 9
Payless Cashways, Inc., 11
Pearle Vision, Inc., 13
Petrie Stores Corporation, 8
PETsMART, Inc., 14
Phar-Mor Inc., 12
Pier 1 Imports, Inc., 12
The Price Company, V
PriceCostco, Inc., 14
Quelle Group, V
R.H. Macy & Co., Inc., V; 8 (upd.)
Raley's Inc., 14
Recoton Corp., 15
Revco D.S., Inc., V
REX Stores Corp., 10
Riklis Family Corp., 9
Rite Aid Corporation, V
Rose's Stores, Inc., 13
Roundy's Inc., 14
Schottenstein Stores Corp., 14
Sears plc, V
Sears, Roebuck and Co., V
Seibu Department Stores, Ltd., V
The Seiyu, Ltd., V
Service Merchandise Company, Inc., V
Shaklee Corporation, 12
The Sharper Image Corporation, 10
Shoe Carnival Inc., 14
Spiegel, Inc., 10
Sportmart, Inc., 15
Stanhome Inc., 15
Staples, Inc., 10
Stinnes AG, 8
Stride Rite Corporation, 8
Sun Television & Appliances Inc., 10
Takashimaya Co., Limited, V
The Talbots, Inc., 11
Target Stores, 10
Tech Data Corporation, 10
Thrifty PayLess, Inc., 12
Tiffany & Co., 14
The TJX Companies, Inc., V
Tokyu Department Store Co., Ltd., V
Toys "R" Us, Inc., V
TVI, Inc., 15
The United States Shoe Corporation, V
United Stationers Inc., 14
Uny Co., Ltd., V
Urban Outfitters, Inc., 14
Value Merchants Inc., 13
Vendex International N.V., 13
Venture Stores Inc., 12
Viking Office Products, Inc., 10
W H Smith Group PLC, V
W.W. Grainger, Inc., V
Waban Inc., 13
Wal-Mart Stores, Inc., V; 8 (upd.)
Walgreen Co., V
Wherehouse Entertainment Incorporated,
   11
Wickes Companies, Inc., V

Woolworth Corporation, V

RUBBER & TIRE

The BFGoodrich Company, V
Bridgestone Corporation, V
Carlisle Companies Incorporated, 8
Compagnie Générale des Établissements
   Michelin, V
Continental Aktiengesellschaft, V
Cooper Tire & Rubber Company, 8
General Tire, Inc., 8
The Goodyear Tire & Rubber Company, V
The Kelly-Springfield Tire Company, 8
Pirelli S.p.A., V; 15 (upd.)
Sumitomo Rubber Industries, Ltd., V
Tillotson Corp., 15
The Yokohama Rubber Co., Ltd., V

TELECOMMUNICATIONS

Acme-Cleveland Corp., 13
ADC Telecommunications, Inc., 10
AirTouch Communications, 11
Alltel Corporation, 6
American Telephone and Telegraph
   Company, V
Ameritech, V
Ascom AG, 9
AT&T Bell Laboratories, Inc., 13
BCE Inc., V
Belgacom, 6
Bell Atlantic Corporation, V
Bell Canada, 6
BellSouth Corporation, V
British Columbia Telephone Company, 6
British Telecommunications plc, V; 15
   (upd.)
Cable and Wireless plc, V
Canal Plus, 10
Carlton Communications plc, 15
Carolina Telephone and Telegraph
   Company, 10
Centel Corporation, 6
Century Communications Corp., 10
Century Telephone Enterprises, Inc., 9
Chris-Craft Industries, Inc., 9
Cincinnati Bell, Inc., 6
Comverse Technology, Inc., 15
DDI Corporation, 7
Deutsche Bundespost TELEKOM, V
Directorate General of
   Telecommunications, 7
DSC Communications Corporation, 12
Executone Information Systems, Inc., 13
France Télécom Group, V
General DataComm Industries, Inc., 14
GTE Corporation, V; 15 (upd.)
Havas, SA, 10
Hong Kong Telecommunications Ltd., 6
IDB Communications Group, Inc., 11
Illinois Bell Telephone Company, 14
Indiana Bell Telephone Company,
   Incorporated, 14
Infinity Broadcasting Corporation, 11
Koninklijke PTT Nederland NV, V
LDDS-Metro Communications, Inc., 8
LIN Broadcasting Corp., 9
Lincoln Telephone & Telegraph Company,
   14
McCaw Cellular Communications, Inc., 6
MCI Communications Corporation, V
Mercury Communications, Ltd., 7
Metromedia Companies, 14
MFS Communications Company, Inc., 11
Michigan Bell Telephone Co., 14
Multimedia, Inc., 11
Nevada Bell Telephone Company, 14

Nippon Telegraph and Telephone
    Corporation, V
Northern Telecom Limited, V
NYNEX Corporation, V
Octel Communications Corp., 14
Ohio Bell Telephone Company, 14
Österreichische Post- und
    Telegraphenverwaltung, V
Pacific Telecom, Inc., 6
Pacific Telesis Group, V
Paging Network Inc., 11
PictureTel Corp., 10
Posti- ja Telelaitos, 6
QVC Network Inc., 9
Rochester Telephone Corporation, 6
Schweizerische Post-, Telefon- und
    Telegrafen-Betriebe, V
Scientific-Atlanta, Inc., 6
Società Finanziaria Telefonica per Azioni,
    V
Southern New England
    Telecommunications Corporation, 6
Southwestern Bell Corporation, V
Sprint Communications Company, L.P., 9
Swedish Telecom, V
SynOptics Communications, Inc., 10
Telecom Australia, 6
Telecom Eireann, 7
Telefonaktiebolaget LM Ericsson, V
Telefónica de España, S.A., V
Telefonos de Mexico S.A. de C.V., 14
Telephone and Data Systems, Inc., 9
Tellabs, Inc., 11
U S West, Inc., V
United States Cellular Corporation, 9
United Telecommunications, Inc., V
Vodafone Group plc, 11
Watkins-Johnson Company, 15
Wisconsin Bell, Inc., 14

TEXTILES & APPAREL

Adidas AG, 14
Albany International Corp., 8
Amoskeag Company, 8
Angelica Corporation, 15
Benetton Group S.p.A., 10
Birkenstock Footprint Sandals, Inc., 12
Brown Group, Inc., V
Burlington Industries, Inc., V
Cato Corporation, 14
Charming Shoppes, Inc., 8
Coach Leatherware, 10
Coats Viyella Plc, V
Collins & Aikman Corporation, 13
Cone Mills Corporation, 8
Courtaulds plc, V
Crystal Brands, Inc., 9
Danskin, Inc., 12
Delta Woodside Industries, Inc., 8
Dominion Textile Inc., 12
Donna Karan Company, 15
Edison Brothers Stores, Inc., 9
Esprit de Corp., 8
Fieldcrest Cannon, Inc., 9
Fruit of the Loom, Inc., 8
The Gitano Group, Inc. 8
Greenwood Mills, Inc., 14
Guccio Gucci, S.p.A., 15
Guess, Inc., 15
Guilford Mills Inc., 8
Gymboree Corporation, 15
Hartmarx Corporation, 8
The Hartstone Group plc, 14
Hermès S.A., 14
Interface, Inc., 8
Irwin Toy Limited, 14
J. Crew Group Inc., 12

Jockey International, Inc., 12
Johnston Industries, Inc., 15
Kellwood Company, 8
Kinney Shoe Corp., 14
L.A. Gear, Inc., 8
L.L. Bean, Inc., 10
Laura Ashley Holdings plc, 13
Lee Apparel Company, Inc., 8
The Leslie Fay Companies, Inc., 8
Levi Strauss & Co., V
Liz Claiborne, Inc., 8
Milliken & Co., V
Mitsubishi Rayon Co., Ltd., V
Nike, Inc., V; 8 (upd.)
OshKosh B'Gosh, Inc., 9
Oxford Industries, Inc., 8
Polo/Ralph Lauren Corporation, 12
Reebok International Ltd., V; 9 (upd.)
Rollerblade, Inc., 15
Russell Corporation, 8
Shelby Williams Industries, Inc., 14
Springs Industries, Inc., V
Starter Corp., 12
Stone Manufacturing Company, 14
Stride Rite Corporation, 8
Teijin Limited, V
The Timberland Company, 13
Toray Industries, Inc., V
Tultex Corporation, 13
Unifi, Inc., 12
United Merchants & Manufacturers, Inc.,
    13
Unitika Ltd., V
Varsity Spirit Corp., 15
VF Corporation, V
Walton Monroe Mills, Inc., 8
The Warnaco Group Inc., 12
Wellman, Inc., 8
West Point-Pepperell, Inc., 8
Williamson-Dickie Manufacturing
    Company, 14

TOBACCO

American Brands, Inc., V
Brooke Group Ltd., 15
Brown and Williamson Tobacco
    Corporation, 14
Culbro Corporation, 15
Dibrell Brothers, Incorporated, 12
Gallaher Limited, V
Imasco Limited, V
Japan Tobacco Incorporated, V
Philip Morris Companies Inc., V
RJR Nabisco Holdings Corp., V
Rothmans International p.l.c., V
Standard Commercial Corporation, 13
Tabacalera, S.A., V
Universal Corporation, V
UST Inc., 9

TRANSPORT SERVICES

Air Express International Corporation, 13
Airborne Freight Corp., 6
Alamo Rent A Car, Inc., 6
Alexander & Baldwin, Inc., 10
Amerco, 6
American President Companies Ltd., 6
Anschutz Corp., 12
Atlas Van Lines, Inc., 14
Avis, Inc., 6
BAA plc, 10
Bekins Company, 15
British Railways Board, V
Budget Rent a Car Corporation, 9
Burlington Northern Inc., V
Canadian National Railway System, 6
Canadian Pacific Limited, V

Carlson Companies, Inc., 6
Carnival Cruise Lines, Inc., 6
Carolina Freight Corporation, 6
Chargeurs, 6
Chicago and North Western Holdings
    Corporation, 6
Coles Express Inc., 15
Compagnie Générale Maritime et
    Financière, 6
Consolidated Freightways, Inc., V
Consolidated Rail Corporation, V
Crowley Maritime Corporation, 6
CSX Corporation, V
Danzas Group, V
Deutsche Bundesbahn, V
DHL Worldwide Express, 6
East Japan Railway Company, V
Emery Air Freight Corporation, 6
Enterprise Rent-A-Car Company, 6
Evergreen Marine Corporation Taiwan
    Ltd., 13
Federal Express Corporation, V
Fritz Companies, Inc., 12
GATX, 6
Hankyu Corporation, V
Hapag-Lloyd AG, 6
The Hertz Corporation, 9
Illinois Central Corporation, 11
J.B. Hunt Transport Services Inc., 12
Kansas City Southern Industries, Inc., 6
Kawasaki Kisen Kaisha, Ltd., V
Keio Teito Electric Railway Company, V
Kinki Nippon Railway Company Ltd., V
Koninklijke Nedlloyd Groep N.V., 6
Kuhne & Nagel International A.G., V
La Poste, V
Leaseway Transportation Corp., 12
London Regional Transport, 6
Mayflower Group Inc., 6
Mitsui O.S.K. Lines, Ltd., V
Moran Towing Corporation, Inc., 15
National Car Rental System, Inc., 10
NFC plc, 6
Nippon Express Co., Ltd., V
Nippon Yusen Kabushiki Kaisha, V
Norfolk Southern Corporation, V
Ocean Group plc, 6
Odakyu Electric Railway Company
    Limited, V
Österreichische Bundesbahnen GmbH, 6
Overnite Transportation Co., 14
Overseas Shipholding Group, Inc., 11
The Peninsular and Oriental Steam
    Navigation Company, V
Penske Corporation, V
PHH Corporation, V
Post Office Group, V
Preston Corporation, 6
Roadway Services, Inc., V
Ryder System, Inc., V
Santa Fe Pacific Corporation, V
Schenker-Rhenus AG, 6
Seibu Railway Co. Ltd., V
Seino Transportation Company, Ltd., 6
Société Nationale des Chemins de Fer
    Français, V
Southern Pacific Transportation Company,
    V
Stinnes AG, 8
The Swiss Federal Railways
    (Schweizerische Bundesbahnen), V
Tidewater Inc., 11
TNT Freightways Corporation, 14
TNT Limited, V
Tobu Railway Co Ltd, 6
Tokyu Corporation, V
Totem Resources Corporation, 9
Transnet Ltd., 6

TTX Company, 6
Union Pacific Corporation, V
United Parcel Service of America Inc., V
United States Postal Service, 14
Yamato Transport Co. Ltd., V
Yellow Corporation, 14
Yellow Freight System, Inc. of Delaware,
    V

UTILITIES

The AES Corporation, 10; 13 (upd.)
Air & Water Technologies Corporation, 6
Allegheny Power System, Inc., V
American Electric Power Company, Inc., V
American Water Works Company, 6
Arkla, Inc., V
Associated Natural Gas Corporation, 11
Atlanta Gas Light Company, 6
Atlantic Energy, Inc., 6
Baltimore Gas and Electric Company, V
Bayernwerk A.G., V
Big Rivers Electric Corporation, 11
Boston Edison Company, 12
British Gas plc, V
British Nuclear Fuels plc, 6
Brooklyn Union Gas, 6
Canadian Utilities Limited, 13
Carolina Power & Light Company, V
Cascade Natural Gas Corporation, 9
Centerior Energy Corporation, V
Central and South West Corporation, V
Central Hudson Gas and Electricity
    Corporation, 6
Central Maine Power, 6
Chubu Electric Power Company,
    Incorporated, V
Chugoku Electric Power Company Inc., V
Cincinnati Gas & Electric Company, 6
CIPSCO Inc., 6
Citizens Utilities Company, 7
City Public Service, 6
CMS Energy Corporation, V, 14
Cogentrix Energy, Inc., 10
The Coleman Company, Inc., 9
The Columbia Gas System, Inc., V
Commonwealth Edison Company, V
Commonwealth Energy System, 14
Connecticut Light and Power Co., 13
Consolidated Edison Company of New
    York, Inc., V
Consolidated Natural Gas Company, V
Consumers Power Co., 14
Consumers Water Company, 14
Consumers' Gas Company Ltd., 6
Destec Energy, Inc., 12
The Detroit Edison Company, V
Dominion Resources, Inc., V
DPL Inc., 6
DQE, Inc., 6
Duke Power Company, V
Eastern Enterprises, 6
El Paso Natural Gas Company, 12
Electricité de France, V
Elektrowatt AG, 6
ENDESA Group, V
Enron Corp., V
Enserch Corporation, V
Ente Nazionale per L'Energia Elettrica, V
Entergy Corporation, V
Equitable Resources, Inc., 6
Florida Progress Corporation, V
Fortis, Inc., 15
FPL Group, Inc., V
Gaz de France, V
General Public Utilities Corporation, V
Générale des Eaux Group, V
Gulf States Utilities Company, 6

Hawaiian Electric Industries, Inc., 9
Hokkaido Electric Power Company Inc., V
Hokuriku Electric Power Company, V
Hongkong Electric Company Ltd., 6
Houston Industries Incorporated, V
Hydro-Québec, 6
Idaho Power Company, 12
Illinois Bell Telephone Company, 14
Illinois Power Company, 6
IPALCO Enterprises, Inc., 6
The Kansai Electric Power Co., Inc., V
Kansas City Power & Light Company, 6
Kenetech Corporation, 11
Kentucky Utilities Company, 6
KU Energy Corporation, 11
Kyushu Electric Power Company Inc., V
LG&E Energy Corporation, 6
Long Island Lighting Company, V
Lyonnaise des Eaux-Dumez, V
Magma Power Company, 11
MCN Corporation, 6
MDU Resources Group, Inc., 7
Midwest Resources Inc., 6
Minnesota Power & Light Company, 11
Montana Power Company, 11
National Fuel Gas Company, 6
National Power PLC, 12
N.V. Nederlandse Gasunie, V
Nevada Power Company, 11
New England Electric System, V
New York State Electric and Gas, 6
Niagara Mohawk Power Corporation, V
NICOR Inc., 6
NIPSCO Industries, Inc., 6
North West Water Group plc, 11
Northeast Utilities, V
Northern States Power Company, V
Nova Corporation of Alberta, V
Oglethorpe Power Corporation, 6
Ohio Edison Company, V
Oklahoma Gas and Electric Company, 6
ONEOK Inc., 7
Ontario Hydro, 6
Osaka Gas Co., Ltd., V
Pacific Enterprises, V
Pacific Gas and Electric Company, V
PacifiCorp, V
Panhandle Eastern Corporation, V
PECO Energy Company, 11
Pennsylvania Power & Light Company, V
Peoples Energy Corporation, 6
Philadelphia Electric Company, V
Pinnacle West Capital Corporation, 6
Portland General Corporation, 6
Potomac Electric Power Company, 6
PowerGen PLC, 11
PreussenElektra Aktiengesellschaft, V
PSI Resources, 6
Public Service Company of Colorado, 6
Public Service Company of New Mexico, 6
Public Service Enterprise Group
    Incorporated, V
Puget Sound Power and Light Company, 6
Questar Corporation, 6
Rochester Gas and Electric Corporation, 6
Ruhrgas A.G., V
RWE Group, V
San Diego Gas & Electric Company, V
SCANA Corporation, 6
Scarborough Public Utilities Commission,
    9
SCEcorp, V
Scottish Hydro-Electric PLC, 13
Severn Trent PLC, 12
Shikoku Electric Power Company, Inc., V
Sonat, Inc., 6
The Southern Company, V
Southern Electric PLC, 13

Southern Indiana Gas and Electric
    Company, 13
Southwestern Public Service Company, 6
TECO Energy, Inc., 6
Texas Utilities Company, V
Thames Water plc, 11
Tohoku Electric Power Company, Inc., V
The Tokyo Electric Power Company,
    Incorporated, V
Tokyo Gas Co., Ltd., V
TransAlta Utilities Corporation, 6
TransCanada PipeLines Limited, V
Transco Energy Company, V
Tucson Electric Power Company, 6
UGI Corporation, 12
Union Electric Company, V
UtiliCorp United Inc., 6
Vereinigte Elektrizitätswerke Westfalen
    AG, V
Washington Natural Gas Company, 9
Washington Water Power Company, 6
Western Resources, Inc., 12
Wheelabrator Technologies, Inc., 6
Wisconsin Energy Corporation, 6
Wisconsin Public Service Corporation, 9
WPL Holdings, Inc., 6

WASTE SERVICES

Browning-Ferris Industries, Inc., V
Chemical Waste Management, Inc., 9
Roto-Rooter Corp., 15
Safety-Kleen Corp., 8
Waste Management, Inc., V

NOTES ON CONTRIBUTORS

Notes on Contributors

BOYER, Dean. Newspaper reporter and free-lance writer in the Seattle area.

COHEN, M. L. Novelist and free-lance writer living in Chicago.

COVELL, Jeffrey L. Free-lance writer and corporate history contractor.

DERDAK, Thomas. Free-lance writer and adjunct professor of philosophy at Loyola University of Chicago; former executive director of the Albert Einstein Foundation.

GALLMAN, Jason. Free-lance writer.

GASBARRE, April Dougal. Archivist and free-lance writer specializing in business and social history in Cleveland, Ohio.

GOPNIK, Hilary. Free-lance writer.

HALASZ, Robert. Former editor in chief of World Progress and Funk & Wagnalls New Encyclopedia Yearbook; author, The U.S. Marines (Millbrook Press, 1993).

HIGHMAN, Beth Watson. Free-lance writer.

INGRAM, Frederick. Business writer living in Johnson City, Tennessee; contributor to the Encyclopedia of Business, the Encyclopedia of Consumer Brands, and Global Industry Profiles.

JACOBSON, Robert R. Free-lance writer and musician.

KELLEY, Michael. Free-lance writer.

LEWIS, Scott. Free-lance writer and editor.

McNULTY, Mary. Free-lance writer and editor.

McMANUS, Donald. Free-lance writer.

MOTE, Dave. President of information retrieval company Performance Database.

PEIPPO, Kathleen. Minneapolis-based free-lance writer.

PFALZGRAF, Taryn Benbow. Free-lance editor, writer, and consultant in the Chicago area.

RIGGS, Thomas. Free-lance writer and editor.

ROULAND, Roger. Free-lance writer whose essays and journalism have appeared in the *International Fiction Review,* Chicago *Tribune,* and Chicago *Sun-Times.*

SALAMIE, David E. Part-owner of InfoWorks Development Group, a reference publication development and editorial services company.

SCHRECENGOST, Lynda D. Free-lance writer and editor specializing in promotional and educational materials.

WERNICK, Ellen D. Free-lance writer and editor.

WOODWARD, Angela. Free-lance writer.